VOLUME 5

Burma to Cathay

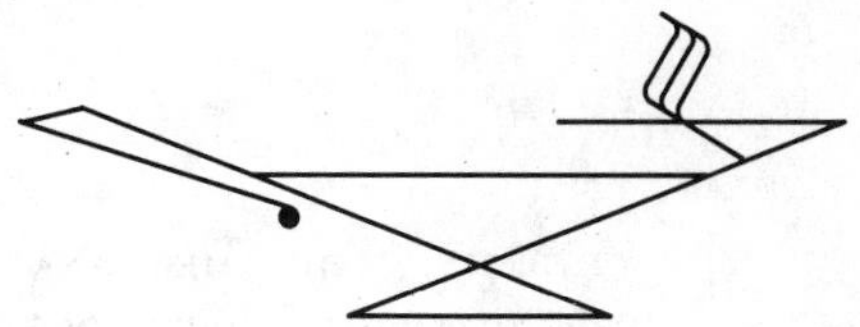

THE ENCYCLOPEDIA AMERICANA

INTERNATIONAL EDITION

COMPLETE IN THIRTY VOLUMES FIRST PUBLISHED IN 1829

AMERICANA CORPORATION International Headquarters: 575 Lexington Avenue, New York, New York 10022

Library of Congress Cataloging in Publication Data
Main entry under title:

THE ENCYCLOPEDIA AMERICANA.

1829–1858 editions published under title:
Encyclopaedia Americana; 1907–1912: The Americana.
Includes bibliographical references.
1. Encyclopedias and dictionaries.
AE5.E333 1973 031 72–89171
ISBN 0–7172–0104–X

MANUFACTURED IN THE U.S.A.

BURMA

JULES BUCHER, FROM PHOTO RESEARCHERS

TEMPLES OF PAGAN, ancient city of the central Burmese plain, are watched over by the mythical half lion, half dog that is Burma's national symbol.

Coat of Arms of Burma

CONTENTS

Section	Page	Section	Page
1. The People	2	**5. Government**	8
Ethnology	2	**6. History**	9
Ethnic Distribution	2	Early Kingdoms	9
Way of Life	4	Coming of the British	10
Religion	4	Kingdom of Ava	10
2. The Land and Natural Resources	5	Nationalist Movement	11
3. Economy	6	Independence	12
4. Education	7		

BURMA, bûr′mə, a country in Southeast Asia sharing land boundaries with India, East Pakistan, China, Laos, and Thailand, seemed destined by location for a critical role in the ideological power struggle underway in Asia in the latter half of the 20th century. Instead, economics and natural environment as well as the character of its political administration have prevented Burma's playing an active part in the world political arena and have made it a country isolated and quiescent.

Burma, like Italy or Spain, is a natural geographical entity. The horse-shoe shaped arc of mountains and hills that encircles Burma on the west, north, and east encloses the plains where most of the people dwell and cuts the country off from its neighbors. Migrations have from time to time changed Burma's culture and the composition of its population, but for nearly a thousand years there has been a continuous history of a Burmese state, drawing its main cultural inspiration from Theravada Buddhism.

Throughout its history, Burma has been inward-looking. Traditionally, the capital was known as "the Center of the Universe." Then for a hundred years Burma was forcibly drawn into a wider political system—the British Empire.

INFORMATION HIGHLIGHTS

Official Name: Union of Burma.

Head of State: Chairman of the Revolutionary Council.

Head of Government: Chairman of the Revolutionary Council.

Legislature: None.

Area: 261,789 square miles (678,033 sq km).

Boundaries: *North,* China; *south,* Andaman Sea; *east,* China, Laos, and Thailand; *west,* Pakistan and India.

Elevations: *Highest point*—Hkakabo Razi, 19,296 feet (5,881 meters); *lowest point*—sea level.

Population: 25,246,000 (1966).

Capital: Rangoon (1963 population, 1,530,000).

Major Languages: Burmese (official), Shan, Karen, Arakanese, Mon, Kachin, Chin.

Major Religions: Buddhism, animism, Christianity, Islam.

Monetary Unit: Kyat (100 pya).

Flag: A red field with a canton of dark blue in the upper left-hand corner. In the canton is a large five-pointed white star, with five smaller white stars between the points.

National Anthem: *Bama Pye* (*The Land of Burma*).

Economically, Burma became an almost classic example of a land under colonialism. Its economy was greatly developed, but primarily to supply raw materials for British trade. The higher echelons of government and business were occupied by Europeans, and there was a huge influx of Indians into the public services and the economy. Much of the feeling in the Burmese nationalist movement was directed against these intruders. After Burma gained independence in 1948 the new democratic government had to contend with violent challenges to its legitimacy, which it successfully resisted until 1962; then the armed forces seized control, announcing that they would proceed along "the Burmese Way to Socialism." Private enterprise, both native and foreign, has been rapidly liquidated. The old inwardness has been deliberately cultivated, and Burma today is largely closed to the outside world and its influences.

1. The People

The last accurate and systematic enumeration of Burma's population took place in 1931. Attempts to calculate growth since independence have depended on samples of uncertain reliability. The growth rate per annum is estimated at 1.9% (one of the lowest rates in Southeast Asia) and the total population (1965) is supposed to number about 24,732,000.

Ethnology. While "Burmese" is a term sometimes loosely employed for all the peoples of Burma, it is (except as a definition of citizenship) usually applied to those 68% of the population who speak the Burmese language. This principal group is also known as Burmans. The Karens are the next most prominent group, forming about 10% of the total population. The Shans, with approximately 8%, are the third most numerous group in Burma. The Burmans are short and slender with brown skin, whereas the Karens are stockier and often lighter in skin color. Among other prominent ethnic groups are the Kachins, Chins, Mons, Arakanese, and Lao. Tribes in the northern hills are frequently rather tall and rosy cheeked and occasionally have wavy hair. Some hold that the aboriginal inhabitants are the Wa of the eastern borderland, who are darker-skinned and short. Burma's various peoples have intermarried in many areas.

The scientific division of Burma's peoples into ethnic groups has been accomplished through the recognition of distinct language groupings. The main language groups are the Tibeto-Burman, the Mon-Khmer, and the Thai-Chinese. The Tibeto-Burman group includes Burmese, Arakanese, Jinghpaw or Chingpaw (Kachin), the Chin and Naga tongues, and the Lolo-Moso (Muhso). The Mon-Khmer group includes Mon (Talaing), Palaung, Wa, Miao, Riang, and others. The Thai-Chinese group includes Shan, Hkun, Lao, and Karen dialects (Sgaw, Pwo, Pa-o, and Kayah), and others.

Ethnic Distribution. The Burmese are the most numerous inhabitants of Burma's central plains, while sizable Karen and Mon communities live in the Irrawaddy-Sittang delta region and in the Tenasserim uplands on the Malay Peninsula. The Arakanese, who live on Burma's Bay of Bengal coast, have an ancient history of separation from Burma proper and of communication with Bengal, accounted for by a mountain barrier between central Burma and the Arakan coast. Although the Arakanese are related to the

BURMA Map Index

Population: 25,246,000 **Area: 261,789 square miles**

INTERNAL DIVISIONS

Name	Key
Arakan (div.)	A4
Chin Hills (special div.)	A3
Irrawaddy (div.)	A4
Kachin (state)	B2
Karen or Kawthoolei (state)	B4
Kayah (state)	B4
Magwe (div.)	A3
Mandalay (div.)	A3
Pegu (div.)	B4
Sagaing (div.)	A2
Shan (state)	B3
Tenasserim (div.)	B5

CITIES and TOWNS

Name	Key
Akyab, 42,329	A3
Allanmyo, 15,580	A4
Alon, 1,932	A3
Amarapura, 11,268	A3
Amherst, 6,000	B4
Athok, 4,819	A4
Bassein, 77,905	A4
Bhamo, 9,821	B2
Bilin, 5,248	B4
Bokpyin, 631	B6
Chauk, 24,466	A3
Danubyu, 9,833	A4
Gangaw, 3,800	A3
Gwa	A4
Gyobingauk, 9,922	B4
Haka	A3
Henzada, 61,972	A4
Hsipaw	B3
Insein, 27,030	B4
Kalemyo, 3,158	A3
Kalewa, 2,230	A3
Kama, 3,523	A4
Kamayut, 23,032	B4
Kanbalu, 3,281	A3
Kani, 2,600	A3
Katha, 7,648	A2
Kawlin, 3,735	A3
Ke-hsi Mansam	B3
Keng Tung	B3
Konglu	B2
Kyaikto, 13,154	B4
Kyangin, 6,073	A4
Kyaukpadaung, 5,480	A3
Kyaukpyu, 7,335	A4
Kyaukse, 8,659	B3
Kywebwe, 3,150	B4
Labutta, 12,982	A4
Lai-hka	B3
Lashio	B3
Lenya	B6
Letpadan, 15,896	B4
Loi-kaw	B4
Lonton	A2
Ma-ubin, 23,362	A4
Madauk, 4,618	B4
Magwe, 13,270	A3
Mahlaing, 6,543	A3
Maingkwan	B2
Maliwun	B6
Man Hpang	B3
Mandalay, 195,348	B3
Mangkyi	B2
Martaban, 5,661	B4
Maungdaw, 3,772	A3
Mawkmai	B3
Mawlaik, 2,993	A3
Maymyo, 22,287	B3
Meiktila, 19,474	A3
Mergui, 33,697	B5
Minbu, 9,096	A3
Minbya, 5,783	A3
Minhla, 6,470	A4
Mogaung, 2,920	B2
Mogok, 8,334	B3
Mong Mau	B4
Möng Pan	B3
Monywa, 26,279	A3
Moulmein, 108,020	B4
Mudon, 20,136	B4
Myanaung, 11,155	A4
Myaungmya, 24,532	A4
Myebon, 3,499	A3
Myingyan, 36,439	A3
Myitkyina, 12,382	B2
Myitnge, 3,888	B3
Myohaung, 6,534	A3
Namhkam	B3
Namlan	B3
Namtu	B3
Natmauk	A3
Nyaunglebin, 12,155	B4
Pa-an, 4,139	B4
Pagan, 2,824	A3
Pakokku, 30,943	A3
Palaw, 5,596	B5
Pantha	A3
Pasawng	B4
Paungde, 17,286	A4
Pegu, 47,378	B4
Prome, 36,997	A4
Pyapon, 19,174	A4
Pyinmana, 22,025	B4
Pyu, 10,443	B4
Rangoon (cap.), 1,530,000	B4
Rathedaung, 2,969	A3
Sagaing, 15,382	A3
Sandoway, 5,172	A4
Satthwa	A4
Shwebo, 17,827	A3
Shwegyin, 5,439	B4
Shwenyaung	B3
Singu, 4,027	B3
Sumprabum	B2
Syriam, 15,296	B4
Taungdwingyi, 16,233	B3
Taunggyi	B3
Taungup, 4,065	A4
Tavoy, 40,312	B5
Tenasserim, 1,086	B6
Tharrawaddy, 8,977	B4
Thaton, 38,047	B4
Thaungdut	A2
Thayetmyo, 11,649	A4
Thazi, 7,531	B3
Thongwa, 10,829	B4
Thonze, 14,443	A4

Population Years: Country total—1966 off. est.; capital (with suburbs)—1963 off. est.; other cities and towns—1958 off. est. or 1953 final census.

Toungoo, 31,589 . . . . A4
Victoria Point, 1,520 B6
Wakema, 20,716 . . . . A4
Yamethin, 11,167 . . . . B3
Yandoon, 15,245 . . . . A4
Ye, 12,852 . . . . B5
Yenangyaung, 24,416 A3
Yesagyo, 7,880 . . . . . . A3

PHYSICAL FEATURES

Amya (pass) B5
Andaman (sea) A5
Arakan Yoma (mts.) . . A4
Ataran (river) B5
Bengal (bay) A4
Bentinck (isl.) B6
Bilauktaung (range) . . B5
Cheduba (isl.), 2,621 A4
Chin (hills) A3
Chindwin (river) A3
Coco (chan.) A5
Combermere (bay) . . . A4
Dawna (range) B4
Diphu (pass) B1
Domel (isl.) B6
Elphinstone (isl.) B5
Great Coco (isl.) A5
Great Tenasserim (river) B5
Heinze Chaung (bay) B5
Heywood (chan.) A4
Hka, Nam (river) B3
Indawgyi (lake) B2
Irrawaddy (river) A4
Irrawaddy, Mouths of the A5
Kaladan (river) A3
Kalegauk (isl.) B5
Khao Luang (mt.) B6
King (isl.) B5
Kumjawng (pass) B2
Launglon Bok (isls.) . . B5
Manipur (river) A3
Martaban (gulf) B5
Mekong (river) C3
Mergui (arch.) B6
Mon (river) A3
Mu (river) A3
Mulayit Taung (mt.) . . B4
Naga (hills) A2
Negrais (cape) A4
Nmai Hka (river) B2
Patkai (range) A2
Pegu Yoma (mts.) A4
Popa Hill (mt.) A3
Preparis (isl.) A5
Preparis North (chan.) A5
Preparis South (chan.) A5
Ramree (isl.), 11,133 . . A4
Ross (isl.) B5
Saint Matthews (isl.) . . B6
Salween (river) B4
Shan (plateau) B3
Shweli (river) B3
Sittang (river) B4
Sullivan (isl.) B6
Taungthonton (mt.) . . . A2
Tavoy (isl.) B5
Tavoy (point) B5
Tenasserim (isl.) B5
Teng, Nam (river) B3
Three Pagodas (pass) B5
Tu, Nam (river) B3
Victoria (mt.) A3

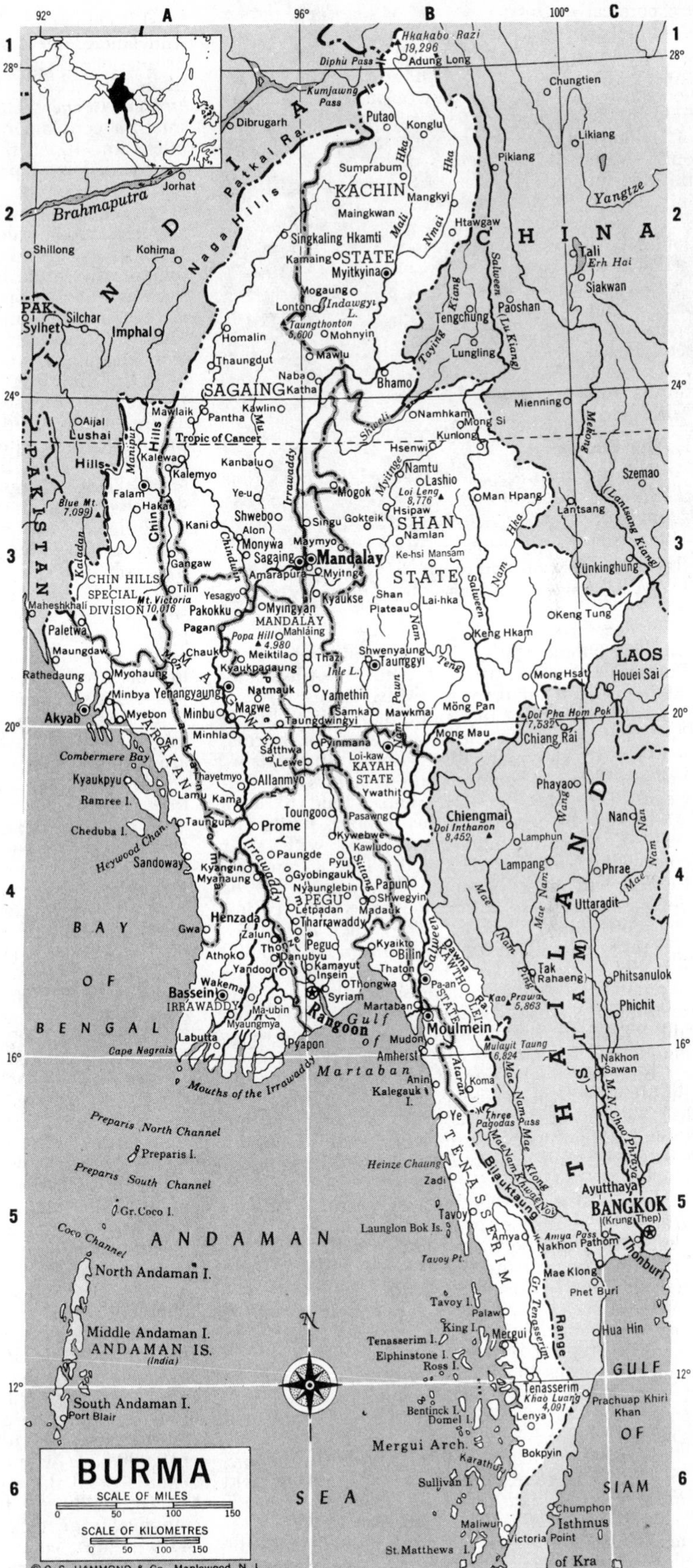

BURMA
SCALE OF MILES
SCALE OF KILOMETRES

A. DEVANEY

HANDICRAFTS are practiced in Burma's villages. In Twante, where this craftsman lives, are many potters.

Burmans, their speech is quite different from Burmese and also many of them are physically taller. Only a minority are Muslims.

The Shans form the traditional ruling elite in the Shan upland in the eastern part of Burma, holding all the cultivable land in the valleys. Because of poor communications across the Salween River, the "western Shans" tend to have established links with Burma proper, while the "eastern Shans" retain associations with their cousins in Laos and Thailand. The Karens, although half their community now lives in the delta and to some extent in the central plains, were originally hill folk. The other hill tribes still reside mainly in the hill country above 3,000 feet (915 meters), though in the eastern hills the population is tending to press southward. The Kachins, the most vigorous and assertive of the hill tribes, have expanded from their northern mountain bastions into the northern plains.

Burmese, Shans, and Mons are predominantly Buddhist, with a developed literary culture. The hill peoples are animists, with an oral culture, though their most progressive elements adopted Christianity and acquired writing and other techniques from missionaries.

Way of Life. The social system of the dominant group, the Burmese, provides the model toward which the other peoples—whether willingly or reluctantly—are moving. The process has gained considerable momentum since independence. Burmese society is fluid and remarkably free of distinctions or degrees, whether of class, caste, or sex. The typical Burmese village is not a tightly knit status-conscious community as in India. In Lower Burma there has been intense mobility, partly because there is no rigidly established social structure.

However, in Upper Burma family distinctions are still important and hereditary offices held under the old kings—such as the office of headman (*thugyi*)—still entitle a person to respect, if no longer to actual leadership. Among the Shans, the princes and aristocrats of ancient family still command obedience from their clansmen. And among the lesser hill tribes there is a clear distinction between those of chiefly and commoner lineage.

The Village. The Burmese village is usually small, a conglomeration of bamboo dwellings on piles. In Upper Burma the village is still often surrounded by a protective thorn hedge which is patrolled at night by village guards. In a land of rivers, many villages are extended, like the crescent moon, along river banks. The fields spread far around the village, and the laborers temporarily reside in field huts before and during the harvest season. Certain villages in Upper Burma are communities of craftsmen. There are villages of weavers, potters, silversmiths, sculptors, and many other specialists.

The Buddhist monastery has a recognized place in any Burmese village which is of any size. There is the traditional stupa or bell-shaped *dagoba* as the center of worship and a monastery where monks dwell.

The City. Many country people have flocked into the towns during the past 20 years. Even in Rangoon, the capital, these people contrive to recreate a village atmosphere in their suburban colonies and temporary hutments. Still, in the late 1960's less than 10% of the population was living in towns. The town dwellers are composed of the nation's traders, factory workers, and almost all of its minute middle class, consisting of government officials, professional people, and business men. Apart from a tiny minority who have two or three generations of Western education behind them, most of the middle class are but one generation away from the villages.

All Burmese, middle classes and masses, find their main enjoyment in the annual cycle of quasi-religious festivals, and in the working of magic and astrology, which make the Burmese accept the changes and chances of life with a gambler's indifference.

In the towns and cities is to be found the small remnant of the foreign population, which once dominated so much of Burma's life. The Indians have been largely expelled. The Chinese, however, still have an honored place in the urban community. Their numbers are usually estimated at 350,000 to 400,000 and many are Rangoon residents.

The Family. The social unit is the family consisting of parents and their children—not the extended family of old China and India. Marriage arises from love matches or from arrangements between parents, but the girl is almost always a willing party to the match. The status of women is high: they have access to education; they have recognized property rights; they do not change their names at marriage; and in the rare instances where a divorce occurs in Burma the woman has equality with the man. Women dominate retail trade, especially in the markets.

Religion. Even after half a century of steady secularization in Burmese society, the Buddhist monkhood, or community (*sangha*), remains the most important single feature of Burmese life. Reliable figures are not to be had, but the best estimates put the total number of monks at about 110,000, of whom about 33,000 are novices (*koyin*) and the remainder are adult monks.

Gradually, the focus of religious life has been moving from Upper Burma to Lower Burma. The greatest concentration of monasteries is still around Mandalay and Sagaing, but increasingly religious activities around Rangoon are assuming importance, especially since the ecumenical council of 1954–1962 led to the foundation of Buddhist centers of higher learning around Rangoon.

Compared to that of other religions, Buddhist ecclesiastical organization is very loose. Within the Theravada school of Buddhism, predominant in Burma, are several sects. *Thuddama* is by far the most numerous; *Shwegyin* is an important but smaller, more "puritan" branch. But religious organization in the various sects is largely dictated by the individual monasteries. The principal monasteries are large, numbering a hundred monks or more, but many monasteries are quite small, containing a dozen monks or less. Standards of discipline, piety, and learning vary considerably according to the code enforced by the abbots and senior monks. See also BUDDHISM—*Theravada*.

2. The Land and Natural Resources

Burma's river valleys and deltas, above all those of the Irrawaddy, and the hills and mountain ranges that form the country's natural boundaries, have played a great part in determining the character and history of the Burmese people and nation.

Topography. The mountains of northern Burma, and the chain of hills that runs down the eastern border forming an extension from the northern massif, are ancient geological formations from the pre-Tertiary era. In the north, the mountains rise to altitudes of nearly 20,000 feet (6,100 meters), and even the passes into Tibet are about 12,000 feet (3,660 meters) high. The eastern hills lose altitude as they run south, diminishing gradually from 8,000 to 3,000 feet (2,440 to 915 meters). The western chain, which extends from the Himalayan foothills to the Arakan Yoma, is of the Tertiary period. Almost in the center of Burma is the conical Mount Popa (4,980 feet; 1,520 meters), the Olympus of Burmese cosmology. Burmese tradition relates that it once rose from the sea.

The southern Burmese plain and its extension, the delta, have been gradually rising, while the sea has receded many miles during historical times. This is due to the silt carried down in large quantities from the mountain country by the great rivers of Burma.

The Irrawaddy, navigable for 900 miles (275 km), provides the main channel of communication and the source of irrigation and fertility for the central plain. Near Mount Popa, the Irrawaddy is joined by the Chindwin, a mighty river from the western hills. In the east of Burma is the Salween River, which rises far away in Tibet and flows parallel to the Mekong through Yünnan province, China, for hundreds of miles before dropping through the Shan States to enter the Gulf of Martaban. Between the Irrawaddy and Salween there is the smaller but faster-flowing Sittang River, also entering the Gulf. The Salween and the Sittang are navigable only in their lower stretches.

The rivers, especially the Irrawaddy, are subject to a considerable variation in level between the rainy and the dry seasons. The lands which are uncovered during the dry season provide some of the most fertile ground for cultivation.

Natural Resources. The soil of the delta is Burma's greatest natural resource, and this area is the major rice-producing region with the densest population. The plain of northern and central Burma was brought under cultivation before the delta region was, partly because it was less densely forested and partly because it lay in the path of immigration. However, the soil in this region is of only medium to low fertility. The soil in the hills is poor. The hill peoples' practice of shifting mountain-cultivation, *taungya* (sometimes called "slash and burn"), whereby the hill forests are quite rapidly denuded, leads to extensive soil erosion and devastation.

FUJIHIRA, FROM MONKMEYER

RANGOON, Burma's capital, was planned in the 1850's so that Sule Pagoda (*at right*) would be at its center.

Mineral resources include petroleum, tin, lead, zinc, wolfram, coal, and precious ores and stones. Among the latter the ruby is famous.

Climate. The greater part of Burma lies in the tropic zone. There is a well-defined rainy season from mid-May to mid-October. The coastal regions of Arakan and Tenasserim and the mountains of the extreme north have a rainfall of about 200 inches (5,080 mm) a year. The Irrawaddy delta has about 100 inches (2,540 mm). The hills of the east and west average about 80 inches (2,032 mm), and the central plain (known as the dry zone) has only 25–45 inches (635–1,143 mm). It seems probable that the deforestation of the central plain has gone hand in hand with a diminution of rainfall.

Burma's hottest season comes in May, immediately before the rains: the shade temperature is then about 100°F (38°C). The minimum temperature in southern Burma (December–January) is about 60°F (16°C), and in the north about 55°F (13°C). The delta and coastlands are humid throughout the year.

Animal Life. The wild animal life of Burma includes elephant, tiger, bear, rhinoceros, deer, and monkey. The elephant has long been employed as a work animal, especially in hauling timber. During World War II, the elephant force was halved, and numbers some 3,000 today. The "white elephant" (albino) was regarded as sacred in old Burma and was much sought after by princes.

The principal domestic work animals are the water buffalo in Lower Burma and the humped bullock in Upper Burma. Fish are plentiful in rivers and seas and (together with prawns) are an important item of diet. In the Mergui archipelago the fishing includes pearling and the collection of edible birds' nests. Burma has many reptiles and insects, some injurious to human life, especially the anophelese mosquito, carrier of malaria, which makes some riverine and submontane tracts uninhabitable.

Forests. Forests cover about 57% of Burma's surface. Tropical evergreen and deciduous forests are found throughout the lower altitudes, while the higher hills are covered with subtropical and temperate forests. Useful trees include the Toddy palm (*Borassus flabeliformis*), the cutch tree (*Acacia catechu*), and the wood oil tree (*Dipterocarpus alatus*). Man has introduced bamboo almost everywhere for domestic purposes. Hardwoods include teak, ironwood or pyinkado, and gyo.

3. Economy

Events in Burma during and after World War II conspired first to wreck and subsequently to deflect the restoration of the formerly prosperous and expanding economy.

Pre-World War II Economy. Before World War II, Burma enjoyed a favorable export trade with India, Europe, and Japan. Roughly half of Burma's exports in terms of money value were made up of rice; about one quarter were the products of the oil refineries; minerals accounted for 12 to 14%; and timber yielded about 7%. Burma led the world in the rice trade. Nearly 54% of the net rice exports of Asia came from Burma, which supplied 90% of India's rice imports, with large quantities also going to Ceylon and Malaya.

The return that Burma received for its exports was composed largely of consumer goods, for Burma produced few manufactures apart from textiles, sugar, and cement. The main industries were the Burmah Oil Company, with its oilfields in middle Burma and its refinery at Syriam, outside Rangoon, and the Burma Corporation, which worked the great Bawdwin mines, producing tungsten and tin.

Communications were served by the 2,060 miles (3,315 km) of the Burma Railways, carrying 4 million tons of freight and 20 million passengers a year, and the Irrawaddy Flotilla Company and Arracan Flotilla Company operating steamship services over some 2,550 miles (4,104 km) of waterways. During the 1920's, an extensive network of local bus and transport services, operated by local people, developed along Burma's 6,800 miles (10,950 km) of metal roads and 10,000 miles (16,100 km) of dirt roads.

Burma probably suffered more devastation during World War II than any other country. A "scorched earth" policy was carried out during the allied retreat of 1942, while heavy allied bombing of the Rangoon docks and the railroads followed for 2½ years. All exports stopped, and the peasants reverted to subsistence farming. After the liberation, much new equipment was imported and railroads, oilfields, and other installations were restored. But even before independence, Burma's leading political party made it clear that it would follow a leftist ideology, and foreign business was hesitant about reinvestment. After 1948, the country was torn by revolts, and the railroads and river steamers subjected to constant attack. However, the rebels allowed a certain amount of rice to reach Rangoon, because they relied upon the tolls they levied from the trade, and Burma's economy survived.

Postwar Agricultural Policies. The underground Communists carried out a program of land reform in areas under their control, and in response the Burmese government rushed through a land nationalization act in 1948. This act was ineffective, and it was replaced by another act in 1953. This provided for the restitution of all agricultural land, compensation being payable to expropriated landlords. Agriculturalist families were exempted from expropriation. Nationalization went ahead very slowly, and there was little actual redistribution of land; but the effect of the measure was to confirm tenants and squatters in permanent occupation of their land and to end all payment of agricultural rents. Government control over agriculture was ensured by setting up a state agricultural marketing board (SAMB) as the sole agency for purchasing rice and establishing prices. The rice was marketed abroad by the SAMB, mainly on a government to government basis, and by fixed long-term contracts.

With the Korean War, there was a boom in prices for several years. Because of fixed price contracts, the SAMB missed the highest prices, but the government's American advisers insisted that prices would remain buoyant, and Burma attempted to realize continuing high prices. But foreign buyers began to be cautious. Sales did not materialize, and stocks accumulated. During the mid-1950's, Burma ran into an acute balance of payments crisis, together with a contraction of traditional markets. It became necessary to lower prices, to search for new customers, and even to trade on a barter basis.

During the early 1960's, Burma largely returned to the former trading pattern. Output was still below prewar figures, though better than in the 1950's. Earnings from rice averaged $160–170 million per annum, and formed 70 to 80% of foreign exchange earnings. Burma's principal customers for rice were Indonesia, India, Ceylon, Britain, and Pakistan. In 1961, China emerged as a leading customer, taking 350,000 tons of rice, but subsequently sales fell to about 100,000 tons per annum, most of which is shipped (on China's account) to North Vietnam and Cuba.

Industrial and Commercial Policies. It was the declared intention of the Burmese government after independence to transform a raw-materials economy into one based on industry. During the 1950's a number of industrial installations were purchased from the United States and Europe. Machinery was imported without regard to its suitability for processing domestic materials or without consideration of the availability of personnel qualified to operate it. Almost every investment was a disaster, and this experience played a large part in turning Gen. Ne Win and his associates against development on Western lines.

Before the military take-over, the army began to gain experience in commercial and industrial operations by acquiring and managing a large number of enterprises: import agencies, retail shops, banks, even a shipping line. Soon after seizing power, General Ne Win ordered an investigation into the actual effect of foreign technical and financial aid to Burma. This inquiry showed that foreign aid had been both expensive and nonproductive. All foreign technicians were dismissed. Technical know-how was obtained on an ad hoc basis from nonaligned or Communist

SHOSTAL

THE MARKET at Inle Lake. Basic dress for both sexes is an ankle-length *longyi,* plus a blouse or tunic.

countries. All remaining foreign business interests were terminated. Although the oil industry was already on a "joint venture" basis, with dual British-Burmese management, the British were bought out. The British stake in the mines came to an end, and the British exchange banks, which still handled most foreign exchange transactions, were nationalized. Burma formally left the sterling area, which meant that its currency and credit was no longer based on London support. There followed a squeezing out of the Indian commercial community. Finally, the general put the squeeze upon the Burmese business community. Currency notes were withdrawn, and assets were required to be declared, so that all wealth had to be exposed to the scrutiny of the government. Gradually all business operations became a government monopoly.

After the mid-1960's all the processes of production and marketing became state monopolies. Emphasis was placed upon the mass market, and quality goods disappeared. New industrialization was restricted, being largely confined to the erection of power plants and other installations for public purposes. The nationalized oil industry produced about 180 million gallons (680,400,000 liters) of crude oil per annum, enough to satisfy domestic needs. However, the oilfields in Chauk and Yenangyaung in middle Burma were drying up and efforts to prospect for new oil deposits in the south failed. Attempts to revive the mining of tungsten and tin were almost entirely unsuccessful.

Transportation. Transportation remains subject to destruction by the rebels, and there is more traffic by water (where this is possible) as being more immune from sabotage. The Union of Burma Airways operates a schedule of services to all parts of the country and to cities in neighboring lands. All communications (railroads, steamships, and airplanes) formerly relied heavily upon foreign pilots and maintenance personnel, but now all foreigners have been discharged, with some adverse effects upon efficiency.

Summary. From a position of relative prosperity in prewar days, Burma has sunk into subsistence. Gross national product per capita (1965) was calculated at $92, compared with $202 for Thailand and $280 for Malaysia. Throughout Southeast Asia, only Laos had a lower GNP, though Indonesia may also have been poorer. The only satisfactory aspect of this situation was that basic food supplies were adequate for the great mass of the people: only a few city dwellers were going short of food. In other ways, Burma represented a condition that one sociologist called "shared poverty."

4. Education

In old Burma, almost all education was based on religion. The village monasteries provided teaching for boys between the ages of 6 and 12. The language of instruction was Pali, the sacred language of Buddhism, and most of the lesson time was devoted to the reading and expounding of the scriptures. Some of the larger monasteries had the character of universities, with famous scholars and sizable libraries.

The British Period. During the British period, there was a long attempt to preserve the monastic schools as the foundation of a secular educational system. However, the monks insisted on maintaining a distinction between religious and secular education, and so during the early 20th century the British administration had to seek other foundations for secular primary education. Government schools were established, as were private schools run by Christian missionaries or by individual Burmese headmasters.

In the 20th century, a career in the administration, the professions, or even in business required a competent knowledge of English. Some secondary schools thus began teaching in English, but most schools still used the vernacular languages for instruction. Higher education was entirely through the medium of English. University education was confined to Rangoon, and an Agricultural College in Mandalay.

Independence. After independence many of the private schools were brought under direct government control, and all teaching was given in Burmese, with English taught as a second language. From 1955 onward the matriculation examination for the university was entirely in the Burmese language, and university instruction was given entirely in Burmese.

A fresh attempt was made to give the monastic schools a place of importance in national education. A Mass Education Council was established to promote literacy and to inculcate higher standards of social behavior. The monks were associated with this program, to which large resources were allocated, but results were meager.

A national campaign of school development concentrated on expansion of enrollment. By 1960, 50% of children of primary school age were in school; 10% of those of middle (junior high) school age were in school; and 3% of senior high school age children were in high (senior high) school. Growth was much more rapid in urban than in rural areas. Enrollment at the university increased from about 3,000 in 1950 to 12,000 in 1960. Mandalay was given the status of a separate university in 1958.

In an attempt to break away from elite concepts of education, a Workers' University was founded in Rangoon from which persons without formal secondary schooling might graduate. However, the length of studies was too long for most of the adult students, studying in their leisure time, to be able to last the course.

Under the military regime all remaining private schools and missionary schools have been nationalized. Institutes set up under foreign auspices for the teaching of languages have been closed, and all foreign language instruction has been centralized in a government institute.

5. Government

From independence until March 1962, the Burmese government functioned under a constitution hastily drafted in 1947. This provided for a parliamentary democracy on British lines.

Constitutional Government. The executive functions of government were exercised by a prime minister and a cabinet, while the president was the titular head of state. A judiciary had a Supreme Court as its apex. The constitution provided for general elections, to be held every 5 years (or more often if necessary) to elect the parliament, the legislative branch. This consisted of two houses, the Chamber of Deputies and the Chamber of Nationalities.

Under the constitution the Shans, the Kachins, and the Karens were permitted to have their own separate states. The new Shan, Kachin, and Karen (Kawthoolei) states were later joined by a fourth state, the Kayah State, set up for a branch of the Karens, the so-called Red Karens, or Karen-ni. These states each had their own governments and state councils. But the councils were composed of members of the all-Burma, or Union, parliament elected from the area of the states, while the head of each state was appointed by the Union prime minister and was a member of the Union cabinet. The Union of Burma was not, therefore, a federation in any meaningful sense.

Between October 1958 and April 1960, the commander in chief of the army, General, or Bogyoke, Ne Win, functioned as head of the government. He was in that period careful to obtain a mandate from Parliament to govern under provisions of the 1947 constitution, and he handed power back to the civilian leaders after the general election of February 1960. However, on March 2, 1962, he intervened again and this time abrogated the 1947 constitution in its entirety. The president, the prime minister, the chief justice, and many other leading citizens were arrested and imprisoned.

Revolutionary Government. In a radio announcement, Gen. Ne Win informed the country that he would become chairman of a revolutionary council, composed of 17 members. This became the government of the Union of Burma.

Ne Win's principal statement of policy and of political philosophy is contained in the manifesto *The Burmese Way to Socialism* issued by him on April 30, 1962. This condemns parliamentary democracy in Burma as having failed to serve socialist development and proclaims "A Socialist Democratic State will be constituted to build up a successful socialist economy . . . . The vanguard and custodian of a Socialist Democratic State are primarily peasants and workers."

The revolutionary government did little to institutionalize and constitutionalize the regime. The anniversary of the military takeover (March 2) was designated Peasants' Day and became the occasion for major policy announcements. Peasants' Day 1966 saw the general issue a promise that what he called "true democracy" would eventually emerge in which power would be transferred to the people. The chief justice and principal consultant on constitutional matters, Maung Maung, was given the task of formulating proposals, but a detailed announcement was long in coming. It seemed probable that a beginning would be made with local peasants' and workers' councils, which could form the base for a "pyramid" system of councils, like the Basic Democracies in Pakistan.

Meanwhile the system of government remained autocratic and bureaucratic. The country is divided into administrative districts, with a deputy commissioner at the head of each district. A number of districts are combined in a division, under a commissioner. Each district is subdivided into "townships," for police and revenue purposes, while townships comprise groups of villages. The district remains the key administrative unit. Its head may be either an administrative civil servant or any army officer seconded to the administration. Other military liaison officers exercise an internal-security and public-relations role at the local level.

After the 1962 revolution, a number of political parties were permitted to operate, but these were gradually suppressed. There remained only the Socialist Programme party (*Lanzin*) as a kind of national rally to facilitate communication between the military government and the people. At the local level, there were a number of "national solidarity associations" designed partly as a means of organizing village guards and local defense forces and also for the purpose of disseminating the political philosophy of the government. The press was brought completely under government control. The public was encouraged to write to the press to ventilate any grievances. The whole emphasis of national life was focused upon the identification of the leaders with the people. University students, officer cadets, and other trainees in the public services were required to participate in labor in the fields,

SHWE DAGON Pagoda in Rangoon, where this family is worshiping, is one of the largest and most famous in the world.

FUJIHIRA, FROM MONKMEYER

or in road-building or some other service to the community.

Armed Forces. The armed forces remained the foundation for the revolutionary regime. The small navy is equipped with coastal patrol boats and river craft. The role of the air force is mainly in support of the army, with aircraft for ground cooperation and some subsonic strike or fighter planes. The army is mainly an infantry force, with supporting arms: artillery, engineers, and some light armor. The field army is supplemented by a force of armed police, also included in the military establishment. Total numbers in the armed forces are approximately 200,000.

For the first decade or so after independence, the armed forces drew most of their arms and equipment from British sources and sent a large number of officers to Britain for training. Later, Burma turned almost entirely to Yugoslavia, eastern Europe, and Israel as military sources of supplies and technology.

Character of the Ne Win Regime. The term "transitional politics" is often applied to the new states of Asia and Africa. Burma remained in a transitional phase after the parliamentary regime was dismissed in 1962. General Ne Win was the antithesis of a charismatic leader. He made frequent visits abroad to other heads of state, but he made few public appearances at home outside of Rangoon. He made few concessions to public opinion and enforced unpopular measures that he deemed necessary. Having neutralized almost all rivals and critics, his regime appeared to be capable of persisting in power indefinitely, unless it suffered a major assault, internally or externally. Although there were a large number of internal revolts—among the Shans, Karens, Kachins, and other minorities—and a persistent Communist underground movement, none of these effectively challenged the regime.

6. History

The first race to people Lower Burma was the Pyu, of whom little is known. Their culture was greatly influenced by Indian culture, and they are the reputed builders of the city Sri Kshetra, whose site (near modern Prome) has been investigated. Circular in shape, with gates marking the points of the compass, the city had an astrological or cosmological significance as "the Center of the Universe."

The Pyu were succeeded by the Mons, a Mongoloid people who settled throughout southern Burma and Thailand. They developed the cultivation of wet rice by techniques of irrigation. They also adopted the Buddhist teaching of the Theravada school.

About the 8th century A. D. the Burmans began to move down into north central Burma via Yünnan. They were followed by a branch of the Thai (Tai) people, known in Burma as Shans.

Early Kingdoms in Burma. The Burmans gradually subjugated the Mons, but they assimilated Mon culture, taking from them economic techniques, religion, and a written script. At first the Burmans settled in Kyaukse ("stone weir") district, near the great bend of the Irrawaddy River where all their later capitals (Ava, Amarapura, and Mandalay) were situated. Then they pushed the Mons down into central Burma, calling a halt at Minhla. They made Pagan the capital of a unified Burma and a center of religion and learning comparable in size and architectural magnificence to Angkor. With King Anawratha (reigned 1044–1077) and Kyanzittha (reigned 1084–1112), his son by an Indian queen, the kingdom established connections with Buddhism in India and Ceylon.

The Pagan Kingdom was overthrown by Mongol invasions from Yünnan, and in 1287 the Mongols sacked Pagan. The next phase of Burmese history saw the emergence of three centers of power. North-central Burma was dominated by Shan dynasties with their capital at Ava. In the south the Mons regained their autonomy with a seaport, Pegu, as their capital. In the foothills of east central Burma, the ethnic Burmese maintained a little kingdom around Toungoo (properly, *Taung-nu*, "sharp hill").

A unified kingdom emerged again in the 16th century under Tabinshwehti (reigned 1531–1550) and his successor Bayinnaung (reigned 1551–1581). Tabinshwehti captured Pegu from the Mons and made it his capital. Bayinnaung (who had been his predecessor's principal military commander) went on to subdue the Shans in the north, and also the Thai principalities, which had been vassals of China and Ayuthia (as Thailand was then called). In 1569 he conquered Ayuthia and brought back its king as his prisoner. However, Bayinnaung's triumph relied upon his personal ascendency alone. Burma did not develop administrative institutions or a standing army or a bureaucracy to provide a structure of organization. After Bayinnaung's death, his successors transferred the capital to Ava, and withdrew into isolationism. The kingdom withered. Bayinnaung's grandson Anaukpetlun (reigned 1605–1628) reunited the kingdom at the price of constant warfare. Thereafter, the kings declined in vigor and ceased to lead their armies in the field. Burma's hill neighbors became more aggressive. Finally, the Mons rose against their Burman overlords and under their able king Binnya Dala (reigned 1747–1757) they became the masters. Pegu once again became the capital, and in 1752 the Mons captured Ava.

Almost immediately, the victorious Mons were challenged by the resistance of a chieftain in whose veins flowed the Burmese blood-royal. Known to history as Alaungpaya ("the coming Buddha"), this hunter-chief proclaimed himself king. He was to reign only 8 years (1752–1760) but he not only destroyed the Mons, capturing their capital, but also set out to conquer Ayuthia. He was fatally wounded while directing his guns before Ayuthia city walls.

Alaungpaya founded the Konbaung dynasty, which ruled Burma until 1885. His successors extended the frontiers; Arakan, which had formed an independent kingdom, was absorbed in 1785. Tavoy and Tenasserim, dependencies of Siam, were annexed. Manipur was conquered (1813) and in what the Burmese called the "creeper-cutting wars," Assam was brought under Burmese rule in 1819.

Coming of the British. Burmese and Mons had already had experience with the Europeans (Portuguese, Dutch, and French) as traders and adventurers, but they were not fully aware that British dominance in India was the opening wedge in a concerted drive by the British for vast imperial power. Various British missions visited the Burmese court but failed to establish effective diplomatic communications. Between British-controlled Bengal and the Burmese provinces of Arakan and Assam there was now a common border, and frontier incidents began to irritate both sides. Finally, in 1824, a Burmese army under General Bandula advanced into Bengal. His troops were ejected, and British forces invaded Burmese territory, occupying the port of Rangoon, which had begun to take over trade from Pegu. Negotiations were rejected by the Burmese until the British had advanced deep into Lower Burma. Then, by the Treaty of Yandabo (1826), peace was restored but at the price of British annexation of the Burmese provinces Assam, Arakan, and Tenasserim.

Relations with the British deteriorated again during the reign (1846–1853) of Pagan Min, a cruel and temperamental Burmese monarch. The European merchants at Rangoon protested their treatment by Burmese authorities, and a squadron of the Royal Navy arrived to demand reforms. Commodore Lambert pursued negotiations in a belligerent manner, and hostilities broke out. Once again a British force occupied Rangoon and advanced up the Irrawaddy. This time there were no peace moves at all from the Burmese side, but a younger brother of Pagan Min, Mindon Min, marched on the capital and deposed the king. Mindon Min (reigned 1853–1878) was an admirable ruler—religious, scholarly, upright, undaunted—but he mistakenly assumed that the British would have no quarrel with him now that his brother was deposed. However, the governor-general of India, Lord Dalhousie, was an expansionist, and he proclaimed the annexation of the province of Pegu (all of Lower Burma) in December 1852.

British Rule in Lower Burma. The territory now under British rule had suffered from centuries of devastation by war, and its population was sparse. However, soil and climate were ideal for the cultivation of rice, and the mid-19th century was a time when a demand for raw materials was growing fast, while improved transport made a world system of trade possible. Under British administration vast areas of land in both Upper and Lower Burma were brought under cultivation: in Lower Burma between 1855 and 1930 the lands under cultivation (most of them in paddy rice) were increased elevenfold.

The vast expansion in peasant farming in Lower Burma was made possible by a continuous migration from Upper Burma. The ethnic Burmese element in the population in the south greatly expanded. Although there was a noticeable increase in the standard of living of the peasants under British rule, the foreigners absorbed much of the profits. British and other European business firms were set up in Rangoon to process and export rice. Indian bankers also entered the rice trade, acting as middlemen between the Burmese peasants and the European exporters. Toward the end of the 19th century Rangoon took on the appearance of an Indian city. Between 1875 and 1900 the population increased from 100,000 to nearly 250,000.

Kingdom of Ava. Meanwhile, in independent Burma (or "the Kingdom of Ava," as the British termed it), King Mindon was attempting to modernize his medieval country. A monetary system was introduced, taxes were payable in money, and officials of the state were paid salaries instead of "eating" the country as of old. Mindon was very interested in religion, and in 1871 he summoned a great council (*sangayana*) of the leading monks of Burma, together with some from abroad, in order to codify and purify the scriptures.

On the death of Mindon, some of the leading ministers proclaimed a lesser son of the late king Thibaw Min as the new ruler. The ministers hoped that this inexperienced and retiring youth would be a tool in their hands, but instead he fell under the influence of one of the queens dowager and his own wife, Princess Supayalat, who persuaded him to evade the pressure of British interests from Lower Burma by obtaining treaties and other kinds of support from France, Italy, and other European powers. This policy had some success during the period when Jules Ferry, foreign minister of France, was pursuing expansionist schemes in Southeast Asia and a pacific Liberal government was in office in Britain. However, Ferry's Vietnamese schemes collapsed and the British Liberals gave way to a Conservative ministry.

At this moment (in August 1885) a dispute between a British firm and the Burmese (Ava) government came to a head. The Bombay-Burmah Trading Company was working a concession for the extraction of teak from Upper Burma, paying a royalty to the King based on numbers of logs felled and cleared down river. Some Burmese foresters alleged that the company was not making a true return of logs exported, and the Hlutdaw, or royal court, ruled that the company must pay the King a compensation of $366,665. The government of India intervened, insisting that the case be submitted to an arbitrator. On October 22 a time limit was imposed, and additional terms were demanded by the British. The ultimatum expired on November 10, and a British flotilla used this pretext to steam up to Mandalay, the Ava capital. Thibaw was rapidly exiled, and on Jan. 1, 1886, Upper Burma was annexed by Britain. Later it was combined with Lower Burma to form a province of the British-Indian Empire.

Burmese Nationalist Movements. Most of the officials of the old royal government took service under the British, and their sons went through the new Western-type high schools and colleges to become lawyers and civil servants. The first organized movement among the new English-educated class was the Young Men's Buddhist Association, founded in 1908 along the lines of the YMCA in order to undertake social service. The first political organization was a branch of the Indian National Congress, established in Rangoon by an Indian, P. J. Mehta. Only one or two Burmese took any interest in the Congress, but Chit Hlaing (1879–1952), a lawyer, was to emerge as the first recognized politician to speak for Burma.

Political action first began in 1920, when Burmese Nationalists proposed the establishment of an autonomous University of Rangoon—but under a wide measure of government control. The British administration ignored this Burmese agitation for an autonomous university, and Burmese leaders called for a national boycott of the whole government system of organization and for the creation of a network of "national schools" to absorb the withdrawn students. The governor of Burma and his superiors in London realized that a new spirit was stirring, and a series of political reforms were hastily applied to Burma. After 1923, Burma had a legislature of 103 members, of whom 79 were selected on a limited franchise. Ministers were appointed from among the elected members to take charge of certain departments of government. A political organization, the General Council of Burmese Associations (GCBA) was set up, led by Chit Hlaing; but almost immediately it split into factions. The lawyer-politicians made little impression on the masses, who found an alternative leadership from monks who aroused the people against the foreigners who had (so they said) cast down Buddhism from its rightful place.

Another form of protest was a rebellion which broke out in 1931 in Lower Burma. A former government clerk, Saya San, proclaimed himself king, asserting that he possessed magical powers to overcome the British. He attracted the support of thousands of rural folk who fought British-Indian troops, believing that magical tatooing had made them invulnerable.

In 1930 a report on constitutional reform was published which recommended that Burma be separated from India and be granted a further installment of self-government. Ba Maw led the movement against separation and emerged with the largest group in the legislature. However, the British government decided to go ahead with separation, and in April 1937, Burma ceased to be administered under the government of India. A general election under an enlarged franchise was held in December 1936. The old GCBA was the largest party, but Ba Maw succeeded in assembling a number of political allies to become the first prime minister of Burma.

MONKMEYER

BURMA ROAD, winding 700 miles over the mountains, was the chief supply line to China during World War II.

A new style in politics was being created in Burma by a party with almost no representation in the legislature—the Thakin (or "Master") party. Its leadership included young men fresh from the university, among whom were "Thakin" Aung San (1916–1947), "Thakin" Nu (1907–), and "Thakin" Shu Maung (1910–), known today as Gen. Ne Win. The Thakins took over the role of the political monks as men of the people. Their main political weapon was the strike. They perfected this weapon in the strike of university students in 1937, but their most important use of it was the general strike of workers in the oil industry in 1938.

The Thakins turned increasingly to nondemocratic ideologies—first to socialism, then to communism and fascism. Many were admirers of Japan, though Nu supported China's struggle against Japanese militarism. When the Japanese invaded Burma in December 1941, they were accompanied by the "Thirty Comrades" from the Thakin, including Ne Win, who raised the Burma Independence Army. The Japanese made Ba Maw head of a puppet administration, and on Aug. 1, 1943, Burma was proclaimed an "independent state," with Ba Maw as Naing-gan daw Adipati, or generalissimo. The Thakins were well represented in his cabinet, while Aung San as defense minister was asked to reconstitute an army, which was commanded by Ne Win.

Meanwhile, a powerful anti-Japanese resistance movement had been created by the Karens. A militant group of ex-Thakin Communists (known as Red Flags) had also gone underground. Late in 1944, the Thakins in Ba Maw's government began to feel that they had backed the wrong side, and made overtures to underground British forces. As a result, the secret Anti-Fascist Organization (AFO) came into being. After the British-Indian army had advanced into Burma and taken Mandalay, the AFO began to "go underground." First, Thakin Than Tun left to organize resistance in middle Burma, and finally Bogyoke Aung San went into the jungle with his Burma National Army (BNA). On May 3, 1945, the British reoccupied Rangoon, and within a few weeks the Japanese army in Burma dissolved.

The allied commander in chief for Southeast Asia, Admiral Mountbatten, issued a directive that those who had cooperated with the Japanese would not be penalized. This left Aung San as the most powerful man in Burma, as Ba Maw had fled to Japan. In August 1945, the AFO was renamed Anti-Fascist People's Freedom League (AFPFL). The struggle from this point on was for independence.

Independence and After. Britain's new Labour government was ready to agree to Burmese independence, and it only remained for Aung San to eliminate rivals and gain the support of the hill peoples. Than Tun, his main rival, the leader of the largest group of Communists (White Flags), was dropped. All the hill peoples except the Karens were conciliated. On Jan. 27, 1947, the Attlee-Aung San agreement was signed, giving Burma full independence within one year. A constituent assembly was elected in April. Former members of the BNA had been incorporated in a quasi-military body, the People's Volunteer Organization (PVO). The PVO ensured an electoral victory for the AFPFL. The assembly met, but before it could ratify the constitution, Aung San, along with five other cabinet ministers, was murdered by a political rival. Thakin Nu took over as prime minister, and independence arrived on Jan. 4, 1948.

Almost at once, the White Flag Communists went into rebellion. Most of the PVO followed, and turned upon the Karens, who formed their own private army, the Karen National Defense Organization (KNDO). In January 1949 the Karens started the largest and most dangerous of the revolts. Slowly, the government of U Nu (he dropped the title "Thakin") regained control of the towns, the railroads, and other communications. The rebels remained at large in the jungles and hills. With the collapse of the Kuomintang in China, some Nationalist troops retreated over the Burma border to add a further warring force to the KNDO, the Communists, and other rebels.

However, Burma's shattered economy revived a little. U Nu resolved to embark on a program of social and economic reconstruction. He hired a team of American economists and engineers who produced a report which became the basis for a socialist program entitled "Towards a Welfare State." Certain ambitious projects were commissioned, but the program accomplished little. Army leaders became increasingly critical of the Nu government, while the more extreme Socialists in his cabinet pressed for more state industrialization and less attention for welfare works. Finally, in 1958, the cabinet split into two factions, the so-called "Clean AFPFL" (because it accused its opponents of corruption) and the "Stable AFPFL" (because it accused its opponents of weakness). Nu led the "Clean" group; the Marxist-Socialists formed the "Stable" faction. In October 1958, power was passed to the army.

The army staged a campaign against corruption and incompetence and an intensified drive against the rebels. Nevertheless, the army regime incurred widespread unpopularity, and Ne Win organized a general election to transfer power back to parliament. Nu won a landslide victory. He placed a great emphasis on religion and in August 1961 amended the constitution to make Buddhism the state religion. In other directions, his regime lacked drive and gave the army the excuse to intervene again, this time decisively.

During his years as prime minister, Nu had been an ardent internationalist. His principal colleague was Nehru, and Nu had espoused Nehru's philosophy of nonalignment. During his premiership, friendly relations were cultivated with all nations. However, Burma had very unfortunate experiences with both the Soviet Union and the United States with regard to economic aid and unlike most Asian countries rejected any further dependence on foreign aid. Increasingly, China came to dominate Burma's international calculations.

Since the time of Bayinnaung, the Burmese and Chinese held entirely opposed views of where their common frontier lay. During the last years of British rule an attempt was made to adjudicate the frontier by agreement, but Chiang Kai-shek withheld his agreement, having large territorial designs in north and east Burma. After the Communists came to power in China, there were protracted negotiations with Burma. Agreement was suddenly attained during the first of Ne Win's military governments, and on Jan. 28, 1960, the general signed a treaty with Chou En-lai whereby China was ceded two small strips of territory previously under the Burmese flag and in return gave up all the vast historical claims of the past.

The price of this concession was the withdrawal of Burma from active relations with all major powers except China. This suited Ne Win's own policies. He was determined that American activity in Burma should cease (he attributed Burma's failures in economic development to faulty American advice and matériel). He wanted the Indians out of Burma, and he compelled the surviving Indian community to close down its firms and leave the country. Finally, the last remnants of British dominance—the banks, and the one or two surviving industrial concerns—were expropriated. In general, the Burmese seemed ready to accept this isolation, though there were signs that the growing Chinese presence was resented. In June 1967, anti-Chinese demonstrations in Rangoon and elsewhere led to protests from Peking.

HUGH TINKER, *University of London*

Bibliography

Andrus, James R., *Burmese Economic Life* (Stanford, Calif., 1948).
Christian, John L., *Modern Burma* (Berkeley, Calif., 1942).
Hall, D. G. E., *Burma*, 2d ed. (London 1956).
Johnstone, William C., *Burma's Foreign Policy: A Study in Neutralism* (Cambridge, Mass., 1963).
Maung Maung, *Burma in the Family of Nations* (Amsterdam, Netherlands, 1956).
Nu, Thakin, *Burma Under the Japanese* (London 1954).
Smith, Donald Eugene, *Religion and Politics in Burma* (Princeton 1965).
Tinker, Hugh, *The Union of Burma: A Study of the First Years of Independence*, 4th ed. (London, 1967).
Walinsky, Louis J., *Economic Development in Burma, 1951–60* (New York 1962).
Woodman, Dorothy, *The Making of Burma* (London 1962).

BURMA ROAD, bûr′mə, a highway opened in 1939 between Kunming, capital of Yünnan province in southwestern China, and Lashio in east central Burma. It follows a trade route at least 2,000 years old. Until the construction of the Burma Road, traffic along this ancient route was confined to mule trains.

Japan's occupation of the Chinese coast during the Sino-Japanese War, in the late 1930's made it necessary for China to find an alternative outlet to the sea and a route for war matériel. For this reason the Chinese conceived the plan to build a highway along the old trail to Burma, which was then under British control. Work began in 1937 to link Kunming with Muse, just across the Burmese border. Thousands of Chinese labored with primitive tools along the 700 miles (1,100 km) of road, which winds snakewise over mountain ridges and along river valleys. The casualty rate among workers was high, but in January 1939 the road was declared open.

The Chinese section of the Burma Road runs from Kunming to Tali, then across the Mekong and Salween rivers to Wanting, the last post in China, and on to Muse. The Burmese section consists of 112 miles (180 km) of mountain road connecting Muse with Lashio, from which there are rail links via Mandalay to Rangoon, on the Bay of Bengal.

Burmese political leaders were not in favor of the road and insisted on the levy of customs dues on goods in transit. The road was closed by the British government, under Japanese pressure, from July 18 to Oct. 18, 1940. During this time the road was much improved and an American transportation expert was placed in charge of truck operations. After the Burma Road was reopened, Japan tried to close the road by bombing the Chinese section, but during 1940–1941 a maximum of 18,000 tons per month was carried into China. Return traffic was about one third of this total.

After going to war with Britain and the United States in December 1941 the Japanese overran Burma, and the Allies had to find a new route into China. During 1943 and 1944 they reconquered part of northern Burma and constructed a military road from Ledo in northeastern Assam (India) to Myitkyina in northern Burma. In January 1945 it was named the Stilwell Road in honor of the American general Joseph W. Stilwell. By way of Bhamo, communication was reestablished with Muse and the old Burma Road. A number of convoys passed over the Stilwell, or Ledo, Road, but the British recapture of Rangoon on May 3, 1945, made it possible to bypass the long overland haul via Assam. The Japanese surrender in August 1945 rendered the Burma Road unnecessary as a supply route into China and traffic over the road became negligible. An agreement signed between Communist China and the Union of Burma in 1954 to promote trade between Yünnan province and Burma had little actual effect on the situation.

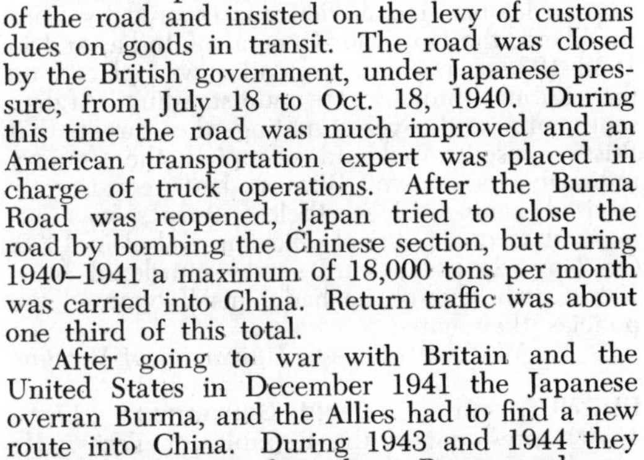

HUGH TINKER, *University of London*

THE BURMA ROAD DURING WORLD WAR II

BURNABY, bûr′nə-bē, is a district municipality in southwestern British Columbia, Canada, on the north side of the Fraser River, between Vancouver and New Westminster. Its area is 36 square miles (93 sq km). Burnaby is an industrial and wholesale-distribution center, with sawmills, paper mills, and oil refineries. Other industries are metal fabrication and food processing.

Simon Fraser University, imaginatively designed on top of Burnaby Mountain, was opened in 1965. The municipality also has a provincial technical institution. The area was named for Robert Burnaby, an early settler. Burnaby was incorporated in 1892. Population: 124,216.

BURNAND, bûr-nand′, **Sir Francis Cowley** (1836–1917), British editor, playwright, and humorist, known for his editorship of *Punch* (1880–1906) and for his burlesques of the works of other dramatists. He was born in London in Nov. 29, 1836, the son of a stockbroker. At Eton he wrote a farce that was performed professionally, and at Trinity College, Cambridge, he founded the A. D. C. (Amateur Dramatic Club). He then studied for the Anglican priesthood at Cuddesdon Theological College until his conversion to Roman Catholicism in 1858. He next studied law, and was admitted to the bar in 1862. By this time, however, he had already achieved some success as a writer and consequently practiced rarely.

Burnand's best-known books are *Happy Thoughts* (1866) and *More Happy Thoughts* (1871), which are collections of his pieces from *Punch*. Of his more than 100 stage burlesques, the most popular was *Black-Eyed Susan* (1866). He also collaborated with Sir Arthur Sullivan on the light operas *Cox and Box* (1867) and *Contrabandista* (1867).

Burnand was knighted in 1902. He died at Ramsgate on April 21, 1917.

OSCAR BROWNSTEIN, *University of Iowa*

BURNE-JONES, bûrn jōnz, **Sir Edward Coley** 1833–1898), English painter and designer, who was a follower of the Pre-Raphaelite brotherhood and a major figure in the arts and crafts movement. His style, which influenced Aubrey Beardsley and the art nouveau movement, has a dreamy elegance akin to the late work of Dante Gabriel Rossetti, but lacks Rossetti's vigor and detail.

Early Life. Burne-Jones was born in Birmingham in Aug. 28, 1833. At Exeter College, Oxford, he became an enduring friend of William Morris, with whom he shared an enthusiasm for medieval legends, especially Malory's *Le Morte Darthur*, and for the artistic theories of John Ruskin. In 1856, Burne-Jones left Oxford for London to study with Rossetti, under whose

THE TATE GALLERY, LONDON

The Golden Stairs (1880), one of the later works of Edward Burne-Jones.

direction he worked on the frescoes for the debating hall at Oxford.

Career. Sienese art, with its linear patterns and rhythms and its jewel-like colors, made a strong impression on Burne-Jones when he visited Italy for the first time in 1859. His own paintings during this period were mostly watercolors. Among the best examples are *Sidonia von Bork* and *Clara von Bork,* both painted in 1860 and now in the Tate Gallery, London.

Gradually Burne-Jones abandoned watercolor for oils. His reputation in this medium was made in 1877, when eight of his paintings were shown at the opening of the Grosvenor Gallery, London. Among his most famous later works are *The Golden Stairs* (1880; Tate Gallery), *King Cophetua and the Beggar Maid* (1884; Tate Gallery), and *The Star of Bethlehem* (1891; Birmingham City Museum and Art Gallery).

In the decorative arts Burne-Jones had a far-reaching influence through his association with Morris and the Kelmscott Press. From 1861 on, he designed many stained glass windows, among the best of which are those at Christ Church, Oxford; Salisbury Cathedral; and the Cathedral of Birmingham. He also designed mosaic decorations for the American Church in Rome and several tapestries. His book illustrations for the Kelmscott Press include the 1897 edition of *Works of Geoffrey Chaucer.*

Burne-Jones died in London, on June 17, 1898. *Memorials of Edward Burne-Jones* was published by his widow in 1904.

WILLIAM GERDTS
University of Maryland

BURNELL, bûr-nel′, **Arthur Coke** (1840–1882), English Orientalist. He was born at St. Briavels, Gloucestershire, and attended King's College, Cambridge. While employed in the Indian civil service, he became interested in ancient Sanskrit manuscripts. His numerous works include *Handbook of South Indian Palaeography* (1874) and *Classified Index to the Sanskrit MSS in the Palace at Tanjore* (1880). He died at West Stratton, Hampshire, on Oct. 12, 1882.

BURNES, bûrnz, **Sir Alexander** (1805–1841), British diplomat and explorer in India and Afghanistan. He was born in Montrose, Scotland, on May 16, 1805, and was appointed to a cadetship in the Bombay Infantry in 1821.

Known for his interest in western and northern India and the surrounding regions, Burnes was sent to Lahore in 1830 carrying gifts from the King of England to Ranjit Singh, leader of the Sikh Confederacy and a British ally. In 1832, Burnes undertook a mission into Afghanistan and then traveled across the Hindu Kush mountains to Bokhara (Bukhara), the Caspian and Turkoman country, and Teheran, from which he made his way south to the Persian Gulf and Bombay. The account of his travels was published in 1834 as *Travels in Bokhara.*

In 1837, while heading a political mission to Kabul in Afghanistan, Burnes recommended negotiations with Dost Mohammed, the dominant Afghan leader. His advice was ignored by Lord Auckland, the Governor-General of India, and in 1838–1839 a rejected pretender was placed on the Kabul throne. Misunderstanding Afghan sentiments and overestimating the threat that Russia posed, Auckland occupied the country militarily, a move Burnes had consistently advised against. Nevertheless Burnes was appointed second political officer in Kabul in 1839. On Nov. 2, 1841, Burnes was murdered by a Kabul mob, though he had himself opposed the policies they hated.

WALTER HAUSER, *University of Virginia*

BURNET, bûr′nət, **David Gouverneur** (1788–1870), president of the Republic of Texas. He was born on April 4, 1788, in Newark, N. J. After working in a New York countinghouse, he joined abortive expeditions (1806 and 1808) to free Venezuela from Spain. Next he entered business in Ohio and Louisiana and then spent two years with the Comanche Indians in Texas.

After practicing law in Ohio for a time, Burnet moved back to Texas in 1826, joined the Texas separatists, and in 1834 was named a district judge. On March 17, 1836, he was chosen interim president of the new Republic of Texas. Plagued by lack of funds and army disorganization, he served only until October 22. But in 1838 he was elected vice president of Texas, and he was president again briefly in 1841 after the resignation of Mirabeau B. Lamar. Defeated for a full presidential term, he farmed until 1846 and then became Texas secretary of state for a year after Texas entered the union.

In 1866, Burnet was elected to the U. S. Senate, but Reconstruction policy barred him from serving. In 1868 he took part in the Democratic National Convention and was a presidential elector. He spent his last years with friends in Galveston, where he died on Dec. 5, 1870. A city and county in Texas are named for him.

WAYNE GARD, *Author of "Rawhide Texas"*

BURNET, bûr'nət, **Sir Frank Macfarlane** (1899–), Australian virologist, who made wide-ranging and imaginative contributions to theoretical biology in the fields of virology and immunology. Burnet shared the 1960 Nobel Prize in medicine and physiology with Sir Peter Medawar for their "discovery of acquired immunological tolerance."

Contributions to Science. Burnet was the first to study in detail the multiplication of bacteriophages, the viruses that grow inside bacteria. This work laid the foundation for many later studies in genetics and molecular biology. In 1932 he perfected the technique of growing viruses in chick embryos. For more than 20 years, until the perfection of tissue culture methods, Burnet's technique was the standard way of isolating and studying viruses. Burnet also learned much about the mechanism of influenza virus growth and its enzymic and genetic properties and isolated a rickettsial organism, *Rickettsia burnetii,* which causes Q fever (q.v.).

In 1949, Burnet published, with F. Fenner, the immunological monograph that was to win him the Nobel Prize years later. In it he predicted that if an antigen (vaccine) were given to an animal in embryonic life, the animal would not form antibodies (proteins that combine with antigens to neutralize the effect of the antigen) against the vaccine, but would instead become tolerant of the antigen and accept it as if it were a normal constituent of its body. This prediction was experimentally validated by Peter Medawar and his colleagues in 1953. The discovery of acquired immunological tolerance had important implications for organ transplantation and cancer research.

Burnet's next major contribution to immunological theory came in 1957, when he enunciated the controversial "clonal selection" theory of antibody formation. According to this theory, there are many different sorts of lymphocytes (a kind of white blood cell), each genetically predestined to form the antibody for a particular antigen. The invasion of an antigen stimulates the corresponding sort of lymphocyte to begin reproducing, and results in the creation of a clone (a group of genetically identical descendants of a single cell) of lymphocytes, all capable of producing the antibody that neutralizes the invading antigen. The clonal theory helped scientists, who had previously concentrated on the antibody molecules in the bloodstream, to direct their attention to the antibody-forming cells.

After 1960, Burnet became progressively more interested in human disease processes, especially autoimmune diseases—those diseases in which the white blood cells of an organism attack certain of the organism's own tissues.

Life. Burnet was born in Traralgon, Victoria, Australia, on Sept. 3, 1899. He received his M. D. from the University of Melbourne in 1923 and joined the staff of the Walter and Eliza Hall Institute in Melbourne. He served as assistant director (1928–1944) of the institute and then as director (1944–1965). He was knighted in 1951 and received the Order of Merit in 1958. He was elected president of the Australian Academy of Science in 1965. He wrote hundreds of technical articles and numerous books—many of them classics in their field.

G. J. V. Nossal, *Walter and Eliza Hall Institute, Melbourne, Australia*

BURNET, bûr'net, **Gilbert** (1643–1715), English bishop and historian. He was born in Edinburgh, Scotland, on Sept. 18, 1643. He graduated from the University of Aberdeen, and devoted himself to the study of law and theology. In 1673 he was made chaplain in ordinary to Charles II, who held him in high esteem for his able defense of the role of bishops in the church. Several bishoprics were offered him, all of which he refused. In London, during a period of public alarm over the growth of Roman Catholicism in England, Burnet began work on his *History of the Reformation in England.* The first volume appeared in 1679, at the time of the popish plot, and gained for Burnet the thanks of both houses of Parliament. Two more volumes followed in 1681 and 1714.

Burnet opposed Charles II both for his mishandling of government affairs and for questionable aspects of his private life. He was associated with the Whig opposition party and actively supported the Prince of Orange, whom in 1689 he accompanied to England as chaplain. Soon thereafter he became bishop of Salisbury. He denounced the ecclesiastical courts as the most corrupt in the land; he opposed parliamentary attendance of bishops as inimical to the execution of pastoral duties; and he supported the Act of Toleration of 1689. He upheld against Roman Catholics the validity of Anglican ordinations, wrote a commentary on the Thirty-nine Articles of Religion, and conceived the idea for what became known as Queen Anne's Bounty (aid to the poor out of taxes paid the crown).

Burnet's *History of My Own Time,* published posthumously, is considered a reliable historical memoir. He died in London on March 15, 1715.

BURNET, bûr'net, **Thomas** (1635?–1715), English clergyman. He was born in Croft, Yorkshire. He first became known for his treatise *Telluris theoria sacra* (1681), which he later translated into English as *Sacred Theory of the Earth.* This contains a theory of the earth's structure that philosophers used in attempts to reconcile the Biblical account of the Creation, Paradise, and the Deluge with scientific principles.

In 1685, Burnet became master of Charterhouse, and after the Revolution of 1688 he was appointed chaplain in ordinary and clerk of the closet to King William III. In 1692 he published *Archaeologiae philosophicae,* in which he combated the literal interpretation of the Fall of Man. This work led to his removal from office. Burnet died in London on Sept. 27, 1715.

BURNET, bûr'nət, **William** (1688–1729), English colonial governor in America. He was born in The Hague, Netherlands, in March 1688. His early education was supervised in part by Isaac Newton. After serving as comptroller-general of customs in England, he was appointed governor of New York and New Jersey on April 19, 1720. He urged the New York Assembly to repair provincial defenses, and he forbade the sale of Indian goods to the French, thus keeping the lucrative fur trade and other trade within the empire. Due to pressure from those who resented his establishment of a chancery court and from some who opposed the curtailment of French Canadian trade, Burnet was transferred to the governorship of Massachusetts. He died in Boston on Sept. 7, 1729.

BURNET, bûr-net′, any of the members of the genus *Sanguisorba* of the rose family. Most are perennials native to the north temperate zone. They have pinnately compound leaves with serrate leaflets. The young leaves are sometimes used in salads. The small individual flowers are crowded into tall spikes that are conspicuous for their long stamens (pollen-bearing organs), which extend from the flowers and give the spikes a feathery appearance. The American or Canadian burnet, *S. canadensis,* reaches 5 feet (1½ meters). It grows in marshes and damp prairies, and its white flowers appear from July to September.

JOAN E. RAHN, *Lake Forest College, Ill.*

BURNETT, bûr-net′, **Carol** (1935–), American comedienne and singer. She is best known for her portrayal of the raucous princess in the off-Broadway musical *Once upon a Mattress* (1959–1960) and her comic performances on television. She was born in San Antonio, Texas, on April 26, 1935, and studied journalism and drama at the University of California at Los Angeles. She first attracted wide notice in 1957 with her night club rendition of the comedy song *I Made a Fool of Myself over John Foster Dulles.* Miss Burnett made many guest appearances on television and played in the Broadway musical *Fade Out–Fade In* and the film *Who's Been Sleeping in My Bed?* (both 1964). She won "Emmy" (1962) and Peabody (1963) awards.

BURNETT, bûr-net′, **Frances Hodgson** (1849–1924), Anglo-American writer, who is best known for the children's book *Little Lord Fauntleroy* (q.v.). Frances Eliza Hodgson was born in Manchester, England, on Nov. 24, 1849, and in 1865 emigrated with her family to Tennessee, where she lived near Knoxville until her marriage to Dr. S. M. Burnett in 1873. Between the ages of 16 and 20 she wrote stories under her family name, Hodgson, for magazines including *Godey's Lady's Book* and *Scribner's.* Her first success was *That Lass o' Lowries* (1877), a novel based on the colliery life she had known in England. She wrote many novels, but it is her books for children that brought her fame. *Little Lord Fauntleroy* (1886) set a fashion in clothes for boys. The book was made into a play and a motion picture. Mrs. Burnett also wrote *Sara Crewe,* later known as *A Little Princess,* which also was dramatized and filmed. She died in Plandome, N. Y., on Oct. 29, 1924.

BURNETT, bûr-net′, **Peter Hardeman** (1807–1895), American pioneer, who was the first elected governor of California. He was born in Nashville, Tenn., on Nov. 15, 1807, and later became a lawyer in Missouri. In 1842 he crossed the plains to Oregon, where he became a leader in the provisional government, serving as a legislator and a judge of the supreme court. Burnett joined the gold rush to California in 1848, and after a time in the gold fields he moved to San Francisco to practice law. In 1849 he was successful in his bid for the governorship. After about one year in office, however, he resigned (1851) because of personal financial problems. In 1857 he was appointed to the state supreme court. He was president of a San Francisco bank from 1863 until he retired in 1880. He died in San Francisco on May 17, 1895.

H. BRETT MELENDY
Coauthor of "Governors of California"

BURNETT, bûr-net′, **Whit** (1899–), American editor, anthologist, and short-story writer, whose *Story* magazine introduced many important American writers. He was born in Salt Lake City, Utah, on Aug. 14, 1899, and attended universities in Utah and California. He worked as a reporter and editor for newspapers and news services in the United States and Europe and organized a foreign news service in Vienna.

It was in Vienna that Burnett, with his first wife Martha Foley, began the magazine *Story* in 1931. Later published in Majorca, then in the United States from 1933 to 1965, *Story* is credited with the first publication and early support of William Saroyan, Carson McCullers, Truman Capote, Tennessee Williams, Norman Mailer, and J. D. Salinger. Burnett also edited numerous short-story anthologies and wrote *A Maker of Signs* (1934) and *The Literary Life and the Hell With It* (1939).

BURNETT, bûr-net′, **William Riley** (1899–), American writer. He was born in Springfield, Ohio, on Nov. 25, 1899. After a year at Ohio State University, he became a statistician for the state of Ohio in 1921. While holding this job he tried to become a writer, but was unable to sell his work. In 1927 he gave up his job and moved to Chicago, where he became imbued with the spirit of the city. His first published novel, *Little Caesar* (1929), reflects this influence. This novel, which became a best seller and was turned into a successful motion picture, is an example of the "hard-boiled" school of fiction, usually involving detectives and gangsters. Many of Burnett's later works are in this vein. They include *High Sierra* (1940), *Nobody Lives Forever* (1944), and *The Asphalt Jungle* (1949).

BURNEY, bûr′nē, **Charles** (1726–1814), English organist, composer, and one of the first music historians. He was born in Shrewsbury, England, on April 12, 1726. His studies, first under the organist of Chester Cathedral and then at Shrewsbury with his half-brother James, culminated in his apprenticeship to Dr. Thomas Arne in London from 1744 to 1747. His first success as a composer was the music for *Queen Mab,* a pantomime produced by David Garrick at the Drury Lane Theatre. Illness obliged Burney to leave London in 1751, and he became organist at St. Margaret's Church, King's Lynn, Norfolk. Here he began his noted *History of Music.*

In 1760, Burney returned to London and in 1769 was awarded the degree of doctor of music at Oxford. He later became a fellow of the Royal Society. The first volume of his *History of Music* appeared in 1776, the second in 1782, the third and fourth in 1789. His second daughter was Fanny Burney (q.v.). He died in London on April 12, 1814.

BURNEY, bûr′nē, **Fanny** (1752–1840), English author, who was the best-known woman novelist of the late 18th century. She was also known by her married name, Mme. d'Arblay. Her novels departed from the coarse-grained language and vulgar situations used by such earlier writers as Fielding and Smollett and helped set a pattern for the more decorous fiction of the Victorian period. Her diaries and letters, published after her death, remain an important source of information about many famous contemporaries.

Life. Frances Burney was born at King's Lynn, Norfolk, on June 13, 1752, the daughter of Charles Burney, a noted organist and music historian. She studied at home, and when her father moved to London, she was introduced to his circle of friends, including Dr. Johnson, Edmund Burke, and Mrs. Thrale. Fanny Burney's novel *Evelina, or A Young Lady's Entrance Into the World,* published anonymously in 1778, won her an even wider circle of notable admirers when its authorship was revealed. Her fame grew with the appearance of *Cecilia, or Memoirs of an Heiress* (5 vols., 1782).

In 1786 the Queen appointed Fanny Burney to the position of second keeper of the robes. Though considered a great honor, this office entailed disagreeable associations and long hours of tedious attendance on the Queen, and after five years Fanny Burney became ill and was allowed to retire from court with a small pension.

Her health gradually improved, she met various French émigrés fleeing the French Revolution, and in 1793, at the age of 42, she married one of them, Alexandre Gabriel d'Arblay, a former adjutant general to Lafayette. She had a son and, to help support the family, resumed writing. From 1802 to 1812 she lived with her husband in France, where he secured a government post under Napoleon. In 1812 the couple returned to England, where she continued to write after her husband's death in 1818. She died in London on Jan. 6, 1840.

Writings. As an 18th century novelist, Fanny Burney knew the predilection of her reading public for sentiment, moralizing, and instruction in manners. Familiar with etiquette books for ladies, she especially appealed to the growing number of women readers by providing examples of decorous behavior in society. Her novels *Evelina* and *Cecilia* also skillfully satirize coarseness, delineate character (the heroines reflect the development of her own personality), and have somewhat natural-sounding dialogue. However, in her two later novels, *Camilla, or A Picture of Youth* (5 vols., 1796) and *The Wanderer, or Female Difficulties* (5 vols., 1814), her artistry was subordinated to an overriding didacticism, which resulted in priggish characters, excessive moralizing, and melodrama.

Fanny Burney was also a diarist and a great hoarder of letters, and her fame may eventually rest on her vivid and often humorous memoirs. In 1832 she published the *Memoirs of Dr. Burney* (3 vols.). Two other important works, appearing posthumously, were *The Diary and Letters of Madame d'Arblay* (7 vols., 1842–1846) and *The Early Diary of Frances Burney* (2 vols., 1889). A great number of her letters, as well as additional diaries, still remain in manuscript.

MAURICE J. QUINLAN, *Boston College*

Further Reading: An outstanding biography is Joyce Hemlow's *History of Fanny Burney* (New York 1958). Others include Emily Hahn's *A Degree of Prudery: A Biography of Fanny Burney* (New York 1950) and Christopher Lloyd's *Fanny Burney* (London 1936).

BURNHAM, bûr'nəm, an English publishing family, descended from Joseph Moses Levy (1811–1888), publisher of England's first penny newspaper.

1ST BARON BURNHAM (1833–1916) was born Edward Levy in London on Dec. 28, 1833, but took his uncle's name of Levy Lawson in 1875. His father, Joseph Levy, acquired the newly founded *Daily Telegraph* in 1855 and soon afterward made Edward its editor.

Fanny Burney, from a portrait by Edward F. Burney.

NATIONAL PORTRAIT GALLERY, LONDON

Their new paper was the first to gain a vast middle-class readership, for it covered more areas of news and art than any paper before and tried to enliven fact with the "human touch" of a Dickens novel. Its early saucy irreverence faded as Edward grew older. He became a baronet in 1892 and, when he retired in 1903, a baron. He died in London on Jan. 9, 1916.

VISCOUNT BURNHAM (1862–1933), son of the preceding, was born Harry Lawson Webster Lawson, on Dec. 18, 1862. He studied at Balliol, Oxford, and was elected to the House of Commons in 1885, serving there for 10 years. He also was a member of the London County Council. He was created a viscount in 1919. He died in London on July 20, 1933.

As a publisher, Lawson lacked his father's shrewd news sense. The *Telegraph* lost ground until it was bought in 1927 and revived by Lord Camrose (William Ewert).

HAROLD R. JOLLIFFE, *Michigan State University*

Further Reading: Burnham, 4th Baron (Edward Frederick Lawson), *Peterborough Court: The Story of the Telegraph* (London 1955).

BURNHAM, bûr'nəm, **Daniel Hudson** (1846–1912), American architect and pioneer in city planning, who was a leader of the "City Beautiful" movement of the early 1900's. Burnham was born in Henderson, Mass., on Sept. 4, 1846. He and John W. Root were partners in Chicago from 1873 until Root's death in 1891, and the works they produced were primarily in Root's free, experimental Romanesque style. Then, as head of D. H. Burnham and Company, Burnham became architectural administrator of the World's Columbian Exposition of 1893 in Chicago, where his more academic inclinations were expressed in the unified classical scheme of the main buildings.

In 1901, Burnham became chairman of the U.S. Senate Park Commission, which restored and adapted the original L'Enfant plan for Washington, D.C. In 1909 he proposed a citywide plan for Chicago—that helped guide the development of lakefront parks, boulevards, and public buildings. His office also made city plans for Cleveland, San Francisco, and Baguio and Manila in the Philippines.

Among Burnham's major architectural works were the Flatiron Building (1902) in New York City; Wanamaker's store (1911) in Philadelphia; and Union Station (1906) in Washington. He died in Heidelberg, Germany, on June 1, 1912.

WALTER KIDNEY, *"Progressive Architecture"*

BURNHAM, bur′nəm, **Sherburne Wesley** (1838–1921), American astronomer, who was known for his work on double stars. In 1894, Burnham was awarded the gold medal of the Royal Astronomical Society for his discovery and measurement of 1,274 new double stars. He also made catalogs of all known double stars visible in the Northern Hemisphere, including more than 12,000 stars. His *General Catalogue of Double Stars* (1906) is one of the most famous catalogs of its type ever published. His photographs were beautiful as well as accurate.

Burnham was born in Thetford, Vt., on Dec. 12, 1838. A reporter during and after the Civil War, he devoted his leisure hours to astronomy. He was a member of the staff of Lick Observatory from 1888 to 1892 and was senior astronomer at Yerkes Observatory from 1897 to 1914. Burnham died in Chicago on March 11, 1921.

BURNIE, bûr′nē, a port in Australia, is on the northern coast of Tasmania, on Bass Strait, about 70 miles (115 km) northwest of Launceston.

Burnie is the export center for agricultural products, zinc and lead concentrates, and timber from the surrounding region. The town has an important paper industry, which uses timber from northwestern Tasmania, and dairy products are processed. Population: (1961) 14,201.

BURNING BUSH, also called *spindle tree* or *wahoo,* is a small tree or shrub of the staff tree family (Celastraceae), native to North America from Ontario and Montana to Texas. Burning bush (*Euonymous atropurpureus*) is a popular garden ornamental and seems to thrive under varied conditions. It usually grows 10 to 12 feet (3–3.5 meters) high but sometimes reaches 25 feet (7.5 meters) in height. Its leaves are 2 to 4 inches (5–10 cm) long, dark blue-green in color, and downy underneath. The rather inconspicuous 4-petaled purple flowers appear in June, followed in the fall by colorful crimson fruits borne drooping on long stems. The fruits are small, dry capsules, which contain 1 or 2 orange-scarlet seeds in a fleshy scarlet covering (aril).

FRANCES SHERBURNE
Massachusetts Audubon Society

BURNISHING is a process of smoothing and polishing that is done by rubbing a surface with a hard, smooth instrument called a burnisher. Burnishing is most commonly used in gilding, to give a deep luster to the gold leaf; in copper engraving, to erase unwanted lines etched in the plate; and in leather work, to create a richly glowing surface.

Burnishers are made in many different sizes and shapes for use on different materials. Agate, steel, and ivory are among the materials most commonly used for the head of the burnisher. Sapphires, emeralds, rubies, and even animal teeth were used for burnishers during the Middle Ages, when the art of gilding reached its apex, especially in manuscript illumination.

In burnishing gilt applied to parchment, leather, or other pliable materials, a burnishing slab of vulcanite, metal, or plastic is placed under the material to provide a hard, smooth backing. Unburnished gilt appears uniformly bright from all angles, but burnished gold appears brilliantly shiny, or very dark, according to the angle at which it reflects the light. See also GILDING.

BURNOUF, bür-nōōf′, a French family of philologists, who lived during the 18th and 19th centuries.

JEAN LOUIS BURNOUF (1775–1844), a classical scholar and philologist, was born at Urville, Normandy, on Sept. 14, 1775. He became a professor of Latin at the Collège de France in Paris in 1817. Burnouf established a wide scholarly reputation with his volumes *Méthode pour étudier la langue grecque* (1813), and *Méthode pour étudier la langue latine* (1838) and also for his translations of and commentaries on Sallust, Cicero, and Tacitus. He died in Paris on May 8, 1844.

EUGÈNE BURNOUF (1801–1852), an Orientalist, son of Jean Louis, was born in Paris on Aug. 12, 1801, and was trained in law. He taught general and comparative grammar at the École Normale in Paris from 1829 to 1833 and later became professor of Sanskrit at the Collège de France. His most noted works were translations of and commentaries on the Avesta, the sacred writings (in the Avestic language) of Zoroastrianism. These works include *Commentaire sur le Yaçna* (1833) and *Études sur la langue et sur les textes zends* (1841). He is also noted for his *Essai sur le pali* (1826), the first European study of Pali, the Indic language in which the sacred texts of the Buddhists of Ceylon and Southeast Asia are written.

Burnouf further advanced the study of Buddhism in Europe with his *Introduction à l'histoire du Bouddhisme indien* (1845) and with his translation of one of the Buddhist texts, *Le lotus de la bonne loi* (1852). He died in Paris on May 28, 1852.

ÉMILE LOUIS BURNOUF (1821–1907), a linguistics scholar and Orientalist, cousin of Eugène, wrote numerous works, including *Dictionnaire classique sanscrit-français* (1863), the first dictionary of its kind, and *L'étude de mythologie comparée* (1872).

M. S. BEELER
University of California at Berkeley

BURNISHING a printing plate with pumice and water precedes the application of the acid used in etching.

BURNS, Anthony (1834–1862), American fugitive slave, whose arrest in Boston inflamed the city and strengthened the abolitionist movement. He was born in Stafford county, Va. He escaped from slavery and made his way to Boston, where he was arrested on May 24, 1854. On May 25 he was taken before U. S. Commissioner Edward G. Loring, but Wendell Phillips and Theodore Parker secured a two-day adjournment. The following evening, after a mass protest meeting at Faneuil Hall, Thomas W. Higginson and others attempted to storm the courthouse where Burns was confined. A deputy was killed before the assailants were repulsed. On May 27, Loring delivered Burns to his claimant under the Fugitive Slave Law.

Burns later gained his liberty, studied theology at Oberlin College, and became pastor of a Baptist church in St. Catherine's, Ontario, Canada. He died there on July 27, 1862.

BURNS, Arthur Frank (1904–), American economist, who contributed significantly to historical and statistical research on economic fluctuations. His studies in this field, beginning in 1930 at the National Bureau of Economic Research, of which he became president and chairman, culminated in the publication in 1946 of his major work (with Wesley Clair Mitchell), *Measuring Business Cycles*.

Burns was born on April 27, 1904, in Stanislau, Austria. He worked his way through Columbia University (Ph.D., 1934) and taught economics at Rutgers University from 1927 to 1944. While holding a professorship at Columbia from 1944, he was consultant to the U. S. Treasury Department and chief economist for the Railway Emergency Board. Under President Eisenhower, he served as chairman of the Council of Economic Advisers (1953–1956). In January 1969 he became counselor to President Nixon with full Cabinet rank, and on Jan. 31, 1970, he took office as chairman of the Federal Reserve Board.

A strong believer in free market capitalism, he advocated encouragement of competition and of small business by tax reform. His published works include *Production Trends in the United States Since 1870* (1934) and *The Management of Prosperity* (1966).

NORMAN A. MERCER, *Union College*

BURNS, Eedson Louis Millard (1897–), Canadian general, who served the United Nations in the Middle East. He was born in Westmount, Quebec, on June 17, 1897, and attended the Royal Military College in Kingston, Ontario. He was an engineer officer in World War I and later evolved new methods of air photography. In World War II he held combat commands, including the 1st Canadian Corps.

In 1954, Burns was named staff chief of the UN Truce Supervision Organization in Palestine. In 1956–1959 he commanded the UN Emergency Force in the Middle East. Burns was promoted to lieutenant general in 1958 and became disarmament adviser to the Canadian government in 1959.

BURNS, George (1896–), American entertainer, who was "straight man" in the comedy team of Burns and Allen. Their continuously successful act was based on Miss Allen's impersonation of a scatterbrained wife and Burns' impersonation of her long-suffering husband.

Burns was born in New York City on Jan. 20, 1896, and began his entertainment career in childhood. He became a dancer and performed in vaudeville acts but did not achieve success until 1923, when he teamed with Gracie Allen (1906–1964). The couple were married in 1926.

In 1932, Burns and Allen became the stars of a radio program and also made their first appearance in motion pictures. In 1950 they began their popular television program, which ran until Gracie Allen's retirement in 1958.

BURNS, James MacGregor (1918–), American political scientist. He was born in Melrose, Mass., on Aug. 3, 1918, and educated at Williams College (B. A., 1939) and Harvard University (Ph. D., 1947). He joined the faculty of Williams in 1941, interrupting his career there during World War II to serve the National War Labor Board and in the U. S. Army.

Burns served in 1948 as a member of the first Hoover Commission on Reorganization of the Executive Branch of the U. S. Government. He was a member of the Massachusetts delegation to several Democratic national conventions and in 1958 was an unsuccessful Democratic candidate for Congress. His books include *Congress on Trial* (1949), *Roosevelt: The Lion and the Fox* (1956), *John Kennedy: A Political Profile* (1960), and *The Deadlock of Democracy: Four-Party Politics in America* (1963). In collaboration with Jack W. Peltason, Burns wrote a widely used textbook, *Government by the People* (1951 and subsequent editions).

MARTIN GRUBERG, *Wisconsin State University*

BURNS, John (1858–1943), British labor organizer and political leader, who was the first workingman appointed to a cabinet post in Britain. He was born in London in the dock area of Battersea in October 1858 and lived there all his life. He began to work as a laborer at the age of 10 and became an engineer's apprentice at 14. Soon thereafter, he manifested an extraordinary gift of rhetoric as a temperance speaker. Burns turned increasingly to labor unionism in the 1870's and acquired the convictions of democratic socialism in the 1880's. He agitated particularly for organization of the unskilled, and he was the principal architect of the successful London dock strike of 1889.

Burns served in Parliament from 1892 to 1918. As chairman of the local government board from 1905 to 1914, he successfully opposed, whether from timidity or stubbornness, the Liberals' enlightened attempts to reform Britain's poor law and to introduce city planning. He joined the cabinet as president of the Board of Trade in 1914 but resigned in protest when the government declared war on Germany. He died in London on Jan. 24, 1943.

BURNS, John Horne (1916–1953), American novelist. He was born in Andover, Mass., on Oct. 7, 1916, and graduated from Harvard College. Burns' first novel, *The Gallery* (1947) depicts the American occupation of Naples in 1944 through sketches of American soldiers and Italians. The novel was a critical and popular success, and Burns turned from teaching to writing. His other novels, *Lucifer with a Book* (1949) and *A Cry of Children* (1952) were not as successful as his first book. Burns died in Livorno, Italy, on Aug. 10, 1953.

BURNS, bûrnz, **Robert** (1759–1796), Scottish poet, who was the most famous poet writing in the Scottish vernacular. However, today he is little read, and less understood. Even the Scots talk about him more than they study him. His greatest patriotic work, the *Songs,* is almost wholly neglected. Even among scholars he is frequently listed as a "preromantic" instead of what he was, the last great exemplar of Scottish vernacular poetry. A first-rate mind among secondraters, a traditional Scot in a day when his countrymen were aping the English, a liberal among Tories, a fiercely proud plebeian in a society based on family and rank, Burns was misunderstood when he was alive and is still misunderstood today.

Early Years. He was born at Alloway, Ayrshire, on Jan. 25, 1759. He was the eldest of seven children of William Burnes—so the father spelled the name—a farmer, and Agnes Brown Burnes. (Robert changed the spelling of his name in 1786, when he published his first volume.)

A native of Kincardineshire, William Burnes had migrated to Edinburgh, and then to Ayr, where he leased land for a nursery. Described by his son as keenly understanding men and their ways, he was also by the same account a man of "stubborn, ungainly integrity, and headlong, ungovernable irascibility." But his irascibility was not vented on his family; in his stern way Burnes was devoted to his wife and children. Largely self-educated, he hoped for better things for his sons. Agnes Burnes was illiterate, but her knowledge of folk literature and music contributed much to Robert's education.

In 1765, Burnes joined with neighbors in employing John Murdoch as a teacher for their children. Two and a half years of Murdoch's training thoroughly grounded the future poet in the elements of grammar. But Scottish vernacular literature was not studied in Scottish education; the gentry regarded their native speech as a relic of a semibarbarous past. The literature taught to Burns was the neoclassicism of Addison, Pope, and Dryden, with Shakespeare and Milton as the sole representatives of earlier periods, and with James Thomson as the standard Scottish poet of the 18th century.

Burns' formal education was brief. In 1765 his father, unable to support his growing family on the 7 acres at Alloway, had rented, at inflated land prices, Mt. Oliphant farm, more than two miles from the school. Though the land at Mt. Oliphant was poor, Burnes lacked capital for anything better. As soon as his sons could work, their labor was needed, although the father managed to send Robert to school again for a few weeks at a time in 1772, 1773, and 1775. By the age of 13 the boy was doing a man's work on inadequate food, which overstrained his heart and implanted the coronary disease that ultimately killed him.

In 1777, Burnes left Mt. Oliphant for Lochlea, between Mauchline and Tarbolton, again acquiring poor land at a high rental. However, the move brought Robert some social life. In 1779 he joined a dancing class (in "absolute defiance" of his father's wishes), and in 1780 he helped organize a debating society, the Tarbolton Bachelors' Club. After experimenting with raising flax at Lochlea, Robert went to Irvine in 1781 to learn flax dressing. Although nothing came of this venture except ill health, he did make the acquaintance there of Richard Brown, a sea captain, who praised his early verses and encouraged him to court the lassies.

At Lochlea things went from bad to worse for William Burnes. He became involved in litigation with his landlord, William M'Lure, who in turn was so in debt that his ownership of the land at Lochlea was doubtful. The legal struggle exhausted Burnes physically and financially. Although on Jan. 27, 1784, the Court of Session (supreme civil court of Scotland) decided in his favor, the strain had been too much, and he died on February 13. He left his affairs so encumbered that his family was saved from ruin only because, as employees on the farm, they were preferred creditors.

Mossgiel. To keep the family together, Robert and his younger brother Gilbert rented Mossgiel farm from Gavin Hamilton, a prosperous Mauchline lawyer. The venture began with high hopes, but they were not fulfilled. Released from his father's surveillance, Robert turned to new interests, amorous and poetical. As a result of the former, Elizabeth Paton, a servant at Mossgiel, bore him a daughter May 22, 1785. As a result of the latter, he established a local reputation.

The churches of the area were rent by quarrels between the Auld Licht (Old Light, or conservative) and New Licht (liberal) factions. Two ministers were squabbling over parish boundaries, the kirk session was prosecuting Gavin Hamilton for Sabbath-breaking. Burns satirized these affairs in such poems as *The Twa Herds, The Holy Fair,* and *Holy Willie's Prayer,* which were circulated in manuscript form, delighting the liberals and infuriating the orthodox.

These poems, the first fruits of Burns' mature genius, were the culmination of several years of literary self-education. As early as 1775, Burns had discovered the fashionable literature of sentiment embodied in the poetry of James Thomson and William Shenstone and in Henry Mackenzie's mawkish novel, *The Man of Feeling* (1771). Early in 1783 he had begun a commonplace book, duly mottoed from Shenstone, in which he recorded some of his poems, as well as sententious comments on life and letters.

But his real awakening came in 1784, when he discovered the poems of his near-contemporary, Robert Fergusson. Here, for the first time, Burns learned that the Scots vernacular could still be a living force, that the speech his schoolmasters had shunned was capable of rich literary use. Instead of the tears of Mackenzie, Fergusson presented a bold, racy interpretation of Burns' own world, and the discovery caused him, he said, "to emulating vigor." He directly imitated several poems from Fergusson—*The Brigs of Ayr* from *The Plainstanes and the Causey, Halloween* from *The Daft Days, The Cotter's Saturday Night* from *The Farmer's Ingle*—and in every instance except the last he improved upon the model in humor, freedom of movement, and the epigrammatic quality that makes Burns' verse so quotable. By 1785 he had also found the verse-epistles of Allan Ramsay and William Hamilton of Gilbertfield. Again he used these poets as models, and again he improved upon the originals.

In short, the period from 1784 to 1786 was the most steadily productive of Burns' life, although his lyric output had scarcely begun. Of the longer poems for which he is remembered—epistles, satires, descriptive pieces, and dramatic monologues—the greater part belong to these years. *Tam O'Shanter* is the only major poem composed after 1786.

But Burns' reckless conduct and his rebellion against the kirk now threatened an untimely end to his career. The birth of Elizabeth Paton's daughter had brought him under kirk discipline. Later in 1785 he fell in love with Jean Armour, the daughter of a Mauchline contractor. By the beginning of 1786, Jean was pregnant, and Burns gave her a written acknowledgement of marriage. But her father would not have Burns for a son-in-law, and the "lines" were repudiated, less because of Burns' morals than for his lack of worldly prospects.

This accumulation of troubles caused Burns to plan to emigrate to the island of Jamaica in the West Indies. First, however, he determined to publish his poems—not to earn passage money, but to leave a memorial behind. Negotiations for printing were already under way, and the poems, printed by John Wilson of Kilmarnock and sold by subscription, appeared on July 31, 1786. Within two weeks all 600 copies had been sold. Of the £40 profits, Betty Paton claimed half; the remaining money derived from the work, together with his share in Mossgiel, Burns signed over to his brother Gilbert, to forestall threatened legal action by James Armour.

During these same months Burns had a passing infatuation for still another young woman, Mary Campbell, the "Highland Mary" of his poetry. The details are obscure, but the notion that Mary was the great love of his life is a fantasy of romantic biographers.

In September 1786, Jean Armour bore twins. During the same month Burns abandoned his plans to go to the island of Jamaica. The Kilmarnock *Poems* had been read by influential gentry who urged the poet to try a larger subscription in Edinburgh. Chief among these advisers were Dugald Stewart, a professor of philosophy at Edinburgh University, and James Cunningham, Earl of Glencairn. In Edinburgh, the novelist Henry Mackenzie praised the poems, but he failed to discern the sound and intelligent reading out of which they had really grown and hailed Burns as a "Heaven-taught ploughman."

Edinburgh. Burns reached Edinburgh at the end of November 1786, and within a fortnight was the lion of the season. Though his reception would have turned most heads, he realized that the adulation sprang from novelty, and that the tide would soon ebb. Nor were all his patrons pleased with his conduct. Scottish society was highly class-conscious, and when its members condescended to receive a plowman, they expected gratitude for their condescension. But Burns, emotional and proud, maintained a bristling self-respect and spoke his mind more bluntly than was thought fitting for a plebeian.

The subscription for the *Poems* went well, however. To the publisher, William Creech, former tutor of Lord Glencairn, Burns sold his copyright for 100 guineas. The subscription itself netted about £500, of which the poet lent £180 to Gilbert. Creech, however, was dilatory in settling accounts, and Burns was forced to spend the next winter in Edinburgh to wind up his affairs.

Meanwhile, during the next few months after publication of the *Poems*, events of major importance occurred in Burns' life. During May 1787 he toured the border with Robert Ainslie, a law student with whom he had formed a rather unfortunate intimacy. On returning to Mauchline, he found the Armours so dazzled by his success that they permitted a renewal of his relations with Jean, although he then had no thought of marriage. After returning to Edinburgh in August he went to the Highlands with William Nicol, a Latin teacher at Edinburgh High School. The tour was of poetic value in acquainting Burns with scenes famous in history and song, but it was a disaster socially because Nicol's rudeness caused estrangement from at least two noble families—Atholl and Gordon—whose patronage might have been useful to Burns.

NATIONAL PORTRAIT GALLERY, LONDON

ROBERT BURNS, from a portrait by Alexander Nasmyth.

During the winter 1787–1788, in Edinburgh, Burns had a silly flirtation with Agnes M'Lehose, a grass widow of vaguely literary yearnings. Because an injured knee kept him housebound for several weeks, Burns conducted the affair mainly in letters full of unreal sentiment. His more basic amorous desires, not ministered to by "Clarinda" (as Mrs. M'Lehose styled herself, from the *Spectator*, with Burns reciprocating as "Sylvander"), were satisfied by a servant lass, Jenny Clow, as in the previous winter they had been satisfied by a certain Meg Cameron. Since Jenny and Meg both bore him children, these liaisons did nothing to lessen Edinburgh gossip. And the Clarinda affair had little relation to the realities of Burns' life. Reality was better served in April 1788, when Burns formally acknowledged Jean Armour as his wife, a few weeks after she again bore him twins, who did not live.

Considering possible futures, Burns decided that the excise service, which collected excise taxes, offered the best assurance of a livelihood. However, his patrons disapproved of his entering this profession. Burns, they believed, was a Heaven-taught plowman and should continue as such. Among these patrons was Patrick Miller, owner of the Dalswinton estate, near Dumfries. At Miller's urging, Burns, against his own better judgment, leased the Ellisland farm in June 1788, on terms that might have been favorable if the soil had not been depleted and if the farm had had proper buildings. For nearly a year Burns had no house of his own.

"Museum" Songs. About this time, Burns became deeply involved in a literary project with an Edinburgh acquaintance, James Johnson. Johnson was a music engraver, imperfectly educated but deeply devoted to the traditional songs of Scotland. In 1787, shortly before meeting Burns, Johnson had prepared the first volume of *The Scots Musical Museum,* in which he proposed to collect all the extant traditional Scots songs with printable words. Burns became so fired by the project that he took over as its editor. Originally planned for two volumes of 100 songs each, the *Museum,* under Burns' guidance, grew to six volumes, of which the last was not published until 1803.

The poet's contributions ranged from collecting folk melodies with traditional words to composing wholly new verses, some to airs that lacked printable words, others to previously wordless dance tunes. Between these extremes, Burns did everything from making minor emendations to fitting new words to old fragments of stanza or chorus. (For his cronies, he also preserved, and sometimes embellished, the bawdy old words that could not be printed.) For the *Museum* and for George Thomson's *Select Collection* (1793–1841), to which he began contributing in 1792, Burns wrote more than 300 lyrics, all composed to specific airs.

Neglected though most of these lyrics are today, their importance to Burns personally cannot be overstated. Without this means of expression, his poetic impulse might have been crushed at Ellisland. The farm, as he had feared, was a losing proposition. Fortunately, however, he knew Dr. Alexander Wood, whom he had met when his knee was injured in Edinburgh. On hearing that Burns still hoped for an excise commission, Wood did what more highly placed patrons had refused to do; he obtained, from Robert Graham of Fintry, chief commissioner of excise, the warrant for Burns to train for the service.

By the summer of 1789 it was obvious that Ellisland could not support a growing family. Burns applied for and received an appointment as rural surveyor in the district to which his farm belonged. Somewhat to the surprise of his superiors, he proved to be an able and conscientious officer. The work, requiring that Burns ride 200 miles a week in all weathers, was hard on his health, and harder on his poetry. Yet, thanks to the *Museum* project, he was able to compose songs as he rode, humming the airs until he was familiar with them, and then finding words to express the spirit of the music.

Dumfries. In 1790, Burns was transferred to duty in Dumfries, and in November 1791 he finally gave up Ellisland. Thenceforth he depended wholly on his excise salary for a livelihood. His songs were a patriotic service for which he refused money, and in 1793 he even permitted Creech to publish an augmented edition of the *Poems* without additional payment. Chief of the new poems in this second edition was *Tam O'Shanter,* composed in 1790, after the poet had met Francis Grose, who was studying the antiquities of Scotland. Burns had suggested the ruins of Alloway Kirk as a subject for an engraving in Grose's forthcoming book. Grose agreed, on condition that Burns supply a witch story to accompany the picture. Burns' single greatest poem was thus written by chance.

Traditionally, the Dumfries years have been called a period of moral and physical decline. The latter was partly true, as Burns' heart ailment worsened, but available evidence offers little confirmation of the former. He continued to fulfill his excise duties and continued writing songs, and he left no debts to indicate heavy dissipation. But he was, as always, reckless in speech, and at the outbreak of the French Revolution his strong radical sympathies caused him trouble more than once. That his superiors thought well of him seems proved by the fact that when Burns was charged with having made seditious utterances, Collector William Corbet investigated in person and exonerated the poet.

Though cleared of charges, Burns was shaken by the ordeal. In addition, he became estranged from several of the gentry, some of whom were angered by his opinions, while others disapproved of his unseemly conduct, perhaps instigated by people who wished him no good. Nevertheless, Burns' professional reputation remained sound. In 1793 he was granted burgess privileges in the Dumfries schools. Earlier, he had been named eligible for promotion to supervisor of excise, and for several months in 1795 he served in that capacity while his chief was ill.

Late in 1795, Burns' health began to fail, and for two months during that winter he was ill with rheumatic fever. He partially recovered during the spring, but thereafter his decline was steady, and on July 21, 1796, he died in Dumfries of heart disease.

A subscription was organized to provide for the maintenance of Burns' widow and the education of his children, seven of whom survived him. Unfortunately, the preparation of the memorial edition of Burns' works was entrusted to Dr. James Currie of Liverpool, a conservative in religion and politics, and a teetotaler, who had never met the poet. Currie's biography, therefore, served to perpetuate a distorted view of the poet's character—a view that was partly dispelled in the 20th century by the recovery of the complete text of Burns' letters.

See also AULD LANG SYNE; COTTER'S SATURDAY NIGHT; JOLLY BEGGARS; TAM O'SHANTER.

DELANCEY FERGUSON
Author of "Pride and Passion: Robert Burns, 1759–1796"

Bibliography

Editions of Burns' works include *Poems,* ed. by William Ernest Henley and T. F. Henderson, 4 vols. (Edinburgh 1896–1897); *Songs,* ed. by James C. Dick and annotated by Davidson Cook (Hatboro, Pa., 1962); *Letters,* ed. by DeLancey Ferguson, 2 vols. (New York 1931).

Crawford, Thomas, *Burns: A Study of the Poems and Songs* (Stanford, Calif., 1960).

Daiches, David, *Robert Burns* (New York 1950).

Ferguson, DeLancey, *Pride and Passion: Robert Burns, 1759–1796,* rev. ed. (New York 1964).

Hecht, Hans, *The Life and Works of Burns,* tr. by Jane Lymburn (Toronto 1936).

Lindsay, John M., *Robert Burns, the Man, His Work, and the Legend* (Chester Springs, Pa., 1954).

Lockhart, John G., *The Life of Burns* (New York 1959).

Pearl, Cyril, *Bawdy Burns* (Hackensack, N. J., 1958).

Snyder, Franklyn Bliss, *The Life of Robert Burns* (New York 1932).

Thornton, Robert D., *James Currie, the Entire Stranger, and Robert Burns* (Mystic, Conn., 1963).

BURNS, William John (1861–1932), American detective, who founded the William J. Burns International Detective Agency, Inc. He was born in Baltimore, Md., on Oct. 19, 1861. While his father was police commissioner of Columbus, Ohio, Burns served as a detective in the department. He joined the U. S. Secret Service in 1889 and earned a distinguished reputation, notably in counterfeit cases. In 1903 he investigated land frauds in the West, and his findings implicated a number of federal and local officials.

Burns formed his own detective agency in New York City in 1909 and established branches across the country. The agency was active on management's side in labor disputes. It investigated a number of sensational murders and other crimes which attracted national attention. Burns was director of the Bureau of Investigation (now Federal Bureau of Investigation) from 1921 to 1924. He died in Sarasota, Fla., on April 14, 1932.

BURNS, in medicine, are the effects produced on living tissue by excessive heat, caustic chemicals, electricity, or various forms of radiation. Burns are usually classified on the basis of their severity. A *first degree* burn is a simple redness (erythema), such as that of a mild sunburn. *Second degree* burn means the simple blistering of the epidermis (the thin superficial layer of the skin), such as occurs in a more severe sunburn. In a *third degree* burn, there is destruction of the full thickness of the skin, both the epidermis and the underlying dermis. In *fourth* and *fifth degree* burns, the bone and adjacent structures are charred. Unless the area is very limited, victims with fourth or fifth degree burns do not usually survive long enough to be treated.

Both the severity of a burn and the percentage of the body surface involved are important considerations in the treatment and prognosis of the patient. People with over 50% of the body surface involved with second and third degree burns have poor chances of survival. Those with more than 75% of the body surface burned have practically no chance at all.

Causes. Burns may be caused by direct heat, flames, smoke, caustic chemicals, electricity, friction, wind, or various forms of radiation. In a broad sense, death of the body tissues is brought about by the precipitation of proteins in the cells. Although each causative agent accomplishes this in an individual manner, the end results are very much the same.

Burns produced by friction are caused by a combination of heat and abrasion. Wind as a causative agent acts in a different manner, removing the protective layer of moisture from the exposed skin surface, thus enhancing the penetration of the sun's ultraviolet rays. This type of burn is not caused by heat but results from injury to the cells due to light waves ranging from 3200 to 2900 angstrom units. These rays initiate complex chemical aberrations that destroy living cells and interfere with the body's normal defenses. Because ultraviolet rays scarcely penetrate the epidermis, the burns they produce are either first or second degree burns.

Like ultraviolet rays, X-rays and particles of atomic radiation cause chemical disturbances of the cells, interfering with their metabolism and reproductive processes. These burns, unlike those caused by ultraviolet rays, are usually very severe, causing the affected tissues to ulcerate (break open and disintegrate), atrophy (waste away), and become scar tissue.

Inhalation burns from smoke, flames, or steam are often immediately fatal. When not fatal, they always cause frustrating complications. In the upper respiratory tract, breathing is affected by the swelling of the air passages, the secretion of mucus, and muscular spasms of the air tubes. In the lungs, the accumulation of fluids (edema) may cause death by drowning. This fluid accumulation in the lungs is often difficult to prevent because the victim is generally in shock and requires transfusions of additional fluids—whole blood, blood plasma, and fluids containing sugars and various salts.

Treatment. In treating first and second degree burns, local therapy is usually all that is needed. Such therapy includes ice baths or the application of butter, olive oil, vinegar, vaseline, special jellies containing extracts from the leaves of aloe plants, or various antiseptic and anesthetic substances.

In the management of more severe burns, keeping the victim alive during the first several days is of greater importance than local therapy. One of the first problems is to alleviate the victim's excruciating pain, usually by administering morphine or other narcotics. The next problem is to prevent or counteract the effects of shock, in which there is a dramatic drop in blood pressure due to the loss of fluids from the larger blood vessels by bleeding or oozing or by dilation (widening) of the smaller blood vessels. If the blood pressure drops too low, brain damage and death may follow. The reestablishment of a blood pressure necessary to keep the patient alive is a difficult task, and various formulas have been devised for estimating the needed amounts of fluids and salts.

Another vexing problem that arises in cases of severe burns is infection, especially by *Pseudomonas aeruginosa* bacteria, streptococci, staphylococci, and bacteria that cause tetanus and gas gangrene. Toxemia, anemia, kidney failure, and a type of ulcer known as Curling's ulcer may also occur.

After a lifesaving regime that may include the use of an artificial kidney and the administration of antibiotics, oxygen, analgesics, whole blood, blood plasma, bacteria antitoxins, and various other substances, attention can be turned to local therapy. A large part of the local therapy consists of using chemicals that further precipitate body proteins to form a crust or scab that covers the wound while the natural healing process takes place underneath. Some of the substances that have been used for local therapy in the past are various dyes, such as scarlet red, gentian violet, and brilliant green. Picric acid preparations and ointments and sprays containing tannic acid have also been used. However, these substances have now been replaced by other chemicals. One of the most popular chemicals for local therapy is a dilute solution of silver nitrate, which is used in repeated applications. Although this solution blackens everything it comes into contact with, it has many advantages. It is easy to apply, produces a soft crust, helps destroy invading microorganisms, and helps ease pain. Another substance used is mafenide hydrochloride, which is very effective against *Pseudomonas aeruginosa* bacteria.

SIDNEY HOFFMAN, M. D.
St. John's Episcopal Hospital, Brooklyn, N. Y.

FROM A PHOTOGRAPH BY MATHEW BRADY—NATIONAL ARCHIVES

GENERAL BURNSIDE, whose whiskers were called "Burnsides" or "sideburns." They were widely imitated.

BURNSIDE, Ambrose Everett (1824–1881), U. S. general who was a commander of the Army of the Potomac in the Civil War. He was born in Liberty, Ind., on May 23, 1824. In 1847 he was graduated from the U. S. Military Academy, but in 1853 he resigned his commission and formed a company at Bristol, R. I., to manufacture a breech-loading weapon that he had invented. When the Civil War began, he returned to active service.

At the First Battle of Bull Run, on July 21, 1861, as a colonel of Rhode Island Volunteers, Burnside commanded the brigade that led the turning movement around the Confederate flank. In August he was commissioned a brigadier general. In January 1862 he led a successful expedition to the coast of North Carolina, seizing several important points. In March he was promoted to major general. During the Antietam Campaign, at the Battle of South Mountain, Sept. 14, 1862, troops under his command attacked Turner's Gap. But three days later, at the Battle of Antietam, Burnside was very slow to advance, and he persisted in directing attacks across Antietam Creek over the bridge that now bears his name, instead of simply fording the stream.

Seven weeks later, President Lincoln offered General Burnside command of the Army of the Potomac. The assignment was accepted, with reluctance, on Nov. 7, 1862. On December 13 he attacked the Confederate army at Fredricksburg, Va. The result was a terrible defeat for the Union, with over 12,600 Northern casualties. Burnside was relieved of command and transferred to the Department of the Ohio. In September 1863 his army occupied Knoxville, Tenn., and Cumberland Gap. In November and December he successfully resisted a siege at Knoxville. In 1864, Burnside commanded the 9th Corps at the battles of the Wilderness, Spotsylvania, and Cold Harbor and at the Siege of Petersburg, until shortly after the Battle of the Crater.

After the war he was elected governor of Rhode Island for three terms (1866–1869). In 1875 he was elected to the U. S. Senate. He served until his death on Sept. 13, 1881, at Bristol, R. I.

JOSEPH B. MITCHELL, *Lt. Colonel, USA*
Author of "Decisive Battles of the Civil War"

BURNSVILLE, a village in eastern Minnesota, in Dakota county, is situated on the south side of the Minnesota River, opposite the twin cities of Minneapolis and St. Paul. Originally an agricultural area, the village is now residential and industrial and is undergoing rapid urbanization. It is near the Minneapolis–St. Paul International Airport and is bisected by an interstate highway. It is served also by rail and water transportation.

The village derives its name from an Irish settler of the early 1850's, William Byrnes. It was organized as a township in 1858. It contains a part of Fort Snelling State Park.

Burnsville was incorporated in 1964. The community is governed by a mayor and trustees. Population: 19,940.

RAY SMITH
Dakota-Scott Regional Library, Minn.

BURNT-OUT CASE, a novel by Graham Greene, published in 1961. *A Burnt-out Case* is set in the Congo in a leper colony run by priests, nuns, and an agnostic doctor. However, Greene, a Catholic, writes of spiritual rather than physical disease. Querry, a famous architect who has fled the world and a succession of women, is the "burnt-out case." By using his talents to construct buildings for the lepers, he expiates his sins and wins new recognition and praise as a saint.

BURPEE, Lawrence Johnston (1873–1946), Canadian public servant and historical writer. He made important studies in early Canadian history.

Burpee was born in Halifax, Nova Scotia, on March 5, 1873, and entered the Canadian civil service when he was 17. He was a private secretary in the ministry of justice from 1890 to 1905; chief librarian of the Carnegie Public Library, Ottawa, from 1905 to 1912; and secretary of the International Joint Commission, which governs the use of United States-Canadian waterways, from 1912 until his death. He died in Oxford, England, on Oct 13, 1946.

Burpee's books, almost exclusively on early Canadian history and exploration, include *Search for the Western Sea* (1907) and *On the Old Athabaska Trail* (1927). In addition to writing books and articles, he edited several of the journals of early French and English Canadian explorers.

BURPEE, Washington Atlee (1858–1915), Canadian-American seed merchant, who was the first to establish a successful mail-order seed business. Starting with a small store in Philadelphia, Burpee built the firm of W. Atlee Burpee & Co. into one of the world's best-known seed houses. He used extensive farms for experiments leading to the development of new plant varieties and succeeded in introducing many new kinds of flower and vegetable seeds. His sweet peas and large lima beans are especially notable contributions.

Burpee was born in Sheffield, New Brunswick, Canada, on April 5, 1858. He studied at the University of Pennsylvania. Besides running his own company, he served as president of two banks. He died at Doylestown, Pa., on Nov. 26, 1915.

BURR, bûr, **Aaron** (1756–1836), American politician and adventurer. Dynamic and ambitious, he built a strong political following and rose to the office of vice president of the United States (1801–1805). But he is remembered more for his duel with Alexander Hamilton, which resulted in the latter's death, and for his schemes of empire, which resulted in his trial and acquittal on charges of treason.

Early Life. Burr was born in Newark, N. J., on Feb. 6, 1756. Of distinguished ancestry, he was the son of the Reverend Aaron Burr, the cofounder and second president of the College of New Jersey (now Princeton University), and Esther Edwards Burr, the daughter of the New England theologian Jonathan Edwards. Both parents died before he was three years old, and his early training was assumed by an uncle, the Reverend Timothy Edwards.

A precocious youth who would rebel against authority throughout his life, Burr escaped the strict discipline of his uncle's home to enter Princeton as a sophomore in 1769 at the age of 13. Graduating with honors in 1772, he studied theology and then abandoned it for law, but he had not progressed far when the Revolutionary War changed his plans.

Burr served on Benedict Arnold's staff, where he met James Wilkinson, who was to figure in his later plans; he then served briefly with George Washington and later with Gen. Israel Putnam. In July 1777, as a lieutenant colonel, he took over command of a regiment. He fought in the Battle of Monmouth the next year and resigned because of ill health in 1779.

When fully recovered, Burr resumed his law studies and was admitted to the New York bar early in 1782. A few months later he married Theodosia Prevost, a widow with five children. Theodosia was 10 years Burr's senior, but he seems to have been devoted to her until her death in 1794. She bore him a daughter, also named Theodosia, whom he idolized.

Political Career. In the bustling, commercial city of New York, Burr soon was competing with Alexander Hamilton for supremacy at the bar. He was adroit rather than profound, with a magnetic personality and a quick mind not overburdened with scruples.

Before the rise of political parties, New York state was divided between Hamilton and Clinton factions. Burr became politically active in 1789, when Gov. George Clinton appointed him attorney general. Two years later he defeated Gen. Philip Schuyler, Hamilton's father-in-law, for a seat in the U. S. Senate. Failing reelection in 1797, he entered the New York legislature. The immediate instrument of his political success was the Tammany Society, founded in 1789 as a social club but converted by Burr into a powerful urban machine.

By 1800, Burr controlled the legislature and thereby the choice of presidential electors in a state whose vote was likely to decide the outcome. To assure his support he was placed on the Republican ticket for vice president. The Republicans won, but in the electoral college Burr and Thomas Jefferson (the intended presidential candidate) tied with 73 votes each, throwing the choice between them into the U. S. House of Representatives. There Federalist votes kept the election deadlocked until the 36th ballot, when Hamilton's influence gave the presidency to Jefferson. Burr became vice president.

There is no evidence that Burr intrigued for Federalist support, although Jefferson believed that he had. Although as vice president Burr was willing to cooperate with the president, he was rebuffed. He was not consulted on appointments nor was he invited to join in party councils. It is not surprising that he began to look to the Federalists for his own future.

Jefferson's administration was bitterly opposed in New England, even to the point of separatist thinking. Burr undoubtedly was sounded out by those who hoped to take the disaffected states out of the Union. It may well have been with the idea of attaching New York to a Northern confederacy that Burr sought the governorship of the state in 1804. He carried New York City, mainly with Federalist votes, but was badly beaten upstate, in part by Hamilton's opposition.

The Duel and the Conspiracy. In the course of the gubernatorial campaign, Hamilton had made derogatory remarks about Burr, who responded with a challenge. On July 11, 1804 the two men exchanged shots at Weehawken, N. J., and Hamilton was mortally wounded.

AARON BURR
Portrait painted in 1809 by the American artist John Vanderlyn.

GRANGER COLLECTION

A fugitive from the law in both New York and New Jersey, Burr fled to Philadelphia, where he and Jonathan Dayton, a former U. S. senator from New Jersey, developed the grandiose scheme that was to prove Burr's downfall. Just what the plans were and whether they were treasonous are uncertain, for Burr told different stories to different people. In its most ambitious form the scheme envisaged a vast empire in the West and South, based on the conquest of Mexico and the separation of the trans-Appalachian states from the Union. This much Burr told the British minister, of whom he asked financial and naval aid.

Burr then proceeded to Washington to finish his term as vice president. Jefferson received him cordially, for Burr as vice president was to preside over the impeachment trial of Supreme Court Justice Samuel Chase, and the President wanted a conviction. The Chase impeachment failed, but Burr's conduct of the trial was a model of decorum and impartiality.

The trial and the vice-presidential term concluded, Burr returned to his schemes. He made a personal reconnaissance of the West in the spring of 1805. It probably was on this trip that he first met Harman Blennerhassett, an Irish expatriate who lived in feudal splendor on an island in the Ohio River. He also visited James Wilkinson, now governor of the Louisiana Territory, and several other government dignitaries.

Burr next acquired title to more than a million acres of land in Orleans Territory, the settlement of which thereafter became his ostensible purpose. Funds were supplied by his son-in-law, Joseph Alston, and by Blennerhassett.

By the summer of 1806, boats, supplies, and men were being procured, mainly at Blennerhassett Island. Satisfied, Burr and some 60 followers set out to join Wilkinson near Natchez, Miss. Coded letters from Burr and Dayton already were on the way to Wilkinson alerting him to be ready to move on Mexico.

The preparations openly being made seemed too extensive for the avowed purpose, giving substance to rumors that approached the truth. To protect himself, Burr demanded an investigation. With young Henry Clay as his attorney, he twice was cleared of any treasonable intent.

Arrest and Trial. At this point, however, General Wilkinson decided to betray his friend. He wrote to the president, who issued a proclamation calling for the arrest of the conspirators. Burr learned of it on Jan. 10, 1807, as he entered Orleans Territory, then saw a newspaper transcript of his coded letter to Wilkinson. He surrendered to civil authorities at Natchez, but jumped bail and fled toward Spanish Florida.

He was intercepted on February 20 and conveyed to Richmond. There he was arraigned before Chief Justice John Marshall, and on June 24 he was indicted for treason. Dayton and Blennerhassett also were indicted, while the chief witness for the government, Wilkinson, barely missed a similar fate. The trial was anticlimactic. Burr was acquitted September 1, after Marshall ruled that acts of treason must be attested by two witnesses.

Later Years. Harassed by creditors and with no prospect of a return to public life, Burr slipped away to Europe. He tried in vain to recoup his fortunes. In June 1812, Burr returned almost unnoticed to New York. In quick succession he received two crushing blows, the death of his grandson and then of his daughter. He spent the remaining years of a long life as a moderately successful New York attorney. In 1833, at the age of 77, he married Eliza Jumel, a wealthy widow. Eliza was granted a divorce on the day that Burr died in Staten Island, N. Y., Sept. 14, 1836.

CHARLES M. WILTSE, *Dartmouth College*

Bibliography

Abernathy, Thomas P., *The Burr Conspiracy* (New York 1954).
Davis, Matthew L., *Memoirs of Aaron Burr,* 2 vols. (New York 1836–1837).
Schachner, Nathan, *Aaron Burr* (New York 1937).
Syrett, Harold C., and Cooke, Jean G., eds., *Interview in Weehawken: The Burr-Hamilton Duel* (Middletown, Conn., 1960).
Wandell, Samuel H., and Minnigerode, Meade, *Aaron Burr,* 2 vols. (New York 1925).

BURRILLVILLE, bur′əl-vil, is a town in northwestern Rhode Island, in Providence county, about 18 miles (29 km) northwest of Providence. It includes the villages of Bridgeton, Glendale, Harrisville (the administrative center), Mapleville, Mohegan, Nasonville, Oakland, Pascoag, Tarkiln, and Wallum Lake. Plastics and textiles are produced here. Apples and dairy cattle are raised. The area became an independent town in 1806. It is named for James Burrill, Jr., state attorney general (1797–1813) and U. S. senator (1817–1820). Government is by town council. Population: 10,087.

BURRITT, bur′it, **Elihu** (1810–1879), American social reformer and pacifist, who was known as "the learned blacksmith." Burritt was born in New Britain, Conn., on Dec. 8, 1810, the son of a poor shoemaker. Studying while at the blacksmith's forge, he became interested in the interrelation of languages and taught himself some 50 tongues. His advertisement for translation work in 1838 brought him to the attention of Gov. Edward Everett and the general public. Henry Wadsworth Longfellow offered him Harvard College aid, but Burritt declared his place to be "in the ranks of the workingmen."

Through lectures and such publications as the newsletter *Christian Citizen* (1844–1851), Burritt urged abolition, temperance, and peace. In England in 1846 he founded the League of Universal Brotherhood. He also advocated "ocean penny postage" to promote international communication. From 1846 to 1851 he organized peace congresses in England and on the Continent. His essays, *Olive Leaves,* were published in 40 newspapers and 7 languages. In America, his hope for a peaceful end of slavery was based on "compensated emancipation." His many writings included *Sparks from the Anvil* (1846) and *Chips from Many Blocks* (1878). He died at New Britain on March 6, 1879.

LOUIS FILLER, *Antioch College*

Further Reading: Curti, Merle, *The Learned Blacksmith* (New York 1937); Northend, Charles, ed., *Elihu Burritt: A Memorial Volume* (New York 1879).

BURROUGHS, bur′ōz, **Edgar Rice** (1875–1950), American novelist, whose Tarzan stories created a worldwide folk hero. He was born in Chicago on Sept. 1, 1875. His education was brief, and, after working at various largely unsuccessful jobs, he began writing stories of fantasy at the age of 36. After selling his first serial, about life on Mars, he turned to a writing career.

In Burroughs' first novel, *Tarzan of the Apes* (1914), Tarzan, the son of an English lord, is abandoned in Africa as an infant and brought up by apes. This novel was followed by dozens of others recounting the extravagant adventures of Burroughs' imaginary king of the jungle. Translated into 56 languages, the Tarzan books sold more than 25 million copies, and Tarzan has appeared in comic strips, on radio and television, and in the movies. Tarzana, Calif., is named for him. Burroughs died in Los Angeles on March 19, 1950.

BURROUGHS, bur′ōz, **John** (1837–1921), American nature essayist, whose writings, particularly about birds, were the best of the nature pieces popular in the late 19th and early 20th centuries. Burroughs was also author of the first biography of Walt Whitman.

Life. Burroughs was born on April 3, 1837, on a farm near Roxbury, N. Y., in the Catskill mountain region. After a sketchy early education, he became a country schoolteacher at 17 and then studied at Ashland Collegiate Institute and Cooperstown Seminary. His earliest essays were published about 1860 in journals that included the *Saturday Press* and the *Atlantic Monthly.* He later described the *Atlantic* as his "university," and he was a frequent contributor to it.

From 1863 to 1872, Burroughs worked as a government clerk in Washington, where he became a close friend of Walt Whitman. After 1872, he lived, studied nature, and wrote in the

John Burroughs

THE BETTMANN ARCHIVE

Catskill region, first on a farm near Esopus, N. Y., and after 1908 on his family farm near Roxbury, where he died on March 29, 1921.

Writings. Burrough's forte was observation of nature with accompanying poetical or philosophical commentary. The sententious style and abstract subject matter of his early *Atlantic* piece *Expression* led readers to ascribe the essay to Emerson. Struggling then to establish his own literary identity, he started to write on rural themes and natural history.

Burrough's early work, influenced by Whitman, shows a poetic appreciation of nature, particularly in such pieces about birds as *Wake-Robin* (1871) and *Birds and Poets* (1877). As a result of his reading Darwin and John Fiske, he turned to scientific speculation about nature, producing such essays as *Locusts and Wild Honey* (1879), *The Light of Day* (1900), and *Leaf and Tendril* (1908). Finally, inspired by the vitalist philosophy of Henri Bergson, he took a more spiritual view of nature in such pieces as *Time and Change* (1912) and *The Breath of Life* (1915). Burroughs' works on Whitman include *Notes on Walt Whitman as Poet and Person* (1867), partly written by the poet himself, and *Whitman, a Study* (1896).

DARRELL ABEL
Author of "American Literature"

Further Reading: Barrus, Clara, *The Life and Letters of John Burroughs,* 2 vols. (Boston 1925); Kelley, Elizabeth B., *John Burroughs* (New York 1959).

BURROUGHS, bur'ōz, **William** (1855–1898), American inventor, who produced the first practical adding machine. Born on Jan. 28, 1855, in Rochester, N. Y., he early moved to Auburn, N. Y., where he worked in his father's shop for making models of castings and new inventions. While there, he developed a calculating machine for solving arithmetical problems, but it proved commercially unsuccessful. In 1882 he moved to St. Louis, Mo., and worked there while perfecting an adding machine that would relieve bookkeepers of some of their laborious tasks. He filed application for his first patents in 1885.

In 1886, Burroughs organized the American Arithometer Co. to market his machine. He then established the Burroughs Adding Machine Co. in Detroit, incorporated in 1905, which is now the Burroughs Corporation. Burroughs died on Sept. 14, 1898, in Citronelle, Ala.

LEONARD M. FANNING
Author of "Fathers of Industries"

BURROUGHS, bur'ōz, **William Seward** (1914–), American novelist. His first novel, *Naked Lunch* (1959), a nightmare fiction based on drug addiction, attempts to examine the place of addicts in modern society. The book was both praised as a work of literary genius and damned as immoral.

Burroughs, a grandson of the inventor of the Burroughs adding machine, was born in St. Louis, Mo., on Feb. 5, 1914. He graduated from Harvard College in 1936. He was a narcotics addict for at least 15 years. His first book, *Junkie: Confessions of an Unredeemed Drug Addict* (1953), published under the pseudonym William Lee, reflected his experiences. (Burroughs claimed to have been cured of his addiction at the age of 45.) His later works include *The Soft Machine* (1961), *The Ticket That Exploded* (1962), and *Nova Express* (1964).

BURROWING OWL, a relatively small ground-dwelling owl found from southern Florida, the West Indies, and the western United States to Tierra del Fuego. It is also sometimes known as the *ground* owl. The burrowing owl is usually 8 to 9 inches (20–23 cm) long. It has a strong hooked bill, long legs, rather broad and rounded wings, and a short tail. It is soft brown in color, somewhat spotted, and has yellow eyes.

Usually found in open prairie country, the burrowing owl is generally solitary, but several pairs may be found in a favorable area. They live in burrows of their own making or dug by animals. The owls often sit near the burrow in daytime and, if approached, will bob up and down rapidly. They sometimes spread their wings and fluff their feathers and fly to a nearby post, fence, or overhead wire.

Although diurnal, burrowing owls feed mostly at dusk. They eat a few small mammals, but their main food is insects. When angered or frightened, they may emit a loud, rattling, hissing scream and snap their bills loudly. At night, particularly during the breeding season, they make a monotonous "coo-coo" cry. Both male and female incubate the 6 to 11 white eggs.

The burrowing owl, *Speotyto cunicularia,* is a "true" or "typical" owl of the family Strigidae, order Strigiformes.

SALLY H. SPOFFORD, *Cornell University*

BURROWING OWLS, shown outside their burrow, have longer legs than tree owls and are active in the daytime.

HUGHES, FROM ANNAN PHOTO FEATURES

BURROWS, bur'ōz, **Abe** (1910–), American librettist, composer, writer, director, and wit. He was born in Brooklyn, N. Y., on Dec. 18, 1910, and was educated in New York City schools. He embarked on premedical studies in 1929 but shifted to accounting. He worked for a brokerage firm from 1931 to 1934, then tried his hand at many jobs, from selling maple syrup to writing radio scripts for *Duffy's Tavern*. In 1939 he went to Hollywood as a gag writer and party entertainer. He collaborated with composer Frank Loesser on the hit record albums *The Girl with the Three Blue Eyes* (1945) and *Abe Burrows Sings* (1950).

Burrows became a writer-director for Paramount Pictures in 1946, and in 1947 he launched his own *Abe Burrows Show* on radio, winning a Radio Critics Award. In 1950 his adaptation (with Jo Swerling) of Damon Runyon stories for the musical *Guys and Dolls* won awards from the New York Drama Critics Circle and the American Theatre Wing. Burrows directed the Broadway musicals *Can-Can* (1953), *Silk Stockings* (1955), and *How to Succeed in Business Without Really Trying*, the latter a Pulitzer Prize and Drama Critics Award winner in 1962.

BURROWS, bur'ōz, **Ronald Montagu** (1867–1920), English classical archaeologist. He was born at Rugby, England, on Aug. 16, 1867. He was educated at Charterhouse and at Christ Church, Oxford. From 1891 to 1897 he acted as assistant to the classical scholar Gilbert Murray in the Greek department of the University of Glasgow. Burrows' excavations at Pylos and Sphactera in Greece provided evidence for Thucydides' accuracy as a historian. In 1905 and 1907 he excavated tombs at Mycalessus in Boeotia and in Crete, and in 1907 he published the first general account of Minoan civilization.

From 1898 to 1913, Burrows was professor of Greek at the University of Cardiff and the University of Manchester. He was principal of Kings College, London, from 1913 until his death in London on May 24, 1920. A champion of Greek independence, Burrows represented the Greek provisional government in London in 1916.

PRISCILLA C. WARD
The American Museum of Natural History

BURSA, bo͝or-sä', a city in northwestern Turkey, the capital of Bursa province, is located about 15 miles (24 km) southeast of Mudanya and 42 miles (68 km) southwest of Yalova—its ports on the Sea of Marmara—at the hub of a good highway system. It was formerly known as Brusa.

Bursa is situated at the base of the 8,179-foot (2,493-meter) Ulu Dağ, in a fertile plain known for its fine fruit, vegetables, and cypresses. The city is a celebrated spa and ski resort and a tourist center with good hotels. There is a cable car that ascends Ulu Dağ. The city is unusually rich in natural fountains and is famous for its hot iron and sulfur springs. It is a favorite place for Turks to retire. Once the silk center of the Ottoman Empire, Bursa now manufactures only a limited amount of silk goods.

The stronghold of Bursa, about 1 mile (1.6 km) in circumference, dates from pre-Ottoman times. The city has a number of noteworthy mosques, which exhibit a variety of influences: Arab (Ulu Cami, or Great Mosque), Persian (Yeşil Cami, or Green Mosque), and even Western (Muradiye Mosque). The mausoleums of early sultans make Bursa the pantheon of the Ottoman Empire; the most famous is the Yeşil Türbe, or Green Mausoleum, built for Mehmed I in 1419.

Bursa stands on the site of ancient Prusa, probably founded by Prusias II (2d century B.C.), king of Bithynia, at the suggestion of the Carthaginian general Hannibal. It later became one of the most flourishing cities of the Byzantine Empire. Upon its capture in 1326 by Orhan, Bursa became the Ottoman capital. In the 14th and 15th centuries the city was the heart of the Ottoman state, and it remained the spiritual center even after the capital was moved to Edirne (Adrianople) during the reign of Murad I (1362–1389). Population: (1960) 153,866.

TIBOR HALASI-KUN, *Columbia University*

BURSA. See BURSITIS.

BURSCHENSCHAFT, bo͝or'shən-shäft, a German student organization formed on June 12, 1815, by 11 students at the University of Jena, most of whom had fought in the Lützow Chasseurs against Napoleon. They advocated the creation of a united Germany on Christian principles and took as their motto "Freedom, Honor, Fatherland." Similar fraternities were soon established at other universities, particularly Protestant ones.

The *Burschenschaften* played a leading role in the political activities at the Wartburg Festival on Oct. 18, 1817, and exactly a year later a national organization (*Allgemeine Deutsche Burschenschaft*) was formed. An inner circle of political radicals, called Blacks (*die Schwarzen*) at the University of Giessen, and Unconditionals (*Unbedingte*) at Jena, came into being. One of the Unconditionals, Karl Sand, on March 23, 1819, assassinated the dramatist August von Kotzebue, an agent of Alexander I of Russia. This deed led to the reactionary Carlsbad Decrees of 1819 and the dissolution of the *Burschenschaften*. Nevertheless, they continued to exist as secret societies. Restrictions against them were lifted in 1848.

In 1883 a reform group, centering their protest against dueling, formed the *Allgemeine Deutsche Burschenbund*. But under Hitler the latter was dissolved in 1934, and the parent federation in 1935. After World War II the *Burschenschaften* again made their appearance, and on June 6, 1950, at Marburg, a national organization was reconstituted.

ERNST C. HELMREICH, *Bowdoin College*

BURSITIS, bər-sī'təs, is an inflammation of a bursa. A bursa, or bursal sac, is a lined sac containing a small amount of fluid and surrounded by a loose fibrous network. Normally there are 52 bursas in the human body, located at friction points, as between tendon and bone; they act as cushions and make for smooth movement. Bursitis is a common human ailment. The bursas most frequently involved are those of the shoulder (subdeltoid), elbow (olecranon), hip (trochanteric), knee (prepatellar), and heel (plantar).

Causes and Symptoms. The inflammation of a bursa may be due to injury, infection, or various diseases such as rheumatoid arthritis, gout, or tuberculosis. Following injury, the bursal sac may become distended with bloody fluid. If infected, the sac may become distended with pus. Many bursas are also often subject to chronic irritation, frequently of mechanical origin, which may cause adhesion—formations of fibrous tissue that cause the inner surfaces of the bursa to become stuck together. Occasionally, calcium salts may be deposited within the bursa.

The symptoms of bursitis vary according to the location of the affected bursa and the severity of the inflammation. Usually bursitis causes pain, limitation of motion, tenderness, and disability.

Treatment. The general treatment of bursitis includes the application of heat, the oral administration of anti-inflammatory drugs, and the injection of cortisone or cortisonelike drugs directly into the bursa. If infected, the bursa may be drained surgically, and under certain circumstances it may have to be removed.

JOHN J. GARTLAND, M. D.
Jefferson Medical College

Further Reading: Beeson, Paul B., and McDermott, Walsh, *Textbook of Medicine,* pp. 1418–1420 (Philadelphia 1967).

BURT, Sir Cyril Lodovic (1883–), British psychologist and a leader in the development of methods of data analysis. He was born in Stratford-on-Avon on March 3, 1883. He received his degree in classics at Oxford but was drawn to the study of psychology by William McDougall, a noted psychologist of the day. After several years of study in Germany, Burt returned to Oxford in 1908 as the John Locke scholar in mental philosophy. He taught at Liverpool University and at Cambridge before joining the faculty of University College, London, in 1924. In 1931 he became professor of psychology there, a post he held until 1950.

In his long career Burt interested himself in a wide variety of subjects, including intelligence testing, juvenile delinquency, and the use of statistics in analyzing data from psychological experiments. His work on factor analysis represents a major contribution to the field of mathematical psychology and brought him many honors. (Factor analysis is a method of analyzing a set of intercorrelated performances into as many independently varying factors as justify the labor of computation.) In 1942 he served as president of the British Psychological Society, and he was knighted in 1946.

Burt's best-known published works include *Mental and Scholastic Tests* (1921), *The Measurement of Mental Capacities* (1927), and *Factors of the Mind* (1940).

MICHAEL G. ROTHENBERG
Columbia University

BURT, Maxwell Struthers (1882–1954), American writer. He was born in Baltimore, Md., on Oct. 18, 1882. He was educated at Princeton University (B. A., 1904), Munich, and Oxford and then taught English for two years at Princeton. In 1908 he went to Wyoming, where he became a rancher. During the Wyoming winters, Burt was able to devote his time to writing, and he produced many books dealing with Western life. These include *The Diary of a Dude Wrangler* (autobiography, 1924), the novel *The Delectable Mountains* (1926), and *Powder River* (1938), a history of Wyoming. Burt also wrote about Philadelphia, where he had spent his youth, in such books as the popular novel *Along These Streets* (1942) and *Philadelphia: Holy Experiment* (1945), which was his last published book. Struthers Burt died in Jackson, Wyo., on Aug. 28, 1954.

BURTON, Harold Hitz (1888–1964), American jurist, an associate justice of the U. S. Supreme Court, who advocated judicial restraint and generally followed the leadership first of Chief Justice Fred M. Vinson and then of Justice Felix Frankfurter. He was born at Jamaica Plain, Mass., on June 22, 1888. Burton graduated from Bowdoin College (1909) and from Harvard Law School (1912) and began practicing law in Cleveland in 1914. He served in World War I and rose to the rank of captain.

Burton was a Republican member of the Ohio House of Representatives in 1929, and in 1930 he was appointed director of law of the city of Cleveland. He was mayor of Cleveland from 1936 to 1940. In 1940 he was elected to the U. S. Senate and served on its Committee on the Conduct of the War, under the chairmanship of Sen. Harry S Truman. Burton was generally more liberal-minded than his party's leadership, supporting lend-lease and sponsoring a bipartisan resolution in 1943 calling for American initiative in establishing a United Nations organization.

In September 1945, President Truman appointed Burton to the Supreme Court. He voted to uphold the non-Communist oath requirement of the Taft-Hartley Act, not merely as to nonmembership but even as to nonbelief in subversion; and in *Bailey* v. *Richardson* (1951) he supported the government's right to dismiss employees suspected of disloyalty on the basis of undisclosed information received from anonymous informers. On the other hand, he voted against the validity of the attorney general's list of subversive organizations and also against the president's power to seize the steel mills. Illness caused him to retire in 1958, but he sometimes served on the court of appeals for the District of Columbia until shortly before his death on Oct. 28, 1964, in Washington, D. C.

LEO PFEFFER, *Long Island University*

BURTON, Richard (1925–), British stage and film actor. He was born Richard Jenkins, in Pontrhydfen, South Wales, on Nov. 10, 1925, one of many children of a Welsh coal miner. At school a teacher and dramatics coach, Philip Burton, recognized the boy's talents and trained him in acting. In 1943, Richard became his teacher's legal ward and changed his last name to Burton. In 1944 he attended Exeter College, Oxford, on a Royal Air Force scholarship and then served in the RAF until 1947.

Before going to the university, Burton had acted briefly in one professional play, *The Druid's Rest.* At Oxford his acting in the O.U.D.S. (Oxford University Dramatic Society) production of *Measure for Measure* attracted the notice of a London producer, Hugh Beaumont. In 1948, Burton resumed his professional acting career under contract to Beaumont and in 1949 played in Christopher Fry's *The Lady's Not for Burning,* starring John Gielgud. Burton starred in Shakespearean plays such as *Hamlet* (1953, 1964) and *Othello* (1957); in the musical *Camelot* (1960); and in many films, including *The Robe* (1953), *Look Back in Anger* (1959), *Becket* (1964), *The Night of the Iguana* (1964) *and The Spy Who Came in from the Cold* (1966).

After a first marriage to Sybil Williams ended in divorce, Burton married actress Elizabeth Taylor, with whom he made the films *Cleopatra* (1963), *Who's Afraid of Virginia Woolf?* (1966), and *The Taming of the Shrew* (1967).

CULVER PICTURES

Sir Richard F. Burton

BURTON, Sir Richard Francis (1821–1890), English traveler and Orientalist, who spent most of his life exploring Asia, Africa, and South America. He is famous for his books on travel and his translation of the *Arabian Nights*.

Early Travels and Works. Burton was born near Elstree, Hertfordshire, on March 19, 1821, the son of an army colonel. As a boy he accompanied his parents on their frequent travels about the Continent. He later attended Oxford, where he was known as "Ruffian Dick" and was expelled.

At 21, Burton joined the army of the East India Company and was posted to Sind, where he lived with the Muslims and learned several Eastern languages and dialects, including Iranian, Hindustani, and Arabic. On leave in 1853 he made a dangerous journey to the sacred Muslim cities of Medina and Mecca disguised as a Muslim pilgrim. His experiences are described in one of his best travel books, *Personal Narrative of a Pilgrimmage to El-Medinah and Mecca* (1855).

On leave again in 1854, Burton went to Somaliland in eastern Africa with John Speke to find the source of the Nile. He then made a trip to the Crimea. On a second expedition in Africa with Speke, Burton discovered Lake Tanganyika in 1858. Another excellent travel book, *First Footsteps in East Africa* (1856), recounts his adventures. A trip to the Mormon settlements in Utah in 1860 was reported in *The City of the Saints* (1861).

Later Travels and Major Works. In 1861, Burton married Isabel Arundell, a devout Catholic aristocrat, who later wrote a "purified" biography of her husband and destroyed those of his writings she considered too unconventional. The same year he accepted the first of several posts as consul. While serving at Fernando Poo, off the west coast of Africa, he explored the Bight of Biafra, Dahomey, and the Gold Coast. From Santos, Brazil, he journeyed throughout South America, travels he related in *The Highlands of Brazil* (1869). While he was consul in Damascus, his favorite post, and in Trieste, he took further trips, described in *Ultima Thule: A Summer in Iceland* (1875), *Sind Revisited* (1877), and *To the Gold Coast for Gold* (1883).

During these years Burton wrote some of his best works—an excellent translation of the *Lusiads* (1880) of Camões, an epic of the Portuguese discovery of the East; the *Kasîdah* (1880), a long poem on the mystic Sufi philosophy of Islam that was his most creative work; and a brilliant, literal translation of the *Arabian Nights (The Thousand Nights and A Night,* 17 vols., 1885–1888).

Burton's more than 50 books reveal his love of wandering, his dislike of convention, and his phenomenal capacity for learning languages. In his work there is always tension between fact and emotion, but because Burton felt that the latter was the most important force in life, he is an artistic rather than a scientific writer. His world view was Oriental in its profound sadness for the misery and sorrow of man; this sympathy, however, was often obscured by his conviction of his personal and racial superiority to those of whom he wrote. Burton died in Trieste on Oct. 20, 1890.

THOMAS J. ASSAD
Author of "Three Victorian Travellers"

Further Reading: Assad, Thomas J., *Three Victorian Travellers* (London 1964); Bercovici, Alfred, *That Blackguard Burton!* (Indianapolis 1962); Brodie, Fawn M., *The Devil Drives: A Life of Sir Richard Burton* (New York 1967); Edwardes, Allen, *Death Rides a Camel* (New York 1963).

BURTON, Robert (1577–1640), English scholar, who is best known for *The Anatomy of Melancholy* (1621). Basically a treatise on various forms of psychiatric disturbance, the *Anatomy* is also the storehouse of Burton's opinions on an extraordinary variety of subjects and is both a fascinating portrait of the author's mind and an invaluable primary source for the study of the intellectual history of the 17th century.

Life. Burton was born at Lindley, Leicestershire, on Feb. 8, 1577, and was educated at the Sutton Coldfield free school, the Nuneaton grammar school, and Brasenose College, Oxford. In 1599 he was elected a fellow of Christ Church College, Oxford, where he took the degree of bachelor of divinity in 1614 and remained as librarian for the rest of his life. He was also vicar of St. Thomas's, Oxford, from 1616, and rector of Segrave, Leicestershire, from 1630 until his death. Burton, a bachelor, seems to have led an entirely uneventful life, with his interests confined to his scholarly studies. He began *The Anatomy of Melancholy,* according to his own account, as a means of relieving his depression, and he spent the rest of his days revising it. Burton died at Oxford on Jan. 25, 1640.

Writings. Burton's first work, *Philosophaster,* a Latin drama written in 1606 and presented at Christ Church in 1617, was a lively satire on charlatanism. In 1621 the first edition of the *Anatomy* appeared, signed with the pseudonym "Democritus Junior." Burton made five revised and enlarged editions of the work, published in 1624, 1628, 1632, 1638, and (posthumously) 1651. His publisher, insisting that Burton write in English instead of the Latin he preferred, is said to have made a fortune from the book. Although the *Anatomy's* popularity declined somewhat in the 18th century, it revived in the 19th. Dr. Johnson, Sterne, Lamb, and Keats were notable among its more ardent admirers.

The *Anatomy* begins with a lengthy preface, "Democritus Junior to the Reader," in which Burton explains his choice of pseudonym; discusses examples of human folly, both ancient and contemporary; and suggests some practical alterations in the social structure for the betterment of mankind. He contends "that all the world is melancholy or mad." In the 17th century the term "melancholy" was used to describe a morbid depression thought to be caused by an excess of the melancholy "humour," one of the four humors, or fluids in the body, that were believed to be the physical determinants of personality. Burton applies the term rather broadly to all forms of mental and emotional disturbance. His chief intent in writing, he says, is not to point out man's imperfections and reform them, but to analyze melancholy in all its causes and manifestations—a step he feels is essential before reform can be effected.

The main body of the *Anatomy* is divided into three "partitions," each with subdivisions into many sections, members, and subsections. The first partition defines the causes, symptoms, and prognoses of various kinds of melancholy; the second describes various cures; the third is devoted entirely to an analysis of love melancholy and religious melancholy, and, like the second, contains a wealth of 17th century medical and psychological knowledge.

A listing of the contents does not, however, give a true picture of the work. As Sir William Osler said, "No book was ever so belied by its title as *The Anatomy of Melancholy*. In reality it is the anatomy of man." Throughout, Burton writes in a leisurely, anecdotal, thoroughly informal and idiosyncratic style, piling up descriptive phrases, citing and quoting at length from innumerable learned sources, eminent and obscure, recounting tales, digressing far from the announced topic, digressing even from his own digressions, and seasoning it all with satire and witty, commonsense comments on every conceivable subject. The book is a vast pudding that defies neat summary, and a thumb thrust in by the reader at any point is sure to pull out an amusing plum.

GEORGIA DUNBAR, *Hofstra University*

BURTON, bûr'ton, **Theodore Elijah** (1851–1929), American public official, who was a Republican congressman and senator for 31 years, the latter part of which he devoted to the cause of international peace. He was born in Jefferson, Ohio, on Dec. 20, 1851, and graduated from Oberlin College in 1872. After studying law and being admitted to the bar, he practiced law in Cleveland for 13 years. In 1888 he was elected to the House of Representatives. Burton was the only person ever to serve alternately in the House (1889–1891, 1895–1909), the Senate (1909–1915), the House again (1921–1928), and the Senate again (1928–1929).

Burton was chairman of the Inland Waterways Commission (1907–1908) and a member of the National Waterways Commission (1908–1912). He also served on the National Monetary Commission (1908–1912). In 1922, President Warren Harding appointed him a member of the World Debt Funding Commission. A pacifist, Burton was president of the American Peace Society in 1911–1915 and 1925–1929. In 1925 he was chairman of the American delegation to the Geneva conference on arms controls. Burton wrote four scholarly books, including *John Sherman* (1906), and was known for his diligent work habits and his opposition to "pork-barrel" legislation. He died in Washington, Oct. 28, 1929.

KEITH W. OLSON
University of Maryland

BURTON, bûr'tən, **William Meriam** (1865–1954), American chemist and industrialist, who in 1913 developed a chemical process that doubled the yield of gasoline from crude petroleum and thus helped to make the automobile practical. Burton was born in Cleveland, Ohio, on Nov. 25, 1865. He graduated from Western Reserve University, received a Ph. D. from Johns Hopkins University in 1889, and joined the Standard Oil Company of Indiana as its first research chemist. Together with Robert E. Humphreys and F. M. Rogers, he developed the Burton process, by which large hydrocarbon molecules of petroleum are broken down into smaller molecules of gasoline.

Burton became president of Standard Oil of Indiana in 1918 and remained in this post until 1927, when he retired. In 1918 he was awarded the Willard Gibbs Medal. He died in Miami, Fla., on Dec. 29, 1954. See also PETROLEUM–6. *Petroleum Refining* (Conversion).

L. PEARCE WILLIAMS, *Cornell University*

BURTON UPON TRENT, bûrtən ə-pon' trent, is a county borough in Staffordshire, England, 23 miles (37 km) northeast of Birmingham. It is situated principally on the left (west) bank of the Trent where the river is divided by several islands. The pleasant scenery of the Trent Valley has lent itself to park development. The Trent and Mersey Canal passes through the northern part of the borough.

Burton is noted for its ale, the brewing of which was started by monks of its ancient abbey. The flavor and keeping qualities of the ale are enhanced by the water, impregnated with calcium sulfate, from wells outside the town. Manufacture of rubber products is another major industry, and engineering is also important.

In the 9th century an Irish nun, Modwen, is said to have founded a nunnery on an island that is still called Andressey, in memory of her chapel to St. Andrew. In 1002, Burton Abbey was founded in Modwen's honor, but the estate was broken up in 1549. Population: (1961) 50,751.

GORDON STOKES
Author of "English Place-Names"

BURU, bo͞o'ro͞o, is the third-largest island of the Molucca group in eastern Indonesia. The name is also spelled *Boeroe*. Roughly oval in shape, the island is 95 miles (153 km) long and 54 miles (87 km) wide with a total land area of about 5,100 square miles (13,200 sq km). Like the other islands of the Moluccas, Buru has a narrow coastal plain and a mountainous interior. Some mountains reach 8,000 feet (2,400 meters).

The people of Buru, estimated in the early 1960's to number anywhere from 30,000 to 100,000, belong to the Alfur stock of the Malayan-Papuan racial group. They are Muslim or Christian, except for elements in the interior that practice tribal religions.

The island's chief exports are cajeput oil, other forest products, and some copra. A primitive subsistence agriculture based on sago and corn is supplemented by hunting and fishing. The only important port is Namles on Kajeli Bay, and there are neither roads nor an airfield.

From the mid-17th century until 1949, Buru was part of the Netherlands East Indies. In 1949 it became part of the independent Republic of Indonesia.

ROBERT C. BONE
Florida State University

WIDE WORLD

THE FLAG OF BURUNDI is raised in Bujumbura at ceremonies marking the nation's independence on July 1, 1962.

BURUNDI, bōō-rōōn'dē, is an independent republic in east central Africa. Before independence it was known as Urundi and was linked with neighboring Rwanda to form the Belgian-administered United Nations trust territory of Ruanda-Urundi. It achieved independence as the Kingdom of Burundi on July 1, 1962. The king was deposed and a republic proclaimed in 1966. Burundi's political instability has been closely related to the unresolved relationship between the Batutsi ruling class and the Bahutu masses.

The People. Burundi, with a population of 3,274,000 (1966), is one of the most densely populated countries in Africa. But it is primarily a rural country, and most of the people live on isolated farms. Bujumbura, the capital and largest city, has a population of only about 75,000 (1965).

Burundi is one of the few Subsaharan African countries to have a single national (Bantu) language—Kirundi. But although linguistically united, the population of Burundi is varied in terms of physical type, cultural values, and socioeconomic relationships.

The Twa, or Batwa, whose average height is 5 feet 1 inch (155 cm), are probably the oldest occupants of the area, but now account for only about 1% of the total population. They specialize in the performance of certain skills and are primarily potters, hunters, entertainers, or bodyguards.

The Hutu, or Bahutu, have an average height of 5 feet 5½ inches (166 cm). They comprise over 86% of the population and live primarily by farming.

The Tutsi, also known as Watutsi or Batutsi, are cattle raisers and warriors. They average 5 feet 9 inches (175 cm) in height. The descendants of an invading group, they account for about 12% of the population and generally stand in a position of social and economic superiority with respect to the Hutu. The Tutsi brought cattle to Burundi and used them to subjugate the more numerous Hutu. A "clientele" system was established that developed into a system of feudalism. The Hutu farmer became a client of the

INFORMATION HIGHLIGHTS

Official Name: Republic of Burundi.
Head of State: President.
Head of Government: President.
Area: 10,747 square miles (27,834 sq km).
Boundaries: North, Rwanda; east, Tanzania; south, Tanzania and Lake Tanganyika; west, Congo (Kinshasa).
Population: 3,274,000 (1966).
Capital: Bujumbura (1965 population, 75,000).
Major Languages: Kirundi and French (both official).
Major Religions: Christianity; tribal.
Monetary Unit: Franc.
Weights and Measures: Metric system.
Flag: Two white diagonal stripes, broken in the center to form a circle. A drum and a stalk of sorghum are in the circle. The panels on the top and bottom are red; those on the left and right are green.
National Anthem: *Cher Burundi, ô doux Pays* (Dear Burundi, o sweet land).

PERMANENT MISSION OF BURUNDI TO THE UNITED NATIONS

COTTON grown on plains near the Ruzizi River in western Burundi is brought to the plantation for processing.

Tutsi by receiving cows and protection in exchange for his services. Under this system the Hutu were reduced to the position of serfs.

Besides these indigenous peoples, there is also a fairly important African immigrant community in Burundi. Nearly 80,000 Tutsi refugees from Rwanda have settled there. A large number of people from Congo (Kinshasa) have settled at Bujumbura, where they actually constitute a majority.

According to missionary claims, over two thirds of the population of Burundi are Christians, and of those more than nine tenths are Roman Catholics. Imported creeds are frequently intertwined with the traditional religion's basically monotheistic concept of God (Imana).

The overwhelming majority of schools, including the University of Bujumbura, are staffed by the Christian missions. Elementary schools enroll approximately 40% of the children of elementary school age. Only a small number are able to go on to secondary school, and few students receive a higher education. Kirundi is the language of instruction in the primary schools, with French as a second language. In secondary schools the language of instruction is French.

The Land. Burundi, which straddles the Congo-Nile watershed, is characterized by an endless succession of hills. Its rugged topography has created serious problems for modern transportation systems and has affected the pattern of human settlement.

Most of the land lies at an altitude of over 5,000 feet (1,500 meters). Only the region of the Ruzizi Valley and the eastern shore of Lake Tanganyika has a narrow alluvial plain lying below 3,000 feet (900 meters). East of this plain, the land rises rapidly to altitudes ranging from 7,000 to 9,000 feet (2,100–2,700 meters) along the north-south axis of the Congo-Nile watershed, in the Mugamba region. The elevation then drops gradually toward Lake Victoria but never falls below 3,000 feet.

Located near the equator, Burundi has two wet and two dry seasons each year. Rainfall varies from about 31 to 57 inches (79–146 cm) annually. Prolonged droughts frequently are responsible for crop failures and famine. Temperatures average about 73° F (23° C) near Lake Tanganyika and about 63° F (17° C) on the Congo-Nile dividing range. The country's generally pleasant year-round temperatures are a result of its high elevation.

The natural vegetation of Burundi is primarily savanna grassland. Much of the country's forested area has been destroyed over the years, but a program of reforestation is in progress. Wildlife, once very abundant, includes elephants, hippopotamuses, crocodiles, leopards, warthogs,

A BASKETBALL GAME outside a modern intermediate (secondary) school in Bujumbura. An increasing number of school-age children are attending secondary school.

PERMANENT MISSION OF BURUNDI TO THE UNITED NATIONS

BURUNDI Map Index

Population: 3,274,000

Area: 10,747 square miles (27,834 sq km)

CITIES and TOWNS	
Bubanza	A2
Bujumbura (cap.), 75,000	A2
Bururi	A2
Gitega, 3,579	A2
Kabezi	A2
Muhinga	B2
Muhenke	B2
Ngozi	A2
Nyanza	A3
Rugombo	A2
Rumonge	A3
Rutana	B2
Ruyigi	B2

PHYSICAL FEATURES	
Kagera (riv.)	B2
Malagarasi (riv.)	B3
Ruvuvu (riv.)	B2
Ruzizi (riv.)	A2

Total Pop.—1966 est.; cap.—1965 est.; Gitega—1959 est.

and several varieties of game birds. Some species have begun to disappear as the area under cultivation has increased.

The Economy. Burundi is predominantly an agricultural country. Over 41% of the total land area is arable, and most of this is under cultivation. Most farming is conducted on a subsistence basis. The major food crops are pulses, bananas, eleusine, sorghum, maize, manioc, peanuts, sweet potatoes, and gourds. The chief cash crop is coffee, primarily of the higher-priced arabica variety. Other export crops include cotton, tobacco, and pyrethrum.

Although cattle raising plays a much more significant role than agriculture in the traditional social order of Burundi, it contributes only a small percentage of the country's income. The social prestige attached to the ownership of cattle has resulted in the frequently uneconomic proliferation of a distinctive, long-horned breed of bovines and in extensive overgrazing.

The principal mineral found in Burundi is cassiterite, which is the chief source of tin. Smaller amounts of gold, amblygonite, and bastnaesite are also mined. Other than mining, industrial activity is limited to some light manufacturing of goods for local consumption, building materials, and primary processing of cash crops.

Burundi's major exports are coffee, cassiterite, cotton, pyrethrum, and hides and skins. The chief imports include fuels, vehicles, clothing and textiles, machinery, and foodstuffs. Belgium and the United States are Burundi's principal trading partners.

Burundi has about 3,700 miles (6,000 km) of roads. The only hard-surfaced road connects Bujumbura around the northern tip of Lake Tanganyika to the Congolese town of Uvira. There are no railroads and no navigable waterways in the country, and development is limited by the rugged terrain. Bujumbura, on Lake Tanganyika, is a good port, the capacity of which has increased fourfold since 1947. It is connected by steamers with Kigoma, the terminal point of the Tanzanian railroad system. Bujumbura has an international airport. There is an airfield at Gitega that can accommodate smaller craft.

History and Government. Burundi was one of several broadly similar states that developed in the great lakes region of central Africa, possibly as early as the 14th century. Other such states included Buganda, Bunyoro, and Ankole in modern Uganda; Buha in Tanzania; and Rwanda. All of them evolved from the more or less peaceful and gradual subjugation of sedentary farmers by invading herdsmen.

There appears to have been comparatively less interpenetration between the two groups in Burundi, and particularly, in Rwanda, than in the northern states. In Rwanda, the Tutsi generally enjoyed privileged status as a group. In Burundi, however, political and economic power was in the hands of the *ganwa* class, a restricted hereditary political elite representing only a small fragment of the Tutsi group. Provincial chiefs, as well as the reigning house, belonged to this class. As a result, Burundi was less centralized than Rwanda, and provincial chiefs apparently enjoyed a good deal of independence from the *mwami*, or king. Traditional rivalries among the *ganwa* have frequently been carried on into modern politics.

European Rule. The first Europeans to explore Burundi were Richard Burton and John Speke in 1858. Henry M. Stanley and David Livingstone landed at the site of Bujumbura in 1871. German explorers entered the area in 1894. Burundi, along with neighboring Rwanda, was incorporated into German East Africa. The Germans attempted to administer the area indirectly through the traditional authorities. However, Burundi was plagued at the time by chronic feuding between the royal line descended from Mwami Mwezi IV (the Bezi) and that descended from Mwezi's predecessor, Mwami Ntare (the Batare). The accession in 1915 of Mwami Mwambutsa IV, of the Bezi line, was an episode in this continuing struggle.

After World War I, Burundi and Rwanda were made the League of Nations mandate of Ruanda-Urundi under Belgian administration. At the end of World War II, the area was made a United Nations trust territory and again entrusted to Belgium. The Belgians applied a policy of indirect rule that had the effect of consolidating Mwambutsa's position to the detriment of the rival line.

Independence. When political parties were first organized in the country in 1959, the two major groups UPRONA (National Unity and Progress party) and PDC (Christian Democratic party), were led by princes of the two contending houses. In elections held under UN supervision

WIDE WORLD

TRIBAL DRUMMERS sound the message of Burundi's independence during the July 1962 celebrations at Bujumbura.

on Sept. 18, 1961, UPRONA, headed by the Mwami's eldest son, Prince Louis Rwagasore, won 58 of the 64 seats in the National Assembly. Less than a month later, however, Prime Minister Rwagasore was assassinated. After Burundi achieved independence on July 1, 1962, several members of the opposition party were executed for their part in the assassination. Under Rwagasore's leadership, UPRONA had attempted to minimize Bahutu-Batutsi differences under the unifying authority of the crown. However, after his assassination the party fell prey to internal rivalries that increasingly followed ethnic lines. As a consequence of the stalemate, the Mwami departed from his supposedly neutral role as a constitutional monarch in order to fill the power vacuum, but in so doing exposed the crown to charges of partiality.

After the assassination of Prime Minister Pierre Ngendandunwe, a Hutu, on Jan. 15, 1965, direct royal intervention became increasingly visible, but could not prevent the May 1965 elections from being fought in terms of Hutu-Tutsi opposition. The Hutu gained 23 of the 33 seats in the National Assembly. At that point the Mwami's interference with the rules of parliamentary government was bound to be interpreted as an anti-Hutu policy.

The Hutu felt their fears were confirmed when Leopold Biha, a *ganwa* of the Bezi line, was appointed prime minister on Sept. 13, 1965. Hutu military personnel attempted a coup d'etat on October 18, and Hutu peasants massacred hundreds of Tutsi throughout the country. The revolt was soon thwarted, however, by loyal army elements led by Capt. Michel Micombero, and widespread reprisals against the Hutu population followed until the early months of 1966.

Mwami Mwambutsa IV nevertheless decided to leave Burundi and eventually elected to remain in Europe, leaving power in the hands of the army. In March 1966, he was persuaded to delegate most of his royal powers to his 19-year-old son, Crown Prince Charles Ndizeye. This awkward situation came to an end in July when Prince Charles deposed his protesting father and appointed Captain Micombero to the post of prime minister.

Tension soon developed between the prime minister and the new Mwami over the limits of royal authority. On Nov. 28, 1966, less than three months after Prince Charles' formal installation as Mwami Ntare V, Captain Micombero deposed the king and proclaimed a republic with himself as president.

Burundi's foreign policy is affected to a considerable extent by its domestic difficulties, primarily the Hutu-Tutsi relationship. Neighboring Rwanda underwent a revolution in late 1959 and early 1960 that resulted in a Hutu takeover and in the physical expulsion of most of its Tutsi population. Relations between the two countries became tense thereafter. The Burundi government walked an uneasy tightrope, wavering between the temptation to help the Batutsi refugees reconquer power in their homeland and the realization that such a policy might precipitate a civil war within Burundi itself. Conversely, Rwanda was accused of encouraging the Hutu insurrection of October 1965. Non-African powers, notably Communist China, attempted to exploit the situation to their advantage, although without any apparent success.

EDOUARD BUSTIN, *Boston University*

Further Reading: Louis, William R., *Ruanda-Urundi, 1884–1919* (London and New York 1963); Stacey, Tom, "Burundi," in *Africa: A Handbook to the Continent*, ed. by Colin Legum (New York 1966).

BURUSHASKI, bo͞o-ro͞o-shas'kē, is a language spoken by about 20,000 persons in the states of Hunza and Nagar in Pakistan-held northern Kashmir. A closely related idiom is Werchikwar, spoken by about 7,500 persons in the Yasin district about 100 miles (160 km) west of Hunza. The language has no written literature. It is recorded only by linguistic fieldwork, and much of the collected material is still unpublished. Burushaski has an extremely complicated grammatical system. Among its most interesting features are four nominal classes and the constant use of possessive prefixes with many words.

Relations between Burushaski and other languages have been much discussed but are still unclear. There is no doubt that it is not related to any of the surrounding Indo-Iranian, Turkic, or Tibetan languages. Various unconvincing attempts have been made to connect Burushaski with the Munda, Dravidian, and Caucasian languages, and connections with Basque have been suggested by Hermann Berger. Probably Burushaski was once current over a larger territory and was spoken by a pre-Aryan population that has survived only in small remnants.

GEORG BUDDRUSS
University of Mainz, Germany

Further Reading: Lorimer, David L. R., *The Burushaski Language*, 3 vols. (Oslo 1935–1938).

BURWELL PAPERS, bûr'wel, a contemporary account of Bacon's Rebellion (1676) against the favoritism and negligence of the governor of Virginia, written by the planter John Cotton. An 18th century copy of the account, owned by the Burwell family of Virginia, was printed in 1814; it was reprinted in 1866 as *The History of Bacon's and Ingraham's Rebellion*. The work is best known for an elegy on Bacon (who died of malaria) and a reply to it, which expresses a less favorable view of him. The two poems, by Cotton or his wife, Anne, have been called the finest examples of poetry written in colonial America. The Burwell Papers were the source for an 18th century burlesque poem on the rising by Ebenezer Cook.

BURY, bū'rē, **John Bagnell** (1861–1927), Irish historian. He was one of the most eminent classical scholars of modern times.

Bury was born in Monaghan, Ireland, on Oct. 16, 1861, the eldest son of an Anglo-Irish minister. He was educated privately and graduated with highest honors from Trinity College, Dublin, where his precocity as a classicist moved Sir John P. Mahaffy, the famous Greek scholar, to enlist his help in publishing an edition of Euripides' *Hippolytus*. Awarded a Trinity fellowship, Bury plunged into the study of classical literature, philology, and ancient history. His interests became more and more historical, and in 1889 he published his widely acclaimed *History of the Later Roman Empire*. The work was notable for its grasp of the sources and substance of the epoch. Bury produced among other things a definitive edition of Gibbon's *Decline and Fall of the Roman Empire* in seven volumes (1896–1900) and a life of St. Patrick (1905).

Bury was regius professor of modern history at Cambridge from 1903 until his death at Rome on June 1, 1927.

L. PERRY CURTIS, JR.
University of California at Berkeley

BURY, Richard de. See PHILOBIBLON.

BURY ST. EDMUNDS, ber'ē sānt ed'məndz, a municipal borough and the county town of West Suffolk, England, is 60 miles (96 km) northeast of London. It is an important agricultural center and processes cattle food and sugar beets. Farm machinery is manufactured, and there is a large brewery. Bury's long ecclesiastical history has given it the character of a cathedral town, and it actually has been one since the foundation of the see of St. Edmundsbury (an alternative name for the town) and Ipswich in 1914. The cathedral was formed from the 15th century Church of St. James, which has been enlarged.

Settlement of Bury St. Edmunds began with a small 7th century monastery on the Lark River. King Edmund of East Anglia, who was martyred by the Danes in 870, was buried there, and the town became known as St. Edmund's Bury (borough). In 1020, Canute II, first Danish king of England, founded an abbey at Bury, and it became one of the most important in Britain. Discontented barons met here in 1214 to voice the grievances against King John that led to the signing of the Magna Carta.

Most of the abbey buildings are in ruins. The splendid 14th century gatehouse leads to remains of the refectory, chapter house, and abbot's bridge. The great abbey church is represented by its west wall and the 12th century Norman tower over its entrance. Moyses Hall, a Norman domestic building, is a museum. The town still has its 11th century street plan and some Georgian buildings of distinction, including the restored Regency Theatre (1815). Population: (1961) 21,144.

GORDON STOKES
Author of "English Place-Names"

BURYAT AUTONOMOUS SOVIET SOCIALIST REPUBLIC, bo͞or-yät', an administrative division of the Russian republic in the Soviet Union. It is located in southeastern Siberia, south and east of Lake Baikal and north of the Mongolian People's Republic (Outer Mongolia). Its area of 135,600 square miles (351,300 sq km) is largely mountainous, with broad intermontane basins and valleys drained by the Selenga River and other tributaries of Lake Baikal. These broad valleys, with a natural wooded steppe and steppe grassland vegetation, are the principal farming districts of the republic. About 70% of the total area, mainly in the north and in the mountains, is forested.

The climate is of the continental type, with a wide seasonal range of temperature from about −16°F (−27°C) in January to 56° (13°C) in July. Precipitation averages from 10 to 15 inches (250–380mm) a year. The severe winters last 7 months, with little snow.

Roughly half of the population consists of indigenous Buryats, a stock-raising people of Mongolic language (Buryat) and Lamaist religion. The other half consists mainly of Russian settlers, with small minorities of Evenki (Tungus) in the north and Tuvinians in the south.

Sheep and cattle raising is the chief occupation. Wheat and animal feed (oats, corn, grasses) are the principal crops. Fur-bearing animals are hunted in the northern forests. Industry is based largely on livestock products (meat, wool, hides) and mineral resources. These include tungsten and molydenum at Zakamensk (called Gorodok until 1959) and brown coal at Gusinoozersk. Sillimanite near Kyakhta is a potential raw material for the aluminum industry of Irkutsk. Manufacturing is concentrated at Ulan-Ude, the capital of the republic, which has a locomotive shop for the Trans-Siberian Railroad, a meat-packing plant, and a glass factory.

Russians reached the Buryat area in the mid-17th century and had completely conquered it by 1727. Under the Soviet regime an autonomous republic was set up in 1923, which was known as the Buryat-Mongol ASSR until 1958. Population: (1966) 771,000.

THEODORE SHABAD
Editor of "Soviet Geography"

BURYING BEETLE, ber'ē-ing bet'əl, a genus of beetles that bury small animals such as mice, moles, frogs, and toads. Burying beetles, also called *sexton beetles,* are found throughout the temperate regions of the world and at higher altitudes in the tropics. Almost all of the species are black with orange markings on their wing covers, but a few species are all black. Burying beetles range from 0.32 inch to 1 inch (0.8–2.5 cm) long.

Soon after the death of a small animal, burying beetles appear from nearby shelters and dig beneath the animal to bury it. The signal to dig is provided by the pressure of the dead animal on the soil above the beetles. Once the carcass is beneath the soil, the beetles lay eggs on it. The beetle larvae that hatch are then able to feed on the buried carcass without having to compete with fly larvae.

The digging behavior of burying beetles has been the subject of a number of experiments. In one experiment, a dead mouse was tied to two twigs to prevent it from being buried. The beetles, in their attempt to bury the carcass, began gnawing at the strings. When the carcass was released, they buried it.

The burying beetle (genus *Nicrophorus*) belongs to the family Siphidae in the order Coleoptera.

R. H. ARNETT, JR., *Purdue University*

BUS. The bus dominates urban transit systems and sight-seeing transportation and shares with railroads and airlines a large portion of public intercity passenger service. The bus has a virtual monopoly on transportation sponsored by schools, hotels, and other institutions.

Throughout the world, nations with modern highways make extensive use of bus service. In the United States, where street and highway systems are highly developed, buses provide convenient and economical transportation in every major city and many smaller communities in all parts of the nation. There is a vast network of intercity bus routes. The United States has more than 20,000 buses engaged in intercity service, about 50,000 in local and suburban transit, and more than 230,000 in school fleets.

Vehicles and Services. The term "bus" is derived from "omnibus" and refers to a large motor-driven vehicle that carries passengers. It does not include taxicabs and limousines. The source of power of a modern bus is a diesel or gasoline engine or an electric trolley.

The modern intercity bus is a large and powerful vehicle usually having a gross weight of 20,000 to 32,000 pounds (9,000 to 14,400 kg). The urban or local bus has a similar range in gross weight but most of them are below 26,000 pounds (11,700 kg). The horsepower rating of the intercity bus is generally between 211 and 272 while for the urban or local bus the range is 170 to 204. The larger buses use diesel motor power and carry from 48 to 64 seated passengers. An urban bus—one that operates within a city for relatively short distances—often carries even more passengers, because it has a seat across the back to increase its seating capacity and because it also carries standing passengers. The intercity bus—one designed for long-distance travel—is a fast vehicle providing comfortable reclining seats, and some have rest rooms. Air conditioning is common in both urban and intercity buses.

Smaller buses that operate between smaller communities and buses used by schools and hotels generally are powered by a gasoline engine. On the upper end of the size scale, large, double-decked buses once were widely used in New York and Philadelphia, but they long since have been replaced in those cities, and they are being phased out in London. Some major cities employ the mini-bus to transport shoppers within the central city area.

A few cities, including New Orleans and San Francisco in the United States and Munich in Germany, make extensive use of electric trolley buses. These buses use the trolley wire routes of abandoned street car operations. American cities employ a single wire, carrying alternate current to trolley buses; Munich uses a two-wire trolley, carrying direct current.

Urban and intercity buses may be engaged in either regular or irregular route service. Charter and sight-seeing buses generally operate over irregular routes.

The minimum standards for school buses in the United States are set by the National Conference on School Transportation and are administered by the National Commission on Safety Education of the National Education Association of Washington, D. C. The capacity varies from 36 to 66. The vehicle must be adequate to handle safely a gross weight of 13,200 pounds (5,940 kg) for the 36-passenger version or 20,-200 pounds (9,000 kg) for the 66-passenger version. All aisles must have a minimum clearance of 12 inches (30 cm). Backs of seats must be slanted away from the aisle to provide a minimum clearance of 15 inches (37 cm). The buses must be equipped with front and rear double-acting shock absorbers. School bus tires must be 10 ply with a rim size between 5 and 7 inches in width. Every school bus must be geared to surmount a 3.7% grade at a speed of 20 miles (32 km) per hour.

Most industrialized countries manufacture buses, but many countries import them from the United States, the largest producer. (General Motors is the world's largest busmaker.) Britain and Japan rank high among the bus-producing nations.

Operators. Most countries have government-owned railroads that often operate buses in conjunction with railroads. However, independent, privately owned bus lines also operate in most nations that have government-owned lines.

In the United States the Greyhound Corporation and Continental Trailways, Inc., affiliated systems operate nationwide and are dominant in intercity bus service. Greyhound management is centralized in a single corporation; Continental Trailways represents an affiliation of about 40 companies, many of which have independent management. There also are scores of bus lines providing localized service in the United States.

AUTOMOBILE MANUFACTURERS ASSOCIATION

EARLY MOTOR BUSES included the 1914 model shown above. This Tacoma Transit Co. vehicle carried passengers the ten miles between Sumner and Tacoma, Wash.

Within U. S. cities, buses often are operated as part of an urban transit system that may include subway and elevated lines or surface railway lines. They may be either privately or publicly owned.

The principal competition to bus service is private automobile transportation, which is increasing steadily. Other competitors for intercity passenger traffic are the railroads, which have encountered a continuing decline, and the airlines, which have shown steady increases. But the passenger traffic of intercity bus lines continues to grow. In part the growth is attributable to express bus service, made possible by extensive expressway development. Intercity bus lines have become large carriers of mail and have entered the package freight business.

Early History. The bus is a 20th century institution. Immediately before the advent of the bus, highway passenger transportation was the work of horse-drawn vehicles. As roads were developed the stagecoach became the principal overland passenger vehicle and was widely used from the 17th century until the late 19th century, when it was succeeded by the hack. Larger than a stagecoach, a hack generally was a wagon equipped with a top for shelter. It carried as many as 20 to 25 persons and operated over improved roads made of broken stone.

A very early effort at developing a large surface vehicle for passengers was the "sailing chariot," built in Holland before 1600 to carry more than 20 persons over a 42-mile (68 km) land route. A predecessor of the bus, with mechanical power, was the steam carriage used in England between 1827 and 1870. Goldsworthy Gurney operated a steam carriage over the 200 miles (320 km) between London and Bath, England, from 1827 until 1829. Other operations were inaugurated between English towns, but in time they gave way to improved steam railroad service.

The Motor Bus. Rapid development of the gasoline engine after 1895 focused attention on the motor bus as the most practical vehicle for carrying a number of persons on the highway. The first regular urban bus services were established in London in 1904, and on Fifth Avenue, New York City, in 1905. The Fifth Avenue Coach Company had imported a London bus for trial. About the same time, intercity bus service began in Oregon between Bend and Shaniko.

Before World War I, the standard bus held some 15 to 25 passengers, operated on solid tires, and often lacked springs. Many of the early intercommunity buses were merely regular or somewhat enlarged touring cars or sedans. These were still common between 1920 and 1930.

The development of bus transportation has been rapid and impressive. It was brought about by the concurrent development of the vehicle's power, chassis, and body, and by the development of tires, fuel, lubrication, and, significantly, streets and highways. This progress has produced today's large and powerful luxury coach that operates over a great highway system. Until a new type of surface vehicle is developed to rival it, the bus will continue to hold an important place in passenger and mail transportation service.

MARVIN L. FAIR
American University

Further Reading: Chilton Co., Inc., *Commercial Car Journal* (Philadelphia, monthly); National Association of Motor Bus Owners, *Development of Intercity Bus Transportation* (Washington 1962) National Association of Motor Bus Owners, *Bus Facts* (Washington, annually); Pound, Arthur, *Transportation Progress* (Garden City, N. Y., 1934); Trussler, David J.; *Early Buses and Trams* (Brattleboro, Vt., 1964).

GREYHOUND CORPORATION

THE INTERCITY BUS common on American highways in the 1960's offered passengers such comforts as air conditioning, rest rooms, and soft, reclining seats.

BUS BAR, an electrical conductor that serves as a common connection between three or more circuits. It generally is a rigid, bare copper bar that is supported on insulators. Bus bars range in size in accordance with the amount of current they are designed to carry. They usually carry large amounts of current, sometimes thousands of amperes. Bus bars commonly are used in power substations, switchboards, and industrial plants that require large amounts of electricity.

BUSCH, bo͞osh, **Adolf Georg Wilhelm** (1891–1952), German-American violinist and composer. He was born in Siegen, Germany, on Aug. 8, 1891, the younger brother of the conductor Fritz Busch. He studied at the Cologne conservatory and in Bonn, and in 1912 became concertmaster of the Vienna Konzertverein. From 1918 he taught violin at the Musikhochschule in Berlin. Busch made many successful concert tours, and in 1919 formed the Busch String Quartette, one of the most famous chamber groups of its time. Refusing to play in Nazi Germany, he settled in Switzerland, where he founded the Busch Chamber Orchestra in 1935. He went to the United States in 1939, reestablishing his chamber orchestra in 1941. He gave outstanding concerts throughout the world with his son-in-law, the Vienese pianist Rudolf Serkin. Busch's compositions include the choral E Minor Symphony, concerti, songs, and various chamber pieces. He died in Guilford, Vt., on June 9, 1952.

BUSCH, bo͞osh, **Fritz** (1890–1951), German conductor. He was born in Siegen, Westphalia, on March 13, 1890, and made his piano debut at seven. He studied at the Cologne conservatory, and at 19 became conductor and chorus director of the municipal theater of Riga. Subsequently he was music director at Aachen (1912), conductor and then music director at the Stuttgart state theater (1918), and music director of the Dresden state opera (1922).

Leaving Germany soon after the rise of Hitler, Busch settled in England in 1934, where, during the summer, he conducted the newly formed Glyndebourne Opera. He also conducted the Danish State Radio Orchestra in Copenhagen and various orchestras in Stockholm, the United States, and South America. Busch, greatly admired as an opera and concert conductor was especially known for his interpretations of the operas of Mozart and of modern composers. He died in London on Sept. 15, 1951.

BUSCH, bo͞osh, **Germán** (1904–1939), Bolivian soldier and president. He was born in San Javier, Santa Cruz, Bolivia, on March 23, 1904. He attended military school in La Paz and, after a distinguished record in the Chaco War, was named chief of staff of the 1st Army Corps. Busch was a member of the military junta that placed Col. David Toro in the presidency in 1936, but he led an army coup d'etat deposing Toro the following year. Elected president in 1938, he settled the Chaco boundary dispute with Paraguay and established the first labor code, a social security system, and a program to end illiteracy. He also sought to regulate the "tin barons," and in April 1939 he suspended the constitution and proclaimed himself dictator. He died of a gunshot wound, officially reported as self-inflicted, in La Paz on Aug. 23, 1939.

BUSCH, bo͞osh, **Niven** (1903–), American novelist and screenwriter. He was born in New York City on April 26, 1903, and went to Princeton University. Between 1924 and 1931 he held editorial positions on the newly founded *Time* and *New Yorker* magazines, for a while simultaneously. In 1931 he began writing novels and screenplays.

Busch adapted his best-known book, *Duel in the Sun* (1944), a novel of the Southwest in the 1880's, for a film of the same name (1946). His other novels, all with strong plots and tempestuous characters, include *The Carrington Incident* (1941), *The Furies* (1948), *The Hate Merchant* (1953), *The Actor* (1955), and *California Street* (1959). Among his original screenplays were *Pursued* (1946), *The Capture* (1946), *Distant Drums* (1951), and *Man from the Alamo* (1952), all psychological dramas with a Western setting, and *The Gentleman from California* (1965).

BUSCH, bo͞osh, **Wilhelm** (1832–1908), German poet and caricaturist, who is considered the father of the modern comic strip. Busch was born in Wiedensahl, Hannover, on April 15, 1832. He studied art in Düsseldorf, Antwerp, and Munich, and from 1859 to 1871 was a member of the staff of the *Fliegende Blätter*, the principal German comic journal. In 1870 he created two famous humorous characters to illustrate his poems for children in *Max und Moritz* (Eng. tr. by Christopher Morley, 1932). Busch's series of drawings, among them *Der heilige Antonius von Padua, Die fromme Helene, Hans Huckebein,* and *Die Erlebnisse Knopps des Junggesellen* were the prototypes of the later comic strips. He died at Mechtshausen on Jan. 9, 1908.

BÜSCHING, büsh'ing, **Anton Friedrich** (1724–1793), German geographer, who laid the foundations of modern statistical geography. He was born in Stadthagen, Lower Saxony, on Sept. 27, 1724, and was educated in Halle. In 1766 he was appointed director of the Gymnasium zum Grauen Kloster in Berlin, where he died on May 28, 1793.

In 1754, Büsching began publication of his *Neue Erdbeschreibung,* of which he completed 11 volumes before his death. The work may be considered the first scientific approach to geography, in that its handling of the political and statistical aspects of geography was based on scientific methods.

BUSH, Alan (1900–), English composer, pianist, and conductor. He was born in London on Dec. 22, 1900, and was trained in music privately and at the Royal Academy, and studied philosophy and musicology at the University of Berlin. In 1925 he became professor of composition at the Royal Academy, where he gave lectures on the history of music. A dedicated Communist interested in making music available to the masses, Bush was adviser and conductor of the London Labour Choral Union (1929–1940) and head of the Workers' Music Association, which he founded in 1936. His early works, such as the string quartet *Dialectic* (1929), are influenced by the 12-tone movement that developed in central Europe. Later works, such as the *Nottingham Symphony* (1949) and the opera *Wat Tyler* (1950), are intentionally more English and harmonic in an effort to reach the people.

BUSH, Vannevar (1890–), American engineer, inventor, educator, and executive, who pioneered in computer technology and led in mobilizing American science during World War II. He was born in Everett, Mass., on March 11, 1890. Bush received B. S. and M. S. degrees from Tufts College (1913) and a doctor of engineering degree from Harvard University and Massachusetts Institute of Technology (1916).

During World War I, Bush did research on submarine detection, and then he returned to Massachusetts Institute of Technology as a professor. While there in 1930, Bush and other engineers invented a differential analyzer, a type of analog computer that solves differential equations. In 1935 he began construction of an advanced model, which handled problems with as many as 18 variables. Modern electronic analog computers are descendants of the analog computers developed by Bush.

Bush became president of the Carnegie Institution of Washington in 1938 and chairman of the National Defense Research Committee in 1940. As head of the Office of Scientific Research and Development, formed in 1941, he directed the most successful and decisive weapons-development program in history. After the war, he devoted his efforts to other national issues, including unification of the armed services, civilian control of atomic energy, and the establishment of the National Research Foundation.

His publication *Science: The Endless Frontier* (1945) formulated new goals for American science and engineering and had a powerful influence on national policy. His other publications include *Principles of Electrical Engineering* (with William H. Timbie, 1922), *Operational Circuit Analysis* (1929), *Endless Horizons* (1946), and *Modern Arms and Free Men* (1949).

J. R. Killian, Jr.
Massachusetts Institute of Technology

BUSH BABY, any of several species of lower primates found in Africa. They are also known as *galagos* or *night apes.* The smallest bush baby, Demidoff's galago, measures 4.5 inches (11.4 cm) from nose to base of tail; the tail is nearly 6 inches (15 cm) long. The largest species, the grand galago, is 15 inches (38 cm) long and has a 16-inch (41-cm) tail. The bodies are clothed in short woolly fur, usually grayish or brownish, and most species have a whitish stripe between the eyes. Bush babies are nocturnal and possess large eyes and ears to aid vision and hearing.

Bush baby

ARTHUR W. AMBLER, FROM NATIONAL AUDUBON SOCIETY

Nimbly hopping in the branches of trees, bush babies capture and eat a variety of insects and other small creatures; they also eat fruits and other plant material. The one or two young may be born in almost any month of the year.

Bush babies belong to the genera *Galago* and *Euoticus*, of the family Lorisdae, suborder Prosimii, order Primates.

Joseph A. Davis, Jr.
New York Zoological Society

BUSH DOG, a small, short-legged member of the dog family, native to forests and savannas from Panama to Paraguay. The bush dog (*Speothos venaticus*) is brownish in color and reaches 15 pounds (7 kg) in weight and 24 inches (60 cm) or more in length, plus a 5½-inch (14-cm) tail; it stands only about 12 inches (30 cm) high at the shoulders. Bush dogs, which are related to the African hunting dog (*Lycaon pictus*) and the Indian dhole (*Cuon alpinus*), live in burrows and come out at night to hunt in small packs for rodents and other animals.

BUSHBUCK, a small forest antelope found throughout most of Africa outside of desert and open plains country. The male bushbuck stands from about 26 to 42 inches (66 to 107 cm) at the shoulder; the female is smaller. The many races vary greatly in color and markings, but typically the animal is a bright reddish tan, darker on the underside. The body is marked by a series of white stripes, vertical and horizontal, interspersed with an irregular series of spots of the same color. The horns, found only on males, are slightly spiraled and rarely exceed 24 inches (60 cm) in length.

Bushbucks prefer to live in the vicinity of water and are most at home in thick growth. They are more often found in pairs than in larger groups and do not appear to wander widely. The single young is born after a gestation period of about 31 weeks.

The bushbuck, *Tragelaphus scriptus,* is one of about half a dozen species of its genus, in the family Bovidae, order Artiodactyla.

Joseph A. Davis, Jr.
New York Zoological Society

BUSHEL, a dry measure containing 32 quarts or 4 pecks. The standard bushel in the United States contains 2,150.42 cubic inches (35,239.07 cu cm) and holds 77.6274 pounds of pure water at a temperature of 39.2° F. The British standard, the imperial bushel, has a capacity of 2,219.36 cubic inches (36,368.70 cu cm) and holds 80 pounds of pure water at 62° F. See also Weights and Measures—*Dry Measures*.

BUSHIDO, bōō-shē-dō, meaning the "Way of the Warrior," was a Japanese code of ethics and feudal behavior often likened to the chivalry of the medieval European knights. The name is a compound of two words: *bushi* (a synonym for samurai), meaning "warrior"; and *do,* meaning "the way."

The term "Bushido" was rarely used by the samurai themselves. It seems rather to have been coined by Inazo Nitobe, the foremost interpreter of Japanese customs to the West, at the turn of the 20th century. The meaning and practice of the code changed as samurai standards evolved, but Nitobe lent the term a romantic coloring which it has retained ever since.

Bushido is actually a blend of two systems of values. The earlier was a reflection of samurai attitudes that developed during the Kamakura period (1185–1333). Japanese politico-military organization and warfare induced members of the warrior class to extol and reward valor on the battlefield, as well as proper relations between superiors and retainers. Obedience was commended, and great stress was placed on honor. Thus, such customs as hara-kiri and the vendetta were glorified. These customs and attitudes are illustrated in *The Tale of the Forty-seven Ronin,* Japan's most famous feudal story.

During the Tokugawa period (1603–1868), Japan entered a long period of domestic peace, when Chinese Neo-Confucianism was officially upheld. The samurai integrated many of its teachings into their code, especially emphasis on loyalty to one's ruler, acceptance of authority, and social harmony. Bushido became the established code until after the Meiji Restoration, when, in 1871, the samurai were legally abolished. As an ideal, it contributed to the growth of Japanese nationalism.

HYMAN KUBLIN
The City University of New York

BUSHING, a thin hollow cylinder designed to line a hole in a bearing or other machine part. The function of a bushing is to reduce the diameter of the hole to the required size and to align a mating part, such as a journal, in the hole. Where required, the bushing is lubricated to reduce friction.

Bushings for bearings are generally of softer material than the journals that fit into them. Brass and other copper alloys and aluminum alloys are the most common materials. Other bushing materials include sintered (fused) metal powder, which is porous and thus easily lubricated; solid graphite, which is itself a lubricant; and nylon, Teflon, and ceramics, all of which provide very little friction. Bushings are inserted in bearings and pressed into place.

Another type of bushing, made of hardened and ground steel, is used in the accurate placement of holes. Such bushings are driven into place and serve as drill guides.

DONALD N. ZWIEP
Worcester Polytechnic Institute

BUSHMAN, Francis Xavier (1883–1966), American film actor, who in the years from 1911 to 1918 made more pictures and earned more money than any other leading man. He was born in Baltimore, on Jan. 10, 1883, and married at the age of 18. After beginning his film career with Essanay in Chicago in 1911, he appeared in some 400 pictures, averaging one a week for several years.

Bushman, who was advertised as having "the handsomest face in the world," symbolized the excitement and extravagance that then characterized Hollywood and the movies. Within a 5-year period before 1918 he is reported to have made and spent $6 million. He lavished money on estates and had the longest car in the world.

Bushman's career was cut short in 1918 when he divorced his wife to marry the actress Beverly Bayne. Overnight, his shocked fans deserted him, and his only subsequent noteworthy role in films was Messala in *Ben Hur* (1926). He died in Pacific Palisades, Calif., on Aug. 23, 1966.

HOWARD SUBER
University of California at Los Angeles

CONSTANCE STUART, FROM BLACK STAR

BUSHMAN of the Kalahari Desert, South Africa, instructs his young son in stalking game with hunting dogs.

BUSHMAN, a member of a nomadic people who live in the Kalahari Desert in southern Africa, especially in adjacent parts of Botswana, South West Africa, and Angola. Bushmen travel in small bands, each of which lives separately and independently from the others. The total Bushmen population is between 50,000 and 60,000. They are culturally and linguistically related to the Hottentots and, together with them, are known by the name Khoisan. The chief difference between these peoples is that the Bushmen live by hunting and food-gathering, with dogs as their only domesticated animal, while the Hottentots subsist by herding and cattle-raising.

Racially, Bushmen are often classified separately from the Negroids, with whom they share certain outward physical characteristics. Bushmen are of short stature (5′2″ for males), have a yellowish brown skin which tends to wrinkle easily, black, tightly spiraled "peppercorn" hair, rather flat faces with wide-set eyes, broad noses, and everted lips. Women especially tend toward plumpness in the buttocks, a normal chaarcteristic, which in its more pronounced form is called steatopygia.

Language. The Bushmen language belongs to the Khoisan, or Click, language family, which is unrelated to any others. The Khoisan languages make extensive use of sounds, the so-called clicks (implosive or suction stops), which are rarely found in other languages. Some subgroups of the Khoisan languages have four varieties of clicks, other five. Like other African languages, they also employ tones as a means of distinguishing between sounds and between meanings. See also CLICK LANGUAGES.

Way of Life. Much of Bushmen culture is specifically designed to adapt to the harsh conditions of life in their semidesert environment. The lack of a permanent water supply is the most severe handicap the Bushmen must face. Water must frequently be carried in ostrich eggshell containers for 20 miles (32 km) or more. On the other hand, the semidesert conditions have proved advantageous for hunting both big and small game.

In this environment the various separate subdivisions of the Bushmen survive best in small groups or bands. Each band consists of a few families led by a headman and usually numbers between 25 and 60 people. The !Kung ("!" symbolizes one of the click sounds) subdivision, for example, has about 1,000 people living in 27 independent bands plus 9 other groups that have entered the employ of neighboring African societies. Each of the nomadic groups continually shifts its camp in the almost never-ending search for food. Material goods, therefore, tend to be of simple design and few in number. Bushmen housing is usually in the form of caves, rock shelters, or semicircular wood and reed windbreaks, quickly constructed and easily abandoned. Their tools, such as the digging stick, weapons, such as the bow and poison-tipped arrow, clothing, ornaments, musical instruments, and other forms of art are also simply adapted to a life of movement in an area of limited resources.

Each dwelling in an encampment is typically occupied by a family consisting of husband, wife, and children, who are joined with the other families by strong ties of kinship and marriage. Together the members of a band exploit the food and water resources of a territory they regard as their own, however vaguely defined its boundaries may be. The property rights of other bands are scrupulously respected, although pursuit of big game into neighboring territories is permitted, and water and food may be shared between bands in a crisis.

Religion. Bushmen religion is also spare in is beliefs and rituals, in keeping with the harsh limits imposed by the environment and with the need to devote great energy to survival in the present life. A greater god, predominantly good in nature, and a lesser god, predominantly, though not solely, evil, and other spirits are thought to be responsible for the fortunes of the band and its members. Medicine men have the power to cure disease and avert misfortune.

Social Structure. Band activities are supervised by a headman, usually an older man skilled in hunting and with great knowledge of the territory. His principal duty is to plan the band's migrations so as to preserve and distribute the resources over the seasons of the year. When the band moves, the headman walks at the head of the line, chooses the new campsite, and has first choice of the place for his own hut and fire. But he carries his own possessions, shares hunger and thirst equally with the other members of the band, and has no other special privileges. Although his eldest son normally inherits his position, the people have the right to turn to another more respected person in the group for leadership.

Thus Bushman politics may be regarded as a kind of simple democracy in which there are no social classes, no special benefits from property ownership, and nearly equal opportunities for leadership. This sense of equality is also found in the lack of desire to accumulate material possessions as marks of high prestige. The rigors of the nomadic life make simplicity more valuable than possessions.

ROBERT A. LYSTAD
Johns Hopkins University

Further Reading: Schapera, Isaac, *Khoisian Peoples of South Africa* (New York 1960); Thomas, Elizabeth M., *Harmless People* (New York 1959); Van der Post, Laurens, *Lost World of the Kalahari* (New York 1958).

NEW YORK ZOOLOGICAL SOCIETY

THE BUSHMASTER, which sometimes grows to a length of 12 feet, is the largest American venomous snake.

BUSHMASTER, the largest of the American venomous snakes. It is known in Trinidad as *magipire d'ananas* ("pineapple viper,") because of its rough scales. The bushmaster ranges from the highland forests of Nicaragua to the lowlands of Ecuador and the Amazon basin of Brazil.

The largest of the pit vipers, the bushmaster usually attains a length of at least 9 feet (3 meters), but specimens reaching 12 feet (4 meters) have been reported. It has a broad, chunky head and small eyes with elliptical pupils. Its body scales are rough, and the tip of the tail is covered with several rows of short spines that serve to differentiate the bushmaster from lance-head vipers found in the same region. The bushmaster is pink or tan with a row of large black or brown diamonds down the back; the dark markings often have light centers.

The bushmaster is active only at night; during the day it retreats into a mammal burrow or some other secluded place in the forest and is very sluggish and difficult to arouse. Its main food in Trinidad is the rodentlike *lappe,* and it probably feeds on moderate-sized mammals as well. It is unique among American vipers in that it lays eggs rather than bearing its young alive. About 15 eggs make up the clutch.

The fangs of a large bushmaster may reach 1.5 inches (3.8 cm) long. Its venom glands are large and contain a strong tissue-destroying venom. Thus the bushmaster is potentially very dangerous. However, the bushmaster, with its tropical forest habitat and nocturnal habits, is seldom encountered by man.

The bushmaster's scientific name is *Lachesis mutus*. Along with rattlesnakes, moccasins, and lance-heads, it belongs to the family Viperidae in the order Squamata.

H. G. DOWLING
American Museum of Natural History

BUSHNELL, Asa (1900–), American athletic commissioner, who formulated the revised college football code nationally adopted in 1945. Asa Smith Bushnell was born in Springfield, Ohio, on Feb. 2, 1900. A graduate of Princeton in 1921, he was named graduate manager of athletics there is 1927. In 1938 he became commissioner of the new Eastern College Athletic Conference (with more than 150 member colleges). He was secretary of the U. S. Olympic Committee from 1945 to 1965. He was named director of the National Football Foundation and Hall of Fame in 1952.

MICHAEL QUINN, *"Sports Illustrated"*

BUSHNELL, bŏŏsh′nəl, **David** (1742?–1824), American inventor, who built the first submarine. He was born in Saybrook, Conn., and graduated from Yale in 1775. While at Yale, he experimented with underwater explosives, and in 1775 he built an underwater craft to place them against enemy ships.

Bushnell's submarine, built of oak, resembled two tortoise shells placed together and was popularly known as "Bushnell's turtle." The craft was manned by one operator, who also turned its screw propellers. It had a tank that was filled for submerged operation and was pumped out for surfacing. It carried a powder magazine with a timer and a drill for attaching the mine to the hull of a ship.

The "turtle" was used during the American Revolution from the winter of 1776 to December 1777, without success. Bushnell joined the Corps of Engineers and became its commander in 1783. After the war he disappeared, but he reappeared in Georgia in 1795 under an assumed name. He died in Warrenton, Ga., in 1824.

JOYCE L. MYERS, *U. S. Naval Academy*

BUSHNELL, bŏŏsh′nəl, **Horace** (1802–1876), American Congregational clergyman. He was born in Bantam, Conn., on April 14, 1802. After graduating from Yale College, he spent some time as a journalist and in the study of law and then entered the Yale divinity school. From 1833 until his retirement in 1861, Bushnell was pastor of the North Church in Hartford, Conn. While in California in 1856, he helped organize the College of California at Oakland (later the University of California at Berkeley). He died in Hartford on Feb. 17, 1876.

Bushnell was one of the most creative and liberal minds in 19th century American theology. Drawing upon German idealism and the American Puritan tradition, he attempted to develop a new theological method that would make dogma once again the servant of the spirit and would present Christianity as a "comprehensive" spiritual view embracing man's personal, family, and social relationships.

In his first book, *Christian Nurture* (1847), Bushnell turned the attention of the church toward religious training for the young. He restated the significance of dogma in *God in Christ* (1849), which affirmed the necessity for belief in the Trinity and atonement, considered outdated by contemporary Unitarian thinkers. In *Nature and the Supernatural* (1858), which attempted to relate theology to discoveries in geology, he presented his view of "Christocentric liberalism" acknowledging Christ as the center and goal of history.

JAMES H. SMYLIE
Union Theological Seminary, Richmond, Va.

BUSHRANGERS, bŏŏsh′rān-jərz, were escaped convicts and other criminals in Australia, who took to the bush and supported themselves by armed robbery. They usually traveled in small gangs, although there were several well known bushrangers who worked alone.

Their depredations became so bold that martial law was proclaimed in Van Diemen's Land (Tasmania) in 1815, and a stringent act was adopted in New South Wales in 1830 to stamp out the bushrangers. The country was not able to rid itself of them, however, until roads, railroads, and telephones opened up the bush country.

BUSINESS CAREERS. In the broad sense, business means the commercial, trade, or financial activities that occupy the time, attention, and labor of men and the investment of capital for the sake of profit or improvement. The term "business careers," however, is used in a more limited sense to refer to two kinds of white-collar occupations: managerial jobs at all levels; and clerical, secretarial, and other office jobs. In the United States, more than 20 million men and women are employed in business careers. They are employed not only by private business but also by government agencies and by nonprofit organizations such as schools, colleges, hospitals, and foundations.

CAREERS IN MANAGEMENT

Management consists of activities undertaken to accomplish results by directing the efforts of others. Management employs more college graduates than any other occupational field except teaching and the social sciences. Many junior college graduates are also entering management. Administration is one of the fastest-growing job fields. In the mid-1960's there were about 5 million salaried managers and administrators in the United States and it was estimated that 8.5 million executives would be needed by American business and government by 1970.

Some middle-management or self-employment opportunities are discussed below.

Accountants. About 500,000 accountants were employed in U. S. business in the mid-1960's, including 80,000–100,000 certified public accountants (CPA's). Ninety percent of all accountants are men; 98% of all CPA's are men. The minimum qualification is a B. A. in accounting. Government agencies require a B. A. with an accounting specialization. A rarer means of achieving an accounting position is through on-the-job training as ledger or cost clerk, entry clerk, or timekeeper, and some large companies offer an internal training program. Even CPA's require additional specialization, particularly in tax and estate work and in computer methods.

This field, which expanded faster than any other profession in the period from 1962 to 1966, was expected to continue to grow at the rate of approximately 10,000 new openings yearly through 1975, with an additional 10,000 needed as replacements. Accountants with advanced degrees were in increasing demand. See also ACCOUNTING—*9. Careers in Accounting*.

Advertising Executives. The field includes advertising managers, account executives, copywriters, media directors, production managers, research directors, and art directors. Although college graduates are preferred, there are no typical training requirements for success; rather, advancement depends on a flair for language and a pictorial sense. Many who have risen to the top entered through routine office jobs.

In the mid-1960's about 160,000 men and women were employed in advertising agencies, in organizations serving agencies, or with large advertisers having their own departments. Only a moderate increase was expected in the field by 1975. See also ADVERTISING—*11. Advertising as a Career*.

Industrial Traffic Managers. Involved in the transport of materials, traffic managers have a broad range of duties, from routine checking to planning major freight movements, by road, rail, water, and air. Although college training is increasingly important, high school graduation is the basic educational requirement. Top jobs go to business administration graduates with transportation majors, or to holders of a B. A. with courses in transportation, management, or statistics. Many men are trained on the job, rising from the shipping room or traffic department.

In the mid-1960's nearly 20,000 traffic managers (almost all men) were employed by manufacturing firms, stores, and freight companies. The field was expected to show steady but moderate growth through 1975, with increasing emphasis on specialization.

Market Researchers. This arm of management collects and interprets masses of data to help in decision-making regarding brand names, packaging, sales forecasts, advertising style, plant location, population and income changes, and consumer credit. Executive-level workers in the field include statisticians, psychologists, and economists. College degrees are required for all nonroutine jobs. Colleges and business schools offer specialized courses and degrees in the field. Entrance positions are usually those of analyst or research assistant. At the next level are senior analysts, and some of them become vice presidents in large companies. There are many independent research firms offering consulting services to industry. The field is expanding, but competition for top jobs is intense.

Personnel Managers. Personnel work involves hiring, testing, and promoting workers, classifying jobs, setting wage scales, and developing safety or morale programs. Personnel experts are employed by private businesses, government agencies, and colleges, and some are in business for themselves as consultants and labor relations advisers. Men comprise 80% of the field, although women predominate in department store personnel positions. College degrees are required, usually with some background in psychology, particularly in jobs that involve testing. About 120,000 men and women were employed in this field in the mid-1960's. Rapid expansion was expected.

Purchasing Agents. More than half of the purchasing agents and buyers work for manufacturing firms; the balance are in government, wholesale and retail trade, schools, hospitals, and utilities. Fewer than 10% are women. College degrees are increasingly in demand, especially degrees in business administration. Some companies, however, make provision for on-the-job training.

About 150,000 men and women were employed as purchasing agents and buyers in the mid-1960's. Boom expansion of the field was expected through 1975.

Top Management. Men and women for the top ranks of management will increasingly be recruited from middle-management ranks, but on a somewhat different basis than in the past. Top executives used to be selected because they had spent years as specialists in sales, finance, or some other branch of a business. The advent of the computer with its ability to present a variety of alternatives from sample solutions based on stored and up-to-the-minute data points to the value of the "generalist" rather than the specialist at the highest level of policy-making management. The well-educated man of broad background who sees his business in the perspective of the larger economic picture will be the best judge of machine-given possibilities.

Salaries for Managers. There is a very wide range in the incomes of men and women employed as managers. In the mid-1960's starting salaries for accountants, traffic managers, purchasing agents, and personnel workers were in the neighborhood of $7,000. Those who reached executive status could expect salaries in the $20,000 to $30,000 range. Much depended on individual ability, particularly in advertising. In general, middle-level managers have incomes comparable to those of professional men such as doctors and lawyers. In the top ranks of management, incomes can rise to $50,000 or $100,000.

CAREERS IN OFFICE WORK

The prospects for office workers have been radically affected by electronic devices. Employers prefer to hire men and women with better than average intelligence and with at least a high school education. The need for the routine clerk-typist and record-keeper is diminishing and the demand for the competent secretary with skill and initiative is at an all-time high.

Stenographers and Secretaries. In the mid-1960's 2 million women were employed in jobs that required stenographic skill, and openings were expected to occur at the rate of 200,000 annually during the next 10 years for workers with the ability to take shorthand. Jobs in this field range from that of entry-level general stenographers, usually assigned to work in the office pool, to college-educated specialists able to record legal, medical, scientific, or foreign language dictation. Some of the most desirable positions are held by those who have shown the ability to organize and supervise office work and to relieve executives of many details of their jobs, thus earning the title of secretary.

Office Machine Operators. This job title covers a range from the worker who operates a simple letter opener through those who run duplicating and tabulating machines and on up to the electronic data processor. As new types of office machines are being developed, business is expected to need some 50,000 operators per year into the 1970's. See also COMPUTER.

Clerk-Typists. In the mid-1960's, there were 650,000 clerk-typists, 95% women. Business will continue to welcome young women with the ability to type the necessary 40–50 words per minute into entry-level jobs into the foreseeable future.

Salaries for Office Workers. The pay of clerk-typists, stenographers, and operators of the simpler business machines tends to be lower than the average wage in manufacturing and well below the income of lower-level managers. Exceptionally qualified office workers, on the other hand, are paid as well as some middle-level managers. Pay prospects are particularly good for executive secretaries and computer programmers.

See also BUSINESS EDUCATION; CAREER PLANNING; VOCATIONAL EDUCATION.

ESTELLE L. POPHAM
Hunter College, New York

Bibliography

Bellows, Roger M., *Executive Skills* (Englewood Cliffs, N. J., 1962).
Goldwin, Roberta, *Toward the Liberally Educated Executive* (White Plains, N. Y., 1957).
King, Alice G., *Career Opportunities for Women in Business* (New York 1963).
Popham, Estelle L., and Farelly, Roberta, *Opportunities in Office Occupations*, 2d ed. (New York 1964).
U. S. Department of Labor, Bureau of Labor Statistics, *Occupational Outlook Handbook* (Washington, biennially).

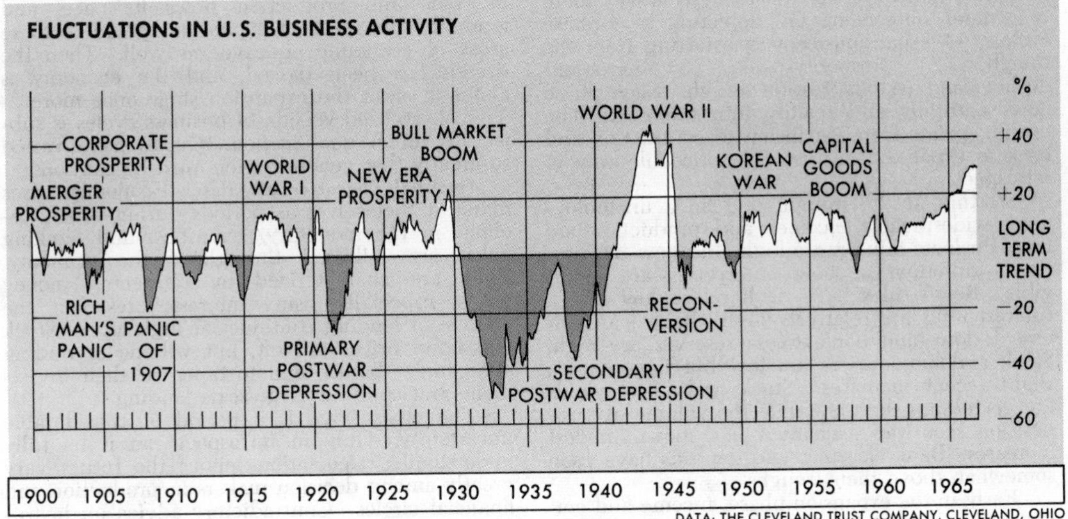

BUSINESS CYCLES have occurred since the Industrial Revolution in industrialized nations with highly developed banking and financial systems. Industrialization involves increased interdependence of the several sectors of a national economy. Uneven rates of growth and development in one sector—especially financial markets or investment—frequently lead to crises and declines that spread throughout the entire economy.

Economic crises are only one phase of the business cycle. They represent the most dramatic aspect of cyclical behavior. An economic crisis is a period of widespread economic and financial stress that shortly precedes the peak of general economic activity. Declines in production, employment, and income follow.

Although early thought tended to regard business cycles as a necessary "price" of industrial growth, attempts to offset or control the cycle have been made since the 1920's. The first efforts were primarily corrective. They sought to counteract declines or depressions already started. After World War II, however, the emphasis shifted to anticipation, and to stabilization of financial activity, production, investment, and consumption. The aim is to stimulate orderly growth in real national income, while sharply diminishing the severity of cyclical swings. The success achieved in approaching this goal has come from greater knowledge of what happens during business cycles and of what areas of economic activity are most sensitive to centralized control.

Nature of Business Cycles. Business cycles are fluctuations in the level of general business, economic, and financial activity. They are usually analyzed in terms of national economies, although international aspects of business fluctuations have long been recognized.

Wesley Clair Mitchell, a founder of the National Bureau of Economic Research in 1920 and the originator of business cycle analysis in the United States, gave the classic definition of the business cycle in *Business Cycles: The Problem and Its Setting* (1927). Mitchell wrote:

> Business cycles are a type of fluctuation found in the aggregate economic activity of nations that organize their work mainly in business enterprises. A cycle consists of expansions occurring at about the same time in many economic activities, followed by similarly general recessions, contractions, and revivals which merge into the expansion phase of the next cycle. This sequence of change is recurrent but not periodic. In duration business cycles vary from more than one year to ten or twelve years. They are not divisible into shorter cycles of similar character with amplitudes approximating their own.

This definition reveals the essential characteristics of business cycles. They are all-pervading and widely diffused over a nation's economy. In this they are distinguished from commercial fluctuations in the preindustrial period and from seasonal or other short-term fluctuations in modern times. Business cycles are also peculiar to private-enterprise industrial societies. In effect, they have been confined to the western European and North American nations.

The business cycle is a complex of many interrelated individual fluctuations. It is general in scope because of the integrated, interdependent nature of modern industrial societies. The cycle is also a constantly repeating, ever-changing phenomenon. The overall pattern recurs, but there are always differences in its makeup. The severity of movement (*amplitude*) and the length of any phase (*duration*) vary from specific cycle to specific cycle.

Empirical evidence is the basis for the indicated duration of more than 1 to 10 or 12 years. The nondivisibility of cycles is similarly based on historical data, for the United States, England, France, and Germany.

The business cycle is measured by an artificial index. This index is obtained by aggregating individual indicators—also called series—such as gross national product and the industrial production index. Each of these indicators has its own pattern and peculiarities. The business cycle index reveals their overall pattern in broad terms, showing the general trend of all the individual indicators taken together. This overall pattern is known as a *reference cycle*. The "normal" level of business is a statistically determined, long-term trend line, against which fluctuations are measured.

The Cycle Pattern. Although individuality and variety are major characteristics of business cycles, there is a fairly typical pattern of movement in them. The usual method of description involves measuring the cycle from trough to trough. While systems of analysis vary, there is general agreement on depicting a 4-phase cycle: (1) expansion-recovery, starting from the trough; (2) prosperity-peak; (3) recession-decline; and (4) depression-trough. Each phase flows naturally and readily into the next. The turning points from expansion to contraction and back to expansion are usually noticeable only in retrospect.

Starting at the trough, one finds unemployment widespread. Incomes and production are low. Business failures are high, and new business starts—formation of new enterprises—are negligible. Retail sales have declined to low levels. Interest rates are relatively high. Bank loan volume is low, and bank excess reserves are high. Stock and bond prices are low but have shown slight recent increases. Stock and bond yields are decreasing slightly, while the volume of business on securities exchanges has shown modest increases. Bank clearings and deposits have risen somewhat above their troughs.

Early in the expansion phase, income and employment characteristically rise. So do such indicators as domestic trade, imports, and commodity prices. Securities prices and volume show rapid improvement. Financial activity quickens markedly, while interest rates at first decline. Bank lending expands rapidly, together with bank clearings and deposits.

The first check in a general advance all along the line is a decline in bond market activity and bond prices, stemming from a switch of funds to stocks. Long-term interest rates begin to rise as the demand for loans catches up with supply and more nearly marginal risks are handled by banks and other institutional lenders.

As general expansion progresses and establishes itself as prosperity, it is the financial sector of the economy that first exhibits fairly general declines: in stock prices and trading volume, in new securities issues, and in bank debits and deposit turnover. This is the statistical and historical record, with no implications as to cause and effect.

The declines and contractions first exhibited in the financial field gradually spread to other areas of the economy. In this period the critical, or crisis, stage occurs. Declining securities prices, declining bank activity, and increasing loan defaults exert stresses on the economy, so that production and employment fall.

Economic crises have often been precipitated by financial panics, stock market crashes, bank failures, or "flights" of money from certain currencies or countries. In every such instance, however, the downward turning point in general business activity has followed such a development only after some lapse of time.

Once the beginnings of recession have permeated the economy, the initial decline in production, employment, income, and prices is usually sharp and rapid. Long-term interest rates continue to rise. Capital goods industries in particular feel the brunt of decline early in the recession.

Gradually bond prices and bond market volume begin to stabilize, because interest rates begin to drift slightly downward. Business failures, in terms of total liabilities, begin to decline in volume, indicating that the worst stage in business liquidations has passed. Then stock prices and trading volume begin to rise, followed by increased securities issues, business incorporations, and turnover of bank deposits. The decline in trade and production slows its pace, and gradually the seeds of expansion spread to these areas of economic endeavor as well. Then the trough has been passed, and the economy is about to enter the expansion stage once more.

This stylized version of business cycles is subject to much qualification. Cycles have varied so greatly that generalization must be cautious.

Financial Character of Crises. Economic crises manifest themselves as periods during which declines in the monetary, securities, and banking fields are reflected throughout the economy. They are characterized by tightening money terms, especially rising interest rates, but the volume of lending continues at high levels. Stock and bond prices fall off, but volume of trading stays high. Banks tend to taper off their investments but continue large-scale lending.

The crisis stage is a period of considerable uncertainty. Only in retrospect can it be fully understood. Expectations about the future vary greatly among decision makers in production and financial circles. Contradictory advice on investments, on inventory policy, and on buying consumers' goods or producers' goods is given on every side. In large measure the uncertainty and hesitancy about the future helps to tip the scales in favor of a general decline.

History of Cycles in the United States. For measuring fluctuations in total business activity in the United States, good data are available for the years since 1919. For some areas of business activity, adequate data are available back to the 1850's or 1860's. Charts of business cycles since 1919 show wider swings in business activity than are shown by charts for earlier cycles. One reason may be simply that more precise information is accessible for the later cycles. Another factor is that each section of the national economy has become more dependent on the rest of the economy, so that all sections are more likely to fluctuate at the same time.

There have been over 35 discernible cycles in general business activity in the United States since 1790. The most severe business declines in American economic life occurred in the cycles that reached their lows in the years 1807, 1837, 1873, 1882, 1893, 1920, 1929, and 1937. Crises in the financial markets occurred in all of these except the 1807 cycle. Lesser business declines took place in 1946, 1949, 1954, and 1958, although activity remained at relatively high levels.

The panic of 1837 began with a suspension of specie payments, widespread bank failures, and wild speculation in commodity markets. Only later did production and employment decline.

The year 1873 produced a "Black Friday" on September 19. Heavy speculation in securities, together with the failure of Jay Cooke and Co., provided the impetus for the panic, which was brief but severe.

The 1882–1884 period witnessed railroad securities speculation and subsequent panics as rail failures occurred. In 1893 a heavy gold flow to the London money market led to a suspension of specie payments. This again precipitated a financial crisis and a stock market break.

The 1920 break was quite severe but shortlived. Speculation during and immediately following World War I set the stage for a spectacular stock and commodity price crash.

By far the most dramatic financial crisis in the entire period was that which began in the United States on Oct. 29, 1929 (Black Tuesday) with the stock market crash. The financial aspects of this crisis were more widespread and lasted longer than in any previous cycle. The bank failures of 1932 and 1933 and the final suspension of the gold standard came at the trough of the cycle, adding greatly to the difficulties of recovery.

In 1937 a combination of tightened monetary controls by the Federal Reserve System, increased margin requirements for securities purchase, and a stock market break produced a less severe—but nonetheless sharp—crisis situation.

The 1946 and 1949 declines also were both preceded by stock market breaks. These were in a technical sense crises also, although in both instances recovery was rapid and complete.

The evidence on cycle activity in the United States indicates that financial crises are connected with, and usually precede, declines in general business activity. The crisis period presages the end of the prosperity phase and the beginning of the recession-contraction phase of the business cycle. It manifests itself through securities market declines, interest rate rises, bank loan stringencies, and general financial contraction.

Causes of Business Cycles. Theories of the causes of business cycles attempt to explain the upper and lower turning points of the cycle. They seek to answer the question: Why does the general level of business activity in the economy change direction and move downward (or upward)? Business cycle theorists have been much more concerned as a group with why and how a decline sets in than with why and how a recovery starts.

Types of business cycle theories include (1) business economy theories, (2) monetary theories, (3) savings and investment theories, and (4) miscellaneous explanations.

Business Economy Theories. The business economy approach holds that business cycles are inherent attributes of an industrial business enterprise economy. The business cycle is said to be a self-generating phenomenon. Each phase contains in it the necessary components of the succeeding phase. These theories are by nature eclectic and inclusive, and are not one-sided in their emphasis. They are essentially realistic and tend to be descriptive rather than analytical.

If Wesley Clair Mitchell's work can be classified under any heading, it belongs here. The British economists Arthur Cecil Pigou and John Maynard Keynes also belong in this category.

Monetary Theories. All business cycles have their monetary aspects. But some economists, notably Ralph George Hawtrey, Knut Wicksell, and the economists of the Austrian school, argue that the chief reason for cycles in total spending is changes in the money supply. These are controlled by banks in a credit-oriented, business enterprise economy. Banks expand and contract the money supply by their creation or destruction of credit money or demand deposits. The controlling mechanism is the interest rate structure.

Empirical evidence in the United States shows that the roles of interest rates and credit are exaggerated in this approach. However, they cannot be ignored entirely as causative factors in the complex of business cycle activity.

Savings and Investment Theories. Theories emphasizing the savings-investment process as the primary determinant of the business cycle may be further subdivided into four groups. In emphasizing the role of fluctuations in investment in causing business fluctuations, however, they all have a common theoretical base. They hold that cycles stem from the inherent instability of long-term investment. The level of investment attained at the peak of prosperity cannot be maintained permanently, and the consequent decline in investment sets off a cumulative decline in business activity.

The *monetary overinvestment* brand of savings-investment approach is most closely associated with Friedrich August von Hayek. Overinvestment occurs during the prosperity phase, according to this explanation, because excessive amounts of credit are made available for investment. Eventually a shortage of capital develops as investment outruns the supply of savings. Investment perforce declines, and recession sets in.

The *partial overinvestment-innovations* theory emphasizes what happens to investment opportunities in particular industries. Stress is placed on the role of innovations in causing cyclical fluctuations in business activity. Investment declines because new investment opportunities created by innovations, which occur sporadically and in bunches, are exhausted. This approach is identified with Joseph Alois Schumpeter, Alvin Harvey Hansen, and Dennis Holme Robertson.

A third savings-investment approach stresses primarily the operational relationships among investment, savings, income, and consumption. The basic point at issue is that as income rises, investment and consumption must keep pace, each also maintaining the proper relationship with saving. The rising volume of saving acts as an increasing drag on continued prosperity because of *underinvestment* of the savings.

The *oversaving*, or *underconsumption*, approach holds that the use of savings in new investment causes production to outstrip consumers' purchasing power periodically. Thus the savings that are necessary for expanded production also lead to overproduction and recession.

Miscellaneous Explanations. Some explanations of the business cycle have been based on agriculture and the weather. Perhaps the most dramatic attempt to show that agriculture is basic to business cycles was made by the 19th century economist William Stanley Jevons. He argued that the entire pattern of cycles depends on sunspots, which affect the weather and therefore crops, which in turn influence prices and business activity. This is now regarded merely as an interesting historical episode in cycle theory.

Of the various attempts to explain the business cycle, all but the business economy type of theory suffer from one-sidedness. Because of the great and growing complexity of national economies, such as those of the United States and Britain, no one simple explanation serves the purpose adequately. The more eclectic, empirical approach has not as yet developed a complete theory of the business cycle. It is in this direction, however, that most effort has been expended since the end of World War II.

Efforts to Control the Cycle. Although there are differences of opinion on the basic causes of the general business cycle, everyone agrees that cyclical fluctuations should be minimized by control of the economic system.

Concentrated, organized interest in controlling business cycles did not exist in the United States until after 1930. The "boom-and-bust" pattern was considered a necessary feature of economic activity before that time. Previous efforts at avoiding crises had relied on increasing the cost of credit and reducing its availability. Following the severe decline of 1930–1933, however, many other kinds of emergency measures were enacted. Although most survived into the post-World War II period, it was not until the 1940's that systematic attempts were made at controlling the cycle in the United States.

Controlling the cycle involves minimizing the severity of fluctuations, but without stagnation. It is recognized that severe recessions stem in large part from excesses committed in the final boom portion of prosperity. Therefore, control of the cycle has taken the form of preventive curbs on many potential excesses, as well as measures to combat fluctuations directly.

The control devices established and employed in the United States emphasize monetary mechanisms and fiscal policy. Securities market speculation is reduced by margin requirements, and the Securities and Exchange Commission has worked to minimize the unfavorable psychological effects of frauds or manipulations. Those stock market breaks that have occurred have been brief, relatively mild, and orderly.

Federal Reserve controls over bank policies have been tightened. Housing credit has become more nearly stabilized and institutionalized. Public works, debt management, and direct credit controls have all been employed in the cause of economic stabilization.

In 1946 the Employment Act was enacted by Congress. It established the Council of Economic Advisers and declared the maintenance of stable, high levels of income and employment to be an integral part of national policy. Both anti-depression and anti-inflation measures are at the disposal of the federal government. By constant collection and analysis of data on the basic components of the national economy, the council can warn of impending declines or inflations.

In the decades since the inauguration of the Council of Economic Advisers, major strides have been made in counter-cyclical programs in the United States. More and better information about the behavior of the various sectors of the economy, coupled with improved understanding of the nature of the business cycle, has led to unparalleled growth at or near full employment levels. Recessions have diminished in magnitude and duration. Recessions have become "dips" in the steady upward movement of economic activity.

Policies have been coordinated among monetary and fiscal authorities in anticipation of excessive upward or downward movement, rather than as a reaction to them. Debate and disagreement still occur over causal relationships in cyclical activity, but the strategic factors for effective control have been identified clearly.

WILLIAM N. KINNARD, JR.
University of Connecticut

Bibliography

Burns, Arthur F., *Management of Prosperity* (New York 1966).
Burns, Arthur F., and Mitchell, Wesley Clair, *Measuring Business Cycles* (New York 1946).
Committee for Economic Development, *Managing a Full Employment Economy* (New York 1966).
Duesenberry, James S., *Business Cycles and Economic Growth* (New York 1958).
Gordon, Robert Aaron, *Business Fluctuations,* 2d ed. (New York 1961).
Levien, J. R., *Anatomy of a Crash–1929* (New York 1966).
Mitchell, Wesley Clair, *What Happens During Business Cycles: A Progress Report* (New York 1951).
Moore, Geoffrey H., ed., *Business Cycle Indicators,* 2 vols. (Princeton 1961).

BUSINESS EDUCATION. Originally, business or commercial education meant training in such skills as arithmetic and bookkeeping. The field has grown, however, and now includes such topics as electronic data processing, corporate management, and economic theory.

Business education may mean strictly vocational training. On the other hand, broader aims may be introduced. One is to give all students the skills they will need to conduct personal business and keep household records. For example, arithmetic with bookkeeping is part of the curriculum in many public schools. Business education may have the still broader aim of helping citizens understand business principles and practices. In such a case, the emphasis is similar to that found in an introductory course in economics.

Commercial education may be given in a specialized vocational school or it may be combined with a program of general education. Some kind of business education is offered in schools and colleges throughout the world, from the elementary clerical training in the post-primary schools of the Democratic Republic of Congo to the doctoral programs of the University of Pennsylvania's Wharton School of Finance in the United States and the London School of Economics and Political Science in England. All levels and varieties of programs can be illustrated by a description of those conducted in the United States.

VARIETIES OF PROGRAMS IN THE UNITED STATES

Business education in the United States is divided into two major segments—secondary and collegiate. In addition, a third segment developed rapidly after World War II in the area of postsecondary education of less than full college grade—the junior college, for example. It shares characteristics of both the secondary and college levels and yet is distinct from both.

Secondary Business Education. There are two major objectives for business education at the secondary level: (1) training students who plan to enter office and distributive occupations and (2) giving all students competence in the use of business services as citizens and individuals. The original goal was job training. Even in colonial times there were simple forms of business education. For example, "merchants accounts" was one of the courses at the Philadelphia Academy, organized in 1751 by Benjamin Franklin. However, the real beginnings of education for the business world date from the development of the private, or independent, business school.

The apprenticeship system so general in Europe did not function well in the United States and especially not in a business office. Therefore, as organized bookkeeping, communication, and computation became more important in American industry, the heads of business firms were willing to pay better salaries to the person who had learned these skills in school before seeking employment.

The development of a functional typewriter in the 1870's furthered the growth of business schools and made shorthand a successful office skill. Moreover, it created an opportunity and a need for the services of young women in the office, for it was soon found that women were especially adept at secretarial work. A parallel growth in the field of accountancy also created opportunities for men. By 1900 a trend that has since become typical had developed: young men specialized in bookkeeping, and young women in typewriting and shorthand.

Parents soon demanded that this type of learning be offered in the public high school and their demand was met. While there had been occasional courses in business in high schools before 1900, it was not until after 1910 that business education, or commercial education as it then was called, became characteristic of the high school program. The demand for office workers was so great, however, that despite the growth of the high school program, enrollment in independent business schools continued to grow. Their enrollments were not seriously affected by the tremendous increase of high school business education until the first post-World War I depression of 1921.

The pattern of high school commercial studies soon became fixed. Special curriculums for business students offered typing, bookkeeping, and shorthand as their three major subjects. Little attention was paid to purely academic subjects since the average business student did not plan on entering college. He and, more usually, she elected two years of typing, bookkeeping, and shorthand and two or three units of social or general business subjects, such as junior business training, business law, business arithmetic, and economics. Only six or eight Carnegie units (credit given for one year's study of one subject at the secondary level, as defined by the Carnegie Foundation for the Advancement of Teaching) of academic work were elected. For completion of this course of study, the student received a commercial diploma.

Enrollment in high school typing classes now far exceeds that in other business courses because typing is elected by both commercial and academic students. Bookkeeping, also a popular subject although not so well attended, is usually offered for one year. Shorthand is often supplemented by courses in transcription. Increasing numbers of schools offer a 1-year business course to bright students, who are found to be as proficient on the job as the less progressive students who require two or more years to complete their studies.

In the 1920's there was a tendency to shift business training down to the junior high school level. This trend has now been reversed. Except on an exploratory basis, bookkeeping, shorthand, and merchandising are rarely taught in the junior high school. However, general business or introduction to business courses are holding their own as 9th-grade, and occasionally as 8th-grade, subjects. These courses are designed to give students an understanding of business for personal use and to serve as prevocational background for skill courses. Typing for personal use is maintaining its enrollment in the junior high school, and several attempts have been made to introduce it into the elementary school as an adjunct to reading and writing.

Changing Emphases in Business Studies. The tendency to require purely business curriculums lessened in the 1950's and 1960's. Instead, students take one or more sequences of business subjects as part of a general curriculum. Office practice is accepted as a finishing course, integrating learned skills with broader job needs and developing initial skills on office machines. Sporadic attempts to make economics and consumer education part of the business program have met with some success. See also CONSUMER EDUCATION.

A growing problem for secondary school educators in business studies is the widening interest of bright commercial students in attending college. This new emphasis has caused an increased demand for the inclusion of academic subjects required for college entrance in the business school curriculum. Even average students have been encouraged to concentrate on academic subjects. Thus, while there are more full-time business students than ever in high schools, such students are often marginal in ability and not so adaptable as their brighter classmates to training for office work. As a consequence, urgent efforts are being made to adapt business curriculums to these less able students. For example, record keeping is replacing bookkeeping, since it eliminates some of the more technical phases of the latter and emphasizes clerical skills.

Distributive or merchandising education has been developed to meet the needs of nonacademic students. A cooperative work-study plan whereby the student spends part of the day working in a store or business office under the direction of the school, is one approach being used to encourage business students. The use of distributive education as a means of developing basic competencies in the three "R's" is another. Visual aids, field trips, and other procedures designed to stimulate interest are a third.

Since electronic data processing has become an integral part of the routine of many offices, the question arises whether students should be taught such simple, easily learned initial skills as key-punch operation on expensive machines in school or should learn them on the job. Teaching data processing at the secondary level also raises the question of whether learning should be limited to an understanding of the process developed by means of a "systems" approach with emphasis on the flow chart as a method of securing understanding. No definite answer to these questions can be provided because learning materials have not been developed to the best level, and teachers have not been trained and adjusted to these newer concepts. The need to incorporate such materials in teacher education is urgent.

Federal Aid to Business Education in Secondary Schools. State and local governments have become aware of the need for improved patterns of vocational education for business. It has also become increasingly clear that funds from the federal government are needed to support such vocational programs.

Since 1917 the federal government has given aid to some phases of industrial and farm job training and, since 1937, to distributive or merchandising education. However, it was not until the passage of the Vocational Education Act of 1963 that specific federal aid for commercial education was provided. The best method of using this aid is still to be decided. New equipment, new course aids, teacher reeducation, and postsecondary programs are typical projects sponsored by federal grants. Funds are being used to provide supervisory personnel at both state and city levels as well as on a federal regional basis. While most states have had supervisors of distributive education for some time, such personnel are now being provided for office education. Cooperative work-experience programs of all types are now being greatly expanded, especially in education programs for dropouts. See also VOCATIONAL EDUCATION.

Training of Secondary School Business Teachers. Those educators involved with the training of business teachers have almost universally directed their curriculums to high school business teaching. State certification of business education teachers for high schools is required in all 50 states. In general, teachers of business classes are required to devote about one half of their undergraduate studies to academic subjects and a little over one quarter to business subject matter. For service in some areas prospective teachers must show competence in both secretarial and bookkeeping specializations. In addition teachers are required to have a fixed number of education courses and to have had student teaching experience, although this requirement may be waived if adequate substitute-teaching experience has been gained.

The trend among state teachers colleges to become general state colleges or universities has offered other outlets for employment to their students, especially to men students. Therefore, there has been a tendency for fewer undergraduate students to plan for careers as business teachers. As a consequence new teachers must sometimes be recruited from among more mature office workers who find the transfer to teaching desirable. Through summer school work and evening study they can meet minimum teaching standards with little difficulty. There is no evidence that teachers with one type of background are materially better than others with different preparation, although each group has its strong advocates.

Permanent certification tends to be given only upon the attainment of a master's degree or its equivalent. California has experimented with a plan that requires all prospective teachers to have an academic major. Business teachers and other vocational teachers may satisfy certification requirements with a minor in their teaching subject. California has also tested a plan that would permit persons with several years of proved job competence to waive all formal subject matter courses. Teachers already in service usually take strong exception to these innovations. However, such moves are worthy of experimentation.

Collegiate Business Education. The aim of business education at the college level may be summarized as the development of competent professional managers for business. To achieve this goal means giving students an understanding of the general nature of business, competence in specialized phases of business activity, ability to provide leadership, and the cultural background necessary to achieve these purposes. The objective of collegiate schools of business has not always been this broad.

Development of Programs. When the Wharton School of Finance and Commerce was established in 1881 at the University of Pennsylvania as the first formal collegiate school of business education in the United States, its program consisted largely of standard academic subjects. Adjunct courses included economics—notably money and banking, the business cycle, and taxation—and business aspects of law. The curriculum was organized in terms of business theory, and there was little attempt to make teaching meaningful in terms of specific managerial problems.

At the beginning of the 20th century an entirely different program was developed for collegiate business education. This approach evolved in response to the needs of the accounting profession. Accounting firms, which formerly had hired accountants trained in Britain, found that their supply of competent professional accountants was diminishing. Moreover, the validity of using British accountants to deal with the unique characteristics of American business became increasingly questionable. Since it was difficult to train accountants on the job, the School of Commerce, Accounts, and Finance was organized at New York University in 1900, purely as an evening curriculum with approximately two years of work. In addition to accounting, sufficient study of business law, economics, banking and finance, and the mathematics of business was provided to give the student the background knowledge he needed to pass the Certified Public Accountant examination. No broad cultural subjects were included in the curriculum.

A few years later specialized training was added in other phases of business, such as banking, marketing, and real estate. Eventually it was found desirable to give the students some general cultural background. As a consequence, in gradual steps and certainly by 1930, the programs at the University of Pennsylvania and at New York University became strikingly similar. This common purpose was fostered by the American Association of Collegiate Schools of Business (primarily an organization of deans of schools of business), which set up accreditation standards with minimal allowances for such areas as cultural subjects and teacher competence. However, the primary aim of the two collegiate schools of business remained specific in terms of training for particular aspects of business, with minimum academic background requirements and a strong tendency toward how-to-do-it courses. The necessity of increasing enrollment brought about a lowering of entrance standards below those of academic schools, and it is possible that lower standards of performance led to a degree of complacency on the part of the administrations of collegiate schools of business.

Criticism and Change. This complacency was dramatically shattered by two occurrences. One was the launching of the first earth satellite, Sputnik I, by the USSR in 1957. The other was the publication of *Higher Education for Business* by R. A. Gordon and J. E. Howell and of *Education of American Businessmen* by F. C. Pierson and others, both in 1959. The launching of Sputnik forced a new appraisal of American teaching in business and technology, and the two foundation-sponsored books presented a severe indictment of collegiate schools of business.

The authors criticized the schools for relatively low entrance requirements and for their failure to require adequate academic background, particularly in the humanities, social studies, science, and mathematics. They were devastating in their criticism of the schools' tendency to emphasize techniques at the expense of an overall understanding of the nature of business. They illustrated dramatically the very considerable amount of duplication in course work in the schools. Possibly the authors' greatest share of criticism was devoted to the proclivity of business schools to offer courses in what was described as clerical work—for example, courses in office practice and procedures and stenography.

While the judgments were by no means universally accepted, they had a major impact. The discussion that followed publication of the critical books brought about a major change in the structure of the American collegiate schools of business.

In general these schools have moved to a new status as senior colleges, offering only a few business courses of a background nature at the freshman and sophomore levels. These first two years emphasize academic background identical with that required for academic degrees.

As a second change, courses in accounting and other business methods are reduced in number and presented from a management point of view.

Third, a systems approach to management, based on the determination of goals and on problem-solving to meet these goals, is emphasized. The spirit of the school is directed toward developing a professional concept of management based on scientific procedures coupled with awareness of the social purpose of business. It is assumed that graduates of collegiate business schools will rise rapidly in the business world, at least to middle management, and that they can learn on the job the relatively few specific skills they will need.

The result of all of these changes has been a stiffening of entrance requirements, and consequently a considerable drop in enrollment. Schools are thus free to select students much more carefully than was possible with older standards.

In the early days of the collegiate schools of business, teachers of economics, businessmen with practical experience, and collegiate school graduates became classroom instructors. The present trend is to hire teachers who have had an extensive academic education at the bachelor's level. Such teachers receive their basic business education at the master's level in a well-known collegiate business school before taking up their classroom duties. Some then gain on-the-job business experience at the managerial level and go on to study for their doctorate before teaching.

Graduate Schools. The graduate school has become a dominating aspect of the work of the collegiate school of business. Here the student with a bachelor's degree can pursue a detailed study of the functions of business under the direction of professors with established reputations. While committed to a certain amount of lecturing, professors emphasize the situational approach; that is, after developing an understanding of the basic nature of the business process, teachers give their students an opportunity to work out solutions to case problems, either individually or as a group.

As electronic data processing and other instruments of control are developed and modified, the case study tends to shift in its organization. For example, in the more progressive schools students function within the limitations imposed by the peculiar nature of electronic data processing. At the same time they are given expanded opportunities to use a vast amount of new evidence for problem solving. This trend makes possible a much wider use of mathematical and scientific instruments for help in providing the materials for problem solving.

The student body often includes business managers in large corporations, who are encouraged by their employers to spend from a month to a semester and even, occasionally, a year in advanced study at collegiate schools of business. Corporations have found that this reorientation at some stage in the professional manager's career gives him a greater understanding of the purposes of the business and of the social environment in which it functions. Younger students profit from the practical problems these executive-students bring to the classroom.

The Postsecondary Level. In many respects the key area of commercial education is the level above the high school but below the 4-year college. Several types of post-high school institutions offer specialized training to the business student, for example, independent business schools, junior colleges, and area vocational schools. There has been a shift upward of some secondary school subject matter to this level and some shift downward, particularly of skill learning, from the collegiate school of business. Some reasons for this change are: (1) awareness of the need for more general education at the high school level; (2) concern that premature preparation in the high school for the job may result in skill training rather than true education; (3) simplification of many office skills, making skill training of marginal value; (4) increased cost and rapid depreciation of office machines, with consequent obsolescence of operating skills; (5) concentration of populations, making area vocational schools, as the post-high school is sometimes called, and similar institutions more feasible; and (6) overcrowding of colleges, forcing many learners into alternate types of schools.

The Independent Business School. Known formerly as the private business school—and still rather generally so titled—the independent business school was the original means of attaining an education for business in the United States.

The subsequent growth of the public high school and the proportionate increase of business subjects in its curriculum reduced the significance of the independent business school as a factor in vocational training. Nevertheless, the demise of this type of school, often prophesied by the ardent public high school advocate, has not taken place. On the contrary the independent business school is far more effective, higher in ethical standards, and probably more prosperous than it was in the early 20th century.

The key motivation of the independent business school is profit. Therefore, such a school is quick to seize upon new training ideas. When, for example, data processing first developed, a number of venturesome teachers set up speed-course schools for training in data processing. Such schools were not always successful, and their students often failed to obtain positions. This phase of enterprise soon passed. The programs that have survived usually are well organized and based on normal job needs.

The rapid increase in demand for vocational education has stimulated government at all levels to use the facilities of independent schools in cases where the need might be transitory or where the student cannot adjust to the typical public high school pattern. Some independent business schools get much of their income from government funds; some seek or get little or none. Financial assistance, or the lack of it, bears no relation to the soundness of the program offered by the individual school.

Some kind of accreditation was needed to measure a private business school's suitability for obtaining government funds. Moreover, the proprietors of independent business schools themselves wished to have a means of identifying the schools that were sound and those that did not meet minimum standards of selection and financial stability. The National Association and Council of Business Schools therefore set up an Accrediting Commission for Business Schools. The commission includes representatives from independent business schools, education associations, and office-executive groups. The establishment of such an agency has helped to police the independent business school program, and the interchange of ideas occasioned by school visitations has probably helped to improve school standards.

Some independent schools have become very similar in format and program to the public high schools or nonprofit-making colleges and have shifted to a nonprofit basis. They are therefore in the strict sense of the word no longer independent schools. However, a number of such schools have avoided this step, despite its advantages for prestige, acceptance of credit by colleges, and tax benefits.

There is a tendency for some 4-year colleges to grant credit for work done in independent business schools, especially those that offer an extended program of from one to two years in skill training and background understanding. This practice complicates to some extent the job training process. However, independent business schools are by their very nature flexible. They have become adept in meeting both the objectives of college-oriented students and those directed to a strict job training situation.

Business Education in Junior and Community Colleges. This type of school, whatever name it adopts, has grown more rapidly than other types of business schools, and now forms an integral phase of the educational process. While the junior college started out as a terminal institution, a strong tendency has arisen to make the junior college serve as a stepping-stone to the senior college. Thus, for many junior college students there has been a reduction in the number of business skill courses taken and an emphasis on those courses that will be accepted as credits for transfer to the senior college. Nevertheless, the goal of educating students for semiprofessional work still predominates, even though this practice means that some students may lose education credits if they transfer to senior college levels.

Whatever their ultimate objective, the immediate aim of students of business in junior colleges is to develop a balanced understanding of the nature of business. Accounting, secretarial work, and salesmanship and marketing are prominent among the subjects studied. There is also an opportunity to develop competence in electronic computer processing. These studies are rounded out by courses in such subjects as business organization, managerial accounting, banking, and business law. See also JUNIOR COLLEGE.

Other Programs. While the junior college will continue to be the standard institution at the post-high school level, a number of other institutions are coming into being to supplement its functions. The need for these new schools arises from the increasing selectivity of the junior college and, more importantly, because of its tendency to bypass training in routine skills in favor of semiprofessional education. Best known of this new type is the area vocational school.

Area Vocational Schools. Because they draw their students from an area that is usually considerably larger than that of the typical high school, area vocational schools offer training in a wider range of subjects. A generally accepted criterion for an area vocational school is that it offer training in at least five different occupational fields on a full-time basis.

Unlike the junior college, the area vocational school accepts dropout students at any level, particularly those for whom some type of job training seems meaningful. Moreover, the vocational school accommodates students at all age levels on a full-time or part-time basis. If enrollment warrants such distinctions, older students are separated from high school dropouts and full-time from part-time students. Some area vocational schools even have a division with junior college status. More frequently, however, a junior college may have an area vocational school as an adjunct, thus providing for better use of equipment, more teacher specialization, and greater opportunity for program diversification.

In some states the area vocational school has become a service school for regular secondary schools, offering occupational training for part of the day to students for whom such programs are not available in their regular secondary curriculum. Such students receive their certificate of graduation from the regular secondary school.

Area vocational schools offer office training in data processing, accounting, secretarial studies, and other clerical duties. In addition they often provide extensive training in distributive skills, with emphasis on retail store operation rather than overall marketing processes.

There are more than 300 area vocational schools in operation, wholly or partly subsidized by federal funds. An additional 1,000 or more schools had curricular characteristics that would justify their being designated as area vocational schools.

In-Service Education for Business. Many commercial firms provide extensive on-the-job training in specific business skills. Insurance companies and banks in particular are likely to have well-defined programs for upgrading the potential competence of their junior workers. Other large firms offer many programs of preparation for managerial work during and after working hours. Smaller firms, and many large firms as well, give full or partial repayment of funds spent by employees on education for advancement.

Rehabilitation Programs. Under the Manpower Act of 1962 and supplementary legislation, programs of business training have been made available for the unemployed and for others who wish to upgrade their competency in business on a short-term, full-time basis. Some of these programs extend for only a few weeks; others continue for a year or more. Among such opportunities are the Job Corps programs.

The Job Corps programs are financed by the federal government and are conducted under direct government supervision or by private companies under contract to the government. Many difficulties had to be met before the corps began to function efficiently. However, its programs are now progressing satisfactorily and give evidence that with careful planning such schooling can be of considerable value in helping youths who were previously unemployable to be fitted for gainful employment.

BUSINESS EDUCATION IN OTHER COUNTRIES

There used to be marked differences between business education in the United States and that in other countries. For example, apprenticeship lasted longer in Europe than in the United States.

As schools developed, most European countries as well as such countries as Australia and New Zealand had a dual system of education. Academic and vocational education were separated, whereas the tendency in the United States was to combine general education with job training. Secondary business schools were not typical in Europe. However, the differences between U. S. practices and those in other countries have decreased.

Germany, Sweden, and New Zealand have strong technical high schools for economics and commerce, often associated with major universities. In Britain the comprehensive secondary school, incorporating academic and vocational training, is coming into prominence. Such school systems also are being explored elsewhere, notably in France, Australia, and Canada. These countries also have private business schools that operate at least as efficiently as those of the United States and have basically similar characteristics. Canadian business education in particular embodies many aspects of U. S. business schools.

In addition the county colleges of Britain and the higher vocational schools of Germany have many similarities with the terminal programs of the American junior college and area vocational school. The USSR has a 3-year secondary technical school, called the *technicum*, for commercial training, that comes under the postsecondary category.

Business technology is spreading so rapidly that educational systems everywhere are being forced to introduce changing patterns of study to meet new developments. As a result all countries, whether they be the technically advanced nations of Europe, America, and Australasia or the developing nations of the Asian continent or Africa, offer business training from the most elementary level to that of the greatest complexity. African nations in particular are combining such training with a strong emphasis on administration. All nations are proceeding with an awareness that the best hope for their economic future lies in the business skills of their individual citizens.

HERBERT A. TONNE
State University of New York at Albany

Bibliography

Douglass, Lloyd V., *Business Education* (Washington 1963).
Gorden, Robert A., and Howell, James A., *Higher Education for Business* (New York 1959).
Miller, Jay W., *The Independent Business School in America* (New York 1964).
Nolan, Carroll A., Hayden, Carlos K., and Malsbury, Dean R., *Principles and Problems of Business Education*, 3d ed. (Cincinnati 1967).
Pierson, Frank C., and others, *The Education of American Businessmen* (New York 1959).
Tonne, Herbert A., *Principles of Business Education*, 3d ed. (New York 1962).
Tonne, Herbert A., Popham, Estelle L., and Freeman, M. Herbert, *Methods of Teaching Business Subjects*, 3d ed. (New York 1967).

BUSINESS INDICATORS, biz'nəs in'də-kā-tərz, also called *economic indicators*, are statistical measures of economic activity. They are used to identify, analyze, and evaluate business and economic performance with the ultimate aim of predicting and controlling the future. Indicators assumed great importance after the Great Depression dramatically demonstrated the need for detailed statistical knowledge of business and economic operations. Currently, business indicators supply crucial information for business and economic decisions.

Measures of Production. National production information is used to study the extent and patterns of economic fluctuations and growth. In the United States the best-known and most widely used measures of production are the national income accounts compiled by the U. S. Department of Commerce and published quarterly in its *Survey of Current Business*. The basic statistic is the Gross National Product (GNP), which measures the current market value of all goods and services produced. Statistics are also published for the GNP components. These components measure production (1) for consumption by individuals, (2) for government purchase, (3) for business capital formation and inventory accumulation, and (4) for net goods purchased by foreigners (exports minus imports).

Important related national account measures are: *net national product*—total output less an allowance for the value of goods consumed by the production process (primarily depreciation); and *national income*—the value of net production measured at factor cost rather than at market prices. National income also measures the total income earned by laborers, businesses, landlords, and lenders.

The Federal Reserve System provides a more sensitive and specific measure of productive activity in the United States with its Index of Industrial Production. This index, published monthly in the *Federal Reserve Bulletin*, is based on production data from 207 basic industries. Separate production indices are computed for three market groups (consumer goods, equipment, and materials) and for three industry groups (manufacturing, mining, and utilities). Construction industry indicators are provided by the F. W. Dodge Corporation's construction contracts index and the Census Bureau's data on new housing starts. See also INDEX NUMBER.

Labor Force Information. The *Monthly Labor Review*, published by the U. S. Bureau of Labor Statistics, contains detailed information about U. S. labor. Policy makers use monthly indicators of population, size of the labor force, and the number of employed workers to assess the growth of the economy's productive capacity. Data for the number and percentage of unemployed workers, average hours worked, and average earnings help

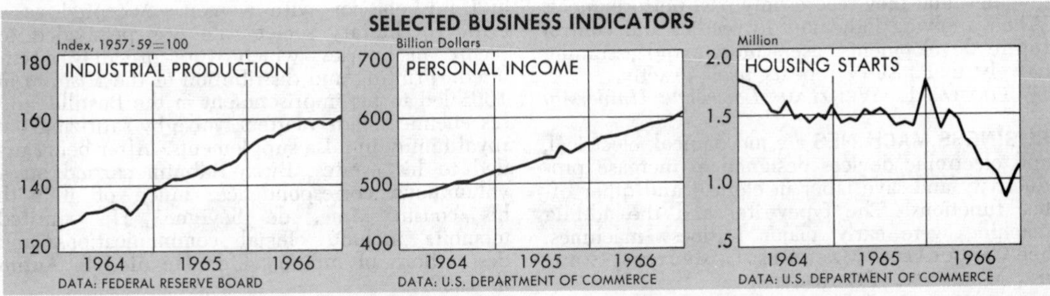

to evaluate underutilization of resources—information of particular value in recessions.

Prices. Because of the problems presented by inflation, measures of the general price level and of prices charged by particular industries are crucial for business and economic decisions. The Consumers Price Index (CPI), calculated monthly by the Bureau of Labor Statistics, measures the changing cost of a fixed market basket of goods purchased by urban wage earners and clerical workers in the United States. "Escalator" clauses in many labor union contracts provide for automatic wage rate adjustments as changes occur in the CPI. The same bureau also calculates the Wholesale Price Index to measure prices charged by producers to wholesalers.

Stock price averages are computed to measure and evaluate stock market behavior. The four Dow-Jones averages—the ones most often employed in financial circles—are calculated from the trading prices of 30 industrial stocks, 20 railroad stocks, 15 utility stocks, and a composite average of the 65 stocks. More comprehensive stock price indices are also compiled. The Standard and Poor's Corporation composite index covers 500 active stock issues, and the New York Stock Exchange index covers all stocks traded on that exchange.

Money and Credit Indicators. The Federal Reserve System supplies indicators of money and credit conditions in the United States. The major monetary indicator is the *money supply*, based on information concerning currency in circulation and checking account deposits. The Federal Reserve also provides data covering various types of credit outstanding, interest rates charged by lenders for different risks and maturities, and bank reserves and operations.

Special Indicators. After years of analysis of business cycles, the National Bureau of Economic Research, in the United States, selected 52 indicators on the basis of their consistent behavior in relation to general economic activity. Thirty have been found to reach peaks or troughs before the peak or trough in economic activity and are called *leading indicators*. The Bureau utilizes leading indicators to predict economic performance. The specific prediction is based on a *diffusion index* (DI). The DI number on any given date is the percentage of the 30 leading indicators that have risen since the previous calculation. A DI number greater than 50 indicates an expanding economy; the larger the DI number, the stronger the basis for predicting expansion.

Business and economic indicators have greatly increased the level of sophistication in the analysis of business performance. The usefulness of indicators, however, depends upon the users' knowledge of their limitations as well as of their applications. Indicators are only averages or aggregates, and they record only past performances. When applying indicators to predict and control future developments, users must avoid assuming naïvely that history repeats itself exactly.

THOMAS E. WENZLAU, *Lawrence University*

BUSINESS MACHINES are mechanical, electrical, and electronic devices designed to increase productivity and save labor in clerical and other office functions. The typewriter and the adding machine were early major business machines. See CALCULATING MACHINES; COMPUTERS; COPYING MACHINES; TYPEWRITER.

BUSKIN, bus′kin, in literature and theater, is a term used figuratively to mean tragedy or the tragic vein. Literally, the buskin is the thick-soled, high-laced, knee-length boot (also called *cothurnus*, from the Greek) worn by tragic actors in ancient Greek drama. The buskin was intended to increase the actor's height and so enhance the dignity of his role. By contrast, comic actors wore a sock (*soccus*) or low shoe. Thus the phrase "to put on the buskins" means to write tragedy. Ben Jonson is described in Byron's poem *Beppo* as one who "was a critic upon operas, too,/and knew all niceties of the sock and/buskin."

BUSONI, bo͞o-zō′nē, **Ferruccio Benvenuto** (1866–1924), Italian composer, pianist, and music theorist, who occupied an important yet isolated and somewhat ambiguous position in early 20th century music. His influence among his contemporaries was as a sort of latter-day Liszt, though as a virtuoso technician and theorist rather than as a composer. As a composer he was the direct antithesis of Liszt, since his art was essentially classical and Liszt's was romantic.

Life. Busoni was born near Florence on April 1, 1866, the son of notable musicians. He gave his first public concert at the age of 7. A year later his playing impressed Anton Rubinstein, and in 1876 the critic Eduard Hanslick devoted a long article to him. Following study at Leipzig, Busoni held teaching posts in Europe and the United States before settling more or less permanently in Berlin, where he died on July 27, 1924.

Works. The two great influences on Busoni's work were Liszt and Bach. The apogee of his Lisztian tendency is the huge Piano Concerto with male chorus (1904); of his Bachian tendency, the Fantasia Contrappuntistica (1910–1912) for solo piano.

The distinctive works of the mature Busoni show a fusion of German formalism with Italian clarity and objectivity. Representative late compositions include the fantasia on American Indian themes for piano and orchestra (1913) and the operas *Arlecchino* (1916) and *Doktor Faust* (unfinished). Perhaps his most frequently performed music is his piano transcriptions of the organ works of Bach.

GERALD ABRAHAM
Author of "A Hundred Years of Music"

BUSSY-RABUTIN, bü-sē′ rà-bü-taɴ′ (1618–1693), French soldier, writer, and member of the Academie Française, who is known chiefly for his *Histoire amoureuse des Gaules*, intimate tales about court ladies told by a well-informed courtier. Roger de Rabutin, Count de Bussy, was born in Burgundy on April 13, 1618. He joined the French Army at 16 and, while a cavalry officer, was often rebuked for his frivolous verse and misbehavior with women. Accepted as a critic by literary society, he was persuaded to record his stories, which were privately circulated. Printing and distribution of the *Histoire* in 1665 led to his imprisonment in the Bastille, and his enemies made matters worse by satirizing the royal family in false supplements. After being exiled to his estates, Bussy-Rabutin carried on a voluminous correspondence, much of it with his cousin Mme. de Sévigné. His spirited memoirs include official communications and descriptions of military life. He died in Autun in 1693.

BUSTAMANTE, bo͞os-tä-män′tä, **Sir Alexander** (1884–), Jamaican political and labor leader. He was born in Blenheim, Jamaica, on Feb. 24, 1884. After serving with the Spanish Army in Morocco and engaging in various occupations in Cuba, Panama, and New York, he returned to Jamaica in 1932. His labor movement activities twice led to his imprisonment. He founded and directed the Bustamante Industrial Trade Union and the Jamaica Labour party. He was a member of the House of Representatives, minister of communications, and chief minister, and was knighted in 1955. When Jamaica became independent in 1962, Bustamante helped prepare the new constitution and became the first prime minister, serving until 1967.

BUSTAMANTE, bo͞os-tä-män′tä, **Anastasio** (1780–1853), Mexican president and revolutionary general. He was born in Jiquilpán de Juárez, Mexico, on July 27, 1780. He fought first on Spain's side but in 1821 joined his 6,000 men to Agustín de Iturbide's revolutionary forces. Rising to commander of the army and vice president under Vincente Guerrero, Bustamante led a military revolt and seized the presidency in 1830. His regime was overthrown in 1832 by Antonio López de Santa Anna. In 1837 he was elected president again, but his prestige declined after France landed troops in Veracruz in 1838 to force settlement of her claims. An army rebellion under Santa Anna forced him into exile in 1841. Returning to fight in the Mexican War, he died in San Miguel de Allende on Feb. 6, 1853.

BUSTAMANTE, bo͞os-tä-män′tä, **Carlos María de** (1774–1848), Mexican historian and soldier. He was born in Oaxaca, Mexico, on Nov. 4, 1774. In 1805 he became editor of the *Diario de Méjico*, the country's first daily newspaper, which favored independence and sought to create a native literature. He held a command in the War for Independence and aided in promulgating the Plan of Iguala, a program of reforms, in 1821. He founded *La avispa de Chilpancingo*, a weekly newspaper, whose articles twice led to his imprisonment. A prolific historian, Bustamante published (1822–1832) a 6-volume account of the Mexican War for Independence and histories of the times of Iturbide and Santa Anna, including much from personal experience. He died in Mexico City on Sept. 21, 1848.

BUSTAMANTE Y RIVERO, bo͞os-tä-män′tä ē rē-vä′rō, **José Luis** (1894–), Peruvian judge and president. He was born in Arequipa, Peru, on Jan. 15, 1894. After practicing law and teaching at the University of San Agustín, he entered the foreign service. From 1934 to 1945 he served successively as minister to Bolivia, minister to Uruguay, and ambassador to Bolivia. He was elected president of Peru in 1945. His administration enacted a press freedom law, extended education, and carried out a program for modernization of the economy, including coastal development, irrigation, and mechanization of agriculture. In 1948, Bustamante's government was overthrown by an army revolt led by Manuel Odría. He became a judge on the International Court of Justice in 1961 and was elected president of the court in 1967.

BUSTAMANTE Y SIRVÉN, Antonio Sánchez de. See SÁNCHEZ DE BUSTAMANTE Y SIRVÉN, ANTONIO.

TONY ANGERMAYER, FROM PHOTO RESEARCHERS

Bustard

BUSTARD, bus′tərd, any of a group of medium to large terrestrial birds found on the plains and in the deserts of the Eastern Hemisphere from southern Europe and Asia to Africa and Australia. Considered a game bird and prized for its flesh, the bustard is becoming rare in the northern part of its range.

Related to the cranes, the 23 species of bustards range from 14½ to 52 inches (37–132 cm) in length. They are stocky birds with long necks, flattened, sometimes crested heads, and heavy bills. Their legs are long and thick; their hind toe is absent, and their other toes are short and stout. Bustards vary in color from gray to brown; they are often barred and spotted with darker colors on the upper surface and white, buff, or black below. The wings of some species have large white patches that are only evident during flight. The males are larger than the females and have better developed ornamental plumes on the head, throat, and flank.

Bustards live mostly on open savannas and arid plains. They travel in small flocks of a dozen or more. Although they are strong fliers, they prefer to walk or run swiftly from danger. They are great wanderers, but only the northern species actually migrate. Bustards fly with their heads and legs stretched to their full extent, and their wing beats are slow and measured. They are omnivorous feeders, thriving chiefly on insects, small mammals, birds, and reptiles.

Bustards nest on the ground in a shallow depression. The female lays from one to five eggs, and she alone cares for the young. Incubation takes from 20 to 28 days, depending on the species.

Bustards are members of the family Otididae in the order Gruiformes, which also includes the cranes, rails, gallinules, sunbitterns, and finfoots.

JOSEPH BELL, *New York Zoological Society*

BUTADIENE, bū-tə-dī′ēn, is the common name for 1, 3-butadiene, a gaseous hydrocarbon with the formula $CH_2 = CHCH = CH_2$. About 90% of the butadiene produced is used in the manufacture of synthetic rubber, largely SBR, or styrene-butadiene rubber. This polymer, which is 75% butadiene and 25% styrene, has proved equal to natural rubber in most respects for use in tires, and in some ways it is superior. The latex material of rubber-base paints is a copolymer of butadiene and styrene containing about 75% styrene. An elastomer of butadiene and acrylonitrile, called NBR, or nitrile rubber, is resistant to the effects of oils and solvents and heat and cold. It is used in fuel hoses, shoe soles, and mats.

Because of the conjugated double-bond structure between its carbon atoms, butadiene is classified as a diolefin. The double bonds make it especially subject to polymerization reactions, or to copolymerization reactions with certain other substances, and because of this property it is used in the manufacture of several types of synthetic rubber. Butadiene solidifies at −108.9° C (−164° F) and boils at −4.4° C (24.1° F).

Between World Wars I and II, research in Germany led to the development of Buna-S, a butadiene-styrene copolymer. This was the first synthetic elastomer that was practical for use in tires. During World War II the manufacture of synthetic rubber became a necessity for the United States, and in 1941 the government began production of butadiene-styrene rubber.

Butadiene can be produced commercially by a number of methods. During the early years of World War II most butadiene was produced from alcohol. However, butane and butylene recovered from petroleum-refining processes proved to be less expensive sources, and these hydrocarbons are now used instead of alcohol. They are catalytically dehydrogenated to yield butadiene and hydrogen.

OTTO W. NITZ, *Stout State University*

BUTANE, bū'tān, is either of two gaseous hydrocarbons, normal butane and isobutane, with the empirical formula C_4H_{10}. The two compounds differ from each other in the arrangement of their atoms—that is, they are isomers. Normal butane (n-butane) has the atomic structure of $CH_3-CH_2-CH_2-CH_3$; isobutane (2-methylpropane) has the atomic structure of

$$\begin{array}{c} CH_3-\underset{\displaystyle \stackrel{|}{CH_3}}{CH}-CH_3. \end{array}$$

Normal butane solidifies at −138.4° C (−216.4° F) and has a boiling point of −0.5° C (31.1° F). Isobutane freezes at −159.6° C (−255.3° F) and boils at −11.7° C (10.9° F). Both n-butane and isobutane, which are members of the alkane family of hydrocarbons, are only very slightly soluble in water but are readily soluble in alcohol and ether.

Like other alkanes, n-butane and isobutane are chemically inert. They form no ions and do not react with acids, bases, or aqueous oxidizing solutions. In excess air they burn readily, yielding carbon dioxide and water. Both compounds react with chlorine gas in strong light. The chlorine atoms replace one or more of the hydrogen atoms on the carbon chains, and hydrogen chloride is also formed as a by-product.

One of the maior commercial sources of n-butane and isobutane is natural gas. Another important source is petroleum refining, particularly the cracking process.

In the production of high-octane motor fuel, n-butane is converted to isobutane, which is polymerized with isobutylene to produce a group of branched chain hydrocarbons. Such mixtures are then blended with motor fuel to give better antiknock properties. Butane is one of the principal sources of butadiene, which is polymerized with styrene to produce one of the most important forms of synthetic rubber.

With the help of certain catalysts, butane or a mixture of butane and propane can be oxidized by air under pressure to form acetic acid, methanol, acetone, acetaldehyde, and other organic compounds. Although this process is not yet in use on a large scale, it appears to be a promising method for industrial syntheses.

OTTO W. NITZ, *Stout State University*

BUTCHER, Samuel Henry (1805–1910), British classical scholar. He was born in Dublin on April 16, 1850, and educated at Trinity College, Cambridge. From 1876 to 1882 he was tutor in classics at University College, Oxford, where he wrote, with Andrew Lang, *The Odyssey of Homer Done into English Prose* (1879). His critical essay *Demosthenes* appeared in 1881.

Butcher occupied the chair of Greek at the University of Edinburgh from 1882 to 1903. His most important work is *Aristotle's Theory of Poetry and Fine Art,* with a critical text and translation of the *Poetics,* published in 1895. Butcher served on two royal commissions for the reform of university education in Scotland and Ireland, and was elected to Parliament for Cambridge University in 1906. A founder of the British Academy, he served as its president in 1909. Butcher died in London on Dec. 29, 1910.

BUTCHERBIRD is the common name for several shrikes found in North America, Britain, and India and for several cracticids found in Australia. These birds are called "butcherbirds" because of their habit of fixing their insect or small vertebrate prey on a thorn or barbed wire, much as meat is placed on a butcher's hook. The thorn holds the prey while the relatively weak-footed butcherbird tears it apart with its hooked bill. Butcherbirds often kill more prey than they can eat, and favorite thornbushes may become larders with a dozen or more impaled carcasses of insects, mice, or birds. When live prey is in short supply, the butcherbird may return to the larder to finish its meal, but much of the impaled prey rots uneaten.

Although the shrike butcherbirds and the cracticid butcherbirds are very similar in habits, they are not closely related. The shrikes belong to the genus *Lanius* in the family Laniidae, while the cracticids belong to the genus *Cracticus* in the family Cracticidae. See also SHRIKE.

GEORGE E. WATSON, *Smithsonian Institution*

Butcherbird (lesser gray shrike)

ERIC HOSKING, FROM PHOTO RESEARCHERS

BUTE, 3d Earl of (1713–1792), Scottish politician, who was friend, counselor, and prime minister to King George III of Britain. Bute was born John Stuart, in Edinburgh, on May 25, 1713, and succeeded to his title when he was nine. Thereafter he was reared mainly in England by his maternal uncles, John Campbell, 2d Duke of Argyll, and Archibald Campbell, Earl of Islay.

Following Argyll into opposition to Sir Robert Walpole, Bute became in the 1740's a friend of the Prince and Princess of Wales. In 1755, four years after the death of the Prince of Wales, he negotiated an agreement between the Princess and William Pitt to combine in opposition to the Duke of Newcastle's ministry. One of his opponents described him about this time as "a fine showy man who would make an excellent ambassador in a court where there was no business." The Princess of Wales entrusted to him the education of her teen-age son George, now, by the death of his father, heir apparent to the British crown. George, an intellectually backward and neurotic youth, fell completely under Bute's influence. With the help of his "dearest Friend," George III set out on his accession to check the corruption of Whig politics and govern with the help of disinterested and patriotic men of all parties. Bute became secretary of state in March 1761, and after Pitt and Newcastle had in turn resigned, he became prime minister in May 1762.

The only notable events in Bute's ministry were the ending of the Seven Years' War, which Bute and the young King agree was "bloody and unnecessary," and the beginning of the controversy over general warrants (see WILKES, JOHN). Against the wishes of the King, Bute, who was on the verge of a nervous breakdown, insisted on retiring from office in April 1763. For another three years he still took some part in politics as "minister behind the curtain." His successors in office naturally resented his continuing influence with the King. Bute's last friends were thus forced out of office, and a complete breach between him and the King followed in 1766. Bute had no discernible influence on policies from then until his death in London on March 10, 1792.

Bute's failure as a politician was due largely to his personal character: he lacked steadfastness. He was the first Scot to hold the prime ministry, and his nationality was a contributing factor to his failure. English resentment at Bute's sudden rise to power as the King's favorite would have been widespread in any event. But it was compounded by the fact that he was regarded as an outsider, if not a foreigner, by the inner circle of English politicians.

Bute was a generous and discerning patron of Scottish scholars and men of letters, and he took a personal interest in several branches of science, especially botany.

D. B. HORN, *University of Edinburgh*

BUTE is a county of western Scotland that comprises several islands in the Firth of Clyde. The county town, Rothesay, is on the island of Bute, 32 miles (51 km) west of Glasgow. It is a busy port and a popular resort. Here in 1398, King Robert III of Scotland bestowed the title of Duke of Rothesay on his eldest son. The title is held by present heirs to the British throne.

The northern half of Bute, the most populous island, is separated from the mainland by the Kyles of Bute, a picturesque narrow strait. Arran Island is larger in area than Bute. It has sandy beaches and mountains—including Goatfell, 2,866 feet (873 meters) high—that are popular with vacationers. Arran's principal town is Brodick. Holy Island in Lamlash Bay rises to 1,030 feet (314 meters). Two other larger islands in Bute County are Great and Little Cumbrae. They lie between the island of Bute and the mainland and have pleasant sandy bays and wooded hills. Millport is the only town in the Cumbraes. Population: (1961) of the county, 15,129.

GORDON STOKES, *Author, "English Place-Names"*

RADIO TIMES HULTON

BUTE ISLAND, in Scotland's Firth of Clyde, has the remains of an 11th century castle standing at Rothesay.

BUTENANDT, bōō'tə-nänt, **Adolf Friedrich Johann** (1903–), German chemist best known for his isolation and study of the sex hormones. For this work, Butenandt shared the 1939 Nobel Prize in chemistry with Leopold Ružička (q.v.).

In 1929, Butenandt isolated estrone, a female sex hormone secreted by the ovaries and vital to the sexual development of women, from the urine of pregnant women and purified it in crystalline form. Two years later, he isolated andosterone, the first male sex hormone to be purified, and shortly afterward, he also isolated progesterone, the female sex hormone essential during pregnancy. Later, Butenandt also contributed substantially both to the elucidation of the chemical structure of these hormones and to their partial synthesis from other steroids.

After 1937, Butenandt directed his attention to the action of the gene, the unit of hereditary material. He demonstrated that eye-color mutations found in several insects could be traced to a metabolic defect. Specifically, he showed that the eye-color mutants were not able to synthesize the eye pigment, omnochrome, from the amino acid, tryptophan. Thus, he concluded that genes act by directing metabolic pathways and that a gene mutation results in a metabolic defect. This idea, expressed by Butenandt in 1944, was later expanded and formulated by George Wells Beadle (q.v.) in the "one gene—one enzyme" hypothesis.

During 1958 and 1959, after 20 years of research, Butenandt and a number of associates succeeded in purifying the sexual attractant of the silk moth, *Bombyx mori.* They also determined the chemical structure of this substance, now known as a "pheromone." Butenandt has also done research on carcinogens, substances that produce cancer, and on viruses.

Butenandt was born in Bremerhaven, Germany, on March 24, 1903. He studied at the universities of Marburg and Göttingen and worked in the laboratory of the Nobel Prize-winning chemist Adolf Windaus. He served on the faculties of the universities of Danzig, Tübingen, and Munich. Since 1936 he has been director of Max Planck Institute for Biochemistry (formerly the Kaiser Wilhelm Institute) and since 1961 president of the Max Planck Foundation for the Advancement of Science. In this position, Butenandt exerts considerable influence on the development of science in West Germany.

PETER KARLSON, *Institute for Physiological Chemistry, Marburg, Germany*

BUTLER, Alban (1710–1773), English Roman Catholic hagiographer whose *Lives of the Saints* has influenced generations of English and American Catholics. He was born in Northamptonshire on Oct. 10, 1710. He attended the English seminary in Douai, France, was ordained in 1735, and taught theology and philosophy at Douai until 1745. After traveling widely in Europe, he became president of the English college at St. Omer, France (1766), where he died on May 15, 1773. Butler labored for 30 years to compile some 1,600 biographies for his *Lives.* Published anonymously in London (1756–1759), it has been revised by Herbert Thurston, S. J. (1926–1939) and by Donald Attwater (1956).

BUTLER, Andrew Pickens (1796–1857), American politician, who defended slavery in the U. S. Senate in the 1850's. Born in Edgefield, S. C., on Nov. 18, 1796, Butler was educated at South Carolina College and was admitted to the bar in 1819. He entered the state legislature in 1824 and became a leader of the faction that supported John C. Calhoun and championed nullification.

After serving as a state judge from 1833, Butler joined Calhoun in the U. S. Senate in 1846. At first he was viewed as the "other senator," but after Calhoun's death in 1850 he established himself as an effective debater in the battle over slavery. The climax of his career came during a confrontation with Sen. Charles Sumner of Massachusetts in 1856. After Sumner verbally attacked Butler in an antislavery speech, Butler's nephew, Congressman Preston Brooks, caned the Massachusetts senator into insensibility. Butler knew nothing of his nephew's intentions, but he later defended Brooks before the Senate. Butler died at his birthplace on May 25, 1857.

JOSEPH LOGSDON
Louisiana State University in New Orleans

BUTLER, Benjamin Franklin (1795–1858), American public official, who was U. S. attorney general under President Andrew Jackson (1833–1838). A gentle, pious man, he seemed out of place in the rough and tumble of politics. William Marcy commented that Butler was "too amiable a man to be a very great one."

Butler was born in Kinderhook Landing, N. Y. on Dec. 14, 1795. Admitted to the New York bar in 1817, he became a partner of Martin Van Buren in Albany, N. Y. Besides practicing law, he served in the state legislature, taught law, helped revise the statutes of New York (1825), and helped settle a boundary dispute between New York and New Jersey (1834).

Friendship for Van Buren drew him into public office and, informally, into the Albany Regency (q.v.). Although he accepted the attorney generalship and also served briefly as U. S. secretary of war (1836–1837), he subsequently declined offers of cabinet posts from Presidents Van Buren and Polk and served instead as a U. S. attorney in New York. The dispute over slavery in the territories led him to support the Free Soil party and ultimately the Republicans. He died in Paris, France, on Nov. 8, 1858.

JOSEPH C. BURKE, *Duquesne University*

BUTLER, Benjamin Franklin (1818–1893), Massachusetts lawyer and politician whose long career was colorful and controversial. He was born in Deerfield, N. H., on Nov. 5, 1818. Reared by a widowed mother in the mill town of Lowell, Mass., Butler was admitted to the bar in 1840 and became active in Massachusetts politics, a Democratic leader in a Whig state. After the secession of the South in 1860–1861, Butler was a vocal advocate of coercion to put down rebellion. Lincoln, grateful for the support of a prominent Democrat, appointed Butler major general of militia in May 1861.

Butler's Civil War career was turbulent and controversial from beginning to end. As a field commander he was a total failure, but his contributions as administrator and pacifier of conquered Confederate territory were genuine. Early in the war, it was Butler with his fertile lawyer's brain who ordered runaway slaves who came within his lines held as "contraband of war" whose labor could be used for the Union cause. As military commander of occupied New Orleans, Butler earned the undying hatred of Southerners and the epithet "Beast Butler" by his notorious General Order No. 28, which declared that any woman showing disrespect for the Union flag or uniform should be treated as a "woman of the town, plying her trade."

Returning to the political hustings in 1866, Butler was elected to Congress as Radical Republican and served influentially until 1875 and again from 1877 to 1879. He was a chief prosecutor during the impeachment trial of President Andrew Johnson and an intimate adviser of President Grant. After several tries for the office of governor of Massachusetts, Butler was elected in 1882 on the Democratic ticket, but his defeat in his bid for reelection marked the effective end of his political career.

In 1884 he ran for president as the nominee of the Greenback party. His autobiography, *Butler's Book,* remarkable for its abuse of his long list of enemies, appeared in 1892. Butler died in Washington, D. C., on Jan. 11, 1893.

JAMES A. BEATSON, *University of Arizona*

Further Reading: Holzman, Robert S., *Stormy Ben Butler* (New York 1954); West, Richard S., Jr., *Lincoln's Scapegoat General* (Boston 1965).

BUTLER, Charles (1750–1832), English Roman Catholic lawyer and writer, who was a leading agitator for Catholic emancipation in England. He was born in London on Aug. 14, 1750, and educated there and in France. He studied law and in 1775 became a conveyance, because Catholics were barred from full participation in other legal fields. From 1782, when he was named secretary to the committee of Catholic laymen that began the agitation for emancipation, he was active as a mediator between British Catholics and the government. He was the first Catholic called to the bar after passage of the Catholic Relief Act (1791) and one of the first appointed king's counsel after the Catholic Emancipation Act (1829). Butler wrote authoritatively on Roman and English law and comparative religion. He died in London on June 2, 1832.

BUTLER, Ellis Parker (1869–1937), American writer. He was born in Muscatine, Iowa, on Dec. 5, 1869. Butler is best known for his *Pigs Is Pigs*, the popularity of which once caused him to complain that his name was never printed without mention of that book. Written in 1906 at the request of a magazine editor, this amusing story of a freight agent who declares that even guinea pigs "is pigs" and, therefore, livestock, not pets, brought Butler fame as a humorist. He wrote more than 30 books, including *The Incubator Baby* (1906), *The Great American Pie Company* (1907), *Mike Flannery* (1909), *Pigs, Pets and Pies* (1927), and *Hunting the Wow* (1934). He died in Williamsville, Mass., on Sept. 13, 1937.

BUTLER, James. See ORMONDE, EARLS, MARQUESSES, AND DUKES OF.

BUTLER, John (1728–1796), American soldier, who served the British during the French and Indian War and, as a loyalist, during the American Revolution. Born in New London, Conn., he moved in 1742 to a tract of land that his father had purchased from the Mohawk Indians on the south bank of the Mohawk River in New York. There his neighbor was William Johnson, who became British commissioner for Indian affairs and whom Butler assisted in this function. During the French and Indian War, Butler commanded all the Indian forces at the siege of Fort Niagara (1759).

A Loyalist, Butler fled to Canada with his son Walter N. Butler (q.v.) at the start of the Revolution in 1775. That year he was appointed deputy Indian commissioner at Niagara by the British, and two years later he joined Col. Barry St. Leger in leading pro-British Indians. Commissioned a major, he recruited a Loyalist corps known as Butler's Rangers. With his Rangers and Indians, Butler raided the Wyoming Valley of northeastern Pennsylvania and was blamed for the massacre there on July 3, 1778. In 1779, Gen. John Sullivan defeated the Rangers and their Indian allies at Newtown (later Elmira), N.Y., but Butler persisted, raiding the Mohawk and Schoharie valleys in 1780. After the Revolution he colonized a grant of land on Canada's Niagara peninsula, where he died in 1796.

HARRISON K. BIRD
Author of "Battle for a Continent"

BUTLER, John (1920–), American dancer and choreographer. He was born in Memphis, Tenn., on Sept. 29, 1920, and studied at Mississippi State College, the Martha Graham School, and the American School of Ballet. He danced with the Martha Graham company and in leading roles in Broadway musicals before forming his own dance company in 1953. As a choreographer, Butler created the ballet for the first production of Gian Carlo Menotti's television opera *Amahl and the Night Visitors* (1951). One of his most celebrated ballets is *The Unicorn, the Gorgon and the Manticore*, which was commissioned in 1956 by the Elizabeth Sprague Coolidge Foundation of the Library of Congress.

BUTLER, Joseph (1692–1752), English theologian and philosopher. He was born at Wantage, Berkshire, on May 18, 1692. He was reared a Presbyterian but became an Anglican and entered Oriel College, Oxford, in 1714. After receiving his degree he became preacher at the Rolls Chapel, where he delivered his famous *Sermons on Human Nature* (published 1726). Ten years later he published an even more famous book, *The Analogy of Religion, Natural and Revealed, to the Constitution and Course of Nature*. He became a friend of Queen Caroline, who at her death left directions that Butler should be promoted. In 1738 he was appointed bishop of Bristol and in 1750 bishop of Durham. He died at Bath on June 16, 1752.

Both his *Sermons* and *Analogy of Religion* had great influence in the later 18th and early 19th centuries. They were used as standard works in the education of Anglican and other clergy until late in the 19th century. Their chief aim was to refute the skeptical and deistic ethics and theology of the time. In ethics, Butler opposed the naturalism of Thomas Hobbes and also the legalistic morality of the deists and the "enthusiasm" of those who relied solely on private conscience.

Butler recognized the historical development of ethical principles, for which he assumed a completely rational explanation, as parallel to the development of science. Man does not possess all knowledge or even the capacity for all knowledge, but he does possess the ability to judge and distinguish right from wrong. As in science, this judgment is often—perhaps always—dependent on the choice not only of the right instead of the wrong, but of the better, not the worse. In a word, man must follow "probability," which Butler described as "the very guide of life." Here Butler relied upon the principle of preferring the more likely and more reasonable view in any crisis demanding choice. His position, however, was not equivalent to the "probabilism" of the Dominicans and Jesuits of the preceding two centuries.

The same test was applied to the whole of religion, in both its natural and revealed stages, against the reduction of religious truth to mere rationality. Aided by reason, we can recognize the better, more reasonable, more probable conception of God, His purpose and will, the nature of man, and his future destiny. Butler defended in the same way the prophecies of the Old and New Testaments, as interpreted in the 18th century, and also the miracles and the whole system designed by patristic and traditional theology. Along with this he included many sage and tersely stated observations on the nature and practice of religion. Like most apologists, he undertook to prove too much. But his effort involved warnings against misinterpretation and false inductions, warnings that deserve perennial recollection.

FREDERICK C. GRANT
Union Theological Seminary

Further Reading: The best edition of Butler's works is the one edited by W. E. Gladstone, 2 vols. (New York 1896, with a supplemental volume of *Subsidiary Studies*).

Consult also Broad, Charles D., *Five Types of Ethical Theory* (New York 1930); Spooner, William A., *Bishop Butler* (Boston 1901).

BUTLER, Nicholas Murray (1862–1947), American educator and political leader. He was born in Elizabeth, N.J., on April 2, 1862. In 1882 he graduated with honors in philosophy from Columbia College, and he earned his Ph.D. at Columbia in the same area two years later. After studying in Berlin and Paris, Butler accepted an appointment as assistant in philosophy at Columbia in 1885. He served as teacher and administrator at Columbia for almost 60 years.

Leadership in Education. Butler was appointed a full professor in 1890 and became the first dean of Columbia's faculty of philosophy. In 1901 he was appointed acting president, and in 1902 he assumed the presidency of the university. During Butler's 44 years of leadership, Columbia grew into one of the world's most renowned universities. New professional schools added during his tenure included the schools of journalism, business, dentistry, social work, public health, and library service.

Butler played a leading role in elevating the position of professional schools of education in American universities. In 1889 the New York College for Teachers was founded with Butler as president. Four years later it changed its name to Teachers College, and six years later it was incorporated into Columbia University, where it became the leading professional school of education of that era. Columbia included on its staff such famous names in professional education as John Dewey, William H. Kilpatrick, E.L. Thorndike, Harold Rugg, and George Counts. Initially, Butler attacked formal educational dogmas, but later he came to be an exponent of what he called "the great tradition in education." He spoke as a classical humanist who opposed many of the newer ideas in education, psychology, and philosophy at the turn of the century.

Butler played a major role in the appointment of the Committee of Ten of the National Educational Association. The committee's report (1894), which reflected many of Butler's conservative views, helped shape the high school curriculum in America into a traditionally oriented college preparatory program. Among his educational contributions was the creation (with President Eliot of Harvard) of the College Entrance Examination Board, an organization that began its activities in 1901.

Leadership in National and International Affairs. Butler became a leader in the Republican party and was an elected delegate to many of its conventions. He was the Republican candidate for the vice presidency in 1912, and in 1920 he received 69½ votes for the presidental nomination.

As president of Columbia, Butler came into contact with important world personalities. Many notable foreign visitors stayed at his home, and he, in turn, was invited to serve as an adviser to foreign governments, gave numerous addresses in foreign nations including several European parliaments, and acted as a special presidential envoy to various nations. He obtained the endorsement of Pope Pius XI for the Kellogg-Briand Peace Pact in 1928, and in 1931 he shared the Nobel Peace Prize with Jane Addams. He served for 20 years as president of the Carnegie Endowment for International Peace, which he and Elihu Root persuaded Andrew Carnegie to endow.

Butler resigned from the presidency of Columbia in 1945. He died in New York City on Dec. 7, 1947.

RICHARD E. GROSS, *Stanford University*

BUTLER, Paul Mulholland (1905–1961), American lawyer and politician. Born on June 15, 1905, in South Bend, Ind., he received a law degree from the University of Notre Dame in 1927. He practiced law, was active in politics, and was elected Democratic national committeeman for Indiana in 1952. From 1955 to 1960 Butler was chairman of the Democratic National Committee. His strong support of civil rights angered southerners, and his formation of the Democratic Advisory Council evoked the opposition of Lyndon Johnson and Sam Rayburn, the Democratic congressional leaders. In 1960, Butler resumed his South Bend law practice. He died in Washington, D.C., on Dec. 30, 1961.

BUTLER, Pierce (1744–1822), American political leader, who signed the U.S. Constitution. He was born in County Carlow, Ireland, on July 11, 1744, and was stationed in America as a major in the British army. In 1773 he resigned his military commission and set up residence in South Carolina with his wife, who was the daughter of a local planter.

A supporter of the patriot cause, Butler served in the South Carolina legislature for most of the period from 1778 to 1789. He represented the state at the 1787 convention and was responsible for the clause in the U.S. Constitution providing for the return of fugitive slaves. Butler was elected to the U.S. Senate as a Federalist in 1789 and reelected in 1792, but he resigned in 1796. In 1802 he was appointed to a Senate vacancy, but he again resigned in 1804. He died in Philadelphia on Feb. 15, 1822.

BUTLER, Pierce (1866–1939), U.S. Supreme Court justice of conservative sympathies. With rare exceptions, such as his dissent in *Olmstead* v. *United States* (1928), in which the majority upheld the use of wiretap evidence in criminal proceedings, he voted to uphold governmental restrictions on civil liberties, particularly in cases of radicals and pacifists. He also opposed governmental regulation of business in the interest of social welfare.

Butler was born in Dakota county, Minn., on March 17, 1866. He soon showed his intellectual capacity and became a schoolteacher at 15. Although a Roman Catholic, he entered Carleton College, founded by Congregationalists. After graduating in 1887, he moved to St. Paul, where he studied law and was admitted to the Minnesota bar (1888). Butler entered politics as a Democrat, was elected county attorney in 1892 and in 1894. Two years later he returned to law practice. He became a highly successful railroad and corporation attorney, whose fame as a trial lawyer spread as far as the nation's capital. In 1921, appearing before an arbitration tribunal in Canada, he made a deep and lasting impression on William Howard Taft, one of the arbitrators, with whom he established cordial relations. Butler was appointed regent of the University of Minnesota in 1907. In this capacity he was responsible for the dismissal of a faculty member he deemed insufficiently loyal to the American cause during World War I. Conservative in economics as he was nationalistic in politics, he was particularly congenial to Taft, who as chief justice worked for his appointment to the Supreme Court. Taft's efforts, which were supported by influential members of the bar, proved successful. Nominated by President Harding, Butler took his seat on the court on Jan. 2, 1923.

Until his death 16 years later, Butler was a member of the conservative phalanx that also included Justices McReynolds, Sutherland, and Van Devanter. However, President Franklin D. Roosevelt's 1937 effort to "pack" the court and subsequent personnel changes brought a radical shift in the court's philosophy; by the time of Butler's death many conservative decisions had been overruled or their authority so weakened that they were not likely to be followed in the future. Butler died in Washington, D. C., on Nov. 16, 1939.

LEO PFEFFER
Author of "This Honorable Court"

BUTLER, Reginald Cotterell (1913–), English sculptor and architect, who was a leading exponent of linear sculpture. He was born in Buntingford, Hertfordshire, on April 28, 1913. Butler lectured at the London Architectural Association School, served as technical editor of *Architectural Press,* taught at the University of London, and became Gregory fellow of sculpture at Leeds University.

His work, most of which is in either forged or cast metal, was exhibited at the Tate Gallery, London; the Museum of Modern Art, New York; Aberdeen City Gallery, in Scotland; and the National Gallery of South Australia. Butler's public commissions included works for the Scottish Festival, the South Bank Festival, and the Hatfield Technical Collection. He also exhibited at the 1951 Venice Biennale and won first prize in the International Unknown Political Prisoner Sculpture competition (1953). His book *Creative Development* was published in 1962.

BUTLER, Richard (1743–1791), American army officer, who negotiated treaties with the Indians after the American Revolution. He was born in Dublin, Ireland, on Aug. 1, 1743. His family settled in Lancaster, Pa. Butler joined the Continental Army when the Revolution began. As lieutenant colonel of Morgan's Rifles in 1777, he took part in the storming of Stony Point, N. Y., and in the Battle of Freeman's Farm (Saratoga). After the war, he was appointed an Indian commissioner by Congress and concluded treaties by which Indian tribes in the Northwest Territory ceded great tracts of land.

In Gen. Arthur St. Clair's expedition against the Miami Indians north of the Ohio River in 1791, Butler held temporary command. His troops were ambushed after he had changed a previous order of his superior. Butler was mortally wounded and died on Nov. 4, 1791.

BUTLER, Richard Austen (1902–), British political leader, who on two occasions missed becoming prime minister. He was born in Attock, India (now Pakistan), on Dec. 9, 1902, the son of a distinguished civil servant. He was educated at preparatory schools and at Cambridge University, from which he graduated in 1925. He was a fellow of Corpus Christi College until elected to Parliament as a Conservative in 1929. He held the seat until elevated to the peerage as Baron Butler of Saffron Walden in 1965.

The great variety of Butler's government offices covered Indian affairs, labor, foreign affairs (as foreign secretary, 1963–1964), education, the treasury (as chancellor of the exchequer, 1951–1955), the home office (as home secretary, 1957–1962), and central African affairs. His reputation was that of a liberal conservative, beginning with his espousal of Indian home rule in the 1930's and continuing through his progressive education act (1944), his opposition to harsh penal measures, and his private opposition to the Anglo-French invasion of Egypt (1956).

As chairman of the Conservative research department, Butler modernized his party's image and machine when the Conservatives were in opposition (1945–1951). Criticism of his liberalism within the party helps explain why he was passed over for prime minister when Anthony Eden (1957) and Harold Macmillan (1963) retired. Many supporters maintained that on these occasions the wishes of the Conservative party were not truly ascertained, but this overlooks the widespread view that in spite of his undoubted administrative qualities Butler did not possess the decisiveness necessary in a prime minister. On retiring from politics, he returned to academic life as master of Trinity College, Cambridge.

A. J. BEATTIE
London School of Economics

BUTLER, Samuel (1612–1680), English poet, whose mock-epic *Hudibras* satirized human folly generally and the Puritans particularly.

Life. Butler was born at Strensham, Worcestershire, on Feb. 8, 1612, the son of a well-to-do farmer. After attending the King's School, Worcester, he became secretary first to Elizabeth, Countess of Kent, and then, despite his Royalist sympathies, to Sir Samuel Luke, a strict Presbyterian, who provided Butler with matter for satire in *Hudibras*.

Butler's activities during the Civil War are not known, but after the Restoration he became secretary to Richard Vaughan, 2d Earl of Carbery, who appointed him steward of Ludlow Castle in 1661. About this time he married a reputedly wealthy woman, who lost her fortune in speculation shortly thereafter. There is little definite information on the rest of Butler's life; he is said to have been given £300 instead of a promised government post and to have been for a while the secretary of George Villiers, 2d Duke of Buckingham. Sarcastic, touchy, poor, and ill, Butler died in London on Sept. 25, 1680.

Writings. The first collection of Butler's works, *Genuine Remains in Verse and Prose of Samuel Butler* (1759), contains 120 prose "characters," a literary form then popular, and *The Elephant and the Moon,* a verse satire on the learned scientists of the Royal Society.

Butler's fame, however, rests incontestably on *Hudibras*. The authorized edition of Part I was published in 1663, having been preceded by a pirated edition. Both editions were instantly popular. Part II, also very successful, was published in 1664, and Part III appeared in 1678. The poem, based on *Don Quixote,* tells the comic adventures of the Puritan knight, Sir Hudibras, and his squire, Ralpho. Its real point, however, is its satirical portrait of human stupidity and hypocrisy, especially that of the Puritans, and it makes the characters unconsciously expose their own failings. The style is mock-heroic, and the heavily stressed meter and often far-fetched polysyllabic rhymes turn the 4-foot iambic couplets into an appropriately grotesque doggerel. Although the poem's topical interest is gone, the commentary on human weakness remains sharp, and the odd rhymes are still surprising and comic.

GEORGIA DUNBAR, *Hofstra University*

NATIONAL PORTRAIT GALLERY, LONDON

Samuel Butler

BUTLER, Samuel (1835–1902), English novelist and essayist, who attacked the complacency, hypocrisy, and ignorance of the Victorian period. His satire is sharp and witty, and his refutation of accepted theories and attitudes of all kinds is scholarly and ingenious. Butler's fame rests principally on *Erewhon* (1872), a utopian novel satirizing English society, and *The Way of All Flesh* (q.v., 1903), a semiautobiographical novel that brilliantly mocks the hidden cruelties of family life. The latter is considered a manifesto of freedom from parental domination—an appropriate final comment on the Victorian age.

Life. Butler, the son of a clergyman, was born in Langar, Nottinghamshire, on Dec. 4, 1835. He was educated at Shrewsbury School, where his grandfather, Bishop Samuel Butler, had for many years been headmaster, and at St. John's College, Cambridge. Despite religious doubts, he prepared for ordination and became lay assistant to a curate in the London slums. His theological studies and his slum experience convinced him that he could not follow family tradition and enter the ministry After months of indecision and disagreement with his father, who frowned on his wish to be a painter, Butler emigrated in 1860 to New Zealand, where, with money advanced by his father, he bought a sheep run.

In 1864, Butler sold the sheep run at a large profit, returned to London, and took rooms in Clifford's Inn, which was his home for the rest of his life. His relations with his family remained permanently strained; he and his conservative father were incomprehensible to each other, and he detested his sisters. Also, having lost his own money through unwise investment, he resented his father's refusal to give him more than a meager allowance from the family fortune.

Butler indulged in few comforts and no luxuries. In London he soon settled into a regular routine of writing, painting, and composing music; study at the British museum; walks in the country; and evenings with one or two friends. The New Zealand venture had made him financially independent for some years, and he was able to ignore his father's disapproval. He enrolled in Heatherley's Art School, and there, in 1871, he met Eliza Mary Ann Savage, who was witty, intelligent, and kind; unfortunately she was also lame, homely, and nearing middle age. She loved Butler deeply, but he was too completely a bachelor ever to respond, although occasionally he seems to have suffered a guilty awareness of responsibility toward her. He thoroughly enjoyed their intellectual relationship, however; and she became his best critic.

Butler's one other close friend was the solicitor Henry Festing Jones. Their friendship began in 1876 and lasted until Butler's death. Together the two men listened to music—especially Handel—and composed music, traveled frequently to Italy, and shared most of their leisure. Jones admired Butler so much that he became virtually his replica in tastes, appearance, and bachelor habits. He later wrote Butler's biography.

Butler had moderate success with his painting (between 1868 and 1876 a dozen of his works were hung in the Royal Academy), but he soon realized that he lacked true talent. Also, as a musician he knew he was only an enthusiastic amateur. His real forte was writing. While in New Zealand he had read Darwin and, as an amateur biologist, had published several newspaper articles on Darwinian evolutionary theories. In 1870 he began to develop these articles into a longer work, *Erewhon.* Over the next 30 years he published a number of iconoclastic works on religious, scientific, and literary topics and worked on *The Way of All Flesh.* He died in London on June 18, 1902.

Writings—"Erewhon." Butler delighted in upsetting accepted ideas of all kinds. *Erewhon* (1872) tells of a visit to an imaginary country, really a satirical duplicate of contemporary England. Its name is an anagram of "Nowhere", and its chief feature is the reversal of all normal values. In *Erewhon* it is a penal offence to be physically ill or unhealthy, but immorality and crime are treated sympathetically as diseases. The narrator's host discusses at length his "attack" of embezzlement and the cure described by the straightening." The English church is satirized in the system of "Musical Banks," whose currency no one believes sound but all profess to admire. At the university the main study is "hypothetics," and there are courses in how to say nothing at great length. All machines have been banished for fear that they might, by evolution, grow powerful enough to enslave men. Privately published, *Erewhon* was warmly received by the public and was the only one of Butler's works to bring him some income, but its outright denial of accepted religious belief horrified Butler's family.

"The Fair Haven." Published in 1873 under the pseudonym John Pickard Owen, *The Fair Haven* parodies confessions of religious doubt and argues on deliberately illogical grounds for belief in miracles. Although intended as a satire, it was taken by many readers as a serious apologetic for religion until Butler admitted his authorship.

Critical Studies. Turning again to Darwin's theory of evolution, Butler this time attacked it as being too mechanistic. He presented his beliefs in *Life and Habit* (1877), *Evolution, Old and New* (1879), *Unconscious Memory* (1880), and *Luck or Cunning As the Main Means of Organic Modification?* (1886). What Darwin considered acquired characteristics Butler held could be inherited, and evolution was not caused by natural selection and chance, as Darwin taught, but by the unconscious memories of previous adaptations transmitted by each sperm and egg cell. This theory, Butler felt, restored purpose and meaning to the universe, but it gained no serious attention from any leading scientist.

Butler next turned to literary detective work. In the *Humour of Homer* (1892), *On the Trapanese Origin of the Odyssey* (1893), and *The Authoress of the Odyssey* (1897), he argued that the *Iliad* was written by a Trojan who hid his real sympathies to gain a wider audience, that Odysseus' voyage from Troy was really a circumnavigation of Sicily, and that the *Odyssey* was written by a woman because no man would have been so ignorant of farming and seafaring and yet so informed on household matters. Robert Graves has recently made these theories the basis of a lively novel, *Homer's Daughter* (1955). In connection with his Homeric interest, Butler also made prose translations of the *Iliad* and the *Odyssey*. Still intrigued by literary mysteries, he wrote *Shakespeare's Sonnets Reconsidered* (1899), in which he rearranged the sonnets to tell a coherent but improbable love story.

Butler's various works of literary research fared no better than his attempts at new scientific and theological theories. Instead of stirring up a storm of controversy for which he longed, they were virtually ignored. Other works were hardly more successful. They included the *Life and Letters of Dr. Samuel Butler* (1896), about his grandfather.

"Erewhon Revisited." In his last book, Butler returned to the subject of his one previous success. *Erewhon Revisited* (1901) is a development of the themes in *Erewhon*, particularly the attack on revealed religion, but the satire is much more biting and the characters lack the redeeming features that in the earlier book made them seem charming despite their folly. Because of his ridicule of the Church of England, Butler could not find anyone to bring out the book until George Bernard Shaw introduced him to his publisher. In 1901, *Erewhon Revisited* and an expanded version of *Erewhon* appeared.

"The Way of All Flesh." All his life Butler strove for recognition as a bold iconoclast. Yet, ironically, to spare the feelings of his family, whom he despised yet faithfully visited, he dared not publish in his lifetime the work on which his fame chiefly rests. *The Way of All Flesh,* begun in 1873 and worked on until 1883, appeared the year after his death. It is a bitter indictment of the Butler family in particular and of the hypocrisy and subtle sadism of the Victorian middle-class family in general. To control young Ernest Pontifex, his clergyman father uses fanatical harshness, his mother guileful sentimentality. They rationalize their lies and betrayals as being for the good of their children. But beneath a self-righteous facade of bigoted Christianity, both are abysmal egoists. Like Butler, young Pontifex gives up a career in the church and, after a series of misadventures brought on by his innocence, gullibility, and longing for affection, finally achieves happiness as a cynical and atheistic bachelor. Butler is at his best in this novel, particularly in the more polished first third. It is a brilliant, witty, devastating portrait of parental hypocrisy, and all subsequent novels of family life are indebted to its honesty.

GEORGIA DUNBAR, *Hofstra University*

Further Reading: Furbank, Philip, *Samuel Butler* (New York 1958); Henderson, Philip, *Samuel Butler: The Incarnate Bachelor* (London 1953); Muggeridge, Malcolm, *The Earnest Atheist* (London 1936); Stillman, Clara, *Samuel Butler: A Mid-Victorian Modern* (New York 1932).

BUTLER, Smedley Darlington (1881–1940), American Marine Corps general, whose outspoken comments on public affairs involved him in controversies. He was born in West Chester, Pa., on July 31, 1881. As a Marine, he won the Congressional Medal of Honor twice and was a major general when he retired in 1931.

Butler caused a sensation in 1930 when he charged that Benito Mussolini, dictator of Italy, had run down a child with his automobile. He barely escaped court-martial, and the United States government formally apologized for his remarks. At the start of World War II, Butler asserted that the United States should be neutral and should withdraw its forces from Hawaii. He died in Philadelphia on June 21, 1940.

BUTLER, Walter (1752–1781), American loyalist soldier, who raided settlements in New York during the American Revolution. He was born in Johnstown, N. Y., the son of John Butler, a large landholder in the Mohawk Valley. As a Tory, at the onset of the Revolution he fled precipitously to Canada with his father, leaving his mother and the younger children behind.

He was commissioned into Butler's Rangers, a corps formed by his father with other loyalist refugees. Captured in 1777 at a clandestine meeting of Tories in Tryon county, N. Y., Butler was tried and condemned as a spy, but he escaped. In 1778 he led a force that pillaged Cherry Valley, N. Y. See CHERRY VALLEY MASSACRE. With prisoners taken there, he effected an exchange for his mother and her younger children.

In his home valley, Walter Butler was hated and feared as a morose, vindictive terrorist. He was shot dead on Oct. 30, 1781, by Continental troops when he made an unsuccessful raid into the Mohawk Valley.

HARRISON K. BIRD
Author of "Battle for a Continent"

BUTLER, William Orlando (1791–1880), American general, who was the Democratic candidate for vice president in 1848. He was born in Jessamine county, Ky., on April 19, 1791, and was educated at Transylvania University. Butler fought in the War of 1812 at the Raisin River (north of the Ohio) and under Andrew Jackson at Pensacola and New Orleans. Brevetted a major, he was on Jackson's staff for two years.

Butler resigned from the Army in 1817 to farm and practice law. He served two terms in Congress (1839–1843) and ran unsuccessfully as a Democrat for governor of Kentucky in 1844.

He fought in the Mexican War as a major general at Monterrey and Mexico City and then commanded the U. S. Army in Mexico. Popular acclaim gave him the Democratic vice-presidential nomination in 1848 with Lewis Cass as presidential candidate. They were defeated by the Zachary Taylor ticket. A Unionist in the secession crisis, he was a delegate in 1861 to the Border Slave States convention at Washington that tried to reach an accord on the slavery question.

Butler expressed his romantic nature in numerous poems. The best known was *The Boatman's Horn*, inspired by boats passing his home along the Ohio River at Carrollton, where he died on Aug. 6, 1880.

ELLIS MERTON COULTER, *University of Georgia; Author of "History of Kentucky"*

BUTLER, Zebulon (1731–1795), American colonizer and soldier. He was born in Ipswich, Mass., and was raised in Lyme, Conn. After serving in the French and Indian War, he led settlers into the Wyoming Valley of northeastern Pennsylvania to establish Connecticut's claim to the land there. In the resulting Pennamite Wars (q.v.) between Connecticut and Pennsylvania, Butler captured Fort Wyoming (1771), defeated Pennsylvania's invasion of the Wyoming Valley (1775), and refused a congressional order to leave (1784).

A colonel in the Continental Army during the American Revolution, he was at his home in the Wyoming Valley in 1778 when John Butler's Loyalist Rangers and Indians invaded the area. He organized a feeble defense and, though defeated in battle, he escaped before the fall of Forty Fort and the ensuing massacre.

HARRISON K. BIRD
Author of "Battle for a Continent"

BUTLER is an industrial borough in northern New Jersey, in Morris county, 22 miles (35 km) northwest of Newark. Its chief manufactures are rubber products and tissue paper. Butler was settled in 1695. Many Hessian soldiers who remained in America after the Revolutionary War settled here. The borough is the site of a Franciscan monastery. It was incorporated in 1901 and is governed by a mayor and council. Population: 7,051.

BUTLER, an industrial city in western Pennsylvania, the seat of Butler county, is 30 miles (48 km) north of Pittsburgh, on Connoquenessing Creek. The city manufactures strip-steel car wheels, plate glass, railroad cars, tubing, oil-well equipment, rubber goods, fishing equipment, fertilizer and clothing. Butler is in an agricultural area and coal, oil, natural gas, and limestone are found nearby.

The site of Butler was originally owned by Robert Morris of Philadelphia, leading financier of the Revolutionary War. It was incorporated as a borough in 1803 and named for Gen. Richard Butler (q.v.). Butler was incorporated as a city in 1917 and is governed by a mayor and council. Population: 18,691.

BUTLER, in English history, an officer of the royal household, who originally had charge of the wine for the king's table and in exchange for his service enjoyed a position of high rank in the government. The office first became prominent at the time of the Norman conquest, when the butler was a leading member of the *curia regis,* or court of the king. At first he served the king wine at royal feasts, but the duty was soon restricted to coronations. In the late 11th century and early 12th century the office was bestowed on the dukes of Norfolk. Thereafter the Belet family held it until its privileges were challenged and usurped by the mayors of London in the 13th century. By that time the office was only nominally connected with the service of wine.

BUTO, bū'tō, an ancient Egyptian goddess, was the guardian of Lower Egypt. She was represented as a serpent and was identified by the Greeks with Leto or Latona. The city of Buto, which took its name from her, is thought to have been on an island in what is now Lake Burullus in the delta of the Nile River.

BUTOR, bü-tôr', **Michel Marie François** (1926–), French writer. The son of a railroad inspector, he was born at Mons-en-Baroeul, Nord department, on Sept. 4, 1926. After receiving the highest diploma in philosophy from the Faculté des Lettres in Paris, he lectured at universities in Europe and the United States. A member of the literary group called the "New Wave," Butor wrote the novels *Passage de Milan* (1954), *L'emploi du temps* (1956), *La modification* (1957), and *Degrés* (1957). His collections of essays include *Le génie de lieu* (1958), *Répertoire* (1960), *Histoire extraordinaire* (1961) *Mobile* (1962), *Réseau aérien* (1963), *Description de San Marco* (1963), and *Répertoire II* (1964). Among his poetry is the volume *6,810,000 litres d'eau par seconde* (1965).

BÜTSCHLI, büch'lē, **Otto** (1848–1920), German zoologist and cytologist, whose work on cell division and the nature of protoplasm contributed to the initial development of cytology. During 1875 and 1876, Bütschli described cell division and conjugation in microscopic organisms (then known as infusoria). Later he studied protoplasm, the living matter of all cells, and concluded that it is a fluid emulsion (a mixture of two mutually insoluble liquids), in which tiny droplets (called "alveoli" by Bütschli) of one liquid are dispersed throughout the other liquid. To illustrate his ideas, Bütschli constructed physical models that exhibited some of the properties of living matter. These models were one of the first attempts to explain the physical functioning of protoplasm.

Bütschli was born in Frankfurt am Main on May 3, 1848. For many years he was professor of zoology at the University of Heidelberg. In addition to his work in cytology, Bütschli also studied and revised the classification of wormlike animals. He wrote *Untersuchungen über mikroskopische Schäume und das Protoplasma* (1892) and *Vorlesungen über vergleichende Anatomie* (1910). He died in Heidelberg on Feb. 3, 1920.

ELDON J. GARDNER, *Utah State University*

BUTT, Dame Clara (1873–1936), English singer. She was born at Southwick, Sussex, on Feb. 1, 1873, and studied at the Royal College of Music and in Paris and Berlin. Renowned for her singing of ballads and her work in oratorio, she had a contralto voice of great range and power. A number of compositions were written especially for her. She gave concerts in the United States in 1899 and toured the world in 1913, and was made a Dame of the British Empire in 1920. She died in Oxford on Jan. 23, 1936.

BUTT, Isaac (1813–1879), Irish scholar, journalist, and political leader. He was born at Glenflin, County Donegal, on Sept 6, 1813, and was a brilliant student at Trinity College, Dublin, where he subsequently taught politics (1836–1841). A Conservative and a Protestant, he wrote for the Conservative press in Ireland and England before entering the British Parliament in 1852. He retired from Parliament in 1865 and at considerable financial sacrifice devoted most of the next four years to defending the Fenian prisoners (see FENIANS). He returned to Parliament as leader of the Home Rule party in 1871 but resigned the leadership to more radical elements in 1878. He died in Dundrum, County Dublin, on May 5, 1879.

BUTTE, būt, a mining city in southwestern Montana, the seat of Silver Bow county, is situated on the western slope of the Rocky Mountains, about 65 miles (104 km) southwest of Helena. Clark Fork, a part of the Columbia River system, flows through the city, where it is known as Silver Bow Creek. Butte is often called "the city that is a mile high and a mile deep." Its elevation above sea level exceeds 1 mile (1.6 km), and some of the ore veins and mine shafts beneath the city are nearly 1 mile deep.

Butte is also known as "the richest hill on earth" because of exceptionally rich deposits of copper and other minerals. Mines at Butte yield approximately 8% of the copper produced in the United States, as well as large quantities of lead, zinc, and manganese. The structures leading to the hundreds of shafts used for vein mining have been disappearing since the 1950's, making way for open-pit mining at or near the surface. The largest of these operations is the Berkeley pit. Low-grade copper ores from the pits are processed at a local concentrator and are smelted at the city of Anaconda, about 25 miles (40 km) to the northwest.

Butte is a trading center for the surrounding area as well as an industrial and commercial city, with livestock markets, packing plants, and a chemical industry. Nearby are recreation areas in the Deerlodge National Forest.

The city is the home of the Montana College of Mineral Science and Technology (formerly the Montana School of Mines). The museum at the college is a showcase of Montana's minerals and its mining industry.

Butte was founded when a gold strike was made in the area in 1864. The gold boom was soon replaced by a silver boom, which gave way to the discovery of the seemingly inexhaustible Anaconda copper lode and its rapid development during the early 1880's. The city, which was named for a nearby butte, was incorporated in 1879. Government is by mayor and council. Population: 23,368.

JOYCE BOUCHARD, *Butte Free Public Library*

JOSEF MUENCH

OVERLOOKING BUTTE, Mont., stands Augustus Saint-Gaudens' statue of the mining tycoon Marcus Daly.

BUTTER is a dairy product consisting chiefly of milk fat, milk curd, and water. One of the oldest dairy products known to man, butter was probably first made by prehistoric nomadic herdsmen, who poured milk or cream into bags made of animal skin and hung them from the backs of horses, camels, or other domestic animals. The movements of the animal shook the bag, agitating the cream or milk until the butter was formed. The ancient Hindus recorded their fondness for butter more than 3,500 years ago, and there are many references to butter in the Bible. The ancient Greeks and Romans used butter as a hair dressing, an ointment, and a medicine, as well as a food. It is also known that the Romans preferred the taste of rancid butter to that of fresh butter.

Kinds of Butter. In the United States, butter is available in three forms. *Sweet butter,* also known as *unsalted butter,* is very popular in many regions. It is made from sweet, pasteurized cream without the addition of salt. *Sweet cream butter* is also made from sweet, pasteurized cream, but for this type of butter salt is added. *Whipped butter* is made from either sweet butter or sweet cream butter combined with air or another inert gas to make the butter spread more easily and to increase its volume.

In the United States, all creamery butter is made from the cream of cow's milk. In many other countries, butter is often made from the milk of other domestic animals, including sheep, goats, horses, and yaks. In India and neighboring countries a semifluid form of butter called *ghee* is usually made from the milk of water buffaloes. After the milk is churned, the resulting butter is heated until the protein precipitates to the bottom. The clear liquid remaining at the top is ghee, or butter oil. In addition to being used as a food, ghee is used in Hindu religious ceremonies and also as a medicine on some occasions.

Composition and Food Value. Butter is a rich source of vitamin A. It also contains vitamin D, vitamin E, calcium, phosphorus, sodium, and potassium. The energy value of butter is 33 calories per teaspoon, the same as that of margarine but less than that of cooking and salad oils.

On the average, the fat content of both salted butter and sweet butter ranges from 80.4% to 81%. The moisture content of salted butter varies from 16% to 17.5%, and in sweet butter the moisture content is 18%. The curd content of butter, which is made up of protein, mineral matter, and lactose (milk sugar), ranges on the average between 0.9% and 1.5%.

Salt is often added to butter to produce a desired flavor and to improve its keeping quality. (Generally, well-wrapped butter will last for about one month under refrigeration. If it is frozen and kept at a temperature no higher than 0° F (about −18° C), butter will keep for as long as 6 months.) The amount of salt added to butter varies from one region to another. Generally, however, the salt content ranges between 1.5% and 2.0%.

In addition to salt, artificial coloring matter is added to butter at certain times of the year in order to produce the characteristic pale yellow color. This is done because seasonal changes often affect the natural color of butter.

COMMERCIAL BUTTERMAKING

In the United States, virtually all commercially prepared butter is made from pasteurized sweet cream. To make 1 pound (0.45 kg) of butter, the cream from slightly more than 10 quarts (about 9.5 liters) of milk is needed.

Whole milk is shipped from the farm to a dairy plant, where it is skimmed, separating the cream from the rest of the milk. Occasionally, the cream is "ripened" to increase its acidity. For ripening, cultures of lactic-acid-producing bacteria are added to the cream. Cultures are sometimes added before churning, and sometimes they are worked into the butter after churning. Ripening improves the flavor and increases the storage life of butter, especially unsalted butter.

Pasteurization. Before it is churned into butter, the cream is first pasteurized. Most often, pasteurization is accomplished by heating the cream to 163° F (73° C) for 30 minutes. However, another method, known as high temperature-short time pasteurization (HTST) is also widely used. In this method, the cream is heated to at least 180° F (about 82° C) for a minimum of 16 seconds.

After pasteurization, the cream is cooled to about 40° F (about 4° C) and held for churning. The temperature of the cream at churning time is important if churning is to be successful.

Churning. In most modern dairy plants, the butter churn is a huge rotating cylinder or drum with shelves inside that serve to raise and drop the cream as it is being rotated. After the cream is agitated in the churn for about 40 to 45 minutes, it becomes a foamy mass. The butter then forms as small granules, each granule consisting of an air bubble surrounded by fat globules. When the air bubbles collapse because of the increasing weight of granule formation, the "breaking point" is reached. The moment this happens, a glass observation window in the churn clears, and the operator sees the butter granules floating on the surface of the remaining liquid, the buttermilk. After the granules have become the size of small peas, the buttermilk is drained off, and the butter then is washed, salted, and worked.

Modern cylindrical or barrel churns are capable of producing as many as 5,000 pounds (2,267 kg) of butter in 1 hour. Early churns, which could produce only about 500 pounds (227 kg) of butter at one time, were made of wood and were so porous that they were difficult to sterilize. Modern churns are made of metal and are easily cleaned.

Working the Butter. After washing, the butter remains in the churn and is worked. The working of butter is essentially a kneading process, similar to the kneading of bread dough. In this process, the butter granules are worked together into a soft mass. It is also at this time that coloring matter and salt (if desired) are added and worked smoothly through the mass.

The moisture content of the butter is also determined at this time. Excess water or buttermilk may be removed; if necessary, additional water may be added. The quality of butter is decidedly affected by its moisture content. High quality butter has good body texture and is not "leaky." Leaky butter does not retain its moisture very well.

Final Steps. The finished butter is packed in parchment-lined corrugated or fiber boxes. Later, converters repackage the butter into smaller units—generally patties, 1-pound (0.45–kg) packages, and ¼-pound (114-gm) sticks. Before it is wrapped, each batch is assigned a grade.

In the U. S. these grades conform to standards set by the federal government. Each grade represents a numerical score that is based on the butter's texture, flavor, and other characteristics. U. S. Grade AA, the grade generally available in most stores, has a score of 93. It has a superior flavor, a smooth, creamy texture, and is easily spread. Its salt is completely and uniformly dissolved throughout the entire mass. Grade A butter has a score of 92, indicating a slightly lower quality. Grade B butter has a score of 90, and Grade C butter a score of 89.

MAKING BUTTER AT HOME

For making butter at home, only a few simple kitchen utensils are necessary. These are: a rotary eggbeater in a fitted bowl (or an electric mixer or blender or a small churn—a jar with a tight-fitting lid will do); a mixing bowl; a wooden spoon or paddle; a measuring cup; salt; and ½ pint (about 180 ml) of whipping cream. The cream must have a fat content of at least 30%. If ripened cream is available, the butter forms more quickly and the buttermilk has a tangy taste.

For making butter, the cream should be removed from the refrigerator and kept at room temperature for about 10 minutes before it is used. The cream is poured into the bowl, mixer, or churn and agitated until small granules of butter are formed throughout the cream. With a rotary eggbeater, this will take about 20 or 30 minutes. With an electric blender or mixer, it will take only about 3 to 5 minutes.

After the butter is formed, the buttermilk is poured off and the butter is placed in a mixing bowl. The remaining buttermilk is worked out of the butter with a wooden spoon or paddle. The butter is washed with cold water, and, if desired, ¼ teaspoon of salt is added. The salt is worked in with the spoon or paddle until it is thoroughly distributed. The finished butter then is ready to be served or stored.

HISTORY OF BUTTERMAKING

The first butter in North America was probably made by early European settlers. There is no evidence that the American Indians ever made butter. The European settlers brought with them their domestic animals and buttermaking practices. For many years all butter was made with wooden churns on farms. The cream was poured into the churn and agitated by the blades of a wooden dasher that was pumped by hand.

As dairy herds became larger, farmers began producing more butter than they could use, and they sold the surplus butter to neighbors or traded it for other commodities at village stores. The first commercial creamery in the United States is believed to have been built in 1856 by R. S. Woodhull in Orange county, N. Y. Soon, other creameries appeared and by 1900 creamery butter was available in most food stores.

The equipment in these early commercial creameries consisted largely of mechanical wooden churns, and the butter was made one batch at a time. A major advance in the buttermaking process was made during the 1930's and 1940's, when several new churning systems were developed. By these new methods, butter could be made in a continuous operation, as compared to making one batch of butter at a time. The first commercial installation of a continuous-process machine was in Australia about 1937. The method was called the "New Way" process. Similar methods were also developed in Germany and the United States.

The type of continuous process most widely used today is known as the Fritz process, which was developed in Germany about 1933. French and Danish versions of this process are also in wide use. A similar process, known as the Meleshin method, is used in the Soviet Union. Although these methods use somewhat different equipment, their basic principles are the same. All these methods start with cream that has been separated from whole milk and use high-speed agitation to form the butter granules in about 1.5 seconds. The granules then are separated from the buttermilk, and the salting and working processes follow. The butter is then extruded from a tube, ready for packaging.

PRODUCTION AND CONSUMPTION

The world's leading butter producers are the United States, the Soviet Union, and West Germany. In the United States, the leading butter-producing states are Minnesota, Wisconsin, and Iowa. Butter represents the second most important use of the U. S. milk supply, accounting for about 20% of all the milk produced.

LEADING BUTTER-PRODUCING COUNTRIES
(Creamery Production)

Country	1956–1960 Average (millions of pounds)	1965 (millions of pounds)
Soviet Union	1,460	2,365
United States	1,385	1,337
West Germany	733	1,067
France	509	794 (est.)
New Zealand	471	550
Australia	424	450
East Germany	349	434 (est.)
Denmark	367	366
Canada	320	342
Poland	184	231
Netherlands	187	228
Finland	169	219
Czechoslovakia	120	184 (est.)
Sweden	184	175
Belgium	107	130

Source: U. S. Department of Agriculture, *Foreign Agriculture Circular*, September 1967.

For many years both the production and consumption of butter have declined in the United States. This has largely been due to the increasing popularity of vegetable oil products competitive with butter and to the declining production of farm-made butter, resulting from the decreasing number of farms.

According to U. S. Department of Agriculture records, average annual production of butter for 1957 through 1959 was 1,476,601,333 pounds, of which 97,261,333 pounds was made on farms. By 1965 total butter production had decreased to 1,337,000,000 pounds, of which only 21,395,000 pounds was produced on farms. The per-capita consumption of butter has also sharply declined from an annual average of 8.2 pounds (3.7 kg) in the 1957–1959 period to 5.7 pounds (2.5 kg) in 1965.

U. S PRODUCTION OF CREAMERY BUTTER

State	1958–1962 Average (pounds)	1965 (pounds)
Minnesota	331,166,000	357,198,000
Wisconsin	290,007,000	290,188,000
Iowa	171,943,000	149,085,000
New York	42,708,000	55,827,000
Nebraska	57,931,000	48,482,000
North Dakota	55,951,000	42,082,000
Michigan	44,954,000	40,421,000
Missouri	47,406,000	35,632,000
South Dakota	38,716,000	35,555,000
California	33,246,000	34,572,000

Source: U. S. Department of Agriculture, *Production of Manufactured Dairy Products*, 1965, and *Agricultural Statistics*, 1966.

WILLIAM S. EPPLE
National Dairy Council

Bibliography

Lampert, Lincoln M., *Modern Dairy Products* (New York 1965).
National Dairy Council, *How Americans Use Their Dairy Foods* (Chicago 1967).
National Dairy Council, *Let's Make Butter* (Chicago 1956).
Newlander, J. A., and Atherton, Henry V., *The Chemistry and Testing of Dairy Products* (Milwaukee 1964).
United States Department of Agriculture, *Production of Manufactured Dairy Products* (Washington 1966).

J. J. SMITH
Butter-and-eggs (*Linaria vulgaris*)

BUTTER-AND-EGGS is a common perennial wild flower of the figwort family that resembles the cultivated snapdragon. It has stems 1 to 3 feet (0.3 to 1 meter) high with narrow leaves 1½ inch (5 cm) long in alternate arrangement. The light yellow flowers, which bloom all summer, are bilaterally symmetrical. They have a 2-lobed upper lip and a 3-lobed lower lip with a deep orange spot. The lower portions of the petals, unlike those of snapdragon, are united into a long spur. Butter-and-eggs, *Linaria vulgaris*, is native to Europe and Asia and naturalized in the northeastern United States and southern Canada. It has become so widespread in fields and along roadsides that it is often considered a bothersome weed. It spreads freely by rhizomes (underground stems) and is difficult to eradicate.

JOAN E. RAHN
Lake Forest College, Ill.

BUTTER TREE is the name commonly applied to at least four different trees whose seeds or fruits contain large amounts of fat or oil. Probably the most important is the shea butter tree (*Butyrospermum parkii*), whose seeds, which may contain 50% fat, are used for food and in manufacturing soap. The shea butter tree is native to tropical Africa where it reaches a height of

35 feet (10½ meters), with a trunk diameter of 5 feet (1½ meters). Its hard wood, which is called ruby wood, is similar in appearance to that of the cedar. Closely related to the shea butter tree is the mahu butter tree (*Madhuca latifolia*), whose fruit pulp has a buttery consistency. The flowers and fruits of this species are used for food.

Another butter tree is the Sierra Leone butter tree (*Pentadesma butyracea*), whose large fruits have a thick rind that is rich in a fatty yellowish substance sometimes used for butter. Another species called butter tree is the *Combretum butyrosum,* whose fruits have a high fat content.

Both the shea butter tree and the mahu butter tree blong to the sapodilla family (Sapotaceae). The Sierra Leone butter tree is a member of the mangosteen family (Clusiaceae) while *Combretum butyrosum* belongs to the combretum family (Combretaceae).

S. C. Bausor, *California State College, Pa.*

BUTTERCUP, any of a number of wild flowers of the buttercup genus *Ranunculus,* in the crowfoot family. Buttercups are probably the best-known flowers. They grow in a variety of habitats throughout the north temperate zone and subarctic regions. Most of them inhabit moist places such as low meadows, marshes, and ponds; hence the generic name, which means "little frog." Alpine species thrive at high altitudes.

Buttercups are herbaceous annuals and perennials. Their leaves are alternate and either simple or compound. The simple leaves are lobed, some so deeply as to be essentially compound. Buttercups are also called *crowfoots* because of the leaf shape of some species.

The flowers are borne singly at the tip of a stalk. Each flower has five (or fewer) green sepals and five yellow (rarely white or red) petals with shiny surfaces that look waxed and polished. The stem rises to a conical tip through the center of the flower, with the stamens positioned spirally around its base and the pistils spirally around its top. Each pistil contains one ovule and, after pollination, matures into a small fruit.

Buttercup flowers share some primitive features with other members of the crowfoot family, which is considered by most botanists to be one of the most primitive families of flowering plants. Unlike flowers that evolved later, buttercups have numerous stamens and pistils and a spiral rather than whorled arrangement of these parts.

Tall buttercup (*Ranunculus acris*)

JOHN J. SMITH

There are some 200 species of buttercup, most of them flowering in spring or early summer. Many of them are cultivated in gardens or indoors in pots. They are propagated by tuberous roots, bulbs, or seeds. Few species have been altered by cultivation, but there are double-flowered varieties in existence.

Buttercups are a problem to farmers because they are poisonous to livestock, causing inflammation of tissues or even death. The strength of the poison varies with the species, the part of the plant, and the season of the year. Because the poison breaks down when the plant is dried, buttercup hay is harmless.

Joan E. Rahn, *Lake Forest College, Ill.*

BUTTERFIELD, Daniel (1831–1901), American general, who composed the military bugle call *Taps.* He was born in Utica, N. Y., on Oct. 31, 1831, and joined the Union Army as a colonel of militia at the outbreak of the Civil War in 1861. Butterfield served in the Peninsular Campaign in Virginia in 1862 and, as a major general, commanded a corps at the Battle of Fredericksburg. He was chief of staff of the Army of the Potomac at the battles of Chancellorsville and Gettysburg. He composed *Taps* in 1862. Seeking a simple, expressive call, he whistled notes that were repeated by his bugler until he was satisfied with the effect. The call is sounded in the armed services when the flag is lowered at sunset, and at funerals. After the war, Butterfield engaged in railroad and steamship enterprises. He died at Cold Spring, N. Y., on July 17, 1901.

BUTTERFISH, a saltwater fish that lives in coastal and offshore waters from Newfoundland to Florida and in the Gulf of Mexico. A thin-bodied, oval-shaped fish, the butterfish grows to a maximum length of 12 inches (30 cm) and a weight of 1¼ pounds (½ kg), but the average weight of those caught is less than 1 pound. It is silvery blue in color and may have dark spots. Butterfish are found from the beaches to a depth of 230 fathoms (1,380 feet, or 420 meters). They often occur in dense schools. They feed on crustaceans, annelid worms, squid, and small fishes.

The flesh of the butterfish is somewhat oily and has a delicious flavor. A large part of the butterfish catch is smoked; some is sold fresh; and some is processed for fertilizer, oils, and other products. The commercial catch is concentrated between Rhode Island and New Jersey.

Young butterfish, up to 3 inches (7.5 cm) long, may have a free-living existence, but they are frequently observed within the tentacles or under the bell of a jellyfish. There they find shelter from predators and are able to eat the small organisms on and around the jellyfish. Occasionally the young butterfish feed on the tentacles of the jellyfish, and rarely the jellyfish eat the young butterfish.

The butterfish (*Poronotus triacanthus*) is a member of the butterfish family, Stromateidae, in the order Perciformes. Close relatives of the butterfish include the harvestfish and the Pacific pompano (which is not a true pompano).

Frederick H. Berry
U. S. Bureau of Commercial Fisheries

X-RAY PHOTOGRAPH OF CECROPIA MOTH, FROM EASTMAN KODAK COMPANY

BUTTERFLIES AND MOTHS

BUTTERFLIES AND MOTHS, but'ər-flīz, môthz, make up the second-largest order of insects, the Lepidoptera. More than 100,000 species are known, with thousands still undescribed. They occur on every continent wherever land insect life is possible, from the far Arctic to deserts and tropical forests. They range in size from minute moths about ⅛ inch (0.03 cm) long to giant moths and butterflies with a wing expanse of 11 inches (27.5 cm).

Butterflies and moths have a complete metamorphosis and develop through four stages: egg, larva (caterpillar), pupa, and adult. The caterpillars have biting mouthparts, while the adults have a tubular proboscis for sucking liquids. The adult wings are typically covered with tiny, flat scales, which overlap like shingles.

Ecologically, butterflies and moths are highly important because of the vast quantities of plants eaten by the larvae, the flower-visiting and pollinating habits of the adults, and the enormous numbers of them eaten by other animals.

Butterflies Versus Moths. The great majority of the Lepidoptera are moths, but the day-flying, brightly colored butterflies are more familiar. No single factor distinguishes moths from butterflies. Most moths fly by night, while butterflies are diurnal; but there are many day-flying, flower-visiting moths. Most moths are relatively dull colored, but some are as brilliantly colored as any butterfly. Moths tend to rest with their wings flat, the fore wings hiding the hind wings; butterflies either hold their wings together vertically over their backs or spread them widely at their sides. Moths' antennae are usually threadlike, tapering to a point, or they bear many close-set branches and look feathery. Butterflies' antennae have a prominent club at or near the tip; however, in some moth families the antennae are clubbed. Finally, most moths have a bristlelike structure, called the frenulum, near the base of the hind wing. It engages a catch, the retinaculum, on the fore wing and joins the wings for flight coordination. Butterflies lack this, but so do some families of moths.

ECONOMIC AND ECOLOGIC IMPORTANCE

Beneficial Types. Relatively few butterflies and moths are definitely beneficial to man. One species, the silkworm (*Bombyx mori*), is the source of nearly all silk. A few other species have been used in weed control; the South American cactus moth (*Cactoblastis cactorum*) was the chief agent in reclaiming millions of acres of Australian agricultural and grazing land overgrown by spiny cacti. Many species of butterflies and moths carry on unrecognized weed control, and flower-visiting adults accomplish much useful pollination. The gypsy, cecropia, and European peppered moths are valuable in research in genetics, physiology, and evolution.

Harmful Types. The order contains a great variety of the most serious agricultural, forest, and household pests. The following are only a small sample. Forest pests include the spruce budworm (*Choristoneura fumiferana*), cankerworms (*Alsophila* and *Palaeacrita*), gypsy moth (*Lymantria dispar*), and leopard moth (*Zeuzera pyrina*). Orchard pests are the codling moth (*Laspeyresia pomonella*) and peach borer (*Sanninoidea exitiosa*). Crop and garden pests are many species of cutworms (Noctuidae), the army worm (*Pseudaletia unipuncta*), European cabbage butterfly (*Pieris rapae*), European corn borer (*Pyrausta nubilalis*), pink bollworm (*Pectinophora gossypiella*) on cotton, corn earworm (*Helicoverpa zea*), tobacco and tomato hornworms (*Phlegethontius*), and sod webworms (*Crambinae*) in grasses. Household and stored-food pests include the clothes moths (*Tineola bisselliella* and others) and Indian meal moth (*Plodia interpunctella*). A beehive pest is the bee moth (*Galleria mellonella*).

Ecological Importance. The general ecological effect of the lepidopterans on land plants and animals is enormous and all-pervasive. Nearly all caterpillars feed on plants and consume an enormous mass. In turn, lepidopterans serve as food for tens of thousands of species of other animals that prey upon them. Their sudden disappear-

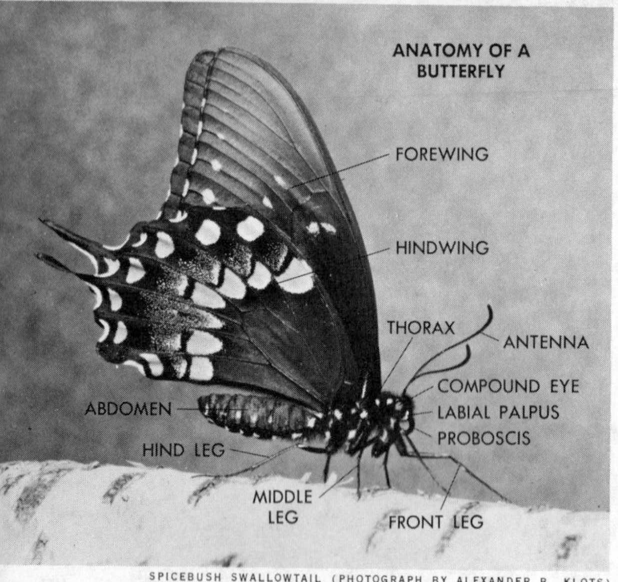

SPICEBUSH SWALLOWTAIL (PHOTOGRAPH BY ALEXANDER B. KLOTS)

ance would cause an almost unimaginable disruption of land life.

Relationships with Plants. The seed plants (Spermatophyta) are the chief source of food for caterpillars, although some ferns, liverworts, and mosses are eaten. The great majority of caterpillars eat foliage, but some families (such as Cossidae and Aegeriidae) are wood and rootstock borers, and many small species bore in the stems of grass and other herbaceous plants. Others bore into fruits or eat seeds or flowers. A few caterpillars cause the formation of galls, in which they live, and many feed on dead leaves on the forest floor. In several families of very small moths (such as Nepticulidae and Gracillariidae) the tiny larvae tunnel within leaves or under bark; small larvae often skeletonize leaves. A few moths are carriers of plant diseases.

Many flowering plants benefit from pollination by adult butterflies and moths; a few such plants—some orchids and morning glories—are dependent upon specific hawk moths (Sphingidae) for pollination. The abundant excretions of caterpillars contribute greatly to soil fertility and especially benefit smaller plants growing under the larger ones on which the caterpillars are feeding. On the whole, however, lepidopterans harm plants more than they benefit them.

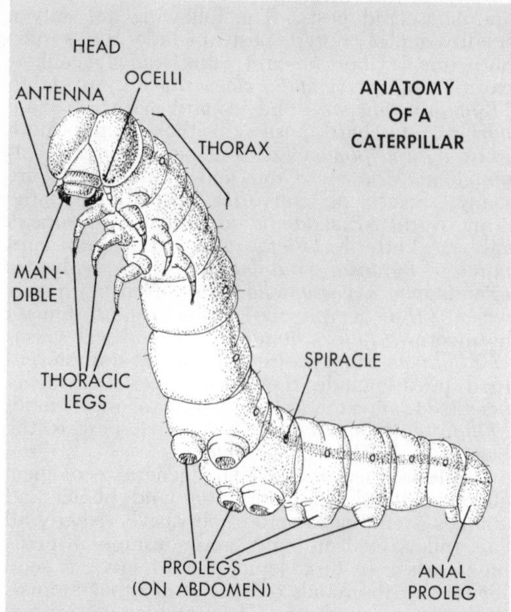

A few cases of obligatory mutualism (Symbiosis) with plants are known. Females of the yucca moths (*Tegeticula*) carry balls of pollen to the stigmata (female organs) of yucca flowers. They also lay their eggs in the yucca seed capsules. Thus pollinated, the plants form fruits in which the moth larvae feed.

Relationships with Other Animals. In all of their life stages lepidopterans are preyed upon by a vast host of other animals. Among the most important of these are centipedes, spiders, and many groups of insects from praying mantids to social wasps. Among vertebrates are frogs, toads and lizards, insectivorous birds, small rodents, bats, and monkeys. Most of these are direct predators which locate their prey chiefly by sight, then seize and overpower it. A few groups of insects, such as the tachina flies (Tachinidae) and many wasp families (Ichneumonoidea, Chalcidoidea, and some Cynipoidea), are parasitoid predators. Females of these insects locate the prey, chiefly by scent, and then lay eggs on or in them. Their larvae then develop slowly within the living hosts like true parasites, and eventually kill the host. Such parasitoids kill far more lepidopterans than the direct predators do.

Lepidopterans are the hosts of very few true parasites. The chief ones are mites (for example, *Myrmonyssus*) that live in the tympanic cavities of noctuid moths and destroy their auditory structures.

Few lepidopterans feed on other animals or animal substances. A few live on the secretions of other insects, and some scavenge in bee, bird, and mammal nests. A few are predatory on scale insects or cannibalistic on other caterpillars. A few lycaenid butterfly larvae have sweet, honeydew secretions that ants relish greatly. The ants often attend these larvae and may take them into their nests, where the larvae sometimes eat the ant brood.

Defenses. The Lepidoptera could never have evolved into the enormous and successful group that they are without efficient defenses against the great variety of predators that attack them. Their first line of defense is a high reproductive rate—50 to 1,000 eggs laid by each female. In addition they have evolved a multitude of special means of protection.

Chemical defenses are many and varied. Many larvae secrete bad-tasting, repellent, or toxic substances such as acids (squirted from gland openings), alkaloids, or even hydrogen cyanide (in the blood). Many moth larvae (for example Notodontidae, Arctiidae, Zygaenidae) and butterfly larvae (such as Danainae, Heliconiinae, some Papilionidae) are noted for such secretions. Still others (Eucleidae, Megalopygidae) have sharp, hollow hairs that cause painful skin rashes. The larval secretions commonly carry over into the pupa and adult. Most of the protected species are very distinctive in appearance and are easily recognized by their bright colors and bold patterns; they also have characteristic poses or actions. Such aposematic appearances—signals of inedibility or toxicity—are easily learned and long remembered by predators after only

BUTTERFLIES AND MOTHS OF THE WORLD

Duomitus leuconotus moth

Pericopis ithomia moth

Saturnia pavonia moth

Pseudophex ichneumoneus moth

Agrias sardanalapus butterfly

Melittia bombyliformis moth

Ancyluris formosissima butterfly

Gonepteryx rhamni butterfly

Morpho cypris butterfly

Egybolis vaillantina moth

Troides paradisea butterfly

Composia fidelissima moth

BUTTERFLIES OF NORTH AMERICA

Approximately ⅔ life size

Leonardus skipper
(Hesperia leonardus)

Tiger swallowtail
(Papilio glaucus)

Pearl crescent
(Phyciodes tharos)

Common alpine
(Erebia epipsodea)

Zebra
(Heliconius charitonius)

Baltimore
(Euphydryas phaeton)

Longtail skipper
(Urbanus proteus)

Regal fritillary
(Speyeria idalia)

Dogface
(Colias cesonia)

Spring azure
(Celastrina pseudargiola)

American copper
(Lycaena phlaeas americana)

Giant swallowtail
(Papilio cresphontes)
with larva

Cabbage
(Pieris rapae)
with larva

Alfalfa
(Colias eurytheme)
with larva

Approximately ⅔ life size

Snout
(Libythea bachmanii)

Red-spotted purple
(Limenitis astyanax)

Great purple hairstreak
(Atlides halesus)

White admiral
(Limenitis arthemis)

Variegated fritillary
(Euptoieta claudia)
with larva

Questionmark anglewing
(Polygonia interrogationis)

Wood nymph
(Minois alope)

Mourning cloak
(Nymphalis antiopa)
with larva

Painted lady
(Vanessa cardui)

Viceroy
(Limenitis archippus)
with larva

Monarch
(Danaus plexippus)
with larva

MOTHS OF NORTH AMERICA

Approximately ⅔ life size

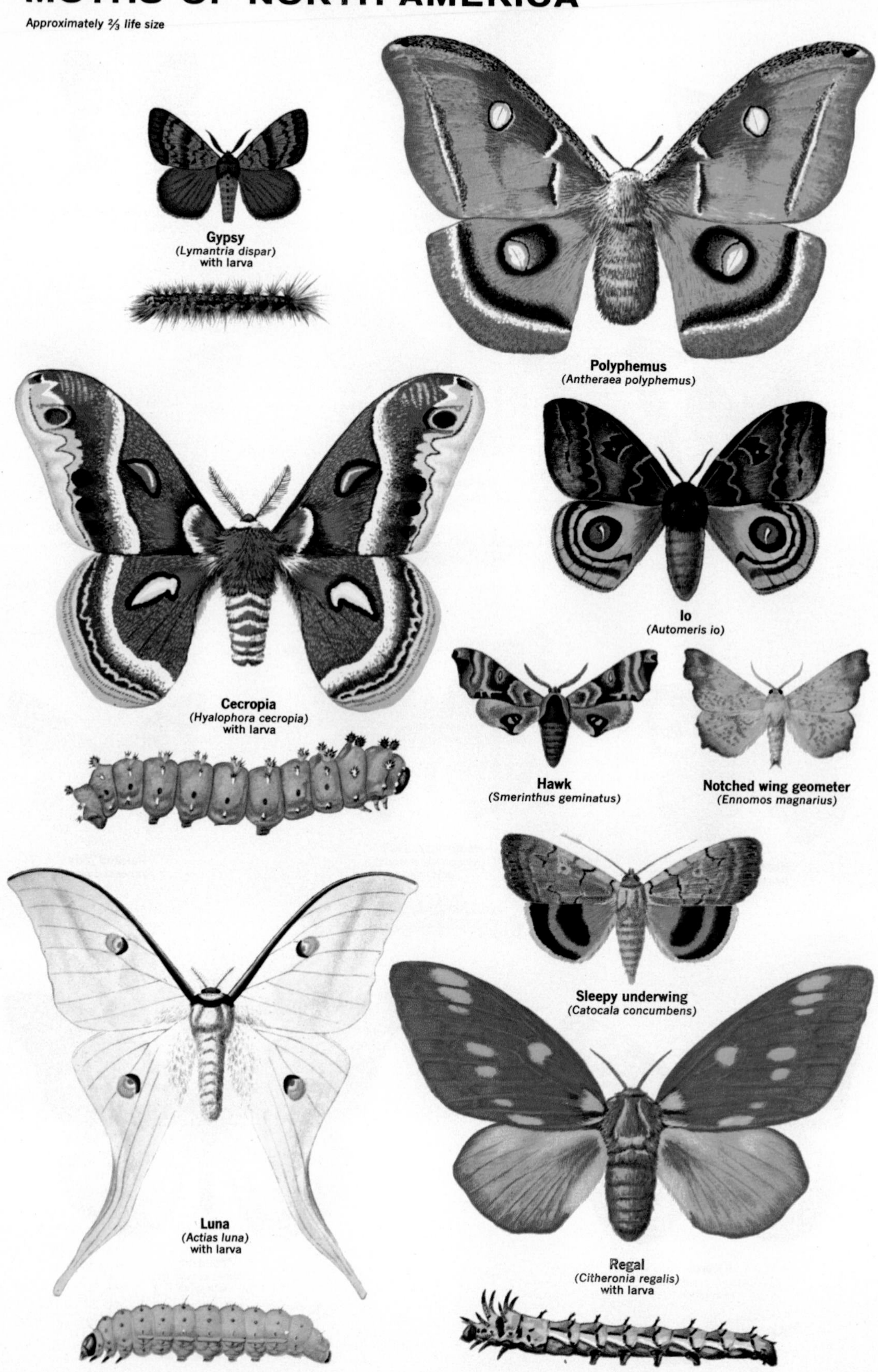

PLATE 4

CLASSIFICATION OF BUTTERFLIES AND MOTHS

The classification of the Lepidoptera is now based on the correlation of many technical characters of the reproductive systems, venation and other wing features, mouthparts, larval setae, pupal structures, tympanic organs, and many other details. Older systems divided the order on the basis of wing features only. Still more superficial divisions into "Heterocera" (moths) and "Rhopalocera" (butterflies) or "Microlepidoptera" (small moths) and "Macrolepidoptera" (larger moths and butterflies) had a certain popular appeal but little scientific merit.

In North America alone, 3 suborders, consisting of 28 superfamilies and over 70 families, are generally recognized. Details of classification may be found in the books in the list of suggested readings. Only the most important families are listed in the classification; those most likely to be encountered are marked with an asterisk. The sequence is from the most primitive to the most highly advanced.

Suborder ZEUGLOPTERA

Superfamily Micropterigoides
Family Micropterigidae (mandibulate moths). A small, widely distributed family of small primitive moths.

Suborder MONOTRYSIA

Superfamily Hepialoidea
Family Hepialidae (ghost moths). Large; worldwide but best represented in Australia and New Zealand.

Superfamily Incurvarioidea
Family Prodoxidae (yucca moths). Small; New World only.
Family Adelidae (fairy moths). Small; widely distributed.

Superfamily Nepticuloidea
Family Nepticulidae (midget moths). Minute; widely distributed.

Suborder DITRYSIA

Superfamily Zygaenoidea
Family *Eucleidae (slug caterpillar moths). Medium-sized; mostly tropical.
Family Megalopygidae (flannel moths). Medium-sized; chiefly New World.
Family Epipyropidae (plant hopper parasites). Small; mostly Indo-Australian.

Superfamily Tineoidea
Family *Tineidae (clothes and scavenger moths). A large, worldwide family of small moths.
Family *Psychidae (bagworm moths). Small to large; widely distributed.
Family Gracillariidae (leaf-mining moths). Small; cosmopolitan.
Family Lyonetiidae (leaf-mining moths). Small to very small; widely distributed.
Family Coleophoridae (case-bearer moths). Small; chiefly northern hemisphere.

Superfamily Gelechioidea
Family *Gelechiidae. Small; worldwide distribution.
Family *Oecophoridae. Small; worldwide distribution.
Family Cosmopterigidae. Small; worldwide distribution.

Superfamily Cossoidea
Family Cossidae (carpenter moths). Medium to large; worldwide distribution.

Superfamily Tortricoidea
Family *Tortricidae (tortricids). Small; worldwide distribution.
Family *Olethreutidae (olethreutids). Small; worldwide distribution.

Superfamily Pyralididoidea
Family *Pyralididae (pyralidid moths). Small to medium-sized; worldwide distribution.
Family *Pterophoridae (plume-winged moths). Small; worldwide distribution.
Family Orneodidae (feather-winged moths). Small; worldwide distribution.

Superfamily Yponomeutoidea
Family *Aegeriidae (wasp, or clearwing, moths). Small; widely distributed.

The foregoing groups are often called the micro-lepidoptera; those below are called macrolepidoptera.

Superfamily Geometroidea
Family *Geometridae (measuring worm moths). Medium-sized; worldwide distribution.

Superfamily Bombycoidea
Family Bombycidae (silkworm moths). Small; mostly Asiatic.
Family *Lasiocampidae (tent caterpillar moths and lappet moths). Medium-sized; widely distributed.

Superfamily Noctuoidea
Family *Noctuidae (owlet moths). Small to very large; worldwide distribution.
Family *Notodontidae (prominent moths). Medium-sized; widely distributed.
Family *Liparidae (tussock moths). Medium-sized; widely distributed.
Family *Arctiidae (tiger moths). Medium-sized; widely distributed.
Family *Ctenuchidae (day-flying mimetic moths). Small to medium-sized; widely distributed.

Superfamily Saturnoidea
Family *Saturniidae (giant silkworm moths and emperor moths). Small to large; mostly tropical.

Superfamily Sphingoidea
Family *Sphingidae (sphinx and hawk moths). Medium to large; worldwide distribution.

Superfamily Hesperioidea
Family Megathymidae (giant skippers). Large; New World only
Family *Hesperiidae (skippers). Mostly small; widely distributed.

Superfamily Papilionoidea (true butterflies)
Family *Papilionidae (swallowtails and parnassians). Medium to large; worldwide distribution.
Family *Pieridae (whites and sulfurs). Medium-sized; worldwide distribution.
Family *Lycaenidae (blues, coppers, and hairstreaks). Small, worldwide distribution.
Family Riodinidae (metalmarks). Small to medium-sized; mostly tropical.
Family *Nymphalidae (brush-footed butterflies)
Subfamily *Danainae (milkweed butterflies and monarchs). Large; mostly tropical.
Subfamily *Satyrinae (satyrs and grass nymphs). Medium-sized; widely distributed.
Subfamily Heliconiinae (heliconians). Medium-sized; mostly tropical.
Subfamily Morphinae (morphos). Large; tropical.
Subfamily *Nymphalinae (checkerspots; fritillaries, tortoiseshells, admirals, and others). Small to medium-sized; widely distributed.

one or two painful experiences, and are thus very efficient visual defenses.

Following the evolution of these protections—chemical and aposematic—came the evolution of the two main types of mimicry for which the Lepidoptera are especially noted. These are Müllerian mimicry and Batesian mimicry. In Müllerian mimicry, protected species mimic each others' appearance and thus simplify the recognition and learning of their inedibility by predators. In Batesian mimicry, unprotected species mimic protected ones and thus gain some immunity from deceived predators. See also MIMICRY.

Most caterpillars that feed in the open and adult moths that rest in exposed places during the day are cryptic in coloration and often also in form; they resemble a background of natural objects such as grass, bark, leaves, twigs, or bird droppings. In this way they may escape detection by predators.

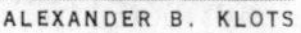

ALEXANDER B. KLOTS

ALEXANDER B. KLOTS

(*Above*) **WHITE-MARKED TUSSOCK MOTH** caterpillars are a pest of shade and fruit trees in the eastern United States.

(*Left*) **TENT CATERPILLARS** eat the foliage of many trees, including fruit trees. The larval stage lasts four to six weeks.

Many other adults and caterpillars have disruptive appearances due to bold, contrasting markings that seemingly break their body outlines into two or more unrelated objects. Leaf-green larvae may thus have white or brown areas resembling holes or dead patches. See also PROTECTIVE COLORATION.

The underwing moths (*Catocala*) combine cryptic, barklike fore wings with brilliant red, orange or white, and black hind wings. Such flash coloration is very effective because the sudden exposure of the hind wings startles an approaching predator and delays it long enough to let the moth escape. Prominent eyespots on the hind wings have a similar startling effect when suddenly exposed.

Nest camouflage is another form of protection. A great many caterpillars live in solitary nests made with silk or rolled or folded leaves. Others, such as the bagworms (Psychidae), make portable silk cases masked with leaves or twigs; they live and pupate in these. Many cocoons, too, are camouflaged with various substances. A few caterpillars (Geometridae) mask themselves with attached bits of leaf or petal.

The tiger moths (Arctiidae) and some relatives have an unusual form of defense. They make very high-pitched noises in the ultrasonic range of bats' flight-orientation apparatus; this seems to interfere with the bats' sonar. These and many other moths can hear the bats' "supersonic" signals, enabling them to evade a bat's attack.

LIFE CYCLE

Egg. Lepidopteran eggs range in shape from very flat disks (Lycaenidae and Eucleidae) to long, spindle-shaped ones (Pieridae). They range in color from whitish to greenish or orange. Most eggs are smooth or granulated, but in some the surface is rough and strongly sculptured. The shell (chorion) is tough and water-resistant. At one side or at the end is an opening called the micropyle, through which the sperm enter as the egg is laid.

Inside the egg, the embryo may develop into a larva in a few days, although the egg may lie dormant for many months of hibernation or estivation (dormancy during a dry season). As the larva develops, its dark colors show through the chorion.

The eggs are usually laid singly or a few at a time, but in some groups the female lays them in a mass, usually covering this with a cement. The hairs of the female's abdomen may be incorporated in the covering. In some groups, such as the silverspot fritillaries (*Speyeria*), the female scatters the eggs while flying, but usually they are laid on or near the food plant.

Larva. The larval stage may last only a few days or as long as two months. Many species spend months in the larval stage in hibernation.

Anatomy. The larva, or caterpillar, has a distinct head, a 3-segmented thorax, and a 10-segmented abdomen. The head bears a curved row of tiny simple eyes (ocelli, or stemmata), usually six in number, low on each side. The head also contains the basic set of chewing mouthparts usual in insects. From front to rear these are: a flaplike front lip, the labrum; a pair of strong, blunt mandibles, usually adapted for rasping plant tissues; a pair of first maxillae, each with a sensory palpus; and a posterior structure, the labium-hypopharynx, which bears a pair of palpi and the spinneret, a median, tubular structure through which liquid silk is extruded. Low on each side of the head is a short antenna. The palpi and antennae have sensory nerve endings by means of which the larva can taste. The ocelli serve for only very simple vision—little more than differentiating degrees of light and dark—with hardly any image formation.

Each of the three thoracic segments (prothorax, mesothorax, and metathorax) bears a pair of short, jointed legs. On each side of the prothorax is a spiracle, an opening into the tracheal respiratory system. Each of the first eight abdominal segments also has a pair of spiracles.

The 3d, 4th, 5th, 6th, and 10th segments of the abdomen each typically bear a pair of prolegs. Each proleg has at the end a patch of many tiny, stiff hooklets, or crochets, and a soft, expansible planta. With these the larva can grasp silk threads or walk on very smooth surfaces.

ALEXANDER B. KLOTS

THE YUCCA MOTH lives symbiotically with the yucca plant, which it pollinates while laying its eggs. When hatched, the larva will feed on the plant's fruit.

The relative size and arrangement of the crochets are very important in larval classification.

Each body segment bears a small number of primary and subprimary setae—short bristles arising from socketed bases. These are also very important in classification. Secondary setae may be sparse and wanting or may be very abundant, long, and hairlike, forming a dense vestiture. In many larvae the body bears protruding, wartlike verrucae and may also have spiny or hornlike projections from the head and body.

The number, shape, and arrangement of the prolegs distinguish lepidopteran caterpillars from similar larvae, such as those of sawflies. Caterpillars never have well-developed prolegs on the 1st, 2d, 7th, 8th, or 9th abdominal segments. They may have lost the first two or three pairs (as in Geometridae) or have the last pair reduced and useless as legs (as in many Notodontidae). Sawfly larvae may also be distinguished from caterpillars by the fact that they usually have only one ocellus on each side of the head.

Most caterpillars are elongate and more or less cylindrical. Some (for example, some slug caterpillars of the family Eucleidae) are very flat, while others (other Eucleidae) are very short, chunky, and boxlike. They are extremely diversified in vestiture, spines, verrucae, warts, and other projections, as well as in color and pattern. Such features are mostly adaptations for defense by aposematism, crypsis, or disruption. Borers and miners are quite plain in appearance, as are many of the night-feeding species and those that live in cases. Leaf miners are usually quite flattened, and often have nearly or entirely lost the legs, prolegs, and eyes.

Internally, larvae are relatively simple. The chief distinctive structures are a capacious stomach (midgut) and the very large silk glands. These are modified labial glands and often extend back far into the abdomen.

The lives of most caterpillars are simple and concentrated on their major function—to eat and grow, while escaping detection if possible. As they grow, they periodically molt the integument (skin), including the head capsule, and quickly harden the new, larger integument. There are normally 5 molts (ecdyses), but some caterpillars molt only twice, others many times more, especially under abnormal conditions.

Larval growth and molting, and also the metamorphosis of the larva to a pupa and of the pupa to an adult, are under the control of a complex interaction of endocrine secretions (hormones). These are formed chiefly in neurosecretory cells of the brain, a corpus allatum behind the brain, and a pair of prothoracic glands. Much of the experimental work on insect endocrinology was done on the silkworm, *Bombyx mori*, and the North American saturniid moths *Hyalophora cecropia* and *Antheraea polyphemus*.

Pupation and Cocoons. The fully grown larva stops eating and empties its digestive tract. Seeking a suitable place, it prepares for pupation. This may be underground, in loose trash, under loose bark, in its mine or burrow, or attached to plants in the open. In most moths the larva forms a cocoon about itself, but many pupate naked in the soil.

Cocoons differ greatly in different groups. Some are of silk alone, but most have some additional substances, such as the excretory secretions or hairs of the larva, chewed wood pulp, or particles of soil or trash. Many are flimsy affairs; others are firm, hard, weatherproof structures. Many have escape valves for the emergence of the adult. Some are spun inside rolled leaves, which may be fastened to twigs. Sometimes the larva pupates almost immediately; sometimes it hibernates as a larva and does not pupate until warm weather comes.

Pupa. The pupa is a resting stage during which the great change occurs—from the slow-moving, voraciously eating larva to the mobile, liquid-sipping, sexually active adult. Although many adult structures have been partly formed in the larva, others must be developed almost wholly in the pupa.

Most pupae are smooth and dull; but some are very shiny, and some are quite hairy. Moth pupae are usually brown and are rarely patterned. Butterfly pupae, often called chrysalids or chrysalides, are frequently brightly colored and boldly patterned, and have bizarre shapes and

THE YELLOW-NECKED CATERPILLAR defends itself by arching and squirting an acid from beneath its thorax.

ALEXANDER B. KLOTS

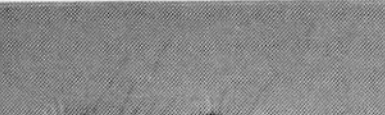

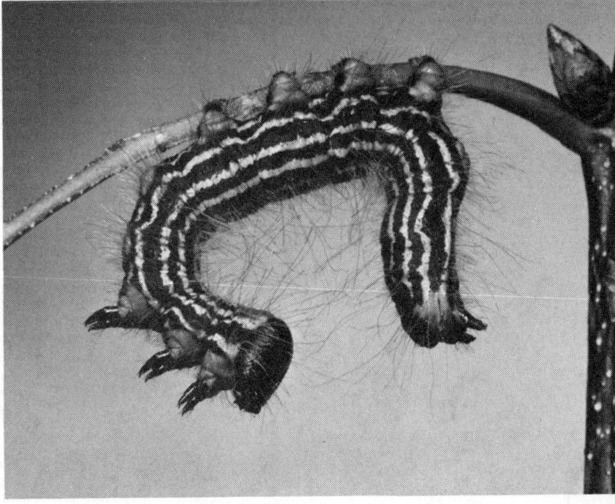

projecting horns and spines. Some are very cryptic, resembling rough bark or dead leaves; others are strikingly aposematic. The pupae of skippers (Hesperioidea) are in a crude cocoon, as are those of satyrs (Satyrinae), but most other butterfly pupae lack any covering.

Most pupae are obtect, having all the appendages fastened immobile to the body. Such pupae can move only a little, by wriggling abdominal segments. Primitive moths have more motile, exarate pupae, with movable appendages and segments; some have movable, functional mandibles used in cutting out of the cocoon or digging up through the soil.

The chief adult structures, such as eyes, fore wings, antennae, mouthparts, and legs are visible in pupae.

At the posterior end of most pupae is the cremaster, a pad or spike bearing hooks or hooklets. This holds a pupa in position inside the cocoon, or suspends a butterfly chrysalis (often head down) from a silk pad. Many chrysalids (for example Nymphalidae) are held by the cremaster alone, but many others (such as Pieridae, Papilionidae) also have a silk girdle about the body.

When the pupa hibernates, this stage may last for many months, although the adult may develop fully in 3 to 10 days. The adult colors develop very late in pupal life. When ready to emerge, the adult cracks the pupal integument by expanding its thorax, and pushes and pulls itself out. Making its way to the open, it crawls up on something and hangs with its wing pads down. It pumps blood into these to expand them, and then hangs until they and its other structures have stiffened, and it is ready to fly.

Adults. The adult structure may be described in terms of the head, thorax, abdomen, and wings.

Head. In most members of the order the chief structures are the paired antennae; one or two pairs of palpi (maxillary and labial); a pair of tiny simple eyes (ocelli); and the coiled, tubular proboscis beneath the head. In many moths the mouthparts are greatly reduced and functionless. In the very primitive Zeugloptera, mandibles are present and there is no proboscis. Other primitive moths (Eriocraniidae, Adelidae) have mouthparts intermediate between those of the Zeugloptera and the higher moths.

Thorax. The first segment, the prothorax, bears a pair of collarlike patagia, a pair of spiracles, and the front legs. The next segment, the mesothorax, bears the fore wings, with a pair of flaplike tegulae overlapping their bases, and the middle legs. The last segment, the metathorax, bears the hind wings and hind legs. In noctuoid moths it has a pair of auditory tympanic organs and in arctiid moths a pair of sound-producing tymbal organs.

Abdomen. This region has 10 segments, but the first and the last two are greatly modified. The first through the seventh segments have a pair of spiracles each. There are no appendages on the abdomen except those of the genitalic structures at the posterior end. These are highly modified for copulation and egg-laying. The structures of the genitalia in both sexes are extremely important in classification. Some families

EGG

LIFE CYCLE OF A BUTTERFLY

The butterfly shown is the clouded sulphur (*Colias philodice*), a common North American species.

PHOTOS BY ALEXANDER B. KLOTS

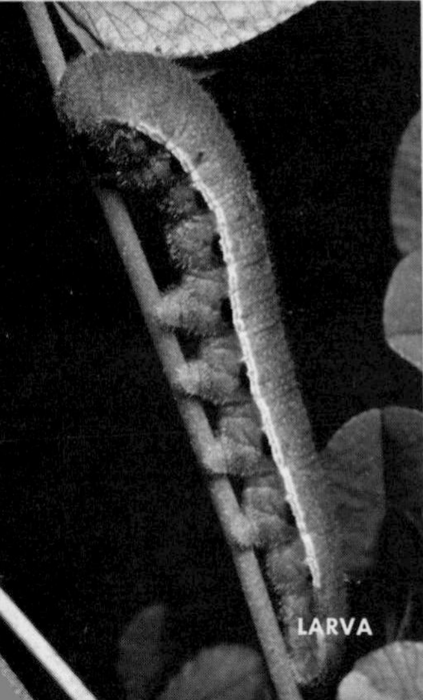

LARVA

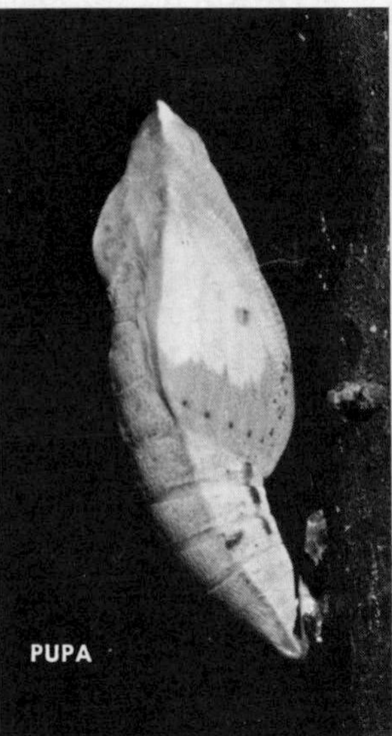

PUPA

ADULT (EMERGING)

of the higher moths (such as the Pyralididae and Geometridae) have paired tympanic organs on the first or second segments. Many moths and butterflies have abdominal sex tufts and hair pencils that are used in courtship.

Internally there is often a very large crop for the reception of liquids sucked in through the proboscis. Paired ovaries and testes are in the abdomen. They connect with accessory glands and the genitalia. The mature ovaries may be very large, distending the female abdomen enormously.

Wings. The wings originate as internal flaps in the larva. In the pupa these evert and lie externally. They are supported by strong, tubular veins, which may branch and rebranch. From front to rear the veins are: costa (C), subcosta (Sc), radius (R), media (M), cubitus (Cu), and three anals (1A, 2A, and 3A). The number and arrangement of the branches are extremely important in classification, both for distinguishing groups and for studying evolution and relationship. In primitive moths (Micropterigidae, Hepialidae) the fore and hind wings are alike in size and venation. In the more advanced groups the hind wings are reduced in relative size and venation, losing most of the branches of the radius. Most moths have a frenulum, but very primitive families have instead a lobe, the jugum, on the fore wing. Many advanced moths and the butterflies lack both.

Adult coloration depends on pigments and structures in the hairs and scales. Most of the colors are due to complex pigments. However, the blues, greens, and iridescent, metallic, and white effects are structural, caused chiefly by very thin, superimposed hair and scale layers that differ in refractive index.

Adult Senses and Behavior. The compound eyes are very sensitive for detecting motion, but not for resolving sharp images of distant objects. In butterflies, color distinction is good, but limited. Most moths see by ultraviolet light (about 3,700 angstroms), invisible to humans. The sense of smell in butterflies and moths is very acute, especially in males that have many small sensitive scent organs called sensilla, on the antennae. Taste, especially for sugars, is very sensitive; receptors are located on the front feet.

Courtships are often very specialized, differing greatly from species to species. In butterflies they are initiated by the sight of specific colors or activities. This is followed by the release of specific aromatic substances (pheromones) distributed by hair pencils and special scent scales. The exact time of day or night may be very important, as well as specific structures of male and female genitalia.

Adult butterflies often form large aggregations while sipping water at wet places. Some of the protected and aposematic species of *Heliconius* form sleeping assemblies night after night in the same spots. The monarch (*Danaus plexippus*) may do the same during migrations.

Migratory swarms are a feature of many butterflies and day-flying moths, especially in the tropics. Pierid butterflies are especially noted for great flocks of millions of individuals, which may fly out to sea and be lost. The painted lady (*Vanessa cardui*) is a famous cosmopolitan migrant. The monarch, however, is the only species that regularly makes a two-way migration, going southward in the fall and northward in the spring.

ALEXANDER B. KLOTS

BUTTERFLY WING SCALES, shown greatly enlarged in a micrograph, grow in overlapping shingled rows.

COLLECTING AND CARING FOR SPECIMENS

A net is essential for butterfly collecting. A 3- to 4-foot (0.9- to 1.2-meter) handle, a ring with a diameter of 12 to 16 inches (30 to 40 cm), and a long nylon mesh bag are best. For moth collecting, lights are used; "black light" fluorescent tubes are best. Butterflies will be seen visiting flowers; females will be seen fluttering about food plants.

Specimens must be treated very delicately. They are best killed in killing jars. Specimens may be "papered," dried, and mounted later. Place each specimen, with its wings above its back, in a separate glassine envelope or paper triangle. Thoroughly dried and stored in a tight box with naphthalene to deter pests that eat them, specimens keep almost indefinitely and can be relaxed and mounted later. Write the data—date, place of capture, environment—on each envelope.

Relax dry specimens in a tight container with wet blotting paper or clean sand. A saturated atmosphere is needed, but do not wet the specimens. Add naphthalene to prevent mold, which is a serious hazard in relaxing.

The relaxed specimen is pinned straight down through the center of the thorax, and then pinned in the groove of a spreading board. The wings are spread flat under paper strips on the sidepieces. They are pulled forward to proper position by delicate pins, which should perforate the wing only just behind a strong vein. The wings must then be kept from curling upward by wide paper or glass strips. Allow 10 days to 2 weeks for the specimen to dry.

Always label each specimen with at least the date and place of capture. Print this on a small label to go on the pin beneath the specimen. Other data, such as food plant, flowers visited, and environment, are very desirable.

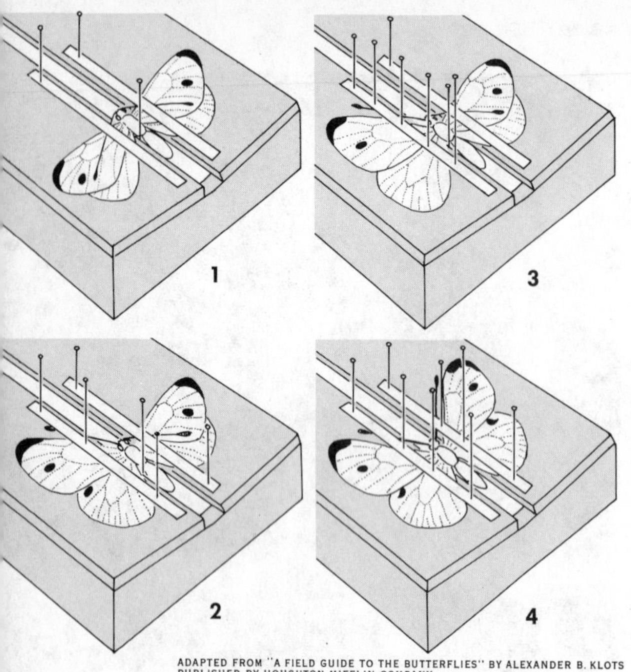

ADAPTED FROM "A FIELD GUIDE TO THE BUTTERFLIES" BY ALEXANDER B. KLOTS PUBLISHED BY HOUGHTON MIFFLIN COMPANY

PINNING A SPECIMEN FOR MOUNTING

Pins are used to extend the specimen's wings and antennae, which are then kept in place by thin paper strips.

Pinned specimens are kept in tightly closed boxes with a pinning bottom of cork or some firm but soft plastic material. The boxes must contain naphthalene or a half-and-half mixture of naphthalene and paradichlorobenzene (PDB) in a container (never loose), to protect the dried specimens against infestation by the small, but very destructive, museum-pest beetles (*Anthrenus*).

Identification is best done by using illustrated manuals. Technical classification, involving the study of many minute characters and often the use of a binocular microscope and dissection, is for advanced students.

For references with detailed instructions on collecting and caring for specimens, see the bibliography. Collecting, preserving, and storing equipment and supplies can be purchased from biological supply companies.

ALEXANDER B. KLOTS
The American Museum of Natural History

Bibliography

Ehrlich, Paul R., and Ehrlich, Anne H., *How to Know the Butterflies* (Dubuque, Iowa, 1961).
Holland, William J., *The Moth Book* (Garden City, N. Y., 1914), on collecting.
Holland, William J., *The Butterfly Book* (Garden City, N. Y., 1931), on collecting.
Klots, Alexander B., *A Field Guide to the Butterflies* (Boston 1951), on collecting.
Klots, Alexander B., *The World of Butterflies and Moths* (New York 1957).

For Specialized Study

Borror, Donald J., and De Long, Dwight M., *An Introduction to the Study of Insects* (New York 1964), on collecting.
Imms, Augustus D., *A General Textbook of Entomology* (London 1957).
Oman, P. W., and Cushman, A. D., *Collection and Preservation of Insects* (Washington 1948).
Peterson, Alvah, *A Manual of Entomological Techniques* (Columbus, Ohio, 1953).
Remington, C. L., in *Classification of Insects,* by **C. T. Brues, A. L. Melander, and F. M. Carpenter** (Cambridge, Mass., 1954).

BUTTERFLYFISH, any of numerous species of salt water fish that exist in most tropical waters around the world. Variously and usually beautifully colored, butterflyfish are popular as aquarium specimens but are little used for food.

Butterflyfish are distinguished from their close relatives, the angelfish, by the lack of a stout spine at the angle of the forepart of the gill cover. They may grow to a maximum length of 7 to 8 inches (18 to 20 cm), but most species are smaller. They have a deep, flat body and strong spines in the fins. Most butterflyfish live in shallow inshore water, but others live in deeper waters, and one was captured at a depth of 100 fathoms (600 feet, or 200 meters). Many feed on small crustaceans and the polyps of corals.

Butterflyfish constitute the subfamily Chaetodontinae. Along with the angelfishes (subfamily Pomacantinae), they make up the family Chaetodontidae. About 11 genera and numerous species of butterflyfish are recognized. The species are most numerous in the Indian and western and central Pacific ocean areas. Only 4 genera and 11 species are known in the tropical Americas and West Indies. The attractive foureye butterflyfish, *Chaetodon capistratus,* of the Gulf of Mexico and the Caribbean Sea is the best known.

FREDERICK H. BERRY
U. S. Bureau of Commercial Fisheries

BUTTERICK, but'ər-ik, **Ebenezer** (1826–1903), American tailor, who devised the first mass-produced patterns for garment making. Butterick was born May 29, 1826, in Sterling, Mass., where he and his wife Ellen later operated a shirtmaking shop. They marketed their first patterns in 1863. Their success with patterns for Garibaldi Suits, children's outfits based on the Italian patriot's uniform, interested the New York businessman J. W. Wilder and his associate A. W. Pollard. In 1867 the firm of E. Butterick & Co., in which Wilder had the controlling interest, was formed, and the factory was moved from Fitchburg, Mass., to Brooklyn, N. Y.

In 1869, on Wilder's initiative, the company began to publish a monthly fashion magazine (the *Metropolitan,* later called the *Delineator*) to promote sales, and by 1871, 6 million patterns a year were being sold in the United States and abroad. In 1881 the company was reorganized as the Butterick Publishing Company, with Wilder as president and Butterick as secretary until his retirement in 1894. Butterick died on March 31, 1903, in New York City.

LEONARD M. FANNING
Author of "Fathers of Industries"

BUTTERMILK. See BUTTER.

BUTTERNUT, a large North American tree that bears sweet, edible nuts. The butternut, also known as the *white walnut,* grows best in rich woodlands, where it may attain a height of 90 feet (27 meters). Its large leaves, which are composed of 7 to 17 leaflets, resemble those of its close relative the black walnut.

The male flowers of the butternut are borne in long, hanging, scaly catkins, while the female flowers grow in small clusters. The fruits are large and ellipsoid, with a thick green rind.

The butternut, *Juglans cinerea,* belongs to the walnut family. The black walnut is *J. nigra.*

S. C. BAUSOR
California State College, California, Pa.

BUTTON, Dick (1929–), American figure skater, who, while a student at Harvard in 1949, held five major titles (Olympic, world, North American, United States, and European)—an unprecedented feat.

Richard Totten Button was born in Englewood, N. J., on July 18, 1929, and began his skating career at the age of 12. He won the U. S. junior championship when he was 15 and the U. S. senior competition at 16, the youngest man ever to hold the title. During his career he held seven consecutive U. S. titles (1946–1952), five world championships (1948–1952), three North American (biennial) crowns (1947, 1949, 1951), and two Olympic games titles (1948, 1952). Among the new feats he introduced in competition was the jump with three midair revolutions.

In 1949, Button received the Sullivan trophy, the Amateur Athletic Union's award for the nation's outstanding amateur athlete; he turned professional in 1952. After graduating from Harvard College (1952) and Harvard Law School, he appeared in and produced ice shows and plays.

HAROLD PETERSON, *"Sports Illustrated"*

WIDE WORLD

DICK BUTTON, twice Olympic figure skating champion.

BUTTON, Sir Thomas (died 1634), English navigator, who was the first to explore the western shore of Hudson Bay, Canada. His family home was in Glamorgan, Wales. He joined the navy about 1589, and in 1612 he commanded an expedition of two ships to search the vicinity of Hudson Bay for a sea passage to the Orient. Button explored the west side of the bay and passed the winter at the mouth of the Nelson River, which he named for the master of one of his ships. Convinced after further exploration that no passage existed to the west, he returned to England in 1613. He was made admiral of the king's ships on the coast of Ireland, and in 1616 he was knighted.

Button Bay, in Hudson Bay, near the mouth of the Churchill River, in Manitoba, was named in his honor.

BUTTON. Buttons are made in an infinite number of designs, some prized highly by wearers, collectors, and museums for their beauty and tradition. They reflect the costumes of many different ages and peoples.

A button may be used merely as an apparel ornament, or it may be attached to a garment to fasten it by passing through a loop or buttonhole. Although slide fasteners have gained acceptance for use as closures on some apparel, the button remains preeminent. The United States annually produces about 12.5 billion buttons.

History of Buttons. Buttonlike discs and knobs were used as ornaments long before they were used as effective fasteners. As long ago at 2500 B. C., Egyptians wore button badges suspended about the neck. Later, Greeks and Romans used ties, pins, and buckles as fasteners, and they used buttons as badges or decoration. The oldest known button ever found was a round disc with holes, which dated back to the early Iron Age; it was found about 1865 in a Danish peat bog.

In Europe buttons were commonly used as ornaments in the 11th century. By the 13th century they were discovered to have practical use in two shapes—a small ball button and a flat, round one. By the 16th century, buttons were widely accepted, and royalty wore the most handsome varieties. King Francis I of France used 13,600 golden buttons on one court costume. The lavish use of gems for buttons encouraged the development of many imitations, and the common people were then able to wear buttons. By the 18th century, the demand for buttons was so great that the button industry became well established in Europe. Originally most buttons were handmade or homemade by skilled artisans, but machines began to take over button-making during the Industrial Revolution.

Although brass buttons had been produced in Philadelphia as early as 1750, the American button industry made no substantial progress until the War of 1812, when it grew after imports from Europe were cut off. A small factory in Waterbury, Conn., then made buttons for the Army and Navy. At the same time, button discs and molds covered with fabric were made in Easthampton, Mass. In 1864 the first factory for manufacturing vegetable ivory buttons was set up in Leeds, Mass. Around 1880 a German immigrant in Muscatine, Iowa, succeeded in making pearl buttons from shells of freshwater mussels. During World War II, chemically impregnated buttons designed to glow during blackouts were introduced as suitable for daytime and blackout wear. After World War II the American button industry captured the market once supplied by Europe and was able to export buttons in quantities. The business tide turned in the late 1950's, however, as U. S. button imports rose and exceeded U. S. button exports. Buttons bearing pictures or slogans have been popular in the United States in the 20th century, particularly in political campaigns. In the 1960's there was a boom in "cause" buttons advocating social action and in novelty buttons bearing absurd legends.

Materials and Manufacturing. Buttons are produced in two classes: (1) those made with a shank that may consist of a loop of metal or other hard substance or a tuft of fabric, and (2) those pierced with holes for threading.

ORNAMENTAL BUTTONS

Buttons in mother-of-pearl that has been carved to render a figure or design in relatively shallow relief.

PHOTOGRAPHS BY A. H. ALBERT

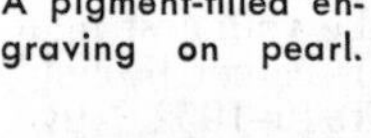

A pigment-filled engraving on pearl.

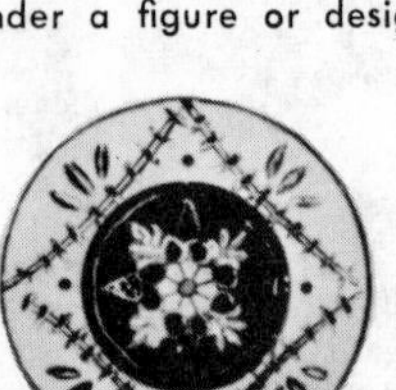

Two pearl buttons decorated with enamel work. The design of the button on the right has been engraved.

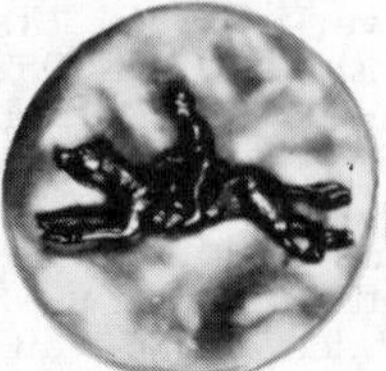

Small metal figures have been affixed to a mother-of-pearl base to make decorative buttons in bold relief.

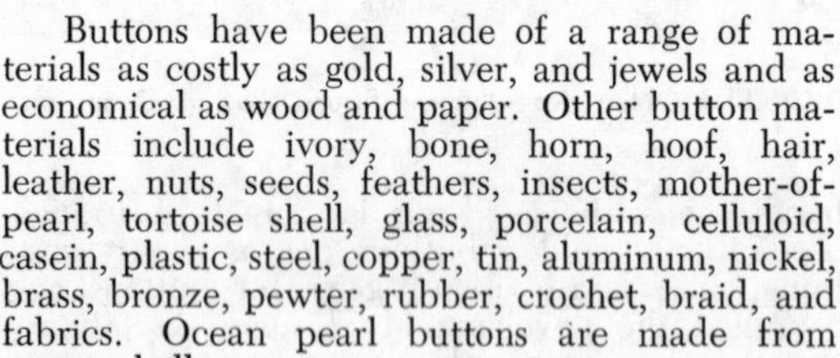

Buttons have been made of a range of materials as costly as gold, silver, and jewels and as economical as wood and paper. Other button materials include ivory, bone, horn, hoof, hair, leather, nuts, seeds, feathers, insects, mother-of-pearl, tortoise shell, glass, porcelain, celluloid, casein, plastic, steel, copper, tin, aluminum, nickel, brass, bronze, pewter, rubber, crochet, braid, and fabrics. Ocean pearl buttons are made from oyster shells.

Buttons made of plastic encompass every color, size, and shape. They imitate shell, ivory, amber, and other expensive materials. Plastic buttons may be cast in sheet form and later shaped mechanically, or they may be molded to final form under heat and pressure. Both processes are highly automated, and they yield products that are uniform in quality and low in cost. Synthetic resins for plastic buttons include polyester, urea, melamine-urea, phenolic, and acrylic. Since 1959, imitation pearl buttons made of polyester have outsold natural pearl by about 30%.

Metal buttons used on high-fashion apparel are desirable also for uniforms and heavy-duty work apparel. Wood, bone, vegetable ivory, leather, and glass continue to be used in limited quantities. In a typical year about 60% to 70% of U. S. button production is plastic, 8% to 10% metal, 5% to 8% pearl, and 10% to 12% other.

Button-producing centers of the United States are situated in Maine, Connecticut, New York, New Jersey, Pennsylvania, and Iowa. The United States exports buttons primarily to Canada, Britain, France, Switzerland, Sweden, West Germany, the Netherlands, and Australia.

Italy, France, and Japan lead in sales of buttons to the United States. Other principal button producers are the Netherlands, Britain, West Germany, Czechoslovakia, and Hong Kong.

Button Collecting. Button collecting has become an enormously popular collecting hobby in the United States. Fifty thousand collectors are served by dealers and museums. They have a nonprofit association, the National Button Society, organized in 1938 to classify the types of buttons and now devoted to promoting the hobby.

The first formal collectors of buttons were girls who in the latter half of the 19th century assembled charm strings. A U. S. army captain, Luis Emilio, started assembling military buttons in 1887 and accumulated a comprehensive collection now at the Essex Institute, Salem, Mass.

Buttons may be classified according to the type of material used, the kind of story depicted on them (such as Bible stories, mythology, children's stories, fables), or by categories such as military and political.

VERNA MOULTON, *University of Connecticut*

Further Reading: Albert, Lillian Smith, and Kent, Kathryn, *The Complete Button Book* (Garden City, N. Y., 1949); Chamberlin, Erwina Couse, and Miner, Minerva, *Button Heritage* (Sherburne, N. Y., 1967); Roberts, Catherine, *Who's Got the Button?* (New York 1962).

Buttonbush (*Cephalanthus occidentalis*)

JOHN J. SMITH

BUTTONBUSH is the common name of a small group of Asiatic and North American shrubs and trees of the madder family. The only cultivated species is the common buttonbush, which usually grows from 3 to 6 feet (1 to 2 meters) tall but occasionally develops as a tree, reaching a height of 20 feet (6 meters) or more. Its leaves are oval or lance-shaped, and its flowers are borne in small, spherical clusters.

Buttonbushes constitute the genus *Cephalanthus*. The common buttonbush is *C. occidentalis.*

S. C. BAUSOR
California State College (California, Pa.)

BUTTONWOOD. See PLANE TREE.

BUTTRESS, bu'trəs, is an architectural element designed to withstand a lateral force, or, used as a verb, the process of withstanding such a force. Buttresses developed simultaneously with arches, vaults, and domes—the principal structural elements that require buttressing. Because arches, vaults, and domes generate a lateral force as well as a downward force, they must be buttressed from the side as well as supported from underneath.

There are two basic kinds of buttressing. One is by means of two or more arches placed side by side in line, as in an arcade or a Roman aqueduct, in which the thrust of each arch equals and counteracts the force from adjacent arches. The other basic kind of buttressing is by means of masses of heavy masonry set against the side of the wall supporting an arch or vault, as in the Arch of Titus, Rome, where the thick walls provide both vertical support and buttressing.

Roman Buttresses. The Romans were the first to make extensive use of the principles of arch and vault. They developed three primary vault forms—the semicylindrical, the hemispherical, and the cross. The semicylindrical, or barrel, vault thrusts outward to either side along the length of the vault, which rests on walls heavy enough to afford both vertical support and continuous buttressing. An example is the so-called Temple of Diana, Nîmes, France. The hemispherical dome also needs continuous buttressing but in a circle, as in the dome of the Pantheon in Rome, which is half-embedded in the 20-foot thick walls that serve as buttressing around its perimeter. The cross, or groined, vault, composed of 2 intersecting barrel vaults, needs buttressing only at its four corners. For example, the central aisle, or nave, of the Basilica of Constantine, Rome, had groined vaults buttressed at the corners by the walls of the smaller barrel vaults over the side aisles. (See also VAULT.)

Romanesque and Gothic Buttresses. Medieval architecture relied heavily on vaults, making buttressing a constant problem. In most Romanesque buildings of the 11th and 12th centuries, the massive walls were strong enough to serve as buttresses. Shallow projecting masses of masonry called pilaster strips were commonly added to give more strength to the wall where needed, such as at points corresponding to each of the main piers holding up the vault of the nave of

GEORGINA MASSON, FROM "ROME REVEALED" BY AUBREY MENEN. THAMES AND HUDSON, LONDON

BUTTRESSES of masonry on both sides of arches or vaults provide support, as in the Arch of Titus, Rome.

the church. Sant'Ambrogio, Milan, has such buttresses alternated with lighter ones corresponding to the piers of the side aisles, which have smaller vaults and thus generate less thrust.

When the full Gothic style emerged in the late 12th and 13th centuries, the great height of buildings and their thin, large-windowed walls made the buttressing problem acute. The pilaster strip gave way to the tower, or pier, buttress, a segment of wall constructed at right angles to the length of the building and projecting from it as much as 8 or 10 feet. A tower buttress, which is thicker at the bottom than at the top, receives the lateral thrust near its top and by its sheer mass converts that thrust into a nearly vertical force.

For churches with a single aisle, such as Ste. Chapelle, Paris, tower buttresses were set directly against the walls supporting the vault. In the usual Gothic churches with three aisles, it was impossible to place tower buttresses against the clerestory walls that upheld the high vault of the nave. To solve this problem,

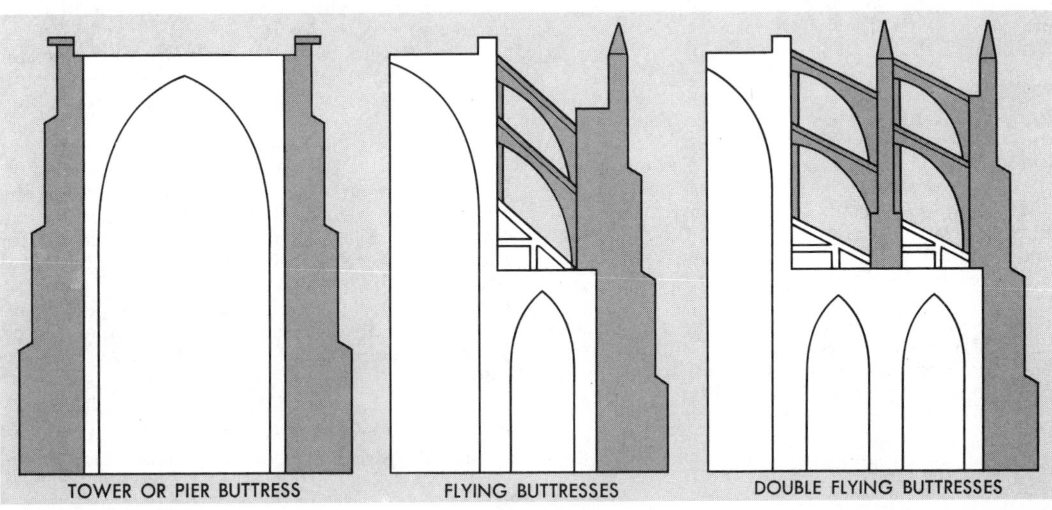

Gothic builders invented the flying buttress, a stone prop that transmits the thrust of the nave vault outward and downward over the roof of the side aisles to the tower buttress against the outside walls. The prop itself consists of a half-arch topped by a row of stones laid so that the joints run at right angles to the direction of the thrust.

In many cases, as at Amiens Cathedral, two flying buttresses, one above the other, rise from each tower buttress to the clerestory wall of the nave. The purpose of the higher flying buttress is to carry the pressure that the roof might receive in high winds out to the tower buttress. However, the upper flying buttress reaches the clerestory wall at a point too high to buttress the main vault.

To support the comparatively rare 5-aisled structure, such as the choir of Reims Cathedral, the flying buttress system had to be doubled. Two flying buttresses rise from the upper part of each tower buttress to a slender buttress on the roof above the piers dividing the inner and outer side aisles; two more flying buttresses ascend from this intermediate buttress to the clerestory wall. In the apse of the Cathedral of Notre Dame, Paris, the intermediate buttress is omitted, and the flying buttress makes a single leap of inordinate length across both side aisles.

The complex buttress system of French Gothic architecture, made necessary in part by the great height of the cathedrals, was accepted in other countries where French influence was strong. In England, however, most cathedrals were substantially lower than in France and more frequently retained the massive walls of the earlier Romanesque style. For these reasons, English Gothic churches usually have tower buttresses rather than flying buttresses.

Buttresses play a less prominent part in the architectural styles that followed the Gothic. New building materials, such as steel and concrete, made possible internal reinforcing, and buttresses in contemporary buildings often exist as decorative rather than structural members.

EVERARD M. UPJOHN, *Columbia University*

BUTUAN, bo͞o-to͞o'än, a municipality in the Philippines, is the capital of Agusan province in the northeast part of Mindanao island. Situated on the Agusan River, the city is a port and trading center for abaca and copra. It was at Butuan in 1521 that Magellan first proclaimed Spanish sovereignty over the Philippines. Population: (1960) 82,485.

BUTUNG, bo͞o'to͝ong, one of the islands of the Republic of Indonesia, in Southeast Asia, lies off the southeastern coast of the major Indonesian island of Sulawesi (Celebes). The name is also spelled *Buton.* The island is separated on the west from the island of Muna by the narrow Butung Strait. Butung is 100 miles (160 km) long and from 10 to 30 miles (16–48 km) wide, the total area being about 2,000 square miles (5,180 sq km).

The island is mountainous, rising to a peak of 2,379 feet (725 meters). Most of Butung is covered by dense forest consisting in large part of teak, which is used for boat building. Coconuts, rice, and corn are cultivated.

The chief town is Baubau. Most of the inhabitants are Bugis (q.v.). Population: (1961) 253,262.

BUXAR, buk'sər, is a town in India, in Shahabad district in the state of Bihar. The name is also spelled *Baxar.* The town is situated on the south bank of the Ganges River, 77 miles (124 km) west of Patna. Rice, wheat, oilseeds, barley, and sugarcane are raised in the area. At Buxar, on Oct. 23, 1764, British forces under Maj. Hector Munro won a decisive victory over Indian forces under Mir Kasim and the nawab of Oudh, thus confirming the British possession of Bengal and Bihar. Population: (1961) 23,068.

BUXTEHUDE, bo͝oks-tə-ho͞o'də, **Dietrich** (c. 1637–1707), Danish-born organist and composer of the North German school. Dietrich (Danish, Diderik) Buxtehude was probably born in Helsingør. He studied organ with his father and later perhaps with Johann Theile, a pupil of Heinrich Schütz. He became organist at St. Mary's, Hälsingborg, Denmark (now in Sweden), in 1657; at St. Mary's in Helsingør in 1660; and at the Marienkirche in Lübeck (Germany) in 1668. He held this last post, with that of *Director Musices* (musical director), until his death, in Lübeck, on May 9, 1707. As director Buxtehude introduced the famous annual *Abendmusiken,* Advent concerts that were attended by such composers as Bach and Handel.

Works. Of Buxtehude's more than 250 known works, almost 100 are for organ; these include preludes, fugues, toccatas, chaconnes, canzoni, a passacaglia, and chorale preludes, fantasies, and variations. The vocal works, numbering more than 120, include more than 100 solo and choral cantatas, as well as hymns, an oratorio, a *Missa Brevis,* a *Magnificat,* and large-scale festive works (notably the *Benedicam Dominum* for two vocal and three instrumental choirs). Buxtehude's chamber music includes 19 suites and 14 sonatas for strings and harpsichord continuo.

Style. Buxtehude's works are usually multisectional. They employ contrasts of timbre, of meter, of instruments and voices, and of contrapuntal, chordal, and improvisational textures, but they are often integrated by repetitions or transformations of themes. His musical lines conform to his texts, which are in both Latin and German, but their rhythms are more regular than those characteristic of early baroque style.

Buxtehude's music is not primarily melodic. Its strength lies in dynamic harmonies generated from a highly active bass line, within a major-minor tonal system reinforced by modulation. His organ style is notable for virtuoso pedal lines, for exploitation of the organ's sonority, and for the development of an abstract (absolute) instrumental style, particularly in the chaconnes and the passacaglia.

Buxtehude's Influence. Buxtehude's abstract organ works were models for Bach, who reworked Buxtehude's discontinuous forms into the acme of formal and thematic integration. From Buxtehude, Bach also absorbed techniques for combining voices and instruments in cantatas and oratories. Finally, Buxtehude's strongly tonal organization and use of modulations helped create the structural basis for the monumental sacred works of the late baroque period that followed him.

ADRIENNE FRIED, *Choral Director*
Dalcroze School of Music, New York City

Further Reading: Hutchins, Farley K., *Dietrich Buxtehude: The Man, His Music, His Era* (Paterson, N. J., 1955).

BUXTON, Sir Thomas Fowell (1786–1845), English philanthropist, prison reformer, and antislavery agitator. He was born at Earl's Colne, Essex, on April 1, 1786. After compiling a distinguished academic record at Trinity College, Dublin, Buxton began his career as a philanthropist by helping to relieve the sufferings of unemployed weavers in the Spitalfields district of London. Turning his attention to prison conditions, he published *An Inquiry Whether Crime and Misery Are Produced or Prevented by Our Present System of Prison Discipline* (1818). The book led to the formation of the Prison Discipline Society, which advocated reform of prison methods.

In 1818, Buxton was elected to Parliament from Weymouth, which he represented until 1837. In Parliament he fought to make the criminal law more humane and became involved in the major project of his life—the fight against slavery in the British Empire. An 1823 proposal by Buxton that slavery be eliminated gradually was thwarted by opposition of the West Indies slave owners. However, in the following year Buxton acceded to William Wilberforce's request and succeeded Wilberforce as chief of the antislavery movement in the House of Commons. Buxton's research on the subject, combined with the efforts of Thomas Clarkson and Henry Brougham, led to success. In 1834 Parliament abolished slavery in the British Empire.

Buxton's efforts for Negroes did not cease at this point. He was successful in improving the living conditions of Jamaican Negroes, and in 1839 published *The African Slave Trade and Its Remedy*. This book urged the British government to strengthen its efforts to end slavery in Africa and also recommended the commercial development of the Niger River area. The failure of the latter scheme was a blow to Buxton, and he retired to his estate. Buxton, who was a deeply religious member of the Evangelical branch of the Church of England, died near Aylsham, Norfolk, on Feb. 19, 1845.

JOHN W. OSBORNE, *Rutgers University*

BUYS BALLOT, bois bä-lot′, **Christoph Hendrik Didericus** (1817–1890), Dutch meteorologist, who was one of the originators of modern weather forecasting. He helped initiate a new system of collecting materials for forecasts, including daily weather reports and simultaneous observations by land and sea. His own observations resulted in the formulation of a general law of winds around a pressure center, known as *Buys Ballot's law*. He invented a system of weather signals and was largely instrumental in bringing about international uniformity in meteorological observations.

Buys Ballot was born in Kloetinge, Zeeland, the Netherlands, on Oct. 10, 1817. He studied at the University of Utrecht, where he became professor of mathematics in 1847 and professor of experimental physics in 1870. In 1854 he became director of the Royal Meteorological Institute at Utrecht. He died there on Feb. 3, 1890.

BUZZARD, the British name for the European broadwinged hawks (*Buteo*). The term "buzzard," however, is commonly and incorrectly applied to two North American vultures: the turkey vulture found from southern Canada to southern South America and the black vulture found from the southern United States to Argentina.

ARTHUR AMBLER, FROM NATIONAL AUDUBON SOCIETY

Black "buzzard"

The "turkey buzzard" is 26 to 32 inches (66–81 cm) long and has a wingspread of 6 feet (1.8 meters); the "black buzzard" is 23 to 27 inches (59–69 cm) long and has a wingspread of less than 5 feet (1.5 meters). Both species have black plumage on their bodies, but their heads are featherless. The turkey buzzard's head is red, while the black buzzard's is black.

Both "buzzards" feed on carrion. The turkey buzzard depends on its sense of smell to find food, while the black buzzard depends on its vision. Both species nest on the ground, in hollow trees, on ledges, or in caves. Their eggs are white, blotched with brown.

The turkey vulture (*Cathartes aura*) and the black vulture (*Coragyps atratus*) belong to the family Cathartidae in the order Falconiformes.

KENNETH E. STAGER
Los Angeles County Museum of Natural History

BUZZARDS BAY is an inlet of the Atlantic Ocean in southeastern Massachusetts. It is 30 miles (48 km) long and 5 to 10 miles (8 to 16 km) wide. On the south, the Elizabeth Islands separate the bay from Vineyard Sound. At the northeast end of the bay is the western end of the Cape Cod Canal, which carries considerable coastwise shipping. The principal harbor on the bay is New Bedford.

BYAM SHAW, bī′əm shô, **Glen** (1904–) British actor and stage director. He was born in London on Dec. 13, 1904. He made his acting debut at the Torquay Pavilion Theatre in 1923 and was a member of J. B. Fagan's Oxford Repertory Theatre Group in 1926 and 1927. In 1929 he married Angela Baddeley, an actress.

Byam Shaw directed plays, operas, and ballets. From 1947 he served as director of the Old Vic Theatre Centre and Old Vic School. He was codirector of the Shakespeare Memorial Theatre, Stratford, England, from 1953 to 1955, and director from 1955 to 1959. He became director of productions of the Sadler's Wells Opera House, London, in 1962, and an administrative director of Sadler's Wells in 1966. He was made commander of the Order of the British Empire in 1954.

BYBLOS, bib'ləs, an ancient town on the coast of Lebanon, 25 miles (40 km) north of Beirut, was an important Phoenician harbor city and commercial center. Its modern name is Jubayl, and in Biblical times it was called Gebal. The settlement goes back at least to 5000 B.C., and some centuries after that it was closely linked with Egypt, serving as the main harbor exporting to Egypt the timber of the hinterland. Among the inhabitants were expert woodworkers and shipbuilders as well as seafarers.

Byblos came under strong Egyptian cultural and religious influence. In its turn, Byblos influenced Egypt, and some of its gods were worshiped there, notably its chief goddess, Baalat ("the lady"), a form of Astarte, whose temple dates from about 3000 B.C. The golden age of the city ended in violent destruction about 2150 B.C. Byblos was later rebuilt and ruled by native princes who were vassals of Egypt.

After the collapse of the major Middle Eastern powers soon after 1200 B.C., Byblos was part of Phoenicia, of which the dominant cities were Tyre and Sidon to the south. In the late 11th century its king was Ahiram, whose sarcophagus, rediscovered in 1922, bears the earliest datable Phoenician inscription.

Later rulers of Byblos came under Assyrian (734–539 B.C.) and then Persian (539–332 B.C.) domination. Captured by Alexander the Great in 332 B.C., the city was soon Hellenized, and it flourished through the Hellenistic and Roman periods – mainly because of its famous cult of Adonis. It was almost abandoned after the Arab conquest in 637 A.D.

The Crusaders captured the site in 1104 and built a castle (later rebuilt in its surviving form). With one short break the site, in this period called Gibelet, was held by Genoese and Franks until the late 13th century.

Papyrus was a principal export from Byblos, and the Greeks used the word *byblos* for "papyrus" and then for "book"; the English word "Bible" derives from this root.

D. J. BLACKMAN
Bristol University, England

BYDGOSZCZ, bid'gôshch, is an industrial city in north central Poland, 143 miles (230 km) northwest of Warsaw. The city, which is the capital of Bydgoszcz province, is located on the small Brda River, a tributary of the Vistula. The Bydgoszcz Canal links the city with the Noteć and Odra (German, Oder) rivers. The city is especially noted industrially for its machine building, chemical, and wood-products industries.

Bydgoszcz grew up during the Middle Ages on the site of a prehistoric fort. It became one of the fortified cities protecting Poland from the German Knights. During the 15th and 16th centuries it developed into an important commercial city, a role which it has since continued to play. It passed to Prussia in 1772, during the partitions of Poland, and was known in German as Bromberg. It returned to Polish rule in 1918.

Bydgoszcz was heavily damaged during World War II, but was rebuilt. It retains very little evidence of its historic past. Population: (1965 est.) 255,000.

NORMAN J. G. POUNDS
Indiana University

BYELORUSSIAN SOVIET SOCIALIST REPUBLIC. See BELORUSSIAN SOVIET SOCIALIST REPUBLIC.

BYELY, byā'lē, **Andrei** (1880–1934), Russian writer. His name, a pseudonym, is also spelled *Bely*. He was born Boris Nikolayevich Bugaev in Moscow on Oct. 14, 1880. By the time he graduated from the University of Moscow, he was already known in Russian literary circles.

Byely became famous for the unique literary innovations in his first major work, *Symphonies* (1902), an experimental symbolist novel. *The Silver Dove* (1910), a novel showing deep psychological insight, linked realism and symbolism, and *Petersburg* (1913–1916) blended fantasy and realism. His important works after the revolution were the novel *Kotik Letayev* (1918), in which he used a Joycean style, and three volumes of memoirs (1929–1933).

Byely also wrote poetry, including the volumes *Gold in Azure* (1903), *Ashes* (1908), and *The First Meeting* (1921). Much of his verse deals with contemporary Russian social and political issues. To achieve new poetic effects, he experimented with many metrical and linguistic devices. He died in Moscow on Jan. 7, 1934.

WAAGENAAR, FROM PIX

AT BYBLOS, in Lebanon, are the ruins of a Crusader's castle, or citadel, built in the 12th century.

BYERS, bī'ərz, **Samuel H.** (1838–1933), American soldier, diplomat, and author. He was born in Pulaski, Pa., on July 23, 1838. He served in the Union Army during the Civil War and was captured at the Battle of Chattanooga and imprisoned at Columbia, S. C. There he wrote the words to the song *Sherman's March to the Sea,* his most famous work. Byers escaped from prison and was on Sherman's staff in the Carolinas.

After the war Byers served about 20 years in the U. S. foreign service, including terms as consul general in Rome and Switzerland. He died in Los Angeles, Calif., on May 24, 1933.

Byers described his diplomatic career in *Twenty Years in Europe* (1896). His books of poetry include *Complete Poems* (1914), *The Pony Express, and Other Poems* (1925), and *In Arcady* (1929).

BYERS, bī'ərz, **William Newton** (1831–1903), American pioneer and newspaperman. He was born in Madison county, Ohio, on Feb. 22, 1831. He became a government surveyor in Iowa, Oregon, Washington, and Nebraska and was elected to Nebraska's first legislature. He then moved on to the Colorado goldfields, hauling a handpress, type, and other printing equipment from Omaha to Denver. In Denver he published and edited (1859–1878) the first Colorado newspaper, the *Rocky Mountain News,* which cost 25 cents a copy because national and international news came by messenger from the nearest post office, at Fort Laramie, Wyo., 220 miles (355 km) away. Byers was also state postmaster of Colorado (1864–1866 and 1879–1883); he died in Denver. The mineral byerite is named for him.

BYLAW, a subordinate rule adopted by an organization or legal body for its own government. The term is derived from the word *byr,* which the Danes applied to townships in England after their invasion in the 8th century. When laws were enacted for these townships, they were called bylaws. In present usage, in the area of municipal government, a bylaw is an ordinance passed by a local legislative body, as differentiated from the general law of the state or country.

Most frequently, the term "bylaws" refers to the rules enacted by a corporation for its internal management. Common examples are the bylaws regulating the conduct of meetings and elections, the number and qualification of officers, and the powers and duties of directors. As a rule, bylaws must be adopted by the shareholders or the board of directors. Once enacted, they are as binding upon the corporation as any public law of the state.

In general, officers, directors, and members of a corporation are presumed to know the bylaws and cannot avoid liability for acts done in violation of them by pleading ignorance. In addition, bylaws are ordinarily binding upon the shareholders, regardless of whether they expressly consent to them. In interpreting corporate bylaws, the primary aim is to give effect to the intention of the parties who adopted them.

Despite their usefulness, bylaws are not essential to the existence or operation of a corporation. The charter creating the corporation may adequately provide for its government, thus removing the need for bylaws.

Peter D. Weinstein
Member of the New York Bar

BYLERT, bī-lərt, **Jan van** (1603–1671), Dutch painter of the Utrecht school. He was born in Utrecht and studied with the mannerist painter Abraham Bloemaert. Bylert traveled to France and to Rome, where he was a pupil of the Utrecht painter Gerhard van Honthorst. Returning to Utrecht about 1625, Bylert became head of the painters' guild there in 1632 and about the same time painted a mural for the Hjobs Hospital.

Bylert's earlier works, like those of other members of the Utrecht school, show the influence of Caravaggio in their religious subject matter, realism, and use of chiaroscuro. Later works after 1630 use lighter, softer colors and are prettier in style; their subjects include mythological and pastoral scenes. Bylert died in Utrecht on Nov. 13, 1671.

BYNG, bing, **George** (1663–1733), English admiral, who won notable victories in the early 18th century. He was born at Wrotham, Kent, on Jan. 27, 1663, and joined the navy at 15. In 1688, as a lieutenant, he persuaded many naval officers to support Prince William of Orange, who was challenging James II for the throne of England. When the prince became King William III, Byng was made a captain. He was promoted steadily, becoming admiral of the fleet in 1718.

Byng turned back a French fleet supporting the landing of James Francis Edward Stuart, the Pretender, in Scotland in 1715 and destroyed a Spanish fleet attempting an invasion of Sicily in 1718. He was named treasurer of the navy in 1720 and first lord of the admiralty in 1727. Byng was knighted in 1704 for his gallantry in the Battle of Malaga and was created Viscount Torrington in 1721. After 1705 he served in Parliament. He died on Jan 17, 1733.

BYNG, bing, **John** (1704–1757), English admiral, who was executed for alleged cowardice. He was born at Southill, Bedfordshire, a son of Viscount Torrington. He served honorably against the Scots and in the Mediterranean. With the threat of renewed war with France, Byng, as vice admiral, was given command of an inadequate fleet to relieve the British garrison on Minorca in the Balearic Islands. He reached the island on May 19, 1756. During an indecisive action with the blockading French Toulon squadron, Byng demonstrated neither tactical skill nor special timidity; he was just incapable of positive action and had to call a council of war even to decide on withdrawal to Gibraltar. The French admiral, who had been equally timorous, was quick with his own vainglorious report of the action, while Byng's dispatch was slow, wordy, and self-justifying.

Byng was brought home as a prisoner and, in the view of some, as a political scapegoat. He was tried by court-martial and sentenced to death. Some members of the court-martial and the admiral's friends pleaded for clemency. All atttempts failed. On March 14, 1757, in a crowded ceremony of great pomp and gravity, Byng knelt upon a silk cushion on the quarterdeck of the *Monarch* at Portsmouth and was shot to death by six marines. The inscription on his monument begins, "To the Perpetual Disgrace of Public Justice . . . ." Voltaire's ironic and timeless comment was that the purpose of the execution was ". . . to encourage the others."

Richard A. Hough
Author of "Admirals in Collision"

THE GRANGER COLLECTION

Byng of Vimy

BYNG OF VIMY, bing, vē′mē, **1st Viscount** (1862–1935), British field marshal and governor-general of Canada. He was born Julian Hedworth George Byng at Wrotham Park, England, on Sept. 11, 1862. In France in World War I he commanded the Canadian Corps that captured Vimy Ridge in April 1917. He also led the British Third Army that scored a striking initial success at Cambrai in November 1917 in the first use of massed tanks and that helped to smash the Hindenburg Line at Cambrai in September 1918.

Byng was governor-general of Canada from June 1921 to September 1926. His popular and successful administration was marred near its close by a controversy that arose from a constitutional crisis.

In the spring of 1926, William Lyon Mackenzie King, the Liberal prime minister, who had been returned to office as head of a minority government after the general election of 1925, decided to appeal to the country in the hope of winning majority support. Byng, however refused King's request for a dissolution of Parliament, in the sincere conviction that Arthur Meighen, the leader of the Conservative opposition, could form a viable government and obviate the need for an election. Byng's refusal compelled King to resign and Meighen became prime minister. Unable to rally a majority in the House of Commons, he was obliged to ask Byng to dissolve Parliament. Byng granted to Meighen the dissolution that he had refused to King, arousing a storm of controversy. A general election returned King as prime minister.

Byng was chief commissioner of the metropolitan police of London, England, from 1928 to 1931. He instituted many reforms. Among these, he retired a number of senior officers to make room for younger men. He inaugurated a network of police telephone call boxes and enlarged the fleet of police cars. Although the Labour party had opposed his appointment, his direction of the police proved so efficient that the Labour government that took office in 1929 would not let him resign. Ill health, however, finally compelled his retirement.

Byng was created a viscount in 1925 and was gazetted a field marshal in 1932. He died at Thorpe-le-Soken, Essex, England, on June 6, 1935.

Allan M. Fraser
Provincial Archivist of Newfoundland

BYNNER, bin′ər, **Witter** (1881–1968), American editor and writer. He was born in Brooklyn, N. Y., on Aug. 10, 1881. After graduating from Harvard, he was an editor for McClure publications and for Small, Maynard & Company. He was president of the Poetry Society of America from 1920 to 1922.

Bynner is known chiefly as a poet. His wide-ranging poetry includes the collections *Grenstone Poems* (1917), *A Canticle of Pan* (1920), *Indian Earth* (1929), *Against the Cold* (1940), *Take Away the Darkness* (1947), *A Book of Lyrics* (1958), and *New Poems* (1960). His plays include *Tiger* (1913), *The Little King* (1914), *Iphigenia in Tauris* (1915; revised 1965), and *Cake* (1926). Bynner knew D. H. Lawrence and his wife, and recorded his memories of them in *Journey with Genius* (1951). He died in Santa Fe, N. Mex., on June 1, 1968.

BYNS, Anna. See Bijns, Anna.

BYRD, Harry Flood (1887–1966), American public official, who became Virginia's foremost political leader in the 20th century. A direct descendant of William Byrd (1674–1744), Harry Byrd was born in Martinsburg, W. Va., on June 10, 1887. His father, Richard E. Byrd, was a newspaper publisher who had influence in the Virginia Democratic organization of U. S. Senator Thomas S. Martin. In 1903, at the age of 15, Harry Byrd left school to manage his father's Winchester (Va.) *Star*. His successful direction of this and other business interests enabled him to obtain extensive apple orchards.

Byrd acquired a political bent from both his father and an uncle, U.S. Congressman Henry D. Flood, a major voice in the Martin organization. Flood's political influence helped Byrd win election to the Virginia senate in 1915, and his death and that of Martin created the leadership vacuum that enabled Byrd to become Democratic state chairman in 1922. In 1925, Byrd won the governorship on a platform pledging ambitious administrative reform. During four years in office he obtained numerous amendments to the state's 1902 constitution, introduced the short ballot, and instituted pay-as-you-go financing.

The reputation and power base Byrd established in the 1920's lasted for four decades. By a sagacious policy of compromise and consensus, his organization gave Virginia a conservative, frugal, and honest government regularly endorsed by the electorate. Byrd entered the U.S. Senate in 1933 as a supporter of President Franklin D. Roosevelt. Within two years, however, he grew disillusioned with what he considered the radical tenor of Roosevelt's New Deal. During his remaining 30 years in the Senate, he tenaciously resisted augmentation of federal power, especially in its welfare state manifestation. As the powerful chairman of the Senate finance committee from 1955 to 1965 he became known to the nation as the "watchdog of the Treasury."

Although nominally a Democrat, Byrd supported no Democratic presidential nominee after 1936. In spite of his party irregularity, he easily defeated all Democratic opponents in Virginia. Even in 1964, when his rural-based organization showed strain, he won reelection effortlessly. In November 1965, Byrd resigned his seat to make way for the appointment of his son Harry Flood Byrd, Jr. Byrd died in Berryville, Va., on Oct. 20, 1966, and two weeks later his son was elected to his Senate seat.

William Larsen, *Radford College, Va.*

BYRD, Richard Evelyn (1888–1957), American naval officer and polar explorer, who led five expeditions to Antarctica and was the first man to fly over the North and South poles. He was born at Winchester, Va., on Oct. 25,. 1888, a direct descendant of William Byrd (1652–1704), one of the earliest plantation owners in Virginia. He was a younger brother of Harry F. Byrd, who was U. S. senator from Virginia from 1933 to 1965. Byrd attended Virginia Military Institute and graduated from the U. S. Naval Academy in 1912.

After four years service in the Navy he was retired in 1916 because of a leg injury. However, in 1917, on the eve of American participation in World War I, he was recalled to active duty and trained as an aviator at Pensacola, Fla. From July to November 1918 he was commander of the U. S. Air Forces of Canada. After the war Byrd was in charge of navigational preparations for the Navy's first transatlantic airplane flight in 1919. He also commanded the aviation unit of the U. S. Navy-MacMillan Polar Expedition in Greenland in 1925.

North and South Pole Flights. On May 9, 1926, with Floyd Bennett as his copilot, Byrd made the first flight over the North Pole. In the following year, with three companions, he made a 42-hour nonstop flight, June 29–July 1, from Roosevelt Field, Long Island, N. Y., to France. Poor visibility made it impossible for him to land at Paris, so he set his plane down in the surf off Ver-sur-Mer in Normandy.

With these experiences behind him, he led his first expedition to the Antarctic in 1928. He established his base camp, Little America, on the Bay of Whales in December 1928.

The first flight over the South Pole was accomplished on Nov. 28–29, 1929, in the trimotored monoplane *Floyd Bennett,* named for Byrd's copilot on his North Pole flight who had died the previous year. Byrd's companions on this privately financed South Pole flight were Bernt Balchen (pilot), Harold I. June (radio operator), and Capt. Ashley C. McKinley (photographer). They took off on the 1,600-mile (2,575-km) flight from Little America. On returning to the United States in 1930, Byrd was advanced to rear admiral (retired) by special act of Congress.

Later Antarctic Expeditions. In 1933–1935, Byrd led a second privately financed expedition to Antarctica and again established his base at Little Amercia. Using modern transportation equipment, the party discovered and photographed vast new areas of the continent. In the winter of 1934, Byrd lived alone for five months at a weather station 123 miles (198 km) south of the base camp. He nearly died of monoxide poisoning and later gave a graphic account of his experience in *Alone,* a book he wrote in 1938.

Named by President Franklin D. Roosevelt to command the U. S. Antarctic Service Expedition of 1939–1941, Byrd for the first time made the trip under government auspices and with government money, thus setting a precedent for future U. S. operations in the Antarctic. On this third expedition, two wintering-over bases were established, and scientific investigation assumed a more important role. During World War II, Byrd served on special assignments for the Navy. Then, in 1947, he was named officer-in-charge of the largest Antarctic expedition in history, the Antarctic Developments Project known as Operation Highjump. Its 13 ships, modern aircraft and tractors, and 4,700 men were under the tactical command of Rear Adm. Richard H. Cruzen.

NAVY DEPARTMENT

ADM. RICHARD E. BYRD, with his dog Igloo, shown on the first of his five expeditions to the Antarctic.

Admiral Byrd made his fifth and last trip to Antarctica in 1955–1956, when he again raised the American flag at the 27-year-old base camp at Little America. This expedition was preparatory to U. S. participation in the International Geophysical Year in 1957–1958. Byrd was named officer-in-charge of the United States Antarctic Programs by President Dwight D. Eisenhower and helped supervise preparations for Operation Deepfreeze, as America's IGY expedition under Adm. George Dufek was called. Before Deepfreeze was carried out, Byrd died in Boston, Mass., on March 11, 1957. He was buried with full military honors at the National Cemetery in Arlington, Va.

George Dufek
Rear Admiral, U. S. Navy (Retired)

BYRD, William (1652–1704), American colonial planter, merchant, and public official, one of the founders of the Virginia gentry society. Born in London, he was sent to Virginia to work with his uncle, Thomas Stegge, Jr., a prominent merchant. Stegge died shortly after his arrival, and the 18-year-old Byrd inherited his estate, including 1,800 acres (728 hectares) at the Falls of the James (Richmond). In 1673 he married Mary Horsmanden, whose family was allied with English mercantile firms; they had a son, William, and three daughters.

Although he apparently sided with Nathaniel Bacon in Bacon's Rebellion of 1676, Byrd unofficially was supporting Gov. William Berkeley by the end of the conflict. Thereafter, he avoided political conflicts even though he held high offices. He was a member of the House of Burgesses from 1677 to 1682 and a councillor after 1683. In 1687 he became auditor and receiver general of Virginia.

William Byrd was a typical 17th century colonial entrepreneur. Diversifying his interests, he invested in the Indian and slave trades, built warehouses, raised tobacco, traded in the West Indies, and speculated in land. He died on Dec. 4, 1704, having amassed estates totaling 26,000 acres (10,500 hectares).

DAVID ALAN WILLIAMS, *University of Virginia*

BYRD, William (1674–1744), American colonial planter, author, and public official. The son of William Byrd (q.v.), he was born in Virginia on March 28, 1674. Educated in England, he observed mercantile methods in Holland and worked in a London tobacco firm. He then studied law at London's Middle Temple and was admitted to the bar in 1695.

Throughout his life Byrd identified with people of influence. Through the support of Sir Robert Southwell he was elected to the Royal Society in 1696. That year he returned to Virginia for the first time since he had left at age six and was promptly elected to a family seat in the House of Burgesses. In 1697 he went to England to defend Gov. Edmund Andros of Virginia, who was accused of hostility to the colony's Anglican Church. Byrd remained there for several years acting as a colonial agent, and he was instrumental in having Andros' successor, Francis Nicholson, turned out in 1705.

After his father's death in 1704, Byrd went back to Virginia, and in 1706 he married Lucy Parke, daughter of Daniel Parke, a Virginia planter and governor of the Leeward Islands. Appointed receiver of royal customs for Virginia in 1705, he was named to the Council of State in 1709. He and his fellow councillors became embroiled in a long conflict with Gov. Alexander Spotswood, who was trying to end the planters' monopoly of vast tracts of land and to withdraw judicial powers from the Council. In 1715, Byrd went to London to protect the councillors and also to defend his Indian trade interests against Spotswood's policy. He was successful on the latter point, but his attempts to have Spotswood ousted almost led to his own dismissal from the Council. Back in Virginia in 1720, Byrd arranged a compromise with Spotswood that opened the way to great land fortunes for the planter gentry. Between 1721 and 1727 he again was in London, where, his wife having died in 1716, he married Maria Taylor.

During the last years of his life Byrd increased his land holdings to 180,000 acres (73,000 hectares), served as a boundary commissioner to North Carolina, promoted schemes for importing Swiss settlers, laid out the town of Richmond (1737), and acted as president of the Council from 1743 until his death on Aug. 26, 1744.

Owner of the largest library in the colonies (4,000 volumes), builder of the magnificent plantation home called Westover, correspondent with the leading scientists in England, Byrd symbolized the elegance and versatility of the colonial planter. His manuscripts and personal diaries establish him as among the foremost literary figures of the era. Edited by Louis B. Wright and others between 1941 and 1966, they are valuable guides to colonial society.

DAVID ALAN WILLIAMS, *University of Virginia*

BYRD, William (1543–1623), English composer and organist, whose genius dominated the "Golden Age" of English music. He excelled in almost every type of composition current during his time, and he was a distinguished performer.

Life. Byrd was born in Lincolnshire. Little is known of his early years. In 1563 he became organist at Lincoln Cathedral, and about 10 years later he was named to the same post at the Chapel Royal. There he was associated with Thomas Tallis, with whom, under royal patent, he was permitted to print and sell music. Although Byrd maintained an allegiance to Roman Catholicism throughout his life, he was professionally engaged in the service of the Church of England until his death, at Stondon Massey, Essex, on July 4, 1623.

Works. Byrd's most famous pupil, Thomas Morley, referred to him as a man "never without reverence to be named of the Musicians." Much of Byrd's work is grave and meditative, but its occasional austerity is mollified by freedom from the commonplace and a wealth of inventiveness. These qualities, together with his exquisite sensitivity to words, make Byrd the most impressive figure in English music before the middle of the 17th century and one of the greatest of all English composers.

Byrd composed much music for both the Catholic and the Anglican liturgy. His masses for three, four, and five voices are works of serene beauty in which "word painting" is effectively employed. His settings for the Anglican service (whether in "Short" or "Great" form) show a comparable melodic and harmonic fluency, although his anthems are less notable. His Latin motets, printed in the *Cantiones Sacrae* (1589, 1591) and the *Gradualia* (1605, 1607), are compositions of great ingenuity, with unexpectedly stark and poignant modulations. In short, as a composer of English ecclesiastical music, Byrd is in a class by himself.

Byrd's secular vocal music includes concerted items and solo songs. His *Psalmes, Sonets and Songs of Sadness and pietie* (1588) and *Songs of Sundrie Natures* (1589) contain some of the earliest madrigal-type compositions published in England. His solo songs are equally innovative, for he replaced the lute accompaniment (as used by John Dowland) with a small string ensemble. The result was rich and satisfying.

Byrd's writing for strings was specifically instrumental in style. The 14 fantasias and 8 *In nomines*, all for a consort of viols, reveal much dexterity in handling fugal passages that are unvocal in character and occasionally of unusual rhythmical complexity. In keyboard composition Byrd's resourcefulness was particularly remarkable. His contributions to *My Ladye Nevell's Booke*, the *Fitzwilliam Virginal Book*, and *Parthenia* were epochal, for, in addition to innumerable dance measures and other short pieces, he contributed the world's finest set of variations. If not in fact the father of keyboard music, he was and is regarded as the greatest keyboard composer of his time.

E. D. MACKERNESS
The University of Sheffield, England

Further Reading: Andrews, Herbert K., *The Technique of Byrd's Vocal Polyphony* (New York 1966); Fellowes, Edmund H., *William Byrd*, 2d ed. (New York 1948); Kerman, Joseph, *The Elizabethan Madrigal* (Philadelphia 1962).

BYRGIUS, Justus. See BÜRGI, JOOST.

BYRNES, James Francis (1879–1972), American public official. Born on May 2, 1879, in Charleston, S. C., he left school early to work. He studied law in his spare time, and was admitted to the bar in 1903. A Democrat, Byrnes served in the U. S. House of Representatives from 1911 to 1925. In 1924 he lost a U. S. Senate bid in the Democratic primary, but was elected in 1930 and reelected in 1936.

Byrnes became one of the most influential senators. During the first years of the New Deal, he supported President Franklin D. Roosevelt, but after 1936 he swung to the right politically, opposing increased relief appropriations and the Fair Labor Standards Act. He remained on good terms with the President, however, and strongly supported his foreign policy. He played an important part in the repeal of the Neutrality Act and approval of Lend Lease.

In 1940, Byrnes backed Roosevelt for a third term. In 1941 he was appointed to the U. S. Supreme Court, but resigned in 1942 at Roosevelt's request to become director of economic stabilization with the job of curbing inflation. In 1943, Roosevelt named him head of the new Office of War Mobilization, which had such power over the economy that Byrnes was known as the assistant president. In 1944 he sought the vice presidential nomination, and thought he had Roosevelt's support. But Northern liberal and labor leaders, including Edward J. Flynn and Sidney Hillman (qq.v.), blocked his nomination.

In 1945, President Harry S Truman, an old friend, named Byrnes secretary of state. He accompanied Truman to Potsdam, and attended other conferences in 1945 and 1946 to work out a peace settlement. His experience with the Russians—notably on the Iranian and German questions—transformed the patient Byrnes into a champion of a hard line against the Soviets.

He left the cabinet in 1947 because of increasing friction with Truman, and he subsequently attacked Truman's Fair Deal and the growth of government. In 1950 he was elected governor of South Carolina. As governor (1951–1955) he staunchly defended states' rights and racial segregation. In 1952 he supported Dwight D. Eisenhower, a Republican, for president. In retirement he lived in Columbia, S. C. *Speaking Frankly* (1947) and *All in One Lifetime* (1958) are accounts of his diplomatic and political careers. He died in Columbia, S. C., on April 9, 1972.

JOHN BRAEMAN, *University of Nebraska*

BYROM, bī′rəm, **John** (1692–1763), English poet and the inventor of a shorthand system. He was born near Manchester, England, on Feb. 29, 1692, and was educated at Trinity College, Cambridge, where he later became a fellow. He also studied medicine at the University of Montpellier, France, but never received a medical degree. He may have lived in France for a time.

Byrom, who was elected to the Royal Society in 1724, taught a system of shorthand he had invented while at Cambridge. He copyrighted the system in 1742, but his book *Universal English Shorthand System* was not published until after his death. Unfortunately, his shorthand was too slow for use by professional stenographers.

Byrom wrote lively epigrams and satirical verse, published as *Miscellaneous Poems* (1773) and a diary, *The Private Journal and Literary Remains of John Byrom* (2 vols., 1854–1857). He died in London on Sept. 26, 1763.

NATIONAL PORTRAIT GALLERY

Lord Byron, from a portrait by Westall.

BYRON, bī′rən, **Lord** (1788–1824), English poet and satirist, whose name became a symbol for the *Weltschmerz* and melancholy of the romantic age, but whose permanent contribution to literature includes much that is in the realistic-satiric mood of the 18th century. The immediate and immense success of *Childe Harold's Pilgrimage,* of which Cantos I and II were published in 1812, channeled Byron's energies into exploiting the romantic vein. In such works as the Oriental tales, which were based on his experiences in the eastern Mediterranean; in the more mature and poetically finer third and fourth cantos of *Childe Harold,* which gave expression to the post-Napoleonic disillusionment; and in the poetic dramas *Manfred* and *Cain,* as well as a number of shorter romantic poems, which voiced the agony and the protest of man "cooped in clay," Byron found an outlet for "the lava of the imagination."

It was only after his self-exile in Italy had encouraged a more relaxed attitude that Byron was able to accept the limitations of life and to point up in poetry, as he had long done in his letters, the amusing aspects of life's ironies and pretensions. It was then, with a wry smile rather than with agonized protest, that he portrayed the imperfections and hypocrisies of the human drama in *Beppo, Don Juan,* and *The Vision of Judgment.* His masterpiece *Don Juan,* a medley reflecting the ever-changing moods of his mobile mind in a "versified Aurora Borealis," alternates between the Childe Harold type of melancholy that was a real part of his "impassion'd clay" and the impulse to be "a little quietly facetious upon every thing."

But Byron's real purpose, which underlies the mocking tone, was not only to expose the follies of the various societies into which he cast his hero, but also to offer a realistic and rational comment on life as he found it. When urged to write some great work such as a serious epic, he replied: "You have so many *'divine'* poems, is it nothing to have written a *Human* one?"

LIFE

George Gordon Byron was born in London on Jan. 22, 1788. His mother, Catherine Gordon, of a proud Scottish family, was the second wife of the poet's father, Capt. John ("Mad Jack") Byron, who was descended from a long line of nobility. The marriage was a tempestuous one. Mrs. Byron took her son, who was born with a clubfoot, to her native Aberdeen, where she lived frugally. Captain Byron had squandered most of her fortune before he died in exile in France in 1791. Byron always retained idyllic memories of his Scottish boyhood. When his great uncle died in 1798, the boy became the 6th Baron Byron and inherited the ancestral estate of Newstead Abbey near Nottingham, which had come into the family by gift of King Henry VIII. After living briefly at Newstead with his mother, he was sent to school in London and went to Harrow in 1801. The rough and tumble of a public school did nothing to lessen his sensitiveness to his lameness, which persisted throughout his life, but in the upper forms he made friends, especially with younger boys. During his holidays at Southwell, near Nottingham, he spent much of his time in an adolescent courtship of his distant cousin Mary Chaworth, who was older and already engaged. This early experience gave a cynical cast to his idealized picture of romantic love.

College and Travel. Byron entered Trinity College, Cambridge, in 1805. There the usual dissipations of the place did not absorb him, but he formed one of the strongest attachments of his life, which he later described as "a violent, though *pure*, love and passion," for a young chorister, John Edleston. He also met and became a lifelong friend of John Cam Hobhouse, who accompanied him on his first pilgrimage to Greece.

Byron's first published volume of poetry, *Hours of Idleness*, appeared in 1807. Two years later, just after he had reached his majority and had taken his seat in the House of Lords, he replied to his critics in *English Bards, and Scotch Reviewers.* His journey to the East, begun in July 1809, which took him to Portugal, Spain, Albania, Greece, and through the Hellespont to Constantinople, had a profound effect on his literary and personal life. The leisurely life of the Greeks—whom he came to know better than did most English travelers—the climate, and the moral tolerance of the people appealed to him. On this voyage he visited Ali Pasha in Albania, saw the site of Troy, and swam the Hellespont.

Byron returned to England a pronounced cosmopolite and thereafter retained a nostalgia for the sunny lands of the Mediterranean. On his travels he had written the first two cantos of *Childe Harold's Pilgrimage*. Its publication in 1812 brought him immediate fame. He frequented the literary circles of Thomas Moore, Samuel Rogers, and Richard Brinsley Sheridan, and the fashionable Whig salons of Holland House and Melbourne House. He was soon involved in a scandalous intrigue with Lady Caroline Lamb and later was captivated with the "autumnal charms" of Lady Oxford, who encouraged his radical stance in Parliament. (His maiden speech in the House of Lords had been a humanitarian appeal against harsh Tory measures to suppress rioting Nottingham weavers.)

Marriage and Separation. Byron's immensely popular Oriental tales, beginning with *The Giaour* (1813), hinted darkly at sins in his past and present life. In 1813 he became dangerously involved in an attachment with his half-sister Augusta Leigh, and after trying vainly to escape his emotional impasse by flirting with Lady Frances Webster, he finally sought safety by marrying Annabella Milbanke, a niece of Lady Melbourne, in 1815. It was a "fatal marriage." Annabella was too much "encumbered with virtue" to make allowances for the vagaries of the Byronic temperament. She left him after a year, following the birth of their daughter Ada, never giving her reasons but hinting at conduct on his part that increased the scandal of their separation.

Switzerland and Italy. In April 1816, Byron went abroad again, never to return to England. After writing, at Waterloo, stanzas for a third canto of *Childe Harold*, he settled for the summer on the shore of Lake Geneva, where he became closely associated with the poet Percy Bysshe Shelley. While in Switzerland, Byron entered reluctantly into a liaison with Claire Clairmont, Mary Shelley's stepsister, finished the third canto of *Childe Harold* (1816), and began *Manfred* (1817).

In September, Hobhouse accompanied him to Italy. In Venice, Byron found solace in the relaxed manners and morals of the Italians, enjoying the carnival, the theater, and Italian society life in the salon of the Countess Albrizzi. He fell in love with Marianna Segati, the wife of a "merchant of Venice," and later with the "gentle tigress" Margarita Cogni, who became his housekeeper at the Palazzo Mocenigo on the Grand Canal. A trip to Rome in the spring of 1817 gave Byron material for the pageant of Roman history in the fourth canto of *Childe Harold* (1818). In the summer he discovered his forte in the light, mock-heroic style of *Beppo* (1818) and followed up this success with the first two cantos of *Don Juan*.

Before the cantos were published in 1819, Byron met and fell in love with the Countess Teresa Guiccioli, a lively girl of 20 married to a man nearly three times her age. Byron followed her to Ravenna, where he became her acknowledged *cavalier servente*. Through her father and brother, the Counts Gamba, he became involved in the secret society of the Carbonari and aided them in their futile plots to overthrow the tyranny of Austrian rule in Italy. After the Guicciolis separated, Byron settled down into a quasi-domestic relationship with Teresa. In 1821, when the Gambas were exiled from Ravenna for their revolutionary activities, Byron followed them and Teresa to Pisa, where he was again associated with Shelley and a circle of his English friends, including Edward John Trelawny, Edward Williams, and Thomas Medwin, who later published Byron's conversations.

A series of events broke up the Pisan circle in 1822—the death of Allegra, Byron's illegitimate daughter by Claire Clairmont; the wounding of a soldier by one of Byron's servants; and finally, the drowning of Shelley. Byron moved to Genoa with his household, which now included the family of Leigh Hunt, who had come to Italy to edit a short-lived periodical, *The Liberal*, with Byron and Shelley.

Byron became increasingly bored with his domesticity and lack of activity in Italy. In 1823, during the Greek war for independence from the Turks, he accepted the invitation of the London Greek Committee to act as their agent in

Greece. He was perhaps drawn to this adventure by the hope of rehabilitating himself in the eyes of his countrymen through some noble action, and by fond memories of his youthful sojourn in Greece. Sailing in the middle of July 1823 and carrying money and supplies for the revolutionaries, he settled at Metaxata on the Ionian island of Cephalonia. He was wary of dissensions in the Greek camp but finally joined Prince Mavrocordatos at Missolonghi in January 1824. Byron gave £4,000 of his own money to activate the Greek fleet, paid the wages of some of the soldiers, and tried to encourage discipline and unity among the Greeks.

But before an offensive could be organized against the Turks, Byron died of a fever on April 19, 1824, at Missolonghi. His body was sent home to England, but in Greece his name became a symbol of disinterested patriotism. Today his statue stands in the center of the "Garden of the Heroes" of the revolution in Missolonghi.

WORKS

Like most young poets, Byron began with imitative verses which nevertheless gave some promise of his later genius. Two opposite but complementary strains appear: a romantic and a realistic interpretation of the human propensity to seek ideal perfection in all the experiences of life. Nostalgia for the lost innocence of youth is a common theme of his early poems. But even when he was imitating the sentimental poetry of Thomas Moore, Byron displayed a preference for truth to the "cold compositions of art." As one modern critic has said, he was "too romantic to refrain from blowing bubbles, and too realistic to refrain from pricking them."

Byron came before the public with the volume *Hours of Idleness* (1807). When the *Edinburgh Review* published a sarcastic critique of that volume, Byron struck back with a Popean satire, *English Bards, and Scotch Reviewers,* attacking most contemporary poets for not following "Pope's pure strain" and "great Dryden's" moralizing song. This first attempt to emulate the Popean model, which he most admired, was followed by other, less successful efforts (notably *Hints from Horace,* which was published posthumously, and *The Age of Bronze,* 1823.) Byron had developed a dual concept of poetry. On the one hand, he wanted most to be a Juvenalian satirist turning his pungent wit against deviations from good sense and good taste and satirizing the errors of the age. On the other hand, he followed perforce the romantic taste for what he considered a lesser genre, the poetry of the feelings, and used it as a safety valve for his emotions.

"Childe Harold's Pilgrimage." The first two cantos of *Childe Harold* take the pilgrim through Portugal, Spain, Albania, and Greece on a foredoomed search. Alternate longing for the ideal and disillusionment in the face of reality form the pattern and set the mood of *Childe Harold.* But in the early cantos the author's zest for travel and new experiences shines through the melancholy. The "satanic pose" and the "lonely soul" themes are interspersed with descriptions of a bullfight in Spain, the kilted Albanians, and the wild Greek dances, or with expressions of sadness over Greece in decay and indignation over the removal to England of the Elgin marbles.

The third canto, which follows the pilgrim from the field of Waterloo up the Rhine to Switzerland, at once expresses the most aspiring and the most melancholy views. The lonely soul confesses that his brain is "A whirling gulf of phantasy and flame," but at times he reaches a tranquillity beyond tragedy and feels that he can momentarily transcend the "clay-cold bond" of reality. It is in the creative process, the "bodiless thought," that he finds escape from the "fleshly chain." The glow of feeling that informs this canto lifts it to the highest reaches of poetic insight into the romantic ego. In his pictures of Waterloo, of Napoleon and Rousseau, of the lake and the mountains, it is evident that his lyre has gained a string. Byron himself said of the canto: "It is a fine indistinct piece of poetical desolation, and my favourite."

The *sic transit gloria mundi* theme of the fourth canto, which follows the pilgrim (now no longer distinguishable from the poet) from Venice to Rome, is interspersed with some of Byron's most poignant and most poetic statements of the romantic agony. The lush rhetoric of the description of the ruins of Rome is dramatic and spectacular, but it does not outshine the poetic brilliance of the evocation of the ineffable longings of the supersensitive romantic mind, "The unreached Paradise of our despair."

Oriental Tales. Byron made the most of his knowledge of Eastern manners and landscapes in the melodramatic poetic tales that he wrote after the publication of *Childe Harold.* Their popularity was due in part to their picturesque descriptions of Greece, such as the passage in *The Corsair* (1814) describing the sun setting over the Morea as "one unclouded blaze of living light." Autobiographical hints added to their interest for Byron's contemporaries. *The Giaour* (1813) was supposed to be based on an episode in which Byron was involved in Athens. *The Bride of Abydos* (1813) hinted at incest in the too close relationship of the lovers. Conrad, the hero of *The Corsair,* that "man of loneliness and mystery," possessed enough Byronic traits to stimulate the suspicion that Byron was portraying himself. *Lara* (1814) was even more self-revealing.

"Manfred." Byron's Faustian drama *Manfred* (1817) carries the romantic quandary to its logical extreme. In the complaint that man is "half dust, half deity," he has reached the ultimate point in his uncompromising revolt against the conditions of life. Nothing less than the bodiless freedom of a deity could satisfy Manfred. But when he calls up the spirits, which are only projections of his own mind, they cannot satisfy him. He is their equal because he has created them. In its fiery protest against the limitations of the mind of man and in its equally fierce affirmation of its invincibility and integrity, Manfred goes beyond the personal problems of the poet to an embodiment of the universal inner conflict of the romantic ego.

"Cain." The poetic drama *Cain* (1821) carries Byron's Promethean defiance and speculative skepticism one step further. When Lucifer takes Cain through the spirit world and shows him things "Beyond all power of my born faculties,/Although inferior still to my desires/And my conceptions," Cain realizes that even deities might not be happy. The tree of knowledge was not necessarily the tree of happiness. Cain remains a three-dimensional character, one that is endowed with a tragic sense of man's limitations yet capable of human sympathy.

"Beppo." Tired of the melancholy voice heard in earlier poems, Byron at last found the perfect medium for the expression of his lighter moods in the mock-heroic ottava rima of the Italian poets, which he employed in *Beppo* (1818), a rollicking satire on Italian life and love. The story itself is slight, but Byron digresses at will upon the absurdities of the carnival, upon Italian women, the *cavalier servente,* the contrast between Italy and England ("Our cloudy climate, and our chilly women"), and every subject that strikes his fancy. He uses facetious rhymes in the final couplets for comic relief in deflating sentiment.

"Don Juan." The success of *Beppo* opened the way for *Don Juan* (1819–1824), a more ambitious project in the same vein, a mock-epic in picaresque form that would allow the freest range for digressive comment in every mood from the melancholy idealization of the sentiments to the satiric exposure of human frailty. Byron chose for his hero the legendary villainous rake, converting him into a well-meaning innocent, more pursued than pursuing, who would act as a norm against which to view the absurdities of the various societies into which he was thrust by his adventures. Byron carries his hero from his native Seville, where he was the victim of an adolescent seduction, to a Greek island where a shipwreck lands him in an idyllic love affair with a pirate's daughter. Then, after Juan is sold in the slave market at Constantinople and carried into the harem for the pleasure of the sultana, he escapes to play an accidentally heroic part in the battle of Ismail. In consequence, he becomes the favorite of Catherine the Great, who finally sends him on a diplomatic mission to England, where he ends in a series of intrigues

In *Don Juan,* as in *Beppo,* the story is only a peg on which to hang the digressive commentary. Although Byron began with the statement that his purpose was only "to giggle and make giggle," he later defended *Don Juan* as "the most moral of poems," a serious satire on abuses in society. The comment runs the gamut in mood from the deepest melancholy of *Childe Harold* to the most hilarious of cynical truisms. The subject matter covers every field of Byronic interest: the vanity of ambition, the pretensions of poets, his distaste for Tory tyrants and the Holy Alliance, the absurdity of "ladies intellectual," the hypocrisy of "Platonism" in love, the paradoxes of love and marriage, the basic savagery of men striving for self-preservation, the beauty of "natural love," the hollowness of glory and the brutality of war, the frailty of women and the inconstancy of men, the hypocrisy and boredom of English society, the prevalence of cant in religion, politics, and education.

In *Don Juan,* Byron did not, as in *Childe Harold,* wholly identify himself with his hero, although there is something of the inner core of what he conceived to have been his innocent youth in the character of Juan. But since Byron reserved the right to step on the stage at will, to voice his comments on the action and to give his own views of life independent of the narrative, the author becomes the real protagonist of the poem.

The colloquial style of *Don Juan* is well suited to Byron's satiric wit and often seems transcribed, in verse, from his vivacious and ironic letters. Although Byron threatened at various times to write 50 or 100 cantos for *Don Juan,* he finished only 16 cantos and 14 stanzas of a 17th before he left Italy for Greece. However, though unfinished, the work has a completeness in itself as a slice of life.

"The Vision of Judgement." Byron's most unified satire is *The Vision of Judgement* (1822), a parody of Robert Southey's laureate praise of King George III. The poem is a masterpiece of sharp wit and scathing irony. The angelic debate for the soul of the late king is turned into farce when Southey starts spouting his verses. The devils run howling back to hell, and St. Peter sends the poet hurtling to earth, while the king, in the confusion, slips into Heaven where he is left "practicing the hundredth psalm."

Shorter Poems. Byron's shorter poems enhanced his reputation almost as much as his longer ones, and some are better known. His most frequently quoted short poems (though not always his best) include *Maid of Athens, The Isles of Greece* (included in *Don Juan*), *"There be none of beauty's daughters," The Prisoner of Chillon, She Walks in Beauty, The Destruction of Sennacherib, So We'll Go No More A-roving,* and *On This Day I Complete My Thirty-sixth Year.* Other short poems that deserve more attention include the Thyrza poems, *Prometheus, Could I Remount the River of My Years,* and *Could Love for Ever.* Many of the *jeux d'esprit* sent in letters to his friends also have a permanent place in his work. These pieces, written in the spirit of outrageous fun, display some of the same wit and exuberance as *Don Juan.* Among the best are *Lines to Mr. Hodgson, Epistle from Mr. Murray to Dr. Polidori,* and *Epistle to Mr. Murray.*

Historical Dramas and Dramatic Narratives. Although much critical effort has been expended to raise Byron's poetical dramas and dramatic narratives to a rank equal to that of his best work, there is little doubt that they will remain, with few exceptions, on a lower shelf than his satires or his most poignant expression of the romantic dilemma. The historical dramas *Marino Faliero, The Two Foscari,* and *Sardanapalus* (all published in 1821) never achieve historical objectivity and are written in an exalted rhetoric which is not Byron's true voice. What merit they have lies in the depth and sincerity of a personal revelation rather than in any genuine dramatic realization of character. In some ways, *Mazeppa* (1819) comes the nearest to objectivity, yet some of its finest touches are overtones of Byronic personal feeling. The same subjectivity obtrudes in *The Island* (1823), a dramatization of the "noble savage" life of the mutineers from the H. M. S. *Bounty.*

Byron's Letters. A great number of Byron's letters, hitherto unknown, have been published in the 20th century, and his reputation has come to rest as much on them as on his poetry. Many of the letters are prose versions of *Don Juan,* with the same sparkling wit and the same willingness to tell the embarrassing truth about himself and others. The degree to which Byron tailored his letters to particular correspondents is strikingly evident. He wrote facetiously to his witty friends Hobhouse and Kinnaird. His epistles to Lady Melbourne, his confidante, were full of cynicism and charm as well as flattery. He could be both tender and witty in addressing his sister Augusta or Teresa Guiccioli. But in writing to his parson friends, Francis Hodgson and Robert C. Dallas, he did not refrain from

CULVER PICTURES

NEWSTEAD ABBEY, near Nottingham, Byron's ancestral home, which he inherited in 1798. (From a 19th century engraving.)

the honest expression of his skeptical religious beliefs.

Some of Byron's most amusing letters were written from Italy to Thomas Moore and to his publisher, John Murray. In these, however, Byron was writing for an audience, for he knew that they showed his letters to a select circle of friends. Whether writing a business letter or a casual note to a stranger, Byron had a directness and a colloquial ease that escapes entirely the artificialities and poses of many 19th century letters.

The Byronic Paradox. The two sides of Byron's character and poetry—the romantic and the realistic—are understandable in terms of his background and temperament. The central problem in all Byron's work is his romantic concern for the disparity between the real and the ideal. Unlike the transcendental romantics, he saw this gap as essentially unbridgeable and perforce felt a deeper melancholy than other romantics, such as Shelley, who believed in the attainability of the ideal dream.

But Byron was too firmly grounded in 18th century rationalism and "common sense" not to see the comedy as well as the tragedy of the discrepancy between reality and appearance, between imperfections and pretensions. And he achieved poetic eminence in both areas. In his intense hatred of sham, as well as in his sense of ironic realism, he seems remarkably modern and congenial to the 20th century, a fact that accounts for the growth of critical esteem for *Don Juan*. Nevertheless, respect for the basic honesty of Byron's exploration of the ineffable longings of the individual ego frustrated by its own human limitations increases with an impartial reading of the last two cantos of *Childe Harold*. Both moods must be recognized as equally important in the Byronic personality.

LESLIE A. MARCHAND
Author of "Byron: A Biography"

Bibliography

The Works of Lord Byron, Poetry was edited by Ernest H. Coleridge, 7 vols. (London 1898–1904); *Letters and Journals* was edited by Rowland E. Prothero, 6 vols. (London 1898–1901).

Borst, William A., *Lord Byron's First Pilgrimage* (New Haven 1948).

Lovell, Ernest J., Jr., *Byron: The Record of a Quest* (Austin, Texas, 1949).

Lovell, Ernest J., Jr., ed., *His Very Self and Voice: Collected Conversations of Lord Byron* (New York 1954).

Marchand, Leslie A., *Byron: A Biography,* 3 vols. (New York 1957).

Marchand, Leslie A., *Byron's Poetry: A Critical Introduction* (Boston 1965).

More, Paul Elmer, ed., *The Complete Poetical Works of Lord Byron,* Cambridge Edition (Boston 1905).

Nicolson, Harold, *Byron, the Last Journey* (London 1924).

Origo, Iris, *The Last Attachment* (London 1949).

Quennell, Peter, ed., *Byron: A Self-Portrait, Letters and Diaries, 1798 to 1824,* 2 vols. (London 1950).

Quennell, Peter, *Byron, the Years of Fame* (London 1935).

Ridenour, George M., *The Style of Don Juan* (New Haven 1960).

Rutherford, Andrew, *Byron: A Critical Study* (Palo Alto, Calif., 1961).

West, Paul, ed., *Byron: A Collection of Critical Essays* (Englewood Cliffs, N. J., 1963).

BYRON, John (1723–1786), English admiral, who was the grandfather of the poet Byron. He was born at Newstead, Nottinghamshire, on Nov. 8, 1723. When he was 17, he was a midshipman on a vessel that was wrecked on the coast of Chile. His written account of his adventures provided material for parts of his grandson's long poem *Don Juan*. As a captain, Byron commanded a frigate dispatched in 1764 by King George III on a voyage of exploration. He sailed around the world on a westerly course in 22 months, but the voyage contributed little to geographical knowledge. Byron was governor of Newfoundland from 1769 to 1772. With the rank of vice admiral, he led a fleet in an indecisive action against the French in the West Indies in 1779. He was known as "Foul-weather Jack" because of the many storms he had encountered at sea. He died on April 10, 1786.

BYTOM, bē'tôm, is an industrial city in Poland, in Katowice province, 160 miles (257 km) southwest of Warsaw. Iron and steel production are Bytom's chief industries. Coal, lead, and zinc mined nearby gave the city its start as an industrial center. In the mid-19th century the processing of these resources was expanded, and iron smelting and steelmaking were introduced.

A fortress was built at Bytom in the 11th century by the kings of Poland, and a city was established there during the 12th century. Bytom was destroyed by the Tatars in 1241, but was rebuilt. Rule of the city passed to the king of Bohemia in the 14th century and, in the 16th century, to the Austrian Habsburgs, along with the other possessions of the Bohemian crown. In the 18th century Bytom became Prussian and was renamed *Beuthen*. It remained part of Germany until 1945, when it was restored to Poland. Population: (1965) 192,000.

NORMAN J. G. POUNDS, *Indiana University*

MARBURG, ART REFERENCE BUREAU

BYZANTINE ARCHITECTURE of the First Golden Age produced its masterpiece in Hagia Sophia, Istanbul. The minarets are 15th century Muslim additions.

BYZANTINE ART AND ARCHITECTURE, bi'zən-tēn, flourished for more than 1,000 years—from 330 A.D. to about 1400—in the Byzantine, or Eastern Roman, Empire. The influence of Byzantine art spread to many areas outside the empire and lingers even today in parts of the USSR.

Diocletian, who ruled the Roman Empire from 284 to 305, first divided its vast territories into eastern and western sections for administrative purposes. In 330, Constantine moved the capital of the empire to the eastern city of Byzantium, which he renamed Constantinople (now Istanbul). While Rome in the West tottered to its fall, the Eastern, or Byzantine, Empire waxed in power, reaching its climax under Justinian, who reigned from 527 to 565. His able generals, Belisarius and Narses, added North Africa, Sicily, and the eastern Gothic kingdom around Ravenna in northern Italy to the already great Byzantine domain.

Since most secular Byzantine buildings have been destroyed, the characteristics of Byzantine style are best studied in the churches that constitute the major surviving monuments of the Empire. The churches are generally dominated by a brick dome, which is often combined with one or more subsidiary domes arranged in various ways. A dome emphasizes and defines the space beneath it, and, when combined with other vaults, it creates a rich spatial organization within the building.

The liturgy of the Eastern Orthodox Church and its allied churches requires a screen, or iconostasis, to separate the chancel from the space for the laity beneath the principal dome. The chancel is flanked by the prothesis, where the elements of the Eucharist are prepared, and by the diaconicon, or vestry. The exterior of Byzantine churches, at least for the first few centuries, was drab. But colored marble columns, slabs of similar material on the lower walls, and mosaics, often with gold backgrounds, made the interior resplendent.

Scholars have long debated the origins of Byzantine style. One group maintains that its sources must be sought in the eastern Mediterranean area, in Egypt, Palestine, Syria, Anatolia, or even farther into Asia. In support of their thesis they point to such qualities as the luxuriant use of color common to Middle Eastern and Byzantine architecture.

Other authorities, with perhaps stronger evidence, trace the roots of Byzantine style to Rome. These scholars cite the unencumbered interior space of Byzantine structures, which is unlike the older styles of the Middle East but similar to the spatial organization originally developed in imperial Roman architecture and carried with the expansion of the empire to most of the Middle East. Rome also produced the first great style of vaulted architecture, which eastern Mediterranean cultures had studiously avoided on a large scale for important buildings. The Byzantine brick dome, lighted by windows around the perimeter, also harks back to Roman precedents, as in the domes of the caldarium in the Baths of Caracalla (211–217) and of the Temple of Minerva Medica (310–320), both in Rome.

Other characteristics of Byzantine architecture that can be traced to Roman sources are the squinch and the pendentive, both devices to support a circular dome on a square plan. A squinch is a flat slab, arch, or arched niche built over the corner of a square structure to convert that shape into an octagon. One of the earliest examples of the squinch is found in the Villa of Hadrian (125–135) at Tivoli.

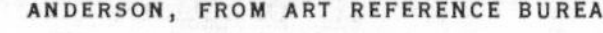

ANDERSON, FROM ART REFERENCE BUREAU

MARBURG, FROM ART REFERENCE BUREAU

THE INTERIORS of the Basilica of San Vitale (*left*), in Ravenna, and Hagia Sophia (*right*) dramatize the play of sunlight against polished marble surfaces.

More important in Byzantine architecture than the squinch is the pendentive, which in fact became the outstanding feature of the Byzantine style. The pendentive is a segment of a hemisphere which has a diameter equal to the diagonal of the square to be covered. In less technical terms, it is a vaulted spherical triangle, whose lower apex rests upon a pier and whose curved upper surface, combined with three other pendentives, provides the circular support on which the dome can be built. Pendentives on a small scale first appear in Roman tombs of the 1st or 2d century and in large sizes in the later Baths of Caracalla.

Early Roman architecture adopted the classic Greek relationships between the column, its support, and what it carried. During the 3d and 4th centuries, however, Roman architecture began to abandon these classical orders of architecture. In the Palace of Diocletian (about 300) at Spalato (Split), arches rest directly on the column capitals, the architrave is bent into the arched form known as an archivolt, and other violations of the rules of the orders are common. This freedom in handling the orders later became typical of Byzantine architecture. The Byzantine use of colored marbles (rarely, if ever, used in eastern Mediterranean countries prior to Roman occupation) has its precedents in the marble floors and sheathing on the lower walls of Roman buildings, such as the Palace of Domitian (about 90), the Baths of Diocletian (305), and the Basilica of Constantine (306–312), all in Rome.

Byzantine architecture, despite its Roman roots, had developed a distinctive character of its own by the 6th century. The same may be said of Byzantine mosaics, manuscripts, and ivories. Roman sculpture in the 4th century abandoned the lifelike realism of earlier Roman art, producing figures that are puppetlike, with naïve modifications of normal body proportions. From this source Byzantine mosaic workers and carvers of ivory had developed by the 6th century a highly sophisticated style. A hieratic and courtly elegance found expression in stylized linear figures with sumptuous details of costume that reflect the semioriental luxury of Justinian's reign.

The First Golden Age. The first flowering of the Byzantine style took place under Justinian in the 6th century. A distinctly Byzantine style had evolved by this time, not only in architecture but in mosaics, manuscripts, and ivory carving.

Architecture. During the First Golden Age, architecture continued to use the basilican plan with its plain timber roof and colonnades dividing the nave from the side aisles. Examples such as Sant'Apollinare in Classe (534–538) and Sant'Apollinare Nuovo (about 500), both in Ravenna, also make use of the typically Byzantine dosseret, a block above the capital that supports the arches and concentrates their weight on the capitals. The first clear structural example of the use of the dosseret is in the Basilica Ursiana (370–384), Ravenna, an otherwise Roman building. The dosserets, coupled with the spiny acanthus motif in the capitals and the gorgeous mosaics, give to the Ravenna churches a decidedly Byzantine flavor.

Even more Byzantine in style is San Vitale, Ravenna, which was completed by Justinian in 547. The central dome rests on squinches, with columnar niches between seven of the eight piers and a vaulted chancel in the eighth. An octagonal aisle surrounds this complex. Windows in the drum light the central area. Colored marbles, mosaics, and the surface carving of the capitals and dosserets are purely Byzantine.

Charlemagne's chapel (796–804) at Aachen (Aix-la-Chapelle) is a much simpler and somewhat naïve restudy of this church, but it lacks entirely the polychromy of its model.

Similar in plan to San Vitale is the Church of Saints Sergius and Bacchus (527–536), Constantinople. An octagon of piers and arches supports a dome whose shape is gored like the rind of a cantaloupe—a form that had a precedent in the Villa of Hadrian. The interior has been so modified as to obscure its Byzantine richness.

Hagia Eirene (St. Irene), Constantinople, which was rebuilt under Justinian but greatly altered since, has two domes over the nave—a hemispherical one with a row of windows around its base, and an elliptical one to the west of that. Thus domical forms were made to cover a longitudinal nave.

The masterpiece of Byzantine architecture of the First Golden Age is Hagia Sophia (meaning "Divine Wisdom"; also called St. Sophia), in Constantinople. It was built under the patronage of Justinian, who, when the older basilican church was burned during the Nika Insurrection in 532, commissioned Anthemius of Tralles and Isidorus of Miletus to build a new church. It was completed in 537. It is almost certain that Anthemius had visited his brother, a noted physician in Rome, and there had mastered the principles of Roman architecture. Anthemius' dome for Hagia Sophia fell after an earthquake in 558, but by 563 it had been replaced substantially in its present form by the younger Isidorus.

Hagia Sophia was preceded by an open court, or atrium, and entered through a double narthex, or vestibule. The church itself measures 308 feet by 236 feet (94 meters by 72 meters). The principal feature of Hagia Sophia, its dome, is about 102 feet (31 meters) in diameter. Such a vault presses outward in all directions, requiring massive support, which is provided in this case by broad arches to the north and south. Four huge piers, themselves buttressed by masses of masonry outside the building, hold the pendentives. Half-domes to the east and west, almost as large as the main dome, extend the length of the nave and help to abut the main dome. These, in turn, are abutted by smaller half-domes over columnar niches. Colonnades between the piers separate the aisles and the galleries over them from the nave.

The Byzantine architects, following the precedent of early Christian basilicas, left the exterior with little or no decoration. However, the structural system of Hagia Sophia itself gives monumentality to the exterior of the building. The system of vaults, niches, buttresses, and half-domes leads up like waves to culminate in the main dome. Blocks of masonry between the windows of the dome weight its base like so many buttresses, leaving only the upper part of the dome's curve apparent from the outside.

The builders of Hagia Sophia lavished their efforts on the interior of the building. Few churches were better lighted; great lunette windows pierce the curtain walls over the galleries to the north and south. Windows around the base of the dome flood it and the area below with light, visually reducing the solid appearance of the supports between the windows and creating the effect of a weightless dome suspended from above instead of supported from below.

To this lightened impression the color scheme is ancillary. Red porphyry and verd antique marble form the columns, while the walls up to the level of the capitals are sheathed in slabs of polychromed veined marble, cut so that the pattern of the veining is reversed in consecutive slabs. Dark blue color applied to the interstices of the patterns carved in capitals and moldings emphasizes the surface decoration by contrast to the white marble. These capitals adhere to none of the traditional orders of Roman architecture but are free designs of a cushion or basketlike shape. They may borrow the convex curve of the Doric echinus, the scroll forms of the Ionic, and the leafage of the Corinthian order (now become the conventionalized spiny acanthus), but all are fused into something new and distinctly Byzantine. Above the level of the columns, the walls, arches, and vaults glitter with gold mosaic, carried around even the edges of intersecting planes. Small wonder then that Justinian prided himself on the building he had erected, and well might he exclaim, "I have surpassed thee, O Solomon!"

After the capture of Constantinople in 1453 by the Ottoman Turks, Hagia Sophia was converted into a mosque. Some of its exterior surfaces were banded alternately light and dark, and four minarets were added at the corners. Hagia Sophia is now a museum.

Mosaics. The medium of mosaic, in which figural or other designs are created from tesserae (small bits of colored marble or colored glass), was extensively practiced in Rome both for floors and for mural designs. The figures in Roman mosaics generally have some indication of three-dimensional solidity. In such early Christian basilicas as Santa Maria Maggiore (5th century), Rome, extensive scenes from the Scriptures appear in the wall mosaics. The mosaic in the apse of Santa Pudenziana (4th century), Rome, shows Christ enthroned, flanked by apostles. The figures, somewhat rounded, are clothed in plain robes; buildings and a clouded sky form the background.

Byzantine mosaic designers, however, were concerned with figures as symbols, rather than as actual human beings, and regarded the design primarily as a chance to use opulent decorative color. They made little use of shading or other indications of three-dimensionality.

In the Byzantine Church of Sant'Apollinare Nuovo, Ravenna, the mosaic on one side above the arcade depicts a long file of male saints approaching Christ, and on the opposite wall a similar line of female saints headed by the three kings approaches the Virgin. The poses of the figures are nearly identical, as are their richly embroidered and bejeweled costumes. There is little attempt to suggest roundness in the figures, and there is no setting except conventionalized palms between the figures. They form, however, a most effective decorative frieze, echoing the colonnade below and leading the eye to the sanctuary ahead.

Two celebrated mosaics face each other across the chancel of San Vitale, Ravenna. One shows the Emperor Justinian holding a patten, Archbishop Maximian with a small cross, priests carrying a book and a censer, and a group of courtiers. The opposite mosaic presents the Empress Theodora with a chalice, priests, and ladies of the court. The figures are almost frontal, in rich draperies at least for the rulers, and with the third dimension indicated more by linear folds than by shaded modeling. No setting is visible in the Justinian mosaic, but Theodora is

BYZANTINE ART

The tendency toward symbolic presentation in Byzantine art is illustrated in the mosaics decorating the apse of the 6th-century Sant'Apollinare in Classe, in Ravenna. The upper part of the apse bowl is almost wholly symbolic and is thought to represent the Transfiguration. In the lower part of the bowl, Saint Apollinare stands with upraised arms in Paradise, with six lambs, symbolizing the faithful for whom he prays, on either side of him.

ART REFERENCE BUREAU

ART REFERENCE BUREAU

The Emperor Justinian, surrounded by clergy and nobles, appears in a 6th-century mosaic in the chancel of the Basilica of San Vitale, Ravenna.

SCALA, FROM SHOSTAL

The seated figure of Christ dominates an 11th-century mosaic in Hagia Sophia, in Istanbul. The mosaic has been greatly altered and restored.

A page from an early 6th-century manuscript, the *Vienna Genesis*, shows Jacob wrestling with the Angel.

EUROPEAN ART COLOR SLIDE CO.

The three kings carry gifts to the infant Jesus in a 6th-century mosaic in Sant'Apollinare Nuovo, Ravenna.

EUROPEAN ART COLOR SLIDE CO.

ART REFERENCE BUREAU

Facing Justinian across the chancel of San Vitale in Ravenna is his wife, the Empress Theodora, and her retinue. Her halo, like Justinian's, indicates rank rather than sanctity. She carries a chalice for the Mass.

PLATES 2 AND 3

The Judgment of Pilate decorates a page of the 6th-century *Rossano Gospels*. The figures of the *Rossano Gospels* exhibit a degree of withdrawn restraint and a lack of interest in three-dimensional modeling that suggests the frontal, linear style that is commonly associated with Bzyantine mosaic art.

EUROPEAN ART COLOR SLIDE CO.

EUROPEAN ART COLOR SLIDE CO.

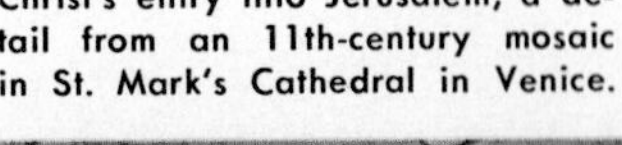

Christ's entry into Jerusalem, a detail from an 11th-century mosaic in St. Mark's Cathedral in Venice.

ART REFERENCE BUREAU

BRITISH MUSEUM

(Left) A page from the *Melissenda Psalter*, a sumptuously bound and illuminated 12th-century manuscript containing scenes from the life of Christ.

PLATE 4

(Right) Charity, one of the allegorical figures of the virtues that decorate St. Mark's.

Richly colored, animated scenes from the life of Christ are spread over the surfaces of the arches supporting the domes of the baptistery in St. Mark's.

SCALA, FROM SHOSTAL

BRITISH MUSEUM

ANDERSON, FROM ART REFERENCE BUREAU

GIRAUDON

BYZANTINE IVORIES. The panel of an archangel (*left*) and the throne of Archbishop Maximian (*center*) are from the First Golden Age. The panel of Christ crowning Emperor Roman IV and Empress Eudoxia (*right*) is from the 10th century.

seen against a shell-like niche with curtains at the sides. The heads have a degree of individuality uncommon in Byzantine mosaics. The Emperor and the Empress are distinguished by halos, used here as marks of rank, not of sanctity.

These mosaics lead up to the fine apse mosaic where Christ is seated on the globe flanked by angels and by San Vitale on one side and by Ecclesius, carrying a model of the church, on the other. The ground, like the draperies, is conventionalized, and the gold background, although laced with symbolic clouds, denies any sense of depth.

With the barbarian invasions of Italy and the west in the 5th century, Constantinople was the major beacon of civilization in Europe for the next two centuries, and Byzantine influence was felt even in Rome. For instance, the 7th century apse mosaic of Sant'Agnese outside the walls in Rome is formal, even rigid, in pose and costume. St. Agnes has become a Byzantine princess dressed in almost Oriental opulence, with a gold crown, gold and precious stones in her hair, a golden stole over her shoulders, and a violet tunic embroidered with gold.

Manuscripts. The three most important Byzantine manuscripts of the late 5th or the 6th century are the *Vienna Genesis* (Imperial Library, Vienna), the *Rossano Gospels* (Cathedral of Rossano, Italy), and the *Sinope Gospels* (Bibliothèque Nationale, Paris).

The *Vienna Genesis* is on purple vellum with silver lettering. The vivacious scenes, set at the bottom of each page, have many Byzantine details of costume and ceremony. Several successive events shown in a single picture preserve something of the "continuous narration" style, familiar from the relief on the Column of Trajan, Rome.

In the *Rossano Gospels,* also in silver on a purple ground, the miniatures may take a full page, or the top half of a page where the lower half is filled with four half-length figures. The figures are quieter and more dignified than those in the *Vienna Genesis.* The arrangement of the scenes, already standardized by the 5th century, persisted in Byzantine art for hundreds of years.

The *Sinope Gospels* are written in gold on purple. Here the miniatures are at the bottom of the page, flanked by two half-length figures rising out of what might be pulpits. In this manuscript, perspective, atmosphere, and setting are avoided even more persistently than in the mosaics of San Vitale.

Ivories. The most important surviving masterpiece of Byzantine ivory carving from the First Golden Age is the throne of Archbishop Maximian (mid-6th century) in the Cathedral of Ravenna. Its side panels have scenes from the life of Joseph in the narrative style. The Scythian or Sarmatian dress of Joseph's guards indicate contact with Asia, as do the tiaras (like those of Persian kings) worn by the sons of Jacob. The Egyptian headdresses of the merchants, and the very choice of the story of Joseph, suggest Egyptian influence. Five panels on the front of the throne show St. John the Baptist and the four evangelists. The figures are stiff, and the drapery is conventionalized. The main scenes and figures are framed by vine patterns, within whose scrolls appear peacocks, deer, lions, and other decorative motifs.

Another masterpiece of Byzantine ivory carving is the panel of an archangel in the British Museum, probably from the 6th century, though dated by some scholars as 4th century. The figure stands on a flight of steps with a staff in his left hand and an orb in his right. The drapery,

ALINARI, FROM ART REFERENCE BUREAU

THE LITTLE METROPOLITAN CHURCH in Athens, built in the 12th century, shows in small scale the late-Byzantine interest in decorating exterior surfaces.

more classical than Byzantine, is conventionalized less than draperies carved in the throne of Maximian. But the decorative effect and some of the architectural details in the archangel panel are characteristically Byzantine.

Some of the best examples of Byzantine ivory carving are consular diptychs, two-leaved panels made for Roman consuls, usually to commemorate the achievements of their office. Examples survive from the Roman period until well into the 6th century. One leaf usually presents figures, a scene, or a decorative motif, such as a wreath with an inscription. The other leaf generally depicts the consul, who is shown standing in the earlier, Roman diptychs but seated in the diptychs of the Eastern Empire. A good example is the diptych of the consul Flavius Anastasius (517; South Kensington Museum, London), which has the formalized style and embroidered costume of the early Byzantine period.

Iconoclastic Age. In 726 an edict of the Emperor Leo III forbade the representation of religious figures in churches and ordered the frescoed walls and mosaics to be whitewashed. The common people had come to attribute miraculous power to these images, a superstition that seemed to the emperor, and to many bishops for centuries before his time, a real menace to Christianity. Although Leo III did not enforce his edict very strictly, some of his 9th century successors were more rigid. Architecture was not directly affected, but for almost two centuries, iconoclasm eclipsed the representational arts of mosaic, fresco painting, and ivory carving. But the Iconoclasts, as the opponents of images were called, met vigorous opposition, particularly from the monks. The Empress Regent Theodora brought the iconoclastic period to an end in 842.

The Macedonian Renaissance. The Macedonian dynasty, which began with Basil I (reigned 867–886), gave Byzantine art and architecture a new lease on life. The art of Byzantium's Second Golden Age, as it is sometimes called, had a far-reaching influence. Venice, by virtue of its strong trade connections with Constantinople, became a cultural offshoot of the Eastern Empire, and the Cathedral of St. Mark in Venice is one of the great masterpieces of the late Byzantine style.

Architecture. The characteristic church plan of the late Byzantine period is a Greek cross whose four, almost equal arms are inscribed within a square. The plan had precedents in Roman tombs and in the 2d century Roman praetorium at Musmiyeh, Syria. Late Byzantine churches frequently have barrel vaults over the four arms of the cross and five domes, over the central crossing and in the four angles between the arms of the cross. The arrangement was quite logical structurally; the four barrel vaults abutted the central dome and were themselves abutted by the domes in the angles. Also during this period at least the central dome was usually raised above the rest of the building and given greater importance by the insertion below it of a masonry drum or cylinder. Eleventh century churches, such as St. Luke's in Phocis, Greece, show a growing concern with external appearance. Molded bands of decoration in stone or brick, some carving, and occasional use of color enrich these buildings. Few of these churches are large in scale; a charming vest-pocket edition is the Little Metropolitan Church (12th century) in Athens, with a dome that measures only 9 feet (2.7 meters) in diameter raised on a slender ornate drum.

The interiors of Byzantine churches of the 9th century and later are generally less impressive than those of earlier times. There is less dramatization of interior space, partly because of the smaller size of the buildings, partly because the cross-in-square plan broke up the interior, and partly because of the greater height of the buildings relative to their length and width. From inside the church these proportions give the viewer the impression that he is at the bottom of a space that extends vertically to the dome, but which is restricted horizontally.

The Basilica of St. Mark in Venice is the best-known example of later Byzantine architecture. It was rebuilt in the Byzantine style between 1063 and 1094. The Greek cross plan of St. Mark's has five domes, but unlike its Byzantine contemporaries, four of these were placed over the arms of the cross instead of between them. The plan was borrowed from the Church of the Holy Apostles (6th century, now destroyed) in Constantinople. The exotic appearance of St. Mark's today is the result of later additions. The domical constructions of wood and lead over the structural domes and much of the complicated detail, especially on the upper part of the building, were added during the Gothic period. But the lower part of the facade, with its multiple colonettes in colored marbles, and at least one of the mosaics above the doors are purely Byzantine, as is the whole interior. Most of the mosaics on the facade are Renaissance or modern in date, but the one farthest left as the viewer faces the church dates from the 13th century. It presents an illustration of St. Mark's as it looked before the Gothic and later additions were made.

Mosaics and Frescoes. The interior glory of these later Byzantine churches lies in their mosaics or in the frescoes sometimes substituted for the mosaics. The churches at Daphne and St. Luke's, Phocis, are excellent examples. A fine, though much later (early 14th century) example of these decorations is St. Saviour in Chora (also called Kahriye Camii or Kariye Djami) in Constantinople.

The arrangement of subjects within the church was dictated by dogma and is therefore nearly the same in all late Byzantine churches. In the center of the main dome is Christ Pantocrator, the all-powerful judge and ruler of mankind, set within a ring of varied colors. Below Him the Virgin, St. John the Baptist, and angels are frequently represented, and below them the prophets. The evangelists generally fill the four main pendentives, serving as intermediaries between the heavenly figures above and the historical or Scriptural themes below. The Virgin and archangels occupy the half-dome of the apse, with Christ below them flanked by angels; beneath these is depicted the institution of the Eucharist and the fathers of the church. Also within the sanctuary may be Scriptural events or figures identified as prototypes of Christ. Elsewhere on the vaults and upper part of the walls in those areas of the church normally open to the laity are the twelve great festivals of the church, from the Annunciation through the Crucifixion and Resurrection, to the death of Mary. Below these may be shown miracles, events from the life of the Virgin, and figures of saints. Near the entrance to the church is pictured the Last Judgment.

Although some latitude was permitted, the general outline of this scheme was so standard that it was incorporated in handbooks for artists. The purpose of the mosaic and fresco decorations was clearly didactic—to give visual reinforcement to the church year and church dogma. Nevertheless, the results at their best are magnificently decorative. The last traces of the Roman past have vanished from these highly stylized figures, which have almost no three-dimensional elements. On the contrary, draperies have become mere patterns of lines, such as concentric circles or ovals to suggest thighs or breasts. In proportion the figures tend to be more elongated than in earlier mosaics and frescoes. The colors were almost as rigidly dictated as the subjects, and a plain gold background denies any sense of space in most of the decorations.

Few buildings anywhere have a more richly colored interior than St. Mark's with its polychromed marble floors, columns, and lower walls, and its mosaics that completely cover the upper walls and vaults, not only within the church itself but in the narthex, or vestibule. In the three domes of the nave and their supporting arches are mosaics from the 11th century; the narthex mosaics are mostly 13th century.

The major devotional panels in St. Mark's, such as the one representing the Madonna flanked by two saints, are as hieratic and dignified as contemporary mosaics, manuscripts, and ivories from Constantinople. The Virgin and Christ Child are impersonal, distant creations, whose slender, curved fingers have become a linear formula. Below them are highly stylized allegorical figures of the virtues, with draperies that express the human body less than they resemble contour maps of hilly country. The inscriptions here are in Latin; in the churches of Constantinople they are in Greek.

Scenes from the life of Christ adorn the arches supporting the domes of the nave in St. Mark's. These narrative panels are more animated though no more realistic in most respects than the other mosaics. One of the most lively

ALINARI, FROM ART REFERENCE BUREAU

ST MARK'S in Venice, the most famous late-Byzantine structure, displays an exuberant exoticism that is partly the result of Gothic and Renaissance decorative additions.

ANDERSON, FROM ART REFERENCE BUREAU

BYZANTINE MOSAICS cover almost all available surfaces of the apse of the 12th-century Norman church in Monreale, Sicily. A half-length image of Christ in benediction dominates the apse.

panels illustrates the Resurrection; the risen Christ, trampling underfoot a grotesque figure of Satan, holds the cross in his left hand, while with his right hand he raises the kneeling Adam from hell.

Another panel illustrates Christ's entry into Jerusalem. Christ's steed walks over garments strewn in his path. Lines suggest the ground, while a palm tree and a conventionalized tower-like form symbolizing a city reveal the setting despite the customary gold background. St. Peter and two other apostles are seen behind Christ; the presence of the other nine apostles is indicated simply by fragments of their halos. Indeed, it was quite common in Byzantine mosaics to suggest a crowd by showing several full-length figures with only bits of other figures appearing above or behind them.

The 13th century mosaics in the narthex of St. Mark's illustrate the building of the Tower of Babel, Noah and the Ark, and other Old Testament scenes that had been more common themes in earlier Byzantine art.

Most of the mosaics of Hagia Sophia were covered by whitewash, plaster, or screens after the Turkish conquest of Constantinople. In 1931 the American archaeologist Thomas Whittemore, with the aid of the Turkish government, began to uncover these mosaics. Some of those in the narthex, jeweled crosses and other designs on a gold ground, date from the 6th century, but most are later in style. The central lunette of the narthex shows Emperor Leo VI (reigned 886–912) kneeling before an enthroned Christ. A 10th century mosaic in the southern vestibule presents the Virgin and Child, with Justinian at the left holding a model of the church and Constantine on the right with a model of the city. The south gallery has two important mosaics. The first shows Christ in the attitude of blessing, flanked by Emperor Constantine IX Monomachus and Empress Zoë, who ruled jointly from 1042 until 1050. The second mosaic depicts the Virgin with Emperor John II Comnenus (reigned 1118–1143) and his mother, Empress Irene. Here also is the important, though fragmentary, 12th century panel of Christ, the Virgin, and St. John the Baptist. In these mosaics the jeweled costumes, stylized folds of drapery, and gold backgrounds are characteristic of the 12th century. The imperial portraits, though far from being realistic, are by no means stereotyped.

Manuscripts. Some manuscripts of the 10th century, such as the *Paris Psalter* (Bibliothèque Nationale, Paris), suggest a classical Renaissance harking back to figure types of late antique origin. But most of the later Byzantine manuscripts are as similar in style to the mosaics of the time as the differences of technique would permit. The principles and the types of Byzantine manuscripts tend to be fixed from the end of the 9th century, and in the 10th and 11th centuries the art reached its apex, with a progressive decline following this period. The figures, which have a majestic hieratic effect, are anti-realistic in their rigidity, their static poses, and their formal linear outlines of body and drapery. Such stately figures as the portraits of Emperor Basil I and Empress Eudocia with her sons in the *Sermons of St. Gregory Nazianzen* (Bibliothèque Nationale, Paris) are reminiscent in their stiffness and their sumptuous jeweled costumes of imperial portraits in the later mosaics of Hagia Sophia.

A very typical 12th century manuscript is the *Melissenda Psalter* (British Museum), its binding adorned with ivory carvings and studded with turquoises and rubies. Its 24 full-page scenes from the life of Christ were drawn and signed by a Greek craftsman, Basileus. The colors are unusually rich but somewhat discordant. The malproportioned figures with their linear draperies are set against a plain gold background with no more details of setting than is absolutely required by the subject.

Ivories. One of the best examples of late Byzantine ivory carving is a fine plaque in the Stroganoff Collection, Rome, probably from the 10th century. It depicts the Virgin enthroned with the Christ Child in her lap and half-length figures of angels in the upper corners. For all the flat linearism of the draperies, the carver has endowed the Virgin with a majestic dignity, austere but impressive.

Another masterpiece is the 10th century panel of Christ crowning Emperor Roman IV and Empress Eudoxia (Cabinet des Médailles, Paris). The composition is rigidly symmetrical; Christ stands on a pedestal in the center and places his hands on the crowns of the two rulers, whose poses are nearly mirror images of each other. The drapery of Christ is linear but has substantial breadth, while the drapery of the royal figures are of the jeweled richness familiar from similar subjects in mosaics and manuscripts.

Diffusion of Byzantine Art and Architecture. The influence of Byzantine art and architecture spread even farther than Venice. The plan of St. Front (about 1120), in Périgueux, in western France, was almost identical with St. Mark's, although the French did not attempt the color decoration. Many buildings in this part of France adopted the Byzantine dome on pendentives.

In the Sicilian Romanesque, too, the Byzantine influence was obvious, less in the plan or structure than in the mosaics and colored marbles of the floors and walls. Fine cycles of mosaics may be seen in the Cathedral of Monreale and in the Church of La Martorana and the Cappella Palatina, both in Palermo.

Byzantine influence also extended to the east of the empire, even before the Macedonian dynasty. The dating of Armenian churches is often uncertain. St. Hripsimeh, in Echmiadzin, may have been built as early as 618, but it has been so much restored that it now appears considerably later in style. The Church of Achthamar (10th century) on Lake Van and the Cathedral of Ani (1001) are typical Armenian Churches of Byzantine style. In the former, tall, V-shaped niches in the outer walls define the limits of the chancel, while flat, pancakelike figures are cut into the volcanic stone facing of the walls. A tall drum topped by a pyramidal roof encloses the dome over the center.

When the Venetians, in 1204, diverted the Fourth Crusade to attack Constantinople, a Latin empire was set up there, destined to last only until 1261. The assault from the west, coupled with the Muslim pressure from the east, permanently weakened the Byzantine Empire, and, although it lingered on for two centuries more, Constantinople never regained its former brilliance. Many of the later buildings were small and were erected in the provinces. No single type of plan was dominant; some churches, like St. Basil in Arta, Greece, were simple wooden-roofed basilicas; others perpetuated the characteristic plan of the Macedonian dynasty, as in the Church of the Holy Apostles, Salonika (early 14th century). The drums beneath the domes were so heightened and the domes themselves so small in some cases that they give the effect of towers. An example is the Grachanitsa Monastery in Priština, Yugoslavia (about 1320). This emphasis on the vertical, perhaps the effect of Gothic influence from western Europe, is also apparent in the monastery (after 1407) at Manasija in Yugoslavia, which has moldings on the vertical angles of the building.

After the conquest of Constantinople in 1453 by the Ottoman Turks, the Byzantine style continued in modified form in Russia. The plans had their basis in earlier precedent, as did the color, but the onion-shaped domes of the Cathedral of the Annunciation (1482–1490) in Moscow and the adjacent Cathedral of the Archangel Michael (1505–1509) are peculiar to Russia and the Islamic countries. These later buildings became, in a sense, baroque versions of the great Byzantine style of earlier days.

EVERARD M. UPJOHN, *Columbia University*

Bibliography

Ainalov, Dmitrii Vlasevich, *The Hellenistic Origins of Byzantine Art* (New Brunswick, N. J., 1961).
Anthony, Edgar Waterman, *A History of Mosaics* (Boston 1935).
Beckwith, John, *The Art of Constantinople* (Greenwich, Conn., 1961).
Council of Europe, *Byzantine Art: An European Art* (Athens 1964).
Demus, Otto, *Byzantine Mosaic Decoration* (London 1953).
Grabar, André, *Byzantine Painting* (Geneva 1953).
Hamilton, John Arnott, *Byzantine Architecture and Decoration,* 2d edition (New York 1956).
Herbert, John Alexander, *Illuminated Manuscripts* (London 1912).
Krautheimer, Richard, *Early Christian and Byzantine Architecture* (Baltimore 1965).
Liddell, Robert, *Byzantium and Istanbul* (London 1956).
MacDonald, William L., *Early Christian and Byzantine Architecture* (New York 1962).
Michelés, Panayotis A., *An Aesthetic Approach to Byzantine Art* (London 1955).
Rice, David Talbot, *Byzantine Art* (Baltimore 1962).
Stewart, Cecil, *Byzantine Legacy* (London 1947).
Stewart, Cecil, *Early Christian, Byzantine and Romanesque Architecture* (New York 1954).
Swift, Emerson Howland, *Hagia Sophia* (New York 1940).

For Specialized Study

Agnello, Giuseppe, *L'architettura bizantina in Sicilia* (Florence 1952).
Cross, Samuel H., *Mediaeval Russian Churches* (Cambridge, Mass., 1949).
Der Nersessian, Sirarpie, *Armenia and the Byzantine Empire* (New York 1945).
Downey, Glanville, *Byzantine Architects, Their Training and Methods* (Brussels 1948).
Hamilton, George Heard, *The Art and Architecture of Russia* (Harmondsworth, Eng., 1954).
Hoddinott, Ralph F., *Early Byzantine Churches in Macedonia and Southern Serbia* (New York 1963).
Lemerle, Paul, *Le style byzantin* (Paris 1943).
Mathew, Gervase, *Byzantine Aesthetics* (London 1963).
Swift, Emerson Howland, *Roman Sources of Christian Art* (New York 1951).
Underwood, Paul A., *The Kariye Djami,* 3 vols. (New York 1966).
Whittemore, Thomas, *The Mosaics of St. Sophia at Istanbul,* 4 vols. (Paris 1933–42).

MARBURG, FROM ART REFERENCE BUREAU

WESTERN INFLUENCE in late Byzantine architecture is discernible in the strong vertical angles of the 15th-century monastery at Manasija, Yugoslavia.

BYZANTINE EMPIRE, biz'ən-tēn, is an expression in use since the Renaissance to identify the Roman Empire after the transfer of imperial administration by Emperor Constantine I (Constantine the Great) from Rome to Constantinople in 334 A. D. The term "Byzantine" is, in fact, a misnomer. The new capital certainly rose on the site of a much earlier Hellenic colony on the European side of the Bosporus, and this colony had been called Byzantium. Moreover, some archaizing Roman Empire writers of the Middle Ages did occasionally use this name for their city. But the successors of Constantine I, right down to the fall of Constantinople in 1453 A. D., never thought of or referred to themselves as "Byzantines." They considered themselves "Romans," the sole heirs to and representatives of the imperial tradition of Augustus Caesar. This tradition implied the stupendous pretension that the empire was divinely ordained and one day would reassert its dominion over all the territories once ruled by Trajan (reigned 98–117 A. D.) or by Constantine the Great himself (reigned 324–337 A. D.). It is now too late to discard the term "Byzantine." But it must never be forgotten that it is a modern, and inaccurate, term for the inhabitants of the Roman Empire as it survived during 11 centuries (334–1453) in the eastern Mediterranean, governed from Constantinople.

During these centuries, as was natural, vast changes occurred in the body of the empire, changes that were territorial, administrative, demographic, mercantile, and military in nature. What never changed was the Christian-imperial idea; and as this was the doctrine, faith, and hope to which every "Byzantine" unquestioningly adhered, and for which he lived and died, it is important to be clear about its axioms.

The Christian-Imperial Idea. Every Roman, at least from the time of Augustus, believed in the divine right of Rome to be the single empire of the world, with a duty to preserve universal peace. This right and duty were deduced from the practical successes of Rome's splendid armies and from the theoretical sanction of its chief god, Jupiter. But the appeal of orthodox paganism was feeble, and in the 3d century A. D. the empire, threatened by barbarian assault and internal economic collapse, seemed in danger of complete disruption for lack of a faith to hold it together. It was the genius or good fortune of Constantine the Great, the founder of Constantinople, that harnessed to the old imperial idea the new and powerful dynamic of Christianity, though, of course, some modifications in the creed of humility and love had to be made to fit it for its new purpose.

The Christian-Roman imperial idea ultimately crystallized as follows. Augustus Caesar and Jesus were contemporaries. That was no accident. The one unified and brought peace to the empire. The other Prince of Peace was sent into this world to interpret the celestial order to the material creation. This celestial order was regarded as a single empire, with a monarch, a governing hierarchy, and an angelic army organized in legions. According to this theory, Jesus said that His Father willed that this temporal world should be similarly organized, that is, it should be a unity under the rule of Rome alone. Hence, successive Roman emperors were considered to be elected by Almighty God Himself, chosen by Him to carry out His will for the government and pacification of the created world. The emperor was, under God, all-powerful. Thus, he was regarded as the supreme governor, the supreme proprietor, the commander in chief, the source of law, the origin of all offices, and the fount of all honors. His duties were to interpret the divine will, to impose and protect orthodox Christian belief, to govern his subjects with mercy and justice, and to advance that moment when all the inhabited world should kneel in homage and offer their riches to the earthly vicegerent of Christ. Emperors so privileged were, in theory, unassailable by malice or treason. In practice, they were very frequently deposed or assassinated. But this did not invalidate the purposes of God; it merely meant that God had withdrawn His favor from an unworthy ruler and conferred it on a new elect. Therefore a successful usurper was the appointed of God, as his predecessor had been before him.

The tenet that Byzantium should one day rule again over the Mediterranean and European possessions of Augustus and Constantine the Great (the *oikoumenē,* or "inhabited world") appeared, especially in and after the 7th century, to be hopelessly chimerical. The empire, except during two centuries of expansion between approximately 850 and 1050, grew ever smaller and weaker. But this did not weaken the prime postulate of empire. If the promised consummation seemed to recede rather than to approach until, in the 14th and 15th centuries, it reached the vanishing point, it was believed that this was due to no change in God's purpose, but to the "sins" of His people. These sins were partly moral, but also, and more important, doctrinal. Thus, the catastrophic decline in Byzantine power between the death of Emperor Michael VIII Palaeologus in 1282 and the Ottoman conquest of Constantinople in 1453 was, in the eyes of church and people, due not to social, economic, or military causes, but to repeated compromises on the part of the Palaeologan sovereigns with Catholic "heresies." The consequent alienation of God (despite His "long-suffering") from His chosen people was inevitable and inexorable.

It is important to note that among the several strands that combined to weave this imperial theory, the Jewish Old Testament, as interpreted by the early Christian Fathers, was by far the strongest. It was from the denunciations of Leviticus and Deuteronomy, and from the messianic utterances of the prophet Isaiah, that the Christian Romans derived their ideas of themselves as the chosen race, of their city as the "new Jerusalem," of their sovereignty as natural and God-given, and, above all, of sin as the direct cause of every setback or disaster. This theory implied a very curious egocentricity. For the Byzantines, foreigners or outsiders had no independent significance or even existence except insofar as they contributed to fulfilling or hindering God's purposes for His earthly empire. They were merely His rods for chastening those whom He loved.

Government and Culture. Two other elements of prime importance that remained constant during all the long life of the empire were the method of government and the cultural background. The method of government was bureaucratic. The later emperors inherited from the earlier the system of administration by a bureaucracy of laymen. Medieval Europe had no comparable system. Indeed, in the empire itself, from the 11th century, the long and eventually success-

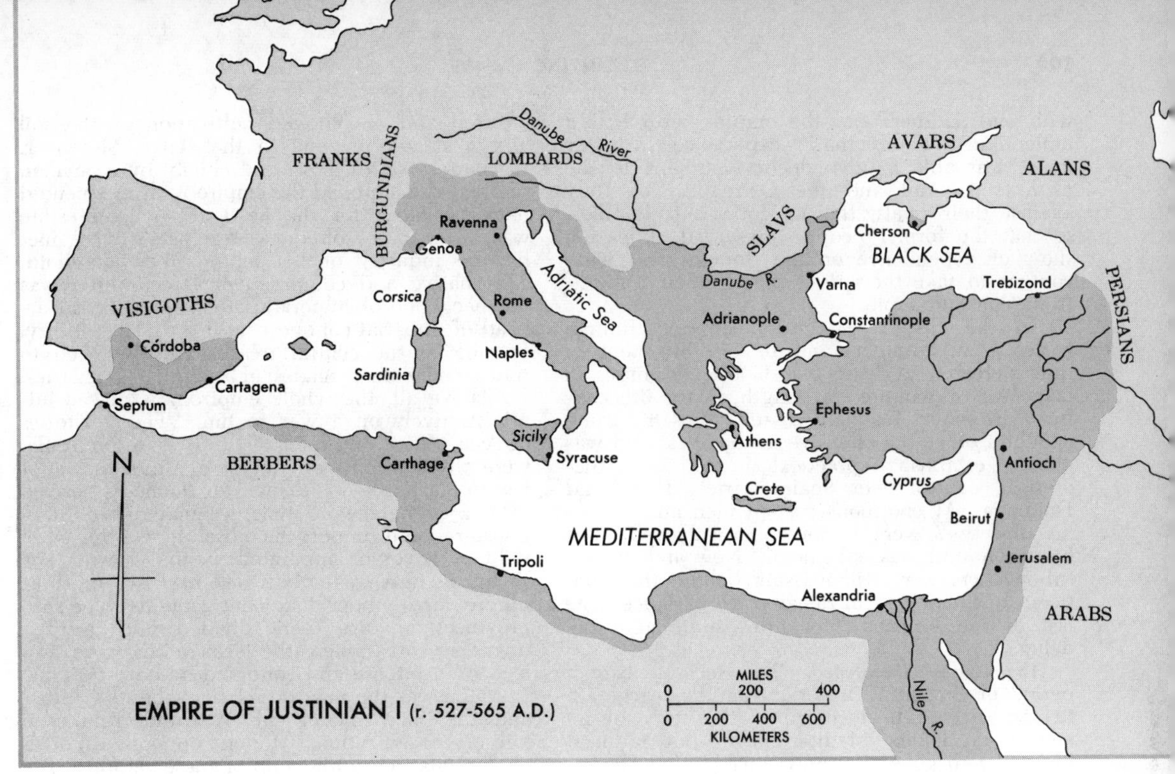

EMPIRE OF JUSTINIAN I (r. 527-565 A.D.)

ful revolt of landed proprietors against government by civil servants was a chief cause of the state's decay and ultimately of its extinction. The departments of the central treasury, of the vast imperial estates, of the war office, and of foreign affairs (which included imperial communications and the secret service) all changed their titles and modified their respective functions from time to time. But in all ages they were manned by a hierarchy of highly educated clerks. These bureaucrats were the most characteristic product of Byzantine civilization. They owed their promotion to their own abilities, were intensely proud of their tradition, and did more than any other class to preserve the Byzantines' conviction of their innate superiority over all other portions of mankind.

Much of their arrogance and self-righteousness was derived from their "Greek" education. The official language of the empire from the 7th century was Greek, and even before then, Greek had been far more commonly spoken than Latin in Asia Minor, the heart of the eastern empire. The backbone of this (Hellenistic) Greek cultural tradition was the study of late Greek rhetoric, which taught its students to be quick and, as they believed, graceful and eloquent of speech. They scarcely understood the cultural heritage of ancient Hellas, as it has been recovered in Western Europe since the Renaissance, and lyric poetry and ancient art were closed books to them. But their pride in their "Hellenic" letters led to the preservation of Greek classical literature, insofar as it has been preserved. And the fact that the New Testament and patristic literature used, in the main, the same language reinforced the Byzantines' belief in their exclusive possession of all that was of value in literary and religious writings.

Orthodoxy. Last, but by far the most important, of the common elements was Christianity. Every Byzantine passionately believed in his "orthodox" version of this creed. Not only did it give him an imperial faith in his own destiny and importance; it also gave him a genuine and inspiring love of the basic Christian qualities—charity, humility before God, a desire to seek after knowledge of Him, and, at the end, to achieve a personal "deification." The true Byzantine, lacking as he was in intellectual genius or originality, pursued, in no merely formal fashion, the virtues of peace, kindliness, purity, and brotherly love. The conduct of the higher clergy, in a church which, politically speaking, had been established by Constantine I as yet one more department of the state, might seem to belie this statement, marred as this conduct all too often was by envy, rancor, and personal ambition. Its lower orders, comprising the secular priests, the monastic communities, and the ranks of popular saints, present a different picture, one which is peopled from age to age by good men who despised worldly things and trod, according to their lights, in the steps of their Master. Christianity was the vital influence, and therewith the saving virtue, of Byzantium.

Thus, in sum, the Byzantine Empire may be depicted throughout its existence as the legitimate heir of the old, bureaucratically governed Roman Empire, but with these modifications. First, its ultimate triumph was thought to be guaranteed by a Christian and messianic, instead of a pagan and fatalistic, sanction. Second, its official, but never its universal, language was no longer Roman Latin but Roman Greek. Third, its culture consequently rested on some of the classical Greek authors and on handbooks of the Hellenistic era.

Political Developments—*Early Period.* Byzantine political developments must next be summarized briefly in order to see how the state confronted its disasters or used its triumphs. In the 4th to 6th century—from about 370 to 570—the chief perils of the Mediterranean empire came from Germanic invaders. Britain and Spain, and for a time Gaul, Italy, and Africa, were wholly lost to the Saxons, the Goths, the Franks, and the Vandals. But these tribes inevitably quarreled with one another; and the empire, with half a millennium of diplomatic experience to draw upon, was able to give decisive support to the Franks of Gaul and the Ostrogoths of Italy against their rivals, the Visigoths and Vandals, so that the former peoples preserved at least a show of dependence on the Romans and were content to take their titles, if not their policies, from Constantinople.

In the eastern Mediterranean the Roman forces were stronger, and in the 5th century they defeated at least two Gothic attempts to take over the empire. At length, in the 6th century, Emperor Justinian I felt himself strong enough to take the offensive in the West and was able to establish a practical, instead of a theoretical, control over Spain, Africa, Italy, and Dalmatia. At enormous cost in men and money his objectives were in the main achieved. But his reconquest was ephemeral. New and powerful invaders were still massing behind the frontiers. Justinian was, in Renaissance parlance, "the last of the Romans"; for after him came the deluge.

The Empire Threatened. The second distinct period of Byzantine history, from the early 7th to the early 11th century, is the story of an empire no longer Mediterranean, but reduced (by 750) to governing only Asia Minor, Thrace, some islands, and the foot of Italy. During the first part of this period, reconquered Italy was mostly lost to the Germanic Lombards; the Greek peninsula to the Slavs; and Syria, Palestine, Egypt, and North Africa to the Arabs, who, converted to Islam (the "Surrender to God"), erupted in 632 from the Arabian Peninsula.

Of these menaces, the last was by far the most formidable, since it threatened the very life and heart of the empire itself. Twice, in 674 and 717, massive Muslim attacks were made on Constantinople itself. They were repelled only by the strength of the Theodosian walls and by the energy and resolution of emperors Constantine IV (reigned 668–685) and Leo III (reigned 717–741). Moreover, from 680 the power of the Bulgarians was permanently established between the Danube River and the Balkan Mountains and for centuries constituted a threat nearly as serious as that of the Muslims. It is astonishing that the empire not only failed to succumb to, but actually surmounted, these traumatic experiences with undimmed faith and vigor and at length, in the Age of Conquest (about 863 to 1025), succeeded in recovering a substantial part of what had been lost.

Imperial Reorganization. Two expedients were adopted to meet the crises. The first of these was the wholesale importation into Asia Minor of Slavs, who restored agriculture on a new system of land tenure, and of Armenians, who by their genius for war and administration rehabilitated the army and government. Second, the Christian-imperial idea was intensified, inspiring the Byzantines, as the upholders of the tradition of ecumenical Rome, with a more mystical notion of Christ's purpose—His empire's ultimate recovery. A discussion of both these phenomena is of the utmost importance in gaining an understanding of the achievements of the period.

The immigrants were settled in villages, or "communes," where they lived as small farmers with free rights of sale or alienation of their properties. In return, they paid taxes to the central treasury at regularly revised rates. This ensured and encouraged cultivation of the soil and a steady revenue to the state. Moreover, the better estates, possessed chiefly by Armenian settlers, also supplied the empire with its splendid native cavalry; for the head of such an estate was a full-time soldier, whose needs were met by the industry of his family and household. This native and comparatively free militia was the backbone of imperial defense and the spearhead of imperial conquest until the 11th century. It relieved the central treasury of the need to rely heavily on brigades of foreign mercenaries.

Above all, the whole empire was placed administratively on a war footing. The territories of Asia Minor, and later of the Balkan Peninsula, were divided into provinces, or "themes," subject to martial law ("theme," or *thema*, is derived from a cognate word that designated a military register), and under the absolute control of a military governor appointed by the crown. The theme in turn was subdivided into two or three subprovinces, under lieutenant generals. The subprovinces in turn were divided into garrison towns, or forts, where the local militia were subject to an intense and continual military training.

Such was the new population, the new order, and the "new model" of Byzantine rural and military organization. Modern opinions differ as to the date and authorship of these reforms. But the Byzantines themselves attributed them, probably correctly, to the house of Heraclius (approximately 610–711).

All this was achieved without any compromise of the "Imperial Faith." The immigrants were systematically Byzantinized by the Christian church and the government machine. Instead of the old tradition of the Fortune of Rome, still strong in the early period of Constantine I and Justinian I, Christ and His divine mother and His saints were believed to be in sole charge of imperial policies and direction. And Christ was understood to make these known through mystical communication to His elect, the Roman emperor.

Some centuries (about 250 years in all) passed before the fusion was complete. Political objectives were, during this period, often frustrated by savage religious disputes, of which the Iconoclast controversy (726–787 and 815–843) was the most disruptive. But at last, in the middle of the 9th century, the whole machine began to operate efficiently. The Muslims were decisively checked in 863. Four years later (867) the gifted Armenian dynasty of the so-called Macedonian, or "Basilid," house was founded by Basil I, and it ruled until 1056.

The Age of Conquest. During this 189 years, the Age of Conquest was consummated. Basil I himself converted and Byzantinized the Slavic settlers of Greece and Dalmatia. John Curcuas, the brave general of Romanus I (reigned 920–944), broke through the Muslim border that ran from Trebizond to Tarsus, and reestablished Byzantine influence in Armenia and Georgia. The usurper Nicephorus II Phocas (reigned 963–969) recaptured Crete, Cyprus, Tarsus, Aleppo, and Antioch. His successor John I (reigned 969–976), the most gifted general in Byzantine history, smashed a powerful Russian (Varangian) invasion of Bulgaria, and then, turning eastwards, put nearly all of Phoenicia and Palestine under Roman protection.

John was succeeded by the legitimate emperor, Basil II (reigned 976–1025), the great-

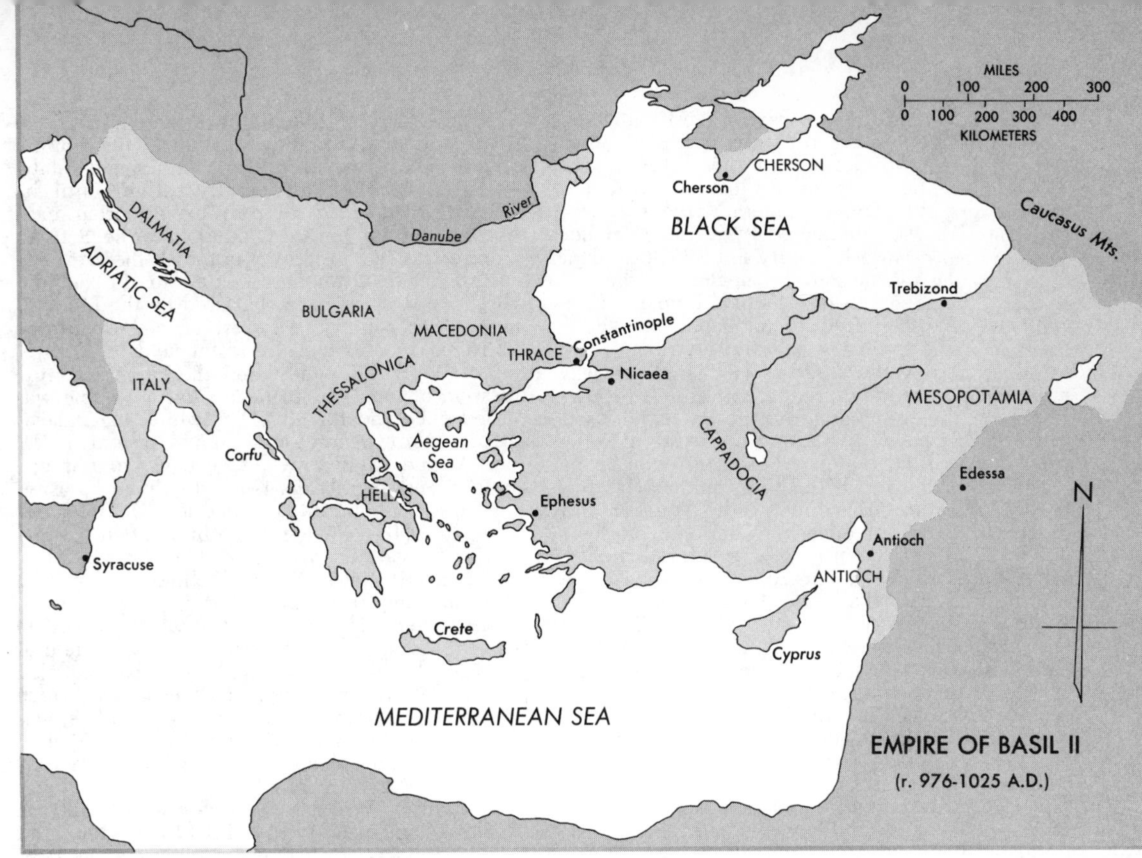

EMPIRE OF BASIL II
(r. 976-1025 A.D.)

great-grandson of Basil I. The energy and ability of this outstanding leader brought Byzantine power to its apogee. With unfailing tenacity he put down the successive revolts of the military aristocrats and succeeded in taking over intact the splendid military machine that they had forged and led to victory. With it he conquered the whole of Bulgaria (991–1019) and pushed the eastern frontier far to the east of Lake Van. There can be no doubt that Basil intended to restore the territorial empire of Justinian I, if not that of Augustus, in the West. He maneuvered unsuccessfully to get the papacy under his control. He next tried, by the expedient of a dynastic marriage, to link the then enormous dominions of Byzantium with those, almost equally large, of the Saxon emperors of the West. But he was frustrated by the death of the Western Emperor Otto III. At last he contemplated the conquest of Sicily and Italy. Time was not on his side, and in 1025 he died at the age of 68. With his death the practical possibility of restoring the old Roman Empire vanished forever.

Decline. The third period in Byzantine history, the period of Byzantium in slow decline, lasted from the 11th to the 15th century—approximately 1025–1453. In this increasingly confused period, certain aspects or trends stand out. First, there was the military decline, due to social conflicts, and the consequent return to dependence on foreign mercenaries, which bankrupted the state. Second, the empire developed a decisively Western orientation once the bulk of Asia Minor had been occupied by the Seljuk Turks (1073 and after). Third, there arose out of the second aspect a native Byzantine reaction against the repeated attempts of the rulers to compromise with Catholic "heresies" in order to prolong, with the aid of Western arms, the life of their state.

The populace of Constantinople and the Byzantine bureaucracy preserved to the last the age-old concept of the *pax Romana*. They hated war, and in consequence everything to do with soldiering. Hence they were in sharp conflict with the military aristocracy, whose trade was fighting. This aristocracy had arisen in and after the 7th century. It was mainly of Armenian stock, and in course of time it had become a dominant caste of intermarrying clans. High command was their monopoly, and the military system of provincial government played into their hands. These two powerful classes—civil and military—were keen competitors for the acquisition of landed properties and estates.

Basil II was the last emperor who was powerful enough to compose their enmities and control their rapacity. After his death, their disastrous feuds, which took no account of the steadily worsening foreign situation, sapped the strength of the empire. This ruin was accelerated by the success of the bureaucrats in continuing to reserve the imperial crown to their nominees during almost all of the next fateful half century (1025–1071). Military appropriations were cut to the bone, the soldiers encouraged to buy exemptions from service, their hereditary leaders vilified and insulted. Yet it would be unjust to put on the bureaucratic party all the blame for Byzantium's decline. The military aristocrats were at least as much responsible for it, since their continual encroachments on the estates of the native militia destroyed the very foundation of the state's war machine. The whole principle of a free soldiery—fighting for, and paying taxes to, the emperor—was crippled when the soldiers' estates were bought up by the "powerful" (as the nobles were called), and the soldiers themselves became serfs.

The splendid edifice of Basil II crumbled into ruin in an unbelievably short space of time. The year 1071 marked the collapse in West and East. The Norman invaders of Italy occupied Bari, the capital of Byzantine southern Italy. On the field of Manzikert, on August 19, a Roman force, painfully scraped together by Emperor Romanus IV, was annihilated by a much smaller force of Seljuk Turkish cavalry led by Alp Arslan. Owing to the dissolution and neglect of the native, or "thematic," brigades, this "Roman" army consisted almost entirely of mercenaries, half of them cowards, the other half traitors.

The irretrievable disaster of Manzikert was a direct cause of the crusading movement (1097–1291), in the sense that Byzantium had ceased to be a great power separating the western European and Muslim worlds. This confrontation of the European powers with Byzantium was fatal to the latter. From the beginning, the Frankish and especially the Norman leaders had had at least one eye on the empire, which offered riches, estates, and plunder far more alluring than those of Muslim Syria or Palestine. The conviction that Byzantium had very little strength to defend its enormous riches grew during the 12th century. And with this conviction came the belief that, as a race of cunning and treacherous swindlers, the Romans had "no right" to continue as possessors of their own lands. The hatred between Byzantines and the "heretical" Franks at length surpassed any that Christians had ever felt for pagans or Muslims. In the notorious Fourth Crusade (1204) Frankish fanaticism, skillfully manipulated by Venetian statesmanship, was turned on Constantinople. The city was stormed, a Frank was set up as emperor of the Latin Empire of Constantinople, and the Byzantine territories were partitioned among the conquerors. In this fearful sack, accompanied by devastating fires, much of the heritage of the ancient as well as of the medieval Byzantine world perished forever.

Following this, an unlikely development took place. The legitimate Byzantine power, instead of becoming extinct, took root in the neighboring city of Nicaea, beyond the Bosporus. Under the brilliant house of Lascaris (1204–1258), the old empire rallied, and evinced a renascent freshness and expansion not seen since the 9th century. It surpassed its only significant Greek rival, the Despotate of Epirus. In half a century, sound economic and military policies and brilliant diplomacy brought this new realm to a commanding position from which it could reclaim the old capital of Constantinople from the remnants of the Western Crusading dynasty (1261).

The recovery of Constantinople by the Greek "Romans" was inevitable, but also, in the long term, probably a disaster. Once more the dead weight of a millennial tradition settled down on the empire; and in recovering the old city, it disinterred also the old illusion of world supremacy. There were no men or money to make good the claim. Michael VIII Palaeologus (reigned 1259–1282), who recaptured the city, was an able man and an adroit diplomatist, the last Roman emperor who had any claim to being a major figure in European history. But he saw, as his far less competent successors also saw, that some kind of religious concordat with Rome was essential if Western support was to be secured against the encroaching Muslims. All efforts at compromise with the Catholics (as in 1274, 1369, and 1439) were denounced by theOrthodox party, which saw clearly that Westerners, if they came at all, would come not as allies but as robbers.

In the 13th to 15th centuries there arose three great contenders for the reversion of the empire. Charles, the Angevin king of Naples and Sicily, headed a coalition against Byzantium until he was forced in 1282 to turn his attention to a rebellion within his own kingdom. The Serbian Empire was left to fight it out with the Ottoman Turks. These Ottomans, related to the Seljuks, whose empire had been shattered by the Mongols in the 13th century, were established in Europe by 1350. In 1389, on the fatal field of Kosovo, Sultan Bayezid I annihilated the Serbs, and the question of who was to have Constantinople was settled once and for all. Meanwhile, the Palaeologan emperors Andronicus II and Andronicus III, John V and John VI Cantacuzenus, fought one another and merely hastened the final disaster. The last emperor, Constantine XI Dragases (reigned 1449–1453), had nothing left to defend but his capital and his honor. On May 29, 1453, the great city fell to Sultan Mehmed II, and the Christian Empire of East Rome ceased to exist.

Evaluation. The history of Byzantium was, in western Europe, long regarded as a sorry tale of political degeneracy, of religious obscurantism, and of debased morality. This estimate, which arose from ignorance and religious prejudice, was altogether unfair and mistaken. The creation of a theocratic idea that could preserve a state during 11 centuries is proof of uncommon ability and vitality. Weakness is certainly the hallmark of Byzantium in and after the 12th century, but a civilization is entitled to be judged at its best, rather than at its worst.

In the 9th to 11th century, Byzantium was the strongest and richest state in the Western world. Byzantium's influence was almost everywhere beneficent. Its missionary work among noncivilized peoples, especially the Slavs, was of the utmost historical importance. It possessed, almost to the end, an artistic genius that today can only be appreciated from the tiny fraction of its products that survive to us; and this artistic genius was placed in the service of the propagation of the Christian religion (see BYZANTINE ART AND ARCHITECTURE). The empire was, it is true, destitute of the poetic faculty; yet even the feeble literary endeavors of Byzantium were productive of a great good: the preservation of some small part of the ancient Greek classics. The people to the last preserved a tincture of the old Greco-Roman civilization; and Byzantine manners were, in comparison with those of the medieval West, mild and even humane. Above all, the Byzantine Empire stood firm when its collapse would probably have meant the extinction of Christian Europe. When at last Byzantium fell, the modern world was already far advanced on its course of achievement and progress. Dying, Byzantium passed on its imperial heritage to Moscow—the Third Rome.

ROMILLY J. H. JENKINS, *Harvard University*

Bibliography

Baynes, North H., *The Byzantine Empire,* rev. ed. (London 1943).

Hussey, Joan M., ed., *The Byzantine Empire,* vol. 4 (2 parts) of *The Cambridge Medieval History,* (New York and London 1966–1967).

Hussey, Joan M., *The Byzantine World* (New York 1957).

Jenkins, Romilly J. H., *Byzantium: The Imperial Centuries,* A. D. *610–1071* (New York 1966).

Ostrogorsky, George, *History of the Byzantine State,* tr. by Joan Hussey (New Brunswick, N. J., 1957).

Vasiliev, Alexander A., *History of the Byzantine Empire,* 2 vols., (Madison, Wis., 1952).

BYZANTINE MUSIC, biz'ən-tēn, is the music of the Byzantine Empire (q.v.) that survives as the music of the Eastern churches, both Catholic and Orthodox. As is the case with the great bulk of Byzantine visual art, most extant Byzantine music is sacred. Much the same can be said of western European music contemporary with Byzantine music, since in both East and West it was almost exclusively in monastic and other ecclesiastical centers of culture that music, largely intended for ritual purposes, was preserved.

In the Byzantine Empire, music adorned nonsacred aspects of life, but little of the secular music survives, except for a few rather stereotyped acclamations (ceremonial chants to the emperor), which are still used to greet bishops. Secular instrumental music, of which none is extant, was probably played on Greco-Roman musical instruments, including portable organs for great ceremonies.

Byzantine church music is choral music bearing a superficial resemblance to Gregorian chant (q.v.). Like Gregorian chant, it is monophonic (not harmonized, but sung in unison); its rhythm is free (having no regular succession of measures, as is usual in most music of the West); and it is modal, although it uses melodic patterns somewhat different from the major and minor scales to which the Western ear is accustomed. Also, there is considerable similarity between Jewish synagogue music and Byzantine church music.

Byzantine Hymns. An important part of the Byzantine rite, as of the Western, is the chanting of psalms and canticles and the intoning of lessons from the Scriptures. Byzantine hymns however, are closely related to ancient Greek poetry in structure and accentual pattern, and tend to rely less on Biblical texts than do the hymns of the Western church. The corpus of Byzantine hymns thus represents a distinctive contribution to both music and poetry.

Troparion. Probably of Syrian origin, the earliest form of Byzantine hymn is the *troparion,* a hymn in one strophe sung between the verses of Psalms. Among the oldest of these is the celebrated *Phōs hilaron* ("O Gladsome Light"), which dates from at least the 4th century and is still used as a hymn for Vespers in the Orthodox church. All feast days had special *troparia,* which occasionally developed to considerable size and acquired great importance, growing in much the same way that Western liturgical drama grew. There is some resemblance between the *troparion* and the Western trope (a textual addition, or intercalation, placed within liturgical texts), but the trope seems to have come later.

Kontakion. The *kontakion* (literally "scroll") form of hymn was introduced toward the end of the 6th century. Using the strophic system, the *kontakion* often consists of 20 or more stanzas. Because each stanza is modeled on the leading stanza (*heirmos*), they all use the same number of syllables and the same meter. In this respect, *kontakia* are somewhat like Western hymns, especially hymns patterned after Ambrosian music (q.v.). The initial letters of each stanza of the *kontakion* form an acrostic, sometimes spelling the name of the author of the hymn. The stanzas are further linked by the repetition of a short refrain at the end of each.

Because it is based on the Scripture lesson read during the liturgy, the *kontakion* might be called a poetic homily. Like the *troparion,* the *kontakion* probably had a Syrian origin. St. Romanos (c. 490–c. 560), a Syrian and the greatest of the Byzantine hymn writers, excelled in the *kontakion.* Many of his hymns are translations of hymns by St. Ephraem (306?–?373), also a Syrian; yet, even when translating, Romanos is more poetic than his source. The British musicologist H. J. W. Tillyard has compared the hymns of St. Romanos with the odes of Pindar.

The most celebrated Byzantine *kontakion* is the *Akathistos,* attributed to Sergius, patriarch of Constantinople from 610 to 638. He is said to have composed it in 626, when Constantinople was threatened by the Avars, though much of the hymn seems to be of earlier origin. The term *akathistos* indicates that the hymn is to be sung while standing. Its text praises the Blessed Virgin Mary for saving Constantinople by a miracle. It salutes her in the kind of rhapsodic language that became popular in the West some centuries later: "Hail, O bride and spotless maiden! Hail, for by you joy will shine forth! Hail, for through you the curse was erased!"

Many scholars consider the period of Romanos and Sergius the golden age of Byzantine hymnody, but no manuscripts of scores from this early period exist, and no one can be certain what the music of these *kontakia* sounded like. The music was probably syllabic (that is, containing roughly one note for each syllable) and rather simple.

The disappearance of the *kontakion* toward the end of the 7th century seems to be connected with a decree of the Quinisext Council (Council in Trullo, 692) requiring sermons at the liturgy. Since the *kontakion* was itself a kind of sermon set to music, it was considered redundant and therefore was abolished.

Kanon. A new form of hymn appeared about 700: the *kanon* (not to be confused with the *canon* of the Roman liturgy, which is the fixed Eucharistic prayer used at Mass). The *kanon,* which remains in use in the Byzantine liturgy, consists of nine odes, each having a different meter and each containing several stanzas.

The rise of the *kanon* (nothing definite is known about its origin), with its variety of meters and melodies, considerably enriched the Byzantine liturgy. The *kanon* was particularly appropriate to the people it served, exemplifying the principles of reiteration and variation admired by the Eastern mind. St. Andrew of Crete (died about 740) traditionally is considered the first writer of *kanons,* but the form almost certainly existed well before his period of activity.

Andrew's contemporaries, the foster brothers St. John Damascene (c. 675–?749) and St. Kosmas of Jerusalem (died about 760), were monks at the monastery of St. Sabas, between Jerusalem and the Dead Sea, where a school of *kanon* writers flourished. At this time the Iconoclastic controversy was under way, and John Damascene was the leading supporter of the cause of sacred images and the champion of Orthodoxy (see ICONOCLAST). His influence as a hymnographer was paramount.

After John's death the center of hymnography moved from St. Sabas to a stronghold of anti-Iconoclastic forces, the Studion monastery in Constantinople. The leading Studite composers were St. Theophanes (759–c. 842) and St. Theodore (759-826); a number of the latter's *kanons* continue to be used in the Byzantine liturgy. Another important hymnographer at the Studion, St. Joseph (died 883), was a Sicilian by birth, an indication of the considerable amount of Byzantine influence even in that section of Christendom traditionally considered part of the West.

From the 11th century, when the Orthodox church forbade the composition of new hymns, *kanons* and *troparia* continued to be written in the Greek monasteries in Sicily and southern Italy. Outstanding among these monasteries is the Abbey of Grottaferrata, near Rome, now a center for the study of Byzantine music.

Sticheron. Another form of hymn, the *sticheron* (from *stichos*, meaning "Psalm verse"), was composed in single strophes and usually had an elaborate melodic structure. A *sticheron* whose meter and melody were original was called an *idiomelon;* one whose metrical pattern and melody were borrowed from another *sticheron* was called a *prosomoion;* and the *idiomelon* that was used as a basis for later *stichera* was called an *automelon.* The most important of the extant *stichera* were composed by Theodore and Joseph at the Studion monastery. Although there is some similarity between the *sticheron* and the sequence of the Roman Mass, no connection between the two forms has been proved.

Later Byzantine Chant. During the period of the Byzantine Empire's gradual disintegration, and following the fall of Constantinople in 1453, Turkish and other Oriental influences crept into Byzantine music. This was especially apparent in the greater stress that was placed on melismatic (highly ornamented) chants. In some instances, simple melodies were embellished; in others, original hymns were composed in an extremely ornate style. The composers or embellishers, called *maistores* (masters), flourished in the 13th and 14th centuries, but the practice of writing new hymns or adding *fioriture* to old ones continues.

Byzantine Musical Notation. For music to be preserved, a system of musical notation must be developed. Two systems were used by the writers of Byzantine music. The first, called "ecphonetic," notation, goes back to the 4th century. It uses simple signs to indicate musical formulas for the chanting of the scripture readings.

The second system, used for hymns, shows a development similar to that of Western notation. It had three phases: (1) an early period, beginning about the 10th century, in which the signs were simply indications of the way in which the melody was to be fitted to the words, but gave no precise indication of the intervals between notes; (2) a middle period, beginning in the 11th or 12th century, in which the intervals and rhythm were indicated more clearly; and (3) a final period, beginning in the 15th century, in which a great many signs, not all of which have been deciphered, were added.

C. J. McNaspy, S. J.
Author of "A Guide to Christian Europe"

Bibliography

Hughes, Dom Anselm, ed., *Early Medieval Music,* vol. 2 of *The New Oxford History of Music,* rev. ed. (London 1955).
Reese, Gustave, *Music in the Middle Ages* (New York 1940).
Tillyard, Henry J. W., *Byzantine Music and Hymnography* (London 1923).
Tillyard, Henry J. W., *Handbook of the Middle Byzantine Musical Notation* (Copenhagen 1935).
Verlimirovic, Miloš, *Studies in Eastern Chant* (London 1966).
Wellesz, Egon, *A History of Byzantine Music and Hymnography,* 2d ed. (New York 1961).
Wellesz, Egon, *The Music of the Byzantine Church* (Cologne 1959).

BYZANTIUM, bə-zan′shəm, was an ancient Greek city on the European shore of the Bosporus. Located at the apex of the promontory that is bounded on the south by the Sea of Marmara and on the north by the Golden Horn and that projects eastward into the Bosporus, Byzantium occupied a small part of the area of modern Istanbul. The location of Byzantium provided the city with some excellent advantages: a position permitting the control of all trade between the Aegean and Black seas; a deep harbor free of tides and capable of accommodating large ships; and extremely abundant fisheries. Throughout its history Byzantium exploited all these advantages.

Byzantium was founded by a group of Greek colonists from Megara, according to tradition, in 659 B. C. Modern research places the founding date not earlier than the 2d half of the 7th century B. C. The city was conquered, damaged, and occupied by the Persians under Darius I (reigned 521–486 B. C.). After the Battle of Plataea in 479, it was liberated by the Greeks led by Pausanius of Sparta. Pausanius returned to Sparta but soon came back to rule Byzantium as a tyrant. However, some time before 476 the city definitely came under the political control of Athens. Despite revolts in 440 and 411, Byzantium remained under Athenian domination until it was taken by Lysander of Sparta after the defeat of Athens at Aegospotami (405 B. C.). In 390, Byzantium again came under the political influence of Athens, and although it switched its allegiance some years later, the threat of Philip of Macedon made it once more turn to Athens. Philip besieged Byzantium in 340 but failed to take it. His failure was attributed to the goddess Hecate, sometimes equated with Selene. To commemorate this event Byzantium issued coins stamped with the symbol of the Crescent and Star.

Byzantium acknowledged the supremacy of Macedon during the reign of Alexander the Great (336-323 B. C.), but regained its independence as Macedonian power declined. The city later sided with Rome in its wars against Philip V of Macedon, Antiochus III of Syria, and Mithridates VI of Pontus. At first a free ally of Rome, Byzantium was eventually reduced to the status of an ordinary Roman colony, finally losing under Emperor Vespasian (reigned 69–79 A.D.) whatever remnants of independence it still possessed. In the civil war between Pescennius Niger and Septimius Severus, Byzantium espoused the cause of the former, and as a consequence Severus, who took it in 196 A. D., demolished its fortifications, razed a considerable portion of the city to the ground, and massacred most of the inhabitants. Although it was partially rebuilt, the city was pillaged by Roman soldiers and by barbarians in the 260's.

The city was in a state of decay when Constantine the Great decided to rebuild it and make it the capital of the Roman world. The new city was officially dedicated on May 11, 330. Renamed New Rome by Constantine, it came to be known more popularly as Constantinople, meaning the city of Constantine. But the name "Byzantium" was sometimes also used to designate the new city, and modern scholars, looking for a term to designate the medieval phase of the Roman empire, decided upon the term "Byzantine." See also Istanbul.

Peter Charanis
Rutgers—The State University

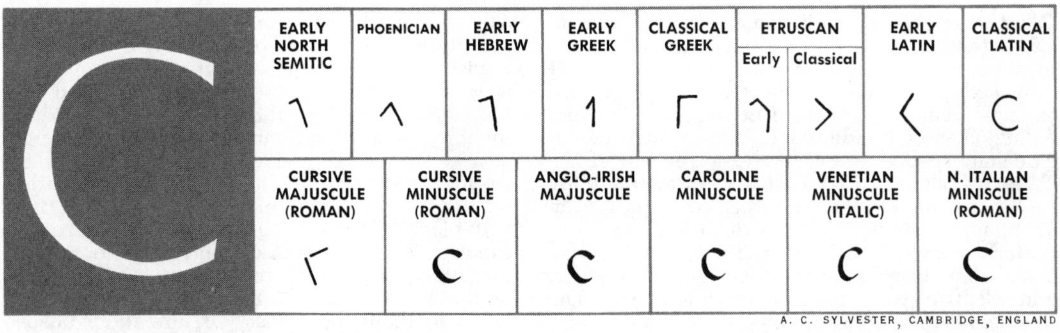

C

EARLY NORTH SEMITIC	PHOENICIAN	EARLY HEBREW	EARLY GREEK	CLASSICAL GREEK	ETRUSCAN Early	ETRUSCAN Classical	EARLY LATIN	CLASSICAL LATIN
								C

CURSIVE MAJUSCULE (ROMAN)	CURSIVE MINUSCULE (ROMAN)	ANGLO-IRISH MAJUSCULE	CAROLINE MINUSCULE	VENETIAN MINUSCULE (ITALIC)	N. ITALIAN MINISCULE (ROMAN)
	c	c	c	c	c

A. C. SYLVESTER, CAMBRIDGE, ENGLAND

DEVELOPMENT OF THE LETTER C is illustrated in the above chart, beginning with the early North Semitic letter. The evolution of the majuscule (capital) C is shown at the top; that of the minuscule (lower-case) at bottom.

C, sē, is the third letter of the English alphabet. It also holds the same position in all the other West European alphabets, including those derived from the classical Latin, or Roman, alphabet. C was the third letter in the ancient North Semitic alphabet, the Greek alphabet, and the Etruscan alphabet, into which it subsequently passed. C, known in the Semitic alphabet as *gimel* and in the Greek alphabet as *gamma,* was originally a sonant guttural, that is, a hard *g* as in "gather," "gear," and "go." However, the Etruscans, who did not distinguish between the voiced *g* and the unvoiced *k* stop, used the letter C for the sound *k.* The letter C retained this sound in the early Latin alphabet, in which it originally served for both *k* and *g* sounds; indeed, the abbreviations C and CN stood for Gaius and Gnaeus.

At a later period, the Romans recognized the distinction between the *g* and *k* sounds and realized that there was a need for two separate letters. Unaware that the original sound of C was *g,* the Romans created a new letter G (about 312 B.C.) by adding a stroke to the letter C. They retained the letter C for the sound *k.*

The form of the letter C has altered very little through the passing centuries. The minuscule character has also survived with practically no variation in its form. It is merely a smaller variation of the capital character.

Pronunciation. When the Latin alphabet was introduced into Britain, the letter C was used only to represent the hard sound of *k.* Thus the Old English words *cyn* and *brecan* are "kin" and "break" in Modern English. Because of French influence, however, the letter C in English has retained the sound *k* only when it is followed by the vowels *a, o, u,* or by a consonant other than *h.* This accounts for the pronunciation of such words as "cat," "come," "cute," and "cloud." When the letter C precedes the vowels *e, i, y,* it has the sound of a sharp *s* as in "center," "circle," and "cypress." The palatalized C before *e, i,* and *y* is written *ch,* as in French. Thus *rice* and *cild* in Old English have become "rich" and "child" in Modern English.

The sound *k* before *e, i,* and *y* is represented by the letter K. This accounts for the spelling of such words as "key," "king," and "kyle." Only in words of Greek derivation is the *k* sound used with the combination *ch.* Examples of such words are "character," "chronology," and "chromosome."

In some words, such as "muscle," the letter C is mute. It is also silent when it precedes the letter K as in "pack." The combination *ch* is mute in words like "yacht." In Scotland, *ch* is a guttural aspirate. Thus the pronunciation of the word loch has the guttural quality of the *ch* sound in German.

C as a Symbol. In numerical notation the letter C represents the Roman numeral for "hundred." It is also a symbol in algebra for the third known quantity $(a+b+c)$.

In music, C is the keynote of one of the most important scales, the "natural" scale. In addition, the note C is one of the three signs, or *clefs,* inscribed at the beginning of the musical staff to indicate the pitches of the lines and spaces.

In academic usage, the letter C indicates only a fair grade because it holds the third place in the alphabet, following A (excellent) and B (good). As a symbol of measurement for shoes, the letter C designates a wide width as opposed to A (narrow) and B (medium).

C is also used as an abbreviation for various words and concepts. For example, C stands for such terms as "cape," "carbon," "centigrade," and "center" (stage). The minuscule character *c* stands for such words as "cent," "centime," *circa* (Latin for "about"), *contra* (Latin for "against"), "contralto," "copyright" (©), "cubic," and "current."

DAVID DIRINGER, *Author of "The Alphabet"*

Further Reading: See the bibliography for the article ALPHABET.

ÇA IRA, sȧ′ ē-rȧ′, was a popular song of the French Revolution, first heard, according to contemporary accounts, on the night of Oct. 5, 1789, when the people of Paris marched on Versailles and took Louis XVI prisoner. The tune had been composed not long before as a dance, *Le carillon national,* by a theater-orchestra violinist named Bécourt. The original words were supposedly written by a street singer called Ladré. According to one tradition, the title was suggested to Ladré by the marquis de Lafayette, who recalled that Benjamin Franklin repeatedly used the expression (which means freely, "We shall succeed") in reference to the American Revolution. The first verse of the original version goes:

Ah! ça ira, ça ira, ça ira!
Le peuple en ce jour sans cesse répète
Ah! ça ira, ça ira, ça ira!
Malgré les mutins, tout réussira.

During the Reign of Terror an alternate version was sung, including the lines:

Les aristocrat' à la lanterne;
Les aristocrat' on les pendra.

CABAL, kə-bal′, a small eminent group of conspirators. The term acquired a somewhat sinister meaning in England after 1667, when Charles II bestowed power on an informal cabinet of intriguers (Clifford, Ashley-Cooper, Buckingham, Arlington, and Lauderdale) whose initials coincidentally spelled "cabal." The secret part of the Treaty of Dover (1670) with France, providing for French military aid in return for a profession of Roman Catholic faith by Charles, was supported by two Catholic sympathizers within the Cabal. The three other members were Protestant, and all five favored religious toleration. The pro-Anglican Parliament opposed toleration and forced the breakup of the Cabal in 1673.

CABALA, kə-bä′lə, is a historical and literary term usually associated with Jewish mysticism. The term, also spelled *kabala,* can be translated "tradition." While cabalistic speculation and mystical symbolism were crystallized in the 13th century, the origins of cabala date back to antiquity. From the 12th century, Jewish mystics have used the term to denote this continuity of thought from the beginnings of Judaism. Jewish history reveals that from early times there was a trend in Judaism toward speculation about the mysteries of God and the universe. In the days when the Talmud was being compiled (edited 500 A. D.) there were warnings against the tendency to delve into uncontrolled speculation that might lead to a misinterpretation of true religious knowledge and understanding. Although the term "cabala" is not specifically used in the Bible or the Talmud, there is evidence that its spirit pervaded some sections of the Bible, notably the books of Ezekiel and Daniel, as well as the schools and academies of post-Biblical days.

"The Zohar." For centuries, the currents of mysticism and religious ecstasy were fused with other metaphysical doctrines including Gnosticism and Neoplatonism as the cabalistic tradition of divergence from formalistic, legalistic modes of religious thought was extended from the Middle East to Germany, Italy, and Provence. In these centers, the teachings of the renowned 12th century cabalists, Abraham ben David and his son Isaac the Blind, were established in the forefront of cabalistic thought. Cabala reached its greatest expression, however, in a 13th century work called *The Zohar* (Book of Brightness).

It is generally acknowledged that *The Zohar* was compiled in Spain by Moses de Leon at the end of the 13th century. De Leon was influenced by the 12th century mystics who viewed cabala as an unbroken tradition in Jewish thought. Thus, in order to give an aura of sanctity and acceptance to the cabalistic speculation of *The Zohar,* he ascribed its philosophy to Rabbi Simon ben Yohai, who lived during the 2d century A. D. Legend tells that Rabbi Simon, forced to hide from the Romans in a cave for 13 years, occupied himself with the mysteries of heaven and earth. It is clear, however, that Simon ben Yohai was not the author of *The Zohar,* nor was Moses de Leon its sole author. Rather, de Leon gathered together the mystical knowledge of several generations, and added his own thinking. That this greatest of all cabalistic books contains chapters varying in style and content is cited as proof of multiple authorship.

Purposes of the Cabalistic System. Cabala, then, is an attempt, in spite of man's limited knowledge, to peer beyond the seen, the touched, the heard. All peoples have such cravings and seek to penetrate the mysteries of heaven and earth. The Jewish mystics, who were part of this movement, wanted to understand the nature of God and how man relates to the Deity. As a result of their meditation and inner groping, they sought answers to questions that to this day perplex the world. How does an infinite being deal with a material world, with men and women of flesh and blood? What is the destiny of human existence? Are the historical and legal contents of the Bible, as well as the essence and practices of the Jewish religion, the only keys to the answers to these questions? Or, are there deeper, hidden teachings that go beyond the Torah (both the laws of Moses and the moral foundation of Judaism), which they passionately loved and to which they were so intensely devoted? These mystics concluded that there are esoteric and mystical values inherent in the Bible, in Jewish law, and in Jewish religious practice that they must seek out.

The cabalistic system dealt with the nature of God and his contacts with man. This relationship could be established and maintained through 10 intermediary emanations, or *Sefirot.* These *Sefirot,* among them *Keter* (highest thinking or striving), *Hokhmah* (wisdom), and *Binah* (understanding), are manifestations of the power of God. When these three are harmonized with the moral qualities *Hesed* (kindness), *Gevurah* (inner strength and discipline), and *Tiferet* (glory or a sense of worth) that operate in the natural universe consisting of *Nezah* (victory or fruition), *Hod* (beauty), and *Yesod* (the natural foundations of the tangible world), and when all of them are joined together by *Malkhut* (the kingship of God), then creation from earliest times to the end of days is continual. And in all the aspects of creativity, including the lives of saintly people and those who carry out *Mitzvot* (divine commandments), God reveals Himself.

Cabala delves also into the nature of God's emissaries, sometimes called angels; what happens when people die; the magical significance of numbers and letters of the alphabet; and the coming of the Messiah, one whose talents are so spiritually superior as to eliminate the evils of war, disease, and destruction, and to herald a glorious era for all mankind. Indeed, men claiming this messianic mantle through understanding of the wonders of cabala arose in different ages. The most famous of these mystical leaders, one who attracted many followers, was the 17th century leader Sabbatai Tzevi.

Cabala tried to establish the thesis that reason alone cannot give us all the answers to questions about God and physical existence. It is obscure in parts, and not accepted by all Jews, but it points up the role of emotion and poetry in any understanding of religion. Through some of its symbolism and imagery it intensified faith and gave those Jews who subscribed to its ideas a sense of the divine and a feeling of purpose. Its influence is felt in dynamic fashion by the modern Hassidic movement and in a lesser way by all forms of modern Jewish religion.

EDWARD T. SANDROW
Rabbi, Temple Beth el, Cedarhurst, N. Y.

Further Reading: Cahn, Zvi, *The Philosophy of Judaism* (New York 1962); Roth, Leon, *Judaism—A Portrait* (New York 1961); Scholem, Gershom, *Major Trends in Jewish Mysticism* (New York 1946); *The Zohar,* tr. by Harry Sperling and Maurice Simon (London 1931).

CABALLÉ, kä-bä-lā′, **Montserrat** (1933–), Spanish operatic soprano. She was born on April 12, 1933, in Barcelona into a music-loving family, entered the Conservatorio del Liceo there at the age of 9, and then studied privately. Miss Caballé made her operatic debut in *La Bohème* in Basel in 1957 and thereafter sang an unusually wide range of roles in various European opera houses. She won immediate acclaim in the American Opera Society production of *Lucrezia Borgia* in 1965, in which she was a substitute in the title role. In the same year she appeared as Queen Elizabeth in the society's *Roberto Devereux* and as Marguerite in a Metropolitan Opera production of *Faust*. Her seductive, disciplined voice and her dramatic power were highly praised.

CABALLERO, kä-bä-lyā′rō, **Fernán** (1796–1877), Spanish writer, who initiated a renaissance in Spanish fiction with the publication of her first novel, *La gaviota* (1849). She was born Cecilia Böhl von Faber in Morges, Switzerland, on Dec. 25, 1796, and was educated in a French school in Germany. After 1813 she spent most of her life in Andalusia, whose customs and landscapes are mirrored in her novels. She died in Seville, Spain, on April 7, 1877.

Fernán Caballero wove the plots of her novels around the *cuadros de costumbres* (literary sketches depicting customs), which had been in vogue during the romantic period immediately preceding her time. Her novels successfully reflect contemporary life, but the characters are stereotypes and the plots romantic.

La gaviota (Eng. tr., *The Sea Gull*, 1864) is a sentimental novel of a peasant girl turned opera singer. Other novels include *Clemencia* (1852) and *La familia de Alvareda* (1856; Eng. tr., *Castle and Cottage in Spain*, 1861).

DONALD W. BLEZNICK
University of Cincinnati

CABBAGE, a low, stout, head-forming food plant. The common cabbage is a biennial that forms cabbage heads one year and flowers the next. The large, shiny leaves that form the head are at first spaced well apart, but they grow into a tight ball as the plant matures. If the head is cut, smaller lateral heads, often no bigger than Brussels sprouts, develop in most varieties. These, or the original cabbage head if left unharvested, will bolt into an extended flowering stalk the second growing season after cold weather. In certain climates with hot summers, cabbage may bolt in the first year of growth and form a flower stalk instead of a head.

Cabbage occurs in a widely diversified array of special types, in many shapes, and in many shades of red and green. It is raised extensively in Europe and in North America, where well over a million tons is consumed annually. It is eaten raw, boiled, or as sauerkraut, which is made by immersing cut cabbage in brine and allowing it to ferment.

Cultivation. For good head formation, cabbages should be grown in well-fertilized soil and amply watered. They grow best in areas that have cool weather. In most cases, seedlings are started under glass and transplanted to the garden or field in early spring. The plants resist light frost well. In warm climates the seeds may be sown directly outdoors. They may be sown in autumn in the southern United States.

GRANT HEILMAN

Cabbage

Early varieties of cabbage develop heads about two months after the seedlings have been set out, while late varieties take about four months. The large-headed varieties, which reach a weight of 10 pounds (4½ kg) or more, are generally slower to mature.

Harvesting and Storage. Cabbage heads are cut for market by hand and may be stored through winter in cold cellars or pit houses. They keep best under moderate humidity and at a constant temperature just above freezing. Home gardeners can store cabbages in trenches covered with mulch, or they can pull up the plants and hang them by the roots in an unheated shed. Gardeners having limited space may wrap the heads in wax paper and store them for many weeks in a cool basement.

Cultivation Problems and Breeding. Serious cabbage diseases include a "yellows" caused by a *Fusarium* fungus that attacks through the roots when the soil temperature is above 65°F (18°C), blocking sap transfer; a debilitating mosaic disease caused by a virus that is transmitted by aphids; and the notorious clubroot, caused by the *Plasmodiophora* fungus in the soil. Varieties more or less resistant to such diseases have been developed as the most effective means of combating them. However, insecticides must be used to prevent the larvae of the cabbage butterfly (cabbage worm) from consuming and mutilating the leaves.

Widespread breeding has produced types of cabbage suitable for almost any climate. Notable breeding programs in Japan have produced many adapted varieties, and plantings there are now almost entirely of hybrids suited to spring, summer, or autumn sowing, and adapted to different elevations. Types that resist bolting in hot weather have especially been sought and propagated for seed production by vegetative cuttings.

Kinds of Cabbage. Cabbage, *Brassica oleracea capitata* L., belongs to the mustard family (Cruciferae). Variations in cabbage are numerous. Cabbages are often classified according to head shape (oval, pointed, round, drumhead, and so on), as well as by color and growth cycle. Common early (quick-heading) cabbage varieties include Copenhagen Market, Badger Market, and Golden Acre; winter cabbages that mature late and store especially well include Premium Flat Dutch, Wisconsin Hollander, and Danish Roundhead. There are several red cabbage types, including Mammoth Red Rock and Red Acre (a smaller type especially suited to the home garden). Crinkly-leaved Savoy cabbages include Perfection and the heat-resistant Savoy King Hybrid.

Related Plants. The familiar cabbage and the other species of economic plants in the cabbage genus are known collectively as cole crops. Other varieties of the cabbage species are Brussels sprout, broccoli, and cauliflower. Species in the same genus include kohlrabi, rape, rutabaga, turnip, various mustards, and Chinese cabbage. Chinese cabbage, also called celery cabbage, is either of two Asian cabbages: pai-ts'ai, which has a compact head of light green leaves, and pakchoi, with a loose head of dark green leaves.

History. The original wild cabbage closely resembles collard, a large kale that is erect and leafy-stemmed rather than squat and head-forming. Today wild cabbage is found mostly in Europe, but it was apparently domesticated in the eastern Mediterranean region, where several varieties of cabbage were in general use 4,000 years ago. One of the first vegetables to be domesticated, cultivated cabbage may have been brought to Europe in pre-Christian times by Celtic warriors who had invaded the Near East. The heading types recognized as cabbage today probably were developed in Europe, especially in northern Europe.

ROBERT W. SCHERY
Lawn Institute, Marysville, Ohio

CABBAGE BUTTERFLY, a butterfly whose larva is a common pest of cabbage, radish, turnips, and cauliflower. The cabbage butterfly was accidentally introduced into Quebec, Canada, in 1860, and within 20 years it has spread rapidly over the eastern half of the United States. It now is found throughout most of North America.

The cabbage butterfly caterpillar, or larva, often called the *imported cabbageworm,* is velvety green and grows to over 1 inch (2.5 cm) in length. The adult butterfly is almost completely white, except for three or four black spots on the wings.

The cabbage butterfly (*Pieris rapae*) belongs to the family Pieridae of the order Lepidoptera.

DON R. DAVIS, *Smithsonian Institution*

CABBAGE MAGGOT, a fly larva that attacks the roots of cabbage plants and other garden vegetables. The adult fly is similar in appearance to the common housefly but is only about half as large. The adult flies deposit their eggs on cabbage plants near the ground level or in cracks in the soil. The small maggots emerge three to seven days later and begin feeding on the cabbage roots. The mature maggots pupate in the ground, and the adult flies emerge from the pupae and deposit their eggs on late cabbage.

The cabbage maggot (*Hylemya brassicae*), a native of Europe, belongs to the family Anthomyiidae in the order Diptera.

ROSS HUTCHINS
State Plant Board of Mississippi

CABBAGE MOTH. See CABBAGE BUTTERFLY.

CABBAGE PALM. See PALMS.

CABBAGE ROSE. See ROSES.

CABBAGES AND KINGS is a series of 19 connected short stories by O. Henry (see PORTER, WILLIAM SYDNEY) published in 1904. The stories form a novel linked by the same group of characters and a single loosely constructed plot about revolution and adventure in the fictional Central American republic of Coralio. O'Henry's first book, it is a mixture of romance and realism based on his life in Honduras, where he had fled from a charge of embezzlement in Texas.

CABELL, kab'əl, **James Branch** (1879–1958), American author, who wrote more than 50 works of fiction, essays, and reminiscences, of which the novel *Jurgen* (1919) is the most celebrated. He was born in Richmond, Va., on April 14, 1879, graduated from the College of William and Mary in 1898, and spent most of his life in Virginia. His first book, *The Eagle's Shadow,* was published in 1904. He did not become famous, however, until New York City censors attempted to suppress *Jurgen* on the grounds of its extreme sexuality. He died in Richmond on May 5, 1958.

Cabell avoided the contemporary scene in his fiction. In the 18 novels that comprise his major work, he invented complex dreamlike adventures set in the Middle Ages in the imaginary country of Poictesme. These novels, which include *The Eagle's Shadow* and *Jurgen,* were assembled in 1927–1930 as a kind of history of a Dom Manuel and his descendants. After *Jurgen,* the most successful works in this series are *The Cream of the Jest* (1917), *Figures of Earth* (1921), and *The Silver Stallion* (1926).

Cabell insisted that he despised realism, and he encouraged his admirers to think of him as a writer of escapist fantasies. Literary critics, however, have found that his allegories have a serious moral purpose. In them, Cabell seems to suggest that though man might strive for perfection, he is bound to a limited existence and to mortal compromises. Only art, in its triumph over time, offers the hope of survival.

JEROME STERN
Florida State University

Further Reading: Davis, Joe L., *James Branch Cabell* (New York 1962); Rubin, Louis, *No Place on Earth* (Austin, Texas, 1959).

CABER TOSSING, kā'bər tôs'ing, is the Gaelic sport of heaving a 16- to 18-foot, 100- to 120-pound tapered log, or caber. It has been a trial of strength between rival Scots ever since, in a Highland forest long ago, a woodcutter felled a tree, picked up the trunk, leaned it against his shoulder, ran a few steps, then heaved it to a waiting wagon. Once another Highlander challenged his friend, rivalry was inevitable. Contests are featured in Scotland and also at Highland Games and police athletic meets in the United States and Canada.

The caber, with a diameter at one end about twice that at the other, is balanced on the ground, small end down. The contestant seizes this end, runs a short distance, and tosses the log so that the large end hits the ground and topples over. Tosses, judged on form and distance, are measured from the toe of the tosser's forward foot to the log's small end. If no one manages a valid toss in three tries, a piece may be cut off the thick end and the contest repeated.

HENRY H. ROXBOROUGH
Author of "Great Days in Canadian Sport"

CABESTANH, kȧ-be-stoɴ′, **Guilhem de,** Provençal troubadour. He is said to have fought the Moors at Navas de Tolosa, Spain, in 1212. According to a widespread 13th century legend, he fell in love with Marguerite, wife of Raymond of Château-Roussillon. Through jealousy, Raymond had Cabestanh murdered, tore out his heart, and served it as a meal to the unsuspecting Marguerite. It is thought that the ninth tale of the fourth day of Boccaccio's *Decameron* is based on this legend. In it, after the wife has eaten her husband's heart, she leaps to her death from a castle window. The "eaten heart" story, however, originated in Oriental literature and was later told of the Châtelain de Coucy, a French troubadour, and of Reinmar von Brennenberg, a German minnesinger.

The poems of Cabestanh, intense and passionate in character, were first published in full in *Les chansons de Guilhem de Cabestanh* (1924) by Arthur Långfors.

CABET, kȧ-be′, **Étienne** (1788–1856), French-American socialist, who founded the Icarian movement and established a utopian community in America based on its principles of pacifism and communism. Cabet was born in Dijon, France, on Jan. 1, 1788. Educated as a lawyer, he moved to Paris in 1820 and joined the republican opposition to the restored Bourbon monarchy. He participated in the Revolution of 1830, which brought Louis Philippe to the throne, and was awarded the post of *procureur général* (prosecuting attorney) in Corsica. However, his continued republican agitation soon resulted in his dismissal.

In 1833, Cabet launched a vigorous attack against the monarchy in his newspaper *Le Populaire*. Threatened with imprisonment, he chose exile in London (1834–1839), where he studied utopian writers, especially Robert Owen. After returning to France he published his own utopian romance, the widely read *Voyage en Icarie* (1840). Icaria was Cabet's vision of a perfect communist society. There all men worked, and all property was owned in common; production was regulated according to a national plan, and goods were distributed according to need.

Cabet has been classed among the "utopian socialists," who, unlike the Marxists, believed that the classes of capitalist society could be persuaded to live in harmony under socialism and that communism could be established through peaceful democratic change. However, Cabet soon became impressed by the bourgeoisie's unyielding hostility to socialist goals. Reluctantly he abandoned his belief in peaceful propaganda and formulated a doctrine of class antagonism. Yet, rather than advocate class war, he chose to establish an Icaria in America.

After an unsuccessful start in Texas, Cabet's Icarians founded a settlement in Nauvoo, Ill., in 1849. Cabet was elected its president, and in 1854 he became an American citizen. Patriarchal and authoritarian, he was deposed in 1856 following a violent schism. With a band of followers he moved to St. Louis, Mo., where he died on Nov. 8, 1856. Icarian communities later were established in Missouri, Iowa, and California, but all were abandoned by the late 1890's.

Richard Bienvenu, *University of Colorado*

Further Reading: Johnson, C., "Cabet and the Problem of Class Antagonism," *International Review of Social History*, vol. 11, pp. 403–443 (Assen, Netherlands, 1966).

CABEZA DE VACA, kä-bā′thä ~~the~~ vä′kä, **Álvar Núñez** (1490?–1557), Spanish explorer of what is now the southwestern United States. He was born in Jérez de la Frontera, Spain. His name, Cabeza de Vaca ("cow's head"), had been made famous by a distant ancestor who marked an unguarded pass in the Sierra Morena with the skull of a cow and thus contributed to the Christians' victory at Las Navas de Tolosa (1212).

Cabeza de Vaca sailed to America in 1527 as second in command with the expedition of Pánfilo de Narváez. Narváez' attempt to conquer Florida proved as unsuccessful as that of Ponce de León in 1521. Deserted by their ships and having found nothing but disappointment, the adventurers constructed makeshift rafts and headed from the northern Florida coast for Pánuco (Tampico, Mexico). Some reached the Texas coast, but in time death took all but four—Cabeza de Vaca, Alonso del Castillo, Andrés Dorantes, and the Negro Estevánico (or Estevan).

Finally united in 1534 after several years as captives and slaves of Indian tribes in Texas, the four men made their remarkable trek through Texas, through a corner of New Mexico and of Arizona, and on into Sonora and Sinaloa in Mexico. In Mexico City in 1536 they told their story to Viceroy Antonio de Mendoza, and interest in the north flamed.

Cabeza de Vaca went to Spain, where he was made governor of Paraguay. In 1540 he went off to his new post. The rough conquerors of Río de La Plata rebelled against him and shipped him back to Spain in irons in 1543. In 1551 he was censured by the Council of the Indies and condemned to exile in Africa. But King Charles I (Emperor Charles V) cleared him and allowed him to live in well-deserved honor until his death in Spain in 1557.

John Francis Bannon, S. J.
St. Louis University

Further Reading: Hallenbeck, Cleve, *Álvar Núñez Cabeza de Vaca* (Glendale, Calif., 1940); Núñez Cabeza de Vaca, *Adventures in the Unknown Interior of America*, ed. and tr. by Cyclone Covey, paperbound (New York 1962).

CABEZONE, kab′ə-zōn, a medium-sized fish found off the west coast of North America from the Queen Charlotte Islands in British Columbia to Turtle Bay in Baja California. It is probably most abundant off central California. The cabezone is popular with sports fishermen.

The cabezone is not an attractive fish. It has a prominent fleshy flap above each eye, large pectoral fins, and sharp spines on some of its fins. Adult males are reddish, while adult females are mainly greenish. The cabezone lacks scales. Rare specimens almost 2½ feet (75 cm) long and weighing 20 pounds (9 kg) have been caught, but cabezones about 1½ feet (45 cm) long and weighing about 6 pounds (3 kg) are far more common.

During their early life, cabezones live offshore in drifting plankton and migrate inshore only after they reach a length of about 1½ inches (4 cm). Young cabezones are often found in rocky tide pools, while larger specimens may be found at depths up to 50 fathoms (300 feet or 90 meters). Adult cabezones feed on crabs, abalone, limpets, clams, chitons, and fishes.

The cabezone, *Scorpaenichthys marmoratus*, is in the family Cottidae, order Perciformes.

Daniel M. Cohen
U. S. Fish and Wildlife Service

CABILDO, kä-bēl′dō, an autonomous town council in Spanish American colonies. The cabildos originated in the 16th century as elective bodies, composed mostly of local property owners. They had wide legislative, executive, and judicial powers at first. Within their jurisdiction were taxation, trade regulation, maintenance of town militia and police, supervision of public works, hospitals, and jails, and the granting of citizenship were in times of emergency *cabildos abiertos,* or open town meetings, were convened.

Under increasingly autocratic Spanish administrations, the cabildos lost much of their early importance as organs of self-government. By the 17th century they became closed bodies; and members were appointed by the crown, or offices were bought and sold. They remained influential, however, in developing civil traditions and nationalistic spirit, and later served as rallying points for movements of independence.

CABIMAS, kä-vē′mäs, a city in northwestern Venezuela, is situated in Zulia state, on the northeast shore of Lake Maracaibo. It lies about 20 miles (30 km) southeast of Maracaibo, with which it is connected by a highway across a bridge spanning the mouth of the lake. Cabimas is an oil-producing and refining center. Its population increased rapidly after World War II because of the development of the oil fields in the Lake Maracaibo area. Population: (1961) 92,656.

CABINDA, kə-vēnn′də, is a Portuguese territory on the west coast of Africa. The name was formerly spelled *Kabinda.* Located north of the Congo River, Cabinda is bordered by Congo (Kinshasa) on the east and south, Congo (Brazzaville) on the north, and the Atlantic Ocean on the west. It is administered by Portuguese officials as part of Angola, from which it is separated by a narrow corridor of Congo (Kinshasa) territory.

Cabinda covers an area of 2,807 square miles (7,270 sq km). It has a tropical climate, with humidity averaging over 80%. Vegetation is mainly thick, equatorial rain forest. The territory is drained by the Chiloango River.

Cabinda has a population of more than 58,000. Most of the people are members of the Bantu-speaking group, including a sizable community of Bakongo. They are known as skilled seamen and carpenters in Angola, where they have played an important part in the economy.

The seaport of Cabinda, located just north of the Congo River estuary, is the most important town in the territory. The interior has few towns and remains largely undeveloped. The traditional economy of Cabinda is agricultural and is based on such tropical crops as fiber, wood, and palm oil. Large offshore oil reserves discovered off Cabinda in 1966 promised to revolutionize the economy in the future.

Portugal acquired formal control over Cabinda at the Berlin Conference (1884–1885), but it had previously exercised influence over groups of the coastal inhabitants. The territory is now surrounded by countries that have achieved independence. African nationalist activity was first felt in Cabinda in 1961, when guerrilla units began to attack Portuguese installations from neighboring independent states.

DOUGLAS L. WHEELER
University of New Hampshire

CULVER PICTURES

PRESIDENT GEORGE WASHINGTON'S CABINET, as pictured by Currier and Ives in 1876. *Left to right:* George Washington; Henry Knox (war); Alexander Hamilton (treasury); Thomas Jefferson (state); Edmund Randolph (attorney general). Cabinet membership has grown with the creation of more executive departments.

CABINET AND CABINET GOVERNMENT. The term "cabinet," derived from the French, referred in the 17th century to a small, private apartment or "closet" in which the king met privately with aides and advisers. Hence a "cabinet meeting" was a secret meeting, and the word still retains something of that old flavor. Today a cabinet is that body of high officers of state, surrounding and presided over by the president, prime minister, or head of state, who meet to discuss, advise on, or decide high policy. Its importance and functions vary considerably, depending on the character of the nation's constitution and political system.

Individually its members usually hold high administrative positions, but the cabinet collectively exercises policy-making functions beyond the separate responsibilities of its members. The presence of an institution called a cabinet, however, does not betoken a system of cabinet government. In the United States, for example, the cabinet performs almost no collective responsibilities, deriving its powers exclusively from those of the president. In Britain, which possesses the archetype of the cabinet system, the cabinet is the focus of both executive and legislative power; it exercises those powers collegially; and it stands accountable to the House of Commons for its performance.

THE BRITISH CABINET

The British cabinet came into being in the late 17th and early 18th centuries. Like most British institutions, it was a creation of circumstance, not of plan. It emerged out of the privy council when that body grew too large for effective discussion. Charles II (reigned 1660–1685) and Anne (reigned 1702–1714) standardized the practice of consulting the leading ministers before the meeting of the larger privy council in order to discuss and settle matters more effectively. Though the practice was much complained of in the beginning, and though the group that advised Charles for several years was reproached as a "junto" or "cabal," its obvious utility led to the rapid decline of the privy council and the growth of the cabinet's power. Through the 18th century the cabinet took the form and acquired most of the characteristics that mark it today.

Factors in the Growth of the Cabinet. Perhaps the greatest impetus to its growth was provided by the accident that brought the Hanoverians to the throne. The first two Georges were not much interested in British affairs and spoke little English. After 1717 the king ceased to meet with his ministers, and during Robert Walpole's lengthy ministry (1721–1742), the cabinet developed into an institutionalized decision-making body centered around a chief or prime minister, though Walpole himself always denied being a "prime" minister. His long tenure established the principles (further strengthened under the Pitts) that the cabinet should be politically homogeneous and that it had to find adequate support in the House of Commons. His opponents' failure to impeach him as a criminal when he was forced out of office in 1742 also demonstrated that political opposition could be accepted as loyal and legitimate rather than proscribed as treasonous—a principle essential to modern democracy but one that was difficult to conceive while the monarch personally presided over the government.

A party system was also developing during this same period. What had been in the early 18th century a mere alignment of personal factions, loosely grouped under the labels Whig and Tory, became by the early 19th century two fairly clear-cut and stable political organizations—in Parliament if not in the country at large. The two developments went hand in hand: party provided a means by which the cabinet could organize its support, and the cabinet provided a center around which the party could coalesce.

Composition of the Cabinet. The cabinet today consists of about 20 ministers, chosen by the prime minister, who in turn is chosen by the monarch on the basis of his ability to command the confidence of the House of Commons. In effect the monarch has no discretion in the matter and merely summons the leader of the majority party. It is the prime minister's task to appoint persons to ministerial office, to determine which ministers shall sit in the cabinet and to dismiss them if necessary, to preside over the cabinet, and to act as its principal spokesman.

In forming his government, the prime minister has considerable discretion but is limited by a number of factors. All ministers must be members of Parliament, and if a man is needed who is not a member, he must qualify within a reasonable time by winning a seat at a by-election or accepting a peerage. The law requires a few cabinet ministers to be drawn from the House of Lords. Certain ministers, such as the foreign secretary, home secretary, and chancellor of the exchequer, must always be included in the cabinet by virtue of the importance of their offices. Members must have at least a minimal understanding of the work of their departments. If two men can't get along, they must not be put in positions where their functions will overlap. Leaders of important factions in the party must be included. In short, the prime minister must put together a cabinet that can work together, govern effectively, and command the confidence of the House. He himself takes the sinecure office of first lord of the treasury.

The Cabinet and Parliament. There is a close correspondence between the cabinet and Parliament, for the cabinet members are the leaders of the majority party in the House of Commons. Hence the executive and legislative powers are "fused," rather than separated as in the United States, and there is a clear focus not only of power but also of responsibility. Along with the prime minister, the cabinet gives general direction to administration, but it also controls the work of Parliament. It prepares the monarch's "Speech from the Throne" announcing legislative plans for the session; its members are pres-

CENTRAL PRESS

BRITISH CABINET during World War II. (*Seated left to right*): Sir John Anderson, Prime Minister Winston Churchill, Clement Attlee, Anthony Eden; (*Standing*): Arthur Greenwood, Ernest Bevin, Lord Beaverbrook, Sir Kingsley Wood.

ent in the House to lead debate and answer questions; it initiates all major legislation; it arranges the schedule of the House; and only ministers may propose public expenditures.

The opposition party is given full opportunity to be heard and to criticize the government and debate its policies, but it does not make decisions. It is the cabinet's prerogative to govern, and the system is designed to enhance its power to do so. The opposition's function is not to make policy or obstruct the government but to debate and criticize and to offer itself as an alternative. So long as the government maintains its majority, it remains in power, limited only by the requirement of an election every 5 years.

The cabinet is responsible to the Commons in the technical sense that it must give way if it loses a motion of confidence or censure or if it loses a vote on a major bill. Given the disciplined two-party system, this could happen only as a result of a split in the majority party, and the necessity of avoiding such a split forces the leadership to conciliate and accommodate opinion in the party. If confidence should be lost, however, the government must either resign and allow the opposition to form a government (most unlikely these days) or dissolve Parliament and hold a general election. This is the ultimate sanction of responsibility, for the ultimate power of the Commons to force the issue to the test of popular approval is the clearest rationalization of democracy in Great Britain.

Responsibility and Power. The responsibility of the cabinet is both individual and collective. The cabinet stands or falls together. Disagreements may be aired within the cabinet, but once a decision has been reached, every member must accept that decision and be prepared to defend it in the House and on the hustings. If a member cannot do that, he must resign his office and risk ending his political career. On the other hand, if a minister is forced to take unpopular measures in his individual capacity, the cabinet will close ranks around him, unless his action runs counter to the cabinet's policies or prior decisions. On a few occasions a minister has been disavowed and dismissed to save the government, but such instances are rare.

The essence of the cabinet system in Britain is that power and responsibility are concentrated in one set of hands—the cabinet's. The vast enlargement of government functions in recent years, however, has raised serious questions about the cabinet's ability to perform all the tasks the system assigns to it. The work of the cabinet is increasingly done through committees whose members include persons from outside the cabinet. The nationalized industries have been placed in the hands of various boards outside the day-to-day control of ministers, and special courts and commissions on which membership is by no means confined to cabinet members, have been created to recommend—and in effect determine—policy.

In consequence there appears to be taking place a diffusion of the power that is theoretically concentrated, and the function of the cabinet is coming to be that of coordinating a number of policy-making agencies rather than concentrating all governmental power in its own hands. Another consequence is to place on the prime minister an ever-greater responsibility to guide, control, and coordinate the work of the cabinet and other instruments of power.

CABINET GOVERNMENT ELSEWHERE

Cabinet systems in other countries have largely been modeled on that of the British, with variations produced by local conditions. The nations of the Commonwealth have for the most part carried on the British traditions of responsible government even when they have abandoned the monarchy for a republic. The older Commonwealth members tend to retain more of the British practices than do the newer ones, owing to the greater stability of their party systems. New Zealand's system is almost a copy of the British. The same is true of Canada's and Australia's, except as the adoption of federalism has produced modifications.

The Canadian Cabinet. The Canadian cabinet is somewhat smaller than that of the British, usually numbering 16 to 18, and fewer ministers are left outside the cabinet. There is no requirement that a minimum number of senators be included, and some cabinets include none at all. In Canada, as in all the monarchical dominions, the prime minister is appointed by the governor-general acting in the queen's name, and the cabinet is appointed in British fashion by the prime minister. The same rules of solidarity and collective responsibility apply as in Britain.

The most distinctive feature of the Canadian cabinet is its composition, which is calculated to reflect the federal structure of the nation. The conventions that govern the composition are quite rigid. Each of the 10 provinces is entitled to at least one member, party distribution permitting, and certain ministries go to certain regions. The results have been to restrict severely the prime minister's discretion and to produce a cabinet that is often more representative than competent. The rigidity of these rules has been declining somewhat in recent years, but the principle has by no means been abandoned. Indeed the cabinet has largely replaced the Senate as a means of representing provincial interests. When both dominion and provincial governments are held by the same party, the province conceives its members of the cabinet to be special representatives of the province in the political life of the dominion.

The Australian Cabinet. The same sort of federalization has taken place in the Australian cabinet. The rules are not nearly so restrictive, but a state not represented will protest loudly, and there has been a striking correlation between a state's share of cabinet posts and the state's seats in Parliament.

Continental Cabinets. European cabinet systems have often been affected by the existence of multiparty systems, which produce coalition governments and uncohesive oppositions. In the French Third and Fourth republics the instability of governments was such that power shifted overwhelmingly to the assembly, and the system was more properly described as a *régime d'assemblée*, or parliamentary government, rather than cabinet government. The Fifth Republic produced a considerable strengthening of the French ministry, attributable in part to the heightened power of the presidency, in part to the prestige of President de Gaulle, and in part to the greater (if temporary) stability of the party system.

West Germany has adopted an ingenious device to solve some of the problems of cabinet instability that earlier plagued both France and Germany. The requirement of a "constructive

HARRIS & EWING

THE FRANKLIN D. ROOSEVELT CABINET in 1937. *Left to right around the table:* President Roosevelt; Henry Morgenthau, Jr. (treasury); Homer S. Cummings (attorney general); Claude A. Swanson (navy); Henry A. Wallace (agriculture); Frances Perkins (labor); Vice President John N. Garner: Daniel C. Roper (commerce); Harold L. Ickes (interior); James A. Farley (postmaster general); Harry H. Woodring (war); Cordell Hull (state).

vote of no-confidence" means that once elected by a majority of the Bundestag (the lower house), the chancellor may be forced out only if the Bundestag simultaneously and by an absolute majority deposes him and elects a successor. This, coupled with the fact that ministers are responsible to the chancellor and not to the Bundestag, produces a strong executive.

THE CABINET IN THE UNITED STATES

The American cabinet has almost nothing in common with the British. Its members may not hold seats in Congress, and it exercises no collegial responsibility. It is not mentioned in the Constitution, which refers only to the heads of the executive departments; the framers of the Constitution apparently intended that the Senate serve as the president's advisory body. But Congress, beginning in 1789, has created executive departments (12 in number in the late 1960's) whose heads have by custom served as an advisory council to the president. Many administrative functions are performed outside the regular departments, and some presidents occasionally include some of these agency heads in the cabinet as well. The cabinet meets regularly (usually weekly) at times determined by the president and considers such matters as he wants discussed. Votes are seldom taken. Though many presidents have given the secretaries wide discretion in running their own departments, only rarely has the cabinet itself served as a real decision-making body. Dwight D. Eisenhower gave it more authority than most presidents, but there are inherent weaknesses that impair its effectiveness.

The president does not have complete discretion in appointing cabinet members. His campaign or other obligations, the claims of important factional leaders, the need for geographical distribution, the appointee's acceptability to the Senate, which must approve cabinet appointments, as well as to major interest groups—all these factors help produce a cabinet whose members are political figures in their own right, with little coherence and no sense of mutual obligation. Because each derives his authority from the president, the members often prefer to work with him directly in planning policy, with the result that only lesser matters are dealt with in cabinet meetings.

Members in effect become rivals for the president's favor, for congressional appropriations, and for political power. Some become so closely identified with their special clienteles, such as commerce, agriculture, or labor, that they are considered the virtual captives of major interest groups. This fragmentation means that the cabinet cannot view government problems and policies from the president's broad perspective and leaves him still in need of advisers and aides who can share his viewpoints and interests.

It is this need that has led most presidents to rely on an informal group of private advisers (Jackson's "kitchen cabinet" is a notable example), who serve him directly without any continuing personal connection with the government. It is this need also that led to the establishment of the White House Office and the Executive Office of the President.

Essentially the American cabinet is a body of administrators rather than an advisory council. It is quite consistent with the pluralist character of American democracy, and it stands in sharp contrast to the system of cabinet government described above.

WILLIAM S. LIVINGSTON
University of Texas

Bibliography

Bagehot, Walter, *The English Constitution* (London 1867).
Birch, Anthony H., *Representative and Responsible Government* (London 1964).
Daalder, Hans, *Cabinet Reform in Britain, 1914–1963* (Stanford, Calif., 1963).
Dawson, Robert M., *Government of Canada,* 2d ed. (Toronto 1954).
Encel, Solomon, *Cabinet Government in Australia* (London and Melbourne 1962).
Fenno, Richard F., *The President's Cabinet* (Cambridge, Mass., 1959).
Horn, Stephen, *The Cabinet and Congress* (New York 1960).
Jennings, Sir Ivor, *Cabinet Government,* 3d ed. (London 1959).
Mackintosh, John P., *The British Cabinet* (London 1962).

CABINET OF DR. CALIGARI, a classic horror film made in Germany in 1919. It was one of the first films to use expressionistic techniques such as distortion in props, costumes, and acting. *The Cabinet of Dr. Caligari* was based on a story by Robert Wiene, who also directed the film. Werner Krauss played the mad physician Dr. Caligari, operator of a carnival concession exhibiting the somnambulist Cesare, played by Conrad Veidt.

CABINETMAKING. See FURNITURE; FURNITURE, AMERICAN; WOODWORKING.

CABLE, kā'bəl, **George Washington** (1844–1925), American author, who was one of the best local color writers to emerge after the Civil War. He was also a social reformer and an early advocate of rights for the freed Negro.

Cable was born in New Orleans, La., on Oct. 12, 1844, and served in the Confederate army during the Civil War. From 1865 to 1879, while on the staff of the New Orleans *Picayune,* he discovered a wealth of romantic material in the history of his native city. Encouraged by Edward King, a journalist then touring the South for *Scribner's Monthly,* Cable published his first story, *'Sieur George,* in October 1873.

Cable was prominent as a public speaker. In 1884 he and Mark Twain billed themselves as the Twins of Genius and toured the United States. In 1885, Cable settled his large family in Northampton, Mass., where he became involved with several reform movements and where he mainly lived for the rest of his life. He died in St. Petersburg, Fla., on Jan. 31, 1925.

Cable's best fiction recreates the picturesque world of the Creoles in antebellum New Orleans. His first book was a collection of stories entitled *Old Creole Days* (1879). The novels *The Grandissimes* (1880), *Madame Delphine* (1881), *Dr. Sevier* (1884), *John Marsh, Southerner* (1894), and *Gideon's Band* (1914) established his literary reputation. Cable also wrote historical nonfiction, including *The Creoles of Louisiana* (1884) and *Strange True Stories of Louisiana* (1889). In essays later collected in *The Silent South* (1885) and *The Negro Question* (1890), he discussed the betrayal of Negro aspirations by the denial of social and civil equality, and the duty of the government to protect civil rights.

JEROME STERN, *Florida State University*

Further Reading: Butcher, Philip, *George W. Cable* (New York 1962); Turner, Arlin, *George W. Cable: A Biography* (Durham, N.C., 1956).

CABLE. See CHAIN.

CABLE, a conductor that provides a path for transmitting electrical energy from one place to another. A cable has one or more current-carrying conductors surrounded by an insulating material that isolates the current. Sometimes a cable also has a protective covering, or sheath, to prevent damage to the insulator.

One basic function of cables is to transmit information, particularly speech. Communication cables, which transmit messages in the form of electrical signals, are designed for low voltages and small currents. The signal power (voltage times current) in a telephone cable circuit, for instance, may be as small as a few millionths of a watt. Communication cables are widely used for transmission of telegraph messages, telephone calls, and pictures (as in closed-circuit television), and they make it possible to send information rapidly between two points that are far apart.

The other basic function of cables is to transmit electrical power. Electric power cables are designed for high voltages and large currents; some massive power cables carry currents of many thousands of amperes. Power cables, which carry direct current (dc) or low-frequency alternating current (ac), transmit electricity from power generating plants for distribution to residential, commercial, and industrial users.

COMMUNICATION CABLES

Development of Land Telegraph Lines. The first long-distance electrical communication system was the telegraph, invented in the late 1830's. This invention led to the birth of the wire and cable industry. Telegraph messages usually were sent over bare wires that were supported on insulators mounted on poles. By about 1860, most major American cities were linked by telegraph lines. Messages were sent in Morse code, which is still used in telegraphy, and these messages could be sent over long distances in minutes. See also TELEGRAPH.

Development of Land Telephone Cable. After Alexander Graham Bell invented the telephone in 1876, it became necessary to develop satisfactory cables for telephone lines. Early telephone lines usually were constructed like the telegraph lines, using bare wires and insulators mounted on poles. However, transmission of speech over relatively long distances presented new problems in designing telephone cable because loss of signal strength and distortion made speech signals unintelligible at the receiving end.

The importance of the electrical properties of the cable, such as capacitance and inductance, was stressed by the mathematical work of Oliver Heaviside of England in 1885–1887, and in 1899 an American scientist and engineer, Michael I. Pupin, saw that adding induction coils to telephone cables would provide strong and clear voice transmission. This method and other ways of loading the cable to counterbalance its capacitance provided improved reception of telephone conversations at the low voice frequencies then in use. See also TELEPHONE.

Modern Land Telephone Cable. After the invention of diode and triode vacuum tubes by John A. Fleming and Lee De Forest in the first decade of the 20th century, speech signals could be amplified, and carrier frequencies could be used to carry simultaneous conversations on a single cable. Tuned filters were used to separate the conversations on the different carrier frequencies.

With the use of high-frequency carrier waves for transmitting telephone messages, loaded cables became obsolete because they were not sufficiently efficient at high frequencies. For carrier frequency transmission, multipair cable constructions were developed in the following order: (1) paper insulation, multiple twin conductors or groups of four conductors, and lead sheath; (2) paper and plastic insulation, multipair conductors, and plastic, metal, or composite sheaths; and (3) plastic insulation, multipair conductors, and plastic sheaths, using plastics such as polyvinyl chloride and polythene (polyethylene).

The unloaded coaxial cable, which was developed to supersede the loaded cable and the multipair cable, has an inner conductor, insulation,

A SUBMARINE CABLE providing telegraph communication between Ireland and North America was successfully laid in July 1866. The cable can be seen paying out over rollers at the stern of the British steamship *Great Eastern.*

CULVER PICTURES

and a surrounding concentric outer conductor. This construction makes it suitable for transmission of high carrier frequencies. Coaxial cable was developed by Bell Telephone Laboratories and the Western Electric Company. The first commercial coaxial cable installation, laid between Stevens Point, Wis., and Minneapolis, Minn., in 1941, had a bundle of four coaxial cables that provided 480 voice channels.

In the United States there is wide use of 0.375-inch-diameter (0.953-cm) coaxial cables bundled together in one protective covering that surrounds as many as 20 coaxial cables. These coaxial cables are used in pairs, one cable in a pair for messages in one direction, and the other for messages in the other direction. With appropriate carrier systems, such cables provide as many as 3,600 voice channels per pair. A line containing 20 coaxial cables provides 32,400 voice channels (9 × 3,600), with one pair kept as a spare.

Since the invention of the telephone, American transcontinental telephone lines and cables were developed in the same sequence as long-distance overland telephone systems elsewhere in the world. This sequence of development was: (1) bare-wire lines; (2) loaded audio-frequency cable; (3) multipair cable for carrier frequency transmission; and (4) coaxial cable for carrier frequency transmission.

The first telephone route across America was opened in 1915. The first intercontinental telephone cable, linking Europe and North America, was laid in 1956, after the development of repeater amplifiers for submarine cable.

SUBMARINE CABLE

Before 1848, many attempts were made to find a suitable insulation for undersea cables; tarred rope, impregnated cotton, split rattan, and india rubber were tried, but none of these was suitable for long periods of immersion in seawater. The first successful insulation for an underwater line was gutta-percha (a gum from a Malayan tree), which was used by Ernst Werner von Siemens of Germany in 1848 in a line to detonate mines in the harbor at Kiel.

Submarine Telegraph Cable. The first underwater telegraph cable, which had a single conductor and gutta-percha insulation, was laid from the tug *Goliath* on Aug. 28, 1850, between Dover and Calais. The cable failed, but its pioneers, Jacob and John W. Brett of England, succeeded with a second cable, 25 miles (40 km) long, laid in 1851 between Dover and Calais. This cable, which had four copper wires and gutta-percha insulation, remained in use until 1875. The electrical and mechanical properties of gutta-percha were so good that for 70 years it had no rival as an insulator in submarine cables.

The first successful transatlantic cable (in use for six years) was laid by the *Great Eastern* starting from Valentia, Ireland, on July 13, 1866, and ending at Heart's Content, Newfoundland, on July 27, 1866. The 693-foot-long (211-meter) *Great Eastern*, by far the largest ship in the world at that time, laid 1,852 nautical miles (3,432 km) of cable from a drum at its stern. The ship carried 2,400 nautical miles (4,447 km) of a single cable coiled in three cylindrical tanks in its hold, and it laid cable at a rate of about 6 nautical miles (11 km) per hour. The 1.1-inch-diameter (2.8-cm) cable, which was laid in waters sometimes more than 2 miles (3.2 km) deep, had a seven-strand copper conductor, four layers of gutta-percha insulation, five layers of a compound containing gutta-percha, a wrapping of tarred hemp, and protective armor of 10 steel wires, each wrapped in impregnated hemp. From the start of the voyage and thereafter, the *Great Eastern* maintained telegraphic communication with Valentia by sending messages through the whole length of the single cable.

On July 27, 1866, a telegram sent on completion of the cable laying read simply, "All right." Within the next few days, a message from Queen Victoria to President Andrew Johnson and a reply from him to the Queen were sent over the cable at a rate of about eight words per minute.

The cable laid in 1866 was the fifth attempt to lay a transatlantic cable. One earlier expedition was made in 1857, two were made in 1858, and one was made in 1865. The broken end of the 1865 cable was retrieved about 600 miles (965 km) off Newfoundland shortly after the 1866 cable was laid, and so there were two transatlantic cables in operation in 1866.

The second 1858 expedition laid a cable from Valentia to Newfoundland that operated successfully from August 5 to September 1. During that period, Queen Victoria sent a cable message to President James Buchanan, and he sent a reply over the cable. On August 20 the first news message was sent across the cable; it was a report of a collision of two ships off Newfoundland.

The enterprise of laying a transatlantic cable

CON EDISON

A HIGH-VOLTAGE POWER CABLE is laid underground in pipes filled with oil to keep it from overheating.

took 13 years of effort and financing. Cyrus W. Field and William Thomson (later Lord Kelvin) participated in all five expeditions, and they played vital roles in achieving the first telegraphic link between Europe and North America.

By the end of the 19th century, there were at least 12 telegraph cables across the Atlantic and several others across the Pacific, including one laid in 1902 from Vancouver Island to Brisbane, Australia. In 1903, President Theodore Roosevelt participated in an experiment—the sending of the first round-the-world telegraph message. His message was sent around the world in nine minutes.

Submarine Telephone Cable. By 1890 the striking success of the submarine telegraph cables had led to keen interest in developing submarine telephone cables. Early submarine telephone cables, such as one laid by the Danish government in 1902, provided underwater telephone communications only over short distances. With the development of amplifiers and other equipment, it became possible to use repeater amplifiers in submarine telephone cable and thus obtain transmission of telephone messages over long distances. The first submarine cable with repeater amplifiers was laid from the Isle of Man to Wales in 1943.

Seven years later Bell Telephone Laboratories produced a repeater amplifier encased in a hollow flexible steel container, which could withstand the high pressure at the ocean bottom and could be laid with the normal gear of a cable-laying ship. (The first ship designed for cable laying was the *Great Western*, launched in 1873.) The repeater amplifiers were inserted in the cable at intervals, and each repeater made a characteristic bulge in the cable.

Because of severe restriction on space, only one-way amplification could be provided by vacuum-tube amplifiers; consequently two cables had to be laid to handle messages in opposite directions. The two coaxial cables laid in 1950 between Key West, Fla., and Havana had repeaters in cables lying at depths ranging down to 950 fathoms (1,820 meters). This system provided 24 telephone circuits that have operated successfully since 1950.

In a joint venture by American, British, and Canadian organizations, the first transatlantic telephone cable system was completed in 1956, using repeaters spaced at intervals of 40 miles (64 km). Two cables, about 25 miles (40 km) apart, were laid for voice messages in each direction between Oban, Scotland, and Clarenville, Newfoundland. Following this success, similar systems were installed, including one between San Francisco and Honolulu (1957) and another between the United States and France (1959).

In the period 1950–1963, about 45,000 nautical miles (83,400 km) of coaxial telephone cable and 1,600 one-way repeaters were laid in European, Alantic, and Pacific waters. In 1963 the first single coaxial cable with two-way repeaters was laid between Florida and Jamaica; this cable provided 128 telephone channels for conversations in both directions. In the same year a single coaxial cable with two-way repeaters was laid between Tuckerton, N. J., and England. In 1964, Hawaii and Japan were linked by a single coaxial cable with two-way repeaters.

POWER TRANSMISSION CABLE

Power cables became important in the early 1880's, only a few years after Thomas Edison developed an incandescent lamp in 1879 that was suitable for commercial use. Edison demonstrated the first experimental overhead line for lighting incandescent lamps at Menlo Park, N. J., on Jan. 1, 1880, and he demonstrated the first direct-current underground power transmission system on Nov. 2, 1880, using about 6 miles (9.66 km) of rigid conductors.

Early DC Power Cable. The Edison underground power cable used in 1882 had two metal rod conductors, each with a semicircular cross section. The rods were slid into an iron pipe and were kept in place by cardboard spacers. A hand pump was used to fill the pipe with a liquid compound that cooled and solidified, creating a rigid cable. Early cables, such as the Edison tubes, transmitted direct current at low voltages (about 100 volts). With this low-voltage, direct-current system, transmission was limited to ¾ of a mile.

Early AC Power Cable. Transmission of electric power using alternating currents occurred shortly after the introduction of the transformer in 1882, and the first commercial ac service was established in Buffalo, N. Y., in 1886. During the period 1885–1890, there was a struggle between the protagonists of low-voltage dc and the protagonists of high-voltage ac as to which method was best for transmitting electric power. Edison favored dc transmission, whereas Sebastian Z. de Ferranti of England favored ac transmission. The chief advantages of low-voltage dc were its safety and its well understood technology. The chief advantage of high-voltage ac was the transmission efficiency resulting from the high voltages, which could be stepped down to low voltages by means of transformers located near the point of use.

In 1890, Ferranti transmitted 10,000-volt ac over a 6.5-mile-long (10.5 km) cable between Deptford and central London. This cable had two concentric copper tubes; one was 13⁄16 inch (2.06 cm) in diameter and the other was 1 15⁄16 inches (4.92 cm) in diameter. The two tubes were separated by 0.5-inch-thick (1.27 cm) wax-impregnated paper; the outer tube was wrapped with 3⁄16-inch-thick (0.48 cm) wax-impregnated paper. The whole assembly was slid into an iron pipe, and the space between the insulation and the pipe was filled with bitumen. In operation, the outer tube was grounded, and transformers were used to step down the voltage.

Ferranti's cable showed that the use of ac could greatly increase the distance over which electrical power could be transmitted, and its success led to the adoption of paper-insulated power cable. Flexible paper-insulated power cables came into use in 1892, and by 1899, London had 90 miles (145 km) of this cable in use.

High-Voltage Power Cable. Before Ferranti developed cable for operation at 10,000 volts, cable was limited to voltages no greater than 3,000 volts. Since 1890 the voltage for electric power transmission has increased steadily upward to take advantage of lower power losses at higher transmission voltages. However, operation of insulated power cables at voltages greater than about 33,000 volts presented the problem of providing strong insulation that will not break down under high electrical stresses. Several kinds of power cables were developed especially for high-voltage transmission.

In 1920, the Italian Luigi Emanueli developed an *oil-filled cable*. It had a thin oil that flowed easily along ducts that connected oil reservoirs within the cable. In 1925, Henry W. Fisher and Ralph W. Atkinson, both Americans, obtained a patent for a *gas pressure cable*. In this cable, dry compressed air or nitrogen at a pressure of 15 atmospheres is applied on the insulation to raise electrical strength. This principle also was utilized by an American, C. E. Bennett, who developed a cable called an *oilostatic cable* in 1931. This cable had a steel-pipe protective cover.

High-Voltage Overhead Lines. The transmission of electrical energy from a power station may be by overhead lines supported on towers or by underground insulated cables, and various design considerations and physical conditions govern the choice. For example, the effect of inductance is predominant in overhead lines, and the effect of capacitance is predominant in underground cables. Apart from technical considerations, overhead transmission is generally favored for long-distance lines across open country because the cost is lower. Usually, in deciding whether overhead transmission should be adopted, many factors have to be taken into account, including the lay of the land, the population density, and the cost of obtaining a right-of-way.

For overhead construction, hard-drawn copper, aluminum and steel, and various combinations of copper and aluminum have been used as conductors. Overhead transmission lines with bare conductors fixed to insulators have given satisfactory service at 250,000 volts. Insulated pressure cables sometimes are used for higher voltages.

Underground Cable. In one commonly used method for laying underground cables, heavily armored cables are laid directly into the ground. In a second commonly used method, less heavily armored cables are run through pipes or ducts, which protect them. In laying the heavily armored cable, a trench is excavated a few feet deep, the drum of cable is taken alongside the trench, and the cable is unreeled and laid along the prepared bottom of the trench.

For very high voltages, oil-filled or gas-pressure cables are used. However, the power transmission capability of all underground power cables is limited by the transfer of heat from the cable to its surroundings. When the heat transfer is not sufficient, the cable overheats and can be damaged. Short cable runs have been cooled by using water or an oil to carry the heat from the cable.

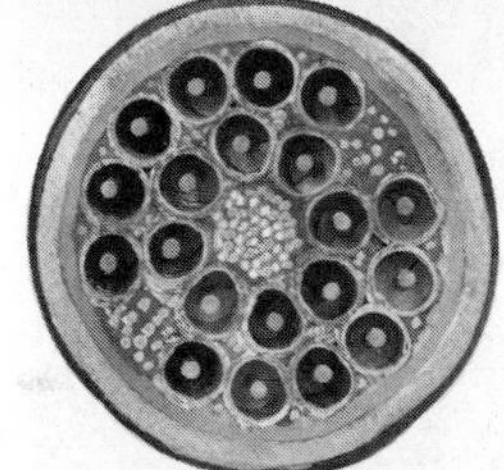

TWENTY COAXIAL CABLES contained in one protective covering can handle 32,400 voice channels at one time.

BELL TELEPHONE LABORATORIES

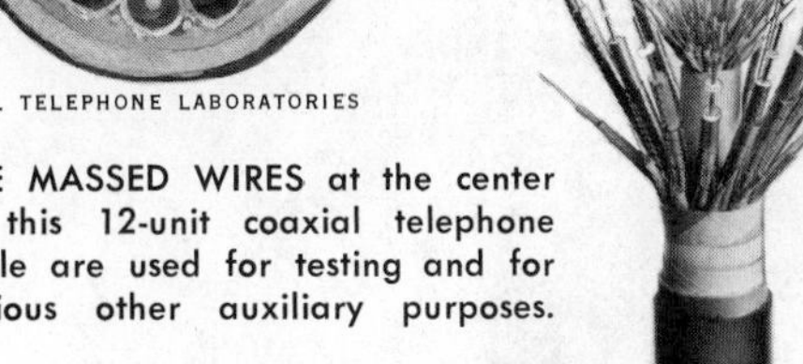

THE MASSED WIRES at the center of this 12-unit coaxial telephone cable are used for testing and for various other auxiliary purposes.

AMERICAN TELEPHONE AND TELEGRAPH

AERIAL TELEPHONE CABLE contains wires bound in an undulating core with enough slack to provide flexibility.

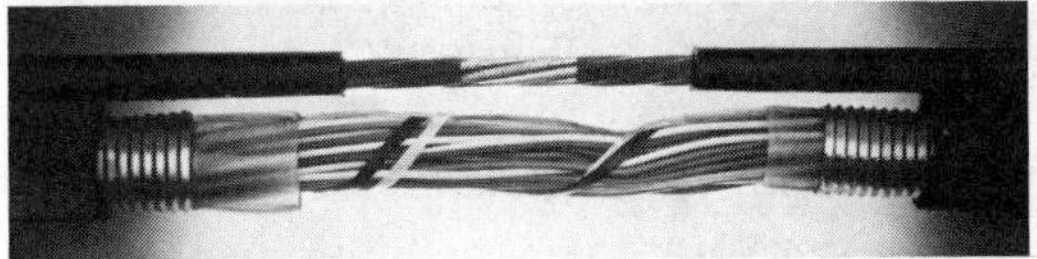

BELL TELEPHONE LABORATORIES

CABLE DESIGNS FOR CLOSED-CIRCUIT EDUCATIONAL TV TRANSMISSION

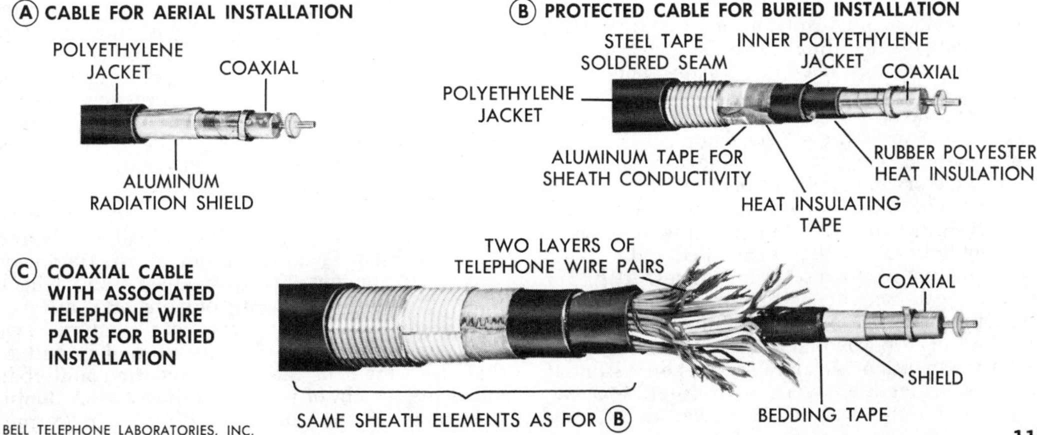

BELL TELEPHONE LABORATORIES, INC.

BOB AND IRA SPRING

ONE TYPE OF CABLE CAR, the aerial tramway, is best known in the ski lifts used in winter resorts.

Underwater Power Cable. In underwater power cable installations, the seawater helps to keep the cable from overheating. Submarine power cables over short distances are installed between the mainlands of Japan, the United States, France, Italy, and Great Britain and islands off their coasts, using oil-filled or gas-pressure cable. The longest underwater cable in the world, between the island of Sardinia and the Italian mainland, was completed in 1965; it transmits 200 megawatts dc from Sardinia to the Tuscany area.

Power Cable Research. Considerable research is being done to attain new and improved methods of transmitting power by cables. Experimental work on superconducting cables indicates spectacular possibilities, since such cables would have no electrical resistance, but many technical problems still remain. Experiments have also been made with cables consisting of a tube of polyethylene filled with a sodium conductor. The electrical conductivity of sodium ranks just below copper and aluminum.

CABLE CONSTRUCTION

Conductors and insulators are the two main constituents of all cables. The use of copper for the conductor has been practically unchanged since the earliest cables, but the materials for insulation have changed considerably with the development of improved insulators.

Conductors. Copper is an ideal material for the conductor; it has high conductivity and will carry current through its length with very little loss. It is ductile and can be drawn down to very fine wires, and it is easily soldered.

Aluminum also is useful for cables. It has an electrical conductivity of 62 compared with 100 for copper, but it is lighter. Silver has a conductivity of 106 compared with 100 for copper, but it is expensive and only used where essential. Where considerable mechanical strength is necessary, as in long suspended power cables and modern submarine cables, steel wires are often used in conjunction with the copper wires.

Insulators. The initial insulation for cables was gutta-percha. Rubber was used for many years as a general-purpose insulator, but it is subject to deterioration, mainly caused by oxygen in the atmosphere, and it is also affected by severe environments. However, vulcanized rubber is more stable. Several synthetic rubbers, such as neoprene, also are used; each has characteristics that make it suitable for certain types of applications. Paper is a useful insulator when it is impregnated with oil and sealed in a protective covering.

Modern insulating materials generally are plastics, such as polyvinyl chloride and polyethylene. The discovery of polyethylene by Imperial Chemical Industries, Ltd., in England in 1933 marked a large step forward in dielectrics for cables that operated at very high frequencies. Since this discovery, other plastics, such as Teflon, have been developed and are in wide use. Insulating materials are also being developed for cables that must operate under severe conditions imposed by a spacecraft environment, extremes of temperature, severe vibrations, or nuclear radiation.

G. W. A. DUMMER, *Coauthor of "Radio and Electronic Components"*

Further Reading: Barnes, C. C., *Electric Cables* (New York 1964); Dibner, Bern, *The Atlantic Cable* (Norwalk, Conn., 1957); Hunter, Philip V., and Hazell, James T., *Development of Power Cables* (London 1956).

CABLE CAR, a cable-drawn passenger vehicle used especially for transportation across hilly or mountainous terrain. Motive power is provided by a moving cable driven from a remote station. Two kinds of cable cars—cable railroads and funiculars—are surface vehicles. A third kind—the aerial tramway—moves on a suspended cable.

The *cable railroad* was invented and patented in 1867 by Andrew S. Hallidie (1836–1900), a San Francisco cable manufacturer and mechanic, who had made his start by designing and building ore cableways for gold mines. The first cable railroad, built by Hallidie's "Clay St. Hill RR Co." in San Francisco, began operation on Aug. 1, 1873. The line was 2,800 feet (853 meters) long with a climb of 307 feet (33.6 meters).

The equipment used in San Francisco's cable cars is basically the same as the equipment of the first cable railroad. Each car is equipped with a grip device that extends through a slot to a moving continuous subsurface cable between the rails. To move the car forward, the operator clamps the "Hallidie grip" on the cable; to stop, he releases the grip and applies brakes. Other features include a turntable at each end of the line to reverse direction and emergency stop devices on each end of the car. By 1877, cable railroads using Hallidie's patented devices were operating in 20 American cities as well as in several foreign countries. Toward the end of the 19th century, the development of practical electric power led to the decline of cable railroads.

A *funicular* is used for rail transportation on very steep inclines. The car chassis and wheels match the angle of ascent, but the seats are parallel to the horizon for safety and comfort. Two cars connected by cables are normally used so that the weight of the ascending car counterbalances the weight of the descending car. A double track may be used, but more often a single track is supplemented by double track at mid-grade so cars can pass each other. In Los Angeles, a notable funicular, called Angels Flight, ascends a 33% grade on a 315-foot-long (96-meter) trestle.

The *aerial tramway* has cars supported by cables suspended between two or more towers. The most common design utilizes two cables. The car is suspended below a truck fitted with grooved wheels that ride on the supporting cables. A separate moving continuous cable propels the car. Tramways are commonly used for long mountain ascents or to cross canyons or rivers. The world's highest tramway, in Venezuela, ascends from the village of Mérida to the summit of Pico Espejo, which is 15,633 feet (4,765 meters) high. The world's longest passenger tramway, near Palm Springs, Calif., rises 5,873 feet (1,830 meters) over a 13,200-foot-long (4,023-meter) cableway on Mt. San Jacinto. The car rides twin cables supported by five towers.

The best-known tramways are ski lifts. In a ski lift, the car usually is fastened to the moving cable. The 21 cable lifts near Aspen, Colo., provide one of the world's most extensive ski-lift facilities. Other major ski lifts in the United States include those at Winter Park, Colorado; Squaw Valley, California; Alta, Brighton, Snow Basin, and Park City, Utah; Big Mountain, Montana; Gore Mountain, New York; Franconia Notch, New Hampshire; Mt. Snow, Vermont; Sun Valley, Idaho; Mt. Baker, Washington; and Jackson Hole, Wyoming.

ROBERT L. MOUNT, *Science Writer*

PHIL PALMER, FROM MONKMEYER

CABLE CARS, as famous for their charm as for their convenience, have become a symbol for San Francisco.

CABOT, kab'ət, a Massachusetts family prominent in America from the early 18th century. The Cabots distinguished themselves by their abilities to make and increase their fortunes. They also produced noted politicians, physicians, and philanthropists. The founder in America, John Cabot, went to Salem, Mass., from the island of Jersey in the English Channel about 1700. The early Cabots made their money in general trade, in slaves, in rum and opium, in privateering, and by marriage. Moving from Salem to Beverly and then to Boston, they intermarried with other Boston Brahmin first families. Prominent scions included George Cabot, Francis Cabot Lowell, Henry Cabot Lodge, Richard Clarke Cabot, and Godfrey Lowell Cabot.

Astute in trade, unself-conscious, prickly, proud, and often puritanical, they provoked envy as well as admiration. It was commonly said, "The Cabots are a Massachusetts tribe known to have many customs but no manners." Their reputation as snobs was spread by the verse:

> And this is good old Boston,
> The home of the bean and the cod,
> Where the Lowells talk to Cabots,
> And the Cabots talk only to God.

However, the Cabots also were known for their support of such local institutions as Massachusetts General Hospital, the Boston Athenaeum, the Boston Symphony, and Harvard University.

LEON HARRIS, *Author of "Only to God: The Extraordinary Life of Godfrey Lowell Cabot"*

CABOT, kab'ət, **George** (1752–1823), American merchant and politician. He was born in Salem, Mass., on Jan. 16, 1752. After attending Harvard for two years, he went to sea, and by 1773 he was in command of a ship owned by his brothers. He became a member of the family mercantile and shipping firm in Beverly, Mass., in 1777.

In the same year he was elected to the provincial congress of Massachusetts, and in 1788 he was a member of the state convention that adopted the federal Constitution. A Federalist, he served in the U. S. Senate from 1791 to 1796. In 1793 he introduced the first of the fugitive slave acts. Weary of politics, he resigned his seat in 1796. Two years later he declined an appointment by President John Adams as the first U. S. secretary of the navy. A member of the group of wealthy Massachusetts Federalists known as the Essex Junto, he presided in 1814 over the Hartford Convention (q.v.) of New England Federalists, which opposed the War of 1812. He died in Boston on April 18, 1823.

LEON HARRIS, *Author of "Only to God: The Extraordinary Life of Godfrey Lowell Cabot"*

CABOT, kab'ət, **Godfrey Lowell** (1861–1962), American manufacturer. A member of the prominent Cabot family, he was born in Boston, Mass., on Feb. 26, 1861, and graduated from Harvard in 1882. Cabot began to manufacture carbon black and developed the world's largest business of its kind. A pioneer in aviation, he tried to interest the government in military aircraft as early as 1903. During World War I, he was appointed to the U. S. Naval Reserves Flying Corps, and he perfected a method of picking up burdens in flight.

A prime mover in Boston's Watch and Ward Society, he also was a vigorous opponent of municipal corruption, and he effected the dismissal of several dishonest politicians. He died in Boston on Nov. 2, 1962.

LEON HARRIS, *Author of "Only to God: The Extraordinary Life of Godfrey Lowell Cabot"*

CABOT, kab′ət, **John** (died ?1498), Italian explorer in the service of England, who led voyages of discovery from Bristol, England, to North America in 1497 and 1498. These were the first recorded landfalls on the North American continent since the voyages of the Norsemen in the 11th and 12th centuries.

A merchant and citizen of Venice, John Cabot (Italian, *Giovanni Caboto*) had, by his own later account, been engaged in the spice trade with the Levant. This experience, and his reading of Marco Polo's description of the Far East, probably led him to formulate his project for a westward voyage to "the Indies." Cabot went to England with his sons in or before 1495 with a plan for sailing westward to Cathay by a more northerly, and therefore shorter, route than the route through the trade-wind zone that Columbus had followed across the Atlantic in 1492–1493.

First Voyage. For about 15 years Bristol seamen had made regular voyages into the western ocean in search of new fishing grounds and of the "Island of Brasil" shown in contemporary maps, and at some date before 1494 they had discovered a mainland in the west. It was in Bristol therefore that Cabot looked for a ship and a crew. Letters patent from King Henry VII dated March 5, 1496, authorized Cabot and his sons to discover and possess lands "unknown to all Christians." In the same year Cabot set out with one ship from Bristol, but was forced to turn back.

In May 1497 he sailed again from Bristol in the ship *Matthew* (named for his Venetian wife, Mattea). After a run of 35 days he made land on June 24, probably in Maine or southern Nova Scotia. Here he went ashore and made a formal act of possession. From this point he turned back and coasted "eastward" for 300 leagues, apparently to Cape Race in Newfoundland, whence he made a fast crossing of 15 days and was back in Bristol early in August.

Although the Bristol seamen were excited by the wealth of fish observed off Newfoundland, Cabot was preoccupied with greater things. His reconnaissance had convicted him that the land he had found was "a part of Asia" or "the country of the Great Khan." This claim was accepted at the English court. A Venetian in London wrote home that Cabot was "called the Great Admiral . . . and these English run after him like mad."

Second Voyage. In December 1497, Cabot presented to the King his proposals for a second voyage. From his original landfall he intended to follow the coast to the southwest until he came to the realm of the Great Khan, in East Asia—the source (according to Marco Polo) of "all the spices of the world." In February 1498 he received royal letters patent allowing him to impress ships and to recruit crews. Early in May Cabot sailed with five ships.

It appears that Cabot himself perished on this voyage, although one or more of his ships may have come back. If he or his companions followed his plan, they found neither Cathay nor a westerly sea-passage to East Asia. In this sense, they may have made (in the words of the historian James A. Williamson) "the intellectual discovery of America," for subsequent English explorers did not confuse America with Asia.

R. A. SKELTON, *Former Superintendent of the Map Room, British Museum*

Further Reading: Williamson, James A., *The Cabot Voyages and Bristol Discovery Under Henry VII* (London 1962).

CABOT, kab′ət, **Sebastian** (c. 1482–1557), Italian explorer and cosmographer. Born in Venice, the son of John Cabot (q.v.), Sebastian went to England with his father during or before 1495.

After John Cabot's second voyage, in 1498, Sebastian became interested in the discovery of a route "by the north to Cathay." In 1508–1509, with two ships, he made a voyage by way of Iceland and Greenland to Labrador. After coasting north and west, he found before him open sea, which (if his account is to be credited) must have been the mouth of Hudson Bay. Here his crew refused to go on, and he turned south along the North American coast to about the latitude of Virginia before returning to England. Cabot believed that he had found the opening of the Northwest Passage to the Pacific and East Asia, and the search for a seaway to Cathay dominated his later career in Spain and England.

In 1512, Cabot entered Spanish service, and in 1518 he was appointed pilot-major in the House of Trade at Seville. He was one of the Spanish experts in the diplomatic exchanges with Portugal (1522–1524) concerning the location of the Spice Islands. In the years 1526–1530, Cabot commanded a fleet promoted by Seville merchants and the Spanish crown to make a commercial voyage to the Pacific by way of South America. The expedition got no farther than the Río de la Plata (between Uruguay and Argentina), and Cabot returned to Spain with little credit. He resumed his duties as pilot-major, which involved him in the construction and revision of charts and in the study of navigational problems, particularly the determination of longitude.

Cabot seems to have become increasingly dissatisfied in the Spanish service. As early as 1520–1521 he had been in secret correspondence with the English authorities, and in 1522–1523 with Venice. In 1548 he fled to England, where he was granted a royal annuity for services "done and to be done" as a geographical adviser, especially in the English search for a northeast passage. Cabot was the first governor of the Muscovy Company and assisted in preparing its expeditions of 1553 and 1556. He died in London before December 1557.

Maps prepared or revised by Cabot in England to illustrate his concept of the Northwest Passage, which he supposed himself to have discovered, gave an impulse to English enterprise in search of this passage in the later years of the 16th century.

R. A. SKELTON, *Former Superintendent of the Map Room, British Museum*

CABRA, kä′vra, is a town in southern Spain, in Córdoba province. It is situated in the valley of the Cabra River, 34 miles (55 km) southeast of the city of Córdoba. The town lies in the midst of a fertile agricultural region. Chemicals, food products, and bricks are manufactured there, and marble is quarried. The handsome parish church was at one time a Muslim mosque, and there is also a ruined Moorish castle.

The town was called Igabrum by the Romans. It was long in the hands of the Moors. Ferdinand III of Castile and León, who conquered large areas of southern Spain, took Cabra from the Moors in 1244, but the Moors recaptured it in 1331. Cabra finally passed into the possession of Spain in the 15th century. Population: (1960) 15,688.

CABRAL, kə-bräl′, **Pedro Álvares** (1460?–?1526), Portuguese navigator. In 1500 he received command of a fleet bound for the East Indies around Africa, and he sailed from Lisbon. But he took a westerly course, and on April 22, 1500, he reached the coast of Brazil, which he claimed for King Manuel I of Portugal. He then continued his voyage east, losing several of his 13 ships in a storm off the Cape of Good Hope. With the remainder he gained Mozambique and continued on to India. He had difficulties establishing a trading post at Calicut but succeeded at Cochin. Cabral, having made the first sea voyage from Europe to India after that of Vasco da Gama, returned to Portugal with highly profitable cargoes.

Cabral is usually credited with discovering Brazil, but this claim has been contested. In any event, his expedition spurred subsequent exploration of the region.

CABRILLA, kə-brē′yə, any of a number of small sea basses. The name "cabrilla" is probably best restricted to the spotted cabrilla (*Epinephalus analogus*) of the Pacific coast of tropical America. This species, a valuable food fish, is common along the coast of Mexico, where it is known as "cabrilla pinta." It reaches a length of 1 foot (30 cm). Its greenish brown body is covered with dark spots, and three or four dark bars are sometimes apparent across its back.

The kelp bass (*Paralabrax clathratus*), found along the California coast, has also often been called a "cabrilla." This fish reaches a length of 1½ feet (45 cm) and is an excellent food fish.

The name "cabrilla" has also been used for several sea basses in the West Indies, most notably the common red hind (*Epinephalus guttatus*), and for other members of the genera *Epinephalus, Paralabrax,* and *Mycteroperca,* all of which are in the family Serranidae in the order Perciformes.

JAMES C. TYLER
Academy of Natural Sciences of Philadelphia

CABRILLO, kä-brē′yō, **Juan Rodríguez** (died 1543), early explorer of the California coast. Little is known of Cabrillo before his appearance in Mexico in 1520. He was probably of Portuguese birth. At Vera Cruz he deserted Pánfilo de Narváez and joined fortunes with Cortés in the conquest of Mexico. Later he was with Pedro de Alvarado in Guatemala and Honduras. He was closely associated with Alvarado when the latter built a fleet of 11 vessels and planned extensive Pacific explorations.

When Alvarado met his death in the Mixton War (1541), Antonio de Mendoza, viceroy of New Spain, sent Cabrillo with two ships to explore the Pacific coast of North America. Cabrillo was the first European (1542) to see San Diego and San Pedro harbors, Santa Catalina Island, the islands of the Santa Barbara Channel, and Monterey Bay. He went as far north as Point Reyes, but missed the Golden Gate. Dropping back to winter on San Miguel Island, in early 1543, he died of injuries sustained in a fall. His pilot, Bartolomé Ferrelo, went north again that year and probably saw the Oregon coast.

Cabrillo is memorialized in Cabrillo National Monument on San Diego Bay.

JOHN FRANCIS BANNON
Saint Louis University

CABRINI, kə-brē′nē, **Saint Frances Xavier** (1850–1917), Italian-American religious foundress. Born at Sant'Angelo, near Lodi (Milano), Italy, on July 15, 1850, Frances (Francesca) was the youngest of 13 children of Agostino and Stella (Oldini) Cabrini. Agostino Depretis, Italian prime minister (1876–1879, 1881–1887), was her paternal cousin. After studying (1863–1868) at the school run by the Daughters of the Sacred Heart in nearby Arluno, she obtained a teacher's certificate and applied for admission to the Daughters. Because of her frail health, however, the Daughters refused her as did the Canossians in 1872. Frances engaged in domestic chores until 1872, when she began teaching at the public school in neighboring Vidardo.

On the recommendation of her spiritual adviser, Monsignor Antonio Serrati, she accepted employment in a small orphanage, the House of Providence, in Codogno in 1874. In 1877 she took religious vows and became directress of the institution. Due to the hopeless mismanagement of the orphanage by its eccentric benefactress, Antonia Tondini, Bishop Gelmini of Lodi finally closed it in 1880. Frances, heeding Bishop Gelmini's advice, gathered around her seven sisters and founded the Missionary Sisters of the Sacred Heart (M. S. C.) on November 14, 1880. She continued as superior general of the order until her death. Mother Cabrini, as she came to be called, composed the rules and constitution of the order which Rome approved definitively in 1907.

ST. FRANCES XAVIER CABRINI CHAPEL, FORT WASHINGTON, N. Y.

St. Frances Xavier Cabrini

Urged by Bishop Scalabrini of Piacenza and Pope Leo XIII, she directed her apostolate toward the Italian immigrants in the Americas rather than to the non-Christians of China, as she had originally planned. She arrived in New York City on March 31, 1889 with six sisters. Eventually she established orphanages, nurseries, hospitals, and schools throughout the United States and opened houses in France, England, Nicaragua, Argentina, and Brazil. These 67 foundations of over 1,500 sisters primarily, but not exclusively, aided Italian immigrants. She died in Chicago, Ill., on Dec. 22, 1917. The "saint of the immigrants," as she is called, was the first American citizen to be canonized (1946). Her feast is November 13.

JOHN F. BRODERICK, S. J.
Weston College, Mass.

JOHN J. SMITH

LEON V. KOFOD

CACAO pods grow on the tree trunk and branches (*left*) and contain the seeds (*right*) from which cocoa is made.

CACAO, kə-kou′, also called *cocoa,* is a small tropical tree that is the source of chocolate. The name "cacao" is derived from the Mayan Nahuatl dialect, in which the plant was known as "cacahuatl" or "chocoatl". The tree had apparently been cultivated by Indians in the region from southern Mexico through northern South America for centuries before the Spanish conquest.

Spanish explorers of the early 1500's found cacao highly esteemed by the indigenous Central American peoples. When Cortés invaded the Aztec empire, Montezuma honored him by serving a chocolate drink. Tribute was often paid to the rulers in cacao beans rather than in precious metal.

The Spanish, and later the Portuguese, soon spread cacao widely through their colonies. Cacao was introduced into Trinidad and other Caribbean islands very early, and not much later into islands in the Gulf of Guinea off the west coast of Africa. Eventually it was taken to Africa and the Far East.

Cacao is seldom more than 25 feet (7½ meters) tall, and it naturally grows in the shade of taller trees. It is important for its beans, or seeds, which occur 30 to 50 in a pod. The seeds are surrounded by a mucilaginous pulp, and the pulp is covered by a fairly hard outer shell something like that of a melon. The pod, technically a berry, is football-shaped and weighs about ¼ pound (⅒ kg). It grows from leafless "cushions" on the lower bare branches and trunk.

Cultivation. Cacao trees require shade. Thus a scattering of taller shade trees is usually planted or left standing when a forest is cleared to protect cacao plantings. The most desirable amount and type of shade for cacao is uncertain. Certain species of shade trees inhibit the growth of cacao, while others encourage it.

Shade trees serve several functions. For one thing, cacao has many feeder roots near the soil surface; under normal forest conditions these draw nutrients from the decomposing leaves that have fallen to the forest floor. Shade trees left or planted supply something of this natural condition. Also, many tropical soils lose their organic content and bake hard when exposed to full sun.

Cacao is adapted to regions of heavy rainfall and equable temperature. For successful growing, rainfall should be 80 inches (200 cm) or more annually, and temperature variations should not exceed a range of about 65° F to 95° F (18° C to 35° C) both daily and seasonally.

Harvesting and Processing. Vigorous trees yield many dozens of pods through the course of a year, and per-acre yields may run as much as two tons of dry cocoa annually. Ripened pods can be discerned by their purple color. They are in harvestable condition for about two weeks, during which they are cut by hand from the trunks and branches of cacao trees and piled in convenient locations for subsequent removal of the seeds.

The pods are cut open with a bush knife (which may damage a few of the seeds) or cracked with a mallet, and the pulpy seeds are scooped from the husks. The familiar chocolate taste and aroma is not found in the fresh bean; it must be developed by processing that involves fermentation. Under primitive circumstances, the fresh seeds are piled in small mounds atop banana leaves, covered with more leaves, and left to ferment. About a week is needed to develop the flavor and aroma, during which time the kernels change color from purple to brown. Larger farms and plantations have a series of fermentation boxes, insulated to retain heat. The seeds are stirred about three times, at intervals of two days. Yeasts and bacteria attack the sweet pulp surrounding the seeds, heating the slimy mass and causing unpleasant odors. The fermentation kills the seeds.

After fermentation the beans must be dried, sorted, and cleaned. Usually this is done by exposing them to the sun over a period of several weeks. Drying beds may be equipped with a portable roof to protect them from rain. In some cases the beans are dried by artificial heating.

Further processing takes place at commercial centers. The shell of the bean is cracked and removed. The oil, or cacao butter, is expressed from the kernels and the remaining "cake" treated to retrieve theobromine, a stimulant that is rather easily transformed to caffeine (much used in cola). The oil may not be completely extracted, but instead the kernels may be ground and compounded with milk, sugar, and other ingredients to make milk chocolate, cocoa, and other products.

The kernels are especially rich in oil, or cacao butter; some 50% of the bean is cacao butter. The starch and protein contents of the bean are about 15% each. The beans contain up to 3% theobromine, small quantities of caffeine, and traces of various aromatic oils that contribute to the flavor of chocolate.

Production. About a million tons of cacao beans are exported annually: about 80% from Africa (mainly Ghana and Nigeria) and most of the remainder from Latin America (mainly Brazil). They are imported chiefly into western Europe and North America. Formerly cacao was produced mostly on plantations; in recent years the trend has been towards small-farm growing, especially in Africa. This affords some greater flexibility in adjusting to market gyrations (though relaxing control over quality).

Kinds of Cacao. Cacao, *Theobroma cacao,* belongs to the Sterculiaceae family. The cultivated races of cacao are not classified authoritatively, but generally two subspecies are recognized: the *cacao* group, including most of the original high-quality "criollo" varieties; and the *sphaerocarpum* group, containing the more vigorous but often less distinctively flavored types. The latter have gradually dominated cacao plantings because of their greater vigor and higher yield. "Criollo" signifies cacao originally grown in western Venezuela. When later introductions were made from Trinidad (from uncertain sources), they were called "forasteiro" (foreign). The forasteiro types have been spread throughout the world and today constitute the main source of commercial chocolate. The Amelonado type predominates.

Robert W. Schery
Lawn Institute, Marysville, Ohio

CACCIA, kach'ə, **Baron** (1905–), British diplomat. He was born Harold Anthony Caccia, of English parents, in Pachmarhi, India, on Dec. 21, 1905. Educated at Eton and Oxford, he entered the foreign service in 1929. Before World War II he served in Peking and Athens, and during the war he held important posts in North Africa, Italy, and Greece. He was British high commissioner in Austria from 1950 to 1954.

Named ambassador to Washington in 1956, he could not immediately present his credentials because of the strained relations over Suez between Britain and the United States, which later were much ameliorated by his pleasant, experienced realism. His final post, permanent undersecretary of state (1962–1965), was the highest in the foreign service. On retiring, he became provost of Eton College. Knighted in 1950, he was created Baron Caccia of Abernant in 1965, a life peerage.

Henry V. Hodson
Ditchley Foundation, England

CACCINI, kät-chē'nē, **Giulio** (c. 1550–1618), Italian composer and singer. He was born in Rome. By 1589, Caccini, a skilled singer and lute player, was associated with a Florentine group of music theorists known as the Camerata. Their theories involved the application of monodic music to dramatic subjects and led to the invention of the *stilo rappresentivo,* the germ from which opera developed.

Besides collaborating with Jacopo Peri and other composers, Caccini wrote several operas himself, including *Euridice* (1600) and *Il rapimento di Cefalo* (1600). He published some of the arias and choruses from the latter work in *Le nuove musiche* (1602), a book of songs. Caccini's daughter Francesca (c. 1581–c. 1640) was the first prima donna and probably the first woman composer of operas. Caccini died in Florence on Dec. 10, 1618.

William Ashbrook, *Author of "Donizetti"*

CACERES, kä'sā-rās, **Andrés Avelino** (1836–1923), president of Peru. He was born in Ayacucho on Nov. 10, 1836. He was a general in the War of the Pacific with Chile (1879–1883), fought over the nitrate-rich border provinces. When the victorious Chilean army occupied and looted Lima, Cáceres led guerrilla forces from the Andes against the Chileans. Another Peruvian general, Miguel Iglesias, made peace with the Chileans, gave them the nitrate provinces, and set himself up as dictator-president in Lima.

Patriotic Peruvians rallied to Cáceres' guerrilla government, and a civil war resulted. Entering Lima in victory, Cáceres was declared president (1886–1890) by the Peruvian congress. Peru was bankrupt, and Lima partly in ruins. Cáceres attempted economic improvement, bringing in a British company to work the guano deposits on the offshore islands and to maintain railroad service into the highlands. Peacefully replaced as president by Morales Bermúdez, Cáceres remained a powerful figure and regained the presidency in 1894 when Bermúdez died. In 1895, Cáceres was overthrown by Gen. Nicolás de Piérola, dictator before the Chilean War. Cáceres was forced into exile but returned in 1903. He later served as envoy to Italy and in other diplomatic posts. He died on Oct. 10, 1923.

Helen Miller Bailey
East Los Angeles College

CÁCERES, kä'thā-rās, is a city in western Spain, the capital of Cáceres province. The city is a market for livestock and grain and manufactures cloth, tiles, leather goods, and corks.

Cáceres was founded in the 1st century B. C. by the Romans. It was taken by the Arabs in the 8th century A. D., and after passing back and forth between the Moors and the Christians, the city was finally retaken in 1229 by King Alfonso IX of León. Relics of the city's past are seen in the Roman walls and statuary; the medieval gates and narrow streets of the old city; and the Gothic churches of Santa María la Mayor and San Mateo, the latter built over an Arab mosque.

The Province. Cáceres province, which together with Badajoz province forms the region of Estremadura, has an area of 7,701 square miles (19,945 sq km) and is second only to Badajoz in size among the provinces of Spain. The Gata and Gredos mountains in the north and the Guadalupe range in the south are separated by a high central plain, through which the Tagus River runs from east to west. The province is largely devoted to agriculture: grains, cotton, tobacco, grapes, olives, and the cork oak are grown. Livestock raising is also of major importance. In the south there is limited mining of phosphate, tin, zinc, and graphite. Population: (1960) city, 42,903; province, 544,407.

M. M. Lasley, *University of Florida*

CACHE, kash, a hiding place, especially one used by explorers, frontiersmen, and trappers for concealing stores while they are away from camp. In unsettled parts of North America and the Arctic the cache was usually a hole that was neatly covered in such a way that it revealed no trace of the excavation. The owner of the hidden store would locate it on his return by means of a nearby landmark. The term may also apply to the store that is hidden and by extension to any secret hoard. Used as a verb, the term means to hide something or put it away for safekeeping.

CACIQUE, kə-sēk′, was a title given to an Indian chief in the Spanish-dominated cultures of Central and South America, Cuba, and Haiti and among the Pueblo Indians of New Mexico. The term is Spanish and was formed from a native Haitian word.

The cacique was a headman or regional governor with a specified territory under his jurisdiction. He served as military chief and civil ruler and performed religious duties as well. Usually he held the office of head of state for life, but his prestige rested on his personal conduct. His authority was virtually absolute, though he was supposed to seek the advice of his council of elders.

CACIQUE, kə-sēk′, a large blackbird that inhabits the forests of tropical America from Mexico to Argentina. It is from 8½ to 11 inches (22–28 cm) long and has black plumage with patches of yellow on the tail and wings or red on the back. The cacique's bill is sharp-pointed and yellowish in color. The female is smaller and duller in color than the male. Both sexes feed on forest fruits and berries.

The female cacique weaves a large nest hanging from the branch of a tree, often over water. Caciques nest in colonies. The female lays four or five white or pale blue eggs marked with violet or red, incubates the eggs, and cares for the young.

Caciques make up the genus *Cacicus*. Along with the blackbirds, meadowlarks, and New World orioles, caciques belong to the family Icteridae in the order Passeriformes.

KENNETH E. STAGER
Los Angeles County Museum of Natural History

CACOMISTLE, kak′ə-mis-əl, either of two raccoonlike carnivores (family Procyonidae) with slender bodies, short legs, pointed faces, and bushy, ringed tails. Both species hunt at night and feed on rodents, birds, insects, and fruit.

The more common species, *Bassariscus astutus*, is found in mountainous areas from Oregon to southern Mexico. Its general color is yellowish brown, with white undersides, blackish eye rings, and a tail with bands of black and white. *B. astutus* ranges from 24 to 32 inches (60–80 cm) in length, including its 12- to 17-inch (30- to 44-cm) tail, and from 2 to 2½ pounds (about 1 kg) in weight.

Jentinkia sumichrasti, the Central American cacomistle, is found in the tropical forests of southern Mexico and Central America. It is brownish gray in color, with a tail banded with black and buff. It grows from 30 to 39 inches (77 cm–1 meter) in length, including its 15- to 20-inch (39- to 53-cm) tail. *J. sumichrasti* differs from the common cacomistle in having rounded ears, naked soles, and nonretractile claws.

FERNANDO DIAS DE AVILA-PIRES
Universidade do Brasil

CACOPHONY, kə-kof′ə-nē, is a harsh or inharmonious combination of sounds. The term, used most often in reference to music and literature, is from the Greek *kakos* (bad) and *phōnē* (sound or tone). In music, cacophony is discordant sounds, false harmony, or noisy and inharmonious combinations of sounds. In literature it applies primarily to poetry, in which it may be unintentional and therefore a flaw, or intentional, to achieve a special effect.

CACOYANNIS, kä-kō-yän′ēs, **Michael** (1922–), Greek director, producer, and writer, noted for his films and plays with Greek subjects, casts, and settings. He was born in Limassol, Cyprus, on June 11, 1922. After taking a law degree at Grey's Inn, London, he practiced law. In his spare time he studied theater and directed a British radio program for Greece. After World War II he played leading stage roles in London and in 1953 moved to Athens to make films. Outstanding among them were Stella (1954), *A Matter of Dignity* (1958), the Cannes Festival prizewinner *Electra* (1961), and the popular *Zorba the Greek* (1964). His New York (off-Broadway) productions of *The Trojan Women* (1963–1965) and *Iphigenia in Aulis* (1967) received wide critical acclaim.

CACTUS, kak′təs, any of a family of flowering plants generally characterized by fleshy stems, clustered spines, and flowers with many petals. The cactus family (Cactaceae) comprises more than a thousand species that commonly inhabit dry to desert areas in the New World from Canada to southern Chile. A small number of these plants grow in tropical rain forests, and a few of these in the genus *Rhipsalis* are found in Africa and Ceylon. Cacti have been introduced to various parts of the world, and in Australia the prickly pear (*Opuntia*) became a serious weed pest until brought under control by certain moths (*Cactoblastis*), which were imported from South America.

Several other plant groups with either or both spines and fleshy parts are often confused with cacti. Century plants, some ornamental milkweeds, and the yuccas, with which cacti are most often confused, have flowers with few petals.

Stems. Cacti are basically like most other flowering plants, but with considerable specialization of parts. With the exception of two genera (*Pereskia* and *Pereskiopsis*), persistent, functional leaves are not produced, although small, short-lived leaves appear at the stem joints of many cacti. The function of photosynthesis has been almost entirely taken over by the fleshy, green stems, which have well-developed water-storage tissue making up most of their bulk. The surface of the stem has a waxy coating that retards evaporation from the plant, and masses of spines and hairs often clothe the stem, further restricting water loss by evaporation.

The stem may be barrel-shaped or otherwise unbranched, but more commonly it is jointed and branched either from the base or at various points along its length. The joints, or segments, of the stem are sometimes rounded, but those of the prickly pears are flattened and referred to as *pads*. Sometimes the terminal (top) joint is so loosely attached to the joint below that even the slightest contact causes it to become detached from the plant and its spines imbedded in an animal or person that brushes against it. This is the basis of the popular term "jumping cactus." Cactus stems may be smooth, as in most of the prickly pears, but more often they have well-developed longitudinal ridges or spirally arranged bumps (*tubercles*). Spines, which are really modified leaves, are produced in clusters at the tips of the tubercles or at regular intervals along the ridges in special localized regions called *areoles*. Areoles are modified branches. Many cacti also have minute, barbed bristles, known as *glochids*, which also arise in the areoles. Although

CACTUS

SAGUARO GROUP

1. Queen of the night *(Peniocereus greggii)*
2. Giant saguaro *(Carnegiea gigantea)*
3. Giant saguaro, full view

R. C. AND CLAIRE MEYER PROCTOR

R. C. AND CLAIRE MEYER PROCTOR

JOHN J. SMITH

PINCUSHIONS AND FISHHOOKS

4. Fishhook cactus *(Ferocactus wislizenii)*
5. Mexican pincushion *(Mammillaria magnimamma)*

PHOTOS BY R. C. AND CLAIRE MEYER PROCTOR

BARRELS

6. Chartreuse pineapple *(Echinomastus johnsonii lutescens)* **7.** Blue barrel *(Echinomastus horizonthalonius)* **8.** Elephant tooth cactus *(Coryphantha elephantidens)*

PHOTOS BY R. C. AND CLAIRE MEYER PROCTOR

PRICKLY PEARS

1. Beavertail prickly pear (*Opuntia basilaris*)
2. Desert prickly pear (*Opuntia engelmannii*)
3. Porcupine prickly pear (*Opuntia hystricina*)

BOB AND IRA SPRING

JOHN J. SMITH

R. C. AND CLAIRE MEYER PROCTOR

HEDGEHOGS

4. Mojave hedgehog (*Echinocereus mojavensis*)
5. Crimson hedgehog (*Echinocereus rosei*)

PHOTOS BY R. C. AND CLAIRE MEYER PROCTOR

CHOLLAS

6. Cane cholla (*Cylindropuntia spinosior*)
7. Teddy bear cholla (*Cylindropuntia bigelovii*)
8. Cane cholla, full view

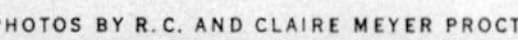
PHOTOS BY R. C. AND CLAIRE MEYER PROCTOR

contact with cactus spines is unpleasant, people are more often bothered by the irritating and hard-to-remove glochids.

Cactus stems, which vary among the species from about 2 inches (5 cm) to more than 50 feet (15 meters) tall, are often an important part of the desert environment in which they grow. Several animal groups are closely associated with cacti: some birds nest in hollows in the stems, and certain species of fruit flies have evolved in such close association with them that they breed only in stem cavities of a single species. Cattle graze on cactus pads in some arid areas where range grasses are insufficient to support herds. The wood of the stems of some of the giant cacti occurs in the form of a hollow, latticelike cylinder; it is useful for the construction of simple shelters, animal corrals, and for novelty furniture.

Flowers and Fruit. The flowers of cacti vary in color from white or creamy to red, purple, orange, and copper. They are usually borne singly on the fleshy stems and arise from the areoles that produce the spines or from special areoles nearby. The sepals, the outermost flower parts, are often not distinguishable in form or color from the petals, as they are in most flowers, and there is sometimes a gradual transition in color from sepals to petals. Both sepals and petals occur in large numbers in overlapping spirals. The bases of the petals and sepals are joined in a common tube of varying length; the tube is attached to the top of the ovary and bears numerous stamens (pollen-producing organs) on its inner surface. Cactus flowers open under a variety of conditions: some open only at night and die in the early hours of the next morning, while others last just through the daylight hours of one day.

The stigma, the pollen-receiving surface of the pistil (seed-producing organ), has 5 or 10 rays that arise from the tip of a single style, or stalk, of the pistil. The ovary has a single chamber within which large numbers of seeds are attached to the inner walls. The fruits vary in size from that of currants to that of large pears, and many not only have a pleasant taste but are highly nutritious. They are eaten by many animals, and prickly pear fruits are a secondary food source in desert areas; in the southwestern United States, they also appear in the market.

Varieties. Botanically, the cactus family is divided into more than 100 genera. But for convenience, the commoner species of North American cacti may be placed into 5 groups: the prickly pears, the saguaro cactus group, the hedgehog cacti, the barrel cacti, and the pincushion and fishhook cacti.

The prickly pears (*Opuntia*) have stems composed of a series of cylinderlike or flattened joints, and the areoles produce glochids and a fleshy leaf at their base. The remaining four groups lack glochids and the leaf at each areole; generally, the stems of the other genera are not composed of a series of joints.

The stems of the saguaro cactus group are cylindrical, up to 50 feet (15 meters) tall, and furnished with a number of longitudinal ribs along the crest of which the spine-bearing areoles are regularly spaced. Included in this group, in addition to the giant saguaro cactus (*Carnegiea gigantea*), are the clambering night-blooming cereus (*Hylocereus undatus* and others), and the organ-pipe cactus (*Lemaireocereus marginatus*). The saguaro and the organ-pipe form extensive forests in many arid localities in the southwestern United States.

The hedgehog cacti (*Echinocereus*) grow either as solitary plants or in low clumps up to 3 feet (1 meter) or more in diameter and up to 1 foot (30 cm) tall. The stem is cylindrical or pear-shaped and is covered by a series of longitudinal, continuous ribs bearing areoles with spines.

The stems of the barrel cacti (*Echinocactus*) vary from columnar to egg-shaped and sometimes grow in clumps; they range in size from about 2 inches (1 cm) tall to as much as 12 feet (3½ meters). The flowers arise from special areoles just above spine-bearing ones, and the fruits are covered by scales rather than spines, unlike those of the genera described above.

Stems of the pincushion (*Mammillaria*) and fishhook (*Ferocactus* and *Ancistrocactus*) cacti usually form low clumps not more than 1 foot (30 cm) tall. Instead of longitudinal ribs, large numbers of cylindrical, pyramidal, or conical tubercles cover the stem surface. Areoles at the tips of each tubercle produce spines that are either straight or shaped like fishhooks; the fishhook-shaped spines were actually used for fishing by Indians and frontiersmen. The flowers arise from between tubercles or along their sides, but not from the tips, and the fruit lacks spines, scales, or hairs.

Cultivation. Cacti are frequently cultivated, either outdoors in specially prepared garden plots or indoors in greenhouses or on window ledges. They require a sunny location and either a neutral or slightly alkaline soil, although in other respects they show a wide tolerance of soil conditions. Standing water or waterlogged soil around the base of the stem usually results in rotting and death of the plant.

Cacti may be propagated from seed collected fresh from the fruits. By careful tending, many new plants can be obtained from a single fruit. Some kinds grow readily from cuttings, others from stem joints, as with prickly pears. Many cacti transplant readily from the natural habitat either into gardens in arid areas or into pots indoors. Pots of the appropriate size should be filled with a layer of coarse gravel for drainage, followed by a 3-inch (1-cm) layer of ordinary potting soil, and finally coarse, clean sand with small quantities of hydrated lime mixed in it to fill the pot. Since the root systems of cacti are shallow, only a few inches beneath the soil surface, it is important to avoid more than the most superficial disturbance of the soil around each plant. The broken surfaces of cuttings and plants taken from the wild should be dried for several days in a well-ventilated shady place before planting.

Seedlings must be watered daily, but older plants may be watered at much longer intervals. Cacti in gardens should not be watered at all following the onset of low winter temperatures.

In the case of such large, columnar species as the saguaro and similar forms, it is advisable to secure root stubs of the transplanted cactus to steel rods driven into the soil. Large rocks around the stem base will also help to prevent overturning by wind.

Richard S. Cowan
Museum of Natural History, Smithsonian Institution

CACTUS WREN. See Wren.

CADALSO Y VAZQUEZ, kä-thäl′sō ē väth′kāth, **José de** (1741–1782), Spanish writer, who is best remembered for his mordant satires on 18th century Spanish decadence. He was born in Cádiz on Oct. 8, 1741. As a youth he traveled through much of western Europe and on his return to Spain about 1761 began a military career. He had achieved the rank of colonel when a grenade killed him on Feb. 27, 1782, during the Spanish siege of Gibraltar.

In his prose satire *Los eruditos a la violeta* (1772), Cadalso lampooned the superficial erudition of his contemporaries. Probably his most celebrated work is *Cartas marruecas* (published posthumously in 1789), a collection of 90 essays inspired in form if not in ideology by Montesquieu's *Lettres persanes* (1721). *Cartas marruecas* is a criticism of the Spaniards' indolence, anachronistic customs, self-defeating pride and backwardness in education and science. Cadalso is considered a precursor of romanticism because of his sentimental autobiographical prose work *Noches lúgubres* (1792).

DONALD W. BLEZNICK
University of Cincinnati

CADAMOSTO, kä-dä-mōs′tō, **Alvise da** (1432?–1488), Italian navigator, who explored the coast of West Africa. He was born in Venice but entered the service of Prince Henry the Navigator of Portugal in 1455. He sailed along the African coast and then explored the Senegal River. Cadamosto next visited the mouth of the Gambia River, famous for supposed riches.

The following year he set out again from Portugal to reach the Gambia River. On route he discovered the Cape Verde Islands. He returned to Venice in 1463. His account of his voyages, posthumously published in 1507, was praised for its descriptions of West Africa.

CADDIS FLY, kad′əs, is the common name for any member of an order of aquatic insects whose larvae live on the bottoms of freshwater lakes and streams. They are distantly related to moths.

The life cycle of a caddis fly consists of four stages—egg, larva, pupa, and adult. After mating, the adult female caddis fly deposits her eggs in or near water. After hatching, the larvae usually build elaborate cases, which protect them from most of their enemies. The cases are built of small pebbles, sticks, pieces of bark, or grass stems. Silk, secreted by the larvae, is used to bind these materials together.

The larvae crawl about on the bottom of the lake or stream with only their heads and legs protruding from their cases. Their food consists of small plant or animal life, depending on the species of caddis. When fully grown, the larvae seal the entrances to their cases and are transformed into active pupae. Eventually, the adults break out of the cases and swim to the water's surface, using their long legs as oars. At the surface they crawl up on plants, and after their wings expand, they fly away to mate. The mothlike adults, whose wings are covered with fine hairs, are often seen clinging to vegetation or flying about in the vicinity of water.

Caddis flies belong to the order Trichoptera, whose name means "hairy winged." Members of different families usually build different kinds of cases. A few caddises build no cases at all.

ROSS HUTCHINS
State Plant Board of Mississippi

CADDO INDIANS, kad′ō, a leading tribe of the North American Caddo confederacy. They settled on the lower Red River of Louisiana and later spread into Arkansas. They first became known in 1687, when they were encountered by the explorer La Salle and his company. From earliest times the Caddo Indians lived a sedentary existence based on agriculture and hunting. Their fields surrounded the villages. Their homes were conical in shape and made of framework of poles covered with thatched grasses. These were grouped around an open space used for ceremonies and meetings. The Caddo population was so divided that at no time could it successfully resist intrusion by white settlers. Wars against the Spanish as well as other Indian tribes seriously reduced their population. After many appeals to the federal government and after strenuous efforts on their behalf by the Indian agent Robert Neighbours (q.v.), the Caddo were led at last to a reservation in Oklahoma.

CADE, kād, **John** (died 1450), Irish-born leader of the revolt known as Cade's rebellion against King Henry VI of England in 1450. Jack Cade spent most of his life in obscurity. In 1449 his involvement in the murder of a Sussex woman forced him to flee to France, but he soon returned and settled in Kent, posing as a physician under the name of Aylmer. He married a squire's daughter, and rose to national prominence by leading a protest of the Kentish commons against royal exactions and fines.

Adopting the influential pseudonym of Mortimer, Cade raised the standard of revolt in the spring of 1450. His followers were not rabble but men of small property who resented high prices and hated some of the King's councillors. Although the rebels were principally Kentish, their cause enjoyed widespread sympathy.

Cade led his army to Blackheath in June and issued a proclamation demanding the recall from France of Richard, Duke of York, Henry's rival for the throne. After a bloody skirmish with the King's army, Cade forced his way across London Bridge and into the city, where his men looted stores and executed the King's unpopular treasurer, Lord Saye. The King finally agreed to redress the rebels' grievances, and the Kentishmen were allowed to return home. But Cade was seized near Lewes and died of wounds on his way to London on July 12, 1450. His rebellion brought England to the verge of civil war and marked the onset of the Wars of the Roses.

L. PERRY CURTIS, JR.
University of California at Berkeley

CADELL, kad′əl, **Francis** (1822–1879), Scottish navigator, whose explorations contributed to the opening up of Australia. He was born at Cockenzie, Scotland, on Feb. 9, 1822. At the age of 14 he entered the service of the East India Company, and he became a commander in 1844.

On a visit to Australia in 1848 he became convinced of the navigability of the Murray River. In 1853 he formed a navigation company and traveled by steamship to a point 1,300 miles (2,100 km) from the mouth of the river. In 1853 he explored the Murrumbidgee River as far as the town of Gundagai, about 2,000 miles (3,200 km) from the sea. The following year he reached Mt. Murchison on the Darling River. Cadell was murdered by his crew while sailing from Amboina to the Kai Islands in June 1879.

CADENCE, kā′dəns, a sequence of notes or chords closing a musical phrase, section, or composition. A cadence is a fall that derives from the natural habit of dropping the voice at the end of a spoken phrase and usually satisfies the ear's tendency to return to the tonic of the music.

In the classical music of the 18th and 19th centuries, cadences are harmonic progressions usually ending on an accented beat. A composition generally ends with a *perfect* (*full*) cadence, which is an *authentic* cadence if it progresses from a dominant chord to a tonic chord and a *plagal* (*amen*) cadence if it moves from a subdominant chord to a tonic. A phrase or section may end with an imperfect cadence (*half-close*), which moves from the tonic or other chord to the dominant, or with an *interrupted* (*deceptive* or *broken*) cadence, which moves from a dominant or other chord to a chord other than the tonic. A *feminine* cadence ends on an unaccented beat.

CADENZA, kə-den′zə, in music, a brilliant exhibition of virtuosity or improvisation at a pause in a composition or just before the cadence (close) of a movement or whole work. It is supposed to use the themes of the movement in artful modifications and combinations and yet suggest spontaneity.

Originally the cadenza was introduced into arias in 18th century Italian opera to provide a singer with an opportunity to show off his skill and powers of invention. The custom was adopted for instrumental pieces, especially those for solo instruments. The singer or instrumentalist improvised his own cadenza. Mozart and Beethoven, however, wrote cadenzas for their piano concertos, an example followed by most later 19th century composers, including Brahms, Schumann, and Tchaikovsky.

CADILLAC, kȧ-dē-yȧk′, **Antoine Laumet de la Mothe** (1658–1730), French colonial administrator. Born in Les Laumets, Languedoc, France, on March 5, 1658, he saw service as a military cadet and lieutenant before going to Canada in 1683. He took part in La Barre's expedition against the Iroquois in 1684, and in 1687 fought under Denonville against the Senecas. He left Port Royal in 1688 to act as pilot for a French sea expedition against Boston and New York City, but adverse winds forced its return to France. Arriving in Quebec in 1691, he was made a lieutenant in the colony troops by Governor Frontenac. Cadillac unsuccessfully urged an attack by sea on New York, which he regarded as responsible for all the Iroquois wars. Having been promoted to captain, he commanded the post at Michilimackinac (1694–1697).

Returning to France in 1699, he drafted proposals for establishing a post at Detroit that would protect the Western fur trade monopoly against Iroquois and English attacks. Despite the opposition of the Intendant Jean Bochart de Champigny and the Company of Canada, Cadillac was sent out in 1701 to found Detroit and was made its commandant in 1704. In 1710 he was named governor of Louisiana, filling this post until 1717, when he was recalled to France. He was thrown into the Bastille for opposing John Law's financial scheme for developing Louisiana, but was released in 1718. He died in Castelsarrasin, Gascony, on Oct. 15, 1730.

MASON WADE, *University of Western Ontario*

CADILLAC, kad′əl-ak, a city in western Michigan, the seat of Wexford county, is 70 miles (113 km) north of Grand Rapids, on Lakes Cadillac and Mitchell. Cadillac manufactures castings, rubber and plastic goods, boats, lumber, and women's clothing. Situated in a farming and forest region, the city is a year-round resort and headquarters for Manistee and Huron National Forests.

Settled by timber crews in 1875, Cadillac was named for Antoine de la Mothe Cadillac, an early explorer of Michigan. Government is by city manager and council. Population: 9,990.

CADILLAC MOUNTAIN, kad′əl-ak, on Mount Desert Island off the coast of Maine, is the highest point–1,532 feet (467 meters)–on the Atlantic coast of the United States. It is situated near the summer resort of Bar Harbor, in one of the sections of the island included in Acadia National Park.

The highway leading to the summit of Cadillac Mountain is noted for views of mainland, ocean, and island scenery. The mountain was named for Antoine de la Mothe Cadillac who received the island as part of a grant issued by Louis XIV in the 1680's.

CÁDIZ, kä′thēth, is a city in southern Spain and the capital of Cádiz province. The city occupies the tip of a narrow peninsula–actually the island of León–which separates the Bay of Cádiz from the Atlantic Ocean. The city's advantageous location near the entrance to the Mediterranean Sea has accounted for its importance as a port. Its mild climate, cooling breezes, and sparkling whiteness make it a tourist center.

The brilliance of the city is sustained in its plazas and parks, and there are many points of interest, both ancient and modern. These include the city walls, the old cathedral, dating from the 13th century, the new cathedral, archaeological and art museums, the docks, and sports and entertainment facilities. Nearby are modern beaches and ruins of ancient civilizations.

In addition to its activities in fishing and international commerce, Cádiz joins with the nearby town of San Fernando to form a port and manufacturing complex that produces textiles, chemicals, paper, glass, ceramics, salt, and both naval and merchant ships.

History. In the 11th century B.C. the Phoenician trading settlement of Gadir existed at the site of Cádiz. The city continued its thriving commerce under the Carthaginians and their conquerors, the Romans, who called the port Gades. Declining under the Goths, the city resumed its activity under Moorish occupation. Cádiz was captured from the Moors by Alfonso X the Wise in 1262 and was rebuilt.

Columbus left from Cádiz on his second voyage to the New World. The fact that the port shared some of Seville's authority in the registering of ships bound for America attests to its importance in that era. After having repulsed attacks by pirates and Muslim raiders from North Africa, the port was attacked by Sir Francis Drake in 1587. The presence of treasure ships from America attracted an English expeditionary force in 1596, led by the Earl of Essex, which sacked the city. As a port of entry, the city suffered plagues and epidemics on several occasions, and in 1755 an earthquake added to the disasters inflicted upon the inhabitants.

SPANISH NATIONAL TOURIST OFFICE

CÁDIZ, in southern Spain, is a city of lovely plazas and parks. In the Plaza de España stands a monument to the Cortes, or assembly, that drew up the liberal but short-lived Constitution of 1812.

Cádiz was the center of resistance to the French when Napoleon attempted to put his brother Joseph on the Spanish throne. Early in the Spanish Civil War (1936–1939) it became a part of Nationalist (Franco) Spain.

The Province. Cádiz province, which has an area of 2,853 square miles (7,389 sq km), is one of eight provinces making up the region of Andalusia. It is the southernmost peninsular province and contains Europe's southernmost town (Tarifa) and cape (Punta Marroquí). Less than 20 miles (32 km) to the east of Tarifa is the British-held sandspit and Rock of Gibraltar; 30 miles (48 km) west of Tarifa is Cape Trafalgar, near which Nelson won his important naval victory over the combined French and Spanish fleets in 1805. Ceuta, the tip of the Moroccan coast across the strait from Gibraltar, is an administrative part of the province of Cádiz.

In the northwestern corner of the province is the grape and wine producing area around Jerez de la Frontera, whose name was pronounced *shere(t)s* at the time its prized wines became known in England as "sherries." The western part of the province is fairly level, the south and east somewhat mountainous. The province contains the Guadalete River, which empties into the Bay of Cádiz, and the lower part of the Guadiaro River in the east. In the northwest it shares the lower Guadalquivir River with the provinces of Huelva and Seville.

Grains, olives, grapes, and some citrus fruits are grown in the province, but productive intensified farming is possible only in the few small areas where irrigation systems have been developed. The thin pasture grass supports widespread stock raising. The mountain slopes have abundant stands of cork oak. Cádiz has both Atlantic and Mediterranean seacoasts, and fishing is important. Population: (1960) of the city, 117,871; of the province, 818,847.

M. M. LASLEY, *University of Florida*

CADMAN, kad′mən, **Charles Wakefield** (1881–1946), American composer. He was born in Johnstown, Pa., on Dec. 24, 1881, and studied music privately in Pittsburgh. He was an organist in Pittsburgh churches for several years and served as music critic for the Pittsburgh *Dispatch* from 1908 to 1910. During a visit to the Omaha Indian Reservation in 1909 he began his lifelong study of American Indian folklore and music. He later lived in California, where he helped found the Hollywood Bowl Concerts. He died in Los Angeles on Dec. 30, 1946.

Cadman's best-known work is the song *From the Land of the Sky-Blue Water,* included in *Four American Indian Songs* (1909). Among his other works are the operas *Shanewis* (first performed at the Metropolitan Opera House in New York City in 1918) and *A Witch of Salem* (1926) and the orchestral suites *Thunderbird* (1917) and *Dark Dancers of the Mardi Gras* (1933).

CADMIUM, kad′mē-əm, is a metallic element (symbol Cd) that was discovered and named by the German chemist Friedrich Stromeyer in 1817 while he was investigating the cause of the yellowish color of zinc carbonate. The name "cadmium" was derived from the old name for zinc ore, *cadmia.*

Uses. One of the most important uses of cadmium is in plating steel. Cadmium is used because it is easily plated and forms a stable surface that resists oxidation. The plating is done either by electrolytic or vapor plating techniques. Because there is a low coefficient of friction between cadmium and other metals, parts such as ball bearings and bearing raceways are often cadmium-plated to decrease friction.

The metal is used in the construction of nickel-cadmium storage batteries and Weston standard cells and as a control rod material in nuclear reactors. Cadmium serves as a hardener in the preparation of certain copper and brass alloys, and it is also important in various casting alloys and solders with low melting points.

Cadmium oxide is used in catalytic reactions, plating baths, and in the preparation of high-purity cadmium compounds. In the ceramics industry, cadmium sulfides are used as yellow pigments and the sulfoselenide as a permanent red pigment. Other cadmium salts are used in soaps, pharmaceuticals, and photosensitive devices.

Properties. Cadmium is a soft, bluish white metal that oxidizes slowly in air to form a stable protective oxide coating. Cadmium is located in column IIB of the periodic table. Its atomic number is 48, and its atomic weight is 112.40. The electronic configuration of the cadmium atom is $2s^2$, $2s^22p^6$, $3s^23p^63d^{10}$, $4s^24p^64d^{10}$, $5s^2$, indicating typical valence of +2. There are isotopes of cadmium ranging from ^{104}Cd to ^{118}Cd. In nature the most abundant isotopes are ^{110}Cd to ^{114}Cd. Each is present in a concentration of from 12 to 24% in a typical test sample.

Cadmium melts at 321°C (610°F), with a latent heat of fusion of about 13.2 cal/gram and a volume of expansion of about 4.7%. The metal boils at 767°C (1413°F), with a latent heat of evaporation of about 286.4 cal/gram. The density of cadmium is 8.65 g/cc (0.313 lb/cu in). The pure metal is about as hard as lead solder and has a tensile strength of 10,000 lb/sq in.

Compounds. Although at low temperatures cadmium is only slightly oxidized by moist air, at red heat the metal burns in air to form brown cadmium oxide, CdO. The metal is rapidly converted to soluble mineral salts, such as chlorides, nitrates, and sulfates, through reactions with acids. Bright yellow cadmium sulfide is precipitated from solution in the presence of hydrogen sulfide. This reaction is used to identify the presence of cadmium ions.

Insoluble cadmium hydroxide is precipitated from solution by the addition of alkali hydroxides. The behavior of cadmium is very similar to that of zinc, but since zinc hydroxide is soluble in excess alkali hydroxide, cadmium can be separated from zinc by this process. Carbonates, arsenates, phosphates, ferrocyanides, and oxalates also form insoluble precipitates with cadmium ion solutions. The cadmium ion is capable of forming complex ions with ammonia, halogens, and cyanides. Many cadmium compounds are photoelectric in nature, and others are phosphorescent and fluorescent.

Occurrence. Cadmium minerals make up less than 0.01% of the earth's crust, and they are usually found associated with zinc ores. The most important mineral of cadmium is the sulfide greenockite, which is always dispersed in zinc sulfide ore in concentrations of 2% or less. Cadmium ores have also been found in the zinc-containing minerals of lead and copper. Since pure cadmium is never found in a natural state and cadmium minerals are not found in concentrated form, metallic cadmium is always prepared commercially as the by-product of primary metal industries, principally the zinc industry.

Production. The starting material for cadmium production is a residue from zinc processing found as a flue dust. The residue usually contains 8 to 20% cadmium, 30 to 45% lead, 10 to 25% zinc, and small amounts of sulfur, copper, and silver. Most of these elements are present in the form of oxides.

The first step in the purification of cadmium involves the conversion of the oxides to sulfates, which are then ball-milled with water into very fine particles. The highly soluble cadmium and zinc sulfates, along with small amounts of copper sulfate, are thus separated from the almost insoluble lead sulfate. The sulfate solution is then acidified slightly, and zinc dust is added. Some of the zinc metal goes into solution, and the copper ions from the solution then plate on the remaining zinc metal. When the excess zinc metal dust is filtered off, the copper is removed with it.

More zinc dust is then added to the cadmium and zinc sulfate solution. Cadmium precipitates out in a chemical exchange reaction similar to that which was used to remove the copper. The cadmium sponge precipitate consists of about 99.6% cadmium and 0.2% zinc with traces of lead, copper, silver, and thallium. The sponge is pressed into blocks and melted at 390°C (740°F) under a flux of sodium hydroxide that both protects the cadmium from oxidation and removes the zinc impurities. Small amounts of ammonium chloride are added to the hydroxide flux to remove thallium. Upon removal of the flux the liquid cadmium is cast into ingots that are 99.99% pure cadmium. The use of zone refining techniques or distillation, or both, makes it possible to produce cadmium that is 99.9999% pure.

DOUGLAS V. KELLER, JR.
Syracuse University

CADMUS, kad'məs, in Greek mythology, was the founder of Thebes. He was the son of Agenor, king of Phoenician Tyre. When Zeus carried off his sister Europa, Cadmus and his brothers were sent to look for her. Consulting the Delphic oracle, he was instructed to cease his search, but to follow a cow marked in a certain way and to build a city where she stopped. In Boeotia (cowland), Cadmus founded the city of Thebes and the citadel, Cadmea. A dragon guarded the local spring and killed his men, whereupon Cadmus slew the monster. On the advice of Athena, he sowed the dragon's teeth, from which warriors sprang up, who fought and killed one another, when Cadmus threw a stone in their midst. The five remaining Sparti ("sown men") became the ancestors of the Theban aristocracy.

Cadmus was forced to do penance to Ares for the death of his dragon-son. He then married Harmonia, daughter of Ares and Aphrodite. At the ceremony, attended by all the gods of Olympus, Harmonia received a necklace which was to bring bad luck to all who possessed it. Among their children and descendants were such mythologically troubled personages as Actaeon, Pentheus, and Oedipus. Cadmus and Harmonia emigrated to Illyria and ultimately were metamorphosed into holy snakes and transported to Elysium. Cadmus has been credited with introducing the Phoenician alphabet into Greece.

URSULA SCHOENHEIM
Queens College, New York

CADMUS, kad'məs, **Paul** (1904–), American realist painter. Working slowly in egg tempera, he turned out few paintings but many drawings and prints, chiefly nudes and portraits.

Cadmus was born of artist parents in New York City on Dec. 17, 1904, and studied at both the National Academy of Design and the Art Students League. In a meticulously realistic style, he portrayed vice and ugliness in *The Fleet's In* (1933), *Greenwich Village Cafeteria* (1934), *Coney Island* (1934), and *Sailors and Floosies* (1938). Also in 1938, he designed sets and costumes for the ballet *Filling Station* and painted a mural for the Richmond, Va., post office. His later paintings include *The Shower* (1943) and *Fantasia on a Theme by Dr. S.* (1946), which depict forms with such perfect fidelity that Cadmus has been called a "magic realist." In 1961, he received a grant from the National Institute of Arts and Letters.

CADOGAN, kə-dug′ən, **Sir Alexander George Montagu** (1884–1968), British diplomat. Born in London on Nov. 25, 1884, he was educated at Eton and Oxford. He joined the foreign service as a diplomatic attaché and was assigned to Constantinople (1909–1912). After a year in the foreign office, he was assigned to Vienna, where World War I in 1914 sent him back to Britain.

Following the war, Cadogan was made a first secretary at Paris in 1919. In 1928 he became a counselor in the foreign office. For the League of Nations he did special work on the Manchurian dispute (1931), and he was ambassador to China in 1935–1936. At first deputy undersecretary, he served as permanent undersecretary of state, the highest post in the foreign office, from 1938 to 1946.

With the U. S. undersecretary of state, Sumner Welles, Cadogan drafted the Atlantic Charter in 1941. He helped to found the United Nations and was Britain's permanent representative on the Security Council from 1946 to 1950. Cadogan died in London on July 9, 1968.

CADOGAN, kə-dug′ən, **William** (1675–1726), British army officer, who was the Duke of Marlborough's quartermaster general and his virtual chief of staff. Cadogan was born at Lismullen, Ireland, the son of a Dublin lawyer. While serving in Ireland and Flanders he won the trust of Marlborough, and when Marlborough was appointed to supreme command in Holland in 1702, he took Cadogan on his staff.

The burly, energetic Cadogan was prominent in Marlborough's principal battles, sieges, and marches, displaying outstanding skill, daring, loyalty, and judgment. After 1712 he shared his chief's exile, but later he became British envoy to the States General of Holland. He commanded the troops that put down the Jacobite rebellion in Scotland in 1715. He was created Earl Cadogan in 1718 and made head of the army in 1722. He died at Kensington, England, on July 17, 1726.

ANTONY BRETT-JAMES
Royal Military Academy Sandhurst
Author of "The Hundred Days"

CADUCEUS, kə-dōō′sē-əs, in classical mythology, a staff or wand around which two serpents were entwined in opposite directions with their heads facing each other and surmounted by two wings.

Caduceus

EWING GALLOWAY

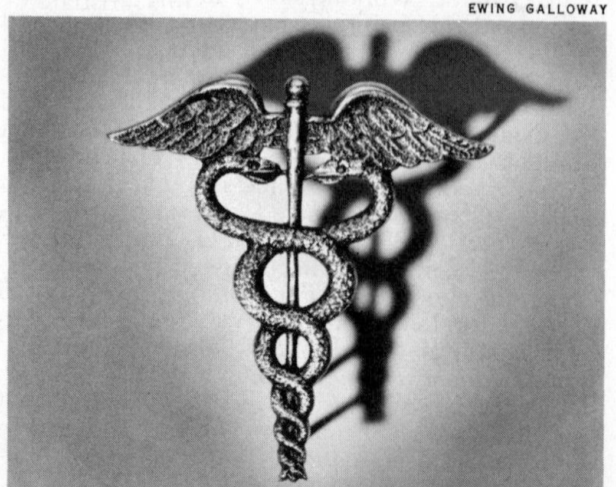

It was commonly associated with the Greek god Hermes (Roman, Mercury), the messenger of the gods, who carried it as a symbol of peace.

The caduceus, with a single snake coiled around it, came to be a symbol for Aesculapius, the god of medicine, and subsequently for the medical profession itself. The U. S. Army Medical Corps uses a caduceus on its insignia.

In the best-known account of its origin, Apollo gave his staff to Hermes as a reward for allowing him the honor of inventing the lyre. According to Apollo, the staff had the power to unite all beings divided by hate. When Hermes came to Arcadia, he saw two serpents fighting; he threw the staff between them, and they wound around it in friendly association.

In antiquity, the caduceus was an olive branch decorated with green wreaths or with ribbons and was carried by heralds and public criers.

CADWALADR, kad-wol′ə-dər (died 1172), Welsh chieftain, was the younger son of Gruffudd, King of Gwynedd (North Wales). When his father died, Owain, the elder brother, inherited Gwynedd, and Cadwaladr received Meirionydd and northern Ceredigion, lands that he had conquered earlier. He became involved in feuds and, repudiated by his brother, fled to Ireland. He returned with a group of Irish Danes to attack Owain, but made peace without fighting. Disgusted by this, the Irish pirates blinded him before ransoming him. Constant friction between Cadwaladr and his nephews led to his eventual flight to England. In 1157, Henry II restored Cadwaladr's lands.

CADY, kā′dē, **Josiah Cleveland** (1837–1919), American architect. He was born in Providence, R. I., and began practicing as an architect in 1870. His noteworthy buildings include the American Museum of Natural History and the Metropolitan Opera House (demolished, 1966) in New York City, as well as various structures at Yale University (including Dwight Hall) and at Williams, Trinity, and Wesleyan colleges. Cady also designed churches, hospitals, mansions, and commercial buildings. He died in Providence on April 17, 1919.

CAECILIAN, si-sil′yən, a family of obscure, limbless amphibians that live in tropical forests and forests bordering rivers flowing through savannas. They are widely distributed. Most are found in North and South America, but some are also found in Africa and Asia.

Most caecilians are about 1 foot (30 cm) long, but they may range from 7 inches to 4½ feet (18 to 140 cm). Some are very slender. Except for a few aquatic species, caecilians are easily mistaken for gigantic earthworms. However, close examination will show that they have vertebrate characteristics such as firm bodies and well-developed mouths and teeth. They also move their throats when breathing. The few aquatic species have narrow bodies and dorsal fins.

Caecilians have certain primitive characteristics, such as scales, that indicate a great geological age. In fact, caecilians may have had an evolution independent from and longer than that of the more familiar amphibians—frogs (including toads) and salamanders (including newts). Unfortunately, no fossil caecilians are known.

Caecilian scales, when present, are embedded in the skin. Numerous grooves, ranging in number from about 60 to almost 300, encircle the body. On each side of the head there is a groove into which a tentacle is retracted when it is not in use as a sense organ. At most a mere rudiment of a tail is present, and in some species there is no sign of an eye.

Little is known about the behavior of caecilians. The sexes look alike externally; however, the male has a concealed copulatory organ, which he uses for internal fertilization. Development is varied. Some species lay eggs, while others give birth to living young. The young may go through a larval stage. For example, the sticky caecilian of Asia lays her eggs in a moist site near water. She then coils around the eggs and drives predators away. The larvae have laterally compressed tails that enable them to live in water. However, after they lose their tails and transform into adults, they will drown in water.

Caecilians make up the family Caecilidae in the order Apoda, or Gymnophiona.

CLIFFORD POPE
Author, "The Reptile World"

CAECILIUS, sē-sil′ē-əs, Greek scholar of Calacte in Sicily, who lived in the 1st century A. D. With the exception of Dionysius of Halicarnassus, Caecilius was considered the foremost critic and rhetorician of the Augustan age. He wrote many books, only fragments of which remain. Among his works were *On the Sublime; On Rhetoric and Rhetorical Figures; On the Style of the Ten Orators; and Alphabetical Selection of Phrases* (a lexicon guide to correct Attic style).

CAECILIUS STATIUS, sē-sil′ē-əs stā′shē-əs (219?–?166 B. C.), Roman comic poet and dramatist. He was known also as *Statius Caecilius.* His contemporaries ranked him with Plautus and Terence. He revealed his talent by adapting Greek plays for the Roman stage from the comedy writers of his period, especially Menander. Fragments of his plays are preserved in Aulus Gellius' *Noctes Atticae.*

CAEDMON, kad′mən, has traditionally been considered the first English religious poet. He lived in the last half of the 7th century A. D. Caedmon composed his verses on Christian themes in Old English, the language of the Anglo-Saxons before the Norman conquest in the 11th century.

From Caedmon's time through the 10th century, the Anglo-Saxons produced a considerable quantity of religious verse, the extant portion of which forms the largest known corpus of early medieval Christian vernacular literature. Caedmon's precise role in the birth and maturation of this type of poetry is currently the subject of lively scholarly debate.

Life. The only source of knowledge about Caedmon is the *Historia ecclesiastica gentis Anglorum* by the medieval English scholar-monk Bede (q.v.). In Book 4, chapter 24, of the *Historia,* Bede relates how Caedmon, an illiterate, elderly lay brother attached to the abbey of Streoneshealh (now known as Whitby) during the time of the Abbess Hild (658–680), was suddenly blessed, through God's grace, with the power to render the Christian Scriptures into beautiful English poetry. Before this divine intervention, Caedmon was so ignorant of poetry that when the harp was passed around the table, as was customary, for the guests to accompany themselves in song, he retreated from the gathering rather than receive the instrument in his turn.

One night after such a withdrawal, Caedmon dreamed that he saw a shining stranger who asked him to sing of the origin of the world. The astonished Caedmon complied. Upon awakening he still had his newfound skill, and when Abbess Hild heard of it she invited Caedmon to become a monk so that he could be instructed in the Scriptures and turn the sacred narrative into vernacular poems. Bede's account adds a list of the subjects treated by Caedmon, praises the poet's own virtue and the power of his verse to promote virtue in others, and concludes with a description of his saintly death at the abbey.

Works. Caedmon's first *Hymn* to God was translated into Latin and paraphrased by Bede in the *Historia.* The old English original was also copied into various manuscripts and is thus preserved. Formerly, other extant Old English poems on subjects mentioned in Bede's list of Caedmon's works were attributed to the poet. (For example, many of the poems in the Junius manuscript written about 1000 and now in the Bodleian Library, Oxford, were thought to be by Caedmon.) However, divergences in style and dating in these works have caused this hypothesis to be discarded. Now only the nine extant lines of the *Hymn* are considered authentic.

The structure of the *Hymn* and its poetic diction—especially the many epithets for God, such as *heofonrices weard* (guardian of the heavenly kingdom) and *wuldorfaeder* (father or glory)—reveal the Germanic influence that pervades Anglo-Saxon literature. They also support Bede's testimony that Caedmon was an oral poet who improvised his verses.

Scholarship. Since Bede, numerous interesting but equally unverifiable explanations of Caedmon's transformation from illiterate lay brother to poetic genius have been offered. More concrete is the evidence, obtained by modern research, that within an oral culture improvisatory verse evolves slowly and without decisive innovations by individual singers. On the basis of this evidence some scholars question the traditional assumption, introduced by Bede, that Caedmon alone was the father of Old English poetry. It may be that Bede wanted to use Caedmon's story—the divinely accomplished "conversion" of a simple man to a great Christian poet—as a microcosmic analogy to the conversion of the pagan Anglo-Saxons to Christianity, an event that was for Bede the central occurrence in his nation's history.

In Bede's work, Caedmon emerges as an exemplary figure whose career illustrates the link between divine grace and the ever wider diffusion of the Gospel message, in this case through song. Indeed, the aim of Caedmon's poetry—to turn the listener from evil toward good—is, as Bede points out, his own aim as a historian as well. Given Bede's use of Caedmon's career in this fashion, it follows that precise evaluation of Caedmon's contribution to English literature will never be achieved.

ROBERT W. HANNING, *Columbia University*

Further Reading: Gordon, Robert K., ed. and tr., *Anglo-Saxon Poetry* (New York and London 1954); Smith, Albert H., ed., *Three Northumbrian Poems* (London 1933); Wrenn, Charles L., *The Poetry of Caedmon* (London 1947).

CAELUM. See CONSTELLATION.

CAEN, käɴ, a port and manufacturing city in France, in lower Normandy, is the capital of the department of Calvados. It is on the Orne River about 9 miles (14 km) from the English Channel, to which it is connected by a canal.

Caen is a major port and the main trade center for the prosperous agricultural region surrounding it, which specializes in grains, horticulture, and dairying; many famous and excellent cheeses are produced in abundance in the countryside of Calvados, among them Camembert and Pont-l'Évêque. Caen's manufacturing activities include shipbuilding, chemicals, textiles, cement, glovemaking, and metallurgy. The city is close to large quarries that have yielded fine building stone for centuries. "Caen stone," a hard limestone, was used by the Norman kings to build St. Paul's Cathedral in London. The relatively good quality of iron ore deposits near Caen fostered the growth of an iron and steel industry just before World War I. These deposits now constitute France's second major source of iron ore. Destroyed in World War II, the iron and steel establishments have been rebuilt along modern lines.

Caen is often called the "Athens of Normandy" in tribute to its cultural, historical, and intellectual importance. Its most renowned monuments are the St. Étienne Church, called the Gentlemen's Abbey (Abbaye aux Hommes), founded by William the Conqueror; the Church of the Trinity, called Ladies' Abbey (Abbaye aux Dames); and St. Pierre Cathedral.

The nucleus of the old city of Caen was an island at the confluence of the Orne and the Odon rivers, which was fortified by the Normans. In the 11th century Caen became the preferred city of William, Duke of Normandy (William the Conqueror), and the capital of his duchy. It was sacked by the English in 1346, and held by them from 1417 to 1450; its great university was founded by Henry VI of England in 1431. The city was a Protestant stronghold briefly in the late 1700's. In World War II, Caen was severely damaged during the liberation of France in 1944. About three quarters of the city was destroyed, and many historical monuments were either ruined or gravely damaged. The city has since been extensively rebuilt. Population: (1962) 88,449.

HOMER PRICE, *Hunter College, New York*

CAENE. See QENA.

CAERE, sē'rē, was one of the wealthiest and most important cities in ancient Etruria. It was located about 22 miles (35 km) northwest of Rome. Remains of Caere's Villanovan culture date back to the 8th century B. C., and there are important Etruscan finds from as early as the 7th century B. C. A vast necropolis surrounds the city. Tombs are frequently cut into the tufa with tumuli heaped above. The interiors of the tombs, obvious reproductions of the abodes of the living, are laid out along regular routes like houses on a street. Objects found attest to Caere's thriving trade with both Carthaginians and Hellenes through the city's ports at Alsium and Pyrgi.

Caere, at its height in the 6th century, allied itself with Carthage in attacks against the Phocaean settlers on Corsica and the western Greeks. After being attacked by the Syracusan tyrant Dionysius in 384 B. C., Caere began to decline. Caere was generally friendly toward Rome and even protected the Vestal Virgins during the Gallic sack (about 390 B. C.). Caere was swiftly defeated after joining with the city of Tarquinii in battle against Rome in 353 B. C. and signed a peace for 100 years. At some unknown date Caere received *civitas sine suffragio* (citizenship without vote) from Rome; if awarded early it was an honor, if late, a punishment.

RICHARD E. MITCHELL, *University of Illinois*

CAERLEON, kär-lē'ən, an urban district and ancient town in Wales, is in Monmouthshire on the Usk River, adjoining Newport, which is to the southwest. Caerleon has the remains of a Roman legionary fortress, from which it took its name, a corruption of "camp of the legions." The fortress has been excavated and its main feature is an amphitheater enclosing an arena 184 feet by 136 (56 by 41 meters). The 12th century historian Geoffrey of Monmouth professed to find in the remains the true setting for some of the Arthurian legends, a romantic view later revived by Alfred, Lord Tennyson, in *Idylls of the King*. Population: (1961) 4,184.

GORDON STOKES
Author of "English Place-Names"

CAERNARVON, kär-när'vən, a municipal borough and the county town of Caernarvonshire, is the most northwesterly town on the Welsh mainland. It is situated at the westerly end of Menai Strait and is a busy administrative, tourist, and trading center. In Caernarvon are the remains of a Roman fortress built in 70–80 A. D. and called Segontium. The Normans built a castle here in the 11th century; in its place, in 1283, Edward I of England began building a castle whose walls are still almost intact. A son, later Edward II, born here in 1284, was crowned the first Prince of Wales in 1301. Successive heirs to the British throne have been invested with the title Prince of Wales at Caernarvon. Population: (1961) 8,998.

GORDON STOKES
Author of "English Place-Names"

CAERNARVONSHIRE, kär-när'vən-shir, is the northwesternmost county on the mainland of Wales. Llandudno, in the northeast, is the largest town. The county town is Caernarvon.

The eastern part of the country is mountainous. Snowdon, the highest peak in England and Wales, rises to 3,560 feet (1,085 meters), and Snowdonia National Park occupies 45% of the county's area. The western part, comprising the Lleyn Peninsula, is mostly broken hill country with two notable peaks, Yr Eifl (1,849 feet; 563 meters), probably known as The Rivals, and Carn Fadryn (1,217 feet; 371 meters).

Sheep and cattle are the principal agricultural products of eastern Caernarvonshire. In the west, black cattle are raised, and there are small general farms. Slate quarries at Bethesda and Llanberis are among the largest in the world, but demand for building slate has declined. There are notable castles at Conway and Caernarvon and smaller ones at Criccieth and Llanberis. Near Penmaenmawr are some remains of prehistoric structures. The University College of North Wales is at Bangor. Population: (1961) 121,194.

GORDON STOKES
Author of "English Place-Names"

CAESAR, sē′zər, **Julius** (100–44 B. C.), one of the most famous men of antiquity, who was dictator of Rome, a renowned general, and man of letters.

Gaius Julius Caesar was born on July 12, 100 B. C. His family, the *gens Julia,* was ancient and patrician, but at the time of his birth it was only beginning to reemerge as an influential family in Roman politics. Caesar's aunt Julia married Marius, the successful general and leader of the *Popularis* party. Caesar's anti-Senatorial attitude was at least partially the result of his relationship to Marius.

Early Career. In 84 B. C. the Marian faction appointed the young Caesar as *Flamen Dialis,* a priest of Jupiter. Somewhat later Caesar strengthened his attachment to the Marians by marrying Cornelia, the daughter of Cinna (the leader of the popular party after Marius' death in 86). When the Roman general Sulla returned from the east and defeated the Marians, he ordered Caesar to divorce his wife. But Caesar refused, and Sulla confiscated his property and deprived him of his priesthood. Caesar's life was spared only when his friends interceded with Sulla on his behalf. But Sulla was still skeptical and is reported to have said, "In this Caesar there is more than one Marius."

Because Caesar could not feel safe in Rome while Sulla was alive, he went in 81 to the province of Asia. Later he served under the proconsul of Cilicia, but in 78, after he heard of Sulla's death, he returned to Rome. In Rome he sought popularity through his oratory in the law courts; and finally, to improve his oratory, he left Rome again in 75 and went to Rhodes to study under the famous rhetorician Apollonius Molon.

Nothing of great historical significance happened to him after that until his election to the quaestorship in 69 (for the year 68). He served in Farther Spain. In 66, Caesar ran for the aedileship, and his campaign was financed by one of the richest and most powerful men in Rome, Crassus. As aedile, Caesar was responsible for supervising the public games, and with Crassus' money he sponsored spectacular contests to gain the favor of the populace. In 63 he was elected pontifex maximus. Then, in 62, he became praetor. In 61, Caesar became propraetor of Farther Spain, and after some military expeditions he returned to Rome to celebrate a triumph and run for the consulship.

The First Triumvirate. This was the great turning point in his career. According to Roman law a general had to stay outside the city until the day of his triumph, but a candidate for the consulship had to present himself before the magistrates in the city. Caesar asked permission to stand for the consulship while remaining outside Rome so that he could celebrate his triumph. The Senate refused. Caesar then gave up his triumph to seek the consulship, but he was now alienated from the Senate. He began to negotiate with Pompey the Great, who was seeking land for his veterans and ratification of the arrangements he had made in the east after his successful campaign against Mithridates. The Senate had also alienated Pompey by refusing his requests. Crassus, who had recently been rebuffed by the Senate, joined Caesar and Pompey. The three formed an unofficial political coalition, called the First Triumvirate, and decided to control Roman politics. Pompey could provide the soldiers and Crassus the money, and Caesar had popularity.

In 59, Caesar became consul with Bibulus, an ineffective colleague. He proposed a land bill for Pompey's veterans, and when the Senate refused to act on it, he took it directly to the people in the Tribal Assembly. Three tribunes vetoed it, and Bibulus declared the omens unfavorable, but with the support of Pompey and Crassus, Caesar called in some troops and the bill was passed. In addition, Caesar secured the ratification of Pompey's arrangements in the east. Then he rewarded Crassus by supporting a bill that Crassus desired. To cement the triumvirate, Pompey married Caesar's daughter, Julia.

Caesar was determined to do something for himself. By the terms of the *Lex Vatinia de Caesaris provincia* he secured as his proconsular provinces Cisalpine Gaul and Illyricum; his proconsulship was to last for five years. After this law was passed, the governor of Transalpine Gaul died, and that province was added to Caesar's other two. The acquisition of these provinces was of great advantage to Caesar. It gave him an opportunity to recruit and train an army, and he would be in an ideal location to march on Rome whenever he wished. Until this time he had had only popularity; henceforth he had popularity and armed might.

The Gallic Wars. For the next eight years (58–51) Caesar was occupied by the Gallic Wars, although he was always in close contact with developments in Rome. When Caesar became proconsul of Transalpine Gaul, the province included only southern Gaul. But Gallic tribes soon asked him to intervene to protect them against other tribes, and at the end of 58 he set up winter quarters in northeastern Gaul. In 57 what are now northern France and Belgium fell to the Roman troops. The tribes along the Atlantic coast were conquered in 56, and in 55 and 54 Caesar campaigned in Germany and Britain. Gaul had not been completely pacified, but Caesar's army seemed everywhere victorious.

However, in 52 the tribes of central Gaul rose in revolt under Vercingetorix. This was the most serious challenge Caesar ever faced in Gaul. Finally he cornered Vercingetorix in Alesia, where the Gallic chieftain ultimately surrendered. By 51, except for occasional local rebellions, the conquest of Gaul was complete. Caesar's army was highly trained and well disciplined and fanatically loyal to him. His military exploits, particularly the invasion of Britain, made him even more popular with the people.

The Dissolution of the Triumvirate. Meanwhile in Rome political events of great magnitude were taking place. The First Triumvirate was falling apart because of the quarrels of Pompey and Crassus. There was rioting in the city, and members of the Senate were beginning to attack Caesar. Therefore, in 56 he called a meeting of the First Triumvirate in the city of Luca (now Lucca) in his own province of Cisalpine Gaul. The triumvirs met secretly, patched up the Triumvirate, and made certain decisions that were to determine the fate of the Roman republic.

It was agreed that Pompey and Crassus should be consuls in 55, and afterward Pompey was to receive the two Spains as his provinces, while Crassus would get Syria. Each of them received his provincial commands for a five-year period. Caesar's own commands were extended for five years (until March 1, 50). Pompey was given the privilege of remaining in Italy and governing his Spanish provinces through legates.

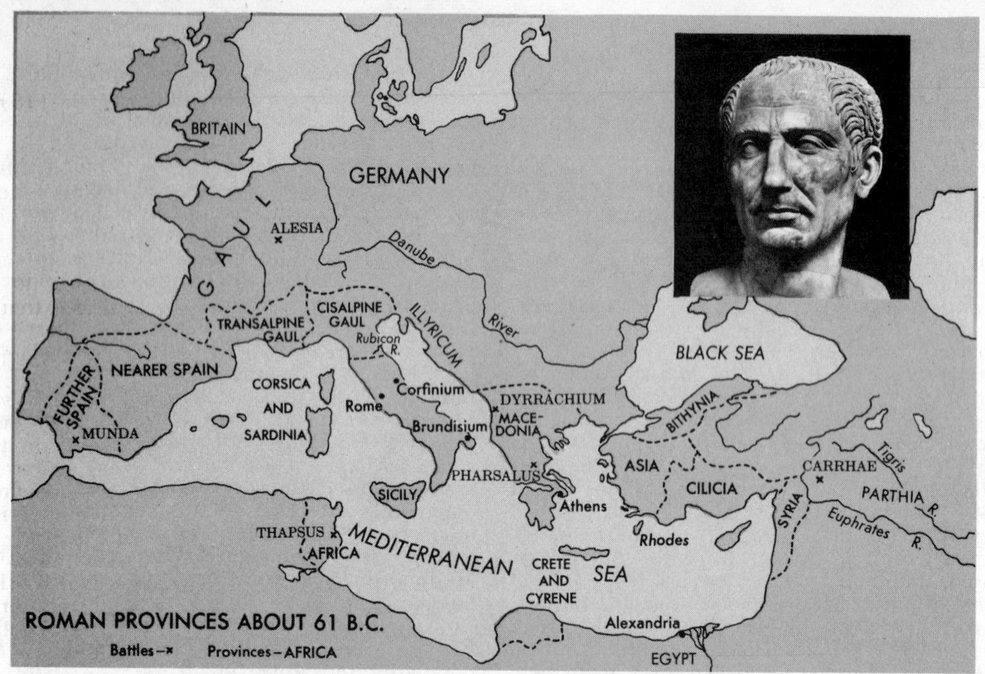

BUST OF JULIUS CAESAR IN THE MUSEO NAZIONALE, NAPLES, ITALY (PHOTO FROM ALINARI: ART REFERENCE BUREAU)

At this point the First Triumvirate seemed to be strong again. But the appearance was deceptive. In 54, Julia, Pompey's wife and Caesar's daughter, died, and one real bond between the two men was lost. In the following year Crassus was killed at the Battle of Carrhae, during his attempted invasion of the Parthian Empire. Only Caesar and Pompey remained, and the senators at Rome immediately began to drive a wedge between them.

Because of rioting in the city it was impossible to hold the consular elections for the year 52. The Senate, which preferred Pompey to Caesar, secured a sole consulship for Pompey and gave him extraordinary powers to protect the city. At this time Julius Caesar was concerned about a constitutional matter: his command in Gaul was coming to an end, and he did not want to lay it down to become a private citizen. If he did so, he would be liable to prosecution in the courts for any illegal acts he had committed as a magistrate, but as long as he held public office he could not be sued. He wanted to be elected to a second consulship while he was still proconsul of Gaul. However the holding of both offices was illegal.

Although Pompey was moving more and more into an alliance with the senatorial faction, he was not prepared to break with Caesar. Thus, in 52 he sponsored a bill that permitted Caesar to run for the consulship in absentia. This did not, however, give Caesar the right to retain his proconsular command until he became consul, so the senators sought to force him out of Gaul before his second consulship. At the same time Caesar tried to prolong his command until after the elections of 49, and Pompey neither gave his support to this scheme nor denied it.

The consuls of the year 51 opposed Caesar's request for an extension, and two anti-Caesarean consuls were elected for 50. Caesar's opponents insisted that he lay down his command, and his partisans replied that he would be willing to do so if Pompey did the same. Pompey refused, and the Romans began to prepare for civil war. In December 50, Caesar was bitterly attacked in the Senate, and he moved with some of his legions close to the border of Italy. To avoid war, Caesar made one last offer to lay down his command if Pompey would also. This was again refused, and on January 10, Caesar crossed the Rubicon, the river that separated his province from Italy, and the Civil War began. Caesar is reputed to have said, "The die is cast."

Civil War. Caesar moved with lightning rapidity down the east coast of Italy. He took Picenum and Corfinium while Pompey withdrew with his entire force to Brundisium and sailed to Greece. Almost overnight, Caesar became the master of Italy. But he was by no means in an enviable position. Pompey controlled Spain on one side of Italy and secured a stable base in Greece on the other side. In addition he had control of the sea. Caesar was virtually surrounded.

He decided to strike first at Pompeian forces in Spain. After a short but difficult campaign he was successful and finally could begin plans to defeat Pompey in Greece. Early in 48 he sailed across the Adriatic and faced Pompey at Dyrrhachium. But Pompey cut off his supplies, and after several difficult weeks Caesar was forced to break away and head east toward Thessaly, where he could feed his army.

Pompey followed and camped opposite Caesar at Pharsalus. In the battle that followed, Caesar was victorious, and Pompey fled to Egypt, where he was murdered by the Egyptians. Caesar arrived three days later to find Egypt in political chaos. The young Ptolemy XIII and his advisers were quarreling with his sister Cleopatra. Ptolemy's advisers turned against Caesar and besieged him in the palace quarters of Alexandria during the winter of 48–47. Caesar championed Cleopatra's cause, and when his reinforcements arrived, he defeated Ptolemy. Cleopatra became the real ruler of Egypt. Caesar lingered with her for a while, obviously enchanted by her charms, but eventually he had to leave for Asia Minor where Pharnaces, the son of Mithridates, was in revolt. Caesar defeated him within five days; this victory was the occasion for his famous "*Veni, vidi, vici*" ("I came, I saw, I conquered").

The Consolidation of Victory. In the summer of 47, Caesar was able to return to Italy. By that time the remnants of the Pompeian forces were gathering in North Africa, and Caesar decided to put them down. He sent his own men over during the winter of 47–46, and defeated the Pompeians at the Battle of Thapsus. It was after this battle that Cato the Younger, the spokesman of senatorial conservatives, committed suicide. But Caesar's task was not yet over. Some of the Pompeians escaped to Spain, and Caesar, after returning to Italy, set out in pursuit. In 45, at the Battle of Munda, he eliminated them. He had now become the sole ruler of Rome.

Throughout this period and in the few months remaining to him after his final victory over the Pompeian forces, despite his preoccupation with warfare he effected numerous reforms in Rome and Italy. In 46 he reformed the Roman calendar; the Julian calendar is still the basis of our calendar today. To ease economic burdens, he remitted approximately one quarter of the principal of debts, and later all of the interest that had accrued since the beginning of the Civil War. He cut the number of citizens eligible for the grain dole from 320,000 to 150,000. He inaugurated a building program and passed laws to regulate traffic and open spaces and to provide for the upkeep of roads. The system of taxation in some of the provinces was reformed, and Roman citizenship was generously bestowed on many provinces. Colonies were founded for his veterans and the surplus population of the city.

Actually, at this time, Caesar was planning another major military campaign. The Roman defeat at the Battle of Carrhae had never been avenged, and Caesar hoped to conquer the Parthian Empire. In 44 he planned to march east, and he began recruiting an army for that purpose, but on the Ides of March (March 15), he was assassinated in the Senate.

The Assassination. It is impossible to understand why Caesar was assassinated without first reviewing his position in government. When he crossed the Rubicon he had been merely the outlawed governor of several provinces. After his initial victories he was appointed dictator in 49. He held the office for only 11 days, long enough to supervise the consular elections for 48, in which he was elected himself. Then he was named dictator again for one year beginning in October 48. When his term expired, he was elected to his third consulship (for the year 46). In the spring of 46, after the Battle of Thapsus, he was *praefectus morum,* which gave him censorial powers for three years, and dictator again for 10 years. He was also elected consul for 45.

After the Battle of Munda (45) many further honors were voted to him. He was given the title *Liberator* and elected to his fifth consulship (for 44). Early in 44 he received the dictatorship for life. His name was given to a month of the year (our July), and he was called *Parens Patriae.* His statue appeared in various places in the city, and a temple was erected to his clemency. Some people tried to hail him as king, and this trend toward monarchical power led to his assassination. The senators could not tolerate any man who made such a show of his power.

Historians are divided on the question of whether Caesar intended to be king, but it is irrelevant. He definitely intended to act like a king, and that was unacceptable to the aristocratic senators. The members of the conspiracy, led by Brutus and Cassius, stabbed him to death at a meeting of the Senate on the Ides (15) of March, 44 B.C.

Personal Characteristics. Julius Caesar was one of the most remarkable men in antiquity or in any period. He was a highly successful general. As a strategist and tactician he fell short of greatness, but he made up for that with speed and boldness as well as courage. His ability as a statesman did not have the opportunity to develop, but all signs indicate that he was extremely sensitive to social and economic problems and was also bold enough to attempt new solutions. As a politician, however, he became too overbearing. The poet Lucan compared him to a bolt of lightning, saying, "Nothing may stand against it, either during that furious progress through the clouds, or when it bursts against the earth and at once recomposes its scattered fires."

Caesar is important not only as a statesman and a general, but also as a man of letters. His *Commentaries* on the Gallic and Civil wars are still widely read today. They were written in a very clear and direct prose style famous for its affected objectivity. In them Caesar referred to himself as "he" or as "Caesar," but not as "I." The simplicity and directness of their style have made the *Commentaries* popular with teachers of beginning Latin classes. In the field of oratory he was regarded as second only to Cicero.

Caesar was married three times. His first wife was Cornelia, the daughter of Cinna, leader of the Marian faction in the mid-80's B.C. The marriage was a political one, but he seems to have been truly devoted to her. They had one child, a daughter, Julia (who later married Pompey the Great). Cornelia died in 69, and not long afterward Caesar married Pompeia, a granddaughter of Sulla. In 62 he divorced her because of a scandal. In that year the religious festival of the Bona Dea was celebrated in Caesar's house under the direction of his wife. It was a ceremony open only to women, but Clodius, Pompeia's lover, dressed himself in woman's clothing and went into Caesar's house, where he was discovered. The sacrilege shook Rome, and Clodius was brought to trial, but he was acquitted through generous bribery. Caesar, however, divorced his wife, saying, "Caesar's wife must be above suspicion." He married his third wife, Calpurnia, in 58 and remained with her until his assassination.

Caesar was generally regarded as very much a ladies' man. He had many illicit affairs. One of the best known was with Servilia, the mother of Brutus; but by far the most notorious was his affair with Cleopatra, by whom he had an illegitimate son, Caesarion. His reputation as a rake was so widespread that his own soldiers sang this line while celebrating the Gallic triumph: "Men of Rome, guard your wives . . . the bad adulterer is coming." He also had a reputation for homosexuality and once was called "every woman's man and every man's woman."

Caesar had no direct male heirs, so in his will he adopted his grandnephew Octavius, much to the chagrin of Mark Antony. Octavius had accompanied Caesar to Spain and at the time of the assassination was in Illyricum, waiting to go with the dictator on the Parthian campaign.

We know something about Caesar's personal appearance. According to Suetonius he was tall and had a fair complexion. His eyes were black. A vain man, he was greatly troubled by his bald-ness and combed what hair he had forward over his head to conceal it. He apparently was quite happy to wear the laurel wreath for this reason. He was regarded as a fashionable dresser. His health was excellent except for infrequent attacks of epilepsy.

Evaluation. All in all, Caesar was an imposing figure. He made a profound impression on his contemporaries, and every subsequent age has found excitement and fascination in the man. Opinions about him are quite divided. Some see him as a power-hungry, self-seeking politician, others as a brilliant statesman. Perhaps the most famous scholarly treatment of him is that of the great German historian Theodor Mommsen, who in his *History of Rome* presented Caesar as a superman, the political genius of the late Roman republic. In the 20th century, however, scholars have tended to direct more attention to his heir and successor, Emperor Augustus. But Caesar's place in English literature is far more secure than that of Augustus, owing to Shakespeare's *Julius Caesar* and Shaw's *Caesar and Cleopatra.*

The name "Caesar" soon became a title. Originally it was simply a family name of the Julian clan, but because of Julius Caesar's success and that of his immediate successors the name became magic. The first five Roman emperors (from Augustus through Nero) used it as a family name. When the Julio-Claudian dynasty died with Nero, succeeding emperors retained the nomenclature. The emperors themselves were always called Augustus, but as time went by it became fashionable to give the name "Caesar" to the heir designate. When the Roman Empire declined and fell, the title "Caesar" lived on even into the 20th century. The German "kaiser" and the Russian "czar" are both derived from "Caesar."

ARTHER FERRILL, *University of Washington*

Further Reading: The basic sources for Julius Caesar are Appian, Plutarch, and Suetonius. Consult also Baldson, J. P. V. D., *Julius Caesar and Rome* (New York 1967); Fuller, J. F. C., *Julius Caesar: Man, Soldier, and Tyrant* (New Brunswick, N. J., 1965); Syme, Ronald, *The Roman Revolution* (London 1939); Taylor, Lily R., *Party Politics in the Age of Caesar* (Gloucester, Mass., 1961).

CAESAR AND CLEOPATRA, sē'zər, klē-ə-pat'rə, is a drama by George Bernard Shaw, first performed at the Theatre Royal, Newcastle-on-Tyne, on March 15, 1899, and published in *Three Plays for Puritans* (1900). In the play Shaw establishes the essential dramatic conflict at the mental, not the emotional, level, with Cleopatra's undisciplined impulses contrasted with Caesar's cool intellectual tolerance. Shaw rationalizes his own shrinking from passion by finding "a technical objection to making sexual infatuation a tragic theme. Experience proves that it is only effective in the comic spirit." He therefore omits Caesar's love affair, and depicts that ruler as a political philosopher vainly trying to educate a spoiled and kittenish young woman. Though neither protagonist follows traditional interpretations of the historic originals, the essence of Shaw's treatment has some scholarly support. Among Shaw's major plays, *Caesar and Cleopatra* probably ranks second only to *Saint Joan.* Despite occasional prolixity, it contains superb wit and theater. A spectacular film version was directed in 1946 by Gabriel Pascal, starring Claude Rains and Vivien Leigh.

DELANCEY FERGUSON
Author of "Selections from Fifty-two Authors"

CAESAREA MAURETANIAE, sē-zə-rē'ə mô-rə-tā'-nē-ē, was an ancient seaport in North Africa, on the Mediterranean Sea. The city was founded by the Carthaginians, who called it Iol. Juba II, King of Mauretania, renamed it Caesarea in honor of Augustus and made it his capital in 25 B. C. During Juba's rule the city became a center of Greco-Roman culture.

Caesarea was annexed by Rome in 42 A. D., and it became one of the provincial capitals of Rome in the 1st century. It had an estimated population of 100,000 and was outranked as an African seaport only by Alexandria and Carthage. Caesarea was sacked by the Vandals in the 5th century and rapidly declined.

The French occupied the site in 1840 and called it Cherchell. Today it is a small seaport in Algeria. The modern town is much smaller than ancient Caesarea. Roman ruins include an amphitheater and baths. The ancient statues have been placed in museums. Population: (1961) 10,943.

CAESAREA PALESTINAE, sē-zə-rē'ə pal-əs-tī'nē, was an ancient city in Israel, 22 miles (35 km) south of Haifa, on the Mediterranean Sea, also known as *Caesarea Maritima.* In 30 B. C., Octavian (later Emperor Augustus) gave the city (then called *Turris Stratonis*) to Herod the Great, king of Judaea, who reconstructed it, built a massive breakwater for the port, and renamed it Caesarea. The surname Palestinae distinguished it from the ancient Syrian city, Caesarea Philippi, a city also belonging to Herod. Caesarea Palestinae later became the metropolis see of the province of Palestina Prima. St. Paul was imprisoned there for two years (Acts 23:23 to 27:1). The Jewish inhabitants who rioted to demand Roman citizenship were massacred there in 66 A. D., but by 81, Caesarea was relieved from various taxes. The Crusaders restored and fortified Caesarea, but the city was seized and destroyed by the Saracens in 1291.

The site, occupied in part by the kibbutz (settlement) of Sdot Yam, is archaeologically important. A Roman theater (now restored and used for performances) was dug up, together with a tablet bearing the name of Pontius Pilate. There are also Crusader and Byzantine remains.

P. R. COLEMAN-NORTON, *Princeton University*

CAESAREAN SECTION. See CESAREAN SECTION.

CAETANI. See GAETANI.

CAETANO, kä-yə-tä'nō, **Marcelo** (1906–), Portuguese premier. He was born in Lisbon on Aug. 17, 1906. Educated at Lisbon University, he became a law professor there. Early in his career he joined the Integralistas, a right-wing political group, and became an adviser and confidant of dictator António de Oliveira Salazar.

Caetano formulated the authoritarian doctrines that served as the basis of Salazar's corporate state. He was minister for the colonies from 1944 to 1947, president of the corporative chamber from 1949 to 1955, and assistant premier from 1955 to 1958, when he became rector of Lisbon University. In September 1968 he was named to succeed the ailing Salazar as premier. While continuing many of his predecessor's policies, Caetano allowed greater freedom to the political opposition, relaxed press censorship, and granted women the right to vote.

CAFÉ, an establishment serving food and drink. The word comes from the French word *café,* meaning "coffee," and referred originally to a coffeehouse (q.v.) offering coffee and light refreshment. In Europe such cafés have flourished since the 17th century. Gradually they came to offer meals and alcoholic drinks. Often they extend out onto the sidewalk.

In the United States the word "café" may mean a coffeehouse, unpretentious restaurant, barroom, or nightclub offering entertainment. Persons in the public eye who frequent nightclubs are sometimes referred to as "café society."

CAFETERIA, a self-service restaurant that provides selective food service to large numbers of people within short periods of time. Cafeterias are particularly suited to the demands of mass feeding because they are characterized by low costs, fast service, and menu variety. They may be divided into four general groups: industrial, commercial, educational (for mass feeding of students), and automatic vending machine operations. Many private cafeterias are operated as a service to employees, and some are subsidized to reduce costs. Cafeterias have a large share of the mass feeding market, but because of the many types and varied ownerships, precise data are difficult to determine.

Cafeterias of all types use similar operating principles. A kitchen area is the center of all food preparation and storage; customers go to a serving and display area to select their food and then carry it to the dining area. Each cafeteria caters to the needs of its particular clientele through variations in equipment layout, service, decor, prices, and menu. Trends in cafeteria operations are toward more automatic vending units supplied from central kitchens and more advanced refrigeration and heating techniques.

KIRBY M. HAYES, *University of Massachusetts*

CAFFARELLI, käf-fä-rel′lē (1710–1783), Italian castrato. He was born Gaetano Maiorano in Bitonto, Apulia, on April 12, 1710, and took the name of a benefactor. He was a student of Porpora in Naples and is said to have spent six years on one page of vocal exercises. Caffarelli, notorious for his rudeness and egotism, made his debut in Rome in 1726 and thereafter sang female roles in major Italian and other European cities. He made a fortune and bought a dukedom. He died in Naples on Jan. 13, 1783.

CAFFEINE, kaf′ēn, is a stimulant that occurs in several plants widely distributed throughout the world. It is an important ingredient in many common beverages and in several drugs. The average cup of coffee or tea contains 100 to 150 milligrams of caffeine, while a 12-ounce (360 ml) bottle of a cola drink contains about 35 to 55 mg of caffeine.

Source. Caffeine is obtained from the seeds of *Coffea arabica* and *Theobroma cacao* and from the leaves of *Thea sinensis*—plants from which coffee, cocoa, and tea are made, respectively. The nuts of the tree *Cola acuminata,* from which various cola-flavored drinks are made, also contain about 2% caffeine.

Physiological Effects and Medical Uses. Caffeine is an alkaloid. It is useful both socially and medically because it has important effects on the brain, kidney, heart, and respiratory system. Caffeine stimulates the central nervous system and therefore is useful in treating cases of poisoning caused by central depressants such as alcohol and morphine. Caffeine is also used, usually in conjunction with an ergot alkaloid, to relieve the pain of migraine; it does this by reducing the diameter of the cerebral blood vessels, thus reducing the flow of blood to the brain.

Although caffeine increases the flow of urine, it is not much used medically for this purpose because its diuretic action is weak and much better diuretics are available. The drug also stimulates the heart and relaxes smooth muscle, especially bronchial muscle, but other alkaloids are more effective for these purposes.

Toxicity and the Caffeine Habit. The toxic effects of excessive amounts of caffeine include insomnia, overexcitement, mild delirium, sensory disturbances such as ringing in the ears and flashes of light, restlessness, and disordered beating of the heart. Extremely large doses of caffeine given to animals lead to convulsions and death because of the stimulation of the central nervous system; in man, however, no deaths from overdoses have been reported.

The stimulation of the central nervous system produced by caffeine sometimes poses a medical problem, particularly in small children, who probably should not be given large amounts of these beverages. A certain degree of physical dependence on caffeine-containing beverages may develop. However, except for persons with peptic ulcers, who must avoid gastric irritation, which caffeine may cause, there is no evidence that the caffeine habit is harmful.

J. M. RITCHIE
Albert Einstein College of Medicine

CAFFIERI, kȧ-fyā′rē, a family of French sculptors and decorative artists of Italian descent, important in the development of the rococo style. The name is also spelled *Caffiéri.*

FILIPPO CAFFIERI (1634–1716), a decorative sculptor of Neapolitan origin, was founder of the family. In 1660, after working for a time in Rome for Pope Alexander VII, he went to France, where he entered the service of King Louis XIV, for whom he executed decorative commissions in many media.

JACQUES CAFFIERI (1678–1755), the son of Filippo, was the most celebrated member of the family. Known especially for his work in bronze, he was employed primarily in decorating Versailles, Fontainebleau, and other royal residences. His chandeliers and furniture mounts have a liveliness and originality that mark a high point of the French rococo style. Many examples of his work are in the Wallace Collection, London.

PHILIPPE CAFFIERI (1714–1774), a son of Jacques, worked with his father for many years and later succeeded him in gaining royal commissions. Among his most important commissions were the cross and candlesticks for the main altars of Notre Dame Cathedral in Paris (lost during the Revolution) and of Bayeux Cathedral.

JEAN JACQUES CAFFIERI (1725–1792), another son of Jacques, won the Prix de Rome in 1748. He was primarily a sculptor, working in marble and terra-cotta. His portraits of the major French dramatic poets are in the Salon de l'Opéra, Paris, and a bronze *Cupid and Pan* is in the Wallace Collection, London. He also designed ornamental metalwork, notably the staircase for the Palais Royal in Paris.

WILLIAM GERDTS, *University of Maryland*

CAGAYAN ISLANDS, kä-gä-yän', seven islets in the Philippines, in the northern Sulu Sea, 70 miles (112 km) west of Negros. The islands constitute the municipality of Cagayancillo, in Palawan province. Population: (1960) 3,880.

CAGAYAN RIVER, kä-gä-yän', the longest river in the Philippines. Rising in the mountains of Nueva Vizcaya province on Luzon island, about 35 miles (55 km) southeast of Bayombong, it flows 220 miles (354 km) north through Isabela and Cagayan provinces to empty into the Babuyan Channel at Aparri. Although the river is navigable by steamers for only 13 miles (21 km), during the wet season small boats are able to travel more than 150 miles (240 km) upstream. The river's large and fertile drainage area yields tobacco as its chief crop. Major tributaries are the Magat and Chico rivers.

CAGAYAN SULU ISLAND, kä-gä-yän' sōō'lōō, one of the Philippine Islands, lies in the Sulu Sea, 65 miles (105 km) northeast of Borneo. Tobacco, sugar, shell, and pearls are exported. With its islets, it forms the municipality of Kagayan, in Sulu province. Cagayan Sulu and Sibitu islands were sold by Spain to the United States in 1900. They had been overlooked in the treaty of 1898 that ended the Spanish-American War and placed the Philippines under United States control. Population: (1960) 10,789.

CAGE, John (1912–), American composer of modern music, noted for his highly unconventional ideas and techniques of composition and performance. He was born in Los Angeles, Calif., on Sept. 15, 1912. After studying with Henry Cowell and Arnold Schönberg in the 1930's, Cage left the West Coast and moved to New York in 1943. There his concerts for percussion only, his "prepared piano" (in which various objects such as rubber bands and coins are attached to the piano strings), and experiments with electronic media, attracted attention in advanced musical circles.

Among Cage's many original ideas was the concept of a "total soundspace" that might incorporate any or all sounds, musical or otherwise, premeditated or accidental. Another radical idea was his notion that the composer need not necessarily "control" sound, but instead might "discover means to let sounds be themselves." Reminiscent of certain oriental philosophies, this concept in its most far-reaching consequences questions the traditional responsibility of the artist toward his work.

Cage's innovations in respect to timbre and form show a logical and consistent development. A pattern can be traced from *Inventions* (1934), in which no instruments were specified, through the use of taped and electronically manipulated sounds in the early 1950's, to the inclusion, in some works, of *all* available sounds, recently with extreme mechanical amplification. A similar pattern of development in terms of rhythm and form has led to their virtual dissolution in some of his compositions. His *4 Minutes and 33 Seconds* (1954) requires a pianist to sit silently before his instrument for that period of time. However unorthodox and occasionally bizarre Cage's works may be, they have left an indelible mark on 20th century music.

GUNTHER SCHULLER, *President New England Conservatory of Music*

CAGGIANO, käd-jä'nō, Antonio (1889–), cardinal of the Roman Catholic Church in Argentina. He was born in Coronda, Santa Fe province, Argentina, on Jan. 30, 1889, and ordained to the priesthood in 1912. When the Argentine Catholic Action Movement was begun in 1931 he became its general ecclesiastical counselor. Two years later he was named military vicar of Argentina and in 1935 was consecrated bishop of Rosario. Caggiano received the cardinal's hat in 1946, and since 1959 has been archbishop of Buenos Aires. He is a member of three sacred congregations of the Roman Curia: the Congregations of Rites and of the Basilica, and the Congregation for the Oriental Churches.

CAGLIARI, käl'yä-rē, is the largest city and a commune on the island of Sardinia, in Italy, and the capital of the autonomous region of Sardinia. Known to the ancient Greeks as Caralis, Cagliari is situated at the southern end of the island, on the Gulf of Cagliari. In addition to its governmental functions, Cagliari is the center of commerce for the entire island, its busiest port, and one of the few industrial centers on Sardinia. Chemicals as well as textiles are manufactured in Cagliari. Handicrafts, especially the making of the characteristic handmade Sardinian woolens and rugs, pottery, and furniture are also important to the economy of the city.

Cagliari is a colorful city. Its most interesting district is the upper town, where the first settlement was made long before the Christian era. The National Museum of Archaeology in Cagliari, one of the most important archaeological museums in Italy, has a series of unique displays illustrating the long history of Sardinia, from its Neolithic beginnings to the Renaissance. Especially noteworthy are the small bronze statuettes found in the *nuraghe* (the Bronze Age towers that ring the heights of the island). The cathedral, originally Gothic in style, has undergone many modifications; in its interior two superb Romanesque pulpits, originally in Pisa Cathedral, stand out as its chief ornaments. The Church of San Saturnino is one of the oldest surviving Christian churches, built in the 5th century, with later additions in Romanesque style.

Because of its good harbor, Cagliari was coveted by the many rulers of Sardinia. In Roman times it was a major civil and naval port. It has remained a part of Italy since the 18th century. In World Wars I and II, it was an Italian naval base. Population: (1961) of the city, 172,925; (1966) of the commune, 211,126.

GEORGE KISH, *University of Michigan*

CAGLIOSTRO, kä-lyôs'trō, **Count Alessandro di** (1743–1795), the most renowned charlatan of the 18th century. His real name was Giuseppe Balsamo. He was born in Palermo, Sicily, on June 2, 1743, and grew up as a street urchin. Admitted to a monastery, he was expelled when, ordered to read aloud from a martyrology, he substituted names of well-known harlots for those of the martyrs. After his expulsion he visited Greece, Egypt, Arabia, Persia, and Rhodes, where he studied alchemy and the occult sciences.

Cagliostro returned to Italy and married Lorenza Feliciani, the beautiful daughter of a Calabrian glovemaker, in 1768. Aided by his wife, he played alternately the roles of alchemist, forger of documents, dispenser of love philters and elixirs of youth, prestidigitator, healer, medium, soothsayer, and procurer. Moving from town to town, the couple took the earnings they obtained from "changing" hemp to silk, pebbles to pearls, and powder to roses, and invested them in a splendid equipage. They acknowledged the plaudits of crowds in London, the Hague, Paris, Strasbourg, Lyon, and Toulouse. They also visited centers in Germany, and even Russia. Despite a coarse and plain appearance, Cagliostro captured the imagination of the best minds of his time, including Goethe, Schiller, and Tieck.

In 1785, during a sojourn in Paris, Cagliostro became implicated in the scandalous Affair of the Diamond Necklace and was imprisoned in the Bastille. On his release, Cagliostro and his wife visited London, where they succeeded only temporarily in their fraudulent practices. Leaving England, the pair traveled again on the Continent. In 1789, Cagliostro was arrested in Rome and condemned to death by the Inquisition as an arch heretic and a Freemason; the sentence was later commuted to life imprisonment. He died in confinement in San Leone on Aug. 26, 1795.

LIONEL ROTHKRUG
University of Michigan

CAGNEY, kag'nē, **James** (1904–), American film actor, who helped transform the traditional movie villain from a two-dimensional evildoer to a fully rounded, flamboyant, sometimes sympathetic gangster hero. Cagney was born in New York City on July 17, 1904, began his acting career as a chorus boy in a Broadway musical, and then turned to vaudeville and motion pictures. Film stardom came with *Public Enemy* (1930), the first of the many gangster and "tough guy" pictures he made in the 1930's. In the 1940's, Cagney appeared in mediocre films, with the exception of *Yankee Doodle Dandy* (1942), in which his impersonation of George M. Cohan won him an Academy Award as best actor.

After acting in *Mister Roberts* (1955) and *Man of a Thousand Faces* (1957), Cagney turned to directing with *Short Cut to Hell* (1957). He both directed and starred in *Shake Hands With the Devil* (1959), and *The Gallant Hours* (1960).

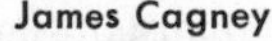
James Cagney

THE BETTMANN ARCHIVE

CAGNIARD DE LA TOUR, kȧ-nyȧr' də lȧ to͞or', **Charles** (1777–1859), French scientist and inventor. He was born in Paris on May 31, 1777. After graduating from the new École Polytechnique in 1794, he became a prolific inventor. He used the principle of the Archimedean screw to make a blowing machine, devised a portable cornmill for Napoleon's armies and invented a gas-lighting apparatus. In 1819 he devised a siren that was an important means of measuring sound vibrations. He also determined the critical temperature for the transformation of certain liquids into gases. In 1838 he advanced fermentation studies by showing yeast to be a living organism. He died in Paris on July 5, 1859.

THOMAS KINGSTON DERRY
Coauthor of "A Short History of Technology"

CAGOT, kȧ-gō', is the name of an outcast people who inhabited parts of the Basque provinces of Spain, and the French regions of Béarn, Gascony, and Brittany during the Middle Ages. Believed to be heretics, lepers, or cretins, these outcasts were denied all political and social rights and were confined to ghettos in towns. Their status was designated by a distinctive costume to which a red cloth in the shape of the foot of a duck or goose was attached. The Cagots were required to worship apart. They entered through a special door, had their own holy water, and were passed the sacramental wafer on a stick. Even burial was segregated.

Their origins have been debated. Some believe they were descendants of the Visigoths, Saracens, or Albigensians. Others have regarded them as lepers. The most recent suggestion is that the Cagots were descendants of persons who for some reason had taken refuge in a leper colony. The French word "cagot," meaning hypocrite, lends credence to this interpretation. Recent studies of a community in Navarre have shown that descendants of the Cagots have no unusual physical characteristics. They were eventually absorbed into the general population.

EDMUND H. DICKERMAN
University of Connecticut

CAGOULARDS, kȧ-go͞o-lȧr', a derisive nickname given to members of the Comité Secret d'Action Révolutionnaire (Secret Committee of Revolutionary Action), a right-wing conspiratorial group active in France in 1937. The name Cagoulard, meaning "hooded one," is derived from the French *cagoule,* the hooded cloak worn by monks.

This clandestine, subversive organization, similar to other fascist leagues in France at the time, actively plotted the overthrow of the Third Republic and the establishment of a rightist dictatorship. It was headed by Eugène Deloncle, a naval engineer and industrialist, and a former royalist. Several high ranking army officers were also involved in it. The Cagoulards were found to be responsible for the bomb explosions in the *Étoile* quarter of Paris in September 1937 and were discovered to have stored huge quantities of arms and ammunition in various parts of the city. Deloncle eventually collaborated with the Germans during the occupation. Marx Dormoy, the Socialist minister of the interior, who had uncovered the plot, was murdered in 1941, a victim, it was widely believed, of Cagoulard vengeance.

JOEL COLTON, *Duke University*

CAGUAS, kä′gwäs, is a town in east central Puerto Rico 22 miles (35 km) by highway southeast of San Juan, in the Cordillera Central. It is situated in an agricultural region where sugarcane, tobacco, vegetables, and bananas and plantains are the chief crops. The town is a center for sugar milling and refining. Cigars, sportswear, and paper products are among its manufactures. Caguas was founded in 1775. Population: 32,015.

CAHAN, kä′hän, **Abraham** (1860–1951), Russian-American newspaper editor and writer, who as editor of the influential New York Yiddish newspaper the *Jewish Daily Forward,* led Jewish immigrant workers in the struggle against sweatshop conditions and for the establishment of strong labor unions.

Cahan was born at Pabradė, near Vilna, Lithuania, on July 6 or 7, 1860. In 1882 he emigrated to New York City, where he worked as a journalist. Cahan edited the Yiddish literary monthly *Die Zukunft* from 1894 until 1897, the year he helped found the *Jewish Daily Forward.* He became editor of the *Forward* in 1902 and headed the paper for almost 50 years. He died in New York City on Aug. 31, 1951.

Cahan wrote several fictional works in English, including the novels *The Rise of David Levinsky* (1917), a realistic masterpiece about a Jewish immigrant's attaining wealth, and *Yekl: A Tale of the New York Ghetto* (1910); and a collection of short stories, *The Imported Bridegroom* (1918). He wrote his autobiography, *Blätter von mein Leben* (5 vols., 1916–1936), in Yiddish.

SOL LIPTZIN
Author of "The Flowering of Yiddish Literature"

CAHOKIA, kə-hō′kē-ə, is a village in southwestern Illinois, situated on the Mississippi River, in St. Clair county. It is just south of East St. Louis, of which it is a residential suburb. The first permanent white settlement in Illinois, Cahokia originated in 1699 as a French mission, named after a nearby Indian tribe. The village passed to the British in 1765 and to the United States in 1778. It was a county seat from 1790 to 1814. Cahokia Court House, the oldest courthouse west of the Allegheny Mountains, has been restored and is a state memorial. Cahokia Mounds State Park is 7 miles (11 km) to the northeast. Government is by mayor and council. Population: 20,649.

CAHORS, kȧ-ôr′, a city in southwestern France, is the capital of Lot department and the principal city of the region of Quercy. It is about 60 miles (97 km) north of Toulouse and is almost surrounded by a meander of the Lot River. Cahors lies at the southwestern edge of the great Massif Central in a rather sparsely populated area that produces grains, fodder crops, and a variety of fruits and vegetables, with some specialization in truffles. Among the city's monuments are the fortified Valentré Bridge, dating from 1308, and the Cathedral of St.-Étienne, with its two cupolas and Romanesque north portal.

The site of Cahors was occupied by the ancient Gallo-Roman town of Divona. In the late Middle Ages Lombard bankers briefly made Cahors a financial center. Its university, outstanding in the Middle Ages, was merged with that of Toulouse in 1751. Population: (1962) 15,528.

HOMER PRICE, *Hunter College*

CAIAPHAS, kā′yə-fəs, **Joseph,** in the New Testament, Jewish high priest of Jerusalem. Caiaphas was a high priest from about 18 to about 36 A. D. He was a son-in-law of the high priest Annas, who probably shared some responsibilities with him.

Caiaphas became an opponent of Jesus. After the raising of Lazarus from the dead, it was Caiaphas who said to the Pharisees, alarmed at the popularity of Jesus, "It is best for us if one man is put to death for the sake of the people" (John 11:49–52). He presided over a meeting of the Sanhedrin at which he showed great determination to have Jesus found guilty and condemned to death. Later Caiphas took part in the examination of the apostles Peter and John (Acts 4:5–21).

CAIBARIÉN, kī-vä-ryān′, is a city on the north coast of Cuba, in Las Villas province, 32 miles (51 km) by road northeast of Santa Clara. It is a fishing port and center for sugarcane, tobacco, and fruit grown in the area. Sawmilling, sugar refining, and fish canning are the main industries. Population: (1953) 23,142.

CAICOS ISLANDS, an island group in the Caribbean Sea at the southeast end of the Bahamas chain. The group is part of a British colony (see TURKS AND CAICOS ISLANDS).

CAILLAUX, kȧ-yō, **Joseph Marie Auguste** (1863–1944), French statesman. He was born on March 30, 1863, at Le Mans. A member of the Radical Party, he was elected to the Chamber of Deputies in 1898 and served as finance minister in the Waldeck-Rousseau and Clemenceau cabinets.

Made premier in 1911, Caillaux arranged a peaceful solution to the Agadir (Morocco) crisis, but he was widely denounced for yielding French territory in Africa to the German protectorate of Kamerun. In 1914, after *Le Figaro* printed a number of his personal letters to his wife, she shot and killed the editor. Although she was acquitted, Caillaux resigned his ministerial post.

During World War I his advocacy of a negotiated peace antagonized Premier Georges Clemenceau and led to Caillaux's arrest, imprisonment, and eventual conviction for wartime communication with the enemy. In 1925, his political rights restored, he was elected to the Senate. He again served as finance minister during the currency crises of 1925 and 1926 and subsequently became chairman of the Senate finance committee. He helped overthrow the Popular Front government in 1937, and voted for full powers to Marshal Pétain, the head of the Vichy government, in 1940. He died at Mamers on Nov. 21, 1944.

JOEL COLTON, *Duke University*

CAILLETET, kȧ-yə-te′, **Louis Paul** (1832–1913), French physicist, who is known for his pioneering work in low-temperature physics. Cailletet was born in Châtillon-sur-Seine, France, on Sept. 21, 1832. Originally a metallurgist working in his father's iron foundry, he became interested in physical research. His most important work (1877–1878) was the liquefaction of oxygen, nitrogen, and other gases, previously considered unliquefiable. He worked independently of the Swiss physicist, Raoul Pictet, who accomplished this feat about the same time. Cailletet became a member of the Académie des Sciences in 1884. He died in Paris on Jan. 5, 1913.

CAILLIÉ, kà-yā′, **René** (1799–1838), French traveler, who was the first European to visit Timbuktu and live to tell about it. He was born in Mauzé, France in 1799. At the age of 16 he sailed to Senegal and the West Indies. He joined an expedition to explore parts of Senegal and Guinea in 1818.

After recovering in France from a tropical fever, he returned to Senegal in 1824 with the aim of visiting the then mysterious trading center of Timbuktu, from which no non-Muslim had ever returned alive. Caillié spent a year among the Moors to learn Arabic, desert customs, and Muslim religious practices. He then disguised himself as an Arab merchant named Abdullahi, claiming to be a freed slave seeking to return to Egypt. In 1827 he joined a caravan of Mandingo merchants and traveled overland across Futa Jallon to Djenné on the Niger River. He then sailed to Timbuktu, where he stayed from April 13 to May 4, 1828.

It took Caillié three months to cross the Sahara to Morocco. He received a hero's welcome in France, although the Timbuktu that he described had clearly seen better days and was far from mysterious. He died in 1838 of a disease contracted in Africa.

ROBERT L. HESS
University of Illinois at Chicago Circle

CAIMAN, kā-man′, an aquatic reptile, closely related to alligators. It is the dominant type of crocodilian in the American tropics. Caimans are widely distributed from southern Mexico to Paraguay and very abundant in some areas.

Like an alligator, the caiman has a long body protected above by heavy armor. It also has a long, broad head, a powerful jaw with sharp teeth, and strong legs. It feeds on animals of many types and sizes, including fishes, birds, and mammals.

The black caiman, *Melanosuchus niger,* is the largest caiman and the only one that is a threat to domestic animals and even man. It is normally about 11 feet (3.3 meters) long, but it may reach a length of 15 feet (4.5 meters). The black caiman is commonly found in the Amazon Basin. It prefers quiet water and frequents swamps, lagoons, flooded forests, and other habitats where the current is not strong. Unfortunately, little is known about the habits of the black caiman. Since it is often hunted for its hide and to eliminate it as a menace to domestic animals, its numbers are decreasing.

The spectacled caiman, *M. sclerops* or *M. crocodilas,* is perhaps the most familar and abundant of the caimans. It is usually about 5 or 6 feet (1.5–1.8 meters) long; its maximum length is a little less than 9 feet (2.8 meters). The spectacled caiman has a curved, bony ridge connecting its eyes. It ranges over the Amazon and Orinoco regions and prefers sluggish water.

In choice of habitat, the smooth-fronted caiman, *Paleosuchus trigonotus,* and its close relative, the dwarf caiman, *P. palpebrosus,* prefer running water and often live in streams with rocky banks and bottoms. They are small caimans, usually only 3 or 4 feet (90–120 cm) long.

The caimans are so closely related to alligators that most herpetologists classify the two groups as a separate family, Alligatoridae, apart from other crocodilians in the order Crocodilia.

CLIFFORD H. POPE
Author of "The Reptile World"

CAIN, kān, in the Old Testament, was the firstborn of Adam and Eve. He became a tiller of the ground, while his younger brother Abel became a shepherd. When the brothers offered up sacrifices to God, Abel's offering was accepted and Cain's was rejected. Enraged, Cain slew Abel, despite a warning from God. As punishment, God cursed Cain by reducing the fertility of the soil and by making him a "fugitive and wanderer." However, upon Cain's entreaty, God put a mark on Cain's forehead as a sign of protection against those who would kill him. Cain then moved to the Land of Nod (Hebrew for "wandering"), to the east of Eden; there his wife bore him a son, Enoch, after whom he named a city he built (Genesis 4).

The Biblical narrative raises problems. After the death of Abel, only Adam, Eve, and Cain were left; yet the need for a "sign" presupposes a large human society, as do the appearance of Cain's wife and his building of a city. Also, the progress of Cain from cultivator to nomad to city-builder is problematical; one would expect nomad to precede cultivator.

A tribe of Cainites (Qeni) is mentioned in the Bible as living to the south of Israel and elsewhere. In view of this, it is tempting to see the possible historical basis of the Cain myth in the early experiences Israelites had with the inimical Cainites. The Cain-Abel conflict is also viewed as the archetypal struggle between agricultural and pastoral societies.

RAPHAEL PATAI, *Theodor Herzl Institute*

CAIN, kān, **James M.** (1892–), American author, noted for his "hard-boiled," fast-moving crime novels. He was born in Annapolis, Md., on July 1, 1892. After working as a reporter on the Baltimore *American* and *Sun* and as a teacher of journalism, he joined the staff of the New York *World.* In 1930 he published *Our Government,* a book of political satires.

In 1931, Cain gave up journalism to concentrate on fiction and motion picture scenarios. His best-selling detective novel *The Postman Always Rings Twice* (1934), which he adapted for the stage in 1936, was also made into a successful film, as were *Double Indemnity* (1936) and *Mildred Pierce* (1941). His other novels include *Serenade* (1937), *The Embezzler* (1940), *Past All Dishonor* (1946), *The Butterfly* (1947), *The Moth* 1948), *Jealous Woman* (1950), *Galatea* (1953), and *Mignon* (1962).

CAINE, kān, **Sir Hall** (1853–1931), English novelist and dramatist. Thomas Henry Hall Caine was born at Runcorn, Cheshire, England, on May 14, 1853, and grew up on the Isle of Man. After working on the Liverpool *Mercury* for six years, he went to London. He became a close friend of Dante Gabriel Rossetti and, after that poet's death in 1882, published his *Recollections of Rossetti.*

Caine's first successful novel was *The Deemster* (1887). His later novels, most of which he adapted for the stage, include *The Bondman* (1890), *The Scapegoat* (1891), *The Manxman* (1894), *The Christian* (1897), *The Prodigal Son* (1904), and *The Women of Knockaloe* (1923). His best novels show a realistic and intimate picture of life on the Isle of Man. His *Life of Christ* was published posthumously in 1938.

Caine was knighted in 1918. He died at Greeba Castle, Isle of Man, on Aug. 31, 1931.

CAINE MUTINY, a novel by Herman Wouk, published in 1951. The action of *The Caine Mutiny* takes place on a World War II minesweeper, the *Caine*, whose officers rebel against Queeg, their overbearing, cowardly, and inefficient captain. It is a novel of considerable narrative power, written in a precise yet graphic style.

The book, an immediate best seller, was later, dramatized for the stage, motion pictures, and television. The play, *The Caine Mutiny Court Martial,* an adaptation of the first part of the book, opened on Broadway in January 1954. The film, *The Caine Mutiny,* covering the entire book, was released in September of that year.

CAIRN, kârn, in archaeology, denotes a mound of stones used as a marker or memorial. The term is derived from the Gaelic word *carn,* meaning "heap."

Cairns are usually conical in form and date from the New Stone or Bronze ages. The use of cairns as burial places was a worldwide custom. Frequently they were used as family vaults. The burial chamber often held urns and chests as well as the dead. Stones were used to protect the dead from mutilation or desecration, and additional stones were piled on the mound to create a marker.

Cairns were also used as road markers or to commemorate important events. Particularly in medieval times, cairns often served as altars at which offerings were made.

See also BARROW.

CAIRN TERRIER, kârn, a small breed in the terrier group of dogs. The cairn is a hardy, active working terrier with balanced proportions, neither leggy nor too close to the ground. It stands about 10 inches (25 cm) at the shoulder and weighs about 14 pounds (35 kg). The head is broad, with a pointed muzzle and strong jaws. The hard outer coat is sandy to near-black; any color except white is permissible.

The cairn was bred to resemble the old-time working terrier of the Isle of Skye and it has characteristics common to other breeds of terriers. It was developed in western Scotland, where it gained favor for its ability to wriggle between the rocks of Scottish cairns in the pursuit of foxes and vermin. The cairn has become popular in the United States since the arrival of the breed in 1913.

WILLIAM F. BROWN
Editor of "American Field"

Cairn Terrier

I. DONALD BOWDEN

CAIRNES, kârnz, **John Elliot** (1823–1875), Irish economist, who made important contributions to the theories of competition, international trade, and labor markets. He developed the concept of "noncompeting groups" to explain immobility between occupational groups but mobility within groups. Cairnes held that craftsmen do not compete for jobs with engineers, nor do engineers compete with doctors and other professional men, but that craftsmen do compete with one another. He extended this thesis to labor and capital mobility in international trade.

Cairnes was born in County Louth on Dec. 26, 1823. He attended Trinity College, Dublin, and studied chemistry and, later, engineering and law. Cairnes was noted as a "pure theorist," and although he was a strong supporter of laissez-faire doctrine, he criticized the extremist position exemplified by Frédéric Bastiat. His *Character and Logical Method of Political Economy* (1857) is considered a landmark in the methodology of economics; his *Slave Power* (1862), an analysis of slavery in America, testifies to his interest in the practical problems of his day. His major work, *Some Leading Principles of Political Economy Newly Expounded* (1874), restated the analytics of the classical theory of value.

He served as professor of political economy at the University of Dublin and at Queens College, Galway, and completed his career at the University of London. He suffered ill health much of his life as the result of a hunting accident. He died at Blackheath, London, on July 8, 1875.

NORMAN A. MERCER, *Union College*

CAIRNS, kârnz, **Hugh McCalmont** (1819–1885), British political leader. He was born in County Down, Ireland, on Dec. 27, 1819, of Scottish Anglican stock. He graduated from Trinity College, Dublin, and in 1838 embarked on a law career in London. Elected to Parliament as a Conservative from Belfast in 1852, he was appointed solicitor general and knighted in 1858 and named attorney general in 1866. A lieutenant of both Disraeli and Lord Derby, the Conservative leader in the House of Lords, he played an important part in steering the party's electoral reform bill through Parliament in 1867 and in getting bipartisan support for the Judicature Act of 1873, which effected basic reforms in British law and equity. Raised to the peerage as a baron in 1867, he succeeded Derby as Conservative leader of the House of Lords in 1869. He was created 1st Earl Cairns seven years before his death at Bournemouth on April 2, 1885.

CAIRNS, kârnz, is a port city in Australia, in northeastern Queensland. It has a good harbor on Trinity Bay and is the northern terminal of the coastal railroad. The center of a large sugar-producing district, Cairns has mills and extensive wharf facilities to process and ship the sugar. The city also exports tobacco, peanuts, pineapples, and corn. Plywood and veneerboard are manufactured.

The city's tropical climate attracts large numbers of tourists. Many visitors are drawn by Green Island, a coral cay on the Great Barrier Reef, 17 miles (27 km) offshore.

The settlement began as a customs collection outpost in 1876. Sugar-planting began in the early 1880's. Population: (1966) 26,555.

R. M. YOUNGER
Author of "Australia and the Australians"

J. ALLAN CASH FROM RAPHO GUILLUMETTE

CAIRO, the capital and largest city of the United Arab Republic, stands on the Nile River. The view here is from Gezira Island, looking south toward the modern city.

CAIRO, kī'rō, is the capital and largest city of the United Arab Republic (Egypt). It is also by far the largest population center in Africa and the Middle East. The Arabic name of the city is *El Qahira,* meaning "the victorious."

Located near the head of the Nile delta, where the river branches into several northward-flowing distributaries, Cairo is a focus of land, river, and air transportation. The main city is on the east bank of the Nile, while extensive suburbs lie on the west bank. Rail lines and motor roads connect Cairo with Alexandria to the northwest, with the Suez Canal cities of Port Said and Suez to the northeast and east respectively, and with Aswan and other cities to the south. River transport, from the Nile to the south and from the delta streams to the north, centers on Cairo. Many air routes that connect Europe to Asia and Australia or to southern Africa use Cairo as an intermediate stop, making it the greatest air terminal in the Middle East.

Plan of the City. The modern portion of Cairo is located along the east bank of the Nile. Here a number of squares and gardens form open places in the overall pattern of irregular small streets, which are crossed at intervals by wider thoroughfares. The Nile Corniche runs right along the river. Farther east and roughly parallel to some of the major streets are Sharia (street) Kasr el-Nil, Sharia Mansour, Sharia Mohammed Farid, and Sharia el-Gumhuria. Sharia el-Tahrir is a major thoroughfare that winds in a westerly direction through the modern city, across the el-Tahrir bridge to Gezira Island and across el-Gala bridge to the west bank. Farther north, Sharia July 26 (formerly Sharia Fouad el-Awal) runs in a northwesterly direction through the modern city and also crosses Gezira Island to the western suburbs. Many places in the city have been renamed for modern heroes or events.

The older part of Cairo, to the east of the modern section, has a traditional Near Eastern atmosphere with winding narrow, alleylike streets, small workshops, marketplaces and curio shops, and many historic buildings. Much of this section was built between the 11th and 16th century. Sharia el-Muski and Sharia al-Azhar are wider streets that run eastward from Opera Square in the modern quarter through the old section to famous al-Azhar mosque. The Citadel, with the mosque of Mehmet Ali, lies on a spur of the Mokattam Hills in the southeast. Several wide streets cut through the old section and connect the Citadel with modern Cairo.

To the south of modern Cairo is Old Cairo, with a port on the Nile and a number of ancient buildings. Nearby, to the east, are the ruins of a Roman fortress. Farther south are the attractive residential suburb of al-Maadi and the industrial district of Helwan.

The Nile River has two islands that form part of the city. Gezira Island, almost a mile wide, has its southern end opposite modern Cairo and extends northward for almost 4 miles (6 km). It has gardens, an exhibition ground, facilities for horse racing, golf, tennis, polo, and other sports and, in the north, clubs, schools, villas, and residences. Roda Island, farther south, opposite Old Cairo, is not quite so large as Gezira. A large government hospital, the former palace and gardens of Prince Mehmet Ali, el-Maniel Museum, and apartment houses take up most of the area. At the southern tip of Roda is the Nilometer, dating from 716 A.D., which measures the annual rise and fall of the river.

On the west bank, opposite Roda Island, is the suburb of Giza with the ancient Sphinx and pyramids, as well as modern Cairo University. Farther north along the western shore are the Zoological Gardens, embassies, residences, and, opposite Gezira Island, the Museum of Agriculture. The modern residential suburb of Heliopolis, the ruins of ancient Heliopolis, and the airport lie northeast of the city.

Points of Interest. Cairo has about 400 mosques, mausoleums, museums, palaces, and other buildings that are of interest to the historian and tourist. The old section of Cairo contains a greater collection of Arab architectural treasures than can be found in any other city in the world. The mosque of Sultan Hasan, built about 1361, has graceful proportions typical of classical Islamic architecture. The university-mosque of al-Azhar was founded in the 970's. A center for the study of Islamic law as well as Arabic language, philosophy, and history, it attracts students from as far as Morocco and Indonesia. The mosque of Ahmad ibn Tulun, built between 876 and 879, has the oldest mosque plan, consisting of an open courtyard enclosed by arcades. The large mosque of Mehmet Ali overlooks the old section from the heights of the Citadel and has the dome, tall minarets, and other features of Ottoman architectural style.

In the northern part of modern Cairo is Rameses Square, which faces the railroad station and has the great ancient statue of Rameses II. Opera Square, about a mile to the south, has the opera house (a copy of the one in Paris) on one side and the Continental-Savoy hotel on the other. In the middle of the square is an equestrian statue of Ibrahim Pasha, the son of Mehmet Ali Pasha. Nearby are sidewalk cafes and restaurants and the Ezbekieh public gardens. A short distance to the southwest is Mustafa Kemal square, named for the Egyptian nationalist whose statue dominates the center.

The largest open place in the city is el-Tahrir ("Liberation") Square near the Nile at El-Tahrir bridge. Ten streets converge on the square, which is criss-crossed by sidewalks with lawn and flower beds between them. On the southern side of the square are large, modern government office buildings, and opposite stands the great Egyptian museum, which contains priceless works of ancient Egyptian art and the treasures from the tomb of Tutankhamen. A short distance away is the Museum of Modern Art, which was founded in 1928. The massive Nile Hilton hotel stands on the western side of the square, between it and the river. Farther south, facing the river, are the Semiramis and the new Shepheard's Hotel. (The old Shepheard's Hotel, a landmark and tourist center for decades, was located about a mile farther east. It was destroyed by fire during the riots of January 1952.) Near el-Tahrir Square there are numerous airline offices, hotels, curio shops, the American University of Cairo, the British and American embassies, and the Parliament building.

Cairo has many secondary and professional schools in addition to the Cairo University, al-Azhar University, Aim Shams University, and the American University. Museums at some distance from el-Tahrir Square include the Museum of Islamic Art, the Coptic Museum in Old Cairo, the Babylonian Museum, the Abdine Museum, and others with collections pertaining to agriculture, hygiene, geology, geography and ethnology, ornithology and entomology, and transport and communications.

The greatest attractions of all are the Sphinx and pyramids at Giza. Nearby is a famous luxury hotel, the Mena House. It was built in 1869 to enable Empress Eugénie of France to visit the pyramids in comfort while she was in Egypt for the celebration of the opening of the Suez Canal.

Economy. The major manufacturing industry of Cairo is textile making based on Egyptian cotton. There are also plants using wool, rayon, jute, and linen. Piece goods, clothing and hosiery, and carpets are the major products. There is also some heavy industry, such as an iron and steel plant and a cement factory at nearby Helwan. Smaller and older industries are tanning and shoe manufacturing, sugar refining, and the making of cigarettes. Consumer oriented industries include baking, printing, furniture making, and the bottling of soft drinks. Traditional handicrafts survive in Cairo with coppersmiths, silversmiths, carpenters, and sandal makers in some parts of the old city. Since 1926, Cairo has had a motion picture industry that makes almost all of the Arab language pictures. The center of the movie industry is in the suburb of el-Jizah.

Commerce, the professions, education, government services, and construction and repair account for the employment of many more people than manufacturing. Cairo is primarily a political, commercial, and cultural center and has wide international influence. Radio Cairo broadcasts to the entire Middle East, and the city has a large publishing business. Cairo is the headquarters of the Arab League. Many leaders from other Arab states have been trained in the city's educational institutions. The flow of tourists to points of interest in Cairo supports numerous hotels, restaurants, curio shops, museums, and travel agencies.

Transport facilities include numerous taxis, as well as streetcar and bus lines to many parts of the city. Both luxury and low-cost rail and

F. RICHARD HSU

THE SPHINX AND GREAT PYRAMID at Giza, a suburb of Cairo, date from about 3000 B. C. They are visited by thousands of tourists each year.

THE CITADEL was built by Sultan Saladin in the 12th century. The mosque of Mehmet Ali crowns the Citadel and looks out over the old city of Cairo.

F. RICHARD HSU

bus service is available to most other cities in Egypt. Air services include local and international lines. Passenger boats on the Nile have landings in the modern city, but freight boats and barges use the port facilities in Old Cairo.

History. The Sphinx and the pyramids of Giza, dating from about 3000 B.C., are among the oldest structures in the vicinity of Cairo. The settlement of Heliopolis, as the Greek named it, and a Roman fortress existed in the pre-Christian era, but only ruins are left of these settlements. During the Arab period, after 640 A.D., several small fortified towns, serving as local capitals, also rose and fell in the locality. One of these, Old Cairo (Misr el-Atika), still exists. The present Cairo was established in 969 A.D. by General Gohar, who had conquered Egypt for the Fatimid Caliph and wanted to establish a capital that would rival the Abassid capital of Baghdad. The Fatimid Arabs later declined in influence, but Cairo continued to grow in cultural, economic, and political importance and eventually replaced Alexandria as the major city of Egypt.

Cairo was built on high ground near the Mokattam Hills to avoid floods. In the 10th century the Nile was broader and spread uncontrolled over the land for a mile or two farther east than the present course of the river. Several islands facilitated crossing the river at the site of Cairo, and across the river and 3 miles (5 km) upstream were the Sphinx and pyramids of Giza. The city's market center served both banks of the river as well as the delta to the north and the long valley to the south.

In the 12th century the ruler Saladin (Salah el-Din) replaced the old brick wall surrounding Cairo with one of stone, constructed the Citadel, extended the city to the south, and built a number of mosques and other public buildings. Bazaars and the workshops of potters, goldsmiths, and silversmiths lined the narrow streets. In later Arab times, especially the 14th century, additional notable mosques were built.

During most of the period when Cairo was dominated by the Turks, from 1517 to 1767, Cairo retained about the same area, and only a few mosques and other important buildings were added. The French under Napoleon I occupied Cairo in 1798 but were expelled by Anglo-Turkish forces in 1801, when the Ottoman Turks resumed nominal control. Under Mehmet Ali, pasha of Egypt from 1811 to 1848, canals were built, new agricultural products introduced, and Cairo gained new buildings and a modest start as a manufacturing center.

The first railroad in Africa was built to connect Cairo to Alexandria in 1855. However, modern urban construction dates from the rule of Khedive Ismail (1863–1879). The capital was moved from Alexandria to Cairo in 1863. Railroads were built linking Cairo to other cities in northern Egypt and to the Suez Canal. The completion of the canal in 1869 was celebrated by many events, including the commissioning of Verdi's *Aida* for the new opera house. (It was not presented until two years later.) A new business district, with broad streets and European style shops and hotels, was laid out along the Nile at the foot of the old city. Boulevards were cut through some parts of the old city, parks and public squares were added, and new residential areas spread outward from the city center. Suburbs rose to the west of the Nile, connected by bridges to the main city.

After World War I, Cairo grew very rapidly, especially between 1937 and 1947 when the population increased from 1,312,000 to 2,100,000. The increase in Egyptian population and in cotton production and manufacturing, all serviced by a growing commercial element in Cairo, caused the rapid urban expansion. Foreigners, including English, Turks, French, Italians, Greeks, Syrians, and Lebanese, and a small group of middle-class Egyptians gave new life to the city. Cairo experienced further industrialization during World War II, when Egypt was a major Allied base, cut off from European industry.

Industrial establishments, research institutes, schools, gardens, and residential areas have spread out from the city center. Today Cairo is surrounded by a vast suburban area, including both banks of the Nile as well as places like Giza and Heliopolis that were once separate centers. Population: (1960) 3,348,779.

BENJAMIN E. THOMAS
University of California, Los Angeles

Bibliography

Devonshire, Henriette Caroline, *Moslem Builders of Cairo* (London 1944).
Dodge, Bayard, *Al-Azhar: A Millennium of Muslim Learning* (Washington, D.C., 1961).
Nelson, Nina, *Shepheard's Hotel* (New York 1960).
Russell, Dorethea, *Medieval Cairo* (Camden, N.J., 1963).
Stewart, Desmond, *Cairo* (London 1965).
Wiet, Gaston, *Cairo* (Norman, Okla., 1964).

CAIRO, kâr′ō, the southernmost city in Illinois, the seat of Alexander county, is situated at the confluence of the Ohio and Mississippi rivers. A system of levees protects it from floods. Cairo is a trade, processing, and shipping center for fruit, grain, and cotton grown in the surrounding area that includes nearby sections of Kentucky and Missouri. The city manufactures lumber, fiber-glass boats, workmens' apparel, and polyurethane foam.

Settlement of the site was attempted in 1818, but of the projected city, only the name "Cairo" survived. The name was chosen because the site and its environs were thought to resemble the geographical situation of Cairo, Egypt. A second settlement was founded in 1837, but it was not until 1855, when the Illinois Central Railroad opened a track between Cairo and Chicago, that the city developed into a busy cotton port. During the Civil War, Cairo was a concentration point for the Union army. Gen. Ulysses S. Grant established headquarters here in 1861; troops were quartered just south of the city at Fort Defiance, now a state park. The city has many fine old homes. Magnolia Manor, built in 1869, is maintained as a museum. Incorporated as a city in 1857, Cairo is governed by Commission. Population: 6,277.

EVELYN J. SNYDER, *Cairo Public Library*

CAIRO CONFERENCE, kī′rō, a meeting of U. S. President Franklin D. Roosevelt, British Prime Minister Winston Churchill, and Chinese Generalissimo Chiang Kai-shek in Cairo, Egypt, on Nov. 22–26, 1943, during World War II. The three statesmen issued a declaration disavowing all desire for territorial expansion and affirming the intention of their countries to demand an unconditional surrender from Japan. They pledged that Japan would be deprived of all Pacific islands occupied since 1914; that all territory seized from China would be restored; and that Korea would be granted independence.

CAISSON, kā′son, a boxlike structure that is sunk to provide an integral part of the foundation of a bridge pier or a building. A caisson is built of timber, metal, or concrete.

A *box caisson,* open at the top, is filled with concrete or stone and sunk to the bottom of the water; it is used when no excavation is required to reach a firm bed.

An *open caisson,* which has no top or bottom, is a thick-walled shell. Soil beneath the caisson is removed with hoisting machinery or by directing a high-pressure air stream at the soil. The walls of the caisson are built upward as the caisson goes deeper. The increase in its weight and the removal of soil force the caisson downward until a firm stratum is reached. The caisson is then filled with concrete. Open caissons are used underwater and on land.

A *pneumatic caisson,* open at the bottom, is filled with air under pressure to prevent water from entering. Workmen enter the caisson through an air lock and excavate to a firm stratum; excavated material is removed through a shaft and air lock. After the men leave, the caisson is filled with concrete. The pneumatic caisson, used at depths as great as 100 feet (30 meters), was developed in England in the 1850's.

ALBERT H. GRISWOLD, *New York University*

CAISSON DISEASE. See BENDS.

CAITHNESS, kāth′nes, in Scotland, is the northernmost county on the mainland of Britain. It occupies the northeastern tip of Scotland, across Pentland Firth from the Orkney Islands, and it is bordered on the west by Sutherland county. The land is a windswept almost featureless plain broken only by the mountains of Morven and Scaraben in the south. Sheep and cattle raising and dairying are pursued in the county.

Wick, on the east coast, is the county town and also a royal burgh. It has a good harbor much used by fishing boats. The most important town is Thurso, on the north coast. Nearby, at Dounreay, the United Kingdom Atomic Energy Authority began experimental work in 1954, and its reactors have been generating power since 1962.

The northernmost point on the British mainland is Dunnet Head, on Pentland Firth. It is not, as is commonly thought, John o'Groat's, about 10 miles (16 km) to the east and slightly south, where in the 1400's a Dutchman named Jon de Groot is said to have built an octagonal house. However, in measuring the length of the British mainland, reference is commonly made to the 876-mile (1,410-km) journey from Land's End in the southwest to John o'Groat's in the northeast. About 5 miles (8 km) west of John o'Groat's, on Pentland Firth, is the Castle of May, which was built in the 1500's and in 1952 was restored as a residence for Elizabeth, the Queen Mother. From earliest times, Caithness was visited by Norsemen, and there are many remains of their stone towers and mounds. Population: (1961) 27,345.

GORDON STOKES
Author of "English Place-Names"

CAIUS, kā′yəs, **Saint,** pope from 283 to 296. Also known as *Gaius,* he has been called a relative of Emperor Diocletian; however, modern scholars dispute the source of this information. As pope, he decreed that a man must go through minor orders successively and the subdeaconate, deaconate, and priesthood before becoming a bishop. It is said that Caius died a martyr during the persecution of Diocletian, but the dates do not substantiate this: Caius died in 296, and the persecution occurred some time later. At any rate he is honored as a saint. His feast is kept with that of Pope St. Soter on April 22.

JAMES S. BRUSHER, S. J.
University of Santa Clara

CAJAMARCA, kä-hä-mär′kä, is a city in Peru, 530 miles (850 km) northwest of Lima. It lies in the Andean highlands, about 9,000 feet (2,750 meters) above sea level. It is the capital for Cajamarca department and the chief commercial center for an agricultural region (grain, dairying) and mining area (gold, silver, copper, coal). Its industries produce textiles, leather goods, straw hats, flour, and silver products.

The city is one of the oldest in Peru. It has the ruins of the palace where the Inca Atahualpa, after his seizure by the Spanish in 1532, is said to have filled an entire room with gold as ransom to buy his freedom. He was executed the following year. (See ATAHUALPA.) The city's cathedral, begun around 1600, was completed in 1960. About 10 miles (16 km) southeast of Cajamarca are hot sulfur springs used by the Incas for therapeutic bathing and still in use. Population: (1961) 22,705.

CAJETAN, kaj′ē-tan, **Saint** (1480–1547), Italian founder of the Theatines. Cajetan or Gaetamo of Thiene was born in Vicenza, Italy, in October 1480, the son of Count Gaspare da Thiene. He earned a doctorate in civil and canon law at Perugia (1504) and began a career in the Roman Curia. In 1516, Cajetan became a priest and joined the Oratory of Divine Love, a pious confraternity. Aided by Gianpietro Carafa, bishop of Chieti (Latin, Theatinus), who later became Pope Paul IV, and by two other members of the Oratory, Cajetan in 1524 founded in Rome the Order of Clerics Regular, or Theatines, a religious order dedicated to the reform of the priesthood and the service of the faithful. After serving as superior general (1527–1530), he became superior in Naples (1533), where he labored until his death, except for a term as superior in Venice (1540–1543).

Cajetan died in Naples on Aug. 7, 1547, and was canonized on April 12, 1671. His feast day is observed on August 7.

JOHN F. BRODERICK, S.J., *Weston College, Mass.*

CAJETAN kaj′ē-tan (1469–1534), Italian cardinal and theologian. He was born at Gaeta, Italy, on Feb. 20, 1469. His real name was Giacomo de Vio, but he changed his baptismal name to Tommaso in honor of St. Thomas Aquinas and adopted the surname Cajetanus or Gaetanus (Italian, Gaetano) from the name of his birthplace.

Cajetan entered the Dominican order in 1485 and was ordained in 1491. He received his bachelor of theology degree from the University of Padua in 1493 and later taught there, developing into a profound metaphysician. In 1508 he was elected master general of his order, and in nearly 10 years in this office proved his gift for constructive reform.

In 1517, Pope Leo X created him cardinal and the following year sent him to Germany as papal legate to unite the princes against the Turks. While there he undertook the most dramatic and historic mission of his career – to seek Martin Luther's recantation and try to win him back into fellowship with the church. Though his meeting with Luther at Augsburg in October 1518 proved fruitless, Cajetan later won praise from church authorities for his handling of an exceedingly subtle and difficult situation. The cardinal's influence is seen in the papal condemnation of Luther in 1520.

He was involved in other noted events of his time. In the sack of Rome by the Spanish in 1527, Cajetan was imprisoned and forced to pay a ransom of 5,000 gold crowns for his liberty. As one of the 19 cardinals who met in consistory with Pope Clement VII in March 1534 in the case of Henry VIII and Catherine of Aragon, he upheld the validity of the marriage and opposed the divorce. He died in Rome on Aug. 9, 1534.

Between 1507 and 1522 Cajetan published the first commentary on the *Summa theologica* of Aquinas. This defense of St. Thomas is considered Cajetan's most notable work and places him among the greatest exponents of the Thomestic School of theology. Cajetan also wrote economic works, particularly on exchange and usury.

EMMET T. GLEESON, *Catholic University of America*

Further Reading: Lindsay, T. M., *History of the Reformation*, vol. 1 (Edinburgh 1906); and the Cajetan centenary issues of the following periodicals: *Angelicum* (Rome, Oct.–Dec. 1934); *Révue Thomiste* (Paris, Nov. 1934–Feb. 1935); *Rivista di filosofia neoscolastica* (Milan, March 1935).

CAJIGAL DE LA VEGA, kä-hē-gäl′ dā lä vä′gä, **Francisco Antonio** (1695–1777), Spanish colonial administrator and soldier. He was born in Hoz, Santander, Spain, on Feb. 5, 1695. After serving as military commandant of Caracas, Venezuela, he was governor of Santiago, Cuba, from 1738 to 1747. He successfully repelled an attack there in 1741 by Adm. Edward Vernon's English fleet and was promoted to brigadier and then field marshal. As governor general of Cuba from 1747 to 1760, he expanded fortifications and built an arsenal and navy yard at Havana. In 1760–1761 he was acting viceroy of Mexico. He died in Hoz on April 30, 1777.

CAJORI, kä-yō′-rē, **Florian** (1859–1930), Swiss-American mathematician, who is known for his writings on the history of mathematics. Cajori was born in St. Aignan, Switzerland, on Feb. 28, 1859. He went to the United States in 1875. After teaching mathematics at Tulane University and mathematics and physics at Colorado College, where he was also dean of engineering, he became the first American professor of the history of mathematics, a post he held at the University of California from 1918 until his retirement in 1929. He died in Berkeley, Calif., on Aug. 14, 1930. Cajori's most important work was *A History of Mathematical Notation* (2 vols. 1928–1929).

CAJUNS, kā′jənz, are French-speaking people who live in southern Louisiana. The name "Cajuns" is a corruption of "Acadians," the ancestors of the Cajuns, who lived in Acadia, French Canada.

Although the British acquired Acadia in 1713, the pastoral Acadians were not molested until 1755, when those who refused to swear allegiance to the British crown were expelled from their homes and repatriated to various British-American colonies. By 1790 about 4,000 Acadians had found their way to southern Louisiana, settling in the fertile bayou lands in the vicinity of the Gulf of Mexico.

In this area their descendants, the Cajuns, still raise cattle and small crops of cotton, corn, sugarcane, and sweet potatoes, and practice home arts such as spinning and weaving. Their speech combines archaic French forms with words taken from English, Spanish, German, Indian, and Negro neighbors. The Cajuns are noted for their industry and hospitality.

CAKCHIQUEL INDIANS, käk′chə-kel, Central American Indians of Mayan stock found east and northeast of Lake Aitlan in the highlands of Guatemala. In pre-Columbian times they were almost constantly at war with their neighbors, the Quiché and the Tzutuhil. All three peoples spoke closely related Mayan dialects and shared with other highland groups a well-developed culture. In art, architecture, astronomy, and hieroglyphic writing, however, the highland groups were far behind the lowland Maya. The Cakchiquel economy was agricultural, based on maize. The women were noted for their colorful costumes.

The Cakchiquel received the Spanish peacefully and allied with them in war against the Tzutuhil. However, Spanish demands for tribute, labor, and treasure finally forced them to revolt. They were subjugated, and their capital, Iximché, was destroyed around 1524. The ruins confirm the importance of these people.

Several thousand Cakchiquel still lived in Guatemala in the 1960's.

CAKE AND PASTRY. Cakes, cookies, and pastries are among the most popular desserts. Rich and fancy or plain and simple, they are equally appropriate to an elaborate tea table or to a lunch box. Cakes and cookies have the same basic ingredients: sugar, shortening, eggs, liquid, flour, leavening (lightening ingredient), and flavoring. The proportions of these ingredients are varied to form thin or thick batter for cakes and soft or stiff dough for cookies.

Cakes typically are high, with a light delicate texture. Cookies are usually small and thin, ranging from crisp and tender to moist and chewy. Both cakes and cookies may be made in a variety of flavors and with fruits and nuts added. Because of their tenderness and moistness most cakes are eaten with a fork, while cookies are usually eaten with the fingers.

Pastry differs from cakes and cookies in being thin and flaky. Flour, shortening, salt, and liquid are combined to form a stiff dough, which is rolled thin and fitted into a pie pan for its most conventional use as pie crust. A richer pastry may be made by layering additional shortening between thin layers of the dough. The resulting puff pastry is so named because the layers separate and "puff" during baking.

CAKES

There are two categories of cakes: shortening type and foam type; both may be prepared from home recipes or from packaged dry mixes.

Shortening Cakes. Shortening cakes are the kind most frquently baked, and the home recipe may be prepared by either the conventional or the one-bowl method. In the conventional method, shortening and sugar are creamed together until light and fluffy, and eggs are then added, beaten or unbeaten, according to the recipe. A flour, salt, and leavening mixture is then added alternately with the required liquid, and well blended.

The one-bowl method is the most popular technique, since all the ingredients called for are combined in one utensil for blending. Recipes for the one-bowl technique usually call for a soft shortening because it blends more easily. The mixing-time directions in the recipe should be followed carefully.

In shortening-cake mixes, the shortening, sugar, flour, salt, leavening, and flavoring are carefully premeasured in the packaged dry mix. Eggs and liquid are added and blended according to directions.

The texture of shortening cakes should have a fine to medium-fine grain with a light and velvety "feel," tender enough to break easily but not crumble. Moistness will vary with the kind of cake, but the cake should not be gummy.

Foam Cakes. For their leavening, foam cakes depend on air beaten into the eggs. The eggs in turn are folded (overturned, not stirred) into the batter. Part of the sugar in the recipe is usually beaten into the egg foam to help stabilize it. Whipped egg whites serve as leavening for angel food cakes as well as for chiffon cakes. However, chiffon cakes differ from angel food in that they also contain egg yolks and liquid shortening. Whipped egg yolks form the leavening for sponge cakes.

Some foam cake mixes require only a liquid additive and a short beating time. Others have a dry egg white mixture that is reconstituted and whipped before being added to the batter.

Angel food cakes have a crisp golden crust with deep cracks and a light delicate interior texture. Chiffon and sponge cakes have a soft tender top with shallow cracks and a light texture that has slightly more body than angel food.

Utensils. Correct utensils and equipment are important for baking results. Standard household measuring cups and spoons are necessary for accurate measurements. Standard or portable electric mixers may be used, but portables must be used at a higher speed and for a longer beating time. If the ingredients are mixed by hand, 150 vigorous spoon strokes are equivalent to one minute beating with a standard-mixer at medium speed. Bowls and beaters must be free from grease for foam-type cakes. Porous plastic bowls or scrapers should never be used because grease will cling to these and the egg white will not form a stable foam.

The size of the pan affects baking results. The most frequently used pans for shortening cakes are 8- or 9-inch x 1½-inch layer pans, 9- x 13- x 2-inch rectangular pans, 8- or 9-inch square pans or loaf pans. They should be of medium weight with a dulled outside bottom finish. Foam cakes are usually baked in a tube pan 10 inches in diameter and 4 inches deep, with a 4½-quart capacity. Shortening or foam batters may be baked in paper baking cups, ½ to ⅔ full.

Ingredients. For best results in cake baking, use the ingredients called for in the recipe and measure accurately. When butter or margarine are stipulated, a whipped form of the product should not be substituted since the air incorporated will change the shortening power. Liquid shortening should not be substituted in a recipe calling for other shortenings.

The majority of home recipe cakes are made with all-purpose flour. Since this flour is presifted, it may be used successfully without further sifting, by spooning into the measuring cup and leveling off with a spatula. However, results will be more accurate for very delicate cakes if flour is sifted before measuring. Most angel food and some sponge cake recipes require cake flour, since these cakes are more delicate. The best eggs to use are large ones, which measure five to the cup. Eggs should be at room temperature before whipping to obtain the greatest volume.

Baking. Pans should be prepared as directed in the recipe. Some shortening cake recipes require the bottom and sides of pans to be greased and floured; others, that the bottom be lined with paper. Foam cake pans must not be greased.

The oven must be preheated to the temperature specified in the recipe. The oven rack should be in the center for shortening cakes, and pans arranged at least 1 inch apart and 1 to 1½ inches from the oven walls to allow an even circulation of heat. Foam cakes should be baked with the oven rack at the lowest position.

When baked, a shortening cake should spring back lightly if touched near its center and be drawn slightly away from the edge of the pan. A wooden pick or cake tester inserted in the center of the cake should come out clean. Foam cakes must be completely baked or they may fall from the pan during cooling. The top crust should be firm and a deep golden brown, and the cracks or crevices should be dry in appearance.

A shortening cake should first be cooled in the pan on a wire rack for about 10 minutes. Then, to remove the cake from the pan, the sides of the cake should be loosened with a knife and

1. Sift and measure flour. Add salt, and cut in shortening with a pastry blender or two knives until the crumbs are coarse and granular, the size of small peas.

2. Add cold water, and with a fork stir the dough quickly until it just holds in a ball. The dough may then be chilled slightly before it is rolled out.

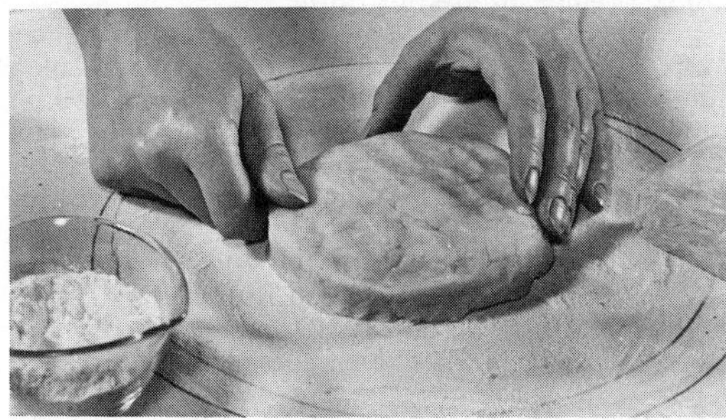

3. Shape the dough into rounds on a lightly floured cloth or breadboard. Each round should consist of dough for one crust; make two rounds for a two-crust pie.

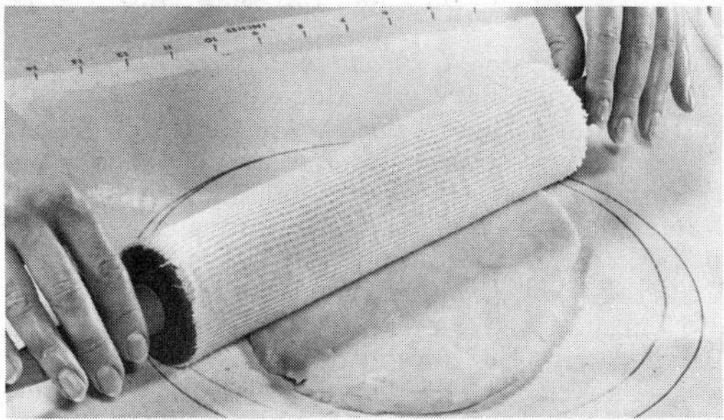

4. Using short light strokes with a lightly floured rolling pin, roll out the dough from the center to the edge to form a circle that is about ⅛-inch thick.

5. Roll the dough for the bottom crust, which must fit into the pie pan, into a circle that is about 1½ inches larger than the outside edge of the pan.

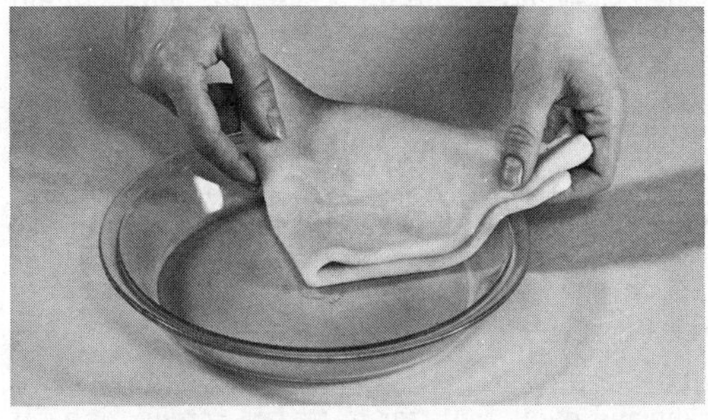

6. When transferring it to the pie pan, be careful not to stretch the thinly rolled dough. One method is to fold the dough into quarters that are unfolded in the pan.

7. Press the dough gently into the pan, making sure that no air remains trapped under the dough. Then trim the dough to within ½ inch of the edge of the pan.

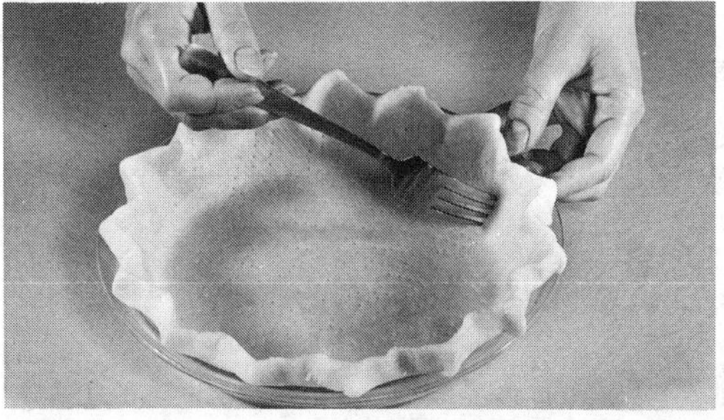

8. Crimp the dough for the bottom crust. If it is to be baked without a filling, the crust should first be pricked with a fork to ensure that no air bubbles form.

PHOTOS COURTESY OF PILLSBURY COMPANY

the bottom loosened by tapping the pan. The wire rack should then be placed on top of the pan, and the pan and cake inverted. If a shortening cake sticks to the pan, placing it over a surface unit at low heat to warm the bottom of the pan slightly will usually release the cake.

Foam cakes should be inverted and permitted to cool in the pan for about 1½ hours. Then the cake can be released.

Frosting. Cake layers must be cooled before frosting. The bottom layer should be placed top-side down on the plate and spread to the edge with frosting. Then the top layer can be placed bottom-side down on the under layer. The sides should be frosted before the top.

COOKIES

There are six basic types of cookie dough—drop, bar, rolled, molded, pressed, and refrigerator doughs.

Cookie Doughs. *Drop-cookie dough* is usually mixed in one bowl and dropped by spoonfuls onto a baking sheet. *Bar-cookie dough* is baked in a shallow square or rectangular pan; the cookies may be chewy or cakelike in texture. *Rolled-cookie dough* is rolled thin and cut with cookie cutters, a knife, or a pastry wheel. *Molded-cookie dough* can be shaped by hand into balls, sticks, or crescents; the shapes may be flattened with the bottom of a glass or tines of a fork. *Pressed-cookie dough,* usually a very rich mixture, can be forced through a cookie press into a variety of shapes. *Refrigerator-cookie dough* is shaped into rolls and well chilled before it is thinly sliced and baked. Packaged refrigerator dough is ready to slice or shape and bake.

Cookie dough usually contains all-purpose flour, shortening, liquid (eggs or milk), and leavening; these ingredients vary in proportion to the type of cookie being prepared. Butter, margarine, or other shortening may be used; some butter is desirable because of its flavor. Recipes for rich cookies may require all butter.

Equipment and Baking. Cookie-making equipment should include standard measuring utensils, rolling pin, breadboard, cookie cutters, and baking sheets. An electric mixer may be used to mix soft doughs.

Cookies should be baked in a preheated oven, allowing sufficient space between cookie sheets or pans and oven walls for good heat circulation. It is wise to bake a few samples first, to test for spreading. If they spread too much, the dough should be chilled or partially frozen before continuing the baking. Baking time must be watched closely. The cookies should be removed from the oven when they are lightly browned and set in the center and cooled immediately on a wire rack. Soft cookies should be stored in a tightly covered container; crisp cookies in a loosely covered container. Cookies may be recrisped by placing them in a 300° oven for about 5 minutes.

PASTRIES

There are two basic types of pastry: *plain pastry,* for pie crusts, and *puff pastry.*

Plain Pastry. Plain pastry is usually a combination of all-purpose flour, salt, shortening, and liquid, which are blended to form a stiff dough. Shortening or lard is used in conventional recipes; liquid shortening in special recipes. Butter or margarine as well as eggs may also be used, but are usually restricted to specialty recipes. Cold water is the conventional liquid that binds the ingredients together; hot water is used only in special recipes. For conventional pastry the shortening must be cut into the flour-salt mixture until the resultant crumbs are coarse and like small peas in size. (Cutting may be done with two knives, a pastry blender, or an electric mixer at low speed.) Water sprinkled over the ingredients is mixed in quickly with a fork until the dough just holds together. Too much water makes the baked crust tough; too little makes it crumble.

With a liquid shortening, the shortening and water are blended into the flour-salt mixture. The hot water method requires that a measured amount of boiling water be added to the shortening and stirred until the shortening melts; then it is blended into the flour-salt mixture. Packaged pie crust can be obtained in both a dry mix and a premeasured stick form.

Pastry dough should be rolled out on a lightly floured breadboard or pastry cloth about ⅛-inch thick, with short light strokes with the rolling pin, working from the center to the edge. The circle of dough should be about 1½ inches larger than the outside edge of the pie pan. To transfer the rolled dough to the pie pan, it may be folded in quarters or rolled up on the rolling pin, with care being taken not to stretch it or it may shrink in the baking. Liquid shortening and hot water pastry is easier to roll between sheets of waxed paper. After rolling, the top sheet can be removed, the pastry inverted over the pie pan paper-side up, and the remaining sheet removed. The less handling the more tender is the pie crust. The dough should be pressed gently into the pan to eliminate air bubbles, the edge trimmed and crimped, and the bottom pricked if it is baked without a filling.

Puff Pastry. Puff pastry also is prepared from flour, salt, shortening (at least half should be be butter), and cold water. A basic puff paste has part of the shortening cut into the flour-salt mixture. The dough, prepared like conventional pastry, is well chilled, then rolled out and dotted with butter, and folded three times and chilled. This process is repeated—chilling, rolling, and chilling—before using the dough in recipes for such pastries as turnovers, Napoleon slices, patty shells, cream horns, Venetian pastry, or strudel.

Danish pastry requires the addition of yeast and eggs to the basic dough mixture before layering with butter. The dough must be allowed to rise before baking.

Cream puff dough is made by melting the shortening (at least half should be butter) over boiling water, stirring in the flour-salt mixture, and beating in the eggs, until a stiff dough is formed. The dough is dropped by spoonfuls on greased baking sheets. Cream puffs are usually split and filled with whipped cream. They may be made smaller and filled with savory fillings for appetizers or baked in strips for éclairs.

Baking. Pie crusts are usually baked in 8- or 9-inch pie pans; puff pastries on cookie sheets or in specially shaped pans. The oven must be preheated, and the baking pan should be in the center of the oven for the even circulation of heat.

HELEN WOLCOTT HORTON, *Consultant Consumer Food Marketing and Communications*

Further Reading: Better Homes and Gardens, *Better Homes and Gardens Pies and Cakes* (Des Moines, Iowa, 1966); Claiborne, Craig, ed., *The New York Times Cook Book* (New York 1961); Peck, Paula, *The Art of Fine Baking* (New York 1961).

CAKES AND ALE is a novel by W. Somerset Maugham (q.v.), published in 1930. The novel is a satire that exposes sham in the English literary world. Two writers, Ashenden and Alroy Kear, reexamine the life of a noted but not very talented Victorian writer, Edward Driffield, who has recently died. Kear plans to write the biography of Driffield, whom Ashenden had known as a young man. Ashenden was based on Maugham himself, while Kear was based on Hugh Walpole. Driffield was said to have been based on Thomas Hardy, but Maugham denied it. Throughout the book Maugham interjects trenchant comments on literary matters.

CAKEWALK, kāk'wôk, a dance originated by American Negroes, which became popular on the stage. On Southern plantations before the Civil War, the cakewalk was a contest in which Negro couples walked in a square formation, men on the inside, taking exaggerated high steps and turning corners precisely in mimicry of the white man's artificial manners. Couples were gradually eliminated until the most elegant and graceful one received a richly decorated cake as a prize.

In the late 19th century the cakewalk was popularized by white performers in minstrel and variety shows. Modern adaptations of the cakewalk include the ballet *Cakewalk* (1951) with choreography by Ruthanna Boris and music by Louis Moreau Gottschalk. The expression "to take the cake" comes from the old cakewalk.

CALABAR, kal'ə-bär, a seaport in southeastern Nigeria, is located at the mouth of the Calabar River, on the Bight of Biafra, an inlet of the Atlantic Ocean. It is about 350 miles (560 km) east southeast of Lagos.

The town is a major center for the export of palm oil, cacao, rubber, timber, and benniseed from the surrounding region. Cotton goods are the principal imports. Industries in Calabar include rubber and palm-oil processing, woodcarving, and fisheries. The town is served by an international airport.

Calabar was an important center for the export of slaves during the 18th and 19th centuries. Population: (1953) 46,705.

CALABASH GOURD, kal'ə-bash gôrd, a rapidly growing tropical annual vine whose fruits are sometimes used as ornaments or utensils, such as cups and bowls. The fruits range in length from 3 inches to 3 feet (7.5 to 90 cm) and are often round, disk-shaped, bottle-shaped, or dumbbell-shaped. They are usually greenish or tan and are sometimes striped or mottled.

The calabash gourd, sometimes called bottle gourd, is technically known as *Lagenaria vulgaris* or *L. leucantha* and belongs to the gourd family. It reaches a length of 30 to 40 feet (9 to 12 meters) and bears large sticky rounded leaves that have a musky odor. The flowers are white and the staminate (male) flowers are borne on long slender stalks while the pistillate (female) flowers are short-stalked. The calabash gourd grows well in almost any light loamy garden soil. For planting in northern regions the seeds should be started indoors.

Frances Sherburne
Massachusetts Audubon Society

CALABASH TREE, kal'ə-bash, a tropical American tree cultivated primarily for its large fruits, which are used as water gourds and bowls. It grows to a height of 20 to 40 feet (6 to 12 meters). The branches extend outward horizontally with practically no secondary branching. The shiny dark-green leaves are bunched, with wide spaces between the clusters. The leaves, which are almost 6 inches (15 cm) long, are lance-shaped, and taper to the base.

The flowers are bilaterally symmetrical, with five fused petals constricted in the middle and usually four stamens. They appear singly and droop and have a disagreeable odor when they decay. The pistil matures into a large capsular fruit about 20 inches (50 cm) in diameter and almost spherical.

The wood is soft and flexible, with a homogeneous grain, and is used for making small objects, such as shoemaker's lasts.

The calabash tree's scientific name is *Crescentia cujete*. It is a member of the Bignoniaceae family.

S. C. Bausor
California State College, Pa.

THE CALABASH TREE (*right*) bears edible fruit (*left*) in a hard shell that can be used as a container.

J. J. SMITH

ROBERT EMMETT BRIGHT, FROM RAPHO GUILLUMETTE

LIFE IN CALABRIA is simple and close to the land. From plum tomatoes a girl makes tomato paste by hand.

CALABRIA, kä-lä′brē-ä, the southwestern extension of the Apennine peninsula, is one of the administrative regions of southern Italy. It is composed of three provinces: Cosenza, Catanzaro, and Reggio di Calabria.

Most of Calabria is mountainous or hilly. In the north, Calabria is connected to the Apennine system by the massif of Monte Pollino, which continues southward as the Coast Range. The wide valley of the Crati River separates the range from the wide, high plateau of the Sila. A narrow isthmus between the Gulf of Sant'Eufemia in the west and the Gulf of Squillace in the east connects southern Calabria and the rest of the region; the south is dominated by the Serre and Aspromonte uplands.

Economy. Until the 1960's Calabria was one of the poorest regions in Italy. Much of the soil on the lower hillsides and in the coastal lowlands was heavily eroded and supported only meager crops of cereals. The few areas of orchards and citrus and olive groves were separated by wide expanses of poor grazing land. There was some lumbering in the mountains, but the slopes were used primarily for pasturing sheep and goats. A large part of the land was held by large landowners. However, in the land reform program of the 1950's much of this land was redistributed to form small peasant farms. Heavy governmental investment brought a measure of prosperity to the coastal areas, where farmers began to grow early fruit, vegetables, and flowers. The uplands, especially the Sila plateau, were slowly developed into resort areas, and the same trend was later followed in some of the coves and bays of the west coast.

Industry is severely limited in Calabria by the lack of mineral resources. However, hydroelectric power is generated in the Sila, and small chemical plants are operating in the town of Crotone, on the east coast.

History and Culture. Calabria entered recorded history during the era of Greek colonization of southern Italy. The Greek settlements that arose on the eastern shore of Italy along the Ionian Sea were among the most prosperous of the Mediterranean. Rome conquered the region, but limited its control to the coastline and to the main road that connected the Naples region with Reggio and the Strait of Messina.

After the decline of the Roman Empire, Calabria knew all the conquerors that swept across Italy: Goths, Lombards, Byzantines, Normans, Germans, Angevins, and Aragonese. From the 14th century onward Calabria was part of the Kingdom of Naples and remained so until 1860, when Garibaldi united Calabria and the rest of the Neapolitan kingdom with Italy.

Although remote and relatively inaccessible until recent times, Calabria nonetheless offers both scenic beauty and artistic treasures to the traveler. The successive conquerors in its long and stormy history have all left something behind: thus some of the finest remaining examples of Byzantine architecture are found in small hill towns of Calabria.

Calabria is noted for the presence, within the region, of a substantial non-Italian minority, the Albanians. The ancestors of this group fled their native land to escape Turkish conquest in the 15th century. The Albanian language is spoken in the homes and taught in the schools. Population: (1966 est.) 2,081,484.

George Kish, *University of Michigan*

Caladium

R. A. SCHLEGEL

CALADIUM, kə-lā′dē-əm, a genus of tropical American plants widely grown for their brightly colored triangular or arrowhead-shaped leaves that are borne on long stems from an underground tuber. The principal species is *Caladium bicolor,* with its many varieties. The leaves of these plants are veined and mottled in various shades of red, green, and/or yellow. *C. schomburgkii* is another popular species. Its leaves are not peltate (attached parasol-like to the leafstalks) as in other species.

In growing caladiums, the tubers are potted early in the spring in soil consisting primarily of leaf mold and some sand. They should be repotted several times, adding well-rotted manure, peat, and loam each time until a combination of equal parts (omitting the sand) is attained. When the weather is warm, the plants are transplanted outdoors in a shady area. They may also be grown indoors as houseplants.

Caladiums belong to the arum family. A related plant, the elephant's ear (Colocasio), is sometimes also known as caladium.

Frances Sherburne
Massachusetts Audubon Society

CALAH, kā'lə, the second capital of Assyria, was located on the east bank of the Tigris River, several miles above its confluence with the Upper Zab. The Assyrian forms of the name were *Kalkhu* and, later, *Kalakh.* The site was occupied intermittently for over 1,000 years before it was expanded and fortified by Shalmaneser I (about 1250 B.C.), who was considered the city's founder. King Ashurnasirpal II (883–859 B.C.) founded it anew, on a much larger scale. It was finally destroyed by the Medes (614 B.C.).

Archaeological work at the site—now called Nimrud and located in present-day Iraq—was begun in 1845 and continued intermittently until 1854. In 1949 it was resumed by M. E. L. Mallowan, who explored the more important remains that had not been cleared previously. The most important building is the Northwest Palace, built in the early 9th century B.C. Other major buildings are the Shalmaneser Fort, built by the founder, and the Ninurta Temple with the adjacent temple tower. Art historians have learned much from hoards of carved ivories, dating from the 9th and 8th centuries B.C. Royal inscriptions and tablet archives, mainly from the reign of Tiglath-pileser III (745–727 B.C.), throw light on the history of Palestine and Syria.

WILLIAM F. ALBRIGHT
Johns Hopkins University

CALAIS, kȧ-le', is a historic French city on the Strait of Dover, in the department of Pas-de-Calais. It is a seaport, a manufacturing city, and a beach resort. Located near the narrowest stretch of water separating England and France, Calais has long been important for its ferry service across the English Channel; regularly scheduled trips to the English ports of Dover and Folkestone are made several times daily.

The hinterland of Calais is a highly productive agricultural region. The industrial suburb of St.-Pierre lies to the south of the city. The manufacture of textiles is the most important of Calais' industries. Fine lace and embroidery are the city's specialties. Fishing vessels and equipment are also manufactured here, and a sizable trawler fleet operates out of the port. Calais' fine beaches make it a popular bathing resort.

An ancient city belonging to the Count of Boulogne, Calais was conquered by the English in 1347. After 1450, it was the last remaining possession of the English in France. They were finally expelled in 1558 by the Duke de Guise. The British used Calais as a naval base during World War I. In that war, the city was severely damaged. In World War II, Calais was overrun by the swift German advance in the spring of 1940 and was not recaptured until Sept. 30, 1944. Heavily bombed, the old city was almost entirely razed by the end of the war. It has since been completely rebuilt. The new city was skillfully planned to combine compatible architectural styles. The austere newness of its buildings is offset by their planted balconies, dormered roofs, porticoes, arcades, and varied shapes and colors.

Though most of Calais' historic monuments have been destroyed, some places of interest remain, notably the city museum, which has a fine collection of laces and a few good Flemish tapestries; the Hôtel de Ville, built in Renaissance style in 1922; and Rodin's *Bourgeois de Calais* monument. Population: (1962) 70,127.

HOMER PRICE, *Hunter College, New York*

CALAIS, kal'is, is an industrial city in eastern Maine, in Washington county. It is situated on the St. Croix River, opposite St. Stephen, New Brunswick, Canada, with which it is connected by a bridge. Calais' industries use resources of the surrounding region to produce millwork, woodenware, and processed foods, especially blueberries. Shirts are manufactured.

The site of the city was settled in 1779. It was incorporated as a town and named for the French city of Calais in 1809. It was incorporated as a city in 1850. Government is by council and manager. Population: 4,044.

CALAMATTA, kä-lä-mät'tä, **Luigi** (1801–1869), Italian engraver. He was born in Civitavecchia, on July 12, 1801. He was educated in Rome, then went to Paris, where he studied under Jean Auguste Ingres. In 1837, Calamatta became professor at the École des Beaux-Arts in Brussels; he also founded a school for engravers in Brussels. In his later years Calamatta was professor of drawing at the Academy of Milan. Among his noteworthy engravings are the head of Napoleon from the death mask and portraits of Ingres, Niccolò Paganini, François Guizot, and George Sand. He died in Milan on March 8, 1869.

CALAMIAN ISLANDS, kä-lä-myän', a Philippine island group 677 square miles (1,753 sq km) in total area, including the main islands of Busuanga, Culion, and Coron and 100 islets. The group lies 200 miles (320 km) southwest of Manila between Mindoro and Palawan, in Palawan province. The islanders practice subsistence farming (rice and coconuts) and fishing.

Although the largest settlement in the Calamians is Coron (1962 population, 11,354) on Busuanga, the place of principal interest is the Culion Leper Colony, founded in 1906. The colony's inhabitants, who usually number between 3,000 and 5,500, are self-governing; here, in 1908, woman suffrage was first practiced in Asia. Population: (1960) 21,975.

CALAMIS, kal'ə-mis, Greek sculptor of the 5th century B.C. He lived in Athens and was a contemporary of Phidias. He worked in marble, ivory, bronze, and gold. Pliny said that Calamis' horses were unsurpassable. Among his most celebrated works were a statue in metal of Apollo Alexicacos, in Athens, in 429 B.C. (erroneously supposed to be the Apollo Belvedere); a colossal statue of Apollo in bronze, more than 40 feet (12 meters) high, which was taken to Rome by Lucullus; and a Jupiter Ammon consecrated by Pindar at Thebes.

CALAMITE, kal'ə-mīt, is the common name for a group of extinct woody trees, typified by the genus *Calamites* of the subphylum Sphenopsida (the horsetails). Calamites came into existence in the late Devonian period, about 360 million years ago, and became extinct at the end of the Permian, about 225 million years ago. These plants, which grew to an estimated 90 feet (27 meters) high, had erect, jointed stems with hollow centers crossed by a partition (nodal diaphragm) at each joint, or node. Whorls of upright branches, originating at the nodes, bore whorls of generally very narrow leaves. Spore-bearing cones were produced at the ends of the branches.

THEODORE DELEVORYAS, *Yale University*

Calamity Jane

CULVER PICTURES

CALAMITY JANE, kə-lam′ə-tē jān (1852?–1903), American frontier adventuress. Her real name was Martha Jane Burke (née Cannary). She was born in Princeton, Mo., on May 1, ?1852, the eldest of six children. In 1865 the family moved by wagon to Montana, where Jane's mother died the next year. After the death of her father in 1867, she roamed about the West, frequenting bars and dance halls. Of medium height, with rawboned features, she dressed like a man, in buckskin suits and wide-brimmed hats and could drink and swear with the roughest frontiersmen.

Jane was in Wyoming in the early 1870's. In May 1875, in man's attire, she attached herself to the Newton-Jenney geological expedition, which left Fort Laramie for the Black Hills, escorted by 400 soldiers. Soon afterward she became a camp follower of the Black Hills force led by Gen. George Crook, but an officer discovered that she was a woman and drove her out.

In Deadwood, S. Dak., in 1876, during the gold-mining boom, Jane knew James B. (Wild Bill) Hickok in the few months that he was there. No evidence has been found, however, to support legends that they were sweethearts or that they married. Hickok, already married, was writing endearing letters to his wife in Ohio.

How Calamity Jane received her nickname is uncertain. One explanation is that it stemmed from her hard-luck experiences. Another claims it resulted from her willingness to help victims of disaster. In Deadwood's smallpox epidemic in 1878, Jane stayed in a crude log cabin pesthouse to care for the patients.

After the Deadwood mining boom subsided, Jane resumed her wandering about the West. In El Paso, Texas, she met a cab driver, Clinton Burke, to whom she was married on Sept. 25, 1891. He soon left her, however. In her last years she drifted from place to place, peddling a small leaflet, full of errors, about her life that she had written or dictated. She died in Terry, S. Dak., on Aug. 1, 1903, and was buried in Mount Moriah Cemetery in Deadwood.

WAYNE GARD, *Author of "Rawhide Texas"*

Further Reading: Aikman, Duncan, *Calamity Jane and the Lady Wildcats* (New York 1927); Horan, James D., *Desperate Women* (New York 1952); Jennewein, J. Leonard, *Calamity Jane of the Western Trails*, a pamphlet (Huron, S. Dak., 1953).

CALAMY, kal′ə-mē, **Edmund** (1600–1666), English Presbyterian clergyman. He was born in London and educated at Cambridge, and obtained a curacy in London in 1639. During that year the controversy between High Churchmen and Presbyterians over the office of bishop and its place in the church became acute. In reply to writings that upheld political rights for bishops, Calamy and several others produced in 1641 *An Answer to a Booke entituled An Humble Remonstrance . . . written by Smectymnuus* (a pseudonym for the group). This work became known as *Smectymnuus*.

Calamy disapproved of the execution of Charles I and did not support Cromwell and the Protectorate. In these matters he was not unlike many other English Presbyterian clergy. He took part in the Savoy Conference of 1661, called by Charles II to enable Puritans and High Churchmen to settle their differences. Nevertheless, he was ejected from his parish under the Act of Uniformity (1662). In 1663 he became the first Nonconformist to be imprisoned for disobeying the act, but he was released after a brief confinement. He died in London on Oct. 29, 1666.

CALAS, kȧ-läs′, **Jean** (1698–1762), French Protestant merchant from Toulouse, who became a judicial martyr. He was born in Lacabarède, near Castres, on March 19, 1698. On Oct. 13, 1761, his eldest son, Marc Antoine, was found hanged in his father's warehouse, and Calas was accused of murder. The prosecutor charged that Jean Calas, along with his wife, his son Pierre, a servant, and a visitor, had killed Marc Antoine out of hatred for the Roman Catholic religion, to which, it was alleged, the eldest son had been secretly converted. The *parlement* (sovereign court) of Toulouse found Calas guilty and sentenced him to be tortured, broken on the wheel, and burned. The sentence was executed on March 9, 1762. His son Pierre was exiled and the three other defendants released.

To Voltaire and his like-minded contemporaries, no hypothesis was more absurd than the supposition that M. and Mme. Calas, Pierre, a Catholic servant long attached to the Calas children, and a friend who had arrived on that very day had all dined calmly with the deceased and subsequently murdered him in cold blood. They led an extraordinarily energetic press campaign to reverse the Calas decision. The movement was successful: after reviewing the entire case, 50 judges reversed the decision on March 9, 1765, rehabilitating Calas' memory. The King sought to recompense the family for losses incurred through the injustice done them.

Voltaire's press campaign, which transformed the affair into a *cause célèbre*, drew a picture of a grossly unfair trial conducted by a *parlement* of religious bigots. Yet the fact remains that relations between Calas and his son were so bad that one can argue that Calas strangled his dissolute son in a fit of anger with as much reason as the defense argued for Marc's suicide. But the *parlement* never considered a nonreligious motive, and in this regard Voltaire's indictment of the tribunal was correct. The Calas case was a powerful stimulus for the reform of French criminal law that was achieved in 1788.

LIONEL ROTHKRUG, *University of Michigan*

Further Reading: Bien, David D., *The Calas Affair* (Princeton 1960).

CALAVERITE, kal-ə-vâr′īt, is a gold-tellurium mineral and an ore of gold. Silver usually replaces the gold to a small extent; if the silver content exceeds 13.4%, the mineral is known as *sylvanite.* Calaverite is named for Calaveras County, Calif., where the mineral was first discovered.

Calaverite occurs in massive form as opaque, very brittle crystals that are pale brass-yellow to silver-white and have a metallic luster. Although calaverite is a rare mineral, important deposits also occur at Cripple Creek, Colo., and at Kalgoorlie, West Australia.

Composition, $AuTe_2$ (Au 44.03%, Te 55.97%); hardness, 2.5; specific gravity, 9.3; crystal system, monoclinic.

CALCAR, käl′kär, **Jan Stevenszoon van** (1499?–?1550), Dutch painter. He was born in Calcar, in the duchy of Cleves, and studied in Venice in 1536–1537 under Titian. Calcar imitated Titian's style so well that their pictures cannot always be distinguished. Later he imitated Raphael with equal success. Rubens so admired Calcar's small *Nativity* that he carried it with him on his travels.

Calcar did mostly portraits. Examples are in museums in London, Berlin, and Florence. He drew almost all the portraits in Giorgio Vasari's *Lives* and some of the figures for Vesalius' anatomical work, *De humani corporis fabrica* (1543).

Calcar died in Naples, Italy, about 1550. The painter's name is also sometimes spelled *Kalkar* or *Kalcker*.

CALCEOLARIA, kal-sē-ə-lâr′ē-ə, a large genus of plants and shrubs several of which are cultivated for their showy flowers. In each flower, the corolla is divided into a large pouchlike lower lip and a similar but smaller upper lip. Because the flowers resemble tiny slippers, the plants are also known as *slipperworts*.

Calceolarias belong to the figwort family (Scrophulariaceae) and are chiefly native to South America. They generally range between 1 and 2 feet (30–60 cm) in height, and their leaves, which are usually hairy, are sometimes composed of several leaflets. Some shrubby forms have solid white or yellow flowers, while many herbaceous forms have been hybridized to produce exotic spots in varying shades of yellow and red on the lower lip.

FRANCES SHERBURNE
Massachusetts Audubon Society

Calceolaria

R. A. SCHLEGEL

CALCHAS, kal′kəs, in Greek legend, was venerated as the wisest of the Greek soothsayers. His predictions and advice were instrumental to the success of the Greeks in the Trojan War. He predicted that the Greeks would never capture Troy without the aid of Achilles and that the siege of Troy would last ten years.

Calchas foretold that the Greek fleet, delayed at Aulis by contrary winds, would not be able to set sail unless Agamemnon agreed to sacrifice his daughter Iphigenia. Agamemnon agreed, but the girl was spared by the goddess Artemis (Roman, Diana).

When Agamemnon refused to return the Trojan captive girl Chryseis to her father, the god Apollo inflicted a pestilence on the Greeks. Acting on Calchas' advice, Agamemnon gave up the girl, and the pestilence was withdrawn.

Calchas is said to have died of sorrow, having been bested by a rival soothsayer, Mopus, who guessed the exact number of figs on a branch.

CALCIFEROL is a form of vitamin D known as D_2. See VITAMINS—*Fat-Soluble Vitamins* (Vitamin D).

CALCIFICATION, kal-sə-fə-kā-shən, is the process by which calcium salts, especially calcium carbonate and calcium phosphate, are deposited in body tissues. Calcification occurs normally in the formation of bone. It may also occur in weakened, degenerated, or diseased tissues. In older people, calcium may be deposited in the walls of arteries. It may also be deposited in chronically irritated or infected tendons or bursas. Occasionally, when large amounts of calcium are excreted through the kidneys, calcification may occur in the kidney tissue (nephrocalcinosis) or in the tubes leading out from the kidneys, forming kidney stones.

Sometimes, calcification occurs simultaneously in many tissues throughout the body. This may be a result of diseases affecting calcium and phosphorus metabolism or from taking excessive amounts of vitamin D, which facilitates the absorption of calcium from the intestinal tract.

LOUIS J. VORHAUS, M. D.
Cornell University Medical College

CALCIMINE. See WHITEWASH.

CALCINATION, kal-si-nā′shən, is the process of heating a material below its melting point to drive off moisture and other volatile materials, such as carbon dioxide. It is often the first step in the beneficiation of ores after grinding. In a broader sense the term includes the roasting of metallic ores to remove sulfur prior to smelting. Ores are roasted by heating them in the presence of air at high temperatures but below the melting point.

In the manufacture of plaster, pure gypsum is calcined to drive off most of the water of combination, which results in the formation of plaster of paris. Cement and hard wall plasters are made in the same way, using impure gypsum. Portland cement is made by calcining mixtures of limestone with shale or cement. In the burning of limestone the water in the stone evaporates, and the carbon dioxide is given off as a gas, leaving the oxides of calcium and magnesium. Cements are calcined in large kilns, usually of the rotary type.

ALVIN S. COHAN
Scientific Design Company, Inc.

CALCITE, kal′sīt, or hexagonal calcium carbonate, is one of the commonest minerals. It is the principal constituent of limestone. The mineral is found in well-defined crystals and crystalline crusts and masses, in stalactites, in aggregates of small spherical particles, and in granular and sometimes fibrous or tabular masses. In the number of its crystal forms and the variety of their combinations, calcite is unsurpassed among minerals. It is usually colorless, white, or amber, but may be any color. Pure crystals have the composition calcium oxide 56% and carbon dioxide 44%, but in impure crystals some of the calcium may be replaced by small amounts of iron, magnesium, and manganese.

Calcite is formed in nature as a vein mineral, often in association with lead, zinc, silver, and other ores. It is also formed as spring-deposited travertine or as the more porous calcareous tufa, as cave deposits (stalactites and stalagmites), as limestones (sedimentary rocks of marine or fresh-water origin), and as the principal constituent of marbles (metamorphic rocks formed from sedimentary limestones by heat and pressure).

Calcite has many varied and important uses. *Iceland spar* is a form of calcite sufficiently transparent and flawless to be used in the manufacture of optical instruments. *Cement limestones* are certain impure limestones used in the making of portland cement; the ideal sources are those that yield natural "cement rock" containing approximately 70 to 80% calcium carbonate and 20 to 30% clayey matter. *Lime rock* is the term used for limestones that are roasted to produce quicklime (CaO). *Chalk* is a white earthy limestone, a chemical precipitate of calcium carbonate and the shells of minute organisms such as foraminifera. It is used in making cements, powders, and crayons. *Marl,* a soft pure limestone deposited in lakes by streams or springs, is used for making portland cement and as fertilizer. *Lithographic limestone* is an unusually fine-grained limestone used for fine engraving.

An important application of limestone is as a flux in metallurgical furnaces, particularly iron furnaces, where it helps to form a slag that collects and retains impurities separated from the metal. Agricultural liming materials include ground limestone, lime, marl, and oyster shell. The chief purposes of agricultural lime are to correct soil acidity, to granulate heavy soil, and to provide plant food. An important use of limestone and marble is as both an exterior and an interior building stone.

Composition, $CaCO_3$; hardness, 3; specific gravity, 2.72; crystal system, hexagonal.

GEORGE SWITZER
Smithsonian Institution

CALCITE GROUP, kal′sīt, an important group of metal carbonate minerals. The group is characterized by its crystals, which are classified in the rhombohedral division of crystal systems. Layers of carbonate ions and metal ions alternate within the crystals.

The calcite group includes the carbonates of calcium (calcite), calcium and magnesium (dolomite), magnesium (magnesite), manganese (rhodochrosite), and zinc (smithsonite). Pure carbonates are uncommon, however, and there are many intermediate minerals, some of which have been given names of their own. See also separate articles on the minerals cited.

CALCIUM, kal′sē-əm, symbol Ca, is a chemical element belonging to the alkaline earth family of metals. Its name was derived from the Latin word *calx,* meaning lime, which was the name by which the oxide of the element was known to the early Romans. Although calx was known and used in ancient times, it was not until 1808 that Sir Humphry Davy isolated elementary calcium as a product of the electrolytic decomposition of calcium hydroxide.

Properties. Calcium is a white, silvery metal that tarnishes readily in air to form a gray or slightly yellow surface. Its melting point is 845° C (1550° F), and its boiling point is 1420° C (2590° F). It has a specific gravity of 1.55 at 20° C (68° F), and its is a good conductor of electricity. Although brittle, it is a soft metal; its hardness is intermediate between sodium and aluminum. It is ductile and malleable to some extent. Its tensile strength is 6900 pounds per square inch (438 kg per sq cm).

Calcium is characterized analytically by the insolubility of its carbonate, phosphate, and oxalate salts, and by the brick red color imparted to a flame when volatile salts of the metal are heated. Most of the compounds of calcium are ionic.

Calcium is located in column IIA of the periodic table along with the other alkaline earth metals—beryllium, magnesium, strontium, barium, and radium. Calcium has an oxidation number of +2. Its atomic number is 20 and its atomic weight is 40.08. There are six stable naturally occurring isotopes of the element: ^{40}Ca, ^{42}Ca, ^{43}Ca, ^{44}Ca, ^{46}Ca, and ^{48}Ca. The most abundant isotope is ^{40}Ca, which comprises about 97% of the calcium found in nature. There are several synthetically produced radioactive isotopes. One of these, ^{45}Ca, is used in research for studying the uptake and deposition of calcium in bone, water purification processes, detergent action, and surface wetting phenomena.

Occurrence. Calcium is the fifth most abundant element in the earth's crust; about 3.63% of the earth's igneous rocks consist of the element. Because of its high chemical reactivity, calcium is not found in a free, uncombined state in nature. Most of the earth's calcium is found in the form of limestone, marble, and calcite, $CaCO_3$; dolomite, $MgCO_3 \cdot CaCO_3$; fluorspar, CaF_2; silicates such as asbestos, $CaMg_3(SiO_3)_4$; rock phosphate, $Ca_3(PO_4)_2$; gypsum, $CaSO_4 \cdot 2H_2O$; and as dissolved salts in seawater and in deposits formed by the evaporation of seawater. The element is also found in various animal structures; it is found in bones in the form of calcium phosphate and in the shells of crustaceans as calcium carbonate.

Production. Production of calcium in the United States began in 1939 after the outbreak of World War II halted imports of the metal from France and Germany. Two major processes are used in the manufacture of the metal. The first is based on the electrolysis of either fused calcium chloride or calcium fluoride. The chloride or fluoride is melted in an electrically heated graphite container; the graphite serves as the anode, or positive electrode. A water-cooled iron bar dipping just below the surface of the melt serves as the cathode, or negative electrode. During electrolysis, calcium is deposited on the iron cathode, resulting in the formation of a stick of metal known as a *carrot.* The deposited calcium thus serves as the cathode during electrolysis. The carrots are remelted in an inert atmosphere of argon or are vacuum-distilled to purify the product.

When calcium is to be produced in large quantities, graphite anodes are suspended in a melt of fused calcium chloride. The metallic calcium is deposited either on the top of an iron cathode, which is continuously raised as electrolysis proceeds, or it is liberated on an iron cathode in the bottom of the cell. Globules of the molten calcium rise from the cathode and are solidified and collected on a block of calcium which is slowly raised out of the bath.

The second process for the manufacture of calcium involves the aluminothermic reduction of calcium oxide, CaO. The oxide, which is obtained from a high-grade limestone, is reduced by treatment with metallic aluminum at a high temperature and a low pressure. The product is then purified by vacuum distillation.

Industrial Uses. Calcium is very useful for the removal of undesirable substances in metallurgical and chemical procedures because it reacts so readily with other elements. Thus it is used to remove bismuth during the purification of lead; it is also used in the removal of carbon, sulfur, and gaseous impurities in the manufacture of steel and other alloys.

Calcium is used as an alloying agent for many metals. Calcium-silicon alloys control the grain size of crystals and inhibit carbide formation in steels. In aluminum alloys, calcium improves the mechanical and electrical properties of the metals. Calcium-lithium alloys are used as deoxidizers for steel, copper, and nickel and their alloys. Calcium-germanium alloys are used as rectifier materials, and an alloy of 98% lead and 2% calcium known as Frary metal is used to prepare bearing metals.

Because calcium metal loses electrons so easily, it is an excellent reducing agent. Although it is more expensive than metallic sodium for this purpose, it is used extensively in the production of some of the less common metals such as zirconium, hafnium, vanadium, tungsten, chromium, thorium, uranium, yttrium, scandium, and cesium, as well as the rare earths. The production of these metals is achieved by the reduction of their oxides or fluorides.

Because of its marked tendency to react with water, calcium is also used to dry organic solvents such as alcohol. Its use in deep-sea sounding devices depends on its reaction with water to liberate hydrogen gas. Calcium metal can be used to purify argon and other rare gases.

Physiological Importance. Calcium plays an important role in the physiological chemistry of living organisms. About 99% of the calcium content of the human body is found in the bones and teeth. However, it is also present in body fluids.

The presence of calcium is essential for the clotting of blood, and calcium is very important in the control of muscle and nerve cell responses because of its influence on the permeability of cell membranes. Calcium is also found in some enzyme systems.

Calcium Compounds. The compounds of calcium are more important than those of other members of the alkaline earth family. The most significant calcium compounds are limestone, lime, gypsum, fluorspar, calcium carbide, calcium chloride, calcium phosphate, and calcium sulfate. Each is discussed in detail in separate articles. *Limestone,* or *calcium carbonate,* is the most abundant naturally occurring compound of calcium. *Lime,* or *calcium oxide* (also called *quicklime*), produced by the thermal decomposition of limestone, is the usual starting material in the manufacture of other calcium compounds. Lime is produced in large, chimneylike furnaces, called kilns. If lime is overheated during production, "dead burned" lime, a relatively inert product, results. Although pure lime is white, commercial lime is slightly brown or yellow because of iron impurities. Pure lime, which has a melting point of 2850° C (5160° F), emits an intense light called "limelight" when heated to a high temperature. When lime is reacted with water, the result is a product called "slaked" lime, which is important in the production of cement.

Because of its vigorous reaction with water, lime is used as a drying agent. When mixed with solid sodium hydroxide, the resulting soda-lime is used to dry gases and to remove carbon dioxide from gases. Lime is also used as a flux in the smelting of metal ores, in the manufacture of glass, and in polishing powder (Vienna lime).

Other calcium compounds of commercial importance include *calcium acetate,* which is used in the manufacture of acetone and acetic acid, in textile dyeing and printing, and in baked goods as an antimold agent. *Calcium bromide* is used in photography, as a dehydrating agent, and as a preservative for food and wood. *Calcium cyanamide* is used in fertilizer, as a weed killer, and in the hardening of iron and steel, while *calcium cyanide* is used as a pesticide for ants, mice, and moles and for fumigating grain and seeds. *Calcium cyclamate* is used as an artificial sweetener in some soft drinks and in low calorie and diabetic diets. *Calcium hypochlorite* is used to kill algae, fungi, and bacteria and as a deodorant and disinfectant. *Calcium tungstate* is used in luminous paints and fluorescent lamps, and synthetic crystals of this compound are used in scintillation counters and as starting materials for lasers and masers.

HERBERT LIEBESKIND
The Cooper Union, New York

CALCIUM CARBIDE, kal'sē-əm kär'bīd, CaC_2, is a chemical compound manufactured by heating lime with coke in an electric furnace at about 2000° C (3630° F). The main use of calcium carbide is in the manufacture of acetylene, which is used extensively in the synthesis of organic compounds, resins, and plastics and in oxyacetylene torches. Calcium carbide is also used in the synthesis of calcium cyanamide and lampblack and as a reducing agent in the preparation of metallic copper.

Properties. At room temperature, pure calcium carbide is a colorless, transparent, tetragonal crystalline solid. However, commercial-grade calcium carbide is a gray-black, lumpy, porous solid containing many impurities. The specific gravity of calcium carbide is 2.22, and its melting point is about 2300° C (4170° F).

The carbon in calcium carbide exists in its most highly ionized form—that is, as C_2^{-2} ions. Carbide ions combine with hydrogen ions to form acetylene, C_2H_2; therefore, calcium carbide rapidly decomposes in water to form acetylene gas and a lime precipitate:

$$CaC_2 + H_2O \rightarrow C_2H_2 + CaO.$$

HERBERT LIEBESKIND
The Cooper Union, New York

CALCIUM CARBONATE, kal'sē-əm kär'bə-nāt, $CaCO_3$, is the most abundant of all calcium compounds. It may occur either as a white powder or as colorless crystals. The crystals occur in two forms—in calcite they are hexagonal, and in aragonite they are rhombic.

The most familiar form of calcium carbonate is limestone, which is found in stratified rock layers in all parts of the world. Other forms of calcium carbonate are chalk, marl (which is a mixture of calcium carbonate and sand), Iceland spar (which is almost pure calcite), marble, pearls, and coral (which is composed of shells of invertebrate marine animals).

Properties. Calcium carbonate is odorless and tasteless. It decomposes at 825° C (1515° F). Although only slightly soluble in water, it dissolves readily in water containing dissolved carbon dioxide, to form calcium bicarbonate:

$$CaCO_3 + H_2O + CO_2 \rightleftarrows Ca(HCO_3)_2.$$

When water evaporates from a solution of calcium bicarbonate and the dissolved carbon dioxide escapes into the atmosphere, the reaction is reversed, and calcium carbonate is deposited.

Uses. Calcium carbonate is used to build macadam roads and concrete structures, to manufacture polishes, pigments, and putty, and to make dental powders and pastes. It is the source of lime, which is used in metallurgical fluxes, water purification, sugar refining, glass and cement manufacture, the pulp and paper industry, and the manufacture of many chemicals.

HERBERT LIEBESKIND, *The Cooper Union*

CALCIUM CHLORIDE, kal'sē-əm klôr'īd, $CaCl_2$, is a salt formed as a by-product of many chemical reactions. However, between 50 and 60% of the calcium chloride produced commercially comes from natural brines.

Properties. At room temperature, calcium chloride is a white solid that occurs in the form of crystals, lumps, or flakes. It is most commonly found as the anhydrous salt ($CaCl_2$), as the dihydrate ($CaCl_2 \cdot 2H_2O$), and as the hexahydrate ($CaCl_2 \cdot 6H_2O$). The anhydrous salt can be prepared by heating the hexahydrate to remove water molecules from the crystals. These salts are all hygroscopic (they absorb moisture from the atmosphere) and deliquescent (they absorb enough water from the atmosphere to dissolve completely). When the anhydrous crystals dissolve in water, a great amount of heat is liberated.

Uses. Because of their strong tendency to absorb water vapor, the calcium chloride salts are used as desiccants to dry and dehydrate organic liquids and to dry gases. During the drying operations, the anhydrous salt is converted by steps to the dihydrate, the hexahydrate, and if enough water vapor is available, to a liquid solution. The salts are also used to reduce the quantity of dust on highways.

Calcium chloride is used to prevent too rapid drying of setting concrete, and it is used in the manufacture of cement. It is also used to preserve wood and stone, in the fireproofing of fabrics, and as a coagulant in the manufacture of rubber. A 29.8% solution of anhydrous calcium chloride in ice lowers the freezing point of water to −55° C (−67° F); therefore, calcium chloride-water mixtures are used as brines in cold storage and refrigeration plants and to control snow and ice on streets.

HEBERT LIEBESKIND, *The Cooper Union*

CALCIUM HYDROXIDE. See LIME.

CALCIUM OXIDE. See LIME.

CALCIUM PHOSPHATE, kal'sē-əm fos'fāt, is a common mineral salt. It is the principal mineral constituent of bones and teeth and accounts for about 60% of the average human skeleton. It also occurs as the very insoluble mineral phosphorite, $Ca_3(PO_4)_2$, which is found in phosphate rock.

Calcium phosphate is derived from orthophosphoric acid, H_3PO_4. Because there are three replaceable hydrogen atoms in the acid, there are three different calcium salts that can be formed from the acid. These are tricalcium phosphate (tertiary calcium phosphate), $Ca_3(PO_4)_2$; dicalcium phosphate (secondary calcium phosphate), $CaHPO_4 \cdot 2H_2O$; and monocalcium phosphate (primary calcium phosphate), $Ca(H_2PO_4)_2 \cdot H_2O$.

Commercially, the most important of the calcium phosphates is primary calcium phosphate, which is commonly known as *superphosphate*. Superphosphate is used as a fertilizer ingredient to replenish soils deficient in phosphorus and calcium. It is manufactured by mixing finely ground insoluble phosphate rock with sulfuric acid. This results in the formation of a mixture of superphosphate and gypsum, $CaSO_4 \cdot 2H_2O$. Since gypsum does not affect the fertilizer capacity of the superphosphate, the mixture is sold as "superphosphate of lime." If the sulfuric acid is replaced by phosphoric acid, the product is not diluted by gypsum, and its phosphate content is doubled or nearly tripled; this product is known as *double* or *triple superphosphate*. Primary calcium phosphate is also used as a leavening agent in baking powders, as a stabilizer for plastics, and in the manufacture of glass.

Dicalcium phosphate is used in animal feed, in dentifrices, in glass, and as a stabilizer for plastics. Tricalcium phosphate is used in ceramics, polishing powders, dentifrices, and rubber, as a mordant in dyeing, and as a stabilizer for plastics.

HERBERT LIEBESKIND
The Cooper Union, New York

CALCIUM SULFATE, kal'sē-əm sul'fāt, is a chemical compound that may occur in an anhydrous form, $CaSO_4$, known as anhydrite, or in a hydrated form, $CaSO_4 \cdot 2H_2O$, commonly known as gypsum. Anhydrous calcium sulfate is white and odorless and is found either as a powder or in crystalline form. It is very slightly soluble in water, and its melting point is 1450° C (2640° F). Gypsum is found in large deposits in New York, Ohio, Iowa, Michigan, Texas, and Nevada.

Naturally occurring gypsum is used in the manufacture of Portland cement, in fertilizers, paints, pharmaceuticals, insecticides, and in the treatment of soil and water. Pure dehydrated calcium sulfate is used in polishing powders, in production of paper, in dyeing and printing of textiles, and as a drier for industrial compounds. See also GYPSUM.

When calcium sulfate is partially dehydrated by heating to about 125° C (255° F), it forms $2CaSO_4 \cdot H_2O$, which is known as plaster of paris. This compound hardens with the addition of water, and it is used for surgical casts, for models, molds, and statues, and to cover interior walls of buildings. See also PLASTER OF PARIS.

HERBERT LIEBESKIND
The Cooper Union, New York

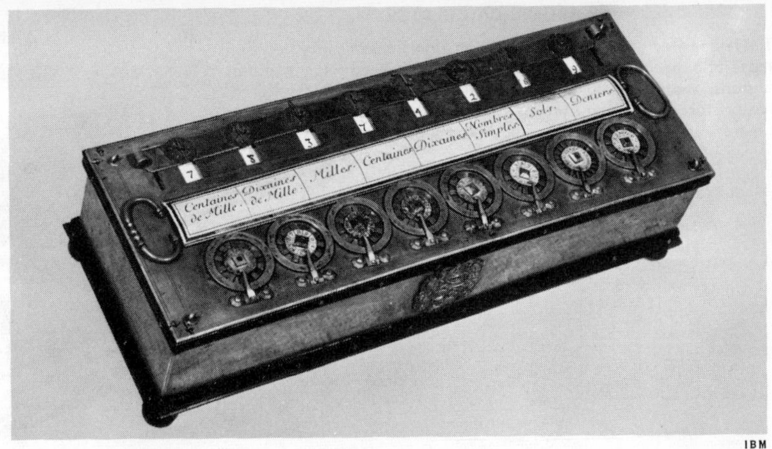

IBM

THE CALCULATING MACHINE invented in 1642 by Blaise Pascal could add and subtract. Each of the eight rotatable wheels has the numbers 0 to 9 on its circumference. The wheels show values from hundreds of thousands (far left) to units (third from right), plus two decimal places at far right.

CALCULATING MACHINE, kal'kyə-lāt-ing mə-shēn', a mechanical, electromechanical, or electronic device that performs arithmetic operations. The simplest kind of calculating machine is an adding machine, which mainly performs addition and subtraction operations. Machines that can automatically repeat addition and subtraction operations in such a way as to multiply and divide are called calculators. Adding machines and calculators are classed as digital devices because the numerical quantities in the machine are represented by a sequence of digits.

The first mechanical calculating aid, the abacus, has been used since ancient times (see ABACUS). The first true mechanical calculator, however, was an adding machine designed by Blaise Pascal in 1642. This machine, which had a series of wheels with the numbers 0 to 9 engraved on their circumferences, could perform addition with carry. In 1671, Gottfried Leibniz designed a calculating machine that could add and multiply, with multiplication being performed by repeated addition. This machine finally was built in 1694. In England in 1822, Charles Babbage built a small six-decimal-place adding machine. Eleven years later he conceived a mechanical device that was designed to perform addition, subtraction, multiplication, and division, but this machine was never completed. The first practical adding machine for business use was designed by the American William S. Burroughs, who received a patent for it in 1894.

MECHANICAL CALCULATING MACHINES

The basic part of a mechanical calculating machine is a *register,* consisting of a set of wheels, each of which has ten positions around its circumference, corresponding to the digits 0 to 9. A number can be represented by positioning each wheel to correspond to the digits in the written decimal representation of the number. The register can be made into a *counter* by providing a *carry* from one wheel to the next. For example, when one wheel changes from the 9 to the 0 position, a partially toothed gear on the wheel causes the wheel for the next higher decimal place to turn to its next digital position, say, from 0 to 1. All mechanical calculators must contain at least one counter that gives the result of the computation; this register is called an *accumulator*.

If the operation of addition is performed by moving the wheels simultaneously by amounts corresponding to the digits in the addend, the accumulator is said to have an *addition feed*. There are an enormous number of types of addition-feed mechanisms, using various combinations of racks, pinions, gears, and stops. A characteristic of these mechanical devices is that a complete arithmetic operation requires a cycle of actions in which each action initiates the next action.

Under certain circumstances, a simple addition feed will lose the carry, but several ways for getting around this difficulty have been devised. In very inexpensive machines, the machine operator enters the digits of the addend one at a time, so that no carry is lost. This method has the disadvantage that it is not possible for the machine operator to check his entry as a complete number, and so it is usually preferable to enter the complete addend on a separate mechanism and then feed it into the accumulator in one operation (addition feed).

One solution of the carry problem for an addition feed was given by Leibniz, who invented a method for storing the carry during the addition feed and then successively adding the carries in a *carry wave*. A variation of this procedure, developed by Babbage, is used to shorten the time required for the carry wave, especially when electric impulses are used to produce the carries.

Another method for producing a carry is to use two input shafts and one output shaft connected so that the amount of rotation of the output shaft is the sum of the rotations of the two input shafts. With this arrangement, the addition feed and the carry are performed simultaneously because the output shaft's feed to a wheel is the sum of the two input shaft motions representing the addition feed and the carry.

Full-Keyboard Adding Machine. The simplest mechanical adding machine with addition feed has an accumulator register, a full keyboard for entering the addend, and an addition-feed and carry mechanism that is activated by a lever on the side of the machine. The full keyboard is a rectangular array of keys, sometimes with 10 rows and 10 columns of keys (100 keys). The 10 keys in each column have the numerals 0 to 9 printed on them. Each column represents a decimal place, so there are 10 keys for each decimal place. Addition is performed by entering the addend at the keyboard and moving the lever in one direction. Subtraction is performed by moving the lever in the reverse direction to reverse the effect of the addition-feed and carry mechanism. The result of the computation is displayed in the accumulator register dials as a sequence of digits.

The addition feed and accumulator mechanism also can be associated with a set of type wheels to obtain an adding machine that provides

ELECTRONIC CALCULATOR

The Friden electronic calculator performs functions midway between those of a mechanical desk calculator and an electronic computer. It adds, subtracts, multiplies, and divides, and it also automatically stores intermediate answers for further calculation. The answers are displayed on a cathode ray tube above the keyboard.

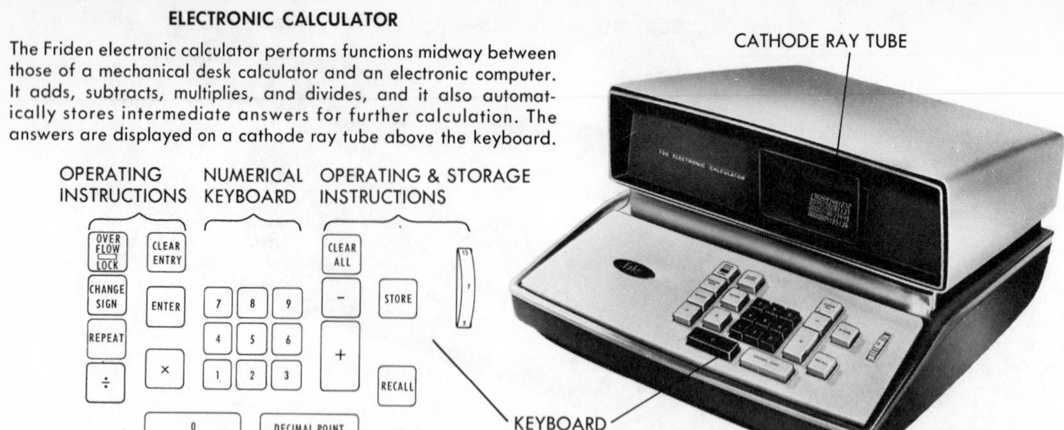

FRIDEN, INC.

figures printed on a paper tape. Such a machine prints the various addends in a sum together with the total itself. Adding machines of this type have a special key that causes subtotals to be printed out at intervals, before the final total is printed. They also contain a mechanism that resets the accumulator register to zero after the final total is printed.

Most full-keyboard printing machines and full-keyboard nonprinting machines are now electrically operated instead of manually (lever) operated. The operator presses a key for the arithmetic operation to be performed, and thereby activates a motor for a cycle corresponding to a complete computational operation.

Ten-Key Adding Machine. In a full-keyboard machine, the use of 10 keys for each decimal place usually makes it necessary for the operator to look at the machine when entering quantities, and thus he must glance from the figure data sheet to the keyboard and back repeatedly. However, it is desirable for an experienced operator to use a touch system similar to touch typing to obtain rapid machine operation. One way of overcoming this difficulty with full-keyboard machines is to use specially shaped 0 and 5 keys. A more fundamental solution to the problem is to have just 10 keys on the keyboard, permitting a touch system for one hand.

In a 10-key machine, the addend normally is entered digit by digit from right to left, with additional zeros entered if necessary to position the number relative to the decimal point. As each digit is entered, it is stored in an addition-feed mechanism, which shifts to receive successive digits. The entered addend is displayed in register dials for visual checking before it is fed to the accumulator. In case of an error, the addition-feed mechanism can be cleared without affecting the previously obtained total. Ten-key machines normally are equipped with printing mechanisms that print the addends, subtotals, and totals. Ten-key and full-keyboard adding machines that print are used in stores and for small-scale accounting activities.

Printing Calculator. Ten-key and full-keyboard adding machines that print can be modified to provide multiplication. For this purpose, the addition-feed mechanism is designed to retain the multiplicand, which is fed into the accumulator once for each unit in the first digit of the multiplier. The addition feed is then shifted one decimal place in preparation for multiplication by the next digit of the multiplier.

In a 10-key machine, the shifting required for multiplication and that required for addition are compatible and are easily realized in one mechanism. Division is accomplished by subtracting and shifting in the reverse direction from that for multiplication. Some of the less sophisticated machines print out each addend in the repeated addition procedure that corresponds to multiplication. In early versions of these machines, the repeated additions were obtained by holding down the add key until the correct multiplier digit was registered on a counter.

Mechanical Rotary Calculator. The mechanical rotary calculator, which is used for general computational operations often required in scientific and engineering work, normally does not have any printed output. The keyboard has a rectangular array of digit keys. There are also operation keys marked to indicate the operations of addition, subtraction, multiplication, and division. In computation, the various operands are entered into the machine, the appropriate operation key is pressed, and the answer automatically appears in accumulator register dials mounted on a carriage similar to a typewriter carriage. Shifting the carriage and the accumulator and counter registers on it moves the registers to the proper decimal place position for the addition feed.

The rotary calculator has storage registers in which a multiplier can be stored and retained for repeated use, and some machines automatically transfer a number from the accumulator to the storage registers. A number can also be retained in the keyboard by keeping keys depressed.

Modern rotary calculators invariably use repeated addition and shifting for multiplication and repeated subtraction and shifting for division. Some rotary calculators can perform the operation of taking a square root.

The Future of Mechanical Calculating Machines. Although mechanical calculating machines have been valuable for progress, they are being replaced by more versatile equipment. In accounting, automatic data-processing machines perform a far wider range of routine services, and they have become standard equipment for large-scale accounting activities. For scientific purposes, the large, automatic stored-program computer can handle far larger problems than can the mechanical calculator. In other applications, small electronic calculators with capabilities similar to mechanical machines have advantages in reliability, ease of maintenance, and silence.

The mechanical and electrical principles that are used for calculating machines will continue to be useful, however. These principles are used in a tremendous variety of devices, such as supermarket scales that weigh meat and print labels giving the weight, the price per pound, and the total price; gasoline pump facilities that do a similar job in terms of gallons of gas; control devices that count or measure manufacturing processes; and time clocks with printed outputs.

ELECTRONIC CALCULATORS

Two difficulties had to be overcome in developing small-scale electronic calculators that could replace the rotary mechanical calculators. One was that normal decimal notation results are very desirable for the purposes of the user, but the binary number system is more suitable for electronic computation. This difficulty was overcome by providing circuits that made conversions from decimal to binary form for use within the calculator and from binary to decimal form to provide a decimal output for the user.

The second difficulty was in providing a suitable output device for the results of computations. One solution to this problem was to use an electrically operated typewriter with auxiliary paper-tape punch facilities, such as a teletypewriter or a Flexowriter. The other solution to the problem was to use a cathode-ray tube, which provides a visual display of numbers on a screen that is like a television screen.

Output Devices. With electronic calculators that use a teletypewriter or Flexowriter as the output device, the computational results appear as a punched paper tape, providing data storage on paper. Holes in the tape are a coded form of the computational data. With electronic calculators that have a cathode-ray tube as the output device, the computational results appear on the cathode-ray tube screen, which can display as many decimal places as are provided in the calculator. Several lines of digits can be displayed simultaneously. Electronic calculators with cathode-ray tube displays have more storage registers than have rotary calculators, so that intermediate results can be stored and need not appear in the visual display. Additional keys are provided to control the transfer of data between these storage registers and the usual active accumulator and counter registers.

Programs. Some electronic calculators are programmed externally. In this case, a sequence of operations that is to be used repeatedly is expressed as a set of instructions and then encoded by punching holes in cards or paper tape. An auxiliary device connected to the calculator reads the encoded instructions and automatically activates the operation keys on the machine to perform the desired sequence of operations.

Other electronic calculators have internally stored programs. In this case, electronic storage is provided for programs that do not exceed a certain fixed length. These programs usually are shorter than the programs of the large automatic computers, and they also are characterized by a provision to stop in order to permit a manual introduction of data.

As electronic calculators increase in capabilities, the gap closes between the capabilities of a calculator and the capabilities of an electronic computer. See also COMPUTER.

F. J. MURRAY, *Duke University*

Further Reading: Bernstein, Jeremy, *Analytical Engine* (New York 1964); Murray, F. J., *Mathematical Machines* (New York 1961).

CALCULUS

CALCULUS, kal′kyə-ləs, is the branch of mathematics designed to represent and study continually changing quantities. Though the word "calculus" is sometimes used to mean any procedure for calculating some quantity, usually when one speaks of "calculus" or "the calculus," one means the particular branch of mathematics created in the 17th century and expanded and perfected in the next two centuries. The basic laws of science and engineering are expressed in terms of concepts of the calculus, and the deduction of knowledge about the physical phenomena so represented makes intensive use of the techniques of the calculus.

CONTENTS

Section	Page	Section	Page
Types of Problems Treated by the Calculus	163	The Calculus of Functions of Several Variables	173
The Limit Concept	165	Analysis	175
The Derivative	166	The Completion of the Calculus	176
Antidifferentiation or Integration	169		

TYPES OF PROBLEMS TREATED BY THE CALCULUS

As an object falls from some height to the earth its distance from the starting point and its speed are continually changing. The temperature and pressure of the air around us, the cost of living, and the amount of oil stored in the earth are continually changing. As a wave travels through the water, the height of the water at any fixed point rises and falls.

Insofar as the representation of changing quantities is concerned, in simple situations it is often possible to write down a description at once. Thus, if an automobile travels at a constant speed of, say, 40 miles per hour, the distance traveled in miles is 40 times the amount of time traveled measured in hours. The relation between the distance and time is called a function. This relation can also be described in symbols. Thus if we let d stand for the distance traveled in miles and t the time traveled in hours, the formula $d = 40t$ represents the function. The quantities d and t are called variables, and because in using the formula one would usually assign values first to t and then calculate d, t is called the independent variable and d the dependent variable.

Even if it is possible to write down the formula that represents the relation between two variables, there are many questions one can raise about such a relation that are not readily answered. Suppose an automobile travels at a varying speed. Then the relation between the distance and time traveled is no longer as simple as $d = 40t$. But let us suppose that we know it, whatever it may be. We might be interested in determining from this relation the speed of the automobile *at a particular instant*, say at 3 o'clock. One must appreciate that determining this speed is quite different from determining the average speed. If the automobile travels 200 miles in 5 hours, then its *average* speed is 40 miles per hour. However this average speed is not necessarily and usually will not be the speed at a particular instant during its journey. How does one find the speed at an instant?

On the other hand, instead of the relationship between distance and time, suppose we know the formula for the speed of an object at each instant of the time during which it travels. For example, if an object is dropped near the surface of the earth, and if the resistance of the air is negligible, the speed it possesses t seconds after it is dropped is given by the formula $v = 32t$, where v is the velocity, or speed. How far does an object fall in 5, 10, or any other number of seconds? We cannot multiply the speed at, say, 5 seconds by the time of fall to obtain the distance because the object does not possess that speed throughout the five seconds.

We have described two fundamental problems in terms of motion, wherein the basic variables are distance and time. However, though motion is indeed a common phenomenon, in many problems the basic variables represent other physical entities. Thus the pressure of the air varies with height above the surface of the earth. One might wish to know the rate of change of pressure with respect to height at a particular height. A large rate of change at a particular height might affect seriously the performance of an airplane. Conversely, if one knew not the variation of pressure with height but the rate of change of pressure with height at any height, one might wish to know the total change in pressure from one height to another.

In more general terms we may pose the two problems thus: suppose one variable changes continually when another does. What is the rate of change of the first with respect to the second at a particular value of the second quantity? Conversely, suppose we know the rate at which one variable changes with respect to another at each value in some range or interval of the second variable. What is the total change in the first variable over this range of the second one? These problems and the difficulties they involve will become sharper as we work with them.

Historical Origins of the Calculus. The 17th century origins of the calculus, of interest in themselves, will at the same time give further indication of the variety of problems that are treated by means of the techniques of this subject. In the 17th century scientists were especially concerned with four types of problems. Chief of these was the study of motion. The scientists of the times had accepted the heliocentric theory, developed by Nicolaus Copernicus and Johannes Kepler, and its concepts of an earth rotating on its axis and revolving around the sun. The previously accepted theory of planetary motion, which dated back to Claudius Ptolemy and which presupposed an earth absolutely fixed in space as the center of the universe, was discarded. The adoption of the theory involving an earth in motion invalidated the laws of planetary motion and the explanations of motion that had been accepted since Greek times and that were being questioned for other reasons also. New answers were needed to such questions as: Why do objects stay with the moving earth? What is the path of a projectile shot from a cannon? Furthermore, Kepler had shown on the basis of observations that the path of each planet around the sun is an ellipse. But no theoretical explanation of why the planets moved on such paths had been offered. In the 17th century the notion that all bodies in the universe attract each other in accordance with a force called gravitation had gained some vogue and had suggested to scientists that the paths of the planets about the sun and the paths of moons around planets could be deduced from the proper laws of motion and gravitation. The motion of celestial bodies became the dominant scientific study. All these motions have variable velocity.

The second major scientific problem of the 17th century was to determine the tangents to curves. This problem was of some interest as a matter of pure geometry, but the deeper significance of the problem is that the tangent to a curve at a point represents the *direction* an object moving along a curve has at that point. To know how a light ray will proceed after striking the surface of a lens, one must know the angle the light ray makes with the lens, and this means the angle between the light ray and the tangent to the lens (Fig. 1). Since the study of

Fig. 1

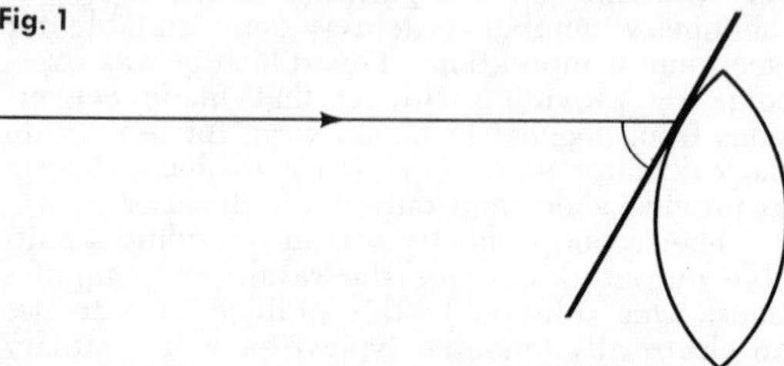

the behavior of light, stimulated by the creation of the telescope and microscope, was, next to motion, the most active scientific field in the 17th century, the study of lenses was of great interest and the tangent problem vital.

A third class of problems besetting the 17th century scientists may be designated as maxima and minima problems. For example, one of the pressing questions concerning projectiles was to determine the maximum range. As the angle of elevation of a cannon (angle A in Fig. 2) is

Fig. 2

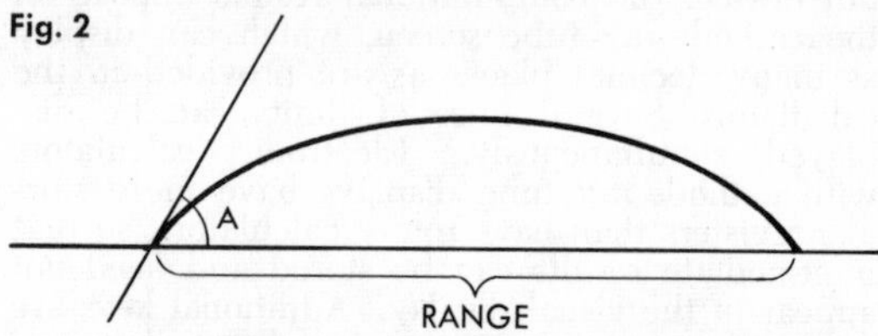

varied, the range, that is, the horizontal distance from the cannon to the point where the projectile hits the ground, also varies. At what angle of elevation is the range a maximum? Other maxima and minima problems of considerable importance arise in planetary motion. As a planet moves about the sun its distance from the sun varies. What are the maximum and minimum distances of the planet from the sun? Some simple maxima and minima problems can be solved by the methods of elementary algebra and elementary geometry. But the most important problems are beyond the power of these elementary branches.

Still another class of problems concerned lengths of curves, the areas of figures bounded by curves, and the volumes of figures bounded by surfaces. Here, too, elementary mathematics suffices to determine the areas and volumes of simple figures. It enabled the Greeks of the period from 600 B.C. to about the time of Christ to obtain the formula for the area of a circle, $A = \pi r^2$. However, the techniques they were able to employ were totally inadequate to handle the problems that arose in the 17th century. For example, the shape of the earth is what is called an oblate spheroid, that is, a sphere somewhat flattened on the top and bottom. The calculation of the volume of this figure cannot be performed with elementary geometry. It can be done with the calculus. Closely connected with the problems of area and volume was the problem of finding the gravitational attraction exerted by, say, the earth on the moon.

The efforts to treat these four classes of problems led the mathematicians to methods that are now embraced under the term "calculus." Though it is at the moment by no means obvious, all four classes can be treated by solving the two general problems we have already described, namely, given a relationship expressing change, to determine the rate of change, and given the rate, to determine the total change. Of course, problems similar to those that are included in the four classes continue to be important, or else the calculus would have only historical value.

The calculus has proved to be the richest lode mathematicians have ever struck. And like almost all branches of mathematics, it is the product of many men. In the 17th century, Pierre de Fermat, René Descartes, Blaise Pascal, Gilles Personne de Roberval, Bonaventura Cavalieri, Isaac Barrow, James Gregory, Christian Huygens, John Wallis, and, of course, Isaac Newton and Gottfried Wilhelm Leibniz all contributed. The names of Newton and Leibniz are most often mentioned as the creators of the calculus. Without deprecating their contributions, it is fair to say, as Newton himself put it, that they stood on the shoulders of giants. Newton and Leibniz saw more clearly than their predecessors the generality of the methods that were gradually being developed, and in addition they added many theorems and processes to the stock built up by their predecessors. But even Newton and Leibniz did not complete the calculus. Throughout the 18th century new results were obtained by, among others, Jakob Bernoulli, his brother Johann Bernoulli, Brook Taylor, Leonhard Euler, Jean Le Rond d'Alembert, and Joseph Louis Lagrange. Moreover, the final clarification of the concepts of the calculus was achieved only in the 19th century by Bernhard Bolzano, Augustin Louis Cauchy, and Karl Weierstrass.

THE LIMIT CONCEPT

When mathematicians began to tackle the problems we have described, they had available to them a fair amount of elementary algebra, plane and solid geometry, trigonometry, and analytic, or coordinate, geometry. However, all of these tools were insufficient. These problems are resolved by one basic operation, the differentiation of a function, and this in turn is defined in terms of a new mathematical concept, the limit of a function. Let us see why a new concept is needed.

We shall consider again the basic phenomenon of motion and the problem of finding speed at an instant of time. By way of preparation, let us be clear about the notion of an instant. As a person travels, time elapses. To reach one place from another requires an interval of time. However, in addition to events that take place over an interval of time, there are events that happen at an instant. A lightning flash happens at an instant, and a bullet strikes a target at an instant.

Normally when one uses the notion of speed, he means average speed. As we have noted, if a car covers 200 miles in 5 hours, its average speed, 40 miles per hour, is obtained by dividing the distance of 200 by 5, the interval of time. Let us suppose that one wanted to know the speed of the car at the instant 3 hours after starting out. It would seem that all one has to do is divide the distance traveled at that instant by the time elapsed and so obtain the speed at the instant. However, at an instant, no time elapses, or, one can say, 0 time elapses. This is the very meaning of "instant." Moreover, at an instant the car covers 0 distance. Hence if we divide the distance traveled at an instant by the time elapsed, we obtain 0/0. Now division by zero is not permitted anywhere in mathematics because there is no meaningful answer. Thus we cannot obtain the instantaneous speed by dividing the distance traveled at an instant by the amount of time in one instant. Yet physically there is no question that the automobile has a speed at any instant during the period it is in motion.

The successful approach to the calculation of instantaneous speed is unavoidably somewhat roundabout. If one knows exactly how far the automobile has traveled from the starting point at each instant during the period of travel, which means knowing the formula for the distance in terms of the time, then he can adopt the following approach. Suppose that the automobile started at 12 o'clock and traveled 50 miles during the 4th hour. Then the average speed during that hour was 50 miles per hour. This average speed is an approximation of the speed at 3 o'clock. However, the automobile may have varied its speed during that 4th hour, and so the approximation need not be the speed at the instant in question. We can do better. Suppose the automobile traveled 28 miles in the half hour from 3 o'clock onward. Then its average speed during that half hour was 56 miles per hour. Although this average may be a better approximation of the speed at 3 o'clock than the preceding one, nevertheless, during the half hour, the automobile may have changed its speed. Suppose that the automobile covered 14½ miles in the fifteen minute interval starting at 3 o'clock. Then the average speed during this interval is 58 miles per hour. This again may be a better approximation of the speed at 3 o'clock, because the automobile had still less time in which to change its speed. Nevertheless the previous objection still applies to this interval of time. Suppose then that we calculate the average speed during 10 minutes, 1 minute, ½ minute, ¼ minute, and so on, each interval starting at 3 o'clock. Let us suppose that by calculating the average speeds for these intervals we obtain the sequence of numbers: (1) 50, 56, 58, 58¾, 59½, 59¾, 59⅞. . . . The dots at the end merely indicate that we can continue the process of calculating average speeds for smaller and smaller intervals of time.

Let us note two facts about this sequence. Each member is an average speed for some interval of time. Hence each can be computed. Second, because the intervals of time over which these average speeds are computed are smaller, these averages should tend toward the speed at 3 o'clock, because there is less time during which the automobile can change its speed. We also observe that the sequence of numbers is getting closer and closer to 60. The decisive step is to take the number 60 as the speed of the automobile at 3 o'clock. The number 60 is called the limit of the average speeds. We should note that the instantaneous speed is not defined as the quotient of distance and time. Rather it is the limit approached by average speeds as the intervals over which these average speeds are computed approach 0.

One might indeed question the right to take the number 60 as the speed at 3 o'clock. All we do know is that as the intervals of time starting at 3 o'clock become smaller and smaller the average speeds approach 60, but nothing seems to force us to conclude that the instantaneous speed at 3 o'clock is 60. However, the automobile is traveling at speeds near 60 for smaller and smaller intervals of time, and if its motion is smooth (the mathematician says "continuous") it has almost no time to change its speed from a value arbitrarily close to 60 in time intervals of a millionth or a billionth of a second. The choice of 60 as the speed at 3 o'clock makes good physical sense. Since mathematics seeks to represent what happens physically, it has adopted a definition in accord with the physical facts.

We see in the above resolution of the problem of finding speed at an instant that a new concept is introduced, namely, the notion of limit. This is the central idea in the calculus and distinguishes the subject from the earlier developments in mathematics. The notion is subtle and is learned best not by grasping at some definition but by working with it.

As a step toward understanding the notion, let us consider a related but somewhat different situation. Suppose a man walks from point A toward a point B and first walks ½ the distance, then ½ of the remaining distance (or ¼ of the original distance), then ½ of the remaining distance (or ⅛ of the total), and continues according to this pattern. Let us set aside the question of how rapidly the man walks and therefore the question of whether he ever arrives at B. We can nevertheless say that the man does come closer and closer to the point B and that B is the limit of his motion, or that B is the point that he is approaching more and more closely. In this same sense the numbers of the sequence (1) above approach 60.

It is true that in taking the number 60 to be the limit of the sequence (1) we were guessing a bit. There is the possibility that the limit might be 59.999 or 60.001. Hence our process of determining the instantaneous speed seems to be no better than a good guess. Moreover, the process is cumbersome, because it calls for calculating a great number of average speeds in order to foresee what the limit might be. Both of these objections are obviated by the definitive mathematical process called the method of increments, which we shall now examine.

THE DERIVATIVE

In order to calculate the instantaneous speed or the instantaneous rate of change of distance with respect to time, one must know the formula that relates the distance traveled to the time traveled. Just how such formulas are obtained will be clearer later. Let us calculate the instantaneous speed of a body that is dropped near the surface of the earth. Such a body falls with increasing speed. If air resistance is neglected, the formula that relates the distance d (in feet) that the body falls and the time t (in seconds) that it falls is

$$d = 16t^2. \tag{2}$$

Let us calculate the instantaneous speed at the end of the 4th second of fall, that is, when $t = 4$.

The distance the body falls in four seconds is denoted by d_4 and is given by substituting 4 for t in the formula. Thus $d_4 = 16 \cdot 4^2$ or

$$d_4 = 256. \tag{3}$$

The generality of the method of increments consists in calculating the average speed, not over a specific interval of time such as 0.1 of a second, but over an arbitrary interval of time. That is, we introduce a quantity h, called an increment, which is to represent any interval of time beginning at $t = 4$ and extending before or after $t = 4$.

We shall first calculate the average speed in the interval 4 to $4 + h$ seconds. To do this, we must find the distance traveled in this interval of time. We therefore substitute $4 + h$ for t in (2) and obtain the distance fallen by the body in $4 + h$ seconds. This distance will be denoted by $d_4 + k$, where k is the additional distance fallen, or the increment in distance, in the interval of h seconds. Thus

$$d_4 + k = 16(4 + h)^2 = 16(16 + 8h + h^2)$$

or

$$d_4 + k = 256 + 128h + 16h^2. \tag{4}$$

To obtain k we have but to subtract equation (3) from equation (4). The result is

$$k = 128h + 16h^2. \tag{5}$$

The average speed in the interval of h seconds is

$$\frac{k}{h} = \frac{128h + 16h^2}{h} \tag{6}$$

When h is *not* zero, it is correct to divide the numerator and denominator on the right-hand side of (6) by h. The result is

$$\frac{k}{h} = 128 + 16h. \tag{7}$$

To obtain the instantaneous speed at $t = 4$, we must determine the number approached by the average speeds as the interval h of time over which these speeds are computed becomes smaller and smaller. From (7) we can now readily obtain what we seek. If h decreases, $16h$ must also decrease, and when h is very close to zero, $16h$ is also close to zero. In view of (7), then, the fixed number that the average speed approaches is 128 feet per second. This number is the instantaneous speed at $t = 4$.

The process we have just examined, the method of increments, is basic in the calculus. It is more subtle than appears at first sight. One should not expect to note and appreciate the finer points on first contact. As a step in the right direction, however, we shall make one or two observations. First, we wish to emphasize the fact that we sought the number or limit approached by average speeds as the intervals of time during which the average speeds were computed became smaller and smaller. The correct expression for the average speed in any time interval h is given by (6), and, since h is not zero, also by (7). Because (7) happens to be especially simple, we can easily determine what the limit of the average speeds is.

Second, as one looks at the right-hand side of (7) in order to determine what the limit of $128 + 16h$ is as h approaches 0, he might note that he can obtain the result of 128 by letting h *be* zero in the expression. But the agreement of the results should not cause us to lose sight of a basic point. We are interested in the limit of k/h as h approaches 0. Step (7) gives a correct expression when h is *not* zero. Hence, we may not use (7) to determine what k/h is when h is 0. Indeed k/h has no value when h is 0 because then k is also 0, as (5) shows us, and so k/h becomes the meaningless expression, 0/0. We can use (6) or (7) to determine what happens to k/h as h *approaches* 0, and this is all we need to know. As a matter of fact, when working with more complicated functions than (2), one does not have any choice. He must find the limit of k/h as h approaches 0.

The main point that emerges from this discussion is the possibility of finding instantaneous speed by a general process, that is, by the method of increments. No tedious arithmetical calculations are necessary, nor is there any doubt about what the limit approached by the average speeds is. Let us also note that k/h is a function of h and that the instantaneous speed is the limit this function approaches as h approaches 0.

We have calculated the instantaneous speed at the end of the 4th second for an object that falls according to the law $d = 16t^2$. Let us investigate the possibility of generalizing the procedure and see whether it might apply to any instant of time and perhaps to other formulas. We shall consider the formula

$$y = ax^2\,, \tag{8}$$

where a is some constant and y and x are any variables related by (8). (After all, the fact that d represented distance and t time in the formula $d = 16t^2$ played no role in the purely mathematical process of calculating the rate of change of d with respect to t at $t = 4$.) By using the letters y and x and the constant a, we emphasize the fact that we are considering a strictly mathematical relationship, and we shall calculate the rate of change of y with respect to x at a given value of x. Such rates, incidentally, are also called instantaneous rates, even though x does not always represent time. The word "instantaneous" has been carried over because many applications of the calculus contain time as the independent variable.

Let x_1 denote the value of x at which we are to compute the instantaneous rate of change of y compared to x. Thus, x_1 is analogous to the value 4 of t used above. To compute the desired rate of change, we shall repeat the process employed there. We first compute y_1, the value of y when x has the value x_1, obtained by substituting x_1 for x in (8). Then, taking increments h in x and k in y, we carry out computations analogous to (4) through (6) to arrive at

$$\frac{k}{h} = \frac{2ax_1h + ah^2}{h}. \tag{9}$$

Equation (9), which gives the average rate of change of y with respect to x in the interval h, is the generalization of equation (6).

To secure the instantaneous rate of change of y compared to x at the value x_1 of x, we must now determine the limit of the right side of (9) as h approaches zero. We are again fortunate in that we may divide the numerator and denominator of (9) by h and obtain

$$\frac{k}{h} = 2ax_1 + ah. \tag{10}$$

As h becomes smaller and smaller, the quantity ah, which is merely a constant times h, also becomes smaller, and the quantity k/h approaches the value $2ax_1$. This last quantity is the limit approached by the average rates of change, k/h, and thus is the rate of change of y with respect to x at the value x_1 of x. Just to check our result, we note that when $a = 16$ and $x_1 = 4$, the quantity $2ax_1$ is 128, and this is the limit we obtained in the special case treated earlier.

Since y and x are variables which have no physical meaning, we cannot speak of the limit $2ax_1$ as an instantaneous speed. Instead we must describe it as the instantaneous rate of change of y compared to x at the value x_1 of x. To avoid this lengthy phrase, the quantity is called the *derivative* of y with respect to x at the value x_1. It is denoted by y', the notation introduced by Lagrange (Newton used $\dot{y}$). Thus, we have established that at the value x_1 of x the derivative y' of y is given by

$$y' = 2ax_1. \tag{11}$$

Actually we have arrived at a more general result. The quantity x_1 was any value of x. Hence we might as well emphasize this fact by dropping the subscript and writing

$$y' = 2ax. \tag{12}$$

Equation (12) states that when $y = ax^2$, the derivative of y with respect to x is $2ax$. Since (12) holds at any value of x, it is a function; that is, the derivative of y with respect to x is itself a function of x and is also called the *derived function*. The process of deriving (12) from (8) is called *differentiation*.

Before we explore further the concepts and techniques, it is advisable to consider the matter of notation. We have used h and k to denote the increments in x and y respectively. The standard notation in modern calculus texts is Δx for h and Δy for k. The Δx must be considered as a single symbol standing for an increment in x. An analogous remark applies to Δy. In place of Newton's notation $\dot{y}$ and Lagrange's notation y' for the derivative or derived function, Leibniz used dy/dx. This symbol is both good and bad. It makes explicit that x is the independent variable. Moreover it suggests that the derivative comes from considering average rates of change, which are quotients. However, it is too suggestive, because though the symbol is meant to be taken in its entirety, the use of the division sign leads one to believe that the derivative is a quotient. This, of course, is not correct. The derivative itself is not a quotient but a limit of a function, k/h, which is a quotient.

The result (12) holds regardless of the physical meaning of y and x. Hence, in any situation in which the formula $y = ax^2$ applies, we may conclude at once that the instantaneous rate of change of y compared to x is $2ax$. The generality of this result is immensely valuable, since a general mathematical result can always be applied to many different physical situations. To illustrate this point for the derivative (12), let us reconsider $d = 16t^2$. In this case, d plays the role of y, t plays the role of x, and 16 is the value of a. Hence,

$$(13) \qquad d' = 2 \cdot 16t = 32t\,,$$

or, since the instantaneous rate of change of distance compared to time is the instantaneous speed, v,

$$(14) \qquad v = 32t.$$

Knowing the formula that relates distance and time of a dropped object, we have derived the formula for the instantaneous speed. Thus from one formula we may derive another significant formula by applying the process of determining the instantaneous rate of change, that is, by differentiation.

To make effective use of the calculus, one must learn how to determine the instantaneous rate of change for many types of formulas. Since our purpose is primarily to gain some idea of what the calculus has to offer, we shall merely note a few results. Thus,

$$(15) \qquad \text{if } y = ax^n,\ y' = nax^{n-1}\,;$$
$$(16) \qquad \text{if } y = \sin x,\ y' = \cos x\,;$$
$$(17) \qquad \text{if } y = e^x,\ y' = e^x\,;$$
$$(18) \qquad \text{if } y = \log_e x,\ y' = 1/x\,.$$

In these last two formulas e is the base of a system of logarithms called natural, or Naperian, logarithms and is an irrational number approximately equal to 2.718. Once formulas have been derived, as we derived $y' = 2ax$ from $y = ax^2$, one uses them without having to repeat the method of increments in each case.

The calculus does not deal only with the simple functions $y = ax^2$ or $y = \sin x$. Indeed the applications call for the use of combinations of functions such as $y = 3x^3 + 5x^2$, $y = x \log x$, $y = x^2/\sin x$, and a great variety of other combinations. Fortunately, to obtain the derivative or derived function of a combination of functions one does not have to go through the method of increments in each case. Suppose that u and v are two functions of x, say $u = x^2$ and $v = \sin x$. Then there are theorems on differentiation that state that

$$(19) \qquad \text{if } y = u + v \text{ then } y' = u' + v'\,;$$
$$(20) \qquad \text{if } y = u - v \text{ then } y' = u' - v'\,;$$
$$(21) \qquad \text{if } y = uv \text{ then } y' = uv' + vu'\,;$$
$$(22) \qquad \text{if } y = u/v \text{ then } y' = \frac{vu' - uv'}{v^2}.$$

The significance of these theorems is simply that if a given function is the sum, difference, product, or quotient of two other functions, then the derivative of the given function can be obtained in terms of the derivatives of the component functions. If one knows the derivatives of the latter, simpler functions, he can obtain the derivative of the given function by using one or more of theorems (19) to (22).

The Geometrical Meaning of the Derivative. The instantaneous rate of change of y with respect to x can be interpreted geometrically. This interpretation not only clarifies the meaning of such a rate but at the same time points the way to new uses of the concept. Let us consider the function

$$(23) \qquad y = x^2,$$

and let us interpret geometrically the instantaneous rate of change of y with respect to x at $x = \frac{1}{2}$. To obtain this interpretation we must utilize the major idea of coordinate, or analytic, geometry, namely that each pair of x and y values that satisfies the formula (it is usually called an equation in coordinate geometry) can be plotted as a point in a rectangular coordinate system and the collection of all such points is a curve that represents the formula.

Fig. 3

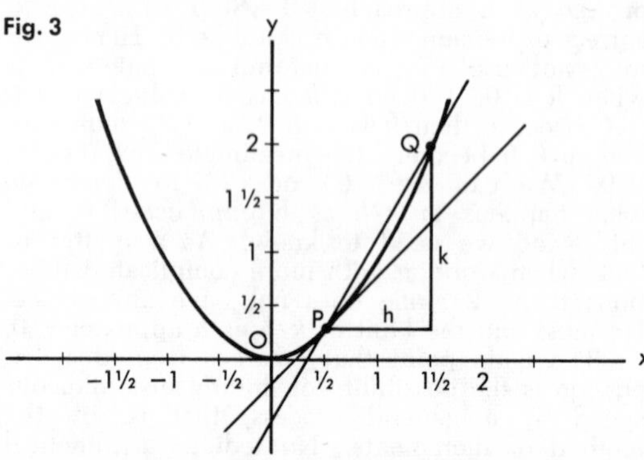

We proceed with the geometrical interpretation of the instantaneous rate of change. To find this rate of change by the method of increments we first calculate y at $x = \frac{1}{2}$. This value of y is $(\frac{1}{2})^2$ or $\frac{1}{4}$. The values $\frac{1}{2}$ for x and $\frac{1}{4}$ for y are, of course, the coordinates $(\frac{1}{2}, \frac{1}{4})$ of a point, denoted by P in Fig. 3 on the curve that represents $y = x^2$. The second step is to increase the independent variable by an amount h so that its value becomes $(\frac{1}{2}) + h$. The dependent variable then changes by an amount k so that its new value is $(\frac{1}{4}) + k$. Now the quantities $(\frac{1}{2}) + h$ and $(\frac{1}{4}) + k$ can be interpreted as the coordinates of another point on the curve, which is shown as the point Q in Fig. 3. Next we calculate the average rate k/h. As the figure shows, k is the difference in the y-values of P and Q, whereas h is the difference in the x-values of P and Q. Thus, the ratio k/h is the slope of the line PQ, which, as in plane geometry, is called a secant. We see, then, that for any value of h and the corresponding value k, the ratio k/h is the slope of the secant through two points of the curve representing $y = x^2$.

Finally, we consider the limit approached by the ratio k/h as h gets closer and closer to zero. As h decreases, the point Q on the curve of Fig. 3 moves closer to the point P. The secant through P and Q changes position, always, of course, going through the fixed point P and the point Q, wherever the latter happens to be. As h approaches zero, the point Q approaches the point P, and the secant PQ comes closer and closer to the line that just touches the curve at P; that is, PQ approaches the tangent at P. Since k/h is the slope of PQ, the limit approached by k/h must be the slope of the line approached by PQ. In other words, the instantaneous rate of change of y with respect to x at $x = \frac{1}{2}$ is the slope of the tangent to the curve at P, the point whose coordinates are $(\frac{1}{2}, \frac{1}{4})$. Of course, the value of $\frac{1}{2}$ for x has been arbitrarily chosen to present a concrete yet typical example. We could have been more general and have carried through the entire discussion for any value of x and obtained the result that the rate of change of y with respect to x at any given value of x is the slope of the tangent to the corresponding curve at the point having that given value of x

as abscissa, or horizontal coordinate.

We see, therefore, that the derivative of a function has a precise geometrical counterpart: the slope. Since slope is the rise (or fall) of a line per unit of horizontal distance, the geometrical meaning is a rather simple one. Thus, since the value of the derivative of $y = x^2$ at $x = \frac{1}{2}$ is 1, the slope of the tangent at $x = \frac{1}{2}$ is 1. The slope of a curve at a point on that curve is very reasonably defined to be the slope of the tangent at that point.

From the standpoint of application, the fact that the derivative is the slope of the tangent or the slope of the curve is significant. To get some idea of how useful this is, suppose a pro-

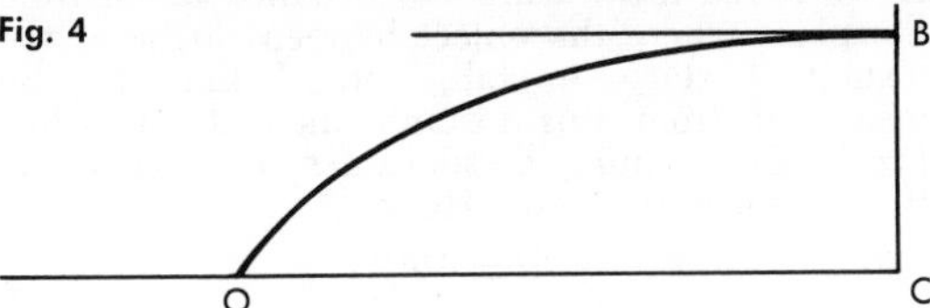

Fig. 4

jectile, shot up and out from the point *0* (Fig. 4), is to strike the wall *BC* at the point *B*. Knowing the equation of the path of the projectile we can calculate the slope at the point *B*. This slope amounts to the direction that the projectile possesses at the point *B*, for the slope is the rate at which the curve (or its tangent) is rising or falling. One might want the direction of the projectile at *B* to be perpendicular to the wall because such an impact would damage the wall more effectively than a hit in a glancing direction. If necessary one could adjust the angle of fire and initial velocity to achieve the desired direction at *B*.

Another example illustrating the usefulness of knowing the slope is furnished by the phenomenon of reflection of light. Suppose one wishes to design a mirror in such a way that all rays of light coming from some source, are reflected to one point. Let us consider a plane cross-section of the mirror which contains the

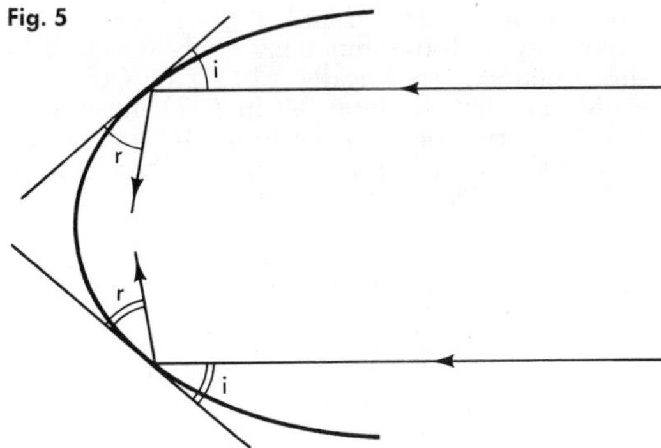

Fig. 5

incident and the reflected rays (Fig. 5). This plane section is a curve. The angle that the incident ray makes with the mirror is, in fact, the angle *i* between the incident ray and the tangent. To discuss this angle as well as the corresponding angle of reflection *r*, we must know the direction, and hence the slope, of the tangent. It is a physical fact that angle *i* always equals angle *r*. Hence by choosing the curve whose slope has the right properties, we can arrange to have all the reflected rays go through one point.

Maxima and Minima. We shall now see how the use of the derivative enables mathematicians to solve problems of the third class described earlier, namely, maxima and minima problems. Let us consider the problem of finding the maximum height to which a ball thrown up into the air with a speed of 128 ft/sec will rise before returning to the ground. The formula that describes the height of the ball at any time *t* is

$$d = 128t - 16t^2. \tag{24}$$

Let us look at the graph (Fig. 6) of the formula (24). At the maximum value of *d*, the slope of the curve is 0. But the slope of the curve is the derivative d'. By applying the appropriate theorems on differentiation, (20) and (15), to the formula (24) we find that $d' = 128 - 32t$. We set $d' = 0$ so that $128 - 32t = 0$, and we see that $t = 4$ when $d' = 0$. If we substitute this value of *t* in (24), we find that the maximum height is 256 feet.

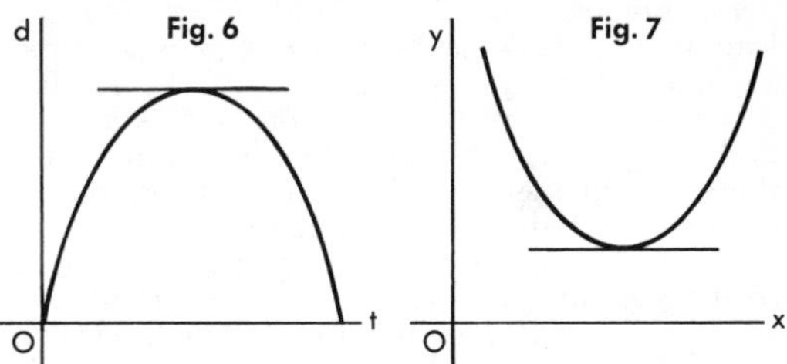

Actually, the derivative of a function is 0 at a minimum as well as a maximum (Fig. 7). In physical problems such as the one we just did, one can usually tell whether the result is a minimum or a maximum. If not, there are mathematical tests to determine whether the value at which the derivative is 0 furnishes a maximum or a minimum value of the function.

ANTIDIFFERENTIATION OR INTEGRATION

The material examined thus far belongs to the differential calculus, whose basic process starts with the formula relating two variables and finds the instantaneous rate of change of one variable with respect to the other. Suppose, however, that one began with the rate of change of one variable with respect to another and wished to find the formula that relates the two variables. For example, if we should happen to know that $y' = 2x$, could we find the relation between *y* and *x*? One might expect that the answer is affirmative, because it would seem that among the various functions whose derivatives have been obtained, there should surely be one whose derivative is $2x$. Except for a minor difficulty, which we shall consider later, this expectation is correct.

The process of finding the formula from the derivative is called *antidifferentiation* or *integration*, and the resulting formula is called the *indefinite integral*. As we shall see later, there is another kind of integral obtained from quite different considerations. The mathematics that treats both notions of integral is usually called the *integral calculus*.

The process of finding the function from its derivative is immensely valuable—indeed, even more valuable than the basic process of finding derivatives from given formulas, because in numerous physical problems the most readily available information is an instantaneous rate of change, whereas the information sought can be best obtained from the function that relates the variables in question. Before we can see how useful this idea is, we must examine and learn a few facts concerning the mathematical process itself.

Suppose we happen to know that the instantaneous rate of change of some variable y with respect to another variable x is $2x$, that is, $y' = 2x$. What formula relates y and x? The mathematician's method of answering this question is to survey all the rates of change of functions obtained in the past and to locate the function whose rate of change he has found to be $2x$. In this case, the function $y = x^2$ is the indefinite integral, or antiderivative, of $y' = 2x$.

However, the formula $y = x^2$ is not the only integral of $y' = 2x$. The presence of a constant term in a formula has no effect on the instantaneous rate of change because the constant does not change when the independent variable does. For example, $y = x^2$ and $y = x^2 + 5$ both lead to $y' = 2x$. Hence $y = x^2 + 5$ is as much an integral of $y' = 2x$ as $y = x^2$ is. In fact, $y = x^2 + C$, where C is any constant, is an integral of $y' = 2x$. It may seem unfortunate that there should be more than one answer, but we shall see that the reverse is the case.

The general problem of finding the formula relating y and x when we are given y' as a function of x is handled by the method illustrated in our example of $y' = 2x$; that is, we must examine the formulas whose rates of change we have previously determined and try to locate among these derivatives the rate of change we are concerned with. Since this rate of change has been previously derived from some formula relating y and x, that formula is the answer to our problem. Also, we can add any constant to the formula and still have the correct answer. The process of searching among all formulas whose rates of change have previously been found may seem to be haphazard, but in practice mathematicians tabulate these formulas according to distinctive properties, so that a little experience with the tables usually enables one to find the desired formula. Since we are limiting the variety of formulas and their derivatives to a few cases, we shall not bother to become acquainted with a table.

Let us consider some examples of the usefulness of integration in physical problems. Galileo had found that if air resistance is neglected, all objects falling to earth from points near the surface of the earth possess the same acceleration, 32 ft/sec^2. This acceleration is the same at each instant of the fall. Since the acceleration at any instant is the instantaneous rate of change of speed with respect to time, we can write

(25) $$v' = 32.$$

The physically important question is: what formula relates v and t? By reviewing the formulas for derivatives, namely (15), one finds that

(26) $$v = 32t + C,$$

where C is any constant.

In a particular physical problem, the quantity C can be chosen to fit the situation. Thus, suppose that the object is merely dropped to earth; that is, at the instant it begins to fall its speed is zero. If time is measured from this instant, then to make the formula (26) fit the physical fact that v must be 0 when $t = 0$, we must have $C = 0$. Hence

(27) $$v = 32t.$$

Physical problems often require knowledge of the distance an object falls. Since $v = d'$,

(28) $$d' = 32t.$$

To find the formula that relates d and t, we again appeal to experience with derivatives and note that the formula $d = 16t^2$ has the derivative given by (28). However, the formula

(29) $$d = 16t^2 + C,$$

where C is any constant, also has this derivative. If we agree to measure the distance fallen from the point where the object happens to be at the instant it starts to fall, and if time is also measured from this instant, then $d = 0$ when $t = 0$. Substituting these values in (29) shows that C must be zero. Hence

(30) $$d = 16t^2$$

gives the distance the dropped object falls.

We have been able to reverse the process of finding the rate of change of a function and thus proceed from a knowledge of acceleration to speed as given by (27) and from speed to distance fallen as given by (30).

Let us consider some other situations. Suppose that an object is thrown downward and leaves the hand with a speed of 100 ft/sec. The acceleration is still given by (25), and so the speed is still given by (26). However, if time is measured from the instant the object leaves the hand, then at the instant $t = 0$, $v = 100$. To make (26) fit this new situation, we must have $C = 100$. Hence

(31) $$v = 32t + 100$$

is the formula for the speed of an object thrown downward with an initial speed of 100 ft/sec.

Now let us seek the distance covered in time t. Since $d' = v$, from (31) we have

(32) $$d' = 32t + 100.$$

What formula relates d and t? By reviewing the derivatives and the functions from which they were obtained, specifically (19) and (15), we would find that the term $32t$ in (32) must come from the term $16t^2$ and the term 100 must come from $100t$. The formula for d, therefore, is $d = 16t^2 + 100t$. However, we must recall that

(33) $$d = 16t^2 + 100t + C,$$

where C is any constant, also has the derivative (32). Hence (33) is the general formula for distance fallen. If we agree to measure distance from the point at which the object happens to be when it begins to fall, and if time is measured from the instant the object begins to fall, then $d = 0$ when $t = 0$. Substituting these values in (33), we have $C = 0$, and

(34) $$d = 16t^2 + 100t.$$

We see from the examples already presented that the occurrence of the constant C in the integral is not a disadvantage but rather an advantage. It permits us to adjust the formulas for speed and distance to the specific situation we wish to describe, although the basic fact in all instances is $v' = 32$.

The process of integration is more useful than differentiation because in physical problems we usually are given information about a derivative, and from this, by integration, we obtain the formula we really want, such as the formula for the distance a body falls. This same point will be illustrated in the next application.

Areas By Integration. One of the four major classes of problems which motivated the work on the calculus was the calculation of areas bounded by curves and of volumes bounded by surfaces. We shall now see how these can be obtained by considering a typical area problem.

Let us try to determine the area *DEFG* of Fig. 8. This area is bounded by the vertical line segments *DG* and *EF*, by the segment *DE*, and by the arc *FG* of the curve whose equation is, say, $y = x^2$. We may think of this area as being swept out by a vertical line segment *PQ*, which starts at the position *DG* and moves to the right, varying in length as it moves. Let us suppose that *PQ* has reached the position shown in the figure. The area swept out by this moving segment depends, of course, upon the position it has reached, which can be specified by the x-value of the point *P*. Hence the variable area, which we shall denote by *A*, is a function of x, the abscissa of the point *P*. We now propose to find the formula that relates *A* and x.

Our procedure is as follows: we begin by determining the rate of change of *A* with respect to x at any given x and integrate this derivative to arrive at the desired formula. To find the rate of change of *A* with respect to x, let us suppose that *PQ* has moved a little farther, to the position *P′Q′*. The abscissa of *P′* is somewhat larger than that of *P*; let us denote it by $x + h$. Obviously the variable area *A* also increases when *PQ* moves to *P′Q′*. Let us use k to denote this increase, which geometrically is the area *QQ′P′P*. It is immediately evident from the figure that the increase is equal to the area of a rectangle whose base is h and whose height is an ordinate, $\bar{y}$, which is larger than *PQ* and smaller than *P′Q′*. (We do not know how large $\bar{y}$ is, but we shall see in a moment that this does not matter.) We have, then,

$$(35) \qquad k = \bar{y}h.$$

Let us divide both sides of (35) by h. Then

$$(36) \qquad \frac{k}{h} = \bar{y}.$$

Now k/h is the average rate of change of area with respect to x in the interval h. By the very definition of an instantaneous rate, the rate of change of area with respect to x at the x-value of *P* should be the limit of the average rate of change as h approaches zero. But as h approaches zero, $\bar{y}$ approaches the y value of Q, or the length *PQ*. Thus

$$(37) \qquad A' = y.$$

Since the y in (37) is the ordinate of the point Q and Q lies on the curve $y = x^2$, it follows that

$$(38) \qquad A' = x^2.$$

We now have the rate of change with respect to x of the variable area *A*. To find *A* itself, we must ask ourselves what formula has the derivative x^2. A review of previously obtained derivatives, specifically equation (15), tells us that the derivative of x^3 is $3x^2$ and that therefore $A = x^3/3$. We know, however, that the integral may also contain a constant term. Hence

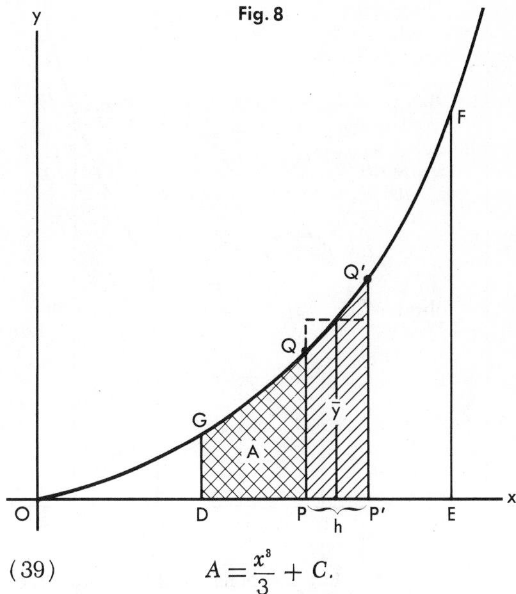

$$(39) \qquad A = \frac{x^3}{3} + C.$$

To determine the value of *C*, we make use of the fact that when *PQ* is at *DG*, the area is zero because *DG* was the starting position of *PQ*. Suppose that the x-value of *D* is 3. Then by substituting 0 for *A* and 3 for x in (39) we obtain $C = -9$. Thus

$$(40) \qquad A = \frac{x^3}{3} - 9,$$

and this formula gives the area between *DG* and the variable position of the moving line segment *PQ*. If we wish to determine the area from *DG* to *EF*, we may assume that *PQ* has reached the position *EF*. Let us suppose that the x-value of *E* is 6. If we now substitute 6 for x in (40), we obtain

$$(41) \qquad \text{area } DEFG = \frac{6^3}{3} - 9 = 72 - 9 = 63.$$

Thus we have found the area bounded by a curve through the process of antidifferentiation, or integration. We have used the equation of the curve, which, by virtue of coordinate geometry, is known to us. This method can be used to find lengths of curves, areas bounded entirely by curves, and volumes bounded by surfaces.

The Integral as a Sum. We have mentioned that there is another notion of integration. Let us first survey this notion by reconsidering the previous problem. We shall, in fact, find the area *DEFG* of Fig. 8 by a totally different approach, which is a modification of one used by the Greeks. We subdivide the interval *DE* (Fig. 9) into three equal parts, each of length h, and denote the points of subdivision by D_1, D_2, and D_3, where D_3 is the point *E*. Let y_1, y_2, and y_3 be the ordinates at the point of subdivision. Now y_1h, y_2h, and y_3h are the areas of three rectangles shown in Fig. 9, and the sum

$$(42) \qquad y_1h + y_2h + y_3h$$

of the three rectangular areas is an approximation to the area *DEFG*.

We can obtain a better approximation to the area *DEFG* by using smaller rectangles and more of them. To illustrate this point, suppose that we subdivide the interval *DE* into 6 parts.

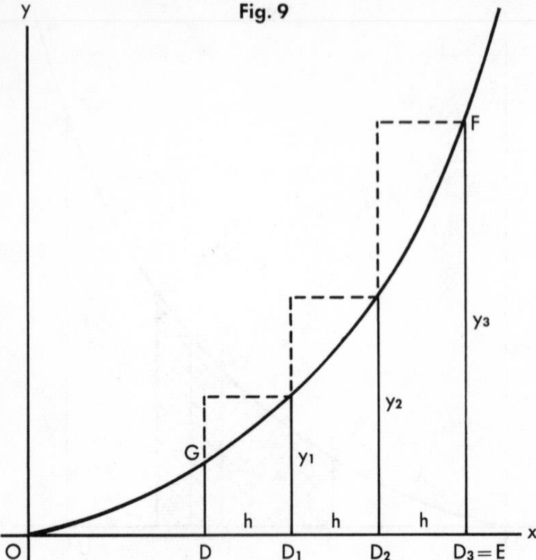

Fig. 10 shows what happens to the middle rectangle of Fig. 9. This rectangle is replaced by two, and because we use the y-value of each point of subdivision as the height of a rectangle, the shaded area in Fig. 10 is no longer a part

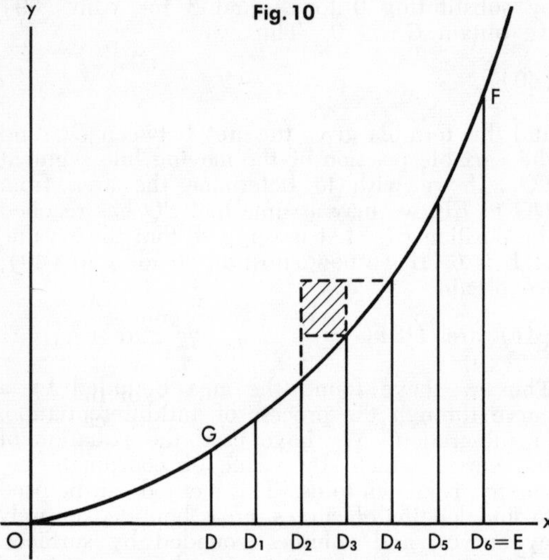

of the sum of the areas of the six rectangles, which now approximates the area $DEFG$. Thus,

(43) $y_1h + y_2h + y_3h + y_4h + y_5h + y_6h$

is a better approximation than the sum (42).

We can make a more general statement concerning this process of approximation. Suppose that we divide the interval DE into n parts. There would then be n rectangles, each of width h. The ordinates at the points of subdivision are $y_1, y_2, \ldots, y_n$, where the dots indicate that all y-values at these points are included. The sum of the areas of the n rectangles is then

(44) $$y_1h + y_2h + \cdots + y_nh.$$

In view of what we said above about the effect of subdividing DE into smaller intervals of width h, the approximation to the area $DEFG$ given by the sum (44) improves as n increases.

We see so far how figures formed by line segments—rectangles in the present case—can be used to provide better and better approximations to an area bounded by a curve. The set of approximations obtained by subdividing DE into more and more subintervals is called a sequence. Its members are denoted by S_1, S_2, and so forth, and its typical term (44) by S_n. The sequence

$$S_1, S_2, \cdots, S_n, \cdots,$$

then, has an infinite number of terms, each successive one providing a better approximation to the area $DEFG$. We take the limit of this sequence, that is, the number approached by the numbers $S_1, S_2, \cdots$, to be the area $DEFG$. Thus

(45) $$\text{Area } DEFG = \lim_{n\to\infty} S_n = \lim_{n\to\infty} (y_1h + y_2h + \cdots + y_nh),$$

where h is equal to DE/n.

It is helpful to shorten the writing of an expression such as (45). The notation used in calculus books is

(46) $$\text{area } DEFG = \int_a^b y\, dx.$$

This notation must not be taken too literally. The symbol $\int$ is an elongated S and is intended to denote that we are dealing with the limit of a sequence of sums. The number a is the abscissa of the left-hand end point of the interval DE, and the number b is the abscissa of the right-hand end point. The entire expression on the right side of (46) is called the *definite integral* of the function represented by y. The words "definite integral" denote that we are interested in the integral as the limit of a sequence of sums as opposed to the indefinite integral that results from antidifferentiation.

The area $DEFG$ has been approximated by a sum of rectangles, and the area itself is a limit of a sequence of sums. Now given the equation of the curve FG and definite values for the x-values (abscissas) of D and E, it is sometimes possible to calculate directly the limit of the sequence of sums and so obtain the area $DEFG$. However, we know from our previous treatment of area that it can be obtained in the following way: If the equation of the curve FG is $y = x^2$, we find the formula whose derivative is x^2, or in other words we find the antiderivative of x^2. This happens to be $x^3/3$. We substitute the abscissa of the point E and obtain a number. We next substitute the abscissa of the point D and obtain a number. Finally, we subtract the latter result from the former. We see, then, that limits of the kind expressed in (46) can be determined by antidifferentiation. This fact that the definite integral can be evaluated by antidifferentiation is called the *fundamental theorem of the calculus*. It is written symbolically as

(47) $$\int_a^b f(x)dx = F(b) - F(a).$$

Equation (47) uses the notation $f(x)$ for a function of x; the left side is the definite integral, as in (46), except that we now write $f(x)$ in place of y. On the right side we understand first of all that there is some function $F(x)$

which is an antiderivative of $f(x)$; $F(b)$ is the value of that antiderivative when b is substituted for x; and $F(a)$ is the analogous value when a is substituted for x.

We have introduced the definite integral and the fundamental theorem by treating the problem of finding the area bounded by a curve. But we knew before we introduced this notion that we could find areas by antidifferentiation, and even after introducing the definite integral, we learned from the fundamental theorem that we evaluate this too by antidifferentiation. For the purpose of calculating areas bounded by curves, the concept of the definite integral and the fundamental theorem add nothing to the power of the calculus. However it is often easier to formulate some desired quantity as a limit of a sequence of sums, and then the fundamental theorem tells us that we can evaluate this limit by antidifferentiation. In such cases the definite integral and the fundamental theorem are basic tools. We shall see shortly where the summation concept is indispensable.

THE CALCULUS OF FUNCTIONS OF SEVERAL VARIABLES

Elementary calculus deals with functions wherein there is one independent variable and one dependent variable, as in $y = x^2 - 7x$ and $y = \sin x$. However, real phenomena more often involve several independent variables. In elementary geometry we learn that the formula for the area A of a rectangle is the product of the length x and the width y; that is, $A = xy$. The area A, then, depends upon two quantities, and if either one or both vary, A varies. Thus the dependent variable A is a function of two independent variables, x and y. Here x and y are both independent variables, and A is the dependent variable. To study the behavior of the area as the two dimensions of the rectangle vary we must then treat A as a function of both variables.

Fig. 11

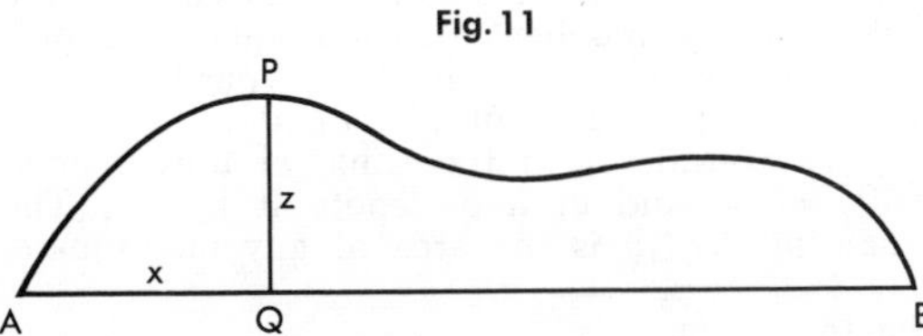

Consider an elastic string, for instance a violin string, which is fixed at the two ends and which occupies the position AQB (Fig. 11). If one plucks this string, it will vibrate. To describe the behavior of this vibrating string, one could specify the displacement z of any point P on it from its rest position. However, the value of z will depend upon which point P we select and, since the string is vibrating, the instant at which we ask for the position of the string. We can agree to let x represent the distance from A to the point Q directly below P and thereby describe the position of any point on the string in terms of its x-value. We can also introduce the time t measured, say, from the instant the string begins to vibrate. Then the displacement z is a function of x and t.

Functions of three or more independent variables also are needed in geometrical and physical studies. To consider a physical example, suppose we have a long metal plate so thin that we can idealize it as a rectangle. Let

Fig. 12

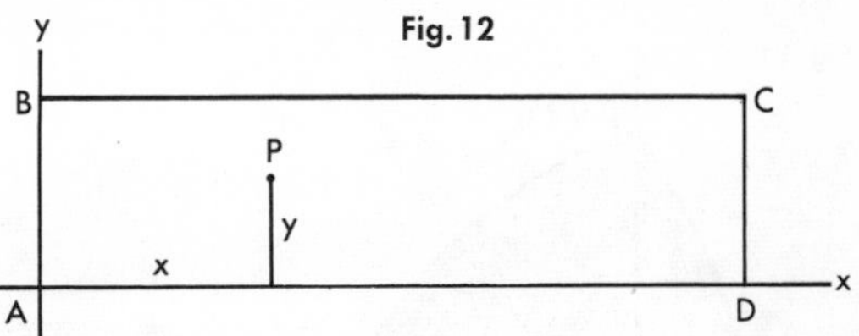

$ABCD$ (Fig. 12) be this rectangle. If we should apply heat to the edge AB, the heat will travel along the plate. Suppose we wish to study the temperature at any point P of the plate. We could specify the position of P by introducing the coordinates x and y. The temperature T will then depend on x and y, but it also varies with the time t. Thus T is a function of three independent variables—x, y, and t.

It is possible to represent geometrically functions of two variables by utilizing the techniques of solid analytic geometry, and the representation will usually be a surface. Functions of three or more variables cannot be represented geometrically.

Partial Differentiation. The derivative of y with respect to x gives the instantaneous rate of change of y with respect to x at a value of x. With functions of two or more independent variables there are several different such rates.

Let us consider the function for the area of a rectangle,

$$(48) \qquad A = xy.$$

Since x and y are independent variables, we can consider changes in the value of x while y is kept at a fixed value. In this circumstance A becomes a function of just one variable, x, and the familiar notion of instantaneous rate of change, or the derivative, applies to A as a function of x only. To indicate that we are considering the rate of change of A as a function of x only, we use the notations $\frac{\partial A}{\partial x}$ or A_x, and we speak of this derivative as the *partial* derivative of A with respect to x. For the function (48), $\partial A/\partial x = y$. Likewise we can consider the rate of change of A with respect to y, while x is kept at any fixed value.

Since a partial derivative, insofar as the actual differentiation process is concerned, amounts to no more than an ordinary derivative, no new technical knowledge is needed to calculate partial derivatives. We have but to remember that in calculating a partial derivative with respect to x, y is to be treated as a constant, and vice versa.

The notion of a partial derivative is readily extended to functions of three or more variables.

Fig. 13

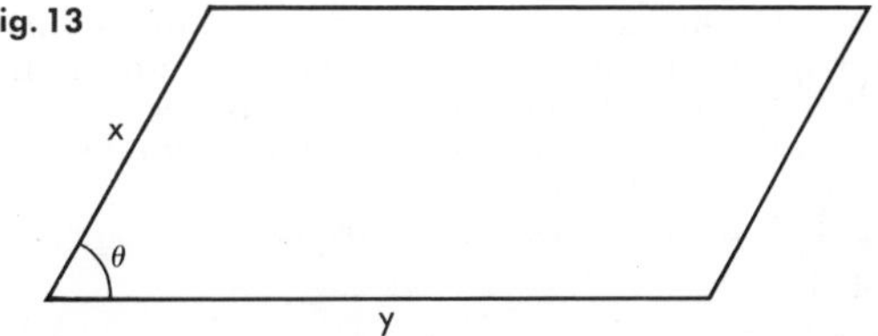

Thus let us consider the formula for the area of a parallelogram (Fig. 13),

$$A = xy \sin \theta.$$

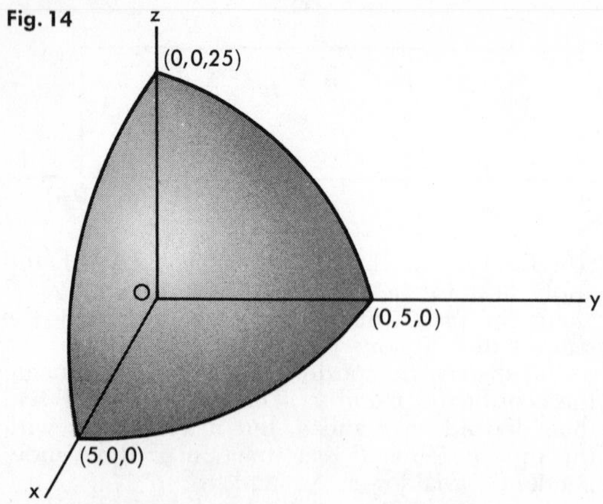

Fig. 14

We can consider the rate of change of A with respect to x, y or θ, where the other two variables are held constant as each derivative is calculated. We find then that $\frac{\partial A}{\partial x} = y \sin \theta$, $\frac{\partial A}{\partial y} = x \sin \theta$, $\frac{\partial A}{\partial \theta} = xy \cos \theta$.

Finally, the notion of partial differentiation is extended to higher derivatives. Thus if $z = x^2 + xy + y^2$, then $\partial z/\partial x = 2x + y$. The derivative of $\partial z/\partial x$ with respect to x, denoted by $\partial^2 z/\partial x^2$ or z_{xx}, is 2. Likewise we can find $\partial^2 z/\partial y^2$ and $\partial^2 z/\partial x \partial y$, the latter meaning the derivative of $\partial z/\partial x$ with respect to y, which in the present case is 1.

Integration of Functions of More than One Variable. Corresponding to antidifferentiation in the calculus of functions of one independent variable there is the analogous process for functions of more than one variable. For example, one might be faced with the equation $\partial z/\partial x = 3x^2 y$ and be obliged to find z. Since y is treated as a constant in the differentiation, it may also be treated as such in reversing the differentiation, and knowing this technique, one would conclude that $z = x^3 y$. However, where in the case of functions of one variable it was necessary to allow for a constant in the integral, in the present case one must allow for the possibility that the original function contained a function of y only, because such a function would "disappear" in the differentiation with respect to x. Hence the correct integral is $z = x^3 y + g(y)$ where $g(y)$ indicates some unknown function of y, which might be determinable from additional information.

Corresponding to the integral as a limit of a sequence of sums in the case of functions of one variable, there are what are called double integrals in the case of functions of two independent variables, triple integrals for three variables, and so on. The prototype of these multiple integrals, as they are called, is the double integral, which gives the volume bounded at least in part by a surface.

Let us start with the surface

$$(49) \qquad z = 25 - x^2 - y^2.$$

A knowledge of solid analytic geometry enables us to recognize that the equation represents a paraboloid (Fig. 14) that opens downward and has its vertex at (0,0,25). The surface cuts the xy-plane in a circle; this is evident from the fact that when $z = 0$, the points on the surface satisfy the equation $x^2 + y^2 = 25$. Because the surface is symmetric with respect to the xz-plane and the yz-plane, the portion of the volume in the first octant is one-fourth of the entire volume bounded by the surface and the xy-plane. Let us find the volume of this quarter, which is bounded by the surface and by parts of the xz-plane, the yz-plane, and the xy-plane.

To obtain this volume we shall follow the procedure used to obtain the area under a curve. In the case of the curve, we approximated the area by a sum of rectangles and then let the widths of these rectangles approach zero while increasing the number of them to fill out the area as much as possible. In the present case we shall use columns with rectangular cross sections. Specifically, we break up the x-interval from 0 to 5 into k equal parts of length Δx and the y-interval from 0 to 5 into k equal parts Δy (Fig. 15). At each point of subdivision on one axis we draw lines parallel to the other axis, thus covering the quarter-circle in the xy-plane by squares. Not all of the area in the quarter-circle is covered by squares lying entirely within the quarter-circle. We shall consider only those which do, and assign a number to each of them from 1 to l so that each square has a unique number. In each square we pick any one point. Thus in the typical, or ith, square we pick a point $(x_i, y_i, 0)$.

Fig. 15

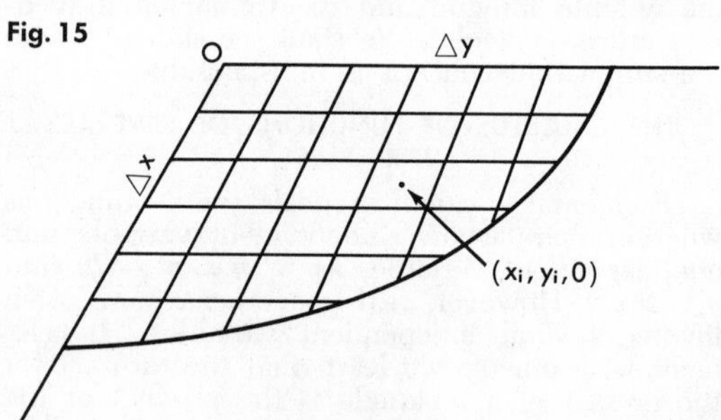

We consider next the value of the function (49) at x_i and y_i and denote it by z_i. The quantity $\Delta x \Delta y$ is the area of any one square,

Fig. 16

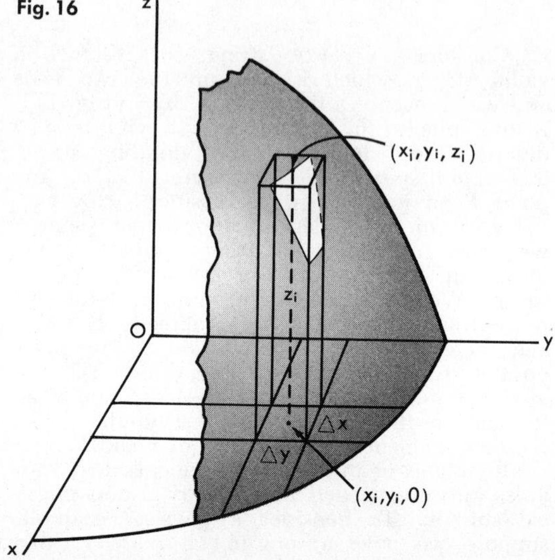

and the quantity $z_i \Delta x \Delta y$ is the volume of a column (Fig. 16) with base $\Delta x \Delta y$ and height z_i. This column is an approximation to the volume underneath that part of the surface (49) that lies directly above the ith square. The column is only an approximation, because the top surface of the column lies in part above the surface and in part below. Thus we may obtain an approximation of the total volume we are seeking by forming the sum

(50)
$$S_1 = z_1 \Delta x \Delta y + z_2 \Delta x \Delta y + \cdots + z_l \Delta x \Delta y.$$

Our next step is to decrease the size of Δx in the x-interval from 0 to 5 by increasing k, and do the same thing with Δy. Consequently there will be some large number of squares $\Delta x \Delta y$ that lie entirely within the quarter-circle of Fig. 15, and in fact these will fill out more of the quarter-circle than the previous set. We again number the squares from 1 to m, say, where m is the number of squares now present, and choose any point $(x_i, y_i, 0)$ in each square. Let z_i be the value of z above each pair x_i and y_i and form the sum

(51)
$$S_2 = z_1 \Delta x \Delta y + z_2 \Delta x \Delta y + \cdots + z_m \Delta x \Delta y.$$

The sum S_2 is a better approximation than S_1 to the volume we are seeking, because the smaller squares $\Delta x \Delta y$ fill out more of the quarter-circle and because any column with base $\Delta x \Delta y$ and height z_i approximates more closely the volume under that part of the surface.

We can continue the process of making Δx and Δy smaller by increasing k, and at the n-th stage of this process we shall have, say, p squares and the sum

(52)
$$S_n = z_1 \Delta x \Delta y + z_2 \Delta x \Delta y + \cdots + z_p \Delta x \Delta y.$$

As with functions of one variable, we let the number of squares become larger and larger, each time securing a new S_n and a better approximation to the volume being sought, thus obtaining the sequence

$$S_1, S_2, \cdots, S_n, \cdots.$$

Since the approximations furnished by the successive terms of the sequence seem to come closer and closer to the volume under the surface, the limit of this sequence should be the volume we seek. This limit, that is $\lim_{n \to \infty} S_n$, is expressed in calculus notation as

$$(53) \quad \iint_A z \, dxdy \text{ or } \iint_A (25 - x^2 - y^2) \, dxdy.$$

The two integral signs show that we are dealing with a function of two variables. The letter A below the two integral signs denotes the region or domain of x and y values to be considered. In the present problem it refers to the region in the quarter-circle of the xy-plane. The $z \, dxdy$ is symbolic of the columns formed to obtain the approximate volume.

The expression of the limit of the sequence of approximating volumes as the double integral (53) does not, of course, determine what the volume is. The double integral is merely a symbol, and the problem of calculating the volume still remains. We faced precisely the same difficulty when we approached the problem of obtaining the area under a curve as a limit of a sequence of sums of rectangles. The essential technique, as in the earlier situation, is antidifferentiation, or finding the indefinite integral.

The consideration of triple integrals involves similar details, except that the domain of integration is itself a volume and we break this up into little cubes. Double and triple integrals are used to calculate volumes, masses, centers of gravity, moments of inertia, the gravitational attraction exerted by an extended body on another localized or extended body, the total heat contained in a volume, and hundreds of other physical quantities.

ANALYSIS

The techniques of the calculus can indeed be used to solve the four classes of problems described at the outset and thousands of similar problems. However, the greater value of the calculus lies in the fact that at least a dozen major branches of mathematics utilize the basic concepts of the calculus, the derivative and the definite integral. The calculus and these newer branches built on it are known collectively as *analysis,* a term used to distinguish this area from algebra and geometry.

Differential Equations. Of the branches of analysis, the most extensive and the most useful for science and engineering is differential equations. The step from the calculus to differential equations is a direct one. Suppose one knows that the rate of change of some variable y with respect to t is $32t$, that is, $y' = 32t$. One can say that the equation $y' = 32t$ is a differential equation, that is, an equation involving the derivative of some function. Solving the differential equation calls for finding the function whose derivative is involved in the given equation. This particular differential equation and all those which are treated in the calculus proper are simple in that the solution can be found by reversing differentiation.

The given physical information can lead to much more complicated differential equations. If we neglect air resistance, then for motions near the surface of the earth we know that the fundamental physical fact is $v' = 32$. If we wish to consider motions at greater distances from the earth, we must utilize the law of gravitation, and in this case the fundamental physical fact is that the acceleration, or the instantaneous rate of change of velocity, that the earth's attraction imparts to any object is given by the differential equation

$$\frac{d^2r}{dt^2} = \frac{GM}{r^2},$$

where G is a constant, M is the mass of the earth, r is the distance of the object from the center of the earth, and d^2r/dt^2 is the second derivative, or the derivative of the derivative of r as a function of t. Here it is no longer possible to find r as a function of t merely by reversing differentiation.

The preceding differential equation describes the motion of an object that moves directly up or down in a straight line. The planets move in curves about the sun, and the curves are paths in a two-dimensional space, in this case a plane. Since the planets, too, move under the gravitational attraction of the sun, the law of gravitation is involved. However, one must write down two differential equations that must be solved simultaneously to obtain the path of a planet, and the same applies to the motion of a satellite around the earth. One of Newton's greatest achievements was to solve just such a pair of differential equations and thus show that the path of each planet is an ellipse.

The differential equations thus far mentioned are called ordinary differential equations because only one independent variable, the time in the above examples, is involved. However, as we noted earlier, to describe the motion of the vibrating string, we must treat z as a function of x and t. The differential equation that describes this motion is

$$\frac{\partial^2 z}{\partial x^2} = \frac{1}{c^2}\frac{\partial^2 z}{\partial t^2}.$$

This is a basic partial differential equation, and solving it calls for finding z as a function of x and t. The theory of partial differential equations is both extensive and complicated.

The basic physical principles of light, sound, motion, electricity, heat, the flow of liquids and gases, atomic structure, and a dozen other branches of physics and chemistry, when mathematically formulated, are differential equations. However, the physical laws that contain the most usable information are solutions of these differential equations. This is why the subject of differential equations is so vital in engineering and science.

Other Branches of Analysis. If an object moves in three-dimensional space, it can take many directions. To describe the velocities and accelerations of such objects and the forces acting on them one must include not only the magnitudes of these quantities but also their directions. The most useful relevant mathematical notion is that of a vector. These vectors are themselves functions of time and of position in space. To study the rate of change of vectors or to obtain the limit of the sum of vector quantities analogous to the areas of the rectangles we considered earlier, we must have a calculus of vectors. This branch has been developed and is known as *vector analysis*.

The study of curves and surfaces wherein the properties change from point to point, unlike the straight line and the plane, must utilize the techniques of the calculus, because as we have already noted, the calculus is the instrument for studying quantities that change from instant to instant or geometrically from point to point. This advanced geometrical study is known as *differential geometry*.

Suppose an object moves along some path from a point A to a point B lower down, just as a child slides from the top to the bottom of a playground slide. The shapes of such slides, that is, the curves in which they are formed, can be quite varied. One can raise the question: What should the curve be so that the time required to go from top to bottom is least? The answer to this problem, unlike the maxima and minima problems we considered earlier, is not a number that yields the maximum value of a function, but a curve. The determination of paths or curves that maximize or minimize some quantity—time, in our example—is the subject of another branch of analysis known as the *calculus of variations*.

These few examples of the branches of mathematics built upon the calculus are just a small portion of the vast domain of analysis.

THE COMPLETION OF THE CALCULUS

The two basic operational ideas of the calculus are differentiation (together with its inverse, antidifferentiation) and the definite integral. Underlying each of these is a limit concept. The derivative rests on the notion of a limit of a function, and the definite integral rests on the notion of a limit of a sequence. Let us reconsider the first of these limit notions, though much of what we shall say applies to both.

The description given earlier of the limit of a function is admittedly vague. In particular the word "approach" is suspect. If for smaller and smaller values of h the ratio k/h should have the values $1/4$, $3/8$, $7/16$, $15/32 \ldots$, are these values approaching 1? They are indeed getting closer to 1, but it is also clear that they are always less than $1/2$, and so the limit might very well be $1/2$. How closely must the values of k/h approach a particular number before we can decide that that number is the limit of k/h? Though we had no difficulty in determining the limit in the cases of particular functions, we have used loose language to describe what we mean by a limit. That we were obliged to do so will be apparent in a moment.

The history of the efforts of mathematicians to grasp the limit concept properly is extensive and instructive as to how mathematics develops. We have already mentioned that many mathematicians of the 17th century made contributions to the calculus even before Newton and Leibniz began to work on the subject. These forerunners realized that they were unable to give satisfactory expositions of their ideas and, in fact, hardly comprehended the significance of what they were creating. Despite the long tradition of rigorous proof in mathematics, the early workers in the calculus did not hesitate to defend their work in ways that are outlandish for mathematicians. Rigor, said Bonaventura Cavalieri, a pupil of Galileo and professor at the University of Bologna, is the concern of philosophy and not of geometry. Pascal argued that the heart intervenes to assure us of the correctness of mathematical steps. Proper finesse rather than logic is what is needed to do the correct thing.

Although Newton and Leibniz made the most significant advances in the formulation of the ideas and methods of the calculus, neither contributed much to the rigorous establishment of the subject. Yet they were sure that their ideas were sound because they made sense physically and intuitively and because the methods gave results that agreed with observations and experiments. Both gave many versions of their ideas in the attempt to hit upon the precise concepts, but neither was successful.

The work of Newton and Leibniz was criticized even by their contemporaries. Newton did not reply to the criticisms, but Leibniz did. In addition to defending the methods by an appeal to the agreement of the results with experience, he attacked the critics as overprecise—a strange stand for a mathematician. He also said that excessive scruples should not cause us to lose the fruits of an invention. Of course, such replies did not provide the missing clarity and rigor.

Later writers attempted to supply better foundations for the calculus, but their efforts were blocked in two ways. First of all, the formulations presented by Newton and Leibniz were somewhat different; hence the rigorous construction of the calculus had to reconcile the two formulations. Second, the whole situation became complicated by an argument between Newton and Leibniz on the question of whether Leibniz had stolen ideas from Newton. Newton's friends, and English mathematicians in general, sided with him, while Continental mathematicians defended Leibniz. The quarrel between the two groups became so bitter that correspondence between English and Continental mathematicians was stopped for about 100 years.

Two of the greatest mathematicians of the 18th century, Leonhard Euler and Joseph Louis Lagrange, worked on the problem of clarifying the calculus, but without success. Others arrived at the conclusion that as it stood, the calculus was unsound, but somehow errors were offsetting one another so that the results were correct. A more drastic opinion was offered by the mathematician Michel Rolle. He taught that the calculus was a collection of ingenious fallacies. Voltaire called the calculus "the art of numbering and measuring exactly a Thing whose existence cannot be conceived." All 18th century attempts to supply rigorous foundations for the calculus failed.

In the first quarter of the 19th century, Augustin Louis Cauchy, the leading French mathematician, gave the first somewhat satisfactory definitions of limit of a function and limit of a sequence. After pointing out that the calculus deals primarily with continuous functions, which means loosely that the values of the function change gradually as the values of the independent variable change gradually, he then defined the derivative, the definite integral, the sum of an infinite series, and other notions.

Cauchy's definitions seemed satisfactory to his contemporaries, and it appeared that the logical foundations of the calculus were secured. However, Karl Weierstrass, a distinguished German mathematician, showed that even Cauchy's definitions were loose and gave more precise definitions, which are now standard, although they are generally presented in a second course in the calculus because they are difficult to grasp. This task of building the foundations of the calculus was finished by about 1900.

In all areas of mathematics, as in the calculus, ideas are first grasped intuitively and are extensively explored before they become fully clarified and precisely formulated, even in the minds of the best mathematicians. In the instance of the calculus, mathematicians recognized the crudeness of their ideas, and some even doubted the soundness of the concepts. Yet they not only applied them to physical problems but used the calculus to evolve new branches of mathematics, such as differential equations, differential geometry, the calculus of variations, and others. They had the confidence to proceed so far along uncertain ground because their methods yielded correct physical results. Indeed, it is fortunate that mathematics and physics were so intimately related in the 17th and 18th centuries—so much so that they were hardly distinguishable—for the physical strength supported the weak logic of mathematics.

It may be clear from this account of the difficulties mathematicians experienced with the concepts of the calculus that the above exposition does not provide a rigorous description of the concepts and all their ramifications. The reader may justifiably feel some vagueness and uneasiness about what has been presented. But the ideas of the calculus are the most profound that mathematics contains, and one cannot expect to comprehend them fully on his first contact with them.

MORRIS KLINE, *New York University*

Bibliography

Ball, W. W. Rouse, *A Short Account of the History of Mathematics,* chaps. 16–17 (New York 1960).

Bell, Eric T., *Men of Mathematics,* chaps. 6–10 (New York 1937).

Boyer, Carl B., *Concept of the Calculus* (New York 1959).

Courant, Richard, and John, Fritz, *Introduction to Calculus and Analysis,* vol. 1 (New York 1965).

Kline, Morris, *Calculus, an Intuitive and Physical Approach,* 2 vols. (New York 1967).

Osgood, William F., *Advanced Calculus* (New York 1925).

Sawyer, W. W., *What Is Calculus About?* (New York 1961).

Toeplitz, Otto, *The Calculus, A Genetic Approach* (Chicago 1963).

CALCULUS OF VARIATIONS,

CALCULUS OF VARIATIONS, kal′kyə-ləs vâr-ē-ā′shənz, a branch of analysis in which one maximizes or minimizes a given relationship between two or more variables. The variational calculus differs from the ordinary calculus in that it concerns an expression whose value depends not simply on one or more variables but on some arbitrary relation among the variables. For example, in an isoperimetric, or equal-perimeter, problem, the area bounded by a closed plane curve of fixed length but undetermined form is not a function of coordinates x and y, but is determined by a relation between x and y which represents the curve that bounds the area. An example of an isoperimetric problem appeared in the proof by the Greek mathematician Zenodorus (about 180 B.C.) that the area of any polygon is smaller than the area of a circle of equal perimeter.

The birth year of the calculus of variations sometimes is taken to be 1696, when the brothers Jakob and Johann Bernoulli quarreled about the brachistochrone—the curve along which an object will slide in the shortest time from one point to a lower point not directly beneath the first. Newton and the Bernoulli brothers showed that the curve is a cycloid. In 1698, Johann Bernoulli discussed with Leibniz another variational problem, geodesics—the shortest curves that can be drawn on a surface between pairs of points on the surface. A solution was published by Euler in 1732.

Variational problems had no collective name when Euler in 1744 wrote the first systematic treatise on the "Art of Finding Curved Lines Which Enjoy Some Property of Maximum or Minimum." In 1756, however, Euler used the concise phrase "calculus of variations" to describe the elegant methods invented the year before by Lagrange for finding the "variation" δ in a relationship in integral form. Gauss and Cauchy later found the variation of multiple integrals, and Weierstrass, using the "second variation," gave a fundamental theorem to distinguish maxima from minima. Sufficient conditions for the existence of extreme values were first systematically considered in the 20th century by Hilbert and generalized by Carathéodory.

CARL B. BOYER, *Brooklyn College*

MARILYN SILVERSTONE, FROM MAGNUM

DOWNTOWN CALCUTTA centers on the Esplanade, which is flanked on one side by the park known as the Maidan and on the other by offices and government buildings.

CALCUTTA, kal-kut'ə, is the largest city in India and one of the largest cities in the world. Capital of the state of West Bengal, in eastern India, it is a major industrial center and port, situated on the Hooghly River, 60–80 miles (97–129 km) from the Bay of Bengal. The East Pakistan border is only 40 miles (64 km) east of the city. Calcutta proper occupies an area of drained marshland along the east bank of the Hooghly River in the western, drier (moribund) section of the Ganges-Brahmaputra delta. Industrial suburbs stretch west of the river and along both banks for 40 miles (64 km) upstream and 20 miles (32 km) downstream, giving the urban region a total area of about 500 square miles (1,300 sq km).

Calcutta has a humid subtropical climate strongly influenced by the monsoons. While its winters are cool and relatively dry, the spring is hot (temperatures often rise above 100° F, or 38° C), and during the summer monsoon (from about mid-June to September) most of its annual average of 62.5 inches (159 cm) of rain falls. Although the humidity remains high, rain is not continuous through the summer months, and rainless periods of several days are common.

The People. The population of the Calcutta urban area in 1961 was 6,500,000. In 20 years it had more than tripled, and it continued growing after 1961 at such a rapid pace that within half a dozen years it probably contained over 8 million people. In 1961 there were about 3 million people living within the municipal limits of the city; the remainder lived in 35 suburbs and satellite cities including Howrah (512,598), South Suburbs (185,811), Bhatpara (147,630), South Dum Dum (111,284), Baranagar (107,837), and Bally (101,159).

Most of Calcutta's people are Indian Hindus who speak the Bengali language, but there are also many minority peoples and languages to be found in the city. Indian Muslims numbered 1 million in 1961, and at that time Calcutta also contained 1.5 million Hindu refugees from East Pakistan. Communal difficulties between Muslims and Hindus in East Pakistan have continued, and the chief destination of refugees fleeing them has always been Calcutta. Besides Hindus and Muslims, there are considerable numbers of Christians, Sikhs, and Jains in the city, and Bihari, Hindi, Oriya, Assamese, and English are languages that are frequently heard.

Calcutta's area is extremely compact, and it has been estimated that if the parks and streets were excluded, the population density in the city proper would be in the neighborhood of 135,000 people per square mile (about 52,000 per sq km). Yet, except in the center of Calcutta, buildings of over three stories are rare, and most people live in what are surely some of the most miserable residences on earth. About 3 million people occupy *bustees,* abject single-room huts without running water or proper sewage disposal. Fifty thousand or more people are without any housing at all and sleep in the alleyways and streets. Disease is rampant and epidemics frequently sweep the city. Cholera, spread by open sewers that often drain into the water system, is a constant menace. Everything in Calcutta is overwhelmingly crowded: thus, Calcutta University was reported to have registered 125,000 students in a recent year.

The Modern City. The center of Calcutta is Fort William (built by the British in the mid-18th century) and the adjoining Maidan, a vast open park 2 miles (3 km) long and about 1 mile (1.5 km) wide. Southeast of the Maidan is the

Victoria Memorial, a huge white marble structure in which there is a historical museum. To the north, and on adjoining streets are a large number of massive stone government and commercial buildings built for the most part by the British. The government buildings in this inner city core include the Raj Bhavan, residence of the governor of West Bengal; the High Court; the General Post Office; the Legislative Assembly House for West Bengal; and the Writers' Building. Nearby are churches, temples, mosques, colleges, hospitals, the university, and imposing stone buildings housing the offices of banks and the principal commercial and industrial firms.

Bordering the Maidan on its east is Chowringhee Road, the city's most fashionable thoroughfare with the best shops, hotels, theaters, and restaurants, and the great Indian Museum and the museum of the Asiatic Society. West of the Maidan, along the Hooghly River, are dock and warehouse areas, which extend downstream for several miles. Across the river is Howrah, an industrial city.

Economy. Calcutta is India's greatest industrial city. Foremost among its diversified industries is jute milling, which employs over a quarter of a million workers. Calcutta is the world's largest jute-milling center, and many of the sprawling riverside mills, originally built by European, especially Scottish, interests, are still owned and managed by foreigners. Other industries employing many workers are engineering (metalwares, machinery, electrical goods), cotton textiles, chemicals and drugs, and food processing. There are more than 600,000 workers in large industrial establishments. In addition, a large number of people work in small plants, workshops, and cottage industries.

As the major transportation center of eastern India, Calcutta has port facilities ranking with Bombay's as the nation's largest. Major rail lines converge from the north, west, and southwest. Formerly rail and riverboat transport served eastern Bengal, but since the creation of East Pakistan, trade with that area has been reduced sharply. Through Calcutta's port go large exports of manufactured jute goods (burlap, gunny), mica, manganese ore, coal, hides, and tea in exchange for all manner of imported manufactured goods and food.

History. The founding of the East India Company's trading base at Sutanati (on the site of present-day Calcutta) resulted from the Company's expulsion by the Mughuls (Moguls) in 1686 from its base of many years at Hooghly. In the fall of 1687, Job Charnock, the Company's agent, secured permission from the Mughuls to found a new base at Sutanati; but renewed hostilities between the Mughuls and the English delayed its actual establishment until 1690. In 1696 Old Fort William was built to secure the base, or "factory," and in 1698 the English were granted proprietorship of the villages of Sutanati, Govindapur, and Kalikata (of which the name Calcutta is a corrupted version), whose lands the base encompassed.

The new base flourished under the name Fort William, and almost from its founding was the seat of the new Presidency of Fort William (Bengal). Its growth was gradual and steady until 1756, when it was captured by the Indian Nawab of Murshidabad, a principality to the north along the Hooghly River. Most of the British fled southward, and many of those who remained became victims of the Black Hole incident. (See also BLACK HOLE INCIDENT.) Six months later Col. Robert Clive retook the city, and soon after, the fort was rebuilt on its present site; it protected Calcutta from many future attacks.

Warren Hastings was made first governor-general of Fort William in 1774, and he was given such powers over Bombay and Madras that Calcutta in effect became the first British capital of India. When the British government finally took over the rule of India from the East India Company in 1857, Calcutta became the formal capital and remained so until 1912. It was the capital of Bengal province until 1947, when the eastern two-thirds of the province was detached to form East Pakistan.

Calcutta occupies an extremely favorable site for trading with the wealthy Ganges-Brahmaputra valley as well as for tapping the mineral-rich valleys and hills to its immediate west. In its early years it was chiefly a warehousing point for the transfer of goods between ocean vessels and the river craft serving the valley. Later, in the middle and late 19th century, British-built railroad links with the Ganges Valley replaced the river craft, and other railroad lines reached westward to the Damodar Valley coalfields and central India. As trade flourished banking institutions were founded in Calcutta, and industries based on local raw jute, plentiful

PHILIP GENDREAU

IN A CALCUTTA PARK, vendors squat by circular trays and wait for passersby to sample their food.

TED POLUMBAUM, FROM PIX

CALCUTTA OFFICE WORKERS on their way to work pass homeless sleepers on the Howrah Bridge.

supplies of inexpensive coal, and other raw materials were established.

The rapid growth of the city since independence has brought appalling problems of housing, employment, transportation, and health. The port is rapidly silting up, the railroads are overburdened, the local transit system has almost collapsed under the strain of serving the burgeoning population, and traffic on the narrow, poorly maintained streets is so heavy it sometimes scarcely moves at all. Unemployment is high. Food, clothes, and other essentials are often in short supply and always more expensive than the typically poor resident can afford. Population: (1961) 2,927,289.

ROBERT C. KINGSBURY, *Indiana University*
Author of "An Atlas of South Asian Affairs"

CALCUTTA, kal-kut'ə, **University of,** one of India's major institutions of higher education, located in Calcutta, India. It was incorporated in 1857 as a "federal" university, on the model of the University of London, with jurisdiction over constituent colleges in northern India and affiliated colleges as far away as Rangoon. Under the Indian Universities Act of 1904, it developed as a teaching institution. In the reorganization of states following Indian independence in 1947, its control was limited to colleges in the state of West Bengal.

The present university comprises 6 university colleges, 7 constituent colleges, and 120 affiliated colleges and recognizes 3 medical institutes. There are 36 departments grouped under 12 faculties: agriculture, arts, commerce, education, engineering, fine arts and music, law, journalism, medicine, science, technology, and veterinary science. The university offers bachelor's, master's, and doctor's degrees to an average of 120,000 students, of whom 30,000 are women. The university library has special collections of Bengali, Sanskrit, and Tibetan manuscripts.

ANAND MOHAN
Author of "Indira Gandhi"

CALDARA, Polidoro. See CARAVAGGIO, POLIDORO DA.

CALDECOTT, kôl'də-kət, **Randolph** (1846–1886), English illustrator and painter, who is noted especially for his delightful drawings for children's books. He was born in Chester, England, on March 22, 1846. His artistic career began with drawings that he submitted to periodicals while he was employed as a bank clerk, and in 1871 he had illustrations published in the magazine *London Society*.

In 1872, Caldecott visited Germany with Henry Blackburn, for whose book *The Harz Mountains* he furnished pleasantly humorous illustrations. Other works illustrated by Caldecott include Washington Irving's *Sketchbook* and *Bracebridge Hall*. His colorful illustrations for some 16 children's books—including *John Gilpin* and *The Grand Panjandrum Himself* became popular. He died at St. Augustine, Fla., on Feb. 12, 1886. The Caldecott Medal of the American Library Association, presented annually "for the most distinguished American picture book for children," is named for him.

CALDECOTT MEDAL, a prize awarded annually for the most distinguished American picture book for children. It was established in 1937 by Frederic G. Melcher in honor of Randolph Caldecott (q.v.). See LITERATURE FOR CHILDREN.

CALDER, kôl'dər, **Alexander** (1898–   ), American sculptor, whose fame originally rested on his "mobiles," the first successful attempts to incorporate movement into sculpture. In these works, many on a monumental scale, free-form shapes of plate metal joined by wires and rods are delicately balanced to nod and sway with the motion of the air or are motor-driven to move in regulated patterns. Later, his nonmoving sculpture, called "stabiles," were equally admired. Calder also painted and designed toys, jewelry, furniture, and tapestries.

Life. Calder was born in Philadelphia, Pa., on July 22, 1898, the son and grandson of distinguished sculptors. After graduating from the Stevens Institute of Technology, he practiced engineering for several years before turning to art. He enrolled at the Art Students League in New

BOTH PHOTOS, PERL GALLERIES, NEW YORK

ALEXANDER CALDER'S standing mobile at the left is called *The Yellow Sled,* and his stabile (*above*) is named *Flaming.* Both of the sculptures are constructed of metal.

York City in 1923, and from 1924 to 1926 he worked as an illustrator for the *National Police Gazette.* After his first trip to Paris in 1926, he divided most of his time between the United States and France.

Work. An important influence on Calder's early work was the Ringling Brothers and Barnum and Bailey circus, which inspired his book *Animal Sketching* (1925) and many of the paintings in his first exhibit (1926), as well as his own miniature *Circus* of wire marionettes that could be manipulated by hand. These marionettes were followed by wire portraits of celebrities, including Josephine Baker and Fernand Léger, and by several crank-operated pieces representing goldfish in bowls.

About 1930, Calder's friendship with Miró and Mondrian directed him toward abstraction. He wanted the abstract colored shapes of these artists to move, and the moving sculptures that he created under this inspiration were dubbed "mobiles" by Marcel Duchamp. The earliest ones were mechanically driven; later, wind-moved forms predominated. Some mobiles were designed to hang from ceilings; others were balanced on stands. Among Calder's best-known mobiles are *Lobster Trap and Fish Tail* (1939; Museum of Modern Art, New York City) and *Spiral* (1958; UNESCO headquarters, Paris).

Monumental stabiles received a larger share of Calder's attention in the 1950's and 1960's. These include *Ticket Window,* which was installed at Lincoln Center, New York City, in 1965.

NICHOLAS GUPPY

Further Reading: Guppy, Nicholas, "Alexander Calder," in the *Atlantic,* vol. 214, no. 6 (New York 1964); Sweeney, James Johnson, *Alexander Calder* (New York 1951); Solomon R. Guggenheim Museum, *Alexander Calder* (exhibition catalog, New York 1964).

CALDERA, kal-der′ə, a large circular or oval basin, of volcanic origin. The terms "crater" and "caldera" are sometimes confused, but a caldera is distinguished by its larger size—often several times the diameter of a single volcanic vent. Calderas are formed on the summit areas of many major volcanoes, and if their rims are unbroken, they are often filled by beautiful lakes. Crater Lake in Oregon is a famous example of a lake-filled caldera. It has a diameter of about 6 miles (10 km), and a depth of about 3,000 feet (1,000 meters).

The formation of a caldera involves volcanic explosion or volcanic collapse, or a combination of these processes. The composition of most of the material ejected by the explosion of the Indonesian volcano Krakatau in 1883 is distinctly different from the composition of the remaining rocks of the former summit. This indicates that the ejected material came from deep within the volcano, and that the top of the volcano then collapsed into the void below. On the other hand, little or no volcanic explosion was involved in the formation of the calderas on the summits of Mauna Loa and Kilauea in Hawaii. Apparently they were formed by the draining out of lava through vents on the sides of the volcanoes, followed by a collapse of the summits into the partly emptied underground lava storage chambers. See also VOLCANO.

ROBERT W. DECKER, *Dartmouth College*

CALDERÓN DE LA BARCA, käl-dä-rôn′ dā lä bär′kä, **Fanny** (1804–1882), Scottish-American author. She was born Frances Erskine Inglis in Edinburgh. After living in Normandy, France, she and her family moved to Boston, Mass., where her intelligence and charm won her the friendship of Henry Wadsworth Longfellow and the historian William H. Prescott. In 1838 she married the Spanish diplomat Don Angel Calderón de la Barca, whom she accompanied to Mexico in 1840. Her book *Life in Mexico* (1843) supplied Prescott with much local color for his works.

Later, while her husband was minister of foreign affairs in Madrid, she related her impressions of Spanish politics in *Attaché in Madrid —Sketches of the Court of Isabella II.* After her husband's death in 1861 she served as tutor to the Infanta in the household of ex-Queen Isabella. On the return of the Bourbons to the Spanish throne, she was created a marchioness by King Alfonso XII. She died in Madrid on Feb. 3, 1882.

CALDERÓN DE LA BARCA, käl-dā-rôn' dā lä bär'kä, **Pedro** (1600–1681), Spanish playwright, who was one of the leading dramatists of Spain's Golden Age of literature and the arts—a period that extended from about the mid-16th to the mid-17th century. His stylized dramatic technique, superb poetic diction (notably his rich metaphorical imagery), and brilliant and complex symbolism represent the culmination of the involved and elaborate baroque style that marked the closing decades of the Golden Age. Calderón is best known outside Spain for his play *La vida es sueño* (*Life Is a Dream,* q.v.), about man's struggle to discover the realities of existence. It is one of the unquestioned masterpieces of Spanish literature.

Life. Pedro Calderón de la Barca Henao de la Barrera Riaño was born in Madrid in January 1600, of distinguished parents. After attending a Jesuit school in Madrid, he continued his studies at the University of Alcalá de Henares in 1614–1615. In 1616 he transferred to the University of Salamanca, where he studied canon law. Four years later he participated in a poetry tournament organized as part of the festivities surrounding the beatification of San Isidro Labrador in Madrid. Calderón's literary career began at about this time; his first known play, *Amor, honor y poder,* is dated 1623.

After traveling to Italy and Flanders, where he may have served in the Spanish military, he returned to Spain and became attached to the court of Philip IV as a kind of official playwright. His reputation soon spread throughout the country, and after the death of the great popular playwright Lope de Vega in 1635, Calderón became the chief Spanish dramatist. In that year one of his plays, *El mayor encanto amor,* was chosen to inaugurate the splendid new Palacio del Buen Retiro in Madrid, and Calderón was honored for his distinguished service with initiation into the Order of Santiago in 1636.

From 1640 to 1642, Calderón fought for the crown in a war resulting from Portugal's and Catalonia's secession from Spanish rule. He was forced to withdraw from military duty after being wounded, and in 1645 he was employed by the Duke of Alba, probably as a secretary. About two years later he became the father of an illegitimate son.

Calderón took the vows of priesthood in the order of San Francisco in 1650 and assumed the post of chaplain in Reyes Nuevos in Toledo in 1653. Ten years later he returned to Madrid, where he was named honorary chaplain to the king. He also became chaplain to the Congregación de Presbíteros (natives of Madrid) in 1666. After his ordination Calderón continued to write dramas, mostly on religious themes, until the end of his life. Many of these plays were expressly written for performance in the Palacio del Buen Retiro. His last work, *Hado y divisa de Leonardo y Marfisa,* is dated 1680. Calderón died in Madrid on May 25, 1681.

Works. Calderón was a prolific author who wrote over 200 works. These fall into three major categories: *comedias, autos sacramentales,* and minor works, including *entreméses* and *zarzuelas.*

His largest group of plays are the *comedias* (over 100). In Spanish usage the term *comedia* includes all kinds of plays, ranging from comedy to tragedy. Many of Calderón's *comedias* reflect his highly intellectual bent in their thoughtful and objective treatment of philosophical, religious, and social themes. His religious *comedias* include *El mágico prodigioso* and *El príncipe constante.* Those on philosophic themes are headed by *La vida es sueño.* In such tragic *comedias as A secreto agravio, Secreta venganza,* and *El médico de su honra,* he dealt with love, honor, and jealousy. Contemporary manners in a light-hearted vein are the subject of *La dama duende* and *Mañanas de Abril y Mayo.* Among his comedies on historical themes are *La cisma de Inglaterra,* and those on mythological subjects include *Eco y Narciso.*

Calderón also wrote over 70 *autos sacramentales,* religious dramas in one act, which were usually performed on the Catholic feast day of Corpus Christi in order to dramatize the mystery of the Eucharist. These plays were on pagan as well as religious themes and were usually allegorical, personifying such concepts as the Senses, the Earth, and Guilt. Calderón was the acknowledged master of this form of drama. His most important *autos* are *El gran teatro del mundo, La cena de Baltasar, La siembra del Señor,* and *La devoción de la misa.*

The *entreméses,* or farces, and the *zarzuelas,* or musical stage pieces for which Calderón provided the dialogue, number about 20. His *entreméses* include *El dragoncillo* and *La casa de los linajes.* Among his outstanding *zarzuelas* are *El laurel de Apolo* and *La púrpura de la rosa.*

Criticism. It is ironic to note that Calderón was condemned by his countrymen in the 18th century, both as a corrupter of the theater and as an inventor of absurd theatrical machinations. This censure reached such proportions that his *autos sacramentales* were banned from performance in 1765. Calderón's genius, however, was recognized outside his own country by about 1800. He was greatly admired by many German romantic writers, notably Friedrich Schlegel and Goethe. Several 19th century English authors, including Shelley, also held him in high esteem. Today, Calderón's place as a foremost and influential Spanish dramatist is acknowledged in his own country as well as in the rest of the world.

ALVA V. EBERSOLE
Adelphi University

Bibliography

Calderón's complete works in Spanish have been collected by Angel Valbuena Prat and Angel Valbuena Briones, 3 vols. (Madrid 1952–1959).

Hilborn, Harry W., *A Chronology of the Plays of Don Pedro Calderón de la Barca* (Toronto 1938).

Parker, Alexander A., *The Allegorical Drama of Calderón* (New York 1943).

Sloman, Albert E., *The Dramatic Craftsmanship of Calderón: His Use of Earlier Plays* (Oxford 1958).

Wardropper, Bruce W., ed., *Critical Essays on the Theatre of Calderón* (New York 1965).

CALDWELL, Erskine Preston (1903–), American novelist and short-story writer, noted for his grotesque tragicomedies of life among the poor whites of the Deep South. He was born at White Oak, Ga., on Dec. 17, 1903, the son of an itinerant minister. As a young man, Caldwell took odd jobs throughout the South and intermittently attended the University of Virginia. In the 1920's he moved to Maine to devote himself to writing. For a time during World War II he was a newspaper correspondent in Russia.

Caldwell's fiction uses degradation and depravity both to evoke humor and to explore Southern realities. His most famous novel, *Tobacco Road* (1932; dramatic adaptation, 1933), about a family of Georgia sharecroppers, has become a part of American folklore. But his best work is the similar but more comic *God's Little Acre* (1933). Among Caldwell's other books are the novel *Claudelle Inglish* (1959); *Complete Stories* (1953); the documentary *You Have Seen Their Faces* (1936), for which his second wife, Margaret Bourke-White, supplied the photographs; and *In Search of Bisco* (1965), a travel book with social commentary.

ANTHONY CHANNELL HILFER, *University of Texas*

CALDWELL, James (1734–1781), American clergyman and patriot. He was born in Charlotte county, Va., in April 1734, and was ordained in 1761, becoming pastor of the First Presbyterian Church of Elizabethtown (Elizabeth), N. J. In 1776 he joined the New Jersey regiment as chaplain and later served in Washington's army as assistant commissary general. In the course of the American Revolution his church was burned by Tories and his wife was killed in a British invasion. During an attack on Springfield, N. J., on June 23, 1780, he used hymn book pages as wadding for guns. He was killed in a dispute with an American sentry at Elizabethtown on Nov. 24, 1781.

CALDWELL, Taylor (1900–), American novelist. Janet Taylor Caldwell was born in Manchester, England, on Sept. 7, 1900. She emigrated to the United States in 1907 and graduated from the University of Buffalo in 1931. In collaboration with her second husband, Marcus Reback, she wrote a number of best-selling novels, beginning with *Dynasty of Death* (1938).

Her own books, generally intricately plotted and suspenseful, have narrative drive and great vitality, but some critics have found her characters somewhat lacking in credibility. Her most important novels include *This Side of Innocence* (1946), *The Devil's Advocate* (1952), *Never Victorious, Never Defeated* (1954), *Dear and Glorious Physician* (1959), *The Listener* (1960), *A Prologue to Love* (1962), *The Late Clara Beame* (1964), and *A Pillar of Iron* (1965). She wrote other books under the pseudonym Max Reiner.

CALDWELL, a city in southwestern Idaho, the seat of Canyon county, is 28 miles (45 km) west of Boise. Situated on the Boise River, in a rich irrigated farming area, it is a trading and shipping center for farm produce and has creameries, meat-packing plants, stockyards, and fruit-packing and dehydrating plants. Caldwell is the site of the College of Idaho, a 4-year coeducational institution. Government is by mayor and council. Population: 14,219.

CALDWELL, a borough in New Jersey, is in Essex county, 9 miles (14 km) northwest of Newark. It has a few light industries but is chiefly a residential community. The birthplace of President Grover Cleveland is located here and has been maintained as a state museum since 1913. The borough is also the site of Caldwell College for Women. Caldwell is governed by a mayor and council. Population: 8,719.

CALEB WILLIAMS, kā′ləb, is the best-known novel of the English writer William Godwin. It was published in 1794 under the title *Things As They Are, or The Adventures of Caleb Williams.* The title character, a devoted servant of the respected country gentleman Falkland, discovers that his master has committed murder and allowed an innocent man to be executed for the crime. Williams leaves his job and, although he has no intention of revealing Falkland's secret, he is followed and persecuted by a henchman of the fearful and suspicious Falkland. Ultimately, Williams is forced to reveal the truth to protect himself, and Falkland confesses to his crime. Throughout the novel Godwin explores the psychology of class and contrasts the power of the privileged with the helplessness of the lowly.

CALEDONIA, kal-ə-dōn′yə, the ancient Roman name for the Scottish Highlands. The name was applied to the region north of the Antonine Wall, a defensive rampart built by the Romans in 142 A. D. from the Firth of Forth to the river Clyde. In poetry, the name *Caledonia* has been used to refer to the whole of Scotland.

CALEDONIAN CANAL, kal-ə-dō′nē-ən, a waterway that runs northeastward through the Great Glen of Scotland from the Atlantic Ocean to the North Sea. Designed to provide an alternative to the stormy route around the north of Scotland, the canal was begun in 1803 and opened in 1822, although it was not completed until 1847. It is now little used. Of its total length of 60 miles (96 km), only 22 miles (35 km) had to be dug to connect the Scottish lochs of Linnhe, Lochy, Oich, and Ness. Differences in altitude required the installation of 29 locks. The canal's minimum width is 110 feet (33 meters) and its depth, 14 feet (4 meters).

GORDON STOKES, *Author, "English Place-Names"*

CALEF, kā′ləf, **Robert** (1648?–1719), American writer on witchcraft. He was said to have been born in England about 1648 and to have become a cloth merchant in Boston, Mass., by 1688. His book *More Wonders of the Invisible World,* completed in 1697, was published in 1700 in London after being rejected by Boston printers. The work is not only a well-annotated account of the Salem witchcraft trials of 1692 but also a virulent attack on Cotton Mather, whom it accuses of having instigated the trials. The book's title satirizes the title of Mather's own book *Wonders of the Invisible World* (1693). Calef's work caused a furor in Boston, prompting a reply on Mather's part in the pamphlet *Some Few Remarks upon a Scandalous Book* (1701). Calef's work may have been an important factor in ending the already dying witchcraft craze, although he probably intended it primarily as a personal polemic against Cotton and Increase Mather. Calef died in Roxbury, Mass., on April 13, 1719.

BRITISH MUSEUM

The Babylonians used a lunar calendar. This tablet (shown in part) records the intervals from new moon to new moon during a 25-month period from 103 to 101 B. C.

CALENDAR, kal'ən-dər, any of a number of systems for keeping track of the days. A calendar is a collection of rules on which a convenient chronology can be based. In practice, a calendar may be in the form of a table, a book, or a series of sheets indicating the day of the week and the month and often the numerical position of the day within the year. A calendar often provides additional information, such as the dates of holidays and historical anniversaries, as well as astronomical data such as the phase of the moon, the length of the day, and times of sunrise, sunset, eclipses, and tides.

The term "calendar" derives from the Latin word *Kalendae,* which designated the first day of the month in Roman times. The efforts of various civilizations to create calendars have marked the beginnings of their astronomical studies. Once a calendar is established and it is used for a long time in recording events, it comes to be cherished by its users and is an integral part of their history. It is therefore difficult to revise a calendar system; even the best suggestions meet strong resistance.

1. The Measurement of Time

The basic calendar units are the day, month, and year, derived from the movements of the earth, the moon, and the sun, respectively.

Day. A day is measured by the rotation of the earth on its axis; the duration of one complete rotation with respect to the stars is called a *sidereal* (from the Latin *sidus,* "star") *day,* a unit of time that is important in astronomy. However, man's daily life is tied in most closely with the cycle of night and day and hence with the apparent motion of the sun in the sky; therefore, the *solar day* is the basis of the civil calendar. The solar day is longer than the sidereal day by about 4 minutes because the sun's position in the sky moves about 1 degree each day in the opposite direction to that of the apparent motion of the stars. This change in the sun's position is not uniform, so the calendar is based on the mean length of the solar day. The term "day," as henceforth used, will mean *civil* day—that is, the mean solar day, beginning at midnight. See also DAY.

Month. A *lunar month* (or *lunation*) is the time it takes the moon to complete a cycle of phases (1 synodical revolution of the moon). The lunar month has an average length of 29.5 days, but it may actually be 6 hours longer or shorter than this average. Observations of a great number of consecutive lunar months make it possible to determine the average length very precisely. The value obtained—29.5306 civil days—has been used in devising various calendars. There are several other kinds of months, such as the *sidereal, anomalistic,* and *draconitic months,* which have different lengths. See also MONTH.

Year. A year is a cycle of time that is less easy to determine. It corresponds to the cycle of the seasons and is the result of the sun's apparent motion through the constellations of the zodiac as the earth moves around the sun.

In ancient times, a year was thought to contain 360 days, but men came to realize that it actually averages about 365 days. The astronomical year is now defined by the passing of the sun over the earth's equator, from the Southern to the Northern Hemisphere. The instant when the center of the sun's disk crosses the equator is known as the *vernal equinox,* and the time interval between two vernal equinoxes is known as the *seasonal* or *tropical year.* Observation of two equinoxes a large number of years apart makes it possible to obtain a satisfactory determination of the average number of days in a year. This average—365.2422 days—will be considered as invariable. See also YEAR.

CONTENTS

Section	Page
1. The Measurement of Time	184
Day	184
Month	184
Year	184
Week	185
2. Kinds of Calendars	185
Lunar	185
Lunisolar	185
Solar	185
3. Ancient Calendars	185
Egyptian	185
Babylonian, Assyrian, and Chaldean	186
Hebrew	186
Chinese	186
Mayan	186
4. Western Calendars	186
Greek	186
Roman	187
Moslem	188
5. Eras	189
Christian Era	189
Julian Period	189
6. Calendar Reform	190
Fixed	190
Universal	190
Perpetual	190
7. Church Calendar	191

Week. The week is another calendar unit that is in use today in almost all civilized nations. Its length of 7 days relates it to the phases of the moon, but in reality it is an artificial unit of time. It was once thought that the week was in universal use in the ancient world, but actually the Hebrews were the first to employ this unit (although they may have borrowed it from Chaldean astrologers). Thus, according to the book of Genesis, the world was created in 6 days, and God rested on the 7th. In the Western world, the use of the week dates only from the 3d century A. D. In most languages the names of the days of the week are associated with the 7 moving celestial objects that were known to the ancients: the sun, the moon, Mars, Mercury, Jupiter, Venus, and Saturn. See also WEEK.

2. Kinds of Calendars

Three basic kinds of calendars have been developed by man. These are the lunar, lunisolar, and solar calendars, based on the phases of the moon or the apparent motion of the sun.

Lunar Calendars. The oldest kind of calendar, and formerly the most widely used, is the lunar calendar. In this calendar, the civil month is approximately the same length as the actual lunar month, and the first day of each civil month is approximately the day on which the new moon occurs. A person who is unable to read a calendar can still tell the day of the month fairly accurately by observing the phase of the moon. There is no tropical year in lunar calendars.

To establish agreement between the civil month—composed of a whole number of days—and the lunar month of 29.5306 days, an early solution was to have civil months that were alternately 29 and 30 days long. This made for an average civil month of 29.5 days—a lag of 0.0306 day behind the actual lunar month. Later lunar calendars generally grouped 12 civil months in a *lunar year* of 354 days; the year, therefore, lagged behind the cycle of the moon's phases by 12 times 0.0306, or 0.3672 days. One way to compensate fairly precisely for this lag was to insert 1 day in the calendar—that is, to *intercalate* 1 day—every 3 years. Alternative solutions were to intercalate 3 days over a period of 8 years, or 7 days in 19 years, or 11 days in 30 years. All of these solutions were utilized; and the last, which remains in favor among Muslims, leaves almost nothing to be desired in terms of precision. The choice of the lengthened year or years in any of these cycles was fairly arbitrary; the intercalated day was usually added to the last short month of the year to make it easier to remember.

Lunisolar Calendars. Once the significance of the solar year of 365.25 days came to be recognized, an exact relationship was sought between the solar year and the lunar month. The problem was how best to establish a periodic relationship, since the lunar year is approximately 11 days shorter than the solar year. One of the first solutions was to add a month to the year every 3 years. Alternatively, if 3 months are added to 8 lunar years, or 7 months to 19 lunar years, the adjustment closely approximates 8 or 19 solar years, respectively. Both the 8-year, or *octennial*, cycle and the 19-year, or *Metonic*, cycle were employed by the Greeks. The Metonic cycle is fairly precise and is still used in ecclesiastical calendar computations.

Solar Calendars. In modern times the lunar month has been largely rejected, in order to obtain better agreement between the civil month and the solar year. The 12 months are retained but are no longer lunar, and the phases of the moon may fall on any day of the month. Only the value of 365.2422 days as the average length of the year is fundamental to the establishment of a solar calendar.

The fraction 0.2422 is close to 0.25. Therefore, a year of 365 days came to be used, with an additional day intercalated every 4th year to compensate for the fraction (4 times 0.25 day); the intercalary year is known as a *leap year*. This solution was the one adopted in the Julian calendar. However, since the fraction being compensated for is actually 0.2422, not 0.25, the addition of 1 whole day every 4 years makes for an excess of 0.25 minus 0.2422, or 0.0078 day per year, or about 3 days every 4 centuries. The Gregorian reform, which resulted in the modern calendar, consisted of eliminating this remaining discrepancy. There is a residual error of 0.0003 day per year, but it is considered negligible.

3. Ancient Calendars

The kind of calendar adopted by a civilization had a great influence on the development of astronomy in that civilization. If a lunar calendar was used, it sufficed to determine the length of the lunar month fairly exactly; if a solar calendar was used, it sufficed to know the approximate length of the year. Slight alterations of such calendars could easily be made empirically, as needed. To develop a lunisolar calendar, however, it was essential to estimate these units of time much more precisely. Only those ancient civilizations that adopted a lunisolar calendar made real advances in astronomy.

Egyptian Calendar. During the first stages of Egyptian civilization, more than 10,000 years ago, a crude calendar consisting of 12 months of 30 days each was developed. The calendar year thus contained only 360 days. About the year 4000 B. C., however, 5 supplementary days were added at the end of each year; the resulting 365-day year, or *vague year*, fell behind the solar year 1 day every 4 years. This calendar made no use of intercalations and constituted a scale of unvarying length; this was most important, for it served the Greek astronomers and was still used by Copernicus in the 16th century A. D.

Sothic Period. However, the calendar was inconvenient in that a holiday with a fixed date (such as New Year's day) had to make a complete cycle of the seasons over a period of nearly 15 centuries. That is, since the holiday moved back 1 day every 4 solar years, it came back to its original position in the seasons only after a period of 4 times 365.25, or 1,461 years. This period was called the Sothic period, from the Egyptian name Sothis for the star Sirius, because the Egyptians had observed that the flooding of the Nile began each year at the time of the heliacal rising of Sirius. (The heliacal rising of a star is the first day the star can be seen before sunrise, in the light of dawn.) The Egyptian calendar was divided into 3 seasons of 4 months each, and every 1,461 years the heliacal rising of Sirius fell on New Year's day—thus marking the beginning of a new Sothic period.

In 238 B. C. an edict of King Ptolemy III attempted to correct the vague year by adding another supplementary day every 4 years (the solution later adopted by the Romans and known as the Julian reform). However, the Egyptian people refused to accept the new regulation; for when a third Sothic period ended in Egypt in 139 A. D., the vague year continued to be used afterward.

Babylonian, Assyrian, and Chaldean Calendar. For the civilizations of the Tigris-Euphrates valley, the year began in the spring with the month Nisannu and consisted of 12 lunar months. Each month began in the evening, as soon as the crescent of the new moon appeared. The months were alternately 30 and 29 days long, and the 354-day calendar year fell approximately 1 month behind the solar year by the end of 3 years. Consequently, an extra month was usually added at such times by order of the reigning king. The time for such an intercalation was determined by observing a star whose heliacal rising occurred—at least in principle—in a designated month. Unfortunately, the intercalations were often poorly regulated; it is not uncommon to find records of 2 consecutive 13-month years. Above all, the intercalations were unreliably recorded. Starting in 380 B. C., however, they were codified, with 7 intercalations being made during a 19-year period—the same period as the Metonic cycle that had been developed in Greece 50 years previously. It is not known whether the Babylonians discovered the cycle themselves or borrowed it from the Greeks.

Hebrew Calendar. The ancient Hebrews were not very interested in astronomical studies and seem to have adopted their empirical lunisolar calendar from that of their Babylonian neighbors. The months in the Jewish calendar were either full (30 days) or deficient (29 days) and were regulated as much as possible by lunar events. Intercalations were, for a long time, arbitrarily decided upon by government authorities or, in the first 3 centuries A. D., by the Sanhedrin (the supreme judicial tribunal of the Jews). It was not until the 4th century A. D. that the Jews adopted the 19-year period—the Metonic cycle—in which 7 months are intercalated in order to maintain agreement with the solar year.

This cycle is still used today in the Jewish religious calendar. The additional months are added to the 3d, 6th, 8th, 11th, 14th, 17th, and 19th years of the 19-year period. They are inserted in the middle of the year and repeat the 6th month. Ordinary years may have 353, 354, or 355 days; intercalary years may be 383, 384, or 385 days long. The system offers some other inconvenient complications, in that for religious reasons the year cannot begin on a Sunday, Wednesday, or Friday. The day begins at sunset of the preceding civil day.

The Hebrews can be considered to have established the week as a unit of time. The pivot of the week is the sabbath, or day of rest, which corresponds to the Saturday of the modern calendar.

Chinese Calendar. The ancient Chinese calendar was lunisolar, and the ordinary year contained 12 lunar months. When a 13th month was added in order to reestablish agreement with the solar year, the intercalary year was called a *full year*. The Chinese year began with the lunar month during which the sun entered the zodiacal sign of Pisces; thus, New Year's day could fall between January 20 and February 19. For recording historical events, two cycles were used, both of them 60 years long; but in civil life, years were dated from the time the reigning emperor ascended the throne.

Mayan Calendar. One of the rare preserved manuscripts from the Mayan civilization in the Western Hemisphere provides dates for certain eclipses that occurred in antiquity. These dates, however, were probably the result of calculations rather than actual observations, and the antiquity of Mayan astronomy is therefore not proven by such documents. On the other hand, the very existence of the calculations implies a high level of astronomical achievement, which in turn indicates a long tradition behind it.

Most of the stone-engraved Mayan inscriptions relating to astronomy are dates. The dates extend from the middle of the 3d to the middle of the 6th centuries A. D., but the Mayan method of calculating time was still in use in Mexico when the Spaniards arrived. The days were placed in groups of 20 to make a kind of month, or *uinal;* and 18 consecutive uinals formed a vague year, or *tun*, of 360 days. A group of 20 such years was called a *katun*, and katuns were in turn grouped in 20's. Alternatively, the Mayans also arranged their days within a year that was rounded out to 365 days by adding 5 supplementary days. Finally, days were also arranged within a *tzolkin*, a 260-day period made up of 13 units of 20 days each. The Mayans did not attempt to link up all these different cycles but allowed the 3 different chronological systems to follow their respective courses.

4. Western Calendars

Many ancient civilizations contributed to the development of the calendar that is in worldwide use today, but its basic form may be said to derive from the calendar used by the Romans. Two other Western calendars, the Greek and the Muslim, should also be considered.

Greek Calendar. The early Greeks first used a lunar calendar in which months of 30 and of 29 days were alternated. For a long time the adjustment of the calendar to the cycle of the seasons was considered unimportant. The course of agricultural events and the probabilities of rain or fair weather were ascribed to the heliacal rising or setting of various easily recognized constellations. For centuries such practical everyday calendars, or *parapegms*, successfully served the needs of the Greeks.

The Greek day began at sunset. Ten days constituted a decade; but in deficient (29-day) months, the 3d decade of the month contained only 9 days. When the Greeks did adjust their calendar in order to obtain periodic agreement with the seasons, by intercalating a 13th month, the intercalation was made arbitrarily. Each community had its own calendar.

Starting in the 6th century B. C., however, Greek astronomers proposed a number of increasingly precise cycles that would adjust the month to the year. The most famous was the octennial cycle, a period of 8 years in which 3 months were intercalated; this cycle remained in use for a long time. In 433 B. C. the Athenian astronomer Meton published his discovery that 19 solar years contain 235 lunations, or lunar months. The admiring Athenians had the Metonic cycle engraved in gold on the temple of Athena, and the unit of 1 year in the cycle took the name *golden number*. It seems, however, that the precise discoveries of Greek astronomy—either of

Meton or of Hipparchus (who was the first to observe, in 130 B. C., that the solar year is not exactly 365.25 days long)—were not incorporated into the Greek civil calendar. The octennial cycle continued to be used instead.

Roman Calendar. The early Romans used a lunar month in the calendar. It alternated between 30 and 29 days in length. The civil year was composed of only 10 months and therefore of 295 days. The first month of the year was March. The 7th, 8th, 9th, and 10th months were logically named September, October, November, and December, respectively—Latin words indicating the position of these months in the year.

According to legend, it was during the reign of Numa Pompilius (about 700 B. C.) that the months of January and February were added as 11th and 12th months to the year. February contained only 28 days. Later in Roman history the months ceased to be lunar. The 2d, 4th. 7th, and 9th months were allotted 30 days, and the rest (except for February) were 31 days long.

The months of the Roman calendar were divided in a singular fashion, and the naming of these divisions was amazingly illogical. The *calends* occurred on the 1st day of the month, the *nones* on the 5th or 7th day, and the *ides* on the 13th or 15th day. Like schoolboys counting the days before a vacation, the Romans characterized each day by its distance from the period that would follow. Thus, as soon as the calends were over, the days were referred to in terms of the nones; and when the nones were passed, the days were counted in terms of the ides. After the ides, the days then referred to the calends of the following month. The day that preceded a period was called an *eve*; but, peculiarly enough, the day preceding the eve was not numbered as the 2d but as the 3d day before the period, and so forth.

ROMAN NOMENCLATURE FOR JANUARY

Date	Name
1	Calends
2	4th day before the nones
3	3d day before the nones
4	Eve of the nones
5	nones
6	8th day before the ides
7	7th day before the ides
13	Ides
14	19th day before the calends
15	18th day before the calends
31	Eve of the calends of February

Compounding all these singularities, Roman emperors also had the right to interfere as they pleased with the calendar. Such interventions became a means of shortening or prolonging certain magistracies. Eventually, the tabulation of the days in Rome reached a state of extraordinary disorder.

Julian Reform. The reformation of the Roman calendar was undertaken by Julius Caesar, who sent for the Greek astronomer Sosigenes to serve as an adviser. The calendar was changed in 46 B. C., which came to be known as "the last year of confusion." First of all, it was decided that the vernal equinox would fall on March 25; to achieve this, 85 days were added to the year 46. The civil year was thereafter fixed at 365 days. The reformers realized that the solar year had 365.25 days, but they felt that the year would remain in agreement with the seasons if an additional day was intercalated every 4 years. The extra day was not added to the end of February, as it is in the modern calendar, but was inserted after February 24. The 24th was, in Roman terminology, the 6th of the calends of March, so the intercalated day was in effect a second "6th"—hence the Latin term *bissextile* for the added day.

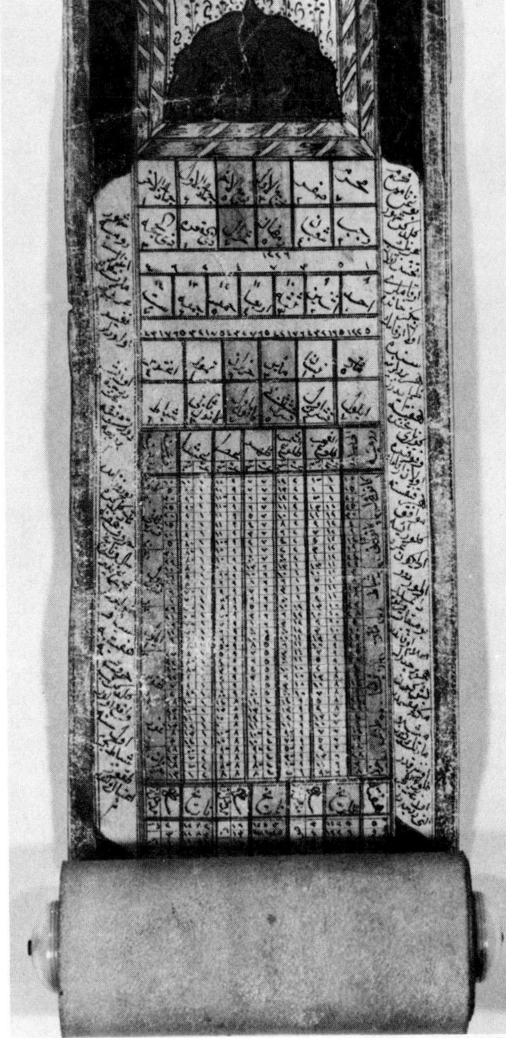

EDWARD CLARK STREETER COLLECTION OF WEIGHTS AND MEASURES, YALE MEDICAL LIBRARY

A 19th-century Muslim calendar. Months and weeks are listed above; sunrise, sunset, and prayer times below.

The Julian reform also reestablished January 1, the day on which the consuls took over their duties, as the first day of the year; January 1, 45 B. C., thus inaugurates the Julian calendar. A discrepancy in names was retained, however, in that the months of September through December still had their former names although they were now the 9th through the 12th months of the year.

Council of Nicaea. The Julian year of 365.25 days, of course, is actually a little longer than the solar year of 365.2422 days. The difference amounts to 0.0078 day per year, or about 3 days every 4 centuries. It is now apparent, therefore, that by the time the first ecumenical council was held at Nicaea in 325 A. D., a lag of about 3 days in the Julian calendar was to be expected. (As the actual lag was 4 days, Sosigenes must have made an error of 24 hours in his determination of the vernal equinox in 46 B. C.) Since the actual length of the solar year was not yet known, however, the council attributed the entire lag of 4 days to Sosigenes; and when it moved the date of the equinox back from March 25 to March 21, it believed that this date would henceforth be stable. The celebration of Easter was then determined on the basis of March 21.

Gregorian Reform. Naturally enough, the Julian calendar continued to deviate. Easter, a spring holiday, eventually would have ended up in the middle of summer. By the time of Pope Gregory XIII in the late 16th century, the deviation amounted to 10 days; the equinox of 1582 fell on March 11.

The true length of the solar year was by that time known, and Gregory undertook to reform the calendar accordingly. He cut 10 days from the year 1582 so that, starting the following year, the equinox would again fall on March 21. The day after Thursday, October 4, 1582, thus became Friday, October 15. (Note that the continuity of the days of the week was maintained.) This gap continued to separate the Julian from the Gregorian calendar where the latter was not adopted. Gregory then promulgated an edict establishing that 3 days would be dropped from the calendar every 400 years, thus correcting the discrepancy between the Julian calendar and the solar year. It was decreed that years with a date ending in two zeros would not be leap years, except when the first two digits were divisible by 4. Thus, in the old Julian calendar, 1600, 1700, 1800, 1900, 2000, and so forth would be leap years. In the Gregorian calendar, 1700, 1800, and 1900 were not leap years; but 1600 was, and so will be 2000. This elimination of 3 days every 4 centuries is clear and simple.

There is a remaining inexactness in that the Gregorian year is equal to an average of 365.2425 days and is therefore longer than the solar year by 0.0003 day per year. The excess amounts to 3 days every 10,000 years. But other factors come into play over such long periods. The solar year has been taken here as being exactly 365.2422 days long, but in reality it varies in length (although very slowly). The law governing this variation is imperfectly known. In addition, the rotation of the earth on its axis is subject to variations, some of which cannot be predicted. It would be futile to anticipate the calendar corrections that might be necessary in 3,000 to 4,000 years, when far greater disparities may intervene in the meantime. The Gregorian calendar therefore leaves nothing to be desired in its precision.

Application of the Gregorian Calendar. Not all countries applied the Gregorian reform simultaneously. France and the Netherlands adopted it in December 1582; the Catholic states of Germany, in 1584; and Poland, in 1586. The Protestant states in Germany and Switzerland accepted the reform in 1700, and England (and its colonies) and Sweden in 1752—by which time 11 days had to be eliminated, rather than 10. Lastly, the orthodox countries preserved the old style Julian calendar until the 20th century, by which time there was a 13-day lag. Thus a date would be written January 10/23, 1920—the 10th in old style, the 23d in new style.

PERPETUAL CALENDAR

Table 1 shows which calendar is to be used in Table 2 to find the weekday of a given date. (Note special calendars for January and February of leap years.) For example: what day will Nov. 23, 2013, be on the Gregorian calendar? On Table 1, read *across* from the year number in hundreds (20) and *down* from the last 2 digits (13). Calendar No. 2 is indicated. Using this heading in Table 2, it is found that Nov. 23, 2013, will fall on Saturday.

TABLE 1

YEAR 2nd 2 Digits

00	01	02	03		04	05
06	07		08	09	10	11
	12	13	14	15		16
17	18	19		20	21	22
23		24	25	26	27	
28	29	30	31		32	33
34	35		36	37	38	39
	40	41	42	43		44
45	46	47		48	49	50
51		52	43	54	55	
56	57	58	59		60	61
62	63		64	65	66	67
	68	69	70	71		72
73	74	75		76	77	78
79		80	81	82	83	
84	85	86	87		88	89
90	91		92	93	94	95
	96	97	98	99		

YEAR 1st 2 Digits

JULIAN CALENDAR			4 OCT. 1582	GREGORIAN CALENDAR 15 OCT. 1582				No. of Calendar						
0	7	14			17	21	25	5	6	7	1	2	3	4
1	8	15						4	5	6	7	1	2	3
2	9	16			18	22	26	3	4	5	6	7	1	2
3	10	17						2	3	4	5	6	7	1
4	11	18		15	19	23	27	1	2	3	4	5	6	7
5	12	19		16	20	24	28	7	1	2	3	4	5	6
6	13	20						6	7	1	2	3	4	5

By now, every country has accepted the Gregorian calendar, at least for civil usage. The Gregorian calendar can therefore be considered universal today; and, in relation to possible new reforms, it would be wise to ensure that this unanimity—which took more than 4 centuries to realize—is preserved.

Muslim Calendar. Finally, mention should be made of the Muslim calendar. It had 12 lunar months of 29 or 30 days each, with no intercalated months. No attempt was made to adjust to the solar year. As a result, a fixed holiday such as New Year's day went through a complete cycle of the seasons over a period of 33 years. The calendar was adjusted to the exact lunar month, however, by the intercalation of 11 days over a period of 30 calendar years. Thus, there were 19 common years with 354 days each, and 11 intercalary years with 355 days each; the 2d, 5th, 7th, 10th, 13th, 16th, 18th, 21st, 24th, 26th, and 29th years of the 30-year cycle were the intercalary years. This fixed cycle of 360 lunar months contained 10,361 days and erred by only 1 day every 2,500 years.

However, this fixed calendar is not used for religious purposes by the Muslims. The religious month starts when the crescent of the new moon appears. This occurrence is usually 2 days after

TABLE 2
The Seven Possible Calendar Arrangements of Dates and Days

	Days of the Week		Days of the Week		
Calendar 1	M T W T F S S	M T W T F S S	M T W T F S S	M T W T F S S	M T W T F S S
Calendar 2	T W T F S S M	T W T F S S M	T W T F S S M	T W T F S S M	T W T F S S M
Calendar 3	W T F S S M T	W T F S S M T	W T F S S M T	W T F S S M T	W T F S S M T
Calendar 4	T F S S M T W	T F S S M T W	T F S S M T W	T F S S M T W	T F S S M T W
Calendar 5	F S S M T W T	F S S M T W T	F S S M T W T	F S S M T W T	F S S M T W T
Calendar 6	S S M T W T F	S S M T W T F	S S M T W T F	S S M T W T F	S S M T W T F
Calendar 7	S M T W T F S	S M T W T F S	S M T W T F S	S M T W T F S	S M T W T F S
	JANUARY	APRIL	JULY	OCTOBER	LEAP YEARS
	1 2 3 4 5 6 7 8 9 10 11 12 13 14 15 16 17 18 19 20 21 22 23 24 25 26 27 28 29 30 31	1 2 3 4 5 6 7 8 9 10 11 12 13 14 15 16 17 18 19 20 21 22 23 24 25 26 27 28 29 30	1 2 3 4 5 6 7 8 9 10 11 12 13 14 15 16 17 18 19 20 21 22 23 24 25 26 27 28 29 30 31	1 2 3 4 5 6 7 8 9 10 11 12 13 14 15 16 17 18 19 20 21 22 23 24 25 26 27 28 29 30 31	CALENDARS OF JAN. & FEB. TO BE USED FOR LEAP YEARS
	FEBRUARY	MAY	AUGUST	NOVEMBER	LEAP JANUARY
	1 2 3 4 5 6 7 8 9 10 11 12 13 14 15 16 17 18 19 20 21 22 23 24 25 26 27 28	1 2 3 4 5 6 7 8 9 10 11 12 13 14 15 16 17 18 19 20 21 22 23 24 25 26 27 28 29 30 31	1 2 3 4 5 6 7 8 9 10 11 12 13 14 15 16 17 18 19 20 21 22 23 24 25 26 27 28 29 30 31	1 2 3 4 5 6 7 8 9 10 11 12 13 14 15 16 17 18 19 20 21 22 23 24 25 26 27 28 29 30	1 2 3 4 5 6 7 8 9 10 11 12 13 14 15 16 17 18 19 20 21 22 23 24 25 26 27 28 29 30 31
	MARCH	JUNE	SEPTEMBER	DECEMBER	LEAP FEBRUARY
	1 2 3 4 5 6 7 8 9 10 11 12 13 14 15 16 17 18 19 20 21 22 23 24 25 26 27 28 29 30 31	1 2 3 4 5 6 7 8 9 10 11 12 13 14 15 16 17 18 19 20 21 22 23 24 25 26 27 28 29 30	1 2 3 4 5 6 7 8 9 10 11 12 13 14 15 16 17 18 19 20 21 22 23 24 25 26 27 28 29 30	1 2 3 4 5 6 7 8 9 10 11 12 13 14 15 16 17 18 19 20 21 22 23 24 25 26 27 28 29 30 31	1 2 3 4 5 6 7 8 9 10 11 12 13 14 15 16 17 18 19 20 21 22 23 24 25 26 27 28 29

the occurrence of the new moon according to the fixed lunar calendar. The Muslims also indicate the name of the day along with the date, however, so the disparity is not too inconvenient. The religious day of the Muslims begins at sunset on the night preceding the civil day. Years in the religious calendar are numbered from the Hegira—the flight of Mohammed—starting with Friday, July 16, 622 A. D. Ramadan, or fasting, begins on the 273d day of the fixed calendar.

5. Eras

Calendar years may be numbered according to their position within one of the broader chronological systems called *eras*. That is, an era starts at a fixed point in history, and the years preceding or following are numbered from that point. Numerous eras have been used throughout history, and several—such as the Christian era—are still in use. They have one common characteristic: they came into actual use long after the time of their theoretical starting points. Therefore the dates of events at the beginning of, and especially prior to, an era are convenient expedients but have no historical validity.

Christian Era. For example, the Christian era was proposed in 532 A. D. by a monk, Denys le Petit, who died in Rome in 540. It did not come into general use in the West until 3 or 4 centuries later. The fixed point of this era is the birth of Christ. From his research, Denys fixed this date at December 25 of the Roman year 753. However, chronologists have moved the beginning of the Christian era to Saturday, January 1. Moreover, the church now places the birth of Christ several years before the date adopted by Denys, in accordance with texts relating to Herod's death.

It should be noted that for historians there is no year 0 in the Christian era. The year preceding the era is called 1 B. C. Leap years would then occur in 1 B. C., 5 B. C., 9 B. C., and so forth, and the rule of divisibility by 4 would no longer apply. Astronomers therefore employ an algebraic notation in order to avoid errors that otherwise might be made in calculations. Unlike historians, they indicate a year 0; the preceding years 5, 9, 13, and so forth then become -4, -8, and -12. The leap year rule is once again applicable, and calculations are simplified.

Among the many other known eras are those of Rome, the Olympiads of Greece, and the Muslim era, which dates from the Hegira.

Julian Period. In order to compare distant dates it is often convenient to use the Julian period of 7,980 Julian years. This cycle of time was devised by the French scholar Joseph Scaliger in 1582, by multiplying the three numbers 28, 15, and 19. These numbers represent the periods, in years, of three elements of the ecclesiastical calendar (see Section 7). The 3d number, 19, is of course the length of the Metonic cycle, by which agreement is maintained between the phases of the moon and the dates of the year. The period of 15 years is the Roman cycle of *indiction,* and the 28-year period is called the *dominical* cycle; neither is of astronomical significance.

The Julian period begins in the year 4713 B.C. (or −4712, as written by astronomers), when the three variables involved had a value of 1. In the course of the period, one and only one year can be expressed by the same numbers in the three cycles. The Julian day begins at midday, starting on Monday, January 1, −4712 (Julian). The period will end on Monday, January 1, 3268, at noon. (The Gregorian date will be January 23.) The days that have been completed since the beginning of the period are numbered, and most almanacs indicate the Julian day corresponding to each date. For example, on November 21, 1967, at noon Greenwich time, 2,439,816 Julian days within the period of 7,980 Julian years were completed.

6. Calendar Reform

The present calendar, despite its accuracy, still has several defects. For example, the number of days in a month varies by about 12%. Business and industrial statistics, in order to be comparable from month to month, must therefore be adjusted constantly. Also, the day of the week of a given date changes from year to year. Conversely, the date of a given day, such as the third Tuesday of the month, varies according to the month and the year. The determination of a past date or day is difficult without the calendar of the year concerned. Many reforms have been proposed to remedy these defects. Two such reforms still have many supporters: the fixed calendar and the universal calendar. In both reforms, the calendar year contains 52 weeks and only 364 days. The 365th day is blank. It is not named or counted, and would be a general holiday. Every 4 years a second blank day has to be added.

Fixed Calendar. In the fixed calendar, the year consists of 13 equal months of 28 days. The months are identical, and each contains 4 weeks. The simplicity (and the monotony) of this calendar is extreme. However, the addition of a 13th month and the shortening of the others are, for many, too radical to be accepted. There is also the superstition about the number 13, but, more important, the number is not convenient for calculations because it is not evenly divisible. Religious and civil groups have opposed the abandonment of the 12-month system. Astronomers and navigators, who associate the 12 months of the year and the 24 hours of the day (1 month corresponds to 2 sidereal hours), also reject the 13-month proposal of the fixed calendar.

Universal Calendar. In the proposed reform known as the universal calendar, the year also has 52 weeks, but the month is no longer an exact multiple of the week. There are 12 months and 4 identical quarterly periods of 13 weeks or 91 days. Each quarterly period includes one month of 31 days.

A UNIVERSAL CALENDAR

	S	M	T	W	T	F	S
January	1	2	3	4	5	6	7
April	8	9	10	11	12	13	14
July	15	16	17	18	19	20	21
October	22	23	24	25	26	27	28
	29	30	31	.	.	.	.
February	.	.	.	1	2	3	4
May	5	6	7	8	9	10	11
August	12	13	14	15	16	17	18
November	19	20	21	22	23	24	25
	26	27	28	29	30	.	.
March	.	.	.	.	.	1	2
June	3	4	5	6	7	8	9
September	10	11	12	13	14	15	16
December	17	18	19	20	21	22	23
	24	25	26	27	28	29	30

Every month in the universal calendar has 26 working days. The fact that the months of each quarterly period begin with Sunday, Wednesday, and Friday, respectively, is no inconvenience, because the day of the week of any date can still be immediately determined. These advantages are obtained with minimal calendar changes.

The disadvantage of the proposed reform lies in the use of blank days. Also, some nations and groups are strongly opposed to any such reform, and it would seem unprofitable to substitute an annoying diversity for the unanimity that currently exists in civil usage. Actually, the rapidity of jet airplane travel, the time-zone differences, and the conventions relating to date changes during voyages all make such objections less valid. However, the use of blank days would still present dangers to chronological exactitude, because the intercalations of blank days in various countries might be poorly synchronized.

Finally, one of the greatest annoyances of the current calendar is that Easter vacillates between March 22 and April 25. This variation is inconvenient because school and other vacation periods are generally tied in with Easter. However, the church could easily eliminate this inconvenience without waiting for any calendar reform, by making Easter fall on the first Sunday in April or some other fixed day.

Perpetual Calendar. The term "perpetual calendar" is given to any system that makes it possible to determine the day of the week for any given date, whether in the Julian or Gregorian system. In drawing up such a calendar, there are only 7 possible calendar variations needed for ordinary years; for leap years, special months for January and February are substituted in these variations. In the simplest form of universal calendar, the entire year of the date that is being sought is shown at a glance, along with the 7 possible calendars of days of the week.

PAUL COUDERC, *Paris Observatory*

Bibliography

Bureau des Longitudes, *Annuaire,* pp. 153–169 (Paris 1967).
Chamberlain, Joseph M., *Time and the Stars* (New York 1964).
Colson, F. H., *The Week* (New York and London 1926).
Couderc, Paul, *Le calendrier,* 3d ed. (Paris 1961).
Ginzel, Friedrich K., *Handbuch der mathematischen und technischen Chronologie,* vol. 3 (Leipzig 1914).
Kubitschek, Wilhelm, *Grundriss der antiken Zeitrechnung* (Munich 1928).
Nautical Almanac Offices of the United Kingdom and the United States of America, *Explanatory Supplement to the Astronomical Ephemeris and the American Ephemeris and Nautical Almanac,* pp. 407–442 (London 1961).
Nilsson, Martin P., *Primitive Time-Reckoning* (Lund, Sweden, 1920).
Parker, Richard A., *The Calendars of Ancient Egypt* (Chicago 1950).
Parker, Richard A., and Dubberstein, Waldo H., *Babylonian Chronology, 629 B. C.–A. D. 45* (Providence, R. I., 1956).

7. Church Calendar

The church calendar is a method of dividing time into certain periods to express the rhythm in the celebration of Christian faith and to assure some regularity in Christian worship. Like the earliest religious calendars of ancient agricultural civilizations, the church calendar has links with nature cycles. Ancient peoples determined these cycles by lunar and solar calculations, and later, in order to facilitate the spread of Christianity, the church set many of its festivals on the dates of pagan celebrations of seasonal changes.

Early Christian Calendars. Because Christianity is rooted in Mosaic traditions, the most primitive church calendar derived in large measure from the Hebrew calendar. The Hebrew 7-day week ending on the Sabbath and the Passover festival celebrated at the full moon following the spring equinox were focal points of the early Christian calendar. The Crucifixion and Resurrection of Jesus occurred during Passover, and Easter became the pivotal festival of the early church. Christians shifted the sacred character of the Hebrew Sabbath on Saturday to Sunday, the first day of the week and the day of the resurrection of Jesus, known as the "Lord's Day." Easter, like Passover, was a movable feast, occurring as early as March 22 and as late as April 25. Two other days, Pentecost, a movable holiday falling 50 days after Easter, celebrating the descent of the Holy Spirit, and Epiphany, a feast fixed on January 6, commemorating the visit of the Magi, the baptism of Jesus, and the working of Jesus' first miracle, became important for early Christians.

Throughout the Roman Empire, various congregations developed their own calendars and established days to commemorate their own particular martyrs and saints. Confusion arising from the diversity of calendars was compounded by the Roman practice of governing civil life by the Julian calendar. Christians established fixed festivals by this imperial calendar, and at the Council of Nicaea (325 A.D.) the church accepted the Julian calendar as the basis for reckoning ecclesiastical dates. At Nicaea it was also decided that Easter should always fall on a Sunday, the day of the Resurrection.

By the mid-4th century A.D., the earliest celebrations had begun to expand into the seasonal cycles that are now the division points in the church calendar. An entire Easter cycle including Ascension and preceded by a Lenten season developed around Easter and Pentecost, and Epiphany became the pivotal point of a Christmas cycle preceded by an Advent season, with Christmas set on December 25 on the Julian calendar. At about the same time, Eastern and Western churches began to differ on the subject of which holidays were major, and this difference has continued.

Gregorian Reform and Aftermath. Inaccuracies in the Julian calendar led to the promulgation of calendar reform by Pope Gregory XIII in 1582. Confusion persisted, however, both between East and West and within Western churches themselves. Because of the importance of the Council, the Orthodox church in the East continued to set fixed feasts by the Julian calendar, 13 days behind the Gregorian calendar, and the Greek and most Orthodox churches did not adopt Gregorian reform until 1924. The Russian Orthodox and some Old Calendarists, however, still celebrate fixed feasts according to the Julian calendar.

MAJOR DATES IN THE CHRISTIAN YEAR

Advent Season—from the Sunday nearest St. Andrew's Day, November 30 to Christmas
Immaculate Conception of the Virgin Mary—December 8 (December 21 in Julian Calendar)
Christmas Season—from Christmas to January 13
Christmas—December 25 (January 7)
Feast of the Circumcision—January 1 (January 14)
Epiphany—January 6 (January 19)
Septuagesima Sunday—9 weeks before Easter
Lenten Season—from Ash Wednesday, 40 days before Easter, to Easter
The Annunciation to the Virgin Mary—March 25
Holy Week—from Palm Sunday to Easter
Good Friday—the Friday before Easter
Easter Season—from Easter to Ascension Day
Easter Sunday—the first Sunday after the full moon on or next after the 21st of March
Ascension Day—Thursday, 40 days after Easter
Pentecost or Whitsunday—Sunday, 50 days after Easter
Trinity Sunday—the Sunday after Pentecost
Corpus Christi—Thursday after Trinity Sunday
Assumption of the Virgin Mary—August 15 (August 28)
All Saints Day—November 1

Note: The dates shown are selected from the Western calendar. The Roman Catholic and Eastern churches observe many other days, including numerous saints' days. The Anglican and Lutheran churches retain some saints' days in their calendars. See references listed under *Further Reading*.

In the West, the Protestant Reformation in the 16th century encouraged a desire to develop particular Protestant festivals in an atmosphere of hostility to Roman Catholicism. Because of this, the Gregorian reform was not adopted in England or the American colonies until 1752 and in Germany until 1775. Among Anglicans and Lutherans, the older ecclesiastical celebrations were continued, with the elimination of festivals considered unwarranted by the teachings of Jesus, and with a wide variation in days celebrating the Virgin Mary, martyrs, and saints. Within other Protestant churches, such as Reformed, or Presbyterian, churches and the more radical Congregationalist, Baptist, and Quaker churches, the church calendar was almost completely discarded. Primarily, Protestants celebrated the "Lord's Day" after the custom of the early Christians. Some employed a church calendar to assure the systematic reading of Scripture and preaching of basic Christian doctrines. Feasts of thanksgiving and fasts of repentance were often set aside as the occasion demanded.

Gradually, however, Protestants returned to the use of a regular, rhythmic church calendar, and as liturgical renewal among Protestants has proceeded, there has been an increasingly greater utilization of the older church calendar. In the United States, a programmatic church calendar has been developed to mark special ethical concerns, such as Race Relations Sunday, and ecumenical responsibilities, such as World Day of Prayer.

While the calculations of the Gregorian calendar are almost totally accurate, some discrepancy still remains, and movements for further reform have continued. The idea of a perpetual calendar making each date fall on the same day of the week would be acceptable to many Christians, and the proposal to fix Easter on a definite Sunday has received some support.

JAMES H. SMYLIE
Union Theological Seminary, Richmond, Va.

Further Reading: *Book of Common Prayer* (any ed.); Boyle, Leonard E., "Calendar, Christian," in *New Catholic Encyclopedia*, vol. 2, pp. 1062–1064 (New York 1967); Denis-Boulet, Noële, M., *The Christian Calendar*, tr. by P. Hepburne-Scott (New York 1960); McArthur, A. Allen, *The Evolution of the Christian Year* (London 1953).

CALENDER, kal′ən-dər, a machine that is used in the finishing of textile fabrics and paper and in the production of plastic and rubber sheeting. It consists of long, rigid, heated rollers mounted horizontally in pairs between which the sheets being formed are squeezed.

In the finishing of textile fabrics, calendering is similar to the ironing of clothes. The pressure applied by the rolls closes the pores in the threads, removes creases from the cloth and flattens it to the required thickness, and imparts a luster. In the plastics and rubber industries, calendering is used in making sheets. Resins, such as vinyl, are blended into a hot plastic mass and passed through the calender. The plastic emerges as a flat film, or sheet, whose thickness is determined by the gap between the rolls. The paper industry uses calenders to compact the paper and to give it either a smooth or a textured finish.

JOSEPH DATSKO, *University of Michigan*

CALENDULA, kə-len′jə-lə, a small genus of annual or perennial plants that often bear large yellow or orange flower heads. Calendulas are native to the tropics but also thrive in temperate regions, in sunny or partly shaded areas.

Probably the best-known species is the pot marigold (*Calendula officinalis*), a favorite garden plant. It ranges in height from 1 to 2 feet (30 to 60 cm) and its flower heads, which are composed of flat spreading rays, may grow 6 inches (15 cm) across. The leaves are oblong; like the stem, they are covered with hairs. The pot marigold is sometimes cultivated as a house plant, and its dried flower heads are sometimes used as a flavoring for soups and stews. In southern regions it may be grown outdoors where, like other calendulas, it blossoms all year long.

Calendulas are readily grown from seeds planted in the spring. For early blooming they may be started indoors and then transplanted to the garden bed.

FRANCES SHERBURNE
Massachusetts Audubon Society

Calendula

ROCHE

CALEXICO, kə-lek′sē-kō, is a border city in southern California, in Imperial county, 95 miles (153 km) southeast of San Diego. It is a port of entry from Mexico into the United States and a shopping center for residents of Mexicali in Baja California. Calexico is a trading center for the Imperial Valley, where livestock is raised and cotton, grains, fruits, and vegetables are grown. Water for irrigating the crops is brought from the Colorado River by the All-American Canal. Municipal government is administered by a city manager. Population: 10,625.

CALGARY, kal′gə-rē, a city in Alberta, Canada, is situated at the junction of the Bow and Elbow rivers in the southwestern part of the province. It is the oldest city in Alberta and, next to Edmonton, which is 160 air miles (260 km) to the north, it is the largest. The metropolitan areas of these two cities contain half the population of the province.

Calgary's altitude of 3,483 feet (1,062 meters) and its proximity to the Rocky Mountains, about 50 miles (80 km) to the west, give it a dry, bracing atmosphere. On below-zero winter days, the warmer chinook wind from the eastern slopes of the Rockies can raise the temperature appreciably in a matter of hours. Calgary is surrounded by seemingly limitless prairies and rangelands. Rich oil and gas fields lie to the north and south. The city's population increased by 1,000 a month during the 1960's. Its land area is now more than 150 square miles (400 sq km).

The Economy. In the present state of its economic development, Calgary is undecided whether it is a "cowtown" (a favorite description), an oil capital, or a financial and industrial center. Actually, it is a combination of all three. Its stockyard auction sales in the late 1960's totaled about $125 million annually.

The city has a centrally located flour mill and grain elevators licensed to handle more than 6 million bushels (211 million liters) of mostly high quality wheat. It also has offices of 300 oil and gas companies. Calgary's industrial parks ship out a great variety of products, from trailers for industrial housing, which are used around the world, to artificial limbs. The city's chief industries are food processing, metal products, chemicals, wood products, and oil refining.

As the trading center for a large area of southern Alberta and southeastern British Columbia, downtown Calgary is building up rapidly. Multistory office buildings attract more traffic to the narrow streets of the old city and the resultant air pollution has become a problem. Calgary claims to have more cars per capita than any other city in Canada, second on the continent to Los Angeles. In the residential areas, single-family dwellings predominate. Most houses are of frame construction and the rambling ranch type of design is popular. There are also a number of modern high-rise apartment houses and convenient shopping centers.

Educational and Cultural Life. In 1966, the Calgary campus (established 1945) of the University of Alberta became the independent University of Calgary. Mount Royal Junior College, founded in 1910, is affiliated with the University of Alberta. Calgary is also the home of the Southern Alberta Institute of Technology, established in 1916. The Glenbow Foundation, originally privately endowed but supported by the provincial government since 1966, has a historical library,

CALGARY, Alberta, in an aerial view, has a backdrop formed by the eastern foothills of the Rocky Mountains.

GEORGE HUNTER, NATIONAL FILM BOARD OF CANADA

art gallery, and history museum in Calgary and an Indian and natural history museum at Banff, a well-known resort in the Rocky Mountains 65 air miles (105 km) to the west. The Calgary Allied Arts Centre offers art exhibitions and theatrical productions.

Recreation and Places of Interest. The city's greatest summer attraction is the Calgary Exhibition and Stampede, a famous rodeo. Because it is celebrated with people dancing in the streets, it has been called "a rangeland Mardi Gras." The Southern Alberta Jubilee Auditorium houses indoor entertainments; McMahon Stadium, the largest in Canada, accommodates football games; and the lawns of Riley Park are used for cricket matches. At Glenmore Dam, Heritage Park presents a frontier village complete with original buildings, steam train, blacksmith shop, and general store. Associated with Calgary's well-populated zoo is a natural history park featuring models of dinosaurs that roamed the badlands northeast of Calgary some 60 million years ago. Reader Rock Gardens are planted with trees and shrubs from all over the world. The Sarcee and Stoney Indian reserves are located on the outskirts of the metropolitan area.

History. Calgary was established in 1875 as a post of the North West Mounted Police (now the Royal Canadian Mounted Police). The first settlers were ranchers from the United States, followed by homesteaders from eastern Canada and Britain who arrived after the Canadian Pacific Railway reached Calgary in 1883. The city was incorporated in 1893. The discovery of natural gas in 1914—and crude oil in 1937—in the Turner Valley field about 25 miles (40 km) southwest of Calgary determined the city's future growth.

Government. Calgary has a commission and council form of government, with a mayor who is a member of the council. The city and its Census Metropolitan Area (C. M. A.) are coextensive. Population: 403,319.

KEN LIDDELL
Calgary "Herald"

CALHOUN, kal-hōōn′, **John Caldwell** (1782–1850), American statesman and political philosopher. From 1811 until his death he served in the federal government, successively as congressman, secretary of war, vice president, senator, secretary of state, and again as senator. Always he was at the heart of the issues of his time, notably the nullification crisis and the conflict over slavery. Loyal to his nation, to his state of South Carolina, and, above all, to his principles, he sought to preserve the union while advancing Southern interests.

Early Career. Calhoun was born in Abbeville district, S. C., on March 18, 1782. He grew up in an atmosphere of controversy and social change. The extension of cotton culture was bringing slavery into the up-country, where small farmers like his father were challenging the political dominance of the low country planters. Calhoun was largely self-educated before he entered Yale as a junior in 1801. He graduated with honors in 1804, went on to attend the Litchfield, Conn., law school, and was admitted to the South Carolina bar in 1807.

Practicing in his native district, he quickly gained the reputation that took him to the state legislature. There, from 1809 to 1811, he helped establish an enduring balance of power between South Carolina's tidewater planters and piedmont farmers.

Calhoun's own future, both socially and economically, was assured by his marriage in 1811 to a wealthy cousin, Floride Bonneau Calhoun. The couple settled at Abbeville, moving in 1825 to the Fort Hill plantation near Pendleton, the future site of Clemson University.

National Politics. Calhoun entered Congress in 1811. He was one of the group of young nationalists urging war with Britain to redeem America's honor. Calhoun introduced the war report of 1812, and throughout the contest he urged measures to strengthen the armed forces and to finance the war. When hostilities were over he proposed reconstruction measures and supported what came to be known as the "American System"—a

NATIONAL ARCHIVES (BRADY COLLECTION)

John C. Calhoun

combination of protective tariff, internal transportation, and national bank. As secretary of war in James Monroe's cabinet, he contributed significantly to the reorganization of the Army and to the extension of the Western frontier.

In 1824, Calhoun was elected vice president of the United States with support from both the Adams and Jackson factions. He served under the victorious John Quincy Adams, but in 1828 he supported Andrew Jackson and was again elected to the vice presidency as Jackson won the presidency.

Between the close of the War of 1812 and the election of 1828, the American scene had changed radically. A postwar depression had aroused a hard core of hostility against the Bank of the United States and had brought the first of a long series of increases in the tariff. The perennial question of state versus national power had been reopened by a series of centralizing Supreme Court decisions, while the Missouri Compromise of 1821 revealed an unsuspected depth of sectional cleavage over slavery.

Although the cultivation of new lands contributed to overproduction and falling prices, the Southern cotton planters blamed their misfortunes on the tariff, which by raising the cost of manufactured goods tended to depress the foreign market for their own staple. In South Carolina, men talked ominously of calculating the value of the union. The very high Tariff of 1828 drove the cotton states to the verge of rebellion. Calhoun had turned against the tariff after 1824, but Jackson's position was equivocal. To advise the incoming president of what the South expected of him, the South Carolina legislature asked Calhoun to prepare a report. The resulting document, known as the *South Carolina Exposition* (1828), was the first explicit statement of Calhoun's unique political philosophy.

Nullification. The theory that a state might nullify—that is, refuse to obey—an act of Congress it believed unconstitutional had been implied as early as 1798 by Madison and Jefferson in the Kentucky and Virginia Resolutions against the Alien and Sedition laws. The doctrine of states' rights, based on the concept that each of the states originally had been sovereign and independent, had been expounded for a generation. From these theories Calhoun derived his remedy. If the tariff were not reduced, he argued, the individual states might "interpose their sovereignty" to arrest the application of the law.

Congress failed to reduce the duties, and some South Carolinians were ready to put the theory to the test. To restrain the hotheads, Calhoun issued a further exposition of his doctrines, the *Fort Hill Address* of 1831. But when the Tariff of 1832 declared protection to be the fixed policy of the country, revolt broke out anew. Calhoun again amplified his doctrine, in a letter to Gov. James Hamilton, Jr., of South Carolina, but the time for words had passed. In November 1832 a special convention declared the tariff null and void within the state.

Calhoun resigned the vice presidency to reenter the Senate, where he could better defend South Carolina's action. Ultimately a compromise tariff was negotiated largely by Henry Clay.

By this time Jackson and Calhoun were sharply at odds. The President had now learned that Calhoun, when secretary of war, had opposed Jackson's pursuit of marauding Seminoles into Spanish Florida. Early in 1829, Mrs. Calhoun's refusal to receive as a social equal the tavern keeper's daughter who had married Jackson's friend and secretary of war, John H. Eaton, opened the rift between the President and the Vice President. After the nullification episode the gulf became unbridgeable, as Jackson fervently opposed that doctrine. When Jackson removed the government deposits from the Bank of the United States in 1833, Calhoun, though not a strong Bank supporter, joined the Whig opposition in censure of the president. He did not return to the Democratic party until the late 1830's.

Sectional Strife. By that time, party politics, for Calhoun, had been superseded by sectional interests. As the antislavery crusade gained momentum in the North, he became preoccupied with the political defense and intellectual justification of the "peculiar institution" on which Southerners generally believed their whole economy to rest. He supported the Independent Treasury plan proposed by President Martin Van Buren as an alternative to a national bank and opposed Whig attempts to restore the tariff, but for the most part the last 15 years of his life were devoted to the promotion of Southern unity.

In the Senate, Calhoun engineered passage of the gag rule that precluded discussion of slavery. As secretary of state in the last year of John Tyler's administration (1844), he arranged the annexation of Texas, which he justified on the ground that it would enlarge the area open to slavery and so help preserve sectional balance in the union. Back in the Senate in 1846, he led the battle against the Wilmot Proviso, which would have excluded slavery from territories acquired as a result of the Mexican War.

He was still insisting upon the right of the slaveholders to take their human chattels into any territory of the United States when he denounced the Compromise of 1850 almost with his last breath. Too ill to speak himself, Calhoun sat in the Senate while his final exhortation was read on March 4, 1850. His last appearance there was on March 7, when he heard and approved Daniel Webster's appeal for sectional peace. He died in Washington on March 31, 1850.

Philosophy. The substance of Calhoun's last speech was an argument for restoration of the sectional equilibrium that had existed from the earliest days of the republic by giving to each section, through its own majority, a veto on the acts of the federal government. This doctrine of the concurrent majority had been implicit in his nullification papers. It was amplified in the 1840's in a *Disquisition on Government* intended as an introduction to a larger *Discourse on the Constitution and Government of the United States*. The *Discourse* and its prologue were published by the state of South Carolina shortly after his death.

Although he was one of the intellectual progenitors of the Southern Confederacy, Calhoun never sought that solution. His tragedy was that his defense of an indefensible institution led him to reject democracy itself. His doctrine of representation by major interests groups influenced the functional federalism of a later day but in his own time only prepared the way for the destruction of the Union he loved.

CHARLES M. WILTSE, *Dartmouth College*

Further Reading: Capers, Gerald M., *John C. Calhoun, Opportunist* (Gainesville, Fla., 1960); Coit, Margaret L., *John C. Calhoun: American Portrait* (Boston 1950); Spain, August O., *The Political Theory of John C. Calhoun* (New York 1951); Wiltse, Charles M., *John C. Calhoun*, 3 vols. (Indianapolis 1944–1951).

CALI, käl′ē, a city in southwestern Colombia, the capital of Valle del Cauca department, is situated in the fertile Cauca Valley. The Cali River, a tributary of the Cauca River, flows through the city.

Cali is the chief industrial and commercial center of the Cauca Valley, where sugarcane, the traditional crop, is still grown but is supplemented by a variety of products, including coffee, tobacco, cotton, rice, tropical fruits, and livestock. The industrial output of the city is varied. Among the significant manufactures are rubber products (chiefly tires), paper, construction materials, chemicals pharmaceuticals, beer and alcohol, electrical equipment, and processed foods.

Cali is the headquarters of the Cauca Valley Authority (Corporación Autonoma Regional del Cauca, or CVC), initiated in 1954 to develop the natural resources of the valley. In scope and purpose it is similar to the Tennessee Valley Authority (TVA) in the United States. Special emphasis has been given to development of electric power, reclamation of land, and flood control.

The city also is an educational and cultural center, with two universities—the Universidad del Valle and the Universidad Santiago de Cali. It was the birthplace of the 19th century novelist Jorge Isaacs.

Cali was founded in 1536 by Miguel López Muñoz, a follower of the conquistador Sebastián de Belalcázar (or Benalcázar), who came north from Ecuador. In 1885 it suffered serious damage from an earthquake, and subsequent rebuilding has given it a modern appearance. Cali's recent growth (the population doubled in the decade 1951–1961) has been due to an influx of former rural dwellers and rapid industrial expansion. Population: (1964) 618,215.

GREGORY RABASSA, *Columbia University*

CALIBAN, kal′ə-ban, is a character in Shakespeare's *The Tempest* (q.v.) and later literature. In *The Tempest* he is the deformed, half-human son of the witch Sycorax, original owner of the unnamed island in the play, and a devil. He has been said to personify the elements of earth and water or to represent brute force or natural man. Enslaved by the magician Prospero, he mutters his way through 12 years of hard labor and plots escape. When Prospero and his daughter Miranda depart, Caliban is left alone on the island.

In Robert Browning's poem *Caliban upon Setebos* (1864), Caliban speaks a long soliloquy on Setebos, his god. In his superstitious fear of Setebos and his characterization of him as neither a kind nor a cruel being who made the world as a toy and sends storms to chasten man, Caliban reveals the nature of his own mind and that of man in general.

CALIBER. See GUNS; SMALL ARMS.

CALICO, kal′ə-kō, is a lightweight cotton fabric that originated in Calicut, India. The fabric was originally block printed by hand in very attractive designs, and many people bought it for its bright colors and patterns rather than for the quality of the fabric or the fastness of the dye.

Calico was manufactured in Europe in the late 18th century and then spread to the United States. During the 19th century, settlers in the Western states, instead of spinning their own cotton yarn and weaving it into cloth, preferred to buy the factory-woven printed fabric shipped from factories in the East. This fabric was used mostly for making dresses, and soon the word "calico" was used to refer to any dress made out of this material. Today the term calico is used occasionally in stores, but it is not a technical term denoting a particular kind of fabric.

ERNEST B. BERRY, *School of Textiles North Carolina State University*

CALICUT, kal′ə-kut, is a seaport in India, in Kerala state, on the Arabian Sea. "Calicut" is the Anglicized form of *Kozhikode* (meaning "cock fort"), the name of the city in the Malayalam language of Kerala. Calicut is the capital of Kozhikode district and was once the leading port of southern India. Calico cloth, first exported to England in the 17th century, was named after the city, which was also an important center for spice. Calicut declined as a port in the 19th century, but it continues to export rubber, spices, lumber, tea, coffee, and coconut products.

Calicut was ruled by Hindu chiefs called *zamorins* and owed its prosperity to the Arabs who settled there in the 7th century A.D. and traded with Southeast Asia, Arabia, China, Africa, and Persia. The city was Vasco da Gama's first Indian port of call in 1498 and soon became a center for European traders. A Portuguese trading post was established in 1510 but was abandoned in 1604, and in 1664 the British East India Company set up a trading establishment in the city.

Much of Calicut was destroyed by Haidar Ali in 1765 and by his son, Tipu Sultan, in 1788, but was subsequently rebuilt. Ceded to Britain in 1792, it remained under British control until 1947, when India became independent. In 1956 it was transferred from Madras state to the new state of Kerala. Population: (1965) 207,168.

CALIFORNIA

DE WYS, INC.

San Francisco and a section of the 8-mile Bay Bridge to Oakland seen from an island in San Francisco Bay.

Great Seal of California

CONTENTS

Section	Page	Section	Page
1. The People	197	Manufacturing	204
2. The Land	200	Research and Development	204
Major Physical Divisions	200	Mining	205
Rivers and Lakes	201	Entertainment Industry	205
Climate	202	4. Government and Politics	205
Plant Life	202	5. Education and Culture	207
Animal Life	202	6. Recreation	209
Mineral Resources	203	National Areas	209
Water Resource Development	203	State Areas	209
3. The Economy	204	The Missions	210
Agriculture	204	7. History	210
Fisheries and Lumbering	204		

CALIFORNIA, kal-ə-fôr′nyə, one of the Pacific states of the United States, is situated in the extreme west of the country, on the Pacific Ocean. It is a state of extremes and paradoxes, which are evident in its geography and climate and in the activities of its people. Its great area embraces a variety of topography, with snowcapped mountains, dense forests, fruitful valleys, and scorching deserts. Its population, the largest of any state in the Union, is expanding so rapidly as to put enormous demands on the vast resources of the state.

One of California's mountain peaks, Mt. Whitney, is higher than the peaks in any other state except Alaska. Death Valley, only some 60 miles (97 km) southeast of Mt. Whitney, contains the lowest and hottest point in the nation. California's earthquakes, rains, floods, and fires can be catastrophic; yet the most populous areas of the state are known for their mild climate and generally agreeable conditions for living. The ancient redwoods of California are the tallest trees in the world, and the California condor is the largest land bird in North America.

California seems new and yet old. At first a remote outpost of Spain, the area emerged from its mission background to become, by the 1830's, a mellow land of huge Mexican ranchos known for hospitality and gentility. Less than two decades later came acquisition by the United States and the frenzied gold rush, which changed California into an Anglo-American pattern. The gold of the Sierra Nevada transformed California's sleepy pueblos into bustling metropolises.

The agricultural potential of California's soil, the diversity of its natural wealth, the beauty of its landscapes, and its mild climate were advertised long before modern chambers of commerce were organized. Beyond the boosterism found in the letters of hide and tallow traders, whalers, and gold seekers lay other qualities, intangible yet real. These gave California a romance and glamour that exerted a magnetic influence even in distant countries. Visitors in the early days came under the same spell that, through the years, has turned tourists into permanent residents.

In the present age of commuting motorists and traffic roar, a solid megalopolis has begun to stretch northward from San Diego to Los Angeles, then to Santa Barbara and beyond. In northern California a second sprawling complex is being formed around San Francisco Bay. Although this growth creates many problems, the planning of the supercities of the future goes forward. Californians hope that their expansive "shuttle living" can be accompanied by reclamation of decayed areas in central cities and suburbs and that new forms of local government can be evolved to meet urban complexities. Other pressing and complex problems include the unmet needs of minority groups, especially California's Negro and Mexican-American citizens; the diminishing supply of pure air and water; chronic transportation congestion; and growing fiscal demands, particularly for education and for crime control.

Californians are concerned both with the present and the future. Their intricate political differences and their contending social and economic philosophies generate attention far beyond the borders of the state. But these internal conflicts have not diminished the people's pride in California. This is reflected in such diverse forms as the Sierra Club's struggle to protect the wilderness areas, the preservation of such symbols of the past as San Francisco's cable cars, and the vigorous economic, educational, and cultural expansion that animates Los Angeles and San Francisco.

1. The People

Before the arrival of European explorers in California in 1542, there was an Indian population estimated at 150,000. Simple in culture, these natives literally lived off the land. The arrival of the first explorers, and especially of the first colonizers in 1769, signaled the ultimate decline of California's native population. Under three governments (Spanish, Mexican, and United States), the Indians of California were to lose their lands, largely without compensation, and they were to diminish steadily in numbers through disease, starvation, and extermination at the hands of soldiers and settlers.

During the approximately 80 years of Spanish and Mexican tenure in California (1769–1848), there was relatively little immigration from either Spain or Mexico. When the United States acquired California in 1848, the number of persons of European descent or birth was estimated at less than 15,000. Up to 10,000 of these were Spanish-speaking. The rest were of various nationalities, but the majority were traders, trappers, and overland settlers from the United States.

The gold rush of 1849 brought an end to Spanish predominance. By 1850, Anglo-Americans (United States citizens of English descent or origin) made up a majority of the population. Thereafter, California became increasingly Anglo-American in character, although the successive waves of newcomers always included people from many countries of the world.

Components of the Population. People from the New England states, New York, and Pennsylvania predominated in the migration of the gold-rush years. The southern California real estate boom of the 1880's brought the first large migrations from the Middle West. But during these periods and since, people from all parts of the nation—farmers, health seekers, merchants, real estate promoters, fruit pickers, engineers, and industrial workers—have streamed into California, looking for new beginnings and new opportunities. World War II brought tremendous numbers of industrial job seekers, including a large influx of Negroes. Since the 1950's, California's growing research and educational facilities have brought increasing numbers of scientists, technicians, educators, and students.

Indicative of the other states' contribution to California's population is the fact that only about 45% of California residents are born in the state. Less than 10% of the total population is foreign-born. The state's foreign stock includes large numbers from Mexico, Canada, the British Isles, Italy, and Germany. Other countries that have contributed substantial numbers to the population are the USSR, the Scandinavian countries, the Philippines, China, Japan, and Poland.

California's non-Caucasian population in 1970 totaled 2,192,102, of which 1,400,143 were Negro. Other nonwhite residents of the state include substantial numbers of Japanese, Chinese, Filipinos, and American Indians. Next to the

INFORMATION HIGHLIGHTS

Location: On the western coast of the United States, bordered north by Oregon, east by Nevada and Arizona, south by Lower California (Mexico), west by the Pacific Ocean.

Elevation: *Highest point*—Mount Whitney, 14,494 feet (4,418 meters); *lowest*—Death Valley, 282 feet (85.95 meters) below sea level; *approximate mean elevation*—2,900 feet (883.9 meters).

Area: 158,693 square miles (411,015 sq km); rank, 3d.

Population: 1970 census, 19,953,134; rank, 1st (attained 1st ranking in 1964). Increase from 1960 to 1970: 27.0%.

Climate: Generally mild winters and agreeable summers in heavily populated areas; extreme ranges of precipitation and temperature elsewhere.

Statehood: Sept. 9, 1850; the 31st state admitted.

Origin of Name: Probably from the fabled island of California in the Spanish romance *Las Sergas de Esplandian* (1510), by García Ordóñez de Montalvo.

Capital: Sacramento.

Largest City: Los Angeles.

Number of Counties: 58.

Principal Products: *Manufactures*—machinery, transportation equipment, food and products, fabricated metals; *farm products*—vegetables, fruits and nuts, cattle, dairy products; *minerals*—petroleum, natural gas, sand and gravel, boron minerals.

State Motto (adopted 1849): "Eureka" (from Greek *heurēka*, "I have found [it]"), referring to the settlement in California of successful gold seekers.

State Song (adopted 1951): *I Love You, California.*

State Nickname (unofficial): The Golden State.

State Bird (adopted June 12, 1931): California valley quail.

State Flower (adopted March 2, 1903): Golden poppy.

State Tree (adopted 1937): California redwood.

State Animal (adopted 1953): California grizzly bear (long symbolic of the state; now extinct).

State Fish (adopted 1947): South Fork golden trout.

State Insect (unofficial): California dog-face butterfly.

State Flag (officially adopted Feb. 3, 1911): A white field with a red star in upper left corner, a grizzly bear on a green patch in center, the inscription "California Republic" below the bear, and a solid red border at bottom; patterned after the Bear Flag designed and flown by American settlers in California when they revolted against Mexico in 1846. (See color plates under FLAG—*Flags of the States.*)

ROBERT W. YOUNG, FROM D. P. I.

LOS ANGELES living has a vibrant quality. A vivid side of the city at night shines in a brilliant gate of Chinatown, an area popular with visitors.

Indians, the Chinese represent the group of longest residence in California.

Population Trends. Most decades between 1850 and 1960 brought increases in California's population averaging 50%, with a resultant doubling of the population every 20 years for more than a century. Californians viewed the censuses of 1950 and 1960 with special satisfaction. Congressional apportionment after the 1950 census increased California's seats in the U. S. House of Representatives from 23 to 30. After the 1960 census the number rose to 38, making California second only to New York, which had 41.

The 1970 census revealed that California had a resident population of 19,953,134. This represented an increase of 4,235,930, or 27%, from the 15,717,204 inhabitants of the state in 1960. As a result of the 1970 census, California gained five seats in the U. S. House of Representatives effective in January 1973 with the 93d session of Congress.

Los Angeles county, in the south, once was known as the "Queen of the Cow Counties." But today the north is the rural part of the state, and Los Angeles county is the focal point of the state's growth. By the mid-1960's, 37 of every 100 Californians resided in Los Angeles county, and well over 9 million (about half the population of the state) lived within a 60-mile (96-km) radius of Los Angeles' old Spanish plaza. Other southern counties with exceptional rates of growth are Orange, Santa Barbara, and San Diego.

Population experts predict that there will be more than 25 million persons in California by 1975, up to 30 million by 1980, and from 38 to 42 million by the year 2000.

Largest Centers of Population. California has 16 areas known as standard metropolitan statistical areas. Each such area contains at least one central city of 50,000 or more inhabitants, and each includes the county in which the central city is situated as well as adjoining counties, if any, that are urban in character and economically integrated with the central county. The most populous standard metropolitan area is the Los Angeles–Long Beach area, followed by the San Francisco–Oakland, and Anaheim–Santa Ana–Garden Grove areas. The population of California is heavily concentrated in urban centers. By 1970, 91 of every 100 Californians lived in urban areas.

Los Angeles, the largest city in the state, and Long Beach are the central cities of a metropolitan area that includes Glendale, Burbank, Pasadena, Santa Monica, Beverly Hills, and approximately 70 other incorporated cities and towns.

San Francisco, the second-largest city, and Oakland are the central cities of the "Bay area," which includes Alameda, Berkeley, Richmond, and numerous smaller communities. This coastal region in the northern half of the state and the Los Angeles–Long Beach area in the southern half are California's most important centers of commerce, industry, research, education, and cultural activity.

GROWTH OF POPULATION SINCE STATEHOOD

Year	Population	Gain	Year	Population	Gain
1850	92,597	...	1920	3,426,861	44%
1860	379,994	310%	1930	5,677,251	66%
1870	560,247	47%	1940	6,907,387	22%
1880	864,964	54%	1950	10,586,223	53%
1890	1,213,398	40%	1960	15,717,204	48%
1900	1,485,053	22%	1970	19,953,134	27%
1910	2,377,549	60%			

Gain between 1960 and 1970: 27.0% (U. S. gain, 13.3%). **Density (1970)**: 125.7 persons per square mile (U. S. density, 50.5 persons per square mile).

URBAN-RURAL DISTRIBUTION

Year	Percent Urban	Percent Rural
1920	67.9 (U. S., 51.2)	32.1
1930	73.3 (U. S., 56.1)	26.7
1940	71.0 (U. S., 56.6)	29.0
1950	80.7 (U. S., 64.0)	19.3
1960	86.4 (U. S., 69.9)	13.6
1970	90.9 (U. S., 73.5)	9.1

LARGEST CENTERS OF POPULATION

Metropolitan Areas[1]	1970	1960	1950
Los Angeles-Long Beach	7,032,075	6,038,771	4,151,687
San Francisco-Oakland	3,109,519	2,648,762	2,135,934
Anaheim-Santa Ana-Garden Grove	1,420,386	703,925	216,224
San Diego	1,357,854	1,033,011	256,808
San Bernardino-Riverside-Ontario	1,143,146	809,782	451,688
San Jose	1,064,714	642,315	290,547
Cities[2]			
Los Angeles	2,816,061	2,479,015	1,970,358
San Francisco	715,675	740,316	755,357
San Diego	696,769	573,224	334,387
San Jose	445,779	204,196	95,280
Oakland	361,561	367,548	384,575
Long Beach	358,633	344,168	250,767
Sacramento	254,413	191,667	137,572
Anaheim	166,701	104,184	14,522
Fresno	165,972	133,929	91,669
Santa Ana	156,601	100,350	45,533

[1] Standard metropolitan statistical areas. [2] Most of the larger cities form part of the metropolitan areas listed above.

CALIFORNIA

5,000 m.	2,000 m.	1,000 m.	500 m.	200 m.	100 m.	Sea Level	Below
16,404 ft.	6,562 ft.	3,281 ft.	1,640 ft.	656 ft.	328 ft.		

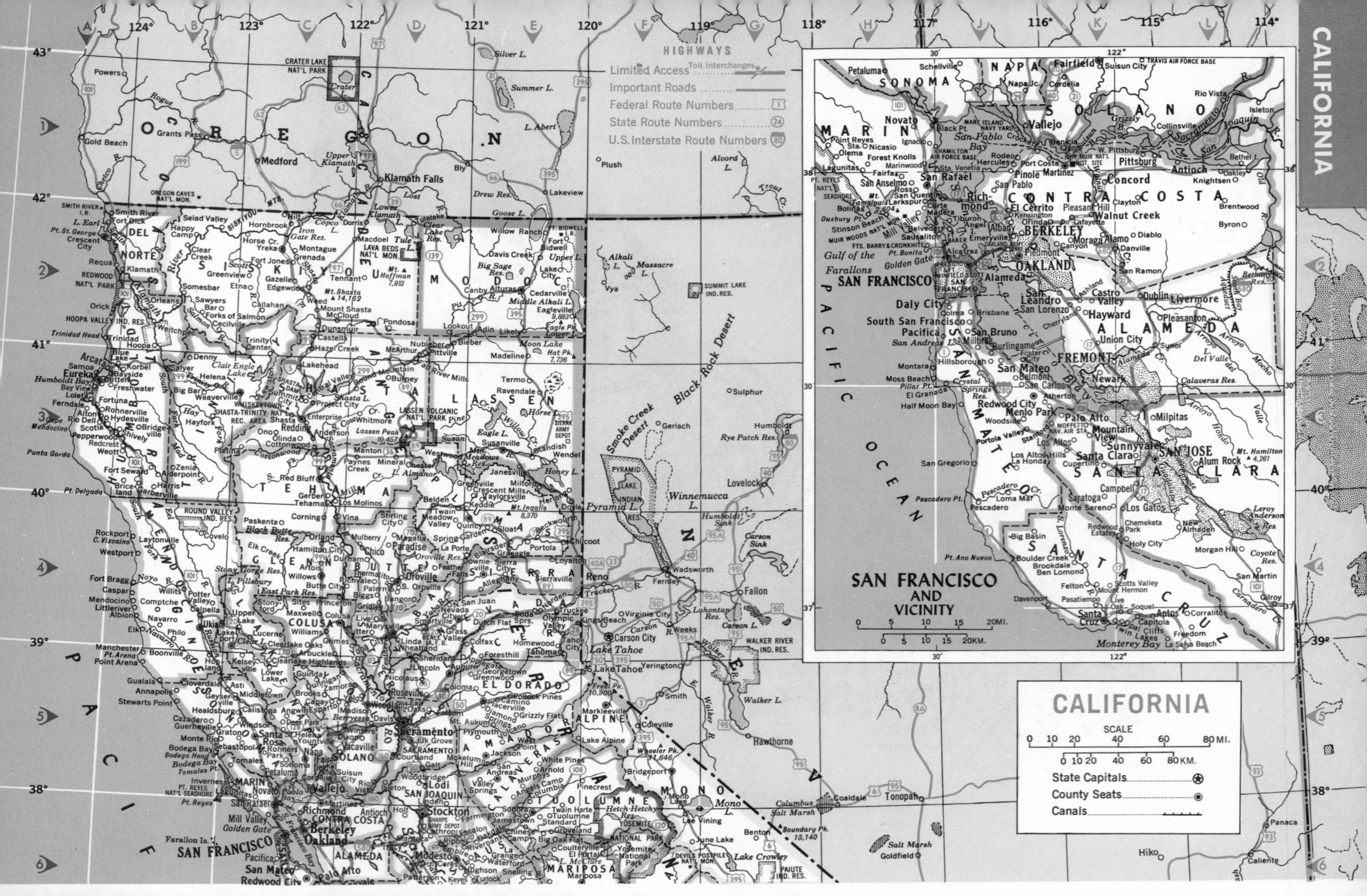
HIGHWAYS
Limited Access
Toll Interchanges
Important Roads
Federal Route Numbers
State Route Numbers
U.S. Interstate Route Numbers
OREGON
NEVADA
PACIFIC
SAN FRANCISCO AND VICINITY
0 5 10 15 20 MI.
0 5 10 15 20 KM.
PACIFIC OCEAN
CALIFORNIA
SCALE
0 10 20 40 60 80 MI.
0 10 20 40 60 80 KM.
State Capitals
County Seats
Canals

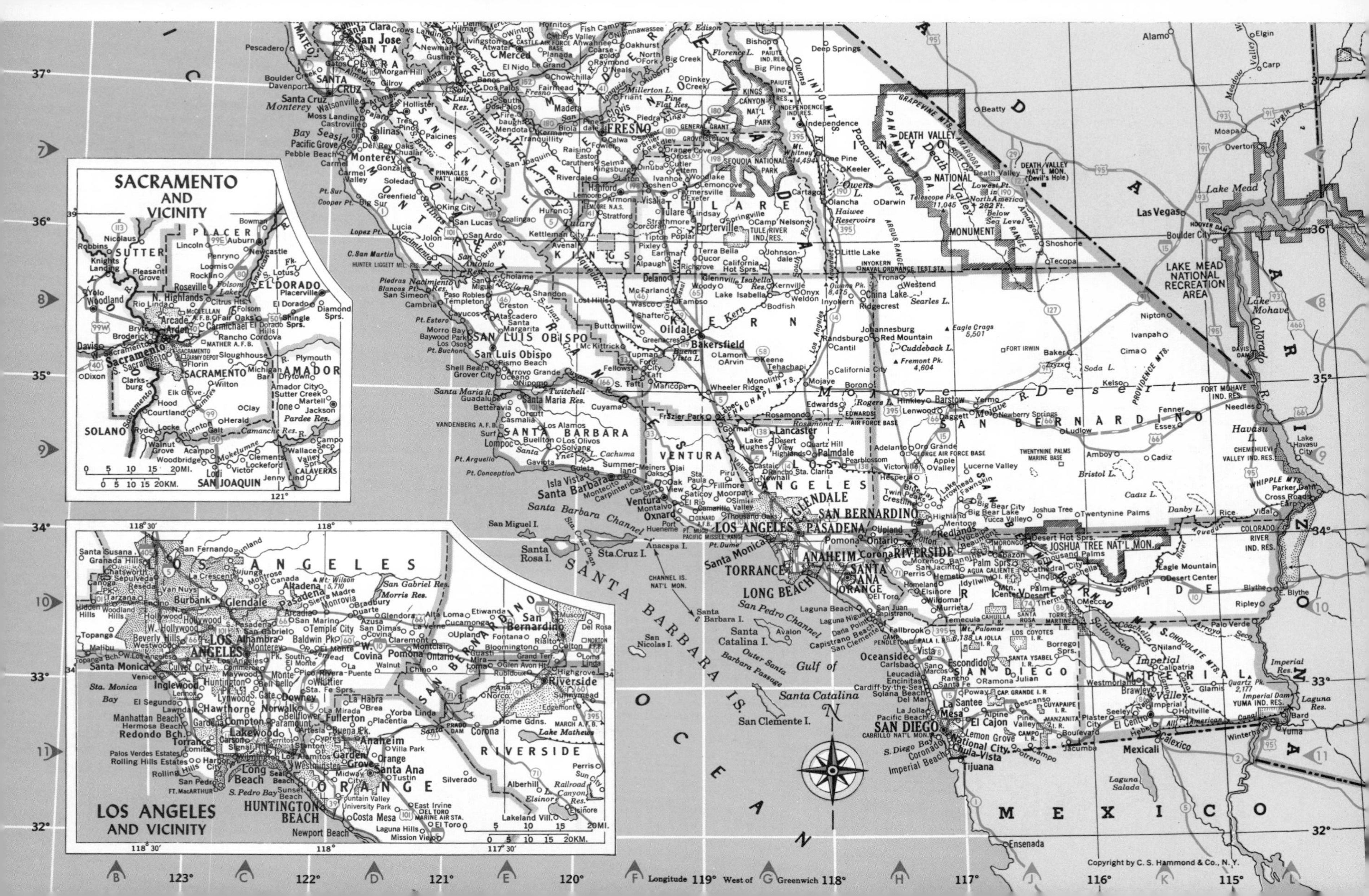
SACRAMENTO AND VICINITY
LOS ANGELES AND VICINITY
PACIFIC OCEAN
SANTA BARBARA IS.
MEXICO
ARIZONA
NEVADA
Mojave Desert
Death Valley National Monument
LAKE MEAD NATIONAL RECREATION AREA
JOSHUA TREE NAT'L MON.
SEQUOIA NATIONAL PARK
KINGS CANYON NAT'L PARK
Gulf of Santa Catalina
San Pedro Channel
Santa Barbara Channel
Salton Sea
SAN DIEGO
LOS ANGELES
LONG BEACH
SAN BERNARDINO
RIVERSIDE
PASADENA
GLENDALE
ANAHEIM
SANTA ANA
TORRANCE
FRESNO
Bakersfield
San Luis Obispo
Santa Barbara
San Jose
Las Vegas
Longitude 119° West of Greenwich 118°
Copyright by C. S. Hammond & Co., N. Y.

CALIFORNIA

COUNTIES

Alameda, 1,073,184 ....D 6
Alpine, 484 ....F 5
Amador, 11,821 ....E 5
Butte, 101,969 ....D 4
Calaveras, 13,585 ....E 5
Colusa, 12,430 ....C 4
Contra Costa, 558,389 ....D 6
Del Norte, 14,580 ....B 2
El Dorado, 43,833 ....E 5
Fresno, 413,053 ....E 7
Glenn, 17,521 ....C 4
Humboldt, 99,692 ....B 3
Imperial, 74,492 ....K 10
Inyo, 15,571 ....H 7
Kern, 329,162 ....G 8
Kings, 64,610 ....F 8
Lake, 19,548 ....C 4
Lassen, 14,960 ....E 3
Los Angeles, 7,032,075 ....G 9
Madera, 41,519 ....F 6
Marin, 206,038 ....C 5
Mariposa, 6,015 ....E 6
Mendocino, 51,101 ....B 4
Merced, 104,629 ....E 6
Modoc, 7,469 ....E 2
Mono, 4,016 ....F 5
Monterey, 250,071 ....D 7
Napa, 79,140 ....C 5
Nevada, 26,346 ....E 4
Orange, 1,420,386 ....H 10
Placer, 77,306 ....E 4
Plumas, 11,707 ....E 4
Riverside, 459,074 ....J 10
Sacramento, 631,498 ....D 5
San Benito, 18,226 ....D 7
San Bernardino, 684,072 ....J 9
San Diego, 1,357,854 ....J 10
San Francisco (city county), 715,674 ....J 2
San Joaquin, 290,208 ....D 6
San Luis Obispo, 105,690 ....E 8
San Mateo, 556,234 ....C 6
Santa Barbara, 264,324 ....E 9
Santa Clara, 1,064,714 ....D 6
Santa Cruz, 123,790 ....C 6
Shasta, 77,640 ....C 3
Sierra, 2,365 ....E 4
Siskiyou, 33,225 ....C 2
Solano, 169,941 ....D 5
Sonoma, 204,885 ....C 5
Stanislaus, 194,506 ....D 6
Sutter, 41,935 ....D 4
Tehama, 29,517 ....C 3
Trinity, 7,615 ....B 3
Tulare, 188,322 ....G 7
Tuolumne, 22,169 ....F 5
Ventura, 376,430 ....F 9
Yolo, 91,788 ....D 5
Yuba, 44,736 ....D 4

CITIES and TOWNS

Adelanto, 2,115 ....H 9
Alameda, 70,968 ....J 2
*Alamo-Danville, 14,059 ....K 2
Albany, 14,674 ....J 2
Alhambra, 62,125 ....C 10
Alondra■, 12,193 ....C 11
Altadena, 42,380 ....C 10
Alta Loma, 6,100 ....E 10
Alturas⊙, 2,799 ....E 2
Alum Rock, 18,355 ....L 3
Anaheim, 166,701 ....D 11
Anaheim-Santa Ana-Garden Grove, ‡1,420,386 ....D 11
Anderson, 5,492 ....C 3
Angwin, 2,690 ....C 5
Antioch, 28,060 ....L 1
Apple Valley, 6,702 ....H 9
Aptos, 8,704 ....K 4
Arcade-Arden, 82,492 ....B 8
Arcadia, 42,868 ....C 10
Arcata, 8,985 ....A 3
Arden-Arcade■, 82,492 ....B 8
Arroyo Grande, 7,454 ....E 8
Artesia, 14,757 ....C 11
Arvin, 5,090 ....G 8
Ashland, 14,810 ....K 2
Asti, 50 ....C 5
Atascadero, 10,290 ....E 8
Atherton, 8,085 ....K 3
Atwater, 11,640 ....E 6
Auburn⊙, 6,570 ....C 8
Avalon, 1,520 ....G 10
Avenal, 3,035 ....E 8
Avocado Heights■, 9,810 ....D 10
Azusa, 25,217 ....D 10
Bakersfield⊙, 69,515 ....G 8
Bakersfield, ‡329,271 ....G 8
Baldwin Park, 47,285 ....D 10
Banning, 12,034 ....J 10
Barstow, 17,442 ....H 9
Bayview, 2,340 ....A 3
Baywood Park-Los Osos, 3,487 ....E 8
Beaumont, 5,484 ....J 10
Bell, 21,836 ....C 11
Bellflower, 51,454 ....C 11
Bell Gardens■, 29,308 ....C 11
Belmont, 23,667 ....J 3
Belvedere, 2,599 ....H 2
Benicia, 8,783 ....K 1
Ben Lomond, 2,793 ....K 4
Berkeley, 116,716 ....J 2
Beverly Hills, 33,416 ....B 10
Big Bear Lake, 5,268 ....J 9
Bishop, 3,498 ....G 6
Bloomington, 11,957 ....E 10
Blythe, 7,047 ....L 10
Bonnyview■, 4,882 ....C 3
Boron, 1,999 ....H 8
Boulder Creek, 1,806 ....J 4
Bowman, 2,089 ....C 8
Boyes Hot Spring■, 3,558 ....C 5
Brawley, 13,746 ....K 11
Brea, 18,447 ....D 11
Brentwood, 2,649 ....L 2
Bridgeport⊙, 525 ....F 5
Brisbane, 3,003 ....J 2
Broderick-Bryte, 12,782 ....B 8
Bryte-Broderick, 12,782 ....B 8
Buena Park, 63,646 ....D 11
Burbank, 88,871 ....C 10
Burlingame, 27,320 ....J 2
Burney, 2,190 ....D 3
Calexico, 10,625 ....K 11
Calipatria, 1,824 ....K 10
Calistoga, 1,882 ....C 5
Calwa, 5,191 ....F 7
Camarillo, 19,219 ....F 9
Camarillo Heights■, 5,892 ....F 9
Cambrian Heights■, 5,316 ....K 3
Campbell, 24,770 ....K 3
Canoga Park, 109,127 ....B 10
Capistrano Beach, 4,149 ....H 10
Capitola, 5,080 ....K 4
Cardiff-by-the-Sea, 5,724 ....H 10
Carlsbad, 14,944 ....H 10
Carmel, 4,525 ....D 7
Carmel Valley, 3,026 ....D 7
Carmichael, 37,625 ....C 8
Carpinteria, 6,982 ....F 9
Carson, 71,150 ....C 11
Castro Valley, 44,760 ....K 2
Castroville, 3,235 ....D 7
Cathedral City, 3,640 ....J 10
Central Valley, 2,361 ....C 3
Ceres, 6,029 ....D 6
Cerritos, 15,856 ....C 11
Chatsworth, 24,000 ....B 10
Cherryland, 9,969 ....K 2
Cherry Valley■, 3,165 ....J 10
Chico, 19,580 ....D 4
China Lake, 11,105 ....H 8
Chinese Camp, 150 ....E 6
Chino, 20,411 ....D 10
Chowchilla, 4,349 ....E 6
Chula Vista, 67,901 ....J 11
Citrus Heights, 21,760 ....C 8
Claremont, 23,464 ....D 10
Clearlake Highlands, 2,836 ....C 5
Cloverdale, 3,251 ....B 5
Clovis, 13,856 ....F 7
Coachella, 8,353 ....J 10
Coalinga, 6,161 ....E 7
Colton, 19,974 ....E 10
Colusa⊙, 3,842 ....C 4
Commerce, 10,536 ....C 10
Compton, 78,611 ....C 11
Concord, 85,164 ....K 1
Corcoran, 5,249 ....F 7
Corning, 3,573 ....C 4
Corona, 27,519 ....E 11
Coronado, 20,910 ....H 11
Corte Madera, 8,464 ....J 2
Costa Mesa, 72,660 ....D 11
Covina, 30,380 ....D 10
Crescent City⊙, 2,586 ....A 2
Crestline, 3,509 ....H 9
Crockett, 2,900 ....J 1
Cucamonga, 5,796 ....E 10
Cudahy■, 16,998 ....C 11
Culver City, 31,035 ....B 10
Cupertino, 18,216 ....K 3
Cutler, 2,503 ....F 7
Cutten, 2,228 ....A 3
Cypress, 31,026 ....D 11
Daly City, 66,922 ....H 2
Dana Point, 4,745 ....H 10
Danville-Alamo, 14,059 ....K 2
Davis, 23,488 ....B 8
Del Aire■, 11,930 ....C 11
Delano, 14,559 ....F 8
Delhi, 2,063 ....E 6
Del Mar, 3,956 ....H 11
Del Rey Oaks, 1,823 ....D 7
Del Rosa, 8,000 ....E 10
Desert Hot Springs, 2,738 ....J 9
Desert View Highlands, 2,172 ....G 9
Diamond Bar■, 12,234 ....D 10
Dinuba, 7,917 ....F 7
Dixon, 4,432 ....B 9
Dominguez■, 5,980 ....C 11
Dos Palos, 2,496 ....E 6
Downey, 88,445 ....C 11
Downieville⊙, 375 ....E 4
Duarte, 14,981 ....D 10
Dublin, 13,641 ....K 2
Dunsmuir, 2,214 ....C 2
Eagle Mountain, 2,453 ....K 10
Earlimart, 3,080 ....F 8
East Compton■, 5,853 ....C 11
East La Mirada■, 12,339 ....D 11
East Los Angeles, 105,033 ....C 10
East Palo Alto■, 17,837 ....K 3
East Porterville■, 4,042 ....G 7
El Cajon, 52,273 ....J 11
El Centro⊙, 19,272 ....K 11
El Cerrito, 25,190 ....J 2
El Dorado Hills, 2,000 ....C 8
El Encanto Heights■, 6,225 ....F 9
Elk Grove, 3,721 ....B 9
El Monte, 69,837 ....D 10
El Rio, 6,173 ....F 9
El Segundo, 15,620 ....B 11
Elsinore, 3,530 ....F 11
El Toro, 8,654 ....E 11
Emeryville, 2,681 ....J 2
Empire, 2,016 ....D 6
Encinitas, 5,375 ....H 10
Encino, 40,000 ....B 10
Enterprise, 11,486 ....C 3
Escalon, 2,366 ....E 6
Escondido, 36,792 ....J 10
Eureka⊙, 24,337 ....A 3
Exeter, 4,475 ....F 7
Fairfax, 7,661 ....H 1
Fairfield⊙, 44,146 ....K 1
Fair Oaks, 11,256 ....C 8
Fallbrook, 6,945 ....H 10
Farmersville, 3,456 ....F 7
Felton, 2,062 ....K 4
Fillmore, 6,285 ....G 9
Firebaugh, 2,517 ....E 7
Florence-Graham■, 42,895 ....C 11
Florin, 9,646 ....B 8
Folsom, 5,810 ....C 8
Fontana, 20,673 ....E 10
Ford City, 3,503 ....F 8
Fort Bragg, 4,455 ....B 4
Fortuna, 6,443 ....A 3
Foster City, 9,327 ....J 2
Fountain Valley, 31,826 ....D 11
Fowler, 2,239 ....F 7
Freedom, 5,563 ....L 4
Fremont, 100,869 ....K 3
Fresno⊙, 165,972 ....F 7
Fresno, ‡413,053 ....F 7
Fullerton, 85,987 ....D 11
Galt, 3,200 ....C 9
Gardena, 41,021 ....C 11
Garden Acres■, 7,870 ....D 6
Garden Grove, 122,524 ....D 11
Gilroy, 12,665 ....D 6
Glen Avon Heights, 5,759 ....E 10
Glendale, 132,752 ....C 10
Glendora, 31,349 ....D 10
Goleta, 3,500 ....F 9
Gonzales, 2,575 ....D 7
Granada Hills, 50,000 ....B 10
Grand Terrace, 5,901 ....E 10
Grass Valley, 5,149 ....D 4
Greenacres, 2,116 ....F 8
Greenfield, 2,608 ....D 7
Gridley, 3,534 ....D 4
Grossmont-Mount Helix■, 8,723 ....J 11
Grover City, 5,939 ....E 8
Guadalupe, 3,145 ....E 9
Gustine, 2,793 ....D 6
Hacienda Heights■, 35,969 ....D 11
Half Moon Bay, 4,023 ....H 3
Hanford⊙, 15,179 ....F 7
Harbor City, 17,500 ....C 11
Hawaiian Gardens■, 8,811 ....C 11
Hawthorne, 53,304 ....C 11
Hayward, 93,058 ....K 2
Healdsburg, 5,438 ....B 5
Hemet, 12,252 ....H 10
Hermosa Beach, 17,412 ....B 11
Hesperia, 4,592 ....H 9
Highgrove, 2,158 ....E 10
Highland, 13,290 ....H 9
Hillsborough■, 8,753 ....J 2
Hollister⊙, 7,663 ....D 7
Hollywood, 85,047 ....C 10
Holtville, 3,496 ....K 11
Home Gardens, 5,116 ....E 11
Hughson, 2,144 ....E 6
Huntington Beach, 115,960 ....C 11
Huntington Park, 33,744 ....C 11
Ignacio, 4,500 ....H 1
Imperial, 3,094 ....K 11
Imperial Beach, 20,244 ....H 11
Independence⊙, 748 ....H 7
Indio, 14,459 ....J 10
Inglewood, 89,985 ....B 11
Ione, 2,369 ....C 9
Isla Vista, 13,441 ....E 9
Jackson⊙, 1,924 ....C 9
Kensington, 5,823 ....J 2
Kerman, 2,667 ....E 7
Keyes, 1,875 ....E 6
King City, 3,717 ....D 7
Kingsburg, 3,843 ....F 7
La Canada, 20,652 ....C 10
La Crescenta-Montrose, 19,594 ....C 10
Ladera Heights■, 6,079 ....C 11
Lafayette, 20,484 ....K 2
Laguna Beach, 14,550 ....G 10
Laguna Hills, 13,676 ....D 11
Laguna Niguel, 4,644 ....H 10
La Habra, 41,350 ....D 11
La Jolla, 30,000 ....H 11
Lake Arrowhead, 2,682 ....H 9
Lakeport⊙, 3,005 ....C 4
Lakeside■, 11,291 ....J 11
Lakewood, 82,973 ....C 11
La Mesa, 39,178 ....H 11
La Mirada, 30,808 ....D 11
Lamont, 7,007 ....G 8
Lancaster, 30,948 ....G 9
La Palma■, 9,687 ....C 11
La Puente, 31,092 ....D 10
Larkspur, 10,487 ....H 1
Lathrop, 2,137 ....D 6
La Verne, 12,965 ....D 10
Lawndale, 24,825 ....B 11
Lemon Grove, 19,690 ....J 11
Lemoore, 4,219 ....F 7
Lennox, 16,121 ....B 11
Lenwood, 3,834 ....H 9
Leucadia, 5,900 ....H 10
Lincoln, 3,176 ....B 8
Lincoln Village■, 6,722 ....D 6
Linda, 7,731 ....D 4
Lindsay, 5,206 ....F 7
Live Oak, 2,645 ....D 4
Live Oak, 6,443 ....K 4
Livermore, 37,703 ....L 2
Livingston, 2,588 ....E 6
Lodi, 28,691 ....C 9
Loma Linda, 9,797 ....F 10
Lomita, 19,784 ....C 11
Lompoc, 25,284 ....E 9
Long Beach, 358,633 ....C 11
Los Alamitos, 11,346 ....D 11
Los Altos, 24,956 ....K 3
Los Altos Hills, 6,865 ....J 3
Los Angeles⊙, 2,816,061 ....C 10
Los Angeles-Long Beach, ‡7,032,075 ....C 10
Los Banos, 9,188 ....E 6
Los Gatos, 23,735 ....K 4
Los Osos-Baywood Park, 3,487 ....E 8
Lynwood, 43,353 ....C 11
Madera⊙, 16,044 ....E 7
Malibu, 15,000 ....B 10
Manhattan Beach, 35,352 ....B 11
Manteca, 13,845 ....D 6
Marinwood, 6,000 ....H 1
Mariposa⊙, 900 ....F 6
Martinez⊙, 16,506 ....K 1
Marysville⊙, 9,353 ....D 4
Maywood, 16,996 ....C 10
McFarland, 4,177 ....F 8
Meiners Oaks, 7,025 ....F 9
Mendota, 2,705 ....E 7
Menlo Park, 26,734 ....J 3
Mentone, 2,900 ....H 9
Merced⊙, 22,670 ....E 6
Midway City, 5,900 ....D 11
Millbrae, 20,781 ....J 2
Mill Valley, 12,942 ....H 2
Milpitas, 27,149 ....L 3
Mira Loma, 8,482 ....E 10
Mission Viejo, 11,933 ....D 11
Modesto⊙, 61,712 ....D 6
Mojave, 2,573 ....G 8
Monrovia, 30,015 ....D 10
Montalvo, 2,400 ....F 9
Montclair, 22,546 ....D 10
Montebello, 42,807 ....C 10
Montecito, 4,900 ....F 9
Monterey, 26,302 ....D 7
Monterey Park, 49,166 ....C 10
Monte Sereno, 3,089 ....K 4
Montrose-La Crescenta, 19,594 ....C 10
Moorpark, 3,380 ....G 9
Morada■, 2,936 ....D 5
Moraga, 14,205 ....K 2
Morgan Hill, 6,485 ....L 4
Morro Bay, 7,109 ....D 8
Mountain View, 51,092 ....K 3
Mount Shasta, 2,163 ....C 2
Mulberry, 1,795 ....D 4
Muscoy, 7,091 ....E 10
Napa⊙, 35,978 ....C 5
National City, 43,184 ....J 11
Nebo Center■, 1,828 ....J 9
Needles, 4,051 ....L 9
Nevada City⊙, 2,314 ....D 4
Newark, 27,153 ....K 3
Newhall, 9,651 ....G 9
Newman, 2,505 ....D 6
Newport Beach, 49,422 ....D 11
Nipomo, 3,642 ....E 8
Norco, 14,511 ....E 11
North Fair Oaks■, 9,740 ....J 3
North Highlands, 31,854 ....B 8
North Hollywood, 190,000 ....B 10
Norwalk, 91,827 ....C 11
Novato, 31,006 ....H 1
Oakdale, 6,594 ....E 6
Oakland⊙, 361,561 ....J 2
Oak View, 4,872 ....F 9
Oceano, 2,564 ....E 8
Oceanside, 40,494 ....H 10
Oildale, 20,879 ....F 8
Ojai, 5,591 ....F 9
Olivehurst■, 8,100 ....D 4
Ontario, 64,118 ....D 10
Opal Cliffs, 5,425 ....K 4
Orange, 77,374 ....D 11
Orange Cove, 3,392 ....F 7
Orangevale■, 16,493 ....C 8
Orcutt, 8,500 ....E 9
Orinda, 6,790 ....J 2
Orland, 2,884 ....C 4
Orosi, 2,757 ....F 7
Oroville⊙, 7,536 ....D 4
Otay-Castle Park■, 15,445 ....H 11
Oxnard, 71,225 ....F 9
Oxnard-Ventura, ‡376,430 ....F 9
Pacifica, 36,020 ....H 2
Pacific Beach, 35,000 ....H 11
Pacific Grove, 13,505 ....C 7
Palermo, 1,966 ....D 4
Palmdale, 8,511 ....G 9
Palm Desert, 6,171 ....J 10
Palm Springs, 20,936 ....J 10
Palo Alto, 55,966 ....K 3
Palos Verdes Estates, 13,641 ....B 11
Palos Verdes Peninsula■, 39,616 ....B 11
Paradise, 14,539 ....D 4
Paramount, 34,734 ....C 11
Parlier, 1,993 ....F 7
Pasadena, 113,327 ....C 10
Paso Robles, 7,168 ....E 8
Patterson, 3,147 ....D 6
Pebble Beach, 5,000 ....C 7
Perris, 4,228 ....F 11
Petaluma, 24,870 ....H 1
Pico Rivera, 54,170 ....C 10
Piedmont, 10,917 ....J 2
Pinedale, 1,900 ....F 7
Pinole, 15,850 ....J 1
Pismo Beach, 4,043 ....E 8
Pittsburg, 20,651 ....L 1
Placentia, 21,948 ....D 11
Placerville⊙, 5,416 ....C 8
Planada, 2,056 ....E 6
Pleasant Hill, 24,610 ....K 2
Pleasanton, 18,328 ....L 2
Pomona, 87,384 ....D 10
Porterville, 12,602 ....G 7
Port Hueneme, 14,295 ....F 9
Portola Valley, 4,999 ....J 3
Poway, 9,422 ....J 11
Quartz Hill, 4,935 ....G 9
Quincy⊙, 3,343 ....E 4
Ramona, 3,554 ....J 10
Rancho Cordova, 30,451 ....C 8
Rancho Rinconada■, 5,149 ....K 3

⊙ County seat.   ‡ Population of metropolitan area.   ■ Name not shown on map.

All figures available from 1970 final census are supplemented by local official estimates.

CALIFORNIA

Rancho Santa Clarita, 4,860 G 9
Red Bluff⊙, 7,676 C 3
Redding⊙, 16,659 C 3
Redlands, 36,355 H 9
Redondo Beach, 56,075 B 11
Redwood City⊙, 55,686 J 3
Reedley, 8,131 F 7
Reseda, 60,862 B 10
Rialto, 28,370 E 10
Richmond, 79,043 J 1
Ridgecrest, 7,629 H 8
Rio Dell, 2,817 A 3
Rio Linda, 7,524 B 8
Rio Vista, 3,135 L 1
Ripon, 2,679 D 6
Riverbank, 3,949 E 6
Riverside⊙, 140,089 E 11
Rocklin, 3,039 B 8
Rodeo, 5,356 J 1
Rohnert Park, 6,133 C 5
Rohnerville, 2,781 B 3
Rolling Hills, 2,050 B 11
Rolling Hills Estates, 6,027 B 11
Rosamond, 2,281 G 9
Roseland■, 5,105 C 5
Rosemead, 40,972 C 10
Roseville, 17,895 B 8
Ross, 2,742 H 1
Rossmoor■, 12,922 C 11
Rowland Heights■, 16,881 D 10
Rubidoux, 13,969 E 10
Ryans Slough■, 3,922 A 3
Sacramento (cap.)⊙, 254,413 B 8
Sacramento, ‡800,592 B 8
Saint Helena, 3,173 C 5
Salinas⊙, 58,896 D 7
Salinas-Monterey, ‡250,071 D 7
San Andreas⊙, 1,564 E 5
San Anselmo, 13,031 H 1
San Bernardino⊙, 104,251 E 10
San Bernardino-Riverside-Ontario, ‡1,143,146 E 10
San Bruno, 36,254 J 2
San Carlos, 25,924 J 3
San Clemente, 17,063 H 10
San Diego⊙, 696,769 H 11
San Diego, ‡1,357,854 H 11
San Dimas, 15,692 D 10
San Fernando, 16,571 C 10
San Francisco⊙, 715,674 H 2
San Francisco-Oakland, ‡3,109,519 H 2
San Gabriel, 29,176 C 10
Sanger, 10,088 F 7
San Jacinto, 4,385 H 10
San Jose⊙, 445,779 L 3
San Jose, ‡1,064,714 L 3
San Juan Capistrano, 3,781 H 10
San Leandro, 68,698 J 2
San Lorenzo, 24,633 K 2
San Luis Obispo⊙, 28,036 E 8
San Marcos, 3,896 H 10
San Marino, 14,177 D 10
San Mateo, 78,911 J 3
San Pablo, 21,461 J 1
San Pedro, 91,000 C 11
San Rafael⊙, 38,977 J 1
San Ramon, 4,084 K 2
Santa Ana⊙, 156,601 D 11
Santa Barbara⊙, 70,215 F 9
Santa Barbara, ‡264,324 F 9
Santa Clara, 87,717 K 3
Santa Cruz⊙, 32,076 K 4
Santa Fe Springs, 14,750 C 11
Santa Maria, 32,749 E 9
Santa Monica, 88,289 B 10
Santa Paula, 18,001 F 9
Santa Rosa⊙, 50,006 C 5
Santa Susana, 2,900 B 10
Santa Venetia, 2,500 J 1
Santee, 21,107 J 11
Saratoga, 27,110 K 4
Saticoy, 2,400 F 9
Sausalito, 6,158 H 2
Scotts Valley, 3,621 K 4
Seal Beach, 24,441 C 11
Seaside, 35,935 D 7
Sebastopol, 3,993 C 5
Selma, 7,459 F 7
Sepulveda, 40,000 B 10
Shafter, 5,327 F 8
Shell Beach, 1,900 E 8
Sierra Madre, 12,140 D 10
Signal Hill, 5,582 C 11
Simi Valley, 56,464 G 9
Solana Beach, 5,023 H 11
Soledad, 6,843 D 7
Solvang, 2,004 E 9
Sonoma, 4,112 C 5
Sonora⊙, 3,100 E 6
Soquel, 5,795 K 4
South El Monte, 13,443 C 10
South Gate, 56,909 C 11
South Laguna■, 2,566 H 10
South Lake Tahoe, 12,921 F 5
South Modesto■, 7,889 D 6
South Oroville, 4,111 D 4
South Pasadena, 22,979 C 10
South Sacramento, 28,574 B 8
South San Francisco, 46,646 J 2
South San Gabriel■, 5,051 C 10
South San Jose Hills■, 12,386 D 10
South Taft, 2,214 F 8
South Whittier■, 46,641 C 11
South Yuba City■, 5,352 D 4
Spring Valley■, 29,742 J 11
Stanford, 8,691 J 3
Stanton, 17,947 D 11
Stockton⊙, 107,644 D 6
Stockton, ‡290,208 D 6
Suisun City, 2,917 K 1
Sun City, 5,519 F 11
Sunland, 22,200 C 10
Sunnymead, 6,708 F 11
Sunnyvale, 95,408 K 3
Sunset Beach, 1,900 C 11
Susanville⊙, 6,608 E 3
Sutter Creek, 1,508 C 9
Taft, 4,285 F 8
Taft Heights■, 2,108 F 8
Tarzana, 24,165 B 10
Tehachapi, 4,211 G 8
Temple City, 29,673 D 10
Thermalito, 4,217 D 4
Thousand Oaks, 36,334 G 9
Tiburon, 6,209 J 2
Topanga, 4,800 B 10
Topanga Beach, 4,500 B 10
Torrance, 134,584 C 11
Tracy, 14,724 D 6
Tujunga, 22,000 C 10
Tulare, 16,235 F 7
Turlock, 13,992 E 6
Tustin, 21,178 D 11
Twentynine Palms, 5,667 K 9
Twin Lakes, 3,012 K 4
Ukiah⊙, 10,095 B 4
Union City, 14,724 K 2
University Park, 3,100 D 11
Upland, 32,551 E 10
Vacaville, 21,690 D 5
Valencia, 4,243 G 9
Valinda■, 18,837 D 10
Vallejo, 66,733 J 1
Vallejo-Napa, ‡249,081 J 1
Van Nuys, 231,600 B 10
Venice, 80,500 B 11
Ventura⊙, 55,797 F 9
Victorville, 10,845 H 9
View Park-Windsor Hills■, 12,268 C 11
Villa Park, 2,723 D 11
Visalia⊙, 27,268 F 7
Vista, 24,688 H 10
Walnut, 5,992 D 10
Walnut Creek, 39,844 K 2
Walnut Park■, 8,925 C 11
Wasco, 8,269 F 8
Waterford, 2,243 E 6
Watsonville, 14,569 D 7
Weaverville⊙, 1,489 B 3
Weed, 2,983 C 2
West Athens■, 13,286 C 11
West Carson■, 15,501 C 11
West Compton■, 5,748 C 11
West Covina, 68,034 D 10
West Hollywood, 29,448 B 10
West Los Angeles, 38,805 B 10
Westminster, 59,865 D 11
West Modesto■, 6,135 D 6
Westmont■, 29,310 C 11
West Pittsburg, 5,969 K 1
West Sacramento, 12,002 B 8
West Whittier-Los Nietos■, 20,845 C 11
Westwood, Lassen, 1,862 D 3
Westwood, L. A., 45,000 B 10
Whittier, 72,863 D 11
Willits, 3,091 B 4
Willowbrook■, 28,705 C 11
Willows⊙, 4,085 C 4
Wilmington, 38,000 C 11
Windsor, 2,359 C 5
Winters, 2,419 D 5
Winton, 3,393 E 6
Woodlake, 3,371 G 7
Woodland⊙, 20,677 B 8
Woodland Hills, 56,420 B 10
Woodside, 4,731 J 3
Yorba Linda, 11,856 D 11
Yountville, 2,332 C 5
Yreka⊙, 5,394 C 2
Yuba City⊙, 13,986 D 4
Yucaipa, 19,284 J 9
Yucca Valley, 3,893 J 9

OTHER FEATURES

Agua Caliente Ind. Res., 78 J 10
Alameda (creek) K 3
Alamo (riv.) K 10
Alcatraz (isl.) J 2
Alkali (lakes) E 2
All American (canal) K 11
Almanor (lake) D 3
Amargosa (range) J 7
Amargosa (riv.) J 7
American (riv.) C 8
Anacapa (isl.) F 10
Angel (isl.) J 2
Arena (pt.) B 5
Arguello (pt.) E 9
Argus (range) H 7
Arroyo del Valle (dry riv.) L 3
Arroyo Hondo (dry riv.) L 3
Arroyo Mocho (dry riv.) L 2
Arroyo Seco (dry riv.) K 10
Beale A.F.B., 9,354 D 4
Berryessa (lake) D 5
Bethany (res.) L 3
Big Sage (res.) E 2
Black Butte (res.) C 4
Bodega (bay) B 5
Buena Vista (lake) F 8
Cabrillo Nat'l Mon. H 11
Cachuma (lake) F 9
Cadiz (lake) K 9
Cahuilla Ind. Res., 62 J 10
Calaveras (res.) L 3
California Aqueduct E 7
Camanche (res.) C 9
Campo Ind. Res., 53 J 11
Capitan Grande Ind. Res. J 11
Cascade (range) D 1
Castle A.F.B., 1,903 E 6
Channel Islands Nat'l Mon. F 10
Chemehuevi Valley Ind. Res. L 9
Chocolate (mts.) K 10
Clair Engle (lake) C 3
Clear (lake) C 4
Clear Lake (res.) D 2
Coachella (canal) K 10
Coast (ranges) B 2
Colorado (riv.) L 8
Colorado River Aqueduct K 10
Colorado River Ind. Res. L 10
Conception (pt.) E 9
Cooper (pt.) D 7
Copco (lake) C 2
Cosumnes (riv.) C 9
Cottonwood (creek) C 3
Coyote (creek) L 3
Coyote (res.) L 4
Cuyama (riv.) E 8
Cuyapaipe Ind. Res., 1 J 11
Danby (lake) K 9
Death (valley) H 7
Death Valley Nat'l Mon. H 7
Delgada (pt.) A 3
Del Valle (lake) L 3
Devils Postpile Nat'l Mon. F 6
Dume (pt.) G 10
Duxbury (pt.) H 2
Eagle (lake) E 3
Eagle (peak) E 2
Edison (lake) F 6
Edwards A.F.B., 10,331 H 9
Eel (riv.) B 4
Elsinore (lake) E 11
El Toro Marine Air Sta., 6,970 D 11
Estero (bay) D 8
Estero (pt.) D 8
Estrella (riv.) E 8
Farallon (isls.) B 6
Farallons, The (gulf) H 2
Feather (riv.) D 4
Florence (lake) G 6
Folsom (lake) C 8
Fort Baker J 2
Fort Bidwell Ind. Res., 104 E 2
Fort Independence Ind. Res., 32 G 7
Fort Irwin, 2,991 J 8
Fort MacArthur C 11
Fort Mohave Ind. Res., 277 L 9
Fort Ord D 7
Forts Barry and Cronkhite H 2
Fort Winfield Scott J 2
Freel (peak) F 5
Fremont (peak) H 8
Fresno (riv.) E 7
Friant-Kern (canal) F 8
General Grant Grove Section (King's Canyon Nat'l Park) G 7
George A.F.B., 7,404 H 9
Golden Gate (chan.) H 2
Goose (lake) E 1
Grapevine (mts.) H 7
Grizzly (bay) K 1
Guadalupe (riv.) K 3
Haiwee H 7
Hamilton (mt.) L 3
Hamilton A.F.B. J 1
Hat (peak) E 2
Havasu (lake) L 9
Hetch Hetchy (res.) F 6
Hoffman (mt.) D 2
Honey (lake) E 3
Hoopa Valley Ind. Res., 992 A 2
Humboldt (bay) A 3
Hunter Liggett Mil. Res. D 8
Imperial (res.) L 10
Imperial (valley) K 10
Ingalls (mt.) E 3
Inyo (mts.) G 6
Inyokern Nav. Ordnance Test Sta. H 8
Iron Gate (res.) C 2
Isabella (res.) G 8
John Muir Nat'l Hist. Site K 1
Joshua Tree Nat'l Mon. J 10
Kern (riv.) G 8
Kings (riv.) F 7
Kings Canyon Nat'l Park G 7
Klamath (riv.) B 2
Laguna (res.) L 11
La Jolla Ind. Res., 76 J 10
Lassen (peak) D 3
Lassen Volcanic Nat'l Park D 3
Lava Beds Nat'l Mon. D 2
Lemoore N.A.S., 8,512 F 7
Leroy Anderson (res.) L 4
Lopez (pt.) D 7
Los Angeles Aqueduct G 8
Los Coyotes Ind. Res., 29 J 10
Lost (riv.) D 1
Lower Alkali (lake) E 2
Mad (riv.) B 3
Manzanita Ind. Res., 19 J 11
March A.F.B., 2,002 E 11
Mare Island Navy Yard J 1
Mather A.F.B., 7,027 C 8
Mathews (lake) E 11
McClellan A.F.B. B 8
McClure (lake) E 6
Mendocino (cape) A 3
Merced (riv.) E 6
Middle Alkali (lake) E 2
Millerton (lake) F 6
Moffett Nav. Air Sta. K 3
Mojave (des.) H 9
Mojave (riv.) J 9
Mokelumne (riv.) C 9
Mono (lake) G 5
Monterey (bay) K 4
Moon (lake) E 2
Morongo Ind. Res., 257 J 10
Mountain Meadows (res.) E 3
Muir Woods Nat'l Mon. H 2
Nacimiento (riv.) D 8
Navarro (riv.) B 4
Nevada, Sierra (mts.) E 4
New (riv.) K 11
Norton A.F.B. F 10
Noyo (riv.) B 4
Oakland Army Base J 2
Old (riv.) L 1
Oroville (res.) D 4
Owens (lake) H 7
Owens (riv.) G 6
Oxnard A.F.B. F 9
Paiute Ind. Res. G 6
Pala Ind. Res., 215 H 10
Palomar (mt.) J 10
Panamint (range) H 7
Pendleton, Camp, 25,495 H 10
Pescadero (creek) J 3
Pescadero (pt.) J 3
Piedras Blancas (pt.) D 8
Pillar (pt.) H 3
Pillsbury (lake) C 4
Pine (creek) D 3
Pine Flat (res.) F 7
Pinnacles Nat'l Mon. D 7
Pit (riv.) D 2
Point Mugu Pacific Missile Range, 3,351 F 9
Point Reyes Nat'l Seashore H 1
Presidio J 2
Providence (mts.) K 8
Punta Gorda (pt.) A 3
Quartz (peak) L 11
Railroad Canyon (res.) E 11
Redwood Nat'l Park A 2
Reyes (pt.) B 6
Rogers (lake) H 9
Rosamond (lake) G 9
Round Valley Ind. Res., 1,115 B 4
Russian (riv.) B 4
Sacramento (riv.) D 5
Sacramento Army Depot B 8
Saint George (pt.) A 2
Salinas (riv.) D 7
Salmon (riv.) B 2
Salton Sea (lake) K 10
San Andreas (lake) H 2
San Antonio (res.) E 8
San Benito (riv.) D 7
San Bernardino (mts.) J 10
San Clemente (isl.) G 11
San Diego (bay) H 11
San Francisco (bay) J 2
San Gabriel (res.) D 10
San Joaquin (riv.) E 6
San Joaquin (valley) D 6
San Lorenzo (riv.) K 4
San Luis (res.) E 7
San Martin (cape) D 8
San Miguel (isl.) E 9
San Nicholas (isl.) F 10
San Pablo (bay) J 1
San Pedro (bay) C 11
San Pedro (chan.) G 10
Santa Ana (riv.) E 11
Santa Barbara (chan.) E 9
Santa Barbara (isl.) G 10
Santa Catalina (isl.) G 10
Santa Cruz (chan.) F 10
Santa Cruz (isl.) F 10
Santa Maria (riv.) E 9
Santa Monica (bay) B 11
Santa Rosa (isl.) E 10
Santa Rosa Ind. Res., 15 J 10
Santa Ynez (riv.) E 9
Santa Ysabel Ind. Res., 136 J 10
Scott (riv.) B 2
Searles (lake) H 8
Sequoia Nat'l Park G 7
Sharpe Army Depot D 6
Shasta (lake) C 3
Shasta (mt.) C 2
Shasta (riv.) C 2
Sierra Army Depot E 3
Sierra Nevada (mts.) E 4
Siskiyou (mts.) C 2
Smith River Ind. Res., 102 A 2
Soda (lake) K 8
South Bay Aqueduct L 3
South Cow (creek) C 3
Stony Gorge (res.) C 4
Suisun (bay) K 1
Sur (pt.) D 7
Susan (riv.) D 3
Tahoe (lake) F 4
Tamalpais (mt.) H 1
Tehachapi (mts.) G 9
Torres Martinez Ind. Res., 75 J 10
Travis A.F.B. L 1
Trinidad (head) A 2
Trinity (riv.) B 3
Truckee (riv.) F 4
Tulare (lake) F 7
Tule (lake) D 2
Tule River Ind. Res., 325 G 7
Twentynine Palms Marine Base, 5,647 J 9
Upper Alkali (lake) E 2
Vandenberg A.F.B., 13,193 E 9
Vizcaino (cape) B 4
Walnut (creek) K 1
Wheeler (peak) F 5
Whipple (mts.) L 9
Whiskeytown-Shasta-Trinity Nat'l Rec. Area C 3
Whitney (mt.) G 7
Wilson (mt.) D 10
Yosemite Nat'l Park F 6
Yuba (riv.) D 4
Yuma Ind. Res. L 11

MONTEREY CYPRESS trees, gnarled by the ocean winds, border the white sandy beach at Carmel. The southern part of the state's Pacific coast abounds in similar beaches.

J. J. SMITH

San Diego, which ranks third in size among California cities, is situated on the far southern coast, near the Mexican border. It is a port of entry, one of the major Pacific bases of the U. S. Navy, and a center of aircraft manufacturing and fishing.

Santa Barbara, on the coast 100 miles (161 km) northwest of Los Angeles, remains primarily a residential community. Monterey, the old Spanish capital, about the same distance south of San Francisco Bay, is a city of exceptional historical interest. It is also a major center of the fishing industry. The adjoining community of Carmel is widely known as an art and literary center. Farther north, San Jose is the hub of a rich agricultural region.

Most of the other urban centers in California lie in the great Central Valley. Sacramento, the state capital, at the junction of the Sacramento and American rivers, and Stockton, on the San Joaquin River have access to river transportation —a unique distinction among California cities. Fresno, at about the center of the San Joaquin Valley, and Bakersfield, near its southern end, are supported by agriculture, petroleum, and local manufactures.

Mt. Shasta, in the Cascade Range in northern California.

JACK ZEHRT

2. The Land

California occupies about two thirds of the United States' Pacific coastal area between Mexico and Canada. If it were situated at comparable latitudes in the Atlantic coast, it would extend approximately from Cape Cod, Mass., to Charleston, S. C. The state has a general coastline of 840 miles (1,352 km), a medial length of 780 miles (1,255 km), and a width of 150 to 350 miles (241 to 563 km). It is extremely varied in topography, climate, and natural resources.

Major Physical Divisions. California's chief physiographic regions are the narrow coastal area between mountains and the sea; the great Central Valley, walled by the Coast Ranges on the west and the Sierra Nevada on the east; the desert basins of the southern interior; and the rugged mountainous areas of the north.

The coast varies from the low, sandy beaches of the south to the rock-girt, sharply uplifted headlands of Cape Mendocino and the Monterey Peninsula. San Francisco Bay is one of the most capacious harbors in the world. Other, smaller bays include Humboldt, Monterey, and San Diego bays. Two groups of islands lie off the coast. These are the Santa Barbara Islands (known also as the Channel Islands) in the south and the small Farallon Islands west of San Francisco.

Numerous mountain chains, broken into ridges and spurs, extend along the California coast. Although the entire system often is referred to as the Coast Ranges, the Coast Ranges proper extend only from Cape Mendocino in the north to Point Conception in the south. Above Cape Mendocino are the Klamath Mountains, which continue northward into Oregon. Below Point Conception is a complex of narrow, generally east-west ranges known as the Los Angeles Ranges. These include the San Gabriel, San Bernardino, and the San Jacinto mountains.

Within the spurs of the Coast Ranges and the Los Angeles Ranges, and between the mountains and the sea, lie many of the most fertile valleys of California. Among these garden spots are the Napa-Livermore, Santa Clara-Santa Rosa, Salinas, San Luis, Santa Clara of the South, San Bernardino, and San Fernando valleys. The coastal area also contains the state's largest cities, most densely populated areas, and chief industrial centers.

JOSEF MUENCH

LAKE TAHOE, shared by California and Nevada (*in background*), is notable among lakes in the Sierra Nevada.

The part of southern California east of the Los Angeles Ranges and south and east of the Sierra Nevada, as well as the northeastern corner of the state, belongs to the Basin and Range province (a region of the western United States characterized by short mountain ranges separated by desert basins). The chief features of this region in California are Death Valley and the Mojave Desert.

The Tehachapi Mountains, a short connecting link between the Coast Ranges and the Sierra Nevada, mark the northern rim of the Mojave Desert. The same mountains form the southern boundary of the rich agricultural region known as the Central Valley of California. This valley, which is drained by the San Joaquin and Sacramento rivers, extends some 400 miles (644 km) from north to south and has an average width of about 50 miles (80 km). The San Francisco Bay area is the only gap in the Coast Ranges, which form the western border of the valley. On the east the valley is walled in throughout its length by the rampart of the Sierra Nevada.

The western slope of the Sierra Nevada is gradual, but on the eastern side the uplift is defiantly sheer. Mount Whitney, near the southern end, reaches an elevation of 14,494 feet (4,418 meters), and many other peaks approach that height. The Sierra's valleys, canyons, lakes, evergreen forests, and other natural grandeurs make it one of the nation's best-known recreation areas.

The northern end of the Central Valley is enclosed by the coming together of the Klamath Mountains and the Cascade Range. The Cascade Range, an extension of the Sierra Nevada, is a volcanically formed range that continues northward through Oregon and Washington. The two best-known peaks in the California section are Lassen Peak and Mount Shasta.

Rivers and Lakes. The northern part of California is drained by such seaward-flowing streams as the Klamath (with its chief tributary, the Trinity), the Mad, Eel, and Russian rivers, and by the Sacramento and its many tributaries, chief of which are the Pit, McCloud, Feather, and American rivers.

The Sacramento runs southward through the upper part of the Central Valley, and the northward-flowing San Joaquin River drains the lower part. The two rivers converge northeast of San Francisco to form a joint delta, from which they empty into Suisun Bay, an arm of San Francisco Bay. They are the major rivers of California, draining the interior country into the ocean. Of the numerous streams that flow into the San Joaquin Valley from the Sierra, the most important, besides the San Joaquin River itself, are the Stanislaus, Tuolumne, and Merced (tributaries of the San Joaquin), and the Kings and Kern rivers.

The rivers of the southern California coastal area are useless for navigation but important for flood control and domestic and industrial use. Frequently they flow down denuded canyons, and in winter sometimes become devastating torrents. The absence of rain and melting snow reduces their summer flow, at least beyond their canyon walls, and their beds become only bone-dry stretches of sand and boulders. The Colorado River forms California's southeastern boundary with Arizona.

Freshwater lakes are rare in southern California but exist in large numbers elsewhere, especially in the Sierra Nevada. Lake Tahoe, in the northern part of this range, is shared by California and Nevada. Clear Lake, in the Coast Ranges north of San Francisco, is the largest freshwater lake wholly within California. The largest lake in the state is the brackish Salton Sea. Artificial lakes have been created throughout the state for water conservation, flood control, and the generation of hydroelectric power.

Climate. What is usually thought of as the characteristic climate of California actually is typical of only a portion of the state—the narrow plain between the ocean and the mountains southward from the San Francisco area. There virtually no snow falls, the thermometer rarely drops to the freezing point, and the annual rainfall, confined in the main to late fall, winter, and early spring, ranges from an average of 10.3 inches (26.2 cm) at San Diego to 22 inches (56 cm) at San Francisco. The mean average tem-

DE WYS, INC.

CITRUS ORCHARD near Fresno. With annual farm income of $4 billion, California is the leading agricultural state.

perature is 56.1° F (13.4° C) at San Francisco, 63° F (17° C) at Los Angeles, and 61.4° F (16.2° C) at San Diego. Growing seasons reach 365 days along the coastal belt. Cool nights, ocean breezes, and early morning fogs are noticeable features of the summers along the entire coastline.

Elsewhere, the climate of California is as varied as the topography. One spot near the coast of northern California receives almost 100 inches (254 cm) of rain a year, while certain desert regions of the southwest experience little or no measurable rainfall in an entire season. In parts of the state a difference of 50° F (10° C) between day and night temperatures is not uncommon. The state's lowest recorded temperature was −45° F (−43° C) at Boca (just north of Lake Tahoe) in 1937; the highest, 134° F (57° C) at Greenland Ranch, Inyo county, in 1913.

The northern coast is a region of heavy rainfall, frequent summer fogs, and even temperatures. Above the 2,000-foot (610-meter) level in the Sierra Nevada and parts of the Coast Ranges, there is a zone of winter snows, moderate rainfall, and marked fluctuations of temperature. The great Central Valley experiences meager to heavy rainfall and greater extremes of temperature, both winter and summer, than do the coastal areas. The southern interior is a land of little rain, extreme summer heat and unusually mild winters in the low Imperial and Coachella valley regions of the extreme southeast, and relatively severe cold at higher elevations.

Plant Life. Forest lands cover about two fifths of California's total area. They lie chiefly in the Sierra Nevada and in the northern coastal counties and contain large stands of ponderosa pine, Douglas fir, spruce, redwood, hemlock, cedar, maple, and oak. But the state is noted especially for the big tree, or giant sequoia (*Sequoiadendron giganteum*) of the Sierra slopes, its redwood empire (forests of redwood, *Sequoia sempervirens*, stretching northward from San Francisco), and the rare stands of Monterey pine and Monterey cypress (probably indigenous to the Monterey area). Also typical are the piñon-juniper woodlands along the lower Sierra and the Coast Ranges as well as the widespread chaparral, mesquite, and sagebrush of the foothills and deserts.

Many imported fruit, ornamental, and shade trees have adapted themselves to California's climate and soils. Among these are the pepper tree (from Peru), Canary Island date palm, the cedar of Lebanon, the East Indian crape myrtle, the East Indian deodar, the camphor tree from China, and the Australian eucalyptus.

Among the wild flowers, different species of lupine, violas, and California poppies crowd the valleys and the mountainsides. Cacti, desert poppies, and Joshua trees (*Yucca brevifolia*) break the monotony of arid expanses.

Animal Life. Naturalists have identified at least 400 species of mammals and 600 types of birds in the state. The most distinctive creatures inhabit the more arid regions—the desert tortoise, horned toad, kangaroo rat, sidewinder (a small rattlesnake), and (in decreasing numbers) the pronghorn antelope. Squirrels, chipmunks, and jackrabbits are the desert's most common animals. Woodland and forest mammals include deer, black bear, bobcat, weasel, and the California ring-tailed cat. In mountainous areas roam mountain lion, coyote, wolverine, and cougar. Bighorn sheep, once fairly common, are now rare, and the California grizzly bear is extinct.

Distinctive birds of the state include blue-fronted and California jays, the California thrasher, the junco, grouse, hermit thrush, and mountain bluebird. Valley quail, mourning dove, wood duck, and mallard tempt the hunter.

In California's reservoirs and freshwater streams, fishermen find trout of a dozen kinds, salmon, and many other fish. Shoreline fishing yields such saltwater varieties as rockfish, striped bass, perch, and tuna. Offshore fish frequently include shark, halibut, tuna, and marlin.

Mineral Resources. The gold of the Sierra Nevada, the borax deposits of Death Valley and the Mojave Desert, and the petroleum of the Los Angeles area have been California's best-known minerals, but almost every area of the state has some mineral resources. Fortunately, the known deposits include a variety of minerals most needed in the construction, chemical, and metalworking industries of the present day. Some of these are gypsum, asbestos, cement, an abundance of sand and gravel, borax, boron, and tungsten.

Water Resource Development. Since the early 1900's, city, state, and federal agencies have engaged in water development projects that are notable for their size no less than for their vigorous approach to California's pressing water problems. The central feature of the projects is that they transfer water from one section of the state to another by means of aqueducts or canals supported by intricate systems of dams, storage reservoirs, hydroelectric plants, and pumping stations.

In 1913, Los Angeles completed the construction of a controversial aqueduct about 215 miles (346 km) long, to bring the water to the Owens River across the Mojave Desert and the San Gabriel Mountains to the city. In 1931, San Francisco completed a similar aqueduct to the Hetch Hetchy Valley (in Yosemite National Park) to tap the waters of the Tuolumne River. The dispute over the impact of these two projects upon conservation of mountain areas continues.

Another undertaking of great benefit to California and adjoining states was the construction by the federal government in the mid-1930's of Hoover Dam (formerly Boulder Dam) on the Colorado River near Las Vegas, Nev. One purpose of this project was to curb the turbulent Colorado and thereby to protect the Imperial Valley against the recurrent threat of flood. In the meantime, Los Angeles and a group of other cities had formed the Metropolitan Water District of Southern California to seek new sources of water supply and bring the water to the area. After construction of Hoover Dam had begun, the district obtained rights to Colorado River water, erected Parker Dam (downstream from Hoover Dam) to store water, and constructed an aqueduct to bring the water westward to the Los Angeles area. The main aqueduct, called the Colorado River Aqueduct, is 242 miles (389 km) long. Branch aqueducts carry water to the San Diego area. The Imperial Irrigation District diverted another large flow of water from the Colorado at Imperial Dam and carried it through the All-American Canal, 80 miles (129 km) to the farms and towns of the Imperial Valley. A branch of this canal serves the Coachella Valley. Most of these projects were completed in the 1940's.

Two other undertakings dwarf all the rest in complexity and size. These are the Central Valley Project (an undertaking of the U. S. Bureau of Reclamation), and the state-financed California Water Project (known also as the Feather River project). Both of these transfer water from the generally well-watered but lightly populated northern third of the state to the arid but evergrowing central and southern thirds.

The Central Valley Project, which was begun in the 1930's, has been constructed under a master plan that provides for extensive water storage in both the Sacramento and the San Joaquin valleys and the transfer of water from the Sacramento and Trinity river basins to the arid parts of the San Joaquin Valley. The earliest key structure was Shasta Dam, with its reservoir (Shasta Lake) and hydroelectric installation near the northern end of the Sacramento Valley. Water from the lake is released to the delta area of the two rivers northeast of San Francisco and from there is conveyed southward by the Delta-Mendota Canal. Another early unit, the Friant Dam near the headwaters of the San Joaquin River, stores water that is carried southward to Bakersfield by the Friant-Kern Canal. These are only some of the units in a water-development program that has transformed the Central Valley into a sprawling agricultural and industrial empire.

The California Water Project was initiated in 1960, when voters of the state authorized a bond issue of $1.75 billion. This multibillion-dollar project is designed to produce hydroelectric power and convey water from the north to various water districts as far south as the San Diego area. The key structure is the Oroville Dam on the Feather River, northeast of Sacramento. Other plans for meeting California's anticipated water shortages include a nuclear desalting plant for southern California.

Other Conservation Agencies. The state operates numerous fish hatcheries (the largest is near the town of Mount Shasta), chiefly for stocking lakes and streams. Waterfowl, birds of many kinds, and game are protected in more than 15 national wildlife refuges. These include the Tule Lake, Salton Sea, and Clear Lake national wildlife refuges. The many lakes created by the Bureau of Reclamation's Central Valley Project enhance fish and wildlife resources and add greatly to recreational facilities. The Sierra Club, the Save-the-Redwoods League, and other organizations help guard irreplaceable resources against the encroachment of commercial interests.

3. The Economy

California's economy benefits from its many natural resources as well as from a mounting population. These resources have enabled California to lead the nation in agriculture and fisheries and have placed it near the top in manufacturing, mineral and lumber production, and tourism. (See the color map *Agriculture, Industry, and Resources* accompanying this article.) The state's remarkable economic growth also has enabled it to solidify its leadership in foreign trade and in wholesaling and retailing.

California ranks among the first five states in per capita income. Employment in manufacturing industries is the leading source of personal income, with government, wholesale and retail trade, and service occupations following in that order. Although agricultural employment is decreasing steadily as a source of personal income, farm activities engage more than half a million persons during seasonal peaks.

PERSONAL INCOME IN CALIFORNIA

Source of Wage and Salary Disbursements	1965	1960	1950
	(Millions of Dollars)		
Farms	626	1,407	1,145
Mining	255	233	159
Contract construction	2,627	2,336	1,209
Manufacturing	10,591	8,991	3,154
Wholesale and retail trade	6,950	6,420	3,329
Finance, insurance, and real estate	1,968	1,886	871
Transportation, communications, and public utilities	2,905	2,411	1,262
Services	5,344	5,158	2,204
Government	8,908	4,808	1,844
Other industries	105	132	116
		(Dollars)	
Per capita personal income	3,258	2,710	1,852
Per capita income, U. S.	2,746	2,215	1,496

Source: U. S. Department of Commerce, *Survey of Current Business.*

Another economic pursuit in which California has made rapid and significant progress is banking. In the early 1920's a number of California banks began to develop branch banking on a large scale. One of these, the Bank of America (formerly the Bank of Italy), with headquarters in San Francisco, was founded by A. P. Giannini and became one of the world's largest privately owned banks. Branch banking resulted in a vast extension of credit, particularly in agricultural regions.

Agriculture. California's preeminence as an agricultural state, with an annual cash farm income of about $4 billion, depends on several factors. The climate permits crops such as vegetables to be grown in California over a longer period than elsewhere, or during the off-season, and thus to find ready markets. There are more than 7 million acres (2.8 million hectares) of irrigated farmlands. Mechanization and specialization are widespread. Many farms specialize in only one or two crops, and some are so highly mechanized that they resemble factories in the fields. Cooperation between farmers and state university experiment stations is close. The range of products is wide, including livestock (meat animals, dairy cows, and poultry), feed crops, food grains (rice and wheat), cotton, vegetables, and fruits and nuts.

Among the states, California ranks first in cash value of all farm commodities combined, first in value of crops, and second in value of livestock. It produces virtually every crop (more than 200) grown in temperate zones and is a major source of the nation's truck crops. These include tomatoes, lettuce, potatoes, celery, broccoli, and avocados. With Florida, California produces the bulk of the nation's citrus crop, although one fourth of California's citrus lands have been lost to highway developments and real estate subdivisions since World War II. Other fruits that California supplies in large quantity are grapes (wine, table, and raisin), peaches, pears, apricots, dates, and plums. Among products that in the United States come almost exclusively from California are artichokes, olives, almonds, and figs.

California also ranks high among the states (first to third) in production of such varied commodities as dairy products, eggs, turkeys, cotton, sugar beets, barley, hay, sheep and lambs, and nursery and greenhouse products.

Fisheries and Lumbering. California is the leading state in commercial fishing and fish canning. Its fishing boats range as far north as Alaska and as far south as Peru. Canneries and processing plants—located principally at San Francisco, Monterey, San Pedro, and San Diego—are supplied with shellfish, skipjack, yellowfin, albacore, and tuna, as well as sardines, anchovies, mackerel, and salmon. Although California is second to Oregon in lumber production, it still must import lumber to meet its needs, chiefly for construction purposes.

Manufacturing. Manufacturing expanded rapidly in the first two decades of the 20th century. Before World War I, the major development was in food processing (such as meat packing and fruit and fish canning), lumber production, and oil refining. During the war and in the postwar years the establishment of new fabricating plants, such as automobile assembly and rubber factories, brought the state far along toward industrial maturity. A pioneer in the manufacture of airplanes, California met the demands created by World War II. Wartime shipbuilding at Oakland and San Pedro accelerated industrial expansion, especially in the southern half of California and in the San Francisco Bay area. New factories were established throughout the state because of favorable climate, ample power, labor, transportation, and markets.

Following World War II, the production of automobiles, airplanes, and ships displaced food processing as the state's leading manufacture. More recently, the engineering and production of aircraft, missiles, and television and communications equipment, including computers, have contributed increasingly to California's economic progress.

Other leading manufactures are industrial and oil field machinery, fabricated metal products, electrical apparatus, chemical and petroleum products, paper and fiber, cement, home furnishings, and clothing.

The first California steel mill began operations at Fontana in 1943, utilizing iron ore mined at Eagle Mountain in Riverside county and tungsten from the Rand Mountains in the Mojave Desert. Since that time metal-processing plants have grown in number, especially at Los Angeles and Oakland.

Although other industries have surpassed food processing in value, California remains the leading state in canning, freezing, and drying of foods. It also produces about 85% of the nation's wines.

Research and Development. The Jet Propulsion Laboratory of the California Institute of Technology at Pasadena has been a center of research for the U. S. space program in conjunction with the National Aeronautic and Space Administration. The RAND Corporation at Santa Monica does strategic and tactical research for the armed forces and other government departments. The name

VALUE OF FACTORY, FARM, AND MINE PRODUCTION

	1965	1960	1950
	(Millions of Dollars)		
Value added by manufacture	17,163[1]	14,174	5,121
Cash farm income	3,751	3,211	2,315
Value of mineral production	1,560	1,422	1,056

[1] 1963.

Sources: U. S. Department of Commerce, *Census of Manufactures;* U. S. Department of Agriculture, *The Farm Income Situation;* U. S. Department of the Interior, *Minerals Yearbook.*

RAND was coined from the words "research and development." RAND is one of the many so-called "think tanks," or "idea factories," for which California has become well known. The major universities all utilize government grants for basic scientific research. Laboratories of industrial corporations also carry on research in telecommunications, space technology, and development of industrial by-products, such as petroleum derivatives. The Department of Viticulture and Enology at the Davis campus of the University of California makes notable contributions to California's internationally known wine industry.

Mining and Minerals Extraction. From the time of the gold rush, American mining law was developed largely in California, and many mining techniques were first perfected in the state. California usually ranks among the first three states in annual value of mineral output, and it leads in the number of commodities produced and in the quantity of mineral raw materials consumed. Although California ranks third in production of petroleum, large imports annually enter the state. Substantial quantities of natural gas come by pipeline from Texas, New Mexico, and Canada.

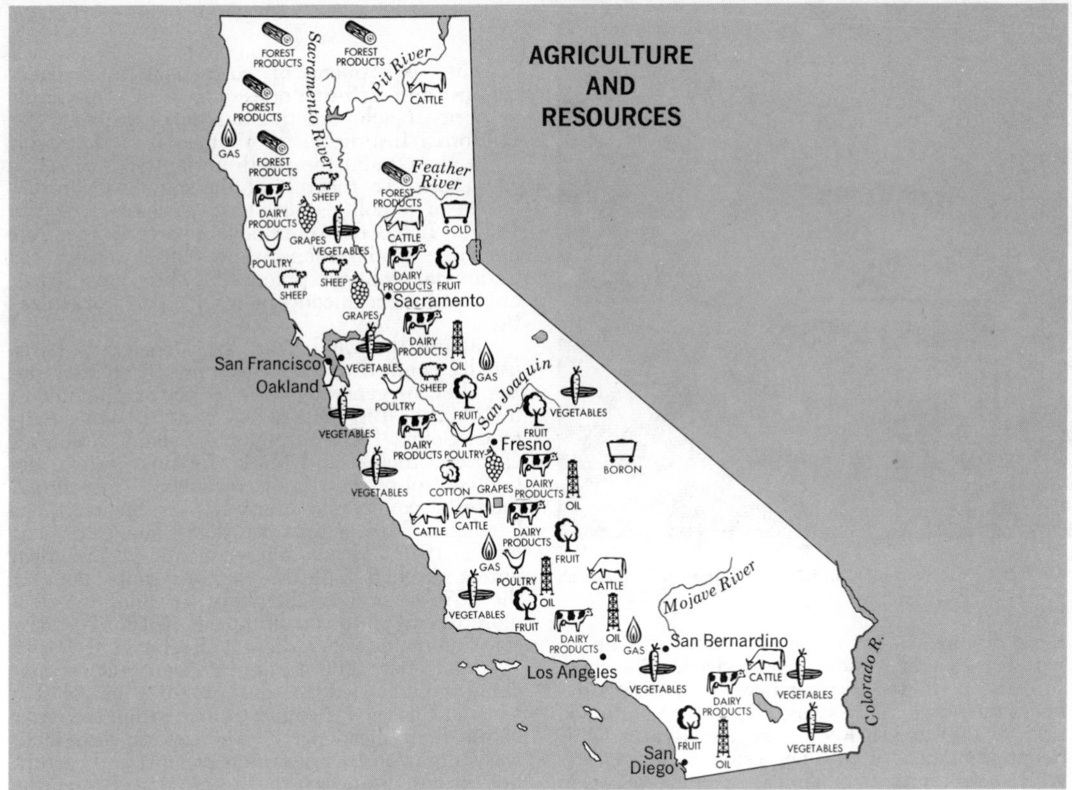

California is the only domestic source, as well as the leading world supplier, of boron minerals and compounds. These come from deposits in Kern and Inyo counties and from the brines of Searles Lake in San Bernardino county. California also is a chief producer nationally of asphalt, borate minerals, diatomite, mercury, rare-earth concentrates, sand and gravel, sodium sulfate, and tungsten concentrates.

Entertainment Industry. The motion picture industry has been one of the state's most distinctive and widely known enterprises. Since World War II, this industry has declined, but many establishments in the Hollywood area still engage in motion picture production or allied pursuits. Many studios are devoted to production of television films, and television broadcasting has become an important new industry as the major networks have concentrated significant new investments in southern California and the San Francisco Bay area. Other by-products of the motion picture industry are as important as the industry itself. These include the development of Los Angeles as a style and sports apparel center.

Transportation. Isolated for centuries from the rest of the world by distances and natural barriers, California found the development of transportation facilities essential to its progress. The completion of the first transcontinental railroad in 1869 gave California its first direct rail connection with the rest of the nation, and the many rail lines built after that time contributed immeasurably to California's development. Some 30 railroads continue to operate in the state, although other forms of transportation have assumed major importance in moving people and goods.

As one of the most air-minded of the states, California has approximately 900 airports. Several dozen scheduled airlines furnish domestic, interstate, or international service.

The ships of numerous steamship lines visit California ports, carrying passengers and cargo to the Orient, along the coast from Alaska to Cape Horn, and through the Panama Canal. The port of Los Angeles–Long Beach is one of the most active in the nation. The San Francisco Bay area, including Richmond and Oakland, ships and receives substantial foreign tonnage.

Automobile transportation began on a large scale in California with the construction of the first paved highway in 1912. Since that time state, municipal, and federal agencies have built some 160,000 miles (264,000 km) of roads in an attempt to relieve congestion. For additional statistics, see THE AMERICANA ANNUAL.

4. Government and Politics

California is governed under its second state constitution, adopted in 1879. The first constitution was prepared during September and October 1849 and was used immediately to set up a state government, almost a year before statehood was granted officially.

Through the years the 1879 constitution has been amended and revised extensively. Among notable amendments were the provisions for initiative, referendum, and recall, adopted in 1911. In 1966 the voters of the state approved a measure revising about one third of the document, the result of lengthy work by a constitutional revision commission.

Structure of Government. The governor and other executive officers of the state are elected to 4-year terms and are eligible for consecutive reelection. The governor is responsible for the state budget. A two-thirds majority of the legislature is necessary to override his veto.

The constitutional revision measure of 1966 provided for annual legislative sessions of unlimited length. Formerly the legislature had met

WILLIAM M. GRAHAM, FROM PHOTO RESEARCHERS

CAPITOL, at Sacramento, resembles the U. S. Capitol.

for a 30-day budget session in even years and a 120-day general session in odd years. The measure also permitted the members of the legislature to set their own salaries, and these were increased from $6,000 to $16,000 a year, effective in 1967. Reapportionment of both houses of the legislature, which was carried out under a court order in 1965, resulted in a transfer of control of the legislature from the northern to the southern counties. Under reapportionment, eight southern counties hold more than half the seats in both the Senate and the Assembly.

The state judicial system consists of a supreme court of seven justices, four district courts of appeal, and superior and municipal courts. There are hundreds of other minor courts. All trial court judges are elected. Appellate court judges are appointed to their original terms by the governor, with approval of the commission on judicial appointments. They run for reelection on their records.

Political Divisions. California's 58 counties and its several hundred cities are administrative agents of the state, performing in its name the basic functions of law enforcement, fire control, and sanitation. The city is less an arm of the state and more a unit of local self-government than the county.

Public Finance. State income is derived chiefly from sales taxes, gross receipt taxes, corporate and individual income taxes, licenses, and property taxes. Federal aid for highways and for water development has helped California's financial progress greatly.

Social Services. In 1927, various bureaus, including a separate board for children's aid, were merged into a department of social welfare, which supervises activities ranging from aid to the aged and the blind to investigation of petitions for adoption. The California department of public health performs traditional public health functions, including coordination of local, state, and federal activities. The department of mental hygiene disseminates mental health information and oversees hospitals for the mentally ill, centers for short-term therapy, and institutions for the mentally deficient and the epileptic. During 1966, California instituted a state Medicare plan, which expands the coverage of the federal program.

The department of corrections administers prisons and reformatories for men, the adult authority (including the bureau of parole), the California Institution for Women (a state prison for women), and the youth authority.

Politics. To the rest of the nation, California has been a political mystery, at least since the 1930's. It has the traditional 2-party system, but numerous Californians show little regard for traditional political practices. They cross party lines and seem unconcerned with party organization.

Before the Civil War, the Democratic party usually controlled state elections. Thereafter the Republicans generally were in power. Beginning in 1869, the Big Four of the Central Pacific Railroad—Collis P. Huntington, Leland Stanford, Charles Crocker, and Mark Hopkins—gained virtual control of the state government. The railroad interests, commonly referred to as the Southern Pacific machine, maintained that influence until as late as 1910. Meanwhile, economic and political unrest reached especially serious proportions in the 1870's and brought about the adoption of a more liberal state constitution in 1879. The new constitution, however, did not effect major reforms.

Soon after 1900 a popular revolt against machine politics led to the organization of the Lincoln-Roosevelt League, at first within the ranks of the Republican party. This reform movement was stimulated by revelations of graft and corruption in San Francisco, both before and after the catastrophic earthquake and fire of 1906. The Lincoln-Roosevelt League eventually identified itself with the Progressive party. In 1910 the Progressives undertook to "kick the Southern Pacific out of politics" and elected Hiram W. Johnson (nominally a Republican) as governor. The next year the California legislature carried through a notable program of social, economic, and political reform, including approval of woman suffrage, formation of a new railroad commission, and adoption of the initiative, referendum, and recall. Johnson's administration also placed certain state and local offices under civil service and established a system of cross-filing (abolished in 1959) under which candidates were permitted to run in both the Democratic and the Republican primaries. These measures were designed to curb political machines and discourage strong party organization. They give the people a direct power of decision and have been partly responsible for an unorthodox approach to politics.

During the depression of the 1930's, California turned Democratic in national politics and gave enthusiastic support to the New Deal. In state politics Upton Sinclair, novelist and social reformer, won the Democratic gubernatorial nomination in 1934 and almost won the governorship as head of the EPIC ("End Poverty in California") movement. Support of the "Thirty Dollars Every Thursday" plan, better known as "Ham

GOVERNMENT HIGHLIGHTS

Electoral Vote—45. **Representation in Congress**—U. S. senators, 2; U. S. representatives, 43. **State Legislature**—Senate, 40 members, 4-year terms; Assembly, 80 members, 2-year terms. **Governor**—4-year term; may succeed himself; salary, $44,100 annually. **Voting Qualifications**—Age, 18; residence in state 1 year, in county 90 days, in district 54 days. **Elections**—General and state, Tuesday after first Monday in November of even year; primary, Tuesday after first Monday in June of even years.

JOHN J. SMITH

CALIFORNIA

(Above) A brilliant carpet of ice plant colors the shoreline of Monterey Bay at Pacific Grove, a resort town southeast of San Francisco. *(Right)* Giant redwoods, the tallest trees in North America, grow at Jedediah Smith Redwoods State Park, near Crescent City, in the extreme northwest corner of California.

CHUCK ABBOT, FROM DE WYS

RAY ATKESON, FROM DPI

JOHN J. SMITH

(Above) Sand dunes cover 60 square miles of Death Valley, the hottest and the lowest land in the United States. *(Right)* California State Highway 1 winds around the precipitous mountains of the Santa Lucia Range where they meet the Pacific near the town of Lucia, south of Monterey.

AL GREENE, FROM SHOSTAL

(Above) An almond orchard blooms in the early spring at Palmdale, northeast of Los Angeles. *(Right)* Enclosed chair lifts carry skiers up the slope of a mountain named K.T. 22 at the winter resort of Squaw Valley. Lake Tahoe can be seen in the distance.

RAY ATKESON

JOHN J. SMITH

(Right) Yosemite Falls, the highest waterfalls in North America, drops nearly half a mile in a series of cataracts to the valley floor. *(Below)* Golden Gate Bridge spans the entrance to San Francisco Bay.

RAY ATKESON, FROM DPI

GOVERNORS		
Peter H. Burnett	Democrat	1849–1851
John McDougal (acting)	"	1851–1852
John Bigler	"	1852–1856
John N. Johnson	Know-Nothing	1856–1858
John B. Weller	Democrat	1858–1860
Milton S. Latham	"	1860
John G. Downey (acting)	"	1860–1861
Leland Stanford	Republican	1861–1863
Frederick F. Low	Union	1863–1867
Henry H. Haight	Democrat	1867–1871
Newton Booth	Republican	1871–1875
Romualdo Pacheco (acting)	"	1875
William Irwin	Democrat	1875–1880
George C. Perkins	Republican	1880–1883
George Stoneman	Democrat	1883–1887
Washington Bartlett	"	1887
Robert W. Waterman (acting)	Republican	1887–1891
Henry H. Markham	"	1891–1895
James H. Budd	Democrat	1895–1899
Henry T. Gage	Republican	1899–1903
George C. Pardee	"	1903–1907
James N. Gillett	"	1907–1911
Hiram W. Johnson	"	1911–1917
William D. Stephens	"	1917–1923
Friend W. Richardson	"	1923–1927
C. C.Young	"	1927–1931
James Rolph, Jr.	"	1931–1934
Frank F. Merriam	"	1934–1939
Culbert L. Olson	Democrat	1939–1943
Earl Warren	Republican	1943–1953
Goodwin J. Knight	"	1953–1959
Edmund G. Brown	Democrat	1959–1967
Ronald Reagan	Republican	1967–

and Eggs," helped Culbert L. Olson win the governorship for the Democrats in 1938. But with this one exception the Republican party maintained control of state politics and held the governorship in unbroken succession for 60 years (1899–1959).

From the mid-1930's onward, the Democrats held an advantage in registration over the Republicans, but until the late 1950's they were relatively unsuccessful in electing candidates, partly because of weak party organization, local conservatism, and poor financial support. Republican Earl Warren, first governor in California's history to be elected to three successive terms (1942, 1946, 1950), was nominated by both major parties in 1946. Governor Warren resigned in 1953 to become chief justice of the United States.

In 1959 the Democrats began an 8-year tenure with Edmund G. ("Pat") Brown as governor, a Democratic slate of state officers, and heavy majorities in both houses of the state legislature. The elections of 1966 were held in an atmosphere of mounting concern over an increased crime rate, high property taxes, and civil disturbances, including riots in the Negro sections of some cities and student rebellions at the state university at Berkeley. Governor Brown sought a third term, but the Republican candidate, actor Ronald Reagan, swept into office with a conservative Republican administration. The Democrats maintained narrow majorities in the state legislature.

5. Education and Culture

California's educational and cultural growth has matched its material progress. The state spends more money for education than for any other purpose, and more people in California are engaged in education than in any other pursuit. The University of California, chartered in 1868, has been rated among the distinguished universities of the nation. It stands at the head of a system of public education notable for progressiveness and high standards. In addition, California is the home of numerous major privately endowed institutions of higher education.

A. DEVANEY, INC.

BERKELEY CAMPUS of the University of California.

San Francisco led the way in the cultural development of the state. After the gold rush, it founded (1853) the California Academy of Sciences, the first such institution in the West, and established museums, libraries, theaters, and opera companies. The city attracted opera stars, artists, and writers.

Later, as the population spread southward, a second center of cultural activity developed at Los Angeles. Musicians and writers were drawn especially to Hollywood, the world's film capital during the early decades of the 20th century. Through the years many noted writers, artists, and musicians have made their home in California. Although California is comparatively young as a state, its efforts in the arts have made it one of the major cultural areas of the nation.

Educational System. The school system of California is under the direction of an elected superintendent of public instruction. Compulsory attendance dates from 1874 and applies to children between the ages of 8 and 16. California ranks high among the states in certification standards for teachers, average teacher's salary (above $8,000 per year), and per pupil expenditure (more than $600 per year). School enrollments in public schools—nursery school through junior college—exceed 5 million.

The state system of higher education, like California's population, is ever growing. It is composed of a state university so far-flung and complex in structure and functions that it has been called a "multiversity" (see CALIFORNIA, UNIVERSITY OF); 4-year state colleges, which are independent of the university; and junior colleges, which numbered about 80 in the late 1960's. The 4-year state colleges include those at Arcata, Chico, Dominguez Hills, Fresno, Fullerton, Hayward, Los Angeles, Long Beach, Northridge, Pomona, Rohnert Park, Sacramento, San Diego, San Francisco, San Jose, San Luis Obispo, and Turlock.

Among privately endowed institutions are the University of Southern California, at Los Angeles; California Institute of Technology, at Pasadena; Stanford University, near Palo Alto; Mills College, at Oakland; the University of the Pacific, at Stockton; Occidental College, at Los Angeles; Whittier College, at Whittier; University of Redlands,

R. BRADLEY, FROM DE WYS, INC.

CIVIC CENTER in Los Angeles includes the beautiful Music Center (*right*) and a 32-story city hall.

at Redlands; and the Associated Colleges, at Claremont. Catholic institutions include the University of San Francisco, the University of Santa Clara, and Loyola University of Los Angeles.

Research Centers. The Lick Observatory of the University of California, on Mt. Hamilton east of San Jose, was one of the first major astronomical observatories established in the United States. The Mount Wilson and Palomar Observatories are sponsored jointly by the Carnegie Institution of Washington, D. C., and the California Institute of Technology. The Mount Wilson observatory is on Mt. Wilson near Pasadena; the Palomar observatory, on Palomar Mountain in northern San Diego county, is noted for its 200-inch (504-cm) reflector. Research centers of the University of California, other than the Lick Observatory, include the Lawrence Radiation Laboratory at Livermore and the Scripps Institution of Oceanography at La Jolla (a part of the San Diego Campus). Located at Palo Alto is the Center for Advanced Study in the Behavioral Sciences and, at Santa Barbara, the Center for the Study of Democratic Institutions.

Libraries and Museums. Facilities for scholarly research are offered by the California State Library at Sacramento, with a branch, the Sutro Library, at San Francisco; the Hoover Library of War, Revolution, and Peace at Stanford University; the many libraries of the University of California, with specialized collections; and the Henry E. Huntington Library and Art Gallery at San Marino. There are more than 200 municipal library systems in California, and many of the county libraries maintain branches or provide bookmobile service.

The major historical societies are the California Historical Society at San Francisco and the Historical Society of Southern California at Los Angeles. Museums in Los Angeles include the Southwest Museum (principally Indian culture), the Municipal Art Gallery (partly designed by Frank Lloyd Wright), the California Museum of Science and Industry, and the Los Angeles County Museum of Art. Among San Francisco's museums are the M. H. de Young Memorial Museum (American, European, and Asian art), the California Palace of the Legion of Honor (art museum), the San Francisco Museum of Art, and the museum of natural history, planetarium, and aquarium of the California Academy of Sciences. Other leading museums include the San Diego Natural History Museum and the Fine Arts Gallery at San Diego, the J. Paul Getty Museum at Malibu, and the E. B. Crocker Art Gallery at Sacramento.

Specialized museums are maintained by the major colleges and universities and by the numerous county historical societies. Many of the state and national park areas also have museums or exhibits, as do some of the old Spanish missions.

Architecture. In the 1890's the adobe, or Mexican ranch-style, house inspired an imitation "mission revival" architecture. From 1910 to 1930 this style shared popularity with the California redwood bungalow of architects Charles Sumner Greene and Henry Mather Greene. Modern architects—among them, Frank Lloyd Wright, Rudolph M. Schindler, and Richard Neutra—built some of their first experimental structures in California. But to a great extent architecture in California presents a fascinating hodgepodge of styles. Within a small area it is not unusual to find structures showing such varied influences as Hawaiian or Oriental, Tudor or Jacobean, French château, Georgian, Cape Cod, or Hopi Indian.

Music and Theater. Music in California flourishes at the War Memorial Opera House at San Francisco, the Los Angeles Music Center, and the Hollywood Bowl. The founding of the San Francisco Symphony Orchestra dates from 1909, and the Philharmonic Orchestra of Los Angeles from

NATIONAL AREAS

AREAS ADMINISTERED BY NATIONAL PARK SERVICE:[1]

National Parks—Kings Canyon; Lassen Volcanic; Sequoia; Yosemite

National Monuments—Cabrillo; Channel Islands; Death Valley; Devils Postpile; Joshua Tree; Lava Beds; Muir Woods; Pinnacles

National Historic Site—John Muir

National Recreation Area—Whiskeytown-Shasta-Trinity

National Seashore—Point Reyes

NATIONAL FORESTS (administered by Forest Service, U. S. Department of Agriculture):[1]

Angeles; Calaveras Big Tree; Cleveland; Eldorado (shared with Nevada); Inyo (shared with Nevada); Klamath (shared with Oregon); Lassen; Los Padres; Mendocino; Modoc; Plumas; Rogue River (shared with Oregon); San Bernardino; Sequoia; Shasta-Trinity (two forests under one supervisor); Sierra; Siskiyou (shared with Oregon); Six Rivers; Stanislaus; Tahoe; Toiyabe (shared with Nevada)

[1] For a brief description of each area, see articles *National Parks and Monuments; National Forests;* and separate articles as listed in Index.

1919. Repertory theaters include the Center Theater Group at the Los Angeles Music Center, the Stanford Repertory Theater at Stanford University, and the Pasadena Playhouse at Pasadena. The Old Globe Theater at San Diego is the home of a community theater and a summer Shakespeare festival.

Communications. The "big three" of California's more than 700 newspapers are the San Francisco *Chronicle*, Oakland *Tribune*, and Los Angeles *Times*. Also serving the state are dozens of AM and FM radio stations and television studios. California's first television station, KTLA, went into operation in 1947.

6. Recreation

From the dawn of the automobile era California, which came to be called "a state on wheels," has attracted hordes of tourists. Persistent and effective private and public advertising has kept the annual flow of tourists high. Despite the detractions of air pollution and congestion in some parts of California, it ranks among the leading states in money earned from tourists' accommodations, amusement centers, and recreation facilities that include beaches, ski slopes, alpine lakes, and the wildest of wildernesses.

California's outdoor recreational resources are among the most varied and extensively developed in the nation. More than one fourth of the total land area of the state is included in national and state recreational areas. These are supplemented by county and city parks and by private agencies. Yet the demand for recreational facilities continuously outruns the supply, and California is pressed to meet the needs of residents and guests noted for their commitment to the outdoor way of life.

National Areas. Agencies of the federal government maintain in California 22 national forests, 4 national parks, 8 national monuments, 1 national historic site, 1 national recreation area, and 1 national seashore, as well as more than 15 national wildlife refuges and numerous areas surrounding water-resource reservoirs.

National forest lands, covering approximately one fifth of California's land area, stretch through the Sierra Nevada and the mountainous northern third of the state. Others are situated in the coastal mountains between Monterey and the southern border of the state. In addition to their chief function in conservation of water, forest, and wildlife resources, they render invaluable service as recreation centers.

Three of the national parks are in the Sierra Nevada. Yosemite National Park, best known of all California parks, is situated in the heart of the Sierra, due east of San Francisco. It is an area of sheer cliffs, domes, and waterfalls. Kings Canyon and Sequoia national parks occupy adjoining but separately administered areas in the lower Sierra, east of Fresno. Sequoia contains hundreds of specimens of the giant sequoia, or big tree. Kings Canyon is noted for wild areas and canyons, especially the canyon of the Kings River. Lassen Volcanic National Park is situated at the southern end of the Cascade Range. It takes its name from the pioneer Danish trapper Peter Lassen (1792–1859). Besides Lassen Peak, it preserves spectacular lava formations and hot sulfur springs.

The national monuments include such diverse scenic spots as Lava Beds in the northeastern part of the state, scene of a war with the Modoc Indians in 1872–1873; the grove of redwoods known as Muir Woods, in Marin county; and Death Valley, desolate, fantastically colored and eroded, in the Mojave Desert. Other scenic and scientific national monuments include Joshua Tree, Pinnacles (towering spirelike rock formations, in the Coast Ranges southeast of Salinas), Devils Postpile (basaltic columns in the Sierra, southeast of Yosemite National Park), and Channel Islands (sea lion rookery and other animal and plant life on two of the Santa Barbara, or Channel Islands). Cabrillo National Monument commemorates the landing of Juan Rodríguez Cabrillo at San Diego in 1542.

JOSEF MUENCH

SQUAW VALLEY, site of the 1960 Winter Olympics, is on the western Sierra Nevada, near Lake Tahoe.

The John Muir National Historic Site at Martinez, authorized in 1964, preserves the residence of John Muir in commemoration of Muir's contribution to conservation and literature. The Whiskeytown-Shasta-Trinity National Recreation Area was established in 1965 to provide a three-unit recreation area at water-resource lakes in northern California. Point Reyes National Seashore, authorized in 1962, preserves the seashore of a peninsula north of San Francisco.

State Areas. The state park system comprises more than 170 units, variously identified as parks, beach parks, recreation areas, reserves, and historic sites, memorials, and monuments. Beach state parks are situated all along the coast, but they are especially numerous south of Monterey. Among the largest or most popular areas designated as state recreation areas are Millerton Lake, surrounding the lake impounded by Friant Dam; Squaw Valley, site of the 1960 Winter Olympics, near Lake Tahoe; and Salton Sea, on the northeast shore of Salton Sea.

Anza Desert State Park in Imperial and San Diego counties is one of the largest state parks in the United States. Other parks, in various parts of the state, are McArthur-Burney Falls Memorial State Park, northeast of Shasta Lake; Mount Diablo State Park, east of Oakland; and Point Lobos Reserve State Park, a preserve of Monterey cypress in Monterey county. Among the more than

25 parks that contain stands of redwoods are Big Basin Redwoods State Park, south of San Francisco, and Humboldt Redwoods and Del Norte Coast Redwoods state parks on or near the northern coast.

Places of historical interest preserved by the state include the Old Customs House in Monterey; Sutter's Fort in Sacramento; Fort Tejon near Lebec; Fort Ross, once a Russian trading post, near Jenner; and the site near Truckee where the Donner party became stranded in 1848. The Hearst-San Simeon State Historical Monument near San Simeon preserves the Hispano-Moorish castle and estate of publisher William Randolph Hearst.

The Mother Lode Country. The principal gold-bearing vein in the western foothills of the Sierra Nevada, known as the Mother Lode country, is traversed by state Route 49. Starting at Mariposa in the south, it takes the traveler through the old gold-rush towns—Sonora, Columbia, Angels Camp, Placerville, Coloma, and others—to Grass Valley and Nevada City in the north. The many places of interest include the Marshall Gold Discovery State Historic Park at Coloma and the Columbia State Historic Park, which preserves a large area of Columbia's old business district. Angels Camp, in Calaveras county, was immortalized in the stories of Bret Harte and Mark Twain, especially Twain's *The Celebrated Jumping Frog of Calaveras County.*

The Missions of California. The 21 Spanish missions founded under the leadership of the Franciscan father Junípero Serra (see section 7. *History*) were spaced out along what became known as El Camino Real ("The Royal Road"). The missions are listed in the order of their location from south to north and their chief features are noted in the list on page 212.

Indian Reservations. At the time of Spanish occupation, the Indians of California were divided into 21 linguistic families and into scores of villages, in which different dialects were spoken. Among the better known tribes were the Hoopa or Hupa, Pomo, Modoc, Maidu, Mono, Yurok, and Yuma. Many smaller tribes have become extinct. Indian lands of California are included in 11 principal reservations and many smaller holdings known as rancherias. About half the area of the famed Palm Springs resort in southern California has been developed on Indian-owned lands of the Agua Caliente Reservation.

Other Places and Activities. Among California's special events, perhaps the best known is the annual Tournament of Roses, held each January 1 or 2 at Pasadena, scene also of the Rose Bowl football game played the same day. The annual state fair has been held at Sacramento since 1861, and the National Orange Show is headquartered at San Bernardino. Santa Barbara holds its Old Spanish Days Fiesta in August. The Ojai Music Festival is held in May, and the Laguna Beach Festival of Arts in late summer. The *Ramona Pageant,* based on Helen Hunt Jackson's novel *Ramona,* is presented annually near Hemet.

Disneyland, opened at Anaheim in 1955, has become one of the nation's most popular tourist centers. Similar in its attraction is the more recently established Pacific Ocean Park, a 30-acre "oceanic wonderland" at Los Angeles. A popular oceanarium overlooks the sea at Palos Verdes.

The state is rich in offerings to sports fans. National League baseball has been played by the Los Angeles Dodgers and San Francisco Giants since the 1958 season. Professional football is represented by the Los Angeles Rams and the San Francisco Forty-niners of the National Football League. Nationally known horse racing tracks include Bay Meadows at San Mateo and Santa Anita at Arcadia.

For other places and activities of special interest, see separate articles on California cities.

7. History

The European discovery of California accompanied the growth of the Spanish empire in the New World. In 1540, Antonio de Mendoza, first viceroy of New Spain (Mexico), sponsored an extensive program of conquest and discovery that included the expedition of Francisco Vásquez de Coronado into what is now the southwestern United States, the exploration of the Gulf of California by Hernando de Alarcón, and a voyage along the coast by the Portuguese-born navigator Juan Rodríguez Cabrillo. Cabrillo left the port of Navidad on the west coast of Mexico in June 1542 and reached San Diego Bay on September 28. Some months later the commander died of an injury on the small island of San Miguel in the Santa Barbara Islands, but his chief pilot, Bartolomé Ferrelo (or Ferrer), sailed as far north as Cape Mendocino before turning back to Navidad.

During the next 60 years, numerous Spanish ships, many of which sailed from the Philippine Islands, visited the California coast. The English navigator and sea raider Francis Drake, on his renowned voyage around the world (1577–1580), entered a harbor of northern California in 1579 and there reconditioned the treasure-laden *Golden Hind.* He also took possession of the land for England, naming it Nova Albion ("New England"). A brass plate, thought to be the plate that Drake and his men inscribed and supposedly nailed to a post as evidence of their claim, was found on the seacoast of Marin county in 1936. In 1602–1603, Sebastián Vizcaíno made an extensive survey of the Monterey Bay area as a possible site for a Spanish colony.

Spanish Settlement. Although known to the Western World long before the English landed at Jamestown, Va., in 1607, California was not actually colonized until 1769. Its exploration and settlement finally were undertaken partly because of the threat of Russian or British advance down the Pacific coast toward the mines and cities of New Spain. Other factors were the missionary zeal of the Franciscan order of friars, the need for a port of refuge and supply for galleons trading with the Philippines, and the zeal of royal officials for a renewed expansion of the Spanish empire. The leading figures of this enterprise were José de Gálvez, visitor-general of New Spain under the energetic King Charles III; Gaspar de Portolá, governor of Lower California and commander in chief of the undertaking; and the Franciscan father Junípero Serra. Two expeditions went by sea to San Diego (a third ship was lost), and two marched overland from the frontier ports of Loreto and Velicatá in Lower California. The overland expeditions reached San Diego without major difficulties, but the maritime parties suffered greatly from disease.

From their base at San Diego, Portolá and a company of 64 priests, soldiers, muleteers, and Indians marched northward on July 14, 1769, to find the harbor in Monterey Bay surveyed much earlier, in 1602, by Vizcaíno. After breaking a

JACK ZEHRT

DAVID MUENCH

HISTORY of California begins in 1542 with its discovery by Cabrillo (*above*). Spanish occupation was commenced in 1769. Father Junípero Serra founded Mission San Carlos Borromeo (*right*), near Carmel, in June 1770.

trail as far north as San Francisco Bay and suffering intensely from hunger and cold, the explorers returned to San Diego on Jan. 24, 1770. But within the next few months, Portolá succeeded in establishing a settlement at Monterey. In 1776, Juan Bautista de Anza, a Spanish frontier captain, led a large overland expedition from Sonora (Mexico) to Monterey. Continuing northward, he selected a site for a settlement, called Yerba Buena, on San Francisco Bay.

As in the case of other border provinces, the Spaniards relied on three frontier institutions—the presidio, the pueblo, and the mission—for the occupation of California. Presidios, or military garrisons, were located at San Diego, Santa Barbara, Monterey, and San Francisco. Pueblos (communities designed for a colonizing or civilian population) were established at San Jose (1777), Los Angeles (1781), and Santa Cruz (1798). Twenty-one Franciscan missions were founded about a day's journey apart between San Diego (1769) and Sonoma (1823). The mission, though designed primarily to convert the Indians to the Christian faith, was also a cultural and agricultural center. Junípero Serra was the founder of the mission system in the province.

Mexican Control. The province of California took virtually no part in Mexico's successful struggle for independence from Spain in 1821, but early in 1822 the Californians declared their allegiance to Mexico. In 1833 a secularization law began the process by which the princely landholdings of the Franciscan missions were reduced to only a few acres. Under Mexican law private citizens could petition for former mission lands. The provincial government, during both the Spanish and the Mexican eras, issued nearly 800 grants, called ranchos. These ranged in size from about 4,500 to 50,000 acres (1,821 to 20,235 hectares). The country then was devoted almost entirely to stock raising. Tradition has given a romantic aura to this Arcadian period of California's history.

United States Acquisition. Under Mexico, the province was subject to various revolutions, but these outbursts, usually bloodless, had a relatively minor effect upon the tranquil life of the Californians. Early in the 19th century, however, the commercial and smuggling activities of New England whalers, sea-otter hunters, and hide and tallow traders called attention to California on the part of United States authorities. The establishment in 1812 of a Russian colony at Fort Ross, north of San Francisco, directed further attention to the province. In 1826, Jedediah Strong Smith led a trapping expedition from the Salt Lake valley to San Gabriel and ushered in a decade of overland exploration by fur trappers. Overland settlers from the United States, notably the Bidwell-Bartleson and Workman-Rowland companies of 1841, pressed hard on the heels of fur traders. Within the next few years, John C. Frémont, explorer and U.S. army officer, led three historic expeditions across the Great Basin and the Sierra (1842–1845), and the publicity given the province by prominent early settlers made the resources of California widely known in the United States. Chaotic political conditions both in Mexico and California presaged an early end of Mexican control, and the possibility of British annexation led the United States government to assert a greater interest in California.

After futile efforts by Presidents Andrew Jackson, John Tyler, and James K. Polk to purchase the territory and following a "revolution" by United States settlers known as the Bear Flag Revolt (June 14, 1846), United States naval and military forces occupied California early in the Mexican War. Mexico ceded the province to the United States at the end of the war.

The Gold Rush and Statehood. On Jan. 24, 1848, less than 10 days before the signing of the treaty, James W. Marshall discovered gold in the tailrace of the sawmill of his employer, John A. Sutter, on the South Fork of the American River at Coloma (northeast of Sacramento). Within a few months one of the great migrations of all time was on—by land and sea to California. Between 1848 and 1852 the population increased from approximately 15,000 to 250,000.

Prior to California's admission to statehood, its society was politically and socially turbulent. Robbery, murder, Indian forays, and the depredations of bandits on outlying ranches and small communities called attention to the need for corrective action. As Californians grew restless over

WELLS FARGO BANK

GOLD RUSH of 1849 brought California a "population explosion." Here are three miners, and a visitor, with a "long tom," a device used in washing out gold.

their unstable society, they undertook what the law had yet failed to do. The military governor, Gen. Bennett Riley, called a constitutional convention. Delegates met at Colton Hall in Monterey on Sept. 1, 1849, and on October 10 they adopted a constitution. California's voters ratified it on November 13 and at the same time elected a governor and state legislators. Without waiting for Congressional approval, the legislature met in December and inaugurated the first governor.

California's action in assuming statehood without federal permission precipitated lengthy debate in Congress, complicated by a struggle between proslavery and antislavery forces (see COMPROMISE OF 1850). Eventually, on Sept. 9, 1850, California entered the Union as a free state.

After admission to statehood, California remained beset by social unrest. The new state covered a vast territory, much of it still a wilderness. Most of the population was concentrated in the northern mining districts and in the boom cities of San Francisco, Stockton, and Sacramento, which was designated the capital in 1854. The problem of maintaining peace and order was especially acute. San Francisco met the situation by organizing vigilance committees (1851, 1856).

Economic Diversification and Growth. Until about 1870, southern California remained a thinly populated cattle frontier, much as it had been under Spanish-Mexican rule, and the life and customs of the people underwent little change. Not until prolonged drought in the 1860's made cattle raising unprofitable did the ranches give way to diversified farming.

Isolation, the controlling factor in California history prior to the Gold Rush, still influenced the state's economic and cultural development. The Butterfield Overland Mail (1857) and later the Pony Express (1860) furnished regular but unsatisfactory overland communication with the Mississippi Valley. The telegraph reached California in 1861. Eight years later the junction of the Union Pacific and Central Pacific railways at Promontory, Utah, gave California direct rail connection with the rest of the nation and marked the beginning of the modern state.

Spanish Missions of California

Mission San Diego de Alcala (July 16, 1769), San Diego; the first of the missions, often called the Mother Mission; moved to present site 1774; restored.

Mission San Luis Rey de Francia (June 13, 1798), near Oceanside; one of the largest of the missions; now a Franciscan seminary. (**San Antonio de Pala,** on Pala Indian Reservation, San Diego county, not one of the 21 original missions but of historic interest; chapel built 1816 as an auxiliary of Mission San Luis Rey de Francia; restored.)

Mission San Juan Capistrano (Nov. 1, 1776), San Juan Capistrano; unusual in having two churches, its stone church (partly destroyed by earthquake in 1812) and an adobe church, called Padre Serra's Church, restored; mission renowned for legend that swallows return every St. Joseph's Day, March 19, and leave on St. John's Day, October 23.

Mission San Gabriel Arcángel (Sept. 8, 1771), San Gabriel; moved to present location in 1776; restored church.

Mission San Fernando Rey de Espana (Sept. 8, 1797), San Fernando; church and monastery completely restored.

Mission San Buenaventura (March 31, 1782), Ventura; restored; state historic site.

Mission Santa Barbara (Dec. 4, 1786), Santa Barbara; sometimes called the Queen of the Missions; the church one of the best preserved of all the mission churches.

Mission Santa Ynez (Sept. 17, 1804), Solvang; restored church serves as parish church.

Mission La Purísima Concepción (Dec. 8, 1787), near Lompoc; one of the most complete restorations; state historic monument.

Mission San Luis Obispo de Tolosa (Sept. 1, 1772), San Luis Obispo; restored church serves as parish church.

Mission San Miguel Arcángel (July 25, 1797), San Miguel; church used as parish church and Franciscan seminary.

Mission San Antonio de Padua (July 14, 1771), near Jolon; mission noted for its site in the "Valley of the Oaks"; chapel restored and entire mission rebuilt.

Mission Nuestra Señora de la Soledad (Oct. 9, 1791), near Soledad; restored chapel.

Mission San Carlos Borromeo (June 3, 1770), near Carmel; called Carmel Mission; founded near presidio of Monterey, transferred to present site 1771; residence, headquarters, and burial place of Father Serra.

Mission San Juan Bautista (June 24, 1797), San Juan Bautista; mission and other buildings in the old plaza preserved as a state historic park.

Mission Santa Cruz (Sept. 25, 1791), Santa Cruz; present church a reproduction of the original.

Mission Santa Clara (Jan. 12, 1777), Santa Clara, on the campus of the University of Santa Clara; present building a replica of original.

Mission San José de Guadalupe (June 11, 1797), Fremont; only an adobe building (quarters of the padres) remains.

Mission San Francisco de Asis (Oct. 9, 1776), San Francisco; known as Dolores Mission; one of the oldest buildings in San Francisco.

Mission San Rafael Arcángel (Dec. 14, 1817), San Rafael; present building a replica of original.

Mission San Francisco Solano (July 4, 1823), Sonoma; restored mission a part of Sonoma State Historic Park, which includes the plaza where the Bear Flag was raised, June 14, 1846.

Extensive railroad construction during the last quarter of the 19th century contributed greatly to California's growth in wealth and population. Gold mining had declined, but the basic wealth of California lay in the rapid expansion of diversified agriculture and the development of irrigation. Southern California profited from a real estate boom that reached its peak in 1887 and from a large-scale development of the citrus fruit industry. Before 1900 the discovery of rich oil fields in the south opened a new economic era.

Oriental Immigration. During the 1860's and 1870's, California vigorously and at times hysterically opposed the immigration of Chinese laborers into the state, even persuading Congress to pass the federal Exclusion Act of 1882. By 1900, Japanese had begun to take the place of the Chinese in California's labor market. In 1907, therefore, the United States entered into an agreement with Japan to reduce the immigration of Japanese laborers. This "gentleman's agreement" proved ineffective from California's standpoint, however, and in 1913 the legislature passed the Alien Land (or Webb) Act to restrict Japanese landholdings in California. This measure was opposed by the administration of President Woodrow Wilson and was sharply criticized by the Japanese government. Nativist agitation against Orientals in California impaired Japanese-American relations, and the situation was not improved by the federal Immigration Act of 1924, which almost shut off the entrance of Japanese nationals into the United States. Then came World War II. After the Japanese attack on Pearl Harbor in 1941, military authorities evacuated all Japanese from the coastal zone and interned them in special camps. Although citizens of Japanese ancestry were authorized to return in 1944, some never came back to California.

In 1962, President John F. Kennedy issued a directive permitting refugees from Hong Kong and Taiwan to join family members in the United States, and many of these came to San Francisco's Chinatown. In 1965, President Lyndon B. Johnson signed into law a bill amending the Immigration and Nationality Act. The new law provided for gradual abolition of the national origins quota system and elimination of it by July 1, 1968.

The Depression. The state's growth in wealth was interrupted in the 1930's by the depression. In 1932, California, traditionally Republican, supported the New Deal of Democratic President Franklin D. Roosevelt, and groups within the state attracted wide attention through proposals aimed at relieving the distress of the period. These included Upton Sinclair's EPIC plan, Dr.

FAMOUS RESIDENTS OF CALIFORNIA

Atherton, Gertrude (1857–1948), author, whose works deal extensively with California.

Belasco, David (1854–1931), playwright and producer, who began his career in his native San Francisco.

Bierce, Ambrose (1842–?1914), author and journalist, who lived and wrote in San Francisco in the late 1800's.

Bolton, Herbert E. (1870–1953), historian, associated with University of California, 1911–1940.

Burbank, Luther (1849–1926), horticulturist, who lived and worked at Santa Rosa from 1875.

Coolbrith, Ina Donna (1842–1928), poet, associated with Bret Harte in editing the *Overland Monthly*, 1868.

Derby, George H. (1823–1861), pen name, John Phoenix; humorist, whose works include *The Squibob Papers*, 1859.

DiMaggio, Joseph Paul (1914–), baseball player; elected to National Baseball Hall of Fame, 1955.

Duncan, Isadora (1878–1927), dancer, known for interpretive and barefoot dancing.

Frémont, John Charles (1813–1890), explorer and U. S. army officer; active in Bear Flag Revolt, 1846.

Frost, Robert (1874–1963), poet, identified with New England but born in San Francisco.

George, Henry (1839–1897), economist, whose works include *Progress and Poverty*, 1879; newspaper editor in San Francisco, 1866–1868.

Giannini, Amadeo Peter (1870–1949), financier and founder of the Bank of America.

Gonzales, Richard A. (1928–), known as Pancho; tennis champion; professional since 1949.

Hale, George Ellery (1868–1938), astronomer; organizer and head of Mount Wilson Observatory, 1904–1923.

Haraszthy de Mokcsa, Ágoston (1812?–1869), Hungarian-American viticulturist, whose work in importing new varieties of grapes initiated large-scale winemaking in California.

Harte, Bret (1836–1902), writer, editor of *Overland Monthly*, 1868–1870; known especially for stories of the gold camps.

Hearst, William Randolph (1863–1951), publisher, editor, and political figure.

Hoover, Herbert Clark (1874–1964), 31st president of the United States; graduate of Stanford University, 1895.

Howard, Sidney (1891–1939), playwright, whose works include *They Knew What They Wanted*.

Huntington, Collis Potter (1821–1900), financier, one of the "Big Four" transcontinental railroad builders.

Jackson, Helen Hunt (1830–1885), author of the novel *Ramona*, 1884, and of *A Century of Dishonor*, 1881, indictments of the treatment of the Indians of California.

Jeffers, Robinson (1887–1962), poet; graduate of Occidental College, 1907; resident of Carmel from 1913.

Johnson, Hiram Warren (1866–1945), reform governor, 1911–1917; U. S. senator, 1917–1945.

Jordan, David Starr (1851–1931), biologist; first president and chancellor, 1891–1916, of Stanford University.

Le Conte, Joseph (1823–1901), geologist, known for studies of the Sierra Nevada and the Cascade Range.

London, Jack (1876–1916), author, whose home near Santa Rosa is preserved as a state historical park.

Lummis, Charles Fletcher (1859–1928), writer and editor; founder of the Southwest Museum at Los Angeles.

McPherson, Aimee Semple (1890–1944), evangelist, at Los Angeles during the 1920's and 1930's; founder of the International Church of the Four-Square Gospel, 1927.

Markham, Edwin (1852–1940), poet and reformer, known especially for the poem *The Man with the Hoe*, 1899.

Muir, John (1838–1914), Scottish-born naturalist, explorer, conservationist, and writer.

Nixon, Richard Milhous (1913–), U. S. vice president, 1953–1961; Republican presidential nominee, 1960, 1968; 37th president of the U. S., 1969– .

Norris, Frank (1870–1902), novelist, known for social and reform themes; brother of the writer Charles Gilman Norris.

Norris, Kathleen Thompson (1880–1966), novelist; wife of the writer **Charles Gilman Norris** (1881–1945).

Otis, Harrison Gray (1837–1917), U. S. army officer; publisher of the Los Angeles *Times*, whose antiunion stand led to dynamiting of the *Times*, 1910.

Patton, George S., Jr. (1885–1945), U. S. army general; commander of the Third Army, World War II.

Royce, Josiah (1855–1916), philosopher, educator, and writer.

Saroyan, William (1908–), author and playwright, whose works include *The Time of Your Life*, 1939, and *The Human Comedy*, 1942.

Serra, Junípero (1713–1784), Spanish Franciscan missionary; founder of the first California missions.

Sinclair, Upton Beall (1878–1968), novelist, Socialist, reformer; Democratic gubernatorial candidate, 1934.

Stanford, Leland (1824–1893), railroad magnate; governor of California; founder of Stanford University.

Steffens, Lincoln (1866–1936), journalist, author, and political reformer.

Steinbeck, John (1902–1968), author; winner of Pulitzer Prize for *The Grapes of Wrath*, 1939; winner of Nobel Prize in literature, 1962.

Stevenson, Adlai (1900–1965), statesman, identified with Illinois but born in Los Angeles.

Sutter, Johann Augustus (1803–1880), German-born pioneer in California, whose large landholdings included the present site of Sacramento.

Warren, Earl (1891–), governor of California; 14th chief justice of the United States.

Wilbur, Ray Lyman (1875–1949), U. S. secretary of the interior, 1929–1933; president and chancellor of Stanford University, 1916–1949.

HISTORICAL HIGHLIGHTS

1542 Juan Rodríguez Cabrillo explored California coast for Spain.
1579 Francis Drake landed on northern California coast and took possession of the land for England.
1602 Sebastián Vizcaíno surveyed Monterey Bay area as possible site for Spanish colony, 1602–1603.
1769 Spanish colonization began with founding of first Alta California mission at San Diego.
1776 Juan Bautista de Anza led overland expedition to select site for settlement on San Francisco Bay.
1781 Pueblo (civilian community) established at Los Angeles.
1812 Russians established Fort Ross north of San Francisco.
1822 Province of California declared allegiance to Mexico (which gained independence from Spain, 1821).
1833 Secularization law deprived Franciscan missions of much of their lands.
1842 John C. Frémont led U. S. government expeditions into California, 1842–1845.
1846 United States settlers in California protested Mexican rule in abortive Bear Flag Revolt.
1848 Mexico ceded California to United States by Treaty of Guadalupe Hidalgo, February 2; gold discovered on Sutter property at Coloma, January 24.
1849 Citizens set up state government, independent of Congressional action.
1850 California entered the Union, September 9, as the 31st state.
1854 Sacramento designated as state capital.
1869 Completion of transcontinental railroad gave California direct connection with eastern United States.
1879 Second state constitution adopted.
1887 Southern California experienced the peak of a real estate boom.
1890 Yosemite National Park established.
1906 San Francisco devastated by earthquake and fire.
1907 "Gentleman's agreement" with Japan reduced number of Japanese immigrants to California.
1910 Hiram W. Johnson elected as reform governor.
1911 Important reform measures passed by legislature.
1930 Dust Bowl refugees began immigration from Midwest.
1934 Upton Sinclair, under EPIC ("End Poverty in California") movement, conducted unsuccessful campaign for governorship.
1935 First phase of Central Valley (water) Project authorized by federal government.
1941 World War II made California a leading area in military construction.
1945 United Nations founded at San Francisco.
1953 Gov. Earl Warren resigned to become chief justice of the United States.
1960 California Water Project initiated.
1964 California attained first rank in population.
1966 Actor Ronald Reagan elected governor.

Francis E. Townsend's old-age pension movement, Technocracy, the Utopian Society, and the "Thirty Dollars Every Thursday" plan. Although the plans were generally visionary, some of them contained aspects that presaged the national Social Security Act of 1935.

Widespread immigration of poverty-stricken settlers from the Dust Bowl region of the Midwest—the "Okies" depicted in John Steinbeck's novel *The Grapes of Wrath* (1939)—greatly aggravated the already difficult problem of migrant agricultural laborers. The depression finally ended in California with the approach of World War II.

World War II and Later. World War II accelerated movements already under way—the shifting weight of wealth and population from northern to southern California, the rapid industrialization of agricultural areas, and the elimination of cultural, economic, and geographic isolation. Perhaps symbolic of the end of isolation was the founding at San Francisco in 1945 of the United Nations Organization.

The era since World War II has surely been California's most complicated historical period, an era characterized by the building of freeways, airports, and many more factories and schools. This period has seen continuing change from an agricultural to and industrial society. A new problem of great public concern accompanying California's industrialization has been the increase of air pollution, or smog, in the largest cities, especially Los Angeles and San Francisco. To rid the atmosphere of noxious fumes, various air pollution control districts have been created.

California's future is contingent not only on solving such pressing problems as smog, which has damaged the state's climatic reputation, but also on expanding the water supply, attracting new industry and investment capital, and providing sorely needed educational and mass-transportation facilities. In addition, inequalities affecting minority groups must somehow be remedied.

The "Negro Revolution" that swept across America in the 1960's had awesome repercussions in California. Rioting broke out in August 1965, in Los Angeles' predominantly Negro suburb of Watts. Hundreds of crazed rioters shouting anti-white epithets looted stores, burned buildings, and shot at firemen and police. Governor Brown ordered National Guard troops into Los Angeles to help restore order, but the riots lasted for several days, causing the death of 35 persons, injury to several hundred others, and property damage estimated at $40 million. Some 4,000 persons were arrested. Rioters charged the arresting police with brutality in Watts and in other cities such as Oakland and San Francisco, where "aftershocks" of these riots were felt for some time. A commission appointed by the governor to study the causes of the riots recommended massive education and job-training programs, new procedures for dealing with complaints involving the police, and other measures to increase employment opportunities for Negroes. Attention to the problems of the Mexican-Americans also resulted from the Watts disturbances as that minority pressed increasingly for greater equality, economically and socially.

Great changes have enveloped the state as it has moved from a rural to an urban culture. Without conforming to rigid patterns, Californians seem to be building a vital center of political and economic life. Favored by climate, geography, and an indefinable ambition, the state daily grows in population, economy, and power. Its expansion, however, needs to be accompanied by cultural and social sophistication and by flexible experimentation. To serve the interminable stream of tourists who daily become residents, California has changed itself. Much of this change suggests a future of limitless opportunity.

ANDREW ROLLE, *Occidental College*
Author of "California: A History"

Bibliography

American Guide Series, *California: A Guide to the Golden State,* rev. ed. (New York 1954).
Bancroft, Hubert H., *History of California, 1542–1890,* 7 vols. (San Francisco 1884–1890).
Cleland, Robert G., *From Wilderness to Empire: A History of California,* ed. by Glenn S. Dumke (New York 1959).
Engelhardt, Zephyrin, *The Missions and Missionaries of California,* 4 vols. (San Francisco 1908–1915).
Lantis, David W., Steiner, Rodney, and Karinen, Arthur E., *California: Land of Contrast* (Belmont, Calif., 1963).
Richman, Irving B. *California under Spain and Mexico, 1535–1847* (New York 1911).
Rolle, Andrew F., *California: A History* (New York 1963).

CALIFORNIA, kal-ə-fôr′nyə, a residential borough in Pennsylvania, is in Washington county, 26 miles (42 km) south of Pittsburgh, on the Monongahela River. California State College, a 4-year coeducational institution, is here.

The borough was named by pioneers on their way to California Territory in the 1849 gold rush. It was laid out about 1850 and incorporated in 1863. Government is by mayor and council. Population: 6,635.

CALIFORNIA, Gulf of, kal-ə-fôr′nyə, an arm of the Pacific Ocean on the northwest coast of Mexico. Over 700 miles (1,100 km) long and from 40 to 150 miles (65 to 240 km) wide, it has an area of 60,000 square miles (155,000 sq km) and is up to 8,520 feet (2,597 meters) deep.

The gulf is separated from the Pacific by the peninsula of Lower California, called "the fleshless arm of Mexico" because of its rugged terrain and aridity. The gulf has several islands. One of the largest, Tiburón, is peopled by aboriginal Seri Indians. There is abundant fishing, both sport and commercial. There are also sponge and pearl fisheries and extensive oyster beds.

Violent storms menace navigation, but tidal bores, caused in part by the influx of the Colorado River, have been greatly reduced by Hoover Dam, upstream. The gulf was first explored by Francisco de Ulloa, for Cortés, in 1539. For a time the gulf was called the Sea of Cortés.

FERDINAND C. LANE
Author of "The Mysterious Sea"

CALIFORNIA, University of, kal-ə-fôr′nyə, a coeducational state and land-grant institution with nine campuses and numerous installations, including the Lick Observatory and the Lawrence Radiation Laboratory, in the state of California. The campuses are at Berkeley, San Francisco, Davis, Riverside, Los Angeles, Santa Barbara, San Diego, Irvine, and Santa Cruz. All except the San Francisco Medical Center offer undergraduate liberal arts instruction and graduate and professional training.

The university, which was founded in 1868, is administered by a president and governed by a 24-member board of regents. Because of its rapid growth, the university's administration has been decentralized to campus chancellors.

Berkeley was the first permanent site of the university, occupied in 1873. The campus comprises 14 colleges and schools and more than 60 research centers covering every major field of knowledge. Its research units include institutes of governmental and international affairs, urban planning, higher education, and industrial relations. In 1966 the American Council on Education judged it the nation's most distinguished center of graduate training.

San Francisco, first opened in 1873 as a department of the university, comprises schools of medicine, dentistry, nursing, and pharmacy. Clinical and teaching facilities include Herbert T. Moffitt and University of California hospitals and the Clinics Building. The medical school and the state department of mental hygiene operate the Langley Porter Neuropsychiatric Institute. Special research units are: a biomechanics laboratory, cancer and cardiovascular research institutes, the Hooper Foundation (ecology and tropical medicine), a hormone research laboratory, and the Proctor Foundation (ophthalmology).

Davis, established as a farm school in 1905, became a general campus in 1959. Its schools and colleges include letters and science, agriculture, engineering, medicine, veterinary medicine, and law. Davis is the site of the National Center for Primate Biology.

Riverside, begun in 1907 as a citrus experiment station, became a general campus with a graduate division in 1959. There are schools and colleges of letters and science, agriculture, engineering, and administration, among others. Special units include an air pollution research center and institutes of citrus, desert, and drylands research.

Los Angeles has been a part of the university since 1919. It comprises a medical center and schools and colleges of letters and science, engineering, applied arts, agriculture, business administration, education, law, public health, social welfare, architecture, urban planning, and library service. Research units include African studies, geophysics and planetary physics, an eye institute, and a Latin American studies center.

Santa Barbara was made part of the university in 1944 and a general campus in 1958. Its colleges and schools include letters and science, engineering, education, and creative studies. Santa Barbara has a computer center and research units in environmental stress and religious studies.

San Diego evolved from the renowned Scripps Institution of Oceanography, which in turn developed from a gift to the university in 1912 from the Marine Biological Association. It became a general campus in 1958 and is being developed on a cluster college plan. The two colleges in operation offer undergraduate and graduate studies. A medical school was opened in 1968. San Diego has research units in marine resources, sea water conversion, and space sciences.

Irvine, opened in 1965, has programs from the undergraduate to the post-doctoral level emphasizing preparation for the needs of a highly urbanized society. Its schools and colleges include arts, letters, and science, engineering, administration, and medicine.

Santa Cruz, developed on a residential cluster college plan, admitted its first students in 1965. The three operating colleges provide liberal arts programs in humanities, social sciences, natural sciences, and engineering. There are doctoral programs in astronomy, biology, and the history of consciousness. Santa Cruz administers the Lick Observatory at Mount Hamilton.

California's commitment to public higher education has attracted distinguished scholars. The faculty in the late 1960's included 13 Nobel laureates and 99 members of the National Academy of Sciences. They served a full-time student body of over 95,000. Library exchange facilities made a total of 7.5 million volumes available to students on all nine campuses. Special collections include California and Spanish-American history, Lincolniana, and oceanography.

MARGARET CHENEY, *University of California*

CALIFORNIA CURRENT, kal-ə-fôr′nyə, a current in the North Pacific Ocean. Fed in the north by the North Pacific current, it carries cool waters southeast off the U. S. and Mexican coasts, then turns west and joins the waters of the North Equatorial current. The California current is the eastern portion of the clockwise motion of water in the North Pacific.

CALIFORNIA INSTITUTE OF TECHNOLOGY, in Pasadena, Calif., is a privately supported technical university devoted to undergraduate and graduate instruction and research, principally in science and engineering. It was developed from Throop Polytechnic Institute, a trade and crafts school, founded in Pasadena in 1891 by Amos G. Throop.

Astronomer George Ellery Hale, who established Mount Wilson Observatory above Pasadena, was the first to envision Throop's future as a center of scientific and engineering research. With Arthur Amos Noyes, a noted chemist, and physicist Robert Andrews Millikan, who later won a Nobel Prize, Hale adopted the institute's present name in 1920 and initiated the educational philosophy that has made the school a world-famous center of teaching and research.

The institute is organized into six divisions: biology; chemistry and chemical engineering; engineering and applied science; geological sciences; humanities and social sciences; and physics, mathematics, and astronomy. Opportunities for research in these fields are extensive, and as many as 900 projects may be under way in a single year.

In addition to the numerous research units on campus, there are a number of outstanding institute facilities nearby: the Jet Propulsion Laboratory, operated by the institute for the National Aeronautics and Space Administration; Mount Wilson and Palomar observatories, operated by the institute and the Carnegie Institution of Washington, D. C.; Owens Valley Radio Observatory; Kerckhoff Marine Laboratory at Corona del Mar; a hydraulics and coastal engineering laboratory at Azusa; and a seismology laboratory.

Library facilities are available for all major disciplines. They have been supplemented by a new nine-story unit, the Robert A. Millikan Memorial Library.

In the late 1960's the institute had a student body of almost 1,500, including about 30 women in the graduate school (the only unit open to women students). The faculty numbered about 600. Six alumni have been awarded the Nobel Prize. Another five Nobel laureates are, or have been, on the faculty.

James R. Miller
California Institute of Technology

CALIFORNIA LAUREL, a beautiful evergreen tree of the laurel family, is native to the West Coast of the United States. California laurel (*Umbellularia californica*), also called pepperwood, California bay, and myrtle, adapts itself to a wide variety of environmental conditions. In dry areas it grows as a shrub in chaparral thickets, while on fog-drenched mountain slopes it may exceed 75 feet in height.

The California laurel's shiny dark-green leaves are lanceolate to oblong in shape, from 3 to 5 inches (7½ to 13 cm) long, and remain on the tree from 2 to 5 years. The yellow-green flower, which is borne in a spraylike umbel, contains a pistil that ripens into a large purple drupe, ½ to 1 inch (1.25 to 2.5 cm) in diameter. The wood, sometimes called Oregon myrtle, is hard and heavy and often mottled, and it will take a high polish. It is used to make novelties and fine furniture.

S. C. Bausor
California State College, Pa.

JOHN J. SMITH

California poppy

CALIFORNIA POPPY, a summer-flowering perennial native to semiarid areas of western North America. The California poppy (*Eschscholzia californica*), a member of the poppy family (Papaveraceae), grows to about 12 inches (30 cm) high and has fernlike, blue-green leaves and large, solitary orange blooms. Cultivated forms, raised as annuals, may bear semi-double or double flowers, from white to almost red.

R. C. Allen
Kingwood Center, Mansfield, Ohio

CALIFORNIA QUAIL. See Quail.

CALIFORNIA TRAIL was the name applied to routes to California used by pioneers traveling from Mexico, Texas, or the Missouri River. To most travelers it meant the main road from Council Bluffs or other Missouri River points. It followed the Platte Valley of Nebraska and then cut across southern Wyoming and into southern Idaho. Its eastern half, to that point, was identical with the Oregon Trail, and both were sometimes called the Overland Trail. Along the Snake River west of Fort Hall, the Oregon and California trails parted. The latter veered southwest across Nevada, over what later became known as the Donner Pass, and continued across central California to Sacramento and San Francisco Bay.

In 1841 the John Bartleson party tried to open the first wagon road across the mountains to California, but failed. In 1843, Joseph B. Chiles, from the Bartleson party, and Joseph R. Walker led another attempt without success. The Elisha Stevens party was the first (1844) to get wagons across the high passes to California.

Use of this rough and hazardous road increased after the discovery of gold in California. In 1849 the trail was used by about 22,500 people, at least 21,000 of whom reached California. Their horses, mules, and oxen numbered about 60,000. Parts of the trail were used by stagecoach lines and the Pony Express. Completion of the first transcontinental railroad in 1869 lessened use of the trail, sections of which were followed later by U. S. Highways 26, 30, 40, and 50.

Wayne Gard
Author of "The Chisholm Trail"

CALIFORNIUM, kal-ə-fôr′nē-əm, symbol Cf, is the synthetic (man-made) element with atomic number 98. It was discovered by S. G. Thompson, K. Street, A. Ghiorso, and G. T. Seaborg at the University of California's Lawrence Radiation Laboratory in February 1950 and was named in honor of the state of California. Isotopes of californium ranging in mass from 244 to 254 are known; all are radioactive, with half-lives ranging from 20 minutes to about 1,000 years.

The chemical properties and methods of production of Californium are in many respects similar to those of element 97. (See BERKELIUM.) The nuclear properties of the californium isotopes, however, are very distinctive because spontaneous fission becomes for the first time an important mode of decay, a trend which continues in heavier elements. The isotope Cf^{252} (half-life 2.6 years) decays partially by spontaneous fission and is produced primarily in high-flux nuclear reactors. It is very useful for the study of fission and for the development of counters and electronic systems, with applications not only in nuclear physics but in other fields such as medical research. The isotope Cf^{254} undergoes spontaneous fission with a half-life of about 60 days and has been assumed to be responsible for the decay of the light intensity of supernovae, which is observed to occur with a similar half-life.

Californium is the 9th member of a series of elements usually called actinides, whose chemical properties are analogous to those of the rare-earth, or lanthanide, series. Californium, like its homologue the rare-earth element dysprosium, has a very stable tripositive oxidation state, and the stabilities of its complex ions and the solubilities of its compounds are similar to dysprosium. Californium is usualy separated from other elements, including its neighbors, by the application of ion exchange methods similar to those used for separating rare-earth elements.

STANLEY G. THOMPSON
Lawrence Radiation Laboratory

Further Reading: Seaborg, Glenn T., *The Transuranium Elements* (New Haven 1958).

CALIGULA, kə-lig′ū-lə (12–41 A. D.), nickname of the Roman emperor Gaius Julius Caesar Germanicus. He was born at Antium (modern Anzio) on Aug. 31, 12 A. D. His father was Germanicus, the nephew and adopted son of Emperor Tiberius; his mother was Agrippina Major (the Elder). As a child he accompanied his father on military campaigns and wore his own military boots. The name Caligula means "Little Boots," and it was given to him affectionately by the soldiers under his father's command.

After his father's untimely death in 19 A. D., Caligula lived with his mother in Rome until she was arrested for conspiracy in 29. After a brief interval he joined Emperor Tiberius, who then resided on the isle of Capri. After 33 he was the only surviving son of Germanicus and was named by Tiberius as joint heir to his property along with Tiberius Gemellus, the Emperor's young grandson.

The Emperor. When Tiberius died in 37 A. D., the Roman senate declared his will invalid, and Caligula became the sole heir. He then adopted Tiberius Gemellus but executed him the following year. The first year of Caligula's reign was relatively peaceful and prosperous, but soon the power of the Roman emperorship began to warp his young mind. As madness set in, he became more despotic. Because of his ancestry (traced back to the deified Julius Caesar and Augustus), he became convinced that he was a god and demanded to be worshiped as such. After the death of his favorite sister, Drusilla, he insisted that she be deified.

Many of his actions were extravagant. He built a bridge from his palace on the Palatine to the Capitoline Hill to enable him to consult more easily with Jupiter in his temple. In less than a year he squandered all the money that Tiberius had saved. He provided his favorite horse, Incitatus, with a marble stable, an ivory stall, and a jeweled collar. There were rumors that he planned to make the horse a consul.

As time went on, a number of conspiracies were formed against him. One, involving Livilla and Agrippina, Caligula's two remaining sisters, and Gaetulicus, the legate of Upper Germany, was discovered and ruthlessly crushed. Finally, on Jan. 24, 41 A. D., Caligula was assassinated in his palace by a member of the Praetorian Guard whom he had insulted.

Evaluation. Very little good was accomplished during Caligula's reign. Some modern historians have attempted to challenge the hostile presentation of the man in the ancient sources, but their efforts have been, for the most part, unconvincing. He did repair some roads and begin the construction of two new aqueducts. He dabbled in foreign affairs but with little success. His visit to the Rhine for a proposed invasion of Britain was a major failure. He almost caused rebellion in the East when he insisted that his statue be placed in the Temple in Jerusalem, but he was assassinated before this order could be carried out. In the final analysis, he must be regarded as the most grotesque figure ever to serve as emperor of the Roman Empire.

ARTHER FERRILL, *University of Washington*

Further Reading: Balsdon, J. P. V. D., *The Emperor Gaius (Caligula)* (New York and London 1964); Suetonius, *The Twelve Caesars*, tr. by Robert Graves (Baltimore 1957).

THE EMPEROR CALIGULA, from a Roman portrait bust.

METROPOLITAN MUSEUM OF ART, ROGERS FUND, 1914

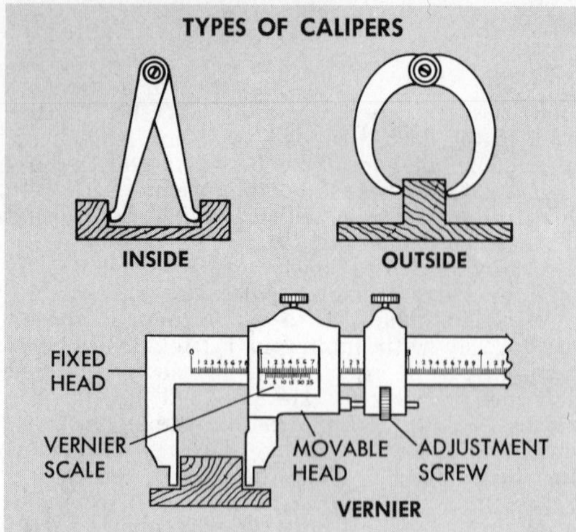

CALIPERS are a device for determining the dimensions of machine parts. Calipers are not usually precision instruments but are sufficiently accurate for the fabrication of many parts. Simple calipers consist of two movable legs joined at one point, with the separation between them usually controlled by a spring-loaded screw.

In *inside calipers,* the ends of the legs turn outward to measure widths of grooves, interior diameters, and similar dimensions. *Outside calipers* have curved legs with turned-in ends suited to measuring outside diameters. *Scribes* are calipers with straight legs and sharp points, used for marking off distances on flat surfaces. *Hermaphrodite calipers* have one inside or outside leg and one straight scribing leg. They are used to scribe a line parallel to a curved shoulder. In simple calipers the opening must be placed against a scale to read the dimension.

Vernier calipers incorporate a scale plus a vernier and are capable of precise measurement. They are shaped something like an adjustable wrench, with points at the end of the jaws that are suited to both inside and outside surfaces.
DONALD ZWIEP, *Worcester Polytechnic Institute*

CALIPHATE, kā'lə-fāt, the office of the Caliph, who was the ruler of the Muslim community. The office was established on the death of the Prophet Mohammed in 632 A. D. in order to provide for the continuation of organized community life among the diverse peoples whom Mohammed had converted to the new faith of Islam. The first caliph was Abu Bakr, one of Mohammed's companions, who was designated *imam*, or prayer leader, arbitrator of disputes and guardian of the laws and precepts bequeathed by Mohammed. The caliph had no prophetic or religious authority; his function was to uphold Islam.

The Arab conquests endowed the caliphate with new and crucial characteristics. The caliphs became both generals of the Arab armies with the duty of waging the *jihad*, or holy war, and administrators, indeed emperors, in the territories they conquered. However, violent disputes over the shifting emphasis from communal and religious to political and secular leadership rocked the early Muslim community. Under the Umayyad dynasty (661–750) the military and governmental aspects of the caliphate overwhelmed the communal and religious legacy, in the eyes of many contemporaries. Though still clinging to the notion of succession to the Prophet and the maintenance of Muslim traditions as the basis for the caliphate, the dynasty sought to legitimize its power by claiming divine selection and fusing the concept of the state with Islamic symbols.

The Caliphate Under the Abbasids. The conflict between political power and religious leadership helped bring an end to Umayyad rule, but the conflict was not resolved by the advent of the Abbasid dynasty (750–1258). The Abbasids sought to establish deeper foundations for the caliphate. They justified their tenure on the grounds that as descendants of the Prophet they had the right to rule the community. They legitimized their rule by taking the lead in the defense of the Muslim faith and the organization of Muslim community life. The Abbasids patronized Muslim religious activities and suppressed heresy. They waged the holy war on behalf of Islam. Most important, they organized a Muslim judicial and religious hierarchy under their control. For a time, the Abbasids also claimed the right to define religiously acceptable doctrines, but they were ultimately forced to concede that only Muslim scholars and divines might determine Muslim law and belief.

Insofar as the Abbasids stressed the descent of the caliphate from Mohammed and their duties and prerogatives in the maintenance of religious community life, they stood in the original tradition of the caliphate. In addition, however, following the Umayyad practice, they claimed that they had been divinely selected to rule. Under the Abbasids the caliphate became a sacral kingship.

From the point of view of religious thinkers, however, the caliphate had related, though slightly different, implications. To the Sunni Muslims (who formed one of the main branches of Islam) the caliph was the successor to the Prophet in the leadership of the community and the executor of the divine law; but in no sense was doctrinal authority or divine qualification attributed to him. Sunni theory specified that the caliph had to be elected by the community and must meet certain personal qualifications; nevertheless, these theoretical requirements were reconciled with the actualities of dynastic succession.

Other Views of the Caliphate. The Sunni view, with its close historical attachment to the existing caliphate, was not universally accepted. The Shiite Muslims (who formed another branch of Islam) held that only Ali, Mohammed's son-in-law and nephew, was the Prophet's rightful successor; the leadership of the community, or the imamate, should devolve only on his descendants. The Alid family claim was thus justified by family descent, by Mohammed's designation of Ali as his successor, and by the spiritual virtue of the Alid family. Shiites believe, though in forms differing among Shiite sects, that an esoteric knowledge of the true Islam is vested in the imam by a divine spirit and that the imam is the ultimate source of the true meaning of Islam. An almost contrary view of the imamate was held by the Kharijites (the members of an early Islamic sect), which held that the caliph could not be confined to any particular family, but was elected to office and could be deposed by the community. He had no religious significance. The Shiite view was theocratic as opposed to the virtually anarchic Kharijite position.

The Caliphate During the Abbasid Decline. Such theories of the religious meaning of the caliphate persisted even after caliphal political domination ceased. From the middle of the 10th

GEORGE ZIMBEL, FROM MONKMEYER

CALISTHENICS, rhythmic exercises performed individually or in groups, improve strength and flexibility.

century the Abbasid caliphs were deprived of all effective imperial power, though they retained their title. In principle, authority was delegated by the caliph to the various princes who in fact governed Muslim lands; the caliphs continued to be responsible for the maintenance of the Muslim faith and Muslim religious institutions.

The Abbasids, however, were no longer alone in claiming the august title. In 909 the Fatimids in Egypt, who belonged to the Ismaili sect, laid claim to the caliphal title. The Fatimid dynasty held it until 1171 and with it they set forth a counterclaim to the worldwide leadership of the Muslim community. In Spain the ruling Umayyad dynasty also adopted the title in 928, to offset the rival Fatimid claim.

The Post-Abbasid Concept of the Caliphate. With the extinction of the Abbasid house in Baghdad in 1258, the title was widely adopted by petty potentates throughout the Muslim world. Most famous of these claimants were the Mamluks, who reestablished the Abbasid caliphate, and the Ottoman sultans. The concept of the caliphate remained alive in Ottoman thinking until the demise of the Ottoman empire at the end of World War I. At that point efforts were made to recreate the unity of Muslims under a single religious and political authority. Caliphal congresses were held in 1919 and 1926. Various rulers were persuaded to adopt the title, but in an age when national feeling precedes religious identification, the effort to reestablish the caliphate proved to be hopeless if not meaningless. But the persistence of the concept into modern times can be understood as the persistence of a fundamental concept of a community that holds itself to be divinely ordained and provided with rulers to sustain its intrinsic purposes.

IRA M. LAPIDUS
University of California at Berkeley

CALISTHENICS, kal-əs-then′iks, are exercises that stress strength, endurance, flexibility, and coordination. The purpose of doing them is to attain and maintain a desired level of physical efficiency and skill. They are free exercises, that is, without apparatus, and are performed with varying degrees of intensity and rhythm. Calisthenics may be prescribed for personal health or for individual or group athletic training and precompetition warmup. Motions include arm swinging, jumping and hopping, twisting and turning, bending and stretching, and pushing and pulling. Movements that are rhythmic and maintained long enough make demands on the circulation, respiration, and other bodily functions that contribute to the individual well-being.

Exercises may be performed separately with rest periods after each one. They also may be done consecutively and in rhythmic continuity, without a rest; performed in this manner they are called *polyrhythmic exercises* and are often demonstrated by large groups in sports festivals.

Early History. Ancient China is credited with categorizing exercises for therapeutic reasons; as early as 2500 B.C. the Chinese used exercises as aids in overcoming disease and prolonging life. In ancient Greece, athletic contests were held widely, and individuals participated to some extent in calisthenics. Among the Romans, calisthenics were used largely to prepare men for the army.

European Revival. During the Dark Ages, a period of asceticism, the body was neglected, and physical training was mainly preparation for the bearing of arms. However, the humanistic philosophies in the 17th and 18th centuries stimulated the revival of physical activity as a part of education. Johann Bernhard Basedow, the German educational reformer, introduced exercises with other forms of instruction at his model school in Dessau in 1774. But it was not until the early 19th century that they became incorporated to any great extent in school programs.

Among the early leaders in the development of systems of exercises and gymnastics were Friedrich Ludwig Jahn and Adolf Spiess of Germany and Per Henrik Ling of Sweden. Jahn opened the first outdoor gymnasium in Berlin in 1811 and founded the first *Turnverein* (gymnastic society). Spiess broadened Jahn's program of strengthening exercises, thus popularizing the *Turnverein,* which spread throughout the world.

Meanwhile, Ling devised a scientific system of exercises for therapeutic purposes. The *Gymnastic Free Exercises of Per Henrik Ling* (1834; Eng. tr., 1853) showed the effects of free exercises on posture and on the functioning of the body organs. The Swedish system was taught largely by command rather than demonstration.

CALISTHENICS

Calisthenics are designed to give tone and firmness to muscles, enable the joints to move readily, and increase general vigor. Circulation and respiration will be greatly stimulated with vigorous performance and rapid movements. Continue each exercise here until a state of mild fatigue is experienced; reduce the time interval between exercises as endurance improves. Before starting an exercise program, a thorough physical examination by a physician is recommended. Movements include swinging, jumping, hopping, twisting, turning, bending, stretching, pushing.

HIGH JUMP: Start with feet apart and knees bent, arms extended backward.
1. *Jump* upward, keeping head high, and *swing* arms vigorously overhead.
2. *Return* to start.
Repeat often. Increase cadence, in moderate to fast time, as flexibility and endurance improve.

HOP AND BALANCE: Start with feet together, arms at sides, body erect. *Hop* to each position.
1. *Hop* on left foot and *extend* right leg and both arms forward, arms parallel to floor.
2. *Swing* right leg sideward and *spread* arms to the side.
3. *Extend* right leg and arms to the rear.
4. *Return* to start.
Repeat on opposite side. Repeat entire exercise. Increase speed as coordination and rhythm improve.

JUMP AND STRETCH: Start with feet together, arms at sides, body erect.
1. *Jump* to a stride and *swing* arms sideward and overhead. 2. *Return* to start. Repeat often. Increase cadence as coordination and rhythm improve with practice.

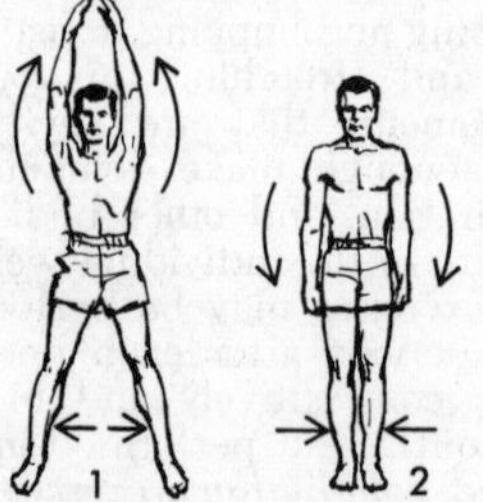

TRUNK TWIST: Start with feet apart, hands behind head, body erect.
1. *Twist* and *bend* upper body, touching left elbow to right knee.
2. *Return* to start.
3. and 4. *Repeat*, right elbow to left knee.
Repeat, increasing speed.

SHUFFLE: Start with feet together, arms flexed, hands clenched.
1. *Hop* on right foot and *extend* left leg and left arm slightly forward.
2. *Return* to start.
3. and 4. *Repeat*, on opposite side.
Repeat, increasing speed as coordination improves. Rotate shoulders in moves.

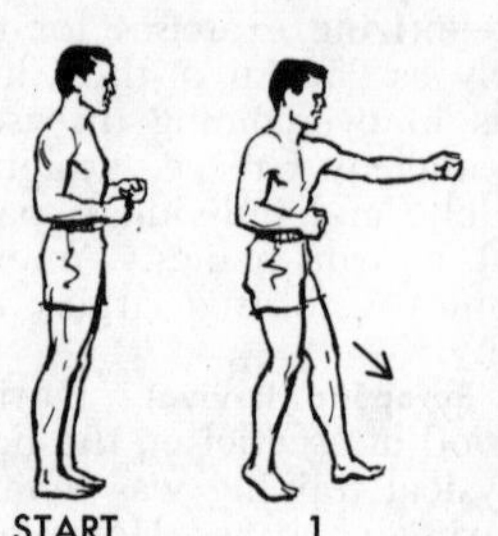

LEG LIFT: Lie on back, feet together, hands on hips.
1. *Raise* both legs off floor, keeping feet together, toes pointed. 2. *Spread* legs to the side. 3. *Bring* legs together. 4. *Lower* legs to start.
Repeat, back pressed to the floor. Increase height of legs off floor.

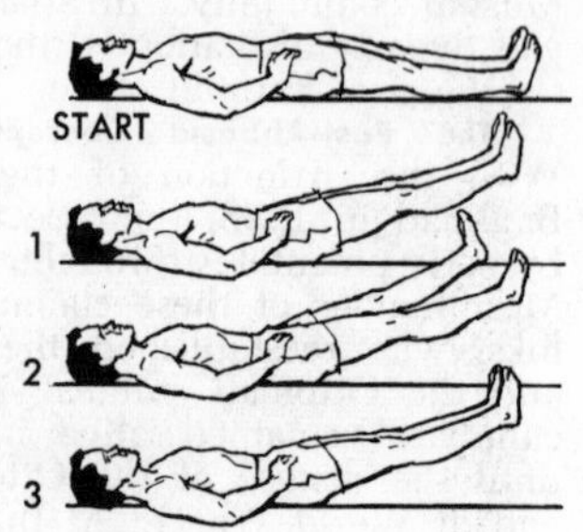

SIT-UP AND LEG STRETCH: Lie on back with feet together, arms extended above head. 1. *Flex* hips and *stretch* arms to feet, fingers touching toes. 2. *Return* trunk and arms to start. 3. *Raise* and *extend* legs backward, touching toes to floor above head. 4. *Return* hips and legs to the starting position.
Repeat, keeping legs straight throughout. Increase speed as strength improves.

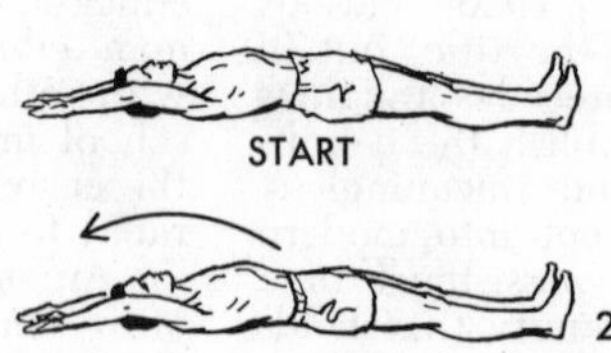

PUSH-UP: Lie face down, hands under shoulders, fingers forward. 1. *Extend* arms full length, keeping the body rigid. 2. *Bend* arms and *lower* body until face almost touches floor. Repeat often, relaxing between each push-up at first. Increase cadence.

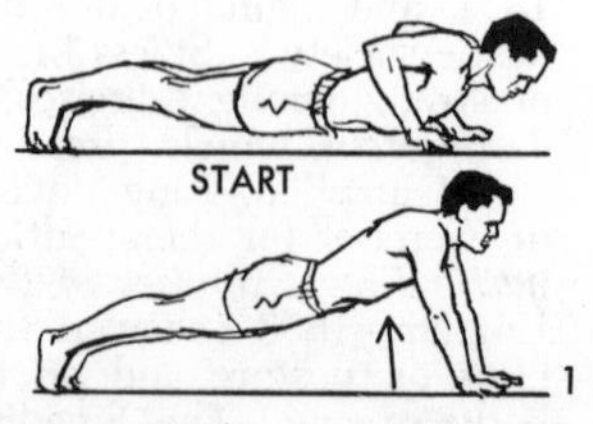

PLACE RUNNING: Start on one foot, arms flexed, hands loose, body relaxed. 1. *Raise* left knee to hip level, swinging arms. 2. *Lower* left leg and simultaneously *raise* right knee, swinging arms. Repeat, running on balls of feet. Lift knees high, changing cadence as desired.

Development in the United States. The German and Swedish gymnastic systems, heavily oriented toward calisthenics, were taken to the United States during the second half of the 19th century. Modifications of both systems were made by such leaders as Dioclesian (Dio) Lewis, Nils Posse, and Dudley Allen Sargent. Lewis introduced more flexibility into Ling's exercises, using dumbbells, clubs, and wands; Posse developed Swedish exercises into a systematic progression, or "day's order"; and Sargent stressed building up deficient parts of the body by especially prescribed "corrective" exercises. Calisthenics continued to be a popular means of exercise until the 1930's, when a greater interest in sports and recreation activities caused a decline.

The attitude of the American people toward exercise and fitness changed sharply after studies of physical achievement indicated a distinct lowering of the general vitality of youth after World War II. This lack, coupled with the modern tendency toward sedentary living, led to a renewed interest in exercises for health and body conditioning. Programs were promoted in newspapers and books and on radio and television for body building and figure improvement; and isometric, or "no movement" exercises (those involving the production of tension in motionless muscles) became popular as strength builders.

D. Verdelle Parker
Purdue University

Bibliography

Guild, Warren R., *How to Keep Fit and Enjoy It* (New York 1962).
Kiphuth, Robert, *How to Be Fit: Exercises for Men and Women,* rev. ed. (New Haven 1963).
Prudden, Bonnie, *Bonnie Prudden's Fitness Book* (New York 1959).
Royal Canadian Air Force, *The Five BX Plan for Physical Fitness* (Ottawa 1960).
Wallis, Earl, and Logan, Gene A., *Figure Improvement and Body Conditioning Through Exercise* (Englewood Cliffs, N. J., 1964).

CALIVER, kal'ə-vər, **Ambrose** (1894–1962), American educator. He was born in Saltville, Va., on Feb. 25, 1894. He received a diploma in cabinetmaking at Tuskegee Institute in 1916 and studied personnel management at Harvard University. He received his M. A. from the University of Wisconsin and his Ph.D. from Columbia University in 1930. Caliver began his long career in the field of education in 1916, serving as principal of a high school in Rockwood, Tenn. The next year he went to Fisk University in Nashville, where he eventually became dean. He remained there until he was appointed to the U. S. Office of Education in 1930.

During his 32 years in the Office of Education, Caliver specialized in adult education and educational opportunities for Negroes. At a time when Negro leaders were divided over the importance of vocational education, he encouraged emphasis on liberal education. In 1950 he became assistant to Earl McGrath, commissioner of education. Caliver recognized the importance of adult education as a means to help the nation make full use of its human resources. He advocated the use of local and state government funds to strengthen adult education programs. As a result of his extensive work, in 1955 he was made head of the newly created Adult Education Section. He also served as educational adviser to the United Nations committee on non-self-governing territories. Caliver died in Washington, D. C., on Jan. 29, 1962.

CALIXTUS, popes. See Callistus.

CALIXTUS, kä-liks'to͞os, **Georg** (1586–1656), German Protestant theologian. He was born Georg Callisen in Medelby, Schleswig, on Dec. 14, 1586. His studies at universities on the Continent and in England exposed him to the leading religious thinkers of the Reformation. In 1614 he became professor of theology at Helmstedt in Brunswick, a position he held until his death.

At Helmstedt, Calixtus worked unceasingly for the peace of the Protestant Church. His writings on the authority of Scripture, transubstantiation, marriage of priests, papal supremacy, and other disputed topics were notable for their scholarly impartiality. This trait, however, led in 1639 to the accusation of latent popery and heresy from the Lutherans. Among the issues were that good works were necessary for salvation and that points of disagreement between Calvinists and Lutherans were less important than points of agreement. Such matters occasioned a series of disputes over efforts to unify the Protestant churches, known as the Syncretistic Controversy, in which Calixtus and his followers were accused of confounding Lutheran with Calvinist beliefs.

After the Diet of Ratisbon in 1653, Calixtus was left in peace, mainly through the efforts of his protector, the Elector of Brandenburg. Calixtus created a reawakening of studies of the church fathers and of church history and established Christian ethics as a discipline separate from dogmatic theology. He died at Königslutter, Braunschweig, on March 19, 1656.

CALL, kôl, **Richard Keith** (1791–1862), American soldier and politician. Born near Petersburg, Va., he was a member of a distinguished military family, and he joined the army in 1814. He served under Gen. Andrew Jackson at Pensacola and New Orleans and became a member of Jackson's staff. After a year in Congress (1824–1825) representing the Florida territory, he became involved in building the third railroad in the United States, from Tallahassee to St. Marks, Fla. (1832–1834).

In 1836, Call was appointed governor of Florida. That year he also served in the army, but he lost his command after an unsuccessful campaign, and, following a dispute with the War Department, he was relieved of the governorship (1839). Before the Civil War he tried to prevent Florida's secession. He died in Tallahassee on Sept. 14, 1862.

CALL OF THE WILD, a novel by the American writer Jack London, first published in 1903. Generally considered London's best work, the novel tells the story of the dog Buck, a mongrel of St. Bernard and Scotch shepherd stock. After enduring unfortunate adventures and a series of cruel masters, Buck is adopted by John Thornton, an Alaskan, who shows him kindness and affection for the first time. When Thornton dies, his dog escapes to the woods, where he becomes the leader of a wolf pack.

In *The Call of the Wild,* London utilized for the first time one of his favorite literary themes: primitive emotions lying just beneath the surface of civilized behavior. The novel has occasional flashes of brilliant writing and has long been popular as an animal adventure story. A sequel, *White Fang,* was published in 1905.

MIKE ANDREWS, FROM BELL HOWARTH LTD.—BLACK STAR

CALLAO, the principal seaport of Peru, harbors seagoing freighters and a large fishing fleet.

CALLA LILY, kal'ə lil'ē, a perennial South African plant grown for its ornamental blooms. The calla lily has long-stalked, arrow-shaped leaves that arise from the rootstock, or corm. The blooms, borne singly on stems reaching 3 feet (1 meter) or more in length, consist of a showy spathe (modified leaf) surrounding a prominent yellow spadix (fleshy flower spike).

Calla lilies belong to the genus *Zantedeschia,* a member of the arum family (Araceae), and are therefore not true lilies; nor should they be confused with the true *Calla,* a North American bog plant.

Five species of calla lilies are commonly grown in the United States: Z. *aethiopica,* the common white calla; Z. *albo-maculata,* the spotted calla; Z. *rehmanni,* the red, or pink, calla; and Z. *elliotiana,* the golden calla. Improved varieties and hybrids also have been developed. The species may be propagated by seed, but the hybrids and varieties are best propagated by offsets from rhizomes (underground stems) and corms.

R. C. Allen
Kingwood Center, Mansfield, Ohio

J. J. SMITH

Calla lily

CALLAGHAN, kal'ə-hən, **Morley Edward** (1903–), Canadian writer. He was born in Toronto, graduated from the University of Toronto, and took a law degree at Osgoode Hall. In 1925 he met Ernest Hemingway in Toronto, and in 1929 he went to Paris, where he became acquainted with many American expatriates (recalled in his memoir *That Summer in Paris,* 1963), and contributed stories to *This Quarter* and *transition.* He became a disciple of Hemingway, though his style is less blunt.

Callaghan's writing, which is intense and clinically observant, often describes an individual who is unable to adjust to society. His novels include *Strange Fugitive* (1928); *Such Is My Beloved* (1934); *They Shall Inherit the Earth* (1935), which most critics consider his best novel; and *A Passion in Rome* (1961), which was praised for its description of the period between the death of Pius XII and the election of John XXIII. Among his collections of short stories are *Native Argosy* (1928), *No Man's Meat* (1931), and *Morley Callaghan's Stories* (1959).

CALLAO, kä-yä'ō, the principal port of Peru, is situated on Callao Bay of the Pacific Ocean, about 8 miles (13 km) west of Lima, the capital of the country, to which it is connected by rail and road. Physically Callao and its environs merge into the Lima metropolitan area. Politically they comprise a constitutional province (as distinct from the departments into which the rest of the country is divided), with departmental status. The province includes Callao (the capital), the suburbs of La Punta, Bellavista, and and Chucuito, and small islands. The dry, cool climate of the region (average annual temperature 66°F, or 19°C) is due chiefly to the presence offshore of a cold-water current known as the Peru (or Humboldt) Current.

The port of Callao handles more than half the country's exports and imports. The harbor is sheltered by the island of San Lorenzo, and the port is modern and well equipped. The Lima-Callao area is also Peru's chief commercial and industrial district. Industries of Callao include fisheries, flour mills, breweries, meat-packing plants, and sugar refineries. La Punta is a popular resort and the seat of Peru's naval academy.

Callao was founded in 1537 by the Spanish conqueror of Peru, Francisco Pizarro, who had selected the site and founded Lima two years earlier. As the chief shipping point of riches from the Inca empire, Callao was frequently attacked by pirates and European rivals of Spain. The English navigator Francis Drake sacked the city in 1578. During the wars for independence, Callao was held by Spanish loyalists until 1826, although Peru's independence was proclaimed in 1821. During the War of the Pacific (also called the Chile-Peruvian War), Callao was occupied by the Chileans in 1881 but was returned two years later. The center of present-day Callao occupies a site a short distance from the site of the original city, which was destroyed by earthquake and tidal waves in 1746. Population: (1961) city, 155,953; province, 213,540.

Gregory Rabassa, *Columbia University*

CALLAS, kä'läs, **Maria** (1923–), Greek-American soprano, one of the outstanding opera singers of the post-World War II era. A superb actress as well as an artist of scrupulous musicianship, she has excelled in a wide variety of roles, notably in the early 19th century *bel canto* operas.

She was born Maria Kalogeropoulos in New York City on Dec. 4, 1923. At the age of 14 she went with her mother to Greece, where she studied voice with the coloratura singer Elvira de Hidalgo at the Conservatory of Athens. Her rise to stardom began in 1947 in Verona, Italy, where she appeard in the title role of Ponchielli's *La Gioconda.* This performance led to her friendship with the conductor Tullio Serafin, who became her artistic mentor. At this time she also met the Italian industrialist Giovanni Battista Meneghini, whom she married in 1949, and from whom she was subsequently separated.

During the Italian appearances that followed the Verona debut, the brilliant and determined young artist sang roles ranging from Bellini to Wagner. In 1949 she made her debuts at the Rome Opera, the Teatro Colón in Buenos Aires, and at the San Carlo Opera in Naples. Her debut at La Scala in Milan, in Verdi's *I vespri siciliani,* took place in 1951. Bellini's *Norma* was her debut vehicle in London's Covent Garden in 1952, at the Chicago Opera in 1954, and at the Metropolitan Opera, New York in 1956.

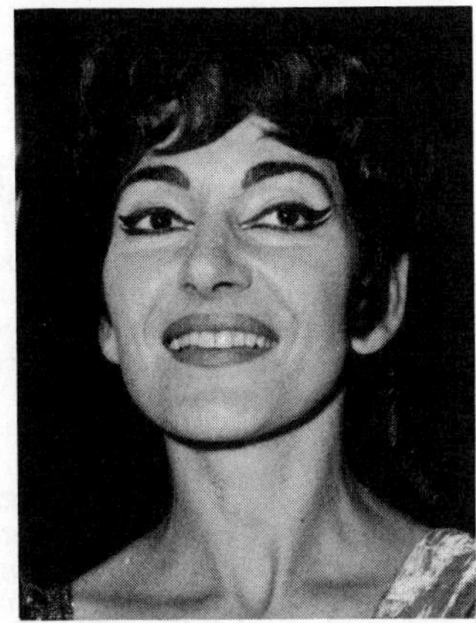
Maria Callas

MIRRORPIC, LONDON

Mme. Callas' artistic successes were accompanied by an extraordinary number of headlines devoted to her personal life. Her professional feuds led to her gradual withdrawal from the major opera houses, and after 1960 her appearances were infrequent.

Recordings by Mme. Callas include more than 20 complete operas, among them the first complete recordings of such works as Bellini's *I Puritani.* On stage she appeared in about 40 operas.

Mme. Callas cannot be considered a "perfect" vocalist because her scale was uneven and her sustained notes in the high register were often wavery. However, her singing gained beauty through her acting and expressive phrasing and meaningful projection.

George Jellinek
Author of "Callas, Portrait of a Prima Donna"

CALLEJA DEL REY, kä-ye'hä thel re'ē, **Félix María** (1750–1820), Spanish general, who was known as "the Butcher" for his severity in crushing a rebellion in Mexico in 1810–1815. He was born at Medina del Campo, Spain, in 1750. As a commander in Mexico, he led troops against the followers of the priest Miguel Hidalgo y Costilla, who had revolted against Spanish rule. Calleja won a victory at Calderón Bridge on Jan. 17, 1811, and six months later he captured and executed Hidalgo.

Calleja was named viceroy of Mexico in 1813 and defeated a rebel army led by another priest, José María Morelos y Pavón. Morelos was tried and shot. Calleja was recalled to Spain in 1815 and was created Count of Calderón. While preparing an expedition to Paraguay in 1820, he was imprisoned by mutinous soldiers. He died at Cádiz, Spain, in 1820, after his release.

CALLENDAR, kal'ən-dər, **Hugh Longbourne** (1863–1930), English physicist, who is known for his many contributions to experimental physics, particularly to thermodynamics. He was born in Hatherop, Gloucestershire, on April 18, 1863. He graduated from Cambridge in 1885, excelling in classics, mathematics, medicine, and law. As professor at McGill University, Montreal, Canada, Callendar did important work on steam engines, using his patented thermometers and recorders. He received an appointment in 1901 as professor of physics at the Imperial College, London, and he retained this position until his death on Jan. 23, 1920. A great inventor of apparatus for science and industry, Callendar was elected a fellow of the Royal Society.

L. H. Callendar
Fellow, Royal Institute of Chemistry

CALLES, kä'yās, **Plutarco Elias** (1877–1945), Mexican military leader. The ablest organizer of the Mexican Revolution, he gave it two basic institutions, the Revolutionary party and a professional army.

Calles was born at Guaymas, Sonora, on Sept. 25, 1877. At the age of 17 he became an elementary schoolteacher. His interest in social reform was awakened at that time, and in 1910 he joined the revolutionary movement led by Francisco Madero. His capacity for organization and leadership brought him the rank of general in the civil war that followed the overthrow of Madero by a military coup in 1913.

Under President Venustiano Carranza (1917–1920) Calles was secretary of commerce, labor, and industry. Under Provisional President Adolfo de la Huerta (1920) he was secretary of foreign relations, and under President Álvaro Obregón (1920–1924) he was secretary of the interior.

As president of Mexico (1924–1928) he was involved in conflicts with the Catholic Church, which opposed new laws limiting the number of clergy and prohibiting church schools; with foreign owners of the petroleum industry, over a law of 1925 regulating the industry; and with owners of expropriated land.

For six years after the assassination of President-elect Obregón in 1928, Calles was the strong man behind three interim presidents. He supported the election of Lázaro Cárdenas in 1934, but broke with the new president a year later over the latter's more radical revolutionary policies and went into exile in the United States. He returned to Mexico City in 1942, where he died on Oct. 19, 1945.

Harold E. Davis, *The American University*

CALLET, kȧ-le, **Antoine François** (1741–1823), French historical and portrait painter who was one of the foremost decorative artists of his day, known chiefly for his paintings of scenes from classical mythology. He was born in Paris. In 1764 he was awarded the Prix de Rome for *Biton and Cleobis Dragging the Chariot of Their Mother to the Temple of Hera,* which was purchased by the Académie Française. In 1780 he was elected to the Académie.

Spring, one of his best classical canvases, is in the Louvre, which also owns some of his portraits, including three of Louis XVI and one each of Louis XVIII and the Count d'Artois. Callet died in Paris.

CALLIAS, kal'ē-əs, was a common name in ancient Athens, the best-known bearers of which were three members of a wealthy, aristocratic family. In the 6th century B. C., Callias (I), son of Phaenippus, opposed Pisistratus and alone dared to buy the exiled tyrant's confiscated property. His grandson, Callias (II), son of Hipponicus, won three chariot races at Olympia. He married the general Cimon's sister but assisted Cimon's rival Pericles in his foreign policy, negotiating peace with Persia in 449 and the Thirty Years' Peace with Sparta in 445.

His grandson, Callias (III), son of Hipponicus, was attacked by the comic poets and the orator Andocides but was depicted sympathetically by Plato in his *Protagoras.* As a general he participated in the victory of Iphicrates' light-armed troops over Spartan hoplites (heavy-armed infantry) in 390. In 371 he was a member of the embassy sent to Sparta in an unsuccessful effort to conclude a common peace.

DONALD W. BRADEEN
University of Cincinnati

CALLICRATES, kə-lik'rə-tēz, Greek architect of the 5th century B. C. He was one of the architects of the Parthenon (q.v.; about 440 B. C.). He collaborated on its design and construction with the architect Ictinus and the sculptor Phidias.

Callicrates, who probably was one of the official architects of Periclean Athens, is also credited with building the Temple of Athena Nike between 427 and 424 B. C., which also stood on the Acropolis. He may have taken part in the building of the walls between Athens and Piraeus (443–442 B. C.) and may also have restored the city walls of Athens itself.

CALLIÈRES BONNEVUE, kȧ-lyâr' bon-vü', **Chevalier Louis Hector de** (1646–1703), French soldier and colonial administrator in New France (Canada). Born in Normandy, he became an army officer and was appointed governor of Montreal in 1684, taking up his duties there in the following year. He fortified the settlement and in 1687 led a division of the French and Indian forces who unsuccessfully attacked the Five Nations in what is today New York State.

Callières became governor of New France in 1699, succeeding the Count de Frontenac, and was an able and popular administrator. He fought the Indian tribes, chiefly the Iroquois, and concluded with them the peace treaty of 1701, which was his most important achievement. He also sent out the expedition under Antoine de la Mothe Cadillac that founded Detroit, in present-day Michigan. Callières died in Quebec on May 26, 1703.

CALLIGRAPHY, kə-lig'rə-fē, is a branch of penmanship in which alphabetical symbols are considered as a means of artistic expression. The word derives from the Greek *kalligraphia,* which means "beautiful writing." The subdivision of writing into two categories—functional and decorative—has been recognized from early times. Philostratus, in the 3d century A. D., wrote that when Apollonius of Tyana set out on a journey, he was attended by two servants who were expert scribes. One was noted for the speed with which he wrote, the other for the beauty of his handwriting.

Purpose and Characteristics. Primarily, the purpose of calligraphy is to please the eye, and this may sometimes be effected at the expense of legibility. Oriental scripts can be admired by people ignorant of the languages concerned. But generally, the ideal form of calligraphy combines beauty and legibility.

The study of the historical development of various types of European handwriting, from classical to Renaissance times, belongs to the science of paleography. Paleography takes into account the broad social, intellectual, and economic factors that modify scripts and determine their regional character. Calligraphy by definition is one of the fine arts. Its course mirrors the fluctuations of artistic taste in various countries, and its study is a function of aesthetic criticism.

Calligraphy results from the unhurried operation, on stabilized alphabetical forms, of superior skill and invention. In any art, the services of a craftsman who has these qualifications will be reserved for the more imaginative forms of expression, and he will assist, consciously or unconsciously, in maintaining tradition and style. A good handwriting style is always distinguished by uniformity, economy of means, and the accurate adjustment of alignment and spacing. The calligrapher in postclassical and medieval times filled a demand for excellent and durable liturgical texts. His less accomplished associates devoted their efforts to the mass of trivial tasks —"clerical work" in the modern sense—required to transact the daily business of organized societies. Thus there arises the distinction (not always clear-cut or easy to define) between formal and informal versions of the same script, and between the calligrapher and the scrivener or copyist. Between these extremes there are many gradations, according to the nature of the work to be done and the competence of the worker. Moreover, formal scripts have degenerated under cursive influence; cursive scripts have been elevated to calligraphic status; and the history of calligraphy has been a long alternating process of loss and recovery.

Early History. The gradual transformation of the written Roman square capital into the half uncial of the 6th–8th centuries is an illustration of the change in writing. The half uncial (the first fully developed minuscule or "small" letter of the Western world) is important for three reasons: its design is fundamental; it inspired a school of calligraphy unsurpassed in brilliance; and it has had a lasting influence on the art of writing.

The evolution of the half uncial owed much to the tendency of a pen to make rounded forms more naturally and easily than square forms. The perfection of the script may be traced to the replacement of papyrus by vellum as a writing material and to improved methods of dressing the skins. The eminent fitness of vellum to fine writing also encouraged the use of the broad-edged reed or quill pen, trimmed obliquely and finished like a chisel, giving maximum definition to the letters. It also encouraged the use of contrasting thick and thin strokes, qualities still sought after by modern practitioners of calligraphy. The union of high-grade tools and materials with an inherently appropriate model made possible the triumph of the half uncial in the Insular scripts (Irish and English) of the 7th-8th centuries. The 20th century calligrapher Edward Johnston attributed to these scripts "a degree of perfection since unrivalled." Johnston's remark referred particularly to the *Book of Kells* (Trinity College, Dublin) and the *Lindisfarne Gospels* (British Museum). Giraldis Cambrensis, who saw the *Book of Kells* at Kildare in the 12th century, said: "If you had but looked into the delicate and subtle forms, you would have said that these things had been put together by the industry of angels rather than of human beings."

No historian has ventured to imagine a supernatural origin for the Caroline minuscule (9th-12th centuries), so important for its influence on humanistic scripts. Compared with the Insular minuscule it is pedestrian, but in its simplicity, clarity, and fitness to purpose it cannot fail to please. The characteristic contribution of the Middle Ages to calligraphy is Gothic or "black-letter" text, the close, if scarcely recognizable, derivative of the Caroline minuscule. More than one writer has drawn the analogy between scripts and architecture—uncials and half uncials suggesting the Romanesque churches, black letter corresponding to the Gothic cathedrals of Europe. Gothic text is the artist's script *par excellence*. As such it was esteemed by Petrarch, who objected only to its extreme forms, on practical grounds. A modern critic, Stanley Morison, has described it as "a monument witnessing to the creative ability of medieval craftsmen . . . the most majestic . . . the most logical minuscule that has ever been evolved." Black letter lends itself to the sort of exuberant treatment that is the legitimate privilege of the artist to confer upon his material. But excess may lead to mere "fancy" writing, splendid when seen in isolation, but fatiguing if extended throughout the pages of a long book.

The Renaissance. The rejection of Gothic as a book script by the Italian humanists at the beginning of the 15th century was not based, as has often been suggested, on purely aesthetic considerations, but rather on the belief that an inherently ornamental script was inappropriate to the purpose of the scholar. His purpose was the transcription of the newly found texts of the classics, the first fruits of the revival of learning.

Humanistic script, the prototype of printed roman, was itself a revival, and in its early development it was a close imitation of the Caroline minuscule. The humanistic reform in writing was therefore a calculated act of archaism. The humanists themselves named the script of their adoption *lettera antica,* the old letter; the abandoned Gothic script, which to the 20th century eye at once suggests the "antique," was to them *lettera moderna,* not the "new" letter, but the characteristic "black" letter of their own time. The chief purpose of the humanistic scribe was to write clearly, expeditiously, and neatly, with beauty being a secondary consideration. Although the neo-Caroline scripts of the first half of the 15th century are often beautiful, they are seldom impressive as examples of calligraphy. However, with the growth of wealth and power in Italy, learning became fashionable and a demand was created for *éditions de luxe* of the classics. With the full momentum of the Renaissance behind it, writing kept pace with rapid and far-reaching technical developments in the other arts.

By the middle of the 15th century, Italian calligraphy had gained the supremacy it was to enjoy for 150 years. The period from 1450 to 1500 was the heyday of the great Italian *amanuenses,* or manuscript copyists. The long tradition of anonymity was broken. The sumptuous manuscripts of that half century bear the names of such masters as Antonio Sinibaldi, Gianrinaldo Mennio, Matteo Contugi, Sigismondo de' Sigismondi, and Pierantonio Sallando.

Simultaneously, the formal development of calligraphy received a new impetus. This derived from the general awakening of the historical sense, and the particular interest of the Renaissance scholars and artists in classical Roman inscriptions. The design of incised capitals was studied and their proportions were accurately measured. About 1463 the Veronese antiquary and scribe Felice Feliciano embodied the results of his investigations in a manuscript (Vatican Library MS. Lat. 6852) containing geometrical diagrams of the Roman alphabet. From that time, some of the conventions of the classical capital (that is, those governing serif formation) were assimilated to both the majuscules and minuscules of the humanistic alphabet. To this formalizing influence was added that of the printing press, which narrowed the field of scribal activity and made it an increasingly specialized profession.

Felice Feliciano's example inspired numerous printed treatises on the technical aspects of letter design, the earliest of which was written by Damiano Moille and published at Parma about 1480. The Moille treatise was followed by those of Hartmann Schedel (1482), Fra Luca Pacioli (1497), Sigismondo Fanti (1514), Francesco Torniello (1517), Albrecht Dürer (1525), Giambattista Verini (1526), Geoffroy Tory (1529), and Urban Wyss (1553). The systematic study

LETTER FORMS following the designs of the ancient Roman stonecutters were the basis of an early Renaissance treatise on calligraphy by Felice Feliciano of Verona.

VATICAN LIBRARY

LITERA DA BREVI

Aabcdeefgghiklmnopqrsstuxyz

~: Marcus Antonius Casanoua :~
Pierij vates, laudem si opera ista merentur,
Praxiteli nostro carmina pauca date.
Non placet hoc; nostri pietas laudanda Coryti est;
Qui dicat haec; nisi vos forsan utrumque mouet;
Debetis saltem Dijs carmina, ni quoque, et istis
Illa datis. iam nos mollia saxa sumus.

Ludouicus Vicentinus scribebat Romae anno
salutis MDXXIII

THE EARLIEST COPYBOOK, published in 1522 by Lodovico Arrighi, presented a script that combined perpendicular majuscules and slightly slanted miniscules.

of calligraphy, and its recorded history, may be said to begin with these and other works in which mathematical principles are brought to bear upon the structure of the Roman alphabet.

After 1500, when the use of the printing press was firmly established throughout Europe, the formal humanistic *lettera antica* declined in importance and vitality. But its informal analogue—the cursive script of the humanists—acquired a new lease of life. This flexible and expeditious script had scarcely altered in essential structure since the beginning of the 15th century. It was given calligraphic status approximately between the years 1470 to 1480, when it became a book hand in its own right. It later served as the basis for the italic typographical characters of Aldus Manutius and his successors. But its original intention was utilitarian. It was as a script for letter writing that it commended itself to Renaissance artists and men of letters and found favor with the chanceries of Rome and Venice for the dispatch of diplomatic business. For the latter reason, it acquired its Italian vernacular name *lettera cancelleresca*, or chancery writing. *Lettera antica* reached its zenith in the mid-16th century, by which time the writing of books by hand was falling into disuse. The highly skilled professional calligrapher of the 16th century faced a shrinking market. He therefore had to seek his livelihood more with the wage-earning public than with the princely patron. In 1522, Lodovico degli Arrighi of Vicenza, a papal scribe who later turned to printing, published at Rome his *Operina. . .da imparare di scrivere littera cancelleresca.* Printed from engraved wood blocks, it was the first manual or copybook to be addressed to the nonprofessional writer.

With Arrighi begins the long hierarchy of the Italian writing masters and the merging of calligraphy with the common business of mankind. His pioneer venture was successful and found many followers whose models influenced, and finally standardized, the form of European handwriting. At Venice in 1525, Giovanni Antonio Tagliente published a manual of similar character, *Opera. . .che insegna a scrivere.* The most versatile and popular of the 16th century Italian masters was Giovambattista Palatino. His *Libro nuovo d'imparare a scrivere* (Rome 1540; enl. ed. 1545) had an immense, if transient, vogue that extended beyond Italy. It was imitated in Spain

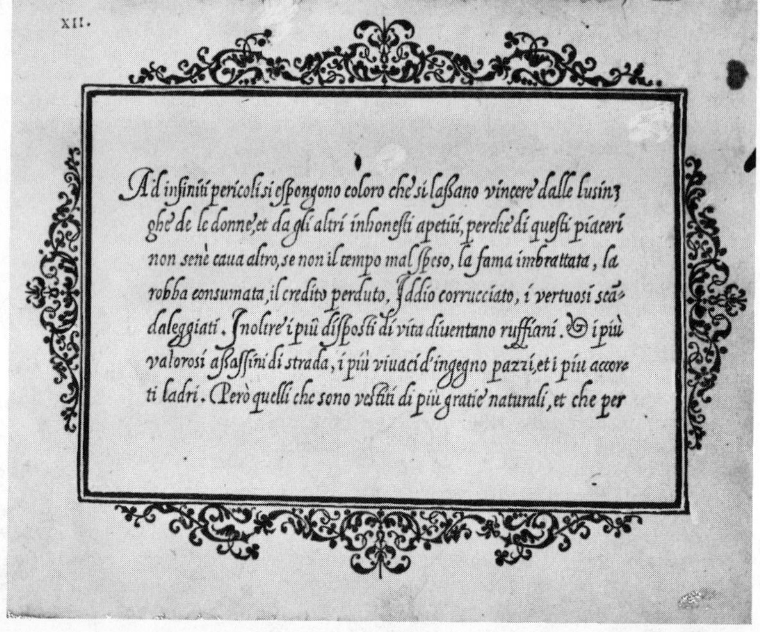
XII.

Ad infiniti pericoli si espongono coloro che si lassano vincere dalle lusinghe de le donne, et da gli altri inhonesti apetiti, perche di questi piaceri non se ne caua altro, se non il tempo mal speso, la fama imbrattata, la robba consumata, il credito perduto, Iddio corrucciato, i vertuosi scandaleggiati. Inoltre i più disposti di vita diuentano ruffiani. Et i più valorosi assassini di strada, i più viuaci d'ingegno pazzi, et i più accorti ladri. Però quelli che sono vestiti di più gratie naturali, et che per

A SCRIPT for more rapid writing was developed by Gianfrancesco Cresci in 1560. Cresci's characters are sloping and well-rounded, with a distinctive decorative blot at the terminals of ascending letters.

by Juan de Icíar in his *Recopilación subtilíssima* (Saragossa 1548). A script based on the Palatino model caught the fancy of court *litterati* in Elizabethan England. Palatino's chancery script had the defects already implicit in the work of Arrighi and Tagliente, of overcompression and angularity. His general tendency as an artist was to set a standard beyond the reach of ordinary people; whereas the need of the times, conditioned by the spread of commerce, was not for art but for speed.

As early as 1548 the Franciscan friar Vespasiano Amphiareo, in his book *Un nuovo modo d'imparare a scrivere,* published at Venice, had offered "chancery" models that allowed for loops and running ligatures. But it was not until the appearance, at Rome in 1560, of Gianfrancesco Cresci's *Essemplare* that the new demands were successfully met. Cresci, a scribe in the Vatican Library, favored the use of a harder, narrower pen, with a rounded point. He demonstrated convincingly the superiority of round to angular forms as aids to speed, and increased the slope of the writing line. Although a rationalist in precept and in practice, he was not opposed to ornament; the clubbed terminals of his ascending letters reflect the baroque taste of his age and anticipate the flourished loops of Victorian copperplate. Calligraphic models engraved from copperplates were first shown in the manual of Giuliantonio Hercolani: *Essemplare utile* (Bologna 1571). In the same year the first writing book to be printed in England was published under the title *A booke containing divers sortes of hands,* by John Baildon and Jean de Beauchesne.

Post-Renaissance Decline of Calligraphy. By the 17th century, the pursuit of writing as an end in itself, and the profession of *scriptor librarius,* had virtually ceased. Only in France did the art of writing and illuminating books on carefully prepared vellum win any renown. The manuscripts of Nicolas Jarry, Étienne Damoiselet, and Jean-Pierre Rousselet, though mechanical and tenuous in point of style, are much prized by collectors; and the doubtful credit of having done supremely well what was scarcely worth doing will not be denied to Jacques Leclabart, the author of *"Écrivain imitateur de caractères d'imprimerie à Paris."*

The pedagogic copybook tradition that flourished in Europe and America into the late 19th century derives from the example of Hercolani and his successors. By confusing the functions of pen and burin, the practitioners of this form reduced the national handwritings of the two continents to the same level of competent mediocrity.

Modern Era. The revival of calligraphy in England, Germany, and the United States is one of the artistic phenomena of the 20th century. Precursors of the movement in the 19th century were the architect Owen Jones and the poet and master craftsman William Morris. Both were collectors of medieval manuscripts. Owen Jones experimented with black-letter text, first building up the outlines of the letters with a fine steel pen,

A COPYBOOK ENGRAVED IN COPPERPLATE was produced in 1571 by Giuliantonio Hercolani. Engraving techniques encouraged a line of uniform thickness.

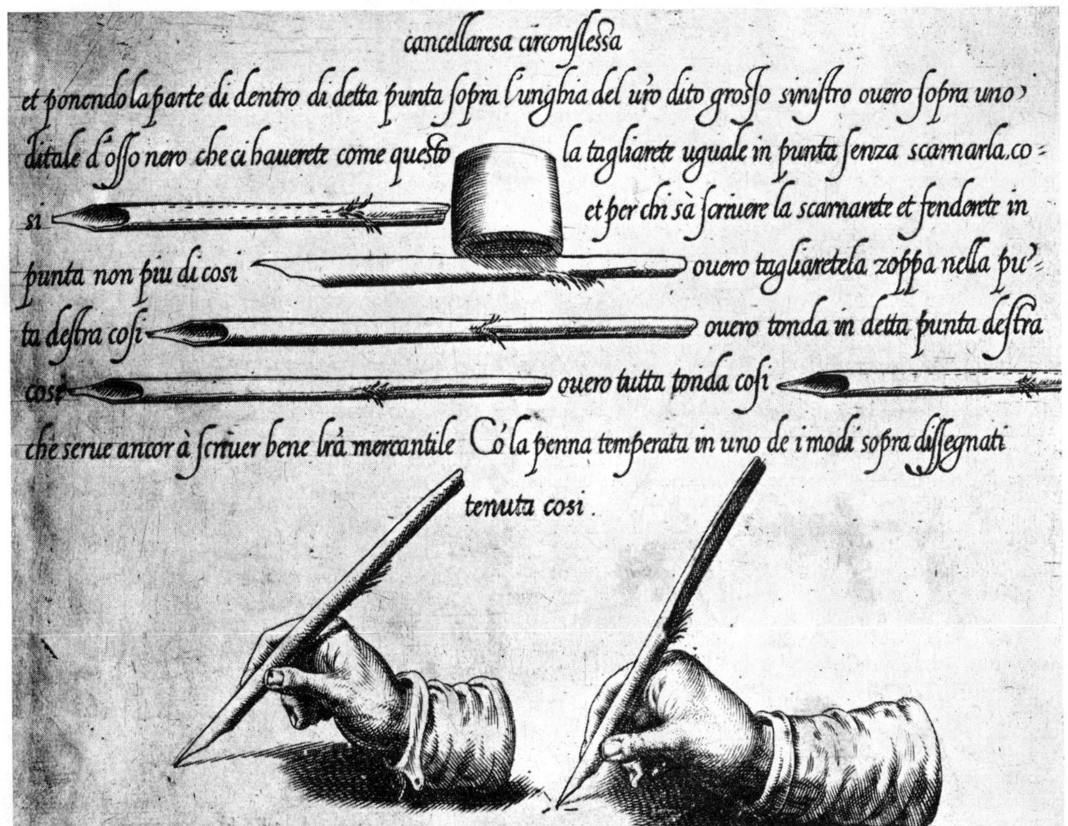
cancellaresca circonflessa
et ponendo la parte di dentro di detta punta sopra l'unghia del uro dito grosso sinistro ouero sopra uno
ditale d'osso nero che ci hauerete come questo la taglierete uguale in punta senza scarnarla, cosi et per chi sà scriuere la scarnarete et fenderete in
punta non piu di cosi ouero taglieretela zoppa nella pu-
ta destra cosi ouero tonda in detta punta destra
cosi ouero tutta tonda cosi
che serue ancor à scriuer bene lrã mercantile Cõ la penna temperata in uno de i modi sopra dissegnati
tenuta cosi.

that went to the battle were Eliab the firstborn, and next unto him Abinadab, and the
third Shammah. And David was the youngest: and the three eldest followed Saul. Now
David went to and fro from Saul to feed his
father's sheep at Beth-lehem. And the Philis-
tine drew near morning and evening, and
presented himself forty days.

AND JESSE SAID UNTO DAVID
HIS SON, Take now for thy brethren an
ephah of this parched corn, and these ten
loaves, and carry *them* quickly to the camp
to thy brethren; and bring these ten cheeses
unto the captain of their thousand, and
look how thy brethren fare, and take their

VICTORIA AND ALBERT MUSEUM

FORMAL CALLIGRAPHY in recent times has been reviewed largely through the work of Edward Johnston (1872–1944), an Englishman who spent years studying the tools, papers, and techniques of the medieval calligraphers. Johnston's script attains a balance between broad and fine lines.

and then filling in the skeleton forms with a brush. Morris began to write books by hand about 1870. With surer instincts than Jones, he worked directly with the quill. His scripts were based on Italian Renaissance models, a surprising choice for one who in everything else showed a preference for the medieval. His example had no immediate following. The true revival in letter design owed everything to Edward Johnston.

Johnston, who abandoned a medical career in 1897 because of ill-health, spent the next two years in the systematic study of pen shapes in early manuscripts at the British Museum. The revolutionary nature of Johnston's teaching at the Central School of Arts and Crafts, London, from 1899 to 1912, depended not so much on his artistic genius as on his inspired recovery of the lost technique of writing. Johnston perceived that the nature and form of a script are determined by the way in which the pen is cut and held and that the proportions of a letter are in direct ratio to the breadth of the pen's edge which, if trimmed chiselwise, gives that range of gradation from the thickest of strokes to the subtlest of hairlines which characterizes the best medieval work. "It is the broad nib," wrote Johnston, "that gives the pen its constructive and educational value. It is essentially the letter-making tool." Johnston's first class at the Central School, which included among its members Eric Gill, T. J. Cobden-Sanderson, Noel Rooke, and Graily Hewitt, became a focus of technical research and experiment. The accumulated experience of his teaching there and at the Royal College of Art was embodied in his textbook *Writing and Illuminating and Lettering*, first published in 1906. The book has since become a classic in its field. In the previous year he had been invited by the Prussian government to give a course of lectures in the art schools of Germany. One of his most brilliant pupils at the Royal College was a German woman, Anna Simons, who did much to propagate Johnston's teaching methods in Germany, Austria, Switzerland, and the Netherlands.

Johnston combined a keenly analytical mind with a phenomenal dexterity of hand. His manipulation of the Roman alphabet, in all its variations, is without parallel in modern times. Stylistically, his early preference was for the rounded contours of the half uncial. It was on English (Winchester) writing of the 10th century and on the Insular minuscule of earlier date that he modeled his so-called "foundation hand." In later life he performed an astonishing series of *tours de force* with a script based on the 15th century *lettre bâtarde.* Both these preferences, and his theory of writing in general, have been criticized as too retrospective; and he has been charged, a little unfairly, with bypassing the Renaissance. There is no doubt that as an artist, Johnston was impatient of restraints. The necessarily small scale of humanistic scripts was unsuited to his genius. He thought of writing, as the Chinese do, pictorially. His calligraphic legacy consists, for the most part, of single leaves.

The balance was to some extent restored by William Graily Hewitt, assistant and afterwards successor to Johnston at the London Central

School of Arts and Crafts. Hewitt was an influential teacher but a less gifted artist than Johnston. He more nearly approached the ideal of the *scriptor librarius*. Unlike his chronically ill master, he was capable of long hours of consistent, and often monotonous, work, and his output was correspondingly greater. Beginning as an imitator of Johnston, he soon developed a distinctive personal style, based on the writing of the Florentine scribe Antonio Sinibaldi. Hewitt consciously hearkened back to the Italian Renaissance. He had hoped to promote a general revival of the manuscript book, and at its best, his own neat humanistic script does not fall short of the 15th century model. He excelled in the difficult art of gilding, and it is probable that his reputation will rest upon the few Greek and Latin texts that he transcribed entirely in gold. The finest among these is the Epistle of St. James from the Vulgate, which is in the graphic arts department of the Harvard College Library.

Since the deaths of Johnston and Hewitt, the practice of fine writing has attracted an increasing number of professional and amateur devotees on both sides of the Atlantic. Noteworthy in London is the Society of Scribes and Illuminators, and a permanent calligraphic exhibit at the Victoria and Albert Museum. There are flourishing schools of calligraphy in New York City and in Chicago, where especially the Newberry Library assists students of this art.

See also ALPHABET; HIEROGLYPHICS; MANUSCRIPTS, ILLUMINATED; PALEOGRAPHY; and WRITING.

JAMES WARDROP
Victoria and Albert Museum, London

Bibliography

British Museum, *Guide to the Exhibited Manuscripts,* part 2, 2d ed. (London 1923).
Child, Heather, *Calligraphy Today* (New York 1964).
Fairbank, A. J., *A Book of Scripts* (London 1949).
Filby, P. W., *Calligraphy and Handwriting in America* (Caledonia, N. Y., 1963).
Heal, Ambrose, *The English Writing Masters, 1570–1800* (Cambridge, England, 1931).
Hewitt, W. Graily, *Handwriting* (London 1938).
Hewitt, W. Graily, *Lettering* (London 1932).
Icíar, Juan de, *Arte Subtilissima,* tr. by Evelyn Shuchburgh (New York and London 1960).
Johnston, Edward, *Manuscript and Inscription Letters* (London 1909).
Johnston, Edward, *Writing and Illuminating and Lettering* (London 1906).
Morison, Stanley, *American Copybooks* (Philadelphia 1951).
Morison, Stanley, *"Black-Letter" Text* (Cambridge, England, 1942).
Morison, Stanley, *Fra Luca de Pacioli* (New York 1933).
Morison, Stanley, *Notes on the Development of Latin Script* (Cambridge, England, 1949).
Ogg, Oscar, ed., *Three Classics of Italian Calligraphy* (New York 1953).
Pickering, Charles L., *Tributes to Edward Johnston* (Maidstone, England, 1948).
Schwandner, Georg, *Calligraphy* (New York 1959).
Thompson, E. M., *An Introduction to Greek and Latin Paleography* (London 1912).
Ullmann, Berthold L., *Ancient Writing* (New York 1932).
Verini, G. B., *Luminario,* ed., by Stanley Morison (Cambridge, Mass., and Chicago 1947).

VICTORIA AND ALBERT MUSEUM

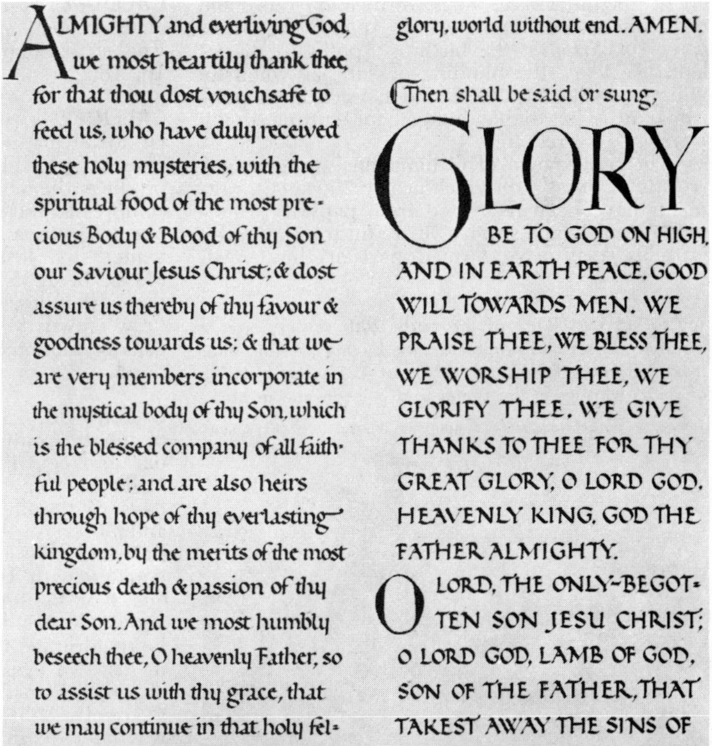

ALMIGHTY and everliving God, we most heartily thank thee, for that thou dost vouchsafe to feed us, who have duly received these holy mysteries, with the spiritual food of the most precious Body & Blood of thy Son our Saviour Jesus Christ; & dost assure us thereby of thy favour & goodness towards us; & that we are very members incorporate in the mystical body of thy Son, which is the blessed company of all faithful people; and are also heirs through hope of thy everlasting kingdom, by the merits of the most precious death & passion of thy dear Son. And we most humbly beseech thee, O heavenly Father, so to assist us with thy grace, that we may continue in that holy fellowship, and do all such good works as thou hast prepared for us to walk in; through Jesus Christ our Lord, to whom, with thee and the Holy Ghost, be all honour and glory, world without end. AMEN.

¶Then shall be said or sung,

GLORY BE TO GOD ON HIGH, AND IN EARTH PEACE, GOOD WILL TOWARDS MEN. WE PRAISE THEE, WE BLESS THEE, WE WORSHIP THEE, WE GLORIFY THEE. WE GIVE THANKS TO THEE FOR THY GREAT GLORY, O LORD GOD, HEAVENLY KING, GOD THE FATHER ALMIGHTY.

O LORD, THE ONLY-BEGOTTEN SON JESU CHRIST; O LORD GOD, LAMB OF GOD, SON OF THE FATHER, THAT TAKEST AWAY THE SINS OF THE WORLD, HAVE MERCY UPON US. THOU THAT TAKEST AWAY THE SINS OF THE WORLD, HAVE MERCY UPON US. THOU THAT TAKEST AWAY

THE HUMANISTIC SCRIPT of Edward Johnston's pupil and assistant, William Graily Hewitt, is based on styles developed in the Italian Renaissance. Hewitt is noted for his skill in gilding and decorating manuscripts.

CALLIMACHUS, kə-lim′ə-kəs, Athenian sculptor of the late 5th century B. C. He was famed as the designer of the "golden lamp" of Corinthian bronze in the Erechtheum of the Acropolis. Pausanias reported that the lamp could burn for a year without refilling and that its chimney was in the shape of a palm tree. Callimachus is important historically as the reputed originator of the Corinthian capital which followed the design of the "golden lamp." He also invented a drill for use on marble. His sculptures, while accurately and meticulously detailed, nevertheless were considered by many critics to be ill-conceived in their overall design.

CALLIMACHUS, kə-lim′ə-kas (c. 310–c. 240 B. C.), Greek poet and scholar. In ancient times he was regarded as the most distinguished figure of the Alexandrian period of Greek literature.

Callimachus came from a prominent family in Cyrene, the Greek colony in North Africa. After being educated in Athens, he went to Alexandria. It is extremely doubtful that he ever became the head of the great Alexandrian library, as was once thought, but it is certain that his long labors there resulted in the earliest work of systematic bibliography, the *Pinakes* (*Catalogs*). The *Pinakes,* no longer extant, was substantially a list of authors and their works, along with biographical and literary data.

The reputation of Callimachus today rests chiefly on his poetry, of which only 6 hymns and 64 epigrams survive intact. The subjects of the hymns, which vary in length from about 100 to about 300 lines, are: Zeus' birth and youth, the description and functions of Apollo, the early career of Artemis, the birth of Apollo on the island of Delos, the blinding of Tiresias when he glimpsed Athena bathing, and Erysichthon's punishment by insatiable hunger for cutting down Demeter's sacred tree.

The best-known of Callimachus' other poems is *Aitia* (*Causes*), of which nearly 200 small fragments have been recovered from papyri. (*Berenice's Hair,* which survives in Latin translation by Catullus, may have formed part of this.) Another poem, *Ibis,* extant in Ovid's Latin adaptation, is an attack on Apollonius of Rhodes, Callimachus' one-time pupil. Callimachus carried on a literary feud with Apollonius and his partisans, in which he contended that the day of the long poem was past and praised the qualities typical of Alexandrian poetry: brevity, wit, polish, erudition, and verbal virtuosity.

RICHMOND Y. HATHORN
Author of "Tragedy, Myth, and Mystery"

Further Reading: Couat, Auguste H., *Alexandrian Poetry Under the First Three Ptolemies,* tr. by James Loeb (New York 1931); Körte, Alfred, *Hellenistic Poetry,* tr. by Jacob Hammer and Moses Hadas (New York 1929).

A CIRCUS CALLIOPE of the early 20th century was a fancifully decorated wagon drawn by horses—this one, from the Adam Forepaugh Circus of 1910, has a series of steam whistles in the center and a large one in back.

FROM THE COLLECTION OF THE RINGLING MUSEUM OF THE CIRCUS

CALLINUS, kə-lī′nəs, Greek poet, who lived in Ephesus about the middle of the 7th century B. C. He was one of the earliest writers of elegiacs and was probably influenced by Homer. His only extant works are an exhortation to the young men of Ephesus to fight in defense of their homeland and several poetic fragments dealing with raids of nomadic peoples on Greek colonies in Asia Minor.

CALLIOPE, kə-lī′ə-pē, in Greek mythology, was the muse of eloquence and epic poetry. She was the most distinguished of the nine muses, daughters of Zeus and Mnemosyne, who presided over the arts and sciences. Calliope, whose name means "beautiful voice," was the mother of several children associated with the arts, notably the singer Orpheus.

CALLIOPE, kə-lī-ə-pē, in astronomy, is the name of asteroid No. 22, which was discovered by the English astronomer John Russell Hind on Nov. 16, 1852.

CALLIOPE, kə-lī′ə-pē, a musical instrument, similar to an organ, whose groups of steam whistles give out piercing tones. The whistles, pitched to produce the notes of the scale, are sounded by compressed air made by steam boilers and are played from a keyboard. The calliope was invented by Joshua C. Stoddard of Worcester, Mass., in 1855. Because it can be heard more than 10 miles, it has traditionally been used to draw crowds to fairs and circuses. The calliope is usually mounted on wheels and gaudilly decorated.

CALLIPPUS, kə-lip′əs, was a Greek astronomer, of the 4th century B. C., who improved the calendar and contributed to astronomical theory. In Callippus' time, the month was reckoned as 29½ days, with alternate months receiving 29 days and 30 days. A cycle of 235 months, of which 125 had 30 days and 110 had 29 days, was equated with 19 years. This equation contained one day too many in 76 years, as was shown about 330 B. C. by Callippus' observations. Hence, he quadrupled the previous cycle of 19 years, and in his own cycle of 76 years he reduced one 30-day month to 29 days, while curtailing the year to exactly 365¼ days. The Callippic cycle itself was later quadrupled to shorten the year in even closer agreement with nature. These two improvements over the established 19-year cycle were used only by professional astronomers. Callippus also contributed to a better understanding of the observed solar and planetary motions.

EDWARD ROSEN
The City College, New York

CALLISTO, kə-lis'tō, in Greek mythology, was the daughter of Lycaon, king of Arcadia. She was one of the nymphs in the hunting cult of Artemis (Roman, *Diana*) and had vowed never to marry. When she was ravished by Zeus (Roman, *Jupiter*) and became the mother of Arcas, the jealous Artemis changed her into a she-bear.

As a youth, Arcas came upon Callisto while hunting in the woods. Callisto recognized her son and tried to embrace him. Arcas raised his spear to kill her, but Zeus intervened and transported them both to the heavens where they became the constellations Ursa Major and Ursa Minor (Great Bear and Little Bear).

CALLISTUS I, kə-lis'təs, **Saint** (died c. 223), pope from about 217 to 222 or 223. Callistus, also known as *Calixtus*, ordered a fast from corn, oil, and wine three times a year, built a cemetery famous as the shrine of martyrs on the Appian Way, and condemned Sabellius, the leader of the Monarchian heresy. Apparently a kind and merciful man, Callistus opposed the rigorists who held that murderers, apostates, and adulterers should be excommunicated for life. He died a martyr. His feast is October 14.

Joseph S. Brusher, S. J.
University of Santa Clara, Calif.

CALLISTUS II, kə-lis'təs (died 1124), was pope from 1119 to 1124. Born Guido or Guy, he was the fifth son of Count William of Burgundy. In 1088 he became archbishop of Vienne. Long before he ascended the papal throne, Guido was in controversy with Emperor Henry V. When Henry came to power, he had extorted a so-called *privilege* from Pope Paschal II, his prisoner, by which the activities of ecclesiastics throughout the empire were severely curtailed. Guido vigorously opposed the *privilege*, first at the Lateran Synod (1112) and later at the Synod of Vienne, over which he presided. Composed of French and Burgundian bishops, the Vienne synod condemned lay investiture as heretical and excommunicated the Emperor. When Paschal II died, his successor Gelasius II refused to confirm the *privilege*. Henry retaliated by installing an antipope and forced Gelasius to flee to Cluny, where he died. Guido was elected as his successor and was crowned at Vienne on Feb. 9, 1119.

Although Henry and Callistus set the stage for peace talks scheduled to be held at Mousson, negotiations broke down, and Callistus again excommunicated Henry at the Council of Reims (October 1119). Callistus then proceeded to Rome, where he quickly allied himself with the Normans. Henry's antipope, Gregory VIII, was imprisoned at Sutri, and Henry was brought to terms. A truce was completed at Würzburg in 1121. Thus Christendom was restored to a temporary peace by the Concordat of Worms (Sept. 23, 1122), which acknowledged that the investiture of clergy was forever conceded to the church, although the emperor retained certain juridical rights; he also guaranteed the security of church property. The First Lateran Council ratified the Concordat in 1123.

A reforming pope, Callistus condemned clerical marriages, simony, violations of the Truce of God, and forgers of ecclesiastical documents. He also helped restore peace between France and England. He died at Rome on Dec. 13, 1124.

Francis X. Murphy, C. S. S. R.
Accademia Alfonsiana, Rome

CALLISTUS III, kə-lis'təs (1378–1458), was pope from 1455 to 1458. He was born Alonso Borgia near Valencia, Spain, on Jan. 13, 1378. He was a well-known canon lawyer when he refused to serve as Aragonese envoy to the schismatic Council of Basel; he also convinced King Alfonso V of Spain to separate from the council. For this service Pope Eugene IV raised him to cardinal in 1444. He worked in the papal curia for some years before being selected to succeed Nicholas V as pope in 1455. An old man when elected, Callistus nevertheless displayed great energy, especially in his efforts to start a crusade against the Ottoman Turks who had taken Constantinople in 1453. His grand design failed, but he had the satisfaction of seeing Hungary's great leader János Hunyadi (q.v.) save Belgrade from Mohammed II in 1456. Callistus was a good, even austere man, but he had the defect of nepotism. One of the nephews he raised to cardinal, Rodrigo Borgia, later became Alexander VI. Callistus died on Aug. 6, 1458 at Rome.

Joseph S. Brusher, S. J.
University of Santa Clara, Calif.

CALLISTUS III, kə-lis'təs, was antipope from 1168 to 1177. Known as John, Abbot of Struma, he was elected to succeed antipope Paschal III by cardinal-supporters of Frederick I (Barbarossa). The Emperor was struggling with Pope Alexander III for political supremacy in Italy but submitted to him after losing the Battle of Legnano in 1176. Callistus III also paid homage to Alexander, who received him graciously and appointed him governor of Benevento.

Joseph S. Brusher, S. J.
University of Santa Clara, Calif.

CALLOC'H, kä-lokh, **Jean Pierre** (1888–1917), Breton poet, considered by some critics to be Brittany's greatest lyricist. He was born on the island of Groix. His verse and prose, written in the Vannes dialect, combine enormous sensitivity with rustic simplicity and reflect his affinity for the sea, his preoccupation with death, his religious passion, and a strong sense of Breton nationalism. His most important work, *War an Daoulin* (1921), centers on the life of Breton fishermen. Calloc'h was also known under the pen name "Bleimor." He was killed in action during World War I.

CALLOT, kȧ-lō', **Jacques** (1592?–1635), French engraver and etcher, who was notable for both his technical and his artistic achievements in printmaking. He produced nearly 1,500 etchings and engravings, and more than 2,000 drawings survive. Callot's style evolved from the elegant mannerism of his time to a powerful realism.

Early Life. Callot was born at Nancy, in the Duchy of Lorraine, the son of the herald and master of ceremonies at the ducal court. In 1607 he was apprenticed to a silversmith and engraver of Nancy, but he soon left for Rome, probably in 1608. In Rome he worked for the printmakers Philippe Thomassin and Antonio Tempesta.

Florence. From 1612 to 1621, Callot lived in Florence, where he was hired by Duke Cosimo II to make a visual record of court ceremonies and fêtes. It was probably during this period that he developed the hard ground material (a varnish of mastic and linseed oil) that made it possible to produce finer lines and more subtle details. This development—Callot's great contribution to

CULVER PICTURES, INC.

CAB CALLOWAY in a scene from the motion picture *Stormy Weather.*

the technique of etching—was an important step toward the tonal refinements of the great 17th century master etchers.

The prints of Callot's Florentine period have many mannerist elements—the elongated limbs, small heads, poses, and costumes of his courtly figures, and the elegant and grotesque ornamentation that frames such prints as *Florentine Fête* (1619). But Callot also drew figures from everyday life, even from low life, and his large print *The Fair at Impruneta* (1620) should perhaps be credited as the first real attempt to depict a cross section of society. This print, containing over 1,300 figures, demonstrates Callot's remarkable ability to unify vast areas and great numbers of figures in a sweeping composition.

Nancy. After the death of Cosimo II in 1621, Callot returned to Nancy. There the realistic tendencies of his style began to dominate his work. *Gypsies* (1621), *Italian Comedians* (1621), and *Hunchbacks* (1622) are among the important series of prints made soon after his return to France. He also developed an interest in religious themes, some treated in the deeply shadowed manner of the tenebrist followers of Caravaggio, and he abandoned all picturesque formulas in many of his beautiful landscape drawings and prints of this period. Gaining international recognition, Callot received a number of major commissions. For the regent of the Spanish Netherlands he made six large prints that combine to form a panorama in the *Siege of Breda* (1627); for Louis XIII of France he made similar prints, the *Siege of Île de Ré* (1631) and the *Siege of La Rochelle* (1631).

Callot's greatest masterpieces are the series *Miseries of War* (1633–1635) and *Miseries and Disasters of War* (1633), based on his own observations during the French invasion and annexation of Lorraine. For the first time in the history of Western art, war was stripped of glamour and romance, and the miseries of the common people caught in the conflict are precisely shown. In his last years, Callot concentrated on religious themes, as in *Life of the Holy Virgin* (1633) and *The New Testament* series (1635). He died at Nancy on March 24, 1635.

GUY WALTON
New York University

CALLOWAY, kal'ə-wā, **Cab** (1907–), American singer, bandleader, and actor. He was born Cabell Calloway, 3d, in Rochester, N. Y., on Dec. 25, 1907. He was raised in Baltimore but settled in Chicago after attending Crane College there. He enjoyed a limited success in Chicago with his group, Cab Calloway and His Alabamians, then rose to fame in 1928 when he introduced the song *Ain't Misbehavin'* on Broadway as a member of the all-Negro cast of *Connie's Hot Chocolates.* Calloway became known as the "King of Hi De Ho" because one night, during a performance, he forgot the lyrics of a song and sang "hi de ho" instead. His recordings of the *St. James Infirmary Blues* and of his own song *Minnie the Moocher* achieved great popularity. Calloway appeared in several films during the 1930's and 1940's, and interrupted a nightclub career in 1952–1954 to play the role of Sportin' Life in the world tour of Gershwin's *Porgy and Bess.* Thereafter he appeared principally in nightclubs.

CALLUS, kal'əs, a hardening and thickening of the skin at a place subject to prolonged rubbing or pressure. Calluses occur most frequently on the soles of the feet, but they may also appear on the hands or other parts of the body. As a callus develops, it gradually rises above the surrounding normal skin. Calluses are not necessarily painful. When a callus appears on the ball of the foot, it may indicate an abnormality of one or more of the metatarsal arches.

Calluses can best be treated by eliminating the causative irritation or correcting the underlying abnormality. Removal of calluses should be done under professional supervision.

SIDNEY HOFFMAN, M. D.
St. John's Episcopal Hospital, Brooklyn, N.Y.

CALMETTE, kȧl-met', **Albert Léon** (1863–1933), French physician and bacteriologist, who is best known for his discovery with Camille Guérin of the BCG tuberculosis vaccine. In collaboration with Guérin, Calmette found that virulent bovine tubercule bacilli lost their virulence when cultured on a medium containing bile. More important, he found that these weakened bacteria were still capable of conferring immunity against either human or bovine tuberculosis, although they could no longer cause the disease.

The weakened bacterial strain was named bacillus Calmette-Guérin and subsequently became known as BCG vaccine. Its use, beginning in 1921, spread quickly throughout the world, and it greatly decreased the number and severity of tuberculosis cases. However, Calmette was forced to defend his findings in numerous scientific publications, and his discovery was not internationally recognized until after his death.

Calmette was born in Nice, France, on July 12, 1863. After studying and practicing medicine in the French Navy, he returned to France to complete his medical education. In 1890 he was sent by Pasteur to organize the new Pasteur Institute in Saigon. There he produced smallpox and rabies vaccines that were adapted to tropical conditions and began his first major research—the development of snake-bite serum. In 1894 he organized the Pasteur Institute in Lille and soon afterward began his association with Guérin and turned his attention to tuberculosis. He became director of the Pasteur Institute in Paris in 1919. He died in Paris on Oct. 29, 1933.

DAVID A. OTTO, *Stephens College*

CALONNE, kȧ-lôn′, **Charles Alexandre de** (1734–1802), French statesman, who was controller general of France before the Revolution. He was born in Douai on Jan. 20, 1734, the son of a leading magistrate. Although he was important in his Flanders *parlement* (sovereign court), Calonne waged war for the crown against the entire Breton *parlement* in 1765. This service won him the intendancy at Metz the following year. Calonne's superior abilities, his intimacy with the highest financial circles, and the continued good favor of the crown were all factors in Calonne's candidacy as controller general. In 1776 he won the intendancy of Flanders, and in 1783 he became controller general of France.

Calonne attempted to restore France's finances and avert a disastrous treasury crisis, but all his measures were opposed by the *parlements*. In 1787 he proposed a plan for radical financial reorganization. It called for the suppression of the fiscal privileges of the nobility, the clergy, and the magistracy. In an attempt to circumvent the *parlements* he presented his program to a national assembly of "notables" that he had convened for the purpose. But the powerful and well-born, especially the clergy, defeated the plan and caused Calonne's dismissal and exile to England. During the Revolution, Calonne remained a zealous royalist. He devoted his energies and his wealth to the cause until, poverty-stricken, he returned to Paris in 1802. He died there on Oct. 29 of that year.

Lionel Rothkrug
University of Michigan

CALORIC, kə-lôr′ik, is a word widely used in the first half of the 19th century to refer both to a hypothetical substance closely related to heat and to certain theories about the nature of heat. The term is the English equivalent of *calorique,* which was coined by Guyton de Morveau in 1787 from the Latin *calor* (heat).

Although modern science now treats heat as a secondary property arising from the rapid molecular motion of matter, most chemists and physicists during the late 18th and early 19th centuries maintained that heat, or caloric, was an independent entity, which, like a weightless fluid, flowed through all material objects. The chemist Antoine Lavoisier included caloric among his list of elements. Many scientists believed that particles of caloric mutually repelled one another and used this repulsion to explain the flow of heat from warm bodies to cold bodies and to explain the general dissipation of heat. The theory of caloric played a major role in the early development of thermodynamics.

The earliest important experimental refutation of the caloric theory was made by Benjamin Thompson, Count Rumford, in 1798. Noticing that an inexhaustible amount of heat was generated in the boring of cannon, Rumford argued that caloric could not be a substance since no substance could be indefinitely generated as heat seemed to be. Although most of his contemporaries disagreed with his analysis, several prominent physicists shared his suspicions of the caloric theory, especially Laplace, Thomas Young, and Humphry Davy. The caloric theory persisted until the 1860's, when studies on the mechanical equivalent of heat and the conservation of energy firmly established the modern kinetic theory of heat.

L. L. Laudan, *University College, London*

CALORIE, kal′ə-rē, the amount of heat required to raise the temperature of 1 gram of water 1° C at normal atmospheric pressure. A calorie is equivalent to approximately 4.2 joules of energy. The several units that have the name "calorie" (abbreviation, cal) differ slightly from one another since the heat capacity of water is different at different temperatures. Thus the 15° C calorie is defined as the amount of heat that will raise the temperature of 1 gram of water from 14.5 to 15.5° C, measured to be 4.1855 joules. Similarly the 4° C calorie, the 20° C calorie, and the mean calorie (over the range 0° to 100° C) are defined in the same operational terms and are 4.2045, 4.1816, and 4.1897 joules, respectively. In addition to these operationally defined calories, the thermochemical calorie and the I. T. (International Steam Table) calorie are defined as exact multiples of the unit of energy, 4.1840 and 4.1868 joules respectively.

The large calorie or kilocalorie (abbreviation, Cal) is used in nutrition to indicate the energy-producing potential of food. Commonly the term "calorie" is used for this unit also, although 1 Cal equals 1,000 cal. See Diet for a listing of the caloric content of many common foods.

Michael McClintock, *University of Colorado*

CALORIMETRY, kal-ə-rim′ə-trē, is the measurement of quantities of heat. The apparatus in which heat is measured is called a *calorimeter.* Quantities of heat may be measured indirectly by observation of the effect of the heat on various substances. The best-known of these effects are (1) rise in temperature of a mass of known heat capacity; (2) change of state of a substance of known latent heat; and (3) transformation of energy.

In order to measure heat it is first necessary to adopt some convenient and accurate unit in terms of which the quantities of heat that are to be measured can be expressed. Several such units have been proposed.

Ice Calorimeter. One of the simplest units suggested is the quantity of heat required to melt a kilogram or a pound of ice. The earliest form of calorimeter based upon this idea was invented by the Scottish chemist Joseph Black, about 1760. It consisted of a block of ice in which a cavity was made, the cavity being closed by a slab of ice laid upon the main block. To determine the quantity of heat given off by a piece of platinum in cooling from 100° F (38° C) to the freezing point, the chamber in the block of ice was first wiped dry. This platinum, heated to 100° F, was placed in the chamber, and the lid of ice was laid in place. The platinum gave up its heat to the ice, with the result that a certain weight of ice was melted and a corresponding weight of water collected in the chamber. When the platinum had attained the temperature of the ice, the cover was lifted off, and the water that had collected about the platinum was removed and weighed. The quantity of heat given out by the platinum was then known, if the accepted unit of heat was the quantity required to melt one pound of ice.

The French scientists Antoine Lavoisier and Pierre Laplace improved Black's calorimeter. Their instruments consisted of three distinct concentric chambers. The object to be tested was placed in the inner chamber, and the ice, in the form of broken lumps, in the intermediate chamber, surrounding the first test object. In the outer chamber broken ice was also introduced to prevent conduction of heat into the apparatus from outside. The quantity of ice melted was determined by observing the amount of water formed in the middle chamber, this being drawn off by a tube and tap.

The ice calorimeter of Robert W. E. Bunsen was a greater advance. This apparatus had an inner chamber, for the test material, and an outer enveloping one, which was entirely filled with a mixture of ice and water, and from which a graduated capillary tube led away. The whole instrument was surrounded by broken ice, as in the Lavoisier-Laplace form, to protect the interior parts from external thermal influences. When the apparatus was in perfect working order, the mixture of ice and water in the intermediate chamber was neither melting nor freezing, but in exact equilibrium. Upon the introduction of the object into the central chamber, the ice in the intermediate chamber began to melt, as in the calorimeters already considered. But with Bunsen's instrument the quantity of ice that was melted could be deduced by observing the change of volume of the contents of the intermediate chamber. This change was shown by the motion of the water in the capillary tube. Because the ice diminished in volume upon melting, once the exact diminution in volume of the contents of the intermediate chamber was known, the quantity of melted ice could be calculated with considerable precision.

Steam Calorimeter. Another unit of heat that suggests itself quite naturally is the quantity of heat given out by a pound of steam when it condenses into a pound of water at the same temperature. A calorimeter based upon this idea was also used by Bunsen, but the steam calorimeter was brought to its present excellent form largely through the efforts of the Irish physicist John Joly. In his type of instrument the object to be studied is suspended from one arm of a delicate balance. After being accurately counterpoised, the object is bathed in an atmosphere of steam, with the result that it absorbs a certain amount of heat as its temperature rises to that of the steam. But the heat thus absorbed by the body under examination can be obtained only from the steam itself; and since saturated steam cannot part with heat in this way without condensing, it follows that there is deposited upon the body a weight of condensed moisture that corresponds precisely to the quantity of heat that has been absorbed. The amount of this moisture is determined by careful weighing; and it is evident that the quantity of heat absorbed by the experimental body in passing from its original temperature to the temperature of the steam is then immediately known, if we take, as the unit of heat, the quantity of heat that is given out by a pound of steam in condensing into a pound of water at the same temperature.

Bomb Calorimeter. Another and more familiar unit of heat is the quantity of heat required to change the temperature of a given weight of water 1° on a given thermometer scale. Thus in general engineering practice in the United States and England it is customary to define a heat unit as the quantity of heat that is required to raise the temperature of a pound of water 1° on the Fahrenheit scale. This definition is good enough for rough purposes, because it conveniently happens that there is no great difference between the quantity of heat required to warm a pound of water from 32° to 33° and the quantity required (for example) to warm it from 99° to 100°. This, however, we can only regard as a fortunate accident; and for accurate scientific purposes we must recognize that the equality is only approximate, and we must adopt some particular temperature range as a part of our definition. Thus it is common to define the British thermal unit (Btu), when great accuracy is desired, as the quantity of heat required to raise the temperature of a pound of water from 59° to 60° F. In accurate scientific work the unit of heat is usually taken as the quantity of heat required to warm a kilogram of water from 15° to 16° C. It is now almost universally agreed that the most logical unit for expressing quantities of heat is that of the centimeter-gram-second (cgs) system, as it is independent of temperature. The unit now in use for such expression is the joule, equal to a watt per second, or 10^7 ergs.

In measuring the quantity of heat emitted by a body by observing the change of temperature produced in a given mass of water when the water absorbs the heat so emitted, the heated body may be placed into the water directly, the water being kept well stirred and its tempera-

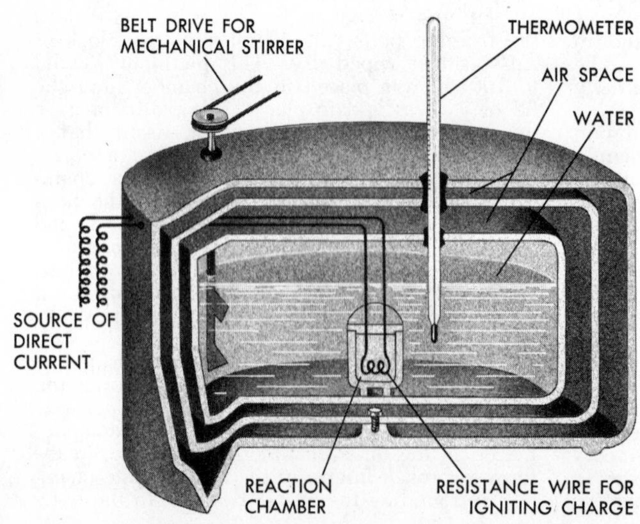

Bomb calorimeters are used for measuring the caloric value and the heat of combustion of fuels. Heat from the resistance wire ignites the test substance in the reaction chamber. The heat from the burning fuel raises the temperature of the water surrounding the reaction chamber, and this change is indicated on the thermometer.

ture taken at the beginning and end of the experiment. In other cases it is necessary to enclose the experimental body in a watertight envelope of some kind, and afterward make due allowance for the heat capacity of the envelope. For example, in cases in which the heat generated by the combustion of fuel is to be measured, the fuel must be enclosed in an airtight bomb containing an oxygen-rich atmosphere. The bomb is surrounded by a mass of water that is disposed in such a way as to intercept and absorb the heat that is produced. A direct observation of the temperature of the water in the calorimeter is made before and after the combustion, and the change of temperature so obtained gives a first approximation of the amount of heat that has been liberated. In all cases it is imperative that no heat be lost or gained by the calorimeter from its surroundings or in any other way than from the combustion alone, and a correction must be made for the thermal capacity of each part of the colorimeter that has been warmed during the experiment.

HERBERT G. BAROTT, *Former Biophysicist*
U. S. Department of Agriculture

CALORIZING, kal′ə-rīz-ing, is one of the earliest commercial processes developed for aluminum coating of steel. The aluminum coating is applied in order to protect carbon and alloy steels against corrosion and scaling at high temperatures. By protecting the base metal from reduction in cross section through oxidation, the useful working range at elevated temperatures of many low-priced steels with poor oxidation resistance is extended. The basis of the calorizing process is the formation of a surface iron-aluminum alloy by diffusion, that is, intimate contact of the base metal and aluminum at an elevated temperature.

In preparing a part for calorizing, the surface of the steel part is sandblasted to remove all scale. Parts are then packed with a calorizing powder into gas-tight retorts, which are sealed and heated at temperatures of 845° to 925° C (1,550° to 1,700° F) for several hours. Calorizing powders vary widely, but a typical mixture is 49% aluminum powder, 49% alumina, and 2% ammonium chloride. The alumina serves to keep the aluminum grains from fusing together.

When the parts are removed from the retort, after about five hours, the aluminum-iron surface alloy formed is in the order of 0.0025 to 0.015 cm (0.001 to 0.006 inch) thick. The thickness is dependent upon the original composition of the steel—some alloying ingredients tend to retard the diffusion of aluminum. To increase the depth of the coating, and increase its toughness and ductility, the parts are usually heat-treated for 12 to 48 hours at temperatures of 815° to 980° C (1,500° to 1,800° F). The resulting coating will range from 0.0635 to 0.10 cm (0.025 to 0.040 inch) in depth.

The formation of an aluminum oxide surface film in service renders the calorized parts highly resistant to oxidation and corrosion at elevated temperatures. Calorized steel and cast iron parts are serviceable at temperatures up to 955° C (1,750° F). Where temperatures do not exceed 760° C (1,400° F), parts have a useful life of many years. Above 955° C, however, the protecting alloy begins to break down because of the diffusion of iron from the base material into the coating, and heat-resisting steels are recommended.

In addition to its oxidation resistance, and of important commercial significance, is the immunity of calorized steels to attack by sulfur-containing gases. Calorized steels can be used in contact with furnace flue gases, at elevated temperatures, that contain hydrogen sulfide, sulfur dioxide, and sulfur trioxide, and in furnaces using high sulfur fuels. Calorizing also has extended the service life in sulfur-bearing atmospheres of some nickel-chromium-iron heat-resisting alloys.

Calorized steel parts are not easily fabricated. Cold working is not generally practicable, and bending and forming are usually done at a bright red heat. Even then, large bending radii must be used or cracking will occur in the coating. The maximum elongation that can be obtained before cracking starts is about 5 per cent. However, the coating is sufficiently ductile to bend with the steel base when hot, and cracks do not develop under the stresses usually encountered in commercial service.

Calorized steel and iron parts find considerable application in the metallurgical, chemical, and oil industries. Typical uses are in pots for salt, cyanide, and lead; case-hardening boxes; annealing pans and trays; conveyor chains; service in ore-roasting furnaces; bolts to be used at elevated temperatures; and tubes for air heaters, radiant steam superheaters, and oil and gas polymerizers.

There are several other commercial methods by which steel can be protected with aluminum. Among these are spraying, electroplating, cladding, casting, and hot dipping. Each method has certain advantages and limitations, and the decision as to which process should be used is based on many economic and performance considerations.

ALVIN S. COHAN
Scientific Design Company, Inc.

CALOTROPIS, kə-lot′rə-pəs, a genus of shrubs and small trees, up to 15 feet (4.5 meters) in height, bearing simple leaves and bell-shaped, 5-petaled flowers. The genus, a member of the milkweed family (Asclepiadaceae), is native to tropical Africa and Asia.

The floss from the downy seeds of the madar (*Calotropis gigantea*) and the akund (*C. procera*) is of commercial value, and these two species are cultivated in South America and the West Indies, as well as in their homelands, for this product. The floss, similar to kapok but inferior in quality, is often used mixed with kapok as an insulating material and as a filler for life preservers and jackets.

CALOTYPE, kal′ə-tīp, is a photographic process invented by William Henry Fox Talbot in England, and patented in 1841. It is important in the history of photography as the first method to produce a negative image. Calotype, also known as *Talbotype*, thus offered two advantages over the contemporaneous Daguerrotype process, in which a positive print was produced directly: it corrected for left-to-right reversal of image, and it permitted the production of any number of positive prints from the negative. The negative was formed on sensitized paper, however, and the definition that could be achieved in making prints was limited by the diffusing action of the negative's paper backing. See also PHOTOGRAPHY —*1. Early History* (Calotype).

CALOYERS, kə-loi′ərz, is the Western derivative of the Byzantine Greek word *kalogēroi,* which designates monks, both male and female, of the Christian Orient. Originally from the Greek *kalos gēros,* which meant venerable old man, it was used in early monastic literature to describe the ascetics, who had turned pale and hoary from their austere practices. The Byzantine Rite Slavs corrupted the word to *kaloger* or *kaluger* and applied it to monks generically. Greek historians and chroniclers also applied the word to anyone following the monastic life. The Turks designate Muslim dervishes as caloyers. The word was introduced into the West in the 14th century by the French, who applied it solely to monks who were members of the Orthodox Church.

Modern Orthodox monks who follow the monastic rule derived from St. Basil and St. Theodore the Studite are described as caloyers. This monastic life, especially as it is lived on Mt. Athos, Greece, and Mt. Sinai in the Sinai Peninsula, has three forms of expression: the *coenobium,* a monastery in which many monks live under a communal rule; a *skete,* a small house in which one or two monks live together under the guidance of a spiritual father; and a *hermitage,* a type of dwelling in which a recluse lives alone in seclusion.

George A. Maloney, S. J.
Fordham University

CALPRENÈDE, Gautier de Costes de La. See La Calprenède, Gauthier de Costes de.

CALUMET, kal′yə-met, a long peace pipe of the North American Indians of the Great Plains and Eastern Woodlands. It was used as a safe-conduct for guides and emissaries, for ratifying agreements between tribes, to bring rain or ensure good weather for trips, and, above all, in formal peacemaking ceremonies. The calumet was regarded as sacred, and any obligations contracted with one were inviolable. Early explorers like Marquette sometimes carried a calumet as a passport in country that was inhabited by potentially hostile Indians.

The name is not Indian in origin but is derived from the Norman-French word *chalumeau* and refers to the elaborately carved wooden stem of the pipe. The bowl was usually carved from an easily shaped stone called catlinite. Sometimes the pipes were decorated with red paint and feathers as a symbol of war. When peace was sought, white feathers were used to decorate the pipes.

Richard A. Gould
American Museum of Natural History

CALUMET CITY, kal′yə-met, is an industrial city in northeastern Illinois, in Cook county, about 20 miles (32 km) south of Chicago, on the Indiana border.

Situated on the Little Calumet River, in the midst of the outlying steel mill districts of Chicago, the city has meat packing plants, an oil refinery, and chemical-manufacturing plants. Lake Calumet Harbor is just north.

The city was incorporated as West Hammond in 1911 and developed as a suburb of Hammond, Ind., during the real estate boom of the 1920's. It was renamed Calumet City in 1924. The city has a mayor-council form of government. Population: 32,956.

CALUMET PARK, kal′yə-met, is a village in north eastern Illinois, in Cook county, 15 miles (24 km) south of downtown Chicago. It is in Calumet township, on the Calumet Sag Channel, 3 miles (5 km) west of Lake Calumet. The village is a residential suburb in a heavily industrial section of the county.

The community was incorporated as Burr Oak in 1912 and was renamed Calumet Park in 1925. The village has the mayor-council form of government. Population: 10,069.

Nathan R. Levin
Chicago Public Library

CALVADOS, kȧl-vȧ-dôs′, a department in northwestern France along the south coast of the English Channel, between the departments of Manche on the west and Seine-Maritime on the east. It is exceptionally rich agricultural country, producing cereals, apples, and a variety of dairy products. The famous cheeses of the areas, which are of excellent quality, include Camembert and Pont-l'Évêque, both of which take their names from small villages in Calvados. Cider and Calvados (an apple brandy) are also made in the department.

The western part of the coast of Calvados, between the Orne and Vire rivers, containing the Calvados Reef, was the scene of most of the Allied "D-Day" landings in World War II, made at dawn on June 6, 1944. Beaches where the landings took place—given the code names Omaha, Gold, Juno, and Sword beaches—are all along the western Calvados coast. There are a number of beach resorts in the department, the most important being Cabourg. The eastern coast of Calvados, called the Flowered Coast (Côte Fleurie), has the advantages of good beaches and proximity to Paris and is, after the Riviera, the most popular beach resort area of France.

Caen is the capital of the department. Other major cities are Honfleur, Trouville, Deauville, Bayeux, and Lisieux.

Homer Price, *Hunter College, New York*

CALVAERT, käl′vȧrt, **Denis** (1540?–1619), Flemish artist, who established a school for painting in Bologna, Italy. His name is also spelled *Calvert;* he was called *Denis le Flamand* (Dionisio Fiammingo, in Italy).

Born in Antwerp, Calvaert studied painting there, and in 1570 went to Italy, where he studied with Prospero Fontany and Lorenzo Sabbatini. In Bologna he was the teacher of Guido Reni, Il Domenichino, and Francesco Albani. Calvaert was a careful student of anatomy, architecture, and history, and a master of color, perspective, composition, and design. His principal works are in Bologna, where he died on March 17, 1619.

CALVARY, kal′və-rē, is described in the New Testament as the site near Jerusalem where Jesus Christ was crucified. Both St. Matthew (27:33) and St. John (19:20) refer to the site as *Golgotha,* which means "place of the skull" in Aramaic. This was translated as *locus calvariae* in the Vulgate Bible and transliterated as Calvary in the English Bible. The origin of the name is obscure: St. Jerome suggested that it was so called because there were skulls lying about unburied; a 19th century theory attributed the name to the skull-like shape of the hill.

Although archaeologists have not completely reached accord concerning the location of Golgotha, the site is traditionally associated with the area near which St. Helena, Emperor Constantine's mother, found the "true cross" in the 4th century. Constantine delegated the Bishop of Jerusalem, Macarius, to clear the temple of Aphrodite that Hadrian had built on the spot and to erect, at imperial expense, a fitting monument to mark the sites of Calvary and the Holy Sepulchre. The rock of Calvary was carefully preserved; it was surrounded by a grille which rose 12 feet above the ground in the court behind the basilica.

Constantine's magnificent basilica, which came to be known as the Church of the Holy Sepulchre and Resurrection, has undergone repeated devastation and reconstruction. It was destroyed by the Persian emperor, Khosrau the Victorious, in 614 and by Caliph Hakim in 1009, and it was gutted by a fire in 1808. A major restoration of the church, which is basically that which the Crusaders erected in the Romanesque style during the 12th century, was begun in 1958. Little, however, remains of the ancient rock of Calvary.

C. J. McNaspy, S. J.
"America Magazine"

CALVÉ, kȧl-vā′, **Emma** (1858–1942), French soprano, who was one of the most celebrated and glamorous operatic personalities of her time. Mme. Calvé was born in Décazeville, France, on Aug. 15, 1858. After completing her education at the Convent of the Sacred Heart in Montpellier, she studied voice in Paris with Jules Puget. In 1882 she made her debut in Brussels as Marguerite in Gounod's *Faust.* From 1885 to 1887 she appeared at the Opéra-Comique in Paris and also toured Italy, where she sang at La Scala, Milan, in Ambroise Thomas' *Hamlet.*

In 1891, in Rome, Mme. Calvé created the role of Suzel in Mascagni's *L'amico Fritz.* At Covent Garden, London, in 1892 and at the Metropolitan Opera, New York City, in 1893, she made her debuts as Santuzza in Mascagni's *Cavalleria Rusticana.* She created the role of Anita in Massenet's *La Navarraise* (London, 1894), and the title role in his *Sapho* (Paris, 1897).

Mme. Calvé's most widely admired characterization was Carmen. This role, which she first sang at the Metropolitan Opera in 1893, was admirably suited to her limpid and sensuous voice. She was also a vital and spontaneous actress. After 1910, Mme. Calvé retired from the operatic stage and limited herself to concert appearances. She died in Millau, France, on Jan. 6, 1942.

George Jellinek
Author of "Callas, Portrait of a Prima Donna"

Further Reading: Calvé, Emma, *My Life* (New York and London 1922); Pleasants, Henry, *The Great Singers* (New York 1966).

CALVERLEY, kal′vər-lē, **Charles Stuart** (1831–1884), English poet and humorist. He was born at Martley, Worcestershire, on Dec. 22, 1831. He attended Harrow and Balliol College, Oxford, and Christ's College, Cambridge. Calverley won the chancellor's prize for Latin verse at both universities. He studied law, but gave up a legal career for poetry, becoming famous as a writer of light verse. His published works include *Verses and Translations* (1862), *Translations into English and Latin* (1866), *Theocritus Translated into English Verse* (1869), and *Fly Leaves* (1872). His complete works were published in 1901. He died in London on Feb. 17, 1884.

CALVERT, family. See Baltimore.

CALVIN, kal′vin, **John,** French theologian and reformer. He was born at Noyon, Picardy, France, on July 10, 1509. He was the fourth son of Gérard Cauvin, notary and secretary to the chapter of Noyon Cathedral, and his wife Jeanne, daughter of Jean LeFranc, a retired Cambrai innkeeper resident in Noyon. John's mother, reputed to have been pious and beautiful, died when he was a small child, and his father remarried. Two of his three elder brothers died very young; the other, Charles, became a cleric of Noyon but died excommunicate in 1537. His one younger brother, Antoine, and one of his two half-sisters, Marie, adopted the Protestant faith of Calvin and followed him to Geneva. Calvin Latinized the family name as Calvinus; it was thereafter written in French as Calvin.

Early Life and Education. As a boy Calvin had good educational opportunities. He was a school companion of the sons of noblemen of the de Hangest family, relatives of the bishop of Noyon, Charles de Hangest. Tutored in the house of Adrien de Hangest, he became a warm friend of the latter's son Claude, later an abbot at Noyon, to whom Calvin dedicated his first book. With others of this connection he attended the Collège des Capettes, a boys' school in Noyon. Gérard Cauvin planned to have his brilliant son enter the priesthood. From his twelfth year the boy was aided by a succession of small ecclesiastical benefices without duties attached. At the age of 14, in the company of three de Hangest boys and their tutor, he went to the University of Paris (1523).

He enrolled in the Collège de la Marche. There he was attracted and stimulated by the distinguished Latinist Mathurin Cordier, who was to spend the last years of his long life at the reformer's side in Geneva. Calvin soon moved to the more celebrated Collège de Montaigu. Noël Beda, the former head of this school, continued to teach in it and exercised a powerful conservative influence on the faculty of theology in the Sorbonne, which two years earlier under his leadership had condemned Luther. From Beda's classes in logic Calvin learned the art of argumentation, but he turned away from Beda's anxious conservatism in theology.

Calvin was a highly gifted and exceptionally hard-working student whose associates were somewhat senior to him and men of outstanding talent. His admiring biographer and successor, Theodorus Beza (Théodore de Bèze), states that he was a severe critic of the faults of his fellow students, but the legend that for his censoriousness he was called the "Accusative Case" cannot be traced earlier than 1633. Despite his undoubted austerity, his friends were numerous and select, and probably few of his fellow students had a more remarkable circle of trusted friends, to some of whom he remained loyal even after religious separation.

Early in 1528 he received the master of arts degree. Instead of continuing in theology, he began the study of law at Orléans, where Pierre de l'Étoile, one of the greatest of French jurists, was teaching. The change of plan was dictated by Calvin's father, who had become involved in a dispute with the cathedral chapter where he was employed. He desired for his son the rewards of a legal career, and Calvin, aged 18 at the time, dutifully obeyed and pursued the study of law with distinguished success. At the same time he began to learn Greek under Melchior Wolmar, a German of Lutheran inclination, and

BETTMANN ARCHIVE

JOHN CALVIN, from a portrait by Lucas Cranach.

the interests of the new humanism dominated his study. When the Italian humanistic interpreter of the law Andrea Alciati was appointed to the faculty of Bourges, Calvin was among those who traveled from Orléans to hear him. But when Alciati unfairly assailed de l'Étoile, Calvin, in a preface he wrote for a book by his friend Nicolas Duchemin, defended and lauded the Orléans scholar.

It is likely that Calvin never inwardly committed himself to the law as a career, and the death of his father in May 1531 left him free to make his own choice. He completed the doctorate in law but afterward devoted himself ardently to the language and literature courses of the newly appointed royal lecturers in Paris. In this environment he published (April 1532) his first independent book, a commentary on Seneca's *De clementia.* This work showed a mature familiarity with classical authors, both Latin and Greek. While it resembled in method his later commentaries on the books of Scripture, it made exceedingly little use of the Bible. The view that it was intended to induce King Francis I of France to exercise "clemency" toward the Protestants seems to be an inference from Calvin's later attitudes. The Seneca commentary yields the impression of a somewhat detached moral humanism, admiring Stoicism but showing a preference for Christianity. It was written in polished Latin, but since it had little application to current issues, it received almost no notice.

Conversion. Calvin's life was soon to take a new direction, in an experience that, in an introduction to his *Commentary on the Psalms* written in 1557, he speaks of as a "sudden conversion":

> Since I was more stubbornly addicted to the superstitions of the Papacy than to be easily drawn out of so deep a mire, God subdued my heart—too stubborn for my age—to docility by a sudden conversion.

The change is simply ascribed to God, and nothing of the circumstances is given. Other sources indicate some of the possibilities and identify some of the personalities whose influence helped to transform the young humanist into an ardent and uncompromising Protestant.

Calvin had had ample opportunity to learn about the religious issues of the age and to observe their growing intensity in France. He had moved in circles of the younger scholars and clerics, disciples and admirers of Jacques Lefèvre d'Étaples, who had anticipated some of Luther's doctrines and had been forced to leave Paris when Luther was condemned there. His young followers had hoped, with the favor of Margaret of Angoulême, the King's sister, to institute a process of reform in the French church. Margaret had been censured by the Sorbonne, but Nicolas Cop, a friend and confidant of Calvin, chosen rector of the university for the term beginning in the autumn of 1533, had won for the Princess a favorable vote in the other faculties. On November 1, Cop delivered as his rectorial address an attack on the censors of the Sorbonne, in which were incorporated passages from Erasmus and Luther. It is unlikely that Calvin, as has been sometimes claimed, had written Cop's oration, but his known association with Cop exposed him to prosecution. Cop and his abettors were at once forced to flee. This incident marked the failure of the party of Lefèvre's followers and Margaret's defenders to get a hearing, much less to defeat the Sorbonne. The hopelessness of the cause of reform by the party of tolerant Christian humanism was now apparent, and the incident may well have had a profound effect on Calvin's mind.

Taking flight from Paris, Calvin spent a period in Angoulême, where he had access to an ample library and the company of scholarly clerics. Early in April 1534 he visited the aged Lefèvre, who was at Nérac under the protection of Margaret. Following this conference Calvin crossed the country to Noyon and there resigned his benefices (May 4, 1534), an act that signalized his breach with the unreformed clergy. The "sudden conversion" should probably be connected with this chain of events and dated not long before or after his visit to Lefèvre.

Calvin had repudiated the papacy and wholeheartedly committed himself to the cause of the zealous minority of persecuted evangelicals. He was now 25 and had 30 years to live. At first he had no thought of public leadership, craving rather the opportunity to read and think, and he seems to have accepted himself as a timid man. Yet he could not be silent. Those who knew of his views thronged to inquire about "the purer doctrine." Short periods in Paris, Poitiers, Angoulême, and Orléans brought him no escape for the concentrated study he most desired. Ardent prefaces written at this time for the French Bible translation made by his cousin Pierre Robert Olivier, known as Olivétan, for the Waldenses testify to his new scriptural faith. Early in 1535 he was in Basel, city of printers and asylum for scholars; and there, in March 1536, appeared the first edition of his *Institutio religionis christianae* (*Institutes of the Christian Religion*), written in Latin for scholarly readers in all lands. Its twofold purpose he describes in the eloquent dedication to Francis I:

> First, to vindicate from undeserved insult my brethren whose death was precious in the sight of the Lord, and secondly, since the same sufferings threatened many pitiable men, that some sorrow and care for these should move foreign peoples.

Before the book was off the press its author was in Italy visiting Renée, the Duchess of Ferrara, a French princess who was temporarily protecting religious refugees, and who was to come permanently under Calvin's influence. He soon returned to Paris, and there he made a settlement of the family inheritance. He set out for Strasbourg, planning to resume his writing tasks, but the war between Francis I and Charles V compelled him to detour through Geneva, and there, suddenly and much against his inclination, he was enlisted in the public leadership of the Reformation.

Influence of Farel. The agent of this fresh change of Calvin's plan of life was Guillaume Farel, a pupil of Lefèvre, more ardent even than his master and one who had left the influence of the Zwinglian Reformation. With the support of powerful elements in Bern, he had aggressively led an evangelical mission in the French-speaking districts then in the process of becoming attached to Switzerland, and he had won striking success in Geneva. That city had long been engaged in a struggle for independence from the dukes of Savoy and the bishops who relied upon their favor. The bishop of Geneva had taken flight, and the efforts of Savoy to restore him were successfully resisted. During this conflict, Farel had entered Geneva and preached so effectively that by August 1535 the churches had been secured for evangelical preaching. In the following May, the assembled citizens pledged themselves to abandon idolatry, to maintain a school for all children, and to live according to the Word of God. It was two months later, in July 1536, that John Calvin arrived. Farel, in need of help, called upon the traveler at his lodging and laid upon his conscience the work of reform in Geneva with such compelling urgency and spiritual threats that Calvin dared not refuse. It was, said Calvin long afterward, as if God from on high had reached forth His hand. By September, having brought his books from Basel, he began to lecture in the Cathedral of St. Pierre on the Epistles of St. Paul. He was at first designated professor of sacred letters and soon became a member of the group of ministers, though by what procedure is uncertain.

The following January 16 the Little Council, the city's chief governing body, adopted a set of articles for the reform of religion prepared by Calvin and Farel. In order to prevent profanation of the Eucharist by the participation of scandalous offenders, "certain persons of good life and repute" were to be appointed to supervise discipline. The document also proposed the use of a short confession of faith and of a little book of instruction (*Instruction in Faith,* 1537), the training of children in psalm-singing, and a commission on marriages. In these provisions many characteristics of later Calvinism are evident.

Resistance to the discipline, and an attempt by those in Bern to impose certain Bernese rites in Geneva, brought on a crisis in April 1538 that forced Calvin and Farel to leave the city. Some months later Calvin was induced to serve the French refugee colony in Strasbourg. In a fruitful three-year period there he organized the French congregation, taught in Johannes Sturm's famous school, lectured in theology, and published numerous writings, including a liturgy that became the basis of Calvinist worship and a little book of French psalms with tunes. He accompanied his friend Martin Bucer, the Strasbourg reformer, at three conferences of Lutheran and Roman Catholic theologians (1540–1541). In August 1540 he married Idelette de Bure (d. 1549), widow of Jean Stordeur, a refugee from Liège. She had two children by her former husband; Calvin's only child died in infancy.

Leader of the Geneva Church. In Geneva the situation was unstable. When Jacopo Cardinal Sadoleto endeavored by a persuasive letter to bring the city back to the Roman obedience, it was to Calvin that the Genevese turned to secure an effective reply to the cardinal (1539). The magistrates of that city now urgently requested Calvin to return and resume his work. "There is no place under heaven that I am more afraid of," he wrote, but a year after the first invitation he finally acquiesced. On Sept. 13, 1541, he was welcomed back to the city, to spend there, as it proved, the rest of his life.

The *Ecclesiastical Ordinances* of November 1541, prepared by Calvin and revised by the Little Council, erected a system of discipline, preaching, worship, and instruction, with a ministry of pastors, teachers (doctors), elders, and deacons. The elders and ministers were joined in the consistory, which met weekly as a court of discipline. All cases involving serious penalties, however, went to the council. Calvin had no officially assigned place in the consistory; ordinarily one of the four syndics (chief magistrates) presided there. Yet Calvin's personal eminence and constant activity made him the leader, and ultimately the master, of the Geneva church, and to a large degree of the city itself.

The discipline of offenders began with "amicable" and "fraternal" admonition. Yet it was watchful and severe, and all ranks were subjected to it. The city's many sumptuary laws and moral regulations, enacted in pre-Reformation decades and intensified shortly before Calvin first came, were now elaborated and rigidly enforced. Such offences as gambling, drunkenness, and even dancing and singing flippant songs drew grave penalties. Citizens of easy morals and free opinions strongly resented this dicipline, and opposition to Calvin grew, making his position far from secure. He was often insulted and often expected dismissal or physical harm as he survived crisis after crisis, continually preaching, lecturing, writing, and contending, often angrily and harshly, with his opponents. He also encouraged the burning of witches. Only in 1555 did he attain a permanent victory. The battles were fought in the consistory and the council and in the annual elections that were a feature of the city's life. Calvin took no direct part in the political government and used no police protection, yet his success was partly due to political changes, since at this time a great influx of refugees, mostly French-speaking and already Calvinist by persuasion, had become a considerable factor in the voting citizenship.

The victims of Calvin's purposeful leadership included many eminent men. The humanist Sebastianus Castellio, schoolmaster, was refused admission to the ministry for what were then very startling views of the *Song of Solomon.* The struggle ended in Castellio's departure with a letter of recommendation for his former service and a complaint of his handling of the Bible. Jacques Gruet was beheaded for blasphemy, treason, and a threat to the ministers. Jerome Bolsec, a physician who assailed Calvin's doctrine of predestination, was banished. His *Life of Cal-*

vin (1577) became the source of many defamatory misstatements. One heretic, the renowned Spanish anti-Trinitarian, Michael Servetus, was burned at the stake (1553). He had clashed with Calvin long before, written against him, and engaged in controversial correspondence with him. He came to Geneva when Calvin's position seemed weak. Calvin had indicated earlier that if Servetus should come there he would do what he could to prevent his getting away alive. Servetus was brought to trial, during which Calvin sought the penalty of death by the sword rather than the flames; the council, however, ruled otherwise. The incident moved Castellio to write a notable treatise against persecution, but Calvin defended the death penalty for heresy, and thereafter always wrote of Servetus and his doctrines with loathing. There was perhaps no spot in Europe where Servetus would have been safe, yet Calvin's reputation justly suffers from his part in the affair.

The defeat of powerful opponents of the policy of admitting the refugees to citizenship left Geneva virtually under Calvin's sway (1555). The consistory became more independent of the councils. The laws became more exacting. Free elections were maintained, but political authority was more centralized in the Little Council. The repressive aspects of the regime were balanced by great attention to education. From 1558 the Academy of Geneva became a nursery of Calvinism, sending alumni to all parts of Europe.

Until his health failed Calvin occasionally played games or took short excursions for recreation, and despite his intensity and hot temper (the "wild beast," he called this defect), he could be a genial companion. In his forties he was assailed by a series of painful diseases that increasingly sapped his vitality. He toiled on with all his strength writing commentaries, treatises, and pamphlets and corresponding with rulers, bishops, ministers, students, and troubled men and women everywhere, all the while giving detailed attention to the people and church of Geneva. He continually enlarged the *Institutes;* the final Latin edition (1559) is nearly five times the bulk of the original of 1536. His works in Latin and in translations were widely circulated and highly influential during and after his lifetime. He died in Geneva on May 27, 1564.

Theology. Calvin's theology rests closely upon the Bible and is everywhere supported by scriptural evidence. It has been charged that he relied almost exclusively upon the Old Testament. But this is widely erroneous, as is shown, for example, by the preponderance of New Testament references in the *Institutes.* According to a meticulous count made by F. L. Battles, these number 4,330 as against only 2,474 references to the Old Testament. Calvin habitually thinks of the superiority of the New Testament over the Old; yet undoubtedly he did at times employ arguments drawn from a primitive stage of the Hebrew religion.

Calvin frequently explains passages by viewing revelation as a progressive process or by supposing that the sacred writer is accommodating his words to an audience not yet illuminated by the Gospel. He sometimes writes in grateful wonder of the grace of God toward undeserving men. But in Calvin's view the characteristic idea of God is of awe-inspiring majesty and sovereignty. God is in the spendor of the stars, in all events of history, in every experience of every man. By the dread decree (*decretum horrible*) of predestination, He appoints to each soul eternal happiness or woe. Calvin is here indebted to Augustine and to certain 14th century Augustinians.

His doctrine of the church may be described as antipapal catholicity. He stresses the universality of the visible as well as of the invisible church and warns of the sin of willful schism. He cooperated with Bucer and with Heinrich Bullinger of Zürich and corresponded with the English archbishops Thomas Cranmer and Matthew Parker in support of ecumenical aims. The triumph of the Lutheran opponents of Melanchthon cut off his relations with official Lutheranism. His doctrine of the Eucharist, in contrast with that of transubstantiation as well as that which prevailed in Lutheranism, lays stress on the real presence spiritually appropriated by the worshiper through a mysterious activity of the Holy Spirit. Important in the eucharistic experience are mystical union with Christ and the sense of corporate communion.

His permission to charge interest on money, despite the Old Testament prohibition, was qualified by extraordinary safeguards against oppressive greed. In government he favored a representative system stabilized by an element of aristocracy, and he sought to establish fruitful interaction of church and state. He exercised a ministry of personal counseling both directly and by letter. He did much to develop psalmody and the training of the young in church singing.

Calvin takes high rank as a writer in both Latin and French. His 1541 version of the *Institutes* is a landmark in early modern French prose. His style in descriptions of God's handiwork in creation glows with eloquence, and in general he treats theological themes with unusual clarity.

CALVINISM

Calvinism is a term used mainly in two senses. In its more limited sense it refers to beliefs derived from John Calvin and held by the Calvinistic churches. In a broader sense, Calvinism applies to a set of ethical and social attitudes that have influenced world culture since Calvin's day.

Doctrine and Practice of the Calvinistic Churches. The system of doctrine, church polity, discipline, and worship derived from the teachings of John Calvin as professed in the Calvinistic (Reformed and Presbyterian) churches throughout their history. The word is commonly applied in a restricted sense to the body of Calvinist doctrine centering in the sovereignty of God and the divine predestination of every human being either by election to an eternal state of bliss in God's presence or by reprobation or preterition to a state of misery in alienation from Him. Calvin taught this double predestination, while urging "that we ought to be humble and modest in the treatment of this profound mystery," learning from it "reverence for the majesty of God." He was, however, engaged in animated controversy over this doctrine with the Dutch Pelagian Albert Pighius (1543) and others. His position on the *ordo salutis*, the sequence of decrees in predestination, is sometimes described as "sublapsarian"; that is, election is regarded as decreed in view of the fact of the fall of man through Adam's sin. But there are passages in which he speaks of election before the fall. Awed by the mystery involved, he does not pursue the issue systematically as did succeeding theologians.

Theodorus Beza put forth the "supralapsarian" doctrine that the decree of election is prior to that of man's creation and to that of the permission of the fall; the fall thus becomes necessary to give effect to the prior decree of election. Jacobus Arminius (1560–1609) recoiled from this teaching and made election conditional on foreknowledge of faith. The Synod of Dort (1618–1619), in accord with Augustine, declared that election is the unchangeable purpose of God whereby He chose some to salvation "before the foundation of the world," but it avoided an explicit statement of supralapsarianism. The Westminster Confession (1647) uses similar language.

The prevailing view of the 17th century Calvinist theologians was "sub-", or "infralapsarianism." As expounded by François Turretin (*Institutio theologiae elencticae,* 1680–1683), it placed the decrees in this order: creation; permission of the fall; election of some and passing over of others; the work of Christ as mediator; effectual calling of the elect. Controversy over these points tended to discredit Calvinism by suggesting arbitrariness in God. The revival of Calvinism in 20th century Swiss, German, and French Reformed theology has been in part a recovery of Calvin's own teaching, stressing the vivifying power of the Word of God and the witness of the Holy Spirit as against the rationalism of scholastic Calvinism.

Calvinism as a Social and Political Force. The term "Calvinism" is also used in the historical and sociological sense of the entire complex of Calvinistic churches and their impact on society during the last four centuries. Calvin has been described by E. Choisy as "educator of consciences" and by E. G. Léonard as "founder of a civilization." His works have been read and are being read today in many languages, and in this century have been industriously reinterpreted by scholars. The Reformed and Presbyterially organized churches of Switzerland, France, Scotland, the Netherlands, various German states, and other parts of Europe and their Congregational and Baptist collateral branches have had a profound influence upon the course of Western cultural history including that of the British dominions and of the United States. They produced a distinctive type of life, marked by family piety, conscientious diligence in one's vocation, business integrity and enterprise, political and social meliorism and activism, and a concern for education at all levels. Typical Calvinism cultivates a somewhat austere morality and recoils from ostentation, waste, and all undisciplined behavior. In some puritans this characteristic has reached extreme expression, to the loss of moral freedom. In general it means the control of personal, social, and economic behavior by considerations of conscience and with the intention of service to God and man. The Calvinist economic philosophy is not one of profit but of service—in Calvin's words, "to serve our neighbor with a good conscience," both by the work we do and by what we earn in doing it. If through thrift and restricted expenditures Calvinists have acquired wealth and yielded to the temptation to use it for profit or wasteful pleasure rather than service, this is a secularization, indeed a reversal, of Calvinist teaching. Even where this tendency is strong it is usually limited by a willingness to use a generous portion of surplus wealth in the support of religious and philanthropic enterprises. Calvinism prizes the church not only as the fellowship of the saints but also as the generating center of community service and regards all human activity and enterprise as answerable to God.

Politically, Calvinism has played a role of some importance. International in its early propagation, it has never been narrowly nationalistic, and many of its political figures and writers have been deeply concerned with international law and peace. In Scotland a new religious dimension was given to the advocacy of limited monarchy, and the reformed church waged a long fight against the absolutist pretensions of the Stuart kings. A similar attitude prevailed in colonial New England and formed a preparation for the Revolution in which monarchy itself was swept away. After the Cromwellian revolution and the Stuart restoration in England came the era of limited monarchy introduced under a Calvinist king and marked by widening liberty in the modern era. In many instances Calvinism has supplied leadership to movements of resistance to despotic governments and worked for the establishment of representative institutions. Calvinist piety involves no detachment from the political scene but rather requires responsible participation in public affairs. A religiously motivated critical restraint has governed the attitude of Calvinism to pictorial art, music, the theater, and the whole field of belles-lettres. Yet it has nourished a few first-rank geniuses in these fields. Calvinists have been particularly active in the promotion of schools and have esteemed the teacher's calling as closely allied to that of the ministry. Believing with Calvin that truth wherever it appears is given by God, they have usually been appreciative of scientific studies and have given them due place in academic institutions. They have supplied much of the leadership in Christian missions and in the ecumenical movement. A recognized social and cultural dynamism is characteristic of historic Calvinism.

JOHN T. MCNEILL
Union Theological Seminary

Bibliography

The standard edition of Calvin's works is in the Corpus Reformatorum series, *Joannis Calvini opera quae supersunt omnia,* ed. by G. Baum, E. Cunitz, E. Reuss, and continuators, 59 vols. (Brunswick and Berlin, Germany, 1863–1900); additional items, chiefly sermons, are *Supplementa Calviniana,* ed. by E. Muhlhaupt and associates (Neukirchen, Germany, 1961–). *Calvini opera selecta,* ed. by P. Barth and Wilhelm Niesel, 5 vols. (Munich 1926–1936), has useful apparatus. An annotated English translation of the *Institutes* was edited by J. T. McNeill, tr. by F. L. Battles, 2 vols. (Philadelphia and London 1960). The *Commentaries* are included in the 48 vols. issued by the Calvin Translation Society (Edinburgh 1843–1855), and there are later translations by T. H. L. Parker and others (Edinburgh and Grand Rapids, Mich., (1959–).

Bieler, A., *La pensée économique et sociale de Calvin* (Geneva 1959).

Bratt, John H., *Rise and Development of Calvinism* (Grand Rapids, Mich., 1964).

Breen, Quirinus, *John Calvin, a Study in French Humanism* (Hamden, Conn., 1967).

Duffield, Gervase E., ed., *John Calvin* (London and Grand Rapids, Mich., 1966).

Fuhrmann, Paul T., *God-Centered Religion* (Grand Rapids, Mich., 1942).

McDonnell, Kilian, *John Calvin, the Church and the Eucharist* (Princeton 1967).

McNeill, John T., *The History and Character of Calvinism* (New York 1967).

Stauffer, Richard, *L'Humânité de Calvin* (Neuchâtel and Paris 1964).

Wallace, Ronald S., *Calvin's Doctrine of the Christian Life* (Edinburgh 1959).

Wendel, François, *Calvin, the Origins and Development of His Religious Thought,* tr. by Philip Mairet (New York 1963).

CALVIN, Melvin (1911–), American chemist, who worked in research areas ranging from metal-organic chemistry to the chemical origin of life and made his greatest contribution in the study of photosynthesis in green plants. In 1961, Calvin was awarded the Nobel Prize in chemistry "for his investigations in the carbon dioxide assimilation of plants."

Contributions to Science. Calvin's early scientific interests in the theoretical aspects of organic structure and properties were reflected in his first book, *The Theory of Organic Chemistry,* coauthored with Gerald E. K. Branch in 1941. His studies of organic compounds that bind metal ions led to his writing, with Arthur E. Martell, *The Chemistry of Metal Chelate Compounds* (1952). His mastery of these subjects proved to be a keen tool for investigations of the chemistry of living cells.

In 1945, Calvin and his associates began to use the radioactive isotope carbon-14 as a tracer element for studying photosynthesis in green plants (the formation of food and oxygen from sunlight, carbon dioxide, water, and minerals). They described radiocarbon tracer methods in the book *Isotopic Carbon* (1949).

By arranging for green plants to use radioactive carbon dioxide, and then identifying the minute amounts of radioactive compounds at the intermediate stages of photosynthesis, Calvin and his group were able, by 1957, to establish most of the reactions used by plants in making sugar and other substances. Calvin and an associate, James A. Bassham, reviewed the discovery of the path from carbon dioxide to the final product of photosynthesis in two books, *The Path of Carbon in Photosynthesis* (1957) and *The Photosynthesis of Carbon Compounds* (1962).

Calvin went on to suggest that plants may convert light energy to chemical energy by transferring electrons through an organized array of pigment molecules and other substances. He also formulated theories concerning the chemical evolution of life. He supported these theories with studies of the organic substances found in ancient rocks, and of organic compounds formed during the irradiation of gas mixtures under conditions that are thought to simulate the atmosphere of the earth as it existed billions of years ago.

Life. Calvin was born in St. Paul, Minn., on April 8, 1911, the son of Russian immigrant parents. He received a B. S. degree from the Michigan College of Mining and Technology in 1931 and a Ph. D. in chemistry from the University of Minnesota in 1935. He became interested in biochemistry while working as a postdoctoral fellow at the University of Manchester, England, during the years 1935–1937.

Beginning in 1937, Calvin taught chemistry at the University of California at Berkeley. He formed the bio-organic chemistry group of the Lawrence Radiation Laboratory there in 1946 and became director of the university's Laboratory of Chemical Biodynamics in 1960.

Calvin was elected to several distinguished societies, including the National Academy of Sciences and the Royal Society of London, whose Davy Medal he received in 1964 in recognition of his pioneering work in chemistry and biology, particularly his photosynthesis studies.

JAMES A. BASSHAM
Lawrence Radiation Laboratory
University of California

CALVINISTIC METHODIST CHURCH, a Protestant denomination centered in Wales and closely allied to Presbyterianism. The denomination originated in 1743 under the influence of the Wesleyan revival. Its primary inspiration derived from the Calvinistic evangelism of George Whitefield. The movement was at first thought of as a reform effort within the Church of England, but a separatist tendency developed when preachers were forced to have their meeting places registered as dissenting chapels under the Toleration Act.

Today the outlook of the Calvinistic Methodist Church is strongly nationalistic; The Welsh language is used in many of its services. The denomination maintains a keen interest in education, politics, and social service. It has about 150,000 members.

CALVINO, käl-vē′nō, **Italo** (1923–), Italian writer, best-known for his adaptations of chivalric romances. He was born of Italian parents at Santiago de las Vegas, near Havana, Cuba, on Oct. 15, 1923. His early books are realistic, but his later writings are a blend of realism and richly imaginative fantasy, showing the influence of the Italian Renaissance writer Ariosto.

Calvino's novels, having little plot but filled with ideas, include *Il sentiero dei nidi di ragno* (1947; Eng. tr., *The Path to the Nest of Spiders,* 1957); *Il barone rampante* (1957; Eng. tr., *The Baron in the Trees,* 1959); and *Il cavaliere inesistente* (1959; Eng. tr., *The Nonexistent Knight,* 1962).

CALVO, käl′vō, **Carlos** (1824–1906), Argentine jurist, diplomat, and writer, for whom the Calvo Clause and Calvo Doctrine in international law are named. He was born in Buenos Aires on Feb. 26, 1824. Calvo began a distinguished diplomatic career in 1852 as Argentine vice-consul at Montevideo, Uruguay, and as consul general there and diplomatic representative of Argentina to Uruguay from 1853 to 1858. From 1860 to 1864 he represented Paraguay as chargé d'affaires at Paris and also was accredited to Britain. At later periods in his career he served as the Argentine minister plenipotentiary to Germany, Russia, Austria, the Holy See, and France. Calvo died in Paris on May 4, 1906.

Although by profession a diplomat, Calvo is best known as the author of numerous scholarly works that greatly influenced the development of international law. His most famous work, which became a standard reference in international law, is a 6-volume treatise that was published originally in French, *International Law in Theory and Practice* (1896). Calvo's publications provided the theoretical basis for the so-called Calvo Clause, a stipulation inserted in a contract between a government and a foreign national (or corporation) whereby the latter promises not to seek the diplomatic assistance of his government in any controversy or claim arising in connection with the contract. Calvo also gave his name to the so-called Calvo Doctrine, a view in international law that no nation has the right to intervene in the affairs of another state, and that foreigners are entitled to only the same rights and privileges accorded to nationals and are therefore barred from appealing to their own governments to seek redress for grievances.

DONALD R. SHEA, *University of Wisconsin*

CALWELL, kôl′wel, **Arthur Augustus** (1896–), Australian politican, who was leader of the Federal Labour party from 1960 to 1967. He was born in Melbourne on Aug. 28, 1896. Active in the Labour party for many years, he was elected to the House of Representatives in 1940. Calwall became minister of immigration in 1945 and thereafter worked assiduously for public acceptance of large-scale immigration. Under his direction, elaborate arrangements were made to select, receive, and train immigrants.

When Calwell became leader of the Labour party in 1960, it had been out of office since 1949. He supported his country's alliance with the United States but was adamantly opposed to military involvement in Vietnam. He retired from the Leadership in January 1967. His publications include *How Many Australians Tomorrow?* (1945) and *Immigration Policy and Progress* (1949).

R. M. YOUNGER
Author of "Australia and Australians"

CALYCANTHUS, kal-ə-kan′thəs, also called *sweet-scented shrub,* is a genus of aromatic shrubs of the family Calycanthaceae. Calycanths are sometimes grown in gardens for ornament and fragrance. There are four species of *Calycanthus,* all of which are native to the United States.

The most frequently cultivated is Carolina allspice (*Calycanthus floridus*), a southeastern species, 4 to 6 feet (about 1½ meters) high with a fragrance, when crushed, similar to that of strawberries. The ovate, opposite, entire leaves are dark green on the upper surface and grayish green and downy on the underside. The flowers are dark red and about 2 inches (5 cm) across. Because it has numerous stamens and numerous free pistils, *Calycanthus* is considered to be a primitive genus. The pistils are on the inside of a hollow receptacle. A western species, *C. occidentalis,* is taller and has larger flowers than *C. floridus.*

S. C. BAUSOR, *California State College, Pa.*

Calycanthus

ROCHE

CALYDON, kal′ə-don, was an ancient city of southern Aetolia, in west central Greece. Its ruins occupy a site about 6 miles (10 km) east of Mesolóngion (Missolonghi). The city played a more prominent part in legend—Meleager hunted the Calydonian boar nearby—than in history. It was held by Achaeans from 391 to 371 B.C. Although Emperor Augustus moved all its inhabitants to Nicopolis in 31 B.C., Calydon continued to be mentioned as a historical site by geographers and historians of the classical period.

CALYDONIAN BOAR HUNT, kal-ə-dō′nē-ən, in Greek legend, a hunt for a giant boar that had been devastating the fields of Calydon. The boar had been sent as punishment by the goddess Artemis (Diana) who was incensed because Oeneus, king of Calydon, had neglected to offer up the annual sacrifice to her.

Meleager, the son of Oeneus and Althaea, called on the Greeks to join him in a hunt for the monster. When Meleager was born, the Fates decreed that he would live only as long as a certain piece of wood burning on the hearth would last, and his mother took it from the fire and preserved it.

Many legendary heroes came to join the hunt, including Theseus, Jason, Peleus (father of Achilles), Telamon (father of Ajax), Nestor, and the huntress Atalanta. In the usual version of the story, Meleager killed the boar and gave its head and hide to Atalanta, who was believed to have been the first to wound it. When Meleager's uncles, his mother's brothers, disputed this, he killed them. In revenge, Althaea caused Meleager to die by throwing the piece of wood in a fire, and allowing it to burn to ashes.

The Calydonian boar hunt, a favorite subject in Greek art, was notably executed by the Greek sculptor Scopas on the pediment of the Temple of Athena Alea at Tegea.

CALYPSO, kə-lip′sō, in Greek legend, was a sea nymph who lived on the island of Ogygia. Homer, in the *Odyssey,* identified her as a daughter of Atlas. When Odysseus (Ulysses) is shipwrecked on his way home from the Trojan War, he makes his way to Ogygia. Calypso falls in love with him and promises him immortality if he will remain with her. Although he is bent upon returning to his wife and son, Odysseus stays with her for seven years. Finally, Zeus (Jupiter) orders Calypso to let Odysseus go, and she supplies him with the materials to build a raft and with provisions for use on his homeward voyage.

CALYPSO, kə-lip′sō, is the traditional carnival music of Trinidad. It has spread to other islands of the Caribbean and has been commercially imitated and exploited elsewhere. Authentic calypsos have words that allude, often in a humorous, satirical, or scandalous manner, to local events and personalities or to international events viewed from a local angle. Trinidadian slang terms and Creole words, such as *craf* (girl) and *bobol* (graft) are often used.

From the end of the Christmas holidays until the beginning of Trinidad's pre-Lenten carnival, "tents" are set up in Port of Spain, where musicians appear each night to test their new songs. Those songs that receive the most applause are used during the carnival season, and one or two of them are chosen by acclamation to be the carnival theme song, or "road march." Each year, also, one calypsonian is chosen as "king" by a jury made up of local and foreign personalities. Professional calypsonians assume flamboyant names, such as Sir Lancelot, Duke of Iron, Attila the Hun, Lord Eisenhower, Lion, Panther, and the Spoiler.

Calypso tunes are based on about 50 traditional melodies. The music is in 2/2 or 4/4 time, with offbeat phrasing, and when used for ballroom dancing it resembles a fast rumba. For carnival "jump dancing" in the streets a "steel band" made up of tuned steel oil drums is favored. Otherwise, the music is usually played by a band of strings and wind instruments, including saxophones, clarinets, and trumpets.

GILBERT CHASE
Tulane University

CALYX, kā′liks, the outermost set of flower parts. These flower parts, individually known as sepals, are commonly small, green, leaflike structures that may be separate or fused to form a tube. Their usual function is the protection and enclosure of the other flower parts in the bud. The number of sepals is generally the same as the number of petals. In some plants the form of the calyx is greatly modified. For example, the calyx of most lilies is large and petaloid and differs from the set of true petals only by its outer position, and the calyx of the dandelion is reduced to a set of hairlike bristles, called the pappus.

DOUGLAS M. FAMBROUGH, JR.
California Institute of Technology

CALZABIGI, käl-tsä-bē′jē, **Raniero da** (1714–1795), Italian poet and librettist, known chiefly for his collaboration with Christoph Willibald Gluck. He was born in Livorno on Dec. 23, 1714. Calzabigi wrote the librettos for three of Gluck's finest operas—*Orfeo ed Euridice* (1762), *Alceste* (1767), and *Paride ed Elena* (1769). Until his time, opera had a stiff, artificial form, but Calzabigi and Gluck tried to reform opera by unifying its dramatic and musical aspects. They thus set off a long controversy, but later composers, notably Mozart, accepted their principles. Calzabigi died in Naples in July 1795.

CAM, koun, **Diogo,** Portuguese navigator of the 15th century, who discovered the mouth of the Congo River. His name is also spelled *Cão*. Early in 1482 he sailed to the Gold Coast (present-day Ghana) and then continued eastward along the coast. After turning south and crossing the equator, he came upon the mouth of the Congo River. The inhabitants of the area were subjects of the Manikongo, ruler of the kingdom of the Kongo. Cam sent two emissaries to the Manikongo and continued south to latitude 13° 26′ S. He took several Kongo hostages with him on his return to Portugal.

In August 1484, King John II of Portugal sent him to open diplomatic relations with the Manikongo. On this second voyage Cam sailed as far as latitude 22° 10′ S. He then returned to Congo and visited the Manikongo's capital at Mbanza. He was well received by the African monarch, who willingly sent an embassy to Portugal. Cam and his Congolese guests arrived at Lisbon in April or May 1486.

ROBERT L. HESS
University of Illinois at Chicago Circle

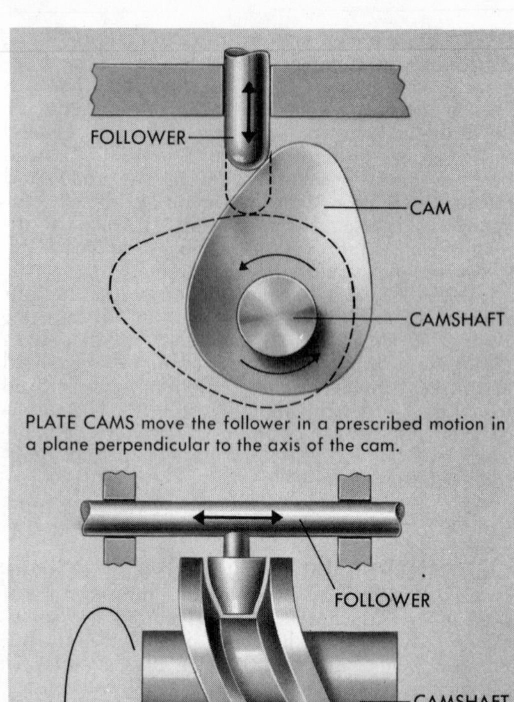

PLATE CAMS move the follower in a prescribed motion in a plane perpendicular to the axis of the cam.

CYLINDRICAL CAMS move the follower in a prescribed motion in a direction parallel to the axis of the cam.

CAM, kam, a mechanical device with surface projections or depressions that impart a repetitive, prescribed motion to a contracting part called the follower. Cams were the first devices used for the automatic control of motion or operations and are used in most machines today. In addition to cams, hydraulic, pneumatic, and electric devices are employed for the automatic control of motion.

Although cams are made in a variety of sizes and shapes, most cams are of one of two principal types: *plate* (sometimes called *disk*) *cams* and *cylindrical cams*. The plate cam moves the follower in a plane that is perpendicular to the axis of the cam, or in the plane of the cam profile. The cylindrical cam moves the follower in a direction that is parallel to the axis of the cam. *Positive-action cams* are cylindrical cams that act on two sides of the follower so that it is moved both backward and forward by the action of the cam surface. The *nonpositive-motion cam* moves the follower in one direction only; it is returned to its starting position by a spring or gravity.

Cams are also classified on the basis of the motion they impart to the follower. A *straight-line cam* raises the follower with constant velocity. To avoid the shock or jerk at the beginning and end of the follower's path, smooth curves are often added to make the cam a *modified straight-line cam*. A *harmonic cam* moves the follower so that its motion represented on a graph as displacement from its starting position, plotted against time, is a sine curve.

JOSEPH DATSKO
University of Michigan

CAMACHO, Manuel Ávila. See ÁVILA CAMACHO, MANUEL.

CAMAGÜEY, kä-mä-gwā′, is a city in Cuba, 310 miles (500 km) southeast of Havana. The capital of Camagüey province, it is situated on a broad plain watered by the Tínima and Jatibonico rivers and is connected with Havana and Santiago by the Central Highway.

The city was founded in 1515 by Diego Velázquez, who named it Santa María de Puerto Príncipe. Originally it was on the coast, near the site of modern Nuevitas, but it was later moved inland to its present location on the site of an Indian village called Camagüey. In its early years it prospered from illegal trade with the English and Dutch colonies in the Caribbean, and its wealth caused it to be raided by the pirate Henry Morgan in 1668.

During the 19th century, Camagüey resisted the movement for Cuban independence. Several fierce battles were fought in the vicinity, and in the central plaza are four palm trees planted in honor of Cuba's first four independence martyrs, who were executed by the Spanish in 1851.

Camagüey has a colonial atmosphere, with winding, narrow streets and several churches, convents, and other colonial buildings of architectural interest. The city is a distribution center for a cattle-raising and sugar-producing region. Local industries include dairying, sawmilling, sugar milling, distilling, and tanning. Population: (1960) 191,379.

GREGORY RABASSA
Columbia University

CAMALDOLITES, kə-mal′dō-līts, or *Camaldolese,* a branch of the Roman Catholic Order of St. Benedict. Because of their distinctive white woolen garments, they are often called "White Benedictines."

The Camaldolites originated in 1012, when St. Romuald, a Benedictine monk, and his companions went to the Apennines near Arezzo, Italy, to live as hermits. Since the mountain where they lived was a gift of Count Maldolo, it was called Campus Maldoli; thus they came to be known as "Eremiti Camaldolesi." Around 1015, St. Romuald opened a hospice nearby, which Blessed Rudolf, the prior from 1074 to 1087, converted into a novitiate and monastery for the sick and aged monks. The Camaldolites were united under one superior until 1534, when they separated into congregations, or groups of houses, but they reunited in 1935.

The Camaldolites have a history both of scholarship and evangelization. They founded hermitages and monasteries outside Italy in France, Poland, Germany, Austria, and Hungary. In the 17th and 18th centuries there were five autonomous congregations with 2,000 members. Of these, two continued to flourish in the late 1960's: Camaldoli, the original house, with 160 members; and Monte Corona, with 100 members. Some 25 monasteries, mostly in Italy, are also operative. A house was founded in Brazil in 1899, and a foundation of the Camaldoli Congregation was established at Big Sur, Calif., in 1958; another, of the Monte Corona Congregation, was founded at McConnelsville, Ohio, in 1959.

MARION A. HABIG, O. F. M.
St. Augustine Friary, Chicago, Ill.

Further Reading: Bede, M., *The Hermits of New Camaldoli* (Big Sur, Calif., 1958).

CAMARGO, kà-màr-gō, **Marie Anne de Cupis de** (1710–1770), French ballerina. She was born in Brussels on April 15, 1710. She made her immensely successful Paris debut in 1726 and performed in more than 78 ballets and operas. She is credited with having the heels removed from ballet slippers and shortening the ballet skirt to its present regulation length. She died in Paris on April 28, 1770.

The Camargo Society, named in her honor, was founded in London in 1930 to revive interest in the ballet. It was disbanded in 1936 after aiding in the establishment of the Vic-Wells (now Royal) Ballet.

CAMARILLO, kam-ə-rē′ō, a city in southwestern California, in Ventura county, is 47 miles (76 km) northwest of downtown Los Angeles. It is the principal commercial center of the Santa Rosa, Pleasant, and Las Posas valleys. Its chief industries are electronics manufacturing and the processing and shipping of citrus fruits and nuts. Beans, celery, lettuce, cabbage, oranges, lemons, strawberries, walnuts, and flowers for seed are cultivated in the area. Camarillo is the seat of St. John's College, a 4-year Roman Catholic institution for men, and of Camarillo State Hospital. The city, incorporated in 1964, is governed by a city manager, mayor, and council. Population: 19,219.

CAMAS, kam′əs, an industrial city in southwestern Washington, is in Clark county, 13 miles (21 km) east of Vancouver, on the Columbia River. The city is in a farming area and produces paper, pulp, and machinery. Camas was settled in 1860 and incorporated in 1906. Government is administered by mayor and council. Population: 5,790.

CAMAS, kam′əs, a showy flowering plant of the lily family (Liliaceae) native to western North America from British Columbia to California. The camas (*Camassia quamash*), also called *bear grass,* has a large underground bulb and narrow grass-like leaves. Its star-shaped purplish flowers, 1 to 2 inches (2.5–5 cm) in diameter, are borne in elongated clusters (racemes) on stems 1 to 3 feet (30–90 cm) high.

The bulbs of this plant were once used as food by Indians, and the name "camas" is derived from Indian word *quamash.*

R. C. ALLEN
Kingwood Center, Mansfield, Ohio

ROCHE

Camas (*Camassia quamash*)

CAMBACÉRÈS, kän-bȧ-sā-res′, **Jean Jacques Régis de** (1753–1824), French political leader, who became archchancellor and prince of the empire under Napoleon I. He was born in Montpellier on Oct. 18, 1753, of a famous legal family. Before the French Revolution he served as counselor to the court of accounts and finances in Montpellier. Elected to the National Convention in 1792, he demonstrated his moderation: he favored suspending Louis XVI's death sentence until the end of hostilities, and he remained aloof from the battle between the Jacobins and the moderate Girondists in the Convention in June 1793.

Elected to the Council of Five Hundred under the Directory, Cambacérès quietly supported Napoleon Bonaparte's coup d'etat of 18 Brumaire (Nov. 9, 1799) and became second consul in 1800. His brilliant oratory helped Bonaparte win the life consulate in 1802, and Cambacérès became archchancellor of the empire in 1804. During the late Consulate and the empire, he devoted himself primarily to legal and administrative questions. Although he served the emperor loyally, he did not agree with Napoleon's aggressive policies toward Spain and Russia. Even so, his services received the highest recognition in 1808, when he became a prince of the empire and Duke of Parma. As life president of the Senate, he favored the retirement of Napoleon after the French collapse in 1814. Yet he served the emperor again during the hectic Hundred Days. Exiled unjustly as a regicide by Louis XVIII, he was allowed to return to France in 1818. He died in Paris on March 8, 1824.

RICHARD M. BRACE, *Oakland University*

CAMBALUC, kam′bə-luk, is the name by which Peking, China, was known in Europe during the Middle Ages. Cambaluc was the form used by Marco Polo for the Mongol name Khanbalik. Under the Ming dynasty, which succeeded the Mongols, Khanbalik was given its present name, Peking.

CAMBAY, kam-bā′, is a seaport in Gujarat state, India. It is situated at the head of the Gulf of Cambay, 76 miles (122 km) northwest of Surat. As the capital of the former princely state of Cambay, it was once a place of importance, but owing to the silting up of the gulf and the bore, or rushing tides, it has greatly declined. The tides run in at from 6 to 7 knots an hour, rising as high as 33 feet (10 meters), and are very dangerous to shipping.

In Cambay are several mosques and Hindu temples and many religious structures of the Jains. The town is noted for its jewelers and goldsmiths, and agate, carnelian, and onyx ornaments are exported. Trade is chiefly in cotton, ivory, and grain, the last shipped to Bombay. Population: (1961) 51,291.

CAMBAY, Gulf of, kam-bā′, a large inlet of the Arabian Sea on the northwestern coast of India between the Kathiawar peninsula and the Gujarat coast. About 125 miles (200 km) wide at its mouth, the gulf narrows toward its head. Monsoon rains and winds cause very high spring tides and a rapid tidal velocity. Sediments carried to the gulf by rivers have caused silting, and shifting sandbanks and shoals make navigation difficult. Several ancient ports, among them Cambay, have declined, but Bhavnagar, with a modern harbor, is still important.

H. J. STEWARD, *University of Toronto*

CAMBERT, käɴ-bâr, **Robert** (c.1628–1677), French composer, whose opera *Pomone,* with libretto by Pierre Perrin, is the first French opera. Before *Pomone,* Italian had been considered the only "operatic" language. By adapting the mode of Italian recitative to the declamatory style of the French classical theater, Cambert and Perrin created a form for French opera that Jean Baptiste Lully later made more dramatic.

Cambert was born in Paris and studied with the harpsichordist and composer Jacques Chambonnières. In 1659 he and Perrin wrote *Pastorale d'Issy,* the first French comedy in music. In 1669, Perrin obtained from Louis XIV the exclusive privilege to produce operas, and in 1671 he and Cambert staged *Pomone,* based largely on *Pastorale d'Issy. Pomone,* of which only the prologue and the first act survive, was an immediate success. In 1672, Lully gained the opera concession from Perrin, thus ending Cambert's career in Paris. The next year Cambert went to England, where he produced operas and wrote a ballet. He died in London early in 1677, possibly poisoned by a servant.

ADRIENNE FRIED, *Choral Director*
Dalcroze School of Music, New York City

CAMBERWELL is a metropolitan borough of London, England, south of the Thames River, between Lambeth on the west and Deptford and Lewisham on the east. The borough is mainly residential and includes the villages of Dulwich and Peckham. Among its many parks are Dulwich Park and Peckham Rye Common and Park. The South London Art Gallery is in Camberwell. Population: (1961) 175,304.

CAMBIASO, käm-byä′zō, **Luca** (1527–1585), Italian painter. He was born in Moneglia, near Genoa, on Oct. 18, 1527. Trained by his father, Giovanni Cambiaso, a fresco painter, he worked under Giovanni Battista Castello and succeeded the latter as the most popular painter in Genoa. His frescoes, admired for their fluent composition and rich color, may be seen in many churches and mansions in or near the city. In 1583 Philip II invited him to Spain to execute frescoes in the Escorial. The most famous of these, painted on the ceiling, is an immense composition representing the gathering of the blessed in Paradise. Cambiaso died in Madrid on Sept. 6, 1585.

CAMBIO, Arnolfo di. See ARNOLFO DI CAMBIO.

CAMBIUM, kam′bē-əm, a zone of actively dividing cells responsible for the growth in diameter of the stems and roots of woody plants. (The apical meristem, or growing point, produces growth in length.) After each cell division, one of the two resulting daughter cells remains a part of the cambial layer, while the other differentiates into an element of the plant's vascular tissue — either a water-conducting *xylem* element interior to the cambium or a food-conducting *phloem* element exterior to the cambium. Though cambial activity produces most of the tissue in woody plants, cambium is lacking in most herbaceous plants and in all monocots, the group of plants containing the lilies and grasses.

Cork cambium, a tissue in the outer layer of woody plants, produces the thick-walled protective cells making up most of the bark.

DOUGLAS M. FAMBROUGH, JR.
California Institute of Technology

FREDERICK AYER, FROM PHOTO RESEARCHERS

The Royal Palace at Phnom Penh, with the Music Pavilion at the right.

CAMBODIA, kam-bō′dē-ə, a nation located in Southeast Asia, is one of the three states of the entity formerly known as Indochina (the other two are Laos and Vietnam). Today an underpopulated, predominantly agricultural country, Cambodia was formerly the seat of the Khmer empire (802–1432 A. D.), which fostered a glorious architecture. The remains of this period, for which Cambodia is still renowned, were uncovered by the French and can be seen in the ruined city of Angkor (q. v.).

After obtaining independence from France in 1953 during the Indochina war, Cambodia pursued a neutralist foreign policy. This policy veered, during the 1960's, toward support of Communist China and North Vietnam. In early 1970 it veered in the opposite direction and precipitated a Vietnamese Communist invasion of Cambodia. This engulfed the country in war.

1. People

Eighty percent of Cambodia's population is engaged in agriculture, notably rice culture. The population is one of the youngest in the world, with 54.5% under 20 years of age and less than 4% over 60. The average family has five children. Despite a high mortality rate, estimated at 22 per 1,000 inhabitants, population growth is 2.2% annually. Life expectancy is short, averaging 44 years for the Cambodian male and 43 years for the female. Cambodia is quite sparsely settled except along its waterways, and the country is unique in Southeast Asia in being seriously underpopulated in relation to arable land area. Over the years this condition has opened Cambodia to encroachments by its neighbors to the east and west and still makes Cambodians fear the annexation of their border provinces.

Ethnology. The people of Cambodia are remarkably homogeneous. Khmer (Cambodian) stock makes up approximately 85% of the total population. Other ethnic groups include the Chinese (435,000), Vietnamese (400,000), Cham-Malays (90,000), Malayo-Polynesian and Austro-Asian hill tribes (50,000), and Europeans, mainly French (6,000).

The modern Khmer are the end product of centuries of intricate cultural and racial blending, already complex before their descent prior to 200 B. C. into the fertile Mekong delta from the Korat plateau in what is now Thailand. Successive waves of Indian immigration at the beginning of the Christian era brought about Indianization of the Khmer, and in the 8th century A. D. the Khmer suffered an Indo-Malay invasion from Java. This was followed by Thai

INFORMATION HIGHLIGHTS

Official Name: Khmer Republic (proclaimed Oct. 9, 1970.

Head of State: Chief of State.

Head of Government: Prime Minister.

Legislature: National Assembly and Senate.

Area: 69,898 square miles (181,035 sq km).

Boundaries: *North,* Thailand and Laos; *east and south,* South Vietnam; *southwest,* the Gulf of Siam; *west,* Thailand.

Elevations: *Highest point*—Mount Aural, 5,948 feet (1,813 meters); *lowest point*—sea level.

Population: 6,701,000 (1969).

Capital: Phnom Penh.

Major Languages: Khmer, also called Cambodian (official); French.

Major Religion: Buddhism.

Monetary Unit: Riel.

Weights and Measures: Metric system.

Flag: Blue, with large red field in upper left-hand corner on which is a representation of the main temple of Angkor; three white stars are evenly spaced across the top.

CAMBODIA Map Index

Total Population: 6,701,000

Angkor Wat (ruins)	A 1	Mekong (river)	B 1
Battambang, 38,846	A 1	Pailin, 15,536†	A 1
Kampot, 12,558	A 2	Phnom Penh (cap.), 403,500*	B 2
Kompong Cham, 28,534	B 1	Prey Veng, 8,792	B 2
Kompong Chhnang, 12,847	A 1	Pursat, 14,329	A 1
Kompong Som, 6,578	A 2	Siem Reap, 10,230	B 1
Kompong Speu, 7,453	B 2	Stung Treng, 3,369	B 1
Kompong Thom, 9,682	B 1	Takeo, 11,312	B 2
Kratie, 11,908	B 1	Tonle Sap (lake)	A 1

† Population of sub-district. *City and suburbs. Total population—1969 official estimate; others—1962 preliminary census.

migrations from the 10th to 15th centuries, Vietnamese, beginning in the 17th, and Chinese, in the 17th and 19th centuries. As a result, the Khmer show great variation in physical traits. A typical Khmer male is about 5 feet 4 inches (152 cm) tall and has bronze skin, a flat nose, oval eyes, and a robust physique. Khmer assimilation of the Chinese has been extensive. The Khmer's traditional distrust of the Vietnamese has made intermarriage with that group much less frequent. The Cham-Malay group, known in Cambodia as *Khmer Islam,* maintains a rigorous Muslim orthodoxy that discourages assimilation into the overwhelmingly Buddhist Khmer ethnic majority. The primitive tribal groups, designated *Khmer Loeu* (upland Khmer), include the Jarai, Rhade, Stieng, Kui, Pear, and Saoch.

Way of Life. In Cambodia, as in other Southeast Asian countries, the Chinese minority has traditionally controlled economic life, serving as moneylenders, entrepreneurs, merchants, and transporters, and working as part of tightly knit family and dialectal organizations. This pattern is now changing, mainly as a result of the government's policy of protecting and encouraging Khmer commercial activities.

The majority of the Khmer are agriculturalists who live in a rural society composed mostly of small landowners holding from 2.5 to 10 acres (1–4 hectares) of rice land or 1.2 to 2.5 acres (0.5–1 hectare) of fertile riverbank property. Two and a half acres (1 hectare) of rice land provide sustenance for a family of five persons, while additional holdings may be used for supplemental crops or animals. People without land are rare, and life in the countryside is noticeably egalitarian and democratic.

Cities. Military insecurity during the Indochina war started an urbanization movement that has continued under the stimulus of modest industrialization. Important cities are Phnom Penh, the capital since 1866 (1962 population, 403,500); Battambang (38,846), located in the western rice bowl adjoining the Thai border; Kompong Cham (28,534), seat of the rubber plantation area; Kompong Som, formerly called Sihanoukville (6,578); and Siem Reap (10,230), near which are Angkor Wat and the ruined temples of the Khmer empire period.

Religion. Buddhism in its Theravada form is the state religion of Cambodia, and Buddhist concepts profoundly permeate Cambodian life, although the traditional custom that all males enter the monkhood for varying periods now is breaking down as a result of the rapid development of secular educational facilities. There are over 65,000 Buddhist monks living in 2,750 *wats* (temples).

2. Land and Natural Resources

One half of Cambodia is forested and one tenth is covered by water. The 900 miles (1,450 km) of navigable waterways define the pattern of population settlement.

Topography. Cambodia's dominant topographical feature is the Mekong River, which rises in Tibet and empties into the South China Sea some 2,600 miles (4,185 km) away, flowing broadly and majestically through Cambodia in a north–south direction. The annual flood of the Mekong is a major geographic phenomenon. Swollen by melting snow in Tibet and southwest China and by torrential rains of the southwest monsoon upon the mountains of China's Yünnan province and upper Laos, the Mekong from May to September rises approximately 45 feet (14 meters); at Phnom Penh it backs water up the Tonle Sap River to the Tonle Sap Lake in central Cambodia, expanding it from a dry season area of 100 square miles (260 sq km) to a rainy season area of 770 square miles (1,995 sq km). The fall of the Mekong at the end of the monsoon reverses the process. Mainly as a result of this annual inundation, the Tonle Sap Lake is one of the richest fish sources in the world.

Cambodia's central region is an alluvial plain stretching over three fourths of the country. The plain has a southeast–northwest orientation and is rarely more than 10 feet (3 meters) above sea level. To the southwest rises the densely forested Cardamom mountain range, and to the north is the Dang Raek chain, consisting of a steep, flat-topped sandstone scarp, which falls abruptly to the plain. In the northeast are high plateaus extending into Laos and Vietnam.

Plant and Animal Life. Cambodia's alluvial plain supports a wide variety of plant life. Growing in profusion are coconut palm, rubber, and orange trees, kapok, bananas, pepper, tobacco, cotton, sugarcane, indigo, and many kinds of vegetables. Animal life includes elephants, wild oxen, tigers, panthers, leopards, bears, and innumerable small game. Among the more common birds are herons, cranes, grouse, pheasant, peacocks, pelicans, cormorants, egrets, and wild duck.

Climate. The climate is typically tropical, with temperatures ranging from the 90's F (30's C) in April to the high 70's (mid-20's C) in January. The rainy season brought by the southwest monsoon lasts from May through October and the dry season of the northeast monsoon from November through April.

3. Economy

In seeking rapid economic development, Cambodia after 1955 followed a socialistic policy that increasingly introduced extensive state planning, financial participation, and control into sectors heretofore dominated by private enterprise. In 1963 this policy brought about nationalization of the banking system, creation of a state monopoly of all imports and exports, and the establishment of a number of state organizations responsible for commodity distribution, paddy (rice) collection and conditioning, and agricultural credit. In 1958 the government had begun the establishment of state enterprises of an industrial nature, some wholly state-owned and others allowing minority private investment.

Agriculture. Rice and rubber play dominant roles in the economy. Some 630,000 out of 800,000 rural families are engaged in rice culture, producing annually an average of 2,250,000 metric tons of paddy rice. Approximately 40% is consumed by the growers and 60% is commercialized, one third going to nonrice areas and urban centers within Cambodia. The remainder is available for export.

The cultivation of rubber was introduced into Cambodia by the French in 1921, and the basaltic plateaus of the provinces of Kompong Cham and Ratanakiri have proven especially suitable, resulting in an average output of 1,218 lb per acre (1,300 kg per hectare), among the highest in the world. By the mid-1960's some 83,000 acres (33,600 hectares) were being exploited out of a total planted area of 118,600 acres (48,000 hectares).

Other agricultural commodities produced in limited commercial quantities include cotton, pepper, corn, beans, kapok, and tobacco. As a Buddhist country, Cambodia is a low consumer of meat, and animals are utilized mainly for work purposes. Some 174 varieties of freshwater fish exist in Cambodia, but export is negligible because of large domestic consumption. Maritime fish production is about 50,000 metric tons annually.

Industrial Development. Cambodia has no large-scale industry, and until the 1960's what little industry did exist was devoted to processing agricultural products. Processing plants included distilleries, rice mills, latex plants, and fish processing plants. During the 1960's, however, Cambodia embarked upon an industrial development program, its own contribution being supplemented by foreign economic assistance. Communist China provided aid to build plants for textiles, plywood, glass, cement, and paper. Czechoslovakian loans helped equip tire and tractor factories and a sugar refinery. France helped to build the port at Kompong Som, and the United States provided funds for a highway linking Kompong Som to Phnom Penh. Before being terminated by Cambodia in 1963, U. S. economic and military aid totaled $403,700,000 over a 10-year period. Soviet Union and Yugoslav loans were earmarked for hydroelectric projects.

PHNOM PENH, capital of Cambodia since 1866 and the nation's largest city, is also a major port by virtue of its location on the Mekong River.

Trade and Commerce. In the commercial sector, Cambodia's major trading partners have been France, Japan, Communist China, Singapore, Hong Kong, Czechoslovakia, and the Soviet Union. In a typical year, imports totaled $102,937,000 in value and exports totaled $105,428,000. Cambodia's principal exports are rice, rubber, and maize, and the chief imports are metals and machinery, textiles, mineral products, foodstuffs, and pharmaceuticals.

Transportation. Cambodia's inland waterways provide an important supplement to the country's 3,181 miles (5,119 km) of road. A railroad line 240 miles (386 km) in length links Phnom Penh with Poipet on the Thai frontier, and another line, opened in 1967, connects Phnom Penh with Kompong Som. Pochentong Airport, near Phnom Penh, handles jet aircraft. Cambodia's national airline offers flights to and from Hong Kong as well as various points in Southeast Asia.

4. Education and Cultural Life

Educational development has been especially significant since independence from France, and by 1965 some 5.3% of the national income was being invested in school facilities, equipment, and personnel. The rush to the schoolroom reflects a basic change of attitude in the average Cambodian, and education is now the most important social mobility factor in contemporary Cambodian society. Between 1955 and 1965 elementary school enrollment rose from 250,000 to 723,000 and secondary school enrollment from 5,500 to 81,200. During this period three public universities were created—in Phnom Penh, Takeo, and Kompong Cham—and a fourth was to be established in Battambang. A law voted by the National Assembly in 1965 obliges all Cambodians between the ages of 10 and 50 to learn how to read, and the government claims that the literacy level has reached 80%.

Cambodia's great cultural heritage goes back to the architectural and sculptural achievements of the Khmer empire period, visible in the ruined temples of the Angkor complex. Here between the 9th and 13th centuries successive Khmer god-kings built a series of great royal cities, whose remains now cover some 230 square miles (600 sq km). Many of the temples have been restored, and Angkor is normally one of the foremost tourist attractions in Southeast Asia.

Cambodian art forms have been strongly impregnated by Indian influence, and generally speaking, the country's eastern border marks the frontier between Indian and Chinese culture and civilization on the Southeast Asian mainland.

5. Government

Cambodia became a constitutional monarchy in May 1947, during the reign of King Norodom Sihanouk, who in 1955 abdicated in favor of his father, Norodom Suramarit. Following succession difficulties after Suramarit's death in 1960, a constitutional amendment created the office of chief of state, to which Prince Sihanouk was named by the National Assembly. The throne was therefore regarded as temporarily vacant. In 1970, after Sihanouk was removed from office, Cambodia was proclaimed the Khmer Republic.

The chief of state promulgates laws, convokes and dissolves parliament, designates the prime minister, names ambassadors, and signs foreign treaties. Executive power is vested in a 16-member Council of Ministers selected by the prime minister but collectively and individually responsible to the National Assembly. The legislative function belongs to the National Assembly, elected every 4 years by direct universal suffrage, and to the Senate, an upper house, which serves as a consultative body.

AT ANGKOR THOM, the "Giant's Causeway" leads to the Victory Gate built by Jayavarman VII (1130–1219).

FREDERICK AYER, FROM PHOTO RESEARCHERS

6. History

Modern Cambodia can be traced back to Funan, a small Indianized kingdom.

Funan and Chenla. Funan, during the first four centuries A. D., came to dominate the Mekong delta. Little is known about this kingdom, but its inhabitants probably were Indian colonists and traders who intermarried with the indigenous Khmer population. In the 6th century A. D. Funan was overcome and annexed by Chenla, a vassal state in what is now southern Laos. About 705, Chenla became divided, and the southern portion fell under Javanese suzerainty. A new king, Jayavarman II, was placed on the throne, and the capital was moved to the Angkor site near the Tonle Sap Lake.

Khmer. In 802, Jayavarman II declared Khmer independence from the Javanese, reunited the two Chenlas, and initiated the Angkor period of Cambodian history (802–1432). The Khmer empire reached its greatest extent under Jayavarman VII (1130–1219), who ruled a collection of conquered states, colonies, and vassal states circumscribed by northern Laos, the South China Sea, the Malay peninsula, and the Chao Phraya river valley. It was more than the Khmer could hold, and, drained by the building frenzy of the *devaraja* (god-king) cult, they were unable to resist Thai encroachment. Angkor was sacked in 1431 and in 1432 was abandoned as the capital.

Decline. The next four centuries were characterized by internal strife, division, and increasingly unsuccessful efforts to resist subjugation by the Thai in the west and the Vietnamese in the east. Beginning in the 14th century the latter had moved progressively southward from Tonkin and by the second half of the 18th century had consolidated control of the Mekong delta at Cambodian expense. Vietnamese confrontation with the Thai took place in Cambodia during the early part of the 19th century, and in 1846 a peace settlement left Cambodia a vassal state of both Siam and Annam (part of present Vietnam), economically prostrate, seriously depopulated, and reduced to its smallest territorial extent. These circumstances led King Ang Duong (1796–1859) to seek protection from a European power, a decision which coincided with the arrival of France in Indochina.

French Domination. The French viewed Cambodia as a buffer state separating their new colony of Cochin-China from British influence in Siam. On the assumption that Annam's suzerainty had devolved to them by conquest, the French signed a protectorate treaty with King Norodom (1834–1904) in 1863. By an accord negotiated in Paris in 1867, Siam surrendered its suzerainty in return for French recognition of Thai rights over Battambang and part of Siem Reap. These provinces were given back to Cambodia in 1907, lost again after the Franco-Siamese war of 1940–1941, and returned once more in 1946.

France's domination of Cambodia lasted until 1953. The early years of the protectorate were benevolent, but in 1884, Norodom was forced to sign a new treaty, which deprived the monarchy of much of its power. In 1898, Cambodia was brought into close alignment with the colony of Cochin-China and the protectorates of Annam, Tonkin, and Laos.

Japanese forces occupied Cambodia during

(LEFT) CATHERINE URSILLO; (CENTER) KATHLEEN VAN WYCK, FROM MONKMEYER; (RIGHT) FREDERICK AYER, FROM PHOTO RESEARCHERS

CAMBODIAN STREET SCENES (*left to right*): A fish market in Phnom Penh; a Cham-Malay carpenter; and, in Siem Reap, a market for bananas, sold wrapped in their leaves.

World War II and declared it independent following the *coup de force* against the French in March 1945, but French administrators returned after the surrender of Japan. In January 1946 a *modus vivendi* ended the protectorate and granted Cambodia autonomy within the French Union, and a 1949 treaty recognized it as an associated state. However, a desire for full independence persisted among intellectuals.

Independence. In 1952, King Norodom Sihanouk took over the government and launched a crusade to achieve independence through negotiation. This objective was attained on Nov. 9, 1953, mainly as the result of Sihanouk's skill in dealing with the French at a time of increasing difficulties in their war against the Viet Minh (Vietnamese Communists). Sihanouk abdicated in 1955 in order to form the Sangkum Reastr Niyum (Popular Socialist Community), a broad-front political organization, which by 1958 had absorbed all parties but the Communist.

The Sangkum, under Prince Sihanouk, dominated Cambodia's political life and attempted to foster a foreign policy based on neutralism and peaceful coexistence. However, the cold war alignment on the Indochinese peninsula infringed upon such a policy, and after 1954 relations with Thailand and South Vietnam progressively worsened, reaching the diplomatic rupture point in 1961 and 1963, respectively. Relations with the United States were severed in 1965–1969 over problems resulting from the Vietnam War.

Convinced that the Communists would win in South Vietnam, Prince Sihanouk increasingly oriented Cambodian policy to accommodate North Vietnam and the National Liberation Front of South Vietnam. He permitted Vietnamese Communist forces to use Cambodian territory for sanctuary and redeployment, and in a secret agreement with Communist China in 1966 he authorized the entry of Chinese war material by sea for delivery to Vietnamese Communist base areas in eastern Cambodia. By 1969 some 40,000 to 60,000 Vietnamese Communist troops were on Cambodian territory. Sihanouk's cooperative attitude played a significant role in the Communist effort to sustain military operations in South Vietnam.

Fall of Prince Sihanouk. In August 1969, faced with a growing economic crisis provoked by the inefficient nationalization program, Sihanouk named Gen. Lon Nol, head of the armed forces, as prime minister. The new cabinet was largely rightist. The threat to national sovereignty posed by the extensive Vietnamese Communist occupation rapidly became a national issue, and Sihanouk sought to persuade the USSR and Communist China to apply pressure on North Vietnam and the Provisional Revolutionary Government (PRG) of South Vietnam to withdraw their forces to prescribed areas. Lon Nol sought a more direct means to compel withdrawal. In January 1970, while Sihanouk was absent in France, Cambodian military forces began limited operations against the Vietnamese in northeast Cambodia. On March 11, mobs in Phnom Penh sacked the North Vietnamese and PRG embassies. From Paris, Sihanouk threatened to dismiss the cabinet and dissolve the National Assembly. On March 18 the legislature deposed Sihanouk by unanimous vote. Cheng Heng, president of the National Assembly, was named acting chief of state. On October 9, Cambodia became a republic.

Beginning in early April 1970, Vietnamese Communist forces moved out of their sanctuaries to begin an invasion of the entire country. In Peking, to which he had traveled immediately after his deposition, Sihanouk formed an exile government with the support of Communist China and North Vietnam. In a limited campaign extending from April 30 to June 30, U.S. forces from South Vietnam struck across the border in an effort to destroy Communist supply depots.

LEONARD C. OVERTON, *The Asia Foundation*

Bibliography

Armstrong, John P., *Sihanouk Speaks* (New York 1964).

Briggs, Lawrence Palmer, *The Ancient Khmer Empire*, Transactions of the American Philosophical Society, New Series, vol. 41, part 1 (Philadelphia 1951).

Delvert, Jean, *Le paysan Cambodgien* (Paris 1961).

Gour, Claude-Gilles, *Institutions constitutionnelles et politiques du Cambodge* (Paris 1965).

Lacouture, Simonne, *Cambodge* (Lausanne 1963).

LeBar, Frank M., ed., *Ethnic Groups of Mainland Southeast Asia* (New Haven 1964).

Smith, Roger M., *Cambodia's Foreign Policy* (Ithaca, N.Y., 1965).

Steinberg, David J., ed., *Cambodia: Its People, Its Society, Its Culture*, rev. ed. (New Haven 1959).

CAMBON, käɴ-bôɴ′, **Joseph** (1756–1820), French politician, whose financial ability served the French Revolution. Pierre Joseph Cambon was born in Montpellier on June 10, 1756. In 1789 he gave up direction of a lucrative cotton-merchandising business and entered political life, later founding a Jacobin chapter in Montpellier. He was elected to the Legislative Assembly in 1791 and soon established himself as a fiscal expert. He cautioned against the overissue of assignats, the government's inflated paper currency, and urged long-range fiscal planning. He took no part in the characteristic infighting in the National Convention.

Marat's irresponsible radicalism offended Cambon, as did Danton's careless ways with public money. Robespierre disliked Cambon's demand that the state cease paying the clergy. Cambon defended the moderate Girondists in June 1793 and joined in the attack of Robespierre on July 26, 1794. In 1795 he retired to his estate, and he did not return to public life until 1815, when he opposed the Bourbon restoration. He was exiled as a regicide in 1816 and died at St.-Josse-ten-Noode, near Brussels, on Feb. 15, 1820.

RICHARD M. BRACE, *Oakland University*

CAMBON, käɴ-bôɴ′, **Jules Martin** (1845–1935), French diplomat. He was born in Paris on April 5, 1845. Admitted to the Paris bar in 1866, he served in the Franco-Prussian War and entered the civil service. From 1891 to 1897 he was governor-general of Algeria. Later, as ambassador to the United States, Cambon represented Spain in the negotiations that ended hostilities in the Spanish-American War, and in 1902 he was made ambassador to Madrid. In 1907 he was moved to Berlin, serving as ambassador there until the outbreak of World War I. The successful solution of the Agadir dispute between France and Germany, which threatened to erupt into European war, was largely due to his efforts. He died in Vevey, Switzerland, on Sept. 19, 1935.

CAMBON, käɴ-bôɴ′, **Paul** (1843–1924), French diplomat. Pierre Paul Cambon was born in Paris on Jan. 20, 1843, the brother of Jules Cambon. After graduating from the École Polytechnique in 1863, he studied law and was admitted to the bar in Paris. In 1870 he entered the civil service and held several prefectural posts. Cambon served as French resident-general in Tunis from 1882 until 1886, when he was appointed ambassador to Madrid. In 1891 he was transferred to Constantinople and in 1898 to London. His 22-year tenure as ambassador to Great Britain was notable for the evolution of the Entente Cordiale between the two countries, embodied in the agreement of 1904, and the subsequent Triple Alliance with Russia. Cambon died in Paris on May 29, 1924.

CAMBRAI, käɴ-brā′, an industrial city in France, is a road and rail center on the Scheldt (Escaut) River, 34 miles (55 km) south of Lille. The linen cloth known as cambric derived its name from Cambrai (Flemish, Kamerijk). The city is famous for the manufacture of cambric and other linen goods, cotton, and lace thread; leather goods, sugar, and beer are also produced.

Cambrai's beautiful cathedral and the tomb of its celebrated Archbishop François Fénelon were razed in 1793 during the French Revolution. Many buildings were later damaged during World Wars I and II. There is a new monument to the memory of Fénelon in the present cathedral, which was built during the 19th century.

In Roman times the city was called Cameracum. In 1508 the League of Cambrai was formed here by Emperor Maximilian, Louis XII of France, the Pope, and Ferdinand of Aragón, who united against Venice. Population: (1962) 32,601.

CAMBRELENG, kam′bər-leng, **Churchill C.** (1786–1862), American politician, who was the administration leader in the U. S. House of Representatives for Presidents Andrew Jackson and Martin Van Buren. Always in the forefront of political controversy, he was considered a paragon by his friends and a demagogue by his enemies.

Born in 1786 in Washington, N C., Cambreleng achieved success in business after moving to New York City in 1802. In Congress from 1821 to 1839 he preached free trade and hard money in speeches characterized by clarity and common sense. Among his House posts were chairmanship of the ways and means, commerce, and foreign affairs committees. In 1840 and 1841 he was U. S. minister to Russia. He followed Van Buren to the Free Soil party in 1848, having been chairman of the Barnburners (q.v.) convention in 1847. He died in West Neck, Long Island, N. Y., on April 30, 1862.

JOSEPH C. BURKE, *Duquesne University*

CAMBRIA, kam′brē-ə, was the Medieval Latin name for Wales. It was derived from *Cymry* (Celtic for "fellow countrymen"), the name under which the Welsh first achieved a common identity. The Welsh still refer to themselves by this name.

CAMBRIAN PERIOD, kam′brē-ən, in geology, the first period of the Paleozoic era. It is estimated to have begun about 600 million years ago and to have lasted 80 to 100 million years. The name derives from a rock system studied by the English geologist Adam Sedgwick—initially with the assistance of his student Charles Darwin—in northern Wales, which in Roman times was called Cambria. In 1835, Sedgwick named the exposed rocks the Cambrian system.

The Silurian system of rocks that was being studied at the same time in southern Wales by another geologist, Roderick Murchison, was originally thought to be more recent than the Cambrian system of Sedgwick. However, the Upper Cambrian of Sedgwick was later determined to be the same as the Lower Silurian of Murchison, and the latter name was applied for a while to the rocks in question. The succession was renamed as the separate Ordovician system in 1869 by the English scientist Charles Lapworth, and the term "Cambrian" is now applied to the lower part of Sedgwick's original system.

Geology of the Period. The Cambrian system of northern Wales is composed of about 10,000 feet (3,000 meters) of sedimentary rocks, primarily sandstones and shales. The rocks contain a distinctive succession of the fossil crustaceans known as trilobites. The presence of an identical or similar sequence of trilobite forms in rocks found in Sweden and along the Atlantic Ocean border of North America (in eastern Newfoundland, St. Pierre and Miquelon islands, Nova Scotia, New Brunswick, and Massachusetts) establishes that these rocks are Cambrian as well.

CAMBRIAN SEAS contained life forms such as those shown in the museum model at right. The key to the numerals is as follows:

1 Trilobites
2 Crustaceans
3 Arachnids
4 Annelid worms
5 Jellyfish
6 Spongelike growths

FIELD MUSEUM OF NATURAL HISTORY

Forms of trilobite have also been found in North Carolina and in South America, particularly in northwestern Argentina. Somewhat different trilobite successions found in other parts of North America (such as western Newfoundland, the Appalachian region, Nevada, and the Canadian Rocky Mountains) are also considered to be of Cambrian age, because they are associated with typical trilobite forms in some areas, and because they are succeeded by fossils that are found in Ordovician rocks in Wales and elsewhere.

Cambrian Rock Series. The Cambrian system in North America provides a good record of the physical history of the interior of the continent. The system is divided into three series: Waucoban, Albertan, and St. Croixan. (Younger rocks classed as Cambrian in Wales, and known as the Tremadocian series, are usually considered to be Ordovician in North America, in conformity with Scandinavian practice.)

The Lower Cambrian, or Waucoban, sediments are restricted to rather narrow belts. In the west they extend from eastern Alaska, through eastern British Columbia and western Alberta, to western Utah, eastern Nevada, and northwestern Sonora in Mexico. In the east they extend from the southern coast of Labrador through the Gaspé Peninsula, Vermont, and southern Pennsylvania, to Alabama. The rocks are shallow sands and silts that were eroded from the interior continental land and carried and deposited by water.

The later Cambrian rocks—Albertan and St. Croixan—are predominantly limestones. They are thickest in the same belts as the early Cambrian rocks. These regions therefore subsided more rapidly than the rest of the continent, although seas were spread over much of the area of the United States during the later Cambrian. The subsided belts, with thicknesses of up to three miles, form the Cordilleran and Appalachian geosynclines on the west and east of the continent. The rather stable, shield-shaped central region of the continent subsided only along the southern part, and in late Cambrian time.

ERA	PERIOD	
CENOZOIC	QUATERNARY	
	TERTIARY	
MESOZOIC	CRETACEOUS	
	JURASSIC	
	TRIASSIC	
PALEOZOIC	PERMIAN	
	CARBON-IFEROUS	PENNSYLVANIAN
		MISSISSIPPIAN
	DEVONIAN	
	SILURIAN	
	ORDOVICIAN	
	CAMBRIAN	
PRE-CAMBRIAN TIME		

Cambrian rocks are not known along the Pacific Ocean coast of North America, and the only Cambrian rocks along the Atlantic shore from Newfoundland to South Carolina are those that contain the same fauna as the Cambrian rocks in Wales.

Sedimentary rocks of Cambrian age appear in many prominent North American landforms. In the west, Mt. Wheeler in eastern Nevada and the House Range in western Utah consist largely of Cambrian rocks, as do some of the highest peaks in the Canadian Rocky Mountains. The Dalles gorge of the Wisconsin River, the gorge of the St. Croix on the Minnesota border, and Ausable Chasm in New York have been produced by the erosion of rocks of the Cambrian system. Many of the rocks of the Great Smoky Mountains in eastern Tennessee and the Green Mountains in Vermont are altered Cambrian sediments.

Cambrian Minerals. Few important mineral products come from the Cambrian period. Roofing slates are derived from the Lower Cambrian in Vermont and eastern New York, and Cambrian marbles occur in Georgia. The lead deposits in southeastern Missouri and the lead and zinc in southeastern Nevada are later emplacements in Cambrian rocks.

Flora and Fauna. The variety of life forms found in Cambrian strata is not as great as that found in the strata of later periods. Calcium-depositing algae were significant rock builders during the Cambrian, and trilobites and brachipods are the only animals that are found frequently in marine Cambrian sediments. It was the consistent order of their appearance that substantiated the use of fossils to determine geological time.

The occurrence of highly organized life forms such as trilobites in the Cambrian rocks, along with associated impressions of structures similar to such living forms as worms, jellyfish, and echinoderms, show that life had evolved considerably by Cambrian time. Although fossils are not found in profusion in most Cambrian rocks, life forms of great variety and in a remarkable state of preservation occur in the shales of Mt. Stephen in eastern British Columbia. Life in the Pre-cambrian era, on the other hand, is known only from structures that resemble primitive plants and from bacteria found in sediments more than 2 billion years old. A number of explanations have been offered for the limited fossil record before the Cambrian period, but the evidence suggests an explosive evolution of life in the early stages of the Cambrian period.

The contrasts between the Cambrian faunas of Wales and the Atlantic Ocean margin of North America, and those of the rest of North America, have been attributed to ecological factors. For example, muddy sediments were predominant in the former areas, and sandy sediments in the latter. Other factors of physical environment that have not been measurably recognized, such as temperatures, may also be involved. At one time, landforms were postulated that would have kept the faunas in segregated provinces, but the faunas have since been found interbedded in some rock successions and somewhat mixed in others. See GEOLOGY–*Geologic Time Scale.*

MARSHALL KAY, *Columbia University*

CAMBRIC, kām'brik, originally a plain-woven linen fabric worn by the clergy in Cambrai, France, is a term now applied to a variety of fabrics finished in the same way as the original. The finest cambric, *typewriter cambric,* is very dense but light enough to register the impressions of typewriter keys. Another fine cambric is made from lawn, a sheer cotton or linen fabric. It is used mostly for handkerchiefs and infant's wear. A coarse cambric made from printcloth is used in making hats and upholstery.

ERNEST B. BERRY, *School of Textiles North Carolina State University*

CAMBRIDGE, kām'brij, the name of several earldoms and dukedoms and a marquessate in the English peerage.

Earls. In 1362, Edmund of Langley (1341–1402), the fifth son of Edward III, was created Earl of Cambridge. His younger son, Richard (died 1415), succeeded to the earldom, but the title was forfeited when he was beheaded at Southampton for conspiracy aaginst Henry V.

Henry (1640–1660), the fourth son of Charles I, was created Earl of Cambridge and Duke of Gloucester in 1659. He died unmarried, and the title became extinct again. In 1698 it was revived as a dignity for the dukes of Hamilton.

Dukes. The dukedom of Cambridge was created for each of four sons of James, Duke of York (afterward James II of England), all of whom died in infancy between 1661 and 1677.

In 1706 a new dukedom of Cambridge was created for George Augustus, prince elector of Hannover, the only son of George I of England. When George Augustus ascended the throne as George II in 1727, the dukedom was merged with the crown. It was created again in 1801 for Adolphus Frederick (1774–1850), the seventh son of George III. He was succeeded as duke by his only son, George William Frederick Charles (1819–1904), who was commander of the British Army from 1856 to 1895. He married a commoner in opposition to the Royal Marriage Act of 1772. Their three sons were denied the hereditary title, and it became extinct.

Marquesses. Adolphus Frederick's second daughter, Mary Adelaide Wilhelmina Elizabeth, married Francis, Prince and Duke of Teck in 1866. Their daughter Mary became the queen consort of George V. Their eldest son, Adolphus Charles Alexander (1868–1927), was created Marquess of Cambridge in 1917 and took the surname of Cambridge. His son, George Frederick Hugh (1895–   ), succeeded him as 2d Marquess.

LESLIE G. PINE, *Former Editor, "Burke's Peerage"*

CAMBRIDGE, kām'brij, a city and municipal borough in England, and the county town of Cambridgeshire, is on the Cam River about 50 miles (80 km) north and slightly east of London. It is the home of Cambridge University, and one of the distinctive features of the city is the intermingling of the academic, residential, and commercial buildings. Supplementing the landscaped university grounds are extensive commons or public open spaces, notably the areas known as Christ's Piece, Parker's Piece, Jesus Green, and Sheep's Green.

After Cambridge became a city in 1951, strict planning controls were instituted to keep it primarily a university city and to prevent the population from exceeding 100,000. (In the late 1960's it had approached that figure.) Within a radius of about 10 miles (16 km) from the city, industrial expansion has been limited, and surrounding villages have been enlarged to accommodate excess population. Cambridge is the main shopping and business center for about 350,000 people living in East Anglia, the region northeast of London. The city has a number of small science-based industries and one large electronics firm. An ancient street plan creates severe traffic problems, but it is felt that drastic alterations would destroy the city's unique character.

History. Cambridge owes much of its historic development to the river Cam. This area became the site for prehistoric settlements when travelers between the regions of East Anglia and the Midlands found a good river crossing at this point. Following the earliest settlers came the Romans and later the Anglo-Saxon invaders. William the Conqueror built a castle here in 1068 of which only the castle mound remains. Cambridge was chartered by Henry I at the beginning of the 12th century and by King John in 1201 and 1207. A mayor is first mentioned in 1231. The university itself probably originated in the early part of the 13th century.

Cambridge developed as an important trading center because the Cam, or Granta River as it is also called, flows north into the Ouse and thence to the North Sea at King's Lynn, about 40 miles (64 km) northeast of Cambridge. During the Middle Ages, King's Lynn (also called Lynn or Lynn Regis) was an important seaport for ships from the continent of Europe and Cambridge was the head of navigation on the Cam.

The oldest secular building in the city, the School of Pythagoras dating from the late 12th century, was owned between 1200 and 1240 by the mayor of Cambridge. At the end of the 15th century, the buildings and grounds of the monasteries were still more extensive than those of the colleges. John Siberch set up the first printing press in Cambridge in 1521 and the first printer for the university began work in 1583. Oliver Cromwell became member of Parliament for Cambridge in 1640. In 1642 he armed the county of Cambridge and secured it for Parliament against the king in the civil war that followed. The great Stourbridge Fair, best known of the medieval fairs and an important element in the mercantile system of eastern Britain until the 18th century, was held in neighboring Barnwell. Addenbrooke's Hospital was opened in 1766 and frequently enlarged until 1966, when its rebuilding began.

In 1801 the population of Cambridge was only 9,276, plus about 800 students. In the half century before the reforms of 1835, the municipal corporation was corrupt and inefficient. The building of the Great Eastern Railway in 1845 disrupted the activities of many of the merchants, who were dependent on the river trade, and caused unemployment and economic distress. The population was now increasing rapidly and in one parish it quintupled in the years between 1821 and 1862.

Historic Churches. There are many ancient and noteworthy churches in Cambridge. The tower of St. Bene't's (or St. Benedict's), dating from the Anglo-Saxon period, is the oldest building in the county. The 12th century Norman Church of the Holy Sepulchre draws many visitors because it is one of only five round churches in England. St. Edward's Church was begun early in the 13th century, and during the 16th century it provided a pulpit for Hugh Latimer, Protestant martyr of the Reformation. The Church of St. Mary-the-Less, erected 1340–1352, has a beautiful east window and a tablet commemorates the Rev. Godfrey Washington (1670–1729), a relative of George Washington. Holy Trinity Church was extensively altered in the 14th century. The parish and university church, Great St. Mary's, stands on the Market Square across from the new Guildhall. Its rebuilding is known to date from 1478. It is one of the finest examples of the Late Perpendicular Gothic style in East Anglia. The melody of its famous quarter-hour chimes, later copied for London's Big Ben and for other clocks throughout the world, was composed in the late 18th century. Population: (1961) 95,527.

F. A. REEVE, *County Councillor, Cambridge*

CAMBRIDGE, kām'brij, a city in eastern Maryland, is the state's second-largest port. It is situated on the south bank of the Choptank River, near the eastern shore of Chesapeake Bay, about 55 miles (88 km) by road southeast of Annapolis. It has extensive fruit, vegetable, fish, oyster, and crab canneries. Other industries include shipbuilding, lumbering, printing, and the manufacture of wire cloth, electronic equipment, clothing, and fertilizer.

Cambridge is the seat of Dorchester county. It was settled in 1684 and incorporated as a city in 1900. It has a mayor and council form of government. Population: 11,595.

CAMBRIDGE, kām'brij, a city in northeastern Massachusetts, in Middlesex county, is just west and north of Boston and separated from it only by the Charles River. From the air the two seem to make up one large metropolitan area, and it is difficult to realize these are two distinct cities, each with its own government, institutions, and character.

Cambridge is the home of Harvard University, the Massachusetts Institute of Technology, Radcliffe College for women (affiliated with Harvard), and the Episcopal Theological School. Its industrial activities, some of which are academically oriented, include research organizations, the manufacture of instruments, photographic equipment, machinery, and electrical equipment, the making of confectionery and food products, and diversified light industries.

History. Cambridge was first referred to in the records of the Massachusetts Bay Colony in 1631 as "the newe towne." It was selected in 1637 to be the seat of a new college that had been authorized the previous year. In 1638 the town was named Cambridge because founders of the college were graduates of that English university. The next year the college was named for John Harvard, a young minister who bequeathed it his small library. In 1639, too, Stephen Day (or Daye) set up the first printing press in the American colonies in Cambridge.

TOM HOLLYMAN, FROM PHOTO RESEARCHERS

A VIEW OF CAMBRIDGE, ENGLAND, with the round Norman Church of the Holy Sepulchre in the foreground.

During the colonial period the town was entirely distinct from Boston. Its farms and handsome country places centered around the college. On Cambridge Common, on July 3, 1775, Gen. George Washington took command of the Continental Army. At the end of the 18th century the population of Cambridge just exceeded 2,000.

The building of the West Boston Bridge in 1793 shortened the 8-mile (13-km) journey between Boston and Cambridge by 5 miles (8 km) and placed Cambridge on the direct route from the farms of Middlesex county to the Boston markets. Other villages—East Cambridge and Cambridgeport—grew up along the road to Boston. Old Cambridge, as it was called, ceased to be the only significant settlement. During the 19th century, however, its population increased by more than 40 times. Cambridge was incorporated as a city in 1846. It continued to expand haphazardly as its farmlands were taken over by industry. In 1912, when Cambridge was connected with Boston by subway, it began to be a "dormitory" suburb for workers in Boston.

Because of the rapid and accidental nature of its growth, Cambridge has little architectural coherence. However, there are a number of historic buildings in the city. Massachusetts Hall,

CAMBRIDGE, Mass., faces the Charles River. Residence buildings for Harvard College students extend along the shore.

HARVARD UNIVERSITY NEWS OFFICE

erected in 1718–1720, is the oldest building in Harvard Yard. Christ Church (1759–1761), facing Cambridge Common, is noted for its fine colonial interior. Along Brattle Street are some handsome 18th century houses. The Craigie-Longfellow House (1759) was Washington's headquarters in 1775 and the home of the poet Henry Wadsworth Longfellow for 45 years until his death in 1882. Elmwood, built in 1767 for the last British lieutenant governor, was the birthplace and home of the poet and diplomat James Russell Lowell (1819–1891). Beautifully landscaped Mount Auburn Cemetery is one of the few green areas in what has become a largely industrial city.

Cambridge has a council-manager form of government. Population: 100,361.

WALTER MUIR WHITEHILL
The Boston Athenæum

CAMBRIDGE, kām'brij, a manufacturing city in east central Ohio, the seat of Guernsey county, is 75 miles (120 km) east of Columbus, on Wills Creek. The surrounding agricultural region produces corn, wheat, and oats and has deposits of coal, pottery clay, oil, and natural gas. Among the city's industries are strip mining and the manufacture of plastics, pottery, glass and glassware, furniture, wood articles, kitchen utensils, spark plugs, small motors, and metal alloys.

About the end of the 18th century, settlers arrived in the area from the island of Guernsey in the Channel Islands, after which the county is named. Cambridge itself was settled and laid out in 1806. It was incorporated as a city in 1837. Manufacturing was established there in the 1880's. Under the charter of 1893, Cambridge is governed by a mayor and council. Population: 13,656.

CAMBRIDGE PLATFORM, a plan of church government agreed upon by representatives of New England churches at a synod held in Cambridge, Mass., in three sessions from 1646 to 1648. It was drawn up by the colonists, who in their new and uncertain environment felt the responsibility to establish positive and unifying standards of church life. The platform served to offset a tendency among dissident church members to appeal to the English Parliament, which until 1647 was predominantly Presbyterian and hostile to the ecclesiastical forms developing in New England. Based on a draft by Richard Mather, and with a preface by John Cotton, the platform was the first church constitution produced in America, and it remained the basis of American Congregationalism for two centuries. See also CONGREGATIONALISTS.

The platform was not designed to describe the true faith, which, as the preface indicates, was believed to have been well set forth in the Westminster Confession, published in 1648. But in contradistinction to Anglicanism and Presbyterianism, the Cambridge constitution holds that the chief temporal authority in the church resides in the local congregations. At the same time, it provides for a fellowship of churches ("The term Independent, wee approve not") for mutual consultation, criticism, and intercommunion. Emphasis is placed on the church covenant, the reciprocal promise that, in response to Christ's presence in their midst, the members of a local church make to Him and to one another. The writers of the platform held strongly to the idea that although the exercise of church power lies with the duly elected officers, the power itself belongs under Christ in the church members.

In the text the ministers of a local church are called *elders*. These are of three kinds: pastors, teachers, and ruling elders. *Deacons* are temporal helpers, who assist at the Lord's Supper and care for the poor.

The Cambridge Platform takes for granted a close relationship between church and state. See also COTTON, JOHN; MATHER, RICHARD.

DOUGLAS HORNTON
Former Dean, Harvard Divinity School

CAMBRIDGE PLATONISTS, kām'brij plā'tə-nists, is the name given to a group of philosophical and religious thinkers that flourished between 1633 and 1688, chiefly at Cambridge University in England. Their center was mainly at Christ's and Emmanuel colleges. The founder of the movement was Benjamin Whichcote. Other leaders were Henry More, Ralph Cudworth, John Smith, Richard Cumberland, Joseph Glanvill, John Norris, and Nathaniel Culverwel.

Beliefs. The point of view of the Cambridge Platonists was liberal, tolerant, and comprehensive. They recognized the merits of opposing schools—Puritan and Catholic, Laudian sacramentalists and Independent Separatists—and even the positive affirmations of non-Christian religions, ancient and modern. They were by conviction Platonists, or even Neoplatonists, and aimed to reconcile faith and reason. The new philosophy of Descartes appealed strongly to some of them, especially its reliance on reason and its use of the simplest postulates (for example, "I think, therefore I am") and its firm rejection of materialism. They completely rejected the political-social views of Thomas Hobbes. Their tendency was toward mysticism and the inner light of immediate religious experience.

The ethical views of the Cambridge group assumed the priority of the distinction between right and wrong, apart from any divine revelation or mandate. The divine revelation is innate in human nature and experience: "The spirit of man is the candle of the Lord," Whichcote wrote. The influence of Plato is obvious: God does what is just; justice is not merely what God commands or does. Nicolas de Malebranche and Jakob Böhme were also favorite contemporary authors, in addition to Descartes. Rejecting the overly rational systems of the Schoolmen, the Platonists also avoided the rigid theological logic and legalistic Biblicism of both Catholicism, as influenced by the Council of Trent, and the current Protestant scholasticism.

They believed in the unity of all truth. They held that faith and reason, if sound, cannot lead to divergent ends, nor can there be one truth in religion and another in science. Human reason can be the voice of God, echoing and interpreting the truths of revelation. Right and wrong are forever opposed, not by divine decree but in the nature of things, like truth and falsehood. They rejected the doctrine of predestination and also that of irresistible grace, believing that free will is indispensable to morality. The redemption takes place within us. Holiness is the only way to God, "without which no one shall see the Lord" (Hebrews 12:14). Characteristically Anglican, they insisted that the essential Christian doctrines are few in number and can be sufficiently understood by reason and therefore need not be accepted implicitly or on faith, relying upon some external authority. Some contemporaries misunderstood this position and labeled them "latitudinarian". The charge was baseless, however; these men were deeply serious and profound believers.

Influence. The academic retirement and composure of 17th century Cambridge—despite the roaring tides of political, social, and religious change and even civil war, in which, by contrast, Oxford was deeply involved—made possible the literary and philosophical writings of the Platonists. But their failure to share in the struggles of the time brought upon them false charges, all the way from Socinianism to atheism. Their legacy to posterity was not a strong and widespread influence but an assured place for toleration and comprehension in the Church of England and elsewhere. The influence of Platonism upon Anglican thought and upon English religious thought in general has long been observed. It still survives wherever English religious thought has spread.

FREDERICK C. GRANT
Union Theological Seminary

Bibliography

Cassirer, Ernst, *Platonische Renaissance in England und die Schule von Cambridge* (Leipzig 1932; Eng. tr. Austin, Tex., 1953).

Colie, Rosalie L., *Light and Enlightenment* (New York 1957).

Inge, William R., *The Platonic Tradition in English Religious Thought* (London 1926).

Powicke, F. J., *The Cambridge Platonists* (Cambridge, Mass., 1926).

Tulloch, J. N., *Rational Theology and Christian Philosophy in England in the 17th Century,* 2 vols., 2d ed. (Edinburgh 1872).

CAMBRIDGE UNIVERSITY, kām′brij, one of the two oldest universities in England, is situated in the municipal borough of Cambridge. Its founding cannot be ascribed to any particular date, although certain historical factors would assign it to the early years of the 13th century.

Origin of the University. In 1209 a number of scholars moved to the town of Cambridge from Oxford because their classes had been suspended. At Cambridge they found an established academic body. Members of several monastic communities—the canons of St. Giles, the convent of St. Radegund, and a number of Augustinian canons—had preceded them and already had attracted a number of students to their monasteries. Certainly by 1226, when first documentary mention is made of a chancellor, there was an organized body of scholars at Cambridge. In 1229 there was an influx of students from the University of Paris.

The students were sufficiently numerous by 1231 for King Henry III to issue writs governing their behavior. Despite these regulations there were serious riots in 1261 involving the university and the town, and new rules had to be set up in 1270 giving the university and the town joint responsibility for maintaining order. Other serious town and gown disturbances, notably in 1381, occurred throughout the Middle Ages.

The earliest students, whose age averaged 14 or 15 years, were first lodged in private houses. Later, they were gathered into hostels, each controlled by a master. Large assemblies were held in Great St. Mary's Church.

A knowledge of elementary Latin was the only requirement for admission. Students began with a three-part course, or *trivium,* comprising grammar, rhetoric, and logic. Each year ended with a disputation on the subject covered. The students then proceeded to the *quadrivium,* or four-part course, in arithmetic, geometry, astronomy, and music. At the end of this program the scholar became a Master of Arts and was qualified to teach.

The student hostels were in time succeeded by colleges, endowed originally to provide accommodations and a small stipend for teachers but expanded by the 16th century to include student residents. Each college was separately endowed and administered. Student academic and social life came under the guidance of tutors, who served as a link between the individual and the university. This concept of a university whose colleges function as independent entities, subject to a very limited control by the university, is still a distinctive feature of Cambridge and Oxford.

Development of the University. Official recognition of Cambridge as a university came in 1318, when a papal bull issued by Pope John XXII decreed that Cambridge should be a *studium generale.* The university was made independent of diocesan jurisdiction, and executive power was vested in the chancellor.

The founding of King's Hall in 1337 by Edward III probably influenced other benefactors to favor Cambridge over Oxford, although the latter was more renowned. Within 35 years seven colleges were established at Cambridge, as opposed to two at Oxford. The divinity school, the first specifically teaching facility, was begun about 1350 and is the oldest existing link with university teaching in the Middle Ages. From the end of the 14th century the general architectural plan of the colleges followed a set pattern, with each college arranged around a court.

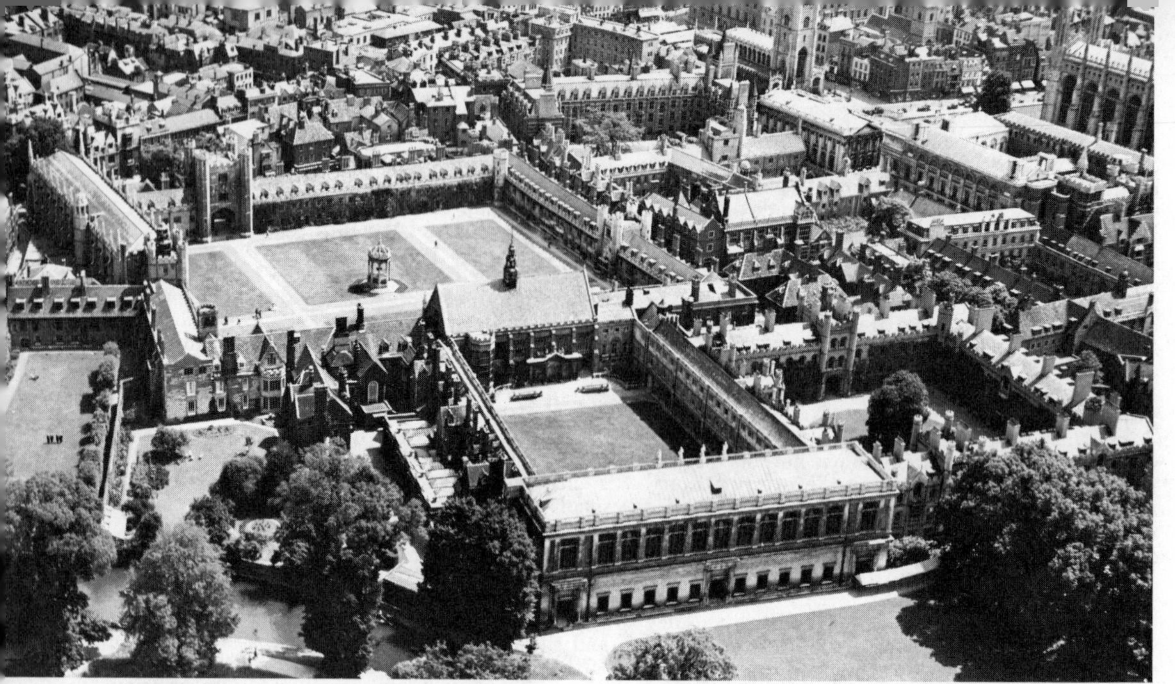

CENTRAL PRESS

CAMBRIDGE UNIVERSITY consists of more than 20 semiautonomous colleges. Trinity College, whose buildings and courtyards are in the center of the photograph, is one of the newer colleges, founded in 1546 by Henry VIII.

In 1441, Henry VI decided to found a college and laid the first stone of King's College chapel in 1446. This chapel is the most magnificent edifice in Cambridge, with superb fan vaulting, the finest woodcarving of its period north of the Alps, and 25 stained-glass windows. The first court of Queens' College, begun in 1448, is the earliest existing quadrangle of real architectural beauty. From 1496, when the convent of St. Radegund was converted into Jesus College, until the early 19th century, subsequent colleges appropriated the sites, buildings, and revenues of suppressed religious houses.

The University and the New Learning. About 1500, John Fisher, master of Michaelhouse, became chaplain to Lady Margaret Beaufort. Fisher persuaded her to enlarge God's House (which became Christ's College in 1505) and to convert the Hospital of St. John to St. John's College in 1511. When he was made the first professor of divinity in 1502, Fisher induced Erasmus to come to Cambridge. Fisher made St. John's the center of Renaissance learning at Cambridge. The university also played a key role in the Reformation in England.

When, in 1546, Henry VIII founded Trinity, the college absorbed Michaelhouse and King's Hall. Trinity's Great Court is the largest of any college in Cambridge or Oxford. Its library is one of Sir Christopher Wren's masterpieces, and its treasures include the first draft of Milton's *Paradise Lost* and manuscripts of William Makepeace Thackeray, Tennyson, and others. Sir Isaac Newton was Lucasian professor of mathematics at Trinity (1661–1696). During his tenure mathematical studies made such advances that they became the sole means of earning an advanced degree. Many innovations were made by Richard Bentley, master of Trinity, and an influential figure during the early 18th century.

In 1570 the university was incorporated and given a constitution, embodied in the Elizabethan Statutes. During the nearly 300 years they remained in force, the statutes dictated the form of government at Cambridge. Power was vested in the heads of the colleges and the vice-chancellor. Membership in the university was limited to students who were affiliated with a college.

The Modern University. By 1760 the average age of entering students had risen to 18 years. Most classes were taught by college tutors. An honors examination was introduced in 1822. The changing pattern of political life in England was reflected in the permission granted to Dissenters in 1858 to take the bachelor's degree. While women students were admitted with the opening of Girton College in 1869, their lectures were given separately. Honors examinations were not opened to women until 1881, and women could not receive degrees until 1923. Full membership was granted them in 1948.

Although Cambridge had been preeminent in mathematics and science since the days of Newton, no college granted a fellowship in science until 1867. From that time on, however, full recognition was given to the sciences. The Cavendish Laboratory for Experimental Physics was built in 1872–1873. Here Joseph J. Thomson presided for 34 years and discovered the electron. Here also J. D. Cockcroft and Ernest Rutherford opened up the new field of nuclear physics.

A new library was built in 1934 to house the university's main collection, including works bequeathed to Cambridge from 1415 on. It has over 2.5 million volumes, 12,000 manuscripts, and 250,000 maps. There are also numerous college libraries and more than 50 special libraries.

Government. Cambridge's first constitution, the Elizabethan Statutes, was promulgated in 1570. As mentioned above, these statutes placed the governing power in the hands of the vice-chancellor and the heads of the colleges. The code was effective until the Cambridge University Act of 1856. The new act shifted effective government to the council of the senate, comprising the chancellor, the vice-chancellor, and 16 graduates elected by regent house (the teaching staff), and it provided for the writing of new

THE COLLEGES OF CAMBRIDGE UNIVERSITY
(Listed in order of founding)

Peterhouse: founded in 1284 by Hughe de Balsham, Bishop of Ely.
Clare: founded in 1326 by Richard de Badew as University Hall; refounded in 1336 by Lady Elizabeth de Burgh, granddaughter of Edward I.
Pembroke: founded in 1347 by Mary de St. Paul, widow of the Earl of Pembroke.
Gonville and Caius: founded in 1348 by Edmund Gonville as Gonville Hall; removed to its present site in 1353 by William Bateman, Bishop of Norwich; enlarged in 1558 by John Caius.
Trinity Hall: founded in 1350 by William Bateman.
Corpus Christi: founded in 1352 by the Cambridge guilds of Corpus Christi and the Blessed Virgin Mary.
King's: founded in 1441 by Henry VI.
Queens': founded in 1446 by Andrew Dockett as the College of St. Bernard; refounded and renamed in 1448 by Queen Margaret, consort of Henry VI; refounded in 1465 by Elizabeth Woodville, consort of Edward IV.
St. Catharine's: founded in 1473 by Robert Wodelarke, provost of King's.
Jesus: founded in 1496 by John Alcock, Bishop of Ely.
Christ's: founded by Lady Margaret Beaufort, mother of Henry VII; Christ's College was the enlarged successor to God's House, which had been established in 1448 by Henry VI.
St. John's: founded in 1511 by Lady Margaret Beaufort; it absorbed the Hospital of St. John, founded about 1135.
Magdalene: founded in 1542 by Thomas, Baron Audley of Walden.
Trinity: founded in 1546 by Henry VIII; it absorbed both Michaelhouse, founded in 1324 by Hervey de Stanton, and King's Hall, founded in 1337 by Edward III.
Emmanuel: founded in 1548 by Sir Walter Mildmay, privy councillor to Queen Elizabeth I.
Sidney Sussex: founded in 1596 under the will of Lady Frances Sidney.
Downing: founded in 1800 by Sir George Downing.
Fitzwilliam: founded in 1869 as Fitzwilliam Hall and later known as Fitzwilliam House.
Girton: founded in 1869 at Hitchin and moved to Cambridge in 1873.
Newnham: founded in 1871.
Selwyn: founded in 1882 in memory of George Augustus Selwyn, first Anglican bishop of New Zealand.
Hughes Hall: founded in 1885.
New Hall: founded in 1954.
Churchill: founded in 1960 as a memorial to Sir Winston Churchill.

There are other student centers for those not directly affiliated with a college. Darwin (founded in 1964), University (1965), and Clare Hall (1966) are approved foundations for graduate students of either sex. The Lucy Cavendish Collegiate Society (1965) is for women graduate students only. St. Edmund's House (1896), a resident foundation, was given collegiate status in 1965, which gave its students the privilege of membership in the university, a status previously reserved to members of a college.

statutes. By 1871, religious tests, except for divinity degrees, had been eliminated.

At the suggestion of a commission, appointed in 1919 to resolve the question of funding, a statutory commission was named in 1923 to revise the financial structure and effect other reforms. As approved in 1926 and revised in 1927 and 1928, the statutes proposed by this commission now govern the university.

The university now receives an annual grant from the Treasury. All legislative power rests with regent house. University functions have been more rigidly organized. Most teaching comes from the university rather than the colleges.

Organization and Programs. The nominal head of the university is the chancellor, usually a distinguished nonresident member, elected for life. The senate, comprising the doctors and masters of all faculties and bachelors of divinity, is the supreme governing body, acting through regent house. The colleges are self-governing. In addition to the master and fellows, college officials include lecturers and directors of studies, bursars, deans, a praelector, and tutors.

Candidates for the university apply to the particular college they wish to attend. The college accepts or rejects students on the basis of character and ability to pass the "previous," or entrance, examination.

Each entering student is assigned to a tutor, who is the keystone of the college system at Cambridge. He serves as the chief link between the student and the college, and is both his mentor and personal guardian.

The student can work toward an ordinary or an honors degree. For an ordinary degree he must pass a general and a special examination. For an honors degree he must pass a tripos (so called because originally the examiner sat on a three-legged stool during the examination). The tripos may consist of one part (as in Anglo-Saxon) or as many as four parts (as in the Natural Sciences).

Six years after entering the university, the scholar can obtain a master of arts degree simply by paying certain fees and by being presented to the vice-chancellor by the praelector. No examination is required and no academic advance is achieved. The only stipulation is that at least two years have elapsed since the B. A. was obtained. For a doctoral degree, however, the scholar must "give proof of distinction by some original contribution to the advancement of Science or of Learning," and prepare a thesis.

The academic year covers three terms: Michaelmas (October 1–December 19), Lent (January 5–March 25), and Easter (April 16–June 24). Students who plan to take a degree must spend nine terms in residence. Affiliated students from other institutions can obtain a shortened residence requirement and, in certain subjects, omit the first part of their tripos.

Faculties. There are 20 major faculties and 4 independent departments. They comprise: classics, divinity, English, fine arts, modern and medieval languages, music, Oriental studies, economics and politics, history, law, moral science, engineering, geography and geology, mathematics, physics and chemistry, agriculture, archaeology and anthropology, biology A (botany and zoology), biology B (anatomy, biochemistry, pathology), and medicine. The independent departments are education, estate management, chemical engineering, and the observatories.

Student Body. In a student population of about 10,000 there are ten times as many men as women. Graduate students compose one fifth of the student body.

F. A. Reeve, *Author of "Cambridge"*

Further Reading: *Commonwealth Universities Yearbook* (London, annually); Reeve, F. A., *Cambridge* (New York 1964); Roberts, Sydney C., *Introduction to Cambridge*, 5th ed. (New York 1948).

CAMBRIDGE UNIVERSITY PRESS

CAMBRIDGE UNIVERSITY PRESS, kām-brij, the printing and publishing house of the University of Cambridge, England. A university department, the press is governed by the vice chancellor of the university and a group of senior faculty members.

Books were first printed at Cambridge under the university's aegis in 1521 by John Siberch, a friend of Erasmus. In 1534, Henry VIII formally authorized the university to publish books, and the press has operated continuously since 1583. Offices were established in London in 1873 and in New York in 1949.

Throughout its long history, in fulfillment

of the university's function of serving "education, religion, learning, and research," the Cambridge University Press has published textbooks, Bibles, works of scholarship, and journals. It brought out the Geneva Version of the Bible in 1591, and in 1629 the King James Version, which it has published ever since. In 1707 the press began publishing the work of Isaac Newton under the guidance of Richard Bentley, master of Trinity College, who greatly expanded the scope of the press. Since then it has maintained a tradition of publishing outstanding scientists, such as Rutherford, Whitehead, Russell, Eddington, and Gamow.

CAMBRIDGESHIRE, kăm'brij-shir, a county of eastern England, was formerly two administrative counties, Cambridgeshire (south) and the Isle of Ely (north). They were united in 1965.

The south is a gently rolling country of mainly chalky soils to the south and east, and Cretaceous, Jurassic, and glacial clays to the west. The north, or fenland, is a dead level of peaty and silty alluvium, broken by low islands of Jurassic clay. It was once waterlogged and desolate, but drainage works begun in the 17th century and extended between 1954 and 1964 have made it a land of rich fertility. The principal rivers of the county are the Nene and the Great Ouse and the Cam.

Predominantly arable, Cambridgeshire is one of the foremost agricultural regions of Britain. Principal crops are wheat, sugar beet, barley (in the south), and potatoes (in the north). Fruit and vegetables, especially carrots and celery, are grown in many sections. Thoroughbred horses are raised near the Newmarket racecourse. Industries include the manufacture of bricks, cement, paper, containers, pesticides, jams, sugar, and canned goods. There are also various highly skilled science-based industries.

The principal towns of the county are Cambridge, Wisbech, and March. The university city of Cambridge is the county town. Although the county is wholly inland, Wisbech, on the tidal Nene, is a seaport. Ely, with its magnificent Norman cathedral, is the seat of a bishop. Population: (1966) of the county, 294,010.

JOHN SALTMARSH, *Cambridge University*

CAMBYSES, kam-bī'sēz, was the name of two monarchs of the Achaemenian dynasty of Persia.

CAMBYSES I was king of Anshan, ancestral home of the Achaemenid kings, from about 602 to 559 B.C. A vassal of Media, he was married to the daughter of Astyages, the Median king. His son was Cyrus the Great (q.v.).

CAMBYSES II was king of Persia from 529 to 522 B.C. He was the son of Cyrus the Great and during Cyrus' reign ruled Babylon (538–530). After succeeding his father, Cambyses in 525 carried out the invasion of Egypt that Cyrus had planned. He defeated Psamtik (Psammetichus) III at Pelusium and captured Memphis and Heliopolis, whereupon Egyptian resistance collapsed. Cambyses treated Psamtik leniently at first, but executed him after an Egyptian revolt (523 B.C.).

Cambyses planned a number of further expeditions. He led one against Ethiopia that conquered large areas but had to withdraw for lack of supplies. He sent a force to conquer the oasis of Ammon, but it perished in a sandstorm. He organized an expedition against Carthage that never set out because the Phoenician sailors refused to attack their kinsmen.

Herodotus says that Cambyses in fits of madness committed atrocities in Egypt. But Egyptian sources of that time paint a different picture, suggesting that Herodotus' account was hostile to Cambyses. He certainly placated the Egyptians and their gods initially, but may have become less tolerant later. He probably was vain, cruel, and violent-tempered.

According to Darius, Cambyses on his accession had his brother Bardiya (Smerdis) murdered and concealed his death. In 522 a Magian priest named Gaumata seized the Persian throne, claiming to be Bardiya. Cambyses set out for Persia, but died in Syria, by accident or suicide (accounts differ). Gaumata was soon overthrown by seven Persian nobles led by Darius (q.v.).

D. J. BLACKMAN, *Bristol University, England*

CAMDEN, Earls and Marquess of. See PRATT, SIR CHARLES.

CAMDEN, William (1551–1623), English authority on ancient Britain, who is best remembered for his *Britannia,* a work of topographical and antiquarian research that both illustrated and nurtured the new interest in British antiquities that was one of the results of the Renaissance. His interests, travels, and friendly disposition made him the focus of a circle of like-minded acquaintances that developed into the first English Society of Antiquaries.

Camden was born in London on May 2, 1551, and, despite family poverty, received a good education at Christ's Hospital, St. Paul's, and Oxford. Later he taught at Westminster School, and in 1593 he became its headmaster. In 1597 he was appointed Clarenceux king of arms, a state office that gave him financial independence, until his death at Chislehurst, Nov. 9, 1623.

The *Britannia* was first published in 1586 in Latin; after five further successively enlarged editions, an English translation by Philemon Holland was published in 1610. It is difficult to overrate the book's influence during the next two centuries. It illustrated a scientific approach to history based on evidence rather than legend; the Trojan theory of British origins was thus finally buried. Camden was particularly interested in the evidence of existing place-names and their relationship with those recorded in classical texts. But he added to his sources by recording the inscriptions on Celtic coins and by collecting Roman inscriptions as well as genealogical and other information. His tours in search of material give his work a freshness and authority much in contrast to the cloistered compilations of earlier writers. He was also author of a history of Elizabeth's reign, a Greek grammar, and an edition of chronicles. In 1622 he founded the Camden chair of ancient history at Oxford.

S. S. FRERE, *Oxford University*
Author of "Britannia"

CAMDEN, a city in southern Arkansas and the seat of Ouachita county, is situated at the head of navigation of the Ouachita River, 83 miles (139 km) southwest of Little Rock. Camden manufactures paper products, bottled soft drinks, furniture, and pottery. It is the trading center for an area producing oil and natural gas and raising cotton, corn, and poultry. Government is by mayor and council. Population: 15,147.

CAMDEN, kam′dən, is a resort and industrial center on the coast of Maine, in Knox county. It is situated on the western shore of Penobscot Bay. A picturesque harbor, filled with yachts and other pleasure boats in summer, and a waterfront park with an outdoor theater are prominent features of the town. The Camden Hills, which rise in a semicircle around it, are noted for recreation areas, including Camden Hills State Park. Skiing and other winter sports are popular. Industrial products include boats, millwork, leather, and yarns and textiles.

Camden was settled in 1769 and incorporated as a town (township) in 1791. Government is by town manager. Population: 4,115.

CAMDEN, kam′dən, is an industrial city and port in southwestern New Jersey, the seat of Camden county. It is situated on the Delaware River, opposite Philadelphia, Pa., with which it is connected by two highway bridges. Camden is a major commercial, industrial, and transportation center. Leading industries include soup canning, shipbuilding, and the manufacture of radio, television, and phonograph sets, missile and communications systems, chemicals, paints, and fountain pens. The College of South Jersey, a coeducational division of Rutgers, is in the city.

Camden was the home of the poet Walt Whitman from 1873 until his death in 1892. His house, now a museum maintained by the state, contains original furnishings, mementos, and writings of the poet. Whitman is buried in Harleigh Cemetery, Camden. The Camden County Historical Museum, in Charles S. Boyer Memorial Hall, has exhibits of local history.

The site of Camden was discovered in 1631 by David Pietersen De Vries, a Dutch colonizer. A Swedish colony was established here in 1638, and in 1680, William Cooper, a Quaker, settled on a bluff at the point of the river and called it Pyne Poynte. One of the Cooper houses, built in 1709, still stands in Pyne Poynt Park. Jacob Cooper, a descendant of William, platted the community in 1773, naming it after Charles Pratt, the first Earl of Camden, who opposed taxation of the American colonies. Camden was incorporated as a city in 1828. It is governed by a mayor and council. Population: 102,551.

MARGARET M. HEWITT
Camden Free Public Library

CAMDEN, kam′dən, a city in north central South Carolina, is on the east side of the Wateree River, about 30 miles (48 km) northeast of Columbia. It is the seat of Kershaw county. Diversified industries, tourism, agriculture, and forestry are the economic base of the area. Camden's industries produce clothing, chemicals, textile fibers, watches, building stone, lumber products, fabricated steel equipment, cement blocks, sand, and gravel. The city is a horse-training center and has long been a winter resort for fox hunters and other equestrian sportsmen.

Camden is the oldest inland city in South Carolina. It was named Fredericksburgh in 1732 and Pine Tree Hill in 1758 and was renamed in 1768 for Lord Camden (Charles Pratt), a champion of colonial rights in the British parliament. As the principal British garrison in the interior, it had a major role in the American Revolution; two battles took place in the immediate vicinity. Camden has a mayor and council form of government. Population: 8,532.

CAMDEN, Battle of, kam′dən, an engagement in the American Revolution, fought on Aug. 16, 1780, about 25 miles (40 km) northeast of Columbia, S. C. The American troops were crushed by the British in the battle. The defeat halted Gen. Horatio Gates' counteroffensive against the British, who had overrun Georgia and South Carolina.

Gates, who had become American commander in the South on July 25, decided to march against Rawdon's 1,300-man force at Camden, S. C. Gates had 3,052 men, more than two thirds of whom were militia. Unknown to Gates, however, Lord Cornwallis reached Camden on August 13 and brought the British forces there to 2,239. As day broke on August 16, Gates saw the British advancing toward his right wing. He ordered the Virginia militia on his left to attack, but they were soon routed. Then the American regulars on his right were overwhelmed by the superior British forces. The patriots suffered nearly 1,000 casualties and the British only about 300.

PAUL C. BOWERS, JR., *The Ohio State University*

CAMEL, kam′əl, a large, humpbacked ungulate mammal, first domesticated by man in prehistoric times. Two species are recognized: the heavily built, two-humped Bactrian camel, which inhabits the deserts of central Asia, and the single-humped Arabian camel, or dromedary, which is widespread throughout the Middle East, India, and North Africa. Neither species has been much modified by man. The Bactrian camel, living in regions where the winters are very cold, has a longer, darker winter coat, and its legs are shorter. An adult Bactrian seldom measures more than 7 feet (2 meters) from the ground to the top of the humps—about the height of the shoulder in the taller and more slender dromedary.

Physical Characteristics. Camels have even-toed, digitigrade feet (that is, the posterior of the foot is raised). The third and fourth toes are united by thick, fleshy pads and tipped with nail-like hooves. Horny pads on the chest and knees support the body when the camel kneels; these pads are present in the newborn calf. The limbs and neck of the camel are elongated, the upper lip is cleft, and the ears are small.

Although they chew the cud, camels differ from most true ruminants in that the adults retain two incisor teeth in the upper jaw. They also differ in the lack of an omasum, or third section, to their stomach. The smooth-walled rumen, or anterior section of the stomach, has diverticula (small sacs) opening out from it. The diverticula were formerly called "water sacs" because of a now-discarded theory (which appeared in Pliny's *Natural History*) that the camel stores water in them. Actually, the fluid in these glandular sacs has the same salt content as the rest of the body, looks like green pea soup, and is quite repulsive. To the desert traveler without water, however, any fluid seems attractive, and it is quite possible that the many tales of people who have saved their lives by killing their camels to drink this fluid are true. Other internal differences of the camel include the absence of a gall bladder and the presence of oval red blood corpuscles, which are not found in other mammals.

The hump of the camel is a food store which, because it is concentrated in one large deposit and not distributed as a subcutaneous layer of fat, allows the rest of the body to lose heat more rapidly. The notion that the camel stores water in its hump, or that the fat of which the hump is composed is itself a water store, is erroneous. On oxidation the fat does produce metabolic water, but the extra oxygen used in the process involves in turn an extra loss of water through the lungs, just about canceling any water gain from oxidation.

Behavior. The camel is a very phlegmatic animal and has a reputation for stupidity and obstinacy. The males are quarrelsome during the rutting season and bite savagely when they fight. The dromedary has a pronounced rutting season at the time of the rains in winter; pregnancy is prolonged for nearly a year until the following rainfall. The Bactrian has an even longer gestation period of 370 to 440 days. In both species the young are born singly and suckled for three or four months, and the interval between births is two years. Camels are full-grown at 16 or 17 years; the normal life span is about 25 years.

Droves of wild Bactrian camels in the Gobi desert consist of one or two males and three to five females. They sleep at night in open spaces and graze during the day on grasses, brushwood, and scrub, migrating to the northern part of the range in spring and returning southward in autumn. Camels mate in January and February.

Pace. When moving fast, camels pace. That is, they raise both legs on the same side of the body and advance them simultaneously. A speed of about 6 mph (10 kph) may be achieved, but it cannot be maintained for more than a few hours. The normal walking speed of a fast dromedary used for racing by Bedouins is 3.5 mph (5.5 kph), and its maximum speed is approximately 10 mph (16 kph). A camel cannot gallop for more than a few yards, however. In order to keep a racing camel at its fastest pace—the long trot—the rider must cultivate a rankling sore on its neck and prick it constantly.

Body Water and Heat Regulation. Besides the heavy eyelids and lashes and the slit nostrils that protect it against desert winds, a camel's body exhibits many special adaptations to life in hot, dry regions. Thus, camels have unusually low metabolic rates. They can exist on dry food for two weeks or more, depending on the temperature, because they tolerate a much greater depletion in body water than most other mammals. A camel may lose about 30% of its weight in body water without ill effects, as compared to about 12% in man. During periods of desiccation the blood of most mammals becomes increasingly viscous; it therefore circulates more and more slowly, until it cannot carry away metabolic body heat to the skin quickly enough, leading to "explosive heat death." This is avoided in camels by a physiological mechanism that ensures that water is lost from the body tissues alone, while the blood's water content remains fairly constant.

THE BACTRIAN CAMEL lives in central Asia.

GEORGE HOLTON, FROM PHOTO RESEARCHERS

The camel does not lose its appetite during periods of desiccation, and can graze over a wide area away from water. When presented with water after a moderate dry period, it takes in, at one time, as much water as was lost—a camel can drink 25 gallons (100 liters) or more in a very short time. The body fluids rapidly become diluted to an extent that could not be tolerated by other mammals, which would die from water intoxication even if they took in a much smaller amount.

Because of its ability to lose water from body tissues alone, and because of its relatively small surface area, the camel can afford to sweat. The coarse hair on the back is well ventilated, allowing the evaporation of sweat to occur on the skin and provide maximum cooling. (The hair also acts as a barrier to the sun's radiation and slows the conduction of heat from the environment.) Undue water loss from sweating is avoided because the camel's temperature can vary over a range greater than that of other mammals. In the North African summer a camel may have a morning temperature of 34° C (93° F), and an afternoon maximum of 40.7° C (105.3° F). Sweating does not commence until the higher temperature is reached; therefore the camel is able to store heat during the day, which can be lost at night without expense of water.

The rate of urine flow is low in camels, and little water is lost with the feces. Moreover, investigations of kidney function in the camel have revealed an extremely low secretion of urea when its food is low in protein. The camel, like most ruminants, can utilize urea for microbial synthesis of protein—a valuable asset to animals that have to exist on low-grade diets in deserts.

Thus, the adaptations of the camel to its hot environment do not involve independence from drinking water but the ability to economize the water available and to tolerate wider variations in body temperature and water content. In winter, when the temperature is comparatively low and water is not needed for heat regulation, camels become independent of drinking water for periods of several months.

Domestication. The dromedary had been domesticated on the borders of Arabia by 1800 B.C., a fact confirmed by the finding of Middle Bronze Age remains of camels at ancient urban sites in Israel. Dromedaries were subsequently introduced to North Africa, the Nile Valley, and the Middle East as far as northwestern India. They appeared in the Roman arenas about 29 B.C. and were later used in chariot races. In modern times 20 of the animals were imported into Australia as carriers for the ill-fated Burke-Wills expedition which crossed the Australian continent

DROMEDARY CAMELS on parade in the Republic of Chad, in equatorial Africa. The dromedary camel, which has one hump, can carry two riders at a rapid pace.

CARL FRANK

in 1860–1861, and the descendants of these camels still live there. Dromedaries were also used in the United States after the Mexican War of the 1840's, on mail and express routes across the newly acquired arid regions, but they were later killed.

Less is known of the history of the Bactrian camel. Remains found at Shah Tepe in Iran and at Anau in Turkestan, dating from about 3000 B.C., have been tentatively assigned to this species. It probably had a wide distribution as a wild animal in central and northwestern Asia in prehistoric times. By the 6th century B.C., Bactrians were domesticated in Persia.

Camels have often been used militarily. For example, a military camel corps was formed for the Gordon relief expedition of 1884–1885, and the French Saharan Camel Corps was largely responsible for the pacification of Algeria during the 19th century. About 3 million camels were used in World war I, and 50,000 in World War II.

Camels are still of great importance in desert countries as beasts of burden. A dromedary can carry 600 pounds (270 kg) for 30 miles (50 km) in a day, and a bactrian can carry up to 1,000 pounds (450 kg). Camel hair is used for making clothes, tents, and carpets. The milk is nutritious, the flesh tastes somewhat like beef, and the liver is considered a delicacy.

Evolution. Unlike other mammals of the order Artiodactyla, camels and llamas (suborder Tylopoda, family Camelidae) have remained a separate stock since Upper Eocene times, 43 million years ago. The Eocene *Protylopus* was small and short-limbed, but camel-like animals became more numerous during the Oligocene. Increase of size and development of special features can be traced through such later types as *Procamelus* of the Upper Miocene, the gazelle-camel *Stenomylus*, and the long-necked giraffe-camels *Oxydactylus* and *Alticamelus*.

The camel family originally flourished in North America but became extinct there in the Middle Pleistocene, less than 2 million years ago. The suborder was unknown in other continents until the coming of desert conditions in the Pliocene, about 10 million years ago, when forms with digitigrade and padded feet entered South America, Asia, and Africa.

Living members of the Camelidae (genera *Camelus, Lama,* and *Vicugna*) include *C. bactrianus*, the Bactrian camel; *C. dromedarius*, the dromedary; *L. glama*, the llama; *L. pacos*, the alpaca; *L. guanicoe*, the guanaco; and *V. vicugna*, the vicuña.

J. L. CLOUDSLEY-THOMPSON
University of Khartoum, Sudan

Further Reading: Cloudsley-Thompson, John L., and Chadwick, Michael J., *Life in Deserts* (London 1964); Lull, Richard S., *Organic Evolution*, rev. ed. (New York 1959); Schmidt-Nielsen, Knut, *Desert Animals* (New York 1964); Zeuner, Friedrich E., *A History of Domesticated Animals* (London 1963).

CAMEL CRICKET. See CAVE CRICKET.

CAMELIDAE. See CAMEL.

CAMELLIA, kə-mēl'yə, an evergreen shrub or small tree of the tea family (Theaceae) native to Asia and cultivated extensively in mild climates.

Camellia (C. *japonica*)

LEWIS P. WATSON, FROM BLACK STAR

In North America camellias are grown outdoors in the states along the Atlantic and Gulf coasts from Virginia to Texas and along the Pacific coast from California to British Columbia.

Camellias are prized for their bright glossy foliage and their showy, waxy, long-lasting blooms. They are unsurpassed as flowering shrubs in lightly or even densely shaded areas. Flowering may occur from September into April.

The three species commonly cultivated—*Camellia japonica, C. sasanqua,* and *C. reticulata*—are native to Japan and China. *C. japonica,* which may grow 30 feet (9 meters) high in its native forests, has many varieties and, horticulturally, is the most important species. *C. sasanqua,* a hardier plant, also has many horticultural varieties; it blooms from September into December. *C. reticulata,* which may grow 20 feet (6 meters) high and bears dark rose-colored blooms, is less widely grown.

Camellia seed germinates readily, and varieties of *C. japonica* and *C. sasanqua* are propagated easily by cuttings. *C. reticulata* varieties are usually grafted onto *C. japonica.*

R. C. ALLEN
Kingwood Center, Mansfield, Ohio

CAMELOT, kam'ə-lot, in the Arthurian legends, was the place where King Arthur of Britain held his court and where the Round Table was located. Some versions say that both Camelot and another site called Caerleon were capitals of Arthur's court at different times of year.

The legends of Arthur's court have been used by many writers, notably by Tennyson in *The Idylls of the King.* A popular retelling of the story is T. H. White's *The Once and Future King,* on which Alan Jay Lerner and Frederick Loewe based their musical comedy *Camelot.* See also ARTHURIAN ROMANCES.

Whether the legend of Camelot has any basis in fact is disputed. Some amateur archaeologists have claimed that excavations show that a court center was located in South Cadbury, southwest of London, which may have been the site of Camelot.

CAMEMBERT. See CHEESE.

CAMEO, kam'ē-ō, a gemstone with its surface carved in relief. Cameos are usually made of stratified stones or shells because these give the relief cut in the top layer a background of a contrasting color. The best materials for cameos are various forms of chalcedonic minerals (chalcedony, sardonyx, onyx, agate), though they are also made of shells, glass, or porcelain.

Cameo cutting is believed to have originated in the ancient Middle East. It achieved unusual artistic distinction in classical Rome and during the Renaissance, in the baroque 17th century, and in the late 18th and early 19th centuries.

Classical Rome. The art of cameo cutting flourished in the first half of the 1st century A. D., particularly in the work of Dioskourides. Among the outstanding cameos surviving from this period are portraits of Roman emperors and empresses and representations of mythological themes. Large cameos were favored; the *Gemma Augustea* (1st century A. D.; Vienna Kunsthistorisches Museum) is about 7 by 9 inches (18 by 23 cm).

Renaissance. A revival in cameo cutting, both of hard stone and of shell, took place in the 15th century in Italy, particularly in Rome, Florence, and Milan. Artists of this period emulated the cameo cutters of classical antiquity so successfully that Italian Renaissance work is frequently difficult to date. Pagan themes were much more popular than Christian ones. Old cameos, especially portraits, were sometimes reworked, making dating particularly difficult.

THE METROPOLITAN MUSEUM OF ART—THE MILTON WEIL COLLECTION

A CAMEO, on which is portrayed *The Education of Bacchus,* carved in Italy in the early 19th century.

The Italian style of cameo cutting spread throughout Europe. Matteo del Nassaro (1515–1547), who settled in France, trained several of the leading French cameo cutters. Spain, Austria, Germany, and England also developed skilled cameo cutters through contact with Italy.

Baroque Period. Baroque cameos are generally larger than those of the Renaissance, with a more expressive style and greater movement. The baroque predilection for naturalism and its disdain for the confines of a frame had little effect on cameo cutting, however. Portraits and classical themes continued to dominate the art.

Late 18th Century. In the late 1700's and early 1800's, cameo cutting enjoyed a short but brilliant revival, dominated in Italy by Giovanni Pichler (1734–1791) and in England by Nathaniel Marchant (1755–1812) and Benedetto Pistrucci (1784–1855), the last great specialist in this medium. Most of the cameos of this period are, strictly speaking, intaglios (the design is incised in, or hollowed out of, the top layer of stone, rather than carved in relief). This period also produced many copyists, imitators of the antique, and forgers. These supplied the innumerable collectors and patrons, many of whom were satisfied with hackneyed shell cameos of a kind that persist in commercial production.

CAMERA

CONTENTS

Section	Page	Section	Page
1. Still Cameras	265	2. Motion-Picture Cameras	272
Parts of a Camera	265	Parts of a Motion-Picture Camera	272
Kinds of Still Cameras	270	Kinds of Motion-Picture Cameras	275
Equipment and Accessories	271	3. Special-Purpose Cameras	276
Selecting a Camera	272		

CAMERA. The basic function of a camera is to record a permanent image on a piece of film. When light enters a camera, it passes through a lens and converges on the film. It forms a latent image on the film by chemically altering the silver halides contained in the film emulsion. When the film is developed, the image becomes visible in the form of a negative. From the negative a positive image, or print, can be made.

Since the time of the invention of the first camera, all cameras have operated on the same fundamental principles. As photographic technology developed, however, various camera functions underwent improvement. Thus, while the basic concept of the camera remains the same today, a wide range of accessories have been created to cope with special situations. In addition, special-purpose cameras have been developed that meet a variety of needs.

1. Still Cameras

All still cameras are designed to do one thing: to capture one single instant in time and space on film. Although there are many different kinds, they all have the same basic design.

PARTS OF A CAMERA

The basic parts of a camera are a lighttight body, or box, and a lens. In addition to the fundamental lens and body, a camera has a shutter, a film-holding and -transport system, focusing and viewfinding systems, and sometimes a system for determining length of exposure.

Camera Body. The simplest camera body is the one designed for the snapshot camera. It holds the lens in a fixed position at one end and the film, under lightproof conditions, at the other. In simple cameras the distance between lens and film remains fixed, but in more advanced cameras it is possible to vary the distance between the lens and film plane for precise focusing. The camera body can range in size from the minute subminiature, the inside diameter of which may measure less than 1 inch (2.5 cm), to extremely large special-purpose machines used for cartography and engraving.

Lens. The function of the lens is to gather light and focus it on the film. A lens provides an angle of view that depends on its focal length (the distance between lens and film plane when the camera is focused on a distant object) and on the film size. On a 35mm camera, for example, a 50mm lens will provide an angle of view of 45° on the horizontal. A 100mm lens has an angle of view of 22°, while a 500mm lens covers a scant 5°. Conversely a 35mm lens covers an area of about 62° and a 28mm lens encompasses 74°. One of the most fascinating is the 8mm fisheye with a coverage of 180°.

Normal Lenses. The normal lens for a 35mm camera—a camera that uses 35mm film and pro-

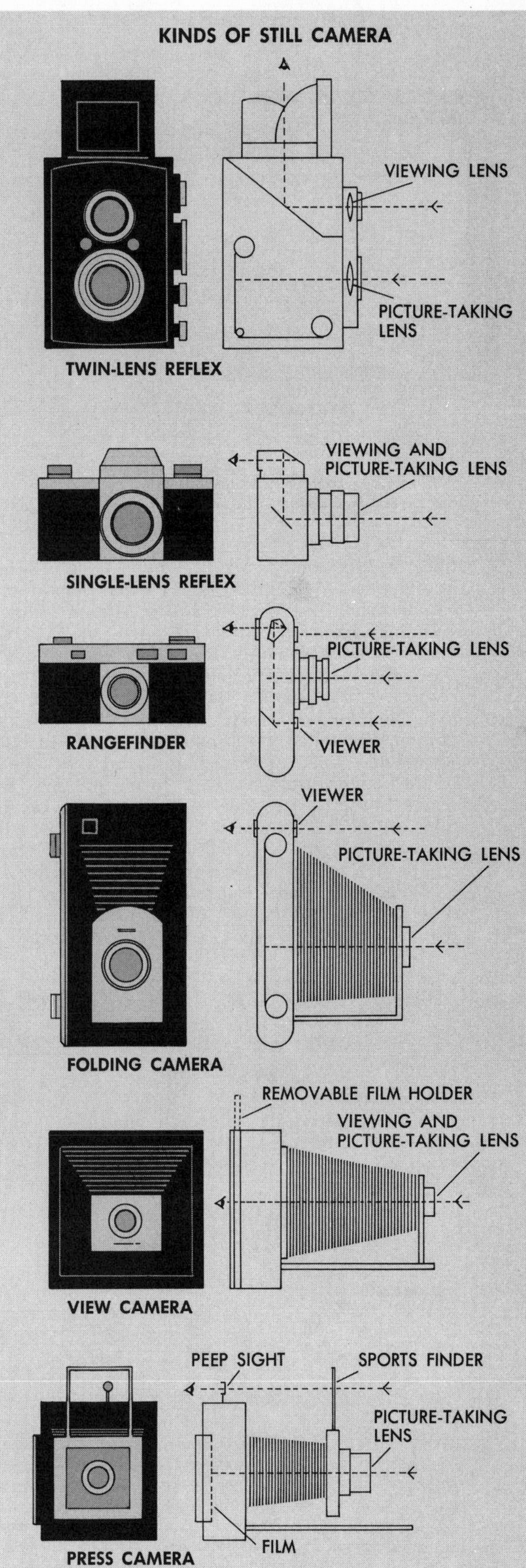

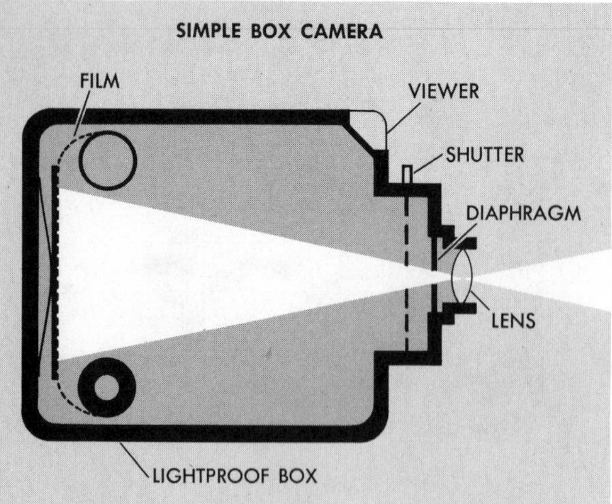

A simple box camera has one lens opening and one shutter speed; the distance between lens and film is fixed.

duces a 24 x 36mm (1 x 1½ inch) negative—has a 50mm focal length. The normal lens for a camera using 4 x 5 inch (100 x 125mm) film is 135mm. Since the angle of view of the two lenses is approximately the same, they provide the same area coverage of the image on their respective film sizes. The image on the 4 x 5 inch film will, of course, be larger than on the 35mm. But when a 135mm lens is used in both 35mm and 4 x 5 inch cameras, and the subject is the same distance away in each case, the image of the subject will be the same size on the films in both cameras. The 135mm lens will, however, provide a much wider angle of view on the 4 x 5 camera than on the 35mm camera.

Wide-Angle and Telephoto Lenses. Any lens with a focal length that is shorter than is normal for a given film size is considered a wide-angle lens. Thus, a 35mm lens for a 35mm camera would be a wide-angle, as would a 90mm lens for a 4 x 5 inch camera. A wide-angle lens produces a smaller image of a subject at a given distance than does a normal lens, but it provides a wider angle of view. A telephoto lens, on the other hand, is one of greater than normal focal length; it produces a larger image of a subject at a given distance than does a normal lens, but its angle of view is narrower. A 135mm lens, for example, would be considered a telephoto for a 35mm camera, while a 250mm lens would be considered a telephoto for a 4 x 5 inch camera.

Zoom Lenses. A zoom lens provides a wide range of focal lengths within a single lens. A control on the outside of the lens allows the photographer to choose a particular focal length by changing the relationship of the lens elements. Zoom lenses usually offer a range of focal lengths of about two or three to one. Typical ranges are 36 to 85mm (1½ to 3⅓ inches).

Relative Aperture. Practically all modern lenses are equipped with a variable diaphragm that controls the amount of light admitted to the film. The opening, or aperture, of the diaphragm is expressed as a fraction of the focal length of the lens. The resulting fractions, or relative apertures, are marked in a series of numbers, such as f/1.9, f/2.8, f/4, f/5.6, f/8, f/11, and f/16, around the rim of the lens mount. All lenses set at the same aperture provide the same image brightness at the film. At a diaphragm setting of f/5.6, for example, a 135mm lens permits the same amount of light to reach the film as a 50mm lens set at the same opening designation. The sequence of numbers is devised so that the next highest number (and therefore smaller lens opening) allows only half as much light to pass as the previous opening does. Thus the light admitted at f/5.6 is half of that admitted at f/4, and at f/8 the amount of light admitted is only half of that admitted at f/5.6.

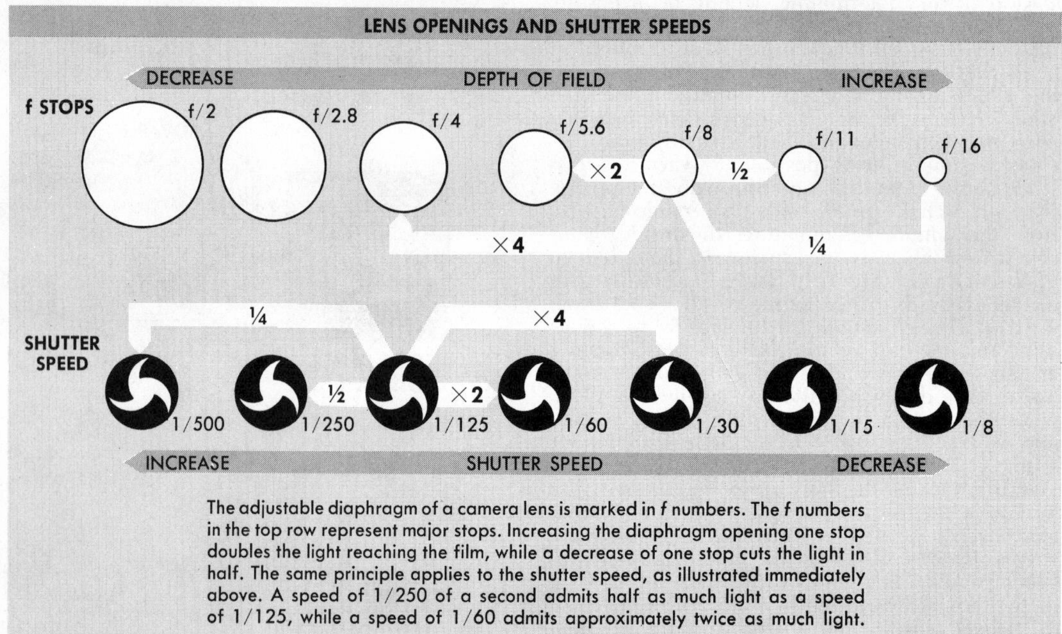

The adjustable diaphragm of a camera lens is marked in f numbers. The f numbers in the top row represent major stops. Increasing the diaphragm opening one stop doubles the light reaching the film, while a decrease of one stop cuts the light in half. The same principle applies to the shutter speed, as illustrated immediately above. A speed of 1/250 of a second admits half as much light as a speed of 1/125, while a speed of 1/60 admits approximately twice as much light.

Depth of Field. When a camera is focused on a particular object, other objects in the image area that are nearer or farther away from the camera may not be as sharply defined.

This change in sharpness is gradual rather than abrupt; there is a zone in front of and behind the exact point of focus where the actual difference in sharpness is too small for the human eye to see. The extent of this zone of sharp focus is called the depth of field. It depends on the lens aperture, the focal length of the lens, and the distance between camera and subject. At a given distance from camera to subject, the smaller the aperture and the smaller the focal length, the greater will be the depth of field. For example, with a 135mm lens set at f/11 and focused on a subject 30 feet (10 meters) away, the depth of field is approximately 26.5 to 34.7 feet (7.9 to 10.4 meters). With a 50mm lens at the same focus and aperture setting, the depth of field is 15 feet (4.5 meters) to infinity. At larger apertures the depth of field for both the 135mm and the 50mm lenses would be shallower, but it would still be relatively larger for the 50mm lens than for the 135mm lens. In addition, at a given aperture for a given lens, the depth of field narrows as the point of focus moves nearer to the lens.

Shutter. The shutter is the other light-regulating mechanism on a camera. It controls the amount of light that reaches the film by regulating the actual exposure time. Two major types of shutter—leaf and focal-plane—are in use in most cameras. In addition, there are other shutter types for motion-picture cameras and special types of still cameras.

Leaf Shutter. This type of shutter usually consists of either three or five interleaved blades, each pivoted on the outer end. The blades form a diaphragm controlled by a ring. When the shutter release of the camera is depressed, a spring moves the ring, which in turn opens the blades. On completion of exposure a second ring closes the blades. The duration of the opening can be set by adjusting the spring's tension. On most advanced cameras that use such a shutter, the speeds with which the shutter opens and closes range from 1 second to 1/500 of a second. In such shutters the slow speeds are controlled by geared timing mechanisms. The leaf shutter can be mounted in the camera behind or in front of the lens or between its elements.

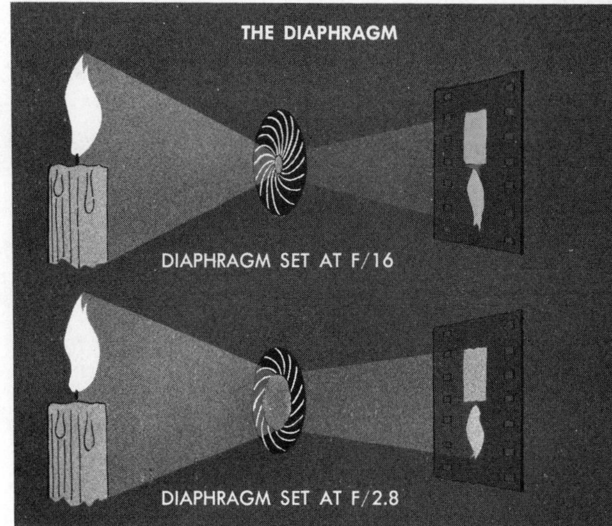

At higher diaphragm settings, less light reaches the film.

Focal-Plane Shutter. The focal-plane shutter is actually a blind with a slit in it. The shutter travels across the film plane, either up and down or from side to side. In focal-plane shutters used on press cameras, both the size of the slit and the tension on the blind can be regulated to control the duration of exposure. However, the modern focal-plane shutter found in 35mm cameras is under constant tension. Exposure time is adjusted only by adjusting slit size. In actual practice the time required for the slit to travel across the film may be much longer than the time a particular section of the film is exposed by the light passing through the slit. For example, with a setting of 1/1000 of a second, the shutter may take as long as 1/100 of a second to traverse the film area. These shutters are usually made of rubberized cloth or thin metal.

Other Shutters. Among other types of shutters is the *electronic* shutter, essentially a leaf shutter that is electronically controlled for accuracy

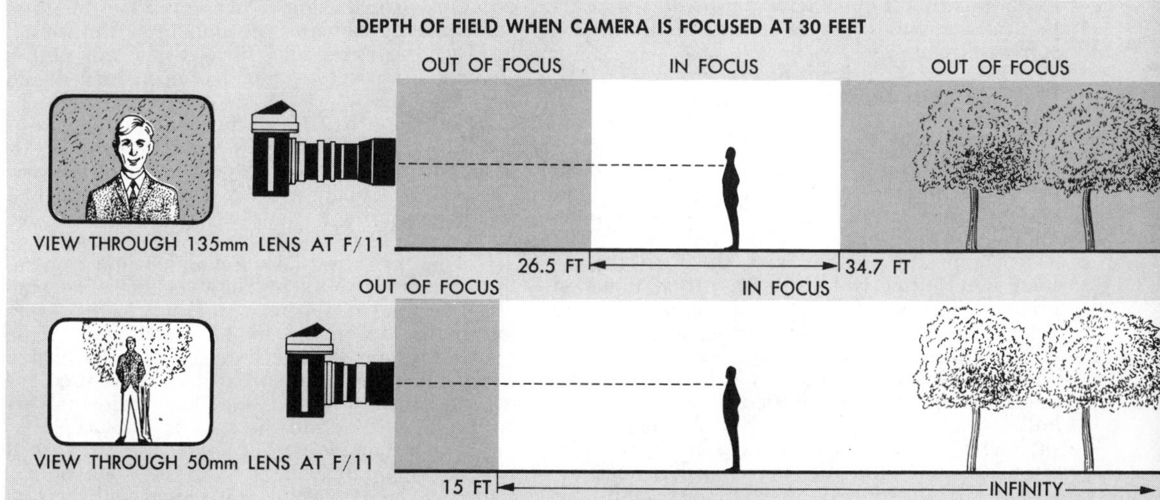

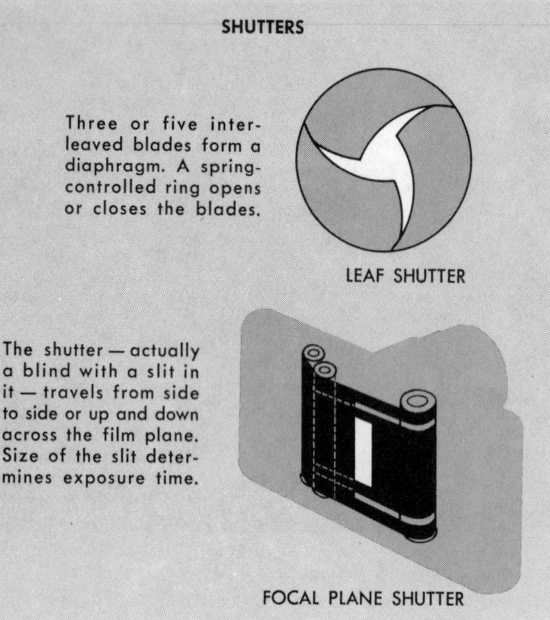

of exposure timing. The *rotary* shutter is a semicircular disk with a wedge-shaped opening. Primarily used in motion-picture cameras, it has also been applied to still cameras–particularly to machines designed to shoot fast bursts of exposures at the rate of several a second. The *prism* shutter is employed primarily for high-speed camera work, where hundreds or even thousands of images must be recorded in a second. As the prism rotates it synchronizes with the travel of the film across the film plane and forms an image on each frame.

Synchronization. One of the most important attributes of the modern shutter is its ability to synchronize with the flash attachments. Of the two main types of shutters, the leaf-type works best with both electronic flash and flashbulbs, which can be used at all speeds with these shutters. When a flash is synchronized with a leaf shutter, the flash reaches its peak of light output at precisely the same time that the shutter reaches its fullest opening. A flash contact inside the camera closes the electrical circuit at the correct instant.

There are three types of synchronization: M, F, and X. The M-synchronization setting on the shutter is used with medium-peak bulbs; the firing circuit closes before the blades of the shutter begin to move and about 1/60 of a second before the shutter opens fully. The F setting is designed for fast-peak bulbs; the circuit fires the bulb when the shutter is about half open. The X-synchronization setting fires the flash the instant the shutter is fully open. It is intended primarily for use with electronic flash with zero delay. X-synchronized shutter speeds are restricted to 1/30, 1/50, or 1/125 of a second.

When a camera has a focal-plane shutter, the flash must be synchronized to coordinate the bulb's peak of light output with the instant the slit starts to move across the film. The flash must last until the entire film area has been exposed. There are FP (focal-plane) bulbs for just this purpose; they work best at higher shutter speeds. Focal-plane shutters also have X synchronization for electronic flash.

Self-Timer. Another feature of many focal-plane and leaf shutters is the self-timer, a device for automatically tripping the shutter after it has been cocked. With leaf shutters the self-timer is usually located on the shutter assembly itself. On focal-plane-shutter cameras it is most often found on the camera body. The self-timer allows a delay of about 10 to 15 seconds after it is tripped before the shutter opens and closes. In most cases the self-timer is used to permit the photographer to get into the picture himself after focusing and setting the exposure. It is also used occasionally in the absence of a cable release when extreme closeups are being made with a tripod-mounted camera, in order to prevent a jarring effect when the finger depresses the shutter release.

Film-Transport System. A primary function of the camera box is the accurate seating of film. In addition, the photographer must be able to go as rapidly as possible from one exposure to the next. The modern film-transport system has been developed to meet these and other needs.

Sheet Film. Sheet film systems are still widely used in view cameras and some press cameras. The sheet film, a single piece of film, is loaded into a lightproof holder. One sheet is placed in each side of the holder and masked with a dark slide. The holder is placed in the rear of the camera and held in the correct film plane by a spring-loaded back. The dark slide is removed prior to exposure. After exposure the slide is replaced, and the film holder is removed and reinserted with the other side facing the lens. Sheet film sizes range from 2½ x 3½ to 11 x 14 inches (6 x 9 to 27.9 x 35.5 cm in European films).

Roll Film. The most popular roll film today is the 120 type, which can produce negatives of 2¼ x 2¼ to 2¼ x 3¼ (6 x 6cm to 6 x 9 cm in European films) depending on the camera in which it is used. The 2⅜-inch film is rolled on a spool with a protective paper backing. When used in a 2¼ x 2¼ camera–a camera that produces 2¼ x 2¼ inch negatives–it yields 12 exposures. However, special long rolls yield as many as 24 exposures.

The film is wound through the camera from the feed spool to the take-up spool. In the more expensive cameras the film-transport mechanism automatically regulates the amount of film wound for each exposure and stops when the proper amount of unexposed film has been moved into the film plane.

The 35mm cartridge works in a similar fashion, but the film comes wound inside a lightproof cartridge. Unlike 120 film, which need not be rewound after it is fully exposed, 35mm film usually must be wound back into its cartridge for removal from the camera.

In both the roll-film and the 35mm camera, the shutter is automatically cocked when the film is wound to the next exposure. This serves to prevent accidental double exposures. Some 2¼ x 2¼ and 35mm cameras have detachable backs that may be preloaded and used as needed. Dark slides prevent any accidental exposure to light before the back is in place.

The Instamatic-type camera uses a special film cartridge that drops into the back of the camera. The camera back is closed and the film advanced to the first exposure. In more advanced models, the film automatically moves to the next frame after each exposure. After the film has been exposed, the cartridge is removed without rewinding.

Viewfinder. The viewfinder provides the photographer with an image of the subject that is identical—or nearly so—with the image that the camera lens will project upon the film. It makes it possible for him to "frame" the photographic subject within a desired background by changing camera angle or position, and it gives a preview of the photograph he is about to take. Viewfinders are standard parts of nearly all cameras except view cameras, which have a ground-glass back on which the image formed by the camera lens can be viewed before the film holder is inserted.

In all viewing systems except the ground-glass back and the single-lens reflex viewfinder, inaccuracies in viewing and framing may be caused by a phenomenon known as parallax. Parallax results from a difference between the viewpoint of the camera lens and that of the viewfinder, and it is most noticeable in the case of nearby subjects. Many viewfinders are designed to compensate in part for parallax.

Sports. The simplest type of finder is the sports, or frame, finder. It consists of a wire frame in the shape of the film format and is designed to frame an area equal to the camera's angle of view. A sports finder may be attached to the side or top of the camera.

Bright-field. The bright-field finder is somewhat more advanced than the sports finder. It is usually found on less expensive cameras, such as box and inexpensive twin-lens cameras. The finder consists of a simple lens that directs an image to a mirror set at a 45° angle inside the camera. The mirror in turn directs the image to another lens where it is brought to focus, producing a very bright image. Bright-field images are rather difficult to view, and usually the camera must be held at waist level. The image is seen reversed from right to left.

Optical. The optical viewfinder is based on the Galilean telescope and provides a less distorted, unreversed image, and one that is easier to see. It consists of two lenses, one concave and the other convex. The separation between the two lenses determines the size of the subject area shown. The optical finder is most often mounted inside and near the top of the camera, for eye-level use. A masking system makes it possible to use the optical finder with a variety of focal lengths, providing different angles of view to match different lenses. Some optical finders incorporate a bright frame, a reflection of a white rectangular line drawn on the sight. In this case, the finder covers a greater area than the lens does, for easier viewing, while the frame provides the exact field of the lens.

Reflex. The twin-lens reflex camera employs two lenses, one for taking the picture and the other for viewing the subject. While similar in principle to the bright-field finder, the typical twin-lens reflex incorporates a ground glass and field lens combination that greatly improves ease and accuracy of viewing.

Another reflex viewing system, the single-lens reflex, does not have a separate lens for viewing. Instead, the light enters the camera lens and strikes a mirror, which directs it to a ground glass. The image formed on the ground glass is viewed by means of a pentagonal prism, or *pentaprism,* and an eyepiece lens. The pentaprism returns the reversed image to the correct right-to-left orientation and directs it through the eyepiece to the viewing eye. During exposure the mirror moves up and out of the way, permitting light to pass to the film and momentarily blacking out the finder.

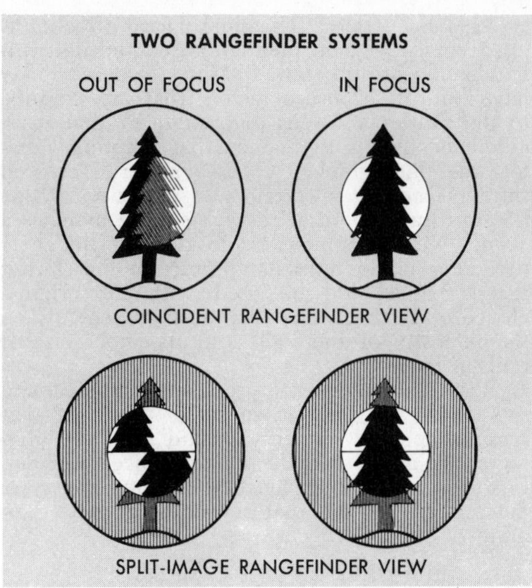

In the coincident coupled range finder, a second image is superimposed on the viewfinder image. In the split-image type, the unfocused image appears unaligned.

Range Finder. In addition to being framed correctly by the viewfinder, the image should be properly focused on the film plane. A range-finder or other focusing system is considered essential for serious photography, therefore, although some cameras do dispense with such systems. The systems fall into two general categories: reflex focusing aids, in which focusing is done by means of the ground glass viewing screen, and coupled range finders.

The two types of coupled range finders in general use are the coincident and the split-image. Both are based on the fact that when an object is viewed from two different positions, the lines of sight converge on the object. The convergence angle increases as the object grows nearer and decreases as the object moves farther away. In the coincident range finder the two viewing points are provided by separate windows, one of which is the viewfinder window. A second image is introduced through another window by means of mirrors and prisms. The images are superimposed, and a double image is seen as long as the lens is out of focus. In the split-image range finder, the unfocused image appears unaligned, or split. When focused, the image is aligned, and the split disappears. The range finders are coupled to the focusing ring of the lens; hence the name.

While split-image range finders are often used in single-lens reflex cameras, the ground glass is most often used for focusing in both single-lens and twin-lens reflex cameras—except the relatively few that do not have ground-glass screens. The ground glass is the same distance from the lens as the film plane is; when the lens is not focused, the image appears fuzzy.

Exposure System. The final factor in obtaining technically good photographs is the determination of exposure times. Many cameras today have built-in exposure meters that are coupled to the shutter and lens diaphragm or that work automatically. If the camera has a coupled meter, the photographer chooses either a desired shutter speed or a certain lens aperture. When he aims the camera at the subject, he matches a needle with a pointer inside the viewfinder to determine either the lens aperture or the shutter speed that should be used with his original choice of setting. The final setting depends on the intensity of the light and its effect on the built-in meter.

With automatic exposure systems, the camera sets either the shutter speed or the lens diaphragm opening without any aid from the photographer other than the initial choice. Further, in some systems both lens and shutter speed are determined by the meter according to a programed system.

KINDS OF STILL CAMERAS

The camera, as it is known today, grew from the work of the French inventors Louis Daguerre and Joseph Nicéphore Niepce in the 19th century. These men were the first to develop methods by which to record, or "fix," the image obtained in the earlier camera obscura.

Box and Folding Cameras. The simple box camera and folding camera are closest in form to the original cameras. Designed for taking snapshots, the box camera needs only to be aimed and the shutter release pushed to expose the film. Most box cameras have one shutter speed and one lens opening; they continue to be used today with little change in mechanism from the earliest models. The folding camera in its simplest form is a box camera with a collapsible bellows that permits the camera to be stored easily because of its small size when collapsed. Some folding cameras, however, have range finders, advanced shutters, and fast lenses.

35mm. The invention of the 35mm range-finder camera was an important turning point in photography. Originally designed to test motion-picture film, the 35mm camera was responsible for the development of the candid photograph and photojournalism. Small, compact, and inconspicuous, it is the ideal camera where speed and versatility are needed. The lenses can often be interchanged, and the camera can take 36 exposures or more on a roll of film. Modern films and developers yield high-quality results.

Twin-Lens Reflex. The twin-lens reflex—primarily a 2¼ x 2¼ camera—provides a reasonably large film image and good operational speed. Modern TLR's incorporate automatic film advance and shutter cocking, fast lenses, and bright viewing images. The cameras are designed for waist-level operation, but accessory prism housings make it possible to use them at eye level. In addition, some TLR's can shoot 35mm and other formats on 120 film. The twin-lens reflex is particularly adaptable to baby and portrait photography, as well as to news work.

Single-Lens Reflex. The 35mm single-lens reflex (SLR) combines the flexibility of the 35mm format with eye-level reflex viewing. It also offers unlimited lens interchangeability. With its fast lenses and fast shutters, the camera can handle a wide range of tasks, from photocopying and photojournalism to portraiture and laboratory work. Accessories permit waist-level shooting, rapid-sequence photography, and macro- and microphotography. Most of these advantages also characterize the 2¼ x 2¼ SLR. The more cumbersome SLR's designed for larger film sizes are generally less versatile.

Instamatic. The Instamatic camera, which uses a special cartridge loaded into the back of the camera, represents one of the first important film-loading innovations in many years. The design of the Instamatic has been incorporated into simple snapshot cameras as well as the more advanced single-lens reflex camera. Many Instamatics incorporate completely automatic electric-eye exposure systems. The film cartridges are keyed to automatically set meters to obtain the proper film speed.

View. The view camera is designed essentially for still-life photography, whether outdoors or in a studio. The ground-glass back provides an image of the same size and shape as the image on the film. After the subject has been framed and focused on the ground glass, a film holder is inserted, and the exposure is made. The film sizes range from 2¼ x 3¼ to 11 x 14 inches. The larger cameras can be modified to accept smaller film. Front and rear standards (lens and film supports) of the view camera may be raised, lowered, and tilted to adjust for depth of field or area coverage, or to correct for distortion. While they generally use sheet film, smaller view cameras may be equipped to use roll film. Because of the long bellows extension, extremely close focusing is possible.

Special Cameras. A number of still cameras have been devised that offer unique advantages or serve special purposes.

Polaroid. The chief attribute of the Polaroid Land Camera is its ability to deliver a completely processed print almost immediately after exposure. The film carries its own developing agent in pods that are activated by rollers inside the camera. Black-and-white film takes 10 seconds, and color film takes 50 seconds to develop. Polaroid Land cameras are designed to accept either roll or film packs.

Press. The press camera is a modified view camera with bellows and ground-glass back. It usually has only a rising and tilting front standard. A range finder is incorporated for rapid focusing. Most press cameras use 4 x 5 inch sheet film to obtain the greater sharpness required for the coarse screen used in newspaper engravings. The subject is viewed through either an optical finder or a frame finder.

Panoramic. Panoramic cameras—also called banquet cameras—are used to encompass large areas on a single exposure. Both the film and the lens move during such an exposure. The lens rotates around its nodal point (the point behind the lens where light rays converge) while the film is drawn past a slit. Both operations are motorized. Larger panoramic cameras use special narrow-width film; there are also cameras that use 35mm film. The angle of view may range from 180° to 360°, depending on the camera.

Process. Process cameras resemble view cameras to some extent. They are used to make halftone and line engravings. Because they accept film formats as large as 24 x 36 inches (60 x 90 cm), the process cameras are extremely large and are usually mounted on rails. The line screen, mounted at the rear of the camera in

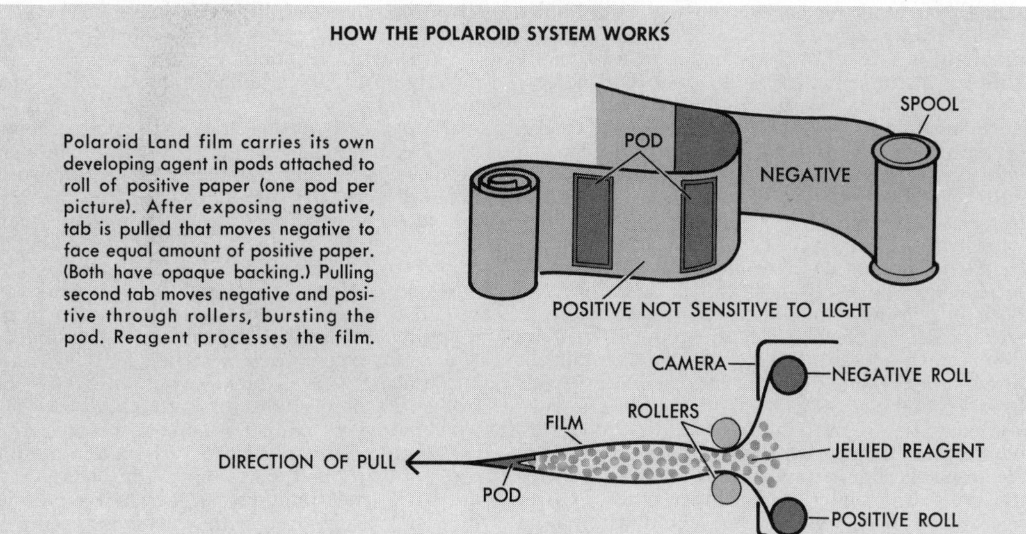

Polaroid Land film carries its own developing agent in pods attached to roll of positive paper (one pod per picture). After exposing negative, tab is pulled that moves negative to face equal amount of positive paper. (Both have opaque backing.) Pulling second tab moves negative and positive through rollers, bursting the pod. Reagent processes the film.

front of the film or plate, breaks the image up into a series of dots. The negative is used to make the copper or zinc engraving.

Aerial. Aerial cameras, in general, are equipped with lenses having a long focal length and a fixed focus, since practically all shooting is done at "infinity." The cameras are stressed to withstand vibration, and in some cases the film is held flat by a vacuum device. Film sizes may range from 2¼ x 3¼ to 9 x 18 inches (6 x 9 to 22.5 x 45 cm) or even larger. Specially modified 35mm cameras have also been used for aerial photography. Many aerial cameras use a system whereby film speed is synchronized with airplane speed. A modern technique employs electronics to accomplish synchronization.

Ultraminiature. The ultraminiature camera is designed to handle extremely small format films ranging from 9.5 to 16mm (.37 to .63 inches). Such cameras are therefore quite small; they fit easily into pocket or purse. Most have fixed-focus lenses and a capacity for a large number of exposures. More recent varieties have built-in exposure meters. These tiny cameras have also been fitted into watches, canes, and cigarette lighters for use as spy cameras.

EQUIPMENT AND ACCESSORIES

Auxiliary Lenses. A camera equipped with an interchangeable lens mount can accept other lenses besides the lens normal for that camera. Thus, the normal lens can be completely removed and one of a different focal length—shorter or longer—can be substituted to deal with particular photographic situations. For example, the normal lens when used indoors may not provide the subject-area coverage desired, because of wall restrictions. A wide-angle lens would be required. Conversely, for photographing sporting events, a telephoto or longer-than-normal-focus lens may be needed. Moderate telephoto lenses are favored for portrait work to minimize apparent distortion.

If the camera lacks interchangeability, moderate wide-angle and telephoto effects are still possible with converter lenses that reduce or magnify the image. The converters are mounted over the regular lens.

Supplementary Lenses and Extension Tubes. All lenses have a minimum focusing distance short of which they will not deliver a sharp image. However, this minimum distance can be shortened by the use of supplementary lenses (also called portrait attachments or close-up lenses) rated in diopters (1 diopter is the refractive power of a lens with a 1-meter focal length). The higher the diopter number, the closer the lens may be focused. They are normally available in strengths from +1 to +10 diopters. No exposure adjustment is required.

Extension tubes can be used only with a camera that has an interchangeable lens mount and a focal-plane shutter that is part of the camera, or with an interchangeable-lens camera in which the lens and shutter are combined. Placing the tube between the lens and the camera increases the lens-to-film distance. This permits extremely close focusing. The degree of closeness depends on the length of the extension tube. The use of the tube changes the values of the lens diaphragm opening; exposure correction therefore is required.

Lens Shades. When photographing takes place in bright light, there is a danger that stray light will enter the lens and produce internal reflections that will cause flare (bright patches on the print). The lens shade is designed to block this stray light; it fits over the front of the lens itself.

Filters. At times a photographer will wish to change the contrast or tonal values that he can normally expect from the light, the subject, and the exposure. Filters are used for this purpose, since they allow more of one part of the spectrum than another to reach the lens. For example, a red filter allows red light, rather than other colors, to pass to the film. Filters are made in various colors to achieve different results. In order to add contrast to sky portions of an image, and to emphasize cloud formations, yellow filters are used. Red filters serve to darken the sky. A green filter helps to enhance skin tones. Filters may also be used to change the color response in color films.

Flashbulbs and Electronic Flash. The basic reason for the use of flash is to provide enough light to photograph when the existing illumination is too weak for the film in use. Flashbulbs are used once and then discarded. The modern flashbulb is small, but it is capable of adequately lighting a subject that is 10 feet (3 meters) from the camera. Larger bulbs, of course, produce more light. Flashbulbs are normally used in battery-operated guns that are synchronized with the camera shutter. Two additional flash guns can be used simultaneously to light extremely large areas. Flashbulbs may be filled with wire or foil and come in clear or blue-coated form (for daylight-balanced color films).

Electronic flash is basically a tube that can be fired literally thousands of times before it wears out. An electronic flash produces light by discharging a medium- or high-voltage current through a gas-filled tube. The charge passes between two electrodes inside the tube. The voltage may range from about 250 to 2,000, depending on the size of the unit. Small portable electronic flashguns use the lower voltages; studio units are usually in the upper range. Power may come from regular household alternating current, or from dry batteries or wet cells.

Electronic flash is of extremely short duration, on the order of 1/1000 of a second or faster. It is used when a moving subject is being photographed. In addition, electronic flash has a color temperature approximating that of daylight, which makes it a good choice for use with daylight-balanced color films.

Tripods and Other Accessories. Tripods are primarily designed to support the camera in order to obtain maximum image sharpness. Any motion of the camera will result in a blurring of the image. While shooting with a hand-held camera is reasonably safe at fast shutter speeds (since the speeds overcome camera shake), tripod use at slow shutter speeds is essential. Tripods are available in various sizes and weights. However, the more substantial the tripod the more certain the results. Similarly, a *cable release* is a plunger-type device that eliminates the camera jarring that can occur when the shutter release is depressed by hand.

Finally, mention might be made of the accessory exposure meter. Many hand-held or accessory exposure meters have a greater sensitivity to light than meters that are built into the camera itself. Such meters therefore are favored by professionals.

SELECTING A CAMERA

The first consideration in the selection of a camera is the use to which the camera will be put. For casual photography, a box or Instamatic camera may be sufficient. However, even among Instamatic cameras there are various kinds; they range from simple cameras with fixed-focus lenses to more advanced units with range finders and fast, variable-focus lenses.

The photographer interested in photographing somewhat more complicated subject matter must think in terms of greater versatility in his equipment. For sports, theatrical, portrait, nature, or documentary photography, interchangeable lenses are perhaps essential. If portability is a necessity, the chosen camera may well be a 35mm. However, range finder 35mm cameras are limited in lens choice unless an accessory reflex housing is employed. The 35mm single-lens reflex with focal-plane shutter has virtually unlimited lens interchangeability. In addition, some 35mm reflexes offer finder and viewing-glass interchangeability; this makes them adaptable to a wide range of photographic tasks.

Film size is another consideration. Larger negatives, under certain conditions, offer greater detail and permit more freedom in selecting only small portions of the negative for enlargement. The 2¼ x 2¼ inch format offers a medium-sized negative, lens interchangeability, and the same range of accessories as that offered by the 35mm format. The 2¼ x 2¼ camera is small enough to be used in the field and flexible enough for studio work. Both the 2¼ x 2¼ and the 35mm are good choices for extreme close-up work.

View cameras hold a special position in photography. Although they are slow-working, and are cumbersome when designed for film formats larger than 2¼ x 3¼ inches, they offer great control over composition for studio and landscape work. A view camera is almost a necessity for architectural photography. When tall buildings are photographed close up with nonadjustable machines, the buildings appear to be falling in the final print; but with the swings and tilts available in the view camera, this distortion can easily be corrected. View camera lenses tend to be expensive, however, since each lens must have its own shutter, and the use of the wrong lens can limit the use of swings and tilts.

In summary, the prospective camera purchaser must take into account his photographic interests. In selecting the camera, he must consider whether the lens, shutter, viewfinder, focusing system, and (in the case of a camera with a built-in meter) exposure system are adequate to his needs. Exposure meters require an added note. The modern 35mm camera offers behind-the-lens exposure meters that read only the light that reaches the film, and the user must be certain that the system he chooses is compatible with his photographic interests. The choice usually lies between a system that reads only a small area of the subject and one that reads the entire area. In general, the camera must fit the photographer if both are to be successful.

2. Motion-Picture Cameras

A strip of motion-picture film consists of a series of still photographs. When motion-picture film moves through a camera, its travel is not continuous. Instead, each frame of the film comes to a complete halt behind the lens. The shutter opens, the exposure is made, and the film moves to the next frame. The standard exposure rate for silent films is 18 frames per second, whereas the rate for most sound films is 24 frames per second. A motion-picture projector operates in a way similar to the camera. The illusion of motion is dependent on the human characteristic of persistence of vision. The eye actually retains an impression of an image for a short period after the image has been removed from sight. Thus, when motion-picture images are presented in rapid succession but on an intermittent basis, one image appears to flow into another, and the illusion of movement on the screen is created. The projector employs a 3-bladed shutter; as a result, one frame is actually projected twice. This reduces the appearance of flicker on the screen.

PARTS OF A MOTION-PICTURE CAMERA

A motion-picture camera consists basically of a body, lens, transport system, shutter, and viewfinder.

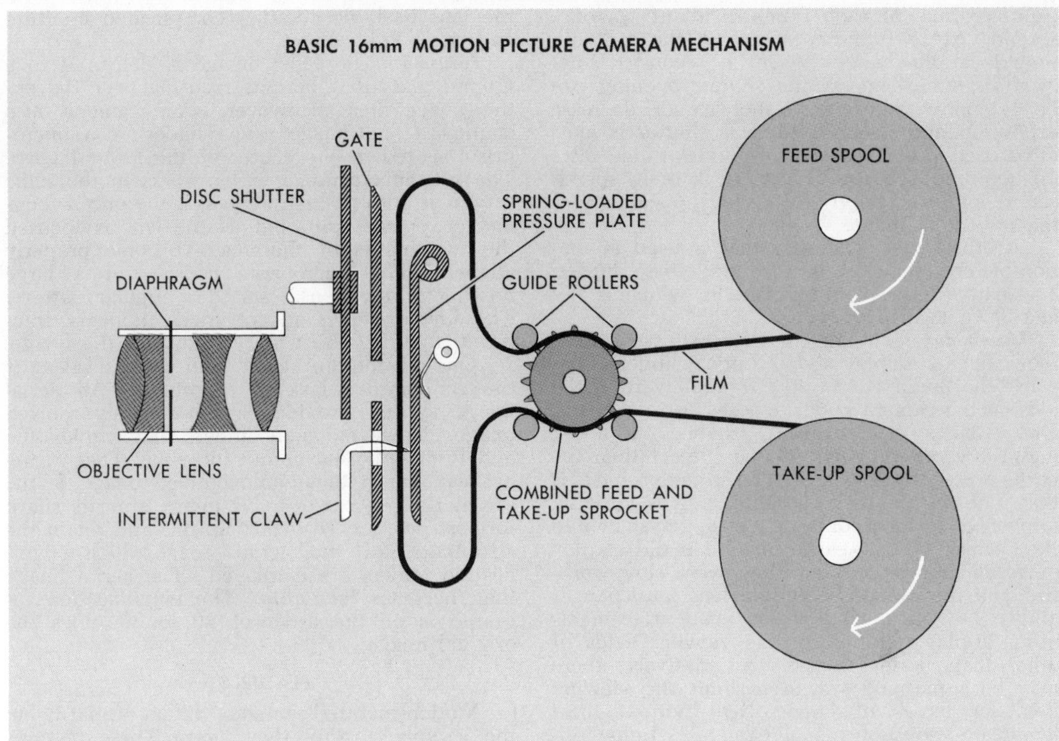

Body. The size and type of motion-picture film that is used determine the dimensions of the camera body. Cameras that use magazine or cartridge-loading systems tend to be smaller than those that use roll film. In either case, the outlines of the camera body conform to the requirements of the film. However, the film-transport system, lens, viewfinder, and controls add to the overall size. A few professional cameras use external magazine systems and therefore do away with internal film loading.

Lens. A motion-picture camera may use one, two, three, or four lenses. If a single lens is used, it may be permanently mounted on the camera; this is most often true of amateur machines. If more than one lens is used, the lenses are mounted on a rotating turret that permits a quick positioning of the desired focal length. In addition, many motion-picture cameras use zoom lenses—variable-focal-length lenses that provide, in one single optic, a range from wide-angle to telephoto. Professional cameras usually have a thread-type or bayonet mount that provides for lens interchangeability.

The standard, or normal, focal length of the lens depends on film size. An 8mm camera will usually have a 13mm lens as the standard optic. A 16mm machine usually employs a 25mm lens, while a 50mm lens is standard for 35mm cameras. The standard lens for a super 8 camera—a camera that uses 8mm film but that obtains a 35% greater image area—is 13 to 15mm.

Transport System. The film-transport system consists of a feed spool, take-up spool, sprocket wheels, motor, gate, and pulldown claw. (The motor drives the claw, sprocket wheels, and take-up spool.) The rotating sprocket wheels enter perforations along the edge of the film, pulling the film off the feed spool and directing it to the camera gate. The gate consists of side rails that keep the film in correct horizontal and vertical alignment behind the lens. A pressure plate in back of the film maintains the correct film plane position.

The claw is inside the gate; it has an up-and-down, in-and-out motion that is regulated by a cam system. At the height of its up movement the claw enters the film sprocket holes, pulls one frame down into position in the camera gate, and disengages. After the frame is exposed the claw starts upward again and repeats the pulldown movement, replacing the exposed frame with a new one. This cycle may take place as little as 1 or 2 times a second, or as often as 64 or more times a second. Once the frame has been exposed, it is pulled toward the take-up spool by a second sprocket wheel, below the gate. The exposed film is stored in the take-up spool until the entire roll is completed and removed from the camera. Most 8mm and super 8 cameras have eliminated the sprocket wheels entirely. The pulldown claw takes film directly from the feed spool, while exposed film is taken out of the gate simply by the combined action of the push of the pulldown claw and the pull of the rotating take-up spool.

Shutter. Most amateur cameras and a number of professional ones employ the rotary, or 180°, shutter, which has the form of a half circle. The shutter is pivoted on the flat, or straight, side of the half circle. When the claw is pulling down the film, the half circle covers the film gate and prevents light from reaching the film. When the frame is motionless in the gate, the half circle moves out of the way and permits light from the lens to reach the film.

Because the opening on most circular shutters is fixed, the exposure time is dependent on the number of frames per second that are exposed. Thus at 24 frames per second, the exposure time of each frame is about 1/50 of a second. At 18 frames per second, the exposure time is approximately 1/35 of a second. However, in some cameras the shutter opening can be externally adjusted to increase or decrease exposure times. Such a *variable* shutter is most often used when higher-than-normal frame rates are required. Its use at normal running speeds can result in a choppy, flickering appearance of the projected image.

Another type of shutter that is used in motion-picture cameras is the guillotine shutter. The name derives from its action, which is up-and-down instead of rotary.

Viewfinder. Some of the least expensive amateur cameras employ simple optical finders. Because the finder is mounted separately from the lens on the camera body, it poses two problems. One is that at close focusing distances the finder may see a different part of the subject than the part covered by the lens. The other problem is that with a separate optical finder it is virtually impossible to incorporate a focusing system into the camera. (Some earlier machines did employ range-finder systems; but they were slow-working, and they seriously limited lens interchangeability.) Optical finders on amateur cameras often display outlines for the viewing fields of other than normal lenses. Alternatively, there may be a masking system to limit the viewing field for lenses of longer than normal focal length. Some professional cameras employ optical finders, but they have interchangeable elements that correspond to the fields of view of a variety of focal lengths.

Through-the-Lens Reflex Systems. Professional cameras were the first to employ through-the-lens viewing and focusing systems, in order to obtain maximum accuracy in both areas. There are two distinct approaches to the design of reflex finders: the mirror and the prism system.

In the mirror system, a small mirror is mounted on the shutter. The shutter is mounted at a 45° angle. When the shutter is closed, the image is reflected to the viewfinder; when the shutter is open, the image reaches the film, and the viewfinder is temporarily blacked out. Since the exposures are taking place at a rapid rate, this blacking out appears as a slight flickering in the finder; the flicker becomes less noticeable as the frame rate increases. The mirror system may be used with either rotary or guillotine shutters, and it permits complete freedom of lens interchangeability.

Most amateur cameras employ the prism, or beam splitter, system. In this system, the light enters the lens and reaches a prism. Most of the light is allowed to pass to the film, but a small percentage is "split off" and redirected to the viewfinder. One advantage of this system is that it provides an extremely bright viewing image; the beam splitter is usually placed ahead of the diaphragm, and the effect is that of viewing the image at maximum lens aperture. On most amateur cameras that have permanently mounted lenses, the lens diaphragm is located inside the camera body because of the requirements of the automatic electric eye system. The beam splitter idea also has been applied to more advanced machines that permit lens interchangeability. However, at small apertures the image in the finder can be difficult to see. Furthermore, if an automatic electric eye system is incorporated into the lens, it requires either a servomotor on the lens itself or a rather complicated aperture and speed adjustment.

Focusing. The reflex image is delivered to a ground glass that permits focusing over the entire image area. However, some cameras also employ a split-image range finder or a microprism seated in the center of the ground glass. The split-image range finder works in the same way as it does on a still camera: the out-of-focus image appears split, but as the lens is focused the two halves of the image become properly aligned. The microprism consists of a large number of tiny lenses set in a circular pattern. The image, when out of focus, appears fractured; focusing the lens reconstitutes the image.

One of the problems with ground glass is the comparative lack of brightness. An aerial image system provides a more easily viewed image. However, many finders that employ the aerial image do not permit focusing. That is, the eye can adjust to an unmagnified image to the extent that an out-of-focus image appears sharp to most people. To overcome this and retain the advantages of the aerial image, high-magnification finders are employed. The aerial image then becomes focusable. The magnification required is on the order of 20 to 30 times the original image.

FEATURES

Motion-picture cameras differ primarily in the various features they offer. These features determine the flexibility and adaptability of the particular camera. An amateur camera may consist of nothing more than a body, lens, motor, and a single shooting speed. More advanced cameras may offer advanced motor design, multiple speeds, and facilities for special effects.

Motor Drive. A number of cameras in use today are still equipped with spring motor drives similar to clock motors. They provide only a limited amount of shooting time and must be rewound periodically. On 8mm cameras, one full wind will usually transport about 6 to 8 feet (2–2.5 meters) of film. On some 16mm cameras, spring motors will run long enough to transport about 16 feet of film (5 meters); other models provide for 23 or even 40 feet (7–12 meters) of film on one wind. Their operation is controlled by a governor.

Electric motor drives have become increasingly popular, particularly on super 8 cameras. Driven by penlight batteries, these motors can transport an entire film load through the camera without pause. Battery life is usually long enough to expose six or more rolls of film. The electric motor is virtually essential for the filming of motion pictures with sound. Professional cameras often have a system of interchangeable motors to meet various needs, which may range from animation (single frame exposures) to sound to slow-motion shooting.

Choice of Frames per Second. The normal frame speed for silent shooting is 18 frames per second (fps); sound films are usually filmed at 24 fps. Higher or lower speeds may be called for, however. For example, a speed of 8 fps may be required to speed up movement. An extremely slow-moving subject shot at 8 fps and then projected normally will appear to move much more quickly than in real life. Conversely, shooting a fast-moving subject at slow motion speeds—such as 64 fps—will have the effect of slowing down the action when the film is projected at normal speed. More advanced cameras may offer speeds of 8 to 64 fps, and some range down to as little as 2 fps. In addition, some cameras can accept special motors for shooting for sound at 24 fps, as well as at higher and lower speeds. Animation motors are designed to expose one frame at a time. They may also be used for time lapse work, in which single frames are equally spaced over long periods of time—for example, to record the blossoming of a flower.

Fading Devices. The "fade" is a kind of cinematic punctuation. That is, a scene may gradually "fade in" (grow to normal brightness from a totally dark screen) or "fade out" (go from a normal image to a totally dark screen). In professional filming this effect is most often added in the laboratory, but some cameras can fade in or out during actual shooting.

Backwind. The backwind permits the winding of exposed film back onto the feed spool. The device can be used to double-expose footage for special effects or to make lap dissolves in which one scene fades out while a superimposed scene fades in.

Footage and Frame Counter. The footage counter keeps track of the amount of film that has been exposed and that remains to be exposed. The frame counter provides the same information, but on a limited basis. While the footage counter is calibrated for the complete film load, the frame counter is not. It keeps track of a limited number of frames and repeats itself when that limit is reached. The frame counter is employed primarily for animation filming and to provide a means for determining the start and stop of fades and dissolves. It also is used in time-lapse photography.

Automatic and Semiautomatic Exposure. Most 8mm and super 8 and some professional cameras have automatic exposure, or electric eye, determining systems. Once the film emulsion speed and frame rate have been set, the lens aperture is determined automatically by either a selenium or a cadmium sulfide cell system. When light strikes such a cell, an electric current is generated, either in the selenium cell itself or in batteries controlled by the cadmium sulfide cell. The amount of current is determined by the amount of light striking the cell. The current travels to a diaphragm control system and determines the lens opening. In semiautomatic systems the current deflects a pointer; the photographer matches a needle to the pointer to open or close the lens opening.

External Magazine Systems. For professional work, the usual 100-foot (30-meter) film loads used in 16 or 35mm cameras are often not sufficient, because involved shooting schedules may require thousands of feet of film. The normal film load can be greatly increased by using magazines. The magazines fit outside the regular camera body, and the film is threaded through ports to the gate of the camera. Magazines are often used for sound shooting and other types of location work.

Magazines are available in 400-, 800-, and 1,600-foot (120-, 240-, and 480-meter) sizes for 16mm cameras, and there are larger sizes for 35mm cameras. Additional torque motors are required for these large sizes, to transport the film from the feed core to the gate and then back to the take-up core in the camera. When the loads are 400 feet or more in size, the magazines are loaded in the darkroom.

KINDS OF MOTION-PICTURE CAMERAS

Motion-picture cameras may be most aptly categorized by the kind of film used. The most widely used films are 8mm, super 8, single 8, 16mm, and 35mm.

8mm. The 8mm film size is primarily an amateur film designed for home movie making. However, it has also found professional application in high-speed motion pictures, in the medical and audiovisual fields, and to a very minor extent in television news work. The 8mm frame measures 0.314 inch (7.97mm) from edge to edge; the actual image area recorded by the camera is 0.192 x 0.003 inch (4.87 x .076mm). The film is obtainable in 25-foot and 100-foot (7.5- and 30.5-meter) double-8 spools and 25-foot double-8 magazines. The film is actually 16mm wide, and on its first trip through the camera only half the film is exposed. The take-up spool is then removed, turned over, and placed in the feed spool position to expose the second side.

Cameras that use 8mm film range from simple machines with a permanently mounted 13mm lens to units that offer through-the-lens viewing and focusing, speeds of from 8 to 64 fps, interchangeable lenses, automatic electric eyes, fading devices, backwinds, and other features.

Super 8 and Single 8. Super 8 and single 8 are enlarged formats on the regular 8mm width. Both films are characterized by smaller sprocket holes than those found on regular 8mm, and by a 35% larger camera image area. The actual projection area is 50% larger than on 8mm. Both films have camera image areas measuring 0.295 x 0.404 inch; the projection area is 0.158 x 0.211 inch (it is 0.129 x 0.172 inch for 8mm).

Super 8 emulsions are coated on a triacetate film base, and the film is loaded into cartridges that hold 50 feet (15 meters). Unlike regular 8, super 8 can be exposed without its having to be turned over. That is, the film is actually 8mm wide. The cartridges are keyed to set the camera's electric eye automatically for the correct emulsion speed. The cartridge itself must be destroyed in order to process the film.

In comparison, single 8 film employs a thin polyester base and therefore has a much smaller, flatter cartridge. There is one other major difference between the two systems. The super 8 cartridge employs a reverse curl and built-in pressure pad to maintain the correct film plane and flatness. The gate in the camera serves only to help position the cartridge. The single cartridge has no pressure pad, and the film must pass through a regular camera gate.

16mm. The 16mm format was once considered a film suitable only for amateurs. Today it has gained wide acceptance for professional use, particularly in the documentary, advertising, educational, and television fields. The image area is large enough to provide excellent quality and a sharpness suitable for large audience presentation. The 16mm camera is used extensively for theatrical films where the 35mm is impractical; the film is enlarged to 35mm for release.

The 16mm film size is available in 50-foot (15-meter) magazines for magazine cameras, in 100- and 200-foot (30.5- and 61-meter) spools, and in 400- to 1,600-foot (122- to 488-meter) loads for 16mm roll film cameras that are equipped to accept external magazine loads. There are 16mm camera designs for every variety of movie task, from home movies to space

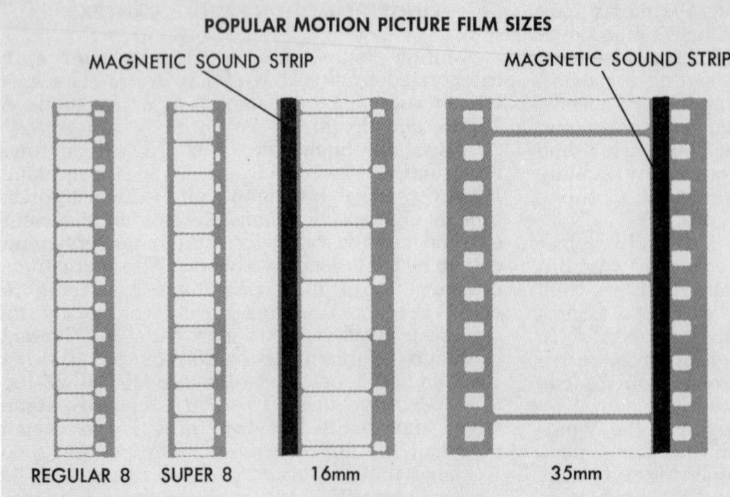

The standard film for theatrical motion pictures is the 35mm format, but 16mm film is also widely used professionally as well as by amateurs. The 8mm format actually is 16mm film that is run through the camera twice to expose both sides.

films. Laboratory facilities provide tremendous latitude in film making. In addition to regular color and black-and-white emulsions, there are films that can handle tasks ranging from oscilloscope recording to high-speed film studies.

35mm. The 35mm film is the standard film for theatrical motion pictures; in addition, many advertising films for television are made on 35mm. The cameras tend to be extremely large and are designed for stationary operation. In production centers such as Hollywood, huge cranes and wheeled dollies are employed to hold and move the cameras. In addition to shooting screen images with a normal aspect ratio (width to height ratio), 35mm cameras are also used to film wide-screen, or *anamorphic,* motion pictures, with an aspect ratio of 2.55 to 1. An anamorphic lens squeezes the image onto the film, and another anamorphic lens on the projector restores the wide-screen image.

Other Film Sizes. The 55mm camera is also used for anamorphic screen processes. The 55mm negative is used to make 35mm release prints. The 65mm camera is employed for a wide-screen process called Todd AO. The original is shot in special cameras and, in this case, release prints are made on the same size film.

Sound Cameras. Virtually any motion-picture camera may be used to shoot a sound film. Depending on the type of motion picture, the sound may be recorded when the film is shot or added later. In the first case, there are the single and the double system to choose from.

In single-system sound, special cameras are employed that record both image and sound on the same film. The sound may be optical; that is, a photographic image of the sound is recorded on the edge of the film. On the other hand, the sound may be magnetic. In this case a sound head, similar to the type found in tape recorders, records the sound on a magnetic stripe (iron oxide coating) along the edge of the film. This striping is applied when the film is in its raw stock form. In double-system sound, the sound recording is made separately and added to the film later as an optical track.

3. Special-Purpose Cameras

While the principles that govern photography are the same for practically all cameras, there are some cameras that are designed or specially modified to perform special tasks. These tasks range from high-speed motion pictures for time studies to tracking missiles and satellites. There are cameras that are used to store huge amounts of information in relatively small containers. Aerial photography requires a camera totally unsuitable for everything but the task for which it was designed. The differences between these cameras and those employed for more conventional photography may be found in the lens, film transport, box, or viewfinder, or in the means by which the cameras are mounted. For example, a camera designed for astrophotography is, in essence, a telescope equipped with a film carrier. In microphotography, the camera body may be quite conventional; the difference is in the lens mount. A television camera bears some resemblance to photographic cameras and is used to record an image. However, its principle is quite different.

In general, form follows function in special-purpose cameras. That is, the machine is designed to do a specific job, and any feature not applicable to the task is eliminated. For example, a special-purpose camera may have only one shutter speed or no shutter at all in the conventional sense; or it may not have a viewfinder, if the viewfinder serves no purpose.

High Speed. The conventional motion-picture camera is capable of taking no more than 250 frames per second. At higher frame rates the pulldown claw tears the film sprocket holes. However, cameras have been built that are capable of exposing film at the rate of 100 million frames per second by using entirely different means. One system employs a compensating moving prism instead of a shutter. The prism may be a cube, a parallel-sided glass plate, or even an octagon. As the film travels across the focal plane, the rotating prism projects a sharply focused image on the film. This system may use 8, 16, or 35mm film; the 8mm provides the highest frame rate, on the order of 16,000 frames per second. Another system employs multiple lenses; in this case, each lens deposits an image on the film through a hole in a rotating disk. The pulldown claw is eliminated completely.

One kind of high-speed camera, called an image-dissecting camera, is used to film lightning and explosions. It breaks the image into small elements that are photographed by a moving grid on a 4 x 5 inch (10 x 27cm) film sheet. The negative image is then converted to conventional motion-picture film. The rate of exposure is 100 million frames per second, but the camera operates for an extremely limited period. If it were to photograph for a full second, it would take days to project the resulting motion-picture film at normal speed.

Astronomical. An astronomical camera is designed to overcome the aberrations common with Newtonian telescopes. One such installation is a Mount Palomar Observatory telescope that is equipped with a 72-inch (783-cm) mirror. The spherical mirror is designed to correct for the various aberrations. The Palomar unit has a field of 6° x 6° and an opening equal to f/2.5. The field is purposely large to facilitate the performance of stellar surveys.

Astronomical cameras, however, need not be on the order of the Palomar telescope. Any telescope with an equatorial mount (to compensate for the movement of the stars in relation to the film) may be used. The camera body may accept 35mm film or larger plates. A shutter is of no particular importance in such a camera, because the exposures are extremely long; any device to open and close the lens will serve.

Aerial Photography. The aerial photographer is concerned primarily with recording information that can be used in map making or perhaps in regional planning. (However, several photographers have recognized that aerial photography also has aesthetic value, and have pioneered in creating a new kind of landscape imagery.) In wartime, of course, aerial photography plays an important role in supplying information on troop movements and emplacements.

Most modern aerial cameras have fixed focus lenses of rather long focal length, because practically all photographing takes place at "infinity." On some cameras a registration glass holds the film flat against the pressure plate. In other cameras the film is held flat by a vacuum system. Flatness of film is extremely important; minor deviations can cause errors that will show up as inaccuracies in the maps made from the photographs. The lenses are designed to be as distortion-free as possible—again, to guard against error. The film format is usually 9 x 9 inches (23 x 23cm); however, some cameras use 4 x 5 inch (10 x 27cm) film.

In general, aerial cameras are equipped with between-the-lens leaf shutters. Shutter speeds are relatively fast, but the lenses are rather slow; apertures of f/4 are the maximum. The camera mounting is designed to prevent vibrations from degenerating the image, and compensation is also made for the sideways movement of the airplane. Finally, heating units may be included in the bodies of the cameras, because the cameras are often required to work at fairly high altitudes. Film loads permit the shooting of 250 to 500 photographs. In addition to the normal aerial camera, 35mm cameras have been specially adapted to aerial work because of their large film load and lens interchangeability.

Stereo. A stereo photograph, in a sense, is the closest the photographer has come to re-creating reality, in the form of an apparently three-dimensional representation of a subject. Early stereoscopic photographs consisted of two positive images photographed in separate cameras and viewed in an open-type viewer equipped with a pair of lenses.

Although a single conventional camera may be used to take stereo photographs, the arrangement is rather cumbersome. Because the stereo effect is based on the interocular distance—the viewpoint separation of two normal eyes (about 2½ inches)—a special "rackover" device must be used. This arrangement is suitable only for still life subjects. The modern stereo camera is equipped with two separate lenses that are fixed at the interocular distance. Two photographs are made simultaneously. In most cases the photographs are made on color slide film. The processed images may be viewed in a special stereo viewer equipped with lenses that make it possible to bring the stereo pairs close to the eyes. For the best effect, the viewing lenses should be of the same focal length as the lenses on the camera.

Stereo camera shutters are of critical importance. The release must be synchronized so that both shutters open and close together. This is particularly true for action pictures, where a delay of one shutter will result in unmatched pairs that show two different stages of the movement. Stereo cameras use leaf shutters, either behind the lens or built into the lens elements. More advanced stereo cameras incorporate range finder systems, although there have been several cameras with fixed focus lenses.

Missile and Satellite. Cameras used in space programs are involved with two distinct areas: photography from the ground and photography from a satellite or missile.

Photography from the ground is designed to record what takes place on the ground, such as a launch, and also to provide information on the flight behavior of the vehicle being launched. Ground-to-air cameras employ either extremely long telephoto lenses or telescopes that range up to 500 inches (1,270cm) in focal length and that are mounted on a motion-picture camera using 70mm film. This setup provides sequence photographs of great sharpness. These cameras are mounted high above the ground to avoid atmospheric problems. The cameras used to obtain more critical information concerning flight characteristics are usually motion-picture cameras to which modified theodolites, or angle-measuring devices, have been attached; the film may be 35mm. Satellite tracking cameras provide information over greater distances. The camera may be a ballistics camera (a type that exposes a moving film through a slit) equipped with a long focal length mirror optic of extremely large aperture.

Television cameras with wide-angle lenses are used in satellites to relay information on weather and cloud formation, and other pertinent data, to the ground. The arrangement involves a 35mm camera-kinescope combination. Astronauts use more conventional machines, usually precision still cameras that are stripped of through-the-lens focusing mechanisms and other nonessentials for air-to-ground shooting. The cameras range in size from 35mm to 70mm, and the lenses used range from wide-angle to telephoto. Some cameras have gas systems that maintain film flatness during exposure; when the shutter is pressed, gas is released which exerts pressure on the film. The cameras may be permanently mounted inside the space capsule; this necessitates aiming the capsule itself to frame the subject. In addition to still cameras, ultrawide-angle movie cameras are also placed inside the capsule.

Television Cameras. There are some resemblances between conventional cameras and television cameras. Both employ lenses, a light-proof box, and a sensitive surface. The principle on which television operates, however, is electronic rather than photographic. The subject image is converted into an electronic signal, the potential of which determines the brightness of the television image.

The television camera has a light-sensitive surface that is made up of 2 million elements. This collection of elements is located on a mica surface that has a metal coating on the opposite side; the surface is built into a tube that resembles a cathode ray tube. The image formed by the lens of the camera is thrown on the light-sensitive screen. The light generates a small electrical charge; the brighter parts of the image produce charges with a higher potential. The result is an electrical interpretation of the subject.

An electron "gun" converts the image into a continuous signal that results in a pattern of horizontal lines. The potential built up by the image is discharged, producing a change in potential in the metal coating. This change is transmitted in the form of a shortwave signal to the receiver; there it becomes a visible image.

Television cameras are used to record and transmit images to the home or to magnetic tape recorders, from which the image can be played back and retransmitted. The advantage of the television camera is its immediacy; the image can be played back immediately after it has been recorded. The recorded image, unlike one on film, can be erased, and a new image recorded on the same tape. Professional cameras and recorders are huge affairs, but small units have been developed that are used in industry for the production of training films, for closed circuit broadcasting, and for surveillance. Camera and recorder units have been designed for home use as well, making it possible to create instant home movies. These smaller units are also used for instructional purposes.

Photo Finish. The photo finish camera is used to determine the winner in speed events such as track, car racing, and horse racing. The camera is aimed at the finish line. The film moves counter to the direction of the action, at a speed approximating as closely as possible the speed of the competitors across the focal plane. At first the image is only a blurry view of the finish line. However, as the competitors cross the line, their images are recorded sharply.

Simon-Wide. The Simon-Wide camera is not actually a wide-angle camera. It is, rather, a machine that provides a large area image on a 2¼ x 7 inch (67 x 178mm) negative, using 120 or 220 roll film. The lens is of normal focal length, and the image has a normal perspective.

MYRON MATZKIN, *"Modern Photography"*

Bibliography

Eastman Kodak Company, *How to Take Better Pictures* (Rochester, N. Y., 1967).

Feininger, Andreas, *The Compleat Photographer* (New York 1966).

Keppler, Herbert, *Keppler on the Eye-Level Reflex* (New York 1960).

Kingslake, Rudolph, *Lenses in Photography* (New York 1951).

Mascelli, Joseph V., ed., *American Cinematographer Manual* (Hollywood, Calif., 1966).

Pitman Publishing Corp. (Focal Press), *Focal Encyclopedia of Photography* (New York and London 1965).

CAMERA LUCIDA, lo͞o′sə-də, an optical device, invented around 1807, that is used by artists to facilitate sketching. Strictly speaking, the camera lucida is not a camera at all. Rather, it consists of a prism held in place over a plane surface, either by hand or mounted in a bracket. One face of the prism has a 90° angle, while the other face has a 135° angle. The prism delivers a virtual image of an external object to a paper or screen placed at the plane surface. The image can then be traced in order to obtain an exact reproduction of the object's perspective. The device is available in more refined forms and also as a rather inexpensive toy.

MYRON MATZKIN, *"Modern Photography"*

CAMERA OBSCURA, əb-skūr′ə, the forerunner of the modern camera. It is essentially like a conventional camera, except that it lacks a shutter. The term "camera obscura" first appeared in the 11th century, but the concept of the device dates back to antiquity.

In its earliest form the camera obscura consisted of a darkened room with a small aperture —later replaced by a lens—in one wall. Through this aperture an inverted image of a daylight scene was projected on the opposite wall. The viewer was inside the room. Artists used the device to attain realistic perspective in their work. For this purpose, portable camera obscuras were developed that utilized canopy arrangements.

Today's camera obscura contains a mirror that is set at a 45° angle to the lens. The mirror reflects the image to another, vertically mounted lens, which in turn projects the image onto a flat table or viewing screen.

MYRON MATZKIN, *"Modern Photography"*

A camera obscura is used by the artist to aid him in drawing the model of a castle. The image is reflected right-side-up through glass onto the underside of the paper.

CAMERARIUS, kam-ər-âr′ē-əs, **Rudolph Jacob** (1665–1721), German botanist and physician, who was the first to prove experimentally the sexuality of plants. Camerarius found that when he removed the staminate flowers of the castor oil plant (*Ricinus communis*) before pollen was emitted, he never obtained a perfect seed. He also found that removal of the styles of the corn plant (*Zea mays*) also prevented seed formation. These and other experiments convinced him that the stamen functions as the male part of the flower and the pistil as the female part. He concluded that pollen must be transferred from the anthers to the stigma if fertile seed is to be produced.

In 1694, Camerarius published his work in *De sexu plantarum epistola,* candidly including some facts that then seemed to contradict his view of plant sexuality. His work directed attention to the study of floral structure and indirectly led to Linnaeus' classification system and to plant breeding experiments.

Camerarius was born in Tübingen, Germany, on Feb. 12, 1695. He received his doctor of medicine degree from the University of Tübingen in 1687 and became professor of botany and director of its botanical garden. He died in Tübingen on Sept. 11, 1721.

WILLIAM T. STEARN
British Museum (Natural History)

Further Reading: Sachs, J. von, *History of Botany,* pp. 385–390 (London 1890).

CAMERON, kam′ər-ən, **Andrew Carr** (1834–1890), American labor leader and publisher, who was the greatest labor editor of the post-Civil War decade. He was born at Berwick-on-Tweed, England, on Sept. 28, 1834, and went to the United States at the age of 17 with his father, who was a printer. Soon active in the Typographical Union, he rose to head the Chicago Trades Assembly and the Illinois State Labor Association. In 1866, Cameron became a founder of the National Labor Union, the first national labor organization of any scope, and the editor of its official organ, the *Workingman's Advocate.* Cameron wrote most of the important theoretical and political documents of the organization.

The labor movement in the post-Civil War period was utopian and reformist in outlook, stressing Greenbackism, land reform, cooperatives, and an 8-hour-day law. Cameron ably espoused these views. In the 1870's, however, the labor movement turned from political reformism to economic action through trade unions, and the National Labor Union disappeared. Cameron discontinued his paper in 1880. He died at Chicago, Ill., on May 28, 1890.

HUGH G. CLELAND
State University of New York at Stony Brook

CAMERON, Donald, and Cameron, Sir Ewen. See CAMERONS OF LOCHIEL.

CAMERON, kam′ər-ən, **Duncan** (1764?–1848), Canadian fur trader. He was born in Glen Moriston, Scotland, and taken to New York as a child by his parents. In 1785 he joined the North West Company as a clerk; by 1800 he had become a partner and was in charge of the Nipigon district until 1807. He was stationed at Lake Winnipeg (1807–1811) and at Rainy Lake (1811–1814). In 1814 he was made *bourgeois,* or director, in the Red River district to hinder the development of Lord Selkirk's Red River colony. In April 1816, Cameron was arrested by the rival Hudson's Bay Company and sent to England for trial. He was released, however, and granted damages for false arrest. He retired from the North West Company about 1820 and settled in Williamstown, Upper Canada (Ontario), where he died on May 18, 1848.

JOHN S. MOIR, *University of Toronto*

CAMERON, kam′ər-ən, **Sir Gordon Roy** (1899–), Anglo-Australian pathologist, who is best known for his study of the effects of prolonged disease on the structure and function of the liver. The unifying thought behind Cameron's research was the response of cells to injury or disease.

During his lifetime research on the liver, Cameron improved methods of excluding the flow of blood to the liver and preventing the outflow of bile. In addition, he carefully studied the effects of exposing the liver to a vast number of toxic agents. He provided the first body of information on the mechanics and biochemistry of cellular injury and led to the development of a new branch of biology—micropathology.

During World War II, Cameron studied the pathology of intoxication with such gases as mustard gas, lewisite, nitrogen mustard, and phosgene, and suggested possible first aid treatments for such intoxications. He also studied the toxicology of insecticides, and as a result of his studies, DDT was adopted as a safe insecticide. Cameron also investigated regeneration in mammalian spleen, skin, adipose tissue, and alimentary canal linings.

Cameron was born in Echuca, Victoria, Australia, on June 30, 1899. He was educated at the University of Melbourne, served as a junior lecturer in pathology there, and in 1925 became deputy director of the Walker and Eliza Hall Institute for Medical Research in Melbourne. He later studied in Germany and then accepted a post at the University College Hospital Medical School in London. From 1945 to 1964 he was director of the Graham Laboratories in London. Cameron was knighted in 1957, and in 1960 he was awarded the Royal Medal of the Royal Society of London for his contributions to cellular pathology. Among his writings are *Pathology of the Cell* (1952) and *Biliary Cirrhosis,* with P. C. Hou in 1962.

DAVID A. OTTO, *Stephens College*

CAMERON, kam′ər-ən, **James Donald** (1833–1918), American industrialist, secretary of war, and Republican senator. The son of Simon Cameron (q.v.), he was born in Middletown, Pa., on May 14, 1833. After graduating from Princeton in 1852, he engaged in banking and in supervising the Northern Central Railroad.

Cameron first demonstrated his political sagacity during the Pennsylvania senatorial contest of 1867, when he helped his father defeat former Gov. Andrew Curtin. In 1876, President Grant finally rewarded the Cameron political machine for its backing by making James Cameron secretary of war. Using the war office as an adjunct of the Republican party, Cameron arrayed troops in Florida and South Carolina in support of Hayes over Tilden at the polls in 1876.

When President Hayes failed to retain James Cameron in the cabinet, Simon resigned his Senate seat in 1877 and obtained the election of James in his place. The younger Cameron was reelected three times, serving until 1897. Hoping to defeat the reformers of his party and to secure patronage, he fought hard but ineffectually for Grant's nomination for a third term in 1880.

Cameron's stand against the Force Bill of 1890, a measure that would have helped the Republican party in the South, lost him many supporters. He advocated free silver in the expectation that it might secure him the presidential nomination.

In 1897, Cameron relinquished to Matthew Quay the leadership of the political machine that he had inherited. He engaged in farming on his country estate near Harrisburg until his death there on Aug. 30, 1918.

ERWIN S. BRADLEY
Union College, Barbourville, Ky.

CAMERON, kam'ər-ən, **Julia Margaret** (1815–1879), British photographer, noted for her portraits of celebrities, including Tennyson, Longfellow, and Carlyle. She was born in Calcutta, India, on June 11, 1815. In 1848, 10 years after her marriage to Charles Hay Cameron, she and her husband went to England.

Given a camera as a gift by her son in 1864, she mastered the difficult wet plate, or collodion,

ART INSTITUTE OF CHICAGO—ALFRED STIEGLITZ COLLECTION

JULIA CAMERON made subtle photographic studies of such famous personages as Sir John Herschel.

photographic process. She then began to produce striking portraits, using an unconventional technique in which the heads of her subjects almost filled the plate, were harshly lighted, and lacked sharp focus. Her work, although somewhat severely criticized, was admitted to have great power. Mrs. Cameron also made highly sentimental costume pieces and did illustrations for the 1875 printing of Tennyson's *Idylls of the King*. She and her husband went to Ceylon in 1875, where she resided, photographing occasionally, until her death on Jan. 28, 1879.

BEAUMONT NEWHALL
George Eastman House, Rochester, N.Y.

CAMERON, kam'ər-ən, **Malcolm** (1808–1876), Canadian public official. He was born on April 25, 1808, in Trois-Rivières, Lower Canada (Quebec). At Perth, Upper Canada (Ontario) he founded the *Courier* (1834) and was elected in 1836 to the assembly for Lanark. Breezy, vigorous, and influential among western Reformers, he became assistant commissioner of public works in the Liberal ministry of 1848. But ambition and discontent with the government's moderation led him to resign in 1850 and help found the "Clear Grit" movement to make the Canadian constitution fully democratic.

When the new Liberal premier, Sir Francis Hincks, reached terms with the Grits, Cameron joined the cabinet in 1851. He found his influence there small and lost office in 1854, and the Grits began looking to a new Reform critic, George Brown. When Cameron returned to Parliament (1858–1863), he supported the Macdonald Conservative forces, but he never regained his old prominence. He withdrew to become queen's printer (1863–1869). He was elected to Parliament again in 1874. He died in Ottawa on June 6, 1876.

J. M. S. CARELESS, *University of Toronto*

CAMERON, kam'ər-ən, **Richard** (1648–1680), Scottish Covenanter leader. At first a schoolmaster in a church-sponsored school at Falkland in Fife, Cameron was converted by field preachers and became an outspoken supporter of the Covenanters, a Nonconformist sect of Presbyterians in Scotland. Although he had no university training, Cameron possessed a powerful eloquence and, as a field preacher, moved hundreds of his listeners to join him. Many left him, however, when in 1678 the English government granted toleration to Nonconformists, obviating the need for separate sects.

With a few remaining followers Cameron framed the Sanquhar Declaration, which disowned the authority of Charles II, declared war against him, and resolved to resist the succession of his brother, the Duke of York. As a result a price was put on the head of Cameron and his associates. He continued his itinerant preaching but, with his followers, was ambushed at Airds Moss in Ayrshire, on July 22, 1680. After offering a prayer, "Lord, spare the green and take the ripe," Cameron was killed. His head and hands were hung on Nether Bow Gate, Edinburgh. His followers became known as Cameronians.

CAMERON, kam'ər-ən, **Simon** (1799–1889), American politician, who was secretary of war at the start of the Civil War and later became state political boss in Pennsylvania. He was born in Maytown, Pa., on March 8, 1799. At 17 he became a printer's apprentice and began a career as a journalist. Cameron entered national politics as a Jacksonian Democrat and was appointed commissioner to settle Indian claims. Dissatisfied with his secondary position in the Democratic party and with its tariff policies, Cameron turned to the Whigs and, with their aid, was elected to the U. S. Senate in 1845. When the Republican Party was formed in the mid-1850's, he joined it. His ability to win election to the Senate in 1857 despite a Democratic majority in the Pennsylvania legislature secured him the Republican leadership in the state.

Cameron's strength in 1860 was not sufficient to secure the presidential nomination that he desired but his managers received, unknown to Lincoln, the promise of a cabinet post for him. He became secretary of war in the new cabinet. Even if the exigencies of the period are considered, Cameron's record as secretary is mediocre. Apparently, Army contracts enriched his friends though Cameron personally derived no profits. In January 1862, Cameron resigned under pressure to become minister to Russia. Within a year he was back in the United States, seeking political rehabilitation by becoming Lincoln's man in Pennsylvania and making an unsuccessful bid to win election again to the Senate. He also supported Lincoln's successor, Andrew Johnson, as long as he considered it expedient.

For more than a decade Cameron struggled against Gov. Andrew Curtin for control of the state party organization in Pennsylvania. His victory over Curtin for the senatorship in 1867 revealed the great strength of his political machine. His rule was now undisputed in the state, and he was easily reelected senator in 1873. Cameron's influence secured the appointment of his son James Donald Cameron (q.v.) to Grant's cabinet. When President Hayes refused to retain James Donald as secretary of war, the elder Cameron resigned his seat in the Senate and easily arranged the election of his son in his place.

Simon Cameron's political machine passed into the hands of his son and Matthew Quay. During most of the years after his retirement in 1877, he managed his beautiful estate at Donegal Spring, near Maytown, where he died on June 26, 1889.

A historian said of Cameron that "No politician of his generation understood the science of politics better than . . . [he]; none enjoyed greater power." He had a pleasing and genial personality, and he would go to great lengths to perform a favor for a friend. But the thesis that his career was based upon corruption is unfounded.

ERWIN S. BRADLEY
Union College, Barbourville, Ky.

Further Reading: Bradley, Erwin S., *Simon Cameron: Lincoln's Secretary of War* (Philadelphia 1966); Crippen, Lee L., *Simon Cameron: Ante-Bellum Years* (Oxford, Ohio, 1942.)

CAMERON, kam'ər-ən, **Verney Lovett** (1844–1894), British explorer, who was the first European to cross equatorial Africa from east to west. He was born at Radipole, Weymouth, England, on July 1, 1844, and joined the navy when he was 13. The Royal Geographical Society commissioned Cameron to find David Livingstone and to explore central Africa in 1872. While crossing Tanganyika the following year, he met servants carrying Livingstone's body to the coast. He then circumnavigated Lake Tanganyika and went in search of the main stream of the Congo River. Meeting with hostility from the local peoples, he veered south to the Congo-Zambezi watershed and then west to the coast of Angola, where he arrived on Nov. 28, 1875.

Cameron traveled with Richard Burton to West Africa on a purely commercial mission in 1882. After retiring from the navy in 1883, Cameron promoted the commercial penetration of Africa and wrote adventure stories for children. He died in England on March 27, 1894.

ROBERT L. HESS
University of Illinois at Chicago Circle

CAMERON, kam'ər-ən, is a city in Texas, 52 miles (84 km) southeast of Waco. It is the seat of Milam county. Cameron has a cotton mill, a meat-packing plant, creameries, and a hatchery. First settled in the 1830's and incorporated in 1888, the city was named for Capt. Ewen Cameron, who fought in the Texan war of independence from Mexico. Cameron has a mayor-council form of government. Population: 5,546.

CAMERONIANS, kam-ə-rō'nē-ənz, a sect of Scottish Presbyterian dissenters named for Richard Cameron (q.v.). The Cameronians were an outgrowth of the rebellion against the liturgy that had been imposed on all his subjects by James I. These rebels, who came to be known as Covenanters, fiercely opposed any usurpation of religious freedom by the king. They supported Cameron in his declaration at Sanquhar, Scotland, which renounced both the authority of Charles II, declaring war against him, and the succession of his brother the Duke of York. They followed Cameron on his preaching tours, and some were taken prisoner when he was killed at Airds Moss by forces loyal to the king.

For a while the Cameronians supported William and Mary when they assumed the crown. They strongly resisted the union of Scotland and England in 1709. In 1743 an act of toleration was secured in favor of the Cameronians and a presbytery was organized.

Although the name "Cameronian" was cherished after the death of Cameron, it came generally to be applied to bodies with unusual or avant-garde opinions. It was particularly applied to Reformed Presbyterians, who rejected the church-state settlement of Willam and Mary (1690). Although this body has declined the name "Cameronian," the name has popularly been applied to them in Scotland, Ireland, and the United States.

CAMERONS OF LOCHIEL, kam'ər-ənz lokh-ēl', Scots chieftains, who were loyal supporters of the Jacobite cause.

Sir Ewen, or Evan, Cameron of Lochiel (1629–1719) was born at Kilchurn Castle, Argyll, Scotland in February 1629. At the age of 11 he was made the hostage of the Marquess of Argyll against the good conduct of the Camerons. Six years later he was allowed to return to his clan. In 1652, with about 700 clansmen, he joined the Earl of Glencairn's rising on behalf of Charles II. After Glencairn had come to terms, Cameron held out, hiding with 32 followers. When English soldiers approached, Cameron attacked, and in the following struggles sank his teeth into the leader's throat and killed him. This furnished Sir Walter Scott with his description of the fight between Roderick Dhu and James Fitz-James in *The Lady of the Lake.*

Cameron eventually made peace with the English and visited London for the Restoration of Charles II in 1660. Knighted by Charles in 1681, he supported James II in 1689 when he led a victorious charge at the Battle of Killiecrankie. He was too old to fight in the Jacobite rising of 1715, but his sympathies were with the Stuarts, and he sent his clansmen to Sheriffmuir to fight under the leadership of his son John.

The elder Cameron, whom Lord Macaulay called the "Ulysses of the Highlands," reputedly killed the last wolf in Scotland. He died at Lochaber in February 1719.

Donald Cameron of Lochiel (c. 1695–1748), called "gentle Lochiel," was born at Achnacarrie, Inverness, Scotland. In 1719 he succeeded his grandfather Sir Ewen as chieftain. In 1745 he rallied the Highlanders to support Prince Charles' attempt to regain the British throne for the Stuarts. He was a Jacobite leader at the disastrous Battle of Culloden (April 1746). Severely wounded, he hid until the following September, when he escaped with Charles to France, where Cameron died in 1748.

MARC AND EVELYNE BERNHEIM, FROM RAPHO GUILLUMETTE

FISHERMEN of the Bananas tribe set out their nets on the Logone River near the village of Gémé. The river, in the northern region of Cameroon, borders Chad.

CAMEROON, kam-ə-rōōn', is a federal republic in Africa. It was formed in 1961 by a merger of the Cameroun Republic, which was a United Nations trust territory under French administration until 1960, and the southern half of the British-administered trust territory of the Cameroons. The two areas are now component states of the Federal Republic of Cameroon, called East Cameroon and West Cameroon, respectively.

Cameroon is one of Africa's most diverse countries. Not only are there two official languages, English and French, but there are over 150 different ethnic groups. Extreme differences in geography and climate are found within the country, which has a cultural variety ranging from forest-dwelling Pygmies to nomadic desert tribesmen.

INFORMATION HIGHLIGHTS

Official Name: Federal Republic of Cameroon.
Head of State: President.
Head of Government: President.
Legislature: Federal National Assembly.
Area: 183,568 square miles (475,442 sq km).
Boundaries: *North and west,* Nigeria; *north and east,* Chad; *east,* Central African Republic; *south,* Congo (Brazzaville), Gabon, Río Muni.
Highest Point: Mt. Cameroon, 13,350 feet (4,070 meters).
Population: 5,229,000 (1965).
Capital: Yaoundé (population, 1962 census, 93,269).
Official Languages: English and French.
Major Religions: Animism; Christianity; Islam.
Monetary Unit: Franc CFA.
Weights and Measures: Metric system.
Flag: Green, red, and yellow vertical stripes, with two yellow five-pointed stars on the green stripe representing the union of East and West Cameroon.
National Anthem: *O Cameroon, Land of Our Ancestors.*

The People. Cameroon is primarily an agricultural country, and most of its people live on the land. The population density average is approximately 23 persons per square mile (9 per sq km), but 80% of the federation's total population (1965, 5,229,000) is in East Cameroon. The population density is highest in the western highlands of East Cameroon in the areas surrounding the capital, Yaoundé; in areas in the north of East Cameroon, around the towns of Garoua and Maroua; and in the grassfields of West Cameroon. The three administrative regions of Diamaré, Bamiléké, and Nyong et Sanaga contain about 42% of the population.

The major ethnic groups in East Cameroon are the Fulani and Kirdi in the north and the Bamiléké, Bulu, Bamoun, Ewondo, Beti, Bassa, and Douala in the south. West Cameroonian ethnic groups are divided between the coastal groups, which include the Bakweri and Douala, and the grasslands populations of the Tikar and related groups. In addition, West Cameroon has substantial numbers of southern Nigerians, including Ibo, Ibibio, Ijaw, Ekoi, and Edo, many of whom work on West Cameroonian plantations.

The capital of the federation is Yaoundé. Douala, with a population of about 187,000 (1964), is the largest city and the principal port and commercial center. Other important cities include Nkongsamba, Garoua, Kumba, and Victoria.

The religion of almost 60% of all Cameroonians, including in particular the Kirdi people, is tribal animism. Roman Catholics, who make up 22% of the population, and Protestants, about 7% of the population, mainly inhabit the southern part of the country. Muslims, about 14% of the

CAMEROON Map Index

Population: 5,229,000

Area: 183,568 square miles

CITIES and TOWNS

Abong-Mbang, 2,000 . . . B3
Bafia B3
Bali, 18,277 . . . . A2
Bamenda, 1,455 . . . . B2
Banyo, 3,000 . . . . B2
Batouri, 8,000 . . . . B3
Bertoua, 2,500 . . . . B3
Bétaré-Oya, 1,400 . . . . . B2
Bonabéri A3
Buea, 7,990 . . . . A3
Campo, 2,000 . . . . B3
Djoum B3
Douala, 187,000* A3
Dschang, 6,000 . . . . A2
Ebolowa, 10,000 . . . . B3
Edéa, 12,000 . . . . B3
Eséka B3
Fort-Foureau, 2,000 . . . . B1
Foumban, 20,000 . . . . . . B2
Garoua, 20,000 . . . . B2
Guidder, 4,500 . . . . B2
Kaélé B1
Kontcha B2
Kousseri (Fort-Foureau), 2,000 . . . . B1
Kribi, 3,000 . . . . B3
Kumba, 10,000 . . . . A3
Kumbo B2
Lomié, 10,000 . . . . B3
Mamfe, 10,000 . . . . A2
Maroua, 20,000 . . . . B1
M'Balmayo, 5,500 . . . . . B3
Meiganga, 2,000 . . . . B2
Mokolo, 3,000 . . . . B1
Moloundou C3
N'Gaoundéré, 15,000 . . B2
N'Kambe, 2,145 . . . . B2
N'Kongsamba, 31,991 . . B2
Poli, 700 . . . . B2
Rei-Bouba B2
Sangmélima B3
Tibati, 3,000 . . . . B2
Tiko, 15,000 . . . . A3
Victoria, 15,000 . . . . A3
Wum, 9,710 . . . . A2
Yabassi B3
Yaoundé (cap.) 93,269 . . B3
Yokadouma B3
Yoko B2

* 1964 est.

PHYSICAL FEATURES

Adamawa (region) B2
Benue (river) B2
Biafra (bight) A3
Cameroon (mt.) A3
Chad (lake) C1
Cross (river) A2
Dja (river) B3
Donga (river) B2
Guinea (gulf) A3
Ivindo (river) B3
Kadei (river) C3
Logone (river) C2
Lom (river) B2
Mbéré (river) B2
Sanaga (river) B3
Sanga (river) C3
Shari (river) C1

Population Years: Country total—1965 UN est.; capital—1962 census; others—1957 off. est.

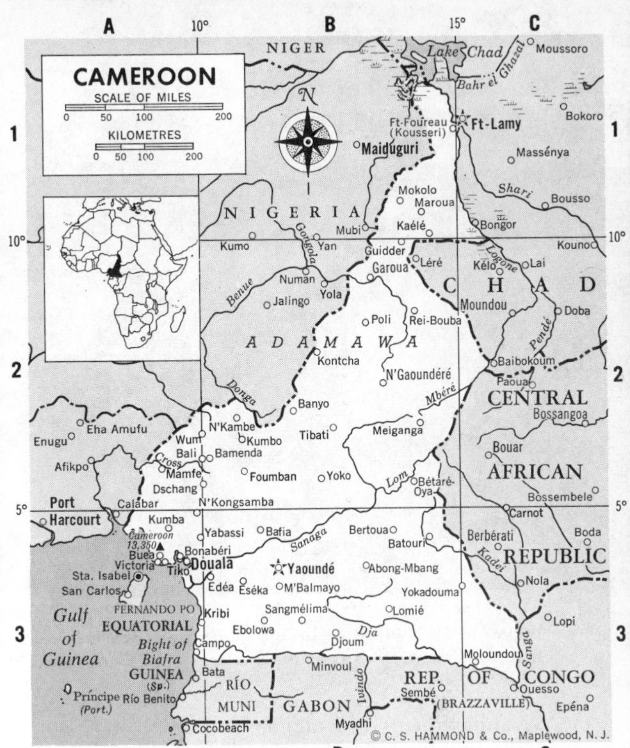

population, primarily include the Fulani and other groups in the north.

Two educational systems are used in Cameroon. West Cameroon's system is based on the British model; East Cameroon's is based on the French. It is expected that the two systems will be gradually merged.

In the southern areas of the country, almost all school age children are enrolled in classes. However, in the north, which has always been the most isolated part of the country, only a little over 10% attend school. Christian mission schools are an important part of Cameroon's education system. Most students do not go beyond the primary grades, although many attend the country's secondary schools. There are also institutions for teacher training and technical education. At the top of Cameroon's educational structure is the Federal University in Yaoundé, which has an enrollment of over 1,000 students. In addition, there are about 1,500 Cameroonians studying in colleges and universities in Europe and the United States.

The Land and Natural Resources. Cameroon can roughly be divided into five geographic zones according to dominant physical, climatic, and vegetative features. The mountain region of West Cameroon includes an irregular chain of mountains, hills, and plateaus that extend north almost to the edge of Lake Chad. This region has a pleasant climate, particularly in the Bamenda, Bamiléké, and Mambilla highlands. The region also has some of Cameroon's most fertile lands. Plantations are set in the volcanic soils of Victoria division, near the sea. Mt. Cameroon, which rises to 13,350 feet (4,070 meters), is the highest peak in West Africa.

The coastal plain extends 10 to 50 miles (16 to 80 km) inland from the sea to the edge of the forest region. Exceedingly hot and humid, the coastal plain contains some of the wettest places on earth. For example, Debuncha, on the seaward slope of Mt. Cameroon, has recorded an annual rainfall of over 360 inches (9,000 mm).

The inland forest plateau, dominated by the tropical rain forest, has an average elevation of about 1,500 to 2,000 feet (460 to 610 meters) and extends about 300 miles (485 km) inland. It is less humid than the coastal plain.

The Adamawa plateau region is an extension of the western mountain region. Running east-west across Cameroon, the rugged plateau forms a barrier between the north and the south. Average elevation is 3,400 feet (1,036 meters), and the plateau has a relatively pleasant climate.

The northern savanna plain extends from the edge of the Adamawa plateau region to Lake Chad. Its principal vegetation is scrub and grass cover. Sparse rainfall and high median temperatures are characteristic of this region.

Cameroon has several important rivers, including the Sanaga, whose lower falls generate hydroelectric power for the Edéa aluminum works; the Dja, which flows southwest into the Congo River; the Logone, which drains into Lake Chad; the Benue, the eastern tributary of the Niger River; and the Wouri.

Douala, located on an estuary of the Wouri River, is the principal seaport. The town of Garoua on the Benue River is accessible from Nigeria for about six weeks during the rainy season (mid-July to mid-September), making it one of the country's most important river ports. Victoria and Tiko are West Cameroon's principal outlets to the sea.

Cameroon's natural resources are best suited to agriculture rather than to industry. Soils and climate in the southern part of Cameroon encourage extensive cultivation of such plantation crops as cocoa, coffee, and bananas. In the north, natural conditions favor such crops as cotton and peanuts. An area that has considerable potential for growth is the tropical rain forest, with timber reserves estimated to cover some

MARC AND EVELYNE BERNHEIM, FROM RAPHO GUILLUMETTE

WOMAN SHOPPING at an outdoor market, containing shoes and sandals, at Yaoundé, the capital of Cameroon.

39 million acres (16 million hectares), of which only 5 million acres (2 million hectares) are accessible under present conditions.

An exceptionally large deposit of bauxite has been discovered near Tibati on the Adamawa plateau. However, the deposit is too far from the sea to be commercially exploitable before the Transcameroon railroad reaches the area.

The Economy. Cameroon has enjoyed one of the highest rates of economic growth in French-speaking Africa. About 75% of its economic activity is agricultural, mostly subsistence farming and production for local markets. Grown almost exclusively for local consumption are manioc, millet, cassava, and various tuberous vegetables. Almost all of the palm oil produced in East Cameroon is consumed locally, but palm oil is West Cameroon's fifth most valuable export crop. Peanuts and bananas, which are important items in the local diet, are also produced in both states in important quantities for export. Cocoa is Cameroon's most important agricultural export. Cotton, coffee, and rice are also major cash crops.

Plantation agriculture is an important part of the economy, especially in West Cameroon. Bananas and rubber are the major crops grown on the large plantations, which are generally owned by joint-stock corporations in which Europeans and Cameroonians both hold shares. Livestock raising is important in the Adamawa plateau region.

Agricultural commodities are the principal exports of the country. Aluminum is the only nonagricultural product exported. Imports are mainly finished consumer goods; capital goods are second in importance, followed by semiprocessed raw materials for local industry. Cameroon's principal trading partners are the countries of the European Common Market, especially France, followed by the United States, Japan, Britain, and Guinea (which provides most of the bauxite processed at Edéa).

The Edéa aluminum plant, which produces over 50,000 tons (45,000 metric tons) of aluminum annually, dominates Cameroonian industry, which ranks third in volume among the French-speaking African states. However, Cameroonian industry other than the production of aluminum is modest and consists mostly of the production of locally sold and consumed articles. A number of local enterprises produce such goods as hats, shoes, cigarettes, plastic articles, soap, aluminum utensils, and beer. In addition, cotton oil, peanut by-products, palm oil, and cocoa are processed on a small scale for both domestic and export markets.

Improvement of Cameroon's rail and road networks is one of the country's most important development priorities. In East Cameroon rail links extend only from Douala east to Yaoundé, a distance of about 187 miles (311 km), and north from Douala to Nkongsamba, about 107 miles (172 km). The latter link was extended west from Mbanga to Kumba, in West Cameroon, in 1965. The Transcameroon railroad, financed by a consortium of American and European funding agencies, was planned to reach Nkongsamba in the north, 397 miles (639 km) from Yaoundé. Cameroon has only about 8,500 miles (13,680 km) of roads, but extensive road construction is under way.

Government. The constitution of Cameroon became effective on Oct. 1, 1961, the date of the formation of the federation, which consists of two states—East Cameroon and West Cameroon. Federal authority is vested in the president and the National Assembly. The federal government has exclusive jurisdiction over defense, foreign affairs, development planning, national economic coordination, external economic relations, money and banking, higher education, the status of aliens, immigration, information services and radio, and foreign financial and technical assistance. Also under federal jurisdiction are personal status and property laws, judicial organization, interstate transportation, public health, and civil service.

The president of the federal republic is the head of state and the chief executive of the federal government. The president and vice president, who under the constitution may not be from the same state, are elected on the same slate by universal suffrage for 5-year terms. The president names federal ministers and deputy ministers, all of whom serve at his pleasure. The National Assembly is elected by universal suffrage and serves for 5 years. There are 50 deputies, 40 from East Cameroon and 10 from West Cameroon.

In areas other than those reserved for federal jurisdiction, the states may choose their own institutions and pass their own laws. The president of the federal republic designates the prime minister of each state, who in turn selects his own cabinet. However, both state prime ministers must be endorsed by their respective legislatures. The legislative assembly of East Cameroon is composed of 100 deputies. West Cameroon's legislative assembly is composed of 41 representatives, and the state has a 20-member house of chiefs as well. The latter house has only consultative powers and is presided over by the speaker of the legislative assembly. The members of each legislative assembly are elected by universal suffrage for 5-year terms.

All of Cameroon's active political parties were merged to form the Cameroon National Union (CNU) on Sept. 1, 1966. Although any party may withdraw from the CNU whenever it wishes and new parties may still be organized,

MARC AND EVELYNE BERNHEIM, FROM RAPHO GUILLUMETTE

ALUMINUM SECTIONS are packed at the aluminum plant in Edéa, Cameroon, before shipment to France for processing into sheet form. The plant was opened in 1955.

the merger effectively transformed Cameroon into a single-party state.

History. Some historians maintain that Carthaginian sailors may have reached the Cameroon coast in the fifth century B.C. The area entered modern history in 1472, when Portuguese mariners visited the Bight of Biafra and sailed up the estuary of what is now called the Wouri River. The Portuguese caught many small crayfish in the river and, mistaking them for prawns, named the river Rio dos Camarões ("River of Prawns"). Transformations of "Camarões"—Camarones (Spanish), Kamerun (German), Cameroun (French), and Cameroons (English)—identified the area thereafter and gave the country its present name.

From the beginning of the 16th century to early in the 17th century, Cameroon's coast was a principal source of supply first for European and later for American slave traders. Britain's attempts to put an end to the West African slave trade during the first half of the 19th century greatly increased British influence in the area. A British missionary settlement, the first permanent settlement in the area, was established at Victoria, at the foot of Mt. Cameroon, in 1858. Although British interests had an advantage over French and German traders who were active in the area, Britain failed to take advantage of its opportunity to impose its rule on the Cameroon coast. Germany signed a treaty with the Douala chiefs, establishing a German protectorate over what came to be called the Kamerun, on July 12, 1884. The German protectorate lasted for 30 years, during which time the Germans developed the basic economy and communications network of the country.

During World War I, Allied forces overwhelmed German resistance in the protectorate, and in 1916 the Kamerun was divided between Britain and France. France received four fifths of the territory and Britain one fifth. Under the terms of the peace settlements, the two territories became mandates of the League of Nations in 1922 and were administered respectively by France and Britain.

Britain's administration of its mandate was relatively uneventful, with little visible material progress except in the southern region, where most of the German plantations were repurchased by their former owners after the war. French administration of its mandate was subjected to considerable criticism, particularly because of the use of forced labor on public projects and also because France did little to improve social and political conditions. During World War II, both territories remained loyal to the Allies, and after the war British and French administrative policies changed considerably. The two mandates were made United Nations trust territories and again placed under British and French administration. Britain and France in turn agreed to foster political growth within their territories toward the goals of self-government and/or independence.

Many political parties and groups were formed in the two territories. These parties were stimulated by the encouraging terms of the trusteeship agreement, by the changes in the colonial policies of both England and France, and by the creation of local representative institutions in which native Cameroonians could participate. Of the political parties that arose in the French-administered territory, three were of particular importance. The Union des Populations du Cameroun (UPC), created in 1948 by Ruben Um Nyobé, was the first party actively to demand independence from France and reunification of the two Cameroons. The Démocrates Camerounais was organized in 1957 by André-Marie Mbida, the first premier of the French-administered Cameroons. The Union Camerounaise (UC) was organized in 1958 by Ahmadou Ahidjo, who later became president of the federal republic.

The UPC led an unsuccessful revolt against the government in 1955 and was subsequently banned. The UPC revolt continued to flare up in the southern and western parts of the territory until 1962, when it was finally put down by the government. The party was legally reinstated in 1960.

but never regained its previous strength. Mbida's Démocrates, together with representatives from the UC and two minor parties, formed the first French Cameroonian government in 1957. In 1958 the Mbida government fell, and Ahmadou Ahidjo became premier. By 1959 the French Cameroons had been accorded full internal self-government and it became fully independent as the Cameroun Republic on Jan. 1, 1960.

In the British Cameroons, which was in turn divided into Northern Cameroons and Southern Cameroons, three main political parties finally emerged to contest for power, each advocating its own special solution to the problem of terminating the UN trusteeship. The Cameroon Peoples' National Convention (CPNC), founded by Dr. E. M. L. Endeley, advocated merger with Nigeria. The Kamerun National Democratic Party (KNDP), led by John N. Foncha, who later became vice president of the federal republic, advocated union with an independent Cameroun Republic. The One Kamerun, a UPC faction led by Ndeh Ntumazah, also favored reunification of British and French Cameroons.

The United Nations conducted two plebiscites to determine popular sentiment on the issue. One was held in August 1959, exclusively in the Northern Cameroons (the northern division of the British trusteeship), and another in both Northern and Southern Cameroons on Feb. 11, 1961. The 1959 plebiscite, asking voters to choose between joining Nigeria or deferring a decision, was inconclusive. In the 1961 plebiscite the Northern Cameroons voted to join Nigeria, while the Southern Cameroons voted to merge with the Cameroun Republic.

On Oct. 1, 1961, in accordance with this second plebiscite, the British Southern Cameroons trusteeship came to an end and the Federal Republic of Cameroon was created. Northern Cameroons had become part of Nigeria in July 1961.

Since 1961 the federal republic has sought to find ways of effectively merging the separate educational, legal, administrative, and economic systems of the two states. A common currency has been introduced for both states, weights and measures have been standardized, and various measures have been taken to integrate the economies of the states. By the mid-1960's, problems of communication still existed: both French and English were official languages; the educational systems, based on different models, had not yet been integrated; the legal systems, based on different principles, had not yet been completely unified; and unrestricted movement between the two states had not yet been accomplished. Suspicion of and fear of being dominated by larger, stronger East Cameroon still could be found among many West Cameroonians. Despite these problems, however, the federation has functioned quite well and with relatively little tension between the partners.

VICTOR T. LE VINE
Washington University, St. Louis, Mo.

Bibliography

Ardener, Edwin, and others, *Plantation and Village in the Cameroons* (London 1960).

Gardinier, David E., *Cameroon: United Nations Challenge to French Policy* (London 1963).

Johnson, Willard R., *"The Cameroon Federation," in French-Speaking Africa, the Search for Identity,* ed. by William H. Lewis (New York 1965).

Le Vine, Victor T., *The Cameroons, from Mandate to Independence* (Los Angeles 1964).

McCullough, Merran, and others, *Peoples of the Central Cameroons* (London 1954).

Welch, Claude E., Jr., *Dream of Unity: Pan-Africanism and Political Unification in West Africa* (Ithaca, N.Y., 1966).

CAMEROON MOUNTAIN, kam-ə-rōōn′, a volcanic massif, is the highest point in West Africa. It is located in the western part of Cameroon, along the coast of the Gulf of Guinea. It extends 14 miles (23 km) inland and nearly 500 miles (805 km) into the Gulf of Guinea in a series of volcanic islands.

The mountain is composed of a double chain of volcanic peaks separated by a graben, or trench. The highest is double-crested Mt. Cameroon (13,350 feet, or 4,069 meters). It was active when seen by Hanno, a Carthaginian explorer, in 470 B.C., and it is still active.

Around the base of the mountain the volcanic soils are rich. Rainfall averages over 400 inches (1,000 cm) annually, making the area the wettest in Africa.

HUGH C. BROOKS
St. John's University, New York

CAMIGUIN, kä-mē-gēn′, is an island in the Philippines with an area of 96 square miles (249 sq km). A part of Misamis Oriental province, Camiguin lies in the Mindanao Sea about 7 miles (11 km) north of Talisayan on Mindanao island. Camiguin has volcanic mountains rising as high as 5,619 feet (1,708 meters). One of them erupted in 1948 and forced the evacuation of the island. The chief agricultural products of Camiguin are cocoa, rice, sugar, and tobacco. Population: (1960) 40,717.

CAMILLA, kə-mil′ə, is a city in southwestern Georgia, the seat of Mitchell county, 93 miles (149 km) southeast of Columbus. Situated in a farming area, Camilla is a processing center for pecans, peanuts, cotton, and poultry. Its manufactures include feeds, fertilizer, and clothing. The city was named in 1857 for the granddaughter of David Mitchell, governor of Georgia (1809–1813, 1815–1817). Government is by mayor and council. Population: 4,987.

CAMILLE, kə-mēl′, is the usual English title of a play by Alexandre Dumas fils (q.v.), *La dame aux camélias* (1849), which was based on his novel (1848) of the same name. The play, first performed in 1852, became the greatest success of 19th century French theater.

Camille is largely autobiographical, presenting the story of Dumas' affair with Marie Duplessis, a well-known Parisian courtesan who died of consumption in 1847. The central character of the play, Camille Gautier, has had several affairs but has never experienced true love before meeting Armand Duval, a young man of good family. They leave Paris together, but their idyllic country life is ended by a visit from Armand's father, who, in Armand's absence, persuades Camille to leave her lover for the good of his family. She tells Armand that she has lost interest in their life together and sadly returns to her former life. Her sacrifice and Armand's denunciations, together with her consumption, hasten her death, and Armand, finally disabused of his bad opinion of her, reaches her only in time for her to die in his arms.

Camille owes its success largely to its romantic pathos and the authenticity of its portrayal of Parisian life. The play inspired Verdi's opera *La Traviata* (1853), and a film version, starring Greta Garbo, appeared in 1936.

KENNETH DOUGLAS, *Author of "A Critical Bibliography of Existentialism"*

CAMILLUS, kə-mil′əs, **Marcus Furius** (died c. 365 B. C.), Roman soldier and statesman, who delivered Rome from the Gauls. He is often called the "second founder" of Rome.

Made dictator of Rome in 396 B. C., Camillus successfully concluded the 10-year siege of Veii in Etruria. In 394 he besieged and forced the surrender of Falerii, another Etruscan city. The approach of Gallic invaders in 388 caused the Romans to recall Camillus from Ardea in Latium, where he had resided after either an enforced exile for misappropriation of military booty or after a self-imposed retreat from those who envied his successes. Again serving as dictator, he rescued Rome from its Gallic captors in 387, rebuilt the devastated city, and gained new victories over the Volscians. Though he was named dictator for a third term in 386, Camillus declined the office. In 381 he led Roman armies victoriously against towns in Latium.

He accepted in 368 a fourth nomination as dictator. A Gallic incursion in 367 led to Camillus' being called for the fifth time to the dictatorship; once again he defeated the invaders. In the same year he aided the passage of the Licinian-Sextian laws, which improved the political status of the plebeians. Modern scholars believe that some fiction has crept into the tradition of Camillus' military and political activities.

P. R. COLEMAN-NORTON, *Princeton University*

CAMILLUS DE LELLIS, kə-mil′əs də lel′lis, **Saint** (1550–1614), Italian founder of the Camillians. He was born in Bucchianico, Italy, on May 25, 1550, the son of an army officer. He served in the Venetian army against the Turks (1571–1574). Twice (1575, 1579) he joined the Capuchins as a lay brother but was forced to leave because of an ulcerated foot that tormented him until his death.

In 1579 he became superintendent of San Giacomo Hospital in Rome, from whose employ he had been dismissed in 1571 for gambling. After studying at the Roman College, he was ordained in 1584. About 1582, Camillus founded a religious order, the Camillians, to tend the sick in hospitals. He served as superior general until 1604, and thereafter as a nurse. He died in Rome on July 14, 1614, and was canonized in 1746. With St. John of God, he is copatron of hospitals, nurses, and the sick. His feast day is July 18.

JOHN F. BRODERICK, S. J.
Weston College, Mass.

CAMISARD, kȧ-me-zȧr′, is the name given to the French Protestants of the Cévennes region who rose in rebellion against Louis XIV in 1702.

Systematic persecution of Protestants in Languedoc, culminating in the King's revocation in 1685 of the Edict of Nantes (which had granted a large measure of religious freedom to the Protestants), had led at first to widespread renunciation of Protestantism among the Cévennes population. Subsequently, however, they returned to their faith, believing that the Protestant powers, if victorious in the Nine Years' War (1688–1697), would help them.

But in forming the Treaty of Ryswick, which ended the war, England and the United Provinces failed to insert any provision protecting French Protestants. In their profound disillusion the Cévennes Protestants, long deprived of trained ministers, became increasingly radical in the face of continued brutal persecution. When hundreds of children, called *les petits prophets,* traveled from village to village reciting the more terrible of Biblical prophecies, 300 were judged guilty of "fanaticism" and sentenced to imprisonment at Uzès.

Open revolt exploded on July 24, 1702, with the assassination of the Abbé du Chayla and the release of Protestants whom he had imprisoned. Favored by rugged terrain and loyally supported by the local population, the Camisards, never numbering more than 1,500 men, waged a guerrilla war of unprecedented ferocity against the armies of Louis XIV. Composed entirely of common people inexperienced in warfare, the guerrilla bands nevertheless fought off 25,000 regular troops for over 3 years. Their most important leader, Jean Cavalier, was the son of a peasant and a baker's assistant; others were peasants, wool carders, and shepherds. They were so successful at first that the crown concluded a peace treaty with Cavalier in May 1704, granting some concessions to the Camisards. The majority of the Camisard army insisted, however, that the Edict of Nantes be restored. Negotiations broke down and the war continued in full force until January 1705. Sporadic hostilities continued until 1711. By this time most of the leaders were dead or in exile, and Protestantism had all but disappeared from the Cévennes.

LIONEL ROTHKRUG, *University of Michigan*

CAMMAERTS, käm′ärts, **Émile** (1878–1953), Belgian poet, who is noted for his impassioned patriotic verses prompted by the carnage of World War I. He was born in Brussels on March 16, 1878. He moved to England in 1908 but retained his Belgian citizenship.

During World War I, Cammaerts wrote many patriotic poems, including *Chants patriotiques et autres poèmes* (1915; Eng. tr., *Belgian Poems*), *Les trois rois et autres poèmes* (1916; Eng. tr., *New Belgian Poems*), and *Messines et autres poèmes* (1918; Eng. tr., *Messines and Other Poems*). He also wrote the plays *Les deux bossus* (1917) and *La veillée de Noël* (1917). Later works, written in English, are mostly on political and historical themes. They include *The Child of Divorce* (1938), *The Keystone of Europe* (1939), *The Prisoner at Laeken* (1941), *Upon This Rock* (1943), and *The Devil Takes the Chair* (1949). Cammaerts died at Radlett, England, on Nov. 2, 1953.

CAMMARANO, käm-mä-rä′nō, **Salvatore** (1801–1852), Italian poet and librettist, who wrote texts for operas by such composers as Donizetti and Verdi. Cammarano was born in Naples on March 19, 1801. After studying under Dante Gabriel Rossetti, he began to write prose plays (among them *Baldovino* and *Un ritratto e due pittori*) that were performed in Florence. At the age of 33 he became interested in lyric drama and subsequently wrote librettos for many operas. He is probably best known for his libretto for Donizetti's *Lucia di Lammermoor* (1835), based on Sir Walter Scott's novel. He also wrote the librettos for Donizetti's *Don Pasquale* (1843); for several operas by Giovanni Pacini, including *Saffo* (1840), *Buondelmonte* (1845), and *Merope* (1846); for Verdi's *Alzira* (1845), *La battaglia di Legnano* (1849), *Luisa Miller* (1849), and *Il Trovatore* (1853); and for works by other composers. He died in Naples on July 17, 1852.

CAMÕES, kə-moinsh′, **Luís Vaz de** (1524–1580), Portuguese poet, the most famous poet to have written in Portuguese. He was probably born in Lisbon, the son of Simão Vaz de Camões, a petty nobleman, and Ana Sá e Macedo, a native of Santarém. The family descended from the Galician Vasco Pérez de Camoens (*Camoens* is the Castilian, and *Camoëns,* the English, spelling of the name), who had fled political persecution in Spain in 1369. The explorer Vasco da Gama, celebrated in Camões' magnum opus, *Os Lusíadas,* or *The Lusiads,* was a distant relation of the family.

Early Life. When Luís was three years old, a plague in Lisbon forced his family to retreat to Coimbra. There he spent most of his childhood and youth with his mother and grandparents after his father returned to a government position in Lisbon. In 1538, Camões entered the University of Coimbra, an important center of learning in the 16th century, where he possibly studied under the tutelage of his uncle, Dom Bento de Camões. Camões read widely in Latin literature and acquired the broad knowledge of classical culture that he frequently displays in his later work. He also learned Italian and Castilian. Camões is said to have been a contentious student, and it is uncertain whether he actually graduated. During his university days he fell in love with a cousin, Isabel, and when she rejected him, he left Coimbra for Lisbon.

In Lisbon, Camões became the tutor of Antônio de Noronha, son of the Count of Linares. This position, and his own aristocratic background, gave him access to the court of King John III. The court had a lively cultural life despite the severe, solemn influence of John's Spanish consort, Catherine, and Camões became a part of the circle surrounding the clever Princess Maria. At the court he met and fell in love with Catarina de Ataíde, a lady-in-waiting to the Queen. Though Camões was rejected by Catarina's family, probably because of his poverty, there is a critical tradition that she served as the poet's inspiration throughout his life.

Possibly because of the influence of the Ataídes, or perhaps because his play *El-rei Seleuco* contained satire dangerously relevant to the Portuguese royal family, Camões was banished in 1546 to Santarém, his mother's native city. He remained there until he volunteered in 1547 for military service in Ceuta, Morocco, for a campaign against the Moors, during which he lost the sight of his right eye.

Camões was back in Lisbon in 1550, but his continued ostracism at court and the newly introduced Inquisition made life there difficult. In 1552 he was in a street fight in which he wounded a minor aide to the King. He was thrown into jail but was pardoned a year later on the condition that he go to India as a soldier.

Years in the Orient. The voyage was difficult, and Camões was unhappy in the hot, unhealthy, and corrupt atmosphere of Goa, the capital of the Portuguese empire in the Orient. The poetry he wrote during this period was highly nostalgic and recalled Coimbra and Catarina de Ataíde. During his participation in punitive expeditions against the natives and in a naval engagement off Ormuz, Camões was revolted by the cruelty of the Portuguese; his revulsion is reflected in his later writings, particularly in *The Lusiads.*

Camões' luck changed when his comedy *Filodemo* was produced in Goa in 1555 on the arrival of a new viceroy. The play so pleased the viceroy, Francesco Barreto, that he adopted Camões as a favorite and later secured for him an official position in the Portuguese possession of Macao. In 1558, Camões arrived in Macao, where his nostalgia for Portugal, reflected in his writings, became even greater than in Goa, though his life was better. After a few years, complaints were made against Camões' official actions, and he was ordered back to Goa to stand trial. However, he was shipwrecked off the Mekong delta (in what is now South Vietnam). He managed to swim to shore, miraculously saving his incomplete manuscript of *The Lusiads.*

Two years later, after returning to Goa, Camões learned of the deaths of Catarina de Ataíde and John III and of the succession of the young King Sebastian, whose mother reigned as regent. The new viceroy in Goa was the Count of Redondo, who had known Camões in Lisbon and who gave the poet a clerkship. During this period, Camões became friendly with the historian Diogo do Couto.

Return to Portugal. In 1567, Camões arranged passage home but quarreled with the Count of Redondo and was stranded without money in Mozambique. He finally was rescued in 1569 by Couto and Heitor da Silveira, who took him with them to Portugal. It was an eventful voyage. A number of manuscripts of Camões' lyrics were lost or stolen, and plague, which had broken out in Lisbon the year before, infected some of those on board, including Silveira, who died before the ship reached Lisbon in April 1570.

Camões energetically set about publishing his life's work, *The Lusiads.* He sought and won the King's patronage for the poem and also gained the approval and friendship of the chief Inquisition censor, Frei Bartolomeu. *The Lusiads,* a highly patriotic epic, which was probably published sometime in 1572, brought Camões immediate fame. However, the royal pension he received was meager. In 1580 the plague again struck Lisbon, and Camões was among the victims. He died on June 10, 1580, and was buried in a mass grave in the Church of Santa Ana.

Interest in the Camões' life was renewed in 1825 with the publication of the long poem *Camões,* by the poet Almeida Garret. In 1880 what was thought to be Camões' remains were entombed in the monastery of Belém, near the tombs of King Sebastian and Vasco da Gama.

Writings. Camões' work marks the highest achievement in Portuguese literature, and his writings enriched the Portuguese language. He was master of many lyric forms and wrote perfectly constructed sonnets, elegies, Portuguese *redondilhas,* and Renaissance *canções* of exquisite expressiveness. His lyrics were first published in 1595; however, a number of the sonnets in that edition were later found to be erroneously attributed to him, and the Coimbra edition of 1953 accepted only 147 of his.

Camões' most famous work is *The Lusiads.* ("Lusiad" refers to the ancient Roman region of Lusitania, which included the territory that is now Portugal.) Written in 10 cantos in the *ottava rima* of Ariosto's *Orlando Furioso* (1516), the poem is closely modeled on Virgil's *Aeneid.* Ostensibly about Vasco da Gama's discovery of the sea route to India in 1497 and 1498, *The Lusiads* recounts great events in Portuguese history, including the founding of the Portuguese empire in the East. It pays tribute to the supposed superiority of Portugal's Latin heritage over the heritage of the "uncivilized" East, which, despite its riches, lacks a humanist tradition. Unlike Virgil, however, Camões does not spare criticism of his own people: their voluptuousness creates disorder and their strict justice verges on cruelty. And unlike Virgil's hero Aeneas, da Gama is not godlike, but an earthy, straightforward protagonist.

The Lusiads is a Christian epic, but mythological figures play an important role in it as well. (Possibly to satisfy the Inquisition censors, Camões explained that the gods in *The Lusiads* were merely symbolic). The three major divinities are Jupiter (Divine Providence); Venus (Divine Love); and Bacchus (The Spirit of Discord), who is the enemy of the Portuguese, having been traditionally associated with India, and whose role corresponds to that of the adversary goddess Juno in Virgil's *Aeneid*. In the same mythological vein, Camões invented the giant Adamastor, the spirit of the Cape of Good Hope, who represents the old chaotic state of the world before it was brought under control by Jupiter.

The story line of the poem follows the voyage of da Gama along the East Coast of Africa, to Mozambique, Mombasa, and finally Melinde. Bacchus tries to destroy the fleet in the Indian Ocean, but Venus calms the sea, and da Gama arrives safely in India. The best-known and most touching episode of the poem is the story, related by da Gama, of the tragic death of Ines de Castro, the mistress of the 15th century heir to the Portuguese throne, Dom Pedro (later Pedro I), whose father, King Alfonso IV, ordered her put to death. The episode, which corresponds to that of the death of Dido in the *Aeneid*, has become one of the great romantic traditions of Portugal. The last canto of the poem contains prophecies by Venus concerning the future of Portugal, whose mission it is to be a great and saving nation because the other countries of Europe have become corrupt and greedy.

The first English verse translation of *The Lusiads* was made by Sir Richard Fanshawe in 1655. Good modern translations include one in verse by Leonard Bacon (1950) and one in prose by William C. Atkinson (1952).

GREGORY RABASSA, *Columbia University*

Further Reading: Bowra, Cecil M., *From Virgil to Milton* (New York 1962); Hart, Henry H., *Luis de Camoëns and the Epic of the Lusiads* (Norman, Okla., 1962).

CAMOMILE. See CHAMOMILE.

CAMORRA, cä-môr-rä, an underground organization, active in the 19th century, that flourished particularly in Naples. Of uncertain origin, it was well established by 1830, giving "protection" to gamblers, smugglers, beggars, and prostitutes, and also to shopkeepers and landowners. A looser organization than the Sicilian Mafia, the Camorra was organized in a three-level structure reminiscent of medieval guilds: apprentices were called *garzoni di mala vita;* later they became *picciotti,* and finally *sgarri.*

The Neapolitan police apparently tolerated and at times made use of the Camorra. But with the unification of Italy in 1861, Italian authorities decided to suppress it. There were mass arrests in 1862, 1864, 1874, and 1883. After 1883, the Camorra ceased to function as a unitary, cohesive organization.

M. SALVADORI, *Smith College*

WIDE WORLD

CAMOUFLAGE for soldiers fighting in the jungle may include clothing dyed in a random pattern of natural colors and daubs of camouflage paint on exposed skin.

CAMOUFLAGE, kam'ə-fläzh, is the art of concealment or deception and the use of decoys as applied to military personnel, matériel, and structures. The simplest camouflage is the use of imitative color and texture and the distortion of outlines to make an object blend into the natural background. Modern camouflage also includes decoy emissions of radio, radar, heat, light, and sound, designed to muddle enemy navigation and to confuse the sophisticated sensors that are used both for surveillance and to steer weapons to their targets.

On land, nature is imitated by use of netting, artificial foliage, paint, dummies, and substitutes. Troops may wear green jungle uniforms, without metal rank badges, that blend with the natural background. Polished metal may be made dull. Equipment may be painted with dots, stripes, or patches. Dummy airfields and cities may be built. Guns are usually difficult to conceal because of the blast marks they leave in front of their muzzles. Installations such as airfields cannot be hidden, but the number and types of aircraft present may be falsified with dummies. Matériel may be housed in buildings that are not what they seem.

At sea, submarines can escape pursuit by dropping cartridges that give off large screens of gas under water. The gas returns a signal on enemy sonar like that of the submarine itself. Self-propelled small decoy submarines simulate the noises made by real submarines and realistically reflect sonar signals. Surface craft may be imitated by inflatable rubber dummies equipped with radar reflectors, or by thermal devices to attract infrared heat-seeking rockets. Torpedo boats are painted black for night attack. Submarines are also black for surfacing at night, and are covered with a soft substance designed to absorb rather than reflect sonar signals. Ships are painted gray so as to blend with the sea and the horizon. The smoke screen, an old camouflage device, may still be used to conceal the composition or maneuvers of a naval force.

In the air, stratospheric bombers and reconaissance aircraft are likely to dispense with camouflage paint in order to fly faster. But low-flying fighters and bombers are usually painted light underneath and dark above, so as to be hard to see against either sky or ground. Naval aircraft are often painted sky-color beneath and sea-color above. Helicopters and parachutes used in jungle war are green or greenish brown.

WIDE WORLD

AN AIRCRAFT FACTORY in Seattle, Wash., was elaborately camouflaged during World War II by having an artificial town complete with houses, trees, and chicken-wire lawns and shrubs built on top of it.

Since atomic warfare became possible, deep installations have been created, using natural cover as camouflage and as protection against attack. It has also been assumed that in a missile attack hundreds of decoy missiles might be launched to attract defensive weapons, so genuine missiles might slip through to their targets.

Camouflage Detection. Detection and surveillance have become as much an art as camouflage. At first limited to acuteness, instinct, and good eyesight, they increasingly have become matters for skilled analysts working in special units near headquarters. The analysts may handle black-and-white or color photographs, radar, sonar, laser, infrared, and other data. The speed with which they can process this information has become vital, and computers are moving close to the front lines. But, at the same time, the detection of camouflage may remain a matter of painstakingly observing every enemy movement and of fitting together many bits of information until a true picture of activities is built up, in which man-made tracks, flaws, and accidents reveal what has been falsified. Modern surveillance includes the difficult mission of discriminating between actual targets and decoys.

United States involvement in the Vietnam war accelerated work on electrooptical sensors including lasers, low-light television and forward-looking infrared cameras, and identification of electromagnetic and sonic radiation. The U. S. Navy's use of these sensors in all-weather aircraft in Vietnam reduced the number of Vietcong torpedo boat attacks, which were usually made under the natural camouflage of bad weather. Means of analysis were also improved: steromicroscopes, computer presentations, pattern recognition techniques, and even direct presentation from aircraft sensors to the battlefield commander's headquarters. Computers produce, within minutes of the return of a surveillance aircraft, complete maps showing targets such as routes, supply dumps, troops, and heavy weapons.

This has made the job of camouflage much more difficult, for such is the sensitivity of these devices that they detect not only trucks but also individual persons. In a war such as that in Vietnam, where Communist guerrillas used all their natural cunning to blend with the surroundings, continuous surveillance by aircraft with

WIDE WORLD

CAMOUFLAGE against visual spotting from above has been painted on a World War II German fighter, flying low over North African desert.

modern technological devices could make a guerrilla band relatively ineffective. There remains, however, a constant struggle between concealment and detection.

History. Various forms of camouflage and concealment are as old as nature itself. The ancient Greeks hid troops in the Trojan Horse to enter Troy. For many centuries a standard ruse was to light campfires, blow bugles, and make other indications of a camp in being while in fact the army was stealing away. Inferior forces, especially guerrillas, have used many clever deceptions.

Land operations by the British in India in the 19th century caused them to change from brilliantly colored uniforms to khaki, since the ability to blend with a barren landscape offered some chance of surprise and protection. At the end of the 19th century the introduction of smokeless powder made it possible to fire without revealing an exact position.

The start of aerial reconnaissance and photography in 1914 made all ground forces vulnerable and caused immediate emphasis on camouflage. Dummy guns had been used for years and forts had been painted to blend into the landscape, but in 1914 a French battery commander sought the aid of artists to hide his guns. Soon the French army had a camouflage section. The British and Germans followed suit.

Camouflage developed in naval warfare also. By 1908 the British had started to paint their ships a plain gray all over, but at the height of the U-boat campaign in 1917 the Admiralty accepted dazzle-paint schemes designed to confuse the aim of torpedomen. These designs were used by the British at the start of World War II, until radar reduced their value.

On aircraft a variety of camouflage appeared in World War I, from the plain green above generally used by the Allies to a polka-dot dapple favored by the Germans. Night aircraft were usually painted black below, a custom early adopted for zeppelins to prevent reflection of searchlight beams. But the effectiveness of this was spoiled by large national markings on many aircraft to identify them during dogfights.

With rearmament in the 1930's naval and air brightwork was again camouflaged. On aircraft it tended to various sky shades for the underside and variations of brown and green above for use over Europe, with other colors elsewhere. National markings were smaller, since pilots identified themselves by radio and aircraft had to be invisible when on the ground. U. S. Navy aircraft generally were a deep blue on the upper surfaces. But the U. S. Army Air Forces abandoned camouflage paint when by 1944 it became obvious that contrails and radar made camouflage useless. In World War II combat uniforms that blended with the terrain were developed, and the bright metal rank badges that had made officers obvious targets were eliminated.

Developments in electronic detection came rapidly in the years 1939 to 1945. Radar made older systems of camouflage no longer effective. Objects could be identified and their exact range noted. On a radar screen, the ground could be read like a map; submarines could no longer hide at periscope depth. The only counter was "window," metallic foil strips dropped from the air, that fogged enemy radar reception.

Other breakthroughs in countercamouflage were made in World War II. Infrared photography, flares, and searchlights pierced the night. Soon came air-to-air missiles steered by infrared heat-seeking devices. Infrared was further developed in the Korean and Vietnam wars. While the principles of camouflage and detection remain the same, the technology becomes ever more complicated.

ROBIN HIGHAM, *Kansas State University*
Coauthor of "A Short History of Warfare"

Bibliography

Addison, G. H., *The Work of the Royal Engineers in the European War, 1914–1918* vol. 3. (Chatham, England, 1927).

Barkas, Geoffrey, and Barkas, Natalie, *The Camouflage Story: From Aintree to Alamein* (London 1953).

Chesney, Clement H. R., *Art of Camouflage* (Hollywood, Fla., 1952).

Haymont, Irving, *Combat Intelligence in Modern Warfare* (Harrisburg, Pa., 1961).

Kleber, Brooks E., and Birdsell, Dale, *The Chemical Warfare Service: Chemicals in Combat* (Washington 1965).

Robertson, Bruce, *Aircraft Camouflage and Markings, 1907–1954* (Letchworth, England, 1961).

Solomon, S. J., *Strategic Camouflage* (London 1920).

CAMP, Walter Chauncey (1859–1925), "the father of American football." Camp was born in New Britain, Conn., on April 7, 1859. He entered Yale University in 1876 and played halfback there for six years, the last two while at Yale Medical School. He made football history in his first season by throwing the first forward pass (legalized in 1906). As Yale captain, Camp made suggestions on rules that led in 1880 to the reduction of men on a side from 15 to 11; the reduction of the size of the field from 140 by 70 yards to 110 by 53; and the substitution of the scrimmage (ball being put into play by one side) for scrum (a scramble for the ball). In 1882, before an injury retired him as a player, he had instigated the system of downs.

After a business venture in New York, Camp was football coach at Yale (1888–1892) and Stanford University (1894–1895). From 1889 to 1924 he named All-America football teams, and these were accepted as the last word on the subject. (He later said that Caspar Whitney, a New York City sports authority, chose the teams through 1896.) In 1917 Camp was chairman of the athletic department, U. S. Commission on Training Camp Activities (for Navy personnel), out of which came the famous "Daily Dozen" exercises. Among his books are *Football: How to Coach a Team* (1886) and *American Football* (1891). He died on March 14, 1925, in New York City.

HAROLD PETERSON, *"Sports Illustrated"*

CAMP is a catchword for something aesthetically "so bad that it is good." The word meant "pleasantly ostentatious" in England about 1900 and "homosexual" later. Its present meaning in the United States was defined by Susan Sontag in 1964 in the *Partisan Review*. The connoisseur of camp, who is likely to live in New York and is generally anti-Establishment, finds amusing and delightful what others consider boring, banal, trivial, outmoded, or absurd. He has, as Miss Sontag put it, a "love of the unnatural: of artifice and exaggeration," of things that are "too much" or "not to be believed," taking pleasure in "the contrast between silly and extravagant content and rich form." Examples of camp are the grandiose musical films of Busby Berkeley in the 1930's, Batman comic books, Andy Warhol's 8-hour film *Sleep*, Tiffany lamps, and fur-covered refrigerator doors.

CAMP AND CAMPING. See CAMPING.

CAMP FIRE GIRLS is a national, nonsectarian, interracial youth organization that provides an educational and recreational program for girls from seven through high school age. It has over 400 councils and associations throughout the United States, serving a membership of more than half a million girls. These groups carry out the organization's program under policies laid down by the National Council of Camp Fire Girls. Assisted by paid local and national staff workers, about 129,000 men and women volunteers serve as group leaders, sponsors, and members of local and national committees to administer the programs.

Activities. The organization comprises four age groups: Blue Birds (7 and 8 years old), Camp Fire Girls (9 through 11 years old), Junior Hi (12 and 13 years old), and Horizon Club (14 years old through high school age). The activities for the older girls are designed to broaden their outlook in career exploration, community service, and social responsibility.

At each age level the Camp Fire program combines group activities with individual achievement. It includes day and resident camping, intergroup and service projects. Many councils offer extended services to disadvantaged and handicapped girls, to minorities such as Indians, Eskimos, Negroes, and foreign-language groups, or to children of migrant workers.

Objectives. The National Council seeks to make available programs designed to encourage in every girl: the application of her religious, spiritual, and ethical beliefs to her daily living; a love of home and family that grows as she grows; pride in woman's traditional qualities—tenderness, affection, and skill in human relationships; deep love of country, the practice of democracy, and readiness to serve; the capacity for fun, friendship, and happy group relations; the formation of healthful habits; the ability to take care of herself, to do her work skillfully, and to take pleasure in it; interests and hobbies she can enjoy, with others and alone; love of the out-of-doors and skill in outdoor living; and a happy heart that will help her find beauty, romance, and adventure in the common things of daily life.

History and National Service. The oldest organization of its kind in the United States, Camp Fire Girls was founded in 1910 by Dr. Luther Halsey Gulick (q.v.), a national leader in recreation for youth, and his wife, Charlotte Vetter Gulick. Much of the early program of the Camp Fire Girls was worked out at their Sebago-Wohelo camp in Maine, started in 1909 as one of the first girls' camps in the United States. Camp Fire Girls was incorporated in 1912. WOHELO (made up of the first two letters of "work," "health," and "love") is the watchword. Crossed logs and a flame within a convex triangle, symbolizing the hearth fire of the home and the campfire of the outdoors, constitute the insignia.

National headquarters, located in New York City, prepares operational and program materials for regional offices and local councils. It also publishes *The Camp Fire Girl*, a monthly magazine for leaders. Local councils receive financial support from community chests or united funds, individual contributions, and special money-raising activities. Individual membership is in the national organization.

ALICE H. SMOLENS
Camp Fire Girls, Inc.

CAMP HILL, kamp, is a borough in south central Pennsylvania, in Cumberland county, about 4 miles (6 km) southwest of Harrisburg, from which it is separated by the Susquehanna River. It is a residential community in the Cumberland Valley, a rich agricultural region where dairy cattle, poultry, grains, hay, market vegetables, apples, and peaches are raised.

Camp Hill was founded in 1756. The borough has the council-manager form of government. Population: 9,931.

CAMP MEETING, kamp mē'ting, is the name usually given to the large, open-air gatherings held for religious purposes on the American frontier. Camp meetings did not achieve popularity or standard form until after 1800. Development of these gatherings is usually associated with the work of the Presbyterian minister James McGready, who was largely responsible for what is called the beginning of the second Great Awakening in the trans-Allegheny West during the years 1800–1805. Assisted by Methodists John and William McGee, McGready conducted an intense 4-day revival on the Gasper River, in Logan county, Ky., which set a pattern for the camp meeting as a "new measure," fit to match the spiritual needs of the environment. At the start, Baptists, Methodists, and Presbyterians united to hold meetings,

CAMP FIRE GIRLS gather around a blazing fire at dusk, near the close of a camping day.

CAMP FIRE GIRLS, INC.

but as time went on the Methodists and Baptists accepted camp meetings more readily than the Presbyterians.

The meetings became known for providing social contacts for the lonely frontiersmen. They were also marked by fervent preaching, praying, and singing, which often lasted for days. There was criticism of the "nervous" behavior caused by the religious excitement. At a meeting at Cane Ridge, Ky., in 1801, attended by an estimated 10,000 to 25,000 people, observers noted such manifestations as jerking, rolling, dancing, running, singing, laughing, and barking.

For the sake of decency and order, some patterns and procedures began to emerge to organize the activity of the thousands of persons who often attended. For example, encampments of tents and other facilities were arranged in rectangular, horseshoe, or circular shapes, enclosing the open-air auditorium. Within the outdoor auditorium were places for pulpits, benches, and "anxious seats" for those particularly concerned about their religious condition. Often, out of these meetings, religious classes and societies were organized, and these sometimes provided the only means of moral discipline found in an otherwise unruly West.

As towns grew and church buildings began to multiply, camp meetings began to lose their popularity, despite attempts to revive the fervor of earlier times and to keep the meetings going. For the most part, camp grounds were transformed toward the end of the 19th century into permanent conference centers and resorts, such as the Chautauqua Assembly, which provided for the recreational and cultural as well as the religious development of those who attended.

JAMES H. SMYLIE
Union Theological Seminary, Richmond, Va.

Further Reading: Johnson, Charles A., *The Frontier Camp Meeting* (New York 1955).

CAMPA INDIANS, kăm′pə, a South American Indian nation of Arawakan linguistic stock, located in the eastern Andean foothills of central Peru. Their name for themselves is *Asháninka.* They live dispersed in semipermanent villages and hamlets. Subsistence activities combine slash-and-burn agriculture with hunting, fishing, and gathering. The main crop is sweet manioc. The chief weapon in hunting and warfare is the bow and arrow. Dress consists typically of a woven cotton robe and, for the men, a wicker crown. Stable political organization is lacking, as are lineages, clans, and moieties. Polygyny is practiced. The Campa believe in good and evil spirits. Their principal deities are the sun and a transformer-trickster called Avíreri. First contacted by the Europeans in 1635, the Campa have been pacified only recently. At present, though still numerous, they are undergoing a slow process of acculturation and assimilation.

GERALD WEISS, *Florida-Atlantic University*

CAMPAGNA DI ROMA, kăm-pä′nyä dē rō′mä, is a historic region around Rome, Italy. Modern cartographers usually consider its borders to be the Sabatine Hills to the north, the Sabine Mountains to the east, the Alban Hills to the south, and the Tyrrhenian Sea on the west. The region is a volcanic plain, grassy in most areas, but somewhat sandy as it slopes toward the sea. Since much of the Campagna's soil is arid, irrigation is required to raise crops of cereals, fruit, grain, and vegetables. However, most of the plain's rural inhabitants are breeders and herders of cattle and sheep.

Apart from Rome and its immediate suburbs, the principal towns of the Campagna are Albano Laziale, Frascati, Tivoli, Ostia Antica (a notable archaeological site and once the port of ancient Rome), and Lido di Roma, a fashionable summer resort on the coast.

In classical antiquity the Campagna, which then comprised the southern portion of Etruria (modern Tuscany) and the northern portion of Latium, was reasonably fertile, and it supported many thriving towns famous in Roman history. However, progressive overgrazing before the end of the Roman republic in 31 B.C., abandonment of irrigation in imperial times, and the barbarian invaders' indifference to restoration of drainage in the marsh areas after the collapse of the Western Roman Empire in 476 A.D., impoverished the land.

In the area known as the Pontine Marshes —25 miles (40 km) southeast of Rome, near the Tyrrhenian Sea—continued neglect of drainage caused stagnation of the water that collected in the rainy season. This situation allowed the area to become a breeding ground for malarial mosquitoes, and the disease became endemic in the area; as a result the district became depopulated in the Middle Ages. It was not until 1926 that the Italian government was able to make the area habitable again through drainage and spraying programs, followed by land reclamation.

The Campagna has long been a favorite subject for painters, who portray the majestic ruins of its aqueducts, temples, tombs, and villas along and near the Appian Way.

P. R. COLEMAN-NORTON
Princeton University

CAMPAGNOLA, kăm-pä-nyô′lä, **Domenico** (1500?–?1563), Italian artist, who is famous for his superb pen-and-ink drawings, especially of landscapes. Little is known about his life although he is believed to have been born in Padua and probably died there. The earliest established dates associated with him, 1517 and 1518, appear on signed engravings. It may be assumed, therefore, that his first training was as an engraver, perhaps with the artist Giulio Campagnola, who may have been a relative. The firm, clear lines and rich shading of such prints as *Assumption,* however, indicate that he also must have received early training as a painter.

Many of Campagnola's drawings, skillfully executed in light and open strokes, were once attributed to Titian, with whom he studied, and also to Giorgione. The largest collection of Campagnola's drawings is in the Uffizi Gallery, Florence.

Campagnola also produced numerous paintings, the first documented ones dating from the 1530's. His best-known paintings include the *Holy Family* (Pitti Palace, Florence) and the *Miracle of the Ass* and *Resurrection of the Drowned Child* (both in the Scuola del Santo, Padua). His fresco *Meeting at the Golden Gate* (Scuola del Carmine, Padua) clearly reveals a debt to Titian in its large figures, deep landscape, relaxed composition and warm, gracious color.

MILTON LEWINE, *Columbia University*

CAMPAÑA, Pedro de. See KEMPENER, PETER DE.

CAMPANELLA, kam-pə-nel′ə, **Roy** (1921–), American baseball player, who was voted the National League's most valuable player by the Baseball Writers Association in 1951, 1953, and 1955. Campanella was born in Philadelphia on Nov. 19, 1921. At the age of 15 he played with a barnstorming all-Negro semiprofessional team as a catcher. In 1946 he signed with the Brooklyn Dodgers organization and played with Nashua, N. H., in 1946, Montreal in 1947, and St. Paul in the first part of 1948.

Campanella was brought up to the Dodgers in 1948, and from then until 1957 he was the first-string catcher for the club. In 1953 he set major league records for a catcher with the most runs batted in (142), the most putouts (807), and the most home runs (41). His baseball career ended on Jan. 28, 1958, when he was paralyzed in an automobile accident.

MICHAEL QUINN, *"Sports Illustrated"*

CAMPANELLA, käm-pä-nel′lä, **Tommaso** (1568–1639), Italian philosopher and poet. He was deeply religious but like his contemporaries Giordano Bruno and Galileo, he sought to establish the independence of natural philosophy from revealed theology. His plan for a utopian society echoes Plato and Sir Thomas More, and his metaphysics anticipates Descartes.

Life. Giovanni Domenico Campanella was born to a poor family in Stilo, Calabria, Italy on Sept. 5, 1568. Early in life he joined the Dominicans, taking the name Tommaso. Rejecting Aristotelian philosophy, he became interested in astrology and defended the mechanistic theories of Bernardino Telesio. He was imprisoned for these views in 1591 by the monastic authorities. After his release, Campanella taught and wrote in Rome, Florence, and Padua, but was again imprisoned in 1593. Abjuring heresy before the Inquisition in Rome, he was freed in 1595 and forced to return to Calabria, where he led a conspiracy to overthrow its Spanish rulers. In 1599 he was condemned to death for treason and heresy but had his sentence commuted to life imprisonment in Naples by pretending insanity.

During nearly 30 years in prison, at times subjected to torture, Campanella continued to write. In 1628 he was liberated by Pope Urban VIII, but his fear of another trial by his enemies caused him to flee to France in 1634. He died in Paris on May 21, 1639.

Works. Campanella is best known for his *Città del sole* (1623; *City of the Sun*) depicting a utopian, communistic, totalitarian society under a philosopher-priest. His many other treatises and his poems reflect his religious and humanistic scheme of the universe.

Anticipating Descartes, Campanella believed true knowledge comes not from the senses but from the mind's awareness of itself. The mind is also aware of being part of a larger whole, which is pantheistically infused with varying degrees of power, wisdom, and love, the attributes of God. Campanella saw no death in the universe, but only "mutation of being," and what seems evil to the individual is enveloped in a providential cosmic design. To the innate movement of all nature toward God (*religio indita*), man's intellect, aided by grace, adds the positive content of Christianity (*religio addita*), which is a fulfillment, rather than a contradiction, of natural religion.

JOHN CHARLES NELSON, *Columbia University*

CAMPANIA, käm-pä′nyä, one of the regions of southern Italy, extends from the Garigliano River in the north to the Gulf of Policastro in the south. Its eastern boundary runs along the Apennines, which separate it from the regions of Abruzzi, Molise, Apulia, and Basilicata. Campania has two distinct types of landscapes. Along and near the coast there are lowlands, facing the Gulf of Gaeta, the Bay of Naples, and the Gulf of Salerno. These lowlands are interrupted by volcanic formations, still partly active, including Mt. Vesuvius and the lesser volcanic forms west of Naples, called the Phlegrean Fields. The other type of landscape is hilly.

Economy. The best-developed agricultural area of Campania is the lowland that runs from the lower Volturno Valley past Vesuvius as far as the coast near Castellamare. Called Terra di Lavoro ("Land of Work"), this densely settled district produces fruit, vegetables, grapes, olives, citrus, tobacco, and hemp. Many of the farms engaged in truck gardening, selling their produce in Naples or shipping it to urban centers in northern Italy. Fishing is important, especially in the gulfs of Naples and Salerno.

Large-scale manufacturing in Campania is concentrated mostly in and around Naples, the largest city and port of the region. Industries range from iron and steelworks to shipbuilding and the manufacture of business machines, precision instruments, textiles, and petrochemicals. Equally important in terms of the number of workers employed are the artisan industries, producing articles made of coral, tortoiseshell, and mother-of-pearl. Campania has good railroad connections and is connected by express highway with Rome and Milan.

History. Campania was settled by Greek colonists as early as the 8th century B. C. During the Roman period it was a flourishing region, as is attested by the important archaeological finds at Pompeii, Herculaneum and elsewhere. After the decline of Roman power, much of inland Campania was under Lombard rule. The Normans established themselves in Campania during the 11th and 12th centuries; they in turn were followed by the Angevins and the Aragonese. From about 1200 onward Campania was part of the Kingdom of the Two Sicilies, later called the Kingdom of Naples. In 1860, Naples, including Campania, joined the united kingdom of Italy. In World War II the first Allied landings on the European mainland were made in Campania. Population: (1966) 5,066,322.

GEORGE KISH, *University of Michigan*

CAMPANILE, kam-pə-nē′lē, in architecture, a bell tower, particularly one that is free-standing. The most notable campaniles are in Italy, where they became popular during the early Middle Ages and continued to be a common part of church complexes until the Renaissance. They often served as watch towers as well as bell towers to indicate hours of worship.

The top story or stories of most campaniles are open windows or arcades that allow the bells to be heard clearly. Below that level, the tower may be quite plain, or it may be distinguished by some structural or decorative form.

The 6th century campanile of Sant'Apollinare in Classe, Ravenna, like most early campaniles, is round, with no indication of any stories within. Later campaniles are commonly square, such as the campanile of San Giorgio in Velabro,

Rome, dating from the 7th century. Each story of this tower is terminated by a cornice; the upper floors have open arcades on all four sides, and the lower floors have similar blind arcades.

A particularly graceful example of a campanile is that of San Zeno, Verona (12th century), whose sides, instead of being straight, have the slightly convex curve known as entasis. The tallest campanile in Italy, that of the Cathedral of Cremona (13th century) is about 400 feet (about 122 meters) high. Each story is marked by a favorite decorative motif of the Lombard Romanesque style—the arched corbel table, which is a frieze of small arches resting on corbels, or brackets. The two highest stories are octagons; the top one, capped with a pyramid, is smaller than the one below. The most famous campaniles are the Leaning Tower of Pisa, in the Romanesque style, "Giotto's Tower" of the Cathedral of Florence, in the Gothic style, and the Renaissance campanile of the Cathedral of St. Mark in Venice.

Pisa. The celebrated Leaning Tower at Pisa, begun, probably by Bonanno of Pisa, in 1174 and finished in 1350, is 179 feet (about 55 meters) high. The lowest of its cylindrical stories has a blind arcade with lozenge-shaped panels in each arch. The six stories above have open arcades with small arches resting on slender colonnettes. The top story is a continuation of the circular wall inside the arcades and is thus slightly smaller; it provides a platform that is accessible from the spiral stairs within the tower.

The tower of Pisa owes its fame largely to its deviation of 14 feet (about 4.3 meters) from the perpendicular, the result of the unequal settling of the foundations. This tendency to list was noticeable even before the structure was completed. Therefore, in an attempt to correct the tendency, the circular wall within the arcades was made somewhat thicker, and thus heavier, on the higher side of the tower, and the upper stories were slightly tipped away from the prevailing tilt toward the vertical. The process of settling was very slow, but 20th century engineers claim that they have finally stopped the tilting and that no further lean will occur.

Florence. The campanile of Florence Cathedral, 292 feet (89 meters) high, was built mostly between 1334 and 1387. Because it was probably designed by the great painter Giotto di Bondone it is frequently called "Giotto's Tower." Like other Florentine buildings of its time, it is sheathed in white marble set with panels of red and green marble. Its traceried windows and pointed arches are characteristic of Gothic architecture. Near its base is a range of 26 hexagonal panels, which contain small scenes in low-relief sculpture by such leading artists as Andrea Pisano and Luca della Robbia, and some, perhaps, by Giotto himself. Full-length sculptured figures, some carved by Donatello in the early 15th century, fill niches above these panels.

Venice. The campanile of St. Mark's, Venice, was begun in 888. A continuous ramp winds up the interior of the tower to the belfry, above which a pyramidal spire brings the whole structure to a height of 325 feet (99 meters). The belfry and spire, as well as the Loggetta around the base, built by Jacopo Sansovino, are 16th century additions. The campanile collapsed in 1902 but was rebuilt in 1908 from careful, measured drawings of the original.

EVERARD M. UPJOHN, *Columbia University*

PHILIP GENDREAU, N. Y.

The campanile of St. Mark's, in Venice, Italy.

CAMPANULA, kam-pan'yə-lə, a genus of some 250 species of annual, biennial, and perennial herbaceous plants of the bellflower family (Campanulaceae). Campanulas, which are widespread throughout the Northern Hemisphere, range from very low, mat-forming plants to tall, upright herbs, and even vines. The petals of the flowers are joined at the base to form bell-like blooms, giving the genus its scientific name *Campanula* (Latin for "little bell"). The predominant flower color throughout the genus is violet, but cultivated varieties include pink, white, and intermediate hues. Canterbury bells (*C. medium*) and the bluebells of Scotland (*C. rotundifolia*) are well-known examples of the genus.

R. C. ALLEN
Kingwood Center, Mansfield, Ohio

CAMPANULACEAE, kam-pan-yə-lā'sē-ē, the bellflower family, comprising some 40 or more genera of mostly herbaceous plants distributed throughout the tropical, temperate, and subarctic regions. The leaves are usually alternate and simple. The flowers are regular (vertically divisible into equal halves along at least two different lines) and perfect (with both stamens and pistils). They are borne either solitary or in clusters. The five petals of the flower are united at the base to form a cuplike corolla, which is usually blue, violet, or shades of purple. The seeds are borne in a dry capsule.

The genus *Campanula* (see CAMPANULA) is the most widely cultivated. *Platycodon,* the balloon bellflower of northern Asia, is a hardy border plant and probably next in popularity. The flowers are swollen and balloonlike in appearance just prior to opening. *P. grandiflorium,* the most common species, grows to 3 feet (1 meter) tall and produces blue-violet, pink, or white flowers up to 3 inches (75 mm) across.

Other genera that are horticulturally important include *Adenophora,* the lady bellflowers; *Ostrowskia,* the giant bellflowers; and *Wahlenbergia,* the tufted bellflowers.

R. C. ALLEN
Kingwood Center, Mansfield, Ohio

CAMPBELL, Scottish noble family. See CAMPBELLS OF ARGYLL.

CAMPBELL, kam'bəl, **Alexander** (1788–1866), American religious leader and a founder of the Disciples of Christ, a Protestant denomination also known as the Campbellites. He was born in Ballymena, County Antrim, Ireland, on Sept. 12, 1788. His father, Thomas Campbell, was a clergyman and teacher in the Church of the Covenanters and Seceders, a reform branch of the Presbyterian Church.

Alexander stayed in Ireland when his father sailed to the United States in 1807. He joined his father in 1809 and became a member of the Christian Association of Washington County, Pa., a church founded by his father. In 1811 the Campbells founded a church in Brush Run, Pa., with Alexander as its pastor. Although the new church was a member of a Baptist association, the liberal views of the Campbells displeased the Baptists, who moved to oust them from their organization. The churches differed in particular about the function of baptism. In 1830, Alexander and his followers withdrew from the Baptist association and formed the Disciples of Christ, an independent organization. In the same year Alexander changed the name of his successful periodical, the *Christian Baptist,* to the *Millennial Harbinger,* reflecting his growing interest in the Second Coming.

Alexander became well known as a speaker and debater, and he toured the United States, Canada, and Britain. He was known especially for his debates with Presbyterian spokesmen, and he once addressed the U. S. House of Representatives by invitation. In 1840 he founded Bethany College, in Bethany, W. Va. He served as president of the college until his death in Bethany on March 4, 1866. He was the author of *The Christian System* (1839) and *Memoirs of Elder Thomas Campbell* (1861). See also DISCIPLES OF CHRIST—*Campbell Movement.*

Further Reading: Humbert, Royal, ed., *A Compend of Alexander Campbell's Theology* (St. Louis 1963); Richardson, Robert, *Memoirs of Alexander Campbell* (Nashville 1956).

CAMPBELL, kam'bəl, **Sir Alexander** (1822–1892), Canadian public official. He was born in Hedon, Yorkshire, England, on March 9, 1822, and was brought as a baby to Canada. Educated in Kingston, Upper Canada (Ontario), and called to the bar in 1843, he formed a law partnership with John A. Macdonald (q.v.).

In 1858, Campbell was elected as a conservative to the legislative council of the old province of Canada for the Kingston area. In 1864 he became commissioner of crown lands in the Macdonald-Brown-Cartier coalition cabinet formed to seek Confederation, and he attended the Quebec conference that planned the scheme that year. At Confederation in 1867, Campbell was named to the Canadian Senate and made postmaster general in Macdonald's federal cabinet. When the government fell in 1873, he led the Senate opposition. When Macdonald regained power in 1878, Campbell held a succession of cabinet posts. In 1887 he was appointed lieutenant governor of Ontario. He died in office on May 24, 1892, in Toronto.

J. M. S. CARELESS, *University of Toronto*

CAMPBELL, Archibald. See CAMPBELLS OF ARGYLL.

CAMPBELL, kam'bəl, **Sir Colin** (1776–1847), British soldier and colonial administrator. Born in London, Campbell ran away from school at the age of 16 and signed on a ship headed for the West Indies. Brought home from Jamaica by his brother, he became a midshipman.

In 1795, Campbell entered the army and distinguished himself under Sir Arthur Wellesley in India. He returned to England with Wellesley in 1806 and accompanied him to Hannover and Denmark, and then to Portugal in 1808 as his senior aide-de-camp. During the Peninsular War (1808–1813), he served as assistant quartermaster general and in 1815 was on the staff of the Duke of Wellington at the Battle of Waterloo. Sir Colin Campbell was the lieutenant governor of Tobago, of Portsmouth, and in 1833 of Nova Scotia. From 1840 to 1847 he was governor of Ceylon. He died in London on June 13, 1847.

CAMPBELL, kam'bəl, **Sir Colin** (1792–1863), British field marshal, who was one of Britain's greatest soldiers in the 19th century. He was born Colin Macliver in Glasgow, Scotland, on Oct. 20, 1792. When he joined the army in 1808, his name was entered erroneously as Campbell, after his mother's family, and he kept the name.

Campbell served in the Peninsular War in Spain (1810–1813) and took part in many colonial campaigns. In the Crimean War he commanded the Highlands Brigade in 1854. His leadership was credited with winning the Battle of the Alma River and with repelling a strong attack at Balaklava. As a major general commanding the British army in India, Campbell quelled the Indian Mutiny. He was knighted in 1848 and was created Baron Clyde of Clydesdale in 1858. He was made a field marshal in 1862. Campbell died in England on Aug. 14, 1863.

CAMPBELL, kam'bəl, **Colin** (died 1729), Scottish architect of English country houses. Nothing is known about his life until he was commissioned by the Earl of Burlington to remodel Burlington House in London in 1717. Campbell was very strongly influenced by Palladio and Inigo Jones.

His best-known houses are Newby in Yorkshire (1720); Mereworth Castle in Kent (1720–1723), based on Palladio's Villa Rotunda at Vicenza; Wanstead in Essex, built in 1720 and razed in 1822; and Houghton Hall in Norfolk, built in 1722 for Sir Robert Walpole. Campbell published a 3-volume work *Vitruvius Britannicus* (1717–1725), a series of plates of English architectural works. He died in London on Sept. 13, 1729.

CAMPBELL, Donald. See CAMPBELL, MALCOLM.

CAMPBELL, kam'bəl, **Sir George** (1824–1892), British statesman and politician, who was lieutenant governor of Bengal in 1871–1874. Campbell was born in Fifeshire, Scotland, the grandson of George Campbell, the Scottish theologian. Young Campbell was educated at St. Andrews University and was appointed to the Bengal civil service of the East India Company in 1842.

Campbell established an excellent record in the Punjab, Oudh, and the Central Provinces and was commissioned to write the official account of the Indian Mutiny (1857). From 1863 to 1866 he was judge of the Calcutta high court.

In 1866, Orissa suffered a devastating famine, and Campbell was named president of a commission of inquiry. The commission's report was a landmark, for Campbell maintained that it was not acceptable to allow people to die of famine, rejecting the laissez-faire concepts of earlier political economists. The Bengal administration came unfavorably into public view because of the famine, and Campbell was made lieutenant governor in 1871. He undertook his task with great vigor, and was considered one of the company's foremost lieutenant governors, although one of the least popular. His most important reforms were in finance and taxation, education, and tribal administration. Campbell died in Cairo, Egypt, on Feb. 18, 1892.

WALTER HAUSER, *University of Virginia*

CAMPBELL, kam'bəl, **John** (1653–1727?), American journalist, who published the first known regular newspaper to appear in colonial America. He was born in Scotland in 1653. Sometime before 1695 he emigrated to Boston, where he became postmaster in 1702. The post office was then the news center of the New England provinces, and in 1703, Campbell began to write newsletters, relating foreign developments, to Governor Winthrop of Connecticut and others who were interested in this service. Soon Campbell decided to put these newsletters into print and offer them for sale. On April 24, 1704, with official authorization, he began to publish his half-sheet weekly, the Boston *News-Letter*. Campbell lost his position as postmaster in 1718, and in 1722 he turned over control of the *News-Letter* to its printer Bartholomew Green. Campbell died in Boston on March 4, 1727 or 1728. See also BOSTON NEWS-LETTER.

CAMPBELL, kam'bel, **John** (1708–1775), Scottish historian, biographer, and political writer. He was born in Edinburgh on March 8, 1708. His initial work was *A Military History of the Late Prince Eugene of Savoy and the Late John Duke of Marlborough...*, a compilation published anonymously in 1736. His first major original work was *The Travels and Adventures of Edward Bevan, Esq.* (1739), a fictitious autobiography. His other works include *Concise History of Spanish America* (1741), *Lives of the Admirals and Other Eminent British Seamen* (1742–1744), and a *Political Survey of Great Britain* (1744).

In 1765, Campbell went to Georgia, in North America, as a British government agent. He is believed to have died there on Dec. 28, 1775.

CAMPBELL, kam'bəl, **John** (1779–1861), British lord chancellor and legal biographer. He was born on Sept. 15, 1779, at Cupar, Fifeshire, Scotland, and educated at St. Andrews University in Scotland and Lincoln's Inn. He was called to the bar in 1806. Campbell was elected to the House of Commons as a supporter of the Whig party in 1830 and was appointed solicitor general in 1832. From 1834 to 1841 he served as attorney general, except for two brief periods when the Whigs were out of office. During his 11 years in the House of Commons, Campbell was instrumental in the passage of much progressive legislation. This included the reform of laws relating to real property and imprisonment for debt, as well as the Municipal Corporations Act of 1835. He was raised to the peerage as Baron Campbell and made Irish lord chancellor in 1841. Nine years later he was appointed lord chief justice, and in 1859 he was made lord chancellor. He died in London on June 22, 1861.

Campbell's most important achievement was his 7-volume book *Lives of the Lord Chancellors* (1845–1847). It was well-researched and written in a colorful style but contained numerous inaccuracies. It was followed by *Lives of the Chief Justices* (3 vols., 1849–1857). Both books remain standard works of reference on their subjects.

JOHN W. OSBORNE, *Rutgers University*

CAMPBELL, kam'bəl, **John Archibald** (1811–1889), American Supreme Court judge, whose main contribution was his concurring opinion in the Dred Scott case (1857). This decision denied Negroes the right to citizenship and held unconstitutional the 1820 Missouri Compromise forbidding slavery north of the line 36° 30′.

Campbell was born on June 24, 1811, at Washington, Ga. A child prodigy, he graduated from Franklin College (now the University of Georgia) with first honors at the age of 14 and entered the U. S. Military Academy. However, his father's death ended his military career. He studied law and at the age of 18 was admitted to the bar by special act of the Georgia legislature. Soon he moved to Alabama, married, and started a very successful law practice. His national reputation induced members of the U. S. Supreme Court to urge his appointment to the court by President Pierce.

Campbell upheld on principle the South's right to secede, but he still sought reconciliation with the North. When he failed and war came, he resigned from the court, and in 1862 he became assistant secretary of war in the Confederacy. After spending four years in a federal prison at the end of the war, he moved to New Orleans and again established a successful practice. He appeared unsuccessfully before the U. S. Supreme Court in the Slaughterhouse (antimonopoly) cases in 1873 and successfully in *United States* v. *Cruikshank* (1876). In the latter, the court practically nullified the Reconstruction Congress' 1870 civil rights laws by dismissing indictments charging outrageous violation of Negroes' rights. Campbell died in Baltimore, Md., on March 12, 1889.

LEO PFEFFER, *Long Island University*

CAMPBELL, kam'bəl, **Joseph** (1879?–1944), Anglo-Irish poet, who was a leading figure in the Irish renaissance in the early 20th century. Campbell, who also wrote under his Gaelic name *Seosamh MacCathmhaoil*, was born at Belfast and taught for a time at Fordham University in New York City. He died in County Wicklow on July 14, 1944.

Campbell's writings were based on an intense interest in religion and the folklore and life of the Irish country people. He adopted traditional lyric and ballad forms, with an emphasis on simplicity of structure and clarity of expression. His best poems, such as *The Old Woman*, have feeling, grace, and dignity. Among Campbell's works are the volumes of poetry *Rushlight* (1906), *Mountainy Singer* (1909), and *Irishry* (1913).

JAMES REEVES
Author of "A Short History of English Poetry"

Further Reading: Gwynn, Stephen L., *Irish Literature and Drama in the English Language* (London and New York 1936); O'Hegerty, P. S., *A Bibliography of Joseph Campbell* (London 1940).

(ABOVE) UPI; (BELOW) CENTRAL PRESS

SIR MALCOLM CAMPBELL *(above)* in his *Bluebird* racer at Daytona Beach, Fla., where he set several speed records; and his son, DONALD CAMPBELL *(below)*, also a racer.

CAMPBELL, Sir Malcolm (1885–1949), British automobile and speedboat racer, who in 1937 held the world speed record both on land and on water. He was the first driver to average more than 300 miles per hour on land.

Campbell was born in Chislehurst, Kent, on March 11, 1885. Educated at Uppingham, in Rutland, England, and in Germany and France, he began a business career at Lloyd's of London as a broker and underwriter. In World War I he was a dispatch rider and then pilot in the Royal Flying Corps, retiring from the service with the rank of captain. He first began to race automobiles in 1910, and finally set a land speed mark in 1927 at Pendine Beach, Wales, with 174.22 mph. In competition with other famous racing men, he continued to break records, and at the Bonneville Salt Flats in Utah on Sept. 3, 1935, he achieved his aim of averaging more than 300 mph with a mark of 301.1292 in *Bluebird*, a car he designed.

Meanwhile, Campbell took up speedboat racing. In his 12-cylinder boat, also named *Bluebird*, he broke Gar Wood's hydroplane mark of 124.86 mph by averaging 129.4164 mph on Lake Maggiore near Locarno, Switzerland, in 1937. He beat his own record in 1939 in *Bluebird II*, at 141.74 mph on Coniston Water, Lancashire. He was knighted in 1931. Sir Malcolm died in Reigate, Surrey, on Jan. 1, 1949. His published works include *My Greatest Adventure*, *Speed* (1931), *Romance of Motor Racing* (1936), and *Key to Motoring* (1938).

DONALD MALCOLM CAMPBELL (1921–1967), his son, broke both land and water speed records in 1964 in vehicles named *Bluebird*. He was the first to average better than 200 mph in a speedboat, with 202.32 mph at Lake Ullswater, Cumberland, in 1955. He hit his top speed of 276.33 at Dumbleyung, Western Australia, in 1964.

Campbell was born at Povey Cross, Surrey, on March 23, 1921. He was educated at Uppingham, and enlisted in the Royal Air Force in 1939. An engineer with Norris Brothers, Ltd., he became chairman of the firm in 1954. In competing for the land speed mark, he set a record for 4-wheeled vehicles in 1964 at Lake Eyre, South Australia, averaging 403.1 mph. He was killed on Coniston Water on Jan. 4, 1967, when his hydroplane became airborne and crashed at about 320 mph.

BILL BRADDOCK, *New York "Times"*

CAMPBELL, Mrs. Patrick (1865–1940), English actress, who, in a career of more than 50 years, was famous on stage and off for her caprices and extravagances. She is also remembered because of her celebrated correspondence with George Bernard Shaw.

Life. She was born Beatrice Stella Tanner, in London, on Feb. 9, 1865, the daughter of an English father and an Italian mother from whom she inherited a dark, Italianate beauty. While still a young girl, she married Patrick Campbell, a Scot, who was killed in the South African War. After some theatrical appearances as an amateur, she was suddenly chosen for the title role in Pinero's play *The Second Mrs. Tanqueray* (1893). The opening performance was one of the great first nights of the theater, and next morning Mrs. Campbell awoke to find herself famous. She then played many leading roles—in Pinero's *The Notorius Mrs. Ebbsmith* (1895), Sudermann's *Magda* (1896), Maeterlinck's *Pelléas et Mélisande* (1900), Ibsen's *Hedda Gabler* (1907), and Shaw's *Pygmalion* (1914)—but she always returned to portray Paula Tanqueray, even when she reached old age. Toward the end of her life she had a few small roles in Hollywood that were unworthy of her talent. She died at Pau, France, on April 9, 1940.

Personality. Mrs. Campbell was notoriously "difficult" in the theater and quarreled with almost all her managers and fellow actors. She had no control over her mordantly witty tongue and regularly bit the hand that fed her. (For example, when she toured the United States, she asked everybody she met whether they thought Columbus' journey was really necessary in the first place.) Shaw, who declared himself in love with her for several years, never forgave her for going off on a honeymoon with her second husband, George Cornwallis-West, in the midst of rehearsals for *Pygmalion*. Thereafter, he never offered her any parts in his own plays, though he confessed (in letters to her) that he had her talent and personality in mind when he wrote *Heartbreak House* (1917) and *The Apple Cart* (1922).

Such drama critics as James Agate and Desmond MacCarthy granted that Mrs. Campbell, even when she was at her most impish, careless, and incalculable, had the rare quality of greatness. In 1922 she published *My Life and Some Letters* (most of the latter from Shaw), which is accurate and honestly self-critical.

ALAN DENT
Author of "Mrs. Patrick Campbell"

Further Reading: Dent, Alan, ed., *Bernard Shaw and Mrs. Patrick Campbell: Their Correspondence* (New York 1952); Dent, Alan, *Mrs. Patrick Campbell* (London 1961).

CAMPBELL, kam'bəl, **Robert** (1808–1894), Canadian fur trader and explorer. He was born in Glenlyon, Perthshire, Scotland, on Feb. 21, 1808. He joined the Hudson's Bay Company in 1830 and in 1834 was sent to the Mackenzie River district. Here, his urge to explore resulted in his establishing a post on Dease Lake in 1838; his discovery and naming in 1840 of Lake Francis, Lake Finlayson, and the Pelly River; and his discovery of the Lewes River in 1843. In 1846 he built the Pelly Banks post and in 1848, Fort Selkirk. In 1851 he explored the Pelly River and proved that it was the upper reaches of the Yukon River. In 1852 he left the Yukon and in 1854 returned to the Mackenzie River district. In 1856 he was appointed chief trader at Fort Chipewyan, and in 1867 he was promoted to chief factor. The company dismissed Campbell for an administrative irregularity in 1871. In 1880 he began ranching in Manitoba, where he died on May 9, 1894.

JOHN S. MOIR, *University of Toronto*

CAMPBELL, kam'bəl, **Roy** (1901–1957), South African poet, whose early poetry was remarkable for rhetorical power and striking imagery. He was born Ignatius Roy Dunnachie Campbell in Durban, South Africa, on Oct. 2, 1901, and studied at Oxford University in England. He fought for General Franco during the Spanish Civil War (1936–1939) and served with the British Army in Africa during World War II. Campbell was killed in an automobile accident at Setúbal, Portugal, on April 22, 1957.

Campbell's personality and work recall Byron. His combative, individualistic temperament kept him apart from literary movements of the day, and some of his lyrics express his sense of isolation and independence amid the hostile forces of nature. Campbell's reputation rests on two early volumes of verse, *The Flaming Terrapin* (1924) and *Adamastor* (1930). Other works include the long poem *Flowering Rifle* (1939), a Byronic satire; and two autobiographies, *Broken Record* (1934) and *Light on a Dark Horse* (1952.)

JAMES REEVES
Author of "A Short History of English Poetry"

CAMPBELL, kam'bəl, **Thomas** (1777–1844), British poet, who was a conservative in the romantic era and whose lasting fame rests on a handful of moving war poems. He was born in Glasgow, Scotland, on July 27, 1777, and studied at Glasgow University. Campbell's first literary success came in 1799, with the publication of his long heroic poem, *The Pleasures of Hope*. The next year, while traveling in Germany during the Napoleonic Wars, he witnessed some military action, on which he based many of his war lyrics. After 1803 he lived in London, where from 1820 to 1830 he was editor of the literary *New Monthly Magazine*. Despite his absence from Scotland, Campbell was elected several times to the honorary position of lord rector of Glasgow University, once in preference to Sir Walter Scott. Campbell died in Boulogne, France, on June 15, 1844.

Campbell is remembered chiefly for such fine martial lyrics as *Hohenlinden, Battle of the Baltic, Ye Mariners of England,* and *The Harper*. His 7-volume anthology, *Specimens of the British Poets* (1819), contains essays on poetry revealing some critical acumen. Except for *The Pleasures of Hope,* his longer poems in the outdated Augustan style were not successful. Campbell's failure in this regard has been attributed to too great a care for correctness and a fear of offending the "polite" reading public. Thus, such poems as *Gertrude of Wyoming* (1809) and *Theodoric* (1824) contain little more of interest than occasional pleasing descriptive passages and brief insights into character.

JAMES REEVES
Author of "A Short History of English Poetry"

CAMPBELL, kam'bəl, **Wilfred** (1858–1918), Canadian poet. William Wilfred Campbell was born at Berlin (now Kitchener), Ontario, on June 1, 1858, and studied at the University of Toronto and the Episcopal Divinity School in Cambridge, Mass. He was ordained in 1886, but his religious beliefs were affected by Emersonian transcendentalism and in 1891 he left the Episcopal ministry for the Canadian civil service. Campbell was elected a fellow of the Royal Society of Canada in 1893. He died at Ottawa on Jan. 1, 1918.

Campbell's best poetry, found mostly in his early collections, strikingly depicts the moods and changing seasons of the countryside around Lake Huron. His later verse was more somber. Collections of Campbell's poetry include *Lake Lyrics* (1889), *The Dread Voyage* (1893), *Beyond the Hills of Dream* (1899), and *War Lyrics* (1915). He also wrote verse dramas, collected in *Poetical Tragedies* (1908), and two novels—*Ian of the Orcades* (1906) and *A Beautiful Rebel* (1909).

MICHAEL GNAROWSKI
Sir George Williams University, Montreal

Further Reading: Klinck, Carl F., *Wilfred Campbell: A Study in Late Provincial Victorianism* (Toronto 1942).

CAMPBELL, kam'bəl, **Lord William** (died 1778), last British governor of South Carolina. Youngest son of the fourth Duke of Argyll, Campbell entered the navy, rising to captain in 1762. In 1763 he married the daughter of a wealthy South Carolina planter-merchant. The next year he was elected to the British House of Commons. He resigned in 1766 to become governor of Nova Scotia.

In 1773 he was transferred to South Carolina. By the time he reached Charleston, in June 1775, the American Revolution was under way. Hostilities had broken out, and a patriot committee—his wife's family among the leaders—had taken over the government. Campbell was unable to revive the royal assembly or to rally Tory elements on the frontier. Learning that a British fleet was descending on Charleston, he fled and joined the invasion. He was taken wounded to England, where he died in Southampton on Sept. 5, 1778.

DAVID ALAN WILLIAMS
University of Virginia

CAMPBELL, kam'bəl, **William Wallace** (1862–1938), American astronomer. Born in Hancock county, Ohio, on April 11, 1862, he received his formal education at the University of Michigan, graduating in 1886. His first position was with the mathematics department at the University of Colorado, but in 1888 he returned to the University of Michigan as instructor in astronomy. After working as a volunteer summer assistant at the Lick Observatory of the University of California in 1890, he was called in as astronomer there in

BANCROFT LIBRARY, UNIVERSITY OF CALIFORNIA

Wm. W. Campbell

1891. A decade later he was promoted to director of the observatory. In 1923 he was elected president of the university.

Campbell's move to California marked the turning point in his approach to research. Previously concerned with such classical pursuits as the observation of comets and the determination of their orbits, he turned to the relatively new field of astronomical spectroscopy. Working with the 36-inch Lick refractor, the largest telescope of its day, and the D. O. Mills spectrograph, a specialized instrument constructed to his own specifications, he devoted himself to the task of determining radial (or line-of-sight) velocities, by measuring the Doppler shift of spectral lines. Results of dubious accuracy had been reported from as early as 1868, but Campbell perfected the techniques and provided the first trustworthy values. In 1913 he published *Stellar Motions*, the classic text on the subject, and issued "The Radial Velocities of 915 Stars," which was the first major catalog in this field. Campbell also inaugurated the statistical analysis of radial velocity data, led a number of solar eclipse expeditions, and conducted qualitative investigations into the constitution of novae and planetary atmospheres. Studies of Mars' spectrum, in particular, led him to announce in 1894 the then heretical but eventually accepted finding that Mars' atmosphere contains little of the oxygen and water vapor that are presumably necessary to support the intelligent life that was generally supposed to exist on Mars.

On retiring from the presidency of the University of California in 1930, Campbell became president of the National Academy of Sciences. He died in San Francisco on June 14, 1938.

VICTOR E. THOREN
Indiana University

CAMPBELL, an industrial city in western California, is in Santa Clara county, about 40 miles (64 km) southeast of San Francisco. Its industries include fruit canning and dried-fruit packing and the manufacture of aluminum products, electrical supplies, dies and other tools, and upholstered furniture. The city is a center for electrical research. Fruits and vegetables are grown and poultry is raised in the area.

Campbell was founded in 1885 by Benjamin Campbell and named for his father, a Kentuckian, who established a sawmill nearby in 1848. The city was incorporated in 1952. It is governed by a city manager. Population: 24,770.

CAMPBELL, a city in northeastern Ohio, is in Mahoning county, on the Mahoning River. It adjoins Youngstown on the southeast. Campbell is an industrial city with extensive iron and steel works. Incorporated in 1914, it was known as East Youngstown until 1926. The city was renamed for James A. Campbell, founder and first president of the Youngstown Sheet and Tube Company. Campbell is governed by a mayor and council. Population: 12,577.

CAMPBELL-BANNERMAN, Sir Henry (1836–1908), British prime minister from 1905 to 1908. He was born in Glasgow, Scotland, on Sept. 7, 1836, and educated at Glasgow University and at Trinity College, Cambridge. Campbell-Bannerman entered politics as a Liberal and from 1868 until his death sat as member of Parliament for the Stirling Burghs of Scotland. Between 1871 and 1885 he served his apprenticeship as financial secretary of the war office, secretary of admiralty, and chief secretary for Ireland. In 1886 he joined the cabinet as secretary of state for war; he supported the fight by William Ewart Gladstone, the Liberal leader, for Irish home rule, and served again at the war office from 1892 to 1895.

During the complicated struggle to succeed Gladstone, Campbell-Bannerman slowly emerged by 1899 as the compromise leader of the Liberal party. He supported the South African war, but pleaded for an early peace and the cooperation of the British and Boers. He became concerned with the failure of the Conservatives to propose a generous South African peace, and in 1901 he created a sensation by referring to "methods of barbarism" in the conduct of the war. Imperialists in the Liberal party opposed his position, but in the long run his stand made it possible for his party, when it took office, to grant self-government to the defeated Transvaal and Orange Free State (1907).

When the Liberals won a sweeping election victory in 1905, Campbell-Bannerman became prime minister. His government set down the principles for constitutional development in South Africa, passed a trades disputes bill extending the rights of trade unions, began the reorganization of the British army, and raised the question of curbing the veto power of the House of Lords. Patient, sensible, conciliatory but tough-minded, Campbell-Bannerman presided over a brilliant ministry with shrewdness and courage. He was one of the most underrated prime ministers of recent times. He retired a few weeks before his death, in London, on April 22, 1908.

HENRY R. WINKLER, *Rutgers University*

CAMPBELL ISLAND is an uninhabited volcanic island in the South Pacific Ocean, about 450 miles (725 km) south of Invercargill, New Zealand. It is semicircular, and is about 30 miles (50 km) in circumference. Although very mountainous, Campbell Island has several good harbors.

CAMPBELL RIVER, a village in southwestern British Columbia, Canada, is on the east shore of Vancouver Island about 160 miles (257 km) northwest of Victoria. It is at the mouth of the Campbell River, on which the large John Hart hydroelectric plant is located. The village is the center of logging and paper mill operations. Strathcona Provincial Park is about 20 miles (32 km) to the southwest. Population: 7,825.

CAMPBELLFORD, kam'bəl-fərd, is a town in southern Ontario, Canada, in Northumberland county, about 80 miles (128 km) northeast of Toronto. It is in a dairying district. Its manufactures include flour, pulp, woolens, and furniture. It was settled in the late 1850's by officers from the Crimean War, who received land grants in the area. Population: 3,522.

CAMPBELLITES. See DISCIPLES OF CHRIST.

CAMPBELLS OF ARGYLL, kam'belz, är-gīl', the leaders of one of the largest Scottish clans.

Sir Ian Douglas Campbell (1903–) succeeded his cousin as head of the clan as the 11th Duke of Argyll in 1949. His full titles conveyed an idea of the widespread interests of Clan Campbell. The Duke was also Marquess of Kintyre and Lorne; Earl of Campbell and Cowall; Viscount of Lochow and Glenyla; Lord of Inverary, Mull, Morvern, and Tirie; Earl of Argyll, Lord Campbell; Lord Lorne; Lord of Kintyre; Lord Sundridge of Coomb Bank; and Lord Hamilton. The Duke was hereditary master of the royal household in Scotland, admiral of the western coasts and isles, keeper of Dunstaffnage and other castles, and hereditary sheriff of Argyllshire.

Early Campbells. Sir Gillespie Cambel founded the family fortunes in the 13th century by marryhis cousin Eva O'Duin, heiress of the barony of Lochow in county Argyll. She was the daughter of Paul an Sporran, the royal treasurer and last of the Clan O'Duin, descended from Diarmid.

Sir Colin Campbell of Lochow (died 1296), their son, was a renowned chieftain and unsuccessful candidate for the throne of Scotland in 1291. He gained the surname Mor, or Great, and the chiefs of the clan still bear the patronymic MacCalein Mor (of Colin the Great). Sir Colin was killed in 1296 at a battle with the Lord of Lorne, the head of a powerful rival barony, and a consequent blood feud between the two families lasted more than 150 years.

Neil Campbell (died c. 1316), Colin's son and successor, was knighted by Alexander III shortly before the king's death in 1286. Sir Neil was a staunch adherent of Robert Bruce, whose sister Lady Mary he married.

Sir Duncan Campbell of Lochow (died 1453), Neil's great-great-grandson, offered himself as a hostage for the release from English captivity of James I of Scotland in 1424 and was created Lord Campbell by James II in 1445.

Earls of Argyll. Colin Campbell (died 1493), Duncan's grandson, succeeded him as 2d Lord Campbell and was created 1st Earl of Argyll in 1457. He held several important positions, including that of chancellor of Scotland. In 1465 he married Isabel, heiress of the barony of Lorne, and thereby ended the blood feud begun in 1296. The lordship of Lorne passed to the *Campbells*. and the galley insignia of Lorne became part of the Argyll coat of arms.

Archibald Campbell (died 1513), the 1st Earl's son, succeeded as 2d Earl of Argyll. He died commanding the vanguard of the Scottish army at the battle of Flodden on Sept. 9, 1513.

Archibald Campbell (died 1558), 4th Earl of Argyll, was the first prominent Scot to become a Protestant and one of the first to agitate for the Reformation in Scotland. However, his son Archibald (1530–1575), the 5th Earl, took the side of the Catholic Mary, Queen of Scots, and commanded her army when it was defeated at the Battle of Langside in 1568. He married Jane, the illegitimate daughter of James V and half sister of Mary.

Archibald Campbell (1576–1638), 7th Earl of Argyll, earned a black reputation for the clan by his merciless persecution of the MacGregor and MacDonald clans. His son Archibald (1597–1661), the 8th Earl, was created 1st Marquess of Argyll in 1641. However, the Marquess wavered between King Charles I and Parliament during the Civil War and paid for his indecision with his head immediately after the Restoration.

Archibald Campbell (1628–1685), the Marquess' son, was restored to the family honors as 9th Earl in 1663. However, he sided with the Scottish Presbyterians in opposing repressions of the Church of Scotland in the 1680's and, after attempting an insurrection in Ayrshire in 1685, was captured and executed.

Dukes of Agyll. Archibald Campbell (1651?–1703), the 9th Earl's son, was a zealous supporter of William of Orange and, after the latter had become William III, was restored to his father's honors and created 1st Duke of Argyll in 1701.

John Campbell (1678–1743), the 1st Duke's son and successor as 2d Duke, was a gifted military commander and leader in the British House of Lords. He supported the succession of George I in 1714 and commanded the royal army that defeated the forces of the Stuart pretender at Sheriffmuir in 1715. Alexander Pope memorialized the 2d Duke of Argyll as:

> Argyll, the State's whole thunder born to wield
> And shake alike the senate and the field.

Archibald Campbell (1682–1761), John's brother, who succeeded as 3d Duke, was a distinguished judge. With his death without issue the Argyll title passed to a cousin, John Campbell of Mamore (died 1770), 4th Duke, from whom the subsequent dukes were directly descended.

The family seat of the Dukes of Argyll is Inverary Castle in Loch Fyne, Argyllshire, Scotland.

L. G. PINE
Former Editor of "Burke's Peerage"

CAMPBELLSVILLE, kam'bəlz-vil, a city in central Kentucky, the seat of Taylor county, is situated 65 miles (105 km) southeast of Louisville. It is a trade and processing center in a farming district where tobacco, corn, hay, and wheat are grown. Livestock is raised in the vicinity. The city has a bottling works and produces furniture, ready-mixed concrete, men's clothing, dairy products, and livestock feeds.

Campbellsville is the home of Campbellsville College, which was established as Russell Creek Academy in 1906 and is now a 4-year coeducational institution under Southern Baptist auspices. Government of the city is by mayor and council. Population: 7,598.

CAMPBELLTON, kam'bal-tən, a city in northern New Brunswick, Canada, is on the Restigouche River, 15 miles (24 km) west of Dalhousie. Ocean-going vessels may ascend the river to Campbellton, and the city is a shipping port for pulpwood. A highway bridge crosses the river to Quebec province. The salmon fishing on the Restigouche above the city is famous. Sugar Loaf Mountain, nearly 1,000 feet (304 meters) high, is southwest of the city. The last sea fight of the Seven Years' War in North America was fought in 1760 in the river above Campbellton. Population: 10,335.

CAMPECHE, käm-pā'chā, is a state in southeastern Mexico, on the Gulf of Mexico. Its area is 21,666 square miles (56,114 sq km). Campeche comprises the southwestern part of the Yucatán Peninsula and the eastern portion of the Tabasco alluvial plain. Shrimp fishing, agriculture (maize, coconuts, henequin, sugarcane, beans, and oranges), and exploitation of forest products (chicle and tropical woods) dominate the economy. Most of the population is mestizo, but about a quarter are Maya Indians.

The capital and largest city is Campeche, founded in 1540 on the site of the Maya settlement of Kimpech. It is a trade center and the seat of the state university. Campeche is known as the "City of Walls" from fortifications built in 1686–1704 as a protection against pirate attacks.

Hernández de Córdoba discovered Campeche in 1517, and European settlement began in 1540. The Campeche district seceded from Yucatán in 1857 and became a state in 1863. A railroad linked Campeche with the rest of Mexico in 1951, and a highway in 1961. Population: (1960) of the state, 168,219; of the city, 43,874.

DONALD D. BRAND, *University of Texas*

CAMPECHE, Gulf of, käm-pā'chā, the southernmost part of the Gulf of Mexico, lying west of the Yucatán Peninsula. Its entire shoreline is Mexican territory. The gulf extends a maximum distance of about 440 miles (710 km) from east to west and 200 miles (320 km) from north to south. Its waters are shallowest in the east, where the continental shelf is 135 miles (215 km) wide. The gulf is fished for mackerel and shrimp. Its chief ports are Veracruz, Coatzacoalcos (Puerto México), and Campeche. The shoal formed in the Gulf of Mexico by the continental shelf north of Yucatán is known as *Campeche Bank.*

CAMPEGGIO, käm-pād'jō, **Lorenzo** (1472–1539), Italian cardinal, canonist, and diplomat. He was born in Milan on Nov. 7, 1472, the son of an eminent lawyer. He studied law, sired five children, and after his wife's death in 1509 entered ecclesiastical life. In 1512, Julius II named Campeggio bishop of Feltre and member of the Rota, the church's highest court of appeal. Pope Leo X, in an effort to unite Christendom against the Turks, sent him as papal legate to the Emperor Maximilian I in Germany, and while there he was made a cardinal (1517).

Campeggio supported Pope Adrian VI (reigned 1522–1523), who sought to reform the abuse of indulgences, the Curia, concordats, and ecclesiastical patronage. With Adrian's premature death, the reforms failed, but Pope Clement VII appointed Campeggio to the bishopric of Bologna and sent him as papal legate to Germany. Lutheran and anti-imperialist forces and the Peasants' War frustrated further attempts at reform.

In 1527, in the Pope's absence, Campeggio ruled a sacked Rome, and a year later he was in England with Cardinal Wolsey to judge the validity of Henry VIII's marriage to Catherine of Aragon. Diplomatic but unbribable, Campeggio referred the case to Rome on July 23, 1529.

In 1530 he returned to Germany as papal legate and attended the Diet of Augsburg. He sought the suppression of Protestantism as a prerequisite for the proposed general council. Campeggio died in Rome on July 25, 1539.

THOMAS A. BRESLIN, S. J.
Loyola Seminary, Shrub Oak, N.Y.

CAMPEN, käm'pən, **Jacob van** (1590–1657), Dutch architect, who was one of the masters of 17th century Dutch classicism. He was born in Haarlem. As an architect he always left the technical side of construction to others. His buildings, which show a strong Palladian influence, include the Mauritshuis (1633–1635), The Hague, and the huge town hall (1648–1662), now the royal palace, Amsterdam. The latter edifice, one of the few Dutch buildings constructed entirely of stone, is somewhat heavy and unimaginative. However, it gives a feeling of power that reflects the self-assurance of the people of Amsterdam at that time. Campen also designed the Nieuwe Kerk (New Church; 1645) in Haarlem, which, with its Greek-cross-in-square style, was imitated several times in England, and it is quite probable that Christopher Wren knew of it, perhaps through his older contemporary Hugh May. Campen also had a strong influence on his Dutch contemporaries. He died in Randenbroek in 1657.

CAMPER, käm'pər, **Pieter** (1722–1789), Dutch physician and naturalist, who is best known for his anatomical studies of man and other animals. Camper was the first to attempt to differentiate people of different races on the basis of their skull shape. His findings, published in his *Dissertation on the Natural Varieties,* were the first to point out concrete anatomical differences among the varieties of the human species. Camper also studied orangutans, elephants, and other animals. While studying birds he was the first to discover the air chambers inside their bones.

In addition to his contribution to natural history, Camper also contributed to the fields of surgery and obstetrics. He was also interested in medical jurisprudence and aesthetics. In studying the works of painters and medieval manuscript illustrators, he formulated the theory that intelligence is related to the facial angle. This theory was published in his *Treatise on the Natural Differences of Features in Persons of Various Countries and ages.*

Life. Camper was born in Leiden, the Netherlands, on May 11, 1722. He received his medical degree from the University of Leiden in 1746 and became professor of medicine at the University of Franeker four years later. He remained there until 1755, when he took a position at the Athenaeum in Amsterdam. In 1763 he accepted a professorship at the University of Groningen, where he remained until his retirement in 1773. He died at The Hague on April 7, 1789. His collected writings were published in Paris in 1803.

DAVID OTTO
Stephens College

CAMPERO, käm-pā'rō, **Narciso** (1815–1896), Bolivian president and soldier. He was born in Tojo (now in Argentina). He entered the Bolivian Army, where he rose to the rank of brigadier general, and in 1872 served as minister of war.

Campero was a leader of the conservative group that ousted Hilarión Daza, and he replaced Daza as president of Bolivia in 1880. He served until 1884. Under his leadership a new conservative constitution was adopted, consolidating the power of the aristocracy and clergy.

During Campero's presidency Bolivia lost its seacoast to Chile in the War of the Pacific. Campero commanded the allied forces of Peru and Bolivia in that war but was defeated at Tacna on May 26, 1880. He died in Bolivia in 1896.

CAMPHOR, kam'fər, is a common organic substance with a characteristic fragrant, penetrating odor and the molecular formula $C_{10}H_{16}O$. It belongs to a class of compounds known as the bicyclic terpenes. Camphor has been used in the Orient since the earliest times both as incense and as a pharmaceutical. It was probably introduced into Europe by the Arabs, who called it *Kafer*. Although camphor is now known to have little therapeutic value, it has been used medicinally in the West for centuries. Children in some rural areas of the United States still wear small bags of camphor around their necks to ward off colds and other ailments.

Properties. Camphor is a colorless or white solid substance. It melts at about 178° C (350° F) and boils at 209° C (408° F). It sublimes readily at room temperature. When fragments of camphor are dropped onto the surface of water, changes in the surface tension of the liquid cause them to gyrate wildly. Camphor is insoluble in water, but it does dissolve in organic solvents such as alcohol, ether, chloroform, and carbon disulfide.

Sources and Production. Camphor is found in the wood and leaves of *Cinnamomum camphora,* a tree native to the coast of China and its offshore islands; Taiwan in particular has extensive stands. The tree also grows widely in the region from southern Japan to Vietnam and is now cultivated in California and Florida.

The camphor tree takes from 45 to 50 years to mature, reaching a height of up to 40 feet (12.2 meters). It bears small white flowers and red fruits. On plantations, the leaves and twigs of the tree are harvested several times a year after the tree is three or four years old. The twigs and leaves are ground up and distilled with steam for several hours to isolate crude camphor, which is then purified further before it is marketed. One tree may yield up to 3 tons of crude camphor during its lifetime.

The product of steam-distillation is known as *natural camphor* and is a dextrorotatory chemical. However, about 75% of the camphor sold in the United States today is *synthetic camphor,* and this substance is optically inactive. It is made largely from the turpentine component pinene, $C_{10}H_{16}$. In the production of camphor, pinene is converted to camphene, which is then converted to camphor by treatment with acetic acid and nitrobenzene. Camphor was first made in the laboratory in 1859, but commercial production did not begin until after World War I, when the Japanese monopoly of natural sources forced the price of camphor to exorbitant levels.

Uses. As a medicine, camphor is used externally as a liniment and as a mild antiseptic and counterirritant. In the past it was taken internally as a cardiac and circulatory stimulant and antidiarrhetic. However, camphor is no longer taken internally because it is toxic and may produce harmful effects, especially in infants.

Industrially, camphor is used as a plasticizer for Celluloid, other cellulose nitrate products, lacquers, and smokeless powder. It is also used as a moth repellent. The decreasing use of Celluloid and substitution of new plastics, the replacement of cellulose nitrate photographic film by safety film, and the widespread use of naphthalene and *p*-dichlorobenzene as a moth repellant have all caused a reduction in the commercial importance of camphor.

ALVIN I. KOSAK, *New York University*

CAMPI, käm'pē, a family of Italian painters, who were members of the school of Cremona in the 16th century. The family included Galeazzo Campi (1475?–1536); his sons Giulio (1500?–?1572), Antonio (1530?–1591), Vincenzo (1536?–1591); and Bernardino Campi (1522?–1592), who may have been Galeazzo's nephew.

GALEAZZO CAMPI, a pupil of Boccaccio Boccaccino, was an accomplished painter in a fully developed Renaissance style. A characteristic work is the altarpiece *Madonna with St. Anthony and St. Biagio* (Brera, Milan).

GIULIO CAMPI (as well as his brothers and his cousin) was closer to the new manneristic tendencies of the 16th century than to the stable and balanced Renaissance style. A pupil of Romanino, Giulio was influenced by the Venetian school, by Giulio Romano, and by the leading mannerist painter, Parmigianino. Characteristic of Giulio's style are elongated, active, turning figures and a strong interplay of light and shade. An example is the *Purification of the Virgin,* a fresco in the Church of Santa Margherita, Cremona. His portrait of his father is in the Uffizi Gallery, Florence.

ANTONIO CAMPI, who studied painting chiefly with his father, was also an architect and the author of a history of Cremona. He worked in Piacenza, Brescia, Mantua, Rome, and Madrid (in the service of Philip II), as well as in Cremona. His best work is the stucco decoration in the Church of San Sigismondo at Cremona.

VINCENZO CAMPI, a pupil of Giulio, specialized in still lifes, genre paintings, and portraits. His portrait of Giulio Boccamozzo is in the Accademia at Carrara, and two characteristic still lifes are in the Brera Gallery at Milan.

BERNARDINO CAMPI was the son of Pietro Campi, a goldsmith whose trade he followed for a time. He is known for his portraits and for religious paintings, especially the series of frescoes in the Church of San Sigismondo, Cremona. In 1584 he published a treatise on painting, *Parere sopra la pittura.*

MARTICA SAWIN
Parsons School of Design, New York City

CAMPIN, Robert. See FLÉMALLE, MASTER OF.

CAMPINA GRANDE, kaNm-pē'nə graNn'də, is a city in northeastern Brazil. It is situated in the interior of Paraíba state, on the eastern edge of the drought region known as the *caatinga,* about 115 miles (180 km) by road northwest of Recife. Campina Grande is the commercial and industrial center of a cotton-growing district that also produces agave fiber, sugarcane, tobacco, livestock, fruit, and vegetables. The city's main industries are based on cotton. Population: (1960) 116,226.

CAMPINAS, kaNm-pē'nəs, is a city in Brazil, in the state of São Paulo, 57 miles (91 km) northwest of the city of São Paulo. It is situated in a diversified farming region that produces coffee, sugarcane, cereals, and cotton. Its industries include sugar refining, metal casting, tanning, coffee processing, and the manufacture of soap, cosmetics, and agricultural machinery. Campinas was Brazil's leading coffee-producing center in the late 1800's, when its important agricultural institute was founded. The city is also the home of the Catholic University of Campinas and the Penido Bournier Institute of Ophthalmology. Population: (1960) 179,797.

CAMPING is an activity that involves living out-of-doors temporarily. It is enjoyed by individuals searching for solitude in wilderness areas and by families and organized groups sharing experiences in the open country.

The American concept of camping owes much to the North American Indian who, during the course of his everyday primitive living, evolved skills and implements that have been adopted by modern outdoorsmen. Early explorers, trappers, and traders recognized the superiority of the Indian's ways and adopted his techniques, living in crude camps, cooking over open fires, and sleeping in fur robes. As the United States grew, the Indian's ways were no longer essential to survival. However, so deeply had thousands of Americans become imbued with a love for the outdoors as a result of this heritage that camping developed into a sport, usually as an adjunct to hunting and fishing.

In Europe, camping developed as an adjunct to the bicycle, and in the early 1900's cycling, hiking, and camping clubs began to become popular. Thus the camping concept grew slowly. But after World War II it mushroomed to the point where close to 30 million persons in the United States and other millions throughout the world were enjoying camping.

The cause of this phenomena is difficult to pinpoint. Undoubtedly the tensions of modern living, the desire to travel inexpensively, the holding together of the family with a common interest, and the appeal of colorful equipment are prime factors. The byproducts of war—such as the four-wheel-drive car, lightweight tents, and practical sleeping bags—also contribute.

INDIVIDUAL AND FAMILY CAMPING

Campers seek various avenues of enjoyment, some searching for solitude in remote areas, traveling on foot, by canoe, trail bike, or boat. However, it is among family campers that the greatest growth in numbers has occurred. The family camper's philosophy varies from that of his wilderness-loving counterpart. He is gregarious, rarely seeking a true wilderness experience but, rather, the company of his own kind on well-established, and sometimes crowded, campgrounds. As a result, the ultimate destination and the techniques of the wilderness camper and the family camper are quite unlike, and so is much of their equipment.

Camping Areas and Services in the United States. In the late 1960's, more than 135,000 miles of trails were open to backpackers in the United States, the best known being the 2,000-mile Appalachian Trail and the 2,300-mile Pacific Coast Trail. Some 24,000 miles of trails on federal land were open to trail bikes. Canoe camping is usually identified with Minnesota and Maine waterways, but thousands of miles of canoe water exist in other states. See also CANOE AND CANOEING.

Some 450,000 campsites were available in wilderness areas or in more than 12,000 campgrounds. In the latter, a campsite consists of a tent or trailer pad, parking space, table, and fireplace and grill. In remote sections, a campsite may be only a small, undeveloped clearing. Within 154 national forests, the U. S. Forest Service could accommodate 52,000 families in 6,400 camp and picnic grounds, while the National Park Service maintained 28,000 sites in 571 campgrounds. At the state level, more than 1,400 parks and forests included one or more camping areas.

Commercially operated private campgrounds numbered about 3,500, mostly in the East and upper Midwest. The trend among these was to highly developed, resortlike facilities, supplying water and electricity to individual sites, sewerage disposal outlets for recreational vehicles, modern toilets, hot showers, and coin laundries.

The Land and Water Conservation Fund Act of 1965 provided for entrance fees and for nominal special-user fees (for services such as hot water, electricity, firewood, and boat ramps) at designated charge areas on federal lands. A Federal Recreation Area Entrance Permit (available yearly for a small fee) admitted the camper's car and its occupants to all national charge areas. Nominal charges were also made for the use of state and private campgrounds.

Camping in Europe. All European countries, especially those in western Europe, catered to campers after World War II. The production of camping equipment developed into a large industry. Governments and commercial interests opened up thousands of campsites on the continent. Millions of hitchhikers, cycle campers, vacationing canoeists, fishermen, and mountaineers roamed the European countryside.

To camp in western Europe, a *carnet* (permit) is essential; it can be obtained through recognized camping clubs or the Fédération Internationale de Camping et de Caravanning.

Campsite and Shelter. In choosing a campsite, safety and comfort should be considered. The ideal campsite should be situated on high ground, with ready access to pure water and firewood. It should be away from swamps, tall grass, and brush, which harbor insects; from tall trees, which might drop limbs or attract lightning; from a dry creek bed, which might be flooded by a heavy rain; and from sharp dropoffs along a shoreline. The tent should be on a flat and elevated spot, with the camper's kitchen near his tent. The backpacker depends for his fire on wood he gathers on the spot. The car camper may bring his fire with him in the form of charcoal and a grill, a two-burner gasoline-burning stove, or a propane campstove. The latter operates from disposable cylinders or refillable 6- to 20-pound tanks.

The primary shelter for every outdoorsman is a tent. A two-man nylon hiker's tent, equipped with a sewed-in floor, insect netting, and a plastic-coated nylon fly, is sufficient for a short trip. For families who do not have a wheeled (truck or trailer) camping shelter, the umbrella or high-walled cottage type tent—with a sewed-in floor as well as a screened door and window—offers the most protection and comfort. These range in size up to 10 by 20 feet and can accommodate large families through the use of double deck, folding aluminum bunks. A 6- by 8-foot tarpaulin will provide cover for equipment and firewood at night and shelter for eating and cooking in rainy weather.

Equipment and Supplies. Equipment for the backpacker must be limited to essentials. The trail biker and canoeist may take a few more belongings in the bicycle carrier and canoe, respectively. With packhorses, the camper may add items of convenience and bulk. Family campers with recreational vehicles have few restrictions on equipment.

The backpacker needs an aluminum packframe

KINDS OF TENTS

TENTS are available in various sizes and styles. The choice may depend on the number of people to be accommodated, the type of site chosen for camping, the climate and the presence or absence of insects or snakes, and also the amount of storage room in the type of transportation used.

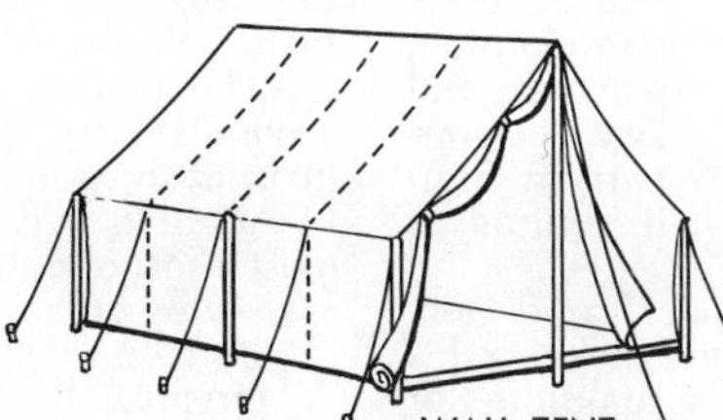

WALL TENT

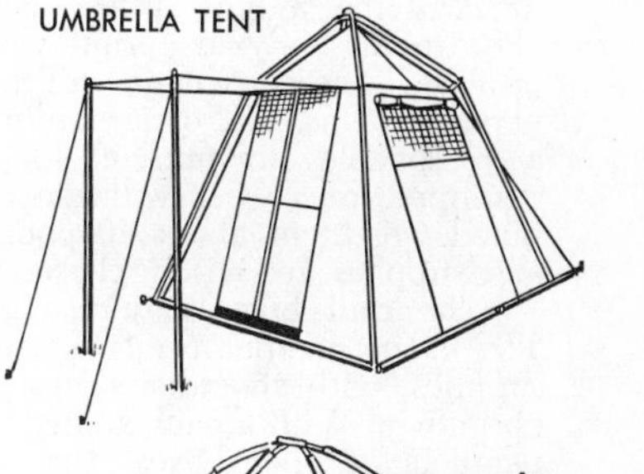

UMBRELLA TENT

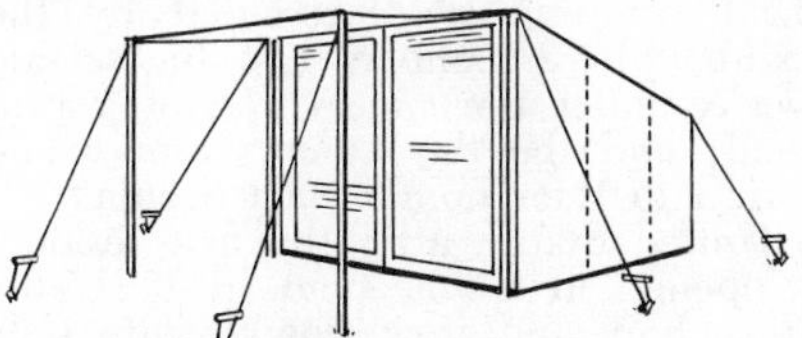

BAKER TENT

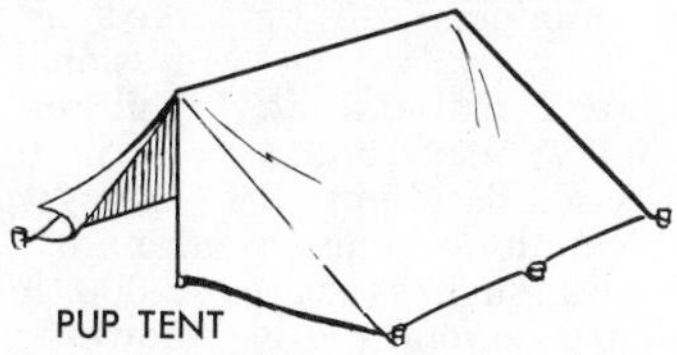

PUP TENT

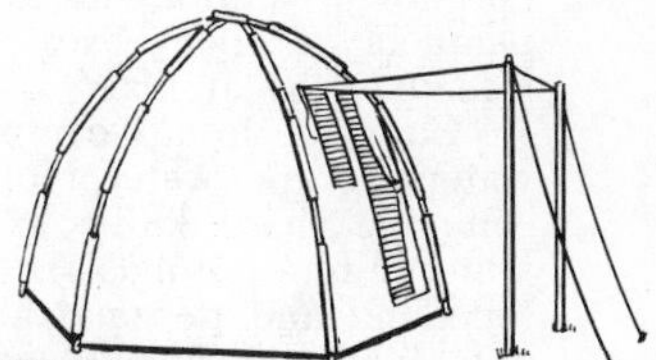

POP TENT

IMPORTANT EQUIPMENT

BASIC EQUIPMENT for camping in the outdoors includes all of the articles illustrated, except for a choice between the sleeping facilities, plus food and other personal items.

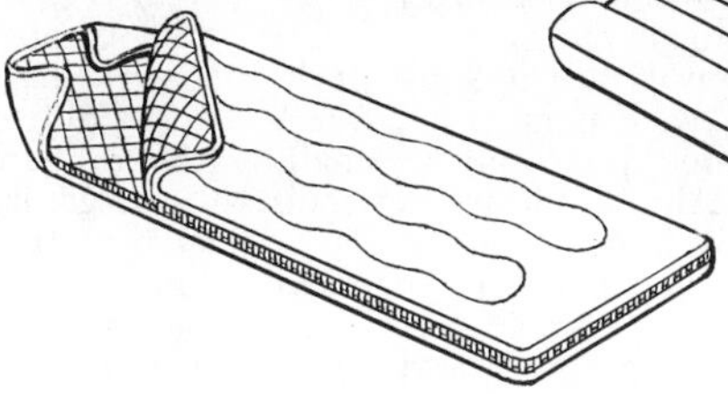

SLEEPING BAG

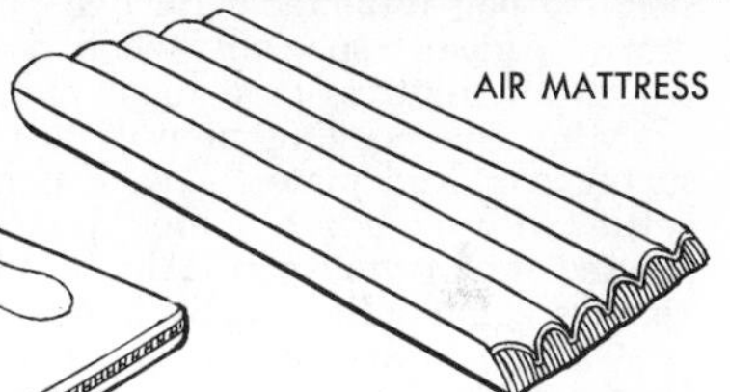

AIR MATTRESS

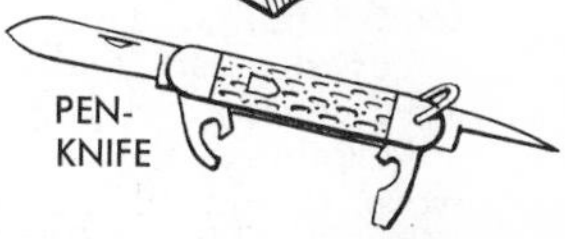

PEN-KNIFE

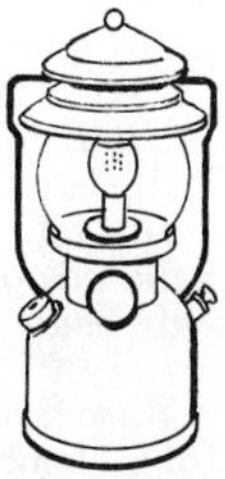

GAS LANTERN

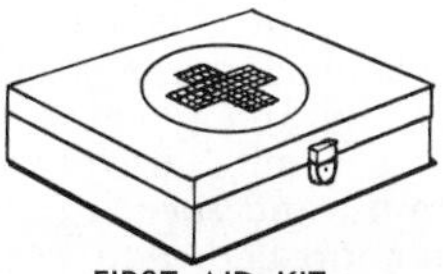

FIRST AID KIT

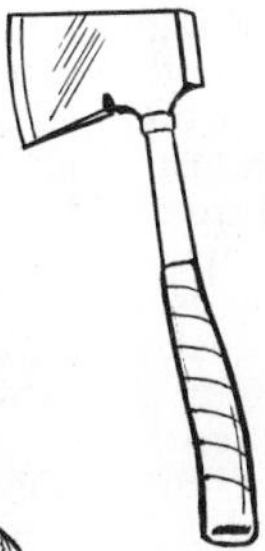

CAMP AX

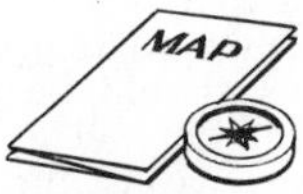

MAPS AND COMPASS

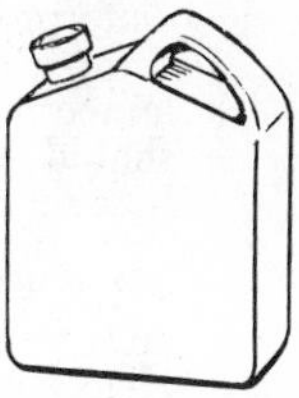

PLASTIC WATER JUG

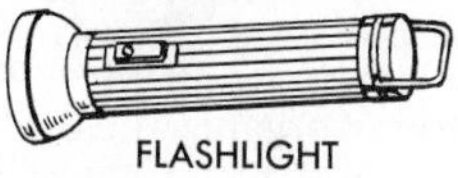

FLASHLIGHT

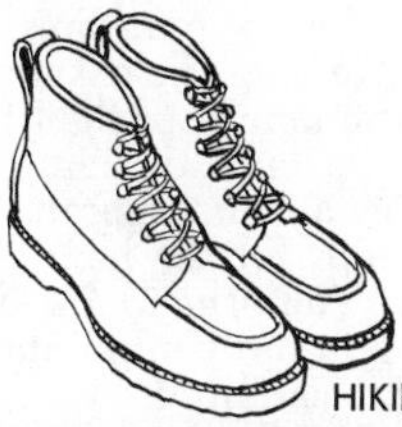

HIKING SHOES

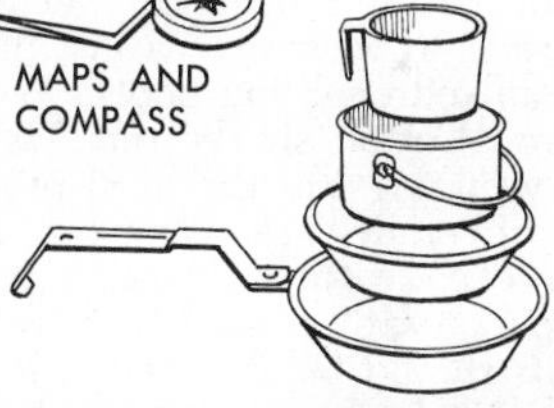

COOKING UTENSILS

CAMP PACKS

PACKS are chosen for their usefulness in carrying different amounts of equipment on the back. For long hikes a pack and a rolled sleeping bag can be carried comfortably on a pack frame.

PACK FRAME

DULUTH PACK

RUCKSACK

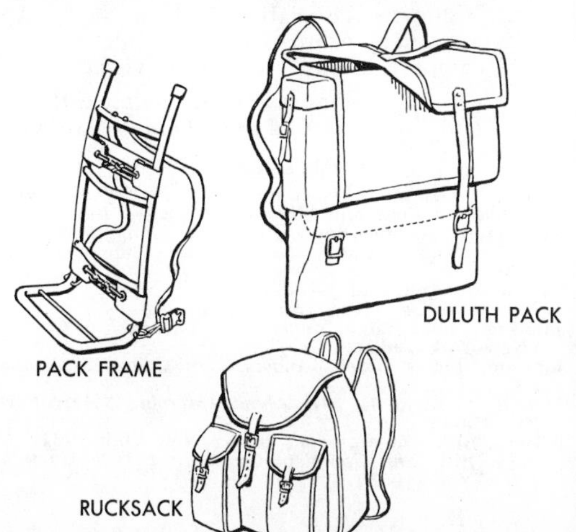

TYPES OF FIRES

FIRES in camps may be needed for cooking and for warmth and may be constructed in some of the ways illustrated, depending on the type of wood available and on the location of the camp site.

TEPEE FIRE

CRISSCROSS FIRE LAY

HUNTERS' FIRE

INDIAN STAR FIRE

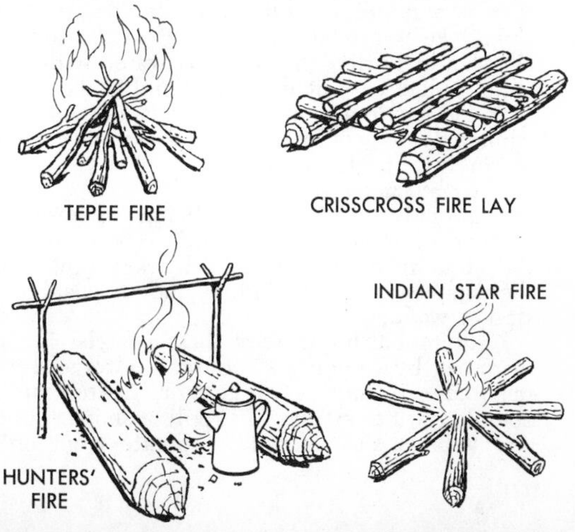

to carry the weight of his equipment high and close to his body to permit walking in an erect position. The packframe will take extra clothing, personal items, tent or tarpaulin, cooking kit, and a reasonable amount of food. Two persons equipped for a week will generally carry a combined weight of about 40 pounds, if equipment and supplies are wisely chosen.

The trail biker may use a packframe, too. The canoe camper needs a canvas pack for his supplies, with shoulder straps and tumpline for portaging. With a pack animal, the camper needs panniers or fiber boxes; the containers can be lashed to the animal.

Common to all campers are a first-aid kit; water jug and waterproof matches; maps and a compass; sharp knife, ax, or saw; flashlight or lantern; rope; sunglasses and sun lotion; insect repellent; and personal necessities, such as soap and shaving cream. In addition, everyone needs a compact sleeping bag. For summer hiking, a sleeping bag insulated with two pounds of goose down is ideal, especially when used with a ¾-length air mattress or a foam pad.

Minimum cooking utensils are a knife, fork, spoon, cup, and plate for each person, a 2-quart kettle with a lid, a coffee pot, and a small, pressed-steel frying pan. Aluminum nesting cook kits are commonly used by family campers.

Canned meats, butter, and jams are practical food supplies. Dried or concentrated foods and juices are tasty and easy to prepare, and packaged cereals and prepared mixes can be used.

Clothing requirements vary, but anything worn should be durable and comfortable, and items should include apparel that can be put on and removed in layers according to temperature and exertion. Shoes or boots should be sturdy, waterproof, and well broken in. The canoe camper may prefer to wear moccasins; the mountaineer needs caulked climbing boots. Wool socks should be worn. Cotton shorts and T-shirts are best for warm weather. For the most protection—and useful at any time—are jeans or slacks, an old felt hat or cap, leather gloves, a windproof jacket or rain parka with a hood, and wool shirts. Heavy garments should be shunned.

Sanitation and Safety. A camper's health and happiness depend on cleanliness and safety precautions. He should confine all camp fires to fireplaces and extinguish them completely each time he leaves the area. Before leaving a campsite, he should burn his waste and bury his cans or put them in a space set aside for trash disposal. He should check all swimming areas for hazards. He should protect his ax and paddle so that porcupines cannot chew the handles. He should keep his food supply safe from animals. He should purify questionable water with halazone tablets or boil it. He should make certain that he assembles a first-aid kit adequate for common emergencies such as blisters, burns, cuts, poison ivy, and toothache.

Recreational Vehicles. In 1966 several million recreational vehicles were being operated by campers throughout the world. These included the large travel trailers and truck campers and the smaller vans, including motor coaches or station wagons.

Equipment for some of these vehicles is often luxurious by camping standards. A travel trailer may have a range, refrigerator, heater, and a complete water system to supply a shower, toilet, and kitchen sink. Utilities operate from either bottled propane gas or 110-volt electricity. Dining areas are provided, and bedding consists of foam mattresses, sheets, and blankets.

The tent trailer, whose canvas top opens to accommodate up to 10 persons, is usually less luxuriously equipped. Most units have at least two double beds with foam mattresses on which most use polyester-filled sleeping bags.

ORGANIZED CAMPING

Organized camping is represented by the resident camp, where campers live for several days or weeks under the supervision of a professional staff; and the day camp, from which children return to their homes each evening.

In the United States, after the first resident camp was opened in Connecticut in 1861, the number of such camps grew slowly, with only 2,000 in operation as late as 1920. By 1966, however, there were 11,200 resident and day camps. The 8,000 resident camps were attended by 3,840,000 persons; day camp attendance totaled 1,676,000. Commercially operated private camps numbered about 2,700, located primarily in New England, Wisconsin, Minnesota, and California. For the handicapped there were 180 resident camps and 75 day camps.

Organized camps are conducted by agencies such as the Boy Scouts, Girl Scouts, Girl Guides (Britain), YMCA, YWCA, and 4-H groups. Camps may be sponsored by service clubs, industry, churches, municipalities, schools, and private groups. In Australia, South Africa, and Japan, school-sponsored camping activities are subsidized by the government. There are also educational, family, travel, health, tutoring, and music camps; and special camps for the crippled, the undernourished, and persons with heart ailments.

Camp programs may include nature study, swimming, field sports, riding, boating, shooting, astronomy, pack trips, canoe trips, dramatics, crafts, and dancing. Traditional camping activities are incorporated in the programs for special camps for the handicapped when possible.

The principal agency serving organized camping in the United States is the American Camping Association; in Canada, the Canadian Camping Association; in Britain, the Camping Club of Great Britain and Ireland; in Germany, the Deutscher Camping Club; and in France, the Fédération Française de Camping et de Caravanning. Other countries have similar organized groups. In the United States there are several large clubs and associations, such as the North American Family Campers Association, and the Sierra, Appalachian, and Adirondacks Mountain clubs, where camping is the foremost activity.

WILLIAM A. RIVIERE, *Author of "The Complete Guide to Family Camping"*

Bibliography

American Camping Association, *Directory of Accredited Camps for Boys and Girls* (Martinsville, Ind., 1966).
Bier, James A., and Raup, Henry A., *Campground Atlas of the United States and Canada* (Champaign, Ill., 1966).
Grifalcone, Ann, and Jacobson, Ruth, *Camping Through Europe by Car* (New York 1963).
Johnson, James Ralph, *Anyone Can Backpack in Comfort* (New York 1965).
Johnson, James Ralph, *Anyone Can Camp in Comfort* (New York 1964).
Merrill, William K., *All About Camping* (Harrisburg, Pa., 1963).
Riviere, Bill, *The Camper's Bible* (New York 1961).
Riviere, Bill, *The Complete Guide to Family Camping* (New York 1966).

CAMPION, kam′pē-ən, **Blessed Edmund** (c. 1540–1581), English Roman Catholic martyr. He was born in London. His father and mother were Catholics until the reign of Elizabeth I (1558–1603). The London Grocers' Company supplied Campion with a scholarship to Bluecoat School, London, and in 1555 to St. John's College, Oxford. He took the required oath recognizing royal supremacy in religious matters when he received his M. A. in 1564, and became an influential and popular teacher at Oxford. Because of his oratorical prowess, he had been chosen to address Queen Mary upon her solemn entry into London in 1553; and when Elizabeth I visited Oxford in 1566, Campion's Latin speech and subsequent disputation induced the Queen's friend, the Earl of Leicester, to be his patron.

A brilliant future in the Anglican Church lay before Campion when he took deacon's orders in 1568, but at the end of his term as junior proctor, his belief in Anglicanism was wavering. He journeyed to Dublin, where he hastily composed the short, and much admired, *History of Ireland.* In 1571, suspected of crypto-Catholic leanings, he fled Ireland. After a brief stay in England he went to Douai, in the Spanish Netherlands, where the English seminary in exile had opened in 1568. Campion became reconciled to Catholicism, joined the Jesuits in 1573, and was ordained in 1578.

In June 1580, Campion returned to England, where, with Robert Persons, he inaugurated a Jesuit mission. He composed a "Letter to the Lords of the Council" ("Campion's Brag"), in which he stated his intention to minister to English Catholics. His preaching, zeal, and winning personality made his ministry most effective.

In July 1581, an apostate Catholic revealed his hiding place to the authorities. He was arrested and taken to the Tower of London. When he spurned all enticements to apostatize, he was severely tortured. Although he recognized Elizabeth as lawful ruler, he was tried on a trumped-up charge of treason and found guilty. He was taken to Tyburn where he was hanged, drawn, and quartered on Dec. 1, 1581. His feast is celebrated on December 1.

John F. Broderick, S. J.
Weston College, Mass.

CAMPION, kam′pē-ən, **Thomas** (1567–1620), English poet and composer, who was one of the masters of the Elizabethan lyric. His genius was singularly well suited to his time, an era that conceived of lyric poetry as inseparable from music and saw English vocal music achieve its greatest triumphs. As a writer of poetic texts for music, Campion has no peer in his age; as a composer of songs, he ranks just below Dowland and Morley.

Life. Campion, son of a prosperous court clerk, was born in London on Feb. 12, 1567. He was educated at Peterhouse College, Cambridge; studied law at Gray's Inn; and may have served in the Earl of Essex's French campaign of 1591–1592. His versatility is suggested by the fact that he obtained a degree in medicine some time between 1602 and 1606 and later practiced in London. Campion seems to have been converted to Catholicism during the latter half of his life. He died in London on March 1, 1620.

Works. Campion's first printed poems formed an anonymous appendix to the pirated first edition of Sidney's *Astrophel and Stella* (1591). Primarily interested in music, he wrote, with Philip Rosseter, the musical accompaniment and perhaps some of the verse in *A Booke of Ayres* (1601) and the four additional books of airs that followed between 1613 and 1617. He also wrote a treatise on counterpoint, some masques that were performed at court, and some skillful Latin poetry.

Campion's fame, however, rests on his lyrics, which he himself considered relatively unimportant. A humanist, he turned to antiquity for his inspiration. In his *Observations in the Art of English Poesie* (1602), he advocated the use of unrhymed "quantitative" meters (based on duration of sound) derived from classical examples, rather than the rhymed accentual meters (based on natural syllabic stress) traditional in English poetry. His position, opposed by Samuel Daniel in *A Defence of Ryme* (1603), was not so simple or crude as that of some earlier humanists since he recognized the value of both the accentual and quantitative potentialities of English rhythm. But he was arguing a lost cause. Although his *Rose-cheekt Laura, Come* is one of the very few successful lyrics in English quantitative verse, most of his own lyrics are accentual and rhymed.

Unlike much poetry written for music, Campion's lyrics are capable of standing by themselves. As C. S. Lewis observed, Campion's poems have "a rhythmical life of their own," apart from the music for which they were intended. (An example is *When to her lute Corinna Sings.*) Although Campion's lyrics do not equal those of his contemporaries Spenser and Donne, lacking the sensuousness of the former's and the dramatic intensity of the latter's, they have a sensitivity, flexibility, and delicacy that charm both the ear and the imagination.

Frank J. Warnke, *Coeditor of "Seventeenth Century Prose and Poetry"*

Further Reading: Kastendieck, Miles Merwin, *England's Musical Poet: Thomas Campion* (New York 1938).

CAMPISTRON, kän-pēs-trôɴ′, **Jean Galbert de** (1656–1723), French playwright. He was born in Toulouse. He began his career with *Virginie* (1683), which, like most of his plays, was a weak imitation of Racine's neoclassical tragedies on classical subjects. His best tragedies are *Andronic* (1685), a drama that presented contemporary life disguised as classical history, and *Tiridate* (1691), the story of an incestuous passion. His plays are fraught with intrigue and melodrama, and their verse is flat. Of his works, nine tragedies, two comedies, and librettos for three operas survive, among them the libretto for Lully's *Acis et Galatée* (1686). He died in Toulouse on May 11, 1723.

CAMPO GRANDE, kaɴm′pōō graɴn′də, is a city in southwestern Brazil, in the hilly region known as the Serra de Amambaí or Serra de Maracaju. The largest and fastest-growing urban center in Mato Grosso state, Campo Grande is the commercial and transportation center of a huge frontier region of cattle ranges and developing agriculture. The city has slaughterhouses, meat-packing plants, and tanneries. It ships meat, hides, coffee, and cereals eastward to São Paulo over the Noroeste railroad, which also extends westward into Bolivia and southward to the Paraguayan border. These rail lines and the airways are the chief means of transportation in the area. Population: (1960) 64,934.

CAMPOAMOR Y CAMPOOSORIO, käm-pō-ä-môr′ ē käm-pō-ō-sō′ryō, **Ramón de** (1817–1901), Spanish writer, who was the first important Spanish poet to break with the romantics. His contemporaries thought him a literary genius comparable to Homer, Shakespeare, Calderón, and Goethe, but later critics considered him outside the mainstream of world literature.

Campoamor was born on Sept. 24, 1817, in the village of Navia in Asturias. He was orphaned at an early age and for a time planned to join the Jesuit order. He studied Latin in Puerto de Vega, philosophy in Santiago de Compostela, and logic, mathematics, and medicine in Madrid. Without having completed any course of studies, he decided on a career in literature. In 1845 he became editor of the newspaper *El Español.* He was governor of Alicante in 1854 and of Valencia in 1856. In 1861 he became a member of the Spanish Royal Academy. He died in Madrid on Feb. 12, 1901.

Writings. Campoamor claimed to have invented two new poetic forms—the *dolora* and the *humorada*—but both forms existed before his time; he merely gave them new names. The *dolora* (as exemplified in his *Fábulas morales y doloras,* 1846), consisting of two (or sometimes four) verses in dramatic or dialogue form, contain clever and humorous moral reflections or philosophical judgments on contemporary mores. The *humorada* (*Humoradas,* 1886–1888) is the *dolora* minus the dramatization. The *pequeño poema* (*Los pequeños poemas,* 1872–1874) is essentially an expanded *dolora* in which the poet satirizes human foibles.

Campoamor wrote several long narrative poems, including *Colón* (1853), a symbolic work based largely on Columbus' discovery of America, and *El drama universal* (1869), which purports to summarize the entire history of mankind. Among his philosophical prose works are *El personalismo* (1855) and *Lo absoluto* (1865). He also wrote a number of verse plays that are more suitable for reading than for staging. His *Poética* (1883), which discusses his poetic precepts, reveals his aversion to art for art's sake and his approval of art founded on ideas.

DONALD W. BLEZNICK, *University of Cincinnati*

Further Reading: Hilton, Ronald, *Campoamor, Spain, and the World* (Toronto 1940); Pineyro y Barry, Enrique, *The Romantics of Spain* (Liverpool 1934).

CAMPOBASSO, käm-pō-bäs′sō, a city and commune in Italy, is the capital of the Molise region. It lies near the center of the Italian peninsula, in the Neapolitan Apennines. The city is difficult to reach as it is served only by a branch railroad and by roads that connect it with the Adriatic coast, with the lowlands of northern Apulia, and with distant Naples. Besides public administration and local trade, the city's activities include the making of knives and scissors.

The city, some 2,300 feet (700 meters) above sea level, comprises a modern section, built mostly during the 19th century, and an old castle that stands on a hill above the city. There are few works of art of any interest, except in the local archaeological museum, which displays a good collection of antiquities of the Roman period. The castle of Campobasso, built in the 15th century, now serves as a water reservoir.

According to tradition Campobasso was founded by the Lombards. It was ruled by a succession of local feudal lords throughout medieval and early modern times. The modern city dates from the beginning of the 19th century, when Joachim Murat, Napoleon's puppet king of Naples, laid out its present plan. Population: city (1961) 27,568; commune (1966 estimate) 37,934.

GEORGE KISH, *University of Michigan*

CAMPOBELLO ISLAND, kam-pō-bel′ō, is in southwestern New Brunswick, Canada, at the entrance of Passamaquoddy Bay, an arm of the Bay of Fundy. It is less than a mile (1.6 km) from the coast of Maine, opposite Eastport and Lubec. It is 9 miles (14 km) long and about 3 miles (5 km) wide. The Roosevelt Memorial Bridge, completed in 1962, connects the island with Lubec.

Campobello was the summer home of President Franklin D. Roosevelt for many years. The Roosevelt Campobello International Park, administered by a joint U. S.-Canadian commission, was established on the island in 1964. The principal settlement is Welshpool.

The island was granted in 1770 to Captain William Owen of the British Navy. His family owned it until 1880, when it was sold to a group of American businessmen, who developed it as a summer resort. The main occupation of the permanent residents is fishing.

IN CAMPOBELLO, the summer home of President Franklin D. Roosevelt is now part of an international park.

I. DONALD BOWDEN

CAMPOS, kaNm'poos, is a city in Brazil, 145 miles northeast of Rio de Janeiro. It is the leading industrial center of Rio de Janeiro state. The chief industries are sugar refining, alcohol distilling, leather working, and fruit, coffee, and tobacco processing. The city was founded in 1634. Population: (1960) 131,974.

CAMPRA, käN-prà', **André** (1660–1744), French composer. Campra was born in Aix-en-Provence on Dec. 4, 1660. He began his career as a clerical musician and became choirmaster of Notre Dame, Paris, in 1694. Three years after the triumphant presentation of his divertissement *L'Europe galante* (1697), Campra left the church for the theater. In 1722, however, he succeeded Marc Antoine Charpentier as master of the Royal Chapel. Campra continued to write sacred music and popular operas until his death, at Versailles, on June 29, 1744.

Campra's numerous and diverse works combine lyricism and theatricality with masterful use of vocal, choral, and instrumental color. He pioneered in the application of the continuous-music technique of tragic opera to works including "comic" characters drawn from contemporary life. Campra is regarded as the outstanding French composer of operas in the interim between Lully and Rameau.

ADRIENNE FRIED, *Choral Director*
Dalcroze School of Music, New York City

CAMRANH BAY, käm'räng', one of the finest natural harbors in Southeast Asia, is situated on the coast of South Vietnam, some 180 miles (290 km) northeast of Saigon. An inlet of the South China Sea, it is deep enough to provide safe anchorage the year round for large seagoing vessels.

Although the Russian fleet anchored at Camranh Bay in 1905 before sailing out to its defeat by the Japanese at Tsushima, the harbor was not much used either commercially or militarily until the United States intervened massively in the Vietnamese war in the 1960's. From 1965, Camranh was built up as the largest U. S. military and supply base in South Vietnam.

ELLEN J. HAMMER
Author of "Vietnam: Yesterday and Today"

CAMROSE, kam'rōz, is a city in central Alberta, Canada, 60 miles (96 km) southeast of Edmonton. It is the rail distribution center of a large and prosperous mixed farming area. Camrose has a cereal plant, a creamery, and a pasteurizing plant. Seamless transmission pipe is manufactured there. Population: 8,673.

CAMUS, kà-mü', **Albert** (1913–1960), French novelist, dramatist, essayist, and journalist, whose writings had a profound influence in the mid-20th century on the conscience of Western man. Both his personality and his work were deeply marked by the historic struggles that shook European civilization during his lifetime. A man of great personal integrity, Camus sought to define not a dogma but a way of life that would respect in equal measure the logic of the heart, the logic of the mind, and the limitations imposed on the individual by reality.

The marked changes in mood in Camus' work and his great diversity in literary technique accentuate rather than mask the inner coherence and continuity of his writing. These unifying characteristics are evident in the recurrence from

THE GRANGER COLLECTION
Albert Camus

work to work of certain images—sea, sky, light, and desert—and of basic themes—exile, revolt, happiness, and man's responsibility in a meaningless world. Camus early defined his own realm of concern and explored it with intellectual and artistic integrity. Like Jean-Paul Sartre and other existentialist thinkers with whom he was familiar, he examined the fundamental dilemmas of modern man, who is shorn of traditional structures of religious belief and explanation and who sees human existence as "absurd," that is, purposeless and incomprehensible in rational terms.

Camus, however, was more optimistic than many existentialists in the value he accorded man. He sought, through the fictional characters he created, to define a positive ethic based on happiness, solidarity, and a respect for human life. This humanistic ethic rejected absolutes and stressed the continual effort, without falling into extremes, to balance the legitimate yet paradoxically contradicting aspirations of the individual for personal freedom and social justice, self-realization and solidarity, the happiness of love and a lucid understanding of the hopelessness of man's fate.

Camus had a demanding conception of the artist's responsibility in a time of crisis. He called upon man to face the crucial issues raised by the convulsions of the time—communism and World War II, for example—and elucidated them in works of sustained intellectual and stylistic excellence. Camus was awarded the Nobel Prize for literature in 1957.

Early Life. Camus was born in Mondovi, Algeria, on Nov. 7, 1913. His father, a farm laborer of Alsatian descent, was fatally wounded in action during World War I. His mother, to whom Camus was devoted, was of Spanish origin and worked as a servant. Camus' poverty-stricken childhood in a working-class section of Algiers inspired his unwavering commitment to social justice, his simple ethical code, and his sense of the violence and fatalism that characterized the illiterate working class. To his environment he also owed his basic fictional milieu, the landscape of the North African Mediterranean coast.

Through education, Camus was able to move beyond the limitations of his environment. At the University of Algiers, under the influence of the philosopher Jean Grenier, he developed a lifelong interest in literature and philosophy. To these fields he added a passion for the drama in all its aspects. Knowledge that he had tuberculosis, a disease that dogged him all his life, forced him to give up an academic career and stimulated him to become a writer.

The 1930's and Early World War II. In the 1930's, Camus became committed to the three-pronged activity—politics, theater, and writing—that shaped his whole career. After briefly belonging to the Communist party, he became a nondoctrinal socialist. As a young journalist in Algiers, he incurred the hostility of the local authorities because of his vigorous and scrupulously documented campaigns for economic and political reforms on behalf of the Algerian Muslims. He participated in an amateur theatrical group as an actor and director, thus acquiring firsthand experience with the stage. Camus also traveled in Europe and was for a short time a journalist in Paris. After the fall of France in 1940, he returned to Algeria, where he taught in a private school.

Throughout this period Camus was hard at work writing. The ambience and imagery of *L'envers et l'endroit* (1937) and *Noces* (1938), two small volumes of essays, reflect Camus' early lyrical commitment to life, beauty, and happiness in this world, especially the world of the North African coast that he knew. The essays also express Camus' revolt against the burden of suffering, death, and solitude that estranges human beings from the plenitude of life.

The theme of revolt dominates Camus' next three works. The novel *L'étranger* (1942; Eng. tr., *The Stranger,* 1946) is narrated by Meursault, a clerk in Algiers, who blindly commits murder, then, confronted by his own execution, realizes the unique value of life and the solidarity of all men in the face of unjust condemnation to death. In the essay *Le mythe de Sisyphe* (1943; Eng. tr., *The Myth of Sisyphus and Other Essays,* 1955), Camus uses Sisyphus, who in Greek mythology is condemned eternally to push a boulder uphill only to have it roll down again, as a symbol of man's fate and possibilities in a purposeless world. The play *Caligula* (written in 1938 and published in 1945; Eng. tr., 1958), presents the Roman emperor as so driven by his sense of the absurdity of life that he indulges in excessive cruelties that destroy even himself.

Later War Years and Postwar Period. In 1942, Camus returned to France, where he took an active part in the Resistance against the German army of occupation. He wrote leading articles and editorials for various underground journals, including the left-wing paper *Combat,* which he edited from 1944 to 1947. In these articles, and in the novels, plays, and essays of this period, Camus expressed his revulsion to the public's cynical acceptance of wholesale violence and murder. He attempted to translate the bitter experiences of the German occupation and of the political disappointments of the post-liberation years into a general philosophy about man's tragic situation.

One of the most important of these somber works is the novel *La peste* (1947; Eng. tr., *The Plague,* 1948). *La peste,* considered at one level to be an allegory of occupied France and at another level an allegory of the human situation, is a sparely written account of an epidemic of bubonic plague in the Algerian town of Oran and of the reaction of various individuals. Dr. Rieux, the central figure, who has no faith in God or the rationality of the universe, devotes himself wholeheartedly to helping his fellow men.

In the essay *L'homme révolté* (1951; Eng. tr., *The Rebel,* 1954), Camus studies the concepts of personal and historical revolutions in Europe since the 18th century, concluding that revolution carried to its logical extreme justifies war and murder, as for example in Stalin's Russia, and thus destroys the very freedom it had set out to win. This view caused great controversy among leftists, and led to a split between Camus and the pro-Communist Sartre. Other works concerned with the troubled war and postwar years include *Lettres à un ami allemand* (1945) and the dramas *Le Malentendu* (1944; Eng. tr., *The Misunderstanding,* 1958) and *Les Justes* (1949; Eng. tr., *The Just Assassins,* 1958).

Among Camus' later works is the novel *La chute* (1956; Eng. tr., *The Fall,* 1957), a powerfully satiric work in which the author frees himself from an obsessional involvement with history to indict those who take an intellectual delight in denouncing the corruption of Western man. Clamence, a former Parisian lawyer, reveals his guilty conscience as a man who has spent his life professionally seeking justice for others but who when personally confronted with a woman's attempt at suicide does nothing to save her.

With *L'été* (1954), a collection of personal, lyrical meditations, and *L'exile et le royaume* (1957, Eng. tr., *Exile and the Kingdom,* 1958), a collection of short stories, Camus returned to his Algerian inspiration. He also adapted and directed plays taken from the works of William Faulkner and Dostoyevsky. However, his new ventures were cut short by his death in an auto accident near Sens, France, on Jan. 4, 1960.

GERMAINE BRÉE, *Author of "Camus"*

Bibliography

Brée, Germaine, *Albert Camus* (New York 1964).
Brée, Germaine, *Camus,* rev. ed. (New York 1964).
Brée, Germaine, ed., *Camus: A Collection of Critical Essays* (Englewood Cliffs, N. J., 1962).
Cruikshank, John, *Albert Camus and the Literature of Revolt* (London 1959).
Hanna, Thomas, *Thought and Art of Albert Camus* (Chicago 1958).
Parker, Emmett, *Albert Camus, the Artist in the Arena* (Madison, Wis., 1965).

CANA, kā'na, or *Cana of Galilee,* in the Bible, is a village in Galilee, Palestine, and the scene of the first two miracles performed by Jesus. Etymology and tradition are the basis for identifying the place as the ancient village of Khirbet Qana, 9 miles (14.5 km) north of Nazareth. The name, meaning "place of reeds," is appropriate to this site, which overlooks a marshy plain. As long ago as the 12th century A. D., pilgrims reported that they visited the site as the scene of events in the Gospels. Although much of the territory remains unexcavated, shards and coins have been found there that supposedly date back to the 1st century A. D.

As reported in the Gospel According to St. John, Cana was the place where Jesus turned water into wine at a wedding feast (2:1–11). There, too, he healed the son of the nobleman from Capernaum (4:46–54).

CANAAN, kānən, was the name of the land later called Palestine. Its original inhibitants were called *Canaanites*. The names occur in cuneiform, Egyptian, and Phoenician sources from the 15th century B. C. on, and in the Bible. They are derived from *Kinakhkhi,* a Semitic term that originally meant "crimson wool trader," and that, in turn, is derived from the Semitic root kna'. This seems originally to have meant "murex," a sea mollusk producing purple or crimson dye. The land of Canaan included the area later known as Phoenicia, and the Semitic term is paralleled by the Greek *Phoinikē* (Phoenicia). The primary meaning of this Greek word might have been "land of crimson wool," since it derives from *phoinix,* sometimes translated as "crimson wool." Phoenicia became the center of a crimson dye industry because of the abundance of murex along the coast, and the existence of this industry is the probable reason for designating the area the "land of crimson wool."

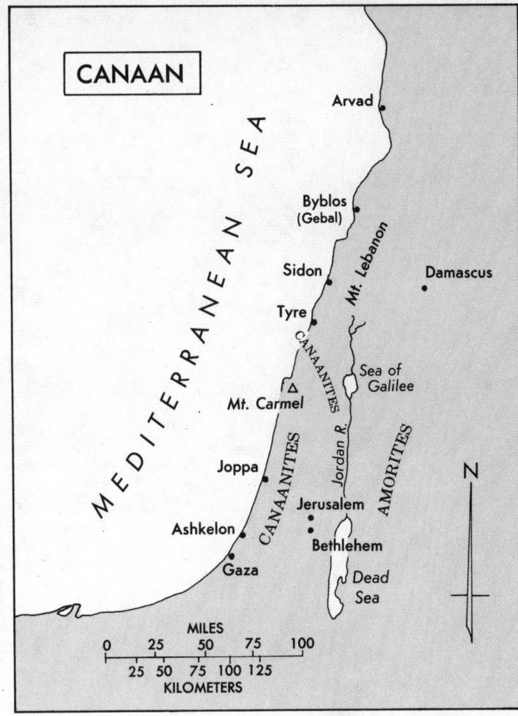

The Land of Canaan. The area referred to as Canaan in the early Egyptian sources extended along the entire eastern coast of the Mediterranean Sea, from Tripoli (in present-day Lebanon) in the north to Gaza in the south, and eastward to the Jordan River and the Dead Sea. After the Israelite conquest of Canaan about the 13th century B. C., the tendency developed to consider only the coastal strip and the Jordan Valley as the "Land of Canaan" (Numbers 13:29; Joshua 11:3). In Hellenistic and Roman times the name "Canaan" was still recognized as the old name of Phoenicia, and as late as the 2d century A. D. the descendants of the Carthaginians in North Africa called themselves Canaanites. The first settlers of Carthage were Phoenician voyagers from Tyre.

In Biblical usage the term "Land of Canaan" is a generic name referring to the entire Promised Land, and its boundaries are described in detail in Numbers 34:1–12. On the other hand, the name "Canaanite" also designates in the Bible one of the nations whose territory God promised to the Children of Israel (Genesis 15:19–21). These same two meanings, one general and one specific, are implied by the name "Amorite," since "Land of the Canaanite" and "Land of the Amorite" appear in the Bible as synonyms.

The Canaanites. The Table of the Nations (Genesis 10) enumerates as Canaanites 11 "sons" of Canaan—forming together with Canaan himself a group of 12 nations, paralleling the 12 tribes of Israel. The Canaanites spoke Semitic languages, and one might thus expect them to be counted among the progeny of Shem, from whose name the term "Semite" comes. However, Canaan, their ancestor, is said to have been a son of Ham (another son of Noah) and a younger brother of Mizraim (Egypt). This genealogy seems to reflect the political situation during most of the 2d millennium B. C., when the land of Canaan was under Egyptian rule. At the time of the invasion of the Hebrew tribes, Canaan had been inhabited by these Semitic-speaking peoples for several centuries. The conquest of the hill country of Canaan by the Hebrews was followed closely by the conquest of the seashore by the Philistines, one of the so-called "sea peoples," between about 1200 and 1170 B. C., and by the invasion of what is today Lebanon and the Syrian coast by desert Aramaean tribes.

Thus, by the 11th century B. C., the Canaanites had lost some nine tenths of their former domain and were concentrated in a small area on the seashore between Arvad and Mount Carmel. Their main port cities, which developed into kingdoms, were Byblos (the Biblical Gebal) and Sidon. Arvad and Zemer were of lesser importance, and Tyre was just beginning to develop. By the 10th century B. C., Sidon was the dominant kingdom. Its capital was moved to Tyre, which became the great seafaring and commercial center under Abiba'al and Hiram I. From this time on, the Canaanites of Phoenicia were called Sidonians in the Bible. Since the Biblical Table of the Nations does not mention Tyre among the Canaanite nations, it appears that this list was drawn up prior to the 11th century B. C.

The Canaanites had rich and sensuous religious rituals, and from the religious point of view they constituted a danger for the Children of Israel. This explains the repeated prohibition against entering into a covenant or intermarrying with them and against serving their gods, and the command to destroy them (Exodus 23:23–24; Deuteronomy 7:1–6; 20:16–18). In the early patriarchal period however, intermarriage between the Israelites and the Canaanites was practiced, and this is recorded without any reproach (Genesis 38:2; 46:10).

The old meaning of Canaanite as "merchant," or "trader," reappears in the prophetic and poetic books of the Bible (for example, Isaiah 23:8; Zephaniah 1:11; Proverbs 31:24; and Job 40:30).

Starting in the time of King Solomon, about the 10th century B. C., the Canaanites who lived in the territory of the Hebrew monarchies gradually assimilated into and merged with the Hebrew nation. During the days of the Roman Empire, the term "Canaanite" came to denote a member of a Jewish sect that was intensely anti-Roman. This interpretation is the origin of the usage of Canaanite to mean zealot, or fanatic.

RAPHAEL PATAI
Theodor Herzl Institute

CANAANITES. See CANAAN.

GEORGE HUNTER, FROM NATIONAL FILM BOARD

TINY VILLAGES perpetuate the older living pattern of Canadians. The dwellings of Chéticamp, in Nova Scotia, face the Gulf of St. Lawrence of the Atlantic Ocean.

CANADA

Canada is the largest country in area in the Western Hemisphere and the second largest in the world, exceeded only by the USSR. It covers more than half the continent of North America, extending from the Atlantic Ocean to the Pacific and from the northern boundary of the main portion of the United States to the polar regions. The state of Alaska bounds it on the northwest.

This huge land is the home of more than 20 million people. They constitute an independent sovereign state that formerly was the senior Dominion of the British Empire and now is a member of the Commonwealth. Canada is a young nation—it celebrated its 100th birthday in 1967—but its influence in world affairs is much greater than the size of its population would indicate.

The country's topography is extremely varied. In the east, the land is generally undulating, with hills and low mountains, few of which exceed 4,000 feet (1,200 meters) in height. The central portions of the country are vast plains. The west is rugged mountain terrain, where the ranges of the Rocky Mountains run north and south. The subarctic north is rolling or level. Hundreds of lakes are scattered through this region; nearly 8% of Canada's total area is fresh water. North of the continental mainland are the bleak islands of the Arctic Archipelago.

Since Canada, except for southern Ontario and part of Nova Scotia, lies wholly north of latitude 45° N, its climate is often rigorous. Summers in much of the country are short, and the winters are long and bitter, with deep snowfall in most sections.

The country possesses rich natural resources. The great forests are one of Canada's prime assets. The central plains are one of the world's most fertile farming regions. Abundant water power potential is available in the rapid rivers. Beneath the land's surface lie huge deposits of minerals. The exploitation of this wealth in a way that will best benefit the whole nation is one of the challenges that face Canadians.

Canadians can draw upon a pioneer heritage that should enable them to face whatever challenges arise. In the 15th and 16th centuries, fish and then furs attracted hardy Europeans to a land sparsely populated by Indians and Eskimo. Fish drying and fur gathering led to white settlement, which in turn led to the tilling of the soil and the cutting of the forests. These were the bases upon which the country grew and prospered until it emerged in the 20th century as a modern industrial nation. Canadians, in their small but increasing numbers, have had half a continent to occupy and develop, and with the tools and skills of modern technology they are making notable progress.

Canadian society displays an ethnic pattern that is largely the heritage of the tumultuous 18th century, when Britain and France contended for sovereignty in the New World. The Seven Years'

ANNAN PHOTO FEATURES

VAST URBAN AREAS typify the new environment of an increasing number of Canadians. Vancouver, British Columbia, is the nation's great Pacific Ocean harbor.

War ended with a British victory in 1763. Settlers from the British Isles and Loyalists from the United States (following the Revolutionary War) moved into the eastern colonies and pushed westward. British influences have been dominant in Canada as the country evolved through several stages from a group of British colonies to a sovereign state.

But for some 150 years before 1763 the French had been established in Canada, principally in and around the valley of the St. Lawrence River. Despite the British victory in the Seven Years' War, their lodgment became the nucleus of a power that has profoundly affected the country's history and will contribute profoundly to the shape of its future.

Today about 45% of Canada's population traces its origin to the British Isles. About 30% is of French origin. The remainder of the people are of various European, native, and Asian stocks. But virtually all Canadians use either English or French as the language of daily business and social life, and the nation is broadly composed of two linguistic and cultural groups—English and French. Inevitably this division has caused over the years tensions and strains that have led since the 1950's to more vigorous attempts to evolve a national pattern that would allow more adequate expression of this "French fact." For instance, the Official Languages Act, passed in 1969, makes French and English the official languages of the federal administration and requires

INFORMATION HIGHLIGHTS

Origin of Name: Probably derived from the Huron-Iroquois *kanata,* meaning "village" or "community"; it first appeared in the narrative of Jacques Cartier in 1534.

Form of Government: Constitutional monarchy, which consists of a federation of 10 provinces and 2 territories.

Head of State: Queen of Canada, represented in Canada by the governor general, whom she appoints on the advice of the Canadian government.

Head of Government: Prime minister.

Legislature: Parliament, consisting of the crown, the Senate, and the House of Commons; each province has its own legislature.

Capital: Ottawa, Ontario (1971 population, 302,-341).

Area: 3,851,809 square miles (9,976,185 sq km), second-largest country in the world after the USSR.

Highest Elevation: Mt. Logan, Yukon Territory, 19,850 feet (6,050 meters).

Population: 21,568,311 (1971 census).

Major Languages: English and French.

Monetary Unit: Canadian dollar (100 cents).

Weights and Measures: Based on the pound and yard for general use; on the metric system in science fields.

Flag: A red flag with proportions of two for length and one for width, containing in its center a white square the width of the flag, bearing a single red maple leaf.

Anthems: National anthem, *O Canada;* royal anthem, *God Save the Queen.*

its departments and agencies to provide services in both languages in designated districts.

The structure of the Canadian nation rests on firm foundations. The country has a tradition of democracy that is embodied in its democratic institutions. It has a flexible governmental system, responsive to the will of the people. Its economy is expanding, and there are great opportunities for development of resources and technology to invite further ventures. Its intellectual life is forceful and questing. In the arena of world affairs, the nation has accepted responsibilities, in war and in peace, that have stimulated the growth of political maturity at home.

The Canadian nation is a federation of 10 provinces and 2 territories. The central authority is the government of Canada. Each province has its own government, which exercises a large degree of autonomy in specifically defined spheres.

CONTENTS

Section	Page
The People	315
1. The Pattern	315
English-Speaking Canadians	315
French-Speaking Canadians	321
Royal Commission on Bilingualism and Biculturalism	324
2. Population	325
The Land	330
3. Area and Boundaries	330
4. Physiography	330
5. River Systems	334
6. Climate	335
7. Soils	338
8. Flora and Fauna	339
9. Natural Resources	343
The Economy	345
10. Manufacturing	349
11. Electric Power	353
12. Mining	355
13. Forest Products	359
14. Agriculture	362
15. Fisheries and Furs	366
16. Trade and Tariffs	369
17. Tourism	375
18. Transportation and Communications	375
19. Labor	380
20. Banking and Currency	382
Government and Politics	386
21. Structure and Function	386
22. Political Parties	391
23. Public Finance	392
24. Defense	396
25. Health and Welfare	400
Education	402
26. Elementary and Secondary Education	402
General Pattern	402
Quebec System	406
Independent Schools	408
27. Higher Education	408
28. Vocational and Adult Education	411
29. Government Aid to Education	412
30. Libraries and Museums	413
31. Research Facilities	414

Section	Page
Religion	415
32. Protestant Churches	415
33. Roman Catholic Church	419
34. Other Religious Groups	422
Culture	423
35. Art and Architecture	423
36. Literature	431
37. Theater	435
38. Music	437
39. Mass Communications	440
Publishing	440
Broadcasting	442
Film	443
Recreation	445
40. Parks	447
National Parks	447
Provincial Parks	450
41. Sports	452
History	454
42. Prehistory and Period of Early Exploration	454
43. Founding and Development of French Canada 1604–1752	459
1604–1662	459
1663–1752	461
44. Canada in the Reorganization of North America, 1752–1818	466
1752–1763	466
1764–1791	469
1792–1818	472
45. The Northwest, 1763–1869	474
46. British North America, 1815–1857	480
Atlantic Provinces	480
Lower Canada, 1815–1840	484
Upper Canada, 1815–1840	486
United Canada, 1841–1857	489
47. The Canadian Confederation, 1857–1914	491
48. World Wars and Depression, 1914–1945	497
49. Modern Canada, 1945–	503

Prepared under the general supervision of J. Cromwell Young, Executive Editor of the *Encyclopedia Canadiana*.

The territories are administered by the federal government, although they have local elected councils. The electorate chooses the House of Commons (the lower house of the bicameral national Parliament) and the unicameral provincial legislatures (except in Quebec, which has two houses, one with appointed members). Canada's leading political parties are the Liberals and the Progressive Conservatives.

Canada's economy is broadly diversified. Agriculture, which was its base for many years, is still a major factor, although its share in the total economy has tended to diminish. Since World War II, Canada has become an industrial nation, with a manufacturing establishment that compares favorably with that of any highly developed nation in the world. The industrial centers are largely concentrated in the eastern provinces, but a thriving nexus has been developed on the Pacific coast of British Columbia, and the midwestern plains, long the heartland of farming, have been invaded by industry, based notably on the oil fields of Alberta and the potash mines of Saskatchewan.

The resources of the Canadian land—its rich soil, its timber, and its minerals—provide much of the raw material for the nation's industry. They also are the base of its foreign trade, which is characterized by specialized exports of grains (especially wheat), wood products, and industrial products using native minerals.

The intellectual life of Canada has been growing wider and richer. The broad-based educational system is improving its facilities and techniques, while the churches are increasingly concerned with the problems of the diverse cultures. In the arts, a uniquely Canadian mode of expression is becoming more evident.

One handicap to be overcome has been the longstanding feeling of many Canadians that their neighbor, the United States, with greater wealth and a population ten times that of Canada, is an overshadowing influence. This influence has been demonstrated in practical terms. About 70% of Canada's manufacturing industry is owned and directed by United States interests, and the heavy influx of books, magazines, motion pictures, and TV programs has inevitably made more difficult native Canadian development in these fields. But Canadians are more and more coping with this situation and refusing to allow it to obstruct their purpose to mold a Canadian nation.

Canada is changing rapidly. Technology is pushing back the last frontiers, opening even the Arctic islands to exploitation. Industrial development is drawing the bulk of the population from the countryside and the small towns into the cities and their environs, and Canada is becoming a country focused around urban centers. In the web of metropolitan life, a new sophistication is manifest in the thinking of the people. As Canadians become more involved in world affairs, their outlook is broadening to become more global in scope.

Against this background the Canadian people are working out their destiny. Many saw in the success of Expo 67, created at Montreal through the efforts of all Canadians, a symbol of what might be accomplished. For the sake of their nation, they are acknowledging that their rich and diverse cultures must learn to live together.

J. Cromwell Young
Executive Editor
"Encyclopedia Canadiana"

CANADA: The People

Canada, generally speaking, has not become a "melting pot" for its citizens so much as the provider of a home for a "mosaic" of population. Its more than 20 million people trace their ancestry to many lands. About 45% are of British Isles ethnic origin, 30% are of French origin, 20% are of other European origins, and the remainder are of native Indian and Eskimo or Asian origin.

1. The Pattern

In the linguistic and cultural sense, the mosaic presents a more sharply defined pattern. Despite the multilingual and multicultural origins of its people, Canada is composed in the main of two linguistic and cultural groupings, the one English, the other French. Thus, the two languages in common use, either of which all Canadians may be expected to use in public if not in their private lives, are English and French.

The English-speaking population, notwithstanding its diverse components, shares a culture whose salient features are those of the Anglo-Celtic world. The culture of the French-speaking population, almost entirely of French descent, is more specific and consequently more intense. This pattern has both enriched Canadian life and created problems and tensions.

ENGLISH-SPEAKING CANADIANS

The total number of people in Canada who do not give French as their first or maternal tongue was, according to the 1961 census, 12,697,928 of a total population of 18,238,274. The portion of the population that is English in the linguistic sense is, therefore, 67.35%. But those of British stock, even when taken as a whole, form less than 45% of the total population. Thus the English-speaking people of Canada are a coherent society only in terms other than that of common or related descent.

What, then, has made English-Canadian society coherent in the past? What makes it coherent today—the same or other factors? Before attempting to answer these questions, it is necessary to consider the facts of settlement.

Regions of English Settlement. The fact that the English-speaking population is to a considerable degree not of British stock has come about historically by a long process of settlement by people of diverse backgrounds. The people of diverse origins, moreover, settled in different regions. It seems best to describe the elements of the English (or English-speaking) people of Canada by regions of settlement and by the history of the occupation of the different sections.

Atlantic Provinces. *Newfoundland,* the oldest of English dependencies in America and the newest of Canadian provinces, was settled and abandoned as a colony in the 16th century. It then became in official policy a "fishery" only, in which settlement was forbidden. Settlement occurred, however, in what was known as a "residency"—that is, fishermen wintered in the island, contrary to imperial policy, until the beginning of the 19th century. As there were some women in the fishing crews, population grew, and the island became not just a wintering place for fishermen but a colony, although it was denied that status.

I. DONALD BOWDEN

CITIES, which are attracting the bulk of Canada's population, offer chances for gracious living. (*Above*) Strollers on the promenade of the Château Frontenac at Quebec. (*Below*) A sidewalk cafe in downtown Montreal.

PIERRE GAUDARD, FROM NATIONAL FILM BOARD

MONTREAL CANADIENS

NFB

GAR LUNNEY—NFB

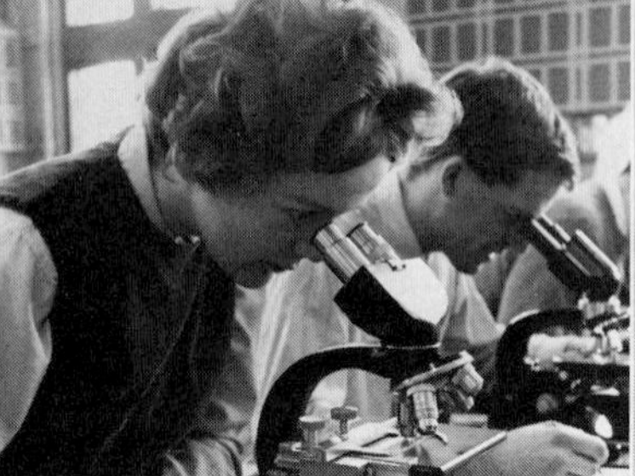

CHRIS LUND—NFB

MALAK, OTTAWA FROM MILLER SERVICES LTD.

The "residents" were west-county English from Devon and Dorset and Irish from southern Ireland. The two groups, separated by religion, remained distinct until recent times. A third group was made up of the "factors" or outfitting merchants, of St. John's, the principal port and later the capital. These people also were largely west-county English. By 1816 the population was estimated to be 52,672.

Nova Scotia received its first English-speaking settlers in 1749. They were sent out by the English government as part of the deliberate foundation of the fortress and naval base of Halifax. They numbered 2,544.

As part of the same policy of imperial colonization, some 1,500 German settlers in 1751–1753 were located at Lunenberg, southwest of Halifax. They began the long and continuous history of German settlement in Canada, which was to make German Canadians the third-largest group of English-speaking Canadians.

Both the English and German settlers were soon outnumbered by the great influx of New Englanders who replaced the Acadians expelled in 1755. The New Englanders settled on the former Acadian lands in the sea marshes of Minas Basin and in the Annapolis River valley on the Bay of Fundy side of the peninsula. Some settled also at the mouth of the St. John River in the part of Nova Scotia that later became the province of New Brunswick. Others settled around the many harbors of the west and south shores. The number of the New England settlers is unknown, perhaps 10,000 to 12,000 persons of a population of 17,000 in 1775. New Englanders remained the principal English element in Nova Scotia for many years and made the geographic ties between that province and New England a demographic one.

Other small groups of English settlers came to Nova Scotia before 1783, notably the Ulster and Yorkshire settlements in the Cobequid area, which may have numbered some 1,800 by 1775. To them was added the beginning of the Scottish element, when in 1779 the emigrant ship *Hector* landed some 200 Highland Scots at Pictou on the Gulf of St. Lawrence shore of Nova Scotia. This was the beginning of the movement of Scots—some Highland, Catholic, and Gaelic-speaking, some Lowland and Presbyterian—who were to become the second great element of the English-speaking people in Nova Scotia. They were in the long run to give the province the Scottish flavor its name suggested; some were to make Cape Breton the largest Gaelic-speaking community in the world today.

The American Revolution was to give Nova Scotia the third chief element of its English

SPOKEN LANGUAGE DISTRIBUTION AMONG THE POPULATION OF CANADA
(1961 Census)

Province or Territory	English Only		French Only		English and French		Neither English nor French	
	Number	%	Number	%	Number	%	Number	%
Newfoundland	450,945	98.5	522	0.1	5,299	1.2	1,087	0.2
Prince Edward Island	95,296	91.1	1,219	1.2	7,938	7.6	176	0.2
Nova Scotia	684,805	92.9	5,938	0.8	44,987	6.1	1,277	0.2
New Brunswick	370,922	62.0	112,054	18.7	113,495	19.0	1,465	0.2
Quebec	608,635	11.6	3,254,850	61.9	1,338,878	25.5	56,848	1.1
Ontario	5,548,766	89.0	95,236	1.5	493,270	7.9	98,820	1.6
Manitoba	825,955	89.6	7,954	0.9	68,368	7.4	19,409	2.1
Saskatchewan	865,821	93.6	3,853	0.4	42,074	4.5	13,433	1.5
Alberta	1,253,824	94.1	5,534	0.4	56,920	4.3	15,666	1.2
British Columbia	1,552,560	95.3	2,559	0.2	57,504	3.5	16,459	1.0
Yukon Territory	13,679	93.5	38	0.3	825	5.6	86	0.6
Northwest Territories	13,554	58.9	109	0.5	1,614	7.0	7,721	33.6
Total	12,284,762	67.4	3,489,866	19.1	2,231,172	12.2	232,447	1.3

Source: Canada Year Book 1966

M. SEMAK—NFB

CHRIS LUND—NFB

BOB BROOKS—NFB

CHRIS LUND—NFB

B. LINGARD—NFB

population. These were the United Empire Loyalists, like the New Englanders, Americans, but political refugees from the United States. Most of these men were officials in the old royal governments or officers and men of Loyalist regiments who had fought to maintain the connection with Britain. The number of those who came to Nova Scotia in 1782–1783 is estimated at over 30,000 men, women, and children.

Some of the Loyalists went to the territory that was to become the province of New Brunswick, and a few to the separate colony of *Prince Edward Island*. The latter had been partly settled already by English, Scottish, and New England immigrants. To these were added the Scottish settlers sent out at the beginning of the 19th century by Lord Selkirk, who was later to sponsor the Red River settlement in the West. This mixed character the English population has retained.

New Brunswick was separated from Nova Scotia in 1784. There were then some 10,000 Loyalists settled mainly in the St. John River valley with the prerevolution New Englanders, for a total of 12,000. When the timber trade developed during the Napoleonic War, English and Scottish timber factors and workers were added to the population. But the great addition to the population was made when the timber ships returning to Canada without cargoes began to bring immigrant Irish, mainly from the south of Ireland. Many of these settled in the St. John River valley, but the greater number settled along the rivers of the north shore on the Gulf of St. Lawrence. Their numbers are unknown, but those who remained in the province added a large and different element to its population.

Quebec. Quebec was entirely French when it became part of the British Empire. After the fall of Quebec in 1759, however, a number of traders—American, English and Scottish—moved to Quebec, Trois Rivières, and Montreal. The Quebec Act of 1774, nevertheless, was based on the premise that Quebec was likely to remain French, and confirmed the use of the French language, French civil law, and the freedom of the Roman Catholic religion. But the coming of Loyalists, though only 6,000 in number, ended in a decade this policy of a wholly French Quebec. The result was the division of the province into Upper and Lower Canada.

There was to be no return, moreover, to a policy of a wholly French Quebec, or Lower Canada. On the contrary, English settlement was encouraged. Not only did the English communities grow with the development of trade, but special provision for English settlement was also made by the creation of the Eastern Townships in which English land law prevailed.

The first settlers in the townships were from New England. They crossed the open frontier and established New England-style settlements along the southern border of the province eastward from Montreal. Their numbers are not recorded, but their coming helped ensure that the population of the province would be English as well as French.

The timber trade, as in New Brunswick, had the same effect. It brought English and Scottish managers and many southern Irish to work in the shanties in the woods, the timber coves at Quebec, and in the harbor of Montreal.

The Irish migration was both forerunner and part of the great British migration to Canada and the United States that began in the 1820's. As a result of this sustained movement, the holders of lands, as well as other capitalists, were inspired to attempt the systematic settlement of the townships and other parts of the province. The consequence was a large body of English and Scottish settlers. The English population today is largely urban and concentrated in western Montreal.

Ontario. Ontario, or Upper Canada as it was first called, began as a Loyalist province. Its people were of English, Scottish, Dutch, and German descent. Some groups were distinctive, such as the Gaelic-speaking Scots who settled Glengarry county on the St. Lawrence River at the present western boundary of Quebec. The so-called "Pennsylvania Dutch" were German Americans, some of them of Mennonite and other pacifist and quietist faiths.

To these between 1783 and 1812 were added an even larger number of American settlers, some of whom were relatives of Loyalists although most were simply landseekers in a country of fertile soil free of the Indian menace. These Loyalists and "late" Loyalists made up the population of Upper Canada almost wholly until 1812 and continued in the majority until 1830. Some British settlement, mostly of disbanded soldiers, began after 1815. It was not, however, until the mid-1820's that the great British migration began. It was spurred by various aids to migration, by unemployment in Britain and Ireland, and by the opportunities in Canada for retired half-pay officers to live inexpensively. By midcentury the expanded migration had made Upper Canada an overwhelmingly British province.

Most of these people were English, Scots, Scots-Irish, and Anglo-Irish. Many of them were people of some means and education, and they gave to the province not only population, but its leading men after 1840.

With them came many southern Catholic Irish, particularly to Ottawa (then Bytown), Peterborough and Toronto, but also to rural settlements. Unlike the American Irish Catholics, they were not outspokenly anti-British, and they blended well with other British stocks. But they were Catholics and, with the Catholic Scots, were the cause of the creation of "separate," that is, state-supported denominational schools, mostly Roman Catholic, in the common school system of Upper Canada. They were English Canadians, but with a difference.

To this fundamentally British stock, however, have been added other groups from other countries and from within Canada. Since 1881, and particularly since the Great Depression and World War II, perhaps the largest distinctive group of internal migrants has been that of the Ukrainian Canadians, largely from western Canada, but partly from overseas. Ontario has also received the greater part of the immigration since World War II to Canada from the Netherlands.

A large and rapidly growing group is the Italian, particularly in the construction industry of Toronto and the steel mills of Hamilton. With them are scores of other groups from Europe—Polish and Russian Jews, Czechs, Poles, Greeks—with the effect that urban Ontario now has a polyglot population. But its British complexion at the same time has been sustained by the large postwar influx of English and Scottish people drawn by the prolonged boom in provincial growth since the war.

Prairie Provinces. Settlement of the Prairies had begun before incorporation into the Dominion in 1870, and this continued on a large-scale in the following decade. Most of the settlers were Canadians, the next largest group English, Scottish, and Irish.

Almost from the beginning other ethnic groups joined the movement to the West. In 1874 the migration of Icelanders to Manitoba began. About this time the first of the Mennonites emigrated from Russia. Many other groups came with them—Jews, Hungarians, Poles, and Ukrainians. Thus the population of the Prairies, originally British-Canadian, came to have a diversity and flavor that has distinguished it from all other parts of Canada, except Ontario in recent times. In the Prairies, the term "English" obviously meant assimilation into English-Canadian society.

British Columbia. Before it joined the Dominion in 1871, British Columbia had been sparsely settled by fur traders and gold miners. The growth of its population after that date was marked by immigration drawn largely from the British Isles. A novel feature was the beginning of Chinese immigration.

Then, in 1921, depression and drought on the Prairies brought many from that and other parts of Canada to the most favored of Canadian provinces in climate and prospects. Despite checks imposed on it, Oriental immigration also continued—Chinese, Japanese, and some Indians.

Because of its growth since World War II the province has attracted many of the immigrants entering Canada, as well as many Canadians. British Columbia remains, however, the most English of the Canadian provinces, a result helped by the dispersion inland of Japanese Canadians during World War II. Here is a population in structure much like that of Ontario, but with a stronger English element, and with the Oriental strain only thinly represented.

Indian and Eskimo Population. It is proper to consider the Indian population of Canada apart from other elements and also in connection with the English people of Canada. In so far as Canadian Indians have assimilated to the general body of Canadian society, most of them—all those outside of Quebec except for the Métis and some Mission Indians of the Northwest—have assimilated to the English population.

The Canadian Indian played a role different from that of the American Indian. He was not the warlike opponent of agricultural settlement but an indispensable partner in the fur trade. Although the Indian did not contest agricultural settlement, the farmer and the town dweller were content to leave him aside on reserves until recent times. Today, the inadequacy of the reserves, his own aspirations, and his growing numbers make it necessary for the Indian to work out his relations anew with Canadian society. He must join it or create a distinct society parallel with it. The size of the Indian population makes some such outcome imperative. Estimated to be about 220,000 when the white man came, it is now believed to be in the neighborhood of 210,000.

The same observations on the whole apply to the Eskimo population of Canada, approximately 12,000 in number. In the instance of Eskimo in the Ungava district of Quebec, the assimilation to English society has been challenged by the government of Quebec by having Eskimo children taught French in school, but some kind of assimilation, direct or indirect, of Indians or Eskimo with the English or French people of Canada seems inevitable.

Nature of English-Canadian Nationality. It is now appropriate to return to the two questions asked earlier. What made English-Canadian society coherent in the past? What makes it coherent today—the same or other factors?

The Past. With all the ethnic and religious diversity of the past, and in spite of the scattering of English people across a transcontinental domain, there was a bond of unity. The strength it had for most English Canadians in the past, and still has for many, may be difficult to imagine now. But there can be no doubt of its reality and its strength. It was the tie furnished

CANADA

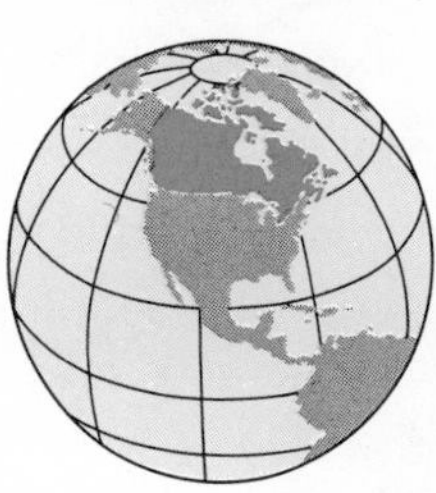

AGRICULTURE, INDUSTRY and RESOURCES

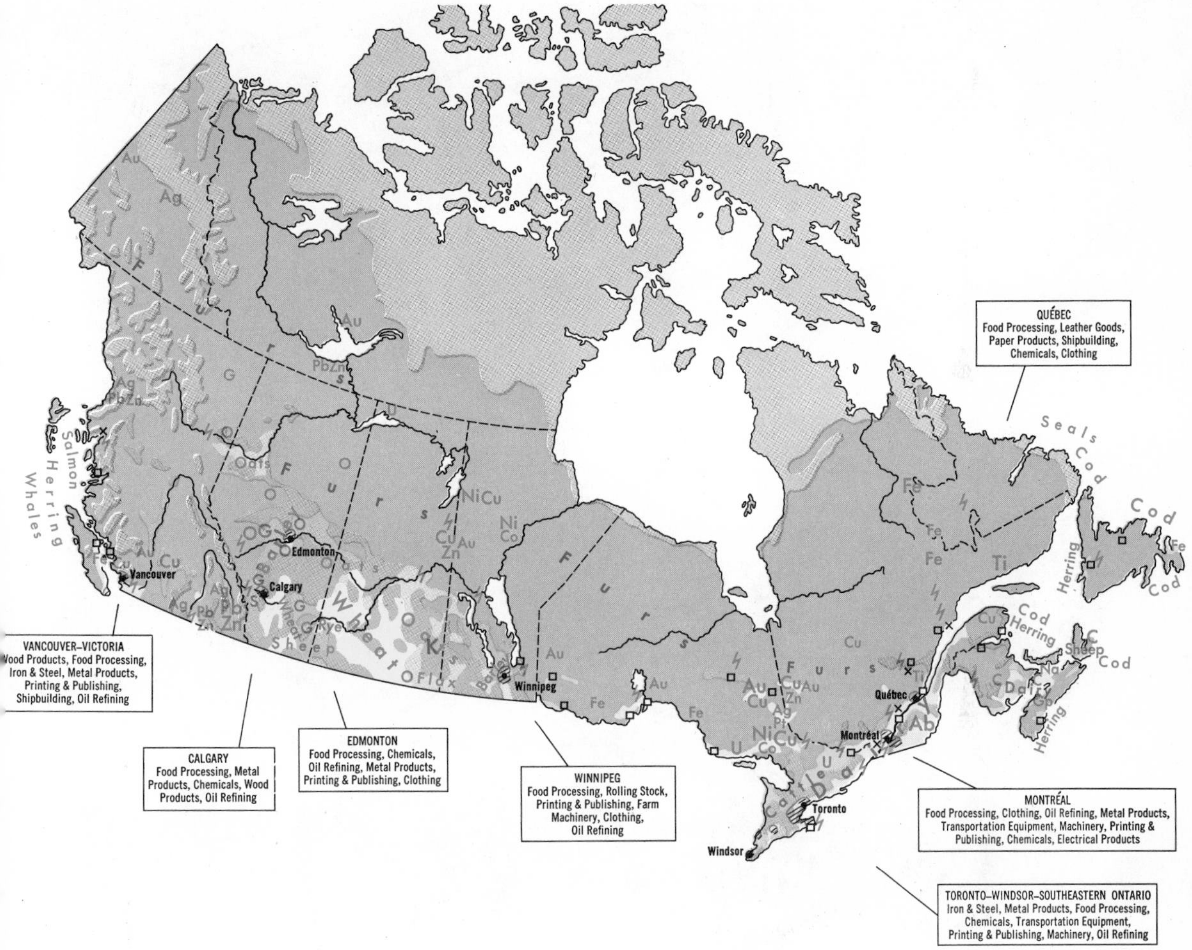

QUÉBEC
Food Processing, Leather Goods, Paper Products, Shipbuilding, Chemicals, Clothing
VANCOUVER–VICTORIA
Wood Products, Food Processing, Iron & Steel, Metal Products, Printing & Publishing, Shipbuilding, Oil Refining
CALGARY
Food Processing, Metal Products, Chemicals, Wood Products, Oil Refining
EDMONTON
Food Processing, Chemicals, Oil Refining, Metal Products, Printing & Publishing, Clothing
WINNIPEG
Food Processing, Rolling Stock, Printing & Publishing, Farm Machinery, Clothing, Oil Refining
MONTRÉAL
Food Processing, Clothing, Oil Refining, Metal Products, Transportation Equipment, Machinery, Printing & Publishing, Chemicals, Electrical Products
TORONTO–WINDSOR–SOUTHEASTERN ONTARIO
Iron & Steel, Metal Products, Food Processing, Chemicals, Transportation Equipment, Printing & Publishing, Machinery, Oil Refining
Vancouver
Edmonton
Calgary
Winnipeg
Québec
Montréal
Toronto
Windsor
Salmon
Herring
Whales
Seals
Cod
Furs
Wheat
Oats
Sheep
Rye
Flax
Cattle

DOMINANT LAND USE

- Wheat
- Cereals (chiefly barley, oats)
- Cereals, Livestock
- General Farming, Livestock
- Dairy
- Fruit, Vegetables
- Pasture Livestock
- Range Livestock
- Forests
- Nonagricultural Land

MAJOR MINERAL OCCURRENCES

Ab Asbestos	Cu Copper	Na Salt	S Sulfur
Ag Silver	Fe Iron Ore	Ni Nickel	Ti Titanium
Au Gold	G Natural Gas	O Petroleum	U Uranium
C Coal	Gp Gypsum	Pb Lead	Zn Zinc
Co Cobalt	K Potash	Pt Platinum	

- ϟ Water Power
- ▫ Major Pulp & Paper Mills
- Major Industrial Areas
- × Aluminum Smelters

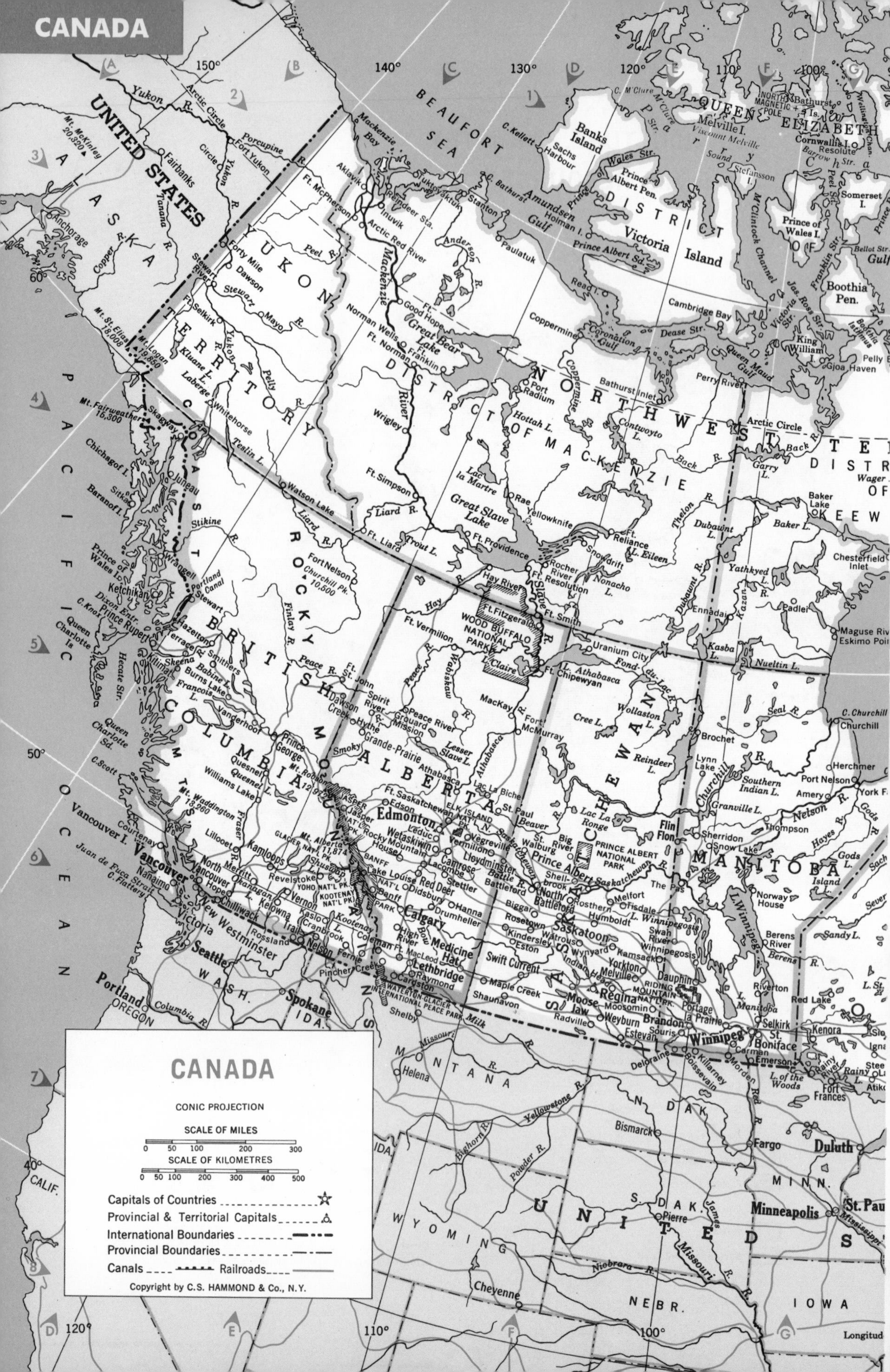
CANADA
CONIC PROJECTION
SCALE OF MILES
0 50 100 200 300
SCALE OF KILOMETRES
0 50 100 200 300 400 500
Capitals of Countries
Provincial & Territorial Capitals
International Boundaries
Provincial Boundaries
Canals
Railroads
Copyright by C.S. HAMMOND & Co., N.Y.
150°
140°
130°
120°
110°
100°
60°
50°
40°
BEAUFORT SEA
PACIFIC OCEAN
UNITED STATES
ALASKA
YUKON TERRITORY
BRITISH COLUMBIA
ALBERTA
SASKATCHEWAN
MANITOBA
NORTHWEST TERRITORIES
DISTRICT OF MACKENZIE
DISTRICT OF FRANKLIN
QUEEN ELIZABETH Is.
ROCKY MTS.
COAST MTS.
Banks Island
Victoria Island
Melville I.
Prince of Wales I.
Somerset I.
Boothia Pen.
King William I.
Amundsen Gulf
Great Bear Lake
Great Slave Lake
L. Athabasca
L. Winnipeg
Mt. McKinley 20,320
Mt. St. Elias 18,008
Mt. Logan 19,850
Mt. Fairweather 15,300
Mt. Waddington 13,260
Mt. Robson 12,972
Mt. Alberta 11,874
Churchill Pk. 10,500
Fairbanks
Anchorage
Fort Yukon
Circle
Dawson
Whitehorse
Skagway
Juneau
Sitka
Ketchikan
Prince Rupert
Prince George
Vancouver
Victoria
New Westminster
Kamloops
Seattle
Spokane
Portland
Edmonton
Calgary
Jasper
Banff
Lethbridge
Medicine Hat
Red Deer
Saskatoon
Regina
Moose Jaw
Prince Albert
Flin Flon
Brandon
Winnipeg
St. Boniface
Churchill
The Pas
Yellowknife
Aklavik
Inuvik
Norman Wells
Ft. Simpson
Ft. Smith
Hay River
Uranium City
Cambridge Bay
Coppermine
Baker Lake
WOOD BUFFALO NATIONAL PARK
PRINCE ALBERT NATIONAL PARK
ELK ISLAND NAT'L PK.
JASPER NAT'L PK.
BANFF NAT'L PK.
YOHO NAT'L PK.
KOOTENAY NAT'L PK.
GLACIER NAT'L PK.
RIDING MOUNTAIN NAT'L PK.
WATERTON-GLACIER INTERNATIONAL PEACE PARK
WASH.
OREGON
IDA.
MONTANA
WYOMING
N. DAK.
S. DAK.
NEBR.
IOWA
MINN.
CALIF.
Helena
Bismarck
Pierre
Cheyenne
Fargo
Duluth
Minneapolis
St. Paul
Missouri R.
Yellowstone R.
Mackenzie R.
Yukon R.
Peace R.
Athabasca R.
Saskatchewan R.
Nelson R.
Churchill R.
Arctic Circle
Longitude

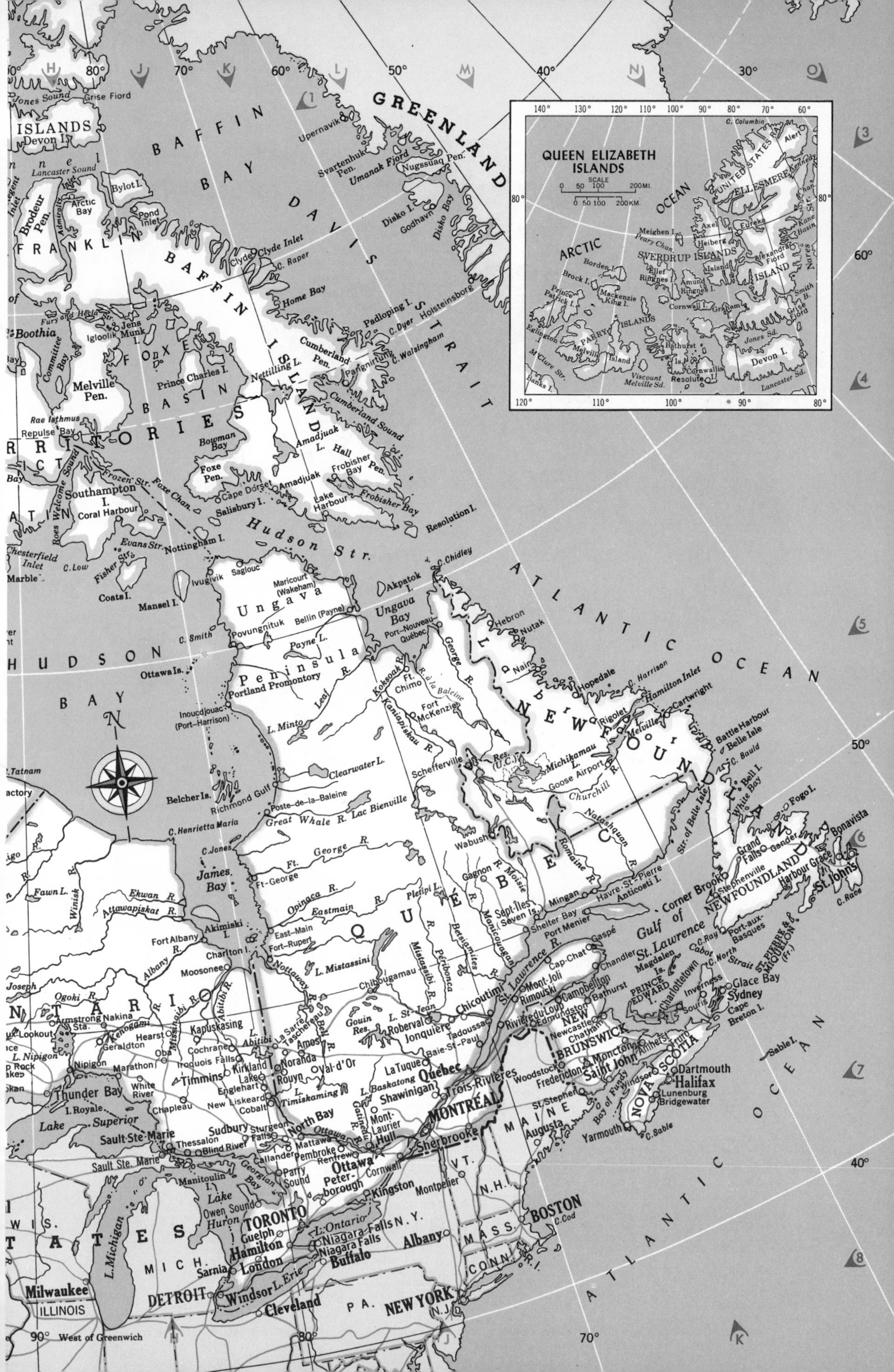

GREENLAND
BAFFIN BAY
DAVIS STRAIT
BAFFIN ISLAND
FOXE BASIN
Hudson Str.
HUDSON BAY
Ungava Peninsula
Ungava Bay
NEWFOUNDLAND
QUEBEC
ONTARIO
ATLANTIC OCEAN
Gulf of St. Lawrence
James Bay
Lake Superior
NOVA SCOTIA
NEW BRUNSWICK
PRINCE EDWARD I.
MAINE
ST. PIERRE & MIQUELON (Fr.)
TORONTO
MONTRÉAL
Québec
Ottawa
Hamilton
London
DETROIT
Cleveland
Buffalo
Albany
NEW YORK
BOSTON
Milwaukee
Halifax
Saint John
St. John's
Sydney
Thunder Bay
Sault Ste. Marie
Sudbury
North Bay
Kingston
Sherbrooke
Trois-Rivières
Chicoutimi
Sept-Îles (Seven Is.)
Goose Airport
Schefferville
Ft. Chimo
Frobisher Bay
Resolution I.
Southampton I.
Coats I.
Mansel I.
Nottingham I.
Belcher Is.
Akimiski I.
Anticosti I.
Sable I.
QUEEN ELIZABETH ISLANDS
ARCTIC OCEAN
ELLESMERE ISLAND
SVERDRUP ISLANDS
PARRY ISLANDS
Devon I.
Melville Island
Bathurst Is.
Cornwallis I.
Resolute
Alert
Eureka
Grise Fiord
West of Greenwich

CANADA

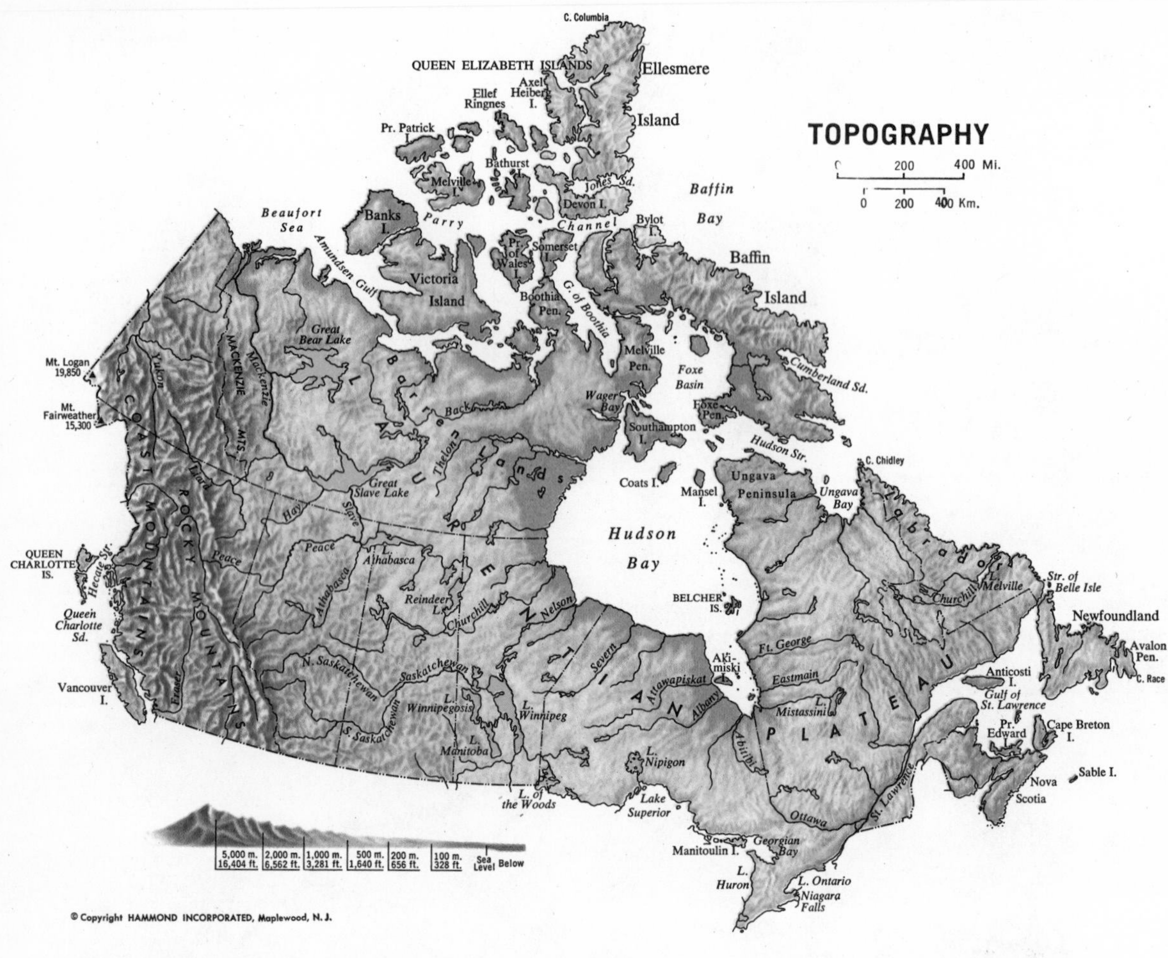

CANADA
Total Population, 21,568,311

ALBERTA
Total Population 1,627,874

CITIES and TOWNS

Athabasca, 1,765 ....E 5
Banff, 2,896 ....E 5
Calgary, 403,319 ....E 5
Calgary, †403,319 ....E 5
Camrose, 8,673 ....E 5
Cardston, 2,685 ....E 6
Coleman, 1,534 ....E 6
Didsbury, 1,821 ....E 5
Drumheller, 5,446 ....E 5
Edmonton (capital), 438,152 ....E 5
Edmonton, †495,702 ....E 5
Edson, 3,818 ....E 5
Fort Chipewyan, 717 ....F 4
Fort Fitzgerald, 68 ....E 4
Fort Macleod, 2,715 ....E 6
Fort McMurray, 6,847 ....E 4
Fort Saskatchewan, 5,726 ....E 5
Fort Vermilion, 768 ....E 4
Grande Prairie, 13,079 ....E 4
Grouard Mission, 328 ....E 4
Hanna, 2,545 ....E 5
High River, 2,676 ....E 5
Hythe, 487 ....E 5
Jasper, 2,360 ....E 5
Lac La Biche, 1,791 ....E 5
Lacombe, 3,436 ....E 5
Lake Louise, 113 ....E 5
Leduc, 4,000 ....E 5
Lethbridge, 41,217 ....E 6
Lloydminster, 4,738 ....E 5
MacKay, 230 ....E 4
Medicine Hat, 26,518 ....E 6
Peace River, 5,039 ....E 4
Pincher Creek, 3,227 ....E 6
Raymond, 2,156 ....E 6
Red Deer, 27,674 ....E 5
Rocky Mountain House, 2,968........E 5
St. Paul, 4,161 ....E 5
Spirit River, 1,091 ....E 4
Stettler, 4,168 ....E 5
Vegreville, 3,691 ....E 5
Vermilion, 2,915 ....E 5
Wainwright, 3,872 ....E 5
Wetaskiwin, 6,267 ....E 5

†Population of metropolitan area.

OTHER FEATURES

Athabasca (river) ....E 4
Banff National Park, 3,532 ....E 5
Bow (river) ....E 5
Claire (lake) ....E 4
Elk Island National Park, 46 ....E 5
Hay (river) ....E 4
Jasper National Park, 3,064 ....E 5
Lesser Slave (lake) ....E 4
Peace (river) ....E 4
Wabiskaw (river) ....E 4
Waterton-Glacier International Peace Park, 259 ....E 6
Wood Buffalo Nat'l Park, 186........E 4

BRITISH COLUMBIA
Total Population, 2,184,621

CITIES and TOWNS

Burns Lake, 1,290 ....D 5
Chilliwack, 9,135 ....D 6
Courtenay, 7,152 ....D 6
Cranbrook, 12,000 ....E 6
Fernie, 2,715 ....E 6
Fort Nelson, 954 ....D 4
Hazelton, 403 ....D 4
Hope, 2,948 ....D 6
Kamloops, 26,168 ....D 5
Kaslo, 940 ....E 6
Kelowna, 19,412 ....E 6
Kitimat, 11,803 ....D 5
Lillooet, 1,379 ....D 5
Merritt, 5,289 ....D 5
Nanaimo, 14,948 ....D 6
Nelson, 9,400 ....E 6
New Westminster, 42,835 ....D 6
North Vancouver, 31,847 ....D 6
Prince George, 33,101 ....D 5
Prince Rupert, 15,747 ....C 5
Quesnel, 6,252 ....D 5
Revelstoke, 4,791 ....E 5
Rossland, 3,896 ....E 6
Smithers, 3,135 ....D 5
Stewart, 1,357 ....D 4
Terrace, 9,991 ....D 5
Trail, 11,149 ....E 6
Vancouver, 426,256 ....D 6
Vancouver, †1,082,352 ....D 6
Vanderhoof, 1,507 ....D 5
Vernon, 13,283 ....E 5
Victoria (capital), 61,761 ....D 6
Victoria, †195,800 ....D 6
Williams Lake, 4,072 ....D 5

OTHER FEATURES

Babine (lake) ....D 5
Coast (mts.) ....C 4
Columbia (river) ....D 6
Dixon Entrance (strait) ....C 5
Finlay (river) ....D 4
Francois (lake) ....D 5
Fraser (river) ....D 5
Hecate (strait) ....C 5
Juan de Fuca (strait) ....D 6
Kootenay (lake) ....E 5
Liard (river) ....D 4
Okanagan (lake) ....D 6
Peace (river) ....D 4
Portland (canal) ....D 4
Queen Charlotte (isls.), 3,365........C 5
Quesnel (lake) ....D 5
Robson (mt.) ....E 5
Rocky (mts.) ....D 4
Scott (cape) ....D 5
Skeena (river) ....D 5
Stikine (river) ....C 4
Vancouver (isl.) ....D 6
Waddington (mt.) ....D 5
Yoho National Park ....E 5

MANITOBA
Total Population, 988,247

CITIES and TOWNS

Amery, 25 ....G 4
Berens River, 212 ....G 5
Boissevain, 1,473 ....G 6
Brandon, 31,150 ....F 6
Brochet, 612 ....F 4
Carman, 1,922 ....G 6
Churchill, 1,678 ....G 4
Dauphin, 8,891 ....F 5
Deloraine, 910 ....F 6
Emerson, 834 ....G 6
Flin Flon, 8,873 ....F 4
Killarney, 1,836 ....G 6
Morden, 3,097 ....G 6
Norway House, 676 ....G 5
Portage la Prairie, 12,950 ....G 5
Riverton, 817 ....G 5
St. Boniface, 46,714 ....G 6
Selkirk, 9,331 ....G 5
Sherridon, 100 ....G 4
Souris, 1,829 ....F 6
Swan River, 3,470 ....E 5
The Pas, 6,062 ....F 5
Thompson, 19,001 ....G 4
Winnipeg (capital), 246,246 ....G 6
Winnipeg, †540,262 ....G 6
Winnipegosis, 908 ....F 5
York Factory, 331 ....G 4

OTHER FEATURES

Berens (river) ....G 5
Churchill (river) ....F 4
Gods (lake) ....G 5
Island (lake) ....G 5
Manitoba (lake) ....G 5
Nelson (river) ....G 4
Riding Mountain Nat'l Park, 210 ....F 5
Winnipeg (lake) ....G 5
Winnipegosis (lake) ....F 5

CANADA: All figures available from 1971 final census are supplemented by local official estimates. **ST. PIERRE & MIQUELON:** 1967 final census.

NEW BRUNSWICK
Total Population, 634,557

CITIES and TOWNS

Bathurst, 16,674 K 6
Campbellton, 10,335 K 6
Chatham, 7,833 K 6
Edmundston, 12,365 K 6
Fredericton (capital), 24,254 K 6
Moncton, 47,891 K 6
Newcastle, 6,460 K 6
Saint John, 89,039 K 6
Saint John, †106,744 K 6
St. Stephen, 3,409 K 6
Woodstock, 4,846 K 6

NEWFOUNDLAND
Total Population, 522,104

CITIES and TOWNS

Battle Harbour, 104 L 5
Bonavista, 4,215 L 6
Cartwright, 752 L 5
Corner Brook, 26,309 L 6
Gander, 7,748 L 6
Goose Airport, 1,591 K 5
Grand Falls, 7,677 L 6
Harbour Grace, 2,771 L 6
Hopedale, 375 L 4
Nain, 708 K 4
Port-aux-Basques, 5,942 L 6
Rigolet, 90 L 5
St. John's (capital), 88,102 L 6
St. John's, †131,814 L 6

OTHER FEATURES

Bell (isl.) L 5
Belle Isle (strait) L 5
Chidley (cape) K 3
Churchill (river) K 5
Fogo (isl.), 4,094 L 6
Labrador (reg.), 28,166 K 4
Melville (lake) L 5
Race (cape) L 6
White (bay) L 5

NORTHWEST TERRITORIES
Total Population, 34,807

CITIES and TOWNS

Aklavik, 599 C 2
Alert, 50 N 3
Alexandra Fiord, 25 N 3
Arctic Red River, 140 C 2
Baker Lake, 596 G 3
Bathurst Inlet, 73 E 2
Cambridge Bay, 531 F 2
Cape Dorset, 336 J 3
Chesterfield Inlet, 253 G 3
Clyde, 99 K 1
Coppermine, 536 E 2
Coral Harbour, 298 H 3
Eskimo Point, 464 G 3
Eureka, 75 N 3
Fort Franklin, 196 D 2
Fort Good Hope, 308 D 2
Fort Liard, 177 D 3
Fort McPherson, 129 C 2
Fort Norman, 209 D 2
Fort Providence, 353 E 3
Fort Reliance, 698 F 3
Fort Resolution, 586 E 3
Fort Simpson, 495 D 3
Fort Smith, 2,364 E 3
Frobisher Bay, 2,000 K 3
Gjoa Haven, 162 G 2
Grise Fiord, 98 N 3
Hay River, 2,406 E 3
Igloolik, 127 H 2
Inuvik, 2,669 C 2
Lake Harbour, 97 K 3
Norman Wells, 297 D 3
Pangnirtung, 376 K 2
Pelly Bay, 171 G 2
Pond Inlet, 178 J 1
Port Radium, 412 E 2
Rae, 779 E 3
Read Island, 75 E 2
Reindeer Station, 76 C 2
Repulse Bay, 116 H 2
Resolute, 254 M 3
Rocher River, 130 E 3
Sachs Harbour, 112 D 1
Snowdrift, 140 F 3
Tuktoyaktuk, 512 C 2
Wrigley, 109 D 3
Yellowknife (capital), 6,122 E 3

OTHER FEATURES

Akimiski (isl.) H 5
Akpatok (isl.) K 3
Amund Ringnes (isl.) M 3
Amundsen (gulf) D 1
Axel Heiberg (isl.) N 3
Back (river) G 2
Baffin (bay) J 1
Baffin (isl.) J 1
Banks (isl.) D 1
Barrow (strait) G 1
Bathurst (isl.) M 3
Belcher (isls.), 176 H 4
Boothia (pen.) G 1
Brodeur (pen.) H 1
Coats (isl.) H 3
Columbia (cape) N 3
Cornwallis (isl.) M 3
Coronation (gulf) E 2
Cumberland (sound) K 2
Davis (strait) K 1
Dease (strait) F 2
Devon (isl.) M 3
Dubawnt (river) F 3
Dyer (cape) L 2
Ellef Ringnes (isl.) M 3
Ellesmere (isl.) N 3
Foxe (basin) J 2
Foxe (pen.) J 2
Franklin, District of, 7,747 H 1
Fury and Hecla (strait) H 2
Garry (lake) G 2
Great Bear (lake) D 2
Great Slave (lake) E 3
Kane (basin) N 3
Kazan (river) F 3
Keewatin, District of, 3,403 G 3
Kennedy (channel) N 3
King William (isl.) G 2
La Martre (lake) E 3
Lancaster (sound) H 1
Liard (river) D 3
Mackenzie, District of, 23,657 E 3
Mackenzie (river) C 2
Mansel (isl.) H 3
M'Clintock (channel) F 1
M'Clure (strait) E 1
Melville (isl.) E 1
Nares (strait) N 3
Nettilling (lake) K 2
North Magnetic Pole F 1
Padloping (isl.) K 2
Parry (channel) E-H 1
Parry (isls.) M 3
Prince Charles (isl.) J 2
Prince of Wales (isl.) G 1
Prince Patrick (isl.) M 3
Queen Elizabeth (isls.) M 3
Rae (isthmus) H 2
Resolution (isl.) K 3
Roes Welcome (sound) H 3
Slave (river) E 3
Somerset (isl.) G 1
Southampton (isl.) H 3
Sverdrup (isls.) M 3
Victoria (isl.) E 1
Viscount Melville (sound) F 1
Wager (bay) G 2

NOVA SCOTIA
Total Population, 788,960

CITIES and TOWNS

Amherst, 9,966 K 6
Bridgewater, 5,231 K 7
Dartmouth, 64,770 K 7
Glace Bay, 22,440 L 6
Halifax (capital), 122,035 K 7
Halifax, †222,637 K 7
Inverness, 2,022 K 6
Lunenburg, 3,215 K 7
Sydney, 33,230 L 6
Truro, 13,047 K 6
Windsor, 3,775 K 7
Yarmouth, 8,516 K 7

OTHER FEATURES

Cabot (strait) K 6
Cape Breton (isl.), 162,359 K 6
Fundy (bay) K 7
North (cape) K 6
Sable (cape) K 7
Sable (isl.), 12 L 7

ONTARIO
Total Population, 7,703,106

CITIES and TOWNS

Armstrong Station, 342 H 5
Atikokan, 6,087 G 6
Blind River, 3,450 H 6
Bowmanville, 8,947 F 6
Callander, 1,236 H 6
Chapleau, 3,389 H 6
Cobalt, 2,197 H 6
Cochrane, 4,965 H 6
Cornwall, 47,116 J 7
Englehart, 1,721 H 6
Fort Frances, 9,947 G 6
Geraldton, 3,178 H 6
Guelph, 60,087 H 7
Hamilton, 309,173 H 7
Hamilton, †498,523 H 7
Hearst, 3,501 H 6
Iroquois Falls, 7,271 H 6
Kapuskasing, 12,834 H 6
Kenora, 10,952 G 5
Kingston, 59,047 J 7
Kirkland Lake, 15,205 H 6
London, 223,222 H 7
London, †286,011 H 7
Marathon, 2,456 H 6
Mattawa, 2,881 J 6
Moosonee, 975 H 5
Nakina, 667 H 5
New Liskeard 5,488 H 6
Niagara Falls, 67,163 J 7
Nipigon, 2,637 H 6
North Bay, 49,187 J 6
Oba, 75 H 6
Ottawa (cap.), Canada, 302,341 J 6
Ottawa, †602,510 J 6
Owen Sound, 18,469 H 7
Parry Sound, 5,842 J 6
Pembroke, 16,544 J 6
Peterborough, 58,111 J 7
Rainy River, 1,196 G 6
Renfrew, 9,173 J 6
Sarnia, 57,644 H 7
Sault Sainte Marie, 80,332 H 6
Sioux Lookout, 2,530 G 5
Sturgeon Falls, 6,662 H 6
Sudbury, 90,535 H 6
Sudbury, †155,424 H 6
Thessalon, 1,879 H 6
Thunder Bay, 108,411 H 6
Timmins, 28,542 H 6
Toronto (capital), 712,786 H 7
Toronto (met. city), 2,086,017 H 7
Toronto, †2,628,043 H 7
White River, 953 H 6
Windsor, 203,300 H 7
Windsor, †258,643 H 7

OTHER FEATURES

Abitibi (lake) H 6
Albany (river) H 5
Attawapiskat (river) H 5
Ekwan (river) H 5
Georgian (bay) H 6
Henrietta Maria (cape) H 4
Kenogami (river) H 5
Manitoulin (isl.) H 6
Missinaibi (river) H 5
Nipigon (lake) H 6
Ogoki (river) H 5
Ottawa (river) J 6
Rainy (lake) G 6
St. Joseph (lake) G 5
Severn (river) G 5
Woods, Lake of the (lake) G 6

PRINCE EDWARD ISLAND
Total Population, 111,641

CITIES and TOWNS

Charlottetown (cap.), 19,133 K 6
Souris, 1,393 K 6

QUEBEC
Total Population, 6,027,764

CITIES and TOWNS

Amos, 6,984 J 6
Baie-St-Paul, 4,163 J 6
Bellin, 95 J 3
Cap-Chat, 3,868 K 6
Chandler, 3,843 K 6
Chibougamau, 9,701 J 6
Chicoutimi, 33,893 J 6
Chicoutimi-Jonquière, †133,703 J 6
Fort-Main, 257 J 5
Fort-Chimo, 480 K 4
Fort-George, 1,074 J 5
Fort-Rupert, 528 J 5
Gagnon, 3,787 K 5
Gaspé, 17,211 K 6
Havre-Saint-Pierre, 2,407 K 5
Hull, 63,580 J 6
Jonquière, 28,430 J 6
La Tuque, 13,099 J 6
Maricourt, 112 J 3
Mont-Joli, 6,698 K 6
Mont-Laurier, 8,240 J 6
Montréal, 1,214,352 J 7
Montréal, †2,743,208 J 7
Noranda, 10,741 J 6
Payne (Bellin), 95 J 3
Port-Menier, 438 K 6
Poste-de-la-Baleine, 718 J 4
Québec (cap.), 186,088 J 6
Québec, †480,502 J 6
Rimouski, 26,887 K 6
Rivière-du-Loup, 12,760 K 6
Roberval, 8,330 J 6
Rouyn, 17,821 J 6
Saglouc, 317 J 3
Schefferville, 3,271 K 5
Sept-Îles (Seven Isls.), 24,320 K 5
Shawinigan, 27,792 J 6
Sherbrooke, 80,711 J 7
Tadoussac, 1,010 J 6
Taschereau, 162 J 6
Trois Rivières, 55,869 J 6
Wakeham (Maricourt), 112 J 3

OTHER FEATURES

Anticosti (isl.), 419 K 6
Baleine (river) K 4
Baskatong (lake) J 6
Betsiamites (river) K 5
Gatineau (river) J 6
George (river) K 4
Gouin (res.) J 6
Kaniapiskau (river) K 4
Koksoak (river) K 4
Magdalen (isls.), 13,303 K 6
Manicouagan (river) K 5
Minto (lake) J 4
Mistassibi (river) J 5
Mistassini (lake) J 5
Natashquan (river) K 5
Nottaway (river) J 5
Péribonca (river) J 5
Pletipi (lake) J 5
St-Jean (lake) J 6
St. Lawrence (river) K 6
Timiskaming (lake) J 6

SASKATCHEWAN
Total Population, 926,242

CITIES and TOWNS

Battleford, 1,803 F 5
Biggar, 2,607 F 5
Big River, 836 F 5
Estevan, 9,150 F 6
Eston, 1,418 F 5
Flin Flon, 471 F 4
Humboldt, 3,881 F 5
Indian Head, 1,810 F 5
Kamsack, 2,783 F 5
Kindersley, 3,451 F 5
Lloydminster, 3,953 E 5
Maple Creek, 2,268 F 6
Melfort, 4,725 F 5
Melville, 5,375 F 5
Moose Jaw, 31,854 F 5
Moosomin, 2,407 F 5
North Battleford, 12,698 F 5
Prince Albert, 28,464 F 5
Radville, 1,024 F 6
Regina (cap.), 139,469 F 5
Regina, †140,734 F 5
Rosetown, 2,614 F 5
Rosthern, 1,431 F 5
St. Walburg, 656 F 5
Saskatoon, 126,449 F 5
Saskatoon, †126,449 F 5
Shaunavon, 2,244 F 6
Shellbrook, 1,048 F 5
Swift Current, 15,415 F 5
Tisdale, 2,798 F 5
Uranium City, 2,209 F 4
Watrous, 1,541 F 5
Weyburn, 8,815 F 6
Wynyard, 1,932 F 5
Yorkton, 13,430 F 5

OTHER FEATURES

Athabasca (lake) F 4
Cree (lake) F 4
North Saskatchewan (river) F 5
Prince Albert Nat'l Park, 182 F 5
Reindeer (lake) F 4
Saskatchewan (river) F 5
Wollaston (lake) F 4

YUKON
Total Population, 18,388

CITIES and TOWNS

Dawson, 747 C 3
Fort Selkirk, 270 C 3
Mayo, 479 C 3
Whitehorse (capital), 11,217 C 3

OTHER FEATURES

Kluane (lake) C 3
Logan (mt.) B 3
Peel (river) C 2
Pelly (river) C 3
St. Elias (mt.) C 3
Stewart (river) C 3
Teslin (lake) C 3

ST. PIERRE & MIQUELON
Total Population, 5,235

St. Pierre & Miquelon (isls.), 5,235 L 6

by the fact that everyone was a British subject and owed allegiance to the British Crown. The concept or sentiment of subjects united in a common allegiance had, according to the degree with which the sentiment was held, immense use. It traversed geographical distance, no matter how broad. Moreover, the notion of a common allegiance, being personal to each subject, had nothing to do with politics, class, race, or nationality. It gave a common basis for political community, a common focus of patriotism.

It was this deeply felt and rarely defined sentiment that made possible the Canadian concept of a mosaic of population. People of whatever origin, it was asserted, had no need to cut the ties with their past or cease in any way to be themselves, provided the concept of a common allegiance was acceptable to them. As the status of British subjects was perhaps the freest the world has ever known in both civil and political liberty and rights, the concept was generally acceptable until recent times.

Changing Concepts. To a good many Canadians, however—until, say, 1959—the concept of common allegiance ceased to be entirely satisfactory. There were sometimes special reasons for this. Some Canadians, like some Englishmen, were republicans in theory. It was not surprising that many Irish Canadians could not wholly forget what British rule had meant to Ireland. It was no less surprising that many French Canadians, those of a liberal turn of thought, could not wholly accept a monarchy by which their ancestors had been conquered or the status of subject rather than that of citizen.

Even more important, however, was the fact that the idea of "subject" and "allegiance"—the terminology, if nothing more—failed to satisfy the growing national feeling of Canadians of most origins, including British, during the 20th century, and particularly as a result of Canadian participation in two world wars. It was partly that Canada had interests of its own to preserve which sometimes differed from those of the United Kingdom and other parts of the British Empire. It was partly that Canadian soldiers insisted on fighting as Canadian formations and were often critical of British direction of the wars. It was partly the rapidly growing influence of the United States in business, entertainment, politics, science, and literature. But above all, Canadians responded like all young developing countries to the influence of national feeling in the present century.

Much was done to reshape the empire and the concept of allegiance to the monarch in order to accommodate the growing national sentiment of Canada and other members of the empire. The British Empire was transformed into the Commonwealth of Nations. Yet this was not enough for many, no doubt the majority, of Canadians.

The Present. Since the end of World War II a number of attempts have been made to state more clearly the position of the Canadian nation in the Commonwealth. The most fundamental of these was the Canadian Citizenship Act, which was passed in 1947. The root effect of this act was to create a specific, legal Canadian citizenship and, moreover, to end the old practice by which, unless specifically prohibited, any British subject could become a Canadian by personal choice and without legal formality. Since 1947 a British subject who is not a Canadian may become a Canadian citizen only by application. Canadians remain British subjects by custom, but by the law of the land they are Canadian citizens, and the status of British subject has only such legal meaning as other members of the Commonwealth may choose to give it.

In short, the concept of Canadian nationality has prevailed over that of British subject with a general allegiance to the crown. Canadians are citizens of Canada with allegiance to the king or queen of Canada, a basic republicanism united with a formal allegiance.

Canadian political society, therefore, rests on the idea of nationality. But what is Canadian

SOLITUDE of life in the Canadian Arctic region is embodied in this figure trudging across a snow plain.

NATIONAL FILM BOARD, FROM MILLER SERVICES LTD.

nationality? The answer is: a common citizenship for Canadians. Yet what is the basis of common citizenship in a country of two language groups? What is it, moreover, when one language group, the French, is an ethnic and cultural group of extraordinary intensity, and the other, the English, is a collection of groups? No English-speaking group is dominant numerically, and the concept of the melting pot, as it is accepted in the United States, is not a popular and national policy. The English-speaking people of Canada are neither ethnically nor culturally a nation like the French people of Canada, and the concept of citizen in the two groups rests on somewhat different bases. A common nationality has not yet replaced a common allegiance for all Canadians.

Among English-speaking Canadians, thought and opinion on the subject varies widely. In the Atlantic provinces change of sentiment from British allegiance to Canadian nationality has been least. In Quebec the English, long a dominant minority, are seeking accommodation with the French majority. In Ontario, Canadian nationality and British allegiance are still in balance, as they are perhaps in British Columbia. Only in the Prairie Provinces, despite the origin there of the concept of a mosaic of population, has there been a true assimilation, very much in the American manner, and the creation of a society that is cohesive, not ethnically and culturally as among the French people of Canada, but socially and politically.

It is in fact towards this kind of society that English-speaking Canadians are moving, although at varying rates of speed in the different regions. True, there is, or will be, an English-Canadian social nationality, much like the American. How to create a common, political nationality between it and the French people of Canada has become the chief matter of Canadian public life.

W. L. MORTON
Champlain College, Trent University

FRENCH-SPEAKING CANADIANS

The history of Canada is, to a large extent, the history of the tensions, conflicts, and compromises between its two contesting partners—English-speaking and French-speaking Canadians. Their relationship has been the cause of a constant, often dramatic dialectic. As early as 1839, the Earl of Durham in his famous *Report* acknowledged that he had found in Canada "two nations warring in the bosom of a single state." After more than a century, in 1963, the Canadian government was giving to a Royal Commission on Bilingualism and Biculturalism the mandate of determining "what steps should be taken to develop the Canadian Confederation on the basis of an equal partnership between the two founding races."

Areas of Settlement. The French-speaking population of Canada is descended from the French who discovered more than half of the North American continent and pioneered the St. Lawrence Valley in the 17th century. After 1760, and chiefly after the Rebellion of 1837–1838, the culture of the French Canadian shaped itself according to the outlook and the needs of a society that was obsessed with survival. This society retired within itself and engaged almost totally in rural pursuits. Its culture, based on the Catholic faith, the French language, and the values of rural life, was also carried by French Canadians who migrated from their original habitat around the St. Lawrence into various Canadian regions in the 19th century, or by the Acadians who obstinately returned to their homeland in the Maritime provinces from which their ancestors had been exiled in 1755.

The French migrations within the continent followed two main directions. First, an abundant stream started as early as 1830 for the United States, and the flow followed almost without interruption until the 1920's. The total French-Canadian population in the United States is estimated at more than a half million.

TORONTO is Canada's second-largest city. Urban centers now hold over two thirds of the country's population.

GEORGE HUNTER, FROM NATIONAL FILM BOARD

The movement within Canada itself was mainly toward the west at successive stages during the second half of the 19th century. The main French concentrations resulting from these displacements are now to be found, in decreasing numerical order, in the following Canadian areas: in New Brunswick and the other Maritime provinces, in southern and northern Ontario, in communities along a northern strip of the Prairie provinces, and in Greater Vancouver. These French nuclei are organically linked by many transcontinental associations, such as the Canadian Association of French Teachers (Association Canadienne des Éducateurs de Langue Française). They regard Quebec as their source of inspiration and their cultural center of gravity. They constitute a diaspora, and each has had to live through identical struggles for the recognition of its rights to the French language and to French schools.

Quebec, the Heartland. Although the French fact is thus alive in each of the Canadian provinces and at the level of the central government, numerous historical, geographical, and political factors have concentrated its main significance in Quebec. One is justified in restricting the term "French Canada" to that province. More than three-fourths of all French-speaking Canadians live in Quebec. Over four-fifths of its population are of French origin. Quebec is more than just one of the ten provinces of Canada, and it is not interchangeable with any other. Although its population is almost 20% non-French, it is in the minds of French Canadians their province.

The British North America Act, which created the Canadian Confederation, recognized Quebec's status as a French province. In more ways than one, it is the home of French Canadians. It is both the geographical milieu that has belonged to them since the early days of French colonization and the political structure that enables them to fulfill their collective ambitions. They have come to consider it as their state, the political expression of themselves as a people. Consequently, any account of the characteristics and achievements of French-speaking Canadians can be rightly focused on Quebec.

Quebec has now assumed a fuller stature and more dashing attitudes than at any time in the past. It has been compared to a young giant awakening after a two-century-long sleep. This awakening is manifest in its political, economic, and cultural life. Politically, not only does Quebec uphold claims similar to those of other provinces, in contradistinction to the centralizing policies of the federal government, but it asserts itself as the national state of French Canadians. To that extent, it must struggle, more than the other provinces, against the political superstructures of the Canadian Confederation. Economically, Quebec must proclaim and carry out the duties entailed in its planning role as a modern state. It must become "master in its own house," in the words of Errol Bouchette, an economist, writing about 1900. To that extent, it must confront the network of foreign financial and industrial superstructures that have long dominated the province's economic activities. Culturally, Quebec has acquired a more vivid consciousness of its "Frenchness," and it has had to create institutions that would give fuller expression to this identity.

Origins of French-Canadian Nationalism. There is nothing magical about Quebec's awakening. It is the outcome of a long process of cumulative experiences, ambitions, and hopes. The history of French Canada since the early 19th century is that of the gradual elaboration of a national spirit. As early as 1845, F. X. Garneau's first *Histoire du Canada* emphasized the necessity of a national revival.

National Aspects. During the first decades of Confederation, the French Canadian's political interest crystallized on the federal level where his leaders tried to obtain equal status and responsibility in governing the country. Confederation, however, thwarted the hopes which had been set on it by proving unable to provide a rightful solution to the claims of French minorities outside Quebec. Successive crises arose—in Manitoba in 1870, in the Northwest provinces in 1905, in Ontario in 1913—in regard to the establishment of French schools.

French-Canadian resentment was further accentuated by a federal foreign policy that was felt to be too directly submissive to British imperialistic aims. Three other major crises broke out in this connection: in 1900, on the occasion of Canada's participation in Britain's South African War against the Boers; in 1910, around the project of creating a Canadian Navy; and in 1917, with the famous "conscription crisis" after Canada's decision to enter World War I.

It was at the time of the first of these crises, around 1900, that there came to the fore the ardent patriotic leader Henri Bourassa, whose diatribes inspired new schools of French-Canadian nationalism. Their more influential spokesmen were Olivar Asselin, Armand Lavergne and, above all, Abbé Lionel Groulx. For more than 40 years the writings of this outstanding historian exercised the deepest influence of all. They continually illustrated the failure of the Confederation "compact" between French and English in Canada and urged a French-Canadian rebirth.

Provincial Aspects. Actually, from 1920 on, French-Canadian political preoccupations shifted from the federal to the provincial scene. Two main factors stimulated the Quebec government to define more explicitly and then assume its responsibilities. The Great Depression of the 1930's prompted it to develop social legislation on a wide scale. Later, to counteract the increase in federal fiscal powers stemming from the defense necessities of World War II, Quebec was compelled to stress its autonomy with renewed vigor.

Yet, autonomy for the time being remained chiefly rhetorical and defensive. It was not until the 1960's that the Quebec government defined its autonomy in a positive, aggressive manner and set up new economic, educational, and cultural institutions needed by an expanding and exploding French-Canadian society. If the Quebec state is the modern embodiment of a century-old wish expressed by the nationalist schools of thought, it is also the concrete answer to structural needs felt from within the society.

Features of French-Canadian Society. French-Canadian society is both related to the larger Canadian society and different and apart from it. One can hardly understand its present features without referring to its traditional traits.

Traditional Attitudes. It has already been pointed out that French Canada reduced itself to an essentially rural society after the first third of the 19th century. Soon after the British conquest, trade and business activities became the exclusive domain of English-speaking entrepreneurs. Among French Canadians, the clergy—even more than the rising bourgeoisie of professionals and politicians—was the dominant elite, for it formulated the ideology that molded the life of the society until the first third of the 20th century. This ideology entwined with the nationalist thought and often conditioned it. Of a quasi-theocratic, messianic character, it stated that the French-Canadian people had a special spiritual mission. Faithfulness to this mission required faithfulness to religion and to the rural values. It stressed the frugal moral values of rural life as above material success.

Factors Influencing Change. The consequences of this ideology were such that, for a long time, French-Canadian society looked like an iceberg, with only a small portion visible above waters. Or, to repeat the often-quoted aphorism from Louis Hémon's novel *Maria Chapdelaine: "Au pays de Québec, rien ne change."* Yet, below this ideological fixity, striking social changes were occurring. French-Canadian society could not escape the industrial fate predetermined by its geographical position and its natural resources. A first phase of industrialization, about the end of the 19th century, gave rise to pulp-and-paper and textile centers and a few mining towns. The rural population, which represented almost two thirds (60.3%) of the Quebec population in 1901, had declined to half of it (51.8%) in 1911, and to little more than a third (36%) in 1921. A second phase of industrialization, geared to the exploitation of hydroelectric resources and accelerated by World War II, multiplied industrial areas and communities. Quebec is now more than 70% urban, and over half of its urban population is concentrated in the Montreal metropolitan area.

Industrialization in Quebec has been achieved by foreign—that is to say, British, American and Anglo-Canadian—capital, management, and technicians. It has in its way constituted for French-Canadian society another type of invasion and domination. There were few French Canadians among the dominant figures of finance and industry. For a long time, secondary and university education kept orienting the students towards liberal professions. The whole educational system was slow in establishing technical schools that would provide adequate training for commercial and industrial occupations. Industry, as it was established, absorbed French Canadians in its lower ranks as unskilled workers.

The prevailing ideology kept depreciating industrial and urban life and, to counteract its effects, the clergy, still playing its role of dominant and ruling élite, inspired and organized the first social movements at the beginning of the 20th century. Most conspicuous of them was the Catholic worker's unions, which the clergy permeated with a philosophy of submissiveness to employers and to social authority.

The Awakening. Essentially the 20th century started for the French-Canadian only in the 1920's. One can reckon from this period the beginning of the awakening from the long, hibernal sleep. The universities of Quebec (Laval) and of Montreal entered a phase of development. Their departments multiplied and blossomed; the teaching of science in particular became solidly organized.

The depression years brought to light the existence of socioeconomic classes. Increasing unemployment emphasized the existence of a large urban proletariat that had been engendered by industry. There also appeared a new middle class, composed of clerical workers, civil servants, small merchants, and entrepreneurs who were to appropriate to themselves some of the social status and prestige hitherto reserved for the clergy and the professional. The depression years were also the occasion of an intellectual and literary outburst. They stimulated criticism of the educational system. Above all, they stimulated programs of social and political reform.

Social protest—criticism of the traditional clerical ideology and of political empiricism—attained its peak after World War II and during the 1950's. Universities then acquired full maturity. French-Canadian society found the ways and means of fully expressing itself. The establishment of a true state involved reorienting nostalgic, restrospective nationalist views toward the future. The coming of age of the society meant that French-Canadian citizens had to discard many worn-out, unrealistic moral imperatives of church ideology and become more secular in their outlook.

In no field has this phenomenon been more dramatically noticeable than in the arts, especially literature. Poetry, drama, and the novel have since long gone beyond the stage of lyrical complacency, of abstraction, of refuge in the past. They testify to the anguishes and to the inner rebellions of the younger generations, to the quest for new values, and to the need for social restructuring. Many of them could bear the title of Émile Borduas' pathetic manifesto *Refus global* (*Global Refusal*) in 1948. Contemporary French-Canadian poets and writers give voice to the rejection of traditional controls, to the wish for emancipation, to the need of overcoming alienations. They bear witness to the fact that not only *"Au pays de Québec,"* many things have changed, but that these changes point to a global reorientation of society.

New Orientation. This new orientation, indeed, is far from complete, but some of its lines of development are already manifest. One of its extreme forms is the separatist movement, espousing a breakaway from Canada.

An area of already impressive progress is that of French-speaking organized labor. The former Canadian and Catholic Confederation of Labour (Confédération des Travailleurs Catholiques du Canada) has become nondenominational. Under its new name of Confederation of National Trade Unions (Confédération des Syndicats Nationaux), it has widened its membership far beyond the ranks of industrial workers to include white-collar and professional wage earners.

The new orientation is also manifest in the radical transformation of the educational system, in the creation for the first time of a Department of Education and in the further advancement of higher education. It is again manifest in such events as the gigantic power achievements of Hydro-Quebec, the creation of the Quebec Economic Advisory Council and the establishment of the General Investment Corporation (Société Générale de Financement). It is manifest too, in the cultural field, in the concluding of agreements between France and Quebec with a view to intensifying exchanges of professors, technicians, students, and artistic works.

PUBLIC ARCHIVES OF CANADA

IMMIGRANTS arriving in Quebec were among the 1.5 million persons entering Canada between 1901 and 1911.

Thus, notwithstanding its motto *Je me souviens* (I remember), Quebec no longer looks to the past for fulfillment, but to the future. The province remains peculiar in that its French-Canadian society has never quite had the benefit of a truly democratic experience. It has been rushed, as it were, from the stage of a tradition-oriented society to the stage of a technological-bureaucratic society. French Canadians, since their destiny was in the past defined by a too abstract and too dogmatic ideology, have had to disentangle themselves from it and to shape their destiny by trial-and-error. This destiny is partly predetermined by geographical conditions, which make French Canada a North American nation as well as a cultural bridge between the French-speaking and the English-speaking worlds. Other conditions that must be realized if French Canada and French-speaking Canadians are to fulfill their destiny have yet to be defined and established.

JEAN-CHARLES FALARDEAU
Laval University

Bibliography

Bergeron, Gérard, *Le Canada français: après deux siècles de patience* (Paris 1967).
Bernard, Michel, *Le Québec change de visage* (Paris 1964).
Blanchard, Raoul, *Le Canada français, province de Québec* (Paris 1960).
Cook, G. Ramsay, *French Canada and the Canadian Question* (Toronto 1966).
Dumont, Fernand, and Martin, Yves, *Situation de la recherche sur le Canada français* (Quebec 1962).
Groulx, Lionel, *Histoire du Canada français,* 4 vols. (Montreal 1950–1951).
Hughes, Everett C., *French Canada in Transition* (Chicago 1943).
Rioux, Marcel, and Martin, Yves, eds., *French-Canadian Society* (Toronto 1964).
Sylvestre, Guy, ed., *Structures sociales du Canada français* (Toronto and Quebec 1966).
Wade, Mason, *The French Canadians, 1760–1945* (New York and Toronto 1955).
Wade, Mason, ed., *Canadian Dualism—La dualité canadienne* (Toronto and Quebec 1960).

ROYAL COMMISSION ON BILINGUALISM AND BICULTURALISM

In July 1963 the federal government appointed a royal commission to investigate the problems posed by Canada's linguistic and cultural dualism, and instructed the ten commissioners to "recommend what steps should be taken to develop the Canadian Confederation on the basis of an equal partnership between the two founding races, taking into account the contribution made by the other ethnic groups to the cultural enrichment of Canada and the measures that should be taken to safeguard that contribution." The commission was instructed to consider in particular the federal public service; public and private organizations, including the mass media; and, in consultation with the provinces, education.

The "B. & B." Commission was composed equally of bilingual English-speaking and French-speaking members, including two foreign-born citizens. The cochairmen, A. Davidson Dunton, president of Carleton University, Ottawa, and André Laurendeau, editor in chief of the Montreal daily *Le Devoir,* and the cosecretaries, one from each language group, shared equal responsibility and authority.

The task proved greater and more complex than anyone had foreseen. The inquiry became the largest, most expensive, and most controversial in Canadian history. The commission undertook broad historical, legal, and socioeconomic research into Canadian problems and practices, and made comparative studies of other countries.

The commission stressed its belief in the value of a continuous, free, and frank dialogue among the Canadian people as a source of insight about the problems and as a necessary first step leading to their solution. In the initial phase the commission attempted to assess public attitudes through direct citizen confrontation by means of preliminary hearings and informal public regional conferences. Visits were also made to all provincial governments to enlist their cooperation, and many private meetings and confidential hearings were held.

Preliminary Report. The commission reviewed its own experience and assessed the existing tensions in a preliminary report published in 1965. This volume analyzed the various "concepts of Canada" and documented the existence of "two societies" within the one country. One of its principal conclusions was that "Canada, without being fully conscious of the fact, was passing through the greatest crisis in its history."

The vigorous public dialogue for which the commission acted as catalyst and focus continued unabated. In 1965–1966, the commission once again traveled across the country, holding formal public hearings on some 400 written briefs that had been submitted.

Final Report. The final multivolume report of the commission began to appear in December 1967. The first volume proposed measures to establish nationwide equality in language and education for English and French. Other volumes consider the principle of equal partnership in the federal public service, the armed forces, business and industry, education, the mass media, political and cultural institutions, the other ethnic groups, and the federal capital.

NEIL M. MORRISON, *Royal Commission on Bilingualism and Biculturalism*

2. Population

The 1971 census of Canada recorded a population of nearly 21.6 million. This represented an 8% increase since the 1966 census and an 18% increase since 1961. The ten-year figure compares with an increase of 30% during the period 1951–1961, revealing a substantial drop in the rate of growth of the Canadian population.

The slowing of population growth was due to a decline in the birthrate, which dropped steadily after 1961. In that year the birthrate was 26.1 per 1,000 of the population. By 1968, it had declined to 17.6, a rate as low as any recorded during the Depression years of the 1930's. Annual immigration totals fluctuated widely from year to year during the 1950's and 1960's but seldom exceeded 200,000. Natural increase (the excess of births over deaths) accounted for at least 85% of the population gain in both decades.

POPULATION OF CANADA (1966–1971)

Province	1966	1971	Percentage increase
Newfoundland	493,396	522,104	5.8
Prince Edward Island	108,535	111,641	2.9
Nova Scotia	756,039	788,960	4.4
New Brunswick	616,788	634,557	2.9
Quebec	5,780,845	6,027,764	4.3
Ontario	6,960,870	7,703,106	10.7
Manitoba	963,066	988,247	2.6
Saskatchewan	955,344	926,242	—3.0
Alberta	1,463,203	1,627,874	11.3
British Columbia	1,873,674	2,184,621	16.6
Yukon	14,382	18,388	27.9
Northwest Territories	28,738	34,807	21.1
Total, Canada	20,014,880	21,568,311	7.8

Historical Factors in Growth Rates. In response to changing economic and political developments the population of Canada has grown at varying rates over the decades since the first post-Confederation census was taken in 1871. The 1871 census recorded a population of 3,689,000. In the last 30 years of the 19th century, population growth in Canada was on a modest scale—a little over 1% per year over this period. By contrast, the decade 1901–1911 was one of record population growth. During this decade, which

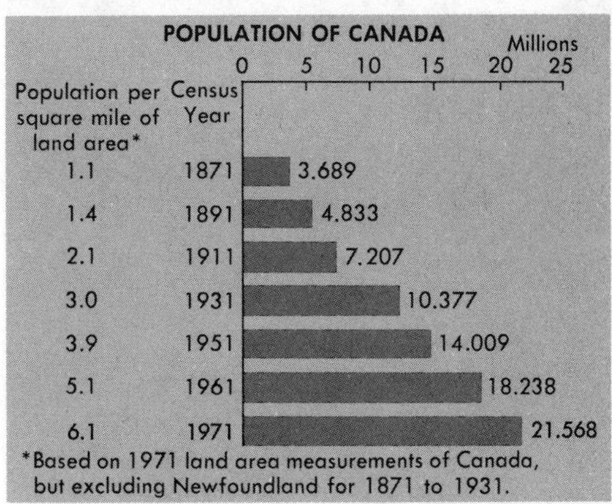

witnessed the opening of the Prairie region to agricultural settlement, well over 1.5 million immigrants arrived in Canada. The population, which had reached a figure of 5,371,000 by the date of the 1901 census, rose to 7,207,000 by 1911, despite the apparent substantial emigration of this period, due in part to losses of population to the United States. The heavy annual movements of immigrants to this country reached a maximum in 1913 when just over 400,000 entered Canada, far exceeding the record post-World War II flow of 282,000 in 1957. Hence, although immigration declined sharply during the World War I period (1914–1918), aggregate inflow to Canada in the 1911–1921 decennial period again exceeded 1.5 million persons.

Births, Deaths, Migration. Statistics of births and deaths have been collected in Canada on a national basis since 1921. It has thus been possible since that year to arrive at an approximate estimate of the relative contribution of natural increase and net migration to population growth. There are no official statistics of emigration from Canada. But data on immigration from Canada to the United States, the United Kingdom, and to certain other countries have made it possible to obtain a rough estimate of total emigration on an annual basis since World War II. Earlier estimates of emigration have indicated that dur-

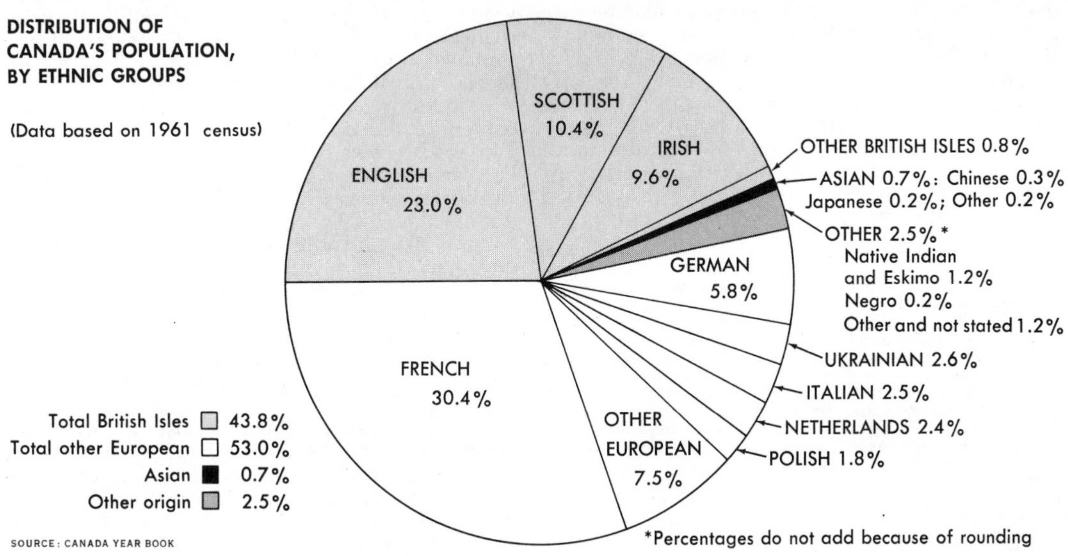

ANNAN PHOTO FEATURES

ARTS may reflect the people's life. An artist in a Quebec village paints a wooden figure of a fisherman.

ing most of the decades of the 20th century, emigration has been on a substantial scale, so the contribution of net migration to the total population growth between most censuses has not been a significant factor. Thus, although about 1.2 million immigrants arrived in Canada between the 1921 and 1931 censuses, net immigration appears to have been only about 230,000. However, due to a rather high rate of natural increase the population of Canada rose to 10.4 million by 1931 or by somewhat more than 1.5 million over this 10-year period. Thus in the first 30 years of the 20th century, Canada's population almost doubled.

Depression Years. The depression years of the 1930's were characterized by a marked falling off in population growth. The gradual decline in the birthrate of the previous decade was accelerated over the 1931–1941 period, when for the first time since vital statistics were compiled the crude rate fell to about 20 per 1,000 of the population. Widespread unemployment was associated with a substantial reduction in marriages which, of course, contributed to the drop in the annual number of births. Perhaps most dramatic was the fall in immigration which, amounting to a little more than 150,000 over this decade, was only about one tenth of the volume of immigration to Canada in the decennial period 1921–1931. As a result of the combined effect of these factors population growth in Canada during the 1931–1941 period was only a little more than a million, bringing the total to 11.5 million in 1941.

After World War II. Although there was little recovery in immigration in the first half of the 1940's, since this was the period of World War II, the second half of this decade saw a resumption of immigration on an expanded scale. In addition, the annual number of births rose steadily during this period following the record registration of marriages in 1946 with the return of large numbers of armed forces personnel to Canada after World War II. Finally, the entry of Newfoundland to the Canadian Confederation on April 1, 1949, accounted for roughly 360,000 of the total population in Canada at the 1951 census.

By this date the population had risen to 14 million or by 2.5 million over the 1941–1951 period. In the decade following the 1951 census, large-scale resource developments were accompanied by a rapid growth in population to 18.2 million in 1961. In absolute terms, the 4.2 million increase was the largest ever recorded in Canada during a ten-year period. In the decade 1961–1971, the population increased to 21.6 million, a gain of 3.3 million—nearly a million less than the gain of the preceding ten years.

Provincial Growth Rates. Over the postwar period fastest growth rates have occurred in the provinces of British Columbia, Ontario, Alberta and Quebec. Although birthrates in Canada are at their lowest in British Columbia and Ontario these two provinces have experienced substantial additions to natural increase as a result of immigration. In the case of British Columbia net migration accounted for over half of its population increase in the period 1951–1961, and the principal type of migration in respect to this province was internal migration, that is, net gains in population at the expense of other provinces of the nation.

On the other hand, although 40% of Ontario's population increase over this period was due to migration, 80% of this represented net immigration and only 20% net gain from other provinces. With the discovery of large resources of oil in Alberta just after World War II, population growth in this province became rapid, with an increase in 1951–1961 of 40%—the greatest of any province—and a 1961–1971 gain of 20%, a rate second only to that of British Columbia (30%).

Modest growth rates in this period were recorded in the other prairie provinces, Manitoba and Saskatchewan, though the latter, in particular, experienced an appreciable net loss of people to other provinces. Quebec's population growth during the 1950's and 1960's was appreciable (about 30% and 15% respectively). Natural increase in this province was greater than that in Ontario, though net immigration was much less.

Among the Atlantic provinces only Newfoundland, with a rather high birthrate, recorded a marked population growth, increasing by 25% in the 1950's and 14% in the 1960's. The Maritime provinces of Prince Edward Island, Nova Scotia, and New Brunswick, though registering increases during both decades, actually experienced, as in the past, considerable net losses of population to other provinces. In other words, they have continued to lose part of their natural increase to other provinces as well as to the United States.

The official source of information on Canada's population is the census. At each 10-year period since 1871, a comprehensive census of the population and agricultural data has been taken. The decennial censuses of population cover such demographic topics as sex, age, marital status, birthplace, language, ethnic origin, education, and religion, as well as inquiries on occupation, employment, and earnings. In 1956 and in 1966 a census of Canada's population was taken, restricted to such basic subjects as sex, age, marital status, and place of residence. A quinquennial census of the Prairie provinces was taken from 1906 to 1946 at each 5-year date following the decennial census.

Rural-Urban Distribution. One of the most striking demographic phenomena throughout the world, in developing countries as well as in more highly industrialized countries, has been the migration of people from rural to urban areas. Canada has been no exception. It is impossible to measure the full magnitude of this movement from census to census over the present century owing to changes in the definition of urban population since 1951.

Previous to the 1951 census the urban population of Canada was defined as the population residing in incorporated cities, towns, and villages. With the rapid expansion of industry in urban centers since World War II much of the growth of population has taken place in built-up areas surrounding the incorporated city or town boundaries. For this reason the definition of "urban" was changed at the 1951 census in order to include such urbanized areas as part of the urban aggregate of each province. However, for purposes of long-term trend comparisons the population of Canada in 1951 and also in 1961 was compiled on the basis of the earlier definition of rural and urban. On the former definitional basis the division of the Canadian population into rural and urban, which at the 1901 census was 62% rural and 38% urban, had by 1961 completely reversed itself, with 38% rural and 62% urban.

Urban Centers. On the basis of the census definition of urban population, which comprises, in the main, the population in cities, towns and villages of 1,000 and over, including the urbanized areas outside incorporated cities and towns of 10,000 and over, the 1961 census revealed that about 70% of Canada's population was living in urban communities on June 1, 1961. The rural population lost much of its natural increase in the 1950's to urban centers, as is evident from the negligible population growth of about 1% in the 10 years from 1951 to 1961. The urban population held most of its natural increase and gained substantially from internal migration and postwar immigration. All this was reflected in a spectacular 47% growth in this period.

It is, therefore, to be expected that the more rapidly growing provinces since World War II in terms of population would also be the most urbanized. Almost four fifths of Ontario's population in 1961 was urban, with Quebec and British Columbia next with three fourths living in urban centers. The slower growing agricultural provinces of Prince Edward Island and Saskatchewan had one third and just over two fifths, respectively, residing in urban areas in 1961.

Metropolitan Areas. About two thirds of Canada's urban population reside in the large metropolitan areas. The slightly more than 8 million residents of metropolitan areas in 1961 constituted 45% of the total population. The fastest growing metropolitan areas from 1951 to 1961 were Calgary and Edmonton in Alberta, both of which almost doubled in population in this decade. Population increase over this decade in the 17 census metropolitan areas of Canada was 2.5 million, or 60%, of the total population increase in Canada between 1951 and 1961.

Farm Population. Despite increases in the volume of farm production the farm population declined steadily from a figure of 3.2 million in 1931 to just over 2 million in 1961. The rural-farm population in Canada in the late 1960's was only about 10% of the total population, compared with a little more than 30% in 1931.

J. SPROAT, FROM NATIONAL FILM BOARD

ESKIMO enjoy some refinements of modern living. A group moves an igloo made of plastic to a new site.

Age Distribution. In the 1961 census, one third of the population of Canada, or about 6 million, were children under 15 years of age. This segment of the "child" population would all be considered as part of the dependent population, since they were under working age. Since more young persons were remaining longer in school, an appreciable proportion of those from 15 to 19 years old could also properly be included in the dependent child population. Between the 1931 and 1961 censuses the proportion of young persons from 15 to 19 years attending school rose from one third to almost three fifths.

Approximately one half of Canada's population in 1961 was between 20 and 64 years of age. This proportion has remained almost stable during the first half of the 1960's. This broad age period covers the bulk of the population at working ages. A little more than 7% comprised the population at retirement ages—65 years and older. The percentage of older persons in the Canadian population has risen since the turn of the century, when it was 5%. The percentage of dependent children under 15 years, which had declined between 1901 and 1941, rose steadily between 1941 and 1961. Thus the proportion of the total population who were in the working age-group of 20 to 64 had fallen off in this period. Although there were some decline in the percentage of males 20 to 64 in the labor force, the opposite occurred with respect to the female population in this age group. The rising proportion of women in the labor force has been associated with the spectacular increase in the number of married working outside the home. Between the close of World War II and 1961 the number of married women in the labor force increased roughly three times, and in the mid-1960's it approached the 1.2 million mark.

Child Population Changes. The long-term effects of past wars, periods of high employment with attendant large-scale immigration, and the great depression of the 1930's upon the age structure of the Canadian population have been significant. For example, the sharp decline in births during the 1930's, when there was also a drastic reduction in family immigration, resulted in an actual decrease in the number of children under 10 years of age in Canada at the 1941 census as compared with that of 1931. This abnormally small number of children born in the 1930's resulted in an unexpected lower number of children entering high schools or the labor force during the 1940's or becoming of marriage age in the 1950's. By contrast, the sharp rise in the birthrate immediately following World War II, together with the substantial immigration of this period, brought about a heavy enrollment of children in primary and, later, in secondary schools during the 1950's and early 1960's. As many of this postwar generation reach marriage age, an increase in family formation may be expected and some recovery from the steady decline in births during the first half of the 1960's, even if the fertility rates of married women by age group, which have been falling in recent years, show no observable tendency to recover.

Older Persons. Part of the increase in the proportion of older persons in the population, especially since 1931, has been due to the aging of persons who came to Canada during the period of heavy immigration up to World War I. Though there have also been improvements in life expectancy for persons, say, 40 years and older, especially among women, it is not clear what ultimate effects improvements in the treatment of diseases of middle and old age may have in prolonging life and thus in bringing about a further probable rise in the proportion of older persons in the Canadian population in the future years.

Marital Status. Two thirds of Canada's population in the late 1960's was of marriageable age, roughly 15 years and older. At the 1961 census about 8 million persons, or two thirds of the population over 15 years of age was married, just over one fourth was single, and 7% were widowed or divorced. Divorced persons accounted for less than 1% of the total population 15 years and older.

A striking characteristic of marital status changes in Canada since 1941 has been the trend to early marriage. This trend is evident in the census data on marital status by age. For example, comparative statistics from the census reveal that 39% of the female population 20–24 in 1941 was married, as compared with 59% in 1961. This period also was characterized by a marked rise in the birthrate from 22.4 per 1,000 of the population in 1941 to 28.0 in 1956, leveling off to 26.1 in 1961. Studies have indicated that the increase in the percentage of married women, and especially the rise in the marriage rate among women under 25 years of age, was a much more important factor in the upward movement in the birthrate in Canada over this period than higher fertility within marriage.

Changes in age structure will, of course, affect the marital status distribution of the population. To illustrate, a rapidly increasing proportion of older persons (over 60 years of age) in the population might be expected to produce a rise in the proportion of widowed persons. In Canada, the percentage of widowed in the population 15 years and older increased only slightly between 1941 and 1961 because, though the percentage of older persons in the population showed a rising tendency, the percentage of widowed in each age group tended to decline. The improvement in life expectancy was more marked among females than among males, thus reducing the risk of widowhood among married males to a greater degree than among married women. This factor, together with the considerably higher remarriage rate among widowers than among widows, largely accounts for the fact that the number of widows 65 years and older in Canada at the 1961 census was 340,000 as compared with only 134,000 widowers. This imbalance in the relative numbers of widows and widowers, which has been increasing in recent decades, is a factor of some significance to those concerned with the problems of aging among the Canadian population.

Birthplace and Ethnic Origin. Though more than 2 million immigrants entered Canada between the close of World War II and the 1961 census, native-born persons still constituted 85% of the total population in the 1961 census. The foreign-born population in 1961 was 2.8 million.

The considerable volume of immigration since World War II has resulted in marked increases in the numbers of foreign born from such countries as Italy, Germany, the Netherlands, and Hungary. In terms of absolute figures, immigrants from the United Kingdom constituted by far the largest group of postwar arrivals, but the increase in the number of persons born in the United Kingdom in the 1951–1961 period was only 10%, while for most of the countries mentioned there were three and four times as many in 1961 as in 1951. Over the 20-year period 1941–1961, the proportion of the total of foreign-born persons with a continental European birthplace rose from one third to just over one half. Over the same period the number of persons in Canada who were born in the United States had a 10% loss to 284,000 in 1961.

About three fourths of Canada's population are of British Isles or French ethnic origin. At the 1961 census the former accounted for just over two fifths, or 8 million, of the population and the French for 5.5 million, or about 30%. More than one fifth is of various other European origins, and the remainder is of native Indian and Eskimo and of Asian origin. The proportion of the population of British Isles ethnic background has declined from one half to two fifths in the period since World War II. The percentage of French origin has remained unchanged over this period. Among the other ethnic groups of European origin, the German group in 1961 slightly exceeded one million, with the Ukrainian, Italian, and Netherlands groups each approaching the half-million mark. For census purposes, ethnic origin is defined as the cultural group to which each person belongs as determined, in the main, by the language spoken, if born outside of Canada, or by the linguistic background on the father's side, if Canadian-born.

Assimilation of the various ethnic groups among the post-World War II immigrants may be expected to proceed more rapidly than in earlier periods of immigration, owing to the heavy concentration of immigrants of the 1946–1961 period in urban centers. Unlike the past, this immigration has been largely confined to large urban centers, close to 70% being residents of cities of 100,000 and more at the 1961 census.

Almost all persons of Jewish origin were resident in large urban communities, as were the Italian group with 95% and the Asian group with

90%. Ethnic groups having the highest percentage of their numbers in rural areas were the Netherlands with 45% and the Scandinavian with 40%.

Regional Distribution. The distinctive regional distribution of certain ethnic groups is worth noting. More than three fourths of the French group reside in the province of Quebec, and about half of the remainder live in the adjacent province of Ontario. The British Isles group is widely distributed in Canada, though close to one half are resident in Ontario. More than two fifths of the German ethnic group are found in the Prairie provinces, with a slightly smaller proportion in Ontario. The Italian group is highly concentrated in Ontario and Quebec. Four fifths of the Jewish group reside in Quebec and Ontario, mainly in Montreal and Toronto. More than two fifths of the Netherlands and Polish groups are located in Ontario, and a similar proportion are in the four western provinces. Close to two thirds of the Russian and three fourths of the Scandinavian ethnic groups reside in the four western provinces. Almost three fifths of the Ukrainian group are located in the Prairie provinces. Roughly one third of the Asian group reside in British Columbia and Ontario.

Language. The decennial census of Canada provides information on the extent to which one or both of the official languages, English and French, are spoken in various parts of the country. In addition, a census inquiry on the mother tongue of each person in the Canadian population supplements the question on official language. Mother tongue is defined as the first language learned in childhood and still understood at the time of the census. Mother tongue statistics suggest the cultural diversity of the population as measured by specific languages still understood besides English and French.

Official Languages. Of the two official languages, "English only" was spoken by 12.3 million, or by just over two thirds of the population of Canada, at the 1961 census, and "French only" by 3.5 million, or about one fifth of the population. Another 2.2 million persons, or 12%, were bilingual in the sense of speaking both official languages, while a little more than 1% spoke neither official language. The latter group was composed mainly of recent arrivals to Canada at the time of the 1961 census. A number of native Indians and Eskimos did not speak either of the official languages.

A high percentage of the French-speaking population is located in the province of Quebec, with relatively small percentages in eastern Ontario, New Brunswick, and other provinces. Most of the French-speaking persons outside Quebec province are of French ethnic origin. Partly because a high percentage of foreign-born persons in Canada reside in Ontario and the western provinces, more than 90% speak English and only about 10% speak French.

Bilingualism. Bilingualism, or ability to speak both official languages, has not made significant progress over the 100 years since Confederation. The percentage of the bilingual population has remained about 12% in recent censuses. About three fourths of the bilingual population are of French ethnic origin. About 80% of bilingual Canadians reside in urban centers.

Other Tongues. More than 10 million Canadians reported English as their mother tongue at the 1961 census, 5 million French, almost 2.5 million a variety of other tongues, of which German, Ukrainian, and Italian were the numerically largest linguistic groups. Only in the Prairie provinces was the proportion of the population reporting a mother tongue other than English or French significant. In these provinces this percentage ranged from 25 to 30%.

Rural segregation, low rates of intermarriage between the English and French ethnic groups, and the desire to retain native tongues are factors contributing to the persistence of various European mother tongues into second and later generations in Canada. For example, although over three fourths of the population of Ukrainian origin in 1961 were born in Canada, only one third reported English or French as their mother tongue. Similarly, 78% of the population of Japanese ethnic origin in 1961 were born in Canada, but only about two fifths reported English or French as their mother tongue.

Among the ethnic groups with over two thirds of their number reporting a mother tongue other than English or French in the 1961 census were the Chinese (83%), Italian (74%), native Indian and Eskimo (71%), and Finnish (68%). As previously stated, a substantial proportion of the Italian ethnic group had immigrated to Canada in the period 1951–1961.

Educational Level. The census provides comprehensive information on the level of educational attainment of the whole population and relates this information to other demographic characteristics such as sex, age, marital status, and ethnic group, by provinces, rural and urban. In the 1961 census, for the first time, an inquiry on actual grade of schooling completed for both the adult population and for children at school was included in the population document. Despite the difficulties inherent in an inquiry of this sort applied to a population educated under different school systems in Canada and abroad, it was felt that a broad classification of educational attainment—elementary, secondary, college, and university—would offer a useful measure of the educational status of the population.

Less than 2% of the population 15 years and older not at school reported no formal schooling. A considerable number of those with no schooling were elderly persons. Among the native Indian and Eskimo populations the percentage with no schooling was higher than elsewhere.

About 45% of the population 15 years and older not at school had received an elementary education; 47%, secondary; 6%, university education. Among the provinces, the percentage with only elementary education was highest in Newfoundland, at roughly one half, and lowest was in the province of British Columbia, at slightly more than 30%. By contrast, the highest percentage (58%) with secondary education occurred in British Columbia and the lowest in Newfoundland, New Brunswick, and Quebec. Secondary education was more common in urban than rural areas. The lengthening of school life was indicated in the fact that in 1961, 60% of the population from 15 to 24 years old not at school had received a secondary education, as compared with only 40% among those from 45 to 60.

The 1960's saw a dramatic reduction of student-teacher ratios in Canadian schools, promising gains in the quality of education. This was due to an increase in the total number of teachers from 175,000 in 1961 to over 300,000 in 1971.

ALLEN H. LENEVEU
Dominion Bureau of Statistics

CANADA: The Land

3. Area and Boundaries

Canada's area is 3,851,809 square miles (9,976,197 sq km). It is the largest country in the Western Hemisphere, exceeded in the world by only the USSR. Of this area, 3,560,238 square miles (9,221,027 sq km) is land, and 291,571 square miles (755,169 sq km) is fresh water.

Canada extends over more than 40 degrees of latitude and over nearly 90 degrees of longitude. From the southernmost to the northernmost point is nearly 3,000 miles (4,800 km). The greatest distance from east to west is about 3,500 miles (5,600 km).

Canada covers all the northern part of the mainland of the North American continent except Alaska, a state of the United States, and includes the islands to the north apart from Greenland, which is part of Denmark. St. Pierre and Miquelon, two small islands in Cabot Strait south of Newfoundland, are French.

The boundary between Canada and Alaska runs south from the Arctic Coast near Demarcation Point along the 141° W meridian to a point about 20 miles (32 km) from the Pacific Ocean on the western shoulder of Mt. St. Elias. From there it runs to the peak of the mountain and then roughly parallel to the coast toward the southeast along an irregular line between 20 and 30 miles (32–48 km) inland, as far as the head of Portland Canal, which it follows to Pearse Canal and on to the Pacific Ocean. The offshore islands from latitude 54°40′ N to the Strait of Juan de Fuca are Canadian.

The southern boundary of Canada passes through Juan de Fuca Strait, Haro Strait, and the Strait of Georgia to latitude 49° N, which it follows eastward across the Cordillera and the prairies to a point in Lake of the Woods. Here it turns due north for about 25 miles (40 km) along the 95°09′ W meridian to the northwesterly point of the lake and then runs irregularly through the lake to the mouth of the Rainy River. It follows the course of the river and then crosses the watershed by a chain of lakes to the Pigeon River, which flows into Lake Superior.

In Lake Superior the boundary passes north of Isle Royale. In St. Mary's River, between Lake Superior and Lake Huron, it passes north of Sugar Island, south of St. Joseph Island, north of Drummond Island, and south of Cockburn Island, to continue across Lake Huron and along the St. Clair River and the Detroit River. In Lake Erie it passes south of Pelee Island and Middle Island, the southernmost part of Canada, and then through the lake, along the Niagara River and through Lake Ontario to the St. Lawrence River.

Passing south of Wolfe Island and through the Thousand Islands, the boundary follows the St. Lawrence to latitude 45° N, which it follows east to the 71°30′ W meridian southeast of Sherbrooke. From here it runs approximately northeasterly as far as the southern end of Lake Pohengamook. It then follows the course of the St. Francis River and the upper St. John River to longitude 57°48′ W near Grand Falls, where it turns due south to the source of St. Croix River, which it follows to Back Bay, part of Passamaquoddy Bay, in the Bay of Fundy. The boundary then passes between the state of Maine and Deer Island, Campobello Island, and Grand Manan Island to the limits of territorial waters.

The eastern boundary of Canada is formed by the Atlantic Ocean and the Labrador Sea and by Davis Strait, Baffin Bay, Smith Sound, Kane Basin, Kennedy Channel, Hall Basin, and Robeson Channel, which separate Canada from Greenland.

GRAHAM W. ROWLEY
Canadian Department of Indian Affairs and Northern Development

4. Physiography

There are five main natural regions in Canada, determined by the surface bedrock and the ways in which the earth's crust has been folded and eroded through the ages. Overlying these rocks and commonly modifying the local physiography are sedimentary deposits formed during the Pleistocene age, when ice sheets covered nearly the whole of Canada at one time or another. The action of the ice itself also changed the physiography, both by erosion and by altering drainage patterns.

The tree line, dividing the Arctic tundra from the subarctic taiga (swampy coniferous forest), runs across the natural regions from the Mackenzie Delta southeast to Churchill and then around southern Hudson Bay to Richmond Gulf whence it crosses the Labrador Peninsula to the Chimo area and on to the Atlantic Coast near Hebron.

Roughly parallel to the tree line and 200 to 600 miles (320–967 km) to the south is the southern limit of permafrost. North of this line the ground remains frozen throughout the year with only the top few inches thawing each summer. This causes poor surface drainage and soil movements, resulting in the development of

BOW RIVER VALLEY NEAR BANFF, ALBERTA (CANADIAN PACIFIC PHOTO)

characteristic stripes and polygons in the ground.

The five main natural regions are the Canadian Shield, the Interior Plains and Lowlands, the Appalachian Region, the Cordillera, and the Innuitian Region. Paralleling the coast line is the Continental Shelf.

Canadian Shield. The Canadian Shield is much the largest of the natural regions and covers about half the total area of Canada. It forms an incomplete ring around Hudson Bay and consists of Precambrian sedimentary and volcanic rocks, commonly altered to gneisses and granitic rocks, and numerous intrusions of igneous rocks. Originally the site of high mountain ranges, the Shield has been worn down and now forms an area of comparatively low, rounded hills and valleys, with numerous lakes and rivers and with many eskers and drumlins radiating from old centers of glaciation. There is a striking uniformity in the topography of great areas of the Shield, and the scenery of much of the Northwest Territories would be practically indistinguishable from that of northern Ontario and Quebec except for the different vegetation.

Heights are usually between 600 and 1,200 feet (180–360 meters) above sea level, but in some places, such as the Haliburton Highlands in Ontario, and Quebec's Laurentian Mountains where Mt. Tremblant rises to 3,150 feet (1,260 meters), the relief is greater. The greatest heights, however, occur along the eastern margin, where the Shield is tilted up to the east, especially in Baffin Island and Labrador. Here, a typical fjord coast provides spectacular scenery with mountains 7,000 feet (2,100 meters) high, sheer cliffs, and numerous glaciers and ice caps.

Interior Plains and Lowlands. The Interior Plains and Lowlands consist of sedimentary rocks of Cambrian and later ages which overlie the Shield and once covered much more of it but have since been eroded away. Today, they lie mainly on the sides of the Shield and in basins within it, where they result in a featureless horizontal topography in striking contrast to the adjacent Shield and to the Cordillera to the west.

The Great Plains form the largest area and can be divided into the first prairie level, or Manitoba Plain, 600 to 900 feet (180–275 meters) above sea level; the second prairie level, in western Manitoba and eastern Saskatchewan, at about 2,000 feet (600 meters); the High Plains of western Saskatchewan and Alberta, up to 4,300 feet (1,300 meters); and the Mackenzie lowlands to the north, with elevations from a few hundred to 4,000 feet (1,200 meters). The Shield slopes down gradually to the west under the Great Plains at about 15 feet per mile (2.9 meters per kilometer) so that in the west the overlying strata reach a thickness of some 10,000 feet (3,000 meters). The boundary between the Shield and the Great Plains is marked by a number of large lakes, including Great Bear Lake, Great Slave Lake, Lake Athabasca, Lake Winnipeg, and Lake Huron.

North of the Shield are the Arctic lowlands, which in the east are better described as plateaus, since they occur at heights up to 4,000 feet (1,200 meters) or more and are deeply incised by river valleys and gullies.

The Hudson Bay lowlands, along the southwest shore of Hudson Bay, are very similar to the Foxe Basin lowlands farther north and some of the islands in Hudson Bay. All of this area has recently emerged from the sea because the land, relieved of a heavy load by the melting of the last ice sheet, has risen as much as 600 feet (180 meters). The sea has left numbers of raised beaches, now often far inland.

The St. Lawrence lowlands, to the south of the Shield, cover southern Ontario and form a narrow belt that extends east into Quebec on both sides of the St. Lawrence River, with Anticosti Island as an outlier.

Grenville Channel near Prince Rupert, B. C.

BOB AND IRA SPRING

I. DONALD BOWDEN

Hopewell Caves Rocks, New Brunswick.

THE FACE OF THE LAND

Canada's physiographic regions (*map below*) display characteristic features that have been shaped by geological forces. Climatic conditions have played a part in creating a landscape of infinite variety over the vast country that borders on three oceans.

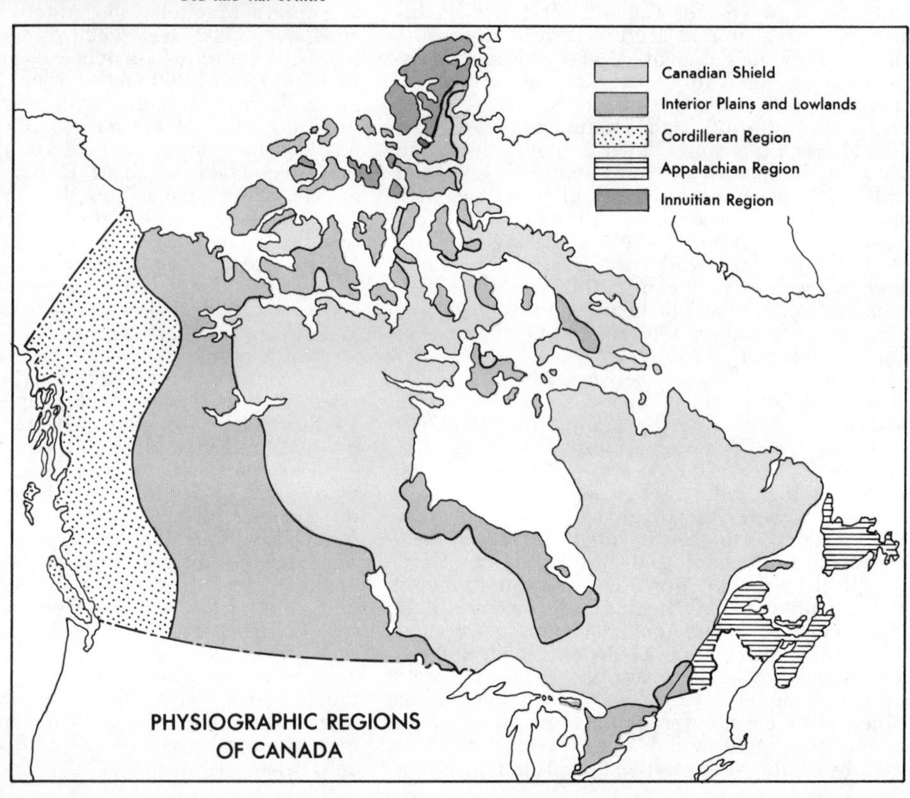

GEORGE HUNTER, FROM NATIONAL FILM BOARD

Farmland in the plains near Moose Jaw, Saskatchewan.

H. TAYLOR, FROM NATIONAL FILM BOARD

(*Above*) Ellef Ringnes Island in the Arctic. (*Right*) The broad delta of the Mackenzie River near Inuvik, Northwest Territories.

GAR LUNNEY FROM NATIONAL FILM BOARD

The Rocky Mountains in British Columbia.

JACK LONG, FROM NATIONAL FILM BOARD

Appalachian Region. The Appalachian Region extends over the whole of Nova Scotia, New Brunswick, Prince Edward Island, and the island of Newfoundland, and into Quebec, where it covers Gaspé and the eastern part of the Eastern Townships. It is the northern end of a long belt of old mountains running northeasterly along most of the Atlantic seaboard of North America. The rocks are mainly sediments and volcanics of Paleozoic age, but some are Proterozoic and some Triassic. They were laid down in a great geosyncline (a downward bend of the earth crust). Although extensively folded and faulted, the mountains have been worn down.

The greatest heights that remain in the Canadian Appalachians are in Gaspé, where Mt. Jacques Cartier reaches 4,160 feet (1,267 meters), and in the Eastern Townships in southeastern Quebec, where there are peaks that rival Mt. Tremblant in the Shield north of Montreal.

Cordillera. The Cordilleran Region lies west of the Great Plains and extends to the Pacific Ocean and into Alaska. It consists of high mountain ranges, running roughly parallel to the coast with many valleys and plateaus, and forms three fairly distinct zones, known as the Western, the Interior, and the Eastern systems.

The high, rugged Coast Mountains of British Columbia and the St. Elias Mountains in the Yukon Territory, which include Mt. Logan (19,850 feet, or 6,050 meters), the highest mountain in Canada, are the major features of the Western System. The Interior System is a complex of plateaus and mountain ranges that widens in the north to form most of the Yukon Territory. The Eastern System consists, in the north, of mountain ranges along the Arctic coast of the Yukon Territory and to the west of the lower Mackenzie River, and the Franklin Mountains that lie to the east of the river. Farther south, and separated from the northern ranges by a plateau and plain through which the Liard River flows, and from the Interior System by the Rocky Mountain Trench, are the Rocky Mountains and the Foothills.

The sedimentary rocks of the Cordillera were laid down in a geosyncline from the late Precambrian era to the Cretaceous period. The Interior System includes large areas of folded sedimentary and volcanic strata locally intruded by massive igneous rocks. Some of the volcanic rocks are flat-lying and are only a few hundred years old. Massive intrusive rocks form much of the Western System, particularly the Coast Range, and elsewhere the rocks are similar to those of the Interior System. The mountains of the Western and Interior Systems were formed by folding in the early Mesozoic era. They were largely worn down before the Tertiary period, when they were uplifted, and the younger mountains of the Eastern System were formed by folding. The Western and Interior Systems are characterized by the old erosion surface. The Eastern System is composed almost entirely of folded sedimentary rocks.

Innuitian Regions. The Innuitian Region, the least known of the regions, forms a band trending to the northeast across the Queen Elizabeth Islands in the Arctic Archipelago. It consists of sedimentary, volcanic, and metamorphic rocks dating from the Proterozoic era to the Tertiary period and folded at various times and in different directions.

The whole region is hilly or mountainous, with the highest land in the north. In Axel Heiberg Island and northern Ellesmere Island there are mountains nearly 8,000 feet (2,400 meters) high, and large areas are covered with ice caps and glaciers.

The remains of an ice shelf lie along the northern coast of Ellesmere Island. It appears to have been more extensive, but pieces have broken off to form ice islands which may drift in the polar pack ice for several years before breaking up in the channels of the Archipelago or being carried to the south to melt in the North Atlantic Ocean.

Continental Shelf. Along the Atlantic coast of Canada, the Continental Shelf is broad with many shoals and banks, especially in the area of the Grand Banks of Newfoundland, where its edge is up to 300 miles (480 km) from the coast. North of Newfoundland the Shelf narrows, and depths of nearly 3,000 feet (900 meters) have been charted within Hudson Strait, although Hudson Bay and Foxe Basin are shallow and are included within the Shelf. On the east coast of Baffin Island the Shelf is only about 10 miles (16 km) wide and is broken by troughs cut by glaciers in the ocean bed, bringing deep water often close inshore. East of Cumberland Peninsula a ridge on the ocean floor runs across Davis Strait to Greenland and separates the Baffin Basin from the Atlantic, although it does not form part of the Shelf. Farther north, however, in Kane Basin the Shelf merges with that around Greenland.

In the Arctic Ocean, the Continental Shelf is wide but irregular. Its edge lies generally about 70 miles (112 km) from the perimeter of the Arctic Archipelago, and it is rather narrower in the north than off Banks Island and adjacent to the mainland coast, where it is almost 100 miles (160 km) wide. Deep channels run into Amundsen Gulf, M'Clure Strait, and some of the passages between the Queen Elizabeth Islands.

In the Pacific, the edge of the Continental Shelf is 50 to 100 miles (80 to 160 km) from the mainland coast of Canada, but it approaches to within a few miles of Vancouver Island and to only a mile from the shore of the Queen Charlotte Islands.

GRAHAM W. ROWLEY, *Canadian Department of Indian Affairs and Northern Development*

5. River Systems

Canada is rich in rivers and lakes with nearly 300,000 square miles (780,000 sq km) of fresh water, representing 7.6% of the total area of the country. The waterways were the routes by which the canoes of the explorers penetrated the interior, and they played a vital role in the fur trade and the opening of the country to settlers.

There are four great drainage basins. Their rivers flow into Hudson Bay and into the Arctic, Atlantic, and Pacific oceans. In addition, a small area of some 12,365 square miles (32,249 sq km) in the extreme south of Alberta and Saskatchewan drains by the Mississippi River system into the Gulf of Mexico.

Hudson Bay Drainage Basin. Many large rivers flow into the Hudson Bay drainage basin, which includes the area draining into Hudson Strait, Foxe Basin, James Bay, and Ungava Bay, making this the largest of the basins (1,421,350 square miles or 3,695,510 sq km). The Nelson, its largest river, drains Lake Winnipeg which itself

CANADA

Comprising ten provinces and two northern territories, Canada is the largest country in the Western Hemisphere and the second largest (after the Soviet Union) in the world. Its territory covers more than 3.8 million square miles, and extends from the Atlantic Ocean to the Pacific, and from the frozen reaches of the Arctic Ocean to the Great Lakes. Although Canadians have become an increasingly industrial, urban people, much of the land remains rural and unsettled. Some of the variety of this vast country is suggested in the photographs that follow.

Coat of Arms of Canada

The federal Parliament buildings in Ottawa, Ontario, overlooking the Ottawa River.

ANNAN PHOTO FEATURES

LAURENCE LOWRY, FROM RAPHO GUILLUMETTE

Ste. Marthe de Gaspé, a farming community, lies in a gentle valley on the north shore of the Gaspé Peninsula.

PLATES 2 AND 3

THE EAST COAST— THE APPALACHIAN AND ACADIAN REGIONS

Canada's east coast opens upon the Atlantic Ocean and the Gulf of St. Lawrence. Here are situated the largest of the provinces (Quebec), the youngest (Newfoundland), and the smallest (Prince Edward Island). The Appalachian and Acadian land formations are very old. Their weathered surfaces—rugged in some places, gentle in others—are in harmony with the character of the hardy, vigorous people who inhabit these picturesque shores.

AVERY SLACK, FROM SHOSTAL

A Nova Scotia fisherman stands beside barrels used in salting fish. Most of Nova Scotia's fresh fish catch is frozen and processed into fish sticks.

ANNAN PHOTO FEATURES

Shediac Beach is one of several popular beaches along New Brunswick's east coast.

Sandy Cove, a village on Digby Neck, lies between the Bay of Fundy and St. Mary's Bay on the western coast of Nova Scotia.

ANNAN PHOTO FEATURES

(Below) The lighthouse on Wood Island, off Prince Edward Island's southeastern coast, with piles of lobster traps in the foreground. *(Right)* St. John's, the capital and business center of Newfoundland, is an important Atlantic port.

CHARLES R. BELINKY, FROM PHOTO RESEARCHERS

DE VISSER, FROM CANADIAN GOVERNMENT TRAVEL BUREAU

Percé Rock forms a cliff 288 feet high off the village of Percé on the Gaspé Peninsula's eastern shore.

NATIONAL FILM BOARD OF CANADA

ANNAN PHOTO FEATURES

GIANNI TORTOLI, FROM PHOTO RESEARCHERS

(Above) A ceremonial changing of the guard outside the Parliament buildings in Ottawa makes a colorful spectacle.

PLATES 4 AND 5

THE ST. LAWRENCE AND GREAT LAKES REGION

The most populous provinces, Ontario and Quebec, together form the commercial and industrial heart of Canada. Since the arrival of the first settlers, the St. Lawrence River and the Great Lakes have played a major role in their development. Along these waterways, the great cities of Quebec, Montreal, and Toronto do business with the world, while the surrounding countryside provides some of Canada's best recreational areas and much of its wealth of natural resources.

(Left) Ships making passage between Lake Ontario and Lake Erie on the St. Lawrence Seaway pass through triple locks in the Welland Ship Canal at Thorold, Ontario. *(Below)* The lights of downtown Montreal illuminate the night sky.

ANNAN PHOTO FEATURES

The turrets and steep gabled roofs of the Château Frontenac, one of the most famous luxury hotels in Canada, overlook the St. Lawrence River at Quebec.

MICHEL SERRAILLIER, FROM RAPHO GUILLUMETTE

ANNAN PHOTO FEATURES

ACE WILLIAMS, FROM SHOSTAL

(Above) Toronto's modern City Hall complex occupies a 12-acre square. *(Left)* Mount Tremblant provides a background for winter sports in the Laurentian Mountains of Quebec.

A mill near Port Arthur processes wood pulp into paper, one of Ontario's leading commodities.

ANNAN PHOTO FEATURES

Vast grain fields stretch out behind a row of wheat elevators at Kronau, near Regina, Saskatchewan.

PLATES 6 AND 7

THE PRAIRIES

The fertile farms and broad, flat grazing lands of Manitoba, Saskatchewan, and Alberta provide Canada with much of its meat and grain. But increasingly important to the economy and way of life of the Prairie Provinces is mining, both for metals and for fuels. One of the world's largest petroleum reserves has been found in the Athabasca tar sands of northeastern Alberta.

One of the six bridges that cross the Saskatchewan River at Saskatoon, a transportation hub in the Prairie Provinces.
OTTO DONE, FROM SHOSTAL

An oil drilling rig near Calgary is reflected in a pool of crude petroleum. Since oil was discovered in the area in the 1930's, Alberta has become a major producer.

NATIONAL FILM BOARD OF CANADA

GEORGE HUNTER, FROM SHOSTAL

(Right) **The chapel of St. Paul's College, University of Manitoba, Winnipeg. Lionel Thomas designed the building.**

ANNAN PHOTO FEATURES

ANNAN PHOTO FEATURES

Urban and rural Canada meet in Regina, Saskatchewan. Part of Regina's business district may be seen beyond Wascana Lake.

The McIntyre ranch near Cardston, Alberta, is the second largest in Canada. Covering some 64,000 acres, the ranch maintains about 3,000 head of beef cattle.

KRYN TACONIS

PLATES 8 AND 9

THE WEST—

FROM THE ROCKIES TO THE PACIFIC

The Pacific Ocean and the great North American mountain ranges influence Canada in the west. Dozens of provincial and national parks in Alberta and British Columbia preserve the spectacular beauty of the Coast and Rocky Mountains. Inland, the alternating mountain slopes and plateaus contain enormous forest, water, and mineral reserves, while the deeply indented coastline provides both shelter for navigation and a base for the fishing fleet.

A canoe crosses the waters of Moraine Lake in the Valley of the Ten Peaks, part of spectacular Banff National Park in Alberta.

BOB AND IRA SPRING

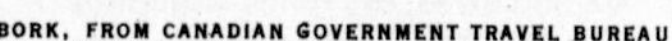
BORK, FROM CANADIAN GOVERNMENT TRAVEL BUREAU

Waterton Park is the headquarters for Waterton Lakes National Park in southwestern Alberta. Mount Crandell rises over Upper Waterton Lake.

SHOSTAL

Vancouver, largest city of British Columbia, lies between the Pacific Ocean and the Coast Mountains.

SHOSTAL

BOB AND IRA SPRING

Forestry and fishing are major sources of British Columbia's wealth. *(Above)* Fishing boats crowd the docks at Prince Rupert. *(Upper left)* A logger participates in a spring logging drive. *(Left)* Salmon in the Adams River are tagged for identification.

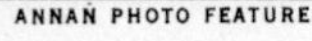

ANNAN PHOTO FEATURES

Rich farmlands lie between the mountain ranges that run from north to south through most of British Columbia.

SHOSTAL

J. L. STAGE, FROM PHOTO RESEARCHERS

SHOSTAL

(Above) An Eskimo family sets up its summer quarters on Baffin Island. *(Top right)* An Eskimo woman of Ungava Peninsula on Hudson Bay scrapes sealskin.

PLATES 10 AND 11

THE ARCTIC AND SUBARCTIC NORTH

Canada's sparsely populated northland embraces the arctic and subarctic regions of the Yukon Territory, the Northwest Territories, Quebec, and Labrador. Much of the land is barren and icelocked, forcing a nomadic hunter's existence on its native Eskimo inhabitants. Late in the 19th century, gold was discovered in the Yukon Territory, and for a short time Dawson and the surrounding area flourished. More recently new mineral deposits have been found in the north, and the territories have begun to play a greater role in Canadian economy.

ANNAN PHOTO FEATURES

On Spence Bay in the Northwest Territories, an Eskimo loads himself and his dog with supplies for a hunting trip.

Dawson, in the Yukon Territory, lies at the junction of Yukon and Klondike rivers.

BOB AND IRA SPRING

BOB AND IRA SPRING

(Above) A canoe rests on glaciated rock on the shore of Great Slave Lake at Rae, a mission and trading post in the Northwest Territories.

ANNAN PHOTO FEATURES

(Above) An outpost on Spence Bay, Northwest Territories, is silhouetted by the light of the midnight sun. *(Right)* Glaciated outcroppings form islands in an ice-covered inlet of Boothia Peninsula, above the Arctic Circle in the Northwest Territories.

GEORGE HUNTER, FROM SHOSTAL

BOB AND IRA SPRING

(Above) A huge old wooden dredge, one of the few remaining, operates near Dawson, center of the Klondike gold-mining area in the Yukon Territory.

(Below) A tour boat carries vacationers through the turbulent rapids of Miles Canyon on the Yukon River, near Whitehorse. Whitehorse is a transportation center and the Yukon Territory capital.

BOB AND IRA SPRING

GRANT COLLINGWOOD, FROM DE WYS

Provincial shields decorate the House of Commons door in Ottawa.

PLATE 12

SHIELDS OF THE PROVINCES AND TERRITORIES OF CANADA

ALBERTA

BRITISH COLUMBIA

MANITOBA

NEW BRUNSWICK

NEWFOUNDLAND

NOVA SCOTIA

NORTHWEST TERRITORIES

YUKON TERRITORIES

ONTARIO

PRINCE EDWARD ISLAND

QUEBEC

SASKATCHEWAN

FLAGS OF CANADIAN HISTORY

VIKINGS

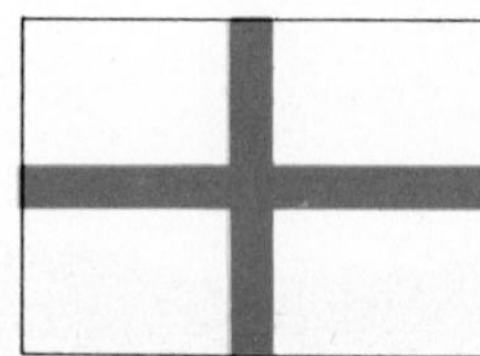
ST. GEORGE'S CROSS

FRANCE (FROM 1534)

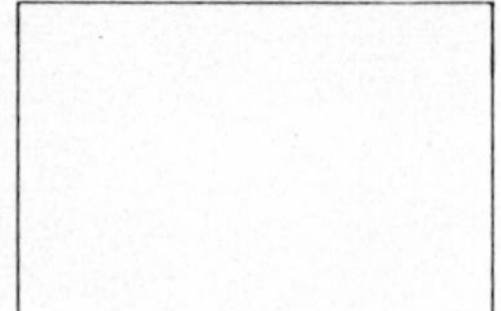
FRANCE (UNTIL 1763)

ST. ANDREW'S CROSS

BRITISH UNION (1763-1801)

BRITISH UNION (1801)

CANADIAN RED ENSIGN (1924-1965)

ST. LAWRENCE RIVER carries the vast flow of water draining from the Great Lakes. This view is from Quebec city.

J. ALLAN CASH, FROM RAPHO GUILLUMETTE

receives the waters of the North Saskatchewan, South Saskatchewan, Red, Assiniboine, and Winnipeg rivers. This river system provided access to the interior for British explorers, became the main artery for the fur traders of the Hudson's Bay Company, and was followed by the Red River settlers early in the 19th century.

Arctic Drainage Basin. The Arctic drainage basin (1,380,895 square miles, or 3,590,327 sq km) is dominated by the Mackenzie River system, which includes Lake Athabasca, Great Slave Lake, and Great Bear Lake. From the head of the Finlay to the mouth of the Mackenzie is 2,635 miles (4,240 km), making this the longest river in Canada; the lower 1,700 miles (2,735 km) is navigable for tug boats and barges, except for a 16-mile (25 km) portage around the series of rapids at the Alberta-Northwest Territories border.

Atlantic Drainage Basin. In the Atlantic drainage basin (580,097 square miles or 1,508,252 sq km) the St. Lawrence River, with the Ottawa River as its most important tributary, is preeminent. The flow of the St. Lawrence, which drains the Great Lakes, is exceeded in North America only by that of the Mississippi River. Apart from Lake Michigan, which is wholly in the United States, the Great Lakes lie partly in Canada and partly in the United States. They cover an area of nearly 100,000 square miles (260,000 sq km) and contain 5,500 cubic miles (22,800 cu km) of water, which is about one fourth of the fresh surface water supply of the world.

The St. Lawrence system was followed by the French explorers and the Montreal fur traders and became the main commercial highway of Canada serving its industrial heartland. Since the opening of the St. Lawrence Seaway in 1959, ocean-going vessels can sail to the head of the Great Lakes, a distance of 2,388 miles (3,842 km) from the Atlantic Ocean at the Strait of Belle Isle.

Pacific Drainage Basin. The Pacific drainage basin (400,730 square miles, or 1,041,898 sq km), the smallest of the basins, includes the areas with the highest precipitation in Canada. It has three major rivers, the Fraser, Columbia, and Yukon. The Fraser, which lies wholly within Canada, and the Columbia, which flows for over one-half its length in the United States, rise in the Cordillera and empty into the Pacific Ocean. Numerous falls and rapids make them unsuitable for navigation. The Yukon, flowing from Canada through Alaska to the Bering Sea, is the fifth-largest river in North America. It is navigable for 1,777 miles (2,858 km) from Whitehorse to its mouth, and was used by river steamers at the time of the Klondike gold rush for supplying Dawson City.

GRAHAM W. ROWLEY, *Canadian Department of Indian Affairs and Northern Development*

6. Climate

Canada's climates are reflected in its forests, grassland, agricultural land, and barren landscapes. Many physiographic features result from past climates while present climates largely determine today's natural vegetation and land use. Because Canada is in the northern half of the continent, its climates are generally cool to cold, although in the interior many days each year have tropiclike conditions. The areas of heavy precipitation lie near the source regions of moisture—the oceans—while the central interior exhibits the dryness common in the middle of large continents.

Climatic Patterns. To explain Canada's climates it is necessary to consider both the general circulation of the atmosphere on a global scale and the physical geography.

Atmospheric Influences. Low-latitude areas to the south of Canada receive an excess amount of heat from the sun each year, while the northern regions lose more heat to space than they receive. To preserve the heat balance, a general pattern of atmospheric circulation transports heat northward, and large masses of cold air frequently move out of the polar regions. The net result is an atmospheric flow from west to east over most of Canada. Within this general circulation, migratory weather systems also move from west to east, associated with the outbreaks of arctic air and the northward surges of relatively warm air. These weather disturbances, low-pressure areas and their associated fronts, are responsible for much of the cloudy, windy, and wet or snowy weather of Canada.

Geographic Influences. The physical geography of Canada has a marked influence on its climate. The mountains of the Cordillera force the westerly air stream to rise, producing copious rain along the Pacific coast, which the mountains also protect from outbreaks of cold arctic air from the interior. The Prairie provinces are part of a broad, flat corridor from the Arctic Ocean to the Gulf of Mexico, along which cold air masses can flow southeastward unchecked, and in the summer hot dry air can move northwestward. The Great Lakes modify the weather and climate of southern Ontario; and Hudson and James bays have a similar effect on the climate of northern Ontario and northern Quebec. In the Atlantic provinces, although the general circulation of the atmosphere usually moves continental air eastward over the coast, frequent short reversals of the air currents result in damp, cloudy, rainy weather from the Atlantic Ocean.

Climatic Regions. The country can be divided into seven climatic regions:

Pacific. Air moving off the Pacific Ocean to the shores of British Columbia gives a narrow coastal band the most equable and moderate climate in Canada. Storms from the Pacific are frequent in winter and, because the incoming air is forced to rise over the coastal mountains, this season is cloudy, dull, and rainy, although mild. Temperatures, even in midwinter, usually average above freezing and neither Victoria nor Vancouver has experienced temperatures below 0°F (−18°C), partly because the mountains effectively block most outbreaks of cold arctic air from the interior. Summers are cloudy and cool on the northern coast, while on the southwestern coast and in the lower Fraser Valley they are usually pleasant and warm, with abundant sunshine and temperatures seldom exceeding 90°F (32°C). In summer the southwestern coast is under the influence of a large Pacific high-pressure area, which provides fine dry weather, as disturbances are kept well to the north. Because of heavy winter rains, however, annual precipitation is generally in the 60- to 100-inch (152- to 254-cm) range throughout the region. There are some sheltered rain-shadow areas, such as southeast Vancouver Island, where the average annual totals are less than 30 inches (76 cm), while at Henderson Lake on the western coast of the island annual precipitation averages 262 inches (665 cm).

Cordillera. Cordillera climates, found in the physiographic region of mountains, plateaus, and valleys, are continental in character, with fairly uniform precipitation throughout the year, cool to cold winters and moderate to warm summers, depending on latitude. Because of the rugged and complex terrain, climate often varies rather markedly within short distances—valleys, for instance, are usually colder in winter and warmer in summer than nearby slopes. In general, annual precipitation decreases inland and is greater on the west windward slopes (30 to 100 inches or 76 to 254 cm) than on east lee areas and in the valleys (10 to 15 inches or 25 to 30 cm). In the central part of the Yukon, precipitation averages only about 10 inches. Annual snowfalls of a depth greater than 800 inches (2,032 cm) have been reported from some localities along the westward-facing slopes of the coast mountains.

Low rainfall and high summer temperatures give the southern interior valleys almost desert-like conditions. Here winters are relatively short, but in the northern areas they are long and cold and the summers only moderately warm at best. The coldest temperature ever recorded in Canada, −81°F (−63°C) occurred at Snag, Yukon Territory. While temperatures over 95°F (35°C) have never officially been reported from the Yukon, temperatures above 100°F (38°C) are quite common in the southern interior valleys of British Columbia.

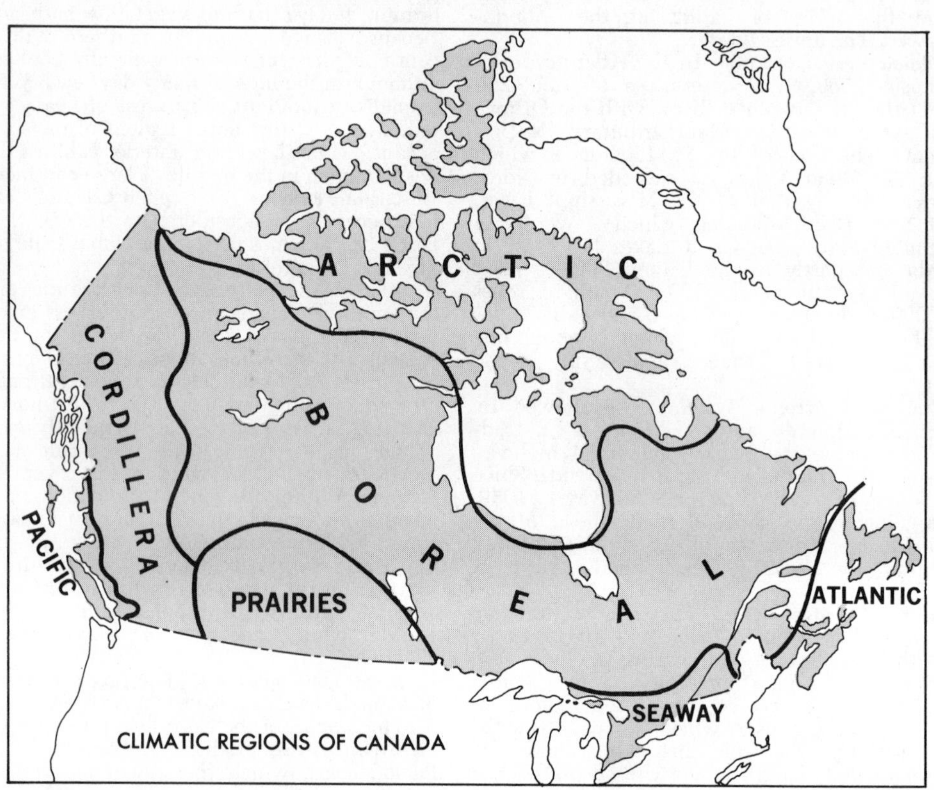

CLIMATIC REGIONS OF CANADA

Prairies. The southern portion of the Prairie provinces has an extremely continental-type climate, with warm summers and long, cold winters. Blocked by the mountains from the Pacific, the prairies are dry, with average annual precipitation generally between 12 and 20 inches (30 to 50 cm). Snowfall is light, usually less than 50 inches (127 cm), and about half the annual precipitation falls during the May to August agricultural season. Temperatures average in the 60's F (about 18°C) in midsummer, but extremes of over 100° F (38° C) are not unusual. The highest official temperature reported in Canada, 113° F (45° C), occurred at Midale and Yellowgrass, Saskatchewan, in July 1937. Even in midsummer, nighttime temperatures can drop dangerously close to freezing and agriculture is often hampered as much by the limited frost-free season as by lack of precipitation. Average temperatures are usually near zero in January, but temperatures below −50° F (−46° C) have been recorded throughout most of the region.

Two remarkable weather phenomena occur during prairie winters—chinooks, when warm, dry "snow-eating" winds descend to lift temperatures in southern Alberta from sub-zero to above freezing, and blizzards, when snow-filled driving winds and sub-zero temperatures can bring outdoor activities to a standstill across large areas.

Seaway. The climate of southern Ontario and the St. Lawrence River valley of Quebec may be classed as humid, somewhat modified continental. A steady progression of high- and low-pressure areas moves from west to east, producing an alternating pattern of weather in which particularly good or bad periods do not usually last more than a few days. The effect of the Great Lakes is particularly noticeable in southwestern and south-central Ontario, giving more snowfall and milder winter temperatures than might otherwise be expected. Winters are more severe in the Ottawa and St. Lawrence valleys, averaging 12° to 15°F (—11° to —9°C) in January, compared with 22° to 25°F (—6° to —4°C) along the lower Great Lakes. Midsummer temperatures average nearly 70°F (21°C) throughout most of the region with short periods of hot, humid weather.

Precipitation is remarkably uniform, both from year to year and from one season to the next, most months averaging about 3 inches (8 cm). Although precipitation is generally slightly heavier in the lee of the lakes than elsewhere, there is a general increase from the upper Great Lakes to the Atlantic coast.

Atlantic. Despite its location, this region (covering Nova Scotia, Prince Edward Island, part of New Brunswick, and the Island of Newfoundland) has a continental rather than a maritime climate because of the usual eastward movement of interior air masses. Most weather systems originating in the central or eastern United States move northeastward over the Atlantic provinces, giving some of the most variable weather from day to day anywhere in the country. January temperatures average in the low 20'sF (nearly —7°C), but frequent influxes of moist Atlantic air produce mild spells. In the early summer, cool foggy periods are common, but midsummer temperatures generally average in the low 60'sF (nearly 16°C). Precipitation is usually abundant, with a maximum in early winter. Average annual precipitation increases from around 40 inches (102 cm) in the west to over 50 inches (127 cm) along the immediate Atlantic coast.

Boreal. The boreal or subarctic climatic region extends south of the tree line in a broad arc from the Mackenzie River basin southeastward across the north of Alberta, Saskatchewan, Manitoba, Ontario, and Quebec to Labrador. Usually snow-covered for more than half the year, the region has a severe continental-type climate, modified in the southeast by Hudson and James bays and the Atlantic. Despite summer temperatures averaging nearly 60°F (16°C) during the warmest month of the year, agriculture is limited by the short frost-free season of about two months, with frost not unusual in every month of the year. Temperatures over 100°F (38°C) have occurred in summer but winters are bitterly cold and long with temperatures averaging between 10° and 20° below zero F (—23° to —29°C) during the coldest months. Precipitation is light in the northwest, but in central Quebec-Labrador more snow falls during most winters than in any other comparable area of Canada.

Arctic. The Arctic islands and the northern fringe of the mainland do not have a summer season as it is known farther south. Midsummer temperatures average below 50°F (10°C) stunting or prohibiting the growth of trees. Temperatures up to 90°F (32°C) have been reported as far north as the Arctic coast, but on the northern islands temperatures over 65°F (18°C) are infrequent. In the central part, temperatures average below zero F (—18°C) for six months of the year, although just enough heat escapes through the ice to keep minimum temperatures from dropping as low as at continental stations several hundred miles to the south. Eureka, on northern Ellesmere Island, is Canada's coldest weather station: February, the coldest month, has an average temperature of —36°F (—38°C), and the mean annual temperature is but —3°F (—19°C). These northern islands constitute the real desert area of Canada, as most stations report under 6 inches (15 cm) of precipitation a year, but because of the low temperatures only about three months are without snow cover, and ponds are common in summer owing to the low evaporation rate. On the Baffin Island coast, Atlantic storms moving up Davis Strait leave from 8 to 16 inches (20 to 41 cm) of precipitation a year.

Climatic Change. Canada's climates have not always been the same. Underground deposits of salt indicate that parts of Ontario were once much hotter and drier, while the petroleum fields of western Canada are the legacy of lush tropical vegetation unknown in Canada today. On the other hand, in comparatively recent times most of Canada lay under great ice sheets. Modern science is only beginning to reveal the secrets of past climates.

In Canada, weather data have been recorded for nearly a century in parts of the southeast, for 80 years in the west, and for nearly 50 years in the north, showing some minor fluctuations over the past several decades.

Temperature. In common with many parts of the Northern Hemisphere, the 1880's were cold. During the next few decades temperatures rose perhaps 1 to 3 degrees F all across Southern Canada. The 1930's and early 1940's were relatively warmer than any other periods on record in most of Canada, but lower temperatures again prevailed in the late 1940's and 1950's, especially in the west. By the mid-1960's the trend had recovered, with temperatures in western Canada averaging as high as in the 1940's. In eastern Canada, temperatures in the 1950's were higher than ever before. At Toronto, where data are available since 1840, the general increase has amounted to about 3 degrees over the past century, and heat produced in the city and the increase in pollution have been responsible for an additional increase of perhaps 1 to 2 degrees during the century in the metropolitan area. In the 1960's the trend has been toward slightly lower temperatures in eastern Canada. In the Yukon, temperatures averaged 3 to 4 degrees warmer during the 1940's than in earlier decades, but in the 1960's they returned to levels of the first decade or two of this century. In the Arctic, there are indications that, after the relatively warm 1940's, temperatures had fallen a degree or two by the mid-1960's.

Precipitation. Records from the Pacific coast fail to reveal any significant change in precipitation. In the Prairie provinces a period of relatively high precipitation shortly after 1900 was followed by a steady decrease until, by the mid-1930's, precipitation averaged 2 to 3 inches (5 to 8 cm) less than 30 years before. The 1950's were again relatively wet, with a subsequent decrease. In southern Ontario there has been a general decrease of precipitation of some 3 to 4 inches (8 to 10 cm) over the past century, and the Atlantic provinces have had a gradual increase, amounting to 4 inches (10 cm) at some stations, since early in the century.

M. K. Thomas, *Climatology Division*
Canada Department of Transport

Further Reading: Boughner, C. C., and Thomas, M. K., "The Climate of Canada," *Canada Year Book* 1959, pp. 23–51 (Ottawa); id., "Climatic Tables," *Canada Year Book* 1960, pp. 31–77 (Ottawa); Canada Department of Mines and Technical Surveys, *Atlas of Canada*, weather and climate section (Ottawa 1959); Thomas, M. K., *Climatological Atlas of Canada*, National Research Council Publication No. 3151 (Ottawa 1953).

7. Soils

Nearly all the mineral soils of Canada have developed from materials left by the melting ice sheets which covered most of Canada during the Pleistocene age. These materials, derived mainly from the underlying rocks and having a wide range in texture, color and composition, were mixed, transported, and deposited as glacial till or as alluvial, lacustrine, or aeolian sediments.

The soils of Canada result from the interaction of the soil-forming factors—climate, vegetation, topography, and time—with these materials. Over broad areas having a particular kind of climate and vegetation the soils tend to develop a few common characteristics, and it is possible to group the dominant soils into a number of zones that reflect these regional influences. Not enough is known to draw the boundaries between all soil zones, particularly in the Precambrian, Cordilleran, and Subarctic areas, which are tentatively referred to as soil regions. Local variations within each zone or region may result in small areas of soils having characteristics similar to the dominant soils in other zones.

The soil zones can be grouped into three major types—soils developed under grass, under forest and under tundra. The boundaries of these zones follow climatic and vegetational patterns, except in British Columbia and the Yukon where topography has a dominating influence.

Grassland Soils. These soils have dark colored, mineral-organic surface horizons and brownish, usually prismatic-structured subsoils lying on calcareous parent materials. They are divided into three zones on the color of the surface soil which reflects the effect of climate.

The soils of the *Brown Soil Zone* occur in the semiarid, open treeless prairies of southern Saskatchewan and Alberta. Because of the low rainfall there is little leaching and the total amount of organic matter in the soil is low. Drought and wind erosion are always serious problems and only the better types of soil are suitable for farming. Cattle ranching is an important industry.

The *Dark Brown Soil Zone* has a slightly moister climate than the Brown zone. Natural vegetation is somewhat more dense and the soils contain slightly more nitrogen and organic matter, resulting in better fertility. The best wheatlands in Canada are found in this zone.

In the *Black Soil Zone,* which lies between the open prairies and the forest, the climate is subhumid with low evaporation. The natural vegetation consists of tall grasses, with poplar and willow along the river valleys. An outlier of this zone occurs in the Peace River region. The soils, rich in organic matter and nitrogen, are probably the most fertile in Canada. They are used predominantly for cereal crops and mixed farming.

In each of these zones there are large acreages of solonetzic soils overlying saline parent materials.

Forested Soils. The forested areas of Canada can be subdivided into nine main soil zones or regions. In general, the forested soils are more strongly leached than the grassland soils.

The *Grey Wooded Soil Zone* covers much of Alberta and parts of British Columbia, Saskatchewan, and Manitoba north of the grasslands. The soils are developed under a cool subhumid to subarid climate, but with low evaporation, and a forest cover of poplar, willow, white spruce, and jack pine. They have a greyish colored surface low in organic matter and nitrogen, and subsoils enriched in clay. These soils have a lower fertility than the grassland soils, but with suitable cropping practices and the addition of fertilizers many of them can be used for mixed farming and cereal crops. Small, but important, areas of Grey Wooded soils occur in the Precambrian soil region and in central British Columbia. Organic soils cover large areas in the soil zone.

A *High Lime Soil Zone* occurs around Lake Manitoba, where the calcareous nature of the bedrock or drift has influenced soil development more than the climate. The soils are usually shallow and somewhat stony. Some mixed farming is possible in the better soil areas.

The soils of the *Grey Brown Podzolic Soil Zone* of southern Ontario are developed under a humid temperate climate and deciduous forest cover. They appear somewhat similar to the Grey Wooded soils, but have a well decomposed organic surface horizon and are not as strongly leached. The parent materials are calcareous. Their fertility combined with the favorable climate makes these soils suitable for a wide range of crops, including tobacco and fruit.

In the *Dark Grey Gleisolic Soil Zone* the climate is cooler and more humid than in the Grey Brown Podzolic zone. The dominant soils are developed under poorly drained conditions and have dull colored, mottled subsoils. They are reasonably fertile, and mixed farming is widely practiced.

The *Podzol Soil Zone* occupies a large part of eastern Canada. The soils are developed under a mixed or coniferous forest and a humid climate. They have strongly leached surface soils, and subsoils in which organic matter and sesquioxides are the main accumulation products. They are low in natural fertility but respond to fertilizers and lime. The smoother, less stony areas are used for mixed farming, potatoes and fruit. Organic soils are widespread.

The *Precambrian Soil Region* is dominated by Podzols, organic soils, and rock outcrops. Except along the southern edge, the natural forest is coniferous. The topography, stoniness, soil pattern, and climate limit agricultural development to the valleys and a few small clay plains, where Grey Wooded, organic, and (to a lesser extent) Gleysolic soils form the soil pattern.

The *Subarctic Soil Region* is characterized by soils with perennially frozen subsoils, extensive peat deposits, and rock outcrops. The trees, except in favorable locations, are stunted. Agriculture is possible in certain limited areas.

In the mountainous *Cordilleran Region* there is a correlation between vegetation, altitude, and soil development resulting in a wide range of soils, including grassland soils, Podzols, Grey Brown Podzolic, Brown Wooded, and Alpine soils. Agriculture is confined mainly to the valleys.

The soils in the *Pacific Coast Soil Zone* are developed under mild winters with heavy rainfall, and summers that are comparatively dry and warm. The native forest, unlike any found elsewhere in Canada, consists of heavy stands of Douglas fir, western red cedar, and western hemlock. The soils are low in organic matter, generally quite acid, and characterized by brownish subsoils. Only a small percentage of the land is suitable for agriculture, but in a few favorable areas intensive development has been possible.

Tundra Soils. The Tundra Soil Region differs from the Subarctic region mainly in the kind of vegetative cover—primarily lichens, mosses, and low creeping shrubs. The subsoils are perennially frozen, and soil development is very slow. On the Precambrian Shield the soils are generally coarse textured and acid, but in limestone areas they are finer textured and more neutral or alkaline. Organic soils are less prevalent than in the Subarctic region. The climate does not permit agriculture.

Soil Conservation. About 25% of the arable land of Canada has been more or less severely damaged by water or wind erosion. Erosion has been particularly serious in the Brown soil zone where early misuse of land resulted in soil drifting. Forested regions have not been so badly affected.

Enough is now known about soils to permit their use without serious erosion. The building of dams, use of windbreaks, terracing, and cropping practices reduce water losses and promote conservation of soil moisture. Soil moisture will continue to be the most important limiting factor in crop production in western Canada.

Soil conservation also involves the proper use of land. The Agricultural Rehabilitation and Development Act passed by the Government of Canada in 1961 provides for an inventory of land resources to determine their suitability for agriculture, forestry, wildlife, and recreation. This information will be used to guide policies on the proper and efficient use of land with a view toward conserving the soil as a natural resource.

D. B. Cann
Canada Department of Agriculture

Further Reading: Agricultural Institute of Canada, "A Look at Canadian Soils," *Agricultural Institute Review*, vol. 15, no. 2 (Ottawa 1960); Jenny, Hans, *Factors of Soil Formation* (New York 1941); Millar, Charles E., Turk, L. M., and Foth, H. D., *Fundamentals of Soil Science*, 4th ed. (New York 1965).

H. ROWED, FROM NATIONAL FILM BOARD

BIGHORN SHEEP in the high Rocky Mountains in Alberta.

8. Flora and Fauna

By "flora" is meant the total mass of different kinds of plants, from the lowest to the highest forms, that compose the entire plant cover of an area. Similarly, fauna includes all animal life. In Canada, where the climate, topography, and soils vary greatly from north to south and from east to west, the composition of the plant cover naturally changes with the environment. The total flora or plant cover can therefore be subdivided into floristic provinces occupied by plants adapted to the climate, topography, and soil which characterize the "province." Their boundaries are bands rather than lines and may alter with such influences as local changes of climate and acts of man—for example by burning in the past or by logging, draining, and pesticides today. Despite some minor changes, the floristic provinces remain remarkably distinct for very long periods. For instance, the effect of the Pleistocene Ice Age can still be recognized in the distribution of some plants and animals.

In this account only the major floristic provinces will be mentioned. These will be used as a division for both animals and plants because, since plants are stationary, the floristic provinces are better defined than the faunal provinces and less susceptible to change. There are many species of animal life—over 80,000 of insects, 780 of fishes (of which 580 are marine), 82 of reptiles and amphibians, 518 of birds and 193 of mammals—only the higher forms will be considered.

There are three main floristic provinces in Canada: grassland, forest, and tundra. They run roughly from west to east, except in the western mountains where the trend is north-south.

Grasslands. There has been much speculation on whether these nearly treeless areas have resulted from too dry a climate, from early burnings, or from grazing of buffalo herds. In southwestern Alberta, southeastern Saskatchewan, and the Okanagan Valley of British Columbia, where temperature extremes of summer heat and winter cold are very marked and lack of rainfall is acute, the vegetation is a *Short-grass Prairie*. The typical

plants are drought-tolerant forms, such as common spear grass, western wheatgrass, June grass, prickly pear, hoary sagebrush, and the shrubs, thorny buffalo berry and winter fat. Around many alkaline lakes without outlets sea milkwort, spike-grass, and sea crowfoot flourish. The lance-leaved cottonwood and narrow-leaved cottonwood trees are found along the river valleys.

Farther north, and to east and west, in southwestern Manitoba and southeastern Alberta, there is a belt of *Mixed Grassland* where many of the plants are the same as those to the south, but with the slightly wetter climate, longer grasses occur, such as northern wheatgrass, green spear grass, and rough fescue. Along streams there may be well-developed groves of poplar and willow.

The characteristic mammals of the grasslands are the pronghorn antelope, Nuttall's cottontail, Richardson's ground squirrel, white-tailed jackrabbit, western harvest mouse, kangaroo rat, pocket mouse, and badger, though some are restricted to the Short-grass Prairie. Of the typical birds, the sage grouse is confined to the Short-grass, and the desert horned lark, chestnut-collared longspur, Sprague's pipit, and burrowing owl are characteristic of the region.

Forests—*Deciduous, or Carolinian, Forest.* Like the Short-grass Prairie, the Deciduous, or Carolinian, Forest is an extension of a southern flora. This specialized deciduous forest occurs in a small strip of very mild climate along the shore of Lake Erie. The dominant trees are maple and beech, but several species are found in Canada only in this region—black walnut, mockernut hickory, pignut hickory, black oak, scarlet oak, honey locust, tulip tree, and cucumber tree. Among the shrubs are the flowering dogwood, deerberry and poison sumac and many herbaceous plants such as the wild bergamot, white adder's-tongue, yellow-fringed orchid, and flowering spurge are confined to this region.

The fauna is also distinctive, with the opossum, eastern mole, least shrew, and pine mouse reaching their northern limit, as well as the hooded warbler, Carolina wren, orchard oriole, cardinal, and several other species of birds.

Eastern Forest. This mixed deciduous and coniferous forest covers a large area, extending from Lake of the Woods in the west to Baie de Chaleur in the east and stretching south to the Carolinian Forest. This province is frequently divided into a northern *Great Lakes-St. Lawrence* region and a southern *Acadian* region, based on the dominance of the red spruce and other adaptations of the Acadian Forest to its moister, cooler maritime climate.

In the Eastern Forest northern hardwoods are dominant, with sugar maple, red oak, white oak, beech, and yellow birch on the upland soils, and red maple, white elm, and ash on the lower ground, but the southern conifers, white pine, red pine, and hemlock, are often economically important, and cedar is common on swampy ground. The underbrush is rather scanty, except in clearings where shrubs such as staghorn sumac, serviceberry, and purple-flowering raspberry may flourish. Herbaceous plants often make a magnificent display with trillium, dog's-tooth violet, jack-in-the-pulpit, bloodroot, and many other species in the woods in spring; and asters, goldenrods, and mulleins on the borders of the woods in the fall.

NATIONAL FILM BOARD

MOOSE near Banff on the Icefields Highway in Alberta.

The fauna is transitional, including both northern and southern forms. Gray and red squirrels, striped skunk, woodchuck, chipmunk, white-tailed deer, black bear, beaver and smoky shrew are all common mammals. Some birds that reach their northern limits in this forest are the white-breasted nuthatch, black-throated blue warbler, Blackburnian warbler, and wood thrush.

Aspen-Grove or Parkland. In this narrow transitional belt between the prairies and the Boreal Forest trees occur mainly along the river valleys or in clumps separated by open grassland. Aspen and black poplar are dominant, with some Manitoba maple, elm, and burr oak, especially in the southeast. Shrubs, such as the Saskatoon berry and highbush cranberry, are common, and in early summer milk vetch, anemones, cinquefoil, and other herbaceous plants make a colorful display. The taller grasses, including spear grass, wheatgrass, bromegrass, and reed grass are typical. The fauna is similar to that of the northern prairies.

Coast Forest. The Coast Forest, which has developed in the wet mild Pacific climate, is the densest and most luxuriant in Canada, with very tall conifers of exceptionally hard wood. The western red cedar and western hemlock are dominant, with large stands of Douglas fir and western white pine. Yellow cedar, Sitka spruce, and red alder are confined to this region and two southern species, the madroña and Garry oak, are found in the south. The undergrowth is dense with shrubs such as salal, devil's club, red-flowered currant, and salmonberry, and the herbaceous vegetation is rich with western buttercup, skunk cabbage, western wake-robin, western wild ginger, cut-leaved goldthread, and many other plants.

The typical mammals are the mule deer, mountain beaver, northern flying squirrel, Townsend's vole, coast mole, and western spotted skunk. Some characteristic birds are the band-tailed pigeon, chestnut-backed chickadee, black-throated warbler, Hutton's vireo, and northwestern crow.

Montane Forest or Dry Interior Belt. In this belt in British Columbia, the vegetation is controlled by lack of summer precipitation and is very varied. In the extreme south and along the valley floors there is Short-grass Prairie. On the slopes of the mountains, clumps of ponderosa pine are interspersed with the grassland. Farther north the ponderosa pine is replaced by rather stunted Douglas fir, aspen, and lodgepole pine, and in the extreme north by Engelmann spruce. There are few shrubby plants, the commonest being sagebrush and antelope brush. Herbaceous plants are mainly xerophytic, such as bunchgrass, bitterroot, balsam root, and bladderpod.

In the south the mammals and birds are those of the Short-grass Prairie. In the north the bighorn sheep, northern flying squirrel, golden-mantled ground squirrel, yellow-pine chipmunk, and heather vole are typical mammals. The pygmy nuthatch, poorwill, and Bullock's oriole reach their northern limit in this region.

Columbia Forest. This has developed in a belt of more abundant rainfall in the Selkirk and Monashee mountains. The forest is somewhat similar to the Coast Forest with smaller forms of western red cedar and western hemlock and some grand fir and western white pine in the south and Engelmann spruce and alpine fir to the north. It

POLAR BEAR mother and two cubs on an Arctic ice floe.

DONALD B. MACMILLAN

has a restricted range, with Subalpine Forest above 4,000 feet (1,200 meters) and Interior Dry Belt flora in the lower valleys. Above the timber the alpine meadows are rich in plant species.

White-tailed deer and mule deer are abundant, and other typical mammals are mountain goat, marten, and striped skunk. Birds, particularly waterfowl, are very varied and interesting as one of the main fall migration routes runs through the area.

Subalpine Forest. The Cordilleran equivalent of the Boreal Forest, the Subalpine Forest covers the slopes of the Rocky Mountains and the higher parts of the interior and coast ranges. Engelmann spruce is dominant, with alpine fir and Douglas fir on the upper slopes. In the south, alpine larch and whitebark pine may be important, and in the north, black and white spruce. Above the tree line there is a rich alpine flora with shrubs such as red heather and moss heather, and many herbaceous plants, such as alpine hair grass, white marigold, and mountain pink.

The typical mammals are the bighorn sheep, mountain goat, moose, wapiti, grizzly bear, caribou, hoary marmot, rocky mountain pika, and least chipmunk. Bird life is very similar to that of the Boreal Forest to the north and east, but there are a few characteristic species such as the mountain chickadee, Townsend's solitaire, varied thrush, and Clark nutcracker.

Boreal Forest. This stretches from Newfoundland to Alaska and covers a greater area of Canada than any other forest belt. The country is mainly rolling, with many lakes and bogs. Throughout, the forest is remarkably homogeneous and is a major source of Canadian pulpwood. It is primarily a region of conifers, but deciduous trees, mainly poplars and white birch, become more common toward the south and southwest. The white spruce is the characteristic tree, but this forest belt can be divided into a wetter eastern section, where black spruce and tamarack are locally most important, and a drier western section, where jack pine flourishes and broad-leaved species are more common. In the northwest, lodgepole pine and alpine fir are dominant. The most typical shrubs are willows, pembina, junipers, bearberry, rock cranberry, Labrador tea, ground birch, and shrubby cinquefoil. Common herbaceous plants are tall cotton grass, holy grass, stitchwort, and baked-apple berry.

SALMON is seen in a respirometer as a researcher tests its energy consumption under various conditions.

TED GRANT, FROM NATIONAL FILM BOARD

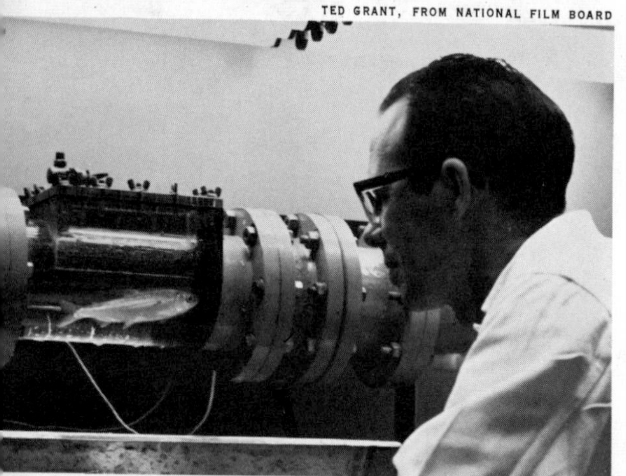

RICHARD HARRINGTON

COTTON GRASS blossoming in a black spruce swamp.

Among the many mammals are moose, woodland caribou, black bear, beaver, red fox, lynx, marten, muskrat, porcupine, snowshoe hare, and redbacked vole. Characteristic birds include some of the warblers, the white-throated sparrow, boreal chickadee, gray jay, and pine grosbeak.

Subarctic Forest. Farther north there is a transitional belt of Subarctic Forest where scattered patches of the Boreal Forest are interspersed with tundra vegetation of mosses, lichens, and creeping shrubs. The dominant trees are white spruce, black spruce, and white birch, with tamarack and black spruce particularly well developed in the bog-like muskeg.

The fauna is also transitional, with both boreal and tundra species overlapping, for example, the woodland caribou with the barren-ground caribou, the spruce grouse and the sharp-tailed grouse with the willow ptarmigan, and the tree sparrow with the Lapland longspur.

Arctic Tundra. In the far northern mainland and the Arctic islands, where the growing season is very short and precipitation very low, most of the country is underlain by permafrost, or perennially frozen ground. The climate prevents tree growth, most of the plants are perennial, and none is poisonous. Large areas of mosses, lichens, and grasses are interspersed with bunch-like plants such as alpine poppy, saxifrages, and sedges, or mats of buttercup, mountain avens, or cotton grass, and small prostrate forms of woody plants, such as willow dwarf birch, mountain cranberry, and Labrador tea.

Here the typical mammals are the barren-ground caribou, musk-ox, Arctic fox, gray wolf, Arctic hare, Arctic ground squirrel, and brown and varying lemmings. In the spring, vast numbers of waterfowl, shorebirds, and other migrating

I. DONALD BOWDEN

WATERPOWER for electricity is abundant in Canada.

CHRIS LUND, FROM NATIONAL FILM BOARD

TIMBER cut finds many uses in the nation's economy.

birds fly north to breed in the tundra, where some of the typical species are the snowy owl, willow ptarmigan, rock ptarmigan, and Lapland longspur.

Aquatic Fauna. Bordering on three oceans and with one quarter of the world's supply of fresh water, Canada is rich in sea mammals and fishes. Three major groups of fishes are found, the lampreys (12 species), the sharks (49 species) and the bony fishes (719 species). The number of species increases markedly from north to south, both in fresh and in salt water. See *15. Fisheries and Furs.*

DIANA ROWLEY
Arctic Institute of North America

Bibliography

Britton, Nathaniel L., and Brown, Addison, *Illustrated Flora of the United States and Canada,* 3 vols. (New York 1913).

Clemens, W. A., *Fishes of the Pacific Coast of Canada,* Canada Fisheries Research Board Bulletin No. 68 (Ottawa 1949).

Cowan, I. McT., and Guiguet, C. J., *The Mammals of British Columbia,* British Columbia Provincial Museum Handbook No. 11, 3d ed. (Victoria 1965).

Gray, Asa, *Manual of Botany,* 8th ed., largely rewritten and expanded by Merritt L. Fernald (New York 1950).

Godfrey, Earl T., *The Birds of Canada,* National Museum of Canada Bulletin 203 (Ottawa 1966).

Hall, Eugene Raymond, and Kelson, Keith, *The Mammals of North America,* 2 vols. (New York 1959).

McAllister, D. E., *Keys to the Marine Fishes of Arctic Canada,* National Museum, Natural History Paper 5 (Ottawa 1960).

Peterson, Randolph Lee, *The Mammals of Eastern Canada* (Toronto 1966).

Porsild, A. E., *Illustrated Flora of the Canadian Arctic Archipelago,* National Museum of Canada Bulletin 146 (Ottawa 1957).

Rowe, J. S., *Forest Regions of Canada,* Canada Forestry Branch Bulletin 123 (Ottawa 1959).

Scott, W. B., *A Checklist of Canadian Atlantic Fishes,* Royal Ontario Museum Life Sciences Contribution 66 (Toronto 1965).

Scott, W. B., *A Checklist of the Freshwater Fishes of Canada and Alaska,* Royal Ontario Museum (Toronto 1958).

Soper, J. Dewey, *The Mammals of Alberta* (Edmonton 1964).

9. Natural Resources

Nature has endowed Canada generously with resources. The plains, mountains, forests, rivers, and seas have all contributed in good measure to the nation's wealth.

Renewable Resources. The riches of the seas were the first to be discovered. In the late 15th century, Sebastian Cabot found "so great multitudes of certaine bigge fishes much like unto Tunies that they sometime stayed his ships." The fish of the Atlantic Coast, especially cod and lobster, are still a very valuable resource and to these have been added those of the Pacific, where salmon are preeminent, and substantial freshwater fisheries. The great whale fisheries, however, which flourished in the eastern Arctic in the 19th century, were destroyed by overexploitation.

Forests cover nearly half of Canada. They sheltered the fur-bearing animals that were the basis of the fur trade, so important a resource in former days and one that led to the exploration of so much of the country. Fur trapping is now of little significance except in the far north, but forestry has long been a major Canadian industry, and today the forests are one of the greatest sources of wealth and employment, in which all the provinces share.

In the prairies, climate and soil have combined to make a granary for the world and, elsewhere in southern Canada, dairy farming, stock rearing, fruit growing, and other agricultural pursuits contribute to the national prosperity. Farther north and over much of the rocky Canadian Shield, poor soils, cold climate, and low precipitation prevent agriculture except in a few favored locations, such as the Peace River area and the clay belt of northern Ontario and Quebec.

The great Canadian rivers provide important waterpower potentials in almost every part of the country except the Prairies, and by good fortune the power sites are often conveniently close to prospective users. As a result, the total installed power capacity of Canada is second only to that of the United States, while Norway alone has a greater capacity on the basis of population. Throughout the North American continent demands for water for both domestic and industrial use are increasing rapidly and water itself is becoming recognized as an extremely valuable resource, one with which Canada is bountifully supplied.

Nonrenewable Resources. The wealth of the country in renewable resources is complemented by nonrenewable resources of great value. Metallic ores, industrial minerals, and petroleum are found in great abundance, and have made Canada a leading producer of several minerals, including copper, iron ore, nickel, zinc, asbestos, uranium, gold, and silver. Geologically, both the Canadian Shield and the Cordillera are exceptionally favorable for the occurrence of metals, and there are great quantities of coal in the eastern Cordillera. In the Great Plains and the Foothills, oil, natural gas, and potash are recovered from the earth and the Athabasca oil sands contain the world's largest known reserves of oil. The Appalachian region is also an important productive area. This is true particularly of industrial minerals such as asbestos, while both the Continental Shelf and the Arctic islands are considered to have good prospects for oil.

Conservation. Small countries with large populations must husband their resources. In Canada, in contrast, resources may appear inexhaustible and the need for conservation is not so immediately compelling. But even the richest resources can be quickly destroyed if they are recklessly exploited. Wildlife is particularly vulnerable as its habitat is often disturbed by man at the same time that more effective hunting methods are introduced. Whales, sea otters, and caribou are among many examples in Canadian history where a valuable species has been endangered by uncontrolled slaughter. Such profligacy has not been restricted to the animal kingdom. In 1871 Sir John A. Macdonald, first prime minister of the Dominion of Canada, wrote that "the sight of the immense masses of timber passing my windows every morning continually suggests to my mind the absolute necessity there is for looking at the future of this great trade. We are recklessly destroying the timber of Canada, and there is scarcely a possibility of replacing it."

In the development of Canadian resources there have frequently been conflicts between different exploiting interests, as when a salmon river is dammed for waterpower, when mining encroaches on an area of natural beauty, or when a city spreads over good agricultural land. Sometimes the interests are incompatible and a choice has to be made, but careful planning can often resolve the difficulties or a satisfactory compromise can be reached. A particular problem arises when the traditional livelihood of the Indians and Eskimo is endangered by resource development or by competition for the same resources by professional hunters and trappers.

Overexploitation and the conflicting requirements of developers are not the only factors that jeopardize renewable resources. For a long time the scale of Canadian resources obscured the dangers of pollution just as it did those of excessive use, but they are now causing great concern. The problem of radioactive fallout depends on international agreement for solution. Its direct effect on human life is well recognized, but it can also affect resources in unexpected ways, such as the absorption of radioactive cesium by lichens on which caribou feed, resulting in high radiation levels in those native people to whom caribou are an important food.

At the same time, the increasing population and greater industrialization are being reflected in pollution of the air, the land, the fresh water, and even the sea. Local pollution can be prevented or diminished, but usually only at great expense. Sometimes a happier solution can be found. The Trail smelter in British Columbia once poured each month 10,000 tons of sulfur as sulfur dioxide into the atmosphere, doing great damage to crops and forests. Now, as a result of research, the sulfur is converted into ammonium sulfate and sold as fertilizer.

Another problem lies in the use of chemical weed killers and pesticides, which help to increase agricultural yields and control biting flies. The effects of these chemicals on soils, fish, animals, and people are not fully understood or adequately assessed.

It is now widely recognized that renewable resources will not be renewed unless effective conservation accompanies exploitation. Conservation goes beyond preservation to embrace the maximum utilization of resources and takes many forms. Multiple use of land, avoidance of waste, control of forest fires, restoration of conditions to allow renewed production, planning of sustained maximum yields, prevention of erosion, and especially research into more productive varieties, and new methods are some aspects of the effective management of resources that is essential if the full potential wealth of the country is to be realized.

GRAHAM W. ROWLEY, *Canadian Department of Indian Affairs and Northern Development*

ASBESTOS DEPOSITS are blasted at a Quebec mine.

MARCEL COGNAC, FROM NATIONAL FILM BOARD

CHRIS BRUUN, FROM NATIONAL FILM BOARD

OIL REFINERY on a snowy plain at Edmonton, Alberta, symbolizes the vigor of Canadian industry.

CANADA: The Economy

The Canadian economy's performance since World War II has been markedly different from that of the 1930's. This difference can be attributed partly to differing economic circumstances and partly to deliberate government intention, as set out in the 1945 "White Paper" on employment and income. However, while the postwar economy has been different from the prewar, the postwar record has been very uneven. Indeed, the whole postwar period must be divided into three main segments, separated by the bench-mark years 1957 and 1961.

Since World War II—*1945–1957*. The first 12 years following World War II witnessed a rapid rate of growth and sustained high levels of employment. The product of many forces, this early postwar upsurge was supported by the deliberate expansionary monetary and fiscal policies of the federal government. The urge to meet the backlog of consumers' and business needs that had accumulated during the war, and the relatively strong position of Canadian exports were other important contributing factors. This expansion was reinforced as well by a substantial net immigration and by the largest "baby boom" of any Western industrial nation.

In the early and mid-1950's several specific developments helped to sustain these general economic trends. Defense expenditures, particularly after the onset of the Korean War, greatly stimulated such industries as aircraft and electrical equipment; the construction industry was given an enormous boost by the start of construction on the St. Lawrence Seaway in 1954. As well, the mid-1950's witnessed massive investment in the mineral resource industries, especially uranium and prairie oil and gas. It should be noted that the bulk of this mineral investment was by nonresidents: between 1946 and 1953 approximately one half of Canada's net capital imports from the United States went into Canadian petroleum development, and by the end of 1953 over 56% of the capital employed in Canadian mining, smelting, and petroleum exploration and development companies was nonresident owned.

During this first postwar period, despite pauses in 1949 and 1954, Canadian national income (in constant prices) grew at a rate of 3.5% per annum. Similarly, population increased from slightly more than 12 million in 1949 to approximately 16.5 million in 1957, at a rate greater than 2.5% per annum. This first phase culminated in the investment boom of 1956–1957.

***1957–1961*.** In the last quarter of 1957, the economy slid into a severe recession that extended throughout 1958 and petered out into the brief recovery of 1958–1959. This recovery did little to offset the increasingly high rates of unemployment from 1957 to 1961. In fact, the highest unemployment rate of the postwar era was registered in June 1958 at 7.8% (seasonally adjusted). Moreover, throughout the 1957–1961 period, the economy's growth of real national income was relatively low—about 2% per annum. This position was further complicated by a relatively slow adjustment in Canada's balance of payments—the result, in part, of large capital inflows caused by the deliberate maintenance of high interest rates.

The reasons for the Canadian economy's slowdown are many. However, the recession in the United States in 1958, the completion of both the St. Lawrence Seaway and trans-Canada pipeline in the winter of 1958–1959, as well as the stretch-out of U.S. and British orders for Canadian uranium, were all primary contributing factors.

***Since 1961*.** Recovering from this trough of recession in early 1961, the Canadian economy then embarked on five years of steady business expansion. Unlike the expansion of the 1950's, mining and utilities did not play a central role; most sectors of the economy, instead, grew at more uniform rates with manufacturing growing slightly faster and greater roles being played by agriculture, forestry, and fisheries. From 1961 through the mid-1960's Canadian real income rose at an extremely high rate of 6.5%. One reason for this rapid rate of growth was an upsurge in immigration, beginning in the early 1960's (especially since 1963) and reaching a peak of 195,000 in 1966. Since emigration has remained virtually constant since 1960, net immigration has increased from virtually nothing at the start of 1960 to approximately 70,000 in the middle and late 1960's.

During late 1961 and early 1962, Canada experienced balance of payments shortages that culminated in the abandonment of the flexible exchange-rate system, which had been in effect for more than a decade. In return for international support of the Canadian dollar, Canada adopted the International Monetary Fund's pegged exchange-rate system, and by May 1962 the Canadian dollar was pegged at 92.5 cents (U.S.). This decline in the external value of the Canadian dollar improved the competitive position of Canadian producers in both domestic and export markets; in particular, Canadian manufactured exports approximately tripled in value by the mid-1960's. This momentum was accelerated by the strong world market for wheat after 1962, especially by large sales to the USSR and China. Canadian motor vehicle production received special stimulus from official efforts to improve the industry's competitive position, which led to the Canada-United States automotive agreement signed in 1965.

Although the 1960's were a period of unrivaled expansion, this is not to say that the economy's growth and prosperity were evenly distributed. There has been a general tendency since World War II for regional per capita incomes to diverge. In Ontario and British Columbia per capita income growth was slightly above the Canadian average, while in the Atlantic region it was at a rate significantly below the national average. These trends, however, were being countered by federal programs such as the Area Development Program and provincial policies such as the Atlantic Development Board to balance regional development.

Industrial Development in Retrospect. Canada has not always been an advanced industrial nation. Indeed, it would be difficult to find a contrast more striking than that between the rural economy of the Confederation provinces and the Canadian industrial complex in the second half of the 20th century.

In Canada's transformation from a rather backward area into a fast-growing industrial power, two distinct phases can be discerned. The first, or "staples" phase, reached its peak in the first decade of the 20th century; the second, the modern industrial phase, had its roots in the new industries that began to dominate the Canadian economy at the turn of the century and in the changing pattern of investment and trade highlighted by World War I.

Nascent Industrialism: The First Phase. The economy of the 1850's bore the stamp of more than two centuries of concentration on a few export staples destined for European markets. Fish, fur, and lumber had successively provided income and drawn manpower in modest volume to Canada. Reliance on these staple products had strengthened ties with Europe and ensured a weak, undiversified development that ruled out any prospect of an early, easily won economic or political independence. Energies were expended on the search for new sources of supply and on costly transportation systems necessary to the continued exploitation of Canada's resources. Geographic and market factors encouraged an early drive to continental interiors and in the process had brought Canadian enterprise face to face with the vastly greater expansive powers of the United States. By the mid-19th century it had become quite apparent that the northern transcontinenal economic system could be held in the face of U.S. economic penetration, but only by strenuous effort. The need for a national policy with aggressive developmental measures was made clear by the decline of the fur trade and the loss of British preferences.

National Policies. This national policy took shape in the 1850's and relied heavily on a combination of industrial protection and railroad construction to build a transcontinental economy. The decade following 1850 was a prosperous period in which railroad construction, reciprocal trade with the United States, a large influx of labor and capital, and an expansionary fiscal policy strengthened the St. Lawrence area as a base for transcontinental expansion. Industry responded to the stimulus of population growth, transportation improvements, and slightly greater tariff protection (after 1859). Although industry remained subordinate to agriculture, a strong nucleus of industrial growth emerged. Flour, grist and paper mills, brewing and distilling plants, lumber and woodworking industries, and factories producing agricultural implements, boots, shoes, woolens and cotton textiles, furniture, paint, and glass all contributed in Ontario and Quebec to an industrial output which at the time of Confederation employed approximately 150,000 workers. Coal mining in Nova Scotia, gold in British Columbia, iron mining in Ontario and Quebec, and copper mining in the Eastern Townships created a diversity of production.

For six years following Confederation in 1867, Canada continued to experience prosperity with relatively low tariff barriers. In 1873, however, with the slump in world markets and depressed economic conditions in both the United States and Britain, Canada's export-producing industries were particularly hard hit. Moreover, with the failure of reciprocal trade negotiations with the United States and with transportation costs declining, Canadian manufacturers felt that home markets should be reserved exclusively for themselves. Thus, to help bolster already declining public revenues, to cater to anti-United States sentiment, and to satisfy the pressures of Ontario and Quebec manufacturers, the higher tariff National Policy of 1879 was implemented.

In the National Policy of 1879, in which tariff, transportation, and land policies were coordinated, industrial protection was accepted as a necessary condition for economic growth. The general tariff level was raised from 17.5 to 20%, but was in the neighborhood of 25% for industrial equipment and machinery and even reached as high as 30% on a wide range of finished consumer goods. The trend to higher protection continued until 1887, with higher duties on iron and steel, farm machinery, and textiles and administrative changes that reinforced the protective features of tariff legislation.

It seems clear that Canadian growth over these decades was much slower than had been anticipated and that the National Policy had failed in its objectives of attracting capital and immigrants in great quantities. In spite of federal land policy, railway construction, and immigration propaganda, more people emigrated from Canada than entered it during this period. Similarly, British foreign investment flowed freely to the United States in the 1870's and to South America during the 1880's, but did not move in volume to finance Canadian economic development until after 1903. Canada's trade position was scarcely more encouraging; despite the fact that prices of imported manufactured goods fell more than those of Canada's nonmanufactured exports, Canada's higher tariffs diluted most benefits that might have accrued to the economy.

If the rate of Canadian growth prior to 1896 was not spectacular, it was at least substantial. The tariff had afforded Canadian manufacturers sufficient protection to enable them to dominate the growing domestic market, and the construction of the Canadian Pacific Railway acted as a strong stimulus to further expansion. Despite a cyclical depression in the 1880's, the gross value of the domestic manufacturing sector increased 50% in this decade, and the transition from local to national industries was well under way.

Prosperity. After 1896 a combination of rising world prices for Canadian exports (especially wheat) coupled with declining transportation costs and significant technological changes in agriculture, mining, and manufacturing helped to bring prosperity to Canada. Population increased by over 500,000 from 1891 to 1901 and by nearly 1.6 million from 1901 to 1911; about half of the latter gain was an increase in prairie population. Immigrant arrivals per year averaged 36,000 for the 1891–1901 decade, climbed to approximately 180,000 per year from 1901 to 1911, and exceeded 400,000 in 1913. The flow of foreign capital to Canada increased significantly after 1902–1903 and averaged almost $400 million per year from 1900 to 1913. Canadian transportation, agriculture, manufacturing, and mining all provided outlets for the British and Continental investor. By 1913 over $2 million had been invested in Canadian railroads alone and 7,500 miles (12,000 km) of rail had been added to Canada's 1901 total of 4,100 miles (6,600 km). Owing to the high level of foreign demand, on the one hand, and innovations such as the chilled steel plow or new wheat varieties, on the other, Canadian wheat production increased from approximately 56 million bushels in 1901 to 231 million bushels in 1911.

With a protected domestic market, massive expenditures on social overhead capital, and thriving prairie farmers, Canadian manufacturers were given an enormous boost in the pre-World War I decade. Over this period the net value of manufactured production grew 250%. The stimulus given to the production of textiles, iron and steel, paper, coal, and hydroelectricity had placed Canadian industry on roughly the same footing as agriculture in the economy, with Ontario and Quebec at the hub of this industrial activity.

It would appear, then, that by 1913, despite various setbacks, the policies that had been formulated during the difficult years of the 1870's had been attained in development, if not in income per capita. A well-balanced east-west complex based on the flow of manufactured products from central Canada to the protected markets of the Prairie provinces, and of western wheat to world markets seemed to be the solution to those seeking an independent unified nation.

Weaknesses. There were, however, weaknesses in this pre-World War I economic structure. Canadian development prior to 1913 had depended heavily on a strong and prosperous European economy; World War I served to destroy this dependence. Prior to 1913, Canadian national policy centered on staple production, and exports had perpetuated an economic structure inherited from the fur trade, which like its predecessor was extremely vulnerable to changes in external demand. Also, the east-west alignment of trade, even by the turn of the century, was being undermined by increasing economic interaction between Canada and the United States. These tendencies, however, are part of the new industrialism, and they lead to the second or modern phase of Canada's industrial development.

The New Industrialism: The Second Phase. The new industrialism had its roots in a changing pattern of trade and investment and a changing technology,

CANADA'S GROSS NATIONAL PRODUCT

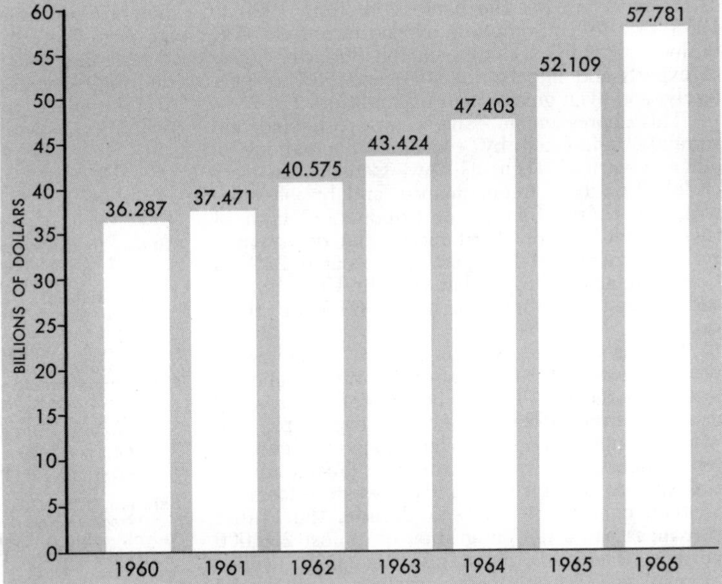

The value of Canada's Gross National Product increased dramatically from a figure of $36.287 billion in 1960 to $57.781 billion in 1966.

DATA: DOMINION BUREAU OF STATISTICS.

whereby an abundance of iron and coal was no longer a sufficient precondition for industrial growth. Even before 1900, Canada's imports from the United States exceeded those from any other country (including Britain), and by World War I, the United States supplied two thirds of Canada's imports. Canada's continued trade deficit with the United States was balanced by a large export surplus to Britain; however, such a triangular relationship of trade and capital flows raised few balance of payments adjustment problems. The overall Canadian balance of payments situation was very similar to that experienced by Canada since World War II, except that Britain was the main source for external borrowings.

This changing pattern of investment and trade is clearly typified by the growth of new industries such as pulp and paper, mineral production, and hydroelectric power. Growing United States interest in Canadian natural resources gave new impetus to Canada's economic growth, strengthened provincial autonomy, and pulled Canada away from dependence on its east-west transcontinental complex.

Impact of World War I. The economic impact of World War I, while perhaps less striking than that of World War II, nevertheless ushered in significant changes in the structure of the Canadian economy. Nonferrous metal refining, particularly copper, zinc, and nickel, was considerably expanded. Wartime demands for steel increased the output of the Canadian steel industry by 125% from 1914 to 1919. Similarly, aircraft and shipbuilding and a wide range of secondary industries were stimulated by wartime demands, so that by 1919 the output of the manufacturing sector contributed 44% of total product, while the agricultural sector contributed 32%.

The Depression. Prior to 1929 the Canadian economy had experienced two periods of depression and adjustment—1913 to 1915 and late 1920 to 1924. With regard to the severity of the downswing, however, neither of these periods could compare with the 1930's. In almost every year of this decade, the Canadian unemployment rate hit 10%, and in 1933 alone it reached 20%. In fact, from 1929 to 1933, Canadian national income was cut in half, and it was not until 1940 that the 1929 level of income was again reached. Every segment of the economy felt the depression: from 1929 to 1933 private consumption expenditure fell 35%, business gross fixed investment fell 80%, the value of exports and imports fell 49% and 53% respectively, and even government expenditures fell 28%.

This depression in Canada was paralleled and certainly influenced by economic fluctuations in other countries. Then, as now, Canada was very closely linked by trade, finance, and business ties with the United States and Britain, and both of these countries were hard hit by the downswing. In 1928 merchandise exports represented 22% of Canadian output, and in that year the United States and Britain together purchased 60% of these exports.

Canada's chief exports in this period were wheat, newsprint, and nonferrous metals, and all three exports were extremely vulnerable in world markets. From 1929 to 1933 the export price of wheat dropped 50%; moreover, the prairies encountered successive years of drought. This combination spelled ruin for thousands of western farmers. In fact, over the 1931–1941 decade, the Prairie provinces had a net emigration of almost 250,000 persons. The newsprint industry began to decline as early as 1926 due to overexpansion and the industry's unstable organization and pricing policy. The nonferrous metal industry enjoyed a boom in the last half of the 1920's, owing especially to the rapid growth in the world automobile and electrical machinery industries, but incurred sharp price and volume declines due to overexpansion, United States tariffs, and the general downturn in industrial production.

It is evident that declines in export prices and volumes and their effects on other sectors of the economy (such as transportation) were important factors in the Canadian depression of the 1930's. It should be noted that there were also other reasons that helped account for the length and severity of this downturn. By 1929 the major phase of western settlement was completed, and the great surge of autonomous investment based on railroads and wheat had lost most of its impetus. The 1920's witnessed the development of several large new industries; investment opportunities were exploited at a very high rate and essentially there was little backlog of investment opportunity left with which to cushion the depression.

Finally, there was little effective government contracyclical policy to help soften the blow of the depression. Government monetary policy was conspicuously absent. Fiscal policy was ineffective as both overall spending and deficits fell as the depression lengthened, and tariff action (the Ottawa Agreements) only threw more of the burden of the downswing on the export industries. Recovery after 1933 was very uneven, and it was certainly far from complete at the beginning of World War II.

Impact of World War II. World War II acted as a catalyst to Canadian industry. By 1945 over half of the value of Canadian output consisted of manufactured goods, and despite a 60% increase in the value of farm production the agricultural sector accounted for only 20%. Industrial growth was most marked in the electrical, chemical, and aluminum industries; aircraft and shipbuilding were stimulated (as in World War I); steel output increased approximately 120% from 1939 to 1943; and aluminum output increased 500% over this same period. New industries, such as synthetic rubber, optical glass, and high-octane gasoline, appeared, and new resources, particularly metallic minerals and mineral fuels, helped to further revolutionize the economy.

All these developments contributed to setting the stage for the spectacular changes that were to take place in the Canadian economy in the post-World War II era.

ANTHONY SCOTT
JAMES D. RAE
University of British Columbia

Bibliography

Aitken, Hugh George J., Deutsch, J. J., Mackintosh, W. A., and others, *The American Economic Impact on Canada* (Durham, N.C., 1959).

Caves, Richard Earl, and Holton, Richard Henry, *The Canadian Economy: Prospect and Retrospect* (Cambridge, Mass., 1959).

Easterbrook, William Thomas, and Aitken, Hugh George J., *Canadian Economic History* (Toronto 1965).

Economic Council of Canada, *First Annual Review: Economic Goals for Canada to 1970* (Ottawa 1964).

Economic Council of Canada, *Fourth Annual Review: The Canadian Economy from the 1960's to the 1970's* (Ottawa 1967).

Firestone, O. John, *Canada's Economic Development 1867–1953* (London 1958).

Safarian, Albert Edward, *The Canadian Economy in the Great Depression* (Toronto 1959).

Stovel, John A., *Canada in the World Economy* (Cambridge, Mass., 1959).

Urquhart, M. C., and Buckley, K. A. H., *Historical Statistics of Canada* (Toronto 1965).

PUBLIC ARCHIVES OF CANADA

RED BRICK FACTORIES, like this at Woodstock, New Brunswick, housed Canada's early national industries.

10. Manufacturing

Canada's manufacturing plants are run by an impressive array of thousands of firms ranging from General Motors of Canada—employer of more than 30,000 Canadians and maker of over half of all the cars bought in Canada each year—to small Canadian owned and operated companies begun by young executives after World War II.

About 70% of Canada's manufacturing capacity is owned or controlled by U.S. companies. Canada is the only major industrial nation whose manufacturing industries are largely controlled from outside the country.

Industries. Canada has an abundant variety of manufacturing industries to serve the needs of a modern society. Among the industry groups, the food and beverage segment accounts for the largest dollar volume of manufacturing shipments. Other leaders include transportation equipment, which soared after the Canada-United States auto agreement was signed in 1964, and paper and allied industries, which in the late 1960's exported more than $800 million worth of newsprint annually.

Canada has about 33,000 manufacturing establishments and over 1.2 million employees in manufacturing. In 1966 total manufacturing shipments first passed $30 billion.

The 1964 auto pact—a move in the direction of economic union between the United States and Canada—stimulated Canadian automotive production dramatically. The agreement set minimum levels of Canadian auto production (requiring increased production in Canada), required that U.S. auto companies increase their outlays in Canada by $260 million in three years, and gave assurance that new cars or parts could be exported free of duty. Canadian assemblies of cars and trucks rose sharply and so did Canadian car exports to the United States (from $99.3 million in 1964 to $845 million in 1966).

The percentage of manufactured goods among Canada's exports has increased rapidly. In 1967, for the first time, automobiles outpaced the country's traditional export leaders—wheat and newsprint—in dollar volume. The dollar volume of exports of industrial and farm machinery also increased in the late 1960's. There was a steady outflow of aircraft and select defense products manufactured in Canada under licensing agreements with U.S. defense industries.

Industrial Achievements. Since 1940, when the expansion attending World War II began to change Canada into an industrial state, Canadians have excelled in several major manufacturing areas. These accomplishments have been achieved against the strong influence of U.S.-designed consumer and industrial products on the market.

Some unique successes have come in industries that are geared to the mastery of Canada's harsh environment. Some of these have worldwide application, such as the volume production of STOL (short take-off and landing) aircraft, built to operate in bush country and in the tundra, and several models of snowmobiles devised to penetrate the snowbound regions of the Arctic. Some of the snowmobiles are huge vehicles that are capable of remaining a week from their base with a crew of six men.

For shipping on the Great Lakes, the pencillike lake carriers, which have been built from time to time in greater numbers in Canada than in the United States, are natural descendants of the historic Canadian "caller." The callers were small lake carriers built just long and wide enough to pass through the Lachine Canal locks at Montreal. The callers became obsolete when the St. Lawrence Seaway was constructed but the modern Great Lakes freighters inherited their shape.

The seagoing collapsible helicopter hangar was invented by a Toronto engineer who became president of a firm—Dominion Aluminum Fabricating, Ltd.—that has sold it to the U.S. Navy and Coast

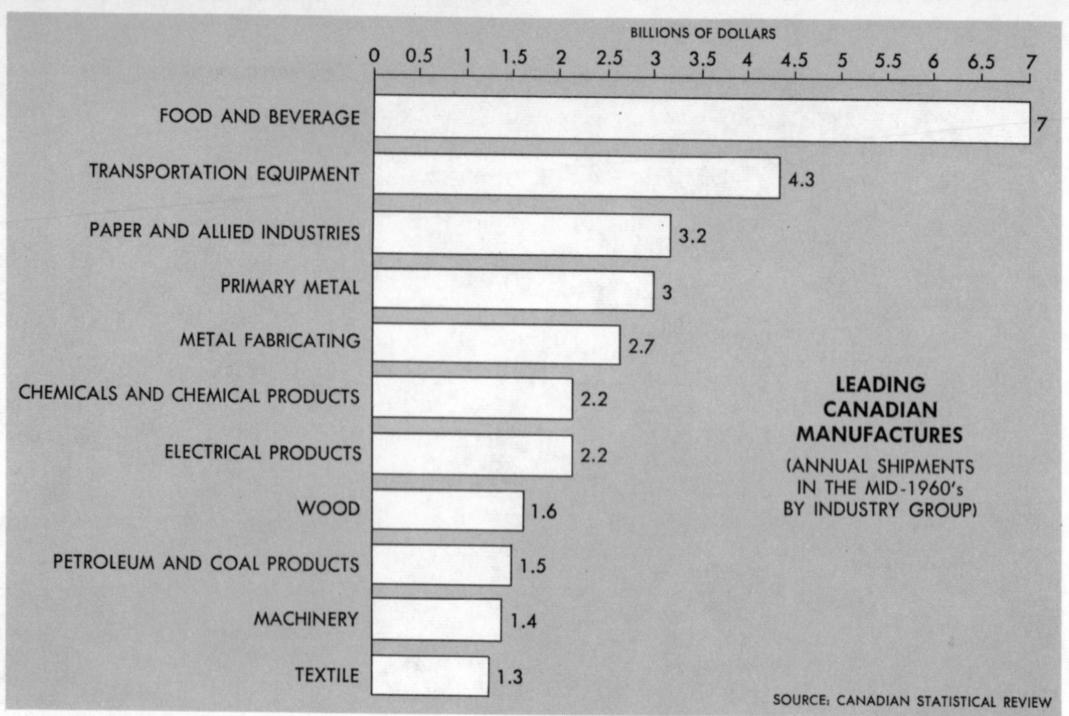

Guard, the navies of France and West Germany, and the permanent Antarctic expeditions of Chile and Japan.

Canadian achievements in navigational aids and radar, first applied to the needs of the Royal Canadian Air Force, and the design and manufacture of the destroyer escort, a unique anti-submarine warship created from a synthesis of British and U. S. naval architecture, have impressed the world.

Distribution of Manufacturing. Canada's manufacturing industries are heavily concentrated in areas of the country close to the U.S. border. The major regions are southern Ontario; the St. Lawrence River basin of Quebec province, especially around Montreal; and the lower mainland of British Columbia and Vancouver Island. Important new industrial developments have arisen in the prairie provinces of Manitoba, Saskatchewan, and Alberta, made possible by the exploitation of the oil and natural gas resources and the successful programs of aggressive provincial development agencies designed to lure new industry.

Ontario, with a population of mixed ethnic groups, largely European, is a vast technopolis where sweeping industrial areas dominate and shape society. Arrayed along the north shore of Lake Ontario, across from New York State, a "golden horseshoe" of plants stretches eastward from Niagara Falls. On the eastern end, this horseshoe extends up the St. Lawrence River to Cornwall. Clockwise around the lake, manufacturing cities in the complex include St. Catharines, Hamilton, Oakville, Toronto, Oshawa, Belleville, Kingston, and Brockville. Industrial giants such as the Steel Company of Canada and Dominion Foundries and Steel Company make Hamilton a steel center.

Another manufacturing concentration extends from Toronto through southwestern Ontario to Windsor and Sarnia. Its chief centers are Brantford, London, St. Thomas, and Chatham.

Another industrial complex spreads across the lower regions of Quebec. Montreal, Canada's largest city, makes railroad equipment, airplanes, metal products, shoes, clothing, and a variety of other products. Trois Rivières, on the St. Lawrence River, is a leading manufacturer of pulp and paper products, including newsprint.

In British Columbia, a rapidly growing industrial base is centered on Vancouver and fans out into the interior of the province and north along the Pacific Coast. Besides Vancouver, major manufacturing cities are Victoria, on Vancouver Island, and New Westminster, both of them large producers of wood products.

In addition to its newsprint, lumber, and fishing industries, British Columbia has an aluminum industry—its first major new industry after World War II. Initially the aluminum industry was concentrated at Kitimat, a new town at the end of a long northern inlet, where Aluminum Limited and the Aluminum Co. of Canada Limited built a $450 million, 212,000-ton aluminum smelter between 1951 and 1954. Most of Kitimat's bauxite comes by sea from Guyana and Jamaica. At Kemano, about 50 miles from Kitimat, stands a large hydroelectric installation to supply power to the smelter. When opened in 1954, Kitimat became the embodiment of the Canadian "company town" of the early 1950's and was called "the saga of Canada."

This huge processing complex has done well, although it has suffered from the overcapacity that the primary aluminum industry has experienced at times since the demand years of the Korean war emergency. Originally expected to be a city of at least 100,000, Kitimat has a population of about 15,000. Unlike the "company towns" built for the uranium industry—some of which have become ghost towns—Kitimat has had steady growth, even if slower than its builders expected. This massive aluminum complex has brought British Columbia several billions of dollars of new industry in pulp and paper, lumber, hydro power, tourism, and fishing.

In the prairie provinces, Winnipeg, Manitoba, has important manufactures of food and beverages, clothing, and iron and steel products. Saskatchewan, once a wheat producing province with no major industry, has become a leading source of the world supply of potash. A giant plant at Esterhazy, wholly owned by U.S. interests, is the largest of 13 potash plants in the province. Manufacturing plants in Alberta produce foods and beverages, chemical fertilizers, and equipment needed in the province's expanding oil fields.

In the Maritime provinces—traditionally Canada's "have-not" region—there has been a stimulating growth of industries. Nova Scotia's Industrial Estates Limited, a provincial crown corporation for the development of industry, has created the province's first integrated industrial base. The corporation has brought a Swedish automobile plant, producers of construction material and of food, and a heavy water plant to Nova Scotia.

In Newfoundland, the major entrepreneur has been Joseph Smallwood, the provincial premier whose energy has brought major manufacturing plants to the province. In New Brunswick, the efforts of Kenneth C. Irving have largely fostered the expansion of manufacturing enterprises. New Brunswick and the small province of Prince Edward Island conduct provincial industrial development programs that have brought in new plants.

Investments. Visitors to Canada are surprised by the wide array of U.S. consumer and industrial products they see. Canadian cities and towns burgeon with neon displays advertising U.S. products ranging from cake mixes to cars. Household goods bearing U.S. trade names, and even motels and restaurants owned by U.S. chains, give thousands of American visitors the impression that Canada is, in all but name, an industrial appendage of the United States. Although it is true that many U.S. trademarks appear in Canada, and that Canada is the largest customer of the United States, nevertheless these products are made, promoted, and distributed by a Canadian work force. Manufacturing in Canada remains entirely Canadian in character.

The pattern of ownership by which U.S. companies own and control about 70% of Canada's manufacturing industries dates back to the 1920's. Even in 1923, before the great boom of the 1920's had gained strong impetus, the *Canadian Historical Review* noted that there were "over 700 branch factories, fully owned by parent companies in the United States." This trend has continued, much to the concern of many Canadians. Foreign ownership of manufacturing is difficult to assess with complete accuracy, because the plants are divided into extractive, assembly, semifabricating, and fully processing concerns. But the Canadian automobile industry is almost 100% U.S. owned. The oil and gas industry is about 80% foreign owned, largely by U.S. interests. Other manufacturing industries, such as plumbing and heating supplies, are dominated by a few U.S. giants.

But other industries, such as Canada's primary steel and aluminum producers, are largely Canadian owned. A few Canadian industries are dominated

JOHN REEVES, FROM NATIONAL FILM BOARD

VTOL AIRCRAFT, for vertical takeoff and landing, in a Montreal plant. This type is useful in wild land.

TED GRANT, FROM NATIONAL FILM BOARD

NEWSPRINT is one of Canada's valuable manufactured products. This mammoth roll is in a mill at Alberni, British Columbia.

GAR LUNNEY, FROM NATIONAL FILM BOARD

PROCESSED FISH is packed at Lunenberg, in Nova Scotia. Food products are significant in the economy.

by Canadian-owned international concerns, such as Massey-Ferguson Limited in farm machinery and the Polymer Corporation in synthetic rubber and plastic powders. The latter, owned by the Canadian government, produces about 10% of the non-Communist world's synthetic rubber.

Management. A large part of the Canadian success in building an industrial democracy was the result of the training in management that began in earnest during the postwar booms of the 1950's when business became an operation requiring many new skills. Management techniques developed so broadly between 1950 and 1965 that distinct lines were drawn between the functions and roles of senior management (company presidents and vice presidents) and "middle management" (directors of sales, marketing, industrial relations, and production). The days had passed when the president or proprietor of a Canadian factory combined all these responsibilities in one person.

Schools of business, which as late as 1949 were limited to one (at the University of Western Ontario, London), expanded widely in the 1960's to serve manufacturing. Their curriculum and teaching reflected a strong influence from the Harvard Graduate School of Business Administration of Harvard University.

But unique Canadian situations have given management its own peculiar cast in Canada, even if the technology and plant that it serves are largely imported from the United States. These Canadian differences include a more conservative business class, isolated and smaller markets, and the special needs of French-speaking Quebec within the Canadian national market.

History. Canada's manufacturing was begun by Canadians in the years immediately following Canadian Confederation in July 1867.

Behind the present modern factories, industrial parks, and supermarkets of Canada still stand the high, brick-walled buildings of the small local industries where Canadian manufacturing began. Their old, often picturesque frames, inevitably raised beside rivers and railroads—the two major transport arteries of 19th century Canada—recall the Victorian era when the legislative basis for a domestic Canadian manufacturing sector was established.

This was the "National Policy" of Sir John A. Macdonald, Canada's first prime minister, and of his Conservative regime. It emerged throughout the 1880's as a tariff structure designed to satisfy the demands from infant, struggling Canadian companies—which were not always efficiently operated—for protection against the growing industrial giant of the United States.

The brick-and-mortar symbols of the old manufacturing ways are the physical embodiment of a process that not only created a national market in Canada but is the basis for the nation's tariff structure now. Canadian manufacturers were relieved that the Kennedy Round of the General Agreement on Tariffs and Trade, completed in 1967, did not result in deep tariff cuts for Canada as it did for the larger industrial countries. They indicated this relief within the spirit of the National Policy.

The great paradox of modern industrial Canada is that the large American, British, and European corporations, seeing the advantage of Canada's tariff wall for manufacturing in its domestic market, leaped over the wall to found local subsidiaries, fully protected under Canadian law as Canadian companies. The National Policy of tariffs became a servant of the Canadian subsidiaries of the foreign international corporations that it meant to restrict. Meanwhile the smaller Canadian-owned companies found themselves serving a reduced portion of their own market as a result of the new competition.

The new money supplied by foreign investment and the manpower supplied by Canada's first waves of immigration between 1896 and 1913 provided the kind of economic impetus that was implicit in Macdonald's National Policy.

The growth of foreign investment was spectacular. The $168 million of U.S. capital invested in Canada in 1900 jumped to $880 million by 1914, and to $1.6 billion after World War I. By 1930, with the Great Depression just begun, the United States had invested $4.6 billion in Canada's industries.

In contrast, the figure of British investment, which was $1.1 billion in 1900, leveled off through the 20th century and was only $3.2 billion in 1959, after Canada's substantial postwar booms of the 1920's and the 1950's.

During World War II, when British investment in Canada ceased and U.S. investment eased off, the stimulus of government as the entrepreneur for wartime needs moved Canadian industry ahead. This came about through the output of about 40 "crown corporations" or government concerns set up hastily and managed by executives called in from private enterprise. These firms supplied huge amounts of war materials, merchant ships, warships, aircraft, and weapons to Britain and its allies. In their production Canadians developed new technology and skills.

The driving force behind wartime industrial expansion was Clarence Decatur Howe, an American-born engineering genius who entered the Liberal government in 1936 as transport minister and served during World War II as minister of munitions and supply. After the war, Howe feared the onset of a depression like that of 1921, which almost wiped out Canada's gains in creating manufacturing industries during World War I; so he sold or leased hundreds of war plants to U.S. and British subsidiaries that were eager to manufacture goods for the pent-up Canadian consumer demand of the early postwar years.

This action of Howe's imparted an early stimulus to the rapid entry of foreign-owned companies into Canada. But the funds that built their postwar plants were generated from the Canadian wartime tax system. The crown corporations, with the technology that they developed, changed Canada from a basically agrarian nation to an industrial nation.

The Future. A basic problem of the future for Canadian manufacturers is to adjust the size of the manufacturing sector to the relative smallness of the Canadian market. In the late 1960's there were too many manufacturers—too many units of output for the small size of the nation's population. The deep tariff reductions expected by many industries as a result of the Kennedy Round did not take place. These reductions would have cut out many inefficient or high-cost producers.

Therefore Canada, even more than smaller industrial states that do not possess Canada's high concentration of industry, must find formulas to trim its manufacturing sector. This will be difficult for Canadians because so many decisions to rationalize industry must be made by parent corporations situated beyond the nation's borders.

More serious has been the rising wave of opposition from all of Canada's leading political parties to the fact that major decisions about Canadian subsidiaries still were being made abroad. Political methods of dealing with the extensive foreign control have been proposed by the government. The proposals include the creation of a large federal government development corporation to "buy back" foreign-owned companies or to prevent more Canadian concerns from being taken over.

On the other hand, many Canadians yearn for U.S. products at the lower U.S. prices in what would be a wider, virtually continental market. They would like to see economic union with the United States even though it might threaten Canada's political freedom.

Thus Canada has a dilemma in manufacturing: more prosperity comes from closer economic ties to the United States, but with the prosperity comes less freedom of economic movement. A major problem in its second century of existence will continue to be the future ownership and control pattern of her manufacturing industries.

JOHN D. HARBRON, *Toronto "Telegram"*

Bibliography

Aitken, Hugh G. J., *American Capital and Canadian Resources* (Cambridge, Mass. 1961).
Canadian Trade Committee, *Canadian Economic Policy Since the War* (Montreal 1966).
Dominion Bureau of Statistics, *Canadian Statistical Review* (Ottawa, monthly).
Dominion Bureau of Statistics, *Canada Year Book* (Ottawa, annually).
Easterbrook, W. T., and Aitken, Hugh G. J., *Canadian Economic History* (London, England, 1958).
Lougheed, W. F., *Secondary Manufacturing Industry in the Canadian Economy* (Toronto 1961).
Safarian, A. E., *Foreign Ownership of Canadian Industry* (Scarborough, Ontario, 1966).

11. Electric Power

The development of electric power in Canada has undergone remarkable and sustained growth since the beginning of the 20th century. From a modest 150,000 kilowatts in 1900, Canada's total installed electric generating capacity rose to nearly 30 million kw in 1965 and was expected to exceed 40 million kw by 1970.

GAR LUNNEY, FROM NATIONAL FILM BOARD

COKING OVENS flare at a steel plant in Hamilton, Ontario, a huge center of the nation's heavy industry.

Sources of Electric Energy—*Waterpower.* Although thermal developments are providing an increasingly larger part of the total each year, waterpower continues to be the main source of electric energy in Canada. In 1930, some 98% of the nation's electric energy was obtained from waterpower. This proportion had registered a decline to 82% by 1965.

In terms of waterpower, Canada is one of the most richly endowed nations in the world. Quebec and British Columbia are the provinces most favored with waterpower resources. Quebec, Ontario, and British Columbia have the largest installed capacities. Most of the waterpower resources in Ontario have been developed.

WATERPOWER RESOURCES OF CANADA
(Jan. 1, 1967)

Province or Territory	Undeveloped waterpower: Available continuous power at 88% efficiency at Q50[1] kw	Undeveloped waterpower: at Qm[2] kw	Developed waterpower: Installed generating capacity kw
British Columbia	16,635,000	24,665,000	2,695,000
Alberta	3,244,000	4,866,000	617,000
Saskatchewan	1,298,000	1,559,000	397,000
Manitoba	5,501,000	5,853,000	1,074,000
Ontario	1,102,000	1,663,000	6,194,000
Quebec	27,788,000	36,576,000	10,746,000
New Brunswick	221,000	497,000	262,000
Nova Scotia	112,000	165,000	143,000
Prince Edward Island	1,000	2,000	—
Newfoundland	3,635,000	4,871,000	466,000
Yukon Territory	3,237,000	5,689,000	28,000
Northwest Territories	2,232,000	3,322,000	35,000
Canada, Total	65,006,000	89,728,000	22,657,000

[1] Power equivalent of flow available 50% of the time.
Power equivalent of arithmetical mean flow.

GEORGE HUNTER, FROM NATIONAL FILM BOARD

ATOMIC POWER plant at Douglas Point, Ontario, marks increasing growth of this new source of energy.

Canada's waterpower has contributed in no small measure to the nation's level of industrial development and to the high standard of living enjoyed by Canadians. Although the abundance of waterpower has caused it to become the main source of electric power in Canada, there are many considerations that prompted developers to choose waterpower over other sources of electric energy. The efficiency of operation, long life of plant, dependability and flexibility of operation, the low maintenance and operating costs which more than offset large capital costs—all are distinct advantages offered by waterpower. Of even greater importance, perhaps, is the fact that the water that drives the hydroturbine is a renewable resource.

Thermal Power. In the early years, thermal stations in Canada were built to provide electricity for remote areas or to supply standby services in the event of a breakdown in regular service. This accounts for the relatively small size of the earlier thermal plants.

After World War II, the sharp increase in power requirements could not be satisfied by hydro sources alone, and this period marks the beginning of an extensive program of thermal station construction.

It was not until 1951 that the first large thermal unit was brought into service—a 100,000-kw steam unit fueled by coal. Continuing research has brought improved efficiency to thermal power production and has resulted in the design of increasingly large steam units, both conventional and nuclear.

In Ontario, conventional steam units rated at 300,000 kw have been in operation since 1961, and 500,000-kw units were being constructed for service in the late 1960's. The 20,000-kw Nuclear Power Demonstration station at Rolphton, Ontario, produced Canada's first nuclear electric energy in 1962. By 1966 the country's first full-scale nuclear power station, housing a 200,000-kw unit, was brought into service at Douglas Point on the shore of Lake Huron. Two 540,000-kw units were under construction for service in the early 1970's and two other similar units were planned for the Pickering nuclear power station on the shore of Lake Ontario. In Quebec, a 250,000-kw nuclear power station was being constructed near Gentilly, on the south shore of the St. Lawrence River, for service in 1971.

The magnitude of the loads carried by thermal stations has steadily increased, not only because thermal power has been the principal source of electric energy in some provinces but also because waterpower resources within economic transmission distance of load centers are rapidly being developed. The fact that a thermal-electric station can be located close to a demand area, with a consequent saving in transmission costs, is probably its most important advantage. However, with the trend to large steam stations, a certain amount of the flexibility of locations of thermal stations is being lost since large steam units require considerable quantities of water for cooling purposes, making it essential that they be situated close to an adequate water supply.

New Techniques. Hydro development has been enhanced as a result of recent advances in extra-high-voltage transmission techniques that have brought many hydro sites previously considered remote within the range of economic development. At the same time, however, important technological development has enlarged the role of thermal stations in the nation's central electric systems.

Electric Power Production. In Canada, electric power is produced by publicly and privately operated utilities and by industrial establishments. Publicly operated utilities, almost all provincially owned, produce some 70% of the nation's electric power requirements. Most of the remainder is produced by industrial establishments.

Canada's power producers entered the second half of the 1960's with major development programs. Touching briefly on some of these programs, an announcement in 1966 signaled a start on the construction of the 4 million-kw Churchill Falls hydroelectric development in Labrador, the largest single source of waterpower in Canada;

INSTALLED ELECTRIC GENERATING CAPACITY IN CANADA
(Jan. 1, 1967)

Province or Territory	Installed generating capacity—kw		
	Hydro	Thermal	Total
British Columbia	2,695,000	1,083,000	3,778,000
Alberta	617,000	1,096,000	1,713,000
Saskatchewan	397,000	662,000	1,059,000
Manitoba	1,074,000	338,000	1,412,000
Ontario	6,194,000	3,923,000	10,117,000
Quebec	10,746,000	441,000	11,187,000
New Brunswick	262,000	433,000	695,000
Nova Scotia	143,000	525,000	668,000
Prince Edward Island	—	57,000	57,000
Newfoundland	466,000	113,000	579,000
Yukon Territory	28,000	4,000	32,000
Northwest Territories	35,000	27,000	62,000
Canada, total	22,657,000	8,702,000	31,359,000

elsewhere in the Atlantic Provinces, another 1.7 million kw of generating capacity, shared equally between hydro and thermal capacity, was under construction. In Quebec, work on the Manicouagan-Outardes hydroelectric complex continued; ultimately a total of 6 million kw at 10 sites will result from the combined harnessing of the two rivers.

Projected into the early 1970's, the electric energy needs of Ontario point to the installation of some 7 million kw of thermal and more than 500,000 kw of hydro capacity. In northern Manitoba, construction to provide 400,000 kw at first, and 1 million kw ultimately, at Kettle Rapids on the Nelson River, was progressing favorably in the late 1960's. In Saskatchewan and Alberta, new thermal facilities were to provide about 500,000 kw and 1 million kw, respectively. In British Columbia, the first units in the Peace River Portage Mountain hydroelectric station were scheduled for service in 1968 and the entire 2.2 million kw will be developed by the mid-1970's. Altogether, a total of 24 million kw of new electric generating capacity was being built or planned for installation in the last of the 1960's and the early 1970's.

Utilization of Electric Power. In 1960, electric energy production in Canada was slightly in excess of 114 billion kilowatt hours. It is estimated that production in 1970 will grow to 210 billion kw-hr, almost double the 1960 production.

Industry uses approximately 55% of the total electric energy made available in Canada; residential and farm use accounts for 21% and commercial use, 15%. The rest is lost or unaccounted for.

Electricity is now used in virtually all of the nation's households. By comparison, only 60% of the nation's households were electrified in 1940. At the same time, the average consumption per household has undergone a fourfold increase, rising from 1,445 kw-hr in 1940 to 6,360 kw-hr in 1960.

Trends. In the years 1950–1965 the average rate of installation of both hydro and thermal generating capacity totaled some 1.4 million kw per year, with hydro contributing two kilowatts of new capacity for each kilowatt of thermal. In the five years from 1960 to 1965, however, the average increase in thermal generating capacity equaled the average increase in hydro capacity and promises to surpass it in the near future.

Large thermal plants require relatively long starting-up times and, therefore, are most efficient when meeting conditions of continuous loads. In contrast, hydro stations can put generating units on line with a minimum of delay and hence are admirably suited to supply power to meet the peak loads that may occur several times each day. By combining the advantages of both hydro and thermal stations in integrated supply systems, power producers have for some time been achieving a markedly greater flexibility of operation.

If Canada's energy requirements continue to double every 10 years as is forecast, it is inevitable that the waterpower resources will be unable to continue to provide the major portion of the nation's electric power needs. Undoubtedly, waterpower will be superseded in this role by thermal power, or some other source of electric power.

ALAN T. PRINCE
Canadian Department of Energy, Mines and Resources

12. Mining

Canada's record of mining exploration and development dates from 16th century accounts of discoveries of gold, silver, and copper. Minerals always have been a dominant factor in the nation's growth, both geographically and economically. Canada is in third place, following the United States and the USSR, in value of mineral output, and is the world's leading exporter.

National Production. Canada produces more than 60 mineral commodities. It leads the non-Communist world in the production of asbestos, nickel, zinc, and platinum; is second in the production of uranium, molybdenum, sulfur, potash, cobalt, titanium, and cadmium; and ranks high in the production of many other minerals, including iron ore, copper, silver, lead, gold, and platinum.

HYDROELECTRIC POWER is generated on many rivers. Below is the Shipshaw Dam at Arvida, Quebec.

GEORGE HUNTER, FROM NATIONAL FILM BOARD

SUN OIL COMPANY

OIL-BEARING SANDS are exploited in Alberta. A bucket wheel excavator digs its teeth into a sandbank.

W. VOLLMANN, FROM NATIONAL FILM BOARD

NATURAL GAS is sought in British Columbia by exploratory drilling. Here, workers change a drill bit.

The value of mineral production in the mid-1960's was some $4 billion, eight times that in the mid-1940's; mineral output value was over 7% of the country's gross national product, compared with 4% 20 years earlier.

About 70% of nonferrous mineral production is smelted and refined in Canada prior to domestic use or export; a smaller portion of ferrous metals output, sufficient for domestic needs, is processed in Canada; and practically all petroleum product requirements west of Montreal are met by the processing of domestic crude oil. The value of mineral exports in the crude and fabricated stage in the mid-1960's reached $3 billion, with about two thirds going to the United States, about 15% to Britain, and the remainder to over 40 countries. Mineral exports accounted for more than 30% of all Canadian exports in the 1955–1965 period.

Provincial Leaders. Ontario is Canada's leading mineral province with about 25% of the total output value. It is followed by Alberta with about 22%, Quebec 19%, Saskatchewan 9%, and British Columbia 8%. Generally, the 10 provinces and 2 territories register annual gains in mineral output; the largest absolute gains in the mid-1960's were by Alberta, Quebec, British Columbia, and Saskatchewan.

Although Ontario is the leading province, its share of output has declined from 37% in 1958 because of the more rapid gains of the three western provinces. Production of petroleum, natural gas, and elemental sulfur in Alberta, base metals in British Columbia, and potash in Saskatchewan has been particularly rapid.

Production by Sector. The metallics sector of the mineral industry in the mid-1960's accounted for nearly 50% of the total value of output; the industrial minerals sector, for just over 20%; and the mineral-fuels sector, for the balance. The 20 leading minerals in terms of output value—topped by crude petroleum, copper, iron ore, nickel, zinc, natural gas, and asbestos—were worth about 93% of the total.

Production Incentives. Many significant developments in Canada and throughout the world since 1950 have contributed to making Canada a prominent and sometimes dominant producer of minerals. The domestic economy, a large consumer of mineral products, has grown rapidly and has frequently outpaced the economies of many other industrial nations. There has also been a significant rise in the economies of many industrial nations, particularly Japan, the United States, and West Germany—all large consumers of mineral raw materials and metals. Canada is blessed with abundant mineral resources. Many mineral deposits have been discovered, but vast mineral-bearing areas still remain to be thoroughly explored.

The policies of both the federal and provincial governments provide a favorable environment for capital investment in mineral exploration, development, and production, thereby attracting the venture capital necessary for progressive mineral development. Many countries of Africa, South America, and Asia also have substantial mineral deposits, but few of them offer the advantages and stability that exist in Canada. The country's mineral development is assisted also by many government services at all levels.

Metallic Minerals. Copper was Canada's leading metallic mineral in the mid-1960's. Its annual production of over 500,000 tons places Canada fifth as a world producer after the U. S., Zambia, the USSR, and Chile.

Iron-ore production was second, with an output of over 40 million net tons. Output is expected to increase to between 45 and 50 million tons a year by 1970, and as iron and steel output in North America increases, to perhaps 60 million tons in the following decade.

Nickel, which had been either in first or second position for many years in value of output, had reached a productive capacity of 550 million pounds a year (275,000 tons). The world's two largest producers, both with operations in Canada, were engaged in expansion programs in Ontario and Manitoba designed to raise capacity to 700 million pounds (350,000 tons) a year by 1970.

Zinc mine production, nearly 1 million tons a year, is the world's largest. Molybdenum output of over 20 million pounds (10,000 tons) a year is second only to that of the United States. Reserves of zinc, lead, and molybdenum are sufficient to increase capacities much above the levels of the mid-1960's. New mines will be developed as market conditions warrant.

The outlook for gold continues to be bleak because of rising costs of production in relation to a fixed price of $35 (U. S.) per ounce.

Silver output, about 35 million ounces (1,089,000 kg) in the mid-1960's, had nearly reached that of Mexico and the United States, the world's two largest producers. About 80% of Canada's silver is recovered as a by-product of base-metal operations, and by the 1970's Canada might well be the world's leading silver producer because of the foreseeable increase in base-metal production.

The outlook for uranium production, which had been in serious decline from a high of 16,000 tons of uranium oxide in 1959, brightened considerably in the late 1960's as a result of the plans of many nations to base future electric power development on nuclear power rather than on hydro or thermal plants. Production of uranium oxide, about 4,000 tons a year in the mid-1960's, is expected to approach 20,000 tons a year by the late 1970's.

Industrial Minerals. Growth in the industrial minerals sector of the mineral industry, in both the nonmetallics and structural materials, is related largely to requirements of the domestic economy, in contrast to metallic and, in part, mineral fuels, both of which are largely dependent on exports.

Nonmetallics. Of the nonmetallics, only asbestos, potash, and sulfur are dependent for production growth on export markets. Canada and the USSR since 1960 have vied for first position as the world's leading asbestos producer, each contributing about 40% of the 3.8 million tons of asbestos-fiber output.

Two outstanding nonmetallic developments in the 1960's were related to potash and elemental sulfur. By the mid-1960's, Canada had overtaken many countries to become second only to the United States in the non-Communist world as a producer of these important basic minerals.

Canada possesses the world's largest and highest-grade potash deposits. Lying in beds at depths ranging from 3,000 to 4,000 feet (900–1,200 meters) in south central Saskatchewan, these deposits were discovered during oil drilling in the 1940's. Once certain mining problems were solved in the late 1950's, the deposits were rapidly developed. Canada is expected to become the world's leading producer of this important fertilizer ingredient in the 1970's.

Elemental sulfur is recovered in Canada from the processing of natural gas, from which the sulfur and natural-gas liquids must be removed before the gas is transported by pipeline. Canada produces many other nonmetallics, including salt, gypsum, sodium sulfate, and mica.

Structural Materials. The output of cement ($160 million), sand and gravel ($150 million), stone ($100 million), clay products, and lime, which comprise this group, is related closely to construction activity. Their use is directed to highway, industrial, residential, and other building projects. The value of structural materials output should increase at about 6% a year from the $470 million of the mid-1960's.

GEORGE HUNTER, FROM NATIONAL FILM BOARD

URANIUM is mined in northern Saskatchewan. A mine geologist studies a Geiger counter by a diamond drill.

Mineral Fuels. Mineral fuels, which embrace petroleum, natural gas, natural-gas liquids, and coal, increased in value more rapidly in the 1955–1965 period than did either of the other mineral sectors.

About 90% of petroleum and natural-gas output comes from the four western provinces, with Alberta supplying some 75% of the total. Exploration has been widespread in Alberta, northern British Columbia, and southern Saskatchewan. Successes have been particularly significant in Alberta. Since the Leduc oil discovery of 1947, resource development has continued undiminished, and by the late 1960's oil reserves stood at 10 billion barrels and natural-gas reserves at almost 50 trillion cubic feet (1.4 trillion cu meters). In addition, there is a huge petroleum reserve in the Athabasca oil sands.

A network of oil transmission pipelines has been built from western Canada to markets in Ontario, British Columbia, and the northwestern and north central United States. Gas pipelines reach markets as far east as the Montreal area of Quebec and southward on the Pacific coast to California.

In the mid-1960's output of liquid hydrocarbons in Canada averaged over 1 million barrels a day, and daily output of natural gas was over 4 billion cubic feet (113 million cu meters). Exports of oil and gas to the United States approached $500 million a year.

Output of coal declined from 19 million tons in 1950 and leveled off at about 11 million tons a year, valued at about $75 million, in the 1960's. Many of coal's traditional markets have been taken over by other sources of energy. Production of coal is confined almost entirely to Nova Scotia and southern British Columbia and Alberta near the common boundary of these provinces.

CHRIS LUND, FROM NATIONAL FILM BOARD

COPPER is a major Canadian mineral. This mine smelter is at Murdochville, Quebec, in the Gaspé Peninsula.

Growth of the Industry. The mineral industry has long been the most dynamic sector in the Canadian economy. Much of the growth in output value has taken place since the mid-1940's. However, since Canada achieved nationhood in 1867 there have been many significant mineral developments that have played very important roles in the country's development, both economically and geographically.

The value of mineral production for the first time reached $1 billion in 1950, approached $2.5 billion in 1960, and exceeded $4 billion annually by the mid-1960's. The growth rate of 8 to 10% a year experienced in the first half of the 1960's is expected to continue well into the 1970's.

MINERAL PRODUCTION VALUE BY CLASSES
($ millions)

	Metals	Non-metals	Structural Materials	Mineral fuels	Total
1950	617.3	94.7	132.3	201.2	1,045.5
1955	1,007.9	144.9	228.2	414.3	1,795.3
1960	1,406.6	197.5	322.6	565.8	2,492.5
1965	1,907.6	327.2	434.2	1,076.5	3,745.5

Source: Dominion Bureau of Statistics.

With the Canadian economy so dependent on the export market, it is revealing to note the importance of minerals to Canadian exports. From less than 5% of total exports in 1870, mineral commodities, including aluminum, have grown until they represent one third of Canada's total exports.

Contributions to the Economy. The growth of the mineral industry has benefited many parts of the Canadian economy. All new railway construction since World War II has been associated with mineral development. The St. Lawrence Seaway owes its beginnings and, in large measure, its sustenance to mineral traffic. The building of many ports and enlargement of others on the Seaway, St. Lawrence River, and in British Columbia, has also been based on mineral traffic. Mining is the mainstay of most northern communities. The construction industry reaps large benefits from mineral industry expansion (capital and repair expenditures average $700 million a year), as do the supply industries.

On the social side, mineral development has led to the opening of vast new territories through the establishment of new communities and communications media. Historically, mineral development has provided an important part of the pioneering activities of a young nation, of the country's great expansion after the turn of the century, of the supply of vital raw materials to Canada and its allies during two world wars and other near-war crises, of the support of the economy in recessions, and of the stimulus to economic activity during great industrial growth.

Forecast. Canada has proved reserves of most minerals sufficient for more than 30 years' operation at the mining rate of the mid-1960's. Large areas of the country remain relatively unexplored, and of the more than two thirds of the total area that is favorable for mineral deposition only a very small portion of this has been explored in detail. New discoveries are made each year in long-established mining areas as well as in the more distant and remote areas. The world's industrial nations are becoming ever hungrier for minerals to meet the requirements of their economies and to increase their output of industrial and consumer goods. It is probable that Canada will, as the years go by, play an ever-increasing role as a major supplier of mineral materials. The Canadian mineral industry base is strongly established, and the continuing development of mineral deposits in all parts of the country assures steady growth.

T. H. JANES, *Canadian Department of Energy, Mines and Resources*

Further Reading: Department of Energy, Mines and Resources, *Canadian Minerals Yearbook* (Ottawa, annually); bulletins and reports on mineral commodities and on mineral economic matters; Department of Mines (of each province), *Annual Report;* Dominion Bureau of Statistics, *Canada Year Book* and *Canada Handbook* (Ottawa, annually).

MALAK, FROM NATIONAL FILM BOARD

TIMBER LOGS are gripped by a loader in a clearing.

ANNAN PHOTO FEATURES

DEFT WORKERS prepare logs to be moved downriver.

13. Forest Products

The vast forests of Canada are one of the nation's most valuable economic resources. The forest products industry account for more than 9% of the net value of production of all commodity-producing industries. It employs 3% of the total labor force and contributes nearly 5% of all salaries and wages. It also contributes almost one fourth of the total value of Canada's export trade.

The most important forest industries are pulp and paper, logging, lumber, and veneer and plywood. Pulpwood, sawlogs, and veneer logs are the principal products removed from the forests, and their combined values represent more than 90% of the total harvest. Other forest products include poles, piling, fence posts and rails, fuelwood, round mining timbers, and hewn ties.

Realizing that the forests are not limitless, and aware of the dangers of overcutting, leaders of the industry have adopted conservation and management practices to ensure the preservation of the forests as a vital national asset.

Forest Land. The total area of forest land in Canada is 1.7 million square miles (4.4 million sq km). The area of productive forest land is 967,000 square miles (2.5 million sq km), making Canada the fifth-largest forested region in the world after the USSR, Asia outside Siberia; South America, and Africa. Total growing stock comprising both hardwoods and softwoods is 752 billion cubic feet (21.2 billion cu meters), ranking Canada third behind the USSR and South America. If softwood volume alone is considered, Canada with 611 billion cubic feet (17.3 billion cubic meters) is second in importance only to the USSR. In Canada, there is an average annual harvest of approximately 3.2 billion cubic feet (90.6 million cu meters).

Approximately 82% of the forest land is publicly owned and administered by the 10 provincial governments. The timber is rendered available for harvesting to forest industries by a variety of methods of tenure, but chiefly through long-term leases and licenses. The provincial governments retain full jurisdiction and control over these forests, and their principal objective is to ensure a perpetual yield of timber through appropriate forest management and protection practices. The remaining 18% of the forest land is composed of farm woodlots, wooded land owned by companies and by individuals, and forest areas belonging to the federal government.

The forests of British Columbia, Ontario, and Quebec contain 597 billion cubic feet (16.9 cu meters) of timber and comprise 80% of the total volume of standing merchantable timber in Canada. The province of British Columbia accounts for about 39% of the total net value of forest products. Ontario and Quebec combined contribute almost 50%.

Pulp and Paper. The manufacture of pulp and paper is one of Canada's leading industries. It contributes almost $1 billion to the approximately $23 billion net value of production of all commodity-producing industries; employs about 65,000 persons and pays out over $350 million in salaries and wages; is responsible for about 72% of the value of exports of all forest products; and earns close to $1.4 billion in foreign exchange. The operations of the industry generate about $1 of every $8 of income for all Canadians.

Newsprint paper is by far the most important product exported in both value and volume. The United States is the most important foreign market not only for newsprint but for practically all pulp and paper products. However, products of this industry enter virtually every country in the Western world.

There are more than 150 pulp and paper mills in Canada. Over 60 mills are located in Quebec, 40 in Ontario, and 25 in British Columbia. Only the province of Prince Edward Island does not have a pulp mill. The combined annual output

ANNAN PHOTO FEATURES

RAFT of logs is towed to a mill for processing.

consists of 16 million tons of newsprint, 8.4 million tons of multipaper and paperboard products, and 4.6 million tons of market pulp and pulp to make rayon, photographic film, cellophane, nitrocellulose, and a variety of plastics. By-products include yeast, turpentine, road binders, and commercial alcohol.

Spruce, balsam fir, jack and lodgepole pines, and hemlock are the principal species used in the manufacture of pulp for paper.

The conversion of trees to pulp and paper is one of the most productive uses of Canada's vast forest resource. Excluding the losses caused by insects and disease, the pulp and paper mills account for only one third of the annual drain on the forests, yet they create more new wealth for Canada than all other forest product industries combined. In addition, pulp and paper industry has been responsible for the development of much of the nation's hydroelectric power potential, and it uses about one fifth of all the electricity consumed in Canada.

Logging. The logging industry, or "woods operations" as it is sometimes called, is the second most important forest industry on the basis of net value of production. It accounts for about $400 million in salaries and wages and provides the equivalent of 80,000 year-round jobs. As an employer, it is the most important forest industry.

This industry is responsible for the harvesting of the timber from the forests and transporting it to the manufacturers. It also supplies timber to the export market, and pit props, poles, posts, and other round timber to the domestic market.

It is a heterogeneous segment of the forest economy and cuts across the boundaries of several industrial groups. The pulp and paper companies provide approximately two thirds of their wood supply by operations that they direct. The nation's sawmills obtain well over half of their sawlogs by logging standing timber owned, controlled, or leased by mill operators. The remaining volume is produced by a large number of independent operators and farmers.

Logging techniques vary from region to region. In British Columbia, the rough terrain and large-sized trees favor more extensive use of heavy mechanical equipment. In eastern Canada, however, logging has rapidly developed from hand and horse methods to highly mechanized systems.

Lumber. The lumber industry employs about 46,000 persons and has an annual payroll of nearly $190 million. The sale value of its products is almost $720 million. Spruce, Douglas fir, hemlock, cedar, white and red pines, jack and lodgepole pines, and yellow birch are the chief kinds of trees used in the manufacture of lumber.

Exports, mostly softwoods, are close to $500 million and account for almost 24% of the value of all wood products exported. Canada's share of the world softwood lumber trade is nearly 35%, making it the largest exporter of softwood lumber in the world. The United States is the chief export market for lumber. The major woods exported in order of importance by value are spruce, hemlock, Douglas fir, and western red cedar. Canadian lumber enters most countries in the Western world.

The industry comprises over 8,000 mills, the greater number being small mills although the medium and larger mills are responsible for the greatest part of the total lumber production. Some of the largest mills are located on the coast of British Columbia, and these account for nearly 75% of the volume of softwood lumber produced in Canada each year. Being part of a highly integrated industry, most companies produce such products as plywood, shingles, or pulp and paper as well as lumber.

Until about 1900 the lumber industry was one of the most important manufacturing industries in Canada, based on the value of factory shipments. Its importance, however, has since declined, and numerous other products now compete with lumber.

Veneer and Plywood. The veneer and plywood industry is of more recent origin in Canada than the lumber industry and has shown a much more rapid rate of growth since World War II. It uses poplar, yellow birch, Douglas fir, spruce and pine. The industry, totaling about 80 mills, employs over 12,000 persons and has an annual payroll of almost $60 million. The annual sale value of its products is over $200 million.

Exports of veneer and plywood approximate $70 million annually and are rising. Douglas fir plywood, shipped chiefly to Britain, is the most important product exported, accounting for over 45% of the total value of exports of all veneer and plywood. Birch veneer from eastern Canada follows Douglas fir plywood in importance and accounts for about 36% of the total export value of veneer and plywood. The birch veneer goes chiefly to the United States.

On the basis of value shipments, the manufacture of softwood plywood, used chiefly for rough construction, is more important than the manufacture of hardwood veneer and plywood. The former centers on the coast of British Columbia, the latter in Ontario and Quebec.

Other Forest Products. Forest products such as fuel wood, poles and piling, round mining timber, fence posts, rails, hewn ties, and miscellaneous round timber products constitute only about 8% of the value of total forest production in Canada. Fuel wood and round mining timber are the two most important components.

History of the Industry. Canada's early forest history was closely identified with the production of masts, spars, and planking for the British Navy and later, in the 1800's, with the white-pine square-timber trade with Britain.

The development of the sawmill industry supplied local needs prior to the 1800's. Lumber became an important export commodity about 1825. A gradual decline in British prejudices against any wood except squared timber permitted export across the Atlantic of sawn deals 2 to 4 inches (5 to 10 cm). This supplemented the timber trade and allowed the use of smaller pine trees and of the abundant Quebec and Maritime spruce.

After 1850 the sawmill industry was favored even more by newly developing markets in the United States. Trade in lumber was hastened by the prevalence of local wood shortages in the rapidly expanding communities of the Atlantic coast; the construction of the great canal systems of New York state and the St. Lawrence region; the decline and eventual lifting of the preferential tariffs of Britain; the investment of American capital; and the agreements of the Reciprocity Treaty of June 1854. These events provided the chief impetus to the development of a powerful lumber industry in eastern Canada.

Lumber for the building of the Prairie provinces initially was supplied from the western edge of the pine belt in northwestern Ontario. It was in British Columbia, however, that the Canadian lumber industry reached its latest and greatest development. The first recorded exploitation of the province's forests occurred toward the end of the 18th century with the export of small quantities of masts and spars. It was the building of the Canadian Pacific Railway and the resultant link with the expanding settlements of the Prairie provinces which gave the industry its first spurt of rapid growth. From then on British Columbia lumber production shot upward at a phenomenal rate, approximately doubling in quantity every decade until the depression of the 1930's. Today, the lumber industry is centered in British Columbia.

The first pulp mill in Canada was built in 1803 in St. Andrews, Quebec. This mill was run by waterpower and used linen and cotton rags as raw material to produce wrapping paper, printing paper, paperboard, and blotting papers. It was not until the 1860's and 1880's that mills using wood as the raw material were built. After the repeal in 1911 of the U. S. tariff on newsprint, the production of such paper rapidly increased, since conditions in Canada for the manufacture of the principal component, groundwood pulp, were particularly favorable. Then as now, the United States was the chief market for newsprint and most Canadian paper products.

Conservation. The Forestry Study Group of the Royal Commission on Canada's Economic Prospects pointed out in 1967 that, though market factors have had a great deal to do with the shaping of Canada's forest industry, technology and the ever-present threat of resource depletion have also had far-reaching implications. One such implication has been the profound change in organization. Nomadic enterprises have given way to more or less permanent institutions. The early philosophy of "cut and get out" has been replaced by the idea of management in perpetuity. Without timber limits sufficient to support several decades of production, it would be impossible to finance a modern pulp mill. Likewise, a well-integrated lumber, plywood, woodpulp and composition-board industry requires limits whose sustained yield is commensurate with its ability to turn out salable products. Vast tracts of Canada's forest lands are being managed in this way.

VICTOR STEWART
Economics Research Institute, Canadian Department of Forestry and Rural Development

Further Reading: Canadian Pulp and Paper Association, *From Watershed to Watermark* (Montreal 1967); Davis, John, and others, Forestry Study Group of the Royal Commission on Canada's Economic Prospects, *The Outlook for the Canadian Forest Industries* (Ottawa 1967); Department of Forestry and Rural Development, Economics Research Institute, *Canada's Forests 1965* (Ottawa 1966).

STACKED by a railroad siding at a mill, pulp logs are awaiting processing and shipment.

I. DONALD BOWDEN

CHRIS LUND, FROM NATIONAL FILM BOARD

HUGE COMBINES move over the wheat fields during the harvest in the rich farmlands of Saskatchewan.

14. Agriculture

On a commercial scale, farming in Canada is practiced over a span of some 4,000 miles (6,400 km) in a discontinuous belt along the border with the United States. Because of the rough and rocky terrain, farming is precluded from a vast portion of the Canadian Shield which makes a break in the belt north of lakes Huron and Superior and extending westward to the Manitoba-Ontario border. In British Columbia the mountain ranges intercept the belt. In other places, as in western Alberta, farming extends northward a distance of about 400 miles (640 km) from the United States border.

Across this broad expanse, there are approximately 430,000 farm units with a total cultivated area slightly exceeding 100 million acres (2.47 acres-1 hectare). In addition, mainly in the drier parts of Saskatchewan, Alberta, and British Columbia, there are an estimated 55 to 60 million acres of native grass used for ranching and farm pastures.

More than two thirds of the present cultivated acreage was brought into use for farming in the 20th century. This resulted from the major settlement of the four Western provinces early in this century. It is primarily in these provinces that the cultivated acreage continues to expand. Because of encroachment by industry and urban and highway expansion, and of the cessation of farming on land of low productivity, elsewhere the acreage of cultivated land has been declining. It is estimated that an additional 42 million acres of mineral soils exist that are potentially arable. Most of such land, however, does present difficulties for development and use. There are also a few million acres of peat soils that many be exploited in the future.

General Characteristics. Farming, though it is the nation's major primary industry, has been in a declining position in the total economy because of the very rapid industrial development in recent decades. In part, at least, the industrial expansion has been made possible by the mechanization of farming operations which released manpower to industry and allied functions. Although it has a lesser place in the total economy, farming still plays a very essential and important role in national life.

The contribution of agriculture amounted to from 5% to 6% of the total value of all goods and services annually during the 1960's. The share of mining and oil wells was slightly over 4% and that of forestry 1%. The contributions of other segments of the economy were about as follows: manufacturing, 26%; services, 15%; finance, insurance, and real estate, 10%; retail trade, 9%; construction, 6%; and transportation, 6%.

In export trade, products of the farm, in original or processed form, annually amounted to about 22% of the value of Canada's total export trade. Because the value of agricultural products imported into Canada amounts to about 50% of the value of such products exported, agriculture makes a very important contribution to the country's balance of payments.

Besides furnishing an abundance of food for domestic needs, farmers produce a number of commodities that are exported in considerable volume.

Chief among these is wheat, in the export of which Canada ranks second (after the United States) among the nations of the world. Canada also exports substantial quantities of barley, oats, rye, flax, rapeseed, tobacco, grass and legume seeds, potatoes, fresh fruits (particularly apples), dairy products, poultry products, cattle, and hogs. These exports contribute in a very significant way to the overall economy of the nation.

About 9% of all employed persons are engaged in farming, but the proportion has been declining, and the decline is expected to continue.

In spite of a decreasing proportion of the labor force engaged in farming, overall agricultural productivity and farm output since 1935 has increased at an estimated annual rate of about 2%. These increases in efficiency and productivity have resulted from a combination of factors, chief of which have been the enlargement of farm size, the specialization and mecha-

J. ALLAN CASH, FROM RAPHO GUILLUMETTE

COWS AND CALVES are driven in from the range to be branded on a cattle ranch in Alberta.

nization of production, and the utilization of technological developments. These developments include new breeds, new varieties, chemicals for control of weeds and insect pests, chemical fertilizers, antibiotics, and hormones.

Size of Farms. Average farm size has been increasing at a fairly rapid rate in all regions of Canada. With this increase in size has been associated a substantial decrease in the number of farm units. This trend is likely to continue. In the mid-1960's the average number of acres per farm was as follows: Prince Edward Island, 145; Nova Scotia and New Brunswick, each about 200; Quebec and Ontario, each about 160; Manitoba, 480; Saskatchewan, 763; Alberta, 706; and British Columbia, 277. These averages include noncultivated as well as cultivated acreage.

Specialization. Coupled with the increase in farm size has been a definite trend toward specialization or intensification of production in one enterprise or, at most, a few enterprises rather than several. For example, many more farmers have been concentrating on dairying alone. An associated process has been that of reducing the number of functions performed in connection with the specialized enterprise. For example, the large-scale poultry producer buys most of his feed requirements instead of producing them. These developments have increased efficiency of production very considerably.

Mechanization and Technology. Many of the farm operations are highly mechanized. By and large, the various operations involved in production of all crops are mechanized, and particularly so on the larger farms. The mechanization of livestock production has been somewhat slower in development, but recently progress in this area has been rapid.

Productivity on the farms has been substantially increased due to the application of improved technology arising from research. A high proportion of the more successful farmers utilize the latest technological developments.

Other Factors. In spite of overall improved efficiency and productivity, many farmers were experiencing financial difficulties in the late 1960's. On a considerable proportion of farms the size of operation is too small to provide an economic unit. Equally important is the fact that the cost of items required for farm operation has increased progressively and substantially whereas the prices received for commodities have not advanced in proportion.

From the east to the west coast a very wide variation exists in the soil and climatic conditions and in the density of the population. These are the chief factors that determine the type of farming that is practiced. These factors, in a general way, are common over fairly large geographical areas and distinct from one area to another. On such a basis, four fairly distinct agricultural regions may be delineated.

Atlantic Region. Included in this region are the provinces of Nova Scotia, New Brunswick, Prince Edward Island, and Newfoundland. However, there are differences among the provinces of this region. The agriculture of Newfoundland, in particular, is quite distinct in that the total arable acreage is small, a high proportion of the farm units are very small, and many farms are managed as a part-time operation. The discussion that follows pertains mainly to the three other Atlantic provinces.

Although locally important, the agriculture of this region is comparatively unimportant in the national picture. This is illustrated by the fact that the production of livestock, livestock products, grains, and some vegetables is insufficient to supply the region's market needs. The production of potatoes and apples are the chief exceptions to this general situation.

Although it has about 10% of the nation's population, only about 1.8% of the improved land of the nation is located in this region. The average improved acreage per farm is lower than elsewhere, and farm land is being abandoned more rapidly than in other parts of the country. However, the average size of farm units has been increasing very rapidly. In spite of the trend to the contrary, there is a potential for considerable expansion of farming activity in this region.

Resource Base. The soils of this region are low in natural fertility. Heavy applications of fertilizers and lime are essential for optimum crop production. While much of the landscape is rolling, the elevations are low and generally do not present obstacles to cultivation.

Climatically, the region is generally favorable for the production of a number of crops. Precipitation is moderately high, generally ranging annually from 40 to 50 inches (101–127 cm), of which 15 to 18 inches (38–45 cm) falls from April to July. The July average temperature is 65° F (18° C), and the frost-free period generally ranges from 120 to 140 days. Although the winters are fairly cold, there are local valleys with sufficiently temperate climate for the growth of certain fruit trees, notably apple.

Production. The region has a reputation for the production of potatoes and apples because these are produced in large enough quantities to permit export. Between them, Prince Edward Island and New Brunswick produce about 40% of Canada's potatoes. Nova Scotia grows about 15% to 18% of Canada's apples. New Brunswick and Nova Scotia, and to a lesser extent Newfoundland, are important producers of blueberries.

However, livestock and poultry production constitute the major enterprise of this region. Over half of the farm-cash income of Prince Edward Island and New Brunswick, and 80% of that of Nova Scotia, is derived from livestock and poultry. Dairying is the major enterprise, and beef production is of lesser importance. Poultry production is second in importance to cattle, and hogs are of lesser significance. Cattle raising is an appropriate endeavor since the climatic conditions are very favorable for grasses and legumes, and about 70% of the arable land is sown to such crops. With adequate fertilization heavy yields of grass-legume mixtures are obtained. Oats are the principal grain crop. The production of grain crops is not sufficient to supply the needs of the livestock and poultry in the region. The deficiency is met by imports from the Prairie region.

Central Canada Region. The provinces of Quebec and Ontario make up the region designated as Central Canada. From an agricultural standpoint, the designation of this area as a region is somewhat artificial in that the soils of the southeastern portion of Quebec are fairly distinct from those of the rest of the area. But in a general way the type of agriculture practiced is reasonably similar throughout the area.

Although secondary in importance to mining, forestry, and manufacturing, agriculture in this region is of substantial size and of great importance. As about 65% of the people of Canada live in this region, the agricultural production is highly important in the region's economy as well as in that of the nation as a whole. Roughly 40% of Canada's total farm-cash income is derived from this region.

Resource Base. The region's improved land amounts to about 21 million acres. This is about 21% of the improved land of Canada.

About 3 million acres of improved land are in eastern Quebec where the soils are strongly acid and leached, so that the natural fertility is low. In the lowlands of the St. Lawrence and Ottawa rivers and in the area between the Great Lakes are located about 16 million acres of improved land with soils of fair-to-good natural fertility. This area possesses the most important agricultural soils of the region. Within the area, however, a considerable acreage is stony and rocky and is of marginal value for agriculture. Some of this land, farmed in the past, has been abandoned. The demands of industrial development and urban expansion have also decreased the arable acreage.

The vast Canadian Shield, lying to the north of these areas, while generally unsuitable for agriculture, does contain about 2.5 million acres of improved land located in scattered pockets of varying sizes. Two thirds of this land is in Quebec. The soils range from moderately fertile to rather infertile, and generally the cooler temperatures and shorter frost-free periods place limitations on the choice of crops. It is estimated that within the Canadian Shield area there are about 10 million acres of potentially arable land.

Throughout the region south of the Canadian Shield the moisture supply is favorable for crop production with a fairly uniform monthly distribution of the 30 to 40 inches (76–101 cm) of total annual precipitation. Occasionally there are fairly severe droughts. Summer temperatures, averaging 65° F (18° C) in July in much of the area and 70° F (21° C) in southwestern Ontario, are conducive to good growth of many crops. These summer temperatures, coupled with fairly mild winters and frost-free periods of up to 180 days in some districts, permit a greater variety of crops to be grown here than in most other parts of Canada. In the Canadian Shield area, summer and winter temperatures and the frost-free period are less favorable.

Production. The agricultural production of the region hinges on livestock and poultry. About two thirds of the nation's dairy cattle are in Ontario and Quebec, with about equal numbers in each province. Beef cattle production is a major enterprise in Ontario but of lesser importance in Quebec. In addition, about 35% to 40% of Canada's hogs are produced in Ontario and 20% in Quebec. Eggs and poultry meats are also major enterprises.

With the emphasis on cattle production, it follows that a high proportion of the arable land is in grass for hay and pasture. In Quebec and in the St. Lawrence lowlands of Ontario about 70% of the land is sown to grass. In the area between the Great Lakes the proportion is slightly over 50%. Oats and mixed grains are grown extensively in rotation with the grass-legume mixtures. Corn for grain has come into use on a substantial scale, particularly in southwestern Ontario. Corn is also grown for silage on a large acreage.

A considerable proportion of the beef cattle production is based upon imports from the Prairie region of feeder cattle and the fattening of these in Ontario and to a lesser degree in Quebec. Large quantities of feed grains are shipped from the Prairie region.

Winter wheat is a minor crop in Quebec. In Ontario it occupies slightly less than one-half million acres. The grain is used for milling and in feeding livestock and poultry.

A number of special crops are produced on a substantial scale, and some of these have a high market value per acre. Included in this group are tobacco, sugar beets, soybeans, and canning crops such as peas, tomatoes, corn, and cucumbers. In addition there is a large and important production of fruit and market garden crops.

From 90% to 95% of Canada's approximately

100,000 acres of tobacco is grown on sandy soils in the warmest part of Ontario. The balance of the acreage is found in Quebec. The bulk of tobacco production is of the flue-cured type, with the balance of the burley and dark types.

Around 20% to 25% of Canada's sugar beet acreage is in Ontario. Quebec has about 10%. The sugar refining companies control the acreage and arrange contracts with the farmers.

Ontario is the only province in which soybeans are grown to any extent. The warm, long growing season of southwestern Ontario is suitable for this crop.

Production of fruits, including apples, pears, peaches, cherries, grapes, strawberries, and raspberries, is on a substantial scale. Although orchards are dispersed rather generally between the Great Lakes in Ontario, there is an area of very concentrated production in the Niagara peninsula. In Quebec, production is situated south and southeast of Montreal and generally on the slopes of hills.

The concentration of population in the region creates a heavy demand for vegetable crops. Thus it is natural to find considerable market gardening. In Ontario, the area of concentrated production is in a band along the north shores of lakes Erie and Ontario. In Quebec, production is concentrated around Montreal, and particularly south from there to the United States border. These are the areas of highest average temperatures and with the longest frost-free period.

Prairie Region. The provinces of Manitoba, Saskatchewan, and Alberta comprise the Prairie region. A large part of the agricultural area was prairie grassland in its natural state. Forests surround the grassland on the east, west, and north, and between the prairie and forest is a transition zone of mixed tree-and-grass cover. Agricultural settlement has extended into the transition zone and, to a lesser extent, into the forest land.

Over 75% of Canada's improved land is located in this region. In addition, there are 25 to 30 million acres of native grassland used for ranching and farm pastures. The region contributes over three fifths of the gross physical output and about half of the total output value of Canadian farming. It is from this region that the deficit requirements of other parts of Canada for milling wheat, feed grains, oil seeds (excluding soybeans), beef cattle, hogs, and sheep are met. This region also supplies Canada's export trade in small grains and oilseed crops.

Resource Base. The soils of this region are predominantly of high fertility. The primary deficiency for grain production is phosphorus. In the forested area the soils are of lower natural fertility. Even these soils are not seriously lacking in fertility, but they do require heavier fertilizer applications and rotations, including legume crops, to attain optimum productivity.

A large part of this region is semiarid, with total annual precipitation of about 14 to 16 inches (35–41 cm). About 7 to 9 inches (18–22 cm) of precipitation occurs from April to July. A small part of southeastern Manitoba and of western Alberta has precipitation of 18 to 20 inches (45–50 cm) annually. Associated with the relatively low precipitation is low humidity and frequent and fairly strong winds. Drought is a major hazard. Irrigation on a fairly extensive scale has been developed in Alberta and is being developed in Saskatchewan.

MARCEL COGNAC, FROM NATIONAL FILM BOARD

MAPLE SAP is collected on a Quebec farm. Such scenes are familiar in eastern Canada in early spring.

Temperatures are warm and the days long in summer. Except in comparatively small areas in southern locations, heat-loving crops such as grain corn and soybeans cannot be grown. Winters are long and cold, and only the more cold- and drought-hardy crops will survive in a large part of this region. For most of the region the frost-free period averages about 100 days, but for certain areas it ranges from 80 to 100 days. This factor limits the selection of crops and varieties.

Production. The nature of agricultural production on the prairies is distinct from that of the rest of Canada. It rests on extensive production on large farms of small grains and oilseed crops. A comparatively small proportion of the cultivated land is sown to grasses and legumes. Furthermore, land management involves extensive summer fallowing. This is a process of leaving the land uncropped for a year during which weeds and volunteer grain are destroyed by repeated cultivation. In the drier portions of this region 50% of the land is summer-fallowed annually, and in many other parts 30% to 40% is so handled. The purpose of this practice is to conserve moisture and nitrogen during the summer-fallow year for use by the crop the following year. Wheat is the crop mainly grown on summer-fallow.

Wheat is king on the prairies. Over 95% of Canada's 27 to 30 million acres of wheat is grown in this region, and Saskatchewan is the major producer. Most of the wheat grown is of the hard red spring variety with high milling and baking qualities. A small acreage of winter wheat, and an even smaller acreage of white pastry flour wheat, is grown in Alberta. About 1 to 2 million acres are devoted to producing durum wheat for the macaroni trade.

Over 90% of Canada's acreage of barley, flax, rapeseed, sunflower, and rye are grown in this region. Oats are a major crop but less dominant in the total Canadian picture. Sugar beets are grown on 60,000 to 70,000 acres, over half of which is on irrigated land in Alberta and the balance on dry land in the Red River Valley of

Manitoba. Potatoes and such specialized canning crops as peas, sweet corn, carrots, and tomatoes are grown on irrigated land in southern Alberta. Grass and legume seeds are produced considerably in excess of regional and domestic requirements.

Although its reputation is based on grain production, this region is also an important producer of livestock. It has about 45% of the total cattle population of Canada, more than 70% of the beef cows and heifers, 35% to 40% of the hogs, and over 50% of the sheep. Fluid milk production is located around the major urban centers, and a substantial volume of cream is produced over a more extensive area. Beef cattle from farm herds and from ranches supply the deficit in eastern Canada and provide for some export. Feedlot finishing of beef cattle is increasingly practiced in this region. Hogs, of which Alberta is the largest producer, also are produced in excess of regional needs.

West Coast Region. This region includes only the province of British Columbia. It has an agriculture which, although limited in extent, includes a wide range of products from the ranch, orchard, and market garden. The entire province is mountainous, and arable agriculture is limited to valleys, islands of alluvial deposits, and a few plateaus.

Aside from tree and small-fruit products, practically all of the production is directed to dairying, poultry products, vegetables, and beef cattle to supply the requirements of the urban population of the province. Grain requirements for the cattle and poultry have to be supplemented by imports from the prairies. The tree and small-fruit production is on a scale that permits a substantial volume to be sold elsewhere in Canada and also to be exported.

Resource Base. The mountainous terrain limits the availability of arable land. Approximately 1 million acres of improved land is in use, and the potentially arable acreage is estimated at 3 million. A considerable portion of the improved land is highly fertile alluvial deposits in river valleys or adjacent to large lakes.

In the southern portion of the central plateau about 20 million acres of native grassland are used for ranching. Some irrigated production of forage crops supplements the native range, particularly for winter-feed supplies.

The climate of the province is a complex mosaic. The most variable factor from area to area is the amount of precipitation. The southern coastal area receives 40 to 60 inches (101–152 cm) annually, with a concentration occurring in the fall and winter. In contrast, the central interior receives annually 12 to 16 inches (30–40 cm), of which a high proportion is received during the growing season. A large part of the agricultural producing area has July temperatures averaging 65° F (18° C) with some isolated blocks as high as 70° F (21° C). Winter averages above 20° F (− 6° C) prevail over the area generally. The southern coastal and adjacent interior areas enjoy a frost-free period exceeding 160 days. In addition, a large block in the southern-eastern section has a frost-free period of 120 days. In specific locations, elevation and patterns of air movement cause wide variations from the general pattern.

Production. Agricultural production may be best discussed with respect to three geographical areas in the province. These are the coastal, the central-interior, and the southern-interior areas.

Dairying is the major enterprise in the coastal area. Over two thirds of the cultivated land is in grass for hay and pasture. Small grains and corn are grown on a limited scale. The poultry industry is an important segment of the economy. Approximately 10% of Canada's production of eggs and 7% to 8% of its poultry meats are produced in the province, mainly in the coastal area. Market gardening and small-fruit production are major enterprises.

The southern-interior area is famous for its fruit production. In the main, production is concentrated along the shores and in the vicinity of Okanagan Lake and to a lesser degree along a portion of Kootenay Lake. The major crops are apples, cherries, pears, peaches, apricots, and plums. Because of the semiarid climate, production depends on irrigation. Packing and storage facilities and canning plants are associated with the primary production.

In the dry, interior-plateau region, the native grasslands are used for ranching. In the drier areas the sparse, short-growing grasses necessitate the use of extensive acreages per animal. Where precipitation improves with elevation, the cattle move up to higher levels as the season advances and trek back to lower elevations or valleys for the winter. Irrigation, where feasible in the valleys, provides hay for winter feed.

W. J. WHITE, *University of Saskatchewan*

Bibliography

Agricultural Institute of Canada, "Agricultural Opportunities for Atlantic Canada," *Agricultural Institute Review* (Ottawa, July–August 1964).

Alberta and Canada Departments of Agriculture, *Alberta Farm Guide* (Edmonton).

Canada Department of Agriculture, Economics Branch, *Canadian Farm Economics,* vols. 1 and 2 (Ottawa 1966, 1967).

Canada Department of Agriculture, Economics Branch, *Current Review of Agricultural Conditions in Canada* (Ottawa, bimonthly).

Canada Department of Mines and Technical Surveys, Geographical Branch, *Atlas of Canada* (Ottawa 1957).

Canada Department of Northern Affairs and National Resources, *Resources for Tomorrow Conference Background Papers,* vol. 1, section 1 (Ottawa 1961).

Saskatchewan and Canada Departments of Agriculture, *Guide to Farm Practice in Saskatchewan* (Regina, revised every 3 years).

University of Manitoba Faculty of Agriculture and Home Economics, *Principles and Practices of Commercial Farming* (Winnipeg 1965).

15. Fisheries and Furs

The abundant wildlife of Canada's waters and lands has been a source of strength to the economy for centuries. In spite of intensive exploitation, its resources have been sustained and have been increased in some aspects by conservation and development measures.

FISHERIES

The fishery resources available to Canada are extensive and varied. Approximately 12,000 miles of coastline on the east and 7,000 miles on the west are in the north temperate zone, and large areas of the continental shelf off both coasts lie within the 250-fathom (457-meter) depth contour. In such areas the sea floor, the chemical constituents of the water, and conditions of temperature, light, and ocean current combine to provide a suitable environment for a wide variety of fish species. A large number of species find a similar environment in the freshwater areas of Canada, 290,000 square miles (751,000 sq km) in extent. Of the numerous species of fish in these waters, some 150 were of importance commercially in the 1960's.

Stocks of Fish—*Saltwater Fish*. The largest resource, that of groundfish (fish that live on the sea bottom), is dominated by Atlantic species. The "standing stocks" of this group of species are estimated to be in excess of 5 million metric tons, 10 times the amount of the known Pacific stocks of related species, exclusive of those of the somewhat more distant waters of the northeast Pacific. About 65% of the Atlantic stocks consist of codfish and about 20% of redfish. The other important stocks, in order of quantity, are those of the flatfishes (5 species) other than halibut, haddock, the hakes (3 species), and pollack. Chief among the Pacific stocks of groundfish are the flatfishes (5 main species other than halibut), lingcod, and the rockfishes (10 main species), in that order. The stock of Pacific halibut approximates 300,000 metric tons; there is also an Atlantic stock about one tenth that size.

In terms of value, the most important group of stocks in the Canadian fisheries has been that of the Pacific salmons, of which there are five major species: sockeye, coho, pink, chum, and spring. The Atlantic species is of relatively minor importance. In total, the stocks of these species amount to approximately 200,000 metric tons. Because the species are anadromous (reared at the early stage in stream systems), the stocks are subject to reduction from the encroachment of industrialization (power dams, pollution, and the like) upon the habitat and for the most part are considered to be in a depleted condition. Since the early environment is amenable to control, however, it is possible to augment the stocks by positive measures of fish culture, and prospective developments in this direction indicate a doubling of total stocks over the next decade or two.

Although the stock of Atlantic lobster is relatively small, being estimated at slightly more than 30,000 metric tons, it supports a major fishery. This fishery draws heavily from the stock and, in the absence of more effective management of the resource, a gradual decline is projected. As in the case of the salmons, a growth in demand for products derived from lobster may encourage development of improved fish raising techniques to increase the lobster stock.

The stock of Atlantic herring is estimated to be at least 1,750,000 metric tons and that of Pacific herring at about 350,000 metric tons. Among the miscellaneous group of sea fish stocks, those of greatest contemporary and potential importance appear to be the mackerel, swordfish, and scallop stocks of the Atlantic coast, and the crab, shrimp, and oyster stocks of both coasts and some others. Knowledge of the extent of all these stocks is imperfect. The same may be said of the stocks of sea mammals, such as whales (both baleen and toothed species) and seals, and of seaweeds, all of which support hunting and gathering operations of relatively minor significance.

***Freshwater Fish*.** Because of the large number and diversity of the bodies of water involved, an estimate of the stocks of freshwater fish is also wanting. The most productive lakes are those in the southern and central parts of Canada; lakes in the Canadian Shield tend to be low in nutrients. Moreover, in general, the shallower and warmer lakes support denser stocks. Thus, of the total physical yield (landings) from these stocks, one third is obtained from the Canadian sections of the 5 Great Lakes (one fourth from Lake Erie alone), one third from 6 large lakes in the prairie and northwest regions of the country, and one third from all the rest of some 600 lakes actually fished. The major species in both quantity and value in order of importance are: whitefish, walleye (pickerel), yellow perch, gray trout, and pike.

Exploitation. A number of the resources are heavily exploited—in some cases possibly beyond an optimum level. Certain of the groundfish stocks, such as those of redfish and haddock and perhaps even those of cod, are approaching this state. In the case of these stocks, located mainly in international waters, the fisheries are shared

NATIONAL FILM BOARD

SALMON FISHERIES are a major industry on the coast of British Columbia. The catch keeps canneries operating often on a 24-hour production basis.

GEORGE HUNTER, FROM NATIONAL FILM BOARD

LOBSTER BOAT leaves a Prince Edward Island port for a day's haul. Atlantic lobsters are famed for quality.

with other countries. The Canadian fishery takes only one fifth of the catch from northwest Atlantic cod stocks, for example. On the other hand, many stocks, such as Atlantic herring, have been underutilized or neglected altogether. In the future the industry may be expected to turn progressively to these alternative resources.

Industry and Trade. Approximately 80,000 men are reported to be engaged in commercial fishing in Canada, perhaps two thirds of this number being occupied more or less on a full-time basis. Of this total, 60% live on the Atlantic coast, with the remainder distributed about evenly between the Pacific coast and the central region (inland lakes). The primary industry comprises 30,000 fishing enterprises, ranging in size from a one-man operation to a division of an integrated firm operating a fleet of vessels. Investment is estimated to be substantially in excess of $200 million, 70% of which is in fishing craft, 20% in gear, and the remainder in installations ashore.

The secondary (fish processing) industry includes about 350 firms. Investment in this industry has been calculated to approximate $250 million, 60% of which is in plant and equipment. The regional distribution of the processing industry is roughly, 50% on the Atlantic coast, 40% on the Pacific coast, and 10% on the inland lakes. As in the case of the primary industry, operations in fish processing tend to be seasonal, employment varying from 5,000 in February to 15,000 in July and August.

The annual production of the primary industry—landings of raw fish—approaches 1,250,000 metric tons. The regional distribution is 65% on the Atlantic coast, 30% on the Pacific coast, and 5% on the inland lakes. The value of the products marketed annually by the fish processing industry exceeds $300 million, about half of which represents the value of raw fish. This is distributed regionally on the average in the same proportions as are landings.

The distribution among product groups is as follows: chilled and frozen dressed fish (derived mainly from Pacific salmon and halibut, Atlantic lobster, and freshwater species), 30%; chilled and frozen filleted fish (derived mainly from Atlantic groundfish species), 25%; canned fish (derived from Pacific salmon and Atlantic herring), 25%; cured fish (derived mainly from Atlantic cod), 10%; and miscellaneous fish products (chiefly meal and oil from Atlantic and Pacific herring), 10%.

Exports of fishery products each year amount to about two thirds of total production and are valued at well over $200 million or roughly 10% of the total world trade in fishery commodities. The principal export market is the United States, where most chilled and frozen products are sold and which purchases 70% of all Canadian exports of fishery products. The remainder, comprising the bulk of exports of canned and cured products, is shipped chiefly to the countries of western Europe and the Caribbean.

Administration. The commercial fisheries are the oldest industry in Canada, having been established on the Atlantic coast early in the 16th century and expanded gradually westward with the settlement of the country. The modern fishing industry developed after the beginning of the 20th century, however, and the current phase of modernization and expansion dates from the end of World War II. The development of fishery administration has paralleled that of the industry.

Under the Constitution (the British North America Act of 1867), the Parliament of Canada has exclusive legislative authority over "sea coast and inland fisheries." This authority has been abridged somewhat, however, as a result of subsequent judicial interpretation. The federal powers are exercised through a department of government under a minister of fisheries. This department is charged with the responsibility of administering the statutes enacted by Parliament for the regulation of the fisheries and those which are designed from time to time specifically for the development of the fishing industry.

Legislation. The basic statute in the first category is the Fisheries Act, under which regulations are made for resource management, including those imposed on the recommendation of the eight international fishery-management commissions of which Canada is a member. The Coastal Fisheries Protection Act permits control of foreign fishing craft in the national ports and territorial waters. The Territorial Sea and Fishing Zones Act establishes a 12-mile exclusive national fishing zone in coastal waters. The Fish Inspection Act provides for control of the quality of fishery products.

The major piece of legislation in the second category probably is the Fisheries Research Board Act, creating an organization for research in oceanography, aquatic biology, and food technology. The Fisheries Development Act joins certain programs or measures to encourage the modernization and expansion of the industry, such as exploratory fishing services, demonstration of improved equipment and methods, and grants-in-aid for innovations. Several other federal agencies, such as the Rural Rehabilitation and Development Administration, the Area Development Agency, and the Atlantic Development Board, as well as most of the provincial governments, are also involved in this field. The activities of all are coordinated through a system of interdepartmental and federal-provincial committees.

W. C. MacKenzie, *Director, Economic Services Canadian Department of Fisheries*

Further Reading: Innis, Harold A., *The Cod Fisheries: the History of an International Economy*, rev. ed. (Toronto 1954); Royal Commission on Canada's Economic Prospects. *The Commercial Fisheries of Canada* (Ottawa 1956).

FURS

The fur industry is one of Canada's traditional industries, and fur production is still important in the national economy. Each year some 40,000 full- and part-time trappers participate in trapping activities, and mink are raised on farms in all the provinces.

Wild Fur-Bearers. Although much of the wildlife has retreated northward before the spread of settlement, substantial catches of beaver, muskrat, mink, wolf, colored fox, weasel, and squirrel are still made in partly settled areas of bush and farmland. Farther north these same species are taken, along with lynx, marten, otter, fisher, and wolverine, while in the barren grounds and Arctic areas Eskimo hunters trap the Arctic fox. Most important of the fur-bearers is the beaver. The annual beaver catch, averaging about 400,000 pelts and worth about $5.3 million, accounts for about one third of the total value of wild fur production.

Despite almost three centuries of trapping, the numbers of fur-bearers are being well maintained, and in some instances catches in the 1960's exceeded those made in the 1920's.

Fur Farming. This industry originated in the 1890's with the raising of silver foxes on farms in eastern Canada. Fox farming progressed rapidly until in the peak year of 1939 production amounted to 240,827 pelts. By then the heavy world output together with an easing of the demand had caused pelt prices to drop to unprofitable levels. When, in the early 1950's, a pronounced fashion swing away from the long-haired furs developed, production dropped off rapidly.

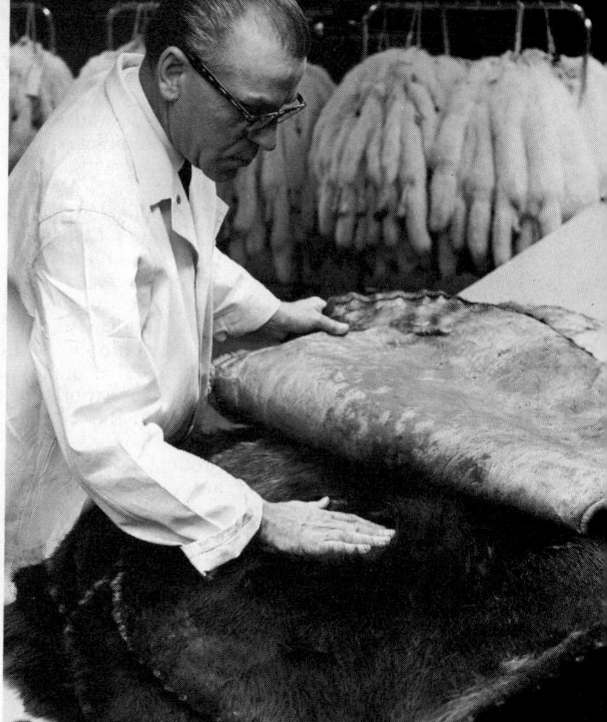

HUDSON'S BAY COMPANY

BEAVER PELTS are inspected by a Montreal expert.

Mink farming began in the early 1900's and developed steadily until over 1.6 million pelts worth $28.4 million were being produced on 1,500 farms in the mid-1960's. Originally, all the mink raised were dark brown in color. However, in 1936 the first color mutation, the silverblu or platinum, was introduced. This mutation was soon followed by others, and the advent of a wide range of attractive, natural colors gave an impetus to the industry. For many years mink has been the world's dominant fur.

The chinchilla was introduced into Canada in 1937, and by the mid-1960's raisers were marketing more than 17,000 pelts annually.

Marketing. Most Canadian furs are sold through fur auctions located in six cities. The fine quality of Canadian furs attracts buyers from many countries, who attend the auctions and buy the furs through competitive bidding.

A. Stewart, *Chief, Fur Section Canada Department of Agriculture*

Further Reading: Fuchs, Victor, R., *Economics of the Fur Industry* (New York 1957); Innis, Harold A., *The Fur Trade in Canada*, new ed. (New Haven, Conn., 1962).

16. Trade and Tariffs

Canada's external trading performance and policy have been and will continue to be among the most important determinants of the country's prosperity and economic structure.

Present Structure and Basis. Canada is relatively specialized as a producer and exporter of temperate-climate grain products, particularly wheat; a small number of other agricultural products; wood products, particularly lumber, plywood, and newsprint; and industrial materials of mineral origin, particularly aluminum, copper, nickel, zinc, lead, uranium, iron ore, and asbestos.

To these should be added a small list of highly manufactured end products including farm implements, automotive products, electric power generation equipment, and a few chemicals, including fertilizers.

For the industrial materials of mineral and wood origin, the Canadian specialization involves quite a high degree of processing. The items within this structure which have notably expanded since World War II include uranium, petroleum, aluminum, iron ore, nickel, plywood, and certain chemicals; and in the 1960's exports of highly manufactured end products expanded at a very rapid rate.

In some respects the Canadian specialization is complementary within the North American continent, and in these respects Canada would be best viewed as a region within a continental economy. This is most notably so for Canadian exports of certain wood products and minerals to the United States, and for the two-way Canada-United States trade in certain manufactured products, particularly agricultural implements and automotive products. However, the principal exports of grain are to the United Kingdom and western Europe. The United Kingdom, European, and Japanese markets are particularly important for some wood products, and take more than half of Canada's exports of aluminum, copper, lead, nickel, and asbestos.

Canada continues to be an importer of tropical and semitropical foodstuffs and raw materials. For a very long time, the main concentration in imports has been in manufactured products, particularly in machinery and equipment; parts and components for both investment goods and consumer durables; and fuels. For industrial products, the concentration on U.S. sources of supply has been very great for a long time, though for some items the United Kingdom and western Europe are either dominant or major suppliers.

Specialization. The fundamental basis of this pattern of Canadian specialization and trade is a combination of the resource structure, location and climate of the country, and the technological, organizational, and input requirements for certain types of manufactured products. The climate implies advantages in temperate-climate agricultural and forest products, but a disadvantage in tropical and semitropical products. Even though Canada is a very large land mass, Canadian resource advantages are somewhat asymmetric; geology has equipped the country with a relatively large supply of well-located nonferrous and nonmetallic minerals. Since World War II outstanding discoveries of commercially exploitable deposits of petroleum, uranium, iron ore, and potash have provided the basis for the new developments in production of staples.

For many of Canada's materials, a combination of factors encourages considerable processing activity in Canada, some of it being technologically very sophisticated indeed. Among these factors are the economies of processing resources that are embodied in considerable waste material, close to the point of primary extraction; the intensive requirement for energy in the processing activities either for heat or power or electrometallurgical processes; and the requirements of masses of capital and high levels of engineering skills. For footloose manufacturing activities, Canadian locations are reasonably good, from a continental point of view, in the area north of the St. Lawrence River and lakes Ontario and Erie. These areas also have good agricultural hinterlands that permit and encourage a considerable manufacturing activity.

Influence of Tariffs. Canadian specialization in trade has been substantially influenced by Canadian and foreign tariffs and related trade and payments policies. For nearly a century Canada has had a protective tariff for a broad range of products, and the country has faced a fairly high set of foreign barriers to trade, particularly with respect to manufactured products. Canada has taken on a very broad range of production activities for home consumption, partly because of these barriers. Canada produces a little of a very large number of products for its own consumption, particularly manufactured products, rather than specializing in a large output of a comparatively small number of products for internal and external markets. Both the Canadian and foreign tariffs contribute to this situation; other restraints on trade and payment also work in this direction. Since the end of the war, Canada has been a persistent participant in the efforts of the General Agreement on Tariffs and Trade (GATT) to reduce barriers to trade and payments on a multinational reciprocal basis. Canada's interests in this respect have ebbed and flowed a little from time to time but always within a general framework of enthusiasm for reductions in trade barriers, provided the government could obtain what it regarded as good deals.

Historical Background. For more than a decade after Confederation in 1867, Canada's trade relations were rather uncertain. The Reciprocity Treaty with the United States, signed in 1854, was abrogated in 1866. The end of reciprocity greatly restricted U.S. markets for Canada. Enlarged markets within and outside of Canada were sought. At Confederation a general tariff rate of 15% on imported manufactures was adopted, somewhat more a revenue duty and less a protective duty than the Galt tariff in 1859. After Confederation, Canada made major efforts to negotiate a new Canada-United States reciprocity treaty, but the U. S. government was eventually unwilling. After disappointments in economic development, in trade and in trade negotiations, the government of Sir John A. Macdonald adopted in 1879 and the 1880's a National Policy of high protective duties for manufactures in Canada. The Liberals, despite their hopes and expectations, did not essentially reduce these barriers in the 1890's and early 1900's. A system of reduced Canadian duties on imports from those countries that gave low duty entry to Canadian exports was added in 1897 and generalized into a British preferential schedule in the Canadian tariff in 1900. But this did not substantially undermine the protection afforded manufacturers by the Canadian tariff. Canada faced free entry into the British market for virtually all goods, low trade barriers for exports of raw materials and foods in many but not all countries, and generally higher duties on Canadian exports of manufactures.

The Golden Age. The six decades prior to World War I were the golden age of growth in world specialization and trade. While Canada was not an outstanding participant in this growth experience prior to the mid-1890's, it actually experienced more rapid expansion in trade than did the world as a whole thereafter. To a fairly strong staple base of timber and lumber, dairy products, fish, and furs, the new major export staple of wheat was added and the production of the staples of later significance, pulp and paper and mineral products, was started. Canadian manufacturing activity grew rapidly too, partly reflecting the protected environment carried forward from Macdonald's national tariff policy. Except for some elementary processing of natural products, the bulk of Canadian manufacturing was for the domestic market.

Canada negotiated a reciprocity treaty with the United States in 1911 which the U.S. Senate ratified. The Liberal party lost the Canadian election

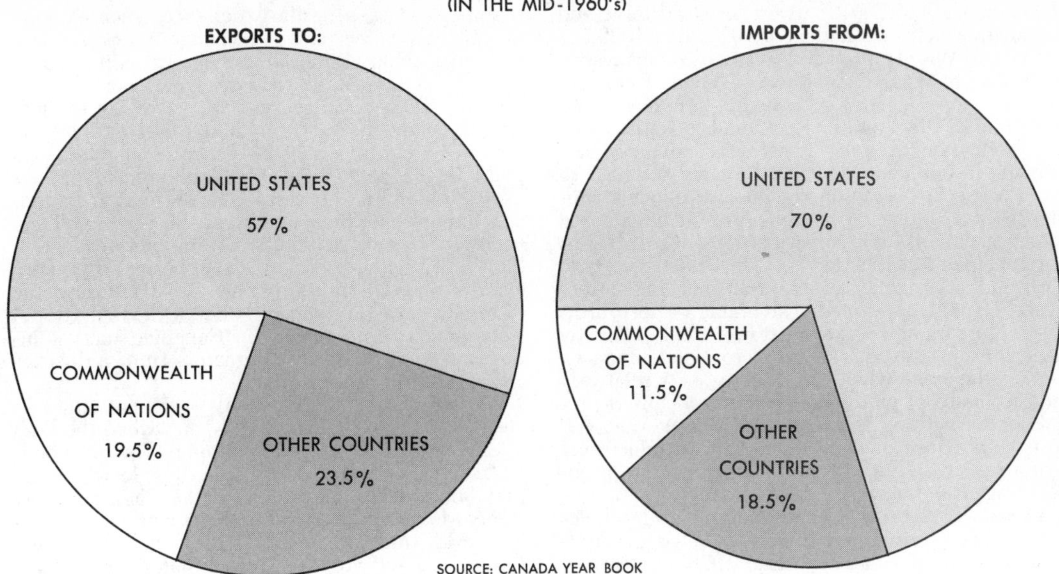

of 1911, and the Canadian Parliament did not ratify the treaty.

World War I and the 1920's. In the two decades ending in 1930, the growth of world trade was much slower than it had been since 1850, and much slower than the growth in world output. Canada's experience was quite different, its trade increasing about as rapidly as before World War I. Thus Canada's share of world trade increased quite substantially, both for primary products and for manufactures, particularly for processed industrial materials. The fulfillment of the promise of the wheat economy, and the production and export of pulp and paper goods and minerals in large quantities, were the outstanding features in Canadian exports.

United States and United Kingdom tariffs on imports of manufactured products were increased significantly in the early 1920's, a change of potential significance for Canada. Canada's tariffs on industrial products were not substantially altered. Canadian industry did not suffer the disadvantages of wartime disruption and of postwar overvaluation of currencies as did the United Kingdom and several European countries. Canadian industrial development during the two decades was rapid and highly diversified. The Canadian tariff was quite substantially differentiated, and some manufactured goods, particularly capital goods, for some purposes (particularly for mining and other resource industry developments), and in some circumstances (items of a class or kind not made in Canada or components for advanced manufacturing) entered Canada at low rates of duty.

Depression and World War II. Canada suffered severely from the destruction of world trade by the Great Depression and by the enormous, complex increase in barriers to world trade and payments in the 1930's. The Smoot-Hawley tariff in the United States, increased United Kingdom and European protection, the breakdown of the international monetary system, the intense use of quantitative trade restrictions, the Ottawa agreements (which established preferential status for British Commonwealth countries in 1932), the buildup of autarky, beggar-thy-neighbor or economic warfare nearly everywhere — all of these had destructive effects on world trade and payments that reinforced and interacted with the trade-reducing effects of the depression itself.

Canada was hit badly, particularly because of the low prices of primary products, the drought on the Canadian prairies, and the heavy burden of fixed external debt service to be met out of lower export values. Canada managed to balance its external payments essentially by restricting production and employment and thus restricting imports. As well, Canada had a depreciated exchange rate and a much higher set of barriers against imports. Among the few hopeful signs later in the decade were the U.S. Reciprocal Trade Agreements Acts and the two Canada-United States trade agreements which cut back the Canada-U.S. tariff levels toward those

LUMBER is loaded aboard a German freighter at Halifax.

GAR LUNNEY, FROM NATIONAL FILM BOARD

of the later 1920's. But barriers to world trade and payments were much higher in 1939 than 1929.

World War II provided a stimulus but also a distortion to Canadian trade. While European markets were cut off, a virtually unlimited need arose outside the country for Canada's staples, and the production of some items was expanded abnormally. Canadian industrial activity was also given a special expansionary push, producing munitions and replacing supplies of manufactured products cut off from other sources. Canada was not a recipient of U.S. lend-lease. Under the Hyde Park and other international war-financing agreements, Canada developed a favorable balance in its basic international economic transactions offset by reductions in Canada's net external indebtedness. During the war, when the country had relatively large volumes of production and a rationalized production structure, the comparative international cost performance of many Canadian manufacturing industries, even for complex manufactured products, was astonishingly good.

Since World War II. Canadian hopes and policies in the early postwar period were directed toward a restoration of the nation's basic 1920's pattern of specialization and trade. Primary emphasis was placed on the creation of international monetary and trade conditions favorable to a high level of international specialization and trade. Canada was a leading contributor to the development of the IMF, International Monetary Fund, the ITO, International Trade Organization, the GATT, the World Bank, and to postwar reconstruction loans. The postwar reconstruction went less well than Canada had expected or hoped for, particularly in the British and European recovery. For this reason and because of internal difficulties of Canadian economic policy, the country experienced a balance-of-payments deficit crisis in 1947 and reoriented its policy a little more toward expanding exports to the United States and temporarily toward a more cautious, restrictive approach to imports by using import controls in 1947 and devaluing the Canadian dollar in 1949. Taking the whole period from 1929 to 1949, the volume of Canadian trade grew absolutely, though at a much slower rate than before 1930, and Canada's share in world trade was much larger in 1949, both in total and for manufactured goods.

Canadian tariffs were reduced in the multilateral tariff-cutting negotiations of the Geneva round under the GATT. Canada negotiated toward a new reciprocity treaty with the United States, but the negotiations were aborted before a treaty was agreed to. The desirability of reciprocity and the attractiveness of an early postwar move in this direction were indicated by (1) the economic successes of continental rationalization of production during the war; (2) the successful experience of continental specialization and trade in a number of products in which trade had been comparatively free of barriers for quite some time, including pulp and paper and agricultural implements; (3) the extremely good working relations between Canada and the United States during the war in dealing with many complex problems of mutual interest; and (4) the possibility of combining the structural readjustments of reciprocity with the structural adjustments of postwar reconstruction.

Attitudes in the 1950's. Canadian attitudes to trade in the 1950's swung from excessive optimism to excessive pessimism, swings only party based on actual experience. In the first part of the 1950's, Canada developed a balance-of-payments surplus position, and, as a result, experienced such extreme upward pressure on the exchange rate, reserves, and expansionary internal monetary conditions that an appreciation of the country's currency was required. The exchange rate was allowed to float freely for the period from mid-1950 until late in 1960. An improvement in the terms of trade took place in the early 1950's, as well as an enormous expansion, with the assistance of foreign capital and foreign entrepreneurship, in the productive capacity of resource industries. Imports reached a high level, both absolutely and by comparison with exports or with the output in Canada during the extremely large investment boom of the mid-1950's. The share of imports in the Canadian market increased, giving rise to complaints from industries about the lack of protection.

When the export potentials were not immediately realized in the late 1950's, and when the high rate of capital inflows and importation of goods and services continued, a generally gloomy interpretation of Canada's position in the world economy emerged. Canada's share both in world trade and in world trade in manufactures had decreased. Canada shared with the United States a reputation for economic stagnation during the late 1950's, and both were thought to have worsened their competitive positions in the world economy quite substantially relative to continental western Europe and Japan. A special factor in Canada's case was alleged to be the enormous increase in capital inflows — notably inflows which increased the foreign ownership and control of activities and resources in Canada. The special U.S. problem was the mounting doubt about the capacity of the (U.S.) dollar to carry the "key currency" burdens. For Canada, a particularly noteworthy feature was the continued high external value of the Canadian dollar, a situation which discouraged Canadian exports and encouraged Canadian imports when the opposite trend appeared desirable.

Policies of the 1960's. Canadian attitudes toward trade and some actions in foreign economic policy changed. The most notable feature was the attempt by the government from late 1960 through early 1962 to intervene directly in the exchange markets in such a way as to decrease the external value of the Canadian dollar, an intervention which, along with other economic and political factors, led toward an exchange crisis for Canada in the first half of 1962. Canada returned to the IMF system of pegged exchange rates, devalued its currency in the process—which intensified the exchange crisis—and eventually adopted emergency measures to reinforce the pegged, devalued dollar.

Several important factors for the subsequent development of Canadian commerce, trade, and tariffs followed from this crisis. First, the country had for a time, after the exchange crisis of confidence was overcome, an undervalued currency. Second, for a time the country also had a surcharge on import duties, which reinforced the effect of the devalued (and undervalued) Canadian dollar in limiting imports into Canada. Third, the country was committed to a program of long-run policies to correct the alleged deficit in the balance of payments.

Measures to stimulate exports and to reduce imports were mooted and some were implemented. The most notable development was Canada's export subsidy scheme for Canadian automotive products that eventually was developed into the Canada-U.S. auto pact that took effect in 1965. Under this pact, Canada took the initiative, and the

U.S. government agreed to arrangements, in direct agreements with the major auto companies to rationalize auto production on a continental basis, but in such a way as to increase the Canadian proportion of the total North American auto goods production. For auto companies, a conditional two-way free trade in autos and parts emerged. The Canadian productivity in automotive products was to be markedly improved relative to that in the United States, and Canadian costs of production of automotive products were to be thereby reduced substantially toward the lower U.S. levels.

Other ideas about promoting Canadian exports were also mooted or implemented, including improved export financing, increased official trade promotion activities, and efforts to improve Canadian productivity and cost competitiveness in certain lines of export production. Even the design of Canada's offers in the Kennedy Round negotiations (1964–1967) was shaped by these considerations.

Regarding imports, Canada seems to have followed a somewhat ambivalent policy in the 1960's. It clearly dragged its feet in the Dillon Round of GATT negotiations. Canada's offer in the Kennedy Round negotiations under the GATT looked somewhat smaller from certain points of view than the typical offer of the major countries. Canadian dumping laws appeared to have been relatively restrictive of imports, though major changes were forecast in the Kennedy Round agreements.

However, Canada has recognized that expansion of its exports of manufactured goods is probably conditional on an enlarged two-way trade in manufactured products — that is, on a Canadian participation in a general program of increased world specialization. Also, a variety of two-way Canadian-U.S. deals to reduce trade barriers within the continent, to rationalize production on a continental basis, and incidentally to intensify Canadian specialization and reduce the gap between Canadian and U.S. productivity have been mooted and one or two tried.

Issues of the 1960's. Among the enduring and fundamental developments in Canada's contemporary trade relations are the remarkable expansion of Canadian exports in the 1960's, the Kennedy Round of tariff-cutting, the post-Kennedy Round issues in world trade policy, and the general problems of Canadian growth in the world economy.

Export Expansion. Economic specialization and trade in the world continued to grow astonishingly in the 1960's, more than was expected even by optimistic forecasters at the start of that decade. The growth was very large even after allowances were made for the expansion in intra-European trade due to the EEC and EFTA. But Canada's export performance was even more astonishing; Canadian trade has expanded even more than world trade. Canadian exports have increased in nearly every broad category: wheat, cheese, and tobacco; minerals; pulp and paper and lumber; and, particularly noteworthy, in highly manufactured end products for which, since 1962, the rate of growth has been much higher even than the average for Canadian exports.

Up to a point, this expansion reflected transitory factors enlarging Canadian exports, such as the combination of extraordinary needs of the Soviet bloc and mainland China for cereals when Canada had a large stockpile carried forward, the extraordinary requirements for metals in the mid-1960's in the United States, the switch from Rhodesian to Canadian tobacco, and the buildup of effects of Canada's devaluation. Both exports and imports have expanded greatly by the buildup of two-way trade in automotive products that has emerged from the Canada-U.S. auto pact. Canada continued to benefit from special treatment in defense sharing, the oil policy, and the external capital policies of the United States. But many enduring features of expansion in Canadian trade were also recognized, such as the likelihood of intense world requirements for food in the future, the increasing efficiency and use of atomic power, the opportunities for improved

Grain elevators near Thunder Bay, Ontario, on Lake Superior, store wheat for export shipment.

GEORGE HUNTER, FROM NATIONAL FILM BOARD

GEORGE HUNTER, FROM NATIONAL FILM BOARD

MONTREAL HARBOR, on the St. Lawrence River, 1,000 miles from the sea, ranks among the foremost cargo ports of the world.

Canadian competitiveness in many lines of manufacturing if production can be rationalized and new techniques and organization put into operation, the high level of two-way trade in manufactured products such as automotive goods after the buildup to the new levels takes place, and the new resource developments in Canada. The outcome depends on events, some of which are under Canadian influence, and on the trade-expanding or contracting nature of Canadian and foreign trade policies.

Tariff Cuts. The Kennedy Round of tariff cuts and other trade agreements under GATT was concluded at the end of June 1967, after four years of negotiations. The agreements were heralded as the greatest bout of multilateral tariff slashing ever undertaken. Their implementation in annual steps from 1968 through 1972 reduces tariffs on industrial products. The Kennedy Round did not result in major reductions in the high levels of agricultural protectionism that existed in the world at the mid-1960's. But the cuts in industrial tariffs were an application, with some qualifications and modifications, of the linear-cut principle, by which equal percentage reductions were made by all countries for all products. The variations from the principle were substantial, but even so about three fourths of the world trade in industrial products came under the tariff-cutting knife. The average cut of tariffs on the items affected was between 35 and 40%, and more than half were at least 50%.

Canada participated in the Kenndy Round of trade negotiations but did not follow the principle of linear cuts. Canada adopted a selective approach to its tariff cuts, under an agreed negotiating principle by which the countries for which the equal linear-cut approach was not appropriate worked out negotiations as a balance of advantages between the concessions they received and made.

When Canada's Kennedy Round concessions are counted up in the usual way, they appear to be smaller than those of other industrial countries; the proportion of the dutiable trade subject to tariff cuts appears to be less and the average depth of cut to be less also. The balance of advantages given and received in Canada's negotiations has to be judged by its structure, timing, and effects, particularly on Canadian imports and exports. The negotiators for Canada and other countries agreed that there was a balance of advantages given and received, having regard for these factors, and particularly considering the very substantial reduction in Canadian import duties on industrial machinery, the immediate implementation of some of the Canadian tariff reductions rather than the gradual five-year implementation, and the major restructuring of Canada's anti-dumping laws to conform with the new code, despite Canadian contentions of special dumping problems.

Canada still has a substantial level of protection for many lines of manufactures after the Kennedy Round is implemented. Further opportunities still exist for significant reductions in Canadian trade barriers if the Canadian government has the opportunity and wishes to participate in partial or general reciprocal reductions of trade barriers in the future.

World Trade Problems. For the world in general, much remained to be done in reducing trade barriers after the Kennedy Round. Industrial protection was greater than the common measures of the heights of tariffs indicated. Agricultural protectionism was still on a very high level. Many nontariff barriers to trade remained. The problems of improved trade opportunities for the developing countries and of improved ability for many countries in dealing with instabilities and balance-of-payments difficulties remained.

Canadian Problems. For Canada many of the traditional problems of trade and commerce, perhaps appearing in slightly different form, continue to demand attention. The gaps between average levels of productivity in Canada and the United States are still large. If wage rates and other elements in the levels of living in Canada are to be raised toward those in the United States, so must levels of Canadian productivity. Some of the closing of the productivity gap can be undertaken by improved education in Canada, improved research and development programs, and other internal Canadian measures.

But much of the closing of the gap appears to depend on more complete economic integration of specialization and trade of Canada into the continental economy. A major, but not the only, step required in this direction is by reduction of the mutual Canada-U.S. trade barriers. However, even then much of Canada's comparative advantage would be relative to western Europe, Japan, and developing countries. Thus, effective exploitation of Canada's production and trading potentials appears to be, indefinitely into the future, through mutual reductions of trade barriers between Canada and countries other than the United States.

Canada's interests in trade expansion, particularly for manufactured goods, are accentuated by its extraordinarily rapidly growing labor force and, therefore, the need for a rapid expansion of high productivity jobs for an urban labor force. Canada's trading policies are intertwined with its policies regarding the continued utilization of foreign capital, and the participation of foreigners in the ownership and control of activities in Canada. If Canada decides, as a matter of policy, to reduce the role of foreign ownership and control in Canada, the need for policies to expand trade would be even greater, but the resulting change in Canada's opportunities are difficult to foresee. Another complicating factor in Canada's trade developments is the tendency toward economic regionalism within Canada, each region desiring a broad range of industrial development. Policies to promote regional preferences for products manufactured within each region, if developed vigorously, could erect another layer of barriers to Canadian trade.

Canadian trade, however, has turned out to be remarkably expansive, a powerful engine of Canadian economic growth, with great capacity of adaptation to changing world opportunities.

DAVID W. SLATER
Queen's University, Kingston, Ontario

Bibliography

Caves, Richard Earl, and Holton, Richard Henry, *The Canadian Economy* (Cambridge, Mass., 1959).
Downs, J.R., *Export Projections to 1970*, Staff Study, Economic Council of Canada (Ottawa 1964).
Economic Council of Canada, *Fourth Annual Review: The Canadian Economy from the 1960's to the 1970's* (Ottawa 1967).
GATT, *Trends in International Trade* (Geneva 1958).
McDiarmid, Orville John, *Commercial Policy in the Canadian Economy* (Cambridge, Mass., 1946).
Mackintosh, William Archibald, *Economic Background of Dominion-Provincial Relations,* Rowell-Sirois Commission (Ottawa 1939).
Maizels, Alfred, *Industrial Growth and World Trade* (Cambridge, Mass., 1963).
Organization for Economic Cooperation and Development, Economic Policy Committee, *Economic Growth, 1960–1970* (Paris 1966).
Royal Commission on Canada's Economic Prospects, *Final Report* (Ottawa 1957).
Slater, David W., *World Trade and Economic Growth: Trends and Prospects* (Toronto 1967).
Wonnacott, R. J., and Wonnacott, Paul, *Free Trade Between the United States and Canada* (Cambridge, Mass., 1967).
Young, John H., *Canadian Commercial Policy* (Ottawa 1967).

17. Tourism

As Canadians entered the early years of their second century of nationhood, they became increasingly aware of the economic importance of tourism. In the 10 years prior to 1967, Canada's annual income from visitors had increased by $500 million. In 1967, Centennial celebrations, highlighted by a magnificent world exhibition, EXPO 67, helped attract a record number of visitors and a record billion dollar income. Its rapid rate of increase suggests that tourism may be assuming first place as a source of foreign currency for Canada.

Tourist Spending. As transportation systems improve, travel by Canadians in Canada is also growing rapidly, with spending estimated at $1.5 billion or more each year.

Half of each tourist dollar is spent on food and lodging, but people on the move—the great majority using the family car—also spend heavily on goods and services. The rising tide of tourism benefits the construction industry, the oil companies, and those who build or service cars, boats, and recreational equipment.

Foreign Tourists. Canada has an enviable position for a vacation destination, sharing its southern border for 4,000 miles (6,400 km) with the United States, which is 10 times as populous. The two countries have excellent road, rail, water and air connections, and to attract visitors Canada has rich recreational resources, a wide variety of natural and man-made attractions, winter sports in abundance, good touring weather in spring and fall, and a temperate summer climate.

Most visits to Canada are made by United States citizens in the summer months. They cross the border about 40 million times a year, with 15 million visitors staying a day or more. As Canadians make almost as many visits, in all seasons, to their southern neighbor, and several million stay for at least one day, this cross-border exchange of visitors and of the money they spend is the largest in the world.

Canada is also benefiting from the increasing mobility of the world's peoples, many of whom—as air fares go down and plane capacity goes up—can now afford to see the New World. In the late 1960's more than 400,000 visitors a year came from other continents to enjoy the hospitality of Canada.

Canadians as Tourists. With per capita expenditure of nearly $50 a year, Canadians spend more on travel abroad than any other people. For many years Canada has had a deficit on travel account, reaching a record $207 million in 1959 and 1960, but Canadians expect, by the 1970's, to attract more spending from visitors than they themselves will spend on travel in other countries.

Facilities. To provide for Canadians on the move and for many millions of visitors, Canadian tourist facilities are steadily expanding. There are many thousands of restaurants, 300,000 accommodation units, and 300,000 miles (487,000 km) of surfaced roads, of which 60,000 miles (80,400 km) are paved. There are many resort areas, convention centers, parks, and campsites.

The money spent by visitors to Canada provides employment for more than 100,000 people, and it returns hundreds of millions of dollars in taxes. There is every reason to expect increasing travel by Canadians within their own country. It is also anticipated that spending by visitors will reach $2 billion a year by 1977.

DAN WALLACE, *Director*
Canadian Government Travel Bureau

18. Transportation and Communications

Canadian interest in transportation has always been keen. Canada occupies more of the earth's surface than any other country except the Soviet Union. It is divided into six economic regions: Newfoundland, the Maritime Provinces, the St. Lawrence Valley, the Prairies, British Columbia, and the North. These are separated from each other by physiographic barriers such as Cabot Strait, the Laurentian Shield, and the Rocky Mountains.

Although parts of southern Ontario and Quebec have as many people per square mile as western Europe, many Canadians live in widely scattered lumber camps, mining communities, and fishing villages. A major objective of Canadian

GEORGE HUNTER, FROM NATIONAL FILM BOARD

PIPELINES carry oil and natural gas for enormous distances. This gas line crosses the Rocky Mountains.

policy is to weld these various regions and communities into a single nation and a prosperous economy.

Early History. During the French regime, settlers clung to the banks of the St. Lawrence River, but explorers and fur traders penetrated the interior by using the birchbark canoe. This Indian invention, made of local raw materials, drew only a few inches of water and could be easily portaged. It was ideal for moving men and limited quantities of essential supplies, trading goods, and furs over long distances.

English-speaking settlers along the Atlantic Coast relied on sailing vessels, but those in Upper Canada (Ontario) found that neither sails nor canoes were practicable along the upper St. Lawrence whether for bringing in needed supplies or exporting their farm produce. Consequently, they developed large flat-bottomed boats, called *bateaux*. These were laboriously pulled or poled upstream by men, though in time horses were used. Logs for export were floated downstream.

In 1809, merchants in Montreal built a steamship that cut the traveling time between that city and Quebec from 15 to 3 days. This event occurred only two years after Robert Fulton ran North America's first successful steamer on the Hudson River. Obviously, even in the early 19th century, Canadian businessmen were alert to the latest technology.

Canals. The usefulness of ships was severely limited by rapids on the St. Lawrence and by Niagara Falls. Attempts to overcome these obstacles included abortive efforts under French rule: the Lachine Canal (just above Montreal, 1825), the Welland (between Lakes Erie and Ontario, 1829), the Rideau (Ottawa-Kingston, 1832), and the St. Lawrence canals (various places between Prescott and Montreal, by 1849).

These facilities were soon made semiobsolete by railways. Even so, they continued to provide cheap transportation for bulky goods where speed was not important. Rapid settlement of western Canada in the early 20th century and the growing industrialization of southern Ontario and Quebec in mid-century led to insistent demands for an improved channel. The new Welland Canal was opened in 1932 and the St. Lawrence Seaway in 1959.

In the treaty governing construction of the Seaway, Canada and the United States agreed to set up Authorities to manage their share of the works and to levy tolls adequate to cover operating costs and amortize the investment over 50 years. Traffic did not reach the anticipated volume until 1966. By that time both Authorities had accumulated large deficits, but the United States objected to higher charges on ships and their cargoes. In 1967, Canada announced that it would collect tolls on the Welland Canal, which was built entirely with Canadian funds. Although more deep-sea vessels enter the Great Lakes than before the Seaway was opened, most transoceanic freight is transshipped at Montreal.

Railways. Although Canada's first railway (near Montreal) was opened in 1835, a shortage of capital and the preoccupation with canals resulted in only 66 miles (106 km) being finished by 1850. In the next decade many schemes were advanced and a few completed, chiefly the Grand Trunk (Portland, Me., through Montreal and Toronto to the foot of Lake Huron), the Great Western between the Detroit and Niagara rivers, and short lines northerly from Lake Ontario.

Many of these roads got into financial trouble in the 1860's, and the failure of the Grand Trunk badly hurt the reputation of Canadian securities in London, then the undisputed center of world finance. In 1879 the Dominion completed building the Intercolonial to connect Nova Scotia and New Brunswick with railways in Quebec. In 1885 the Canadian Pacific Railway was finished with generous public aid to connect British Columbia with the East. At about the same time most of the smaller roads were absorbed by the Canadian Pacific or the Grand Trunk.

Early in the 20th century another railway boom got under way, mainly in answer to the rapid development of agriculture in the West. The Canadian Northern was cheaply built by a group in Toronto. The Grand Trunk Pacific (Winnipeg-Prince Rupert) was the child of the old Grand Trunk, which feared it would be

PUBLIC ARCHIVES OF CANADA

GOLDEN SPIKE, completing the rail line across the continent, was driven in (*above*) on November 7, 1885.

CANADIAN PACIFIC RAILWAY

CANADIAN PACIFIC Railway, with streamlined trains (*above*) runs from sea to sea.

strangled by the thriving Canadian Pacific. The National Trans-Continental (Winnipeg-Quebec City-Moncton) was built by the Dominion to provide a relatively direct route between the West and the Intercolonial. During or just after World War I all these lines, except the Canadian Pacific, became virtually bankrupt. They were taken over by the federal government and consolidated into the Canadian National Railways in 1923.

After engaging in a reckless competitive battle in the 1920's and struggling through the depression of the 1930's, the Canadian Pacific and Canadian National both made large profits during World War II. Wage rates and the cost of supplies were frozen, traffic expanded enormously, and the operation of automobiles, buses, and trucks was restricted.

Railway Rates. Shortly after hostilities terminated, price and wage controls were lifted. As the level of freight rates had remained substantially unchanged since 1922, railway net revenues dropped. By 1960 the Board of Transport Commissioners had allowed railways to raise most tolls 155% above the level of 1939. But carriers were not able to reap the full benefit of the authorized increases because of intensive competition from trucks and because rates on grain exported from western Canada were exempt. All things considered, the increases that could be made to "stick" raised the general level of rates by only about 55%.

In 1897 the Canadian Pacific Railway had agreed with the Dominion to cut rates on grain and grain products moved from the West to ports on Lake Superior and on settlers' effects hauled in the opposite direction. In return, it got a subsidy of roughly \$3.4 million to build a line through the Crow's Nest Pass into southern British Columbia. Though the reductions in rates were technically made without limit of time, the government set them aside during and after World War I, reinstated them on grain but not on settlers' effects in 1922 and 1925, and applied them on all railway lines in the West, not merely on the Canadian Pacific as it existed in 1897. Moreover, Crow's Nest Pass rates were applied on grain exported through Vancouver by virtue of an order of the Board of Transport Commissioners (1925) and by legislation (1967).

Railways claim these statutory rates are below the costs of handling the traffic. In 1961 a royal commission recommended that the federal government pay to the railways the difference between what they charged shippers (the Crow's Nest rates) and the cost of moving export grain. This proposal was defeated in the House of Commons in 1967. Western farmers dislike being subsidized, and they argue that improved methods of handling grain are rapidly reducing the cost of moving this freight to the level of the Crow's Nest Pass rates.

The Dominion also subsidizes freight rates in "select territory." This includes Nova Scotia. New Brunswick, Prince Edward Island, and the Gaspé Peninsula of Quebec (since 1927) and Newfoundland after it joined Confederation in 1949. The subsidy is 20% of the normal rate on purely local traffic and 30% of the toll east of Lévis, opposite Quebec, on traffic moved from select territory to other parts of Canada.

Effects of Competition. Canadian railways, like those elsewhere, face increasing competition from trucks, pipelines, and inland ships for the carriage of freight, and from private passenger cars, airplanes, and to a minor extent buses, for the movement of passengers. Their traffic in coal has been ruined by the growing use of fuel oil in domestic heating and of hydroelectricity for power. The demand for rail transportation is further reduced by the better location of plants, more efficient use of raw materials, rural depopulation, and the propensity of people to spend

TED GRANT, FROM NATIONAL FILM BOARD

TRANSPORT RIG with tractor treads moves goods through the miry ground of the Northwest Territories.

relatively less on foodstuffs and durable goods and rather more on services, such as entertainment, which are not heavy users of transportation. On the other hand, railways have gained from the rise in the standard of living, the growth in population, and the rapid industrialization of Canada.

To protect their earnings, Canadian railways have introduced diesel locomotives, the latest methods of operating yards and controlling traffic, competitive rates, agreed charges (low rates that apply when a shipper agrees to send all or a large percentage of his traffic by rail), and incentive rates that encourage shippers to load cars more heavily. The gains anticipated from these measures tend to be offset by rising rates of wages, rising prices, and continued loss of traffic to competitors.

Railways have also tried to cut losses by abandoning unprofitable passenger trains and branches, cutting out small stations, and accelerating the introduction of technological advances. These changes are often opposed by labor unions and the public generally. In 1967 the Railway Act was amended to facilitate abandonments wherever advisable and to provide for federal subsidies in the event that a nonpaying service was required in the public interest, that is, where alternative transportation by highway was nonexistent. The same legislation forbade railways to charge excessive rates on "captive" traffic—that which can be moved only by rail. It also required that every rate be compensatory, thus forestalling the danger that a railway, in its zeal to take business from competitors, might make unsound judgments. Any rate that is below the out-of-pocket cost of handling the traffic in question throws an unfair burden on other kinds of freight.

Mileage. Since 1945 new lines have been built to serve mines and agriculture, but numerous branches have been abandoned. Total mileage has risen from 43,730 (70,370 km) to more than 45,000 (72,232 km). The Canadian National has over half and the Canadian Pacific three eighths of the total. The two companies jointly own Northern Alberta Railways, 790 miles (1,272 km) from Edmonton to Waterways and to Dawson Creek. The White Pass and Yukon joins Skagway, Alaska, with Whitehorse in the Yukon by 90 miles (145 km) of narrow-gauge line (3 feet 6 inches, or 106 cm, standard-gauge being 4 feet 8½ inches, or 143 cm). The Pacific Great Eastern runs from northern Vancouver to Fort St. John, 789 miles (1,270 km) to the northeast. It is owned by the province of British Columbia. Another provincially owned system is the Ontario Northland. Its main line stretches from North Bay to the foot of James Bay, and with branches is 727 miles (1,169 km) long.

The main job of the Sydney and Louisbourg, 70 miles (113 km) long, is to serve the coal mines of Cape Breton Island in Nova Scotia. The Quebec, North Shore, and Labrador (330 miles, or 531 km) and the Wabush Railways (42 miles, or 68 km) bring iron ore to Sept-Îles, a port on the Gulf of St. Lawrence. American railways run across southern Ontario to join the states of Michigan and New York. They also enter Montreal, Winnipeg, and Vancouver, giving them a total of about 400 miles (644 km) within Canada.

Highways. The history of motor vehicles in Canada has followed the same general pattern as in the United States—few cars up to 1914, rapid growth during the 1920's, some reduction in the 1930's and early 1940's because of depression and war, and then a sharp increase.

The quality of Canada's roads compares favorably with those in nearby American states. The federal government maintains roads in national parks and in the Yukon and Northwest Territories. It owns the Canadian portion of the Alaska Highway, which it bought from the United States after World War II, and it subsidized the Trans-Canada Highway. This was completed across mainland Canada in 1963 and across Newfoundland in 1965. The federal government also helps build "roads to resources," such as potential mines and tourist attractions.

All other roads come under provincial and municipal governments. For all practical purposes taxing and regulating highway vehicles is a provincial responsibility.

Water Transport. In the days of wood and sail, vessels built and manned by Nova Scotians sailed the seven seas. After the introduction of steel and steam, Canada's oceanic fleet quickly shrank. By about 1914 its vessels were confined to inland and coastal waters. The Canadian Pacific Railway operated liners across both the Atlantic and the Pacific, but under British registry.

Toward the end of World War I the federal government began to build and operate a mer-

FREIGHTER PLANES serve the northern lands. A cargo is transferred on a desolate snowy plain.

H. TAYLOR, FROM NATIONAL FILM BOARD

chant marine. When losses mounted, the ships were sold. In World War II the government tried to avoid earlier mistakes, but again found that Canadian-built vessels could not compete with ships of other countries where costs of construction and operation were much lower. In addition, work at sea was unattractive when well-paying jobs and good living conditions might be found at home.

By the late 1960's Canada's merchant navy consisted of ships plying the Great Lakes, the St. Lawrence and Mackenzie rivers, and coastal waters. In addition, Canada had the world's second-largest fleet of icebreakers and a coast guard to patrol its shores and to supply isolated settlements in the Arctic Archipelago. Shipbuilding is not a major industry, notwithstanding federal subsidies. Canada's ports are well-equipped.

Air Transport.—Canada's size, the progressiveness of its people, the difficulty of reaching many remote settlements by surface transportation, flying experience in two world wars, and the continued need for alertness in defense have combined to stimulate civil aviation. After 1920 the so-called bush pilots helped uncover and exploit the wealth of the Laurentian Shield. In the 1930's many of these operators were consolidated into Canadian Pacific Airlines, a subsidiary of the railway. In 1937, Parliament chartered Trans-Canada Air Lines (called Air Canada since 1964). Though technically affiliated with the government's Canadian National Railways, it is essentially a separate entity.

Air Canada has the primary responsibility for all scheduled services under the Canadian flag to Britain and northern Europe, the Caribbean, and the United States (except Vancouver-San Francisco). Canadian Pacific Airlines flies regularly across the Pacific, to Mexico, and to Amsterdam, the Netherlands, and southern Europe. Prior to 1963, Air Canada had the sole right to fly between Vancouver, Montreal, and intermediate points. Then Canadian Pacific was permitted one flight a day each way on this transcontinental route. By 1971 it will be allowed to carry up to 25% of the passengers along this route, with Air Canada having the remainder.

Both major systems, especially Air Canada, provide regular service to many smaller cities throughout the country. In addition, five regional carriers—Eastern Provincial (formerly Maritime Central), Quebecair, TransAir, Saskair and Pacific Western—schedule flights that in the main, follow a north-south pattern, whereas the two major

JET AIRLINERS load passengers at Dorval International Airport, Montreal. Air Canada has overseas routes.

AIR CANADA

carriers generally fly east-west. Several operators are licensed for nonscheduled services, such as carrying prospectors and their equipment into the north, flying sportsmen on hunting and fishing expeditions, and dusting crops with insecticides and fungicides.

Pipelines. In the 1860's and 1870's pipe was used to move crude oil from wells near Petrolia, 20 miles (32 km) directly south of Lake Huron, to a local refinery. Later, pipelines distributed natural gas to cities in southwestern Ontario. In the 1920's they were used to gather petroleum from wells near Calgary, Alberta. During World War II a line built between Portland, Me., and Montreal saved tankers the long and hazardous trip around Nova Scotia and up the St. Lawrence. After the discovery in 1947 of enormous reserves of petroleum and natural gas near Edmonton and elsewhere in Alberta, pipelines were laid to provide cheap transportation throughout the West and into Ontario and British Columbia.

Communications. Telephone services are privately owned except for provincial systems in the three Prairie Provinces and along the Ontario Northland Railway. Telegraphic communication is supplied by the railways in thickly settled areas while the federal government has both wire services and wireless stations for public use in northern Canada and along both coasts. Cables connect Canada with Britain, Australia, and New Zealand. Submarine telephone or telegraph cables, or both, connect mainland Canada with the provinces of Newfoundland and Prince Edward Island, and with numerous other islands, including the French possessions of St. Pierre and Miquelon in the Gulf of St. Lawrence. The post office is a basic and cheap means of communication.

In all, Canadian communication facilities, in proportion to population, are among the most extensive in the world. See also section 39. *Mass Communications*.

A. W. Currie, *University of Toronto*

Further Reading: Currie, A. W., *Canadian Transportation Economics* (Toronto 1967); Glazebrook, George P. de T., *A History of Transportation in Canada* (Toronto 1937); Skelton, O. D., *The Railway Builders* (Toronto 1920); Stevens, George R., *Canadian National Railways* (Toronto 1962).

19. Labor

Canada began its second century in 1967 with a population of 20 million and a labor force of about 7.7 million, of whom approximately 6.3 million were wage and salary earners. Almost two thirds of the labor force was located in Ontario and Quebec. Less than 10% of the labor force was engaged in agriculture, compared to 20% in 1950. Service industries, including finance, trade, transportation, government, schools, and hospitals, accounted for over 55%, compared with 42% in 1950.

While the participation rate—the ratio of labor force to population of working age—for men declined from 84% in 1950 to about 78% in 1965, it increased from 23% to 31% for women. The rapid growth of the female labor force has been one of the more notable labor force developments since 1940.

Labor Organizations. Trade union membership in the mid-1960's was approximately 1,750,000. Hence, about 25% of the total labor force and about 31% of all nonagricultural paid workers were members of the union movement. About 85% of all union members in Canada were in unions affiliated with one of the two central labor organizations; about 74% in unions affiliated with the Canadian Labour Congress, the larger of the two central bodies; and about 11% in unions (*syndicats*) affiliated with the Confederation of National Trade Unions, which operates almost exclusively in Quebec.

International Character. A unique feature of the Canadian labor movement is its international character. About 70% of Canadian union members belong to international unions with headquarters in the United States. This international connection has brought many benefits to Canadian union members, and has had also a significant impact on the historical development of central labor bodies in Canada.

In addition to the purely Canadian initiatives that helped shape the Canadian labor movement, the various mergers and splits in American labor federations have had a significant impact on Canadian developments. For example, the Trades and Labour Congress of Canada, formed in 1886, was composed mainly of unions affiliated with the American Federation of Labor, founded the same year. When a number of international unions broke away from the American Federation of Labor in the mid-1930's to form the Congress of Industrial Organizations, those same international unions operating in Canada joined with a number of purely Canadian unions to form the Canadian Congress of Labour in 1940. Although unity talks between the two Canadian bodies had begun prior to the merger of the AFL-CIO in 1955, it was only after the merger in the United States that the two Canadian bodies, along with two of the four independent railway-running trades, united to form the Canadian Labour Congress in 1956. In contrast, the Confederation of National Trade Unions, the Quebec-based central labor body which was known as the Canadian and Catholic Confederation of Labour until 1960, has had a continued existence since its formation in 1921.

Canadian union members belonging to international unions enjoy almost complete autonomy. In most cases, however, the international headquarters has the power to veto strikes for which it would have to pay strike benefits—a veto power that is seldom exercised. The Canadian Labour Congress is completely independent of its counterpart in the United States.

Extent of Organization. The extent of union organization varies considerably by province and industry. The most reliable data available suggest that organization among nonoffice employees varies from over 65% in British Columbia to less than 30% in Prince Edward Island. Organization among nonoffice employees in some industries, including railways, motor vehicles, pulp and paper, iron and steel, meat packing, rubber products and electric apparatus, ranges between 75% and 95%; in other industries, such as clothing, printing and publishing, bakery products, wood products, and chemical products, it is only slightly over 50%. Organization among office employees is still very low in most industries.

Working Conditions. The Canadian worker enjoys a standard of living—made possible through a combination of favorable economic conditions and trade union activities—second only to that of the worker in the United States. Average weekly wages and salaries are close to $100 per week. More than 75% of all workers work a standard workweek of 40 hours or less, and over 85% work a 5-day week.

About 75% get 8 or more paid statutory holidays a year, and 3 to 4 weeks of vacation a year are becoming fairly common. The vast majority of workers are covered by health benefit plans, with the employer paying all or part of the total cost.

Labor Legislation. Among the more important statutes in the labor field are those that provide for collective bargaining, unemployment insurance, minimum wages, maximum hours, and workmen's compensation.

The federal government in Canada, in contrast to those of most advanced industrialized countries, exercises jurisdiction over only about one tenth of the nonagricultural labor force. Since Canada's written constitution, the British North America Act (1867), gives to the provinces jurisdiction over property and civil rights as well as local works and undertakings, the courts interpreted these provisions as giving the provinces jurisdiction over labor relations and labor matters generally. Consequently, federal jurisdiction is confined to interprovincial and international operations such as railways, trucking, pipelines, ferries, telephone and telegraph service, air transport, radio and television broadcasting, uranium mining and processing, and works declared by the Parliament of Canada to be for the general advantage of Canada—for example, grain elevators.

Collective Bargaining. The federal Industrial Relations and Disputes Investigation Act (1948) governs collective bargaining in federal industries. The act guarantees both workers and employers freedom of association and the right to organize, provides machinery for the certification of unions as bargaining agents, and requires the parties to negotiate with the object of reaching a collective agreement. It also provides for a two-stage compulsory conciliation procedure, first by a government conciliation officer and, if he fails, by a tripartite board. Strikes or lockouts are prohibited until seven days after the board has reported, as well as during the life of a collective agreement.

All of the provinces have labor relations acts similar to the federal act. The Saskatchewan Act, however, has never contained the compulsory conciliation requirement, and a number of provinces have made adjustments in their dispute settlement procedures.

In 1967 the federal government enacted the Public Service Staff Relations Act, which gives collective bargaining rights to over 200,000 federal civil servants. The act is similar to the labor relations acts that apply to other workers, but it contains two special features. First, the act gives employee organizations a choice between two methods of dispute settlement: one provides for binding arbitration and the other for reference of disputes to a conciliation board, with the right to strike if conciliation fails. Second, the act denies the right to strike to employees whose services are essential to the safety and security of the public. A number of the provinces have also enacted legislation that gives their public servants the right to bargain collectively.

Unemployment Insurance. The Unemployment Insurance Act, a federal statute passed in 1940 after a constitutional amendment, covers about 80% of all nonagricultural workers in Canada. The compulsory contributory program is financed by equal contributions from employers and employees, the amount of the contribution depending on the employee's wages, plus a contribution by the federal government. Duration of benefits depends on the length of the employee's contribution. Their amount, which varies with earnings, goes to a maximum of $36 a week for workers with one or more dependents.

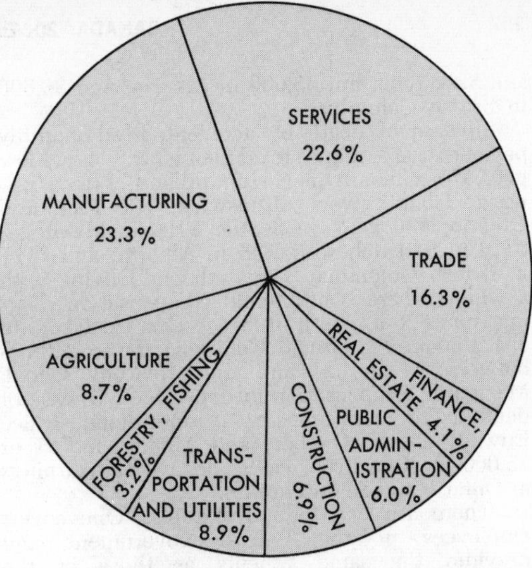

CANADIAN LABOR FORCE, BY INDUSTRY

Hours and Wages. Federal law sets a standard workweek of 40 hours and a maximum of 48. Alberta and British Columbia set a maximum workweek of 44 hours, and Ontario 48. Manitoba sets a standard workweek of 48 hours (44 for women); Saskatchewan 44; and Newfoundland 40 for shop employees. New Brunswick limits the hours of women and boys to 48 a week, while Quebec limits the hours of women and boys to 55 a week in factories and to 60 in commercial establishments in towns with more than 10,000 people.

Federal and provincial legislation, except in Newfoundland and Prince Edward Island, provides for annual vacations with pay, as follows: federal, British Columbia, Alberta, and Manitoba, for two weeks after one year's service; Quebec, Nova Scotia, and New Brunswick, for one week after one year's service; Ontario, for one week after one year's service and two weeks after four years' service; Saskatchewan, for two weeks after one year's service and three weeks after five years' service.

Minimum wage laws are in effect in the federal jurisdiction and in all 10 provinces. The federal rate is $1.25 an hour, and the most common rate under provincial jurisdiction is $1.00 an hour. Only Newfoundland and New Brunswick have rates below $1.00 an hour. With the exception of Newfoundland, Nova Scotia, and Prince Edward Island, the same rates apply to both men and women.

Workmen's Compensation. All provinces have workmen's compensation laws that provide both medical care and compensation. The cost is borne completely by employers through contributions to a provincial fund, based on the accident and disease record of their industry. Disability compensation is 75% of earnings. up to maximum earnings of $5,000 a year in Newfoundland, Prince Edward Island, Nova Scotia, New Brunswick, and Quebec; $6,000 in Ontario, Manitoba, and Saskatchewan; $5,600 in Alberta; and $6,600 in British Columbia.

In case of death by accident, fixed monthly payments are made to dependents. A widow gets $75 a month in Newfoundland, Prince Edward Island, New Brunswick, Quebec, and Ontario; $90 in Nova Scotia; $100 in Manitoba; $110 in Saskatchewan; $85 in Alberta; and $117 in British Columbia. For each child living with a widow, there is additional compensation ranging from $20 a month in Prince Edward Island to $51 a month in British Columbia if the child is between 18 and 21 and still attending school. Maximum compensation to dependents in case of death is 75% of earnings in Newfoundland, Prince Edward Island, Quebec, and Manitoba; 75% of $5,000 in New Brunswick; and average earnings in Ontario and Saskatchewan.

There are two federal statutes. One covers employees of the federal government and provides the same benefits as those of the province in which the federal government employee is usually employed. The other federal statute, covering merchant seamen, holds the individual employer liable for the payment of compensation and requires him to carry accident insurance to cover his liability.

Other Labor Laws. There are other laws covering the minimum age for employment, equal pay for men and women, paid public holidays, and fair employment practices.

Government Manpower Programs. In response to rapid economic and technological changes, a number of manpower programs have been strengthened and new ones introduced to better match the supply of and demand for labor. During the 1960's the National Employment Service was completely reorganized, strengthened, and renamed the Canada Manpower Division of the federal Department of Manpower and Immigration. Under the Federal-Provincial Technical and Vocational Training Program, substantial training facilities have been constructed and generous training allowances made available to those enrolled in training courses.

The Manpower Mobility Program provides financial assistance designed to encourage unemployed workers to move to areas where employment is available. In addition, substantial incentives are available to industries that move into areas of low income and high unemployment, thus providing jobs for workers in these areas.

ALTON W. J. CRAIG
Chief, Industrial Relations Research Division
Economics and Research Branch
Canada Department of Labour

Bibliography

Canada Department of Labour, *Labour Organizations in Canada* (Ottawa, annually).
Canada Department of Labour, *Labour Standards in Canada* (Ottawa, annually).
Canada Department of Labour, *Working Conditions in Canadian Industry* (Ottawa, annually).
Crispo, John H. G., *International Unionism: A Study in Canadian-American Relations* (Toronto 1967).
Jamieson, Stuart, *Industrial Relations in Canada* (Toronto 1957).
Woods, Harry D., and Ostry, Sylvia, *Labour Policy and Labour Economics in Canada* (Toronto 1962).

20. Banking and Currency

The Canadian banking system is characterized by a high concentration of ownership and widespread branch operations. These structural characteristics, which permit large-scale commercial banking, reflect the distinctive historic needs of financing Canadian economic development.

Canada has eight chartered banks (privately owned commercial banks granted charters by Parliament), and in the late 1960's they operated more than 5,700 banking offices. This oligopoly—a market structure consisting of "few sellers"—has been encouraged by public policy. High capital requirements and the necessity of obtaining a federal charter present difficulties in starting a new bank, and the government in the past has taken a tolerant attitude toward bank mergers and amalgamations. The oligopoly is also, however, a reflection of basic economic forces, including the difficulties faced by new firms in competing with established banks that benefit by the economies of large-scale business.

The country's central bank is the Bank of Canada, founded in 1934 as a privately owned institution but converted to public ownership by 1938. The Bank of Canada regulates credit and currency, and it promotes the general economic and financial welfare of the country.

Banking History—*Pre-Confederation.* Like all social institutions, banking is evolutionary, and the present structure and operation of the Canadian banking system can therefore be understood only in terms of the particular circumstances that have conditioned it. Following the British conquest of New France in 1763, complaints about the chronic scarcity of money in the rudimentary economy of that colony became increasingly widespread. The solution was thought to lie in the introduction of a paper-money issue, to be effected in the form of bank notes through the founding of a commercial bank. Thus, in 1817, nine Montreal merchants signed articles of association to conduct, without statutory authority, a banking business to be known as the Bank of Montreal.

The beginning of Canada's present chartered banking system dates from the founding of this institution, which was incorporated in 1822, along with two other banks which had begun operations in the meantime. The Bank of Montreal was the first bank of discount, deposit, and note issue to be established anywhere in the colony. Its articles, taken directly from the constitution of the First Bank of the United States, served as the model for all banks subsequently founded both in Upper and Lower Canada. Despite this similarity in charters, it is not surprising that the structure and practices of commercial banking in Canada and the United States have differed so widely. Each represents the product of its environment. In Canada there have been three major influences.

The first of these influences was the Scottish background of many of the earliest Canadian bankers, which led to the introduction of branch banking, the issuing of notes, payment of interest on deposits, and the maintenance of joint clearing facilities. A second influence lay in the particular problems that arose as the banks sought to adapt their operations to the requirements of an expanding pioneer economy; lessons were learned from commercial banking practices in the United States. The distinctive pledge provisions of section 88 of Canada's Bank Act of 1859 and the use of an unsecured note issue illustrate this background. A third and very important factor in Canadian bank development before Confederation was the guidance and supervision exercised by the British Colonial Office, which was empowered to revise or disallow colonial legislation, especially where matters of banking and currency were involved.

Experimentation in Canadian banking thus tended to be minimized, and this conservatism was further reinforced by the fact that the early banks were established by mercantile and trading interests, able and willing to provide the large amounts of capital essential in financing costly undertakings in an economy where capital was scarce. This concentration of banking funds likewise made possible the development of branch banking from the beginning.

By the time of Confederation in 1867, the Canadian commercial banks had achieved greater stability, versatility, and diversification of risks. Expansion of credit by these banks was of course closely related to the basically extractive processes of production, such as wheat growing, lumbering, and shipbuilding. The total volume of credit fluctuated directly with changing economic conditions. The marked pattern of seasonal variation in Canadian bank credit had already become apparent with the peak note-issue occurring in the late autumn and the low point being reached in late winter. Until after Confederation, the importance of deposits remained relatively small.

Basic Features Developed. By 1867 the Canadian chartered banks had developed many of the basic features which have remained to the present day. Among these should be noted:

(1) The incorporation of banks by specific legislative enactments, and the granting of charters to govern their operations (hence the name, chartered banks).

(2) The relatively high minimum capitalization ($1 million) required to establish a new bank in the late 1960's).

(3) The requirement of a decennial renewal of all bank charters, which provides the opportunity for periodic discussion and study of the operations of the banks and of the need for revisions in banking legislation.

(4) The "pledge" provisions of the Canadian Bank Act, which have basically been related to the financing of primarily extractive production, but which in recent times have been broadened, reflecting the growing diversification of the Canadian economy.

(5) The unsecured note issue of the chartered banks (until the privilege of issue was withdrawn when the central bank began operations in 1935). No specific collateral was required as backing for bank notes, in contrast to the provisions of the National Bank Act in the United States. The total note issue was merely limited to the total of the bank's paid-in capital (plus reserves). Such an issue was relatively inexpensive to provide, but its elasticity, while lauded by the bankers, was frequently perverse, and by no means an unmixed blessing.

(6) The branch banking system, which undoubtedly made possible a wider dissemination of credit facilities than could otherwise have been possible, and at a reasonably uniform cost throughout the country. The other principal advantage claimed for the branch banking system is its greater financial strength and stability, resting upon the wide diversification of assets that it is able to accomplish.

Post-Confederation. In the decades following Confederation, chartered banking continued to expand, its uneven rate of progress reflecting the cyclical fluctuations in the Canadian economy. From the turn of the century to World War I, the development of Canada's western wheat economy was accompanied by a rapid expansion of chartered banking facilities on the prairies. As in earlier periods of frontier settlement, the arrival of these large branch banking institutions was preceded by private banks which provided valuable and extensive financial services before being either bought out or crowded out by their powerful eastern competitors. Numerous mergers occurred in this period and by 1914 only 24 banks were in operation. This trend toward concentration of ownership continued until the early 1930's, by which time the systems had been reduced to 10 banks.

Chartered Bank Activities. The Canadian banks, throughout their development, have been strongly influenced in their lending operations by the commercial loan theory of banking. This theory asserts that banks should confine their credit to the financing of short-term, self-liquidating, "real" transactions. It has long been erroneously contended that such a lending policy would guarantee bank liquidity, provide an appropriate elasticity for the country's money supply, and prevent any excessive expansion or contraction of credit.

The Canadian banks have nevertheless acquired a diversity of assets far removed from the dictates of the commercial loan theory, since they extend credit not only to business but to the government and personal sectors of the economy. Moreover, they lend not only at short term but over a broad distribution of maturities. It is nevertheless true that they have strongly preferred the acquisition of short-term assets to a degree by no means dictated by their liquidity requirements, and they have not invested extensively in areas accommodated by savings banks elsewhere. It is apparent, however, that the chartered banks, particularly in the light of the Bank Act revisions of 1967, will continue to broaden their concepts of appropriate forms of lending, including term-lending, and that innovations here, as well as in their borrowing, are to be expected.

Of the banks' total assets in the late 1960's, cash and other liquid assets represented approximately 15%, general and other Canadian loans 55%, insured residential mortgages 3%, Government of Canada and other Canadian securities 16%, and all other assets 11%. In their general loans, the banks have achieved a very broad diversification—personal loans, farm improvement and other farm loans, business and industry loans, and loans to religious, educational, and welfare institutions. Traditionally, the Canadian banks have not engaged extensively in "term" lending—that is, loans with an original maturity exceeding two years.

In addition to their commercial banking activities, the chartered banks also operate as savings banks, but these two aspects of their business are fully integrated in the sense that not even a "notional" segregation of assets is attempted, in relation to current and savings deposits. Savings deposits are legally "notice" deposits, because the banks may require 15 days' notice of withdrawal, but in practice savings deposits, like current deposits, are cashable on demand. Canadian savings bank facilities, other than those provided by the chartered banks, are of only minor importance. The banks, in their continuous competition with other financial intermediaries for the attraction and retention of cash, create deposit liabilities, all of which in practice represent demand claims and which, being completely liquid, by definition constitute money.

Bank deposits constitute a large proportion of the Canadian money supply in the late 1960's. The relatively small currency component includes

A. SIMA, FROM NATIONAL FILM BOARD

MONTREAL STOCK EXCHANGE, in modern quarters, is a center of securities trading in Canada.

notes, issued solely by the Bank of Canada, and coinage.

CANADIAN MONEY SUPPLY, JUNE 1967

(In millions of dollars)

Currency:			
Bank of Canada notes.......	$2,266		
Coinage....................	306		
Total currency..............................			$2,572
Bank Deposits:			
Chartered banks:[1]			
Personal savings deposits...	$10,961		
Demand deposits........	5,264		
Nonpersonal term and notice deposits.....	2,982	$19,207	
Bank of Canada:			
"Other" deposits[2]....................		10	
Total bank deposits........................			19,217
Total currency plus bank deposits..............................			$21,789

Data derived from Bank of Canada, *Statistical Summary*. [1] Government of Canada deposits are excluded. [2] Deposits other than those owned by the chartered banks and the Bank of Canada.

Canadian Bank Act. The statutory authority that governs the operation of the chartered banks is the Canadian Bank Act. It was significantly revised in 1967 in the course of the decennial renewal of the banks' charters. The revisions reflect much of the philosophy contained in the 1964 Report of the Royal Commission on Banking and Finance. This commission had been instructed "to enquire into and report upon the structure and methods of operation of the Canadian financial system," and in particular, to study the country's banking and monetary system and the institutions and processes involved in the flow of funds through the capital market.

The pervasive theme of the report was that all financial institutions should be permitted to compete as freely as possible for business, subject to the minimum regulation necessary for the protection of their customers.

In the movement toward greater competitive freedom, the Bank Act revisions of 1967 freed the chartered banks from the interest-rate ceiling (for many years fixed at 6%) long imposed on their loans and advances. Another rigidity, the long-standing general prohibition against the banks' engaging in conventional mortgage lending, likewise was removed in 1967. Freed from those restrictions upon the choice and yields of their assets, the banks appear likely to be able to compete much more effectively with other financial intermediaries for the savings of the public, and also to shift the distribution and lengthen the maturity of their assets.

Bank of Canada. The Bank of Canada is directed by statute to "regulate credit and currency in the best interests of the economic life of the nation, to control and protect the external value of the national monetary unit and to mitigate by its influences fluctuations in the general level of production, trade, prices and employment, so far as may be possible within the scope of monetary action, and generally to promote the economic and financial welfare of the Dominion."

The Bank of Canada possesses a monopoly of the note issue, and its notes are, except for limited amounts of subsidiary coinage, the only form of legal tender in Canada. Although the act requires the Bank of Canada to redeem its notes in gold, this provision has been in continuous suspension since 1934. The requirement that the bank maintain a minimum 25% gold reserve against its notes and deposits has likewise been suspended since 1940. In that year its holdings of gold and foreign exchange were transferred to the newly created Foreign Exchange Control Board to facilitate the financing of the Canadian war effort.

Since the beginning of World War II all decisions relating to the determination of foreign exchange rates and to the buying and selling of foreign exchange have been made directly by the Canadian government, through the bank's Exchange Fund Account. The Exchange Fund was first utilized by the government during the war to support the fixed rates established in September 1939 and maintained without change until 1946. An approximate 10% appreciation in the external value of the Canadian dollar at the latter date was followed by an equivalent devaluation in 1949, and in the following year the system of fixed rates was abandoned. For more than a decade, until May 1962, the Exchange Fund was employed in smoothing out disruptive short-term fluctuations in Canada's floating rate. No effort was made, until the end of the period, to influence basic market trends. In the midst of the severe exchange crisis in the spring of 1962, the Canadian government moved into conformity with the general postwar fashion by returning to a fixed parity.

Assets and Liabilities. All but a very small proportion of the Bank of Canada's assets are held in the form of government securities. These encompass a broad distribution of maturities – a circumstance that furthers their effectiveness as instruments of open-market trading. The bank's note issue constitutes its major liability. Its deposits are owned mainly by the chartered banks, for which these balances make up their major holdings of cash reserves.

Statutory Powers. The main legislative powers that support the Bank of Canada's ability to influence general credit conditions include:

(1) The requirement placed upon the chartered banks to maintain a minimum ratio of cash to their Canadian deposits. The 1967 Bank Act provides that, for demand deposits, this ratio will be 12%, and for time deposits, 4%. Beginning in 1968, the calculation of these required ratios was altered, from the basis of monthly averaging to that of two-weeks averaging.

(2) A requirement in the Bank of Canada Act, new in 1967, that the chartered banks maintain a minimum "secondary" reserve (the ratio of treasury bills plus day-to-day loans to Canadian deposits) at levels prescribed from time to time by the Bank of Canada, but not to exceed 12%. The previous arrangement initiated in 1955 rested on the reluctant agreement of the banks rather than on any statutory authority, and involved the holding of a minimum 7% ratio.

(3) The Bank of Canada's authority to buy and sell Canadian government securities, provincial securities, bills of exchange and banker's acceptances, foreign exchange, securities of the United States, and short-term securities of the United Kingdom. The Bank of Canada may also acquire securities issued by its wholly owned subsidiary, the Industrial Development Bank. In practice, however, it has confined its open-market transactions to Canadian government securities, in which it has usually, but by no means always, dealt in short-term issues, where the market is broadest, in order to minimize the direct "price" effects of its own operations.

(4) The Bank of Canada's preparedness, as a leader of last resort, to make temporary advances, within specified limits, to the chartered banks in response to their requests for accommodation, the minimum rate charged being known as the Bank rate; and its readiness to provide the same facilities for approved securities (money market) dealers.

It is the Bank of Canada's view that "provided that arrangements for access to central bank credit are subject to adequate restrictions and involve paying a penalty rate of interest, they need not in practice appreciably weaken the central bank's control over the total cash reserves" of the banks.

Nonstatutory Powers. In addition to its statutory powers, the Bank of Canada continues from time to time to employ the technique of moral suasion. Because the concentration of ownership of the chartered banks is so great, this approach has proved particularly effective in the Canadian banking system. Further useful monetary effects are achieved by the Bank of Canada when the Canadian government, cooperating with the bank, alters the distribution of its cash balances as between the central bank and the chartered banks.

It is nevertheless true that, in seeking to exercise monetary control through the management of the chartered banks' cash reserves, the Bank of Canada places its basic and continuous reliance on open-market transactions. It possesses no authority to impose selective or qualitative – as contrasted with general or quantitative—credit controls. The Bank of Canada takes the view that only in urgent circumstances might the use of such direct measures be justified, and then only as the instrument of specific government policy as reflected in appropriate legislation.

Debt Management. The Bank of Canada also acts as debt manager for the government. As fiscal agent, it advises the government on the maturity distribution of the debt and the terms on which securities are issued, redeemed, and refunded.

In mid-1967, the gross Canadian government debt outstanding approximated $21.3 billion, or about one quarter of the total Canadian public and private debt. Because decisions in this area strongly influence the composition and price structure of financial assets, it is obvious that debt management must be closely integrated with monetary management, and with government fiscal policies, if they are to contribute most effectively to the attainment of broad economic objectives. In this connection, Canadian postwar experience has been one of frequent conflict rather than of continuing harmony in the use of these instruments.

During the 1960's the structure of the Canadian financial system was significantly broadened through the development of an active short-term market in Canadian government securities and in other public and private issues. These instruments are characterized by their high liquidity, and the growth of this market enabled lenders to employ short-term balances more profitably and borrowers to acquire such funds more readily or more cheaply. It also provided the Bank of Canada with an improved mechanism for transmitting to the economy the effects of its monetary policies.

Financial Intermediaries. Although ultimate borrowers and lenders may deal with one another directly, the well-known and serious limitations of this process have stimulated in Canada, as elsewhere, the evolution of an expanding range of intermediaries. The major objective of the intermediaries is the efficient transfer of funds from "surplus" to "deficit" economic units.

Since World War II, Canadian financial development has included not only a substantial expansion of the assets and liabilities of the older established intermediaries (the chartered banks, life insurance companies, trust companies, and mortgage loan companies), but an even more rapid growth and diversification of the operations of newer forms of financial institution (such as investment funds, sales finance and small-loan companies, pension funds, and credit unions). The relative rates of growth of these financial intermediaries, each with its lending preferences, affect directly the pattern of allocation of real resources within the economy. Because these preferences have been conditioned in part by historic legislative restraints, the fundamental revisions embodied in the 1967 Canadian Bank Act presage a changing role for the chartered banks, the social consequences of which remain to be assessed.

R. CRAIG MCIVOR, *McMaster University*

Further Reading: Government of Canada, *Report of the Royal Commission on Banking and Finance* (Ottawa 1964); McIvor, R. C., *Canadian Monetary Banking and Fiscal Development* (Toronto 1958): Neufeld, E. P., *Bank of Canada Operations* (Toronto 1964).

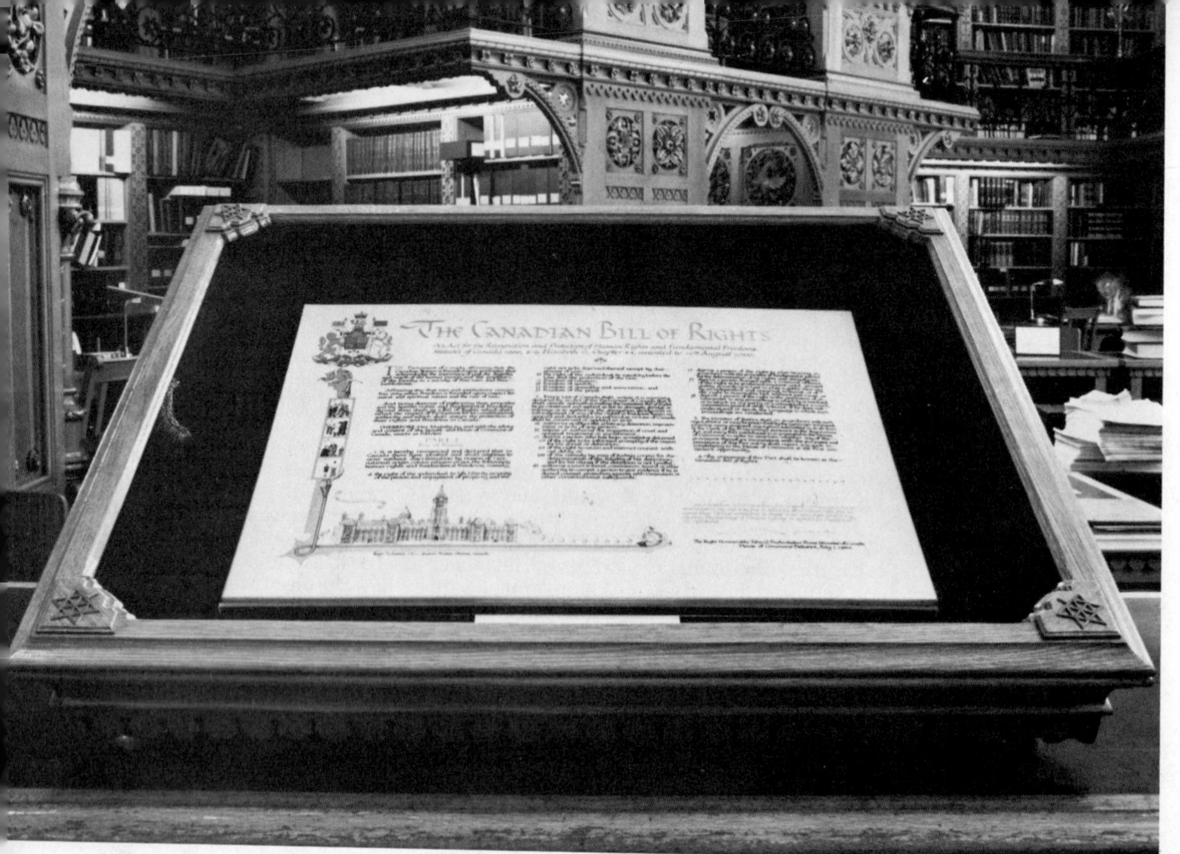

CHRIS LUND, FROM NATIONAL FILM BOARD

THE CANADIAN BILL OF RIGHTS, displayed in the Parliamentary Library, Ottawa.

CANADA: Government and Politics

Canada, because of its union of two distinct cultures—Anglo-Saxon and French—and because of its federal system establishing three elected levels of authority, is of especial interest to students of government and politics. Here, the field is surveyed in five dimensions: structure and functions of government, political parties, public finance, defense, and health and welfare.

21. Structure and Functions of Government

A study of government in Canada must embrace the constitution, the national institutions of monarchy, executive, Parliament, public service and judiciary, and provincial and local governments.

Constitution. The basic written document of the Canadian constitution is the British North America (B.N.A.) Act of 1867. Because Canada was a colony at the time, the act is an ordinary statute of the United Kingdom Parliament, and no provision was written into it for its amendment by any other body. This fundamental part of the Canadian constitution has thus remained a statute of the legislature of another country, and while agreement has been sought within Canada for years on the terms on which the act could become a purely Canadian document, Canada reached its first centennial without its constitution having been brought home. The act itself permits the provinces to amend their own constitutions, and in 1949 the Canadian Parliament enacted a statute to ensure that Parliament could amend the purely federal parts of the act. But important sections of the act, including the distribution of powers between the national and provincial legislatures, can still be amended only by an act of the United Kingdom Parliament.

The U.K. Parliament has never sought to amend the B.N.A. Act on its own initiative, nor has it ever refused to pass an amendment requested by Canada. The problem of amending the act has been a purely Canadian one, and there has been much discussion about how one properly asks the United Kingdom Parliament to amend the act. The settled technical process now is for a joint address to be passed through both houses of the Canadian Parliament, formally requesting an amendment; but behind that lie prolonged debates about when and how, if at all, the provinces have a right to be consulted in the amending process, and the circumstances under which majority or unanimous consent of the provinces may be requested. The long delay in making the act purely Canadian has been caused in part by further disagreement about how the act will be amended after it is brought to Canada. That the act will be brought to Canada is certain, but the terms on which it will be remain unsettled.

Provisions and Practices. Amendments to the act are not numbered, since they too are technically ordinary statutes, and there have been at least eighteen of them; there is room for disagreement among experts as to what constitutes an amendment. The act consists of 147 clauses in 11 sections, and establishes Canada as a monarchy, and as a federal state with a governmental system based on the British parliamentary model. It provides for the use in Parliament of English and French, both of which are official languages in Canada. It creates not only Canada, but also the four original provinces (On-

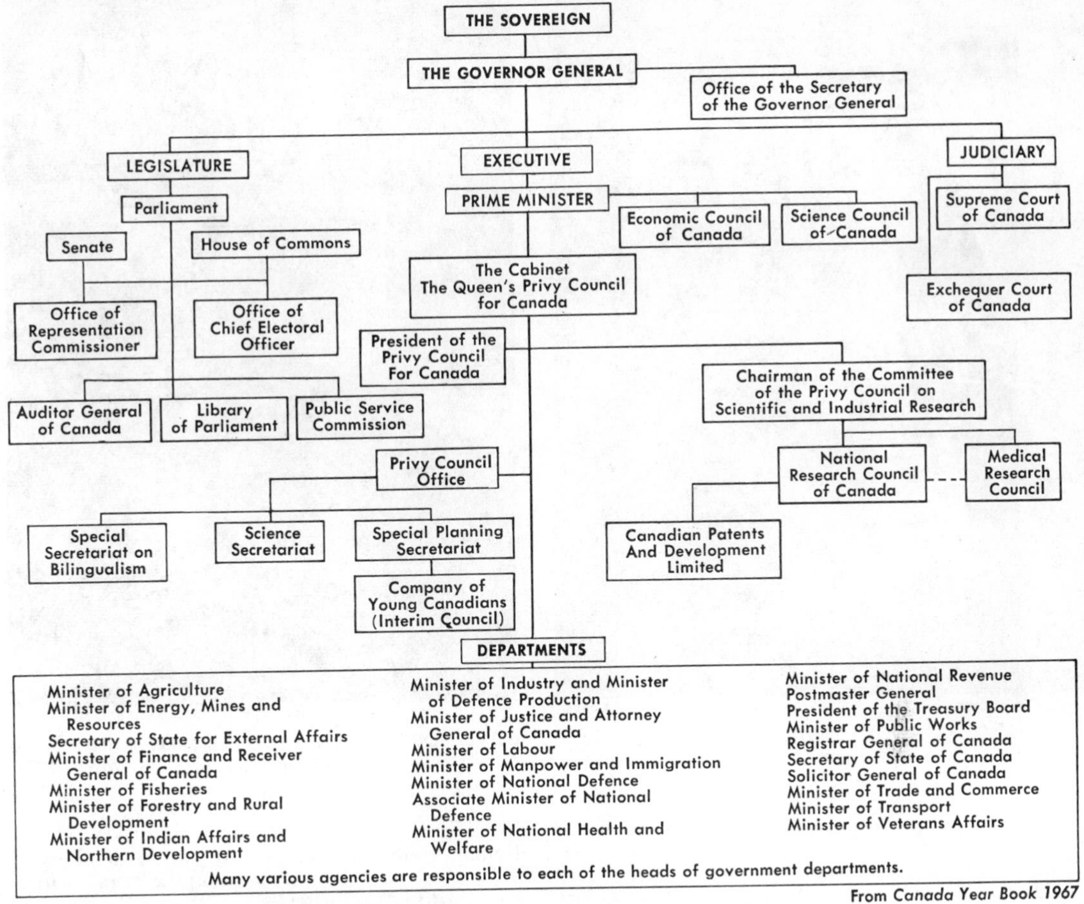

From *Canada Year Book 1967*

tario, Quebec, New Brunswick, Nova Scotia) as as part of it, and provides for the admission of new members.

The original financial relations between Canada and the provinces, since altered many times, are part of the act. The act also distributes legislative powers between Parliament and the provincial legislatures in a manner intended to give the preponderance of influence to the central government. The Parliament of Canada is authorized "to make laws for the peace, order, and good government of Canada"; in addition, the central executive may disallow any provincial statute within a year of its passing (a power not used since 1943, but 112 times before that), and appoints provincial lieutenant governors, the judges of all higher provincial courts, and senators, who were originally intended in part to be special representatives of the provinces in the national government.

The constitution of Canada also includes a variety of institutions and practices which are not spelled out in the B.N.A. Act. The relationships between the ministry and the monarch (or the monarch's representative, the governor general), between the prime minister and his colleagues, and between the ministry and Parliament are all fundamentally customary rather than statutory, and the same is true of such factors as the separation of church and state, the absence of a military tradition, and the use of public enterprise to influence the economy, all of which profoundly affect the nature of government.

Monarchy. The main national institutions of government can be described simply: the executive power is vested in the monarch; the legislative in Parliament; and the judicial in the supreme court and the exchequer court. Vesting the executive power in the monarch, even in 1867, meant something very different from what the words might seem to convey. It is understood by everyone in a position of influence that the monarch (as represented by the governor general) does virtually nothing of political or constitutional significance without the advice of the prime minister, who with his colleagues holds the real executive power.

But the monarch is not a nonentity: the King (Queen) of Canada has his own title as such and is distinct from the King (Queen) of the United Kingdom. It is a mistake to think that the holding of both positions by the same person means that Canada is in any way subordinate to the United Kingdom. As head of state the monarch and his representative enjoy great prestige, take part in many ceremonials, and relieve the prime minister of many onerous public duties. There are great advantages in having a nonpartisan head of state distinct from the leader of government.

The governor general is now appointed by the monarch on the advice of the Canadian prime minister. Prior to 1926, when Canada ceased even technically to be a colony, the governor general represented the government of the United Kingdom rather than the monarch personally and was sent from the United Kingdom for a term of five to seven years. In 1926 the nature of the office changed and the choice became Canadian, but the practice of selecting governors general from the United Kingdom continued until 1952. Since 1952 the gover-

CANADIAN GOVERNMENT TRAVEL BUREAU

HOUSE OF COMMONS meeting before an audience in its chamber in the Parliament Buildings at Ottawa.

BILL CADZOW, FROM NATIONAL FILM BOARD

GOVERNOR GENERAL Roland Michener is installed as the representative of the monarch in April 1967.

nor general has been himself Canadian, and the practice has begun of alternating the position between English- and French-speaking citizens. Canada pays the full cost of the governor generalship, but makes no other financial contribution to the upkeep of the monarchy.

Executive, or Cabinet. The operative part of the executive, the cabinet, consists of two dozen or more ministers, almost all of them members of the House of Commons, and almost all of them heads of government departments. It is customary, but not binding, for one senator to sit in the cabinet; or a minister may be chosen from outside Parliament and be temporarily without a seat until he gets one. It is also common for a person to be "minister without portfolio," that is, in the cabinet but attached to no department.

The prime minister, the head of government, is chosen by the governor general, and ordinarily the choice is not difficult: he is the man leading the party with a majority of seats in the House of Commons, or, if there is no such party, the man who can otherwise win the support of a majority of the members of the Commons.

Choosing a Cabinet. The prime minister chooses all the other ministers (all of whom take oaths as members of the privy council, which is provided for in the B.N.A. Act and from which the cabinet derives its legal powers; the active Privy Council comprises, in effect, the monarch's confidential advisers), and this in itself marks him off from the rest of the cabinet, as do his positions as party leader, and special adviser to the crown. A prime minister's resignation resigns the entire cabinet. Theoretically, the prime minister may choose anyone for his cabinet, but practical politics limits him severely. He must consider his own position in the party, and balance cabinet representation as among the provinces, between English- and French-speaking, Protestants and Roman Catholics, senior and junior members of the party, and conservative and liberal wings. Every prime minister finds that his first real baptism of fire is forming his first cabinet.

Status of Ministers. All ministers are legally equal, but an informal hierarchy always exists in a Canadian cabinet. Some portfolios, of which finance is perennially the most important, invariably outrank others; some individuals, because of their personal or party stature, are closer to the prime minister. Whatever his status, each minister is responsible to Parliament both for his department and for his government policy as a whole; ministers attend in Parliament, explaining and defending policies, answering questions and, at least once each year, piloting their departmental estimates.

Outside Parliament, ministers administer their departments, attend cabinet and other important meetings, and make countless speeches; since each is a parliamentarian, an executive, and a leading party member, a minister's duties can be onerous. Both in and out of Parliament, the cabinet (which meets in secret) acts as a unit, the ministers having both individual and collective responsibility. The executive has no fixed term, and a prime minister can remain in office as long as the Commons supports him. In addition to the remuneration of members of Parliament, the prime minister receives $25,000 annually, a departmental minister $15,000; each also receives a car allowance of $2,000.

Parliament. The Parliament of Canada is defined in the B.N.A. Act as "consisting of the Queen, an Upper House styled the Senate, and the House of Commons." The parliamentary role of the monarch, performed by the governor general (or his deputy) except on the rare occasions when the monarch is in Canada, is limited to opening and closing sessions of Parliament with a formal speech written by the prime minister, and giving royal assent to bills; all statutes are enacted in the monarch's name. The governor general never appears in the House of Commons but discharges his duties in the Senate chamber.

Senate. Although the equal legislative partner of the Commons (except in that all money bills must originate in the lower house), the Senate is immeasurably the weaker of the two. In the late 1960's, it consisted of 102 members: 6 each for the 4 western provinces, 24 each for Ontario and Quebec, 10 each for Nova Scotia and New Brunswick, and 4 for Prince Edward Island; plus 6 for Newfoundland, which entered the federation after the Senate's regional representation had been settled. Originally it was intended to give special representation to the provinces to counterbalance a Commons based on representation by population. It was also meant to represent property: senators (who are appointed by the governor general on the recommendation of the prime minister, originally for life although they must now retire at 75), must be 30 years of age and possess a property qualification of $4,000 in the province which they represent and in which they must also be resident at appointment.

The Senate from the first was undermined by the fact that the cabinet was responsible only to the House of Commons, and the assumption by the cabinet of the role of regional representation. The first cabinet was made larger than it needed to be to give a voice to all provinces and major interests, and every cabinet since has fulfilled the same function, thus greatly reducing the Senate's area of possible influence. At the same time, the appointing system left the senators without electorates, and without incentives, for from the start senatorships were used to reward party workers for what they had done, rather than what they might do in the future. The result is a house with many elderly members who feel no great urge to distinguish themselves further. Senators receive $12,000 annually, plus a tax-free allowance of $3,000, and traveling expenses to and from Ottawa.

House of Commons. The House of Commons, on the 1966 reapportionment of constituencies, had 264 members distributed as follows: Ontario, 88; Quebec, 74; Nova Scotia 11; New Brunswick, 10; Newfoundland, 7; Prince Edward Island, 4; Manitoba, 13; British Columbia, 23; Saskatchewan, 13; Alberta, 19; Yukon and Northwest Territories, 2. The seats are divided among the provinces after each decennial census on a population basis, except that every province is guaranteed as many M.P.'s as it has senators.

The actual drawing of constituencies was done in 1966 for the first time by independent commissions, one for each province, each headed by a judge; before 1966, constituencies were drawn by a Commons committee. In general, though there are some disqualifications, every citizen or resident British subject over 18 is eligible to vote and seek election. The Canadian federal election system is a national one, and is supervised by a chief electoral officer responsible only to Parliament.

Each House of Commons has a maximum life of five years, but the prime minister may advise the governor general to dissolve Parliament at any time; once, in 1926, a governor general refused, precipitating a constitutional crisis. The House, like the Senate, determines its own rules, and is presided over by a speaker chosen from among its members. The Senate speaker is appointed on the advice of the prime minister. Both speakers are expected to be nonpartisan.

The most important single characteristic of the House of Commons is that it is partisan. The strongest party forms a government. Always an opposition is ready to form an alternate government.

The chief single function of the House of Commons, apart from the usual debating of issues and policies, the questioning of ministers, and the passing of legislation (most of it introduced by the cabinet), is the annual granting of money to the executive for all the various public policies that Parliament is willing to support. The granting of supply is done in considerable detail and members of Parliament have thus many opportunities to query the administration, both on the floor of the House and in committees to which the government's proposals are often referred. To assist in its scrutiny the House has an invaluable officer, the auditor general, whose function is to audit the public books and report critically on them, independently of the cabinet, to Parliament. His report is also examined by a committee, presided over by a member of the opposition.

The dominant element in every House of Commons is the cabinet. The ordinary M.P.s are handicapped by having no research assistants, and committees have no technical staffs. The cabinet, by contrast, has at its disposal the knowledge and skill of the civil service for whose acts it is responsible, and is sustained further by its political powers as committee of a victorious party. All significant patronage is in the ministers' hands, and the M. P. on the government side who seeks advancement has good reason to support his leaders. Parliamentary committees reflect the governing party's strength. The cabinet dominates the parliamentary timetable, and only its members initiate money bills. The House of Commons is by no means a rubber stamp, and a determined opposition can criticize the government's act at great length and sometimes win concessions; but the House rules provide for closure of debate on sufficient notice. Some cabinets have resorted to it.

Members of Parliament receive $12,000 annually, plus a tax-free allowance of $6,000 and traveling expenses. Those who are parliamentary secretaries (assistants to ministers), receive an additional $4,000, as does any leader of a smaller party with 12 or more M.P.s.

The Public Service. One of the chief preoccupations of both the cabinet and Parliament is the public service. The federal public service is divided loosely into two main categories: the civil service under the Public Service Act, which in general consists of roughly 150,000 people organized into two dozen departments under ministers, and a few agencies; and an additional and somewhat larger number employed in crown corporations (public businesses organized like private ones), and other organizations outside the act. The total public service of Canada, both in Ottawa and outside the capital in local offices, numbers well over 350,000.

The difference between the departments, on the one hand, and the crown corporations on the other, is more than one of name. They recruit personnel differently, the departments through a civil service commission which enforces a strict merit system of examination, the corporations substantially through their own arrangements as laid down in their own governing statutes. They are organized differently, the departments in a hierarchical pattern with a minister at the head of each, the corpo-

CHRIS LUND, FROM NATIONAL FILM BOARD

THE SUPREME COURT of Canada building, Ottawa.

rations like a business under a board of directors in whose affairs ministerial influence may vary from a great deal to almost none. They enjoy different relations with Parliament: a minister heading a department is subjected to endless questioning and criticism in the House of Commons; some crown corporations are all but ignored in Parliament while others, which may touch affairs in many constituencies (such as Canadian National Railways or the Canadian Broadcasting Corporation), receive much parliamentary attention.

Departments and corporations are also established for different reasons. In general, the departmental form is chosen to administer statutes for which direct accountability to Parliament is desired, while some corporations are established for precisely the opposite reason—to take administration out of politics, as with the two already mentioned. Corporations are also used for public enterprises which are really businesses, such as Eldorado Mining and Refining Limited, and sometimes to attract into the public service business executives who would not be attracted into civil service as such. Ministers in Parliament frequently refuse to interfere in the affairs of corporations, or even to answer questions. Questions about the Canadian Broadcasting Corporation, which operates radio and television networks in both English and French, are, for example, commonly transmitted to the corporation by a minister who accepts no responsibility for the answers. Nonetheless, both departments and corporations are created by law, and Parliament can review legislation, or establish committees of inquiry into the affairs of any establishment set up by law, and also debate the annual granting of funds to any establishment financed through Parliament.

Overseeing of the public service is not left solely to the ministers and the public service commission. The treasury board, which is a special financial subcommittee of the cabinet with a president who is a minister, is specifically charged with responsibility for terms and conditions of employment in the public service (including collective bargaining), and for administrative policy generally, and thus enjoys the largest share of influence in operating the public service as a going concern. The public service commission mainly recruits; the Treasury Board manages.

Royal Commissions. One additional branch of the executive of considerable significance is the royal commission, in effect an ad hoc committee of inquiry set up by the executive with its own terms of reference, and normally its own budget and staff. The royal commission is so widely used in Canada that it almost qualifies as another branch of the government. A commission has obvious advantages over a parliamentary committee: it is smaller and more mobile; it can sit when Parliament is not sitting, and committees normally cannot; it can hire whatever technical staff it desires; it is not distracted by anything outside its terms of reference, whereas parliamentarians have multifarious claims on their time; and, perhaps, best of all, the cabinet can pick its personnel and thus "load" a commission any way it likes.

Royal commissions, which are purely executive agencies and, once set up, virtually a law unto themselves, are used for a variety of purposes. They may examine some extremely complex matter which cuts across the jurisdictions of many branches of government. They may investigate some contentious matter on which the government is unprepared or reluctant to take a stand immediately, and thus facilitate the postponement of a decision while a thorough inquiry is held. They may be used to prepare, or even create, public opinion in connection with a difficult issue over which a government may genuinely not know which policy is best. A royal commission can only recommend, and the government is free to accept or reject a report.

Judiciary. Standing apart from the executive and legislative branches of the government is the judiciary. Canada has both provincial and federal courts: each province has its own hierarchy of courts from justices of the peace and magistrates' courts up to provincial high courts and courts of appeal, which the provinces maintain except for the judges' salaries in the higher courts; and at the apex is the Supreme Court of Canada, established under federal law, sitting in Ottawa, and the last court of appeal in both civil and criminal cases. It consists of nine justices, including a chief justice. The governor general, on the advice of the prime minister, appoints all judges above magistrates, who are provincial appointees; federal appointees are paid by act of Parliament. No Canadian judges are elected. The criminal law is a federal matter in Canada, while the administration of justice is under provincial jurisdiction.

Both the nomenclature and the organization of provincial courts vary widely in Canada. In general, the lower courts hear minor disputes, the higher courts the more important, measured either by the nature of the case or the amount of property involved. But since the administration of justice is a provincial matter, even lower courts may handle at least the preliminary stages of serious cases, and a magistrate may in the same day sit on cases involving local bylaws, provincial civil cases, or federal criminal charges. An appeal may be made from the highest provincial court to the Supreme Court in any case where the amount in controversy exceeds $10,000; permission to appeal any other case may be granted by the highest court in each province, and if the provincial court refuses leave the Supreme Court itself may grant it.

Considerable effort is made to ensure the independence and integrity of all judges in Canada. They are well paid, receive good pensions, and may remain on the bench until 75, when they must retire. Judges are all but impossible to remove from the bench; those of the higher courts can be removed by the governor general on the address of the Senate and House of Commons, but Parliament has made only one such recommendation, in 1967.

Provincial Government. The structure of each provincial government is superficially like that at Ottawa. At the head in each province is a lieutenant governor, appointed by the governor general on the advice of the prime minister; each province has a premier who corresponds to the prime minister; each has a cabinet, and an elected assembly to which the cabinet is responsible. These similarities can be very misleading; each province has its own traditions, some having roots that go back to the earliest days of settlement on the continent, others having been created well after Confederation; and provincial political mores differ considerably across Canada.

Two factors make the provinces as a group differ from the federal government. Whereas Parliament is now in session most of the time, the provincial assemblies tend to have much shorter sessions, thus leaving the executive free of legislative scrutiny for much of each year; provincial government is thus a more executive than a parliamentary government, although the provinces have civil services structured much the same as the federal government's. And provincial jurisdiction is different from Parliament's: Parliament's powers are national in scope, and were designed in part to create a national economy; the provincial powers are more narrow, and their scope may be summarized in a clause from the B.N.A. Act as "generally all matters of a merely local or private nature in the province."

Nonetheless, a number of topics assigned to the provinces, such as education and roads, have grown enormously in importance since 1867, and judicial review of the B.N.A. Act has further enlarged provincial powers. Since the provinces vary sharply in wealth, the poorer ones have encountered profound problems in meeting their obligations. Parliament can raise money "by any mode or system of taxation" while the provinces are limited to "direct taxation within the province."

Inevitably, the provinces began early to turn to Ottawa when in need, and the record of Dominion-provincial financial relations is one of the most complex in Canadian history; so much so, indeed, that ad hoc Dominion-provincial conferences meeting outside of Parliament and the assemblies form a major part of the government of Canada. The record became increasingly complex in the 1960's when some of the provinces began to want to "opt out" of shared-cost programs with Ottawa in order to operate their own programs, while still retaining grants from federal funds. Apart from financial matters, Dominion-provincial cooperation covers a myriad of subjects, and there always are many consultative and advisory committees engaged in work.

The northern territories are not provinces, and while they have local elected councils they are still strongly under the sway of the national government.

Local Government. Municipal government in Canada is exclusively the responsibility of the provinces, and again nomenclature and practices vary greatly. Unlike the structure of the federal and provincial governments, which are based on the British model, municipal government in Canada follows more closely American models, and a typical Canadian city council has a mayor elected independently of the council. As is common in the United States, responsibilities in municipal government are generally diffused throughout a series of boards and commissions supplementing the elected council, and school government in Canada is almost everywhere separate from the rest of the local government.

Some of Canada's largest cities, led initially by Toronto, began in the 1950's to experiment with the federal principle at the local level, uniting several contiguous municipalities into a metropolitan government for some purposes. Most of the provinces (six of which are very large geographically) have vast, thinly settled areas which require no municipal organization of any kind.

NORMAN WARD, *University of Saskatchewan*

Bibliography

Ashley, Charles A., and Smails, Reginald George, *Canadian Crown Corporations* (Toronto 1965).

Beck, James Murray, *The Government of Nova Scotia* (Toronto 1957).

Dawson, Robert MacGregor, *The Government of Canada,* 4th ed., rev. by Norman Ward (Toronto 1963).

Donnelly, Murray S., *The Government of Manitoba* (Toronto 1963).

Hodgetts, John E., and Corbett, David Charles, *Canadian Public Administration* (Toronto 1960).

Kunz, F. A., *The Modern Senate of Canada, 1925–1963* 2d ed. (Toronto 1967).

MacKinnon, Frank, *The Government of Prince Edward Island* (Toronto 1951).

Rowat, Donald C., *Your Local Government* (Toronto 1962).

Royal Commission on Government Organization, *Report* (Ottawa 1962).

Saywell, John T., ed., *Canadian Annual Review* (Toronto, annually).

Ward, Norman, *The Public Purse* (Toronto 1962).

22. Political Parties

In the more than 100 years since Confederation, national political office in Canada has been monopolized by two parties, the Liberals and Conservatives (officially the Progressive Conservatives since 1942), although minor parties have been represented in all 14 parliaments elected since 1921.

The Two Major Parties. The continued preeminence of these two parties is directly attributable to the fact that they alone have maintained a sufficiently pragmatic approach to policy making to enable them to draw wide support from the diversity of regional, economic, language, and religious groups that form Canadian society.

The broad principles of Liberal and Conservative policy have not been wholly alike. The Liberals, for example, have always harbored a lingering fondness for free trade; and Conservatives, for protection. But both parties have never failed to realize the importance of commanding the middle ground. Thus differences between them over specific issues at any given time probably can be assumed to derive from their differing interpretations of how best to put together or maintain a broadly based national coalition.

Paradoxically, while the two older parties have been able to preserve their preeminence because of their success as conciliators, the rise of new parties was a response to their failures at conciliation. The development of western Canadian agriculture, initiated by Sir John A. Macdonald, a Conservative prime minister who held office for all but five years from 1867 to 1891, and successfully pursued by the Liberal administrations of Sir Wilfrid Laurier from 1896 to 1911, bred conflicts between farm and industrial-commercial interests. Responding to this pressure, the farmers were driven to independent political action. In 1921 the populist, farmer-supported Progressive party won 65 seats in the Federal Parliament, but disagreements among its members led to its exhaustion, and by 1930 it was not an effective political force.

Minor Parties. During the Great Depression two new parties arose, both in the West. One of these, the Social Credit party, was founded on a mixture of utopian economic ideas (among them the notion that the economy could be restored to health by paying all citizens a "social dividend") and fundamentalist religion. Social Credit won control of provincial governments in Alberta (1937) and British Columbia (1952), but it achieved no significant success in federal politics until 1962, when it won 30 seats in the Federal Parliament, 24 of them from Quebec.

On the face of it, the Quebec success suggested that the party might free itself of its sectional bonds, but the Quebec vote was equally sectional. Those French Canadians who turned to "les Créditistes" did so out of frustration with the failure of the Liberals and Conservatives to accord sufficient recognition to their cultural and economic demands as French Canadians. What is more, the rise in Social Credit support in Quebec coincided with declining strength for the party at the federal level in the West. When, in the elections of 1963 and 1965, Social Credit support in Quebec began to recede and, in 1964, the bulk of the Quebec wing of the party splintered off, Social Credit's chances to become a national party appeared to have died.

The prospects of the other Depression-born heir to the Progressives, the New Democratic party (formerly the Co-operative Commonwealth Federation), seemed rather brighter in the late 1960's. Formed with working class as well as farm support, the party's appeal from the outset has extended beyond its sectional birthplace. Although in 1964 it lost control of the government in Saskatchewan where (as the CCF) it had been in power for 20 years, by the late 1960's the NDP had substantial strength provincially in British Columbia, Saskatchewan, Manitoba, and Ontario, and it appeared to be winning support in Quebec. Federally, as late as the 1965 election, the party was still able to win only 21 of 265 parliamentary seats, but it did manage to poll 18% of the popular vote. The party's program originally was one of Fabian socialism, but in 1961, when the new name was adopted and formal ties were established with the Canadian Labour Congress, NDP leaders began to call themselves "liberals." In fact, as the NDP has made an effort to win a share of the middle ground, it has drawn away from ideological prescriptions.

Political Trends. Ultimately the future of the NDP is likely to be determined as much by what the Liberals and Conservatives do as by its own actions. Of the two older parties, the Liberals have been significantly more successful over the half century to the late 1960's. Since 1921 they have held office for all but a few months in 1925, five years from 1930 to 1935, and six years from 1957 to 1963. Their long tenure had its roots in Conservative alienation of Quebec, which began with Macdonald's decision to permit the execution of Louis Riel, the French-speaking leader of a rebellion among the Métis in the Northwest in the 1880's. A number of other issues, notably the question of religious and language rights in schools outside Quebec and French-Canadian opposition to conscription in the two World Wars, have served to keep Quebec and the Conservatives well apart. The Liberals under Laurier and his successor, W. L. Mackenzie King, ably exploited the situation by scrupulously avoiding the kind of involvement in cultural and religious matters that might give offense to Quebec while offering social and economic policies that would be expected to win support from all sections of the country.

In 1958 the Conservatives were afforded an opportunity to repair their mistakes in relations with French Canada when Quebec joined the rest of the country in giving an overwhelming majority to the new Conservative leader, John Diefenbaker, who had won enough support in 1957 to form a minority government. But the opportunity was lost when the Diefenbaker ministry failed to understand or respond to the renaissance of French-Canadian nationalism. In the election of 1962, Quebec returned only 14 Conservative M.P.'s, 36 fewer than in 1958. In fact, disillusionment with Diefenbaker extended well beyond Quebec, but his party retained sufficient support to enable it to form another minority government. In a new election in the following year the Liberals, under Lester B. Pearson, picked up enough additional seats to return to power, but they too lacked a majority. Both parties, in fact, were regionally isolated—the Conservatives in the Maritimes and the Prairies, the Liberals substantially in Ontario and Quebec.

When this pattern of results was repeated in the 1965 election it seemed unlikely that either party in the near future would be able to rebuild a national coalition. In the meantime, both had to be wary of the NDP. The future shape of relations in the Canadian party system appears most uncertain.

GEORGE C. PERLIN
Queen's University, Kingston, Ontario

Bibliography

Courtney, John C., *Voting in Canada,* rev. ed. (Scarborough, Ontario, 1967).
Englemann, F. C., and Schwartz, Mildred, *Political Parties and the Canadian Social Structure* (Scarborough, Ontario, 1967).
MacPherson, Crawford B., *Democracy in Alberta* (Toronto 1962).
Meisel, John, *The Canadian General Election of 1957* (Toronto 1960).
Meisel, John, ed., *Papers on the 1962 Election* (Toronto 1964).
Porter, John, *The Vertical Mosaic* (Toronto 1965).
Thorburn, H. G., *Party Politics in Canada,* rev. ed. (Scarborough, Ontario, 1967).
Zakuta, Leo, *A Protest Movement Becalmed: A Study of Change in the CCF* (Toronto 1964).

23. Public Finance

The influence of public spending on the Canadian economy is an increasingly important one. Total government expenditure in 1965 (national accounts basis) was equal to 31% of the gross national product. Disregarding intergovernmental transfers, the federal share made up 13% of the GNP with the balance more or less divided evenly between provinces and municipalities. This compares with 16% in total in 1929 and a peak of 50% in 1944 at the height of wartime activity. In the postwar years, the trend has been slowly upward from 22% in 1951 to a high of 32.3% in 1961.

Division of Responsibilities. The division of responsibilities for the public services is set out in the British North America Act, largely in Sections 91 and 92. In broad terms, the federal government has the responsibility for functions that are primarily related to the country's national status. Such matters as banking, currency and coinage, defense, criminal law, postal services, trade and commerce and national public works are specifically allocated to it. Responsibility for agriculture and immigration is shared with the provinces.

In addition to those responsibilities that are specifically allocated to it, the federal government by constitutional amendment has assumed authority over unemployment insurance and certain pensions. By exercising its powers of spending on national objectives it has also entered into such fields of income redistribution as family allowances, which are not specifically allocated in legal terms.

In 1867, when Canada was formed, the provinces were granted a relatively minor part in the structure of governmental responsibility. But, over the first 100 years of the nation's existence, events and a changing social structure have occasioned important changes in the nature of the demand for government services. Under section 92 of the British North America Act, the provinces were made responsible for purely local matters, such as health, welfare, protection of persons and property, property and civil rights, public lands, local public works, and municipal government. Most of these were relatively unimportant 100 years ago, but as conditions have changed so has the focus of public expenditure. However, the costs of provinces and municipalities have become substantially higher than those of the federal government, despite the continuing heavy burden of national defense.

NET GENERAL EXPENDITURES OF ALL GOVERNMENTS, 1963
(in millions of dollars)

	Federal	Provincial	Municipal	Total
Defense services	1,717	..	..	1,717
Veterans' pensions	336	..	..	336
Health	492	692	238	1,422
Social welfare	1,666	310	46	2,022
Education	206	1,089	888	2,183
Transportation and communications	450	790	404	1,644
Natural resources and primary industry	421	208	..	629
General government	299	154	189	642
Protection of persons and property	99	172	299	570
Debt charges (excluding debt retirement)	823	123	201	1,147
Other	751	133	288	1,172
Total[1]	7,260	3,671	2,553	13,484
	53.9%	27.2%	18.9%	100%

[1] After elimination of intergovernmental transfers (budgetary basis).

Division of Revenue Sources. The division of revenue sources is also provided for under sections 91 and 92 of the British North America Act. Here the emphasis is on strong central government, which was the aim of the country's founders. Under section 91, the government of Canada is given the right to impose and collect funds by the "raising of money by any Mode or System of Taxation." The provinces are more limited and under section 92 may only impose direct taxation for provincial purposes.

Over the years a complex tax structure has gradually developed, but the demands for public expenditure were not such that any really serious conflicts developed until the demands for revenue in World War I required the entry of Canada into the income tax field in 1917. After that time, increasing pressure of public demand so influenced the tax system that a serious overlapping of federal and provincial interests developed. These reached a climax in the Depression years of the 1930's when the tax system approached chaos.

Since that time a series of intergovernmental financial adjustments, originally stimulated by World War II needs, has provided a working relationship that has permitted a sharing of the various direct tax fields in a manner reasonably consistent with the needs of the federal and provincial governments.

The demands of the provincial governments for additional revenue sources have continued to grow with the increasing pressure of public demand for services. The result has been a growing trend toward a relinquishment of some of the taxing powers by the federal government in favor of greater provincial participation. It is important to remember that most of the important revenue sources are legally open to both levels of government, and if uneconomic taxation is to be avoided cooperation is essential.

The federal government relies to a substantial extent on four main sources of revenue: personal income tax, corporation income tax, customs duties, and excises (including a sales tax at manufacturers' level). The provinces have a somewhat more diversified field of interest that includes not only the minor share of the personal and corporation income taxes, but also general retail sales taxes, gasoline taxes, motor vehicle taxes, revenue from liquor monopolies, natural resource revenues and fees and licenses. They are also in varying degrees dependent on transfers from the central government. Succession duties (estate taxes) are shared 25–75 between federal and provincial governments. Municipalities are heavily dependent on taxes on real property, with some assistance from fees and licenses. Provincial government grants-in-aid to local governments are also of importance in most provinces. Federal revenue in 1965 made up 54.8% of the total, provincial 30.3%, and municipal 14.9%. Government revenue at all levels as a percentage of the gross national product in that year was 31.5%, of which 17.3% was federal, 9.5% provincial, and 4.7% municipal.

NET GENERAL REVENUE OF ALL GOVERNMENTS, 1963
(in millions of dollars)

Taxes	Federal	Provincial	Municipal	Total
Corporation income	1,375	412	..	1,787
Personal income	2,168	389	..	2,557
General sales	1,278	562	58	1,898
Motor fuel and fuel oil	..	539	1	540
Other sales	..	70	3	73
Excises	666	..	..	666
Customs	581	..	..	581
Real and personal property	..	9	1,622	1,631
Business	..	..	52	52
Estate and succession duties	91	86	..	177
Other	124	198	17	339
Total taxes	6,283	2,265	1,753	10,301
Nontax Sources				
Liquor control	..	56	..	56
Motor licenses	..	211	..	211
Natural resource charges	5	367	..	372
Sales and services	67	54	..	121
Fines and penalties	2	11	..	13
Grants in lieu of taxes	..	..	24	24
Other	498	296	204	998
Total[1]	6,855	3,260	1,981	12,096
	56.7%	26.9%	16.4%	100%

[1] After elimination of intergovernmental transfers (budgetary basis).

Public Debt. Governments in Canada, as in most countries, have less trouble spending public funds than raising revenues. Hence the public debt is an important factor in any examination of public finance. Canada, over the years, has accumulated an increasing total of public debt at all levels of government. While to some extent this has been the result of overspending in relation to the revenues available for ordinary expense, the main burden of it has come from special requirements. Historically, in the case of the federal government, the cost of national development has been high, particularly for railway building. The relief of unemployment and agricultural distress has also been important in certain periods, as has the financing of two world wars. Of these the costs of war finance have been by far the most important.

Over the years nearly all the provinces have accumulated substantial debt, either directly or through guaranteeing the loans of subsidiary units. While there has been some deficit financing on ordinary account, this has become much less usual in the postwar years. Generally the situation has been one of indebtedness incurred for developmental purposes. Highways have been a consistent user of capital funds, but more recently in most provinces there has been heavy emphasis on public utility financing for electricity production and in Western Canada for telephones. In the Depression years, some provinces incurred substantial debt for relief purposes. To a considerable extent this was owed to the government of Canada and is now written off or repaid.

Municipal debt has continued to be incurred at a fairly high rate, and it is an important factor in municipal finance. As municipalities are not generally permitted to operate in a deficit position, nearly all this debt has been for municipal facilities. Utilities, education, and urban redevelopment have become important factors in some cases.

Too much emphasis can be placed on the debt position of governments. Government debt, however, is an essential factor in the whole Canadian financial-investment structure and increasingly in the U. S. foreign exchange situation due to large borrowings in New York by provinces and municipalities.

In Canada today, at both the federal and provincial levels, the burden of debt in relation to total revenues is very low and in many cases (where the debt is incurred for development) produces the funds necessary for its own support. The municipal situation is less favorable.

PUBLIC DEBT
OF ALL GOVERNMENTS, 1963
(in millions of dollars)

Direct	Federal	Provincial	Municipal	Total
Debenture debt	16,510	4,651	5,527	26,688
Treasury bills	2,230	133	1	2,364
Trust and other deposits	5,157	208	7	5,372
Other	1,854	552	882	3,288
Subtotal	25,751	5,544	6,417	37,712
Less sinking funds	..	686	228	914
Total direct debt	25,751	4,858	6,189	36,798
Dollars per capita	1,339	253	321	1,913
Indirect				
Guaranteed bonds and debentures	1,378	5,516	11	6,905
Guaranteed bank loans	219	65	..	284
Others	4,892	101	..	4,993
Subtotal	6,489	5,682	11	12,182
Less sinking funds	..	214	..	214
Total indirect debt	6,489	5,468	11	11,968
Dollars per capita	337	281	1	619
Total net direct and indirect debt	32,240	10,326	6,200	48,766
Dollars per capita	1,676	534	322	2,532

Federal-Provincial Fiscal Relations. When the Canadian provinces were formed in 1867 it was not considered likely that they would have large requirements for revenue. Further, it was the intention of the founders of the country that a strong centralized authority should prevail. Consequently, the widest powers of taxation were given to the central government, which assumed the debts of the new provinces and most of the responsibilities of government as they were known at that time.

The provinces were compensated for the loss of many of their revenue sources, particularly customs duties, by subsidies from the central government. These made up a substantial part of provincial revenues, particularly in the Maritime Provinces of Nova Scotia and New Brunswick.

Early Adjustments. It was not long before it became clear that the subsidy arrangements were inadequate. A series of adjustments, each hopefully of a final nature, began. These have been characteristic of the federal-provincial relationship.

Prior to the first formal conference on fiscal matters between the central and provincial governments in 1906, subsidy adjustments had been negotiated bilaterally, although the advantage gained by one province often had to be extended to others. But since that first conference it has been the policy to carry out these negotiations on a broader basis with all governments being involved in the process.

Use of Grants. In the period just before World War I, Canada began a rather halting approach to a new form of grants—conditional program grants. Federal aid was given for special purposes under defined conditions. The first of major importance came in 1927 with the joint federal-provincial old-age pensions.

During the Depression years of the 1930's, the federal government of necessity had to take an increasing part in the relief of unemployment, although legally this was a provincial-municipal function. Much of this relief was through grants, but there was a substantial volume in loans, both long- and short-term.

Unusual Problems. The Depression found the federal government the only one with sufficient financial power to carry on the business of government effectively, although the degree of distress varied from province to province. This was the beginning of a long period in which centralized authority was consolidated by the demand of wartime finance (1941–1945) and the reconstruction that followed.

A Royal Commission on Dominion-Provincial Relations (the Rowell-Sirois Commission) was appointed in 1937 to examine the economic and financial structure of the Canadian federation. The commission in 1940 made financial recommendations that would, if adopted, have resulted in the principal taxation powers being concentrated in the central authority. However, when the report was presented in 1941, wartime conditions made consideration of its proposals inappropriate. Three provinces—Alberta, British Columbia, and Ontario—refused to discuss implementation of a permanent solution.

The federal government was determined, however, to finance the war to the greatest extent possible from current revenue and made it quite clear to the provincial governments that it was going to raise all the revenue it could, largely from personal and corporation income taxes, regardless of provincial views. To avoid conflict it offered to rent exclusive use of the two tax fields from the provinces for the duration of the war and one year thereafter for a fixed annual fee. This was accepted by all the provinces for the period 1942–1947.

Postwar Reconstruction. As the end of the war approached, a full-scale federal-provincial conference was called in 1945 and 1946 to discuss the problems of reconstruction. While the conference failed in that many of its far-reaching proposals, especially in health and social welfare, were not completed, the first of the tax-rental agreements was signed after lengthy negotiation. Neither Ontario nor Quebec was prepared to accept the federal offer and resumed levying their own taxes on corporations, although neither reentered the personal income tax field.

As these agreements came up for renewal, a further conference was called in 1950, but owing to the outbreak of the Korean War little new was accomplished. An updating and revision of the 1947 agreements were proposed, and as a result of improved terms, Ontario reentered the agreements. Quebec alone remained on its own. In 1954 that province announced its intention of reentering the personal income tax field at levels that exceeded the allowable credit against federal tax. Eventually a compromise was worked out that stood until the agreements came up for renewal in 1957.

Income Tax Sharing. At federal-provincial conferences in 1955 and 1956, new proposals were put before the provinces that provided for a specific share of the personal income tax (10% of the federal tax), the corporation income tax (9% of taxable income), and succession duties (50% of federal duty) to be set aside for provincial use. In addition a new concept of fiscal aid called "equalization" was introduced. This provided for federal payment to each province of an amount sufficient to bring its per capita revenue from the three tax fields involved up to the average of that in the two wealthiest provinces, Ontario and British Columbia.

Thus, all provinces except Ontario received a supplementary payment based on deficiency in revenue capacity. While under the tax-rental agreements there had been a subsidy element in the scale of payments, these had been tied into the surrender of taxing powers and so had not been available to any province that was not prepared to withdraw from those taxes for the period required by the agreements. As a result, under the new proposals, Quebec was enabled to receive equalization assistance even though it was still imposing its own personal and corporation income taxes. Ontario for its part resumed the imposition of its own corporation income taxes but rented the personal income tax field to the federal government. All other provinces rented their rights to Canada in all three areas.

The government changed in 1957, and new offers were made to the provinces. The rate of provincial participation in the personal income tax was increased to 13% of the federal tax. The other shares were unchanged. After a conference in 1960, new terms were finally negotiated. These saw the end of the tax-rental system, and provinces were given tax room to impose their own taxes by way of a staged withdrawal by the federal government starting at 16% of the federal personal income tax in 1962, increasing by 1% each year to reach 20% in the final year of the 5-year agreement in 1966. There was no change in the rate of corporation income tax assigned to the provinces. It remained at 9% of taxable income; succession duties were at 50% of the federal tax. The federal government collected provincial taxes when imposed on a standard base where this was requested, without charge to the provinces.

The basis of equalization was broadened in one respect by introducing a factor for one half the three-year average of natural resource revenues, one of the most unevenly distributed of provincial revenue sources, but was narrowed by lowering the application to the per capita national average from the level of the average of the top two provinces.

Following another change of government in 1963, further alteration was made, and the rate of provincial participation in the personal income tax was increased to 24%. Equalization was returned to the level of the top two provinces, and a readjustment was made in the application of the natural resource revenue by deducting this factor from equalization otherwise payable.

Other Developments. A number of important fiscal developments took place in 1964 and 1965. Arrangements were made to coordinate the new federal contributory old-age pension plan, which was to apply in all provinces except Quebec, with the plan of that province. Reserve funds of over $500 million a year were to be invested in provincial securities. Further, as a result of Quebec pressure, the federal government agreed to allow provinces to withdraw from certain conditional-grant programs in return for increased tax room in the personal income tax field. These conditional grants had grown rapidly in the postwar years and by the 1960's substantially exceeded the unconditional grants in importance. Only Quebec accepted the federal offer.

The result of this change was a different level of federal taxation in Quebec from that prevailing in other provinces, although the net effect on the taxpayer was the same. This, along with concern as to the effect of the progressive loss of federal control of the personal income tax field and therefore control of fiscal policy, led the minister of finance to propose discontinuance of federal participation in certain of the joint programs in the health and social welfare fields after 1970. In this way all provinces would be restored to an even footing as far as federal tax rates were concerned.

A new 5-year financial arrangement was provided for the period commencing April 1, 1967. Under it the provinces have 24% of the personal income tax field (except Quebec, which has 28%), 10% of corporation taxable income, and 75% of succession duties. After federal withdrawal from some of the shared-cost programs in 1970, the provincial share of personal income tax will increase to 45% (Quebec 49%). A new equalization formula gives weight to all elements of provincial taxation and brings them up to the national average per capita for each province.

Influences for Change. The state of public finance in Canada is fluid and unsettled. With rapid growth in provincial responsibilities exceeding their revenue capabilities, there is unavoidable and continuing pressure from provincial governments on the federal government and from municipal governments on provincial governments for greater access to revenue sources or for large subsidies. The situation is complicated by the militant and independent attitudes of some of the more powerful provinces, particularly Quebec.

Efforts were made in the late 1960's to resolve some of the problems. At the 1963 Federal-Provincial Conference a tax structure committee of federal and provincial ministers examined the whole question of federal-provincial finance. This committee in its first report forecast substantial increases in provincial and municipal deficits under the existing tax system. The essential difficulty appeared to lie in trying to reconcile the needs of the provincial governments for revenue with the acknowledged need for strong central control of the tax system for fiscal purposes.

A royal commission on taxation appointed in 1962 reported to the government of Canada in February 1967. Its report recommended some fundamental changes in the Canadian tax system that would have important influences on the whole structure of public finance. Emphasis was laid on the importance of a continuing strong central influence. Whether this is possible under traditional provincial attitudes is difficult to foretell.

R. M. BURNS
Queen's University, Kingston, Ontario

Bibliography

Bank of Canada, *Statistical Summary* (Ottawa, monthly and annually).
Canadian Tax Foundation, *The National Finances* (Toronto, semiannually).
Canadian Tax Foundation, *Provincial Finances* (Toronto, semiannually).
Canadian Tax Foundation, *The Financing of Canadian Federation 1966* (Toronto 1966).
Dominion Bureau of Statistics, *National Accounts—Income and Expenditure* (Ottawa, annually).

24. Defense

Fundamental changes have taken place in the Canadian military system since World War II. Prior to 1939 the principal role of the Canadian armed forces was to cooperate with other countries of the British Commonwealth in major wars. By the mid-1960's, however, Canadian defense policy was based on four quite different roles—the fulfillment of Canadian obligations under the North Atlantic Treaty Organization (NATO); cooperation with the United States in North American air defense (NORAD); the support of United Nations peacekeeping commitments; and the defense of Canadian territory.

Unification of Forces. By far the most dramatic result of the change of role was the creation in 1967 of a single unified force, which was called the Canadian Armed Forces, replacing the former Royal Canadian Navy, Canadian Army, and Royal Canadian Air Force. After prolonged and often bitter debate, the Canadian Forces Reorganization Act, Bill C-243, was passed by the Canadian House of Commons in April. The process of unification was scheduled to be completed by the early 1970's. All Canadian servicemen would wear the same uniform, probably a dark green one.

The first step toward unification was taken in 1946 with the appointment of a single minister of national defense to replace the three ministers who had been responsible for the navy, army, and air force during World War II. In 1947 the Defence Research Board of Canada was established as a single scientific organization to serve the fighting forces. In 1950 a new National Defence Act unified the codes of military law, and the following year a Chairman Chiefs of Staff Committee was appointed. The Canadian Services Colleges were reorganized on a unified basis, and during the 1950's the legal, medical, and chaplain services were integrated.

Headquarters Reorganization. These preliminary moves fell far short of complete unification. In 1964, however, a single chief of the defense staff replaced the former three service chiefs of staff, thus making one man instead of a committee responsible for the control and administration of the Canadian Forces. The reorganized Canadian Forces Headquarters was divided into four branches: the vice chief of the defense staff branch, primarily responsible for military operations; the chief of personnel branch, responsible for personnel policies; the chief of technical services branch, responsible for engineering and development activities; and the comptroller general's branch, responsible for the financial and general management of the forces.

A reorganized defense council—consisting of the minister of national defense as chairman, the associate minister as vice chairman, the chief and vice chief of the defense staff, the chairman of the defense research board, and the deputy minister—began to play a much more vital role in the formulation of defense policy.

Commands. The number of commands was reduced from 11 to 6. The mobile command, with headquarters at St. Hubert, Quebec, is responsible for maintaining combat-ready land forces and tactical air forces. The maritime command, with headquarters at Halifax, Nova Scotia, is primarily responsible for antisubmarine tasks. The air defense command, with headquarters at North Bay, Ontario, contributes to the defense of the continent in concert with United States forces. The training command, with headquarters at Winnipeg, Manitoba, is responsible for the individual training of all members of the Canadian Forces. The air transport command, with headquarters at Trenton, Ontario, is responsible for providing strategic airlift capability, and the matériel command, with headquarters at Rockcliffe, Ontario, provides the necessary supply and maintenance support to the other commands. In addition, Canada maintains an infantry brigade group and an air division of six squadrons in Europe, both under NATO operational command.

Strength. Just before unification the approximate strengths of the fighting services were: Royal Canadian Navy, 18,500; Canadian Army, 43,900; Royal Canadian Air Force, 45,100. These levels were kept after unification.

Although there was some opposition within the services to so radical a change, there is little evidence that unification has seriously impaired service morale or motivation. In spite of steadily rising costs, unification has resulted in considerable financial savings, thus providing more money for military equipment, construction, and development than otherwise would have been possible.

Peacekeeping Commitments. By the late 1960's, Canada had been the only country to have contributed military personnel to every United Nations peacekeeping operation throughout the world. About 1,900 Canadian officers and men were continually employed in this type of duty. Canadians have served in Palestine, Kashmir, Indochina, Egypt, Lebanon, the Congo, West Irian (West New Guinea), Yemen, and Cyprus.

History to World War I. Although Canadians have never been a military people, war has often played a decisive part in their lives.

This badge is worn by members of the unified armed services.

Canadian troops near Normandy beachhead on D Day, June 6, 1944.

(LEFT) DEPARTMENT OF NATIONAL DEFENCE; (ABOVE) PUBLIC ARCHIVES OF CANADA

Colonial Period. Both under the French regime and the British colonial government that succeeded it in 1763, every able-bodied male in the colony was liable for compulsory military service, and in 1775 British soldiers and French-Canadian militia fought side by side to repulse an American attack on Quebec. The American War of Independence dragged on for another six years and left behind it a continuing hostility, so that for the next century Canadian defensive efforts were directed exclusively against the United States. The War of 1812 saw American armies invade Canada, and British armies invade the United States. The war ended with the restoration of the *status quo,* but the Treaty of Ghent which brought peace did nothing to eradicate old antagonisms. Until about 1850, Britain maintained in the Canadas a garrison of regular soldiers approximately equal to the entire regular army of the United States.

During this period the defense of the colonies rested always upon the British regular garrison. Native Canadians were organized into a "sedentary militia" that held only one muster parade a year and did no training. By 1851, however, the British government began to withdraw its troops, and during the Crimean War the Province of Canada established a small volunteer force. For the first time these men were armed, uniformed, and trained. As the British regular garrisons were progressively reduced, the Canadian volunteers came to supplant the old militia. The last British garrisons (except for small forces at Halifax and Esquimalt) were withdrawn from Canada in 1870–1871 over the protests of the Canadian government.

Confederation to 1914. The Fenian Raids, which began in 1866 (and were responsible in no small measure for the confederation of the British colonies into the Dominion of Canada in 1867), were largely defeated by the Canadian volunteer militia. The new Militia Act of 1868 in theory still required compulsory service from every able-bodied male, but an active militia was established, recruited solely by voluntary enlistment. A considerable number of militiamen accompanied Lord Wolseley on the Red River Expedition of 1870, and the Northwest Rebellion of 1885 was suppressed entirely by the militia. See also section *47. The Canadian Confederation, 1857–1914.*

By this time a small Canadian Permanent Force had been organized. Two batteries of artillery were formed in 1871, and cavalry and infantry units were raised in 1883–1884. In 1876 the Royal Military College of Canada was opened at Kingston, Ontario, for the training of cadets. In 1898 a Yukon Field Force was dispatched to Fort Selkirk and Dawson City to aid the Northwest Mounted Police in maintaining law and order in a territory which had been flooded with prospectors because of the gold rush to the Klondike.

When the South African War broke out in October 1899, the Canadian government reluctantly recruited a contingent—a notable event, since this was the first time in history that Canadian soldiers had been employed outside North America. Before the war was over, Canada had contributed about 8,000 men, of whom 7,000 were dispatched overseas, while the remainder relieved the British troops of the Halifax garrison. The Canadians fought at Paardeberg, Wolve Spruit, Leliefontein and in numerous guerrilla engagements, suffering 224 fatal casualties, including those who died by accident and disease, and 252 wounded.

Militia reforms were undertaken after 1900, both in Britain and the Dominions. In Canada, permanent engineer, army service, and ordnance corps units were formed, as was a signal corps and an intelligence branch. The number of artillery units was increased, and some cavalry was converted to mounted infantry. Training facilities were improved and rifle ranges and armories constructed.

World War I. In August 1914 the Canadian permanent force consisted of 3,000 of all ranks, and the militia had a strength of about 59,000. Most of the 32,665 officers and men who flocked to join the colors at Valcartier Camp feared that the conflict might be over before they could play a part in it. On Oct. 3, 1914, the first Canadian contingent, 30,808 strong, sailed in convoy to England. The Canadians spent that winter on Salisbury Plain under conditions of extreme misery, but there, in spite of rain and mud, the 1st Division was trained and equipped.

1915–1916. The division arrived in France in the middle of February and held quiet sectors of the line until, on April 22, 1915, it found itself involved in the bitter fighting of the Second Battle of Ypres, where the Germans employed poison gas for the first time on the western front. When French colonial and territorial troops on their left broke and fled, the Canadians took over and held the line. They were continuously engaged until April 26, by which time they had suffered 6,035 casualties (dead and wounded). Their tenacious defense had restored a critical situation and firmly established the reputation of Canadian arms.

After launching bloody and unsuccessful attacks at Festubert and Givenchy in May and June, the Canadian force was expanded to a corps of two divisions in September. A British officer was corps commander but both divisions were commanded by Canadians. The 2d Canadian Division suffered heavily at St. Eloi in April 1916, but in a brilliant counterattack at Mount Sorrel in June the Canadians proved that they were as effective in attack as in defense.

The great Battle of the Somme began in July, and by September the Canadians had been committed to the holocaust. Vicious fighting dragged on until the end of November. The Canadians had suffered 24,029 casualties. By the end of 1916, 265,000 Canadian soldiers had been dispatched overseas, and enlistments numbered nearly 400,000.

A 3d Canadian division had joined the Canadian Corps at the end of 1915 and a 4th division in August 1916. By mid-1916 voluntary recruitment had slackened off in Canada, and in 1917 the government imposed conscription. However, only 24,132 conscripts saw active service in France.

1917–18. The Battle of Vimy Ridge was the first major Allied victory of the war. On April 9, 1917, the Canadian Corps attacked and captured the ridge which previously had resisted all Allied assaults. The battle cost Canada 3,598 fatal casualties but had important psychological effects and materially assisted Canada's evolution to full nationhood.

In August the Canadians struck again, this time at Hill 70, and again were victorious, although at a cost of 9,198 casualties. However, in mid-October they were committed to the Third Battle of Ypres, better known as Passchendaele, and for the next month struggled forward over a sea of mud to reach Passchendaele Ridge. Between October 18 and November 14 the corps suffered 15,654 casualties, gaining in exchange a few acres of devastated and useless ground.

At the Battle of Amiens on Aug. 8, 1918, the Canadian Corps broke cleanly through the German line for the first time in the war, but hard fighting remained before the Armistice. In the final months the Canadians fought their way through the Drocourt-Quéant and Hindenburg lines, across the Canal du Nord and into Cambrai. When the war ended on November 11 the Canadians were in Mons, the same town where, four and a half years previously, the British Army had first seen action.

Service Figures and Casualties. A total of 619,636 men and women had served in the Canadian Army; 59,544 had been killed, and another 172,950 wounded. The population of Canada in 1914 had been about 8 million.

The Royal Canadian Navy had been formed in 1910, but in 1914 it consisted of only two old cruisers, the *Niobe* and the *Rainbow*. During the war the RCN helped defend Canadian coastal waters against submarine attack, and by November 1918 it had grown to a force of 115 small vessels and 5,500 officers and men.

In World War I some 22,000 Canadians joined the British Royal Flying Corps or Royal Naval Air Service. By 1918, 24% of the flying personnel in the Royal Air Force were Canadians. Nearly 1,600 Canadian airmen lost their lives in the conflict.

Interwar Period. In the years after 1918 militia strength shrank to somewhat less than it had been in 1914. But an important addition to the forces was made. In February 1920 the government authorized the formation of a Canadian Air Force, originally designed as an air militia with no permanent component. On April 1, 1924, the Royal Canadian Air Force was established as a separate service on a permanent basis.

From 1935 on, as the shadow of another German war grew steadily darker, Canada began slowly to rearm. The nonpermanent active militia was reorganized in 1936 to produce a more balanced force. The naval budget was doubled in 1936–1937 and thereafter continued to increase sharply, but the Royal Canadian Air Force was given the highest priority in rearmament. By the summer of 1939 the RCAF consisted of eight permanent and three auxiliary squadrons.

World War II. Canada's contribution in World War II was larger and much more diversified than in World War I. In addition to the First Canadian Army, which consisted of an army headquarters, two corps headquarters, three infantry divisions, two armored divisions, two independent armored brigades, and many ancillary units, substantial naval and air forces were committed to operations, and the country's industrial effort far surpassed that of 1914–1918.

Canadian Army. Because the Allied armies had been driven off the continent of Europe in 1940, the role of the Canadian Army for a long period was the defense of Britain and the colonies. Two Canadian battalions fought in the unsuccessful defense of Hong Kong in September 1941, and a large-scale Canadian raid at Dieppe, France, on Aug. 19, 1942, suffered a bloody repulse. It was not until July 1943 that a major Canadian formation was committed to battle. In that month the 1st Division took part in the invasion of Sicily and fought its way up the island and onto the Italian mainland, where it captured Ortona in December.

The decision was taken to commit more Canadian forces to the Mediterranean theater, and by the end of 1943 a Canadian Corps was in Italy. The 1st Canadian Corps took part in breaking the Adolf Hitler Line in May 1944 and the Gothic Line in August and September. In December the Canadians captured Ravenna, but in February 1945 the 1st Canadian Corps rejoined the First Canadian Army in northwest Europe.

The 3d Canadian Division was one of the assault formations that stormed ashore on the coast of Normandy on June 6, 1944, for the invasion of northwest Europe. During July the remainder of the 2d Canadian Corps arrived in France, and by the end of the month the First Canadian Army, commanded by Lt. Gen. H. D. G. Crerar, became operational. The Canadians were committed to very heavy fighting around Caen and Falaise in July and August. After the enemy had been driven back in disorder across the Seine, the Canadian Army cleared the coast. Dieppe, Ostend, Boulogne, and Calais were successively captured, and the Canadians pressed northward to Antwerp. In October and November 1944 the Battle of the Scheldt to open the port of Antwerp resulted in bitter fighting. South Beveland and the island of Walcheren were captured; the Breskens Pocket was cleared; and the first Allied convoy entered the port of Antwerp on November 28.

Winter on the Maas River was reasonably quiet, if uncomfortable, but with the coming of spring the Canadians saw hard fighting in the Rhineland, breaking through the Siegfried Line in the Reichswald, clearing the Hochwald, and pushing the Germans back over the Rhine. As German resistance everywhere crumbled, the Canadians advanced through the Netherlands and into the northwest corner of Germany. The last German forces surrendered on May 5, 1945, ending the war in Europe.

A Canadian Army Pacific Force, consisting of a division and ancillary troops, was raised for the war against Japan, but on August 10, Japan sued for peace and the Canadian Pacific Force was disbanded.

A total of 730,625 Canadian men and women served in the Army during World War II. Of these, 22,917 were killed and 52,679 were wounded.

As in World War I, conscription for overseas service was imposed relatively late in the conflict. Until 1944, conscripts were employed only on home defense duty, but in November of that year they began to be sent overseas. However, by the end of hostilities only 2,463 had actually joined the strength of field units.

Royal Canadian Air Force. During the war the Royal Canadian Air Force expanded into the fourth-largest air force of the Allied powers, and 232,632 men and 17,030 women served in it. The Canadian government administered the British Commonwealth Air Training Plan that was formally established on Dec. 17, 1939. At the peak of its operations, 97 units and 184 ancillary units were functioning under the plan and over 3,000 students were graduating each month. The BCATP produced 131,553 airmen, more than 55% of whom were members of the RCAF.

In spite of the gigantic size of the BCATP, three RCAF squadrons were sent overseas in 1940, and one of them fought in the Battle of Britain. By the end of the war the RCAF had 48 squadrons overseas, but more Canadian airmen served in Royal Air Force units than in RCAF units. The largest Canadian formation overseas was the No. 6 (RCAF) Group attached to RAF Bomber Command from Jan. 1, 1943. A total of 9,980 Canadians in the Bomber Command were killed—almost as many as died in the army's 11-month campaign in northwest Europe.

Of the 48 squadrons overseas, 15 were in Bomber Command, 18 with the 2d Tactical Air Force in northwest Europe, five in Fighter Command, five in Coastal Command, three in Transport Command (one in northwest Europe and two in Burma), one with the Desert Air Force in Italy, and one in Ceylon. Some 17,100 Canadian airmen and airwomen lost their lives in the military service.

In addition to the units overseas, some 23 RCAF squadrons served in the North American zone on home defense and seaward patrol duties. These participated in the air offensive against the Japanese in the Aleutian Islands in 1943 and conducted antisubmarine patrols over the North Atlantic.

Royal Canadian Navy. In World War II the Royal Canadian Navy expanded to a force of 106,522 of all ranks. The 15 vessels in commission at the beginning of the war grew to 404 warships and 566 auxiliary vessels.

The main role of the RCN was the protection of Allied shipping in the North Atlantic, and by March 1943 it was responsible for 48% of United Kingdom convoys. At the Atlantic Convoy Conference in that month the RCN assumed command of all escorts in the area north of New York and west of 47° west longitude.

When the Allies landed in North Africa in November 1942 the RCN was represented by corvettes and landing craft flotillas, and it later took part in other amphibious operations in the Mediterranean. On D Day, June 6, 1944, it was represented by 110 ships and 10,000 men. The war against Japan ended before the RCN could redeploy in the Pacific, and only one Canadian ship, the HMCS *Uganda,* saw action in that ocean.

During the war the Canadian Navy destroyed, or shared in destroying, 27 enemy submarines. It lost 24 of its own ships, and suffered 1,797 fatal casualties.

Industrial Effort. The Canadian industrial record during World War II was remarkable. Although organized by the department of munitions and supply, Canada's war production was largely the work of private firms. More than 800,000 transport vehicles and 16,000 aircraft were produced, in addition to 487 warships, 391 cargo ships, armored vehicles, and all kinds of military equipment, including guns, radar devices, and small arms. Much of this equipment was surplus to Canadian requirements and was exported to other Allied nations.

Postwar Developments. After World War II, Canada maintained considerably larger regular forces than ever before in peacetime. In 1946 the strength of the Royal Canadian Navy was fixed at about 10,000 officers and men, that of the Army at approximately 25,000 men, including an air transportable brigade group, and that of the Royal Canadian Air Force at about 16,000, with eight operational squadrons. In 1948 a National Defence College was established in Kingston, Ontario, for the instruction of senior officers, and army and air force staff colleges remained in operation. Nevertheless, the tendency was to economize, and in 1947–1948 the defense budget fell to a postwar low of $195 million. By 1948, however, the Cold War had begun, and Canada began slowly to rearm, a process greatly accelerated by the outbreak of the Korean War in June 1950.

Korean War. In July 1950 three Canadian destroyers were dispatched to Korean waters, and one RCAF transport squadron was assigned to operate between the United States and Japan. In August recruitment was begun for a Canadian Army Special Force of brigade size to fight under United Nations command.

A single infantry battalion went to Korea in November 1950, where it took part in the recapture of Seoul and the liberation of South Korea. By the spring of 1951 the Canadian brigade was in action; it served in the 1st Commonwealth Division for the remainder of the war. Canadians remained in Korea until early 1956. They had suffered 1,557 casualties, all but 14 of them in the army.

Forces in Europe. While Canadian soldiers were fighting in Korea, the Royal Canadian Air Force continued its program of expansion. Between 1950 and 1958 it trained aircrews for NATO, and in November 1951 it sent an air division, originally of 12 squadrons, to Europe. In the summer of 1951 a Canadian brigade was raised for NATO and was sent to Germany late that year. These Canadian forces have since been maintained on the continent of Europe.

D. J. GOODSPEED
Lieutenant Colonel, Canadian Armed Forces
Senior Historian, Canadian Forces Headquarters

Bibliography

Goodspeed, D. J., ed., *The Armed Forces of Canada 1867–1967* (Ottawa 1967).
Hamilton, Charles F., "Defence 1812–1912," *Canada and Its Provinces,* vol. 7 (Toronto 1914–1917).
Nicholson, Gerald W. L., *Canadian Expeditionary Force 1914–1919* (Ottawa 1962).
Nicholson, Gerald W. L., *The Canadians in Italy 1943–1945* (Ottawa 1956).
Preston, Richard A., *Canada and Imperial Defense 1867–1919* (Durham, N. C., 1966).
Stacey, Charles P., *Canada and the British Army 1846–1871* (Toronto 1963).
Stacey, Charles P., *Six Years of War* (Ottawa 1955).
Stacey, Charles P., *The Victory Campaign* (Ottawa 1960).
Stanley, George F. G., *Canada's Soldiers, 1604–1954* (Toronto 1954).
Wood, Herbert F., *Strange Battleground* (Ottawa 1966).

25. Health and Welfare

The British North America Act of 1867, adopted when social services represented a very small part of governmental activity, places major responsibility for health and welfare upon the provinces. Over the years, however, the federal government has come to play the major role in these fields. It always has had responsibility for certain groups —Indians and Eskimos, service and ex-servicemen, mariners, immigrants, residents of the territories, and inmates of penitentiaries. Progressively, it has assumed full or partial responsibility for the unemployed, the aged, the permanently disabled, and the surviving dependents of insured persons. In addition, it pays family allowances.

The federal government, because of its revenue-raising powers, also makes grants to the provinces for various health and welfare programs. (Since 1965 this has been less true in the case of Quebec, which has been given special status, with consequent financial adjustments.) Federally, the department of national health and welfare has the main responsibility. Each of the provinces has its own departments of health and welfare and generally uses local government to carry out some functions. There are also a number of voluntary organizations, many of them receiving grants from the government.

Income Maintenance. Social security measures provide some coverage for all the major threats to income except maternity and temporary illness. Demogrants (universal grants, provided without a means test), insurance benefits, and public assistance give this coverage.

Allowances. Federal demogrants (introduced in 1951) of $75 a month are paid to the aged with 10 years' residence. Family allowances (1945) of $6 to $8 a month are given to mothers of most children under 16 years of age. Youth allowances (1964) of $10 a month are available for those 16 and 17 years old who are in school or are mentally or physically infirm.

Insurance. Federal government annuities (1908) provide voluntary group insurance for retirement. The Canada pension plan (1965) is a universal, compulsory, earnings-related insurance for retirement, permanent disability, and survivors. Compulsory unemployment insurance (1941) is financed by employer and employee contributions and a 20% federal subsidy. Provincial workmen's compensation, which started in 1914, provides for the victims of industrial accidents and diseases through the compulsory contribution of employers.

Public Assistance. Public assistance provides for needy people not covered or not adequately covered by the above measures. The federal government initiated programs for certain categories by offering to share with the provinces the cost of assistance to the aged (1927), the blind (1937), and the permanently and totally disabled (1954). The provinces administer these uniform programs and receive reimbursement of 75% of the assistance given to the blind and 50% to the other groups. The latter percentage was also made available toward payments made to other needy persons (payments frequently administered by local government) under the Unemployment Assistance Act (1956) with the minimum of federally imposed conditions. The existing provincial programs for needy mothers with dependent children were not included in the sharing arrangements.

The federal Canada Assistance Plan (1966) is designed to prevent and remove the causes of poverty and help dependent persons achieve self-support. It offers the provinces 50% of the costs of services to people, regardless of the cause of need. No residence can be required. This program is gradually replacing the above categories.

Old-Age Supplements. In 1967 the federal government took another revolutionary step in establishing a guaranteed income for the aged. When the taxable income, including the demogrant, is less than a set sum, a supplementary payment is made. The sum, first set at $105 a month, is adjusted according to changes in the cost of living.

Health Services. The federal government is responsible for food and drug control, national statistics, and international obligations. Provincial health departments carry major responsibility for public health, delegating this in part to local governments and regional health units. The provinces set standards, help financially, and provide laboratory service.

Hospitals. The federal government has provided hospital facilities for veterans and Indians, but it is increasingly using community facilities, except in remote areas. Special health programs are provided in the Far North through traveling clinics, air ambulance, and other services.

Provincial responsibility for hospital care for tuberculosis or mental illness has been assumed directly or through voluntary organizations. Many provinces have given special attention to alcoholics and the retarded.

Hospitals for acute cases are generally under voluntary boards, but in some provinces they are partly provincial and municipal undertakings. Facilities for convalescent and chronic patients are mainly under voluntary or commercial auspices.

The trend in treatment of mental illness stresses the use of local facilities, including psychiatric units in acute hospitals.

Home Care. Increased emphasis is placed on home care for both the physically and mentally ill. Visiting nursing is provided by the public health department or a voluntary organization. Community services of many kinds are mobilized to make home care practical.

Health Grants. The federal government uses financial incentives to encourage provinces to expand their programs of preventive and treatment services. The national health grants (1948) provide substantial assistance for buildings and equipment, research, training, and specific programs. The federal Hospital and Diagnostic Services Act (1957) provides about 50% of the costs of provincial hospital plans, excluding treatment for mental illness and tuberculosis. The plans are financed by individual premiums, sales taxes, and general revenue.

Medicare. The Medical Services Act, passed in July 1967, took effect in July 1968. It provides for the federal subsidy of universal provincial plans to cover the costs of doctors' services and other medical requirements. Some provinces had already established plans which covered the total (Saskatchewan) or part of their population (Newfoundland), subsidized lower-income groups (Alberta, British Columbia, and Ontario), or paid the costs for indigents.

Training and Research. The Health Resources Fund (1966) makes federal money available for the capital costs of facilities for training health personnel. The Medical Research Council and the National Research Council, both set up by the federal government, allocate research funds, and some of the provinces have established foundations. National voluntary health organizations also allocate research funds.

Welfare Service—Housing. The Central Mortgage and Housing Corporation, established by the federal government, provides research and consultation in housing, assists financially in land assembly, urban renewal, and low-cost housing projects, and makes money available at a reasonable interest rate. It has concentrated on private home ownership. Providing enough low-rental public housing remains a major problem.

Child Welfare. Provincial legislation regarding child welfare follows a common pattern, except in Quebec, and includes the protection of children and the transfer of guardianship, public assumption of maintenance costs, provision for foster-home or other care, adoption, and assistance to unmarried mothers. The administration is by the province or shared with local government or a children's aid society. Voluntary organizations provide institutional care, although the traditional institution is slowly giving way to treatment centers for disturbed children and group homes for adolescents.

The importance of the family to the child is emphasized, and efforts are made to strengthen the home through community services for family counseling, day care, child guidance, homemaking, and recreation. Most of these are provided by local public or private organizations. The provinces provide leadership and frequently extensive financial assistance. Licensing of facilities is divided between provincial and local authorities.

Voluntary organizations have succeeded in arousing public interest in retarded, emotionally disturbed, and physically handicapped children, and have induced local and provincial governments to provide more adequately for their special needs.

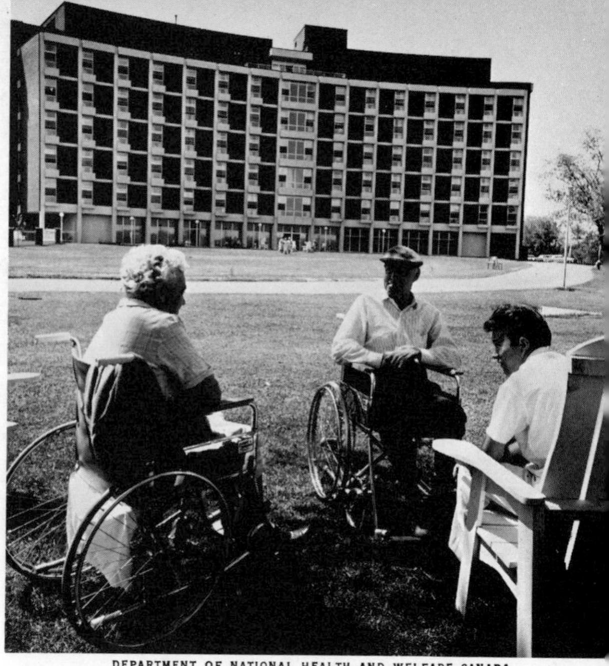

DEPARTMENT OF NATIONAL HEALTH AND WELFARE CANADA

HOUSING for the elderly is supported by municipal and provincial fund grants. This lodge is at Ottawa.

The Handicapped. The rehabilitation of handicapped adults places emphasis upon vocational training, but it also includes restorative services. Federal leadership and grants support the provincial administration. Many of the services are under voluntary auspices. Retraining is provided for the technologically displaced, with the federal government assuming the costs of vocational education. The war on poverty has concentrated on impoverished rural and depressed urban areas, and involves all levels of government.

The Aged. Interest in the problems and needs of the aged has resulted in public hearings at federal and some provincial levels. Improved income maintenance has been accompanied by more and varied living accommodation under public and voluntary auspices. The aged, with assistance from other citizens, have organized local clubs and developed a national organization for recreation and social action.

Youth. Youth has been receiving a great deal of attention. Public hearings have resulted in reports for action regarding delinquency. The Company of Young Canadians (1965) was established as an independent corporation and financed liberally by the federal government to organize volunteers for service at home and abroad.

ELIZABETH S. L. GOVAN
University of Toronto

Bibliography

Canada Department of National Health and Welfare, *Provincial Health Services by Provinces,* Health Care Series No. 20 (Ottawa 1966).

Canada Department of National Health and Welfare, *Social Security in Canada,* Memorandum 17, Social Security Series (Ottawa 1967).

Canadian Welfare Council, *Social Policies for Canada,* Part I (Ottawa 1969).

Defries, Robert Davies, ed., *The Federal and Provincial Health Services in Canada,* 2d ed. (Toronto 1962).

Dominion Bureau of Statistics, *Canada One Hundred: 1867–1967* (Ottawa 1967).

Dominion Bureau of Statistics, *Canada Year Book* (Ottawa, annually).

Paltiel, Freda L., *Poverty: An Annotated Bibliography and References,* Canadian Welfare Council (Ottawa 1966).

Woodward, Agnes, *Poverty,* Supplement 1, Canadian Welfare Council (Ottawa 1967).

TED GRANT, FROM NATIONAL FILM BOARD

SIMON FRASER UNIVERSITY, in Burnaby, British Columbia, opened in 1965, is an arresting example of the imaginative design of some educational institutions.

CANADA: Education

26. Elementary and Secondary Education

Canada is committed to the principle of publicly supported, publicly controlled systems of education, with compulsory schooling and free elementary and secondary education operating under provincial school laws. This principle recognizes that education is an important factor in educational advance, in safeguarding democratic institutions, and in the self-realization of the individual.

GENERAL PATTERN

The acceleration of social change since World War II has had considerable impact on educational institutions and has disturbed their traditional functioning. Almost everyone has been concerned with ways of changing the roles of elementary and secondary education whether in relation to vocational education, further education, higher education, society, or the world of work. Additional stimuli have come from outside Canada.

The schools are changing as are the education systems. Many schools use computers and programmed instruction, overhead projectors, television, radio, films, language laboratories, and reading devices and may be organized for team teaching, individual study, seminars, and large-class instruction. Yet there are other schools where a teacher from the 1920's would feel at home in a familiar teaching pattern — prepare, tell, assign, test, and possibly reject; and for the pupils — listen, follow example, review, and prepare for final examinations. Generally, however, there is a new emphasis on individual development, creativity, productive thinking, and group dynamics. Education from cradle to grave and the lighted schoolhouse are becoming more of a reality year after year.

Canadian education can perhaps be understood best through going back to its several beginnings, which for the French-language segments began in Quebec and Acadia early in the 18th century; and for the English-speaking, in the 16th century in Newfoundland, in the early part of the 18th century in Nova Scotia, and in the last half of the 19th century in the four western provinces—Manitoba, Saskatchewan, Alberta, and British Columbia.

French Heritage. It is estimated that about one third of the settlers in the French colony were literate, with many more having been taught the essential prayers of the Roman Catholic Church. These colonists generally wished that their children should receive education comparable with their own. Some colonists became *coureurs de bois,* adopting certain carefree aspects of Indian life and accepting no responsibility for their behavior. This fact, added to some licentiousness connected with frontier life, influenced the church authorities to be extraordinarily strict in the patter of life they designed to ensure security and happiness.

Most of the authorities in the French colony were interested in providing at least elementary education for both Indian and white children. The schools that developed were, for the most part, patterned after France's schools of the 18th century, and it is of interest that many of the practices introduced at that time continued until the "quiet revolution" in education during the 1960's.

Through direct teaching and by government action, a definite though limited objective was achieved in the colonial period. Some 30 elementary schools were established for boys; of these, 3 provided practical training. There were also 2 seminaries and 1 college for boys at the secondary level, and some 15 convent schools for girls. The broad program as set out, in addition to the command of fundamentals, strengthened faith and provided a deep-rooted sense of religion. It fostered a distinctive, homogeneous, cohesive society that changed little to the middle of the 20th century.

British Heritage. The beginnings here must include, first, Newfoundland, which began as a base for fishing ships, with some 350 families settled by 1650. Second is the Maritime area, where there were few English-speaking residents from 1713 to 1763. Third is Upper Canada, whose history under British rule began about 1791, and fourth, the West, which was opened up by fur traders and developed more than a century later.

Newfoundland. Newfoundland, unlike the mainland provinces, did not feel the North American influences that promulgated economic enterprise, social democracy, political responsibility, and local control of the schools. For many years it remained Old World, depending on charity schools and the clergy. Little formal education was provided until the 18th century, when education for the poor was conducted by school societies financed by people of means in England or on the island. The upper classes employed private tutors or sent their children abroad.

Maritimes. British rule in Nova Scotia began in 1713 and embraced all of the Maritimes by 1763. In addition to the Acadians, four groups — English Protestants, Highland Scots, continental Europeans, and Loyalist emigrants from the United states — helped determine the pattern of education in the areas where they settled. For the first century of British rule in the Maritimes there were only private, parish, and charity schools, many conducted under the Society for the Propagation of the Gospel in Foreign Parts, which ensured that teachers sent out from England met specified requirements of character, knowledge, patriotism, and religious conformity. The private schools included Latin grammar schools, academies, and entrepreneur establishments. All charged fees, and most had annual or semiannual public examinations.

The Latin grammar schools generally provided courses for the select few, stressing Latin, Greek, and mathematics for university entrance. Many provided elementary instruction as well. The academies, cooperative enterprises by well-to-do parents in a locality, were secondary-level institutions offering both classical and practical subjects. Most private schools were established as business ventures. Elementary and secondary courses selected according to the staff competency ranged from classics to music, dancing, and practical courses. Some were boarding institutions; a few offered evening courses.

Upper Canada. The pioneer period in Upper Canada, from about 1759 to 1841, marked the transition for schools from private to public control. New settlers during the last decades of the 18th century were disbanded officers, United Empire Loyalists, some Dutch, Germans, and Quakers, and immigrants from Scotland and England. This intermingling of individuals of different origins made it easier to overcome extreme positions and to obtain provincewide agreement on school organization. Moral and religious aims permeated all school efforts including apprenticeship, the Sunday School movement, the teaching of reading and spelling, and even the common schools established by the parents.

Government revenues were first used to support people's schools under an act in 1807 that provided grants to grammar schools and the Common School Act of 1816. Amounts of up to £25, to a total of £6,000 per year were provided. After 1824, new legislation continued to provide limited resources for schools, but now included provision for control of books, tracts, the examination of teachers, and Indian education.

The West. The West was opened up chiefly by the Hudson's Bay Company and the North West Company (which united with Hudson's Bay Company in 1821), which governed the area until after Confederation. Manitoba was formed in 1870, and the 1871 census reported 1,656 whites, 5,757 French-speaking half-breeds, and 4,083 English-speaking half-breeds. The first schools were established by Catholic priests, followed by schools organized by the Hudson's Bay Company and some Anglican clergymen. In the territories from which Alberta and Saskatchewan were formed in 1905, the first institutions were mission or private schools. With the coming of thousands of homesteaders after 1872 and the construction of the trans-Canada railway, a beginning of local responsibility for schools patterned on the Ontario system was made.

Although settlements began in British Columbia in the middle of the 18th century, the first schools were not established until about a century later by the Hudson's Bay Company and an Oblate priest, first in Victoria, then in Nanaimo and Craigflower. Later the first common or colonial school, financed in part by grants from the government or company, was established at Victoria. Other church or private schools were also provided there. The Common School Act (1865) established a general board of education. It was hampered by a depression following the gold rush, with the government being unable to meet its generous promises. Yet the number of schools and pupils increased.

On the mainland the Rev. Robert Jamieson started the first school and persuaded the citizens of New Westminster to accept responsibility for operating it by grants and local levies.

In 1869 "an Ordinance to establish Public Schools throughout the colony of British Columbia" made the government the central authority, provided for elected boards, and required local support for education. An amendment provided for an inspector general and the appointment of a committee to examine and certify teachers. A poll tax rather than a land tax was generally used, and the municipal council became the education board as well. Private schools continued. This was the situation when British Columbia entered Confederation in 1871.

Stages of Development. The colonial period thus provided for the settlers' children a wide variety of schools. These included church or parish schools, charity schools, Sunday schools, infant schools, some Latin grammar schools, academies, community schools, and other special schools supported by subscriptions, government grants, and fees. One of the more unusual types was the monitorial schools, which represented the last major effort of philanthropy to provide education on a massive scale. Here large rooms were used, with one section for desk work and another where groups were instructed by pupils (monitors), who had been instructed by the master.

The second stage in the development of Canadian education was marked by the establishment of strong central authorities, local taxation, free elementary schools, and secondary schools that were either free or charged low fees, with the taxpayers accepting responsibility for maintaining schools. This marked the beginning of provincial systems of education. At this time from one third to two thirds of the children received some schooling: generally two to four 6-month stints at irregular intervals.

In Upper Canada (Ontario), Egerton Ryerson adapted what he found good in European and American education for use in Ontario schools, which were largely copied by the Western provinces in their development.

In Lower Canada (Quebec), the period was marked by the efforts of a small minority of English-speaking and a large majority of French-speaking persons with different political, social, and educational backgrounds to work out a mutually beneficial, peaceful coexistence. The French Canadians clung tenaciously to their religion, language, and agricultural economy. The act of 1801 attempted to establish free common schools, but was inoperative until 1818 when a central authority was established, only to find itself up against a variety of vested interests. Two committees were established in 1829, but it was not until 30 years later that a type of divided authority was worked out that proved workable and satisfactory to the people of Quebec.

During the third stage, from the time of Confederation to the beginning of the 20th century in the East, and somewhat later in the West, the provincial departments assumed essentially their present form. Quebec developed a somewhat different pattern, as did Newfoundland, each providing for a denominational organization. By the turn of the century most elementary and secondary schools were supported by local land taxes and provincial grants. Schools were generally free, although low fees were charged in some high schools, and eight or more years of education was made compulsory.

Administration—*Education Departments.* The British North America Act gives the provincial governments jurisdiction over education.

The federal government has responsibility for the education only of its wards, the Indian population on reserves, Canadians living outside the provincial boundaries including members of the armed services, Eskimo, Indians, and others. There is no federal minister or department of education.

Each province designates a cabinet member to serve as minister of education and may appoint an advisory committee. The minister presides over a department of education and represents education on the floor of the legislature. Under him, the deputy minister, who is a civil servant and senior professional educator, administers the department, advises the minister on policy, and gives a measure of permanency to the undertaking. In general, he carries out departmental policy and enforces the provincial school act.

From the beginning, each provincial department of education has undertaken (1) training and certification of teachers; (2) inspection directed toward maintaining specified standards; (3) financial assistance to the schools through grants and services; (4) provision of courses of study and prescribing of school texts; and (5) setting out of rules and regulations for the guidance of trustees and teachers. Each department requires regular reports from the schools.

Personnel of most departments include a chief inspector of schools; high school and elementary school inspectors or superintendents; directors or supervisors of curricula, technical education, teacher training, home economics, guidance, physical education, audiovisual education, correspondence instruction, and adult education; directors or supervisors of a limited number of other services (according to the needs of the provinces); and technical personnel and clerks. In Newfoundland there are superintendents for the five denominations recognized by the School Act; and in Quebec there are two deputies, one in charge of the French-language and the other of the English-language system.

For many years schools were established and operated under close supervision of the provincial department; responsibility for competent instruction and uniform standards throughout the province fell on provincial inspectors. In recent years the trend has been to decentralization. As city schools have become more integrated and larger units have been organized in rural and semiurban areas, district superintendents have been employed. They with local principals now supply leadership and direction to the schools in their district. Decentralization is also seen in a reduction over the years of the number of departmental or external examinations, which now are generally limited to the final, or last two years, of high school. Some provinces permit the schools to select textbooks or reference books from a fairly extensive list and to try out experimental classes.

Local Boards. In all provinces local boards of education function as legal corporations operating under the provincial school act and regulation. They establish and maintain a school or schools, select qualified teachers, prepare a budget for the annual meeting, and present it to the municipal authorities. The original boards were of three members, but as towns and cities grew provision was made for larger elected or appointed boards.

In the rural areas where school districts were generally four miles square, except in Quebec parishes, life changed as farms became larger and more highly mechanized, and as automobiles and trucks replaced horses and oxen. There were shortages of teachers, many of whom lacked security of tenure and were discontented, and great inequality in the financial ability of districts to support schools. These and other reasons were behind the movement toward larger units of administration with more decentralized authority.

It was hoped that larger units would provide a greater degree of equalization, better facilities at a lower rate, and greater control of teacher shortages. Larger units were introduced by acts of the legislatures in Alberta and British Columbia, and by acts providing for local option in Saskatchewan and the Maritime provinces. Manitoba introduced legislation making it beneficial for areas to organize as larger units. Under "Operation 55" Quebec reorganized its schools, including vocational, into 55 larger units for the Roman Catholic schools and 15 for the Protestant.

Separate and Private Schools. All Canadian provinces permit private academic and vocational schools to operate. Private academic schools include many established to provide a richer and more cultural education for those able to afford it, and others operated by and for persons of a specific faith or even language. About 5% of elementary-secondary schools are private, but the percentage of pupils is lower. At the high school level, pupils in private schools generally write the provincial departmental, final examinations. The trade and vocational schools generally prepare out-of-school youths and adults for occupations, but some prepare students for the arts. Most provinces require that independent schools be registered.

Newfoundland and Quebec have denominational systems. (In Quebec the Protestant-run schools are known as "separate schools.") Ontario, Saskatchewan, and Alberta provide by law for "separate schools" run by Catholic school boards. The Maritime provinces and Manitoba, by gentlemen's agreement, allow local autonomy to determine if a school should be, for example, Roman

I. DONALD BOWDEN

A SCHOOLROOM in an Ursuline convent in Quebec city. Quebec province also has schools that are operated by Protestants. They are called "separate schools."

Catholic or nondenominational. British Columbia has no provision for separate schools. Separate schools come under the jurisdiction of the provincial department of education.

The School Ladder. In September of each year 6-year olds enter elementary school. There they remain for 6 to 8 years before entering a junior, academic, commercial-vocational, or composite high school. After 12 or 13 years of school, those in the college-preparatory course may continue to a university. Others may enter postsecondary institutes of technology or take professional training in nursing schools, teachers' colleges outside the universities, business, or other private schools.

Almost 90% of all boys and girls who begin the first grade later enter high school. About 22% enter the final year of high school, and 18% of boys and 8% of girls go on to a university, from which 13% of boys and 6% of girls graduate. Less than 2% of the total receive a second degree, and only 16 out of 1,000 graduate with a doctorate.

The 8–4 plan (8 years of elementary school, 4 of secondary) was for many years the basis for organizing the curriculum and classes other than in the Quebec Catholic school system. It is still followed in many rural, village, and town schools and in some cities. This plan, however, has been modified over the years in cities, groups of schools, or provinces for it appeared inadequate to meet demands coming out of new aims of education. There are a number of variants in Canada's school system. For example, one or two kindergarten years are added to the beginning of the system. An extra year has been added to the secondary division. Junior high schools have been introduced and the resulting organization changed to 6-3-3, 6-3-4, 7-3-3, or 7-4-2 plans. The trend is more toward an ungraded school, especially at the elementary level. Also, junior colleges are being organized, overlapping secondary and university years as well as providing terminal courses.

Teachers. About 4% of Canada's work force are teachers who instruct the more than one fourth of the total population enrolled full-time in formal education courses. More than 5 million pupils are enrolled full time in elementary-secondary schools, a figure that is increasing by over 3% per year, with the secondary school enrollment increasing by more than 5%. In times of prosperity there has generally been a shortage of teachers, the shortage being most evident for specialists at the secondary level and for university professors. The trend is toward raising the requirements for certification, extending the length of training, and providing all teacher training at a university.

In the Western provinces combined arts, science, and education courses leading to degrees are provided, although teachers may, after two years, withdraw from the course to teach. Elsewhere, most high school teachers are university graduates with a year of professional training, and elementary teachers have a high school education or better and one year of professional training. Special training is provided for teachers of vocational subjects and of special subjects.

Many teachers in addition to their regular courses teach night classes for out-of-school youths and adults.

Over two thirds of the female teachers are 25 to 45 years of age, and almost 40% are married. Male teachers are usually married, and, apart from principals and vice principals, most of them are in secondary schools. There is considerable teacher mobility, with about 16% having taught in more than one province and about 2% recruited from outside the country. Almost 25% are university graduates, and another 53% have at least senior matriculation (first year university) and one year of professional training.

Canadian teachers are about equally divided among city, town and village, and rural schools, with the number in the city increasing most rapidly.

Most teachers are paid according to a local salary schedule, although one province, at least, has a provincial schedule. Most teachers belong to professional associations and have reasonable security.

Costs. The share of Canada's gross national product spent on education rose from 1.4% in the early 1940's to an estimated 6% in the mid-1960's. Almost one half of municipal, one third of provincial, and 2.3% of federal expenditures go for formal education, of which the estimated cost is $2.75 billion or more. The federal government makes grants to provincial trade and technical schools, university education, and a variety of manpower programs. Although its contribution is under 14% of the total, its influence on directing education is disproportionately high considering its contribution.

The provincial governments have provided either flat or incentive grants of one sort or another and special grants. Several have adopted some sort of foundation program under which a minimum level of services is guaranteed, with local authorities providing the proceeds from a tax on an equalized assessment and the province making up the balance. A district may levy to provide additional services. The foundation program may replace a variety of grants, such as those for salaries, maintenance, supplies, administration, transportation, capital, and other special grants.

Schoolhouses. A few old-timers still reminisce nostalgically about the "little red schoolhouse." Modern school buildings are built to serve a variety of community purposes, avoid early obsolescence, provide facilities necessary to house the new teaching aids, and exhibit good quality. Building design has gotten away from the egg-crate type of building and now provides classrooms for the emotionally disturbed, vocational workshops, science laboratories, larger and better libraries, shops, and makes provision for team teaching. Emphasis is on adaptability in constructing functional buildings for the new curricula.

Current Situation. Present growth and development are related to economic, political, and social forces for change; development has also been influenced by scholars from abroad, Canadians educated abroad, and by a flood of literature from other countries, especially the United States.

The 4-mile-square districts, each with a single one-room, one-teacher school, have generally given place to larger rural units and town and city systems. This change has gone hand in hand with greater decentralization, with urban units accepting greater responsibility for curricula, organization, examinations, research, and innovations such as electronic aids. The trend is toward ungraded schools, team teaching, self-study, and improvement of quality. There is increased interest in social-economic-psychological problems related to disadvantaged youth and the physically and mentally handicapped. There are exciting developments in the construction of functional buildings, including the development of complexes in Quebec with academic, trade, technical, and teacher-training units on the same campus and using libraries, auditoriums, and playing fields in common.

FRED E. WHITWORTH
Canadian Council for Research in Education

Bibliography

Audet, Louis-Philippe, *Le système scolaire de la province de Québec*, 6 vols. (Quebec 1950–1956).

Dominion Bureau of Statistics, *The Organization and Administration of Public Schools in Canada*, 3d ed. (Ottawa 1966); *Canada Year Book* (Ottawa, annually); *Canada, the Official Handbook of Present Conditions and Recent Progress* (Ottawa, annually); *A Bibliographical Guide to Canadian Education* (Ottawa 1964).

Frecker, George Alain, *Education in the Atlantic Provinces* (Toronto 1957).

Phillips, Charles Edward, *The Development of Education in Canada* (Toronto 1957).

Rowe, Frederick William, *The History of Education in Newfoundland* (Toronto 1952).

Toombs, M. P., *The Control and Support of Public Education in Rupert's Land and the North-West Territories to 1905 and in Saskatchewan to 1960* (Saskatoon, Saskatchewan, 1962).

QUEBEC SYSTEM

Following the recommendations of a Royal Commission (the Parent Commission) made public in the mid-1960's, the educational system of the province of Quebec entered a period of complete reorganization that was expected to last for several years. In the late 1960's most institutions could be described only in approximate terms, for several of their features were either about to disappear or were mere innovations adopted on a tentative basis.

While this was taking place, schooling was making headway, especially among the French-speaking group. The proportion of students completing high school in Quebec more than doubled during the 1960's, and budgets multiplied approximately fourfold. This sudden expansion has been a response to the urgent needs created by the industrialization of Quebec. The radical changes in both structure and content of education imply a flat rejection of several principles hitherto considered sacrosanct in French Canada and must be interpreted in the context of a broad cultural evolution, of which such reforms are in turn a most efficient agent.

Department and Superior Council. The most decisive step was the long-discussed creation in 1964 of a department of education headed by a cabinet minister who is responsible to the legislature for all educational matters. The new department replaced two autonomous committees, one dominated by the Roman Catholic hierarchy, the other being nominally Protestant, whose decisions were executed by a politically independent superintendent. The system was rigid and uncoordinated, operating with little concern for public opinion and without any jurisdiction over the numerous and important institutions under private control.

The jurisdiction of the new department extends to all levels of education, although universities preserve a very large measure of autonomy. Alongside the minister is a Superior Council of Education, the members of which are appointed by the government after consultation with churches and representative associations. The council may make any recommendations concerning education, and such matters as curricula and regulations must be submitted to the council for adoption. Although the department and council are not denominational, the new system retains several of the traditional Roman Catholic and Protestant features: a certain proportion of the members of the council have to belong to each religious group, and there are denominational committees having final authority over matters related to religion and ethics in denominational schools. The council also includes several advisory commissions established by law for the different levels of education.

The council was created as an intermediary between the department and public opinion and as a safeguard for traditional values in the school. In practice, the new system has operated smoothly, the council tending to put pressure on the government to accelerate long-needed reforms. The department has actually undertaken the organization of a comprehensive system to integrate the two denominational divisions and absorb a large proportion of the private institutions.

Expansion Plans. Public kindergartens are to be made available to all. Elementary education will be gradually reduced to six years, while secondary education will be extended to five years. All schools eventually will adopt active pedagogical methods and a very flexible system of promotion. High school will combine liberal and vocational training with maximum possibilities to pass from one curriculum to another. Vocational training is to be graduated and integrated in such a way that no student will leave school without some specific preparation for the labor market. This integrated vocational training will replace the present system of government-operated technical schools independent of high schools.

School Boards. Public schools are administered either by local boards, whose members are generally elected by property owners and parents, or by regional boards with members appointed by local boards. The Royal Commission, later endorsed by the Council of Education, recommended that the province maintain only large regional or municipal nondenominational boards, responsible for all public schools, whether denominational or secular, French or English. This is a radical departure from the traditional system in which most school boards have been small local units, Catholic or Protestant, either legally or by custom. This strict denominational duality has been the most typical feature of the Quebec system and it has been widely criticized for several reasons. From the beginning, the situation proved unsatisfactory both for non-Christian groups and for English or French minorities within each denomination. Moreover, the dual system has meant higher costs for all and a financial handicap for the less prosperous Roman Catholic group, whose boards could scarcely raise adequate taxes.

More important, however, is the fact that a small but vocal French-speaking group has insisted on the necessity of nondenominational public schools. The need for at least a certain number of such institutions is now widely recognized. In order to avoid further divisions within the public system, the Royal Commission recommended unified boards. Committees of parents would supervise the religious and ethical aspects of education in denominational as well as in secular schools, religion being taught as an optional subject in the latter. These proposals have raised bitter opposition in several quarters.

Meanwhile, denominational divisions have already become less rigid. The evolution of religious thinking toward ecumenism, the gradual secularization of French Canadian society, and the need for larger and more expensive schools all contribute to put the emphasis on academic and administrative rather than religious considerations in education. For instance, all Roman Catholic public high schools have already dropped compulsory religious instruction.

New Colleges. A third level of education was created in 1967. It is intermediate between secondary and higher education and consists of two or three years in a "college of general and vocational education." As the name suggests, the new college prepares for both admission to university and to professions requiring less than a full university course. In arts and science, it is intended to correspond roughly to a junior college. Its graduates entering a university take three years for either an honors' degree or a general degree, or else are admitted directly into any professional school.

This third level of education serves many purposes. It gives a better preparation for a university to students coming from public schools, who will be admitted into all faculties, a privilege traditionally reserved to the graduates of private institutions in French-speaking Quebec. The new school will also initiate an extensive program of vocational training intended to meet the growing need for specialists in many fields. Curricula are very flexible, allowing students to shift from general to vocational education and vice versa, and the school operates the year round, favoring more extensive work for students who need or desire it.

GAR LUNNEY, FROM NATIONAL FILM BOARD

ESKIMO AND INDIAN pupils around a teacher in a Federal school at Inuvik, Northwest Territories.

The new college is administered by a board on which an important proportion of members are appointed by the government and others by the faculty, students' parents, and students. Tuition is free, and the college is financed by the department of education, which exercises a large measure of control over most aspects of college life.

In most cases, the college begins as an amalgamation of a variety of traditional institutions. In French-speaking Quebec, the new schools absorb parts of the traditional classical colleges (*collèges classiques*), junior teachers' colleges (*écoles normales*), senior vocational schools, and others. In English-speaking Quebec, the creation of "colleges of general and vocational education" is also a revolutionary step, since students have always been admitted to a university after high school. The reactions to the new institution have been rather unfavorable, and there is a tendency to minimize the change through plans to relate the new colleges as closely as possible to universities.

Vanishing Institutions. Among the vanishing institutions, the *collège classique* deserves special mention. There used to be in Quebec approximately 100 such colleges, all of them controlled by the Roman Catholic clergy. They offered an 8-year course beginning after the 7th grade. The curriculum was strongly influenced by the traditional secondary schools of continental Europe, with the last two years corresponding roughly to the first two years of a general arts course in North America. For generations, the classical colleges have trained the bulk of the typical French Canadian elite of churchmen, professionals, politicians, and magistrates. After World War II, new and more modern curricula, the gradual replacement of clerical by lay teachers, and a growing dependence upon public funds substantially altered their character, and the rapid development of public education has been fatal to them. Most have been disbanded and integrated to various degrees with the public secondary schools and the newly created colleges.

The virtual disappearance of the old junior teachers' colleges is also significant. Like the *collège classique,* they were very numerous, often very small and strictly denominational. The Royal Commission recommended that teachers receive their general education in the new colleges and their professional training in the universities. The latter proposition has produced strong resistance, a possible alternative being the development of a few *écoles normales* along the lines of regular North American teachers colleges.

The Future. It is of course too early to evaluate the sweeping reforms taking place in Quebec education. In many cases there is an inevitable tendency to retain much of the old content under new names. Moreover, certain recommendations of the Royal Commission are naturally open to criticism, especially as to their practicability. Above all, a genuine application of the reforms will require a degree of competence among administrators and teachers that will be found only gradually.

However, it may be taken for granted that the Quebec system of education will be predominantly public, increasingly unified and secularized, and more and more conditioned by the needs of the industrial society.

PAUL LACOSTE, *University of Montreal*

Further Reading: Audet, Louis-Philippe, *Histoire du Conseil de l'Instruction publique de la Province de Québec, 1856–1964* (Montreal 1964); Government of Quebec, *Report of the Royal Commission of Inquiry on Education,* 5 vols. (Quebec 1963–1966); Miller, P.-A., *Administration et législation du système scolaire de la Province de Québec* (Quebec 1956); Tremblay, A., *Les collèges et les écoles publiques: Conflit ou coordination* (Quebec 1954).

INDEPENDENT SCHOOLS

Although Canadian education falls under the jurisdiction of the 10 provincial departments of education, many Canadians assert their democratic right of having their children educated in private or independent schools. Such schools are found in every province and in every category, such as elementary, secondary, Protestant, Roman Catholic, Jewish, day schools, boarding schools, boys' schools, and girls' schools.

Origins. Originally, these schools were founded because of a strong desire to pass on to the sons and daughters of the next generation the faith of their fathers. This was particularly true of the 19th century, when many Protestant and Roman Catholic educational institutions came into being. The major distinction, therefore, of the independent school is its concern for religion and the religious convictions of whatever group conceived it. From this concern grows the school's need to emphasize the importance of moral and spiritual values and the development of a philosophy of life based on the faith of the founders.

Curriculum. From the point of view of academic curriculum the independent school differs very little from its provincial counterpart. It too prepares its students for the same high-school-leaving certificates and entrance to the same universities as the government school. The curriculum set forth by the department of education in each province is followed by the independent school. So that students may earn provincial high-school-leaving certificates, the school is inspected by the department and must satisfy the provincial government that suitable standards are maintained.

The meaning of "independent," therefore, is significant in terms of philosophy of education, enrichment of program, the right to choose and engage a teaching faculty, and to select student personnel according to the school's own standards. Independence also implies the necessity to finance the school on the basis of fees and endowment without the advantage of government grants. Independent schools, in the main, offer academic programs leading to university entrance and are not involved with technical or commercial courses.

Advantages. Because classes in independent schools are small, considerable individual attention is possible. Although many such schools were founded out of religious conviction, parents have come to seek out private or independent education, not only for religious reasons, but also for the more personal nature of the education offered. In this way they hope to avoid the disadvantages of mass education.

The independent school is not necessarily better than the provincial school, but it enjoys the advantage of being small enough to permit teachers and students to get to know one another. If the religious basis is to mean anything, there must be emphasis on character development, and a close relationship between teachers and students makes this possible. The student in the independent school may benefit from a personal interest on the part of the teacher in his progress in academics, in athletics, and in cocurricular activities of a cultural nature. Opportunity, therefore, is given to the student to come closer to his true potential in many aspects of modern school life.

Affiliations. The largest proportion of independent schools belong to the Roman Catholic faith. Many Protestant schools of high standing and with roots in Canada's early history are members of the Canadian Headmasters' Association and the Canadian Headmistresses' Association. Of the total student population in Canada approximately 4% of the students attend elementary or secondary independent schools.

HARRY M. BEER
Canadian Headmasters' Association

27. Higher Education

Canada has about 50 universities. Although the earliest colleges, forerunners of the universities, were established by the churches (one in the 17th century, two in the 18th, many in the 19th), the majority are public foundations—provincial or provincially assisted universities. In some the language of instruction is English; in others, especially in the province of Quebec, it is French; and there are a few bilingual universities that teach in both languages.

Universities vary in size and complexity, from those with one faculty and fewer than 1,000 students to others with many faculties and professional schools, enrolling more than 20,000 full-time candidates for degrees and diplomas.

Admission. Students enter a university after 11, 12, or 13 years of primary and secondary schooling, at levels known as senior matriculation (12 or 13 years) and junior matriculation (11 or 12 years). In most provinces admission is based on examinations set and graded by a provincial examining board. The universities decide who shall be admitted.

The Service for Admission to College and University was established in 1966, jointly by the universities and the provincial departments of education. Its headquarters are in Ottawa.

THE UNIVERSITY OF TORONTO is an important center of graduate studies and research enterprises.

J. ALLAN CASH, FROM RAPHO GUILLUMETTE

Its first task was to provide objective admission tests, in both French and English, for use throughout Canada.

Curricula. In English Canada the course most commonly chosen is one leading to the degree of bachelor of arts (B. A.). After senior matriculation a general B. A. course may be completed in three years of full-time study, an honors (specialized) course in four. If entrance is at the junior matriculation level (which is becoming less common), an extra year is required. Courses leading to the degree of bachelor of science (B. Sc.) are organized in a similar fashion. Those providing preparation for entrance into the professions are usually four or more years in length (six in the case of medical doctors).

Graduate studies and research lead to advanced degrees, of which the master of arts (M. A.) and doctor of philosophy (Ph. D.) are typical.

In French Canada the traditional route formerly was from the *école primaire* (primary school) to an 8-year course of humanistic education in a church-related *collège classique* (classical college) affiliated to a French-language university. The successful scholar was awarded the *baccalauréat ès arts* (B. A.), and this admitted him to the university for advanced humanistic or professional studies.

Changes introduced in the late 1960's made the pattern of courses more like that in English Canada. The degrees, however, are designated *licence, diplôme d'études supérieures,* and *doctorat* rather than B. A., M. A., and Ph. D.

In addition to courses leading to degrees and diplomas, most universities offer extension programs in general, cultural, and vocational education as additional services to their communities.

Sessions. In addition to regular 2-term winter sessions (September to April) for full-time students, most universities have summer sessions (primarily for school teachers) and offer evening courses for part-time students. Correspondence courses are available from some universities and television courses began to be introduced in the 1960's. A few universities offer instruction in three terms of about 15 weeks each (so-called year-round operation) and a few have cooperative or work-study programs in which students alternate between classroom and job every four months.

Teaching. Those who teach in the universities normally hold at least one advanced degree, and about half of them have a doctorate. The usual ranks are professor, associate professor, assistant professor, and lecturer. Men outnumber women about seven to one. Persons in these ranks are assisted by instructors, demonstrators, teaching assistants, and technicians.

The most common teaching method is the lecture, which is sometimes delivered to as many as 300 or 400 students in one auditorium, sometimes to even more, in several auditoriums, by closed-circuit television. Lectures are complemented by laboratory experiments in many courses, especially in the biological and physical sciences, and by group tutorials in the humanities and social sciences. Smaller groups often are taught in seminar rather than by classroom lecture.

Students. The typical university student enters at the age of 18 and takes his first degree at 21—unless he is the one in three who drops out before graduating. Student numbers increased rapidly after World War II, rising from 63,000 in 1952–1953 to more than four times that number in the late 1960's.

In 1952–1953, full-time university enrollment was equal to 4% of the population 18 to 24 years of age. By 1967–1968 that percentage had risen to 12%. In the late 1960's the ratio of men to women was about two to one.

Most students attend a university in their home province. About 6% of total enrollment is from other countries. One student in five lives in a student residence on campus.

Administration. A university is usually governed by two bodies: a lay board of governors concerned primarily with financial management, and an academic senate concerned with instruction and research. Until the late 1960's virtually the only communication link between them was the chief administrative officer of the university (president, principal, or *recteur*). However, as a result of the report *University Government in Canada*, published in 1966, there has been a trend toward cross-representation between these two bodies.

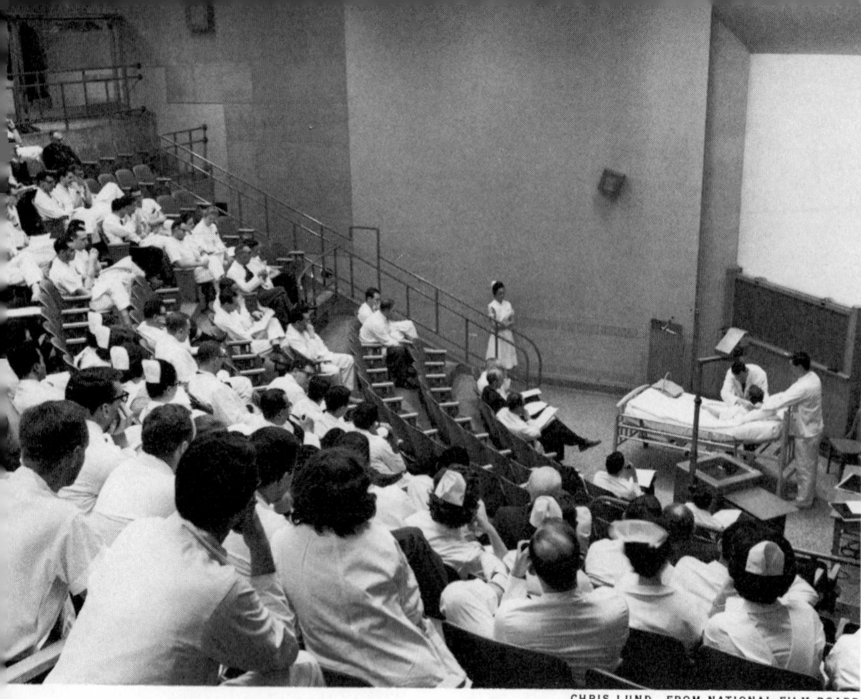

CHRIS LUND, FROM NATIONAL FILM BOARD

STUDENTS AND STAFF MEMBERS hear a lecture at McGill University Medical School, situated in Montreal.

Finance. In the mid-1960's about 60% of university operating costs, totaling more than $400 million a year, were being met by government grants. Students' tuition fees were providing about 25%. The remaining 15% came from endowments, gifts, and other sources. Capital expenditures were over $200 million a year, with approximately 70% being met by governments.

The role of governments in the financing of universities was relatively insignificant until after World War II. Then provincial government assistance increased markedly. Federal grants were introduced in 1951, and in 1967, federal grants were combined with provincial grants. The government of Canada gave the provinces additional taxing powers and supplementary grants to enable them to meet the operating and capital costs of all postsecondary education. The federal government continued, however, to support research, both in and outside the universities.

Agencies. During the 1960's most provinces established agencies—governmental or quasi-governmental—to encourage and coordinate university development and to advise on government financial support. For example, Alberta has a universities commission; Ontario, a ministry of university affairs and an advisory committee on university affairs; Quebec, a directorate-general of higher education within its ministry of education; and Nova Scotia, a university grants committee. A small secretariat concerned with federal support of higher education was established in 1966 in the department of the secretary of state of Canada.

Interuniversity Organizations. The universities of all Canada are served by the Association of Universities and Colleges of Canada. Grouping the universities of the most easterly provinces is the Association of Atlantic Universities. In Quebec there is a Conférence des Recteurs et des Principaux des Universités, and in Ontario a Committee of Presidents of Universities of Ontario.

There is a Canadian Association of University Teachers, with provincial counterparts, and a Canadian Union of Students which also has provincial counterparts, including the Union Général des Étudiants du Québec and the Ontario Union of Students.

Other Institutions of Higher Education. Nonuniversity institutions of postsecondary education include junior colleges, institutes of technology, teachers colleges (for the training of elementary school teachers), hospital schools of nursing, and colleges of art.

During the 1960's great strides were made toward the addition of a new dimension to postsecondary education in Canada—the community college. This concept caught on, and in one province after another provision was made for a system of institutions offering courses of two or three years from the junior matriculation level, some leading on to university with advanced standing, some preparing for semiprofessional occupations.

These colleges operate alongside the universities, except in Quebec, where they are an integral stage in the educational system between the secondary school and the university. Such colleges are called by different names in the various provinces: district and regional colleges in British Columbia; junior colleges in Alberta; colleges of applied arts and technology in Ontario; and *collèges d'enseignement général et professionnel* (colleges of general and vocational education) in Quebec.

EDWARD F. SHEFFIELD, *University of Toronto*

Bibliography

Association of Universities and Colleges of Canada, *Canadian Universities and Colleges* (Ottawa, annually).

Association of Universities and Colleges of Canada, *University Affairs* (Ottawa, quarterly).

Canadian Association of University Teachers, *C.A.U.T. Bulletin* (Ottawa, quarterly).

Commission on the Financing of Higher Education, *Financing Higher Education in Canada* (Toronto 1965).

Dominion Bureau of Statistics, *Survey of Higher Education* (Ottawa, annually).

Dominion Bureau of Statistics, *Survey of Vocational Education and Training* (Ottawa, annually).

Duff, James, and Berdahl, Robert O., *University Government in Canada* (Toronto 1966).

Harris, Robin S., and Tremblay, Arthur, *A Bibliography of Higher Education in Canada* (Toronto 1960); *Supplement,* by Robin S. Harris (Toronto 1965).

Harris, Robin S., ed., *Changing Patterns of Higher Education in Canada* (Toronto 1966).

28. Vocational and Adult Education

Since the early 1960's there has been a marked and widening acceptance of the concept that education is a lifelong process and not just the formal, institutionalized operation, organized by the state, for the training of the young. The term "continuing education," now widely used in Canada, assumes that learning is a normal activity for an adult. This growing acceptance has meant that adult education is no longer seen as mainly remedial in purpose.

Although many programs are designed to upgrade the education of adults who left school before completing their primary or secondary courses, it is generally believed that adult education has a much broader function than that of making up for what was missed in youth. Increasingly, it has been recognized that men and women, no matter what their background, want and need to go on learning throughout their lives as a means of both improving their earning capacity and enriching their lives. Programs are provided by a variety of agencies, government and voluntary, to serve both these ends.

Contributions of Existing School Systems. A result of this changing attitude is that responsibility for the adult population has been assumed by Canadian school systems. School boards across the country offer extensive evening programs. In such centers as Vancouver, Winnipeg, and metropolitan Toronto, diploma courses in academic and vocational subjects are offered during evening hours. The scale of some of these evening programs can be gauged from the fact that in a typical year the Toronto board of education, one among six metropolitan borough boards, carried some 250 courses. Approximately 52,000 adult students registered in these courses, with about 45% of them working for credit.

School board involvement in vocational and adult education is by no means restricted to major urban centers. By the mid-1960's, approximately 200 officials across Canada had responsibility, either part- or full-time, for school board adult programs. The classes cover a wide range of vocational, recreational, and liberal subjects. School systems also have developed informal programs that are offered in the community outside school buildings. Development has been greatest in British Columbia and Ontario, although provision for adult education at the school board level has been extended in most regions.

Vocational Education. Formal vocational education is carried on in Canada chiefly in three types of institutions: technical or composite schools, which are part of the regular secondary school systems; trade schools, for those who are past provincial school-leaving age and have a standing of grade 8 to 10; and institutes of technology, which provide a much higher level of training, principally for high school graduates.

In addition, there is on-the-job apprenticeship training, with classes held at trade schools, as well as a variety of courses offered by private trade schools and business colleges. An important aspect of vocational training is that conducted by private industry, designed both to upgrade skills and to improve management quality. Although there is little statistical information, the volume of such training is known to be large.

As the pace of technological change in Canadian industry began to quicken in the late 1950's, it became clear that large numbers of both young people and adults had acquired neither the basic education nor the skill to obtain and hold a job. It was decided that a new approach to the training of manpower must be taken. Only by a program of education could Canada build a sufficiently large and well-trained labor force.

Government Legislation. The result was the passing of the Technical and Vocational Training Assistance Act of 1960 and the signing of the Federal-Provincial Training Agreements. Through this cost-sharing plan, amended and broadened in 1963, the federal government agreed to reimburse the provinces, up to 75%, for expenditures on technical and vocational training programs, and to provide capital assistance for the construction of new or the extension of old training facilities. By the mid-1960's, building projects valued at over $800 million had been approved, providing more than 250,000 new places for students.

An important section of the program was designed for adults who had left the regular school systems, both those currently employed and unemployed. The purpose was to upgrade skills, to increase basic education, as well as trade, technical, and occupational competence.

In 1967 the Adult Occupational Training Act was passed by the federal Parliament. This retained the basic purposes of the former legislation, but radically altered dominion-provincial arrangements for manpower training.

Under the 1967 act, the individual deals directly with the federal manpower center in his locality, which can pay up to 100% of the cost of training and provide a living allowance, if that is required. Federal manpower officials contract with provincial governments to provide the needed training services directly or through local school boards. To qualify for training under the program, a man or woman must have been a member of the labor force for not less than three years, or have one or more persons totally or substantially dependent upon him for support.

Community Colleges. During the 1960's there were developed what are widely, though unofficially, called "community colleges." The provinces most active in establishing these post-secondary institutions have been British Columbia (regional colleges); Alberta (junior colleges); Ontario (colleges of applied arts and technology); and Quebec (institutes). Other provinces have considered similar action.

The colleges vary widely from province to province in administrative structure and in admission requirements. But with the exception of Ontario, which offers no university credit program, the colleges will provide both vocational and technical courses based on community needs and a 2-year academic program that will permit transfer to a university.

To what extent community colleges will undertake programs of adult education in the broad sense is not yet certain. However, it is expected that a gocd many will offer educational activities having no admission requirement for adults other than interest.

Adult Education. In both volume and range of activity, there has been a phenomenal growth in adult education conducted by universities and colleges since the 1930's. In 1935 only 9 universities had extension departments. By the mid-1960's, owing both to the increasing acceptance of a wider responsibility and to the establishment of many new campuses, some 70 institutions were providing educational services to other than full-time students. Some 135,000 men and women were enrolled in part-time courses for credit and nearly 172,000 in part-time, noncredit study. Regular full-time student enrollment at the university level was slightly under 176,000.

Some extension departments, such as those at the universities of British Columbia, Alberta, and Saskatchewan, consider the whole province to be their field of operation, and St. Francis Xavier University in Antigonish, Nova Scotia, works even more widely in the Maritime Provinces. Extension staffs use study groups, short courses, seminars, special institutes, and conferences to encourage community interest in such diverse subjects as parent education, cooperative theory and practice, farming methods, community development, discussion techniques, public affairs, music, drama, and human relations.

Community programs of a similar character are carried on by some provincial governments through adult education divisions of their departments of education. Regional field workers assist in organizing programs and activities to meet local needs and interests. Provincial governments with such divisions or special sections within their departments of education are Nova Scotia, Quebec, Ontario, and British Columbia.

Professional Training. By the late 1960's adult education had emerged as a profession. Several universities—British Columbia, Saskatchewan, Toronto, Guelph, St. Francis Xavier, and Ontario Agricultural College—offer graduate and summer courses leading to diplomas and degrees in adult education. Many Canadians have studied at American institutions. Men and women have received special training in such fields as extension teaching, adult learning, residential adult education, labor education, agricultural extension, family relations, rural and urban leadership, counseling and guidance, group development, and industrial training. These professional specialties indicate the range of subject matter in programs for adults and the variety of settings in which such programs are offered.

Canadian Association for Adult Education. The CAAE was founded in the mid-1930's as a national clearinghouse for the movement. At that time, most workers in adult education had had no specific training in that field. The association brought these people together for consultation and the exchange of information and experience.

Much of the effort of the CAAE and its French-speaking counterpart, *l'Institut canadien d'éducation des adultes,* is spent on providing services, in seminars, conferences and publications, for an increasingly professional membership.

A pioneer effort of the CAAE was its use of national radio to promote the discussion of public affairs. The techniques worked out in the National Farm Radio Forum and Citizens' Forum programs, developed with the Canadian Broadcasting Corporation in the early 1940's, are regarded as a major Canadian contribution to adult education. This combination of printed study material, radio broadcasts, group discussion and group reporting is being adapted in many countries of Asia and Africa and of the Caribbean.

In the late 1940's the CAAE developed a joint planning commission for carrying out its coordinating function. Representatives of the many voluntary organizations engaged in some form of adult education meet to report on their current programs and publications and to discuss emerging needs. The meetings provide a means for the Canadian Broadcasting Corporation and the National Film Board to maintain contact with program users.

ISABEL WILSON
Canadian Association for Adult Education

29. Government Aid to Education

Under the terms of the British North America Act of 1867, responsibility for the organization and administration of public education in Canada is exercised by each of the provinces. Canada has never had a federal ministry of education, although the federal government does assume responsibility for education in the Yukon and Northwest Territories; for educating certain groups such as Indians, Eskimo, children of armed forces personnel employed at defense establishments at home and overseas, and penitentiary inmates; and for the full costs of the three Canadian Services Colleges.

Sources of Funds. Costs of public elementary and secondary education are met, in the main, by local taxation on property and by provincial legislative grants to school boards. Direct governmental assistance to higher education has been, since 1967, primarily in the form of provincial government grants for current and capital purposes. In the late 1960's, the ultimate responsibility for financing education in Canada seemed to be falling more and more on provincial governments. As an example, certain federal grants for higher education, for some years paid through the Association of Universities and Colleges of Canada and its predecessor organizations directly to eligible institutions, were paid, beginning in 1967, in the form of tax transfers and supplementary equalization and adjustment payments directly to the provinces, for distribution by the provinces to postsecondary institutions. At the same time, the provinces were tending to assume certain costs for elementary and secondary education, formerly borne by local governments, through expanding programs designed to give common province-wide basic levels of financial support.

In the mid-1960's, sources of funds for formal education (including vocational education) were about 30% from local government taxation, 50% from provincial and territorial governments, 10% from the federal government, and the balance of about 10% from private nongovernmental sources.

Expenditures. About half of the total revenue of local governments and one third of the revenue of provincial governments were expended on education in 1965, as estimated by the Dominion Bureau of Statistics. Total expenditures on education in 1965 amounted to an estimated 6.3% of the gross national product, with the percentage rising by about 0.4% per year.

For 1966, expenditures on education by the three levels of government were estimated by the Economic Council of Canada to be $3.3 billion — the largest single component of government spending, and close to one fifth of total government outlays during the year. The council estimated, perhaps conservatively, that total government expenditures on education would increase by an annual rate of over 6% per annum, to approach $4.3 billion (in 1966 dollars) by 1970.

Problems. Local government support of education is concentrated primarily at the elementary and secondary levels. Because of increasing demands on locally collected taxes for other purposes and because of varying degrees of affluence in different areas of a province, local authorities have become increasingly convinced of the necessity of expanded provincial support for education. The provinces, in turn, faced with many demands on their tax revenue, are demanding a further share of federal tax revenue for all levels of education within their borders.

It is within this context, and within the framework of the British North America Act, that the dilemma of acceptable forms of governmental support of education in Canada is being debated, and is slowly being resolved. Rapidly expanding enrollment, especially at the postsecondary level, increased costs made higher by the enrollment expansion, and the fact that in one form or another governments must be the main source of revenue for education, all point to the need for active cooperation among the various levels of government.

Federal Aid. The role of the federal government in financing education, apart from those responsibilities noted previously, has been primarily through assistance to vocational and technical training, to universities, and through grants for research. In addition, it administers through several of its departments and agencies programs of graduate scholarships and fellowships. In 1964 it began the Canada Student Loans Plan whereby postsecondary students could receive loans up to $1,000 a year for a maximum of five years, which would be interest-free while the borrower remained a student and for six months thereafter.

Funds for Higher Education. From 1951–1952 to 1966–1967, annual grants were paid by the federal government to universities and colleges for current operating purposes. Originally on the basis of 50 cents per capita of population in each province, the rate was raised to $1.00 per capita beginning with the 1956–1957 academic year, to $1.50 for 1958–1959, and to $2.00 from 1962–1963. For 1966–1967, the last year in which grants were paid in this form, the rate was raised to an average of $5.00 per capita for each province, based on a weighted formula taking into account different levels of studies and the number of out-of-province students in each province.

Beginning on April 1, 1967, a new form of federal postsecondary assistance replaced the per capita grants and certain other forms of postsecondary assistance. Through the unconditional transfer of 4 personal and 1 corporate tax points, and additional equalization and adjustment payments, funds were made available to each province equal to either 50% of eligible operating expenditures of postsecondary institutions (or $15 per capita of provincial population whichever figure was higher). About $350 million (as opposed to about $100 million at $5 per capita) was expected to be transferred to the provinces for the first fiscal years under the new plan.

Canada Council. The per capita university grants were one recommendation contained in the 1951 *Report of the Royal Commission on National Development in the Arts, Letters and Sciences.* Another recommendation led to the formation of the Canada Council for the Arts, Humanities and Social Sciences in 1957. The council was granted $100 million, half of which, with accrued interest, was to be distributed to universities and colleges over a 10-year period for capital construction or equipment projects in the council's fields of interest. The interest on the other half was to be used for graduate scholarships and grants to individuals and organizations in these fields. Later the federal government gave more money to the council, and it has received private donations from time to time. In its own fields, the council complements the grants and awards made in science fields by the National Research Council, the Medical Research Council, and several other federal bodies.

R. HALIN, FROM NATIONAL FILM BOARD

THE PARLIAMENTARY LIBRARY in Ottawa contains a vast collection of Canada's historical records.

R. D. MITCHENER, *Education Support Branch Department of the Secretary of State, Ottawa*

Further Reading: Best sources of additional information are the numerous publications of the Education Division, Dominion Bureau of Statistics, Ottawa; of the Canadian Education Association, Toronto; of the Canadian Teachers' Federation, Ottawa; and of the Association of Universities and Colleges of Canada, Ottawa.

30. Libraries and Museums

Canada has several thousand libraries and more than 400 museums to meet various needs.

Libraries. The country's libraries are staffed by about 2,500 professional librarians and 5,000 supporting personnel. Professional graduate training is given at Dalhousie, Montreal, McGill, Ottawa, Toronto, Western Ontario, Alberta, and British Columbia universities.

Public Libraries. All of the larger cities have public libraries. Many of these libraries are also resource centers for regional systems, serving small communities and rural areas. By the mid-1960's, public libraries served about 70% of the total population, and further extension was under way.

Provincial governments create public libraries by law. They provide grants for, and supervise these libraries, which are operated by municipal and regional boards. General tax funds support public library service, and nationwide payments amount to about $30 million annually, or $1.50 per capita. Additional expenditures for buildings and equipment total several million dollars more each year.

In the 20 years after World War II, the book stock of public libraries rose from under 6 million volumes to over 20 million volumes, and circulation increased from 20 million to approximately 100 million. Library collections expanded to include films, video tapes, sound recordings, and materials for programmed learning.

The Toronto Public Library is outstanding for its history, fine arts, and business collections. The

GAR LUNNEY, FROM NATIONAL FILM BOARD

NEW PUBLIC LIBRARY at Regina, Saskatchewan, has a reading room that features space and light.

Bibliothèque Saint-Sulpice, in Montreal, contains many rare and historic books and manuscripts.

Other large urban centers have excellent libraries, especially Regina (Saskatchewan), Edmonton (Alberta), and Vancouver (British Columbia), which have built new headquarters. Several regional libraries have modern, functional headquarters buildings to serve predominantly rural areas. The Prince Edward Island libraries headquarters is in the Fathers of Confederation Memorial Centre, Charlottetown, with a provincial art gallery, theater, and other cultural facilities.

Academic Libraries. University libraries contain more than 10 million volumes, or about 65 per student served. Expenditures are about $25 million annually, or about $100 per student. The University of Toronto library has collections of associated and affiliated institutions and a humanities and social sciences research center. Distinguished libraries may be found at almost every degree-granting institution.

Centralized school libraries exist in almost all secondary schools and in about one fifth of the elementary schools. The total book stock amounts to over 8 million volumes, or about 5 books per student served. Expenditures for library materials total about $4 million annually or about $3 per student served.

Special Libraries. Canada has more than 600 special libraries to serve federal and provincial government departments, business, technical and industrial firms, and members of private professional and other associations. Total stock includes more than 7 million books and extensive holdings of other materials.

The Parliamentary Library and the National Research Council Library, in Ottawa, are the outstanding federal government libraries. Nova Scotia, Manitoba, and Saskatchewan have excellent provincial libraries. The Bell Telephone Company library, in Montreal, has a modern technical collection, and the Academy of Medicine Library, in Toronto, contains many valuable works.

National Library. Operated by the federal government, the National Library of Canada provides bibliographic, reference, and interlibrary loan facilities to all libraries. In 1967 it moved into spacious new quarters in Ottawa, along with the Public Archives. Its facilities may be used by any student.

Library Associations. The Canadian Library Association, in Ottawa, and provincial associations are independent groups that provide members with opportunities for exchange of views, publications, and information. Members include librarians, library trustees, publishers, and other interested persons, who meet at annual conferences and other sessions to review needs and set standards for libraries in Canada. See also LIBRARIES—9. *Canadian Library System.*

Museums. Of the more than 400 museums in Canada, only 6 were founded before Confederation in 1867. More than 60% were established after World War II. Some were anniversary projects, marking milestones in provincial history; others commemorate the Centennial of Confederation, in 1967.

Government authorities at federal, provincial, and local levels operate more than half the museums, and government grants assist many of the private institutions. Total expenditures are estimated at $15 million annually, and about 75% of the funds are from government sources. More than 1,000 full-time employees and an almost equal number of part-time employees staff the museums.

Major Institutions. The National Museum and the National Gallery, in Ottawa, specialize in Canadiana. The National Gallery also has a small but growing international art collection.

The Royal Ontario Museum, in Toronto, has important Chinese, Egyptology, and Canadiana collections, and the Art Gallery of Toronto specializes in older, modern, and Canadian painting and sculpture. The Ontario Museum of Science and Technology, in the Toronto area, is a Centennial project. The Montreal Museum of Fine Arts has a fine collection of Oriental and Occidental art. See also ART GALLERIES.

Historic sites with museums include Fort Louisbourg and the Halifax Citadel, in Nova Scotia; the Plains of Abraham, in Quebec City; Fort York, in Toronto; Fort Henry, at Kingston, Ontario; and Fort Garry at Winnipeg, Manitoba.

Provincial museums in Winnipeg, Regina, Edmonton, and Victoria (British Columbia) are rich in Indian and pioneer material, as is the Glenbow Foundation, a private institution in Calgary. The Art Galleries of Vancouver, Edmonton, and Regina have fine modern collections.

The Canadian Museums Association, in Ottawa, advises on government grants, conducts courses and field surveys, issues publications, and holds annual conferences.

EDITH ADAMSON, *Library Consultant*
Indian Affairs Branch, Canadian Department of Indian Affairs and Northern Development

Further Reading: Dominion Bureau of Statistics, *Museum and Art Galleries 1964* (Ottawa 1966); id., *Survey of Libraries, Part I: Public Libraries; Part II: Academic Libraries* (Ottawa, annually); *Part III: Library Education, 1960–1965* (Ottawa 1966). Consult also publications of the Canadian Museums Association, the Canadian Library Association, provincial associations and provincial governments, and individual institutions.

31. Research Facilities

Research has become an important part of every aspect of life in present-day Canada. Pure research, without reference to its possible applications, centers mainly in the universities. But applied research, concerned with the practical problems of industry, defense, government, medicine, welfare, and education, is an ongoing concern of a great variety of organizations.

National. Research workers in the universities have drawn their main support from the National Research Council of Canada, established in 1916. As its area of concern is only the natural sciences, pure and applied, its work has been supplemented by creation in 1957 of the Canada Council for the arts, letters, and social sciences. Both organizations conduct large-scale programs of scholarships and fellowships to train research workers in the universities and programs of grants to faculty members. Support in the areas of concern to the Canada Council before 1957 was provided for 15 years by the Social Science Research Council of Canada and the Humanities Research Council of Canada, using funds from American foundations.

The National Research Council established its own laboratories in Ottawa in 1924. These have been several times expanded, and regional laboratories have been established in the Atlantic and the Prairie provinces.

Most federal government departments maintain research branches. In 1947 the Defence Research Board was created to provide scientific advice and assistance to the armed forces. It maintains laboratories in various parts of the country. In 1964 the government established a Scientific Secretariat in the office of the prime minister with the duty of assembling and analyzing information related to the government's many-sided scientific and technological activities.

A medical division of the National Research Council became the Medical Research Council in 1960. It assists the research work of hospitals, medical schools, and other institutions. Specialized national voluntary organizations concerned with particular types of disability conduct annual campaigns to raise funds for research.

Provincial. Most of the provinces have followed the lead of the federal government in their creation of provincial research councils or foundations. Their main concern is developing natural resources and aiding the efficiency of provincial industries. Some, notably the Ontario Research Foundation, founded in 1928, do a good deal of contract research that is paid for by industry.

Industrial. Many larger industries operate important research enterprises, though some that are branches of companies based in the United States rely heavily on the research done by the parent concern. The Ontario government in the 1960's took an important initiative in inducing numerous industries to build their research laboratories at a central location, the Ontario Research Community at Sheridan Park.

Educational. Research in educational methods and programs has become the focus of more attention. Most provinces have an educational research council.

In 1961 the Canadian Council for Research in Education was established with an office in Ottawa, under the multiple sponsorship of most major educational organizations whose interests are national in scope.

JOHN E. ROBBINS, *President*
Brandon University, Brandon, Manitoba

CANADA: Religion

The Christian faith is dominant in Canada. The vast majority of its adherents are divided almost evenly between the Roman Catholic Church and various Protestant churches, of which the United Church of Canada and the Anglican Church of Canada are the largest. A number of sects and groups claim the allegiance of small numbers of people.

32. Protestant Churches

The most striking feature of Canadian Protestantism is its preoccupation with the nation's cultural and ethnic backgrounds. This is due, to a large extent, to the bicultural tension within the Canadian nation, the most determinative factor in Canadian national and ecclesiastical development. It is this factor that provides a sense of continuity to Canadian history both before and after the British conquest, for it was present in the first French settlements on the North American continent when Huguenot and Catholic attempted to cooperate in the foundation of a French Empire in the New World. After this brief attempt at

RALPH GREENHILL FROM MILLER SERVICES, LTD.

THE UNITED CHURCH OF CANADA church in Edgeley, Ontario, bears the date 1877 over its doorway

cooperation between Protestant and Catholic, Cardinal Richelieu came to the conclusion that no satisfactory colony could emerge in America amid the clamor of religious controversy and so in 1628 all Protestants were banished from New France.

Similar emotions of distrust and fear prevailed in the English-speaking colonies in America, where Roman Catholicism was a proscribed religion. Whenever they could persuade the British authorities to cooperate, New Englanders were foremost in attempting to remove all traces of French colonization from the New World. This desire was made evident in 1755 when some 10,000 Acadians were uprooted from what is now Nova Scotia and dispersed throughout the Thirteen Colonies to be replaced mostly by New England Congregationalists. With the capture of Quebec by the English in 1759 and the subsequent Treaty of Paris in 1763, it seemed almost a certainty that the long religious and cultural struggle between New France and New England was at an end and that 65,000 French-Canadian Roman Catholics would lose their identity within a British North America already peopled by 2 million English-speaking Protestants.

The strenuous struggle for ethnic survival by the French Canadians which, as the historian Mason Wade points out, "still continues, long after survival has been assured," explains the present-day preoccupation of the Canadian churches with cultural affairs.

Cultural Religions. Since the conventional churches have, rightly or wrongly, been regarded as the guardians of the cultures of the founding ethnic groups of Canada, they have responded by allowing themselves to be molded by the cultures they are supposed to protect: the larger Protestant denominations have become closely identified with Anglo-Saxon and Celtic cultures; the Roman Catholic Church, particularly the French-speaking sector, has been regarded as the true bulwark of French-Canadian nationalism. With the arrival in Canada in the mid-20th century of ethnic groups unrelated to either of the major cultures there has been a tendency on the part of the churches closely identified with these new Canadians to foster Old-World cultural activities, and thus to transform Canada into a multicultural society. Whatever may be the defects of culture religions, and there are many, they seem to be the inevitable outcome of Canadian national development.

Religious Census. Because of the close identity of culture and religion, Canadians show great interest in the decennial religious census. The 1961 census was of unusual interest; it revealed that Protestants (46.5%) and Roman Catholics (45.7%) were nearly equal in numbers. (Ten years earlier the Roman Catholic proportion was 43.3%.)

The United Church of Canada (20.1%)—a blend of Methodist, Presbyterian, and Congregational traditions—was the largest Protestant denomination, the Anglican Church of Canada (14.7%) second, and the Presbyterian Church (4.5%) third. The country's fastest-growing religious groups were the Lutherans (3.6%) and Pentecostals (0.8%); in 10 years the former had increased memberships by about a half and the Pentecostals by slightly more.

Canada is still fruitful soil for sectarian movements. (The Dominion Bureau of Statistics lists well over 200 types of religious affiliations.) However, the gains made by the Pentecostal and allied fundamentalist groups such as the Adventist and Holiness churches will not much alter the Canadian social scene.

Common Pattern. There can be little doubt that the three churches that dominate the Canadian scene are the Roman Catholic, the United, and the Anglican, and that they follow a common pattern peculiar to Canada, evident most strikingly in their deep sense of responsibility for national development, but also in similar social activities and in the formation of church societies for historical, theological, and biblical research. Nor should it be overlooked that 8 out of 10 Canadians belong to one or other of these three churches. That this common pattern will be followed more vigorously in the future than in the past seems evident from the fact that two of these churches announced in the mid-1960's their intention to proceed toward organic union on the basis of a document entitled *The Principles of Union between the Anglican Church of Canada and the United Church of Canada.*

Toward a National Protestant Church. These principles are regarded by the negotiating churches as a restatement of the faith which "the Church has always held in Jesus Christ," and it is hoped that they will become the basis of an organizational structure both episcopal and reformed. They were confirmed by the General Synod of the Anglican Church in 1965 and by the General Council of the United Church of Canada in 1966. A commission on union composed of 20 representatives of each church was later set up to be "responsible for and supervise other commissions on constitutional, legal, doctrinal and liturgical matters." When this union is consummated, either this united church or the Roman Catholic Church will be numerically dominant in each province of Canada.

Such a union as that contemplated by the United Church and the Anglican has been opposed by some churchmen because of the fear that it will produce a "closed society" in contrast to a progressive society. Despite these fears, there seems little doubt that the proposed union will be consummated, since it represents a long-standing deep-felt urge in Canadian development—a national Protestant church.

At the time of the British conquest the Church of England had aspired to displace the Roman Catholic Church in the newly acquired province and to take on the responsibility of creating a homogeneous society in British North America. The Scottish Kirk was not adverse to such a project, but it wanted a share in the establishment since it was also an established church within the British Empire. Among the Wesleyan Methodists there was some support for such an establishment.

An upsurge of frontier sectarianism made all attempts for an established Anglican church futile; nevertheless the ideal of a Protestant national church as a balance to French-Canadian Catholicism never quite faded from Canadian consciousness and was greatly stimulated after Confederation in 1867.

Nationhood. Behind Confederation was the desire on the part of both French- and English-speaking colonists to move out of the colonial stage and become citizens of a self-governing dominion. This desire became so strong that even religious controversy was stilled in its presence. Next to the desire of nationhood was the fear of absorption into the United States, which weighted the scales on the side of Confederation in the final debate in the united legislature of Upper and Lower Canada.

Territorial Churches—*Presbyterian*. Immediately after Confederation, leading churchmen undertook to create territorial churches coterminous with the national boundaries of the new nation.

The first to take the lead in this direction were the Presbyterians. In the early days of settlement there had been an awareness among competing Presbyterian sects of the incongruity of continuing in North America the divisions that had arisen out of special political circumstances in Scotland. In 1836 the Kirk synods of the Maritime provinces opened negotiations for a union of all branches of Presbyterianism. A similar offer was made in the Canadas and the secession churches were not unresponsive.

Thus, it appeared that, by mid-century at least, Presbyterianism would become one church. But the Great Disruption in Scotland changed such rosy hopes into the blackest despair. In a remarkably short time, however, disruptions came to an end, and the movement toward union resumed its course. By 1875 all the independent Presbyterian churches were incorporated into the General Assembly of the Presbyterian Church in Canada, with the basis of union including a reaffirmation of the Westminster Confession of Faith and the longer and shorter catechisms.

Methodist. First among the other larger groups to follow the Presbyterian example were the Methodists. Their path to unity, however, was strewn with far greater obstacles than those encountered by the Presbyterians. One of the worst of these was the ill feeling generated between two traditions that looked back to either British or American origins: the latter had come to Canada during the great religious revivals on the Western frontier; the former arrived during the War of 1812, when the loyalty of American circuit riders was under great suspicion. The tensions that arose over the many issues that troubled the Methodist conscience finally led to a separation of the rival traditions into two conferences; but this was of brief duration and reunion was brought about in 1847.

Reunion of these two major branches was a preliminary step toward the creation of an autonomous Methodist Church in Canada, which included the Wesleyan Methodist churches of the Maritimes and such splinter groups as the Primitive Methodist, the Bible Christian, and the New Connexion churches. By 1884, it was the largest Protestant church in Canada, representing about 17.8% of the population. The Methodists were for the most part Arminian and pragmatic and were deeply interested in the improvement of the social order. They developed what the Methodist historian Goldwin French has called "a Canadian Methodist mind," which explains their unusual influence in shaping the cultural and social outlook of English-speaking Canada.

Anglican. Surprisingly, the Anglican was the last of the larger denominations to create a territorial church. The delay was due to the fact that as the Church of England in Canada it had depended upon the Imperial parliament as the basis of its presence in the colonies. When that parliament withdrew support, the church had to find a new apologetic for its claim for loyalty on the part of its membership. There now emerged in many quarters a strong emphasis upon historical continuity with the primitive church, with particular stress upon apostolic succession. These high-church views were shared by most of the bishops appointed by the crown in the middle of the 19th century, but many of the clergy and the laity were still strongly evangelical.

It was in the midst of suspicion and recriminations of high- and low-church factions that the Anglicans had to face the crisis of disestablishment.

D. ASHLEY, FROM NATIONAL FILM BOARD

CHRIST CHURCH ANGLICAN CATHEDRAL in Ottawa blends dignity with simplicity in its interior design.

To meet this crisis the bishop of Quebec called a conference in 1851 which was attended by most of the colonial bishops. The conference called for the formation of diocesan synods with lay representation as a substitute for the authority that had formerly been exercised by the Crown; it also called for an observance of Prayer Book formularies and an adherence to the Thirty-nine Articles. Thus the groundwork was laid for the formation of a territorial church, which came to pass with the creation in 1893 of the General Synod of the Church of England in Canada (now the Anglican Church of Canada).

Newlights and Baptists. The next-largest group after the Anglicans to attempt to create a national church were the Baptists. They had more disunity to contend with than any of the other conventional churches because of the conception that each local church must be an independent democracy. But Baptists also had behind them, especially in the Maritimes, a most disruptive history, associated with a doctrine of Newlightism. At the center of the Newlight movement in Nova Scotia was a rather boisterous farm boy, Henry Alline, whose spiritual and mental turmoil preceding his determination to become a preacher is told in vivid detail in his *Journal* (1836), and was probably typical of the religious experience of many young men and women of New England Puritan background living in the out settlements of Nova Scotia during the American Revolution. The mystical gospel which he preached with much vehemence throughout Nova

Scotia did not long survive his death, but his demand to bring religion to the test of feeling and experience was taken up by other sects and became a determining influence in the social and political development of the Maritimes.

Before Newlightism disappeared as an organized church it had destroyed New England Congregationalism in Nova Scotia. The chief beneficiary from this disintegration of Congregationalism was the Baptist Church. An attack by Bishop Charles Inglis, the first Anglican bishop of British North America (consecrated in 1787), upon the Newlights as "engaged in a general plan of total revolution in religion" and civil government, persuaded the Newlights to find a name less suspect to the ruling authorities. They began to call themselves the Baptist and Congregational Association of Nova Scotia; soon Congregational disappeared from the title and they were designated as the Nova Scotian Baptist Association. During the transference they became more conservative and dogmatic, adhering to the same faith "as set forth by upwards of one hundred congregations in Great Britain in the year 1687, and adopted by the Association of Philadelphia in 1742."

Not all Newlights were happy about this transference into a rigid creedal religion but, despite the internal stresses, there was finally organized a Maritime Baptist Convention which put forward in 1908 a plan for uniting all Free Baptists of Canada into one national church. When it was submitted to the Baptist Convention of Ontario and Quebec, which was oriented toward the Regular Baptist tradition of unqualified election and close communion, it did not receive a very enthusiastic welcome; nevertheless, the plan continued to be discussed year after year until at last, in 1944, there emerged a very loosely formed Baptist Federation of Canada, representing some 4.2% of the population of Canada.

Lutheran and Congregational. The other denominations that attempted to organize themselves on a territorial basis, with even less success than the Baptists, were the Lutheran and Congregational.

The latter, as we have seen, were practically wiped out in the Maritimes; in the Canadas they hardly appeared as distinct from the Presbyterians. Congregations did emerge, however, here and there across Canada and did achieve a very fragile federation about 1906. Surprisingly, this federation played an important role in the formation of the United Church of Canada.

In the early stages of settlement in the British colonies Lutherans were inclined to identify themselves with Anglicanism. A distinction began to emerge when the Evangelical Synod of Pittsburgh started a mission in Canada in 1850. About 1879 the very conservative and vigorous Missouri Synod began work in Canada, and this was the beginning of the extension of the work of several American synods across the northern border. These were strengthened by a continuous immigration from Europe of ethnic groups adhering to the Lutheran church. With the exception of the Missouri Synod, the many varieties of Lutheranism in Canada are all now fraternally associated with the Canada Lutheran Council, which has asserted an extremely conservative theological position.

Church Union. The mixing of a great variety of ethnic groups in western Canada has enforced a necessary toleration of creeds and cultures in that part of the country. Thus the west became fruitful soil for moral and religious experiments and an arena for one of the most significant developments in ecumenism—the creation of the United Church of Canada. As early as 1904 a joint Committee of Union, consisting of representatives from the Presbyterian, Methodist and Congregational churches, was set up. A basis of union, completed in 1908, attempted to create a delicate balance between the Calvinism of the Westminster Confession and the Arminianism of John Wesley.

Because of much hesitation on the part of the Presbyterians, actual union by act of Parliament was not achieved until 1925, with a goodly number of Presbyterians remaining outside and continuing under the old title of the Presbyterian Church of Canada. Nor was the opposition to church union confined to the Presbyterians alone; in point of fact all the remaining major churches viewed the United Church with considerable apprehension, fearing its attraction as a national church, particularly to new Canadians.

Sectarian Revival. At first these fears appeared to be ill founded, for a fresh outbreak of sectarianism in western Canada blunted the appeal of the new church. For the origin of this latest outbreak of sectarianism it is necessary to look beyond the borders of Canada to Europe and perhaps more immediately to the United States. A Holiness movement within the membership of the Methodist Church of the United States was at first welcomed by Canadian Methodists. Ralph Horner, a Methodist evangelistic preacher, took it up with great fervor, but soon found himself at odds with the newly organized church of 1884. In 1886 he broke with his church and organized a considerable following into a Holiness Movement Church, popularly known as the Hornerites. For a time the new sect entered upon a very expansive career, but dissensions among the Hornerites led to a rather rapid decline of the movement.

The Salvation Army. A major contribution to this decline was the appearance in Canada in 1883 of the Salvation Army. It made a strong appeal to uprooted people in urban centers. At first municipal authorities were horrified by the army's unorthodox methods of preaching and tried to suppress out-of-doors religious services. Persecution only served to add to its popularity among social outcasts. Within a short time after its arrival there were few urban centers where a local army had not been organized. Its mass appeal as a conversion religion has considerably diminished in the mid-20th century; nevertheless, it still has a following of some 92,000 members in Canada, representing 0.5% of the population.

Urban Sects. With the decline of the Hornerites and the Salvation Army as evangelizing forces, the way was opened for a large influx of sects from the United States. Among the new arrivals were several varieties of Holiness sects, the most conspicuous being the Nazarenes. A serious rival to the Holiness movement was the Pentecostal Church, whose rapid growth in recent years has been noted. Although Ontario still continues to lead all the other provinces in the variety and number of sect religions, their greatest influence is in western Canada, simply because they represent a higher percentage of the population. A fundamentalist interpretation of the Bible seems to be their greatest asset, particularly in winning converts from the conventional churches.

Fundamentalism. Fundamentalism had become a serious issue in most churches in the first quarter of the 20th century, but it seems to have fragmented the Baptist Church more than others. It was particularly strong in western Canada where it offered —and still does—greater security to disturbed

NOTRE DAME CHURCH in Place d'Armes, Montreal, was erected in the 1820's.

J. ALLAN CASH, FROM RAPHO GUILLUMETTE

people than the cultic movements that also were attempting to convey "peace of mind" through an eclectic combination of spiritual healing, mysticism, metaphysics, and various other comforts. Fundamentalism in the west is creating a sense of unity among the sects not enjoyed by the cults, particularly in the political and social life of the area. It was on this common interest in an inerrant Bible that William Aberhart, with his slogan "Back to the Bible" was enabled to organize a political party and became premier of Alberta.

Social Reform. The modern-day sects, in contrast to earlier sects in Canada, are far to the right politically and offer little hope for social reform. Any serious attempts at social reform initiated by religious groups, with the outstanding exception of the Quakers and Unitarians, must come from liberal groups within the conventional churches. It is now recognized, however, that in a highly specialized society church pronouncements in the fields of industry and agriculture must be based upon research by competent experts.

As it is difficult for churches with limited budgets to secure such services, it was decided to emulate the churches of the United States and to set up a central church council similar to the National Council of the Churches of Christ in the United States of America. Thus came into being the Canadian Council of Churches, which was commended to the Anglican Synod in 1943 on the basis "that we must have sufficient organization to examine more closely into industrial and economic matters." Up to the present the Canadian Council has not obtained the same prestige as the mouthpiece of Canadian Protestantism as has the National Council of the United States. Part of the failure is due to the lack of fervor for cooperative denominationalism in Canada. And so the search for a national church of Canada goes on, the latest phase being the current attempt to unite the Anglican and the United churches.

H. H. WALSH, *McGill University*

Bibliography

Armstrong, Maurice W., *The Great Awakening in Nova Scotia* (Hartford, Conn., 1948).
Clark, Samuel Delbert, *Church and Sect in Canada* (Toronto 1949).
Dawson, Carl Addington, *Group Settlements; Ethnic Communities in Western Canada* (Toronto 1936).
Grant, John Webster, ed., *The Churches and the Canadian Experience* (Toronto 1963).
Latourette, Kenneth S., *Christianity in a Revolutionary Age* (New York 1961).
McNeill, John Thomas, *The Presbyterian Church in Canada, 1875–1925* (Toronto 1925).
Pascoe, C. F., *Two Hundred Years of the S. P. G.* (London 1901).
Saunders, E. M., *History of the Baptists of the Maritime Provinces* (Halifax, Nova Scotia, 1902).
Silcox, Charles Edwin, *Church Union in Canada* (New York 1933).
Walsh, Henry Horace, *The Christian Church in Canada* (Toronto 1956).
Walsh, Henry Horace, *The Church in the French Era* (Toronto 1966).

33. Roman Catholic Church

The Roman Catholic Church is the largest of all religious denominations in Canada. The 8.5 million Catholics comprise approximately 46% of the total population. They are found in every province, but more than 30% of all Catholics reside in the province of Quebec.

Administration. For administrative purposes, the church is divided into 61 archdioceses and dioceses headed by the same number of archbishops and bishops. In some dioceses there are assistant coadjutors and bishops. The apostolic delegate is the official representative of the pope in Canada. The post was first established in 1899 by Pope Pius X. In the late 1960's, Canada had three cardinals. The first cardinal in Canada, Monsignor Taschereau, was consecrated in 1886.

There are over 9,000 diocesan priests, about 6,000 priests in religious orders, and more than 6,000 brothers. The religious orders are engaged in parochial ministry, teaching, preaching, and charitable work. Some of the longest established and well known orders are the Franciscans, Jesuits, Sulpicians, Cistercians, Oblates, Basilians, Resurrectionists, Dominicans, and Redemptorists. The 185 communities of women religious in Canada have over 52,000 members, and are devoted to work in hospitals, education, orphanages, and other forms of charity. The church in Canada provides more overseas missionaries per capita than any other country with the possible exception of Ireland.

Roles of the Church. The church plays an important role in social and economic fields, such as labor relations, development of cooperatives, and social welfare. One can mention here only the

Antigonish Movement in Nova Scotia which has had worldwide repercussions and has served as a training ground for community leaders from many countries.

Education is another major interest of the church. There are 20 Catholic colleges and universities with degree-conferring powers, and many federated Catholic colleges. There are also a great number of Catholic schools meeting the high standards demanded in each province.

Roman Catholicism serves also as a unifying force between English and French Canadians, with large numbers of both of the great founding peoples sharing membership in the church. But Canada is more than a nation of two cultures. Since the turn of the century other ethnic groups (with large Catholic percentages) have increased in size and number to the point where 23% of Canada's population is of neither French nor English origin. Here again the Catholic Church is a unifying force, and uses more languages in its parish work than any other religious group. In the English, French, Polish, and Hungarian parishes of a large metropolitan center like Toronto, one may see all the rich varieties of Canada's cultural mosaic.

Ecumenical Movement. In recent years the church has been closely involved in the ecumenical movement in Canada. Interfaith services are common, and in 1963 an ecumenical center was established in Montreal. The *Ecumenist,* a bimonthly journal for encouraging Christian unity, is published by the Centre of Ecumenical Studies at St. Michael's College, Toronto. The ecumenical spirit was demonstrated in the decision of the Roman Catholic Church and six Protestant churches to cooperate in a Pavilion of Christian Unity at Expo 67 in Montreal. Father Martucci, the secretary of the project, summarized this interfaith spirit of cooperation and understanding: "Sharing the same faith, the same hope and the same charity [we] want to bear the same witness to Christ and his Gospel."

History Under French Rule. The extension of the Catholic faith was a part of France's policy from the time that explorers and settlers were first sent to North America in the 16th century. Missionaries worked in the ill-fated settlement of Acadia even before the founding of Quebec (1608), which marked the first significant French achievement in colonizing Canada. The Franciscan Récollets were the first missionaries at Quebec (1613) but were soon followed by the Jesuits, who came to be the backbone of the missionary efforts in Canada.

The church provided for the spiritual needs of the few settlers but worked mainly in the interior among Algonquin and Huron-Iroquois tribes. Work was interrupted when the English captured New France in 1629, but recommenced immediately after restoration of the colony in 1632. The Jesuits concentrated their efforts among the settled Hurons in the Georgian Bay district, where native conversions seemed most promising. However, in the 1640's these missions were destroyed along with most of the Huron nation when the Iroquois launched an all-out offensive to eliminate the French and their Indian allies as competitors in the fur trade. This was the occasion of the heroic deaths of eight Jesuits (the North American Martyrs), including Jean de Brébeuf and Gabriel Lalemant.

Elsewhere, the church continued its missionary work as priests sought to make new converts and to maintain contact with the scattered remnants of the Huron nation. Preceding and accompanying the explorer and fur trader, they crossed to Hudson Bay, the Lake of the Woods, the Mississippi River, and Illinois country, winning fame not only as devoted and energetic men of God, but also as explorers. Although they made few converts, their heroism was an inspiration to the early church and society in Canada. Fathers Joseph Le Caron, Jean Dolbeau, Paul Le Jeune, René Ménard, Claude Allouez, Jacques Marquette, and many others well earned their eminence in Canada's history.

Serving the Colonists. Toward the end of the 17th century the great age of missions passed. The missionary zeal of the church in Canada was in part an extension of the religious fervor generated by the Catholic Reformation in Europe, and this phenomenon of religious enthusiasm was still a vital force in France when colonizing efforts first began. However, as the century progressed, the energies of the Catholic Reformation ebbed. Moreover, the population of New France continued to grow and the church was asked to provide a widening range of services for the colony.

The Jesuits continued the educational work begun by the Récollets, serving both French and Indians. A college was opened at Quebec in 1635, the first north of Spanish America. In 1639 Marie de l'Incarnation and her Ursuline nuns established a school for Indian girls at Quebec. In the same year the Hospitaller sisters began work at a Hôtel Dieu (hospital). At the site of the present-day city of Montreal a mission was established in 1641 by the courageous Sieur de Maisonneuve under the direction of the Society of Our Lady of Montreal. Here a hospital was founded by Jeanne Mance, a member of that society, and a school was opened by the Congregation of Notre Dame under their founder Marguerite Bourgeoys. In 1657 the Sulpicians arrived to become the dominant order in Montreal and contribute to missionary work in Canada.

As the population continued to grow, the services of the church steadily expanded. Elementary, secondary, post-secondary, and technical schools were founded. Many fine libraries were established. Charities for the needy and indigent were provided. The church aided and initiated local industries through loans and gifts. The fine arts were encouraged and many orders established model farms. The annual reports of the Jesuits, the *Relations,* kept interest alive in France and encouraged the sending of immigrants and assistance to the colony. Furthermore, missionaries served New France by acting as diplomatic agents and encouraging Indians in political and economic loyalty to the colony. The church was aided in its work by large grants of land and the collection of tithes. The historian Marcel Trudel asserts that the allotment to the church of one quarter of all land granted during the French regime was only a just share for the services rendered. By the time of the first census in Canada (1666) there were 3,215 inhabitants, a bishop, 18 secular priests, 31 Jesuits, 19 Ursulines, 23 Hospitallers, and 4 Sisters of the Congregation.

Church-State Relations. The first bishop, François de Montmorency-Laval, had arrived in 1659. A dynamic and aggressive leader, he contributed to the vitality of the church, centralized control of the clergy, and opened seminaries, but he also came into conflict with civil authorities.

Mutual esteem and cooperation were most characteristic of church-state relations in New

France, although friction occasionally developed. The liquor trade with the Indians was one source of chronic difficulties. The moral and physical harm to the natives was self-evident and led to forthright church opposition. However, the economic factor was inextricably entangled with the moral issue and many in government and society supported the brandy trade in spite of the church's position. Nonetheless, society always deeply appreciated the presence of the church. Moreover, with French Protestants (Huguenots) excluded since the 1620's, there naturally developed a striking similarity of religious outlook which contributed to the cohesiveness of society.

Later Years. In 1713 a long period of peace, steady growth, and general prosperity began for the colony of over 18,000 inhabitants, 56 priests, and 182 sisters. In the three main centers of Quebec, Montreal, and Trois Rivières, and in each parish was to be seen the familiar and beloved church steeple and related school. Bishop Henri Marie Dubreuil de Pontbriand, who occupied the see after 1741, reorganized clergy retreats, and restored and enlarged the cathedral at Quebec. By this time, however, the "golden age of New France" was drawing to a close.

In 1755 the French settlers were expelled from Acadia, which had been ceded to England in 1713. Shortly after, priests were excluded. In 1756 the final clash between two empires competing for sovereignty of a continent began. Bishop Pontbriand, the last bishop of New France, died in 1760. By the Treaty of Paris (1763) the colony and the church passed under the direct control of England.

History Under British Rule—*Early Uncertainty.* After the conquest, the church in Canada viewed the future with justifiable uncertainty. Many of the leaders of society had returned to France and the church remained as the one organization able to offer strength and direction to the 65,000 vanquished people. But could it survive in a hostile empire? Admittedly, the peace treaty granted freedom of religion but only "as far as the laws of Great Britain permit." This was a dubious concession since little toleration of Catholicism was permitted under British law.

Fortunately, England's hostile policy of anglicization of language and religion was applied with neither consistency nor determination. All connections with Rome were made illegal, and repressive actions were taken against the male religious communities which led to the extinction of several religious orders in Canada. But a vast influx of English-speaking Protestants, essential to the success of British policy, was not forthcoming, and in 1766, Britain permitted Bishop Jean Olivier Briand to fill the vacant see in Canada. However, the British withheld official recognition of the title of bishop. In the 1790's clerical exiles were permitted to come from France following the anticlerical excesses of the French Revolution. By this time relations had improved between the church and the British government.

Path to Survival. The Catholic Church, while asserting its rights, had counseled acceptance and loyalty to the new regime after 1763 and the British were appreciative. The Quebec Act (1774) reflected a more conciliatory attitude toward the church and the French Canadians by extending to them many of the rights enjoyed under the French regime. British policy was partly prompted by concern over mounting unrest in the Thirteen American Colonies. The concessions to the church in Canada proved timely. When the American Revolution came, the church ensured the loyalty of French Canada to the British Crown, and, as A. R. M. Lower says, "sealed the alliance between the two authorities, secular and spiritual."

The coming of the English-speaking Loyalists to Canada led to demands for changes in the colony. The Constitutional Act (1791) altered the system of government and separated the English and French into Upper and Lower Canada, but the guarantees of religious liberty in the Quebec Act were not repealed. Nevertheless, the arrival of Loyalists in Canada encouraged some authorities to attempt to weaken the church's position. Bishops Jean François Hubert (1788–1796) and Pierre Denault (1796–1806) struggled to maintain church independence from the state, and their efforts were crowned by the successes of Bishop Joseph Octave Plessis, one of the most courageous, capable and respected leaders of the period.

The outbreak of the War of 1812 was fortunate for Bishop Plessis' purposes. French-Canadian loyalty was again a prized commodity, and the hierarchy ensured that it was forthcoming. Britain showed its gratitude by officially recognizing the title of bishop, by assigning him a seat on the Legislative Council, and by granting an annual stipend to the church. Meanwhile, Bishop Plessis took action to meet the needs of the expanding church in Canada.

Expansion. In the Maritime provinces a steadily increasing Catholic population of Scots, Irish, and returned Acadians made many demands on the few English- and French-speaking priests in the area. Bishop Plessis visited the region, and the vicariates apostolic of New Brunswick and Nova Scotia were erected in 1817 and 1819, respectively. In 1818, Father Edmund Burke became the first bishop of the Maritimes at Halifax.

An appeal for priests from the small settlement of Red River in the Northwest led Bishop Plessis to dispatch Fathers Joseph Norbert Provencher and Sévère Dumoulin to the area. In 1820, Father Provencher was consecrated bishop of the newly created suffragan see of the Northwest, and until his death in 1853 performed herculean tasks for his church and country in opening up the territory.

In 1819 the province of Upper Canada was made a Vicariate Apostolic. Father Alexander Macdonell had first come to Glengarry county in 1803 to serve the Scottish Catholics in the area. In 1826, when he was made bishop of the newly erected episcopal see at Kingston, there were 15,000 Catholics in Upper Canada.

Years of Tension. The 1830's were years of increased immigration, epidemics, and political discontent which culminated in rebellions. The unsanitary conditions in overcrowded vessels bringing immigrants to Canada led to periodic outbreaks of cholera among the new arrivals and colonists. Many priests and nuns sacrificed their lives in ministering to the sick and dying. When rebellions broke out in Upper and Lower Canada in 1837–1838, the hierarchy denounced the appeal to violence and thereby limited the scope of the risings. The church in Lower Canada had cooperated with the reformers for a time, but when leaders like Louis Joseph Papineau became more violent in their demands, the church withdrew its support and thereby guaranteed the failure of the rebellion.

Survival Assured. After the union of Upper and Lower Canada in 1841, legislation provided for separate schools for religious minorities. The church was further gratified by legislation in 1851 which affirmed "the free exercise and enjoyment of . . . religious worship in the Canadas."

Thus, by the 1860's, the fears of a century earlier were completely dissipated and the church stood as a powerful and dynamic force in society. New dioceses were created. Religious communities increased in size and numbers. The Oblates of Mary Immaculate had already commenced their heroic endeavors in the Northwest, and the Grey Nuns had gone to the same area. Bishop Ignace Bourget of Montreal encouraged many religious orders to come to Canada and, by the time of Confederation, Jesuits, Sulpicians, Christian Brothers, Franciscans, Fathers of the Holy Cross, and the Clerics of St. Viateur were all contributing to the vigor of the church in Canada. Many new Catholic colleges were opened before 1867.

After Confederation. In the years after Confederation in 1867, the hierarchy continued to grow. By the early 1900's there were 8 archdioceses, 23 dioceses, three vicariates apostolic, 3,500 priests, about 30 men's religious communities, 70 communities of women religious, and over 2 million Catholics, comprising 42% of the total population of Canada.

Unfortunately these years of growth were occasionally marred by outbursts of religious and racial antagonism. The close identification between French Canada and the Catholic Church make it virtually impossible to delineate clearly between racial and religious emotions at play during the various disputes. In 1885, Louis Riel was executed for his part in leading a rebellion of French-speaking Métis of Saskatchewan. Despite church efforts to moderate the passions of the time, many in Quebec viewed Riel as a martyr to religious and racial bigotry in English Canada. In 1890, Manitoba followed the earlier example of New Brunswick and abolished separate schools. Bishop Louis Philippe Adélard Langevin fought vigorously for the continuation of separate schools in Manitoba, but was forced to accept what he viewed as an unsatisfactory compromise after Wilfrid Laurier became prime minister in 1896.

Since the turn of the century, Protestant-Catholic relations have steadily improved, and the spirit of compromise, conciliation, and cooperation characteristic of Canada's history has prevailed.

THOMAS K. CAVANAGH
St. Patrick's College, Ottawa

Bibliography

Brown, George W., ed., *Canada* (Toronto 1950).
Bull, William P., *From Macdonell to McGuigan: History of the Growth of the Roman Catholic Church in Upper Canada* (Toronto 1940).
Dominic of St.-Denis, *L'église catholique au Canada* (Montreal 1956).
Lanctôt, Gustave, *A History of Canada*, 3 vols. (Toronto 1963–1965).
Lower, Arthur Reginald Marsden, *Canadians in the Making* (Toronto 1958).
Sissons, Charles B., *Church and State in Canadian Education* (Toronto 1959).
Walsh, Henry Horace, *The Christian Church in Canada* (Toronto 1956).

34. Other Religious Groups

Canada has a number of sects and religious groups outside the general framework of the Protestant or Roman Catholic traditions. The most important of these are treated briefly below.

The faith with the largest number of adherents apart from the Protestant and Roman Catholic traditions is Judaism. Jews, most of them descended from exiles from Spain and Portugal, began to arrive in Canada soon after the British conquest. Following the serious outburst of anti-Semitism in eastern Europe about 1880, there was an increasingly large influx of Jewish refugees to Canada. The figure reached about 75,000 in 1911. More recent immigration has increased the Jewish population to more than 250,000, or about 1.4% of the Canadian population. Judaism in Canada is fragmented into Orthodox, Conservative, and Reform groups.

Next numerically are groups of Christians allied in spirit to Eastern Orthodoxy. The Russian Orthodox Church, because of its political divisions, passed through a confusing period. The old Orthodox autonomous church, which refuses to recognize the patriarch at Moscow, has its representatives in Canada, as does a pro-Soviet group. There are also Russian émigrés who are in communion with the patriarch of Constantinople.

Much the largest of the ethnic groups from eastern Europe are the Ukrainian (Greek) Catholics, a Uniat church, which for a time was under the direction of the Presbyterian Church. The group broke with both the Roman Catholic and Presbyterian churches (1918) to form a very democratically based church with a bishop of its own.

The Mennonites, originating out of the Anabaptist branch of the Reformation, began as a brotherhood attempting to carry out literally the principles of the Sermon on the Mount. They developed strong economic communities that were in continual conflict with state authorities, and this to some extent has been their history in Canada. Their divisions, a complicated story, have produced six varieties of the Mennonite religion in Canada.

Closely allied to them are the Hutterites and the Doukhobors. The former have established firmly knit communal settlements; the latter have been less successful in maintaining their own peculiar way of life and have broken into many rival groups.

According to the 1961 official census, there are about 20,000 Christian Scientists in Canada, with more than 200 registered healing practitioners. Most of these are concentrated in the larger cities.

The Mormons are now a considerable sect with a following of about 50,000, principally concentrated in southwestern Alberta. Economically they have been very successful and have built a huge granite temple at Cardston, Alberta.

Jehovah's Witnesses, directed by the Watch Tower and Bible Tract Society in Brooklyn, N. Y., are a rapidly growing sect, asserting with vigor what they believe to be Christianity as it was practiced during the first two centuries of the Christian era.

Oriental religions form small minority groups. There are about ten Buddhist temples in Canada and a few Islamic mosques. Since the establishment in 1952 of the Institute of Islamic Studies at McGill University, a number of Muslim professors and research students have resided in Montreal.

Other Groups. Among the psychical comfort religions, there are many different forms of expression, ranging from Father Divine's Peace Mission Movement to Bahaism, which stresses the oneness of mankind, world peace, and universal language. Both these, along with Unity Truth, Church of Truth, Divine Science, Spiritualists, Rosicrucians, Christadelphians, and several others, have their missions in Canada.

H. H. WALSH, *McGill University*

"NORTHERN LIGHTS," BY TOM THOMSON, 1877-1917 (MONTREAL MUSEUM OF FINE ARTS).

CANADA: Culture

Canada's cultural life lagged behind other aspects of national development for more than 200 years and it was not until the mid-20th century that a sudden and comprehensive growth occurred in the complex pattern of Canadian painting and architecture, literature and the theater, music, publishing, broadcasting and films. The growth was directly influenced by economic, political and social factors and it reflected the emerging spirit of national pride and confidence seen throughout the contemporary Canadian picture. Canada now enjoys a cultural life which is vigorous in manner and universal in outlook and the arts are generously encouraged by both government and private patronage—notably by the Canada Council for the encouragement of the arts, humanities and social sciences, established by the federal government in 1957.

35. Art and Architecture

The story of the visual arts in Canada, from the early days of exploration and pioneering through the period of settlement and development, against the background of two world wars and into the contemporary scene, was marked by two periods of notable vitality. The first was from 1910 to 1930, when the vigorous and rebellious painters who were known as the "Group of Seven" introduced a strong nationalistic flavor, and during the 1960's, when contemporary international standards characterized the work of most Canadian painters. In relation to painting, the arts of architecture, graphics, sculpture, and fine crafts have been of secondary importance in Canada.

Early Painting. The earliest painting in Canada was the work of self-taught, unimaginative French settlers and clergymen who, encouraged by their church, produced works of great religious and moral value and minor artistic merit. The early English artists were mainly military men and land surveyors whose reportorial drawings and topographical sketches were fastidiously correct. Most of this early work was purposeful and functional and involved little of the "self-expression" factor that became the main concern of later painters. Substantial collections of early Canadian paintings and drawings are found in leading museums and art galleries throughout North America, and to a lesser extent in France and Britain.

Not until the middle of the 19th century did Canadian painters gain personal recognition beyond their immediate home localities. The first whose names appear in the records were Paul Kane (1810–1871), a young Irishman who settled in what is now Toronto, and Cornelius Krieghoff (1812–1872), who came from either Amsterdam or Düsseldorf to French Canada.

Between 1845 and 1860, Kane distinguished himself as a traveler and as a painter of the Indian peoples throughout Canada. His most notable

NATIONAL GALLERY OF CANADA, OTTAWA

PORTRAIT OF SOEUR SAINT-ALPHONSE, by Antoine Plamondon (1804–1895), a painter of Quebec.

journey took him from Toronto to the Pacific coast, when he accompanied a group of Hudson's Bay Company *voyageurs* through the midcontinent system of lakes and rivers, across the prairies and over the Rocky Mountains and back. He made more than 500 careful sketches of the countryside and of the Indians and later completed a large number of full-scale oils and published a book, *Wanderings of an Artist.*

His noted contemporary, Krieghoff, was a prolific portraitist and genre painter whose work was concerned almost entirely with the life and people of French Canada. He was a *bon vivant* intimately acquainted with both the fashionable urban scene and the day-to-day joys and tragedies of the country people, and his eager brush found subject matter wherever he happened to be. The works of both these men are notable collectors' items on both sides of the Atlantic Ocean today, and their names are probably the first to appear in art histories as representative Canadian painters.

Before and after Kane and Krieghoff, chronologically, a number of Canadian painters won local acclaim, and their names are milestones in all the histories of Canadian art. François Beaucourt (1740–1794), Joseph Légaré (1789–1885), and Antoine Plamondon (1804–1895) were early French Canadians whose works have lasted well and are prized by museums and galleries today. Daniel Fowler (1810–1894), Otto Jacobi (1812–1901), Lucius O'Brien (1832–1899), and Paul Peel (1859–1892) are notable names among the early English Canadian painters who lived and worked in central Canada. In Nova Scotia, Robert Field (1769–1819) and William Valentine (1798–1849) were portraitists whose works are still exhibited by galleries in Canada and New England.

Many painters of those times were Canadian only in the geographical sense, having been born or raised in the country. Their painting was not Canadian in any sense. Young Canadians, of both the French-speaking and English-speaking areas, in the era prior to 1900, with ambitions to become painters, followed a well-established pattern. They learned the rudiments of painting skill at the studio of a local artist and then proceeded to England or the Continent for advanced training in artistic mannerisms and fashions. They absorbed the attitudes of European teachers and returned to Canada to paint the Canadian scene in the European manner. Some went to art schools in New England, where they learned European methods of painting at second hand. A number of able painters of Canadian origin became recognized by the patrons and galleries of Europe, but none of their work was recognizably Canadian.

NATIONAL GALLERY OF CANADA, OTTAWA

BLACKFOOT CHIEF AND SUBORDINATES, by Paul Kane (1810–1871), who worked from sketches which he made on journeys through the Canadian Indian country.

New Attitudes. Between 1900 and 1910 an important change of attitude was noted among painters in Toronto and Montreal, and a Canadian art movement was beginning to simmer. In Toronto, four well-established painters and teachers, William Cruikshank, Robert Holmes, Charles Jefferys, and Fred Brigden—were boldly advocating "a new approach to painting suited to the Canadian Scene." In Montreal, followers of Maurice Cullen and James W. Morrice were advocates of "a Canadian Manner of painting."

Leading critics and collectors in both cities were outspokenly opposed to the burgeoning new attitude, regarding it as "ostentatious nonsense." But many of the young Canadian painters became excited by the prospect of "liberation" from the formalities and rigidities of European painting. A most important group of Canadians at the time were the middle-aged art teachers who found that their European training and experience gave them virtually no inspiration or leadership for their young students, and who stimulated a spirit of rebellion and defiance in the Canadian art world. Another factor was the travel between the Canadian cities and New York, where artists had espoused novelty in every form.

In 1913 the first effective challenge to the conventionality of Canadian painting was seen when a small group of Toronto-based painters, led by J. E. H. MacDonald, inspired by Tom Thomson, and subsidized by Dr. J. M. McCallum, set out to reflect the magnificence of Canada's northland on canvases which would show a new, free Canadian spirit. The outbreak of World War I, a year later, was a solid setback to their eagerness. Immediately after the war, however, the painters came together again, without Thomson, who had died in 1917, and renewed their project. Concentrating on the flamboyantly rugged wilderness of the Algoma country and the north shore of Lake Superior, they traveled and painted tirelessly and produced an eloquently bold collection of canvases that shocked and dismayed the established critics.

The Group of Seven. The name "Group of Seven" was first used in 1920 by Frank Carmichael, Lawren Harris, A. Y. Jackson, Franz Johnston, Arthur Lismer, J. E. H. MacDonald, and Frederick Varley, who held their first bold and provocative exhibition at the Art Gallery of Toronto. Violent disapproval came instantly from the conventional critics and from the relatively unsophisticated public of Toronto. Abuse and scorn were showered upon the painters, individually and as a group, and there was widespread belief that the first exhibition by the Group of Seven would also be its last.

But the open-minded directorate of Canada's National Gallery stood by the bold new group, bought some of their canvases, and arranged for an important showing in London, England. Unexpectedly favorable reactions came from many of Britain's most respected art critics. In Paris the art fraternity enthusiastically admired the Group's powerful paintings. A number of art opinion leaders from the United States liked what the Group was exhibiting. This kind of praise could not be ignored by Canadians, and during the five years following the 1920 show a gradual, almost reluctant, acceptance of the Group of Seven took place. This was the greatest development in Canada's art history. The Group continued vigorous and effective for 10 years.

It seems unlikely that the influence of the Group of Seven upon Canada's cultural life will ever be forgotten, even though changing times and changing fashions may label their formidable canvases anachronisms. During its few active years the Group inspired many young Canadians to attempt to speak for Canada in art, music, theater, and creative writing; and the reverberations of that original inspiration are still felt. It broke down forever in Canada the rigidities of colonialism in art appreciation and brought a fresh approach to the concept of what Canada's participation in the art world should be. The Group of Seven came and went, and some critics argue that its overall influence was bad because it inspired a "school of Christmas Card Art" for young Canadians to revere. But such criticism should not be taken seriously. By 1950 the direct impact of the Group upon young and maturing Canadian paint-

NATIONAL GALLERY OF CANADA, OTTAWA

THE SOLEMN LAND, painted by J. E. H. MacDonald (1873–1932), a member of the "Group of Seven," who found many of his subjects in the Ontario wilderness.

ART GALLERY OF ONTARIO, TORONTO

BARNS, a typical work of A. Y. Jackson (1882–), who favored bold colors and flat designs in his paintings.

ers had dwindled notably, and during the 1960's there was virtually no imitation of the Group's mannerisms in the major exhibitions.

Outside the Group. Several painters who flourished simultaneously with the Group, but were not associated with it, deserve recognition in any account of Canadian art for they were men and women of outstanding artistic independence who provided important inspiration and leadership for young painters. In Quebec, the names of Clarence Gagnon, Albert Robinson, Lilias Newton, and John Lyman stand out. In British Columbia, the name of Emily Carr was monumental. David Milne, in Ontario, was unforgettable. In Winnipeg, Manitoba, Lemoyne Fitzgerald was a great teacher and painter whose originality and initiative won him a permanent place in Canada's art annals.

Contemporary Painting. Mounting excitement, change, and controversy marked the Canadian art scene during the 1930's through the 1960's. These decades saw Canadians experiencing the pleasures and joys and agonies and quarrels and despairs associated with periods of representational painting, nonobjective painting, regional painting, propaganda painting, hard-edge painting, and "pop" and "op" and psychedelic art, and intermediate forms of infinite variety. During these years it became obvious that Canada had become a full fledged member of the world art fraternity and was willing to meet the challenge of international standards and fashions. Achieving membership was not an easy process.

Increased Support and Instruction. Patronage of the arts was remarkably niggardly in Canada, at both the public and private levels, until well into the 1950's, when the federal government's decision to set up the Canada Council primed the pump for cultural subsidy throughout the country. At the same time greatly enlarged federal grants to the long-failing National Gallery of Canada and to the cultural division of the department of external affairs made it possible for Canada to take part, in a serious way, in the international art scene. By 1965 the visual arts in Canada presented a scene of unprecedented activity and variety, with public interest, governmental involvement, and professional excitement at high levels.

Canada's art schools have become jammed with students, and the demand for new teaching facilities has been insistent. At the university level, departments of fine arts are hard-pressed to supply the art historians, teachers, and museologists sought by institutions in all the provinces. Hundreds of adult courses in painting are thriving in all the cities and towns and in many villages throughout the land, and the terms "amateur" and "Sunday painter" are used as respectful designations. Awards and scholarships for artists are multiplying

Well-patronized exhibitions are frequent. International art exchanges between Canada and other countries are prestigious affairs. Sales of canvases and sculptured works are increasing in volume and value, and profitable commissions are common among most front-rank Canadian painters and sculptors. Reportage of art matters, which for more than a century was of little or no concern to most Canadian newspapers and journals, showed notable improvement during the 1960's, and indications are that a corps of trained and perceptive art critics is developing in Canada. At all levels of government the public purse has been opened to encourage the arts. In 1967, when Canadian artists stood at their country's centennial vantage point, looking back into the record of the years past and forward into the future's promise, it was said that they could not refrain from admitting that "things looked good."

Internationalism. Canadian artists are deeply involved in the world art scene. They paint like their contemporaries in New York, San Francisco, London, Paris, Warsaw, and Tokyo; not consciously influenced by the others, but definitely motivated by the same events and feelings and developments. They participate in international art shows, and they enter art competitions. They are represented by agents and dealers in other countries. They travel widely. They are citizens of the vast contemporary art world, an unbelievably far cry from the Canadian painters to whom they are linked in historical perspective.

Notable Teachers. Distinguished men and women and schools in all parts of Canada influenced the gradual, but inevitable, development from the

VISITORS ARE INVITED TO REGISTER, painted by Alex Colville (1920–). It represents the interior of the Old Covenanters' Church (built 1790), at Grand Pré, a village in Nova Scotia.

SASKATOON GALLERY AND CONSERVATORY CORPORATION

Canadian painter of 1930 to his modern counterpart. On the Pacific coast, for instance, a powerful, nonconformist Vancouver school of art was led by Fred Amess and Jack Shadbolt, whose influence upon the young artists of the day is seen clearly in many of the contemporary painters in all parts of Canada. Other West Coasters whose inspiration of young painters was notable included B. C. Binning, Bruno and Molly Bobak, Gordon Smith, and Lionel Thomas. The Prairie provinces nourished their own art movement, which brought to prominence the names of Joseph Plaskett, Takao Tanabe, Kenneth Lochhead, Roy Kiyooka, and Janet Mitchell. In the Atlantic provinces the names of Alex Colville, Jack Humphrey, Lawren Harris, Jr., and Robert Annand grew in prestige through the years of post-World War II turmoil and now stand in the grouping of top contemporary Canadian artists.

The rebellious and tempestuous "Montreal school" led by Alfred Pellan was rarely out of the news spotlight during the late 1940's and early 1950's and its radical subschool of Montreal "automatistes," sparked by Paul-Émile Borduas, kept temperatures running high in Quebec art circles. Followers of Pellan have risen to eminence, particularly Jacques de Tonnancour, Léon Bellefleur, and Robert Lapalme. Jean-Paul Riopelle, the eminently successful nonobjectivist who smashed his way into European favor in 1955 and has remained there ever since, was a student of Borduas. English-speaking Quebecers who were on the fringes

PAVANE, a triptych on canvas by Jean-Paul Riopelle (1923–), of the Montreal school of "Automatistes." His nonobjective works have become internationally famous.

NATIONAL GALLERY OF CANADA, OTTAWA

NATIONAL GALLERY OF CANADA, OTTAWA

ST. JOHN THE EVANGELIST (*left*), wood carving ascribed to François Baillairgé (1759–1830). *INDIENNES DE CAUGHNAWAGA* (*right*) by Aurèle de Foy Suzor-Coté (1869–1937).

of the Montreal school, Goodridge Roberts and Stanley Cosgrove, became notable elder statesmen of the Canadian art world.

At Queen's University, in Kingston, Ontario, André Biéler served as resident artist from 1936 to early in the 1960's, combining his talents as a fine artist with vigorous leadership of young painters in all parts of Canada. In Toronto, regarded from early times as the artistic capital of Canada, there was little of the feverish excitement and rebellion that characterized the Montreal school during the 1940's and 1950's, but the city's art development during the period was notable, and a number of top-ranking painters emerged, among them George Pepper, Will Ogilvie, Jack Nichols, Carl Schaefer, and Charles Comfort.

Gallery Activities. The National Gallery of Canada held its first biennial exhibition in 1955; its seventh was scheduled for 1968, having been postponed because of the national centennial exhibition in 1967. The intervening years were crowded with artistic activity in every part of Canada, featuring new developments, new trends, new organizations, new patrons, and, in great numbers, new artists. Engendered by improved communications, a buoyant economy, and a worldwide sense of disturbance, there was an astonishing awakening of public interest in all cultural matters and particularly a new, solid type of encouragement for painters and sculptors.

During this period encouragement of the arts by federal and provincial governments, mainly through specialized agencies, assumed unprecedented importance. The activities of the Canadian Broadcasting Corporation and the National Film Board became deeply involved in all art forms, and these two national bodies became important employers and patrons of Canadian art, music, and theater. During this period Canada's National Gallery was transformed from a dull, pedestrian, financially starved art warehousing agency into a vigorous, forward-looking, and bold and proud art gallery of international stature. The Toronto Art Gallery changed its name to The Art Gallery of Ontario and assumed new responsibilities and new challenges in keeping with these times. The Montreal Museum of Fine Arts grew suddenly, in tune with the spirit of its city, from a sleepy, wealthy, cultural giant to a vigorous gallery determined to keep abreast of the times. In Fredericton (New Brunswick), Charlottetown (Prince Edward Island), Quebec, Hamilton and London (Ontario), Winnepeg (Manitoba), Saskatoon (Saskatchewan), and Vancouver (British Columbia), public art galleries became institutions of pride and enjoyment, and in virtually every Canadian city, art galleries sponsored by private dealers multiplied. With this growth of institutional facilities for art presentation and communication after 1955, there was an amazing development of public interest in art throughout Canada, a development that was a reflection of the new worldwide participation by ordinary people in the world of the artist. If Canadians can look back at the history of art in their country and call the 1920's period the day-of-awakening, it seems only resonable that they should regard the period since 1955 as their day of artistic forward propulsion.

Sculpture. Painting has received most of the attention in the art world of Canada over the years, but sculpture has always been nearby in the background. In the pioneer days, wood carving, mainly for church embellishment, was a notable form of artistic expression in French Canada. Later, in both French Canada and English Canada, a succession of European-trained stone carvers conscientiously produced monuments and decorations for public parks and buildings. It was not until the 1930's that an element of vigor and excitement among Canadian sculptors was noted, although this only reflected new trends in the sculpture salons of New York, London, and Paris.

Since World War II a working relationship has evolved between sculptors and architects and builders in Canada, and today works of sculpture in

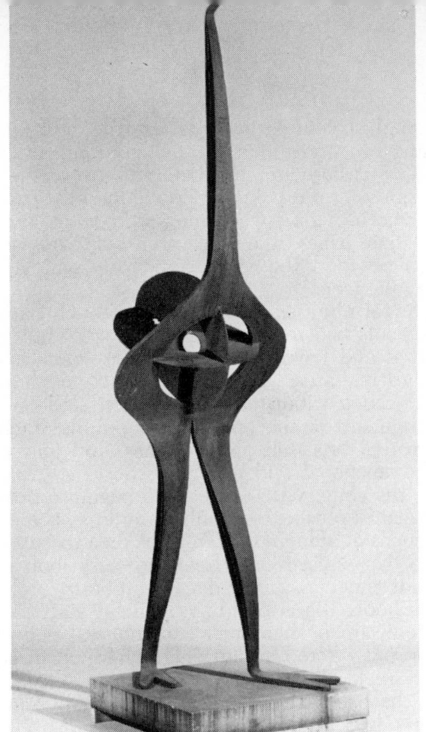

NATIONAL GALLERY OF CANADA, OTTAWA

OISEAU DE FER (*Iron Bird*), by Louis Archambault (1915–), a Montreal sculptor.

CHRIS LUND, FROM NATIONAL FILM BOARD

ESKIMO SCULPTURE of a man poising a fish spear, done by Kalloar, of Baker Lake, Northwest Territories.

stone, wood, metals, and synthetic materials are normally included in plans for public and commercial buildings. The government agencies, which have helped and encouraged the painters in recent times, have also offered support to the sculptors, and "big business" has become an eager patron. Exhibitions of sculpture in Vancouver, Montreal, and Toronto, at Expo 67 and the Stratford Festival have been important art events with an international flavor. The contemporary art of Eskimo stone carvers, now a matter of artistic interest extending far beyond Canadian borders, has become of great importance in the story of sculpture in Canada. Just as there is no distinctive school of Canadian painting, so is there no distinctive Canadian sculpture; however, there is throughout Canada a thriving, successful, modern practice of sculptural art.

Architecture. Very little special consideration has been given to architecture in Canada over the years. If architecture involves the planning of

VILLENEUVE HOUSE, near Charlesbourg, Quebec, a stone cottage built about 1700, is a fine example of French colonial architecture in a Norman medieval tradition.

JEAN-PAUL MORRISET—NATIONAL GALLERY OF CANADA, OTTAWA

GEORGE HUNTER, FROM NATIONAL FILM BOARD

Parliamentary Library, Ottawa (*above*), is an example of the Gothic Revival in High Victorian architecture. The Church of Our Lady of Fatima (*below*), at Jonquière, Quebec, was designed by Desgagné and Coté.

ELLEFSEN PHOTOGRAPHE

areas and structures and making the best use of available materials to suit the environment, then Canada's earliest architectural forms were the ice-block igloos of the Eskimo people, the hide-covered wigwams and the wood-mud-hide longhouses of the Indian tribes, the log cabins of early white settlements, and the sod shanties of some of the prairie pioneers.

The farmhouses of developing French Canada, where roofs had to cope with heavy snowfalls, and the rural and town buildings of early Ontario and the Maritime areas, were purely functional and effective and a tribute to the common sense of the folk architects of the time. Early public structures in Canada, forts, schools, churches, and inns were always functional and never artistic.

As the country developed and began to become somewhat sophisticated, public buildings and the residences of affluent citizens took on a picturesque aspect that indicated a free and easy borrowing from all the classical and contemporary architectural schools. Bank buildings, railway stations, hotels, legislature chambers, courthouses, churches, and prisons offered an amazing exhibition of styles from Greek classical to neo-château. By 1930 things had settled down, and throughout Canada a liking was noted for "modernism" in architecture, emphasizing the light-space-function prejudices of the United States architectural profession.

The contemporary architectural fashion in Canada is that of the Western world, but within that framework Canadian architects have shown notable initiative and enterprise. They have admitted that architectural concepts and devices planned for the mild climate of Atlanta, Ga., for instance, must be substantially varied before they can be used successfully in cities of the Canadian blizzard belt. The Canadian-built "Habitat" multiple-dwelling complex that was exhibited at Expo '67 and Simon Fraser University created on a mountaintop in Burnaby, B. C., a suburb of Vancouver, in the mid 1960's, caught the attention of the worldwide architectural profession.

The vocation and career of architecture is well organized in Canada, and good teaching is available at universities from Halifax to Vancouver. A Canadian government agency, the Central Mortgage and Housing Corporation, gives substantial encouragement to all valid architectural activities throughout the country.

Prospects. For a variety of good reasons, Canada was a slow developer in the areas of art and architecture, and for a matter of two centuries of its evolution the nation was far behind the stream of artistic life that prevailed in the many countries from which its culture sprang. Now Canada has caught up. Its artistic life is interesting, exciting, and vigorous and genuinely a matter of national importance. The prospect for Canada's painters and sculptors and architects seems bright.

WALTER B. HERBERT
Director, Canada Foundation, Ottawa

Bibliography

Dominion Bureau of Statistics, *Canada One Hundred, 1867–1967* (Ottawa 1967).

Gowans, Alan, *Looking at Architecture in Canada* (Toronto 1958).

Harper, J. Russell, *Painting in Canada* (Toronto 1966).

Hubbard, Robert H., *The Development of Canadian Art* (Ottawa, Queen's Printer, 1963).

Kilbourn, Elizabeth, *Great Canadian Painting* (Toronto 1966).

Park, Julian (ed.), *The Culture of Contemporary Canada* (Ithaca, N. Y., Cornell University Press, 1957).

Swinton, George, *Eskimo Sculpture/Sculpture esquimaude* (Toronto 1967).

36. Literature

The history of Canadian literature is interesting chiefly as the record of the attempts of a young nation to establish its own identity, to find its own language, and to come to terms with its own environment. There are as yet no giants, no great world figures, among Canadian writers. A few writers—Thomas Chandler Haliburton (1796–1865) and Louis Honoré Fréchette (1839–1908) in the 19th century, Gilbert Parker (1862–1932), Bliss Carman (1861–1929), Stephen Leacock (1869–1944), and Louis Hémon (1880-1913) in the early 20th century, and most recently Mazo de la Roche (1885–1961), Malcolm Lowry (1909–1957), Ethel Wilson (1890–), Margaret Laurence (1926–), "Ringuet" (Philippe Panneton, 1895–1960). Gabrielle Roy (1909–), and Marie-Claire Blais (1939–)—have earned international reputations, but in most cases their reputations have faded with time. There are other writers whom Canadians cherish, sometimes as much as if not more than those who are internationally known; but no one would claim that any of these writers are in the first rank by world standards. The quantity and quality of Canadian writing have made steady progress, and recently spectacular progress, but it has not yet achieved a level of rivalry with the great literatures of such countries as France, England, Russia, and the United States.

This fact is partly attributable to the youth of Canada, which celebrated its first centennial in 1967. But there are other reasons. The country and its culture have had to grow up in the shadow of its two founding nations—England and France—and of its great neighbor, the United States. It has been difficult to avoid merely imitating these exemplars, and to find a distinctive Canadianism which is not a mere compromise between French, English, and American ways. Futhermore, unlike the United States and France, Canada has had no revolution, has undergone no great national crisis to shock it into self-awareness. The minor crises of Canadian history—the Conquest of 1759, the War of 1812, the Rebellions of 1837, Confederation in 1867, and the two world wars have all stimulated increased cultural activity and hastened the process of self-definition, but none of them stirred the country to its depths.

English and French Literatures. Another important difficulty has been the bilingual nature of the country. Canada has had to create not one literature but two—one in English and one in French. The two literatures have grown up side by side and have shown remarkable similarities, but there has been very little contact between them, and almost no cross-fertilization. The similarities, however, are so strong as to deserve remark.

In both cases, the first writings were those of the explorers such as Samuel de Champlain (c. 1577–1635), Pierre Esprit Radisson (1636–1710), Henry Kelsey (c. 1670–?1730), Samuel Hearne (1745–1792), the two Alexander Henrys (1739–1824; died 1814), Alexander Mackenzie (1764–1820), Simon Fraser (1776–1862), and David Thompson (1770–1857). Native writing began in the late 18th and early 19th century with the establishment of such serials as the *Gazette littéraire* in Montreal and the *Novascotian* in Halifax. The first novels and books of verse began to appear in both languages in the 1820's and 1830's.

A consciously national literature began to establish itself in both languages in the latter half of the 19th century; the prevailing mode was romantic and nostalgic. A more critical, realistic, and technically sophisticated literature developed in both languages in the first four decades of the 20th century; and in both languages the really spectacular progress toward a literature worthy of the world's attention has taken place in the period since World War II.

There have been other marked similarities between Canadian literature in English and French. Poetry has flourished vigorously; only history in the prose forms has rivaled it; the novel lagged until well on into the 20th century; dramatic writing hardly existed until the mid-20th century; and original philosophical writing has been virtually nonexistent. Even the individual forms have resembled each other in emphasis and direction: poetry in both English and French has been until recent years predominantly landscape poetry, strongly influenced by the overpowering presence of a magnificent and varied terrain. In the 19th century the novels in French and English were almost all historical romances; in the early 20th century the regional idyll became the dominant form; and only in the 1920's did the novel turn in the direction of the realistic, satirical, or symbolic exploration of contemporary life.

Search for National Identity. In both literatures, the quest for national identity has been a major factor. The French especially, finding themselves a tiny minority in an English-speaking North America, have sought above all *survivance* (survival). Their historians—such as François-Xavier Garneau (1809–1866), Benjamin Sulte (1841–1923), Thomas Chapais (1858–1946) and Lionel-Adolphe Groulx (1878–1967)—have written their volumes to inculcate in their people a pride in their past and a determination to protect and project their inheritance. Their novelists have with unashamed didacticism sought to teach them to resist American influences, to stay on the ancestral soil, to be true to their traditions.

In English-Canadian writing the nationalistic emphasis has been more diffuse and more subtle, but it is there nonetheless in the glorification of the Canadian landscape, in the dozens of regional novels which treat lovingly the distinctive life patterns of the farms, fishing villages, or small towns, as well as in such obviously nationalistic testaments as the patriotic poems of Charles G. D. Roberts (1860–1943), Wilfred Campbell (1858–1918), and E. J. Pratt (1883–1964) and the identity-seeking novels of Hugh MacLennan (1907–).

Even when, in the modern trend, Canadian writers in both English and French satirize "Canadianism" and its traditional pieties, they do so to promote a higher patriotism. With very rare exceptions, Canadian writers, although they may decry literary or other forms of nationalism, write with at least some modicum of patriotic zeal.

Poetry. Poetry in both English and French Canada began to appear in the late 18th century with the work of Joseph Quesnel (1749–1809) in Quebec and of Henry Alline (1748–1784) in Nova Scotia, but it was not until the latter half of the 19th century that poetry of any quality was produced. Before 1850 there were sporadic pioneer efforts such as Oliver Goldsmith's *The Rising Village* (1825), Michel Bibaud's *Épîtres, satires, chansons* (1830), Peter Fisher's *The Lay of the Wilderness* (1833), the patriotic songs of Jonathan Odell (1737–1818), of New Brunswick and Joseph Howe (1804–1873) of Nova Scotia, and *The Emigrant* (1841) by Standish O'Grady of Sorel, but all these are of historical rather than of strictly literary interest.

The Early Years. The first real poetic flowering in French Canada began as the result of the resentment caused by the observation of Lord Durham (governor general of Canada, 1838), in his famous *Report on the Affairs of British North America* (1839), that the country had no literature and no history. François-Xavier Garneau wrote his *Histoire du Canada* (1845–1848) to disprove part of this remark, and soon he and Abbé Henri-Raymond Casgrain gathered around themselves in Quebec a group of writers who proceeded to disprove the other part. The first important poet was Octave Crémazie (1827–1879), who wrote about the glories of the French tradition in vigorous lyrics such as *Chant du vieux soldat canadien,* which helped restore the pride of his people. He was followed by Louis-Honoré Fréchette, who thrilled his countrymen by winning a prize of the French Academy for *Les fleurs boréales* (1879) and heightened their faith in their traditions by publishing his 3,000-line epic, *La légende d'un peuple* (1888). Other poets of this group, usually known as the school of Quebec, were Pamphile Lemay (1837–1918), Nérée Beauchemin (1850–1931) and William Chapman (1850–1917). All of these poets imitated such French romantic poets as Victor Hugo and Alphonse Lamartine in their style, and were largely orthodox in their religious, moral, and political ideas, but they gave to their people a sense of cultural identity and prepared the way for the more sophisticated poets who were to follow them.

In the last decades of the 19th century the foundations of poetry were also laid in English Canada. In the 1850's and 1860's, Charles Sangster (1822–1893), Charles Mair (1838–1927), and Charles Heavysege (1816–1876) published volumes of poetry that contained a few striking lines or stanzas, but it was the publication of Charles G. D. Roberts' *Orion* in 1880 that really was the sign of the beginning of the new movement.

Roberts went on to publish several more volumes of poetry, including the very fine *Songs of the Common Day* (1893), and many volumes of animal stories and other prose fiction, and in many ways deserves the title sometimes accorded him of "father of Canadian literature." His *Orion* stimulated Archibald Lampman (1861–1899), Bliss Carman, Duncan Campbell Scott (1862–1947), Isabella Valancy Crawford (1850–1887), Wilfred Campbell, and Pauline Johnson (1862–1913).

Each of these poets had a distinctive quality. Roberts was an accurate landscape painter and a master of poetic structure. Carman had a magical power of evoking atmosphere and haunting musical effects. Lampman had an almost mystical sense of the cyclical rhythms of nature and a sharp eye for the ugliness of industrial civilization. Scott could re-create the violence and tensions of the Canadian wilderness and its primitive inhabitants. Isabella Crawford was most ingenious in finding images and symbols to express her awe at the strength of the Canadian physical environment. Wilfred Campbell at his best could evoke the mingled beauty and terror of the violent contrasts of the Canadian climate and topography. Pauline Johnson gave a somewhat melodramatic expression to the character, traditions and aspirations of the Indians from whom she was in part descended.

But they make an impression chiefly as a group—the "Group of the Sixties," as they are usually called—by their successful efforts to give poetic expression to the vastness and variety of the Canadian land. They were not, with the possible exception of Lampman, great individual poets, but collectively they made the Canadian people aware of the fascination of their habitat.

The 20th Century. In the early decades of the 20th century, Canadian poetry in French moved ahead of that in English in the work of the so-called school of Montreal. These poets—chiefly Émile Nelligan (1879–1941), Charles Gill (1871–1918), Albert Lozeau (1878–1924), Paul Morin (1889–1963), René Chopin (1885–1953), and Louis Dantin (1865–1945)—were stimulated by the French symbolists such as Baudelaire, Mallarmé, and Verlaine to write a poetry far more subtle, sophisticated, and experimental than that of Crémazie and Fréchette. Nelligan was the first great poet of French Canada, distinguished by the originality and complexity of his images and symbols, the sensuous suggestiveness of his diction, and the uniqueness of his sensibility. Gill was more traditional, but his *Le Cap Éternité* (1919) had majesty and touches of sublimity. Lozeau was a fresh and sincere poet who wrote of love and nature in a chastely elegiac style. Morin was technically the most dazzling of the group, Chopin the most structurally correct, and Dantin (who was also a leading literary critic, and the chief promoter of Nelligan) the most delicate lyricist.

The first two decades of the 20th century in English Canada were poetically rather barren. There were the rollicking, popular rhymes of Robert Service (1874–1958) and Tom MacInnes (1867–1951) and the wistful, delicate lyrics of Marjorie Pickthall (1883–1922), but nothing to rival the previous achievement of the "Group of the Sixties" nor the contemporary achievements of Nelligan and Morin. It was in the 1920's that English-Canadian poetry began its second birth, in the vigorous narratives and subtle lyrics of E. J. Pratt, the witty, polished lyrics and satires of A. J. M. Smith, A. M. Klein, F. R. Scott, and Robert Finch, and the early imagist verse of Dorothy Livesay and W. W. E. Ross.

Pratt was the most distinguished single figure, and the most original: he owed little to contemporary poetry in Canada or elsewhere, but steeped himself in the English Elizabethans and brought to bear on his narratives of heroism (*The Roosevelt and the Antinoe,* 1930; *The Titanic,* 1935; and *Brébeuf and His Brethren,* 1940), the tough vigor and linguistic exuberance of that era. At the same time, he studied the minutiae of contemporary science and technology, so that he was able to give to his poems a high degree of authenticity. Moreover, he had an overriding philosophy of life, his own distinctive version of Christian humanism, which gave resonance and consistency to his handling of themes.

Smith, Scott, Klein, Finch, and Livesay, however, are also very fine poets. Smith is an exigent craftsman, Scott a witty satirist and grave proponent of social justice, Klein a richly modulated psalmist of the Jewish people in their exultations and agonies, Finch a delicate lyricist and subtle wit, Livesay a musical celebrant now of sexual love, now of human dignity, now of natural beauty. Livesay, indeed, has been the most evolutionary poet of this group, having passed from early imagism through a social revolutionary phase into a highly personal and confessional type of poetry.

After World War II. The period since the beginning of World War II has been the most efflorescent in the history of Canadian poetry in both English and French. The period has been one of material prosperity, stimulating debate about national and international issues, and of progressive cultural maturity. New periodicals have been founded, publishers have become more venturesome, a substantial domestic readership has welcomed Canadian books, and writers in unprecedented numbers have quickly established reputations. The new poetry in both languages has moved away from the traditional preoccupations with landscape and nationalism, has become more and more experimental in the use of free verse and other technical innovations, and increasingly daring in subject matter and attitude.

In English Canada, the chief poets have been Roy Daniells, Earle Birney, John Glassco, Wilfred Watson, Irving Layton, George Johnstone, Douglas LePan, Fred Cogswell, P. K. Page, Miriam Waddington, Margaret Avison, Louis Dudek, Alfred Purdy, Raymond Souster, Elizabeth Brewster, Eli Mandel, Milton Acorn, James Reaney, Phyllis Webb, Jay Macpherson, Alden Nowlan, Leonard Cohen, Daryl Hine, and John Newlove.

Of this sizable group, all of whom are poets worthy of detailed critical scrutiny, the major ones appear to be Birney (*Selected Poems*, 1966), Irving Layton (*Collected Poems*, 1965), Raymond Souster (*Selected Poems*, 1956; *The Colour of the Times*, 1964); James Reaney (*The Red Heart*, 1949; *A Suit of Nettles*, 1958), and Leonard Cohen (*Let Us Compare Mythologies*, 1956; *The Spice-Box of Earth*, 1961; *Flowers for Hitler*, 1964; and *Parasites of Heaven*, 1966).

Birney is something of a virtuoso, capable of narrative and dramatic verse, of lyrics of love and nature, of philosophical and political poems, and of wry satires. Layton is also a poet of great power and variety, a realist with romantic overtones who can celebrate sexual love or curse social hypocrisy with equal vehemence. Souster is notable for his lack of pretension, recording in irony and tenderness his observations of contemporary city life in short and seemingly simple lyrics which usually explode in the mind like a time bomb. Reaney is a poet of a private mythology and of archly ironic portraits of small-town Ontario places and persons. Leonard Cohen, the youngest and in many ways most promising, is at once erudite and impassioned, a master both of the private love lyric and the public tract for the times.

The poetry of French Canada has been equally prolific and distinguished. The chief figures have been Saint-Denys-Garneau (1912–1943), whose *Poésies complètes* (1949) reveals a haunting strain of personal anguish expressed in impeccable form; Alain Grandbois, whose poetry is distinguished by its plastic perfection and rich harmony of sound (*Les îles de la nuit, 1944*); Robert Choquette, whose *Suite marine* (1953) has majestic amplitude and a highly suggestive descriptive accuracy; Rina Lasnier, a virtuoso who writes of love, nature, religion, and art in a style that is at once vigorously incisive and sensuously rich; and Anne Hébert, whose *Poèmes* (1960) are memorable for their incantatory music, symbolic resonance, and emotional poignancy. Younger poets who have demonstrated great promise in their work are Jean-Guy Pilon, Fernand Ouellette, Pierre Trottier, and Gatien Lapointe.

Fiction. The first novels in English and French Canada appeared in the second and third decades of the 19th century—Julia Catherine Beckwith's *Nun of Canada* (1824), Major John Richardson's *Écarté* (1829), and Philippe Aubert de Gaspé's *Le chercheur de trésors* (1837)—but, as with poetry, it was not until the last decades of that century that work of any real distinction began to appear. Canadian society was still in a nascent state, and it is not surprising that most of these 19th century novelists turned for material to the past, which lent itself to romantic glorification. William Kirby (1817–1906) produced his historical romance *The Golden Dog* in 1877. Philippe-Joseph Aubert de Gaspé (1786–1871), father of the novelist, produced *Les anciens Canadiens* in 1863. Joseph Marmette (1844–1895) wrote *François de Bienville* in 1868 and *L'intendant Bigot* in 1870. Napoléon Bourassa (1827–1916) wrote *Jacques et Marie* in 1866; Gilbert Parker (1862–1932), *Seats of the Mighty* in 1896; William D. Lighthall (1857–1954), *The Young Seigneur* in 1888; and Thomas G. Marquis (1864–1936), *Marguerite de Roberval* in 1899. All of these novels were once highly popular but are now almost forgotten; they were, for the most part, merely costume melodramas, but they served to give Canadians a sense of their past and hope for their future.

More realistic novels were few and far between. The chief alternative to the historical romance was the regional idyll, which painted in soft, flattering colors the day-to-day life of farm, village or small town. This genre had its origins in French Canada in *Charles Guérin* (1846) by Pierre-Joseph-Oliver Chauveau (1820–1890) and in *Jean Rivard le défricheur* (1874) and *Jean Rivard économiste* (1876) by Antoine Gérin-Lajoie (1824–1882), and reached its peak there in *Marie Chapdelaine* (1916) by Louis Hémon (1880–1913).

In English Canada the chief practitioners of this genre were Ralph Connor (1860–1937), author of many best-selling novels including *The Man from Glengarry* (1901); Lucy M. Montgomery (1874–1942), author of the classic for girls, *Anne of Green Gables* (1908); Stephen Leacock, who was primarily a humorist but whose *Sunshine Sketches of a Little Town* (1912) is the most delightful of all Canadian regional idylls, in spite of, or perhaps because of, its ironic undertones; and Mazo de la Roche. The triumph of Miss de la Roche's *Jalna* (1927) led to a whole stream of idylls about the Whiteoaks family in rural Ontario.

Realism. The realistic movement in Canadian fiction began in the 1920's and 1930's, chiefly in the work of Frederick Philip Grove (1871–1948), Morley Callaghan, Albert Laberge (1871–1960), Jean-Charles Harvey, Claude Henri Grignon, and Ringuet. Grove's somber, naturalistic novels of pioneer life in the West (*Our Daily Bread,* 1928; *Fruits of the Earth,* 1933) have their urban counterpart in Callaghan's sadly ironic but compassionate studies of outcasts and aliens in the modern city (*Such Is My Beloved,* 1934; *They Shall Inherit the Earth,* 1935; and *The Loved and the Lost,* 1951). Albert Laberge's *La Scouine* (1918) is a kind of French-Canadian version of Émile Zola's bitter work *La terre.* Jean-Charles Harvey (*Les demi-civilisés,* 1934) rebels against the traditional pieties of French-Canadian life and exposes hypocrisy and corruption. Claude Henri Grignon shows the greed and treachery that exist below the idyllic surface of habitant life in *Un homme et son péché* (1933). Ringuet, in *Trente arpents* (1938), for the first time gives a picture of rural life in French Canada which is authentic, accurate, and tragically moving.

Further Developments. Since the early 1940's, Canadian fiction in both English and French has come of age: novelists and short story writers of high quality are almost as numerous in this recent period as the good poets.

In English Canada, there have been a number of distinguished novelists. Hugh MacLennan has sought in full sincerity to plumb the depths of the nation in such novels as *Barometer Rising* (1941), *Two Solitudes* (1945), *Each Man's Son* (1951), *The Watch That Ends the Night* (1959), and *Return of the Sphinx* (1967). Sinclair Ross has written two novels and several short stories about rural Saskatchewan (notably *As For Me and My House,* 1941). Malcolm Lowry (1909–1957) wrote *Under the Volcano* (1947), which seems destined to become a classic in English fiction. Ethel Wilson, in *Hetty Dorval* (1947), *The Innocent Traveller* (1949), *The Equations of Love* (1952), *Swamp Angel* (1954), and *Love and Salt Water* (1956), has demonstrated adroitness of technique and delicacy of perception beyond anything yet accomplished in Canadian fiction. Robertson Davies in *Tempest-tost* (1951), *Leaven of Malice* (1954), and *A Mixture of Frailties* (1958) has brought refreshing gusts of humor and high spirits. Brian Moore resembles Callaghan in his interest in the compassionate study of misfits (*The Luck of Ginger Coffey,* 1960) but has an Irish humor largely absent in Callaghan. Mordecai Richler is primarily a social satirist (*The Apprenticeship of Duddy Kravitz,* 1959). Margaret Laurence has produced two beautifully authentic novels of small-town life in Manitoba, *The Stone Angel* (1964) and *A Jest of God* (1966), as well as two books of fiction set in Africa. The poet Leonard Cohen has also made a brilliant start as an experimental and subtle novelist with *The Favourite Game* (1963) and *Beautiful Losers* (1966).

The recent novelists of French Canada as a group have largely turned away from the country to the city and from traditional affirmation to skeptical questioning or violent denunciation. Gabrielle Roy is the author of perhaps the best two of all French-Canadian novels in *Bonheur d'occasion* (1945) and *Alexandre Chenevert* (1954). Yves Thériault is a prolific writer of novels and short stories, of which *La fille laide* (1950) and *Aaron* (1954) are probably best. Roger Lemelin is a deceptively gentle satirist whose *Les Plouffe* (1948) made the Plouffe family household names in both French and English Canada. André Langevin's taste for strange and violent events and characters can be seen in such examples as *Évadé de la nuit* (1951) and *Poussière sur la ville* (1953). Robert Elie is an acute analyst of the soul, as in *La fin des songes* (1950). Germaine Guèvremont is a belated but honest chronicler of habitant life, as in *Le survenant* (1945) and *Marie-Didace* (1947). Jean Simard is a fierce critic of all the traditional shibboleths such as family, puritanism, and piety in novels such as *Hôtel de la Reine* (1949) and *Les sentiers de la nuit* (1959). Gérard Bessette has written such probing "problem novels" as *La bagarre* (1958) and *Le libraire* (1960). Claire Martin in the short stories of *Avec ou sans amour* (1958) and the novels *Doux-Amer* (1960) and *Quand j'ai payé ton visage* (1962), has shown herself to be a master of ironic analysis. Marie-Claire Blais' violent situations and surrealistic style, in novels such as *La belle bête* (1959), *Tête blanche* (1960), *Le jour est noir* (1962), and *Un saison en la vie d'Emmanuel* (1965), have attracted attention throughout the English- and French-speaking worlds.

Historical Writing. Relatively speaking, historical writing has flourished in both English and French Canada since early in the 19th century.

In French Canada the pioneer work of François-Xavier Garneau has already been noted. He was soon followed by Jean-Baptiste-Antoine Ferland (1805–1865), Étienne Michel Faillon (1799–1870), Henri-Raymond Casgrain (1831–1904), Joseph Edmond Roy (1858–1913), and Benjamin Sulte. All of these historians, like their contemporaries in English Canada, were basically amateurs—priests, journalists, and others—who wrote propaganda designed to persuade their readers that French Canada had a glorious past. In the 20th century, these amateur historians have largely been replaced by professional scholars, who make much greater use of documentary evidence and, with one or two conspicuous exceptions, attempt to achieve a greater objectivity in their interpretations of the evidence.

Pierre-Georges Roy (1870–1953) is a master of the minutiae of church history. Antoine Roy is the author of *Les lettres, les sciences, and les arts au Canada sous le régime français* (1930), a heroic effort at synthesis. Thomas Chapais, author of biographies of Talon and Montcalm, is master of a lively if somewhat ornate prose. Lionel-Adolphe Groulx is a violently nationalistic, eloquent spokesman of his race. Guy Frégault is a very meticulous historian of the War of Conquest and biographer of Iberville and Bigot. Robert Rumilly is the incredibly persistent author of a history of Quebec in 32 volumes. Gustave Lanctot is the biographer of François-Xavier Garneau and author of a singularly unprejudiced *Histoire du Canada* (1960). Marcel Trudel has demonstrated a great gift for documentary research in the preparation of such books as *L'esclavage au Canada français* (1960.)

A similar evolution from amateur, patriotic history to scholarly and relatively objective history can be seen in English Canada. In the 19th century the task of recording the English-

Canadian past was performed by such men as Thomas Chandler Haliburton (1796–1865), better known as a great humorist and author of *The Clockmaker; or the sayings and doings of Sam Slick of Slickville* (1836); George Heriot (1766–1844), deputy postmaster-general of British North America; John Richardson (1796–1852), author of *The War of 1812* (1842) and of several historical novels, of which *Wacousta* (1832) was the best known; John McMullen (1820–1907), a bookseller of Brockville, Ontario, author of *The History of Canada* (1855); Charles R. Tuttle, a journalist and the most prolific historical popularizer of the period; William Kingsford (1819–1898), a civil engineer who devoted his last years to writing a 10-volume *History of Canada* (1887–1898); and a number of other civil servants, clergymen, and journalists.

About 1900, however, George M. Wrong (1860–1948) became professor of history at the University of Toronto and began to promote the academic study of Canadian history, archives were established in Ottawa and some of the provincial capitals, the Champlain Society was founded and began to issue historical documents, and gradually the writing of Canadian history became a much more scholarly process. Valuable constitutional history was written by such men as W. P. M. Kennedy (1881–1963), R. G. Trotter (1888–1951), O. D. Skelton (1878–1941), and Chester Martin (1882–1958).

In the middle decades of the 20th century, Canadian historical writing in English became truly distinguished in the hands of such men as H. A. Innis (1894–1952), Donald G. Creighton, Frank H. Underhill, W. L. Morton, Arthur R. M. Lower, Edgar McInnis, James M. S. Careless, Charles Stacey, G. F. G. Stanley, and William Kilbourn. There was great improvement in the writing of political biographies, prominent among these being Creighton's works on John A. Macdonald, Careless' on George Brown, Stanley's on Louis Riel, and Kilbourn's on W. L. Mackenzie.

Summary. With the exception of drama—and even it has been showing signs of life in the work of Paul Toupin, Gratien Gélinas, Marcel Dubé, Lister Sinclair, Robertson Davies, James Reaney, and Patricia Joudry—the various literary forms may now be said to be well established in Canada. In addition to the creative writers, there are literary critics and historians of the first rank to appraise and foster the work of these writers—critics such as Northrop Frye, Carl F. Klinck, A. J. M. Smith, Milton Wilson, Roy Daniells, Malcolm Ross, George Woodcock, Jean le Moyne, Gérard Bessette, Gilles Marcotte, Guy Robert, Guy Sylvestre, Roger Duhamel, and Gérard Tougas. Out of this very active literary life it is almost certain that, sooner or later, work of the highest quality will emerge. In the meantime, a young nation has found its voice.

DESMOND PACEY
University of New Brunswick

Bibliography

Klinck, Carl F., and others, eds., *Literary History of Canada* (Toronto 1965).
Pacey, Desmond, *Creative Writing in Canada* (Toronto 1961).
Pacey, Desmond, *Ten Canadian Poets* (Toronto 1958).
Park, Julian, ed., *The Culture of Contemporary Canada* (Ithaca, N. Y., 1957).
Tougas, Gérard, *History of French-Canadian Literature* (Toronto 1966).

37. Theater

Theater in Canada has a long history, if not a crowded one. In a wilderness sparsely settled late in the 18th century, the stage was recognized as an attribute of civilization, despite some opposition. Early Roman Catholic attempts to discourage this irreverent offspring of the church were followed, more persistently, by a Puritan disapproval that still holds the stage less respectable than sporting events.

The survival of living theater was threatened more violently by scientific development. For a thinly populated country, the 20th century media of film, radio, and television seemed particularly suited. They obviated both the tours between widely separated communities and the organizing of regional productions for limited audiences.

By the third decade of the 20th century, the stage in Canada was almost entirely deserted as a profession. Most determined talents left the country to seek opportunities elsewhere, although a few eventually remained to create a much-respected, government-supported radio theater, notably in the Canadian Broadcasting Corporation's Stage Series, directed by Andrew Allan.

As the century unfolded, it became apparent that the new media were unique forms of communication and expression, not substitutes for the involvement of actors and audiences in an ancient exchange. Emulating the British acceptance of cultural subsidy by setting up the Canada Council (through the Massey Report, 1951) and other bodies, the country began to develop regional theaters, each serving large areas.

The exchange between these was encouraged by the Centennial Commission, established to celebrate the 100th anniversary of Confederation in 1967. It was planned that such exchanges would be regularized by 1970 with the opening of the National Arts Centre in Ottawa. In addition to housing visiting provincial companies, this was to offer a winter home to the best-known Canadian company, that of the Stratford Festival, and also for a new French-language troupe, to constitute together Canada's National Theatre.

Also in 1967, attention was paid to the state of dramatic writing in Canada, until then largely a borrowing nation. The Dominion Drama Festival, the Canadian Theatre Centre and other bodies advanced the production of new plays by Canadians. Principal dramatists up to this point included Robertson Davies, Lister Sinclair, Marcel Dubé, and Gratien Gélinas.

Historical Development. It was to welcome the Sieur de Poutrincourt, an early colonizer of Nova Scotia, back to Port Royal, N. S., from a tour of exploration, that Marc Lescarbot had devised the *Theatre of Neptune,* the first play written in New France, in 1606. Forty years later a production of Corneille's *Le Cid* was described in a Jesuit journal. In 1694 a bishop's edict stopped the showing of Molière's *Tartuffe* in Quebec. The producer was jailed.

The English regime, especially the military, encouraged theatricals. The garrison theater of the late 18th century staged Shakespeare, Molière, current farces, and original sketches. In 1790, Joseph Quesnel had a full-length comedy produced and published. Le Théâtre du Marche opened in Quebec that same year. In 1786 a group of English players arrived in Montreal from Albany, among them actors who had emigrated to America with Lewis Hallam in 1750. In 1825

PETER SMITH PHOTO, COURTESY OF STRATFORD SHAKESPEAREAN FESTIVAL

STRATFORD SHAKESPEAREAN FESTIVAL THEATRE, at Stratford, Ontario, famed for summer plays.

the Theatre Royal was opened there. As audiences were built up, touring companies and even star performers made their appearances, including Edmund Kean, who appeared in Montreal by 1826. Halifax produced a new three-act comedy, *Acadius, or Love in a Calm,* in 1774. It opened its first theater in 1787, starting with Richard Cumberland's *The West Indian.* Saint John, New Brunswick, had local theater in 1789. Its first theater building was erected in 1806.

The Royal Lyceum was built in Toronto in 1847, first of a series of modest buildings of which the finest was the St. Lawrence Hall, built in 1850. Jenny Lind sang there the next year. Noted names of the era were those of the Nickerson and Tavernier families. The Royal Alexandra was put up in 1907, the O'Keefe Centre in 1960.

As the railroad made the rest of the country accessible, great European players like Sarah Bernhardt, Henry Irving, Ellen Terry, Sir Johnston Forbes-Robertson, and Sir John Martin-Harvey were seen in the Far West as well as in the East. Winnipeg, Manitoba, opened the Bijou Theatre (later the Winnipeg) in 1897, the Dominion (which was to house the successful Manitoba Theatre Centre 45 years later) in 1904, and the Walker in 1907. West Coast theater followed the gold rush in the 1860's, with Barkerville a theatrical center. Victoria, British Columbia, had theater in 1857.

With both stock companies and touring troupes flourishing, the 20th century started off well, but World War I and the depression that followed a decade later forced both contributors out of the Canadian scene. By 1933 the situation was so grave that the Earl of Bessborough, then governor-general, established the Dominion Drama Festival as a bulwark, calling on community and little theaters to fill the gap. This national body has since centered its efforts on annual competition and has served as a training ground for talent. With the Canadian Theatre Centre, it helped establish the National Theatre School in Montreal in 1960. The bicultural school, like the Canadian Theatre Centre and Actors Equity of Canada, evolved with the indigenous professional theater, which has been developing since the end of World War II.

Since World War II. In 1946, the New Play Society was established in Toronto by Dora Mavor Moore and Mavor Moore. From it came *Spring Thaw,* a revue that won a national audience. In 1951, Jean Gascon and Jean-Louis Roux founded Le Théâtre du Nouveau Monde, an extension of Les Compagnons de St. Laurent, which Father Émile Legault had supervised from 1936 to 1952. In this same period, Gratien Gélinas rose to national attention in revues and plays of his own writing. In 1951, Jupiter Theatre opened in Toronto with Bertolt Brecht's *Galileo,* directed by Herbert Whittaker and starring John Drainie and Lorne Green.

Stratford Festival. Two years later the Stratford Festival was established at Stratford, Ontario, by Tyrone Guthrie, at the invitation of Tom Patterson and a group of Stratford citizens. Each summer, the Festival has presented plays by Shakespeare, but it has occasionally included those of Sophocles, Wycherley, Molière, and Rostand. Opera, comic opera, and new plays have been staged at the Festival's second theater, the Avon, a traditional house fully restored by 1967. Alec Guinness and Irene Worth headed the Festival's first company in Shakespeare's *Richard III* and *All's Well That Ends Well.* Its open stage, designed by Tanya Moiseiwitsch, was first set up in a tent, later in a building created around it by Robert Fairfield. Under Guthrie and later Michael Langham, the Stratford Festival won international repute.

Following the appearance of the company at Expo Theatre, Montreal, in October 1967, in *Antony and Cleopatra* with Christopher Plummer and Zoe Caldwell, and in *The Government Inspector* with William Hutt, Langham turned over his 12-year artistic directorship to Jean Gascon and John Hirsch. The company had visited New York with *Tamburlaine the Great* in 1956, London, Ont., Toronto, Montreal, and New York with *The Two Gentlemen of Verona* and *The Broken Jug* (adapted by Donald Harron) in 1956, the Edinburgh Festival in 1956, Chichester in 1964, and made a Centennial tour of Canada in 1967.

Other Theaters. Stratford encouraged two other theaters. In 1954, Toronto's Crest Theatre was set up by Murray and Donald Davis, and the Ca-

JOHN REEVES, FROM NATIONAL FILM BOARD

THE NATIONAL BALLET presents a pattern of grace in a Christmas show in its home city of Toronto.

nadian Players, a touring organization, by Tom Patterson and Douglas Campbell. From the amalgamation of these two in 1966 rose Theatre Toronto, to open at the Royal Alexandra Theatre in January, 1968, with Clifford Williams imported from England as artistic director, and John Colicos, Eric House, and Barbara Hamilton in the company.

Other influential theaters have been the Canadian Repertory Theatre, Ottawa, 1949–1956, Le Rideau Vert, Montreal, 1948; the Manitoba Theatre Centre, Winnipeg, 1958; the Neptune Theatre, Halifax, 1963; the Playhouse Theatre Company, Vancouver, 1963; the Bastion Theatre, Victoria, British Columbia, and The Citadel Theatre, Edmonton, 1965. Important developments have also included the Toronto Workshop Productions, Le Théâtre Populaire du Québec, La Nouvelle Compagnie Théâtrale in Montreal, L'Estoc in Quebec, the Shaw Festival at Niagara-on-the-Lake, Théâtre l'Escale in Montreal, and the Centre Cultural du Vieux Montreal.

Of equal importance, in their own field, have been such community operations as the Montreal Repertory Theatre, 1939–1961; the London Little Theatre; the Cercle Molière, St. Boniface; Workshop 14, Calgary; the Ottawa Little Theatre; and the Winnipeg Little Theatre, from which developed the Manitoba Theatre Centre.

Overshadowed by the Stratford Festival, other summer theaters nevertheless were important in their day, mostly as a training ground for talent. Among these were Montreal's Mountain Playhouse; the Straw Hat Players of Port Carling, Ont., from which sprang The Crest Theatre; the Brae Manor Theatre, Knowlton, Quebec; the Red Barn, Jackson's Point; the Garden Centre Summer Theatre, Vineland, Ontario; and the Open-Air Playhouse, Montreal. The latter staged a series of individual Shakespearean productions, one under the direction of Theodore Komisarjevsky. An annual Shakespearean enterprise was the Earle Grey Festival in Toronto's Trinity College quadrangle from 1947 to 1958.

Major contributions have been made by Toronto's Hart House Theatre, especially under the direction of Robert Gill. From it emerged Kate Reid, Stratford and Broadway star. It became the Centre for the Study of Drama at the University of Toronto in 1966. Numerous other university drama departments have been set up, the most advanced being those at the University of Alberta and at Simon Fraser University, Burnaby, British Columbia.

HERBERT WHITTAKER
Drama Critic, Toronto "Globe and Mail"

38. Music

The development of music in Canada has clearly been shaped by historical and geographical circumstances, principally its size and its proximity to the overpowering United States. Except for the Quebec "chansonniers," virtually all popular music is foreign; the serious budding artist must make "the debut" in New York. However, such international stars as Glenn Gould, pianist, Lois Marshall, soprano, Maureen Forrester, contralto, Louis Quilico, baritone, Jon Vickers, tenor, Theresa Stratas, soprano, and Mario Bernardi and Wilfrid Pelletier, opera conductors (all trained in Canada), help to belie the myth of a nonmusical Canada.

National Organizations. The Canadian Broadcasting Corporation is the most important national organization in the field of Canadian music. It carries the music of Canadians from coast to coast and also is the largest single employer of musicians on the continent. It maintains studio or chamber orchestras in at least five cities and also carries broadcasts of most major Canadian city orchestras and special musical events. "CBC Talent Festival," an annual nationwide competition, provides a major opportunity to discover young talent.

The Canadian Music Council (member of the International Music Council) was formed in 1945 by Sir Ernest MacMillan and functions as the national voice of the profession. Its membership includes many individual musicians as well as national musical organizations such as the CBC, the Canadian Folk Music Society, Canadian Music Educators' Association, National Youth Orchestra, Royal Canadian College of Organists, Canadian Music Centre, and virtually every other national musical organization. The Council initiates many projects and holds annual meetings on many topics.

All professional instrumentalists (except many

E. ROSEBOROUGH, FROM NATIONAL FILM BOARD

TORONTO SYMPHONY ORCHESTRA plays in a rehearsal that is conducted by Seiji Ozawa.

church organists) are members of the American Federation of Musicians of the United States and Canada. Of the federation's 660 locals, 37 are Canadian (24 in Ontario alone).

The Department of National Defence maintains 17 full-time service bands and a tri-service music school, which contribute to the musical lives of their communities. The Royal Canadian College of Organists (essentially an examining body) has centers across Canada but mostly in Ontario.

Performance. Except for CBC broadcasts most musical activity is essentially local or regional. Canada has some 30 symphony orchestras, of which the leaders are those of Toronto, Montreal, Vancouver, and Winnipeg. Although these are all composed of professional musicians, none yet pays its members year round. Few of the leading orchestras are conducted by Canadians, and their programs are essentially of the established European repertoire.

Each summer the National Youth Orchestra convenes for a few weeks of intensive professional training prior to touring. The players (14 to 24 years old) are carefully chosen from all parts of the country, and each need pay only $50 toward the costs of training and travel.

There are fewer than ten "permanent" chamber orchestras, of which the oldest and most active is the McGill Chamber Orchestra (Montreal) under Alexander Brott. Also widely known is Toronto's Hart House Orchestra formed and conducted by Boyd Neel.

Canada is not rich in chamber groups. The most promising string quartet is the Orford Quartet, its nearest rival being the Gabora Quartet in Montreal. Leading wind groups are the Toronto and Quebec Woodwind Quartets, the Cassenti Players of Vancouver, and the Montreal Brass Quintet. Likewise the Montreal Baroque Trio (oboe, flute, harpsichord) has continued over the years.

Most eminent of the large choirs (about 200 voices), are the Toronto Mendelssohn Choir, the Bach-Elgar Choir (Hamilton, Ontario) and the Elgar Choir of Vancouver, which still initiate their own programming. A few cities have excellent chamber choirs, the most eminent being The Festival Singers of Toronto, the Tudor Singers of Montreal, and the Winnipeg Choristers.

Opera. Opera is a late-comer in Canada. All the permanent companies have been formed since 1945. Foremost is the Canadian Opera Company (Toronto) under Herman Geiger-Torel. However, even by the mid-1960's its season (6 productions) lasted only four weeks (although a nucleus company tours some 15,000 miles (24,000 km) during the early spring). The oldest company is the Vancouver Opera Association, which gives some three productions spaced through the winter season. The Edmonton Opera Company gives two. Montreal has no permanent company, but the Montreal Symphony presents four productions during the season and Pauline Donalda's Montreal Opera Guild, two. The most recent company is the Théâtre Lyrique de Nouvelle-France of Quebec City, its repertoire being rather on the lighter side. The summer music festivals of Stratford (Ontario) and Vancouver feature opera productions of high caliber.

For the most part opera in Canada leans heavily on standard European repertoire, with *Traviata, Trovatore,* and *Carmen* not lacking in exposure, although the Canadian Opera Company during the 1960's began to feature original large-scale Canadian operas.

Ballet. Ballet likewise is a newcomer to Canada. The Royal Winnipeg Ballet and Toronto's National Ballet have been in existence only a generation and Montreal's Les Grands Ballets Canadiens an even shorter time. All three companies have founded ballet schools and during the 1960's developed extensive touring circuits. All these companies have shown a strong interest in developing a Canadian repertoire, but it was not until 1966 that the first full-length ballet (Harry Freedman's *Rose Latulippe)* was commissioned by the RWB under Brian Macdonald.

Jazz. Jazz has always sounded irresistibly in Canadian ears and there have been several excellent jazz groups in Canada, although the slow decline of Toronto as a jazz center since the late 1950's seems to stem from the failure of a jazz music school (Oscar Peterson and Phil Nimmons) after only a few seasons. The cities of Montreal and Vancouver fare no better.

Composition. The composer needs a performer, and not until the last couple of generations has Canada had a large professional fraternity of good players. As late as 1930 the most advanced musical organization in the country, the still fledging Toronto Symphony Orchestra, was able to present hour-long "Twilight Concerts" only; the Montreal Symphony Orchestra was not founded until 1935. Their audience had (indeed still have) much repertoire "catching up" to do, and the prospects for serious composers were not promising.

TED GRANT, FROM NATIONAL FILM BOARD

WILFRID PELLETIER, leading opera conductor.

KARSH, OTTAWA, FROM RAPHO GUILLUMETTE

ERNEST MacMILLAN, eminent teacher of music.

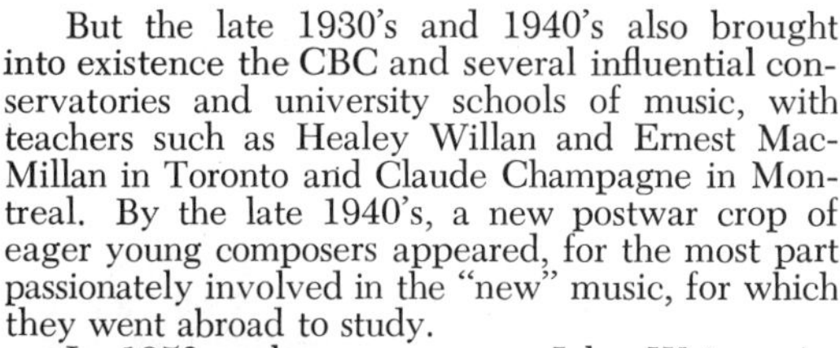

But the late 1930's and 1940's also brought into existence the CBC and several influential conservatories and university schools of music, with teachers such as Healey Willan and Ernest MacMillan in Toronto and Claude Champagne in Montreal. By the late 1940's, a new postwar crop of eager young composers appeared, for the most part passionately involved in the "new" music, for which they went abroad to study.

In 1952 such composers as John Weinzweig, Jean Papineau-Couture, John Beckwith, Murray Adaskin, Violet Archer, Barbara Pentland, Pierre Mercure, Harry Freedman, Clermont Pépin, and Harry Somers formed the Canadian League of Composers to press for more recognition; a decade later, the League numbered some 60 members. accepted only on the basis of established professional competence and serious intent. By the mid-1960's a second generation of "new music" composers had arisen (Norma Beecroft, Serge Garant, Irving Glick, Jacques Hétu, Bruce Mather, Murray Schafer), several of them venturing along the trails of the avant-garde. The body of native Canadian composers has been distinctly stimulated by the immigration of several from Europe, such as István Anhalt (Hungary), Eckhardt-Gramatté (Austria), Otto Joachim (Germany), Udo Kasemets (Estonia), Oskar Morawetz (Czechoslovakia), and others. Canada can also boast of many excellent film composers (Louis Applebaum, Maurice Blackburn, Robert Fleming, Eldon Rathburn), and composers for radio and television work (Morris Surdin, Lucio Agostini), and for school music (Keith Bissell).

Many universities now teach composition, and several maintain electronic music studios, notably Toronto, McGill, Simon Fraser, and the University of British Columbia.

Publication. Publication of serious music in Canada is scattered at best, most publishers being subsidiaries of foreign companies. However, Canadian composers can look to three organizations for some assistance: the performing right societies CAPAC (Composers, Authors, and Publishers Association of Canada, which sponsors various recording and other promotional projects) and BMI Canada, which is also the most active of Canadian publishers, and the Canadian Music Centre founded in 1959 to provide a central library and information center on Canadian music.

Recording. Recording in Canada is still dominated by foreign firms (RCA Victor, Columbia, Capitol, London), although in the early 1960's the Quebec popular "chansonnier" movement heralded a swing to a more indigenous product. More serious (and expensive) music has found several sponsors (CBC International Service, CAPAC, the government's Centennial Commission, and a few industrial firms), and some form of government recording agency may be established.

Music Education. The Canadian Association of University Schools of Music now numbers 17 members, the most prominent of which are the universities of Toronto, Montreal (French), McGill (English, also in Montreal), British Columbia (in Vancouver), and Alberta (in Edmonton). During the 1950's and 1960's several of these have leaned more and more toward the United States pattern of degree courses in performance.

The most prominent conservatory is the School of Music of the University of Toronto's Royal Conservatory of Music, which annually still sends examiners throughout the country. In Quebec, the Conservatoire de Musique is free to all deserving students of the province, with large branches in Montreal and Quebec City and smaller branches in Trois-Rivières, Val d'Or, Hull, Chicoutimi, and Sherbrooke.

School music varies greatly across the country but secondary schools particularly have made great strides in the past generation, especially in instrumental music. Specialist teachers, however, are scarcely to be found in the elementary schools. Each province has its Music Educators' Association, and together these have formed the national Canadian Music Educators' Association. There are some 12,000 private teachers in Canada, each province having its Registered Music Teachers' Association (although the conditions of "registration" do not ensure a high standard). The national body, the

A. SIMA, FROM NATIONAL FILM BOARD

PLACE DES ARTS in Montreal, a performing arts center, has two auditoriums besides that shown above.

Canadian Federation of Music Teachers Association, provides a useful, though loose, point of contact for its scattered membership.

Like several European countries, Canada has its "Jeunesses Musicales (du Canada)," claiming some 90,000 young members. These attend recitals and concerts patterned especially for young people and given by leading European and Canadian artists. Annual competitions by JMC demand the highest standards, and winners are launched on the JM International circuits. JMC also operates a summer music camp at Mount Orford, Quebec, for particularly deserving students.

The competitive festival movement is very vigorous in Canada, some 200 taking place each year across the country.

Folk Music. The variegated sources of Canada's population have resulted in a rich heritage of folk music. Songs of French Canada and of the Atlantic provinces are known around the world. There is much of beauty, too, in Eskimo and Indian music. Marius Barbeau, in the 1920's and 1930's, collected some 12,000 Indian, French, and Maritime songs. Helen Creighton and Kenneth Peacock have also added substantially to our knowledge of east-coast songs, while in recent years Edith Fowke also has revealed unexpected treasures in Ontario.

Patient scholarly work proceeds, much of it under the aegis of the Canadian Folk Music Society (affiliated with the International Folk Music Council), while the installation of the ethnomusicologist Dr. Mieczyslaw Kolinski at the University of Toronto in the mid-1960's promises a deeper examination of our musical folk heritage.

On the livelier entertainment level, the recently formed Canadian Folk Arts Council arranges for the international exchange of singers and colorful folk troupes of Ukrainians, Scots, Poles, Hungarians, and of course French Canadians.

Instrument Building. By 1900, Canada supported about 50 piano factories. Now there are very few. The new Sabatil harpsichord company in Vancouver is well established, but usually for the best instruments of other kinds the Canadian musician must look abroad. One great exception still thrives in St. Hyacinthe, Quebec—the organ building firm of Casavant Frères, whose name is still respected throughout the world.

KEITH MACMILLAN
Canadian Music Centre

Further Reading: Kallmann, Helmut, *A History of Music in Canada, 1534–1914* (Toronto 1960); Lasalle-Leduc, Annette, *La vie musicale au Canada français* (Quebec 1964); MacMillan, Sir Ernest, ed., *Music in Canada* (Toronto 1955); Saywell, John, ed., *Canadian Annual Review,* chapters on "Music" (Toronto, annually).

39. Mass Communications

Because of its relatively small population and its proximity to the highly developed media of mass communications in the United States, Canada has often found itself at a disadvantage in building a flourishing native industry in mass communications. Since World War II, however, there has been marked growth, both in quantity and quality, in publishing, broadcasting, and film production.

PUBLISHING

After more than two centuries of growth, publishing has been transformed from a weak pioneer venture of unassociated and isolated units into a centralized and consolidated segment of the national life, powerful commercially and important culturally.

By the late 1960's, Canadian readers were served by about 110 dailies, more than 900 weeklies, and about 500 trade and business papers, as well as national weekend newspapers and farm, labor, political, religious, cultural, and other special-interest magazines. Book publishing, although slower to develop, has displayed particular vigor since World War II.

Newspapers. Although daily newspaper circulations have risen steadily since 1900 and the number of daily newspapers has grown gradually since the low year of 1945, the number of publishers in the daily field has decreased. In 1930, 99 publishers owned 116 dailies; in the late 1960's, 4 major publishing groups owned 42 of the 110 dailies. The groups' share of total circulation had risen from 25% in 1958 to more than 40% in 1965.

Economic factors are the chief cause of such consolidation and centralization. The costs of operating a daily newspaper have accelerated so much that publishing units must be wealthy and stable if they are to survive. In some cases, even the rich entrepreneur has had to join larger groups to protect his paper from destructive competition and the sometimes disastrous effects of death duties.

The foremost daily newspaper publishing groups are Free Press Publications, Southam Company, and Thomson of Canada in the English-language field, and Les Journaux Trans-Canada Limitée in the French-language field. Although a colossus on the world scene, the Thomson chain is less important in Canada than Free Press Publications and Southam, because its Canadian operation is limited to small papers in small population centers. Except for *La Presse* of Montreal, one of Canada's largest dailies, Les Journaux Trans-Canada consists of small units.

Because weeklies are mainly concerned with regional matters, they are less disposed than dailies to join under common ownership, so that Canadian weekly publishing groups are few and small.

Magazines. Canadian mass circulation publishers are particularly subject to foreign competition. Three out of four popular-appeal periodicals bought by Canadians are American. Understandably, therefore, only two Canadian companies are large-scale publishers. These are the Maclean-Hunter organization and Southam Business Publications, each the producer of more than 50 magazines in the late 1960's. Maclean-Hunter relies heavily on profitable trade and business publications to subsidize its general-interest magazines *Chatelaine* and *Maclean's*. The Southam organization and Canada's many small publishers, being more exclusively concerned with special-interest periodicals, are not subject to significant American competition and enjoy success within their specialized field.

In 1965, Canadian magazines and newspapers were given legislative protection from real and potential foreign competition. A federal act disallowed as income tax deductions advertising aimed at the Canadian market and placed in a non-Canadian newspaper or periodical. "Canadian publications" were defined as those of which three fourths or more of the voting shares were owned by Canadians. The purpose of the legislation was to discourage foreign ownership of the printed media by so raising advertisers' costs for advertising placed in non-Canadian publications that they could not compete for advertising against Canadian newspapers and periodicals. However, *Time* and *Reader's Digest,* long established in Canada, shared Canadian privileges inasmuch as they are considered "Canadian magazines" for purposes of the act.

Weekend Papers. Weekend supplements help to make up for the lack of Canadian consumer magazines. Much of their strength derives from the fact that they are assured of the established circulations of the newspapers in which they are inserted. The main national weekend newspapers are *Weekend* (inserted in more than 40 papers), *Perspectives* (French-language; 6 papers), *The Canadian* (12 papers), *Globe Magazine,* and *SW Magazine* (formerly *Star Weekly.*)

Books. Book publishing is another aspect of Canadian activity long overshadowed by the enterprise of other countries. The domestic book market, particularly before World War II, was kept weak and fragmented by the smallness of a population scattered over a wide geographic area and divided into two disparate parts by bilingual differences. Canadian publishers found it risky to issue titles of narrow national interest. They also faced difficult competition from American, British, and French publishers who could treat Canada as an overflow market after their home markets had paid basic costs.

Until 1962, Canada subscribed only to the Bern Copyright Convention, which did not protect Canadian books in the United States. By an amended 1924 copyright agreement, American publishers had to respect the copyright on a Canadian book only if it were wholly manufactured in the United States, or on a Canadian-manufactured book for five years provided that not more than 1,500 copies of the book were exported to the United States. The situation was remedied in 1962 when Canada signed the Uni-

TELEVISION STUDIOS of the Canadian Broadcasting Corporation in Montreal are source of performance by the Chorale de Lameque during *L'Heure du Concert.*

A. LE COZ, FROM NATIONAL FILM BOARD

NATIONAL FILM BOARD

FEATURE-LENGTH motion picture, *Waiting For Caroline*, produced by Canadians, is filmed in Quebec city.

versal Copyright Convention, of which the United States is a member.

Repeal of the "manufacturing clause" intensified an upsurge in Canadian publishing that had begun immediately after World War II when Canadian titles increased spectacularly. French-language publishing made its most impressive gains during the war, suffered a postwar setback, then became lively again. In the late 1960's about 100 Canadian and 650 foreign publishers attested to the health of publishing in Canada.

W. H. Kesterton
Carleton University, Ottawa

Further Reading: Irving, John A., ed., *Mass Media in Canada* (Toronto 1962); Kesterton, W. H., *A History of Journalism in Canada* (Toronto 1967).

BROADCASTING

Of all the mass media of communication in Canada, broadcasting has experienced the most rapid and costly development, as well as the most abrupt transformations in technology under the impact of the electronics revolution. This medium of communication could hardly be expected to be absorbed into the community without dramatically reshaping its culture, economy, and politics. Consequently, it is not surprising that since the start of publicly owned or regulated sound broadcasting in the early 1930's and the start of television at the end of World War II these media have been the center of constant agitation and virtually unceasing inquiry into the policies, programs, and administrative structure deemed most appropriate for a country of continental dimensions.

The fact that Canada, faced by a wealthier and more populous nation on its southern border, has deliberately sought through these media to identify and preserve its national image has accentuated the significance of broadcasting to the community. The price of achieving a peculiarly "Canadian" broadcasting system has been high. And the special form assumed by that system is a strictly Canadian solution that, in broadcasting as well as other means of communication, has evolved into a genuinely "mixed" enterprise, with publicly owned components operating in parallel with privately owned establishments, sometimes complementing, but often competing with, one another. Thus, Canadian broadcasting falls somewhere between the nationalized British system and the regulated free-enterprise arrangements in the United States.

Government Regulation. Presiding over this mixed system since 1958 has been the Board of Broadcast Governors (BBG), a body of 11 members appointed by the cabinet and vested with comprehensive regulatory and licensing powers over broadcasting, akin to those of the Federal Communications Commission in the United States. The state-owned portion of the broadcasting enterprise is managed by the Canadian Broadcasting Corporation (CBC), which is also government appointed. This agency originally was vested in 1936 with both an operating monopoly of the national network and regulatory powers over all broadcasters—its own and private stations alike.

Ostensibly, the amendments to the broadcasting legislation that brought the separate, regulatory BBG into being in 1958 also stripped the CBC of all but its operating responsibilities. In practice, the BBG has concentrated its regulation on private broadcasters and has sought to arbitrate between the public and private sectors of the industry. Under the auspices of the BBG the private broadcasting sector has grown. This is true particularly of television, where the monopoly of network radio broadcasting originally conferred on the CBC has been adjusted to recognize the legal right of private television stations to form a limited network (CTV).

Coverage. Canadian broadcasting is conducted by the publicly owned CBC with over 30 radio and 16 television stations, together with some 130 private stations, that are affiliated under set contracts with the CBC to provide full national coverage; and by 231 private radio stations and 59 private television stations, 11 of which are joined to form the CTV private network. Together, these facilities reach practically the entire population, beaming at an estimated 4.5 million households with radio and television sets. In fact, television has grown so rapidly that householders with television sets far outnumber those with telephones in their homes.

Thus it may be said that one of the major objectives of the early policy makers—attainment of virtually total coverage—has been achieved. Room for expansion has been found largely through the frequency modulation (FM) channels for sound broadcasting with limited range; by resorting to ultrahigh frequency channels for allocation to educational broadcasters; in community-antenna television services; and in space communication via artificial satellites.

Programs. In implementing a policy of providing a varied choice of high quality programs in two languages and with a sense of national responsibility, public and private broadcasters have tended to place undue stress on light entertainment, and up to half of the prime viewing time is filled with programs from the United States. News and information account for about one third of the broadcasting fare; sports occupy about 8% of the time, and arts, letters, and science average a low 1.6 broadcasting hours.

Financing. The financing of broadcasting has raised serious problems in a mixed system such as Canada's, particularly when the policy of government regulation has been directed to achieving a balance between commercially sponsored programs and sustaining programs.

For the public sector with a special responsibility for preserving such a balance as well as promoting Canadian talent and vitalizing Canadian culture, a simple policy of financing all costs from commercial revenues could not be followed. Moreover, such an exclusively commercial operation would have failed to provide the desired coverage in sparsely populated (and from a market point of view, uneconomic) areas, and would have encouraged the importation of "made in U. S." programs across an open communications frontier. On the other hand, if the financing of the publicly owned broadcasting system had to depend on annual parliamentary handouts, the political independence of the CBC from the government would be jeopardized.

This dilemma was met initially by a variety of expedients, such as a license fee, borrowing, or an excise tax on television receivers; but in recent years the CBC has been financed by annual appropriations, supplemented by commercial revenues. Its rapidly mounting budget (increased sixteenfold between 1950 and 1965) has brought renewed attention to the best method of financing operations, which by the 1970's are expected to cost close to $200 million.

Proposals for Change. The government-sponsored inquiry into broadcasting, conducted in 1965, proposed financing the public system in such a way that it could plan beyond the range permitted by the existing practice of doling out money on an annual basis. But more significant and controversial was its recommendation to place the entire field of broadcasting under a single broadcasting authority, which would be responsible for ensuring that the public and private operating components worked together as part of a more integrated system, in which the highest standards of programming would be required. A government white paper on broadcasting, issued in 1966, indicated preference for retention of the "double board" arrangement, and by the late 1960's no official action had been taken to amend the arrangements that were made in 1958.

It is clear that no matter what changes are made, broadcasting is still in such a state of flux and has such a striking impact on a democratic society that renewed inquiries and constant public agitation will give no respite to the public or private operators of this vital medium of mass communication.

J. E. Hodgetts
Victoria College, University of Toronto

Further Reading: Fowler, Robert M., Lalonde, Marc, and Steele, Granville G. E., Report of the Committee on Broadcasting (Ottawa 1965).

FILM

Canada is known as a film-making nation largely through the work of the National Film Board (the NFB), a federal government agency established in 1939, which, until the early 1960's, made purely functional and instructional documentary short subjects. The production of the more important feature-length films for cinemas was largely neglected by both private interests and the government.

Production. In the mid-1960's a restlessness and frustration among young film makers caused the NFB to start a limited program of feature films, of which Don Owen's *Nobody Waved Goodbye* (1964), Gilles Groulx's *Le chat dans le sac* (1965), and Gilles Carle's *La vie heureuse de Leopold Z* (1965) were notable examples. At the same time, NFB short subjects (about 100 a year running from 5 to 60 minutes) became more adventurous, experimental, sophisticated, and outspoken. By the late 1960's the NFB's reputation at home and abroad had never been higher.

Outside the NFB, eager independent film makers such as Pierre Patry in Montreal, Larry Kent in Vancouver, and David Secter in Toronto, short of funds and under incredible difficulties, produced several films of note. Kent made *Sweet Substitute* (*Caressed*) and *When Tomorrow Dies;* Patry, under a cooperative arrangement, made *Trouble-Fête* and three others; and Secter made the student film *Winter Kept Us Warm* and *The Offering.* During this period, F. R. Crawley, Canada's leading producer of sponsored commercial shorts, made two excellent and unusual features: *Amanita Pestilens,* directed by René Bonnière; and the U. S.-Canada coproduction *The Luck of Ginger Coffey,* with Robert Shaw and Mary Ure, directed by Irving Kershner.

At the same time, lack of opportunity drove Sidney Furie, Norman Jewison, Arthur Hiller, Ted Kotcheff, and Silvio Narrizano, among oth-

J. MARSHALL, FROM NATIONAL FILM BOARD

FEDERAL ELECTION RETURNS are tabulated in the Canadian Broadcasting Corporation news center.

ers, to London and Hollywood, where they achieved recognition. All received their training in Canadian Broadcasting Corporation television. Others who worked for the CBC managed to branch out at home: Allan King with *Warrendale,* Ron Kelly with *Waiting for Caroline,* and Paul Almond with *Isabel.*

Development Fund. Continuity of production, however, was impossible. This resulted in concerted demands on the part of film makers for government assistance in the financing of feature films. With a new mood of vigorous Canadianism sweeping the country, coinciding with the country's Centennial, the government established the Canadian Film Development Fund which makes $10 million available to Canadian film makers. It may be well into the 1970's before Canadian features become accepted as a natural part of programs in Canadian cinemas or a publicly recognized fact abroad, but the promise is there.

U. S. Control. In all spheres of motion picture endeavor (the NFB excepted) Canada, like many other nations, is dominated by Hollywood companies and their New York offices. The Americans recognize that countries other than Canada are different in many ways from the United States and will even partly finance and accept for distribution films made in those countries. But Canada is treated as part of the U. S. domestic market.

Almost all the distributing companies are American owned and are controlled from New York. They earn some $40 million a year, most of which leaves the country. None of them has invested any of this in native production. One reason why Canadian financiers have refused to put money into productions is that no distributor will guarantee distribution by doing the same. Columbia Pictures has a good record of distributing Canadian films in which it has no financial interest, but (like the others) it does not have permission from its corporate headquarters to put up money for production.

Canada's 1,400-odd theaters are largely controlled by Famous Players (owned by Paramount Pictures) and Odeon Theatres (part of the Rank Organization). Few exhibitors show any interest in promoting Canadian films, although Odeon takes more interest in Canadian activity than does its competitor. It took almost 15 years for the NFB's shorts to find significant playing time in Canadian theaters, and most Canadian-made features have never been shown except in a few special cinemas. This has brought demands for a Canadian quota law, which have not been heeded. But the threat of legal compulsion, and the delay, give exhibitors the opportunity to change their policies.

Non-Theatrical Films. There is, however, a strong element of Canadian control in nontheatrical and noncommercial film activity. The Montreal International Film Festival, with its Festival of Canadian Films, is recognized as one of the finest film festivals held anywhere. Vancouver's International Film Festival has done much to make British Columbia film minded and film active.

The Canadian Film Institute (CFI) in Ottawa services some 80 film societies across the nation and distributes educational, scientific, and art films for many groups and companies. It also has a large library and reference section, and its National Film Theatre in Ottawa and Toronto holds ambitious programs illustrating the history of the cinema and new developments in film making. The Canadian Film Archives is part of the CFI and has grown rapidly in recent years.

The Cinémathèque Canadienne in Montreal (which, like the CFI, is not a government institution) also collects films and periodicals and holds regular series of film showings devoted to the work of individuals and nations. The film councils and public libraries in towns and cities throughout Canada are the NFB's nontheatrical means of reaching the people on film, although the impact of television, in which the NFB plays a considerable role with its films, has diminished audiences over the years.

Censorship. Much has been made of the narrowness and profuseness of Canadian censorship, but this is no longer the retrogressive force it once was. While 8 of the 10 provincial governments insist on maintaining their own censor boards, the majority of them have come to realize the absurdity of their position: while they snip, any film can be shown across the country on television without submission to censor boards.

All censor boards, following Ontario's lead, have a classification that prohibits persons under 18 from seeing certain films. Nevertheless, with the exception of Ontario, Quebec, and British Columbia, provincial boards continue to cut even the films restricted to adults.

The question of setting up one censor board for all of Canada has often been raised, and just as often has been buried because of jealousies over provincial rights. The legality of provincial censorship has never been challenged in the courts.

GERALD PRATLEY
Film Critic and Commentator
Canadian Broadcasting Corporation

CANADA: Recreation

With its great variety of landscape, the diversity of its cities and towns, and the vibrant life of its people, Canada offers notable opportunities for enjoyable and enriching experience. Canadians, absorbed in the natural beauty of their land and the history of their nation, are eager explorers of their country. They are joined the year round by millions of visitors from the United States and overseas.

The range of recreational attractions is as broad as the continent. Foremost among them are those of outdoor Canada. From rocky headlands and sandy beaches through rolling country covered with great forests and sprinkled with lakes and rivers, farmland and vast prairies to jagged snow peaks, the scenery is enthralling. For the sportsman, this country offers camping, fishing, hunting, hiking, canoeing, and skiing and other winter sports.

These opportunities are available to visitors, especially in Canada's 19 national parks, which lie in every province except Quebec. Hundreds of provincial parks are scattered through all 10 provinces. The national and provincial parks provide campsites and other facilities for tourists, but many contain large areas of primeval wilderness. Outside the parks there are vast areas throughout Canada that will reward the venturesome traveler.

Landmarks in every province trace the march of Canadian history from the earliest English and French settlements in the East to the western frontier. Nineteen national historic parks and a number of historic sites are maintained by the federal government. Many other historic sites are marked by various authorities.

Canada's cities and towns display a wide variety of characteristics. The metropolises of the East, with their shops and fine restaurants, still reflect the tone of an older culture. The great cities of the West are attuned to the life of the plains. Fishing villages along the Atlantic coast, hamlets in Quebec, where the French influence is dominant, and logging towns in the western mountains all have a distinctive flavor of their own.

Throughout Canada the performing arts and other cultural activities are reflected in festivals and fairs. Among the notable annual events are St. Jean Baptiste Day in Quebec; the daily Changing the Guard ceremony in Ottawa; the summer Shakespeare Festival at Stratford, Ontario; the Canadian National Exhibition in Toronto; Pion-Era Days in Saskatchewan; the Calgary Stampede in Calgary, Alberta; and the Pacific National Exhibition in Vancouver, British Columbia. Dominion Day, July 1, is marked by celebrations everywhere. Scottish games and other folk gatherings are favorite attractions. There are many museums, art galleries, zoos, aquariums, and planetariums. In summer and winter, visitors may watch or participate in various sports.

Travel in Canada. Most visitors from the United States live only one or two days' drive from the border. Visitors from other continents can come by sea, but the great majority come by air.

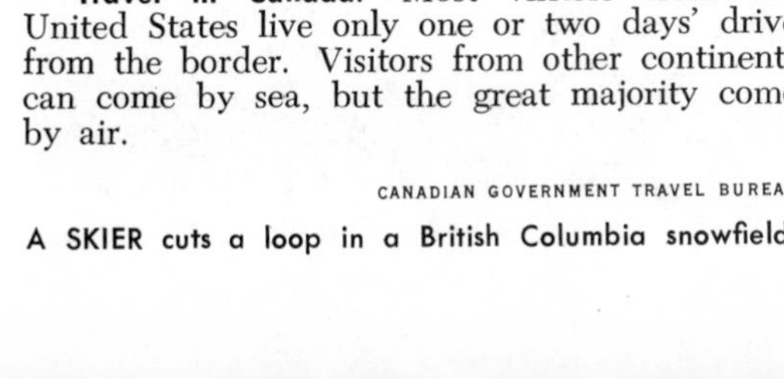

CANADIAN GOVERNMENT TRAVEL BUREAU

A SKIER cuts a loop in a British Columbia snowfield.

Twenty major world airlines fly to Canada's international airports. Inside the country there are two giant airlines—Air Canada and Canadian Pacific Airlines—that provide regular daily transcontinental runs, and a number of small airlines that provide frequent intercity flights. Airports are generally modern and are able to handle the newest jet planes.

Within Canada, most people, including visitors, travel by automobile—often a rented vehicle. The major route is the Trans-Canada Highway, 4,800 miles (7,700 km) of paved road traversing the 10 provinces. More than 60,000 miles (96,500 km) of paved roads provide easy access to the more densely settled parts of Canada. The remote rural areas are made accessible by thousands of miles of surfaced roads. Regular bus lines serve the larger communities, with intercity and interprovincial connections.

The Canadian National Railways and the Canadian Pacific Railway manage most of the 40,000 miles (64,300 km) of railroad lines. They provide daily transcontinental trains, frequent runs between major cities, and less frequent service between smaller communities. For longer trips, there are dining and sleeping facilities and observation cars. Some railroads reach far into the north country.

There are regular ferry services to Vancouver Island, Newfoundland, and Prince Edward Island, all favorite areas with visitors. Ferries also cross the St. Lawrence River at many points.

Accommodations. Canada has a varied range of accommodations. In the late 1960's these provided space for 600,000 persons. There are resort hotels, large metropolitan convention hotels, and other hotels and motels of all sizes situated in or near most communities. The two major railways operate extensive hotel systems, and other hotel chains are well represented in Canada.

For hunters and fishermen, accommodations are available in areas easily reached by automobile. There are many "fly-in" wilderness camps beyond the reach of road or rail, where guides and equipment are available. Reservations may be made by mail or through travel agents.

Motor campers and travelers by trailer will find ample accommodations throughout the country. The national and provincial parks and many smaller campsites and trailer parks can accommodate 200,000 persons overnight.

Rules for Foreign Tourists. Visitors who are citizens or permanent residents of the United States can cross their border to Canada with little difficulty or delay. While they need not have passports or visas, they should carry some identification. Visitors from other countries need a valid national passport and a Canadian visa. However, visas are not required for British subjects of Commonwealth countries, citizens of Ireland or South Africa, persons born in Western Hemisphere countries who come directly from those countries to Canada, or citizens of Japan and some 18 countries in Europe who visit Canada for not more than three consecutive months.

A visitor's personal effects and reasonable amounts of goods for his use are admitted free of duty. Sporting outfits and other equipment for the visitor's own use may be brought in by declaring them on entry. A visitor does not require a federal permit to possess rifles, shotguns, or fishing tackle in Canada. Special licenses must be obtained to hunt or fish.

The entry of automobiles and trailers for touring purposes and of tourist aircraft is generally a quick routine matter, but motorists from the United States who are planning to travel in Canada should obtain from their insurance company a Canadian nonresident interprovince motor vehicle liability insurance card. Pleasure boats may enter by permit for up to 12 months.

DAN WALLACE
Canadian Government Travel Bureau

RED DEER RIVER valley in Dinosaur Provincial Park, Alberta, shows the sweep of the western plains.

J. ALLAN CASH, FROM RAPHO GUILLUMETTE

40. Parks

Canada contains some 500 national and provincial parks besides many conservation areas and public green sites provided by municipal governments. The total area of national and provincial parks is about 100,000 square miles (259,000 sq km). Of this, at least 30,000 square miles (78,000 square km) is regarded as available for full use by the public. The larger figure includes vast areas awaiting development. Many such reserves already are designated as parks.

The parks reflect the varied topography of Canada. They embrace rocky ocean shores and sandy beaches, inland lakes, turbulent rivers, marshes, mountains, icefields, glaciers, prairies, forests, sand dunes, and deserts. Every type of Canadian wildlife, except possibly the polar bear and the musk-ox, is found in the parks. This is true also of species of birds, trees, and flowers.

Above all, the parks, especially those in the western mountains, are beautiful. Few places in the world can equal the scenery in the national parks in the Rocky and Selkirk mountains. The visitors enjoy manifold attractions: camping, fishing, boating, canoeing, hiking, skiing, mountain climbing, golfing, and picnicking. There are unlimited opportunities for nature students, photographers, and artists. All the parks are wildlife preserves, and no hunting is allowed.

More than 25 million persons visit Canada's parks annually, and this figure is expected to increase at least fivefold before the end of the 20th century. The number of visitors to national parks alone has increased at a rate of 10 to 17% annually. In the late 1960's, the annual figure was about 10 million.

Federally operated areas include 19 national parks and 19 national historic parks. A total of more than 500 national historic sites have been noted by markers throughout Canada. Wood Buffalo Park, a half-tamed wilderness of over 17,000 square miles (approximately 45,000 sq km) astride the Alberta-Northwest Territories boundary, is the largest national park in the world.

To accommodate the increasing pressure on the parks, it is estimated that a total of 40 to 60 national parks will be required. One was being prepared in the late 1960's in Kent county, New Brunswick, containing 160 square miles (414 sq km) of coast, sand dunes, waterways, and marshland. The expansion of the national parks system almost certainly will include new parks in the Yukon and Northwest Territories. Land is readily available, and transportation changes may bring remote regions within easy reach of people in all parts of Canada. For one possible site, the greatest interest has been shown in an area in the Yukon that contains the St. Elias Range, including Mt. Logan, the highest in Canada (19,850 feet, or 6,050 meters). Around Mt. Logan are peaks over 15,000 feet (4,600 meters). Icefields and glaciers spread for miles.

The growing population and abundance of leisure time have created serious problems of overcrowding in Canada's parks. There also is constant pressure by commercial interests to open wild or protected areas to development. Measures to ease the crowded conditions are being considered by the government and conservationists.

NATIONAL PARKS AND NATIONAL HISTORIC PARKS

Canada's national park system had its origin in what is now Banff National Park in Alberta. Among the unique features of the region are mineral hot springs that bubble from the slopes of Sulphur Mountain. The springs were discovered in 1883. Three railroad workers staked the land and planned to build bathhouses on the site. The government felt that the springs were a national nature asset and in 1885 made them a preserve of 10 square miles (26 sq km). In 1887, the preserve became a national park, and the Banff reservation was quickly expanded.

FORT HENRY, which was built in 1813 to defend the harbor of Kingston, Ontario, has been restored.

GEORGE HUNTER, FROM NATIONAL FILM BOARD

All the national parks and historic parks are directly under the jurisdiction of the government of Canada through the Department of Indian Affairs and Northern Development in Ottawa. The annual budget for operation and maintenance of the national parks is about $28 million, and the value of these parks to Canada's tourist industry is estimated at about $200 million a year.

Each of Canada's 10 provinces has at least one national park, except Quebec. The Northwest Territories shares Wood Buffalo Park with Alberta. There is no national park in the Yukon Territory. Each province except Alberta has at least one historic park. There is none in the Yukon or in the Northwest Territories.

Following is a listing of these areas in the provinces and territories, from east to west:

Newfoundland: Terra Nova Park (153 square miles, or 396 sq km) on Bonavista Bay, 162 miles (259 km) north of the provincial capital of St. John's. Here is a prime example of a coastal park—rocky and rugged, with deep bays and fjords. Inland, the terrain is gently rolling forested hills separated by ponds, lakes, and marshes. Even in summer, which is pleasantly mild, several species of animals and birds from the low Arctic zone are present, and icebergs commonly are seen offshore. Moose and black bear are regular inhabitants of the park, and seabirds are abundant.

Historic Park: Signal Hill (243 acres, or 98 hectares) at the entrance to St. John's harbor, the site where the first transatlantic wireless signal was received by Guglielmo Marconi on Dec. 12, 1901.

Nova Scotia: Cape Breton Highlands Park (367 square miles, or 950 sq km), a rocky Atlantic shoreline with a mountain background reminiscent of the Highlands of Scotland. In some places cliffs tower 1,500 feet (460 meters) above the ocean. The Cabot Trail, a highway that traverses the park, offers magnificent ocean views.

Kejimkujik Park (140 square miles, or 363 sq km), 150 miles (241 km) southwest of Halifax, embracing an area of lake, stream, and forest characteristic of the beauty of Nova Scotia's inland country. It was established in 1967.

Historic Parks: Fortress of Louisbourg (20 square miles, or 52.6 sq km), a remarkably detailed and accurate reconstruction of the walled city built by the French in the early 18th century; Halifax Citadel (20 acres, or 8 hectares), the early 19th century stone fortress that guarded the province's capital; Grand Pré (20 acres), where the expulsion of the Acadians took place; Fort Anne (31 acres, or 12.5 hectares) at Annapolis Royal; and Port Royal (20 acres), a restoration of the first fort built in 1605 by the French.

Prince Edward Island: Prince Edward Island Park (7 square miles, or 18 sq km), largely a coastal strip of sand beaches extending 25 miles (40 km) along the Gulf of St. Lawrence.

Historic Park: Fort Amherst (222 acres, or 90 hectares), site of a French settlement of 1720 captured by the British in 1758.

New Brunswick: Fundy Park (80 square miles, or 207 sq km). It skirts the Bay of Fundy, noted for its swift and exceptionally high tides, for 8 miles (12 km) and extends inland some 9 miles

CANADIAN PACIFIC

RESORTS such as the Banff Springs Hotel in Banff National Park, Alberta, are set in scenic wilderness.

(14 km). Fundy's tides, which rise up to 42 feet (13 meters), have sculptured the coast's sandstone cliffs into masses of rugged grandeur.

Historic Park: Fort Beauséjour (93 acres, or 38 hectares), an early French fort near Sackville.

Quebec—*Historic Parks:* Fort Lennox (210 acres, or 85 hectares) on Île-aux-Noix in the Richelieu River near St. Jean, an island fort built by the French; Fort Chambly (2.5 acres, or 1 hectare), a 1665 French strongpoint rebuilt in 1710 by the British; and Cartier-Brébeuf (5 acres, or 2 hectares) in Quebec city to commemorate the camp of Jacques Cartier and his men there in the winter of 1535.

Ontario: Canada's most populous province contains only three national parks, with a total area of 12 square miles (31 sq km). They are: St. Lawrence Islands (12 in number) among the Thousand Islands of the St. Lawrence River in the vicinity of Kingston-Gananoque; the Georgian Bay Islands, largely for recreation and camping, which include tiny Flowerpot Island with its unique rock pillars; and Point Pelee, a forested area on Lake Erie with fine beaches and unusual flora for the region. The point is a resting place for migratory birds. The first of a chain of national parks nature centers was opened at Point Pelee in 1966. The aim of this center is to provide information for visitors, present film programs and talks, and conduct nature hikes.

Historic Parks: Woodside (11.5 acres, or 4.7 hectares), in Kitchener, boyhood home of the prime minister William Lyon Mackenzie King; Fort Malden (10 acres, or 4 hectares), a defense post built between 1797 and 1799 facing the Detroit River at Amherstburg; Fort Wellington (12 acres, or 5 hectares), at Prescott, site of a military garrison from 1812 to 1866.

Manitoba: Riding Mountain Park (1,148 square miles, or 2,973 sq km), west of Lake Manitoba, on a vast rolling plateau that rises to 2,200 feet (670 meters) above sea level. Many of the natural features of this park were shaped by Ice Age glaciers that retreated about 10,000 years ago. Evidence of the glacial bulldozing remains in the plateau's depressions, now filled by small lakes, and by moraines and boulders found in many parts of the park. The forest cover is predominantly white and black spruce, while wildlife includes mule and white-tailed deer, elk, moose, coyote, lynx, wolf, and beaver, and an exhibition herd of bison.

Historic Parks: Lower Fort Garry (13 acres or 5 hectares), a fort built by the Hudson's Bay Company between 1831 and 1839 on the Red River about 20 miles (32 km) north of Winnipeg; and Fort Prince of Wales (50 acres, or 20 hectares), a partial restoration of a stone fort built between 1733 and 1771 at Churchill on the shore of Hudson Bay.

Saskatchewan: Prince Albert Park (1,496 square miles, or 3,875 sq km), in the central part of the province, 100 miles (161 km) north of the city of Saskatoon. This territory was a favorite hunting and fishing ground of the Indians. Grey Owl (George Stansfeld Belaney), author and conservationist, wrote his nature tales in a cabin at Lake Ajawan, where he died and is buried. The park has many lakes with good sand beaches. Larger animal residents include wolf, black bear,

GAR LUNNEY FROM NATIONAL FILM BOARD

BOW RIVER in Alberta is one of Canada's famous fishing streams. Here an angler nets a cutthroat trout.

mule and white-tailed deer, and woodland caribou. Some 175 species of birds have been counted, among them the bald eagle. At Lavallee Lake are the nesting grounds of the American white pelican and the double-crested cormorant.

Historic Park: Fort Battleford (37 acres, or 15 hectares), a North West Mounted Police post built in 1876, 4 miles (6 km) south of North Battleford.

Alberta: Wood Buffalo Park (17,300 square miles, or 44,807 sq km), straddling the boundary of the Northwest Territories. It is a nesting ground of the whooping crane, a species that is fighting to avoid extinction. This park is an important refuge for bison, which has been saved from extinction. Because of its remote location, Wood Buffalo Park is regarded more as a land bank for future use than as an active park.

Elk Island Park (75 square miles, or 194 sq km) near Edmonton, the first area to be set aside primarily as a wild animal preserve. It has two fenced areas with a large herd of bison, as well as elk, deer, and moose.

Waterton Lakes Park (203 square miles, or 526 sq km), in a scenic mountain region that rises abruptly from the prairie in the southwestern corner of the province. The park shares the international boundary with Glacier National Park of the United States, in Montana. These two compose Waterton-Glacier International Peace Park, formed in 1932, the first of its kind in the world. The highest peak in the Canadian park is 9,600-foot (2,930-meter) Mt. Blakiston. Geological formations in the park are colored purple, red, green, and gray as a result of mineral particles in the rocks. A conspicuous feature of the park is the main chain of lakes, of which Upper Waterton is 7 miles (11 km) long, a half mile (0.8 km) wide, and, in places, more than 450 feet (137 meters) deep. The lakes, for which the park is named, were named in honor of Charles Waterton, an early 19th century English naturalist. Cameron Creek is noted for its picturesque waterfalls and rainbow trout. Waterton Park contains plants characteristic of zones from prairie to alpine—Indian paintbrush, larkspur, wild geranium, avalanche lily, mariposa lily, bear grass, and many others. Among its large animals are black and grizzly bear, cougar, elk, moose, bighorn sheep, and mountain goat. Among the bird species, golden eagles often are seen.

Banff Park (2,564 square miles, or 6,641 sq km), on the eastern slopes of the Rocky Mountains. It is probably Canada's best known park, with superlative mountain scenery. Banff has many lakes, big and small, winding rivers and turbulent creeks. Among the notable lakes are the turquoise-colored Moraine Lake, set in the majestic Valley of the Ten Peaks; the mountained-ringed Lake Louise; and Mirror Lake, called the Goat's Looking Glass by the Indians because, it was said, mountain goats went there to comb their beards. Icefields cover large areas in the high mountain country and send out tongues of glaciers that are visible from the highway connecting Banff Park with Jasper National Park to the northwest. Mt. Norquay on the outskirts of Banff townsite is a fine skiing spot. The ski lift carries summer visitors to the top of the mountain for panoramic views.

Jasper Park (4,200 square miles, or 10,878 sq km), adjoining Banff Park on the northwest, where the awesome Columbia Icefield lies among the peaks at an elevation of 8,500 feet (2,590 meters). One point on this rugged sea of ice is said to be a three-pronged watershed where a drop of rain falling can split and go in three directions—to the Atlantic, Arctic, and Pacific oceans—after flowing for thousands of miles in three river systems. Tongues of ice flow from the Columbia Icefield into valleys on several sides. One of these, the Athabasca Glacier, moves about 50 feet (15 meters) a year. It can be explored by tourists in snowmobiles.

Jasper offers panoramas of magnificent mountain scenery. Mt. Edith Cavell, seen across the lake in front of Jasper Park Lodge, is one of the finest sights in the Rockies, especially at sundown or dawn. At timberline (about 7,000 feet, or 2,130 meters) and above is a wealth of plant life—red and pink mountain heath, white heather, rhododendron, and an ever-changing carpet of alpine meadow flowers. There is excellent skiing.

British Columbia: Kootenay Park (543 square miles, or 1,406 sq km), situated in southeastern British Columbia, on the western slopes of the Rockies. It extends about 5 miles (8 km) on each side of a section of the Banff-Windermere highway for about 60 miles (96 km). It possesses scenic valleys (especially those of the Kootenay and Vermilion rivers), deep canyons, spectacular waterfalls, and mineral-bearing hot springs. The park abounds in vivid masses of wild flowers. The name Kootenay is all the white man's tongue could do with the Indian word *K'tunaxa,* meaning "strangers" or "people from the hills."

Yoho Park (507 square miles, or 1,313 sq km), situated just north of Kootenay. It is a region of lofty peaks, breakneck cliffs, gorges, and waterfalls. Yoho Park sometimes is called the "Roof of the Rockies." The highest point in the park is Mt. Goodsir (11,685 feet, or 3,660 meters). Yoho attracts mountain climbers, and for hikers there are more than 200 miles (321 km) of trails. In this park is Mt. Burgess, which has been pictured on the back of Canadian $10 bills for many years, rising behind Emerald Lake. Yoho's first 10 square miles (26 sq km) were established as a scenic reserve in 1886.

Glacier Park (521 square miles, or 1,349 sq km) in the Selkirk Mountains, west of the Rockies, within the great northern bend of the Columbia River. From some peaks in this park more than 100 glaciers can be seen threading their way down into the valleys. The mountainsides are clothed with thick forest and marked by waterfalls born of the melting ice. Mountaineering and skiing are excellent in Glacier.

Mt. Revelstoke Park (100 square miles, or 259 sq km), a mountaintop plateau on the western slopes of the Selkirks. It has good skiing. A lookout, served by road, offers vistas from the top of Mt. Revelstoke itself.

Historic Parks: Fort Langley (11 acres, or 4 hectares), a reconstruction of a Hudson's Bay Company post of the 1850's; and Fort Rodd Hill (44 acres, or 18 hectares), a 19th century British fortification on Vancouver Island.

PROVINCIAL PARKS

Each of the 10 provinces has its system of provincial parks. These parks cover every type of terrain. The parks of some provinces—notably Quebec, Ontario, and British Columbia—are outstanding for scenery and recreational opportunities. Ontario has 17,000 campsites, twice the number in the nine other provinces combined. Fees for use of the provincial parks are nominal.

TED GRANT, FROM NATIONAL FILM BOARD

CALGARY STAMPEDE, where rodeo performers show their skill, is held annually at Calgary, Alberta.

Following is a listing of the parks established and operated by the provincial governments, from east to west:

Newfoundland: More than 30 parks operating, containing some 600 campsites.

Nova Scotia: Many small camping and trailer sites; more than 30 large-scale picnic grounds. A 14-acre (5.7-hectare) wildlife park at Shubenacadie displays native birds and animals.

Prince Edward Island: 24 provincial campgrounds and 32 privately operated sites. These range in size from 5 to 250 acres (2–101 hectares) and are centered principally on the fine beaches. Some 150,000 campers, more than the population of the province itself, use the parks each year.

New Brunswick: A wide selection of small camping and picnic sites.

Quebec: 23 parks and reserves with a total area exceeding 52,000 square miles (134,680 sq km). Some of the parks—such as Mt. Orford, a skiing, golf, music, theater and fine arts center south of Montreal—are small, but most are large tracts of wilderness or semi-wilderness, attractive to sportsmen and canoeists. Almost without exception, the parks offer excellent fishing for brook trout, lake trout, walleye, northern pike, and, in the Gaspé, salmon. La Vérendrye, nearly 5,000 square miles (12,950 sq km), north of Ottawa-Hull, is the largest park. It was named after Pierre Gaultier de Varennes, Sieur de la Vérendrye, discoverer of the Rocky Mountains. Laurentides, northeast of Quebec city, sprawls across 4,000 square miles (10,360 sq km) of forested ridges, lakes, and rivers. Chibougamau and Mistassini (home of prize brook trout) are other notable parks in the northern wilderness. Mt. Tremblant Park in the Laurentian Mountains north of Montreal is easily accessible and is famous for skiing. In general, Quebec's parks are not quite so fully tailored for family campers as those in some other provinces.

Ontario: 96 provincial parks, more than any other province. The largest is Algonquin Park (2,910 square miles, or 7,536 sq km), with more than 1,500 campsites. About 125 miles (201 km) north of Toronto, it is within easy reach of population areas and is visited by about 500,000 persons annually. This park contains an excellent nature museum, a pioneer logging display, and is a popular center for nature talks and hikes. Quetico Park, in the northwest part of the province, is second in size—1,750 square miles (4,531 sq km). This park is almost primeval wilderness, with many canoe routes. Ontario's parks range from highly developed areas to near-wilderness regions.

In addition to the provincial parks, a number of other public parks called "conservation areas," have been developed by the conservation authorities of several river watersheds in Ontario. These are regional government projects (most of them in or close to urban areas) primarily designed for flood control or land use experimentation. The result has been a series of fine parks that in many cases provide facilities for public camping, picnicking, swimming, fishing, and nature study.

Manitoba: In the late 1960's nine provincial parks had been developed or were in the development state. There were also more than 40 recreation areas, ranging from 2.5 to 2,000 acres (1–809 hectares). Whiteshell Forest Reserve, 100 miles (160 km) east of Winnipeg, an area of forest, lakes, rivers, and rocks just before the prairies begin, is one of Manitoba's best.

Saskatchewan: Nine provincial parks and 19 smaller regional parks, plus scores of local campgrounds.

Alberta: 42 established parks extending in size from 4-acre (1.6-hectare) Ma-Me-O Beach near Wataskiwin to 49,629-acre (20,085-hectare) Cypress Hills Park near Medicine Hat. Alberta's parks cover 197 square miles (510 sq km) and receive more than 3.5 million visitors a year.

British Columbia: 226 park reserves, of which more than 170 have been developed for public use. About 90 of these have camping facilities. The variety of the parks ranges from oceanside to mountain and forest. Some parks have all three types of terrain. The total area of the parks is more than 9,375 square miles (24,282 sq km).

Tweedsmuir Park (3,125 square miles, or 8,094 sq km), in the wilderness 300 miles (483 km) northeast of Vancouver, is the largest. One of the most popular tourist sites is Barkerville Historic Park, 60 miles (97 km) east of Quesnel. A gold rush town that became a ghost town, Barkerville has been restored by the province as a showplace of pioneer days. Strathcona Park, more than 781 square miles (2,023 sq km) of wilderness in the center of Vancouver Island, was the first park established in the province.

FUTURE OF THE PARKS

While many of the parks are among the world's best for scenery and public facilities, the pressures of population and leisure are placing tremendous demands on the quiet places. Conservationists are greatly concerned, especially over the national parks.

Nearly a century ago the government of Canada promised that these preserves "shall be maintained and made use of so as to leave them unimpaired for the enjoyment of future generations." Conservationists argue that "unimpaired" means just that—no deep penetration by blacktop highways, widening campsites, shopping centers, and similar evidences of modern civilization. The government agrees that national parks are not intended to fill every recreational need or interest; their purpose, rather, is to provide opportunities for rest, enjoyment of nature, and aesthetic inspiration.

The likelihood is that Canada will introduce a system of areas set aside exclusively for recreation. These would be different in character from national parks, which are basically intended to be nature conservancies. The recreation areas would include water frontage, ski slopes, and other parcels of land suited to specific outdoor activities. Such areas, it is hoped, would greatly reduce the pressures on other parks and preserve them as near-wilderness places. See also articles on individual provinces.

ROBERT TURNBULL, *Travel Editor Toronto "Globe and Mail"*

Information Sources

National Parks

Canadian Government Travel Bureau, Ottawa, Ontario.

Department of Indian Affairs and Northern Development, National Parks Branch, Ottawa.

National and Provincial Parks Association of Canada, Toronto, Ontario.

Provincial Parks

Alberta: Parks Division, Department of Lands and Forests, Edmonton, Alberta.

British Columbia: British Columbia Government Travel Bureau, Parliament Buildings, Victoria, British Columbia.

Manitoba: Trade and Publicity Branch, Department of Industry and Commerce, Legislative Building, Winnipeg, Manitoba.

New Brunswick: New Brunswick Travel Bureau, Fredericton, New Brunswick.

Newfoundland: Newfoundland and Labrador Tourist Development Office, Confederation Building, St. John's Newfoundland.

Nova Scotia: Nova Scotia Travel Bureau, Halifax, Nova Scotia.

Ontario: Department of Lands and Forests, Parliament Buildings, Toronto; Department of Tourism and Information, Parliament Buildings, Toronto.

Prince Edward Island: Prince Edward Island Travel Bureau, Charlottetown, Prince Edward Island.

Quebec: Department of Tourism, Fish and Game, Quebec City, Quebec.

Saskatchewan: Tourist Development Branch, Power Building, Regina, Saskatchewan.

41. Sports

Canadians are a sports-minded people. Men and women engage the year round in a variety of competitive and noncompetitive sports, outdoors and indoors. As spectators, they flock in thousands to tournaments and games. Their zest for vigorous living, their various racial origins, the diversity of their country's climate and terrain—all have contributed to the multiplicity of sports that distinguishes the nation's recreation.

Ice hockey is perhaps the premier Canadian sport. It was originated and developed wholly in Canada, and is played throughout the nation. Other winter sports include curling, skiing, tobogganing, and ice-skating—figure skating, speed skating, and skating for fun. Canada is a regular participant in the Winter Olympic Games.

In summer the variety of sports ranges from archery to automobile racing. Almost every sport popular in other lands has its counterpart in Canada. Other seasons also have their special sports: rugby football, fishing, and hunting.

Special Sports Centers. While all sports have a national following, especially in the more populous areas, there are certain places where one sport is highly favored. New Westminster, British Columbia, and Cornwall, Ontario, are centers for lacrosse. Scottish games thrive in Nova Scotia. Rowing is featured at St. Catharines, Ontario, where an annual regatta draws oarsmen from all North America. The Winnipeg, Manitoba, curling bonspiel is Canada's oldest event in that sport.

Horse racing, popular everywhere, flourishes especially in metropolitan Toronto, where the Queen's Plate, the oldest continually run racing event in North America (since 1860), is conducted annually. Automobile racing is popular at Mosport, a specially designed track near Bowmanville, Ontario. The Calgary Stampede, famous for its rodeo competition, is perhaps the best annual show of its kind in the world.

Winter Sports—*Ice Hockey*. Ice hockey began in military garrisons in the 19th century as a game for the long Canadian winters. The rules varied widely until the late 1870's, when a group of students in Montreal drew up a code that was generally adopted. The game has spread until it now is played in at least 25 countries and is the principal winter sport in the Olympic Games.

Across Canada, more than 250,000 youths play in organized leagues, and thousands more play informally on frozen ponds and outdoor rinks. Canada's Hockey Hall of Fame, in Toronto, honors famous players and leaders of the sport.

In Canada, professional hockey is so popular that the two largest hockey arenas—the Forum in Montreal and the Maple Leaf Gardens in Toronto—have not had an unsold seat at a National Hockey League game since the end of World War II.

***Curling*.** Curling attracts thousands of Canadians in the winter. Each province holds a series of games for men and women to determine the provincial champion rink. The provincial title winners compete annually to decide the Canadian champion. The men's winning rink represents Canada in the world competition.

Summer Sports—*Lacrosse*. The native Indians taught lacrosse to the white man and were so generous that they allowed their opponents to play 25 men on a side against their 20. The game finally was codified with 12 men on a team

ANNAN PHOTO FEATURES

ICE HOCKEY is Canada's premier sport. Professional games in indoor arenas draw thousands of spectators.

and became a rage. In the 1860's, when Montreal's population was about 100,000, an important lacrosse match often drew 10,000 spectators. Lacrosse was called Canada's national game and was introduced successfully in the British Isles, the United States, and Australia. It attained its peak of popularity in Canada in the early 1900's and was featured in the Olympic Games at St. Louis, Mo., in 1904.

Suddenly its popularity declined. Some attributed this to the excessive roughness of the game; others, to the encroachments of professionalism. But in 1930, a new form of the game called "box-lacrosse" was developed. This is played by six men on a side and can be adapted to outdoor or indoor play, especially in arenas originally designed for hockey.

Baseball. Baseball is another sport that has known both fame and ill fortune in Canada. The game was introduced from the United States in the 1860's and for many years competed with lacrosse and cricket for public favor. Canada has been linked to professional baseball in the United States. Some Canadian cities have had teams in leagues with U. S. teams, notably Montreal and Toronto in the International League. In the mid-20th century, baseball has been largely replaced by softball, which requires only a small area and is played more quickly.

Golf. As a sport for participants and spectators, golf is popular throughout the country. Many local and regional tournaments are held. The annual Canadian Open, in which the world's best players have competed for stakes totaling $200,000, may draw 20,000 watchers on one day.

Track and Field. Track and field athletics are a favorite sport with Canadians. National and provincial championships are held annually. Hamilton, Ontario, was the site of the first British Empire games in 1930, and Vancouver, British Columbia, was the host city for the fifth games held in 1954. The 1967 Pan-American Games were held in Winnipeg. Canada has competed in all the Olympic Games since 1904.

Canadians in World Sport. Through more than a century of competition, many Canadians have achieved international fame. Ned Hanlan was a world champion sculler late in the 19th century. Louis Rubenstein was the first world's champion figure skater (1890). Louis Cyr was a celebrated weight lifter. Tommy Burns and Jimmy McLarnin were world champion boxers. Bill Sherring was a noted distance runner, and Percy Williams won the 100- and 200-meter sprints at the 1928 Olympic Games. Many Canadian teams, especially in hockey and curling, have ranked as the world's best.

Many women athletes also have excelled. Barbara Ann Scott won the world and Olympic figure skating titles and two others in one month. Marlene Stewart, then a teen-ager, won the Canadian and British women's open golf championships. Marilyn Bell, another teen-ager, swam across Lake Ontario, the Strait of Juan de Fuca, and the English Channel. Ann Heggtveit and Nancy Greene won women's skiing titles. The Edmonton Grads women's basketball team was internationally famous for 20 years.

Financial Support. Canadian athletes formerly were handicapped by lack of funds to travel to compete in distant international events. In the 1960's this problem was remedied by contributions from the federal government that will enable Canadian athletes to enjoy the coaching, training, and competitive opportunities comparable to those in many European countries.

HENRY H. ROXBOROUGH
Author of "Great Days in Canadian Sports"

Further Reading: Bull, W. Perkins, *From Rattlesnake to Hockey* (Toronto 1934); Reed, Thomas A., *The Blue and White* (Toronto 1944); Roxborough, Henry H., *Canada at the Olympics* (Toronto 1963).

PUBLIC ARCHIVES OF CANADA

JACQUES CARTIER, who staked France's claim to Canada, views the future site of Montreal from Mount Royal in 1535, as portrayed by L. R. Batchelor.

CANADA: History

42. Prehistory and Period of Early Exploration

Of Canada's human and physical geography before 1615, when Samuel de Champlain made the first exploration of the country's interior, two factors must be considered. First, human geography had a history of at least 15,000 years (perhaps much more), and it has been in process of slow and steady change. Second, such change reflected not only the introduction and spread of ideas, methods, tools, and weapons, or variations in the number and distribution of people, but also as sweeping a transformation of the geography of nature as any comparable area may have experienced in so short a time.

The major landforms themselves underwent little change. The mighty Rocky Mountains and towering coastal ranges to the west, and the alpine or subalpine mountains of Ellesmere and Baffin islands, the rugged Torngat Mountains of Labrador, the Laurentian hills, and the Appalachian rough lands, to the east, formed the framework. Between these marginal highlands stretched a great mid-continent expanse of low elevation and subdued relief. Most of it comprised the Canadian (or Laurentian) Shield of ancient crystalline rock in a great horseshoe around Hudson Bay. To its west lay the Prairie plains and the Mackenzie River lowlands. The western cordilleran area was broad and largely uninterrupted; to the east, Hudson Strait and the St. Lawrence Valley cut wide trenches through the more subdued upland areas.

Land of Ice. Between 20,000 and 15,000 years ago, however, this variety was largely obscured by widespread mantles of ice. The undulating glacial surface had its own domes and troughs. Near Hudson Bay one or more of the domes may have reached a height of 2 miles (3 km). Yet there were ice-free areas in the western Arctic and, usually, a nearly continuous ice-free corridor east of the western mountains, which were capped by another vast glacier. Probably the only use any human inhabitants could have made of the Canadian lands in those icy millennia was for passage through that corridor from the unglaciated basin of the lower Yukon River (which had dry-land connections with Siberia) to beyond the southern margins of the continental ice sheet, which followed approximately the courses of the Missouri and Ohio rivers.

The Glaciers Leave. The period of deglaciation over the continental lowlands (there is still much ice left in the mountainous west and extreme northeast) extended roughly from about 15,000 to at least 7,000 years ago. For the ice to melt, summers must have warmed and lengthened and winter snows much decreased. As the ice edges retreated through wastage, many of the continental margins were far seaward of present coastlines. The masses of water tied up in ice sheets in many parts of the world had depressed the ocean surface by hundreds of feet. Thereafter, the position of the coastline represented a delicate balance between rising sea level and the delayed "rebound" of land from which the ice had been removed. Meanwhile, the steady dissipation of continental ice broke it up into distinct masses, isolated or interconnected, that went through their own cycles of growth and decline within the general process of ice wastage.

So rapidly did the ice melt at times that great volumes of water were released, often to be dammed up between elevations of land and the ice fronts themselves. Thus large areas, especially in the present Northwest Territories, Saskatchewan, Manitoba, Ontario, and Quebec, were covered by lakes, some much larger than the present Great Lakes, for hundreds or even thousands of years. On their floors great depths of silt settled, forming the famed Red River plains and the vast Ontario-Quebec clay belt. Over most of the land, however, the disappearance of the ice left indiscriminately dumped glacial debris or bare rock expanses that interrupted preglacial drainage patterns so as to leave over much of the surface an intricate, variegated pattern of lake, stream, and bog.

Plant and Animal Life. The evidence of vegetation and soils buried by the moraines of minor, local, and temporary readvances of the ice during the general deglaciation indicates that a robust vegetation of some variety established itself rapidly and close to the edge of the ice. Indeed the climate often was warmer than today's for most of the time between 9,000 and 3,000 years ago; from about 7,000 to 5,000 years ago this warming (sometimes also drying) trend reached a peak in a so-called "climatic optimum." Where the ice had disappeared, many kinds of plants and animals lived farther north and, on mountain slopes, higher than their present ranges.

Some changes in plant and animal life may have resulted from the additional forces of genetic change, competitive advantage, or of burning or hunting by man. Contemporaneous with the first good evidence of man in the central continent are the bones of many late Pleistocene species of animals: elephants, mammoths, huge bison, giant beaver, horses, camels, sloths, and many others long since extinct or now geographically far removed. Slowly they disappeared and, by 5,000 years ago, if not before, the plants and animals were, in kind and location, not too different from those reported by the first European observers.

Evidence of Man. This is a picture in broad sweeping strokes, of the changing natural environment in which man must have lived in the Canadian lands during deglaciation and postglacial times. No doubt, men had made their way far to the south from the continental "doorway" in Alaska through a largely ice-free corridor while most of the Canadian lands were still ice covered. Then, as the ice receded, evidence of human life began to appear on its fringes, certainly in the present Maritime Provinces and probably on the shores of the ancestral Great Lakes and the southwestern grasslands of the west as well, more than 10,000 years ago.

From 15,000 to 10,000 years ago most of the people who inhabited the present American or Canadian lands probably were unspecialized hunters, food-gatherers, and fishermen. But there have been sporadic finds, scattered widely over the continent and representing a period of thousands of years, of large, beautifully chipped stone blades; these may be taken as evidence of the existence of groups of men as specialized in hunting large game animals (such as elephants) as were the bison hunters on the Great Plains in historical times. After these groups disappeared, there was little significant cultural change for several thousand years, although it is believed that the Canadian lands were occupied continuously and that the occupation became increasingly widespread as vegetation and animals closely followed the retreating ice margin.

By 5,000 years ago most of the northern forest area of present Canada from Newfoundland to the Rockies may have been occupied thinly by people living very much as those in the same areas were four centuries ago — eating the same kinds of berries, meat, and fish, wearing the same kinds of skins and furs, perhaps using essentially the same kinds of tools and weapons. It is not known when the division of most of the people into two major language families—Algonkian in the center

HISTORICAL HIGHLIGHTS

1000 (c.)	Norsemen reach North American coast.
1497	John Cabot, in service of Britain, lands on Atlantic coast, in Newfoundland, Cape Breton Island, or southern Labrador.
1534	Jacques Cartier enters the Gulf of St. Lawrence.
1535	Cartier ascends the St. Lawrence River to sites of Quebec and Montreal.
1605	First permanent colony founded at Port Royal.
1608	Quebec founded by Champlain.
1610	Henry Hudson, in search of Northwest Passage, discovers Hudson Bay.
1615	Samuel de Champlain penetrates interior to Georgian Bay.
1627	Louis XIII grants part of New France to Company of One Hundred Associates to promote colonization.
1642	Sieur de Maisonneuve founds Montreal.
1663	Louis XIV cancels One Hundred Associates charter and restores New France to royal rule.
1670	Founding of Hudson's Bay Company by royal charter brings British and French into conflict.
1713	Acadia (Nova Scotia), Newfoundland, and the Hudson Bay region are ceded by France to Britain.
1759	Wolfe defeats Montcalm at Quebec.
1760	French surrender Montreal to British.
1763	Britain gains control of New France by terms of Treaty of Paris; Seven Years' War ends.
1774	Quebec Act extends boundaries of Quebec province and guarantees religious freedom.
1783	Montreal traders form North West Company.
1791	Constitutional Act divides Quebec into Upper and Lower Canada.
1792–93	Mackenzie completes first crossing of the continent North of Mexico.
1812–14	Invading American forces are repulsed.
1837–38	Rebellions occur in Upper and Lower Canada.
1840	Act of Union joins Upper and Lower Canada under one government.
1846	Oregon Territory boundary is fixed along 49th parallel.
1856	Gold is discovered in Fraser River basin.
1858	Crown colony of British Columbia is proclaimed.
1864	Charlottetown and Quebec conferences held.
1867	Confederation. Self-governing Dominion of Canada is established by union of provinces of Canada (divided into Ontario and Quebec), Nova Scotia, and New Brunswick.
1869	Louis Riel's first rebellion is quelled.
1870	Northwest Territories are transferred to Canada and province of Manitoba enters Confederation.
1871	British Columbia enters Confederation.
1873	Prince Edward Island enters Confederation.
1885	Main line of transcontinental Canadian Pacific Railway is completed; Riel hanged after second rebellion.
1896	Klondike gold rush begins.
1905	Alberta and Saskatchewan enter Confederation.
1914	Canada enters World War I.
1920–21	Insulin is discovered by Banting and Best.
1931	Statute of Westminster is passed by British Parliament.
1939	Canada enters World War II.
1949	Newfoundland enters Confederation; Canada joins NATO; appeals to Privy Council are abolished.
1952	First Canadian is appointed governor general.
1959	St. Lawrence Seaway opens.
1967	Canada celebrates first centenary of Confederation.

and east, and the Athapaskan in the northwest —may have begun. There must have been a relatively frequent shifting of individual groups and a constant diffusion of various elements of culture.

Arctic Culture. At some time more than 4,000 years ago, there spread out, even more thinly, along the Arctic coastlands a people and culture (probably derived from northeastern Asia) that reached Greenland by about 2000 B.C. and dominated the area for another thousand years. These people, living in small, isolated bands, made typically small and delicate stone tools and lived chiefly on sea mammals, fish, caribou, and musk-ox. Succeeding them (probably their cultural and biologic descendants) were people with a culture that has been given the name "Dorset." A little skeletal evidence and the descriptions in the Viking sagas (for these were the "Skraelings" whom the Icelanders and Greenlanders encountered on North American shores) suggest that they were the direct ancestors of the historical Eskimo. The latter, however, had a culture (the "Thule" to archaeologists) that seems to have spread, perhaps, from 1000 to 1300 or 1400 A.D., over all the same Arctic shores from the northern coasts of Alaska.

By this time a full panoply of intricate equipment for coping with the severe environment had developed: tailored clothing, blubber lamps, harpoons, kayaks and umiaks, dogsleds, domed snow houses, and the rest.

Since the Eskimo followed the seals and subarctic climate south to Newfoundland and the Strait of Belle Isle, and since both Indian and Eskimo hunted caribou and migratory waterfowl in the tundra barrens, there were some, though not very frequent, contacts between the two sharply contrasted peoples and cultures.

Woodland Culture. Meanwhile, slow changes occurred on the southern margins of the northern forest area. When these changes were striking enough in the archaeological record (as with the introduction of pottery, although it was not very important to their way of life), they denoted a transition from an Archaic to a Woodland culture. This was what most Europeans encountered in the Canadian lands before 1615. However, it is known that by about 1000 A.D. there was some geographic variety in Canadian Indian cultures.

West Coast Indians. On the western seaboard, by then, and probably long before, the ancestors of the rather spectacular Northwest Coast tribes, with their striking variety of languages, must have been well established. Concentrated here and there on patches of gently sloping hinterlands amid steep-sided fjords were impressive village buildings of red cedar and, drawn up on shore, beautifully fashioned, huge, seagoing dugouts hewn from the giant trees of the lush west coast rain forest. The climate was benign, the resources of salmon, seal, whale, and otter apparently limitless. There may have been a larger population in that area in 1615 than there was to be of Europeans in all of New France even a full century later.

Plains Indians. Historians are less certain of conditions on the western grassland plains in 1615. Before that time these plains were occupied or utilized only by Algonkian-speaking peoples as far south as the 49th parallel of latitude. The Siouan-speaking Assiniboines were later arrivals from the southwest. Projectile points, peculiar to plains areas, have been found in prairie sites that are dated roughly from 2,500 years ago. In prehorse days, hunting of bison was chiefly a matter of driving herds (perhaps aided by setting prairie fires) over precipitous stream bluffs or other cliffs. The result was usually an untidy but temporarily rich supply of meat, as well as hides, sinews, bones, and horn, that could supply most of the needs of any group for a long period.

Iroquoians. The most significant variation from the cultural patterns of the boreal forest was found by Jacques Cartier in Hochelaga (Montreal), to which he had penetrated in 1535, when he discovered a substantial stockaded village surrounded by flourishing fields of maize. Here he had touched the northeastern corner of a great triangle (largely the present Ontario interlake peninsula south of the Canadian Shield) where, some five or six centuries before, plant husbandry had become established for corn, beans, and squash. In part, this was but the northern flank of a large area of Iroquoian-speaking people with an economy in which agriculture played a sur-

PUBLIC ARCHIVES OF CANADA

CHAMPLAIN defeats the Iroquois at Lake Champlain in 1609, as pictured in a story of his voyages, dated 1613.

prisingly large role, considering that this was on the extreme northeastern edge of the diffusion of plant husbandry from its source areas in Mesoamerica. With good resources of game and fish in addition, the Iroquoian tribes occupying these southernmost Canadian lands, the Huron and their allies, the Petun and Neutrals, lived in greater density, with a richer resource base, than did any other pre-European Canadians, except possibly those on the Pacific Coast.

East Coast Indians. In maritime Canada, too, there were lesser variants from the northern forest culture. The Malecites of New Brunswick had some agriculture, but it was far less important than that of the Iroquois. The Micmac of Nova Scotia and Gaspé exploited many of the resources of the sea. Little is known about the Beothuk of Newfoundland, who disappeared before there were adequate descriptions of them and whose archaeological relics have yet to be interpreted (or perhaps even discovered).

Advent of Europeans. This was the background of the human geography of the Canadian lands in the period before 1615. European contacts were to seriously disrupt the native cultures and economies. Through Old World diseases that proved deadly (measles and smallpox in particular), vastly more destructive weapons, and the widespread distribution of cheap alcohol, their numbers declined rapidly. But the entry of Europeans was to be much slower in the higher latitudes of North America than in the lower, and up to 1615 these were still Indian and Eskimo lands.

If the human geography of northern North America underwent only a relatively slow metamorphosis in the steady succession of the first 15 centuries of the Christian era, that of Europe, the Mediterranean, and the Near East had experienced vast and revolutionary changes. As the centers of political activity and cultural diffusion moved northwestward in Europe in the later Middle Ages and the Renaissance, western Europe became the chief source of geographical expansion and discovery or rediscovery.

Viking Landings. The first movements toward the Western Hemisphere came with a push from Norway and Denmark to the Faeroes, the British Isles, and Iceland in the 8th and 9th centuries. Before the end of the 10th century the momentum of the westward push was running out, but Greenland had been reached and settlements made there, at the beginning of a two-century phase of warmer climates. North American shores had been coasted, and about 1000 A.D. these westernmost Vikings had wintered in different places on present Canadian lands, probably chiefly (or entirely) in Newfoundland's northern peninsula.

To anyone comparing the coasts these Vikings saw, or may have seen, perhaps as far south as Nova Scotia, with the coasts of Greenland that they occupied for more than four centuries thereafter, their failure to extend permanent settlement to North America may seem inexplicable. Partly it must have been the dissipation of energy at the outer margins of a diffusion process, but the continental winters were far colder than those of Iceland or Greenland, the small numbers of these Scandinavians were too vulnerable to Indian and "Skraeling" attack, and the new lands offered nothing for trade or exploitation that the lands they already knew did not have in plentiful supply.

At any rate, the first European footholds in North America were abandoned, if not forgotten. It is apparent that the new lands ("Helluland," "Vinland," and "Markland") could have been considered only another part of a vast and none-too-attractive archipelago stretching vaguely westward from Scandinavia. Lacking any satisfactory way of determining longitude, the voyagers would not have concluded from the shortened east-west distances in high latitudes that in Newfoundland they were one sixth of the way around the world from Norway. Just as this land was on the very edge of diffusion from the higher culture centers of Mexico and Central America, so it proved to be for Europe. Perhaps only in Australia and isolated parts of Africa and the Pacific Islands were there parts of the inhabited earth comparably so isolated from world streams of new ideas and techniques.

John Cabot's Landfall. The first European wave that had lapped at Canadian shores having receded, no more contacts would appear to have been made for another five hundred years until, close on the summer solstice of the year 1497, Giovanni Caboto (John Cabot), a Venetian sailing for interests in Bristol, England, landed on what is believed to have been Cape Breton Island and coasted the peninsula of Nova Scotia and southwestern Newfoundland. He returned the next year to explore perhaps as far north as Labrador and as far south as New Jersey. His most important report dealt with the wealth of cod on Newfoundland's Grand Banks, although his sponsors, seeking precious metals and, especially, a western route to the Indies, considered his voyages largely failures.

Growth of the Fisheries. During the early 15th century European trading voyages to Greenland persisted, although they became more sporadic and ceased altogether with the end of settlement there before mid-century. About mid-century the Azores were occupied, and Portuguese interests in the Atlantic became more widespread from Iceland (and probably Greenland) to the Southern Hemisphere coasts of Africa (and probably Brazil). Iceland's cod-rich waters were being fished by Europeans from many nations. So widely was the Atlantic known, and so many were the probes into its northern basin, at least by the 1480's, that pre-Columbian knowledge of the incomparable fishing resources near Newfoundland is highly likely.

At least by the turn of the 16th century, the annual fleets of fishing ships in dozens, scores, and then hundreds, as the century progressed, sailed across the Atlantic to reap the great marine harvest. First they came principally from Portugal and Spain, but soon also from France and England. At the same time came explorers to map the coastlines: the brothers Gaspar and Miguel Corte-Real from Portugal in 1501 and 1502, Denys and Thomas Aubert (perhaps) from France in 1506 and 1508, and João Alvares Fagundes (Portuguese), Giovanni da Verrazano (a Florentine in French service), and Estevan Gomez (Portuguese) in the 1520's. By the end of the third decade it became discouragingly clear to those who sought a westward passage from Asia that the continent was relatively continuous from Florida to Labrador.

France Stakes a Claim. Still it was believed that some of the great drowned estuaries that had been noted (the St. Lawrence, Hudson, Delaware, or Chesapeake Bay) might be, if not straits between islands, at least routes to short portages to a more westerly ocean. In 1534 and 1535, Jacques Cartier, acting on knowledge of the Gulf of St. Lawrence brought back by cod fishermen based on his home port of St. Malo, France, explored that great gulf and reached far into the continent at the site of Montreal. Thus France staked the first European claim to the land then first called Canada—the St. Lawrence Valley heart of the future New France. With Jean François de la Rocque, Sieur de Roberval, he attempted a more ambitious scheme of settlement and exploitation in the years 1541–1543. But neither precious stones nor metal nor an easy passage to the "Ocean of the Indies" was found, and further interest in the area rested on furs and the vast opportunity for Christian missionary work.

At the time, neither was sufficient motivation for official action from France, nor for competition from its European rivals, in this area of the new continent. For more than half a century the exploitation was left chiefly to steadily increasing fleets of the cod fishery that extended their fields of operation into the Gulf of St. Lawrence and along the Labrador coasts. From time to time, as ships put into coves to get wood and water, to make a base for fishing the coastal waters, or to cure their catch, they picked up bales of furs. As these proved profitable a few ventures specifically for fur trading were undertaken, and the economic basis for the 17th century development of New France was laid.

Settlement in Newfoundland. In 1583 an English expedition under Sir Humphrey Gilbert gained for that nation its first temporary foothold in North America, in St. John's Harbor on Newfoundland's southeastern Avalon Peninsula. Gradually the English came to dominate Newfoundland and the fishery in the outer areas, while the French moved increasingly into the waters of the Gulf of St. Lawrence itself. Spain and Portugal largely abandoned the fishery after the capture of their cod-fishing fleet by Sir Francis Drake in 1585.

Northwest Passage. But beyond the profitable cod fishery, the imagination of the English, too, had been seized by the twin magnets of a passage to Asia and the possibility of a northern Mexico or Peru. In 1576, 1577, and 1578, Martin Frobisher made three epoch-making expeditions to Arctic waters, known hitherto only to the now defunct Greenland settlements, seeking a Northwest Passage and bringing some tons of supposed ores of precious metals from Baffin Land (Frobisher Bay). In 1585, 1586, and 1587 the English effort was renewed by John Davis, who finally sailed up the strait that bears his name well beyond the Arctic Circle to 72° 12′ north latitude. But his only yield was sealskins and furs bartered from the Eskimo. Ice prevented discovery of the passage north of Baffin Island, and Hudson Strait, to its south, was missed.

The strait was first recognized by George Weymouth in 1602, but it remained for Henry Hudson to make the final discovery and exploration of Hudson Bay, where he lost his life. Two years later Sir Thomas Button explored the bay; but expeditions by Edward Gibbons in 1614, by Robert Bylot and William Baffin in 1615 and 1616 (they reached 76° north latitude), and by others in the next decade or two all failed to solve the maze of islands and ice. There the search for the Northwest Passage was to rest for many years.

New French Interest. The English interest in areas so close to Cartier's Canada, signalized by the abortive settlement of Newfoundland by Sir Humphrey Gilbert and other earlier expeditions of Frobisher, finally spurred official French interests to make more formal establishments in the region. A governorship of New France, first assigned to Jean François de la Rocque, Sieur de Roberval, in the early 1540's, was renewed for the Marquis de La Roche-Mesgouez in 1578. His first effective expedition, delayed by France's religious wars, set out in 1597. The only settlers obtainable were convicts; when they mutinied en route they were dumped on Sable Island off Nova Scotia's southwestern coast (a few survivors being rescued in 1603), and another French settlement venture had failed.

Growth of the Fur Trade. Meanwhile, the incidental fur trade had been growing steadily. A particularly absorptive market had opened for beaver. That fur, shaved from the skins, made an incomparably tight, long-lasting and lustrous felt, and a fashion for beaver hats demanded far greater supplies than could be obtained from northern and eastern Europe. More ventures for fur trading alone were mounted from France in the 1580's and 1590's, and barter for tools, weapons, cloth, metal pots, and baubles took place at dozens of places around the shores of the gulf and up the St. Lawrence River itself as far as Montreal Island. There were occasional winterings-over; one such, in 1600–1601, associated with the names Pontgravé (Sieur du Pont, a veteran fur trader in the area) and Pierre du Guast (Sieur de Monts, a Huguenot nobleman) lost 11 of 16 men to scurvy.

Two years later, in 1603, Pontgravé employed Samuel de Champlain as cartographer and draftsman to explore and chart the coast on an expedition to Tadoussac. Champlain pushed up to Montreal, made the first sophisticated geographic and ethnographic survey of Cartier's Rivière St-Laurent and heard the exciting story of great bodies of water to the west that might be the China Seas.

Acadian Settlement. Champlain's enthusiastic reports on his return to France led to the expedition of 1604 to Acadia (roughly the present Canadian Maritime Provinces and the coast of New England) with the Sieur de Monts as lieutenant general and monopolist of trade in what was to be a new colony. The first winter, which was disastrous because of scurvy, was spent on an island at the mouth of the St. Croix River; the next summer the settlers shifted to the Port Royal (present Annapolis Royal) basin of Nova Scotia, where one of the gentlemen associates, Sieur de Poutrincourt, was granted a seigneury.

The de Monts monopoly was canceled in 1607, and the settlement was abandoned except for some desultory fur trading until 1611. A new settlement there lasted only until 1613, when it was sacked by a colonial English freebooter, and for some 15 years Acadia was once again left to the fur traders. Some skeleton settlement, probably without European women, was maintained at Port Royal by one of them, Poutrincourt's son and heir.

Opening the Interior. Meanwhile, the geographer Champlain associated himself with de Monts in a new trading-settlement enterprise, this time back in the traditional French area of interest on the St. Lawrence. In 1608, on the site of the old Indian village known to Cartier as Stadacona, where a rock promontory overlooks the meeting point of river valley and estuary, Champlain founded the settlement of Quebec. Despite scurvy, mutiny, and temporary English occupation, continuous settlement was to be maintained here.

In 1609, Champlain went up the river to extend his surveys made six years before. The Iroquoian peoples who had lived in the area in Cartier's time long since had withdrawn west and south, but were a constant threat to the Algonkian tribes that had replaced them. One of Champlain's first efforts was an expedition into the lands of the Five Nations' Iroquois, up the Richelieu River, to impress them with the terror of French firearms. In 1610 he sent a lieutenant, Étienne Brulé, to the Huron country; he was the first European to see one of the Great Lakes. Faced with competitive traders, Champlain managed to secure the virtual governorship of the area and a trading monopoly for his group, and in 1613 he himself pushed up the Ottawa River beyond the site of Canada's present capital.

In 1615, the year of the arrival of the first missionaries on the St. Lawrence, Champlain made his first great interior reconnaissance by the Ottawa River and Lake Nipissing to Georgian Bay of Lake Huron. Then, with a band of Huron Indians, he crossed the peninsula to Lake Ontario, traversed the lake, and attacked an Onondaga fort near present Syracuse, N.Y., before retiring. He thus assured the future New France the friendship of the Hurons and the Algonkians, and the enmity of the Iroquois, in the fur trade on which its economy was based. This expedition established the French deep in the interior and laid the basis for a future continental nation.

Intertwinings of Destiny. A number of possibilities were always present for the exploitation of North America by Europeans after the first Viking contacts. The Norsemen might have colonized it had the winters been warmer and the natives fewer or less combative. Had they done so, the four centuries of European contact with Greenland well might have extended to Canada. Had Cabot, Cartier, or Frobisher really discovered easily processed precious metals or a route to the Indies, a very different history would have resulted. One may speculate on the probability of English or French interests had there been no codfish or fur or no market for them in Europe. What did eventuate required the peculiar combination of European interests and both the cultural and physical geographical characteristics of the Canadian lands in the 15th and 16th centuries.

Andrew Hill Clark, *University of Wisconsin*

Bibliography

Biggar, Henry P. (ed.), *The Voyages of Jacques Cartier* (Toronto 1924).
Brebner, John B., *The Explorers of North America 1492–1806* (New York 1933).
Burpee, Lawrence J., *The Discovery of Canada* (Toronto 1946).
Clark, Andrew H., and Innis, Donald Q., "The Roots of Canada's Geography," *Canada: A Geographical Interpretation* (Toronto 1967).
Innis, Harold A., *The Cod Fisheries*, rev. ed. (Toronto 1954).
Innis, Harold A., *The Fur Trade in Canada*, rev. ed. (Toronto 1956).
Jenness, Diamond, *The Indians of Canada*, 5th ed. (Ottawa, National Museum of Canada, 1960).
Jones, Gwyn, *The Norse Atlantic Saga* (Toronto 1964).
Neatby, Leslie H., *In Quest of the North West Passage* (Toronto 1958).
Oleson, Tryggvi J., *Early Voyages and Northern Approaches 1000–1632* (Toronto 1963).
Spencer, Robert F., Jennings, J. D. et. al., *The Native Americans: Pre-history and Ethnology of the North American Indians* (New York 1965).

43. Founding and Development of French Canada, 1604–1752

From the founding of Port Royal in 1605 and of Quebec in 1608 the French in America struggled to form viable settlements, based largely on the fur trade. By 1663 colonial rule by trading companies had failed, and the French crown established New France as a royal province. But still the problems of the wilderness, of Indian attacks, and of expanding English colonies to the south persisted and finally led to all-out conflict for supremacy in North America.

THE PERIOD 1604–1662

During the last half of the 16th century, cod fishermen and fur traders had ensured a constant link between France and Cartier's territory. The profit-earning capacity of the fur trade—inexhaustible wealth acquired for a minimum of manpower and investment—had given rise among enterprising traders to the desire to hold a monopoly and to exploit it on a vaster scale.

Fur Monopolies. Granted as early as 1588, monopolies had never been fully utilized. For one reason, they were too tenuous; the French court, under pressure from excluded merchants, revoked monopolies as easily as it conceded them. Besides, obligations on monopoly holders to colonize for the vague ideal of glory to God and the king—contrary to the interests of a settlement devoted solely to the fur trade—retarded French development in North America.

In 1603, following the death of Aymar de Chaste, lieutenant general of New France, the trade monopoly passed to Pierre du Gua, Sieur de Monts, of Saintonge, who in 1600 had made a voyage to Tadoussac with the expedition supported by Pierre Chauvin, predecessor of de Chaste.

Not having been greatly impressed by the St. Lawrence territory up to the mouth of the Saguenay River, de Monts decided to attempt a settlement in Acadia, where mineral deposits had just been discovered. After a fruitless attempt at settlement at the mouth of the St. Croix River, Port Royal was founded in the Annapolis region of present-day Nova Scotia in 1605. But the post had not time to take root. De Monts lost his monopoly in 1607. For lack of financial security he abandoned the enterprise. Thanks to a few adventurers, Port Royal was to remain on the map. But its fate was linked in part with English colonization of the Atlantic coast until 1670.

Quebec Founded. In 1608, de Monts, who had been granted a new monopoly for a year, was again tempted by the lands of North America. This time he entrusted the settlement to Samuel de Champlain. The latter had appeared on the Canadian scene in 1603, when on de Chaste's behalf he had sailed up the St. Lawrence River as far as Montreal, noting the characteristics of the region, in particular the hydrographic system of the river, of which the Indians had made a creditable sketch. From 1604 to 1607 he was in Acadia with de Monts, where he scrutinized the Atlantic coast from the Bay of Fundy to beyond Cape Cod.

Champlain chose to establish de Monts' new post on the St. Lawrence River in order to ensure the security of the monopoly against French and foreign smuggling and to permit easier access to the West by means of river networks.

Quebec was founded by Champlain in 1608. It was both a strategic post commanding access to the upper St. Lawrence and a stopping place for a floating population made up mainly of interpreters and clerks. At this time, besides the one at Tadoussac, trading agencies were already taking shape on the sites where later would be founded the posts of Trois Rivières and Montreal.

Fur Trade Organized. From 1608 to 1627 the organization of the fur trade came into being. It is with this primary activity, which was to remain the economic basis of New France, that the main endeavor—if not the thinking—of Champlain was associated.

The aim of this endeavor was to establish stricter control over the Indians, who were necessary intermediaries in the fur trade. To this end Champlain became diplomat, traveler, and warrior. Through diplomacy he tried to enroll the Indian tribes by supporting chiefs whose loyalty to him was assured or by assigning to them Frenchmen who would help to keep them in the French orbit. By means of what he called "les descouvertures"—his voyages on the Richelieu River, Lake Champlain, the Ottawa River, Georgian Bay, and Lake Ontario—he tried to increase the area of French influence, at the same time continuing his search for the western sea. His economic alliance with the Algonquins and Hurons, which involved him in attacks on the Iroquois, led to a military alliance as well.

Company of Merchants. But all this effort had meaning only if the colony could endure, and for this a trade monopoly had to become a permanent reality. In 1609, on the expiration of de Monts' monopoly, trade became free along the St. Lawrence River. This was a cause of disorder, or at least of stagnation, which hindered the progress of commercial planning. In France, Champlain was busy arranging creation of a permanent viceregal post in Canada, with the sole right to trade. He was successful in 1613. The assured monopoly was to be exploited by the Company of Merchants.

In 1627, with the small post at Quebec City numbering some 50 persons associated mainly with the trading company and its seasonal arrival of cargoes of pelts, and with its missionaries, New France offered a picture of a trading agency that had finally taken root and whose orientation provided a glimpse of the future development of a vast trade empire.

Diversification. But Champlain's ideal was very different. For him, New France should not be merely a colony for exploitation but a colony for settlement based on a diversified economy made up of agriculture, fisheries, lumbering, and mining. He had, moreover, found in the missionaries faithful allies who called for a French agricultural settlement as a model to the nomadic tribes that they were trying to induce to settle in one place, the better to convert them.

But the merchants who held the monopoly were not well disposed toward this reorientation of the colony. For them settlement did not pay because it could not contribute to trade profits. On the contrary, it risked diminishing profits by creating on the spot eventual competitors of the monopoly holders.

In 1627 the creation of the Company of New France (the One Hundred Associates) marked the triumph of the thesis of Champlain and the missionaries. Previously, it would have been necessary for them to overcome the hostility of the shareholders of the Company of Merchants (1613–1621) and of the Company of Caen (1621–1627) which succeeded it.

The Company of New France was formed, thanks to the intervention of Cardinal Richelieu, with shareholders from all over France among whom the merchants figured as a minority. The company's first duty was to send to Canada 4,000 colonists in 15 years.

Circumstances rendered it financially incapable of fulfilling its obligations. In 1628 the English appeared in the St. Lawrence valley. The following year they seized Quebec City. Canada was to remain under English control until 1632 when it was to be given back to France. The most serious consequence was the loss sustained by the Company of New France, which had recruited in 1628 and 1629 two convoys of colonists who never reached their destination. To this financial setback was added the expense of a lawsuit that the company lost to the former Company of Caen.

In 1632 the company did not have the means to assume the cost of founding a settlement. However, from 1632 to 1662 some 1,000 immigrants came to Canada, and by the latter date the population numbered about 2,300.

This first migratory current—however weak it may have been—can be traced especially to the financial, propaganda, and recruitment capacities of the missionary organizations.

The Missions. The years between 1632 and 1662 for the missions in Canada were a golden age that reached its peak during the decade 1640–1650. And this was not only the accomplishment of the Jesuits at Tadoussac, Quebec, Sillery, Trois-Rivières, and in the territories of the Hurons and Iroquois. Around them in Quebec City the Ursulines and the Hospitalières had founded a convent and a hospital. Then came Montreal, founded by la Société de Notre Dame from strictly missionary motives. A few years after its founding were established the Hôtel-Dieu (hospital) of Jeanne Mance and the school of Marguerite Bourgeois. In 1657 arrived the Sulpicians, who also were concerned with missions, and in 1659 Bishop Laval, apostolic vicar responsible to the Sacred Congregation for the Propagation of the Faith.

This enumeration alone is evidence of an ensemble whose elements of permanence, dynamism, and, in certain cases, of financial affluence were considerably in advance of the colonial milieu, whose political and economic structures were still quite rudimentary. This well-rooted religious and missionary society attracted to Canada, directly or indirectly, probably the majority of the immigrants between 1632 and 1662. The recruiting of the "Montréalistes" alone amounted to more than 400 persons, to whom must be added the colonists who settled in the religious seigneuries, the manpower in the employ of diverse communities, and the spiritual secular assistants.

The Colony Matures. In 1645 the Company of New France consented to transfer its trade monopoly to the colonists. This was the birth of the Community of Habitants, a kind of cooperative that grouped together all the heads of families. This event was important because henceforth the only profitable economic activity in New France was to benefit the colonists themselves.

The year 1645 also marked the beginning of the social and political formation of the colony. A small bourgeois elite—later called "the aristocracy of the beaver"—made up of intelligent and audacious men was before long to dominate the Community of Habitants and apparently use it for its own benefit. This was the first appearance in the colony of a secular ruling class, which to maintain its privileges sought to dominate political life.

In 1647, as a result of complaints concerning the management of the Community of Habitants,

LA SALLE, who explored North America's interior in the 17th century, builds a vessel for a voyage in this print of 1697.

PUBLIC ARCHIVES OF CANADA

there was set up a vigilance council—the Council of Quebec—the composition of which was to vary over the years, but whose role was to exercise control over the economic life of the colony. Little by little, however, its powers were to become broadly administrative and political.

Nevertheless, it was the fur trade—the colony based on exploitation—and not the missionary ideal and the settlement it could promote, that gave rise to the first viable structure of colonial society. In fact, in the 1660's this colonial society presented a curious picture of duality. On the one hand, the old trading agency that had extended its field of exploitation to the Great Lakes and Hudson Bay had come to exercise its influence over Quebec and was soon to control Montreal. On the other hand was the agricultural colony established laboriously in the seigneuries of the Montreal-Quebec region, but which visibly lacked the vital impulse. Between the two there was no unity or organic ties.

Iroquois Menace. Both, however, were menaced by the Iroquois Indians. Tribal wars already existed at the time of Champlain's arrival. They set the Algonquins of the north shore of the St. Lawrence River and the Huron of Georgian Bay against the Iroquois to the south of Lake Ontario. Little by little the conflict took on an economic meaning, the Iroquois acting as suppliers of furs to the Dutch of the Hudson River Valley, the Huron and Algonquins to the French.

Owing to their marked superiority, the Iroquois in the 1660's succeeded not only in mastering their Indian adversaries but also in bringing New France to the brink of ruin. They controlled the tributaries of the St. Lawrence, considerably reducing the consignments of pelts to the colony and thus rendering untenable the financial situation of the Community of Habitants. They had in a few years reduced to nothing all the missionary labor undertaken by the Jesuits in Huron country. Finally, by their incessant raids, they hindered the progress of French settlement and discouraged immigration.

More and more desperate appeals were made to Paris. Only the king of France could remedy the situation.

JEAN BLAIN, *University of Montreal*

THE PERIOD 1663–1752

In 1663, in response to urgent appeals from the colonists, New France was taken over by the crown from the moribund Company of New France and made a royal province. Louis XIV and Jean-Baptiste Colbert, comptroller general of France, then launched an ambitious scheme for colonial development.

Under the Crown. A new administrative system was established consisting of a governor-general, an intendant, a sovereign council, several junior officials, and royal law courts in the three towns. The Carignan Salières regiment was sent out and in three quick campaigns forced the Iroquois Confederacy to cease their devastating raids on the settlements. Over a million livres was invested in the colony, and a massive, subsidized emigration program provided labor, both skilled and unskilled.

By these means the population grew from 2,500 in 1663 to nearly 8,000 by 1675. Virgin forest land on both sides of the St. Lawrence River was cleared and brought into cultivation. New industries were established and Canadian-built ships began transporting surplus food and timber to the West Indies. With the river routes to the West made safe, the fur trade prospered.

Western Expansion. Jean Talon, the intendant, began sending exploration parties north to Hudson Bay and west through the Great Lakes. These parties claimed the lands they traversed for Louis XIV and returned with their canoes heavily laden with furs. The Canadian settlers were quick to follow the example. Within a very few years hundreds of the more hardy men departed to trade with the western Indians.

This had a deleterious effect on the colony's economic development. The seigneurs, who were required to clear and settle the lands granted them or forfeit their concessions, complained that they lacked the labor to comply. Colbert, although he had no desire to restrict the fur trade, could not allow it to undermine his long-range plans for the colony's economic diversification. He thus became a firm opponent of western expansion, forbade the Canadians to leave the confines of the central colony, and gave strict orders that the fur trade was to be confined to Montreal, Trois-Rivières, and Tadoussac.

The Canadians, however, refused to pay heed. Despite Colbert's injunctions, western expansion continued. In 1674, Louis Jolliet returned from his voyage down the Mississippi River, opening up a whole new area for expansion. Before the end of the 17th century, fur trade posts and Jesuit missions had been established all through the Great Lakes, west over the height of land in the Lake Winnipeg area, and down the Mississippi, at the mouth of which a new colony, Louisiana, was being founded.

Although the French claimed title to all these lands, they did not really occupy this vast area. They held only the isolated trading posts in or near Indian villages, manned by a handful of traders, with here and there a missionary. The West was still the country of the Indians who, because they had become dependent on European goods, permitted the French to establish posts and to voyage along the waterways. The French and certain of the Indian tribes thus became commercial partners in the fur trade. Other Indian nations, however, were dissatisfied with this arrangement.

Iroquois Hostility. The powerful confederacy of the five Iroquois nations occupied lands between New France and New York. The merchants of Albany were their commercial partners. Their hunting lands were stripped of beaver, and they looked with covetous eyes on the furs flowing from the West to Montreal. In 1675 they terminated a long war with hostile tribes on their flanks and immediately challenged the French for the role of middlemen in the fur trade. They began attacking tribes allied to the French, then attacking the French themselves. It was with great difficulty, and only after several hundred regular troops had been sent to the colony, that they were brought to terms in 1688.

The following year England and France were at war. The Iroquois immediately reopened the conflict. For the next 10 years New France had to withstand constant attacks from the Iroquois and one large-scale seaborne assault on Quebec launched by New England. This last was easily repelled, but the Canadians suffered heavy losses before they subdued the Iroquois. In 1701 the Five Nations finally came to terms and agreed to remain neutral in any future conflict between the English and French.

Acadia and Hudson Bay. On the eastern flank of New France, Acadia, seized by the English of Massachusetts in 1654, had languished since its return to the French crown in 1670. A royal governor had been appointed, some settlers had been sent out, but no real attempt had been made to develop its resources. The French population was less than 400; by the end of the century it had barely doubled. The settlers had much closer ties with New England than with either France or Quebec. That it had managed thus far to remain under the French flag merely indicated that New England did not yet regard the province as a threat or a potential asset worth seizing.

Far to the north, in Hudson Bay, the French contested the hold of the Hudson's Bay Company on the area. Expeditions by both land and sea were launched to drive the English out. Everything depended on which side got its ships into the bay first after the breakup. One year the French would seize the main posts scattered around the shores of the inland sea, the next the English would recapture them. A major weapon in this struggle was scurvy. When the war ended, the English held the posts at the foot of James Bay, the French the main post to the north (York Factory) at the mouth of the Nelson and Hayes rivers.

France vs. England. In 1701, England and France were again at war. In North America, however, hostilities were limited. The Iroquois, for the most part, remained neutral and insisted that the entire area between New York and New France be maintained as a neutral zone. The governor of the colony, Philippe de Rigaud de Vaudreuil, informed the minister of marine that it was in Canada's interest to remain at peace with the Iroquois as long as possible. From bitter experience he declared, "The five Iroquois villages are more to be feared than the whole of the English colonies." Thus, until the closing years of the war, peace continued on that frontier, and a thriving smuggling trade developed between the merchants of Albany and Montreal.

To the east, however, on the frontier of Acadia and New England there was constant warfare. With their pitifully small population in Acadia the French had to depend on the Indian tribes of the region to prevent the New Englanders, now pushing their settlements northward, from seizing the entire province. The French, therefore, kept the New England frontier aflame with devastating raids on the settlements as far south as the outskirts of Boston. Lacking Indian allies and tough guerrilla fighters, as the Canadians had become, the New Englanders were hard pressed to defend themselves. For them to launch similar raids on the Canadian settlements in reprisal was out of the question. A maritime expedition, however, succeeded in capturing Port Royal in Acadia in 1710. Encouraged by this, naval aid was obtained from Britain for an assault up the St. Lawrence River on Quebec. At the same time a land army was mustered at Albany to attack New France by way of the Richelieu River. The fleet, commanded by Sir Hovenden Walker, came to grief in the Gulf of St. Lawrence (1711) and withdrew. The land army retired to Albany and disbanded.

Peace of Utrecht. The following year hostilities ended and in Utrecht, the Netherlands, the diplomats began negotiating the terms of the peace treaty, signed in 1713. In North America the French gave up much. Acadia, with its limits to be settled by a commission, was ceded to England, as was Hudson Bay. Article 15 of the treaty, however, proved to be the most dangerous for Canadian interests. By it, the French recognized British sovereignty over the Iroquois, and the British were granted equal rights to trade with the western Indians in the areas long claimed as belonging to France. With their cheaper trade goods, the British thus threatened to eliminate the French from the Western fur trade and gain control of the interior.

Aftermath. The French had no intention of allowing this to happen. With their chain of posts in the West and control of the waterways they continued to exclude the British. They were able to do this with little trouble because the merchants of Albany dominated the English fur trade, and they saw no need to contest the French hold on the West. They obtained ade-

LA VÉRENDRYE explored the West. C. W. Jefferys depicts the party sighting mountains.

PUBLIC ARCHIVES OF CANADA

quate supplies of furs from the Iroquois and, clandestinely, from the French at Montreal and Detroit without venturing far afield. The colonial authorities, fully cognizant of the benefits derived by both parties from this contraband trade, made only feeble efforts to curb it. The Montreal traders, men such as the La Vérendryes, well supplied with the English woolen cloth that the Indians preferred, now pushed westward across the prairies, seeking a route to the western ocean. They established trading posts on the Red, Assiniboine, and Saskatchewan rivers, thereby diverting much of the trade from English posts on Hudson Bay.

To the east, however, there was conflict. The French chose to define the Acadia that they had ceded as consisting only of the peninsula southwest of Chignecto Bay. The English claimed the whole area north of New England to the St. Lawrence River at a point below Quebec. The French, however, in close alliance with the resident tribes, were able to retain control of the territory as far south as the Kennebec River and of Cape Breton. On this island they set to work constructing a fortified naval base at Louisbourg to protect their fisheries and guard the entry to the Gulf of St. Lawrence. The French maintained their position in Acadia mainly because the English did not choose to contest it with vigor. In both France and England the governments were unstable and needed peace to consolidate the regency of the Duke of Orléans and the Hanoverian succession. And in the ceded section of Acadia, renamed Nova Scotia, the Acadian people remained on their lands undisturbed, although as an alien population in a British province.

Years of Peace. Following the Peace of Utrecht there ensued on the whole a 30-year period of peace (1713–1743), during which Canada began to prosper. The fur trade, which had been extremely depressed for nearly 15 years owing to a glut of beaver, began to revive, and after 1716 it flourished. The Canadian population increased from less than 19,000 in 1713 to over 48,000 by 1739—these census figures may well be too low.

With the construction of Louisbourg, begun in 1713, an important new market was created for Canadian agricultural produce. New seigneuries, with their narrow strip farms running back from the river, were conceded by the crown, and a second range of farms, behind the first river concessions, came into production. The few old industries such as lumbering and fishing expanded, and new ones were established. Among these were the iron forges of St.-Maurice near Trois-Rivières. The extraction of oil from seals, walruses, and whales in the gulf provided an important item for export. Shipbuilding, with large ships at Quebec and coastal vessels at smaller yards along the river, assumed sizable dimensions. The manufacture of goods for the Indian trade kept artisans in the towns busy, for furs still remained the colony's staple product. The Canadians thus enjoyed during these years considerably higher living standards than did their social equals in Europe.

Political and Social Framework. During the preceding half century of almost constant war, the institutions and the social framework of New France had taken their peculiar form. Although the colony was governed by the minister of marine and his aides at Versailles, and merely administered by the royal officials at Quebec, policy decisions were almost invariably made only on the advice of the governor and intendant. However, legislation on purely local matters was enacted after consulation with the people. Public assemblies were frequently called to discover the views of the people on issues that affected them directly, and in country districts parish assemblies were held before decisions were made. Since the colonists paid no direct taxes, only import duties on certain goods and export levy on beaver pelts and moose hides, there was no need for the type of assembly that existed in the English colonies. Yet the regime was quite democratic, in its own peculiar way.

Justice. Similarly, the crown took steps to safeguard the civil liberties of the people against infringement by the senior officials. In 1679 a royal edict forbade the governor-general and the local governors of the three towns to imprison anyone arbitrarily except for sedition and treason. This edict had the same intent and effect as the Habeas Corpus Act passed in England's Parliament that same year. As for op-

PUBLIC ARCHIVES OF CANADA

BRITISH NAVAL EXPEDITION attacks Cape Breton Island in 1745, when the French fortress of Louisbourg was captured. From a contemporary engraving.

pression by minor officials, in such matters the intendant was expected to take action.

In the administration of justice, Louis XIV and Colbert introduced reforms that vested legal interests had prevented them making in France. They made it plain that justice had to be equitable, impartial, swift, and cheap. No one was to be barred from seeking justice for lack of means. To prevent the abuses that had made a mockery of the law courts in France, lawyers were not allowed to practise in the colony. The fees that officers of the courts could charge were strictly regulated at low rates. The Sovereign Council heard all cases without fee, and in civil cases, if both parties agreed, the intendant could adjudicate without fees of any sort. In short, the inquisitorial legal system of New France compared quite favorably with the adversary system of England and its colonies. There were plenty of complaints and abuses but they were caused more by human failings than by any serious flaw in the system.

The Church. Similarly the role played by the church underwent change during these years. Its power in secular affairs was considerably reduced, and it became subservient to the crown. The Canadian people were anything but priest ridden; in fact, just the reverse. As the 18th century wore on, the intendant frequently had to censure the *habitants* for bad behavior during mass or religious processions, and by the 1750's the bishop was concerned about the presence of Freemasons among his flock. Yet most Canadians were deeply attached to their religion; the absence of any threat to it allowed them to wear it lightly.

In the social field the clergy played a very important role, for New France was virtually a welfare state. Nursing sisters cared for the sick, the indigent, and orphans in the colony's well-run hospitals and almshouses. For those without means, care was free. On orders of the intendant, offices to minister to the needs of the poor and curb mendicancy were established in the towns. Poverty was not regarded as a crime but as a weakness in the social fabric that had to be rectified. In these poor law offices, the clergy were required to act in concert with the lay authorities. Education was another responsibility of the clergy. Schools were established in the towns and in many country districts, and the Jesuits had an excellent college at Quebec, founded in 1635, one year before Harvard College at Cambridge, Mass., but the Canadians were not noted for intellectual activities, and the colony never possessed a printing press.

Society. Although the basis of the social framework was imported from France, the Canadian environment imposed significant modifications. The dominant values of 17th century French society were aristocratic. The bourgeoisie sought to emulate the nobility in all things and to gain entry into its ranks. In New France this was made easier by the relaxing of the ban on the nobility's engaging in trade, by the existence of abundant free land, and by the presence of a sizable body of regular troops in the colony wherein the Canadians could obtain commissions.

It was thus possible for a talented, ambitious Canadian of humble origins to acquire wealth in the fur trade, obtain a seigneury, a commission in the Troupes de la Marine, and eventually be elevated to the nobility for valiant service. Although few achieved the last, many did make it a dominant social aim to emulate the way of life of the *noblesse*. They thereby earned a reputation for ostentatious living, for squandering their wealth on luxury goods, and for lavish entertainment. Visitors from Europe were much impressed by the urbane society of Montreal and Quebec.

Military Spirit. The main formative influences on Canadian society, however, were the military

PUBLIC ARCHIVES OF CANADA

JESUITS' COLLEGE AND CHURCH at Quebec, drawn by Richard Short, a naval officer with the British army holding the city in the winter of 1759–1760.

and the Indians. Throughout the 17th century and into the 18th the Canadians had had to fight for their existence in the cruel wars against the Iroquois, and later the English colonies. The presence of a large body of regular troops in the colony, and the requirement that all men from 15 to 70 serve in the militia, fostered a military spirit, making New France the Sparta of North America.

These values were reinforced by the constant contact of the Canadians with the Indian nations. Every year, hundreds of men voyaged to the West to trade, living among the Indians for months and years on end. In the wilderness, they acquired their techniques for survival and their methods of waging war. And in their voyaging, from the far Western plains to the Gulf of Mexico, amid nations with strange ways, they became men of very broad horizons, quite unlike their parochial counterparts in Europe. Just as the merchant ships and fishing fleets were regarded as the training schools for the navies of the maritime powers, so the Western fur trade was the harsh training school for the frontier soldiers of New France.

Renewed Conflict. When, in 1744, France and England resorted to war to settle their differences, it was once again the frontier settlements of the English colonies that bore the brunt of it. In the east, a New England expedition captured Louisbourg, but at the conclusion of the war it was returned to France in exchange for Madras. In 1749, however, the British began constructing their naval base, Halifax, and British immigrants began to arrive in force.

Although in North America, the war appeared to have changed nothing, appearances were deceptive. Traders from the English colonies had recently flooded over the Allegheny Mountains into the Ohio Valley. This was an area that Canadian fur traders had neglected; their posts were to the north and west. By 1748 the English had gained the allegiance of the resident Indian nations by commercial ties.

The French government was not willing to let this go unchallenged. It was feared that the English would consolidate their hold on the valley, then threaten the French settlements on the Illinois, and ultimately sever communications between Canada and Louisiana. For reasons mainly to do with imperial policy, it was decided that the English must be driven back over the Alleghenies. In 1749 an expedition led by Céleron de Blainville was sent down the Ohio River to reclaim possession of the region for France and drive out the English traders. He discovered the Indian nations to be solidly in the English interest and was obliged to withdraw rather hurriedly.

The French, however, refused to abandon their aim of gaining control of the region. If force was required, it would be used. That such measures could be effective was demonstrated by Charles Michel Langlade, who in 1752 swept down from the north with some 240 Chippewa and destroyed the English trading post at Pickawillany. This caused the Ohio nations to question the advantage of a commercial alliance with the English. It also marked the beginning of the Anglo-French conflict for supremacy in North America.

W. J. ECCLES, *University of Toronto*

Bibliography

Brebner, J. Bartlet, *New England's Outpost: Acadia Before the Conquest* (New York 1927).

Eccles, W. J., *Canada Under Louis XIV, 1663–1701* (Toronto 1964).

Eccles, W. J., *The Government of New France*, Canadian Historical Association booklet No. 18 (Ottawa 1965).

Frégault, Guy, *La civilisation de la Nouvelle France* (Montreal 1944).

Gipson, Lawrence Henry, *The British Empire Before the American Revolution*, vols. 4, 5 (New York 1936–1942).

Lanctôt, Gustave, *A History of Canada*, tr., Margaret M. Cameron, vol. 3 (Cambridge, Mass., 1965).

44. Canada in the Reorganization of North America, 1752–1818

The Peace of Utrecht, in 1713, had seriously weakened the position of New France in North America. Henceforth, Britain was firmly established to the north on Hudson Bay and to the east in Newfoundland and Acadia at the entrance to the St. Lawrence River. Everywhere along the entire frontier, which the treaty failed to define with precision, from Cape Breton through Canada to the Illinois River and the upper Mississippi River and from there south to New Orleans, Englishmen and Americans were pressing inward upon the territories claimed by France. And as they pressed, they were convinced more and more of the need to enlarge their foothold on the Atlantic littoral and to reach westward to the interior of the vast continent with its wealth of furs and lands.

Fundamentally, French and English and Canadian and American rivalry in North America was economic in origin. That is not to say that there were no other factors. Religion was one. But even the struggle between Catholics and Protestants was subordinate to the Indian trade and the exploitation of the continent's resources. The Peace of Utrecht was no more than an episode, albeit an unfortunate episode as far as New France was concerned, in the two-centuries-long contest between France and Britain for North America that began with Samuel Argall's destruction of the French post on Mount Desert Island, Maine, in 1613. The French surrendered Montreal in 1760, and their venture terminated with Napoleon's sale of the Louisiana Territory to the United States in 1803 for $12 million.

After several years of peace and recuperation, following the Peace of Utrecht, fighting broke out again in North America in 1744. The fact that the war, known in Europe as the War of the Austrian Succession and in America as King George's War, was ostensibly the result of a dynastic dispute in Europe, was of little moment. The real reason for the resumption of hostilities was Britain's imperial economic ambitions. But even more than England, the English colonies were anxious to renew the struggle for mastery of North America, and in 1745 William Pepperell's amateur soldiers demonstrated their resourcefulness and strength by seizing Louisbourg, the great French naval base built on Cape Breton to guard the entrance to the St. Lawrence.

THE PERIOD 1752–1763

The war ended in 1748 with the Treaty of Aix-la-Chapelle, but not the Anglo-French struggle in North America. For both Canadians and Americans the peace was only a truce, and while the French and English international commission in Paris argued over the location of the frontiers between New France and the thirteen colonies, French and English colonists began to fight again. When their respective mother countries formally exchanged declarations of war in 1756, Canadians and Americans had been engaged in hostilities for a year.

Situation in Early 1750's. The Treaty of Aix-la-Chapelle had restored the *status quo ante bellum*, and in 1749 Louisbourg was handed back to its original owners in return for Madras, a French conquest in India. The French garrison returned to Cape Breton, and other troops from Canada were established at Beauséjour and Gaspereau on the narrow isthmus linking Nova Scotia with Canada. Their task was to encourage the Acadians to maintain their old loyalties to France and to induce them to leave Nova Scotia to take up new lands in Cape Breton and in the Île Saint Jean (Prince Edward Island).

To the west, along the St. Lawrence and the Great Lakes, new Canadian posts were established at La Présentation, at Rouillé, and at the Niagara Portage. Farther west, to the south of Lake Erie, still more posts were built at Presqu'Isle, Rivière aux Boeufs, and at the forks of the Ohio River known to the Canadians as "La Belle Rivière."

In the minds of the French and Canadians, there was never any doubt of their rights to the valley of the Ohio River. From the days of its discovery by the Sieur de La Salle, the Ohio had been looked upon as part of New France. At first there was some question as to whether it came under the jurisdiction of Canada or Louisiana; but in the end the region was divided by the judgment of Solomon and the eastern part became the responsibility of Canada and the western that of Louisiana.

Prelude to Formal War. In 1749, as a result of this division, La Galissonière, governor of Canada, sent Céloron de Blainville to show the flag in eastern Ohio and warn off American interlopers, traders and land seekers. Blainville planted lead plates along the line of the Allegheny and Ohio rivers. But more effective than Blainville's action was that of Charles Langlade and a force of Ottawa Indians, who in 1752 attacked Pickawillany, the Miami town that had become the center of American trade and political intrigue. In a single blow Langlade put an end to American influence in the Ohio region and made it possible for the Sieur de Contrecoeur to build Fort Duquesne at the junction of the Allegheny and Monongahela rivers in 1754.

The Virginians were not prepared to stand idly by and watch their rivals extinguish their trade and occupy the western lands they hoped to annex for themselves. Accordingly, Governor Robert Dinwiddie of Virginia sent a force under a militia officer, George Washington, to assert the American claims. But Washington's expedition ended in the mud and surrender of Fort Necessity (1754) and Contrecoeur was left master of the Ohio. This was not something that the English and Americans would supinely accept. Reinforcements of British regulars were hurried to Virginia from Britain, and under the direction of the Duke of Cumberland in London a master plan was prepared calling for offensive action against New France at Beauséjour, Lake Champlain, Niagara, and Fort Duquesne. The French, too, responded to the deteriorating situation by sending reinforcements to Canada and to Cape Breton.

The fourfold attack, launched in 1755, ambitious though it was in concept, was poor in execution. Sir William Johnson ran foul of the Baron Dieskau's troops at Lac St. Sacrément (Lake George) and never reached Lake Champlain; Governor William Shirley of Massachusetts did not get beyond Chouaguen (Oswego); and Gen. Edward Braddock marched his men into death and humiliation at the hands of Liénard de Beaujeu's Indians and Canadians at Fort Duquesne. Only Gen. Robert Monckton at Beauséjour achieved anything in the way of success. His capture of the Chignecto forts made it pos-

QUEBEC city is taken by British troops in assault on Sept. 13, 1759, as shown in a contemporary engraving.

PUBLIC ARCHIVES OF CANADA

sible for Governor Charles Lawrence of Nova Scotia to carry out the plans, which he and Governor Shirley had concocted, of seizing the bewildered Acadians and sending them off to the other English colonies. (See ACADIA.) At least there would be no more neutral French to complicate the situation in Acadia, and the vacated farmlands might attract the English and American immigrants who thus far had fought shy of moving to Nova Scotia.

Early Stages of Seven Years' War. The formal declaration of war in 1756 and the arrival of the Marquis de Montcalm with further reinforcements of regulars encouraged the governor of New France himself, the Marquis de Vaudreuil, to take the offensive. Although there were differences of opinion on general strategy between Vaudreuil and his military commander, a Franco-Canadian force successfully liquidated Chouaguen on Lake Ontario and, a year later, in 1757, captured Fort William Henry, Johnson's old base camp at the south end of Lac St. Sacrément. An operation planned by the Earl of Loudoun and Adm. Francis Holburne against Louisbourg bogged down in military red tape, and when Holburne's ships were dispersed by storms, like those which had wrecked the Duc d'Anville's attempt to recover Louisbourg for France in 1746, Louisbourg survived to guard the entrance to New France for another year.

New France, with a militia system better than that of the Thirteen Colonies, with the superior mobility afforded by the east-west water system of the St. Lawrence and the Great Lakes, and with a sound strategic approach to the problems of defense, could reasonably hope for victory in a short defensive war, but not in a long one. The country lacked men, arms, and foodstuffs, and with France unwilling to depart from its traditional policy of fighting on the continent of Europe and reluctant to risk its fleet in conflict with that of Britain, little help could be expected from Canada's mother country. Food rationing had been introduced, but monetary inflation was uncontrolled and the Intendant François Bigot and his unscrupulous associates, "La Grande Société," were lining their pockets at the administration's expense. Was it surprising that the Canadian high command looked forward to the campaign of 1758 with apprehension? Once the Anglo-Americans should undertake to make full use of their overwhelming advantage in manpower and strike at Canada's long, lightly held frontier at widely divergent points, defeat would become inevitable. The Franco-Canadians might successfully withstand one enemy blow, but they could never parry all of them.

Campaign of 1758. For 1758 the Anglo-Americans planned a land and sea assault upon Louisbourg to be carried out simultaneously with a major drive north along Lake Champlain and with subsidiary operations involving the recovery of Chouaguen and moves against Fort Frontenac and Fort Duquesne. A British fleet under Adm. Edward Boscawen and an army under Gen. Jeffrey Amherst carried the Cape Breton fortress in July, after a six-week siege; but Gen. James Abercromby's unimaginative efforts to take Carillon (near present Ticonderoga, N.Y.) on Lake Champlain by hurling waves of regulars against Montcalm's positions yielded nothing more than casualties and frustration.

Nevertheless, in mustering their strength at Carillon the French had robbed their other posts of men, and the Anglo-Americans had no difficulty in reoccupying Chouaguen and in taking both Fort Frontenac and Fort Duquesne. The sea approaches to Quebec were now open, and communications with Louisiana were no longer safe. The ring was steadily closing in upon French power in North America.

Campaigns of 1759–1760. In June 1759 a large fleet under Adm. Charles Saunders and an army under Gen. James Wolfe sailed up the St. Lawrence. At the same time Amherst set in motion an even larger army against Carillon and along the backdoor route to the St. Lawrence. It was the classic strategy that had been used by the Anglo-Americans against Canada ever since the days of William Phips. The town of Quebec was the vital point, a fact which both Vaudreuil and Montcalm fully appreciated. An effort during the winter of 1758–1759 to obtain help from France had yielded only good wishes, promotions, and medals, and Montcalm faced his task of meeting the twofold threat to Canada with a dwindling number of French regulars and Canadian militia.

Fall of Quebec. Relying upon the strong natural defensive position afforded by Quebec, Montcalm made the invader come to him. And come he did, on July 31, with an attack upon Montcalm's trenches at Montmorency. But the attackers were thrown back, and Wolfe was, for the moment, devoid of any tactical ideas save that of frontal attack. Finally, in September, his briga-

NATIONAL GALLERY OF CANADA, OTTAWA

THE DEATH OF WOLFE **in the Battle of Quebec, on September 13, 1759, painted by Benjamin West in 1770. Wolfe's French rival, Montcalm, also was mortally wounded.**

diers suggested a flanking move, which the English commander adopted. Although the plan was not his, he at least accepted responsibility for it, and on the night of September 12–13, British troops crossed the St. Lawrence from the south shore, above Quebec, under cover of the darkness. By good fortune, rather than by good management, they made the top of the cliff and drew up in battle order before the French had realized what had happened. Montcalm launched a too-hurried attack. Wolfe was killed in the exchange of shots, and Montcalm himself, at the head of his troops, was fatally wounded.

Following the French defeat, Vaudreuil withdrew the demoralized Franco-Canadian army up the river, and on September 18, Quebec surrendered to the British. In the following spring, the Chevalier de Lévis gained a victory over the British at Ste. Foy and laid siege to the British-occupied Quebec. However, the arrival of a British naval squadron forced him to withdraw to Montreal. The ships sent from France to cooperate with Lévis were forced to seek shelter in Chaleur Bay, where they were later destroyed by Commodore John Byron. The fall of New France was now only a matter of time.

Articles of Capitulation. Meanwhile, Amherst plodded methodically northward along the Lake Champlain route. The small French force opposing him fought a series of delaying actions that stalled the ponderous British commander until the late summer of 1760. Finally, on September 8, almost a year after the surrender of Quebec, Vaudreuil signed the Articles of Capitulation. The war was over, although there was further fighting in 1762 at St. John's in Newfoundland, and in the western regions the Sieur de Bellerive did not surrender Fort Chartres on the Mississippi River until 1765.

End of the French Regime. Few tears flowed in France with the collapse of the French North American empire. The *philosophes,* like Montesquieu, Voltaire, and Raynal, had written that colonies were more often a source of economic weakness than of strength; and intellectuals, like the Marquise de Pompadour, who adopted these ideas and whose influence was paramount over Louis XV, saw no reason why strong protests should be made to the peace conference at Paris against the cession of Canada to Britain. Neither did the commercial interests in La Rochelle, Bordeaux, Saint-Malo, Le Havre, Dunkirk, and other coastal towns which, presumably, might have been most anxious to hold fast to the colony on the St. Lawrence.

At the same time, in Britain, there were men who viewed the return of Canada to France with equanimity. They believed that the West Indian sugar island of Guadeloupe would be more of an economic asset than Voltaire's "few acres of snow." That Canada, rather than Guadeloupe, did become a British possession by treaty in 1763 was due largely to William Pitt, who sought territorial dominions as well as economic dominion and whose hatred of France was a compulsive thing that led him to demand every possible concession from Britain's erstwhile enemy.

The cession of Canada to Britain was a traumatic experience for the people of New France. Not that the occupying British troops were harsh or cruel—the evidence is all to the contrary. But the mental agony of defeat and conquest struck deeply. Canada had, during the *ancien régime,* acquired many of the attributes of nationhood, religious and ethnic homogeneity, and political, judicial, and social institutions of its own. After the conquest these were submerged in the domination of the conqueror. Deprived of its military, social and economic elite, New France looked for leadership to the church and to the clergy. Thus, from an active, commercial society, independent and proud according to Peter Kalm, the Swedish scientist who visited New France in 1748, French Canada became the rural, peasant society, withdrawn and strongly dependent upon its religious faith so familiar to observers in the 19th century. Such was the legacy of the defeat of French arms in North America during the Seven Years' War.

George F. G. Stanley
Royal Military College of Canada, Kingston, Ont.

Bibliography

Bird, Harrison, *Battle for a Continent* (Oxford 1965).
Casgrain, Henri R., *Montcalm et Lévis*, 2 vols. (Quebec 1891).
Frégault, Guy, *La Guerre de la Conquête* (Montreal 1955).
Gipson, Lawrence Henry, *The Great War for the Empire*, 9 vols. (New York 1939–56).
Hamilton, Edward P., *The French and Indian Wars* (New York 1962).
Pargellis, Stanley, ed., *Military Affairs in North America* (New York 1936).
Parkman, Francis, *Montcalm and Wolfe* (Boston 1884).
Stacey, Charles P., *Quebec* (Toronto 1959).
Stanley, George F. G., *New France, the Last Phase, 1774–1760* (Toronto 1968).

THE PERIOD 1764–1791

The Treaty of Paris (1763), which had for all practical purposes eliminated the presence of France in North America, left Britain serious problems. Those who drafted the Royal Proclamation (Oct. 7, 1763) and the instructions sent to Gen. James Murray (Dec. 7, 1763), governor of the new British colony of Quebec, seem to have been unaware of these problems.

Post-Conquest Problems. Problems ensuing from the British victory were of two types: those involving the mother country and its former American colonies, and those of administrative transition in what had been New France. The enlarging of Nova Scotia, the extension of Newfoundland's jurisdiction over maritime fisheries, and the creation of a fifteenth North American colony (Quebec)—all under Royal Proclamation—did not constitute a valid answer.

The complete shift in balance of power had transformed the relationship between the imperial government and the former colonists. With the enemy expelled, survival was no longer in question. Moreover, the government in London was now likely to become an opponent insofar as it created restrictions; this, in fact, it did, both in the colonies that later revolted and in Canada. The decisions to place under direct authority of the home government the vast territories of the hinterland under the pretext of reserving them for the Indians, and to maintain a permanent army on the North American continent provoked the anger of the majority of the colonists. This imperial policy hindered the progress of settlement westward and prejudiced commercial expansion. The presence of an army, now that the French threat no longer existed, led the colonists to wonder whether the mother country was not seeking to make the weight of its authority felt because it distrusted them and judged them insufficiently docile.

In the Laurentian colony a particularly complex situation developed. The Royal Proclamation ignored the fact that the French-speaking and Catholic inhabitants (some 65,000) made up more than 99% of the white population. Did the ministers and the agents of the imperial government anticipate that with massive immigration the British colonists would quickly become the majority, or that the Canadians would suddenly be transformed into English-speaking and Anglican subjects of His Majesty King George III? It is not easy to understand exactly what they thought.

The Victors Compromise. The British authorities were not slow to note the lack of realism in the Royal Proclamation. From the earliest years numerous compromises became essential. Murray refused to convene an Assembly that would have been entirely at the service of the tiny British minority of the colony, and there could be no question of placing legislative power in the hands of the Franco-Catholic majority. The Canadiens received permission to serve on juries without taking the Test Act oath, which would have required them to repudiate Catholicism. In certain cases French laws remained in force. In 1766, Bishop Jean Olivier Briand became head of the episcopal center in Quebec. London had given him permission to go to France for his consecration and return to Canada.

The conquerors had realized that it was not in their interest to persecute the church and its ministers, who had been trained to respect the authority of an absolute monarchy and had given proof that they were willing to collaborate. Closely watched by the governor, the clergy formed an indispensable link between the conquered population and the British administration. The emigration to France and to other French colonies of several leading families altered the old social balance and broadened in abnormal fashion the role of the clergy.

These compromise measures favored by a group of colonial administrators whom their adversaries dubbed the French Party, aroused the indignation of several hundred British businessmen, professionals, small shopkeepers and farmers who lived in the colony. Their spokesmen formed an antigovernment coalition known as the English, or British, Party. The latter insisted upon the strict application of English laws and convocation of a Legislative Assembly that would be wholly dedicated to the interests of the British minority since the Franco-Catholics could not sit in it. The less fanatic or more conciliatory members of the English Party would have conceded to the Canadiens the right to vote and to elect some of their own people as members of the Assembly. The imperial government and its representatives in Quebec City did not want to be party to such an arbitrary policy.

Quebec Act. The London ministers, relying on the advice of Governor Sir Guy Carleton, had the Quebec Act passed by the British Parliament (1774). Its aim was to solve the problems of the province of Quebec at a time when the agitation of the American colonies was severely taxing the patience and the lucidity of the rulers of the empire. Although English criminal law remained in force, French civil law was restored in order to end the disorder which reigned in the administration of justice. Seigneurial rule, officially recognized since 1771, was retained. The Catholic clergy achieved almost the status of an established church since it received the right to levy the tithe and to prosecute the recalcitrant faithful. Finally, by the abolition of the Test Act, Franco-Catholics were no longer excluded from public office. All legislative powers were vested in a council appointed by the king. According to the expectations of Carleton himself, only a few Canadiens who had given proof of their devotion to the British authorities would be permitted to sit in it.

If the Quebec Act satisfied most leading Canadiens and in particular the ecclesiastical administrators—a veritable political alliance, reinforced by reciprocal feelings of friendship, had been established between Carleton and Bishop Briand—it aroused the ire of the English Party. The Anglo-Protestant minority of the colony accused the king of having abandoned it.

American Revolution. The American Revolution brought to light the tensions and contradictions that existed in the Laurentian colony and in Nova Scotia.

Effects in Quebec. The alliance concluded between the British administrators and the official spokesmen of the Franco-Catholic community—members of the seigneurial class, a few merchants and professionals, ecclesiastical directors—did not have the spontaneous support of the population. The latter remained in a state of passive resistance. To the mass of the people, its own notables, forced to collaborate with the British authorities, seemed to be emissaries of a foreign power rather than real leaders. Nevertheless, historians who denounce the sociopolitical order sanctioned by the Quebec Act by calling it the "system of the generals" or the "aristocratic pact" ignore the imperatives to which every conqueror must submit. A foreign power cannot establish itself peacefully in a country if it does not obtain the collaboration of the former leaders, or if it does not at least succeed in neutralizing them. Deprived of their natural leaders and unable to replace them immediately, the conquered people realize that nothing remains but to submit in the hope that future circumstances will permit them to show their dissatisfaction.

The American invasion (1775–1776) gave the Canadiens the opportunity to dissociate themselves from those who called themselves their chiefs. The seigneurs and the clergy were unable to rally the majority of the population to defend the colony against the invaders, who received in several regions the support of the population or at least benefited from its neutrality. Nevertheless, the loyalty of the seigneurs and clergy and the weakness of the invaders facilitated Carleton's task. The arrival of a British army in the spring of 1776 convinced the people that submission to the government was the most prudent policy to follow. The intervention of France (1778) in the American Revolution raised high hopes among the whole Canadien population. Governor Sir Frederick Haldimand who succeeded a disappointed and frustrated Carleton in 1778, had reason to be nervous and suspicious.

The leaders of the English Party and the English-speaking minority of the Laurentian colony likewise lived through tense years between 1775 and 1783. The agitation of the American colonies had aroused some sympathy among them. Dissatisfied with the Quebec Act, they did not appear eager to defend the colony. A few members of the English Party even encouraged the mass of the Canadien people in their neutralism and in their opposition to the orders of the colonial government. But just as the Canadiens were recalled to more realistic sentiments by the defeat of the Americans at the walls of Quebec and the arrival of an army of His Majesty, so the British businessmen of the colony were convinced by their economic interests that they had everything to gain by supporting the imperial cause, because they were, after all, in competition with their southern rivals for the trade of the hinterland.

Between 1760 and 1775, British traders and merchants who came from former colonies or from Britain to settle in the St. Lawrence valley, prospered rapidly and secured control of the colonial economy without difficulty. The few Franco-Canadian merchants—the least rich and least influential—who had remained in their conquered country, had been inevitably placed in a position of inferiority in the face of the competition of the newcomers, who benefited by private and official support in Britain and in the colony.

The colony had developed rapidly owing to the initiative of British contractors, who knew how to profit by the combination of circumstances: postwar reconstruction, public expenditures, extension of the fur trade, development of the maritime fisheries of the Gulf of St. Lawrence, new requirements created by the American Revolution, upkeep of a larger army, and the settling of Loyalist immigrants. The Canadiens themselves, in particular the peasants who sold their produce at a better price, obtained some advantage from this generally favorable economic situation, which greatly aided the British in getting their rule accepted.

Effects in Nova Scotia. In Nova Scotia the American Revolution provoked distressing discords within the population and decisively influenced the evolution of the region. At least half its inhabitants, through their origins and families, identified themselves with New England. In addition, Governor Francis Legge, who had arrived in 1773, was unpopular. However, the presence of the British fleet obliged the majority of the population to be prudent in the expression of their innermost feelings. George Washington himself realized that it was wiser for the Americans not to attempt the invasion of Nova Scotia. Its inhabitants received the nickname of "Neutral Yankees" and only a few extremists came to blows.

The war itself helped to strengthen the ties between Nova Scotia and Britain. The blockade of the port of Boston, the arrival of military transports, and the commercial expansion created by the needs born of the struggle developed Halifax. Business circles in the colony were not slow to comprehend that it was in their interest to make common cause with the empire.

After the Revolution. The arrival in the Maritime colonies of some 35,000 Loyalists and disbanded soldiers to whom the imperial government granted land and indemnities radically altered the composition of the population. In 1784, in order to comply with the demands of the colonists, it was decided to create two new colonies. New Brunswick and Cape Breton Island were detached from Nova Scotia. Prince Edward Island, detached from Nova Scotia in 1769, continued its separate existence. Newfoundland remained a fishing center and port of call for His Majesty's navy. In New Brunswick a few hundred Acadians, principally from New England, had settled since the removal by the

PUBLIC ARCHIVES OF CANADA

LOYALISTS, who fled to Canada during the American Revolution, encamped on the St. Lawrence River in 1784, as shown in a contemporary watercolor by James Peachey.

imperial government of every interdiction against them (1764) along the Restigouche River and on the banks of its estuary. In Nova Scotia itself bitter conflicts developed between the Loyalists, who believed they had special rights, and the colonists who had arrived before the War of Independence. The former accused the latter mainly of having lacked loyalty to the crown. At least a generation was necessary to end these rivalries.

In the province of Quebec the return of peace permitted leaders and spokesmen for communities and business groups to manifest their dissatisfaction face-to-face. The Quebec Act, which the English Party had never accepted, satisfied only partially the deep-seated aspirations of the majority of Canadien leaders who, noting not without bitterness that France, having helped the Americans to free themselves from British rule, had abandoned them to their fate, concluded that it was up to them to take their fate in their own hands. Even the few Canadien families who had benefited from the protection of governors Carleton and Haldimand judged that the situation was greatly in need of improvement.

The Canadiens were always a minority without influence in the administration or in the Council. The greatest confusion reigned in the administration of justice. The Catholic Church lacked priests and the imperial government obstinately refused their entry from France. All attempts to reopen the College of Quebec and to bring over a few French professors had failed.

Voices of Reform. A veritable war of petitions broke out in the colony between 1783 and 1788. The English Party called for the repeal of the Quebec Act and the adoption of a constitution that would at last make of Canada a real British colony. Its leaders could now speak in the name of some 7,000 Loyalists whose arrival had augmented the English-speaking and Protestant population of the St. Lawrence Valley. The economic difficulties of some British businessmen after the prosperity of the easy and inflationary war years and the consequences of the Treaty of Versailles (ending the American Revolution in 1783), which limited the expansion of their trade toward the interior of the continent to the advantage of their competitors of the American Confederation, had made them particularly aggressive.

For their part the Canadien leaders, conscious that they still spoke in the name of a majority, had no intention of renouncing the advantages which political power bestows. On the contrary, they believed to be inadequate the rights and privileges acquired since the Quebec Act. The sudden increase of the Anglo-Protestant population made them especially uneasy. However, there was no unanimity on the measures to be taken to ensure the liberty and progress of the Canadiens. The conservative element confined itself to proposing a generous application of the existing constitution by calling for a greater participation of the Canadiens in the government of the colony in order to protect the established order against the introduction of English laws and institutions. The return of Carleton, now Lord Dorchester, in 1786, aroused great hopes among the more and more restricted group of traditional leaders, who still relied on the paternalism of the king's representative. The Canadien community now had new spokesmen, who perceived the advantages they and their compatriots would derive from the representative system. Since the Franco-Catholic population formed the majority of the electors, would not the Assembly comprise a majority of Canadien representatives?

As early as 1784 an alliance was formed between the heads of the English population and the reformist Canadiens who had separated from the conservative elements of the old ruling seigneurial and military class. In Quebec and Montreal, citizens' committees were organized, with the aim of grouping together all those—English-speaking and French-speaking—who advocated constitutional reform. These committees drew up a petition to the king in November 1784 and held meetings in support of their requests. Their adversaries did the same. As for the clergy, it was itself divided.

Constitutional Act (1791). Invited to advise the imperial government, and deemed to be a specialist on the Canadian question, Dorchester was in a delicate situation. He was shrewd enough to note that his own policy between 1767 and 1774 had been a partial failure. He realized that Quebec was not a simple colony-fortress; on the contrary, the St. Lawrence Valley, coupled with the colonies of the Gulf of St. Lawrence, could become the center of another British empire in North America. Canada's future appeared to him in a new perspective. Unfortunately he was not permitted to ignore totally the presence of the Canadiens and the political alliances he had concluded with their rulers 20 years before, more especially as Monsignor Briand, although he had resigned as bishop of Quebec in 1784, was still alive. The reports he sent to London sought to put the imperial authorities on guard against any decision that would compromise the future of British colonization in North America. However, his personal links with a recent past, of which he was partly prisoner, prevented him from being as explicit as he ought to have been.

Under the most contradictory pressures, the imperial government adopted the Constitutional Act (1791). This act did not cancel the Quebec Act. It stated quite simply that the colony in the future would have an elective assembly and would exercise legislative power in collaboration with a legislative council appointed by the king. It also gave notice of the king's intention to divide the St. Lawrence Valley into two colonies. An imperial decree, signed August 24, 1791, created the colonies of Upper and Lower Canada.

The king and his counselors had fancied that this division would do justice equally to the British minority and the Canadien community. They had simply forgotten that the English bourgeoisie lived in Lower Canada. The province of Quebec at that time numbered some 160,000 inhabitants of whom 21,000 were English-speaking. The majority, about 14,000, had settled in the western section of the territory that came to be called Upper Canada. Nevertheless, the real leaders and founders of English Canada, still in embryo, lived in the towns of Quebec, Trois-Rivières, Sorel, and Montreal. The leaders of the English Party and their representatives in London tried in vain to prevent this division.

Their confusion further convinced reformist Canadiens that the new constitution would be advantageous for them and for their compatriots, who had only to learn how to use it efficiently. It was in doing this apprenticeship that they came to grips with the British minority and the bureaucrats of Lower Canada. A new epoch had begun in the history of the Canadiens and of British colonization in the St. Lawrence valley.

MICHEL BRUNET
University of Montreal

Bibliography

Brebner, John Bartlet, *North Atlantic Triangle* (New Haven, Conn., 1945).

Brunet, Michel, *French Canada and the Early Decades of British Rule, 1760–1791,* Canadian Historical Association Booklet No. 5 (Ottawa 1955).

Brunet, Michel, *La Présence anglaise et les Canadiens* (Montreal 1958).

Burt, Alfred Le Roy, *Guy Carleton, Lord Dorchester, 1724–1808,* revised version, Canadian Historical Association Booklet No. 5 (Ottawa 1955).

Burt, Alfred Le Roy, *The Old Province of Quebec* (Minneapolis, Minn., 1933).

Graham Gerald S., *British Policy and Canada, 1774–1791* (London 1930).

Graham, Gerald S., *Empire of the North Atlantic,* 2d ed., (Toronto 1958).

MacNutt, William S., *The Making of Maritime Provinces, 1713–1784,* Canadian Historical Association Booklet No. 4 (Ottawa 1955).

Neatby, Hilda, *Quebec, the Revolutionary Age, 1760–1791* (Toronto 1966).

Ouellet, Fernand, *Histoire économique et sociale du Québec, 1760–1850* (Montreal 1966).

Rothney, Gordon Oliver, *Newfoundland: From International Fishery to Canadian Province,* Canadian Historical Association Booklet No. 10 (Ottawa 1959).

THE PERIOD 1792–1818

In 1792, with the main constitutional arrangements for British North America completed for the next 50 years, there were seven governments representing the British part of the continent.

Forms of Government. Newfoundland, although it was given its first regular system of courts in 1791 and a governor resident the year round in 1818, was not formally acknowledged as a colony until 1824. Cape Breton Island, reopened for settlement by the imperial authorities in 1784 when the Loyalists founded Sydney, remained under its own lieutenant governor from that date until it was made part of Nova Scotia again in 1820. The other five colonies—Upper and Lower Canada, Nova Scotia, New Brunswick, and Prince Edward Island—each had an assembly, elected on a wide franchise, with no special property qualification for candidates.

In the two Canadas and in Prince Edward Island there were bicameral legislatures: each had an appointed legislative council in addition to the elected assembly, each distinct from the usual executive council of officials subordinate to the governor. In the Canadas the legislative council was intended to strengthen the governor's position by acting as a check on the assembly, and also to encourage "connection, order, gradation and subordination" in a continent where democracy had recently proved itself unruly. The Clergy Reserves—land provided for under the Constitutional Act (1791) to support Church of England clergy in the Canadas—and the creation of Anglican bishoprics for Quebec and Nova Scotia, had in part the same purpose. In the main, British North America had the old representative system of colonial government, extended in spite of its failure in the Thirteen Colonies. For the moment, the most important difference was probably that no attempt was made to have the colonies help to pay the salaries of the officials who governed them.

Some Loyalists had suggested a central government for the British North American colonies. Lord Dorchester, given the title of governor-in-chief at Quebec, hoped that he would have some power in the other colonies; but he was not able to exercise it even over Upper Canada. Apart from the imperial government, there was no civil authority common to all the colonies. Only in his military capacity as commander-in-chief of British North America was Dorchester able to extend his authority outside Lower Canada.

Political Climate. In Lower Canada, the French Canadian professional class, which had joined in the demand for an elected assembly, controlled it immediately. Rejecting the leadership of both the seigneurs and the English-speaking merchants, they began the movement of Canadien nationalism. Resisting the blunt anglicization intended by Governor Sir James Craig and Bishop Jacob Mountain, they defined most of the issues that were to lead to the Rebellion of 1837. In 1809 their first spokesman, Pierre Bédard, clearly forecast the need for responsible government.

In the other colonies, political discontent was minor until the 1820's. Before Robert Gourlay's survey of grievances in Upper Canada in 1817–1819, no critic of the administration there was at all formidable. In Prince Edward Island, Lieutenant Governor J. F. W. Desbarres spent eight years (1805–1813), in almost continuous conflict with the assembly. Loyalist and pre-Loyalist factions divided the island, and appeared more gradually in Nova Scotia. In New Brunswick, the American settlers of Sunbury county disturbed the harmony of a Loyalist government until their Scottish assemblyman, James Glenie, left in 1805.

Population Growth. Even in Upper Canada, where Lieutenant Governor John G. Simcoe was an unrestrained prophet of conservatism and British loyalty, political issues were secondary to material growth. British North America had some quarter of a million inhabitants in 1792, and about twice that number 20 years later. Upper Canada grew most rapidly, quadrupling its original 20,000 by 1812; but Nova Scotia's population rose from about 30,000 by 1790 to 86,668 by the first census in 1817, and New Brunswick's 35,000 in 1806 had doubled by 1820. Lower Canada, with about 250,000 people by 1806, remained much the most populous colony; and its increase of roughly 100,000 since 1792 had been accomplished with an immigration of only some 15,000 "Yankees and Yorkers" into the Eastern Townships. The other colonies, especially in Upper Canada, were growing because of American immigrants, seeking good land with little attention to political boundaries.

Trade Development. Farmers might be indifferent to boundaries, but trade was not. British North Americans had no quarrel with the laws regulating colonial trade; their problem was to develop a trade that could take advantage of them. Hopes that British commerce with the American West would be channeled through the St. Lawrence River were destroyed in 1794 by Jay's Treaty, which removed obstacles to direct trade between Britain and the United States. In 1802, Canadian exports of wheat to Britain reached 1 million bushels but this was a temporary peak. With the fur trade declining and agricultural staples not yet ready to take its place, the commercial empire of the St. Lawrence valley needed a new commodity; the Maritimes were in the same position. Facing American competition on their own fishing grounds, they were having only fitful success in the attempt to replace New England as the supplier of provisions, livestock, and lumber to the British West Indies. The disappointing measure of the colonies' trade can be found in the records of their shipping: the port of Quebec received less than one third as many British ships as went to the Newfoundland fisheries.

Timber was the new staple that fulfilled British North American commercial ambitions. In 1807, Napoleon's "continental system" cut off Britain's main source of naval timber in the Baltic, just three years after a critical shortage of English oak had opened the way for a trade in timber from Quebec, and 30 years after Halifax had established a modest trade in pine masts. It no longer mattered that transport from Halifax cost three times as much as from Riga, in Russia, or that New Brunswick and Canadian timber was not yet skillfully selected, cut or handled. A high preference in tariff was given to colonial timber; even when it began to be reduced in 1821, it stood at 275%. At its peak the Maritimes' timber trade employed 1,520 ships and 17,600 men.

The Canadas benefited even more. Beginning with the establishment of Hull in 1800, timbering spread to the Ottawa Valley, which was to prove its most enduring home. American as well as British capital was attracted. By 1815 the United States was becoming a growing market and the way was open for extensive sawmilling.

War of 1812–1814. The United States was more than a source of immigrants, a market, and a commercial competitor: it was an enemy. In September 1794, the uneasy border, with British troops still posted on American soil and Indian resistance to American settlement still thought to have British support, almost flared into open war. Jay's Treaty smoothed over the conflict, provid-

BATTLE OF QUEENSTON HEIGHTS, Ontario, on October 13, 1812, a British victory over the invading Americans, from a contemporary aquatint by Major Dennis.

PUBLIC ARCHIVES OF CANADA

ing for the withdrawal of the troops; but British control of Upper Canada still aroused some American fears and stood in the way of some American ambitions. When in 1812 war broke out between Britain and the United States over neutral rights, Upper Canada was the obvious American target.

With only 10,000 regular troops in all of British North America, defense against a nation of more than 7 million was based on the strategy of holding Quebec, the one point that could be reinforced by sea. But the Americans, relying mainly on western militia, did not try to cut Upper Canada off from the east. Their first fumbling attempt at western invasion was turned back at Queenston Heights (Oct. 13, 1812). There, and in the war's hardest-fought battle, at Lundy's Lane (July 25, 1814), the invaders threatened only the settlements west of York (Toronto). Even when York fell in April 1813, the British forces for a counterstroke were left intact.

The war was an object lesson in the strategic importance of the St. Lawrence and the Great Lakes, which were both Upper Canada's border and its line of communications. York fell because the Americans were the first to build a naval squadron on Lake Ontario. The main British counterattack by way of Lake Champlain was similarly defeated by the loss of its accompanying flotilla in Plattsburg Bay. The naval war was as decisive as the presence of the British regular troops (many recruited in British North America) who bore the brunt of the land fighting.

Results of the War. When the Treaty of Ghent was signed in 1815, the United States was on the defensive: Washington had fallen and a British force was before New Orleans. The British government was, however, more interested in a durable peace than in pressing the territorial and commercial claims of British North America. The treaty merely ended the war; a settlement was worked out in subsequent agreements.

By the Rush-Bagot agreement of 1817, each side limited itself to four small armed vessels on the Great Lakes and Lake Champlain. In the following year, a convention settled the 49th parallel as the boundary from Lake of the Woods to the Rockies, with joint occupation of the disputed Pacific watershed for 10 years. The Maine-New Brunswick boundary was left to be the object of negotiation, arbitration, and occasional violence until 1842. Only one of the colonies' special demands was supported in the convention of 1818. American fishermen were excluded from the inshore waters of British North America, except to seek wood, water and shelter or to make repairs. The exclusion was not complete: the inshore fisheries of Labrador, and of southern and western Newfoundland, were left open. Since the main fishing grounds were outside the 3-mile limit, the Americans did not lose anything vital by the convention. What British North America gained from the war was simply the right to remain British. Since even this might still be questioned, defensive preparations were necessary. Most of the defenses surviving along the border were built in the years following 1815.

STANLEY R. MEALING
Carleton University

Further Reading: Burt, Alfred Le Roy, *The United States, Great Britain, and British North America ... 1775–1820* (New Haven and Toronto 1940); Craig, G. H., *Upper Canada: The Formative Years, 1789–1841* (Toronto 1965); Hitsman, J. Mackay, *The Incredible War of 1812* (Toronto 1966).

45. The Northwest, 1763–1869

The British victory in the Seven Years' War (1756–1763) profoundly affected the future of the vast territory lying between Hudson Bay and the Pacific Ocean, which was to become part of the new Dominion of Canada a little more than a century later. France was no longer able effectively to assert its claim to the northern continental interior, for it had lost its base on the St. Lawrence River. The terms of the Treaty of Paris, ending the war, shattered the dream of the explorer Sieur de La Vérendrye of a French empire founded on the fur trade, although France did not give up easily. In 1782 a French squadron under the Count de La Pérouse captured York Factory and Prince of Wales's Fort, two key establishments of the Hudson's Bay Company. However, it was the last time the French ever attacked in Hudson Bay. Even the British reverses in the American Revolution did nothing to restore the old position of France.

With the American victory, the continent was once again divided. As Britain's new rival for the dominance in the Northwest, the United States was to prove quite as formidable as the old, but in an economic and cultural rather than a political or military sense. The ambitions of Spain and Russia on the Pacific coast, though posing a more immediate threat, were checked by the Nootka Sound Convention of 1790 between Britain and Spain, and by treaties in 1824 and 1825 between Britain, the United States, and Russia that fixed the southern boundary of Russian territory on the Pacific coast at latitude 54°40′ north. Conflicts between British and American interests were to take longer to resolve and played an important part in the history of the Northwest from 1763 to 1869.

Advance into the Interior. The Northwest in 1763 was still virtually an unknown land to the European, except to the fur traders who had followed the trails of La Vérendrye and Anthony Henday, both of whom traveled almost as far west as the Rocky Mountains. The pace of the expansion of geographic knowledge accelerated rapidly under the pressure of fur trade rivalries. At first the French had made much more rapid progress both in exploration and in trade, but the expedition by Henday, a Hudson's Bay Company employee, to the Saskatchewan country was the spearhead of a more aggressive policy on the part of the company—a recognition that it was no longer possible to wait for the Indians to bring their furs to the posts by Hudson Bay.

The French defeat in the Seven Years' War and the consequent disorganization of the fur trade of New France brought only a brief and local advantage to the English company. Even before the peace treaty was signed, traders like Alexander Henry the elder began to fill the void left by the conquest in the fur trade of Montreal and Quebec. Under the stimulus of their challenge the Hudson's Bay Company was to resume the advance into the interior for which Henday's journey had been the preliminary reconnaissance.

Rivalry for Furs. Governmental efforts to restrict the trade and the expansion of settlement into the interior were ineffective; by 1768 the Indian trade was officially as well as practically open. By then the Hudson's Bay Company was feeling the effects of the competition of the Pedlars, as they called their rivals from the St. Lawrence River. Sending inland men like Isaac Batt, Louis Primeau,

A FUR TRADER of the Canadian West bartering in an Indian council tepee, as depicted in a wood engraving after Frederic Remington.

THE GRANGER COLLECTION

and Matthew Cocking to persuade the Indians to bring their furs to Hudson's Bay Company was not enough; if the company's trade were to survive it would have to build a post in the Interior.

This task was entrusted in 1774 to Samuel Hearne, recently returned from his famous journey with the Chipewyan Indian leader Matonabbee to the Coppermine River and the Arctic Ocean that had so much enlarged geographic knowledge of the northern interior. Hearne's Cumberland House stood 60 miles (96 km) above The Pas, on Pine Island Lake. Here the company could command the Saskatchewan River and take advantage of its base on Hudson Bay and the route this gave to the interior, which was much shorter than the one its rivals had to follow.

The Pedlars countered this move by a closer organization of their own: their shifting partnerships after 1776 began to merge into the North West Company. It was very different in structure from its opponent, but a formidable enterprise nevertheless, able to take full advantage of the old skills of the French in the trade and the thrusting energy of the merchants who moved into the fur trade of Montreal, Quebec, and Michilimackinac.

The American Revolution gave Montreal an advantage over New York and Albany in trade with England. At the same time the use of Grand Portage and later Fort William to outfit the canoes for the West rapidly extended the range of the Montreal traders. By 1778, Peter Pond, a future partner in the North West Company, had passed over Methy Portage and down the Clearwater and Athabasca rivers to build a post near Athabasca Lake. The post, in what is now northern Alberta, stood in the heart of one of the richest, fur-bearing areas of the West.

Though sharp competition between the Canadian traders continued, the North West Company by 1784 had emerged to bring together the Montreal interests, who provided the capital and sold the furs abroad, and the "winterers" inland, who gathered the furs. This effort at coordination was not wholly successful and three-cornered competition between the Hudson's Bay Company, the North West Company, and independent interests continued.

Violence, which frequently marked the fur trade competition, reached a peak after 1800, when Alexander Mackenzie, who had been associated with the Nor'Westers, took his high prestige and his uncommon talents into a "New North West Company," usually known as the XY Company. The violence did not subside until the union of the North West and Hudson's Bay companies in 1821.

The Pacific Is Reached. Competition for the furs of the Northwest brought about the rapid exploration of the region. Hearne's journey to the Arctic demonstrated how illusory were hopes of a commercially feasible northwest passage by sea. Pond dreamed of an overland passage to the Pacific by the rivers and lakes of the interior.

Alexander Mackenzie put that dream to the test. His voyage down the Mackenzie River (named for him) was a bitter disappointment, for it led only to the icy waters of the Arctic. His journey up the Peace River and over the mountains was crowned by the magnificent understatement he daubed on a rock by the Pacific: "Alexander Mackenzie, from Canada, by land, the twenty-second of July, one thousand seven hundred and ninety three."

Simon Fraser of the North West Company made the perilous passage down the Fraser River to its mouth in 1808. David Thompson of the North West Company (once in the employ of the Hudson's Bay Company) completed his more leisurely journey down the Columbia River by 1811, only to find John Jacob Astor's Pacific Fur Company already established at its mouth.

The Pacific coast was already well known through the exertions of the Russians who pressed down from the north in the wake of Vitus Bering, Spanish explorers like Juan Josef Pérez Hernández and Juan Francisco de la Bodega y Quadra, and Englishmen like Capt. James Cook and George Vancouver. Knowledge of the geography of the interior owed much to men like Thompson, Philip Turnor, and Peter Fidler (the last two of the Hudson's Bay Company). They were not only explorers but also surveyors whose scientific observations served both the commercial interests of their companies and the growing curiosity of educated Europeans about the New World. By 1814 the state of geographic knowledge enabled Thompson to complete the remarkable map that hung in the North West Company partners' dining hall at Fort William.

Visions of Settlement. Competition in the fur trade led not only to an increase in geographic

PUBLIC ARCHIVES OF CANADA

CAPTAIN GEORGE VANCOUVER, British navigator, explores Burrard Inlet, near the present city of Vancouver, in 1792, as depicted in a print by artist J. D. Kelly.

knowledge but also to the beginning of settlement. The vision that led Mackenzie to the Arctic and the Pacific embraced the continent and its neighboring oceans and reached as far as Europe and the Orient. The organization of the trade, as he conceived it, would be based on the wealth and business acumen of London, with which the Canadian traders had close links; it would take advantage of Montreal's driving energy and grasp of American realities; and it would use the Hudson's Bay Company's short route to the interior. Thus it would command not only the furs of the interior and the Pacific coast but also the lucrative exchange of goods with the Far East.

Such a scheme would succeed not by competition but only by close cooperation between the Hudson's Bay Company and the St. Lawrence. To this end Mackenzie tried to persuade his Montreal associates to buy a controlling interest in the English company. He did not succeed; although the Nor'Westers in the "Columbia enterprise" carried their trade to the Pacific coast, it was left to the united companies after 1821 to achieve something of what he had dreamed.

Red River Settlement. An even broader vision of the future of British North America was that of Thomas Douglas, Earl of Selkirk. Selkirk, a Scottish nobleman of philanthropic disposition, was interested in the settlement overseas of the Scottish crofters evicted by Highland landowners.

GOVERNOR OF RED RIVER COLONY, in present-day Manitoba, traveling in a light canoe (1824). This lithograph is by Peter Rindisbacher, a colony resident.

PUBLIC ARCHIVES OF CANADA

To Selkirk the lands along the Red River, in what is now southern Manitoba, presented promising possibilities. As these lands under the Hudson's Bay Company's charter in 1670 were part of Rupert's Land, cooperation with the company was as essential to Selkirk as to Mackenzie, and he too began to acquire stock in the company, in which his relations by marriage were already heavily interested. The company, under the pressure of competition that was catastrophically reducing its returns, accepted a scheme of reorganization that involved a settlement, under Selkirk's direction, at the forks of the Red and Assiniboine rivers, embracing the present site of Winnipeg.

Selkirk's first settlers reached their destination in 1812. The North West Company saw it as a threat to the future of its trade and launched a bitter attack that almost destroyed the colony. The company's campaign reached its climax in the Massacre of Seven Oaks and the murder of Governor Semple in 1816. Selkirk led an expedition to its rescue and, in an action of doubtful legality, seized the Nor'Westers' headquarters at Fort William. Selkirk's Swiss and German veterans of the War of 1812, though they did not prove very satisfactory settlers, were too much for the Nor'Westers. Although the colony's survival was assured, it was to undergo a succession of ordeals by flood, famine, and drought.

End of the Fur War. The survival of the colony was proof of the waning power of the North West Company and the hardened resolve of its older rival not to be driven out of the Northwest. The latter stiffened its resistance, renewed its challenge in the fur-rich Athabasca country and prepared to do battle west of the mountains, where the Nor'Westers had enjoyed a monopoly after they had acquired the Astor posts during the War of 1812. To the wintering partners and the British agents of the North West Company it became increasingly evident that amalgamation with their rival was the least of evils. The two companies united under the name of the older (the Hudson's Bay Company) in 1821. The chief casualties of the union were the Montreal merchants, for their role in the trade ceased to exist, and the links the fur trade had forged between the Northwest and the Canadas very largely ceased to exist. The short route to the interior proved an advantage that all the trading expertise of Montreal could not overcome.

After the union, the reorganization of the fur trade was carried out largely by George Simpson, who was named governor of the Northern Department in 1821, governor of the Southern Department as well in 1826, and governor-in-chief of all the company's territories in 1839. He remained in this office until his death in 1860. For 40 years the able and energetic "Little Emperor" dominated the Northwest, always serving what he saw as the interests of the company. Superfluous posts were closed, officers of both companies were ruthlessly retired, and the profits of the company rose steadily. On the periphery of the trading area, whether in the interior or on the coast, he executed a skillful strategy of sterilization that discouraged rival traders from attempting to penetrate the heartland of the company's monopoly. Minute attention to detail, an infinite capacity for work, and a flinty hardness, tempered only by his desire to please his superiors, made Simpson the most effective of the company's servants.

Under Simpson's rule the violence of competition disappeared almost instantaneously. The fur trade still dominated the Northwest, but settlement had begun on the Red River and on the Pacific coast. Simpson fully realized the incompatibility of trade and settlement and did nothing to encourage the latter, but even he realized its inevitability. Settlement would certainly bring tensions in relations with the Indians, but for the moment the absence of competition made possible a rigid control of the use of liquor in trade. The fur trade exploited the Indians, but it ceased to debauch them. Not until the very end of the period, in the late 1860's, did the appearance in what is now southern Alberta of whiskey traders from Fort Benton threaten to destroy the equilib-

UPPER FORT GARRY was built in 1835 on the Red River. Its site is now in Winnipeg. This lithograph by H. J. Warre shows the fort as it appeared in 1845.

PUBLIC ARCHIVES OF CANADA

rium established under Simpson between the Indians and the company as the representative of the white man.

Growth at Red River. The Red River settlement grew slowly but steadily, an island of civilization rather than a frontier, for its contact with the outside world was through the waters of Hudson Bay with the United Kingdom rather than through the Great Lakes with the Canadas or the United States. It was a bicultural and even a multicultural society, partly French-speaking and Roman Catholic, partly English-speaking and Protestant, but predominantly of mixed white and Indian ancestry.

The retired officers of the fur trade brought their Indian wives and their children to the Red River in preference to the United Kingdom or the eastern colonies. They formed a relatively well-to-do element, able to take advantage of the opportunity for the assimilation of their children offered by the schools established by English missionaries.

The Kildonan Scots, the first real agricultural settlers, maintained their identity as Gaels and Presbyterians and, like the handful of French Canadians at St. Boniface, resisted intermarriage.

The largest group was the *métis*, the descendants of the *voyageurs* and Indian women; they were French-speaking and Catholic, but generally less remote from their Indian cousins than the English-speaking "native born." Their missionaries also established schools but, perhaps because of the economic difference between the officers and the servants of the company, these seem to have been less effective as instruments of assimilation. The *métis* became increasingly a people apart, with their own tradition and a way of life centering in the buffalo hunt.

The various groups in the settlement were physically as well as culturally isolated, but there was little friction between the groups. The Red River settlement seems to have been singularly law-abiding for a colony so isolated from any focus of order.

The tranquillity of the colony was disturbed by the resistance of the *métis* to the company's monopoly of trade, for increasingly they saw themselves as having a special position as the real owners of the country. In this they enjoyed the general sympathy of the native born, and in 1849 it became apparent that, no matter what the legality of the company's position might be, its monopoly of trade could no longer be enforced against the opposition of the half-breeds. Thus, without serious violence the Northwest passed into a new stage of development, although the company continued to maintain its dominant position.

Work of the Missions. In the life of the settlement the missionaries played a part second in importance only to that of the company and its officers. Selkirk was sympathetic to the request of the Kildonan settlers for a Presbyterian minister and encouraged the bishop of Quebec to send Joseph Norbert Provencher and Sévère-Joseph-Nicolas Dumoulin to minister to the Roman Catholics of the Red River settlement. Provencher arrived in 1818; John West, the first Anglican missionary, in 1820; the Presbyterians, however, did not receive their missionary, John Black, until 1851. The missionaries were as active in the school as in the church and thus wielded a double influence.

Simpson and some other company officers were less than enthusiastic in their support of missionary work. But the missionaries could depend upon influential members of the company's London committee like Benjamin Harrison, staunch adherents of the Evangelical movement as they were.

Provencher became bishop of the Northwest in 1822, David Anderson first Anglican bishop of Rupert's Land in 1849. Their churches did not confine their work to the settlement. Catholic missionaries followed their *métis* flocks into the interior and worked among the Indians; the Angli-

MC CORD MUSEUM, MC GILL UNIVERSITY, MONTREAL

DISMANTLED WAGONS of westbound travelers are ferried over the Battle River (now in Saskatchewan), as pictured in a watercolor by William G. R. Hind (1833–88).

CARIBOO ROAD, near Yale, in the Fraser River Valley, British Columbia, built in 1862–1865 in the gold rush.

PUBLIC ARCHIVES OF CANADA

cans by 1869 had established their work as far north and west as the Yukon. The Methodists entered the field in 1840 and through the work of James Evans developed the use of syllabics to provide the Indians with a written language.

West Coast Settlement. The Red River remained the only important center of settlement east of the mountains and west of the Great Lakes, although little communities did grow up around important posts like Edmonton and elsewhere in the Saskatchewan Valley. Missions like St. Albert were also serving as focuses for settlement toward the end of the period.

The mountain and Pacific coastal region had a rather different development, although it too was dominated by the fur trade until the gold rush began in 1857. What might happen not only to the West coast region of British North America but also to its interior had been foreshadowed in 1846 by the fate of the Oregon territory. There, in spite of British claims, American settlement had determined that the region south of the 49th parallel of latitude should be part of the United States.

The Hudson's Bay Company accordingly had retired northward to develop its colony of Vancouver Island, established in 1849. The colony's governor, James Douglas, acted decisively to prevent a repetition, farther north, of the events that had carried the Oregon territory into the American union. The mainland colony of British Columbia was established in 1858, law and order were more or less established, and the crisis was surmounted.

As the gold rush receded, both colonies languished. They were united in 1866 and immediately plunged into a discussion of the advantages and disadvantages of joining the wider Canadian federation of 1867.

Growing Unease. The pressure from the South was felt not only in the Pacific and Western mountain regions of British North America. In what was to be southern Alberta, whiskey traders from across the border were threatening to disturb the relations with the Indians that had been so generally satisfactory since the union of the companies in 1821. In the Red River the movement of American settlement into Minnesota had changed the lines of communication with the outside world. It became much quicker and easier to reach London by way of St. Paul, Minn., than by way of York Factory. A few Americans in the colony and a rather larger number south of the border showed an ominous disposition toward northward as well as westward expansion.

Canada was showing a renewed interest in the Northwest. English Canadians were moving into the colony and not always behaving tactfully in that sensitive and isolated society.

In Britain the Hudson's Bay Company came increasingly under fire as an anomaly in the laissez-faire atmosphere of the later 19th century. Its ownership had changed hands in 1863. The new owners had interests that went far beyond the fur trade, and they were viewed with considerable suspicion and distrust by the officers and servants of the company in the Northwest. The *métis* more and more regarded themselves a "new nation," highly sensitive to any infringement of what they held to be their rights. Throughout the Northwest, from the Great Lakes to the Pacific, a sense of unease prevailed, at once excited by, and suspicious of, the prospects for the future.

LEWIS G. THOMAS, *University of Alberta*

Bibliography

Boon, Thomas Charles Boucher, *The Anglican Church from the Bay to the Rockies* (Toronto 1962).

Galbraith, John S., *The Hudson's Bay Company as an Imperial Factor* (Berkeley and Los Angeles 1957).

Morton, Arthur Silver, *History of the Canadian West to 1870–71* (London 1939).

Morton, William Lewis, *Manitoba: A History* (Toronto 1957).

Ormsby, Margaret A., *British Columbia: A History* (Toronto 1958).

Rich, Edwin Ernest, *Hudson's Bay Company, 1670–1870,* 3 vols. (Toronto 1961).

46. British North America, 1815–1857

After the War of 1812 the six colonies of British North America—Newfoundland, Prince Edward Island, Nova Scotia, New Brunswick, Lower Canada, and Upper Canada—faced a period of growth bedeviled by constitutional and financial problems. For five of them—all but Newfoundland—the problems of the period led within a few years to acceptance of the Confederation idea.

THE ATLANTIC PROVINCES

The period after 1815 in the Atlantic Provinces was, broadly speaking, one of considerable economic progress. It was also one of stormy politics. However, by the mid-1850's the political turbulence had abated, and each of the four colonies had achieved responsible government.

Nova Scotia. The War of 1812 brought unprecedented prosperity to Nova Scotia. Privateering became a lucrative pursuit. Trade with the New England states continued to flourish because of the neutralist sentiment of the region. Fisheries, lumbering, and shipbuilding remained the basis of Nova Scotia's maritime economy. Timber was king. A staple export, it was used also to build ships. In 1830 more than 1,320 ships were owned by Nova Scotians; by 1846, this number had grown to 2,843, compared with only 604 for Canada. Nova Scotia's ships dominated the West Indian trade and carried on a profitable commerce with New England. A steady stream of immigrants, some 55,000 between 1815 and 1851, stimulated the economy. Most of them were Scots or Irish, but 2,000 Negroes arrived at the close of the War of 1812 and some 200 Welshmen in 1818–1819.

Peace, however, was followed by an economic depression, all the more serious because of a succession of poor harvests. Discontent expressed itself in protests against the Convention of 1818, which permitted the United States to share in the fisheries of British North America and in the West Indian trade. This grievance festered until recovery set in. The postwar depression aggravated latent political controversy and generated the struggle for responsible government, which convulsed the colony in the 1830's and 1840's.

This contest reflected a clash of economic interest between the banking and mercantile establishment in Halifax on the one hand and the farmers, small shopkeepers, and mechanics on the other. The conflict also had ecclesiastical overtones, with Anglican ranged against Dissenter and Roman Catholic. The wealthy, office-holding Anglican establishment was solidly entrenched in the appointed Council of Twelve, which had monopolized political power for years. The spearhead of reform was the elected house of assembly, increasingly representative of rural interest and religious dissent.

The struggle between the council and the assembly coincided with an intellectual awakening reflected in the writings of Thomas McCulloch, Thomas Chandler Haliburton, and Joseph Howe. The establishment of Pictou Academy (1816) marked the extension of educational benefits to the working class. This, in turn, made possible the appearance of a number of popular newspapers and magazines, notably the *Acadian Recorder* and the *Novascotian*, both of Halifax, the *Colonial Patriot* of Pictou, and the Yarmouth *Herald*. The new press strongly advocated the cause of reform. It also encouraged the founding of public libraries and literary and debating societies, all of which helped to create an intelligent public opinion well disposed to reform. Moreover, the press appealed to "the stout yeomen of the counties," notably in 1818 in John Young's *Acadian Recorder* series published later as a book, *Letters of Agricola*. The Central Agricultural Society, founded in the same year, did much to bring together the scattered local farmers' organizations and thereby develop a farming class well informed on current issues, political as well as economic. Thus, the intellectual awakening strengthened the hands of the assembly in its struggle with the council and gave the Reformers their foremost champion, Joseph Howe.

Joseph Howe's Struggle. The son of the king's printer, Howe was born in Halifax of Loyalist ancestry and by 1828 had become proprietor and editor of the *Novascotian*. His indomitable courage and shrewd political intuition were first revealed in his *Legislative Reviews*, a series of Reformist articles, the first of which appeared in his paper in 1830. Thanks largely to Howe's efforts, the legislative council, or upper house, was separated from the executive council (1833) and, for the first time, four members of the latter were chosen from the assembly, where they would be answerable for the policies of the government. Two years later, Howe defended himself successfully in a libel suit brought against him on account of his attacks on the government. It was a *cause célèbre*, which gained him public prominence and election (1836) to the assembly as one of the members for Halifax.

Now the acknowledged leader of the Reform party, Howe demanded that the executive council be changed if it failed to retain the confidence of the assembly. His agitation for responsible government was temporarily checked, however, by the outbreak of the Papineau-Mackenzie Rebellion in Canada (1837), which aroused the fear that advocacy of self-government might lead to revolution. This reaction occurred despite Howe's deliberate dissociation of Nova Scotia from the insurgent cause, and the assembly's demonstration of its loyalty to the crown by unanimously voting £100,000 and calling out the Nova Scotia militia for the defense of New Brunswick in the Aroostook War (1839).

Later that year, however, Howe returned to the attack with his *Letters to Lord John Russell*, in which he ridiculed the colonial secretary's doctrine of "colonial government based upon an Executive Council" under a "Governor receiving instructions from the Crown on the responsibility of a Secretary of State." Howe argued that this device would make the governor a mere tool of the latter, responsible to neither the colonial office nor the people of the colony. He maintained that the only means by which the governor could shake off this "thraldom" to the council was for Britain to grant responsible government.

Howe's arguments, backed by the impact of the Durham Report and Buller's *Responsible Government for the Colonies*, induced Russell to authorize (Oct. 16, 1839) the lieutenant governor to change the executive council for reasons of public policy—a declaration which Howe promptly put to the test by carrying in the assembly a vote of no confidence in the council. Upon Lieutenant Governor Sir Colin Campbell's refusal to dismiss the council, the assembly, led by Howe, petitioned successfully for his recall. Russell decided to temporize and, at his request, Governor-General Lord Sydenham visited Halifax to win over Howe. By playing upon Howe's imperial loyalty and his willingness to introduce responsible government "by degrees," Sydenham persuaded him to become a member of the council. Despite the earnest efforts of Lord Falkland, the new lieutenant governor, the obstructionist tactics of the establishment encouraged by the return of the Conservatives to power in Britain (1841) made the coalition unworkable, and Howe, in consequence, resigned (1843).

Responsible Government, 1848. In 1847, Howe led the Reform party to victory at the polls. Profiting from his previous experience and heartened by the electoral success of the Whigs in Britain (1846), he spurned the proposal of Falkland's successor, Sir John Harvey, that he enter a new coalition. Howe now demanded the immediate grant of full responsible government, as defined in November 1846 and March 1847 in dispatches to Harvey from Lord Grey, the new colonial secretary. In January 1848, the assembly voted "no confidence" in the executive council, and this time the latter resigned. A new cabinet, with James Boyle Uniacke, a veteran Reformer, as prime minister, and Joseph Howe as provincial secretary, took office in February—the first responsible government in the British Empire overseas.

The new administration addressed itself to the economic development of the colony, especially railway construction and trade with the United States. Although 6 miles (9.6 km) of railway had been opened at the coal mines of Pictou county in 1839, large-scale railroad construction did not begin until 1854. In that year, Nova Scotia became a party to the Reciprocity Treaty with the United States, a treaty that proved beneficial to the colony until its abrogation by the Americans in 1866.

New Brunswick. New Brunswick, like Nova Scotia, benefited from the War of 1812, and for similar reasons. The colony's population increased owing to the influx of immigrants, a large proportion of whom, including many veterans of the Napoleonic Wars, came from the British Isles; by 1824 it had risen to 74,000 and by 1855 to 250,000. Under the stimulus of British tariff preferences, the timber trade became the predominant economic activity. This produced lasting social and economic results. As capital and labor poured into the timber industry, agriculture was neglected and failed to produce a politically powerful farming interest. The colony's need of the British timber market reinforced its Loyalist ties.

Partly because of its close commercial and sentimental links with Britain, the agitation for responsible government developed more slowly and less vigorously in New Brunswick than in Nova Scotia. Moreover, the class conflict that embittered the struggle for responsible government in Nova Scotia was much less pronounced in New Brunswick. For one thing, Saint John, the chief mercantile center but not the political capital, never aspired to monopolize the government as Halifax did. For another, wealth was much more evenly distributed throughout New Brunswick, with the result that the leaders of the elected assembly, like the members of the appointed council, were men of means, and there was no sharp cleavage of economic interest between the two bodies. Nevertheless friction did develop, and the British government granted the assembly's demand for the separation of the executive council from the legislative council in 1832.

Crown Lands Issue. Ironically enough, the most contentious issue arose, although indirectly, from the timber trade. It concerned the control of the crown lands, which were vital to the timber industry. As early as 1825, the commercial panic of that year focused public criticism on the abuses in the crown lands department. In 1832, the assembly's offer to authorize a civil list in return for control of the crown lands was rejected by the British government.

In 1836, however, the British government agreed to transfer the crown lands revenues to the assembly, although retaining the administration of the crown lands for itself and also refusing to admit members of the assembly to the executive council. Even this limited concession was anathema to the reactionary lieutenant governor Sir Archibald Campbell, who resigned in protest. In 1837 his successor, Sir John Harvey, was instructed to grant the assembly full control of the crown lands and their revenues in exchange for a fixed civil list. Furthermore, on his own initiative, Harvey admitted several members of the assembly to the executive council.

Thus, the assembly not only emerged victorious from the long controversy over the crown lands but also gained a voice in the determination of executive policy. On his visit to the colony in 1840, Lord Sydenham, the governor-general, reported that, in contrast to the rest of British North America, "there reigns in New Brunswick the most perfect tranquillity and an entire harmony between the Executive and the Legislative."

This, however, did not mean that the colony had attained full responsible government. On the contrary, the assembly, out of gratitude for the satisfactory settlement of the crown lands question, decided to "repudiate the claims set up by another colony" (Nova Scotia) for the accountability of the council to the assembly "at all times." Moreover, the general election of 1842 resulted in a severe rebuff to the Reform party while in 1843 its leader, Lemuel Allan Wilmot, entered the executive council, and the assembly recorded its support of the resistance by the governor-general, Sir Charles Metcalfe, to the "extravagant demands" being made by his Canadian ministers upon crown patronage.

Responsible Government, 1854. A reaction set in, however, in 1845 as the result of the blatant nepotism of the lieutenant governor, Sir William Colebrook, in appointing his son-in-law, a complete stranger to New Brunswick, as provincial secretary. Wilmot and four of the seven Tory members of the executive council resigned in protest. The assembly denounced the appointment. Lord Stanley, the British colonial secretary, hurriedly canceled it, but the damage had been done. By a vote of 24 to 11, the assembly carried a resolution endorsing the principles of responsible government outlined in Grey's famous dispatches to Harvey.

But no effective action was taken to implement this resolution despite Howe's crowning victory in Nova Scotia. Coalition governments of Tories and Reformers followed each other in kaleidoscopic succession. Wilmot himself reentered the executive council as attorney general in 1851 and accepted appointment to the supreme court of New Brunswick the following year. It was not until 1854 that the Reformers, under their new leader, Charles Fisher, were able to win a decisive triumph at the polls and form New Brunswick's first fully responsible government.

Maine Border Dispute. Meanwhile, soon after the crown lands controversy had ended, the long-standing dispute over the Maine-New Brunswick boundary entered a decisive phase. After an abortive attempt at arbitration in 1831 the question slumbered until 1839, when it became acute. In February of that year, a crew of New Brunswick lumbermen cut timber on disputed territory and resisted the efforts of a Maine sheriff's posse to expel them. The governor of Maine sent Sen. Rufus McIntire to the Aroostook River to investigate. The senator and two of his officers were captured; although they were speedily released on parole, tension mounted on both sides. The governor of Maine called for 10,000 troops to uphold the claims of his state. Sir John Harvey dispatched 500 regular troops and 1,000 militiamen to the scene, and Nova Scotia hastened to the aid of its sister colony.

Fortunately, the old friendship between Harvey and Gen. Winfield Scott, the commander of the U.S. forces, led to an agreement on a joint occupation of the disputed area. Eventually, the dispute was settled amicably by the Webster-Ashburton Treaty of 1842, which awarded the Aroostook Valley to the United States and opened the St. John River to navigation by both countries.

The settlement of the boundary dispute, combined with the abrogation of the British timber preferences in 1846, revived New Brunswick's interest in railway construction as a pathway to new markets. A railroad from Halifax to Quebec was projected, and an imperial guarantee of £7 million was promised, but the scheme fell through when the British government excluded from the guarantee the line to the American border—the part of the project in which New Brunswick was chiefly interested.

Prince Edward Island. Largely because of immigration, mainly from Scotland, the population of "the Garden of the Gulf" (of St. Lawrence) increased from 10,000 in 1815 to more than 62,000 in 1848. With the arrival of increasing numbers of settlers, new roads were opened and shipbuilding was started. The felling of timber for shipbuilding led to the clearing of land and thus stimulated agriculture. Prince Edward Island ships took local products abroad, and the resulting trade, continuing until the decline of sailing ships after the mid-19th century, was the chief factor in the colony's growth.

Absentee Landlords. The island's economic progress would have been greater and more rapid had it not been for the curse of absentee proprietorship, a system of landownership imposed on the colony by Britain in 1767. The land question also gave rise to a chronic contest between the "Snatchers," as the absentee landlords were called, and the "Escheaters," whose aim was to expropriate them.

The conflict between the rival interests had political ramifications. The colonial office was responsive to the proprietors, who also were strongly represented on the appointed council. Their opponents dominated the elected assembly and through it made repeated attempts to escheat the lands on the ground that the absentee proprietors and their successors had failed to fulfill the original conditions of the land grants. Thus, the land question further embittered the relations between the council and the assembly, already strained by their quarrel over the control of public revenue.

The influence of the proprietors with the British government secured the appointment of Charles Douglas Smith as lieutenant governor (1813–1824). Smith's unabashed championship of the "Snatchers" involved him in a collision with the assembly, which eventually led to his being cashiered. The struggle continued even under the conciliatory rule of his successor, John Reedy (1824–1831), the assembly persisting in its demand for either a court of escheat or penal taxation of absentee estates to support local services. The assembly gained its first success in 1839 when it obtained the separation of the legislative council from the executive council—a concession that it had been demanding since 1834. This proved to be a hollow victory, however, since the assembly soon discovered that both new councils contained most of the former members of the old, many of them officials and proprietors or their agents.

Responsible Government, 1851. The assembly, whose membership now included an increased proportion of recent immigrants, decided that the only way to remove the burden of absentee proprietorship was to achieve responsible government. Accordingly, in April 1846, the assembly for the first time carried an address urging the adoption of "the principles of responsible government," and on March 18, 1847, approved by a vote of 18 to 3 a resolution declaring that if the executive council failed to "retain the confidence of the majority.... [it] ought to resign." The March 18th resolution was backed by the lieutenant governor, Sir Henry Vere Huntley, partly to win the support of the house in his personal vendetta with the speaker, Joseph Pope, and partly because of the return of the Whigs to power in Britain.

Despite Huntley's able series of dispatches in favor of responsible government, Lord Grey, the colonial secretary, rejected the 1847 resolution on the grounds that the colony lacked the numbers, wealth, and administrative skills necessary for self-government. As an alternative, Grey proposed a constitution on the Jamaican model, with a multiparty executive council, a system which he believed would afford adequate protection to the rights of the proprietors. He also refused the assembly's petition that Huntley's term of office be extended.

The consequent delay in the grant of responsible government aroused the assembly's indignation and caused it to resort to obstructionist tactics. The lieutenant governorship of Sir Donald Campbell (1847–1850) was a contentious period, punctuated by votes of no confidence and the stopping of supplies. For his part, Grey disallowed a civil list bill because it included a proviso calling for the establishment of responsible government. Though now aware that self-government had become inevitable, he took the stand that it must be based not upon statutory conditions laid down by the assembly but "on the faith of the Crown." The assembly met his objections by granting the civil list unconditionally, whereupon Grey implemented his implied pledge. On April 24, 1851, the new lieutenant governor, Sir Alexander Bannerman, called on George Coles, the leader of the Reformers in the assembly, to form the first responsible government in Prince Edward Island.

The new government addressed itself to the land question, and in 1853, Premier Coles introduced a policy of purchase and resale to the tenants which, however, affected only a small fraction of the total. The problem was not finally solved until after Confederation. One of the first measures of the Coles adminstration was to pass a Free Education Act in 1852. Two years later, on Oct. 7, 1854, the colony ratified the Reciprocity Treaty with the United States.

Newfoundland. Like its maritime neighbors, Newfoundland prospered during the War of 1812. Its exports of fish and oil fetched high prices, and St. John's, in particular, benefited from the naval prizes brought into port. One effect of the war and of the conflict with Napoleonic France was to enable Newfoundland to rid itself of the repressive imperial legislation that had retarded colonization. Its naval governors, engrossed in their wartime responsibilities, neglected to enforce the antisettlement law; French privateers, by increasing the dangers of the annual Atlantic fishing voyage, induced many transient fishermen to winter in the island; and the war-engendered shortage of imports forced the settlers to grow their own farm produce. The growth of the resident population gave birth to the increasingly profitable seal fishery and shore cod fishery; bank cod fishery, however, remained the jealously guarded preserve of the West of England merchants.

Problems After the War of 1812. When peace came, economic depression followed. Fish prices collapsed. The slump, combined with a number of disastrous fires and the bitterly cold winter of 1817–1818, reduced the colony to the verge of starvation. In an attempt to cope with the desperate situation, Britain ordered that the naval governors from 1818 onward reside in the island throughout the winter months. The first civil governor, Sir Thomas Cochrane, was appointed in 1825, and a supreme court was established a year later. Under Cochrane's wise and vigorous leadership, roads were built, public buildings erected, farming encouraged, and education promoted.

Despite these improvements, there were persistent demands for an elected legislature, especially on the part of the growing merchant class of St. John's. They were convinced that locally elected representatives were needed to protect Newfoundland's economic interests against the political influence of the West Country firms in London. Moreover, they believed that local representation was necessary to counter the danger to the island's fishery implicit in the Treaty of Paris (1815), which confirmed French fishermen in their previous rights on the "French Shore," and in the Convention of 1818 with the United States, which granted American fishermen rights in certain sections off the coasts of Newfoundland and Labrador.

Representative Government. The agitation for representative government was spearheaded by Dr. William Carson and Patrick Morris. Thanks to their tireless and courageous efforts, the Whig government of Lord Grey granted representative government to Newfoundland in 1832. A bicameral legislature, consisting of an elected house of assembly and an appointed legislative council was established.

Unfortunately, friction similar to that in the Maritimes soon developed between the two chambers over the control of revenue. The struggle was embittered by conflicting economic interests and sectarian animosities. After a serious election riot at Carbonear in 1840, Britain instructed Governor Henry Prescott to dissolve the legislature, and in 1841 the constitution was suspended. Two years later, representative government was revived, but in a modified form involving an "amalgamated legislature." This constitutional experiment failed to stop the political wrangling, and in 1848 representative government was restored in its original form.

Paradoxically, these years of political controversy were also years of substantial material progress. The seal fishery was revitalized after 1830 and did much to raise the standard of living in the fishing settlements of Conception Bay and north to Fogo and Twillingate. The success of the seal fishery furnished capital for the expansion of the cod fishery, not only offshore but also off Labrador. In 1834 the Government Savings Bank was established and two years later the Bank of British North America opened a branch in St. John's. A geological survey was undertaken between 1838 and 1840. In 1842 steamship communication was inaugurated between St. John's and Halifax, Nova Scotia.

Responsible Government, 1853. Newfoundland's economic progress generated a new spirit of self-confidence that expressed itself in a demand for responsible government. Representative government had proved to be unworkable. Roman Catholics, in particular, complained that they were being discriminated against under the existing regime. Their numbers were growing fast as a result of large-scale immigration from Ireland, and in 1848 they acquired a new and forceful leader, John T. Mullock, bishop of St. John's. Together with Philip Francis Little, an able lawyer from Prince Edward Island, Bishop Mullock organized the Catholic Liberal party, which campaigned energetically for self-government.

The chief opposition to the movement came from the wealthier merchants, who were well satisfied with their powerful influence in the executive council and wished to preserve the status quo, and from many Protestants who looked askance at the new party's Roman Catholic leadership. Fearful that responsible government would be a divisive factor, the British government at first refused to grant it, but the tide of events flowed strongly in its favor. Responsible government had already been conceded to Canada and the Maritime colonies; the Cape of Good Hope and Australia were about to achieve it. In these circumstances, it was difficult to deny it to Newfoundland. Accordingly, in 1853, the new governor, Sir Charles Darling, appointed Newfoundland's first responsible government with Little as prime minister.

French Shore Question. The new government soon was confronted by a crucial challenge to its constitutional autonomy and its territorial integrity. This arose out of the French shore question and took the form of the Pigeard-Merivale Convention (January 14, 1857), an agreement reached by Britain and France in an attempt to solve the difficulties stemming from conflicting interpretations of the Treaty of Paris. By the terms of the convention the French, among other gains, would have secured an exclusive fishery on the northern extremity and the northeast coast of Newfoundland and also on five strategic locations on its west coast, in return for the grant of a concurrent fishery on a section of the west coast, a right already claimed by Newfoundland.

When the convention was presented to the assembly on Feb. 6, 1857, it provoked a storm of protest. An appeal for support was made to the mainland colonies, and a delegation was dispatched to London. The outcome of Newfoundland's determined resistance was the Labouchere Dispatch, in which Henry Labouchere, the colonial secretary, declared the convention null and void. This document became famous as the Magna Carta of Newfoundland because of its solemn pledge that "the consent of the Community of Newfoundland is regarded by Her Majesty's government as the essential preliminary to any modification of their territorial or maritime rights."

ALLAN M. FRASER
Provincial Archivist, Newfoundland

Bibliography

Brebner, John B., *The Neutral Yankees of Nova Scotia* (Toronto 1937).
Chadwick, St. John, *Newfoundland: Island into Province* (Cambridge, England, 1967).
Clark, Andrew H., *Three Centuries and the Island* (Toronto 1959).
MacKinnon, Frank, *The Government of Prince Edward Island,* Canadian Government Series (Toronto 1951).
McLintock, Alexander H., *The Establishment of Constitutional Government in Newfoundland, 1783–1832* (London 1941).
New Brunswick Government Bureau of Information, *An Historical Guide to New Brunswick* (Fredericton 1948).
Raddall, Thomas H., *Halifax: Warden of the North* (Toronto and London 1950).
Thomas, Llewellyn O., *The Province of New Brunswick* (Ottawa 1930).

LOWER CANADA, 1815–1840

The years 1815–1840 were among the most troubled in Canadian history. It is the political and constitutional conflicts of those years that have attracted the most attention. Historians have described these struggles broadly either as an episode in the winning of ministerial responsibility and political autonomy or as another stage in the battle for the national survival of French Canadians.

However, the agitation was rooted not only in politics but also in economics. In the rural community, discontent was accentuated by the increasing scarcity of land and by the fears aroused in the French Canadian *habitant* by British immigration. Just as serious was the fact that the three dominant classes—the clergy, merchants, and professionals—were engaged in a conflict in which the control of society was at stake. To crown it all, nationalism was winning over certain of the elite and was penetrating the masses. The insurrections of 1837 were the direct consequence of these diverse conditions.

An Economy in Difficulty. For some 15 years the Lower Canadian economy had been in the process of transformation. Traditionally, it was based on two extensive main activities—the fur trade and wheat. As the basis of nourishment, wheat was more and more in demand in external markets. Its cultivation, in spite of backward techniques and a rapid growth in population, had yielded an ever-increasing surplus. Centered on the market of the metropolis, the collecting of furs ensured permanent relations between the Canadian West and the lowlands of the St. Lawrence Valley.

By 1815 this traditional economy was in the process of disintegrating. The fur trade was entering its last phase of decline. In 1821 the annexation of the North West Company by the Hudson's Bay Company put an end to the time-honored relations that had existed between Lower Canada and the West. In the agricultural districts, where 85% of the population was employed, quite radical changes were taking place. Gradually the production of wheat fell off to such an extent that by 1832 Lower Canada had become a heavy importer of wheat from Upper Canada and the United States. Though the *habitant* concentrated on producing potatoes and livestock, he could not resolve his fundamental problem created by the need of a revolution in agricultural techniques. In 1832 the crisis affected not only substitute crops but also the raising of livestock. Thus the Lower Canada farmer was cut off from his contacts with the external market and became more and more isolated, impoverished, and in debt. His discontent made him receptive to the nationalist message.

The decline of the fur trade and the agricultural crisis created unfavorable economic conditions. Fortunately, there occurred during this period an extraordinary expansion of the lumber trade and, to a lesser degree, of shipbuilding. Though these two activities were not sufficient to restore prosperity, they were nevertheless the salvation of the Lower Canadian economy. All classes of the population benefited.

Added to the long decline in agricultural prices, these conditions brought to light the existence of new problems. The agricultural crisis, massive immigration, and increasing American competition, as a consequence of the construction of the Erie Canal, demanded the development of new land. It was also necessary to establish routes connecting the townships of Lower Canada with the urban markets and to stimulate the development of Upper Canada by the canalization of the St. Lawrence River. But the realization of these plans necessitated a redefinition of fiscal policy and the role of the state in the economy. A stable banking system was essential. The elimination of certain institutional obstacles to economic progress—for example, seigneurial rule and French common law—was also imperative.

Demographic Pressures. Since the beginning of the 18th century French Canadian population had been increasing at an astonishing rate. From 1700 to 1840 it at least doubled every 28 years. Until the beginning of the 19th century it grew in a context of liberty. In spite of the almost complete cessation of the granting of seigneuries, the seigneurial territory comprised enormous tracts of unoccupied land. After the turn of the century this context changed. In certain seigneuries the population reached the saturation point, and the overpopulation soon extended to all regions. To complicate the situation, the majority of seigneurs, instead of granting lands on demand, retained the control over good lands and over the timber resources. All this created serious tensions in the rural community. Seigneurs and tenants quarreled over portions of land allocated to pasture. To resolve their difficulties, some *habitants* subdivided their lands into extremely small lots; others emigrated to the towns and to the United States. The average farmer, therefore, was in a serious state of moral and material insecurity.

At this time massive immigration from the British Isles took place. The immigrant was regarded by the rural French Canadian as a competitor in the search for land and employment. He represented a danger both economic and cultural. There was a bitter struggle for control of the waste land outside the seigneuries. This question, which had been given a highly political character, brought two groups, the nationalists and the merchants, into opposition. The nationalists desired the conversion of the cantons (townships) into seigneuries and their allocation to French Canadians only. The merchants saw in the townships an outlet for the surplus population of the seigneuries and for the immigrants. They also considered the township system an instrument for developing

MC CORD MUSEUM, MC GILL UNIVERSITY, MONTREAL

LA RUE NOTRE-DAME, Montreal, a watercolor by R. A. Sproule, about 1829. The column was erected by English and French townsfolk to honor Lord Nelson, the famed British admiral.

agrarian capitalism. This confrontation set one against the other—two ethnic groups, two dominant classes.

Social Tensions. This economic background coupled with demographic pressures was a prime source of social instability. It is certain that the rural communities were most sharply affected, especially in places where forest exploitation was of little economic importance. The average *habitant,* who had not adopted new methods, was always most sensitive to propaganda that represented the English, the government, and the immigrants as the principal authors of his misfortunes. Furthermore, the elite were divided. From the beginning of the century the struggle for leadership was remarkably keen.

Bureaucrats. The bureaucrats, for their part, lived in fear of losing their power and privileges. As a threat to these perquisites, the liberal professions (such as law), which provided the greatest number of candidates for administrative positions, were the most menacing, because of their political conceptions. Moreover, they dominated the legislative assembly. They were in a position to affect the standing of the bureaucrats by their legislative action.

The bureaucrats drew their strength from the support that came to them from business circles, and this business bourgeoisie was predominantly English; French Canadians were active only in small enterprises. In the domain of landed property a better balance existed between the ethnic groups, but on the whole economic power belonged to the English element.

Merchants. Nevertheless, the business bourgeoisie lived in a state of insecurity. Not only did it suffer from economic difficulties, but its program for improvements came up against the opposition of the professionals. The future of the lumber trade, despite its prosperity, remained uncertain. In England, the advocates of free trade were fighting mercantilism and the tariffs that protected colonial lumber and wheat, while in Canada French Canadian professionals were declaring in favor of free trade. They also objected to any reform of traditional institutions.

Politically, the merchant class, for whom political power is an economic instrument, suffered serious setbacks. After the beginning of the 19th century it was downgraded in the assembly by the professionals of French Canadian origin. The business bourgeoisie, reformist in the economic and social fields, was conservative in politics.

Clergy. The Catholic clergy, another dominant group, was obsessed by fear of the French Revolution. With the decline of the ancient nobility, the rise of the middle classes, and the intrusion of liberal ideas, the position of the clergy became less certain. A change of strategy was imperative. Even if the clergy did not have absolute confidence in a government that intervened in education, a strengthening of ties with the latter became a necessity. Although the clerics defended the seigneurial regime and the *coutume de Paris* (the common or unwritten law of Paris), they found more safeguards in the political conservatism of government officials and merchants.

For the clergy, the principal danger came from the liberal professions, which according to the clergy incarnated the spirit of revolutionary France. The members of these professions, many of lower-class origin, had a profound influence on the masses. All this did not prevent the clergy, which was beginning to be affected by nationalism, from supporting on occasion certain political measures advanced by the professionals.

Professional Class. The aspirations of the people were infinitely better understood by the professionals, whose numbers continued to expand as the classical colleges developed. Economically, the professions were in a precarious position, and officialdom interested them keenly. Their growth surpassed that of the population in a context of economic difficulty. Still little appreciated for their professional activity, and little esteemed socially, they nonetheless aspired to social leadership. They saw in political power the key to social control.

Nationalism served as a link between the professions and the less favored elements of the masses. Instead of promoting a revolution of a liberal and bourgeois type, the professions, espousing the reactionary tendencies of the rural community, took up the defense of the French Canadian nation and its causes. It must be said that the professionals were the first to become aware of the economic inferiority of French Canadians and to consider it a deliberate injustice. Doubtless, anticlericalism and unbelief were on the increase in this group, but most of them looked on the church as a national institution and a bulwark against the English. Although the profes-

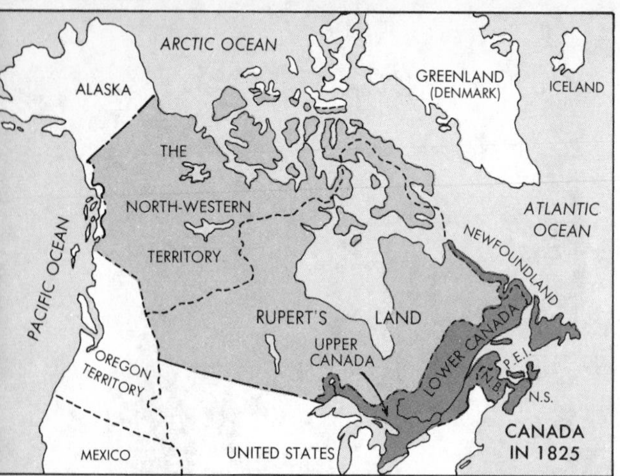

sionals were reactionaries in the economic and social fields, they stood in politics under the reformist, liberal and, after 1830, democratic colors.

Political Conflicts. In and behind the political parties there were social groups with their own ideals, interests, and ambitions, who had grown restive. Between the Canadian party (Patriot party after 1826) and the bureaucratic party the cleavage was doubtless ethnic in the first place, but also economic and social. Hence, the bitterness of the conflicts. In 1815 the struggle began, and strategies were outlined. The Canadian party dominated the legislative assembly for a long time. Since the time of Pierre Stanislas Bédard, leader of the Canadian party until 1810, the theory of ministerial responsibility as a basis for the demands of the party had been proclaimed. This reform, besides giving the professionals power, aimed at providing them with the means of realizing their nationalist, agrarian, and feudal dream.

With the advent of Louis Joseph Papineau as party chief, in 1815, their strategy was modified. While continuing to speak of responsibility, the leaders of the party demanded above all control by the assembly of public funds. Thus they attempted to establish their hold on economic policy and to give themselves an effective instrument with which to blackmail the administration. After 1830, when Papineau became convinced that London was in connivance with the British of Lower Canada to keep French Canadians in a state of inferiority, he became republican and modeled his program of reform on the American Constitution. Many of his party talked of revolution and independence.

This growing intransigence was also found in the opposing group. The merchant party had lost ground with the electorate, and French Canadians who collaborated with it were called traitors. The economic interests of the merchants demanded total attachment to the old colonial system and to the principles of political equilibrium basic to the constitution of 1791. That is why this party sought dominance in the executive and legislative councils, whose function was to counter-balance an assembly crowded with nationalist elements.

Political stability doubtless made it possible to check nationalist and democratic tendencies; but in business circles it did not provide the political means of realizing their economic objectives. Frustrated by the resistance of the assembly, these groups sought more radical solutions in moments of crisis. In 1810 and 1822 they appealed directly to London to unite the Canadas and to establish a property qualification for the franchise, so that the extremists would be eliminated from the political arena. All this evidently aroused the fears and resistance of the Patriot party.

Faced with a rapidly deteriorating political situation, the governors tended to waver between one party and the other, and this complicated the problems. Although the British government remained neutral, it showed until 1831 most interest in the majority of the Assembly. From then on, this attitude changed. The resolutions of Lord John Russell in March 1837 implied that London had decided to check the patriot movement. The conflicts had taken such a turn that a revolution was foreseeable.

Rebellion of 1837–1838. Between May 1837 and November 1838 two insurrections broke out in Lower Canada. These two uprisings, limited to the region of Montreal, failed lamentably, as did a plot fomented in Quebec City in 1838. Despite their unquestionable efficacy, the interdicts issued by the clergy against the insurrectionists do not suffice to explain the failure. The causes of the setbacks may be found principally in the organization of the patriot movement. It was essentially a problem of leadership. The adulated head of the movement, Papineau, was a rousing orator but a pitiable man of action, always undecided and fearful. He fled on the eve of the battle at St. Denis (Nov. 23, 1837). With few exceptions the same weakness was found in most of the principal leaders of the insurrections. Events took place as though the leaders believed that the badly led peasants could do the whole job by themselves. The Quebec-Montreal rivalry also played a role in these somewhat inglorious performances.

Between the two insurrections occurred the mission of Lord Durham, who inquired into Lower Canadian problems. Having left before the second uprising, he submitted to London a report recommending assimilation of the French Canadians by the union of the Canadas and the recognition of the principle of ministerial responsibility. The first suggestion was accepted in 1840, and the second was rejected.

FERNAND OUELLET, *Carleton University*

Further Reading: Bruchési, Jean, *Histoire du Canada* (Montreal 1954); Wade, Mason, *The French Canadians, 1760–1945* (Toronto 1955).

UPPER CANADA, 1815–1840

Although Upper Canada recovered from physical damage suffered during American invasions of the province in the War of 1812, the war left its mark on the minds and emotions of the people and strongly influenced government policy in later years. Not only did the three years of fighting lead Upper Canadians to feel a greater sense of separation from their American neighbors in the years immediately after 1815, but in later years the war was to be remembered as a great epic of valiant defense against overwhelming odds and as a main focus in the development of Canadian national feeling.

Conservatism After War of 1812. The war also influenced government leaders to take steps to strengthen the British character of the colony. Authorities in England provided assistance to emigrants to encourage them to go to Upper Canada and other British colonies rather than to the United States. Moreover, the colonial secretary instructed the lieutenant governor to discourage any further influx of American settlers

FIRST WELLAND CANAL, linking Lakes Erie and Ontario, opens on Nov. 27, 1829. The event is pictured by artist J. D. Kelly.

PUBLIC ARCHIVES OF CANADA

into Upper Canada. Within the province, government leaders strove both to eradicate American influences and to shape educational, religious, and other policies along British lines. These leaders, who were later (about 1830) to be given the condemnatory epithet of the "Family Compact," were highly critical of the rising tide of political democracy, strong believers in an established church, and ardently attached to the British connection. The most prominent figures in this group of leaders were John Strachan, a Church of England clergyman, later (1839) first Anglican bishop of Upper Canada, and John Beverley Robinson, attorney general, later (1829) chief justice of the province.

For some years there was no effectively organized opposition to the conservative leaders of Upper Canada. There was some excitement in 1817–1819 when Robert Gourlay, who had recently come from England, mounted a campaign of criticism against the provincial government and sought to assemble a popular convention to protest against "misrule." But after his arrest and banishment, the province remained quiet. There was another period of uncertainty in the early 1820's, when a bill was introduced in the British House of Commons to unite Upper and Lower Canada. Strachan and Robinson were much relieved when this project came to nothing; they were ready to envisage a union of all the British North American colonies, but not a dual union with the more numerous French Canadians. Apart from these two episodes the history of Upper Canada in the decade after 1815 is similar to that of many another pioneer community: the story of clearing the forest, improving land, building roads and other internal improvements, erecting schools, churches, sawmills, and gristmills.

Sources of Tension—*Alien Question*. Nevertheless, as the 1820's wore on, the political life of Upper Canada was increasingly marked by bitter controversy, as opposition was organized against the conservative leadership. This opposition was fed from several sources.

First, the provincial executive antagonized the numerous settlers of American origin who had come into the colony in the previous quarter century. These people had taken up land, voted and held office, and otherwise acted as equal members of the community. A few years after the War of 1812, however, the colonial secretary ruled that American-born settlers did not have the rights of British subjects in Upper Canada until they were naturalized, a lengthy and rather antiquated procedure. The question was given a still sharper turn in 1821 when the Massachusetts-born Barnabas Bidwell was expelled from the assembly and his son, Marshall Spring Bidwell, was rejected as a candidate for election on the ground that he was an alien.

Throughout most of the 1820's the "alien question" was the leading political issue in the province. Public opinion was so strongly in favor of granting American-born settlers who had lived in Upper Canada for seven years or longer the rights of British subjects without any naturalization proceedings that both the colonial office and the provincial executive had to give way. Marshall Spring Bidwell was subsequently elected to the assembly, where he served twice as speaker and as leader of the emerging Reform party.

***Land Reserves*.** Second, there were controversies relating to land policy, and especially to the crown and clergy reserves. Settlements were widely dispersed, and road communications between them were poor. Many critics felt that progress was retarded by the existence of the reserves, and this criticism continued even after an active program for selling and leasing the reserves was instituted in the late 1820's.

The crown reserves were conveyed to the Canada Company, which in turn was to make various payments, including an annual grant to defray the costs of civil government. But the Canada Company was unpopular for many reasons, including the fact that its payments reduced the provincial executive's financial dependence upon the assembly. As for the clergy reserves, there was a growing feeling that the proceeds from their sale should be used for the support of education and not for the support of one or more religious denominations.

***Church and Education*.** Third, the sharpest disputes were, in fact, in the realm of religion and education. Conservative leaders frequently deplored the fact that some of the largest Protestant denominations had close organizational ties with their sister churches in the United States, ties that were thought to bring harmful American or "republican" influences into Upper Canada. In particular, John Strachan leveled sharp criticism against the largest denomination, the Methodists, for their American associations, and he in turn was stingingly answered by Egerton Ryerson, a rising young clergyman, soon to be editor of the important Methodist newspaper, the *Christian Guardian*.

Strachan's efforts to secure the entire proceeds of the clergy reserves for the Church of England heightened sectarian feeling, as did his success, in 1827, in securing a charter for a provincial university. The latter was to be endowed with provincial land, but only Anglicans would be eligible to be members of its governing body or to be trained in its divinity school.

Economic Controversy. Fourth in this cluster of controversies were those associated with economic development. Aroused by the building of the Erie Canal across New York state (1817–1825), merchants and others in Upper Canada strove to improve the St. Lawrence-Great Lakes route. Like most such large works in Canadian (and U. S.) history, canal building required support from government. The imperial government confined its role to a defense project, the Rideau Canal, the costliest military work ever undertaken by the British government in North America. This canal linked the Ottawa River and the eastern end of Lake Ontario, thus joining the latter with Montreal by a route that was remote from the American border. It was left to local enterprise to overcome the greatest obstacle to Great Lakes navigation—Niagara Falls—and in the early 1820's, William Hamilton Merritt undertook the construction of the Welland Canal. Within a few years, however, this canal was too expensive for private enterprise to finance, and provincial loans were necessary to help complete the work. The "Family Compact" favored these loans, but its opponents were often critical.

The chartering of the Bank of Upper Canada (1821) led to similar criticism, for the bank, receiving government support, enjoyed a virtual monopoly for several years. By the end of the 1820's, opponents of the "Family Compact" asserted that the government of the province was not only exclusive and oligarchic in character but also was managed for the pecuniary advantage of a small and unrepresentative clique.

Struggle for Reform. In 1828 these opponents, calling themselves Reformers, secured a majority in the assembly after a clear-cut electoral victory. One of their most vocal members was William Lyon Mackenzie, a Scottish-born newspaper editor, who had been attacking the provincial "oligarchy" for several years in his *Colonial Advocate*. As he became more attracted by the example of Jacksonian democracy in the neighboring American republic, Mackenzie placed strong emphasis on the need to extend the elective principle, in particular to make the legislative council elective.

Two more moderate Reformers were W. W. Baldwin and Robert Baldwin, who argued for "responsible government"—that is, for an executive council composed of men who had the confidence of a majority of the legislative assembly. As it was, in the 1820's and 1830's, the "Family Compact" kept control of the executive, even when the Reformers had a majority in the assembly.

Nevertheless, Conservative politicians also had considerable support among the voters, and were able to defeat the Reformers in the election of 1830. As a member of the Reform minority in the assembly, Mackenzie now redoubled his vitriolic campaign against "Tory rule," with the consequence that on several occasions he was expelled from the assembly, only to be triumphantly reelected each time in his own electoral district. In 1832 he took the Reform case to England, and for a time it seemed that the colonial office might act favorably on his petitions. In the end it did not, and Mackenzie returned to Upper Canada in an increasingly radical frame of mind.

In 1834, when the Reformers were again victorious at the polls, Mackenzie became chairman of an assembly committee to investigate the workings of the provincial government and in the following year produced the violently partisan "Seventh Report on Grievances." Much of the material in it was so unfair and inaccurate that moderate Reformers refused to endorse it. The document, however, did convince the colonial office that changes were necessary in Upper Canada, and at the end of 1835 a new lieutenant governor, Sir Francis Bond Head, was selected as an agent of conciliation and reform.

Head proved to be a poor choice. Although he began by appointing some Reformers to the Executive Council, it was soon clear that he did not intend to follow the Council's advice in governing the province. A stormy quarrel between the lieutenant governor and the assembly followed, culminating in 1836 in a new election. In the campaign, Head appeared openly as the partisan leader of the Conservative side, denouncing Reformers of all stripes as republicans and asserting that Upper Canada might cease to enjoy the advantages of British protection and support if the latter should win. The large numbers of recent British immigrants, the role of the Orange Order (a militantly Protestant society, introduced from the British Isles a few years earlier), and memories of the War of 1812 were some of the factors that made Head's appeal a potent one. The Reformers were routed in the 1836 election.

Rebellion. The result so discouraged moderate Reformers that many of them retired from politics. But Mackenzie, who had lost his seat, was consumed with a furious determination to hit back at the "oligarchy," or Family Compact. Believing that the election had been unfairly rigged against the Reformers, thus closing peaceful avenues to reform, and turning his back on the British connection as a buttress of the oligarchy, Mackenzie became increasingly convinced that an armed uprising to establish an independent, democratic state, probably in close association with the neighboring American Union, was both feasible and essential. The business panic of 1837, rebellion in Lower Canada, and Head's dispatch of most of the troops there provided further incentive.

Early in December 1837, Mackenzie and a few hundred followers, poorly armed and trained, set out to capture the provincial capital, Toronto, from the north. The result was a miserable fiasco. Within a day the rebel forces were scattered, and Mackenzie was fortunate to escape across the American border. His rash action threw the Reform cause into disarray and for some months Conservatism, or Toryism, was more solidly entrenched than ever.

Durham's Report. Nevertheless, political change could not long be postponed, and after a few months moderate Reformers began to regroup their forces. They were greatly helped by the British government's decision in 1838 to send out Lord Durham as governor general and as high commissioner to recommend changes in the government of Upper and Lower Canada. His famous *Report on the Affairs of British North America*, published early in 1839, gave powerful support to the doctrine of responsible government, long advocated by Robert Baldwin and other moderate Reformers. At first, the British government was not ready to accept this doctrine, arguing that a governor could not both obey his instructions from England and act on the advice of local ministers. But during the regime of Poulett Thomson (Lord Sydenham), 1839–1841, Tory Family Compact rule came to an end, men of moderate and practitical outlook were drawn into the government, and the air cleared for an era of achievement on many fronts under the Union that came into effect in 1841.

GERALD M. CRAIG, *University of Toronto*

Further Reading: Craig, Gerald Marquis, *Upper Canada: The Formative Years, 1784–1841* (New York and Toronto 1963); Creighton, Donald Grant, *The Empire of the St. Lawrence* (Toronto 1956); Dunham, Aileen, *Political Unrest in Upper Canada 1815–1836* (Toronto 1963); Kilbourn, William, *The Firebrand: William Lyon Mackenzie and the Rebellion in Upper Canada* (London 1956).

UNITED CANADA, 1841–1857

In the Province of Canada, proclaimed in February 1841, cultural and social differences inevitably persisted between English-speaking, largely Protestant Upper Canada (renamed Canada West) and predominantly French and Catholic Lower Canada (renamed Canada East). But since Canada East and Canada West had been given equal representation in the united legislature, they also formed two distinct sections in politics. Equal representation had been prescribed in the Union Act of 1840, of course, to put the French Canadian element in more populous Canada East decisively in the minority, looking to its eventual assimilation. Yet the real result was to embed sectional division in the political system and to embitter the French against a union meant to swamp them.

Responsible Government. Lord Sydenham, first governor-general of a union he had done much to effect, promoted economic progress and efficient administration—but not responsible government, which the imperial authorities still held inadmissible in a colony. Instead he used his energy and political skill to satisfy United Canada with everything short of it. He constructed a coalition ministry able to work in harmony with the majority in the assembly, elected in the spring of 1841. He announced an imperial loan of £1.5 million for the construction of canals on the St. Lawrence River. And under his shrewd influence a cooperative assembly passed measures establishing municipal institutions, a rudimentary public educational system for both Canadas, and more besides.

Yet when Sydenham died in September 1841, he had only postponed demands for responsible government. His coalition of Conservatives and moderate Reformers was threatened on the right by disgruntled Tories and on the left by leading Reformers like Robert Baldwin and Louis Lafontaine seeking a united Reform front. Above all, he had not won over the French Canadians. His successor, Sir Charles Bagot, a veteran diplomat, strove to strengthen the government, fearing that his ministers might be defeated when Parliament met again. At length, in September 1842, Bagot offered places in the ministry to Lafontaine, to his French colleagues and—on Lafontaine's insistence—to Baldwin. This assured him of assembly support. Yet, far from being assimilated, French Canadians now had party leaders in the government itself.

It was not yet responsible government. While Reform party chiefs had entered the ministry, it still contained members of the former administration, all under Bagot's direction. The latter died in the spring of 1843. Sir Charles Metcalfe, the distinguished civil servant who replaced him, was determined to defend the governor's authority, indeed was instructed to do so. Quarrels arose with his Reform ministers, who resigned late in 1843. Metcalfe gradually rebuilt a government headed by William Draper, a capable Conservative prominent under Sydenham, and in the fall elections of 1844 took his case before the people. After a hot campaign and fervent appeals to loyalty, Metcalfe's adherents swept Canada West, where Baldwin's Reformers had evidently pressed too far ahead of public opinion. But as Lafontaine's Liberals won Canada East, the Draper ministry had only a bare majority in Parliament.

A period almost of marking time ensued. Metcalfe, courageously devoted but to little effect, returned to England in 1845, nearly blind, to die of cancer. Meanwhile, the Draper ministry was operating practically as a responsible cabinet, managing its own affairs during Metcalfe's illness. The succeeding governor, Lord Cathcart, who was the commander of the forces, was preoccupied with military affairs in the Anglo-American crisis over the Oregon territory, which was settled by the Oregon Treaty in 1846. Meanwhile, too, Canada prospered, as the canals were built, staple exports of timber and wheat flourished in a protected British market, and the spread of settlement, road construction, and manufacturing marked the passing of frontier times.

In Britain, the repeal of the protectionist Corn Laws in 1846 brought to office a Liberal government determined to institute full free trade. But if imperial controls were to be lifted from the colonies' trade, there was little reason to control their internal political affairs either. A new governor-general of Canada, the resourceful, judicious Lord Elgin, was instructed to take as his ministers whatever party leaders had "command of the confidence of the legislature."

Arriving in Canada early in 1847, Elgin first gave cordial support to the existing Tory-Conservative ministers who held their slight parliamentary majority. But in elections at the close of the year, the Reformers carried both East and West, and when Parliament met, they defeated the government. Elgin promptly called on Lafontaine and Baldwin as the majority leaders to form a new administration. In March 1848, a wholly Reform party cabinet took office. Clearly, this was the beginning of responsible government.

Depression and Other Problems. The Lafontaine-Baldwin ministry faced serious problems: above all, a spreading world depression that had begun to cripple Canadian trade. The newly completed canal system remained half used. Bankruptcies mounted in Montreal. And Britain's adoption of free trade confronted St. Lawrence Valley merchants with ruin. A crisis developed in 1849, when the government put before Parliament major reform legislation, including the Rebellion Losses Bill.

This bill was designed to compensate any who suffered damages in the Lower Canadian Rebellion of 1837. French Canadians insisted on it as a salve for old sufferings; but Tories deemed it a veritable payment for treason. The latter, led by fiery Sir Allan MacNab, fought it strenuously in Parliament, and when the bill passed they looked to the governor to refuse it. Elgin, however, gave it assent. At once Tory political anger and commercial bitterness burst in Montreal, the capital. Elgin's carriage was attacked, while a violent mob set fire to the Parliament building. Rage soon ebbed, and responsible government was confirmed anew.

Later in 1849, gloom over continuing depression and the loss of protected British markets inspired a mounting agitation for annexation to the United States, as Canada's only economic hope. Annexation notably attracted Montreal Tories, who were sure that Britain had abandoned them both politically and commercially. Yet emerging radical elements—especially a young French Canadian group of democratic nationalists, to be termed *Rouges* – also adopted the cause, in a belief in American republican liberty. An eloquent Annexation Manifesto appeared in Montreal in October 1849. The antiannexation reaction proved far stronger. French Canadians were generally satisfied with Lafontaine's party and achievements; Upper Canadians were vigorously pro-British and anti-American; western Tory-Conservatives firmly rejected annexation.

New Growth. In any case, world trade revived in 1850, and Canada entered a new period of growth. Its staples of wheat and square timber found substantial British markets. An expanding market for sawn lumber emerged in the United States; agricultural exports also went increasingly across the border. Then in 1854 the Reciprocity Treaty was secured with the United States, providing reciprocal free trade in natural products. It contributed markedly to the growing north-south traffic, enhancing a Canadian prosperity that was fast becoming a boom.

Railway building in the 1850's particularly encouraged the boom. With canals completed and capital available in good times, railway construction barely begun in Canada in the 1840's now went rapidly ahead. Tracks linked Montreal and the Atlantic at Portland, Me.; Toronto and Lake Huron; Hamilton and the Detroit River. The greatest enterprise was the through east-west line across the province, the Grand Trunk, chartered in 1852 and opened between Montreal and Toronto in 1856. Railways—above all the Grand Trunk – brought waste, heavy public debt, and close, often dubious entanglements between politics and promotion. Yet before the railway boom collapsed in 1857, it had united Canada, stimulated urban and industrial growth, and made possible a circulation of people, goods, and newspapers unknown in the old days of inland isolation and winter freeze-up.

While Canada advanced, however, new political problems appeared. In 1850 there arose in Canada West the radical Clear Grit movement, somewhat akin to the eastern *Rouges* in its demand for American-style democracy, but also expressing western farmers' desires for cheap, simple government. "Grittism" made such headway in Upper Canadian Reform ranks that Baldwin, a believer in British parliamentary institutions, retired affronted in mid-1851, and Lafontaine soon followed. Their longtime associates Francis Hincks and Augustin Morin took over as copremiers in the double-headed governments made necessary by the sectional division of the union. Hincks brought two Clear Grit leaders into the cabinet, deftly muting their thunder; and the Hincks-Morin Liberal ministry successfully carried the elections of late 1851.

Sectionalism. But forces more disturbing than Grit or *Rouge* radicalism were also arising. In Canada West, Protestant voluntarism, which sought the complete separation of church and state, was renewing attacks on the clergy reserves. In French Canada, Catholic conservatism was advancing, seeking to strengthen ties of church and state, and sympathetic to demands of the Catholic minority in Canada West for state-aided Catholic separate schools. A Canada West School Bill in 1850 had enlarged separate school rights. Yet this invited a growing conflict between western voluntarists, concerned to defend the public school system, and eastern Catholics concerned to protect religious rights. Voluntarism spread among Grits and western Reformers, voiced particularly by the editor of the powerful Toronto *Globe,* George Brown, who entered Parliament in 1851.

In the session of 1852–1853, sectarian issues were at the fore, as Brown and his allies fought a new separate school measure and attacked "state church" power. French Canadian Liberals grew more defensive and conservative to guard the interests of Catholicism. The sharpest kind of sectional conflict, involving culture and religion, was disrupting union politics, as Catholic East confronted Protestant West. Consequently, party structure was breaking down. The ruling Reform party was now a tangle of Grit radicals, Brownite voluntarists, and Hincksite moderate Liberals, as well as a fringe of *Rouges* and Morin's increasingly conservative followers, who were to become known as *Bleus.*

Emerging Parties. Meanwhile, Tory-Conservatives had been recovering from their woes of 1849. Though the old Tory MacNab nominally led the party, younger men like astute John A. Macdonald were increasingly rendering it "progressive conservative," as Macdonald put it. The way was open for party reorganization. In 1854, after new elections and the defeat of the crumbling Hincks-Morin ministry, a MacNab-Morin coalition, backed by Tory-Conservatives, Hincksite moderates, and Morin's *Bleus,* took office in September. This Liberal-Conservative coalition proved capable of lasting; indeed, it was to become the national Conservative party of the future. Committed to railway development (especially the Grand Trunk), it also showed readiness to carry strongly sought reforms, such as the abolition of clergy reserves and Lower Canadian seigneurial tenure in 1854. Moreover, it renewed an Anglo-French political alliance vital to any major Canadian party, which was notably expressed in the partnership of John A. Macdonald and George Etienne Cartier, the two ablest party spokesmen, who became copremiers in 1857.

But in opposition, a new Liberal party was emerging, also to endure; its leaders were A. A. Dorion for the *Rouges* and George Brown for the Upper Canadians. Brown massed an increasingly powerful western force, linking Toronto urban leadership with Grit rural strength. He fought still another separate school bill, carried by French Canadian votes in 1855. He urged representation by population (for Canada West had passed Canada East in population after 1850) to gain more western seats and end "French Catholic domination." In 1857, at a Reform convention in Toronto, Brown and the Grit Liberals demanded the acquisition of the vast Northwest beyond the Great Lakes, as well.

The Situation in 1857. In 1857, then, the Canadian union was far from calm, with sectional and sectarian turmoil and angry talk of "rep by pop" (representation by population) or Grand Trunk corruption. Yet broader issues were already emerging, such as the question of the Northwest. Moreover, this vexed union had already witnessed striking accomplishments: not only in economic development or the attainment of responsible government, but also in the growth of distinctive Canadian institutions. These included political parties, public and separate school systems, an organized civil service, and municipal governments — no slight record for United Canada.

J. M. S. CARELESS, *University of Toronto*

Further Reading: Careless, J. M. S., *Brown of the "Globe": The Voice of Upper Canada* (Toronto 1959); id., *The Union of the Canadas, 1841–1857* (Toronto 1967); Creighton, Donald G., *John A. Macdonald: The Young Politician* (Toronto 1952); Tucker, G. N., *The Canadian Commercial Revolution, 1845–1851*, reprint (Toronto 1964).

47. The Canadian Confederation, 1857–1914

Confederation (1867), the watershed of Canada's history, was preceded by a decade of ferment involving many complicated issues. It was succeeded by many more years of stress and strain — and accomplishment.

Causes. The causes of Canadian Confederation were to be found in the province of Canada itself, in the Atlantic provinces, in British imperial policy, and in events in the United States.

In the province of Canada, Confederation offered a solution to two pressing needs: to expand as good land was running out; to resolve the conflict between English and French in the legislative wedlock of the Canadian Union of 1840.

Expansion pressures were the least recognized but perhaps the most important cause of Confederation. To expand on British soil, it was necessary to acquire the lands of the Hudson's Bay Company to the far northwest. To develop those lands it was necessary to build a railway to them. To have such a railway pay it was necessary to reach the Pacific Ocean and its trade. To expand at all, therefore, Canada had to become a transcontinental dominion. Apart from satisfying the need for more land, expansion was also likely to relieve internal pressures between English and French.

Having become a majority, English Canadians of Canada West were demanding more and more representation by population. Representation, they said, should be based on population and not, as hitherto, on the equal representation of the two sections of the Union. But the French of Canada East, having been underrepresented from 1841 to 1851, insisted on maintaining the Union as it was. Representation by population in the Union would make them a minority subject in all matters to an English majority. If the Northwest were added to the Union, their position as a minority would only be made worse, as the Northwest would be largely settled from English Canada West.

Such would be the fact unless the Union were merged in a larger union that would give local self-government to Canada East, and to the Northwest. It was the genius of George Etienne Cartier that he saw this in 1858. He began the slow task of persuading his followers, the Bleus, the larger political party in Canada East, to see it too.

In the Atlantic provinces of Newfoundland, Prince Edward Island, Nova Scotia, and New Brunswick there was need for change, also, although not necessarily for expansion. Newfoundland's population, spreading along the coast, had reached the French shore. Troubles had resulted which the imperial government had failed to remove. Perhaps a united British North America might. Prince Edward Island wished to buy out its absentee landlords, but the imperial government had objections to every scheme to do so. Again a British North American Union might help. Nova Scotia, prosperous, proud, and content with its shipping within the empire, needed credit to build railways and had some men at least who saw the need for a continental hinterland. New Brunswick, too, was hungry for railways, which would give its merchants continental as well as maritime trade. From these causes chiefly Confederation was to spring.

Obstacles. The stumbling block was defense. The colonial governments insisted that defense was an imperial responsibility, since the only war would be one with the United States. The British government was increasingly aware, nevertheless, of the danger of a war with the United States in defense of the colonies.

Relations with the United States were not, indeed, reassuring. Border disputes, over the Oregon Territory in the 1840's and over San Juan Island in 1859, revealed an obvious danger. And there were those who saw that the colonies had an affinity with the northern states in that they both advocated the policy of free soil. Their security rested on the fact that the Southern states were flatly opposed to the annexation of free soil territories. But what if the growing tension between North and South in the United States should result in the breakdown of the American Union? That breakdown, when it came, would quicken the pressures for Confederation.

The year 1857 was a watershed between the great period of political reform under the Union government in Canada and the achievement of responsible government in all the Atlantic provinces. Political issues had dwindled; practical matters, especially railway building, had taken over, and provincial politics without issues were petty to the depths of boredom. In the province of Canada the fact was underlined and intensified by a steady drift to sectional politics.

The result was that Canada was to be governed by a majority from one section and a minority from the other, each of the opposite races. Whichever way, it was racial domination of one section by the other. In these circumstances accidents could happen, and one did — in the fall of the Macdonald-Cartier ministry on a private member's motion on the seat-of-government question in 1858. After a vain attempt by the Liberals and Rouges (French Canadian liberals) to take over power, an escape from the growing sectional deadlock was sought by making Alexander Galt's proposal for a federal union of British North America a policy of the Cartier-Macdonald ministry.

The commitment of the Canadian government to Confederation was met, however, by the scornful skepticism of the Opposition and the anger of the colonial secretary, Edward Bulwer-Lytton, who had not been consulted. The skepticism was not without warrant, as it took some time for the policy of the leaders to be accepted by the followers. As imperial policy became one of insisting that union of the Maritime Provinces must precede a wider union, but only on colonial initiative, the policy of Confederation dragged on in repeated conferences in London and became submerged in other events.

The chief of these events was the outbreak of the Civil War in the United States, followed by the Trent Affair in late 1861. (See CIVIL WAR, AMERICAN.) The immediate result of the threat of an Anglo-American war was a return to the old order of a Britain ready to defend the colonies

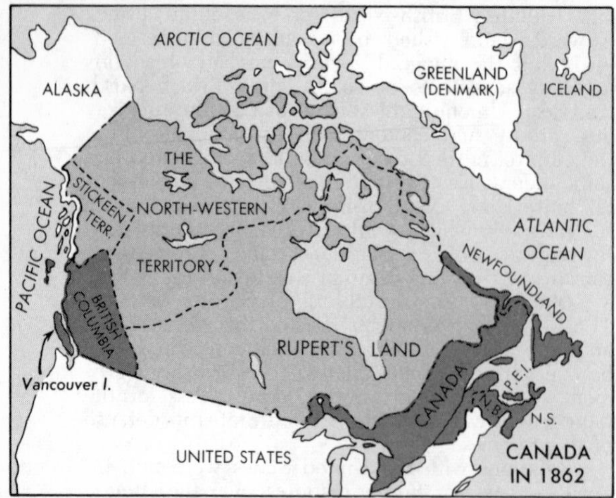

The geographic outlines of modern Canada existed by 1862 *(above)*. The boundary with the United States was fixed in 1846. The political subdivisions had changed. The Province of Canada was created in 1840 by joining Upper and Lower Canada. British Columbia was a British colony by 1858. The Dominion of Canada was formed in 1867 by uniting Canada, New Brunswick, and Nova Scotia *(below)*. Canada was divided into Ontario and Quebec. By 1912, there were 9 provinces *(bottom)*. Newfoundland joined the Confederation in 1949.

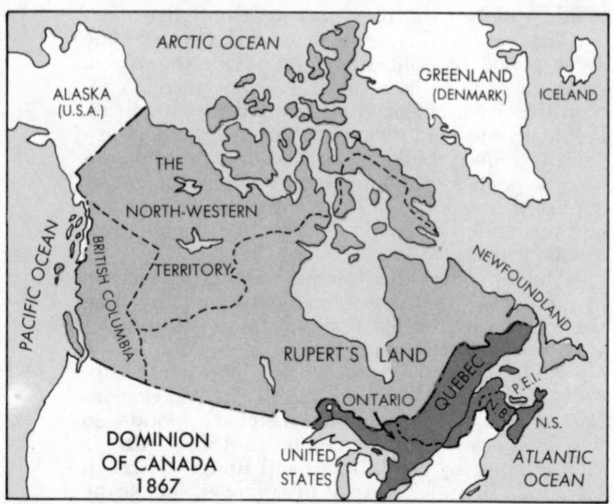

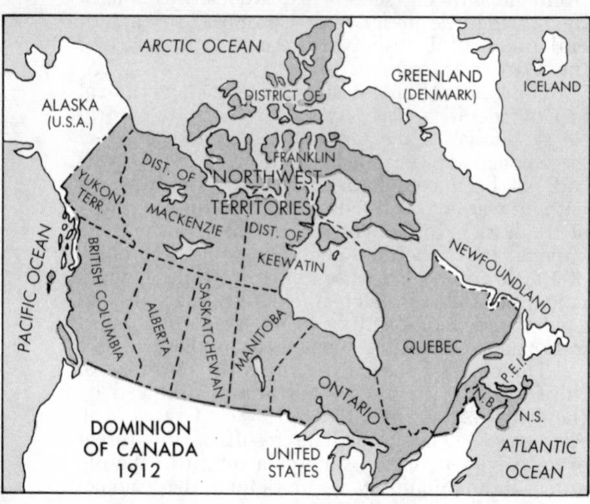

against American attack. Emphasis passed from long-range political plans to hurried military measures, and on new proposals for the Intercolonial Railway. Thus an event that eventually underlined the need for Confederation stopped consideration of it for three years. The fact was stressed by the Cartier-Macdonald government's defeat in 1862 on its militia bill, a bill precipitated by the Trent Affair.

The result was a return to the sterile politics of the last years of the Union. Government by double majority (a majority in each section of the province) was attempted, and proved impossible. The two ministries of John Sandfield Macdonald (joint premier of United Canada, 1862–1864) were lukewarm on matters of defense, thinking American attack unlikely. Committed to economy, they were reluctant to cooperate in building the Intercolonial railway.

Coalition Achieved. Two men were the principals in overcoming the inertia of John S. Macdonald. One was the governor-general, Lord Monck, who was convinced of the need of an improved militia and a union of British North America. He was prepared to use all his power and influence to obtain them. The second was George Brown, editor of a powerful Toronto newspaper, the *Globe*, and one-time leader of the Liberals. Between 1861 and 1864, Brown became convinced of the need for a change in the Union. He was prepared to accept a wider union as one way to end the moribund province of Canada. The outcome of their efforts, after the fall of the J. S. Macdonald-Dorion and the Taché-John A. Macdonald ministries was a coalition ministry of Cartier's Bleus, Brown's Liberals, and John A. Macdonald's Conservatives.

The purpose of the new government was to bring about the union of all British North America. If it failed to do that, it was to make the union of the Canadas a federal one. A scheme of legislative union with federal features, drafted in the summer of 1864, and based on Galt's project of 1858, became the basis of Confederation.

Confederation Realized. Meantime, politicians in the Maritime Province had been prodded by the colonial office into a conference at Charlottetown, Prince Edward Island, to discuss a legislative union of the Maritimes. The Canadian government asked to attend and persuaded the Maritimers to attempt a general and federal union at a conference in Quebec.

There, in October 1864, delegates of the five colonial governments worked out a scheme of union. The chief issue was how to protect minorities, the small provinces, and the French against a powerful central government. The solutions proposed were equality for the two Canadas and the Maritimes in the upper house, explicit guarantees for the r rench language in Quebec and the federal Parliament and courts, and making civil law a provincial matter. But the central government was to be given all the great powers of government; the provinces were to be subordinate. The union was to be essentially a legislative union, although a quasi-federal one. It was to be modeled not on the American system, then in discredit, but on the British Empire as it was after 1849.

The scheme was adopted unanimously by the delegations, and the hope was to have it made law by the Imperial Parliament in 1865. The need for it was emphasized by the raid from Canadian soil against St. Albans, Vt., by agents of the American Confederacy in October 1864, which revived the fear of worse Anglo-American relations.

PUBLIC ARCHIVES OF CANADA

QUEBEC CONFERENCE (October 1864) on the union of the provinces drew delegates from Canada, Nova Scotia, New Brunswick, Prince Edward Island, and Newfoundland. Their decisions provided a base for Confederation in 1867.

Serious delays then arose. New Brunswick repudiated the government of S. L. Tilley that had accepted the Quebec scheme. Canada had to work out a guarantee for Protestant schools in Quebec. The serious Fenian Raids of 1866 kept Canadian ministers at home all the summer of 1866. But pressure from the imperial government changed the electoral decision in New Brunswick and avoided obstruction in Nova Scotia. Newfoundland and Prince Edward Island withdrew from the project, but in December 1866 the Westminster Conference approved the Quebec scheme as it was, except for changes to avoid deadlock in the Senate and to make general the power of the central government to protect the school rights of religious minorities. In May the British North America Act, the constitution of the Dominion of Canada, became law, and was proclaimed on July 1, 1867.

Expansion. The new Dominion of Canada at once set itself to complete the territorial expansion provided for in the act. A repeal agitation in Nova Scotia had to be quieted by the grant of better terms in 1869. By then, however, terms had been worked out for the transfer to the Dominion of all the vast Hudson's Bay Company territory from Labrador to the Rocky Mountains. Resistance to the transfer, without terms agreed to by the inhabitants, was made by the *métis* of Red River during the uprising of 1869–1870 under Louis Riel. This was overcome by concessions in the Manitoba Act of 1870 by which that province was created, notably denominational schools and the official use of French as well as English. But the territories and all public lands were held "for the purposes of the Dominion." These purposes were settlement and the building of a railway to the Pacific.

The year 1871 saw three events, two of which confirmed the work of Confederation and one which was ominous for the future. The last was the New Brunswick School Act, which revealed much weakness in the power of the Dominion to intervene in the affairs of a province. The *parti national* of Quebec, inspired by the Red River troubles, was to feed on this. The other events were union with British Columbia, which made feasible the building of the Pacific railway, and the Treaty of Washington (1871), which ended the strained relations with the United States.

The triumph of Confederation then encountered a grave check, partly caused by the difficulties of deciding the eastern terminus of the railway and of preventing American control. The result of this and of some opposition to the Treaty of Washington was undue reliance on funds from an interested capitalist by the Macdonald government in the election of 1872. From this burst the Pacific Scandal of 1873, which led to the fall of the government that had carried Confederation. Its fall was paralleled by the great economic slump of the same year. The Liberal party, the critics, and even opponents of expansion and Confederation took power.

Consolidation. The speed of Confederation now slowed, and as a result the provincial was to surmount the national, the prudent the bold.

There was, however, one positive benefit gained from the change of ministry. Confederation, planned and carried by a coalition in each of the three original provinces, was not a party measure. Although the Liberals had become its critics (as the Rouges had always been), in office they became the trustees and upholders of the new order. Confederation resumed and thereafter retained, outside certain circles in Quebec, its original character.

This is not to say that the Liberal concept of Confederation was the same as that of the Conservatives. Inevitably the Liberals governed Confederation at a slower pace and with different emphasis than their predecessors in office. The collapse of the Pacific railway made it impossible to fulfill one of the terms on which British Columbia had entered Confederation — completion of the railway within 10 years of the union. That term had to be negotiated again. The difficult business was also complicated by the action of the colonial secretary, Lord Carnarvon, in putting forward the Carnarvon terms. These put off the completion of the railway until 1890, but they had to be accepted by British Columbia and by the Liberal government of Prime Minister Alexander Mackenzie.

Similarly, the government inherited the fruits of the Red River troubles. One was the denial of an amnesty to Riel, the hero of the *métis* and a symbol to Rouge nationalists and ultramontanists. After an inquiry by Parliament, Riel was banished, and he retired to the United States. But the clash of French and English interests in the Northwest had given rise to the *parti national* in Quebec, a party that combined extremes in French politics under the stimuli of the Red River troubles and the New Brunswick school question. It was the beginning of Quebec's withdrawal from support of Confederation to a position of provincial defense and nationalist politics.

One further step the ministry took in building Confederation—the creation by the North-West Territories Act of 1875 of the office of commissioner and of the council of the territories. The act incorporated a provision for separate schools similar to those in Ontario, thus continuing something of the pattern of Anglo-French relations established in the Manitoba Act.

In all this, however, the Mackenzie government was only carrying on in its own way the work of its predecessor. But it did introduce reforms of its own, such as the Ballot Act of 1874. It also set up the Supreme Court of Canada in 1875. A distinct nationalist tinge infused the insistence by Edward Blake, minister of justice, that on all matters internal to Canada the governor-general should speak and act only on the advice of his ministers.

The characteristic measures were democratic and nationalist in spirit. They were nothing more. The Liberals did not believe that government should be used for national development. What distinguished them from the Conservatives was that they refused to use government to support private enterprise when serving public ends.

This reticence was revealed by the tariff issue. The newly founded industries of Canada had received a degree of protection since 1859. Under the competition of American dumping in the depression (1870–1880), the industrialists clamored for outright protection. But the minister of finance, Richard Cartwright, was a free trader on principle; Mackenzie himself concluded that the Canadian tariff must be one for revenue only. This decision gave Macdonald his opportunity, and he came out boldly for a National Policy of protection. The election of 1878 returned him to office.

The Railway Goes Through. The Macdonald government, aided by a revival of business, resumed power with much of the dash and daring of Confederation times. It applied the new National Policy at once, and the budget of 1879 gave greatly increased tariff rates on a wide range of commodities. While pushing on with public construction, it soon revised the railway policy of its predecessors. Construction by a private company was decided on, and in 1880 a company was formed and given a charter of sweeping powers, privileges, and obligations. In 1881 the route of the line was pulled south from the northern parkland; and from the low and known Yellowhead Pass of the Rockies to the southern plains and the high Kicking Horse Pass and the unknown ranges beyond. At once the rate of progress was speeded up; the line pushed up the Fraser and was driven west across the prairies and east across the Precambrian Shield. The Canadian Pacific Railway Company was at last binding Confederation together.

The sweep across the continent soon encountered obstacles. The boom of the early 1880's was violent and brief. In 1883 the Canadian Pacific had to make the first of repeated visits to the government for aid. Hard times brought on by drought and frost on the prairies drove the farmers to the first of many revolts in the Farmers' Union of Manitoba. In 1884 the *métis* who had retreated from the Red River to the Saskatchewan before the coming of settlement, rose again under Louis Riel. Some Indians, made destitute by the passing of the buffalo herds, joined them.

This unwise and unnecessary rebellion was easily put down by Canadian militia rushed to the Northwest on the yet uncompleted railway. Riel, captured after the defeat of his people, was tried, convicted, and hanged for treason. As the result, an all-but-forgotten exile became a martyr of French Canadian nationalism.

Federalization. The execution of Riel led to an outburst of racial feeling that seemed to shake the Dominion. It did so, however, because the structure of Confederation, as reared in 1867, was undergoing a radical reshaping. The decade of the 1880's saw both a political assertion of provincial powers and a judicial interpretation of the British North America Act that was to make the provinces no longer subordinate to the Dominion but coordinate with it. The constitution, that is, was made by judicial review much closer than it had been to a classic federal system.

The judicial committee of the Privy Council of the United Kingdom had been since 1833 the final court of appeal for Canada. At first it was cautious in assuming the power of judicial review over the one constitution in the empire that at the time was in any way federal. On the whole it supported the paramountcy of federal powers stated in the general clauses of section 91 of the British North America Act. The fullest affirmative of this trend was made in the case of *Russell* v. *The Queen* in 1882.

In the very next year, however, the judicial committee reversed that trend in the case of *Hodge* v. *The Queen*. This victory for Ontario's Premier Oliver Mowat and the provinces was confirmed by succeeding cases, until in 1892, in the case of the *Liquidators of the Maritime Banks* v. *the Attorney General of New Brunswick*, the provinces were declared to be in no way subordinate to the Dominion in respect to their proper powers. It remained only for the Local Prohibition case of 1896 to diminish the power of the Dominion to legislate for "peace, order and good government" to an emergency power, in effect; transformation of the constitution into something very close to a federal one was complete.

The same year, 1896, saw the completion of a course of political events that paralleled and strengthened the same development. Honoré Mercier, a former Rouge nationalist, led a combination of Rouge and ultramontane nationalists to victory in the Quebec election of 1886. Mercier sought to voice and to lead provincial resistance to the powers and policies of the federal government. At Quebec City, in 1889, he called a provincial conference that was attended by six provincial governments.

Jesuits' Estates Question. The action of his government, which provoked a reaction in English Canada, however, was a sound and necessary piece of legislation. This legislation settled in 1888 the question of the Jesuits' Estates, which had been confiscated at the conquest and held by the crown since 1801. The act divided the proceeds of the property equitably between the Catholic and Protestant schools of Quebec. What gave offense was the provision that in event of dispute the pope should be requested to arbitrate. This invocation of the papacy in Canadian affairs offended Protestant sentiment. In Ontario a Conservative politician, D'Alton McCarthy, formed the Protestant Protection Association and began a crusade against Roman Catholic denominational schools in Canada. In 1890 he carried his crusade into Manitoba.

Rail Competition Issue. That province had already been at odds with the federal government. The charter of the Canadian Pacific Railway Com-

DAWSON, in Yukon Territory, was a boom town in the gold rush during the late 1890's. A pack train is seen.

PUBLIC ARCHIVES OF CANADA

pany had prohibited the building of railways in a southerly or southeasterly direction from the main line of the railway. The legislators of Manitoba, seeking access to American lines that might compete with Canadian Pacific rates, had repeatedly been disallowed by the federal government. Finally in 1889 the federal government withdrew its opposition to the Manitoba railway charters, and compensated the Canadian Pacific. The Liberal Manitoba government of Premier Thomas Greenway then made an arrangement for the Northern Pacific Railway to come into Winnipeg, and the railways promptly charged equal rates.

Manitoba School Question. A political diversion from such an acute embarrassment was necessary. This Greenway found in the Manitoba School Question. Since 1870 no dissatisfaction had been expressed with respect to either schools or languages, yet immigration into Manitoba since 1870 had been almost wholly English and largely Protestant. Roman Catholic schools and the French language were used by the diminishing minority.

Greenway and his attorney general, Joseph Martin, were both considering taking up the school question when McCarthy aroused English and Protestant feeling on his tour of Manitoba. The legislature at once abolished both the denominational school system and the official status of French.

The School Act (1890) went to the courts. The act was sustained by the Manitoba courts, declared unconstitutional by the Supreme Court of Canada, and finally upheld by the judicial committee of the privy council in 1893. The pressure from the Catholics of Manitoba and from Quebec for remedial legislation then became intense. The federal government was divided between the need to hold its followers in Quebec and to avoid offending those elsewhere.

The embarrassment of the Conservatives was the opportunity of the Liberals. Not only did the federal Liberals enjoy close relations with the Liberal governments of Manitoba, Ontario, Nova Scotia, and New Brunswick, they also had an able and attractive leader in the Quebec politician Wilfrid Laurier. A onetime Rouge, a Liberal of the "English school," Laurier handled the situation with easy mastery. He refused to commit himself on the legalities of the matter. He simply argued that it was a matter to be settled not by the courts or the political coercion of remedial legislation, but by the "sunny ways" of federal-provincial diplomacy.

From 1891 to 1896 the Manitoba School Question repeatedly dominated political debate at Ottawa. It was not, of course, the only controversy of the times. Relations with the empire had become a new issue, by the organization in Canada of the Imperial Federation League, the British response to the growth of a unified Germany and a reunified United States. In Canada the league became a forum for British Protestant nationalism and a response to French and Catholic nationalism in Quebec.

The Conservative government, concerned to restore its position in Quebec without falling into the hands of the nationalists, and plagued by the repeated loss of leaders, tried to stave off dealing with the Manitoba school issue by referring to the courts the question of the extent of its obligations to act. Assured in 1895 that it must act, it introduced a remedial bill to restore the Catholic schools of Manitoba. A Liberal filibuster held up the bill until the life of Parliament expired. In the ensuing general election the Manitoba School Question was therefore one of the chief issues. The result was a sweeping victory for Laurier and the Liberals.

The Liberal victory confirmed the trends of the quarter century since 1882. The constitution became a standard federal one in practice. The paramountcy of Confederation was little more than a war power. Quebec would rely no more on the federal government to protect its rights or those of French Canadians in other provinces. It would rely on its rights as a province and on its leverage in Canadian politics. The nature of Confederation was transformed.

Reaffirmation of Confederation. The depth and bitterness of the controversy over the Manitoba School Question, and the extent of the reshaping of the constitution seemed to have reduced Confederation to impotent fragments. Actually, it was on the eve of one of its strongest and most prosperous periods. What in fact had happened was that again the Liberal party had taken over the federal government and the national policies of its predecessors. But at this time it had done so with its own concept of the nature of the constitution and in circumstances of renewed and multiplied prosperity. As a result, the original and national purposes of Confederation were at last realized as never before. What the Conservatives had sought to do, the Liberals now did.

Compromises. The first considerable measure of the Laurier government was the arrangement of the Laurier-Greenway compromise of 1897. The compromise left the public school system of Manitoba intact, but it established conditions for teaching in a language other than English and reserved time for religious instruction.

On the other great matter of the election, the tariff, an even subtler compromise was desired. No significant lowering of the tariff was attempted, but a preferential rate was set for British goods. In effect, the Liberals, as both their later modifications and elaborations of the tariff showed, had taken over the National Policy of protection.

U. S. Relations. They had done so, it must be said, to a greater degree than they had intended. Relations with the United States had been difficult for a decade, and Laurier attempted to have them dealt with collectively by a joint commission of the two governments. The commission had some success, but in two leading matters it failed. One was reciprocity. The United States government rebuffed the approach of the Canadian members of the commission, and Laurier was forced to say that there would be no more journeys to Washington in search of reciprocity.

The other failure was in an attempt to determine the American-Canadian border of the Alaskan panhandle. The great gold rush to the Yukon had made a decision on this neglected subject a necessity. The disputed territory might itself contain gold, and the Canadian claim, if allowed, would have given access by the great Pacific inlets to Canadian territory. But the border remained in dispute.

Imperial Relations. With difficulties with the United States not wholly resolved, Canada had to face the question of its relations with the British Empire. In the South African War (1899–1902) the imperial government adopted the novel policy of urging its major colonies to participate. The invitation brought forth a warm response from the British elements in English Canada. In Quebec, however, it provoked outspoken resistance from a young Liberal member of Parliament, Henri Bourassa. Caught between English and French Canada, the government compromised by sending a force of volunteers to serve in British pay.

At the time, however, it seemed only a parliamentary, even a personal, episode. Far more dramatic was the outcome of the Alaskan boundary dispute. It was referred to a special joint commission of three United States, one British, and two Canadian representatives. A majority of the commission—the three Americans and the British member—found in favor of the American claims; Canadian anger was deep and lasting.

The anger was turned against Britain, however, rather than the United States. The result was an upsurge of Canadian as distinct from British nationalism that was to affect a generation of influential Canadians. The first specific result was the creation of the department of external affairs in 1909. After a time for tempers to cool, remarkable progress was made in improving relations with the United States. In 1910 the Permanent Joint Commission on Boundary Waters was set up; in 1911 the long-established fishery rights of the United States in Canadian waters were ended. Canada was assuming the conduct of its own affairs, in North America at least.

Economic Boom. In yet another way besides tariff policy was the Liberal government assuming the policies by which Confederation was to be made good. It too became involved in the politics of expansion. The great boom that followed the long depression (1883–1896) was swelling year by year. The Yukon gold rush turned all eyes to Canada; the closing of the American frontier turned the tide of immigration to the yet open frontiers of the Canadian West. American, British, and European settlers poured into the prairies.

As more and more wheat came off the newly broken sod, the Canadian Pacific Railway found itself unable to keep pace with the demand for freight cars to move the harvests. Already a new private line, the Canadian Northern Railway, was making its way to the twin Ontario ports of Fort William and Port Arthur on Lake Superior. The demand for more railways was economic, of course, but it was also political. The Canadian Pacific had been a great supporter of the Conservative party. The Liberal party, now national and accustomed to power, sought a similar ally. But what was its associate to be, the Grand Trunk or the new Canadian Northern? A fierce struggle ensued, from which emerged a government plan to have a subsidiary of the Grand Trunk, the Grand Trunk Pacific, build a line across the prairies and the Rockies to a port in northern British Columbia, while the government itself built the National Transcontinental from the prairies across Ontario and Quebec to the winter ports of the Maritimes. But the Canadian Northern also set out to become a transcontinental line, and by 1914 Canada was feverishly completing two more lines from sea to sea.

The overbuilding was not as apparent then as it became later. The rush of population to the prairies and repeated mineral finds on the Canadian Shield seemed to warrant the expansion. In 1905 the rapid growth led to the creation from the southern territories of the new provinces of Saskatchewan and Alberta. Their creation, however, led as expansion had always done to a renewal of the old controversy over separate schools. As a result, Bourassa began to be a plain French nationalist.

Military Dilemma. That the ancient rift should have reappeared was ominous, because the pressure from the imperial government on the Dominions, first evident in the South African War, to take an active part in imperial defense, was kept up in the imperial conferences that had become a new institution of the empire. Britain was itself moving into line with France and Russia in opposition to the exuberant strength of Germany. It wished to have support from all possible sources — military, naval, and political. Military support it did get in coordination of training, tactics, and command among the Dominions. Naval support was more difficult to obtain for the world's greatest navy, but the matter was soon to arise. Loyally, there was no question of the unity of the empire, but Laurier declined to admit that this carried any support for imperial policy before the event. In the event, the Canadian Parliament would decide whether it would vote money to participate in any war.

It was a politic compromise, but on one point it failed in practice, that of naval aid. The sudden intensification of the Anglo-German naval race in 1907 led to a great pressure for and from the Dominion in the shape of money contributions to the building program of the United Kingdom. The Canadian government again compromised by undertaking to create a Canadian navy which in time of war would come under British command. The amount to be spent under the Naval Bill of 1910, however, came under fierce assault from the imperialists of English Canada as absurdly little, and the Quebec nationalists as too much.

French nationalism now achieved its final form in a closed nationalism, restricted to French Canadians and, in practice, to the province of Quebec.

Farmers' March. The year 1910 was in fact one of growing agitation. For quite other reasons, the organized farmers of Canada, led by the Canadian Council of Agriculture, marched on Ottawa to demand reforms favorable to agriculture. One of their demands was for reciprocity with the United States.

Reciprocity Fails. At this point, with surprising irony, the protectionist United States offered to make an agreement for reciprocity. The Laurier government accepted the prize it had sought in vain a decade before, and its fortunes seemed to be restored. But for a moment only. Resistance began, as the Opposition in Parliament realized that the magic of reciprocity, particularly when sought by the Americans, had worn off.

When the government called an election, the great railway interests, faced with a loss of east-west traffic, mobilized their formidable political influence. All the latent anti-Americanism of the country, still sore over the Alaska boundary, came to the surface and was inflamed by the fervid oratory of the campaign, and 18 leading Liberals of Toronto resigned from the party. The Conservatives under Robert L. Borden, and allied with the nationalists of Quebec, won the 1911 election.

World Involvement. The new government had the old issues to deal with, but in altered circumstances. The boom was drawing to its close, the defeat of reciprocity had angered Western farmers, the new railways were feeling the costs of mounting construction, the crises in Europe were sharper and more frequent. The government had not really established itself in Quebec. Borden reversed the naval policy of his predecessor and decided to give money contributions as the only effective aid in the circumstances. The Liberal majority of the Senate voted down the money bill to grant $35 million to the Royal Navy. A stalemate resulted.

The soldiers, however, to a great extent without the knowledge of government, were completing the plans for an expeditionary force. When World War I broke out, an all-but-unanimous Parliament voted to send troops overseas. Canada was committed to the revolutionary events of the 20th century.

W. L. MORTON
Trent University, Peterborough, Ontario

Bibliography

Creighton, Donald G., *The Road to Confederation* (Toronto 1964).
Morton, William Lewis, *The Critical Years: The Union of British North America, 1857–1873* (Toronto 1964).
Trotter, Reginald G., *Canadian Federation: Its Origin and Its Achievement* (Toronto 1924).
Waite, Peter B., *The Life and Times of Confederation* (Toronto 1962).
Winks, Robin W., *Canada and the United States: The Civil War Years* (Baltimore 1960).

48. World Wars and Depression, 1914–1945.

The two world wars and the Great Depression between them cost Canada dearly in human terms. But the challenges posed and successfully faced made very important contributions to its evolution as a nation and to its material progress.

World War I. As part of the British Empire, Canada was automatically a belligerent when Britain declared war in 1914, and plans to raise 25,000 troops were immediately set in motion. Within two months the 1st Division of the Canadian Expeditionary Force, the largest military force that had yet crossed the Atlantic Ocean, was on its way to further training in England. This was only the first installment of a contribution in manpower which eventually saw more than 600,000 men in the uniform of the Canadian army. Of the more than 400,000 who served overseas, some 60,000 were killed and 173,000 wounded. In addition, some 9,000 men served in an expanded Canadian naval service and some 22,000 Canadians enlisted in Britain's Royal Flying Corps, since Canada had no air force of its own.

Agricultural Expansion. From the outset of the war Canada was a major supplier of food to the Allies and their armies. This steadily growing demand greatly stimulated agricultural production. In the years 1913 to 1919 wheat acreage in Canada increased by over 80%, livestock production by more than one third, and cheese and other dairy production by almost 50%. Owing to the depletion of American forest resources and the cutting off of Scandinavian sources of supply, Canadian pulp and paper found greatly increased markets in both the United States and Britain and the total value of exports of these commodities rose from $19 million in 1913 to $105 million in 1919.

Industrial Growth. The most far-reaching effect of the war on the economy was in the growth of industry. Until this time Canada had had little heavy industry, except in the production of railway equipment and farm implements. Now, under the direction of the Canadian government and the Imperial Munitions Board, a large ammunitions and small arms industry was developed. Before the end of the war nearly one third of all shells being used by the British forces in France were manufactured in Canada. While overseas demands for munitions accounted for most of the increase in manufacturing, the reduction of imports from Europe due to wartime conditions prompted Canadian manufacturers to claim an increased share of the home market and to manufacture a wide variety of consumer goods. In the last three years of the war total employment in manufacturing rose by 32%, a shift of the greatest importance for the future of the economy.

The demands of the armaments plants in Canada and in other allied nations furnished a powerful impetus to mineral production and to the improvement of techniques for extracting and refining minerals. During the war the production of nickel in northern Ontario, which had the largest known deposits of that mineral in the world, rose by 86%, while the total value of nickel, copper, lead, and zinc mined increased from $29 million to $74 million a year. Between 1913 and 1920 the value of all Canadian exports rose from $355 million to $1,239 million.

War Measures Act. The organization of the war effort involved the federal government in the economic life of the nation as never before, although both government and public were reluctant to abandon traditional *laissez-faire* attitudes. The War Measures Act, passed by Parliament at the beginning of the war, gave the government broad powers to mobilize the nation in almost every area of its life. Although most of these powers were never used, a cost-of-living commissioner appointed in 1916, food and fuel controllers appointed in 1917, and the War Trade Board of 1918 made modest attempts to control the cost of living, stimulate production, and supervise the distribution of raw materials and consumer goods. In

1919 a board of commerce was established to administer the new Combines and Fair Prices Act in a further attempt to control prices and profits.

These measures can scarcely be said to have been effective, for the cost of living rose by 60% during the war, and for a brief period in 1920 was double the prewar figure. The most drastic intervention of government in economic activity came with the appointment of a board of grain supervisors in 1917 to fix domestic and export prices of wheat; in 1919 the Canada Wheat Board became the exclusive agent for marketing the Canadian wheat crop.

Financing the War. At first, the war was financed by increased duties on certain services and on articles of consumption, including liquor and tobacco, and later by an increased general customs tariff. In 1916 Parliament decided to abandon this reliance on its traditional methods of raising revenues and to enter the field of direct taxation—which had until then been the preserve of the provinces—with the imposition of a business profits tax and a personal income tax, both at moderate rates. With increased taxation the federal government was still able to raise only one quarter of its requirements, and the remainder was secured by borrowing. Most of the $2 billion acquired in this manner was borrowed within the country; at the beginning of the war some funds were obtained in Britain but by the end Canada was supplying Britain with credit, a dramatic illustration of the wartime transformation of the Canadian economy.

Canadian National Railways. A major economic issue of the war years developed from the over-expansion of railways in the preceding decade. Even before the war the Canadian Northern and Grand Trunk systems were in grave difficulties, but after 1914, when the entry into Canada of both settlers and capital almost ceased, the two companies faced bankruptcy, and in 1916 a commission of enquiry recommended that the federal government take over the railways. Not through any conviction about government ownership of public utilities, but out of concern for Canada's credit abroad and the stability of leading financial institutions at home, the government nationalized the Canadian Northern, the Grand Trunk Pacific, and the Grand Trunk and combined them in the new Canadian National Railways system.

Prohibition and Female Suffrage. Under the social conditions arising from the war two movements with a long history in Canada came to fruition, movements which were not altogether unrelated. Proponents of the prohibition of the sale of beverage alcohol and supporters of the enfranchisement of women both found new arguments for reform during the war. To their old strictures against the evils of drink the "temperance" forces now added patriotic pleas for the conservation of grain and money for war purposes. During the war all the provinces except Quebec enacted prohibition laws and these were reinforced by federal laws to prevent the importation and interprovincial shipment of beer, wine, and spirits.

During 1916 and 1917 women in Ontario and the four Western Provinces—Manitoba, Saskatchewan, Alberta, and British Columbia—were granted the provincial franchise and in 1918 a bill granting the franchise in federal elections was passed by Parliament.

Tensions. The Canadian contribution to the Allied war effort was an enormous one for a nation of only 8 million population, and it was made at the price of acute racial and social tension. The national unity that had been so evident in 1914 was brief as differences in French and English Canadian responses to the conflict became evident. At the outset the French Canadian leader of the Liberal opposition in the House of Commons, Sir Wilfrid Laurier, pledged full suport to the Conservative administration of Sir Robert L. Borden in the prosecution of the war. But it was perhaps inevitable that Canadians of Anglo-Saxon origin, and especially the many who had migrated from Britain in the past decade and a half, would feel stronger emotional involvement and would prove readier to enlist than French Canadians who tended to view the war as another manifestation of British imperialism. Moreover, the French Canadians had long since ceased to have any strong ties of sentiment to France, and French Canada was greatly agitated by Ontario's persistent adherence to the terms of Regulation 17, issued originally in 1912 and designed to limit the use of French as a language of instruction in the schools of Ontario.

Henri Bourassa, who emerged as the spokesman of French Canadian antiwar nationalist feeling, encouraged Quebec to give its first attention to "the Prussians of Ontario" before doing more to defeat the Prussians of Europe. The government's ineptness in dealing with recruitment in Quebec, and its tardiness in creating French Canadian regiments and in promoting French Canadian officers did nothing to improve matters.

Conscription. By 1916 it was evident that the government faced a manpower crisis in its attempts to recruit the 500,000 men it had promised to send overseas. A movement for conscription arose in English Canada, and gained force after Borden made a trip to England in the spring of 1917 and returned convinced that the military situation was critical and that Canada must honor its commitments and maintain the strength of its four divisions in France.

The vast majority of French Canadians were strongly opposed to conscription. In an attempt to prevent a destructive racial cleavage, Borden invited Laurier and the Liberals to join a coalition government. Although Laurier had consistently supported the war and had urged his fellow countrymen to enlist, he was also on record as being opposed to compulsory service; he believed that if he now joined a coalition for the purpose of enforcing conscription he would hand the province of Quebec over to Bourassa and the Nationalists, with consequent damage to both unity and the war effort.

When Laurier refused the coalition proposal, a number of Ontario and western Liberals, and in due course representatives of the Maritime provinces, joined with the Conservatives in a Union government pledged to the enforcement of conscription. The government appealed to the voters in the "khaki election" of December 1917 amid racial cries of unprecedented bitterness.

The victory of the Unionists was assisted by extraordinary electoral laws, enacted before the formation of the coalition, giving the vote to soldiers overseas and to their female relatives in Canada, and disenfranchising Canadian citizens who had migrated from enemy alien countries and had been naturalized since 1902. The Laurier Liberals won 82 seats, all but 20 of them in Quebec, while the government carried 153 seats, only three of them in Quebec. The popular vote was not as one-sided as the distribution of seats suggested, since Laurier received 42% of the votes cast, including many from farmers and trade unionists in English Canada.

IN WORLD WAR I in France, Canadian infantry goes over the top in October 1916. They were rated as strong attack troops.

PUBLIC ARCHIVES OF CANADA

But the fact remained that Canada was more politically divided on racial lines than ever and the country was left with an inheritance of bitterness which the passage of many years did not erase. Slightly less than 122,000 men were raised by conscription, but only about 47,000 of these were sent overseas, since the war ended within 10 months of the adoption of conscription.

By the summer of 1920 most of the Liberal Unionists had left the administration, Borden had resigned, and a new Conservative party under the leadership of Arthur Meighen had begun to prepare to go to the polls against a Liberal party which was reorganizing under William Lyon Mackenzie King, who had been elected leader in 1919 following Laurier's death.

Post-war Growth. A brief boom immediately at the conclusion of the war was followed by a three-year trade slump, but then economic expansion continued steadily until "the great crash" of 1929. The chief advances were no longer in agriculture, but in manufacturing, mining, pulp and paper, and the development of hydroelectric power. Much of this economic growth depended on the riches of the Canadian Shield, and to a lesser extent on the first serious attempts to exploit the resources of the Arctic region. Canadians were beginning to be aware that, although the old agricultural frontier of the prairie was gone, they now had a new northern frontier.

The new staples drawn from rock and forest increasingly found their market in the United States, and Canada's dependence on trade across her southern border and on American capital to develop her resources showed a sharp increase during the 1920's. Not all sections of the country experienced the prosperity of the 1920's in equal measure. Ontario, Quebec, and British Columbia were booming, but the Prairie provinces were less flourishing. The shipment of grain from Alberta and parts of Saskatchewan to Europe via British Columbia and the Panama Canal added greatly to the prosperity of the port of Vancouver, but in disrupting earlier patterns of shipment by rail through eastern Canada it did nothing for Winnipeg. The Prairies had their own scheme for a short-water route to Europe in the Hudson Bay Railway to Churchill, but when it was completed in 1929 the short season and high freight charges rendered it much less useful to the prairie economy than had been anticipated.

The Maritime provinces profited little if at all from the prosperity of the rest of the country for there was no solution to their perennial problem—the absence of the natural resources that would enable them to prosper in an industrial age.

Farmers' Movements. The political developments of the postwar decade reflected both the new class consciousness that was a product of the war and the developing sectionalism created by the inequalities of economic growth in the various regions of the country. The emergence of the farmers as a distinctive political force was the most noteworthy feature of the political scene in the years immediately after the war. The United Farmers of Ontario surprised even themselves by capturing the provincial legislature in 1919 in the most heavily industrialized province in the nation. In 1921 the United Farmers of Alberta came to power, and in the following year a farmers' government took office in Manitoba.

Federally, the farmers organized as the Progressive party under the leadership of T. A. Crerar and pledged themselves to the implementation of the "New National Policy," the platform adopted by the Canadian Council of Agriculture during the war. In the federal election of 1921, when the tariff was the main issue, Mackenzie King's Liberals won the largest number of seats, but the Progressives emerged as the second-largest group, their support coming almost entirely from the Prairies and Ontario. The Progressives declined to form a coalition with the Liberals, or to act as the official opposition in Parliament, a role they left to the now weakened Conservatives. Rather, they determined to support King on policies to their liking and won some moderate concessions in the form of lower tariffs and freight rates.

From the outset the Progressives were weakened by internal divisions; some members, mainly from Manitoba and Ontario, looked on themselves as being indeed what Mackenzie King called them, "Liberals in a hurry"; another wing, led by Henry Wise Wood of Alberta, was more radical and favored "group government" based on occupational groups, a form of parliamentary representation that would have destroyed cabinet government. A further weakness of the Progressives was their complete lack of representation from Quebec. From 1925, the party declined rapidly, and the federal party system seemed to have been restored almost to its traditional pattern.

The Depression. Few countries were more vulnerable to the effects of a world depression than Canada. An economy so heavily dependent on exports of wheat, dairy produce, newsprint, lumber, minerals, and fish was bound to suffer from a contraction of world markets after the crash of October 1929. At the same time the economy labored under heavy fixed costs in transportation and borrowed capital. Some regions suffered more from the depression than others; the Prairie provinces, so dependent on one staple export, wheat, and afflicted also by drought, were hardest hit. In the province of Saskatchewan the per capita income fell by 72% in the period 1929–1933, compared with 44% for Ontario and Quebec, and 48% for Canada as a whole.

In the federal election of 1930, Prime Minister King assured the voters that the depression would be short lived and could be met by belt-tightening measures to produce a balanced budget. The Conservatives, led by the millionaire lawyer R. B. Bennett, advocated jobs through public works projects and a higher tariff that would enable Canada to "blast her way into the markets of the world."

Bennett's "New Deal." The electorate chose the Conservatives, and for the next four years the Bennett government sought to alleviate the impact of the depression with the highest tariff in Canadian history, a system of imperial preference worked out at the Imperial Economic Conference of 1932 in Ottawa, and a program of payments to the provinces for the growing bill for unemployment relief. Early in 1935, Prime Minister Bennett, greatly to the surprise even of his own cabinet members, revealed in a series of radio addresses his belief that more radical measures were now necessary. "The old order is gone. It will not return," Bennett told the nation, and proceeded to outline proposals for a Canadian "New Deal."

Subsequently, Parliament passed a series of measures to reduce farm debt, regulate certain business practices, introduce unemployment insurance, establish minimum wages and maximum hours of work, and control export trade. Capitalism was to be reformed to meet changed conditions, and on this platform the Conservatives fought the federal election of 1935. King and the Liberals countered with claims that most of the "New Deal" legislation was beyond the constitutional power of the federal government, while their own prescription for healing the nation's ills remained obscure.

In the meantime, as increasing numbers of young men were "riding the rods" across the country in search of jobs, and the lines of the hungry outside the city soup kitchens grew longer, many Canadians began to look for more radical solutions to their economic ills than any offered by either of the two traditional parties. Thus, in the election of 1935, three new political parties sought the support of the voters.

Three New Parties. The most important of these was the Co-operative Commonwealth Federation (CCF), the first attempt at the formation of a national socialist party in Canada. Many of the founders of the new party had been members of the Progressive party or of provincial labor parties during the 1920's. In its inspiration the new party owed much to the western agrarian protest tradition, to the British Labour Party, and to the Fabian ideals current among some of the Canadian academic community.

Its leader, J. S. Woodsworth, was a former Methodist minister whose political thinking had been shaped by the social gospel movement, and by his experiences in the East End of London, among the immigrants of western Canada, and in the Winnipeg strike of 1919.

The CCF platform, the Regina Manifesto adopted in 1933, declared: "We aim to replace the present capitalist system with its inherent injustice and inhumanity by a social order from which domination and exploitation of one class by another will be eliminated, in which economic planning will supersede unregulated private enterprise and competition, and in which genuine democratic self-government based upon economic equality will be possible." To achieve this end the party endeavored to appeal to farmers, labor, and middle-class voters of reforming spirit.

An even more distinctly western political movement was the Social Credit party, born in Alberta under the leadership of William ("Bible Bill") Aberhart, a Calgary school principal and fundamentalist preacher. Possessed of great oratorical powers and the capacity to simplify and dramatize complex issues, Aberhart was one of the first Canadian politicians to use radio effectively in a political campaign. He already had a large audience for his religious broadcasts and in 1934, when he combined revivalism with the expounding of Social Credit economic theory, he started a movement which enlisted a distraught people under his banner.

Basing his political teaching on the social credit theories of an English engineer, Major C. H. Douglas, Aberhart promised an end "to poverty in the midst of plenty" by increasing purchasing power through "social dividends" to be paid to all citizens; initially, Albertans were to receive a dividend of $25 per month. In a landslide victory in the provincial election of 1935, Aberhart and his followers defeated the United Farmers of Alberta to become the world's first Social Credit government. After he took office Aberhart's somewhat reluctant attempts to implement his monetary theories soon came up against the constitutional barrier of the federal government's control over banking and finance. While Social Creditors resigned themselves to giving Alberta "sound business government," they endeavored to become a national party that could capture the citadel of financial control in Ottawa.

Yet another party appeared on the national scene under the leadership of a Vancouver business man, H. H. Stevens. As minister of trade and commerce in the Bennett cabinet, Stevens had urged and then chaired a royal commission on price spreads in 1934. The committee's revelations of high profits and starvation wages in retail merchandising did much to color public thinking about the operation of the business system. Stevens' forthright attacks on the business community led to dissension within the cabinet and to his resignation. Shortly afterward he launched the Reconstruction party on a platform designed to appeal to the small business man and to ensure his survival within the capitalist system.

In the election of 1935 the CCF, Social Credit, and Reconstruction parties all vied with the Liberals to wrest power from the Conservatives. Owing largely to the million votes divided among the three parties, Bennett retained only 39 seats, while the Liberals, with 171 seats, emerged as the government. Mackenzie King held office without interruption from this time until his retirement in 1948.

Constitutional Questions. The proliferation of new parties aiming at federal power during the depression was in part a manifestation of the sectionalism which economic distress fostered. There were also other signs of sectionalism in the emergence of provincial regimes which adopted an aggressive attitude toward the federal government. In Ontario the Liberal Mitchell Hepburn waged war against the Liberal government in Ottawa in defense of Ontario rights never clearly defined, while declaring his intention to save the province from the "communism" of the American CIO, which made its first attempt to organize automobile workers in Canada during the Oshawa (Ontario) strike of 1937. In Quebec, Maurice Duplessis led a Union Nationale government that made radical economic promises before election but adopted an ultraconservative attitude toward social change when it obtained office, while charging the federal government with undermining provincial autonomy and inhibiting French Canadians in the enjoyment of their natural rights. In British Columbia the Liberal T. D. Pattullo found that the "Work and Wages" program which had brought him to power could not be implemented without new sources of funds and by 1935 his government was involved in a bitter controversy with Ottawa over federal financial policies.

A further factor in Dominion-provincial relations arose from the decisions of the Supreme Court of Canada and the Judicial Committee of the Privy Council. In a series of court decisions, most of the social credit legislation passed by the Alberta legislature, as well as the Bennett "New Deal" legislation, was found unconstitutional. It was now clear that while the provinces alone had the constitutional right to pass the kind of economic and welfare legislation that might have alleviated the effects of the depression, they did not have the taxing powers to implement such measures.

The King government responded to this impasse in 1937 by appointing a royal commission on Dominion-provincial relations to investigate the constitutional and financial relations between the federal and provincial governments and to suggest changes to meet some of the nation's difficulties. After three years the commission, popularly known as the Rowell-Sirois commission after its two chairmen, submitted sweeping proposals that amounted to a plan for reconfederation, although the structure of the British North America Act was to be left technically intact. Through a series of "tax rentals" and grants, the provinces were to be put in a position to administer measures providing minimum standards of social and educational services for all Canadians, while the whole burden of unemployment insurance and unemployment relief would be assumed by the federal government. By the time the report was received Canada was at war. Its recommendations were not implemented entirely, but its thinking and some of its specific proposals had great influence for years to come.

Notable Achievements. Although the depression years brought so much friction between Ottawa and the provinces, the federal government instituted several policies of national scope and lasting significance. The Bennett administration reorganized the government railways, reestablished the government wheat board to market the wheat crop, established a Bank of Canada to regulate currency and credit and to advise the government on financial policy, and inaugurated a publicly owned national broadcasting system. All these measures were sustained or extended under the succeeding Liberal government, which then added to the involvement of government in economic life by setting up the publicly owned Trans-Canada Air Lines (now Air Canada). All these measures were in keeping with traditions that went back at least as far as government assistance to the building of the Canadian Pacific Railway.

In the two decades following World War I, Canada developed both the substance and the symbols of full nationhood. The nation's contributions to the allied war effort, and the insistence of Borden and his colleagues on recognition, won for Canada a place at the peace conference and separate representation in the League of Nations. Subsequently, King pressed forward in the same direction; the new British Commonwealth was described in the Balfour Report of 1926 as an association of members "equal in status, in no way subordinate to one another." In 1931 the Statute of Westminster, passed by the British Parliament, made the necessary legal changes to give practical effect to the dominions' position of equality with the mother country. An accompaniment of the new status was the establishment of Canadian diplomatic representation in foreign countries, beginning with the United States, and followed by France and Japan.

Once possessed of the right to pursue an independent foreign policy, Canada used its new freedom with great caution. The necessity to promote good relations between Britain and the United States remained an objective of great priority, as did the maintenance of world peace in the interests of overseas trade. But Canada took no initiative in the efforts of the League of Nations to ensure international amity. Its policy of "no committments" was dictated partly by the feeling that Europe was far away and by an awareness that a nation as small as Canada could not hope to influence world affairs decisively, and partly by the requirements of domestic politics. Canadian politicians, most notably Mackenzie King, were well aware that to take a definite stand on foreign policy, especially on issues that might lead to war, risked the destruction of national unity. King could never afford to forget that his most solid block of support came from the traditionally isolationist Quebec.

World War II. Although King put off the hour of decision with renewed assertions that in due course "Parliament will decide," there was little doubt about the direction Canada would take as war once again threatened Europe and the world. In 1937, Canada began to expand its defenses and then to draw the blueprints for what was to become the Commonwealth Air Training Scheme. At the same time Canada began to draw closer to the United States, a move that was formalized after the outbreak of war in the Ogdensburg agreement of 1940, when Canada and the United States agreed to established a permanent joint board on international Defense to devise plans for the defense of the northern half of the Western Hemisphere.

In the meantime, when Britain and France went to war against Hitler's Germany in September 1939, King had called Parliament to decide on Canada's course. Britain no longer had the power to commit Canada to war automatically, but a majority of Canadians could see a future for their country only within a free British Commonwealth, and they supported the action of a Parliament which, with very little dissent, now committed Canada to the war against fascism.

Canada's Contribution. At first it seemed that Canada's role in this war would be confined mainly to the provision of food and armaments, although the first Canadian army contingent was dispatched to Britain before the end of 1939. Everything was

IN WORLD WAR II, in the Italian campaign, the Princess Patricia Light Infantry lands at Reggio in September 1943.

DEPARTMENT OF NATIONAL DEFENCE

changed by the German advance through the Low Countries and the fall of France in June 1940. For a time, until the United States was forced into the war by the Japanese attack on Pearl Harbor, Canada was second in size only to Britain among the nations opposing the Axis powers. From this time forward the war effort was expanded relentlessly until Canada had over a million men and women in the armed forces and had extended its industrial productivity to become the fourth industrial nation in the world. In the vast expanses of the Dominion the airmen of the Commonwealth, over half of them members of the Royal Canadian Air Force, were trained for service in places as far afield as North Africa, Burma, and the Canadian Arctic. The prosperity brought by the war enabled Canada not only to finance her own war effort but to lend money to Britain and its other allies. Again, as in World War I, a small nation, this time of 12 million people, had made a contribution to victory far out of proportion to its size. Although the casualties were proportionatey lower now, the loss of nearly 42,000 dead and missing was a grim reminder of the worst cost of war.

New Conscription Issue. From the beginning of the war Canadians were mindful of the disagreements, especially over conscription, that had split the nation so badly during World War I, and were determined to avoid a repetition of this domestic tragedy. Mackenzie King's government pledged to fight the war on a voluntary basis, but after the fall of France certain elements in English-speaking Canada began to advocate conscription. In response, the government introduced conscription for service in Canada only, and later, in April 1942, under mounting pressure a national plebiscite was held to ask the voters whether they wished to release the government from its promise not to institute conscription for overseas duty.

Although a majority of voters agreed to release the government from its pledge, the nation was once more divided: 80% of English-speaking Canada favored giving the government a free hand, while 72% of the voters of Quebec were opposed. The result of the plebiscite did not obligate the government to introduce conscription and King managed to resist all demands that he do so until the manpower crisis created by the allied invasion of France in 1944.

After the resignation of the minister of defense, J. L. Ralston, who insisted that conscription was now essential, and the failure of the efforts of his successor, General A. G. L. McNaughton, to secure further enlistments by voluntary methods, King agreed in November 1944 to a limited conscription measure that made 16,000 men already conscripted for home duty eligible for overseas service. This was a decision full of peril both for the King government and the unity of the nation. Thanks largely to the fact that King's leading French-speaking lieutenant, Louis St. Laurent, stood by the decision, no serious rift occurred. In his handling of the conscription issue, King's policies of caution and moderation had their chief vindication.

Effective Administration. On the economic front as well, Canada profited by the lessons of World War I. This time effective government control of strategic materials and a system of rationing and price controls kept the cost of living from rising unduly during the war and limited the accentuation of class consciousness that had characterized the earlier conflict. Moreover, the King government had taken steps intended to assist the country in meeting the social and economic dislocation of the postwar period, including the institution in 1940 of a federal system of unemployment insurance and the payment of children's allowances in 1944. To these were added proposals for the stabilization of agricultural prices, hospital insurance and government-subsidized housing schemes. On this platform the King government faced the voters in June 1945 and found itself one of the few wartime governments in the world returned to office after the war.

MARGARET PRANG
University of British Columbia

Bibliography

Cook, George Ramsay, *The Politics of John W. Dafoe and the Free Press* (Toronto 1963).

Dawson, Robert MacGregor, *William Lyon Mackenzie King: A Political Biography:* vol. 1, *1874–1923* (Toronto 1958).

Graham, William Roger, *Arthur Meighen,* 3 vols. (Toronto 1960–1965).

Irving, John Allan, *The Social Credit Movement in Alberta* (Toronto 1959).

McNaught, Kenneth, *A Prophet in Politics: A Biography of J. S. Woodsworth* (Toronto 1959).

Morton, William Lewis, *The Progressive Party in Canada* (Toronto 1950).

Neatby, H. Blair, *William Lyon Mackenzie King:* vol. 2, *1924–1932* (Toronto 1963).

Pickersgill, John Whitney, *The Mackenzie King Record:* vol. 1, *1939–1944* (Toronto 1960).

Royal Commission on Dominion-Provincial Relations, *Report,* book 1 (Ottawa 1940).

49. Modern Canada, 1945–

Were they to return to life today the Canadians who died on the World War II battlefields of Europe would be as surprised by the Stratford Festival as by the gleaming Montreal skyscrapers; by the oceangoing freighters berthed at Great Lakes ports as by the wells, pipelines, and refineries drawing on the wealth hidden beneath prairie wheatfields; by the serious and passionate advocacy of secession in Quebec as by the remarkable increase in the role of the state in Canadian society. Postwar Canada underwent a revolutionary change in its relation to the outside world, the structure of its population, the taste and temper of the people, and even in the landscape itself.

Toward a Welfare State. Since 1942, Mackenzie King's Liberal government had been planning for postwar domestic reconstruction. Uppermost in its mind was the fear that once the war was over the depression would return, unless effective anti-depression policies were devised and implemented. The Liberals were also acutely aware that the government's future might depend on a dramatic move to the left.

The Reconstruction proposals, made public in the spring of 1945, had three major and interrelated goals: to use the power of the state to maintain high levels of income and employment; to provide increased nationwide health and welfare programs; and to provide minimum revenues to the provinces in order to assure a minimum standard of living throughout Canada. To reach these objectives the federal government proposed to adopt the policies advocated by John Maynard Keynes, the British economist. As a result they recommended that the federal government should have complete control over personal and corporate income taxes and succession duties, in return for which it would pay an annual per capita rent to the provinces. The federal government also would assume wide responsibility for unemployment insurance, old-age pensions, health insurance, and public works, and provide aid to the provinces in the development of natural resources. Taken together the Reconstruction proposals placed the central government in a paramount position in the Canadian federal system.

King's Policy Endorsed. The King government went to the people on its wartime record and its proposed postwar policy on June 11, 1945. There was a sharp decline in Liberal strength in every province, as the party's 181 seats won in 1940 fell to 125, and its popular vote from 51.5 to 41.1%. Although the Conservative popular vote fell, despite its new leader (John Bracken) and its new "Progressive Conservative" label, the party added 27 seats to the 40 it had won five years earlier. The Co-operative Commonwealth Federation (CCF) won 28 seats and 15.6% of the vote. Social Credit won 13 seats in Alberta, and 11 independents were elected.

Since implementation of the proposals needed provincial concurrence the federal government called a Federal-Provincial Conference in August 1945. The two largest provinces made it clear at once that they opposed the federal scheme. Premier Maurice Duplessis of Quebec rejected any suggestion that the powers of the central government should be increased, and Premier George A. Drew of Ontario argued firmly in behalf of provincial fiscal autonomy. After lengthy and heated discussions the conference broke up without any agreement having been reached. But a month later the federal government offered to negotiate tax rental agreements with the individual provinces, and eventually did so with all but Quebec. Since 1945 the federal government has also worked piecemeal at the health and welfare and other proposals, and by the late 1960's most of them had been put into effect through a variety of forms of federal-provincial cooperation.

A New Chief: St. Laurent. Seeing the nation moving toward some of the social reforms he had first outlined in *Industry and Humanity* (1918) and, having seen Canada adopt a bold and positive postwar foreign policy, Mackenzie King concluded in 1948 that the time had come to resign. His successor was Louis St. Laurent, a Quebec corporation lawyer who had entered the cabinet in 1941. King left his successor a legacy of purposeful reform and a booming economy. He also left him with the certainty that Newfoundland would enter Confederation and thus complete the design of 1867. The margin of the 1948 referendum on union was close, but on March 31, 1949, Newfoundland became Canada's tenth province. Joseph Smallwood of the Liberal party, became the first premier of the province.

St. Laurent also completed several other matters that King had started. In 1949 the federal government assumed power to amend the constitution except for certain matters pertaining to the provinces. Appeals to the judicial committee of the privy council, in Britain, were abolished in the same year, and the Canadian Supreme Court became the final court of appeal. Another expression of Canadian nationalism was the appointment in 1949 of a royal commission, known as the Massey Commission after its chairman, Vincent Massey, to inquire into the state of Canadian culture.

The report, published two years later, recommended massive state aid to the arts and sciences in Canada if Canadian culture were to be enriched and flourish and Canadians remain a distinctive society in North America. In subsequent years the federal government increased its aid to the Canadian Broadcasting Corporation, the National Film Board, the Public Archives, and the National Museum. In 1951 it began giving aid to Canadian universities, although education was a provincial responsibility and in the face of strong opposition from the Duplessis government in Quebec, which refused to allow universities in the province to accept the aid. Finally, in 1957, the St. Laurent government established the Canada Council to provide financial support to scholars and artists in the humanities, the fine arts, and the social sciences.

Assuming a World Role. There was no more striking a demonstration of the new sense of national confidence than in the field of external relations. After the war, although Mackenzie King, the engineer if not the architect of prewar isolationism, was still in office, Canada resolutely adopted a clear-cut policy of international involvement. The task was made easier when St. Laurent became secretary of state for external affairs in 1946, and easier still when he became prime minister and was replaced in external affairs by Lester B. Pearson, a career diplomat in the department.

MALAK, FROM CANADIAN INFORMATION SERVICE

CENTENNIAL of Confederation is hailed by throngs on Parliament Hill, Ottawa, at midnight, June 30, 1967.

Role in the United Nations. Although critical of some aspects of the United Nations, and particularly of the role of the great powers on the Security Council, Canada played an active part in the creation of the United Nations. The Canadian attempt to create a special role for the middle powers, of which it saw itself as a leader, met with limited success. However, in 1948 and 1958, Canada served a term on the Security Council, and in 1953 rejoiced in the election of Pearson as president of the General Assembly.

Korean War. The nation soon made it clear that it would back words with deeds when it became the third-largest military contributor to the UN action in the Korean War. For five years Canadians fought in Korea and suffered 1,600 casualties. Canada's role was also important on the diplomatic front where Lester Pearson was instrumental in defining and limiting the aims of UN action, and as president he steered the assembly through key discussions about the settlement of the war.

Suez Crisis. The most dramatic and controversial example of Canadian policy in the United Nations was in 1956 when Britain and France, to secure control of the Suez Canal, intervened during the war between Israel and Egypt. The condemnation of this action was not only widespread, but so strong on the part of the United States and India that Canada feared for the continuation of Anglo-American friendship and the Commonwealth. Pearson's immediate task, as he saw it, was to bring an end to the conflict and, particularly, the Anglo-French intervention. To achieve this he formulated, actually within the space of hours, the plan for a cease-fire and the UN Expeditionary Force. Canadian diplomats played a significant role in repairing the breach in the Western alliance, and there can be little doubt that Canada's action in "regretting" the intervention—the sole white member of the Commonwealth to do so—was in large measure responsible for the fact that the Afro-Asian members did not desert the Commonwealth. For his work during the crisis Pearson was awarded the 1957 Nobel Peace Prize.

Peace-Keeping Policy. It was appropriate that a Canadian, Maj. Gen. E. L. M. Burns, was appointed commander of the UN Emergency Force in the Middle East. Canadian troops formed the largest single contingent. Even before 1956 Canadians had participated in UN peace-keeping operations in Palestine and Kashmir, and Canada was appointed to the Indo-China Truce Supervisory Commission in 1954. But after 1956 peace-keeping became a major plank in the foreign policy of all Canadian governments. Within the next decade Canadians served in Lebanon, the Congo, Yemen, New Guinea, Cyprus, and along the Indo-Pakistani border for the United Nations. Canadian spokesmen at the UN took the lead in attempts to strengthen the UN's capability to deal effectively with threats to security.

Shaping the Commonwealth. Although the action of the Liberal government during the Suez crisis was criticized by many Canadians who felt that Britain should have been supported, it revealed the new stature Canada had assumed and the new role it was to play in the Commonwealth. However satisfying the declarations of 1926 and 1931 had been, prewar Canada was still a very subordinate member of the British Commonwealth and the nationalism of most Canadians was still tempered by the instincts of colonials. The war had made equality a reality, however, and had banished most sentiments of inferiority. The abolition of appeals to the Judicial Committee, the creation of the status of a Canadian citizen in 1947, the appointment of Vincent Massey as the first Canadian governor-general in 1957, and the change in the royal title in 1952 designating the sovereign as King of Canada reflected the new equality.

Moreover, Canada vigorously supported the transition from the old British Commonwealth into the new multiracial Commonwealth of Nations. Canada applauded the independence of India and helped persuade other Commonwealth members that India could be a republic and yet remain within the Commonwealth. Canada also helped organize the Colombo Plan in 1950 to provide economic aid to underdeveloped nations and by 1965 had contributed more than $500 million.

NATO. Perhaps the most striking illustration of the revolution in foreign policy was Canada's permanent involvement in the defense of western Europe. Canada had discovered the nature of postwar diplomacy when, in 1946, Igor Gouzenko, a clerk in the Russian embassy in Ottawa, had revealed the existence of a Soviet spy ring in Canada and other Western countries. When the consolidation of Soviet power in eastern Europe was capped by the coup in Czechoslovakia in 1948, Canada was one of the first Western nations to suggest a treaty of mutual defense. St. Laurent urged that under Anglo-American-French leadership the West establish "an overwhelming preponderance of force over any adversary or possible combination of adversaries." The Western response resulted in the creation in 1949 of the North Atlantic Treaty

Organization (NATO), whose members were pledged to act together in the event of an attack on any one of them. As a member of NATO, Canada has since had troops in western Europe. But while the country fully accepted its position as a North Atlantic power, it refused to join the Southeast Asia Treaty Organization (SEATO) in 1954 and assume similar responsibilities in the Pacific.

North American Defense. The postwar period also saw a confirmation and consolidation of Canadian-American wartime cooperation in the defense of North America. In 1949, after the USSR had exploded its first atomic bomb, work started on three early-warning radar systems across Canada, in great part paid for and manned by the United States. After lengthy discussions the two countries signed the North American Air Defense Agreement (NORAD) in 1958, which placed the air defense of North America under what, in theory at least, was a united command.

Rapid Domestic Expansion. While the government had feared a postwar depression and had taken steps to counter it, it soon became clear that postwar Canada was to enjoy an economic boom. For more than a decade after the war almost every aspect of the economy underwent rapid expansion.

Population. The population soared from 11,500,000 in 1941 to 17,000,000 in 1958 and to 20,400,000 by 1967. Seventy percent of the increase in the 1950's was due to a high birthrate, one of the highest among industrialized countries. But the country also received over 1.5 million immigrants between 1945 and 1957, a peak of 282,000 arriving in 1957. A third came from the British Isles and about 100,000 from the United States. The majority came from Italy, Germany, and other countries in continental Europe. In 1956, after the unsuccessful revolt in Hungary, Canada organized an airlift to bring over 30,000 Hungarian refugees.

Gross National Product. The increase in the gross national product (GNP) provides the clearest illustration of the postwar economic growth. In current dollars the increase in the GNP moved from $11.8 billion in 1945 to $18 billion in 1950 and $31.9 billion in 1957.

Mineral Resources. While there were remarkable advances throughout the industrial sector of the economy, perhaps the most sensational were in the discovery and exploitation of natural resources. In 1947, years of exploration paid off when Imperial Oil "blew in" an oil well at Leduc, Alberta. Hundreds of companies engaged in the search for oil and natural gas, and the estimates of the reserves throughout the West doubled and tripled and tripled again.

Equally exciting in the atomic age, though of less significance, was the expansion of the uranium industry. Exploitation of the rich Beaverlodge field in northern Saskatchewan began in 1953. Soon afterward came the news of sensational discoveries in the Blind River-Elliot Lake district in northern Ontario. By 1958, Canada had become the world's leading uranium producer.

One of the weaknesses in the prewar economy was the absence of iron ore in Canada. During the war, rich deposits were discovered at Steep Rock in Ontario. In 1948, explorations in northern Quebec, near the Labrador boundary, uncovered one of the largest ore bodies in the world. A railway was built from the St. Lawrence River, and the first shipments from the new mines began in 1954. Ten years later, as more mines opened in northern Ontario and in the Quebec-Labrador region, production in Canada was 38.6 million tons.

Power and the Seaway. Despite its great waterpower resources, Canada realized that in time it would need to use nuclear power to supplement hydroelectric power. Planning began in the mid-1950's; in 1962 a small experimental nuclear power station was completed at Rolphton, Ontario, and three years later a full-scale commercial station was completed at Douglas Point, Ontario.

Many postwar developments centered on the stimulus to industrial development provided by the availability of hydroelectric power. The isolated Indian fishing village at Kitimat, British Columbia, became the site of an immense aluminum smelter in 1951 when engineers decided that the waters of the Nechako River, 50 miles (80 km) away, could be used to generate 2 million horsepower. One of the great engineering feats of the 20th century, the Kemano power plant receives its water through a tunnel 250 feet (76 meters) wide and 10 miles (16 km) long through a mountain, and then sends the power the 50 miles to Kitimat over the largest transmission cables then made. The later expansion of the Columbia River capacity and the exploitation of the vast power resources of the Peace River promised to provide British Columbia with adequate power for its growing economy; they also made possible the sale of power to the United States. Throughout Canada there was a sharp increase in the development of hydroelectric and thermal-electric power, and the total capacity increased fourfold between 1945 and 1966.

The construction of the St. Lawrence Seaway made it possible for the iron ore ships, as well as deep-sea freighters, to reach into the heartland of the continent, and the allied power project increased the power supply of eastern Canada. The billion-dollar project was completed in 1959. See SAINT LAWRENCE SEAWAY.

Manufacturing. Less striking than the development of natural resources but equally important was the rapid expansion of Canadian manufacturing. Old industries, such as pulp and paper, the leading manufacturing industry in postwar Canada, and steel expanded rapidly. New ones were created. New factories dotted the landscape throughout Canada, but particularly in southern British Columbia, around Winnipeg, throughout central Ontario, and Quebec. Before the war one Canadian worker in three was employed in agriculture, but by 1960 only one in eight was; two out of every three Canadians lived in urban areas. In the decade after the war Canada completed its transformation into an industrialized urban nation.

Agriculture. Nevertheless, agriculture remained one of the nation's leading primary industries. Yet while its value and volume were substantially above those of the prewar years, agriculture did not share in the postwar boom. Despite higher production, farm income actually declined between 1951 and 1956, and due to a decline in external markets, wheat farmers were faced after 1953 with huge unsold surpluses.

Discontent and Remedies. By the mid-1950's, therefore, the Canadian farmer was becoming disillusioned with the Liberal government in Ottawa, which refused to guarantee him the prices he desired for his goods. The farmer was not alone in his disenchantment. The Atlantic provinces had not shared in the new prosperity, and in 1954 established the Atlantic Provinces Economic Council to seek ways to increase their prosperity. The general prosperity of the boom years, plus the lack of strong opposition parties, enabled the Liberal government to win handily the general elections of 1949 and 1953. In 1949 they won 193 of the 262 seats, leaving the Conservatives with only 41, the CCF with 13, and Social Credit with 10. The election of 1953 saw the opposition parties make scattered gains and the Liberals drop to 173 seats.

However, regional discontent found its political outlet in the provinces. British Columbia elected a Social Credit government in 1952; Alberta remained firmly in the Social Credit camp; Saskatchewan repeatedly reelected the CCF government first placed in office in 1944; Ontario showed no sign of displacing its Conservative government nor Quebec the Union Nationale led by Premier Duplessis; and in the Maritimes both New Brunswick (1952) and Nova Scotia (1956) had replaced Liberal with Conservative governments. Manitoba and Prince Edward Island did the same in 1958 and 1959.

Equalization Payments. While the Liberals tended to overlook regional inequalities in their determination to increase overall prosperity, they did attempt to remedy some in the new tax rental agreements passed in 1956. The new agreements introduced the principle of equalization payments. These were unconditional grants to the poorer provinces, designed to enable them to provide a moderate level of provincial services without resorting to excessively heavy taxation of citizens who could not afford increased taxes. All provinces but the three wealthiest—Ontario, British Columbia, and Alberta—received increased revenues under the agreement.

Dependence on the United States. The boom brought another widespread criticism of the Liberal government. In large part, the expansion of manufacturing and the development of new natural resources were carried on with American capital. In 1945, for example, there was $7.1 billion of foreign capital invested in Canada, of which 70% was American. By 1957 there was $17.5 billion invested, of which 76% was American. By 1957, Americans owned or controlled 39% of Canadian manufacturing, 57% of the petroleum and natural gas industry, and 46% of the mining and smelting industry. In some industries, such as rubber (79%) and automobiles (89%), American control was almost complete. Moreover, by the mid-1950's, 60% of all Canadian exports went to the United States and 70% of Canadian imports came from the United States. Many Canadians began to suggest that a loss of political independence would follow the growing economic power of the United States in Canada, and the increasing Canadian dependence on American capital, markets, and supplies. This criticism was reinforced in English Canada by the growing fear of cultural assimilation and by a distaste for some aspects of American foreign policy that the government seemed unwilling to censure. Some people regarded the Liberal government as virtual annexationists in disguise.

Pipeline Issue. In 1956 an issue arose that not only seemed to confirm the government's pro-Americanism but also suggested that the cabinet had become arrogant, after being too long in office, contemptuous of both public opinion and Parliament. Led by C. D. Howe, the minister of trade and commerce who had played the key role in the wartime and postwar economic development, the government decided to assist a private company to build a much-needed natural gas pipeline from Alberta to central Canada. Criticism of the proposal to lend $80 million to an American-controlled company was immediate. With the opposition parties ready for a long fight in the House of Commons, Howe speeded the bill's passage by persuading the cabinet to adopt closure in an attempt to choke off debate so that work could begin at once. The outcry in the Commons and in the country was intense.

Diefenbaker Heads the Conservatives. George Drew, leader of the Conservative party since 1948, might not have been able to capitalize on the growing opposition to the Liberals. But Drew resigned in 1956, and the party elected John G. Diefenbaker to succeed him. Diefenbaker was a prairie lawyer, with a passion for the underdog and the crusading manner of a criminal lawyer. A member of the Commons since 1940, he had run for the leadership in 1942 and 1948. Elected in 1956 this evangelical orator with a commanding presence brought to the party a vitality it had lacked since Macdonald.

As the election of 1957 approached, which the Liberals were supremely confident of winning, Diefenbaker was able to integrate the discontent with the St. Laurent government. Not only was he able to secure an appreciative hearing in the prairies and the Atlantic provinces, but he was also able to attract the support of the aged who had just been granted by the Liberals a small pension increase that did little to help them meet rising prices. He declared that his party had "an appointment with destiny to plan and build for a greater Canada . . . one Canada, with equality of opportunity for every citizen and equality for every province . . . ." Before enthusiastic crowds he pictured "the shocking contempt" and the "bludgeoning" to which the "arrogant" Liberals had subjected Parliament. Under his leadership the Conservatives became the party of protest—against big business, the intellectual establishment, and big government. It became not only the party of the little man and the have-not, but of many Canadians who were of neither English nor French extraction and who saw him as the personification of the new multiracial Canada that was emerging.

The Conservatives also appeared as the party that traditionally had been pro-British and anti-American, and much of the anti-Americanism, always latent in Canada, found an outlet in a swing toward Diefenbaker. This swing was more pronounced because many Canadians had felt that the Liberals had let Britain down in the Suez crisis and sided with the United States.

Conservative Landslide. On June 10, 1957, the voters returned 112 Conservatives and 105 Liberals. A new era had begun in Canadian history. After a parliamentary session which saw considerable useful legislation passed, Diefenbaker called a second election. The Liberals, meanwhile, had elected Pearson to succeed St. Laurent as the party leader. The election was a rout. The Conservatives won 208 seats, the largest majority in Canadian history, the Liberals were reduced to a rump of 49 members, and the minor parties were virtually eliminated. Even in Quebec the Conservatives were able to win a majority for the first time since 1887.

The first few years of the Conservative government were remarkably productive, as it worked to fulfill promises made during the campaign. To the prairie farmer it gave cash advances against farm-stored grain, increased acreage payments, and the South Saskatchewan dam. An aggressive sales and credit policy abroad, aided by crop failures in China and other countries, found additional markets for Canadian grain. The Western granaries were soon empty and the West was confirmed in its support of Diefenbaker. A roads-to-resources program helped to open up the Northern frontier. Substantial aid was given to the Atlantic provinces. In 1958 an annual subsidy of $25 million was provided to the four provinces for a 4-year period, and in the following year Newfoundland was given $36.5 million to spend over five years. In 1962 the Atlantic Development Board was created and a fund of $100 million established to aid in the economic development of the region.

To meet the demands of all provinces for more money and for more freedom in levying taxes and determining spending priorities, the Conservatives ended the tax rental agreements in 1962. In a complicated piece of legislation the federal government adopted a new policy whereby the principles of equalization and stabilization were retained, further special grants were made to the Atlantic provinces, the federal government withdrew from a part of the income tax field, and the provinces were able to levy their own personal income taxes to the extent, or to a greater extent, than that vacated by the federal government. The poorer provinces were critical and the wealthier were lukewarm. And while the new agreement provided the provinces with increased freedom and responsibility, it also weakened the federal government's power to use fiscal policy to maintain high levels of income and employment.

The government also provided much-needed increases in pensions for the aged, the disabled, and the veterans. A royal commission was appointed to examine the health of Canadian publications and suggest how to strengthen them against American competition. A measure for which the prime minister took personal responsibility was the Bill of Rights passed in 1960.

Recession. But the Conservative government had the misfortune to take office as the postwar boom was losing its momentum. The economic recovery of Europe reduced the market for Canadian goods, while a recession in the United States caused a temporary reduction in the capital available for investment. Since Canada depended so heavily on external markets and foreign investment, the results were serious. The slowdown accentuated certain other basic weaknesses in the postwar economy, such as its unplanned nature, the overinvestment or gambling in speculative stocks, and the relative high-cost and inefficient operation of considerable Canadian manufacturing. For four years Canada suffered a period of recession and readjustment: technological, seasonal, and structural unemployment joined to bring the number of unemployed to over 500,000 in the worst months of the year and to a percentage higher than in any year since the depression period of the 1930's. The average daily number of shares traded on the Toronto Stock Exchange fell from 6 million in 1956 to 2 million in 1960, and the growth of real income per capita on an annual basis dropped to less than 2% a year. The Diefenbaker government had staggering budget deficits, and it seemed unable to develop monetary and fiscal policies to fight the recession and keep welfare legislation and regional aid to which it was committed.

NICK MORANT, FROM NATIONAL FILM BOARD

UNITED NATIONS CHARTER is signed by Prime Minister Mackenzie King at San Francisco in 1945.

By 1962 the commercial and financial community was beginning to turn away from its traditional friend, the Conservative party. Others felt that the government lacked a consistent and purposeful foreign and defense policy and had tarnished Canada's reputation abroad. Finally, the government seemed unable to find a suitable response to the nationalist movement in Quebec.

Meanwhile, the other parties had recovered from their shattering defeat in 1958. At a Study Conference on National Problems at Kingston, Ontario, in 1960, the Liberals drew on Canadian intellectuals in their search for new policies. The CCF had sought to widen its base of support by cooperating with the newly amalgamated Canadian Labour Congress and liberally minded independents to form the New Democratic party. The founding convention of the NDP was held in Ottawa, July 31–August 4.

The origin of the party, however, was implicit as early as 1956, when the CCF convention at Winnipeg adopted a more moderate platform and the Trades and Labour Congress and the Canadian Congress of Labour merged to form the CLC. The CCF move to the right made it more acceptable to trade unionists and independents. The merger of the TLC and the CCL left little doubt that the traditional CCL support of the CCF would win over the traditional nonpartisanship of the TLC. When Stanley Knowles, the defeated CCF candidate in 1958, was elected vice president of the CLC in 1958, the handwriting was on the wall.

Although many socialists in the CCF were unhappy with the move to the right, and although many trade unionists were less committed than their leaders, the party came into being in 1961 and promptly elected T. C. Douglas as its first leader. With a broader basis of support, a new and dynamic leader, and the promise of trade union funds to fill the party's war chest, the NDP was in a much stronger position to fight the election of 1962 than the old CCF had ever been. The Social Credit party had also been reorganized. In 1961 a convention elected Robert Thompson as its national leader and sought to capitalize on the growing Social Credit strength in Quebec and to take every advantage of the reawakened Quebec nationalism by electing Réal Caouette as associate leader of the party.

Prime Minister Diefenbaker called an election for June 18, 1962. Amid the shadows of recession and unemployment, Diefenbaker campaigned largely on his record but did outline a vague "prosperity blueprint" that included additional development policies, more social welfare, and increased aid to industry. The Liberals concentrated on the economic slowdown, as did the NDP, but they also found time to attack Conservative bungling and mismanagement and to charge that Canada had lost respect abroad. Liberal and NDP charges that the country faced an economic crisis were made more credible when in the midst of the campaign the government, faced with an outflow of gold reserves, was forced to devalue the Canadian dollar to 92½ cents. In Quebec, Réal Caouette appealed to Quebec nationalism, demanding increased provincial autonomy, true bilingualism, and respect for minority rights, but his most effective cry in the depressed areas was "you have nothing to lose, vote Social Credit."

Conservative Reversal. The June 18 results were an astonishing reversal of the 1958 sweep. The Conservatives were virtually destroyed in the cities and returned only 116 members, most of whom were from the West, rural Ontario, and the Maritimes. The Liberals swept the cities and won 100 seats. The NDP returned 19 members and showed increased strength in heavily unionized sections of the country. Most surprising of all was the election of 30 Social Credit members, 26 of them from Quebec.

The next nine months were among the most tortured and confused in Canadian history. Six days after the election, the Prime Minister was forced to announce an austerity program to meet the foreign-exchange crisis that included a billion dollar loan from the International Monetary Fund, the United States, and the United Kingdom; increases in the tariff on a wide range of goods; and reductions in the value of goods Canadian tourists could bring back. Legislation was promised to deal with the crisis, but when Parliament met the legislation failed to materialize.

Defeat in the Commons was inevitable. When it came it was triggered by dissatisfaction with the government's foreign and defense policy. On the whole, while that policy followed the same general path as that of the postwar Liberals it differed in some particulars and generally lacked the sophistication of its predecessors. The much-publicized plan to divert as much as 15% of Canadian trade from the United States to Britain met an embarrassingly sudden end in 1958 when the British replied with a proposal for free trade, and the blunt Canadian opposition to British membership in the Common Market did not improve Anglo-Canadian relations.

In the Commonwealth, Diefenbaker implemented a new Commonwealth scholarship scheme. He also was widely supported in Canada when in 1961 he backed the Afro-Asian nations in condemning the South African policy of apartheid, thus making it inevitable that South Africa would leave the Commonwealth.

In the United Nations the Conservatives took a strong stand against communism and in a more practical sense backed the UN action in the Congo in 1960. Particularly after Howard Green became secretary of state for external affairs in 1959, a touchstone of Canadian policy was the advocacy of disarmament, a policy Canada championed at the ill-fated ten-nation disarmament conference at Geneva in 1960 and repeatedly at the United Nations. Although seldom expressed, there was also in Canadian policy a critical approach toward the United States.

Defense Crisis. By 1962 the unresolved tensions between the policy of disarmament, championed by Green, the Canadian commitments to NORAD and NATO that seemed to call for arming Canadian weapons with nuclear warheads (the view of at least Douglas S. Harkness, the minister of national defense), and the alliance with a nation that in the minds of many Conservatives was somehow suspect, had reached the breaking point.

The difficult relations between Diefenbaker and President Kennedy did not make a solution easier. The crisis began on October 22 when Kennedy ordered the quarantine of Cuba and placed the Strategic Air Command on full alert, and on the next day ordered the naval blockade of Cuba. Not until October 24, after many hurried cabinet meetings, did Canada place the NORAD component on a similar alert despite the terms of the 1958 agreement. This crisis served to focus more sharply the debate over Canada's NATO and NORAD commitments, and particularly the question of nuclear warheads. With the cabinet split Diefenbaker sought to postpone a decision and suggest that there was no commitment to accept nuclear weapons. At an Ottawa press conference on January 3, Gen.

GOVERNORS GENERAL

Viscount Monck	1867–1868
Baron Lisgar	1868–1872
Earl of Dufferin	1872–1878
Marquess of Lorne	1878–1883
Marquess of Lansdowne	1883–1888
Baron Stanley of Preston	1888–1893
Earl of Aberdeen	1893–1898
Earl of Minto	1898–1904
Earl Grey	1904–1911
Duke of Connaught	1911–1916
Duke of Devonshire	1916–1921
Baron Byng of Vimy	1921–1926
Viscount Willingdon	1926–1931
Earl of Bessborough	1931–1935
Baron Tweedsmuir (John Buchan)	1935–1940
Earl of Athlone	1940–1946
Viscount Alexander of Tunis	1946–1952
The Rt. Hon. Vincent Massey	1952–1959
Gen. Georges P. Vanier	1959–1967
The Rt. Hon. Roland Michener	1967–

Lauris Norstad, the retired NATO supreme commander, categorically affirmed that Canada was committed to the use of nuclear weapons on its Starfighter squadrons in Europe. On January 12, Pearson reversed Liberal policy and urged that Canada honor its commitments. On January 29 the United States issued an unusual release sharply challenging Prime Minister Diefenbaker's statement about nuclear weapons. Finally, on February 4, Harkness, critical of the Prime Minister's indecisiveness, resigned.

The split on defense policy tumbled the already tottering Conservative government. On February 5, after some Conservatives had vainly tried to persuade the Prime Minister to resign, the government was defeated on a general motion of nonconfidence. Another election was called for April 5. Before the campaign began, however, members of the Diefenbaker cabinet made another attempt to persuade the Prime Minister to resign, feeling that the party was doomed if it went to the people under his leadership. Diefenbaker defeated the rebels in his party, but two members of the cabinet, George H. Hees and Pierre Sévigny, resigned a few days days later.

Pearson's Victory. The campaign was bitter and intense. For the Conservatives it was a personal campaign by the Prime Minister who, lashing out at his enemies—the Liberals, the Tory "traitors," and the Americans—singlehandedly kept his party in the running. The Liberals attacked the government's handling of the economic crisis and its indecision on nuclear arms, and called for stable government. The country returned 129 Liberals, 95 Conservatives, 24 Social Credit members, and 17 New Democrats.

Pearson had promised 60 Days of Decision with his new cabinet team that was described as a "brains trust." But decision turned to indecision as the House of Commons continued to be the forum of petty squabbling. Indecision became disaster when the minister of finance, Walter L. Gordon, was less than open about his use of three outside consultants in drawing up the June budget. To the furor inside the House over the unusual procedure was added a tempest outside as the financial community forced him to withdraw a hastily conceived measure to use taxation as a means to cut down American ownership of Canadian industry. Other measures to stimulate economic growth, however, were more readily received. In 1964 the budget was much more straightforward, as the pace of economic activity quickened to reach its highest point in seven years. With good markets abroad and a strong domestic demand, the buoyant economic conditions continued until mid-1966. Increasing prices then indicated that some sectors of the economy had reached their capacity, and by 1967 Canada faced tight money and inflationary dangers.

Repairing Foreign Relations. Between 1963 and 1965 the Liberal government advanced some new policies and passed some useful legislation. In foreign affairs Pearson quickly sought to repair the breaches in Anglo-Canadian and Canadian-American relations. Soon after his election he visited London and Washington. Reversing their previous position, the Liberals came to an agreement with British Columbia and the United States on the question of power exports, water diversion, and financing and made possible the ratification of the Columbia River Treaty. While Pearson accepted nuclear warheads, his government promised to reappraise the Canadian defense policy. Seven thousand men were sent to Cyprus in 1964, and the government convened a 23-nation conference in Ottawa to discuss the techniques involved in UN intervention and Pearson's proposal for the creation of a permanent standby force.

Concern on Vietnam. Although the Prime Minister insisted in 1965 that good Canadian-American relations were "the very keystone of Canada's foreign policy," he very quickly expressed concern about U. S. bombing in Vietnam. Under pressure from wide sections of Canadian opinion to take a stronger line, Pearson suggested at Temple University in Philadelphia, Pa., on April 2 that negotiations in Vietnam might be facilitated if the United States suspended its air strikes, and he followed his speech with a frank discussion with President Johnson the following day at Camp David, Md. Later, he firmly insisted on the Canadian right to criticize U. S. policies, although he continued to resist pressure from a large and growing body of the public to demand an end to the war in Vietnam and to prevent Canadian industries from providing war materials to the United States. The government also maintained the policy of nonrecognition of Communist China, but while in 1966 it abstained on a UN motion to seat Communist China it called for the membership of both Chinese governments, with Peking sitting on the Security Council.

The Rivard Affair. At home the Pearson government was in almost constant difficulties. An ill-fated attempt to prevent extradition to the United States of Lucien Rivard, accused of narcotics smuggling, revealed the possibilities of corruption in the Liberal party. Although the report of the Dorion Inquiry in June 1965 found Guy Favreau, the minister of justice, innocent of any misdeed it questioned the wisdom of his actions. Favreau immediately resigned as minister of justice.

Domestic Progress. In the domestic field, however, the government made a significant advance in 1964, when it passed a bill for the impartial and more rational redistribution of seats in the Commons, and in 1965, when it implemented reforms in the internal procedure and organization of the House. More controversial was a 1965 act to protect Canadian magazines and newspapers from American competition by making

PRIME MINISTERS

Sir John A. Macdonald	Conservative	1867–1873
Alexander Mackenzie	Liberal	1873–1878
Sir John A. Macdonald	Conservative	1878–1891
Sir John Abbott	Conservative	1891–1892
Sir John Thompson	Conservative	1892–1894
Sir Mackenzie Bowell	Conservative	1894–1896
Sir Charles Tupper	Conservative	1896
Sir Wilfrid Laurier	Liberal	1896–1911
Sir Robert Borden	Conservative (Unionist after 1917)	1911–1920
Arthur Meighen	Unionist	1920–1921
William Lyon Mackenzie King	Liberal	1921–1926
Arthur Meighen	Conservative	1926
William Lyon Mackenzie King	Liberal	1926–1930
Richard Bedford Bennett	Conservative	1930–1935
William Lyon Mackenzie King	Liberal	1935–1948
Louis St. Laurent	Liberal	1948–1957
John G. Diefenbaker	Progressive Conservative	1957–1963
Lester B. Pearson	Liberal	1963–1968
Pierre Elliott Trudeau	Liberal	1968–

advertising in American publications, with the exception of *Time* and *Reader's Digest*, nondeductible. (These magazines have long printed Canadian editions.) Prodded by its left wing, it also proposed new pension and medicare legislation, as well as a wide range of measures in the 1965 speech from the throne for a full-scale "war on poverty." The welfare and poverty legislation, however, immediately involved the government in difficult negotiations with the various provinces.

Nationalism in Quebec. The most important single problem facing the Pearson government and the country by the mid-1960's was that posed by Quebec nationalism and its effect on federal-provincial relations. By the late 1950's criticism of the reactionary social and economic policy and the negative and defensive nationalism of the Duplessis government was mounting in the province of Quebec. Sociologists argued that the old values were hopelessly outdated in a society that was urban and industrial. Educators demanded modernization and an end to church control. Radical nationalists denounced the alien capitalists who, in league with the politicians, allegedly controlled the economy; the federal government, which intruded on the autonomy of Quebec and denied it the fiscal resources to finance the necessary social revolution; and the federal politicians, who seemed insensitive to the unique position of French Canada and its aspirations for a bilingual and bicultural nation. This combination of radicalism and nationalism was held in check during its formative years by the political maneuvering of Maurice Duplessis. But after his death and that of his liberally minded successor, Paul Sauvé, one hundred days later, its success was inevitable.

Emergence of Lesage. In 1960 the Quebec Liberals under Jean Lesage won the provincial election, and a new era in Canadian history had begun. The new government cleared out corruption, introduced a wide variety of social welfare measures, and moved toward secularizing the educational system. Led by René Lévesque, minister of natural resources, it decided in 1962 to nationalize the hydroelectric companies as a first step toward regaining control of the economy and took the issue to the people. Campaigning on the slogan "maître chez nous" the government was easily returned to office.

Terrorism Erupts. By this time it was clear that the forces released in Quebec demanded not only internal reform, but revolutionary changes in the structure of the country. Underlying the new nationalism was the belief that Quebec was not a province like the others, but a homeland of a people, a nation that like other nations had its own history, culture, resources, and institutions. To a small minority the logic of complete sovereignty was irresistible. In 1963 the Rassemblement pour l'indépendance nationale was launched as a political party; Marcel Chaput, a separatist, fasted to secure $100,000 for the cause; and before the year was out young terrorists of the Fédération pour la libération du Québec caused a general reign of terror in Montreal, bombing federal buildings (killing one man) and placing bombs in mailboxes in English-speaking areas.

Quest for Special Status. The majority, while denouncing the status quo, sought more moderate goals. Some advocated the status of an associate state for Quebec in a new confederation of two equal partners with the absolute minimum legislative, economic and diplomatic power vested in the central government. The Union Nationale, Le Ralliement des Créditistes, and the Parti Socialiste du Québec adopted some version of the associate-state concept.

Others demanded a vague "special status" for Quebec in a radically altered federal system. By the mid-1960's, Premier Lesage had worked toward a definition of special status: the right to contract out of shared-cost programs; constitutional amendments to extend provincial powers; a greater share of (and, ideally, all) direct taxes; a voice in the formulation of financial and commercial policy; the right to conduct foreign relations on matters within provincial jurisdiction; and the transformation of Canada into a bilingual and bicultural country. The crux of the matter, he said in 1965, was whether Canada was to be vertically or horizontally structured: "Is it the political division of Canada into ten provinces, or is it the presence across the same vast territory of the two peoples who founded this country? Quebec feels that the second factor is the one that really counts."

Federal Concessions. The Pearson government moved at once to find some accommodation with Quebec. In 1963 it appointed a Royal Commission on Bilingualism and Biculturalism; the first volume of its final report, recommending countrywide equality between English and French language and culture did not appear until late 1967. Sharp opposition to legislation to create a Canadian flag, passed in 1964, did little to improve English-French relations. After acrimonious debate, the government bowed to Quebec on the pension plan, allowing the province to control its own reserves, and backed away from further shared-cost programs that would affect the province. In 1965 any province was permitted to "opt out" of many existing shared-cost programs or not enter new ones and receive a financial equivalent instead. Moreover, the pro-

EXPO 67, created by all Canadians, displayed their pride in the first century of Confederation. From all over the world, thousands of visitors went to Montreal.

vincial share on the return from direct taxes was increased and equalization payments increased. A complete review of the field of federal-provincial relations was promised upon the report of a Royal Commission on Taxation appointed in 1962 and the Tax Structure Committee appointed in 1964.

The Liberals also secured provincial agreement to a formula for constitutional amendment in October 1964. Originally developed by the Conservative minister of justice, Davie Fulton, and altered slightly by Favreau, the Fulton-Favreau formula provided for complete entrenchment of certain clauses relating to provincial and minority rights, amendment of most other sections with the agreement of two thirds of the provinces representing half the population, and the right of any four provinces or the federal government to delegate powers allocated to it by the constitution. Most of the premiers were restrained in their enthusiasm, and some shared the view of the opposition parties that it represented a serious weakening of federal power and bound the country in a straightjacket. Nevertheless they secured the consent of their legislatures. Premier Lesage hailed it as "an historic day," only to find that his enthusiasm was not shared in Quebec. By 1965, Premier Lesage was backing away from the formula, and by 1966 he admitted that it was dead.

"Equality or Independence." Concern over the Fulton-Favreau formula was not the most serious difficulty Premier Lesage faced. The rapid pace of social reform, which increased indebtedness and taxes, had alienated conservative and rural Quebec. At the same time radicals within his party demanded an acceleration of the reform movement and nationalists demanded a stronger line against Ottawa. A reinvigorated Union Nationale, led by Daniel Johnson, championed the cause of the dissaffected Conservatives and hoped to secure the support of the ultranationalists by demanding "equality or independence" and taking a "not necessarily separation, but separation if necessary" position. When Premier Lesage called an election for June 5, 1966, the combination of forces was too strong, and although the Union Nationale secured only 40% of the vote (compared with the Liberals' 47) they won 56 seats to the Liberals' 50. Separatists received the support of 8.6% of the population. By 1967, Premier Johnson was attempting to persuade investors that separatism was improbable, while others like René Lévesque moved beyond special status or associate state to a bold advocacy of secession.

A Time of Uncertainty. The Pearson government had tried to win a parliamentary majority in an election on Nov. 8, 1965. Diefenbaker vigorously denounced the Rivard affair, alleged republicanism in the Liberal party, the fall in the price of wheat, and the Liberal policy of "tearing the nation asunder." The people would not give their full confidence to any party. The Liberals remained a minority government with 131 seats.

Although Diefenbaker had again saved the party, the opposition to his leadership did not diminish. At a leadership convention in September 1967, Robert Stanfield, longtime premier of Nova Scotia, was elected to replace him.

Six months later, Pearson resigned, and a party convention in April 1968 elected Pierre Elliott Trudeau (q.v.) as leader. Articulate, completely bicultural, a staunch supporter of provincial rights, yet an opponent of extreme French Canadian nationalism, Trudeau presented a youthful image that captivated the "new" generation. He called a national election for June 25, in which the Liberals won 155 seats—a clear majority. The Progressive Conservatives were reduced from 94 seats to 72.

Yet after the enthusiasms of its 100th birthday, the nation, sharply divided culturally and regionally, facing the tensions posed by a booming if precarious economy, and with two new national leaders, looked warily to the future.

JOHN T. SAYWELL
York University, Toronto

Bibliography

Careless, J. M. S., and Brown, R. C., eds., *The Canadians* (Toronto 1967).
Dawson, R. MacGregor, *The Government of Canada*, 4th ed. rev. by Norman Ward (Toronto 1963).
Eayrs, James, *The Art of the Possible: Government and Foreign Policy in Canada* (Toronto 1961).
Eayrs, James, *In Defence of Canada* (Toronto 1965).
Saywell, John T., ed., *The Canadian Annual Review* (Toronto, annually since 1960).
Saywell, John T., and Ricker, John C., *How Are We Governed?* (Toronto 1967).

COURTESY OF WOLCOTT, CARLSON AND COMPANY

CANADA BALSAM, bôl′səm, also known as *Canada turpentine,* is a pale-yellow viscous liquid with a pinelike odor. It is an oleoresin obtained from the balsam fir *Abies balsamea.* Canada balsam is insoluble in water but is soluble in benzene, chloroform, and ether. The liquid, which dries slowly to form a transparent varnish, is used in the manufacture of fine lacquers. Canada balsam is also used for cementing lenses together, for mounting objects for microscopy, and as a flavoring agent.

CANADA COMPANY, a colonizing company formed in 1824 through the initiative of the Scottish novelist John Galt. Galt suggested that by selling crown lands to a colonizing company, Upper Canada (Ontario) could raise enough funds to compensate persons who had suffered losses during the War of 1812. The Canada Company was chartered on Aug. 19, 1826, and it purchased nearly 2.5 million acres (about 1 million hectares) of land, almost half of it in the "Huron Tract" in southwestern Ontario. Galt became secretary of the company, and superintendent in 1827. He carried out a program of townsite development (founding Guelph and Goderich) and built roads, schools, and mills. By 1834 the company had settled some 2,500 people on the Huron Tract. It met all its charter obligations by the contract deadline of 1843 and continued in operation until the 1950's.

John S. Moir, *University of Toronto*

CANADA GOOSE, one of the commonest wild geese in the North American region. Its range extends from eastern Greenland west to the Komandorskie (Commander) and Kuril islands in Asia and from the Arctic south to Mexico.

The Canada goose has a long, black neck and head with large, white cheek patches. Its body is brown with black legs and tail. Eastern forms are from 35 to 43 inches (87–107 cm) long and weigh from 7 to 14 pounds (3–6.3 kg). Western forms of the Canada goose are smaller and darker.

Because of its wide range, the Canada goose is found in a variety of habitats, from ocean shores and wooded regions to semiarid land in the interior. It feeds either by grazing or by sounding for aquatic vegetation in streams and ponds. It mates for life and nests on the banks of streams, islands, or open tundra. Four to 10 white eggs are laid and incubation is from 25 to 30 days.

Canada geese are swift fliers and migrate in formations. Their habit of calling constantly during flight has earned them the name *honker.*

The Canada goose (*Branta canadensis*) is a member of the family Anatidae in the order Anseriformes. There are 12 subspecies.

Joseph Bell, *New York Zoological Society*

CANADA JAY, a jay found from the northern portions of North America south to the northern United States. It is also called the *gray jay,* and it has several popular names including *camp robber, whisky jack,* and *meat bird.*

The Canada jay is from 10 to 13 inches (25–33 cm) long. Its fluffy plumage is mostly gray with a white forehead and black nape. The young are almost uniformly dusky until early fall.

The Canada jay is a tame bird, well known to hunters, trappers, and campers for its companionableness—and also for stealing food from their camps. However, during its nesting season in March and April it becomes secretive and quiet. It lays 3 to 5 grayish eggs with brown and buff spots. After the young leave the nest, they travel in noisy family groups. Canada jays rarely migrate.

The Canada jay (*Perisoreus canadensis*) belongs to the family Corvidae in the order Passeriformes.

Sally H. Spofford, *Cornell University*

CANADA THISTLE is a common flowering weed of the composite family. The plant was misnamed for its supposed place of origin; it is native to Europe. Canada thistle, *Circium arvense,* is widespread in the United States and Canada. It is found along roadsides and in waste places and has become a noxious pest difficult to eradicate from cultivated fields.

Canada thistle grows from 1 to 5 feet (0.3 to 1.5 meters) high. The small curling leaves are covered with prickles. The flowers, which bloom throughout the summer and into autumn, are pink to lilac (rarely white) and crowded in dense heads. Several heads are present simultaneously on the plants.

Joan E. Rahn, *Lake Forest College, Ill.*

I. DONALD BOWDEN

THE CANADA GOOSE, which is distinguished by its long black neck and white cheek pouches, gets some of its food by grazing the land.

CANADIAN, kə-nā′dē-ən, in geology, the oldest series of rocks of the Ordovician system in North America. Laid down in the Canadian epoch about 500 million years ago, the rocks succeed the Croixan series of the Upper Cambrian and underlie the Chazyan series. The typical sections of the Canadian series are found along Lake Champlain in southeastern Quebec and in Vermont. Their 2,000 feet (600 meters) of limestone grade westward into the dolomitic Beekmantown group of northeastern New York. The Canadian Shield and its margins remained above the sea as a low land during the Canadian epoch.

Canadian rocks have been correlated by fossils of brachiopods and cephalopods. Similar successions of fossils are found in the Appalachian Mountains, Missouri, and Oklahoma. Progressively changing trilobite forms define zones among Canadian rocks in the west, particularly in Utah. Shales of Canadian age contain graptolites (primitive hemichordates) also found in the Arenigian series in Europe. Rocks of the Arenigian epoch therefore are generally correlated with the Canadian in North America. See also ORDOVICIAN PERIOD.

MARSHALL KAY, *Columbia University*

CANADIAN EDUCATION ASSOCIATION, a voluntary union of autonomous educational authorities concerned with furthering the interests of public education in Canada. Its directors include the deputy ministers of education of the 10 provinces, superintendents of major urban school systems, and representatives of teacher-training institutions. Other national education associations with specialized interests are represented on its board of directors.

Since Canada has no federal office of education, the CEA acts as a liaison between the government and the provinces, providing data and doing special studies on particular aspects of public education. It also serves as a clearinghouse for information on all phases of public education. Through its standing committee of provincial ministers of education (inaugurated in 1960), CEA promotes activities beneficial to school systems, and it arranges, in cooperation with the provinces, for interprovincial and international teacher exchanges and for representation at international conferences abroad.

Founded in 1891 as the Dominion Education Association, the CEA is financed chiefly by grants from the 10 provincial education departments and some 50 urban school systems. Since 1945 it has maintained an office and a permanent secretariat in Toronto. The association holds an annual conference. It also publishes a monthly *News Letter* in both French and English and issues a quarterly, *Canadian Education and Research Digest.*

F. K. STEWART, *Canadian Education Association*

CANADIAN FEDERATION OF AGRICULTURE, a nonpolitical organization of provincial farm bodies and other agricultural groups in Canada. Its purpose is to unify and coordinate the efforts of farmers' organizations of all types to serve the economic and social interests of farmers throughout Canada. Founded in 1935 as the Canadian Chamber of Agriculture, it adopted its present name in 1940. The federation, representing between 350,000 and 400,000 farmers, functions essentially by voluntary cooperation of its autonomous parts.

The membership of the CFA consists of provincial federations of agriculture in the four Western provinces, in Ontario, and in the three Maritime provinces; the Coopérative Fédérée de Québec, the Union Catholique des Cultivateurs, and the Quebec Farmers Association; and the Dairy Farmers of Canada, the Canadian Horticultural Council, and the United Grain Growers Limited. The provincial federations vary in structure according to the nature and historical development of farmers' organizations in each province. Members of provincial federations include general farm organizations and agricultural societies, farmers' cooperatives, commodity associations of producers, and women's guilds.

The CFA is a founding member of the International Federation of Agricultural Producers, representing the farmers of more than 32 countries. The national office of the CFA is in Ottawa.

J. M. BENTLEY
Canadian Federation of Agriculture

CANADIAN FOOTBALL. See FOOTBALL—*Canadian Football.*

CANADIAN LABOUR CONGRESS, the major central labor body in Canada. It has a membership of 1.5 million, about three fourths of the total union membership of the country. Affiliations of the CLC in the late 1960's included 14 national unions, 92 international unions, 5 provincial organizations, 170 directly chartered unions, 10 provincial federations of labor, and 114 local labor councils. Its national headquarters is in Ottawa.

The CLC came into being in 1956 as a result of a merger between the Trades and Labour Congress of Canada and the Canadian Congress of Labour. It acts as the coordinating body for its affiliates on matters of mutual interest and is the Canadian counterpart of the AFL-CIO in the United States.

The CLC is administered by four full-time officers—president, secretary-treasurer, and two executive vice presidents—and by an executive committee and executive council, representing unions and geographic areas. All officers are elected at biennial conventions. These conventions, attended by 1,800 rank-and-file delegates, also determine the CLC's policy objectives.

The CLC represents a major section of the Canadian labor movement in the international field through its active participation in the International Confederation of Free Trade Unions. Domestically, it conducts an active educational program ranging from community weekend institutes to a labor college held annually at Montreal in cooperation with McGill University and the University of Montreal. Other CLC departments deal with research, political education, legislation, government employees, liaison with provincial federations and local labor councils, organization, and public relations.

Politically, the CLC endorses the New Democratic party and urges its unions to give active support to the NDP. There is, however, no formal relationship between the NDP and the CLC.

Each year the CLC meets with the prime minister and his cabinet members to submit a memorandum expressing CLC views on a variety of matters. These range from international affairs to social legislation and usually place emphasis on current economic conditions.

JOHN L. FRYER
Director of Research, Canadian Labour Congress

CANADIAN LEGION, Royal, a patriotic nonpolitical, and nonmilitary Canadian organization, open to all honorably discharged men and women who have served in any of Her Majesty's forces. It operates under a Dominion charter granted in 1926. The Legion serves the needs of those whose lives were affected by war and perpetuates the memory and deeds of the fallen.

The Legion also emphasizes community and national services. It conducts an annual Poppy Day campaign and disburses nearly $300,000 yearly for welfare work on behalf of veterans and their families. It encourages physical fitness through athletic training programs, sponsors scout troops, awards scholarships, and provides recreational facilities. During World War II it sponsored the Canadian Legion War Services and the Canadian Legion Educational Services to provide educational, recreational, and personal services to members of the armed forces.

The Great War Veterans' Association, formed after World War I, was merged into the Canadian Legion in 1925. The new organization was affiliated with the British Legion and similar organizations in other Commonwealth countries within the British Empire Service League, now the British Commonwealth Ex-Services League. The word "Royal" was added to the Legion's name in 1960. By the late 1960's the 284,000 members were organized in 2,000 branches in Canada and 200 posts in the United States, the whole under a Dominion command with headquarters in Ottawa. Most local branches own halls or meeting places; many own club premises. In rural areas the legion hall is often the main community center.

As the veterans' spokesman in Canada, the Legion deals directly with the federal department of veterans affairs or the prime minister in seeking changes in legislation affecting disability pension rates, war allowances, and other matters. The official publication is *The Legionary*.

LORNE MANCHESTER
Associate Editor of "The Legionary"

CANADIAN LIBRARY ASSOCIATION—ASSOCIATION CANADIENNE DES BIBLIOTHÈQUES, a private corporation concerned with the welfare of librarians and with standards of library service in Canada. It was founded on June 14, 1946, at a national conference called by the Canadian Library Council. Its membership is open to any person or institution interested in libraries or librarianship in Canada. In the mid-1960's there were more than 3,000 members in Canada and in 20 other countries.

Major Programs. The founding conference of the CLA-ACB adopted a vigorous program. From the beginning the CLA-ACB became directly involved in the professional welfare of librarians, including education in librarianship, salary standards, and a code of ethics, and in standards for library service. It led the promotional campaign for a national library and was instrumental in the establishment by the government of the National Library Advisory Committee. It also inspired the government to set up the Canadian Bibliographic Centre, a clearinghouse of bibliographic information in Canada.

The CLA-ACB organizes annual conferences and institutes for the exchange of information and ideas concerning books and libraries and for the consideration of action on matters of importance to members. A highlight of each national conference is the presentation of an award known as the Book of the Year Medal, an honor given to encourage the writing of children's books.

Projects and Publications. The CLA-ACB sponsors Young Canada's Book Week, a project of the Canadian Association of Children's Librarians. This event, observed annually since 1949, endeavors to interest Canadians in the best reading for youth. The association also sponsored the Canadian Library Research and Development Council, an independent corporation, and Canadian Library Week, a project of the Canadian Library Week Council, another independent corporation.

One of the most important of the projects undertaken by the association was the microfilming of Canadian newspapers of historic significance and Canadian documents of research value. This effort was climaxed by the filming of all important newspapers current at the time of confederation (1867) and, in cooperation with the Bibliographic Centre, of all documents listed in Marie Tremaine's *The Bibliography of Canadian Imprints, 1751–1800* (1952).

Publications played a vital role in the work of the CLA-ACB from its inception. The most important publication is the *Canadian Periodical Index*, covering the contents of 86 periodicals as well as documentary films. This reference work is offered as both a monthly and an annual service. A publication entitled *Canadian Authors, Artists, and Musicians* provides biographies of outstanding Canadians. *Canadian Library*, published bimonthly, is the official bulletin, and *Feliciter* is the newsletter. Other publications include the *Canadian Library Directory, Canadian Public Library Laws*, and occasional professional papers and miscellaneous items.

History and Organization. Proposals for a national library association were first heard among Canadian librarians attending the meeting of the American Library Association held in Montreal in 1900. The issue was revived at the ALA meeting in Toronto in 1927, but the decision to organize a body that would prepare the way for the formation of a national association was not made until the ALA meeting in Montreal in 1934. From this plan the Canadian Library Council evolved in 1941, its objective being to promote and coordinate the efforts of all groups working for library welfare until a national organization could be formed. Under the aegis of this body, the Canadian Library Association was established in 1946 as a private corporation.

The chief officer of CLA-ACB is the president, who is elected and holds office for one year. A board of directors and a policy-making body (council) represent membership at large and particular interests as expressed through ten organized sections. More than 20 special committees advise the executive and report on numerous matters having to do with libraries.

The general program is financed from membership fees, grants in aid from provincial governments and library associations, and grants given for specific purposes. Projects and publications receive some support from special grants. Scholarships are provided out of gifts and from money raised for that purpose. While much of the formal program is carried on through the sections and committees, all activities are coordinated through the headquarters office in Ottawa.

JOHN H. ARCHER, *Director*
McGill Libraries, McGill University

CANADIAN MILITARY COLLEGES, comprising the Royal Military College of Canada (Kingston, Ontario), Royal Roads (Victoria, British Columbia), and Collège Militaire de Saint-Jean (St.-Jean, Quebec). They constitute a military university for young men and are under the administration of the department of national defense.

University status was achieved in 1959 when the Ontario legislature enacted a provision enabling the Royal Military College to grant degrees. Bachelor's degrees are offered in arts, science, and engineering to an average of about 1,100 students yearly.

For the final two years of study, all degree candidates attend the Royal Military College of Canada, Kingston.

The Royal Military College is served by the Massey Library and the Fort Frederick museum, both of which have valuable collections of military materials.

R. E. JONES
The Royal Military College of Canada

CANADIAN NATIONAL RAILWAYS, North America's longest railway system, extending from St. John's, Newfoundland, westward to Prince Rupert and Vancouver, British Columbia. It has more than 24,000 miles (about 39,000 km) of main track. Canadian National's publicly owned lines serve all 10 of Canada's provinces and 11 states in the United States. The Canadian National's headquarters are at Montreal, Quebec.

The system's earliest ancestor road was the Champlain and St. Lawrence, which started operations in 1856 between Montreal and New York. The present unified system came into being on Jan. 1, 1923, incorporating five separate railways: the government-built Intercolonial and National Transcontinental and the privately owned Canadian Northern, Grand Trunk, and Grand Trunk Pacific. Although government owned, the Canadian National is operated as a competitive business enterprise with minimal government participation.

From 1942 to 1966, gross revenues rose from $380 million to $998 million, but during that 25-year period the system earned profits only eight times. In the late 1960's, Canadian National had assets of about $4 billion and a fleet of 2,200 locomotives, more than 100,000 freight cars, and over 2,500 passenger cars. Freight accounted for over 90% of the system's revenues. But the Canadian National continued to be best known to the public for such premier passenger trains as the *Supercontinental,* running between Montreal and Vancouver; the *Panorama,* between Toronto and Vancouver; and the *Ocean Limited,* between Montreal and Halifax. The system has introduced Rapido trains between Montreal and Quebec and Montreal and Toronto, and it became the first railroad to order TurboTrains designed along aerodynamic lines.

LUTHER MILLER, *"Railway Age"*

CANADIAN PACIFIC RAILWAY COMPANY, a privately owned company with more than 16,000 miles (about 26,000 km) of main track and assets of over $2.2 billion, including a controlling interest in the Soo Line in the United States. The company also has substantial airline, steamship, hotel, and telecommunications interests. Some 56.8% of Canadian Pacific's voting rights is held by Canadian interests, 20.9% in Britain and other Commonwealth countries, and 15.6% in the United States. Its headquarters are in Montreal.

Canadian Pacific's lines extend from Halifax, Nova Scotia, to Vancouver, British Columbia. The system grew out of an 1871 agreement between the dominion government and the province of British Columbia, calling for the development of a transcontinental railway. Construction was started by the government, but the project ran into difficulties, and a private syndicate took over. The main line from Montreal to the Pacific was completed on Nov. 7, 1885.

Unlike its principal competitor, the publicly owned Canadian National Railways, the Canadian Pacific was a profitable carrier in the late 1960's. Passenger revenues were declining, reflecting the discontinuance of a number of passenger trains, and only 5% of the railroad's revenues came from passenger operations. It was investing around $100 million a year in capital improvements. Its rolling stock fleet included more than 1,000 locomotives, 80,000 freight cars, and about 1,000 passenger cars.

LUTHER MILLER, *"Railway Age"*

CANADIAN RIVER, in the southwestern United States, about 900 miles (1,450 km) long. It is sometimes called the *South Canadian River.* It rises in the Sangre de Cristo Mountains in northern New Mexico and flows generally eastward into Texas and central Oklahoma to the Arkansas River. Near the end of its course it receives the North Canadian River. Dams have created the Conchas Reservoir, in New Mexico, for irrigation and flood control, and the Eufaula Reservoir in Oklahoma, for hydroelectric power.

CANADIAN SHIELD, in geology, the part of the continental mass of North America that has remained relatively stable since Precambrian times, more than 600 million years ago. The Canadian Shield has an area of nearly 2 million square miles (5 million sq km). It is centered around Hudson Bay and includes most of Canada, Greenland, and Baffin Island; extensions enter Minnesota, Wisconsin, and northern New York. See also CANADA—4. *Physiography*.

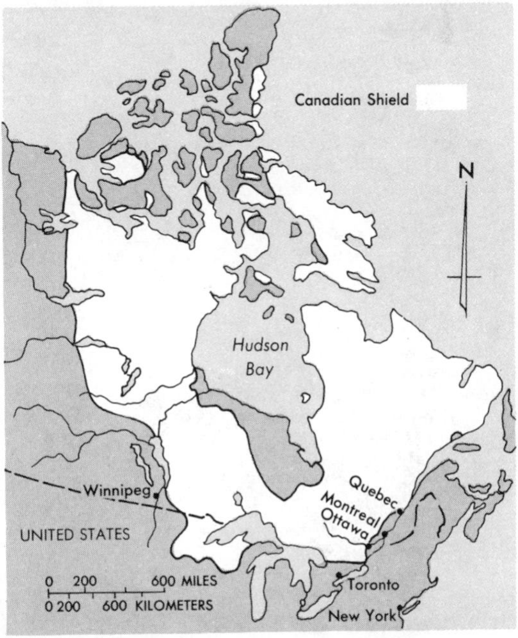

CANADIAN WRITERS FOUNDATION, INC., a benevolent trust operated on a voluntary basis for the benefit of needy Canadian writers who have made a worthy contribution to the nation's literary heritage. Nonsectarian and nonpolitical, the foundation serves writers who reside and produce in Canada and who write in either French or English.

The CWF was founded in 1931, largely through the efforts of Oscar Pelham Edgar, author, editor, and literary critic. It obtained a Dominion charter in 1945. The foundation is financed by an annual grant of $10,000 from the Canada Council and by donations from individuals and corporations. Every contributor of $5 or more becomes a member of the organization and may vote at the annual meeting in February.

Two executive officers—the treasurer and public relations officer and the executive secretary—manage the CWF. The board of directors is composed of 27 distinguished citizens who meet regularly to consider applications for financial assistance and to authorize payments to beneficiaries. The official trustee is the National Trust Company. Headquarters is in Ottawa.

THERESA E. THOMSON
Canadian Writers Foundation, Inc.

CANAIGRE, kə-nī'grē, also called *wild rhubarb*, a perennial herb native to the United States from Oklahoma to California. Canaigre (*Rumex hymenosepalus*), a member of the buckwheat family (Polygonaceae), grows to 3 feet (1 meter) high and bears narrow, crinkled leaves up to 1 foot (30 cm) in length. The roots are thick and fleshy and usually spindle-shaped. The flowers are produced in large panicled clusters. The winged seed pods, known as "valves," are large and showy and turn an attractive rose color.

R. C. ALLEN
Kingwood Center, Mansfield, Ohio

CANAL ZONE. See PANAMA CANAL–2. *Canal Zone.*

CANALETTO, kä-nä-lāt'ō (1697–1768), Italian painter, was one of the most important of the group of painters who, in the 18th century, restored Venetian painting to the greatness it had enjoyed during the 16th century. Like his contemporaries Giovanni Battista Tiepolo and Giovanni Piazzetta, Canaletto returned to the perennial strengths of Venetian painting—light and color. But unlike his major contemporaries, who generally continued to paint traditional figural compositions, Canaletto turned to a subject relatively new and rare in Italian painting, the city view, or *veduta*. He shares this distinction only with his fellow Venetian, Francesco Guardi.

Life. Canaletto was born Giovanni Antonio Canal in Venice on Oct. 28, 1697. His father, Bernardo Canal, who was a designer of elaborate architectural stage settings, gave Giovanni his first instruction in painting and perspective.

After a brief residence in Rome in 1719–1720, Canaletto returned to Venice, where by 1725 he had begun his career as a specialist in views. By 1730 he had established a connection with Joseph Smith, an Englishman, who after 1744 was British consul in Venice. For more than three decades Smith acted as Canaletto's patron, dealer, and adviser.

There is some evidence to suggest that Canaletto made a second trip to Rome in the early 1740's; however, this has not been definitely established.

Canaletto traveled to London in 1746 and lived there (except for eight months in Venice in 1750–1751) until 1756, when he returned to Venice. He was elected to the Venetian Academy of Painting and Sculpture in 1763. Canaletto's last known dated work, a drawing of the interior of St. Mark's (1766), bears a notation that it was done without the aid of glasses.

CANALETTO painted many versions of the Bacino di San Marco in Venice.

MUSEUM OF FINE ARTS, BOSTON (SETH K. SWEETER RESIDUARY FUND; CHARLES EDWARD FRENCH FUND; CASTLE HOWARD COLLECTION; ABBOTT LAWRENCE FUND)

Canaletto died in Venice on April 19, 1768.

Work. Canaletto's most characteristic works, topographical views, developed from the Venetian tradition of commissioning paintings to record important religious and civil ceremonies. These usually took place in the most important and impressive areas of the city, and as the tradition was expanded to include popular festivals and subjects of anecdotal interest, the setting assumed greater importance. The most important single influence on Canaletto's early development was Luca Carlevaris, who painted the first topographical views of Venice. Canaletto probably also studied the Venetian views of the Dutch painter Gaspar van Wittel. Van Wittel, who as a resident of Italy after 1672 became known as Gaspare Vanvitelli, introduced the stylistic conventions of Dutch 17th century city views.

Canaletto's early paintings tend to strong contrasts of light and shadow and to the dark, saturated tonalities that were prevalent in Venetian painting of the early 1700's. He very rapidly acquired the ability to suggest by tonal variations the quality of air and light and their effect on the appearance of objects. He also mastered the grouping of figures, gondolas, and ships in ways that enhance the feeling of animation that permeates even his largest canvases. Canaletto's views appealed especially to the many travelers to Venice, mostly English, who wanted to take home some record of their visit. This accounts for his innumerable repetitions of a few popular subjects. It may also explain the slight loss of freshness and the increasingly conventionalized execution that, about 1740, gradually began to appear in his work. To render the many, small details in his views, Canaletto devised a summary, calligraphic shorthand manner of quickly and solidly placing well-defined areas of even, opaque color. The moist, transparent, and often stormy character of his early views gave way to the harsh sparkle of brilliant noon.

After the outbreak of the War of the Austrian Succession in 1741, there were few travelers in Venice, and the resulting scarcity of commissions prompted Canaletto to try new types of work. Dating from the early 1740's are a series of extremely accomplished etchings of Venetian views and both etchings and paintings of *capricci*, witty, imaginary landscapes that often contain recognizable buildings in new or fanciful settings. Also from the 1740's are a number of Roman views that are sometimes cited as evidence of a second journey to Rome, but which may have been based on material collected on the earlier trip.

Canaletto's move to England in 1746 was a drastic attempt to recover the lost flow of patrons. During his years there he repeated the favored Venetian and Roman subjects and produced a number of very fine views of London and the Thames. However, most of the paintings of this period and later are generally held to have been weakened by a mechanical manner that reduces everything to easily duplicated and quickly repeated forms. But even Canaletto's last paintings are redeemed by their unfailing clarity and precision and by the continuing charm of the scenes that he recorded.

Barry Hannegan, *University of Virginia*

Further Reading: Constable, William G., *Canaletto: Giovanni Antonio Canal*, 2 vols. (Fairlawn, N. J., 1962); Levey, Michael, *Painting in XVIII Century Venice* (London 1959); Moschini, Vittorio, *Canaletto* (Milan 1954); Watson, Francis J. B., *Canaletto* (New York 1950).

CANALS are watercourses constructed to improve and extend natural waterways. They are generally built to facilitate transportation, but from the beginning they have been used for many additional purposes, including draining swamps, irrigating land for cultivation, promoting economic development, and improving communication.

Canals provide valuable short cuts on important trade routes. Many link major river basins and lakes, and others provide better access to rivers than the often silt-clogged river mouths and harbors. An increasing number of waterway projects are planned to include major hydroelectric power plants and extensive water control and distribution programs in addition to transportation facilities.

Canals are often classified by the size of vessel they can accommodate. Some small local canals, which may be able to float only 100- to 300-ton boats or small rafts of timber, may be only 3 feet (.9 meters) deep. Major barge canals range from 6 to 9 feet (1.8 to 2.7 meters) in depth, and some Soviet and U. S. ones are 10 or 12 feet (3 or 3.6 meters) deep. These canals can carry 1,350- to 2,000-ton craft. Ship canals are 25 feet (7.6 meters) or more deep and are capable of accommodating large vessels in the seagoing class.

Canals may also be classified as either water-level or lock canals. Water-level canals do not vary in height along their courses. The best known of these is the Suez Canal, which is at sea level. Lock canals, which include most modern waterways, contain locks, or special devices for raising and lowering boats along their courses.

EARLY HISTORY

Ancient Canals. Canals have been constructed for the past several millennia. The earliest canals in China, Babylonia, and Egypt were probably multipurpose watercourses whose primary objective may well have been drainage or irrigation. The use of these ditches for transportation may have been incidental. As the economy of these areas flourished and political organization and ambitions expanded, more impressive waterways were built to facilitate commerce and to increase the power and efficiency of the emerging empires. The direct relationship between the vitality of interest in canals and the existence of efficient centralized governments is almost universally apparent in Chinese history, in Roman times, and in the Middle Ages.

There also seems to be considerable evidence to support the association between the rise and fall of canal systems and the fluctuation between surplus-producing and market-minded agrarian or maritime states on the one hand and pastoral or essentially land empires on the other. Persia and Rome are good examples of empires which passed successively through periods of canal building and neglect as the character and extent of their realms changed.

China. There is mention of important work on the system of waterways which became the Grand Canal in China as early as the 6th and early 5th centuries B. C. During Wü Ti's reign (about 109 B. C.) there was construction from the Wei Valley in the north to the Han in the south. In the Sui dynasty (581–618 A. D.) the system of canals between the Yellow and Yangtze rivers was developed. By the 8th century, the Grand Canal is said to have been 600 miles (960 km) long and to have been carrying 2 million tons (1.8 million metric tons) of freight a year. Repairs to this historic waterway are recorded in 984 A.D., and Kublai Khan (died 1294) is usually credited with completing the work on the Grand Canal. It then included about 1,000 miles (1,600 km) of river improvements and artificial waterways. Canal interest in China continued to fluctuate throughout the centuries, with considerable activity in the 1800's and a general decline in the 1900's.

Middle East. Canals in the Tigris-Euphrates Valley have a history which is thousands of years old. Nebuchadnezzar, the Biblical ruler of the resurgent Babylonian empire, reportedly restored canals in the Fertile Crescent about 600 B.C. Careful water management in this area made possible a bountiful pastoral and agrarian economy.

The importance of a connection between the Nile and the Red Sea was early recognized—the historical origins of the project are lost. The Persian monarch Darius proposed the rebuilding of this waterway in 510 B.C. The Ptolemies, who reigned in Egypt during the first four centuries B.C., and the Roman emperor Trajan (about 53–117 A.D.) are also credited with efforts to open the short cut for trade between the Mediterranean and the East. However, the blowing sands repeatedly frustrated each attempt to construct the waterway, and interest and energies lagged.

THE CORINTH CANAL, connecting the Ionian Sea and the Aegean Sea, is a deep-ditch ship canal built between 1882 and 1893. Its entire length is at sea-level.

J. ALLAN CASH, FROM RAPHO GUILLUMETTE

Greece and Rome. The commercially oriented Greek city-states showed an awareness of the value of short cuts in sea trade by maintaining the Leukas Canal (originally cut in 640 B.C. to separate the peninsula of Leukas, now an island, from the Greek mainland) and by efforts to cut through the isthmus at Corinth. Imperial Rome also brought its engineering skills to the problem of canal building—at Corinth; in Egypt and North Africa, where careful water management won back many miles of desert; in Italy itself, on the Lombardy plain and in the construction of an improved harbor at Ostia, a port near Rome on the Tiber River; in France, where the Fossa Mariana improved navigation from the Rhône River to the Mediterranean (102 B.C.); in the Low Countries; and in Britain, where the Exe River was canalized and where the Foss Dyke, a canal, was built from the Trent River to Lincoln, on the Witham River.

Middle Ages. The decline of the Romans' administrative vigor and efficiency was paralleled by a decay of their irrigation and navigation canals. Nevertheless, medieval Europe, although ravaged by invasions and politically decentralized after the collapse of Roman authority, was not without its artificial waterways. The Germanic leader Odoacer built a waterway from Mentone, near Ravenna, to the sea in the 5th century A.D. Charlemagne reportedly proposed a connection between the Rhine and the Danube. In England, Henry I reputedly deepened the Foss Dyke in the 12th century. The Low Countries were a natural center for the development of waterways when trade began to revive after 1000 A.D. In Spain, the Moors built canals in Granada which fell into disuse after the reconquest of the region by Ferdinand V at the end of the 15th century. Leonardo da Vinci planned and directed the construction of canals in Milan following his appointment as engineer in 1482.

Mercantile Era. In the age of mercantilism following the Renaissance, there was a noticeable quickening of interest in canals. The emergence of centralized nation-states, the growth of industry and commerce, and the expansion of European horizons all contributed to the revival of canal construction. The Netherlands, present-day Belgium, and Italy were already well aware of the importance of inland waterways. Sweden's first short waterway was completed in 1606. France built the Briare Canal between 1605 and 1642. The French statesman Jean Baptiste Colbert promoted a vigorous internal improvements program for France, including projects such as the Canal of Orléans (completed in 1692), and the Languedoc Canal (Canal of the Two Seas; completed 1692), which joined the Bay of Biscay and the Mediterranean Sea via the Garonne and the Aude rivers. The Languedoc Canal has been described as the greatest engineering feat after the Roman Empire and up to its own time. It required aqueducts, tunnels, reservoirs, and locks to overcome the rugged terrain.

Although Germany, Russia, and southeastern Europe relied primarily on rivers, they were not untouched by the growing interest in canals. A waterway joining the Elbe and Oder rivers dates from 1745. Peter the Great undertook the connection of the Baltic and Caspian seas (via the Volga River), and a waterway of sorts was opened in 1718. He also proposed a canal between the Volga and the Don rivers, but without immediate success. In Britain, John Trew made

GERMAN INFORMATION CENTER

THE KIEL CANAL, Germany, has only two locks, one at either end. It connects the North and the Baltic Seas.

some efforts to improve the canalized Exe River in 1566 during the reign of Elizabeth I, and Newry was connected with Lough Neagh in Northern Ireland in 1742, but most activity was concentrated on extensive river improvements. By 1750, however, there had been a considerable development of canals and improved waterways on the continent of Europe.

THE CANAL ERA

Europe. The major canal era of recent times began in 1761 when the Duke of Bridgewater built a canal, designed by James Brindley, from Worsley to Manchester, in England. Its success prompted the construction of countless other canals. In contrast to the pattern of canal construction on the Continent, where governments planned, built, and maintained the waterways, often with only nominal tolls, in Britain private capital built and operated canals. The close relation of the Industrial Revolution to the building of British waterways is also pronounced. By 1830 there were 1,927 miles (3,101 km) of canals in England and Wales and 1,312 miles (2,111 km) of improved river navigation, plus additional waterways in Scotland and Ireland. All types of improvements were represented: the waterways included lock canals, water-level canals, and canalized rivers. Examples of cross-country canals are the Kennett and Avon, the Thames and Severn, the Grand Union, the Leeds and Liverpool, the Forth and Clyde, and the Caledonian.

Canal building on the Continent revived after 1815 in France, Germany, Italy, the Low Countries, Russia, and Scandinavia. The later start was due in large part to the disturbances of the French Revolution and Napoleonic periods, the slower spread of the Industrial Revolution, and the relatively recent emergence of efficient administrative units in Germany, Italy, and Russia. France added 560 miles (900 km) of canals before 1830 and another 1,200 miles (2,000 km) by 1848.

In Scandinavia, the Danes built the first canal between the North and Baltic seas (1777–1784). Sweden developed an extensive canal system for transport of timber and mineral products. The most famous Swedish waterway was the Gota Canal (completed in 1832, improved between 1877 and 1887), which crosses the country, joining lakes and rivers, from the Baltic to the Skagerrak. Norway devised two systems (the Haldenvassdraget and the Skienvassdraget), only portions of which are fully navigable, primarily for the shipment of timber products. In Finland, Estonia, and Poland, modest series of canals were built, connecting lakes and rivers in the 19th century.

Sporadic work was carried on in the Danube basin, but the political and economic climate of Austria-Hungary and the Ottoman Empire was not stimulating. The Ludwig Canal, which formed part of the long-proposed Rhine-Main-Danube route, was built by 1846.

In Italy the Paderno Canal (completed in 1777) was probably the first waterway opened in this period, but the greatest effort in the 19th century was expended on the Po River valley. In Greece, the most spectacular and most lasting accomplishment was the Corinth Canal (1882–1893), constructed during the period of decline of the old waterways. The few which survived were of obvious strategic commercial importance.

In the 19th century the most complete system of artificial and improved waterways and the one longest in continuous use was in the Netherlands and Belgium. Many of these waterways, such as the Amsterdam-Rhine Canal, the Albert Canal, the Meuse River canalization, and many others, have been repeatedly enlarged to achieve 1,350 and 2,000-ton (1,220 and 1,800 metric ton) standards. Germany finally completed the principal part of the Mittelland Canal in 1915 and gradually extended it as a barge canal in the 20th century.

Russia concentrated its efforts in the 19th century on connections between the heads of navigation on such great river systems as the Volga, Dnieper, Don, Dvina, and Ob. By 1900 there were 29 relatively short canals totaling 500 miles (800 km) in operation. The best-known of these were the Vyshni-Volochek system, the Tikhvinsk and the Mariinsk canals, and the Berezina, Courland, and Brest-Litovsk canals.

Canada. The enthusiasm for canal construction spread from Europe to Canada and the United States. In Canada this interest resulted in the Welland Canal, which opened in 1829. Enlargements were completed in 1887 and in 1932. The Rideau Canal, from Ottawa to Kingston, and the first St. Lawrence waterway were completed by 1848. The Trent Canal, made primarily for small boats, was opened in 1915 from Lake Ontario to Georgian Bay on Lake Huron.

THE ERIE CANAL, opened in 1825, is one of the great 19th-century barge canals still in operation.

PHOTO RESEARCHERS

United States. In the United States progress in canal construction was generally slower and financially and physically more difficult. The major impetus in the 19th century came from growing American trade, agriculture, industry, and capital. Because the Middle Atlantic states and the area around the Great Lakes were developing most rapidly, most of the canal construction occurred in those sections. Waterways were also planned and some were built in the Southern states, but this agriculturally oriented region had many long navigable streams, and lacked the large sums of fluid capital and the substantial markets for trade needed to promote internal improvements. New England, though interested, was physically removed from the mainstream of the trans-Allegheny trade, although hopes for a share of this burgeoning business eventually promoted construction of railroads when canals proved unfeasible. And during the peak canal-building period, the country west of the Missouri River was still largely unsettled.

Proposed Canals. Many suggestions for canals had been made before the 19th century period of canal development. Louis Jolliet proposed a connection of the Illinois and Chicago rivers in 1673; the Cape Cod Canal was first suggested in 1676, surveyed in 1697 and 1776, but not finally opened until 1914; the present Chesapeake and Delaware Canal was first mentioned in 1679–1680 and surveyed in 1764 and 1769; William Penn advocated a better connection between the Delaware and the Susquehanna in 1690; Sieur Antoine de la Mothe Cadillac proposed an artificial waterway between Lake Erie and Lake Ontario in 1707; and tradition says that Gov. Alexander Spotswood recommended a waterway between the James and Kanawha rivers in 1716, but it was not even surveyed until 1762.

Early Canals. Some short canals were actually built before 1815; at South Hadley Falls on the Connecticut River, at Little Falls and Great Falls on the Potomac, and at Richmond on the James. The Dismal Swamp Canal was built from Chesapeake Bay to Albemarle Sound (1787–1794), and the Old Basin Canal (Carondelet) was constructed in New Orleans during the Spanish period in Louisiana. Other smaller canals were constructed in Maryland, Pennsylvania, and New England, primarily around falls as parts of river improvement projects. Finally, in the late 18th century, more ambitious waterways were dug: the Santee and Cooper Canal (chartered 1786, built 1792–1800) near Charleston, S. C., and the Middlesex Canal between Boston and the Merrimac River (chartered 1793, built 1794–1803).

The Erie and Other Major 19th Century Canals. Most of the waterways built during the 19th century were intended to achieve national significance, but some were modest, seeking only to open up timber and mineral lands to urban markets. All the canal companies anticipated great returns from the promotion of economic activity, the opening up of mines and farms, and the rise of industry based on waterpower from the canals and on ready access to both markets and raw materials.

Following numerous disappointing attempts to rely upon river improvements in the 1790's and early 1800's, New York state led the way with its spectacular Erie Canal, which opened in 1825. It was an immediate success in almost every way. It served as a school for canal engineers, in which many problems of construction and maintenance were solved. It established patterns for later waterways in financing, relations with the state government, and solutions to labor and health problems. The impact on the port of New York City, on the settlement and economic development of western New York, and on the traditional routes of trade and migration was so great that many other canal projects followed.

Between 1815 and 1850 several other projects with pretensions to national importance were undertaken. The Pennsylvania Main Line of Public Works, a curious and cumbersome combination of railroad, canals, and inclined planes from Philadelphia to Pittsburgh, was built. The Chesapeake and Ohio Canal, the inheritor of George Washington's interest and activities in the Potomac route to the west, had a grand design,

THE PANAMA CANAL is a lock and lake type of ship canal. Shown here are two ships in the Gatun Locks.

JANE LATTA, FROM PHOTO RESEARCHERS

which was never completed beyond Cumberland, Md., and it eventually became simply another coal carrier. Ohio constructed a comprehensive network of waterways including the Ohio and Erie, the Miami and Maumee, and the Ohio and Pennsylvania canals. Indiana virtually bankrupted itself building the Wabash and Erie Canal from a junction with the Miami and Maumee to Terre Haute. Most of the improvements projected by Michigan and Illinois were not completed, the major exception being the strategic and successful Illinois and Michigan Canal, connecting Chicago with the Mississippi River via the Illinois River.

Some of the waterways constructed during this period were more modest in scope. The Delaware and Hudson, the Lehigh Navigation, the Morris Canal, and the Delaware and Raritan fall essentially into this category. The Schuylkill Navigation was a coal carrier that, it was long hoped, would develop through trade to the West via the Union Canal. The Chesapeake and Delaware, the Susquehanna and Tidewater, and the short canal around the falls of the Ohio at Louisville were financially modest undertakings that produced truly strategic waterways. Virtually all of these waterways started with modest dimensions, frequently about 40 feet (12 meters) wide and 4 feet (1.2 meters) deep. The more successful ones were subsequently enlarged. Entire waterways were widened and deepened. Locks were lengthened and often doubled, and dams and reservoirs were made larger. Constant experimentation went on in an effort to increase the efficiency of the waterways. Many types of canal boats were tried; various methods of speeding loading were sought; and improvements in motive power were encouraged. Also new types of cement were developed, and methods of preserving wood were improved.

Decline. The canal boom which began in the late 18th century lasted, both in Europe and in North America, through the third quarter of the 19th century. The major cause of the close of this canal era was the rise of competing transportation facilities, especially railroads. The occasion for the eclipse of the waterway by the railroad was undoubtedly the onset of commercial and financial difficulties in much of the Western world in the late 1870's and 1880's. As is usually true of historical developments, there were exceptions to this general picture, and there were many additional contributory conditions underlying it.

The rapid expansion of canals became possible when the enormous investments of labor and capital necessary were available, when there was some assurance of long-term profitable operation, and when speed was not yet a vital concern in transportation. The dawn of the industrial age provided these conditions, and the canals flourished as shippers of food and fuel to the urban centers and of bulk commodities to and from the factories. During the heyday of the canals they created and sustained many local economic activities—small towns, local industries and shops, boatyards, feedstores, and wharf and warehouse facilities.

Unfortunately, canals proved to be less susceptible to technological advances than were the competing railroads and highways. As the economy expanded, year-round rather than seasonal transportation was required. The delays in locking and damages in shipping grew increasingly intolerable as the pace of economic life speeded up, and shifting trade patterns found the canals less flexible than other forms of transportation. Most canals were particularly suited to local or regional development; as economies became national in scope, alternative means of communication were sought. Moreover, artificial waterways are expensive to build.

The decline of canals has been relative rather than absolute. The financial advantages of water for the transport of bulk commodities, where speed is not a decisive factor, are still significant. One estimate gives these cost figures per ton-mile: ship, 0.2 cent; pipe, 0.25 cent; barge, 0.4 cent; train, 1.4 cents; truck, 6.5 cents. If modern canalized rivers are included, there has in recent decades been a resurgence of water-borne commerce, especially in Europe.

EWING GALLOWAY

THE SUEZ CANAL, oldest of the modern international ship canals, connects the Red Sea and the Mediterranean Sea. This sea-level canal opened in 1869.

MAJOR MODERN CANALS

Barge Canals. Of the waterways that continue to operate, virtually all have been taken over by governments and maintained as public services. Many are purely for local convenience, such as those in Scandinavia, the British Isles, Spain, and Italy, but the more important ones have been made into barge canals. Among the major barge canals are those of the Rhine River valley in western Europe, the sprawling network of French canals, the ambitious Soviet complexes, the Atlantic and Gulf intracoastal waterways (including the Cape Cod and the Chesapeake and Delaware canals, which are somewhat larger ship canals), the New York State Barge Canal system (including the Erie Canal), and the giant Mississippi River system.

Ship Canals. A few of the surviving watercourses are full-fledged ship canals of considerable capacity. One category of these canals serves to provide access to deep-sea harbors. In Europe, such canals include the Manchester Ship Canal, opened in 1894, and the lower Rhine canals serving Ghent, Rotterdam, and Amsterdam. In North America they include the Houston Ship Canal, the Sacramento Deepwater Ship Canal, the New Orleans Industrial Canal, and the Lake Washington Ship Canal. The second major category of ship canals comprises the great international waterways—the Suez, the Kiel, the Panama, and the St. Lawrence.

The Suez Canal, a sea-level waterway 103 miles (165 km) long, is the oldest of the modern international ship canals. It was begun in 1859 and completed in 1869 under the direction of Ferdinand de Lesseps. Control of the Suez Canal Company came into British hands in 1875; since 1956 the canal has been operated by the Egyptian government. See also SUEZ CANAL.

The Corinth Canal, prompted by the success of the Suez Canal, was constructed between 1882 and 1893. It too is a sea-level canal, 4 miles (6½ km) long. The present Kiel Canal, 61 miles (98 km) long, with only two locks at either end, was opened in 1895 as the Kaiser Wilhelm Canal. See also KIEL CANAL.

The Panama Canal was also directly inspired by the example of the Suez Canal, although it had been suggested as early as the 16th century. In the 19th century a French company undertook to cut a sea-level canal planned by de Lesseps but failed to overcome financial, construction, and health problems. The present canal, opened by the United States government in 1914, is a "lock and lake" type of waterway with a summit level 85 feet (26 meters) above sea level. The waterway is 50 miles (80 km) long, and not less than 41 feet (12.5 meters) deep, and the locks are 1,000 feet (300 meters) long and 110 feet (34 meters) wide. The famous Gaillard (Culebra) Cut is over 8 miles (13 km) long and 500 feet (150 meters) wide. See also PANAMA CANAL.

The newest international waterway of major ship canal proportions is the St. Lawrence Waterway. It has been estimated that 80% of the present salt-water fleet can pass through the 2,342 miles (3,768 km) of channels and 16 locks from Duluth to the Atlantic. The waterway embraces three major improvements: the St. Lawrence Seaway (opened in 1959), which has seven locks to overcome a rise of 226 feet (69 meters) between Montreal and Lake Ontario; the Welland Canal (originally opened in 1829 and recently enlarged), with eight locks to surmount a 326-foot (99-meter) rise between Lake Ontario and Lake Erie, and the Sault Ste. Marie locks which overcome a 28-foot (8½-meter) rise between Lake Michigan and Lake Superior. See also SAINT LAWRENCE SEAWAY.

CANAL CONSTRUCTION

In canal planning, determination of the available water is a primary concern. Canals essentially require an adequate water supply at the summit level. It is often necessary to supplement the impounded natural water flow with water pumped from lower levels to reservoirs. Other considerations in canal engineering include the determination of the route for the watercourse, the width and depth of the canal, the overhead clearance above water level, and the dimensions of permanent structures such as tunnels, aqueducts, and locks.

Variations in the levels of the terrain through which canals pass are the rule rather than the exception. This has led to the development of a variety of imaginative ways to overcome the rise or fall in the canal line. Keeping the force of canal currents low is also of great importance. Bypass canals and other methods for getting rid of surplus water are necessary. Adequate power for moving boats must be available, though most boats are now self-propelled through canals.

Locks. Many ingenious methods have been

devised to transfer boats from one level to another along waterways. One of the oldest, used in England, Scandinavia, and Russia, and probably still in use on isolated small canals, is the flush-lock system. This system employs only a single gate. Water is first accumulated in a pool. The lock gate is then opened and the boat or boats pass to the next level on the swell of the outrush of water. A somewhat more dangerous modification of this method, which was more rarely used, is the chute, down which a boat would be flushed. The ruins of the chute on the Potomac Company canal at Great Falls, Va., are still visible. Obviously, methods such as these made upward navigation virtually impossible.

Modern locks are essentially small sections of waterways that are divided into steps by a series of gates. Valves control the inlet and outlet of water from each section, or lock, and thus regulate the water level of each lock. A boat traveling either upstream or downstream enters the first lock in its course when the water level in the lock is the same as that of the stream. The gate is closed behind it and the water level is then raised or lowered to that of the next lock. The gate is then opened to the next lock and the boat proceeds. This procedure is repeated until the boat passes through the series of locks.

Inclined Planes and Lift Locks. Locking, though the commonest method used for overcoming the rise or fall of canals, has several disadvantages. It is a slow procedure and requires large supplies of water. Inclined planes (including marine railways) and caisson type locks (lift locks) have been used in attempts to meet the objections.

Inclined planes have two distinct advantages over ordinary locks. They do not require water for their operation, and they enable substantial rises and falls to be overcome in relatively short distances. In this system the boats are pulled out of the water and moved on trucks on an inclined plane to either the upper or lower level of the canal. Some of the better-known examples were those on the Pennsylvania Main Line of Public Works (five on the eastern slope of the mountains and five on the western side). Other inclined planes are still in operation at Swift Rapids (47 feet, or 14 meters) and Big Chute (58 feet, or 18 meters) on the Trent Waterway in Canada and on the Brussels-Charleroi Canal in Europe. Lift locking, in which the lock itself is raised or lowered mechanically, is more common in Europe than in North America. The Anderton Lift (50 feet, or 15 meters) in England is electrically operated. Les Fontinettes (43 feet, or 13 meters) in France is hydraulically operated.

WALTER S. SANDERLIN
Washington and Jefferson College, Pa.

Bibliography

Calvert, Roger, *Inland Waterways of Europe* (London 1963).
Fair, Marvin L., and Williams, Ernest W., *Economics of Transportation,* rev. ed. (New York 1959).
Goodrich, Carter, ed., *Canals and American Development* (New York 1961).
Hadfield, Charles R., *British Canals: an Illustrated History,* 2d ed. (London 1959).
Hadfield, Charles R., *Canals of the World* (New York and London 1964).
Harlow, Alvin F., *Old Towpaths* (New York 1926).
Kirby, Richard S., and others, *Engineering in History* (New York 1956).
Lebed, Andrei, and Yakovlev, Boris, *Soviet Waterways* (Munich, Germany, 1956).
Locher, Harry O., *Waterways of the United States,* 2d ed. rev. (New York 1963).
Waggoner, Madeline S., *The Long Haul West: The Great Canal Era, 1817–1850* (New York 1958).

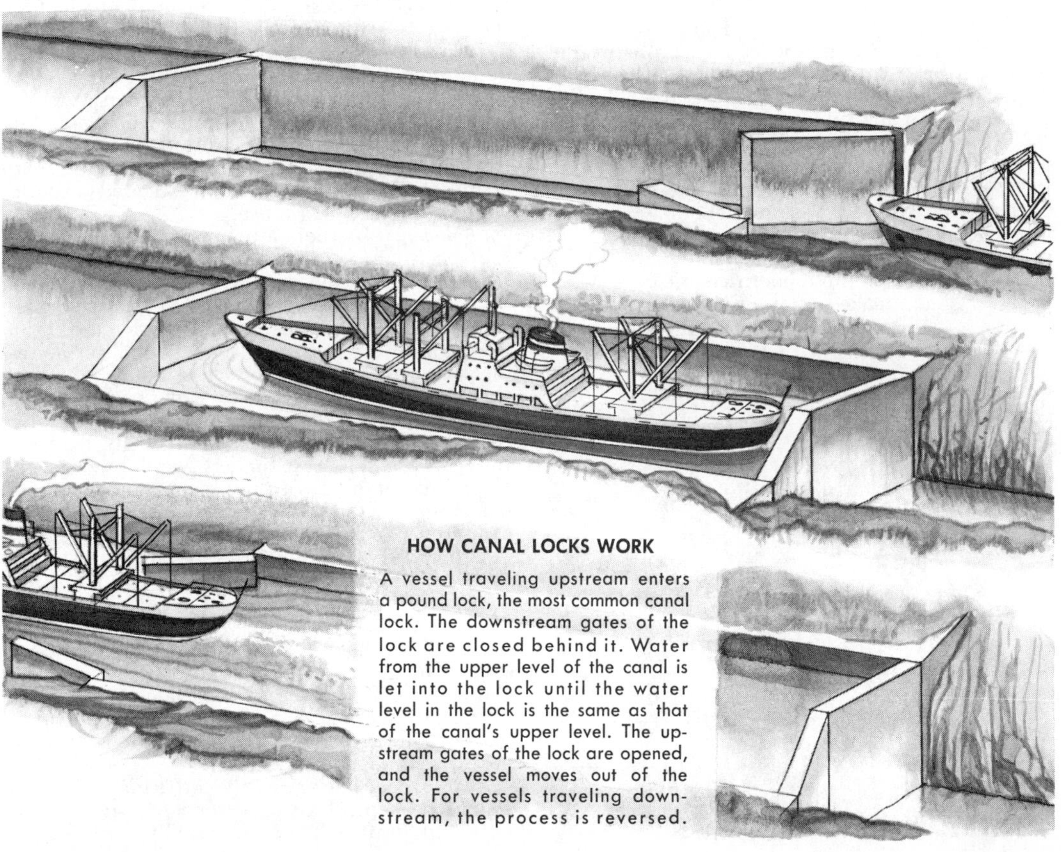

HOW CANAL LOCKS WORK

A vessel traveling upstream enters a pound lock, the most common canal lock. The downstream gates of the lock are closed behind it. Water from the upper level of the canal is let into the lock until the water level in the lock is the same as that of the canal's upper level. The upstream gates of the lock are opened, and the vessel moves out of the lock. For vessels traveling downstream, the process is reversed.

CANANDAIGUA, kan-ən-dā′gwə, a city in western New York, the seat of Ontario county, is at the northern end of Canandaigua Lake, 24 miles (39 km) southeast of Rochester. It is a resort area and a shipping and industrial center. Chief products are typewriter ribbons, labels, plastics, fishing tackle, baby furniture, underwear, and wines. Buildings of historic or architectural interest include the Granger homestead (1815) and the city hall (1824). In 1794 the Pickering treaty with the Six Nations of the Iroquois was signed in Canadaigua. Government is by city manager. Population: 10,488.

CANARIS, kä-nä′ris, **Walter Wilhelm** (1887–1945), German admiral. He was born at Aplerbeck, Westphalia, on Jan. 1, 1887. A naval officer from 1905, Canaris was known for his keen intelligence and sober judgment. In 1935 he was appointed head of counterespionage in the Wehrmacht (armed forces). His new office gave him extensive opportunities for promoting resistance to Hitler, whose regime he opposed. He was torn between his duty as an officer and the demands of conscience, and consequently his attitude toward the German opposition was ambivalent. His connection with it baffled the Gestapo investigators until the end. He never committed himself to an open coup, but provided the military conspirators with information and protection. In February 1944 he was relieved of his office on suspicion of subversive activity. He was arrested after the officers' abortive attempt to assassinate Hitler in July 1944, and he was executed on April 9, 1945.

C. M. Kimmich
Columbia University

CANARY, a small seed-eating finch noted for its lovely song. The domestic canary probably descended from two very similar races of the wild finch *Serinus canarius.* One race is the so-called wild canary of the Canary Islands, Madeira, and the Azores, while the other is the serin of central and southern Europe and northern Africa.

Wild Canaries. The smallest of the seed-eating finches, wild canaries measure about 4½ inches (12 cm) long and weigh about ½ ounce (14 grams.) The ancestral wild canaries are not so brightly colored as the modern cage birds. Their backs are a streaked gray, tinged with olive-green, while their underparts are yellowish and their sides are yellowish streaked with gray-brown. They also have a yellow stripe over each eye and a bright yellow rump patch. The Canary Island bird has more gray and less olive-green on its back and deeper yellow underparts than the mainland serin. The canary's bill is short and stubby. The song of the serin is sweet, powerful, and persistent, but is less varied than that of the cage bird.

A pair of Gloster fancy canaries.

ANNAN PHOTO FEATURES

Since they are avid bathers, wild canaries live near water. They are often found in parks, gardens, vineyards, or other open places bordered with trees or shrubs. They are sociable birds, and in the fall and winter they gather in great flocks. They feed predominantly on vegetable matter such as seeds, fruits, and sometimes figs.

Wild canaries on Tenerife Island in the Canary Islands begin breeding in January, and in mid-Europe breeding begins in May. The male vigorously defends his nesting territory with prolonged singing, erratic flights, and sometimes physical combat with other males. The female builds a small nest 5 to 20 feet (2 to 6 meters) above the ground in a tree or shrub. The well-concealed nest is made of plant stems, fine roots, lichens, and moss woven together with spider webs. Its bowl is lined with fine grasses, hair, and feathers. The female lays three or four bluish eggs with rust-red or purplish markings. A second clutch may be laid later in summer. The female usually incubates the eggs and is fed by the male. The eggs normally hatch in 13 days.

Young canaries are born naked and blind. They are fed regurgitated food by their parents, and they remain in the nest for about 16 or 17 days until they are completely feathered. After they leave the nest, they remain dependent on their parents for several weeks.

Cage Canaries. Canaries probably became domestic cage birds as early as the 14th century. Through artificial selection by breeders, canaries soon became brighter and yellow in color, and completely yellow birds existed in Augsburg, Germany, in 1677. At the beginning of the 18th century, 27 varieties of domesticated canaries were recognized in France.

Breeding. In their attempts to secure desired traits in song, color, feathering, and body form, breeders have hybridized tame canaries with other, closely related, species of European finches. The resulting hybrids, or "mules," are often sterile, but there have been enough fertile interspecific hybrids to produce strikingly different varieties of modern domestic canaries.

For the past three or four centuries canaries have been bred and selected primarily for song. Initially, the choicest singers were bred in the Harz Mountain region of northern Germany. Selection for song in canaries has yielded birds exhibiting great variety in loudness, pitch, and continuity of song. Canaries are apt mimics, and with training they can be taught to imitate the songs of other birds or even the notes of musical instruments. Older trained birds, called "campaninis," are used to teach the younger birds to sing. The songs of females are weaker and less consecutive than those of the males.

Canaries are also bred for their appearance. Such exhibition birds show variations in size, posture, plumage, and color.

Care. Canaries are easily cared for. The birds should be kept clean and protected from dampness and drafts. They are usually fed seeds of

LAS PALMAS, on the island of Gran Canaria, showing a section on one of its bathing beaches.

J. ALLAN CASH, FROM RAPHO GUILLUMETTE

canary grass, hemp, and summer rape, together with small amounts of greens. Lime, an essential element in the diet, is usually provided in cuttlefish bones. In the breeding of canaries, large cages and much equipment are needed. Bowls or boxes fastened to the walls of the cage serve as nests. The young birds are fed soft foods. After they leave the nest, they learn to feed themselves and can be removed from the parents.

Classification. Both wild and domestic canaries belong to the species *Serinus canarius* of the family Fringillidae in the order Passeriformes.

CARL WELTY, *Beloit College*

CANARY ISLANDS, an archipelago in the North Atlantic Ocean, off the northwestern coast of Africa. The name in Spanish is *Islas Canarias*. Located about 70 miles (113 km) west of the Morocco-Spanish Sahara border, the islands are scattered in an arc 300 miles (480 km) long and consist of 7 major islands and 6 islets.

Administratively, the Canary Islands constitute two provinces of Spain. Las Palmas, the easternmost province, consists of Gran Canaria, Fuerteventura, Lanzarote, and the islets of Graciosa, Alegranza, Montaña Clara, Roque del Este, Roque del Oeste, and Las Islas de Lobos. The province of Santa Cruz de Tenerife is made up of Tenerife, Gomera, La Palma, and Hierro.

Many shipping lines make the Canaries a port of call. The islands attract increasing numbers of tourists, who are drawn by the pleasant climate and the variety of scenic attractions—from tropical coasts to mountains, from late medieval churches to modern resort facilities.

People. The islands had a population in 1960 of almost 1 million, divided nearly equally between the two provinces. Las Palmas had 453,793 inhabitants, of whom 400,837 lived on Gran Canaria, including 193,862 in the province's capital city, Las Palmas. Three of the islets are uninhabited. In the province of Santa Cruz de Tenerife (population 490,655) the capital city of the same name had 133,100 of the 387,767 inhabitants of the island of Tenerife.

The original inhabitants of the Canary Islands, called Guanches, are believed to have been of Berber stock. They have merged entirely with the Spanish immigrants to the islands.

Land. The islands cover an area of 2,894 square miles (7,495 sq km). Of volcanic origin, they are very mountainous and have steep coasts. The terrain runs from sea-level valleys to high mountain peaks. The Canaries rise to an altitude of 12,200 feet (3,619 meters) in Pico de Teide, the highest peak on Spanish territory. Most other islands have peaks ranging from 4,500 to 7,000 feet (1,370 to 2,130 meters) Lanzarote and Fuerteventura, the islands closest to the African coast, do not exceed 2,400 feet (730 meters) in elevation, and their dry, crater-scarred surface is less attractive and less populated.

The volcanic slopes are generally steep, but weathering has formed some alluvial plains and beaches. The soil is fertile, and although there are no rivers and the rainfall is scant at best, irrigation systems make possible a high level of agricultural production.

Economy. The islands' economy is based primarily on agriculture. The coastal lowlands are favorable for growing bananas as well as dates and sugarcane. Higher up the climate is more Mediterranean, and tomatoes, oranges, lemons, and figs are grown. Potatoes and tobacco are other important crops. Wheat, barley, corn, peaches, apricots, and almonds are grown less extensively. The major exports are tomatoes and bananas. Grape-producing vines are grown in some quantity, and in the past wine was a major export. Some of the vines grow under apparently impossible conditions on dry, rocky slopes.

The surrounding seas are rich in fish and, as a result, fish salting and canning are major industries. The tourist industry is growing rapidly, with increasing travel service by ship and plane. Las Palmas and Santa Cruz de Tenerife are the major ports of the Canary Islands. They are important fueling stations and regular ports of call for pleasure cruises.

There is little mineral wealth in the Canary Islands, although there are deposits of pumice stones, sulfur, mineral water, and granite.

History. The Romans called the islands *Insulas Canarias*, or "islands of the dogs," because of the many canines found there. The islands were also identified with legends about the lost city of Atlantis. One of the traditional names applied to the islands was Isles of the Blest, or Fortunate Islands (Islas Afortunadas), because of their pleasant scenery and climate. The birds known as canaries received their name because they abound in the islands.

The Canary Islands were known to the Phoenicians, Greeks, Carthaginians, Romans, Arabs, and medieval western Europeans. The modern history of the islands began in 1402 with an expedition led by French explorer Jean de Béthencourt. Failing in his attempt to capture the islands, Béthencourt sought and received help from Henry III of Castile, whom he recognized as sovereign, and Béthencourt was named king of the Canary Islands. The islands were also claimed by Portugal, but by the end of the 15th century they were completely under Spanish control. They have remained under Spanish rule ever since.

The Canary Islands were made two provinces of Spain in 1927. Gen. Francisco Franco began his revolution against the Spanish republic from the Canary Islands in 1936.

M. M. LASLEY, *University of Florida*

CANASTA, kə-nas′tə, is a card game derived from rummy. It originated in Uruguay after World War II, reached the United States by way of Argentina in 1949, and became a popular fad game. By 1953 its popularity had decreased. The word *canasta* is Spanish and means "basket." It probably refers to the tray used to hold the undealt cards and the discards.

Canasta is best played with four persons, in two partnerships, although it may be played with two to six persons. Two regulation decks of 52 cards plus four jokers (108 cards in all) are used. Deuces (twospots) and jokers are *wild* cards and may be designated to be of any rank, at the pleasure of the holder. Each player is dealt 11 cards. The remaining cards are placed face down on the table and form the *stock*. Turning the top card of the stock face up beside it starts the discard pile. If the card turned is a red trey (threespot) or a wild card, the next card must be turned up to cover it.

The object of the game is to make as many points as possible, the winner being the side that first reaches 5,000 or more. Points are scored by forming *melds* (combinations of cards), *laying off* (adding cards to existing melds of partner or self), and *going out* (disposing of all holdings in the hand).

Play is begun by the person on the dealer's left and proceeds clockwise. The routine of each turn includes drawing a card from the stock or the discard pile, melding (optional), and discarding. Red treys are bonus cards. At his first turn, and thereafter, each player must remove any red treys from his hand and face them, drawing another card from stock to restore the hand.

Melding. Melds are combinations of three or more cards of the same rank (not sequences), which are placed face up on the table. The melds of partners are combined, and a partnership may meld only one set of any rank; additional cards of that rank are laid off on the existing meld. The *initial meld* must contain at least two *natural* (not wild) cards of the same rank. Wild cards are used to fill out the combination, but no meld may have more than three wild cards. Black treys can be melded only when the player goes out in the same turn. Red treys are never used in melds. A canasta is a meld of seven or more cards. Seven natural cards form a *natural canasta*. A canasta formed with some wild cards is a *mixed canasta*.

CARD VALUES

Each joker	50
Each deuce or ace	20
Each K, Q, J, 10, 9, 8	10
Each 7, 6, 5, 4, black 3	5

The initial meld of a side must meet a minimum count, dependent on the accumulated total score of that side at the beginning of the current deal. A player may make two or more different melds in the same turn to achieve the minimum.

INITIAL MELD

Previous score	Minimum requirement
Minus	15
0 to 1,495	50
1,500 to 2,995	90
3,000 or more	120

Drawing. In his turn, a player may draw the top card of stock or may elect to draw from the discard pile, under certain restrictions. A discard pile topped by a black trey or a wild card cannot be touched. The discard pile is also *frozen* against a side that has not made an initial meld. It is frozen against both sides at any time that it contains a red trey. If the pile is not frozen, a player must use the top card to lay off or make an immediate meld. However, if the pile is frozen, he must use the top card in a meld with two natural cards from his hand. In any case, the player must take the rest of the discard pile into his hand after he has melded. Then he may meld further.

Going Out. A player goes out and play ends when he melds his last card, providing his side has completed at least one canasta. Play also ends when stock is exhausted or when the stock's last card is a red trey. It also ends if no one can draw further from the discard pile. A player is said to go out with a *concealed hand* when he melds all his cards in a single turn.

To score a deal, items in B should be subtracted from the total of the items due in A.

(A) Card values of all melds by partnership, plus	
For going out	100
For concealed hand (extra)	100
For each natural canasta	500
For each mixed canasta	300
For each red 3*	100
For all four red 3's (bonus)	800
(B) Total of card values left in hand	

*Subtract red 3's if the side has made no meld

Variations. *Samba* is an outstanding variant, especially popular for two players. Three decks plus six jokers are used, and each player is dealt 15 cards. The draw from stock is two cards, and only one is discarded. Melds can have no more than 2 wild cards. Only natural cards from the hand may be laid off on a completed canasta. Sequences of 3 to 7 cards in the same suit may be melded; a sequence of 7 with no wild cards is a *samba*. The pack may be taken only to meld with a natural pair from the hand or, when not frozen, to lay off the top card on a group or sequence meld of fewer than 7 cards. Sambas count 1,500 points; two are needed to go out. Going out counts 200. Initial meld requirements for a side with 7,000 or more is 150. Game is 10,000.

In *Bolivia*, the rules for Samba are followed, except that wild cards (from 3 to 7) may be melded as a separate rank. A set of 7 is a *bolivia* and counts 2,500. A black trey left in the hand counts 100 minus. Game is 15,000.

FRANK K. PERKINS, *Boston "Herald"*

CANASTOTA, kan-ə-stō′tə, is a village in New York, just off the New York Thruway, 21 miles (34 km) east of Syracuse. Situated in a farming district in Madison county, it has canning and milk-processing industries. It manufactures television cabinets, copper wire fabricators, and machine tools. Nearby are Oneida Lake and Chittenango Falls State Park. Settled in 1806 and incorporated in 1835, Canastota was named for an Iroquois Indian Village in the vicinity. Population: (1960 census) 4,896; (1965 special census) 4,971.

DAVID MOORE, FROM BLACK STAR

R. E. LORD, FROM DE WYS INC.

CANBERRA IS A PLANNED CITY, noted for the architectural variety of its public and governmental buildings. A low concrete dome houses the Academy of Science (*above*). In the civic center (*left*) a stylized statue by the Australian sculptor Tom Bass faces modern buildings containing offices of the government.

CANBERRA, kan′ber-ə, is the capital city of Australia. It is located in the Australian Capital Territory (q.v.) in the southeastern part of the country, on the Molonglo River, about 150 miles (240 km) by air southwest of Sydney. Canberra stands about 1,900 feet (580 meters) above sea level, and highlands in the area reach 5,000 feet (1,500 meters).

Plan of the City. Canberra was designated from the outset as a planned city and has been developed on distinctive lines. Capital Hill, in the southern part of the city, is the focal point from which all principal avenues radiate. The central area of the city is reserved for official buildings. It is divided by Lake Burley Griffin, an artificial lake, spanned by two bridges. The main commercial and shopping area is situated north of the lake at Civic Center. Spacious residential suburbs extend along the valley and over the rising ground on its margins, where much of the original tree cover has been preserved. In addition to the garden plantings of householders, more than two million trees and shrubs have been planted along the streets and in public parks.

Points of Interest. National buildings include stately Yarralumla House, which is the residence of the governor-general; Parliament House; the Lodge, home of the prime minister; various administration office blocks; the National Library; the War Memorial; and the Royal Military College at Duntroon. The Australian National University attracts scholars from around the world, as do the modern facilities of Mount Stromlo Observatory. The 258-foot (79-meter) shaft of the Australian-American Memorial, expressing the gratitude of the Australian people for United States assistance during World War II, is a prominent landmark. Another popular attraction is the unique building of the Academy of Science, with a dome 150 feet (46 meters) in diameter.

Population. The federal government is the chief employer in Canberra. Most members of parliament remain in the city for only a few days at a time, either during sessions or when special discussions are in progress. The prime minister is normally in residence at the Lodge. Various organizations representing political and other special groups have set up headquarters in the city. Canberra is an important center of diplomatic activity; nearly 40 nations have established permanent diplomatic missions (involving about 1,200 personnel). A corps of news correspondents is in residence to cover political and other national events. Conventions and conferences of technical, scientific, and education groups are held from time to time. More than 500,000 sightseeing visitors a year are attracted to the city.

History. The district was first occupied as a sheep run in 1826. In 1909 the area was chosen as the site for the national capital of Australia. A worldwide competition was held to choose a plan for the new city, and in 1911 the design of an American architect, Walter Burley Griffin, was selected. Construction work began under Griffin's supervision two years later.

Development of the city proceeded very slowly at first. Even after parliament was transferred from Melbourne in 1927, Canberra's progress continued to be halting. Starting in the late 1940's, however, continuing departmental transfers and the growth of nongovernmental activities contributed to Canberra's physical expansion as well as its stature. The National Capital Planning Commission was established in 1958, and under its guidance construction in the city accelerated. By the early 1960's, Canberra had become Australia's largest noncoastal city. Population: (1966) 93,197.

R. M. Younger
Author of "Australia and the Australians"

Further Reading: Slessor, Kenneth, and Baglin, Douglas, *Canberra* (San Francisco 1966); Wigmore, Lionel, *The Long View* (Melbourne 1963).

CANBY, kan′bē, **Edward Richard Sprigg** (1817–1873), American general, who frustrated a Confederate invasion of the Southwest during the Civil War. He was born in Kentucky in August 1817 and graduated from West Point in 1839. When the Civil War began in 1861, he commanded Union forces in New Mexico Territory. Confederate Gen. Henry H. Sibley entered New Mexico with the objective of reaching California and mobilizing its manpower and resources for the Confederacy. Heading a volunteer force, Canby was able, by harassing tactics, to compel Sibley to withdraw.

Canby maintained order in New York City after the draft riots in 1863. As a major general, he led troops that took Mobile, Ala., in April 1865. While commanding in California after the war, he was murdered by Modoc Indians on April 11, 1873.

CANBY, kan′bē, **Henry Seidel** (1878–1961), American editor and author. He was born in Wilmington, Del., on Sept. 6, 1878. After receiving his Ph. D. from Yale in 1905, he taught there for more than 20 years. In 1920, Canby became the first editor of the literary review section of the New York *Evening Post.* In 1924 he helped found the *Saturday Review of Literature* and served as its first editor until 1936. Under his direction the magazine became the leading literary weekly in the United States. He was also the first chairman (1926–1958) of the board of judges of the Book-of-the-Month Club.

Canby's major books include *Thoreau* (1939); *Walt Whitman, an American* (1943); *Turn East, Turn West* (1951), a comparative study of Henry James and Mark Twain; and the autobiographical *American Memoir* (1947). He died in Ossining, N. Y., on April 5, 1961.

CANCER, in astronomy, is a spring constellation of the Northern Hemisphere. It lies on the ecliptic (the sun's apparent path among the stars) and is the fourth sign of the zodiac. The name means "crab" in Latin. In mythology, the crab was killed when it nipped Hercules as he fought the hydra. The goddess Hera rewarded the crab by placing it in the heavens. The summer solstice (the northern limit of the ecliptic) occurred in Cancer in ancient times; because of precession it has since moved into Gemini.

Cancer lacks bright stars, but it contains the Beehive (Messier 44), an open star cluster that is visible to the naked eye as a hazy patch of light. See also CONSTELLATION; ZODIAC.

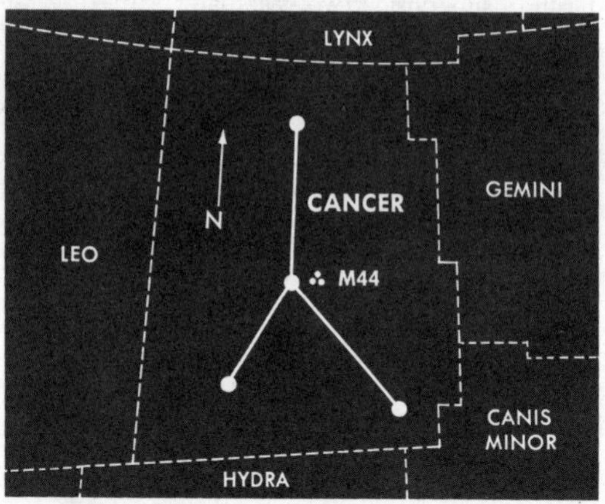

CANCER is the term applied to a group of diseases that are produced when a single cell or a group of cells escapes from the usual controls that regulate cellular growth and begin to multiply and spread. This cellular activity results in a tumor, or neoplasm. Many tumors are benign; that is, the abnormal growth is restricted to a single, circumscribed expanding mass of cells. Other tumors are malignant; that is, the abnormal growth invades the surrounding tissues and may spread, or metastasize, to distant areas of the body. Although benign tumors may produce serious complications, the malignant ones are usually more serious and it is for these tumors that the term cancer is used.

Incidence. In the United States there are about 450,000 new cases of cancer each year. The importance of cancer as a health problem is indicated by the estimated 295,000 deaths caused by cancer in the United States in 1965. In addition, the incidence of cancer appears to be increasing. In 1900, for example, the death rate from cancer was 79.6 per 100,000 people. By 1962, the death rate had risen to 125.6 per 100,000 people. Part of this increase is due to the more accurate reporting of the causes of death. In the past, many deaths from cancer were attributed to other diseases, largely because of incorrect diagnoses. Another cause of the increase in cancer deaths is the decrease in mortality from other causes, such as tuberculosis and other infectious diseases. However, there has also been a true increase in the incidence of certain types of cancer, notably those arising in the lung.

The incidence of cancer varies somewhat according to sex and age. During the last few decades there has been a marked increase in the cancer death rate among men, largely because of the increasing incidence of lung cancer. At the same time, there has been some decrease in the death rate among women, owing to a decline in deaths resulting from cancers of the female reproductive system. This decline can be largely attributed to better methods of detection, resulting in earlier diagnoses and more effective methods of treatment.

Although cancer occurs most commonly after the age of 40, it can occur at any age. By examining a graph showing the age distribution of all cancer deaths in the United States, one sees a sharp peak between the ages of 5 and 10 and a high, broad peak between the ages of 40 and 65. However, there is a difference in the predominant types of cancer between these two age groups. In the older group, cancers of the breast, uterine cervix, colon, stomach, and lung are responsible for most of the deaths. In children, leukemia and neoplasms of the brain and spinal cord predominate.

Although the overall incidence of cancer appears similar in those parts of the world for which accurate information is available, geography appears to influence the incidence of specific types of cancer. For instance, cancer of the stomach is most common in Japan and parts of Scandinavia, and primary cancer of the liver is common in parts of Africa and Asia. The factors that cause these differences in geographic incidence are not definitely known. It is thought, however, that nutritional, racial, and infectious factors may be responsible. For example, the high incidence of liver parasites (called liver flukes) in China may contribute to the high incidence of liver cancer there.

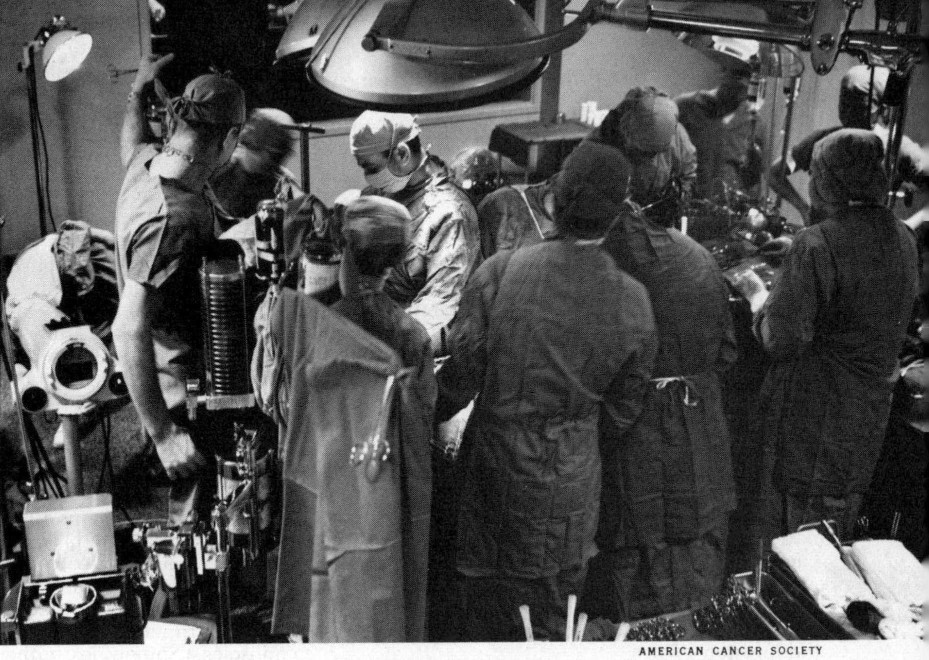

SURGERY is the oldest method of treating cancer. If it is impossible to remove a malignant growth completely, surgery may help to restore bodily functions for a time, relieve pain, and also retard the growth of the cancer.

AMERICAN CANCER SOCIETY

CLASSIFICATION

Cancer may occur in any tissue or organ of the body and the different forms of cancer vary widely in their characteristics. Several methods for classifying the different types of cancer have been devised. One of the simplest but most useful classifications divides all cancers into three groups: carcinomas, sarcomas, and the leukemias and lymphomas. A *carcinoma* is a malignant neoplasm that arises in the skin, the linings of various organs, or in glandular organs or tissues. A *sarcoma* is a malignant tumor arising in bone, muscle, or connective tissue. In the third group, a *leukemia* is a malignancy that arises in bone marrow and a *lymphoma* arises in lymph nodes.

Both the sarcomas and carcinomas may be further classified according to their degree of malignancy as seen through a microscope. They may also be classified on the basis of the kind of tissue in which they originate. The leukemias, neoplastic diseases of the white blood cells, are commonly classified into acute and chronic forms. These two forms are further broken down into groups according to the type of white blood cells involved. Each of these classifications may be valuable in predicting the progress of the disease and in choosing the proper treatment.

CAUSES

No specific cause of human cancer has been identified. All cells divide to produce other cells, and it is thought that the formation of a cancer cell from a normal one is due to a genetic mutation at the time of cell division. Such a mutation can be initiated by many factors. Through studies of single cells and of various animals, including man, scientists have found a number of chemical and physical agents that can initiate a neoplastic change. These cancer-promoting agents are known as carcinogens.

Chemicals. A large number of chemical substances have been shown to produce tumors when applied to the skin of mice and rabbits. Although it is not necessarily correct to assume that the same reaction occurs in man, there are many instances in which a true cause and effect relationship appears to exist between exposure to a carcinogen and the development of human cancer. For example, tars, pitch, and certain industrial oils have been associated with a high incidence of skin cancer. It has also been found that workers in the aniline dye industries who absorb these dyes and excrete them in their urine have a high incidence of cancer of the urinary bladder. The evidence for a relationship between cigarette smoking and lung cancer has been well documented in the 1964 report *Smoking and Health,* by the Advisory Committee to the Surgeon General of the U. S. Public Health Service. Although the exact carcinogenic factor in smoking has not been identified, it has been shown that smokers have a higher rate of lung cancer than nonsmokers. See SMOKING AND HEALTH.

Radiation. The relatively high incidence of skin cancer among the scientists who first worked with X-rays, radium, and other radioactive materials first indicated the ability of ionizing radiation to induce cancer. Subsequently, the development of bone cancer in women who painted radium dials served to confirm this relationship. (The women had ingested the radium by moistening their brushes with their tongues.)

The most recent large-scale study of radioactivity as a cause of cancer has been in the survivors of the atomic bomb blasts at Hiroshima and Nagasaki. The incidence of leukemia in these individuals has been found to be directly related to their distance from the center of the blast. For people who were 2,000 meters (6,500 feet) from the explosion, the incidence of leukemia is three times the normal rate and for those who were only 1,000 meters (3,300 feet) away, the incidence is twenty times the normal rate. Other examples of radiation-induced cancer are seen among people who have received unusually large doses of radioisotopes or X-ray therapy as treatment for other types of cancer.

Viruses. The first evidence to suggest that viruses can cause cancer was demonstrated by the American physician Francis Peyton Rous in the early 1900's. The virus Rous found was in a tumor of a chicken and it is known as the Rous sarcoma virus. Since then, painstaking laboratory work has demonstrated that certain other cancers in laboratory animals are caused by viruses and there has been an enormous effort devoted to investigations of the possibility that human cancers may also be induced by viruses. However, at the present time there is no direct evidence to support the theory that there may be an association between viruses and human cancer.

Other Causes. Under special circumstances many other factors may play a role in the production of cancer. Alcohol, for example, when taken in excess, appears to promote cancer of the larynx. Nutritional deficiencies are believed to promote cancer of the liver and esophagus, and syphilitic lesions of the tongue may lead to cancer of the tongue. In addition, a definite link has been found between skin cancer and prolonged exposure to the sun.

Some factors that were once thought to lead to certain types of cancers have, on closer examination, been found to be unrelated to cancer. The alleged relationship between pregnancy and cancer of the uterine cervix has been disproved as has the relationship between the therapeutic use of hormones and cancers of the breast, uterus, and prostate.

Secondary Factors. It is obvious that not every individual who is exposed to a potentially carcinogenic stimulus actually develops cancer. It appears, therefore, that there must be certain intrinsic factors that influence a person's susceptibility to the extrinsic factors, the cancer-inducing agents. It is believed that the intrinsic factors are related to a person's heredity, immunity, and sex, but very little is known about how these factors are involved.

PROGRESSION

When a cell normally divides, its chromosomal material, consisting largely of a very complex molecule, deoxyribonucleic acid (DNA), also divides, providing each "daughter" cell with chromosomal material identical to that in the original, or "mother," cell. If the chromosomal material is affected by a carcinogen or some other factor, the abnormal chromosomal material will be passed on to succeeding generations of cells. This process may be the beginning of a malignant tumor, which starts as a small localized group of cells but grows and spreads and ultimately destroys its host.

There are several ways in which a cancer may spread. Through *local extension* it infiltrates into the surrounding tissue, continuously expanding and sometimes involving adjacent tissues and organs. Many cancers spread through the bloodstream, a process known as *metastasis*. Small collections of cells break off from the original tumor and are carried to other organs where they are deposited. These secondary deposits, called metastases, also grow and may extend locally into the surrounding tissues. Certain types of cancer metastasize in characteristic ways. For example, cancers of the thyroid gland, lung, breast, kidney, and prostate frequently metastasize to the bones.

Sometimes cancer spreads through the lymphatic system, a process called *lymphatic extension*. In this process, cancer cells from the primary growth enter nearby lymph vessels and are deposited in lymph nodes. From the lymph nodes they are then disseminated throughout the body.

Leukemia does not spread in the same manner as other neoplasms—it is considered to be a generalized disease at the onset. Nevertheless, if seen early, this disease may be first represented by only a few abnormal cells in the blood and bone marrow (the place where many of the blood cells are produced). As this type of cancer progresses, the abnormality of the blood and bone marrow becomes more marked. The cells that form the red blood cells are crowded out of the bone marrow into the blood, as are the precursors of the platelets, the tiny cells responsible for the normal clotting of blood. As a result, the patient progressively deteriorates, developing anemia, infections, and a tendency to bleed.

As cancer progresses, it may affect the patient in many ways. Many forms of cancer are associated with pain and weight loss. Leukemias, as well as other cancers that affect the bone marrow, result in anemia, bleeding, or a deficiency of normal white blood cells. A tumor that originates in a gland, such as the thyroid gland, may cause an overproduction of the hormones normally secreted by the gland, leading to a wide variety of disorders. The involvement of bone tissue may result in the liberation of excess calcium into the blood, a condition that may interfere with the normal functioning of the nervous system and muscles. Sometimes, either by local extension or metastasis, cancer can destroy a vital organ, such as the liver or lungs, resulting in death.

The rate of progression of cancer is influenced by many factors, including the organ of origin, the patient's natural resistance, and his response to treatment. Malignant tumors of the lung, if they cannot be removed surgically, lead to an average survival of less than one year. If a breast tumor is not removed, the average life span of the patient is about 3 years. Skin cancer in most cases can be cured, but even if a complete cure is not achieved, the patient may live for many years.

DETECTION AND DIAGNOSIS

Since the cure of cancer depends on its early treatment, early detection of the disease is essential. The American Cancer Society has widely publicized seven danger signals of cancer. Any person who recognizes one of the following danger signals should consult his physician promptly:

(1) Unusual bleeding or discharge.
(2) A lump or thickening in the breast or elsewhere.
(3) A sore that does not heal.
(4) Change in bowel or bladder habits.
(5) Persistent hoarseness or cough.
(6) Persistent indigestion or difficulty in swallowing.
(7) Change in a wart or mole.

Prompt attention to these symptoms may lead to the effective, uncomplicated, complete removal of a malignant tumor, with an excellent chance for a permanent cure. However, an even greater chance of a complete cure can usually be assured if the cancer is diagnosed at an earlier stage, before the onset of symptoms. This early diagnosis requires a routine cancer detection examination. In women, such an examination includes a careful examination of the breasts. Often, the physician also instructs the patient in the technique of self-examination, an easy and important aid in cancer detection. In all patients over the age of 40, the cancer detection examination includes an examination of the rectum and the lower part of the large intestine with a special instrument called a proctosigmoidoscope.

In addition to the physical examination, a cancer detection examination includes a cytologic examination, in which a few cells are obtained from a body cavity for examination under a microscope. This technique, known as the "Pap" smear after the American physician George Papanicolaou who devised it, has been most widely and successfully used in detecting carcinoma of the uterine cervix. It is also being used in detecting cancer in other areas of the body, including the urinary bladder and the mouth.

Chest X-rays are another part of a routine cancer detection examination. They are extremely useful in the early detection of lung cancer and greatly enhance the possibility of achieving a complete cure. Biopsies of suspicious areas of tissue can form an important and valuable adjunct to the physical, cytologic, and X-ray examinations. In this procedure, a small piece of tissue is removed surgically and examined under a microscope. Very often, a biopsy enables the doctor to make an accurate diagnosis quickly and simply.

Once cancer is diagnosed, certain other specialized techniques are used to determine if and to what extent the disease has spread. These techniques provide a basis for determining the kind of treatment to be used. One such procedure is radioactive isotope scanning, in which a radioactive material is swallowed by the patient or injected into a vein. Because the concentration of the radioactive material will generally be different between cancerous tissues and normal tissues, it is possible to determine if an organ has been affected by the disease. Using radioactive isotope scanning, it is now possible to detect neoplastic growths in the thyroid gland, brain, liver, kidney, pancreas, spleen, lung, and bone.

In another procedure, called lymphangiography, a radio-opaque dye is injected into a lymph vessel, after which an X-ray is taken of the area normally drained by that vessel. Using this technique, the doctor can determine whether the lymph nodes in the area have been affected by the tumor.

(*Top*) **Normal cells lining the uterine cervix.** (*Bottom*) **Early stage of cancer of the same type of cells, showing a disruption of the normal cell architecture.**

DR. LEO KOSS—MEMORIAL HOSPITAL

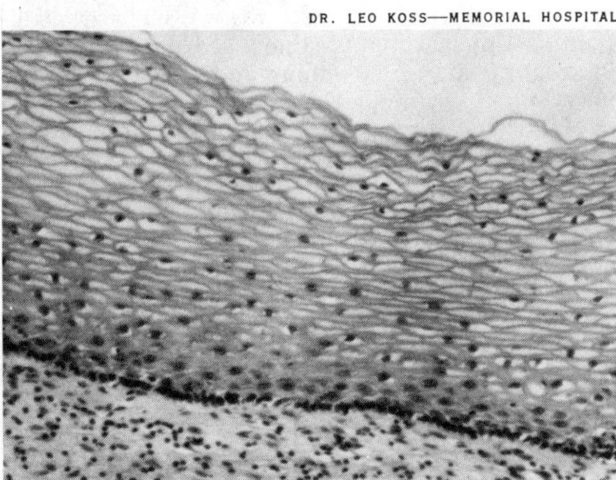

DR. LEO KOSS—MEMORIAL HOSPITAL

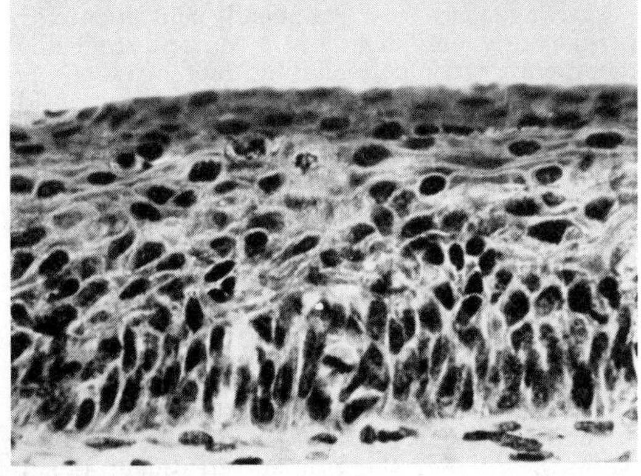

TREATMENT

There are, in general, three basic therapeutic approaches to cancer: surgery, irradiation, and chemotherapy. The use of a particular approach is often determined by the type of cancer and the stage to which it has progressed. Sometimes more than one method is used.

Surgery. The surgical treatment of cancer is the oldest of the three methods. The Ebers papyrus, which is thought to have been written about 1550 B.C., contains references to the surgical removal of tumors. Today, the surgical approach to cancer is very much the same. In many instances it is possible to remove the entire tumor, resulting in a complete and permanent cure. However, surgery also plays a role in the treatment of cancer even though a curative operation may not be possible. In some cases, an operation to relieve an intestinal obstruction, to restore normal urinary flow, or to decrease pain may provide a patient with additional months or even years of comfortable living even though the tumor cannot be completely removed. In addition, surgery may be used to remove glands, such as the ovaries or testes, to change the patient's hormone balance. This operation may result in a temporary but marked regression of certain cancers that are dependent on homones for their continued growth. Cancers of the breast and prostate are particularly affected by the removal of the sex glands.

Radiation Therapy. For some types of localized cancer, such as those originating in the skin, uterine cervix, or larynx, X-rays administered externally can result in complete eradication of the disease without other forms of treatment. In cases where surgical removal cannot be achieved or in cases where the cancer recurs in an area where a tumor had once been removed, external X-ray therapy may be used to relieve pain, prolong the patient's life, or both.

Radiation may also be applied to tumors by the internal administration of radioactive materials. Sometimes, a radioactive material such as radium is implanted directly in a tumor. Another technique of internal radiation is based on the ability of certain organs to absorb and concentrate specific elements. Since the thyroid gland attracts and concentrates iodine, an oral or intravenous administration of radioactive iodine results in its deposition in normal thyroid tissue and the destruction of a thyroid cancer that has retained its normal iodine-concentrating ability. Similarly, because phosphorus is deposited in the bone marrow, radioactive phosphorus can be used to treat certain leukemias.

Chemotherapy. Chemotherapy is the attempt to treat cancer with chemicals that might selectively destroy the cancer cells or inhibit their growth without seriously harming normal cells. Although there are many substances that have

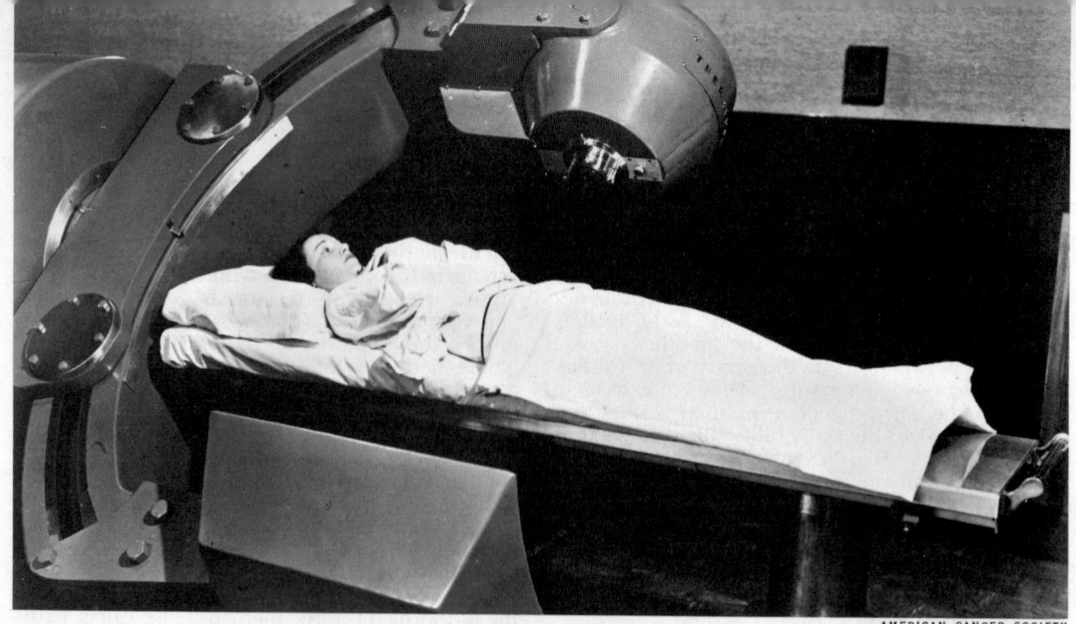

AMERICAN CANCER SOCIETY

RADIATION THERAPY can retard the growth of some cancers, and in certain cases it can entirely eradicate the cancer without recourse to other treatment.

been found to inhibit the growth of cells, the use of these chemicals in treating cancer has been limited by the fact that there is no evidence of the selectivity of any of these substances on cancer cells. For many years, biochemical studies of normal and cancer cells have concentrated on determining possible differences in growth requirements between the two types of cells, but no such differences have been found. As a result, in nearly every instance, drugs that interfere with the growth of cancer cells also adversely affect normal cells. Nevertheless, certain chemicals, when used cautiously, have the ability to impair the growth of neoplastic cells without doing irreparable damage to normal cells.

The modern era of chemotherapy is considered to have begun during World War II, when research on poison gases showed that mustard gas interferes markedly with the growth of cells. The development of a related substance, nitrogen mustard, provided a drug that was and still is of great value in the treatment of certain types of cancer, particularly lymphomas, chronic leukemias, and carcinomas originating in the lung and ovary. Since then, scientists have developed several related drugs that are easier to use and produce fewer undesirable side effects. These newer drugs include busulfan, chlorambucil, and cyclophosphamide.

Another group of drugs used in cancer chemotherapy are the antimetabolites, substances that closely resemble certain essential nutrients of cells. By substituting for the required nutrients, these drugs interfere with cell nutrition and consequently affect cell growth. Although the antimetabolites that affect cancer cells also affect normal cells, it has been possible, through careful regulation of the dosage, for them to temporarily slow down or stop the growth of certain types of cancer, particularly the acute leukemias. The antimetabolites that have been traditionally used in treating cancer are methotrexate, 6-mercaptopurine, and 5-fluorouracil. A more recent addition to this group, arabinosyl cytosine, appears to be contributing to the treatment of patients with leukemias that do not respond to the other antimetabolites.

In addition to the antimetabolites and nitrogen mustard group, other kinds of chemotherapeutic agents have contributed to the treatment of cancer. These include actinomycin D and daunomycin, both of which are antibiotics. These drugs are too damaging to human cells to be useful in treating infections but they can be used in treating certain types of cancer, notably acute leukemia and choriocarcinoma.

Another group of chemicals recently developed are derived from a plant, the Madagascar, or red periwinkle (*Vinca rosea*). These drugs (vinblastine and vineristine) are used primarily in treating acute leukemias and certain lymphomas.

Hormone treatment is another form of cancer chemotherapy. The administration of male or female sex hormones can produce temporary, but sometimes dramatic, improvements in carcinomas of the breast and prostate. Cortisone, which is normally produced by the adrenal gland, and several cortisone-like synthetic drugs have been very useful in the treatment of acute leukemias and certain chronic leukemias and lymphomas.

Although chemotherapy is not usually considered to be curative, there are a few kinds of cancers that can be completely cured through the use of drugs. Choriocarcinoma, a rare, serious, and usually rapidly fatal type of cancer that arises in a remnant of the placenta after childbirth or a miscarriage, has been completely and apparently permanently eradicated by a variety of chemotherapeutic agents, including methotrexate, actinomycin D, and vinblastine. It is now considered that up to 80% of all women with this type of cancer may be completely cured with these drugs. Another type of malignancy that can apparently be cured by chemotherapy is Burkitt's tumor, a kind of lymphoma that occurs predominately in children living in a narrow strip across Africa, below the Sahara Desert. This type of cancer can be completely eradicated by any of several different drugs when the treatment is started early enough.

Supportive Treatment. Supportive treatment is an important part of the management of cancer patients, whether the primary treatment is surgery, radiation, or chemotherapy. The treatment of all forms of cancer has been helped by improvements that have been made in blood transfusion techniques, antibiotics, anesthesia, and pain-killing drugs. Even in cases in which a permanent cure cannot be achieved, it is often possible to prolong the patient's life significantly and nearly always to relieve the patient's symptoms.

CANCER RESEARCH

Since the end of World War II, medical research, particularly cancer research, has expanded enormously. The importance of cancer as a major cause of death and the recognition that the problems of cell growth in cancer are of basic biologic importance have stimulated research into every facet of the disease and it has become apparent that many of these facets are related.

Many laboratories, chemical, radiologic, viral, and genetic, have become concerned with the problems of mutations, trying to discover how mutations are induced and how they affect a cell's activities. Additional information concerning the cause of mutations may be provided by epidemiological studies, which gather evidence from large populations.

The development and improvement of the electron microscope and other instruments have made it possible for scientists to examine the fine structure within cells, stimulating the investigation of viruses as possible carcinogenic agents. Another phase of current cancer research is concerned with the study of immunity. There is evidence that some animals may have an immunity to certain types of tumors, and this has intensified the search for tumor immunity in humans.

An example of a laboratory program designed to develop new chemotherapeutic agents is the current research on L-asparaginase. Based on the observation that a component in the blood serum of guinea pigs could inhibit the growth of experimentally induced leukemia in mice, it was determined that certain leukemic and other cancer cells require a certain amino acid, L-asparagine, for their growth but that normal cells do not. This finding appeared to be the first observation of a specific biochemical difference between normal and cancer cells. L-asparagine is destroyed by an enzyme, L-asparaginase, and it is this enzyme that is responsible for the antileukemic effect of guinea pig serum. Subsequent studies on people with leukemia have indicated that L-asparaginase also has the ability to inhibit the growth of human leukemia cells without damaging normal cells. However, its effectiveness in human leukemia has yet to be fully determined.

In the field of surgery, the development of new techniques and materials is constantly increasing the possibility of removing cancers completely. Current studies of organ transplantation and the use of artificial organs may further extend the limits of surgical removal of cancerous organs without causing severe disability.

IRWIN H. KRAKOFF, M. D.
Sloan-Kettering Institute for Cancer Research

Bibliography

Blakemore, William S., and Ravdin, Isidor S., eds., *Current Perspectives in Cancer Therapy* (Evanston, Ill., 1966).
Greenstein, Jesse P., *Biochemistry of Cancer* (New York 1965).
Homburger, F., ed., *Progress in Tumor Research* (New York 1963).

CANCERROOT is a parasitic flowering plant of the broom-rape family, which lacks chlorophyll and absorbs food from the roots of other plants. The stems of cancerroot grow to 10 inches (25 cm) tall, are tan colored, and bear narrow, tan, scalelike leaves. Clusters of stems frequently grow from a single underground stem. One nodding flower, white or pale lilac with two yellow spots near the center, appears at the tip of the stem in May or June. Cancerroot, *Orobanche uniflora,* is usually found in moist woods throughout much of the United States and Canada. The name cancerroot is sometimes applied to beechdrops and squawroot, members of the same family.

JOAN E. RAHN, *Lake Forest College, Ill.*

CANCIONERO DE BAENA, kän-thyō-nä′rō t͟hā bä-ā′nȧ, an anthology of 14th and 15th century Spanish poetry, compiled about 1445 by Juan Alfonso de Baena (1406–1454) for John II of Castile. It contains the courtly verse of some 50 poets, called *trovadores,* of late medieval Spain, most notably Alfonso Álvarez de Villasandino. Similar collections are the *Cancionero de Stúñiga* (late 15th century) and the *Cancionero general* (1511).

CANCIONEIROS, kaɴn-syō-nā′ē-rōōs, meaning "songbooks" in Portuguese, refers specifically to several anthologies of medieval Galician and Portuguese verse. About 2,000 compositions of the late 12th to the mid-14th century are collected in the *Cancioneiro da Ajuda,* the *Cancioneiro da Vaticana,* the *Cancioneiro Colocci-Brancuti,* and the *Cantigas de Santa Maria.* They include *cantigas de amigo,* a young girl's songs of her lover; *cantigas de amor,* addressed by a lover to his lady, and the satirical *cantigas de escárnio e maldizer.*

The later *Cancioneiro Geral* (1516) includes the work of 286 poets, some of whom also wrote in Spanish. It includes many examples of the *glosar os motes,* a courtly diversion in which the poet was required to follow a specified poetic pattern.

CANDACE, kan′də-sē, was the hereditary title of the queens of ancient Ethiopia. It was mistaken by the Greeks and Romans for a personal name.

The most famous Candace, like other queens of Ethiopia, was most likely queen-regent for her son. She invaded the Roman province of Egypt in 22 B.C. and was defeated by Gaius Petronius, governor of Egypt. Emperor Augustus canceled the tribute that had been imposed on Ethiopia by Petronius.

CANDELA OUTERIÑO, kän-dä′lä ōō-tä-rē′nyō, **Félix** (1910–), Mexican architect and engineer, who pioneered in the design and construction of concrete shell structures. He was born in Madrid, Spain, on Jan. 27, 1910, and was graduated from the Escuela Superior de Arquitectura in Madrid in 1935. During the Spanish Civil War (1936–1939) he served as a captain of engineers in the Republican army. After the war he left Spain for Mexico, where he established a construction firm in Mexico City.

Candela first gained international attention with his design for the Radiation Institute at the University of Mexico (1951), on which he collaborated with J. González Reyna. The building is a hyperbolic paraboloid (saddle-shaped) structure of concrete. Candela's later work includes the Iglesia de La Virgen Milagrosa (1953; Mexico City) and the Los Manantiales restaurant (1958; Xochimilco).

Further Reading: Faber, Colin, *Candela: The Shell Builder* (New York 1963).

CANDELILLA, kan-də-lē′yə, is an important vegetable wax used as a substitute for carnauba wax in many products, especially paste waxes. Candelilla is inferior to canauba in hardness, luster, melting point, and emulsifying ("mixing") properties and therefore is less used for self-polishing waxes. It may be used in carbon papers, inks, cosmetics, lubricants, paint removers, electrical insulation, and crayons, and as a substitute for chicle in chewing gum.

Candelilla is obtained from the wax-covered stems of *Euphorbia antisyphilitica*, a small desert plant of the spurge family (Euphorbiaceae) found in northern Mexico and adjacent areas of the United States. The wax is removed by submerging the plants in a mixture of boiling water and sulfuric acid.

LAWRENCE ERBE
University of Southwestern Louisiana

CANDIA. See IRÁKLION.

CANDIDA, kan′di-də, is a play by George Bernard Shaw, written about 1895 and published in the volume *Plays: Pleasant and Unpleasant* (1898). Although critics immediately hailed it as a masterpiece of satire, it was not performed in London until 1904.

In *Candida,* Shaw took the familiar dramatic triangle of a woman and two men—Candida, her parson husband, and the young poet Marchbanks who loves her—and turned it into something "quite new and strange and diverting," as one critic put it. Candida, forced to choose between her husband and Marchbanks, decides to stay with the former when she realizes he is the weaker of the two men.

Ellen Terry, who may have inspired *Candida,* never played the title role. Famous Candidas in England have been Janet Achurch, who created the role, Sybil Thorndike, and Diana Wynyard. In the United States, Katharine Cornell first appeared in the part in 1924, and revived it many times—most notably in 1946.

ALAN DENT
Author of "Mrs. Patrick Campbell"

CANDIDE, OU L'OPTIMISME, kän-dēd′o͞o lôp-tē-mēsm′, is a philosophical tale by Voltaire (q.v.) published in 1759. Voltaire's most popular work, it is a terse, lucid, and brilliantly witty satire on 18th century optimistic rationalization.

Candide focuses on the problem of evil. Earlier writers, notably Leibniz and Pope, had "solved" this problem by asserting that all apparent evils are necessary steps toward universal good. Voltaire's own *Discours en vers sur l'homme* (1734–1737) reflects Pope's doctrine that "whatever is, is right"; and the hero of his tale Zadig (1747) suffers many misfortunes but finally learns from an angel that all evils lead to good.

By 1758, Voltaire's opinion had changed. The terrible Lisbon earthquake of 1755 had shaken his optimism, and his *Poème sur le désastre de Lisbonne* (1756), despite its prudently qualified conclusion, is bleakly pessimistic.

In *Candide,* Voltaire resolutely avoids coming to terms with evil. Candide, the naïve young hero of the tale, has been brought up in the household of Baron Thunder-ten-tronckh, but he is expelled when he falls in love with the Baron's daughter Cunégonde. Candide wanders around the world, sometimes with and sometimes separated from Cunégonde, her brother, and his own tutor Pangloss, a disciple of Leibniz who unceasingly proclaims that "all is for the best in this best of all possible worlds"—although they experience a great variety of terrible disasters, including war, plague, famine, rape, multilation, the Inquisition, and the Lisbon earthquake. Candide finds happiness only in the South American kingdom Eldorado, but there he soon grows bored. Ultimately the companions are reunited in Constantinople. Cunégonde has grown ugly and foul-tempered, and Pangloss continues to philosophize, but Candide concludes practically, "We must cultivate our garden."

Candide mercilessly derides the many absurd perversions of science, religion, government, and romance. It asserts the futility of philosophical speculation and the necessity of hard work.

KENNETH DOUGLAS, *Author of "A Critical Bibliography of Existentialism"*

CANDIDOSIS, kan-də-dō′sis, is one of the commonest fungal diseases of man. Candidosis, previously known as candidiasis and moniliasis, is caused by *Candida* fungi that live in the mouth and digestive tract. A common form of candidosis, known as *thrush,* involves the skin and mucous membranes. Other forms affect the lining of the heart (endocarditis), the meninges (meningitis), and the blood (blood poisoning, or septicemia). See also BLOOD POISONING; MENINGITIS; THRUSH.

CANDLE. A candle is made largely of solid combustible waxes or fatty substances formed around a fibrous wick. As a candle burns, its flame is fed by a supply of molten wax, which flows up the wick as a result of capillary action. Candles are used chiefly for lighting, especially ornamental lighting, but they are also used as a readily portable source of heat for chafing dishes and similar appliances.

History. The origin of the candle is unknown. The ancient Egyptians used both tapers and candles, and it seems likely that candles were developed from tapers that consisted of fibrous materials impregnated with wax or tallow. The rushlight, for example, was a taper made by saturating the pithy core of reeds or rushes with molten fat. At some later date a fiber wick was dipped in molten tallow, cooled, and redipped until the desired thickness of tallow had solidified around the wick. Beeswax was probably next used in place of tallow and offered the advantages of an aromatic odor without the unpleasant characteristics of burned fats. Much later, candles were made by pouring molten wax or tallow into molds containing wicks.

At the end of the 18th century the fishing industry was expanding, and spermaceti, the wax crystallized from the oil of the sperm whale, became a major constituent of candles. It too produced no acrid odor, and in addition produced candles which did not tend to soften and bend in summer temperatures. The spermaceti candle was the first standard candle. It weighed one sixth of a pound and was so constructed as to burn at the uniform rate of 120 grains per hour. Follow-

WILL & BAUMER CANDLE CO., INC.

CANDLES may be given a final color coating of wax by the hand-dipping method.

ing spermaceti as a candle wax source came ceresin, or ozokerite, a mineral hydrocarbon wax that featured a high melting point and therefore had the power to stiffen or harden the softer tallow or beeswax.

About the middle of the 19th century paraffin wax crystallized from petroleum became a major wax ingredient for candle manufacture. Paraffin required considerable stiffening because of its tendency to soften and become plastic at temperatures well under its melting point. This led to the blending of paraffin with spermaceti and ceresin. By the end of the 19th century the cause of the acrid odor from the burning of glyceride fats had been traced to the glycerin component of the fat. This led to the use of the solid fatty acids, prepared by the splitting of animal fats with subsequent separation of the solid acids by crystallization. The solid fatty acids (palmitic and stearic) were found to impart no acrid odor, to stiffen the paraffin, and to give a brighter light.

Contrary to popular belief, the advent of modern electric lighting did not cause a sharp reduction in candle production. In fact, since the turn of the century candle production has increased because of the popularity of candles for ornamental lighting.

Modern Manufacture. Modern automatic candle molding machinery used today, although embodying numerous improvements, is not unlike the first candle-molding machine invented by Joseph Morgan in 1834.

There are three important phases in the commercial manufacture of candles: preparation of the wicking; preparation of the wax base; and continuous molding of the finished candle.

Preparation of the Wicking. A good grade of cotton or linen is woven or braided in such a way that it will burn in one direction, curling so as to extrude its end into the oxidizing zone of the candle flame for complete combustion. Porosity or capillarity of the wick must be such as to draw the molten wax into the combustion zone as fast as it is melted by the flame. In addition, the wick is impregnated with inorganic salt solutions and dried prior to molding into candles. These solutions retard the combustion of the wicking. If untreated, the wicking would burn too rapidly, and the flame would be quenched by submersion in the molten wax. If wick combustion is retarded excessively, then as the amount of exposed wick increases, the amount of wax obsorbed into the flame increases, and the candle can become a hazard.

Preparation of the Wax Base. Standard commercial candles in the United States, whether decorative or plain white, contains 60% paraffin, 35% stearic acid, and 5% beeswax. Depending upon climatic conditions, small amounts of candelilla or carnauba waxes may be added for the purpose of raising the softening or melting point of the finished wax formula. Beeswax candles may contain only the pure insect wax or may be a blend of beeswax and as much as 50% paraffin, plus a small quantity of stiffening wax and stearic acid.

The wax is carefully blended into a clear, molten mass prior to being fed to the continuous molding machine. In the melting of the wax, direct heating is accomplished in steam-jacketed kettles. Heating by direct flame or prolonged heating is avoided so as not to produce charred, dark-colored wax or small pieces of carbon char. Most wax ingredients are purchased according to specification and require no special purification. In any case, the molten wax mixture is carefully filtered to remove any insoluble impurities that might interfere with wick capillarity.

Continuous Molding of the Finished Candle. Candle-molding machines are designed to mold a series, or multiple charge, of candles. One charge may involve anywhere from 50 to 500 candles per load, and the machines complete a cycle in about 20 to 30 minutes. The molds or tubes are made of tin whose interior surface is highly polished and slightly tapered to facilitate ejection of the finished candle. The tip mold, which shapes the wick end of the candle, is drilled and threaded, with the wicking led from a spool beneath the mold. The wicking is drawn through the mold prior to filling with the filtered molten-wax formula. The wax, previously cooled to a point just above its melting point, is then poured into the trough above the molds, and it runs into the individual molds, all of which are preheated so as to permit the wax to flow into all portions of the mold. The steam or hot water in the jacket around the molds is then vented or drained, and the surrounding chamber is cold-water chilled until solidification of the candle is complete. The candle battery is then ejected upward into the clamp above the machine, thereby drawing the continuous wick through for the next batch. Finished candles are trimmed, the molding tubes are reheated, and the cycle is then repeated. Different temperatures of pouring, molding, and solidification are employed, depending upon the wax formulation used.

HARLAND H. YOUNG
Swift and Company

CANDLE, in physics. See PHOTOMETRY.

CANDLEBERRY. See WAX MYRTLE.

CANDLEFISH, a North Pacific smelt that is found from the Klamath River in California to southeastern and southern Alaska and around the Pribilof Islands in the Bering Sea. The candlefish, which is also known by its Indian name *eulachon,* is esteemed as a food fish and was used by the Indians for food and oil. At one time the Indians also used dried candlefish, with wicks drawn through their oily bodies, as candles (hence "candlefish").

The candlefish is a trim, slender fish with a troutlike appearance. It has no spines in its fins, only soft rays and a small, fleshy adipose fin on the back about midway between the dorsal fin and the tail fin. It is bluish brown along the back and silver on the sides. Specimens reaching about 1 foot (30 cm) long have been seen, but a length of 6 or 7 inches (15 to 18 cm) is more common.

The candlefish spends most of its life in the ocean, where it is preyed upon by salmon and fur seals. After 2 or 3 years in the sea, the fish, now fat and oily, swims into freshwater streams in the spring to spawn, burying its eggs in fine gravel or sand. The eggs hatch in 2 or 3 weeks, and the hatchlings are carried out to sea by the currents. The adults die after spawning.

The candlefish, *Thaleichthys pacificus,* belongs to the smelt family (Osmeridae) of the order Clupeiformes. The family is a small group of fishes, most of which live in the North Pacific.

DANIEL M. COHEN
U. S. Fish and Wildlife Service

Candlefish

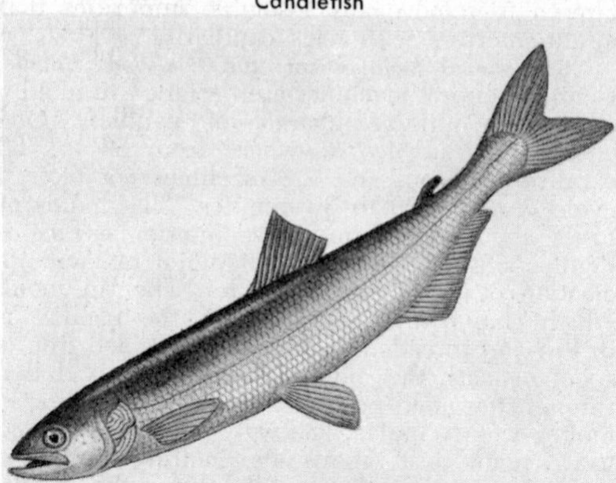

CANDLEMAS, kan′dəl-məs, is a feast of February 2 that, in the Roman Catholic and Anglican churches, commemorates the Purification of Mary; in the Eastern Christian churches it commemorates the Presentation of Christ in the Temple. In accordance with Mosaic law (Leviticus 12:2–8), Mary presented Jesus in the Temple of Jerusalem and made an offering to symbolize her purification 40 days after his birth (Luke 2:22–38). The feast, which can be traced to the 4th century, is marked by a procession and by the blessing of candles, to symbolize Christ as the Light of the World.

CANDLENUT, the seed of the candleberry tree (*Aleurites moluccana*), native to southeastern Asia but now cultivated in many tropical areas. The nuts, which are walnut-sized, yield a drying oil, known as candlenut oil, kekune oil, or lumbang oil, that is used in the making of paints, varnishes, lacquers, and linoleum. The oil cake is poisonous and is used only as a fertilizer.

CANDLEPOWER is the intensity, or *luminous flux,* of a light source, expressed in units called *candles.* See PHOTOMETRY.

CANDLER, kan′dlər, **Asa Griggs** (1851–1929), American manufacturer and philanthropist, who founded the Coca Cola soft drink company. He was born near Villa Rica, Ga., on Dec. 20, 1851. After studying medicine and pharmacy privately, he became a pharmacist in Atlanta.

In 1887 he purchased the formula for Coca Cola, which had been perfected by Dr. J. S. Pemberton, a patent medicine manufacturer. After improving its quality, Candler gave his full time to its production and sale. From 1909 to 1917 his company was the defendant in a federal case under the Pure Food and Drug Act regarding the contents of the beverage. After assertions by the company that the Coca Cola formula had been changed, the case was settled by condemnation of a quantity of the beverage.

Candler sold the business in 1917 for $25 million. In the same year he was elected mayor of Atlanta. He gave generous support to the city's religious and educational institutions, and with his personal credit he bolstered Atlanta real estate and the badly depressed cotton market. His large gifts to Emory College assured its expansion to university status. Candler died in Atlanta on March 12, 1929.

COURTNEY ROBERT HALL
Author, "History of American Industrial Science"

CANDLESTICK, a device designed to hold a candle. A *candelabrum* is a branched candleholder designed for two or more candles. A candleholder attached to a wall is called a *sconce,* and one hung from the ceiling is known as a *chandelier.*

Because candles are more difficult to make—as well as more expensive to burn—than oil or tallow lamps lit with a floating wick, the burning of candles has always been considered a luxury. Candleholders, therefore, became objects associated with wealth, and through history they have commonly been made of costly materials in styles that reflect the prevailing artistic taste.

Early History. The earliest candlesticks were probably designed to serve ecclesiastical and ceremonial purposes. Though there exist a few objects resembling socket candlesticks that date

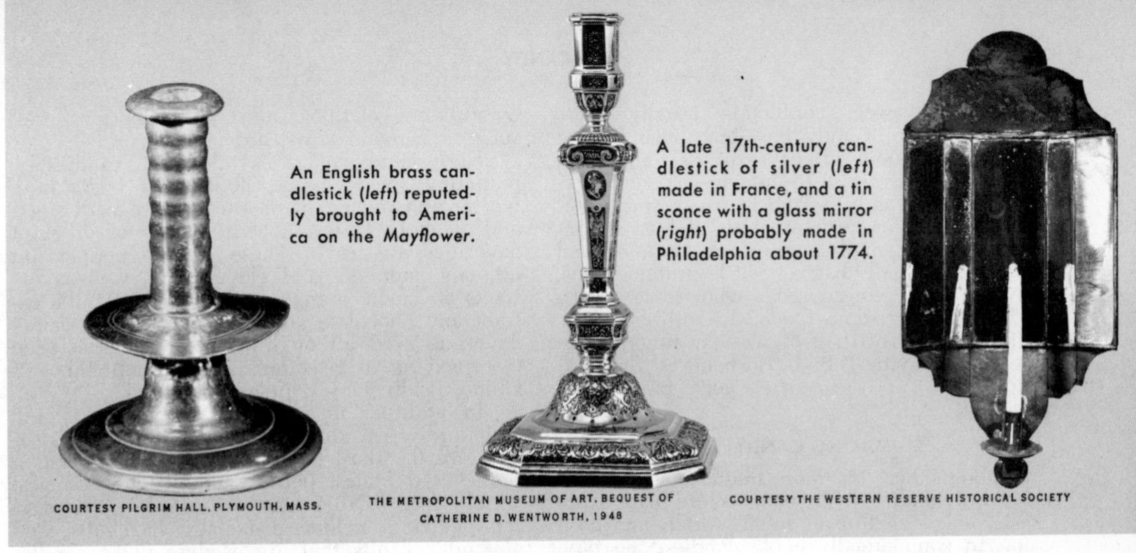

An English brass candlestick (*left*) reputedly brought to America on the *Mayflower*.

A late 17th-century candlestick of silver (*left*) made in France, and a tin sconce with a glass mirror (*right*) probably made in Philadelphia about 1774.

COURTESY PILGRIM HALL, PLYMOUTH, MASS. THE METROPOLITAN MUSEUM OF ART, BEQUEST OF CATHERINE D. WENTWORTH, 1948 COURTESY THE WESTERN RESERVE HISTORICAL SOCIETY

from pre-Christian times, there is reason to doubt that candles were known at that time. (The famous "seven-branched candlestick" that the Jews were commanded to erect before the ark of the Covenant probably consisted of oil lamps rather than true candleholders.) The first firm evidence of the use of candles dates from the 1st century A. D., when Pliny the Younger described threads of flax coated with pitch and rush lights made of peeled rush stems dipped in wax.

The earliest known candlesticks were *prickets,* candleholders with, instead of sockets, thin iron spikes onto which candles could be stuck. Prickets often were made with wide drip pans beneath them to catch melted wax. Since candles were not uniform in size, they often had to be either pared down or surrounded with stuffing to make them fit into socket candlesticks, but any size candle could be stuck on a pricket.

Most medieval candlesticks were prickets. They were made of iron or brass, sometimes incorporating fanciful figures or beasts and dragons as bases. After the medieval period prickets were seldom made for domestic purposes; socket-type candleholders replaced them.

Renaissance and Later. By the 16th century socket candlesticks were in common domestic use among the rich. They usually took the shape of a short stem set above a squat, bell-like base, and were made of brass, silver, or pottery.

In the 17th century, candlesticks took on an architectural character; they were built up of single fluted columns or groups of clustered columns. Often they had wide platforms around the sockets to catch the dripping wax. For stability, the columns were mounted in high plinths above broad flat bases. Later, candlesticks with baluster stems were made of cast brass, a form popular through the early 1700's and often revived.

With the spread of the rococo style in the 1730's, baluster candlesticks were superseded by more elaborate, assymetrical shapes built up of foliage and shell forms. During the classical revival of the 1770's, column forms came back into favor, along with classical decorative motifs such as husks, rosettes, and swags. The early 19th century saw a return to baluster shapes, which gave way briefly at the end of the century to the twisted, vinelike stems of art nouveau (q.v.). Candlesticks of the 20th century include revivals of all past styles, as well as highly imaginative new designs in a wide range of materials – from terra cotta to plastic.

Candlestands. Both single candlesticks and candelabra have had special furniture developed to hold them. Torcheres, or candlestands, were used during the 17th and 18th centuries to hold single candlesticks and candelabra. They were frequently of wood, often gilded, and usually stood about five feet (1.5 m) high. Candlestands were often made in matched sets of two or more to be placed where there might not otherwise be furniture to support the candlestick. They also made it possible to achieve a more even light throughout the room.

Reflectors. Because the light thrown by a single candle is so slight, reflectors of various kinds have long been used to multiply the available light. During the Renaissance candles were set at the ends of arms and hung from wall sconces made of highly polished silver or brass. Later reflectors incorporated mirrors, which might be faceted to give the light a shimmering effect. Rock crystal or cut glass prisms hanging from candelabra or wall sconces gave the same effect.

J. STEWART JOHNSON, *Newark Museum of Art*

Further Reading: Butler, Joseph T., *American Candleholders* (New York 1967); O'Dea, William T., *The Social History of Lighting* (London 1958).

CANDOLLE, kän-dôl', **Augustin Pyrame de** (1778–1841), Swiss botanist, whose system of classifying plants on the basis of structure was an important contribution to the development of botany. Influenced by Antoine Laurent de Jussieu's idea of a natural system of classification, Candolle thought that anatomy alone should be the basis of plant classification. He studied the structure, position, and number of the organs of plants and based his classification on the similarities and relationships that he found. Through his ideas on plant taxonomy and his natural classification system, he exerted considerable influence on later botanists.

Candolle was born in Geneva on Feb. 4, 1778. After studying in Paris, he served as professor of botany at the University of Montpellier from 1808 to 1816. While there, he wrote *Théorie élementaire de la botanique* (1813), in which he outlined his important ideas on plant taxonomy. Later, while teaching in Geneva, he began *Prodromus systematis naturalis*, a monumental attempt to classify and describe all seed plants. He died in Geneva on Sept. 9, 1841 after completing the first seven volumes of his project.

CANDY, Ceylon. See KANDY.

CANDY is a sweet confection usually made largely of sugar. Candy has long been one of man's favorite foods. Because of its high sugar content, candy is also a high-energy food. However, although candy is rich in sugar and sometimes also contains large amounts of fats, it contains only very small amounts of vitamins and minerals and usually has very little protein. Thus, candy cannot be considered a wholesome substitute for more nutritious foods. In addition, some candies, because of their high sugar content, can cause dental cavities. It is also believed that eating too much candy can cause acne, particularly in adolescents.

MAKING CANDY

Although there are more than 2,000 different varieties of candies, many of them are made from a basic boiled mixture of sugar, water, and corn syrup. In commercially made candies, the type of sugar used may be invert sugar (a mixture of glucose and fructose), dextrose, maltose, or sucrose. Other types of sweeteners used include honey and maple syrup. Corn syrup is also used as a sweetener, but its more important function is to control sugar granulation (crystallization).

The length of time the mixture is boiled, the temperature to which it is then cooled, and the way in which it is handled after it is cooled, determine to a large extent the textural characteristics of candy. As the sugar mixture is boiled, it first reaches what is called the soft-ball stage at about 240° F (about 116° C), the temperature at which fondant is cooked. If cooked further, the mixture reaches the hard-ball stage at about 270° F (about 132° C), the temperature at which taffy is made. Between 300° F and 310° F (149° C and 154° C) the hard-crack stage is reached. At this point many mints, lollipops, spun sugar, and barley sugar are made. With the addition of milk, cream, butter, or chocolate to the sugar mixture the range of candies widens to include fudge, which is cooked at low temperatures, and, at higher temperatures, caramels, toffee, and butterscotch. To make divinities and nougats, egg whites are added to the syrup, and by adding a gelatinous substance, smooth candies, such as marshmallows, are made.

Early candymakers flavored their candies by pounding spices, herbs, flowers, or fruits in a mortar and mixing them into a paste with sugar and alcohol. Today, a wide variety of different flavorings are used. These include peppermint oil, cinnamon oil, and clove oil as well as extracts of lemon, orange, and almond. Vanilla extract and chocolate are the most popular candy flavorings used, although licorice, which has been esteemed for its sweetness since ancient times in China, is also very popular.

In addition to various flavorings, nuts and fruits are often added to candies. Although peanuts are the most popular type of candy nut in the United States, pecans and walnuts are also widely used. Other kinds of nuts often used in candymaking include pistachios, hazelnuts, and almonds. Fruits that are used to make candies are sometimes used whole, as in chocolate-covered cherries. More often, however, they are cut into small pieces and added to marshmallows, chocolate bars, or other types of candy.

PULLING TAFFY by machine improves its texture and blends in the various flavorings at the same time.

HISTORY

Beginnings of Candymaking. Probably the first candies made in early civilizations were sweetmeats of fruits and nuts, often bound together with a flour paste, sweetened with honey, and flavored with various herbs and spices. These candies satisfied man's craving for sweets and also served to preserve fresh fruits so that they could be eaten in winter.

One of the oldest hard candies is barley sugar, which was originally—and sometimes still is—made with barley grains. A sugarless form of this confection was eaten by the ancient Greeks and Romans, and in China it was spun into stick form and rolled in toasted sesame seeds. The forerunner of the modern Turkish delight was a boiled grape juice and starch mixture that was cut into strips or squares. Marzipan, the sweetened almond paste that is often molded into the shape of fruits or figures, developed from the almond sweetmeats that were served at lavish Oriental feasts centuries ago.

The earliest recorded references to candies are found in Egyptian papyri that date back to 2000 B. C. In tombs of a later period are illustrations showing various steps in the candymaking process. These drawings show, for example, how the candies were molded into various shapes inside furnaces and how honey, which was the principal sweetener, was culled from honeycombs, strained, and heated in small ovens.

Candy in the Middle Ages. During the Middle Ages the apothecaries were the first to sell sugar candies. Sugar was classed as a drug, and it was blended with bitter-tasting medicines to disguise their flavor. In addition, the apothecary's sugar pill, either with or without medicinal ingredients, was regarded as the cure for many ailments. Sometimes, the pill was made from an herbal infusion boiled with a sugar syrup. More often, however, the sugar pills were made by hard-boiling a sugar syrup, pulling it over a hook until it was opaque, and cutting the hardened sweet into small pieces that were then powdered or pressed into pills.

Although sugar was not uncommon in Europe after the Crusades, it was so costly that it was measured by the ounce and only the wealthiest households could afford it. Despite the pro-

BON BONS are made by dipping centers into a fondant coating with a fork and drying them on trays.

hibitive price of sugar, however, France became famous for its crystallized fruits and sugared almonds as early as the 15th century. In Italy, a popular candy was confetti, small hard sugarplums that carnival revelers pelted at one another. Nougats were probably first made in Spain a few centuries later.

Introduction of Machinery. Although candymaking machines were invented in the late 1700's, confectionary manufacture on a large scale did not begin until the last half of the 19th century. England was the first country to manufacture hard candies in large quantities, and at Prince Albert's Great Exhibition, which was held in London in 1851, European and American confectioners were introduced to a large assortment of boiled sweets, bonbons, chocolate creams, caramels, and many other types of candy. These candies aroused so much interest that other countries soon began candy manufacturing industries of their own. With the development of new machinery for making different kinds of candy and the increasing abundance of sugar (a method of obtaining sugar from the juice of the sugar beet had been devised in 1747), candymaking rapidly grew into a major food industry in many European countries and the United States.

Candymaking in the United States. At the time of the Great Exhibition in 1851, commercial candymaking in the United States was largely confined to candy sticks and lozenges. Machinery had been introduced only 10 years earlier; before then, all candy had been made by hand. The early settlers had made maple sugar and nut confections, and the first candied apples and rock candy probably appeared in the 18th century. The first commercial American candymakers were the Dutch bakers of New Amsterdam who, during the 1700's, made sugar wafers, marchpanes (later known as marzipan), macaroons, and sugarplums.

The days of the penny candy in the late 1800's were probably the most colorful days of candy in the United States. Every grocery store had buckets of such favorites as jawbreakers, licorice ropes, Gibraltars, all-day suckers, heart-shaped sweets with sentimental sayings imprinted on them, and sugar-coated nuts that were known as Boston baked beans.

Although many of the basic types of candies originated in continental Europe and in England, some candies are distinctly American. Although the French had invented the almond praline in the 18th century, candymakers in New Orleans devised a pecan version of this candy. Peanut brittle, according to one legend, came about in the 1890's, when a New England woman absentmindedly added baking soda instead of cream of tartar to a batch of peanut taffy cooking on the stove. Fudge is believed to have resulted from another accident, probably from a ruined batch of caramels. Caramel-coated popcorn balls became popular in the 1870's, and about 30 years later popcorn was combined with caramel and peanuts, resulting in Cracker Jack.

World War I brought about the greatest revolution in the candy industry in the 20th century—the spectacular rise of the candy bar. In 1876 solid milk chocolate had been invented in Switzerland, and by the early 1900's a few candymakers were experimenting with chocolate bars. During the war years, however, many companies began mass-producing candy bars to meet the enormous military demand. By World War II, hundreds of different varieties of candy bars were being manufactured and they are still one of the most popular forms of candy.

PRODUCTION AND CONSUMPTION

In terms of dollar volume, the United States, in the mid-1960's, produced an estimated $1.4 billion worth of candy each year. Great Britain, the largest producer in western Europe, accounted for $900 million, while West Germany was next, with $575 million.

In the United States the candy industry ranks 9th among the food industries. In the mid-1960's, the leading candy-producing states were Illinois, which produced about 31% of the nation's total, and Pennsylvania, which accounted for about 16.5%. New York and New Jersey together produced about 19%.

It is estimated that the annual per capita consumption of candy in the United States was about 19 pounds (8.5 kg) in the mid-1960's. The per capita consumption in Great Britain was about 24 pounds (11 kg). For Belgium and Luxembourg combined it was about 22 pounds (10 kg).

CAROLINE BATES
Former Senior Editor, "Gourmet" Magazine

Further Reading: Austin, Alma H., *The Romance of Candy* (Evanston, Ill., 1938).

ROCHE

Candytuft (*Iberis umbellata*)

CANDYTUFT is the common name for plants of the genus *Iberis,* of the mustard family (Cruciferae). Candytufts are low-growing annuals, biennials, or perennials, seldom attaining more than 1 foot (30 cm) in height. The perennial species are typically evergreen and usually woody near the base. Most candytufts are native to the Mediterranean region.

The small, four-petaled, white to purplish flowers, produced in spring and summer, are borne in showy clusters (corymbs or short racemes). The outer two petals of each flower in the cluster are characteristically larger than the inner two petals.

About 10 species are cultivated. One of the most popular is *I. sempervirens,* the edging, or evergreen, candytuft, an excellent border, rock-garden, and ground-cover plant.

R. C. Allen
Kingwood Center, Mansfield, Ohio

CANE, Melville Henry (1879–), American poet, whose verse ranges from light lyrics to long reflective poems. He was born in Plattsburgh, N. Y., on April 15, 1879. In 1905, after receiving a law degree from Columbia University, he joined a New York City law firm.

Cane's verse first appeared in magazines during the early 1900's, and his first volume of poetry, *January Gardens,* was published in 1926. Later volumes included *Behind Dark Spaces* (1930), *Poems, New and Selected* (1938), *And Pastures New* (1956), *Bullet-Hunting* (1960), *The Golden Year* (1960), and *To Build a Fire* (1964). His major prose work is *Making a Poem* (1953).

CANE, is a term applied to the stems, or stalks, of a wide variety of plants. Horticulturally, the term "cane" usually refers to the stems of certain bush fruits, such as raspberries and blackberries, or to the stems of roses. Certain plants of the grass family (*Gramineae*), for example, the bamboos (*Bambusa*) and reeds (*Arundinaria*), are called "canes," as in cane reed, giant cane, southern cane, switch cane, sugarcane. The term "canebrake" refers to a thicket of cane plants, usually bamboo. The bamboos are mostly native to the tropics, with a few species found in temperate regions. Many are grown for ornamental purposes.

Botanically, the term "cane" should be restricted to a group of climbing, or trailing, plants of the palm family (Palmae), including the genera *Korthalsia, Plectocomia,* and particularly *Calamus:* these are known as the rattans. *C. tenuis* and *C. rotang* are the chief sources of rattan cane used for weaving wicker baskets, mats, and furniture. Another species, *C. scipionum,* furnishes the Malacca canes used for walking sticks.

Rattan palms are native to the Old World tropics, including the Indian Archipelago, the Malay Peninsula, India, and China. The very slender stems, which are seldom over 1 inch (25 mm) in diameter, creep or trail over other vegetation and may reach lengths as great as 500 feet (150 meters). The creeping habit of the rattan palm is facilitated by numerous hooklike structures on a slender continuation of the midrib of the leaves.

Both bamboo and rattan have a great many uses. Bamboo serves as a structural material for dwellings in many parts of the world and for all sorts of utensils, furniture, and equipment from fishing poles to umbrella handles. Rattan may also be twisted into rope or woven into many kinds of ornamental, decorative, and utilitarian objects.

R. C. Allen
Kingwood Center, Mansfield, Ohio

CANES VENATICI, kā'nēz və-nat'ə-sī, also known as the *Hunting Dogs,* is a faint spring constellation of the Northern Hemisphere. The constellation represents two hunting dogs held on a leash by Boötes as they pursue Ursa Major—the Great Bear—across the sky. Canes Venatici contains no bright stars, but the Whirlpool galaxy (the first celestial object in which a spiral structure was observed) is located in the constellation. See also Constellation.

•

CAÑETE, Manuel kä-nyā'tā, (1822–1891), Spanish dramatist, critic, and literary historian. An early advocate of realism, he helped to break the dominance of the romantic tradition in Spanish drama.

Cañete was born in Seville on Aug. 6, 1822. He served for a time as secretary to the Infanta Dona Isabella (later, Queen Isabella II), and from 1883 he was active as one of Spain's most influential drama critics. He died in Madrid on Nov. 4, 1891.

Cañete's plays include *Lo que alcanza una pasión* (1842), *Un rebato en Granada* (1845), and *El duque de Alba* (1845). He also wrote a number of *zarzuelas,* short comic sketches that incorporate music and songs. Gradually, his interest turned from writing plays to dramatic criticism and the history of the Spanish theater. His books on these subjects include *Escritores españoles e hispano-americanos* (1884) and *Teatro español del siglo XVI* (1884). Cañete also wrote verse, collected as *Poesías* in 1859.

CANFIELD, Dorothy. See Fisher, Dorothy Canfield.

CANFIELD, Richard A. (1855–1914), American gambler, Wall Street operator, and art connoisseur, whose gambling houses drew a large sporting public toward the end of the 19th century. He was born in New Bedford, Mass., on June 17, 1855, and early acquired a passion for gambling. In the middle 1880's he began his spectacular career in New York. He had a palatial gambing house adjoining Delmonico's restaurant on 44th Street, and his Saratoga (N. Y.) Club became the

Monte Carlo of America; they were closed by court order in 1904 and 1907, respectively.

For years Canfield was one of the largest operators on Wall Street. His collection of Whistler paintings, sold to the Knoedler Galleries in New York City in 1914, was exceptional. He died on Dec. 11, 1914, leaving an estate estimated at more than $1 million. "Canfield," a variation of the game of solitaire, was named after him.

JACK STRALEY BATTELL
"Chess Review"

CANIDAE. See DOG.

CANIFF, kan′if, **Milton Arthur** (1907–), American cartoonist, who created the popular comic strips "Terry and the Pirates" and "Steve Canyon," which relate the adventures of American heroes in the Orient. Caniff was born in Hillsboro, Ohio, on Feb. 28, 1907. After graduating from Ohio State University in 1930, he began to work as a political cartoonist on the staff of the Columbus *Dispatch*.

In 1932, Caniff was hired by the Associated Press, for whom he created "The Gay Thirties" and "Dickie-Dare" comic strips. In 1934 he joined the Chicago Tribune–New York Daily News Syndicate and began "Terry and the Pirates." This was followed by "Steve Canyon," on which were based a movie serial and a television series. From 1946, Caniff's work was handled by the Publishers Newspaper Syndicate. The National Cartoonists Society presented him with its "Reuben" award in 1946.

CANIS MAJOR, kā′nis mā′jər, is a winter constellation that lies in the Southern Hemisphere. It contains Sirius, the brightest star in the sky, and six other stars of 2d or 3d magnitude. Since ancient times, Sirius has been known as the Dog of Orion because the constellation Orion precedes it across the heavens. Canis Major is known also as the Larger Dog, the English translation of its Latin name. See also CONSTELLATION; SIRIUS.

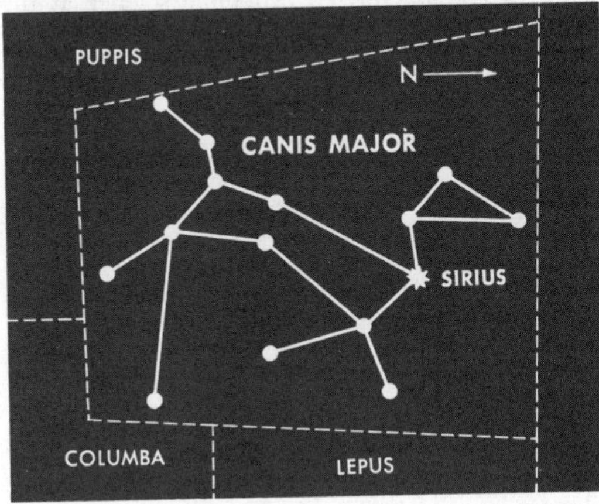

CANIS MINOR, kā′nəs mī′nər, is a small winter constellation of the Northern Hemisphere. Its name is Latin for "Smaller Dog," and it is also known by this name. In mythology it is the second hound of Orion (the first being Canis Major). Procyon, the brightest object in Canis Minor, is the 8th-brightest star in the sky. It is actually a binary, or double star, having a very faint companion. See CONSTELLATION.

CANISIUS, kə-nish′əs, **Saint Peter** (1521–1597), Dutch theologian, writer, and Doctor of the Church. He was born in Nijmegen, Netherlands, then subject to the Holy Roman Empire, on May 8, 1521. His family, the Kanis or Kanijs (Canisius is a Latinized form), were wealthy merchants. He received his M.A. from the University of Cologne in 1540 and remained there three years longer to study theology before he entered the Jesuit order. He was ordained in 1546.

From 1549 to 1560 Canisius labored in Germany, where he became the first Jesuit provincial and founded several colleges. During the crucial period of the Counter Reformation, his effective preaching and writing helped renew and stabilize the church in Germany. His most lasting and widespread influence, however, came through the catechisms he composed, which have gone through hundreds of editions. During his last years he labored in Switzerland, where he died at Fribourg, on Dec. 21, 1507. In 1925, Pope Pius XI canonized the "second Apostle of Germany," as Canisius is called, and also declared him a Doctor of the Church. His feast is April 27.

CANKAR, tsän′kär, **Ivan** (1876–1918), Slovene novelist, dramatist, and poet, who was one of the major figures in modern Yugoslav literature. He was born in Vrhnika, near Ljubljana, Slovenia (now part of Yugoslavia), on May 10, 1876. He went to Vienna in 1896 to study architecture but soon left school to write. He remained in Vienna, however, until 1909, supporting himself as a journalist. Thereafter he lived in Ljubljana, where he died on Dec. 11, 1918.

Cankar's only volume of poetry, *Erotika,* and the sketches *Vinjete,* both published in 1899, set the cynical and irreverent tone of his work, in which poverty and social injustice are the principal themes. His plays, influenced by Ibsen, include *Pohujšanje v Dolini Sentflorjanski* (1908; *Scandal in the Valley of St. Florian*) and *Lepa Vida* (1912; *The Beautiful Vida*). The novel *Hlapec Jernej* (1907; Eng. tr., *Yerney's Justice,* 1926) brought Cankar an international reputation. His other works include *Podobe iz sanj* (1917; *Parables from My Dreams*) and an unfinished autobiography, *Moje življenje* (1914; *My Life*).

CANKER, kang′kər, a small, shallow ulceration of the mouth. The lesion, also called a *canker sore,* usually occurs on the inner surface of the lip or under the tongue, although it may also occur on the palate or gums. Cankers are sometimes recurrent, and although they often occur singly, they also are known occasionally to develop in small groups.

A canker starts as a tiny blister that usually remains unnoticed until it develops into a shallow sore about ⅛ of an inch (3 mm) in diameter. The floor of the ulcer is grayish white and is surrounded by a narrow bright red zone. It is extremely tender and often painful but heals spontaneously within a period of from one to three weeks and leaves no scar.

Some cankers may be caused by eating certain foods or taking certain drugs, but the cause of the vast majority of cankers is still unknown. Although cankers cannot be prevented or cured, a light application of silver nitrate or tincture of benzoin often stops the pain and may hasten the onset of healing.

STEPHEN E. SILVER, M.D.
University of Oregon Medical School

CANKERWORM, a slender moth caterpillar that eats the foliage of fruit, shade, and forest trees, and is often seen swinging from branches on the silken threads that it spins. Because it crawls with a characteristic looping motion, it is also called *measuring worm, inchworm,* or *looper.* Cankerworms occasionally become abundant and cause serious damage.

Two kinds of cankerworm moths—spring and fall—are found in North America. The eggs of both types hatch in May. The larvae are green, with varying shades of brown to black and lighter lengthwise stripes; the fall species is predominantly green. Fully grown larvae are slightly more than 1 inch (2.5 cm) long. In June the larvae burrow underground and pupate. Moths of the fall cankerworm emerge in November and lay eggs that remain dormant during the winter. The spring cankerworm moths do not emerge to lay eggs until late winter or early spring. Adult male moths have delicate, silky, gray wings speckled with dark spots; the fall species is slightly darker. Their wingspread is about 1¼ inches (3 cm). The female moths are wingless.

The spring cankerworm (*Paleacrita vernata*) and the fall cankerworm (*Alsophila pometaria*) belong to the family Geometridae.

RALPH H. DAVIDSON, *Ohio State University*

CANNA, kan'ə, a genus of large, attractive plants mostly native to the tropics and subtropics of the Western Hemisphere. Cannas produce stout, unbranched stalks, 2 to 8 feet (60–240 cm) tall, that terminate in a cluster (raceme) of large, showy flowers. The flowers, each about 6 inches (15 cm) across, vary from pale yellow through many pastel hues to brilliant scarlet.

Root clumps are dug in the fall and stored in a cool cellar until spring. Then the clumps are divided, leaving one or two buds to a division, and started in greenhouse pots or, after the last frost, planted directly in the garden.

Modern cultivated forms have been produced by extensive interbreeding, and it is very difficult to assign any to a given species. *Canna* is the only genus in the family Cannaceae.

R. C. ALLEN
Kingwood Center, Mansfield, Ohio

Canna

J. J. SMITH

CANNAE, Battle of, kan'ē, in 216 B.C., in which the Carthaginians led by Hannibal defeated the Romans. It is the most perfect example in the history of warfare, of the double envelopment of an opposing army.

The Second Punic War fought between Rome and Carthage for the mastery of the ancient world began in 218 B.C. Hannibal crossed the Alps, defeated the Romans at the Ticinus and the Trebia rivers, and in 217 B.C. destroyed a Roman army at Lake Trasimene. His greatest victory occurred in 216 B.C. at Cannae near the coast of the Adriatic Sea. Hannibal with 50,000 men was confronted by an army of over 80,000 led by the consuls Gaius Terentius Varro and Lucius Aemilius Paulus who, according to custom, commanded on alternate days. Hannibal drew up his army, making the center thinner than usual, and moved it forward, inviting attack. With Varro in command, the Romans charged deep into Hannibal's lines. This was exactly what Hannibal had planned. Both wings closed in, enveloping the Romans. Meanwhile, Hannibal's cavalry had routed the Roman cavalry and was attacking from the rear. The entire Roman army was almost annihilated; Hannibal lost 6,000 men. It took Rome nearly a decade to recover.

JOSEPH B. MITCHELL, *Lt. Col., USA*
Author, "Twenty Decisive Battles of the World"

CANNAN, kan'ən, **Edwin** (1861–1935), British economist, who produced notable studies of the theories of the classical economists and also wrote tracts on money and monetary policy. His major work, *A History of the Theories of Production and Distribution in English Political Economy from 1776 to 1848,* often sharply critical of the past masters, remains a valuable reference on the history of economic thought.

Cannan was born at Funchal, Madeira, on Feb. 3, 1861, and was educated at Balliol College, Oxford. He joined the London School of Economics in 1895, its first year, and became professor there in 1907. He disdained the theorizing that characterized economic science at the time. To implement his own bent toward applied economics, he entered into public discussions of local government, taxation, and economic policies. He died at Bournemouth, England, on April 8, 1935.

NORMAN A. MERCER, *Union College*

CANNES, kȧn, is a resort and seaport on the Mediterranean coast of southeastern France, close to the center of the French Riviera, in the department of Alpes-Maritimes. Its port is of some commercial importance, and some fishing is still carried on. Tourism, however, is by far the most important activity of this world-famous playground.

Cannes lies on the board, crescent-shaped Gulf of Napoule, protected by a backdrop of mountains and hills. These make the city's winter climate so mild that subtropical vegetation flourishes. They also afford a splendid scenic accompaniment to the vivid colors of the city and to the deep blue of the Mediterranean.

Cannes' magnificent site has greatly encouraged its rapid development from a tiny fishing village of about 4,000 in the 1830's to its present position as one of France's—indeed, one of Europe's—most popular resorts. In 1834 the British political leader Lord Brougham became charmed by Cannes and built a winter home there, setting an example that was followed by the English aristocracy in increasing numbers. For a century or more Cannes continued to grow primarily as a winter resort for the wealthy British, though increasingly for the well-to-do from other countries as well. In the post-World War II era, the city's attractiveness as a summer resort has been capitalized on, and today it is a year-round center, frequented by vacationers of all social and economic strata.

Cannes has an airport for smaller planes and is served by excellent road and rail connections. Its port accommodates large numbers of large and small pleasure craft, and it is an important port of call for liners of many flags. The environs have abundant points of interest, including the Lérins Islands. Several festivals take place annually in Cannes, and the city's international film festivals are major attractions. Population: (1962) 54,967.

Homer Price
Hunter College, New York

TOM HOLLYMAN, FROM PHOTO RESEARCHERS

CANNES, a popular French resort on the Mediterranean, accommodates many pleasure boats in its harbor.

CANNIBALISM is the eating of human flesh by human beings. The word comes from the name of the Carib Indians of the West Indies, who were called Caribales or Canibales in early reports. At the time of Columbus, they were found to be man-eaters. The fact that the older term *anthropophagy* derives from the classic Greek *anthrōpos* (man) and *phagein* (eat) suggests that from ancient times certain peoples were known to eat human flesh, or at least were accused of doing so.

Extent of Cannibalism. How widespread cannibalism may have been in early times is uncertain. The accusation was freely made to disparage enemies or people who were considered to be barbarians. There is no reason to place much confidence in the reports of ancient writers such as Herodotus (5th century B. C.) and Strabo (63 B. C.?–?24 A. D.) that the Irish Celts, the Scythians, and others were cannibals. In modern times, castaways in small boats or on desert islands, travelers trapped by snow, and the populations of famine-ridden areas have occasionally been driven in desperation to eat human flesh. But as a regular, socially approved practice, cannibalism has been confined in recent centuries to certain tropical and subtropical areas. By the middle of the 20th century, pacification and police control had checked the practice in most regions still inhabited by uncivilized peoples. It is probable that the practice continued only in the most remote districts of the island of New Guinea, perhaps in the northeast Congo, and in inaccessible parts of the Amazon region in South America.

The extent of cannibalism among primitive peoples has been commonly exaggerated. Old maps abound in the legend *Anthropophagi sunt* (there are cannibals), written across the faces of areas that were unexplored and therefore filled with imagined terrors. The celebrated 13th century traveler Marco Polo reported, from hearsay, cannibalistic practices in the lands from Tibet to Sumatra and the Andaman Islands, but the sole case that survives investigation is that of Sumatra. Likewise, in South America, cannibalism was probably less prevalent than some early sources would seem to indicate.

It is possible that the earliest humans fed on human flesh, as on any other. Carnivorous animals often kill and eat those of their own species that are injured or feeble. Some authorities maintain that the first humans were essentially carnivorous, as witnessed by the great accumulation of animal bones in ancient cave dwellings. One of man's precursors, *Sinanthropus pekinensis* (Peking man), apparently took skulls of his fellows into the caves at Choukoutien (near Peking), where the posterior sections were bashed in, presumably to pick out the brains. There is no reason for assuming that the first true humans did not eat other humans also. There is some evidence for cannibalism in Aurignacian times (late Ice Age) in central Europe and among the Early Neolithic peoples of Switzerland. Even so advanced a group as the Bronze Age dwellers of Bohemia (about 2000 B. C.) hacked human bones with knives and split them in order to extract the marrow.

The aversion to eating human flesh is not instinctive; rather, the horror shown by civilized men and by most of the primitive peoples is a specialized development. It is the response to a tabooed food, a revulsion that applies equally to other foods, considered unorthodox, unclean, and unfit for human consumption. It is possible that the abhorrence arose from a combination of factors, including fear of the dead and fear of becoming a victim. As ethical codes developed, people came to believe in the sanctity of human life.

Motives for Cannibalism. The motive of augmenting the food supply does not seem to have been a vital factor in impelling humans to cannibalistic habits. No people made human flesh a staple of their diet. It is noteworthy that many of the people who lived under the most adverse conditions for securing food did not consume human flesh: Eskimos, northern Siberian natives, Indians of the interior deserts of North America, and those of sub-Arctic Canada or Tierra del Fuego. All these people had to struggle for subsistence. On the other hand, cannibalism flourished throughout the Congo Basin and adjacent West Africa where food, both animal and vegetable, was abundant. This was true as well for the Oceanic natives who had good supplies of plants and sea food though they had no large mammals other than the domesticated pig. In Africa and Oceania, cannibalism was motivated to a considerable extent by liking for the food and by desire for variety. But everywhere motives for partaking of human flesh were mixed.

A custom often cited to demonstrate cannibalism among savages is that of eating or biting a part taken from an enemy as a trophy—such as his heart, limbs, or scalp—or of partaking of the corpse or blood of a human sacrifice. This, however, is hardly more than token cannibalism and should not be confounded with the consumption of flesh as food. A common and widely occurring custom, it was an expression of blood-thirstiness or exultation over an enemy's downfall. In many cases, eating a portion of an enemy was motivated by a belief in the possibility of acquiring the enemy's strength or prowess, or certain magical qualities. Where, as among the tribes of East Africa, the flesh of a deceased relative was eaten, the purpose was to conserve his spirit and virtues for the family. Where human sacrifices or headhunting occurred, there was sometimes ceremonial partaking of the flesh, but in most instances this was nor more than a ritual act.

Pacific Islands. The South Pacific islanders had a well-deserved reputation as notorious cannibals. Cannibalism was customary and held in high esteem in most of Polynesia, where it was everywhere connected with warfare. It was of minor importance in Micronesia except in the Gilbert Islands, the group adjacent to Polynesia. The practice was common in the Marquesas, Easter Island, and New Zealand, and limited in Samoa and Tonga. But it was abhorrent to the natives of Hawaii and the Society Islands. In the period of European discovery the practice was dying out in Samoa, but, by reason of Fijian influence, was on the increase in Tonga. The need for a supplementary food source cannot be held accountable for cannibalism in this region since human flesh was generally tabooed to women. The esteem attached to despoiling enemies and a real fondness for the unusual food seem to have been the motives. As a consequence of their dismemberment of corpses, the Maori of New Zealand accumulated a considerable knowledge of human anatomy.

In Melanesia, cannibalism was most common in Fiji. The victims were usually enemies, but sacrificed commoners and shipwrecked strangers were also devoured. So extensive was cannibalism that at one feast 200 bodies were consumed, and one 18th century native chief was credited with having eaten about 900 persons in his lifetime. As in Polynesia, human flesh was cooked separately and handled with special wooden forks, the utensils for its preparation being taboo for any other purpose.

Cannibalism also occurred elsewhere in Melanesia, and in Australia, New Guinea, and, on a lesser scale, in parts of the Malay Archipelago. Among the Batak of Sumatra, for example, prisoners of war and outlawed men furnished the supply.

Africa. Most of equatorial Africa, as well as the regions westward to the Guinea coast and eastward to the sources of the Nile, was a cannibalistic area. The Fan (or Fang) tribes, north of the Congo mouth, were reputed to engage in an extensive trade in captives to eat, fattening them for the market, but the reports seem exaggerated. Ritual cannibalism occurred in central Nigeria, where flesh from trophy heads was eaten. Among the Ovimbundu (or Mbundu) of Angola, slaves were eaten ceremonially at the accession of a new king. The filing of front teeth to points for self-beautification, not uncommon in central Africa, erroneously led to accusations of man-eating. However, there is no relation between the two practices.

America. Cannibalism was widespread in northern South America and the West Indies at the time of discovery, and extended to the Gulf Coast tribes of the present United States. It flourished especially in three regions: among the Carib of the Lesser Antilles and the Orinoco, the Tupi-Guarani of eastern Brazil and the lower Amazon, and the Chibcha of northern Colombia. Half-cooked human flesh, left by Caribs, was found by Columbus' party on Guadeloupe Island. The Arawak of Puerto Rico seem not to have been man-eaters at the time, but adopted the practice in revenge against their Carib enemies.

The Tupinamba of the Brazilian coast elaborated the procedure for feasting on a war prisoner. He was kept captive for a period of a few months to several years, and during this time he was allowed to marry a local girl. Finally he was taken to the plaza to be tormented, in song and dance, with his impending fate and would reply with similar taunts. He was then allowed to defend himself against the appointed executioner. When the victim was struck down, the whole community rushed to the body, at least to dip their fingers in the warm blood.

In the Cauca Valley of Colombia, the Chibchan tribes reveled in the custom of eating their prisoners, and even consumed the flesh raw. On a single occasion, under Spanish eyes, 100 captives were devoured; on another, the 4,000 native auxiliaries of the Spaniards were reported to have eaten 300 enemies. On a more modest scale, cannibalism was known sporadically southward as far as Chile, where it was practiced by the Araucanians.

LESLIE SPIER
Former Professor of Anthropology
University of New Mexico

Further Reading: Hogg, Garry, *Cannibalism and Human Sacrifice* (New York 1966).

CANNING, kan'ing, **Charles John** (1812–1862), British statesman, who was governor-general of India during the mutiny of 1857. The son of George Canning (q.v.), he was born near London on Dec. 14, 1812. He was elected to Parliament in 1836 and succeeded the next year to the title Viscount Canning. He was undersecretary for foreign affairs from 1841 to 1846.

Sent to India in 1856, Canning inherited a condition of unrest among Indian soldiers under British command. When they mutinied, Canning moved slowly to subdue them, and British arms prevailed in 1858. Because he meted out mild punishment to the Indians, the governor-general was derisively nicknamed "Clemency Canning"; but historians now praise his moderation.

On the transfer of the Indian government from the East India Company to the crown in 1858, Canning became the first viceroy of India. He was created Earl Canning in 1859. He retired in 1862, and died in London on June 17, 1862.

Further Reading: MacLagen, Michael, *"Clemency" Canning* (London 1962).

CANNING, George (1770–1827), British political leader, who was prime minister for the last 100 days of his life. He ranks among Britain's greatest statesmen on his record as foreign secretary during the five years preceding his premiership. Canning is known less for his skillful upholding of national interests than as Europe's liberal hero against Metternich, as liberator in Greece and Latin America, and as the orator who said, "I called the New World into existence to redress the balance of the Old."

He was born in poverty in London on April 11, 1770, and educated at his grandfather's expense at Eton and Oxford. His talents and devastating wit developed precociously, and he entered Parliament at 23. But goaded by ambition and supremely self-confident, he consistently overplayed his hand. As foreign secretary in 1807 in the Tory government of the Duke of Portland, Canning aspired to direct Britain's war against Napoleon, but his impatience to establish his control brought him into a bitter conflict with Viscount Castlereagh that cost him the opportunity and his office in 1809. Pretentious miscalculation blocked his return to office in 1812, and he held only minor or peripheral offices for 13 years. The effects were chastening, for Canning was more circumspect when, in 1822, Castlereagh's suicide opened the way to the foreign secretary's post.

As foreign secretary, Canning ingeniously imposed a foreign policy that seemed to Tory traditionalists charged with dangerous liberalism but that succeeded in identifying Britain with popular causes in its own interest. Posturing as the opponent of reactionary ideological alignments in Europe, he actually refurbished them and increased Britain's influence in them. By negotiating the separation of Brazil from Portugal and by recognizing the independence of Spain's American colonies, he hoped to monopolize Latin American goodwill. Outmaneuvered by the Monroe Doctrine, which his policies had invited, he retaliated by exploiting British prejudice against the United States, and with British naval superiority unchallenged, he raised Britain's prestige to a pinnacle.

In domestic politics, Canning managed to project a progressive image at home, despite his consistent opposition to Parliamentary reform. He deliberately appealed to public opinion in speeches outside Parliament and in the press—innovating tactics that enraged both Tory and Whig grandees. When the Earl of Liverpool resigned the premiership in 1827, Canning succeeded him, but he died little more than three months later at Chiswick, on Aug. 8, 1827.

P. J. V. Rolo, *Author of "George Canning"*

CANNING, Stratford (1786–1880), English diplomat. He was created 1st Viscount Stratford de Redcliffe in 1852. Born in London on Nov. 4, 1786, he was educated at Eton and Cambridge. While serving as acting ambassador at Constantinople, he negotiated the Treaty of Bucharest (1812), which ended the Russo-Turkish War and freed Russia to resist Napoleon. After serving as ambassador to the United States (1820–1824), he returned to Constantinople, where he patched up a peace between Russia and Turkey (1826). He was a member of Parliament from 1828 to 1841, and again ambassador to Turkey from 1842 to 1858. Canning died on Aug. 14, 1880, at Frant, Sussex.

CANNING is the method of preserving food by heating it and sealing it in airtight containers. The heat serves to kill microorganisms and to inhibit the activities of enzymes that cause food to spoil. The containers are made airtight to prevent recontamination of food by microorganisms in the air after the canning process is completed.

Canning is the most widely used method of food preservation. Most foods can be preserved by canning, and shipment and storage of canned goods present relatively few problems. Canned foods require no preparation prior to serving other than warming or chilling.

Nutritive Value of Canned Food. Generally, proteins, carbohydrates, and fats are not detrimentally affected by canning. Vitamins A, C, D, and riboflavin are also well retained. Vitamin B_1 retention is dependent upon the amount of heat the vitamin is subjected to during canning. If the acid content of the food containing the vitamin is high, the canning temperature need not be high, and retention is good. Vitamins and minerals often dissolve into the canning liquid, but their nutrient value is not lost if the liquid is consumed.

Causes of Spoilage. The most dangerous microorganism from the standpoint of food poisoning is the bacterium *Clostridium botulinum.* It produces a toxin that causes the disease botulism, which can be fatal. In nonacid foods such as corn, peas, and meat, the causative agent of spoilage is often a putrefactive bacterium known as *C. sporogenes.* This microorganism is not toxic to man but causes economic spoilage. There are also a number of microorganisms that cause spoilage of specific canned foods. These can be species of yeasts, molds, and bacteria that produce undesirable textures, colors, flavors, and odors in foods. Spoilage is also caused by autolytic enzymes, which act to disintegrate dead cells. This action, called autolysis, is allowed to proceed to a limited extent in the aging or tenderizing of meat. Autolysis and the destruction of food by microorganisms is prevented by heat in the canning process.

HISTORY

Canning was the first new and great development in food preservation since about 3000 B.C., when the Egyptians invented sourdough bread. It was the first approach directed toward developing a new method of food preservation not based on an adaptation or modification of the natural process of drying and cooling.

Appert. The invention of canning is credited to Nicolas Appert (1749–1841), although preserving food by a combination of heating, drying, and vinegaring, and sealing in a container was practiced before his invention. Appert learned to be a cook, confectioner, and hotelier while an apprentice in his father's hotel in Châlons-sur-Marne, France. About 1780, after trying his luck as a cook and steward to several noblemen, he set up a confectionery shop in Paris. He became deeply interested in the preservation of foods of all sorts, and he found by experiment that most foods could be preserved by heating them in glass jars for extended periods of time. In 1796, confident of his success, he gave up the confectionery business and settled in Ivry-sur-Seine in order to perfect his method and thus win the prize of 12,000 francs offered by the Directory to the discoverer of a method of conserving the

LIBBY, MC NEILL & LIBBY

In a canning factory, pineapples are carried on conveyor belts to the first processing stage.

MYLES J. ADLER

The pineapples are conveyed to a machine that removes their outer skin and inner core.

freshness and nutritive qualities of meat and vegetables for several months.

In 1804 he set up his first bottling factory (cannery) at Massy (Seine-et-Oise), near Palaiseau, a few miles outside of Paris, where he maintained a store. On Feb. 10, 1809, the *Courrier de l'Europe* stated that "Monsieur Appert has discovered the art of making the seasons stand still: at his shop, spring, summer, and autumn survive the whole year round, just like the delicate plants that the gardener protects under a glass cloche against bad weather."

He was awarded the 12,000-franc prize on Jan. 10, 1810, after his canning process was examined by an official commission that included the chemist Joseph Louis Gay-Lussac. In 1810, Appert published his treatise on canning, which became the definitive textbook on the subject. When France was invaded by the Allies in 1814, during the Napoleonic wars, his factory was ruined and was never restored. In 1822 the Society for the Encouragement of National Industry awarded Appert the title of "Benefactor of Humanity," yet he died a pauper, at Massy on June 1, 1841.

Spread of Canning. While the French failed to exploit Appert's process, called the "Art of Appertizing," the British were not so backward. A copy of Appert's book was brought to London, and Peter Durand took out a patent (1810) for a method of preserving foods that was a copy of Appert's method. Durand's patent was for use of

After the pineapples have been sized, cored, and their ends cut off, they are ready to be sliced by machine.

BOTH PHOTOS FROM LIBBY, MC NEILL & LIBBY

The cans packed with the sliced fruit and juice proceed to the final stage where they are covered and sealed.

a tinned container. Appert did not use metal containers, probably because of the poor quality of the tinplate and the irregularity of its supply in France. Soon the firm of Donkin and Hall of London was supplying the British navy with tinned foods, and the firm of Crosse and Blackwell was using Appert's process.

Appert's discovery reached America via William Underwood and Thomas Kensett. Underwood opened a preserving firm in Boston about 1820, and about the same time Kensett established his company in New York together with his father-in-law, Ezra Daggett.

In 1856, Gail Borden was issued a patent for a milk condensing process and formed the New York Condensed Milk Company in the following year. He used a vacuum pan to concentrate milk that had been scalded at a temperature between 150°F and 200°F (66°C and 93°C) by a continuous-flow process. The milk volume was reduced by 65%–80%. One of the essential requirements of Borden's process was cleanliness in handling the raw milk—still a basic requirement for proper canning.

During the period from 1810 to about 1860 the canning industry grew in Europe and in the United States. However, it was based primarily on the erroneous premise that exclusion of air is the principal requirement to avoid spoilage. In fact, Gay-Lussac, in investigating Appert's process, had pointed out that, by analysis, the air in the bottles in which substances (beef, lamb, fish, mushrooms, and must of grape) have been well preserved does not contain any oxygen, and the absence of this gas is thus a necessary condition for the preservation of animal and vegetable substances. With the discovery, in 1774, of oxygen as a component of air, and its significance to respiration and combustion realized, it can readily be understood how the then-current incorrect view as to its role in spoilage of canned foods arose.

Pasteur. It was only through the research of Louis Pasteur that the basic premise of Appert's invention became understood—that heat serves as the agent to destroy microorganisms that cause spoilage. In 1856, Pasteur began investigating the souring of wine, which caused the loss of great sums of money each year by the French wine industry. He showed that yeast cells are necessary for fermentation and that while one type of yeast cell produces alcohol, another type present produces lactic acid, which causes souring. Pasteur, in applying Appert's methods, found that vigorous heating damaged the quality of the wine, whereas heating it to about 130°F (55°C) was sufficient to destroy the spoilage organisms and yet not adversely affect the quality of the wine. He discovered that after such heating and subsequent stoppering, the wine did not sour. Thus arose the procedure of partial sterilization known as pasteurization.

In 1860, Pasteur began his investigation of the widely accepted theory of "spontaneous generation," and completely upset it by a series of carefully and brilliantly designed experiments. In his decisive demonstration disproving the theory, he boiled meat extract and left it in a swan-necked flask, which bent down, then up. Though the extract was left exposed to the air, dust particles, which carry other contaminants, were trapped in the bend in the neck. The meat extract did not deteriorate, and no organism developed.

Russell. In 1895, Henry L. Russell of the University of Wisconsin demonstrated that the cause of spoilage of canned foods is gas-producing bacilli. He showed that this spoilage could be avoided by heating the products to higher temperatures for longer periods of time.

Prescott and Underwood. Samuel C. Prescott, an instructor in biology at the Massachusetts Institute of Technology, and William Lyman Underwood, grandson of the pioneer American canner William Underwood, studied the fundamental principles of bacteriology and their application to canning technology. Their work was instrumental in changing an industry based upon individual experience to one under scientific control. In a paper presented before the Atlantic States Packers' Association, in Buffalo, N. Y., in February 1898, they described the nature and source of the spoilage organisms in canned corn, and the time-temperature requirements to prevent such spoilage. They pointed out the need for a thorough knowledge of principles involved in canning and of doing away with rule-of-thumb methods.

Growth of the Canning Industry. Since Prescott and Underwood the canning industry has grown to be the largest single segment of the food processing industry. In 1905, 34 million standard cases of canned foods, excluding milk, meat and fish, were marketed. In 1930, 177 million cases, excluding the same items, were produced. In a typical year in the mid-1960's, 787 million cases, including all canned foods, were marketed. The developments in the last six decades have made possible the preserving of all types of gourmet foods, as well as simple vegetables and meats.

CANNING TECHNOLOGY

The modern thermal processing industry is based on the principle that foods can be preserved through proper application of a sufficient quantity of heat to destroy the spoilage microorganisms and enzymic activities, and that sealing the foods in airtight containers prevents subsequent contamination. Industrial canning procedures can be divided into four parts: handling the raw material; blanching the material and filling and closing the containers; sterilizing the canned product; and labeling and warehousing the goods.

Raw Materials. Regardless of the process, the finished product can be of no better quality than the raw material from which it is made. Thus, selection of raw materials of good quality is important. In order to obtain uniform and high quality canned products, it is also important to select varieties that are good for thermal processing. For this reason many of the larger canning organizations supply both seeds and technical know-how to farmers. Specifications depend on the type of fruit or vegetable, but usually include color, degree of ripeness, size, lack of bruises and other defects, and low mold count.

One cardinal rule is to bring fruits and vegetables to the factory for processing as soon after harvesting as possible, to slow down the undesirable changes which begin immediately after harvesting. These changes include, for example, the conversion of sugar to starch in peas.

The preliminary preparation of materials for canning includes cleaning and sometimes peeling, coring, and slicing. Cleaning is done with the help of a detergent, which is subsequently removed so that no residue remains. Peeling is usually done with lye solutions, steam, or hot water, or by abrasion, and it is generally carried out by means of continuous-process rather than batch-process devices.

Blanching. Some fruits and almost all vegetables are blanched, or heated, prior to being put into cans or glass jars. Blanching is usually carried out on a continuous basis in a unit known as a blancher. It brings the product into direct contact with hot water, or in some cases with steam, under controlled conditions of time and temperature. Blanching serves several functions: it softens the tissues and makes them pliable for ease in filling the can; it inactivates the enzymes that might cause harmful changes before canning and removes some oxygen from the tissues; it serves as a final cleaning of the food and washes away some raw flavors; and it reduces the number of microorganisms on the surface of the food and helps preserve the color in some foods, such as that due to carotene and chlorophyll.

Blanching done in hot water causes more loss of nutrients, minerals, and flavor compounds than does steam blanching. However, steam is more difficult to control. The adequacy of the blanching is checked by qualitative tests for either the enzyme catalase or peroxidase.

The cans are washed before filling. Filling is done either by hand or by semiautomatic or fully automatic machinery. If the product is a mixture of vegetables and brine, or fruit and syrup, the containers are filled with the solid constituents as much as possible without injury to the food segments. Brine or other liquid is then added to replace as much of the air as possible.

The filled cans are next passed through an exhaust box, which is a continuous unit with hot water or steam that heats the filled cans for a few minutes to drive out remaining air. The cans next pass to a closing machine (which usually operates at over 300 cans per minute) where lids, coded either by embossing or with special canner's stamping ink, are placed on the cans. The closing machine seals the cans by a "double roll" method, which provides a "hook-over" seam. A small amount of a polymeric compound is deposited on the sealing area to assure airtight closures.

Sterilization. During sterilization the canned foods are given sufficient heat to prevent spoilage. The sterilization process is usually carried out in large pressure cookers known as "retorts." They are equipped with automatic devices for controlling and recording temperature and pressure. The retort is filled with a large basket full of cans, the cover is clamped down, and air is exhausted. Pressure is then built up by steam until the prerequisite temperature is reached and is held for a predetermined period of time. In retorts used in processing glass containers, water is used with superimposed air pressure to keep the lids on the jars.

MILESTONES IN THE DEVELOPMENT OF CANNING

1795 French government offered a 12,000-franc prize for a method of food preservation for the armed forces.

1810 Nicolas Appert won the French government's 12,000-franc prize for the invention of canning. Appert's book on canning was published in France. Peter Durand was granted a British patent for a tin-plated iron food container.

1819–1820 Thomas Kensett and Ezra Daggett began canning in New York City. William Underwood opened a cannery in Boston, Mass.

1839 Underwood and Kensett adopted a tin-plated can to replace their glass container. Isaac Winslow of Maine began experiments in canning corn.

1840 Canning of salmon and lobster began in Maine and Newfoundland, and of oysters in Maryland.

1852 French patents were issued to Appert and Raymond Chevallier for the autoclave, or steam cooker.

1856 Gail Borden patented condensed milk.

1860 Louis Pasteur disproved the theory of spontaneous generation. He also invented pasteurization in the early 1860's.

1861 Gilbert C. Van Camp opened a cannery for fruits and vegetables in Indianapolis.

1862 Winslow was granted a patent on canning corn.

1874 Andrew K. Shriver patented the closed steam pressure kettle, or retort.

1885 John B. Meyenberg of Highland, Ill., introduced canned evaporated milk and applied agitation to milk during sterilization.

1890 Max Ams introduced European inside-coated can in United States.

1891 Pineapple canning in Hawaii began on an experimental basis by John Kidwell.

1895 Henry L. Russell gave the first scientific demonstration of spoilage in a cannery.

1896 Samuel C. Prescott had the first thermometer made for sealing inside a can to record maximum temperature reached during processing.

1897 First of Samuel C. Prescott and William Lyman Underwood's papers on microorganisms as causative agents of spoilage in canned food was published in *The Technology Quarterly* (Boston).

1898 Prescott and Underwood made the first public demonstration of harmful bacteria in canning at the Atlantic States Packers' Association convention in Buffalo.

1899 F. W. Smith of Portland, Me., obtained patents on continuous cookers.

1901 The American Can Company was organized.

1902 E. W. Duckwall established the first canners research laboratory at Aspinwall, Pa., called the Sprague Canners Laboratory.

1903 James D. Dole began pineapple canning in Hawaii.

1905 The Continental Can Company began production.

1907 A. W. Bitting devised a method of reading a thermometer to observe the temperature during cooking, also a thermocouple for recording the temperature of cans in a retort. National Canners' Association was founded in the United States.

1912 Bronson Barlow demonstrated the existence of thermophilic organisms in canned corn.

1920 W. H. Bigelow and J. R. Esty published a bulletin on heat penetration in processing canned foods.

1936 C. O. Ball received the first patent for an aseptic canning unit.

1950 William Martin's aseptic canning system in which food is pumped through the tubing of a heat exchanger, was put into commercial use.

1964 The pressure system of aseptic canning (*Flash-18*) was put into commercial use by Swift & Company.

The amount of heat and time needed for sterilization depends on the type of product, the nature and type of contaminants, and the size of the container. High acidity reduces the temperature necessary to preserve food by canning. For tomatoes and certain acid fruits, boiling for a few minutes is all that is required. Cans of non-acid foods such as corn, spinach, beans, and meat require more intensive treatment. Following the sterilization process, the cans are cooled to 100°F or 120°F (38°C or 49°C) in clean water and are then air-cooled.

Labeling and Warehousing. Labels are usually put on the cans by machines following cooling and before casing. In the case of small companies that pack for others, labeling may be done later.

Proper warehousing is important in order to retain the quality of canned foods. Canned foods that are stored at too high temperatures may undergo undesirable postprocessing chemical changes. They may also develop thermophilic spoilage and display darkening due to a browning reaction. Ideally canned foods should be stored at 75° F (23° C) or less and should not exceed 100° F (38° C).

Improved Processing Techniques. The bulk of the canned foods marketed are sterilized without agitation, as described in the preceding section. The limiting factor in using retorts is the rate at which heat penetrates the cans. For a number of products, especially those packed in large containers, the result is overheating of the food near the surface of the can in order to obtain sufficient heat to sterilize the center, or "cold spot," of the container. The undesirable effects are diminished somewhat by sterilizing the food at relatively low temperatures and for longer periods of time. However, it has been observed that foods treated at high temperatures for short periods of time (H.T.S.T. processing) are usually of better quality in terms of such features as texture, color, and vitamin content than foods treated at lower temperatures for periods of time long enough to make them safe. Several types of equipment have been developed to eliminate overheating by reducing the time-temperature requirements. Such equipment works primarily on two principles: agitation of the container during sterilization, and filling of the cans, in an aseptic environment, with food that has been presterilized.

Agitation. In agitation processing the cans are rotated, turned end-over-end, or agitated in some other way during sterilization, so that a turbulence is produced in the contents. In this way all portions of the contents are heated evenly. The effectiveness of the principle of agitation is most apparent in the "direct flame" sterilizer which rotates cans at 120 rpm and carries them through gas flames without damage to food near the walls of the cans. This device is particularly useful for high-temperature short-time processing of mobile products such as peas in brine and mushrooms in brine.

Aseptic Canning. In aseptic canning the food is brought to sterilization temperatures, usually in the tubing of a heat exchanger. It is held at the desired temperature for as long as needed and is then rapidly cooled in a heat exchanger. The food is filled aseptically into cans which have been previously sterilized. The cans are then sealed aseptically. This type of canning is of particular value for those foods which can be pumped through tubing easily, such as soups, purees, and stews with particle sizes no greater than ¼ inch (0.6 cm) in diameter.

In another form of aseptic canning (*Flash-18*), which involves manual agitation, the sterilization of food and filling of cans is done by workers in a chamber kept at a pressure greater than atmospheric pressure. Pressure locks acclimatize personnel gradually to the greater pressure. Food is stirred while it is sterilized at about 255° F (124° C). Because of the higher pressure, it does not boil. The containers are filled, sealed, cooled, and then discharged from the pressurized room. This method makes it possible to prepare foods made up of large particles, which cannot be processed by the conventional aseptic canning equipment.

Containers. Most food containers used in canning are made of sheet steel coated with a thin layer of tin. Often an enamel coating is applied over the tin to prevent it from reacting chemically with certain foods. Glass containers, which are transparent and do not react chemically with foods, and aluminum containers, which are lightweight and easy to open, are also popular. In addition, both flexible and rigid plastic containers are being developed for thermal processing. Their potential advantages are low cost, lightness, and transparency. All containers must be able to withstand external and internal pressure and a wide range of temperatures and to resist corrosion.

Canned Food Standards. Under the U. S. Food, Drug, and Cosmetic Act, standards for grades of a number of canned foods are specified. These are mandatory standards, and products that do not meet these standards must be labeled "substandard." There are also voluntary standards of quality promulgated by the Agricultural and Marketing Service of the U. S. Department of Agriculture. These are designed to aid processors in packing better and more uniform quality foods.

S. A. Goldblith
Massachusetts Institute of Technology

Bibliography

Ball, Charles O., and Olson, Franklin C. W., *Sterilization in Food Technology* (New York 1957).
Beauvais, M., Thomas, G., and Cheftel, H., "A New Method for Heat-Processing Canned Foods," *Food Technology*, April 1961 issue (Chicago 1961).
Bitting, Arvill W., *Appertizing; or, The Art of Canning: Its History and Development* (San Francisco 1937).
Blanck, Frederick C., ed., *Handbook of Food and Agriculture* (New York 1955).
Joslyn, Maynard A., and Heid, J. S., *Food Processing Operations*, 3 vols. (Westport, Conn., 1963–64).

HOME CANNING

Home canning, or home food preservation, encompasses the production of fruit products (jellies, jams, conserves, marmalades, preserves) by the open-kettle method; the processing of fruits (including tomatoes), pickled vegetables, and other acid foods by the boiling-water-bath method; and the processing of vegetables, meats, and other low-acid foods by the steam-pressure method. (Heating in any type of canner is called "processing.") To keep the quality of the products high and to prevent spoilage, each home canning method has been adapted and designed to fit the products to be preserved.

Jellies are made from fruit or berry juice; the product is clear and firm. Jams, made from crushed fruit or berries, are less firm than jellies. Conserves are jams made from a mixture of fruits; nuts and raisins may perhaps be added. Marmalades commonly hold in suspension pieces of pulpy citrus fruits and fruit rind. Preserves are whole or large pieces of fruits contained in a thick syrup. In the production of these fruit products, sugar serves as the preserving agent, aids in gel formation, and contributes to the flavor. In addition, it has a firming effect on the fruit in preserves.

Fruits, tomatoes, and pickled vegetables must be processed in boiling water for a stipulated period of time to ensure against spoilage from yeasts and molds. Other vegetables and fish, poultry, and meats require high-heat treatment to prevent spoilage by bacteria; these foods must be processed under steam pressure or at temperatures above 212° F (100° C).

Equipment and Utensils. Many utensils available in the average home kitchen—pots, pans, kettles, colanders, bowls, knives, and standard measurers—can be used for canning. In addition, a fruit press or a jelly bag (of cheesecloth, unbleached muslin, or flannel) and a jelly or candy thermometer are important items to have.

For jellies and jams, home canners may use several sizes of tapered or fluted glasses that can be sealed with paraffin and covered with metal lids. But for most other canned products, straight-sided Mason jars, wide-mouth or regular, are preferred. The most popular and easiest jar to seal of the wide-mouth models is the two-piece Mason jar. This has a metal lid with sealing compound and a metal screw band. Other kinds are the standard Mason jar, with porcelain-lined zinc cap and rubber ring; the modified Mason, with glass lid, top-seal rubber ring, and metal screw band; and the wire-bail type, with glass lid and rubber ring. Tin cans, both enameled and plain, may be used for home canning; these require a can-sealing machine.

All glasses and jars must be washed thoroughly and kept hot so that they will not break when they are filled with the hot mixture. The lids must be absolutely clean for a good seal; and manufacturer's directions should be followed closely in the sealing.

For water-bath canning or boiling-water processing, a large kettle with a cover and a perforated rack are standard equipment. The rack allows water to circulate and keeps the glasses or jars from resting directly on the bottom of the kettle. The kettle should be deep enough to permit the water to cover the glasses or jars by at least one inch without boiling over. (If a standard canner is not available, any large vessel or tub that meets the above requirements may be used.)

For pressure canning a steam-pressure canner is essential. This kind of kettle comes equipped with a rack on the bottom, a cover that can be clamped or locked to make the unit steam tight, a safety valve, a petcock (vent), and a pressure gauge.

Open-Kettle Canning. In open-kettle canning, food is cooked in an uncovered vessel, poured boiling hot into glasses or jars, and sealed. This method is best for fruit products, relishes, and some pickles; it should be used only when called for in the canning instructions. The open-kettle method is satisfactory for food products containing a large amount of sugar or vinegar, which help in food preservation. All other food products need a processing period to destroy undesirable microorganisms.

FOUR STEPS IN PACKING SUMMER SQUASH

After the ends of the squash have been trimmed off, it is cut into slices one half inch thick. Large sections may be halved or quartered to make the pieces of uniform size.

The squash is tightly packed into jars to about ½ inch from the top. The jars are then filled to the top with boiling water and the metal lids are screwed on firmly.

The jars are placed in a pressure canner that contains 2 or 3 inches of boiling water. Pint jars of squash need to be processed for 25 minutes and quart jars for 30 minutes, at 10 or more pounds pressure, depending on altitude.

ALL PHOTOS FROM U. S. DEPARTMENT OF AGRICULTURE

The cover is locked and steam allowed to escape for about 10 minutes; then the vent is closed. At 10 pounds pressure the timing starts. At the end of the processing, pressure must drop to zero before cover and jars are removed.

THREE TYPES OF JAR CLOSURES AND HOW TO USE THEM

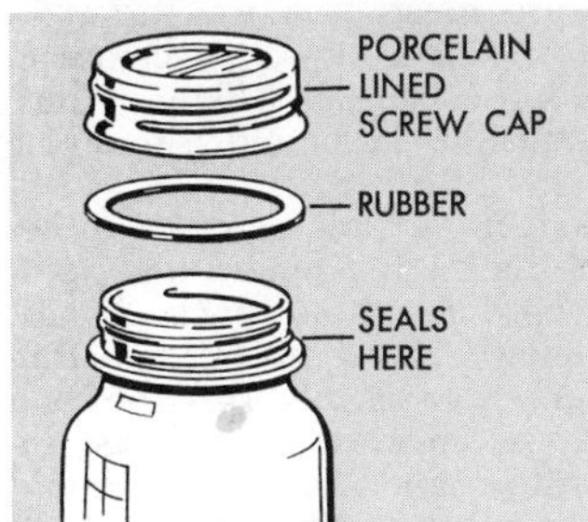

Before canning, fit the wet rubber ring on jar shoulder, stretching no more than necessary. Fill jar; wipe the rubber ring and jar rim clean. Screw cap down firmly and turn it back ¼ inch. After canning, screw cap on tight to complete the seal.

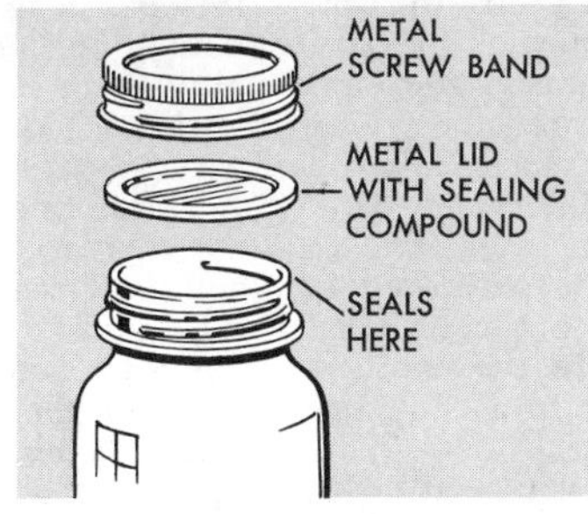

Wipe rim clean before canning. Put lid on with sealing compound next to glass, and screw metal band down tight by hand. The lid has enough give to let air escape during canning. It is self-sealing and needs no tightening after canning.

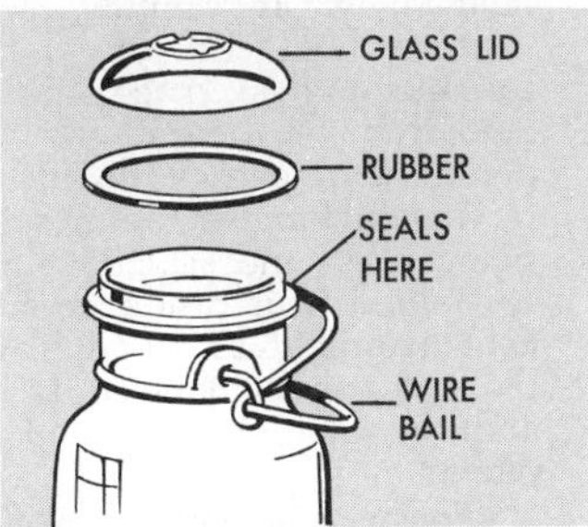

Before filling jar, fit wet rubber ring on ledge at top of jar. After filling, wipe ring and rim clean; put on glass lid and push long wire over top of lid so that it fits into groove; and leave short wire up. Push short wire down after canning.

For good results with a jellied fruit product, proper amounts of fruit pectin (a substance that yields a gel), acid, and sugar are essential. Fruits for jellies and jams should be hard to fully ripe; imperfect mature fruit is highly suitable. Some fruits have adequate natural pectin. Others require added pectin to help the jellied product maintain its shape. Commercial fruit pectins, either in liquid or powdered form, permit the use of fully ripe fruits (these have less pectin than underripe fruits), give a greater yield (more jelly or jam) from a given amount of fruit, and shorten the cooking time that is required for the jelling.

Products such as cucumbers and green tomatoes should be small to medium size for pickling. Other ingredients—cider vinegar, spices, and herbs, for example—must be fresh and of good quality for the best results.

In jelly making, the fruit should be washed thoroughly and then sorted to remove undesirable pieces. It should be prepared for juice extraction as directed in the recipe. Generally, the fruit has to be boiled and the pulp placed in a damp jelly bag or fruit press. The juice is extracted from the pulp by squeezing. This pressed juice must be strained again through a second damp bag, without further squeezing, in order to clarify it. The juice should then be measured according to the recipe.

Jellies made without added pectin require less sugar per cup of fruit juice than do those with added pectin, and accurate control of the boiling is essential to bring the mixture to the proper sugar concentration. (Faster cooking is assured in a kettle with a broad, flat bottom.) Without added pectin the mixture should form a satisfactory gel if cooked to a temperature of 8° F (−13.3° C) above the boiling point of water (the temperature at which water boils should be determined shortly before cooking, since atmospheric conditions may affect it).

Jams, conserves, and marmalades are prepared much the same as jellies, except that the ingredients must be stirred constantly during cooking to prevent scorching. Without added pectin the mixture will be finished at 9° F (−12.7° C) above the boiling point of water. When pectin is used, the manufacturer's directions should be followed exactly for quality results.

The hot mixture should be poured into the glasses to within ½ inch of their tops and immediately covered with melted paraffin about ⅛ inch thick. If canning jars are used, the hot mixture should be poured to the top of the jars, the lids put in place, and the jars sealed immediately. If the jars are to be stored for a long period of time, they should be processed (allowed to remain for five minutes in boiling water after being filled and sealed).

Jellied fruit products should be permitted to cool overnight to avoid breaking the gel. Then the jars can be labeled to indicate the contents and the canning date, and stored in a cool, dry place.

Boiling-Water-Bath Canning. For water-bath canning, all fruits, including tomatoes, should be firm and ripe. Sorting for size, degree of ripeness, and color will result in a more even processing and a more attractive pack.

Sugar helps canned fruit hold its shape, color, and flavor, and a sweetening generally must be added during the canning. Sweetening may be in the form of a sugar syrup (sugar mixed with water or with juice extracted from some of the fruit) or in solutions made by mixing water and noncaloric sweeteners such as Sucaryl or saccharin. Fruits intended for desserts should be canned in a syrup heavy enough to sweeten the fruit for taste. For most fruits, a medium syrup, made by mixing one cup of sugar in two cups of water or juice, is satisfactory. By increasing or decreasing the amount of water by one cup, a light or heavy syrup can be obtained. Oxidation causes fruits such as apples, peaches, and pears to darken during preparation. Surface darkening can be reduced by covering these fruits after peeling with a solution of one gallon of water and two tablespoons each of salt and vinegar. During storage darkening may occur because of air in the jars or as a result of too little processing to destroy enzymes. This can be avoided or controlled by the addition of ¼ teaspoon of ascorbic acid (vitamin C) to each quart of fruit before it is processed.

Fruits may be packed in raw or hot pack style. With raw pack the fruit is placed in the jars, covered with boiling-hot syrup, juice, or water, and then sealed and processed. With the hot pack method the fruit is heated in syrup, water (or steam), or extracted juice; put into jars and covered with boiling liquid; and then sealed and processed. For most fruits and tomatoes the raw pack method is preferred.

Now the filled and sealed jars must be placed in the canner containing the water bath. For raw pack foods in jars, the water in the canner should be hot but not boiling; for the hot pack products, the water must be boiling. In both of these methods the water should cover the jars by an inch or two.

After the canner has been covered and the water has come to a rolling boil, the processing time must be counted. (These times are noted in all detailed directions.) The water should be kept at a gentle, steady boil for the length of the recommended boiling time. Then the jars should be removed from the canner, placed on a cloth or rack, and allowed to cool thoroughly before they are labeled and stored.

Steam-Pressure Canning. Low-acid foods—vegetables, meats, fish, poultry, and specialty foods—should be prepared in a steam-pressure canner. By processing at 10 pounds steam pressure, a temperature of 240° F (115.5° C) is reached. At this temperature bacteria spores will be destroyed. (At altitudes above 2,000 feet, or 600 meters, steam pressure must be raised approximately one pound for each 2,000-foot increase in altitude to reach a temperature of 240° F. Thus, at 4,000 feet, a pressure of 12 pounds should be used.)

Most vegetables can be processed by either the raw or hot pack method; potatoes and spinach, however, must be done by hot pack. Meats, fish, and poultry should be precooked before being packed into jars in order to shrink the food and aid the processing. Specialty products, including chili, meat sauce, and mincemeat, should be cooked and then packed hot into jars to blend the flavors fully prior to processing.

Vegetables selected for canning should be fresh, young, and tender, and sorted for size and ripeness. They must be canned quickly or they will lose their freshness. They should not be prepared in large batches. Meats, fish, and poultry must be fresh and of good quality if the results are to be palatable.

The preparation of foods and the filling of jars for steam-pressure canning differ somewhat from other canning procedures. Raw pack vegetables must be packed tightly in the jars because there will be some shrinkage. The cooking liquid from hot pack vegetables should be used for packing because it contains nutrients dissolved from the food. Meat and poultry should be packed loosely, with a 1-inch headspace in the container; vegetables, however, need only a ½-inch headspace.

A pressure canner is a safe utensil to use, but it should be checked at the beginning of each canning season to make certain that the gauge is correct and that all openings are clean. Before using any pressure canner, the cook should be completely familiar with the instructions for its operation.

The canner should be filled to a water depth of two to three inches and heated; after the filled jars are placed on the rack, the cover must be fastened or locked in place. Then the petcock must be opened and a steady stream of steam permitted to escape for at least 10 minutes. After this, the petcock should be closed and the pressure allowed to reach 10 pounds, at which time the processing timing should begin. (Pressure can be maintained at the proper level by adjusting the heat.) At the end of the processing, the canner should be taken from the heat and the pressure permitted to return to zero. Following a five-minute wait, the petcock may be opened, the cover removed, and the canner and jars set aside to cool.

Spoilage. Foods usually spoil because of the action of microorganisms (molds, yeasts, bacteria), and enzymes. Microorganisms exist in soil, water, and air; they appear in vegetative or growing form, or in spore or dormant form. Enzymes are natural substances found in all fruits, vegetables, and meats. If enzymes are not destroyed by heat, they can change the color, texture, and flavor of the product.

Home canned foods processed correctly will remain in good condition for many months. A careful check should be made of the seal on each glass or jar the day after processing. Each should be turned partially over during the check. If the jar has a flat metal lid, the seal can be tested by tapping the center of the lid with a spoon. If there is a good seal, normally there will be a clear, ringing sound. Leaky jars should be set aside at once and the food used as soon as possible.

At the time glasses or jars are removed from storage a check should be made for signs of spoilage, such as bulging jar lids or rings, gas bubbles, or bulging can ends. When the jar is opened, if liquid spurts or if the color of the product appears to be changed, spoilage might have set in.

Discard any jars showing spoilage. Sulfur in meat may cause metal lids of jars to darken; this discoloration does not affect the condition of the meat. Unless mold growth on fruits, jellies, or jams is heavy, it may be removed and the food used. Although other minor causes of food spoilage occasionally are found, spoilage of home canned food can be eliminated or kept extremely low if proper procedures are followed and utensils are carefully cleaned before use.

KIRBY M. HAYES
Professor of Food Science and Technology, University of Massachusetts

CANNIZZARO, kän-nēd-dzä'rō, **Stanislao** (1826–1910), Italian chemist, who made important contributions to the atomic theory of matter. Cannizzaro was born in Palermo on July 13, 1826. He turned to chemistry in 1845, served with the Sicilian artillery starting in 1847, and after the defeat of the Sicilians by the Neapolitans in 1849, he fled to Paris, where he was accepted in Chevreul's laboratory. He obtained a professorship at Alessandria in 1851, then at Genoa (1855) and Palermo (1861), and finally in Rome (1871). At Rome he also became a senator of the newly united kingdom of Italy. He died in Rome on May 19, 1910.

In 1858, Cannizzaro published an outline for a course in the philosophy of chemistry. Applying the ideas of Avogadro and Ampère on atomic theory, he distinguished between the atom of hydrogen, which he took as unity, and its diatomic molecule, composed of two atoms. The composition of hydrochloric acid, HCl, then furnished the atomic weight of chlorine and its diatomic molecule. For carbon, the molecule was unknown, but he saw that in its compounds its atomic weight is 12. He used this to define the atomic formulas for the molecules of organic compounds. His system was publicly presented at Karlsruhe in 1860, after which it began to be generally accepted.

EDUARD FARBER, *Editor of "Great Chemists"*

CANNON, Annie Jump (1863–1941), American astronomer, who classified the spectra of stars. Annie Cannon was born in Dover, Del., on Dec. 11, 1863. In 1896 she joined the staff of Harvard College Observatory in order to study its rich collection of astronomical photographs. In the early work there, the spectra of stars had been sorted into various categories. Miss Cannon rearranged and subdivided these groups, forming the definitive Harvard system of spectral classification. Her work proved that, with few exceptions, all stars could be grouped into a few basic spectral types arranged in a continuous series related to the colors of stars.

Her greatest achievement was the *Henry Draper Catalogue,* a 9-volume list containing spectral classifications of 225,300 stars, the final volume of which was issued in 1924. Miss Cannon classified over 150,000 more stars before her death in Cambridge, Mass., on April 13, 1941.

OWEN GINGERICH
Smithsonian Astrophysical Observatory

CANNON, Clarence (1879–1964), American congressman. He was born on April 11, 1879, in Elsberry, Mo., and earned a law degree (1908) at the University of Missouri. He went to Washington in 1911 as confidential secretary to Champ Clark, speaker of the House. He was elected as a Democrat to Clark's old seat in 1922 and remained in Congress until he died in Washington on May 12, 1964.

Cannon was chairman of the powerful House appropriations committee (1941–1947, 1949–1953, 1955–1964). His special interest was parliamentary procedure, and he catalogued or devised most of the rules of procedure later used by Congress and many other legislative bodies. His works in this area include *Cannon's Procedure* (1928 and later editions), and *Cannon's Precedents* (1936 and 1949).

WALTER DARNELL JACOBS
University of Maryland

CANNON, George Quayle (1827–1901), American church leader and legislator. He was born in Liverpool, England, on Jan. 11, 1827. He emigrated to Nauvoo, Ill., in 1842 as a convert to The Church of Jesus Christ of Latter-day Saints, crossed the plains as a pioneer to Utah in 1847, and was a missionary to the Hawaiian Islands from 1850 to 1854. In 1860 he became one of the Twelve Apostles of the Mormon Church, and from 1880 until his death served as First Counselor in the First Presidency. He died in Monterey, Calif., on April 12, 1901.

Cannon was a member of the territorial legislative council of Utah and a delegate to Congress (1872–1881), where he was seated after a long fight waged against him because he practiced polygamy. His son, Frank J. Cannon, was one of the first two U. S. senators from Utah.

EARL E. OLSON, *The Church of Jesus Christ of Latter-day Saints*

CANNON, James, Jr. (1864–1944), American clergyman and prohibitionist. Cannon was born in Salisbury, Md., on Nov. 13, 1864. He was educated at Randolph-Macon College and Princeton Theological Seminary. Elected a bishop of the Methodist Episcopal Church in 1918, he served until 1938. Cannon's efforts on behalf of prohibition brought him national prominence. Called the "Dry Messiah," he became active in the Anti-Saloon League, wielding powerful influence on legislative bodies as well as in church circles. He was one of the chief organizers and leaders of the World League Against Alcoholism.

In the 1928 presidential campaign, Cannon helped to defeat the antiprohibition Democratic candidate, Alfred E. Smith. His enemies in politics and the church sought to prove him guilty of unethical and immoral conduct, but church tribunals continued to support him. Although he was acquitted when tried for misusing campaign funds, this charge and others destroyed his influence as a reformer. He died in Chicago, Ill., on Sept. 6, 1944.

ALBEA GODBOLD, *Editor, "Methodist History"*

CANNON, James Graham (1858–1916), American banker, who wrote the standard reference work *Clearing-Houses, their History, Methods and Administration* (1908) and was a pioneer in the development of credit departments in banks. He was born in Delhi, N. Y., on July 26, 1858. He graduated from Packard's Business College in New York in 1875. Entering banking as a messenger, he worked his way up to president of the Fourth National Bank, in New York, in 1910. An organizer and president of the National Association of Credit Men, he introduced the custom of having commercial borrowers provide financial statements periodically. Cannon died in New York City on July 5, 1916.

MARGARET G. MYERS, *Vassar College*

CANNON, Joseph Gurney (1836–1926), American political leader and speaker of the U. S. House of Representatives, whose authoritarian control of House business led to a rebellion against his rule. Cannon was born in New Garden, N. C., on May 7, 1836. Shortly thereafter his family moved to Indiana. After clerking in a country store, he studied law and began practice in 1858. He eventually settled in Danville, Ill., where he lived the rest of his life.

In 1870, Cannon ran for Congress as a Republican but was defeated. He was elected in 1872 and held his seat, except for 1891–1893 and 1913–1915, until his retirement in 1923.

Although his name was associated with no important piece of legislation, Cannon rose rapidly in the House. In the 51st Congress (1889–1891), he was the chief lieutenant of Speaker Thomas B. Reed, and he served as chairman of the powerful Committee on Appropriations. In 1903, he was elected speaker of the House.

As speaker, Cannon ran the House with an iron hand through his power of appointing committee chairmen and members, his chairmanship of the Committee on Rules (which controlled the flow of legislation), and his arbitrary behavior in recognizing or refusing to recognize members on the floor. His archconservatism—most notably his adamant opposition to downward revision of the tariff—led to a revolt by a minority of Republican

Joseph G. Cannon

BROWN BROTHERS

congressmen, who were largely from the Middle West, who became known as "insurgents."

An insurgent-Democratic attempt to break Cannon's power failed at the beginning of the first session of the 61st Congress (1909). But in March 1910, this combination, under the leadership of George W. Norris of Nebraska, pushed through a resolution enlarging the rules committee and providing for its election by the House, election of its chairman by the committee itself from among its own members, and exclusion of the speaker from membership.

At the next session, the Democrats had a majority in the House, which ended Cannon's term as speaker, and he was defeated even for reelection in 1912. But "Uncle Joe" regained his seat in 1914, and he remained highly esteemed as an elder statesman by his fellow Republicans. He died in Danville, Ill., on Nov. 12, 1926.

JOHN BRAEMAN, *University of Nebraska*

Further Reading: Bolles, Blair, *Tyrant from Illinois* (New York 1951).

CANNON, Walter Bradford (1871–1945), American physiologist, who is best known for his introduction of the use of X-rays in physiological studies and for his theory of homeostasis. In 1897, while still a medical student, Cannon introduced the use of bismuth (a substance opaque to X-rays) for X-ray studies of the gastrointestinal tract of animals. This technique became an important diagnostic tool that showed the presence of any tumors or abnormalities of structure or position. Cannon himself used X-rays to study the relation of gastric movements to hunger. He also investigated the mechanical forces of digestion and the relationship of gastric acidity to the control of the pyloric valve, a circular muscle separating the stomach from the beginning of the small intestine.

During World War I, Cannon studied shock resulting from hemorrhage or other causes. This and his later research on the endocrine glands, especially the adrenals, showed how hormones permit the body to meet emergencies. As a result of his experimental work and observations, Cannon formulated the theory of "homeostasis," according to which the body acts to maintain a stable internal environment through the interaction of various physiological processes.

In 1931, Cannon announced the discovery of an adrenalinlike hormone that he called "sympathin." He also worked on the chemical factors related to nerve conduction.

Cannon was born in Prairie du Chien, Wis., on Oct. 19, 1871. He studied at Harvard University, receiving his B. A. in 1896 and his M. D. in 1900. He spent most of his academic career at Harvard, where he was Higginson professor of physiology from 1906 until he retired in 1942. He died in Franklin, N. H., on Oct. 1, 1945.

Among his many books are *Bodily Changes in Pain, Hunger, Fear, and Rage* (2d ed., 1929), *The Wisdom of the Body* (1932), *The Supersensitivity of Denervated Structures* (1949), and *The Way of an Investigator* (1945).

CANNON. See ARTILLERY; FIELD ARTILLERY; GUNNERY; GUNS; HOWITZER; MORTAR; PROJECTILE.

CANNONBALL TREE is the common name for a number of trees with fruits that resemble rusty cannonballs. The name is used for about a dozen species of the genus *Couroupita* of the Brazil nut family, which are scattered throughout tropical America from Brazil to Central America. They produce a hardwood valuable for structural purposes and furniture. They are large forest trees, some reaching 100 feet (30 meters), with large wedge-shaped leaves in clusters at the tips of young branches. Probably the best known species is *C. guianensis*. The wood and decaying fruits give off a nauseating odor.

Cannonball tree leaves, flower, and fruit.

U. S. DEPT. OF AGRICULTURE

A member of the mahogany family, *Xylocarpus granatum*, is also known as the cannonball tree. This plant, sometimes called the sea coconut, is found in Burma, Ceylon, Fiji, and the East Indies.

S. C. BAUSOR, *California State College, Pa.*

CANO, kä'nō, **Alonso** (1601–1667), Spanish painter, sculptor, and architect, who was one of the masters of the Spanish baroque and is considered the founder of the Granadine school. Born in Granada on March 19, 1601, Cano lived and studied in Seville from 1616 until 1638, when he moved to Madrid. Accused of murdering his wife, he fled to Valencia in 1644. He returned to Madrid the next year and, by undergoing torture on the rack, was able to gain acquittal. Cano later served as prebendary at the Cathedral of Granada, for which he designed a new facade. He died in Granada in October 1667.

Among Cano's major paintings are a series of seven canvases illustrating the life of the Virgin (in the Granada cathedral) and the *Madonna of the Rosary* (in the Málaga cathedral). His sculpture includes a number of polychromed wood pieces done for the Granada cathedral.

CANO, kä'nō, **Juan Sebastián del** (1476–1526), Spanish mariner, who commanded the first ship to circumnavigate the globe (1519–1522), after the death of the expedition's original commander, Ferdinand Magellan. Cano, also called *Elcano*, was born at Guetaria, Spain, of parents of the lesser Basque nobility.

Magellan's five ships sailed westward from Sanlúcar de Barrameda, Spain, in 1519 on a voyage to the Moluccas (Spice Islands) in the Pacific Ocean, with Cano as pilot of the *Concepción*. When they reached winter quarters in Patagonia, South America, on March 31, 1520, some Spanish captains mutinied, and Cano was punished as a ringleader. Three ships continued on to the Marianas and Philippines, where Magellan and most of his officers were murdered by Filipinos in April 1521.

On Sept. 6, 1522, Cano returned to Sanlúcar in command of the *Victoria*, the only ship to complete the voyage. He received a pension from Emperor Charles V (who was also king of Spain). Cano died at sea on July 30, 1526.

ROBERT G. ALBION, *Harvard University*

CANO, kä'nō, **Melchior** (1509–1560), Spanish theologian. He was born in Tarancón, Spain, on Jan. 6, 1509, and entered the Dominican order in 1523. As a student at the University of Salamanca (1527–1531), he was influenced by Francisco de Vitoria, a leading authority on natural law and a founder of international law.

Cano was ordained a priest in 1531. After teaching philosophy and theology at Valladolid and Alcalá, he succeeded de Vitoria in the chair of theology at Salamanca in 1546. In 1551 he represented Emperor Charles V at the Council of Trent. He died in Toledo on Sept. 30, 1560. Cano's treatise *De locis theologicis*, published posthumously in 1563, was an important statement of Thomistic philosophy and the dialectic method of scholastic disputation.

CANOE AND CANOEING. The canoe is a light, somewhat fragile water craft, pointed at both ends and propelled by means of a paddle or paddles, although a sail or an outboard motor is sometimes used. Canoes that are open from end to end are often referred to as the *Canadian type;* those that are completely covered, or "decked," except for a well or cockpit where the paddler sits, are known as *kayaks*. The Canadian-type canoe is generally propelled with single-bladed paddles; the kayak, with one or more double-bladed paddles. In both types of craft the paddler faces the bow.

The canoe and kayak are two of the very few primitive or native craft that have survived among modern water craft. Both are characterized by lightness, maneuverability, versatility, ease of repair, silent operation, and relatively inexpensive cost. The canoe is widely used for economic and industrial purposes, including prospecting, mining, lumbering, and surveying, and is valued for a variety of governmental projects relevant to parks and forests. But the canoe and kayak are best known for their application in leisure activities such as touring and camping. They are also used for racing and for formal drills and stunts.

MODERN EQUIPMENT

Canoes vary considerably in shape, size, weight, durability, stability, and ease of propulsion. Construction materials include, with varying degrees of success, cedar planks and ribs, canvas, metal sheath lining, molded plywood, aluminum, rubber, plastic foam, nylon, fiber glass, and steel. The average canoe ranges from 15 to 18 feet (4½–5½ meters) in length, and from 35 to 37 inches (88–93 cm) at its widest, and it weighs from 55 to 85 pounds (20–30 kg). The most common ones have two seats and two thwarts. Some canoes have a square stern to accommodate an outboard motor; some are designed for quick conversion to sailboats. In the racing canoe, balance, stability, and maneuverability are sacrificed for speed. The V-shaped hull of the racing canoe acts like one large keel, helping to keep it on a straight course.

Modern kayaks are made of fiber glass, although some are built of a rubberized fabric over a light wood frame. They range in length from 17 to 36 feet (5–11 meters), depending on whether the craft is a one-, two-, or four-man vehicle. Especially popular in Europe and the United States are folding versions, called foldboats.

Paddles are manufactured in several shapes, depending on application, and most commonly from maple or spruce woods. The beavertail, or oval, blade is commonly adopted by the bowman, and the slightly rounded and square-tipped blade by the stern paddler, because it affords more surface for steering. Racing paddles have a wide and long blade (some racing paddles have a convex blade) to permit maximum thrust, or "catch," in the water. The blades of double-bladed paddles are either spoon-shaped or flat. For racing, a paddle with a one-piece shaft is preferred; for general use, a shaft with a ferrule joint in the middle for convenience in stowing is advisable. Grips are either pear-shaped or T-shaped, the latter being more comfortable and secure for the beginner.

Overall length varies with the height of the paddler, kind of propulsion demanded, type and size of canoe, and number of paddlers. A rule of thumb is that a single-bladed paddle should be almost as long as the paddler is tall (4 to 6 feet). However, for a lone paddler who has to stroke near the center of the canoe, a shorter paddle will make up for his proximity to the water. With two or more paddlers, a shift of weight to the gunwales allows easier access to the water, and a longer paddle is the better choice. Because kayaks are narrower and much lower-sided than canoes, the average length of a double-bladed paddle is about 8 feet (2.4 meters).

CANOEING FUNDAMENTALS

The canoe is usually paddled by two persons, the stern man doing the steering; the kayak is more often a one-man craft.

Paddling Positions. Although some canoeists paddle perched high up on the seat, the ideal paddling position is on well-spread knees, sitting back on the heels with some of the body weight resting against the seat of the canoe. In this position the paddler's center of gravity is lower in the craft, and he also can apply greater power to his paddle. For racing, the position is on one knee, with the leg away from the paddling side extended forward, foot braced against the bottom of the canoe. The paddler rises erect on the one knee, carrying most of his weight on it. (Kneeling pads to protect the knee are a standard part of the conoeist's equipment.) In the kayak, the paddler sits snugly in the bottom of the craft.

In single-blade paddling, the canoeist paddles continuously on one side. With two paddlers, the stern man strokes on the opposite side from the bowman, and both stroke in unison.

Strokes. Fundamental canoeing strokes may be divided into those used primarily for propulsion and those required for steering and maneuvering. Basic strokes in the first group include the straight, or bow, stroke, performed from any paddling position to propel the canoe forward; the J, or stern, stroke, used for forward motion and to counteract the tendency of the bow to swing away from the paddling side; and the draw and pushaway strokes, used to change the direction of the, canoe by pulling or pushing it sideways from the long axis of the canoe. Feathering, which follows the figure 8 pattern, is the most useful stroke for making the canoe travel sideways, however.

Essential strokes for steering and maneuvering include the bow rudders and cuts, for directing the canoe left or right quickly, especially where there is a current; the draws, for turning; and the sweeps, for maneuvering through turns. The quarter sweep is particularly effective for turning the bow.

HISTORY OF CANOES AND CANOEING

The canoe was born when man discovered that he could ride a floating tree trunk on a moving body of water. By using a pole or flattened piece of wood, he then learned that he could propel his log across a still body of water. Later he found that a log to which a limb was still attached tended to be more stable.

To enable it to carry more passengers, man hollowed and shaped the log by hacking and burning it with primitive equipment. Dug out further, the craft became more easily portable and more readily propelled in either calm or swiftly moving waters. This dugout canoe was

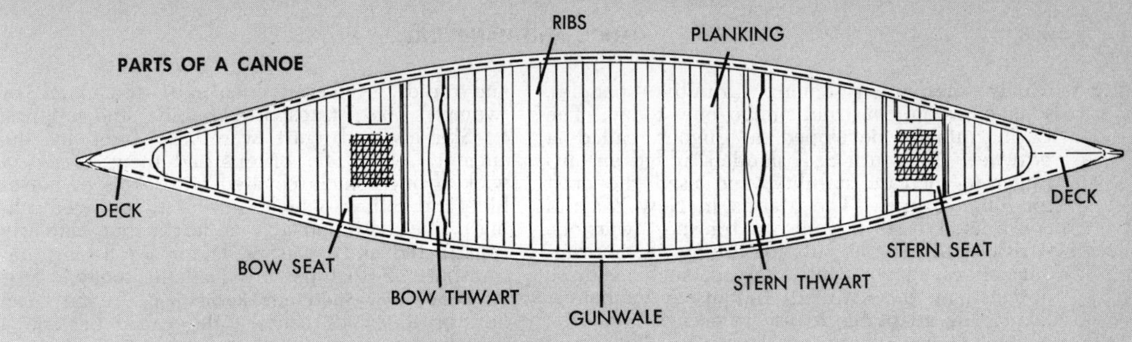

BASIC CANOEING STROKES

STRAIGHT OR BOW STROKE
Dip paddle forward into the water close to the canoe, back of blade facing squarely astern. Pull blade back, parallel to the keel, stopping at the hips.

J OR STERN STROKE
Reach paddle forward into the water about a foot from the canoe. Pull aft, twisting blade toward the canoe then outward vertically, making a hook or "J."

DRAW STROKE
Reach way out and dip blade into the water, parallel to canoe's center line. Pull blade in toward craft. Push blade outward before it reaches side of canoe.

PUSHAWAY
Place paddle vertically into the water close to the canoe, blade forward of the hips and edgeways to the water. Push blade outward and away from the canoe.

BOW CUT
With body well braced, reach forward of the bow and lower paddle into the water, blade at an angle with keel. Hold firmly, resting shaft against gunwale.

QUARTER SWEEP
Holding paddle almost horizontal, thrust blade forward and pull in an arc toward the canoe. Keep two-thirds of blade in the water throughout the sweep.

RECREATIONAL PADDLING POSITION

Paddling on knees separated from 12 to 18 inches gives the canoeist a broad base and helps keep his weight low. Edge of the seat or thwart supports most of his weight. In this paddling position, canoeist gains greater steadiness and control of the craft.

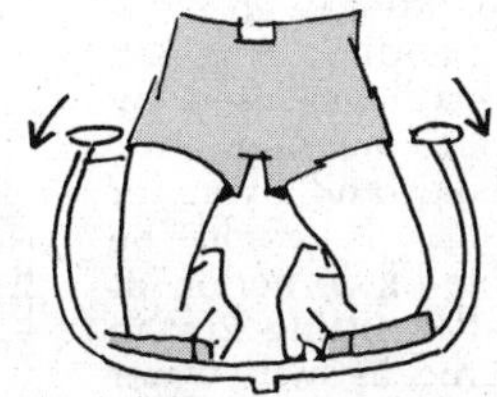

widely distributed among primitive peoples, some of whom construct similar ones today. The Carib Indians developed a dugout called a *pirogue*. The South Sea islanders added an outrigger to increase stability, and used the craft for long voyages. The Maoris in New Zealand constructed huge dugouts to transport warriors. Africans still use dugouts for fishing. Some dugout canoes, magnificently carved, such as those designed by the Kwakiutl Indians of Vancouver Island, are adaptable to use in ocean waters.

Bark Canoes. The North American Indian built a light craft because considerable portaging was necessary in his lands. He covered a wooden shell with bark, and the resulting craft was strong enough to carry cargo and buoyant enough to travel in shallow waters. It could be repaired readily with forest materials and without special tools. The Indians used their canoes for hunting, fishing, trapping, and exploring. They built large models for transporting the warriors to battle. It was this type of bark canoe that impressed the white man when he first began to penetrate the wilderness of the North American continent. The rapid exploration and development of a great part of the United States and Canada were direct results of the white man's adoption of the Indian's bark canoe as a mode of travel.

The white man first began to build canoes in the late 1600's for the rapidly growing fur trade and for exploring new trade routes. The first "factory" was situated at Trois-Rivières, on the St. Lawrence River. About 20 canoes a year were constructed, measuring 36 feet (11 meters) long, 5½ feet (2.3 meters) wide, and 33 inches (83 cm) deep. These oversized versions of the Indian bark canoe transported thousands of bales of pelts annually. They resembled the later *grand canot* or *canot de maître*, which had remarkable carrying capacity and earned an honored place in North American history.

What material was available governed to some extent what was used to construct the canoe. The winter bark of the white, or paper, birch was favored for the frame, but other woods were also employed. The root of the black spruce was used as lashing to secure the bark seams and frame, and resin for pitching the seams came from black or white spruce. White cedar was sought for ribs, white or black ash for keels and gunwales, and hard maple for thwarts and paddles.

The tools used originally included a stone ax, a wedge, and a knife. Wooden mauls (hammers) and driving sticks later became part of the builder's kit. Then the white man introduced the Hudson Bay ax, steel awls, crooked knives, shaving horses, and froes (for cleaving), which accelerated canoe building considerably.

Skin-Covered Craft. Skin-covered canoes originated with the Eskimo. He stretched sealskins over a frame of wood or whalebone and held these together with sinews. He extended the hide across the top, forming a watertight deck with an opening amidships for the paddler, who navigated with a double-bladed paddle. A small craft, the kayak, or hunting boat, was used by hunters who harpooned seals in the open sea, speared swimming caribou in lakes and rivers, or explored territory for trapping. It could be propelled quickly by the double-blade action of the paddle; and with the paddler sitting low in the center it could be maneuvered in swift water and rapids. A larger, open craft, the *umiak*, or "woman's boat," transported families and supplies.

Skin-covered craft were also built by the ancient Celts. The Britons had their *coracle*, a wickerwork vehicle covered with skins or horsehide and tallow, which they used for river fishing. The Irish *curragh*, a larger but similarly constructed craft, was made for sea fishing and transport. Both types are available today.

Canoes for Sport and Recreation. In the latter half of the 19th century the canoe became a vehicle for sport or pleasure, as distinct from business. Interest in the craft for pleasure was stimulated by John Macgregor, a Scottish canoeist, who began in 1865 to make long journeys by water in decked craft he had constructed himself, which he propelled with a double-bladed paddle and sails. Modifications of his design caused sail racing between individuals and newly organized clubs to become a popular event in Britain and the United States. In 1885 the New York Canoe Club, the first local canoe organization in the United States, offered a trophy for international competition in decked canoe sail racing. This International Challenge Cup is still in contention.

Among early canoe enthusiasts in the United States and Canada, an all-wood open canoe, based on the original design of the Indian bark canoe, surpassed the decked sailing vehicle in interest and use. Today's Canadian-type canoe is a modification of the all-wood craft.

ORGANIZED COMPETITION

Canoe racing clubs throughout the world stage competitions and demonstrations that require considerable training and practice in handling the canoe. For uniformity, all competitive canoeing groups and associations have adopted the Olympic standards. In the United States, organized canoeing is governed by the American Canoe Association, founded in 1880. In Canada, dominion championship meets are conducted under the auspices of the Canadian Canoe Association (founded 1900); in Britain, by the British Canoe Union (founded 1936). Other prominent organizations are the North American Canoe Racing Association and the Pan American Canoeing Federation. The world governing body is the International Canoe Federation, formed in 1945. Canoeing for men became an Olympic sport in 1936; women first competed in 1948.

Other canoe activities include white-water (rapids) races and slalom competitions. In a kayak, the paddler covers a slalom course of upstream and downstream "gates" established on a stretch of white water by stringing wire across the river and hanging sets of poles from the wire to create 36- to 40-inch (91–102-cm) openings. Prominent marathon races include England's Devizes to Westminster; the U. S. Bemidji to Minneapolis derby; and Canada's Voyageur Pageant. Canoes have also been used to commemorate and celebrate special events. Canada's Cross Canada Journey from Newfoundland to Vancouver in the 1967 Centenary Year by the youth of that country is a notable example.

KIRK A. W. WIPPER, *University of Toronto*
Director, Camp Kandalore, Minden, Ontario

Further Reading: Camp, Raymond R., *Young Sportsman's Guide to Canoeing* (New York 1962); Perry, Ronald H., *Canoeing for Beginners* (New York 1967); Urban, J. T., ed., *White Water Handbook for Canoe and Kayak* (Boston, no date); Whitney, Peter D., *White Water Sport* (New York 1960).

CANOGA PARK, kə-nō′gə, is an unincorporated community in southwestern California, in Los Angeles county. Although it is 23 miles (37 km) northwest of downtown Los Angeles, it is governed as part of the city. Canoga Park is primarily residential but has several large manufacturing and research firms in the fields of aeronautics and space technology. The area was originally known as Owensmouth because of its proximity to the Owens River Aqueduct, completed in 1913. It was renamed Canoga Park shortly after its annexation by the city of Los Angeles in 1917. Population: 110,600.

MARILYN C. WHERLEY
Los Angeles Public Library

CANON, kan′ən, is an ecclesiastical title that originally referred to certain clergy of the Roman Catholic Church who were members of the official body of diocesan clergy but who lived in groups. The term was applied particularly to those clergy who lived at the cathedral. During the Gregorian reform of the church in the 11th and 12th centuries, a movement to introduce a monastic observance among the canons became widespread. Those who accepted a monastic form of life became known as *canons regular;* those who continued to live without the vow of poverty or a monastic rule came to be called *secular canons.*

Since most of the houses of canons regular adopted the rule of St. Augustine, they became known as Augustinian, or Austin, canons. In England, where there were large numbers of foundations of canons regular, monastic observance rather than clerical service was emphasized. The various orders of canons regular still operative in the Roman Catholic Church include the Canons Regular of the Lateran and the Norbertines (also called the Premonstratensians).

Although there are no chapters of canons secular in the United States and English-speaking Canada, the tradition has been preserved in other parts of the world. The Roman Catholic Code of Law, promulgated in 1917, carefully lists the responsibilities and privileges of secular canons. Basically, they constitute a chapter, or collegiate body, that assists and counsels the bishop and that performs divine services at the cathedral. Where no chapter has been established, diocesan consultors act as advisers to the bishop. Bishops may name honorary canons. The Church of England also has the institution of secular canons.

KEITH J. EGAN, O. CARM.
Mt. Carmel College, Ontario

CANON, kan′ən, in art and literature, a standard of judgment. The term is derived from the Greek *kanōn,* "a straight rod," and it retains this sense of a standard of measurement.

In art, a canon is a standard or model of beauty, often in the sense of a system of proportion. Such a system enables one to use the given dimensions of one part of a figure or building, for example, to compute those of the other parts or of the whole. This use of the term is derived from the *Canon,* written by the Greek sculptor Polyclitus in the 5th century B.C. It sets down a system of ideal human proportions—epitomized in Polyclitus' statue *Doryphorus*—by which a work of art can achieve a perfect balance between moving and motionless parts of the body.

In literature, a canon is also a standard, in the sense that Aristotle set the canons of the literary forms of his day in his *Poetics.* The term has the additional meaning of a body of writings held to be authentic. For example, a canon of scripture comprises those works believed by adherents of a religion to have been divinely inspired, and the canon of an author are those writings that almost certainly were from his pen. For example, the Shakespeare canon includes those works that scholars agree were actually written by him, as distinguished from works erroneously attributed to him, such as many poems in *The Passionate Pilgrim* (1599).

C. HUGH HOLMAN
Coauthor of "A Handbook to Literature"

CANON, kan′ən, in music, a composition in which two or more voices or instruments, usually beginning one after another at equal intervals, render the same melody. The canon (Greek *kanōn,* literally, "rod") is the strictest form of contrapuntal melodic imitation; but it has been developed with some freedom and great variety, and there now exist more than a dozen distinct types. The most familiar is the round (q.v.), such as *Three Blind Mice,* which is technically a "perpetual" canon.

The earliest known canon, *Sumer is icumen in,* dates from the early 13th century. It is a two-in-one canon—a single melody arranged to be sung by two voices. (Analogously, four-in-two canons have four voices singing two harmonized melodies.)

Composers of the 14th and 15th centuries found the canon form challenging, and developed very complex types. These included interval canons, in which a later voice starts the melody at a pitch different from the original; augmented and diminished canons, in which a later voice increases or diminishes the time values of the notes of the original melody; reverse (or "crab") and inverse canons, in which a later voice performs the melody backward or upside down; and canons *al contrario riverso,* in which a later voice both reverses and inverts the melody.

About 1450 it became fashionable to turn canons into puzzles by notating only the basic melody and indicating, by a pun, conundrum, or presa, how it was to be performed. With many composers the canon became a sterile diversion more notable for intricacy than for beauty.

The canon was restored to musical importance by J. S. Bach, whose canons in *The Art of Fugue* and the *Goldberg Variations* are especially noteworthy. Distinguished canons by later composers include passages in Mozart's Overture to *Don Giovanni,* Beethoven's Eighth Symphony, Mendelssohn's *Elijah,* and Franck's Violin Sonata. In the 20th century the canon took on added importance with its frequent use in serial, or 12-tone, music (as in Schönberg's String Quartet No. 4).

HELEN N. MORGAN
North Shore Branch, New England Conservatory

CANON CITY, kan′yən, in Colorado, is on the Arkansas River, 47 miles (75 km) by road southwest of Colorado Springs, at an altitude of 5,330 feet (1,625 meters). It is the seat of Fremont county. The city has brick and tile yards, foundries, and canneries. On the outskirts is Colorado State Penitentiary. The outstanding tourist attraction of the region is Royal Gorge, spanned by a bridge more than 1,000 feet above the Arkansas River. Population: 9,206.

CANON LAW, kan′ən lô, is the body of rules and regulations governing a church. Canon law is not the same as doctrine; rather, the laws are attempts to apply doctrine to the organization and life of a church. Canon law is made by the church and does not involve civil laws that may apply to a church.

This article discusses, first, the canon law of the Roman Catholic Church, which has the most complete and systematic body of ecclesiastical law. Sections on the canon law of the Orthodox and Protestant churches follow.

ROMAN CATHOLIC CANON LAW

The body of laws and constitutional principles of the Roman Catholic Church constitutes the canon law of that church. While the term "canon law" can encompass the laws of the many regional jurisdictions within the church, it is commonly applied to the universal laws of the church, especially those contained in its official juridical compilation, the *Code of Canon Law*.

Etymologically considered, "canon" derives from a Greek word meaning "rule" or "norm." It long has been used in the church to signify the "rule of faith" (Galatians 6:16) and the "norm of Christian life" (Philippians 3:16), and it was adopted by the early councils of the church for the laws ("canons") they issued. From that time canon law has come to mean sacred or ecclesiastical law as differentiated from the the imperial law or "nomos"—the civil law of the Roman Empire and other states.

Church law appears to be like the law of civil society, sharing the forms and borrowing the legal techniques of the latter; in reality, however, the two are essentially different. Civil law is a code for the regulation of external social behavior and the maintenance of personal rights; church law is a complex of regulations governing not only the external but also the internal religious behavior of the church's members. More basically, whereas the force and authority of civil law come from within the community—from the members themselves or from a ruler—the force and authority of church law comes not from its membership or leaders but from Christ, who is at once within and above the community. Like civil society, the church is an institution composed of men; it has human leaders and man-made laws. But these leaders must be submissive to the guidance of Christ and his Holy Spirit if the laws they proclaim are to be authentically Christian. To be authentic, church law must conform to the will of Christ as it is expressed in Holy Scripture and as it is experienced in the inspirations of the Holy Spirit. It must have as its objective not mere social order but the education of the members of the church to a life more nearly like that of their Master.

In the Catholic Church the study of canon law has the status of an academic discipline for which a comprehensive curriculum is prescribed and degrees are granted. Canon law is both a historical and a practical science, looking to the legal traditions of past centuries, the present governing of the church, and the continuing development of its legal structure. An understanding of canon law, then, should include not only a knowledge of the current structure of the Code of Canon Law but an awareness of its history and a concern for its future.

The Past: The History of Canon Law. The New Testament gives evidence, especially in the Acts of the Apostles and the Epistles of St. Paul, that even in the earliest years of the Christian era laws and internal organization, at least of a rudimentary sort, were part of the life of the church. It was, though, several centuries before anything resembling what today we call canon law could be recognized. The development of the church's law depended on the prior development of ecclesiastical institutions; it was only after the flowering of the monarchical episcopate (in which each local church was governed by its own bishop), after the growth of interdependence of the individual churches one upon the other, and after the ascendancy of the major patriarchal sees (those claiming foundation by one of the Apostles) that the beginnings of a universal canon law can be discerned.

Early Canonical Collections. As the centers of the Christian church began to be more closely tied, councils—at first regional but becoming general or ecumenical after the accession of Emperor Constantine—were held by the bishops. From these councils, canons, or rules of worship and principles for the organization of Christian life, emanated and spread throughout the Christian world. Side by side with the authentic canons of the councils were circulated collections of apocryphal canons, often claiming authorship by the Apostles themselves. Popularly accepted as genuine, these pseudo-apostolic collections (*Didache, Didascalia apostolorum, Canones apostolorum, Constitutiones apostolorum*, and *Traditio apostolica sancti Hippolyti*) helped to establish a degree of organizational and juridical uniformity in the early church.

In the late 5th century Pope Gelasius I (reigned 492–496) set about gathering the early canons and collections into an official compilation of laws, and assigned the work to Dionysius Exiguus (q.v.), a Scythian monk living at Rome. Dionysius gathered the canons of local synods and the general councils, and added certain of the "apostolic" canons; thus, he produced the first noteworthy collection of canon law in the western church. Editions of this *Dionysiana*, as the collection was called, were later sent from Rome to other parts of the church and so served as the foundation for a uniform canonical development in the West.

Frankish Influence. Uniform development was temporarily thwarted during the 6th and 7th centuries. The barbarian invasions and the disintegration of the western Roman Empire were followed by a period of anarchy and decadence. Out of these conditions arose national kingdoms governed by their own legal codes, which were based on tribal customs. The church, accustomed to the structure and unity of the Roman legal system, was then faced with the need of adapting itself to the legal codes of these peoples and the local pecularities of the young nations they had founded. Centralization of government and uniformity of laws was, therefore, postponed, and local questions were settled by the decrees of regional synods.

A further complication was introduced into ecclesiastical law when the Irish missionary monks appeared on the continent with their *Libri paenitentiales*. This detailed listing of crimes, sins, and penances, which was based on the tribal laws of their homeland, was imposed on their converts. These "penitentials" were rapidly integrated into local laws.

Out of this confusion, however, emerged a

renewed, though temporary, supremacy of the pope and a strengthened centralization of church authority. The papal cause was championed by Pepin the Short, king of the Franks (reigned 741–768). Requesting a rescript on canon law from Pope Zacharias in 747, Pepin engaged in strengthening the organization of the church. Some time between 754 and 756 he gave the pope the lands which became the Papal States, thereby establishing the temporal power of the papacy and setting the stage for its later claims of wide temporal jurisdiction. About this time, also, a document called the Donation of Constantine appeared. It purported to show that on his departure from Rome for the East, Constantine had conferred on Pope Sylvester I (reigned 314–335) far-reaching temporal rights over the western part of the Roman Empire. Though a forgery, this document was used for many years to bolster papal claims to temporal jurisdiction.

After Pepin, Charlemagne (reigned 768–814) continued the work of reform; he restored ecclesiastical organization as a whole throughout his kingdom, reduced the divergent tendencies and institutions of canon law, and again brought into a place of prominence the general collections of law. In 774, Pope Adrian I gave him a code of law—a version of the Dionysian collection supplemented by later papal legislation—to serve as a basis for his reform of the Frankish church.

Although the work of Charlemagne and the canonists of his time enhanced the prestige of canonical tradition and prevented the dissolution of the Latin Church into a multitude of autonomous local churches, the years following his death did not fulfill the promise of his reign. Under his successors his kingdom was split, and the church, though better organized than before, fell prey to secular rulers who abused the privileges of the clergy, interfered with the power of the bishops, and confiscated ecclesiastical property. A new collection of decretals conveniently appeared containing legislation against just such abuses. The collection was attributed to Isidorus Mercator, and its decretals were said to date from Pope St. Clement and other early bishops of Rome. Now known as the "false" or "pseudo-Isidorian" Decretals, the collection was compiled by well-intentioned churchmen of the day partly from authentic decretals of an earlier day and partly from decretals of their own fabrication. Gaining acceptance as authentic, the false decretals were used to reinforce episcopal power and to deter the seizure of church property. Since they advocated appeal to Rome for the settlement of controversies, they served to strengthen papal jurisdictional claims. See also DECRETALS.

That jurisdiction, however, was once again being weakened by the Roman aristocracy's control over the papacy during the 9th century and by the Germanic emperors' interference with church affairs during the 10th and 11th centuries. More than this, the feudal culture of the day, with its multiplicity of political subdivisions, its predilection for "private" churches, and its attempts at lay dominance of the clergy, minimized the central authority of Rome. This decline of papal authority was accompanied by a decline in canon law as well. Thus any contribution to canonical progress during those times was made by individual compilers of new collections. The most significant of these collections, and one prophetic of the coming of a better age of canonical activity, was the *Decretum* of Burchard, the reform-minded bishop of Worms (died 1025). His was the most complete and systematic collection yet produced and served as the groundwork for the later great collections of Ivo of Chartres and Gratian.

Gregorian Reform. The reform of the abuses of this period (lay investiture and simony, for example) and the return to a strong central authority began in the middle of the 11th century and reached its peak in the reign of Pope Gregory VII (1073–1085). To restore the authentic sources of law and strengthen the measures of Gregory's reform, canonists searched out documents and compiled collections of texts (the most notable collection being the *Dictatus papae*). These collections strengthened the authority of the Roman See by recognizing the pope as the primary and supreme source of ecclesiastical laws with power over all members of the church. Furthermore, by virtue of a kind of papal theocracy, secular rulers were held to be subject to the pope, even in temporal matters.

Although these claims, backed by the arguments of the papal canonists, continued for several centuries and reached their highwater mark in *Unam sanctam* (1302), the bull promulgated by the canonist-pope Boniface VIII, a moderating influence entered canonical literature even at this time. Ivo, bishop of Chartres (Yves de Chartres; 1040?–1116), who accepted the principle of papal primacy in the church but nonetheless respected the rights of secular rulers, sought to restore peace between church and state. Zealous for reform, he was careful to temper the rigor of the law with mercy and charity. Moreover, he tried to update the study of canon law by providing rules for the historical and rational interpretation of its sources. Like the *Decretum* of Burchard (from which he borrowed extensively), the work of Ivo signaled the coming of a new era in the history of canon law.

Gratian and the Classical Period of Canon Law. The new era began in the mid-12th century with the work of Gratian. A monk, he was educated in Bologna, which at that time was the greatest center of legal learning in Europe. It boasted a school of law where, under its founder Irnerius, the newly revived legislation of Justinian—the *Corpus Juris Civilis*—was studied and commented upon. In this setting Gratian applied to the complex and disorganized canon law of his time the form and order of Justinian's Roman law. He adopted a rational method for the selection and interpretation of legal texts similar to the dialectical method Peter Abelard had earlier used in his landmark theological treatise *Sic et non*. Setting out to compile a *summa* of canon law, Gratian gathered all the available legislation of the past from the Sacred Scripture, the writings of the Fathers, and the decrees of councils. First, he discarded apocryphal texts and laws narrowly regional or superseded by later legislation and then added to what remained the most recent papal and conciliar decrees. Finally, he tried to reconcile the often divergent texts into a coherent unity.

Gratian's work was published about the year 1140 and was titled *Concordantia discordantium canonum* (Concordance of Discordant Canons), but it soon came to be called by the shorter and more familiar name *Decretum Gratiani* (Decree of Gratian). Though the *Decretum* was never made an official or authentic source book of ecclesiastical law by the church, it did become the handbook of the Roman Curia and the textbook of canon law in the great university centers of Europe.

Understandably, the scope of such a work, undertaken by one man alone, made textual discrepancies and verbal obscurities inevitable. Very soon, commentators on the *Decretum* appeared who were called "decretists." Some of these were Gratian's own pupils—Paucapalea and Rolando Bandinelli (later Pope Alexander III; reigned 1159–1181). Others—Huguccio (died 1210) and Juan de Torquemada (1388–1468)—came years and centuries after him. The decretists wrote extensively on Gratian's work, trying to resolve its difficult passages and to answer the numerous questions its publication had raised. Their efforts clarified many controverted points, but some of the issues were so involved as to require authoritative answers from the papacy itself. Papal decretals multiplied, accordingly, in the years following Gratian, and these, like his *Decretum,* were in their turn commented on by another group of canonists—the "decretalists." Among these were Raymond of Peñafort (c. 1180–1276), Sinibaldus Fieschi (Pope Innocent IV), and Nicolas de Tudeschis (1389–1446).

The plethora of papal decretals required collection and order. During the 13th and early 14th centuries three major collections were made by the popes: the *Decretals of Gregory IX* in 1234; the *Liber sextus* of Boniface VIII in 1298; and the *Constitutions of Clement V,* promulgated by John XXII in 1317. These official collections, together with two unofficial collections published in 1500 by Jean Chappuis (the *Extravagantes of John XXII* and the *Extravagantes communes;* "extravagantes" means decretals circulating outside official collections), were added to the *Decretum* of Gratian to form the *Corpus Iuris Canonici.*

Conciliarism. During the 13th and 14th centuries canonists were called on to choose sides in a conflict whose repercussions would be felt for centuries in the church—the seemingly perennial question of papal jurisdiction. As might be expected, papal claims of temporal authority created tension between the church and secular rulers. These claims also engendered opposition within the church itself; men like Marsilius of Padua, William of Ockham, and John Wycliffe (qq.v.) opposed them. Likewise, papal claims to total authority within the church led to an ever-increasing centralization of power and consequent strained relations with local churches. The practice of reservation of local ecclesiastical judicial and administrative matters to the pope —a practice often enough made necessary by the less than ideal conduct of some local clergy—similarly created conflicts between the universal papal laws and local rules and customs.

Those who wished to mitigate the exercise of papal power found gratification in the Western schism that divided the church from 1378 to 1417. During this disastrous period, when two and sometimes three claimants to the papal throne split the church into factions and no resolution of the division appeared likely, the theory known as conciliarism gained fairly wide acceptance in some areas of the church. Many theologians and canonists (notably Jean Gerson and Pierre D'Ailly) as well as bishops and cardinals were prepared to accept the thesis that only a general council could end the disunity, and that indeed such a council would be legislative authority superior to the pope. Other canonists, equally renowned—Baldus de Ubaldis and Juan de Torquemada, to name two—argued against the conciliar theory and supported papal authority.

For a time it appeared that the views of the conciliarists were destined to prevail. But the general council of Constance (1414–1417) ended the schism by deposing two of the papal contenders, accepting the resignation of the third, and electing one of its own members to reign as Pope Martin V (1417–1431). Though Martin's actions after the Council of Constance are the subject of some dispute, it appears that, once elected, he repudiated the conciliarist views of his electors and reaffirmed the supremacy of pope over council.

The Reformation and the Council of Trent. One century to the year after the election of Martin V ended the schism, a greater rupture of the unity of western Christianity occurred when Martin Luther and the reformers rejected, among other things, the hierarchical-papal structure of the church. Along with that structure, Luther rejected the canon law that served as its legal justification. The effect of Luther's attack on canon law, though not what he might have hoped for, was considerable in that it occasioned the calling of the Council of Trent. For the next four centuries this great council's decision would regulate the life, structure, and law of the Catholic Church. From the Roman Curia to the smallest parish community, Catholic life was restructured and renewed according to the spirit and laws of Trent, and as the church's life was renewed, so too was its law. The *Canons and Decrees of the Council of Trent* became, with the *Corpus Iuris Canonici,* the law of the church. Its laws on marriage, priestly and religious life, and the government of dioceses supplemented and in many cases supplanted the old law.

The old law was not neglected (though persistent requests for its complete restructuring were not answered). Pope Pius IV (reigned 1559–1565) appointed a commission to correct and revise the *Corpus Iuris Canonici,* and a new edition was published by the authority of Pope Gregory XIII in 1582. For a time following the council there was a lessening of canonical activity when Pius IV forbade the writing of commentaries on Trent's decrees. Official interpretations only were to be allowed, and a committee of cardinals was given the task. By the end of the 17th century, however, this ruling had been allowed to lapse; from that time to the present, hundreds of commentaries have enriched the literature of canon law.

Even though Trent, by way of answer to the reformers, anchored the church more securely than ever in the papacy, theories aimed at limiting papal power still continued to circulate. In 17th century France the movement held that the pope is limited by the general council in matters of spiritual government, by the episcopate in matters of faith, and by special "Gallican privileges" on matters relating to the French church. Predictably, this movement was condemned by Pope Alexander VIII in 1690, and its theories lived on in Febronianism in Germany and Josephinism in Austria during the last half of the 18th and first half of the 19th centuries until the First Vatican Council (1869–1870). The more publicized definition of papal infallibility in matters of faith and morals overshadowed a Vatican I definition of at least equal importance. The council defined that the Roman pontiff has full, supreme, ordinary, and universal power throughout the entire church, in all its parts, and over all its members, bishops as well as laymen. The papal primacy was once again vindicated.

To balance such a strong affirmation of Roman authority the council had intended to make statements on the role of bishops in the church and on their relationship with the pope. The premature closing of the council occasioned by the fall of Rome to Garibaldi's army precluded the discussion of this relationship, and a balanced answer to the perennial question of papal power would have to await the Second Vatican Council nearly a century later.

Thirty-four years after the close of the First Vatican Council, Pope Pius X (reigned 1903–1914) announced that it was his intention to revise canon law in structure as well as content. His revision was the first official collection since the promulgation of the *Constitutions of Clement V* nearly 600 years before. It was also the answer to centuries of requests for a general revision and modernization of the law. Pius X decreed that the *Corpus Iuris Canonici* should be replaced by a modern code of law patterned after the civil codes adopted in many European countries following the publication of the Napoleonic Code in the early years of the 19th century. A commission of cardinals and experts was set up under the presidency of Pietro Cardinal Gasparri to carry out the actual labor of codification. Pius X died before the completion of the new *Codex Iuris Canonici,* and his successor Pope Benedict XV promulgated it on May 27, 1917. It became effective one year later. Although a new revision was in progress in the 1960's, it remained the law of the Catholic Church.

The Present: The Code of Canon Law. The Code of Canon Law is composed of 2,414 concise formulations or canons of law, which are arranged under 5 general headings into "books": 1. General Norms (canons 1–86); 2. Persons in the Church (canons 87–725); 3. Sacred Matters (canons 726–1551); 4. Legal Procedures (canons 1552–2194); 5. Crimes and Penalties (canons 2195–2414).

The Content of the Code. Book 1 (General Norms) is, in effect, a guide for the books that follow. It contains basic principles on the nature and binding force of ecclesiastical laws; rules for their interpretation; and the procedure to be followed in applying for and receiving dispensations from the law.

Book 2 (Persons in the Church) presents the legal aspects of the three states of life—clerical, religious, and lay—which a Catholic may choose to follow as a member of the church. The first part of the book considers the rights and duties of the members of the clergy; the nature of the ecclesiastical offices they hold and the power of jurisdiction they exercise; and the hierarchical structure of the church from pope to pastor. Rules regulating religious life (that is, the freely chosen community life in which a member of the church pledges himself to lifelong observance of the evangelical counsels of chastity, poverty, and obedience) are contained in the second part of this book. The lay state is the subject of comparatively few canons. These deal with religious associations formed by or for laymen.

Book 3 (Sacred Matters) lists the laws governing the sacraments, sacred places and seasons, divine worship, the teaching authority of the church, and the temporal needs of the ecclesiastical mission: the support of its ministers and the administration of its material goods.

Book 4 (Procedures) is a lengthy and detailed outline of the legal process in ecclesiastical trials. Just as the church has its own legal system, so too it has a judiciary system, which consists of local courts or tribunals, courts of appeal, and the equivalent of a supreme court. In past centuries these courts tried cases of all kinds and are still empowered by the church to do so. Today, however, their activity is limited mostly to the adjudication of marriage cases. In addition to the rules of court procedure, this book contains the special directives for the beatification and canonization of saints.

Book 5 of the Code presents the penal legislation of the Catholic Church, defining what constitutes an ecclesiastical crime and specifying what remedies may best be employed in order to safeguard the common good and correct the offender.

Official Interpretation of the Code. The modern compilation of the law can be likened both in its magnitude and its lasting significance to the medieval compilation of Gratian. As with Gratian, it should not be surprising that controverted points, obscure wordings, and textual conflicts might be found in the new law. Not wishing to leave the interpretation of such matters in the hands of unofficial commentators only (though their contribution has been considerable), Pope Benedict XV established the Commission for the Authentic Interpretation of the Code on Sept. 17, 1917. The function of this commission is to give authentic and legally binding interpretations of disputed points and to make modifications in the canons themselves whenever the need arises. In the half-century since the promulgation of the Code, the Commission for Interpretation has changed the Code only slightly, although it has, together with the Roman Congregations and the popes, carried out a constant updating of ecclesiastical legislation.

The medium for the promulgation of new legislation, and the only official publication of the Holy See, is the *Acta Apostolicae Sedis.*

The Future: The Second Vatican Council and The Revision of Canon Law. Simultaneously with his announcement of the convocation of the Second Vatican Council, Pope John XXIII in January 1959 announced a new revision of the Code of Canon Law, which after 50 years was once more in need of modernization. A new commission of cardinals and experts was appointed by John in March 1963 and told to revise the law in the light of the Vatican Council then in progress. In June of that year John XXIII died, but his successor Pope Paul VI pledged himself to carry out the work of revision. Paul reorganized the commission somewhat and appointed an internationally representative body of canonical experts to assist the cardinals.

Like the Council of Trent before it, Vatican Council II was expected to exert a profound influence on the development of canon law. In the light of the council's decrees, certain nearly inevitable changes in church law could be predicted, especially in that area of perennial concern—the relationship of the universal primacy of the pope with the authority of the bishops. The council's teaching on the collegial nature of the government of the church (whereby the bishops, united in a body or "college" headed by the pope as bishop of Rome, govern the church together) would require a new canonical formulation of the papal-episcopal relationship. It could be expected that in such a formulation the principle of subsidiarity (enunciated by Pope Pius XI for civil society and applied by Pope Pius XII to the church) would play a large part. This principle states that what can be accomplished by a lesser social unit should not be taken over by a greater unless there is evident need. Thus, decisions that can be made by the bishops at the diocesan or national level would not need to be reserved to the Roman authorities. Steps to apply this principle were taken by the council in establishing national conferences of bishops, and by Pope Paul VI in lifting many of the restrictions of episcopal power caused by the reservation of cases to the Roman See.

The role of the laity, which in the Code is overshadowed by that of the clergy, was expected to receive more equal legal recognition. The ecumenical spirit of the council, its openness to other churches and ecclesiastical communities, and its concern for Christian unity require the formulation of new norms for intercommunication among Christians.

These and many other changes were expected to be integrated into a new code of canon law. The most profound conciliar modification of canon law, however, had already begun to take its subtle effect. In the years following Gratian, the science of canon law, in developing the techniques that made its progress possible, became, to a degree, separated from its natural roots in the fundamental sources of the church's life—Scripture and the Fathers. Now that the Vatican Council, so Biblical in its teaching, had securely anchored the church in the Word of God, canon law was expected to rediscover its Biblical source and inspiration and become an authentic manifestation of the law of Christ. These ideals were reiterated at the Synod of Bishops held in Rome in October 1967. The bishops gave much attention and time to the problem of revising the code and generally agreed that the code should be simplified and reduced in volume.

ROMAEUS O'BRIEN, O. CARM.
Catholic University of America

CANON LAW IN THE EASTERN CHURCHES

The canon law of the Eastern churches is primarily derived from pseudoapostolic writings, the writings of Church Fathers, and the decrees of ecumenical and local councils. From the earliest times many works attributed to the apostles enjoyed the force of law; only one, however, *The 85 Canons of the Holy Apostles,* has been fully accepted by the Eastern churches. In the 4th century laws began to be properly promulgated by the ecumenical councils. In addition to the canons issued directly by them, the norms of local synods and councils gained universal authority when they were cited at the ecumenical councils; and, by approving the writings of the Church Fathers, the ecumenical councils imparted the status of norms to these as well.

Subsidiary sources of Eastern legislation include the writings of Eastern patriarchs, the canons promulgated by the standing episcopal conference in Constantinople, and the liturgical and penitential books, which list the exact laws for worship, fast and abstinence, observation of holy days, and penances. Custom, another source of law, was applied as a norm as early as the Council of Nicaea (325). The interpretations of unclear laws by prominent canonists have also attained a quasi-legal status.

Because of the symbiosis of church and state in the Byzantine Empire, many ecclesiastical laws were formulated by the emperors who frequently organized them into collections. The most famous imperial collection was Justinian the Great's (483–565) *Corpus Iuris Civilis.* In addition, systematized laws or opinions arranged according to topics were issued in collections. Among these were *Collection of Fifty Chapters, Synopsis of Canons, Nomocanon* (50 chapters), and *Nomocanon of John the Faster.* Nomocanons list the civil and church laws dealing with the same problem side by side. St. Sava (Rastko; 1174–1235) translated a selection of laws from the nomocanon ascribed to Photius into Church Slavonic. Called the *Kormchaja Kniga* (*Book of the Rudder*), this became the most prominent collection of canon law in use in the Slavonic Orthodox churches.

The *Syntagma of Canons,* arranged by Rhalli and Potli (1852–1859), is the most thorough collection of Byzantine church laws, but until officially accepted by pan-Orthodox agreement, it cannot have the force of universal law for all Orthodox churches. The canon law in force for Eastern Catholics is largely based on the Latin rite code. The decree on Eastern Catholic churches promulgated by the Second Vatican Council in Nov. 1964 has, however, prompted the undertaking of a totally new codification.

GEORGE A. MALONEY, S. J.
Fordham University

CANON LAW IN THE PROTESTANT CHURCHES

Repudiation of the traditional canon law was characteristic of the earliest stage of the Reformation. For example, Martin Luther burned the *Corpus Iuris* on Dec. 10, 1520, along with the papal bull that excommunicated him. But as soon as the Lutheran and Calvinist churches came to rely on state support they developed codes of canon law. Other Protestant churches, not supported by the state—that is, the Nonconformist or Independent churches—adopted laws or rules for their internal regulation. Some of these codes were known as books of discipline.

The Church of England retained many of the pre-Reformation canons, though legislation for the church was in the hands of the king and Parliament. At the Convocation of Canterbury in 1604 and that of York in 1606, 141 canons were adopted. At present, new canons may be authorized by the two convocations, with royal assent, or by Parliament. Other churches of the Anglican Communion, such as the Episcopal Church in the United States, devised their own canons, apart from those of the mother Church of England. Equally independent is the Church of Scotland, which is Presbyterian. It recognizes none of the pre-Reformation canons but only those authorized by a national council. Laws set up by the council require approval by Parliament.

See also GREAT BRITAIN AND NORTHERN IRELAND—*13. Religion* (Church of England; Church of Scotland); PRESBYTERIANISM; and articles on other churches.

FREDERICK C. GRANT
Union Theological Seminary

Further Reading: Dawley, Powel Mills, *Chapters in Church History,* rev. ed. (New York 1963); White, E. A., *Annotated Constitution and Canons of the Protestant Episcopal Church,* rev. ed. (New York 1954).

CANON OF SCRIPTURE, kan'ən, skrip'chər, a list of books accepted by a body of believers as containing the truths of their religion. Most major religions have books that are considered to be divinely inspired or to hold the teachings of their founders. See BIBLE—*1. Canon of the Old Testament; 10. Canon of the New Testament;* BUDDHISM; KORAN; VEDIC LITERATURE.

CANON OF THE MASS, the core of the Roman Catholic liturgy. It consists primarily of the Eucharistic prayer, but it is more proper to include the Preface, or special prayer of thanksgiving, and the Sanctus ("Holy, holy, holy . . .") which is recited or sung by the people. Historically these prayers are one, and were sung to the same melody by the presiding priest. In the Eastern rites, the term *anaphora* is used to include the canon as well as the communion service which immediately follows.

The central part of the canon is the consecration when, according to traditional Catholic theology, bread and wine are transformed into the body and blood of Christ at the intonation of the words Christ used at the Last Supper: "This is my body" and "This is the cup of my blood."

Until the Second Vatican Council (1962–1965) instituted liturgical reform, the Roman canon had remained practically unchanged for over 1,000 years. Indeed, the basic prayer can be traced at least to St. Ambrose (339–397). Since Vatican II the canon has been translated into the vernacular. The English version was put into official use in the United States and Canada in October 1967. In some countries, notably Holland, a variety of canons can be heard. All are structured on the Roman canon, however, especially its primitive form, called the "canon of Hippolytus."

C. J. MCNASPY, S. J., *"America" Magazine*

CANONESS, kan'ə-nəs, is an ecclesiastical title for women. It was first used in the Eastern Church and was adopted in the Western Church by the 8th century. The title was applied to women who carried out various works on behalf of the church and had an official capacity as designated by the inclusion of their names in the church's register. Some virgins and widows, although not officially nuns, were known by this title.

From the time of the Gregorian reform of the church in the 11th century there developed a differentiation between *secular canonesses* and *regular canonesses* with "regular" designating those who followed a *regula*, or rule. The secular canonesses were not nuns but women of the higher classes—often of noble and royal families—who lived together in temporary community. Such communities still exist in a few parts of Europe, chiefly as women's residences; some are Protestant establishments. The regular canonesses were and are nuns in the Roman Catholic Church who follow a religious rule and profess the vows of poverty, chastity, and obedience. Their beginnings coincided with the development of the canons regular in the ecclesiastical revival of the 11th and 12th centuries (see CANON).

KEITH J. EGAN, O. CARM.
Mt. Carmel College, Ontario

CANONICAL BOOKS. See BIBLE—*1. Canon of the Old Testament; 10. Canon of the New Testament.*

CANONICAL HOURS, kə-non'i-kəl, the eight times of the day that the Roman Catholic Church has established as periods in which the clergy are to recite the divine office. This is the public prayer of the church and a song of praise of God. It was evolved by the early Christians, who combined the Roman and Jewish traditions of designating certain hours for prayer. The office is arranged so that the whole course of the day and night is holy with prayer.

The canonical hours were divided into Matins (with three nocturns at 9:00 P.M., midnight, and 3:00 A.M.); Lauds (at daybreak); Prime (6:00 A.M.); Terce (9:00 A.M.); Sext (noon); None (3:00 P.M.); Vespers (6:00 P.M.); and Compline (at nightfall). The Constitution on the Liturgy promulgated by the Second Vatican Council (1963–1965) established Lauds and Vespers as the chief hours and suppressed the hour of Prime. It also recommended that the office be read sequentially, in accordance with the canonical hours, rather than all at one time as had become the practice among many priests. See also BREVIARY.

CANONICUS, kə-non'i-kəs (1565?–1647), American Indian, who was grand chief of the powerful Narragansetts, and an important figure in the development of the New England colonies. In 1621, Canonicus threatened Plymouth Colony by sending a rattlesnake skin stuffed with arrows, but Gov. William Bradford returned the skin filled with powder and shot, and there was no war. Instead, in 1631, Canonicus made an alliance with Massachusetts Bay Colony, and in 1636 he granted Roger Williams land for Rhode Island. The neighboring Pequot Indians sought an alliance with the Narragansetts for a war with Massachusetts, but Williams circumvented the move and persuaded Canonicus to join Massachusetts in a war that destroyed the Pequots in 1637.

In 1644 the Massachusetts Bay Colony government, suspecting the Narragansetts of maneuvering for an Indian war, delivered Canonicus' nephew Miantonomo over to the enemy Mohegans. Canonicus appealed to the British Crown, but his claim was disallowed. Thereafter he considered promoting an Indian alliance to war on the New England colonies, but it never came to be. He died on June 4, 1647.

DAVID H. CORKRAN
Author of "The Cherokee Frontier"

CANONIZATION, kan-ə-nə-zā'shən, is the solemn and definitive declaration of the Roman Catholic Church by which a deceased person is inscribed in the catalog of the saints and declared worthy of public veneration by members of the church. The decree of canonization, issued only by the pope, does not promote a person to eternal glory; it merely states that he has attained that glory and that he may be venerated as a saint by the faithful.

Historical Development. The judicial processes preceding the decree of canonization result from a long, complicated historical development. In the early church the veneration, or *cult*, of the martyrs began as a spontaneous response of the Christian community toward those who, having died for the faith, were considered perfect Christians. Because this veneration was expressed in religious acts, it was rooted in the liturgy. Thus the local bishop had both the right and duty to intervene; his approval gave the cult legitimacy.

What examinations were conducted in those times to distinguish true martyrs from imposters and frauds is unknown because the historical sources are scant and noncontemporaneous. The fact that miracles were strongly emphasized as signs of divine sanction does emerge. In the 5th century, bishops and synods intervened increasingly as the cult of confessors (those who had professed the faith through holy lives rather than martyrdom), begun in the preceding century, grew more prominent.

The first recorded papal canonization was that of Ulrich of Augsburg presided at by Pope John XV in 993. Although episcopal canonization did not then end, papal canonizations increased. The procedure for papal canonization, which was to petition the pope and present him with a life and list of miracles, endured for 100 years. When Pope Urban II (1088–1099) refused to grant canonization requests unless witnesses existed who could testify to a person's sanctity, a new element was introduced. Within 30 years of Urban's death, this had become the norm. Episcopal canonizations continued, but a decree of Pope Alexander III (1159–1181) forbade canonization without papal approval. Whether this ruling was definitive or not is unclear, but after its inclusion in Gregory IX's code of canon law (1234), it became official. Since then canonization has been the exclusive right of the Holy See.

The processes for canonization were first documented in the 13th century, when a cause for canonization began to be conducted like a lawsuit. This arose partially because canonization requests were increasing at the very time that the church's judicial and canonical procedures were receiving increased recognition and impetus from the great jurist popes of the 13th and 14th centuries. The judicial processes used in canonization today are substantially the same as those which developed then.

In the 17th century Pope Urban VIII forbade public veneration of those not beatified or canonized by the Apostolic See. He further ordered that no canonization process could begin until it was proved that no veneration had been given in conflict with his decrees. He excepted those around whom a cult had been established from time immemorial.

Procedure. At the present time any Catholic may petition his local bishop to initiate a beatification or canonization process. If the bishop agrees, a tribunal is set up in the diocese. A process (technically called "non-cult," or *de non cultu*) is conducted to prove that Urban VIII's decrees forbidding unauthorized veneration have been observed, or, in the exceptional case, that an immemorial cult already exists. The court then collects all extant writings of the *servant of God*, as the candidate for canonization is called, and finally extensive testimony is taken concerning the candidate's reputation for sanctity or martyrdom. All the proofs thus obtained are forwarded in copy to Rome.

If after appraisal the Holy See wishes to proceed with the case, another tribunal is convened in the diocese but this time by papal authority. Known as the Apostolic Process, this second hearing examines the servant of God's reputation for sanctity or martyrdom; detailed testimony is sought on the particular Christian virtues he exhibited, and submitted data concerning his alleged miracles are compiled. This testimony is then reexamined in Rome. If sanctity to a high degree is substantiated, a decree of "heroicity of virtue" is issued. By this decree the servant of God is given the title *venerable*, which does not, however, inpart permission for public veneration or cult. Important in all these judicial procedures is the "promoter of the faith," an official who, because he must often oppose the beatification or canonization, is popularly known as the "devil's advocate."

After it has been established that miracles—the number required depends on whether the proofs offered in the previous processes were from living witnesses or documentary—occurred through the intercession of the servant of God, the pope may proceed to formal *beatification*. By this the person is given the title *blessed* and restricted cult or veneration is permitted. (See BEATIFICATION.) Beatification is solemnly proclaimed by the pope amid great pomp and splendor in St. Peter's Basilica. Later, after additional miracles have been established and further requests have been made by the faithful, the pope may proceed to *final canonization*. This final decree is jubilantly proclaimed to the universal church in St. Peter's.

Theological Aspect. Catholic theologians generally hold that the decree of canonization is definitive, infallible, and irrevocable and binding on the universal church. The infallible content of the decree pertains only to the fact that the person who is canonized has attained eternal beatitude and is worthy of veneration: it does not pertain to evidence gathered in the process concerning life or miracles. The legends, myths, and tales that have grown up around many of the saints of earlier times are no more than myths and are not validated by the decree of canonization.

While the formal decree of canonization is considered infallible, the catalog of the saints may be revised and names dropped from it. None of the earlier saints were formally canonized, and in many cases the cult surrounding them was local in character. Many of these were merely accorded what is now known as beatification rather than canonization. Modern historical research has discovered errors in the catalog of the saints. Some were cases of mistaken identity, such as Philomena, whose name came from the misreading of a tomb inscription. The decree of beatification is not infallible or definitive; it is not binding on the universal church and is revocable.

At the present time there are many American candidates for sainthood. Among them are Catherine Tekakwitha, the first North American Indian candidate; Junípero Serra, apostle to California; Elizabeth Seton, who laid the foundation of the American parochial school system, and who was beatified in 1963; and John Neumann, an early bishop of Philadelphia, who was also beatified in 1963. Frances Xavier Cabrini, the first American citizen to be proclaimed a saint, was canonized in 1946. In 1930 the eight North American Martyrs were canonized.

DAMIAN J. BLAHER, O. F. M.
Holy Name College
Washington, D. C.

Further Reading: Blaher, Damian J., *The Ordinary Processes in Causes of Beatification and Canonization* (Washington, D. C. 1949); Cicognani, Amleto G., *Sanctity in America* (Paterson, N. J., 1945).

CANONIZATION, The, kan-ən-ə-zā'shən, a poem by the English metaphysical poet John Donne. It was published for the first time in the collection of Donne's verse that appeared in 1633, two years after his death.

The Canonization, one of the great love poems of the English language, is built on a sustained metaphor, or "conceit," of the kind that characterizes metaphysical verse. It argues that the great and pure love of the poet and his mistress makes them the saints of love, destined to be immortalized in poetry.

CANONSBURG, kan'ənz-bûrg, is an industrial borough in southwestern Pennsylvania, in Washington county, 20 miles (32 km) southwest of Pittsburgh. Its principal manufactures are electrical transformers, fabricated metal products, and pottery. Bituminous coal mines are operated in the vicinity.

In 1772, Col. John Canon settled here and in 1788 platted the borough, which was incorporated in 1802. It was the site of Jefferson College before the institution was merged with Washington College in 1865 to become Washington and Jefferson College at Washington, Pa. Canonsburg was a center of the Whiskey Rebellion of 1794.

The borough is governed by a manager. Population: 11,439.

CANOPIC JARS, ka-nō'pik, are large-bellied vessels, found in ancient Egyptian tombs, that contain the embalmed viscera of a mummified corpse. Four Canopic jars were placed in a tomb, each holding one of the internal organs—the liver, intestines, kidneys, or stomach. The tops of the jars represented the four sons of the god Horus, who were depicted with the head of a man, an ape, a jackal, and a hawk.

Canopic jars were made of wood, of basalt, of limestone, or of white alabaster with spiral flutings, or formed of black burned clay. Their name is derived from the town of Canopus.

CANOPIC JARS of limestone. Such jars, in an Egyptian tomb, held the internal organs of a mummified corpse.

UNIVERSITY MUSEUM, PHILADELPHIA

CANOPUS, kə-nō'pəs, was a port in ancient Egypt at the mouth of the Canopic branch of the Nile River. The town is the site of modern *Abukir*. Canopus probably reached its greatest prominence in the 26th dynasty (664–525 B.C), when Greek ships bringing merchandise to the trading center at Naukratis were subject to its control. During the Ptolemaic period (332–30 B.C), when Alexandria was the capital of Egypt, Canopus became a suburb and part of the fleet was stationed there. In Hellenistic and Roman times the temple of Serapis at Canopus was more splendid than the one in Alexandria, and its reputation for healing brought hordes of pilgrims to the town. Wealthy Alexandrians maintained villas with extensive grounds along the canal, and Canopus became known to Greek and Roman writers as a center of licentious revelry.

CAROLINE PECK, *Brown University*

CANOPUS, kə-nō'pəs, is a yellowish-white star of the Southern Hemisphere and the second-brightest star in the sky. Only Sirius, the Dog Star, is brighter. Canopus is located in the constellation Carina (part of the older constellation Argo Navis), and it is never visible above latitude 37° N. It has been estimated to be about 100 light years from the sun, which is relatively distant for a star as bright as Canopus is in the earth's sky. Canopus is therefore probably a supergiant and may be 1,300 times more luminous than the sun.

The star was worshiped in ancient times, and the early Egyptians oriented some of their religious structures on the position where it rose above the horizon.

CANOPY, kən'ə-pē, in architecture, a shelter or covering set above an altar, a statue, or, most commonly, a niche. A canopy serves more for decoration and for emphasizing the object below, than for protection. It may be corbelled out from the top and sides of a niche, or it may be free standing (supported by posts of columns at the corners). Canopies of the former type reached their highest development in Gothic architecture, in which they often accent the sculptured figures lining church portals, and adorn niches on facades and buttresses. Canopies above niches are commonly semipolygonal in plan, with small Gothic arches, sometimes traceried, set in each exposed face, as, for example, on the 13th-century facade of Amiens Cathedral.

A free-standing canopy above the high altar of a church is called a baldachin or ciborium. The Byzantine Emperor Justinian provided one of silver for Hagia Sophia (534 A.D.), Istanbul. In St. Peter's, Rome, Bernini designed the famous 94-foot bronze baldachin (1624–1633), whose spiral columns support four scrolls that converge in an apex topped by a ball and cross.

EVERARD M. UPJOHN, *Columbia University*

CANOSSA, kä-nôs'sä, is a castle in northern Italy, about 17 miles (27 km) southeast of Parma and 12 miles (19 km) southwest of Reggio. It is built at the edge of the Tuscan foothills, on an eminence of whitish rocks of great strategic value that dominates the Lombard plain and the Roman Via Aemelia.

The site was fortified by the middle of the 10th century. During the next 300 years Canossa received many notable guests and refugees, among them Pope Gregory VII (Hildebrand).

ANDERSON—ART REFERENCE BUREAU

ANTONIO CANOVA'S marble figure *Pauline Bonaparte Borghese as Venus Victrix* (1808), in the Villa Borghese, Rome.

The most famous incident associated with the castle occurred during his stay. The Pope was en route to Augsburg to meet with the rebellious magnates of the Emperor Henry IV, the Pope's most powerful enemy. The Emperor, however, crossed the Alps in midwinter and presented himself at the gate of the castle on Jan. 25, 1077, barefoot and in penitent's garb. The Pope was under an ecclesiastical obligation to pardon the repentant, and he finally received Henry after the Emperor had waited outside for two or three days, exposed to the inclement weather.

The incident became a symbol of the power of the church and inspired Bismarck's famous affirmation during the *Kulturkampf* against the Roman Catholics in the 1870's that "to Canossa we shall not go." However, it had the immediate effect of lifting the ecclesiastical sanctions against Henry; it allowed him to restore his position in Germany and to humiliate Gregory, who died in exile from Rome in 1085. The castle of Canossa subsequently fell into the hands of the imperial troops and was razed by the men of Reggio in 1255. Since then it has often been restored.

R. T. McDONALD, *Smith College*

CANOVA, kä-nô'vä, **Antonio** (1757–1822), Italian sculptor, who was one of the greatest exponents of the neoclassic movement that flourished in the second half of the 18th century.

Early Development. Canova was born at Possagno, near Venice, on Nov. 1, 1757. He was apprenticed by his grandfather, a stonecutter, to a local sculptor, who introduced him to the famed collection of casts in the palace of Filippo Farsetti in Venice. After the death of his master in 1774, Canova set up his own studio in Venice. One of his first commissions was a marble *Daedalus and Icarus* (1778; Museo Correr, Venice), done for the Procurator Pietro Pisani. This sculpture, conventional in the unstable grouping of the two moving figures and more original in the decided realism of the nude figure of the old man, has an impressive psychological subtlety in the facial expressions and the poses. The same quality also appears in portrait busts Canova was then carving.

In 1779, Canova moved to Rome, where the Venetian ambassador provided him with a studio. Responding strongly to the classical spirit of Rome and of southern Italy (he visited Paestum, Herculaneum, and Pompeii in 1780) he substantially changed his style in a very short time. One of his earliest Roman works, the *Theseus and the Minotaur* (1782; Collection of Lord Londonderry, London), shows a high degree of neoclassical idealization and a new compositional solidity. The linear severity of the drawings for the *Theseus* recalls the outline drawings of archaeological publications and of the illustrations of John Flaxman.

Maturity. Canova's first major commission, the tomb of Pope Clement XIV (begun 1784; Church of the Holy Apostles, Rome), is a masterpiece of neoclassical simplicity. The female mourners are supremely graceful, with something of Greek pathos, while the image of the seated Pope strikes a pose of imperious power. The success of this work brought Canova a series of commissions for tombs, among them the famous tomb of Pope Clement XIII (begun 1787; St. Peter's, Rome) and the funeral monument of Archduchess Maria Christina (begun 1798; Augustinerkirche, Vienna).

During the 1790's Canova vacillated somewhat between the naturalism of his early works and his later neoclassicism, a conflict that is apparent even in such masterpieces as the *Cupid and Psyche* (1787–1793; Louvre, Paris). However, by 1801, when he executed the *Perseus* for the Belvedere of the Vatican (second version, Metropolitan Museum of Art, New York City) as a companion piece to the famous antique *Apollo Belvedere,* he had decided in favor of the neoclassical style. In this instance the example of the superb grace of the antique figure seems to have led Canova to a certain overrefinement without the psychological strength of many of his other works.

Under the patronage of Napoleon, Canova went twice to Paris to execute portrait statues of Napoleon and other Bonapartes. The *Letizia Bonaparte* (1805–1808; Museo Canova, Possagno), a full-length representation of Napoleon's mother seated and dressed as a Roman matron, brilliantly conveys the intelligence and power of this woman, the matriarch of a family that ruled most of Europe. Canova's most famous sculpture, the reclining semi-nude figure of Pauline Borghese, Napoleon's sister, as *Venus Victrix* (1808; Villa Borghese, Rome), combines the elegant simplicity of neoclassicism with a seductive sensuality.

In 1810, Canova was appointed director of the Accademia di San Luca in Rome. After the fall of Napoleon in 1815, he successfully negotiated the return to Italy of masterpieces taken to Paris during the French occupation. He also went to London and executed commissions for the English nobility. Canova died in Venice on Oct. 13, 1822.

Estimate. Enormously famous during his lifetime, Canova had begun to fall from esteem by the time of his death. As the romantic movement supplanted neoclassicism, the severe simplicity of his style was sharply criticized by younger artists, and eventually he came to be regarded as an unfeeling imitator of antiquity. Only in the mid-20th century did his reputation revive, and he is now generally thought of as one of the great and original figures in the history of sculpture.

GUY WALTON, *New York University*

CÁNOVAS DEL CASTILLO, kä′nō-väs thel käs-tē′-lyō, **Antonio** (1823–1897), Spanish politician and historian. Born in Málaga on Feb. 8, 1828, the son of a poor teacher, he had the good fortune to be adopted at age 15 by his uncle, Serafín Estébañez Calderón, who was a writer and politician in Madrid. Cánovas followed a similar career, and to it added an interest in history. His major works, all on Spain, include *Historia de decadencia de España* (1855) and *Estudios del reinado de Felipe IV* (1888). In these and other works Cánovas argued that there had been a persistent failure to unify Spain; Spanish unity became one of his major political ideals and, in particular, his justification for advocating strong administration.

Cánovas became a deputy to the Cortes in 1854 and a cabinet member in 1864, but his fame as a politician really dates from the Restoration period (from 1874), when he was able to stabilize the government. As premier six times during this period, he reduced military and clerical influence in Madrid. However, he was criticized for his Castilian orientation and for his use of *caciques* (local political bosses) to control political life and limit normal parliamentary debate. After his assassination by an anarchist on Aug. 8, 1897, in the Basque town of Santa Águdeda, Cánovas' Liberal-Conservative party continued to defend the nonclerical right. However, it was hampered by involvement in the disastrous Spanish American War, for which Cánovas had been partly responsible.

Robert W. Kern, *University of Massachusetts*

CANROBERT, kän-rō-bâr′, **François Certain** (1809–1895), marshal of France, who commanded the army in the Crimean War. He was born at St.-Céré on June 27, 1809. He attended the military academy of St.-Cyr and joined the army in 1828. Canrobert was a general commanding a division in the French army sent to the Crimea in 1854. Promoted to command the army, he was an ineffective leader and was relieved because of friction with the allied British command. Later he was made a marshal of France and fought against the Austrians in 1859. In the Franco-Prussian War of 1870–1871 he served with Marshal Achille Bazaine's army besieged in Metz and was captured. After 1876 he was elected a senator three times. He died in Paris on Jan. 28, 1895.

CANT. See Slang.

CANTABRI, kan′tə-brī, a warlike people who in ancient times inhabited the seacoast and mountains of northwestern Spain, an area known as Cantabria. They were so removed from civilization that they were still untouched by Roman arms or influence in the time of Augustus. The mountainous habitat of the Cantabri was ideally suited to guerrilla warfare and very difficult to conquer.

Augustus himself defeated them at Vellica in 26 B.C., but the final conquest and systematic pacification of the Cantabri were undertaken by Augustus' chief aid, Agrippa. Agrippa was particularly ruthless in his treatment of the Cantabri; in his final pacification of the area, in 19 B.C., many lost their lives, and the survivors were separated and resettled in towns that the Romans could control.

Richard E. Mitchell, *University of Illinois*

CANTABRIAN MOUNTAINS, kan-tā′brē-ən, is the name of a mountain range in Spain extending for a distance of over 300 miles (480 km) along the Bay of Biscay coast of Spain to Cape Finisterre on the Atlantic Ocean. The range is called Cordillera Cantábrica in Spanish. The highest peak is Peña (or Torre) de Cerredo; it is 8,794 feet (2,680 meters) high. The range is rich in minerals, especially iron and coal. There are extensive forests on many of the mountain slopes. On the west coast the mountains are very steep and form a rugged seacoast, but their southern and eastern slopes are less rugged and descend gradually to the Castilian plateau.

CANTACUZENE, kan-tə-kū-zēn′, is the name of a Byzantine and later Rumanian family (Latin, Cantacuzenus; Rumanian, Cantacuzino) that included several notable men.

John VI Cantacuzene was Roman emperor of the East from 1347 to 1354. Şerban Cantacuzino (1640–1688), a Greek prince descended from him, was ruler of Wallachia from 1679 to 1688. In 1683 he was forced to join the Turks in their siege of Vienna. He secretly aided the Austrians during the siege and later assisted Habsburg forces as they began their drive to oust the Turks from Europe.

CANTAL, kän-tål′, a department of France, is situated in the west central part of the Massif Central, in the Auvergne region. Rugged in topography, the region is rather poor except for some small protected, and quite fertile valleys.

The department comprises the southern end of the high volcanic country of the Auvergne Mountains. The Cantal Mountains, remnants of an enormous volcanic cone more than 30 miles (48 km) across, culminate in the largest of the Massif Central's many volcanic peaks, Mount Cantal, which is more than 6,000 feet (1,800 meters) high. Though now much eroded, in Tertiary times it stood at more than 9,000 feet (2,700 meters).

Sparsely populated, Cantal has few urban centers larger than villages. The largest towns are Aurillac (the department capital), Murat, Vic-sur-Cère, Saint-Flour, and Le Lioran.

Extensive grazing and cereal cultivation, with some more intensive farming in the more favored valley bottoms, are the principal agricultural pursuits of Cantal. A famous cheese of the Auvergne—called Cantal—is made in the department. The unusual geologic and physiographic features of the region, and its spectacular scenery, as well as the distinctive and authentic rural ways of its people and some development of winter sports facilities, have led to the growth of considerable tourism. Population: (1962) 172,977.

Homer Price, *Hunter College, New York*

CANTALOUPE, a popular name for the muskmelon. See Melon—*Muskmelon*.

CANTATA, kən-tä′tə, a musical composition for soloists and choir with instrumental accompaniment, written in the form of a short oratorio. The term at first denoted a work for one voice accompanied by one instrument. This form of the cantata originated in Italy shortly after 1600 as a monodic adaptation of the polyphonic madrigal: in the cantata one part of the madrigal was sung and the other parts were played on the lute.

The earliest cantatas usually varied the melody from verse to verse while repeating the "strophic bass" accompaniment.

As the cantata developed, its texts became standardized as secular narratives, usually pastoral or dramatic; but cantatas were always performed without costumes, scenery, or action. During the 17th century they gradually incorporated recitatives, ariosos, arias, duets, choruses, and instrumental *sinfonie* and *ritornelli*. The first important cantata composers were Claudio Monteverdi, Luigi Rossi, and Giacomo Carissimi. Carissimi (1605–1674) introduced more elaborate accompaniments, added choral sections, and adapted the cantata to the church. Alessandro Scarlatti (1660–1725) standardized the form to two contrasting arias.

The cantata attained great popularity in the later 17th century and spread beyond Italy. It was introduced to France by Marc Antoine Charpentier (1634–1704), a pupil of Carissimi, but it became popular there only after his death. The sacred cantata was adapted for the Lutheran service by the German composers Heinrich Schütz and Dietrich Buxtehude, who increased its gravity, intricacy, and drama. The sacred cantata reached its highest point in the hands of Johann Sebastian Bach (1685–1750). Bach composed 5 cycles of 59 cantatas each—one for every Sunday and for every Lutheran holiday of the year—of which only about 200 survive. In accordance with the German convention, they generally end with traditional chorales; many are technically chorale cantatas, employing chorales in other movements as well as the last.

After Bach the cantata declined, although secular occasional cantatas were composed by Haydn, Mozart, and Beethoven. After 1800 cantatas became more diverse, including a wide variety of forms. Composers of cantatas included Mendelssohn, Brahms, Debussy, and Benjamin Britten. See also CHORAL MUSIC.

CHARLES N. HENDERSON
Choirmaster, St. George's Church, New York

CANTELLI, kän-tel′lē, **Guido** (1920–1956), Italian conductor, whose intense, lyrical interpretations were compared by Toscanini to his own. Cantelli was born in Novara on April 27, 1920, and studied at the Conservatory of Milan. From 1943 to 1945 he was held in a concentration camp because of his opposition to fascism.

After World War II, Cantelli made his reputation conducting at La Scala and other Italian opera houses and with various symphony orchestras. He made his U.S. debut with the NBC Symphony in 1949; thereafter he appeared with many orchestras in the United States and in Europe. He was killed in an airplane crash, near Paris, on Nov. 23, 1956.

CANTELOUBE DE MALARET, kän-tə-lo͞ob′ də mà-lä-re′, **Marie-Joseph** (1879–1957), French composer, whose dramatic works and vocal music were largely inspired by his study of French folk music. He was born at Annonay on Oct. 21, 1879, and studied with Vincent d'Indy at the Schola Cantorum in Paris. His operas *Le Mas* (1929) and *Vercingétorix* (1933) were produced in Paris. Canteloube's best-known work is *Chants d'Auvergne* (1923–30), four sets of songs with accompaniment scored either for piano or for orchestra. He published *Anthologie des chants populaires français* (4 vols., 1938–1944). Canteloube died in Paris on Nov. 4, 1957.

CANTERBURY is a city in Kent, southeastern England, on the London-Dover road where it crosses the River Stour, 53 miles (85 km) southeast of London. It is the site of Canterbury Cathedral, see of the Archbishop of Canterbury, Primate of all England. The cathedral plays an active part in the city's life.

The city consists of a medieval nucleus within the ancient walls, surrounded by suburbs that extend 3 miles (5 km) along the valley, reaching the hillcrests on both sides. Canterbury stands in an area of intensive agriculture and is a busy shopping center for east Kent. There is a small amount of light industry, but Canterbury's economic base, as it has been much of the time since 1200 A. D., is catering to visitors. An estimated million tourists a year visit the city.

Canterbury is an important educational center. The University of Kent at Canterbury opened in 1965. There are Christ Church (teacher training) College, Canterbury College of Art and Architecture, and Canterbury Technical College. Independent boarding "public" schools are Kent College, St. Edmund's School, and the 7th century King's School attached to the cathedral.

Ancient Period. The city site has been occupied from remote times. Below ground are traces of a heavily stockaded prehistoric town. The Romans made a permanent settlement after one of their invasions of Britain (43 A. D.). They modeled Canterbury, which they called Durovernum (a Latinization of the Celtic name meaning "fort among the alders"), on a squared street pattern and equipped it with fine buildings, including a vast theater. They constructed a town wall of which parts are still visible, although it was largely rebuilt in medieval times. Christianity's early spread to Roman Canterbury is shown by the discovery of pottery and silverware marked with the Greek *chi* superimposed on *rho,* the early Christian monogram for "Christ." There may have been three Christian churches in Roman times. By 400 A. D., Continental tribesmen had seeped into the area and Christianity disappeared.

Medieval Period. After the collapse of Roman civilization a Teutonic kingdom emerged in Kent. It was ruled from about 560 A. D. by Ethelbert, who married Bertha, a Christian Frankish princess, thus paving the way for the reintroduction of Christianity by Augustine, the missionary sent by Pope Gregory the Great in 597. Augustine established Canterbury Cathedral, one of the great buildings of pre-Conquest England, and an abbey outside the walls, which was named for him. Canterbury, as it was now called (Cant-wara-burh, borough of the men of Kent), was preeminent as a home of learning in Anglo-Saxon times, especially under Archbishop Theodore of Tarsus in 668–690. It suffered from Danish raids, principally in 1011, when Archbishop Ælfheah was seized and later murdered.

In 1066, Canterbury was the first inland borough taken by William the Conqueror after his victory at Hastings. In 1067 the cathedral was accidentally burned, but it was rebuilt by Archbishop Lanfranc, who had been brought from Caen by William. The cathedral was enlarged by 1130. In 1174 the choir burned and was rebuilt in the Gothic transitional style. The old Norman nave was demolished (about 1380) and reconstructed in Perpendicular style. The central tower, called "Bell Harry," was remodeled about 1500.

The chief among many historical events in medieval Canterbury was the murder in the cathedral (1170) of Archbishop Thomas à Becket after a long quarrel with King Henry II. The Shrine of St. Thomas à Becket became one of the principal objects of religious devotion in Europe.

Modern Period. At the Reformation, under King Henry VIII, the shrine was destroyed (1538) and the monks expelled (1540), while the cathedral body was refounded as a dean and chapter, as it still remains. Among other monastic establishments in Canterbury dissolved at the same time were the ancient abbey of St. Augustine, the priory of St. Gregory, and Blackfriars, Greyfriars, and Austin Friars.

In the reign (1553–1558) of Queen Mary I, 41 Protestant martyrs were burned at Canterbury, and in the reign (1558–1603) of Elizabeth I, some Catholics were put to death. The city suffered in the English Civil War (1642–1660). The cathedral was damaged by the Puritans in 1642 and 1643, narrowly escaping demolition by Oliver Cromwell's government. In 1660, King Charles II, restored to his father's throne, passed through Canterbury en route from Dover.

Canterbury had fallen into a decayed state in the 16th century, but its prosperity was much revived from about 1570 through an influx of Walloon and French Protestant refugees, chiefly weavers. Fresh waves of refugees came in the next century, and weaving was a mainstay of economic life until about 1800. By this date a large garrison had been established (to meet a threat of French invasion), strengthening the resources of Canterbury. An important event was the opening of the Canterbury-Whitstable Railway (1830), linking the city with the sea (5 miles, or 8 km, distant), the first railroad in southern England. Improved transportation resulted in extensive growth and new tourism.

Great numbers of troops were stationed at Canterbury in World War I. In World War II there were continual air attacks, the worst being on June 1, 1942, when a third of the old medieval city was destroyed. Surrounded by bomb craters, the cathedral survived with only superficial damage. Since the war, replanning and rebuilding have gone on, a major object being relief of the intense traffic congestion.

The cathedral provides a background to the city's cultural activities apart from its religious functions. The Friends of Canterbury Cathedral, who preserve the cathedral's material substance, hold an annual festival of music and drama, and the King's School holds a parallel festival. There is active society and club life in the city, manifested in archaeological, musical, and literary groups. In sports, Canterbury Cricket Week is famous throughout the Commonwealth.

The city is well provided with libraries, having that of the city and those of all the educational institutions and the cathedral. The cathedral library contains extensive collections of archives. Population: (1961) 30,415.

William Urry
Canterbury Cathedral and City Archivist
Author of "Marlowe of Canterbury"

BRITISH TRAVEL ASSOCIATION

Canterbury Cathedral in Canterbury, England

CANTERBURY BELL, a cultivated flowering member of the bellflower family. The Canterbury bell (*Campanula medium*) is a biennial standing 1½ to 4 feet (½–1 meter) tall. Its leaves at the base are 6 to 10 inches (15–25 cm) long; the upper leaves are 3 to 5 inches (8–13 cm) long. The violet-blue, bell-shaped, upright flowers appear singly or in pairs in long open racemes (branched spikes) in late spring and early summer. White, pink, and double-flowered varieties are cultivated. Two varieties have sepals that resemble the petals in color: the hose-in-hose, with sepals and petals that are nearly identical; and the cup-and-saucer, with sepals that form a saucer-shaped structure below the petals.

Joan E. Rahn, *Lake Forest College, Ill.*

Canterbury bells (*Campanula medium*)

ROCHE

CANTERBURY TALES, a collection of stories within a narrative framework by the English poet Geoffrey Chaucer (q.v., 1343?–1400). It is one of the outstanding poetic achievements of both English and world literature. In the *Canterbury Tales,* Chaucer revealed his gift for vivid characterization, his technical skill, and his sympathetic but objective insight into the human condition. The contemporary setting of the work (14th century) has provided readers through the centuries with the character and flavor of late medieval English life and morals.

The verse (predominantly five-stress, rhyming couplets) that ensheathes this "human comedy" is rich, colorful, and concrete, giving the impression of almost casual ease in its conversational tone and juxtaposition of details. Beneath this appearance, however, all is tightly controlled by the poet for purposes of maximum suggestivity, irony, and insight into events and characters.

The *Canterbury Tales* consists of a General Prologue, 24 stories (some fragmentary) with their prologues, and connecting narrative "end-links" set within the framework of a pilgrimage from London to the shrine of St. Thomas à Becket at Canterbury. Chaucer conceived and began to carry out the scheme of the work about 1387. He rewrote some of his earlier tales (such as *The Legend of St. Cecilia,* which became the Second Nun's Tale, and his adaptation of Boccaccio's *Teseida,* which became the Knight's Tale), but also wrote new stories for the work. Why the *Canterbury Tales* was not finished is unknown; perhaps it was interrupted by Chaucer's death. His Retraction (an apology for his works "that tend toward sin"), appended to the last tale, seems to date from the end of his life.

There are over 80 extant manuscripts (including fragments) of the *Canterbury Tales.* However, even the most reliable of these disagree concerning the intended sequence of the tales. This inconsistency corroborates other evidence, furnished by the text itself, that Chaucer had not fully revised the completed part of the work before his death. Modern editors, depending on indications from the text itself, have arranged the tales in various plausible orders.

The Narrative Framework. In the General Prologue, which begins with an evocation of spring, the narrator (Chaucer himself in the role of a character) tells how he sets out on a pilgrimage one April to the shrine of the "holy blissful martyr," St. Thomas à Becket. While staying at the Tabard Inn near London, he encounters 29 pilgrims bound for the same destination. The Host of the inn, Harry Bailly, who plans to accompany the group, proposes that during the journey each pilgrim tell four stories, two going to Canterbury, two on the way back. The teller of the best tale, as judged by the Host, will win a free dinner at the inn. Meanwhile, the narrator has described each pilgrim, and the prologue ends with the party under way and the selection of the Knight to tell the first tale.

The Tales. After the Knight's long, dignified philosophical romance, the drunken Miller shatters the spirit of decorum by "requiting" and parodying the opening story in a bawdy fabliau (q.v.). Thus enlivened, the pilgrimage remains spirited: the scrawny, choleric Reeve (an estate manager) reads a personal insult into the Miller's Tale and replies with another fabliau about a dishonest miller. The Friar ridicules avaricious summoners (process servers from the church courts), and the Summoner, in turn, tells the story of a greedy friar. The Pardoner (a trafficker in ecclesiastical indulgences) and the Wife of Bath confess their personal peccadilloes. The Canon's Yeoman exposes the vices of his master, an alchemist. The Wife of Bath's Tale about the joys and sorrows of marriage touches off discussions of marriage by the studious Oxford Clerk, the egocentric Merchant, and the epicurean Franklin (a country gentleman).

The overly refined and mundane Prioress sentimentalizes the story, then popular, of a pious little Christian boy who is murdered by Jews and avenged through the miraculous intervention of the Virgin. The Monk, who prefers hunting and a fine roast to monastic rigor, nonetheless recounts a dignified and learned collection of medieval tragedies. The Squire, brilliantly depicted in the General Prologue as the embodiment of high-spirited youth, tells a fantastic romance (one of the incomplete tales) into which Chaucer introduced themes from his early poetry. The Nun's Priest tells a beast epic, about a pompous cock and a vain and foolish fox, in which bombastic rhetoric and man's pretensions to understand and control his life are ridiculed.

After the worldliness and bawdiness of many of the tales, Chaucer planned a pious ending. One of the completed tales, delivered by the simple, idealized Parson, is a sermon on the seven deadly sins. This selection, intended as the last of the projected 120 stories, is the final offering in modern versions of the *Canterbury Tales.*

Chaucer's Aim. Chaucer's objective in the *Canterbury Tales* was to present the fascinating relationship between art and reality. His tales, which encompass a great variety of genres and are told by a highly diversified group of people, offer a wide range of contemporary views of society—views that are conditioned by the social status and personal temperament of each pilgrim. The characters of the pilgrims come alive both in their portraits in the General Prologue and in the revealing encounters between them during the journey. The fact that each pilgrim is simultaneously an artist (in his tale) and an object of art (in the portrayal of his character) permits an interplay between the concepts of art and reality that is potentially unlimited in its possibilities for irony and exposure. Often, a tale generally in harmony with its teller can harbor a moment which is "out of character." The brutal and amoral Miller, for example, presents a brutal, amoral, and lively view of the relations between the sexes; yet his pathetic carpenter arouses a sympathy through his devotion to his lecherous wife that the Miller probably never intended to evoke. In the Merchant's Tale (about a repulsive marriage), the teller's intent to show how women dupe men in marriage is undermined by the unappetizing quality of both husband and wife.

Chaucer's concern with the interplay between art and experience is perhaps best seen in his presentation of the Wife of Bath and the Pardoner. The Wife justifies her constant squabbles with the five husbands she has dominated by expounding her theory that female sovereignty (*maistrie*) is the secret of conjugal felicity. She supports this proposition with evidence from her own life and with a tale in which a knight who has raped a woman (an extreme act of male sovereignty) is saved from punishment by an old hag who insists that he marry her. On their wedding night, the mortified groom resigns sovereignty to her and is rewarded by her metamorphosis into a young, beautiful, and faithful wife.

In defending this vision of the happy marriage, the Wife betrays herself by her enthusiastic revelations of how she tormented her husbands; by her quotes from the antifeminist literature (popular at the time) that she opposes but corroborates by her behavior; and by her admission that her character partakes of both Venus and Mars, making her a lover of both sex and combat in marriage. Seen in this light, her tale is a pathetic daydream of rejuvenation at the hands of a sixth husband.

On the other hand, the Pardoner, in his prologue, revels in confessing the corrupt practices by which he intimidates simple folk. He defrauds them of their earnings with his bogus relics and terrifying pulpit rhetoric while preaching that such cupidity is the root of all evil. The morality tale he tells describes how three young men set out to destroy death and, finding a hoard of gold, destroy each other instead, each one seeking the treasure for himself. The inner irony of the tale matches the irony of the Pardoner in telling it. The Pardoner's words confirm the description of him in the General Prologue as a repulsive man but a magnificent performer. Realizing the negative impression he has made on the other pilgrims, the Pardoner decides to satisfy and surpass their most lurid imaginings.

These two confessional figures, the Wife and the Pardoner, are among the liveliest and most interesting of the pilgrims. The Wife, as artist, loses control of her considerable art, which works to undermine and destroy her avowed opinions; the Pardoner, as artist, so controls his art, however perverse, that he can intentionally and credibly destroy himself in public.

Between these two extremes are such characters as the Knight, whose avowed search for simplicity in narration is refuted in the elaborate descriptions of his tale, and whose insistence that providence rules the world for the best is challenged by the long and arbitrary sufferings of his protagonists; the Franklin, whose optimistic, middle-class exaltation of innate nobility ("gentilesse") jars with his disappointment at his worthless son, and whose "simple" tale of the triumph of faithful love elaborately compares art and nature, illusion and reality; and the narrator, whose wretched, popular romance of Sir Thopas, halted by the disgusted Host, is actually a hilarious satire on a decadent literary form, unbeknownst to Host or narrator.

Sources. The narrative forms and techniques of the *Canterbury Tales* are as varied as its sources, or as the characters who recount and inhabit the tales. Sources and analogues, ranging from French and Flemish fabliaux to works of Petrarch and Boccaccio, are known for most of the stories in the *Canterbury Tales.* Chaucer freely combined and reworked these sources. The inspiration for the narrative framework may have been Boccaccio's *Decameron* or the *Novelle* of another Florentine, Giovanni Sercambi, or it may have been the more inflexible frame of Chaucer's earlier work, *The Legend of Good Women.*

Criticism. Critics are generally agreed that Chaucer occasionally attempted to utilize sources too intractable even for his adapting genius. The tale told by the Clerk of Oxford perhaps falls into this category. The Clerk, who is presented as the ideal of devotion to truth and study in the General Prologue, has learned from Petrarch

THE BRITISH MUSEUM

THE CANTERBURY PILGRIMS are depicted in this illuminated manuscript from a page of Chaucer's *Canterbury Tales,* located in the British Museum, London.

the story of the sufferings of a patient and faithful wife, Griselda, whose husband constantly tests her virtue. The Clerk's references to Job and his indignation at the husband's excesses do not make Griselda seem any more believable. However, Chaucer turns even this difficulty to his advantage by adding an "envoy," or comment to the tale, in which the Clerk ironically advises women never to be like Griselda, but rather to imitate the Wife of Bath instead. Here the poet, with typical ingenuity, uses his narrative frame to save its contents.

Dryden's exclamation at Chaucer's variety—"Here is God's plenty"—remains the most just evaluation of the achievement of the *Canterbury Tales.* The collection of pilgrims and their tales will appeal as long as there is interest in the way people react to each other, and in the way in which men transform their experience and reveal the depths of their being through the narrative art.

Robert W. Hanning
Columbia University

Bibliography

The **Canterbury Tales** are available in various editions, including Cogrill, Nevill, *The Canterbury Tales* (Baltimore 1952), a modern English translation; Donaldson, E. Talbot, *Chaucer: An Anthology for the Modern Reader* (New York 1958); Manly, John M., and Rickert, Edith, eds., *The Canterbury Tales,* 6 vols. (Chicago 1940); Robinson, Fred N., ed., *The Complete Works of Geoffrey Chaucer,* 2d ed., (Boston and London 1957).

Bowden Muriel, *A Commentary on the General Prologue to the Canterbury Tales* (New York 1948).

Bryan, William F., and Dempster, Germaine, eds., *Sources and Analogues of Chaucer's Canterbury Tales* (Chicago 1941).

Huppé, Bernard, *A Reading of the Canterbury Tales* (Yellow Springs, Ohio, 1964).

Lawrence, William W., *Chaucer and the Canterbury Tales* (New York 1950).

Lumiansky, Robert M., *Of Sondry Folk: The Dramatic Principle in the Canterbury Tales* (Austin, Tex., 1955).

Ruggiers, Paul, *The Art of the Canterbury Tales* (Madison, Wis., 1965).

Schoeck, Richard, and Taylor, Jerome, eds., *Chaucer Criticism: The Canterbury Tales* (South Bend, Ind., 1960).

Wagenknecht, Edward C., ed., *Chaucer: Modern Essays in Criticism* (New York, 1959).

CANTICLE OF BROTHER SUN, a hymn by St. Francis of Assisi praising God and His creatures. St. Francis created the hymn in 1225 after a night of great pain. Its rugged lines in Umbrian Italian are in assonanced prose with some rhyme. A translation follows:

"Most high, almighty, good Lord, Thine are the praises, the glory and the honor and every benediction. To Thee alone, Most High, do they belong, and no man is worthy to name Thee. Praised be Thou, my Lord, with all Thy creatures, especially Sir Brother Sun, who is the day, and Thou dost give us light through him. And he is beautiful and radiant with great splendor: of Thee, Most High, he bears witness. Praised be Thou, my Lord, for Sister Moon and the Stars: in heaven has Thou formed them, bright and precious and beautiful. Praised be Thou, my Lord, for Brother Wind, and for Air and cloudy and calm and every weather, by which Thou dost give sustenance to Thy creatures. Praised be Thou, my Lord, for Sister Water, who is very useful and humble and precious and chaste. Praised be Thou, my Lord, for Brother Fire, through whom Thou dost brighten the night: and he is beautiful and merry and vigorous and strong. Praised be Thou, my Lord, for our Sister, Mother Earth, who sustains and governs us, and produces divers fruits with colored flowers and herbs. Praise and bless ye my Lord, and give Him thanks, and serve Him with great humility."

Francis later added four verses: "Praised be Thou, my Lord, for those who grant pardon for Thy love, and endure infirmity and affliction. Blessed are they who endure them in peace, for they shall be crowned by Thee, the Most High. Praised be Thou, my Lord, for our Sister Bodily Death, whom no living man shall escape. Woe to those who die in mortal sins. Blessed are they who shall find themselves in Thy most holy will, for the second death shall not harm them."

Despite its lack of formal art, the Canticle is an important literary work. It is fresh, strong, unified, and above all true and sincere. Because of it, St. Francis holds a small but secure place in literature. Many individual words and thoughts have a Scriptural origin, and the entire hymn is related to the Canticle of the Three Children (Daniel 3 in the Douay Bible and to Psalms 146 to 148. It expresses St. Francis' love of God, his fellow men, and nature. It contains no pantheistic identification of God, nature, and the author, but is completely Christian in thought and describes sun, moon, stars, wind, water, earth and fire as creatures that manifest God's goodness and glory. Francis' vision is comprehensive: he speaks of sin, death, and final judgment. Hence the Canticle is a complete prayer and stresses the necessity of sorrow for sin and of the virtues of faith, hope, and charity along with the worship of God and the praise of all nature as the work of His hands.

JOHN K. RYAN
The Catholic University of America

Further Reading: Branca, Vittore, *Il cantico di frate sole, studio delle fonti e testo critico* (Florence 1950); Cuthbert, Father, *Life of St. Francis of Assisi* (New York 1912); Jørgensen, Johannes, *Saint Francis of Assisi*, new ed. (New York 1936).

CANTICLE OF CANTICLES, kan'tə-kəl, a canonical book of the Old Testament. The name derives from the Latin translation of the Hebrew *Shir ha Shirim,* or Song of Songs, as the work is known in the Hebrew Bible. It is also called Song of Solomon, and Solomon is sometimes given as the author. However, there is no scholarly evidence for this theory.

The book, a collection of love poems, is read in synagogues on the Jewish festival of Passover. The poems have been interpreted allegorically to represent the love of God for Israel or the love of Christ for the Church, but many scholars see the work simply as lyrical poetry in praise of love. Individual poems may date back to the 9th century B.C., but the extant version of canticles is usually dated between the 5th and 3d century B.C.

CANTILEVER, kan'tə-lē-vər, a usually horizontal beam or structure that has a support at only one end; the other end is free. A diving board is an example of a cantilever; the wing of an airplane is another example. The largest cantilevers are erected by bridge builders. In a cantilever truss bridge, two piers are built in a river, and the cantilevered trusses are extended from each shore over and beyond the piers. A center span is joined to the free ends to complete the bridge. Cantilever construction is also used in building floors, roofs, and porches.

R. LESAGE, FROM UNESCO

A CANTILEVERED CANOPY of reinforced concrete at an entrance to the UNESCO Secretariat building in Paris.

A cantilever differs from a beam supported at both ends. When a cantilever bends under a load, its upper surface is convex; when a beam supported at each end bends under a load, its upper surface is concave. See also BRIDGE.

ALBERT H. GRISWOLD, *New York University*

CANTINFLAS, kän-tēn'fläs (1911–), Mexican comedian and film star, who created a waifish character that is often compared to Charlie Chaplin's tramp. He was born Mario Moreno, in Mexico City, on Aug. 12, 1911. Noted for his bumbling antics, Cantinflas first became popular in short advertising films. His first full-length films, *Ahí está el detalle* (*Here's the Point*) and *Ni sangre ni arena* (*Neither Blood Nor Sand*), both released in 1941, broke box office records in Latin America. He later appeared in the Hollywood productions *Around the World in 80 Days* (1956) and *Pepe* (1961).

CANTON, kan'tən, **John** (1718–1772), English physicist. Canton was born in Stroud, Gloucestershire, on July 31, 1718. He became a schoolmaster in London, and in 1749 he read a paper before the Royal Society on the making of artificial magnets that won him election as a fellow and the award of the Copley Medal. He invented an electroscope and an electrometer and originated experiments in induction, and in 1762 he demonstrated the compressibility of water. Almost simultaneously with Benjamin Franklin, he discovered that some clouds were charged with positive and others with negative electricity. He died in London on March 22, 1772.

EASTFOTO

AN OPEN SQUARE IN CANTON, CHINA, replaces a crowded business area destroyed during the war with Japan.

CANTON, kan-ton, is the leading metropolis and port of South China and the capital of Kwangtung province. It is situated on the left bank of the Chu Kiang (Pearl River) about 80 miles (130 km) from the sea. A sprawling city of narrow, crowded streets, Canton long ago tore down its ancient city walls to allow its population to spread outward. The Chinese name of Canton is *Kwangchow*.

The People. The city is located in the heart of the densely populated Canton Delta. Because of population pressure and Canton's role as China's southern gateway, the city has long been the leading center for Chinese overseas emigration. Indeed, people from the Canton area account for a large proportion of the overseas Chinese population.

Of Canton's resident population, many are *tanchia* (boat people), who live on riverboats crowding the Chu Kiang for a distance of between 4 and 5 miles (6.4 to 8 km). These people have many distinctive customs arising from the fact that they spend their entire lives on the riverboats.

Economy. The connection between the people of Canton and the overseas Chinese had created a ready-made market for Canton's local handicrafts, especially jade and ivory carving, lacquer ware, and silk embroidery, and thus these have become significant export industries.

Canton had a late start in modern industry, mainly because of prolonged political instability and a shortage of good-quality coal. The establishment of some light industries in the 1920's, the construction of a modern port and shipbuilding facilities in the suburb of Whampoa (Huangpu), and the completion of the Wuhan-Canton railroad were among the significant pre-World War II developments that enhanced the position of Canton as the chief commercial center in South China. In 1960 the Chu Kiang bridge was completed, linking the Wuhan-Canton trunk line with the Canton-Kowloon railway leading to Hong Kong. Since 1961, oceangoing ships have been built at dockyards near Whampoa. The sugar refineries in the delta at Shunteh, Chungshan, Chihni, Nanhai, Tungkuan, and Shihtou are among the largest in the nation. Along with the expansion of the coal mines in northern Kwangtung and of the iron-ore mines in the delta and on Hainan Island, iron and steel industries have been built, making the city and its environs the leading industrial district in China south of the Yangtze.

History. Canton's history dates back to the 3d century B. C., when the first emperor of the Ch'in dynasty dispatched a large army to conquer the Pei Yueh in what is now Kwangtung province. Since the Han dynasty (202 B. C.–220 A. D.), Canton has been known as Kwangchow.

In a later period the city became the destination of migrants from North China, who entered the area by way of two passes, Cheling and Meiling. These passes link the delta with the valleys of the Hsiang and Kan, both of which are tributaries of the Yangtze.

Much of the delta region was settled during the T'ang period, and the Cantonese often identify themselves as "the T'ang people" instead of "the Han people," the latter term usually applied to the Chinese. Canton became the nation's vestibule by the middle of the 8th century, when the T'ang empire lost control of the overland route to western Asia. It replaced Changan (now Sian) as China's chief trading center and was soon frequented by many merchants from India, Persia, and the Arab countries.

At the turn of the 18th century European ships began to visit Canton regularly. By an imperial decree in 1757, foreign merchants were required to deal with a small group of Chinese merchants directly responsible to the government. This so-called Cohong system came to an end after the Opium War (1839–1842), which resulted in British annexation of Hong Kong and the opening of five ports, including Canton, where foreigners could live and conduct business outside Chinese jurisdiction. British and French concessions were established in Shameen, a southwestern suburb of Canton, in 1860.

As a major point of contact between China and the West, Canton became the cradle of the revolutionary movement in modern times. Under Sun Yat-sen, several uprisings were staged on the southern coast. The bloodiest was the abortive uprising in Canton on March 29, 1911, which cost the lives of 72 martyrs to whose memory a towering obelisk was built at Huanghuakang in the northern suburb.

The city of Canton was also the power base of the Kuomintang or Nationalist party in the period following the overthrow of the Manchus. It was here that Sun Yat-sen set up the famous Whampoa Military Academy under the directorship of Chiang Kai-shek. Population: (1965) 2,500,000.

KUEI-SHENG CHANG
University of Washington

CANTON, kan'tən, a town in northern Connecticut, is in Hartford county, about 12 miles (19 km) northwest of Hartford, of which it is a residential suburb. The town has some light industry, including the manufacture of precision metal products, chemicals, and gold leaf.

Settled in 1740 as Suffrage, Canton was incorporated in 1806 from the town of Simsbury. It still has many early saltbox houses. The town includes the villages of Canton, Canton Center, North Canton, and Collinsville. It is governed by a board of selectmen. Population: 6,868.

CANTON, kan'tən, a manufacturing city in western Illinois, is in Fulton county, 25 miles (40 km) southwest of Peoria. The city's largest industrial plant, founded in 1847 and covering 23 acres, produces agricultural implements. Other industries include dairies and plants making kitchen cabinets and overalls. Canton is also the trading center of a rich corn-raising area, and coal mining is an important activity in the region.

Canton is the site of Canton Community College, a 2-year coeducational institution. The community was founded in 1825 by Isaac Swan and was called "Swan's Catch-all" by settlers who stayed in Swan's cabin while building their own homes. Canton was severely damaged by a tornado in 1835. It was incorporated as a city in 1854. Government is by mayor and council. Population: 14,217.

CANTON, kan'tən, a manufacturing town in eastern Massachusetts, is in Norfolk county, 15 miles (24 km) south of Boston. It produces electrical equipment, radio parts, plastics, rubber goods, woolens, and children's wear. The Massachusetts Hospital School for the physically handicapped and the Harvard Blue Hill Observatory are in Canton.

Settled in 1650, the town was first called Ponkapoag. It was a part of Stoughton from 1726 to 1797, when it became incorporated as a separate town. Canton was the site of Paul Revere's brass and bell foundry and, during the War of 1812, of his powder mill. Government is by town meeting. Population: 17,100.

CANTON, kan'tən, a city in central Mississippi, the seat of Madison county, is 22 miles (35 km) northeast of Jackson, between the Big Black and Pearl rivers. It is a trade and processing center in an agricultural area producing dairy cattle and cotton. The city has cotton gins and creameries. Its manufactures include lumber, furniture and furniture parts, fertilizers, pesticides, shirts, and canvas tents and gun covers. Canton was founded in 1824 and incorporated in 1836. It still has some fine houses built before the Civil War. Government is by mayor and council. Population: 10,503.

CANTON, kan'tən, a village in northern New York, is situated on the Grass River, 118 miles (199 km) north of Syracuse. It is a processing center in a dairy- and poultry-farming region. Canton is the seat of St. Lawrence University and of the Agricultural and Technical College at Canton of the State University of New York. Frederic Remington, painter and sculptor, was born here. The village was settled in 1799 and incorporated in 1845. It is governed by a mayor and council and is the seat of St. Lawrence county. Population: 6,398.

CANTON, kan'tən, a town in southwestern North Carolina, is in Haywood county, 20 miles (32 km) west of Asheville. It is on the Pigeon River, at the edge of Pisgah National Forest in the southern Appalachians and 32 miles (51 km) east of Great Smoky Mountains National Park. Canton manufactures lumber, pulp and paper, and other wood products. It was incorporated in 1893 and is governed by a town manager. Population: 5,158.

CANTON, kan'tən, an industrial city in northeastern Ohio, the seat of Stark county, is located 22 miles (35 km) southeast of Akron, in a dairy and poultry-farming area. The city is a leading producer of metal alloys, mechanical and hydraulic metalworking presses, tapered roller bearings, rubber gloves, paving brick, ceramics, water softeners, bank vaults, and safes. It is also a mining center with local resources of clay, coal, and natural gas.

Canton is the seat of several educational institutions including Malone College, a 4-year coeducational Quaker college; Walsh College, a 4-year Catholic college for men; and an extension center of Kent State University. William McKinley, 25th president of the United States, made his permanent home in Canton after 1867. He and his wife are buried in a granite memorial in Monument Park, administered by the Ohio Historical Society. The National Professional Football Hall of Fame, housed in a building shaped like a football, was opened in the city in 1963. Canton was the home, in the early 1900's, of one of the nation's first professional football teams.

The Canton area was first settled permanently in 1805. Incorporated as a village in 1822, Canton soon became a center for the manufacture of agricultural machinery. It received its city charter in 1854. Canton is governed by a mayor and council. Population: 110,053.

MERLIN D. WOLCOTT, *Canton Public Library*

CANTON, kan'tən, a political or judicial division or subdivision in some countries of Europe. The states of the Swiss Confederation are called cantons. In France, cantons are judicial districts comprising a number of communes.

CANTON AND ENDERBURY, kan'tən, en'dər-ber-ē, are islands in the South Pacific Ocean, under joint Anglo-American administration. The largest of the Phoenix Islands, they lie about 2,000 miles (3,200 km) southwest of Hawaii.

Canton is an isolated atoll with an area of about 3½ square miles (9 sq km). It was once known variously as Mary, Mary Balcout, and Swallow. Within its narrow pear-shaped ring of low-lying land is a lagoon, which is more than 8 miles (13 km) long and 4 miles (6 km) wide at one point. Stunted vegetation grows on the island, and there are some coconut palms. Canton, with a population (1961) of about 290, is the administrative center of the Phoenix Islands.

Enderbury, about 37 miles (60 km) southeast of Canton, covers about 2 square miles (5 sq km) and is also of coral formation. Low and flat, it is covered with dense brush and thickets. Enderbury is uninhabited.

The islands were sighted by navigators of various nationalities but ignored when found to be barren and uninhabited. Large guano deposits were worked by British interests after 1860. Companies from the United States claimed guano

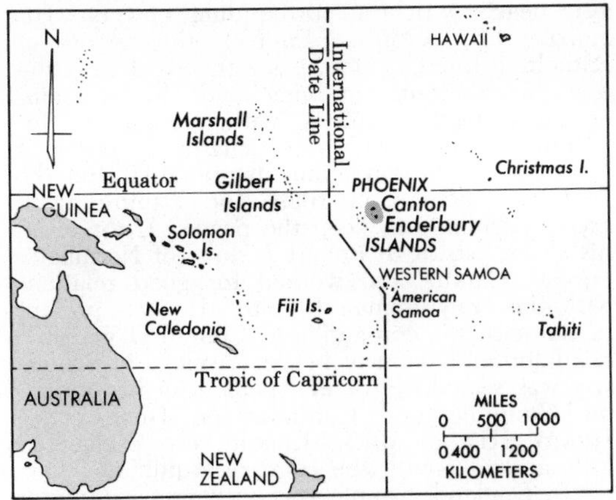

rights on Canton, and in 1872 a U. S. naval vessel surveyed the island.

Because of the potential value of the islands as air-route stopover points, American and British interest quickened in the 1930's. British sovereignty over Canton was claimed in 1936. The following year solar observation expeditions from New Zealand and the United States arrived, and both groups made claims of sovereignty. A permanent British representative was then sent to Canton and a radio station set up; later, officials from the United States arrived.

In an exchange of notes in 1939, the United States and Britain agreed (without prejudice to their respective claims) to establish a condominium over the islands until 1989. Canton was an important fueling station in World War II.

R. M. Younger
Author of "Australia and the Australians"

CANTOR, kan'tər, **Eddie** (1892–1964), American comedian and song-and-dance man, who moved from the stage to a highly successful career in radio, motion pictures, and television. He was born Edward Israel Iskowitz, in New York City, on Jan. 31, 1892. He first appeared in vaudeville after winning an amateur night award when he was 16. He later starred in a number of *Ziegfeld Follies* and musical comedies, including *Kid Boots* (1923) and *Whoopee* (1928).

During the 1930's Cantor achieved nationwide fame through his regular Sunday night radio program. He also starred in many films, including *Roman Scandals* (1933) and *Forty Little Mothers* (1940) and made a brief return to the stage in *Banjo Eyes* (1941). From 1950 to 1953 he appeared on the *Colgate Comedy Hour* on television. Cantor's autobiographical *My Life Is in Your Hands* was published in 1928, and a film, *The Eddie Cantor Story*, was released in 1953. He died in Hollywood, Calif., on Oct. 10, 1964.

CANTOR, kän'tôr, **Georg F. L. P.** (1845–1918), German mathematician, who formulated the theory of sets. Cantor was born in St. Petersburg (now Leningrad), Russia, on March 3, 1845, the son of a well-to-do merchant. His family moved to Germany in 1856, and he received his doctorate from the University of Berlin in 1867. His entire professional career was spent at the University of Halle, where he was appointed a lecturer in 1869 and professor in 1879.

Cantor's early work was on the theory of numbers, but under the influence of Karl Weierstrass he turned his attention to the branch of mathematics known as analysis. His work led to an investigation of the infinite in mathematics, which underlies all questions concerning the concepts of limits, convergence, and continuity of functions. His first paper on the theory of sets—in particular, infinite sets—appeared in 1874. In this and subsequent papers he established a theory of the infinite so revolutionary that, from the beginning, both Cantor and his theories came under strong, even bitter, attack. The principal critic of the new theory was Leopold Kronecker, who believed, as had Gauss, in the traditional view that the actual infinite (the "transfinite") has no place in mathematics. In spite of this, Cantor's ideas gained wide acceptance before his death in Halle, on Jan. 6, 1918.

Cantor's other contributions in mathematics include a definition of irrational numbers based on his theory of the infinite, and papers on trigonometrical series and on the history of the concepts of the actual infinite.

Dirk J. Struik
Massachusetts Institute of Technology

Further Reading: Jourdain, P. E. J., ed., *Contributions to the Founding of the Theory of Transfinite Numbers* (Chicago 1915; paperback reprint, New York 1952); Bell, Eric Temple, *Men of Mathematics* (New York 1937).

CANTOR, kän'tôr, **Moritz Benedikt** (1829–1920), German historian of mathematics. Cantor was born in Mannheim on Aug. 23, 1829. In 1848 he entered the University of Heidelberg where, after a brief interlude at Göttingen, he took his doctorate. He taught at Heidelberg from 1853 until his death on April 10, 1920.

Cantor's greatest work was *Vorlesungen über Geschichte der Mathematik* (4 vols., 1880–1908), a monumental history of mathematics. The first 3 volumes carried the history to 1758. When it became apparent that the author could not continue the project without aid, a plan was worked out at an international congress of mathematics at Heidelberg in 1904 by which nine scholars, working under Cantor's direction, composed the final volume, bringing the account to the end of the 1700's.

Carl B. Boyer, *Brooklyn College*

CANTOR, kan'tər, is an English term derived from Latin *cantor* (singer), usually applied to the leader of prayers in Jewish synagogues. The Hebrew term is *hazzan* or *sh'liah tzibbur* (emissary of the congregation).

The cantor's role is central in all Jewish religious services. He sings or chants the prayers alone, and the congregation responds "Amen" after certain phrases, or it may sing alternate passages. The function of the cantor originated in Palestinian synagogues in the 1st century A. D., when the texts of many prayers were crystallized. Some of the melodies go back to a tradition of the 8th century Babylonian synagogues. Others developed in medieval Europe, influenced by Italian and other musical styles.

In larger Jewish congregations today a professionally trained cantor is employed to lead the prayers all year round; in smaller ones his functions are fulfilled by members of the congregation, and a cantor is called in only for the high holidays (Rosh Hashanah and Yom Kippur). In American Reform congregations, prayers are often led by the rabbi, assisted by a choir.

Raphael Patai, *Theodor Herzl Institute*

CANTOS, kan'tōz, a "work in progress" by the American poet Ezra Pound (q.v.). The unfinished poem, begun in 1916, shows many different facets to different readers. Some find in it a broad analogy to Dante's *Divine Comedy*. Others view it as a social and political document, a protest against the evils of the 20th century. Others regard it as a diary of Pound's poetic evolution from the day he started writing it.

Nine volumes of *The Cantos* were published between 1925 and 1959. The work contains discourses on economics, politics, and aesthetics. The only unifying element is Pound's complex, not always sane personality. Some passages are merely arid or examinatory, but others, particularly those evoking the worlds of Homer and Ovid and the civilizations of China and the European Middle Ages, are of overwhelming beauty.

The Cantos includes *The Pisan Cantos*, written after the U. S. Army imprisoned Pound at Pisa, Italy, in 1945 on a charge of treason. *The Pisan Cantos* received the Bollingen Prize for poetry in 1949.

HORACE V. GREGORY, *Coauthor of "History of American Poetry 1900–1940"*

CANTRIL, kan'tril, **(Albert) Hadley** (1906–), American psychologist, who studied thought patterns and was an expert in public opinion. Cantril was born in Hyrum, Utah, on June 16, 1906. He attended Dartmouth College and received his Ph.D. at Harvard in 1931. Cantril was an instructor of psychology at Harvard from 1932–1935. The next year he became assistant professor at Teachers College, Columbia University. Beginning in 1936, Cantril was professor of psychology at Princeton University and director of public opinion research of the department of psychology.

Cantril was the author of several books, among them *Politics of Despair* (1958), *Human Nature and Political Systems* (1961), and *Adventures in Policy Research* (1966).

CANTUTE II, kə-nyōōt' (died 1035), king of Denmark, England, and Norway, who was the first Danish king of England. He was the son of Sweyn, King of Denmark. Canute accompanied Sweyn on the last of his series of invasions of England (1013–1014). On the death of Sweyn (Feb. 3, 1014) in the course of his campaign, Canute was declared king by his sailors, according to Viking custom. He was not, however, able to hold the country against Æthelred the Unready, so he fled home to Denmark after mutilating his hostages.

Canute's brother Harold accepted him as joint king, and in the autumn of 1015, Canute returned to England. The reconquest was difficult. Æthelred died on April 23, 1016, and his son, Edmund II Ironside, continued the struggle so valiantly that the Danes despaired of victory, despite their considerable successes (especially in the Battle of Ashingdon, Oct. 18, 1016). Accordingly, the two kings came to an agreement: Edmund took Wessex, and Canute took Mercia. Northumbria had already fallen to Earl Eric of Hlathir, a Norwegian supporter of Canute. Edmund died on Nov. 30, 1016, and Canute was accepted as king of the whole country in 1017. Soon afterward the death of his brother left him sole king of Denmark also.

Canute gave England a just rule within the highly developed institutions he found there and also peace with the surrounding powers. His marriage to Ælfgifu (Emma), the widow of Æthelred the Unready, was aimed at creating dynastic continuity at home and also at maintaining smooth relations with Normandy, for Ælfgifu was a sister of Richard II, duke of Normandy. These relations deteriorated after the death of Richard in 1026, and Canute again used matrimony to keep the peace. He married his sister Estrith to Robert I, duke of Normandy (q.v.). Canute also worked for good relations with the Holy Roman Empire. He was present in Rome at the coronation of Conrad II in 1027. His later settlement of border disputes in Schleswig was sealed by the engagement of his daughter Gunnhild and Conrad's son Henry (See HENRY III) in 1035. Canute also exchanged gifts annually with the court of Aquitaine.

In England, Canute was a vigorous supporter and benefactor of the church. In secular government he aimed initially at a fourfold state, with Northumbria ruled by Eric of Hlathir; Mercia by Eadric Streona, an Englishman who had treacherously abetted the Danish conquest; East Anglia by Thorkell the Tall, a Danish adventurer who had been in Æthelred's service; and Wessex by Canute himself. Eric, however, died prematurely, and Eadric and Thorkell soon lost favor with their subjects. Eadric was murdered, and Thorkell was sent to honorable exile in Denmark as guardian of the king's son Hardecanute (q.v.).

Canute's policy in Scandinavia was less peaceful than in England and on the Continent. He aimed at the subjugation of Norway. The death of Olaf II (q.v.) at the Battle of Stiklestad in 1030 left the way open for the establishment of Danish rule, and Canute placed the country in the hands of his mistress Ælfgifu of Northampton and of Sweyn, their son. Their rule was ended by Olaf's son Magnus in 1035. Canute died at Shaftesbury, England, on Nov. 12, 1035.

ALISTAIR CAMPBELL, *Oxford University*

CANUTE III. See HARDECANUTE.

CANUTE IV, kə-nōōt' (1043?–1086), was a king of Denmark. He was canonized in 1099 as St. Canute and is patron saint of Denmark. Canute IV was a grandnephew of King Canute II; he succeeded his brother Harold Hen on the throne in 1080. Canute attempted to assert Danish claims to the English crown and planned an expedition against William the Conqueror. On July 10, 1086, before he could set sail for England, he was killed by rebellious Danes.

CANVAS is a medium-weight to heavy fabric usually made of cotton. Canvas, known also as *duck*, ranges in texture from soft and pliable to stiff. It is the heaviest single-layer fabric made, as well as the strongest and most durable. It also has more uses than any other kind of cloth.

Army duck, so called because it is often purchased by the armed services, is also widely used in civilian trade. Some types of army duck are used as they come from the loom, that is, not finished or dyed. Such off-loom canvas is used to make hammocks, laundry bags, outdoor folding chairs, overcoat linings, and the upper parts of shoes. Army duck that is waterproofed and dyed or printed is used for awnings, tents, hammocks, collapsible wading pools, water buckets, and coveralls. *Flat ounce duck* is canvas that must be sized before it is woven. It is used largely for box spring coverings, upholstery, men's caps, and boot covers. *Number duck,* the heaviest and strongest canvas, is used for making cots, hammocks, mailbags, sailcloth, golf bags, water buckets, and tents.

ERNEST B. BERRY, *School of Textiles North Carolina State University*

CANVASBACK, kan'vəs-bak, a diving duck found on the coastal waterways, inland lakes and streams, and marshes of North America. Its breeding grounds are in Alaska, Canada, and the western United States. It winters as far south as central Mexico, the Gulf Coast, and Florida.

The male canvasback weighs about 3 pounds (1.4 kg), is about 2 feet (0.6 meters) long, and has a wingspread of more than 30 inches (76 cm). He has a rich chestnut-colored neck and head and a long, straight, black bill. His breast, rump, and tail are black, and his back, wings, and flanks are pale gray. After the breeding season, his colors are more subdued. The female canvasback is slightly smaller than the male. She lacks the bright color on the head, and her breast, rump, and tail are dull brown.

The canvasback is an expert diver. Its large webbed feet, set far back on the body are a special adaptation for swimming underwater to feed on the roots of aquatic plants, shrimp, and small fish. After wintering offshore in salt water, the canvasback flies in long V-shaped flock formations to its northern breeding grounds. It arrives in late March or early April and begins nesting by May. There are usually 10 large, greenish eggs per clutch.

The canvas back (*Aythya valisineria*) is a member of the family Anatidae in the order Anseriformes.

JOSEPH BELL
The New York Zoological Society

A. W. AMBLER, FROM NATIONAL AUDUBON SOCIETY

CANVASBACK DUCKS breed in Alaska, Canada, and western United States. The male is shown in this photo.

CANYON, kan'yən, a city in northwestern Texas, is the seat of Randall county, in the Panhandle, 18 miles (29 km) south of Amarillo. It is a trade center in a farming and stock-raising area. West Texas State University, a 4-year coeducational institution, is here. Palo Duro Canyon State Park is to the east. Government is by a mayor and commissioners. Population: 8,333.

CANYON DE CHELLY NATIONAL MONUMENT, kan'yən də shā, is within the Navaho Indian Reservation in northeastern Arizona. It was established in 1931 to preserve the ruins of prehistoric Indian cliff dwellings there. Among the several hundred ruins within the 131-square-mile (339-sq-km) area of the monument are White House, a pueblo begun in the 1060's, and Mummy Cave, a notable example of the 12th–13th century pueblo. Canyon de Chelly was a stronghold from which the Navaho resisted Spanish soldiers and later the U. S. Army under Kit Carson.

CANZONE, kan-zō'nē, a poem, song, or ballad consisting of long stanzas of equal length and a shorter "envoi" or closing stanza. Each stanza except the envoi has the same elaborate rhyme scheme. The length of the stanza, which may be divided into two parts, varies from 7 to 20 lines, and that of the envoi from 3 to 10 lines. Most canzoni deal with love and other emotions, but some deal with nature and politics. The form, which resembles both the madrigal and the *chant royal,* developed during the Middle Ages and Renaissance. Modern poets sometimes use the term "canzone" for poems with long, intricately linked stanzas.

Italian Canzoni. The basic canzone form originated in the 12th century with the troubadour verse of the Provençal poet Giraud de Borneil. It was further refined by the Sicilian poets at the court of Emperor Frederick II in the 13th century. Three Tuscan writers, Dante, Guido Cavalcanti, and Guido Guinizelli, adopted the Sicilian form. Dante defined it in his *Vita nuova* (about 1293), which contained examples of different types of canzoni. The Sicilian canzone, according to Dante, consisted of a series of complex stanzas (to be accompanied by music), usually written in 11-syllable lines, with end rhyme and with rhyming linkage between the first and second parts of stanzas.

Petrarch, in the 14th century, set up a stricter canzone pattern, limiting the poem length to 5 to 7 stanzas of 12 to 16 lines each, with an envoi, and eliminating the division of the stanzas. The *canzone petrarchesca* was popular in Italy through the time of Tasso in the 16th century. Gabriello Chiabrera revived the looser Sicilian canzone in the 17th century, and it was used by the school of Pietro Metastasio in the 18th century. At that time the Petrarchan mode was revived by the poets Vittorio Alfieri and Ugo Foscolo, and it was continued by Alessandro Manzoni, Giosuè Carducci, and Gabriele d'Annunzio in the 19th and early 20th centuries.

Other Canzoni. Outside Italy, the canzone was most popular in Portugal and Spain, where it was introduced in the early 16th century by the Portuguese poet Francisco Sá de Miranda and the Spanish poet Garcilaso de la Vega. In the same period the form spread to England, when Sir Thomas Wyatt translated Petrarchan canzoni into English and Edmund Spenser wrote his own canzoni. In the 17th century, William Drummond of Hawthornden produced accomplished canzoni, as did the German poet A. W. von Schlegel in the 19th century. In the 20th century, W. H. Auden adapted the form, with repeated end words instead of rhyme, for his poem *Canzone.*

C. HUGH HOLMAN
Coauthor of "A Handbook to Literature"

CANZONE, kan-zō′nē, in music, one of the major forms of instrumental music in the 16th and 17th centuries. The term *canzone* (plural, *canzoni*) is variously spelled *canzon* and *canzona*, and means "song" in Italian. The musical form was derived from the French and Flemish vocal *chansons*, or songs, that flourished in the 16th century. In Italy these pieces were transcribed for instruments and inspired the creation of new works, known variously as *canzoni alla francese* (songs in the French style) and *canzoni da sonare* (sound songs).

Early canzoni were usually written for organ or harpsichord, for lute, or for small groups of instruments. Important composers of these canzoni were Marcantonio Cavazzoni, his son Girolamo, and Andrea Gabrieli.

During the 17th century, canzoni underwent a series of modifications and alterations. In the works of some composers, notably Girolamo Frescobaldi, they became fugal in style. In the second half of the 17th century, this treatment of canzoni also appeared frequently in the French or Lullian overture, usually as quick fugal second movements. Canzoni developed in a different direction in the works of Giovanni Gabrieli, an important innovator who added more instrumental parts to the traditional four and infused his compositions with great expressiveness. Through the influence of Gabrieli and others, the canzone, with its emphasis on ensemble playing, contrasting sections, and intimate character, developed into the baroque sonata, the earliest great form of chamber music (q.v.).

The term "canzone" is also applied to a 16th century Italian secular vocal form; a 17th century song with keyboard accompaniment, the *canzone alla villanesca;* and a light song incorporated into an 18th or 19th century opera.

FRANKLIN B. ZIMMERMAN
Author of "Henry Purcell: His Life and Times"

CAOILTE, kēl′tə, was a legendary Irish poet and warrior, who belonged to the Fenians, a band of warriors described in Gaelic sagas as defending Ireland from invaders in the 3d century A. D. His full name is *Caoilte* (or *Cailte*) *mac Ronáin.* Caoilte was one of the close associates of his cousin, the Fenian chief Fionn mac Cumhail as well as of Fionn's son Oisín (Ossian, q.v.). He was renowned for his speed in running, being swifter than the March wind. He ran a race with a magic blacksmith, after which his name was changed from Daolghus to Caoilte.

Caoilte figures in ancient ballads and in two later written texts. In the *Agallamh na Seanórach* (*Colloquy of the Ancients*), a collection of tales compiled possibly in the 12th or 13th century, he and Oisín are represented as traveling about Ireland with St. Patrick in the 5th century, explaining to the saint the origin of place names commemorating the exploits of the Fenians. This use of traditional Fenian lore in a Christian framework was one way of reconciling old pagan beliefs with Christianity.

In the *Duanaire Fionn* (*Anthology of Finn*), a 17th century compilation of earlier poems, Caoilte is one of Fionn's favorite warriors and succeeds him as a professional bard. He is credited with having written the famous lyric *Arran of Many Stags* and a poem on Tara. Finally, St. Patrick converts him to Christianity.

ROBERT T. MEYER
Catholic University of America

Church of Notre Dame du Cap at Cap de la Madeleine.
QUEBEC PUBLICITY OFFICE

CAONABÓ, kä-ō-nä-bō (died 1496), an Arawak Indian chief, who fought against the Spanish conquest of the island of Hispaniola. After the *Santa Maria* was wrecked in December 1492, Christopher Columbus founded a settlement along the northwestern coast of Hispaniola and left 39 men there, commanded by Diego de Harana. Lust and avarice overcame the colony, and mercy and discipline were forgotten in a search for women and gold.

Caonabó, the cacique (chief) of Maguana in the central portion of the colony, became enraged and attacked the Spaniards at their fort, La Navidad, in March 1493, killing all the defenders. When Columbus returned he faced other Indian raids, including one in 1495 in which Caonabó menaced the settlement of Santo Tomás. Alonso de Ojeda then tricked Caonabó into wearing a pair of manacles, which the Spaniard presented as an ornament. Caonabó died en route to Spain to stand trial.

LAURENCE R. BIRNS
The New School For Social Research, New York

CAP DE LA MADELEINE, kåp de lå må-dlen′, a city in Quebec, Canada, is about 80 miles (128 km) southwest of Quebec city on the north bank of the St. Lawrence River where it is joined by the St. Maurice. Although "Le Cap," as it is commonly called, was originally residential, the rich timberlands and hydroelectric power of the St. Maurice Valley are making it an industrial center like its sister city, Trois Rivières, across the St. Maurice. Important manufactures in "Le Cap" are wood pulp, paper, paper bags, plywood, aluminum and aluminum products, and clothing.

"Le Cap" was a fur trading post in 1636. In 1659 a chapel was built by the Jesuits and was replaced later by a small stone church. This is now the sanctuary of Notre Dame du Cap. Adjoining it is a basilica, begun in 1957, for pilgrims who come to worship at the shrine of the Virgin Mary because of favors reported there. Cap de la Madeleine was established as a municipality in 1845; a town, in 1918; and a city, in 1922. Population: (1966) 31,463.

LOUIS-PHILIPPE AUDET, *Université de Montréal*

CAP-HAÏTIEN, kȧp-ȧ-ē-syaɴ′, is Haiti's second largest city and an important commercial center and seaport. It is located on the nation's northern coast, 95 miles (137 km) north of the capital, Port-au-Prince, and is the capital of Nord department. Although migration to the south has resulted in a declining population, the city is still the processing point for such agricultural products of the fertile Plaine du Nord as sugarcane, coffee, cacao, tobacco, pineapples, bananas, hardwoods, and sisal.

The area abounds with historic sights. Cap-Haïtien's history goes back to 1492, when Columbus established the fort of La Navidad a few miles away. The city was the main setting for French culture and commerce in Haiti during the 18th century and was the colony's capital from the beginning of French rule in 1697 to 1770. The great sugar and coffee plantations required large numbers of slaves to work the fields. The scene of slave uprisings in 1791, the city became the center of the Haitian independence movement after the turn of the century. From 1811 until his suicide in 1820, Henri Christophe (q.v.) ruled the northern part of Haiti from Le Cap (as the city is popularly known). He ordered the construction of elaborate public buildings, including his palace of Sans Souci and, at the cost of thousands of lives, built the mountain fortress of Citadelle Laferrière at nearby Milot. Although continuously ravaged by earthquakes (including a particularly severe one in 1842), the city is still considered to be the most pleasant in Haiti, with many balconied colonial houses in pastel colors fronting narrow streets. Population: (1966) 30,500.

Laurence R. Birns
The New School for Social Research

FRITZ HENLE

NEAR CAP-HAÏTIEN, on a mountain top, stands the Citadelle Laferrière, Henri Christophe's famous fort.

CAPA, kap′ə, **Robert** (1913–1954), Hungarian-American photographer, who was noted for his outstanding war photographs. He was born André Friedmann in Budapest, Hungary, on Oct. 22, 1913. He began his career as a photojournalist in 1931, when a picture agency in Berlin sent him to Copenhagen to photograph the Russian Communist leader Leon Trotsky. When the Nazis came to power, he left Berlin and settled in Paris, where he adopted the pseudonym "Robert Capa" in 1936. In the same year he photographed the Spanish Civil War with courage and insight and won instant acclaim. He later lived in the United States and became an American citizen.

Capa documented the Japanese invasion of China, and during World War II he covered the African, Mediterranean, and European theaters as an American correspondent. With Henri Cartier-Bresson and other photographers, he founded the photographers' agency Magnum in 1947. In that year he went to Russia with John Steinbeck, and together they produced *Russian Journal* (1948). In 1949, Capa visited Israel, where he photographed the Israeli struggle to maintain their independence. He was killed in Indochina on May 25, 1954, while covering the war there for *Life* magazine. His other books include *Slightly Out of Focus* (1947) and *Images of War* (1964).

Beaumont Newhall
George Eastman House, Rochester, N.Y.

CAPABLANCA, kä-pä-bläng′kä, **Jose Raoul** (1888–1942), Cuban chess grand master and world champion. Because of his deceptively simple style and extremely small percentage of losses in play, "Capa" became known as "the chess machine," and Capablanca was somehow uniquely an idol of the non-chess-playing public.

José Raoul Capablanca y Graupera was born in Havana, Cuba, on Nov. 19, 1888. A child prodigy, he learned to play chess at the age of four, became the leading Cuban master at 12, and went on to become the most renowned tournament player of his time. His principal international successes included first prizes at tournaments at San Sebastián, Spain (1911), London (1922), New York (1927), and Budapest (1929). Capablanca won the world chess championship in 1921 at Havana defeating the German Emanuel Lasker, who had held the title since 1894. Capablanca lost the world title to Alexander Alekhine in 1927 at Buenos Aires. He was never given a rematch.

An official in the Cuban foreign service from 1913, Capablanca was commercial attaché of the Washington embassy when he died on March 8, 1942, in New York City. His books included *My Chess Career* (1920), *Chess Fundamentals* (1921), and *Primer of Chess* (1935).

Jack Straley Battell, *"Chess Review"*

CAPACITANCE, kə-pas′ə-təns, is the property of an electrical system, consisting of two conductors separated by a nonconductor, that permits the storage of electrical energy when a voltage exists between the conductors. A voltage, V, applied between two electrically insulated conductors produces a positive charge of Q coulombs on the positive conductor and an equal negative charge on the negative conductor. The capacitance, C, of this system is defined as the ratio of charge to voltage: $C=Q/V$.

The unit of capacitance is the farad, named for Michael Faraday. Smaller units, the microfarad and the picofarad, are commonly used because the farad is an inconveniently large unit (1 farad$=10^6$ microfarads$=10^{12}$ picofarads). Capacitance usually is measured by bridge-circuit methods that compare an unknown capacitance to a known value of capacitance.

L. W. Matsch, *University of Arizona*

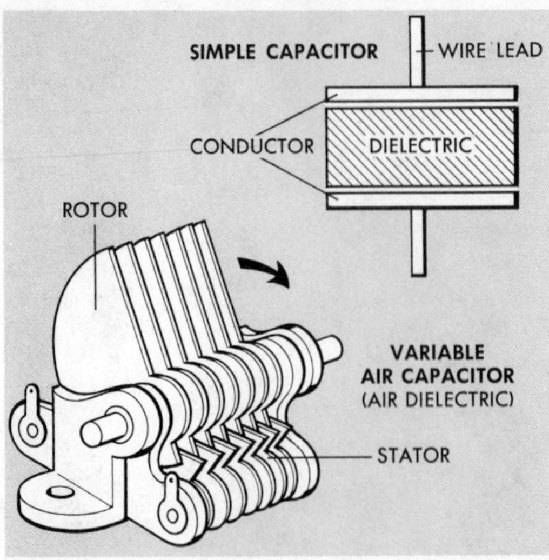

A capacitor consists basically of two conductors separated by a nonconductor, called a dielectric. In the variable air capacitor the dielectric is air, and the conductors are sets of stationary and movable plates.

CAPACITOR, kə-pas′ə-tər, an electric circuit element that consists basically of two conductors separated by a nonconductor. The conductors are called *plates,* or *electrodes,* and the nonconductor is called a *dielectric.*

The capacitor is an important element in modern electrical and electronic equipment, particularly in radio, television, and telephone equipment. For example, a typical home television set has more than 80 capacitors.

Capacitors are widely used for three reasons: (1) they can store electrical energy in a circuit; (2) they pass alternating current in a circuit while blocking direct current; and (3) they are essential elements in tuned circuits. For energy storage, a capacitor can be charged either by using direct current (dc) voltage or alternating current (ac) voltage. The amount of energy it can store depends on its *capacitance,* which is the ratio of the charge on one conductor to the voltage across the two conductors.

The first device capable of storing a large electric charge in a small space was the Leyden jar, invented by Pieter van Musschenbroek in 1745. The next year, John Bevis of England lined the inside and outside of a glass bottle with two sheets of metal, and in this way built the prototype of the modern capacitor.

Design. A primary objective in designing a capacitor is to minimize its size and maximize its capacitance. The capacitance is given by:

$$C = 0.2248\ KA/t$$

where C is the capacitance in picofarads, K is the relative dielectric constant, A is the area, in square inches, of one plate facing the other, and t is the thickness of the dielectric in inches. The capacitance can be increased by increasing the value of K, increasing the value of A, or decreasing the value of t. The value of K depends on the dielectric material that is selected and other factors. The dielectric constant of materials commonly used in capacitors ranges from 1.00 for air to as high as 8,000 for some ceramics. The typical values of K of some other commonly used dielectrics are 2.3 for paper, 2.25 for plastic films, and 7 for mica.

Types and Uses. Each of the many types of capacitors has certain advantages, depending on the application. Considerations of size, precision, cost, and capability to withstand harsh environments also influence the choice of capacitor.

The *variable air capacitor,* which is used for tuning a home radio, for example, has a set of stationary plates and a set of movable plates, usually made of aluminum. Air is the dielectric between the two sets of plates. Turning the tuning knob rotates the movable plates and alters the capacitance of the tuning circuit by varying the area A (see equation above). Altering the capacitance changes the frequency to which the circuit is tuned.

The *ceramic capacitor* has metal plates and a dielectric that is mainly a mixture of titanium oxide and other oxides. It has good dielectric strength, a high dielectric constant, and provides a very high capacitance in a small size.

The *paper capacitor* has layers of kraft paper, from 0.0002 to 0.001 inch (0.05–0.02 mm) thick, between two sheets of aluminum foil. The paper is impregnated with a liquid, such as mineral oil, to increase the capacitance and dielectric strength. Such capacitors can be used at voltages up to 100,000 volts dc and up to 14,000 volts ac. Paper capacitors for use at lower voltages sometimes are impregnated with a solid such as chlorinated naphthalene. Metalized paper capaci-

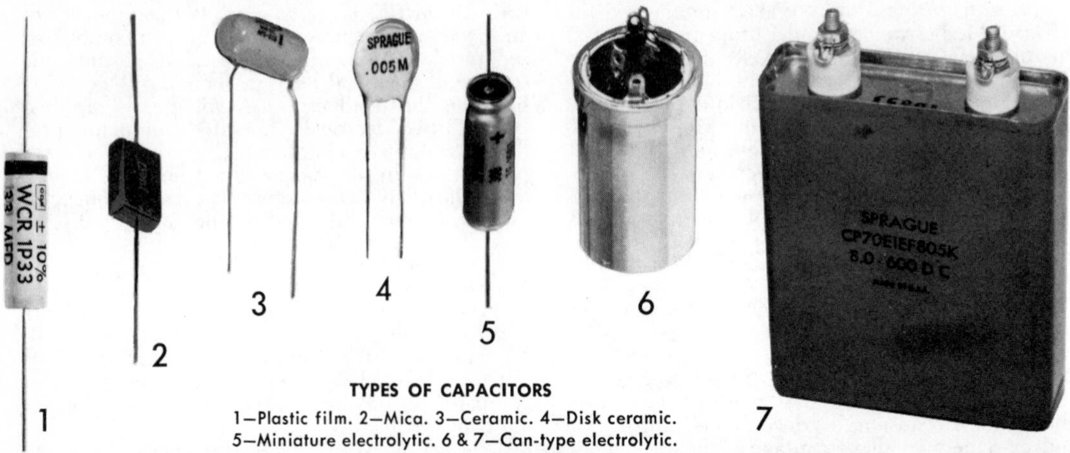

TYPES OF CAPACITORS
1—Plastic film. 2—Mica. 3—Ceramic. 4—Disk ceramic.
5—Miniature electrolytic. 6 & 7—Can-type electrolytic.

(4) FEDERAL PACIFIC ELECTRIC CO.; (OTHERS) SPRAGUE ELECTRIC CO.

tors have paper sheets with an aluminum or zinc coating that may be as thin as 0.0003 inch (0.076 mm).

The *plastic-film capacitor* has metal plates and a dielectric film made of polystyrene, Mylar, or Teflon as thin as 0.00025 inch (0.0064 mm). Film capacitors and paper capacitors are used for power-factor correction in electric power systems; they are used also for energy storage with subsequent rapid capacitor discharge in applications such as nuclear fission studies, hydraulic metal forming, and electric plasma research experiments.

The *electrolytic capacitor* differs considerably from other capacitors. In one kind of electrolytic capacitor, the positive plate is a metal, such as aluminum or tantalum, but the negative plate is an electrolyte. The dielectric is an oxide film coating the positive plate. The capacitor has a very small size relative to its capacitance because the oxide film is about 0.000004 inch thick (t in equation). This kind of electrolytic capacitor, which is suitable only for pulsating dc voltages, is used in filter circuits in radio, television, telephone, telegraph, missile, and computer equipment. Equipped with two oxide-coated positive plates, an electrolytic capacitor can be used for intermittent duty with ac voltages—for example, in starting certain types of alternating-current motors.

A *metal-silicon-dioxide-silicon capacitor* is used in integrated circuits. A silicon dioxide dielectric film and then a metal film, usually aluminum, are deposited on a small piece of silicon, which is the other capacitor plate. Because the metal plate area (A) is only about 0.002 square inch, the silicon dioxide film must be made about 0.000002 inch thick (t in equation). See also CAPACITANCE; ELECTRIC CIRCUITS.

L. W. MATSCH
University of Arizona

CAPACITY. See WEIGHTS AND MEASURES.

CAPE. For geographical features beginning with this word, see also articles under second part of name, such as HATTERAS, CAPE; HORN, CAPE.

CAPE BARREN ISLAND. See FURNEAUX ISLANDS.

CAPE BRETON HIGHLANDS NATIONAL PARK, kāp bret'ən, a national park at the northern end of Cape Breton Island, Nova Scotia, Canada, between the Gulf of St. Lawrence and the Atlantic Ocean. Its area is 367 square miles (950 sq km). The Cabot Trail, a fully paved scenic highway 185 miles (298 km) long, nearly encircles the park. It crosses the summits of French and Mackenzie mountains and cuts through miles of rugged coastal scenery. Campsites are found along the highway.

The park is a recreation center with facilities for golf, swimming, boating, fishing, hiking, and tennis. It is also a wildlife sanctuary inhabited by deer, black bear, beaver, and muskrat. The "Lone Sheiling," a thatched-roofed stone building near Pleasant Bay, is an accurate replica of a crofter's cabin in the highlands of Scotland. It was built in 1942 to commemorate the Scottish ancestry of many Cape Breton residents. Cape Breton Highlands National Park was established in 1936 and was opened in 1941. The main entrances are at Ingonish Beach on the east and at Cheticamp on the west.

R. A. MACLEAN
St. Francis Xavier University, Nova Scotia

CAPE BRETON ISLAND, kāp bret'ən, is an irregular, rocky island in northeastern Nova Scotia, Canada, separated from the mainland by the narrow Strait of Canso. Bounded on the east by the Atlantic Ocean and on the north by the Gulf of St. Lawrence, the island is nearly bisected by the almost landlocked Bras d'Or Lakes. The island has an area of approximately 3,975 square miles (10,295 sq km). The Canso Causeway, completed in 1955, provides road and railway connections with the mainland.

The Scots, most of whom migrated here after 1800, form the largest ethnic group on the island, and Scottish customs are still observed. A few thousand inhabitants are fluent in the Gaelic tongue. Richmond county and the Cheticamp area of Inverness county are populated mainly by people of Acadian stock. The industrial area in the east of the island has a greater diversity of ethnic groups.

The western portion of the island has good agricultural land, and sheep, grain, and truck

CAPE BRETON ISLAND fishing village of Cape North, situated on an inlet of Aspy Bay.

I. DONALD BOWDEN

crops are raised there. The eastern section has mineral wealth in the form of bituminous coal and iron ore. The bulk of the Nova Scotia mining industry is located in Cape Breton Island. Coal, first systematically mined around 1720, is the most profitable mineral produced. Steel manufacture, centered in Sydney, is also a leading industry. In the 1950's and 1960's coal production on the island declined. The 1966 census showed a loss of population for every major town in the industrial area. Diversification of industry has been started, particularly in the Strait of Canso area, where a thermoelectric plant was being planned in the late 1960's and a pulp mill has been established. Fishing and lumbering are old and important industries. Inshore and offshore fishing are carried on in Richmond and Inverness counties.

Tourism is a major industry. The Cabot Trail, which passes through much of Cape Breton Highlands National Park, in the northern part of the island, is a rewarding drive. At Baddeck, on Bras d'Or Lake, is the Alexander Graham Bell Museum, commemorating the inventor of the telephone, who was a summer resident of Baddeck and who died there.

The Fortress of Louisbourg National Historic Park marks the site of the 18th century French fortress. The Canadian government has approved a project to restore it. The Gaelic College at St. Ann's, the only Gaelic college in Canada, is a center of Gaelic cultural activities.

History. Norsemen may have visited Cape Breton Island as early as 1000 A. D. Britain claimed the territory after John Cabot's landing in June 1497. It was ceded to France by the Treaty of St.-Germain-en-Laye (1632). Cape Breton Island played an influential role in French policy after the Treaty of Utrecht (1713) when construction of the Louisbourg fortress was begun to protect the entrance to the Gulf of St. Lawrence. Although the fortress was captured by a New England expedition in 1745, the territory was returned to France by the Treaty of Aix-la-Chapelle (1748). It came under permanent British rule by the Treaty of Paris (1763). It was made a separate province in 1784 but was reannexed to the mainland of Nova Scotia in 1820. Population: 166,943.

R. A. MacLean
St. Francis Xavier University, Nova Scotia

CAPE CANAVERAL. See Cape Kennedy.

CAPE COAST, kāp kōst, a town in Ghana, is a former capital of the British Gold Coast colony. It is located in southern Ghana, on the coast of the Gulf of Guinea. Once a source of slaves, Cape Coast now exports cacao. The Portuguese landed at what is today Cape Coast in 1482. They were followed by the British, Dutch, Swedes, and Danes. The Swedes built a castle on the site in 1652, and the area became known as Cape Coast Castle. The Danes competed with the Swedes for slaves, but the town was seized by the British in 1664. In 1821 the British government took over control of the town from the trading companies and, by 1844, had signed bonds of mutual cooperation at Cape Coast with the coastal chiefs. From this area the colony of the Gold Coast developed and Cape Coast served as its capital until 1876. Population: (1960) 41,230.

Hugh C. Brooks
St. John's University, New York

JOHN J. SMITH

PROVINCETOWN, at the tip of Cape Cod, harbors its fishing fleet in sight of the Pilgrim Monument (*center*).

CAPE COD is a peninsula projecting from the southern coast of Massachusetts like a bent upraised arm. It extends due east to the "elbow" for about 35 miles (56 km) and then curves slightly northwestward about 32 miles (51 km) to Provincetown at the tip of the cape. Within this curving arm lies Cape Cod Bay. Cape Cod and a few small islands adjacent to it make up Barnstable County. It is separated from the mainland by the Cape Cod Canal, which runs southwest from Cape Cod Bay to Buzzards Bay. On the east, Cape Cod faces the Atlantic Ocean and on the south, Nantucket Sound.

The peninsula of the cape, varying in width from 1 to 20 miles (1.6–32 km), covers 399 square miles (1,033 sq km). Formed by glaciers and fashioned by winds and tides, the land is sandy and for the most part flat but with rolling dunes and gentle hills covered with scrub pine, scrub oak, and such low-growing bushes as beachplum, bayberry, blueberry, and shadbush, with bearberry as a ground cover. Sand cliffs 175 feet (50 meters) high rise from the beach on the Atlantic Ocean side. There are many freshwater lakes and hundreds of kettle-hole ponds.

To assure the preservation of the natural beauty of this land, a park known as the Cape Cod National Seashore was established by the U. S. government in 1961. It runs from Nauset Beach off Chatham at the elbow of the cape along the Atlantic coastline to Long Point Light, at Provincetown. Here and in Wellfleet the park covers the entire width of the cape in some spots. A visitor center in Eastham provides exhibits and lectures, and there are guided walks and nature trails throughout the park.

Other outstanding tourist attractions include the Woods Hole Oceanographic Institution and the U. S. Bureau of Fisheries Aquarium at Woods Hole, Cape Cod Museum of Natural History in Brewster, Wellfleet Bay Wildlife Sanctuary in South Wellfleet, Chrysler Art Museum in Provincetown, the Historical Society's Glass Museum in Sandwich, and the Kennedy Memorial (honoring President John F. Kennedy) in Hyannis.

The magnificent shoreline, quiet villages with weathered houses, artists' colonies, summer theaters, gift and antique shops, museums, and a great variety of sports including golf, tennis,

JOHN J. SMITH

THE GREAT OUTER BEACH of the Cape Cod National Seashore is backed by high, grass-covered sand dunes at Newcomb Hollow, near the town of Wellfleet.

riding, bathing, water-skiing, skin diving, surfing, boating, and fishing have long attracted vacationers. Cape Cod's population is nearly quadrupled during the summer months.

The cape is served by direct air and bus connections to Boston, Providence, and New York. There is steamboat service between Boston and Provincetown, and nearby Nantucket and Martha's Vineyard are reached by ferries from Woods Hole and excursion steamers from Hyannis.

History. Cape Cod was named by the English explorer Bartholomew Gosnold for the fish he found most plentiful when he visited its shores in 1602. It is thought that Vikings may have explored the coastline earlier. The Pilgrims landed first at Provincetown, and the Mayflower Compact was signed in 1620 in the harbor there.

From earliest times until the latter part of the 19th century the cape's economy depended mostly on fishing and whaling. Commercial fishing is still practiced, and cape oysters, scallops, and clams are renowned delicacies. The cranberries that are widely grown here are also famous. There was once a flourishing glass factory at Sandwich. Now the cape's main industry is tourism, which brings an estimated annual income of $121 million.

MURIEL G. BATCHELDER
Hyannis Public Library

CAPE COD CANAL, in southeastern Massachusetts, across the western end of the Cape Cod peninsula. The canal, which is 8 miles (13 km) long, connects Buzzards Bay and Cape Cod Bay. Coastal and oceangoing vessels use the canal, avoiding a passage of at least 70 miles (112 km) around the Cape, which often is beset by fog and rough weather. The canal has no locks; its construction was begun by private enterprise in 1909, and the canal was opened in July 1914. The federal government purchased the canal in 1927 and operates it free of tolls.

CAPE COWSLIP, any of a group of bulbous South African herbs belonging to the genus *Lachenalia* of the lily family (Liliaceae). Cape cowslips produce long-lasting, tubular flowers, 1 to 2 inches (2.5–5 cm) long, which are borne hanging from upright stems about 1 foot (30 cm) tall. The flowers vary in color from pale to bright golden yellow and are sometimes flushed, banded, or tipped with red or green. The leaves usually have purple blotches or purple margins.

There are about 50 species of cape cowslips, but only 4 or 5 are cultivated to any extent. They are most commonly used as potted spring-flowering bulbs for greenhouse culture.

R. C. ALLEN
Kingwood Center, Mansfield, Ohio

CAPE ELIZABETH is a resort town in southwestern Maine, in Cumberland county, 7 miles (11 km) south of Portland, on the southern shore of Casco Bay. It is a residential center in a truck-farming area that raises cabbage, lettuce, squash, and strawberries. The town's rocky coastal scenery attracts many tourists. Other points of interest are the Portland Head Light, one of the oldest lighthouses in the United States, built in 1791, and Two Lights and Crescent Beach state parks. Cape Elizabeth was settled about 1630 and incorporated in 1765. It is governed by a town manager and a board of selectmen. Population: 7,873.

CAPE GIRARDEAU, ji-rär′dō, is an industrial city in Missouri, in Cape Girardeau county, on the Mississippi River, about 100 miles (160 km) south of St. Louis. It is the major trade and shipping center for southeastern Missouri. Leading industries include meat packing and the manufacture of cement, electrical appliances, clothing, and shoes. The city is the seat of Southeast Missouri State College, a 4-year coeducational institution, and a library resource center for a wide region.

A trading post was founded here about 1705 by the Frenchman Sieur Jean Girardot, and his name (in a variant spelling) was given to the permanent settlement founded in 1793. Cape Girardeau was incorporated as a town 15 years later and as a city in 1843. Government is by council and manager. Population: 31,282.

CAPE HEN. See FULMAR.

CAPE HONEYSUCKLE. See TRUMPET-FLOWERS.

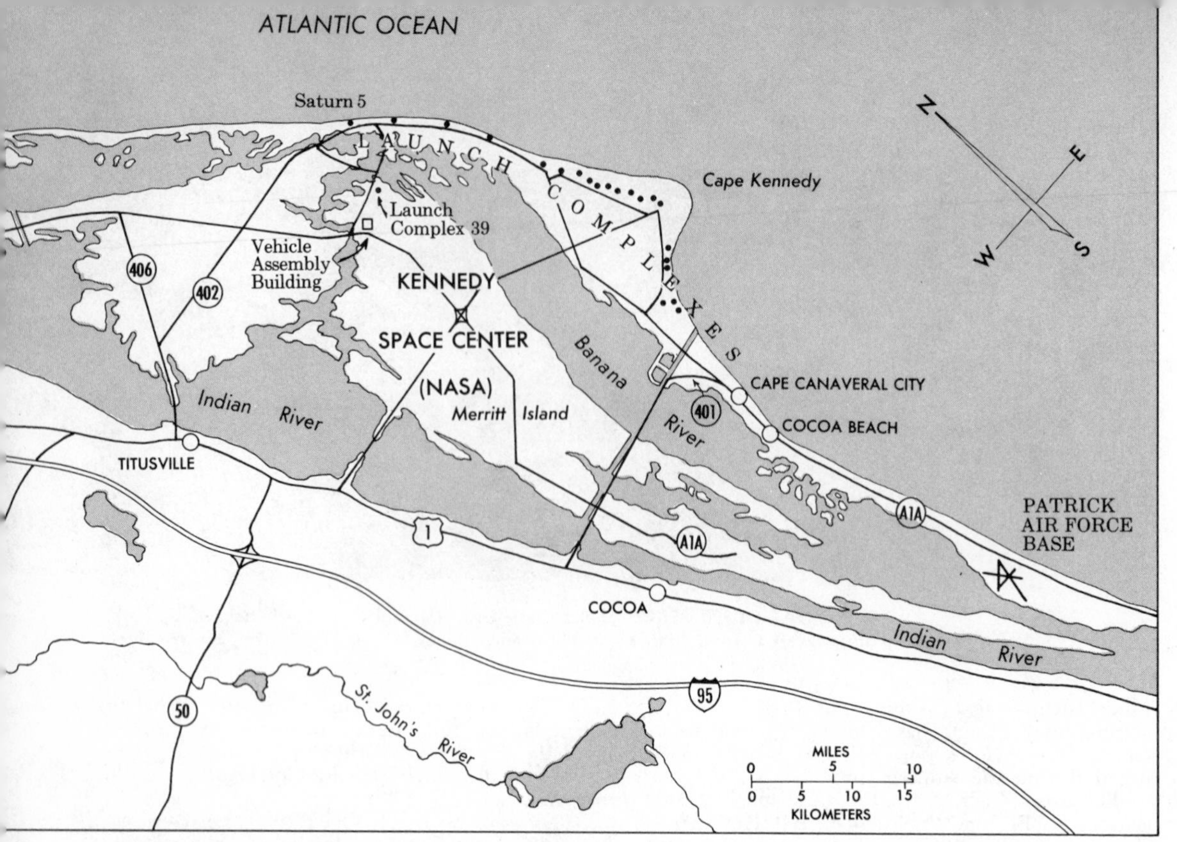

CAPE HUNTING DOG, a large wild dog found throughout most of Africa. It somewhat resembles hyenas, to which it is not related. The head and body are about 40 inches (100 cm) long, and the tail about 18 inches (46 cm). The mottled black, white, and orange color of the body is variable in pattern. The ears are large and erect.

Cape hunting dogs live in packs, usually of about a dozen animals, and hunt at any hour of the day or night. They pursue even the larger kinds of antelope. The dogs do not bark but utter a variety of high-pitched, birdlike sounds.

The single species, *Lycaon pictus*, belongs to the family Canidae, order Carnivora.

Joseph A. Davis, Jr.
New York Zoological Society

CAPE KENNEDY, ken′ə-dē, is the principal launch site for the missile development and space exploration programs of the United States. The cape is located on Florida's Atlantic coast, east of Cocoa and Titusville. Launch operations at Cape Kennedy are conducted by the National Aeronautics and Space Administration (NASA) and the Army, Navy, and Air Force. The Air Force Eastern Test Range, extending down the Atlantic Ocean, provides range support services.

The John F. Kennedy Space Center, a field installation of NASA, has its headquarters on Merritt Island west of Cape Kennedy and has facilities at both the island and the cape. The center manages all NASA launch activities in the area and develops facilities and ground equipment to support space flight missions.

Development. In 1948, Cape Canaveral (the name of Cape Kennedy until Nov. 28, 1963) was selected by the Department of Defense as a missile test site. The site offered the advantages of a temperate climate that allowed operations to take place all year long and a location that permitted spacecraft to be launched eastward (thus benefiting from the velocity of the earth's rotation in obtaining orbit). In addition, a string of islands to the southeast provided bases for stations to track the vehicles being launched.

Activity at Cape Canaveral in the early and middle 1950's centered around flight testing of missiles for use in weapon systems. These missiles included the Army Redstone, Jupiter, and Pershing; the Air Force Thor, Atlas, Titan, and Minuteman; and the Navy Polaris. When the USSR orbited the first artificial satellite in October 1957, the U. S. space exploration program was still a modest one, aimed primarily at placing small satellites in orbit as part of the International Geophysical Year (1957–1958). The program was accelerated after the Russian achievement, and the first U. S. satellite, Explorer I, was sent into orbit from Cape Canaveral by a modified Redstone rocket in February 1958.

Following the creation of NASA in October 1958, a broad program of manned and unmanned space flights was planned. The manned program was initiated in May 1961 by Alan Shepard's suborbital flight from Cape Canaveral down the Eastern Test Range in a Mercury capsule. Meanwhile, many record-setting unmanned flights were also being launched from the cape. In 1961, President Kennedy's announcement of a manned lunar landing by 1970 as a national goal led to the establishment of Project Apollo. Kennedy Space Center was formed to manage the development of facilities and to conduct the launch operations. Project Gemini, a two-man-spacecraft program conducted at the cape as a forerunner to Apollo, provided valuable information and training for the manned lunar flight.

Cape Kennedy Facilities. The shoreline of Cape Kennedy is occupied by a row of concrete launch pads, each equipped with a gantry for the erection and servicing of the space vehicle and with a blockhouse for personnel and instrumentation. Smaller space vehicles are fueled by tank trucks; for larger vehicles there are fixed facilities for storage and transfer of propellants. Tracking stations, located at island bases and on ships, extend 10,000 miles (16,000 km) southeastward from the cape. All range support facilities are managed by the Air Force Eastern Test Range, with headquarters at nearby Patrick Air Force Base.

Kennedy Space Center Facilities. Kennedy Space Center has constructed Launch Complex 39 on Merritt Island. The complex is a unique spaceport planned for the giant Apollo Saturn rocket. Earlier space vehicles were erected and checked out at their launch pads, requiring months of exposure during the process. In contrast, at Complex 39 the Saturn rocket is assembled and checked out inside the huge Vehicle Assembly Building, 525 feet (160 meters) high. It is then lifted and carried several miles on its launcher to the launch pad by means of a tractorlike "crawler" transporter. After connections are made to control equipment and fueling facilities, the vehicle is loaded and final checkout is completed before launch.

Future Plans. Following the conclusion of the Apollo project, extended lunar exploration and the orbiting of large space stations can be accomplished by using adaptations of the Apollo Saturn vehicle launched from Complex 39. The complex itself can be modified to accommodate the nuclear-powered upper stages of future rockets. Such rockets will be needed for manned exploration of the planets. See also NATIONAL AERONAUTICS AND SPACE ADMINISTRATION.

J. P. CLAYBOURNE
John F. Kennedy Space Center

CAPE LEADWORT, led'wûrt, is a cultivated flowering member of the leadwort family. Cape leadwort, *Plumbago capensis,* is native to South Africa. It is used as an ornamental in gardens in the southern United States and is raised in greenhouses in colder areas. It may be trained as a vine or a shrub and must be cut back to prevent its overgrowing other plants. The leaves are oblong and alternate. The flowers are borne in terminal spikes that resemble those of phlox. They are azure blue or sometimes white. The petals are fused into a narrow tube that flares into 5 spreading lobes 1 inch (2½ cm) across. The short sepals are densely covered with glandular hairs.

JOAN E. RAHN, *Lake Forest College*

CAPE MAY is a resort city in southern New Jersey, in Cape May county, at the southern end of Cape May Peninsula, on the Atlantic Ocean. It is 40 miles (64 km) southwest of Atlantic City. Cape May Canal crosses the peninsula from Cape May Harbor, an artificially extended inlet of the ocean, to Delaware Bay. A ferry connects Cape May with Lewes, Del., across the bay. The city has a sandy beach, a boardwalk, and is noted for its Victorian houses and hotels. Victorian Village Museum, founded in 1964, has exhibits of 19th century social history.

Cape May's popularity as a vacation place dates back to 1766 and, before the Civil War, it was one of the most fashionable resorts on the Atlantic coast, visited by several U. S. presidents, including Lincoln and Grant. Government is by commission. Population: 4,392.

CAPE OF GOOD HOPE, at the southwestern extremity of Africa, is both literally and figuratively a landmark in the history of trade and navigation. The hazards of the sea route to India opened around the cape (not the southernmost point of Africa, but the point at which the winds are fiercest) resound in the name Cabo Tormentoso (Cape of Torment, or Storms) given the cape by the Portuguese navigator Bartholomeu Dias, who first reached it in 1487. The riches brought back from the Orient by the dangerous cape route, charted by Vasco da Gama in 1497, caused King John II of Portugal to change its name to Cabo da Bõa Esperança (Cape of Good Hope).

The cape proper is a rocky promontory only about 3 miles (4.8 km) long, lying between the Atlantic Ocean on the west and False Bay on the east. False Bay derives its name from the mistaken belief of early mariners that in rounding the cape they had rounded Africa.

CAPE PROVINCE is the largest and oldest of the four provinces of the Republic of South Africa. It is called *Kaapprovinsie* in Afrikaans and is often erroneously referred to as Cape of Good Hope province although it was never so named. It was called Cape Colony prior to the creation of the Union of South Africa in 1910.

Situated at the southern extremity of Africa, Cape province occupies an area of 278,465 square miles (721,224 sq km). Bordering it on the west is the South Atlantic Ocean, on the south and southeast the Indian Ocean, and clockwise from northwest to east: South West Africa, Botswana, Transvaal, Orange Free State, and Natal.

The Land. The province is essentially a plateau that is depressed in the middle and is bounded by the Great Escarpment. The escarpment, which extends into Transvaal and Natal and at its highest point in the Cape, Compass Berg, reaches 8,215 feet (2,504 meters), parallels the southeastern coast at distances of 30 to 150 miles (48 to 241 km). The plateau area includes sections of the sand-covered Kalahari Basin in the extreme north, the rocky plain of the Cape Middle Veld in the northwest, and the monotonous High Veld which rises from 4,000 to 6,000 feet (1,219 to 1,829 meters). The marginal lands below the Great Escarpment include the erosional basins of the Great and Little Karoo. The major drainage system is the Orange-Vaal River.

Bordering oceans and changes in altitude account for most variations in climate. The southwest has hot, dry summers and cool, rainy winters; the southeast has warm temperatures and year-round rainfall; and inland areas are hot and either arid or semiarid. The interior areas of the High Veld and the karoos are covered with desert scrub, and only in the east and southeast are there extensive stretches of savanna and forest. Much of the indigenous fauna was driven away by settlers and currently can be found only in the national parks and game preserves.

The People. The four main population groups are white, Bantu, Coloured, and Asiatic. According to the 1960 census, there were 1,003,207 whites (18.7%), 3,011,080 Bantus (56.1%), 1,330-089 Coloureds (24.8%), and 18,477 Asians (0.34%). The population is unevenly distributed, with the highest densities in the west around Cape Town and in the southeast in the vicinity of Port Elizabeth, East London, and the Transkei.

The white population, mainly British and Afrikaner—descendants of Dutch settlers with a

LAWRENCE LOWRY, FROM RAPHO GUILLUMETTE

CAPE OF GOOD HOPE, at the southwest tip of Africa.

strong admixture of German and French Huguenot—is 80% urban, half of which lives in the nine largest cities. Over 90% of the republic's Coloured population (people of mixed racial origin) live in Cape Province, especially in Cape Town and its environs. Approximately 66% are urban. About 47% of the Bantu population live in the Transkei, with the remaining in rural areas.

The languages spoken in the province, as in all of South Africa, reflect ethnic origin. Over 90% of the Africans speak one of the three Bantu languages—Xhosa, Tswana, or southern Sotho. English and Afrikaans are the official languages of the province and bilingualism is steadily increasing. More than 38% of the white population speak English; 58%, Afrikaans; and 1.4%, both. The Coloureds speak English or Afrikaans.

Religion, like language, is related to ethnic origin. The Dutch Reform Church has the largest membership among whites and Coloureds, but a variety of Christian denominations are represented. Education is based on language and is compulsory for all white and some Coloured children. Most of the Coloured schools are mission-aided and have a special curriculum that has existed since 1923. There are three universities for whites: Cape Town, Stellenbosch, and Rhodes University at Grahamstown. The Bantus may attend Fort Hare University College, while nonwhites other than Bantu attend University College in Belleville.

Economy. Cape province produces 65% of South Africa's wool, the most important agricultural product in the republic. The province is the country's sole producer of citrus fruits and wine, the largest producer of diamonds, manganese, and copper, and is second in asbestos. Cape Town, the provincial capital, is a major industrial center and port, and is linked with all parts of the republic by a network of rails and roads.

Government. The province is governed by an appointed administrator and by a council of 52 elected white members and 2 representatives of the Coloureds. The province is represented in the national parliament by 54 elected members of the assembly, 4 elected members to represent the Coloureds, and 13 senators—2 nominated by the state president and 11 elected in the province.

In 1963, South Africa granted self-government to the Transkei, the largest single Bantu territory in the republic. It has 16,000 square miles (41,440 sq km) and 1,415,789 people, 98% of whom are Xhosa-speaking Bantus. All Xhosas have Transkei citizenship and vote only for their own parliament. The first session of the legislative assembly met at Umtata, the capital, on May 5, 1964.

History. Although the Cape of Good Hope was sighted in 1487 by Bartholomeu Dias, no attempt at settlement was made until the Dutch explorer Jan van Riebeeck landed in 1652. Slaves were imported in 1658, and in 1687 the first French Huguenots arrived. Expeditions into the interior began in the mid-18th century, and by 1779 the first of many wars with the Bantus began.

The Cape changed hands several times between 1780 and 1814 and was finally ceded to Britain in 1814. In 1820, 5,000 British settlers known as the "Albany Settlers," arrived. The British abolished slavery in 1834, and a result was the Great Trek of 1836, when many Afrikaners left the colony.

The economy improved after the discovery of diamonds in 1867, and by 1872 the colony was granted parliamentary government. Early governors and Cecil Rhodes, who became prime minister of the colony in 1890, foresaw the advantage of uniting the four territories of southern Africa, but this policy was opposed by the South African Republic and the Orange Free State. The conflicting interests of the British and the Afrikaners culminated in the South African War of 1899–1902, which the British won. Cape Colony's leaders pressed for union, and in 1910 the colony was incorporated into the newly founded Union of South Africa. See also SOUTH AFRICA, REPUBLIC OF.

EDWARD J. MILES, *University of Vermont*

CAPE TO CAIRO RAILWAY, a project of the South African statesman and financier Cecil John Rhodes, who dreamed in the late 19th century of building a railroad under the British flag to link Cape Town in South Africa with Cairo in Egypt. However, the effort to realize the dream went against the colonial interests of Portugal, Germany, Belgium, Italy, and France. Serious diplomatic crises arose as a consequence, and the railroad was never completed. German control of East Africa was the most serious obstacle.

By the mid-20th century, the line had been built from Cape Town as far north as Kindu, Congo (Kinshasa). The section beginning in Egypt makes no contact with the railroads in the Sudan, which have an outlet on the Red Sea. Cape Town and Cairo are now connected by airline routes and motor roads.

HARRY R. RUDIN, *Yale University*

SOUTH AFRICAN TOURIST CORP.

CAPE TOWN, in South Africa, has developed new areas on land reclaimed from Table Bay. The older part of the city extends inland to the base of Table Mountain at rear.

CAPE TOWN, a city in the Republic of South Africa, is the legislative capital of the country and the capital of Cape Province. It is considered to be one of the great scenic cities of the world, and is often called the "Mother City of South Africa" because of its historical background. The city is second in South Africa to Johannesburg in size of population and second in importance to Durban as a port and industrial center.

Cape Town is situated in the southwestern part of Cape Province. It lies at the foot of 3,549-foot (1,082-meter) Table Mountain on the shore of Table Bay. Because of Table Mountain and the other mountains in the area, the city has spread out along the coast, its western suburbs fronting on the Atlantic Ocean and the southern suburbs on the Indian Ocean. Since World War II, the reclamation of a large area, known as the Foreshore, from Table Bay has provided 360 acres for the redevelopment of the congested central area. An entirely new city section is being developed on this reclaimed land.

Food processing and clothing manufacture are the city's most important industrial activities. Other manufactures include motor vehicles, shoes, and the products of the printing and engineering industries. Cape Town is the leading port for the export of fruit, wine, grain, and gold and diamonds from the surrounding region. There is an oil refinery on the outskirts of the city.

Cape Town has become a famous holiday resort. It is an attractive city with a magnificent setting and has miles of inviting shoreline. As a winter resort it draws people from all over southern Africa. A tourist attraction is the Table Mountain Aerial Cableway, which enables visitors to reach the top of Table Mountain, whose sheer precipice forms the backdrop for the city. The National Botanic Gardens are located in a suburb of Cape Town.

The city is also an outstanding cultural center. There are carefully preserved examples of the Dutch colonial style of architecture, including early homesteads with their characteristic, gracefully curved gables and thatched roofs. The South African Museum, housing relics dating from the earliest days of discovery and settlement, and the National Historical Museum, opened in 1964, are both located in Cape Town.

The most interesting structures in the city are the Houses of Parliament and the Castle. The original Parliament building was completed in 1886, and a new wing was added in 1910 to house the Union Parliament. The Castle, the most important historic building in South Africa, was begun in 1666. Much of the material for the early construction was brought from Holland. Besides serving as a fortress, the building functioned as a residence for the governor and as the seat of the government and the courts during the 17th century.

Cape Town is also an important education center. The University of Cape Town is in the city, and Stellenbosch University is 31 miles (50 km) away. Numerous other educational institutions are located in the area.

Cape Town was founded on April 6, 1652, by Jan van Riebeeck as a supply station for the Dutch East India Company. It became the center of the colony that developed and has remained the focus and capital of Cape Province. The city was made the legislative capital of the Union of South Africa when it was formed in 1910. Today, the Parliament of the republic meets in Cape Town about five months each year. Population: (1960) 807,211.

EDWARD J. MILES, *University of Vermont*

CAPE TOWN, University of, kāp′toun, a public, coeducational institution of higher education, located in Rondebosch, a suburb of Cape Town, Republic of South Africa. The main campus is on the grounds of Groote Schuur, the estate that Cecil Rhodes bequeathed to South Africa. Other university units are in the city of Cape Town. Founded by the citizens of Cape Town in 1829 as the South African College, the school remained under private control until 1879, when its government was assigned to a council. University status under the present name was conferred in 1918.

Instruction was initially limited to arts and science. These studies were augmented first by law courses and then, between 1900 and 1918, by schools of medicine, engineering, and education. Later additions include faculties of commerce and social science and schools of African studies and fine art and architecture. Music studies were inaugurated with the incorporation of South Africa College of Music, and there is a speech and drama department and a little theater. Cape Town's library includes collections in medicine, music, architecture, law, and botany. Five teaching hospitals are affiliated with the university. The National Botanical Gardens, in nearby Kirstenbosch, contain a collection of South African flora. Full-time student enrollment averages about 5,000

JAMES J. GRANT, *Republic of South Africa Information Service, New York City*

CAPE VERDE ISLANDS, kāp vûrd, an archipelago in the North Atlantic Ocean about 320 miles (515 km) off the coast of West Africa. The islands, called *Ilhas do Cabo Verde* in Portuguese, constitute an overseas province of Portugal. Since their barren island homeland affords little opportunity for employment, Cape Verdians emigrate to other parts of Portuguese Africa or outside the Portuguese-speaking community. Traditionally, educated Cape Verdians have filled posts in other Portuguese territories in Africa.

The province consists of ten islands and five smaller islets covering an area of 1,557 square miles (4,033 sq km). The principal islands are São Tiago, Santo Antão, São Vicente, São Nicolau, Sal, Boa Vista, Fogo, Maio, Brava, and Santa Luzia. Praia, on São Tiago, is the capital.

The islands, of volcanic origin, are arid and mountainous and have poor soil. They rise to 9,281 feet (2,829 meters) in the Pico do Cano, on Fogo, the only active volcano. The climate is hot and humid, and rainfall is sparse.

More than one third of the population of the islands is on São Tiago. Most of the people are mulattoes—a racial amalgam of Portuguese from Europe and Africans from Guinea. An important feature of the population is the disproportion between males and females as a result of the heavy male emigration to North America. Literacy rates are higher in the Cape Verdes than in other parts of Portuguese Africa. The people speak a dialect of Portuguese. Their culture includes a distinctive poetry and balladry.

Despite adverse conditions, the economy of the Cape Verde Islands is based primarily on agriculture. Cash crops include coffee, corn, sisal, oranges, tobacco, and sugarcane. Fish is an important part of the people's diet, and salt abounds on many islands. The archipelago has long suffered from periodic drought, famine, and crop failure.

The archipelago was discovered in 1455 by Alvise da Cadamosto and Antonio Noli, explorers in the service of Prince Henry of Portugal. The islands were uninhabited, but they were soon settled by Portuguese colonies and African slaves from Guinea. The Cape Verdes were administered as one colony with Portuguese Guinea until 1879. Today the islands are administered as a separate province, with a governor-general as Portugal's chief representative. Population: (1960) 201,549.

DOUGLAS L. WHEELER
University of New Hampshire

CAPE VERDE PENINSULA, kāp vûrd, in the Republic of Senegal, is the westernmost projection of Africa. About 20 miles (32 km) from east to west and up to 7 miles (11 km) across, the peninsula is composed of dunes and limestone cliffs and has marshy areas called *niayes.* Cape Almadies is at its western tip. Dakar, chief port and capital of Senegal, is on the southern coast. The peninsula was discovered about 1445 by the Portuguese navigator João Fernandes, who gave it its name, meaning "green cape."

CAPE YORK PENINSULA, kāp yôrk, in Queensland, is the northernmost point of Australia. About 280 miles (450 km) from south to north and 150 miles (240 km) wide, it juts north toward New Guinea, from which it is separated by Endeavour and Torres straits. The Gulf of Carpentaria is on the west and the Coral Sea on the east. The peninsula is largely tropical jungle. The west coast has extensive deposits of bauxite.

CASA DE PORTUGAL

THE CAPE VERDE ISLANDS produce salt. These salt pans are on Sal Island.

ČAPEK, chä′pek, **Karel** (1890–1938), Czech dramatist and novelist, who is best known for his allegorical plays *R. U. R.* and *The Insect Comedy.* In these and other works, he satirized such contemporary social evils as excessive mechanization, undue emphasis on materialism, and totalitarianism.

Life. Karel Čapek was born in Malé Svatoňovice, Bohemia (now Czechoslovakia), on Jan. 9, 1890. In 1909 he began to study philosophy at Charles University, Prague. In 1910 he studied in Berlin, then returned to Charles University in 1911, where he received a Ph. D. in philosophy in 1915.

A champion of modern drama, Čapek was art director of the National Art Theater in Prague for a number of years. Later he established his own Vinohradsky Art Theater, which became a showcase for gifted young Czech playwrights. Čapek died in Prague on Dec. 25, 1938.

Plays. Čapek's most celebrated play, *R. U. R.* (1921; Eng. tr., 1923), expresses his ambivalent attitude toward technology, which makes man its victim and superman its product. The play introduced the world to the word "robot," from *robotit,* meaning to drudge. (R. U. R. stands for "Rossum's Universal Robots.") *The Insect Comedy* (1921; Eng. tr., 1923), written with his brother Josef, satirizes modern materialism. *The Makropoulos Secret* (1922; Eng. tr., 1925) is a comic satire on the quest for immortality. Čapek's last play, *Power and Glory* (1937; Eng. tr., 1938), is a protest against dictatorship.

Other Works. Čapek's important early novel *Factory for the Absolute* (1922; Eng. tr., 1927) has much the same theme as *R. U. R.* His novel *Krakatit* (1924; Eng. tr., 1925) anticipated both the destructive possibilities of nuclear physics and the moral problems these possibilities would raise. His greatest novels constitute a trilogy—*Hordubal* (1933; Eng. tr., 1934), *The Meteor* (1934; Eng. tr., 1935), and *An Ordinary Life* (1934; Eng. tr., 1936). Mystical and philosophical, they are independent of Čapek's other works with respect to subject, characters, and setting. However, they all have the same theme, the search for the ultimate meaning of human life.

Čapek, who worked as a journalist, also wrote nonfiction. A friend of President Tomáš Masaryk of Czechoslovakia, he recorded Masaryk's political ideas in *Conversations with T. G. Masaryk* (1928–1935).

Josef Čapek (1887–1945), Czech painter, art critic, and writer, was Karel's brother and frequent collaborator. He was born at Hronov, Bohemia, on March 23, 1887. In addition to working with Karel on two collections of short stories (1916 and 1918) and the plays *The Insect Comedy* and *Adam the Creator* (1927; Eng. tr., 1930), he wrote a drama of his own, *The Land of Many Names* (1923; Eng. tr., 1926), and several volumes of short stories and two short novels. In much of his fiction he revealed an unusual preoccupation with the subconscious.

As a painter, Čapek developed his own style of primitivism. His books of art criticism include *The Humblest Art* (1920) and *The Art of Primitive Nations* (1938).

Čapek was imprisoned in the concentration camp at Bergen-Belsen, Germany, in 1939 and died there in April 1945.

Oscar Brownstein, *University of Iowa*

Further Reading: Harkins, William E., *Karel Čapek* (New York 1962).

CAPEL, kā′pəl, **Sir Arthur** (1610?–1649), English Royalist leader in the Civil War, who sacrificed his life for the sake of King Charles I and the Established Church. The son of an influential landowner in Essex, Capel entered politics in 1640 and sat in both the Short and Long Parliaments of that year. He was a moderate monarchist at first, but the extremism of John Pym, the Parliamentarian leader, and of his friends made Capel a staunch champion of the King. His loyalty was rewarded in 1641 when the King created him Lord Capel of Hadham.

After the final rupture between king and Parliament in the summer of 1642, Capel accompanied Charles to York, where he raised substantial funds for the Royalist cause. In 1643 he was made lieutenant governor of Shropshire, Cheshire, and North Wales, and he fought in a brief campaign near Chester. He represented the King in the unsuccessful negotiations with the Parliamentarians at Uxbridge in February 1645, and after the surrender of the last of the Royalist forces in April 1646 he accompanied the Queen to Paris. In 1648, after the King's escape to the Isle of Wight, Capel encouraged the Royalists to renew hostilities, and he was in command of a regiment at Colchester when the Royalists capitulated a second time in August 1648.

Capel was impeached on a charge of high treason and imprisoned in the Tower of London. His attempt to escape across the Thames was foiled by a boatman who betrayed him for the sum of £20. Sentenced to death, he died bravely on the scaffold in Westminster Hall on March 9, 1649. Clarendon, the 17th century historian, described Capel as a man "in whom the malice of his enemies could discover very few faults."

L. Perry Curtis, Jr.
University of California at Berkeley

CAPELIN, kap′ə-lin, a saltwater fish found in Arctic and subarctic waters of North America. In the Pacific it ranges southward to Washington and in the Atlantic south to Nova Scotia. It is abundant along Newfoundland, ranking in numbers with the common cod. The capelin is used as fertilizer and for making fish meal.

A slender-bodied fish, the capelin usually grows to a length of 7 to 9 inches (18 to 23 cm). It is covered with minute scales. Spawning males have two ridges of elongated scales on each side of the body. These ridges have a villous, or hairy, appearance. The capelin is olive above, silvery on the sides, and white below; the scale margins are dotted with minute dusky specks.

The capelin, *Mallotus villosus,* belongs to the smelt family, Osmeridae, order Clupeiformes.

W. B. Scott, *University of Toronto*

CAPELLA, kə-pel′ə, is a yellow first magnitude star of the Northern Hemisphere and the sixth-brightest star in the sky. It is in the constellation Auriga and lies closer to the north celestial pole than any other very bright star. In Greek mythology Capella was the Cretan goat or nymph that nursed the infant Zeus.

Capella has been determined spectroscopically to be a binary, or double star. The component stars are 79 million miles (127 million km) apart and rotate about one another every 104 days. Together they are 150 times more luminous than the sun. Both are similar in composition to the sun but more massive, and one is a giant star. Capella lies at a distance of 46 light years.

ANNAN PHOTO FEATURES

A CAPERCAILLIE cock struts and calls for a mate.

CAPER, kā'pər, a prickly shrub, usually known as the *caper bush,* native to the warm, arid and semiarid areas of the Mediterranean regions of North Africa and southern Europe. The plant's pickled flower buds, called *capers,* are used for garnishing or seasoning food. The caper (*Capparis spinosa*), a member of the caper family (Capparidaceae), grows to 4 feet (120 cm) tall and produces quickly fading, 4-petaled, white flowers. The flowers, which bear masses of showy stamens that extend well beyond the petals, mature into berries with numerous seeds. Caper is found on rocky soil and is common on old walls and ruins. It often grows in a creeping, or trailing, manner, similar to blackberries and other common brambles.

Caper is cultivated extensively in France, Sicily, and other parts of southern Europe for its flower buds, which are picked before opening and preserved in vinegar. The quality of capers depends upon the stage of development at the time of picking. Young, tender buds are preferred to those that are nearer the opening stage. The caper is grown to some extent in Florida and California.

There are about 150 species in the genus, some of which occasionally are used as a source of capers.

R. C. Allen
Kingwood Center, Mansfield, Ohio

CAPER flower buds are pickled and eaten as capers.

RUSS KINNE, FROM PHOTO RESEARCHERS

CAPERCAILLIE, kap-ər-kāl'-ē, a turkey-sized game bird found in the northern parts of Eurasia. It once was more widely distributed, but its range has shrunk because of the pressure of hunting and the reduction of the dense and remote evergreen forests that the capercaillie inhabits. An extremely wary bird, the capercaillie is difficult to find and shoot; therefore, it is highly prized by hunters. Its flesh is considered delicious.

The male capercaillie is almost 3 feet (90 cm) long. It is striking black with some green iridescence. It has red wattles over its eyes, a white shoulder patch, and spots of white in its large rounded tail. The female is about 2 feet (0.6 meter) long and is dull brown with a reddish patch on its breast.

Usually found on the ground, the capercaillie roosts in evergreens and spends much time in trees in winter. It flies up suddenly with very explosive wingbeats. It then alternates swift wingbeats with smooth glides and maneuvers easily through the dense trees. The species is nonmigratory, but individuals move around locally. It feeds on shoots and buds of conifers, pine needles, berries and other fruits, mast, and sometimes insects.

During the breeding season, the male capercaillie sets up a display territory and is highly polygamous. During the display, which may take place from some high perch, the male stretches his head and raises and fans his tail conspicuously. His song is a retching noise combined with a clicking and cork-popping sound. The capercaillie nest is a depression in the ground, often at the base of a tree. The female lays five to eight eggs, and she also incubates them.

The capercaillie, *Tetrao urogallus,* is an Old World member of the grouse family, Tetraonidae, in the order Galliformes.

Sally H. Spofford
Cornell University

CAPERNAUM, kə-pûr'nā-əm, a city in ancient Palestine, was the home of Jesus during much of his ministry. It was located on the northwestern shore of the Sea of Galilee on what is now the ruined site of Tell Hum. It was in Capernaum that Jesus chose the first of his disciples, Peter, Andrew, James and John, and a nearby hill is supposed to have been the scene of the Sermon on the Mount. A synagogue that was built in the 2d or 3d century has been excavated and partially restored.

CAPET, kȧ-pe', was the surname given to King Hugh of France (reigned 987–996) and thereafter to his descendants, the subsequent kings of France. The Capet family is notable for its extraordinary genetic accomplishment: for 13 generations each king passed the throne on to his son, a succession unbroken until 1316, when the son of Louis X died in infancy.

During the following 12 years the crown passed to brothers of Louis X. It was decided during this time that French succession law excluded from the throne both women and males deriving from their claim through a woman. Accordingly, when the last brother died in 1328, leaving only daughters, Philip of Valois, first cousin of his predecessor, became king. When the Valois line died out in 1589, another cadet branch of the family, the House of Bourbon, succeeded to the throne. Overthrown by the French Revolution of 1789, the Bourbons were restored from 1814 to 1848. The last reigning king, Louis Philippe of the Orléans branch of the house, was deposed in 1848.

Establishment of Capetian Authority. Historians conventionally apply the name Capet only to the senior branch of the family, which began with King Hugh and ended in 1328 when Philip of Valois became king. The Capets were descended from Robert the Strong, a 9th century count in the Carolingian kingdom of the West Franks, whose son Odo (Eudes) was elected king in 888 when the Carolingian heir was a minor. Two other members of the family also held the royal title in the early 10th century. There were thus precedents for the election of Hugh Capet to the throne in 987.

Hugh and his next five successors gradually managed to transform the elective monarchy into a hereditary one by having the king's eldest son designated and crowned in his father's lifetime. The early Capetian kings exerted effective authority only in the two counties of Paris and Orléans, but they managed to conserve, pacify, and gradually augment this narrow territorial base.

Philip Augustus (reigned 1180–1223), the sixth of Hugh's successors, was the real founder of the French monarchy. He made skillful use of feudal principles, asserting his rights over the great magnates. At his accession all of western France was under the control of the Angevin king of England, but Philip exploited his role as feudal suzerain to dispossess the English King, John, of Normandy, Anjou, and Maine in 1203–1204. Philip's military victory at Bouvines in 1214 guaranteed these acquisitions, which vastly augmented the resources of the Capetian monarchy.

Through war, inheritance, and other means, the Capetians further extended their royal domain in subsequent decades. They also derived immense prestige from the just and saintly reign (1226–1270) of Louis IX, whose example was a great political asset to his successors. Louis IX's grandson Philip IV (reigned 1285–1314) was the last really strong king in the direct line of the Capetian family. Philip has been associated with a new spirit of cynicism, ruthlessness, and administrative innovation, dominated by the rise of an aggressive class of royal bureaucrats and lawyers. In fact, Philip IV appears to have been more conservative than was formerly thought, and many of these changes were more pronounced under Philip V (reigned 1316–1322), who reorganized governmental administration and experimented with representative assemblies.

JOHN HENNEMAN, *McMaster University*

CAPILLARITY, kap-ə-lar′ə-tē, the phenomenon in which the level of fluid inside an open tube of very small diameter is higher or lower than the level of the surrounding fluid. Capillarity, also known as *capillary action,* also occurs in plant fibers, and it is the direct result of the action of surface tension.

When two fluids are in contact with each other, the forces of attraction between the molecules of the different fluids create forces in the surface of separation that make the surface contract to a shape having the smallest area consistent with the shape of the containing vessel and the force of gravity. This tendency of the surface to contract is called *interfacial tension* or, if one of the fluids is a gas such as air, *surface tension.* Thus a drop of liquid in air is spherical because a sphere has the smallest surface area that can contain the liquid.

CAPILLARITY

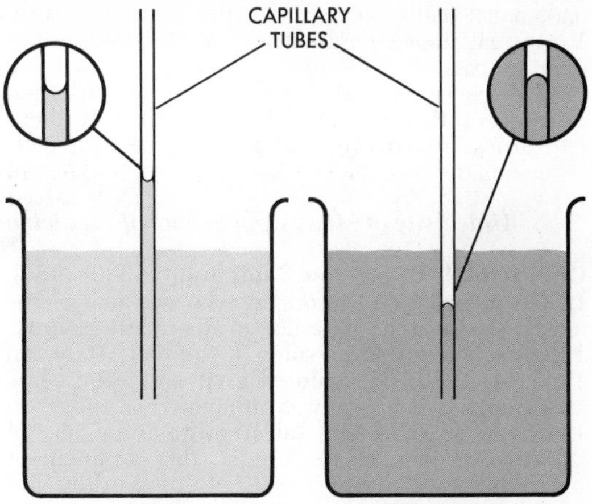

CAPILLARY TUBES

WATER

MERCURY

If r is the radius of a liquid drop, and p_1, p_2 are the pressures on the inside and outside of the drop, respectively, then $p_1 - p_2 = 2\gamma/r$, where γ is the surface tension. Therefore the pressure on the concave side of the surface is greater than that on the convex side.

When a capillary tube, that is, a tube of small diameter, is inserted into a liquid, the surface of the liquid inside the tube is constrained to the shape of a spherical segment. This surface is called the *meniscus,* and for liquids that "wet" glass, that is, liquids that spread without limit over a clean horizontal glass surface, the meniscus is concave; while for liquids, such as mercury, which do not wet glass, the meniscus is convex. Since the pressure under a concave meniscus is less than that at the plane surface of liquid outside the capillary tube, liquid will rise in the tube until the weight of the liquid column equals the pressure difference. Those liquids that form a convex meniscus will be depressed in the capillary tube.

Capillary pressure is pressure developed through capillary action. This pressure can be used to split rocks by driving wooden wedges into crevices and soaking them with water. The water enters the wood fibers through capillary action, and the pressure of the resultant swelling is usually sufficient to split the rock.

HERBERT LIEBESKIND, *The Cooper Union*

CAPILLARY, kap′ə-ler-ē, one of the many microscopic blood vessels that connect the terminal branches of arteries with the beginning segments of veins. Capillaries are the smallest of all blood vessels, having a diameter of about 8 microns. (One micron equals about 1/25,000 of an inch.) They are only slightly wider than red blood cells, which must pass through them in single file.

The human body contains so many capillaries that any living body cell is never more than 50 microns away from one. This close proximity is extremely important because the bloodstream contains the food materials needed by the cells and also serves to remove their wastes. As nutrients pass to the cells through the capillary walls, waste materials pass back through the walls into the bloodstream. Substances that are fat-soluble, such as oxygen and carbon dioxide, appear to diffuse directly through the layer of endothelial cells that forms the capillary wall. Very small molecules that are not fat-soluble appear to pass through tiny slits or pores that are formed where the endothelial cells join each other. Substances that do not fall into either of these categories are actively transported across the cells by enzymatic mechanisms that are as yet unknown.

ELVIN SMITH
University of Mississippi School of Medicine

CAPISTRAN, kə-pis′trən, **Saint John** (1386–1456), Italian preacher and reformer, who was one of the most prominent ecclesiastics of the 15th century. He was born at Capestrano (Aquilia), Italy, on June 24, 1386. He studied civil and canon law at Perugia, where he was appointed a judge in 1413. In 1415 he was taken prisoner by one of the warring factions in Perugia; this confinement led him to weigh the merits of his worldly life against his spiritual inclinations. Consequently when he was liberated he had his unconsummated marriage dissolved and joined the Franciscan Observants in Perugia.

John rapidly became famous as a preacher and served as a higher superior and official visitor of his order. Although he was largely responsible for the rapid growth of the Observants, he attempted, unsuccessfully, to prevent the Franciscan order from dividing permanently into Observants and Conventuals. As papal inquisitor he was severe against the Fraticelli (q.v.) and Jews.

Pope Eugene IV and other popes sought his advice and sent him as papal representative to mediate serious disputes in various parts of Italy. He was also active in Germany, Poland, Austria, Bohemia, and Moravia. The crusade against the Turks occupied him as a diplomat and preacher (1454–1456), and John, as much as Janós Hunyadi. was responsible for the victory of Belgrade in 1456, his last and most memorable accomplishment. He died in Ilok, Yugoslavia on Oct. 23, 1456. His feast day in March 28.

CAPITAL, in architecture, the crowning member of a column or pilaster. The function of the capital is to gather and concentrate on the shaft of the column the weight of the entablature or arch supported by it. Aesthetically, the capital provides a visual transition, through its moldings or sculpture, from the vertical shaft to the horizontal entablature.

The two capitals most common in ancient

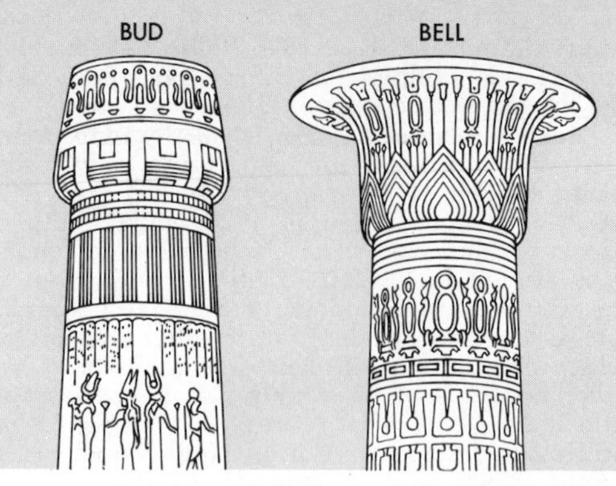

Egyptian architecture largely fail to serve these practical and aesthetic purposes. The tapering, bud-shaped capital, resembling a closed lotus, and the flaring campaniform, or bell-shaped, capital, inspired by the open lotus, support a square block that abruptly raises the entablature above the rim of the capital.

The three types of capitals most commonly used in Western architecture were developed in Greece. The Doric capital is composed of three superimposed sections—the necking, echinus, and abacus. The necking, separated from the shaft by a narrow groove, serves as a bed for the cushion-like echinus, which bulges out from the shaft. The echinus supports the square abacus that provides a larger bearing surface for the entablature. The repeated horizontal lines and the bulging curve of the echinus, afford a fine transition from the vertical to the horizontal. The distinguishing marks of the Ionic capital are the scrolls, or volutes, on either side that give extra support to the entablature. The Corinthian capital is a bell-shaped form adorned with two rows of acanthus leaves below small diagonal scrolls.

Rome adopted these three Greek forms, modified them in some details, and added the Tuscan form, a simplified version of the Doric, and the Composite form, a combination of Ionic scrolls and Corinthian leafage. Medieval capitals were composed of groups of moldings, with leafage derived ultimately from the Corinthian capital or with various animal designs influenced by Eastern styles. Classical forms were revived in the Renaissance and used in later neoclassical periods. See also COLUMN; GREEK ARCHITECTURE.

EVERARD M. UPJOHN
Columbia University

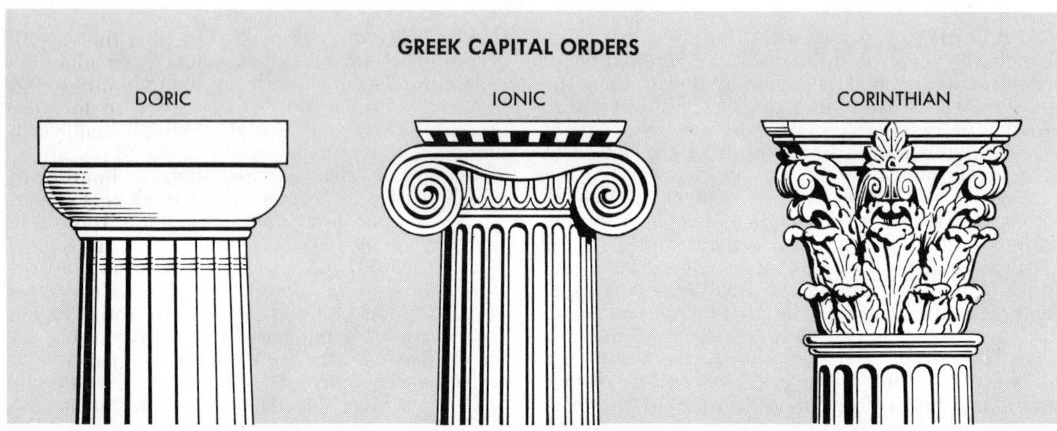

CAPITAL, in economics, has different meanings. Care must be taken, therefore, to indicate the sense in which the term is being used.

Historic Meanings. The term "capital" was used in the 16th and 17th centuries to mean either (1) the stock of money used for the purchase of physical commodities to be sold for a profit in trade and commerce or (2) the stocks of physical commodities themselves. "Capital" was thus given both a financial and a physical meaning, and there was confusion when the intended sense of the term was not clearly indicated. The terms "stock" and "capital" were used more or less synonymously when the English trading companies were established on a share basis in the 1500's and 1600's, and they became known as joint stock or capital stock companies.

Adam Smith, in *Wealth of Nations* (1776), used "capital" in both its financial and its physical meanings. John Stuart Mill, in *Principles of Political Economy* (1848), used "capital" to mean both (1) physical goods used in producing other goods and (2) a fund available for the hiring of labor. By the latter part of the 19th century, capital in the sense of physical goods used in the process of production was viewed as one of four basic factors of production, the others being land, labor, and organization (entrepreneurship). Neoclassical economists such as Alfred Marshall, in *Principles of Economics* (1st ed., 1890), also used this fourfold classification. A similar threefold classification of the productive factors as land, labor, and capital is still widely used in economic analysis.

Current Meanings. Capital as an economic concept is currently used in several different contexts. The broad term "capital goods" covers *fixed (durable) capital* in the form of factory buildings, machinery, commercial transportation equipment and facilities, communications equipment, power plants, distribution facilities, and many other items used to produce commodities or render services; and *nondurable (circulating) capital* in the form of inventories of finished goods and semifinished goods in the process of being fabricated into finished goods.

Fixed capital goods are acquired by business firms in the expectation that over their useful lifetime the added revenues they will contribute will be greater than the added costs involved in their acquisition and use. This relationship for an individual firm can be summarized in the following formula:

$$C = \frac{R_1}{(1+r)^1} + \frac{R_2}{(1+r)^2} + \frac{R_3}{(1+r)^3} + \dots + \frac{R_n}{(1+r)^n}$$

C represents the present *cost* to the firm of an additional unit of fixed capital. R_1, R_2, and so on represent the *anticipated net dollar returns* from the added capital during each year of its useful lifetime, and r represents the *rate of return* (the marginal efficiency of capital) that the capital good is expected to yield. The anticipated rate of return, r, can then be compared with the market rate of interest (cost of funds for investment) to see whether the acquisition of the additional fixed capital is economically justifiable.

Because fixed capital increases the productivity of the firms that use it, why does not an economy keep adding to its stock of this productive factor indefinitely? The answer rests on the fact that the production of fixed capital takes resources that otherwise could have been used for the production of directly consumable goods. Thus possession of more consumer goods in the future requires giving up a smaller amount of consumer goods in the present, and there are limits to the extent to which the public is willing to sacrifice present for future consumption. Because fixed capital increases productivity, a close relationship exists between a country's rate of capital accumulation and its rate of economic growth.

Specialized Current Meanings. There are also several other economic uses of the term "capital." *Social capital* (social overhead capital) means the kinds of capital available for public use in such facilities as highways, schools, and hospitals. *Human capital* is a country's productive population. *Capital stock,* in finance, means equity shares, common and preferred, sold by corporations to raise funds for investment in durable and nondurable capital goods. *Capital account* means the items in a firm's balance sheet that represents claims of the owners to assets of the business; it also means the items in a nation's balance of payments that arise as a result of an imbalance of payments on current account. In the latter balance-of-payments sense, capital account items include capital transfers (financial investment) and sales or purchases of gold and foreign exchange between countries.

WILLIAM P. SNAVELY
University of Connecticut

CAPITAL GAINS TAX, a tax imposed on the increase in the amount for which an asset is sold over its original purchase price, less any allowable depreciation.

Various techniques for taxing capital gains have been used by the countries employing this form of taxation. In the United States, short-term capital gains (gains on assets held no longer than six months) by individuals are taxed as regular income; long-term gains (on assets held over six months) are taxed at a maximum rate of 25%. Both short-term and long-term capital losses are deductible from capital gains within five years of the loss. U. S. corporations are also taxed on capital gains. Total revenue received from capital gains taxes is relatively small.

WILLIAM P. SNAVELY
University of Connecticut

CAPITAL LEVY, a tax designed to transfer to the government part of the value of the assets of individuals and businesses. It differs from an income tax, which is imposed on the income from assets. Proponents have advocated the capital levy primarily as a means of reducing the volume of war debt, easing wartime or postwar inflationary pressures, and reducing the inequities that result when some persons realize large financial gains in wartime while others endure major economic sacrifices.

Difficulties of administration have limited the use of this tax. It was tried in Austria, Czechoslovakia, Germany, Greece, Hungary, Italy, and Poland soon after World War I; in Italy and Hungary again in the 1920's; and in Austria, Ceylon, India, and West Germany in the post-World War II period. In most cases the results were poor. This type of tax is not highly regarded by most specialists in public finance.

WILLIAM P. SNAVELY
University of Connecticut

CAPITAL PUNISHMENT, kap'ə-təl pun'ish-mənt, is the infliction of the death penalty on persons convicted of a crime. As ideas about what crimes should be punishable by death have differed, so have the methods of inflicting this penalty. The criminal has been hanged, burned, boiled in oil, thrown to wild beasts, flayed alive, drowned, crushed, crucified, stoned, impaled, strangled, torn apart, beheaded, smothered, disemboweled, shot, gassed, or electrocuted.

Ancient Times. Capital punishment was common among all ancient civilizations. Egyptians, Babylonians, Assyrians, Hebrews, Persians, Greeks, and Romans prescribed it for a variety of crimes, including acts that today are considered minor offenses or no crimes at all. Thus death was decreed for malpractice in selling beer by the Code of Hammurabi, for idolatry by the law of the ancient Hebrews, for accidentally sitting on the king's throne by Persian law, for sacrilege by Greek law in the days of Pericles, and for stealing the keys to one's husband's wine cellar by the laws of the early Roman republic. The means of inflicting death in ancient times were varied, but they were characterized by a common barbarity. Executions were devised as great public spectacles where crowds might observe any one of a number of methods of killing criminals, including boiling in oil, flaying alive, stoning, or impaling. One of the most horrible ways of inflicting death in ancient times was the Persian method called "the boats." The condemned was put in one boat with another fitted over him. From these his head, hands, and feet protruded. Thus encased, he was forcibly fed with milk and honey, which were also smeared on his face. Exposed to the sun, he was eventually devoured alive by insects and vermin that swarmed about and bred within him.

Middle Ages to 18th Century. Throughout Europe during the Middle Ages, death was the penalty for a great many crimes. Criminals were drawn and quartered, broken on the wheel, burned at the stake, beheaded, hanged, or stretched on the rack. Before execution they were sometimes subjected to the most fiendish and excruciating tortures. Minor offenders were usually given some form of corporal punishment, such as branding, mutilation, or flogging. Imprisonment as punishment for crimes was not used to any great extent until the mid-16th century in England and the beginning of the 17th century on the Continent. Not until the beginning of the 19th century, however, did imprisonment replace capital and corporal penalties for many crimes.

At the end of the 15th century, England had eight major capital crimes: treason (including attempts and conspiracies), petty treason (killing one's husband), murder, larceny, robbery, burglary, rape, and arson. Many more offenses became capital crimes during the Tudor and Stuart periods, and the total increased under the first three Hanoverian kings to about 350 in 1780. Convicted traitors were cut down from the gallows while still alive. After their bowels had been extracted and burned before their eyes, they were beheaded and quartered. Every London district had its gallows, and corpses were sometimes left hanging as a warning to the "wicked." A man might hang for a long time before he died, but usually he was given brandy to dull his senses; and if the hangman felt inclined, he might pull on the legs of the prisoner to send him more quickly to his death. As late as 1819, according to one estimate, English law provided the death penalty for over 220 crimes, including such minor ones as shoplifting articles valued above five shillings, cutting down trees along an avenue or in a park, and shooting a rabbit.

Although the laws were not strictly enforced, courts handed down between 2,000 and 3,000 death sentences a year from 1805 to 1810. The severity of the laws, however, was considerably mitigated by the frequent refusal of judges or juries to convict, by the quashing of indictments on a technicality, by the arbitrary fixing of the value of the stolen article at less than that required for a capital crime, by royal pardon, and by benefit of clergy. As originally designed, benefit of clergy made clergymen subject to the generally lighter penalties of ecclesiastical courts, except in cases of high treason or arson. Gradually this benefit was extended to all who could read, protecting them from death if the crime could come under ecclesiastical jurisdiction and was a first felony offense. By the end of the 18th century, however, this benefit was almost meaningless.

As a result of these mitigating devices, by the 1800's executions apparently never exceeded 70 a year, even though all felonies carried a mandatory death sentence.

The American colonies inherited English jurisprudence but had no uniform criminal law, and the number of capital crimes varied from one jurisdiction to another. The Massachusetts Bay colony imposed death for many crimes, including idolatry, witchcraft, blasphemy, murder, assault, sodomy, adultery, rape, manstealing, perjury in a capital crime, and rebellion. In contrast, during the early days of the Pennsylvania colony, the death penalty was limited to crimes of treason and murder. But it is not known how vigorously early colonial laws were enforced. Benefit of clergy was never widely permitted in America. Hanging was the usual method of execution.

Effects of the Enlightenment. Both in Europe and America during the 18th century Enlightenment, strong social forces were effecting changes in the treatment of criminals. These forces were given added impetus by the French philosophers Montesquieu, Voltaire, Diderot, Turgot, and Condorcet and their British contemporaries David Hume, Adam Smith, Thomas Paine, and Jeremy Bentham. Inevitably, the sanguinary penal codes were condemned in the name of reason and humanity, the two compelling ideas of the 18th century. Expounding this philosophy, Cesare Beccaria's *Essay on Crimes and Punishments* (1764) became the theoretical basis for the great reforms in criminal law that followed in Europe and America. In England, the number of capital crimes was reduced to 15 by 1834, and to 4 by 1861. In America, agitation for abolition of the death penalty increased, and in 1845 the American Society for the Abolition of Capital Punishment was organized. Abolition bills were constantly before state legislatures, and in 1847 Michigan abolished capital punishment for all crimes except treason, becoming the first English-speaking jurisdiction to do so. Other states had meanwhile reduced the number of their capital crimes, and the tendency outside the South was to retain the death penalty only for murder, treason, and one or two other offenses.

20th Century. Capital punishment can be enforced for certain crimes in a majority of jurisdictions throughout the world. Even where it has been abolished for previously capital civilian crimes, such as murder or rape, it can frequently be inflicted for exceptional crimes, such as murder of a prison guard by a convict, or for treasonable offenses during or arising from war.

On June 29, 1972, the Supreme Court of the United States declared capital punishment, as then practiced, in violation of the constitutional prohibition against "cruel and unusual punishment." However, two justices in the narrow five to four majority did not say that the death penalty was inherently unconstitutional but that the discretion given judges and juries in imposing it made it arbitrary and discriminatory and therefore unconstitutional. It remained to be seen whether revised state laws allowing capital punishment would pass judicial scrutiny.

At the time of the historic Supreme Court decision only 16 of the 50 states had abolished capital punishment, and some of these retained it for exceptional crimes. Although the movement toward abolition had accelerated, it appeared that the Supreme Court's stand would not have been reached by even a majority of state legislatures for many years. Controversial executions, such as those of the convicted spies Julius and Ethel Rosenberg in 1953 and of Caryl Chessman, a convicted kidnapper, in 1960, lent fervor to the abolitionist campaign, but notorious crimes, including political assassinations and airplane hijackings, strengthened the arguments of supporters of capital punishment and led to laws increasing the types of capital offenses.

Elsewhere in the Western Hemisphere, the death penalty has been abolished in Canada (1967) and in almost all of the states in Mexico. Only a few Latin American countries retain it. Costa Rica, Ecuador, Nicaragua, and Venezuela abolished the death penalty before 1900.

In Europe the death penalty is in effect in all Communist states and in Greece, Turkey, Ireland, France, and Spain. It was eliminated early in the Netherlands (1870), Portugal (1867), and (de facto) in Liechtenstein (1798) and Luxembourg (1821); in Sweden in 1921 and Denmark in 1930; in Austria, Finland, West Germany, Iceland, and Italy during the 1940's; and as late as 1965 in Britain and 1969 in Vatican City State.

The death penalty has also been abolished in New Zealand (1961), in four of six states in Australia (1922–1968), in Nepal (1931), and in Israel (1954). It still exists in most Asian and African countries.

Criminal homicide and treason are widely classified as capital crimes, but the trend in most countries has been to reduce the number of other crimes punishable by death. Japanese law, for example, inflicts the death penalty for various criminal homicides, rape followed by death, arson causing death, and treason and related acts against the state. France prescribes the penalty for wrongful detention with torture and for perjury resulting in a death sentence, as well as for various criminal homicides, arson causing death, armed robbery, and treasonable act. The Soviet Union has inflicted the death penalty for economic crimes such as profiteering. In the 1970's Iran was executing opium smugglers.

In all countries, enforcement of the death penalty by civilian courts can be mitigated in some cases. Mental incompetence, however defined, generally exempts persons from the death penalty, and many jurisdictions prohibit its infliction on children below a certain age, usually 14, 16, or 18. In addition, some countries forbid its infliction on women. The laws regulating military personnel decree death for treason, espionage, desertion, and looting during war.

Number of Executions. In the 20th century there has been a decline in the number of executions in many countries maintaining the death penalty. In the United States between 1930 and 1972, the year of the Supreme Court decision, 3,859 civilian prisoners were executed. The number of executions had decreased from a high of 199 in 1935 to a low of one in 1966; two prisoners were executed in 1967. None were executed between 1968 and 1972. More than 600 prisoners were under sentence of death in 1972, apparently reprieved by the court. Of the total executed since 1930, 33 (less than 1%) were federal offenders, 3,335 (86.4%) had been convicted of murder, and 455 (11.8%) had been convicted of rape; 2,066 (53.5%) were Negroes, 1,751 (45.4%) were white, and 42 (1.1%) were of other races; and 32 (less than 1%) were women (20 white and 12 Negro). The U. S. Army (including the Air Force) executed 160 prisoners between 1930 and 1972; the Navy carried out no executions between 1949 and 1972.

Discretionary or Mandatory Penalties. The current trend is increasingly toward making the imposition of the death penalty discretionary rather than mandatory. In general, it is mandatory only in very serious offenses, such as murder or crimes against the security or integrity of the state. In the Soviet Union, Poland, and Yugoslavia the penalty is never mandatory.

Type of Execution. For many years governments believed that public executions were necessary to achieve the greatest retributive and deterrent effects. The authorities in some countries still hold to this point of view, but since the second half of the 19th century the general practice has been to exclude the public from executions.

As was seen, in earlier times methods of execution were greatly varied, sometimes attended by cruel tortures. Today the trend is toward relatively swift and painless methods of execution. Military executions are by firing squad almost everywhere, but civil authorities vary considerably in their methods, although most use hanging. Decapitation (by guillotine) is used in France and in a few Asian and African countries. In Spain the method is strangulation by the garrote. The electric chair and the gas chamber were most prevalent in the United States.

Debate on the Value of Capital Punishment. Arguments about the philosophy of punishment and its methods are largely meaningless unless presented in terms of a particular culture. The following discussion applies principally to the countries of Western civilization, especially the English-speaking countries.

Proponents and opponents of capital punishment argue in terms of its deterrent, retributive, economic, and socially protective effectiveness.

Deterrence. The most frequently advanced and widely accepted argument in favor of capital punishment is that fear of death deters people from committing crimes. Opponents contend that any fear of the death penalty is greatly reduced by the decrease in the number of jurisdictions using it, by the uncertainty of detection, the long delays in court procedures, and the unwillingness of many juries to convict in cases where the death penalty is mandatory, by the decline

WIDE WORLD

Capital punishment continues to be used in some nations as a deterrent to crime, especially in times of social or political unrest. Prisoners are sometimes executed in public as examples to potential wrongdoers.

in the number of executions, and by the nonpublic nature of executions. They argue that statistical studies, although not conclusive, indicate that the use of the death penalty has no significant effect on either the frequency of capital crimes or the safety of law-enforcement officers, and that the humanitarianism of modern society would probably defeat any effort to increase the use of capital punishment.

Proponents of capital punishment not only point to the inconclusiveness of statistical studies but also emphasize that the deterrent influence of the death penalty does not depend merely on the fear it may engender. By attaching this penalty to certain crimes, the law exerts a positive moral influence in the educational process. By strongly stigmatizing these acts, the law helps to develop attitudes of disgust and even horror for them. Further, proponents insist that the deterrent influence of the death penalty reaches across state lines into jurisdictions that have abolished it, and so all are benefited by its continued use in some areas.

Retribution. In favor of capital punishment, it has been insisted that the criminal should die because he has perpetrated a horrible crime, and that only his execution will satisfy the public and prevent it from taking the law into its own hands. Opponents of the death penalty argue that all the evidence points to the opposite conclusion. Many jurisdictions have abolished capital punishment; many others have reduced the number of capital offenses; and everywhere authorities have sought to make the method of execution as swift and painless as possible. Opponents also say that studies show no positive correlation between illegal lynchings for revenge and the elimination of the death penalty.

The proponents of capital punishment argue that retribution should not be construed as revenge. The almost universal desire for revenge must be kept in check and regulated in modern society by legal retribution if order is to be maintained. Retribution functions interrelatedly with reformation and deterrence, both of which must be expressed in terms of society's moral code. The principal function of retribution is to support this code and thus help unify society against those who violate it. In supporting the moral code, this argument continues, retribution increases the effectiveness of reformation and deterrence.

The law exacts retribution by attaching a penalty to each crime according to its seriousness as measured by the moral code. Thus, explain the proponents, the value of the life of the criminal, as measured by the moral code, may be less than such values as the security of the state, the sanctity of the home, or the life of the innocent victim. The law has always recognized the necessity of such a choice, and justifies killing in self-defense, in the prevention of a felony, in the lawful arrest of a felon, or in war against the enemies of a state. Indeed, proponents contend, not to kill in these cases would jeopardize the welfare of society. Just as the individual has the right and duty to kill to protect himself, so the state has the right and duty to take the life of a criminal to protect greater values, according to this argument.

Proponents further argue that there is no substitute for the death penalty in giving retribution its maximum effectiveness. Life imprisonment, usually advanced as a substitute, can readily be converted into early parole. Thus the malefactor may soon come to see no difference between the breaking of a window and the fracturing of another's skull. What often parades as humanitarianism is merely public indifference to dealing with delinquents and criminals. Such public lethargy endangers the moral code. Opponents, however, say that the limited enforcement of the death penalty has little effect on upholding the moral code.

Economy. Some proponents of capital punishment argue that it is cheaper to execute a prisoner than to keep him in an institution for life or a long term. Opponents insist that it is increasingly expensive to enforce the death penalty. Since a large segment of the public is against capital punishment, juries are more and more reluctant to convict those who may receive this penalty. For those who are convicted, the commonly used process of appealing the decision is costly to the state. Further, a prisoner committed to an institution may be able to support himself and his dependents and make restitution to his victim or to the surviving relatives. Moreover, say the opponents, the economic argument if carried further might be applied to all prisoners who are not self-supporting. If the argument is valid, all prisoners should be executed to save the taxpayer the expense of institutionalizing them. When extended this far, opponents contend, the absurdity of the economic argument becomes obvious.

Protection. A fourth argument in favor of capital punishment is that it protects society from dangerous criminals by ensuring that they will neither repeat their crimes nor pass on undesirable hereditary traits to their offspring. Opponents, however, adduce the following arguments: (1) The improvement of institutional rehabilitation programs and probation and parole procedures could reduce the possibility of sending dangerous persons back into the community. (2) People who commit noncapital offenses and are not executed may also have mental and physical defects, and the existence of such defects may not be related in any way to the causation of crime. (3) Mental and physical defects may be caused either by heredity or environment, and in many cases scientists are not able to determine the cause. (4) Many persons who are apparently normal may carry recessive defective genes and have defective children. Therefore, even if all persons who have hereditary defects could be identified and killed, the next generation would still have a new group of defective individuals. (5) Only a very small percentage of all criminals are executed, and, again, the number is declining. (6) The wealth, education, or social position of the accused, rather than his potential threat to society, may determine whether he receives the death penalty, and therefore the penalty can be, and indeed has been, applied arbitrarily. Moreover, society sometimes executes persons who are entirely innocent. Proponents agree that such an occurrence should be guarded against but argue that the possibility of executing innocent persons should not blind people to the important protective and retributive effect of the death penalty on persons of criminal intent.

The opponents of capital punishment have achieved some notable victories in recent decades. The death penalty, however, remains in the laws of most jurisdictions throughout the world. Apparently public opinion still strongly supports its use, at least for those crimes that are considered to offer the most serious threat to society.

ROBERT G. CALDWELL
State University of Iowa

Bibliography

Bedau, Hugo Adam, ed., *The Death Penalty in America* (Chicago 1964).
Caldwell, Robert G., *Criminology,* rev. ed. (New York 1965).
Radzinowicz, Leon, *A History of English Criminal Law,* vol. 1 (New York 1948).
Sellin, Thorsten, *The Death Penalty,* report for the American Law Institute (Philadelphia 1959).
United Nations, *Capital Punishment,* Publication No. 62–IV–2 (New York 1962).

CAPITAL SINS, kap′ə-təl sinz, in theology, are the wrongful desires or vicious affections that are the source and origin of habitual vice. Also called the *seven deadly sins,* they include pride, avarice, lust, anger, gluttony, envy, and sloth. These perverted desires, inclinations, or habits are basic to man's capacity for evil. Although the Bible does not list them specifically, one or more of them are described individually in different passages (pride, Ecclesiasticus 10:15; avarice, I Timothy 6:10; in I John 2:16 all the world's evil is attributed to "the lust of the flesh, the lust of the eyes, and the pride of life"). In the *Summa theologiae,* St. Thomas Aquinas enumerates and classifies the capital sins, lists relevant patristic texts, and provides a moral analysis of the sins.

Four of the capital sins involve a perverted pursuit of legitimate objectives. Pride and vanity are the distortions of normal self-respect. Avarice replaces a worthy ambition to succeed. Lust and gluttony destroy proportion and control in the rightful enjoyment of sex, eating, and drinking. The other three sins imply total rejection of legitimate objectives. Sloth is the refusal to produce the personal effort required to achieve one's goal. Envy and anger represent, in opposite ways, a diminution of self in comparison with the qualities or advantages of another person or persons.

CHARLES E. SHEEDY, C. S. C.
Notre Dame University

CAPITALISM, kap′ə-təl-iz-əm, is the type of economy in which capital is privately owned and may be freely used by the owners as they wish in attempting to make profits from their economic enterprises. This type of economy is known also as the *capitalistic system.* Implicit in capitalism is the existence of an effective technique for exchanging goods and services. In all but extremely primitive forms of capitalism this presupposes the existence of a monetary and financial system.

As used by economists, *capital* refers to (1) physical capital—the natural resources and man-made goods of various kinds used in the production of other goods and services; and (2) financial capital—the sums of money available for investment in capital goods.

The use of physical capital involves a "round-about method" of production because the capital goods themselves must first be produced before they can be used in producing other goods. The increase in productivity gained from the use of appropriate types of capital goods makes it worthwhile to devote time and resources to their production.

To avoid confusion of terminology it is important to understand that capital is used in all economic systems, from the most primitive through the most highly developed. But not all economies employing capital can be placed under the heading of capitalism. In the USSR the use and growth of capital are emphasized, but the ownership of capital is public rather than private. Therefore the system is identified as socialistic rather than capitalistic.

Another economic system employing capital is classified as fascism rather than capitalism. In fascism, capital may be privately owned and the owners may be permitted to make profits, but in many parts of the economy the government directs the use to which the capital may be put.

Even among economies classified as capitalistic there may be considerable variation from the conditions that characterize pure capitalism. The contemporary economy of the United States, which is regarded as an outstanding example of modern capitalism, is a mixed rather than a pure capitalistic system.

Historical Development. In the sense that the term "capitalism" may designate any economic system in which capital is privately owned and used by the owner as he wishes, capitalism is not of recent origin. Elements of this type of economic system may be traced to early historical periods. Even in the hunting and fishing stage of society, physical capital (crude weapons and tools) and financial capital (primitive money) were individually owned and used. Further capitalistic developments continued through the pastoral and agricultural stages and into the age of metals.

By the time of the Greek and Roman civilizations, capitalism had become fairly well developed. Productive establishments of substantial size were present in Greece and Rome, and extensive private capital resources were devoted to trade throughout the known world. Financial capital gained increased economic significance, and the techniques of banking became more highly developed.

After the decline of the Roman Empire, capitalistic elements in trade and manufacturing were greatly reduced in western Europe. Several centuries passed before towns, trade, and the production of nonagricultural commodities began to revive and then to expand rapidly. The revival of commercial capitalism in western Europe continued under the form of mercantilism from the 1500's through the latter 1700's as national states replaced towns in political importance.

Mercantilism was characterized by nationalistic economic policies. These were imposed to strengthen the national state by encouraging manufacturing and trade and by stimulating the growth of capital goods and capital funds. The extensive governmental direction given to economic activity under mercantilist capitalism distinguishes this system from pure capitalism. In the latter, capital would not only be privately owned but would also be used within a framework of freedom from governmental controls and regulations.

Economic Liberalism. During the 18th century a doctrine of economic liberalism was developed by a group of French thinkers, disciples of François Quesnay, who were known as *physiocrats*. They believed that the natural laws that Sir Isaac Newton and others had developed to explain the phenomena of the physical world had their counterpart in a natural order that was applicable to economic, social, and political relationships. To achieve this natural order, they believed that it was necessary to eliminate artificial restrictions upon individual behavior. They wanted to reduce the activities of the state to police protection of the individual and his property, the administration of justice, and the performance of certain necessary public works. This philosophy of liberalism, known as the doctrine of *laissez-faire,* was supported by C. M. V. de Gournay, Anne Robert Jacques Turgot, Pierre Samuel du Pont de Nemours, and others. Du Pont edited a collection of Quesnay's writings that was published in 1756 under the title *Physiocratie*. The laissez-faire doctrine was quite at variance with the doctrine of mercantilism, and it provided an important foundation for the development of a more complete philosophy of capitalism by Adam Smith.

In his famous work, *An Inquiry into the Nature and Causes of the Wealth of Nations,* published in 1776, Adam Smith was highly critical of mercantilist economic controls. He applauded the laissez-faire concept advanced by the physiocrats. But Smith went beyond the physiocrats in emphasizing the beneficial economic effects that would flow from the exercising of individual self-interest within the framework of a laissez-faire policy by government. He believed that if each individual sought his own interest, a driving force of competition would develop throughout the economy. This force, he felt, would provide the best answers to the basic economic questions of what commodities should be produced, by what means, how much of each, and how the output of the economy should be distributed. The philosophy of pure capitalism advanced by Adam Smith was thus both simple and optimistic. By reducing the role of government to a bare minimum and by permitting the free play of competition, capitalism would maximize the material well-being of society.

Smith's emphasis upon individual economic self-interest reflected the increasing freedom from religious control that businessmen had gained during the mercantilist period. Before that time religious teachings had been antimaterialistic and had condemned attempts by individuals to climb to a higher level of living through economic activity.

In advocating the laissez-faire competitive economic system, Smith did not call it "capitalism." This name was applied by socialist critics of the system, one of the severest of whom was Karl Marx in the mid-19th century.

Modern Capitalism. Smith's doctrine of laissez-faire and competition was propounded during the early stages of the Industrial Revolution. This revolution produced a rapid capitalistic development—first in England and then in other countries. When the *Wealth of Nations* was written, the profound impact upon industrialization that was to follow the introduction of steam- and water-powered machinery could not be clearly foreseen. Yet Smith's doctrine, when implemented, greatly encouraged the development of the industrial stage of capitalism that replaced the commercial stage in the 19th century.

Serious economic problems accompanied the Industrial Revolution in England as it advanced rapidly during the last quarter of the 18th century and continued into the first half of the 19th century. One was a surplus of industrial labor. The conversion from diversified farming to sheep raising resulted in a marked reduction in the number of agricultural workers required. Workers uprooted from the soil drifted to urban centers in greater numbers than could be easily absorbed into industrial jobs, particularly at a time when machine power was replacing manpower in production. The relatively large supply of labor available during much of the Industrial Revolution period in England led to extremely low wages, long hours, and poor working conditions for men, women, and children.

This oppressive phase of capitalistic development drew much socialist criticism. Marx and others tended to generalize from the unfortunate aspects of the Industrial Revolution and to conclude that the exploitation of labor was an inherent evil of capitalism. Marx predicted that under capitalism cyclical fluctuations in business activity would become increasingly severe. This would cause more and more members of the capitalist class to be reduced to the ranks of the proletariat. Eventually, he predicted, the increasing misery of the proletarian class would lead it to overthrow the capitalistic system and replace it with some form of socialism.

The actual development of capitalism in England during the second half of the 19th century was quite different from Marx's prediction. Under a relatively laissez-faire government policy, industry and commerce prospered greatly, and the earlier surplus of labor was overcome. During this period the level of living of British workers rose substantially as they shared in the general economic expansion.

U.S. Capitalism. In the United States, rapid industrialization followed quickly after the Civil War. Here, too, a relatively laissez-faire policy on the part of government provided an atmosphere favorable to industrial growth. The industrial stage of capitalism that developed in the United States during the last quarter of the 19th century evolved quickly into the financial stage as financiers gained control of large industrial combinations. In oil, steel, and other areas, strong monopoly positions were attained. During the 1890's Congress found it necessary to pass antitrust legislation to protect the public from monopolistic exploitation.

Problems arising from depressions, such as those of 1907, 1920–21, and the 1930's, and from participation in two world wars caused the United States to deviate further from a purely laissez-faire policy during the 20th century. Less than purely competitive conditions developed in much of the business sector and also over much of the labor sector (with the growth of strong unions), and there was increasing government control and regulation of the economy. As a result, the economic system of the United States differs markedly today from the laissez-faire competitive system described by Adam Smith.

Because government intervention in the economy is limited and wide scope for individual initiative remains, and because competition—though not pure—is still extremely vigorous throughout much of the economy, the economic system of the United States is basically one of capitalism. It is classified as a mixed capitalistic system, however, in recognition of its deviation from the model of pure capitalism. Examples of restrictions affecting workers and industrial firms include laws to prohibit child labor, to set safety standards, to protect workers' rights to bargain collectively, to establish minimum wages, to set tariffs and quotas on imports, to regulate rates charged by public utilities, and to enforce pure food and drug standards. Financial institutions also face numerous legal limitations. Banks, for instance, are regulated as to the maximum interest rates they may pay on deposits.

The capitalistic system has proved, particularly in the United States, to be both flexible and durable. It has been possible through a process of adaptation to deal with the problems of war, cyclical fluctuations, and long-continued international tensions that have required large expenditures for armaments. Because the system is dynamic rather than static, further adaptations are to be expected as new problems arise.

See also BUSINESS CYCLES; CAPITAL; ECONOMICS; FREE ENTERPRISE; LAISSEZ-FAIRE; MERCANTILISM; SOCIALISM.

WILLIAM P. SNAVELY
University of Connecticut

Bibliography

Ebenstein, William, *Today's Isms: Communism, Fascism, Capitalism, Socialism,* 4th ed. (Englewood, N. J., 1964).
Friedman, Milton, *Capitalism and Freedom* (Chicago 1962).
Galbraith, John Kenneth, *American Capitalism* (Boston 1956).
Hacker, Louis M., *The Triumph of American Capitalism* (New York 1940; paperback ed., New York 1965).
Hayek, Friedrich A., ed., *Capitalism and the Historians* (Chicago 1954).
Heilbroner, Robert L., *Limits of American Capitalism* (New York 1966).
Hoover, Calvin B., *The Economy, Liberty, and the State* (New York 1959).
Kelso, Louis O., and Adler, Mortimer J., *Capitalist Manifesto* (New York 1958).
Kelso, Louis O., and Adler, Mortimer J., *New Capitalists* (New York 1961).
Marx, Karl, *Das Kapital* ed. by Max Eastman, Modern Library ed. (New York 1932).
Monsen, R. Joseph, *Modern American Capitalism: Ideologies and Issues* (Boston 1963).
Pigou, Arthur C., *Socialism Versus Capitalism* (London 1939).
Rand, Ayn, *Capitalism, The Unknown Ideal* (New York 1966).
Shonfield, Andrew, *Modern Capitalism* (New York and London 1965).
Schumpeter, Joseph A., *Capitalism, Socialism, and Democracy,* 3d ed. (New York 1950).
Tawney, Richard H., *Religion and the Rise of Capitalism* (New York 1926).
Wallich, Henry C., *Cost of Freedom* (New York 1960).
Weber, Max, *The Protestant Ethic and the Spirit of Capitalism* (London 1930).
Wright, David McCord, *Capitalism* (New York 1951).

CAPITALS are the large letters (majuscules) used in writing and printing, as distinguished from the smaller letters (minuscules). From the times of ancient Greece and Rome until about the 10th century A. D., all books were written without any distinction regarding the size of letters. But gradually it became the practice to begin a book (later, also, the chief divisions and sections of a book) with a large capital letter, usually illuminated and often richly ornamented. Today, the initial letters of certain words, particularly proper nouns, and of all words in certain positions (as at the beginning of sentences or as items in lists) are printed or written as capitals. See also ALPHABET; WRITING.

CAPITOL is a name first applied to the southern summit of one of the hills of Rome, the Mons Capitolinus, on which the Temple of Jupiter was built, and later applied to the entire hill. "Capitol" was also the name of the temple.

The southern and northern summits of the Capitoline Hill are separated by a depression that today is occupied by the Piazza del Campidoglio (Capitol Square), designed by Michelangelo and finished in the 17th century. The Arx, or fortified citadel, stood on the northern summit, as did the Temple of Juno Moneta (344 B. C), which was later occupied by the Roman mint. The Temple of Concordia (216 B. C) and the Auguraculum, the primitive hut used by augurs when they took auspices, were also on this summit.

The original Capitoline Hill, once very steep and accessible only from the Forum, was greatly changed by construction and erosion. The hill was always more of a citadel and religious sanctuary than an inhabited area. Here the first sacrifices were offered each year; frequently the Senate held its first meeting of the year on the hill, and triumphant generals advanced to the Temple of Jupiter and made sacrifices.

The Capitoline Temple, begun by Tarquinius Priscus, the fifth king of Rome, was not dedicated until the first year of the republic (509 B. C). Although traditionally associated with Jupiter, the temple was actually dedicated to the Etruscan triad of deities, Jupiter, Juno, and Minerva. The temple was divided into three *cellae* (chambers), one for each of the gods, and within each *cella* stood a statue of the god to which it was dedicated. This was the largest, one of the earliest, and most magnificent of Rome's temples. It stood approximately 200 feet (61 meters) long and 185 feet (56 meters) wide, with 3 rows of 6 columns each across the front and 4 columns along each side. The temple was burned in 83 B. C., 69 A. D., and 80 A. D., and had to be replaced each time. Embellishments were often made upon the old foundation. The "Golden Capitol" was legendary for the wealth of its gilding, gold plating, and rich offerings. Its wealth attracted the attention of the advancing barbarians in the 4th and 5th centuries, and the temple was plundered of all its riches. Today only the tufa platform of the original structure is still partially visible.

According to tradition, the Capitol got its name in the 6th century B. C. when the foundations for the Temple of Jupiter were being dug. A head (*caput*) was uncovered, supposed to be that of a mythical hero, Tollius. Thus the Western world obtained the name that is almost universally used for the political center of a state.

RICHARD E. MITCHELL, *University of Illinois*

FRED WARD, FROM BLACK STAR

THE U. S. CAPITOL in Washington, D. C., stands at the eastern end of a long mall. At the western end rises the obelisk of the Washington Monument, with the Lincoln Memorial behind it, and the Potomac River in the distance.

CAPITOL, United States, kap'ə-təl, the building in Washington, D. C., where the Congress of the United States conducts its legislative sessions. The Senate meets in a chamber in the north wing of the Capitol and the House of Representatives in a similar chamber in the south wing. Visitors are permitted in the galleries of the legislative chambers when Congress is in session. Other important rooms in the Capitol which may be visited by the public include the rotunda, decorated with paintings and statues and rising 180 feet (55 meters) under the Capitol's huge dome, and Statuary Hall, which contains statues of distinguished American citizens.

Because of its great size, central location, and elevated position on Capitol Hill, the Capitol dominates the Washington skyline. Below it, to the west, the broad grassy Mall stretches past the Washington Monument to the Lincoln Memorial on the bank of the Potomac River, about 2½ miles (4 km) in the distance. Just east of the Capitol grounds are the handsome Supreme Court Building and the Library of Congress. Twelve of Washington's major thoroughfares converge on the beautifully landscaped grounds of the Capitol.

The Capitol has been the legislative center of the United States since 1800. It is built of sandstone and marble in the classic style of architecture, principally Roman with some Greek and some Renaissance details. The building itself is 751 feet 4 inches (213.76 meters) long and 350 feet (106.68 meters) wide. It contains 16½ acres (6⅔ hectares) of floor space. The height of the Capitol, to the top of the 19½-foot (6-meter) statue of Freedom on the great dome, is 287 feet 5½ inches (87.65 meters). The dome, which is one of the largest in the world, actually consists of two cast-iron shells, an exterior and an interior one. A steep stairway between the shells leads to the cupola under the bronze statue of *Freedom.*

The Capitol was one of the first two buildings planned for a new "Federal City" in the District of Columbia, when land for the district was acquired by the government in 1791. The other building was to be the President's House, which is now known as the White House. President George Washington and his secretary of state, Thomas Jefferson, selected Major Pierre Charles L'Enfant, a young French engineer and veteran of the American Revolution, to plan the new city.

Major L'Enfant decided to place the Capitol near the center of the city, on what was then called Jenkins' Hill. Approximately 1½ miles (2½ km) to the northwest, L'Enfant located the President's House. He then planned for a mall, 400 feet (120 meters) wide, leading westward to the Potomac. And at the point where a line drawn due west from the center of the Capitol intersects a line drawn due south from the center of the President's House, he fixed the site for a monument to George Washington.

In 1791 the commissioners of the District of Columbia voted to change the name "Federal

City" to Washington, after the President. In March of the following year, Jefferson proposed to the commissioners that a prize of $500, or a medal of that value, be offered for the "most approved plan" for a Capitol and a President's House.

Architects of the Capitol. Of the 14 designs submitted for the Capitol, none was judged satisfactory. But Stephen Hallet (Étienne Sulpice Hallet), a French architect of Philadelphia, was asked to rework a design which the commissioners thought might prove acceptable. The competition for the design of the President's House was won by James Hoban, an architect from Charleston, S. C.

While Hallet struggled to make satisfactory revisions in his plan for the Capitol, the commissioners received a communication from William Thornton, a young physician, painter, and inventor turned amateur architect, who had been born in the Virgin Islands, studied medicine in Edinburgh, lived in Paris, and moved to the United States in 1787. Writing from the Virgin Islands in October 1792—three months after the competition had officially closed—Thornton asked permission to compete. Dissatisfied with the drawings already received, the commissioners agreed to consider his design.

On Jan. 31, 1793, Thornton's still unfinished drawings were submitted to President Washington, who later praised the plan for its "grandeur, simplicity, and convenience." The plan called for a nearly square central section surmounted by a low dome and flanked on the north and south by rectangular wings, each 126 feet (38½ meters) long and 120 feet (36½ meters) wide.

On April 5, 1793, the commissioners accepted Thornton's design. President Washington gave his approval on July 25, and work on construction began that same month. On Sept. 18, 1793, the cornerstone was laid by the President.

Development of the Thornton plan began with the construction of the north wing of the Capitol under the direction of Hoban and Hallet. Virginia sandstone, from nearby Aquia Creek, was selected for the building material. Hoban, who was in charge of work on both the Capitol and the President's House, evidently spent most of his time superintending construction of the executive mansion. Hallet, his assistant at the Capitol, persisted in trying to alter Thornton's design. Eventually it was discovered that Hallet's foundation plan did not match the original drawings and Hallet was discharged. At President Washington's request, Thornton was asked to proceed with the building according to his original plans.

Hoban continued to superintend the work until Oct. 15, 1795, when George Hadfield, a graduate of the Royal Academy in London, arrived to take charge. Hadfield, like Hallet, was not content just to direct the work but soon began to make changes in Thornton's plans. The commissioners allowed him to continue until the expiration of his contract on May 10, 1798, when supervision was again entrusted to Hoban.

The Original Capitol: 1800–1851. The north, or Senate, wing of the Capitol was completed in 1800. Records, archives, and furniture were brought by ship from Philadelphia, the former seat of the federal government, in October 1800. Congress convened in the Capitol for the first time on November 21. President John Adams addressed the members the following noon and congratulated them "on the prospect of a residence

WILLIAM R. BIRCH—LIBRARY OF CONGRESS—U. S. CAPITOL HISTORICAL SOCIETY

THE U. S. CAPITOL OF 1800 actually consisted of no more than the original north, or Senate, wing.

KIPLINGER COLLECTION—U. S. CAPITOL HISTORICAL SOCIETY

A WOODEN DOME sheathed with copper covered the rotunda connecting the wings of the Capitol in 1829.

KIPLINGER COLLECTION—U. S. CAPITOL HISTORICAL SOCIETY

THE CAPITOL IN 1871 looked much as it does today. Recent additions have not altered its basic design.

WINSTON POTE, FROM A. DEVANEY

THE CAPITOL DOME, as seen above the east front, is brilliantly silhouetted against the night sky.

not to be changed." The Senate then consisted of 32 members from 16 states, and there were 105 members of the House of Representatives.

On March 6, 1803, President Jefferson appointed Benjamin Henry Latrobe to be surveyor of public buildings and placed him in charge of construction at the Capitol. Latrobe's qualifications were impressive. He was a trained architect and civil engineer, who once had served as surveyor of public offices in London and had declined the office of surveyor to the crown in 1795 to come to America.

In 1801, while Hoban was still in charge of the work, there was erected within the half-completed south, or House, wing an elliptical one-story brick structure, whose arched roof and inside temperature caused it to be known as the "Oven." After one session, however, the House gave up the Oven and Latrobe dismantled it to build a more satisfactory enclosure. Although Latrobe was aware of deficiencies in Thornton's plan, it was of course necessary that the design of the south wing correspond to that of the already completed north wing.

The House of Representatives occupied its new legislative chamber in 1807, although the entire south wing was not completed until 1811. At this time the House and Senate wings were joined by a wooden arcade, 145 feet (44 meters) in length, spanning the area where the rotunda now stands. Between the wings were two wells of drinking water. Although weather and souvenir hunters damaged the uncompleted building, work on the Capitol continued at a steady pace.

Then a great and unexpected setback occurred during the War of 1812. On the night of Aug. 24, 1814, a British expeditionary force commanded by Adm. Sir George Cockburn set fire to the Capitol. Only the walls of the building were left standing.

When Congress convened in the fall of 1814, it had to meet in the only government building not burned—Blodget's Hotel, at E and 7th Streets, N.W. In order to forestall agitation for removal of the government from Washington, a group of citizens had a meeting place for Congress constructed on the present site of the Supreme Court Building. Known as the Old Brick Capitol, this

CAPITOL FLOOR PLAN AND SOME IMPORTANT ROOMS

1. COMMITTEE ON APPROPRIATIONS
2. HOUSE CHAMBER
3. SPEAKER'S OFFICE
4. COMMITTEE ON WAYS AND MEANS
5. STATUARY HALL
6. HOUSE MINORITY LEADER
7. ROTUNDA
8. SENATE MINORITY LEADER
9. SENATE MAJORITY LEADER
10. SENATE CHAMBER
11. PRESIDENT'S ROOM
12. MARBLE (READING) ROOM
13. VICE PRESIDENT'S FORMAL OFFICE
14. SENATE RECEPTION OFFICE
15. VICE PRESIDENT

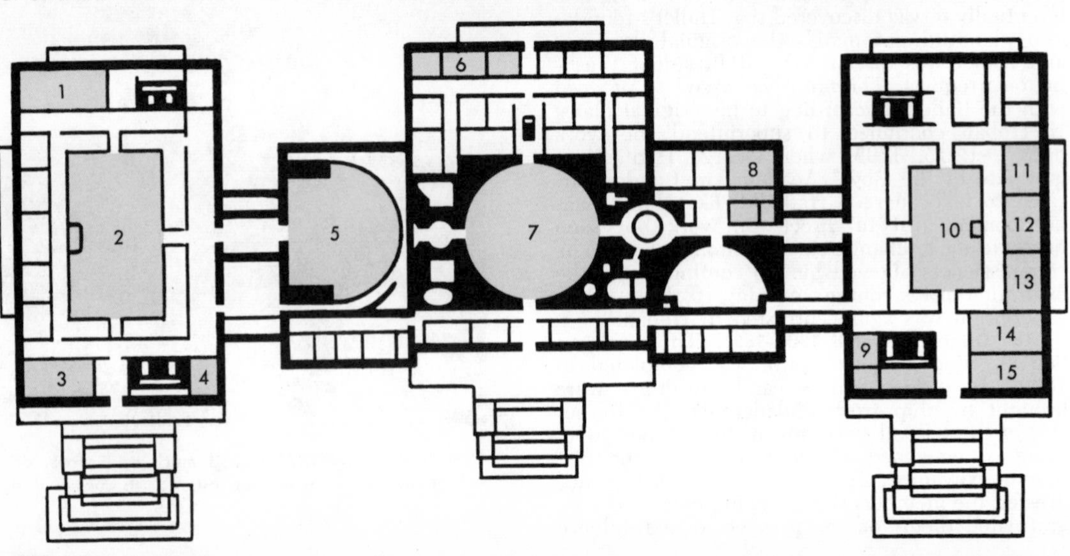

THE ROTUNDA under the great dome contains sculpture and paintings of men and events in American history.

EWING GALLOWAY

structure functioned as the home of Congress from 1815 until the war-scarred Capitol was restored to use in 1819.

In December 1817, Latrobe resigned and was succeeded by New England's leading architect, Charles Bulfinch. Like Dr. Thornton, Bulfinch had had no formal academic training in his chosen profession, but unlike Dr. Thornton, he had devoted himself seriously to the study of architecture. During Bulfinch's tenure of office, John Trumbull, Connecticut artist and Revolutionary War veteran, executed four well-known historical paintings that still hang in the rotunda. Each one measures 12 by 18 feet (3.6 by 5.4 meters) and cost $8,000.

In 1829, Bulfinch completed construction of the original Capitol, which has since been remodeled and enlarged. At that time, the two wings were connected by a rotunda which was 97 feet (30 meters) in diameter and crowned with a wooden, copper-covered dome 150 feet (46 meters) high. The original building had about one half the length and slightly more than one third the width of the present Capitol. It was 351 feet long by 131 feet wide (107 by 40 meters).

Remodeling the Capitol. The appointment of Charles Bulfinch was terminated on June 25, 1829, and there was no architect of the Capitol until June 11, 1851, when President Millard Fillmore appointed Thomas Ustick Walter to be architect for a necessary enlargement of the Capitol. At that time, there were 62 senators and 232 members of the House of Representatives crowded into their respective chambers. To accommodate this greatly increased membership, Walter planned to add new and larger Senate and House chambers onto the north and south wings. To balance the elongated wings, he suggested constructing a larger iron dome to replace the original one of copper-covered wood.

President Fillmore laid the cornerstone for the extensions on July 4, 1851. The present chamber for the House of Representatives was completed and occupied on Dec. 16, 1857. Two years later, on Jan. 4, 1859, the Senate moved into its new chamber. In 1860 the Supreme Court took over the old Senate chamber, and in 1864 the old House chamber became National Statuary Hall by act of Congress. The tumult of the Civil War did not interrupt work on the Capitol. While Union and Confederate armies met in bitter battles not far from Washington, workmen swung into place the sections of the Capitol's huge dome. And on Dec. 2, 1863, a great crowd gathered to watch Thomas Crawford's bronze sculpture of *Freedom* placed on top of the dome.

Walter resigned as architect of the Capitol in 1865 and was succeeded by Edward Clark, who served until 1902. Under Clark's supervision the Library of Congress was moved to its own building in 1897; Constantino Brumidi finished most of his mural decorations; and landscaping of the west, north, and south terraces by Frederick Law Olmsted was completed between 1844 and 1892. Clark's successor, Elliot Woods, supervised construction of the first House and Senate office buildings, which were built between 1903 and 1909.

On Aug. 22, 1923, David Lynn was appointed architect of the Capitol by President Calvin Coolidge. During his 31 years in office, Lynn contributed greatly to the efficient operation of government on Capitol Hill. He directed construction of an additional House Office Building; completed the Senate Office Building; constructed the Supreme Court Building; relocated the Botanic Garden and constructed its new conservatory; built the Library of Congress Annex; and renovated the legislative chambers, adding air conditioning and improving the lighting and acoustics.

J. George Stewart became architect of the Capitol in 1954, by appointment of President Dwight D. Eisenhower. Under provisions of the Legislative Appropriations Act of 1956, Stewart accomplished the Capitol's first major structural change in nearly a century. A new marble east front, faithfully reproducing the design of the old sandstone front, was constructed 32½ feet (9.9 meters) east of the original walls. The latter were retained to serve as interior walls. Work on the new extension began in 1958 and was completed in 1962, adding 100 rooms at a total cost of $11,400,000. Congress then turned its attention to the west central front. After careful study of an engineering survey conducted in 1965, $300,000 was appropriated for preliminary plans, a model, and estimates of cost for an extension in marble of the west central front of the Capitol.

Generally speaking, the plans for remodeling and expanding the Capitol have successfully preserved the character of the original building. In recent years some architects have criticized the widening of the central building and the use of marble instead of the original sandstone. But the Capitol continues to be the preferred attraction in Washington, the tourist capital of America, and the average American seems to approve of changes that make the Capitol appear more imposing.

FRED SCHWENGEL
U. S. Capitol Historical Society

CAPITOL REEF NATIONAL MONUMENT, established in 1937, covers approximately 60 square miles (155 sq km) in south central Utah. The area, traversed by the Fremont River, is notable for weirdly shaped rocks, pinnacles, arches, cliffs, and narrow, high-walled gorges. In the variety of its brilliantly colored erosional formations, Capitol Reef National Monument rivals Bryce Canyon and Zion national parks, which lie to the southwest.

The "reef" that gives the monument its name is a formidable uplift of sandstone cliffs, 20 miles (32 km) long. "Capitol" refers to the dome-shaped white cap rock, resembling a capitol dome, along the Fremont River.

Prehistoric Indian remains, including pictographs and petroglyphs on the cliff walls, and areas of petrified forest also can be seen in the monument. Vegetation of desert and semidesert types and small wildlife are abundant.

CAPITOLINE GAMES, kap'ə-tə-līn, games held annually in ancient Rome in celebration of the deliverance of the city from the Gauls and in honor of Jupiter Capitolinus, to whom the Romans ascribed the salvation of the Capitol in the hour of danger. The games were instituted in 387 B.C., after the departure of the Gauls, on the motion of Marcus Furius Camillus. The guild of the Capitolini, whose members were chosen from those who lived on the Capitol, were in charge of the games. In time the games appear to have been discontinued. However, in 86 A.D., Emperor Domitian reinstituted Capitoline games that were held every four years down to a late period of the empire.

CAPITOLINE HILL. See CAPITOL.

CAPITULARY, kə-pich'ə-ler-ē, a document publishing new laws and administrative rules. Possibly influenced by Lombard practice, Charlemagne introduced this form of promulgation into Gaul with his Capitulary of Heristal, issued in 779. Both Charlemagne and his son Louis the Pious used the capitulary frequently as emperors of the Carolingian Empire. Their descendants used it rarely. Lambert of Spoleto, king of the Lombards, issued the last capitulary in Italy in 898. The name "capitulary" comes from the Latin word for the document, *capitulare*, derived from Latin *capitula*, meaning "chapters" or "articles."

Unlike standard decrees, charters, and privileges, capitularies usually lacked an address, subscription, witnesses, and a statement of date and place of issue. With rare exceptions, capitularies were a series of headings without the chapters (*capitula*) they were meant to introduce.

One major kind of capitulary includes answers to questions from *missi dominici* (royal inspectors) and supplemental instructions to them. Another type of capitulary consists of two kinds of memorandums: rules that modify existing tribal laws, and rules that break new ground, having originative force. Within these limits, distinctions exist between Frankish and Italian capitularies and between ecclesiastical, temporal, and mixed capitularies.

Two things gave capitularies legal force: the king's command to obey the rules (the *bannum regis*), the consensus of the Kingdom's most powerful men, expressed particularly by the king's Diet, which included both clergy and laity.

K. F. MORRISON
University of Chicago

CAPITULATIONS, kə-pich-ə-lā'shənz, was the name given to the trading concessions, embodying extraterritorial privileges, granted by the Ottoman sultan to European merchants resident in the Ottoman Empire. These were in the form of treaties with the respective countries, and the articles (*capitula*) of the treaties defined the nature and scope of the concessions and exemptions.

The precedents for such commercial treaties go back to Byzantine relations with such states as Venice, Genoa, and Pisa. While such privileges were continued under the early Ottomans, the Capitulations assumed a new significance with the treaty of 1535 between the sultan and France. By this treaty French merchants were permitted to trade throughout the Empire, and obliged to pay only such taxes and duties as were levied on Ottoman subjects; moveover, they were recognized as being under the jurisdiction of their own ambassador and, in general, subject only to the laws of their own country. In 1580 the English were granted capitulatory rights couched in similar terms, and there began a rivalry between France and England that was as much concerned with the gaining of influence at the sultan's court as with commerce.

With the accession of each new sultan, these treaties had to be renewed, and as the Ottoman state went into decline, the provisions of the Capitulations were gradually expanded so as virtually to exclude Ottoman Turks from the commercial life of the empire. Merchants belonging to the Christian minorities that were subject to the Ottomans could place themselves under the protection of a foreign embassy and enjoy the same privileges as its nationals; this situation was to lead the foreign powers to regard themselves as the lawful custodians of the rights of these minorities. In 1774 Russia gained its Capitulation and became thereby the protector of the Orthodox Christians and the Slavs within the Ottoman Empire. In the second half of the 19th century Western capitalism, too, exploited the advantages of the capitulatory system by means of loans and investments that reduced the Ottoman Empire to the status of an economic fief. The Capitulations were finally abolished by the Treaty of Lausanne (July 24, 1923) concluded between the Turkish Republic and the Western powers after World War I. See also EXTRATERRITORIALITY.

JOHN R. WALSH, *University of Edinburgh*

CAPODISTRIAS, kap-ō-dis'trē-əs, **Ioannes Antoniou** (1776–1831), Greek statesman, who was prominent in the Russian foreign service and later in the Greek War of Independence. Sometimes known as Count Capo d'Istria, he was born of a noble family on Corfu on Feb. 11, 1776. In 1803 he became secretary of state of the Septinsular Republic, consisting of the Ionian Islands, which was established in 1800 under Russian protection; France regained the islands after the Peace of Tilsit in 1807. Capodistrias left Corfu and entered the Russian diplomatic service in 1809. From late 1816 he shared the direction of Russia's foreign ministry with Count Karl Nesselrode. In 1822, Capodistrias took an indefinite leave of absence from Russian service and spent the next five years in Switzerland, devoting himself to the Greek cause from his retreat in Geneva.

On April 14, 1827, a revolutionary assembly elected him president of Greece. Arriving in Greece in January 1828, he tried to build up a centralized administration. When Prince Leopold of Saxe-Coburg was chosen by the great powers to become sovereign prince of Greece, Capodistrias wrote him deploring conditions in the country and asking that the boundaries of the Greek state be greater than those delineated by the powers. Leopold rescinded his acceptance of the Greek throne, and Capodistrias was accused of deliberately having discouraged the prince in order to maintain his own position. Meanwhile, Capodistrias' authoritarian ways and his pro-Russian attitude antagonized many other leaders of the war of independence, including the powerful Mavromichalis family. On Oct. 9, 1831, two members of the family assassinated him as he was going to church in the revolutionary capital, Nauplia (Návplion).

GEORGE J. MARCOPOULOS
Tufts University

CAPONE, kə-pōn′, **Al** (1899–1947), Chicago gangster, who was the symbol of prohibition era lawlessness. Alfonso (or Alphonse) Capone was born on Jan. 17, 1899, in Naples, Italy, the son of an impoverished barber. He spent his formative years in petty crime in South Brooklyn, N. Y., where he received a razor slash on his left cheek, from ear to lip, the source of his nickname "Scarface." In the 1920's, Capone worked as a bodyguard for Johnny Torrio, a notorious Chicago gangster. After Torrio left Chicago, Capone became undisputed head of an enormous regional criminal syndicate whose operations included such varied underworld activities as gambling, prostitution, and—preeminently—the illegal sale of liquor.

Government agencies later estimated that his wealth by 1927 was close to $100 million. He remained immune to prosecution for his many crimes, including the St. Valentine's Day massacre of 1929, when his gunners, dressed as policemen, killed eight rival gang members. In June 1931, he was finally indicted for income tax evasion. In October he was found guilty and sentenced to 11 years in prison and fined $70,000. He was imprisoned in Atlanta and then on Alcatraz Island, in California. In January 1939 he was released, a slack-jawed paretic. He retired to his Miami Beach, Fla., estate, where he died on Jan. 25, 1947.

JAMES D. HORAN
Author of "The Desperate Years"

CAPORETTO, Battle of, kä-pō-rāt′tō, the Austrian-German offensive of October-December 1917 that nearly caused Italy's collapse in World War I. For two years Italian armies commanded by Gen. Luigi Cadorna had been attacking the Austrians along the Isonzo River, north of the Adriatic Sea. To relieve the pressure, German troops were sent to attack Italy. On Oct. 24, 1917, Gen. Otto von Below's Fourteenth Army, of German and Austrian divisions, surged forward in the first major test of new German tactics. Results exceeded expectations. Other Austrian armies joined the attack. British and French divisions rushed to Italy's assistance.

The attackers had planned to stop at the Tagliamento River but their pursuit continued to the Piave River. In November the Italians, now led by Gen. Armando Diaz, finally stemmed the tide, although fighting continued until December. Italian losses numbered over 300,000 men.

JOSEPH B. MITCHELL, *Lt. Colonel, USA*
Author, "Twenty Decisive Battles of the World"

MIKE SMITH, FROM PIX

Truman Capote

CAPOTE, kə-pō′tē, **Truman** (1924–   ), American author, noted for his graceful and evocative prose style. In 1966 he achieved an extraordinary critical and financial success with the publication of *In Cold Blood,* an account of a multiple murder in Kansas.

Capote was born in New Orleans, La., on Sept. 30, 1924. Critics acclaimed his first novel, *Other Voices, Other Rooms* (1948), as one of the most exciting works of fiction to appear in postwar America. This book, a "Southern Gothic" novel set in a rundown Mississippi mansion, tells of a young boy's discovery of his homosexual identity. It was followed by *A Tree of Night* (1949), a collection of Gothic horror tales. Capote's second novel, *The Grass Harp* (1951; dramatized, 1952), turns away from the Gothic, treating its mild nonconformists with wit and sentiment. His fine short story, *A Christmas Memory* (1965; dramatized for television, 1966), is about an eccentric, lovable lady. In 1958, Capote created the sophisticated waif Holly Golightly in *Breakfast at Tiffany's,* a novel that was filmed in 1961.

Capote turned to reportage in 1956. He accompanied the all-Negro cast of *Porgy and Bess* on their tour of the Soviet Union, and his documentary account of the trip, first serialized in the *New Yorker,* was published in book form as *The Muses are Heard* in 1956. *In Cold Blood,* which also appeared first as a *New Yorker* serial, was written after six years of research. With this book, Capote claimed to have invented a new literary form—the "nonfiction novel."

ANTHONY CHANNELL HILFER
University of Texas

CAPP, Al (1909–   ), American cartoonist, the creator of the immensely popular *Li'l Abner* comic strip. Capp was born Alfred Gerald Caplin in New Haven, Conn., on Sept. 28, 1909. He had some art school training, but was mostly self-taught. He began newspaper art work in 1928, and in 1934 began *Li'l Abner,* which had its major setting in the hillbilly country.

While *Li'l Abner* contains all the elements usually found in a narrative comic strip—menace,

Al Capp

WIDE WORLD

mystery, and cliff-hanger suspense—Capp's unique contribution to the genre is the juxtaposition of these elements with the comic and the burlesque. His stories are satires on human conduct, the mores of the times, and contemporary political affairs. His characters are sketched in a broad comic style—another departure from the more usual, realistically drawn adventure comic. Two of Capp's inventions in *Li'l Abner* achieved international popularity: the benevolent, pear-shaped little animals called "Schmoos," and "Sadie Hawkins Day," when unmarried women are licensed to pursue the bachelors of their choice.

In 1956, Capp was chairman of the cartoonists' committee of the President's People-to-People program. In the 1960's he became a popular lecturer on college campuses and a frequent guest on television discussion programs.

JACK MARKOW, *Author of "Cartoonist's and Gag Writer's Handbook"*

CAPPADOCIA, kap-ə-dō'shē-ə, a mountainous area in the central part of what is now eastern Turkey, was a client kingdom of the Roman Empire and later a Roman province. It extended originally from the Taurus Mountains northward to the Black Sea, and from the Euphrates River westward to the Halys River (now the Kızılırmak River) and Lake Tatta (now Tuz Gölü).

Cappadocia became part of the Persian Empire in the 6th century B. C. and was sometimes divided into two satrapies (areas ruled by Persian governors called satraps): Cappadocia or Greater Cappadocia in the south and Pontic or Lesser Cappadocia in the north. Pontic Cappadocia was later included in the kingdom of Pontus.

Cappadocia long remained uncivilized. Except in the Euphrates plain near Melitene (now Malatya) the soil was poor and the terrain was rugged. Few cities developed, except the capital, Mazaca (from about 10 B. C., Caesarea Mazaca; now Kayseri), Tyana (near modern Kemerhisar, southwest of Niğde), the two temple sites of Comana, and Venasa. The 10 districts of Cappadocia were based mainly on tribal divisions, and many were probably ruled by feudal chiefs.

Alexander the Great bypassed Cappadocia; it was finally conquered by the Macedonian general Perdiccas in 322 B. C. In the 3d century B. C. the area (now only Cappadocia proper, since Pontus had become an independent kingdom) came under the nominal rule of the Seleucid kings, with a native dynasty of fairly independent vassal rulers in Mazaca. In about 255, Ariarathes III proclaimed himself an independent king. However, both Ariarathes III and his successor Ariarathes IV (reigned 220–163) remained allies of the Seleucid dynasty until the final defeat of the Seleucid king Antiochus III in 190. At this time Ariarathes IV became a client king of Rome.

Roman Hegemony. Ariarathes V (reigned 163–130 B. C.) was a loyal supporter of Rome and a great devotee of Greek culture; he did much to Hellenize and civilize his country. During the turbulent reigns that followed, Mithridates VI of Pontus gradually gained control of the kingdom. The Roman senate finally intervened in 95 B. C., compelled Mithridates to withdraw, and installed a Cappadocian chief, Ariobarzanes, as king; his family ruled until 36 B. C., when Antony installed Archelaus (great-grandson of Archelaus, Mithridates' famous general) as king. He was deposed in 17 A. D. by the Roman emperor Tiberius, who made the kingdom a Roman province.

In 72 A D., Emperor Vespasian allotted two legions to Cappadocia because of its strategic position of the Euphrates frontier. Until Trajan's time, Cappadocia's governor ruled much of central and eastern Asia Minor. The province was divided by Diocletian (reigned 284–305) and again by Valens in 371–372.

D. J. BLACKMAN, *University of Bristol*

CAPPELLE, kä-pel'ə, **Jan van de** (c. 1624–1679), Dutch painter famous for his calm seascapes and silvery winter landscapes. He was born in Amsterdam about 1624. A dyer by trade, he was self-taught as an artist. He was a disciple of Simon de Vlieger, a leading Dutch painter of seascapes. Cappelle's paintings are characterized by their low horizons and almost unlimited vistas. His works are exhibited in the National Gallery, London, and the National Gallery, Washington, D. C. A wealthy man, he collected about 500 Rembrandt drawings. He had his portrait painted by both Rembrandt and Frans Hals. Capelle died in Amsterdam on Sept. 22, 1679.

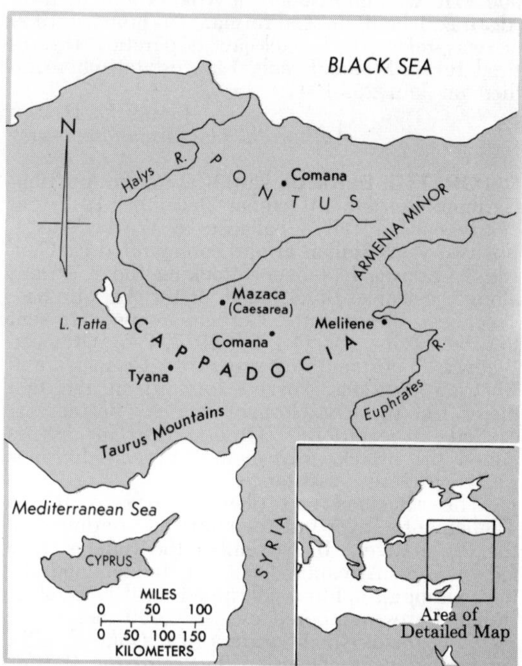

ITALIAN CULTURAL INSTITUTE

THE ISLAND OF CAPRI rises in limestone cliffs from the Gulf of Naples.

CAPPER, Arthur (1865–1951), American senator, governor, and journalist, who served the interests of the farmers. Capper was born in Garnett, Kans., on July 14, 1865. He went from compositor to publisher (1892) of the Topeka *Daily Capital.* He also published the *Daily Kansan* and farm journals such as *Capper's Weekly.* A Republican, he was governor of Kansas from 1915 to 1919, and he served as U. S. senator from 1919 until 1949. With Sen. Andrew Volstead of Minnesota he cosponsored the Cooperative Marketing Act of 1922, which strengthened farm cooperatives. Capper died in Topeka on Dec. 19, 1951.

CAPRA, kap'rə, **Frank** (1897–), American motion picture director. He was born in Palermo, Italy, on May 18, 1897, and emigrated to the United States in 1903, where he became a film director in 1921. He is best known for the Academy Award-winning comedies *It Happened One Night* (1934), *Mr. Deeds Goes to Town* (1936), and *You Can't Take It With You* (1938), and for a number of more serious films, including *Lost Horizon* (1937). A gift for comic improvisation and a strong if sentimental feeling for the lives of ordinary people combined to make Capra's motion pictures especially appealing to American audiences in the 1930's and early 1940's. Among his later films are *Arsenic and Old Lace* (1944) and *Pocketful of Miracles* (1961).

CAPREOL, ka'prē-ôl, is a town in northeastern Ontario, Canada, about 18 miles (29 km) northeast of Sudbury. It is a division point of the Canadian National Railways and the site of some of the railways' general offices. Iron-ore pellets and concentrates are produced in the town and there is a bulk distribution plant for gasoline and fuel oil. Population: 3,470.

CAPRERA, kä-prâ'rä, is a small rocky island in Italy, off the northeast coast of Sardinia. It is connected by a causeway with the island of La Maddalena. Giuseppe Garibaldi died on Caprera in 1882. His house and tomb are national shrines.

CAPRI, kä-prē', is an island in the Gulf of Naples Italy, 17 miles (27 km) south of Naples and 9 miles (14 km) west of Sorrento. It has been a resort for over 2,000 years. The island is a huge limestone block, 4 square miles (10 sq km) in area, with rugged shorelines into which the sea has carved deep caves that are among the island's chief attractions. Capri is noted for its mild climate. It produces citrus fruit, olive oil, and white wine grapes, and many inhabitants engage in fishing. But tourism is the main source of revenue.

Capri has very little level land. Marina Grande on the north shore, the only port, is connected by cable railway to the main town, Capri. The island's principal hotels are located here, and the tiny Piazza Umberto I is the center of island life, with outdoor cafés that are popular with both residents and tourists. A short distance to the east are the ruins of a villa built by the Roman emperor Tiberius in the 1st century A. D. It stands nearly 1,000 feet (300 meters) above the sea, and from its veranda there is a superb view of the Gulf of Naples and the nearby Sorrento peninsula.

The town of Anacapri is on the northern slopes of the island's highest peak, Monte Solaro (1,932 feet, or 589 meters). Like Capri, Anacapri is a tourist center; its most famous visitor in the early years of the 20th century was the Swedish physician Axel Munthe, whose villa, San Michele, with its fine collection of antiquities, charming garden, and excellent view, is a major tourist attraction. The famous Blue Grotto, a limestone cavern created by the sea, is noteworthy. Known in Roman times, it was rediscovered in 1826. Its waters reflect the blue of the sea outside, giving the grotto its name.

Capri was known to the Romans as *Capreae.* In 1806 it was captured by the English, but they lost it to the French in 1808. They regained it in 1813 and ceded it to King Ferdinand IV of Naples. With the rest of the Kingdom of the Two Sicilies, it became a part of united Italy in 1860. Population: (1966 est.) 7,816.

GEORGE KISH, *University of Michigan*

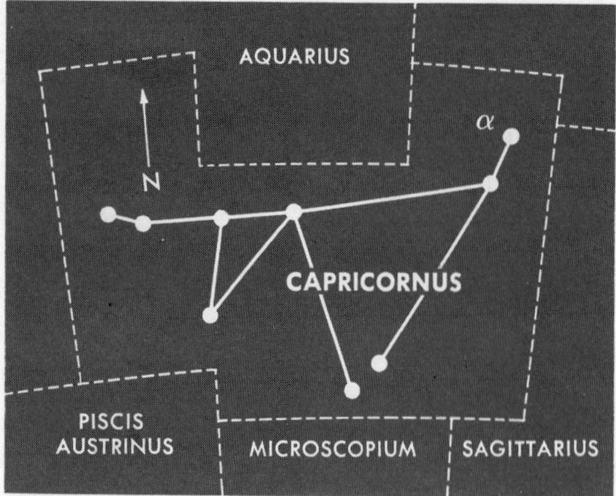

CAPRICORNUS, kap-rə-kôr′nəs, is an inconspicuous autumn constellation that lies along the ecliptic (the sun's apparent path among the stars) in the Southern Hemisphere. Capricornus, the Horned Goat or Sea Goat, is the 10th sign of the zodiac and is usually pictured as having the tail of a fish; according to one Greek fable, this was a shape assumed by Pan or Bacchus.

Despite its lack of very bright stars, the constellation appears in the oldest mythologies. In ancient times the winter solstice (the southernmost limit of the ecliptic) occurred in Capricornus, in a region of the sky that was associated with water and the sea. Because of precession the solstice has since moved into the constellation Sagittarius.

Several binaries, or double stars, are found in Capricornus. The two stars of α Capricornus can be observed with the naked eye. See also CONSTELLATION; ZODIAC.

CAPRIFICATION. See FIG.

CAPRIVI, kä-prē′vē, **Count von** (1831–1899), German general and statesman. Georg Leo von Caprivi was born in Charlottenburg (now part of Berlin) on Feb. 24, 1831. A military officer with a distinguished career, Caprivi was chosen to succeed Bismarck as imperial chancellor and Prussian prime minister on March 20, 1890. He possessed neither the temperament nor the experience to carry on his predecessor's complicated political game. He defined his outlook as "moderately conservative," and he believed firmly in the sanctity of a constitutional monarchy based on Christian principles.

His political program broke various precedents. He embarked on a course of conciliation toward the socialists and the Polish minority in Prussia. He enacted important social legislation, negotiated trade treaties to promote Germany's burgeoning industry, and reduced the term of military service from three years to two. He gave up Bismarck's policy of close relations with Russia and concentrated on the alliance with Austria-Hungary and Italy.

His life in office was never easy. Bismarck sniped at him from retirement. The unexpected initiatives of the impulsive emperor, William II, were a constant source of harassment. Dispirited and out of imperial favor, he resigned on Oct. 26, 1894. He died at Skyren, near Crossen on the Oder, on Feb. 6, 1899.

C. M. KIMMICH, *Columbia University*

CAPRIVI STRIP, kä-prē′vē, a narrow strip of land extending east from northern South West Africa to the Zambezi River. Bordered on the north by Angola and Zambia and on the south by Botswana, it is 300 miles (480 km) long and 50 miles (80 km) wide. It is also known as the Caprivi Concession and the Caprivi Zipfel.

Geographically the Caprivi Strip is part of the northern section of the Kalahari Desert and has a very even surface. Only a few sand ridges extend 60 to 100 feet (18 to 30 meters) above the surface and there are a few isolated rock outcrops. Economically the area is poor because desert conditions prevail from the Okovanggo River eastward. Rainfall averages 25 inches (640 mm) annually, and although evaporation is high, grasses support some animal life. Farming and stock raising are possible in the extreme eastern end of the strip, where the Kwando and Zambezi rivers are used for irrigation. Some timber is cut and taken to Livingstone, Zambia, for milling. No minerals have been found. The area suffers from the tsetse fly and malaria.

The Caprivi Strip was named after German Chancellor Leo von Caprivi, who obtained its concession from Britain in 1890 as part of the Treaty of Heligoland. Caprivi wanted an outlet to the Zambezi River for the German colony of South West Africa. He also hoped to prevent the South African empire builder Cecil Rhodes from moving into Central Africa. Since 1939 the strip has been governed directly by the government of South Africa.

HUGH C. BROOKS
St. John's University, New York

CAPRONI, kä-prō′nē, **Gianni** (1886–1957), Italian aircraft designer and manufacturer, who designed more than 100 types of civilian and military airplanes. Count Giovanni Caproni di Taliedo was born at Massone d'Arco, near Trento, on July 3, 1886. After studying at the Polytechnical Institute at Liège, Belgium, and other European universities, he designed his first aircraft, which he flew in 1910.

During World War I, Caproni designed many planes, including the first Italian 3-engine bomber. He also served as an adviser to Gen. John J. Pershing and is credited with giving Pershing the idea of strategic bombing. After the war Caproni designed several high-speed and heavy-duty long-distance planes used by the Italian air force. His planes set altitude records of 47,360 feet (14,435 meters) in 1934, 51,362 feet (15,658 meters) in 1937, and 56,017 feet (17,073 meters) in 1938.

Caproni also experimented with jet propulsion. Together with Secondo Campini he developed the C.C.2, powered by a 900-hp engine driving a ducted fan. It flew in August 1940, about one year after the world's first jet-propelled flight. He died in Rome on Oct. 27, 1957.

RAMON KNAUERHASE
University of Connecticut

CAPSIAN CULTURE, kap′sē-ən, a Stone Age culture of North Africa, dating from the Upper Paleolithic and Mesolithic eras. The Capsians were among the first people to specialize in making stone blades of a regular form. Characteristic findings include burins or microliths, and other small-blade tools, frequently made of obsidian (volcanic glass). Larger tools of bone and various artifacts made from ostrich eggshells have been discovered as well. The Capsians were food-gatherers and generally camped in the open. The only dwellings of this period were crude rock shelters or shallow caves, on whose walls are drawings of hunting scenes done in a linear manner. Nearby kitchen middens with refuse of their daily lives contain large deposits of land-snail shells. In the later stages of Capsian culture, animals were domesticated, copper and bronze were used, and pottery was made.

The name of the culture is taken from the type-site at Gafsa (Latin: Capsa), Tunisia. In variant forms the culture spread over a large part of North Africa, and traces are found in Kenya and Tanganyika and again in southern Spain. Because few of the sites have been dated, the relationship between the North African, Kenyan, and Spanish forms of the culture is unclear. A late Capsian site at el-Mekta in Tunisia has been dated as early as 7000 B.C., while the Capsian site at Gambles Cave in Kenya contains pottery, which necessarily dates it later than 5000 B.C. Because of this dating, it is surmised that the Capsian people were of a Mediterranean Caucasoid type who migrated from Palestine across North Africa to Tunisia, whence the culture later spread to Kenya.

In southern Spain there was a cultural tradition unlike the Magdalenian culture that entered Spain from Europe. Findings from this, which feature microliths and a linear form of cave art similar to the stick figure noted in the Capsian cave paintings of Africa, have been dated as earlier than the corresponding culture in Africa. Although the Spanish Capsian has closer affinities with North Africa than with European cultures, the nature of the relationship is still obscure.

PRISCILLA C. WARD
American Museum of Natural History

CAPSICUM, kap'si-kəm, is a genus of plants in the nightshade family (Solanaceae), native to Central and South America and widely cultivated throughout the world for its pungent fruits, known as red peppers. The genus is generally considered to contain only one species, *Capsicum frutescens,* with many varieties. *C. frutescens* is a shrubby perennial, 6 to 8 feet (2–2½ meters) high, with small whitish flowers. It is capable of bearing fruit in its first year. Cultivation takes advantage of this early fruiting, and in the more northerly areas this perennial plant is grown as a herbaceous annual.

The cherry pepper, which is classified as the variety *C. f. cerasiforme,* bears pungent, rounded, red, yellow, or purplish fruits, about ¾ inch (20 mm) in diameter. The bell pepper, or sweet pepper, (*C. f. grossum*), the one usually found in gardens, has large, mild-tasting, red or yellow fruits, which are often eaten green and unripe. The chili pepper (*C. f. longum*) bears long, tapering, usually pungent, red or yellow fruits, 4 to 10 inches (10 to 25 cm) in length. Dried chili peppers are ground to make cayenne pepper, or red pepper, seasoning.

DONALD WYMAN
Arnold Arboretum, Harvard University

CAPSTAN, kap'stən, a rotary device used primarily for lifting heavy loads on ships and in shipyards. A capstan consists of a vertically mounted iron drum with a rope wound on it. The drum is sometimes smooth but often has ribs or ridges, called whelps, running up and down its surface to increase traction. It usually is driven by steam or electric power but sometimes is turned by hand with a bar. The load is attached to the rope and is wound in as the capstan turns. The drum moves over a notched rim at the base which prevents it from slipping or turning in the opposite direction. Manually operated capstans sometimes have a reduction gear which reduces the force necessary to turn the drum.

FARRELL LINES INC.

Capstan

The capstan on a tape recorder is a motor-driven spindle that regulates the speed with which the tape moves over the recording, the erasing, and the playback heads.

CAPSULE, kap'səl, in botany, a type of dry fruit that opens to release its seeds. Azaleas, poppies, and tulips are examples of plants with capsule fruits. See FRUIT—*Dehiscent.*

CAPTAIN is a junior military rank, a senior naval rank, and the title of a ship's master. In the U. S. Army, and most armies, a captain may command a company of infantry or a battery of artillery. In the U. S. Air Force a captain may be a flight leader, commanding a flight of 2 to 5 or more aircraft. A U. S. Navy captain, ranking with an Army colonel, may command the largest warships. Regardless of his Navy rank, the commanding officer of a Navy ship or activity ashore is called the captain. The commander of a merchant ship, properly the master, is usually called the captain. In the early Middle Ages in Europe captain was the highest military rank.

CAPTAIN BRASSBOUND'S CONVERSION is a three-act play written by George Bernard Shaw in 1899 and included in the volume *Three Plays for Puritans* (1901). After the birth of her first grandchild, the actress Ellen Terry wrote Shaw that no one would write a play for a grandmother, and Shaw, because of his admiration for Miss Terry, created the heroine, Lady Cicely Waynflete, for her. The moral of the play, which was produced at the Court Theatre, London, in March 1906 with Ellen Terry as Lady Cicely, is that revenge is not wild justice but childishness and that legal justice is frequently only organized revenge.

CAPTAIN OF KOEPENICK, kû'pe-nik, a novel by the German writer Carl Zuckmayer, published in 1931. Its German title is *Der Hauptmann von Köpenick.* The novel satirizes Prussian militarism before World War I. The hero, an ex-convict unable to get work or a passport to leave the country, acquires an army captain's uniform and dupes the town of Koepenick, arrests its mayor, and robs its town hall. Finally he gives himself up, but the townspeople refuse to believe that such a fool could really be an impostor.

CAPTAINS COURAGEOUS is a novel written in 1897 by the English author Rudyard Kipling. It tells the story of Harvey Cheyne, the spoiled 15-year-old son of an American millionaire. While a passenger on a liner bound for Europe, Harvey is washed overboard and picked up by the captain of a fishing boat. Refusing to believe the boy's tale, the captain puts him to work. The novel deals primarily with Harvey's adventures aboard the boat and his transformation from a snobbish boy into a self-reliant young man, who values people for their abilities rather than for their financial worth.

CAPTIVI, kap-tē'vē, is the most serious of the comedies of the Roman writer Titus Maccius Plautus. The title in English is *The Captives.* Adapted from a Greek original, the play was written some time between 205 and 189 B. C. The plot turns, as often in Roman comedy, on a deception (a slave, Tyndarus, and his master, Philocrates, who are prisoners of war, change places) and a discovery of hidden identity (the slave is found to be well-born but to have been stolen and sold into slavery at the age of four). The subject is not, however, treated as a farce; Tyndarus has the soul of a gentleman and acts accordingly, and the elderly man who buys the prisoners of war is not the stock figure of an imbecile or tyrant. The audience therefore is in sympathy with both deceivers and deceived, a most unusual arrangement. The comedy inspired such later plays as Ariosto's *I suppositi* (about 1500), Ben Jonson's *The Case Is Altered* (about 1597), and Calderón's *El principe constante* (1629).

CAPUA, kä'pwä, is a town and commune in Italy, 21 miles (33 km) north of Naples, on the Volturno River. It was originally built as the river port of the Roman town of Capua, some 3 miles (5 km) to the southeast. When the Roman town was destroyed, the present town of Capua came into existence, probably during the 9th century. It is now a business center for the surrounding, densely settled countryside.

The cathedral of Capua was severely damaged in 1943 but was later restored. Begun in the 9th century, it is predominantly in the Romanesque style of the 11th century, with a massive tower and an elegant entrance flanked by late Roman columns. The other principal point of interest in Capua is the local museum, noted for its 13th century statues that once decorated one of the city's gates, including statues of Emperor Frederick II and his courtiers.

Capua has been the site of many battles and sieges. The two most notable in the modern period were the defeat of the Bourbon armies of Naples by the forces of King Victor Emmanuel and Garibaldi in 1860; and the Battle of the Volturno River, fought in World War II by the Allies and the retreating Germans in the fall of 1943.

Santa Maria Capua Vetere, built on the site of the original Roman town of Capua, is a farmers' town, famous for its Roman remains. The Campanian amphitheater, built during the 1st century A. D., was second in size only to the Colosseum of Rome. It measures 548 feet by 449 feet (167 by 137 meters). Next to it is an underground temple of the cult of the sun god Mithras. Population: (1961) of the town, 13,334; (1966 est.) of the commune, 18,979.

George Kish, *University of Michigan*

CAPUANA, kä-pwä'nä, **Luigi** (1839–1915), Italian novelist and critic, who was a leader of the movement toward realism in Italian literature. He was born in Mineo, near Catania, Sicily, on May 28, 1839. He abandoned law studies to pursue a literary career in Florence, Milan, and Rome. Later, from 1902, he was a professor of Italian literature at the University of Catania.

As a literary critic, Capuana was strongly influenced by the aesthetic approach of Francesco de Sanctis. As a novelist, indebted to the psychological works of Balzac and Zola, Capuana became, with Giovanni Verga, one of the founders of *verismo,* the Italian analogue of French realism and naturalism. His novels, which are sometimes objective to the point of aridity, contain impersonal analyses of the psychology of love, jealousy, and eccentricity, joined with a vivid curiosity about the occult. They include *Giacinta* (1879), about a bride who takes a lover on her wedding day, and *Il marchese di Roccaverdina* (1901), the story of a Sicilian noble who kills his mistress' husband and then, out of guilt, kills himself. Capuana also wrote successful folkloristic fables, children's stories, and plays in Sicilian dialect. He died in Catania on Nov. 29, 1915.

John Charles Nelson, *Columbia University*

CAPUCHIN, kap'yə-shən, a medium-size monkey of the family Cebidae, found from Honduras to northern Argentina and Paraguay. It is also known as *sapajou* and *ringtail monkey.*

Capuchins average 27 to 35 inches (685 to 888 mm) in length, including the 15- to 20-inch (380–508 mm) prehensile tail, and from 3½ to 9 pounds (1.5–4 kg) in weight. Coat color is brownish or grayish to yellowish. Capuchins live primarily in the tops of large trees, where they form closely knit clans with definite territorial boundaries. They are active during the day and feed mostly on fruit, but also eat leaves, shoots, insects, eggs, and small animals. In captivity, where they are raised as pets and laboratory animals, capuchins have lived to 37 years.

Four species are generally recognized: the white-faced capuchin (*Cebus capucinus*), the white-fronted capuchin (*C. albifrons*), the brown capuchin (*C. apella*), and the weeper capuchin (*C. nigrivittatus*). There is, however, much variation in these monkeys, and the exact number and definition of species are unclear. The capuchins can be divided further into two distinct groups: one, typified by *C. apella,* has two tufts of hair at the top of the head; the other, typified by *C. capucinus,* lacks the tufts but shows whitish markings on the head and chest.

Fernando Dias de Avila-Pires
Universidade do Brasil

CAPUCHINS, kap'yə-shinz, a religious order of the Roman Catholic Church. Officially known as the Order of Friars Minor Capuchin (O. F. M. Cap.), it began as a reform of the Franciscan order that was initiated by Father Matthew of Bascio, Italy, in 1525. In 1528 the Capuchins received papal approval to become an autonomous branch of the Franciscan order committed to a stricter interpretation of the Rule of St. Francis. The first friars wore what they considered to be the primitive Franciscan garb with a long hood, or capuche, attached. They were, as a result, jocularly called "capuccini," or hooded friars, and this designation became the popular name of the order.

By the late 1960's, the order, composed of priests and brothers living in community and vowed to poverty, chastity, and obedience, numbered more than 15,000 friars. They are engaged in a flexible and varied apostolate in approximately 70 countries, with general headquarters in Rome. Although their apostolate is diversified, the Capuchins have always stressed missionary activity. The friars were instrumental in founding the Congregation of the Propagation of the Faith in Rome in 1622. The congregation's first superior was a Capuchin cardinal; its first martyr was also a Capuchin, St. Fidelis of Sigmaringen. Approximately 20% of the order's personnel is engaged in mission work.

In the United States and Canada there are nine jurisdictions, or geographic divisions, of Capuchins engaged in varied activities: parish work, preaching, retreats and parish missions, teaching, writing, counseling and guidance, running information centers and Newman centers, acting as institutional and military chaplains, and adult education. The Capuchins of the North American jurisdictions staff missions in India, Chad, New Guinea, Guam, the Ryukyu Islands, Nicaragua, and Puerto Rico.

In 1959 Pope John XXIII declared one of the Order's members, St. Lawrence of Brindisi, a Doctor of the Church. Since 1743 a Capuchin has held the position of Apostolic Preacher at the Vatican; at specified times during the year he preaches to the pope, cardinals, bishops, and other church officials.

SIMON R. CONRAD, O. F. M. CAP.
St. Fidelis Monastery, Kansas

CAPULET AND MONTAGUE, kap'yə-let, mon'tə-gyōō, two feuding families of the nobility of Verona in Shakespeare's *Romeo and Juliet* (q.v.). Their enmity leads to the death of their children, which reconciles the families.

The story of the feud goes back to historical families, the Capelletti of Cremona and the Montecchi of Verona, who were famous for their fierce rivalry based on the political factions that divided northern Italy in the late Middle Ages. The Capelletti belonged to the Guelph, or papal party, and the Montecchi to the Ghibelline, or imperial, party. Their conflict was cited by Dante in his *Divine Comedy* (1321; *Purgatorio*, Canto VI) as an example of the violence and confusion of the time. The theme of the families' rivalry, focused upon a legendary tragic love affair, later appeared in a 15th century Italian account and in two 16th century English versions, from which Shakespeare drew.

Shakespeare's drama was the basis for Bellini's opera *I Capuletti ed i Montecchi* (1830) and Gounod's *Roméo et Juliette* (1867).

PHILIP GENDREAU

Capybara

CAPYBARA, kap-i-bar'ə, either of two species of Central and South American semiaquatic rodents resembling giant guinea pigs. Capybaras are the largest living rodents, sometimes exceeding 110 pounds (50 kg) in weight. They have a broad, deep muzzle, short ears and tail, small eyes set far back on the head, and short limbs with partially webbed feet. Because capybaras have a rather sparse coat, the skin is visible beneath the long, coarse hairs. Coloration is reddish brown to grayish above and yellowish brown below.

Capaybaras live in wooded areas, near water, in groups of up to 30 individuals. They feed on grasses and aquatic plants growing on riverbanks and lake shores. These animals are active in the morning and evening, but rest in the forest during the hottest part of the day. Capybaras bear 2 to 8 young once a year after a gestation period of about 4 months. They live to about 10 years of age.

The two species are the only living members of the family Hydrochoeridae. The larger species, *Hydrochoerus hydrochaeris,* is found in South America from east of the Andes Mountains to Uruguay. It grows to 4 feet (1.2 meters) long, 2 feet (60 cm) high at the shoulders, and 110 pounds (50 kg) in weight. The smaller species, *H. isthmius,* is native to Panama; it averages approximately 60 pounds (27 kg) in weight.

FERNANDO DIAS DE AVILA-PIRES
Universidade do Brasil

CAQUETÁ RIVER, kä-kä-tä', the longest river in southern Colombia. It rises in the central range of the Colombian Andes, in Cauca department, and flows southeast some 750 miles (1,200 km) across the equator to the Brazilian border. There it meets the Apaporis River to form the Japurá, which is a tributary of the Amazon.

Most of the country watered by the Caquetá is thick jungle, inhabited mainly by primitive Indians. The forest produces hardwoods, gums, and resins, but in general the region is economically undeveloped.

CARABAO. See BUFFALO.

Caracal

RUSS KINNE, FROM PHOTO RESEARCHERS

CARACAL, kar'ə-kal, a small to medium-sized member of the cat family. The caracal ranges through all the savannas and semidesert regions of Africa, Arabia, Asia Minor, and India.

The body of an adult caracal stands about 16 inches (40 cm) at the shoulder. The head and body are about 28 inches (70 cm) long, and the tail is only 10 inches (25 cm) long. Because of its long legs and short tail, the caracal is often thought to be related to the lynxes. The smooth, short fur ranges from grayish buff to reddish brown, according to subspecies, of which there are 9. The back of the ears is black, there is a dark spot over each eye, and a larger spot appears on either side of the muzzle; shadowy stripes and spots mark the belly and the insides of the legs. The pointed ears are tufted.

The gestation period of the caracal is about 70 days, and there are normally 2 to 4 young in a litter. The caracal is an expert hunter of small antelope, hares, and game birds; it was, in fact, trained for hunting in ancient Egypt.

The single species, *Caracal caracal* (also called *Felis caracal*), is classified in the family Felidae, order Carnivora.

PAUL LEYHAUSEN, *Max Planck Institute For Behavioral Physiology*

RUSS KINNE, FROM PHOTO RESEARCHERS

Caracara

CARACALLA, kar-ə-kal'ə (c. 188–217 A. D.), was Roman emperor from 211 to 217. He was originally named Bassianus, and his throne name was Marcus Aurelius Antoninus. "Caracalla" is a nickname derived from the Gallic military cloak that he introduced into Rome.

The elder son of Septimius Severus and Julia Domna, Caracalla was a pawn in his father's struggles for the throne and consequently was named caesar (junior emperor) in 196 and coaugustus (joint senior emperor) with Septimius by 198. In 202, Caracalla was married to Plautilla, the daughter of the Praetorian prefect Plautianus, but the alliance was dissolved three years later when Plautianus fell from power.

Caracalla, along with his younger brother Lucius Septimius Geta, accompanied Septimius to Britain, where Septimius died in 211. Geta, an augustus since 209, was expected to share the throne with Caracalla, but in 212 he was assassinated by Caracalla, who thereafter ruled alone.

After a campaign against the Germans in 213 and a foray along the Danube in 214, Caracalla arrived in the Middle East, where he provoked a war with Parthia in 216. In the midst of this venture he was assassinated by his praetorian prefect, Macrinus, near Carrhae, in 217.

Caracalla may not have been in complete possession of his faculties during the last years of his reign. It was said that he fancied himself a new Alexander the Great and organized a part of the army into a phalanx, a then outmoded military formation that had been used by Alexander.

Caracalla is chiefly remembered for the Antonine Constitution of 212, a measure that extended Roman citizenship to nearly every person (except slaves and criminals) within the Roman Empire. The purpose of this law was to simplify the administration of justice and possibly the tax structure. This emperor also built the famous Baths of Caracalla in Rome.

TOM B. JONES, *University of Minnesota*

CARACARA, kar-ə-kar'ə, is a genus of long-legged, carrion-eating hawks. Caracaras are found largely in South America, where the carancha (*Caracara plancus*) ranges from the Amazon to the southern tip of South America. The now extinct Guadalupe caracara (*C. lutosus*) was found on Guadalupe Island, off Lower California; it was last seen alive in 1903. The common caracara of the United States (*C. cheriway*) is found from central Florida, Arizona, New Mexico, and Texas south to the Amazon.

The caracara is related to the falcons, although its behavior is more like that of vultures. The common Caracara is about 23 inches (58 cm) tall with a wingspread of 4 feet (120 cm). Its naked face and throat are bright red, and its crested crown is black. Its back, belly, and wings are rusty black. The wings have whitish patches near the tips, and the breast is white.

Although they are good fliers, caracaras also walk and run with agility. They are valued scavengers in removing dead livestock, and they aggressively drive vultures away from contested carrion. Besides carrion, they eat live insects, fish, reptiles, birds, and rodents—especially rabbits. Both sexes help build the nest and incubate the two brown, blotched eggs. The eggs hatch in four weeks.

Caracaras belong to the subfamily Caracarinae in the family Falconidae.

CARL WELTY, *Beloit College*

CARACAS, kä-rä'käs, the capital and largest city of Venezuela, is situated in the north central part of the country, 7 miles (11 km) south of La Guaira, its port on the Caribbean Sea. It lies in a small valley, on the Guaire River, about 3,000 feet (914 meters) above sea level, and is surrounded almost entirely by mountains of twice that elevation that rise abruptly from the dry, hot coastline. Although the mountains create obstacles to transportation, this disadvantage is offset in part by the climate of the valley, which is healthful and generally pleasant, with temperatures rarely above 80° F (27° C) or below 50° F (10° C). Most of the rainfall, averaging 32 inches (81 cm) a year, occurs from May through November. A magnificent superhighway provides swift access to La Guaira and the nearby commercial airport at Maiquetía. Connections with other parts of the country are maintained chiefly by highway and air.

Caracas is the capital also of a political entity of 745 square miles (1,903 sq km) known as the Federal District, which borders the Caribbean Sea and the states of Aragua and Miranda.

Economy. Caracas long has been important politically. With the exploitation of Venezuela's mineral wealth in recent times, it has become the financial and commercial center of the country as well. Many oil companies and iron and steel companies have established offices in Caracas, and a number of industries have been attracted to the city. These include automobile assembly and food processing plants, breweries, and factories that make detergents, textiles, paper products, rubber goods, and pharmaceuticals.

The growth of Caracas since the 1940's has been so rapid that its metropolitan area now sprawls into the state of Miranda. Planning has been essential, and much has been done toward redesigning the city with wide new avenues, great blocks of housing to replace former slums, and handsome new commercial and recreational centers.

Places of Interest. The Plaza Bolívar is still the official center of the city, although it is no longer the geographical center. The old colonial cathedral and an equestrian statue of Simón Bolívar are there. In the vicinity are the national capitol; Miraflores, the presidential palace; and the National Pantheon, burial place of Bolívar and other leaders. The new Centro Simón Bolívar, with its twin skyscrapers and underground parking and shopping center, now houses many government offices. University City is a strikingly designed complex of new structures including office buildings, a medical center, theaters, and stadiums. Caracas' many cultural and educational institutions include historical and fine arts museums, academies of art and music, scientific institutes, the Central University of Venezuela (founded in 1725), and the Universidad Católica Andrés Bello, named for the scholar, author, and statesman Andrés Bello (1781–1865), who was born in Caracas.

History. Caracas was founded in 1567 by Diego de Losada and named Santiago de León de los Caracas, after local Indians known as the Caracas. In the history of Latin America's struggle for independence, Caracas is noted as the birthplace of Francisco de Miranda (1750–1816), precursor of the movement, and Simón Bolívar (1783–1830), revered as "El Libertador." Venezuelans, under these leaders, spearheaded the struggle with a declaration of independence at Caracas in 1811. Spanish loyalists soon retook the city, but it was freed within a decade. Venezuela then was joined with Colombia and Ecuador to form the short-lived republic of Gran (Great) Colombia. By 1830, Venezuela became a separate republic, with Caracas as its capital. Population: (1961) 786,863; Federal District, 1,257,515; metropolitan area, 1,336,464.

CARL FRANK

SIMÓN BOLÍVAR CENTER, in Caracas, Venezuela, houses government ministries in twin 32-story buildings.

GREGORY RABASSA, *Columbia University*

CARACTACUS. See CARATACUS.

CARAGIALE, kä-rä-jä'le, **Ion Luca** (1852–1912), Rumanian playwright, author, and theatrical manager. He was born of a theatrical family in Haimanale, near Ploesti, on Jan. 29, 1852. He wrote his first play in 1878 for the Junimea ("Youth") literary society. His popular comedies, in which he satirized the too hasty modernization of traditional Rumanian urban life, include *Conul Leonida față cu reacțiunea* (1879; *Mr. Leonida Faces the Reaction*); *O noapte furtunoasă* (1880; *The Stormy Night*); and his best play, *O scrisoare pierdută* (1884–1885; *The Lost Letter*). Among his other writings are the peasant drama *Năpasta* (1890; *Calamity*) and three fine short stories—*O făclie de paşti* (1889; *An Easter Torch*), *Păcat* (1892; *The Sin*), and *Kir Ianulea* (1909).

In 1888, Caragiale became director of the Bucharest National Theater. In his last years, he lived in retirement in Berlin, Germany, where he died on June 22, 1912.

CARAJÁ INDIANS, kä-rä-zhä′, an Indian people of eastern Brazil, occupying the Ilha do Bananal (Island of Bananal) in the Araguaia River in the state of Goiás. The name is also spelled *Carayá* and *Karayá*. The Carajá live in permanent villages of rectangular thatched houses and subsist chiefly by farming and fishing. Their surplus animal skins and fish are traded to the Neo-Brazilians of the area, with whom they are generally on friendly terms. The Carajá are famous for the elaborate dance masks with which they impersonate supernatural beings in their religious dances. Their language is classified in a separate family, Carajá or Caraján, and is unrelated to any other. It is made up of three mutually intelligible dialects: Carajá proper, Javahé, and Shambioá. Although early estimates indicate that the group was once numerous, it had shrunk to around 1,500 by the 1940's.

John Howland Rowe
University of California at Berkeley

Further Reading: Lipkind, William, "The Carajá," *Handbook of South American Indians* (Washington 1948).

CARALIS. See Cagliari.

CARAMBOLA, kar-əm-bō′lə, a small evergreen tree native to the East Indies, cultivated for its edible fruit. The carambola tree (*Averrhoa carambola*), a member of the oxalis family (Oxalidaceae), bears small, whitish flowers and smooth-skinned, egg-shaped fruit about 4 inches (10 cm) long. Carambola fruit is juicy and tart. It is eaten raw, preserved, or pickled.

CARAMEL, kar′ə-mel, is a slightly bitter, dark-brown liquid or powder obtained by heating sugar. It is also known as *burnt sugar* and is widely used in cooking as a coloring agent. Caramel is used in making carbonated beverages, baked goods, candies, soups, and sauces. Commercial caramel is made by gradually heating sugar to about 340°–355° F (170°–180° C) and adding small amounts of sodium carbonate while it is heating.

The name caramel is often applied to a chewy brown candy that sometimes contains pieces of fruit or nuts. See also Candy.

CARAN D'ACHE, kȧ-räɴ′ dȧsh′ (1858–1909), French caricaturist and illustrator. He was born Emmanuel Poiré, in Moscow, the grandson of a French soldier who had settled in Russia. At the age of 20 he went to Paris, where, hoping to become a painter of military subjects, he studied with Édouard Detaille. Under his pseudonym (derived from the Russian *karandash*, meaning "pencil"), he began to publish caricatures in *La vie militaire*. In this journal he introduced to France the "story without words," originated by the German caricaturists Wilhelm Busch and Adolf Oberländer.

Caran d'Ache later contributed pictorial ancedotes to many Parisian journals, including *La vie parisienne, Le Figaro, La caricature,* and *Le chat noir*. He also illustrated a number of books and published several albums of sketches. He died in Paris on Feb. 26, 1909.

CARANGIDAE, kə-ran′jə-dē, is a family of marine fishes that contains about 150 species, including the jack crevalles, pompanos, scads, amberjacks, lookdowns, and leatherjacks. Carangids live in all warm seas; a few species exist in temperate seas and in fresh water. The various species differ considerably in body shape, and some species undergo extreme changes in shape during their development.

Most carangids are used for food, although a few species, such as the black jack, have been linked with fish poisoning. Some species are landed in large quantities in commercial catches, and many are prized by sport fishermen.

Frederick H. Berry
U. S. Bureau of Commercial Fisheries

CARAPACE, kar′ə-pās, the tough protective outer covering of certain vertebrate and invertebrate animals. The most familiar example is the shell of a turtle. The turtle's carapace is typically composed of an outer horny layer and an inner bony layer, which in the upper shell incorporates much of the vertebral column. Often, the term "carapace" is used to refer only to the turtle's upper shell.

Clifford Pope, *Author, "The Reptile World"*

CARAT, kar′ət, a unit of measurement used to express the weight of precious stones. The word comes from the Greek name for the carob or locust tree. The dried seed of this tree was originally used by gem traders as the unit for weighing their gems. Because the seeds are not perfectly uniform, variations in the value of the carat developed in different areas. An international or metric carat of 0.2 grams (1 gram equals 0.035 ounces) was proposed in Paris in 1907. This value was adopted by the United States in 1913, and it is now generally accepted in most countries. One carat is equal to about 3.086 grains in the troy system.

The word "carat" is also used to express the purity of gold; in this sense, it is usually spelled *karat*. A karat is not a unit of weight but instead means 1/24th part. Thus, 24-karat gold is pure gold, whereas 18-karat gold contains 18 parts gold and 6 parts alloy.

CARATACUS, kə-rat′ə-kəs, was the leader of the resistance to the Roman conquest of Britain in the reign of Claudius. On the death of his father king Cunobelinus about 42 A. D., Caratacus shared the kingdom with his brother Togodumnus. They indulged in policies provocative to Rome. In 43 the Roman army invaded and decisively defeated the brothers at the Medway River. Caratacus retired to Wales, where for eight years he was the inspiration of resistance. At first he led the Silures in the south, successfully ambushing Roman forces or raiding the Roman province. At length, in 49, Ostorius Scapula began to group forces to conquer the Silures.

Caratacus shifted his activities to North Wales, where the Ordovices also accepted his leadership. In 51 he took a decisive stand in what seemed to be an impregnable position. But the legions broke in, and he fled northward hoping to raise the Brigantes. However, their queen, Cartimandua, was allied to Rome. She arrested Caratacus and handed him over. He was taken to Rome and exhibited to the people; there he asked the famous question "Why do you, with all these great possessions, still covet our poor huts?" He was spared by Claudius and presumably pensioned.

S. S. Frere, *Oxford University*
Author of "Britannia"

CARAUSIUS, kə-rô′zhē-əs, **Marcus Aurelius** (died 293 A. D.), Roman usurper. He became a prominent figure in the Roman Empire during the joint reign of emperors Diocletian and Maximian. Carausius was a Gallic officer who had been given a command over the English Channel for the purpose of suppressing the Saxon pirates. In 287–288 he was suspected of collusion with the enemy. He was charged with catching the pirates on their return journey and then simply forcing them to share their booty with him.

Threatened with disgrace, Carausius proclaimed himself augustus (senior emperor) in Britain. In 289, Maximian built a fleet and attacked him, but Maximian's fleet was wrecked at sea. For several years Carausius was left undisturbed in Britain. Finally, in 293, he was assassinated by one of his officers, Allectus, who assumed his title. In 296 Constantius I regained Britain for the Roman Empire.

ARTHUR FERRILL, *University of Washington*

CARAVAGGIO, kä-rä-väd′jō, **Michelangelo Merisi da** (1573–1610), Italian painter, who was one of the creators of the Italian baroque style. A rebel in both art and life, Caravaggio rejected the elaborate and artificial idiom of the 16th century mannerists. Instead he developed a subjective style that was filled with a magic realism and powerfully charged with emotion. Caravaggio achieved these effects with two innovations—a radical handling of *chiaroscuro* (light and shadow) and a selective but intensely realistic portrayal of figures and detail. His work exerted an enormous and widespread influence, for example, on such painters as Rubens, Rembrandt, Velázquez, and Murillo.

Early Period. The son of a stone mason, Michelangelo Merisi, or Amerisi, was born on Sept. 28, 1573, in the small north Italian town of Caravaggio. At about the age of 11 he was apprenticed to an obscure Milanese painter, and four years later, about 1590, he went to Rome. During his first few years there, he produced genre paintings, still lifes, and mythological and allegorical scenes. They include *A Music Party* (Metropolitan Museum of Art, New York) and the *Fortune Teller* (Louvre, Paris). These are fairly small pictures with one or two half-length figures set in a shallow space and painted in bright colors.

Another early work, a Bacchus (Uffizi, Florence), an allegorical self-portrait, is traditional in its use of classical metaphor and novel in its evocation of a subjective mood of license and narcissism. A light, clear blackground sets off the figure, whose stylized forms convey reality through the solidity of the flagrantly epicene flesh and the precise still-life detail.

In these and subsequent paintings, all in oil on canvas, Caravaggio executed every detail himself without the aid of assistants. He also worked *alla prima,* that is, painting directly on the canvas without careful preparatory drawings.

Middle Period. Caravaggio's work brought him to the attention of a small circle of patrons, one of whom, Cardinal del Monte, probably helped him to obtain in 1597 his first public commission, two paintings—the *Calling of St. Matthew* and the *Martyrdom of St. Matthew*—and an altarpiece—*St. Matthew and the Angel*—for the Contarelli Chapel in San Luigi dei Francesi. These works display his characteristic principles and techniques. The tangible reality of his peasant St. Matthew reflects his belief that it is the simple and humble who receive divine knowledge and grace. His dramatic use of chiaroscuro causes forms and figures to emerge out of space that is *tenebroso,* or filled with mysterious dark shadows, as if the figures were spotlighted by a hard light from no definite source.

In the *Calling of St. Matthew,* for example, an almost anonymous Christ gestures across deep space to Matthew, a simple, provincial tax-collector, seated with companions at a table. Over them broods a vast, empty darkness, illuminated by a shaft of light from the right that is clearly conjoined with Christ's gesture, calling Matthew to his new life. In *St. Matthew and the Angel,* Caravaggio showed the saint as a vigorous peasant awkwardly seated cross-legged, one dirty foot jutting shockingly out of the picture. Beside him an angel patiently guides his clumsy hand in writing the gospel. Caravaggio's attempt to create an imagery of Biblical figures who were everyday, common people illuminated by divine grace was, however, appreciated only by the intellectual elite. The monks who commissioned the altarpiece rejected this first version because they felt Matthew was too plebeian-looking. Caravaggio had to do a second version with a more conventional saint and an angel in the heavens.

Other famous works of Caravaggio's middle period are the *Conversion of St. Paul* (Santa Maria del Popolo, Rome), the *Deposition* (Vatican, Rome), and the *Death of the Virgin* (Louvre).

Late Period. A man of violent temperament, Caravaggio was constantly involved in tavern brawls and street fights. In 1606 he killed a man and had to leave Rome. He went to Naples, where he received several commissions and strongly

CARAVAGGIO painted the *Young Bacchus* about 1590. This work, one of a series on Bacchus painted from the same model, is located in the Uffizi Gallery, in Florence.

ALINARI—ART REFERENCE BUREAU

influenced the Neapolitan school of painting, and from Naples he went to Malta and Sicily.

During his exile from Rome, Caravaggio's style changed. Many of his late works are dark and sinister more and more sacrificing logic and realism for emotional impact. Paintings such as the *Raising of Lazarus* (Messina) and the *Burial of St. Lucy* (Syracuse) are marked by austere, geometric composition, oppressive shadows, a fresh interpretation of gestures, and stiff, disproportionately scaled figures enveloped in tremendous spaces. These late works reached new heights of genius, but were forgotten until recent years.

In 1610, expecting a papal pardon, Caravaggio decided to return to Rome. On the way, he caught malaria and died near Port'Ercole in July.

MILTON LEWINE, *Columbia University*

Further Reading: Friedlaender, Walter, *Caravaggio Studies* (Princeton 1955); Hinks, Roger, *Michelangelo Merisi da Caravaggio* (London 1953); Venturi, Lionello, *Il Caravaggio* (Novara, Italy, 1951).

CARAVAGGIO, kä-rä-väd'jō, **Polidoro da** (1495?–1543), Italian painter. He was born Polidoro Caldara, in Caravaggio, and received his early training from Giulio Romano and Giovanni da Udine. He specialized in chiaroscuro, a type of monochromatic painting simulating relief structure. He was greatly admired for his chiaroscuro ornamentation of palace facades featuring classical themes and imitating the style of Roman sculpture, as in the Palazzo Cesi in Rome.

Although he was long famous and influential, Caravaggio is not highly regarded by modern critics. Many of his decorations are known only through engravings and drawings. His frieze decorations are in the Vatican.

CARAVAGGIO, kä-rä-väd'jō, is a town and commune in northern Italy, 13 miles (21 km) south of Bergamo, on the plain lying between the Serio and Adda rivers. It was the birthplace of two famous Renaissance painters known as Caravaggio, Michelangelo Merisi and Polidoro Caldara. Raw silk, hats, and knitted goods are the chief products; it is also noted for its woodcrafts and wrought iron. Near Caravaggio, on a site where the Virgin Mary is said to have performed a miracle, is an imposing church built in the 16th century, which is visited by thousands of pilgrims every year. Population: (1961) of the town, 9,938; (1966 est.) of the commune, 13,046.

CARAVAN, kar'ə-van. Since ancient times, men traveling through inhospitable territory in various parts of Africa and Asia have sought safety by organizing caravans. The word comes from the Persian *karwan,* meaning "a company of travelers." Caravans differed greatly in size, ranging from half a dozen members to processions of thousands extending from horizon to horizon. The use of pack animals to carry passengers and baggage was a distinct feature of such groups. In desert areas, camels—either the single-humped (dromedary) type of Southwest Asia and North Africa or the double-humped (Bactrian) Central Asian breed—were customarily used. In mountainous, forested, or prairie country, horses and donkeys were preferred, and in some places human porterage was used.

Although caravans were organized for many reasons, the conduct of trade was a primary purpose. Until the growth of large-scale maritime commerce, overland transport by caravan was the main means for the exchange of goods between widely separated peoples. The rise of Islam furnished an additional stimulus to caravan travel, for pilgrims journeying to the sacred city of Mecca often had no other way of travel available to them.

Caravan trips, which often required months or years to complete, were costly enterprises. Men and animals had to be maintained, and hazards from brigands, climate, and terrain were formidable. Caravaners therefore trafficked chiefly in goods of small bulk and high value. Fine cloth, ceramics, glassware, hides, salt, ivory, gems, and rare metals were typically found in caravan shipments.

Caravans apparently first flourished in the ancient Near East and linked the principal urban centers of the region extending from Persia to Egypt. In time these caravan routes reached further, to India, Central Asia, and China. The Great Silk Road through Central Asia is renowned as the path by which the wonders of Chinese civilization became known to the West.

The introduction of the camel from Southwest Asia into North Africa about the 1st century A.D. spurred the growth of communications between the lands along Africa's Mediterranean coast and the sudan and forest regions south of the Sahara. Timbuktu, Gao, Takedda, Walata, and many other African cities flourished as "ports" situated along the trans-Saharan caravan trade.

In the New World, the wagon train, in which people migrated westward, was the counterpart of the Old World caravan. Settlement more than trade, however, was the driving force behind the organization of the American and Canadian version of the caravan.

HYMAN KUBLIN
The City University of New York

CARAVANSARY, kar-ə-van'sə-rē, an inn and way station established on main roads throughout the Middle East to shelter travelers and to provide relays for official postal couriers. Caravansaries were usually spaced about a day's journey apart and sometimes were fortified to protect the highways and the surrounding areas from bandits. They were first built in ancient times throughout the Persian and Roman empires and by Islamic times were to be found in North Africa and eastern Europe as well.

Caravansaries have a characteristic physical form. They are structures with an open central court surrounded by porticoes that give access to rooms for dwellings, storage, and shops. Travelers or caravans unload and tether their animals in the central court and occupy the surrounding rooms. By Islamic times caravansaries were found not only on the highroads but also in towns where they either served as inns for incoming traders or were adapted to related but slightly differing purposes. Buildings (variously called *qaisariya, khan, funduq,* or *wakala*), built in the same physical form as the road caravansary, were used as warehouses, markets, or factories. Such caravansaries usually specialized in a single activity such as selling cloth, manufacturing soap, or even banking. Along with the suqs, they were the all-purpose physical structures for economic activity in the Middle East.

IRA M. LAPIDUS
University of California at Berkeley

CARAVEL, kar′ə-vel, a small 15th century Spanish and Portuguese merchant vessel, extremely broad-beamed, with a round stern and a sharp convex bow. Commonly the caravel carried a forecastle, projecting over the stem, and a small poop aft. The mainmast stood exactly amidships. The only other mast was the mizzen, stepped in a half deck aft of the mainmast. Caravels carried either two lateen (triangular) sails or a square mainsail and a lateen mizzen. The helmsman stood under the half deck and steered with a stern rudder, which was an innovation, and a very long tiller. Christopher Columbus' *Niña* and *Pinta* were caravels.

EDWIN TUNIS
Author of "Oars, Sails and Steam"

BIBLIOTECA NAZIONALE DI BRERA, MILAN

A CARAVEL of the 15th century, after a woodcut that was made from a drawing by Columbus in a letter he wrote to the treasurer of the king of Spain in 1493.

CARAWAY, Hattie Wyatt (1878–1950), American politician, who was the first woman elected to the U. S. Senate. She was born near Bakerville, Tenn., on Feb. 1, 1878. On the death in 1931 of her husband, Thaddeus H. Caraway, U. S. senator from Arkansas, she was appointed by Gov. Harvey Parnell to fill the vacancy. She made history when she retained the seat in a special election in 1932. Twice reelected, she served until 1945, and was the first woman to preside over a Senate session. She supported prohibition, antilobbying bills, equal rights for women, and much of the New Deal legislation. She died in Falls Church, Va., on Dec. 21, 1950.

CARAWAY, an annual or biennial plant from which caraway seeds, used as a food flavoring, are obtained. Caraway (*Carum carvi*), a member of the carrot family (Umbelliferae), is native to Europe and Asia and has become naturalized throughout much of North America. Its leaves, growing mostly from the base of the plant, are compound, finely divided, and fernlike in appearance. The stems are slender, 1 to 2 feet (30–60 cm) tall. The individual flowers, which are very small and white, are produced in small umbels (clusters) that are grouped into larger umbels about 4 inches (10 cm) across. The tiny, dry, oblong fruits are about ⅛ inch (3 mm) long, brownish gray in color, and pleasantly aromatic. The fruit, botanically known as a *schizocarp,* consists of two halves (mesocarps), each containing a single seed. These half fruits, which separate while still attached to the plant, are the caraway seeds of commerce.

Caraway seeds are used in baking, pickling, and beverages. They are grown commercially in northern Europe and parts of North America.

R. C. ALLEN
Kingwood Center, Ohio

Caraway (*Carum carvi*)

CARBARSONE, kär-bär′sōn, an arsenic-containing compound used in the treatment of intestinal infections caused by the ameba *Entamoeba histolytica.* Carbarsone acts to kill motile ameba present in the intestines and thus prevents the formation of encysted amebae. It is not, however, effective against organisms that have penetrated the intestine and entered various other organs such as the liver. Although carbarsone cannot be relied upon to kill all amebae, it is widely used in combination with other drugs. It seldom has serious toxic effects, although it occasionally causes arsenic poisoning; the antidote for such poisoning is dimercaprol. Carbarsone is prepared in tablet form.

ANDRES GOTH, M. D.
University of Texas Southwestern Medical School

CARBERRY HILL, kär′ber-ē, a hill in Midlothian, Scotland, was the site of the surrender of Mary, Queen of Scots, to the Scottish nobles who had been provoked to rebellion by her marriage to James Hepburn, Earl of Bothwell. The nobles sent a force to oppose Bothwell at Carberry Hill on June 15, 1567. There was no battle. Bothwell escaped, and Mary was sent a prisoner to Loch Leven Castle near Kinross, where she remained for 11 months.

Carberry Hill is situated about 7 miles (11 km) east of Edinburgh, between Musselburgh and Ormiston. It is about 500 feet (152 meters) high. Carberry Tower was built near the hill in 1597.

CARBIDE, kär′bīd, is a solid compound formed between carbon and a more electropositive element, such as one of the metals.

Formation and Types of Carbides. Carbides are usually formed at elevated temperatures by the reaction of a metal or a metal oxide with carbon or a carbon-containing gas. The transition metals of the 4th, 5th, and 6th groups of the periodic table form carbides with the general formula MC or M_2C, where M represents the appropriate metal atom. Examples of such carbides, which may be manufactured by the reaction of the metal with carbon, are tungsten carbides (WC and W_2C), tantalum carbide (TaC), and titanium carbide (TiC).

Carbides of nontransition metals, such as aluminum carbide (Al_4C_3) and beryllium Carbide (Be_2C), may also be formed by high temperature reactions of metals with carbon. These compounds liberate methane (CH_4) on reaction with water, and thus are termed *methanides.* Carbides formed with metals of the first group of the periodic table have the general formula M_2C_2, while those of the second group are of the formula MC_2. These compounds may be produced by high temperature reactions of the metals with acetylene (C_2H_2). They liberate acetylene when reacted with water and are called *acetylides*. Common acetylides are sodium carbide, magnesium carbide, and calcium carbide, the last used in the commercial production of acetylene.

Properties. The strong covalent bonding of carbides is responsible for their characteristic hardness, high modulus of elasticity, high boiling and melting points, low impact strength, and low electrical and thermal conductivities compared to pure metals. Zirconium, hafnium, and tantalum carbides all have melting points above 3500° C (6365° F), whereas tungsten, which has a higher melting point than any other metal, melts at 3410° C (6200° F).

Carbides such as silicon and titanium carbides are thermodynamically quite stable. This can be seen in their high heats of formation. However, some of the carbides formed in metal alloys that contain carbon are unstable and will ultimately decompose into metal atoms and graphite. The rate of decomposition of iron carbide in steels is extremely slow, and the phenomenon is not usually observed. However, in gray cast iron (an iron-carbon alloy that contains a higher percentage of carbon than steel) the rate may be rapid and results in graphite particles in the microstructure of the alloy.

The crystal structures of carbides are varied. The carbides with high melting temperatures generally have cubic or hexagonal crystal structures, while those that melt at lower temperatures have orthorhombic and tetragonal structures. The tight atomic packing in the crystalline lattices of carbides and the strong covalent bonding of these materials are responsible for the rigid stoichiometry of these compounds. That is, the ratio of metal to carbon atoms in carbides is fixed, and the solubility of extra metal or carbon atoms in the lattice is low.

Cemented Carbides. One of the most important uses of carbides is in the manufacture of cemented carbides, which are compounds that consist mainly of carbide particles (usually tungsten carbide) bonded to each other, with the interparticle pores filled with a ductile metal such as cobalt. The cobalt is present in concentrations of 3% to 20%, depending on the specific properties desired of the material. Compared to other carbides, cemented carbides show enhanced toughness, shock resistance, thermal conductivity, and compressive strength resulting from the cobalt and its interaction with the carbide.

In the manufacture of cemented carbides, powdered cobalt and powdered carbide are thoroughly blended and consolidated into a dense mass. The consolidation may be carried out by one of several methods: the blended powders may be compacted in a die and sintered above the melting point of cobalt; they may be compacted by hot pressing at elevated temperatures where the cobalt will readily deform; the powders may be extruded through a die at elevated temperatures.

Cemented carbides are used for hard, wear-resistant items such as drill bits, saw teeth, lathe and milling machine tools, wire drawing dies, and balls for the tips of ballpoint pens.

Many metal alloys that contain carbon either as an impurity or as an intentionally added alloying element may contain small amounts of carbides. Proper thermal and mechanical processing of such alloys results in improved mechanical properties due to the presence of the carbides. For example, many steels are basically alloys of iron and carbon processed to provide small particles of iron carbide in a matrix of almost pure iron. In such steels, the size, shape, distribution and amount of the carbide determine the properties of the steel.

Refractory Carbides. Carbides such as silicon and boron carbides not only have very high melting points but are also resistant to chemical attack and extremely hard. They have a hardness between 8 and 9 on the Mohs hardness scale, which means they are softer than diamond and sapphire but harder than quartz and topaz. Silicon carbide is often used in industrial grinding operations because of its hardness. It is used in the manufacture of special grinding wheels and of grinding belts and papers. The compound is also used in the manufacture of electrical resistance heating elements for furnaces.

RICHARD W. HECKEL
Drexel Institute of Technology

CARBINE, kär′bīn, a military firearm, similar to the rifle but shorter. It is fired from the shoulder. A cartridge of standard rifle caliber (diameter) but with a smaller propelling charge is used, resulting in lower muzzle velocity. No carbines currently are standard in the U. S. armed forces. The design of military rifles is tending toward the short barrel of carbines, but the firepower of the rifle is kept by firing smaller bullets at high velocity. Hunting rifles of carbine size are generally used in country with heavy brush or by hunters on horseback.

The carbine came into use toward the end of the 16th century as a short musket designed principally for use by cavalry. It remained so until World War II and the Korean War, when carbine-type weapons were used as an infantry arm, particularly in jungle fighting and by paratroopers, glider forces, and tank crews. Originally semiautomatic or self loading, later models were capable of either semiautomatic or fully automatic fire. Carbines were used by British, German, Russian, and other troops in World War II. See also SMALL ARMS.

JOHN D. BILLINGSLEY, *Colonel, U. S. Army*
United States Military Academy

CARBOHYDRATE, kär-bō-hī'drāt, any of a large class of carbon-hydrogen-oxygen compounds that includes the simple sugars and their polymers (chiefly starch, glycogen, and cellulose). Most carbohydrates are produced by photosynthesis in plants. They are the major food compounds for both plants and animals, and one group of carbohydrates (cellulose) is the chief structural material of plants.

Most carbohydrates are represented by the formula $C_x(H_2O)_n$, where n is three or higher. However, the formula does not apply to all carbohydrates. For instance, deoxyribose ($C_5H_{10}O_4$) does not fit the formula, but it is a carbohydrate; lactic acid ($C_3H_6O_3$) fits the formula, but it is not a carbohydrate. On the basis of their chemical structure, carbohydrates are classified as polyhydroxyaldehydes, polyhydroxyketones, or their derivatives.

Kinds of Carbohydrates. Carbohydrates are divided into four groups, according to the number of simple sugars or their derivatives contained within the carbohydrate molecule. Nearly all are white solids that are soluble in water, and those of low molecular weight are sweet.

Monosaccharides. The monosaccharides are simple sugar molecules made up of three, four, five, or six carbons in chain or ring form. The three-carbon sugars, called trioses, include glyceraldehyde, an aldo-sugar, and dihydroxyacetone, a keto-sugar. Tetroses, or four-carbon sugars, include D-erythrose and D-threose.

The five-carbon sugars are called pentoses. Some, such as D-ribose and D-xylose, occur widely in nature and are of great biological significance. L-arabinose is a five-carbon compound that is the only L-series sugar to occur in appreciable quantities in nature. In some of the five-carbon sugars, a hydrogen atom replaces the hydroxyl group. The resulting compound has one less oxygen atom and is called a deoxy compound. One deoxy compound, 2-deoxy D-ribose, is a major component of biological coding systems.

Six-carbon sugars, the hexoses, are the most important intermediate source of energy to biological organisms (sunlight is the primary source; adenosine triphosphate, or ATP, is the immediate source). Common natural hexoses include D-glucose, D-mannose, D-galactose, and D-fructose.

D-fructose, a common fruit sugar which also is found in honey, is the only sugar besides glucose that is metabolized in any substantial quantity by plants and animals for energy. In the respiratory process in cells, glucose is converted into fructose-1,6-diphosphate—an important step in glucose metabolism for the liberation of energy.

Glucose, fructose, and mannose can be fermented to yield carbon dioxide and alcohol. Some organisms, like lactic-acid bacteria, cannot live in an atmosphere with free oxygen and must rely on fermentation for their energy.

Another important group of monosaccharides, the hexosamines, have an amino group (NH_2) in place of the hydroxyl group on the second carbon atom. These compounds are the monosaccharide subunits in chitin—the exoskeletal material in insects, lobsters, and crabs, and they are found in heparin, a substance in the blood that prevents clotting. The hexosamines also form a large part of hyaluronic acid, a carbohydrate that has adhesive properties in tissue and lubricating properties in the joints. They are the major substance, other than water, in the vitreous humor of the eye and in the umbilical fluid. These substances —chitin, heparin, and hyaluronic acid—also are known as mucopolysaccharides.

Disaccharides. The disaccharides are molecules of two simple sugars linked together. Common disaccharides are maltose, lactose, and sucrose. Maltose (malt sugar) is made up of two glucose units; lactose (milk sugar) consists of one glucose unit linked to one galactose unit; and sucrose (cane sugar) is composed of glucose and fructose. One interesting disaccharide is amygdalin, a component of oil of bitter almonds. When hydrolyzed, it yields two glucose molecules and the poisonous hydrogen cyanide.

Trisaccharides and Polysaccharides. The trisaccharides are raffinose (fructose, glucose, and galactose) and melezitose (glucose, glucose, and fructose). The most commonly known polysaccharides are cellulose, starch, and glycogen. All of these are made of identical sugar molecules linked together in a long chain.

Cellulose is the most abundant polysaccharide and makes up over half of the total carbon in the plant world. It is found in all plant cell walls and in the woody parts of shrubs and trees. Cellulose also makes up the body wall of tunicates in the animal kingdom. The cellulose molecule is a long unbranched chain consisting of 300 to 3,000 glucose units joined together. The molecular weight of cellulose ranges from 50,000 to 500,000. Cellulose is almost totally insoluble in water and thus is difficult to digest. Herbivorous vertebrate animals such as sheep and cattle and invertebrates such as termites digest cellulose by way of enzymes produced by microorganisms living in their intestinal tracts. Man has difficulty in digesting cellulose, so it serves mainly as roughage in his diet.

Starch is a large polysaccharide made up of approximately 500 to 10,000 glucose subunits organized as repeating maltose (glucose-glucose) units. It is the energy storage form in cereal grain, peas, beans, potatoes, green fruits, and other plants. Natural starches contain two components—amylose, which has long unbranched chains, and amylopectin, a shorter, highly branched chain.

Glycogen, or animal starch, is a reserve energy form stored in liver and muscle cells. It is a branched-chain polysaccharide readily dispersed in water. The size of the glycogen molecule ranges from approximately 1,000 to 400,000 glucose units with a total molecular weight of 160,000 to 65,000,000.

Other homogeneous polysaccharides include xylans, dextrans, insulins, pectins, and chitins.

The heterogeneous polysaccharides are large polymers of mixed monosaccharide units. Examples of these are hemi-cellulose, gum acacia, agar, and mucoproteins.

Chemical Representation of Carbohydates. Carbohydrates can be represented by different types of chemical notation. Each of the notations emphasizes certain properties and characteristics of carbohydrates.

Straight Chain Form. Carbohydrate molecules can be represented as straight carbon chains or in some cases branched carbon chains. This method of representation emphasizes the asymmetric carbon atoms in carbohydrates and the resulting stereoisomers (the different possible arrangements in space of the atoms that make up a particular molecule).

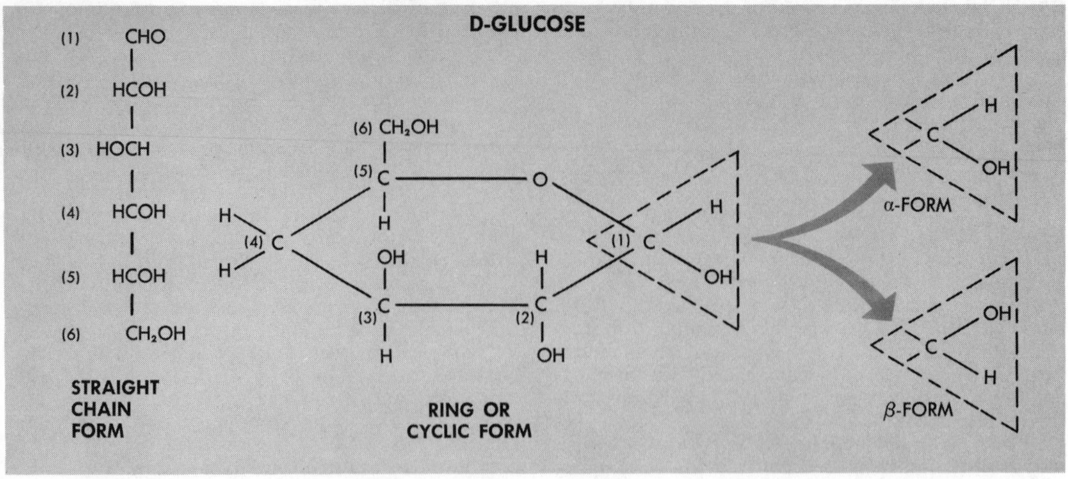

D-GLUCOSE

(1) CHO
(2) HCOH
(3) HOCH
(4) HCOH
(5) HCOH
(6) CH_2OH

STRAIGHT CHAIN FORM

RING OR CYCLIC FORM

α-FORM

β-FORM

Asymmetric Carbon Atoms. A carbon atom, which has a valence of 4, is asymmetric when four different atoms or groups of atoms are bonded to it. The number of stereoisomers for a carbohydrate with n asymmetric carbon atoms is 2^n. Thus if a carbohydrate has three asymmetric carbon atoms, it has 2^3, or eight, stereoisomers.

One example of a carbohydrate with different stereochemical forms is glucose. Of its six carbon atoms, four (numbers 2, 3, 4, and 5) are asymmetric, and thus glucose has 16 possible isomers. The carbon atoms containing hydroxyl (OH) and hydrogen (H) groups can have the groups reversed. This switch changes the molecular form and thus results in a different six-carbon sugar. Glucose also exists in two different forms (α and β) when the compound occurs in ring form. The first carbon becomes asymmetric, and the H and OH positions on this atom may be reversed.

Another dissymmetry in carbohydrate molecules is designated D or L. If the hydroxyl group on the carbon atom farthest from the oxidized carbon (CHO) is to the right when the formula is written or printed on paper, the letter D is prefixed to the compound. In D-glucose, the determining group is at carbon 5. If the hydroxyl group on this carbon is to the left, the letter L is prefixed to the compound, such as L-ribose, in which the determining group is at carbon 4.

Glucose also can be a dextro-isomer or a levoisomer, in which a solution of a glucose rotates a plane of polarized light either to the right or to the left. The plane of rotation and the angle of rotation are measured by an instrument known as a polarimeter. Solutions with this property are called optically active solutions. Compounds shifting the plane of the light to the right are dextrorotatory compounds and are designated with either a *d* or a plus. Those shifting the plane of light to the left are levorotatory compounds are are designated with either an *l* or a minus, as in (−) fructose.

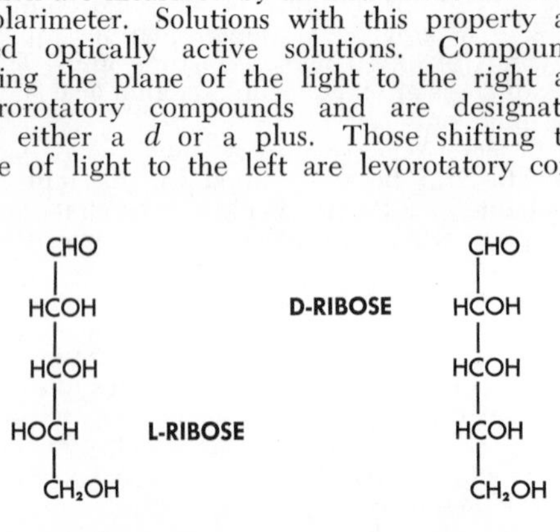

L-RIBOSE: CHO, HCOH, HCOH, HOCH, CH_2OH

D-RIBOSE: CHO, HCOH, HCOH, HCOH, CH_2OH

Ring Form. Carbon atoms are bonded to hydrogen and hydroxyl groups at certain angles. When a three-dimensional model of glucose is built using known angles, the oxygen on carbon 1 is seen to be close to the hydroxyl group on carbon 5. In an actual molecule of glucose, the oxygen would therefore attract the hydrogen atom in the hydroxyl group, and the oxygen can thus connect carbon 1 and carbon 5, producing a ring form. This is the second way in which carbohydrates may be represented. The ring structure is more accurate than the straight-chain in summarizing the properties of sugars. Also, X-ray crystallographic studies have shown that glucose, for instance, is a cyclic compound.

ALFRED NOVAK, *Stephens College*

CARBOLIC ACID. See PHENOL.

CARBON, kär′bən, symbol C, is a nonmetallic chemical element whose compounds are very widely distributed in nature. There are three elementary forms of carbon, of which two—graphite and diamond—are crystalline allotropes. The other, amorphous, form includes several impure substances, such as coal, which originated in plant life. Carbon compounds make up petroleum and natural gas and occur in oil shale. Other carbon compounds are found in limestone and dolomite rock. Still others occur in solution in ground water, lakes, streams, and in the oceans. All organic compounds contain carbon, and large and complicated carbon compounds form the complex structural basis of living matter.

Graphite and diamond, the crystalline forms of carbon, are discussed in separate articles. Some of the less well crystallized forms of carbon, such as charcoal, are used as adsorbents for poisonous gases and for the removal of colored impurities in such materials as oils and syrups. The extremely porous structure of such carbon exposes a very large surface area per unit mass. The unbalanced electronic attraction of surface carbon atoms draws and holds foreign materials, especially those with polar molecules. When the adsorbing surface becomes saturated with foreign matter, it can often be cleaned by heat or the action of steam. Although such forms of carbon may be described as amorphous, they do show some evidence of graphitic structure. Carbon is also a valuable reducing agent for the ores of many common metals.

Properties. Carbon is a nonmetallic element of atomic number 6. It melts at 3550° C (6454° F), although it begins to sublime at 3500° C (6364° F). Its boiling point is about 4827° C (8750° F). The specific gravity of carbon, in the form of graphite, is 2.26. In its chemical reactions, carbon commonly exhibits a valence of 4, although it may show valences of 2 and 3. It is inert to most forms of chemical attack at ordinary temperatures and is virtually insoluble in most common solvents. At elevated temperatures all forms of carbon will oxidize (burn) to form carbon dioxide, although the kindling temperatures of diamond and graphite are quite high.

Isotopes. There are seven isotopes of carbon ranging from ^{10}C to ^{16}C. Only two of these isotopes, ^{12}C and ^{13}C, are stable. Natural carbon, which is a mixture of the stable isotopes, consists of 98.89% ^{12}C and 1.11% ^{13}C, and has an atomic mass of 12.01115. The most nearly stable of the radioactive isotopes is ^{14}C, which has a half-life of 5,770 years and is used in archaeology for dating specimens. (See also CARBON-14 DATING.) In 1962 the isotope ^{12}C became the international unit for atomic mass measurement. It was assigned a mass of 12.00000 units.

Bonding of Carbon. Carbon, which forms only covalent bonds, can form linkages with other carbon atoms or with atoms of other elements. Strong carbon-to-carbon linkages make possible the complicated structures of organic substances. These structures can take the form of chains or rings or combinations of chains and rings. Atoms of other elements sometimes form parts of these structures or branch from them.

The carbon atom has four outer-level electrons, two in the 2s sublevel and one each in two orbitals of the 2p sublevel. The spectral notation for this structure is $2s^2$, $2p^2$. In bonding with other atoms the carbon atom behaves as if one of the 2s electrons moves into the unoccupied 2p orbital. There are then four unpaired electrons in four orbitals which bear the same relationship to the atom. This behavior is called sp^3 hybridization.

Graphite, which is the most stable form of carbon, consists of plates of six carbon atom rings in which each atom forms covalent bonds with three others. Three electrons from each atom are thus bound, and the fourth electron is free to move from atom to atom. These mobile electrons give graphite the property of electrical conductivity.

Diamond has a crystal structure consisting of regular tetrahedra with a carbon atom at each vertex. Each carbon atom is linked to four others by covalent bonds that bind all four outer electrons. Diamond is a nonconductor of electricity.

Carbon Compounds. There are more than a million known compounds of carbon. These may be divided into the inorganic carbon compounds and the organic compounds.

Organic compounds may be divided into two groups—the *aliphatic* compounds, which are in the form of continuous or branched chains, and the *aromatic* compounds, in which carbon atoms in a six-member ringed structure form part of the molecule. One class of organic compounds contains only carbon and hydrogen atoms; these compounds are called *hydrocarbons*. In the simplest saturated hydrocarbon, methane (CH_4), the electron in each outer level orbital of the carbon atom is paired with an electron from a hydrogen atom, and a tetrahedral structure of four hydrogen atoms around the carbon results. The effective angle between any two of these covalent bonds is 109° 28′.

Saturated chain hydrocarbons are formed when two unpaired electrons of each carbon atom are shared with electrons of other carbon atoms and the other two are shared with hydrogen atoms. The two end carbon atoms on such a chain would have only one carbon-to-carbon bond and three carbon-to-hydrogen bonds. There is a distance of 1.54 Angstrom units between centers of adjacent carbon atoms.

Ethene (C_2H_4, or $H_2C{=}CH_2$) is the simplest member of a family of unsaturated hydrocarbons in which double bonding occurs. Three of the unpaired electrons of each carbon seem to be directed toward corners of an equilateral triangle. Two of these form bonds with hydrogen atoms and the third is shared with an electron of the other carbon atom, forming the principal, or sigma, bond between them. The fourth orbitals of the two carbon atoms unite to form a secondary, or pi, bond between the atoms.

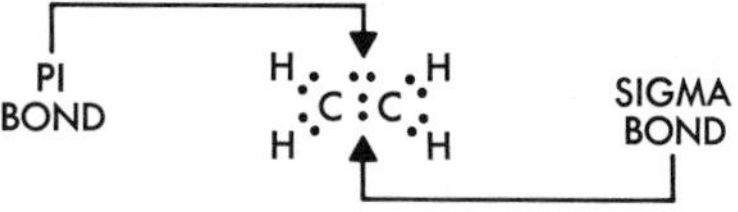

The sigma bond serves to hold the two atoms together, and the pi bond, which is more exposed, is open to chemical attack and seems to account for the increased chemical activity of unsaturated hydrocarbons.

In ethyne (C_2H_2, or $HC{\equiv}CH$), a triply bonded hydrocarbon, one orbital from each carbon atom is combined to produce the sigma bond. An electron orbital, 180° removed, bonds a hydrogen atom on each carbon atom. The two remaining orbitals of each carbon atom produce two pi bonds, which are quite receptive to chemical attack: H:C$\vdots$C:H.

The basic structure of the aromatic hydrocarbons is the six-member carbon ring.

Two orbitals of each carbon atom bond to adjacent carbon atoms, producing sigma bonds, and the third orbital bonds a hydrogen atom. The fourth orbitals of the carbon atom, which are represented in the diagram by the circle, are available to form pi bonds between them. These aromatic pi bonds do not add atoms or groups of atoms as readily as those in chain hydrocarbons.

Inorganic Carbon Compounds. Among the most common of the many inorganic carbon compounds are carbon dioxide and carbon monoxide, carbon disulfide, carbon tetrachloride, the carbonates, the hydrogen carbonates, the cyanides, the cyanates, the thiocyanates, and the carbides. These compounds are covered in separate articles.

OTTO W. NITZ
Stout State University, Menomonie, Wis.

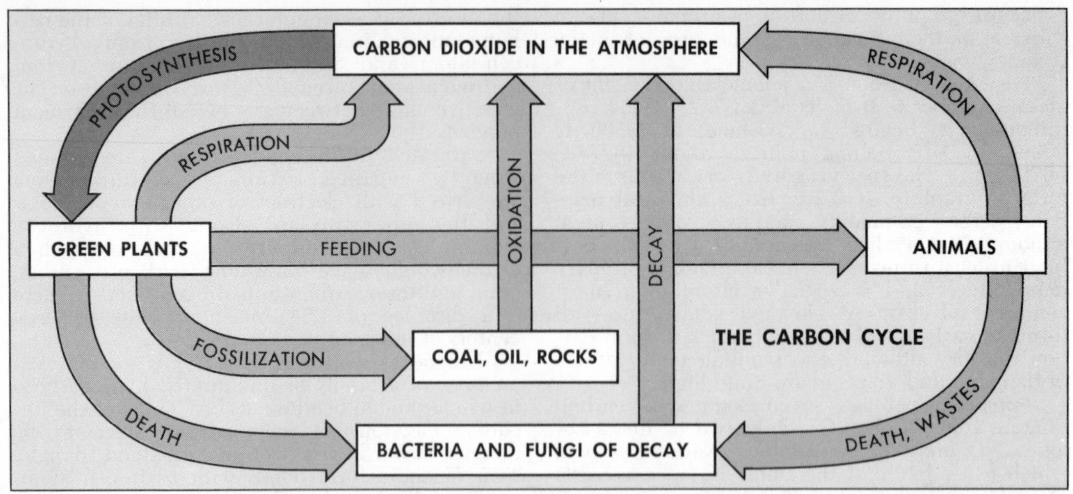

Carbon dioxide from the atmosphere is utilized by green plants in photosynthesis and returned to the atmosphere by animal respiration and the breakdown of organic matter.

CARBON BLACK is the fine particles of elementary carbon formed by the incomplete combustion of hydrocarbon gases and liquids. The particles range in diameter from 25 to 400 millimicrons. About 95% of the carbon black produced in the United States is used in rubber manufacture. Small percentages are used as pigment in printers ink, India ink, and paints.

Carbon black is the most important reinforcing filler used in rubber manufacture. It gives toughness and abrasion resistance to both natural and synthetic rubber. The actual mechanism of the reinforcing action is not fully understood, but it is closely related to particle size; the finer the particles, the greater the reinforcing action.

Most carbon black is manufactured by the incomplete combustion of natural gas or liquid-oil refinery by-products in a special furnace. The combustion gases carry particles of furnace black, a form of carbon black, which are then separated out by means of cyclone separators, electric precipitators, and bag filters, in sequence.

In the channel process, an older method, natural gas, often enriched by oils, is burned with insufficient air in special burners that produce a smoky flame. The flames strike a channeled steel surface, which moves slowly back and forth. The soot deposited in the channels is then scraped off by stationary blades.

Another form of carbon black, called acetylene black, is produced by the thermal decomposition of acetylene, CH_2-CH_2. The reaction, which is exothermic, is started by heating the acetylene to about 800°C (1475°F), after which it continues without the application of further heat.

OTTO W. NITZ
Stout State University, Menomonie, Wis.

CARBON CYCLE, the flow of the element carbon between living and nonliving systems on earth. The cycle is essential for sustaining life.

Using Carbon. Carbon dioxide is the source of almost all the carbon used by living systems. It is stored in "reservoirs" in the waters, rocks, and atmosphere of the earth. The first step in the carbon cycle begins when green plants trap carbon dioxide from the atmosphere along with energy from the sun. In this process of photosynthesis, simple food compounds known as carbohydrates are formed. The plants then may convert these carbohydrates into other complex organic compounds such as proteins or fats.

In the next step, the plants are eaten by animals, which cannot manufacture their own food through photosynthesis and therefore depend on green plants as an energy source. The carbon compounds in the plants are digested by the animals, which then incorporate the digested carbon compounds into their own bodies. Other animals eat the plant-feeding animals, whose carbon compounds are digested, in turn, and incorporated into the protoplasm of the meat-eating animals. Thus the element carbon is transferred from one organism to another through sequences that may become quite long. In the process, any given carbon atom may become an integral part of numerous types of carbon compounds.

Returning Carbon. Eventually most of the carbon that has been bound through photosynthesis is returned as carbon dioxide to the atmosphere or oceans. This return phase is extremely important, because without it all the available carbon dioxide would become bound in compounds of the tissues of plants and animals and life would stop.

There are several pathways that return carbon to the reservoirs. The most direct pathway is cellular respiration, in which plant and animal cells free the contained energy stored in carbon compounds by breaking them into smaller molecules, including carbon dioxide. The carbon dioxide of respiration is then available for photosynthesis.

Another pathway involves carbon compounds contained in waste products eliminated by animals or in the dead tissue of plants and animals. If these materials were not broken down, the face of the earth would become a dunghill littered with dead bodies. Eventually, all the carbon would be tied up in these forms, and life would end. Fortunately the process of decay, or putrefaction, provides a return pathway for such bound carbon compounds. Bacteria and other fungi attack and digest the carbon-containing compounds in waste materials and the tissues of dead organisms. During the process, the bacteria and other fungi are able to utilize the energy released through the degradation of the carbon-containing compounds. As a result of such activities, carbon dioxide and other low-energy compounds are produced. Thus carbon dioxide is released to be used in the cycle again.

Another way in which carbon dioxide is returned to the atmosphere or oceans is the combustion of coal, natural gas, and oil. Combustion of this type returns carbon that has been bound for millions of years in these fossilized remains of prehistoric organisms. Combustion of wood, cloth, or paper results in the freeing of carbon that has been bound for relatively short periods of time.

DAVID A. OTTO, *Stephens College*

CARBON DIOXIDE, dī-ok'sīd, is the commonest and most stable oxide of carbon. It is a colorless, odorless gas with a density about 1½ times greater than air. It dissolves in water, forming a weak acid, carbonic acid, H_2CO_3. Carbon dioxide does not burn or normally support combustion. However, at high temperatures it oxidizes sodium, magnesium, and potassium.

Carbon dioxide is formed by the combustion in excess oxygen of any material containing carbon, and in decay processes and as an end product in animal metabolism. It is present in the air in concentrations of about 0.03%. Although it is not usually described as poisonous, its presence in air in concentrations greater than 10% will produce unconsciousness and eventually death from suffocation, or lack of oxygen; there is also some narcotic action.

At room temperature, carbon dioxide can be liquefied at a pressure of about 56 atmospheres, and it is normally stored and shipped in the liquid form. It has a critical temperature of 98°F (31.1°C) and a critical pressure of 72.8 atmospheres. When liquid carbon dioxide is permitted to evaporate at atmospheric pressure, the consequent absorption of heat by the vapor allows the remaining liquid to freeze and form a solid. The loose white solid that results is compressed into compact cakes and becomes the commercial refrigerant known as "dry ice." Dry ice sublimes, or changes directly from a solid to a gaseous state, at −109°F (−78°C) at atmospheric pressure.

Production. Approximately one million tons of carbon dioxide is manufactured in the United States annually. One of the chief industrial sources is the fermentation of sugars in the production of alcohol:

$$C_6H_{12}O_6 \rightarrow 2C_2H_5OH + 2CO_2.$$

Carbon dioxide is also produced in the combustion of coke and absorbed from the combustion gases in a potassium carbonate solution. It is also recovered as a by-product of the manufacture of quicklime by the thermal decomposition of limestone:

$$CaCO_3 \xrightarrow{\text{heat}} CaO + CO_2.$$

Uses. About half of the carbon dioxide produced is used for refrigeration, mostly in the form of dry ice. Over half the remainder goes into the manufacture of carbonated soft drinks. The carbon dioxide is dissolved in water at pressures of 3 to 4 atmospheres, and after the sugar or artificial sweeteners, flavoring extracts, and coloring materials are added, the solution is bottled under pressure. The carbonic acid that is formed by the dissolved gas supplies the pleasant sharp taste.

In liquid form, carbon dioxide is used extensively in fire extinguishers. A mixture of gas and solid that quickly sublimes dilutes the air and reduces the oxygen percentage below the combustion level, smothering the fire. Carbon dioxide is used in the manufacture of soda ash, Na_2CO_3, an important industrial material, and it is also combined with ammonia in the production of urea, which is used in the manufacture of fertilizers and urea plastics.

OTTO W. NITZ
Stout State University, Menomonie, Wis.

CARBON DISULFIDE, dī-sul'fīd, CS_2, is a flammable, nearly colorless, very toxic liquid. The odor of commercial carbon disulfide, which is reminiscent of rotten cabbage or eggs, is caused by impurities. Carbon disulfide must be stored and handled with care. Its toxicity threshold is only about 20 parts per million, and it forms explosive mixtures with air when present in concentrations of from 2 to 50%. The flash point of such mixtures is low enough for them to be ignited by hot steam pipes.

Carbon disulfide solidifies at −111°C (−168°F), boils at 46.3°C (115.3°F), and has a specific gravity of 1.261. It is only slighty soluble in water but is completely miscible with alcohol, ether, and carbon tetrachloride. It is a good solvent for oils, fats, waxes, rubber, sulfur, iodine, and white phosphorus.

Carbon disulfide is commonly manufactured by heating coke and sulfur in an electric furnace at from 800 to 1000°C (1472 to 1832°F). The product passes out of the furnace as a vapor and is then condensed to a liquid. Annual U. S. production is about 700 million pounds.

The major use of carbon disulfide is in the manufacture of viscose rayon and cellophane. Wood pulp is first treated with a 20% sodium hydroxide solution and then with carbon disulfide. A viscous liquid called cellulose xanthate is formed, which is then forced through spinnerets or slits into an acid bath where the regenerated cellulose forms either a fiber or a sheet.

Carbon disulfide is also used in the manufacture of carbon tetrachloride, dithiocarbonates, thiocyanates, and urea. It is also used in agriculture to fumigate stored grain, to disinfect soil, and to destroy burrowing animals.

OTTO W. NITZ
Stout State University, Menomonie, Wis.

CARBON-14 DATING, or *radiocarbon dating*, is a technique widely used for dating archaeological objects. The isotope ^{14}C is formed in the atmosphere by the bombardment of nitrogen by cosmic rays. It is oxidized to carbon dioxide and taken up by plants. The plants, in turn, are ingested by animals.

In living organisms there is an equilibrium between the intake of ^{14}C and the decay of the isotope. After death, radioactivity slowly decreases; when the level in a specimen is compared with that of living organisms, the period since death can be estimated by calculating the amount of decay of ^{14}C, which has a half-life of 5,700 years. This method can be used for periods up to 60,000 years. See also ARCHAEOLOGY—3.

OTTO W. NITZ
Stout State University, Menomonie, Wis.

CARBON MONOXIDE, mən-ok'sīd, CO, is a colorless, odorless, highly poisonous gas. It is only slightly soluble in water. Its boiling point is − 191.5° C (− 312.7° F), and its freezing point is − 199° C (− 326.2° F). Carbon monoxide is formed by the incomplete combustion of carbon, hydrocarbon fuels, and other carbonaceous material. It normally comprises 10 to 12% of the exhaust gases of internal combustion engines.

The lowest limit of carbon monoxide toxicity is about 100 parts per million in air. This level develops quickly if an automobile engine is allowed to run in a small closed garage. It can also accumulate in a car from a faulty exhaust system or in a house from a defective furnace or a stopped up flue. Because the victim of carbon monoxide poisoning becomes drowsy, he often does not recognize his own danger.

Carbon monoxide is poisonous because it interferes with the ability of the blood to carry oxygen. Normally, oxygen is readily bound to hemoglobin molecules in red blood cells in the oxygen-rich environment of the lungs and is readily released in the oxygen-poor environment of other body tissues. Carbon monoxide interferes with this process by combining with hemoglobin in place of oxygen; since this reaction is not easily reversible, the hemoglobin—once combined with carbon monoxide—can no longer carry oxygen.

Carbon monoxide is a component of several industrial fuel gases. For example, *water gas,* a mixture of carbon monoxide and hydrogen, is made by passing steam through a white-hot bed of coal or coke. *Producer gas,* which contains about 25% carbon monoxide, is formed from coal or coke burned in a deficiency of air. *Synthesis gas,* a mixture of hydrogen and carbon monoxide, is used in the manufacture of alcohols, aldehydes, and synthetic petroleum.

OTTO W. NITZ
Stout State University, Menomonie, Wis.

CARBON-NITROGEN-OXYGEN BI-CYCLE, a group of thermonuclear reactions in which carbon, nitrogen, and oxygen nuclei capture protons. The CNO bi-cycle is important in astrophysics because it is believed to be the principal source of energy in stars more massive than the sun. The first reaction is the capture of a proton ($_1H^1$) by the light stable carbon isotope C^{12} to produce a radioactively unstable nitrogen isotope, N^{13}, with emission of a photon (γ). Emission of a positron (e^+) and a neutrino (ν) by N^{13} produces the heavier of the two stable carbon isotopes C^{13}. In the next reaction C^{13} captures a proton to form stable N^{14}. The remainder of the reactions can be read in the accompanying table.

Usually when N^{15} captures a proton, an alpha particle (nucleus of the helium-4 atom) is emitted and the CN part of the bi-cycle is completed by cycling back to C^{12}. However, in about one in 2,000 proton captures by N^{15}, O^{16} is formed with emission of a photon, and the bi-cycle goes into the NO part. The final reaction cycles back to N^{14} upon formation of the alpha particle.

The net result of the bi-cycle by either route is the synthesis of a helium nucleus from four hydrogen nuclei, the emission of two positrons and two neutrinos, and the release of 26.73 Mev of energy (including the annihilation energy of the two positrons with two electrons). The cycling conserves the total number of C, N, and O nuclei so that this group of nuclei acts as a catalyst in the formation of helium from hydrogen. However, the probability of N^{14} capturing a proton is very small compared to the probabilities of the other CN reactions. Therefore, if the CNO bi-cycle is active in a star at a temperature in the range of 20 million to 100 million °K for a long time in the presence of many protons, the majority (more than 90%) of the C, N, and O nuclei will be processed into N^{14}. Only small amounts of C^{12}, C^{13}, N^{15}, O^{16}, and O^{17} will be left in the ashes of hydrogen burning by the CNO bi-cycle.

GEORGEANNE R. CAUGHLAN
Montana State University

Further Reading: Bethe, Hans A., "Energy Production in Stars," *Physical Review,* Vol. 55, p. 103 and pp. 434–456 (1939); Caughlan, Georgeanne R., "Approach to Equilibrium in the CNO Bi-cycle," *The Astrophysical Journal,* vol. 141, pp 688–717 (1965); Fowler, William A., *Nuclear Astrophysics* (Philadelphia 1967).

CARBON TETRACHLORIDE, tet-rə-klôr'īd, CCl_4, is a heavy, nonconducting, nonflammable, colorless liquid. It yields heavy vapors that have a peculiar odor. Carbon tetrachloride solidifies at − 23° C (9.4° F) and boils at 77° C (170.6° F). Its specific gravity is 1.585. The carbon tetrachloride molecule is a regular tetrahedron with the carbon atom in the center, and it is nonpolar. The liquid is almost insoluble in water, which is polar, but it dissolves readily in nonpolar solvents, such as alcohol.

Carbon tetrachloride is poisonous. It has a toxicity threshold of about 25 parts per million in air. It apparently can also be absorbed through the skin. Excessive breathing of the vapor or contact with the liquid can cause nausea, and with prolonged exposure, it may lead to liver or kidney damage and finally death.

Carbon tetrachloride is widely used an an industrial solvent and degreasing agent and as an intermediate in the manufacture of other materials. It is also used in grain fumigants and in insecticides. Because carbon tetrachloride is a good solvent for grease it was once widely used in dry-cleaning fluids, but it has now been replaced by less toxic chemicals.

Carbon tetrachloride has been used for extinguishing fires. When heated it liberates large quantities of very heavy vapor that acts to dilute the oxygen in the air and tends to smother the flames. It is a nonconductor of electricity

CNO BI-CYCLE

$$_6C^{12} + {}_1H^1 \rightarrow {}_7N^{13} + \gamma$$
$$_7N^{13} \rightarrow {}_6C^{13} + e^+ + \nu$$
$$_6C^{13} + {}_1H^1 \rightarrow {}_7N^{14} + \gamma$$
$$_7N^{14} + {}_1H^1 \rightarrow {}_8O^{15} + \gamma$$
$$_8O^{15} \rightarrow {}_7N^{15} + e^+ + \nu$$
$$_7N^{15} + {}_1H^1 \rightarrow {}_2He^4 + {}_6C^{12}$$

or once in about 2000 times

$$_7N^{15} + {}_1H^1 \rightarrow {}_8O^{16} + \gamma$$
$$_8O^{16} + {}_1H^1 \rightarrow {}_9F^{17} + \gamma$$
$$_9F^{17} \rightarrow {}_8O^{17} + e^+ + \nu$$
$$_8O^{17} + {}_1H^1 \rightarrow {}_2He^4 + {}_7N^{14}$$

and can be used safely on electrical fires. However, a toxicity hazard results in closed areas from high vapor concentration and from the oxidation of some carbon tetrachloride to phosgene, $COCl_2$, which is a highly poisonous gas.

Carbon tetrachloride is manufactured by heating carbon disulfide with dry chlorine gas in the presence of a catalyst:

$$CS_2 + 3Cl_2 \rightarrow CCl_4 + S_2Cl_2.$$

The products are separated by fractional distillation, and sulfur monochloride is recycled with fresh carbon disulfide to produce additional carbon tetrachloride:

$$2S_2Cl_2 + CS_2 \rightarrow CCl_4 + 6S.$$

OTTO W. NITZ
Stout State University, Menomonie, Wis.

CARBONADO, kär-bə-nā'dō, is a dark, tough, compact form of diamond, the hardest known substance. It is also known as "black diamond," or simply as "carbon." Carbonado is of importance as a grinding and cutting material in industry, where it is used on lathes and on steel bits for deep-boring drills.

Carbonado is an aggregate composed of many small particles. It is therefore somewhat less dense than are crystalline diamonds, but it is also less brittle. The aggregate is opaque, ranges from dark gray to black, and has a resinous or diamondlike luster. It is of no value as a gem material.

The commercial supply of carbonado comes from the state of Bahia in Brazil. It occurs in angular fragments that occasionally have a rough cubic outline. See also DIAMOND.

Composition, C; hardness, 10; specific gravity, 3.15–3.29; crystal system, isometric.

CARBONARI, kär-bə-nä'rē, members of a liberal and patriotic secret society, the Carboneria, that was particularly active during the early part of the 19th century in Italy, France, and Spain, with branches in other countries. The name Carbonari signifies "makers of charcoal"—symbolically the purifiers, carriers of liberty, morality, and progress. A relation to medieval guilds cannot be proved, but it is possible that the carbonari were connected with a late 18th century secret democratic association of inhabitants of the French and Swiss Jura. The Carboneria, or Charbonnerie in French, has also been considered an offshoot of Freemasonry, but despite similarities and contacts between the two societies, there were differences and antagonisms.

Evidence of the existence of the society in eastern France in the first decade of the 19th century is not conclusive. However, there is reliable evidence that Carbonari were present in southern Italy soon after the French conquest of the Kingdom of Naples in 1806. There the society acquired a considerable following among those sectors of the middle and upper classes that opposed the rule of Napoleon's brother Joseph and of his brother-in-law Joachim Murat.

The Carbonari developed their program and organization in southern Italy. They favored constitutional government founded on free universal suffrage; national unity and independence; and a moral code based on Christian ethics. Although anticlerical, the Carbonari professed belief in God, the Grand Master of the Universe. Secrecy, pseudonyms, and passwords were essential features of the society. Its members addressed one another as "cousin." Complicated symbolic rituals accompanied initiation into each of the nine ranks of the society's structure. Symbolism was largely borrowed from Christianity and freemasonry. The *vendita* (literally, "sale"; symbolically, the union of co-workers), formed of 20 Carbonari, was the basic group. Twenty *vendite* formed a *vendita centrale* (central union), grouped in turn in *vendite superiori* or *madri* (mother unions), and subordinated to the Alta or Grande Vendita (the High or Great Union), composed of delegates from the *madri*.

When Murat called for Italian unification in March 1815, the Carbonari supported him. At that time many *vendite* were organized in northern Italy. Numerous conspiracies were hatched between 1817 and 1831, three of which led to insurrections in Naples in 1820, in Piedmont in 1821, and in the Papal States and Modena in 1831. In 1820, Saint-Amand Bazard, the future disciple of Saint-Simon, organized *vendite* in Paris. Several conspiracies were suppressed by the French police in 1820–1822. The society was still active in France at the time of the 1830 revolution. In that year the Italian revolutionary Philippe (Filippo) Buonarroti organized the Universal Democratic Charbonnerie in Paris. Carbonarismo, as it was called in Spain, appealed to many Spanish liberals after their 1823 defeat.

By the mid-1830's the society had become ineffectual everywhere and was superseded by more dynamic organizations. Among those who joined the ranks of the Carbonari at one time or another were the Marquis de Lafayette, Lord Byron, Louis Napoleon (later Napoleon III), and Giuseppe Mazzini.

M. SALVADORI, *Smith College*

CARBONATES, kär'bən-āts, a widespread, abundant, and important group of minerals. Some of them are of great economic value. The carbonates are metallic salts of carbonic acid, H_2CO_3, a weak acid that is one of the principal weathering agents of rocks. The metals include calcium, magnesium, iron, manganese, zinc, barium, strontium, and lead.

The carbonates fall into subgroups of different crystal structures. The calcite group has hexagonal crystals. The principal minerals in this group are calcite, $CaCO_3$; dolomite, $CaMg(CO_3)_2$; magnesite, $MgCO_3$; siderite, $FeCO_3$; rhodochrosite, $MnCO_3$; and smithsonite, $ZnCO_3$. Calcite appears in forms such as limestone, marble, and chalk; along with dolomite, it is an important building material. Magnesia is derived from magnesite, and the other carbonates have been used as ores of their respective metals.

The aragonite group (orthorhombic crystals) begins with aragonite, which is also $CaCO_3$, but has a different crystal structure. The other important members of the series are witherite, $BaCO_3$; strontianite, $SrCO_3$; and cerussite, $PbCO_3$. Cerussite is an important ore of lead.

There are also carbonates that crystallize in the monoclinic system. The principal minerals are malachite, $Cu_2CO_3(OH)_2$, and azurite, $Cu_3(CO_3)_2(OH)_2$, both of which are copper ores. See articles on individual minerals.

CARBONDALE, a city in southwestern Illinois, is in Jackson county, about 145 miles (233 km) south of Springfield, in the southern Illinois coal district. The city is a trade and educational center and a rail junction with railroad shops. Its manufactures include gloves, dresses, dairy foods, concrete, treated wood, and tape. Fruits and truck vegetables are grown nearby. Southern Illinois University, a 4-year coeducational institution, is here. Crab Orchard National Wildlife Refuge is just east of the city, and Shawnee National Forest is 1 mile (2 km) south. Carbondale has a commission form of government. Population: 22,816.

CARBONDALE, kär'bən-dāl, is an industrial city in northeastern Pennsylvania, in Lackawanna county, 20 miles (32 km) northeast of Scranton. Its industry is varied and includes the manufacture of perforated metals, tanks, boilers, mobile homes, and wood products. There are also dress factories and silk mills. Dairy, poultry, fruit, and truck farms are nearby. Situated in a mountainous region, the city is a summer and winter resort.

Carbondale is in an anthracite coalfield where some veins are 20 feet (6 meters) thick. The coal was discovered in 1814, and by 1826 it was being mined intensively. Mining became the principal industry of the city, but it is no longer an important activity. Incorporated as a city in 1851, Carbondale has a commission form of government. Population: 12,808.

CARBONEAR, kär-bə-nir', is a town in southeastern Newfoundland, Canada, on Avalon Peninsula, on the western shore of Conception Bay. It is 27 miles (43 km) northwest of St. John's. The town is a trading center, fishing port, and railway terminus. Its industries include fish processing, tanning, and the manufacture of furniture. Population: 4,732.

CARBONIC ACID. See CARBON DIOXIDE.

CARBONIFEROUS PERIOD, kär-bə-nif'ə-rəs, in geology, is the fifth period in the Paleozoic era. It began about 350 million years ago and lasted about 80 million years. The Carboniferous was an age of amphibians and of coal-forming swamps. It was named in 1822 for a system of coal-bearing rocks in Britain by an English geologist, William D. Conybeare.

Two North American rock systems are generally recognized within the span of the Carboniferous period: the Mississippian and the more recent Pennsylvanian. They were originally described as rock series by the American paleontologist Henry S. Williams in 1891, but they are now considered as larger subsystems. The top rock layer of the Mississippian seems a little older than the top of the equivalent Lower Carboniferous in Europe. In western Europe the Lower Carboniferous (also called Dinantian) consists of the marine Tournaisian and the later Visean series. The Upper Carboniferous consists of the Namurian, Westphalian, and Stephanian series, in order of decreasing age; these are mainly nonmarine, coal-bearing rock strata.

ERA	PERIOD	
CENOZOIC	QUATERNARY	
	TERTIARY	
MESOZOIC	CRETACEOUS	
	JURASSIC	
	TRIASSIC	
PALEOZOIC	PERMIAN	
	CARBON-IFEROUS	PENNSYLVANIAN
		MISSISSIPPIAN
	DEVONIAN	
	SILURIAN	
	ORDOVICIAN	
	CAMBRIAN	
PRECAMBRIAN TIME		

GEOLOGY

The Carboniferous rocks exhibit repeating successions of rock types. For example, quartz sandstones may alternate with limestones. More complicated successions are found above erosion surfaces—stream-laid sandstone, nonmarine shale, fire clay, coal, and marine shale and limestone. These repetitions are a record of alternate rises and falls of the sea level in gradually sinking areas of land. Thus, after a withdrawal of the sea and subsequent erosion of the exposed rocks, the forested plains would again be buried beneath an advancing sea, and sediments would be deposited. This cycle of events might be repeated a number of times.

The occurrence of tillite (a rock of nonstratefied sediment) of Carboniferous age in the Southern Hemisphere is evidence that glaciation took place in that period. The freezing and thawing of large water masses may, as a result, have produced an alternating depression and rise of ocean levels. The glaciation culminated in the succeeding Permian period, in Australia, South Africa, and South America.

The Mississippian Subsystem. The Mississippian subsystem of rocks is named for the strata that crop out in bluffs along the Mississippi River in Missouri, Illinois, and southeastern Iowa. The subsystem consists of the Kinderhookian, Osagian, Meramecian, and Chesterian series, in order of decreasing age. In the central states these rocks are predominantly limestone. In the eastern states and maritime Canada, the earliest deposits are coarse nonmarine products of the erosion of mountains formed in the late Devonian. The lands had subsided by the middle Mississippian; the silts and sands that spread westward to Illinois are overlain by limestone—more than 1,000 feet (300 meters) thick in southern West Virginia.

In the east the later Mississippian is sediment that was eroded from lands rising to the east of the geosyncline. Salts that precipitated during Meramecian time in a somewhat isolated basin in southern Michigan are the source of the chemical industry there. Meramecian gypsum occurs in Nova Scotia, and Indiana limestone also derives from this epoch. Zinc ores of Missouri, Oklahoma, and Kansas are found in Osagian limestones, and Chesterian sandstones are a source of Illinois petroleum.

The Pennsylvanian Subsystem. The series of rocks in the area from which the Pennsylvanian took its name are, in order of decreasing age: Pottsvillian, Alleghenian, Conemaughan, and Monongahelan. From a thickness of a few hundred feet in western Pennsylvania and Ohio, the Pottsvillian increases through southern Virginia, eastern Tennessee, and Alabama to a thickness of more than a mile. The rocks are primarily sandstones and shales, with interbeds of coal and a few marine limestones. The greater thickness is caused partly by a more rapid sinking into the geosyncline toward the southeast. Throughout the interior of the continent, the Pennsylvanian system lies on an eroded surface of Mississippian and older rocks.

CARBONIFEROUS LANDSCAPE of the Pennsylvanian subsystem, in an artist's reconstruction. Amphibians leave the water near the enormous fernlike plants that, in the course of millions of years, will become coal.

Some of the greatest geological changes of the period took place in the southern central states. The rocks there are classified in six series: Springerian, Morrowan, Lampasan (or Atokan), Desmoinesian, Missourian, and Virgilian. The first three are approximately equivalent to the Pottsvillian. At the beginning of the period more than a mile of marine and stream-laid sediments accumulated in a geosyncline skirting the Gulf of Mexico through southern Arkansas, southeastern Oklahoma, and Texas. The material was eroded from islands to the south and from the continental interior land. This geosyncline was deformed and raised during later epochs; by Virgilian time the southern shore of an interior sea extended through northern Oklahoma and central Texas. The rocks of the Ouachita Mountains of southeastern Oklahoma were carried northward scores of miles on thrust faults formed during or after the Pennsylvanian, and similar activity affected western Texas at the close of the Virgilian. In addition, the folds of the Arbuckle Mountains in Oklahoma were made within the late Pennsylvanian period.

Colorado and northern New Mexico had been warped only gently in earlier Paleozoic time. In the Pennsylvanian and the succeeding Permian periods, however, a geosyncline subsided more than two miles through central Colorado. It filled with stream-laid sands and gravels derived from highlands to the west, approximately in the position of the present Front Range of the Rocky Mountains. The red sediments spread in a great alluvial plain, with interrupting mountains, over an area of about 100,000 square miles (260,000 sq km) in Colorado and northern New Mexico.

Rocks of the Pennsylvanian period are the major source of coal in the eastern and central states, as well as in maritime Canada. Oil is produced in many regions, and important fields underlie central Texas and Oklahoma.

The Continental Margins. The Carboniferous rocks of the maritime provinces of Canada were laid in deeply subsiding depressions that were separated by rapidly rising headlands. The rocks are not marine, except for about 1,000 feet (300 meters) of fossiliferous limestone and gypsum in the middle Mississippian.

In the western states approximately a mile of limestones passes into shales, sandstones, and conglomerates in a belt that extends through central Nevada and Idaho. Earlier Paleozoic rocks of that region were folded and moved eastward on thrust faults in Carboniferous time. Farther west the record is poor. Mississippian sediments and volcanic rocks are known in many regions, but large areas seem to have been laid in Pennsylvanian times. Thus, Permian rocks lie directly on Mississippian rocks in northern California and the Yukon, but are separated by stream-laid strata in localities in central Oregon and eastern Alaska.

The close similarities in the rocks (and the faunas) of South Africa, southern India, Australia, and South America have led to the theory that these lands once formed a single great land mass, Gondwanaland, that split apart at some time later than the Carboniferous. Comparisons of the Carboniferous rocks of the British Isles and of the Atlantic Ocean provinces of Canada further suggest that the north Atlantic Ocean formed in the rift that developed as the continents subsequently drifted apart.

FAUNA AND FLORA

The fossils of Mississippian time reveal that a variety of beautiful echinoderms existed then, such as sea urchins, sea lilies, and little nut-shaped blastoids (a class of stemmed echinoderms). Although all these forms are known from a large part of the Paleozoic era, and some from later eras, they thrived particularly well in the seas that produced the limestones of the Mississippi Valley. Spiny brachiopods first became abundant during the period, but were more varied during the Permian period, which followed.

Amphibians were prevalent land vertebrates in the Mississippian, but sprawling reptiles became more common in the Pennsylvanian. Plants grew in such profusion that they led to the formation of coal. Fernlike forms that grew to the size of trees and bore seeds were numerous.

LAPIE-PHOTOTHÈQUE FRANÇAISE

CARCASSONNE, in southern France, is famous for its Cité, the medieval fortress that is the outstanding monument of its kind in Europe. Its restoration began in the 19th century under the direction of the famous French architect Viollet-le-Duc.

Among Pennsylvanian invertebrates, the shells of one-celled calcium-producing foraminifera called fusulinids were the most distinctive. The shells were spindle-shaped, spirally coiled, and about the size of a grain of wheat. They are virtually limited to Pennsylvanian and Permian rocks; their changing forms make excellent guides to the divisions of time and rock. The ammonoid cephalopods, which exhibit very complex patterns of junction of interior chamber walls with outer shell, have also been useful in determining the divisions of time in these rocks. The clams that lived in fresh-water environments associated with coal swamps have been classified and found to be of practical value in the correlation of coal seams. Many other forms of invertebrates thrived in the Carboniferous period as well.

See also COAL—*1. How Coal Was Formed;* GEOLOGY—*Geologic Time Scale.*

MARSHALL KAY, *Columbia University*

CARBORUNDUM, kär-bə-run'dəm, is the trade name for silicon carbide (SiC), a substance used mainly as an abrasive. The crystal structure of silicon carbide is similar to that of diamond, and like diamond it is extremely hard. It will cut all substances except diamond and boron carbide. Commercial silicon carbide is iridescent and black; it is made by heating silicon dioxide and coke in an electric furnace.

HERBERT LIEBESKIND, *The Cooper Union*

CARBUNCLE, a group of abscesses with interconnecting pus-filled sinuses. Carbuncles usually occur on the neck, buttocks, or thighs, but sometimes the causative bacteria are spread through the bloodstream to other parts of the body, where they give rise to fresh lesions.

A carbuncle starts as a warm, painful, dark red swelling. The skin there seems thick and firm. Pus forms within one to two weeks, but instead of coming to head as would a simple abscess, multiple drainage points form. By this time, the surrounding skin has a dusky purplish cast or may even appear blackish. There is often considerable death of tissue at and around the drainage points, leaving small cavities that heal with some degree of scarring.

STEPHEN E. SILVER, M. D.
University of Oregon Medical School

CARBURETOR. See AUTOMOBILE—*5. Modern Automobiles;* INTERNAL COMBUSTION ENGINE—*Carburetors.*

CARCASSONNE, kȧr-kȧ-sôn', a city in southern France, is the capital of Aude department. It lies on the Aude River, about 40 miles (64 km) from the Mediterranean Sea. Physiographically, its site is strategic, and the city has historically been a fortress guarding the eastern end of the gap that lies between the Massif Central of France to the north and the Pyrenees to the south. This gap, known as the Toulouse Gateway, has been for centuries a vital transit route connecting Mediterranean France with the Aquitaine Basin and Atlantic France. It was the site of the first canal, the Canal du Midi, which linked the headwaters of the Garonne River to Mediterranean drainage.

Carcassonne is transitional, too, in terms of climate and vegetation, between Mediterranean and Atlantic influences. The summers are less dry and the rainfall greater, for instance, than in eastern Languedoc, where the climate is dry-summer subtropical (Mediterranean). The olive and green oak, so typical of Languedoc, peter out near Carcassonne, heralding the proximity of more Atlantic conditions.

Carcassonne is the chief trade and service city of western Aude department and is surrounded by a moderately prosperous agricultural region. The chief farm commodities are cereals, mostly wheat, wine (though the concentrations of vineyards is much heavier in eastern Aude), livestock products, and fruit. Manufactures include agricultural equipment, rubber articles, clothing, textiles, and shoes.

Carcassonne was a Roman outpost, founded as Colonia Julia Carcaso, in the 1st century A. D. In the 6th century the Visigoths began to construct the walls of the fortress from which Carcassonne's fame stems. This medieval Cité, or walled fortress, lies astride the hill rising from the right bank of the river. The complex, with its high double walls that boast 50 towers and that contain a much-restored medieval village, is the most remarkable fortified walled city of the Middle Ages extant in Europe and one of the architectural wonders of France. Aside from the magnificent walls themselves and the overall impression the visitor gains of a village of that period, the outstanding points of interest in the Cité, which is illuminated in the evening, are the Narbonnaise Gate, the Trésau Tower, the Comtal Palace, and the old St. Nazaire Church, formerly a cathedral. Population: (1962) 37,190.

HOMER PRICE
Hunter College, New York

CARCHEMISH, kär′kə-mish, is an ancient fortified site located at Karkamış, Turkey, on the west bank of the Euphrates, 60 miles northeast of Aleppo. The nearest large town in Jerablus, in Syria. Lying at a strategic point where the main route from northern Mesopotamia (Iraq) to the Mediterranean crosses the Euphrates, the site was occupied from the Neolithic period onward. It is first mentioned, with its king, Aplahanda, in a letter (about 1700 B.C.) found at Mari, and it is mentioned again about 1470 B.C.

Carchemish was a fortress in the kingdom of Mitanni but was finally captured by the Hittite king Suppiluliumas (about 1340), who established one of his sons as ruler. It was destroyed about 1190 B.C., but a new city arose, the center of a small "Neo-Hittite" kingdom. It gradually came under Assyrian control, paying tribute to the Assyrians after the mid-9th century and annexed outright in 717 B.C. Nebuchadnezzar II's victory at Carchemish over Pharaoh Necho II (605) enabled Babylon to take over Assyrian territory in Syria. In the Roman period Carchemish, under the name Europus, was still an important river crossing.

The British Museum conducted excavations at Carchemish in 1878–1881 and 1911–1914. The remains include a citadel, with a palace, temple, and friezes of stone reliefs, and an inner and outer city with fortifications and gates.

D. J. BLACKMAN
Bristol University, England

Further Reading: Gurney, O. R., *The Hittites* (London 1952); Lloyd, Seton, *Early Anatolia* (Harmondsworth, England, and Baltimore, Md., 1956).

CARCINOGEN, an agent that produces cancer. See CANCER.

CARCINOMA. See CANCER.

CARCO, kȧr-kō′, **Francis** (1886–1958), French poet and novelist. The son of Corsicans, he was born François Carcopino-Tusoli on July 3, 1886, in Noumea, New Caledonia, and went to France when he was 14. He became known as the chronicler of Parisian bohemian life in such novels as *Jésus-la-caille* (1914) and *L'homme traqué* (1922; Eng. tr., *The Hounded Man*, 1924). For the latter, he was awarded the Grand Prix of the French Academy.

Carco's volumes of poetry include *La Bohème et mon coeur* (1912) and *Poèmes en prose* (1948). In 1937 he was elected one of the 10 members of the Goncourt Academy, which annually awards an important literary prize. He died in Paris on May 26, 1958.

CARDAMOM HILLS, kär′də-məm, a mountain range in southern India, in the state of Kerala. The hills are named for the large estates of cardamom planted on the hillsides and are sometimes called the *Travancore Hills*. Comprising the southern section of the Western Ghats, the Cardamom Hills extend along the eastern border of what was formerly the princely state of Travancore, and terminate about 10 miles (16 km) north of Cape Comorin. Their average elevation is between 2,000 and 4,000 feet (610–1,219 meters), and in the east ridge there are rises of over 4,500 feet (1,371 meters). Elephants and other big game are found in the thick forests. In addition to cardamom (or cardamon), tea, coffee, teak, bamboo, and tumeric are raised.

CARDAMON (*right*) bears highly aromatic seeds (*below*, bleached and natural) used for centuries in the Orient as a food seasoning.

RUSS KINNE, FROM PHOTO RESEARCHERS

CARDAMON, kär′də-mən, or *cardamom*, is a herb with seeds that are used as a spice and in medicine. Cardamon, *Elettaria cardamomum*, the only species in its genus, is native to India. It grows 5 to 9 feet (1½–2¾ meters) high and has coarse leaves 2½ feet (75 cm) long; the leaves are hairy underneath. The white flowers are borne in loose, irregular spikes about 2 feet (60 cm) long. The rootstock is thick and creeping.

Cardamon grows easily in moist mild climates, especially in shaded situations. It is commercially cultivated in Jamaica and is sometimes raised in greenhouses. It is easily propagated by seeds and division of roots. Supposedly, cardamon becomes exhausted after bearing three or four crops.

The seeds of *Amomum cardamon*, a closely related member of the ginger family, are sometimes substituted for those of the true cardamon, but the seeds of the substitute are decidedly inferior.

DONALD WYMAN, *The Arnold Arboretum*
Harvard University

CARDANO, kär-dä′nō, **Girolamo** (1501–1576), Italian physician, mathematician, and scientist, who is noted for his work on the solution of algebraic equations of the third and fourth degrees. Cardano was born in Pavia on Sept. 24, 1501, the illegitimate son of a jurist and lecturer in geometry in Milan. He was educated at the universities of Pavia and Padua and received a medical degree from Padua. He practiced medicine for some years in nearby Sacco but returned to Milan because his income was insufficient to support his growing family. When he was refused admission to the medical guild in Milan because of his illegitimacy, he responded with a blistering book on the malpractices of the medical profession.

Cardano published his first works in mathematics in 1539, but his chief mathematical work was the *Ars magna* (1545), which constituted a great advance in algebra and became a cornerstone in the subject. It contains the first published method for the solution of cubic equations and also a method, discovered by his pupil Ferrari, for solving equations of the fourth degree. Publication of the latter precipitated a violent priority feud with Tartaglia, climaxed by a public dispute in Milan between Tartaglia and Ferrari in 1548. Both sides claimed victory.

In 1539 the medical guild in Milan relented and admitted Cardano to full membership. Within a few years he became its rector and one of the most famous physicians in Europe. Following the execution of his elder son in 1560, for poisoning his wife, Cardano went to Bologna as professor of medicine in 1562. In 1570 he was arrested there by the Inquisition for heresy, but he was released in 1571 after some months in prison. He died in Rome on Sept. 21, 1576.

OYSTEIN ORE, *Yale University*

Further Reading: Cardano, Girolamo, *The Book of My Life*, tr. by J. Stoner (New York 1962); Ore, Oystein, *Cardano, the Gambling Scholar* (Princeton 1953).

CARDBOARD. See PAPER.

CÁRDENAS DEL RIO, kär-thā-näs del rē′ō, **Lázaro** (1895–1970), Mexican soldier and statesman, during whose presidency (1934–1940) the Mexican Revolution's program of agrarian and national economic reforms was largely fulfilled.

He was born in Jiquilpán de Juárez, in the state of Michoacán, on May 21, 1895. Like most Mexicans, he was a mestizo, with a strong sense of the Indian part of his background. The son of poor parents, Damaso Cárdenas and Felicitas del Río, he received only an elementary education. He was the proprietor of a printing shop in 1913 when Gen. Vitoriano Huerta overthrew President Francisco Madero. Cárdenas joined the fight against Huerta, rose rapidly through the revolutionary ranks, became a brigadier general under President Obregón, and was commissioned a general under President Pituarco Calles.

Gen. Lázaro Cárdenas

UNITED PRESS INTERNATIONAL

As governor of Michoacán after 1928, Cárdenas pushed the construction of rural schools and agrarian reform. In 1930, as head of the PNR (National Revolutionary party), he gained the support of powerful labor and peasant leaders in formulating the 6-year plan to complete the program of the revolution. With the backing of Calles and the PNR, Cárdenas was elected president in 1934. He had campaigned vigorously, traveling more than 16,000 miles to all parts of the country by rail, on horseback, and on foot.

As president, Cárdenas pushed the 6-year plan vigorously. Large-scale expropriation and distribution of farmlands transformed the Mexican agricultural population into a landowning peasantry. He supported the demands of labor organizations for increased wages. A railroad strike was settled by turning over the national railways temporarily to the workers. Official support of the demands of striking petroleum workers brought nationalization of the foreign-owned petroleum industry. New rural schools were built at the rate of some 2,000 a year, and the Pan American highway was constructed from Nuevo Laredo to Mexico City. Eventually these measures provoked a clash with the politically powerful ex-president Calles, and Calles was exiled.

Cárdenas continued to play a leading role in Mexican politics after his presidency—as minister of defense during World War II and as the leader of the left wing of the official party. He died in Mexico City on Oct. 19, 1970.

HAROLD E. DAVIS, *The American University*

CÁRDENAS, kär′thā-näs, is a seaport on the north coast of Cuba, in Matanzas province, 95 miles (150 km) by road east of Havana. It is one of Cuba's leading fishing ports. Its industries include sugar refining, distilling, rice milling, and the manufacture of rope, tile, matches, and brooms. About 15 miles (24 km) southwest of the city is San Miguel de los Baños, a popular spa with white sulfur springs. One of Cuba's best beaches is at Varadero, about 10 miles (16 km) northwest of Cárdenas. In 1965 the Cuban government designated Varadero airport as the departure point for Cubans emigrating to the United States. Population: (1965 est.) 54,600.

CARDIFF, kär′dəf, the capital and largest city of Wales and the county seat of Glamorganshire, is situated on the Taff River at its mouth on the Bristol Channel, about 130 miles (210 km) west of London. It is an important seaport and administrative and industrial center of Great Britain. While the city is of ancient origin, it is in many aspects thoroughly modern. It is noted for its civic center and spacious parks.

Cardiff is on the edge of the largest continuous coalfield in Britain and until recently was the country's most important coal port. It was also the outlet for products manufactured in the ironworks of the neighboring Merthyr Tydfil region. However, diminishing production of Merthyr iron ore and increased dependence on imported ore led to the removal of the works to the coast. Thus Cardiff became an important center for the manufacture of iron and steel. There are also diversified industries in Cardiff, including

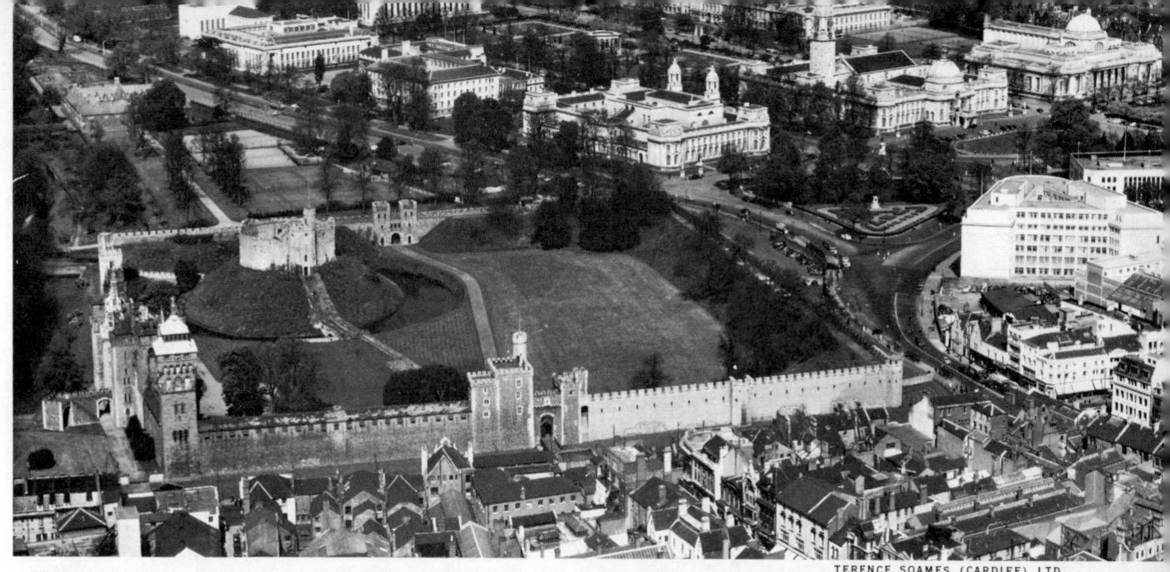

TERENCE SOAMES (CARDIFF) LTD.

CARDIFF grew up around the little Norman castle on a mound *(left center)*, now within the walls of the city-owned Cardiff Castle. In the civic center *(background)* the city hall is the domed building beside the tall tower.

wire-rope making and the manufacture of automobiles, as well as flour mills and biscuit companies. Cardiff is a distributing center for frozen meat, cattle, timber, tobacco, fruit, and vegetables. Its docks cover 165 acres (67 hectares).

Cultural and Educational Life. Through the years Cardiff has established itself as a cultural and civic force in Wales. It has an excellent public library, and its museum became the nucleus of the National Museum of Wales, founded in 1907. It is the center of the University of Wales and the home of the University College of South Wales and Monmouthshire, as well as the Welsh National School of Medicine and the College of Advanced Technology.

Among the city's architectural treasures are the Norman cathedral in Llandaff (begun about 1120), with its handsome modern sculpture of Christ by Jacob Epstein; the 15th century tower of the parish church of St. John; and notably Cardiff Castle (begun about 1090) and its grounds in the center of the city, which were given to Cardiff in 1948 by their owner, the Marquess of Bute. Actually, land for a civic center had been purchased from the Bute estate in 1905.

History. The city's ancient origin is indicated by the foundations of a Roman fort, dating from about 75 A.D., on the site of Cardiff Castle—which was built by the Normans. The Normans also established a walled borough, administered by its burgesses until the union of Wales with England in 1536, when Cardiff became the seat of government of the new shire of Glamorgan. It continued as a small, walled country town until the opening of the rich iron and coal deposits at Merthyr Tydfil, north of Cardiff, in 1760. Thereafter, the streets were paved and the restrictive town gates removed. After the opening of the Glamorganshire Canal in 1794, Cardiff entered on a period of expansion. The first dock for ocean-going vessels was built in 1839, the railway came to Cardiff in 1840, and by 1860 Cardiff was exporting 2½ million tons of coal.

In 1905, Cardiff was declared a city, and in 1922 it extended its boundaries to include the city of Llandaff. It became the capital of Wales in 1955. Population: (1961) 256,582.

WILLIAM REES
Author of "Cardiff—A History of the City"

CARDIGAN, kär′di-gən, **7th Earl of** (1797–1868), British general, who led the Charge of the Light Brigade (q.v.) at the Battle of Balaklava in the Crimean War. He was born James Thomas Brudenell, at Hambleden, Buckinghamshire, England, on Oct. 16, 1797. Rich and handsome, Cardigan showed public spirit by continuous service in the army and by sitting in Parliament for 18 years. But he was quarrelsome, arrogant, and unpopular; he lived loosely and made two scandalous marriages; and he acquired military rank by purchase.

He commanded the 15th Hussars (1830–1834) and the 11th Hussars (1836–1854), spending £10,000 a year on his men's uniforms and equipment, yet he had many quarrels with his officers. In 1840 he was tried in the House of Lords for dueling and was exonerated only on a technicality.

In June 1854, Cardigan went to the Crimean War in command of the Light Brigade that was part of the cavalry division of his brother-in-law and old enemy, Lord Lucan. He was 57 when, on Oct. 25, 1854, near Balaklava, he was ordered to recapture a battery of guns and rode at the head of his men "into the jaws of death," as Alfred, Lord Tennyson wrote in *The Charge of the Light Brigade*. Cardigan was the first to reach the Russian guns, but almost half his men were killed or wounded. He has been condemned because he left the field without re-forming his troops or seeing to their welfare and returned to his yacht to bathe and dine. Yet he had obeyed orders with conspicuous bravery; the shout of a surviving trooper, "We'll do it again, m'Lord!" proclaimed his men's reckless pride. The military historian Sir John W. Fortescue believed that the real tragedy of Balaklava was Cardigan's failure to take the initiative in reinforcing the successful charge of the Heavy Brigade earlier in the day.

Returning to England a hero in January 1855, Cardigan publicly boasted and argued about his military feats. He died at Deene Park, Northamptonshire, after a fall from his horse, on May 28, 1868.

WILLIAM E. D. ALLEN
Coauthor of "Caucasian Battlefields"

Further Reading: Fortescue, John W., *History of the British Army*, vol. 13 (London 1930); Woodham-Smith, Cecil Blanche, *The Reason Why* (New York 1954).

I. DONALD BOWDEN

Cardigan Welsh Corgi

CARDIGAN WELSH CORGI, kär′di-gən welsh kôr′gē, an ancient breed in the working group of dogs. The Cardigan is long-bodied and short-legged and may share a common ancestor with the dachshund, which it resembles. It stands about 12 inches (30 cm) at the shoulder and weighs 15 to 25 pounds (7 to 11 kg). The head is foxlike and the ears are large and erect. The short or medium coat is hard and may be any color except pure white. A longer, bushier tail and a somewhat longer body distinguish the Cardigan from the Pembroke Welsh corgi.

The Cardigan was brought into Wales by the Celts about 1200 B.C. It was developed in Cardiganshire for herding cattle, sheep, swine, and even poultry, and for killing vermin; it drives cattle by nipping at their heels. The breed is less popular in the United States than the Pembroke.

William F. Brown
Editor of "American Field"

CARDIGANSHIRE, kär′di-gən-shīr, is a county of western Wales with a coastline on Cardigan Bay extending from the mouth of the Teifi River at Cardigan to the River Dovey below Machynlleth. Many of the people speak Welsh. It is a county largely of small villages and farms in sheltered valleys. Cardigan is the nominal county town, but Aberystwyth has the county offices. Also in Aberystwyth are University College, the senior college of the University of Wales (1872), and the National Library of Wales. Aberystwyth is the principal resort on the west coast. At Lampeter, famous for its horse fairs, held in March, is St. David's College (1820) for students preparing for the Anglican priesthood. It is affiliated with both Oxford and Cambridge universities.

The shoreline is mostly of shingle, with sandy beaches at Gwbert-on-Sea, New Quay, Borth, and Aberayron. Inland the ground rises steadily to a general average of about 1,800 feet (550 meters), the highest point being Plynlimon (2,468 feet, or 752 meters), source of the Severn, Wye, and other rivers. In general the county is steeply undulating. The main products are cattle, sheep and wool, barley and oats, fish and timber. Population: (1961) 53,564.

Gordon Stokes
Author of "English Place-Names"

CARDINAL, a dignitary of the Roman Catholic Church, who assists the pope in the government of the universal church. The office of cardinal is honorary and is of human origin; it is not an extension or enlargement of the sacrament of Holy Orders, has no particular theological significance, and may be conferred only by a pope. The Code of Canon Law, promulgated in 1917, specified that all cardinals must be ordained priests. Before 1917, especially during the Middle Ages, clerics in minor orders, or even laymen, could become cardinals. The last nonpriest cardinal was Giacomo Antonelli, secretary of state to Pope Pius IX (reigned 1846–1878).

Categories. In 1962, Pope John XXIII decreed that all cardinals must first be consecrated bishops. "Bishop," in this usage, refers to the hierarchical status within the sacrament of Holy Orders and not to one of the cardinalitial categories, of which there are three—bishop, priest, and deacon. These categories are based on the traditional church structure of ancient Rome and, since all cardinals are aggregated to the clergy of Rome by reason of their office, are still applied.

Cardinal bishops are those attached to the suburban dioceses of Rome, namely Ostia, Porto-Santa Rufina, Albano, Palestrina, Sabina-Poggio Mirteto Frascati, and Velletri. The Dean of the College of Cardinals, who must be a cardinal bishop, is titular bishop of Ostia, in addition to his original titular see. Since 1962 cardinal bishops have been relieved of jurisdiction of their titular sees; actual administration is confided to resident bishops.

Cardinal priests, who were originally the pastors of the ancient churches of Rome, are still assigned title to these churches, but generally reside elsewhere. *Cardinal deacons* are the ecclesiastical descendants of deacons once assigned to the papal palace and to the Roman areas called "deaconries" (*diaconiae*). A cardinal *in petto* is one who has been named by the pope but whose nomination has not been publicly revealed. He may not use the title of cardinal nor exercise the rights or duties of the office until his selection is publicly announced.

An exception to the rule that all cardinals automatically become aggregated to the Roman clergy was made in 1965, when four major Eastern Rite patriarchs were created cardinals by Pope Paul VI. Although all were given the title cardinal bishop, they were not assigned titular sees in Rome nor aggregated to the Roman clergy since the title and position of patriarch antedates that of cardinal.

Functions. Collectively the cardinals constitute the Sacred College of Cardinals, or senate of the church. As members of the College they are counsellors and advisers to the pope. This function is exercised through the Curial departments (dicasteries), which are not unlike the ministerial offices of civil governments. The cardinals may act as heads of these departments, or of various commissions and secretariats, or as special consultants to them. Although the daily administration of the church is primarily handled by the cardinals who, as important officials in the Roman Curia, reside in Rome, the cardinals living outside of Rome also hold positions on various bureaus and are consulted on matters of major importance.

The greatest privilege enjoyed by the Sacred College is its power to elect a new pope whenever the papal office becomes vacant. This function was reserved to the college of cardinals by the Third Lateran Council (1179). A two-thirds majority is required for election (if the votes cannot be divided by three, an additional vote is necessary for an election to be valid). In modern times the Sacred College has always elected one of its own members as pope.

History. The title of "cardinal" is found in authentic papal documents dated as early as the 5th century. At that time, however, the term was not attributed solely to the clergy of Rome, but was used throughout the Western church. Scholars disagree concerning the original meaning of the word. Some have concluded that it derived from the Latin word *cardo,* meaning "pivot" or "hinge," and hence designated those clerics who held key positions in particular churches. Others suggest that it was derived from the canonical term *incardinare* which referred to the transfer of a cleric from one church to another. The title, thus, was in connection with bishops, priests, and deacons who were permanently assigned to a church or diocese different from that of their ordination.

Under Pope Stephen III (reigned 768–772) the term began to be applied to the senior priests of the parish churches in Rome and to the bishops of the seven suburban dioceses surrounding Rome. Not until the 11th century were the deacons of the papal palace and of the diaconal churches of Rome designated as cardinals. At this time the functions of the Roman cardinals began to shift from purely liturgical and pastoral duties to participation in church government. The Sacred College of Cardinals was given definite form about the middle of the 12th century, when the three cardinalitial categories were also clearly established.

The number of cardinals fluctuated until 1586, when Pope Sixtus V set the number at 70 in imitation of the 70 elders God assigned Moses to assist him in governing Israel. (As a result of this ruling, some 16th century theologians suggested that the cardinalate was of divine origin; but this idea never took hold in the church.) Sixtus V also decided that there were to be 14 cardinal deacons, 50 cardinal priests, and 6 cardinal bishops. This ruling was incorporated into the Code of Canon Law (1918). It remained the norm until Pope John XXIII raised the number in the College to 79, and then to 87; Pope Paul VI increased the number to 103 in 1965, and to 118 in 1967. These increases were deemed necessary to make the College of Cardinals more international in representation and to meet the growing demands of the church's central administration.

John McCloskey, archbishop of New York, in 1875 became the first American cardinal. James Gibbons, archbishop of Baltimore, followed in 1886. Several ecclesiastics who served in the United States were subsequently raised to the cardinalate. For example, Egidio Vagnozzi, who was the apostolic delegate to the United States for many years, was raised to cardinal in 1967.

Form. When the pope decides to raise clerics to the cardinalate, he usually announces their names at a secret consistory (meeting) attended by the members of the Sacred College. The ceremonies of elevation take place later and follow certain formalities: the conferral of the red hat (*galero*), a symbolic low-crowned, wide-brimmed hat from which are suspended two clusters of 15 tassels each (this is the heraldic device of a cardinal); and the presentation of the scarlet skullcap (*zuchetto*), the scarlet biretta, and the cardinalitial ring. Traditionally the ring had been sapphire, but in 1967, Pope Paul VI decreed that a simple gold band, incised with an image of Christ, was to be used.

In 1630, Pope Urban VIII approved a decision to honor cardinals with the title of "Eminence" or "Your Most Eminent Lord." This form of address is still used. The custom of inserting the title of cardinal between a given name and a surname dates from the time when surnames were little used. Thus, a man signed his given name followed by his title.

DAMIAN J. BLAHER, O. F. M.
Holy Name College, Washington, D. C.

CARDINAL, a finchlike songbird found in North and South America. The well-known American cardinal (*Richmondena cardinalis*), often called the *redbird,* ranges from South Dakota, southern Ontario, and Connecticut south to British Honduras and west to central Arizona. It is especially abundant in the southeastern United States, and it has also been introduced into Bermuda, Hawaii, and southeastern California.

Description. The cardinal is from 8 to 9 inches (20–23 cm) long. The male has bright red plumage and a sharp pointed crest of feathers on its head. Its large bill is orange-red, and it has a black area around its eyes and head. The female cardinal has a red bill and a dull reddish crest, wings, and tail. The rest of her body is yellowish-brown.

Behavior. A relatively nonmigratory bird, the cardinal is often present in a region throughout the year. It feeds on weed seeds, wild fruit, and insects. It is beneficial to man since it kills many insect pests such as the potato beetle, the cotton boll weevil, and the cucumber beetle.

Both the male and the female cardinal are excellent songsters. Their song is basically a series of loud, clear whistles with a repertoire of some 16 variations. The female's song is softer than the male's and is often more pleasing to the ear.

Reproduction. The cardinal's nest, built by the female alone, is cup-shaped. It is loosely constructed of grasses, weed stalks, bark, roots,

Cardinal

KARL H. MASLOWSKI, FROM PHOTO RESEARCHERS

leaves, and twigs and is lined with hair or fine grass. It is well-concealed in bushes, small trees, or vines, usually 5 to 15 feet (1.5–4.5 meters) above the ground.

The female lays 2 to 4 pale blue eggs heavily spotted with reddish brown and lilac. She then incubates the eggs for 12 days. Both parents care for the young while they are in the nest. However, after the young leave the nest, the male alone cares for them, while the female often builds a new nest. As many as three broods may be reared in one year.

Classification. Cardinals, together with grosbeaks, finches, and sparrows, are classified in the family Fringillidae in the order Passeriformes.

KENNETH E. STAGER
Los Angeles County Museum of Natural History

CARDINAL FLOWER, a perennial plant of the lobelia family cultivated for its brilliant scarlet flowers. It is native to North America from New Brunswick, Canada, to Florida and Texas, where it favors moist habitats, such as the edges of ponds and streams.

The cardinal flower (*Lobelia cardinalis*) grows 2 to 4 feet (60 to 120 cm) high and has alternate, short-stalked, oblong leaves 3 to 5 inches (7.5 to 12.5 cm) long. Its vivid scarlet flowers, which bloom between July and September, are borne in racemelike spikes. Each flower is about 1½ inches (40 mm) long and has 3 brightly colored corolla lobes.

Propagation of the cardinal flower can be by seed or cuttings, but dividing the clumps just after they are through flowering in the early fall is the easiest method. Best results are obtained by planting in a partially shaded moist spot.

DONALD WYMAN
The Arnold Arboretum, Harvard University

Cardinal flower (*Lobelia cardinalis*)

J. J. SMITH

CARDINAL VIRTUES, in theology, the principal moral qualities that determine man's goodness. They are generally given as *prudence, temperance, justice,* and *fortitude.* The term "cardinal" is derived from the Latin *cardo,* meaning "hinge"; the cardinal virtues, then, are those qualities on which man's morality turns or is hinged.

Virtues are habits of good conduct. Men make decisions, exercise choice, and carry out actions; in time, they form patterns of behavior that become habitual. Good habits thus formed are strongly established dispositions toward valid human realizations and, as such, are virtues. Bad habits, whether developed from choice of evil ends or of evil means, are vices. Although men always act as individual responsible agents, their actions take place in a variety of moral contexts and involve different kinds of moral decisions. The cardinal virtues represent a set of firm moral dispositions that facilitate right conduct in every major context of moral responsibility.

Prudence is the virtue of discretion and good judgment that presupposes a willingness to do what is right. Justice is rectitude of will, a readiness to give to every man his due. It applies to such social duties as fair housing, payment of taxes, equality before the law, as well as to individual debts. Temperance is moderation in the enjoyment of pleasures of the senses. Fortitude, or courage, is firmness in the face of hardship and danger.

The qualities that make these virtues good—namely, discretion, rectitude, moderation, and firmness—establish a dependable pattern of behavior in the person of good character. The virtues and other qualities are interconnected and mutually dependent. Firmness, for example, is not fortitude unless tempered by moderation. The virtues are said to inhabit a "golden mean" between excess and defect: prudence lies somewhere between folly and craftiness; temperance, between licentiousness and insensitivity; courage, between timidity and rashness. Other moral qualities such as truthfulness, magnanimity, patience, and humility, can be affiliated with one or another of the cardinal virtues.

The fourfold classification of the virtues is found in classical philosophy (Plato, Aristotle, Cicero). The 5th century Church Father, St. Ambrose, was apparently the first to apply the term "cardinal" to the four major moral virtues. Christian theology subordinates the cardinal virtues to the theological virtues of faith, hope, and charity. St. Thomas Aquinas discusses the cardinal virtues in *Summa theologiae.*

CHARLES E. SHEEDY, C. S. C.
University of Notre Dame

CARDING is the process in which textile fibers are disentangled, freed of impurities, and arranged in the form of a fine web. The web is then gathered into a loose strand, called a sliver, which is further processed for spinning. See also TEXTILE MACHINERY.

JOHN F. BOGDAN, *School of Textiles*
North Carolina State University

CARDIOGRAM is a term sometimes applied to an electrocardiogram, a recording of the electrical activity of the heart. Electrocardiograms are often useful in diagnosing heart disorders. See also ELECTROCARDIOGRAPHY.

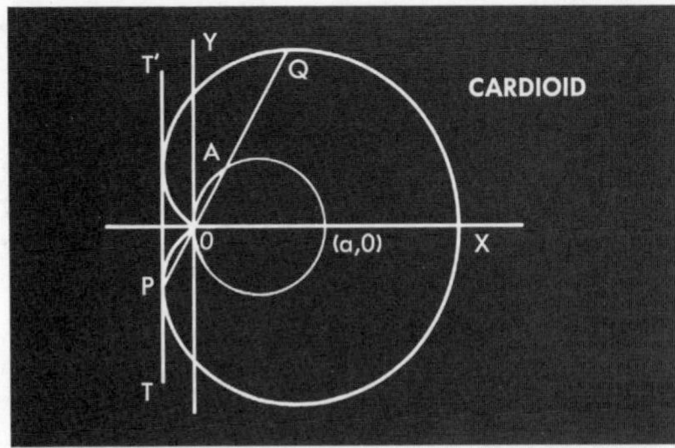

CARDIOID, kär′dē-oid, a heart-shaped curve traced by a fixed point on the circumference of a circle that rolls completely around the circumference of a second circle of equal diameter. If a is the common diameter of the circles, the equations of the curve are

$$(x^2 + y^2 - ax)^2 = a^2(x^2 + y^2)$$

and

$$r = a(1 - \cos \theta)$$

in rectangular and polar coordinates, respectively. The curve is a special case of an epicycloid, and may also be regarded as a special case of the limaçon curve.

CARDIOVASCULAR SYSTEM, kär-dē-ō-vas′kyə-lər, is the collective name applied to the circulatory system, the lymphatic system, the blood, and the lymph. The circulatory system consists of a vast network of blood vessels and the heart, which pumps the blood through the blood vessels.

The lymphatic system consists of vessels containing lymph. Lymph is the watery fluid that has filtered out of the bloodstream, gradually flowed around the body cells, and then filtered into the lymph vessels. Through the lymph vessels it is conveyed to one of several veins, where it again becomes part of the blood.

See also ANATOMY, HUMAN—*Circulatory System;* BLOOD; LYMPH.

ELVIN SMITH
University of Mississippi Medical School

CARDOZO, kär-dō′zō, **Benjamin Nathan** (1870–1938), American judge, who gained an international reputation for his ability to bring legal rules into harmony with social interests and values. His careers as a lawyer (1891–1913), as a judge on the New York court of appeals (1914–1932), and as a United States Supreme Court justice (1932–1938) were marked by the highest achievements. All his life he was fascinated by the problem of finding the right way to reconcile the conflicting demands of stability and change in law. Consequently, his briefs and judicial opinions were marked by a concern for the nature of the law, its mode of evolution, and the limits of its authority.

Born in New York City on May 24, 1870, Cardozo was the youngest son of Albert and Rebecca Cardozo, descendants of Sephardic Jews who had settled in New York before the American Revolution. At the age of 21 he began to practice law, having received bachelor's (1889) and master's (1890) degrees from Columbia University and having been admitted to the New York state bar (1891).

In 1913 he was elected to the state supreme court, and in the following year he was appointed temporarily to the court of appeals. He later was elected to that court for a term of 14 years, beginning in 1918, and served after 1927 as its chief judge. His skill and learning helped make the New York court of appeals the leading state court in the nation. Other courts turned to his opinions as guides in adjusting the laws of an agrarian society to the demands created by industrialization.

Cardozo was appointed to the United States Supreme Court by President Herbert Hoover on Feb. 15, 1932, and served there until his death in Port Chester, N. Y., on July 9, 1938. On the high court his judicial talents were put to a severe test because the justices were divided on the issue of how they should treat New Deal legislation. Cardozo attempted to reconcile the conflict by demonstrating, both in his opinions for the court and in dissent, that the task of fitting traditional principles of law to changed conditions was not certain or easy and that it was useless to search for fixed rules. The meaning of any rule could not be confined within the words in which it was originally cast; its purpose, not its form, was the proper basis for judgment.

For Cardozo, the chief value of the Constitution lay in its ample generality, enabling it to accommodate the differing value systems of successive generations to meet changing circumstances. Working within this view, he sought to stabilize and rationalize legislative actions, to infuse them with principle. Despite his short tenure, he made a lasting contribution to the work of the high court because of his sure touch in joining legal rule and social need. With rare insight he discerned the emergent trends and forces of the nation and made public law more responsive to them.

HENRY M. HOLLAND, JR.
Alfred University, N. Y.

Further Reading: Cardozo, Benjamin N., *Selected Writings,* ed. by Margaret E. Hall (New York 1947); Goodhart, Arthur L., *Five Jewish Lawyers of the Common Law* (New York 1949); Hellman, George S., *Benjamin N. Cardozo, American Judge* (New York 1940); Levy, Beryl H., *Cardozo and the Frontiers of Legal Thinking* (New York 1938; reprinted Port Washington, N. Y., 1965).

Benjamin Cardozo

PICTORIAL PARADE

U. S. PLAYING CARD CO.

(*Left*) one of the early court cards made about 1440 from a wood block.

(*Above*) A numeral and two court cards from an Indian pack picturing the ten avatars of Vishnu.

THE JOHN OMWAKE PLAYING CARD COLLECTION ON PERMANENT LOAN TO THE CINCINNATI ART MUSEUM, FROM THE U. S. PLAYING CARD CO.

CARDS, Playing, small layered-paper devices, sometimes called "pasteboards," generally rectangular, bearing suit marks and numerals on the face side and colorful designs on the back. Used in the playing of numerous games, a standard 52-card deck, or pack, such as for poker or bridge, consists of four 13-card suits called spades, hearts, diamonds, and clubs. Each suit contains three court or face cards (king, queen, and jack) and numeral cards from 1 (ace) to 10. The extra card, called the joker, became a part of the decks used in the United States in 1872. The joker is used as an extra or "wild" card in several American card games.

There is no written record that playing cards were in use until about the 12th century in the Orient, and little is known of their origin and intent. Some historians contend that cards evolved from chess, which emerged from a game played with pebbles by shepherds of western Asia. Others believe that playing cards evolved from divining rods or arrows that were used for conjuring and divination. Communication with the gods was obtained by casting the rods, marked with four different symbols, upon a central altar; the priests interpreted the commands of the gods according to the direction in which the rods fell. Whatever the origin of playing cards—Oriental, Egyptian, or Arabic—they found their way into European countries in the 12th century, perhaps carried there by traveling merchants, professional soldiers, or wandering tribes of Gypsies.

EVOLUTION OF THE DECK

Early European cards were called Tarots (tablets of fate), or *tarocchi.* These were picture cards used for fortune-telling or instruction. The earliest such cards are the rare *tarocchi di Mantegna,* engraved by the artist Mantegna in Lombardy in 1470. This 50-card pack has five groups of 10 cards each, bearing allegorical or mythological subjects representing the different states of life—as the Muses, the virtues, the planets, the liberal arts, and the sciences. These handsome pictures are now ascribed to Botticelli and Baldini, and the Florentine school of painting is evidenced in their design.

From the tarots of Mantegna evolved the 78-card Venetian tarots consisting of four suits of 14 cards each. Each suit has 4 coat (court) cards (king, queen, cavalier, and valet) and 10 numeral cards (1 to 10) bearing suits of swords, cups, money, and batons. In addition, the tarot pack includes 22 numbered *atouts* (high cards or trumps) with various meanings, bearing such symbols as the sun, the pope, justice, and death (the 13th card). The 22d card, which is unnumbered, is *il matto* (the fool), precursor to the modern joker.

In the 15th century this 78-card Venetian pack was increased to 97 cards to form the Florentine minchiate deck. The 19 *atouts* added were 3 virtues, 4 elements, and 12 signs of the zodiac. The later Bologna tarots, or *tarocchino,* reduced the Venetian pack to 62 cards by the elimination of the 2, 3, 4, and 5 of each suit. All three forms of tarots—the original Venetian, Florentine minchiate, and Bolognese *tarocchino*—are still in use in Italy.

Many shorter decks evolved from the original 78-card tarot pack. Trappola contained 36 cards —as a result of discarding the *atouts,* queens, 3's, 4's, 5's, and 6's—until the 18th century, when it was further cut to 32 cards with the elimination of the aces. The French game of piquet also had 36 cards after the dropping of the *atouts,* knights, and the 2, 3, 4, and 5 of each suit. The modern piquet pack has 32 cards, the 6 of each suit having been discarded in the 1700's. The Spanish hombre pack contains 40 cards: *reyes* (kings), *caballeros* (knights), *sotas* (knaves), and numeral cards 1 through 7.

MANUFACTURE AND DESIGN

Earliest European playing cards were handmade and beautifully painted, but because of their exhorbitant cost they were the prerogative of only the wealthy. It was not until the invention of printing that playing cards were brought within the reach of the common people.

Card Manufacture. During the 15th century cards were printed from wood blocks, a form of printing first used by German "kartenmachers" (card makers) of Ulm, Nuremberg, and Augsburg, whose cards were exported to many countries. An old Ulm chronicle (about 1397) states: "Playing cards were sent in small casks into Italy, Sicily, and also over the sea, and bartered for spices and other wares." After complaints by

U. S. PLAYING CARD CO.

Tarot card made in Constance, Germany in 1680.

U. S. PLAYING CARD CO.

French face cards, designed in 1856, depict figures in French history.

Italian artists that their craft was suffering because of excessive importation of cards, an order of the magistracy of Venice in 1441 forbade such practice under heavy penalty. An English petition in 1463 also forbade importation of cards because of similar difficulties.

Progress in card manufacture accelerated after the invention of the printing press, and the slow methods of hand coloring and wood blocking were replaced in the 16th century by copperplate engraving. The revolutionary process of color reproduction known as lithography was first used in the early 1800's to produce many beautiful series of German, Italian, and French cards. Today the photoengraving process used in the manufacture of cards has created an enormous increase in an industry that has had a tremendous influence on the life and history of peoples everywhere.

Court-Card Design. Like other forms of art, the design of the court cards reflected the various whims of artists. Early card makers soon cast aside religious themes for the labors and merriment of the everyday scene. When playing cards were first separated from the original tarot into suits, full-length court figures portrayed various rulers. In some early Italian and Spanish packs, the 4 kings represented the four great world monarchies of the Middle Ages; mounted knights (or *caballeros*) were used in place of the queens, which were still prominent in the French packs. Artists altered the court cards to resemble important rulers or nobility of the day; names, costumes, and weapons were also changed.

During the reign of Henry III of France, costumes reflected the extravagant fashions of the era. When Henry IV of Navarre mounted the throne, card costumes and names were immediately altered. In a pack of engraved English cards of 1780, the kings represented the flourishing monarchies of Britain, France, Spain, and Prussia. During the French Revolution the playing card "royal family" was banished from the pack because of the prevailing antagonism toward nobility, being replaced by philosophers and other important personages. However, by 1813 the card royalty had reappeared, and it has remained on face cards since that time.

Modern double-headed (reversible) court cards first appeared in France in 1827 and were altered representations of the following personages:

	King	Queen	Jack
Spades:	David	Pallas	Hogier
Hearts:	Charlemagne	Judith	La Hire
Diamonds	Julius Caesar	Rachael	Hector
Clubs:	Alexander the Great	Elizabeth I	Lancelot

Back Decoration. With the exception of the foldover woodcuts of the Italian tarots, which carried simple wood-block designs of a figure, flower, or coat of arms, early playing cards had plain uncolored backs. Simple uncomplicated patterns appeared in the early 1800's, but back decoration had its first artistic development under Owen Jones, artist for Thomas de la Rue, London card makers, about 1860. (Jones' book of original designs is retained in the Cincinnati Art Museum.) By the end of the 19th century back design had become an important phase of the playing card industry, and drastic changes were avoided to avert suspicion of a "marked" deck.

Suit Marks. Suit marks likewise passed through many changes in form, number, arrangement, and decoration. Early Chinese cards used suits of coins, strings of coins, myriads, and tens of myriads, resembling the values of Chinese paper money. An old Oriental circular pack contained 10 suits of 12 cards each, emblematic of the ten avatars (incarnations) of the Hindu deity Vishnu. The suits included were such as fish, lions, hogs, tortoises, serpents, dwarfs, apes, dragons, shells, men-horse, and wild boars. The four emblems of the earliest Italian tarots—swords, cups, rings, and batons—were the emblems held in the four hands of the two-headed Indian deity Ardhanari. These were symbolic of the four chief castes of men on the banks of the Ganges and Nile rivers. The suit of swords denoted the kings or soldiers; cups symbolized the church; rings (and coins) signified the merchants; batons (and wands) were emblematic of agriculture. The first known German cards of Stuttgart (1440) were a hunting series with suit marks of dogs, stags, ducks, and falcons. Conventional German suit marks were hawks (or bells) for the nobles, hearts for the clergy, leaves for the citizenry, and acorns for peasants.

Card makers of France simplified the shapes of the suit emblems and divided the cards into a two-color (red and black) system for easy identification. La Hire (Étienne de Vignollès), the

(*Left*) Knave of clubs by Alexandre Lionnet, noted card maker at Montpellier, France, 1730–1750. (*Above*) Five of diamonds (on its side) from a transformation series by Tiffany, New York, 1879.

U. S. PLAYING CARD CO. AND JOHN OMWAKE PLAYING CARD COLLECTION ON PERMANENT LOAN TO THE CINCINNATI ART MUSEUM

famous knight who invented piquet, introduced the suit marks of *piques* (pike heads or lance-points), *coeurs* (hearts), *carreaux* (diamonds or squares), and *trèfles* (clovers). England adopted the French suits, designating them spades, hearts, diamonds, and clubs, and American suits are patterned after the English cards. Manufacturers have attempted to introduce strictly American symbols, such as stars, stripes, shields, and eagles, and to set up 4-color systems, but they have met with little success. Traditional designs and colors still prevail, and today there is a standardization of suit emblems throughout the world.

Special Issues and Uses. Interesting packs of educational cards have been issued for simplification of such subjects as grammar, rhetoric, music, astronomy, history, geography, heraldry, morals, politics, and even military strategy. Unusual packs have highlighted or satirized papal scandals, religious intolerances, political and historical events, and also opera lyrics and scores. Clever transformations, wherein the suit signs form part of the designs, were reflections of sentiments and fashions of the times, and some such issues were quite humorous. Interesting modern souvenir issues depict a country's scenery or a famous historical event.

Playing cards have also served other purposes in time of emergency; for example, the plain backs of early issues were used for written instructions. In 1685 they became the first paper currency of Canada when the French governor, Jacques de Meulles, paid off some war debts with them. During the French Revolution they were used as ration cards by Napoleon. In early America they appeared as invitations to parties and balls or, quartered, as visiting cards. In 1765, the year of the Stamp Act, when every pack of playing cards was taxed one shilling, they were used for class admission at the University of Pennsylvania.

CARD COLLECTIONS AND COLLECTING

Large and valuable collections of playing cards are housed and maintained in various museums of the world, including the Librairie Nationale in Paris; the British Museum and Royal Asiatic Society in London; museums in Dresden, Munich, Nuremberg, Vienna; and the National Gallery of Art in Washington, D. C. Many fine private collections exist throughout the world, one having belonged to the queen of Spain. The most comprehensive collection in the United States is that of the United States Playing Card Company on permanent loan to the Cincinnati Art Museum.

In the United States the hobby of collecting playing cards began about 1900. Today there are thousands of collectors around the world. Advanced deck collectors save full or near-full packs of early issues; they study the types of paper used, the methods of printing, the various inks and dyes, and other technical details that often reveal the date and identity of a deck. Other collectors save single cards with varied back designs in many categories. Particularly appealing classifications in this phase of collecting are reproductions of famous paintings, museum treasures, state historical cards, transportation issues, and topicals such as Indians, flowers, birds, and animals.

Collectors' clubs foster interest in the hobby with meetings, study, and research on playing-card lore; discussions, exhibits, swap sessions, mail trades, and auctions; and informative bulletins and catalog listings. *Hobbies* magazine carries an illustrated article on playing cards in its columns every month, and from time to time articles on the subject appear in various other magazines. New books are constantly being added to library shelves for readers seeking further information on this fascinating subject.

DOROTHY POWILLS
Chicago Playing Card Collectors, Inc.

Bibliography

Benham, W. Gurney, *Playing Cards, Their History and Secrets* (London 1931).
Chatto, W. A., *Facts and Speculations on the Origin and History of Playing Cards* (London 1848).
Hargrave, Catherine Perry, *A History of Playing Cards* (Boston 1930; reprinted New York 1966).
Mann, Sylvia, *Collecting Playing Cards* (London 1966).
Taylor, E. S., ed., *The History of Playing Cards* (London 1865).
Tilley, Roger, *Playing Cards: Pleasures and Treasures* (New York 1967)
Van Rensselaer, Mrs. John King, *The Devil's Picture Books, a History of Playing Cards* (New York 1895).

CARDSTON, kärd′stən, is a town in southern Alberta, Canada, about 15 miles (24 km) north of the United States border. It is a trading center for an agricultural area and has dairying, baking, cabinetmaking, and commercial printing industries. The Blood Indian Reserve borders the town on the north. The only temple of the Church of Jesus Christ of Latter-day Saints in Canada is in Cardston. Population: 2,685.

CARDUCCI, kär-do͞ot′chē, **Bartolomeo** (1560–?1610), Italian baroque painter, architect, and sculptor, who spent most of his active career in Spain. In Florence, his native city, he studied architecture and sculpture with Bartolomeo Ammannati and painting with Federigo Zuccaro, whom he accompanied to Spain about 1585. Carducci assisted in painting the fresco decorations in the library and cloister of the Escorial. He was patronized by Philip II and Philip III. Many of his best works, including the *Descent from the Cross,* are in the Church of San Felipe el Real, Madrid. He adopted the Spanish spelling of his name (Bartolomé Carduco) and stayed in Spain until his death in Madrid, about 1610.

VINCENZO CARDUCCI (1568?–1638), brother and pupil of Bartolomeo, was born in Florence. He accompanied his brother to Madrid and settled there. A prolific artist, he painted in a fluid, brilliant style reminiscent of Florentine and Venetian painting of the early 16th century. With Eugenio Caxès he painted the great altar of the convent of Gerolomitano of Guadelupe. His best-known work is the *Martyrdom of St. Andrew* in the Cathedral of Toledo.

MARTICA SAWIN
Parsons School of Design, New York City

FOTO MAS, BARCELONA
The Descent from the Cross, by Bartolomeo Carducci.

CARDUCCI, kär-do͞ot′chē, **Giosuè** (1835–1907), Italian poet, scholar, and critic. He was born at Val di Castello, Tuscany, on July 28, 1835. After study in Pisa, he taught, edited, and wrote, and from 1860 to 1904 was professor of Italian literature at the University of Bologna. From his father, one of the revolutionary Carbonari, Carducci derived his liberal republicanism and anti-Catholicism. Vivacious and nonconformist, he coupled in his poems and criticism an enthusiasm for the Risorgimento with a strong classicism that opposed both romanticism and Catholicism because he believed they had weakened Italy.

Carducci's chief volumes of poetry are *Giambi ed epodi* (1867–1879), *Rime nuove* (1861–1887), *Odi barbare* (1877–1889), and *Rime e ritmi* (1887–1899). His most famous poem is *Inno a Satana* (1865), in which Satan, symbolizing human science and progress, stands against error and superstition. Carducci's views were later modified to include an appreciation of the new Italian monarchy and of religion. He became a senator in 1890, and in 1906 he was the first Italian to receive the Nobel Prize for literature. He died in Bologna on Feb. 16, 1907.

JOHN CHARLES NELSON, *Columbia University*

CARDWELL, Edward (1813–1886), English politician and military reformer. He was born in Liverpool on July 24, 1813, the son of a merchant. As an expert on financial, commercial, and colonial affairs, Cardwell held high office in the ministries of Aberdeen, Palmerston, and Gladstone from 1852 to 1874.

He contributed much to the building of the Canadian federation, but the achievement for which he is best remembered was his reform and reorganization of the British army as secretary for war in Gladstone's government (1868–1874). Despite much opposition, he finally brought the army under civilian political control, abolished the practice of purchasing commissions, and reformed the terms and conditions of service. A capable administrator, amiable but somewhat colorless, he was unquestionably the greatest British military reformer of the 19th century. He was created Viscount Cardwell in 1874. Cardwell died on Feb. 15, 1886, in Torquay, England.

ANGUS MACINTYRE, *Oxford University*

CARE (Cooperative for American Relief Everywhere, Inc.) is a nonsectarian, private, nonprofit agency for voluntary aid, owned and operated by 26 major American service, religious, labor, and fraternal organizations. The federation annually helps feed 40 million needy people in Europe, Africa, Latin America, and the Middle East. It also aids self-help and community development efforts in these areas, supplying farm implements and other tools; seeds and livestock; textiles; and educational, medical, and scientific equipment. *Medico* (Medical International Cooperation Organization, founded in 1958), a service of CARE since 1962, recruits medical specialists to establish and staff clinics and hospitals in developing areas and to train doctors and other medical personnel. CARE was originally incorporated in November 1945 as the Cooperative for American Remittances to Europe.

FRANK L. GOFFIO, *Executive Director, CARE*

CAREER PLANNING. There are about 25,000 occupations in the United States, and new ones are developing every year. One of the few safe generalizations about the requirements and rewards of jobs is that they will change. Young people face the problem of choosing a career from this large and changing array of possibilities. No one, of course, is forced to pick one job and stick with it forever. In fact, a person may have to change his plans several times in the course of his working life in order to adjust to new ways in business, industry, and government. But it is necessary to make at least a choice of a field of work in time to get whatever training is needed. The boy or girl who wants to go into a profession has to decide in the early years of high school to enroll in the college preparatory course. Once a student has entered college, he may decide to change his career plan and his major field of study. More options are open to him, however, once he has the basic education required for admission to professional schools.

Having a large and growing array of jobs to choose from is both an advantage and a problem. Americans have more freedom of choice in career planning than is found in some other societies. In some countries, members of farm families tend to go on being farmers from generation to generation—a pattern that used to hold true to a considerable extent in the United States also. Choosing is a problem because it is neither completely free nor simple. Many factors limit choices; for example, women are still outnumbered by men in many fields. Many young men and women cannot afford the seven years of college study required for a professional degree. Nevertheless, most people have a considerable range of choice.

There are no simple rules that will guarantee a successful choice, but some general principles can be laid down. The young man or woman should learn as much as possible about the world of work. The next step is to make a realistic assessment of his or her abilities and interests and try to match them up with a field of work. Everyone should get as much education as possible. Risks of unemployment are highest among workers who have not completed high school. Job security is greatest and earnings are highest among those who have completed college. It is important to get a sound general education before starting to specialize.

Surveying Careers. To survey the world of work, it is neither necessary nor even profitable to go down a list of 25,000 separate jobs. It is easier and more efficient to look at groupings of jobs. The table starting on page 643 lists a selection of careers grouped, in general, according to the level of work done and the amount of preparation required: Professional and Administrative Jobs, Semiprofessional and Technical Jobs, Skilled Jobs, Sales Jobs, Clerical Jobs, and Service Jobs. The lists under each category offer a small but representative sample of the opportunities that exist. Descriptions of occupations are necessarily brief. The purpose of the table is to help a man or woman think about the kinds of work people do and consider which area to aim for. The listing of professional and administrative occupations, for example, runs from Accounting to Zoology. All the fields listed are well established and provide rewarding careers.

The capsule descriptions under each title suggest factors to consider in evaluating a field. Among them are the kind of work, the training needed, the probable income, and the prospects for employment.

Nature of the Work. The first thing to find out about a job is exactly what kind of work is done and where and when it is done. If a man is attracted to a sales career, he should ask how much he will have to learn about his product and what kind of customers he will approach. He should realize that his job may involve working evenings and weekends and traveling for weeks on end. A man who likes selling but hates to travel might be happier as a real estate broker than traveling for a manufacturer.

A common mistake is to pick a job because it has one very attractive feature or is described as glamorous. Archaeology, for example, is sometimes described as treasure hunting in exotic places. Actually, archeologists spend only part of their time in the field; they also teach, write, and work on museum collections. Their field operations require meticulous measuring and record keeping, and they may work for weeks to recover samples of broken clay pots.

Training Needed. No realistic career plan can be made without a clear understanding of how many years of training are required to get started in a field. A look through the job descriptions will show that high school graduates get preference for skilled, clerical, and sales jobs. In addition, apprenticeship or another form of on-the-job training is usually required for skilled trades. Printers, for example, spend two to five years in apprenticeship. At the semiprofessional and technical level, the emerging pattern is to require two years of study beyond high school, often in a technical institute or junior college. For professional careers, a bachelor's degree can be called the minimum entrance requirement. As the listing points out, a doctorate is needed for advancement in such fields as anthropology, biology, chemistry, and engineering. To become a full-fledged professional, a man or woman needs the ability, interest, and money to complete seven years of college and graduate study—as much as twelve or thirteen years for some specialties in medicine.

Moreover, even men and women who have become established in their fields have to continue studying to keep up with the "knowledge explosion." Office workers have to learn to use new machines, and teachers have to take summer courses on developments in their fields.

To start work in many fields, a man or woman must be licensed by a state authority or a professional group. All states license teachers, doctors, lawyers, and dentists. Many other jobs, including real estate selling and cosmetology, require licensing. Any candidate for a field that requires a license must make sure he can meet licensing requirements in the state where he wants to work. If he plans to enroll in a professional or technical school, he should be certain that the school's course is acceptable to the licensing authorities.

Income. Money is not necessarily the first factor to consider in choosing a career. Many people who have been asked to give their reasons for liking their jobs rank satisfaction with the work done and security of employment above salary. Still, income is important to most.

To judge how much income can be expected from a field, it is necessary to get current and

(*continued on page 651*)

MAJOR CAREER FIELDS

This 8-page table gives capsule descriptions of more than one hundred representative occupations grouped under professional, semiprofessional, skilled, sales, clerical, and service categories. The categories and descriptions are based on the *Occupational Outlook Handbook* published by the U. S. Department of Labor. Cross references direct the reader to articles elsewhere in the *Encyclopedia Americana* that provide more detailed career information.

Professional and Administrative Jobs

Accountants maintain precise financial records for business and industry. As in many other fields, there are specializations within the profession: for example, cost accountants, tax accountants, machine accountants, and certified public accountants (CPA's). To be a CPA a man or woman must pass a state examination; a college degree is usually a prerequisite for taking the examination. Accounting is one of the largest professions, with more than 450,000 members. The outlook is excellent. See ACCOUNTING—*9. Careers in Accounting.*

Actors who are stars of Broadway, the movies, radio, and TV have been glamorized by the public, but very few men and women reach star rank. Most actors and actresses have supporting roles or "bit" parts, and even small parts are often hard to find. There is no standard preparation, though experience in high school, college, and community theaters is a useful test of talent. Most performers belong to some type of union. Success depends so much on individual factors that no general prediction about the field is worthwhile.

Advertising Copywriters. Advertising makes a client's products or services known through words, very often in combination with pictures. Writers may prepare copy for magazines, newspapers, TV, direct mail brochures, or other media. Most jobs are found in large cities. A college degree in liberal arts is desirable preparation; experience with school publications may help. Competition is keen, but opportunities for well-qualified copywriters are good. See ADVERTISING—*11. Advertising as a Career.*

Aircraft Pilots not only fly but also are responsible for aircraft during flight operations. Best known to the public are pilots for scheduled airlines, but the larger group of commercial pilots is made up of pilots of executive planes, taxi pilots, pilots of charter planes, and flyers of cropdusting planes. All employed pilots must have commercial pilots' licenses. Physical qualifications such as good eyesight are obviously important. Employment opportunities are excellent. See AIR TRANSPORTATION—*4. Airline Careers.*

Archaeologists study man's past by excavating or otherwise recovering evidence of what man did and made. The field is small but has grown. Opportunities will be good for men and women who have the interests and the education the field demands. A Ph. D. (seven years of college and graduate study) is almost essential for advancement in archaeology. Many archaeologists teach and hold posts in museums. Most do fieldwork, which may take them on extended travels. See ARCHAEOLOGY—*6. The Profession of Archaeology.*

Architects plan and design private homes, office buildings, and factories. All buildings of any size or permanence are first sketched out by an architect. After preliminary plans are developed the architect consults with the client to reach agreement on the design before final plans are made. Often architects develop a specialty such as marine architecture or work in a particular area such as school building, office, or factory construction. The employment outlook for architects will be good as long as the construction rate is high. See ARCHITECTURE.

Astronomers make observations on the celestial happenings by means of optical and radio telescopes, photometers, spectrometers, and other instruments. Such observations have traditionally been made from the surface of the earth, but more recently they have also been made from balloons, aircraft, and rockets. From these observations tables are developed which aid in navigation over the surface of the earth and in the future will aid in space navigation by astronauts. The field is small, but the outlook appears good because of the increased need for this type of information.

Biologists study the origins and functions of animal and plant life. Biologists may work for private concerns that specialize in such areas as the development of seeds and new breeds of animals, for government agencies, or in secondary schools, colleges, and universities. Many focus on research — see BIOLOGY. The entry requirement is usually the bachelor's degree in biology. The employment outlook for biologists is good.

Botanists work toward the development of plant life that will be more sturdy and useful to man. They study the hereditary characteristics of plant life crossbreeds and experiment to develop strains that will survive and flourish in many different climates and types of soil. Botanists may work for concerns specializing in the development of new types of plants, for government agencies, or in colleges. Employment outlook is good. See BOTANY.

Business Administrators are the men (and some women) who manage businesses of all kinds from major corporations down to owner-run stores. The title is most often applied to men in the corporate chain of command — presidents, vice presidents, department managers, and so on. Men with similar administrative skills are employed in "non-business" enterprises such as colleges, hospitals, and foundations. College courses in business administration offer one way to start in this profession, and more than 50,000 degrees in business administration are granted each year. Experience is also important. Many executives are trained by their companies after they have shown promise. Outlook, good. See BUSINESS CAREERS.

Chemists. The work of chemists is divided roughly into inorganic and organic fields. Experiments are conducted in order to develop better, more useful products from the natural resources of the earth. Chemical engineers design plants and develop methods of manufacturing products that the research chemist has discovered. Chemists may also teach in secondary schools, colleges, and universities. The entry requirement is the bachelor's degree; a Ph. D. is usually needed for top jobs. The employment outlook for chemists is excellent. See CHEMISTRY.

Commercial Artists develop sketches and layouts to be used in advertisements, in books, billboards, and posters, and other media. Employment is primarily in large metropolitan areas. Much of the training is developed after the initial position is obtained. Early experience with school newspapers and yearbooks is often very helpful in developing samples of work to be shown to prospective employers. The employment outlook for the commercial artist is good. See COMMERCIAL ART.

Computer Programmers prepare instructions for electronic computers. They take such data as census statistics or sales records and put this information in the language of the computer. Programmers are employed by large businesses such as banks and insurance companies, by public utilities, by government agencies, by research centers, and by firms that specialize in computer services. Some programmers work up from such jobs as machine tabulation, but college training is desirable. Outlook, excellent. See COMPUTER.

Dentists repair and extract teeth and treat diseases of the gums. About 4% of dentists are specialists in oral surgery or in orthodontia, the straightening of teeth. Approximately 90% of all dentists are in private practice. The remainder are in the armed forces, public health service, schools, and hospitals. To qualify, a person must graduate from an accredited school of dentistry and pass the state board's examination; 6 to 8 years is needed for training. Prospects for employment are good. See DENTISTRY.

Economists are concerned with how man satisfies his material needs from the natural resources available to him. Economists are employed primarily as teachers in colleges and universities, or as research analysts with the federal government and private industry. The bachelor's degree in economics is the basic entry qualification, with the master's degree and Ph. D. necessary for significant advancement. Outlook, excellent.

Editors are employed by magazines, newspapers, and by publishers of books of all kinds. Some editors are responsible for planning programs and administering staffs. Some concentrate on content and others on style of copy. There is a trend to specialization, as in medical editing or preparation of elementary teaching materials. No general statement can cover preparation; however, many editors got liberal arts degrees and learned at least some of their skills on the job. Prospects are fairly favorable in book editing and in specialties such as science editing.

Engineering is the second-largest professional field, and the largest for men. With nearly one million members, it is exceeded in size only by teaching. Most engineers specialize in one of the ten branches listed below. A bachelor's degree, earned in 4 to 5 years of college, is the basic requirement for getting a job. Both experience and advanced study are needed for the higher salaried positions. See ENGINEERING—*Professional Practice and Training*.

Aeronautical Engineers are vital in the development of military air power and air transport. Minimum requirement for entry is usually the bachelor's degree in aeronautical engineering. Expansion of air transport and the continuing space program make the occupational outlook excellent.

Agricultural Engineers are employed primarily by private industry in the improvement of tractors and other farm equipment necessary for the production of farm products. They are also concerned with the efficient utilization of natural resources of the soil, and with water and soil conservation. Because of the increased demand for farm products that will occur with the increase in population, the occupational outlook is very good. See AGRICULTURAL ENGINEERING.

Ceramic Engineers work in the field of ceramics, improving methods of firing and processing clays and silicas. They design machinery and coordinate testing of finished products. They may specialize in brick, tile, glass, chinaware, or other media. Usually employed by a corporation. A degree in ceramics necessary.

Chemical Engineers are often the link between the new knowledge in the laboratories and the production line for the many chemical products necessary for modern living. Because of the great complexity of the work, this type of engineer often develops a specialty in some particular operation. Most chemical engineers are employed by private industry, others by the government and colleges and universities. Outlook, excellent. See CHEMICAL INDUSTRIES; CHEMISTRY—5. *Careers*.

Civil Engineers plan, design, and oversee construction and maintenance of bridges, buildings, airports, roads, power plants, and water systems. Civil engineers are employed by large industries and corporations and by government agencies, or they may have their own firm. Minimum requirement is a degree in civil engineering. The outlook is very good. See CIVIL ENGINEERING.

Electrical Engineers plan and design electrical equipment and facilities. They oversee installation, construction, and maintenance of these systems. They may be employed by industry or a public utility company, but sometimes are self-employed. A degree in electrical engineering is essential. With new inventions and discoveries, the outlook for qualified people is very good.

Industrial Engineers plan and oversee production and personnel in an industrial plant. They set up training programs to maintain and upgrade profiency, and recommend revisions to increase production. They are usually employed by industry but may be independent. An engineering degree is the minimum requirement. Outlook, good. See INDUSTRIAL ENGINEERING.

Mechanical Engineers design, install, and maintain mechanical equipment. They may specialize in, for example, jet engines, heating plants, steel mills, or machine tools. They are employed by large manufacturing concerns or construction companies or work independently. A degree in mechanical engineering is necessary. Outlook, good.

Metallurgical Engineers are concerned with new processes in refining ores, producing new alloys, and developing better qualities of malleability and strength in existing metal products. They consult with other engineers to develop better products at a minimum cost. They may specialize in radiology, machines, or electrolysis. Many are employed by the steel industry. An engineering degree is required. The outlook for employment is good.

Mining Engineers determine the location and size of ore deposits and best methods of extraction. Oversee construction and layout of tunnels, shafts, access roads, and the like. Coordinate manpower and equipment suitable to terrain at site. They are employed by mining companies or work independently. There are fewer opportunities than in other branches of engineering.

Farm Managers supervise employees of larger farms and ranches. They are responsible for work schedules, often determine when crops should be planted and harvested, and determine the need for fertilizer and insect repellants. They may also have the responsibility for the purchase of equipment and the sale of produce. Some learn on the job; others by college study plus experience. Employment prospects are fair.

Foreign Service Officers represent the interests of the U.S. government abroad and help visiting nationals. Such officers make reports to the secretary of state, and may negotiate with representatives of other countries. A college degree in political science, government, or economics is usually necessary for entry. Competition for posts means that employment prospects are limited.

Foresters work for the U.S. Department of Interior, other government agencies, or lumber companies. The forester develops master plans for the planting and cutting of forests for industrial and recreational uses. This profession is also responsible for developing systems of forest fire prevention and safety measures within the forests. A bachelor's degree in forestry is usually the entry requirement. The employment outlook for forestry is good.

Geographers study the physical characteristics of various regions of the earth and try to determine the relationships of these characteristics to the inhabitants of the region. Many geographers teach in colleges and universities. The entry requirement is usually the bachelor's degree. For advancement in this small field, a doctorate is almost essential. Outlook, fair.

Geologists study the development of earth's crust through examination of rocks, fossils, and minerals; determine locations of mineral or petroleum deposits and water; aid in the construction of dams and tunnels; and prepare reports and maps. They may specialize in engineering, ground water, or mining. A college degree in geology is essential. Outlook, good.

Geophysicists investigate forces affecting the earth, its atmosphere, and hydrosphere. They analyze data as to the earth's shape, ocean tides, activity of glaciers, earthquakes, and volcanoes and compile maps and charts for navigation. They may specialize in glaciology, hydrology, or seismology. Geophysicists are employed by the government and private industry. They may also teach. A starting job requires a master's degree, with a Ph. D. necessary for advancement. Outlook, good.

Guidance Counselors provide advice to individuals or groups on educational and vocational problems. They collect and analyze information on counselees through interviews, tests, and records, and assist individuals to overcome emotional and social problems. They conduct follow-up studies to evaluate techniques. They may be employed in educational institutions or industry; some are self-employed. A graduate degree in guidance is required. Outlook, good.

Home Economists work to improve family living by teaching people to be effective buyers and users of food, clothing, and other products and by other means such as research to improve goods and services. More than half of all home economists are teachers in schools and colleges. Other jobs include education and research programs for manufacturers, food processors, and magazines and newspapers. A bachelor's degree is the minimum requirement, and a master's or doctor's degree is essential for some more specialized jobs such as research or university teaching. Prospects are excellent for women.

Industrial Designers design products to be manufactured, and packaging for products, considering serviceability and eye appeal. They consult research personnel to determine public reaction to new designs and to obtain new ideas. They sometimes make model forms of new designs and working specifications for production. They are employed by manufacturing concerns. A minimum of four years in architecture or design school is the usual background. The outlook for employment is good.

Lawyers counsel clients on personal and business matters, and draw up documents, and represent clients in criminal and civil lawsuits. They may specialize in criminal or civil cases, corporation law, probate, real estate, or patents. They are employed in private law firms or by the government, industry, or individuals. A 4-year college degree plus law school is required; the candidate must pass state bar examinations. Outlook, very good.

Librarians maintain catalog files and collection of books, periodicals, records, and other library materials. They help individuals to find and use these materials, and will compile reference material on request. They instruct in the use of library facilities, prepare collections for groups and schools, and set up displays and readings lists. Librarians can specialize in reference works, research, films, special collections, or a particular age level. Large industry, local and federal government, schools, and colleges are employers. A degree in library science is preferred. Outlook, good for men and women. See LIBRARIES—7. *Library Personnel.*

Market Research Analysts analyze market conditions to detect the success or failure of a service or product, or to predict future success or failures. They study the preferences and buying habits of the public, and collect data on competitors for comparisons of prices and sales. Some specialize in advertising. A degree in economics is required. Outlook, good.

Mathematicians apply mathematical techniques to management, science, government, and other areas. They advise research personnel on methods and applications of mathematics. Some mathematicians teach. Many use and sometimes operate calculators and electronic computers. A basic 4-year college mathematics degree is necessary, and higher degrees are helpful for advancement. Outlook, very good.

Meteorologists forecast changes in weather, both immediate and long-range, by study of atmospheric conditions. They prepare weather maps and forecasts for farmers, pilots, mariners, and others. They are employed at government weather stations, by the armed forces, and by commercial airlines. A degree in meteorological science is required, and graduate study is recommended. Outlook, very bright.

Musicians. A professional musician may be a composer, classical or popular; an arranger; a singer; an instrumentalist; or a teacher. Education for each varies, but years of private lessons are essential, often with a formal educational background in music theory. Some musicians teach privately, or in schools or universities. Some are employed by bands or orchestras. Success depends so much on individual talent that no general forecast can be made.

Oceanographers study the ocean basins and the waters in them. They prepare navigational charts showing depths, currents, channels, and hazards and predict current changes and ocean flow. The field is allied to geology and geophysics. Oceanographers specialize in aquatic science, limnology (similar study in freshwater), or drafting and chartmaking. Some do biological research or teach. They are employed by government or by industries such as oil companies. An advanced degree is desirable but not essential except for college teaching. The field is expected to grow in importance.

Optometrists examine and prescribe eyeglasses and contact lenses. Most optometrists are in private practice; a few are salaried employees in clinics and the armed forces. Entry qualifications are graduation from an accredited school of optometry and passing the state board examination. At least five years of study beyond high school is required. A liking for scientific and delicate precision work is necessary. Outlook, excellent.

Pharmacists are employed in retail pharmacies, pharmaceutical manufacturing research, hospitals, and the U.S. Public Health Service. The minimum entry requirements are graduation from an accredited college of pharmacy and passing an examination by the state board of pharmacy. Because of increased population and demand for medical services, the occupational outlook is excellent.

Physicians are engaged in the treatment and prevention of disease in humans. Doctors are employed by government and business, but the majority are in private practice. About half the physicians in private practice are general practioners, or "family doctors," but there is a trend toward specialization. To become a doctor a man or woman must invest at least 7 years beyond high school, including pre-med school, medical school, and internship, and must pass a licensing examination. Specialization requires additional study—as much as 5 or 6 years for neurosurgery. Because of population increase and a growing investment in medical care, there is a demand for physicians.

Physicists study matter and energy in all forms. The minimum requirement for entry is the bachelor's degree in physics, and the doctorate is becoming more and more standard. Physicists are employed by private industry, academic institutions, research foundations, and government. Employment opportunities will continue to be excellent as the demands for research talent continue to grow.

Political Scientists study the functions of government at the federal, state, and local level. A master's degree is usually required for entry, and the Ph. D. is necessary for advancement. Most political scientists are employed as teachers in colleges and universities; others work for the U. S. Department of State and other government agencies. Employment prospects, very good.

Psychologists study human behavior, often with reference to areas such as juvenile delinquency, old age, social attitudes, and education. They may specialize in counseling, engineering, industrial, educational, or clinical phychology. Some study and treat emotional and mental disorders. Psychologists are employed by schools and institutions, industry, and government, or may be self-employed. A Ph. D. degree in psychology is required, and some internship is preferred. For private practice, many states require a license. Employment prospects, excellent.

Public Relations Counselors plan and conduct public relation campaigns, using newspapers, radio, TV, and other media. They may conduct public opinion polls as a guide to planning favorable publicity for clients. They often write stories for news media, including radio and television. A degree in journalism or English is a usual form of preparation, and knowledge of business administration is helpful. Nearly all businesses employ public relations people, hence the outlook is good.

Registered Nurses give expert care to the sick and injured, under the direction of doctors. They observe and record symptoms and temperatures, bathe and feed the sick, change dressings, prepare operating room, sterilize instruments, and give injections. They may specialize in public health nursing, private nursing, industrial nursing, school nursing, or nursing education. Candidates must successfully complete a 3-year course of study in a hospital, and some take 4-year baccalaureate course in a college or university. To become a registered nurse, a graduate must pass an examination required in all states. Nursing is one of the leading fields for women, with more than 580,000 members. Outlook, very good.

Sanitarians plan and administer environmental health programs. They set sanitation regulations for food processing and serving, sewage disposal, smog control, and control of radiation and other environmental health hazards. They collaborate with officials on health and safety laws. They may specialize in sanitation technology or sanitary engineering. Sanitarians can be employed by government, industry, or public health services. In most cases a degree in engineering is required, and further study in a specialized field helps advancement. Outlook, very good.

Social Workers analyze and try to ease and prevent social problems caused by poverty, unemployment, and physical, mental, and social maladjustments and handicaps. They conduct individual or group case studies. They are employed by governmental agencies, church or ethnic group agencies, schools, and other institutions. They may specialize in individual, group, or organization work, or teach. A master's degree in social work, with some clinical training, is preferred. Candidates often take an undergraduate degree in liberal arts, then an advanced degree in social work. Outlook — because of emphasis on inner-city problems and remedies for poverty — very good.

Sociologists study human groups such as families, communities, political organizations, and religious bodies. Some sociologists specialize — for example, in market research, education, urban problems, or juvenile delinquency. The majority of sociologists are in colleges and universities, combining teaching and research. Others work for government or for private industry or are self-employed. A master's degree is usually necessary for a starting job, and a Ph. D. is required for advancement. The field is small but growing. Outlook, very good.

Speech Therapists diagnose and treat speech disorders. They work with people who are handicapped by mental or emotional disorders, injuries, foreign-speech accents, or stuttering. They often work with psychologists and medical doctors. Therapists are employed in schools, universities, clinics, and in some institutions. A bachelor's degree is essential, and graduate work is needed to advance to research or pathology and psychology. A demand for qualified people is expected to continue.

Statisticians analyze and interpret numerical data with the aid of modern data-processing equipment and calculating machines. They may specialize in one field—for example, agriculture, economics, engineering, education, psychology, or medicine. They are employed by government or industry, or may teach or do research. A 4-year baccalaureate degree is essential, with a trend toward requiring two or more years of graduate work. Outlook, very good.

Surveyors measure distances, locate topographic elevations and contours, determine property boundaries, and compile exact data for mapmaking. They may specialize in geodetics, hydrographics, mining, highways, topography, or general land surveying. They are employed by the government, local and federal; engineering firms; construction companies; and oil or transportation industries. If a man starts work without a college degree, a rigid and extensive on-the-job-training program is required. A junior college or technical school background in engineering and surveying is most helpful. In addition, a surveyor is required to be licensed. Outlook, good.

Teaching is the largest professional field and by far the largest for women. Of more than 2 million full-time teachers in the United States, almost three fourths are women. Duties and requirements vary from one level to another. See EDUCATION—*14. Careers in Education.*

Elementary school teachers often are responsible for teaching a number of subjects to one class of children, although there is a trend toward subject specialization. Willingness to work with young children is important. At the secondary level, teachers usually work in one subject field. The great majority of elementary and secondary school teachers are employed by public schools. All states require that public school teachers hold certificates, and most states make four years of college a criterion for certification. Advanced study may lead to salary increases and promotion. Many subject teachers find that they need refresher courses in order to keep up with the knowledge explosion. The outlook is very good for elementary teachers. Candidates for high school posts will face stiffer competition, and advanced training may become a requirement in many schools.

College and university teachers usually combine instructing undergraduate or graduate students with research in their fields of specialization. The minimum requirement is the master's degree, and a doctorate is needed for advancement. Many college teachers supplement their incomes by consulting work, independent research, and writing. The employment outlook is very good.

Technical Writers interpret the work of technicians and scientists for lay people. They write instructions for new machines such as washers, driers, stoves, refrigerators, and automotive equipment. They also prepare service manuals, repair books, and catalogs and may write articles and publicity. They are usually employed by industry or government agencies. A 4-year college degree is the minimum requirement, plus thorough knowledge of a technical area. A journalism or English background is helpful. A new field with a very favorable outlook.

Urban Planners analyze the patterns of business, housing, traffic, and other aspects of city life in an effort to make communities safer, more convenient, and more attractive. They may, for example, plan the redevelopment of a run-down area. The majority of planners work for government agencies. Young men or women with bachelor's degrees in such subjects as civil engineering, architecture, or public administration can get beginning jobs, but many employers require a master's degree in planning. Outlook, very good. See URBAN PLANNING.

Zoologists study the origin, classification, diseases, growth, and development of animals. They often collect examples for study and often work in laboratories. They may specialize in herpetology, icthyology, ornithology, or mammalogy. Some combine research and teaching. At the minimum a 4-year college or university degree is required; graduate work, preferably a doctor's degree, is necessary for top professional positions. Outlook, good for men and women with graduate degrees.

Semiprofessional and Technical Jobs

Aeronautical Technicians work with engineers and scientists on the design and construction of aircraft, rockets, and space capsules. They assist engineers by collecting data and performing tests and experiments. Sometimes they estimate costs of manufacturing, and they may write instruction manuals or catalogs. They are employed by manufacturers and by government agencies. The minimum requirement is post-high school technical school training with specialization in the field, and on-the-job training is often required. Armed forces technical training is very helpful. Outlook, good.

Agricultural Technicians work with agricultural engineers on such problems as controlling harmful insects and crop diseases and developing better strains and varieties of plants. They are usually employed by farm agencies, government experiment stations, colleges, and other agencies dealing with agriculture. A college education with specialization in a particular area is required. They may specialize in biochemistry, genetics, entomology, bacteriology, plant and animal husbandry, embryology, or pathology. Demand for these technicians exceeds the supply, particularly since many are needed to staff agricultural missions in developing countries.

Airline Dispatchers direct and control commercial air flights. They study weather reports to determine any needed change in flight plans and keep pilots informed of changes in weather and traffic. They instruct pilots in case of emergencies. Controllers must pass an examination by the Federal Aviation Agency (FAA). Because this is a relatively small field, the outlook is limited.

Chemical Technicians assist chemists and chemical engineers in development, production, and sales of chemical products and equipment. They do research and tabulate and analyze the results of testing. They are employed by laboratories, government agencies, and chemical manufacturing concerns. A minimum of technical school or junior college training (two years of each), is needed. Outlook, good.

Dental Hygienists work under the supervision of dentists on such tasks as taking X-rays, cleaning teeth, and massaging gums. School systems employ dental hygienists to examine children and report their findings and recommendations for treatment to parents. All states require licensing, and most require a 2-year training course. Outlook, excellent for women. See DENTISTRY.

Dental Laboratory Technicians make plaster molds for artificial dentures and orthodontal appliances. They often make the appliances and dentures and make bridges and crowns for teeth. Many are employed by commercial dental laboratories and governmental agencies, and some by individual dentists or clinics. They must be high school graduates with on-the-job training for a period of 3 to 4 years. Vocational high school or junior college training work is helpful. Certification by professional associations is desirable. Outlook, good. See DENTISTRY.

Draftsmen devise complete working plans and detailed design layouts from rough drafts and notes by architects or engineers. They are employed by government agencies and in private industry. A high school diploma plus technical institute or junior college study is usually required. Apprenticeship is most helpful. Experience and skill are necessary for advancement. Outlook, very good.

Electronics Technicians assist engineers and scientists with research and design in the field of electronics. They help to design and construct working models. They may service equipment and inspect or test electronic devices. They are employed by electronics manufacturing plants and by government agencies. They must have a background of technical training, and may qualify through a 3- to 4-year apprenticeship program or on-the-job training. They may be required to hold a license, as in radio transmission. Outlook, very good.

Instrument Makers design or repair mechanical or electronic instruments. They read and follow blueprints and use welding and other special equipment. Graduation from high school with technical school training in electronics and mechanics is desirable. On-the-job apprenticeship is helpful — usually a 4- to 5-year program. Usually they must pass an oral and written examination. Outlook, very good.

Medical Technologists make various chemical and microscopic tests to aid the physician in the detection and treatment of disease. Hospitals employ the largest number of these special technicians. The total formal training necessary is approximately four years, and candidates must pass an examination. Outlook, excellent.

Medical X-Ray Technicians or Technologists work under the direction of physicians to diagnose and treat diseases, using X-ray, radium, and other equipment. They are employed by hospitals and clinics and sometimes by individual doctors. The usual training is a 2-year post-high school course in a hospital or medical school. Some schools require a 2-year nursing course as preparation. Registration with a professional association helps advancement. Outlook, excellent.

Tool Designers design tools and machine devices for manufacturers. Make sketches of designs for jigs, tools, dies, and other machine fixtures. Modify existing tools for efficiency and durability. Preparation is a course in a technical training school. Apprenticeship with on-the-job training is often required. Outlook, good.

Skilled Jobs

Air-Conditioning Mechanics install, maintain, and repair equipment used for conditioning air. They may work for air-conditioning, retail firms or manufacturing companies, or be self-employed. Mechanics must be trained by an on-the-job or apprenticeship program; training usually takes 3 to 4 years under an experienced mechanic. Graduation from high school or technical high school is very valuable background, and armed forces technical training is helpful. Outlook, very good.

Automobile Mechanics repair electrical and mechanical parts of all automobiles, buses, and trucks and perform periodic checks on cars to assure proper performance. They may specialize in tune-up, brakes, automatic transmissions, electrical repair, or body work or air conditioning. High school graduates are preferred, and technical high school background is very helpful. On-the-job or apprenticeship training is required in large operations. Outlook, very good.

Bricklayers work with bricks, concrete, cinder or tile blocks, stone, marble, or terra-cotta. They construct walls, floors, fireplaces, archways, partitions, and chimneys from these materials. They repair or replace such construction if necessary. Bricklayers are employed by construction and engineering companies or may be self-employed. Trade school or high school education required, followed by on-the-job training for a period of 3 years. Outlook, good.

Carpenters saw, fit, and assemble wood or its substitutes to make structures of many types. They may also install tiles and linoleum and roofing or ceiling tiles. They are employed by contractors and homebuilders and in highway construction or may be self-employed. A 4-year apprenticeship is required and a high school education is desirable. Outlook, good.

Electricians install, repair, and maintain electrical wiring of all types. They plan new layouts to minimize hazard and cost. They may specialize in airplane, marine, construction, powerhouse, machine, or radio-TV work. Electricians are usually required to be licensed. Trade school background is helpful but not necessary. Practical knowledge gained as an electrician's helper or apprentice is often a deciding factor in employment. Outlook, very good.

Machinists make metal parts to specifications with machine tools, operating all types of machine tools. A machinist may be employed in a job shop, production shop, or maintenance shop. High school or vocational school graduates are preferred, and 4 years of apprenticeship or on-the-job training is required. Outlook, good.

Painters prepare interior and exterior surfaces and then apply paint, stain, lacquer, or similar materials. They must be skilled in handling brushes and must be familiar with the characteristics of paints and finishes. To mix paints, they must have a knowledge of color harmony. Some are employed by construction companies; others are self-employed. Some work on maintenance staffs in factories or public buildings. Apprenticeship is required. About 400,000 men are employed as painters. However, new discoveries in the paint field enable anyone to paint, new paints last longer than older types, and builders now use materials that do not need paint. The outlook is only fair.

Plumbers assemble, alter, install, and repair plumbing fixtures and pipes, heating and air-conditioning units, and hot water tanks; they may work on sewers and septic tanks. They may be employed by construction companies or industry or be self-employed. High school education is preferred plus on-the-job or apprenticeship training, usually for a 5-year period. Licenses are required in most states. Outlook, good.

Printing Pressmen handle the final steps in preparing type forms and press plates for printing and operate printing presses. Sometimes they maintain and repair presses. They are employed by newspapers and by large and small printing plants. Most are union members. A high school education is required, and vocational high school training is helpful. The specific preparation for this craft is usually an apprenticeship of 2 to 5 years. The amount of printing is expected to increase, but improved technology will limit the need for pressmen. Outlook, fair.

Stationary Engineers operate and maintain large stationary industrial equipment — for example, boilers, ventilators, air-conditioners, turbines, and compressors. They also repair equipment. The usual requirements are high school or trade school graduation and a 4-year apprenticeship program. Some small concerns give on-the-job training. Outlook, good.

Structural Ironworkers assemble and install structural metal products, mainly in the construction of large buildings. They may rig heavy construction equipment. They also repair and make alterations on existing buildings. They may be employed by steel-erection contractors, ornamental iron contractors, general contractors on large building projects, large steel companies, or government agencies and public utilities. A high school diploma is desirable, and a 3-year apprenticeship program is necessary. Superior bodily strength and agility are vital. Outlook, good.

Television Repairmen diagnose trouble and make necessary adjustments and repairs in television equipment. They may install and repair antennas. They are employed by repair shops, retail stores, and television manufacturers or are self-employed. Technical or vocational school training in electronics is most helpful. Military training in electronics is an asset. In addition, on-the-job training is required, usually for 2 or 3 years. Outlook, good.

Tool and Die Makers construct jigs and fixtures to hold metal for shaping, make gauges for manufacturing precision parts, and construct metal forms (dies) for shaping metals and plastics. They must be able to read blueprints and operate all types of machine tools. They may work for construction firms, farm machinery or automotive plants, electrical machinery companies, or metal products industries. Vocational or technical high school graduates are preferred and correspondence school courses are valuable. A 4- to 5-year apprenticeship is necessary. Outlook, fair.

Welders join metals together by electric arc, acetylene torch, atomic hydrogen arc, or other heat methods. They may also cut or shape metals. Vocational or technical school graduates are preferred, and they must complete an on-the-job training program — usually of a year or more. They are employed by machine shops, manufacturing plants such as shipyards, and government agencies. Outlook, good.

Sales Jobs

Automobile Salesmen demonstrate new and used automobiles to prospective buyers. They must know how to quote tentative prices and trade-in allowances and write up orders, and may sell financing and insurance. They develop and follow up leads on prospective new customers. On-the-job training is necessary to become familiar with the particular cars handled and to get some knowledge of the strong and weak points of others. At least a high school or technical school education is required. A salesman may advance to sales manager or general manager and in some cases to his own dealership. Outlook for interested men, good.

Clerks in Retail Stores demonstrate merchandise, receive payments, and wrap or arrange for the delivery of purchases. Clerks may advance, through on-the-job training, correspondence courses, or night school, to management assignments. There is a trend toward hiring only high school graduates because mathematical computations are necessary and legible writing and correct spelling are required. Outlook for qualified men and women, good.

Manufacturers' Salesmen describe, display, and demonstrate company products to customers. They call at wholesale houses, retail outlets, and other business concerns. They are employed by the food products industry, chemical products industry, machinery and parts companies, publishing houses, and many others. Men with college degrees are preferred. Some jobs require a college background in a particular field. Outlook, good.

Real Estate Agents are employed on commission by buyers or sellers to arrange rental or sale of property. Agents must be familiar with all aspects of property ownership, such as taxes, zoning regulations, insurance needs, and water supply. They negotiate with seller and buyer, prepare final sales contracts, and may arrange for loan and title search. A high school diploma is usually required, and agents must pass a written examination and get a state license.

Clerical Jobs

Bookkeepers record and summarize the financial transactions of an industry, business, or institution. They keep accounting records on ledgers, journals, and other forms and use adding machines and typewriters. Some bookkeepers advance to supervisory jobs or do teaching. A high school education with business background is required, and business school graduates are preferred. More than 1 million men and women are employed in the field, and the outlook is good. See ACCOUNTING—*Bookkeeping;* BUSINESS EDUCATION.

Cashiers receive money and make change for goods sold to customers, or serve depositors in banks. They are responsible for correct records of transactions. They may handle adding machines or cash registers. Cashiers are employed in all businesses. No special education is necessary, but high school business courses are valuable. Outlook, good.

Computer Operators run electronic computers for such purposes as preparing payrolls, making out bills for customers, keeping stock inventories, compiling personnel records, and sorting census data. The operator may work under the direction of a programmer, who sets up the detailed instructions to be fed into the computer. The operator may insert tapes or punched cards, run the control console, and use other machines to translate the computer's output into words and numbers. At least a high school education is required for starting in the field. Specific computer training is given on the job. The field is expanding, and the outlook is good. See COMPUTER.

Office Machine Operators are especially trained to work with calculating, billing, key punch, tabulating, sorting, copy, and duplicating machines. They are responsible for accuracy of the machine and in some cases perform minor maintenance and adjustment on machines. They must have a general knowledge of the equipment used. High school courses in business or business school background is helpful, and on-the-job training on specific machines is necessary. More than 300,000 men and women are in the field. Outlook, very good. See BUSINESS EDUCATION.

Secretaries handle a variety of duties, including dictation and transcription, answering telephones, operating office machines, acknowledging correspondence, and preparing reports. Secretaries may work closely with executives and handle confidential information. A high school business course is usually the minimum requirement for a starting job. On-the-job performance greatly influences advancement opportunities. There are more than 2 million secretaries and stenographers, 95% women. The employment outlook for secretaries is excellent. See BUSINESS CAREERS.

Stenographers take dictation in shorthand and transcribe it on typewriters. They may transcribe from recordings. Some specialize in court, legal, medical, or technical stenography, and they must be familiar with the language used in the particular job. Stenographers answer mail or telephone, or use business machines. High school business education is necessary, and business school is preferred. Outlook, excellent.

Telephone Operators place calls and make telephone connections for people using telephone services. They aid customers having difficulties or in emergency situations. They work for telephone companies or large businesses on switchboards. On-the-job training is provided. Outlook, good—though automation may lessen the demand for operators.

Typists are clerical workers who type letters, forms, stencils, and other materials from corrected copy or rough drafts. They may operate a duplicating machine or addressograph. About 650,000 people work as typists, 95% women. Outlook, good.

Service Occupations

Airline Stewardesses serve food and beverages, check passenger lists, and generally see that the plane is neat and in order. They also care for invalids and provide other special services for passengers. At least a high school education is required; nurse's training or college is preferred. Stewardesses must attend an airline school and then serve a trial employment of six months' duration. Outlook, very good.

Beauticians (often called cosmetologists) style, cut, shampoo, condition, and color hair and give facials, manicures, and massages. They may shape eyebrows, apply makeup, and care for wigs and hairpieces. Some are self-employed; others work in department stores, drugstores, hospitals, and hotels. Trade or vocational school graduation is required, and beauticians must be licensed by state boards. About 400,000 people (90% women) work as hairdressers and beauticians. Outlook, very good.

Chefs are usually highly skilled cooks who coordinate the work of a kitchen staff. They may plan menus and purchase supplies. Chefs are employed by hotels, restaurants, hospitals, private clubs, railroads, airlines, large manufacturing companies, schools, and government agencies. High school or vocational school graduates are preferred. On-the-job training or courses given by restaurant associations or hotel management groups are valuable. Outlook, excellent.

Protective Service Occupations

FBI Agents investigate violations of federal laws, such as espionage, mail, fraud, and sabotage. They have broad responsibilities for protecting the security of the United States. A candidate must be a graduate of a 4-year law school or 4-year accounting school. A 14-week training period is mandatory after appointment. Because of competition the outlook is fair. See FEDERAL BUREAU OF INVESTIGATION.

Firemen are employed to protect property and life from fire. In addition to fighting fires they conduct inspections at theaters, factories, and other buildings to see that all preventive regulations are adhered to. They may give talks on fire hazards and fire prevention. Most are employed by local governments. A high school education is preferred, and candidates must pass a written intelligence test and a physical examination. Several weeks' training is usual after appointment. Outlook, good.

Policemen are charged with preserving law and order. Their duties may include directing traffic, giving first aid and information, investigating crimes, and arresting criminals. Most are employed by local, state, or federal government, but some are employed by banks and industry and as watchmen. High school graduates are preferred. Candidates must pass physical and written examinations and often have training periods at police academies. Outlook, excellent.

(*continued from page* 642)
specific details. Average figures are not always reliable guides, because the range may be very wide. For example, in the mid-1960's salaries of classroom teachers in the U. S. public schools ranged from $3,300 to $14,100. Starting salaries in some states were double those in others. Top pay usually went to teachers in or near large cities who had more than minimum training.

Maximum salary figures are often misleading. A few professional athletes, for example, draw six-figure incomes in their peak years, but their earnings as players can be expected to drop to zero before they reach middle age. They need to have some other source of income in reserve.

It is also necessary to relate income to the investment that must be made in order to qualify for a high level of income. It is often said that doctors make a lot of money, and some do. But they have to get through many years of training before they can start to earn large incomes. Moreover, many doctors have to invest in expensive equipment before they can start to practice.

Prospects for Employment. Before a young man or woman starts a course of training that may take from two years to seven or more, he or she will want to be reasonably sure that there will be a job open when the time comes to apply. In the listing accompanying this article, the outlook for employment is described by such terms as "fair," "good," and "excellent." These judgments are those of the U. S. Department of Labor and are based on analysis of current employment, population growth, and expected demand for goods, services, and skills. The Department of Labor stresses that any predictions can be upset by such factors as international crises or depressions. Less drastic changes may be caused by automation and by the appearance of new products and new industrial and business methods.

A few trends seem well established. There is a decreasing demand for unskilled workers and a growing need for skilled, technical, and professional workers. As society becomes more mechanized, the manual jobs that once employed the majority of men dwindle, while new jobs requiring special skills open up. Employment in farming has fallen sharply, but the outlook for agricultural engineers is rated very good.

While overall employment in farming and mining is expected to continue to drop, employment in construction, the service industries, and civilian work for government is expected to rise rapidly through the late 1960's and into the 1970's. Government employment—chiefly by state and local agencies—grew by about 75% between the end of World War II and the mid-1960's. People in most professions and other kinds of work are employed by branches of government, usually under civil service regulations. See also CIVIL SERVICE.

Job Families. In planning a career in a time of changing job patterns, it is important to keep in mind the concept of job families. If openings in one type of work decrease, it may be possible to move into a related job. For example, a man with a degree in chemistry might have the following options: teaching in high school or college, doing research in a university, developing products for private industry, testing products in a government laboratory, editing textbooks or a professional journal, and technical writing.

The idea of job families has another value in career planning. Many professions have counterparts at the semiprofessional level. If a man cannot qualify for—or finance—professional education, he may not have to give up his interest in his chosen field. He may find a useful and well paid career as a technician. Dentists, for example, need the help of dental hygienists and laboratory technicians.

Evaluating the Individual. It is easier to analyze the requirements of jobs than it is to assess the abilities and interests of an individual. Psychologists and sociologists have studied thousands of men and women in various careers, but they have not been able to isolate factors that fully explain why one is a success and another is mediocre or a failure. Obviously, talent is an advantage, but ability does not guarantee success. Some machinists, for example, score higher on measures of ability than some mechanical engineers. Such factors as interest, drive, and good health are also involved.

There are no simple ways to gauge abilities and interests, but there are some useful indicators. School grades—particularly a pattern over several years—often point to a promising career area. Hobbies can be evidence of interests and skills. Experience in a part-time job is a practical test of how well a person will match a job. Many tests have been devised in an effort to provide objective measures of aptitudes and interests. The results of these tests can be valuable indicators of the sort of field an individual should aim for, but they are only indicators and should not be taken as decisive evidence. Test scores are more valuable for predicting achievement during training than for predicting success on the job. For example, a law or medical aptitude test is more valid as a predictor of success in law school or medical school than of success in professional practice. See also APTITUDE TEST.

Sources of Information. Career planning should be based on study of the best and latest data about the world of work. Both information and advice can be obtained from high school guidance offices. State employment offices, service clubs, the YMCA, churches, unions, and corporations are other sources.

One of the most comprehensive and objective published sources is the *Occupational Outlook Handbook* issued by the U. S. Department of Labor. This book discusses broad trends and also describes hundreds of jobs in detail.

Many professional groups offer information on jobs in their areas—for example, the American Chemical Society, the National Education Association, the American Anthropological Association, and the American Psychological Association. Professional societies furnish lists of approved training schools.

See also COLLEGES AND UNIVERSITIES—2. *Programs in Higher Education;* JUNIOR COLLEGE; VOCATIONAL EDUCATION; VOCATIONAL GUIDANCE.

GARLAND M. FITZPATRICK
Connecticut State Department of Education

Bibliography

Hopke, William E., ed., *Encyclopedia of Careers and Vocational Guidance* (New York and Chicago 1967).

Roe, Anne, *The Psychology of Occupations* (New York 1956).

Thorndike, Robert L., and Hagen, Elizabeth, *Ten Thousand Careers* (New York 1959).

U. S. Department of Labor, Bureau of Labor Statistics, *Occupational Outlook Handbook* (Washington, biennially).

U. S. Department of Labor, U. S. Employment Service, *Dictionary of Occupational Titles,* 3d ed. (Washington 1966).

CARÊME, kȧ-rem′, **Marie Antoine** (1784–1833), French chef and writer, whose books on culinary art had an immense influence on the development of classic French cookery. He was born in Paris on June 8, 1784, and at the age of 11 he began a kitchen apprenticeship in a cheap tavern. By the time he was 17, he was chief pastry cook in the elegant pastry shop of a Monsieur Bailly. Carême studied architectural engravings and learned to draw, then applied his knowledge and skill to the elaborate pastry constructions (*pièces montées*) supplied by Bailly to Parisian gourmets.

Carême profited from the widespread interest in elegant dining during and after the Napoleonic era. Prince Talleyrand, famed as a host, employed him for 12 years. Carême later became head chef in kitchens belonging to the Prince Regent of England, Alexander I of Russia, and Baron James de Rothschild in Paris.

Carême's books, published under the name Antonin Carême, are storehouses of culinary knowledge. They include *Le pâtissier royal parisien* (1815), *Le pâtissier pittoresque* (1815), *Le maître d'hôtel français* (1822), and the 5-volume *L'art de la cuisine française au XIXe siècle,* which was unfinished at his death, in Paris, on Jan. 12, 1833.

Esther B. Aresty
Author of "The Delectable Past"

CAREW, kə-rōō′, **George** (1555–1629), English soldier, who suppressed revolts in Ireland. He was born on May 29, 1555. Between 1575 and 1583 he fought Irish rebels against English rule, and from 1588 to 1592 he was master of ordnance in Ireland. He accompanied Robert Devereux, 2d Earl of Essex, in his expeditions against Cádiz, Spain, in 1596 and to the Azores in 1597. When Essex was appointed lord lieutenant of Ireland in 1599, Carew returned there with him as president of Munster. Under Essex and his successor, Lord Mountjoy, Carew ruthlessly quelled the rebellion of Hugh O'Neill, Earl of Tyrone.

Carew returned to England in 1603 and held several important places under James I. He was made Baron Clopton in 1604 and Earl of Totnes in 1626. He died in London on March 27, 1629.

CAREW, kar′ē, **Thomas** (1594?–1640), English poet and courtier. One of the Cavalier poets, Carew was endowed with the easy brilliance and courtly polish typical of the poets of his era, but surpassed most of them in the meticulous craftsmanship of his lyrics.

Carew was born in West Wickham, Kent, the son of an important government official. In 1613, after study at Merton College, Oxford, and the Middle Temple, he became secretary to Sir Dudley Carleton, ambassador to Venice and the Hague, but was dismissed in 1616 for writing a satire against Carleton. Carew then entered the service of Sir Edward Herbert (later Lord Herbert of Cherbury), and by 1630 he was attached to the court of Charles I, where he was a great favorite, and took part in its fashionable, dissipated life. Carew died in London in March 1640, shortly before the Puritan Revolution swept away the frivolous, decorative society he had adorned.

Except for *Coelum Brittanicum,* a masque performed at court in 1634, Carew's work is exclusively lyric poetry. His principal subject is love, which he treats in a conventional but graceful manner. In his best lyrics, such as the lovely *Ask me no more,* he shows a genius for combining the sensuousness of the Elizabethans, the clarity of Jonson, and the wit of Donne.

Frank J. Warnke
Coeditor, "Seventeenth Century Prose and Poetry"

CAREY, kâr′ē, **Henry** (1685?–1743), English poet and composer. Born in London, he is said to have been an illegitimate son of George Savile, Marquess of Halifax. His first poems were published in 1713. Between 1715 and 1739 he wrote, for the London stage, farces, burlesques, and nine ballad-operas, for which he composed pleasing and often deeply pathetic melodies. He also wrote many cantatas, ballads, and songs, among them *Sally in Our Alley,* later sung to the borrowed tune of *The Country Lasse.* His *Chrononhotonthologos* (1734) was a burlesque of the theatrical bombast of his time. He also composed *A Wonder, or the Honest Yorkshireman* (1735), a burlesque opera.

More than 50 years after Carey's death, in London on Oct. 4, 1743, his posthumous son, George Savile Carey, made an unestablished claim that his father had composed the words and music of *God Save the King* (q.v.) in 1740.

CAREY, kâr′ē, **Henry Charles** (1793–1879), American economist and publisher, who espoused a protectionist tariff policy, founded the "nationalist" school of economics, and propounded the notion of the ultimate harmony of interests of all social and economic classes.

Born in Philadelphia on Dec. 15, 1793, the son of the prosperous publisher Mathew Carey, he achieved considerable status in the publishing field before withdrawing from it to devote himself to economic studies and writing. He opposed the "pessimistic" rent doctrines of David Ricardo and population theses of Thomas Malthus. However, his own theorizing suffered from his lack of analytical powers, his misreading of history, and his strong ideological commitment to the concept of the ultimate harmony of all classes resulting from the pursuit of self-interest.

His *Essay on the Rate of Wages* (1835) was followed by four other books including *Principles of Social Science* (1858–1859), which John Stuart Mill considered "the worst book on political economy I ever toiled through." Carey nonetheless had numerous supporters in his "nationalist" school. He died in Philadelphia on Oct. 13, 1879.

Norman A. Mercer, *Union College*

CAREY, kâr′ē, **Joseph Maull** (1845–1924), American public official. He was born on Jan. 19, 1845, in Milton, Del., and was educated at Union College and the University of Pennsylvania law school. Appointed by President Grant in 1869 the first U. S. attorney in Wyoming Territory, he later served on the territorial supreme court and three times as delegate to Congress.

A Republican, he was the first U. S. senator from Wyoming (1890–1895). In the Senate he gave his name to the Carey Act (1894), which authorized the transfer of federal desert lands to states reclaiming and irrigating them. Carey's support of President Cleveland against the free coinage of silver cost him reelection. In 1910, as the Democratic nominee, he was elected governor. He promoted extensive state irrigation projects to open land for agriculture. He died on Feb. 5, 1924, in Cheyenne.

CAREY, kâr′ē, **Mathew** (1760–1839), American publisher, bookseller, and economist. He was born in Dublin, Ireland, on Jan. 28, 1760. In 1779, after publishing an attack against English rule, he fled to Paris, where he met Benjamin Franklin. He returned to Ireland in 1780 and edited several politically controversial journals before emigrating to Philadelphia in 1784. There, in 1785, he founded the *Pennsylvania Herald.* Later he published the *American Museum* and helped establish the Hibernian Society and also the first American Sunday school. From 1790 he was closely identified with the Philadelphia book trade. He was a member of the firm of Carey, Lea & Carey, which published the first edition of the *Encyclopedia Americana* in 1829. His political tracts, notably *The Olive Branch* (1814), and economic pamphlets, including *Essays on Political Economy* (1822), were widely read. He was the father of the economist Henry Charles Carey (q.v.). Carey died in Philadelphia on Sept. 16, 1839.

CAREY, kâr′ē, **William** (1761–1834), English Orientalist and Baptist missionary. Carey was born in Northamptonshire on Aug. 17, 1761. He joined the Baptist Church in 1783 and helped organize the Baptist Missionary Society in 1792. He believed that missionaries should study the background and thought of non-Christian peoples and spread the gospel in their language, and he advised missionaries to train an indigenous ministry as rapidly as possible.

Carey went to India in 1794. He quickly mastered Indian languages, taught Sanskrit, Bengali, and Marathi for 30 years, and published dictionaries and grammars as well as a translation of the New Testament into Bengali. He died in Serampore on June 9, 1834.

JAMES H. SMYLIE
Union Theological Seminary, Richmond, Va.

Further Reading: Oussoren, Aalbertinus H., *William Carey* (Leiden, Neth., 1945).

CARGILL, kär′gil, **Donald** (1619–1681), a leader of extreme Scottish Covenanters. He was born in Rattray, Perthshire, Scotland, and was educated at Aberdeen and St. Andrews universities. In 1655 he was appointed minister to the Barony parish in Glasgow, from which he was ejected in 1662 because he criticized the return of Charles II to the throne. He later continued his preachings in private houses and at great field meetings. He was wounded at the Battle of Bothwell Bridge (1679) and fled to Holland where he remained a few months. When he returned, he joined Richard Cameron in publishing the Sanquhar Declaration against Charles II, and in September 1680 he publicly excommunicated the king, the duke of York, and other officials. After avoiding arrest for months, he was captured and brought to Edinburgh, where he was beheaded on July 27, 1681.

CARGO CULT is the name used by anthropologists for a type of religious movement that has developed in Melanesia since 1913. The central belief of such cults is that magic will cause great riches to arrive in the form of cargo on ships or planes. The cults developed among peoples who were impressed by the overpowering material wealth of Europeans, Australians, Japanese, and Americans. The Melanesians had no way of knowing how the many goods of the foreigners were made; they only saw them arrive in quantity. Consequently the native peoples came to believe that these cargoes were sent from the spirit world, and they appealed to their ancestors to supply them also with cargo. The magical practices used in the appeal for goods often involved careful imitation of the foreigners. Cult members drilled with wooden rifles and held flag-raising ceremonies; sometimes they even built piers or landing strips for the expected ships or planes.

The cargo cults illustrate problems that develop when a traditional culture is forced to give way to a foreign style of life. The native peoples turn to magic in an effort to achieve a good life that seems out of reach by other means.

Cargo cults are particularly associated with Melanesia. However, the general phenomenon is not new. Many peoples in many ages have resorted to magical and religious means to change society because they lacked the technological and political power to do so.

ERIKA BOURGUIGNON
The Ohio State University

Further Reading: Lanternari, Vittorio, *The Religion of the Oppressed: A Study of Modern Messianic Cults* (New York 1960); Thrupp, Sylvia, ed., *Millennial Dreams in Action* (The Hague 1962); Worsley, Peter, *The Trumpet Shall Sound: A Study of Cargo Cults in Melanesia* (London 1957).

CARIA, kâr′ē-ə, was a division of ancient Asia Minor, in the southwestern part of what is now Turkey. It was a mountainous region with a coastline on the Aegean Sea. Its border with Lydia to the north was marked by the Maeander River.

Herodotus says the Carians originally inhabited the Greek islands. The Carians, however, regarded themselves as indigenous. They lived in hilltop villages and were famous seamen and mercenaries. Later, Greek cities were founded on the coast, notably Halicarnassus and Cnidus (qq.v.).

In the early 6th century B. C., Caria was ruled by Lydia and from 545 by Persia; it later joined the unsuccessful Ionian revolt (499–493). In the 4th century it formed a separate Persian satrapy ruled by a native dynasty with its capital at Mylasa; the capital was moved to Halicarnassus by Mausolus about 362. The dynasty greatly Hellenized the country. After Alexander's conquest (334 B. C.), Caria was ruled by the Seleucids, then by the Ptolemies, and then in turn by Pergamum and Rhodes. It was incorporated in the Roman province of Asia in 129 B. C. and was made a separate province by Diocletian.

D. J. BLACKMAN
Bristol University, England

CARÍAS ANDINO, kä-rē′äs än-dē′nō, **Tiburcio** (1876–), Honduran president and general. He was born in Tegucigalpa, Honduras, on March 15, 1876. He led the conservatives in the civil war of 1924 and was elevated to the presidency with their support in 1933. Coming to power during an economic depression, Carías Andino established a vigorous dictatorial regime. Opposition was repressed by censorship and armed force, and the 1936 constitution curtailed many former liberties. A major uprising in 1944 was put down harshly, but led to several political and economic reforms. He retired on Jan. 1, 1949, and was succeeded by his minister of war, Gen. Juan Manuel Gálvez. In 1954 he failed in an attempt to return to power.

CARIB INDIANS, kar'ib, a group of American Indians scattered through the Amazon Basin, the Guianas, and the Caribbean. These Indians vary considerably in appearance and culture and are distinguished as a group by the fact that with few exceptions their languages belong to a single stock, the Cariban.

History. When Columbus discovered the New World, the Arawak Indians of Cuba and Haiti told him that they suffered from raids by the *Caribales*, or cannibals, who lived in the Lesser Antilles to the southeast. On his second voyage, Columbus sailed south to visit these Indians and observed evidences of cannibalism among them. The first Spanish settlers raided the Indians in order to obtain slaves for their farms, mines, and fisheries. The King of Spain ultimately prohibited such raids but specifically exempted the Carib on the grounds that they were hostile to both Spaniards and the friendly Indians. This caused the slave raiders to extend the term "Carib" to include all hostile Indians, and so the term came to be applied to many tribes that were not related to the *Caribales*. When the English explored the Guianas at the close of the 16th century, they found Indians living there who called themselves Carib, and it is these Guiana Indians who are now considered to typify the Cariban linguistic stock.

The original home of the Carib was on the mainland, possibly in the Guianas. Shortly before the discovery of America, according to their traditions, they seized the Lesser Antilles from an Arawakan-speaking group known as the Igneri; and if Columbus had not come when he did, they might have continued northward and taken the Greater Antilles as well. They claimed to have killed the Igneri men and married their women, with the result that the men and women spoke different languages. Surprisingly enough, by the 17th century the men's language had largely given way to the women's, and the island Carib spoke Arawakan with only on overlay of Cariban words.

The great mass of Cariban-speaking Indians are now concentrated on the mainland, in the Guianas and the adjacent parts of Brazil and Venezuela. The Island Carib, with their Arawakan language, were decimated in the 17th century struggle for control of the Lesser Antilles among the British, French, and Dutch, and they survived in appreciable numbers only on Dominica and St. Vincent. There is still a group of about 400 Carib on a reserve in Dominica that differs racially from the general population and retains a few native crafts and customs.

On St. Vincent they mixed with shipwrecked and escaped Negro slaves to form a group known as the Black Carib. This group revolted against the British in 1795 and was defeated, and in 1797 the British deported the 5,000 survivors to the island of Roatán off the coast of Honduras. They later migrated to the mainland and spread into Guatemala, British Honduras, Nicaragua, and Costa Rica, where they formed an appreciable part of the coastal population. They are almost wholly Negro in racial type but maintain the language and many of the customs of the Island Carib.

Customs. The Carib were best known for their practice of cannibalism, although many of the mainland Carib did not follow this practice, and it was present among other Indian groups as well. The Island Carib were accustomed to raid the Arawak of the Greater Antilles in order to obtain captives. They kept the women and children as slaves but tortured, killed, roasted, and ate the men to celebrate their victories. They were skilled in building and managing the canoes used on the raids, and some of these, consisting of dugouts with planks built up on the sides, were large enough to hold 50 people. The skill of the Carib in making long sea voyages led some authors to compare them with the Vikings and the Polynesians.

The Island Carib practiced both fishing and agriculture. They went naked, except for a cotton apron worn by the women, painted their bodies red, and wore their hair long to distinguish themselves from their enemies, the short-haired Arawak. Strong individualists, they lacked the relatively elaborate system of rank and government that characterized the island Arawak. Each family, including its married children and other close relatives, comprised a separate village, consisting of a man's house and a series of smaller huts for the women and children. Their religion, too, was simpler than that of the island Arawak. See also ARAWAK INDIANS.

IRVING ROUSE, *Yale University*

Further Reading: Gillin, John, *The Barama River Caribs of British Guiana*, Papers of the Peabody Museum of American Archaeology and Ethnology, vol. 14, no. 2 (Cambridge, Mass., 1936); Steward, Julian, ed., *Handbook of South American Indians*, Bulletin of the Bureau of American Ethnology (Washington 1948). Taylor, Douglas MacRae, *The Black Carib of British Honduras*, Viking Fund Publications in Anthropology, no. 17 (New York 1951).

J. J. SMITH

CARIB INDIANS are believed to have carved these petroglyphs found near Reef Bay on St. John, in the Virgin Islands of the United States.

DANCING to the music of a steel band, costumed residents of the island of Martinique fill the city streets during Carnival.

CARIBBEAN, kar-ə-bē′ən, the region of tropical islands between continental North and South America. Named after the fierce, savage Carib Indians encountered by Columbus on his second voyage to the New World, the Caribbean is the home of a colorful multiracial population of some 25 million.

The heart of the region is the archipelago known as the *West Indies* or the *Antilles,* forming the broken land barrier between the Atlantic Ocean and the Caribbean Sea. These islands consist of two main groups: the Greater Antilles—Cuba, Jamaica, Hispaniola, and Puerto Rico—on the northern side of the Caribbean Sea; and the Lesser Antilles—the Leeward and Windward Islands—on the eastern side. Included in the Caribbean region, but not always considered part of the West Indies, are islands such as Curaçao, Aruba, and Margarita (off the Caribbean coast of Venezuela) and the Bahamas (in the Atlantic Ocean southeast of Florida).

The Caribbean Sea, bounded by the West Indies and the mainlands of South and Central America, extends more than 850 nautical miles (1,574 km) from Cuba southward to Colombia and more than 1,800 nautical miles (3,334 km) from Martinique westward to British Honduras. From the Atlantic Ocean it can be entered through many natural straits, such as the Mona, Windward, and Anegada passages, and from the Gulf of Mexico through the Yucatán Passage. From the west and south, the only entrance is the Panama Canal.

The People. The pre-Columbian population of the Caribbean disappeared long ago. The American Indian inhabitants were replaced rapidly as Europeans settled island after island. The Europeans introduced African slaves, whose descendants have remained to claim most of the region.

THE CARIBBEAN REGION

Political Component[1]	*Population (1965)*	*Capital*
Latin American Republics:		
Cuba	7,631,000	Havana
Dominican Republic	3,619,000	Santo Domingo
Haiti	4,660,000	Port-au-Prince
British Commonwealth:		
Antigua	60,000	St. John's
Bahama Islands	142,000	Nassau
Barbados	245,000	Bridgetown
British Virgin Islands	9,000	Road Town
Cayman Islands	9,000	Georgetown
Dominica	67,000	Roseau
Grenada	94,000	St. George's
Jamaica	1,773,000	Kingston
Montserrat	14,000	Plymouth
St. Kitts-Nevis-Anguilla	60,000	Basseterre
St. Lucia	94,000	Castries
St. Vincent	87,000	Kingstown
Trinidad and Tobago	975,000	Port of Spain
Turks and Caicos Islands	6,000	Grand Turk
French Caribbean Departments:		
Guadeloupe	316,000	Basse Terre
Martinique	321,000	Fort-de-France
Netherlands Antilles	208,000	Willemstad
U. S. Outlying Areas:		
Puerto Rico	2,633,000	San Juan
U. S. Virgin Islands	43,000	Charlotte Amalie
Total Caribbean Area	*23,066,000*	

[1] Excluding insular portions of mainland Latin American states.

LUC BOUCHAGE, FROM RAPHO GUILLUMETTE

The Europeans were rarely in the majority, even on those islands like Cuba and Puerto Rico where the introduction of slaves was severely restricted. The Spaniards mixed with the Africans with relative ease in comparison with the exclusive English. Thus today in these two islands the pure African descendants are a decided minority, as are also the pure descendants of the Spanish colonizers. On other islands, like Aruba and Curaçao, where agriculture never prospered, the descendants of the Dutch are more noticeable, though again the population is heterogeneous.

The island of Hispaniola (Santo Domingo) presents a special case. It was colonized first by Spaniards, who were later forced to recognize the sovereignty of the French over Haiti, the western section of the island. The whole island was caught up in a slave rebellion which produced the first black republic in the New World. Haiti remains a black republic, but the people of the eastern part of the island—the Dominican Republic, independent since 1844—are of mixed extraction. The blending continues, since European immigrants are encouraged to settle in the republic, and black Haitian laborers have often been brought in to cut sugarcane.

Besides the Europeans and their descendants, other racial minorities can be found in the Caribbean. The Chinese were imported in the 19th century to islands like Cuba and Jamaica. Used to build roads and later to cut sugarcane, the Chinese rapidly left the rural areas to take up small businesses in the urban centers. There are 10,000 Chinese in Jamaica and many more in Cuba.

After the abolition of slavery in the West Indies, laborers were imported under contracts of 5 to 10 years from many other sections of the world. Along with the Chinese came Portuguese from the Madeira Islands and Spaniards from the Canary Islands, but the hardest-working and most adaptable to the climate of the Caribbean were the East Indians. Thousands were imported from what are now India and Pakistan, mostly into the Lesser Antilles, right up into the first decades of the 20th century. Their descendants can be found in Jamaica, Martinique, and Guadeloupe, but above all in Trinidad, where, out of an estimated population of about a million, more than one third is East Indian. The East Indian, a faithful believer in his Hindu or Muslim religion, lives apart from other groups, refusing to mix with members of other races.

Natural Resources. The islands of the West Indies are formed by two principal chains of mountains, one running east and west and the other north and south. The Atlantic and the Caribbean have left only the most prominent peaks of these mountain chains visible above the water. On some of the islands, like Cuba and Hispaniola, the mountains are joined together by extensive and fertile inland valleys, while on others, like Puerto Rico and Nevis, the fertile land is limited for the most part to a coastal fringe around the principal elevations.

The mountains reach their highest point in Hispaniola—over 10,000 feet (more than 3,000 meters)—and, in contrast, the sea drops to a depth of about 27,000 feet (about 8,200 meters) just north of Puerto Rico. Some of the more recently formed mountains in the Lesser Antilles are still active volcanos. Other islands in the Lesser Antilles, like Barbados and Antigua, have been formed by geologically older mountains which have been worn away, leaving a comparatively flat and unbroken surface above the water.

The climate of the West Indies is temperate all year. In January and February the temperature drops at night to 70–75°F (21–24°C) in the coastal areas and to 63–66°F (17–19°C) in the high mountains of Haiti and Cuba, but during the day it rises to 80°F (27°C) and above. The months of July and August are the hottest in the Caribbean, but the gentle breezes of the trade winds keep the high temperature below 90°F (32°C). Torrential rains also help to keep the temperature down during June, July, and August. In these months and in September, hurricanes may occur.

With fertile alluvial plains, abundant rain (except perhaps in the dry months of March and April), thick tropical foliage, and an ideal climate, the West Indies seem to combine all the elements necessary for a rich tropical garden. The islands are not blessed, however, with rich mineral resources. The few exceptions of Trinidad, Jamaica, and possibly Cuba only serve to emphasize the plight of the other smaller islands. Petroleum is found in Trinidad, and, since World War II, Jamaica has become one of the largest producers of bauxite, from which aluminum is extracted. In Puerto Rico, copper has been found. Cuba has workable deposits of copper, nickel, manganese, chromium, and iron. Some bauxite is mined in the Dominican Republic.

Pearls have been taken for centuries from the sandy depths off the island of Margarita; lobsters found around St. Martin are flown to gourmets in New York and London; and turtles from the Cayman Islands have been hunted for over 300 years. Caribbean waters abound with fish like the tuna and marlin, which are only a few of the varieties available to commercial and sport fishermen.

The Economy. For centuries the West Indies have been known for the production of sugar, coffee, tropical fruits, and spices. While this

J. ALLAN CASH, FROM RAPHO GUILLUMETTE

THE PITONS, two conical volcanic peaks, rise steeply from the sea near Soufrière on St. Lucia, one of the Windward Islands in the Lesser Antilles.

CARIBBEAN

ANTIGUA
Total Population, 60,000

CITIES and TOWNS
Codrington, 1,145 ... G 3
Falmouth, 239 ... F 3
Saint John's (capital), 21,595 ... G 3

OTHER FEATURES
Antigua (isl.), 54,304 ... G 3
Barbuda (isl.), 1,145 ... G 3
Redonda (isl.) ... F 3

BAHAMA ISLANDS
Total Population, 144,000

CITIES and TOWNS
Nassau (capital), 81,591 ... C 1

OTHER FEATURES
Acklins (isl.), 1,160 ... C 2
Andros (isl.), 7,460 ... B 1
Atwood (Samana) (cay), 32 ... D 2
Berry (islands), 266 ... B 1
Biminis, The (islands), 1,576 ... B 1
Caicos (passage) ... D 2
Cat (isl.), 3,131 ... C 1
Cay Sal (bank) ... B 2
Crooked (isl.), 764 ... D 2
Crooked Island (passage) ... C 2
Eleuthera (isl.), 7,247 ... C 1
Exuma (cays), 220 ... C 1
Exuma (Great Exuma) (isl.), 2,854 ... C 2
Exuma (sound) ... C 1
Flamingo (cay) ... C 2
Grand Bahama (island), 7,847 ... B 1
Great Abaco (isl.), 4,746 ... C 1
Great Bahama (bank) ... B 1
Great Exuma (isl.), 2,854 ... C 2
Great Inagua (isl.), 1,240 ... D 2
Great Isaac (isl.), 5 ... B 1
Gun (cay), 3 ... B 1
Harbour (isl.), 997 ... C 1
Little Inagua (isl.) ... D 2
Long (cay), 22 ... C 2
Long (isl.), 4,176 ... C 2
Mayaguana (isl.), 707 ... D 2
Mayaguana (passage) ... D 2
Mira Por Vos (cays) ... C 2
New Providence (island), 81,591 ... C 1
North East Providence (channel) ... C 1
North West Providence (channel) ... B 1
Old Bahama (channel) ... B 2
Plana (cays), 3 ... D 2
Ragged (isl.), 371 ... C 2
Rum (cay), 77 ... C 2
Samana (cay), 32 ... D 2
San Salvador (isl.), 968 ... C 1
Santarén (chan.) ... B 1
Tongue of the Ocean ... C 1
Verde (cay) ... C 2
Watling (San Salvador) (isl.), 968 ... C 1

BARBADOS
Total Population, 245,000

CITIES and TOWNS
Bridgetown (capital), 11,452 ... G 4
Speightstown, 2,415 ... G 4

BERMUDA
Total Population, 51,000

CITIES and TOWNS
Hamilton (capital), 3,000 ... G 3
Hamilton, *14,156 ... G 3
Saint George, 1,335 ... H 2

OTHER FEATURES
Bermuda (isl.) ... H 3
Castle (harb.) ... H 2
Great (sound) ... G 3
Harrington (sound) ... G 3
Ireland (isl.) ... G 3
Ledge Flats ... G 2
North East Breakers ... H 2
North Rocks ... H 2
Saint Davids (isl.) ... H 2
Saint George's (isl.) ... H 2
Somerset (isl.) ... G 3
West Ledge Flats ... G 3

CAYMAN ISLANDS
Total Population, 9,000

CITIES and TOWNS
Georgetown (capital), 2,573 ... B 3

OTHER FEATURES
Cayman Brac (island), 1,240 ... B 3
Grand Cayman (island), 6,359 ... B 3
Little Cayman (island), 23 ... B 3

CUBA
Total Population, 8,238,000

CITIES and TOWNS
Alto Cedro, 679 ... C 2
Antilla, †38,840 ... C 2
Artemisa, 27,300 ... A 2
Banes, 27,900 ... C 2
Baracoa, †105,070 ... C 2
Batabanó, †18,190 ... A 2
Bayamo, 45,400 ... C 2
Bejucal, †14,410 ... A 2
Bolondrón, †11,580 ... B 2
Boquerón ... C 3
Cacocum, 2,724 ... C 2
Caibarién, 26,400 ... B 2
Caimanera, 8,600 ... C 3
Camagüey, 178,600 ... B 2
Cárdenas, 67,400 ... B 2
Ciego de Ávila, 54,700 ... B 2
Cienfuegos, 91,800 ... B 2
Colón, †37,430 ... B 2
Consolación del Sur, †69,460 ... A 2
Cruces, †26,790 ... B 2
Gibara, †44,890 ... C 2
Guanabacoa, †203,010 ... B 2
Guanajay, †22,920 ... A 2
Guane, †49,680 ... A 2
Guantánamo, 135,100 ... C 2
Güines, 45,000 ... B 2
Havana (capital), 1,008,500 ... A 2
Havana, *1,760,000 ... A 2
Holguín, 100,500 ... C 2
Jagüey Grande, †17,030 ... B 2
Jovellanos, †20,610 ... B 2
Los Palacios, †28,480 ... A 2
Manzanillo, 91,200 ... C 2
Marianao, †350,260 ... A 2
Martí, †17,520 ... C 2
Matanzas, 84,100 ... B 2
Morón, 26,600 ... B 2
Niquero, †86,820 ... C 2
Nueva Gerona, 9,000 ... A 2
Nuevitas, †62,760 ... C 2
Pinar del Río, 67,600 ... A 2
Puerto Padre, †118,010 ... C 2
Remedios, †31,760 ... B 2
Sagua la Grande, 35,200 ... B 2
San Antonio de los Baños, 23,700 ... A 2
Sancti-Spíritus, 62,500 ... B 2
San Luis, †68,870 ... C 2
Santa Clara, 137,700 ... B 2
Santa Cruz del Sur, †77,760 ... B 2
Santa Fé, 2,195 ... A 2
Santiago de Cuba, 259,000 ... B 2
Trinidad, 28,000 ... B 2
Tunas de Zaza, 1,380 ... B 2
Viñales, †18,710 ... A 2

OTHER FEATURES
Batabanó (gulf) ... A 2
Cruz (cape) ... C 3
Florida (straits) ... B 1
Guacanayabo (gulf) ... C 2
Jardines de la Reina (arch.) ... B 2
Largo (cay) ... B 2
Maisí (point) ... D 2
Nicholas (chan.) ... B 2
Old Bahama (channel) ... B 2
Pines (Pinos) (island), 20,630 ... A 2
Romano (cay) ... C 2
San Antonio (cape) ... A 2
San Felipe (cays), 391 ... A 2
Windward (passage) ... C 3

DOMINICA
Total Population, 68,000

CITIES and TOWNS
Portsmouth, 2,238 ... G 4
Roseau (capital), 10,417 ... G 4
Roseau, *13,883 ... G 4

DOMINICAN REPUBLIC
Total Population, 3,889,000

CITIES and TOWNS
Azua, 12,350 ... D 3
Baní, 14,472 ... D 3
Bánica, 633 ... D 3
Barahona, 20,398 ... D 3
Enriquillo, 3,485 ... D 3
La Romana, 24,058 ... E 3
Las Matas de Farfán, 3,585 ... D 3
La Vega, 19,884 ... D 3
Moca, 13,829 ... D 3
Montecristi, 5,912 ... D 2
Neiba, 7,322 ... D 3
Puerto Plata, 19,073 ... D 3
Sabana de la Mar, 4,032 ... E 3
Samaná, 3,309 ... E 3
Sánchez, 4,587 ... E 3
San Francisco de Macorís, 26,000 ... E 3
San Pedro de Macorís, 22,935 ... E 3
Santiago de los Caballeros, 83,523 ... D 3
Santo Domingo (capital), 522,490 ... E 3
Seibo, 4,621 ... E 3

OTHER FEATURES
Beata (cape) ... D 3
Beata (isl.) ... D 3
Mona (passage) ... E 3
Samaná (bay) ... E 3
Saona (isl.), 409 ... E 3

GRENADA
Total Population, 97,000

CITIES and TOWNS
Gouyave, 2,356 ... F 4
Saint George's (capital), 7,303 ... F 5
Saint George's, *26,843 ... F 5

OTHER FEATURES
Carriacou (isl.), 6,958 ... G 4

GUADELOUPE
Total Population, 324,000

CITIES and TOWNS
Basse-Terre (capital), 16,000 ... F 4
Pointe-à-Pitre, 50,000 ... G 3
Port-Louis, 5,000 ... G 3

OTHER FEATURES
Marie-Galante (island), 16,341 ... G 4
Saint-Barthélemy (island), 2,176 ... F 3
Saint-Martin (island), 4,502 ... F 3

HAITI
Total Population, 4,768,101

CITIES and TOWNS
Cap-Haïtien, †33,979 ... D 3
Fort-Liberté, †26,942 ... D 3
Gonaïves, †99,140 ... D 3
Hinche, †63,793 ... D 3
Jacmel, †199,598 ... D 3
Jérémie, †92,500 ... C 3
Lascahobas, †29,760 ... D 3
Léogane, †140,607 ... D 3
Les Cayes, †95,446 ... C 3
Miragoâne, †50,059 ... D 3
Mirebalais, †78,060 ... D 3
Petit-Goâve, †123,157 ... D 3
Port-au-Prince (capital), †352,681 ... D 3

*City and suburbs. †Population of municipality or commune. ‡Population of metropolitan area.

ANTIGUA: Total pop.—1966 off. est.; other pops—1960 final census. **BAHAMA IS.:** Total pop.—1967 off. est.; capital & New Providence I. —1964 off. est.; other pops—1963 final census. **BARBADOS:** Total pop.—1966 off. est.; other pops—1960 final census. **BERMUDA:** Total pop.—1967 off. est.; cap.—1965 off. est.; other pops—1960 final census. **CAYMAN IS.:** Total pop.—1966 off. est.; other pops—1960 final census. **CUBA:** Total pop. & cap. (with suburbs)—1968 off. est.; cap., cities & municipalities (over 10,000)—1967 off. est.; other pops —1953 final census. **DOMINICA:** Total pop.—1966 off. est.; other pops—1960 final census. **DOMINICAN REP.:** Total pop.—1967 off. est.; cap.—1965 off. est.; other pops—1960 prelim. census. **GRENADA:** Total pop.—1966 off. est.; other pops—1960 final census. **GUADELOUPE:** Total pop. & cities—1969 off. est.; other pops—1961 final census. **HAITI:** 1969 off. est.

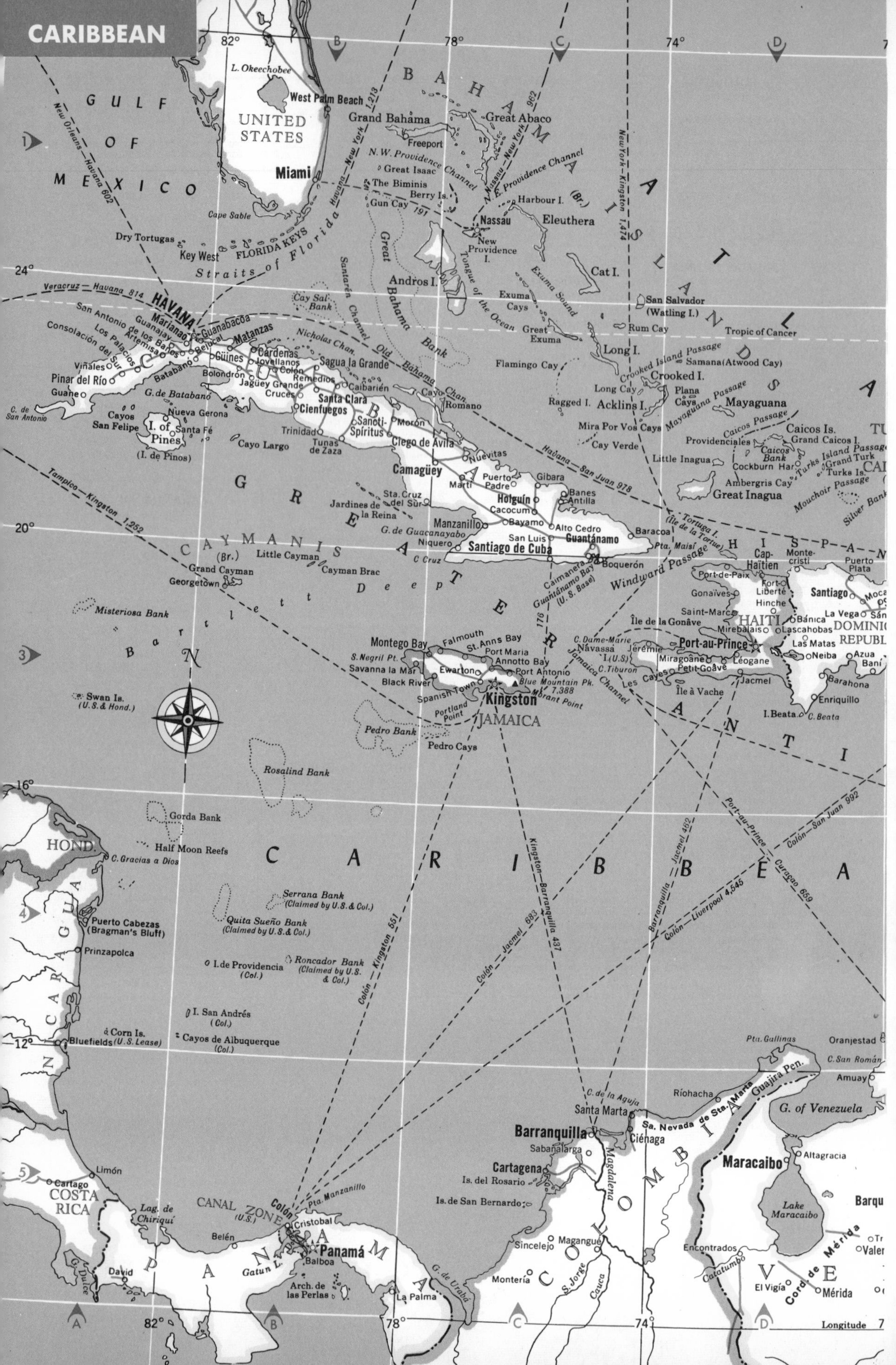
GULF OF MEXICO
UNITED STATES
L. Okeechobee
West Palm Beach
Miami
Cape Sable
Dry Tortugas
Key West
FLORIDA KEYS
Straits of Florida
New Orleans—Havana 602
Veracruz—Havana 814
Havana—New York 1,213
Nassau—New York 962
New York—Kingston 1,474
Havana—San Juan 978
Tampico—Kingston 1,252
BAHAMA ISLANDS (Br.)
Grand Bahama
Freeport
Great Abaco
N.W. Providence Channel
N.E. Providence Channel
Great Isaac
The Biminis
Berry Is.
Gun Cay
Harbour I.
Nassau
New Providence I.
Eleuthera
Great Bahama Bank
Tongue of the Ocean
Andros I.
Exuma Sound
Exuma Cays
Great Exuma
Cat I.
San Salvador (Watling I.)
Rum Cay
Tropic of Cancer
Long I.
Crooked Island Passage
Samana (Atwood Cay)
Crooked I.
Flamingo Cay
Long Cay
Plana Cays
Mayaguana Passage
Mayaguana
Ragged I.
Acklins I.
Mira Por Vos Cays
Caicos Passage
Caicos Is.
Providenciales
Grand Caicos I.
Caicos Bank
Turks Island Passage
Grand Turk
Turks Is.
Cockburn Har.
Ambergris Cay
Mouchoir Passage
Silver Bank
Cay Verde
Little Inagua
Great Inagua
Cay Sal Bank
Santarén Channel
Nicholas Chan.
Old Bahama Chan.
HAVANA
Marianao
Guanabacoa
Matanzas
San Antonio de los Baños
Guanajay
Artemisa
Consolación del Sur
Los Palacios
Bejucal
Güines
Cárdenas
Jovellanos
Colón
Sagua la Grande
Viñales
Pinar del Río
Batabanó
Bolondrón
Jagüey Grande
Remedios
Caibarién
Guane
G. de Batabanó
Cruces
Santa Clara
Cienfuegos
Cayo Romano
C. de San Antonio
Cayos San Felipe
Nueva Gerona
I. of Pines
Santa Fé
(I. de Pinos)
Cayo Largo
Trinidad
Sancti-Spíritus
Morón
Tunas de Zaza
Ciego de Avila
Nuevitas
Camagüey
Puerto Padre
Martí
Gibara
Holguín
Banes
Antilla
Sta. Cruz del Sur
Jardines de la Reina
Cacocum
Manzanillo
Bayamo
Alto Cedro
Baracoa
G. de Guacanayabo
Niquero
San Luis
Guantánamo
Santiago de Cuba
C. Cruz
Pta. Maisí
Tortuga I. (Île de la Tortue)
Caimanera
Guantánamo Bay (U.S. Base)
Boquerón
Windward Passage
GREATER ANTILLES
CAYMAN IS. (Br.)
Little Cayman
Cayman Brac
Grand Cayman
Georgetown
Bartlett Deep
Misteriosa Bank
Swan Is. (U.S. & Hond.)
N
HISPANIOLA
Cap-Haïtien
Monte-cristi
Puerto Plata
Port-de-Paix
Fort Liberté
Santiago
Gonaïves
Hinche
Saint-Marc
HAITI
DOMINICAN REPUBLIC
Île de la Gonâve
Mirebalais
Bánica
Lascahobas
La Vega
Las Matas
Port-au-Prince
C. Dame-Marie
Navassa I. (U.S.)
Jérémie
Miragoâne
Petit-Goâve
Léogane
Neiba
Azua
Baní
C. Tiburon
Les Cayes
Île à Vache
Jacmel
Barahona
Enriquillo
I. Beata
C. Beata
Jamaica Channel
Montego Bay
Falmouth
St. Anns Bay
Port Maria
S. Negril Pt.
Annotto Bay
Savanna la Mar
Ewarton
Port Antonio
Black River
Blue Mountain Pk. 7,388
Spanish Town
Kingston
Morant Point
Portland Point
JAMAICA
Pedro Bank
Pedro Cays
Rosalind Bank
Gorda Bank
Half Moon Reefs
HOND.
C. Gracias a Dios
CARIBBEAN SEA
Serrana Bank (Claimed by U.S. & Col.)
Quita Sueño Bank (Claimed by U.S. & Col.)
Puerto Cabezas (Bragman's Bluff)
Prinzapolca
NICARAGUA
I. de Providencia (Col.)
Roncador Bank (Claimed by U.S. & Col.)
I. San Andrés (Col.)
Corn Is. (U.S. Lease)
Bluefields
Cayos de Albuquerque (Col.)
Colón—Kingston 551
Colón—Jacmel 683
Kingston—Barranquilla 437
Barranquilla—Jacmel 462
Colón—Liverpool 4,545
Port-au-Prince—Curaçao 659
Colón—San Juan 992
Pta. Gallinas
Oranjestad
C. San Román
Amuay
Ríohacha
Guajira Pen.
C. de la Aguja
Santa Marta
Sa. Nevada de Sta. Marta
G. of Venezuela
Barranquilla
Ciénaga
Sabanalarga
Magdalena
Maracaibo
Altagracia
Cartagena
Is. del Rosario
Is. de San Bernardo
Lake Maracaibo
Barquisimeto
COLOMBIA
Sincelejo
Magangué
Encontrados
Catatumbo
Cord. de Mérida
Valera
Montería
S. Jorge
Cauca
El Vigía
Mérida
VENEZUELA
Limón
Cartago
COSTA RICA
Lag. de Chiriquí
CANAL ZONE (U.S.)
Colón
Pta. Manzanillo
Cristobal
Belén
PANAMA
Panamá
Gatun L.
Balboa
G. Dulce
David
Arch. de las Perlas
G. de Urabá
La Palma
82°
78°
74°
24°
20°
16°
12°
Longitude

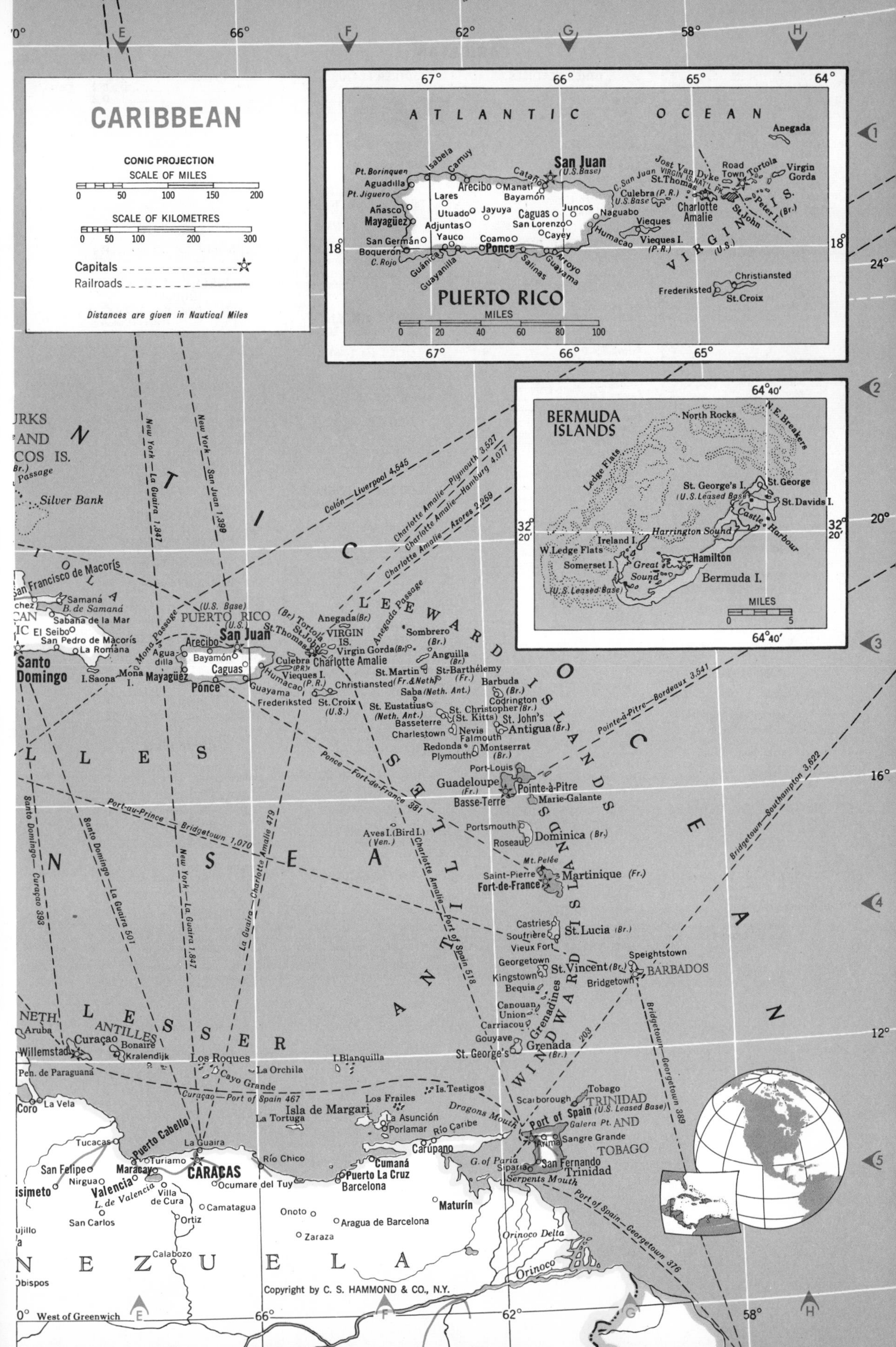

CARIBBEAN
CONIC PROJECTION
SCALE OF MILES
0 50 100 150 200
SCALE OF KILOMETRES
0 50 100 200 300
Capitals
Railroads
Distances are given in Nautical Miles
ATLANTIC OCEAN
PUERTO RICO
MILES
0 20 40 60 80 100
San Juan (U.S. Base)
Pt. Borinquen
Isabela
Camuy
Aguadilla
Pt. Jiguero
Arecibo
Manatí
Cataño
Bayamón
Lares
Añasco
Mayagüez
Utuado
Jayuya
Caguas
Juncos
Naguabo
Adjuntas
San Lorenzo
Cayey
Humacao
San Germán
Yauco
Coamo
Ponce
Boquerón
C. Rojo
Guánica
Guayanilla
Salinas
Guayama
Arroyo
Culebra (P.R.)
U.S. Base
Vieques
Vieques I. (P.R.)
C. San Juan
Jost Van Dyke
St. Thomas
VIRGIN IS. NAT'L PK.
Charlotte Amalie
St. John
Road Town
Tortola
Virgin Gorda
Anegada
Peter I. (Br.)
VIRGIN IS. (U.S.) (Br.)
Christiansted
Frederiksted
St. Croix
BERMUDA ISLANDS
North Rocks
N.E. Breakers
Ledge Flats
St. George's I. (U.S. Leased Base)
St. George
St. Davids I.
Castle Harbour
Harrington Sound
Ireland I.
W. Ledge Flats
Somerset I.
Great Sound
Hamilton
Bermuda I.
(U.S. Leased Base)
MILES
0 5
64°40′
32° 20′
TURKS AND CAICOS IS. (Br.)
Passage
Silver Bank
San Francisco de Macorís
Samaná
B. de Samaná
Sabana de la Mar
El Seibo
San Pedro de Macorís
La Romana
Santo Domingo
I. Saona
Mona I.
Mona Passage
Aguadilla
Mayagüez
PUERTO RICO (U.S.)
(U.S. Base)
Arecibo
San Juan
Bayamón
Caguas
Ponce
Humacao
Guayama
Culebra (P.R.)
Vieques I. (P.R.)
Frederiksted
Christiansted
St. Croix (U.S.)
(Br.) Tortola
St. John
St. Thomas
Charlotte Amalie
Anegada (Br.)
VIRGIN IS.
Virgin Gorda (Br.)
Anegada Passage
Sombrero (Br.)
Anguilla (Br.)
St. Martin (Fr. & Neth.)
St. Barthélemy (Fr.)
Saba (Neth. Ant.)
Barbuda (Br.)
Codrington
St. Eustatius (Neth. Ant.)
St. Christopher (Br.) (St. Kitts)
Basseterre
St. John's
Antigua (Br.)
Charlestown
Nevis
Falmouth
Redonda
Montserrat (Br.)
Plymouth
Port-Louis
Guadeloupe (Fr.)
Pointe-à-Pitre
Basse-Terre
Marie-Galante
Aves I. (Bird I.) (Ven.)
Portsmouth
Roseau
Dominica (Br.)
Mt. Pelée
Saint-Pierre
Martinique (Fr.)
Fort-de-France
Castries
Soufrière
St. Lucia (Br.)
Vieux Fort
Georgetown
Kingstown
St. Vincent (Br.)
Bequia
Speightstown
BARBADOS
Bridgetown
Canouan
Union
Carriacou
Grenadines
Gouyave
St. George's
Grenada (Br.)
LEEWARD ISLANDS
WINDWARD ISLANDS
ATLANTIC OCEAN
LESSER ANTILLES
CARIBBEAN SEA
New York—La Guaira 1,847
New York—San Juan 1,399
Colón—Liverpool 4,545
Charlotte Amalie—Plymouth 3,527
Charlotte Amalie—Hamburg 4,077
Charlotte Amalie—Azores 2,259
Pointe-à-Pitre—Bordeaux 3,541
Bridgetown—Southampton 3,622
Ponce—Fort-de-France 381
Port-au-Prince—Bridgetown 1,070
Santo Domingo—Curaçao 393
Santo Domingo—La Guaira 501
New York—La Guaira 1,847
La Guaira—Charlotte Amalie 479
Charlotte Amalie—Port of Spain 518
Curaçao—Port of Spain 467
Bridgetown—Georgetown 389
Port of Spain—Georgetown 376
NETH. ANTILLES
Aruba
Curaçao
Bonaire
Willemstad
Kralendijk
Los Roques
La Orchila
I. Blanquilla
Cayo Grande
Is. Testigos
Pen. de Paraguaná
Coro
La Vela
Los Frailes
Isla de Margarita
La Asunción
Porlamar
La Tortuga
Dragons Mouth
Scarborough
Tobago
TRINIDAD AND TOBAGO
Port of Spain (U.S. Leased Base)
Galera Pt.
Arima
Sangre Grande
San Fernando
Trinidad
Siparia
G. of Paria
Serpents Mouth
Río Caribe
Carúpano
Cumaná
Puerto La Cruz
Barcelona
Río Chico
Tucacas
Puerto Cabello
La Guaira
Turiamo
Maracay
CARACAS
San Felipe
Nirgua
Valencia
L. de Valencia
Villa de Cura
Ocumare del Tuy
Barquisimeto
San Carlos
Ortiz
Camatagua
Onoto
Aragua de Barcelona
Zaraza
Maturín
Calabozo
Orinoco Delta
Orinoco
Obispos
VENEZUELA
Copyright by C. S. HAMMOND & CO., N.Y.
West of Greenwich
70° 66° 62° 58°
E F G H
1 2 3 4 5
24° 20° 16° 12°

Port-de-Paix, †54,016 ....D 3
Saint-Marc, †61,359 ....D 3

OTHER FEATURES

Dame-Marie (cape) ....C 3
Gonâve (isl.), 45,411 ....D 3
Jamaica (channel) ....C 3
Tiburon (cape) ....C 3
Tortuga (Tortue) (isl.), 13,723 ....D 2
Vache (isl.) ....D 3
Windward (passage) ....C 3

JAMAICA

Total Population, 1,860,000

CITIES and TOWNS

Annotto Bay, 3,559 ....C 3
Black River, 3,077 ....B 3
Falmouth, 3,727 ....C 3
Ewarton ....C 3
Kingston (capital), 123,403 ....C 3
Kingston, *376,520 ....C 3
Montego Bay, 23,610 ....B 3
Port Antonio, 7,830 ....C 3
Port Maria, 3,998 ....C 3
Saint Anns Bay, 5,087 ....C 3
Savanna la Mar, 9,789 ....B 3
Spanish Town, 14,706 ....C 3

OTHER FEATURES

Blue Mountain (peak) ....C 3
Jamaica (channel) ....C 3
Morant (point) ....C 3
Pedro (bank) ....B 3
Pedro (cays) ....C 3
Portland (point) ....C 3
South Negril (point) ....B 3

MARTINIQUE

Total Population, 331,000

CITIES and TOWNS

Fort-de-France (capital), 100,000 ....G 4
Saint-Pierre, 5,556 ....G 4

OTHER FEATURES

Pelée (volcano) ....G 4

MONTSERRAT

Total Population, 14,000

CITIES and TOWNS

Plymouth (capital), 1,911 ....F 3

NETHERLANDS ANTILLES

Total Population, 216,000

CITIES and TOWNS

Kralendijk, 839 ....E 4
Oranjestad, 15,398 ....D 4
Willemstad (capital), 43,547 ....E 4
Willemstad, *94,133 ....E 4

OTHER FEATURES

Aruba (island), 58,868 ....E 4
Bonaire (island), 5,755 ....E 4
Curaçao (island), 196,170 ....E 4
Saba (island), 1,094 ....F 3
Saint Eustatius (island), 1,020 ....F 3
Sint Maarten (Saint Martin) (isl.), 4,970 ....F 3

PUERTO RICO

Total Population, 2,689,932

CITIES and TOWNS

Adjuntas, 5,309 ....F 1
Aguadilla, 21,087 ....F 1
Añasco, 4,402 ....F 1
Arecibo, 35,420 ....G 1
Arroyo, 5,410 ....G 1
Bayamón, 146,363 ....G 1
Caguas, 62,807 ....G 1
Caguas, ‡95,661 ....G 1
Camuy, 3,882 ....F 1
Cataño, 26,056 ....G 1
Cayey, 21,372 ....G 1
Coamo, 11,957 ....G 1
Guanica, 8,538 ....F 1
Guayama, 20,227 ....G 1
Guayanilla, 5,156 ....F 5
Humacao, 12,332 ....G 1
Isabela, 9,884 ....F 1
Jayuya, 3,800 ....G 1
Juncos, 7,911 ....G 1
Lares, 4,505 ....F 1
Manatí, 13,433 ....G 1
Mayagüez, 69,485 ....F 1
Mayagüez, ‡86,267 ....F 1
Naguabo, 4,136 ....G 1
Ponce, 125,926 ....F 1
Ponce, ‡156,498 ....F 1
Salinas, 4,447 ....G 1
San Juan (capital), 444,952 ......G 1
San Juan, ‡839,813 ....G 1
San Lorenzo, 7,699 ....G 1
Utuado, 11,475 ....F 1
Vieques, 2,385 ....G 1
Yauco, 12,880 ....F 1

OTHER FEATURES

Borinquen (point) ....F 1
Culebra (isl.), 726 ....G 1
Jiguero (point) ....F 1
Mona (isl.) ....E 3
Mona (passage) ....E 3
Rojo (cape) ....F 1
San Juan (cape) ....G 1
Vieques (isl.), 7,817 ....G 1

SAINT CHRISTOPHER-NEVIS-ANGUILLA

Total Population, 58,000

CITIES and TOWNS

Basseterre (capital), 15,726 ....F 3
Charlestown, 2,852 ....F 3

OTHER FEATURES

Anegada (passage) ....F 3
Anguilla (isl.), 5,605 ....F 3
Nevis (island), 12,762 ....F 3
Saint Christopher (Saint Kitts) (isl.), 38,291 ....F 3
Sombrero (isl.), 5 ....F 3

SAINT LUCIA

Total Population, 103,000

CITIES and TOWNS

Castries (capital), 4,353 ....G 4
Castries, *15,291 ....G 4
Soufrière, 2,692 ....G 4
Vieux Fort, 3,228 ....G 4

SAINT VINCENT

Total Population, 90,000

CITIES and TOWNS

Georgetown, 1,213 ....G 4
Kingstown (capital), 4,308 ....G 4
Kingstown, *20,688 ....G 4

OTHER FEATURES

Bequia (isl.), 3,148 ....G 4
Canouan (isl.), 542 ....G 4
Union (isl.), 1,274 ....G 4

TRINIDAD & TOBAGO

Total Population, 1,000,000

CITIES and TOWNS

Arima, 10,982 ....G 5
Port of Spain (capital), 93,954 ....G 5
Port of Spain, *120,694 ....G 5
San Fernando, 39,830 ....G 5
Sangre Grande, 5,087 ....G 5
Scarborough, 1,931 ....G 5
Siparia, 4,174 ....G 5

OTHER FEATURES

Dragons Mouth (strait) ....F 5
Galera (point) ....G 5
Paria (gulf) ....G 5
Serpents Mouth (strait) ....G 5
Tobago (island), 33,333 ....G 5
Trinidad (island), 794,624 ....G 5

TURKS AND CAICOS IS.

Total Population, 6,308

CITIES and TOWNS

Cockburn Harbour, 866 ....D 2
Grand Turk (capital), 2,339 ....D 2

OTHER FEATURES

Ambergris (cay) ....D 2
Caicos (bank) ....D 2
Caicos (islands), 2,956 ....D 2
Caicos (passage) ....D 2
Grand Caicos (island), 2,446 ....D 2
Mouchoir (passage) ....D 2
Providenciales (island), 510 ....D 2
Silver (bank) ....E 2
Silver Bank (passage) ....D 2
Turks (islands), 2,760 ....D 2
Turks Island (passage) ....D 2

VENEZUELA

Aves (Bird) (isl.) ....F 4

VIRGIN ISLANDS (British)

Total Population, 9,000

CITIES and TOWNS

Road Town (capital), 891 ....H 1

OTHER FEATURES

Anegada (isl.), 268 ....H 1
Anegada (passage) ....F 3
Jost Van Dyke (island), 178 ....G 1
Peter (isl.), 9 ....H 1
Tortola (isl.), 6,238 ....H 1
Virgin Gorda (island), 564 ....H 1

VIRGIN ISLANDS (U.S.)

Total Population, 63,200

CITIES and TOWNS

Charlotte Amalie (capital), 12,372 ....H 1
Frederiksted, 1,548 ....G 2
Christiansted, 2,966 ....H 1

OTHER FEATURES

Saint Croix (island), 31,892 ....H 2
Saint John (island), 1,743 ....H 1
Saint Thomas (island), 29,565 ....G 1

CARIBBEAN

Antilles, Greater (isls.) ....D 3
Antilles, Lesser (isls.) ....F 4
Bartlett Deep ....B 3
Caribbean (sea) ....D 4
Greater Antilles (islands) ....D 3
Grenadines (islands), 12,040 ....G 4
Hispaniola (island), 8,563,000 ....D 2
Leeward (islands) ....F 3
Lesser Antilles (islands) ....F 4
Misteriosa (bank) ....A 3
Navassa (isl.) ....C 3
Windward (islands) ....G 4

JAMAICA: Total pop.—1967 off. est.; other pops— 1960 final census. **MARTINIQUE:** Total & cap.—1969 off. est.; Saint-Pierre—1967 prelim. census. **MONTSERRAT:** Total pop.— 1966 UN est.; capital—1960 final census. **NETH. ANT.:** Total pop.—1969 off. est.; isls.—1968 off. est.; other pops—1960 final census. **PUERTO RICO:** 1970 prelim. census. **ST. CHR.-NEVIS-ANG.:** Total pop.—1967 off. est.; other pops—1960 final census. **ST. LUCIA:** Total pop.—1966 off. est.; other pops—1960 final census. **ST. VINCENT:** Total pop.—1966 off. est.; other pops—1960 final census. **TRINIDAD & TOBAGO:** Total pop.—1966 off. est.; other pops—1960 final census. **TURKS & CAICOS IS.:** Total & Cockburn Hbr.—1963 off. est.; other pops—1960 final census. **VIRGIN IS. (BR.):** Total pop.—1966 UN est.; other pops—1960 final census. **VIRGIN IS. (U.S.):** 1970 prelim. census.

J. ALLAN CASH, FROM RAPHO GUILLUMETTE

HILLY COUNTRY in Barbados contains the homesteads of many families. This scene is on a slope behind the village of Bathsheba, on the east coast of the island.

continues to be true for most of the islands, industry and commerce are beginning to dominate. Industry first touched the almost deserted and barren islands of Curaçao and Aruba, where oil refineries were built by the Dutch and Americans to refine Venezuelan oil. Trinidad soon followed with its own refineries, but the depression of the 1930's prevented any further development of industry or commerce in the West Indies.

After World War II, Puerto Rico led the way with an impressively successful industrial development program, which facilitated the establishment of over a thousand new industrial plants. Other islands, like Jamaica, Trinidad, Martinique, and Antigua, hoping to imitate Puerto Rico's success, initiated their own industrial development programs with varying degrees of failure or success. Ready and direct access to the vast North American market, which producers in Puerto Rico have, was not available to other islands of the West Indies since they do not lie within the U. S. tariff walls. Nevertheless, industry can be found on the sugar island of Antigua in the form of a modern oil refining plant. St. Croix, one of the American Virgin Islands, has harvested its last sugar crop; its people, who cut cane for 300 years, are now working in chemical plants and in oil and bauxite refineries.

The West Indies received some of the benefit of North American and European prosperity after World War II through the increased tourist trade, which previously had been almost monopolized by Havana. Small islands like St.-Barthélemy (French), St. Martin (French and Dutch), and St. John (U. S.) joined the list of ports of call for tourist ships, which usually put in at the standard colorful West Indian communities of Charlotte Amalie (U. S. Virgin Islands), Port-au-Prince (Haiti) and Willemstad (Curaçao).

Either through industry or through commerce stimulated by tourism, the West Indies were enjoying a certain degree of prosperity in the late 1960's. The average per capita annual income in Puerto Rico, the American Virgin Islands, and Curaçao was coming close to $1,000 a year. There were still pockets of extreme poverty like Haiti, where political instability and uncertainty combined with a high density of population to keep down the standard of living.

Educational and Cultural Life. The first university in the New World was founded in 1538 (nearly a century before Harvard) in Santo Domingo, the present capital of the Dominican Republic. Now the West Indies have at least a dozen universities and colleges, a clear indication of the attention paid to education in the Caribbean. With the notable exception of the island of Hispaniola, illiteracy has been all but eliminated from the West Indies. Popular libraries on all the islands, scientific centers of research (like the nuclear center in Mayagüez, Puerto Rico), educational television (found in Puerto Rico and Antigua), and graduate schools of medicine (in Cuba, Puerto Rico, Jamaica, and the Dominican Republic) are some of the institutions which attest to the intellectual progress of the West Indies.

The West Indies are famous for their popular forms of music such as the calypso and the rumba. Less known are their poets, like Aimé Césaire (Martinique), founder of the school of negritude; their anthropologists, like Fernando Ortiz (Cuba) and Jean Price Mars (Haiti), pioneers in the study of West Indian culture; and their novelists, like Alejo Carpentier (Cuba), V. S. Naipaul (Trinidad), and George Lamming (Barbados), or short story writers, like Juan Bosch (Dominican Republic) and John Hearne (Jamaica). The list could be extended to include many others.

Creole culture is typical of the West Indies, where ancient folkways of expression in speech and art have not been wiped out by modernization. The people of Haiti prefer to speak a French Creole rather than pure French; the multilingual people of Curaçao, fluent in Dutch, English, and Spanish, prefer to use Papiamento (a Spanish-based Creole language) to converse among themselves.

The West Indies present contrasting cultural patterns that reflect the varied European heritage of the colonial period. However, beneath this heterogeneous pattern lies a common cultural base, which serves to identify and in a way bind together all the island communities.

History. Columbus' first landfall was in the West Indies on what is believed to be the island of San Salvador in the Bahamas. The Spaniards explored the whole Caribbean Sea and eventually settled the Greater Antilles. The indigenous Arawaks of the larger islands were either eliminated or absorbed by the Spanish in the first years of the 16th century. The Caribs were confined to the Lesser Antilles, which the Spanish felt were not valuable enough to colonize. Thus, in the 17th century, when the French, Dutch, Danish, and English invaded the Spanish domain, they were at first limited to the islands of Barbados and St. Christopher (St. Kitts), and later St. Eustatius, Antigua, and Martinique. In 1655, under Oliver Cromwell's directives, the English made a major attempt to conquer Hispaniola but, when repelled by the Spanish, were forced to settle for Jamaica. The French, by the end of the 17th century, had succeeded in secur-

JOHN J. SMITH

SUGAR MILL RUINS on St. John, U. S. Virgin Islands, stand as a relic of the days when large plantations in many parts of the Caribbean used slave labor to grind the cane into raw sugar for the export trade.

ing Spanish recognition of their occupation of Haiti.

Spices and productive sugar plantations converted the West Indies into precious jewels in the crowns of European monarchs, and throughout the 18th century, possession of the islands was hotly contested. By the end of the Napoleonic era, however, the lines of control were established. Spain had lost Trinidad and Jamaica to the British; and France had taken Haiti, only to lose it in 1794 to Toussaint L'Ouverture, who led his slave companions to a successful revolt.

At the close of the 19th century the United States wrested from Spain its remaining two colonies in the New World: Cuba achieved nominal independence, but Puerto Rico remained a colony of the United States at the end of the Spanish-American War. In 1917 the Danes sold the Virgin Islands to the United States, thus completing American expansion in the Caribbean.

Cuba, Haiti, and the Dominican Republic, the only independent countries in the West Indies until 1962, have fluctuated between revolutionary anarchy and bloody dictatorship. On various occasions the United States intervened in Cuba under the Platt Amendment (see PLATT, ORVILLE HITCHCOCK), and in 1965 it intervened in the Dominican Republic—on each occasion to prevent bloody civil strife. Some material progress was realized under ruthless dictators like Rafael Trujillo in the Dominican Republic and Fulgencio Batista in Cuba.

Since World War II, the United States and Britain have moved to liquidate their colonial empires in the Caribbean. Puerto Rico enjoys a high degree of prosperity and stability in a voluntary association with the United States that allows complete local autonomy. Jamaica, and Trindad with its satellite island of Tobago, achieved independence in 1962, and Barbados in 1966—all within the Commonwealth of Nations. In 1967, Antigua, Dominica, Grenada, St. Kitts-Nevis-Anguilla, St. Lucia, and St. Vincent became free states in association with Britain. Great political leaders like Luis Muños Marín in Puerto Rico and Eric Williams in Trinidad have headed popular mass movements that have brought political freedom, economic prosperity, and a stable democratic government.

In one respect the West Indies have produced disappointing failures. After World War II attempts were made to bind the West Indies closer together in some type of regional federation or association. These attempts, such as the Caribbean Organization (q.v.) and The West Indies federation, were made both at the national and international levels, but after a few years the organizations were disbanded.

However, in the 1960's steps were being taken in the Caribbean to seek closer cooperation, particularly in the economic field, with the hope that political cooperation would follow.

THOMAS MATHEWS, *University of Puerto Rico*

Further Reading: Bosch, Juan, *The Unfinished Experiment: Democracy in the Dominican Republic* (New York 1965); Lewis, Gordon, *Puerto Rico: Freedom and Power in the Caribbean* (New York 1963); Mathews, Thomas, and others, *Politics and Economics in th Caribbean* (San Juan 1966); Naipaul, V. S., *The Middle Passage* (New York 1962); Parry, John H., and Sherlock, P. M., *A Short History of the Caribbean* (New York 1956); Sherlock, Philip M., *West Indies* (London 1966).

CARIBBEAN ORGANIZATION, kar-ə-bē′ən, a regional organization that dealt with economic and social affairs in the Caribbean area from 1942 until its dissolution in 1965. Essentially an advisory body, it was formed to cope with the region's precarious economy, but became concerned with health, welfare, and education.

The organization was created in March 1942 as the Anglo-American Caribbean Commission, with authority limited to the British and American dependencies in the West Indies. With the adherence of France and the Netherlands at the end of 1945, its name was changed to the Caribbean Commission. At the first meeting of the expanded organization in St. Thomas, V. I., in 1946, the delegates from the 15 dependent entities carried on their discussion free of control from the colonial powers. Significantly, of the 29 delegates in attendance, 23 were native-born and 16 were members of local legislatures. The next step in the evolution of the organization occurred in June 1960, when, at the instance of the territorial dependencies, the four colonial powers signed an agreement in Washington creating a successor body, the Caribbean Organization.

At its height the organization included in its membership France, for its departments of French Guiana, Guadalupe, and Martinique; the Netherlands Antilles and Surinam; British Guiana and The West Indies federation (comprising 10 British territories, including Barbados, Jamaica, and Trinidad and Tobago); and the U. S. dependencies of Puerto Rico and the Virgin Islands. Although the metropolitan nations retained broad powers and unanimity was required on important votes, only the 12 territories had the vote, with the colonial powers having observer status. After Dutch and British Guiana, as well as Puerto Rico, gave notice in December 1964 of an intent to withdraw, the Caribbean Council—the organization's governing body—asked the four signatory nations to dissolve the agency by Dec. 31, 1965.

LAURENCE R. BIRNS
The New School for Social Research, New York

CARIBBEAN SEA. See CARIBBEAN.

CARIBE. See PIRANHA.

ARCTIC CARIBOU, also known as barren-ground caribou, photographed in Alaska. The slaughter of these animals by Eskimos and northern Indians for food and pelts has much diminished the herds.

LEONARD LEE RUE, FROM NATIONAL AUDUBON SOCIETY

CARIBOU, kar′ə-bo͞o, is a town in northeastern Maine, in Aroostook county, on the Aroostook River, about 150 miles (241 km) north of Bangor. It is situated in an area of intensive potato production and is a center for the processing, storage, and shipping of potatoes. Other industries include food freezing and the manufacture of potato pulp, dairy products, fertilizer, starch, burlap bags, and paper products. Caribou was settled in 1829 and was incorporated in 1859. It is governed by a manager and council. Population: 10,419.

CARIBOU, kar′ə-bo͞o, a medium-sized member of the deer family. The caribou of northern North America and the reindeer of northern Europe and Asia belong to a single widespread species, *Rangifer tarandus*. Three clearly distinct North American subspecies of caribou are the woodland caribou (*R. t. caribou*), the barren-ground caribou (*R. t. groenlandicus*), and the Peary caribou (*R. t. Pearyi*) of the Canadian Arctic archipelago and northern Greenland.

Characteristics. An adult caribou is about 5 to 7 feet (1.6–2.5 meters) long, and stands about 42 inches (1.2 meters) at the shoulder. An average-sized male weighs 175 to 350 pounds (81–153 kg), but a woodland caribou may weigh up to 600 pounds (270 kg).

Caribou are unique among deer in that both sexes generally carry antlers. Those of the male are much larger. The main beam of each antler sweeps back gracefully over the neck, then curves forward, and divides eventually into a number of fingerlike terminal tines. Two larger tines branch off close to the base; one points down over the forehead and acts as an eye shield, and the other points to the side.

The caribou possesses a number of special adaptations to its arctic environment. It has a well-furred muzzle and short, furred ears and tail. The unusually large feet and crescent-shaped hooves facilitate travel over snow-covered and boggy ground. The coat is composed of long, brittle guard hairs and close, crinkled undercoat.

The basic clove-brown color of the coat is darker on the face and chest. The creamy white color of the neck and throat mane extends in a band across the lower shoulder and flank. The belly, rump, and undersurface of the tail are white; the legs are brown, except for narrow white socks just above the hooves. The Peary caribou is largely white with a blue-gray saddle, and the woodland caribou is sepia-brown except for white patches on the neck, belly, and rump.

Behavior. Caribou are gregarious and live in herds that may include thousands of individuals during migrations. The sexes are segregated most of the year; the does and young animals are led by an old doe, while the bucks travel in bachelor bands. The sexes reunite during the rutting period (September to November), and the unspotted, dun-brown fawns are born in June after a gestation period of about 240 days. The life span of the animal is about 15 years.

The herds are almost constantly on the move, migrating from one seasonal pasture to another. The forested southern winter ranges of the barren-ground caribou may lie up to 800 miles (1,200 km) from their northern tundra summer ranges. Woodland caribou are more local in their movements. Lichens form the mainstay of the caribou diet, especially in winter; an adult eats about 10 pounds (4.5 kg) of lichens a day. Other plants eaten include grasses, sedges, horsetails, mushrooms, heaths, and twigs of willows and birches, and weeds and berries in the summer.

Caribou are usually quiet animals, but the passage of the herds is marked by the belchlike grunting of the adults, the bawls of the fawns, and the characteristic clicking sound produced by a tendon slipping over bones in the foot. The animals rely mainly on their sense of smell to warn them of danger. They seldom run far when alarmed before stopping and looking back over their shoulders.

Caribou and Man. Caribou were an important economic resource to Eskimos and Indians before the arrival of Europeans. They provided nutritious meat for man and his dogs. The pelts provided light warm clothing, beds, and summer tepees. Thread was made from the sinews, and utensils from the bones; the fat was used to provide heat and light.

Originally the caribou were trapped in enclosures, snared, speared in the water, or hunted with bow and arrow. However, the introduction of firearms greatly tipped the scales against the caribou, and their numbers declined in the face of increased hunting. From an original population of perhaps 5 to 10 million, the number of caribou shrank to about half a million by the mid-20th century; but the number is again on the increase. Besides man, the main hazards that face caribou herds are wolves, spring storms, thin ice, and forest fires.

A. W. F. BANFIELD
National Museum of Canada

DRAWN FOR THE ENCYCLOPEDIA AMERICANA BY DAVID LEVINE

DAVID LEVINE contrasts a more realistic likeness of author Rudyard Kipling *(left)* with a caricature.

CARICATURE, kar′i-kə-choo̅r, in the pictorial arts, a representation, ordinarily of a person or a type of person, made unliteral (and usually grotesque or ludicrous) by the exaggeration of certain features. The term, derived from Italian *caricatura* ("loading," "charging"), is also applied to works in other arts, but these are more often termed "burlesque" or "parody."

Caricature depends for its effect on dissimilarity from a recognizable original; the distortion or simplification, reflecting the artist's point of view, usually comments on the character of the subject. Because exaggeration of the human features is ordinarily uncomplimentary, caricature lends itself to satiric uses, but it is sometimes intended quite innocuously.

ORIGINS

Caricature originated in the Renaissance. Champfleury, in his *Histoire de la caricature antique* (1865), erroneously maintained that caricature goes back to ancient times. He cited classical zoomorphic drawings of people as being caricatures, but these drawings lack the "charge" of caricature since they do not illuminate for the viewer the characters of their subjects. They are merely burlesques, drawings intended only to amuse through incongruity.

The usual simplicity and didactic intent of caricature made it suitable to wide audiences, and its development in the Renaissance coincided with that of various techniques—woodcut, etching, engraving—for producing multiple impressions of a single drawing. Caricature in its most familiar form—the satiric representation of individuals or types—first became important in the 16th and 17th centuries with such artists as Agostino Carracci (1557–1602) and Giovanni Bernini (1598–1680). One of the best caricatures of the 16th century is a German woodcut showing a glutton trundling his own stomach along in a wheelbarrow and vomiting.

Caricatures centering on political issues flourished in the 16th, 17th, and 18th centuries. Among their controversial subjects were the rise of Lutheranism, the Mississippi Bubble, and the antipathy in England between the Hanoverians and the Jacobites. Two of the outstanding caricaturists of the 18th century were Giovanni Tiepolo (1696–1770) and William Hogarth (1697–1764). Both of these artists usually caricaturized types rather than individuals; an exception is Hogarth's portrait of the Jacobite Lord Lovat at his trial in 1745.

EARLY 19TH CENTURY

The 19th century was the golden age of caricature. The popularity of this art form was stimulated by Thomas Bewick's refinement of the art of wood engraving in the 18th century and by Aloys Senefelder's invention of lithography about 1798. These techniques, making it possible to print thousands of impressions of a single caricature, caused a flowering of the art. Both in the quantity and in the quality of their work, the caricaturists of the 19th century have never been equaled.

The finest English caricaturists at the beginning of the century were Thomas Rowlandson and James Gillray. Rowlandson (1756–1827) began his career as a watercolorist and portraitist in oils, but about 1781 he turned to comic drawing. He did not produce many genuine caricatures, being content for the most part to burlesque the manners of the day. The exceptions include his etching of the boxing match between Quirk and Ward (1812), which clearly shows not only the scene but the artist's attitude toward the boxers and the spectators. Rowlandson's works are characterized by imagination and a boisterous humor.

Gillray (1757–1815) was famous for his caricatures on social subjects, especially political questions, to which he devoted himself for the most part from 1780 to 1811 (when he lost his sanity). Gillray's drawings, like those of most other early caricaturists, are crowded with incident: they must be "read" rather than observed. His technique was bold and vigorous and his satire often savage. His brutal drawing of Czar Paul I of Russia was one of the earliest of portrait caricatures, which during the late 19th century became the dominant mode of caricature art in England.

Poverty forced George Cruikshank (1792–1878) to begin drawing professionally at the age of 13, and in the 1810's he was producing caricatures for several English papers. His manner echoed that of Gillray, but Cruikshank was more genial and less skillful. In the early 1820's, guided by the British preference of the comic to the satiric, he turned chiefly to book-illustrating, which brought him considerable fame later in the century.

MIDDLE 19TH CENTURY

France. During the 18th century, caricatures had ordinarily been sold to printsellers; but early in the 19th century caricature became attached to the profession of journalism. The first great journal of caricature was French: *La Caricature,* a weekly founded in 1830 by Charles Philipon. Because *La Caricature* espoused Republican views, it soon acquired a formidable array of caricaturists, among them Jean Grandville, Henri Monnier, C. J. Traviès, Paul Gavarni, and Honoré Daumier. But it also attracted the hostile attention of Louis Philippe's government, which suppressed it in 1834. Its place was taken by a daily, *Le Charivari,* which Philipon had founded in 1832.

Philipon (1800–1862) was the creator of one of the great caricatures. Having used a pear to symbolize Louis Philippe, he was taken to court for libel, and in his defense he produced a four-part drawing. The first part accurately depicted the monarch's broad jaws, heavy jowls, and multiple chins below a head that narrowed toward the crown; in the second and third parts these features were gradually simplified and exaggerated until, in the fourth part, Louis had become nothing but a pear with vestigial eyes, nose, and mouth.

Philipon's most remarkable artist was Honoré Daumier (1808–1879), the greatest of all caricaturists. Daumier's wide-ranging mind detested humbug, hypocrisy, and injustice in all their forms, and he attacked them with superb draftsmanship and composition. He took all of Parisian life as his province, but he concentrated on such evils as fraud in high places and smugness in the body of society. Among his most notable works are the lithograph *Enfoncé Lafayette* and the magnificent series *Le ventre législatif.* Daumier's career continued through the Franco-Prussian War, and his last important work, the *Album du siège,* is a threnody on devastated Paris.

Germany. Caricature became important in Germany about the middle of the century. *Die fliegende Blätter,* the first of many German satirical papers, was founded in 1844 by Kaspar Braun and Friedrich Schneider. Unlike their French counterparts, the German magazines underplayed political and social comment, focusing instead on manners and morals. The German style also differed in two important respects. Whereas the French employed pen, pencil, watercolor, and gouache, the Germans tended to use pen only; thus, most of the German drawings were done in simple line. Further, the Germans generally avoided captions, so that their drawings had to speak for themselves. This convention led to the development of the sequential caricature made up of as many as six different drawings, each illustrating one stage of a story.

One of the early masters of this genre was Wilhelm Busch (1832–1908), who belonged to the staff of *Die fliegende Blätter* from 1859 to 1871. Busch was Germany's finest caricaturist, although his drawings often leaned toward the merely comic. His famous series *Max und Moritz* led to the development of the American comic strip; its influence is especially apparent in the early *Katzenjammer Kids,* which would not have appeared out of place in the 19th century German magazines (see COMICS). Among Busch's colleagues, Adolf Oberländer, Adolf Hengeler, and Emil Reinicke were also influential.

BY SPECIAL PERMISSION OF ALBERT HIRSCHFELD

HIRSCHFELD'S caricature of Franklin D. Roosevelt.

England. *Punch,* the most famous of all humor magazines, was founded in London in 1841. British caricature was then declining, and *Punch* did little to revive it. Clever political cartoons occasionally appeared in its pages—the best-known is Sir John Tenniel's *Dropping the Pilot*—but for the most part its drawings merely illustrated dialogue captions. The magazine never published a caricature that could have disturbed British bourgeois complacency.

LATE 19TH CENTURY

England. Caricature in England was revived by an Italian, Carlo Pellegrini (1839–1889), who went to England in 1864. Pellegrini refined the portrait caricature, purging it of the symbolism that French caricaturists had given it. At first

DAVID LOW'S caricature (c. 1925) of Winston Churchill.

GRANGER COLLECTION

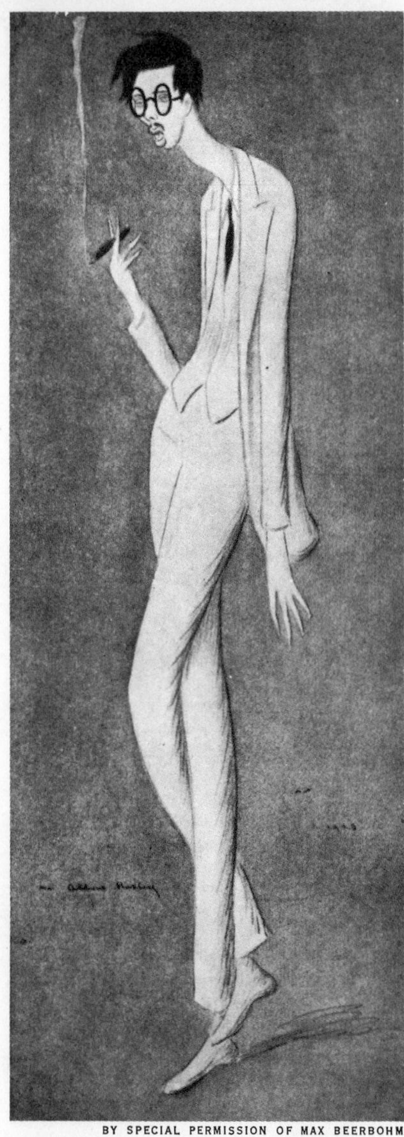

BY SPECIAL PERMISSION OF MAX BEERBOHM

MAX BEERBOHM caricatured British author Aldous Huxley, as a young man, in 1923.

OLAF GULBRANSSON resolved his subject into contrasting masses of light and dark in his caricature pen sketch of the Norwegian dramatist Ibsen.

ALFRED A. KNOPF INC.

ALFRED J. FRUEH caricatured theatrical personality George M. Cohan with a few jaunty lines.

BY SPECIAL PERMISSION OF ALFRED J. FRUEH

he published his drawings over the signature "Singe"; in 1869, when he became a regular contributor to Thomas Gibson Bowles's *Vanity Fair* (founded in 1868), he began to sign himself "Ape."

Vanity Fair boasted other caricaturists, including "Spy" (Sir Leslie Ward) and the most famous of all English caricaturists, Max Beerbohm (1872–1956). Beerbohm, who also contributed to the *Yellow Book* and the *Savoy*, published four books of caricatures, beginning with *Caricatures of Twenty-five Gentlemen* (1896). His work, although it reveals Pellegrini's influence, is unmistakably individual. His graceful drawings possess to a high degree the frivolity he considered essential to the art.

France. After the 1850's a new and more frivolous variety of caricature, social comedy, developed in France. New papers were founded, including the *Journal amusant, Le Rire, Le chat noir,* and *L'assiette au beurre;* and new artists, among them Caran d'Ache, Toulouse-Lautrec, Jean Louis Forain, and Théophile Steinlen, came to the fore. Their favorite target was the *beau monde:* the newly rich bourgeoisie, the nobility, the crowned heads of Europe, the stars of the theater, the mistresses of kings, all were subjected to the caricaturist's pen. Meanwhile, the satirists were gaining sympathy for the lower classes. Shop girls, domestic servants, and working men began to figure in their drawings in the 1870's. The energetic and hardhitting Steinlen, in his *Chansons rouges,* depicted the Parisian proletariat with all its latent power.

United States. Caricature has never been very strong in the United States. Thomas Nast (1840–1902) was a political cartoonist rather than a caricaturist, although there are strong elements of caricature in his famous attacks (1869–1871) on the Tweed Ring at New York City's Tammany Hall. American political cartoons were usually allegorical, and a tendency toward allegory is visible even in the work of Charles Dana Gibson (1867–1944), who approached genuine caricature in his series called *Life's Comedy.*

THE 20TH CENTURY

The best known of all German satirical papers, *Simplicissimus,* was founded in Munich in 1896 by Albert Langen and Thomas Theodor Heine. Heine's and Eduard Thöny's drawings led the paper's vitriolic attacks on German politics, pedantry, and militarism; in 1902 they were joined by the charming and ingenious caricatures of Olaf Gulbransson (1873–1958). *Simplicissimus* continued to be published until 1967, but in recent years its caricatures, with occasional exceptions, were coarse and uninteresting.

After World War I, caricature entered a general decline. This was probably caused by changes in the media of information, particularly the growing use of halftone photoengravings in magazines and newspapers. Another possible cause was the political changes that took place after the war; monarchies toppled and were replaced by multi-party political systems. The caricature of policy, which implies a unified national view, gave way to political cartooning, which implies a party view; and anything so narrow as party politics offers the caricaturist meager scope.

Nevertheless, a number of excellent 20th century artists contributed to the art of the portrait caricature. In France, André Rouveyre (1879–1962) was noted for the felicitous economy of line in his *Visages des contemporains.* In England, portrait caricatures were drawn by "Quiz" (Powys Evans), Aubrey Hammond, and Bohun Lynch; David Low (1891–1963), whose usual work was in the realm of cartooning, occasionally produced political caricatures. In the United States, Ralph Barton (1891–1931) turned from comic art to genuine caricature, especially of literary and theatrical celebrities. Barton also persuaded the American magazine *Vanity Fair* to publish the portraits of Miguel Covarrubias (1904–1957), a Mexican caricaturist.

Today caricature appears to be reviving. There are a number of satirical papers behind the Iron Curtain: the well-known (but artistically thoroughly uninteresting) *Krokodil* in Russia, *Ludas Matyi* in Hungary, *Dikobraz* and *Roháč* in Czechoslovakia, *Jez* in Yugoslavia, *Sturshel* in Bulgaria, and *Eulenspiegel* in East Germany. Much of the work in these papers is pedestrian and predictable; but East Germany has a very genial draftsman in Henry Büttner, and Poland has Jan Lenica, who generally designs posters or works with film animations but occasionally does masterful caricatures.

There are fewer satirical papers in the West. The best are *Nebelspalter* in Switzerland, *Private Eye* in England, and *Le canard enchaîné* in France. The work of Nuez, in Cuba, deserves serious attention. The French cartoonist Siné founded an antiestablishment paper called *Massacre,* but it was short-lived.

American caricature today is carried on the shoulders of Albert Hirschfeld and David Levine. Hirschfeld's weekly theatrical caricatures are an outstanding feature of the New York *Times,* while Levine's works, which have revitalized political caricature in the United States, appear regularly in the *New York Review of Books.* Levine's drawings are equally well known in France, where *Le nouvel observateur* presents them several times a month. Levine's style reflects the strong influence of Tenniel, but the moods of their drawings differ strikingly. Where Tenniel was ordinarily placid and matter-of-fact, Levine is fiery and matter-of-truth. An example of Levine's work, drawn for *The Encyclopedia Americana,* accompanies this article. See also CARTOON.

DOUGLASS PAIGE, *Editor of "The Letters of Ezra Pound, 1907–1941"*

Bibliography

Alexandre, Arsène, *L'art du rire et de la caricature* (Paris 1892).
Ashbee, Charles R., *Caricature* (New York 1928).
Escholier, Raymond, *Daumier* (Paris 1923).
Fuchs, Eduard, *Die Karikatur der europaischen Völker* (Munich 1912).
Fuchs, Eduard, *Der Weltkrieg in der Karikatur* (Munich 1916).
Gombrich, Ernst H., and Kris, Ernst, *Caricature* (New York 1940).
Hofmann, Werner, *Caricature from Leonardo to Picasso,* Eng. tr. (New York 1957).
Larkin, Oliver W., *Daumier, a Man of His Time* (New York 1966).
Low, David, *British Cartoonists* (London 1942).
Lynch, Bohun, *A History of Caricature* (Boston 1927).
Malcolm, James P., *An Historical Sketch of the Art of Caricaturing* (London 1813).
Paine, Albert B., *Th. Nast, His Period and His Pictures* (New York 1904).
Price, Richard G. G., *History of Punch* (London 1957).
Veth, Cornelis, *Comic Art in England* (New York 1930).
Williams, Ronald E., ed., *A Century of Punch Cartoons* (London 1955).
Wright, Thomas, *History of Caricature and Grotesque in Literature and Art* (London 1865).
Wright, Thomas, *Works of James Gillray the Caricaturist* (London 1873).
Wright, Thomas, and Evans, Robert H., *Historical and Descriptive Account of the Caricatures of James Gillray* (London 1865).

CARIES. See TEETH.

CARILLON. See CHIMES AND CARILLONS.

CARINA. See CONSTELLATION.

CARINTHIA, kə-rin'thē-ə, is the southernmost of Austria's nine provinces. Carinthia (German, Kärnten) is nearly 100 miles (160 km) in length from east to west and varies from 28 to 44 miles (45 to 71 km) from north to south, enclosing an area of 3,680 square miles (9,530 sq km). The population is predominantly German-speaking, though about 4% speak Slovene.

The province embraces the upper valley of the Drave (German, Drau) River, and mountains guard most of its perimeters. To the west and northwest are the Hohe Tauern Mountains, through which the Grossglockner Alpine Highway, constructed in 1935, connects Carinthia with Salzburg. On the south the Carnic Alps and the Karawanken form a mountain wall against Italy and Yugoslavia. Carinthia has many beautiful lakes, among them the Wörthersee, the Ossiachersee, and Millstättersee, whose warm waters in summer are popular with vacationers. Carinthia is primarily a rural province; wood is its most important natural product, but its mines produce lead, iron ore, zinc, and magnesite. The cultural and political center is the capital, Klagenfurt, but the chief commercial city is Villach.

Carinthia derives its name from an ancient Celtic tribe, the Carni, who once inhabited the region. In Roman times it became part of the province of Noricum. In the 8th century it came under the rule of the dukes of Bavaria. Emperor Otto II separated it from Bavaria in 976 and made it a separate duchy. It was subsequently held by various families, and in 1286 it came under the jurisdiction of the counts of Tyrol. In 1335 it passed to the Habsburgs.

AUSTRIAN STATE TOURIST DEPARTMENT

Heiligenblut in the province of Carinthia, Austria.

From 1809 to 1813 it was part of Napoleon's Province of Illyria. Returned to the Habsburgs, it was made into a separate crown land of Austria in 1849. After World War I, Yugoslavia laid claim to portions of Carinthia and sent in troops. The disputed Klagenfurt region was divided into two zones and plebiscites were to be held in each. When the zone nearest to Yugoslavia voted 22,025 to 15,279 to remain with Austria, no plebiscite was considered necessary in the other zone. However, Austria was forced to cede the Miess Valley to Yugoslavia and the Kanal Valley to Italy. Population: (1961) 492,226.

ERNST C. HELMREICH, *Bowdoin College*

CARINUS, kə-rī'nəs, **Marcus Aurelius** (died 285 A.D.), Roman emperor from 283 to 285 A.D. He was the elder son of Emperor Carus. When Carus became emperor in 282, he appointed Carinus as caesar (junior emperor) and put him in charge of the Western Roman Empire. Later Carinus was made augustus (senior emperor) and coruler with his father. When Carus was killed in 283, Carinus and his brother Numerian became coemperors. But Numerian was murdered the following year, and the army selected Diocletian to take his place. Carinus, anxious to secure control of the entire Roman Empire for himself, led his army against Diocletian. The campaign culminated with the Battle of the Margus in Moesia (285). Carinus won the battle but was murdered by one of his officers. The armies accepted Diocletian as emperor.

ARTHER FERRILL, *University of Washington*

CARISBROOKE, kar'iz-bro͝ok, is a village on the Isle of Wight, England, just southwest of Newport. On a nearby hill are the ruins of Carisbrooke Castle, where Charles I was imprisoned in 1647–1648 before his trial and execution. The castle, founded on the site of a Roman fortress, was built in the early Norman period. Most of the remaining walls were added in the 1200's and after. Population: (1961) 2,767.

CARISSIMI, kä-rēs'sē-mē, **Giacomo** (1605–1674), Italian composer, who was an important figure in the development of the dramatic oratorio. His most significant contribution was the use of the chorus as a full dramatic participant in oratorios.

Carissimi was born in Marino, near Rome. From 1623 to 1627 he held appointments at Tivoli as a singer and organist. After a year as choirmaster at San Rufino in Assisi, he became choirmaster at Sant'Apollinare in Rome in 1629, a post he held until his death, in Rome on Jan. 12, 1674.

Many of Carissimi's works were written to satisfy the Italian demand for opera during Lent, when operas were forbidden. His surviving works include 16 oratorios with Latin texts based on tragic episodes, usually from the Old Testament, of which the best known are *Jephte* and *Jonas;* 210 sacred motets in the style of cantatas; 12 masses in polyphonic style; and 145 secular cantatas for solo voices, mainly on amorous texts.

Carissimi's cantatas and oratorios owe a clear debt to the earlier operatic style of Monteverdi. While Carissimi's contemporaries made sharp distinctions in style between *recitativo secco* and aria, Carissimi lyrically fused music and text so that there is very little difference between recitative and aria. In his oratorios and cantatas, chromaticism and vocal flourishes are directly related to the text, with whole sections or short arias often devoted to one emotional quality. The harmonies are mainly diatonic, but some modal harmony is present.

Carissimi strongly affected 18th century music through his pupils—including Marc Antoine Charpentier, Giovanni Bononcini, and Alessandro Scarlatti—and influenced the English Restoration composers Purcell and Blow. Carissimi's style is reflected in the oratorios of Handel, who even borrowed entire scenes from Carissimi's works.

ADRIENNE FRIED, *Choral Director*
Dalcroze School of Music, New York City

CARLETON, kärl'tən, **Sir Guy** (1724–1808), British administrator in Canada. He was a longtime governor of Quebec and a controversial civil and military leader during the era of the American Revolution.

Carleton was born in Strabane, Ireland, on Sept. 3, 1724. He possessed sufficient social and economic station to rise in rank in Britain's class-conscious army. After distinguished duty in Canada during the French and Indian War (1754–1763), Carleton became lieutenant governor of Quebec in 1766 and governor in chief in 1768. After 1775 he also served as military commander. He displayed integrity, humanity, and dedication in performing his duties. His vision in dealing with the French Catholic inhabitants led to Parliament's adoption of the Quebec Act (1774), which allowed Britain's new subjects to retain their former rights and liberties. However, Carleton was hostile to the English-speaking mercantile minority and denied them the protection of English law in civil suits contrary to the provisions of the Quebec Act itself.

Carleton found it difficult to work with other British officials, both in Canada and in London. A clash with the colonial secretary Lord George Germain prompted his removal from military operations in 1777, although he had defeated an American invading army under Gen. Richard Montgomery and had pursued the enemy as far as Lake Champlain.

In 1778, Carleton gave up the governorship, but in 1782 he returned as commander in chief of all British forces in Canada. He was governor of Quebec again from 1786 to 1796. In 1786 he was created Baron Dorchester, and in 1793 he was promoted to general. Governor Carleton advanced a startling proposal, prophetic but unacceptable in his time: the federation of all British North America. He died in Stubbings, near Maidenhead, England, on Nov. 10, 1808.

DON HIGGINBOTHAM
University of North Carolina

CARLETON, kärl'tən, **Will** (1845–1912), American poet and journalist. He was born near Hudson, Mich., on Oct. 21, 1845, and graduated from Hillsdale College in 1869. He worked as a journalist for several papers in the Midwest, and in 1871 wrote the poem *Betsy and I Are Out,* which appeared in *Harper's Weekly* and achieved nationwide popularity. *Harper's* also published his next poems, including *Out of the Old House, Nancy, Over the Hill to the Poor House* (his best-known poem), and *Gone with a Handsomer Man,* all sentimental favorites. In 1882, Carleton moved to Brooklyn, N. Y., where in 1894 he founded the illustrated monthly *Every Where,* in which most of his subsequent work appeared. He died in Brooklyn on Dec. 18, 1912.

CARLETON, kärl'tən, **William** (1794–1869), Irish novelist, noted for his colorful portrayals of Irish life and character. He was born in Prillisk, County Tyrone. After moving to Dublin, Carleton temporarily turned from Catholicism to Protestantism and contributed sketches to both Protestant and secular periodicals. He also published *Traits and Stories of the Irish Peasantry* (2 vols., 1830–1833), *Tales of Ireland* (1834), and the popular novel *Fardorougha the Miser* (1839), which was subsequently adapted for the stage. His later works, which frequently championed the cause of the oppressed Irish peasants, include *Valentine McClutchy* (1845) and *The Black Prophet* (1847). Carleton died in Dublin on Jan. 30, 1869.

CARLETON COLLEGE, kärl'tən, is a private, nonsectarian coeducational institution of higher education in the liberal arts in Northfield, Minn. It was incorporated in 1866 as Northfield College and renamed in 1872 to honor William Carleton, a benefactor. Departments include American studies, physical and social sciences, languages, government and international relations, physical education, mathematics, and philosophy. Credit is given for independent study.

Carleton maintains cooperative programs with nine Midwest colleges; shares in the Washington Semester Plan for government study; cooperates with Columbia University and Massachusetts Institute of Technology in engineering studies; and offers a study-abroad program. Enrollment in the mid-1960's averaged 1,400 students.

CARLETON UNIVERSITY, kärl'tən, is a private, coeducational, nonsectarian institution of higher education in Ottawa, Ontario. It was founded by the Ottawa Association for the Advancement of Learning in 1942 as Carleton College and granted university status in 1952, although the present name was not assumed until 1957. Classes were first held in the evening in rented quarters. A building was purchased in 1946, and a full campus was acquired in southeast Ottawa in 1959. The university has faculties of arts, engineering, science, and graduate studies. Distinctive programs include a School of Public Administration, an Institute of Canadian Studies, and a special unit in Soviet studies. University enrollment in the mid-1960's averaged about 2,300 students.

CARLILE, kär-līl', **John Snyder** (1817–1878), American politician, who was instrumental in establishing the state of West Virginia. He was born in Winchester, Va., on Dec. 16, 1817. A Virginia lawyer, he served in the state Senate (1847–1851), as a delegate to the Virginia Constitutional Convention of 1850–1851, and as a U. S. congressman (1855–1857). A strong Unionist, he was a member of the Wheeling Convention of 1861, which established the Reorganized Government of Virginia, and he urged the creation of a new state in western Virginia. He was elected to Congress in 1861 to represent the Wheeling district of the Reorganized Government, but soon moved to the U. S. Senate, where he served until 1865, the last two years as senator from West Virginia. He died in Clarksburg, W. Va., on Oct. 23, 1878.

CARLILE, kär-līl', **Richard** (1790–1843), English publisher, who was an outspoken advocate of freedom of speech and press. He was born in Ashburton, England, on Dec. 8, 1790. While serving as a journeyman tinworker in London, he read the works of Thomas Paine and was inspired to become a political radical and a freethinker himself. He eventually established himself as a publisher, purveying works of Paine and other forbidden free-thought literature.

As a result of his activities, Carlile was imprisoned, fined, and deprived of property several times, and his assistants and members of his family were also prosecuted. While in prison, he supervised the publication of the first 12 volumes of his periodical the *Republican* (1819–1826). He was also the founder and publisher of the radical weekly the *Gorgon.* During the last years of his life he was again imprisoned for more than three years for refusing to pay church taxes. He died in London on Feb. 10, 1843.

CARLING, kär'ling, **Sir John** (1828–1911), Canadian brewer and public official. He was born in London, Upper Canada (now Ontario), on Jan. 23, 1828. He entered his father's business and succeeded him as president of the Carling Brewing and Malting Company. In 1857 he was elected as Conservative member for London in the assembly of the old province of Canada. At Confederation (1867) he was returned for London both to the new Dominion House of Commons and to the Ontario provincial assembly. In addition, he was commissioner of agriculture and public works in the Ontario government from 1867 to 1871.

When dual representation was abolished (1872), he chose to sit in the Dominion house, but he was defeated in 1874. Reelected in 1878, he remained in the house until 1895 and held posts in the Conservative cabinets of Sir John A. Macdonald and Sir John Thompson. Carling died in London, Ontario, on Nov. 6, 1911.

J. M. S. CARELESS
University of Toronto

CARLINVILLE, kär'lin-vil, is a city in western Illinois, the seat of Macoupin county, 38 miles (61 km) southwest of Springfield. The city is a trade center and makes steel pipe fittings, agricultural implements, cotton gloves, and dairy products. It is the seat of Blackburn College. Government is by mayor and council. Population: 5,675.

CARLISLE, kär-līl', **John Griffin** (1835–1910), American public official. He was born in Campbell (now Kenton) county, Ky., on Sept. 5, 1835. Largely self-educated, he studied and practiced law in Covington and served two terms in the state legislature (1859–1861). Elected twice to the state senate, he resigned in 1871 to become lieutenant governor. He was sent in 1877 as a Democrat to the U. S. House of Representatives.

Elected speaker in 1883, he administered parliamentary law and the rules of the House with scrupulous impartiality. In 1890 he resigned to fill an unexpired term in the Senate, and in 1893 he became President Cleveland's secretary of the treasury. He left office in 1897. Carlin died in New York City on July 31, 1910.

CARLISLE, kar-līl', a city and county borough in northwest England, is the county town of Cumberland. Situated on the Eden River, 8 miles (13 km) south of the Scottish border, Carlisle has been for centuries the main gateway between England and Scotland. The city is a major rail center and has textile factories, biscuit bakeries, and varied manufactures. A new civic center was opened in 1964; another modern building (1952) houses the technical college, and there is a college of art and design.

Carlisle's history is a series of sieges, sackings, and rebuildings. Parts of the city wall remain, and also the gateway and keep of the castle founded by William Rufus in 1092 and rebuilt by Henry I in 1122. The cathedral, begun in the 12th century, has a fine 14th century east window. In Tullie House are the city museum, library, and art gallery. Population: (1961) 71,101.

GORDON STOKES
Author, "English Place-Names"

CARLISLE, kär-līl', a borough in southern Pennsylvania, the seat of Cumberland county, is situated in an agricultural valley 18 miles (29 km) southwest of Harrisburg. It is a manufacturing center, widely known for production of crystals for radio and electronic uses.

Carlisle is the home of Dickinson College, founded in 1783, and the Dickinson School of Law (1833). Carlisle Barracks, one of the oldest of U. S. Army posts (established in 1757), has been occupied since 1951 by the U. S. Army War College. From 1879 to 1918 the post was the site of a school for American Indians, the Carlisle Indian School, which became famous for its athletes, especially Jim Thorpe. Among many other points of interest are the First Presbyterian Church (1757) and a monument to Molly Pitcher, Revolutionary War heroine.

Carlisle was laid out in 1751 on land that was part of William Penn's holdings. It was planned as the county seat and was named for Carlisle, the seat of Cumberland county, England. The present form of government, council-manager, was adopted in 1921. Population: 18,079.

ELIZABETH M. HENCKEL
J. Herman Bosler Memorial Library, Carlisle

CARLISM, kär'liz-əm, a Spanish regional movement with political and religious overtones, has produced two civil wars and more than a century of controversy. Its origins were dynastic, centering around who should succeed Ferdinand VII on the Spanish throne. The childless king had married María Cristina of Naples in 1829, and a year later a daughter, Isabella, was born. When Ferdinand died in 1833, María Cristina assumed the regency for Isabella.

However, the king's younger brother, Don Carlos María Isidro, disputed the infanta's claim, asserting that by the Salic law, introduced by Philip V in 1713, women were barred from the throne. Although the Cortes (parliament) had reinstated female inheritance in 1789, the king at that time, Charles IV, had not published this law. Because it had not been made public, the Salic law was generally thought to be the law of the land, at least until 1830 when it was finally made public. Throughout his lifetime, Carlos maintained that the decree had been belatedly promulgated only to prevent him from acquiring the crown. Carlos formalized his claim in 1833 by proclaiming himself Charles V. He gathered dissident political and religious factions under the banner of Carlism.

Behind this movement was a strong reaction to liberalism. Ferdinand himself had twice destroyed liberal regimes, but in his final years bankruptcy had forced him to install liberal businessmen at the court. Fear of secularism and centralism rather than the dynastic squabble attracted support for Don Carlos. He styled himself as an absolute monarch who believed in the "Glory of God and the prosperity and splendour of his Sacred Religion." His attitude was particularly comforting to the intensely Catholic Basques and Navarrese of northern Spain, who identified liberalism with Protestantism and the French Revolution. They feared the loss of their churches and of their *fueros*, or local liberties, and it was the latter issue that became the focus of Carlist struggles and came to be directed against the liberal cabinets during María Cristina's regency.

The Carlist Wars. The First Carlist War began in 1833 in the far northern provinces. Gen. Tomás Zumalacárregui led his small Carlist army to numerous victories, and the Carlist regions soon constituted a state within a state, extending from Galicia on the west to Catalonia on the east, and as far south as lower Aragón. What hurt the Carlists' cause, however, was their rejection by the Spanish propertied classes, who had benefited from liberal confiscation of church lands. By 1838 it was clear that the revolt had been confined to the north, and on Aug. 31, 1839, a truce, the Convention of Vergara, was finally signed.

For some time the Carlists remained inactive. Charles V died in 1855 and was succeeded by his son the Count of Montemolín, known as Charles VI, who unsuccessfully tried to reconcile Queen Isabella and the Carlists. A younger son of Don Carlos, Don Juan, succeeded Charles VI in 1861; and in 1868 a grandson, Don Carlos María de los Dolores, became Charles VII. When Isabella was deposed by revolution in 1868, Charles VII championed northern demands to restore the "legitimate" monarchy. Only the legalist arguments of Cándido Nocedal, the leading Carlist of Madrid, prevented civil war in 1871, when Amadeus, an Italian prince, became king; but after Amadeus' abdication in February 1873, the Carlists could no longer be restrained. Risings in the Basque provinces, Navarre, and parts of Catalonia forced the collapse of Spain's First Republic and the restoration of Alfonso XII, son of Isabella, in 1874. The new king's large-scale offensive finally forced Charles VII and 10,000 followers to flee to France on Feb. 28, 1876.

Modern Carlism. The pretender, Charles VII, lived until 1909, but no strong personality emerged after his death to carry on. Carlist energies increasingly were devoted to the Catholic Union party and various secular regionalist organizations. Only in the years immediately preceding the outbreak of the Spanish Civil War in 1936 did the Carlists reemerge as a separate party. They were an important Nationalist faction for a time under the leadership of Manuel Fal Conde, and the Navarrese militia (*requetés*) gave military support to the rebels in the Civil War. The ultraconservative character of Generalissimo Franco's government favored a more open role for modern Carlism, but it did not spread outside the north, and its persistent monarchist philosophy often brought it into conflict with the regime. The present Carlist pretender is French-born Carlos Hugo de Bourbon-Parma, who married Princess Irene of the Netherlands in 1964. He is not accepted, however, by all Carlists. See Bourbon—*Table III*.

Robert W. Kern
University of Massachusetts

CARLOMAN, kär'lō-man, was the name of several members of the Carolingian dynasty of the Franks, including:

Carloman (715–754), son of Charles Martel. On Charles Martel's death in 741, Carloman and his brother Pepin the Short, succeeded him as mayors of the palace, respectively, in Austrasia and Neustria. As mayors, they controlled the government of these kingdoms. Under pressure of revolts by both the Swabians and the Aquitanians in 743, Carloman and Pepin designated Childeric III king of the Franks, the throne having been vacant since 737. In 747, Carloman ceded his powers to Pepin and became a monk.

Carloman (751–771), second son of Pepin the Short. Pope Stephen III consecrated Carloman king at St.-Denis, in 754, together with his older brother Charlemagne and their father Pepin. On Pepin's death in 768, the brothers divided the Frankish realm. In a diplomatic settlement, Carloman and Charlemagne married daughters of the Lombard king Desiderius in 770. When Carloman died in 771, his widow fled with their children to her father's court. When Charlemagne conquered Lombardy in 774, they vanished without a trace.

Carloman (828–880), son of Louis the German. In 856 and later he defended Bavaria from Bohemian and Moravian attacks. He rebelled against his father several times from 861 until 865, when he took viceregal control of Bavaria and Carinthia. On Louis the German's death in 876, Carloman became king of Bavaria, and in 877 he became king of Italy. He fell ill and was incapacitated until his death in 880.

Carloman (died 884), son of Louis II the Stammerer, West Frankish king. On the death of Louis II in 879, the legitimacy of the birth of Carloman and his brother Louis, and thus their right to the throne, was disputed by partisans of Charles the Simple, their father's son by a later marriage. However, a faction of the kingdom's most powerful men crowned them, exacting an oath that made their title conditional upon their observing established laws and privileges. Generally acknowledged as kings by 880, Carloman and Louis III divided the realm. On Louis' death in 882, Carloman became sole ruler.

K. F. Morrison, *University of Chicago*

CARLOS I, kär'lo͞osh (1863–1908), king of Portugal. Carlos, whose name is sometimes Anglicized as Charles, was born in Lisbon on Sept. 28, 1863. He was the son of Luís (Louis) I of the house of Bragança and Maria-Pia of Savoy. In 1886 he married Marie Amélie of Orléans, daughter of the Count of Paris. A man of wide culture, Carlos was an accomplished painter and oceanographer.

His reign began in 1889 and was fraught with internal and external problems. There were strained relations with Brazil and an uprising in Portuguese India. At home, a deteriorating financial situation and republican agitation brought on a revolt in Oporto in 1891. In an attempt to solve these problems, the king gave dictatorial powers to João Franco, his prime minister, in 1907. Oppressive decrees caused a fresh revolt in Lisbon in 1908, and both he and his eldest son, Luís, were assassinated as they returned to the capital on Feb. 1, 1908. His second son, Manuel, succeeded him as Manuel II.

Gregory Rabassa, *Columbia University*

CARLOS, Don kär'lōs, (1545–1568), crown prince of Spain, who was one of the most enigmatic figures in Spanish history. He was born at Valladolid on June 8, 1545, the son of Philip II and Maria of Portugal. As a boy Carlos was sickly and felt particularly alone after his mother's death. In adolescence he became so pathologically disturbed that his father was completely alienated from him. Matters reached a climax in January 1568 when the King accused Carlos of conspiring against him. Don Carlos was imprisoned on January 18 without being charged with any specific crime. The mysterious circumstances surrounding his death in a Madrid prison on July 24, 1568, gave rise to his legend. William of Orange, in his *Apology* (1581), charged that Philip had poisoned Don Carlos to prevent him from siding with the Protestant rebels in the Netherlands. Schiller in his play *Don Carlos* shows the prince about to flee to Holland to become a Protestant, no longer able to bear the love he felt for his stepmother, Elizabeth of Valois. Verdi's opera *Don Carlos* is based on Schiller's drama.

Robert W. Kern
University of Massachusetts

CARLOS, Don, name of several pretenders to the Spanish throne. See Carlism.

CARLOTA, kär-lō'tä (1840–1927), empress of Mexico. She was born near Brussels, Belgium, on June 7, 1840, the daughter of King Leopold I of the Belgians. At 17 she was married to Archduke Maximilian of Austria. For two years the young couple lived in Milan as the Austrian regents, but when Austria lost Lombardy in 1859, they went into retirement near Trieste. Ambitious and restless, Carlota was delighted when her husband was offered an imperial throne in Mexico, to be backed by French troops as part of a grandiose scheme of Napoleon III.

They landed in Mexico on May 28, 1864, and were welcomed only by the conservative pro-church party that had joined Napoleon III in inviting them. Benito Juárez was actually legal president of Mexico, and he harassed the forces of Maximilian and Carlota for three years. Carlota herself was interested in Mexican history and legend and desired to help the Mexican Indians. She adopted as her son the young grandchild of the former Mexican emperor, Agustín de Iturbide. She remodeled Chapultepec Castle, and established Mexican women's charitable organizations.

When the forces of Juárez began to win, Napoleon III withdrew his troops. Carlota, determined to get help to maintain the throne, returned to Europe alone in August 1866. Napoleon III refused to back Maximilian further, and the pope could not help her financially. On Oct. 7, 1866, in the pope's presence, Carlota lost her mind and never recovered. She never knew of Maximilian's execution in Mexico in 1867 and lived in seclusion near Brussels until her death on Jan. 19, 1927.

HELEN MILLER BAILEY, *East Los Angeles College*

CARLOW, kär'lō, is a small inland county in Ireland, in the southern part of the province of Leinster. It is watered by the Barrow and Slaney rivers. Its main crops are barley and sugar beets. Sheep and cattle are raised, and some coal is mined. The principal manufactures are sugar, footwear, flour, and razor blades.

Carlow town, the county seat, was a Norman stronghold, and one wall remains of the 12th century Norman castle. There is an early 19th century Gothic-style cathedral in the town.

Carlow figured prominently in the great insurrection of 1798. The insurgents attacked the town but were beaten off with heavy losses. Father John Murphy, leader of the rebels, was executed at Tullow, where a monument has been erected to his memory. Population: (1966) of the county, 33,479; of the town, 7,787.

THOMAS FITZGERALD
Department of Education, Dublin

CARLSBAD, kärlz'bad, a city in southwestern California, in San Diego county, is situated on the Pacific coast, 32 miles (51 km) north of San Diego. It is a beach resort and an important center of flower, fruit, and vegetable culture. The Mission San Luis Rey de Francia, founded in 1798, is now a Franciscan monastery. Carlsbad Beach State Park is just south of the city. The Palomar Observatory is 33 miles (53 km) to the east. The Army and Navy Academy, a boarding and day school for boys, was moved to Carlsbad from Pacific Grove in 1937.

Originally known as Frazier's Station, the site was renamed Carlsbad in 1880, when water from its mineral springs was analyzed and found to have a mineral content almost identical with that of one of the wells at the spa of Carlsbad in Europe. Carlsbad was incorporated in 1952 and has a city manager. Population: 14,944.

GEORGINA D. COLE, *Carlsbad City Library*

CARLSBAD, kärlz'bat, a town in Czechoslovakia, is one of the most celebrated health resorts in Europe. Carlsbad (Czech, Karlovy Vary; German, Karlsbad) is on the Ohre River about 70 miles (110 km) west of Prague, in northwestern Bohemia. Famous for its mineral springs, it was once one of the most fashionable watering places of the European aristocracy.

The town is set in lovely scenery at an altitude of about 1,165 feet (356 meters). Its 19 alkaline-sulfur springs have an estimated daily flow of some 2 million gallons (7.6 million liters). Water temperatures in the various springs range from 47° to 165° F (8° to 75° C).

Carlsbad was founded by the Emperor Charles IV in 1349 and was made a free town by Joseph I. in the early 1700's. Besides the spa, it has long-established glass and porcelain industries. Population: (1961) 42,735.

CARLSBAD, kärlz'bad, a city in southeastern New Mexico, the seat of Eddy county, is on the Pecos River, 70 miles (113 km) south of Roswell. It is a trading center in an irrigated farming section producing cotton, grain sorghum, alfalfa, and cattle. Potash mining and refining are important activities. Carlsbad is a tourist center and the gateway to Carlsbad Caverns National Park, 20 miles (32 km) to the southwest. Annual festivals are the rodeo in May and the Pecan Festival in November. A branch of the New Mexico State University is in the city.

Carlsbad was settled in the late 1880's with the formation of the Pecos River irrigation project promoted by the Eddy brothers, cattlemen in the area. The town was originally known as Eddy, but the name was changed to Carlsbad in 1899 when its spring waters were discovered to be similar to those of the German spa, Carlsbad (now Karlovy Vary, Czechoslovakia). Government is by mayor and council. Population: 21,297.

HELEN BOND MELTON, *Carlsbad Public Library*

CARLSBAD CAVERNS NATIONAL PARK, kärlz'-bad, is in the foothills of the Guadalupe Mountains, in southeastern New Mexico, 27 miles (43 km) southwest of Carlsbad. The caverns are a vast complex of underground chambers and corridors, only partly explored.

The deepest explored cavern is 1,013 feet (309 meters) below the earth's surface. The largest, called the Big Room, is at a depth of 750 feet (228 meters). It is large enough to accommodate 14 football fields and high enough to contain a 22-story building. In it are the caverns' largest known formations, including the Giant Dome, which is 62 feet (19 meters) high and 16 feet (5 meters) thick. From the Bat Cave, only 200 feet (60 meters) down and near the caverns' entrance, huge swarms of bats spiral skyward each summer evening at sundown.

The cavern-building process began some 60 million years ago when underground water penetrated hairline cracks in an immense block of limestone, gradually creating chambers and corridors. Between 5 million and 1 million years ago the water table lowered and the caverns filled with air. Calcite and aragonite deposited by evaporating lime-laden groundwater then began building the beautiful cavern formations: glistening red, tan, yellow, and white stalactites, helictites, stalagmites, columns, and flowstone.

The cavern area was set aside as a national monument in 1923 and became a national park in 1930. The park covers 73 square miles (189 sq km). Visitors who wish to see the caverns must join tours, which are conducted by National Park Service personnel every day throughout the year. Tours begin at the visitor center and descend either by elevator or through the natural cave entrance. The complete tour is 3 miles (5 km) long and lasts 3½ hours. The deepest tour descent is 829 feet (253 meters).

George B. Hartzog, Jr.
Director, National Park Service

CARLSBAD DECREES, kärls-bät, the resolutions enacted by the Diet of the German Confederation in 1819 to suppress liberal movements in Europe. On March 23, 1819, Karl Sand, a member of a liberal student organization, the Burschenschaft, assassinated the dramatist August von Kotzebue, an agent of the Russian czar. Shortly thereafter an attempt was made on the life of the minister-president of Nassau. These deeds frightened the authorities, and Prince Metternich, chancellor of Austria, convinced King Frederick William IV of Prussia that measures were needed to curb liberalism.

Metternich met with ministers of various German states at Carlsbad. Here, from Aug. 6 to 31, 1819, the representatives of Austria, Prussia, Saxony, Bavaria, Württemberg, Baden, Nassau, Hanover, and Mecklenburg decided that the Burschenschaft and all other secret societies were to be dissolved; a uniform press censorship was to be established; state commissioners were to supervise instruction at the universities; and a central investigation commission at Mainz was to investigate all revolutionary activity. Laws giving effect to the measures were enacted by the Diet on Sept. 20, 1819. They were finally repealed by the Diet on April 2, 1848. The Carlsbad Decrees have become a byword for extreme police control and censorship.

Ernst C. Helmreich, *Bowdoin College*

CARLSON, kärl'sən, **Anton Julius** (1875–1956), Swedish-American physiologist, who contributed importantly to a better understanding of virtually every body organ and system. In his most important work he demonstrated, by experiments upon himself and his associates, that hunger pangs are caused by contractions of the stomach and that the flow of gastric juices is rhythmic and does not entirely depend on the stimulus of food. He also made basic advances in determining the cause of diabetes, and he elucidated the relationship between nerve conduction and muscle contraction. He clarified many aspects of lymph formation, the heartbeat, nutrition, thirst, salivary secretion, thyroid function, and the parathyroid control of blood calcium.

Carlson was born in Svarteborg, Sweden, on Jan. 29, 1875. He went to the United States at the age of 16, and earned his Ph. D. at Stanford University in 1902. His researches there and at the marine laboratories in Woods Hole, Mass., on nerve conduction, muscle contraction, and the cause of the heartbeat led to his appointment as professor in the department of physiology at the University of Chicago, where he became department head. He retired in 1940.

Carlson wrote some 250 scientific treatises and *Control of Hunger in Health and Disease* (1916). He also coauthored, with Victor Johnson, *Machinery of the Body* (1937). Carlson died in Chicago on Sept. 2, 1956.

Victor Johnson
Coauthor of "Machinery of the Body"

CARLSON, kärl'sən, **Chester F.,** (1906–1968), American physicist and lawyer, who invented xerography. He was born in Seattle, Wash., on Feb. 8, 1906. Carlson was fascinated by graphic arts from childhood. While in high school he published a little magazine for amateur chemists with an old printing press he had acquired by working for a printer. The need for simple copying became very apparent to Carlson when he worked as a patent lawyer in the 1930's. He noted that there never were enough carbon copies of patent specifications. The way to get more copies involved retyping or making photocopies.

Carlson first experimented with employing photoelectric effects for copying in his apartment in Jackson Heights, N. Y. In a key experiment, Carlson made a 2 by 3 inch (5 by 8 cm) sulfur-coated zinc plate and charged the plate in the dark by rubbing it with a cotton cloth. After placing a transparent celluloid ruler having black scale markings on the charged plate, he exposed with an incandescent lamp for about 10 seconds to produce an electrostatic latent image on the plate. He then sprinkled a little lycopodium powder on the plate and gently blew away the loose powder. He obtained a perfect image in powder of the scale of the ruler. The same day he copied a glass plate on which he had printed "Astoria 10-22-38."

His first patent was issued in November 1940. After failing to interest over 20 companies in his invention, he signed an agreement with Battelle Development Corporation in 1944. In 1947, the Haloid Company, now Xerox Corporation, negotiated an agreement with Carlson, allowing Haloid to launch its own program to develop xerography. Xerography is now pursued by more than 50 companies. Carlson died in New York City on Sept. 19, 1968.

John H. Dessauer, *Xerox Corporation*

CARLSON, kärl'sən, **Evans Fordyce** (1896–1947), American Marine Corps officer, who commanded Carlson's Raiders in World War II. Born in Sidney, N. Y., on Feb. 26, 1896, Carlson joined the Army at 16. He was wounded in France in World War I and left the Army at 23 as a captain.

Carlson enlisted in the Marines in 1922. After 1933 he was mostly in China. As an observer with the Chinese forces in the Sino-Japanese War, he studied guerrilla warfare and Japanese tactics. He resigned from the Marines in 1939.

He returned to the Marines as a major in 1941 and was given command of the 2d Marine Raider Battalion (Carlson's Raiders). The Raiders became famous after landing from submarines on Aug. 17, 1942, on Makin Atoll to damage Japanese installations and gather intelligence. On Guadalcanal late in 1942 they killed 500 retreating Japanese, losing only 17 men. On Saipan, while rescuing an enlisted marine, Carlson was wounded. He retired as a brigadier general. Carlson died in Portland, Oreg., on May 27, 1947.

Carlson's Raiders were all volunteers. He chose hard men who liked to fight and taught them ruthless guerrilla methods. He insisted that his men know what they were fighting for. They fought a war of their own, with independent arrogance that sometimes irked Carlson's superiors.

Karl A. Schuon, *Author of "U. S. Marine Corps Biographical Dictionary"*

CARLSTADT, kärl'shtät (c. 1480–1541), was a German theologian and reformer. His real name was Andreas Rudolf Bodenstein; he took the name Carlstadt, or Karlstadt, from his town of birth in Bavaria. Educated at the University of Erfurt (1499–1503), he transferred to Cologne and then to the new University of Wittenberg. At Wittenberg he taught philosophy and championed the philosophical-theological system of Thomas Aquinas against the prevalent nominalism of Occam. In 1515 he went to Rome for further study and a doctor's degree in law.

Carlstadt's visit to Rome had much the same effect upon him as upon Luther; he renounced Thomism and adopted Augustinianism, with its stress on the impotence of the human will and the Pauline-Augustinian doctrine of salvation by grace alone. His 151 Theses, dated Sept. 16, 1516, show that he preceded Luther in challenging the papal system.

Despite their influence upon each other, Carlstadt and Luther were never warm friends. In 1521 the two were included in a papal bull of excommunication. Following this, Carlstadt began attacking the papal "corruptions" in earnest, in a book entitled *Papal Holiness.*

The following year he was invited to Denmark by King Christian II, to share in the reformation of the Danish church. His stay was brief, for his impatient temper antagonized both clergy and nobility. As often happens, the reformer denounced celibacy and at once took a wife. Returning to Wittenberg, he became the leader of the Protestants. But nine months later Luther also returned to Wittenberg and proposed measures, supported by Elector Frederick the Wise, designed to slow down the Reformation and retain the traditional rites and rubrics. The reaction of Carlstadt was to deny the necessity of the clerical order, and even, for a time, to abandon the ministry.

The rest of his life was spent mainly in exile, frequently in Switzerland, and often in poverty. His influence on the Reformation was exerted chiefly from 1518 to 1524. His flaming ardor for reform was never tempered with adequate prudence and practical good sense. He died at Basel on Dec. 24, 1541.

FREDERICK C. GRANT
Union Theological Seminary

CARLSTADT, kärl'stat, is an industrial borough in northeastern New Jersey, in Bergen county, about 8 miles (13 km) northeast of Newark. Its varied manufactures include chemicals, textiles, candles, and paints and varnishes. The land was bought cooperatively and settled about 1850 by German immigrants, who named the site for their leader, Carl Klein. Carlstadt, incorporated in 1894, is governed by a mayor and council. Population: 7,947.

CARLTON, kärl'tən, **Newcomb** (1869–1953), American engineer and executive, who led the expansion of the Western Union Telegraph Co. into a modern, worldwide system. Carlton was born in Elizabeth, N. J., on Feb. 19, 1869. After being associated with the Bell Telephone Company, he joined Western Union in 1910 and became its president in 1914. Although not an inventor, Carlton encouraged the use of many telegraphic devices that were previously considered impractical. He died at White Plains, N. Y., on March 13, 1953.

CARLYLE, kär-līl', **Thomas** (1795–1881), Scottish historian and social critic, who was the most important philosophical moralist of the early Victorian age. Carlyle's famous *French Revolution* (1837), like his other historical works, has a polemical intent and highly dramatic coloring that puts it outside the current of modern analytical historical study. His cult of the hero in history, especially as expounded in *On Heroes* (1841), has influenced modern proponents of authoritarian government.

The more thoughtful of Carlyle's contemporaries responded to his urgent prophetic picture of a materialistic, mechanistic, pauper-haunted England in the throes of the Industrial Revolution and rapidly approaching the brink of chaos. Deeply influenced by the stern morality of his Calvinist upbringing and by German idealism, Carlyle articulated the social and spiritual disorders of an age of declining religious faith, weakening social ties and purpose, and unpredictable change.

In the autobiographical *Sartor Resartus* (1833–1834), Carlyle maintains that the material world is, as it were, only the temporary clothing of a permanent spiritual reality. In *Past and Present* (1843) and other works of social criticism he hurls denunciations at the privileged classes of England—the aristocracy and the new industrial rich. He attacks the uselessness of the aristocracy because it either does not govern or governs only to protect its own special interests, and though he recognizes the energy and social value of the industrial bourgeoisie, he upbraids it for its "Mammonism"—that is, its exclusive faith in the profit motive and unregulated competition and its belief that the chief business of life is to buy cheap and sell dear. Especially effective are Carlyle's descriptions of the brutalized and starving poor, whose hunger and despair gradually turn into an incoherent rage to destroy.

Although Carlyle attacked specific abuses, such as the Corn Laws, which exploited the poor by artificially keeping up the price of grain, and the Poor Laws, which locked them up in workhouses, or "Bastilles" (as he called them), he was less a reformer of individual evils than a visionary moralist calling for a renovation of the spirit in both the individual and society. With the sternness of an Old Testament prophet, he preached renunciation, duty, work, and reverence. This exclusively moral analysis of an economic revolution has left Carlyle outside the mainstream of modern social thought. But he remains a great visionary mystic, who discerned and recorded in compelling language the spiritual and social upheavals caused by the emergence of modern industrial society.

LIFE

Early Years. Carlyle was born at Ecclefechan in Dumfrieshire, Scotland, on Dec. 4, 1795, the oldest son of James Carlyle by his second wife, Janet Aitken. A stonemason and farmer, the senior Carlyle was an "irascible, choleric," highly moral man; his mother, who won her son's lifelong devotion, was more gentle and yielding, but equally upright. They were a typical Scottish Calvinist family: hardworking, frugal, clannish, and pious. Throughout his life, Carlyle reflected his parents' moral earnestness, contempt for pleasure, and belief in the elect. But with his acceptance of self-denial and submission to authority, the hot-tempered Carlyle had had a streak of rebellion and pride, which first showed itself when, breaking his promise to his mother not to resort to violence, he trounced the school bully.

After three years at Annan Academy, Carlyle walked the 100 miles from his home to Edinburgh in order to prepare himself for the ministry at the university. Proud, awkward, silent, and very poor, he kept much to himself, reading omnivorously and distinguishing himself in mathematics. In 1814, disillusioned by the intellectual mediocrity of the university and dubious of his religious vocation, he turned for two years to tutoring in mathematics at his old school, scrupulously performing the hated duties of schoolmaster. Between 1816 and 1818, while he was a tutor at a Kirkcaldy school, Carlyle became a lasting friend of Edward Irving, a fellow instructor who later became a famous London preacher. After reading Hume and Gibbon in Irving's library, Carlyle completely lost his faith in orthodox Christianity. Burdened by religious uncertainty and without a real vocation, he was also rejected in his courtship of Mary Gordon, probably the original of Blumine, the lost beloved of *Sartor Resartus*.

New Interests. The next four years were the darkest in Carlyle's life. He gave up teaching to study for the bar in Edinburgh but soon abandoned that as well, eking out his living by writing articles for Brewster's *Edinburgh Encyclopaedia*. Tormented by dyspepsia and insomnia and suffering from the lack of a settled way of life, he experienced an acute spiritual crisis in the summer of 1822, movingly recorded in "The Everlasting No" and "The Everlasting Yea," chapters of *Sartor Resartus*. Nevertheless, even this gloomy period was a time of preparation. In 1819, Carlyle began to study German, thus fitting himself for his future role as a critic of German literature and philosophy. In 1821 he met, through Irving, his future wife, Jane Baillie Welsh. A wit, a beauty, a bluestocking, a minor heiress, and a writer of letters that have earned her a place in English literature, Jane Welsh found Carlyle both brilliant and bearish. Their five-year courtship finally led to marriage in 1826.

Meanwhile Carlyle was publishing translations and studies of German literature, meeting literary celebrities in London, and beginning a promising career as a writer. Even so he was still poor, and from 1828 to 1834 the couple lived at Mrs. Carlyle's farmhouse at Craigenputtock.

The Carlyles' famous marriage, revealed in his *Reminiscences* (1866), her letters, and J. A. Froude's biography, was characterized by deep love and equally deep conflict. Childless, and compatible chiefly on an intellectual plane, both of the Carlyles were thin-skinned and neurotic; they suffered from indigestion and sleeplessness, were driven wild by slight noises, and were constantly lacerated by each other's presence. Yet genuine tenderness united them, and their strife was lightened by humor and occasional flashes of ironic self-awareness.

Maturity. By 1831, Carlyle had achieved maturity as a writer. He had made something of a name for himself by introducing into England the transcendental thought of the German romantics—Goethe, Schiller, Fichte, and Richter. Now ready for ambitious independent work, he composed his spiritual autobiography *Sartor Resartus* and began work on a history of the French Revolution. In order to be near suitable collections of books, the Carlyles moved to London in 1834, where they remained thereafter.

The publication of *The French Revolution* in 1837 established Carlyle as a leading literary figure, and his subsequent works of social criticism enhanced his reputation. He gave fashionable public lectures and was soon a familiar sight in London drawing rooms, where the Carlyles became famous—he for his impassioned outbursts of eloquence, and his wife, in a lesser way, for her maliciously observant wit. They made many friends among the great, notably John Stuart Mill, Emerson, Dickens, Tennyson, Kingsley, Browning, Ruskin, and Mazzini. Serious-minded young people wrote to Carlyle asking for counsel. With Emerson's help he became widely known in the United States and was for the last four decades of his life a venerated sage and guide—a position formally recognized by his election as Lord Rector of Edinburgh University in 1865.

Despite his fame, Carlyle remained as restless, unhappy, and tormented by nervous disorders as he had been as an obscure young man in Scotland. He was often at odds with his wife, struggled painfully for 14 years with his monumental but comparatively sterile *Frederick the Great* (1858–1865), and took an increasingly gloomy view of the future of English society. After the death of his wife in 1866, Carlyle sank gradually into a gloomy old age, devoting himself to her memory and publishing only occasionally. He died in London on Feb. 5, 1881.

WORKS

Studies in German Literature. Carlyle's articles for the *Edinburgh Encyclopaedia* (1819–1823) are conscientious and intelligent but give almost no hint of his genius or of his flamboyantly personal mature style. The fructifying element of the first ten years of Carlyle's literary life was his absorption in German poetry and philosophy, an involvement that led him to break the mold of convention and formulate his own philosophy and style. His *Life of Schiller* (1825) shows the beginning of the process. Though conventionally and impersonally written, the work reflects Carlyle's immense enthusiasm for his subject and his identification with Schiller's idealism and with his struggles and ambitions as a writer and prophet.

In his essays on Goethe, Fichte, and Richter, Carlyle became the leading exponent in England of the new German romanticism, with its emphasis on individual imagination and emotion, and of German transcendental idealism, which stressed the primacy of mind. But Carlyle was not content merely to transmit the ideas of his masters. Ignoring Goethe's urbanity, liberalism, and epicureanism, Carlyle underscored his doctrine of renunciation. From Kant and Fichte, Carlyle took the idea of the subjectivity of time and space—the idea that the physical world is a mere projection of an inner reality—and transposed it into his own characteristic key. He interpreted Kant's categorical imperative as a sanction for the Calvinistic ethic of work and duty. Following Fichte, he began to formulate his idea of the hero, one who grasps the inner necessities of his times and imposes his vision on men and events by persuasion or force.

German thought gave Carlyle a point of vantage from which to attack the arid rationalism of French thought and, more important, the dominant English utilitarianism of Jeremy Bentham and James Mill. It gave him a philosophical basis for his opposition to empiricism, mechanism, and materialism, and it showed the way to the restoration of intuition, mystery, faith, and sacredness, without a return to orthodox Christianity. The application of this transcendental view directly to problems of modern life occurs first in *Signs of the Times* (1829) and *Characteristics* (1831), in which Carlyle attacks self-consciousness, preoccupation with logical and empirical analysis, and faith in the efficacy of tinkering with the machinery of social institutions —qualities that characterize modern man.

Sartor Resartus. The central book of Carlyle's career, *Sartor Resartus* (1833–1834, "The Tailor Retailored"), was composed in 1830–1831, during his isolation at Craigenputtock. Its first readers received it with "unqualified disapprobation," and Carlyle wrote to his brother, "A very singular piece I assure you! It glances from Heaven to Earth and back again in a strange satirical frenzy, whether fine or not remains to be seen." The basic conception of the book is that all the phenomena of nature and society are merely "clothes," the outward trappings of an invisible reality. The material world is but the covering of the spiritual world, and the institutions of society, being only old clothes, are due to be discarded when they wear out. The social clothing handed down from the past has been patched over and over and is now almost in tatters, a theme on which Carlyle plays pyrotechnical variations that range from explosive humor to tragic seriousness.

Sartor Resartus is narrated by an anonymous English editor who has come into the possession of the manuscripts of the German Teufelsdröckh (devil's dung), who is professor of Allerleiwissenschaft (things in general) at the University of Weissnichtwo (nowhere). The manuscripts, carelessly tossed together in 12 bags, form a book entitled *Clothes, Their History and Influence,* a brilliant chaos through which the editor gropes for the history of the author's life and thought and adds to the confusion with learned allusions, frequent digressions, and flights of fancy and vituperation.

The work is divided into three books. Books 1 and 3 are concerned primarily with general ideas—the spiritual nature of the world, the symbolism of matter, the inferiority of logic to spiritual insight—and the application of these ideas to society and the individual soul.

Book 2 is a disguised autobiography, in which Carlyle freely alters the outward events of his own life but remains faithful to its inner drama. He outlines the stages of this drama in three famous chapters. First, Teufelsdröckh recounts his fall into melancholy negation when he loses his sweetheart Blumine and comes to see the world as a purposeless machine of which he is the passive victim ("The Everlasting No"). Second, in his despair he wanders aimlessly from nation to nation until he discovers that if the world is only a man-destroying machine he can at least hate that fact and thus continue to exist; freed thereby from his paralysis he regains contact with the outside world ("The Centre of Indifference"). Third, he learns to renounce all expectations of personal happiness and regains his soul through work and human fellowship ("The Everlasting Yea"). The morality is close to that of the conventional Christian emphasis on self-sacrifice and duty at the expense of the body and pleasure. But God has been replaced by the abstract principle of transcendence, and the hero's salvation comes through moral rather than religious conversion.

Carlyle's style reached maturity in *Sartor Resartus.* It is a compound of traditional pulpit oratory, the language of transcendentalism, and the homely, forceful speech of Carlyle's boyhood. It is full of jagged idioms, "German" involutions of syntax, odd compound words, and strained grammatical combinations. In its nervous intensity and aggressive individuality, Carlyle's prose represents the breakup of the measured and cadenced prose of the Enlightenment and prepares the way for the stylistic development of such later writers as Dickens and Ruskin.

"The French Revolution." The public acclaim of *The French Revolution* (1839) was preceded by a severe trial of Carlyle's endurance. He loaned the manuscript of the first volume to John Stuart Mill, whose maid accidentally burned it, so that Carlyle had to undertake the agonizing task of rewriting the whole from memory without the aid of notes. The most coherently organized of his works, *The French Revolution* constitutes one of his chief claims to literary merit. Breaking with the older tradition of English historians, Carlyle paid less attention to strictly military and political history than to the great mass movements and tides of opinion and passion that underlie specific events. With epic scope and energy he traced the revolution from its sources in the folly of the aristocracy and royal family, the misery of the poor, and the reforming zeal of men of letters, through the Reign of Terror, and to the rise of Napoleon. The dozens of richly drawn biographical sketches and scenes of mob action are saturated with his nightmare vision of violence and destruction. Carlyle saw the revolution as a necessary purgation of a sick social order and refused to treat the victims of the Reign of Terror with the sentimental pathos usually accorded to them. Although he abhorred the democracy that the revolution heralded, he saw only justice in the destruction of the old order. A tract for the times as well as a history, *The French Revolution* is Carlyle's warning that if there is in England no far-reaching reform from above, there will be irresistible revolution from below.

"On Heroes, Hero-Worship, and the Heroic in History." The last of four series of public lectures, *On Heroes* (1841) has always been popular because of its relatively colloquial and straightforward style. Carlyle treats the hero as divinity (the Teutonic god Odin), as prophet (Mahomet), as poet (Dante and Shakespeare), as priest (Luther and Knox), as man of letters (Johnson, Rousseau, and Burns), and as king (Cromwell and Napoleon). As he presents dramatic, poetically colored narratives of his heroes, Carlyle also elaborates his idea of the hero. The common quality that unites these apparently diverse men is an intellectual ability to pierce through the sham and cant that make up most of ordinary life to expose its underlying significance. The hero as writer expresses the deepest reality of his age, and the hero as man of action expresses its deepest historical necessity for change. Great men create the values by which other men exist, and their fitness to instruct or to rule justifies their claim to obedience and reverence. A great man, in short, is a direct instrument of the Divine Will, and his words and deeds have the quality of revelation. Despite the fact that in discussing his military heroes Carlyle sometimes comes close to asserting that might proves right, it remains that the ultimate source of his heroes' authority is always spiritual.

"Past and Present." The essay *Past and Present* (1843) combines an evocative account of 12th century monastic life with incisive social criticism of modern times. Emerson described the work as an "*Iliad* of English woes," but it is also a celebration of medieval England. Carlyle presents a contrast that fascinated the Victorian imagination: that between an old Saxon serf living in the Middle Ages, with its organic society, unquestioning faith, and virile enforcement of authority, and a workman in the modern age, with its fragmentation, skepticism, and vacillating leadership. The serf was restricted in many ways, but he was guaranteed food, shelter, and protection against enemies and had a permanent and recognized place in society. The modern workman, on the other hand, is free, but he is bound to society only by his exchange of labor for wages, and if he is thrown out of work he loses, at one blow, food, shelter, protection, and his place in society; his freedom is little more than freedom to starve. In opposition to the idea of freedom, Carlyle advocates a society in which all men are bound together in a web of privileges and duties and in submission to authority.

The hero of *Past and Present* is Samson, Abbot of Bury St. Edmunds. He is drawn from Carlyle's reading of the 12th century *Chronicle of Jocelyn of Brakeland* and developed into the purest embodiment of Carlyle's conception of the creative power of the hero. With selfless devotion, Samson gives his life to driving out sloth with energy, replacing chaos with order, and turning waste into productivity. He restores his decaying abbey, courageously and skillfully threads the tangled politics of the time, and supports an impersonal ideal of justice against pressure from both foes and friends.

Although Carlyle does not propose a return to feudalism, he insists that the problem of government—how to achieve the rule of the wise—has not changed. Political democracy, which he pessimistically sees as inevitable, will merely submerge the superior man in mediocrity, and modern society is probably doomed to centuries of degradation until the democratic experiment proves itself bankrupt. Carlyle concludes with a plea for an aristocracy of talent and dedication to come forward to save England.

Later Writings. By 1850, Carlyle had completed the most important part of his work. He had developed his characteristic style as a narrative artist and a thinker, and he had delivered the substance of his message. Although he did valuable work in the latter half of his life, he became increasingly rigid and insistent, so that he often refused to correct even errors of fact in his writings. His early radicalism hardened into a disconcerting attachment to force and authority.

The two major historical works of Carlyle's later life show an increasingly sure faith that history is simply the biography of great men. Both works are concerned with warriors and statesmen in a revolutionary age. His *Oliver Cromwell* (1845) rescues Cromwell from the denunciation conventional among English historians and treats him as a divinely inspired seer who always acted from a passionate conviction that he was doing God's will. If the picture is in the main convincing, Carlyle's deliberate distortion of evidence has done no service to his reputation as an artist and a historian. The massive *Frederick the Great* (1858–1865) turns Frederick into a kind of abstract Ruler and is bloated with uncontrolled detail. Despite splendid passages it is an arid work, ridden by the thesis of Frederick's unwavering rightness in all that he did.

Carlyle's later works of social criticism exhibit the same increasing rigidity. *Latter-Day Pamphlets* (1850) goes over much the same ground as his earlier writings, but with increased asperity. *Shooting Niagara, and After?* (1867) is another fulmination against the spread of democracy, occasioned by the Second Reform Bill, which widened the franchise. Only in the nostalgia and tenderness of some of his *Reminiscences* (1866) is the genius of Carlyle evident in his old age.

MASON COOLEY, *Columbia University*

Bibliography

Carlyle's Works

Carlyle, Alexander James, ed., *Letters of Thomas Carlyle to John Stuart Mill, John Sterling, and Robert Browning* (London 1923).

Carlyle, Alexander James, ed., *Love Letters of Thomas Carlyle and Jane Welsh* (London 1909).

Slater, Joseph, ed., *Correspondence of Carlyle and Emerson* (New York 1964).

Trail, H. D., ed., *Centenary Edition of the Works of Thomas Carlyle*, 30 vols. (London 1896–1899; New York 1896–1901).

Critical Works

Bentley, Eric C., *A Century of Hero-Worship*, 2d ed. (Boston 1957).

Cazamian, Louis, *Carlyle* (Paris 1913).

Froude, James Anthony, *Thomas Carlyle*, 2 vols. (London 1882).

Harrold, Charles Frederick, *Carlyle and German Thought: 1819–1834* (New Haven 1934).

Lehmann, Benjamin Harrison, *Carlyle's Theory of the Hero* (Durham, N. C., 1928).

Neff, Edward Emery, *Carlyle* (New York and London 1932).

Roe, Frederick William, *The Social Philosophy of Carlyle and Ruskin* (New York 1921).

Symons, Julian, *Thomas Carlyle: The Life and Ideas of a Prophet* (New York 1952).

Tennyson, George B., *Sartor Called Resartus* (Princeton 1966).

Young, Louise Merwin, *Thomas Carlyle and the Art of History* (Philadelphia 1939).

CARMACK, kär′mak, **Edward Ward** (1858–1908), American prohibitionist, public official, and journalist. He was born in Sumner county, Tenn., on Nov. 5, 1858. He attended the Webb School in Culleoka, Tenn., studied law, and was admitted to the bar in 1879. Between 1888 and 1896 he edited, successively, the Columbia *Herald*, the Nashville *American*, and the Memphis *Commercial Appeal*.

A popular prohibitionist editor and a Democrat, he served in the House of Representatives (1897–1901) and in the Senate (1901–1907). In 1906 he ran for governor of Tennessee, but lost to Malcolm R. Patterson. Undaunted, Carmack carried the prohibitionist crusade to the state legislature in 1908. In the volatile atmosphere before the legislature met, Carmack was killed in Nashville on Nov. 9, 1908 by supporters of Patterson. The legislature subsequently passed a state prohibition law.

RONALD A. WELLS, *Simmons College*

CARMAGNOLE, kȧr-mȧ-nyôl′, a popular song and dance of the French Revolution. The song contained 12 couplets and the following refrain:

Dansons la Carmagnole,
Vive le son, vive le son,
Dansons la Carmagnole,
Vive le son du canon.

The author and composer of the song are unknown. It first appeared in 1791 and was subsequently sung at festivals and executions and during eruptions of popular discontent. Later, the name "Carmagnole" was applied to the National Guards, to enthusiastic supporters of the Revolution, and to a style of jacket popular with the Revolutionists.

CARMAN, Bliss (1861–1929), Canadian poet and critic. He was born William Bliss Carman at Fredericton, New Brunswick, on April 15, 1861. He received several degrees from the University of New Brunswick and later studied at Edinburgh and Harvard universities. In 1888 he moved to New York City, where he lived most of his life. Carman became literary editor of the New York *Independent* in 1890 and later held editorial positions on several American magazines, including *Current Literature,* the *Atlantic Monthly,* and *Cosmopolitan.* He died at New Canaan, Conn., on June 8, 1929.

Writings. Carman's poetry was impressionistic, filled with strong cadences, powerful—if imprecise—emotions, wistfulness and nostalgia, and sensuous imagery. His most popular work was the exuberantly optimistic *Vagabondia* series, written in collaboration with the American poet Richard Hovey—*Songs from Vagabondia* (1894), *More Songs from Vagabondia* (1896), and *Last Songs from Vagabondia* (1901). Among other collections of Carman's verse are *Low Tide on Grand Pré* (1893), *Behind the Arras* (1895), *April Airs* (1916), and *Wild Garden* (1929). In his theoretical writings, including *The Friendship of Art* (1904), *The Kinship of Nature* (1904), and *The Making of Personality* (1908), Carman spoke of an ideal poetry based on affirmation of universal brotherhood and love of nature.

MICHAEL GNAROWSKI
Sir George Williams University, Montreal

Further Reading: Cappon, James, *Bliss Carman and the Literary Currents and Influences of His Time* (Toronto 1930); Stephens, Donald G., *Bliss Carman* (New York 1966).

CARMARTHENSHIRE, kär-mär′thən-shir, is a county in southern Wales, with a coastline deeply indented by Carmarthen Bay and facing the Bristol Channel. Carmarthen, the county town, is 59 miles (94 km) northwest of Cardiff. The county, which is the largest in Wales (919 sq miles, or 2,380 sq km), is characterized by grassy hills and well-watered valleys with many small dairy farms. Industry is mostly in the southeast, where Llanelli (formerly Llanelly), the largest town, is the center of a great tinplate and steel industry based on nearby iron and anthracite.

The highest point is the Black Mountain (2,460 feet, or 750 meters), part of the Carmarthen Van massif. The coastline is mostly low with long stretches of sand, broken by the estuaries of the Towy, Taf, Gwendraeth, and Loughor rivers. Population: (1961) 167,736.

GORDON STOKES
Author of "English Place-Names"

CARMATHIAN, kär-mā′thē-ən, is the name given to peasant and bedouin revolutionary and terrorist outbreaks in Syria, Iraq, and Arabia in the late 9th and early 10th centuries. These uprisings against the culture, the religion, and the political controls of the Abbasid empire seem to have been crystallized by the work of missionary preachers, who belonged to the Ismaili sect of the Shiite branch of Islam.

Beginning in the 870's, the Ismailis preached political revolution as well as esoteric religious beliefs. The first violent outbursts in Iraq, Syria, and Arabia were named Carmathian after the leading Ismaili missionary in Iraq, Hamdan Qarmat; but in fact the various outbursts do not seem to have been connected to each other. In 900 there were peasant revolts led by Hamdan Qarmat in the region of Kufa, Iraq. From 901 to 906, bedouin tribes terrorized Syria, Palestine, and Mesopotamia. In eastern Arabia, Said al-Jannabi founded a Carmathian state whose inhabitants cut the pilgrimage routes, attacked Basra, Kufa, and even Baghdad (the Abbasid capital), and in 930 seized the sacred Black Stone from the Kaaba in Mecca. The Carmathian danger soon passed as a result of internal quarrels, and its ideological and political threat evaporated, though the Carmathian state in eastern Arabia survived into the 11th century.

IRA M. LAPIDUS
University of California at Berkeley

CARMEL, Mount, a mountain ridge in Israel, extending from the Valley of Jezreel to the Mediterranean Sea, where it forms a cape at the southern end of the Bay of Acre. From the sea the mountain stretches southeast toward the Jordan Valley. Covered with natural forests, it reaches a peak of 1,791 feet (545.5 meters). The city of Haifa is built at its foot.

Mt. Carmel has both historical and religious importance. Prehistoric Carmel man, considered a transitional form between Neanderthal and modern man, lived in caves on the mountain. In the Bible the mount was the site of the Prophet Elijah's victory over the prophets of Baal (I Kings 18:20–46) and of the residence of the Prophet Elisha. In Talmudic times (1st to 5th centuries A.D.) wine from Carmel grapes was famous. The monastery of the Carmelite order, organized in the 12th century, adorns the westernmost promontory of Mt. Carmel. Two villages of the Druzes, a dissident Muslim sect, and several Jewish kibbutzim (communal settlements), as well as the largest cement factory in Israel, are located there.

RAPHAEL PATAI, *Theodor Herzl Institute*

CARMEL-BY-THE-SEA is a residential city in western California, in Monterey county, about 130 miles (209 km) south of San Francisco. Situated south of Monterey Bay on the Pacific coast, at the southern end of the Monterey Peninsula, the city is a vacation spot noted for the natural beauty of its setting.

Carmel-by-the-Sea was founded in 1904 by several artists, as a retreat. It is still an art center and the home of many artists and writers. The scenic 17-Mile Drive runs north along the coast from Carmel to Pacific Grove. The Mission San Carlos Borromeo del Rio Carmelo, established in 1770, is south of the city. Incorporated in 1916, Carmel is governed by a mayor and council. Population: 4,525.

CARMELITES, kär′mə-lītes, a mendicant order of the Roman Catholic Church. It was founded as an order of hermits about 1200 A.D. on Mt. Carmel in Palestine. Gradually the Carmelites turned toward the mendicant way of life. As a result, the members of the order were forbidden to own property and the order as a whole could not have possessions. The members therefore subsisted by begging. The prophets Elijah and Elisha were for a long time considered to have been the founders of the order, but the medieval origin of the order is certain.

Early Years. The order's first authentic document is the brief, simple, and Biblically oriented rule that was approved between 1206 and 1214 by St. Albert, patriarch of Jerusalem. Unsettled conditions in Palestine made it necessary for some of the hermits to migrate to the West from 1238 onward. They went first to Cyprus and Sicily, and in 1242 they settled in England, where there was an important province of Carmelites until the Reformation. In 1247 a general chapter of the then hermit order met at Aylesford in England and petitioned the papacy for a revision of their eremitic rule. The revision of the rule was approved by Innocent IV on Oct. 1, 1247. Though minor in content, the revision set the hermits firmly into the mainstream of the mendicant tradition, principally by allowing the Carmelites to move to the towns. Thenceforth, the Carmelites closely resembled the Dominicans and the Franciscans. In 1274 the Second Council of Lyons decreed the dissolution of some mendicant orders but gave full approval to the Dominicans and Franciscans while suspending judgment on the Carmelites and the Augustinian Friars. In 1298, Pope Boniface VIII gave final and full approval to the latter two orders.

The Carmelites in 1287 gave up wearing the striped cloaks they had brought with them from the East and adopted the white mantle which gave them their popular name, Whitefriars. This white cloak is worn over the brown habit.

Growth. In the late 13th and in the 14th centuries the Carmelites spread rapidly throughout Europe. At the end of the first quarter of the 14th century they numbered about a thousand members in England alone. The Carmelites became noted for devotion to the Blessed Virgin; the official title was Brothers of the Order of Blessed Mary of Mount Carmel, and their churches were invariably dedicated to Mary. This devotion to the Virgin was symbolized in the wearing of the brown scapular. The order of Carmelite nuns began officially in the mid-15th century in the Low Countries during the reform by John Soreth, prior general of the order.

The reform of the order by two Spanish saints, Teresa of Ávila and John of the Cross, created in 1593 a separate order of Discalced (Barefoot) Carmelites, known now by the initials O. C. D. The older branch of the order, Carmelites of the Ancient Observance, have the initials O. Carm. In the mid-1960's the former group numbered more than 4,000 friars and the latter more than 3,000. Although many of their strict observances were modified over the years, they have retained their medieval liturgy.

The friars of the Ancient Observance underwent a reform during the 17th century that originated in France and is known as the Touraine Reform. This reform, like the one that produced the Discalced order, emphasized the interior life. Yet both branches of the order as friars of the church have always actively engaged in apostolic and missionary work. Nuns leading a cloistered life are affiliated with both branches of the order and constitute the Second Order. Their life is one of prayer and penance lived in an atmosphere of seclusion. Various congregations of sisters, affiliated to the order as Third Order members, work in the active apostolates of teaching, nursing, and the like. Laity are also affiliated to the order and are known as Third Order members or as Lay Carmelites.

The Discalced Carmelite nuns of the Second Order were the first women religious to settle in the American colonies when they came to Port Tobacco, Md., in 1790. The most famous Carmelite of recent times is St. Thérèse of Lisieux.

KEITH J. EGAN, O. CARM.
Mt. Carmel College, Ontario

Further Reading: Rohrbach, Peter-Thomas, O. C. D., *Journey to Carith: The Story of the Carmelite Order* (New York 1966); Smet, Joachim, O. Carm., *An Outline of Carmelite History* (Washington 1966).

CARMEN, kär′mən, is an *opéra-comique* composed in 1873 and 1874 by Georges Bizet (q.v.), with libretto by Henri Meilhac and Ludovic Halévy. The work is based on Prosper Mérimée's novel of the same name, dealing with Gypsy life and first published in 1847.

Production. *Carmen* was first produced at the Opéra-Comique in Paris on March 3, 1875. Its reception by the public and the press was cool. Its story of tragic illicit love was considered scandalous in a theater known for propriety and happy endings, and the music was condemned as dull, noisy, and tuneless.

The success of the opera dates from its production in Vienna in October 1875, and *Carmen* has since become a universal favorite with public and singers alike—one of the most popular operas in the French repertoire. (Famous singers of the title role have included Marie Galli-Marié, Minnie Hauck, Emma Calvé, and Risë Stevens.) *Carmen* is also the acknowledged masterpiece of *opéra-comique,* a form that is not the same as comic opera but implies an action and characters founded on everyday life, with spoken dialogue replacing the recitative of grand opera.

Libretto. The libretto, in which Bizet had a hand, ranks very high, although it has been criticized for introducing Micaela, a character not in the novel, as a foil to Carmen, and for the development of Mérimée's shadowy Lucas into the bullfighter Escamillo. But both of these figures throw the main characters, Carmen and José, into high relief and strengthen the theatrical impact of their conflict. Carmen's fascination remains undimmed, and the gradual deterioration of José from the simple peasant to the desperate outlaw and murderer is managed with exceptional skill.

Music. The music of *Carmen* is distinguished by rhythmic vitality, picturesque and subtle orchestration, irresistible melody, and above all by Bizet's ability to project himself into the sufferings of his characters. Whereas earlier *opéra-comique* had been superficial, sentimental entertainment, *Carmen* is a drama of unlimited passion expressed with a classical detachment and refined technique that owe much to Bizet's favorite composer, Mozart. In Bizet's *Carmen* the cool, ironic tone of Mérimée's novel found its operatic counterpart.

WINTON DEAN
Author of "Georges Bizet, His Life and Works"

CARMER, kär′mər, **Carl Lamson** (1893–), American folklorist, writer, and editor, noted for his books about American rivers. He was born in Cortland, N.Y., on Oct. 16, 1893, and took degrees at Hamilton College and Harvard University. His first book, published in 1934, was a collection of Alabamian folk tales, *Stars Fell on Alabama.* His other works include *Listen for a Lonesome Drum* (1936), a book on New York state folklore, and *Genesee Fever* (1941), a historical novel. Carmer edited the Rivers of America series and wrote *The Hudson* (1939) and *The Susquehanna* (1955). He also wrote a number of children's books.

CARMI, kär′mī, is a city in southeastern Illinois, the seat of White county, about 145 miles (233 km) southeast of Springfield, on the Little Wabash River. It is an oil production center and trading point in an agricultural area raising hogs, corn, wheat, oats, and soybeans. Manufactured products include underwear and soft drinks. Government is by mayor and council. Population: 6,033.

CARMICHAEL, kär′mī-kəl, **Hoagy** (1899–), American pianist, composer, and actor. He was born Hoagland Howard Carmichael at Bloomington, Ind., on Nov. 22, 1899. While studying law at Indiana University, Carmichael composed songs, played the piano and organ, and performed with such friends as "Bix" Beiderbecke and the Dorsey brothers. After receiving his law degree, Carmichael became a professional musician.

Following the success of his first big hit, *Stardust* (1930), he played and sang his songs in theaters, nightclubs, and films, and had his own television program. In 1951 he won an Academy Award for the song *In the Cool, Cool, Cool of the Evening.* His most famous songs include *Ole Buttermilk Sky, Georgia on My Mind, Two Sleepy People,* and *Heart and Soul.* He also composed the scores for the films *A Song Is Born* (1948) and *Here Comes the Groom* (1951) and appeared in the movies *To Have and Have Not* (1945), *The Best Years of Our Lives* (1946), and *Young Man with a Horn* (1950). Carmichael wrote two books, *The Stardust Road* (1946) and *Sometimes I Wonder* (1965).

CARMICHAEL, kär′mī-kəl, **Leonard** (1898–), American psychologist and educator. He was born in Philadelphia on Nov. 9, 1898. He graduated from Tufts College in 1921 and received his Ph.D. from Harvard in 1924. During the years before World War II he taught psychology at Brown, Princeton, and Rochester and became dean of arts and sciences at Rochester in 1936. In 1938 he returned to Tufts as its president, a position he held until 1952, when he was appointed director of the Smithsonian Institution in Washington, D.C. He became vice president for exploration and research of the National Geographic Society in 1964.

One of Carmichael's greatest contributions was his research on the development of newborn primates and humans. His best-known books include *Manual of Child Psychology* (1946), which he edited; *Basic Psychology* (1957); and *James Smithson and the Smithsonian Story* (1965).

MICHAEL G. ROTHENBERG
Columbia University

CARMICHAEL, kär′mī-kəl, **Stokely** (1941–), American civil rights leader, who was a leading spokesman for the "black power" (q.v.) philosophy among Negro Americans in the late 1960's. Born in Port of Spain, Trinidad, on June 21, 1941, Carmichael moved with his family to the Harlem section of New York City in 1952. He graduated from Howard University in 1964 with a degree in philosophy. At Howard he was a militant leader in the student government, working mainly through the Non-Violent Action Group.

An early member of the Student Nonviolent Coordinating Committee (SNCC), he was arrested many times while participating in its activities in the South during the first half of the 1960's. In 1964 he directed SNCC's Mississippi summer project, a civil rights and voter-training program. As chairman of SNCC from May 1966 to May 1967, he was closely identified with the organization's shift from a policy of nonviolence. Carmichael was the author (with Charles V. Hamilton) of *Black Power: the Politics of Liberation in America* (1967).

C. ERIC LINCOLN
Union Theological Seminary, New York

CARMICHAEL, kär′mīk-əl, **William** (died 1795), American diplomat of the Revolutionary period. Born into a wealthy Maryland family, he was educated at Edinburgh and then became active in London society. At the outbreak of the American Revolution, he joined the American commissioners (Silas Deane, Benjamin Franklin, and Arthur Lee) in Paris as a secretary. He served in the Continental Congress (1778–1779) and then returned to Europe as secretary to John Jay, minister plenipotentiary to Spain. Carmichael was well liked in Spain, but Jay, rightly or wrongly, believed his secretary sought to undermine his authority. When Jay departed for Paris in 1782, Carmichael remained in Madrid as America's chief diplomatic representative until shortly before his death there on Feb. 9, 1795.

DON HIGGINBOTHAM
University of North Carolina

Further Reading: Morris, Richard B., *The Peacemaker* (New York 1965).

CARMICHAEL, kär′mī-kəl, is a village in central California, in Sacramento county, about 8 miles (13 km) east of Sacramento. It is named for D.W. Carmichael, who developed Carmichael Colony here about 1910 as a residential and agricultural community. The village is now mainly residential. Carmichael is unincorporated and is governed by the supervisors of Sacramento county. Population: 37,625.

CARMINA BURANA, kär′mi-nə bū-ran′ə, is a "scenic cantata" by Carl Orff, first produced in Frankfurt in 1937. The libretto is from the *Carmina Burana,* a 13th century collection of verses found in the abbey of Benediktbeuren in Bavaria. They are the work of the Goliards, *vagantes,* or wandering scholars, who sang and begged their way from one medieval university to another. The texts, in medieval Latin, German, and French, praise wine and love and satirize the corrupt clergy.

The cantata consists of 25 pieces divided among three parts: "Springtime," "In the Tavern," and "The Court of Love." Believing that traditional instrumental forms of music were outworn, Orff tried in *Carmina Burana* and the other two works of the trilogy *Trionfi* to return to the spoken word and to the most basic elements of music by subordinating melody to text, using vigorous, exhaustively repeated rhythms and emphasizing the chorus and percussion.

CARMINE, kär'mən, is a natural dye made from carminic acid ($C_{22}H_{20}O_{13}$) extracted from the dried bodies of the female cochineal insect (*Dactylopius coccus*). The dye is used for biological stains, chemical indicators, an oil-color pigment, and in dyeing. It produces scarlet, crimson, purple, or claret when various metals are added. See also COCHINEAL INSECT.

CARMONA, kər-mō'nə, **António Óscar de Fragoso** (1869–1951), Portuguese general and politician. He was born in Lisbon on Nov. 24, 1869. Descended from a long line of military men, he graduated from the army school with honors and was commissioned in the cavalry in 1894. He became a general in 1922 and war minister of the republic in 1923.

Carmona assumed the post of prime minister six weeks after the coup of May 28, 1926, that established a military dictatorship. In November 1926 he was named provisional president. Elected president in March 1928, he named António de Oliveira Salazar as his finance minister. Salazar became prime minister in 1932. Carmona was reelected president for 7-year terms in 1935, 1942, and 1949, but his functions were mainly ceremonial. In 1947 he received the rank of marshal. He died in Lisbon on April 18, 1951.

GREGORY RABASSA, *Columbia University*

CARNAC, kȧr-nȧk', is an ancient Gallo-Roman town in northwestern France, on Brittany's southeastern coast It is on Quiberon Bay, near the small Quiberon Peninsula, in the department of Morbihan, about 17 miles (27 km) southeast of Lorient It is actually two villages: Carnac-Ville, the old town, about a mile from the shore, and the newer Carnac-Plage, on the water. Carnac-Plage, with its pine groves and ample beach, is an excellent bathing area.

Carnac is famous for the monuments of great stones (megaliths), just northeast of Carnac-Ville, that testify to Brittany's ancient civilization. This culture knew the use of some metals: gold and tin have been found in the sands along the south coast of Brittany, and hard stones, used for shaping tools and ornaments, have been unearthed. Among the thousands of megalithic monuments and mounds in and around Carnac are the long lines and clusters of menhirs (upright stones) of Ménec, Kermario, and Kerlescan; the dolmen (stones set up to form a chamber) of Kergavat; and the tumulus (a mound covering burial chambers) of St. Michel and of Moustoir. Carnac has an excellent prehistoric museum (Miln-Le Rouzic). Population: (1962) 1,606.

HOMER PRICE, *Hunter College, New York*

CARNALLITE, kär'nəl-īt, is a hydrous chloride of potassium and magnesium. It is named in honor of the 19th century German mining engineer Rudolf von Carnall. Carnallite, which is a source of potassium compounds and magnesium, generally occurs in granular or massive form. The transparent to translucent crystals have a greasy nonmetallic luster and are white to reddish. The most important deposit of the mineral is at Stassfurt, Germany. In the United States there are smaller deposits in Texas and New Mexico.

Composition, $KMgCl_3 \cdot 6H_2O$; hardness, 1; specific gravity, 1.6; crystal system, orthorhombic.

CARNAP, kär'nap, **Rudolf** (1891–1970), German-American logician and philosopher of science, who was a pioneer in the development of philosophical analysis and a leading member of the Vienna circle of logical positivists. He was born at Ronsdorf, Germany, on May 18, 1891, and studied at the University of Jena. From 1926 to 1931 he taught at the University of Vienna and then at the German University of Prague. After moving to the United States, he taught at the universities of Chicago and California at Los Angeles. He died in Santa Monica, Calif., on Sept. 14, 1970.

After 1945, Carnap concentrated on the construction of an ambitious system of inductive logic in which the traditional qualitative methods of Francis Bacon, J. S. Mill, and others are replaced by quantitative methods involving mathematical logic and probability theory. Carnap held an evolving series of philosophical positions. Common to all are: the view that philosophical problems are basically problems about language; the attempt to achieve clarity by replacing questions about natural language by corresponding questions about idealized languages formalized within the framework of symbolic logic; insistence upon the "principle of tolerance," recognizing the possibility of alternative adequate explications or "logical reconstructions" of philosophically important concepts corresponding to different choices of idealized languages; and the view that philosophy, like science, is properly an impersonal, cooperative enterprise. *The Philosophy of Rudolf Carnap* (1963), edited by Paul A. Schilpp, presents the range of his views.

RICHARD C. JEFFREY
Author of "The Logic of Decision"

THE MENHIRS OF CARNAC are now the property of the French government. In the past they were quarried for building stone by the people of the commune.

E. BOUBAT—RÉALITÉS, FROM PHOTO RESEARCHERS

CARNARVON, kär-när′vən, **George Edward Stanhope Molyneux Herbert, 5th Earl of** (1866–1923), English Egyptologist. He was born at Highclere, Berkshire, on June 26, 1866, and was educated at Eton and at Trinity College, Cambridge. He first went to Egypt in 1903, because of poor health. His interest in archaeology began when he visited several excavation sites, and he undertook his own excavation in 1906. He soon realized his own limitations, however, and enlisted the help of Howard Carter, an experienced and highly trained archaeologist who became the permanent supervisor of all Lord Carnarvon's excavations. Together they discovered several tombs dating from the 12th and 18th dynasties in the Valley of the Kings. Their most important discovery was in 1922, when they found the entrance to the long-sought tomb of Tutankhamen. The tomb, never before penetrated, consisted of several rooms and passages filled with gold and other treasures. Lord Carnarvon did not live to see the completion of this excavation. He died in Egypt on April 5, 1923.

PRISCILLA C. WARD
American Museum of Natural History

CARNARVON, Earls of. See HERBERT (family).

CARNARVONSHIRE. See CAERNARVONSHIRE.

CARNATIC, kär-nat′ik, European name commonly used for the region of southeastern India between the Eastern Ghats and the seacoast. It extends from Cape Comorin in the south to the northern end of the Coromandel Coast at the Kistna River delta. Wholly within the states of Madras and Andhra Pradesh, the Carnatic is about 550 miles (885 km) long, and its average width is 60 miles (97 km). Sometimes the term is used to include the Malabar Coast. Actually, it should refer to Kanara, which lies between the Eastern and Western Ghats in approximately the same area as the modern state of Mysore. The term was extended in meaning when the Vijayanagars conquered the south in the 14th century.

The coastal strip is divided into two sections. The eastern section is a low, level plain, and in the west is a belt of low hills. The soil is fertile, and the chief crops are rice, cotton, sugar, and coffee. Other commodities include teak and gold. The area is heavily populated, with modern industries in the large cities.

During its early history, the Carnatic was the home of three Tamil kingdoms—the Pandya, the Chola, and the Pallava. The region was unified under the Vijayanagar kings between 1336 and 1565, but a period of disintegration followed. In the early 18th century the Mughul (Mogul) emperor Aurangzeb appointed Zulfiqar Khan nawab, or governor, of the Carnatic. From this time it was ruled as an independent state although it owed allegiance to the Mughul emperors. After 1748, Anglo-French colonial rivalry and uprisings by the Indians dominated the politics of the area. Largely because of the successes of Robert Clive (q.v.), the region was administered by the British East India Company after 1752. British sovereignty, however, did not come until Hyder Ali was defeated in the Second Mysore War (1780–1784). The Carnatic was annexed in 1801, following the victory of Arthur Wellesley (later Duke of Wellington) over Tipu Sultan, and was later incorporated into Madras presidency.

HARRY STEWARD, *University of Toronto*

RUSS KINNE, FROM PHOTO RESEARCHERS

Carnation

Cross section of a carnation

CARNATION, a perennial of the pink family, widely cultivated for its large very double (many-petaled) fragrant flowers. Carnations can be grown for cut flowers in greenhouses or outdoors in some areas. In America the only species popularly called the carnation is *Dianthus caryophyllus*. Of Eurasian origin, this species has been widely modified by hybridization over the years. Today there are over a hundred varieties, all bearing flowers ranging in color from white to yellow, pink, and red. Some varieties have petals with two or three colors.

The carnation is a herbaceous plant with slender stems that arise from the base. It grows 3 to 5 feet (1 to 1½ meters) tall. The narrow opposite leaves are lanceolate in shape, and the flowers are borne at the ends of long stalks. Several flowers are produced on one stalk, but the commercial grower reduces this number to one by pinching off all the buds except the terminal bud. Thus larger flowers are produced.

Carnations are grown commercially from cuttings 3 inches (7½ cm) long, made from side shoots or the middle of the main stalk. They are taken from December to March, and rooted in sand and potted. They are always grown in a cool greenhouse, 50° to 60°F (10° to 15°C), with a comparatively dry atmosphere. Potted plants either are grown outside over summer or are planted directly in a greenhouse bench of newly sterilized soil. They are planted 8 to 10 inches (20 to 25 cm) apart in a row. Carnations bloom from October to June, each plant producing 18 to 24 flowers.

DONALD WYMAN
The Arnold Arboretum, Harvard University

CARNAUBA, kär-nô′bə, is the most important vegetable wax. Its combination of desirable properties occurs in no other commercial wax, natural or synthetic. In addition to an unusually high melting point of 182°–187°F (83°–86°C), carnauba has unsurpassed luster, unexcelled hardness, and superior emulsifying ("mixing") properties. These characteristics make carnauba ideal for self-polishing water-emulsion floor waxes. Carnauba is used for this purpose more than for any other, but it is also a common ingredient of shoe polishes, automobile polishes, and other high-luster polishes. Substantial quantities are used in carbon papers, and carnauba may be used in lubricating greases, electrical insulation, antifouling paints, lipsticks, and candles.

Carnauba, which was introduced in 1846, is produced only in northeastern Brazil, mainly in the states of Ceará and Piauí, where it occurs as a coating on the leaves of the carnauba palm (*Copernicia cerifera*). Carnauba palms grow to a height of about 35 to 40 feet (10.5–12 meters) and bear a crown of fan-shaped leaves at the end of the straight cylindrical trunk. The leaves are cut during the dry season; after being dried and shredded, they are flailed with a stick or by machine to remove the wax, which collects as a powder. Yellowish wax from unopened leaves is best. Older leaves produce inferior greenish waxes with impurities in the form of vegetative matter and dust.

LAWRENCE ERBE
University of Southwestern Louisiana

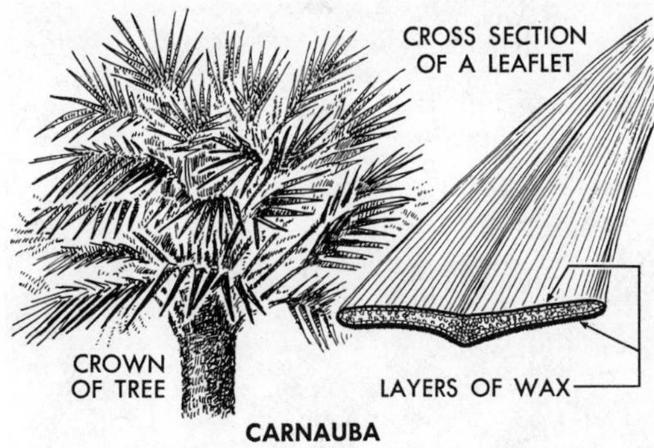

Carnauba, showing layers of wax on the leaf surfaces.

CARNÉ, kär-nā′, **Marcel Albert** (1909–), French film director, producer, and critic. He was born on Aug. 18, 1909, in Paris. He studied film technology, but went into the insurance business. In 1928, however, he turned to motion pictures, becoming assistant director to Richard Oswald for *Cagliostro* (1929), and in 1930 he directed the documentary *Nogent, eldorado du dimanche* and assisted René Clair in the direction of *Sous les toits de Paris*. He also served as film critic for the publication *Ciné-Magazine* from 1929 to 1933.

Carné first became prominent as a director with *Jenny* (1936). This was followed by nearly 20 films, of which the most famous is *Les enfants du paradis* (1944; *Children of Paradise*), a sensitive account of theatrical life in 19th century Paris. The scenarios for many of Carné's films were written by Jacques Prévert; their collaboration resulted in a distinctive style, known as "poetic realism."

CARNEADES, kär-nē′ə-dēz (c.214–c.128 B.C.), Greek philosopher, who, after Plato, was the most distinguished leader of the Academy, Plato's school. Carneades was considered to be the founder of the so-called "New Academy," in which Platonism was redirected toward skepticism in epistemology and eclecticism in ethics and politics.

While on a diplomatic mission from Athens to Rome in 155 B.C., Carneades seized the opportunity to give public lectures. His most adroit performance was two addresses given on successive days, one in favor of justice, one against. The sensation produced by the philosopher's ability to argue on both sides of a question marked the beginning of Roman interest in—and distrust of—Greek philosophy.

Carneades believed only in oral teaching and published no writings. But his opinions were carefully noted down and passed on by his pupils. His influence on Cicero is evident in Cicero's *Republic, On the Nature of the Gods,* and *On Fate.*

Opposing the dogmatism of the Stoic school, Carneades insisted that only probability is attainable, and man, therefore, should cultivate suspension of judgment. On this basis, he criticized the Stoic arguments in favor of the existence of the gods, divine providence and divination, and absolute determinism. He also opposed the notion of an eternal and unbroken chain of causality, maintaining that the self on its own initiative may change many of the conditions imposed from without, and was skeptical of the idea of natural law in politics because of the great variety in human customs.

RICHMOND Y. HATHORN
Author of "Tragedy, Myth, and Mystery"

Further Reading: Bevan, Edwyn, *Stoics and Sceptics* (New York 1913); Patrick, Mary M., *The Greek Sceptics* (New York 1929).

CARNEGIE, kär′nə-gē, **Andrew** (1835–1919), American iron and steel manufacturer and philanthropist, who probably did more than any other individual to bring world leadership in steel production to the United States. To aid education and research, he endowed educational institutions and foundations and gave funds for 2,800 free public libraries.

Early Career. Andrew Carnegie was born in Dunfermline, Scotland, on Nov. 25, 1835, the son of William Carnegie, a handloom weaver. Andrew came from a family with a literary and radical bent, and he early developed a dislike for privilege based on the accident of birth. The introduction of power looms and the depression of 1848 in Britain induced the Carnegies to move to the United States, where they settled at Allegheny, Pa., now part of Pittsburgh. Andrew found work in a cotton factory at $1.20 a week. His father, after brief experience in the factory, returned to his hand loom, selling his product door to door. After firing the furnace and operating a small engine in a bobbin-making shop, young Carnegie went to work in the office as a clerk and attended night school, where he studied double-entry bookkeeping.

In 1850 he took a job as a messenger boy in the telegraph office at Pittsburgh and started on a career that led in the classic tradition "from rags to riches." He systematically prepared himself for advancement by doing each job to the best of his ability and seizing every opportunity to take on new responsibilities. To speed his

BETTMANN ARCHIVE

Andrew Carnegie

work as a messenger boy, for example, he memorized the locations of business houses and the names of their employees. Meanwhile, he practiced telegraphy, sought experience in debating, and became acquainted with Shakespeare's plays in the local theater. In 1852 he got the chance to be a relief telegraph operator and performed so well that he shortly became a regular operator. When Thomas A. Scott went to Pittsburgh in 1853 as division superintendent of the Pennsylvania Railroad, he was so impressed by Carnegie that he hired him as his personal clerk and telegraph operator. From then on Carnegie's rise was rapid.

Scott came to depend heavily on Carnegie, and as the older man rose to be vice president of the Pennsylvania Railroad, the young telegrapher followed in his wake. In 1859, six years after joining the railroad, Carnegie himself became superintendent of the Pittsburgh division. Early in the Civil War he served as an assistant to Scott, who had been placed in charge of military transportation. Carnegie organized the eastern military telegraph and railroad service and had limited experience in the field, supervising the transportation of the wounded after the First Battle of Bull Run. It was during this period that he suffered some form of sunstroke that in later years, so he said, made him seek the coolness of Scotland during the summer months.

Industrial Success. Meanwhile, Carnegie had seen opportunities to augment his salary from other sources connected with the railroad. His first investment was made, at Scott's suggestion, in Adams Express stock. The $500 involved was raised by his mother's mortgaging their home. A one-eighth interest in Theodore Tuttle Woodruff's sleeping car company, whose product Carnegie had called to Scott's attention as desirable for the Pennsylvania Railroad, was financed by a loan from a local banker. Another important venture was an investment with Scott and other railroad officials in a firm that specialized in building iron railroad bridges, the Keystone Bridge Company. Among other enterprises, Carnegie also invested in the Superior Rail Mill and Blast Furnaces, the Union Iron Works, and the Pittsburgh Locomotive Works. In addition, he made highly profitable investments in the oilfields of Pennsylvania.

Although offered the post of assistant general superintendent of the Pennsylvania Railroad, Carnegie resigned in 1865 to devote his attention to the rapidly expanding iron industry. Within three years he had an annual income of $50,000 and was toying with the idea of retiring to a scholarly life. But the same characteristics that had brought him financial success at an early age prevented the early fulfillment of this plan.

Carnegie was one of the largest shareholders in the Pullman Company until 1873 and also served briefly as a director of the Union Pacific Railroad. In these operations, and in others, he was associated with Scott and J. Edgar Thomson, the top officers of the Pennsylvania Railroad. It was Scott who made Carnegie the agent for selling railroad securities in Europe during this period, many of them through Junius S. Morgan & Company. Carnegie's commissions were invested in his Pittsburgh works and helped him to become the dominant partner.

Carnegie did not occupy himself with the details of ironmaking but supplied capital, negotiated major contracts, and made general policy, which was implemented by other able men. It was therefore possible for him to live in New York after 1867, to cultivate acquaintance with men of letters as well as finance, and to travel abroad, whence he brought back new ideas for iron and steel manufacture. He especially encouraged the adoption of innovations to cut manufacturing costs. By concentrating on aggressive selling of quality items and by reducing production costs, Carnegie and his colleagues soon outstripped their competitors. With the erection of the Lucy Furnace in 1870, the Carnegie group also began the integration of production processes by turning out their own pig iron.

The financial panic of 1873, which wiped out many businessmen, was viewed as an opportunity for further expansion by Carnegie, who had refused to engage in speculation and adopted the policy of concentrating his resources in the business he knew best. Impressed by what he had learned of steel production in Britain, he erected a steel mill, the J. Edgar Thomson Works at Braddock, Pa. Captain "Bill" Jones, an exceptionally able steelmaster, was put in charge and was soon breaking one production record after another for Carnegie. By 1877 the Carnegie furnaces were producing about one seventh of the Bessemer steel in the United States, much of it destined for the steel-hungry railroads.

In 1882 the Carnegie firm bought a substantial interest in the H. C. Frick Coke Company, which controlled an important area of good coking coal. Equally valuable, the business talents of Henry Clay Frick were added to Carnegie's resources. Thereafter various plants were acquired, including an important one at Homestead, Pa., the site of a famous strike in 1892 which damaged Carnegie's reputation as an employer. As the output of the Carnegie works rose, the United States in 1890 took the lead from Great Britain as the foremost steel producer in the world.

The process of vertical integration was completed under Frick when the Carnegie interests in 1896 obtained a very favorable lease on Mesabi (Minn.) iron-ore lands. The ore flowed via company-owned steamers and railroads to the Carnegie furnaces and mills in Pittsburgh. The only stage of manufacture not embraced in these operations was the large-scale fabrication of products such as tubing and wire.

Carnegie attributed the success of his business to its organization. Although he had no official title or responsibilities, Carnegie controlled overall policy and spurred production by stimulating rivalry among superintendents and managers. From time to time promising young men who had proved themselves in the mills were made partners at no cost to themselves. At times as many as 40 were included. Among the important active managers were his brother Thomas M. Carnegie, Henry Clay Frick, and Charles M. Schwab. Frick and Henry Phipps, the only one of Carnegie's original partners remaining under the Frick regime, attempted and failed to sell the Carnegie properties in 1899. When Carnegie discovered that they had sought promoters' profits from the sale, he ousted Frick as chairman of the company and kept the option money, amounting to over $1 million.

In the same year the Carnegie Steel Co. was organized as a New Jersey corporation with a capital of $320 million. In 1900 it made a profit of $40 million, of which $25 million went to Carnegie. The next year, as a competitive struggle developed, he sold the properties to J. P. Morgan to form the nucleus of the United States Steel Corporation, receiving as his share more than $250 million in bonds of the new combination.

Systematic Philanthropy. Thenceforth Carnegie attacked the problem of giving away his money as systematically as he had administered his business. In magazine articles and more prominently in *The Gospel of Wealth* (1900) he had expressed the view that the rich should distribute their wealth during their lifetime.

As early as 1869 he gave public baths to his home town in Scotland, and in 1903 he established the Dunfermline Trust for the benefit of the town. Although unsympathetic to organized labor, he had acted paternalistically toward able workers, and one of his first acts upon retiring from business was to establish a pension fund for Carnegie employees. He also established a pension fund for aged professors (1905), and endowed the Carnegie Institute of Pittsburgh (1895), the Carnegie Trust for the Universities of Scotland (1901), and the Carnegie Institution of Washington (1902). In addition, he made many gifts to smaller educational institutions in the United States and for free public libraries.

His Hero Fund, established in the United States in 1904 and subsequently extended abroad, gave material recognition to bravery. His other benefactions ranged from the Peace Palace at The Hague (1903) and the Carnegie Endowment for International Peace (1910) to a grant of $50,000 to aid the radium research of Mme. Curie. Although not a formally religious man, he contributed to the purchase of over 7,500 church organs. After 1911 the distribution of Carnegie money for educational and research purposes was handled by the Carnegie Corporation.

Andrew Carnegie was a complex individual and therefore a controversial one. He was attacked as an exploiter of labor and as an unscrupulous business colleague and competitor. On the other hand, his competitive innovations transformed the steel industry, and his philanthropy has had a lasting impact. He was perennially optimistic about the future of a democratic America. His writings, including numerous books and some 80 articles, evidence his awareness of the problems created by the demands and rewards of a society undergoing industrialization.

Carnegie married Louise Whitfield in 1887, and their daughter Margaret was born in 1897. Until World War I intervened, the Carnegies divided their time between Skibo Castle in the north of Scotland and New York City. Carnegie's best-known works are *Triumphant Democracy* (1886), *The Gospel of Wealth* (1900), *The Empire of Business* (1902), and his *Autobiography* (1920).

ARTHUR M. JOHNSON, *Harvard University*

Bibliography

Casson, Herbert N., *The Romance of Steel* (New York 1907).
Harlow, Alvin F., *Andrew Carnegie* (New York 1953).
Hendrick, Burton J., *The Life of Andrew Carnegie*, 2 vols. (New York 1932).
Hughes, Johnathan, *The Vital Few* (Boston 1966).
Winkler, John K., *Incredible Carnegie* (New York 1931).

CARNEGIE, kär′nə-gē, **Dale** (1888–1955), American author and teacher of public speaking, whose book *How to Win Friends and Influence People* (1936), translated into more than 30 languages, has been called the most popular work of nonfiction in modern times. He was born in Maryville, Mo., on Nov. 24, 1888. After a brief career as a salesman, he went to New York City and in 1912 began to teach public speaking at the YMCA. He eventually expanded his lectures to teach his students how to acquire success through poise, concentration, and self-confidence. Carnegie's other books include *How to Stop Worrying and Start Living* (1948). He died in New York City on Nov. 1, 1955.

CARNEGIE, kär′nə-gē, is an industrial borough in Pennslyvania, in Allegheny county, 12 miles (19 km) southwest of downtown Pittsburgh. Steel manufacturing is the chief industry, and there are coal mines nearby. Of interest is Neville House, the home of Brig. Gen. John Neville (1731–1803), an officer in the French and Indian War and the American Revolution, who was also a central figure in the Whiskey Rebellion of 1794. Carnegie was formed from the boroughs of Chartiers and Mansfield in 1894 and named in honor of Andrew Carnegie. It has the mayor-council form of government. Population: 10,864.

CARNEGIE CORPORATION OF NEW YORK, a philanthropic foundation established by Andrew Carnegie (q.v.) in 1911 for the advancement and diffusion of knowledge and understanding among the people of the United States and certain Commonwealth countries (Britain, India, and Pakistan are excluded). In 1967 the market value of its capital assets was approximately $336 million.

The corporation is primarily interested in education and certain aspects of governmental and international affairs. From time to time it also makes grants for special studies and programs in other fields. Grants are made to colleges and universities, professional associations, and other educational organizations for specific programs. The programs involve basic research as well as more effective use of the results of research. Programs include preschool education; education of the disadvantaged; urban educational problems; and improving government at local, state, and federal levels.

A lifelong interest of Andrew Carnegie's was the establishment of free public libraries to make available to everyone a means of self-education. He and the corporation spent more than $56 million to build 2,509 libraries throughout the English-speaking world. The library building program was terminated in 1917. Since then other major corporation grants have been made for the development of college and university art departments; studies and demonstration programs in adult education; research in the social sciences, including foreign area studies and research on learning and teaching; studies of higher education, including professional fields; and the broadening of education opportunities. In the Commonwealth, the corporation's program has been largely concerned with higher education, particularly in Africa, and with educational exchange.

Presidents of the corporation were James R. Angell (1920–1921), Henry S. Pritchett (acting, 1921–1923), Frederick P. Keppel (1923–1941), Walter A. Jessup (1941–1944), Devereux C. Josephs (1945–1948), Charles Dollard (1948–1955), John W. Gardner (1955–1967), and Alan Pifer (1967–).

Through Sept. 30, 1967, grants—paid or promised—to recipients in the United States totaled $346,633,753. Grants to recipients in Commonwealth countries totaled $27,950,589.

KATE WOODBRIDGE
Carnegie Corporation of New York

CARNEGIE ENDOWMENT FOR INTERNATIONAL PEACE, a trust established by Andrew Carnegie in 1910 with a fund of $10 million to advance the cause of peace. Carnegie intended the money to be administered by the board of trustees "to hasten the abolition of international war, the foulest blot upon our civilization." The endowment's headquarters is in New York City. A European center is located in Geneva.

Objectives. The objectives of the endowment were defined in the charter drawn up by the first board of trustees. Its principal goals included the study of the causes of war and practical means of preventing it, aid in the development of international law, and promotion of friendly relations and understanding among the peoples of the world. Three separate divisions—economics and history, international law, and intercourse and education—were established to carry out the programs of the endowment. Among the activities during the first 36 years of the endowment's existence were the publication of an extensive series of studies on the economic and social history of World War I, on Canadian-American relations, and on international law. During this period the endowment established a large program of fellowships and grants-in-aid to individuals and organizations throughout the world.

In 1948 the endowment decided to shift its emphasis and give up the major part of its fund-granting activities in order to concentrate on the development of its own programs. To implement this new policy, the endowment's structure was reorganized, and the three divisions were abolished.

A major review of programs was undertaken in connection with the 50th anniversary of the endowment in 1960, from which emerged the concept of program areas on which the endowment's activities are now focused. Among the major programs of the endowment are those centered in international organizations, international law, diplomacy, and the changing role of military force.

Programs. The endowment's interest in international organizations antedates the founding of the United Nations, and since 1945 the work of that organization has been one of the primary concerns of endowment programs. Analyses of a wide range of UN issues have been published, and the endowment's periodical, *International Conciliation,* concentrates largely on problems relating to international organizations.

The international law program of the endowment focuses primarily on improving the competence in international law of the newly independent and developing countries through such means as seminars and conferences. A basic textbook on international law for use principally in these areas was prepared under endowment auspices.

Programs in diplomacy were begun in 1960. They are designed to give special training and education in international affairs to foreign service officers from nations that are newly independent or soon to become independent. To provide this training the endowment sponsors a program of fellowships, seminars, and institutes. The program on the changing role of military force seeks to shed light on means of controlling military force and its impact on the relations between great and small powers.

EVA POPPER
Carnegie Endowment for International Peace

CARNEGIE FOUNDATION FOR THE ADVANCEMENT OF TEACHING, an organization established by Andrew Carnegie in 1905 mainly to furnish retirement allowances and free pensions to college and university professors. It was also the aim of the foundation to "encourage, uphold, and dignify" both the teaching profession and the cause of higher education in the United States and Canada. Under the Teachers Insurance and Annuity Association (TIAA), organized in 1918, the foundation set up a self-supporting system of pensions to which professors and administrators in all universities could contribute. The TIAA became an independent organization in 1930, and in 1952 it set up the closely related College Retirement Equities Fund to invest funds in various common stocks in order to ensure retirement incomes for educators.

In line with its aim of strengthening the teaching profession and higher education, the CFAT has had a notable impact nationally and internationally through its surveys and publications on various aspects of education. The foundation's widely circulated annual reports frequently contain valuable information on the problems and development of higher education in the United States and in other countries. Several of the more than 30 CFAT bulletins are credited with having stimulated vigorous discussion, debate, and ultimate reform in education. *Medical Education in the United States and Canada* (1910) resulted in a radical transformation of American medical schools. *American College Athletics* (1929) helped bring academic control to college sports. *The Student and His*

Knowledge (1938) revealed serious flaws in secondary and higher education in Pennsylvania and pointed to reforms with implications for the entire country. Other important reports included *The Professional Preparation of Teachers for American Public Schools* (1930) and *The Quality of the Educational Process in the United States and Europe* (1927).

WILLIAM W. BRICKMAN
University of Pennsylvania

CARNEGIE HALL is a historic concert hall at Seventh Avenue and 57th Street, New York City. For many years it was the home of the New York Philharmonic, and some of the world's finest musicians made their American debuts there, including Jan Paderewski (1891), Jascha Heifetz (1917), Sir Thomas Beecham (1928), and Vladimir Horowitz (1928).

Opening ceremonies for the hall, which was designed by William Burnet Tuthill, were held in May 1891, with Tchaikovsky conducting his own works. Originally known as the Music Hall, the name of the building was changed in 1898 to honor Andrew Carnegie, who had supplied most of the funds for its construction.

Carnegie Hall was threatened with destruction in 1959 when plans were made to move the New York Philharmonic to its new home at Lincoln Center. A citizens' committee to save Carnegie Hall was formed by the violinist Isaac Stern and music patrons Alice and Jacob Kaplan. In June 1960, New York City purchased the building for $5 million, to be repaid by the nonprofit Carnegie Hall Corporation, which also renovated and redecorated the concert hall.

CARNEGIE HERO FUND COMMISSION, manager of an original $5 million endowment established by Andrew Carnegie in 1904, the proceeds of which are used to aid financially those injured in heroic lifesaving acts and the dependents of heroes who lost their lives on such occasions. The commission, a self-electing body of 21 members representing business and professional interests in Pittsburgh, Pa., employs field representatives to investigate all extraordinary heroic acts and to prepare reports for study and appraisal. On recommendations by an executive committee, the members of the commission make the final decisions. Grants are accompanied by a gold, silver, or bronze medal, depending on the degree and duration of the risk involved.

The scope of the Hero Fund includes the United States, Canada, and the immediately surrounding waters. (Carnegie later established similar funds in Britain and Ireland and the Scandinavian and other Western European countries.) By 1966 the commission had considered 49,515 cases and dispensed a total of $10,468,050 to heroes and dependents.

DAVID B. OLIVER
Carnegie Hero Fund Commission

CARNEGIE INSTITUTE is a partially endowed center of science, art, and music, the gift of Andrew Carnegie to the people of Pittsburgh, Pa., in 1895. Its 13 acres of floor space contain a museum of natural history, a museum of art, music and lecture halls, and the Carnegie Library of Pittsburgh, which is operated on municipal funds.

The Carnegie Museum is noted for its collection of Jurassic dinosaurs, including the *Diplodocus carnegiei*, the first of the large dinosaurs to be excavated, mounted, and placed on exhibition. Six million specimens are distributed among nine scientific sections devoted to lower fossils, higher fossils, plants, insects, invertebrates, amphibians and reptiles, birds, mammals, and man (including useful arts, coins, and stamps). The Powdermill nature reserve, a field station near Ligonier, Pa., is operated by the museum.

The Museum of Art maintains a permanent collection of paintings and sculpture, including works by leading artists from the 15th century to the present. There are strong representations of French impressionist, postimpressionist, and contemporary art. On exhibit are works from an extensive collection of drawings, water colors, prints, and decorative arts. A spacious hall of architecture displays the great works of Assyria, Persia, Chaldea, Rome, France, and other cultures and nations of the past. The museum is the home of the Pittsburgh International Exhibition of Contemporary Painting and Sculpture. This exhibition, instituted in 1896, is staged triennially.

Carnegie Music Hall, seating 2,000, is equipped with one of the world's largest and finest organs. It has a spacious foyer lavished with gold incrustation and colorful Mediterranean marbles. The division of education works on a regular curriculum schedule with the public, parochial, and private schools of the area, in bringing to students a foundation in the cultural realm.

The Carnegie Institute Society was formed to obtain additional sources of income for the operation of the Institute. In the late 1960's membership in the society totaled more than 12,000.

ALEXANDER BREVAK
Carnegie Institute

CARNEGIE INSTITUTION OF WASHINGTON, a scientific research foundation established in Washington, D. C., on Jan. 28, 1902, by Andrew Carnegie, with an original endowment of $10 million. The institution's objective is "to encourage, in the broadest and most liberal manner, investigation, research, and discovery, and the application of knowledge to the improvement of mankind." It operates under a charter from the Congress of the United States, which was approved on April 28, 1904. The institution's endowment was increased by $2 million in 1907 and by $10 million more in 1911. Fundamental research is conducted in six centers, each with its own library, laboratory facilities, necessary field stations, and equipment. Participating scientists choose their own fields of investigation. The centers comprise the following:

The Mount Wilson and Palomar Observatories (Pasadena, Calif.) are operated jointly with the California Institute of Technology. These astronomical observatories, situated on separate mountain peaks in southern California, employ two of the world's largest telescopes and many associated instruments, in broad programs on the structure, dimensions, and evolution of the universe. The Geophysical Laboratory (Washington, D. C.) conducts research on the formation and evolution of the earth's crust and on the origin and age of life.

The Department of Terrestrial Magnetism (Washington, D. C.) studies the magnetic and electrical fields of the earth, radio astronomy, the geophysics of the earth's crust and mantle, and nuclear physics and biophysics. The Department of Plant Biology (Stanford, Calif.) investigates photosynthesis and the evolutionary mechanisms by which plants have developed their variation in form, size, and distribution. The chief investigations of the Department of Embryology (Baltimore, Md.) are concerned with the form and function of the human embryo. The Genetics Research Unit (Cold Spring Harbor, N. Y.) studies the mechanisms by which life processes are directed and those by which inherited traits are transmitted.

Executive offices of the institution are in Washington, D. C. Publications include yearbooks for reviews of all investigations in progress and numerous monographs for the presentation of completed studies.

DONALD J. PATTON
Carnegie Institution of Washington

CARNEGIE-MELLON UNIVERSITY, a private, nonsectarian institution of higher education in Pittsburgh, Pa., was formed on July 1, 1967, by a merger of Carnegie Institute of Technology and Mellon Institute, both in Pittsburgh. Carnegie Tech had been endowed by Andrew Carnegie in 1900 and chartered in 1912 to provide undergraduate education and to foster research and creative attainment. Mellon Institute, an endowed nonprofit organization, was founded in 1913 by Andrew and Richard Mellon to conduct comprehensive research in the fundamental and applied natural sciences and to cooperate with industry in sponsored programs of research.

The new university has six divisions: the College of Fine Arts, Carnegie Institute of Technology (engineering and science), Mellon Institute, Margaret Morrison Carnegie College for Women, the Graduate School of Industrial Administration, and the Division of Humanities and Social Sciences. Additional facilities include a nuclear research center in Saxonburg, Pa.; a radiation chemistry laboratory at Bushy Run, Pa.; a computation center for research in computer languages; an education center for curriculum development; the Transportation Research Institute; and the oldest drama department in the United States. All curricula emphasize an interdisciplinary approach.

Carnegie-Mellon offers both undergraduate and graduate degrees. At the time of the merger there were about 3,000 undergraduate and 1,000 graduate students.

DENTON BEAL
Carnegie-Mellon University

CARNEGIE UNIT, a device to determine the nature and amount of subject matter studied in high school by applicants to colleges and universities. As specified by the Carnegie Foundation for the Advancement of Teaching (CFAT), a unit constituted the study of a subject for one year for a minimum of 120 hours, or the equivalent. The unit not only standardized data on secondary school instruction, but also defined the status of a college in terms of its students' previous preparation. This status helped to determine the eligibility of a college for CFAT benefits.

For many years, the Carnegie Unit was a standard in the United States both for college entrance and for the stabilization of high school curricula. With the development of various methods to test qualifications for college, the use of the Carnegie unit gradually decreased.

WILLIAM W. BRICKMAN
University of Pennsylvania

CARNEIA, kär-nē'yə, a festival in ancient Greece in honor of the god Apollo Carneius, who was associated with the flocks and fertility. It was celebrated annually from the 7th to the 15th of the month of Carneius (August–September). Although the celebration was common to all Dorian Greeks, knowledge of its details comes only from Sparta.

The agrarian origin of the festival survived in a race in which one young man was pursued by five others; it was a good omen if he was caught. There was also a military element, probably introduced in 676 B. C.; nine tents were set up, in each of which nine men ate and lived in a military fashion. There was also a musical competition. During the Carneia the Spartans could not wage war; in 490 they had to wait for the festival's end before going to the aid of the Athenians against the Persians and thus did not participate in the Battle of Marathon.

DONALD W. BRADEEN
University of Cincinnati

CARNELIAN, kär-nēl'yən, or *cornelian,* is a reddish quartz mineral used in jewelry. It is generally classified as a special type of chalcedony, a cryptocrystalline quartz—having crystals too small to be observed even with a microscope. Carnelian is sometimes referred to as *sard,* but it is simpler to consider them as two separate types of chalcedony. Carnelian ranges from pale to deep clear red, whereas sard is brownish red to yellowish brown. The colors are caused by traces of ferric oxide.

The mineral, which is widely distributed, has a waxy luster and takes a fine polish. It is used for making beads and similar jewelry, and especially for signets cut in intaglio—that is, with the design cut below the surface of the stone. It was widely used in the ancient world in the form of such seals. Carnelian may be heated or stained to improve its color. Agates from Brazil and Uruguay that are treated in this manner are often sold as carnelian.

Composition, SiO_2; hardness, 7; specific gravity, 2.65; crystal system, hexagonal.

CARNIOLA, kärn-yō'lə, a former Austrian duchy and crownland, now part of Slovenia in Yugoslavia, is a mountainous area at the northern end of the Adriatic Sea. In Roman times it formed part of the province of Pannonia. The present ethnic composition of the region was determined in the 6th century, when Carniola was occupied by the Slovenes, a South Slavic people. The area was a part of Charlemagne's empire and in the 13th century was incorporated into the Holy Roman Empire as the March of Carniola. In the 14th century the territory became a possession of the house of Habsburg. In 1365, Rudolph IV of Habsburg took the title of Duke of Carniola.

Carniola remained under Habsburg rule until 1918, with only one short interruption. From 1809 to 1831 it was joined to Napoleon's Illyrian province. In 1849, Carniola became a separate crownland of the Habsburg empire with Ljubljana (Laibach) as the capital. In 1918 all but a small section of the area was merged into Yugoslavia. The part that was given to Italy at this time was returned to Slovenia after World War II. Slovenia is now one of the most prosperous areas of Yugoslavia.

BARBARA JELAVICH and CHARLES JELAVICH
Indiana University

CHAMBER OF COMMERCE OF THE NEW ORLEANS AREA

New Orleans' Mardi Gras culminates in a series of spectacular parades that attract thousands of spectators.

CARNIVAL, kär′nə-vəl, in the traditional Christian calendar, is a period of feasting and merrymaking immediately preceding Lent. The generally accepted derivation of the term is from medieval Latin *Carnem levare* or *carnelevarium* (*caro* means flesh, and *levare* to put aside) referring to abstinence from meat during the 40 days of Lent of the Christian year.

Origin. The origin of carnival is uncertain, except that it is to be found in pre-Christian customs. Although scholars see links between the pagan Roman Saturnalia and Greek festivals, they regard carnival as an even more ancient agricultural rite connected with the theme of death and resurrection in nature. As such, this spring festival was recorded in ancient Babylonia, Egypt, Greece, and Rome.

The pagan Roman Saturnalia was held in honor of Saturn, who in one of his many forms was the god of sowing. His wife, Ops, was also honored as the goddess of crops and the harvest. This festival in honor of the sowing of the seed for the coming year and commemorating the happy, classless reign of Saturn was celebrated on December 17, and lasted seven days. Social rank was temporarily forgotten, and slaves dined with their masters. Gifts were exchanged between people of different social positions, and feasting, drinking, and sexual activity were unrestricted. Over each Saturnalia reigned a king chosen by lot, who was burned in effigy at the conclusion of the festivities.

The festival called Cronia in ancient Greece corresponded to the Roman Saturnalia. Among his other attributes, Cronus was the god of the harvest. Like his Roman counterpart Saturn, Cronus was believed to have been a king who reigned during the golden age of his people; in his honor, master and slave shared a common meal during the celebration of the festival.

These agricultural festivities were very popular in antiquity, and they continued into the early medieval period. Although the Christian church in Rome permitted the festivities to continue on their usual dates, it endowed them with new, Christian meanings. Saturnalia was reinterpreted as carnival, and many popes became its patrons. For example, Pope Paul II (1464–1471) ordered a variety of races to be held in Rome and introduced masked balls. The church, however, tried to curb excesses. From Italy the festivities spread to Spain, Portugal, France, and other European countries.

Modern Carnivals in Europe. Surviving carnival customs have been modified by local folk traditions and show great variety. These traditions are especially strong in rural areas where magical rites and observances carried over from pre-Christian times mingle comfortably with Christian ritual and precept. The main features that have endured are: (1) dramatizations symbolizing the death of winter and the resurrection of life in the spring; (2) customs and rites to ensure fertility and abundance in man and nature; (3) rich food, drink, and merrymaking; (4) masquerading, songs, folk dancing, and popular plays to symbolize the carnival events; and (5) the temporary suspension or inversion of social roles, rank, and seniority.

The struggle between winter and spring, or life and death, is variously dramatized in many parts of Europe by the staging of symbolic battles between masked representatives of winter and spring, at which winter is defeated and burned in effigy. For example, Hungarian villagers used to perform the symbolic burial of King Marrow-Bone, who represented the indulgences of life. An even more realistic funeral was held in Catalonia, Spain, in which the effigy rode in a hearse attended by masked men.

GERMAN INFORMATION CENTER

German carnival features paraders in traditional masks and feathered costumes depicting "Feather Hans."

SWISS NATIONAL TOURIST OFFICE

Basel's February carnival includes parades by local groups wearing costumes that often carry out a theme.

Rites to ensure fertility and abundance are prominent in carnival. In Poland, Shrovetide paraders wear fantastic costumes with masks of straw, leather, wood, or rags. The agrarian theme behind such gay antics is revealed in a song of the marchers:

Make merry, little horse.
In the green grove
Where our horse walks
There grain will grow.

In parts of eastern and central Europe a dance is performed by married women who try to leap high in the air, in the hope that nature will make hemp or flax grow high. In Bulgaria, carnival used to start with a procession of mummers led by a man dressed as an old woman (Baba). Proceeding from one household to the next, marchers went through the motions of plowing and sowing, for which they received small gifts.

The theme of human fertility is also prominent. Carnival is the time to get married and establish a new family. Marriageable girls and men who failed to choose a mate during the preceding season are penalized on Shrove Tuesday. In Poland chicken feet, turkey windpipes, and herring skeletons are pinned on them. In another custom on Shrove Tuesday, married women dressed in men's hats and overcoats, gathered all the new brides, and took them to the tavern, where the young brides paid a ransom that gave them entry into the society of matrons.

In northern Europe, where the majority of the population is Protestant, only Catholics celebrate carnival in the Latin fashion. This is true in Sweden, Norway, the Netherlands, and Denmark. But the season is set aside as an occasion for children to invert rank and seniority with their elders. In Denmark, on Fastelavn, the Monday preceding Ash Wednesday, children are allowed to use switches decorated with paper flowers on their parents and elders and to demand the traditional Fastelavnsboller, or Shrovetide buns.

In England, although carnival is not as popular as in Latin countries, the Tuesday before Ash Wednesday (Shrove Tuesday) is known as Pancake Day. In some parts of England, after the morning services, "pancake bells" are rung at 11 o'clock to announce the time to begin frying, tossing, and eating the pancakes.

The carnival dramatization played a great role in the development of popular theater, especially in Germany where the *Fastnachtsspiel*, or carnival play, originated in Nuremberg, was popular from the 15th century. According to local tradition, the right of performing the "Dance of Life" during carnival was granted in 1348 to the butchers of the city who remained loyal to the aristocratic council during the short-lived democratic revolution of other artisan guilds. The dance seems to derive from ancient spring festivals and fertility rites. The sons of rich families who wished to join the butchers had to pay for the privilege. In grotesque processions, mummers impersonated vegetation demons and clowns. The special attraction was the Höllen, large floats pulled on sleighs exhibiting dragons, ogres, and other fantastic creatures. At present, the pre-Lenten carnival on Shrove Tuesday is celebrated with costume balls, parades, and hearty eating and drinking.

In France the Mardi Gras ("Fat Tuesday") is celebrated with masked balls, parades and floats, and rich food and drinking. It used to be the tradition in Paris for the butchers' guild to parade an enormous ox festooned with garlands and flowers and ridden by a boy holding a knife in his hand and representing the king of the butchers. As in the German tradition, the butchers perhaps were celebrating their last activity before the meatless fast of Lent.

At the start of the 20th century, this colorful custom disappeared from Paris, but in southern France, especially in Nice, the carnival remains spectacular. Floats carry an enormous effigy of the king of carnival seated on a throne and surrounded by a court of clowns.

HANS MANN FROM MONKMEYER

Rio de Janeiro's carnival (*left*) brings thousands of celebrants into the streets.

Trinidad carnival features grotesque masks such as this devil mask (*below*).

FRITZ HENLE FROM MONKMEYER

The New Orleans Mardi Gras. Carnival probably has been celebrated in the United States since the first French and Spanish settlers came to the South. The gayest and most extravagant celebration of the Mardi Gras season is in New Orleans, where it first started. In 1857, on the night of Mardi Gras, a group of men calling themselves the Mystic Krewe of Comus appeared on the streets of New Orleans. Carrying torchlights and moving on floats, the 1,200 masked figures illustrated the demon actors in Milton's *Paradise Lost.* After the success of this first entertainment, new secret societies, such as the Krewe of Proteus and the Krewe of Nereus, were formed. Carnival was observed continually until 1861, when it was temporarily suspended because of the Civil War. In 1872 the Knights of Momus appeared in their first parade, representing scenes from Sir Walter Scott's romance *The Talisman.*

The Mardi Gras season officially opens on Epiphany with a magnificent procession of floats and costumed marchers wearing beautiful, grotesque, or comical masks representing historical, legendary, or mythological themes. New Orleans is also known for its elaborate balls. Both the procession and the balls are still carefully prepared by the men's secret societies whose members are not supposed to reveal their membership to outsiders. Women in recent years have begun to organize their own Krewes.

There is dancing and pageantry during the afternoon and nights of Monday and Fat Tuesday. Rex, the king of carnival, appears on Monday afternoon; only a few people know his identity. At City Hall he ceremonially receives from the mayor the keys to the city. Afterward, he mysteriously disappears—probably to symbolize the original custom of burning the king in effigy.

In parts of Louisiana where there are people of French descent, the Mardi Gras is often celebrated by men dressed in female attire. Accompanied by musicians, they wander from house to house, receiving good things to eat. Mobile, Ala., and cities in Mississippi and Florida are also known for their pageants on Shrove Tuesday.

The Rio de Janeiro Carnival. In 1966, Rio de Janeiro, Brazil, celebrated its 126th annual carnival. Preparations for each event begin months ahead of time, and interest in competitions organized by societies and clubs runs high. Winning songs are quickly popularized, and their composers become famous. The best costumes receive wide recognition. For high society the merrymaking is climaxed by a costume ball in the Municipal Theater. Streets are packed with enormous crowds, and there is an atmosphere of happy madness. Even the poorest people put together some kind of a costume.

Carnival in Russia. In the USSR, where Ash Wednesday is not observed, carnival lasts seven days and is the gayest season of the year. It is popularly called "Wide-Open Week." The proper names are Maslenitza (Butter Week) or Syrnaia Nedlia (Cheese Week). Each day of the week has a special significance: Monday, meeting day; Tuesday, teasing or playful day; Wednesday, sweet-tooth or gourmand's day; Thursday, free-for-all day; Friday, mother-in-law celebration; Saturday, daughter-in-law celebration; Sunday, farewell—kissing day or the day of forgiveness. The traditional *blini,* pancakes of raised rye flour, are served with butter and sour cream. In olden times a ritual significance was attached to eating *blini,* and the first pancake was given to a beggar in memory of the dead.

In Eastern Orthodox tradition, Saturday evening, the eve of Maslenitza, memorializes one's departed parents. On the other hand, the period from January 6 to carnival week was known as the wedding season, the start of a new life. In the 15th century, January and February were called the "weddings." Eligible young people who failed to get married during this time were subject to pranks. In the Ukraine and in Poland a bit of wood or a stick was hung on the young people, who had to pay ransom to be freed of them. Verses were often pinned on them, such as the following:

If, gracious maiden, you walked in a pair,
You would not now carry this block of wood—
In penance for your spinsterhood,
Bear as your badge this turkey foot.

In central Russia proper, peasants celebrated carnival with prearranged fist-fighting competitions in the outskirts of villages. For Maslenitza, there were also gay masquerades and amusements such as ice hills and swings. A popular superstition warned people to rinse their mouths after the last meal of Maslenitza; otherwise, devils would pull out bits of the remaining food together with the teeth. At the end of Maslenitza it was said that one should quickly forget past indulgences, because "even for the cat, Maslenitza does not last forever."

In Soviet Russia the religious meaning of Maslenitza is gradually dying out, but carnival masquerading, amusements, and especially the preparation of *blini* are still popular.

Carnival had a great influence on the Jewish festival of Purim, which falls on the 14th of Adar, either in February or March. Purim commemorates the deliverance of the Jews from the destruction that was to have taken place in ancient Persia on the 13th of Adar. Although the Old Testament book of Esther is read in the synagogues, the festival is secular and has the character of a European carnival. It is celebrated with masquerades and plays dramatizing the characters of the Esther story. A doll called "Haman" (the name of the Persian prime minister who plotted the death of the Jews) is frequently burned in effigy or beaten. Small honey and poppy-seed cakes called Hamanohren (literally, "the ears of Haman") are sent to friends and given to the poor. On this day Jewish custom sanctions indulgence and noisemaking by children.

Traveling Shows. In the United States the name carnival often means a traveling entertainment featuring ferris wheels, merry-go-rounds, games of skill and chance, and side shows. These carnivals move from town to town. Local organizations such as fire departments raise funds by sponsoring the show and sharing in the money taken in.

SULA BENET, *Hunter College, New York*

Further Reading: Frazer, James G., *The Golden Bough*, 13 vols. (New York 1911–1936); Spicer, Dorothy G., *Festivals of Western Europe* (New York 1958); Sumberg, Samuel L., *The Nuremberg Schembart Carnival* (New York 1941); Tallant, Robert, *Mardi Gras* (New York 1948).

CARNIVAL IN FLANDERS, the English title of a French film, *La kermesse heroïque* (1935), directed by Jacques Feyder and starring Louis Jouvet and Françoise Rosay. Its farcical plot concerns an attempt by the women of a 16th century Flemish town to delude the Spanish soldiers occupying it. The movie is famous for its historical realism and for its elaborate scenery, designed by Lazare Meerson and reminiscent of Flemish paintings, such as Pieter Bruegel the Elder's *La kermesse*.

CARNIVORA, kär-niv′ə-rə, a diverse group of mammals, scientifically classified as an *order*, which are linked by common ancestors and a common habit of living primarily on the flesh of other animals. The term is derived from the Latin root *carn-* (flesh) and *vorare* (to devour). The order's seven families can be divided into two main groups: the dogs, bears, raccoons, and weasels; and the civets, hyenas, and cats. The closely related seals used to be considered a part (that is, a suborder) of the Carnivora, but they are now classed in a separate order, the Pinnipedia.

Although very few of the Carnivora live exclusively on meat and there are other flesh-eating mammals, the name is a good, simple definition since the generally shared anatomical characteristics of this group are all special adaptations to a predatory life.

GENERAL CHARACTERISTICS

The most important general characteristic of the carnivores is the structure of the skull and particularly the teeth. The incisors are small and sharp for cutting. The canines curve inward and are large and pointed for seizing and holding prey. Two of the cheek teeth (the last upper premolar and the first lower molar) on either side are enlarged with a prominent cutting ridge; these teeth, known as carnassials, chop food up quickly by biting against one another in a scissor-like fashion. The digestive tract is specially adapted to deal with food swallowed in lumps.

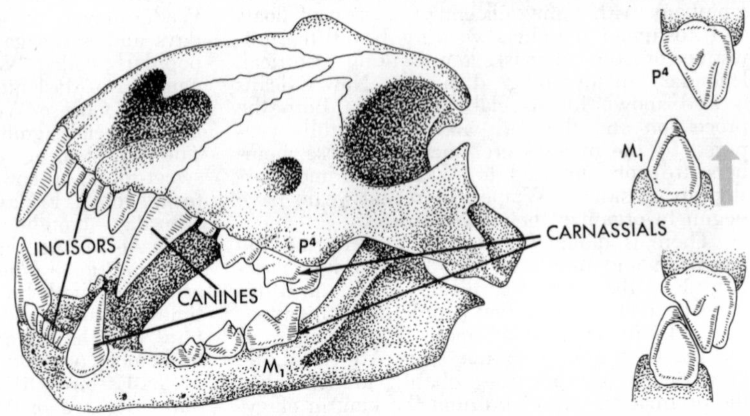

THE CARNIVORA, as a group, are mammals specialized for a meat-eating existence. An example of this specialization is seen in the modification of the last upper premolar (P^4) and the first lower molar (M_1) for the slicing of flesh. These teeth, termed the carnassials, are an identifying feature of the Carnivora. The carnassials and their shearing action are shown in the illustrations (right) of a cat skull and teeth. The cats are highly specialized carnivores, having almost no tooth surfaces suitable for grinding.

There is a development of ridges on the skull to which the necessarily powerful jaw muscles are anchored. Because food is chopped rather than chewed, the lower jaw is attached in such a way as to allow it to move only up and down, and not from side to side.

There are at least four toes on each foot, frequently five; the first toe is reduced or absent and is never opposable like a true thumb, so that carnivores cannot be said to have "hands." The sharp, curved claws are very strong for digging and tearing. The collarbone (clavicle) is either incomplete or absent, depending on the species.

Though all families eat some plant material and insects, the cats and dogs, and to a lesser extent the civets and weasels, exist almost entirely on freshly killed meat and fish. The hyenas are scavengers of carrion; the bears and raccoons are omnivorous, eating both plant and animal food regularly.

Distribution. Carnivores are native to all continents and large islands of the world except Antarctica, Australia, New Guinea, and New Zealand (both wild and domestic species have been introduced to the last three areas). Some, notably dogs and cats, have a geographic range as large as that covered by the whole order; others, such as civets and hyenas, have a very restricted distribution. The greatest concentration of species is in the tropics, and most carnivores inhabit forests.

FAMILY CHARACTERISTICS

The order Carnivora is divided into two main groups, known as superfamilies: the "dog" superfamily (Canoidea) and the "cat" superfamily (Feloidea). The dog superfamily is made up of four families: the dogs (Canidae), bears (Ursidae), raccoons (Procyonidae), and weasels (Mustelidae). The cat superfamily is made up of three families: the cats (Felidae), hyenas (Hyaenidae), and civets (Viverridae).

Dogs have successfully colonized the whole world, mainly because their lack of physical specialization and their adaptable behavior enable them to live in almost any environment. All wild dogs are characterized by long, pointed muzzles; bushy tails; erect ears; blunt, straight claws; uniform and, with a few exceptions, neutral coloring. Their feet are so constructed that dogs actually walk on their toes, of which there are five on the forefeet (the first, or "thumb," does not touch the ground) and four on the hindfeet. Many species live and hunt in packs.

The dog family is made up of 37 species, grouped into 14 genera. The species include the wolves, coyotes, jackals, foxes, and various wild dogs.

Bears include the largest meat-eating land animals. All bears are heavily built, almost tailless, with short, powerful legs and very broad, flat feet, each bearing five toes. Unlike dogs, they walk on the soles of their feet. Their coats are thick and shaggy. Their teeth are adapted more to chewing plant food, the carnassials being flattened. The young are born exceptionally small. Bears are usually solitary and cover large distances in their slow, measured walk. When necessary they can walk on their hind legs. In colder regions they put on excess weight in the summer and then spend most of the winter asleep. This, however, is not the deep coma-like sleep of true hibernation.

The bear family is made up of 7 species, grouped into 6 genera. The 7 species are the Asiatic black, American black, brown (including the grizzly), sun, polar, sloth, and spectacled bears. Bears are found in Asia, Europe, and the New World.

Raccoons, which occur mainly in the New World, are most nearly related to the bears, the closest being the two Asiatic members of the family, the pandas. Most species are small, with long and usually ringed tails. They walk on the soles of their feet, and each foot has five toes. Raccoons climb well and spend a lot of time in trees. Like the bears, they are omnivorous and probably eat more vegetable matter than meat. There is still argument as to whether the very rare black-and-white giant panda should be classed with the bears, which it resembles more in appearance than it does the raccoons.

The raccoon family is made up of 18 species, grouped into 8 genera. The raccoons, cacomistles, coatis, kinkajous, and olingos constitute the larger branch, or subfamily, and are found in most areas of the New World. The pandas, found in Asia, make up the other subfamily.

Weasels are very extensive and varied, but typical forms are small, with long, slender bodies and short legs. The least weasel (*Mustela rixosa*), of North America, is the smallest carnivore. It may be less than 6 inches (150 mm) long, including the tail, and weighs about 1 ounce (28 grams). Weasels live mainly in cold and temperate regions. Most possess valuable fur, which in some northern forms turns white in winter. All have well-developed scent glands. The family is divided into five subfamilies, distinguished by their teeth and claws. The most important subfamilies are the weasels, which walk on their toes and are almost completely carnivorous; the more heavily built badgers, which walk on the soles of their feet and live on a mixed diet; and the otters, which have webbed toes, are primarily aquatic, and live on fish.

The weasel family is made up of 68 species, grouped into 25 genera, and is represented on all continents except Antarctica and Australia.

Civets are uniformly small, with long, pointed faces, long bodies and tails, and short legs. They tend to be spotted or striped. The family inhabits the tropical areas of the Old World and lives on a varied diet, many species eating insects and fruit as much as meat.

The civet family is made up of 82 species, grouped into 35 genera. The species include linsangs, genets, civets, mongooses, and the fossa. All are found only in the Old World.

Hyenas have specialized in living on the abandoned prey of other carnivores, and their very strong teeth and jaws are powerful instruments for crushing bones and gristle. They are heavily built, with short heads and tails, and coarse, shaggy fur; the front legs are longer than the hind legs, and all feet have four toes. When scavenging, they cover large distances, mainly at night. They are usually solitary, but may hunt live prey in loose packs, choosing old or weak animals as their victims. The rare aardwolf, despite its name, is really a hyena. It is mainly insectivorous, and its teeth are correspondingly small and weak.

The hyena family is made up of 4 species, grouped into 3 genera. The 4 species are the spotted, striped, and brown hyenas and the aardwolf. Hyenas are found in Africa and Asia.

Cats represent the furthest evolution of the Carnivora, and they are the most completely adapted to hunting by stalking and ambushing. Despite their greatly varying sizes, all cats look alike: long, lean, and agile bodies; blunt muzzles; long, mobile tails; short, rounded ears; and in most species, marked with dark spots or stripes on a light background color as camouflage in the woods and forests in which they generally live. Cats, like dogs, walk on their toes, with their heels permanently held above the ground. There are five toes on the forefeet and four on the hindfeet. The characteristically stealthy walk of cats is due to soft pads that cushion the soles of the feet. Excepting the cheetah, all cats can retract their claws into sheaths for protection when not in use. Cats are found in most climatic areas but chiefly in warm regions. Though they will eat carrion when very hungry, they usually kill their own prey. Cats tend to lead solitary lives.

The cat family is made up of 36 species, usually grouped into 4 genera. The cats, which occur naturally on every continent except Antarctica and Australia, include the lions, tigers, leopards, jaguars, snow leopards, pumas, lynxes, cheetahs, and many small wild cats.

EVOLUTION

Ancestral carnivores known as *creodonts* ("flesh-teeth") emerged in the Eocene epoch (about 55 million years ago) from a line of small insectivores that had adapted themselves to catching larger prey. Some creodonts grew quite large: *Andrewsarchus,* from Mongolia, was the biggest carnivore that ever lived; its skull was 3 feet (1 meter) or more in length, and in overall size it dwarfed the giant Alaska brown bear. Creodonts did not need to develop much intelligence to prey on the slow, dull-witted herbivores of the time. With a few exceptions, notably the genus *Hyaenodon,* which lived on until about 10 million years ago, creodonts became extinct at the end of the Eocene (about 35 million years ago) when their prey died out. The creodonts, however, had given rise to a more progressive group known as *miacids* ("small cutting teeth"). These were mainly tree-living and must have somewhat resembled the small carnivores that today inhabit the same forest environments: the weasel family of cold and temperate areas and the civets of tropical regions.

From the more weasel-like miacids grew a small group of carnivores with longer legs and bodies and larger brains—*Cynodictis,* from Europe, is a typical example. When these eventually left the trees and spread into open country, their claws became sharper and their legs longer for running. By the Miocene (25 million years ago), there were many varieties of these doglike animals, and their success may be partly due to their early adoption of cooperative, or pack, hunting. They first colonized the Northern Hemisphere, especially North America, and very few reached Africa until the Pleistocene (2 million years ago). Another branch of *Cynodictis,* which is thought to have evolved in North America into the ancestral raccoon *Phlaocyon,* spread south, leading to such forms as the coati and kinkajou, and west (across the Bering Sea land link which then existed between North America and Asia), where it evolved into the pandas. The bears were a later offshoot from the dog tribe, which during the Miocene became larger and heavier, relying less on speed as they adopted a more mixed diet.

The cats were an early development from the civetlike miacids and were a distinct family by the Oligocene (35 million years ago), when the famous saber-toothed tigers such as *Smilodon* arose. A later side shoot of the civet family led to the hyenas, of which the earliest was *Ictitherium.* Marine carnivores (seals, sea lions, and walruses) diverged from the main carnivore stock in Miocene times.

The glaciation of the Pleistocene, the so-called Ice Age, which started 2 million years ago, was the last great test. Only those carnivore species that were able to adapt to the cold or to move to the warmer areas survived, developing into the efficient and successful predators of today.

MARY H. HAYNES
Zoological Society of London

Bibliography

Burt, W. H., and Grossenheider, R. P., *A Field Guide to the Mammals* (Boston 1952).
Morris, Desmond J., *The Mammals: A Guide to the Living Species* (London 1965).
National Geographic Society, *Wild Animals of North America* (Washington 1960).
Sanderson, Ivan T., *Living Mammals of the World* (New York 1955).
Walker, Ernest P., *Mammals of the World,* vol. 2, (Baltimore 1964).

CARNIVOROUS PLANTS, kär-niv′ər-əs plants, are plants that have specialized leaves for trapping and digesting insects. These plants, also known as *insectivorous plants,* obtain some nutrients from their prey, but most of their food materials are manufactured in their leaves by the process of photosynthesis.

See also BLADDERWORT; PITCHER PLANT; SUNDEW; VENUS' FLYTRAP.

CARNOSAURIA. See DINOSAUR—*Order Saurischia.*

CARNOT, kȧr-nō′, **Hippolyte** (1801–1888), French republican politician. Lazare Hippolyte Carnot, the second son of the French revolutionary military leader Lazare Carnot, was born at St.-Omer, on April 6, 1801. For several years he was an active disciple of the social philosopher Saint-Simon. During the 1830's, Carnot took a leading role in the republican opposition to the government of Louis Philippe, serving in the Chamber of Deputies from 1839 to 1848. As a moderate republican he played a part in the campaign against the government that led to the Revolution of 1848.

Carnot was named minister of education by the new republican government but retained his post for only five months. His many progressive proposals, including free and compulsory elementary education and vocational training, were defeated by a conservative legislature. During the last years of the Second Empire, he reentered active politics but by that time he was considered too conservative by a new generation of republicans.

Following the fall of the Empire, he sat with the republican left in the National Assembly and was awarded a life senatorship in 1875. After living to see his son Sadi Carnot elected president of the republic in 1887, Hippolyte Carnot died in Paris on March 16, 1888.

PETER AMANN
State University of New York at Binghamton

CARNOT, kär-nō′, **Lazare Nicolas Marguerite** (1753–1823), French general and minister of war. He was born at Nolay in Burgundy on May 13, 1753, the son of a lawyer and notary. After graduating from the exacting engineering school at Mézières, he became a first lieutenant in the army engineering corps in 1774.

In 1787, as a captain, he joined the Academy of Arras. He studied in depth the problems of military fortification, examining the work of the 17th century military engineer, the Marquis de Vauban, and the views of the new school of perpendicular fortification advocated by the Marquis de Montalembert. He also joined the local Jacobin Club, where he spoke against tyranny. Elected to the Legislative Assembly in 1791 and to the National Convention the following year, he was among those who voted for the death of Louis XVI in January 1793.

But it was above all his military and organizational talents that earned him national attention. His greatest contribution to the First Republic came in the summer of 1793, when besieged France suffered from deep-seated internal troubles and defeats at the front. Carnot's advice, which led to the alteration of the original battle plan, brought victory over the Austrians at Wattignies (Oct. 16, 1793). His position on the Committee of Public Safety resembled that of a modern chief of staff plus secretary of defense. Carnot's direction of the war effort earned him the title of "Organizer of Victory."

More of an expert in his chosen profession than a politician, he steered clear of the cutthroat politics of the National Convention. During the Thermidorian reaction the anti-Robespierre forces tried to bring Carnot down, but they failed. He simply stood on his record. He served on the Directory from 1795, and when it was threatened by a resurgent royalist majority in the elections of 1797, he tried unsuccessfully to restrain the other directors from using force. The coup d'etat of 18th Fructidor (Sept. 4, 1797), agreed to by Napoleon Bonaparte from Italy and executed by General Augereau, resulted in the deportation of more than 50 persons suspected of being royalists, including Carnot. He escaped to Switzerland.

Carnot returned to France to become Napoleon Bonaparte's minister of war in 1800. In this job he concentrated upon reducing military expenses by centralizing procurement, but he soon resigned after differences with Bonaparte. Elected by the Senate to the Tribunate, he opposed the creation of the Legion of Honor and the life consulate for Napoleon. Later he lived on his estate at Presles, but he never allowed himself to be idle. A rich stream of studies on fortification, mechanics, and geometry came from his fruitful mind. Bonaparte understood the value of this intelligent critic and granted him a pension, asking him to prepare a study on fortification for military schools.

In 1814, when the empire was shaken by the onslaught of the coalition against it, Carnot volunteered for active service. Napoleon appointed him general in command of the defense of Antwerp, and he took a heavy toll of the enemy in a brilliant plan. He served as minister of the interior in the Hundred Days, but he was exiled as a regicide after the restoration of Louis XVIII. He died in Magdeburg, Prussia, on Aug. 3, 1823.

RICHARD BRACE
Oakland University, Mich.

CARNOT, kär-nō′, **Nicolas Léonard Sadi** (1796–1832), French scientist, who founded thermodynamics. Sadi Carnot was born in Paris on June 1, 1796, the son of Lazare Carnot, the military genius. He was named for the medieval Persian poet Sadi, whom his father admired.

Carnot was educated at the École Polytechnique, the school for army engineers, which then provided the finest scientific education in the world. In 1824 he produced a short book, *Reflections on the Motive Power of Fire,* ostensibly a study of the design of steam engines. But his insight and ability to simplify made this a classic, far more significant than a mere technical study. Though most of the detailed results are wrong because they were based on the incorrect caloric theory of heat, the theorems he deduced remain among the most important in science.

Carnot simplified a heat engine into its ultimate components: a source of heat, a receiver (or sink) of heat, and a working substance. In a steam engine, these are, respectively, the boiler, the condenser, and water. He visualized an ideal engine without friction of any kind, using a simple cycle of operations that left the working substance unchanged. He showed that the amount of work that could be extracted from any machine for a given consumption of heat did not depend on the working substance, but only on the temperatures of the heat source and the heat sink. Knowing the efficiency of this ideal machine, the efficiencies of all others could be calculated.

Carnot died in Paris on Aug. 24, 1832. His book remained unnoticed for 20 years, until William Thomson (Lord Kelvin) rediscovered it. Thomson used its results to calculate the properties of substances rather than the performance of steam engines and thus completed the founding of modern thermodynamics begun by Carnot.

E. MENDOZA
University College of North Wales

CARNOT, kär-nō′, **Sadi** (1837–1894), French political leader, who was president of the Third Republic from 1887 to 1894. Marie François Sadi Carnot was born on Aug. 11, 1837, in Limoges, the grandson of the military hero Lazare Carnot and son of the political leader Hippolyte Carnot. Sadi served in the National Assembly from 1871 to 1876 and in the Chamber of Deputies from 1876 to 1887. He was also minister of public works and finance minister at various times during these years. Because of his proven statecraft and independent republican views, he was a logical candidate to succeed Jules Grévy when Grévy resigned the presidency after revelations of corruption involving his son-in-law.

Elected fourth president of the republic in 1887, Carnot served with distinction. He supported the government's decision in 1889 to arrest Gen. Georges Boulanger, which quickly ended the antirepublican movement headed by the general. When the scandals over the financing of the Panama Canal broke in 1892, Carnot eloquently defended the regime against charges of corruption. To help create national unity he toured France and presided over many expositions and fairs, including the world exposition in Paris in 1889. At an exposition in Lyon on June 24, 1894, he was stabbed by an Italian anarchist and died that night.

JOEL COLTON, *Duke University*

CARNOT CYCLE. See THERMODYNAMICS.

CARNOTITE, kär′nə-tīt, a hydrous vanadate (vanadium-oxygen compound) of uranium and potassium, is one of the most important ores of uranium. It is named for Marie Adolphe Carnot, a French chemist and mining engineer.

The mineral occurs in sedimentary rock such as sandstone, usually in powdery form or as a loose aggregate. Microscopic crystal plates are seen only rarely in the deposits; they are soft, opaque, have an earthy luster, and are a bright yellow. Unlike many other uranium minerals, carnotite does not fluoresce. It has a strong pigmenting power and will stain sandstone yellow when present even in small quantities.

The most significant deposits of carnotite are in the United States, principally in western Colorado and eastern Utah. The mineral is also found in Mexico, South Australia, and in Katanga in the Congo (Kinshasa). Before uranium was extracted from these deposits, they were already important as a source of radium. Carnotite is a leading ore of vanadium, as well.

Composition, $K_2(UO_2)_2(VO_4)_2 \cdot 3H_2O$; hardness, indeterminate; specific gravity, calculated as 5.03; crystal system, orthorhombic.

CARO, kä′rō, **Joseph** (1488–1575), last and most important codifier of Jewish religious law. His name is also spelled *Karo* or *Qaro.* He was born in Toledo, Spain, in 1488. His family was among the Jews expelled from Spain in 1492, and, after a period of wandering, they settled in Constantinople in 1498. Caro himself finally settled about 1537 in Safed, Palestine, where he founded a yeshivah (Talmudic academy) and became a leader of the Jewish community. In 1559 he completed his *Bet Yoseph* (*House of Joseph*), a commentary on the *Arba 'ah Turim,* the religious code of Jacob ben Asher. His own code, the *Shulhan 'Arukh* (*Prepared Table*), including original legal decisions, was published in 1565. Although this code was opposed at first by some rabbinical authorities, it has become the authoritative standard code of Judaism, still followed by Orthodox and many Conservative Jews.

Caro was also preoccupied with the Cabala (q.v.), the tradition of Jewish mysticism. Caro played a major role among 16th century mystics, who were concentrated in Safed. He claimed that religious secrets were divulged to him by an angel, a so-called *maggid,* whose voice was also heard by others. Caro kept a diary of his mystical experiences, parts of which were published in the *Maggid Mesharim* (1646). He died in Safed in 1575.

RAPHAEL PATAI, *Theodor Herzl Institute*

CAROB, kar′əb, a small, evergreen tree, native to the eastern Mediterranean basin and widely grown in tropical and subtropical regions for its edible pods. It is also known as *St. John's bread, locust bean, algarroba,* and *caroubier.* The carob may grow to 50 feet (15 meters) in height but is usually smaller. It has dark-red bark and glossy, pinnately compound leaves, and bears clusters of small red flowers. Its fruit grows into a flat, dark brown, leathery pod (legume) about 1 foot (30 cm) long. The pods are fed primarily to livestock but are also eaten by humans. Extract of carob seeds is used in curing tobacco, in papermaking, and in foods.

The carob, *Ceratonia siliqua,* is a member of the pea family, Leguminosae.

S. C. BAUSOR, *California State College, Pa.*

CAROL I, kar′əl (1839–1914), the first king of Rumania, was a member of the family of Hohenzollern-Sigmaringen, a Catholic branch of the Prussian royal house. Carol (sometimes Anglicized as Charles) was born in Sigmaringen on April 20, 1839. In 1866, following a coup that removed Prince Alexander Cuza as ruler of the principality of Rumania (technically part of the Ottoman Empire), Carol was chosen as his successor. During his 47-year reign he was to prove a conservative, stable, and patient if not a brilliant monarch.

In 1869, Carol married Princess Elizabeth of Wied. His only child, a daughter, died in childhood, so his successor was to be his nephew Ferdinand.

In 1877, Rumania joined Russia in a war against the Ottoman Empire. Despite previous assurances to the contrary, Russia at the Congress of Berlin (1878) took southern Bessarabia from Rumania, allowing her in return the poorer Dobrudja (Dobrogea). At the same time, Rumania was declared fully independent of the Ottoman Empire. In 1881 Carol became king.

In internal affairs Carol held real personal power. In the first part of his reign, until 1888, he cooperated with the Liberal party leader Ion Bratianu; thereafter, Liberals and Conservatives alternated in office.

In 1914, with the outbreak of World War I, Carol favored a policy of cooperation with the Central Powers, but the parliament insisted on the maintenance of Rumanian neutrality. Carol died at Sinaia on Oct. 10, 1914. Subsequently Rumania joined the Allies.

CHARLES JELAVICH
BARBARA JELAVICH
Indiana University

CAROL II, kar′əl (1893–1953), king of Rumania from 1930 to 1940, was born at Sinaia on Oct. 15, 1893, the eldest son of Ferdinand I. His life was ridden with scandal. In 1926 he divorced his first wife to marry Princess Helen of Greece, who bore him a son, Prince Michael. Throughout most of his career he maintained an open liaison with Magda Lupescu, whom he finally married in 1947.

His personal life had important political repercussions. When Ferdinand I died in 1927, Carol was first excluded from the succession because of his relations with Magda Lupescu and his earlier renunciation of the throne. A regency was formed to rule for Michael until he became of age. But in 1930, Prime Minister Julius Maniu agreed to Carol's assumption of the crown. Later the two quarreled over the king's continued liaison with Magda Lupescu. When Maniu resigned, Carol strengthened his own position and finally established a royal dictatorship. In 1938 a new constitution abolished political parties and gave the king control of the government. In the 1930's a Fascist political organization, the Iron Guard, was formed, but when it became too strong, Carol had it dissolved.

In 1940 after Rumania lost Bessarabia to the Soviet Union, southern Dobrogea (Dobrudja) to Bulgaria, and a part of Transylvania to Hungary, Carol abdicated in favor of his son Michael and went into exile. He died in Estoril, near Lisbon, Portugal, on April 10, 1953.

CHARLES JELAVICH
BARBARA JELAVICH
Indiana University

CAROL, a seasonal religious song with a simple tune, intended for performance by untrained singers. The term (from the French *carole,* a round dance with musical accompaniment) refers almost always to Christmas carols, although there are carols for other liturgical seasons—Advent, Epiphany, Easter.

Early English Carols. The carol originated in the early 15th century. Most of the earliest carols were anonymous works probably written by clerics or court musicians; some of them, such as the *Coventry Carol,* came from mystery and miracle plays. Their text–narrative, lyrical, or dramatic—were not always religious; the words were generally vernacular or macaronic (in a mixture of English and Latin). The carol melodies were generally simple in style, with strong rhythms and a characteristic lilt; their musical form was distinguished by a refrain *(burden)* sung probably at the beginning of the carol and after each stanza of the text.

The earliest printed collection of carols was issued in 1521; it included the *Boar's Head Carol,* which is still sung during Christmas dinner at Queen's College, Oxford. However, most carols were passed on orally from one generation to the next. Many of these were in ballad form, the texts being poems in short stanzas narrating a story; among the earliest carols of this type are The *Cherry Tree Carol, The Seven Joys of Mary,* and *I Saw Three Ships.*

The English Puritans of the 17th century opposed the celebration of religious feast days, and in 1647, at the end of the Civil War, carol singing was forbidden. After the Restoration, in 1660, carols were revived, but their popularity had diminished. The Puritans who colonized America during the 17th century also disapproved of carols, and the practice of carol singing in the United States is relatively recent.

Later English Carols. Many of the most popular carols date from the 18th and 19th centuries. These include *Adeste Fideles,* possibly by John Francis Wade (1711–1786); *Hark! The Herald Angels Sing,* with words by Charles Wesley (1707–1788) and music by Felix Mendelssohn (1809–1847); and *Joy to the World,* with words by Isaac Watts (1674–1748) and music adapted from George Frideric Handel (1685–1759). These songs were written as Christmas hymns, which were more formal and didactic than the traditional carols; but the distinction has since been abandoned.

Carols from Other Countries. Carols began to be written in the United States in the 19th century. American carols include *O Little Town of Bethlehem* and *It Came upon a Midnight Clear.*

Many of the Christmas carols popular in England and America originated as French *noëls* or German *Weihnachtslieder.* The most familiar of the French carols is *Angels We Have Heard on High;* Germany contributed the lovely *Lo, How a Rose E'er Blooming,* by Michael Praetorius (1571–1621), as well as *Silent Night, Holy Night,* with words by Joseph Mohr (1792–1848) and music by Franz Gruber (1787–1863), which is the most popular of all carols.

CHARLES N. HENDERSON
Choirmaster, St. George's Church, New York

Further Reading: Dearmer, Percy, and others, eds., *The Oxford Book of Carols* (New York and London 1928); Greene, Richard L., *The Early English Carols* (New York and London 1935); Nettel, Reginald, ed., *Carols, 1400–1950* (New York 1956); Routley, Erik, *The English Carol* (London 1958).

CAROL CITY is an unincorporated city in southeastern Florida, in Dade county. It is situated about 12 miles (19 km) northwest of Miami, of which it is a suburb. The community, which includes Miami Gardens, is chiefly residential. Some poultry and beef and dairy cattle are raised, and citrus fruits and truck vegetables are grown on farmlands to the west.

The city was originally called Coral City by its developer, but its name was changed to avoid confusion with Coral Gables, Fla. Special Christmas caroling services are held each year in the city. Carol City is governed by a mayor and council. Population: 27,361.

CAROLINA PROPRIETORS, kar-ə-līn'ə, the men who controlled an immense domain in America, including most of modern North and South Carolina, as well as Georgia and part of Florida, under charter from the King of England, from 1663 to 1729. The original eight proprietors were Edward Hyde, Earl of Clarendon; George Monck, Duke of Albemarle; William, Lord Craven; John, Lord Berkeley; Anthony, Lord Ashley; Sir George Carteret; Sir William Berkeley; and Sir John Colleton. On March 24, 1663, they jointly received a charter from King Charles II for a grant of land between the 31st and 36th parallels of north latitude, stretching theoretically from the Atlantic to the Pacific oceans. In 1665 this grant was extended to the area from 36°30′ to 29°. With some changes in personnel, the proprietorship endured in some form until the Carolinas officially became royal colonies in 1729.

Colonization. Although the charter cited a desire to Christianize the natives, the proprietors' interest was primarily economic. This was indicated in their early issue of the *Declarations and Proposals to All That Will Plant in Carolina* (1663), which offered land under a "head right" system to settlers who would establish themselves without cost to the proprietors. Settlers were promised representation in a provincial assembly and freedom of conscience.

Two early colonization attempts at Cape Fear (N.C.) were abandoned before 1667, but the Albemarle settlement, which began as an overflow from Virginia, expanded slowly to become North Carolina. Its economy, like Virginia's, was based on tobacco, but with more diversified farming. An expedition from England in 1670 established a settlement at Charlestown on the Ashley river, which grew to become South Carolina. Here rice became the economic staple after experimentation with wine, silk, cotton, sugar, indigo, olives, and other products.

Government. In March 1669, Lord Ashley (Earl of Shaftesbury) issued the *Fundamental Constitutions,* a plan for a permanent form of government for Carolina. His secretary, John Locke, undoubtedly had a hand in its formulation. This document provided for an essentially aristocratic, somewhat feudal governmental system, including two ranks of colonial nobility–*landgraves* and *caciques.* The common people who fulfilled landholding qualifications were to elect representatives to the parliament, but legislation was to be initiated by a grand council consisting of the governor and the nobility. It is unclear to what extent the proprietors intended to make this system operative, but it did not go into effect.

Problems. In the early days both North and South Carolina had trouble with pirates using their protected waters. South Carolina successfully fought incursions by the Spanish and the French. A serious Indian threat in North Carolina, the Tuscarora War (1711–1713), was suppressed with aid from South Carolina and Virginia. In 1715 the Yamasee uprising in South Carolina took a heavy toll. Several times the colonists appealed to the proprietors for aid, but none was forthcoming because the enterprise was proving unprofitable.

In 1719 rumors of a new Spanish threat combined with a proprietorial repeal of several acts of the colonial assembly to produce a revolution in South Carolina. The assembly repudiated proprietorial control and appealed to the popular governor, Robert Johnston, to join them in a caretaker government until the king's will could be known. When Johnston refused, the assembly turned itself into a convention, appointed another governor, and appealed to the king to take over. This was accomplished in 1720. However, North Carolina governors continued to be appointed by the proprietors. In 1729, King George II agreed to pay £17,500 to extinguish the claims of seven of the proprietors. The eighth, Lord Granville, refused to settle; he retained a strip along the northern border of North Carolina until it was confiscated during the American Revolution.

Appraisal. The establishment of the Carolina proprietorship contradicted the contemporary trend toward more centralized royal control, but probably did little to slow it. The proprietors were not aggressive colonizers, but they did adopt a land policy that encouraged settlement and they sponsored some experimentation that aided the colonial economy. Religious toleration under the proprietorship contributed to the American tradition. The very indecision about the unworkable *Fundamental Constitutions* allowed the development of an assembly with considerable power, as evidenced by its initiative in ending proprietorial rule.

CLARENCE J. ATTIG
Westmar College, Iowa

CAROLINE AFFAIR, kar'ə-līn ə-fâr', a series of incidents that increased tension between Britain and the United States from 1837 until 1842. The *Caroline,* an American-owned steamboat being used by Canadian rebels, was attacked in United States waters by Canadian government troops.

In late 1837, William Lyon Mackenzie (q.v.), a leader of the abortive Canadian rebellion against British authority, sought refuge in Buffalo, N. Y. From American territory he raised funds, recruited volunteers, and directed propaganda against Upper Canada. He and nearly 1,000 followers established a provisional Canadian government on Navy Island, on the Canadian side of the Niagara River, and hired the *Caroline* to bring supplies from the U. S. shore.

On the night of Dec. 29, 1837, a Canadian force set out to destroy the ship. Not finding it in Canadian waters, the raiders crossed to the American shore, where they set the vessel afire and towed it into the river to sink. One American was killed in the attack.

President Martin Van Buren ordered Maj. Gen. Winfield Scott to the border, and a formal protest was issued to the British minister. In the succeeding months Canadian refugees and American adventurers harassed the border. The British steamship *Sir Robert Peel* was attacked on the American side of the St. Lawrence River to the cry of "Remember the *Caroline.*"

The *Caroline* was remembered again in November 1840, when New York officers arrested Alexander McLeod, a deputy sheriff from Upper Canada, for arson and murder in connection with the original raid. Britain refused to recognize the legality of any trial. The British foreign secretary, Lord Palmerston, argued that even if McLeod had been among the raiders, he was acting under orders in a legitimate attempt to defend Canadian shores from American-supplied but Canadian-based potential marauders. The U. S. secretary of state, Daniel Webster, felt the incidents unworthy of war, but he could not interfere with state courts. The trial was held, but McLeod was acquitted in October 1841.

In 1842, while Webster and Britain's Lord Ashburton were negotiating the Webster-Ashburton Treaty (q.v.), Ashburton suggested that Britain should have apologized for the attack on the *Caroline*. Webster took this as an apology, accepted the British contention that the raid had been in self-defense, and, by not demanding an indemnity, closed the *Caroline* affair.

ROBIN W. WINKS, *Yale University*

CAROLINE ISLANDS, kar'ə-līn, an island group lying just north of the equator in the western Pacific Ocean, part of the United Nations Trust Territory of the Pacific Islands, administered by the United States. The Carolines comprise the administrative districts of Palau, Yap, Truk, and Ponape.

There are more than 930 islands in the group, spread over an ocean area of nearly 1.3 million square miles (3.4 million sq km) but with a land area of only about 450 square miles (1,165 sq km). Babelthuap in the Palaus and Ponape in the Eastern Carolines are the two largest islands. Ulithi, Yap, and the Palaus rest on a long volcanic ridge that stretches northward through the Mariana Islands to Japan. The Eastern Carolines consist of numerous coral atolls and volcanic islands that rise from the sea floor. The Caroline Islands have a tropical climate, with annual rainfall averaging above 100 inches (2,540 mm). Typhoons are common in the northwest.

People. The Carolines have an estimated population of 62,048 (1965). Except for Polynesian inhabitants on Nukuroro and Kapingamarangi atolls in the southeast, the people are primarily Micronesian. Although customs differ among the widely scattered islands, ancestor cults, strong political and family ties, and leadership by chiefs are common.

The language of Palau is essentially Malaysian, whereas Micronesian dialects predominate on other islands. Polynesian is spoken on Nukuroro and Kapingamarangi. English is the language of instruction in the public schools and is rapidly becoming the chief means of communication among diverse groups. Public schools are free and compulsory for children from 7 to 13 years old or until they have completed the elementary grades.

Economy. Agriculture and fishing are the principal bases of the islands' economy. On the coral atolls, fish supplements the staple diet of coconuts, pandanus, and breadfruit. Taro, sweet potatoes, yams, arrowroot, cassava, bananas, and citrus fruits are grown on the volcanic islands as additional subsistence crops. Copra is the main cash crop and leading export. Since World War II, attempts have been made to establish cacao and black pepper as commercial crops. Trochus

DEL REY, FROM MONKMEYER

IN THE CAROLINE ISLANDS district of Yap, young men perform a dance interpreting the birth of Christ.

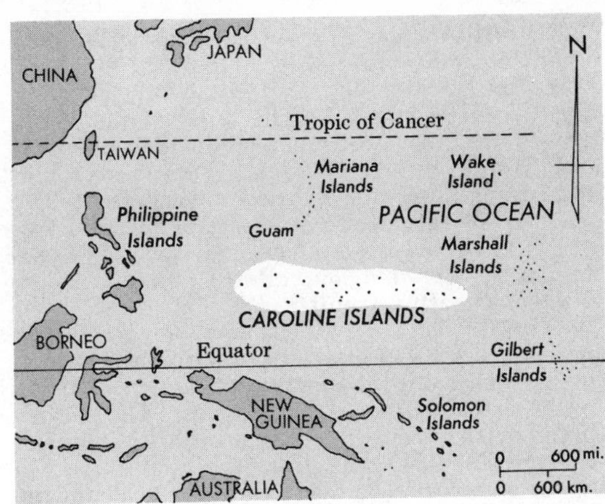

shell is exported from Yap and the Palaus. The principal domestic animals are pigs and poultry.

Manufacturing is limited chiefly to handicrafts, boat building, and, in the Palau Islands, to processing frozen fish.

The Carolines have extremely limited mineral resources. Mining operations in the past virtually exhausted deposits of phosphate, bauxite, and manganese. Small reserves of bauxite remain on Babelthuap and Ponape.

Gradual improvement of airfields, local transportation, and hotel facilities has assisted the development of a small tourist industry. Commercial shipping serves the main islands and makes connections with the Marianas and Marshalls.

History. Portuguese and Spanish explorers visited the Carolines in the early 16th century. The Spanish named the islands "Carolina" after King Charles II of Spain and claimed them for a time in the 19th century before negotiating a treaty of sale with Germany.

During World War I, Germany lost control of the islands to Japan, which held them under a League of Nations mandate from 1920 until World War II. Since 1947 the United States has administered the Carolinas together with the Marianas and Marshalls as the UN Trust Territory of the Pacific Islands. Administrative responsibility was transferred from the secretary of the navy to the secretary of the interior in 1951.

HOWARD J. CRITCHFIELD
Western Washington State College

CAROLINE OF ANSPACH, anz'pak (1683–1737), queen consort of George II of England. She was vivacious and politically astute, and she used her influence to help consolidate the Glorious Revolution of 1688 and the Hanoverian Succession.

Caroline was born on March 1, 1683, the child of the Margrave of Brandenburg-Anspach (or Ansbach), who died in 1687. In 1692 her mother married the Elector of Saxony and moved to Dresden. On her mother's death in 1696, Caroline was brought up by her guardian, the Elector Frederick III of Brandenburg (later King Frederick I of Prussia) and his wife, Sophia Charlotte. Caroline soon became another expensive pawn in the royal game of dynastic matchmaking. After various intrigues and false starts she was married in 1705 to George Augustus, son and heir of the Elector George of Hanover, who succeeded to the English crown in 1714.

Caroline spent nine happy years in Hanover, reading Leibniz and other savants and producing children. As Princess of Wales she aided and abetted her husband in his prolonged breach with his father, and as queen she handled his love affairs and his ministers with almost equal shrewdness. Her support of Sir Robert Walpole as first minister paid dividends to both Walpole and the cause of political stability. English politicians learned to regard her as a powerful ally and a dangerous opponent. She died in London on Nov. 20, 1737.

L. PERRY CURTIS, JR.
University of California at Berkeley

CAROLINE OF BRUNSWICK (1768–1821), wife of the English king George IV. Caroline, the second daughter of the Duke of Brunswick-Wolfenbüttel and Augusta, King George III's sister, was born in Brunswick, Germany, on May 17, 1768. When marriage with Caroline was proposed to the future George IV (then Prince of Wales), he demanded £27,000 for wedding expenses, in addition to an annual increase of £65,000 in his personal income and a further £50,000 each year for his wife.

Caroline arrived in England in 1795, and on the evening of April 8 she and the prince were married. But their union was not happy. Although Caroline gave birth to a daughter (Charlotte Augusta) in January 1796, she and George formally separated three months later. Not long afterward Charlotte was taken away from her mother. Caroline's isolation from the court deepened in 1811 when her husband assumed the regency, and in 1813 she went to Europe.

Having visited her family in Germany, Caroline went to Italy. There the excessive favors she bestowed on one Bartolomeo Bergami gave rise to such scandalous rumors that secret agents were sent from London to investigate the matter. Before deciding (in 1820) to return to England, Caroline journeyed to Constantinople and to the Holy Land. George, now king, offered his wife a handsome stipend if she would remain abroad—but to no avail. Caroline had stubbornly resolved to be crowned. After the divorce proceedings that Parliament initiated on the King's behalf proved abortive, George became equally determined that his wife would never wear the royal crown. Consequently, when she tried to enter Westminster Abbey for her husband's coronation, the way was barred. Caroline did not recover from this crushing defeat; in less than a month she died, on Aug. 7, 1821, in London.

JOHN FERGUSON, *Columbia University*

CAROLINGIAN, kar'ə-lin-jən, a dynasty that governed in France from 754 to 987, in Germany from 754 to 911, and in Italy (with interruptions) from 774 to 901. The family sprang from two 7th century Austrasian landholders, Pepin I and Arnulf, bishop of Metz. Pepin's daughter and Arnulf's son were married to each other. The son born of this marriage, Pepin of Heristal, began the line, which is known variously as *Carolingian* or *Carlovingian,* after Charlemagne, or *Arnulfinger,* after Arnulf.

The Carolingians ruled new kingdoms that marked Europe's progress from barbarism to high civilization, from the anarchy of migratory tribes to the order of feudal monarchies. The history of the dynasty consists of three periods. The first period (613–754) runs from the family's rise to power under the Merovingian kings to Pepin the Short's coronation as king of the Franks. The second period (754–887) saw the Carolingian empire reach its peak under Charlemagne, and gradually splinter into separate kingdoms under different branches of the family. The third period, one of decline, lasted until those branches died out.

The Mayors of the Palace. Pepin I (d. 639) founded his family's fortune by securing governmental power as mayor of the palace of the Merovingian kings of Austrasia (the eastern Frankish lands centering on Metz). His descendants continued as mayors of the palace. The feeble Merovingian kings reigned in title; the Carolingian mayors ruled in fact. Four generations of powerful mayors, sometimes governing without kings on the throne, prepared for the day in 750 when Pepin the Short asked Pope Zacharias if it was not right that the man who did the king's work should have the king's title. Pope Stephen III sealed the Carolingian ascendancy by crowning Pepin and his sons as kings in July 754.

Before the dynasty's first period ended, the mayors had set lines of action that led to the greatness of the second period. They united the Frankish kingdoms and made their people preeminent among the barbarian tribes west of the Rhine. They established their military and cultural influence over pagan tribes to the east of the Rhine and Weser rivers. Armies under the mayors' command and missionaries under their protection extended the frontier of western Christianity into the lands of the Swabians, Thuringians, Hessians, Saxons, and Bavarians.

Pepin's question to Pope Zacharias foretold a fateful development in European history: an alliance between popes and Frankish kings that was to embroil Germanic rulers in Italy's politics for centuries. The alliance was secured in 754 when Pepin and his sons were crowned and the Franks were forbidden ever to seek kings outside the line of Pepin's descendants.

The Carolingian Apogee. Three characteristics of early Carolingian history—strong administration, military and cultural expansion to the east, and alliance with the popes—predominated in the dynasty's second period. For all of his effective innovations, Charlemagne (742?–814), Pepin's son, followed the precedents of his ancestors, the palatine mayors. He followed precedent when he revised forms of government to strengthen and extend the royal power. He followed it when he led armies and established monasteries between the Rhine and Elbe, securing Frankish rule in Saxony, Thuringia, and Bavaria. He also followed family precedent when his intervention in Italy, and particularly his defense of the Roman church, brought him to the supreme moment in his family's rise, his coronation as "Emperor of the Romans" in 800.

When Charlemagne died, the Carolingian Empire united under one ruler all Europe from the North Sea to the Mediterranean, from the Atlantic to the Elbe-Saale-Danube line, and Italy as far south as Benevento, and Spain to the Ebro River.

Decline of the Empire. Still, the union was precarious. Some provinces, especially in Italy, gave only lip service to Frankish rule and waited to revolt. Norse raids on the northern empire began. Neither transport, nor communications, nor the offices of government were developed enough to sustain a far-flung empire.

However, there was a more basic flaw in the Carolingian political structure. There was a confusion of public and private powers. This was critical in successions to the throne. From the earliest Merovingian period, Frankish history was marked by a broken sequence of strong rulers who spent their lives unifying the Franks, only to divide their realms as their own personal estates among their heirs when they died. This alternation of unification and disintegration continued among the Carolingians, both as palatine mayors and as kings.

The sons of Charlemagne prepared to share the empire as dictated by their father's decree *Divisio imperii* (Division of the Empire), issued in 806. Because all of Charlemagne's sons except Louis the Pious predeceased Charlemagne, the realm ultimately descended to him intact. But the divisions of the empire that he executed among his own sons aroused civil wars that shattered the empire's unity. Only by chance, Charles III (reigned from 881 to 887) reunited the empire, for the last time. Even before his death, the kingdoms of Italy, Provence, Burgundy, Germany, and France began their separate histories.

The Feudal Monarchy. Fragmentation into several kingdoms had the effect of resolving some of the problems arising from the confusion between public and private estates. Society had developed to the point where ethnic groupings could not be combined and divided as the personal estates of kings. The state began to emerge as a permanent territorial unit, rather than as the personal entourage of a tribal chieftain.

But this confusion between public and private rights reappeared on the level of the military, landed aristocracy. As Carolingians expanded their realms, they set up military governments with wide administrative powers in the conquered lands. They granted fiefs to their agents in the conquered lands. The fiefs were intended to be held in return for the performance of duties for the king. The fiefs, however, became hereditary. Without solving its own problem of succession, the dynasty had encouraged the growth of regional groupings of great nobles, having political powers independent of the kings. The dynasty fell before those rising feudal or protofeudal classes. The old order of tribal kingship had ended and its place was gradually being taken by the feudal monarchy, which matured in the 12th century.

K. F. MORRISON, *University of Chicago*

Further Reading: Conant, Kenneth J., *Carolingian and Romanesque Architecture: 800 to 1200* (Baltimore 1959); Fichtenau, Heinrich, *The Carolingian Empire* (Oxford 1957); Halphen, L., *Charlemagne et l'empire carolingien* (Paris 1947).

CARON, kä-rôɴ′, **René Édouard** (1800–1876), Canadian public official. He was born on Oct. 11, 1800, in Ste.-Anne-de-Beaupré, Lower Canada (Quebec). Admitted to the bar of Lower Canada in 1826, he served as mayor of Quebec from 1834 to 1836 and from 1840 to 1846.

A Liberal, he was named to the Legislative Council of Canada in 1841 and served as its speaker from 1843 to 1847 and from 1848 to 1853. He became judge of the superior court of Lower Canada in 1853, later was promoted to the court of queen's bench, and from 1873 until his death served as lieutenant governor of Quebec. Caron died on Dec. 13, 1876, in Spencer Wood, Quebec.

CARONDELET, kä-rôn-dā-let′, **Francisco Luis Héctor de** (1748?–1807), Spanish colonial official. Barón de Carondelet was born in Noyelles, Flanders. After serving as governor of San Salvador, Guatemala, he was governor of Louisiana and West Florida from 1791 to 1795 and continued as governor of Louisiana until 1797. By intriguing with dissatisfied American frontiersmen and arousing Indian tribes against the United States, he created great unrest and strained relations between the United States and Spain. Carondelet later served (1799–1807) as governor general of Quito, Ecuador, where he died on Aug. 10, 1807.

CARONÍ RIVER, kä-rō-nē′, the major source of hydroelectric power in Venezuela. It rises in the Guiana highlands and flows 430 miles (690 km) west and north to the Orinoco. On a remote tributary of the Caroní is Angel Falls, with the world's highest single fall, 2,648 feet (807 meters).

Hydroelectric development of the Caroní is planned to furnish electricity to all of Venezuela and parts of neighboring countries. Construction of the Guri Dam on the lower Caroní began in 1965, with a plant designed to generate 6 million kw of electricity. Part of this output is for Ciudad Guyana (q.v.), an industrial center under development at the junction of the Caroní and Orinoco. Downstream from Guri, the Macagua hydroelectric station (375.000 kw) powers a large steel mill near Ciudad Guyana.

The Caroní waters the state of Bolívar, one of Latin America's richest developing regions. It contains iron, manganese, bauxite, nickel, chrome, diamonds, gold, and vast forests reserves. The region is abundant in land suitable for the raising of crops and livestock.

CAROSSA, kä-rōs′ä, **Hans** (1878–1956), German neoclassical writer, whose poems and autobiographical novels express his philosophy that enlightened man can help nature recover from evil. Carossa was born in Tölz, Germany, on Dec. 15, 1878. He became a physician, like his father, and practiced in Nuremberg, Munich, and Passau. He died in Rittsteig on Sept. 12, 1956.

Carossa was influenced by Goethe, Rilke, and Stefan George, and his poetry, collected in *Gesammelte Gedichte* (1949), is in the classical tradition in moderation, balance, and confidence in man. In his prose writings, he sought to reveal that divine order underlies chaos and to promote reverence for individual human life by using stages in his own spiritual development as symbols of the struggle of nature toward renewal and maturity. Among such writings are *Eine Kindheit* (1922; Eng. tr., *A Childhood,* 1930); *Rumänisches Tagebuch* (1924; Eng. tr., *A Roumanian Diary,* 1927), about his experiences as an army doctor in World War I; and *Ungleiche Welten* (1951), which deals with Nazi and postwar Germany in terms of his own experience and of historical and philosophical interpretation.

RANDOLPH J. KLAWITER
University of Notre Dame

CAROTENOIDS, kə-rot′ən-oidz, is a general term for a group of plant-produced pigments ranging in color from yellow to red and brown. The carotenes and the xanthophylls, yellow in color, are the most common. Carotenoids are responsible for the coloration of certain plants (for example, the carrot) and of some animals such as the lobster (the pigments are transferred to animals as an element in their foods). Carotenoid pigments are present in the chloroplasts of all green plants, but their colors are usually masked by the green chlorphylls. Much of the autumn coloration of leaves is due to the loss of chlorophylls and the uncovering of the carotenoids. Carotenoids are composed of isoprene units (usually eight), which may be modified by the addition of other chemical groups.

The functions of carotenoids in plants are not well understood, but the carotenes are important to the higher animals since they are utilized in the formation of vitamin A.

DOUGLAS M. FAMBROUGH, JR.
California Institute of Technology

CAROTHERS, kə-ruth′ərz, **Wallace Hume** (1896–1937), American chemist, who worked on the organic chemistry of synthetic fibers and plastics. Carothers was born in Burlington, Iowa, on April 27, 1896. After receiving a doctor's degree from the University of Illinois and teaching there and at Harvard, he was engaged by the du Pont Company in 1928 for fundamental research in organic chemistry. His first discovery at du Pont was chloroprene, which together with its polymers (large compound molecules) soon became industrially important.

Carothers theorized that certain polymers are produced by condensation through elimination of water or an equivalent substance. The aim of his research was a truly synthetic material that could be spun into strong fibers. He obtained "superpolymers" by the reaction of acids with alcohols, where the acid had two acidic groups at the ends of a long chain of carbon atoms, and the alcohol had hydroxyl groups at the ends of its molecule. A long chain of alternating acid and alcohol residues was formed during heating in a vacuum. The polymeric product, however, was found to be too fusible and soluble.

After other attempts to find the correct reactants, Carothers discovered a combination that gave a product with the desired properties. On Feb. 28, 1935, he made a resin from adipic acid and hexamethylenediamine, both components containing 6 carbon atoms. The product, named nylon, thus was characterized by the number 66. It gained considerably in strength by drawing the fiber under tension, which causes a reorientation of the crystals. Commercial production of nylon 66 was begun in early 1940, about three years after Carothers' death in Wilmington, Del., on April 29, 1937.

EDUARD FARBER
Editor of "Great Chemists"

CAROTID ARTERY, kə-rot′əd är′tə-rē, either of a pair of major vessels that supply blood to the head and neck. The right carotid artery originates from a branch of the aorta, while the left carotid arises directly from the aorta. Both carotid arteries soon divide into two main branches: an *external carotid* and an *internal carotid*. The external carotid divides into cervical branches, which supply the greater part of the neck, and the facial branches, which supply the external parts of the face and the head. The internal carotid supplies the brain and eye. Both the left and right carotid arteries together carry about 20% of the heart's output, about 1 liter (2 pints) of blood every minute.

In addition to transporting blood, the carotids aid in regulating blood pressure and respiration. The *carotid body*, a small structure at the junction of each artery's external and internal branches, is sensitive to the amount of oxygen in the blood. If the oxygen content is too low, the carotid body sends nerve impulses to the brain centers that increase the rate of respiration. The *carotid sinus*, a slight enlargement of the internal carotid near the carotid body, measures the blood pressure and relays this information to the brain.

ELVIN SMITH
University of Mississippi Medical School

CAROUSEL, kar-ə-sel′, is a musical play with book and lyrics by Oscar Hammerstein II and music by Richard Rodgers, first produced in 1945. It was adapted from Ferenc Molnar's drama *Liliom* (1909), and the setting was changed from Hungary to New England in the 1870's. *Carousel*, in a prelude and two acts, centers on the carnival barker Billy Bigelow. It portrays his marriage to Julie Jordan, his suicide to avoid arrest after a robbery, and his attempt to redeem himself during a return from Purgatory.

CARP is the name applied both to a large species of fish (*Cyprinus carpio*) and to the family (Cyprinidae) of which it is a member.

Carp. The largest member of the carp family and the typical form, *Cyprinus carpio*, grows to a length of about 40 inches (1 meter) and a weight of about 70 pounds (32 kg) in Europe and Asia. In Britain and North America, however, its maximum weight is around 45 pounds (20 kg). The carp is a narrow fish with a broad oval cross section and a very long dorsal fin. The dorsal fin and the anal fin have a stout serrated first ray. Four barbels surround a moderate-sized, toothless mouth. The color varies from a muddy brown to olive or coppery brown. The lower fins are often red. Wild carp usually have scales that are regularly arranged and overlapping, but there is considerable variation in scales among the great many varieties of the species. The mirror carp, for example, has a few extremely large scales, while the leather carp has only a few small scales along the base of the dorsal fin.

Carp

TREAT DAVIDSON, FROM NATIONAL AUDUBON SOCIETY

In common with other members of the family, the common carp has a number of interesting anatomical features. For example, it has pharyngeal, or throat, teeth (rather than teeth on the jaws). These grind food against a hard pad on the lower part of the skull. The fish also has a group of unique bones, called Webberian ossicles, that connect the air bladder to the middle ear.

Behavior. The carp thrives best in large bodies of warm, quiet water, but it lives in rapid rivers as well. Large carp are very active in shallow water in the spring. Their activity is usually obvious since they swirl and jump, muddying the water. Carp feed on aquatic insects, snails, crustaceans, aquatic vegetation, organic waste, and to a lesser extent on the eggs and young of other fishes when they are abundant. Because of their omnivorous diet, carp were once used in sewage treatment in Europe.

The carp spawns in late spring. Its eggs adhere to vegetation and are not cared for. Some carp have lived for over 40 years in captivity. However, wild carp probably only live for 12 to 15 years.

Range. The original habitat of the carp was probably the region from the Amur River in northeastern Asia to Burma and westward to the Black, Caspian, and Aral seas. In the hope of providing a readily available and cheap food supply, it was introduced into many other regions. The carp was introduced into eastern Europe before the Christian era. It was then taken to Britain and in the late 19th century was introduced into North America, where it quickly became widely distributed.

Economic Importance. In Europe and Asia, carp are netted in large numbers and cultivated extensively for food. In North America large numbers are captured by commercial fishermen, but carp has never been highly prized for food there except by recent emigrants from Europe. In North America, it has only recenly been angled to any extent. Carp is thought to be destructive to its habitat and harmful to other fishes inhabiting the same area because of its "rooting" behavior (its tendency to dig up the earth with its snout) and omnivorous eating habits.

Carp Family. The carp family, often referred to as the minnow family in North America, comprises some 1,500 species, which occur throughout the Northern Hemisphere. The family is classified in the order Cypriniformes (Ostariophysi). Among the members of the family are the bitterling, bream, bleak, chub, and goldfish. The wild goldfish, *Carassius auratus*, and its many derivatives, such as the crucian carp and the golden carp, are closely related to the carp, *Cyprinus carpio*. Both the carp and the goldfish have been selectively bred for so long—both as food fishes and as ornamental fishes—that a confusing complex of varieties now exists.

E. J. CROSSMAN
University of Toronto

CARPACCIO, kär-pät′chō, **Vittore** (1465?–1526?), Venetian painter, whose career spanned the period of transition from the early to the High Renaissance. Carpaccio's major achievement was his ability to combine an almost Flemish precision of detail with a Venetian sense of scale and love of pageantry, and to organize this wealth of pictorial detail into the logical and coherent space characteristic of the Italian Renaissance. Although he was one of the foremost Venetian painters of his day, Carpaccio's failure to assimilate the High Renaissance stylistic innovations of Titian and Giorgione led to a hardening of his style and a decline in his popularity.

Early Career. Carpaccio was born in Venice about 1465; little is known of his early life and training. The Flemish characteristics of his style indicate a close association with Antonello da Messina, the painter who brought Flemish influence to Italy in the late 15th century.

Carpaccio's earliest (1490–1495) and his most famous cycle of paintings is the series of panels devoted to the legend of St. Ursula, originally painted for the Scuola di Sant'Orsola, and now in the Accademia, Venice. This series, a masterpiece of pictorial narrative, gives a vivid picture of 15th century Venice in the detailed backgrounds of the panels. It is this meticulous rendering of detail, in both outdoor and indoor settings, and his close scrutiny of human appearance that links Carpaccio to Antonello da Messina and the microscopic naturalism of the Flemish.

Later Work. A cycle of nine paintings, depicting episodes from the lives of saints, was painted by Carpaccio between 1502 and 1507 for the Scuola San Giorgio degli Schiavoni, Venice. Of particular interest is *St. Augustine in His Study* (formerly called *St. Jerome*); the room reflects the interests of the cultivated man of his day—relics of classical antiquity, scientific instruments, and musical scores.

Carpaccio's later work includes six scenes from the life of the Virgin (1504) for the Scuola degli Albanesi; five panels on the life of St. Stephen (1511–1520) for the Scuola di San Stefano; and the *Presentation in the Temple* (1510), an altarpiece for the Church of San Giobbe. He died in Venice sometime between Oct. 28, 1525, and June 26, 1526.

MARTICA SAWIN
Parsons School of Design, New York

Further Reading: Zampetti, Pietro, *Vittore Carpaccio* (Venice 1963).

ANDERSON—ART REFERENCE BUREAU

THE ARRIVAL OF ST. URSULA AT COLOGNE, by Vittore Carpaccio (located in the Accademia, Venice).

CARPANI, kär-pä′nē, **Giuseppe Antonio** (1752–1825), Italian librettist and musicographer. He was born in Villalbese, Italy, on Jan. 28, 1752. He was trained as a lawyer but devoted himself to the stage and to music, writing a comedy and translating several opera librettos. His anti-French writings forced him to leave Milan when the French took that city in 1796, and he settled in Vienna, where he died on Jan. 22, 1825.

For years, Carpani's *Le Haydine* (1812) was the only vital account of Haydn's life. The biography was plagiarized by Stendhal (Henri Beyle) for his own music biographies. Carpani's biography of Rossini, *Le Rossiniane* (1824), was also pirated by Stendhal.

CARPATHIAN MOUNTAINS, kär-pā′thē-ən, an important mountain system of eastern Europe. Rising near Bratislava, Czechoslovakia, from the valley of the Danube River, which separates them from the Austrian Alps, the Carpathian Mountains swing in a great arc toward the east through parts of Czechoslovakia, Poland, the Ukraine, and Rumania. Then curving sharply westward through Rumania in what are known as the Transylvanian Alps, they again approach the Danube (near Orşova, Rumania), which separates them from the Balkan Mountains to the south.

With the Danube as a base, the Carpathians outline a tongue-shaped projection into central Europe, enclosing Hungary and erecting a natural barrier between Slovakia and Poland. In width the mountain system varies from about 7 to 230 miles (11 to 370 km) and in length extends some 800 miles (1,300 km).

The Carpathian system may be roughly divided into the western and eastern Carpathians. The western section includes an imposing mountain knot known as the High Tatra. Gerlachovka Štit, the highest peak in the Carpathians, rising to a height of 8,737 feet (2,700 meters), is located in the High Tatra. Several other summits of the group reach to more than 8,000 feet (2,400 meters). Negoiul Peak is the culminating point of the eastern Carpathians.

Structure and Mineral Resources. The Carpathian Mountains were mainly formed during the Tertiary period, with the process largely completed by the Miocene epoch. The outer flanks, generally steeper than the inner slopes, are composed largely of shales and sandstones dating from Cretaceous and Tertiary times. Here is found the characteristic building material known as Carpathian sandstone. The inner flanks are more complex in structure with Permian and Mesozoic strata overlying a foundation of Carboniferous and older rocks interspersed with outcroppings of Jurassic limestone.

The Carpathians are so rich in mineral deposits that some Slovakian peaks are called "ore

mountains. Gold, silver, copper, lead, zinc, mercury, and iron are found there. Coal and petroleum are abundant. There are also pockets of rock salt hundreds of feet thick.

Water Resources. The Carpathians form a natural watershed between such important river systems as the Oder, Vistula, and Dniester to the north and east and the southward flowing tributaries of the middle Danube. The annual rainfall ranges from 24 to 56 inches (610–1420 mm).

Plant and Animal Life. Vegetation, as in other mountainous regions, ascends through definite gradations. Agricultural crops and fruit trees flourish to a height of about 1,500 feet (450 meters), while numerous herds of cattle and sheep find pasturage at higher levels. Forests of oak, beech, and chestnut clothe the slopes to a height of about 4,000 feet (1,220 meters), where they yield to hardier firs and pines. Above an altitude of 6,000 feet (1,800 meters) only desolate outcroppings of barren rock emerge. The Carpathians provide a natural barrier against chill winds from the north and endow regions to the south with an unusually mild climate. Bears, wolves, and lynxes still lurk in the wilder areas, and birds of prey are common.

History. The Carpathian Mountains have played an important part in the history of eastern Europe. Although the range appears formidable on the map, the configuration of the land allows for easy passage through and settlement in areas near to the mountains.

In the 1st century the southern Carpathians were the center of the Dacian kingdom, which was conquered by Emperor Trajan in 106 and added to the Roman Empire. With the withdrawal of the Roman forces in 271, the numerous peoples—Slavs, Magyars, Germans, and others—who were to populate eastern Europe in modern times, passed through the mountains or settled near them. In World War I and World War II the area was the scene of major campaigns.

BARBARA JELAVICH and CHARLES JELAVICH
Indiana University

CARPEAUX, kar-pō′, **Jean Baptiste** (1827–1875), French sculptor, who was one of the creators of the romantic style popular during the Second Empire. He was born at Valenciennes on May 11, 1827. In 1844 he went to Paris to study under François Rude. Carpeaux's *Hector Bearing His Son Astynax in His Arms* (1854; Musée de l'École Nationale des Beaux-Arts, Paris) won him a Prix de Rome, which enabled him to study for several years in Italy. While there he executed the well-known *Neapolitan Fisherboy* (1858; Louvre, Paris) and, under the influence of Donatello and Michelangelo, the more romantic *Ugolino and His Starving Sons* (1857–1861; Louvre).

Carpeaux's later sculpture incorporates some of the elegance of the 18th century rococo style. *The Dance* (1856–1869), on the façade of the Paris Opera House, has a rococo liveliness that harmonizes with the sumptuousness of the building's architecture. Carpeaux's other important works include *Flora with Dancing Cupids* (1863–1866), in the Tuileries; the *Four Continents* fountain in the Luxembourg Gardens; and the monument to Watteau (1869) in Valenciennes. Carpeaux died at his château near Courbevoie on Oct. 11, 1875.

WILLIAM GERDTS, *University of Maryland*

CARPENTARIA, Gulf of, kär-pən-târ′ē-ə, a large gulf in northeastern Australia that is a southern extension of the Arafura Sea. It is named after Pieter Carpentier, a governor of the Netherlands Indies (Indonesia). The gulf is bounded by Queensland's Cape York Peninsula on the east, and by Arnhem Land in Northern Territory on the west. The Torres Strait connects it in the northeast with the Coral Sea.

About 420 miles (675 km) at its maximum width and 480 miles (870 km) long, the gulf is closed off from all oceanic circulation, except for the summer monsoon period when currents enter from the northwest. The largest of the gulf's numerous islands are Groote Eylandt, Sir Edward Pellew Islands, and Wellesley Island. Several large rivers flow into the gulf, including the Roper, Norman, Flinders, and Gilbert, which are navigable for varying distances.

CARPENTER, Edward (1844–1929), English social reformer and author, whose views on such subjects as penal reform, the status of women, and homosexuality exerted an important influence on liberal thought. He was born at Brighton, Sussex, on Aug. 29, 1844, and studied at Trinity Hall, Cambridge, where he was elected a fellow in 1868 and ordained in 1870. In 1874 he resigned his orders and fellowship and became a lecturer in Cambridge's extension program. In 1883 he bought a farm at Millthorpe, near Sheffield, and thereafter was increasingly concerned with the problems of labor. In 1877 and 1884 he visited the United States, where he met Walt Whitman, and in 1890 he went to Ceylon, where he was influenced by Indian mysticism. Carpenter died at Guildford, Surrey, on June 28, 1929.

Carpenter's central work, *Towards Democracy* (1883), is a long, exuberant, unrhymed sequence of poems influenced by Whitman and inspired by the ideal of a society based on brotherly love. Among his prose works are *The Intermediate Sex* (1908), on homosexuality, and *My Days and Dreams* (1916), an autobiography.

J. K. JOHNSTONE
University of Saskatchewan

CARPENTER, John Alden (1876–1951), American businessman and composer. He was born in Chicago on Feb. 28, 1876, the son of a wealthy industrial-supply manufacturer. While attending Harvard (B.A., 1897), he studied composition with John Knowles Paine, and later with Bernard Ziehn and Sir Edward Elgar. He then entered the family business, from which he retired in 1936. He died in Chicago on April 26, 1951.

Carpenter's first notable success as a composer was an amusing orchestral suite, *Adventures in a Perambulator* (1918), which was greatly influenced by French impressionism. This was followed by three successful ballets: *Birthday of the Infanta* (1919), *Krazy Kat* (1921; based on a comic strip), and *Skyscrapers* (1925), commissioned by Diaghilev as "a ballet of modern American life." *Krazy Kat* and *Skyscrapers*, as well as the Concertino for Piano and Orchestra (1915), drew on the idioms of American popular music. Carpenter also wrote song cycles, the orchestral tone poem *Sea Drift* (1933), a violin concerto (1936), and choral and chamber music.

GILBERT CHASE, *Author of "America's Music"*

CARPENTER, Joseph Estlin (1844–1927), English Unitarian minister and scholar. He was born in Ripley, Surrey, England, on Oct. 5, 1844. Carpenter was educated at University College, London, and at Manchester New College (now Manchester College, Oxford). From 1869 to 1875 he was a minister in Leeds, and he taught at Manchester College from 1875 to 1924.

Carpenter was a pioneer in the study of comparative religion and one of the first scholars to introduce the Old Testament into the curriculum of a theological college. He died in Oxford on June 2, 1927.

CARPENTER ANT. See ANT.

CARPENTER BEE. See BEE.

CARPENTER MOTH, the common name of a family of moths (Cossidae) whose larvae are serious pests of forest, shade, and fruit trees. They are also called *goat moths*. The family contains several hundred species and is widely distributed throughout the world.

Carpenter moths are moderately large, with wingspreads ranging from 1 to 7 inches (2.5–18 cm). They are nocturnal and are not able to feed because of their reduced mouthparts. Their larvae, commonly called *carpenter worms*, bore large tunnels in tree wood, causing serious injury to the host tree. The larva of one common North American species (*Prionoxystus robinae*) is a serious pest of black locust trees.

DON R. DAVIS, *Smithsonian Institution*

CARPENTERS AND JOINERS, United Brotherhood of, an AFL-CIO union of carpenters and others who work with wood. Originally a craft union (limited to craftsmen), it continues to function as such in the building trades, but it operates as an industrial union (open to all workers) in logging and furniture manufacturing. It has about 800,000 members in 2,900 locals. Its national headquarters is in Washington, D. C.

Carpenters first organized in America in 1724. The Continental Congress met in 1774 in the hall of the Carpenters' Company of Philadelphia. The present union was founded in 1881 by Peter McGuire, a socialist and the leader of the 8-hour-day movement. In 1915 the more conservative William Hutcheson became president, and in 1952 he was succeeded by his son Maurice Hutcheson. Because of the decentralized and competitive nature of the industry, the local district councils of the union retain much autonomy.

HUGH G. CLELAND
State University of New York at Stony Brook

CARPENTERS' HALL is a historic building in Philadelphia, Pa. It was constructed (beginning 1770) as a meeting hall by the Carpenters' Company of Philadelphia, a guild organized in 1724 by the master craftsmen responsible for much of the city's early design and construction. The hall was the meeting place of the First Continental Congress (Sept. 5–Oct. 25, 1774) and served as a hospital during the American Revolution. The First Bank of the United States was a tenant during the 1790's. Various organizations occupied the hall in the early 1800's.

The Carpenters' Company restored the hall, opened it to the public in 1857, and has maintained it as a historic landmark. It is included within Independence National Historical Park but is owned and used by the Carpenters' Company, which is the oldest organization of builders in the United States.

CARPENTERSVILLE is a village in northeastern Illinois, in Kane county, on the Fox River, 38 miles (61 km) northwest of Chicago. It produces plowshares and steel specialties. There are dairy and grain farms in the vicinity. Charles Valentine Carpenter of Uxbridge, Mass., settled the village in 1837. His son, Julius Angelo Carpenter, platted it in 1851. It was incorporated in 1887 and is governed by a mayor and trustees. Population: 24,059.

CARPENTIER, kär-pen-tyâr′, **Alejo** (1904–), Cuban writer. Alejo Carpentier y Valmont was born in Havana on Dec. 26, 1904, and was educated at the University of Havana. He later was program director of the Havana radio station CMZ, professor of the history of music at the National Conservatory, and a journalist in Havana and in Caracas, Venezuela.

Carpentier's writings mesh vivid exotic description with incisive intellectual commentary. His works include the novels *Ecue-yamba-o* (1933), *El reino de este mundo* (1949; Eng. tr., *Kingdom of This World,* 1957), and *El siglo de las luces* (1962; Eng. tr., *Explosion in a Cathedral,* 1963), and the collection of verse *Poemas de las Antillas* (1932).

CARPENTIER, kär-päɴ-tyā′, **Georges** (1894–), French boxer, who won the world light heavyweight championship in 1920 by knocking out Battling Levinsky. A year later he was knocked out in the fourth round by Jack Dempsey in a heavyweight title fight at Jersey City, N. J.

Carpentier was born on Jan. 12, 1894, in Lens, France. He won the European welterweight title in 1911. During World War I he served as a pilot in the French air force. He lost the light heavyweight crown to Battling Siki in Paris in 1922. He retired in 1927 after 106 professional fights, of which he won 85.

BILL BRADDOCK, *New York "Times"*

LIMESTONE RELIEF, ABOUT 665 B.C.—BROOKLYN MUSEUM

CARPENTRY has for thousands of years found an exacting test in the specialized and intricate craft of building wooden ships. The workman at the left in this ancient Egyptian relief uses an adze, a traditional shipwright's tool for shaping timbers.

CARPENTRY is the art of cutting, framing, and joining timber, chiefly in the construction of buildings and their interior woodwork.

Early History. Primitive carpentry developed fast in forested regions during the Neolithic period of the Stone Age. Improved stone axes of that period enabled men to shape wood for such objects as animal traps, dugout boats, sledges, and shelters. In the 4th millennium B. C., the Egyptians used copper tools to fashion coffers, chests, and bedframes. In the 2d millennium B. C., they had bronze tools and bow drills. Their skills in dovetailing, mitering, mortising, and paneling is exemplified in the beautiful and intricate furniture of the tomb of Tutankhamen.

European peoples produced no such furniture until the Renaissance, but from very early times they used timber to construct their huts and household gear, burial barrows, and henges (sacred enclosures). In the Rhineland and in Denmark, Neolithic man built rectangular timber houses more than 100 feet (30 meters) long. The so-called lake villages of Switzerland, resting on piles or a framework of beams, also imply the existence of the art of carpentry. At Stonehenge, in England, the mortised and fishtailed joints of the trilithons (stone structures consisting of two uprights and a lintel) show that advanced carpentering techniques were available for imitation by masons in Bronze Age Britain. Before the Romans conquered the island, its carpenters handled iron adzes, saws, rasps, awls, gouges, and knives of modern shapes, and turned woodwork on pole lathes.

Medieval Carpentry. In the Middle Ages much carpentry was the work of specialized craftsmen, such as the shipwright, wheelwright, turner, cooper, and millwright. But general-purpose carpenters were still found in most villages and on manorial estates. Carpenters congregated in the larger towns; Paris, for example, in 1300 had 108 carpenters. Such craftsmen could easily travel with their tools to outlying hamlets that had no carpenters of their own, or to wherever some major building enterprise required temporary labor.

Medieval carpenters had many efficient tools, such as the carpenter's brace, which was invented during the Middle Ages; the plane, which was known to the Romans and reappeared about 1200 A. D.; and other steel-edged tools, which were improved by the progress of steelmaking. Wrought-iron nails of uneven shape and sometimes wooden pegs were used to hold work together. Screws were not used until the 16th century.

In northern Europe the first churches and castles were made of timber and the great stone buildings, by which they were gradually replaced, demanded skillful carpentry for floors, doors, and, in the later centuries, paneling. In England large spans were often roofed with timber and required special devices to tie the rafters at a height which did not obstruct the end windows; this roofing technique culminated in the spectacular hammer-beam roof which was first used in Westminster Hall. Large stone buildings also required the erection of scaffolding for walls and towers, framework for the assembling of arches, and often piles to strengthen the foundations.

Houses and other ordinary buildings were still made of timber, with thinner wood or mixtures of clay and other materials to fill the gaps between posts and beams. For a single-story cottage, the frame might consist of only a few pairs of curved timber uprights (crucks) nailed to a roof beam, but usually the thatch or other roofing material was laid upon rafters made fast to two lines of posts rising 8 to 10 feet (2½ to 3 meters) above the foundation.

Furniture consisted mainly of chests, trestle table, benches, and other carpentered pieces. Most of the larger implements of agriculture and industry also were carpentered. Even the catapults and siege towers of medieval warfare were made by carpenters.

Carpentry since the Renaissance. The great Renaissance buildings owed part of their splendor to the art of carpentry. The outer dome of St. Paul's Cathedral in London and the 68-foot (23-meter) roof span of the Sheldonian Theatre in Oxford are two of Sir Christopher Wren's masterpieces in timber construction. More widespread examples of architecture requiring skilled carpentry are the mansard roof with its double slope, used to provide loftier attics, and broad wooden staircases, large panels, and sashed windows.

These features, as well as the humbler clapboards and shingles of southern England, were all incorporated in the timber-built homes of New England, where the carpenter's trade was well established.

With the growth of refinement in woodwork, the term *cabinetmaking* came into vogue for the work on better quality furniture. Other close-fitted nonstructural woodwork, executed generally with lighter tools, became known as *joinery*. The joiner, who appeared first in Italy and was known in England by the 13th century, became established in New York and in the New England towns from the 17th century onward.

The scope of carpentry has been reduced in modern times through the substitution of stronger and less combustible materials for much of the timber construction that was formerly used in buildings. The element of craftsmanship has likewise been reduced through the increasing utilization of machine-made parts and repetitive processes.

In the first decade of the 19th century, for example, the French-English engineer M. I. Brunel began the mass production of ships' blocks at Portsmouth, England, and about 30 years later George Washington Snow introduced balloon-frame building in Chicago. Using machine-made 2-inch (5-cm) studs fastened to plates with machine-made nails, he demonstrated a cheaper and quicker method of construction that largely outmoded the mortise-and-tenon frame, which required the work of skilled carpenters.

At present, carpentry consists mainly in combining pieces of timber that have been shaped by machinery. The work is further speeded up by the use of powered hand tools. But the complex skills that were associated with carpentry's heyday in the post-Renaissance period, and that used to be acquired through long apprenticeship and wide experience, are now nearly extinct. However, carpentry has never lost its fascination for amateurs.

THOMAS KINGSTON DERRY
Coauthor of "A Short History of Technology"

Further Reading: Briggs, M. S., *Short History of the Building Crafts* (Oxford, England, 1925); Burbank, N. L., *House Carpentry Simplified*, 6th ed. (New York 1958); Goodman, W. L., *History of Woodworking Tools* (New York 1966); Rose, W., *The Village Carpenter* (Cambridge, England, 1937).

CARPET, a soft heavy fabric used as a floor covering. See RUGS AND CARPETS.

CARPET BEETLE, a small beetle whose larvae feed on soiled or unprotected rugs, upholstery, padding, and clothing. They are also serious pests of insect collections and other types of museum specimens. Carpet beetles usually enter a building through an open window or door. Once inside, they are difficult to control. Sometimes it is necessary for rugs, upholstered furniture, and other items to be removed for fumigation. Moth crystals and cedar chests are usually adequate repellents, although they do not destroy these pests.

The most familiar species are the common carpet beetle (*Anthrenus scrophulariae*) and the black carpet beetle (*Attagenus piceus*). The adult common carpet beetle is about 1/10 inch (3 mm) long, with a mottled black-and-white pattern marked with red along the middle of the back. Its larva has long bristles that are often seen covered with lint and other particles of debris. The adult black beetle is somewhat longer than the common species and is all black. Its larva has a long tuft of bristles at the end of the body and shorter bristles along the sides.

After mating, the female lays her eggs on material that will serve as food for the larvae. The eggs soon hatch. The larval period may last from 8 months to more than a year. The larvae then pupate, and the adults emerge in the spring.

R. H. ARNETT, JR., *Purdue University*

Constructing a wood-frame, carpenters in this medieval woodcut use axes, saws, hammers, and block and tackle.

THE BETTMANN ARCHIVE

CULVER PICTURES

A CARPETBAGGER, supported by bayonets, bends the back of the South in this Reconstruction era cartoon.

CARPETBAGGER, a Northerner who moved to the Southern states after the Civil War and went into politics. A term of contempt, the word was current during the Reconstruction era to denote Northern-born politicians who played prominent roles in the Republican Reconstruction governments of the ex-Confederate states between 1867 and 1876.

It was charged by both white Southerners and Northerners that these men were so poor that when they went South they carried all their belongings in satchels made of cheap carpeting. The carpetbaggers went into the South for a variety of reasons, although a majority of them seem to have been motivated by a desire to improve themselves economically.

When the great majority of Southern whites boycotted elections to the constitutional conventions held in their states in 1867 because they preferred military rule to Negro suffrage, leadership in these conventions fell into the hands of the Republican carpetbaggers and a small group of native white Southerners called "scalawags." So long as the Republican party controlled the Southern states, political leadership remained in the hands of carpetbaggers and scalawags. Generally speaking, the role of the carpetbagger was more significant in the states of the Deep South, which had Negro voting majorities, while the role of the native scalawag tended to be predominant in the states of the Upper South where white voters outnumbered the Negroes.

Instrumental in shaping the new constitutions of the ex-Confederate states, the carpetbaggers wrote into them certain progressive provisions of their own Northern states. Thus, Robert K. Scott, the dominant figure in the South Carolina convention, modeled the South Carolina constitution of 1868 on the constitution of Ohio, where he formerly lived. In the same state, carpetbagger Gov. Daniel H. Chamberlain conducted his office with integrity and efficiency.

Unfortunately, the careers of such carpetbaggers as Gov. Henry C. Warmoth in Louisiana, Gov. Adelbert Ames in Mississippi, and Milton S. Littlefield in North Carolina and Florida support Horace Greeley's description of the carpetbagger as a person "bent on stealing and plundering, many of them with both arms around Negroes, and their hands in their pockets, seeing if they cannot pick a paltry dollar out of them."

Whatever their merits, the carpetbaggers aroused the bitter hostility of native whites in the South, and they were almost all forced out when conservative Democrats recaptured control of the various ex-Confederate states during the decade of the 1870's.

JAMES A. BEATSON,
University of Arizona

CARPUS. See HAND.

CARQUINEZ STRAIT, kär-kē′nes, in California, connects San Pablo Bay and Suisun Bay, the northern and eastern extensions of San Francisco Bay. It is about 8 miles (13 km) long and 2 miles (3 km) wide at its widest point. Carquinez Bridge, completed in 1927, crosses the western end of the strait south of Vallejo.

Another span was built in 1958 parallel to this bridge to handle increasing highway traffic. A highway bridge between Benicia and Martinez was completed across the eastern end of the strait in 1962.

CARR, Emily (1871–1945), Canadian artist, who was noted for her paintings of Indian village scenes and the forests of British Columbia. She was born in Victoria, British Columbia, on Dec. 13, 1871, and studied art in San Francisco and London and at the Académie Colarossi in Paris. In the late 1890's she began to visit and sketch the Indian villages of Canada's west coast. Toward the end of her life she wrote a number of prose sketches—many about the west coast Indians—collected in volumes that included *Klee Wyck* (1941) and *Book of Small* (1942). She died in Victoria on March 2, 1945.

Emily Carr's paintings, which borrowed from both the cubist and impressionist traditions, has a primitivistic quality. They include *Cape Mudge: An Indian Family with Totem Pole* (1912) and *Woods and Blue Sky* (1932), both at the Beaverbrook Art Gallery, Fredericton, New Brunswick, and *Kispiax Village* (1929), at the Art Gallery of Toronto.

CARR, John Dickson (1906?–), American mystery writer. He was born in Uniontown, Pa., and educated at Haverford College. He began writing mystery fiction in 1930, with *It Walks by Night*. He then moved to England and, under his own name and the pseudonyms "Carr Dickson" and "Carter Dickson," began producing short stories and as many as six books a year. Carr wrote *The Life of Sir Arthur Conan Doyle* (1949) and collaborated with Adrian Conan Doyle on *The Exploits of Sherlock Holmes* (1954), containing new adventures of Sir Arthur's famous detective. In 1948 he returned to the United States, where he was elected to a term as president of the Mystery Writers of America in 1949.

CARR, Robert (1590?–1645), lord chamberlain of England. He accompanied James I to England as a page, but he was soon discharged and went to France. Returning, he happened to break an arm at a tournament before James, who recognized him. He was knighted and rose rapidly in favor. In 1609, James gave him Sir Walter Raleigh's forfeited manor of Sherborne. By 1610 his influence was such that he persuaded the king to dissolve his first Parliament, which was showing signs of attacking James' Scottish favorites.

Carr was created Viscount Rochester in 1611, subsequently became a privy councillor, and began to act as the king's secretary in 1612. In November 1613 he was advanced to the earldom of Somerset, in December made treasurer of Scotland, and 1614, lord chamberlain.

He fell from favor, however, in 1615 when he and his wife, Lady Frances Howard, were implicated in the murder of Sir Thomas Overbury. Lady Frances had previously been married to the Earl of Essex. Overbury had been Carr's confidant in the divorce intrigue, which Overbury violently opposed. Imprisoned in the Tower of London at Lady Frances' contrivance, Overbury died of poisoning.

Two months later Carr and Lady Frances married. It was not until a year later that suspicion was aroused and the couple brought to trial. Four accomplices were hanged. Lady Frances pleaded guilty but was spared, and Carr himself was disgraced. It was later thought that he may have been no more than an accessory after the event. He was pardoned in 1624, after which he lived in obscurity until his death in July 1645.

CARR, Sir Robert (died 1667), British colonial administrator in America. Born in Northumberland, England, he was appointed one of four commissioners to New England by Charles II in 1664. That year he participated in the capture from the Dutch of New Amsterdam, which the English called New York in honor of the duke of York (later James II). Carr then forced the Swedes and Dutch on the Delaware River into a capitulation. That accomplished, he went to Boston in 1665, but met with stubborn opposition from the Massachusetts authorities, who refused to acknowledge his commissionership, as did also the people of New Hampshire. Maine, however, submitted and was governed separately by him from 1666 to 1667. Carr died in Bristol, England on June 1, 1667.

CARRÀ, kär-rä′, **Carlo** (1881–1966), Italian painter, who was a founder of futurism (q.v.) in art. He was born on Feb. 11, 1881, in Quargneto and was educated in Milan. In 1910 he and four other Italian artists in Milan signed the Futurist Manifesto, aligning themselves with the dynamism of the machine age and against the "tyranny" of the past. Attracting great attention for both their works and their extraordinary behavior, the group influenced many aspects of art and decoration. World War I dispersed the group. During his military service, Carrà met the painter Giorgio di Chirico. Together they founded the school of "metaphysical" painting, devoted to expressing the artist's private symbols in a mysterious or ominous manner. Carrà's later works were more conventional, reflecting his studies of early Italian painting. The last survivor of the futurist movement, he died in Milan on April 13, 1966.

CARRACCI, kär-rät′chē, a family of 16th century Bolognese painters, who, with Caravaggio, created the baroque style. Seeking to escape the artificialities and complexities of the prevailing mannerist school, at first they studied Correggio, the Venetian masters, and nature. Gradually they developed a powerful baroque art that blended classical ideals of beauty with naturalistic representation and dramatic color and light. They also founded an influential academy in Bologna, devoted primarily to drawing from life.

Lodovico Carracci was baptized on April 21, 1555, in Bologna. He probably studied with many painters in various north Italian cities before returning to his native city. There, about 1582, together with his cousins Agostino and Annibale, he established an academy of art. The three also collaborated on many commissioned frescoes.

Lodovico developed a painterly and emotional style. His *Madonna dei Bargellini* (1588, Pinacoteca, Bologna) and *Holy Family with St. Francis* (1591, Museo Civico, Cento) show weighty figures engaged in a passionate religious emotion expressed through strong gesture and movement set off by flickering lights and darks. Lodovico later moved from this exciting kind of lighting, which is close to that of Tintoretto, toward Correggio's pearly whites bathed in smoke, as in *Transfiguration* (1593, Pinacoteca, Bologna). Lodovico also abandoned careful preparatory drawings in favor of spontaneous painting. Some of his late work relies on earlier formulas, but the best of it—for example—the *Martyrdom of St. Angelus* (1598 or 1599, Pinacoteca, Bologna)—still reveals a masterful hand. Lodovico died in Bologna on Nov. 13, 1619.

Annibale Carracci, the greatest painter of the family, was born in Bologna on Nov. 3, 1560. He was trained in Bologna and later traveled to Parma and probably Venice. He first looked to the figures of Correggio to free himself from mannerism. In the late 1580's he turned increasingly to the dramatic color and strong composition of the Venetian school. His innate sense of gravity and controlled structure then led him to admire the masters of Florence and Rome. These influences, always restudied from life, may be seen in the works he painted in Bologna, such as *Virgin with St. John and St. Catherine* (1593, Pinacoteca, Bologna), with its triangular organization, weighty architecture, and strong gestures and poses, combined with a rich, glowing Venetian palette.

In 1595, Annibale went to Rome, where his study of the work of Raphael and Michelangelo and antique remains helped him to evolve a rational, baroque classicism. His major commission was the frescoes of the Farnese Gallery (1597–1604), a sumptuous and melodic evocation of classical mythology that was the first of the great baroque ceilings. Notwithstanding its elaborate organization, the ceiling is dynamic and vigorous, and it has a direct appeal through its airy space, solid modeling, rich color, and logical composition.

No eclectic, Annibale was able to absorb the influences of other men's work and transform them into something new and personal. After 1600 he refined his style to a melancholy, heroic grandeur, simplifying his composition while adding further mass and weight to the figures. The sequence can be followed from the *Assumption* (1603, Santa Maria del Popolo, Rome) to the

ALINARI—ART REFERENCE BUREAU

ANNIBALE CARRACCI'S *Landscape with the Flight into Egypt* (about 1600) is in the Doria Gallery, Rome.

Domine, Quo Vadis? (National Gallery, London) and the *Pietà* (Louvre, Paris), both painted about 1605. During the same period Annibale also created a type of ideal landscape—panoramas of nature ennobled by man and his works—exemplified by the *Flight into Egypt* (Galleria Doria Pamphili, Rome).

Another side of Annibale's work is represented by his drawings of everyday life in all its aspects; pure genre paintings of sparkling naturalism, such as the *Bean Eater* (Galleria Colonna, Rome); and caricatures, an art form that he may have invented. About 1606, Annibale fell into a deep melancholia and ceased to paint. He died in Rome on July 15, 1609.

Agostino Carracci was baptized in Bologna on Aug. 16, 1557. He was an engraver as well as a painter. He studied in Venice and Parma and worked in Bologna and Rome. Stylistically he followed his younger brother Annibale, whose influence is apparent in the rational construction and Venetian color and atmosphere of the *Last Communion of St. Jerome* (early 1590's, Pinacoteca, Bologna). In 1597, Agostino collaborated with Annibale on the frescoes for the Farnese Gallery in Rome. His style, drier, harder, and somewhat colder than Annibale's, is seen in *Cephalus and Aurora* and the so-called *Galatea*.

In 1600, Agostino broke with Annibale and went to Parma, where he began a ceiling in the Palazzo del Giardino. He died in Parma on Feb. 23, 1602.

Milton Lewine, *Columbia University*

Further Reading: Friedlaender, Walter F., *Mannerism and Anti-Mannerism in Italian Painting* (New York 1957); Martin, John R., *The Farnese Gallery* (Princeton, N. J., 1965); Wittkower, Rudolf, *The Drawings of the Carracci at Windsor Castle* (London 1952).

CARRANZA, kär-rän′sä, **Venustiano** (1859–1920), Mexican soldier and statesman. After the overthrow of President Francisco Madero in 1913, Carranza emerged as the chief leader of the military uprisings against the usurping president Victoriano Huerta. Under Carranza's leadership the civil war was ended, and a new constitution (1917) established the basic reforms in land ownership, national control of natural resources, labor, and social legislation that Mexicans call their revolution. Carranza was the first president elected under the new constitution.

He was born into a landowning family at Cuatro Ciénegas, Coahuila, on Dec. 29, 1859, and entered politics as a young man. In 1910, as governor of Coahuila, he led his state in joining the Madero uprising, which ended the long dictatorship of Porfirio Díaz, and in 1913 he assumed the leadership of the uprising against Huerta. Several of the rebel leaders opposed him, and he was not securely established in power until his army, under Gen. Álvaro Obregón, defeated the forces of Francisco (Pancho) Villa at Celaya in 1915.

Although rebellion still continued in some areas, Carranza stabilized the nation and was able to govern as constitutional president until 1920. When he tried to impose his own successor as president, however, Obregón led an armed uprising against him. The train on which Carranza was taking government records and treasures to Veracruz was attacked, and he fled overland with a few followers to Tlaxcalantongo, Puebla, where he was murdered on May 18, 1920.

Carranza was a stubborn nationalist and was several times embroiled in controversy with the United States. He opposed U. S. occupation of Veracruz (1914), even though it was directed against his enemy Huerta, and he rejected the friendly mediation of the ABC powers to end the civil war (see ABC Powers). He prevented the U. S. military expedition under Gen. John Pershing (1916–1917) from capturing Villa after his raid on Columbus, N. Mex. The measures of his administration to extend control over the foreign-owned petroleum industry almost brought U. S. intervention in 1919.

Harold E. Davis
The American University

CARRARA, kär-rä′rä, is a city and commune in Italy, in the province of Massa e Carrara in Tuscany. It lies in the foothills of the Apuan Alps and is the world's leading producer of high-quality marble. Marble has been quarried in the uplands near Carrara since Roman times.

Carrara, only some 3 miles (5 km) from the Tyrrhenian Sea, acts as the gateway to the great quarries that lie behind it. The marble is transported from the quarries to the city by a special standard-gauge railroad that also offers the easiest access to the quarries for visitors. For centuries, Carrara marble has been considered the world's best, and its many varieties, ranging from pure white to soft green and beige, have been used for statues and for building purposes. Many great sculptors have come to Carrara to select marble of the right color and texture, as did Michelangelo.

The outstanding artistic feature of the city of Carrara is the cathedral, of Romanesque and Gothic styles, dating to the 13th century. Its facade, in black-and-white stripes of marble, is dominated by a superb rose window; the interior is handsomely decorated with carvings and paintings.

The Carrara (Carraresi) family, which is not connected with the city, ruled the northern Italian town of Padua from 1318 to 1435. The city of Carrara itself knew the rule of a long list of feudal lords; from 1473 to 1790 it was part of a principality, together with the neighboring city of Massa, under the rule of the Malaspine family. Population: (1961) of the city, 37,386; (1966) of the commune, 66,592.

George Kish
University of Michigan

CARREL, kȧ-rel′, **Alexis** (1873–1944), French-American surgeon, who was awarded the 1912 Nobel Prize in medicine for his development of a new technique for sewing up blood vessels end to end. Following the pioneer work of Ross Harrison at Johns Hopkins University, Carrel also successfully refined the techniques of tissue culture research.

Contributions to Science. Carrel developed his new technique for suturing blood vessels end to end in 1902. The method was used to connect blood vessels to transplanted organs in the body. The study of transplants interested Carrel, and in 1913 he removed a kidney from one cat and transplanted it into the body of another cat.

In January 1912, Carrel succeeded in transplanting heart tissue from a chick into an *in vitro* culture. He maintained the culture in an alive, although primitive, state for 38 years. Carrel was especially careful in providing the correct medium for the tissue. He added embryonic chick juice or some other liquid nutrient to the original artificial medium. He also bathed the tissue in fresh nutrient and discarded the used medium to ensure the removal of waste products.

Carrel, working with Henry Dakin during World War I, also devised a successful method for treating wounds with a solution of sodium hypochlorite that was antiseptic but essentially harmless to body tissues. This method prevented many amputations of infected limbs and saved many lives.

As a natural extension of his successful experiments in keeping tissue alive *in vitro,* Carrel turned to the problem of keeping whole organs alive outside the body. In the 1930's he collaborated with Charles A. Lindbergh at the Rockefeller Institute for Medical Research in studying the problem of supplying an *in vitro* organ with a continuous supply of blood. They successfully developed and perfected an apparatus—a germ-proof perfusion pump—that kept whole organs alive outside the body.

Life and Writings. Carrel was born in Ste.-Foy-lès-Lyon, France, on June 28, 1873, the son of a silk merchant. He attended the University of Lyon and in 1900 received his medical degree. After a brief stay in Canada, he moved to Chicago, where he worked at the Hull Physiological Laboratory of the University of Chicago. In 1906 he joined the Rockefeller Institute for Medical Research in New York. There he devoted most of his time to surgical research, especially the study of transplanted organs.

During World War II, Carrel and his wife, Anna de La Motte, one of Carrel's former laboratory assistants, established a laboratory hospital in France. They later returned to the Rockefeller Institute where Carrel worked until his retirement in 1939.

Carrel was acquainted with a large circle of people, including philosophers, artists, poets, and scientists. He also read the works of such physicists as Albert Einstein, Robert Andrews Millikan, and Arthur Stanley Eddington. He himself wrote several books, some of which deal with philosophic and sociologic topics as well as scientific ideas. In *Man the Unknown* (1935), he showed an appreciation for Percy W. Bridgman's concept of operationalism (q.v.). His other books include *The Making of Civilized Man* (1937) and *The Prayer* (1948). He also coauthored, with C. A. Lindbergh, *The Culture of Organs* (1938).

In 1941, Carrel returned to his native France. There he promoted the Fondation pour l'Étude des Problèmes Humains, whose purpose was to study all human problems and attempt to find practical solutions. Carrel died in Paris on Nov. 5, 1944.

Alfred Novak, *Stephens College*

Further Reading: Soupault, Robert, *Alexis Carrel* (Paris 1952); Sourkes, Theodore L., "Alexis Carrel," *Nobel Prize Winners in Medicine and Physiology 1901–1965,* pp. 74–78 (New York 1966).

ROCKEFELLER UNIVERSITY

Alexis Carrel

CARREÑO, kär-re′nyō, **Maria Teresa** (1853–1917), Venezuelan pianist. She was born in Caracas on Dec. 22, 1853. Taught by her father and Julius Hoheni, she appeared as a concert player in New York City in 1862 and attracted the interest of the American pianist and composer, L. M. Gottschalk, whose pupil she became. She later studied under Georges Mathias in Paris and achieved international fame as a pianist.

A woman of many talents, she was also active as an opera singer, a composer, and a conductor. She was acclaimed, from 1890 on, as the foremost woman pianist of the day, for her technique, dramatic intensity, and interpretation. She died in New York City on June 13, 1917.

CARRERA, kär-re′rä, **José Miguel de** (1785–1821), a leader in the movement for Chilean independence. He was born in Santiago, Chile, on Oct. 15, 1785, and educated in Spain. He returned to Chile and in 1811 assumed control of its government, disrupted by the Napoleonic capture of the Spanish throne. He effected some reforms, including the abolition of Negro slavery.

He was deposed in early 1814 after military reverses again brought Chile under Spanish control. Carrera retreated with his political antagonist Bernardo O'Higgins across the Andes into Mendoza, Argentina, where José de San Martín was organizing an army. When San Martín backed O'Higgins, Carrera traveled briefly to the United States for assistance, leaving in Mendoza his brothers Juan José and Luis to support his cause. After they were executed in 1818 by supporters of O'Higgins, Carrera organized an unsuccessful opposing army and was himself executed in Mendoza on Sept. 4, 1821.

JOHN FINAN, *The American University*

CARRERA, kär-re′rä, **Rafael** (1814–1865), Guatemalan political leader, who led an insurrection in the late 1830's and became an ultraconservative dictator. He was born in Guatemala on Oct. 24, 1814, of mixed white and Indian blood, and had no formal education. He became the leader (*caudillo*) of the Indian masses, who idolized him. With a band of 6,000 Indians, he took the city of Guatemala in 1838 and soon overthrew the liberal anticlerical government. Consolidating his rule, he became dictator of the nation in 1840 and president for life in 1854. He was violently opposed to the short-lived Central American Federation and caused its dissolution in 1840.

Until his death on April 14, 1865, Carrera was the most powerful figure in Central America. He repeatedly intervened in the affairs of nearby states to overthrow liberal regimes and shore up conservative ones. Deeply religious, he recalled the Jesuits and reestablished the Roman Catholic Church by means of the Concordat of 1852. He was despotic with his people and ruthless against his enemies. The upper class and clergy deplored his crudity but supported his regime because of its stability, respect of property, and veneration of the Church.

LAURENCE R. BIRNS
The New School for Social Research, New York

CARRERA ANDRADE, kär-re′rä än-drä′thā, **Jorge** (1903–), Ecuadorian poet. He was born in Quito on Sept. 28, 1903, and studied in Quito and in Europe. He was secretary of the Ecuadorian Socialist party in 1927–1928 and of the Senate in 1933.

For Carrera Andrade poetry is the exaltation of man's hope, as shown by the deep concern in his poems for the plight of the Ecuadorian Indian. By experimenting with poetic form, he sought also the most effective means of conveying the stormy experience of poetic inspiration. His work is characterized by an objective yet emotional description of the details of physical objects, expressed in simple vocabulary fused with brilliant metaphorical images. His cosmopolitan background is revealed in his descriptions of various countries and in the influences evident in his work of French symbolism, Spanish classicism, and Japanese haiku. His verse collections include *El estanque inefable* (1922; Eng. tr., *The Secret Country*, 1946), *Registro del mundo* (1940), and *Edades poéticas* (1958). *La tierra siempre verde* (1955) is a collection of essays.

FRANK DAUSTER
Rutgers University

CARRÈRE, kə-râr′, **John Merven** (1858–1911), American architect, the business partner in Carrère and Hastings, which specialized in classical design and was one of the most successful architectural firms of the early 20th century. He was born of American parents in Rio de Janeiro, Brazil, on Nov. 9, 1858, and studied at the École des Beaux-Arts, Paris. In 1883 he went to work for the rising architectural firm of McKim, Mead, and White, where he met Thomas Hastings (q.v.), with whom he formed a partnership in 1885.

Carrère and Hastings' early commissions included two resort hotels in St. Augustine, Fla.—the Ponce de Leon and the Alcazar, both in a romantic Hispano-Moorish style. Hastings, who was primarily responsible for all of the firm's designs, soon abandoned romantic idioms in favor of French-inspired classicism. The most important of the firm's buildings from the period of Carrère's lifetime is the grand but inconvenient main building of the New York Public Library (1911). Carrère was killed in New York by an automobile on March 1, 1911.

WALTER KIDNEY, *"Progressive Architecture"*

CARRHAE, kər′ē, **Battle of,** an engagement between the Romans and Parthians in northern Mesopotamia in 53 B.C. The Roman politician Marcus Crassus sought a military reputation to put himself on a par with his powerful political allies, Caesar and Pompey. Crassus possessed wealth, influence, and eloquence, but he lacked recent military experience.

Having stirred up war against Parthia in 54, Crassus marched his troops not through the mountains of Armenia, the longer though safer route, but directly across the Mesopotamian desert. After a long and exhausting march in the heat, Crassus faced the enemy at the city of Carrhae (modern Harran, Turkey). Parthian tactics relied heavily on cavalry and archery, areas in which Rome was deficient. Crassus assumed that, as in the past, the Parthians would be helpless when their arrows ran out. But this time a special corps of 1,000 Arabian camels brought a seemingly endless supply. The Romans were cut to pieces, their standards were captured, and Crassus himself surrendered and was slain. Of 44,000 Romans, only 10,000 survived. The disgrace embarrassed Rome until Augustus recovered the standards more than 30 years later.

ERICH S. GRUEN
University of California at Berkeley

CARRIAGES, kar′ij-əz, are horse-drawn, wheeled vehicles, especially for carrying passengers. Mankind's first vehicles were sledges that were dragged over the ground. Later, logs or rollers were put under the sledges to facilitate their movement. The origin of the wheel is obscure. It is believed to have been invented in the Middle East about 3500 B.C. Wheels were first used for 2-wheeled carts, and thereafter for 4-wheeled wagons. The earliest wheels seem to have been made of three parts, held together by wood strips or battens. Spoked wheels are believed to have developed about 2000 B.C. The earliest spoked wheels were very small—less than 2 feet (0.6 meter) in diameter—and had 4, 6, or 8 spokes. This type of wheel was most often found on vehicles used for warfare, hunting, or ceremonial purposes. Utilitarian vehicles generally had disc wheels.

Evidence indicates that 2-wheeled chariots and carts were in use in Egypt about 1600 B.C. The Romans, Scythians, Persians, Greeks, and Sumerians also made early use of vehicles, particularly the 2-wheeled kind. The 4-wheeled wagon developed slowly because the inflexible axle did not permit the wagon to be guided along curving roadways. This difficulty was eventually overcome by the Romans with the use of a swiveling front axle. The Romans copied and improved designs of the vehicles they found in all the nations they conquered and thus acquired a wide variety of carriage types.

During the Dark Ages, the general stagnation in man's inventiveness retarded the art of carriage building. Development ceased and wheeled vehicles—excepting carts and wagons—were more rarely used. During this period, too, the science of wheel building, which had progressed almost to the state later reached in the 19th century, slipped backward. Wheels were made with fewer spokes and with very wide and crude rims.

Medieval Carriages. Beginning about the 12th century, historical references to carriages again become common and we may assume that development resumed where it had stopped at the end of the Roman period. An early example of a vehicle with a suspended body was the English hammock wagon, in which a kind of hammock was hung from posts at the ends of the carriage. Like springs, which were later used to support carriage bodies, this type of suspension helped absorb the shocks from rough roads. Another vehicle developed in medieval England was the whirlicote, a long, highly decorated, covered wagon. On the European continent improvements in carriages around the mid-15th century resulted in a new and enduringly popular type of vehicle, the coach.

Carriage Building: 1600–1900. The 17th century brought not only a significant increase in the use of carriages but also the development of several new types. Late in the century 2-wheeled cabriolets were used in both France and Italy. Cabriolets were also built in a 4-wheeled style that could be called an early version of the phaeton. The phaeton carriages grew to be large and varied and remained very popular until the end of the carriage era in the early 20th century. The sociable was developed near the end of the 17th century, probably in Germany. It was an open carriage with transverse seats facing one another as in a coach.

During the last half of the 18th century the art of carriage building reached a high degree of perfection. Suspension had already improved through the use of whip-springs and S-springs, and these evolved into the C-spring shortly before 1800. More effective suspension offered greater comfort, and lessening the jolts caused by poor roads permitted lighter, more tastefully designed carriages to be made. By 1800, coaches, chariots, phaetons, landaus, landaulets, barouches, sociables, cabriolets, gigs, and chaises were in use in Europe and America.

In 1804 an English coachmaker, Obadiah Elliot, invented the elliptical spring. These springs eliminated the need for a bulky supporting framework—a heavy perch (shaft) and cross beds—thereby lessening the weight of the carriage still further. Improved spring suspension combined with another early 19th century invention, macadam road surfacing, to produce a revolution in carriage design. During the 1830's the cabriolet-phaeton and the brougham were designed in England. Originally intended for use by the gentry, these carriages became immensely popular and eventually were used extensively as hackney (or hack) carriages for hire. Another vehicle for public transportation was the omnibus, first used in Paris about 1820 and in England and America by 1830. There was a tendency at this time for vehicle bodies to be hung lower, thus affording easier access.

In the United States, too, there was accelerated activity in carriage building in the early 19th century. Among the designs of that era were the rockaway and the popular American buggy. After 1850 the carriage industry began to modernize. Mechanized manufacture and malleable iron castings instead of hand-forged parts reduced the cost of carriages in the United States so that people of more modest means could afford them. By 1900 an inexpensive buggy could be purchased for $30. Final improvements, near the end of the carriage era, were rubber tires—first solid and then pneumatic—and ball bearings for the axles. For a time the carriage industry coexisted with the manufacture of automobiles, sometimes in the same factories, but following World War I the demand for carriages rapidly declined.

TYPES OF CARRIAGES

The following listing contains most of the more important carriage types. There was great variation in the definition of these terms in the carriage trade.

Ambulance, a 2- or 4-wheeled vehicle used to carry sick or injured persons, equipped with a litter or bed, and characterized by easy suspension. The term was also applied to a type of passenger wagon in the western United States.

Barouche, a 4- or 6-passenger kind of coach, with the running gear of a coach and a body much like that of a landau, except that the folding top covered only the rear seat.

Berlin, a type of 4-wheeled carriage developed in Berlin, Germany, about 1660, with the front and rear portions connected by two perches instead of one and the body resting on leather thoroughbraces running from front to back. The berlin gained in popularity in Europe during the 18th century, and the term eventually came to mean a light coach.

Bike Wagon, a light runabout developed late in the carriage era, having one or several of the following features: wire wheels, rubber tires (cushion type or pneumatic), ball-bearing axles, and tubular steel running gear.

Buckboard

Calèche

Coupé

Hansom

Break, a heavy vehicle that was nothing more than a running gear with a high driver's seat in front. It was used for breaking horses into harness. The term eventually was applied to a kind of heavy phaeton, generally seating four, with a rumble for footmen in the rear.

Brougham, a 2-passenger carriage resembling a coupé, developed in England in the 1830's. It had a paneled boot, or box, for the driver in front and its low suspension provided easy access. It was designed as a gentleman's carriage but was also commonly used as a hack for public hire.

Buckboard, a simple American carriage type, originally with no springs but with a seat or seats placed on risers mounted on one or more flexible springlike boards bolted directly to the axles. Afterward, some types were equipped with springs.

Buggy, a term originally used in England for a chaise or phaeton intended for only one person. Eventually it was applied to the most popular of American carriages, the light 4-wheeled vehicle for one or two passengers, which was generally equipped with a folding top.

Cab, when the cabriolet was introduced from Italy into France, it came into common use as a public hack, and the name was often shortened to cab. Eventually "cab" meant any carriage for hire, whether 2- or 4-wheeled.

Cabriolet, originally a 2-wheeled vehicle, developed in Italy, with a body resembling a nautilus shell. Later it had four wheels, with a folding top over the rear seat and a boot, or box, for the driver in front. In America it was often called a "panel-boot victoria."

Calash (or **Calèche**), originally either of two types of carriages: (1) a Canadian vehicle resembling a chaise, with a driver's seat on top or in front of the dash; and (2) a 4-wheeled vehicle resembling a barouche. The term came to mean simply a folding carriage top.

Cart, a simple 2-wheeled vehicle used to carry moderately heavy loads. The term was applied also to certain types of passenger carriages. See also *Dogcart*.

Chair, a 2-wheeled vehicle of the chaise type, very light, frequently for one passenger, and without a top.

Chaise, a light, 2-wheeled carriage, generally carrying two passengers, frequently so constructed that the elasticity of the supporting shafts provided the resilience of springs. Most were equipped with calash tops.

Chariot, a vehicle equipped and suspended like a coach, but with a shorter body and only one inside seat, generally for two passengers.

Coach. See separate article COACH.

Conestoga Wagon. See separate article CONESTOGA WAGON.

Coupé, a carriage resembling a brougham, with the driver's seat framed to the front of the body. It differed from a brougham in having a hinged seat inside and a rounded or octagon front.

Curricle, a 2-wheeled carriage, heavier and more elaborate than a chaise or gig, and drawn by two horses.

Democrat wagon, a name sometimes applied to a spring wagon.

Depot Wagon, a variety of rockaway, sometimes made with a folding end gate which served as a luggage rack.

Dogcart, a sporting vehicle, usually 2-wheeled, with two transverse seats placed back to back. It was used for hunting, and dogs could be carried in a rear compartment under the seats.

Dougherty Wagon, a variety of passenger wagon, hung on steel springs rather than on braces. It originated in St. Louis, Mo., and was

much used in the American West, particularly by the U. S. Army.

Drag, a heavy coach with roof seats and rumble seat, popularly used as a sporting vehicle and to carry people on picnics and outings. It was generally drawn by four horses.

Gig, a carriage resembling a chaise, but more elaborately suspended; the body was often hung by braces from C-springs.

Germantown, a carriage with two or three seats, resembling a rockaway, that was developed about 1816 in Germantown, Pa.

Hack, shortened name for hackney coach.

Hackney coach, a carriage available for public hire. The term did not indicate a style of carriage so much as its availability for hire.

Hansom Cab, a 2-wheeled closed carriage often used as a public carrier. The driver's seat was high on the rear of the body and entrance for two passengers was gained through the front.

Landau, a heavy vehicle resembling a coach, but with two calash tops that locked together in the center and could be let down in pleasant weather.

Mud Wagon, a popular term for passenger wagons, because they were so often mud-splattered.

Omnibus, a public carrier seating at least 12 passengers. The seats were longitudinal, the door was in the rear, and the driver's seat was frequently on the roof.

Passenger Wagon, a type of stage, generally resting on thoroughbraces. It was less expensive to build than a regular stage coach because of its simplified wagonlike construction.

Phaeton, any of a large number of carriages of various types. A phaeton was a 4-wheeled carriage with a folding top. It had no coachman's seat and was often driven by the owner.

Rockaway, a general American type that developed after 1830. Rockaways were of various designs but each had a standing top that covered it completely, including the driver's seat.

Runabout, generally a buggy without a top.

Spring Wagon, a versatile light wagon with two or three removable seats, popular in rural areas for carrying passengers or produce. A spring wagon might be open or equipped with a canopy top. Its springs were usually of the platform type.

Stage, a coach or wagon providing public transportation. The word derives from the stages into which a long journey might be divided by stops at resting places, or stations, along the way.

Stagecoach. See separate article COACH.

Sulky, a very light, 1-passenger, 2-wheeled skeleton vehicle, designed for trotting races. Early in the 19th century the term was applied also to the type of vehicle called a chair.

Surrey, a comparatively low-cost family carriage, generally with a square body and two transverse seats. It might be without a top, or it might have either a canopy or a folding top.

Victoria, a stately carriage resembling a cabriolet, but in place of the latter's paneled boot it had a skeleton iron boot above a curving leather dash.

Wagon. See article WAGONS AND CARTS.

Wagonette, a light wagon resembling an open omnibus, with longitudinal seats and a back door. Small wagonettes might be used as pleasure carriages and larger ones—in pleasant weather—as omnibuses.

DON H. BERKEBILE, *Smithsonian Institution*

Further Reading: Stratton, Ezra M., *The World on Wheels* (New York 1878); Straus, Ralph, *Carriages and Coaches* (London 1912); Tunis, Edwin, *Wheels, a Pictorial History* (New York 1955).

CARRIER, kȧ-ryā′, **Jean Baptiste** (1756–1794), French revolutionist. He was born in Yolet, a small town near Aurillac, on March 16, 1756. Before the French Revolution he held a provincial administrative post. In the National Convention he sat with the Jacobins, voting death to Louis XVI in January 1793, and leading the attack on the moderate Girondists later that year.

In October 1793, Carrier was sent to Nantes with a commission to suppress the royalists in the Vendée, a center of violent and bloody opposition to the revolutionary government. He aggravated the conflict by his savage measures. Prisoners were swiftly condemned, particularly clergymen who refused to accept the government's civil constitution of the clergy, which removed the French Church from the jurisdiction of Rome. Thousands died in mass executions and *noyades,* in which the prisoners were placed upon sinking barges and drowned. When word of Carrier's atrocities reached Paris, he was recalled and tried by the Revolutionary Tribunal. He was guillotined in Paris on Dec. 16, 1794.

RICHARD M. BRACE, *Oakland University, Mich.*

CARRIER, kar′ē-ər, **Willis Haviland** (1876–1950), American mechanical engineer and industrialist, who developed many of the basic processes of air conditioning. Carrier was born near Angola, N. Y., on Nov. 26, 1876. He graduated from Cornell University in 1901 and worked for the Buffalo Forge Company from 1901 to 1915.

Carrier designed his first air-conditioner in 1902 to control humidity in the Sackett-Wilhelms Lithographing and Publishing Company in Brooklyn, N. Y. It consisted of heat-transfer coils through which he circulated cold water, and a fan to direct air over the coils. The temperature of the coils and the velocity of the airflow were balanced to maintain the desirable humidity for the printing process.

In 1907 the Buffalo Forge Company set up a subsidiary, Carrier Air Conditioning Company of America, to exploit his developments. In 1915, after the company decided to restrict its activities, Carrier and six coworkers founded what is now Carrier Corporation. Carrier was its president from 1915 to 1930 and chairman of the board from 1930 to 1948. Carrier died in New York City on Oct. 7, 1950.

BURGESS H. JENNINGS, *Northwestern University*

CARRIER SHELL, the shell of a marine snail found in tropical and temperate seas. The snail cements pebbles, broken coral, and other shells to its own shell. The cementing medium is a liquid form of calcium carbonate, which is exuded from glands in the edge of the animal's mantle (outer covering). The snail's head, tentacles, and muscular foot are red. Its shell is about 3 inches (7.5 cm) in diameter.

The carrier shell belongs to the family Xenophoridae in the class Gastropoda. There are about 15 species including the Atlantic carrier (*Xenophora conchyliophora*), found in Florida and the Caribbean, which completely covers itself with foreign fragments; the sunburst carrier (*Stellaria solaris*), from the western Pacific, which produces its own shell projections; and the digitate carrier (*X. digitata*), from West Africa, which grows projections and also cements on bits of shells.

R. TUCKER ABBOTT
The Academy of Natural Sciences of Philadelphia

CARRIERA, kär-ryâ′rä, **Rosalba** (1675–1757), Italian painter, the leading Venetian portrait and miniature painter of her day, whose work was often compared to that of Antonio Correggio. She was born in Venice, on Oct. 7, 1675. Also known simply as Rosalba, she was internationally acclaimed for her pastel portraits of Venetian ladies. She also painted royalty, including Elector Augustus II of Saxony, who was one of her early patrons. In 1720–1721 she visited Paris, where she introduced pastels to M. Q. de La Tour and was elected to the French Royal Academy of Painting and Sculpture. Although her paintings were criticized for faulty composition, they have a vivacious charm and elegance. She died in Venice on April 15, 1757.

CARRIÈRE, kȧ-ryâr′, **Eugène Anatole** (1849–1906), French painter and lithographer, whose poetically impressionistic style earned him many awards in the salons of the 1880's and 1890's. His favorite subjects were mothers and children, his own wife and family, and writer and artist friends. The figures in his prints and paintings usually emerge softly shaded from the obscurity of a dark, misty background.

Carrière was born at Gournay, on Jan. 27, 1849. He studied drawing and lithography at Strasbourg and St. Quentin before going to Paris in 1870 to study painting with Alexandre Cabanel. He served in the army during the Franco-Prussian War, then resumed his studies. In 1876 he won the coveted Prix de Rome and began to exhibit regularly in the Paris Salon. Carrière won many honors and awards, notably the Cross of the Legion of Honor in 1890. He knew most of the important figures in Parisian artistic circles, and painted many of them, including Alphonse Daudet, Edmond de Goncourt, Paul Verlaine, Puvis de Chavannes, and Auguste Rodin. He died in Paris on March 27, 1906.

HENRY E. SCOTT, JR.
University of Missouri, Kansas City

CARRILLO Y SOTOMAYOR, kär-rē′yō ē sō-tō-mä′-yôr, **Luis** (1583?–1610), Spanish poet. He was born in Córdoba, the son of a royal councillor. He studied at the University of Salamanca and served as a soldier and naval commander in Italy. As the chief exponent of *culteranismo,* the artificially elegant style later adapted by Luis Góngora, Carrillo held that Spanish should be Latinized and that poetry should be intentionally full of obscure classical allusions and subtleties so as to be comprehensible only to the educated elite. Carrillo's works, the most important of which are *Fábula de Acis y Galatea* and *Libro de la erudición poetica,* were published posthumously from 1611 to 1613. He died in El Puerto, Spain, in 1610.

CARRINGTON, Edward Codrington (1872–1938), American lawyer, who was prominent both in corporation law and on the national political scene. He was born in Washington, D. C. on April 10, 1872. Admitted to the Maryland bar in 1894, he practiced law in Baltimore and New York as a member of the firm of Carrington & Carrington.

Carrington was campaign manager for Theodore Roosevelt in Maryland in 1912 and signed the call for the Progressive national convention that year. He was elected a member of the Progressive national committee and also was chairman of the Maryland Progressive state committee. After the presidential election he sought to unite Republicans and Progressives; he was the Republican nominee for the U. S. Senate, but lost.

In 1934 and 1935, Carrington was president of the Americana Corporation, publishers of *The Encyclopedia Americana.* He died in Baltimore, Md., on Dec. 30, 1938.

CARRINGTON, kar′ing-tən, **Henry Beebee** (1824–1912), American soldier and historian. He was born in Wallingford, Conn., on March 2, 1824. Educated at Yale, he began to practice law in Columbus, Ohio, in 1848. He was active in the antislavery movement and in the establishment of the Republican party. Appointed adjutant general of Ohio in 1857, he reorganized the state militia in preparation for the Civil War. He was commissioned colonel of the 18th U. S. Infantry Regiment in 1861 and became brigadier general the following year. After serving through the Civil War, Carrington fought in the Indian wars on the plains. Later he negotiated treaties with the Indians and set up reservations. He was professor of military science and tactics at Wabash College from 1870 to 1873, and wrote numerous books, including *Battles of the American Revolution* (1876), *The Indian Question* (1884), *The Six Nations* (1892), and *Washington, the Soldier* (1898). He died on Oct. 26, 1912.

CARRINGTON, kar′ing-tən, **Richard Christopher** (1826–1875), English astronomer, who made important studies of the sun. Carrington was born in Chelsea on May 26, 1826. He was educated at Trinity College, Cambridge, and from 1849 to 1852 was observer at the University of Durham. In 1853 he began observations at Redhill, Surrey, and in 1857 published a catalog of circumpolar stars. More important were his observations of sunspots between 1853 and 1861. He found that the farther sunspots were from the solar equator, the longer was their period of rotation, thus indicating that the sun's surface could not be a solid rotating at a constant rate. Carrington died in Churt, Surrey, on Nov. 27, 1875.

CARRION BEETLE. See BURYING BEETLE.

CARRION FLOWER, kar′ē-ən, is a wild herbaceous vine of the lily family. Its small greenish flowers in dense clusters appear in late spring. Blue-black berries are borne in autumn. Its leaves are ovate, tapering at the tip. Male and female flowers appear on separate plants and pollination is effected by flies that are attracted to the putrid odor of the flowers.

Carrion flower, *Smilax herbacea,* trails over the ground or finds support on other vegetation. It grows in moist open woods and thickets in most of the eastern United States. Members of the unrelated genus *Stapelia,* native to South Africa and sometimes cultivated in greenhouses in the United States, are also called carrion flowers.

JOAN E. RAHN, *Lake Forest College, Ill.*

CARRIZO SPRINGS, kə-rē′zō, the seat of Dimmit county, Texas, is 104 miles (167 km) southwest of San Antonio. Situated in an irrigated farming region, the city is an important processing and shipping center for fruits and winter vegetables. There are oil wells nearby and an oil refinery in the city. Government is by a city manager. Population: 5,374.

CARROLL, kar′əl, **Charles** (1737–1832), American patriot and public official. He was known as Charles Carroll of Carrollton (his mansion in Frederick county, Md.), the name he signed on the Declaration of Independence.

Charles Carroll of Carrollton

THE GRANGER COLLECTION

Carroll was born in Annapolis, Md., on Sept. 20, 1737, to one of the most prominent Roman Catholic families in America. Educated in France and England, mainly at Jesuit schools, he completed legal studies at London's Inner Temple. On his return to Maryland in 1764, his father gave him the 10,000-acre (4,000-hectare) estate of Carrollton Manor, where Carroll lived the life of a country gentleman, excluded from holding political office by the Protestant majority because of his religious faith. In June 1768 he married his cousin, Mary Darnall.

Carroll's political interests survived his denial of political rights. His study of law convinced him of the constitutional reality of American rights. The Stamp Act (1765) filled him with alarm. Such legislation, he contended to friends, was the product of British decadence and corruption. But the occasion for Carroll's public political debut was domestic. In 1773, Gov. Robert Eden of Maryland asserted for himself the right of setting Crown officers' fees. The governor later surrendered this claim, but in the meantime he provoked a dispute, carried on in the *Maryland Gazette,* in which Carroll established his reputation as an educated and persuasive patriot at the expense of Eden's supporter, Daniel Dulany.

From 1773 until his retirement in 1804, Carroll was active in public life. In 1775, he was a member of the "Committee of Observation" in Annapolis and was elected to the provincial convention there. In 1776 the Continental Congress named him to a futile mission to persuade Canada to join the Revolution; it was hoped that his Catholic faith would reassure the French. On his return he was elected to the Second Continental Congress on Independence Day, and he quickly voted for the Declaration. He helped draft the Maryland constitution of 1776, although he opposed the confiscation of British property. He declined to attend the federal Constitutional Convention of 1787, but he did urge ratification of the U. S. Constitution. He served in the U. S. Senate (1789–1792) and in the Maryland Senate (1774–1804), and he also was a member of the Maryland-Virginia Boundary Commission of 1797. A Federalist, he opposed the War of 1812. He died in Baltimore on Nov. 14, 1832, the last surviving signer of the Declaration of Independence.

TREVOR COLBOURN
University of New Hampshire

CARROLL, kar′əl, **Daniel** (1730–1796), American public official, who signed the U. S. Constitution and who is credited with drafting its 1st Amendment. He was born in Upper Marlboro, Md., on July 22, 1730. Educated in Flanders, he returned to Maryland in 1748 and three years later married Eleanor W. Carroll of Duddington, an heiress to the fortune of Charles Carroll (q.v.) of Carrollton. A delegate (1781–1783) to the

Continental Congress, Daniel Carroll was the only Catholic to sign the Articles of Confederation. He was appointed to the Constitutional Convention of 1787 and figured prominently in its debates. He was elected to the first U. S. Congress and served from 1789 to 1791, then accepted an appointment as a commissioner of the District of Columbia (1791–1795), charged with establishing plans for the capital. He died at his home, Forest Glen, in Rock Creek, Md., on May 7, 1796.

CARROLL, James (1854–1907), American physician and microbiologist, who helped establish that yellow fever is caused by a virus transmitted by the *Aëdes aegypti* mosquito. After working with Walter Reed (q.v.) in determining that yellow fever was not caused by bacteria, Carroll became a member of the U. S. Army's Yellow Fever Commission in Havana. There in 1900, Carroll let himself be bitten by an *Aëdes aegypti* mosquito that had feasted on the blood of yellow fever victims. He promptly developed a severe attack of the disease. This and further experiments substantiated the theory, expressed earlier by Carlos Finlay (q.v.), that yellow fever was transmitted by the *Aëdes aegypti* mosquito.

Later, with Reed and other associates, Carroll studied the blood of yellow fever victims and found that the agent that caused yellow fever was present in the bloodstream, was sensitive to heat, and was able to pass through a filter that had pores too fine for any bacteria to pass through. These discoveries proved that yellow fever was caused by a virus.

Carroll was born in Woolwich, England, on June 5, 1854. He went to Canada in 1869 and in 1874 joined the U. S. Army. While serving in an army infirmary, he became interested in medicine and in 1891 received his medical degree from the University of Maryland. After additional study in bacteriology at Johns Hopkins, he began his work with Walter Reed. He died in Washington, D. C., on Sept. 16, 1907.

CARROLL, John (1735–1815), the first native American appointed a bishop of the Roman Catholic Church in the United States. Carroll was born at Upper Marlboro, Md., on Jan. 8, 1735. He attended St. Omer's in Flanders and entered the Jesuit order at Walten, France, in 1753. He was ordained probably in 1769.

After the Jesuits were suppressed in Europe (1773), Carroll returned to America. In 1776 the Continental Congress invited him to join Benjamin Franklin, Samuel Chase, and his cousin, Charles Carroll, in an unsuccessful effort to obtain French Canadian support for the American Revolution. In 1784 he was appointed superior of the Maryland mission, and in 1789, Pius VI confirmed Carroll's election as bishop of Baltimore. He was consecrated in England in 1790.

As the first Catholic bishop, Carroll set a precedent of cordial relations with the government: in 1791, for example, he initiated the custom of public prayers for the government. Carroll was instrumental in the founding of several Catholic colleges, including Georgetown University. He consecrated the first bishops of Boston, Philadelphia, and Bardstown (Louisville), and was himself appointed archbishop. He died in Baltimore on Dec. 3, 1815.

THOMAS MCAVOY, C. S. C.
University of Notre Dame

CARROLL, Lewis (1832–1898), English writer and mathematician, who is famous as the author of *Alice's Adventures in Wonderland* (1865; q.v.), in which he developed a high and unique form of "nonsense" literature. Carroll, whose real name was Charles Lutwidge Dodgson, was born at Daresbury, Cheshire, on Jan. 27, 1832. He studied at Rugby and at Christ Church, Oxford, where he graduated with honors in mathematics in 1854, and was ordained a deacon in 1861. However, he did not take further orders, because he considered himself unfit for parochial work largely because of a bad stammer.

Carroll remained at Christ Church as a lecturer in mathematics, becoming much less shy and constrained with adults, but seeking more and more the company of children, with whom his stammer disappeared. He published, under his real name, a number of mathematical works of ephemeral value, including *Euclid and Modern Rivals* (1879), *Curiosa Mathematica* (2 vols., 1888–1893), and *Symbolic Logic* (1896).

CULVER PICTURES

Lewis Carroll

In 1865, Carroll achieved an enormous success with the publication of *Alice's Adventures in Wonderland*, illustrated by Sir John Tenniel. (The pseudonym "Lewis Carroll," used only for the author's lighter works, was derived from the Latinization of his real given names—Carolus Ludovicus.) This book and its sequal evolved from tales told to Alice Liddell, the young daughter of the dean of Christ Church, Henry George Liddell, while she and her sisters were on boating picnics on the Thames.

Carroll's fame during his lifetime was further enhanced by his avocation of photography. He was an outstanding photographer of children, and he also did portrait photographs of Tennyson, Ruskin, and Rossetti. Carroll died at his sisters' house at Guildford, Surrey, on Jan. 14, 1898.

Writings. *Alice in Wonderland*, its sequel, *Through the Looking Glass* (1872), and the long nonsense poem *The Hunting of the Snark* (1876) are unique in literature in combining fantasy and fun, parody and wordplay, and "illogical" logic—logic driven with mathematical precision to impossible extremes. Behind these supremely entertaining children's stories lies light but penetrating satire on the use of language and on character types of the Victorian era both academic and general.

Carroll's other imaginative writings were less successful. They include the long children's story *Sylvie and Bruno* (2 vols., 1889–1893), the puzzles—in story form—*A Tangled Tale* (1885) and *The Game of Logic* (1886), and the collections of light verse *Phantasmagoria* (1869) and *Rhyme? and Reason?* (1883).

ROGER LANCELYN GREEN
Author of "Lewis Carroll"

Bibliography

Editions of Lewis Carroll's writings include *The Complete Works* (Chester Springs, Pa., 1961) and *The Diaries of Lewis Carroll*, 2 vols., ed. by R. L. Green (New York 1953).
Collingwood, Stuart Dodgson, *The Life and Letters of Lewis Carroll* (London 1898).
Gardner, Martin, *The Annotated Alice* (New York 1960).
Green, Roger L., *Lewis Carroll* (London and New York 1960).
Greenacre, Phyllis, *Swift and Carroll: A Psychoanalytical Study of Two Lives* (New York 1955).
Hudson, Derek, *Lewis Carroll* (London 1954).
Lennon, Florence B., *The Life of Lewis Carroll*, rev. ed. (New York 1962).
Taylor, Alexander, *The White Knight* (Edinburgh 1952).
Weaver, Warren, *Alice in Many Tongues* (Madison, Wis., 1964).
Williams, Sidney H., and Madan, Francis F., eds., *The Lewis Carroll Handbook*, bibliography (New York and London 1962).

CARROLL, Paul Vincent (1900–1968), Irish dramatist, whose work helped renew the fame of the Abbey Theatre as a training ground for new Irish playwrights. Carroll was born on July 10, 1900, in the resort town of Blackrock, County Louth, Ireland. He was educated (1916–1920) at St. Patrick's Training College in Dublin. In 1921 he became a schoolmaster in Glasgow, Scotland, but retired from teaching in 1937 to devote himself to writing. In 1943 he helped James Bridie found the Glasgow Citizens' Theatre. He died in Bromley, England, on Oct. 20, 1968.

One of Carroll's earliest plays, *Things That Are Caesar's* (1931), was produced by the Abbey Theatre and received the Abbey Theatre Prize. His reputation rests, however, on his two most successful plays, *Shadow and Substance* and *The White Steed*, both of which preach against reactionary clericalism. *Shadow and Substance*, Carroll's most widely acclaimed play, was produced in Dublin in 1936, in New York in 1938, and in London in 1943. *The White Steed* was refused a production at the Abbey Theatre but was well received in New York in 1939. Both plays won New York Drama Critics Circle Awards.

OSCAR BROWNSTEIN
University of Iowa

CARROLL is a city in west central Iowa, the seat of Carroll county, about 75 miles (121 km) northwest of Des Moines. It is a trading center for the surrounding agricultural area. Important industries include poultry processing and the manufacture of farm machinery, feeds, ladders, and bathroom fixtures. The Swan Lake State Reserve for fish and game is 2 miles (3 km) east. Carroll was settled in 1867. It is governed by a mayor and council. Population: 8,716.

CARROLLTON is a city in western Georgia, the seat of Carroll county, about 40 miles (64 km) southwest of Atlanta. It is a trade center in an agricultural and poultry-raising area and it manufactures textiles, shoes, fertilizers, processed foods, and aluminum and copper cable and wire. West Georgia College, a 4-year coeducational state institution, is in the city. Government is by mayor and council. Population: 13,520.

CARROLLTON, an unincorporated township in east central Michigan, is in Saginaw county, on the Saginaw River. It is a residential suburb of Saginaw, about 2 miles (3 km) south. Carrollton is situated in the fertile Saginaw Valley, where beans and sugar beets are the principal crops. There are beet sugar refineries in the township. Government is by a board of supervisors. Population: 7,300.

CARRONADE, kar-ən-ād′, a short-barrelled light iron naval gun used in the British, U. S., and French navies from 1779 to about 1850. Shooting 12- to 32-pound balls, it was destructive against wooden ships at short range. It was invented by Gen. Robert Melville, a Scotsman, in 1759.

CARROT, a biennial plant grown for its edible, fleshy root, which is usually orange in color, aromatic, and sweet. Carrot (*Daucus carota*), a member of the carrot family (Umbelliferae), is believed to have originated in the Middle East. It is now found worldwide, either as a cultivated plant or a weedy, wild plant with long, dry roots. Wild carrots, which grow to 5 feet (1.5 meters) high, can be seen along roadsides and other waste areas where they produce flattish clusters (umbels) of small, white flowers. These white flower clusters give the wild carrot its common name of *Queen Anne's lace*.

Early development from the wild type occurred in France about 1830, with much of the credit for varietal improvement attributed to the Vilmorin Seed Company, of Paris. The carrot rapidly became an important crop.

Cultivation. Carrots develop best in a deep, sandy loam that is well drained and slightly acid. Muck soils are often used because of their loose texture and water-holding capacity.

The crop is hardy and can be planted as soon as severe freezes are over in the spring. A well-prepared seedbed is essential because the small seeds germinate and grow slowly. Late plantings where the soil is warm and dry are usually unsuccessful.

In the vegetative stage, the plant produces a rosette of finely divided leaves on a compact stem. After exposure to low temperatures, the stem elongates and produces a flowering shoot.

JANE LATTA

CARROTS: roots and foliage.

Carrots may be harvested as soon as the roots are large enough to be used. Medium-size roots are preferred for fresh market, but canners and other processors want them large and well matured.

Carrots are grown commercially in almost half of the United States, with Texas, California, Michigan, and Wisconsin leading in production. The farm value of the carrot crop in the United States has exceeded an estimated $60 million.

In 1939 an average of 284 man-hours was required to grow and harvest an acre of carrots; by 1959 this had been reduced to 105 man-hours. This decrease in labor was due primarily to the use of precision seeders, to herbicides that eliminated thinning and hand weeding, and to machine harvesting.

JOHN P. MCCOLLUM
University of Illinois

CARRUCCI, Jacopo. See PONTORMO, JACOPO DA.

CARSON, Sir Edward Henry (1854–1935), British political leader and judge, who was a leading Ulster Unionist. Carson was born in Dublin on Feb. 9, 1854. After studying and practicing law there, he became queen's counsel at the Irish bar in 1889 and at the English bar in 1894. In 1892 he was elected to Parliament from Ireland and named solicitor general for Ireland. He was subsequently Britain's solicitor general, attorney general, first lord of the admiralty (1917), and a member of the war cabinet (1917-1918).

From 1911, Carson was the most formidable opponent in Ireland of home rule for the counties of Ulster. He led a masterful opposition in Parliament to the Home Rule Bill of 1911 and was principally responsible for the eventual separation of the southern and northern counties of Ireland. In 1921 he was appointed lord of appeal and raised to the peerage as Baron Carson. He retired from the bench in 1929. He died at Minster, Kent, on Oct. 22, 1935.

KIT CARSON, from a photograph by Mathew Brady.

THE BETTMANN ARCHIVE

CARSON, Kit (1809–1868), American frontiersman and scout, who was one of the most skillful and dependable guides in the early West. Christopher Carson was born on Dec. 24, 1809, in Madison county, Ky., to which his parents had migrated from North Carolina. Lindsay and Rebecca Carson were among the restless folk who followed the frontier westward. A year after Christopher's birth they moved beyond the Mississippi to Howard county, Mo., to resume their lives as yeoman farmers. For a time they lived with other families in a stockade, and Kit grew up in an atmosphere of Indian warfare. When he was about 15, he was apprenticed to a saddlemaker, but this occupation failed to hold his interest. In 1828 he joined a party to make his first trip across the plains to Santa Fe, N. Mex.

At Taos, N. Mex., Carson became acquainted with Ewing Young, a western trader and trapper, whom he accompanied into the Rocky Mountain fur country. This expedition ultimately led Carson to California. He now had trailbreaking in his blood, and in 1830 he accompanied a second trapping party to the central Rockies. For the next 12 years he lived as a mountain man and underwent unbelievably rugged experiences. He fought horse and fur thieves, hostile Indians, camp bullies, and rival trappers. In the mountains he met such famous trappers as James Bridger, Thomas Fitzpatrick, the Sublette brothers, and Jedediah Smith (see MOUNTAIN MEN). In 1841 he became hunter for Bent's Fort, in Colorado. Before he left the Rocky Mountain beaver country, he married an Indian girl who bore him a daughter.

Kit Carson's big moment came in 1842 when he returned to Missouri to visit his relatives. There he met Lt. John Charles Frémont (q.v.), who was seeking the services of a mountain guide. On Frémont's first two expeditions (1842, 1843–1844), Carson proved himself a competent guide and adviser.

Carson served ably in California during the Mexican War. After the Battle of Los Angeles, when it was necessary to send dispatches to Washington, D. C., Carson set out for the Potomac in command of 15 men. En route he met Gen. Stephen Watts Kearny and had to turn back to serve as his guide. Nevertheless, he delivered the dispatches in a remarkably short time.

After the Washington trip Carson returned to Taos, where he hoped to lead a quiet life. Indian hostilities prevented this. From 1846 to 1865 he was involved in limited farming activities, sheepherding, fighting Apaches, and scouting for the Army. In 1853 he crossed the mountains with 6,500 sheep for the California market.

During the Civil War, Carson was active in the Southwest. He was at the Battle of Valverde in 1862 and fought Mescalero Apaches and Navahos and later (1864) Kiowas and Comanches. His great military success was in the Battle of Adobe Walls, Tex., on Nov. 25, 1864, when with 400 men he routed a much larger Indian force.

In the later years of his life Carson served briefly as a brevet brigadier general in command of Fort Garland in Colorado. He died at Fort Lyon, Colo., on May 23, 1868.

THOMAS D. CLARK, *University of Kentucky*
Author of "Frontier America"

Further Reading: Carson, Kit, *Kit Carson's Own Story of His Life,* ed. by Blanche C. Grant (Taos, N. Mex., 1926); Estergreen, M. Morgan, *Kit Carson* (Norman, Okla., 1962); Sabin, Edwin L., *Kit Carson Days,* 2 vols., rev. ed. (Elmira, N. Y., 1935).

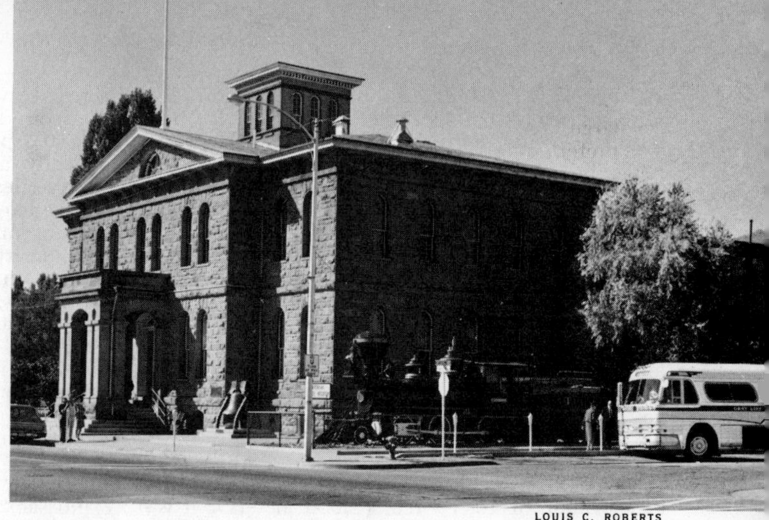

CARSON CITY'S old mint stopped coining silver and gold in 1893. It is now a museum of history and natural science.

LOUIS C. ROBERTS

CARSON, Rachel Louise (1907–1964), American biologist and writer known for her books about the sea and pesticides. Her last book, *Silent Spring* (1962), warned of the possible dangers of the indiscriminate use of pesticides and touched off a controversy that resulted in increased research on the effects of pesticides. In her earlier books, Rachel Carson displayed a sensitive style and a thorough knowledge of the ocean and its life. Her first book, *Under the Sea* (1941), passed nearly unnoticed, but her second book, *The Sea Around Us* (1951), won her much acclaim. It was followed by *The Edge of the Sea* (1955).

Rachel Carson was born in Springdale, Pa., on May 27, 1907. Her love of the outdoors began in childhood. She graduated from Pennsylvania College for Women in 1929, received an M. A. from Johns Hopkins University in 1932, and did postgraduate work at Woods Hole Marine Biological Laboratory. In 1936 she became an aquatic biologist with the U. S. Bureau of Fisheries and in 1947 editor in chief of the publications of the U. S. Fish and Wildlife Service. She died in Silver Spring, Md., on April 14, 1964.

H. CHARLES LAUN, *Stephens College*

CARSON CITY, in western Nevada, near the Nevada-California boundary, is the capital of the state and the seat of Ormsby county. It is situated in Eagle Valley, near the Carson River, about 30 miles (48 km) south of Reno and just east of Lake Tahoe.

In addition to its function as the seat of government, Carson City is a trading center for an area devoted to livestock raising, irrigated farming, and mining. It is also a resort, with a large and growing tourist business. Residents of the city are employed chiefly in government offices, small businesses, and the gambling industry, which was legalized in Nevada in 1931. Points of interest include the Nevada State Museum, with natural science and historical exhibits housed in the old mint, which was operated from 1870 to 1893 as a branch of the U. S. Mint and later, until 1930, as an assay office.

Carson City, named for the frontiersman Christopher ("Kit") Carson, was laid out in 1858 on the site of a trading post established in 1851 by prospectors from the California goldfields. Growth of the new town, a supply point for the surrounding mining area, was stimulated by the discovery in 1859 of the rich Comstock Lode (chiefly silver), the rapid development of Virginia City and other nearby mining camps, and the construction of the Virginia and Truckee Railroad to serve the mining area. Carson City became the capital in 1861 but was not incorporated until 1875. It has a mayor-council form of government. Population: 15,468.

VIRGINIA RULE
Carson City–Ormsby County Library

CARSON RIVER, in western Nevada, about 170 miles (274 km) long. It rises on the eastern slope of the Sierra Nevada in Alpine county, Calif., flows north into Nevada, and continues north and east to the vicinity of Fallon, where its waters are impounded in Lahontan Reservoir and used for irrigation.

CARSON SINK, in west central Nevada, is a shallow saline basin, 15 to 20 miles (24–32 km) wide, left in the bed of a prehistoric lake known as Lake Lahontan. Both Carson Sink and Carson Lake, a similar but smaller formation 25 miles (40 km) south, are terminal basins of the Carson River. Both are dry periodically, but before the river was dammed, its flow maintained water in Carson Lake and at times provided an overflow into the marshlands of Carson Sink.

CARSTARES, kär′stârz, **William** (1649–1715), Scottish clergyman and statesman, who was instrumental in securing Scottish support for William of Orange before the Glorious Revolution of 1688. Carstares was born near Glasgow on Feb. 11, 1649. Because of his family's opposition to the Scottish government under Charles II, he left Scotland after graduating from Edinburgh University in 1667 and continued to prepare for the ministry in the Netherlands. There he shortly began to act as an agent between the discontented Scots party and the Orange party.

On returning to England in 1674, Carstares was imprisoned for five years without trial, and in 1683 he was briefly imprisoned again in connection with the Rye House Plot (q.v.). After his release he returned to the Netherlands and became chaplain and confidential adviser to William. After the latter's coronation as William III of England, Carstares served as his principal adviser on Scottish affairs. As royal chaplain to Queen Anne, he was instrumental in establishing Presbyterianism in Scotland and in securing Scottish support for the union of Scotland and England. He died at Edinburgh on Dec. 28, 1715.

CARSTENS, kär′stəns, **Asmus Jakob** (1754–1798), German painter, who was known for his historical scenes, portraits, and frescoes. He was born in 1754 in St. Jürgens, Schleswig-Holstein, and studied in Copenhagen. In 1783 he went to Italy, where he was profoundly influenced by wall paintings. He settled briefly in Lübeck, where he painted portraits, and then, in 1787, he went to Berlin. Two of Carstens' important frescoes—*Apollo and the Muses,* painted in the von Heinitz house in Berlin, and a grisaille ceiling for the bedroom of the queen of Prussia—are no longer extant. In 1790 he was made a professor at the Berlin academy, but left two years later and returned to Italy. He died in Rome in 1798.

CARSTENSZ, Mount, kär′stenz, in Indonesian West Irian on the island of New Guinea. With an elevation of 16,503 feet (5,030 meters), it is the highest island peak in the entire world. Along with other towering peaks of the Snow Mountains, which form the axis of New Guinea, Mt. Carstensz was one of the last major mountains to be climbed. The first ascent, made by a Dutch expedition under Captain Hendrik Colijn, took place in 1937.

ROBERT C. BONE, *Florida State University*

CARTAGENA, kär-tä-hä′nä, a seaport in northern Colombia, the capital of Bolívar department, is situated on the Bay of Cartagena of the Caribbean Sea, about 65 miles (105 km) southwest of the port of Barranquilla. Cartagena has a good natural harbor and is connected with Colombia's principal river, the Magdalena, by a channel that has been dredged to permit river steamers to reach the port. Although not so important economically as Barranquilla, it ranks among the country's leading ports, especially in total cargo tonnage handled and in export cargo. One of Colombia's longest petroleum pipelines terminates at the nearby port of Mamonal. Among Cartagena's manufactures are chemicals, footwear, cotton textiles, and toiletries. The petrochemical complex at Mamonal includes refineries and plants that make fertilizers, urea, ammonia, and other products.

Cartagena was founded in 1533 and soon became one of the chief strongholds of colonial Spanish America. Although the harbor was guarded by a series of forts and the city was surrounded by high walls, it was assaulted frequently and sacked several times by buccaneers of the Spanish Main. Cartagena declared its independence from Spain in 1811. It was taken by loyalists in 1815 and recovered by rebel forces in 1821. The forts and walls represent the most important single body of colonial military architecture in Latin America. Among many other points of interest are the cathedral, the Church of St. Peter Claver, and the University of Cartagena. Population: (1964) 217,910.

GREGORY RABASSA, *Columbia University*

IN CARTAGENA, a statue in front of the old wall commemorates the 19th century revolt against Spain.

CARL FRANK

CARTAGENA, kär-tä-hä′nä, is a city and seaport in the province of Murcia, on the southeast coast of Spain. The city is located on the edge of a coastal plain with mountains to the west and inland. The sheltered bay provides an excellent harbor for the fishing boats and other vessels that make it a port of call, and fortifications afford it the defense it has required as one of Spain's major naval bases.

The annual rainfall in Cartagena is moderate, and the surrounding hills produce olives, grapes, and some cotton. The cultivated, irrigated fields along the valley to the northeast produce a variety of vegetables and fruits. The nearby hills, famed in Roman times for their minerals (especially gold, silver, and lead), are now mined for lead, iron, zinc, and manganese. The city's factories process metals and fish and produce explosives, pottery, and insecticides. There are also shipyards, a smelting works, and an oil refinery in or near Cartagena.

History. A settlement, built perhaps by the Iberians, existed on the site of Cartagena, but history records the building of the city by Carthaginians from North Africa in the 3d century B. C. It was an important trading and military post for the Carthaginians and for their conquerors, the Romans, who in 210 B. C. took the port, which they called Carthago Nova (New Carthage). During the Muslim occupation of Spain many large ships were constructed at Cartagena. The Reconquest of Spain reached this region in the 13th century under the leadership of King James I of Aragon.

There is a fine view of the coast and sea from the peaks that guard the entrance to the harbor and from many of the fortifications and bulwarks that have been constructed over the centuries. The city has an archaeological museum with many exhibits, especially of objects from Roman times. Of interest also are the arsenal, the naval base installations, and the shipyards. Population: (1960) 122,387.

M. M. LASLEY, *University of Florida*

CARTAGO, kär-tä′gō, is a city in the highlands of Costa Rica, 13 miles (20 km) by road southeast of San José. The capital of Cartago province, it is situated in a coffee-growing district near Mount Irazú, whose destructive eruptions of ash in 1963–1964 were a national calamity.

Cartago, founded in 1563, was the first permanent Spanish settlement in Costa Rica and was its capital until 1823. Earthquakes all but destroyed the city in 1841 and 1910, and there was a severe flood in 1964. Few colonial buildings have survived these disasters. The chief point of interest is the basilica of Our Lady of the Angels, containing a small stone image of the Virgin that is much venerated. Population: (1963) 18,084.

CARTE, kärt, **Thomas** (1686–1754), English historian, who was one of the first to base his work on a comprehensive survey of the royal archives. Carte was born in Warwickshire in April 1686 and received his education at Oxford (B. A., 1702) and Cambridge (M. A., 1706). In 1722 his vociferous support of the exiled Stuarts forced him into temporary exile in France, where he examined many rich manuscript collections.

Carte devoted the years 1738–1744 to a painstaking search of royal records stored in the Tower of London. The catalog of Gascon, Norman, and French rolls (published 1743) that resulted from this study remains a valuable tool of historians. The first volume of Carte's great work, the *General History of England,* appeared in 1747; other volumes followed in 1750 and 1752; and the final section was issued posthumously in 1755. Apart from these works, the author's *History of the Life of James Duke of Ormonde* is still read for its notes. Carte died near Abingdon on April 2, 1754.

JOHN FERGUSON, *Columbia University*

CARTE BLANCHE, kärt blänsh, a blank sheet of paper signed by one person and given to another who has the authority to fill in his own terms or conditions. In securities and commodities trading, a *carte blanche order* gives a broker or agent unlimited discretionary power to buy or sell. In general usage, the term denotes unconditional power or authority to act or decide on a matter.

CARTEL, kär-tel′, an arrangement among business firms to reduce or eliminate competition. The arrangement may be either a formal agreement or an informal understanding. Although the term "cartel" has been applied both to national and international arrangements of this kind, present usage tends to restrict the meaning to arrangements designed to limit or regulate competition in international trade.

Cartels are often considered a category of monopoly, along with trusts. A distinguishing feature of cartels, however, is the relative independence that each component firm retains in its internal operations.

The purpose of a cartel is to limit competition in a given area of business activity, thereby increasing profits. Maintaining prices, or avoiding price competition, is the commonest activity. The result is greater profits for the participating firms.

Techniques. To achieve increased profits through price fixing or price maintenance, cartels control production and distribution. Limiting supply is the best means of assuring price maintenance. Cartels usually employ some form of quota system. The output permitted each member may be set by the arrangement, or the amount to be sold may be limited. Alternatively, a regional monopoly may be established for each of the participating firms. This method is most commonly employed by international cartels.

International cartels often do not create new monopolies but rather strengthen existing domestic national monopolies. The cartel develops among firms dominating their respective national markets. Reciprocal agreements reinforce and confirm this local dominance by eliminating the threat of competition from abroad.

Cartels often exist in areas of business activity where natural monopolies are not readily developed. It is then necessary to permit relatively free entry by any firm that constitutes a threat to the cartel. On the other hand, restricted entry can be enforced if the group has control of raw material sources or of basic patents. Cartels have been particularly successful when they control patents and arrange international cross-licensing.

A general operational principle for cartels is that they are most successful in those areas of production where demand is inelastic and no substitute is readily available. The most successful cartels have developed in such products as fertilizers, chemicals, plate glass, steel, and dyestuffs. I. G. Farbenindustrie, the German supercartel of the 1920's and 1930's, concentrated on dyestuffs and chemicals.

A cartel must be able to enforce its quotas and other limitations. With prices and profits artificially high, a temptation always exists for one or more members to exceed the quotas. A cartel must be self-policing to deter such action. Fines have often been imposed, but they have proved relatively ineffective. Enforcement is more effective when violators can be refused access to patent rights or raw materials.

Objections to Cartels. The basic objection to international cartels is economic. Prices are higher and output lower than would generally be the case under competition. The unlimited-entry cartel is especially inefficient, because too many firms are producing too little. This means improper use of productive resources. A reversion of such an industry to competition would result in a saving, because fewer firms would be producing more units per firm at a lower cost per unit.

The limited-entry cartel, however, encourages productive efficiency. This form of cartel is also more effective in restricting output and maintaining high prices. But such a cartel prolongs a favored market position for its members at the expense of the consumer. It thus impedes the rise of living standards and general economic well-being.

It is often charged that cartel members are more loyal to the cartel than to the interests of their respective countries. Wendell Berge, former assistant attorney general of the United States, in his book *Cartels* (1944), cites the cooperation of United States and German firms in the 1930's as proof that cartels have retarded technological advance and improvement "whenever such developments seemed to threaten their vested interests despite the fact that thereby national security might be jeopardized."

It is further maintained that the cartel has been an important adjunct to the periodic development of the German war machine. In World War I the German government employed domestic cartels to organize the production and distribution of war material. The movement toward international combines in the 1920's and 1930's found German firms again taking the lead. After the outbreak of World War II, investigations by U. S. Senate committees showed that "in the latter stages of rearmament, cartels were widely used by the Nazi government to strengthen German industrial resources for war."

Status of Cartels. For cartels to flourish, as they did in pre-1939 Germany, the government must give at least its sanction, if not active support to their existence and activities. In Nazi Germany the cartel was granted a special legal status of its own. In Britain and the United States, however, basic economic beliefs have been opposed to group monopoly. For most British and American firms, any participation in international cartels has been an extralegal activity. This explains in part the ability of German firms to dominate the pre-1939 cartels.

The discovery of many cartel records after Germany's defeat in 1945 led to a reaction against international cartels in Britain and the United States. Regulation of domestic firms was tightened, and a strong decartelization movement was fostered by the British and Americans in the West German economy. Cartels still exist, however, and they continue to hold attractions for their members. But their disadvantages have become more widely appreciated, and the legal opportunity for their development has been considerably restricted.

WILLIAM N. KINNARD, JR.
University of Connecticut

Bibliography

Berge, Wendell, *Cartels: Challenge to a Free World* (Washington 1944).
Edwards, Corwin D., *Cartelization in Western Europe* (Washington 1964).
Miller, John P., ed., *Competition: Cartels and Their Regulation* (New York 1962).
Newman, P. C., *Cartel and Combine* (Ridgewood, N.J., 1964).
Plummer, Alfred, *International Combines in Modern Industry,* 3d ed. (London 1951).

CARTER, Don (1926–), American bowler, who was considered the greatest in the history of the game. Donald James Carter was born in St. Louis, Mo., on July 29, 1926. After two years in the U. S. Navy, he played Class D baseball with the Philadelphia Athletics organization. On his release in 1947 he took up bowling seriously.

In 1952, Carter won the first of four Bowling Proprietors' Association (BPA) All-Star championships. Between 1953 and 1962 the Bowling Writers Association named him Bowler of the Year six times; he won the World's Invitational singles championship five times between 1957 and 1962; and he was an eight-time American Bowling Congress (ABC) All-American selection (1956–1963). He won the BPA doubles title (with Tom Hennessey) in 1958 and 1959, and the ABC Master's title in 1961. The first president of the Professional Bowlers Association, Carter won six PBA tournaments. For seven years he was the key member of the renowned Budweiser team of St. Louis.

Carter's record included 11 sanctioned 300 games. He used an unorthodox bent-arm delivery from a low crouch.

MICHAEL QUINN, *"Sports Illustrated"*

CARTER, Elizabeth (1717–1806), English poet and translator of classics. She was born on Dec. 16, 1717, in Deal, Kent, and was schooled in languages by her clergyman father. Her poetry first appeared in the *Gentleman's Magazine,* published by a friend of her father's, who introduced her to Dr. Samuel Johnson. Johnson became her lifelong friend and she contributed two essays to his *Rambler. Poems upon Particular Occasions* (1738) and *Poems on Several Occasions* (1762) followed. She was most noted for her translation (1758) of the philosopher Epictetus. Her memoirs and correspondence were published posthumously. She died in London on Feb. 19, 1806.

CARTER, Elliott (1908–), American composer, whose complex and individual works in an advanced style have made him a major figure in 20th century music. Elliott Cook Carter, Jr., was born in New York City on Dec. 11, 1908, the only son of well-to-do parents who left him a substantial income. At Harvard (B. A., 1930; M. A., 1932) he studied music with Walter Piston, Archibald Davison, E. Burlingame Hill, and Gustav Holst. He also studied composition with Nadia Boulanger in Paris (1932–1935). Except for an occasional teaching post, his life thereafter was devoted to composing.

After some early "populist" works, such as the First Symphony (1942) and *Holiday Overture* (1944), Carter's music, beginning with the Piano Sonata (1946), became increasingly complex, difficult, and uncompromising. Yet his circle of listeners and admirers steadily widened. He attracted international attention with his first and second string quartets (1951 and 1959), in which his experiments with speed, rhythm, texture, and independence of parts reached full fruition. Other important works include the ballet *The Minotaur* (1947); Woodwind Quintet (1948); Variations for Orchestra (1955); Double Concerto for Harpsichord and Piano, with two chamber orchestras (1961); and Piano Concerto (1966).

GILBERT CHASE, *Tulane University*

CARTER, Henry. See LESLIE, FRANK.

CARTER, Henry Alpheus Peirce (1837–1891), Hawaiian merchant and diplomat. He was born in Honolulu, of American parents, on Aug. 7, 1837. After a limited education in Boston, he returned to Hawaii in 1849. In 1854 he began to work as an office boy at C. Brewer & Co., a leading commission firm in Hawaii. He rose to partnership by the age of 25 and foresightedly steered the firm's capital from whaling, a declining industry, to sugar, a promising one.

In 1874, wealthy and ambitious, Carter was appointed a privy counselor by King Kalakaua and sent to Washington to secure a reciprocity treaty. The treaty, ratified in 1875 (effective in 1876), admitted sugar and other Hawaiian products to the United States duty free. The remainder of Carter's life, except for service as Kalakaua's minister of the interior and minister of finance, was spent in negotiating trade and immigration agreements in foreign lands. From 1883 until his death he was minister to the United States. In 1887 he obtained a renewal of the 1875 treaty. The extended pact also provided for the leasing of Pearl Harbor as a U.S. naval station. Carter died in New York City on Nov. 1, 1891.

JOSEPH A. BOROMÉ
The City College, New York

CARTER, Henry Rose (1852–1925), American physician and epidemiologist, who is noted for his studies of yellow fever. Carter's investigations of the disease determined that the incubation period lasts from 3 to 6 days. He also pointed out that there is a prolonged "extrinsic incubation" of the disease. Later, it was discovered that yellow fever is transmitted by mosquitoes and that the extrinsic incubation period extends from the time an uninfected mosquito bites an infected person until the time the mosquito can transmit the disease to others.

Carter was born at Clifton Plantation in Caroline county, Va., on Aug. 25, 1852. He graduated from the University of Maryland medical school in 1879. Carter then entered the federal Marine Hospital Service, where he was instrumental in establishing uniform federal quarantine regulations. He remained in the agency, which later became the U. S. Public Health Service, for 40 years. In 1915 he was named assistant surgeon general of the Public Health Service and engaged in a campaign against malaria in the United States. After retiring in 1919, he wrote *Yellow Fever, an Epidemiological and Historical Study of Its Place of Origin.* He died in Washington, D. C., on Sept. 14, 1925.

IRVING SOLOMON, M. D.
Mount Sinai Hospital, New York

CARTER, Hodding (1907–1972), American newspaper publisher and author, best known as the crusading, liberal editor of the Greenville (Miss.) *Delta Democrat-Times.* William Hodding Carter was born in Hammond, La., on Feb. 3, 1907, and graduated from Bowdoin College and the Columbia University School of Journalism. He began his career on Southern papers and news bureaus. Then in 1932, with his wife Betty, he started the Hammond *Daily Courier,* in which he fought the Huey Long machine. In 1936 he moved to Greenville and founded the *Delta Star,* which he merged two years later with the older *Democrat-Times.*

During World War II, while his wife and associates carried on the newspaper, Carter served in the Pentagon and edited Middle East editions of *Yank* and *Stars and Stripes* in Cairo. Returning to Greenville, he won a Pulitzer Prize in 1946 for editorials against racial intolerance. He died in Greenville on April 4, 1972.

Carter's many essays and sketches also fearlessly exposed demagogues, racists, and racketeers; yet they reveal a faith and pride in the South and a deep love of people, His books include the autobiographical *Where Main Street Meets the River* (1953); the discursive journal *Southern Legacy* (1950); *First Person Rural* (1963), a collection of essays; and the novels *Winds of Fear* (1944) and *Flood Crest* (1947).
HAROLD R. JOLLIFFE, *Michigan State University*

CARTER, Howard (1873?–1939), English Egyptologist. He was born in Swaffham, Norfolk, probably in 1873. At the age of 17 he was sent to Egypt as a draftsman for the Egyptian Exploration Fund. He received his early archaeological training while assisting Sir Flinders Petrie (q.v.) at Tell el Amarna. Carter remained with the Fund until 1900, when he was appointed inspector general for the antiquities department of the Egyptian government, working at Abu Simbel and Thebes. He also helped to reorganize the antiquities administration of Upper Egypt. As supervisor of the excavations of Theodore M. Davis in the Valley of the Kings, he was responsible for discovering the tombs of Mentuhotep I, Queen Hatshepsut, and King Thutmose IV. Carter was dismissed from this position in 1903, after a disagreement with the Egyptian government.

In 1906, Carter met George Herbert, 5th Earl of Carnarvon (q.v.), and became supervisor of Lord Carnarvon's excavations in the Valley of the Kings. They uncovered the tomb of Amenhotep I, the Valley Temple of Queen Hatshepsut, and the cemetery of the 18th dynasty queens. Their digging was interrupted by World War I, but in 1922, Carter and Carnarvon made their most important contribution—the uncovering of the tomb of Tutankhamen. The tomb consisted of several chambers filled with treasures of enormous historical significance. The preservation and removal of these art objects took ten years. Carter died in London on March 2, 1939.

PRISCILLA C. WARD
American Museum of Natural History

CARTER, James Coolidge (1827–1905), American lawyer, who markedly influenced the development of American jurisprudence. Taking a philosophical approach, he viewed law as an evolutionary process of social determination—self-regulating, self-creating, and self-executing. He believed that the judiciary should be the spokesman, not the creator, of law, and that it must respect the existing mores of society.

Carter was born in Lancaster, Mass., on Oct. 14, 1827. He graduated from Harvard College in 1850 and from Harvard Law School in 1853. Admitted to the New York state bar that year, he soon became one of New York's most prominent attorneys. In 1871 he participated in the successful prosecution of "Boss" William M. Tweed (q.v.). In 1875 he served on a commission to devise a plan of government for the cities of New York State, and in the 1880's he led a successful fight against a proposed codification of the common law by the state legislature. He was chief counsel for the United States before an international tribunal considering the Bering Sea controversy in 1893. A founder of the New York City bar association, he also served as president of the American Bar Association (1894–1895). Carter died in New York City on Feb. 14, 1905.

LEO HERSHKOWITZ, *Queens College*
The City University of New York

CARTER, James Gordon (1795–1849), American educator, who was a noted advocate of normal schools and an inductive teaching method. He was born in Leominster, Mass., on Sept. 7, 1795. Carter was influenced by the Swiss educator Johann Pestalozzi, who held that students should learn by reasoning and discovery rather than by memorizing. He applied this method to his teaching of geography.

Carter had been known as a promoter of public education since 1821 as a result of articles in Boston newspapers pointing out the weaknesses of the Massachusetts schools. These essays, later published as pamphlets, called for free education through the secondary level, upgrading of schools, centralizing of authority in a state board of education, public supervision of schools, and the establishment of a normal school for teacher training. In 1830, Carter founded the American Institute of Instruction.

Elected to the state senate in 1835, he was able to achieve many of his educational aims, particularly as chairman of the education committee. After the creation of a state board of education, he anticipated being made secretary of public education. When that position went to Horace Mann, Carter's disappointment led him to relax his efforts. He was, however, the first member appointed to the board of education and was responsible for the establishment in Lexington, Mass., of the first state normal school in 1839. He died in Chicago on July 21, 1849.

RICHARD E. GROSS, *Stanford University*

CARTER, Mrs. Leslie (1862–1937), American actress. She was born Caroline Louise Dudley in Lexington, Ky., on June 10, 1862. In 1880 she married Leslie Carter, from whom she was divorced in 1899. She made her New York debut in 1890 in *The Ugly Duckling* under David Belasco's management. Her first great success, in *The Heart of Maryland* (1895), was followed by starring roles in *Zaza* (1898), *Du Barry* (1901), and *Adrea* (1905). She left Belasco's management in 1906 and appeared under other managements in *La Tosca, Two Women, The Second Mrs. Tanqueray,* and *Camille*. In 1921, in *The Circle* with John Drew, she made her last successful New York stage appearance.

She then went on several tours in *The Shanghai Gesture, Stella Dallas,* and other plays, acted in motion pictures, and made her last stage appearance in a revival of *The Circle* in 1934. She died in Santa Monica, Calif., on Nov. 13, 1937.

CARTER, Nick, fictional detective, who was both a character in, and the pen name of authors of, a series of dime novels published in the United States by Street & Smith in the late 19th and early 20th centuries. Carter seems to have been invented by John Russell Coryell, who possibly based the character on the historical detective Allan Pinkerton. Other contributors to the series included T. C. Harbaugh, G. C. Jenks, and E. T. Sawyer. The first of the 1,076 titles in the series was *The Old Detective's Pupil* (1886). The Nick Carter novels, of which some 4 million copies were sold, inspired radio plays and movies.

CARTER, Samuel Powhatan (1819–1891), American officer, who was the only American to hold the ranks of major general in the Army and rear admiral in the Navy. He was born at Elizabethton, Tenn., on Aug. 6, 1819. After graduating from the U. S. Naval Academy in 1846, and after several years' service, he was promoted lieutenant in 1855.

When the Civil War began, Carter wrote a letter home pledging his allegiance to the Union and as a result was assigned the task of raising and organizing Union troops in eastern Tennessee. He was a skillful commander, and in 1862 as a brigadier general of volunteers he led an important cavalry raid at Holston, Tenn. He served in later engagements and was mustered out of the Army in 1866 as a major general.

Returning to the Navy, he commanded ships and was commandant of midshipmen at Annapolis. Carter was promoted to captain in 1870 and to commodore in 1878 and retired in 1882 as a rear admiral. He died on May 26, 1891.

CARTER, Thomas Henry (1854–1911), American legislator and Republican party leader. He was born in Scioto county, Ohio, on Oct. 30, 1854. In 1882 he began to practice law in Montana Territory. When Montana became a state in 1889, he was its first representative in the U. S. Congress, but he lost the election of 1890. As chairman of the Republican national committee, Carter managed President Benjamin Harrison's unsuccessful campaign for reelection in 1892.

In 1895, Carter was elected to the U. S. Senate, where he served for 12 years (1895–1901; 1905–1911). In the Senate he supported bimetallism, a postal savings system, and the civil service and insisted on the inclusion of Montana's raw materials in protective tariff acts. He helped found Glacier National Park. Carter died on Sept. 17, 1911, in Helena, Mont.

CARTERET, kär'tər-et, **Sir George** (1613?–1680), English Royalist governor of Jersey and colonial proprietor of New Jersey. A devout supporter of the Stuart cause during the English Civil War, he was abundantly rewarded for that support after the Restoration.

Sir George belonged to the prominent de Carteret family of St. Owen, Jersey, in the Channel Islands. In 1633 he captained his first ship, and in 1639 he was appointed comptroller of the English Navy. After the outbreak of the Civil War, he supervised shipping to Royalist forces in the west of England, using his own credit in France to provide arms and ammunition. Carteret also helped fortify the Channel Islands.

In 1643, Charles I appointed him lieutenant governor of Jersey, which he used as a base for skillful privateering raids against Parliamentary shipping. Parliament declared him a pirate and refused to grant him amnesty. When Charles II took refuge on Jersey in 1649–1650, he honored Carteret with the lease of some land on the east coast of America, and the area was called New Jersey in Carteret's honor. In December 1651 the Parliamentary Navy finally captured Jersey, and Carteret followed the King to France.

When Charles II was restored to the throne in 1660, he made Carteret a privy councillor and vice chamberlain of the household. In 1663, Carteret was named one of the eight original proprietors of Carolina, and in 1664 he was granted proprietary rights to half of the colony of New Jersey. As treasurer of the navy from 1661 to 1667, he was accused of gross mismanagement, and he was suspended from Parliament in 1669. In 1673, however, he was returned to office as a commissioner of the admiralty. He died in January 1680.

L. PERRY CURTIS, JR.
University of California at Berkeley

CARTERET, kär'tər-et, **John** (1690–1763), English politician, who was chief minister of George II. He was born at Bath on April 22, 1690, and at the age of 5 succeeded his father as 2d Baron Carteret. He was educated at Oxford.

In the closing years of Queen Anne's reign, Carteret took his place in the House of Lords as a Hanoverian Tory and vigorously defended the Protestant succession of George I. After a successful embassy to Sweden (1719–1721), he became secretary of state for the southern department of Europe. After he was ousted by Charles Townshend and Robert Walpole, George I made him lord lieutenant of Ireland (1724–1730), where he spent the happiest years of his life.

Shortly after his return to England, Carteret became a leading opponent of Walpole and succeeded him as the most influential minister of George II. His policy was to form a coalition strong enough to destroy French domination of Europe and as the ally of Austria to take a leading part in the War of the Austrian Succession. Henry Pelham forced Carteret to resign from the ministry in 1744, the year Carteret succeeded in his mother's right to the title of Earl Granville. George II attempted unsuccessfully to reinstate him as chief minister in 1746. The Duke of Newcastle, a former opponent, finally returned him to office in 1751 as lord president of the council—an office he retained until his death at Bath on Jan. 2, 1763.

Carteret has been described as the brilliant failure of 18th century politics. His career proves that his views, summed up in his phrase "give a man the crown on his side and he can defy everything," were out of date. His lack of experience in the Commons and the general belief that he owed office solely to the personal favor of the king ruined his career.

D. B. HORN, *University of Edinburgh*

CARTERET, kär′tər-et, **Philip** (1639–1682), English colonial governor of New Jersey. He was born in Jersey, in the Channel Islands, a relative of Sir George Carteret, joint proprietor of New Jersey. In 1665 he was appointed governor of the province, with the authority to institute an assembly, which first sat at Elizabethtown in 1668. However, settlers who refused to pay quitrents to the proprietors rioted and chose James Carteret, George Carteret's son as governor. The rebellion collapsed, but shortly afterward the Dutch temporarily regained New Jersey. Philip Carteret left for England in 1672, but in 1676 he became governor of East Jersey. In 1680, Gov. Edmund Andros of New York imprisoned him for disobeying New York's customs laws. With Andros' recall in 1680, Carteret reaffirmed his authority but gave up his office in 1682 after William Penn purchased East Jersey.

CARTERET, kär-tər-et′, is an industrial borough in northeastern New Jersey, in Middlesex county. It is situated on the Arthur Kill, opposite Staten Island, 11 miles (18 km) south of Newark. Carteret has heavy industries, including oil refineries, copper smelters, boiler shops, and steel mills, and manufactures paints, varnishes, and chemicals. It was founded in 1906 and was incorporated in 1922, and is governed by a mayor and council. Population: 23,137.

CARTERSVILLE is an industrial city in northwestern Georgia, the seat of Bartow county, 35 miles (56 km) northwest of Atlanta. It is a shipping center for iron ore, barite, bauxite, limestone, slate, potash, manganese, and ocher. Its manufactures include underwear, bedspreads, carpeting, tire cord fabric, and plastics. The Etowah Indian Mounds are 3 miles (5 km) south of the city.

The community was founded in 1832 and was called Birmingham. It was partly destroyed by the Union troops of General Sherman in 1864. It was incorporated as Cartersville in 1872. Government is by mayor, city manager, and council. Population: 9,929.

CARTHAGE, kär′thij, was for almost 1,500 years, from the 8th century B. C. to the 7th century A. D., the most important settlement west of Egypt on the Mediterranean coast of Africa. In its Phoenician period, Carthage was the most difficult foe Rome faced. When refounded by the Romans, it became a large city and a significant center in early Christianity. Its importance was always in commerce and politics.

PHOENICIAN PERIOD

The name Carthage comes from the Phoenician *Kart-hadast,* meaning "new town." In legend, the foundation of Carthage is traced to Elissa, who fled to its site after the murder of her husband in Tyre. In 814 B. C. she bought from the Libyans as much land as an oxhide would contain. She cut the hide in thin strips and used them to encircle the hillock of Byras, which remained the citadel of later Carthage. Although Virgil's *Aeneid* describes the dalliance of Aeneas with Dido, as the Greeks called Elissa, she is probably fictitious. The earliest evidence of settlement, unearthed through archaeological exploration, consists of a votive deposit of Greek pottery, dated shortly before 700 B.C.

The Phoenicians, who settled Carthage, began in the 8th century B. C. to found trading posts in North Africa, western Sicily, Sardinia, the Balearic Islands, and southern Spain. Phoenicia itself came under Assyrian control, and Tyre was besieged by Nebuchadnezzar II in the years 586–573 B. C. The western colonies, menaced by Greek expansion, especially in Sicily, turned for protection to Carthage, the largest and strongest Phoenician city. Thenceforth, it is possible to speak of a Carthaginian "empire." Most available information on Carthage is from the post-6th century period, but it often comes from hostile Greek and Roman sources and does not adequately describe Carthaginian institutions.

The City. Carthage lay on an easily defended peninsula just north of the Lake of Tunis. Its walls, well over 40 feet (12 meters) high, were 22 to 23 miles (35–37 km) long. The triple walls that guarded the land side extended for about 2½ miles (4 km). On the inside of the triple walls, there were stables for 300 elephants and 4,000 horses. The harbor, partly artificial, was a double one: the outer for traders; the inner, circular harbor (called *cothon*) for warships. The inner harbor was walled, and 220 war galleys could be sheltered in its sheds. The houses, which ranged up to six stories in height, were closely packed on narrow, winding streets. The most richly adorned of the Carthaginian religious shrines was that of Eshmoun, the god of healing, on Byrsa. Other shrines were dedicated to Astarte, Demeter and Kore (Persephone), and Melkart (identified with Hercules). The old sanctuary of Tanit near the harbor has revealed thousands of urns with the burned bones of children, for the Carthaginians—to the horror of Greeks and Romans—continued the Phoenician practice of child sacrifice (the "Moloch" of II Kings 23:10).

Although Greek sources mention kings at Carthage, it is doubtful if a regular kingship ever existed. Certainly from the mid-5th century on, Carthage was ruled by an aristocracy. Each year two officials (Latin, *suffetes;* Hebrew, *shophets*) were elected by a popular assembly to be administrators and judges. When necessary, generals were also elected and could be reelected. Their

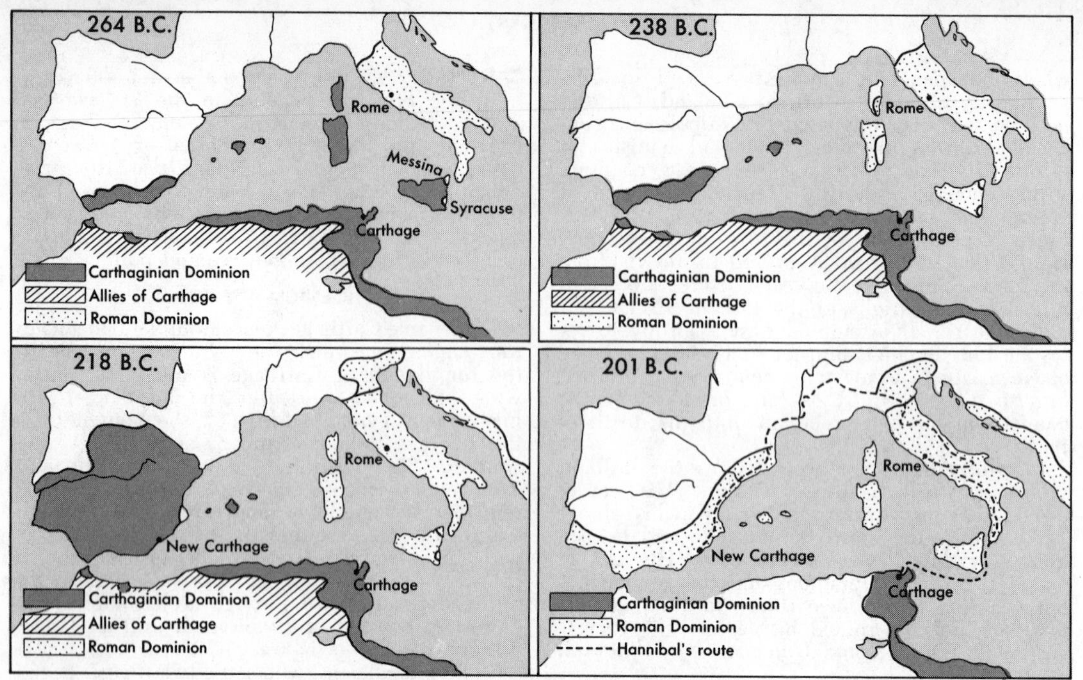

CARTHAGE AND ROME, 264-201 B.C.

troops were mercenary Libyans, Numidians, Greeks, and Spaniards, for the citizens of Carthage did not normally serve in the army.

A senate of perhaps 300 members, elected for life, advised the *suffetes*. From this senate committees were drawn, such as a judicial committee of 104 judges, a group of 30 that watched closely over public affairs, and smaller boards of 5. Only if the *suffetes* and the senate disagreed were matters referred to the popular assembly. The stability of the Carthaginian constitution was praised by Aristotle, and there seem to have been few efforts to overthrow it. No tyrants are known to have ruled Carthage. Modern scholars at times seek to explain Carthaginian policy in terms of conflicts between commercial and agricultural interests, but there is no evidence to support this hypothesis.

Economic Life and Culture. During the 5th century B.C., the aristocrats built up fairly large estates in the Bagradas (modern Medjerda) valley in northern Tunisia, where olives, grapes, and livestock were raised. The Libyans who lived beyond the valley were forced to provide troops and to surrender a quarter of their wheat crops. Apart from nearby Phoenician settlements—such as Thapsus, Leptis (Lepcis), Hadrumetum, and Utica—Carthage dominated trading points from the Gulf of Sidra to the Straits of Hercules (Gibraltar) and on to Gades (Cádiz). Probably early in the 5th century the navigator Hanno established posts on the Atlantic coast of Africa and voyaged around its westernmost tip, Cape Verde, as far south as Sierra Leone. At about the same time the navigator Himilco explored the Atlantic coast of Spain and France as far north as Brittany. All Carthaginian domains were closed to outsiders, who were killed as pirates if caught. By treaties with Rome (509 and 348 B.C.) and other states, foreigners were allowed to trade only in Carthage itself.

From its empire Carthage drew great riches in raw materials—gold, silver, tin, and iron—for which it apparently paid in textiles, olive oil, wine, and various luxuries of Greek and Italian origin. The metals were then exported to the more developed countries of the eastern Mediterranean. Coinage in electrum (an alloy of gold and silver), gold, and silver was used until the Hellenistic period only for paying mercenaries.

Archaeological explorations in Spain and Africa have revealed very little pottery or metalware made in Phoenicia or Carthage; the Carthaginians were traders, not artists. In the earliest levels, objects with Egyptian characteristics are numerous. Later imported wares are mostly Greek. During the 5th century B.C., there was a break in contact with Greek culture, but thereafter the Carthaginians were more and more heavily influenced by Hellenic civilization. The only native literature that is known is a treatise on estate management by Mago that was translated into Latin by order of the Roman Senate.

Wars with the Greeks. During the 6th century B.C., Carthage halted Greek colonization on the African coast west of Cyrene, in western Sicily, and along the eastern coast of Spain. With the Etruscans as allies, the Carthaginians fought a great naval battle about 535 against the Greeks off Corsica; as a result of this battle the Phocaean Greek settlers at Alalia abandoned the island. The Carthaginians remained friendly with the Etruscans.

Thereafter the Carthaginians fought the Greeks in Sicily, with the main objective of holding the western third of the island to protect their homeland and their rule in the western seas. The main Carthaginian bases were Motya (later Lilybaeum), Solus, and Panormus (Palermo). The boundary eventually came to be the Halycus River, west of Acragas (Agrigento). To counteract the power of the Greek city of Syracuse, in Sicily, under its tyrant Gelon, the general Hamilcar landed at Panormus in 480 B.C. and marched to Himera, where he and his army were caught by surprise and wiped out. In 410 B.C., Segesta appealed to Carthage for help. The general Hannibal, grandson of Hamilcar, took Selinus in 409 and destroyed Himera in the same year. His successor, Himilco, sacked Acragas in 406, whereupon the Greeks evacuated Gela and Camarina.

The Carthaginian threat to Syracuse led to the rise of Dionysius I as tyrant of Syracuse. To gain time, Dionysius made a peace treaty unfavorable to Syracuse, then strongly fortified the city, built a large navy, and assembled siege equipment. When he resumed the war, he drove to Motya, which he destroyed in 398, only to be forced back to Syracuse by Himilco. Pestilence and a defeat at the hands of the Syracusans finally ended the Carthaginian siege. After an inconclusive war that lasted approximately from 382 to 375, Dionysius once more resumed hostilities; he was stopped at Lilybaeum in 367 and died in the same year.

In 341 B.C., Timoleon of Corinth, aiding Syracuse, defeated the Carthaginians on the Crimisus River near Segesta. The Carthaginians besieged Syracuse itself in 310, but the city was saved when the Syracusan tyrant Agathocles boldly invaded the Carthaginian homeland in the same year and took nearby Utica. After several victories, Agathocles suffered a reverse in 307 and agreed to peace in 306. Again in 278 the Carthaginians besieged Syracuse but were driven back to Lilybaeum by Pyrrhus of Epirus, who had come over from the Italian mainland. On his departure, peace was arranged in 275.

The Punic Wars. Against the Greek states, which were divided and often unsettled internally, Carthage could hold its own. But the continuing animosities in Spain and Sicily caused its downfall once Rome entered the scene as defender of the Greeks.

The First Punic War broke out in Sicily in 264 B.C. as a result of trouble between Messana (Messina) and Syracuse, in which both Rome (now master of the Italian peninsula) and Carthage intervened. Roman armies quickly gained control of most of Sicily but found it difficult to take Carthaginian strongpoints, which could be supplied by sea. The Romans built a large navy and manned it with Italian rowers and Roman soldiers. The Roman consul C. Duilius won the first battle at sea off Mylae, Sicily, in 260. Thereafter, their military discipline and tenacity enabled the Romans to win all but one of the naval battles of the war.

In 256 the Roman consul Marcus Atilius Regulus invaded North Africa, but he was unexpectedly defeated on land the next year by a Carthaginian army with elephants, trained by the soldier of fortune Xanthippus of Sparta. After losing fleet upon fleet in storms, the Romans built a navy that won the battle of the Aegates Islands, off western Sicily, in 241. Carthage was exhausted and agreed to a peace involving the surrender of all of Sicily and the payment of an indemnity of 3,200 talents.

After the war, the Carthaginian mercenaries revolted because of arrears in pay. The Romans at first were neutral, but in 238 they seized Sardinia and Corsica from Carthage. Carthaginian attention was then directed toward expansion in Spain under Hamilcar Barca, his son-in-law Hasdrubal, and his son Hannibal. This alarmed the Greek city of Massilia (Marseille), which appealed to Rome. Eventually, the Second Punic War broke out in 218. Hannibal surprised Rome by marching across southern Gaul to the Po valley to invade the Italian peninsula in 217. One of the world's great generals, Hannibal won every battle of this campaign, but he could not induce all of Rome's subjects to revolt. The Roman general Scipio Africanus meanwhile conquered Spain by 207, and in 204 he invaded North Africa. Hannibal returned home during a truce and was defeated at Zama, in North Africa, in 202. The ensuing peace of 201 stripped Carthage of its navy and overseas possessions. Even in Africa, Carthage was permitted to fight only on Roman approval. As *suffete* in 196, Hannibal sought to make Carthage more democratic, but he was hounded out in 195 by Roman threats. See also HANNIBAL; HAMILCAR; HASDRUBAL.

Carthage paid its huge indemnity of 10,000 talents but became ever more prosperous. The suspicious Romans finally declared the Third Punic War in 149, and after the Carthaginians surrendered both hostages and arms, ordered them to abandon their homes and settle 10 miles inland. The desperate citizens forged new arms and defended their city against the Romans for three years, but in the spring of 146 the Romans broke through the walls and fought their way house by house for six days to the citadel of Byrsa. Fifty thousand citizens surrendered, the city burned for 10 days, and the Roman commander Scipio Aemilianus sowed salt on its site.

ROMAN PERIOD

For a century, Carthage remained deserted, though the Roman popular reformer Gaius Gracchus tried to resettle it in 122 B.C. Finally a colony was established in 44 B.C., following the plans of Julius Caesar. Carthage was reinforced under the emperor Augustus in 29 B.C. and quickly bloomed into one of the most important centers of the Roman Empire. The seat of the proconsul of Africa, Carthage was adorned by baths, a theater, a long aqueduct, and other buildings of which remains have been found. Carthage became Latin in appearance, but considerable Phoenician influence remained. Among its important gods were Saturn (identified with Baal) and Juno Caelestis (identified with Tanit).

Christianity gained a foothold in Carthage in the 2d century A.D. Tertullian (c. 160–c. 230), the first great Christian writer to employ the Latin language, lived there. The Donatist heresy of the 4th century took its root in a dispute over elections to the bishopric of Carthage. St. Augustine, one of the main opponents of this heresy and one of the great Latin Fathers of the Church, received his higher education at Carthage. In his *Confessions* he describes vividly the bustling, worldly life of the city.

As the Roman Empire declined in the west, the Vandals under Genseric (Gaiseric) invaded North Africa from Spain and took Carthage in 439. In the emperor Justinian I's great effort to regain the west, Carthage was conquered from the Vandals by the general Belisarius in 533, but in 698 the Arabs, rushing across North Africa from Egypt, seized it permanently.

Thereafter, Carthage deteriorated, its ruins becoming a source of stone for buildings, for the Arabs preferred to settle on the nearby site of Tunis. St. Louis IX of France invaded Tunisia in 1270, during the Eighth Crusade. He died of the plague in the citadel of Byrsa, which today is crowned by a cathedral in his memory.

CHESTER G. STARR, *University of Illinois*

Further Reading: Dunbabin, T. J., *The Western Greeks* (New York and London 1948); Harden, Donald, *The Phoenicians* (New York 1963); Warmington, B. H., *Carthage* (London 1960).

CARTHAGE, kär′thij, an industrial city in southwestern Missouri and the seat of Jasper county, is situated on the Spring River, about 130 miles (210 km) south of Kansas City. It is a trade center for a farm area and makes dairy and other food products. Marble and limestone are quarried, and lead, zinc, and coal are mined. Carthage was settled in 1833 and, in 1861, was the scene of a battle between pro- and antislavery forces in Missouri. Government is by mayor and council. Population: 11,035.

CARTHUSIANS, kär-thōō′zhənz, a Roman Catholic order of monks and nuns, whose lives are totally dedicated to contemplation. They are noted for the austerity and solitude of their monastic existence. Each choir monk (priest) lives in a hermitage, or cell, consisting of a living room, workshop, garden, and ambulatory. He spends the greater part of his day in solitude and silence, praying, studying, or laboring. He joins the other monks in church for sung matins, lauds, vespers, and Mass. Once a week the monks break their solitude and silence for three or four hours while they walk together. Lay brothers lead a slightly less exacting life and care for the material needs of the house.

Male Carthusians wear a white habit, scapular, and hood, and a white cowl when in choir. Carthusian nuns, whose lives are also contemplative, though less solitary, wear a white habit, black veil, and linen wimple.

Origin and Development. The order was founded in 1084 by St. Bruno the Carthusian (q.v.) and six companions in the Chartreuse mountains north of Grenoble. Its name is derived from the French *chartreuse,* which the English corrupted into "charterhouse." From the first community, La Grande Chartreuse, a second was opened in 1092 at La Torre, in Calabria, Italy. During the century that followed, 38 charterhouses, including two for nuns, were established throughout England and the Continent. The high point of Carthusian expansion was reached in 1521, when the order included 195 houses.

Reverses. During the Reformation more than 50 monks were killed in England, Holland, France, Austria, and Yugoslavia; the Grande Chartreuse itself was destroyed by Huguenots. In 1676, having recovered many of its losses, the order claimed 173 houses, 2,300 choir monks, 1,500 lay brothers, and 170 nuns. During the 18th century Carthusian houses were suppressed by nationalist rulers or parties in Austria, Tuscany, and the Republic of Venice. The French houses suffered greatly during the Revolutionary and Napoleonic periods, and an antireligious spirit in Spain, Portugal, and Switzerland resulted in the suppression of houses in those countries during the 19th century.

Exiled from France at the beginning of the 20th century, the community of the Grande Chartreuse in Isère established itself at Farneta, Italy. The monks returned to their house at Montrieux in 1929 and to Isère in 1940. In the late 1960's there were about 25 charterhouses in France, Spain, Portugal, Italy, Yugoslavia, Germany, Switzerland, and England, with about 600 choir monks and lay brothers and some 140 choir nuns and lay sisters. A house was founded in the United States at Whitingham, Vt., in 1950.

Rule. St. Bruno produced no written rule for Carthusian life, but Dom Guigo, prior of the Grande Chartreuse from 1109 to 1136, compiled Bruno's monastic customs into a directory, the *Consuetudines,* which Innocent II approved in 1133. General chapters, the supreme authority in the order, have provided further ordinances. The latest revision was published in 1924. The prior of Grande Chartreuse exercises jurisdiction in the two-year intervals between sessions of the general chapter.

MICHAEL V. GANNON, *University of Florida*

CARTIER, kȧr-tyā′, **Sir George Étienne** (1814–1873), Canadian public official, who championed Confederation. He was born at St.-Antoine, Verchères county, Lower Canada (Quebec) on Sept. 6, 1814. Cartier was educated in Montreal and in 1835 was called to the bar of Lower Canada. A follower of Louis Joseph Papineau, he participated in the rebellion of 1837 that sought to keep French Canada separate and autonomous. When the revolt failed, he fled to the United States but returned to Canada in 1838 when amnesty was declared.

In 1848 he was elected to the Legislative Assembly of Canada as a Conservative from Verchères, and he represented that constituency and later Montreal in the Legislative Assembly and the House of Commons until his death. From 1857 to 1862 he was joint premier of United Canada with the Conservative leader, John A. Macdonald. Their administration won the support of the businessmen of Montreal by promising to work for Confederation.

Cartier was active at the Quebec Conference of 1864 and persuaded French Canadians to accept the proposals for federation. Among his other accomplishments were the negotiations leading to the surrender of the Hudson's Bay Company's rights in the Northwest. His work in projecting and chartering the Canadian Pacific Railway was an essential preliminary to the admission of British Columbia into the Confederation in 1871, although it involved him with other Conservatives in the "Pacific Scandal." Cartier died in London on May 20, 1873.

GEORGE M. WRONG, *University of Toronto*

CARTIER, kȧr-tyā′, **Jacques** (1491–1557), French navigator, who was the first explorer of the Gulf of St. Lawrence and the discoverer of the St. Lawrence River. He was born in St.-Malo, France. He probably participated in Breton trading voyages to Brazil and may have accompanied Verrazano in his North American expedition of 1524.

Certainly in 1534, when King Francis I of France commissioned him to search for a route to the Western Sea, Cartier appeared to be familiar with Newfoundland waters. Passing through the Strait of Belle Isle and turning southward from the coast of Labrador, he crossed the Gulf of St. Lawrence to the Magdalen Islands and Prince Edward Island and explored Chaleur Bay before landing at Gaspé Bay, where he took possession of the country for France. Taking two young Iroquois with him, he returned to France by way of Anticosti Island and the Strait of Belle Isle, thus completely circumnavigating the gulf without finding any passage to the west.

Cartier returned to North America in 1535 with three ships and discovered and sailed up the St. Lawrence after again using the Belle Isle entry. As he went he was told tall tales of the kingdoms of Saguenay, Canada, and Hochelaga.

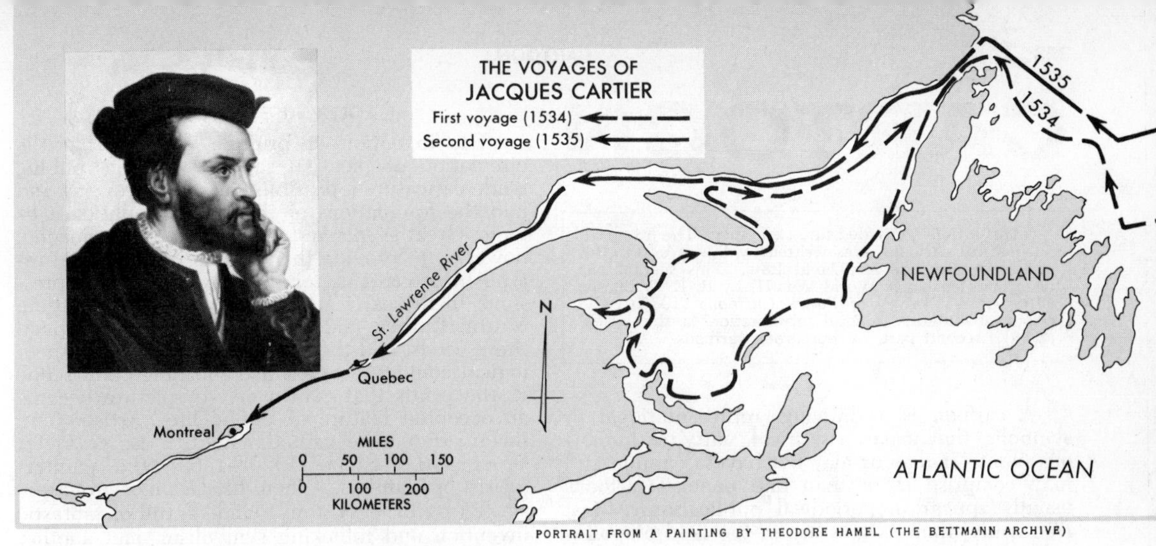

PORTRAIT FROM A PAINTING BY THEODORE HAMEL (THE BETTMANN ARCHIVE)

Despite the efforts of Chief Donnacona, father of the two Indian boys he had brought back from France as interpreters, to dissuade him from going farther, he pressed up the river from Stadacona (Quebec City) to Hochelaga (Montreal), where he climbed and named Mount Royal after finding the way west blocked by rapids. He spent that winter at Quebec, losing many of his men from scurvy, before returning to France.

Because of royal disillusionment about the resources of Canada, he was unable to go again to the New World until 1541, when he was named captain and pilot of a colonizing expedition commanded by the Sieur de Roberval. On his arrival at Stadacona, he found the Indians distrustful of the French, who had failed this time to bring back the Indians they had taken to France, and he established the proposed French settlement at nearby Cap Rouge, naming the place Charlesbourg-Royal. On his way home to France the following spring he encountered the belated Roberval off Newfoundland and ignored his orders to turn back. Roberval's colonizing efforts were a disastrous failure, and his party returned to France in 1543. With France thereafter involved in wars at home and abroad, the French did not return to the St. Lawrence until early in the 17th century.

Cartier, who had established France's claim to Canada, died at St.-Malo on Sept. 1, 1557. The best edition of his narratives is *The Voyages of Jacques Cartier* (1924), edited by Henry P. Biggar.

MASON WADE, *University of Western Ontario*

CARTIER-BRESSON, kȧr-tyā′ bre-sôN′, **Henri** (1908–), French photographer, famous for his portrayals of major social and political events and for his portraits. He was born in Chanteloup, France, on Aug. 22, 1908. After attending school in Paris and in Cambridge, England, he studied painting with André Lhote. In 1931 he traveled in Africa and Europe as a free-lance photographer, determined to "preserve life in the act of living."

After traveling in Mexico, Cartier-Bresson assisted Jean Renoir in making motion pictures, including *The Rules of the Game* (1939). While serving in the French Army during World War II, he was captured by the Germans and, after escaping, joined the French underground movement. In 1945 he directed *Le Retour,* a film documentary of the return of war prisoners.

Cartier-Bresson went to New York City in 1946 for an exhibition of his works at the Museum of Modern Art. While in New York he helped found in 1947 the Magnum agency, a cooperative firm owned and operated by photographers to promote and sell their work. Cartier-Bresson published several books, among them *The Decisive Moment* (1952), *The Europeans* (1955), and *People of Moscow* (1955).

BEAUMONT NEWHALL
George Eastman House, Rochester, N.Y.

CARTILAGE, kärt′əl-ij, is a type of connective tissue characterized by its resiliency and toughness. Like other types of connective tissue, it consists of cells and fibers embedded in a substance called *matrix.* However, unlike other connective tissues, cartilage does not contain blood or lymph vessels or nerves.

Cartilage cells, or *Chondrocytes,* occur either singly or in groups, and they lie within small spaces called *lacunae.* The fibers in cartilage are collagen fibers and elastic fibers. The matrix consists largely of a protein-carbohydrate substance called *chondromucoid.* After a certain age, some cartilage, especially in the larynx and trachea, has a tendency to become calcified. Under such conditions, the chondrocytes usually die while the matrix is replaced by bone.

Surrounding each cartilaginous structure is a membrane called the *perichondrium.* Its outer layer contains blood vessels while the inner layer contains cartilage-forming cells, or *chondroblasts.* These cells are responsible for adding new cells and matrix to the outside of the structure. Cartilage also grows by the enlargement of the existing cells and matrix within the structure.

Types. Structurally, cartilage is divided into three types. *Hyalin cartilage* is the most common. In adults, this glossy translucent cartilage is found in the nose, larynx, trachea, bronchi, and the synovial joints, the fluid-filled joints between certain bones. In an embryo, it makes up the skeleton before it becomes bone.

Elastic cartilage is found in the outer flap (auricle) of the external ear, the Eustachian tube (between the middle ear and the throat), and in some cartilages of the larynx. *Fibrocartilage* is found chiefly in the intervertebral joints.

OTHMAR SOLNITZKY, PH. D., M. D.
Georgetown University School of Medicine

CARTOGRAM. See MAP.

CARTOGRAPHY. See MAP.

CARTOON

This article is divided into two parts. The first part, on political cartoons, was written by the great English cartoonist, the late Sir David Low. This section has been updated (since World War II) by R. E. Williams, editor of *A Century of Punch Cartoons* (1955), who also contributed a general introduction to the article and the second part, on humorous cartoons.

A cartoon is a drawing, representational or symbolic, that makes a satirical, witty, or humorous point. It may or may not have a caption and may comprise more than one panel. Cartoons usually appear in periodical publications. Most frequently, their targets are in the field of political or public affairs, but they may be social customs, fashions, or sports events or personalities.

In its original meaning, in the fine arts, a cartoon (from Italian *cartone,* meaning "paper") is a preliminary sketch for a large canvas or fresco painting, for an architectural drawing, for a tapestry design, or for pictures in mosaic or glass.

"Cartoon" acquired its present meaning in 1843, when a great exhibition of cartoons was given for a competition devised by Queen Victoria's consort Prince Albert to get designs for frescoes for the walls of the new Houses of Parliament. Many of the entries, though lofty in intention, were ludicrous, and John Leech drew a series of imitations in *Punch,* satirizing them and railing at social and political abuses of the day.

POLITICAL CARTOONS

The invention of printing, by ensuring the circulation of pictorial satire to a large public, made caricature a possible arm of controversy and laid the foundations of the modern political cartoon. Great events and great figures were needed, however, to provide the impetus which would establish conventions for the new means of expression. In the early 16th century, the Reformation, Martin Luther, and Pope Alexander VI supplied these needs, and the passions engendered in theological conflicts so extended the range and scope of the prints that controversy-by-picture became an accepted feature of public life. Artistry and imagination were gained with the rise of Pieter Bruegel the Elder (1520?–1569), the painter-satirist of Flanders. When the stream of grotesque started by Bruegel from Flanders, full of fantastic invention and rollicking symbolism, met another stream of graphic moralities, full of mythological allusions and heavy allegory coming from Italy, the political cartoon was on its way. In Italy in the 17th century, it was unsafe to be too openly critical of authority; therefore, to survive, political satire had to be ambiguous or disguised. In France also, Cardinal Richelieu, who dominated the government, severely discouraged comment in caricature. His successor, Cardinal Mazarin, was less sensitive and under his regime the social and political prints multiplied, though their quality remained dull and mediocre.

The Dutch School and Romeyn de Hooghe. At the end of the 17th century, encouragement to growth was found at last in the Netherlands, where the free republican spirit of the Dutch and the pres-

HONORÉ DAUMIER'S "Enfoncé, Lafayette. Attrapé, mon vieux!" A gross Louis Philippe wears mourning clothes but hides a satisfied smirk at the funeral of the famous soldier who had once helped him become King of France.

LIBRAIRIE FLOURY

THOMAS NAST'S "What are you going to do about it?" was an attack on "Boss Tweed" and the Tammany political machine in New York. Tweed is pictured as a Roman emperor at a gladiatorial contest watching the Tammany tiger (Nast's invention) rip apart a young woman symbolizing the Republic. Nast's cartoons helped cause Tweed's overthrow.

ence of many painters and etchers fostered a flourishing center of political caricature. Romeyn de Hooghe (1645–1708) stood out from among Dutch practitioners, not because he was a good artist but because he was a political propagandist of such skill and popularity that his services were in demand outside his own country. William of Orange employed him to advantage during his disputes with Louis XIV, and the latter is said to have competed vainly for his services. Caricatures, with captions suitably translated into various languages, became one of the Dutch exports to France and Britain. Prints on the eccentricities of English politics—from the Restoration (1660) to the South Sea Bubble (1720)—had already won popularity among the English by the time William of Orange crossed the channel in 1689 to become King William III of England.

Gillray and the English School. William Hogarth (1697–1764), the painter and etcher, began to create an indigenous English school. His inspiration was not political. It was his great individuality that most inspired the subject-etchers and engravers of the succeeding generation, among whom were the fathers of the political cartoon of later years, James Gillray (1757–1815) and Thomas Rowlandson (1756–1827). Gillray took the caricatural art of Bruegel, the form and moral purpose of Hogarth, added his genius as a caricaturist of personality, and fashioned them into something recognizably akin to the modern political cartoon. Rowlandson was in some ways his superior as an artist, but preferred to satirize morals and manners, whereas Gillray was a born politician. George III, William Pitt the younger, Charles James Fox, Richard Sheridan, Lord North, and Edmund Burke appear vividly in his gallery of contemporary statesmen. With daring independence and a flow of comic, often grossly indecent, ideas, his wit was directed not only against the political and legislative abuses of his time but also against the morals of the royal family. Gillray favored principles of freedom and at first approved of the French Revolution, but the execution of Louis XVI and the work of the Terror were too much for him. It may be said that Napoleon Bonaparte and Gillray arrived at their highest form together—Napoleon as the raw material for caricature, and Gillray as the caricaturist. The matured artist dealt with the doings of "Boney the carcase-butcher" and his friends in a wide variety of unflattering images, sometimes giving offense to Napoleon.

In France, political caricature, which had been weak under Louis XVI, flourished vigorously just before and during the Revolution. Great numbers of prints, the "flying leaves" of the Revolution, passed from hand to hand. Bitter and forceful, they were mostly anonymous and of little artistry. In Britain, after the fall of Napoleon, passions slowly cooled and the temper of caricature changed. George Cruikshank (1792–1878) became the leading member of a new and more polite school. Cruikshank had been conspicuous earlier

REPRODUCED BY PERMISSION OF THE PROPRIETORS OF PUNCH

JOHN TENNIEL'S "Dropping the Pilot," one of the most famous 19th century cartoons, was a comment on Kaiser William II's dismissal of Bismarck, the Iron Chancellor.

among the fiercer imitators of Gillray, but he abandoned political caricature for pictures of generalized social comedy and book illustration. A series of lithograph *Political Sketches* signed "HB" by John Doyle (1798–1868) reflected a milder mood. In the days when Gillray and Rowlandson flourished, England had been known as the "Home of Caricature". Caricature now quietly moved its home to France.

Philipon's "La Caricature" and Daumier. Following the Revolution of July 1830 events happened in Paris which vitally affected the future of the art. Charles Philipon (1800–1862), in November, founded *La Caricature,* the first distinct type of the modern illustrated satirical weekly. After four years of prosecutions, fines, and imprisonments, it was suppressed, but Philipon had already begun *Le Charivari* (1832), the first daily paper to print a new drawing every day. Philipon was a caricaturist himself and a born journalist with a rare perception of genius in others. Contributors to *Le Charivari* during the five years of its stormy life are of astonishing brilliance, and the campaigns of its famous "Phalanx" of caricaturists had much to do with the downfall of Louis Philippe, the "Citizen King" whose pear-shaped head Philipon exploited to the full in the *Poire Royale* (Royal Pear) series. Among Philipon's political cartoonists were Grandville (pseudonym of Jean Gérard, 1803–1847) and Charles Joseph Traviès de Villers (1804–1859), but his greatest find was Honoré Daumier (1808–1879). Daumier was an artist, a man of feeling rather than a politician, not lively in ideas, but masterly in depiction. His vivacity and strength as a political cartoonist did not mature until after he served a prison sentence for offending the king by presenting him as Gargantua. His lithographs *Enfoncé Lafayette* and *Rue Transnonain* show the simple power of his rendering of situation, and his series of portrait caricatures show his comprehension of individual character. In emulation of Philipon's enterprise many comic and satirical papers arose in France, with brilliant artists to serve them, but most of them sketched the social rather than the political scene. The rise and fall of the Second Empire, the Commune, and fears of Prussia and Russia released a new flood of political caricature. Cham (pseudonym of Amédée de Noé, 1818–1879), not so much the successor as a follower of Daumier, was at his best in his lithographs of the follies of the Commune. André Gill (pseudonym of Louis Alexandre Gosset de Guines, 1840–1885) and Alfred Le Petit (1841–1910) were the most notable of numerous producers of savage cartoons against Napoleon III and his Empress Eugénie. Toward the end of the 19th century, British imperialism and the Dreyfus case were material for better drawing by Jean Louis Forain (1852–1931), Charles Léandre (1862–1934), and Caran d'Ache (pseudonym of Emmanuel Poiré, 1858–1909).

"Punch" and Tenniel. Philipon's example was followed in other countries also, and periodicals publishing caricatures, political and otherwise, began to appear all over Europe. In 1841 *Punch,* the London *Charivari,* appeared in Britain and the establishment of a new tradition based upon the outlook of the middle classes was advanced. The change was reflected in the drawings of John Leech (1817–1864) which, incidentally, were the first "cartoons," in that sense of the word, to be so called. Though some of Leech's earlier cartoons against Catholics and Jews were sufficiently biting and direct to excite anger at home, and others against Napoleon III and Nicholas I of Russia had *Punch* banned abroad, Leech's work later mellowed into social pleasantries. Among his contemporaries was John Tenniel (1820-1914), the apotheosis of a dignified school, who had become the most significant English cartoonist of his day. He scrupulously eschewed vulgarity and specialized in statuesque personifications and symbols such as Britannia, Germania, Columbia, John Bull, Uncle Sam, the British lion, and the Russian bear. He was at his best on national occasions that called for commemoration in sedate treatment and his cartoons, extending over his long life, form an illustrated commentary on virtually the entire Victorian era. The most famous is *Dropping the Pilot,* drawn when the German emperor, young William II, dismissed Prince Bismarck. The relatively minor matters of party warfare were served by Harry Furniss (1854–1925). (Edward) Linley Sambourne (1844–1910), an impeccable draftsman, had a purity of line well suited to carrying on the Tennielesque conceptions, which were meticulously continued into the 20th century by Bernard Partridge (1861–1945), and, somewhat less solemnly, by Leonard Raven-Hill (1867–1942). Other distinguished cartoonists working during the latter half of the 19th century were Matt Morgan of *Tomahawk* and W. Bowcher of *Judy*.

"Simplicissimus" and Gulbransson. Philipon's example, again, inspired the start of *Kladderadatsch* (1848) in Berlin and of *Die fliegende Blätter* (1845), followed by *Punsch* and later by *Simplicissimus*, in Munich. The latter, a colored Socialist weekly, poked scorn at Junkers, Prussians, and the Kaiser. The progress of Bismarck and his aims may be traced through many undistinguished but highly critical German cartoons against Napoleon III and Nicholas I, but by the turn of the century the *Simplicissimus* team of cartoonists, Olaf Gulbransson, Bruno Park, Thomas Theodor Heine, and Blix, had made Munich the most interesting center of European political caricature. The 20th century opened with plenty of subject matter in international fears, scandals in high places, and the Russo-Japanese, South African, and Balkan wars. German caricaturists, including C. Kunze, Feininger, Engert, and Gehrte, dealt particularly hard with Queen Victoria and her son Prince Edward.

United States and Nast. In America, after some importations and imitations of European styles, a more native school of talent emerged in a crop of anonymous lithographs inspired by the election of President Jackson, the Mexican War, the rise of slavery agitation and the Civil War. Popular feeling about the Civil War brought young Thomas Nast (1840–1902), an illustrator-reporter of *Leslie's Weekly*, to national attention with a cartoon

BY PERMISSION, NEW YORK WORLD-TELEGRAM

ROLLIN KIRBY'S "Upsetting an Old-Timer!" indicates the effect that business-control laws have on those who favor a "hands-off" government policy toward industry.

DAVID LOW'S "In Future the Army Will Be Guided by My Intuitions" ridicules Hitler as a military commander.

DAVID LOW

BORIS EFIMOV'S "American Motor of the Latest Type" gives a Soviet view of the motives behind United States financial aid to Europe in the years after World War II.

defending Lincoln's policy. Later, as the graphic inventor of the Democratic donkey, the Republican elephant, the Tammany tiger, the rag-baby of paper currency, the cap-and-dinnerpail of labor, and other symbols familiar in American cartooning, Nast showed that the United States had a master whose imagination, draftsmanship, subtle portraiture, and effective composition were peculiarly appropriate to political cartoons. His most notable political, as distinct from artistic, achievement was his exposure of corruption in Tammany Hall which culminated in the overthrow and imprisonment of "Boss" Tweed. On Nast's retirement, his mantle hovered over his successor, O. G. Bush (1842–1909), who later left weekly for daily journalism, and settled on Joseph Keppler (1838–1894) and Bernhard Gillam (1856–1896). Political cartoons had become so popular that *Puck* was established (1876–1877), a colored comic paper in the German style with doublepage political cartoons by Keppler, one of its founders. Since *Puck* was sympathetic to the Democratic party, a rival, *Judge*, soon followed in support of the Republicans, with cartoons by Gillam. Gillam had been working for *Puck*, but changed sides, which enabled him to perform the peculiar feat of assisting Grover Cleveland and the Democratic party into power with ruthless cartoons in *Puck*, and then attacking both with equally ruthless cartoons in *Judge*.

DANIEL FITZPATRICK'S "Old Politicians Never Die, They Don't Even Fade Away" lampoons campaign oratory.

BY PERMISSION ST. LOUIS POST-DISPATCH

The 20th Century to End of World War II. Before the turn of the century, daily newspapers had solved technical problems of reproduction and the daily "editorial" cartoon arrived as a regular feature of journalism, particularly in the United States. Distinguished early arrivals among the legion of cartoonists fostered by this encouragement were Homer Davenport (1867–1912), O. Cesare, and Frederick Opper (1857–1937). The style of drawing cartoons in chalk, which became a widespread convention among American editorial cartoonists, had its earliest and most talented exponents in Rollin Kirby (1875–1952) and Daniel R. Fitzpatrick. Of those to whom Americans looked for interpretation of news and events leading to the world wars, Ding (J. N. Darling), T. Brown, Nelson Harding (1879–1944), Harold M. Talburt, Carey Orr, Edmund Duffy, and Herblock (Herbert L. Block) have had honorable places, with Art Young (1866–1943), Boardman Robinson, William Gropper, and Robert Minor as thunder on the political left.

The most famous political cartoonist of World War I was a Dutchman, Louis Raemaekers. During the between-wars period in France, Nob, Her-

BASTIAN'S "Who's Burying Who?" uses Soviet Premier Khrushchev's remark in 1957 that the USSR would "bury" the West to comment on worsening Soviet-Chinese relations in the 1960's.

BASTIAN IN THE SAN FRANCISCO CHRONICLE

mann Paul, and Sennep upheld French nationalism in varying degrees, with occasional anger against both their enemies and their friends during the troubled years of the Versailles Peace, the League of Nations, and the Ethiopian, Manchurian, and Spanish wars. In Germany, Gulbransson, supported by E. Schilling, Karl Arnold, Erich Wilke, O. E. Petersen, and Garvens, lent his considerable talent to depicting these events in their relation to the revival of German nationalism. In Italy, Mario Sironi, with his use of a peculiar mechanical style, supported the policies of Mussolini. The international outlook was preserved by Derso and Kelen, a partnership of talents, who "adopted" the League of Nations and, working at Geneva, supplied various papers with good-natured but penetrating cartoons of its doings from "on the spot."

The first British daily newspaper cartoonist was F. C. G. (Francis Carruthers Gould, 1844–1925), a Radical influenced by Tenniel in approach, who exercised his powers against the imperial policies of Joseph Chamberlain. The aggressive Gillray spirit seemed to have died out

HERBLOCK'S cartoons are a pungent appraisal of contemporary affairs. "The Built-In Bomb" (*left*) suggests the explosive urban situation; "Back to the Foreign Legion" (*right*) views France's anti-NATO stand under de Gaulle.

COPYRIGHT 1966, HERBLOCK IN THE WASHINGTON POST

COPYRIGHT 1966, HERBLOCK IN THE WASHINGTON POST

in British cartooning when Will Dyson (1813–1938), an Australian, came to London to prove that it had merely been renewing its youth overseas. Dyson's cartoons established him as a caustic critic of the British social-political order. During World War I his *Kultur Cartoons* against German militarism were of national importance. Poy (P. H. Fearon), S. Strube, and L. Illingworth redressed the balance on the side of amiability in the between-wars period, but another Antipodean, David Low (1891–1963), who was more interested in ideas than in parties, worked in turn for newspapers of all shades of opinion, criticizing their policies as he did so. Outraged by nazism, his work reached a crescendo with the rise and fall of Hitler.

Russian political caricature under the czars was undistinguished, but from the beginning of the Revolution of 1917 the Bolsheviks valued picture propaganda, and made plentiful use of political cartoons in window displays, in newspapers, on leaflets and banners, and as posters. Deni cartooned general events for *Pravda,* Boris Efimov pilloried the capitalist statesmen and their conferences in *Isvestia,* and Moor was the anti-God cartoon specialist for the atheistic papers. Then appeared *Krokodil,* a national comic paper, issued from the office of *Pravda,* printed in color and resembling the Munich *Simplicissimus* in appearance. Although at first there were attempts to develop particular Soviet schools of caricature, the Russian cartoonists soon returned to the styles of the bourgeois past and thereafter there was no discernible departure from the Western traditions in method, technique, or imagery. Restrictions on material, and official political direction, especially after 1946, were impeding circumstances, but there were always the alleged misdeeds of "capitalist warmongers" to inspire a prodigious output of vivacious cartoons by Efimov, by the Kukriniksi, a pen name covering three artists working jointly on the same drawing (Mikhail Kuprianov, Porfiril Krilov and Nikolai Sokolov), and by Broadaty, Eliseyev, and Ganf.

DAVID LOW

POSTWAR CARTOONING

After World War II, political cartoons proliferated as weekly opinion publications adopted them. After 182 years of publication, the London *Times* started running a daily political cartoon in May 1966. The death of the prolific "Vicky" (Victor Weisz, 1913–1966), who reached his peak in the *News Chronicle,* left a gap in English political cartooning not easy to fill. Norman Mansbridge of *Punch* and Leslie Illingworth of the *Daily Mail* were in the great tradition of English cartoon art. Cummings of the *Daily Express* returned to the brutality of the early masters of the genre, and Gerald Scarfe, a free-lancer, drew with a skill, intricacy, and venom that would have been acclaimed in the 18th century.

In the United States, Herblock (Washington *Post*), Fitzpatrick (St. Louis *Post-Dispatch*), Edmund Duffy (Baltimore *Sun*), and Bill Mauldin (Chicago *Sun-Times*) dominated the field for many years. American cartoonists who established themselves somewhat later include Patrick Oliphant (Denver *Post*), Paul Conrad (Los Angeles *Times*), Gib Crockett (Washington *Star*), Hugh Haynie (Louisville *Courier-Journal*), Don Hesse (St. Louis *Globe Democrat*), and Guernsey Le Pelley (*Christian Science Monitor*).

R. E. WILLIAMS

HUMOROUS CARTOON

Although *Punch* dropped the word "cartoon" for a number of years after first using it in 1843, the term remained in popular usage. The public applied it to the pictorial humor emerging in the periodicals of the day. The biting satire and crudity of the independently circulated prints of the 18th and the early 19th centuries gave way to gentler, although somewhat more patronizing, lampoons of social behavior, human ignorance, field sports, snobbery, and man's foibles generally. The one-panel, meticulously drawn and detailed picture with an explanatory caption of as many as 12 lines lightened the dark pages of small print in many publications.

The main bases of cartoon humor are the same as those of any other form of humor: incongruity, misfortune, discomfiture, excess in emotions or behavior, stupefying ignorance, and natural human responses to unusual events or circumstances. Comment on current mores usually fits into one of these classifications.

The highest types of humorous cartoon art are in two categories: the entirely visual cartoon for which no title or caption is necessary or, indeed, desirable; and the cartoon in which picture and caption are inseparable, each adding to the effectiveness of the other. There is a variation in which the illustration is humorous or intriguing in its own right and the caption provides added dimension. The mainstream of cartoon art, however, remains faithful to its beginnings. The picture still sets the scene and mood for the witty caption, but does not necessarily add to the humor of the cartoons.

Historical Development. The Swiss illustrator Rodolphe Töpffer (1799–1846) drew picture story books having a satirical and social point. He was ahead of his time in his understanding of the power of such a medium, and his books, especially the collection of drawings *Histoires en estampes* (1846–1847), were forerunners of the comic strip. Töpffer understood that "more people can look than read" and that "he who uses the direct method [of drawing] will have the advantage of those who talk in chapters."

In France, Honoré Daumier (1808–1879) was influenced by the English school of satirical artists (Hogarth, Gillray, and Rowlandson). In 10 years, Daumier contributed more than 900 lithographs to the Paris daily paper *Charivari,* etching most of them himself. He explored every pictorial device to attract maximum attention to the focal points of his drawings. Daumier's supreme art, tremendous output, and trenchant exploitation of situation and emotion were a major inspiration to cartooning in the Western world for well over a century.

While *Punch* was popularizing the humorous cartoon in England, the genre was almost unknown in the United States, where editorial cartoons still predominated. The pioneers of the American humorous cartoon were two Englishmen, William Newman, who served as a cartoonist for *Punch* for 20 years, and Frank Leslie (1821–1880), who was the publisher of the *Jolly Joker, Comic Monthly, Budget of Fun, Leslie's Weekly,* and other magazines. Social satire appeared in almanacs such as *Davy Crockett's Almanac of Wild Sports of the West.* With the founding of the publications *Puck* (1876), *Judge* (1881), and *Life* (1883), the United States began to produce magazines whose cartoons had a high standard of draftsmanship but a quality of

GEORGE DU MAURIER was a novelist, editor, and artist, who produced satirical cartoons for the magazine *Punch*.

CULVER PICTURES

Fashionable Emulation

Lady (*speaking with difficulty*). "What have you made it round the Waist, Mrs. Price?"
Dressmaker. "Twenty-one Inches, Ma'am. You couldn't *breathe* with less!"
Lady. "What's Lady Jemima Jones's Waist?"
Dressmaker. "Nineteen-and-a-half just now, Ma'am. But her Ladyship's a head shorter than you are, and she's got ever so much thinner since her Illness last Autumn!"
Lady. "Then make it *Nineteen*, Mrs. Price, and *I'll* engage to get into it!"

GIBSON GIRLS of Charles Dana Gibson were models of fashion, as were the du Maurier ladies.

BROWN BROTHERS

JOHN LEECH drew the first cartoons for *Punch*.

CULVER PICTURES

A London Gent Abroad.
Scene—A Café in Paris.

London Gent. "Garcong! Tas de corfee!"
Garçon. "Bien, M'sieu'—vould you like to see zee Times'?"
London Gent. "Hang the feller! Now, I wonder how the doose he found out I was an Englishman!"

wit hardly distinguishable from its counterpart in English periodicals.

In the 1890's process engraving degraded cartooning as an art but paradoxically upgraded it as a skill. The speed with which cartoons now had to be produced to keep their humor topical and to satisfy the capacity of daily papers to print them led to the use of a symbolic shorthand to convey meaning. This style opened the field to draftsmen with technical skill rather than artistic ability, giving the humorous cartoon an increasing monotony of execution only partially balanced by the sharpening of its timing and satirical bite.

The cartoon's characters and settings became progressively less representational and more symbolic, tending to suggest and evoke rather than to portray their subjects in a realistic style. This led to a widening of the cartoon's audience, because most people could immediately and effortlessly take in the simple humorous pictorial shorthand.

With the emergence after World War I of the cinema (and its animated cartoons) and radio broadcasting on a large scale, the cartoonist realized that if he was to keep his place as a mass entertainer he must simplify, speed up, and shed the weight of the multiline caption. In the mid-1920's the *New Yorker* magazine began publication and soon made *Life, Punch, Puck,* and *Judge* seem old-fashioned. The *New Yorker* burlesqued traditional cartoon conventions, notably the long caption, and built a cartoonist elite into which it was difficult to break. The *New Yorker* became the Mecca for American cartoonists, although there was opportunity for them in an increasing number of other publications.

By 1935 the *New Yorker* style of humor was as entrenched as the *Punch* style had been. Other American magazines and newspapers became vast repositories for cartoons and lucrative outlets for cartoonists, but in general they had little influence on cartoon development.

As competition with films, radio, and television put a premium on clever ideas, the humorous cartoonist, instead of relying on his own inventiveness and powers of observation, began to turn to professional "gagmen" and joke merchants. The result, though acceptable, tended to emphasize the caption at the expense of the picture.

One of the most powerful factors in the spread of the cartoon, if not in its development, was the international syndication of single-panel cartoons and comic strips (see COMICS). Syndication is strongest in the United States; consequently, the American style of cartooning also spread to other countries by this method.

Cartoon Clichés. Certain cartoon situations have been used so often and so widely that the viewer may become more intrigued by the achievement of a new variation than by the humor itself. The cartoon clichés used most frequently throughout the world include: the unseated horseman; the unfortunate who has fallen through the ice; the castaway or castaways on a desert island; the fakir's bed of nails; the magic carpet; the psychiatrist's couch; the missionary or explorer in the cannibal's cooking pot; the late arrival home of the drunken husband; the tramp begging for a dime; the men newly arrived from another planet; the computer with human reactions; the woman driver; the department store information- or complaint-window; and the interpretation of Egyptian hieroglyphics.

The majority of these clichés are common to both European and American humor pages. The *New Yorker* invented its own cliché – George Price's drawing of a man in a permanent state of levitation a foot above his bed. For a time this picture appeared regularly, with a different caption on each occasion.

Fantasy Cartoons. The one type of cartoon humor that does not stem from traditional sources or from the happenings of everyday life is found in the so-called "fantasy cartoon." The fantasy cartoon has as its basis a normally representative picture, but its humorous point is that what is happening defies the laws of nature. The most celebrated example of this is Charles Addams' skier whose tracks go on either side of a tree and join again. Another example, which appeared in both *Punch* and the *New Yorker* by different artists, shows a dog with a bone in its mouth looking at its reflection in a pool, then jumping into the pool and emerging with two bones in its mouth. Fantasy humor in general and fantasy cartoons in particular had a striking gain in popularity after World War II.

Notable Cartoon Publications. *Punch,* inspired by Philipon's *Charivari* in Paris, was the biggest influence on the establishment of the humorous cartoon, and on its progress until the *New Yorker* was founded in 1925. From the late 1930's, *Punch* was largely experimental, as were such European magazines as *Simplicissimus* in Germany and *Le Rire* and *Le canard enchainé* in France. In the Soviet Union, *Krokodil's* humor seems ponderous by Western standards, but its drawings are good (in the late 1960's they were curiously akin to American drawings).

Technical Development. When the cartoon became a feature of the periodical publication, the method of reproducing it became tremendously important. In the early stages of development, the newspaper or magazine cartoonist drew his picture directly on a boxwood block (boxwood is hard enough to withstand the printing of a large number of copies). The drawing was made with a brush, pen, or pencil exactly as it would appear in the periodical—even as to size. The engraver then cut away the surface of the block, leaving the drawn lines in relief. This was a slow process; a full page block took about 24 hours to produce (whereas by the 1960's it took the same number of minutes). Detail and shading, easily accomplished by the artist, were difficult and lengthy matters for the engraver—so much so that his skill was acknowledged on the larger reproductions by the inclusion of his initials in the corner opposite that of the artist's name.

In the 1860's, the production of the larger blocks was speeded by cutting them into a number of parts and giving each part to a different engraver. The pieces were then clamped together for printing. In the 1880's, photography freed the artist to draw to any size or scale. The picture was photographed and transferred, in the required size, directly onto the block. (One by-product of this advance was that the original drawing was not destroyed.) The limitations of the engraver, however, had still to be borne in mind.

Although in the majority of English publications cartoons were printed from woodblocks (before the incidence of process engraving), lithography was used in French and American publications. Lithography was expensive and slow, but it allowed the use of color. In the United States, *Judge* carried crude color on its covers and in its middle pages, and *Puck* was printed completely

CULVER PICTURES

"Thought you said your uncle was a-sending you an umbrella."
A Characteristic 'Fragment from France.'

BRUCE BAIRNSFATHER, in his World War I cartoons, found humor in the misery of life in the trenches.

Fresh, spirited American troops, flushed with victory, are bringing in thousands of hungry, ragged, battle-weary prisoners. (News item)

BILL MAULDIN'S World War II cartoons won him a 1944 Pulitzer Prize for his "distinguished service."

in color lithography. Single lithographic cartoon prints, some in color, continued to sell in bookshops and galleries until the 1890's. In England, woodcut cartoon prints costing a penny each flooded the market, but their quality, both of reproduction and content, was so poor that they killed the market for themselves and for their better executed lithographic competitors.

After process engraving was introduced in the 1890's, drawings were photographed and the images transferred to metal blocks by photographic exposure, and all but the black lines were eroded by acid. This left the artist with nothing to inhibit his freedom to use either a bold line or a delicate one; and with the introduction of half-tone printing at about the same time, the artist was assured that his work would be reproduced with a fidelity that extended even to the subtleties of shading.

In the 20th century, although there have been improvements in technical quality, there has been only one vital technical change. This was the introduction of sophisticated printing processes—four-color letterpress, offset lithography, and rotogravure, all giving the cartoonist the opportunity to make the fullest possible use of color. Even so, the bulk of 20th century cartooning was done in black and white, and the possibilities of color cartooning have not been fully exploited. One reason for this neglect may lie in the belief that color cartoons, while they are more pleasing to the eye, are not necessarily wittier than black and white.

A technical development of minor importance resulted from the drastic reduction in the size of publications during World War II—cartoons a single column wide called "pocket cartoons." These proliferated during the war, and continue to be published, especially in British papers.

The Great Cartoonists. Essentially, the singly sold lithographic prints of the pioneers of cartooning (Hogarth, Gillray, and Rowlandson) were propagandistic, antigovernment, and antisocial. They were abusive diatribes, with humor a purely secondary consideration. When cartoons became part of publications with editorial policies and circulation figures to consider, financial and readership commitments influenced a cartooning trend toward respectability. Although editorial (political) cartoons still thundered, they became increasingly surrounded by what were called "social cuts" in *Punch*, the magazine responsible for shaping the early humorous cartoon. Middle class prejudices prevailed. A chronological study of John Leech's drawings illustrates the reduction of fire in the belly and the increase of humor in the mind. There is a dramatic difference in concept between Leech's first picture to be called a "cartoon" (1843) and his stereotyped hunting drawing in 1855 bearing the caption *No Consequence* and the following dialogue:

"I say, Jack! Who's that come to grief in the ditch?"
"Only the parson."
"Oh, leave him there! He won't be wanted until next Sunday."

Punch cartoonists whose careers overlapped that of Leech were George du Maurier (1834–1896) and Charles Keene (1823–1891), artists who sacrificed the freer ranging of their talents to the security they found in weekly publication. These three men were responsible for more than 9,000 social, humorous, or satirical cartoons in *Punch*. All three were fine artists, and their influence was strong on both sides of the Atlantic. Du Maurier's tall gracious ladies found an echo 30 years later in Charles Dana Gibson's "Gibson girls" in the American magazine *Life*, and the young women

DRAWING BY PETER ARNO; COPYRIGHT © 1939, 1967 THE NEW YORKER MAGAZINE, INC.

"Well, that's how it is, men. You just rub two dry sticks together."

PETER ARNO'S sophisticated cartoons have ridiculed some of the institutions Americans have held most dear.

of each period attempted to imitate the cartoon creations.

The captions to the pictures by these men seem long and tedious to the 20th century reader, but to their contemporaries they were substitutes for long anecdotes. Furthermore, that these cartoons were intended to be read aloud is confirmed by the recapitulation in the captions of items in the pictures that are entirely obvious to the eye of the viewer.

Although the American cartoonist Thomas Nast (1840–1902) was concerned almost completely with political cartoons, his influence was great on the progress of cartooning in general in the United States. He was held in high regard throughout the country for the power and technical skill of his drawing and the incisiveness of his message.

The 20th Century. The first quarter of the 20th century produced a number of cartoonists with highly individual styles of drawing. Cartooning as a whole, however, was static and its humor thin. Exceptions in the United States include Art Young (1866–1943) and E. W. Kemble (1861–1933), who were prime examples of comic originality, and Reginald Birch (1856–1943) and John Held, Jr. (1889–1958), who employed wide ranges of cartooning styles.

In 1925 the *New Yorker* started a new and long-overdue genre of cartoon humor. Because the magazine had no stylistic or readership traditions to restrain it, the task of innovation was easier than it would have been for an established publication. Imitation of the *New Yorker* cartoon style was inevitable, and scores of cartoonists of lesser ability profited from the fashion set by the exceptionally good artists contributing to the *New Yorker*. It was nearly a century after Rodolphe Töpffer had said that the comic artist need have only a very basic artistic skill that the truth of his statement was realized.

The early cartoonists in the United States were succeeded by Gluyas Williams, a much-copied artist who, along with Rea Irvin, perfected the use of blobs of solid black to punch home the points of the simple line. But preeminent among *New Yorker* cartoonists was James Thurber (1894–1961), whose use of the smugly childish line was uniquely right, with or without his sophisticated captions. Other cartoonists associated primarily with the *New Yorker* were Alan Dunn, Whitney Darrow, Robert Day, Otto Soglow, George Price, and Richard Taylor.

Three giants of American cartooning were Peter Arno, whose sharp, superficial sex stereotypes achieved world popularity; Charles Addams, who perfected a wildly funny use of the macabre and found humor in the reversal of human emotions; and Saul Steinberg, whose greatest effects were built on the continuous line that flows between person and object with a lucidity in its nonsense that repays repeated study. Among the finest American women cartoonists were Peggy Bacon, Alice Hervey, Mary Petty, and Helen Hokinson (1900–1949). The latter's suburban clubwomen were faintly ridiculous but thoroughly lovable.

In Britain the World War I cartoonist Bruce Bairnsfather (1888–1959) invented the character "Old Bill," who found philosophic humor in the muck of the trenches. (Bill Mauldin was Bairnsfather's American equivalent in World War II.) Britain tended to produce illustrators rather than cartoonists—F. H. Townsend, C. A. Shepperson, E. H. Shepard, Frank Reynolds, and Lewis Baumer. There was a sparse output by W. Bird, a pseudonym known only to a few as that of J. B. Yeats (1871–1957), whose drawings were 25 years ahead of their time.

"Fougasse" (C. Kenneth Bird, 1887–1965), who became editor in chief of *Punch,* was unequaled in his achievement of movement and expression in a very few lines. His drawings consisted of many frames and carried long narrative captions. Other British practitioners include H. M. Bateman, whose energetic expression of emotion and situation rarely needed captions; the very popular Heath Robinson, who produced drawings of zany mechanical contraptions; Rowland Emett, who drew trains as they had never before been drawn; and David Langdon, whose cheeky humor was widely imitated and whose cartoons appeared regularly in both England and the United States. Several women cartoonists were outstanding: "Fish," whose work appeared in both English and American periodicals; Joyce Dennys, who drew for *Punch* and other English publications in the 1930's and 1940's; and Mary Dunn, who was active in the 1940's.

Both "Paul Crum" (Roger Pettiward) and "Pont" (Graham Laidler), English pioneers of the willfully unacademic line and previously untapped sources of humor, died young (during World War II) before their talents were fully realized. Ronald Searle, whose St. Trinian's girls found favor on both sides of the Atlantic, and Gerald Scarfe achieved highly individualistic effects. Other British cartoonists of the postwar period were Bill Tidy, "Larry," and "Anton," the latter a brother and sister using identical drawing styles to express a feminine point of view.

CHARLES ADDAMS uses the macabre to achieve a humorous rather than a sinister effect in his work.

English humor after World War II, though sometimes relying on the stock situation or cartoon cliché, ranged widely in subject matter and treatment. English cartoonists came from many professions and trades, and drew their humor from personal experience rather than from the stock provided by professional gag merchants.

France, the most productive cartoon nation on the Continent, approached a more universal humor in the 1960's after a long period in which the ideas in its cartoons were frequently obscure to Anglo-Saxon minds. The majority of French cartoonists reflecting this newer attitude – men such as Sempé, Chaval, Bellus, Trez, Peignet, Bil, and André François – divorced their work from exclusively French subjects.

See also CARICATURE.

R. E. WILLIAMS
Editor of "A Century of Punch Cartoons"

Bibliography

Alexandre, Arsène, *L'art du rire et de la caricature* (Paris 1892).
Ashbee, Charles R., *Caricature* (New York 1928).
Becker, Stephen, *Comic Art in America* (New York 1959).
Butterfield, Roger, ed., *The American Past*, 2d ed. (New York 1966).
Champfleury (Jules Fleury-Husson), *Histoire de la caricature antique* (Paris 1865).
Champfleury (Jules Fleury-Husson), *Histoire de la caricature au moyen age* (Paris 1871).
Escholier, Raymond, *Daumier* (Paris 1923).
Fougasse (C. K. Bird), *The Good Tempered Pencil* (London 1956).
Gombrich, Ernst H., *Art and Illusion*, 2d ed. (Princeton 1961).
Gombrich, Ernst H., and Kris, Ernst, *Caricature* (New York 1940).
Hofmann, Werner, *Caricature from Leonardo to Picasso*, Eng. tr. (New York 1957).
Larkin, Oliver W., *Daumier, a Man of His Time* (New York 1966).
Low, David, *British Cartoonists* (London 1942).
Lynch, Bohun, *A History of Caricature* (Boston 1927).
Malcolm, James P., *An Historical Sketch of the Art of Caricaturing* (London 1813).
Murrell, William, *History of American Graphic Humor* (New York 1938).
Paine, Albert B., *Th. Nast, His Period and His Pictures* (New York 1904).
Price, Richard G. G., *History of Punch* (London 1957).
Spielmann, Marion H., *History of Punch* (London 1895).
Veth, Cornelis, *Comic Art in England* (New York 1930).
Williams, Ronald E., ed., *A Century of Punch Cartoons* (London 1955).
Wright, Thomas, *History of Caricature and Grotesque in Literature and Art* (London 1865).
Wright, Thomas, *Works of James Gillray the Caricaturist* (London 1873).
Wright, Thomas, and Evans, Robert H., *Historical and Descriptive Account of the Caricatures of James Gillray* (London 1865).

JAMES THURBER'S fencing cartoon gets its humor from the incongruous understatement of its caption.

"Touché!"

MATCHSTICK FIGURES were animated by Émile Cohl in 1908 for his 5-minute *Drama Among the Puppets.*

GERTIE THE DINOSAUR was the heroine of Winsor McCay's pioneering American cartoon, produced in 1909.

SOME EARLY CARTOONS

KO KO THE CLOWN and other characters appeared in Max Fleischer films combining animation and live action.

MICKEY MOUSE made his first appearance in a sound cartoon in Walt Disney's 1928 release *Steamboat Willie.*

FILM LIBRARY, MUSEUM OF MODERN ART

CARTOON, Animated, a motion picture consisting of a series of individual hand-drawn sketches, in which the positions or gestures of the figures are varied slightly from one sketch to another. Generally, the series is filmed and, when projected on a screen, suggests that the figures are moving.

A motion picture film (silent speed, 16 frames per second; sound speed, 24 frames per second) relies on the optical illusion known as "persistence of vision." This is accomplished by "stop-frame" or "stop-motion" photography, which deludes the eye into accepting the projection of a rapid succession of slightly variant still photographs as a single picture involving continuous movement.

An animated cartoon uses this principle, replacing live-action photographs with photographs of drawings. For each second's projection of a sound cartoon film, separate exposures are made of 24 successive drawings or sets of drawings on transparent celluloid sheets. These exposures, placed on top of each other over a static background, make up a composite picture. The stop-frame process of photography is the common basis of all true animation, but even this may be dispensed with in certain kinds of animated films. The films of the Canadian animator Norman McLaren, for example, are made up of patterns and designs painted directly onto a reel of celluloid film.

In addition to drawings, the stop-frame process is applied to a wide variety of animation techniques. These include three-dimensional puppets and flattened marionettes with jointed limbs, whose positions and postures are changed for each motion picture frame; mobile diagrams (in instructional films); silhouette animation; object animation; and typographical animation. Pixilation, which is widely used in television commercials and film titles, is an animation technique in which photographed objects, especially human beings, seem to jerk about at high speed.

As an art form distinct from live action film, animation, with its versatile technical facilities, can be used to great advantage by both education and industry. For example, animation makes it possible to present schematically everything from scientific phenomena and technological processes to the rapid analysis of a complex industrial or commercial balance sheet. Even the art of painting has been explored in animation—by Pablo Picasso, in his film *Le mystère Picasso* (1956).

History of Animation. In the 1880's the seeds of animation were present in the work of two French pioneer film makers, Jean Marey and Émile Reynaud. Marey used a photographic "gun" to film in quick succession the wing movements of birds and the perambulations of men and animals. Reynaud developed the Praxinoscope, a device that projected onto a screen hundreds of hand-painted drawings, thus producing a moving picture.

Animation proper began to develop about 10 years after the introduction of motion picture films in the last decade of the 19th century. From 1908, Émile Cohl of France made simple animated films of highly expressive matchstick figures. Winsor McCay in the United States produced *Gertie the Dinosaur* (1909), a brief film that, in effect, animated a comic strip typical of those already popular in American newspapers. Other early pioneers were Lotte Reiniger of Germany, who began in 1919 to develop the sil-

FEATURE-LENGTH cartoons, often based on well-known literary texts, became a specialty of the Walt Disney studios beginning in the 1930's. *Alice in Wonderland* was made in 1951.

houette film, and Berthold Bartosch of France, who experimented in the 1930's with animated cut-out figures derived from woodcuts.

However, the establishment of the cartoon series as a regular part of the motion picture theater program had started as far back as 1913, and by the early 1920's the first of the celebrated American animators were at work. Max Fleischer (the creator of the *Popeye* cartoons in the 1930's) developed *Ko Ko the Clown,* and Pat Sullivan produced *Felix the Cat.* The drawings for these series were extremely simple: both backgrounds and figures consisted of bare outlines or black silhouettes. But crude as they were, these cartoon animals, notably Felix, had real (if humanized) qualities of wit and character that made them world famous.

The emergence of the cartoon series coincided with a basic refinement in technique. Whereas McCay had produced his silent films by laboriously copying the whole drawing 16 times for each second of action, Fleischer and Sullivan had the advantage of "cell animation," a process that enabled the animator to use single drawings of the static backgrounds of individual shots or scenes, while the mobile figures were traced with black ink onto transparent celluloid sheets (the "cells"). These cells were placed over the same background as the successive exposures were made. Cell animation, simple at first, became more complicated with the addition of such refinements as color. Later innovations included painting directly on film, introduced by Len Lye of Canada in *Colour Box* (1935), and puppet animation, as used by George Pal of Hungary, who began to produce short puppet films in the Netherlands in 1934, and Aleksandr Ptushko of Russia, who brought out the feature-length puppet film *The New Gulliver* (1935).

One of the most important developments toward increasingly elaborate animation was the introduction of sound about 1930. Sound was used with particular effectiveness by Walt Disney of the United States, whose wit and sentiment captivated audiences throughout the world, especially during the 1930's and 1940's, with his *Mickey Mouse, Donald Duck,* and *Silly Symphony* series. Disney eventually produced feature-length cartoons, such as *Snow White and the Seven Dwarfs* (1938). However, his style of animation was generally conventional. Only in *Fantasia* (1940), an ambitious film with animation designed to accompany the music of Beethoven and Stravinsky, among others, did he approach abstract design, a form that had been used much earlier in the post-World War I films of Oskar Fischinger of Germany.

The conventional style of Disney's films, which had become the model for most animation, was challenged in the United States during the 1940's by the UPA company. The freer graphic stylization of UPA cartoons had been anticipated to some extent in France by Hector Hoppin and Anthony Gross with *Joie de vivre* (1934) and in wartime Britain by John Halas and Joy Batchelor with *Dustbin Parade* (1942). A number of UPA members had broken away from Disney's studio, and some of them developed into outstanding animators. These included John Hubley, who was responsible for the first *Magoo* films (beginning in 1949) and *Rooty-Toot-Toot* (1951); Pete Burness, who worked on later *Magoo*'s; and Bob Cannon, who began the *Gerald McBoing Boing* series in 1950 and was responsible for animating the cartoon version of Bemelmans' *Madeline* (1952).

As Disney himself turned increasingly to live-action film making in the 1950's, American film cartooning developed along two distinct lines. One was the hard-hitting and violent cartoons by Tex Avery and Chuck Jones (*Bugs Bunny*),

Gerald McBoing Boing (left), a UPA cartoon hero.

AN ANIMATED CARTOON replaces live-action photographs with photographs of drawings. For each second's projection of a sound cartoon, separate exposures are made of 24 successive drawings or sets of drawings. To produce a feature-length animated cartoon requires possibly hundreds of artists and technicians. The photographs on these pages illustrate some of the steps that are necessary to complete a cartoon musical feature by the Walt Disney studios.

BACKGROUNDS for an animated cartoon are prepared separately from the animated figures. The figures will be photographed superimposed on the backgrounds.

THE ANIMATED FIGURES are first sketched in pencil. Teams of artists are required to sketch the many single drawings needed to make the figures move.

Fritz Freleng (*Tweety Pie and Sylvester*), and William Hanna and Joseph Barbera (*Tom and Jerry* and *Huckleberry Hound*). The other was the imaginative, highly stylized work of such creative experimenters as Hubley and Ernest Pintoff (*Flebus* and *The Violinist*).

After World War II, many individual styles emerged in several countries. In Canada, Norman McLaren was experimenting with such films as *Hoppity Pop* (1946), *Around Is Around* (three-dimensional, 1951), and *Neighbours* (1952). The British team of Halas and Batchelor, who produced the first feature-length cartoon having a serious subject (*Animal Farm,* 1954), animated a long succession of short films in a variety of graphic styles. At the same time, several smaller, highly creative cartoon units were established in Britain. Like their opposite numbers in the United States, they used their profits from television commercials to subsidize their work.

Other important postwar animators included Paul Grimault, Jean Image, and Henri Gruel of France; Jiri Trnka and Karel Zeman of Czechoslovakia; Dusan Vukotic, Vatroslav Mimica, Vlado Kristl, and Boris Kolar of Yugoslavia; and Jan Lenica and Walerian Borowczyk of Poland. Among eastern European animators, those of Czechoslovakia, Yugoslavia, and Poland took the lead in brilliant stylization, whereas those of the USSR tended to retain conventional designs.

Techniques of Animation. The styles used in cartoon animation range from a relatively realistic reproduction of life to the most romantic and impossible fantasy. They can be both dreams and nightmares, and their visual jokes satisfy all extremes in man's taste for violence, sentiment, or wish fulfillment.

Graphic stylization transforms living beings and inanimate objects alike into strange creatures that exist only in the artist's imagination. Cartoon films may be peopled with characters that walk and talk realistically or with creatures that respond exaggeratedly to the law of gravity or even defy it altogether. Cartoon characters levitate, flatten, squash, freeze in the air without visible support, accelerate suddenly into high speed, contract or expand like elastic, and appear and disappear magically.

The preparatory steps for making an animated cartoon must take into account all these qualities if the film is to excite laughter, wonder, or a sense of fantasy. The most important prerequisite for success is a strong graphic style that produces animated creatures with immediately recognizable characteristics. This was as necessary for Felix the Cat, Mickey Mouse, and Tom and Jerry as it was for Mister Magoo and other human figures.

Storyboard. The story told by these graphic beings must consist of a series of situations in which they can function characteristically. It generally originates in a series of continuity sketches rather than in words. These sketches are the first stage of the animated cartoon "storyboard," which represents in an extensive sequence of drawings the full action of the film, with every key shot and movement indicated. When new characters are introduced, they have to be "modeled" in sketches showing them from every angle, so that the animators can visualize them in any body position the action demands. The animators must know the size of each character in relation to the backgrounds and the objects that will appear with them, as well as the overall graphic style and color design to be used.

PAINTING the animated figures is the work of a separate department in the animation studio. The painting is done on sheets of transparent celluloid, called "cells," and great care is taken to ensure even and consistent color within each sequence.

A STOP-MOTION CAMERA photographs the painted cells one frame at a time. The cells are arranged in layers above the previously prepared painted backgrounds.

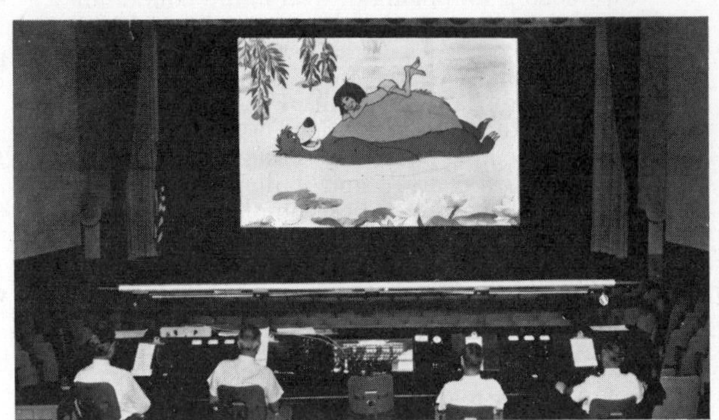

THE COMPLETED CARTOON is shown on a motion-picture screen, while technicians at a mixing panel check the synchronization of sound and picture.

The storyboard also indicates what may be called the "choreography" of the action, for the movements at most stages will have to be closely timed with the music and other sound and vocal effects, whether these are composed and recorded before or after animation is undertaken.

Workbook. Time control, therefore, is of major importance, and it is ensured by means of a "workbook." The cartoon director draws up his workbook in a form that is similar to a musical score, giving shot-by-shot and even frame-by-frame instructions for the animation. The workbook is used by the cartoon's music composer and the animator alike, and if the sound track is prerecorded, the animator will be in an even better position to synchronize the movements with the music. Similarly, the director uses the workbook to prepare details of the "exposure chart," which controls the frame-by-frame photographic recording of the cells and their backgrounds. The equipment normally used is a rostrum camera focusing downward onto a flat surface on which the backgrounds and the cells are firmly pegged.

Animators. The key phases of movement—that is, those most directly related to character and expression—are drawn under the director's supervision by "key animators." In-between drawings are usually completed by assistant animators. If the animation is not made directly on the cells, tracers and painters, in a separate operation, transfer the animators' work onto the numbered cells.

The same basic principles apply to all kinds of stop-frame animation. For silhouette or flat-figure animation, jointed limbs must be fractionally adjusted for frame-by-frame rostrum photography, then posed against their appropriate backgrounds. Usually their movements have to be timed and charted in the same way as those of drawn figures. For puppet animation, three-dimensional dolls or objects are adjusted for each frame and photographed in scale-model sets.

Technical Refinements. Great ingenuity has been applied from the earliest years of cartoon making to save labor in animation. The movements of recurrent characters are now to a considerable extent standardized. This means that cycles of cells reproducing leg movements or facial expressions, for example, are used and reused. In the case of puppets, detachable masks are employed for characteristic expressions. In deliberately staccato animation, the number of movement changes has been reduced to one every other frame or even one every three or four frames. For television cartoons (in commercials), advanced research has been undertaken to speedup the animation process and thus lower production costs. For example, to save time and labor, electronic controls have been applied to the manipulation of cartoon puppets.

Animation has had to adjust to various screen sizes that range from CinemaScope to the 360° screens of the Cyclorama system. Satisfactory three-dimensional animation has also been undertaken.

ROGER MANVELL
Author of "The Animated Film"

Bibliography

Field, Robert D., *The Art of Walt Disney* (Toronto 1942).

Halas, John, and Manvell, Roger, *Design in Motion* (New York 1962).

Halas, John, and Manvell, Roger, *The Technique of Film Animation* (New York 1959).

Manvell, Roger, *The Animated Film* (New York 1955).

Stevenson, Ralph, *Animation in the Cinema* (New York 1967).

CARTOUCHE, kär-to͞osh′, the nickname ("Cartridge") of the French brigand Louis Dominique Bourguignon (1693–1721). As a child he was stolen by gypsies, who trained him as a thief. At the age of 16 he joined a band of highway robbers operating in and near Paris, and in 1717 he became its chief. He was captured in 1721 and broken on the wheel in Paris on November 28. His exploits were celebrated in ballads, popular prints, plays, and films, and *cartouche* has become a French term for "highwayman."

CARTOUCHE, kär-to͞osh′, in architecture and decoration, an ornament representing a partly unrolled scroll on which there is usually some inscription or device. In heraldry, it is an oval shield, used particularly in the coats of arms of popes and other ecclesiastics. In Egyptology, a cartouche is an oblong or oval figure containing a royal personage's or deity's name in hieroglyphics.

CARTRIDGE, a charge for a firearm, in a case of metal, pasteboard, or cloth. For small-arms ammunition the term "cartridge" means the completely assembled cartridge case, primer, propellant powder charge, and bullet. For artillery weapons the corresponding complete unit is called a *round*, of which one component is the *cartridge case* or *bag*.

Cartridges for shotguns, also called *shotgun shell*, have a metal base and paper or plastic sidewalls. The case for a rifle or pistol cartridge may be made of brass or soft steel. It holds the components together for storage and handling and prevents the escape of gas to the rear. Small-arms cartridges are classified as ball, soft-point, armor-piercing, tracer, incendiary, high-pressure-test, blank, and dummy.

Rounds of fixed ammunition used in some flat-trajectory artillery are similar to small-arms cartridges; the projectile is securely crimped into the mouth of the cartridge case. Indirect-fire weapons (howitzers), 105 mm (4.13 inches) or less in caliber, use semifixed ammunition, in which the projectile is loosely fitted into the cartridge case and may be removed in the field to adjust the propelling charge. In the larger cannons' separate-loading ammunition, the propelling charge is in a cloth bag. See also AMMUNITION; ARTILLERY; BULLET; SMALL ARMS.

JOHN D. BILLINGSLEY, *Colonel, U.S. Army*
United States Military Academy

CARTWRIGHT, Alexander Joy, Jr. (1820–1892), American sportsman, who framed the first standard set of rules for baseball and organized the first baseball club. He was elected to the Baseball Hall of Fame in 1938.

Cartwright, born in New York City on April 17, 1820, was a 6-foot 2-inch, 215-pound fireman when he started playing "base ball." In 1845 he formed the New York Knickerbockers, who played the first recorded game on June 19, 1846, in Hoboken, N.J. (against a team called the New York Club), under his list of rules. Cartwright, who was trained as a civil engineer, made the infield diamond-shaped, reduced the bases from 5 to 4, made them flat bases instead of stakes, and eliminated plugging (retiring a runner by hitting him with a thrown ball). In the Hoboken game he enforced baseball's first fine, a 6-cent levy for swearing. He died in Honolulu on July 13, 1892.

HAROLD PETERSON, *"Sports Illustrated"*

CARTWRIGHT, Edmund (1743–1823), English inventor, who is best known for his power loom. He was born in Marnham, Nottinghamshire, on April 24, 1743, the younger brother of John Cartwright (q.v.). Educated at University College, Oxford, he became rector of Goadby Marwood, Leicestershire, where he also experimented in agriculture.

In 1784, while on holiday near Arkwright's cotton-spinning mills at Cromford, Derbyshire, Cartwright saw the need for similar machinery for weaving. In 1785 he patented his first loom, which was unsuccessful. But in 1786, after enlisting skilled help in Manchester, he made a machine that reproduced each of the weaver's movements; the shuttle was propelled by a spring. He set up a factory at Doncaster in which he used a steam engine to drive the looms. Cartwright's looms were also used in a factory in Manchester, which was burned down in 1791, probably by handweavers. His own venture went bankrupt two years later.

Between 1789 and 1792, Cartwright invented and improved the first wool-combing machine. He later worked with Robert Fulton on steam navigation, and from 1800 to 1807 he managed the Duke of Bedford's experimental farm at Woburn. A parliamentary grant of £10,000 in 1809 finally enabled him to buy a farm in Kent, where he spent his last years. He died in Hastings, Sussex, on Oct. 30, 1823.

THOMAS KINGSTON DERRY
Coauthor of "A Short History of Technology"

CARTWRIGHT, John (1740–1824), English humanitarian and advocate of radical political reform, known as the "father of reform." He was far ahead of his time in agitating for radical changes in Britain's government, among them annual elections, universal male suffrage, and the secret ballot. He consistently favored abolition of slavery, and he contributed generously from his substantial personal wealth to the cause of Greek independence in 1821.

Cartwright was born at Marnham, Nottinghamshire, on Sept. 17, 1740. He enlisted in the British Navy at 18 and had a successful career as an officer until his sympathy with the American colonies barred further advancement. He retired in 1775 and accepted a major's commission in the Nottingham militia, but his radical political opinions at the time of the French Revolution led to his dismissal.

During the period of his maximum influence (1810–1820), Cartwright occupied the middle ground between Whig advocates of limited reform and radicals who sought violent overthrow of existing institutions. In 1811 he cooperated with the former in creating the Hampden Clubs, which advocated extension of the franchise to all taxpayers.

He persuaded Sir Francis Burdett to accept the ideas of equal electoral districts and annual elections and William Cobbett to espouse universal manhood suffrage. In the years 1812, 1813, and 1815, Cartwright toured the North of England and later claimed that he had secured 200,000 signatures to petitions urging reform. In 1820, after legislation was enacted to stem the tide of radicalism, he was tried for sedition and fined £100. He died in London on Sept. 23, 1824.

JOHN W. OSBORNE
Rutgers University

CARTWRIGHT, John Robert (1895–), Canadian jurist, who in 1949 was appointed a justice of the Supreme Court of Canada. Cartwright was born at Toronto, Ont., on Mar. 23, 1895. Educated at Upper Canada College and Osgood Hall, in Toronto, he read law with Smith, Rae & Greer. He served in the army throughout World War I (1914–1918), advancing from private (machine gunner) to captain, and was wounded twice, in 1915. He won the military cross.

Cartwright was also called to the bar of Ontario in 1920 with honors and silver medal, was made a K. C. (now Q. C., or Queen's Counsel) in 1933, and became a bencher of the law society of Upper Canada in 1946. Before becoming a justice of the supreme court of Canada in 1949, he practiced law for many years as a member of the firm of Smith, Rae, Greer & Cartwright.

CARTWRIGHT, Peter (1785–1872), American Methodist clergyman. He was born in Amherst county, Va., on Sept. 1, 1787. He was converted to the Methodist Church at a camp meeting when he was 16 years old. Although he received very little formal education, he was a successful exhorter and traveling preacher, and in 1818 he was ordained an elder of the church. In 1824 he moved to Illinois and served as a member of the state legislature for two terms. In the congressional campaign of 1846, however, he was defeated by Abraham Lincoln.

Cartwright's thunderous eloquence and fighting spirit made him a leader in religious activities in the West. He never fully adapted to the intellectual interests of the newer Methodism and deplored the passing of the camp meetings and love feasts. He was the author of several vigorous pamphlets, and although his autobiography is unsatisfactory as an accurate record of his life, it reveals his ability as a storyteller. Cartwright died in Pleasant Hill, Ill., on Sept. 25, 1872.

CARTWRIGHT, Sir Richard John (1835–1912), Canadian political leader, who from 1896 to 1911 was minister of trade and commerce in Sir Wilfred Laurier's administration. He was born on Dec. 4, 1835, in Kingston, Ontario, and was educated at Trinity College, Dublin. He entered the Canadian Parliament in 1863 as a Conservative but later served as a Liberal member of the House of Commons continuously from 1878 to 1904, when he was appointed to the Senate. For nearly 40 years he was chief fiscal spokesman for the Liberal party. On four occasions, he served as acting premier during Laurier's absence.

He did much to promote better relations with the United States, representing Canada on the Anglo-American Joint High Commission at Quebec (1898) and at Washington (1898–1899). He died at Kingston, Ontario, on Sept. 24, 1912.

CARTWRIGHT, Thomas (1535–1603), English Puritan leader, whose reputation as a scholar and forthright advocate of the Calvinist system of church order made him the most influential leader of the Puritans in the Elizabethan church. Cartwright was educated at St. John's College, Cambridge, a center of Puritan discontent, and in 1562 became a fellow of Trinity College. In 1569 he was appointed Lady Margaret professor of divinity at Cambridge. His open attacks on the character of the church settlement of Elizabeth I, however, aroused the hostility of the ecclesiastical authorities, and he was deprived of his professorship in 1570 and of his fellowship in 1571, chiefly through the influence of John Whitgift, later archbishop of Canterbury. In 1572, after a visit to Geneva, Cartwright supported John Field and Thomas Wilcox, authors of *An Admonition to the Parliament,* in their assault on the prayer book and the hierarchy of the established church.

Cartwright fled abroad in 1573, when the court of high commission issued a warrant for his arrest. While abroad, he translated Walter Travers' *Disciplina Ecclesiae Sacra* as *The Book of Discipline.* This concise exposition of the Puritan platform for reform was a standard handbook of the Puritans well into the Stuart period.

Returning to England in 1585, Cartwright suffered a short imprisonment, but largely through the protection of the Earl of Leicester he spent his closing years quietly at Warwick. He died in 1603, after assisting in drafting the Millenary Petition, in which the Puritans presented their grievances to James I.

POWELL MILLS DAWLEY
The General Theological Seminary, New York

CARÚPANO, kä-ro͞o'pä-nō, is a seaport on the Caribbean coast of eastern Venezuela, in the state of Sucre. The city is a commercial and fishing center, with some manufacturing. Its chief exports are cacao, coffee, sugar, tobacco, timber, and hides. Its manufactures include straw hats and other fiber products, soap, rum, sawmill products, and pottery. Silver, copper, and lead are mined nearby. Population: (1961) 37,268.

CARUS, kâr'əs, **Marcus Aurelius** (died 283 A. D.), Roman emperor in 282–283. He was a native of Narbo Martius (Narbonne) in Gaul. He served as praetorian prefect under Emperor Probus, but his troops insisted upon hailing him as emperor while Probus was still alive. Probus, who was a strict disciplinarian, was murdered by his troops. When Carus became emperor, he led a successful campaign against the Persians and captured the city of Ctesiphon. In 283, in the midst of stunning military successes, he died unexpectedly, probably as a result of treachery on the part of his praetorian prefect. After his death his sons Carinus and Numerian were declared coemperors.

ARTHER FERRILL, *University of Washington*

CARUS, kä'ro͞os, **Paul** (1852–1919), American editor and philosopher, who sought a scientific base for philosophy and religion. He was born in Ilsenburg, Prussian Saxony, on July 18, 1852, the son of a Lutheran church official. He was educated at the universities of Greifswald, Strasbourg, and Tübingen. Forced to give up a teaching post in Dresden because of his liberal views, he went to England and then, about 1883, to the United States. In Chicago, Carus edited the *Open Court* and the *Monist* and directed the Open Court Publishing Company, all of which specialized in philosophy.

Carus' own numerous writings reflect his rationalist, monist conviction that the laws of mind and matter are the same, that God is an objective world order, and that a person's immortality is his continuing influence on earth. Carus' major works include *Fundamental Problems* (1889), *The Religion of Science* (1893), and *Philosophy as a Science* (1909). He died in LaSalle, Ill., on Feb. 11, 1919.

THE BETTMANN ARCHIVE

Enrico Caruso as the Duke in *Rigoletto*.

CARUSO, kä-rōō′zō, **Enrico** (1873–1921), Italian operatic tenor, who was one of the most famous, influential, and best-loved singers of all time. His artistry represented a clear departure from the old-fashioned school of vocalism in which beautiful tone and technical agility were all-important. Caruso, who possessed these elements, blended them with a human warmth and an instinctive dramatic sense to create a superbly harmonious artistic whole.

Caruso was born in Naples on Feb. 25, 1873. He studied voice for several years with Guglielmo Vergine and then with Vincenzo Lombardi. He made his debut at the Teatro Nuovo, Naples, in 1894, and later sang throughout Italy. He had his first great success in 1898 when he was in the cast of the premiere performance of Giordano's *Fedora* at Milan's Teatro Lirico. In 1900 he joined La Scala, Milan, and within two years had established an international reputation.

Caruso made his London debut at Covent Garden in 1902. He sang there frequently in succeeding years in operas that included *La Bohème, Les Huguenots,* and *Carmen.* His New York debut at the Metropolitan Opera took place in 1903. He sang over 600 times at the Metropolitan in more than 35 Italian and French operas and was the tenor star of every opening night (with one exception) from 1903 to 1920.

Caruso made recordings of about 250 operatic excerpts and art songs, and many of these have never left the active catalog. Despite technical limitations, these recordings are a true mirror of his art. Caruso had a voice of sensuous richness and great power that grew progressively darker in timbre during his maturing years. His style was emotional and distinctly Italianate, yet he did not indulge in inartistic excesses. An impressive range and technique also contributed to the totality of his interpretative excellence.

Caruso's last appearance in New York was in *La Juive* on Dec. 24, 1920. He was found to be suffering from pleurisy, with complications, and after several operations returned to Italy. He died in Naples on Aug. 2, 1921.

GEORGE JELLINEK
Author of "Callas, Portrait of a Prima Donna"

Further Reading: Caruso, Dorothy, *Enrico Caruso, His Life and Death* (New York 1945); Robinson, Francis, *Caruso, His Life in Pictures* (New York 1957).

CARUTHERSVILLE, kə-ruth′ərz-vil, is a city in southeastern Missouri, the seat of Pemiscot county, 180 miles (290 km) south of St. Louis. Situated on the Mississippi River, in a rich farming area where cotton, soybeans, and alfalfa are raised, it is a trade center and a rapidly growing river port. Industries include shipbuilding, cotton gins, shoe and box factories, and the manufacture of hospital equipment. Founded in 1794, it was destroyed by an earthquake in 1812 and later rebuilt. The city is governed by a mayor and council. Population: 7,350.

CARVER, George Washington (1861?–1943), American botanist, chemurgist, and educator who made significant contributions through his research in agriculture. He developed more than 300 by-products from the peanut and sweet potato, including plastics, dyes, medicines, flour, powdered milk, wood stains, and fertilizer. His extensive experiments in soil building and plant diseases helped revolutionize the economy of the South.

Early Life and Education. Carver was born near Diamond Grove, Mo., the son of Negro slaves. Although the exact date of his birth is not known, it has been deduced that he was born on or about July 12, 1861. While Carver was still an infant, his father was killed, and his mother, along with George and another child, was kidnapped from her master, Moses Carver. Moses Carver bought back the sickly infant George for a horse valued at $300. George remained with the Carvers, whose surname he took, for some years after the Emancipation Proclamation was signed.

Even as a youth he had a keen and inquiring mind and an instinctive knowledge of plants. He left his home with the Carvers when he was 10 to enroll in a one-room school at Neosho, Mo. By hard work and the help of benefactors, Carver was able to continue his education. In 1885 he finished high school in Minneapolis, Kans., but although his credentials were accepted by Highland University, he was refused admittance because of his race. In 1890 he enrolled at Simpson College, at Indianola, Iowa. Despite his talent and interest in painting, Carver's art teacher encouraged him, because of his skill with plants, to enroll the next year at the State Agricultural College in Ames, where he earned his bachelor's degree in 1894. He was then employed at the Ames Experiment Station as assistant to Louis Pammell, a noted botanist and mycologist. After receiving his master's degree at Ames in 1896, he accepted Booker T. Washington's invitation to head the newly organized department of agriculture at Tuskegee Institute in Alabama.

Agricultural Research and Contributions. Carver found the land in Alabama exhausted by single-crop cotton cultivation, eroded for lack of plant cover, and parched by the sun. He found ways of restoring the mineral content of the soil by planting nitrogen-producing legumes, and he discovered that peanuts and sweet potatoes would yield especially productive crops in the Alabama soil. He then taught farmers crop diversification. When many heeded his advice but found no ready markets for their new products, Carver began experiments that resulted in more than 300 by-products of the peanut and sweet potato. His demonstrations of the commercial possibilities of these products virtually changed the economy of the south.

Just as spectacular was Carver's work with

hybrids and various types of fertilizer. On the experimental farm at Tuskegee he evolved a cross between short-stalk and tall-stalk cotton, known as Carver's hybrid, and several other strains. He also grew enormous vegetables. Carver and Henry Ford collaborated on many matters, and together they perfected a process for extracting rubber from the milk of the goldenrod.

Carver instituted a visiting day for small farmers to come to Tuskegee to learn about soil fertilization. For those who were unable to travel to the campus, Carver began a "school on wheels," going into the communities to give demonstrations. His movable school idea was soon adopted by the U. S. Department of Agriculture and in many foreign countries.

The results of Carver's research and the products of his laboratory became known throughout the world. As a consequence, many persons, including Thomas Edison, offered him employment at high salaries, but he would not leave Tuskegee. Moreover, he would not accept a raise in salary above the meager $1,500 a year that Booker T. Washington offered him when he first came to Tuskegee.

Carver's first publication from Tuskegee, a pamphlet called "Feeding Acorns to Livestock" (1898), was followed by 43 other publications. Among the honors he received were election to fellowship in the British Royal Society of Arts in 1916 and awards of the Spingarn Medal in 1923, the Roosevelt Medal in 1939, and the Thomas A. Edison Foundation Award in 1942.

In 1940 the Carver Research Foundation was established at Tuskegee Institute. Carver contributed most of his savings to the foundation. Following his death on Jan. 5, 1943, in Tuskegee, Ala., his entire estate was added to the foundation's endowment. The Carver Museum at Tuskegee, which houses many exhibits of Carver's work, was dedicated in 1941. The George Washington Carver National Monument is at the site of the Moses Carver farm. Congress has designated January 5 as a day to honor Carver each year.

L. H. FOSTER, *Tuskegee Institute*

Further Reading: Elliott, Lawrence, *George Washington Carver: The Man Who Overcame* (Englewood Cliffs, N. J., 1966); Holt, Rackham, *George Washington Carver* (Garden City, N. Y., 1950).

CARVER, kär′vər, **John** (c.1576–1621), a Pilgrim father, who was the first governor of Plymouth Colony. Born in Nottinghamshire or Derbyshire, England, Carver emigrated to Holland in 1609 and joined the Separatist church of English exiles at Leiden, subsequently becoming a deacon. In 1617 some members of the Leiden church began to consider moving to America, and Carver and Robert Cushman were sent to England to negotiate with the Virginia Company of London. Failing to obtain the company's financial support, in 1619 they entered into an agreement with Thomas Weston, who headed a company of London merchants, to underwrite the venture.

As chief organizer of the London group of Pilgrims, Carver played a major role during the final preparations for the voyage. Accompanied by his wife Catherine and six servants, he sailed on the *Mayflower* for America in September 1620. He was a signer of the Mayflower Compact and was elected the first governor of Plymouth Plantation, in November 1620. Weakened by the rigors of life in the wilderness, however, Carver died a few months later, at Plymouth, in April 1621.

GEORGE D. LANGDON, JR., *Vassar College*

GRANGER COLLECTION

GEORGE WASHINGTON CARVER *(second from left)*, **conducting a class at Tuskegee Institute, about 1900.**

CARVER, kär′vər, **Jonathan** (1710–1780), American traveler and writer, who was the author of the most popular book of travels by a colonial American. *Travels Through the Interior Parts of North America in the Years 1766, 1767, and 1768* is a highly readable description of the rich lands and the life of the Indians of the upper Mississippi Valley. First published in London in 1778, it won an enormous audience through more than 30 editions in five languages. A facsimile of the third London edition of 1781 was printed in Minneapolis in 1956. Although the authenticity of the *Travels* was questioned at one time, subsequent research has revealed that the book was based mainly on Carver's firsthand observations combined with some passages copied from earlier travelers.

Carver was born in Weymouth, Mass., on April 13, 1710, and grew up in Canterbury, Conn. He became a private in the Connecticut forces in 1746 and later served in a Massachusetts regiment throughout most of the French and Indian War, rising to captain in 1760. In 1759 he was a selectman in Montague, Mass., where he had moved from Connecticut.

In 1766, Robert Rogers, the controversial leader of Rogers' Rangers who had been appointed governor of the British outpost at Michilimackinac (Mackinac, Mich.), commissioned Carver to chart the regions along the main rivers of Wisconsin and Minnesota in preparation for an expedition to find an overland Northwest Passage to the Pacific. Accordingly, Carver left the Straits of Mackinac on September 3 and proceeded by the Fox-Wisconsin river route to Prairie du Chien and then up the Mississippi and Minnesota rivers to a point west of what is now Minneapolis. There he wintered with the Sioux Indians. In the spring he joined Capt. James Tute, formerly of Rogers' Rangers, and James Stanley Goddard, a Montreal trader, at Prairie du Chien and proceeded to Grand Portage on Lake Superior. When word arrived from Rogers that no further supplies would be forthcoming, they returned to Michilimackinac in August 1767. Rogers, they learned, had no official approval for the expedition, and he was in conflict with his superiors that later resulted in his arrest for treason.

Carver went to London in 1769 to petition for the money Rogers had promised him and to publish an account of his travels. The government paid him on condition that he surrender his maps and manuscripts. The *Travels* finally appeared in 1778. As edited by Alexander Bicknell, the book was an elaboration of Carver's original journals with an appendix consisting of his own notes as well as material from other travelers. (A second edition of the *Travels,* as well as a treatise on tobacco cultivation, appeared in 1779. Carver's account of Indian life was drawn upon by early 19th century romantic writers, and his description of fertile Midwestern lands stirred the interests of settlers and speculators.

Carver died in poverty, in London on Jan. 31, 1780, before his *Travels* gained its greatest circulation. He left several children by his American wife, Abigail Robbins of Connecticut, whom he married in 1746, and a daughter by his English wife, Mrs. Mary Harris on London, whom he married in 1774 while Abigail was alive. A deed to a vast tract in Wisconsin allegedly given Carver by the Sioux was energetically exploited by his American and English descendants and others until Wisconsin became a state in 1848.

Robert C. Davis
Case Western Reserve University

CARVER, Robert (born 1487), Scottish composer of church music, who is considered to be the foremost composer of 16th century Scotland. He is said to have taken monastic vows at Scone Abbey in Perthshire at the age of 16. His only extant works, some masses and two motets, are in a choir book compiled at Scone during the first half of the 16th century. They are similar in style to those in the Eton choir book, which is of earlier origin. Carver's compositions, including one for 19 parts, indicate that he was well-versed in counterpoint and the complicated mensural system of notation.

CARVING, one of the basic techniques of the sculptor, is the art of cutting a material, such as wood, stone, or ivory, to reduce its mass to the desired shape. The opposite technique is building up the mass, as in modeling clay or wax. Both cutting and carving are ways of reducing masses. Cutting is the process used to rough out the general form, and carving creates the specific forms and surfaces.

Tools. Carving tools are highly specialized to fit the requirements of the material to be cut. Both wood and stone are carved with hammers and chisels and finished with files, rasps, riflers, and sandpaper and other abrasives. For stone carving, pointed chisels, flat steel chisels with a beveled cutting edge, and crenellated (toothed) chisels are hammered with a 2-pound (about 1 kg) steel mallet or a lighter wooden maul. A running drill, or bow drill, is used for deeper incisions, and a pneumatic hammer provides greater speed and flexibility. In wood carving, a round mallet, a square maul, or the heel of the hand is used to drive steel gouges and spoon-shaped, fantailed, or flat chisels. Materials other than stone and wood are carved with knives or with specialized variants of the tools described.

History. The earliest carvings, dating from the dawn of man, are fertility symbols and other objects made for magic rites. By 3000 B.C., stone carving as a monumental art appeared in Egypt, Mesopotamia, and the Orient. In Western art the classical Greek and Roman periods produced a rich variety of sophisticated stone carvings. The numerous cathedrals and churches built throughout Europe during the Middle Ages established a great tradition in both stone and wood carving for exterior and interior decoration and objects for liturgical use. In the late Gothic period a specialized art of carving fruit pits and small boxwood figurines flourished in Germany. In the Renaissance and baroque periods, the art of stone carving was again emphasized, although in Spain the medieval tradition of wood carving persisted.

Among the great stone carvers in the history of Western art are Michelangelo, Bernini, and Donatello (who also carved in wood). In the 20th century there has been a revival of interest in stone and wood carving, with styles tending to emphasize the process of carving often by means of tool marks left on the finished piece. Constantin Brancusi and Henry Moore are among the best-known 20th century sculptors who are primarily carvers in stone and wood. See also Woodcarving.

H. Dustin Rice, *Columbia University*

CARY, kâr'ē, **Archibald** (1721–1787), American patriot leader. He was born at Williamsburg, Va., and attended the College of William and Mary. In 1744 he married Mary Randolph, a second cousin of Thomas Jefferson. Cary served in the Virginia House of Burgesses with Patrick Henry and others who protested the Stamp Act of 1765. From 1774 to 1776 he served on several committees of correspondence and attended provincial revolutionary assemblies. In 1776 he was chairman of Virginia's Committee of the Whole, which drew up the Virginia Declaration of Rights, and as such he instructed Virginia delegates to the Continental Congress to vote for the Declaration of Independence. Except for brief intervals, he served in the state senate from October 1776 until his death in Virginia in 1787.

CARY, kâr'ē, **Henry Francis** (1772–1844), English clergyman and translator of Dante. Cary was born in Gibraltar on Dec. 6, 1772. He studied at Christ Church, Oxford, was ordained, and was assistant librarian in the British Museum from 1826 to 1837. He died in London on Aug. 14, 1844.

Cary's blank verse translation (1814) of the *Divine Comedy* of Dante was highly praised and publicized by Coleridge. It preserves the homely simplicity and vividness of the original Italian and is recognized as the standard English translation. Cary also translated Aristophanes' *Birds* (1824) and Pindar's *Odes* (1834).

CARY, kâr'ē, **Joyce** (1888–1957), British novelist, whose best-known works brilliantly depict the struggle of the individual against the restrictions imposed by society. His books have a lively style, a compassion for the human condition, and unforgettable characters, and for these qualities some of his novels have been compared with those of Charles Dickens. Cary's most famous novel, *The Horse's Mouth,* tells the story of a nonconforming artist with gusto and wit.

Early Life. Joyce Cary was born in Londonderry, Ireland, on Dec. 7, 1888. He studied painting in Edinburgh and Paris. Later he attended Trinity College, Oxford, graduating in 1912. In 1913 he went to Nigeria in West Africa, where

Joyce Cary

EUROPEAN—COURTESY OF MICHAEL JOSEPH LTD.

he joined the Nigerian political service. He remained in West Africa as a colonial administrator until 1920.

Later Years. Returning to England, Cary decided to become a writer and spent the next 12 years perfecting his craft. His early novels—*Aissa Saved* (1932), *The African Witch* (1936), and *Mister Johnson* (1939)—were drawn from his experiences in Africa. Cary's reputation grew in the 1940's with the publication of his first trilogy: *Herself Surprised* (1941), *To Be a Pilgrim* (1942), and *The Horse's Mouth* (1944). These books tell about the relationship among a Blakean visionary artist, an inhibited upper-class lawyer, and an alert, charitable cook, who was married, after a fashion, to both. Each of the three novels is told from the point of view of the character most concerned with the events in it, thus enriching and broadening the whole. A second trilogy, on a political theme, comprises *Prisoner of Grace* (1952), *Except the Lord* (1953), and *Not Honor More* (1955).

Cary developed muscular atrophy in 1955 and died at Oxford, England, on March 29, 1957. *Spring Song and Other Stories* was published posthumously in 1960.

ANNE FREMANTLE
Author of "This Little Band of Prophets"

Further Reading: Wright, Andrew, *Joyce Cary: A Preface to His Novels* (New York 1959); Mahood, Molly M., *Joyce Cary's Africa* (Boston 1965).

CARY, kâr'ē, **Lott** (1780?–1828), American Baptist missionary. Cary was born in slavery in Charles City county, Va. He learned to read and write and was able to purchase his freedom about 1813. After being licensed to preach by the First Baptist Church of Richmond, he preached to Negroes on plantations and became a pastor of the African Baptist Church.

Cary helped organize the Richmond African Missionary Society, and in 1819 he was accepted for service in Africa by the Baptist Board of Foreign Missions.

In 1821, Cary sailed for Liberia, where he organized the first Baptist church and taught in the colony's school. He also served as assistant to the agent and governor, and after protests concerning the government of the colony, he helped establish a more representative system. He served as vice-agent of the colony until his death in a powder explosion on Nov. 10, 1828.

JAMES H. SMYLIE
Union Theological Seminary, Richmond, Va.

CARY, Lucius. See FALKLAND, 2D VISCOUNT.

CARY, kâr'ē, a town in central North Carolina, is in Wake county, 7 miles (11 km) west of Raleigh, of which it is a residential suburb. Hogs, corn, cotton, and tobacco are raised nearby. The birthplace of Andrew Johnson, 17th president of the United States, is about 3 miles (5 km) to the south.

Cary was founded in 1852 and incorporated in 1870. It has the council-manager form of government. Population: 7,430.

CARYATID, kar-ē-at'id, an architectural support in the shape of a female figure. Such figures, though not limited to human dimensions, generally adorn buildings or parts of buildings that are small. A 40-foot (about 12-meter) column is not unusually tall, but a caryatid of this height would give an effect of colossal size. A male figure used similarly is called an *atlas* (plural, *atlantes*).

The earliest extant example of the use of caryatids to replace columns is in the porch of the Treasury of the Siphnians at Delphi. They stand on pedestals and bear cushionlike moldings and an abacus (square plinth) on their heads to support the entablature. The patterned drapery, bulging eyes, and frozen smile of these caryatids are typical of archaic Ionian sculpture of the late 6th century B. C.

The most famous caryatids are those on the south porch of the Erechtheum on the Acropolis in Athens, dating from the late 5th century B. C. These six figures support ovolos, or quarter-round moldings, and an abacus that serves to hold the entablature.

Because human figures supporting a heavy architectural load may, through empathy, induce weariness in the observer, it was perhaps to minimize this effect that the frieze, normally the middle third of the entablature, was omitted from the south porch of the Erechtheum. Each figure carries her weight primarily on one leg, with the other leg bent at the knee. The figures on the west half of the porch bend their left knees; those on the east half, their right knees. The straight, or supporting, leg is thus always toward the outside—a detail that helps to give

CARYATIDS on the south porch of the Erechtheum, Athens.

BERNARD SILBERSTEIN, FROM RAPHO GUILLUMETTE

an effect of stability. In style, these caryatids show the influence of the sculptor Phidias in their sturdiness and grace and in the broad idealism of both figure and drapery. Five of the caryatids are original; the sixth is a cast of the figure in the British Museum, London.

Jean Goujon, foremost French sculptor of the early 1500's, used caryatids to support a balcony inside the Louvre. He probably did not know the Athenian work, but his architectural instinct led him to carve figures of comparable character.

EVERARD M. UPJOHN, *Columbia University*

CARY'S REBELLION, kâr′ēz, the popular term for an unstable era in North Carolina history (about 1703 to 1711), in which Thomas Cary figured prominently. The trouble stemmed from religious bodies vying for political power.

Long a haven for religious dissenters during the proprietary period (from 1663), North Carolina developed two distinct factions, a Church of England party and a Dissenter party (principally Quakers). In 1703 the Church party under Gov. Robert Daniel succeeded in legally establishing the Church of England in the colony. The Dissenters then rose up, ousted Daniel, and invited Thomas Cary, a Charleston merchant, to become governor. Cary's religious policies proved equally unsatisfactory to the militant Quakers, and in 1706 they prevailed on the proprietors in London to remove Cary and appoint councillor William Glover in his place. However, Glover never established his authority, and Cary returned to power in 1708. In 1711, Edward Hyde, Queen Anne's cousin, was sent as governor by the proprietors. Hyde nullified all laws signed by Cary, whereupon Cary, aided now by the Dissenters, launched a naval attack against Hyde at Edenton in June 1711. Repulsed, Cary was about to attack again when Gov. Alexander Spotswood of Virginia sent royal marines. Cary surrendered, was sent to England and there was freed.

DAVID ALAN WILLIAMS, *University of Virginia*

Casablanca, the largest city in Morocco

DICK HUFFMAN, FROM PIX

CASA GRANDE, kas′ə gran′dē, is a city in southern Arizona, in Pinal county, 43 miles (69 km) southeast of Phoenix. It is a trade and shipping center in a heavily irrigated region that produces cotton, vegetables, citrus fruits, figs, and alfalfa. There are copper, gold, and silver mines nearby. Clothing and furniture are produced.

The city was named for the Casa Grande ruins, now in Casa Grande Ruins National Monument, 6 miles (10 km) to the northeast. Government is by town manager. Population: 10,536.

CASA GRANDE RUINS NATIONAL MONUMENT, kas′ə gran′dē, is near Coolidge in the Gila River valley of south central Arizona. It was established in 1918 to preserve a ruined 4-story adobe tower, 40 feet (12 meters) high, built between 1300 and 1400 A. D. by Salado (Salt River) Indians who moved into the area from the north at about that time. The tower, used presumably as a watchtower and fort, is the only structure of its kind still standing. It was named Casa Grande (Great House) by the Jesuit missionary Eusebio Francisco Kino when he visited the site in 1694.

The 473-acre (191-hectare) area of the monument includes the crumbling remains of adobe villages that once clustered around the tower. There are traces of the irrigation system developed by earlier farmers, the Hohokam, and adopted from them by the Salado. For reasons not clearly understood, both the Salado and the Hohokam disappeared by about 1450 A. D.

CASABA. See MELON—*Muskmelon*.

CASABIANCA, kȧ-zȧ-byäɴ′kȧ, **Louis de** (1755?–1798), French naval officer. He was born at Vescovato, Corsica. He served in the American Revolution under the Count de Grasse. After returning to France, he sat in the National Convention of 1792. As captain of the flagship *Orient* in the expedition to Egypt, he was fatally wounded in the Battle of the Nile at Abukir, Egypt, on Aug. 1, 1798. When the ship caught fire, Casabianca's 10-year-old son, Giacomo, refused to leave him. The powder magazine exploded, and both were killed. This incident is the subject of Felicia Hemans' poem *Casabianca* (1829).

CASABLANCA, kas-ə-blang′kə, is the largest city and chief port of Morocco, and one of the most populous cities in Africa. It is known in Arabic as *Dar el-Beida*. Located on the Atlantic coast, it has a well-protected harbor, one of the largest artificial ports in the world.

Casablanca is the principal commercial and industrial center of Morocco. Its port handles over three quarters of the country's foreign trade. Phosphates are the leading export, comprising 75% of the total export traffic. The major imports are petroleum products. Most of Morocco's industries are centered in Casablanca, which has textile mills, glassworks, brickworks, and a blast furnace.

Casablanca is connected by road and rail with the major towns of Morocco. An international airport serves the city. It is a port of call for ships linking Europe, Africa, and South America.

Casablanca is spread out along 10 miles (16 km) of the coast. The modern city, built by the French, forms a semicircle around the old town. The center of the business and tourist district is the Place de France. From here, avenues radiate in all directions and lead to every part of the city. The new city is distinguished by its broad avenues, white skyscrapers, luxury hotels, and modern office buildings.

The old medina, which was the original Arab town, is a section of narrow, winding streets that always teem with people. It is still partly enclosed by a high wall. New medinas have been constructed around the French-built section.

Casablanca stands on the site of the medieval town of Afna, which was a pirate's nest in the 15th century. It was destroyed in 1468 by the Portuguese, who built a town on the same site in 1515 and called it Casa Branca (White House). The present name, Casablanca, is the Spanish spelling. Later abandoned, the town was rebuilt in the 18th century by Sultan Sidi Mohammed. In the 19th century, European traders settled in the city in great numbers. It was occupied by the French in 1907.

After the establishment of the French protectorate over Morocco in 1912, Casablanca's port was greatly improved and enlarged, and the city grew rapidly. Terrorism by Moroccan nationalists broke out in Casablanca in 1952, leading to Moroccan independence four years later. Population: (1960) 965,277.

I. WILLIAM ZARTMAN, *New York University*

CASABLANCA CONFERENCE, a meeting of U. S. President Franklin Roosevelt and British Prime Minister Winston Churchill at Casablanca, Morocco, in January 1943, as final Allied victory became a certainty. Two questions needed answers: militarily, where to engage the Allied forces after the North African campaign; and politically, the terms to be imposed on the Axis powers. The decisions were to land in Sicily, defeat Italy, and then demand Japan and Germany's unconditional surrender.

The formula of unconditional surrender has been severely criticized as having united Germany and lengthened hostilities. In fact, since Hitler remained in power until the collapse of Germany, there was never an alternative to unconditional surrender. The formula did fulfill its intended purposes: to ensure that the Soviet Union would not sign a separate peace, leaving the West alone to defeat Germany; and to ensure that Germany would not, as after World War I, feel that it was not defeated and try to attain victory in another war.

JOHN W. SPANIER, *University of Florida*

CASABLANCA GROUP, kas-ə-blang'kə, a bloc of African nations, which was formed at a conference held in Casablanca, Morocco, on Jan. 7, 1961. The members of the Casablanca Group were Algeria, Ghana, Guinea, Libya, Mali, Morocco, and the United Arab Republic. These states supported the position of Patrice Lumumba in Congo (Kinshasa) and Morocco's claim to Mauritania. Another reason for the creation of this bloc was a need to counterbalance the importance of the Brazzaville Group (q.v.) in African and international politics.

The members of the Casablanca Group pledged to follow a policy of nonalignment and called for the independence of all colonies. The establishment of the Organization of African Unity (OAU) in 1963 brought about the dissolution of the group.

ALFRED G. GERTEINY, *University of Bridgeport*

CASADESUS, kä-sä-dē'səs, a family of French pianists, consisting of the world-famous virtuoso Robert; his wife, Gaby; and their son, Jean. They toured the world, performing variously as soloists, in two-piano teams, and as a trio.

ROBERT CASADESUS (1899–), one of the most distinguished French concert artists, was born in Paris on April 7, 1899, into a family of celebrated musicians. He graduated from the Paris Conservatory, where he won the Diémer Prize in 1921. Later that year he married Gaby Hôte, a conservatory student. His concert career began in 1922, and he made his American debut in New York City on Jan. 20, 1935. In 1935 he became head of the piano department of the American Conservatory at Fontainebleau, France, and from 1955 served as that institution's director general. With his wife, Casadesus gave two-piano concerts, presenting the world premiere of his own two-piano concerto in New York City in 1950. A sophisticated pianist, Casadesus placed greater importance on structural logic, refinement, and objectivity than on passion or personal idiosyncrasies.

JEAN CASADESUS (1927–1972), the eldest of their three children, attended the Paris Conservatory, where he won the first medal in piano playing. Jean began playing professionally after receiving first prize at the Geneva International Competition in 1947. From 1965 he was artist in residence at the State University of New York at Binghamton. Jean died in an automobile accident near Renfrew, Ontario, Canada, on Jan. 20, 1972.

DAVID EWEN
Author of "Famous Instrumentalists"

CASAL, kä-säl', **Julián del** (1863–1893), Cuban poet, who was one of the first modernists of Spanish American literature. He was born in Havana on Nov. 7, 1863. Like many other Spanish American authors, he greatly admired Paris and the French. His poetry was influenced by Gautier, Baudelaire, and Verlaine, as well as by the Nicaraguan poet Rubén Darío. Casal suffered from tuberculosis; his illness affected the mood of his poetry, which is pessimistic, elegiac, and morbidly introverted. His verse was published as *Hojas al viento* (1890), *Nieve* (1891), and *Bustos y rimas* (1893). He died in Havana on Oct. 21, 1893.

CASALS, kä-säls', **Pablo** (1876–), Spanish cellist, generally regarded as the greatest cello virtuoso of the 20th century and perhaps of all time. His brilliant technique and infinitely expressive style set a standard that, while widely emulated, remained unsurpassed. Although most famous as a cellist, Casals also won great distinction as a conductor, composer, and pianist.

Early Years. Pau Carlos Salvador Defilló de Casals was born at Vendrell, Catalonia, Spain, on Dec. 29, 1876. (Pau is the Catalonian form of Pablo or Paul.) His first teacher was his father, a church organist, under whom he learned to play the organ, piano, violin, flute, and various other instruments. At the age of 12, Casals decided to become a cellist and went to Barcelona, where he studied with José Garcia at the Municipal School of Music. Soon he started to develop a naturalistic approach to technique and his own theories of cello playing, including exact and expressive intonation and rhythmic and melodic accentuation. While a student in Bar-

HORST TAPPE, CAMERA PRESS: PIX

Pablo Casals

celona, he came upon six unaccompanied cello suites by Bach, thus initiating a lifelong devotion to that composer, of whose works he became a foremost interpreter.

In 1894, Casals went to Madrid. There he was encouraged and helped financially by Count Morphy, secretary to the queen, and by Queen María Cristina herself. After studying at the Royal Conservatory in Madrid, he went to Paris, where in 1895 he became cellist at the Paris Opéra. His career as a cello virtuoso began in Paris in 1899, when he made his concert debut with the Lamoureux Orchestra. He was an instant success and from that time on was recognized as the supreme musician of his instrument.

Casals began to tour widely in Europe and North and South America, as a soloist and as a co-performer with such distinguished musicians as the violinists Fritz Kreisler and Jacques Thibaud and the pianists Harold Bauer and Alfred Cortot. He made his American debut in 1901 and played at the White House for President Theodore Roosevelt in 1904. In 1905 he formed a chamber music trio with Cortot and Thibaud.

Middle Years. Casals' other great interest, in addition to the cello, was the art of conducting. In 1919 he founded the Pau Casals Orchestra in Barcelona and provided the people of Catalonia, notably the working classes of Barcelona, for whom he set special low admission prices, with splendid performances of classical music. Casals also was a guest conductor outside Spain, leading such orchestras as the London Symphony and the Vienna Philharmonic.

When the Spanish Civil War broke out in 1936, Casals made no secret of his sympathy for the Republican cause, giving numerous benefit concerts for the wounded and for refugees. He left Spain in 1939, on the eve of Franco's victory and settled in Prades in southern France. During World War II, he courageously refused to have anything to do with the Germans and gave a number of concerts to raise money for victims of the war. In 1950 he founded the Prades Festival, an annual event that attracted many famous musicians and in which he participated both as cello soloist and as conductor.

Later Years. In 1956, Casals visited his mother's birthplace in Puerto Rico and shortly thereafter settled there. In 1957 he married his third wife, Martita Montañes. In that year he also inaugurated the annual Casals Festival in Puerto Rico, which became one of the major international musical events. Even in old age Casals continued to pursue a very active career, not only as a cellist and conductor but also as a recording artist, teacher, and composer. His compositions include the cantata *La visión de Fray Martín* and the oratorio *El pesebre*. Among his most important single appearances were his performance, dedicated by him to the cause of peace, at the United Nations in New York City in 1958 and his recital at the White House in 1961, when he played for President John F. Kennedy.

Throughout his career, Casals, revered equally as a superb musician and as a great human being, tirelessly used his musical genius and his international reputation to further the cause of peace and harmony. His character is best expressed in his own statement, "I am a man first, an artist second."

ROBERT MANN
Juilliard String Quartet

Further Reading: Littlehales, Lillian, *Pablo Casals* (New York 1948); Taper, Bernard, *Cellist in Exile* (New York 1962).

CASANOVA, kä-sä-nô′vä, **Giovanni Giacomo** (1725–1798), Itallian adventurer and author, who is famous for the bold and libertine life he led and recorded in his memoirs. Casanova was born in Venice on April 2, 1725, of a family of actors. After studying at the University of Padua, he attended the Seminary of St. Cyprian; however, he was expelled for bad conduct, after taking minor orders. In 1744 he became secretary to Cardinal Acquaviva of Rome. A scandal forced Casanova to leave that city, and after visiting Naples, Corfu, and Constantinople, he returned to Venice, making a living as a violinist and, possibly, as a magician, until he won the patronage of a Venetian senator.

Suspected by the Inquisition, Casanova fled Venice in 1749, traveling to Lyon (where he joined the Masonic order), Paris, Dresden, Prague, and Vienna. Wherever he went he won influence with his charm and supported himself by gambling and intrigue. On his return to Venice in 1755, he was arrested on suspicion of being a Freemason and a magician, and was cast into the Piombi, the state prison, from which he made an ingenious escape that he described in his *Histoire de ma fuite* (1788).

In 1757, Casanova returned to Paris, where he instituted and directed the royal lottery and won acceptance into Parisian society. After a trip to Holland, during which he was named Chevalier de Seingalt, he established a mansion in Paris under his new title. Subsequent travels took him to Geneva (where he met Voltaire), London, and St. Petersburg (where he met Catherine the Great).

Casanova's personal charm began to wane with age, and charges against him grew. He was expelled from Vienna in 1766 and from Paris in 1767. In 1775 he was again in Venice, as a spy for the state inquisitors, but he was forced to leave after publication of his libelous *Nè amori nè donne* (1782). He spent his last years as secretary and librarian at the castle of Count von Waldstein in Dux, Bohemia, where he wrote his memoirs "to keep from going mad or dying of grief." He died at Dux on June 4, 1798.

The Memoirs. Casanova's memoirs, written in French, tell the story of his life until 1744. They are his chief work, and the one on which his subsequent reputation (largely as a seducer of women) is based. The memoirs portray the life of a man devoid of moral principles and belong to the erotic literature of the time. But they also give a vast, colorful picture of the life and culture of 18th century Europe.

Until recently, many authorities cast serious doubt on the authenticity of the memoirs because the original manuscript, sold by Casanova's family to the German firm of F. A. Brockhaus in 1821, was not released until 1960. The texts used up to that time were based on a 28-volume German translation (1822–1828) and a highly inaccurate French edition (1838). The integral French text was first published as *Histoire de ma vie* in 1960–1962. The first volume of a projected multivolume English edition, *History of My Life*, translated by Willard R. Trask, was published in 1966.

Casanova's other works include an incomplete translation of the *Iliad* (1775) and a fantasy novel, *Icosameron* (1788), which describes the adventures of two brothers who live in a world made perfect by scientific discoveries.

CHARLES SPERONI
University of California, Los Angeles

Further Reading: Childs, J. Rives, *Casanova: A Biography Based on New Documents* (London and Mystic, Conn., 1961); Dobrée, Bonamy, *Three Eighteenth Century Figures; Sarah Churchill, John Wesley, and Giacomo Casanova* (New York and London 1962).

BROWN BROTHERS (PORTRAIT BY ALESSANDRO LONGHI)

Giovanni Casanova

CASATI, kä-sä'tē, **Gaetano** (1838–1902), Italian explorer, who was the first European to sight the Ruwenzori mountains ("Mountains of the Moon") of east central Africa. He was born at Ponte Albiate, Italy, on Sept. 4, 1838.

Casati volunteered his services to Romolo Gessi, governor of the Sudanese province of Bahr el-Ghazal in 1879. His first task was to explore the Congo-Nile watershed. In March 1883 he reached Lado, the seat of Emin Pasha, governor of the Equatoria province of the Sudan. From Emin he learned of the beginning of the Mahdist revolution in the Sudan.

In May 1884, Emin sent Casati to the kingdom of Bunyoro to see if his small band of Europeans could escape through Uganda. However, Casati was imprisoned by the king of Bunyoro. He managed to escape and fled southward, becoming the first European to see the colossal Ruwenzori range. In April 1888 he rejoined Emin Pasha, and they were rescued by Henry M. Stanley.

After Casati's return to Italy in 1890, he published an account of his travels, which was widely translated. He died on March 7, 1902.

ROBERT L. HESS
University of Illinois at Chicago Circle

CASAUBON, kȧ-zō-bôɴ', **Florence Étienne Méric** (1599–1671), Swiss-English classical scholar and clergyman. He was born in Geneva on Aug. 14, 1599, the son of Isaac Casaubon. Méric Casaubon followed his father to England in 1611 and studied at Eton and at Oxford, receiving the degree of doctor of divinity in 1636. He was ordained a priest in the Church of England but was deprived of his parish by Parliament during the Commonwealth period. After the restoration of King Charles II, Casaubon was reinstated. He died at Canterbury on July 14, 1671.

Méric published a number of editions of classical writings. The most notable was his edition of the *Meditations* of Marcus Aurelius. He also wrote two vindications of his father against Puritan attacks and collected his papers.

CASAUBON, kȧ-zō-bôɴ', **Isaac** (1559–1614), Swiss classical scholar. The son of a French Huguenot minister in exile, Casaubon was born in Geneva, Switzerland, in 1559. His promising work as a classical scholar at the Academy of Geneva brought him an appointment to teach Greek there, and he became widely acquainted with the refugees, scholars, and visitors who were drawn to this center of Calvinism in Switzerland. In 1596, after the Edict of Nantes guaranteed civil rights and a limited freedom of worship to French Protestants, Casaubon accepted a post in France at the University of Montpellier. Presented to King Henry IV by Roman Catholic friends who were eager for Casaubon's conversion, he was given the post of sublibrarian in 1604 at the royal library in Paris. Within a few years his reputation as a scholar had spread throughout northern Europe.

Through his studies of early Christian theology, Casaubon became disenchanted with Calvinist principles of faith and order. He found himself attracted to the doctrines and policies of the church in England. When the death of Henry IV heightened religious tensions in France, Casaubon accepted the invitation of Richard Bancroft, archbishop of Canterbury, to move to England. Warmly welcomed by King James I, and by Launcelot Andrewes and other English bishops, Casaubon was granted a royal pension, and though a layman, he was given the income of a canonry in Canterbury. In 1611 he became a naturalized English subject. His last few years were devoted chiefly to pamphleteering controversy, defending the English Church from Roman Catholic attacks. One of his tasks was the preparation of the refutation of the *Annals*

RAY ATKESON

THE CASCADE RANGE extends from California to British Columbia. Mt. Hood, in the foreground, is in Oregon. Mt. Rainier, the central peak in the distance, is in Washington, and more than 100 miles from Mt. Hood.

of the historian Baronius, largely anti-Protestant history of the Christian church. Casaubon died in London on July 12, 1614, and was buried in Westminster Abbey.

Isaac Casaubon's editions of the works of classical writers are more important than his ecclesiastical polemics. He published commentaries on Suetonius, Theophrastus, Athenaeus, and others. His edition of Polybius was left unfinished. A valuable record of the life of his times is contained in his diary, *Ephemerides*, which was printed for the first time in 1850. Many of his notes and papers were collected and preserved by his son, Méric Casaubon.

POWEL MILLS DAWLEY
The General Theological Seminary, New York

CASBAH, kaz'bä, a walled agglomeration of urban dwellings in North Africa, piled compactly alongside and atop each other. The word *Qasaba* means "metropolis," "capital," or "citadel" in Arabic, and in a few places, such as Algiers, it is used for the entire native quarter.

Modern casbahs more often house hundreds rather than thousands of inhabitants. The buildings are constructed of mud-plastered, sun-baked brick; wood, because of its scarcity, is used only for doors and beams. When the walls weather, the dwellings are abandoned because of the difficulty of repair. The complex is usually three or four stories high, with narrow, irregular dirt streets, if any, and has only rudimentary sanitation. Casbahs of this type are famous in Morocco and in Algeria south of the Atlas Mountains. The well-known casbah in Algiers has a high concentration of people and is also composed of closely built buildings, but it is constructed of fire-clay brick, cinderblock, or concrete.

I. WILLIAM ZARTMAN, *New York University*

CASCADE RANGE, kas-kād', a mountain system in western North America. Though separated from the Sierra Nevada by deep valleys, it is a northward continuation of that system. From northern California, it extends some 700 miles (1,100 km) through Oregon and Washington into British Columbia, where it fans out in an eroded tableland. Rising between the Coast Ranges and the Rocky Mountains, the Cascade Range roughly parallels the Pacific coast, 110 to 160 miles (180 to 260 km) inland.

The loftiest peaks are volcanic cones that are among the most imposing American mountains. The monarch of these is Mt. Rainier (in Washington), which rises 14,410 feet (4,392 meters). Noteworthy also are Mt. Shasta (Calif.), and Mt. Hood (Oreg.), Mt. Adams (Wash.), and Mt. St. Helens (Oreg.). A spectacular scenic spot is Crater Lake (Oreg.), which fills the burnt-out heart of Mt. Mazama.

Several river valleys cut through the Cascades—the Klamath, the Fraser, and most important the Columbia, which has eroded a gorge nearly to sea level. The foaming rapids (cascades) of this river have given their name to the mountains. There are glaciers and snowfields, and the flanks of some mountains are scarred by well-marked avalanche paths.

The Cascades are clothed with extensive forests. There are magnificent stands of Ponderosa pine and Douglas fir—some specimens 250 feet (75 meters) high—together with fir, tamarack, and cedar. Much of this growth is protected by government forest reserves.

FERDINAND C. LANE
Author of "The Story of Mountains"

Further Reading: Wills, Robert H., and Marshall, L., *High Trails: A Guide to the Cascade Crest Trail* (Seattle 1967).

CASCADE TUNNEL, kas-kād′, on the Great Northern Railway in central Washington, in King and Chelan counties, about 55 miles (88 km) northeast of Seattle. It cuts across the Cascade Range, beneath Stevens Pass (4,061 feet, or 1,240 meters), between the small communities of Scenic and Berne. The single-track tunnel, 7.79 miles (12.5 km) long and 16 feet (5 meters) wide, is the longest railroad tunnel in the Americas and one of the longest in the world. The project was started late in 1925, completed in 1928, and opened early in 1929. It included the replacement on the tunnel approaches of 43 miles (69 km) of old, winding lines by 34 miles (55 km) of new high-speed tracks.

CASCARA SAGRADA, kas-kar′ə sə-grä′də, is a drug obtained from dried bark and used as a laxative. Cascara sagrada, or "sacred bark," also known as chittam bark, bitter bark, and bearwood, is obtained from a small buckthorn tree (*Rhamnus purshiana*) found in the northwestern United States and in Canada. The medical value of the bark was first learned from the California Indians, and by 1890 cascara sagrada was an officially listed drug in the *United States Pharmacopoeia.*

Cascara sagrada acts to increase the motor activity of the colon. Evacuation usually occurs within 6 to 8 hours after ingestion. A potential harm of cascara sagrada is excessive catharsis. Prolonged use may cause unusual pigmentation of the lining of the colon, but the pigmentation returns to normal within 4 to 12 months after use of the drug is discontinued.

The active ingredients in cascara sagrada are similar to those in other vegetable laxatives, such as senna and rhubarb. Liquid preparations of cascara sagrada are reportedly more reliable than solid dosage forms. Magnesium oxide often is added to the preparations to remove the bitter taste and reduce irritating action.

George B. Griffenhagen
American Pharmaceutical Association

CASCO BAY, kas′kō, is a bay of the Atlantic Ocean on the coast of southern Maine, between Cape Elizabeth on the south and Small Point on the north. It is about 20 miles (32 km) long and contains about 200 small islands. Many summer resorts are on its shores. The city of Portland, with a fine harbor, is on the western side.

CASE, Clifford Philip (1904–), American public official. Born in Franklin Park, N. J., on April 16, 1904, he graduated from Rutgers University in 1925 and received an LL. B. degree from Columbia in 1928. From then until 1953 he maintained a law practice in New York City. His political career began with service on the Rahway (N. J.) Common Council (1938–1942), from which he moved on to two terms in the New Jersey legislature.

A popular campaigner, he was elected as a Republican to the U. S. House of Representatives in 1944 and then reelected for four succeeding terms. In 1953 he resigned his House seat to serve as president of The Fund for the Republic. New Jersey voters elected him to the U. S. Senate in 1954, and he won reelection twice by successively increasing margins. In the Senate he was a vigorous, effective champion and sponsor of constructive legislation in the fields of civil rights, education, health, and urban affairs. He labored for reform in congressional operations and campaign practices. His concern with foreign policy and international affairs led to his selection as one of two American delegates to the 1966–1967 session of the UN General Assembly.

David Lindsey
California State College at Los Angeles

CASE, Francis Higbee (1896–1962), American public official. He was born in Everly, Iowa, on Dec. 9, 1896, but grew up in Sturgis, S. Dak. He graduated from Dakota Wesleyan University in 1918 and, after service in World War I, became a journalist. He published and edited the Custer (S. Dak.) *Chronicle* from 1931 to 1946. Elected to Congress as a Republican in 1936, he served in the House until 1951, then in the Senate until his death, receiving an increasing number of votes in each election.

Case was a member of the House Appropriations and Armed Forces committees and the ranking Republican on the Senate Public Works Committee. In 1946 the Case labor disputes bill to provide stricter controls on labor was passed but vetoed by President Truman. Case died in Bethesda, Md., on June 22, 1962.

CASE, Jerome Increase (1818–1891), American industrialist and inventor of a threshing machine. Case was born Dec. 11, 1818, in Williamstown, N. Y., and grew up on a frontier farm. His early interest in agricultural machinery led him to sell threshers in Wisconsin. In Racine, in 1844, he produced a practical combined thresher and separator for wheat that eliminated the need for a fanning mill. The Case threshing machine and other farm machinery soon displaced hand methods, and by 1860 mechanical threshing was standard practice on commercial-scale wheat farms. Case's agricultural experience and business sense brought him success, and by 1857 his plant was producing 1600 machines a year. In 1880, Case's company was incorporated as the J. I. Case Threshing Machine Co., and he later formed the J. I. Case Plow Works. He died in Racine, Wisconsin, on Dec. 22, 1891.

Robert S. Woodbury
Massachusetts Institute of Technology

CASE is the term used in grammar for any of the distinctive forms of a noun, pronoun, or adjective that mark the word's particular function in an utterance. One form, for example, might be required for the subject (*He* goes), another for the direct object (They cheered *him*), and yet another to signal possession (*his* hat). Each form is said to be in a separate case, and the usual sign of case is an ending that is added to a generally invariant stem (in English, adjectives have no case endings). Case forms are only one of a variety of means by which such syntactic functions are signaled.

This meaning of the word "case" derives from Latin *casus* ("a fall"), in turn a translation of Greek *ptōsis* ("a fall"). Ancient grammarians considered that each word had some ideal form from which the ordinary forms with case endings had "fallen away."

Indo-European Cases. The reconstructed parent language of the Indo-European family, hence of English, exhibits eight case forms. The following list gives the name of each case, the source of the name, and the phrase with which the French scholar Antoine Meillet (1866–1936) described the use of the case in Indo-European (also called Proto-Indo-European): (1) *nominative* (from Latin *casus nominativus*, "case for naming"); Meillet, "form for the subject"; (2) *accusative* (from Latin *casus accusativus*, "case for accusing," apparently a mistranslation of Greek *aitiatikē ptōsis*, "case of causes"); Meillet, "form for the direct object"; (3) *genitive* (from Latin *casus genitivus*, "case of production or origin"); Meillet, "form for the whole of which one takes a part"; (4) *locative* (from Latin *locativus*, "pertaining to place," first used in the 19th century for describing Sanskrit grammar); Meillet, "form for the noun indicating the place where or the time when something happens"; (5) *ablative* (from Latin *casus ablativus*, "case of removal"); Meillet, "place from which something comes"; (6) *dative* (from Latin *casus dativus*, "case of giving"); Meillet, "indicates at whom or at what the action is aimed"; (7) *instrumental* (from *instrument*, first used in the 19th century for describing Sanskrit grammar); Meillet, "indicates with whom or with what the action is performed"; and (8) *vocative* (from Latin *vocativus*, "pertaining to calling"); Meillet, "designates the person who is called upon or questioned."

Germanic Languages. Old English, spoken from about 450 to about 1050, had noun, pronoun, and adjective inflections for the nominative, genitive, dative, and accusative cases, and sometimes for the instrumental. The word for "boat," for example, was inflected as follows:

	Singular	Plural
Nominative	*bāt*	*bātas*
Genitive	*bātes*	*bāta*
Dative	*bāte*	*bātum*
Accusative	*bāt*	*bātas*

During the Middle English period, from about 1050 to about 1475, distinctive case endings were lost as a result of changes in pronunciation, and in Modern English they survive in the noun only as the "common case" (The *boat* sails; I sail the *boat*) and the "possessive case" (the *boat's* rudder). The old case system survives most fully in English pronouns, most of which have a subject form (*I, you, he*), one or more possessive forms (*my, mine, your, yours*), and an object form (*me, him, her*).

When case distinctions were lost, their role in syntactic signaling was assumed by "function words," especially prepositions, and by very strict and complicated rules for word order.

Of the other Germanic languages, only German and Icelandic retained the old system of case inflections. Modern Danish, Norwegian, Swedish, and Dutch are similar to Modern English in having lost nearly all such inflectional distinctions.

Romance Languages. Although classical Latin had six cases—the nominative, genitive, dative, accusative, vocative, and ablative—spoken Latin (Vulgar Latin) tended to use the accusative form where the classical language required the genitive, dative, or ablative, and thus reduced the 6-case system to a 2-case system (the vocative was usually the same in form as the nominative). The modern Romance languages—French, Spanish, Italian, and Portuguese—have gone on to a common case of the noun and adjective. They have not even retained a possessive form of the noun, as English has. Only Rumanian among the Romance vernaculars has distinctive forms for a nominative-accusative case and a genitive dative case.

Other Indo-European Languages. Many of the remaining Indo-European languages show the same tendency to reduce the ancient case system and to substitute prepositions and word order as syntactic signals. In the Indo-Iranian subfamily, Persian, Hindi, and Urdu have lost case distinctions to about the same extent as English. In the Celtic subfamily, Welsh and Breton have adopted the common case, although Irish and Scots Gaelic retain four cases. Modern Greek has five cases, but the Greek dative is being replaced by a prepositional construction, as in English; ancient Greek had seven cases. Albanian has three cases.

The Balto-Slavic subfamily as a whole is the most faithful inheritor of the ancient structure. Modern Lettish, Lithuanian, Russian, Polish, Serbo-Croatian, Czech, and others retain from five to seven cases (all lacking the ablative).

Non-Indo-European Languages. Syntactic signaling by the use of case forms is uncommon among non-Indo-European languages. It is not found in the Semitic or the Sino-Tibetan families, or in the Japanese, Korean, or American Indian languages, or among the Subsaharan languages of Africa. Deep differences in structure have sometimes been obscured by the tendency of European grammarians to describe these languages with the terms and patterns of Latin or other case-inflected tongues.

The Finno-Ugric family, however, has a case system similar to the Indo-European, but even more complex. Depending upon the mode of analysis, the Finnish language can be shown to have from 15 to 20 cases. See also INFLECTION.

ROBERT L. CHAPMAN, *Drew University*

Bibliography

Bourciez, Edouard, *Éléments de linguistique romane* (Paris 1956).
Meillet, Antoine, *Introduction à l'étude comparative des langues indo-européennes*, 6th ed. (Paris 1930).
Meillet, Antoine, and Cohen, Marcel, *Les langues du monde* (Paris 1924).
Pei, Mario, *The World's Chief Languages*, 5th ed. (New York 1960).
Prokosch, Eduard, *A Comparative Germanic Grammar* (Philadelphia 1939).

CASE, in law, is a general term for an action, suit, cause, or controversy brought before a court of justice. A party's case consists of a set of facts that the law deems sufficient to warrant judicial relief. A party "has a case" when the state of affairs, as proved to the court's satisfaction, gives rise to a cause of action recognized in the law. To constitute a case suitable for judicial determination, the parties' dispute must be concrete and definite; abstract or hypothetical conflicts are generally nonjusticiable.

The word *case* is used in many contexts. Students and practitioners of law use it to denote judicial opinions; thus, volumes of reported opinions are said to contain cases, and the rules of law derived from judicial decisions are said to constitute *case law*, as distinguished from statutory rules.

The term also appears in a variety of more technical phrases. A *case made*, for example, is a statement of facts in relation to a disputed point of law, agreed upon by both parties and presented to the court; *case agreed* or *case stated* have similar meanings. A *case reserved* or *case certified* is a statement of the facts proved at the trial, drawn up by the parties' attorneys under the supervision of the court, for the purpose of having a higher court decide a question of law. A *case on appeal* is a document prepared by appellant's counsel for the appellate tribunal, containing the testimony and proceedings of the trial necessary to an understanding of the matter on appeal.

An *action on the case*—a term more honored in legal history than used in modern jurisprudence—denotes a device for presenting the court with an action that fell outside the existing writs necessary to invoke the judicial power. The plaintiff, or complaining party, was authorized to bring a special action on his own case—hence the term. In time, "actions on the case" came to fit recognized categories of legal disputes; for example, one prominent type involved a suit for damages to persons or property caused unintentionally, or negligently.

Cases *at law*, as distinguished from cases *in equity*, describe the controversies traditionally heard by the law courts, as distinguished from the courts of equity. In modern practice, law and equity have been merged in one court system. However, the distinction remains important, primarily because the right to trial by jury is generally accorded only in cases historically heard at law.

In Anglo-American jurisprudence, cases decided by the highest court of a jurisdiction are binding as precedents on lower courts faced with subtantially similar sets of facts.

DOV GRUNSCHLAG, *Member of the New York Bar*

CASE HARDENING is a process designed to increase the surface hardness, wear resistance, and strength of steel after it has been formed or machined into its final shape. Flame hardening or induction hardening can be used for this process. These techniques are carried out by heating the surface of the steel, quenching to room temperature, and then tempering the steel to improve the toughness. Other techniques such as gas or pack carburizing, carbonitriding, cyaniding, and nitriding are used to case harden steel by the introduction of carbon or nitrogen atoms into the surface of the steel at elevated temperatures. Typical steel parts that are often given case hardening treatments include gear teeth, rifle bolts, splined shafts, and camshafts.

RICHARD W. HECKEL
Drexel Institute of Technology

CASE HISTORY, a detailed study of a person's background and the influences on his life, used by social scientists and clinicians as a means of developing information about human behavior, particularly to understand individuals with mental health problems or who are socially or educationally deviant.

To determine "average" behavior, investigators may observe a carefully chosen sample of people. Sometimes called the *nomothetic* approach, this technique generates reliable statements about the probability of a particular behavior occurring in the group studied, but in order to make predictions about individuals it is usually necessary to seek *idiographic* (individual) knowledge from the interrelated events in a case history.

Two rather different means of obtaining data for a case history are widely used. The first technique involves obtaining answers to carefully devised questions that explore how an individual's problems or symptoms have been expressed in his personal and social life. This procedure is complete in its systematic coverage of all relationships and events considered influential in a person's life, but it may discourage the respondent from offering his own interpretations of his unique experiences. The second technique involves the assumption that the respondent, if encouraged to talk freely with occasional guidance, will report the significant events in his life without prompting.

While psychology and sociology are generally regarded as nomothetic sciences, psychologists such as Gordon Allport and Henry Murray have argued for the idiographic case history approach. This technique, which takes systematic account of the many factors influencing an individual, is uniquely suited for testing generalizations about human behavior derived by other methods.

Criteria necessary for judging the adequacy of a case history technique, established by the American psychologist John Dollard, include the following: (1) the subject's behavior must be viewed in light of the dictates of his culture; (2) motivations must be proven socially relevant and not ascribed solely to inheritance and maturation; (3) the essential role of the family in transmitting culture must be adequately interpreted; (4) the specific process by which biological potentialities are elaborated into social behavior must be shown; (5) life experiences must be shown to be continuous and related; (6) the social circumstances in which particular behavioral sequences occurred must be specified; and (7) the facts of a life history must be organized in terms of a coherent conceptual scheme.

These requirements are designed to be comprehensive, and few case histories fulfill all of them. As actually used, the case history method has many forms, and in any given setting theoretically important facets of the history may be ignored. Nevertheless, Dollard's criteria are a useful standard for evaluating a case history.

RALPH W. HEINE, *University of Michigan*

Further Reading: Allport, Gordon, *Personal Documents in Psychological Science* (New York 1951); Dollard, John, *Criteria for the Life History* (New York 1949); Lewis, Oscar, *Five Families* (New York 1959).

CASE METHOD, a system of teaching law through the analysis of actual recorded cases. Introduced at the Harvard Law School in 1870 by Christopher C. Langdell (q.v.), this method eventually was adopted in virtually all law schools in the United States because of its advantages over the textbook system then prevailing.

The typical "case" consists of an opinion, usually rendered by an appellate court. It includes a statement of the facts that gave rise to the dispute, the procedural steps taken by the parties, the conclusion of the court, and the reasons that persuaded the court to reach the particular decision. The cases are collected in a casebook and arranged according to the categories of rules they illustrate. For example, a homicide chapter in a criminal law casebook might begin with the case of the sleepwalker who, while in a state of somnambulism, shot a man trying to wake him. Another case in the same chapter might deal with a father who killed to save the life of his child, or the man who killed to save himself, and so on. From these various concrete cases, the student will derive his own generalizations as to the applicable rules of law.

More important than the generalizations derived are the legal skills that are learned, for the law student necessarily uses legal materials the way practicing lawyers do in advising their clients and in litigation.

A chief disadvantage of the case method is its inadequacy for the study of the vast volume of legislation as yet uninterpreted by the courts. The growing accumulation of legislative and judicial materials has brought about a freer use of these materials and textual notes to supplement the cases.

LINDA ALDEN RODGERS
School of Law, Columbia University

CASE WESTERN RESERVE UNIVERSITY, a private nonsectarian institution in Cleveland, Ohio, was established on July 1, 1967, through the federation of Western Reserve University (founded 1827) and Case Institute of Technology (1880). All divisions of the university are coeducational except Adelbert College for men and Flora Stone Mather College for women, both undergraduate liberal arts schools. The two other undergraduate units–Case Institute of Technology, for engineering and basic sciences, and Cleveland College, for continuing adult education–are coeducational.

The university has schools of business, dentistry, law, library sciences, medicine, nursing, and applied social sciences. There are also 10 centers for interdisciplinary research in the sciences, engineering, medicine, law, and the humanities. The library has over one million volumes.

The campus of Case Western Reserve is in Cleveland's University Circle, which also contains the buildings of the Cleveland Orchestra, the Museum of Art, University Hospitals, and other museums and research centers. The university's enrollment in the late 1960's was about 12,000, including about 4,500 graduate students.

CASEIN, kā-sēn′, is the principal protein of milk, occurring in varying proportions in the milk of all mammals. It accounts for about one third of the nonaqueous ingredients in whole cow's milk, from which commercial casein is obtained. Being a protein, the casein molecule is constructed of a number of different amino acids linked together to form a chainlike polypeptide structure. The chain possesses amino, hydroxyl, and carboxyl side groups. Casein is insoluble in water, alcohol, or ether, but dissolves easily in alkali solutions. The substance is also soluble in some acids.

Commercial casein is the product of the curding of skim milk. Commercial practice yields about 3 pounds of casein from 100 pounds of skim milk. When curding is done with acids, such as hydrochloric or sulfuric acid, or simply by allowing the skim to sour, the casein is referred as *acid casein.* It is the primary type of casein in commercial use. Curding from skim milk by the enzyme rennet provides a grade of casein used in the manufacture of plastics.

Casein is industrially important because of its sticky nature when dissolved in water containing an alkali. In this state it becomes a colloid of high molecular weight, capable of being dried to form a film. This film constitutes the bond in such important commercial applications as the gluing of wood, the binding of clay in paper coating, and the binding of pigments in water paints. Casein glues provide a water-resistant bond by virtue of the chemical action of lime, which forms insoluble calcium caseinate during the setting of the glue. In paper coating, the casein bond is made water-resistant by treatment with formaldehyde.

Another useful application of casein is as a top coat on the finer grades of leather, where its film clarity provides color depth and its toughness protects the leather. Casein is also used in the coating for lithographic printing plates, as a stabilizer for emulsion paints, as a binder for wallpaper pigments and for artists' colors, in shoe dressings, in clarifying wine and other beverages, and in a number of other ways.

When it is cured with rennet, casein is the base for casein plastics, one major use of which is in the production of buttons. An alkaline solution of casein can be extruded into a coagulating bath to form filaments that subsequently are stretched and hardened to produce a commercial wool-like fiber. Casein produced under sanitary conditions and made soluble with alkali is employed in the manufacture of nutritional and pharmaceutical products. As a source of essential amino acids, casein has high nutritive value.

H. K. SALZBERG
Consultant, Borden Chemical Co.

CASELLA, kä-sel′lä, **Alfredo** (1883–1947), Italian composer, pianist, and conductor. He was born in Turin on July 25, 1883. In 1896 he began study at the Paris Conservatory, where he composed his two symphonies and the orchestral rhapsody *Italia* (1909). Casella returned to Italy in 1915 and taught music in Rome. In 1917 he founded the Società Nazionale di Musica. He died in Rome on March 5, 1947.

Casella classified his works in three periods. Those before 1913 (such as the First Symphony, 1906) are neoromantic, reflecting the influences of Strauss and Mahler; those of 1913–1923 are dissonant and polytonal, verging on atonality (*Notte di Maggio,* 1913); and those following 1923 are neoclassical with an extended tonal range (Concerto for String Quartet, 1923–1924).

CASEMENT, Sir Roger David (1864–1916), Irish patriot, whose execution by the British in World War I made him a martyr of the Irish nationalist cause. Casement was born of Ulster Protestant stock, in Sandycove, County Dublin, Ireland, on Sept. 1, 1864. He left school at 16 to work for a Liverpool shipping company. In 1887 he launched a career in the colonial world that was to bring him international renown. From 1892 to 1895 he served in the British Foreign Office in Nigeria. He then entered the consular service and held posts at Lourenço Marques, Portuguese East Africa (1895–1898), Luanda in Angola (1898–1900), and Boma, then capital of the Belgian Congo (1901–1904). Casement investigated and courageously exposed the existing system of exploitation in the Congo. He reported that Congolese were being slave-driven, mutilated, and murdered on Belgian-owned rubber plantations. His report, published in 1904 and confirmed by a judicial commission established by the Belgian king Leopold, helped end the atrocities.

After a year's leave of absence in Ireland, during which he became deeply interested in Irish politics, Casement went to Brazil as consul at Santos (1906) and Pará (1907) and as consul-general at Rio de Janeiro (1908). In 1910 he was sent to investigate alleged atrocities by the employees of the British-owned Peruvian-Amazon Company rubber plantations along the Putumayo River. He established the truth of the allegations, and, after submitting his report, was knighted in 1911.

Casement retired from the consular service in 1912. Suffering from various tropical diseases, he settled in Ireland the next year and devoted himself almost exclusively to agitation for Irish home rule. He took a leading part in organizing the National Volunteers, and in July 1914 he went to New York to enlist American support for them. After the outbreak of World War I, Casement made his way from New York via Scandinavia to Germany, where he attempted unsuccessfully to recruit a brigade of Irish prisoners of war for service against Britain. Thereafter, convinced that Germany did not intend to furnish sufficient arms for the projected Easter Rebellion of 1916, he returned to Ireland in a German submarine to try to prevent the rising. He landed safely at Banna, in Kerry, on Good Friday, but British authorities, who had been forewarned, arrested him the same day and took him to London to stand trial for treason.

Casement was convicted and sentenced to death, and despite the efforts of prominent Englishmen to obtain a reprieve, he was hanged at Pentonville Jail, London, on Aug. 3, 1916. In his last hours he became a Roman Catholic.

Before his execution, in order to discredit him, British authorities surreptitiously circulated diaries in Casement's handwriting that described homosexual encounters. Casement was never permitted to see them or defend himself. Although the government finally made the diaries available to scholars in 1959, no agreement has been reached as to their authenticity.

Casement's remains were returned to Ireland for burial at Glasnevin in February 1965.

GIOVANNI COSTIGAN, *University of Washington*

Further Reading: Gwynn, Denis R., *Traitor or Patriot: The Life and Death of Roger Casement* (New York 1931); MacColl, René, *Roger Casement, a New Judgment* (London 1956); Parmiter, Geoffrey, *Roger Casement* (London 1936).

CASERTA, kä-zer'tä, a city in Italy 17 miles (28 km) north of Naples, is best known for the great palace and gardens built there by the Bourbon kings of Naples during the 18th century. Caserta's proximity to Naples, as well as the availability of ample level land, inspired King Charles IV of Naples, in 1752, to order the building of a royal palace there to rival Versailles.

The Palace. Luigi Vanvitelli, the leading Italian architect of the time, designed the palace. It was completed in 1774, although the interior took some years more to furnish: on approaching the palace, the visitor faces an immense front, more than 800 feet (250 meters) long; the six wings of the palace form four large interior courtyards. A vast formal staircase in the center of the palace leads to the main reception room. The royal apartments, sumptuously decorated, comprise a series of private and public rooms, a chapel, a charming small theater, and a library. There is a separate apartment in the palace housing a magnificent Christmas crèche, or *presepio,* an outstanding example of this minor art form of Naples.

Behind the palace lies a vast park, extending 2 miles (3 km) from the palace to the Grand Cascade. The Cascade, formed by an artificial river that was made by tunneling through the hill to bring water a distance of 30 miles (50 km), is ornamented with groups of statues of Diana and the hunter Actaeon.

ALINARI-ART REFERENCE BUREAU

CASERTA'S Palazzo Reale was the scene of the surrender of German forces in Italy to the Allies in 1945.

Part of the palace is a museum; the rest is used as a training school for the Italian Air Force. During the last part of World War II, in 1944–1945, the entire palace was occupied by the Allied Forces Headquarters for the Mediterranean theater. Population: city (1961) 36,337; commune (1966 estimate) 56,743.

GEORGE KISH
University of Michigan

CASEY, Richard Gardiner (1890–), Australian statesman and diplomat. Born in Brisbane on Aug. 29, 1890, he was appointed Australia's first liaison officer in London in 1924. He was elected to the Australian House of Representatives in 1931, was federal treasurer from 1935 to 1939, and the country's first minister to the United States in 1940. He became British minister of state resident in the Middle East in 1942, and from 1944 to 1946 was governor of Bengal, India.

Minister for national development from 1949 to 1951 and minister of external affairs for the next nine years, he helped Australia become a bridge between the Western allies and Southeast Asia, and strengthened its ties with the United States. He resigned from Parliament in 1960, when his life peerage as the Baron Casey of Berwick and of the City of Westminster was conferred. In 1965 he was appointed governor general of Australia. His publications include: *An Australian in India* (1947), *Double or Quit* (1949), *Friends and Neighbors* (1954), *Personal Experience 1939–1946* (1962), and *The Future of the Commonwealth* (1963).

R. M. YOUNGER
Author of "Australia and the Australians"

"CASEY JONES" is an American railroad ballad named for its hero, the engineer Casey Jones, who dies in a collision in his effort to deliver the 8-hour-late westbound mail on time. The hero of the ballad is supposedly based on John Luther Jones, an Illinois Central engineer who was born in 1864(?) and died in a wreck in 1900, probably of the "Cannonball Express" on the Chicago-New Orleans run.

The original version of the ballad is thought to have been written by Jones' Negro engine wiper, Wallace Saunders. A revised version by T. L. Seibert and E. W. Newton (1909) was popularized in vaudeville. Other versions followed, and the ballad has become part of American folklore. It inspired Robert Ardrey's play *Casey Jones* (1938).

CASGRAIN, käz-graɴ', **Henri Raymond** (1831–1904), Canadian priest and historian. He was born on Dec. 16, 1831, at Rivière-Ouelle, Lower Canada (Quebec). Educated at the Collège de Ste. Anne and Quebec Seminary, he was ordained to the priesthood in 1856. He started to write early in life; his first important book, *Légendes canadiennes,* appeared in 1861. He also wrote tales depicting the life of the early colonists in Canada and published these in the periodicals *Les soirées canadiennes* and *Le foyer canadien,* which he had helped found.

In 1870, because of ill health, he relinquished his parochial duties and devoted himself to literature, mainly history. A founder of modern French Canadian historiography, Casgrain edited the *Collection des manuscrits du Maréchal de Lévis,* 12 vols. (1889–1895). Among the books that he wrote were *Biographies canadiennes* (1885), *Montcalm et Lévis* (2 vols., 1891), and *Montcalm and Wolfe* (1905). His *Pèlerinage au pays d'Évangéline* (1888) was honored by the French Academy. In 1889, Casgrain was elected president of the Royal Society of Canada. He died in Quebec on Feb. 11, 1904.

CASGRAIN, käz-graɴ', **Marie Thérèse** (1896–), Canadian feminist and politician, who led the fight to obtain political rights for women in Quebec. Marie Thérèse Forget was born in Montreal on July 10, 1896, and was educated at the city's Sacred Heart Convent. In 1916 she married Pierre François Casgrain, a fellow politician. They had two sons and two daughters.

Although Quebec women could vote in federal elections from 1918, they were denied that right in provincial elections. As president of the Quebec League for Women's Rights (1929–1942), Mme. Casgrain struggled to attain full suffrage and finally was victorious in 1940. The following year women became eligible for admittance to the Quebec bar.

In 1942, Mme. Casgrain became the first Quebec woman candidate in a federal election. She lost and never held a popularly elected office, but she became national vice-chairman of the Cooperative Commonwealth Federation (CCF) in 1948 and was its provincial leader in 1951. She retired in 1957.

CASGRAIN, käz-graɴ', **Philippe Baby** (1826–1917), Canadian lawyer, public official, and historian. He was born in Quebec city on Dec. 30, 1826. Admitted to the bar in 1850, he was a Liberal member of the Canadian House of Commons from 1872 to 1891. Later he was clerk of the provincial circuit and revision court. Casgrain earned a reputation as an amateur historian, especially through his articles on the early history of Quebec city. His published writings include *Letellier de Saint-Just et son temps* (1885) and *La vie de Joseph François Perrault* (1898). He was three times elected president of the Literary and Historical Society of Quebec. Casgrain died in Quebec on May 23, 1917.

CASH, Wilbur Joseph (1901–1941), American writer and editor. He was born at Gaffney, S. C., on May 2, 1901, and graduated from Wake Forest College (1922). He taught English at Georgetown (Ky.) College and English and French at a boys' school in Hendersonville, N. C. Then he became a newspaperman in Chicago and in Shelby and Charlotte, N. C. In 1937 he was appointed associate editor of the Charlotte *News.* Cash's book *The Mind of the South* appeared in 1939 and attracted considerable attention. It was a brilliant critical analysis of the social background, psychological temperament, and characteristic customs of the region, which not only showed why the South was what it was but also prophesied the problems that the section would have to overcome in the following decades. A troubled genius, Cash committed suicide in Mexico City on July 1, 1941.

Further Reading: Morrison, Joseph L., *W. J. Cash: Southern Prophet.* (New York 1967).

CASH, in accounting, is money (coins or specie and paper), bank deposits, and any negotiable instruments generally accepted as money, such as bank checks, cashier's checks, traveler's checks, and postal money orders.

To be considered cash, an instrument must be immediately and directly convertible into money. Bank deposits make up the major portion of nonmonetary cash. Only demand deposits (checking accounts) should be considered cash. There is a tendency among some accountants, however, to regard saving deposits and saving certificates as cash.

Cash serves two important functions: (1) as a medium of exchange, and (2) as a standard of value. As a medium of exchange, cash is the most liquid and most active of a firm's assets. As a standard of value, it is the only item valued exactly in a firm's statements.

W. Asquith Howe, *Temple University*

CASH FLOW, in accounting, is the inflow and outflow of cash in a firm. Cash flow is determined commonly by financial analysts by adding to net profit such noncash items as depreciation allowances. This sum constitutes the money generated by a firm for dividends, working capital, and investment in new plant and equipment. In the financial analysis of a firm, cash flow should be used in addition to—and not instead of—net profit.

A cash-flow statement is a limited type of funds-flow statement in which funds are defined as actual cash rather than as working capital or as all financial resources. The statement is used to determine a firm's ability to pay its bills, dividends, and capital expenditures. It is possible for a firm that is profitable and solvent (assets exceeding liabilities), as shown by the income statement and balance sheet, to discover suddenly that it lacks cash to pay maturing debts.

W. Asquith Howe, *Temple University*

CASH REGISTER, a machine that records daily sales, keeps track of the money exchanged, and identifies separate transactions for management audit and control. Simple mechanical registers may be activated by keys, levers, or cranks. Electromechanical registers are motor-driven and are divided into two general classes: conventional and data-input types. Data-input registers are used as part of an electronic data-processing system; some types automatically produce a punched-paper-tape record of transactions while others print figures in a special stylized type font that can be read by people as well as by scanning devices coupled to computers. Conventional-type registers are available with from 1 to 30 mechanical totals, and data-input registers can provide up to 9,999 separate information classifications, with totals broken down by computer analysis.

Hundreds of models of cash registers are available, including designs for virtually every type of retail business. Special features include portion control for cafeterias; selective itemization for check-out counters where some of the items are taxable; subtraction; multiple totals; multiple cash drawers; and automatic change. Many special printing features and other devices are available on sales registers to perform auditing, bookkeeping, itemizing, and analyzing functions. Most sales registers print customer receipts and keep a printed record of every transaction.

LAWRENCE D. MATTHEWS
The National Cash Register Company

CASHEL, kash'əl, is a small market town in Ireland, in the inland county of Tipperary, 48 miles (77 km) northeast of Cork. It is the center of a fertile region known as the Golden Vein.

About 400 A.D. a people called the Eoghanacht conquered the district and erected a fortification on the Rock of Cashel, which dominates the town. By the middle of the 10th century they had become undisputed lords of the kingdom of Munster, but at the time of the Scandinavian invasion they were in disorder. Cashel fell to the Norsemen, but was recaptured by the Dal Chais of Clare, whose leader, Brian Boru, became king of Munster. In 1152, Cashel became the seat of an archbishopric, a status it has retained, although the archbishop's cathedral is now at Thurles.

Cormac's Chapel, an Irish Romanesque church of the 12th century, is one of many buildings of archaeological interest on Cashel's famous rock. Population: (1966) 2,680.

THOMAS FITZGERALD
Department of Education, Dublin

CASHEW, kash'ōō, an evergreen tree native to South America and widely cultivated throughout the tropics for its fruits (cashew nuts). The cashew, *Anacardium occidentale,* is a member of the cashew family (Anacardiaceae). It grows to 40 feet (12 meters) high and has spreading branches and large oblong leaves, 4 to 8 inches (10–20 cm) long. The tree also possesses a system of latex tubes that ooze a milky juice when injured. The plant's yellowish flowers, less than a ½ inch (13 mm) across, are borne in loose clusters (panicles) about 10 inches (25 cm) long. The flower consists of 5 sepals, 5 petals, 10 or usually fewer stamens, and a single pistil enclosing a single ovule.

As the ovary of the pistil matures into fruit, it develops a nutlike shell, becomes comma-shaped, and grows to about 1 inch (25 cm) long. Within the shell of the cashew fruit, or nut, is a single seed. This seed, after roasting, becomes the cashew "nut" we eat. While the fruit is developing, the receptacle (tip of the flower stem) below the ovary enlarges into a red or yellow fleshy structure, called the cashew apple, upon which the cashew nut sits. The cashew apple, which is about 3 inches (7.5 cm) long and more conspicuous than the cashew nut, is sour but edible; in Brazil it is fermented into "cajú" wine.

JANE LATTA

CASHEW NUTS develop in the shells at the end of the enlarged receptacles known as "cashew apples."

The cashew nut has a double shell, between which lies a blackish, irritating oil called *cardol.* Like the oils of certain other plants of the cashew family, such as poison ivy, poison oak, poison sumac, and poison wood, cardol can cause a rash and blistering of the skin. This oil, which is sometimes used as an insecticide, is removed during the roasting process.

S. C. BAUSOR
California State College, Pa.

CASHIER'S CHECK, a check drawn by a bank on itself and signed by its cashier. The check is a direct obligation of the issuing bank, payable upon demand. A cashier's check may be obtained from a bank by paying the face value of the check plus a service fee. This type of check may be used by a person who wants to assure the recipient that the check will be paid. It may be used also to make a remittance by a person who lacks a bank account. Cashier's checks are used also by a bank to pay its own obligations.

CASHIN, kash'in, **Sir Michael Patrick** (1864–1926), Newfoundland public official. He was born in Cape Broyle, Newfoundland, on Sept. 29, 1864. After attending St. Bonaventure's College in St. John's, he became a fish merchant at Cape Broyle.

Elected to the Newfoundland legislature from Ferryland in 1893, he was first an Independent and then a Liberal before joining the People's party in 1907. Two years later he entered the cabinet as minister of finance and customs, a post he held for 10 years. He became acting prime minister in 1918 and prime minister a year later. He lost office that same year, however, and headed the opposition in the House of Assembly until he retired in 1923. In 1918 he was made a Knight of the Order of the British Empire. He died on Aug. 30, 1926, in St. John's.

CASHMERE. See KASHMIR.

CASHMERE, kazh'mēr, is one of the softest and finest natural fibers, second in fineness only to vicuña. True cashmere comes from the cashmere goat, which is raised in China, Tibet, Mongolia, Iran, and the Soviet Union. The goat's fleece consists of two layers: coarse outer fibers, called *beard hairs,* which range in length from 1½ to 8 inches (40–200 mm), and a fine soft undercoat, called *down,* consisting of fibers ranging from 1 to 3¼ inches (25–80 mm). Only the down is used for weaving the luxury cloth.

The natural color of the cashmere goat may be white, off-white, gray, tan, brown, or black. After the fleece is collected, either by shearing or combing the goats, it is sorted according to grade, amount of down, and color. Generally, a single fleece weighs 3 to 16 ounces (90–450 grams) and contains from 20 to 80% down. Cashmere fibers are not very strong (about 10% below the strength of wool and 35% below that of mohair) and because bleaching further reduces their strength, sorting them according to color is very important. After the fibers are sorted, they are scoured and sometimes bleached before being spun into yarn.

Fabric woven from cashmere fiber is light in weight and is used largely for clothing, especially sweaters, scarves, and shawls. Because the fiber is damaged by strong soaps and chlorine, extreme care must be exercised in the home care of cashmere garments. Generally, the best method of cleaning cashmere is with a cold-water soap.

ERNEST B. BERRY, *School of Textiles North Carolina State University*

CASHMERE GOAT. See GOAT, DOMESTIC.

CASIMIR, I, kaz'i-mir (1016–1058), called *Casimir* (Polish, Kazimierz) *the Restorer,* was ruler of Poland from about 1034. After the death of his father, King Mieszko II, in 1034, the Polish state nearly disintegrated as the result of civil war and pagan reaction to its recent Christianization. Casimir wisely refrained from claiming the royal crown, calling himself instead the Duke of Poland. Supported by the German emperors Conrad II and Henry III, whose suzerainty he recognized, and by Yaroslav the Wise of Kiev, with whom he arranged a marriage alliance, Casimir was able to restore unity to his state.

By 1047 he had regained the rebellious region of Mazovia, and by 1050 he had driven the Czechs out of Silesia, a Polish region they had occupied since the civil war. Because of the devastation in parts of Poland in the wake of the Czech invasion, Casimir moved the capital from Gniezno to Cracow. He rebuilt the administrative machinery and the religious organization of the state. Casimir died on Nov. 28, 1058, and his eldest son became king as Boleslav II.

CHARLES MORLEY, *Ohio State University*

CASIMIR II, kaz'i-mir (1138-1194), ruler of Poland from 1177, called *Casimir* (Polish, Kazimierz) *the Just,* was the youngest son of Boleslav III, Duke of Poland. Casimir acquired the duchy of Sandomierz upon the death of his brother Henry in 1166. With the help of dissatisfied nobles, Casimir drove his brother Mieszko III from Cracow in 1177 and installed himself as Duke of Poland, despite the stronger rights of his elder brothers.

Casimir invited Polish magnates and bishops to a congress at Łęczyca (1180) and persuaded them that the supreme authority in Poland should henceforth be hereditary in his family. In return, he granted certain privileges to the clergy, freeing the Polish church from the domination of the Duke. Both the Pope and the Emperor recognized Casimir's new position, but in return the Duke had to acknowledge their right to interfere in Polish affairs. Casimir made territorial gains in the east and took advantage of the division of Russia after the fall of Kiev (1169) to intervene in the principalities of Halicz (Galicia) and Volhynia (Volyn). He died on May 5, 1194.

CHARLES MORLEY, *The Ohio State University*

CASIMIR III, kaz'í-mir (1310–1370), king of Poland from 1333, called *Casimir the Great.* He was born on April 30, 1310, the son of Vladislav IV. As the last of the Piast dynasty, Casimir (Polish, Kazimierz) ascended the throne of a Poland exhausted from numerous wars. He attempted, therefore, to achieve his objectives through diplomacy rather than war.

At the Congress of Visegrád (1335) Casimir recognized the sovereignty over Silesia of the King of Bohemia who, in turn, renounced claims to the Polish throne. Casimir concluded the Treaty of Kalisz in 1343, by which he surrendered the disputed region of Pomerania to the Teutonic Knights in exchange for the return of the Kujavia region with the neighboring town of Dobrzyń to Poland. While making these territorial sacrifices in the west, Casimir acquired Galicia (Halicz) and Volyhynia (Volyn) in 1352 by reinforcing dynastic claims with military action. He received assistance from his nephew, King Louis I of Hungary (Louis of Anjou), who was confirmed at a meeting in Buda (1355) as the childless Casimir's successor to the Polish throne.

Casimir's domestic policy made possible great strides in the economic and cultural development of the country. For his support of the lower classes, Casimir came to be known as "King of the Peasants." He extended privileges to Jews, who settled in Poland in large numbers. He encouraged internal trade and industry. He founded the University of Cracow (1364) on the pattern of Italian law schools. He codified the customary laws of the land and established new courts of law. By the time of Casimir's death at Cracow on Nov. 5, 1370, his policies had made Poland a great power, paved the way for its union with Lithuania, and laid the foundations for its later preeminence under the Jagiello (Jagello) dynasty.

CHARLES MORLEY, *The Ohio State University*

CASIMIR IV, kaz'í-mir (1427–1492), was king of Poland from 1447 and Grand Duke of Lithuania from 1440. The second son of King Vladislav II of the Jagiello (Jagello) dynasty, Casimir (Polish, Kazimierz) was chosen to rule Lithuania at the age of 12. He ascended the throne of Poland after the death of his elder brother, Vladislav III. Casimir was allowed to accept the crown only after he recognized the equality of Lithuania within the Polish-Lithuanian union.

Poland's relations with the Teutonic Knights constituted one of the country's most difficult problems. Nobles and townsmen revolted against the Knights and placed themselves under the suzerainty of Casimir. The war that resulted lasted 13 years. By the Treaty of Toruń (Thorn) in 1466, negotiated with the approval of the papacy, Poland received full sovereignty over the area that came to be known as West, or Royal, Prussia, while East Prussia became a Polish fief. The importance of the treaty was that Danzig Pomerania, which included the mouth of the Vistula River, was returned to Poland.

Casimir's marriage to a sister of the King of Bohemia and Hungary gave him a claim to the thrones of these countries for his sons. He succeeded in placing one of them, Vladislav, on the Czech throne in 1471 and on the Hungarian throne in 1490. In the East, Casimir maintained peace by recognizing the growing influence and strength of Grand Duke Ivan III of Muscovy. Casimir died at Grodno in June 1492. His reign is remembered not only for its territorial gains and for the foundation of what is called the Jagiełło federation, but also as a period of great cultural growth. Jan Długosz, Poland's first historian, and Wit Stwosz (Veit Stoss), a famous sculptor, flourished during this peroid.

CHARLES MORLEY, *The Ohio State University*

CASIMIR-PÉRIER, kȧ-zē-mēr′ pā-ryā′, **Jean Paul Pierre** (1847–1907), French politician. He was born in Paris on Nov. 8, 1847, grandson of Casimir Périer, Louis Philippe's prime minister, and son of Auguste Casimir-Périer, minister of the interior in the 1870's (who added the hyphen to the name). The family was wealthy and held the majority interest in the Anzin coal and iron firm.

Identifying himself with the moderate republicans, Casimir-Périer was elected in 1876 to the Chamber of Deputies, of which he eventually became president. From December 1893 to May 1894 he served as premier. Despite his republicanism, he found himself increasingly at odds with the Radicals and Socialists, who were growing in strength. Following a bomb explosion in the Chamber of Deputies, he won rightist support for strong antianarchist laws.

After the assassination of President Sadi Carnot in June 1894, Casimir-Périer was elected 5th president of the Third Republic. Sensitive about his constitutional rights as president, irritated by leftist personal attacks on him, and resentful of the Dupuy government's intention to isolate him from political developments, he resigned the presidency after only 6 months, in January 1895. Abandoning politics, he occupied himself exclusively with his business affairs until his death in Paris on March 11, 1907.

JOEL COLTON, *Duke University*

CASINO, kə-sē′nō, is a card game of skill for two to four players. Ancestors of the game include *papillon* (butterfly), played in 18th century France, and *callabra,* named for the Calabria region in Italy, and played early in the 19th century.

Casino is played with a standard deck. Cards count their pip value, face cards have no value, and suits are not considered.

In the first deal of a 2-handed game the dealer deals out 12 cards, 2 to his opponent, 2 face up on the table, 2 to himself, and then repeats the round. Thus, when play begins, each player has 4 cards, and there are 4 face up on the table. At each turn the players (beginning with the nondealer) play a single card. After the hand is played, the dealer gives 4 more cards to each person, in rounds of 2 at a time, but no longer deals cards to the table. Play and dealing continue until the pack is exhausted.

Play. The object of play is to *take in,* or *capture,* cards and combinations of cards of scoring value. The total point value taken in determines the winner. A card from the hand may take in any card or cards on the table that match it in rank (this is called *pairing,* and is the only way face cards can be taken); or it may capture two or more cards whose pips total the same as the pip value of the capturing card. For example, a 9 in the hand may take in one or more 9's on the table, or a 4 and a 5, which total 9.

Cards may also be won by *building;* the player places a card from his hand on another card on the table, the pile to be taken later by a second card from the hand. For example, a player may place either a 6 from his hand on a faced 6 or a 2 from his hand on a faced 4; on his next turn he can take the pile with a 6 from his hand. On placing the first card, the player must say "Building 6's." This announcement prevents the opponent from splitting the build and using any of the cards separately. The opponent may, however, capture a build, and he may even increase the build if it is not a "double build." Thus, using the above example, he could capture the build with a 6 in his hand; or he could add a 3 to the 2-4 build and announce "Building 9's" (but he could not do this if it was a double build, that is, if the pile also contained a 6).

When a player is unable or unwilling to take in, he may *trail;* that is, he may face a card from his hand. For example, if the table shows a jack and a 4 and the nondealer holds a 4 as his last card in the next-to-last deal, he may trail with a 4 instead of taking in the 4 on the table. The object may be to avert a *sweep* (taking in all the cards on the table) by his opponent, or to leave a combination of 8 in case he is dealt an 8 in the final deal. When the pack is played out, the last player taking in a card also gets any other cards remaining on the table.

Scoring. At game's end, each player totals his *counting cards:*

Cards (a majority of the 52 cards)	3
Spades (a majority of the 13 spades)	1
Big casino (the 10 of diamonds)	2
Little casino (the 2 of spades)	1
Aces	1 each
Sweeps (not always counted)	1 each

Game is commonly set at 21 points. During any deal, if a player correctly claims to have 21 points, he wins. This is called *counting out.* when four play, the cards taken by partners are counted together in determining the winner.

FRANK K. PERKINS, *Boston "Herald"*

CASIQUIARE RIVER, kä-sē-kyä′rā, a link between the Orinoco and Amazon river systems in South America. It branches from the upper Orinoco in southern Venezuela and flows 140 miles (225 km) southwest into the Río Negro, a tributary of the Amazon.

A

SPECIMEN

OF

Printing Types,

BY

William Caslon, Jun.

Letter-Founders

London.

PRINTED BY

GALABIN AND BAKER,

MDCCLXXXV

TITLE PAGE from William Caslon's sample book of type faces, published in 1785.

NEW YORK PUBLIC LIBRARY

CASLON, kaz′lən, **William** (1692–1766), English typefounder, whose achievement lay in the splendid regularity and proportion of his letters, which combine sensitivity with vigor. Matrices struck from his original types are still in use.

Caslon was born at Cradley, Worcestershire, and began work as an ornamental engraver to a gunsmith. In 1716 he set up his own foundry in London. The earliest known type designed by Caslon is the Arabic used in the *Psalter* (1725) published by the Society for Promoting Christian Knowledge. His first specimen sheet, showing roman and italic type in 14 sizes, appeared in 1734. Caslon quickly established his superiority over his rivals, and for the rest of the century almost all books of importance were set in his types. Their popularity spread to the Continent and America, where one of his fonts was used for the printed Declaration of Independence. Caslon's eldest son William (1720–1778) continued the business after his father's death, at Bethnal Green, London, on Jan. 23, 1766.

GRANT UDEN
Author of "Collector's Case-book"

CASO Y ANDRADE, kä′so ē än-drä′thā, **Alfonso** (1896–), Mexican anthropologist and prehistorian. He was born in Mexico City on Feb. 1, 1896. He attended the University of Mexico, where from 1918 to 1940 he was on the faculty of philosophy and letters. In 1930 he became head of the department of archaeology of the Museo Nacional, and was director of the museum in 1933–1934. He became director of the Instituto Nacional Indigenista in 1950, and was founder of the *Boletín Bibliográfico Antropología Americana*.

Caso excavated numerous sites in northern Mexico. From 1931 to 1944 he was director of explorations at Oaxaca, where he excavated the ancient Zapotec city of Monte Albán. There he found evidence for five major epochs of Zapotec history, dating from the 6th century A. D. to the Spanish conquest in the 16th century. He then was able to establish a chronology for the preconquest history of the locality with which to correlate information from other sites.

In his extensive writings, Caso made a major contribution to the reconstruction of Mexican prehistory. He translated the Mixtec Codices, the historical records of the people who displaced the Zapotecs at Monte Albán.

PRISCILLA C. WARD
American Museum of Natural History

CASPER, Billy (1931–), American golfer. William Earl Casper, Jr., was born in San Diego, Cal., on June 24, 1931. After attending the University of Notre Dame on a golf scholarship for one term and serving four years in the United States Navy, where he played or taught golf at three installations in the San Diego area, he turned professional in 1955.

Through 1967 he had won 37 tournament titles, including the 1959 U. S. Open, his first major tournament victory, and the 1966 Open. In 1961, 1963, 1965, and 1967 he was a member of the Ryder Cup team, which plays the best of the British professionals; and in 1960, 1963, 1965, and 1966 he received the Vardon Trophy, given to the player with the lowest average score in matches approved by the Professional Golf Association (PGA). His best year was 1966, when he won four major tournaments (U. S. Open, San Diego Open, Western Open in Chicago, and "500" Festival Open in Indianapolis), became golf's leading money winner of the year (about $122,000 in 22 events), and was selected as the PGA Player of the Year. Casper owed much of his success to his excellent putting.

MICHAEL QUINN
"Sports Illustrated"

CASPER is the second-largest city in Wyoming and its leading industrial center. It is situated on the North Platte River, 150 miles (240 km) northwest of Cheyenne, and is the seat of Natrona county. Casper is surrounded by large oil fields, including the historic Teapot Dome and Salt Creek fields; it is a business center for oil companies, and oil refining is its chief industry. It is also a shipping and wholesale center for a stock-raising and farming area. The mining and milling of uranium are important. Casper College, a 2-year coeducational college, is in the city.

Fort Caspar, built on this site in 1863, protected travelers on the Oregon Trail and served as a Pony Express depot. It has been restored and is now a museum. Casper was founded in 1888. It is governed by a city manager. Population: 39,361.

CASPIAN SEA, kas′pē-ən, the world's largest inland sea, lying between Europe and Asia. In ancient times it was known as *Caspium Mare* or *Hyrcanium Mare*. Except for its south coast, which belongs to Iran, the sea is surrounded by the territory of the USSR.

The Caspian Sea is about 730 miles (1,200 km) long from north to south and is 180 miles (300 km) wide, on an average. It has no outlet and therefore has undergone fluctuations in level all through recorded history. Between 1930 and 1957 its level dropped from 85 feet (26 meters) below sea level to 92 feet (28 meters) below sea level. Its area shrank accordingly from about 141,400 square miles (424,300 sq km) to about 123,700 square miles (371,000 sq km). The drop in level occurred because evaporation substantially exceeded inflow from tributary streams and precipitation. In addition, stream flow was reduced because water from the Volga River, which accounts for 80% of the inflow, was increasingly diverted for use in irrigation and for industrial needs. Several projects have been proposed to help restore the level, but none has been implemented.

The shallow northern part of the Caspian Sea is an important sturgeon-fishing ground and a major source of caviar, the salted roe of the sturgeon. The sea's greatest recorded depth, 3,209 feet (978 meters), is in the south. Caspian water is salty, with an average salt content of 13 parts per 1,000 by weight, and has a greater sulfate content than ocean water. A vast shallow lagoon on the east coast, the Kara-Bogaz-Gol, has natural deposits of sodium sulfate.

The Caspian Sea is a major transport route, except during the winter, when the shallow northern reaches freeze over for several months. The main Soviet ports on the sea are Astrakhan, in the Volga delta, and Baku and Krasnovodsk, which are linked by a railroad ferry. Oil from the Baku and Krasnovodsk fields (partly offshore) is the principal freight. The main Iranian port is Bander Shah.

THEODORE SHABAD
Editor of "Soviet Geography"

CASS, kas, **Lewis** (1782–1866) American political leader often called the "Father of the Old Northwest," who figured prominently in the major issues of his time, from the War of 1812 to the bitter controversies preceding the Civil War. In a distinguished public career he was a general, a governor, a cabinet officer, a diplomat, a senator, and a presidential candidate.

Cass was born at Exeter, N. H., on Oct. 9, 1782, and was educated at Phillips Exeter Academy. In 1799 he settled in Ohio, where he studied law at Marietta, was admitted to the bar in 1802, and began to practice in Zanesville. He was elected to the Ohio legislature as a Jeffersonian Democrat in 1806.

At the outbreak of the War of 1812, Cass became colonel of an Ohio volunteer regiment. Taken prisoner in the surrender of Detroit, he was later exchanged, and he served as brigadier general under Gen. William Henry Harrison. Cass' war experience resulted in a lifelong distrust of Britain.

In 1813, President Madison appointed Cass governor of Michigan Territory (formerly part of the Northwest Territory, or Old Northwest). His vigorous administration and liberal program encouraged settlement and led to statehood for Michigan and Wisconsin. He was notably successful in negotiating land-cession treaties with the Indians, whose confidence he won by treating them fairly.

Cass' success in Michigan and his understanding of the Indian problem led President Jackson to appoint him secretary of war in 1831. This was at the time of the South Carolina nullification crisis, and Cass reinforced the Charleston defenses to support Jackson's firm stand. As secretary he also directed the Army in the Black Hawk and Seminole wars and he supervised the removal of Indians to territories west of the Mississippi River.

Appointed minister to France in 1836, Cass ingratiated himself with King Louis Philippe and the French people. His popularity enabled him to block French ratification of the Quintuple Treaty, proposed by England, under which a five-power European naval force would police the African slave trade. Cass feared that the treaty would violate American maritime rights. However, Secretary of State Daniel Webster accused Cass of being politically motivated, a charge that led Cass to resign the French ministerial post in 1842.

Back home Cass was hailed as a hero for his stand against the treaty and mentioned for the Democratic presidential nomination in 1844. However, James K. Polk received the party's endorsement, and Cass was elected U. S. senator from Michigan.

Strongly nationalistic and suspicious of British policy, Cass opposed concessions to Britain in the Oregon boundary dispute of the mid-1840's, but as administration spokesman he supported Polk's Mexican War policy. The acquisition of territories as a result of the war brought into full focus the slavery issue, in which Cass was deeply involved for the rest of his political life. His doctrine of popular sovereignty, upholding the right of territorial settlers to decide for themselves if slavery would be permitted, proved acceptable to the Democratic party and won him the presidential nomination in 1848. However, dissident Democrats and abolitionists formed the Free-Soil party, which nominated Martin Van Buren and cut into Democratic strength, assuring the election of the Whig candidate, Zachary Taylor.

Returning to the Senate, Cass supported the Compromise of 1850, but compromise on slavery cost him the confidence of the South and won him the appellation "doughface" (for failing to oppose slavery) in the North. The success of the new Republican party in 1856, particularly in the Old Northwest, which had been his political stronghold, amounted to a repudiation of Cass. In 1857, Michigan refused to return him to the Senate.

President Buchanan compensated Cass for the loss of his seat by naming him secretary of state, but Cass became alarmed at the President's refusal to take a firm stand against secession. When Buchanan failed to reinforce Fort Sumter, Cass resigned in protest in December 1860. He retired to Detroit, where he died on June 16, 1866.

FRANK B. WOODFORD
Author of "Lewis Cass: The Last Jeffersonian"

CASSANDER, kə-san'dər (c. 350–297 B.C.), was a leading statesman during the breakup of the empire of Alexander the Great. His father, Antipater, served as viceroy of Macedonia and Greece during Alexander's conquest of the Persian Empire, and, after Alexander's death (323), as regent of the entire Alexandrian empire from 321 to 319. On his death Antipater left the regency to the general Polyperchon; but the other marshals of Alexander refused to accept this appointment, and Cassander gained their support, enabling him to take Athens in 317 and then Macedonia.

In 316, Cassander seized and executed Olympias, mother of Alexander. He also took into custody Alexander's widow Roxane and infant son Alexander IV, both of whom he put to death in 310. Thereafter his aim was to hold the Macedonian homeland and Greece. His major action was to oppose the ambitious general Antigonus I, who was killed in 301 at the Battle of Ipsus in Phrygia. Cassander, like his allies Ptolemy, Seleucus, and Lysimachus, took the title of king in 305.

Cassander was disliked by many Macedonians for wiping out the Macedonian royal house. However, he remained master of the country and at times expanded its domains to the Adriatic coast. In Greece, where his power was exercised by garrisons and through the support of local despots, he was also unpopular. The son of Antigonus, Demetrius I Poliorcetes, took most of Greece from Cassander in 307 and supplanted his three sons in Macedonia after his death in 297. Personally, Cassander was a cultured man. He rebuilt Thebes and founded two new cities, Cassandreia and Thessalonica.

CHESTER G. STARR, *University of Illinois*

CASSANDRA, kə-san'drə, in Greek legend, was the daughter of Priam, King of Troy, and Hecuba. She was loved by the god Apollo, who endowed her with the gift of prophecy; but when she resisted his advances, Apollo ordained that her prophecies would never be believed.

Cassandra continually foretold the downfall of Troy and warned repeatedly against the dangers of the Trojan horse, but her pleadings were in vain. When Troy was taken by the Greeks, Cassandra took refuge in a temple of Athena (Minerva). There, however, the Greek warrior Ajax found her at the altar and raped her. Cassandra was bound and taken away to be made a slave. After the fall of Troy, in the division of the spoils, Cassandra was awarded to Agamemnon, who took her as his slave and mistress to Mycenae, his kingdom.

During Agamemnon's absence from Mycenae, his wife, Clytemnestra, had been unfaithful to him. Upon her husband's return, Clytemnestra and her lover, Aegisthus, plotted to kill him. Cassandra warned Agamemnon, but as usual her warning went unheeded. Agamemnon was murdered in his bath before a banquet celebrating his return, and Cassandra was killed shortly after.

Cassandra was also known as *Priameis,* for her father, and *Alexandra,* for her brother Paris, or Alexander. The rape of Cassandra by Ajax was regarded as an infamous atrocity by the ancients and was the subject of sculpture and poetry. Her story is told in Aeschylus' *Agamemnon* and Euripides' *Trojan Women,* and she also appears in Homer's *Iliad,* Virgil's *Aeneid,* and Seneca's *Agamemnon.*

CASSANDRE, kä-sänd'rə, **A. M.** (1901–), French poster artist and scenarist, who revolutionized French poster design in the early 20th century. He was born Adolphe Jean Marie Mouron in Kharkov, Russia, on Jan. 24, 1901, and went to Paris in 1915. His posters were first published in 1922, and within a year he had won fame with his poster *Le bûcheron* (*The Woodcutter*), executed for a cabinetmaker. Cassandre's posters, which advertised wines, magazines, travel, festivals, and sports, among other things, are simple and forceful. They wittily combine modern typography with techniques drawn from photography, cinema, and contemporary painting.

CASSATT, kə-sat', **Alexander Johnston** (1839–1906), American railroad executive, who is credited with planning the extension of the Pennsylvania Railroad tunnel and terminal facilities into New York City. He was born in Pittsburgh, Pa., on Dec. 8, 1839. A civil engineer, he spent most of his life in important posts with the Pennsylvania Railroad, rising to president of the road in 1899. He was credited with introducing many advances in traffic and operating conditions, extending the system's lines, and increasing its income.

Cassatt was a key figure in a battle with powerful shippers over rebates, and he helped develop a common policy with other railroads to prevent such special privileges. He supported the Interstate Commerce Commission and legislation to strengthen its powers during the administration of President Theodore Roosevelt. Mary Cassatt, the painter, was his sister. Cassatt died in Philadelphia on Dec. 28, 1906.

COURTNEY ROBERT HALL
Queens College, City University of New York

CASSATT, kə-sat', **Mary** (1844–1926), American painter, who was a leading member of the impressionist school. Working in oils, pastels, and prints, she generally portrayed women and children engaged in the common activities of daily life. Her art, always regarded highly in France, where she spent most of her life, has received increasing recognition in the United States.

Early Years. Mary Cassatt was born in Allegheny City, Pa., on May 22, 1844. In 1851 she went with her family to Paris, and during their five-year residence there she became acquainted with the great art in the museums of Europe. When the Cassatts returned to the United States they settled in Philadelphia, where Mary studied at the Pennsylvania Academy of the Fine Arts from 1861 to 1865. However, she found the curriculum of drawing from plaster casts and copying third-rate old masters uninspiring, and she convinced her father that she should go abroad. For most of the years 1866–1873 she traveled and studied in France, Italy, Spain, and Belgium. In Italy she was especially impressed by the work of Correggio; in Belgium, by Rubens.

Mary Cassatt's genius matured slowly, and her earliest paintings are undistinguished. But in Spain, about 1873, she introduced broad brush strokes, a good deal of color, and fresh, lively effects into her work, to produce her first paintings of real merit.

Impressionist Period. For five successive years, beginning in 1872, Mary Cassatt exhibited in the annual Paris Salon. Her *Portrait of Ida,* exhibited in 1877, so impressed Edgar Degas that he invited her to show with the impressionists. She first joined that group in 1879 at their fourth exhibition, with *The Cup of Tea* (1879; Metropolitan Museum of Art, New York). She remained a faithful member of the impressionists, and her work was seen in their fifth, sixth, and eighth shows. (Following Degas' lead, she refused to enter the seventh because of dissension within the group.) Durand-Ruel Galleries in Paris presented her first one-man show in 1891, and a second, larger show followed in 1893.

The best of Mary Cassatt's impressionist paintings were done in 1879–1880. They include, in addition to *The Cup of Tea, La Loge* (William Coxe Wright Collection, St. David's, Pa.) and *Woman and Child Driving* (Philadelphia Museum of Art). These works, painted in rich, luminous tones with a subtle suffusion of light, show the influence of Degas in the unusual thrusts of the figures and in the way that portions of the composition are cut off by the edge of the canvas.

Later Paintings. About 1882, Mary Cassatt reached a stylistic turning point in the distinguished portrait of her mother, entitled *Reading "Le Figaro"* (Mrs. Eric de Spoelberch Collection, Haverford, Pa.). Painted in broad, fluid brush strokes, the figure is solidly conceived and given great psychological intensity. The *Lady at the Tea Table* (1885; Metropolitan Museum of Art) shows a further change in style. The face is delicately modeled and the figure is more of a silhouette, emphasizing outline rather than solid form. The paintings of the late 1880's achieve firm, well-rounded form by the use of fine parallel strokes, as in *Girl Arranging Her Hair* (1886; National Gallery of Art, Washington, D. C.).

A great exhibition of Japanese prints in Paris in 1890 stimulated Mary Cassatt's interest in the style of that art form. For example, *The Bath* (1891–1892; The Art Institute of Chicago) shows the Japanese influence in the tipped-up plane of the floor and in the interplay of patterns.

Prints and Pastels. Mary Cassatt's prints, which total about 200, are of the highest distinction. About half of them are drypoints, and most of the others are soft ground etchings, aquatints, or a combination of the two. The culmination of her work in printmaking is a series of 10 color aquatints done in 1891 that show a strong Japanese influence.

Mary Cassatt had a great interest in 18th century French pastels and frequently used pastels herself. This medium tempted her to be more adventurous in color, an effect that carried over into her late paintings, such as *After The Bath* (1901; Cleveland Museum of Art).

Last Years. After 1900, failing eyesight caused by cataracts forced a coarse and relatively formless style on Mary Cassatt's work. She first abandoned printmaking and after 1914 was no longer able to paint. Blindness and her sadness about World War I darkened her last years both physically and spiritually. She died on June 14, 1926, at her beloved country house, Château de Beaufresne, near Paris.

FREDERICK A. SWEET
Author of "Miss Mary Cassatt, Impressionist from Pennsylvania"

Further Reading: Breeskin, Adelyn D., *The Graphic Work of Mary Cassatt, a Catalogue Raisonné* (New York 1948); Rewald, John, *The History of Impressionism* (New York 1961); Sweet, Frederick A., *Miss Mary Cassatt, Impressionist from Pennsylvania* (Norman, Okla., 1966); Watson, Forbes, *Mary Cassatt* (New York 1932).

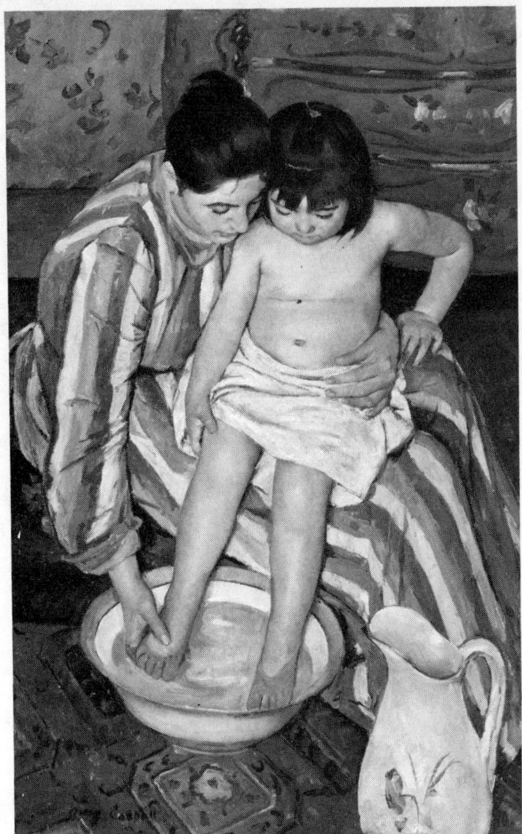

ART INSTITUTE OF CHICAGO—THE A. WALLER FUND

Mary Cassatt's *The Bath*, 1891–1892

CASSAVA, ka-sä'və, is the common name for a starch-producing plant, *Manihot esculenta,* native to South America. A member of the spurge family (Euphorbiaceae), cassava is also known as manioc, mandioca, yuca, and tapioca plant. Because it is an important source of starch, the cassava is of major economic importance in the tropics and is one of the great root crops of the world.

The cassava is a shrubby perennial, about 9 feet (2.5 meters) high, with deeply lobed leaves, rather inconspicuous staminate (male) and pistillate (female) flowers on the same plant, and clusters of cylindrical roots at the base of the stem. The roots, which are the source of the cassava starch, are quite large, reaching a length of 3 feet (1 meter) each and a total weight of more than 20 pounds (9 kgs) per plant. The yield of starch from a cassava crop can be very high. One acre of cassava is capable of producing 10 tons (9 metric tons) or more of starch.

The many varieties of *M. esculenta* under cultivation throughout the tropics are usually grouped into bitter cassavas and sweet cassavas, depending upon the amounts of poisonous hydrocyanic (prussic) acid present in the milky root sap. Though the actual quantities of hydrocyanic acid in the roots vary with the variety and the season, those cassavas classified as bitter are poisonous if eaten raw. To remove the hydrocyanic acid, the cassava roots are grated or otherwise macerated, squeezed in a bag or other container to force out most of the sap, and then heated to expel the remainder. This process produces a coarse meal known as farinha. Farinha may be eaten dry or baked into bread.

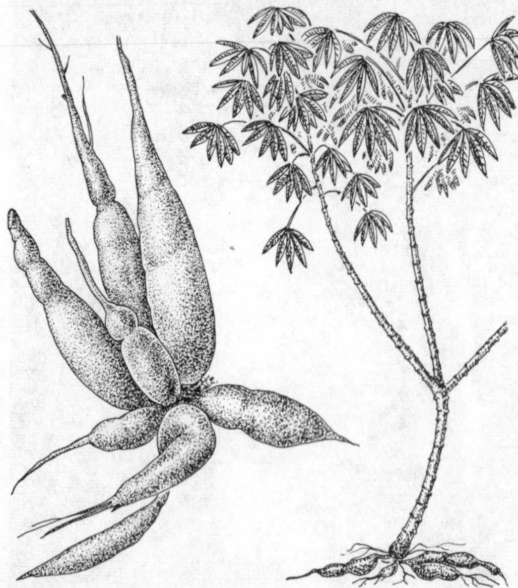

THE CASSAVA PLANT (*right*) has palmate leaves; at the left are shown the plant's fleshy edible rootstocks.

Cassava roots also supply tapioca, a preparation of cassava starch used for a bread or as a thickening in puddings, soups, and other dishes. The production of tapioca is similar to that of farinha, with the addition of soaking the meal in water, straining it to a finer consistency, and heating it over a gentle flame to cause the tapioca flour to round up into little balls.

Cassareep, a flavoring agent used in sauces and spicy stews, is made by boiling cassava juice, which drives off the poison and thickens the liquid into a syrup. Cassava juice, starch, and bread all can be fermented into alcoholic drinks.

The sweet cassavas, which contain negligible amounts of hydrocyanic acid, can safely be eaten raw, but they are usually boiled and served as a table vegetable. Another species, *M. dulcis,* is also grown as a sweet cassava, but it has smaller roots and is generally not as productive as *M. esculenta.* Its roots are sometimes used as food for livestock.

DONALD WYMAN
The Arnold Arboretum, Harvard University

CASSEL, käs′səl, **Gustav** (1866–1945), Swedish economist, who in the 1920's developed the purchasing power parity theory of foreign exchange rates. This theory, which played an important role in the monetary reforms of the period, held that foreign exchange rates are determined mainly by the relative purchasing power of one currency in terms of another. It displaced older less satisfactory explanations of exchange rate fluctuations.

Karl Gustav Cassel was born in Stockholm on Oct. 20, 1866. After studying in Germany and England, he was appointed in 1907 to the chair of political economy at the University of Stockholm. He believed in the efficacy of free market economies, opposed arbitrary controls of the pricing process, and deplored tendencies toward economic planning. He favored a return to the gold standard in the 1920's, supported efforts to reduce trade barriers, and pointed to the harmful economic effects of efforts then being made to collect war debts and reparations. He explained the deflation of the 1930's as the result of a growing scarcity of gold and was convinced of a close connection between gold production and prices.

Cassel's more important works are *The Nature and Necessity of Interest* (1903), *World's Monetary Problems* (1921), *Money and Foreign Exchange After 1914* (1922), *The Theory of Social Economy* (1923), *Postwar Monetary Stabilization* (1928), *The Crisis in the World's Monetary System* (1932), *On Quantitative Thinking in Economics* (1935), and *The Downfall of the Gold Standard* (1936). He died in Stockholm on Jan. 14, 1945.

BENJAMIN HAGGOTT BECKHART
Columbia University

CASSELL, kas′əl, **John** (1817–1865), English publisher, whose name is perpetuated in the publishing house of Cassell & Co. He was born in Manchester on Jan. 23, 1817. As a young man he was deeply committed to the temperance movement, and by 1847, aided by funds from his wife, he had set up an extensive tea and coffee business, partly to provide the poor with low-priced, harmless beverages.

About 1850, when he turned to publishing as well, he also had the working classes in mind. His early periodicals included *The Working Man's Friend, Cassell's Popular Educator,* and *Cassell's Family Paper.* In addition to illustrated editions of standard works such as *Robinson Crusoe* and *Gulliver's Travels,* he published other popular and educational books—often at a loss.

Cassell's fight against newspaper taxes made enemies of his creditors. By 1855 he had nothing left but his name. Two printers, Thomas Dixon Galpin and George William Petter, made him a partner in their publishing firm, but his authority was minimal. The firm, Cassell, Galpin & Petter, later became Cassell & Co. Cassell died in London on April 2, 1865.

HAROLD R. JOLLIFFE
Michigan State University

Further Reading: Nowell-Smith, Simon H., *The House of Cassell* (London 1958).

CASSIA, kash′ə, is a genus of wild flowers, popularly known as senna, belonging to the pea family. Many species of *Cassia* are cultivated as ornamentals and some for the cathartic properties of the leaves. Temperate zone members of the genus are herbs and shrubs, but some tropical members are trees. The irregular flowers are

Apple blossom cassia (*Cassia javanica*)

J. J. SMITH

Cassia fistula, known as "Shower of Gold."

variously colored and resemble slightly those of common peas and beans. The many-seeded pods are flat or cylindrical; some have cross partitions between the seeds. Even when not in bloom, cassias are attractive for their foliage; the pinnately compound leaves have a fernlike appearance. *C. nictitans* and *C. fasciculata* are annuals native to the United States. They are known as "sensitive peas" because their leaflets tend to fold together if disturbed by wind or touch.

JOAN E. RAHN
Lake Forest College, Ill.

CASSIA BARK, kash'ə, is the dark reddish brown bark of the Chinese cinnamon tree (*Cinnamonum cassia*). Cassia bark, also known as *Chinese cinnamon,* contains an aromatic oil similar to cinnamon oil and is sometimes used to scent soaps and perfumes and to flavor candies and medicines.

Most cassia bark is grown in southern China and Indonesia, where it is stripped off young trees and allowed to dry. The young dried fruits of the trees, called cassia buds, are sometimes used for the same purposes as cassia bark.

CASSIANUS, kas-ē-ā'nəs, **Johannes** (360?–?432), ecclesiastical writer and a founder of Western monasticism. John Cassian, as his name has been Anglicized, first settled in a monastery in Bethlehem, and later was drawn to the more rigorous life of the Egyptian monks. At Constantinople he was ordained deacon, and after having been made priest, he established two monastic foundations in Marseille about 415.

Between 419 and 426 he wrote his influential monastic work *De institutis coenobium* (*Of the Rules of Monks,* 12 books), the first four books of which describe the eight principal vices against the spiritual life, adding dejection to the usual seven. Between 426 and 428 he wrote the controversial *Collationes patrum* (*Discourses of the Fathers,* 24 books), which described the spiritual combat man must endure in his progress toward purity of heart.

On the principal question of grace, Cassianus tried to establish a middle ground between the teaching of St. Augustine and that of Pelagius. He attacked Augustine's *De correptione et gratia* (*Of Reproach and Grace*) for allowing no room for man's free will. He insisted that even after the fall there remained in every soul "some seeds of goodness" that must be "quickened by the assistance of God."

Whereas St. Augustine considered the soul completely dead as a result of the fall, and Pelagius regarded the soul as totally unaffected by it, Cassianus considered the soul to be sick and in need of help. He is therefore considered to be the father of Semi-Pelagianism, which, after much controversy, was formally condemned in 529 at the Council of Orange. St. Benedict, however, referred to the *Collationes* as *speculum monasticum* ("a monastic mirror"), and ordered it read daily in his new monasteries. In 430, Cassianus wrote *De incarnatione Domini contra Nestorium,* 7 books). This was one of the earliest attacks against Nestorianism. Cassianus died between 432 and 435.

JAMES A. WEISHEIPL, O. P.
Medieval Institute, University of Toronto

CASSILL, kas'il, **Ronald Verlin** (1919–), American author and teacher. He was born in Cedar Falls, Iowa, on May 17, 1919, and was educated at the University of Iowa, where he later became writer-in-residence at the Writers' Workshop. Cassill began his career as a painter but soon turned to writing; his first novel, *Eagle on the Coin* (1950), describes a Negro's unsuccessful campaign for a seat on a small town's school board. Cassill later published more than a dozen novels and scores of short stories, many of which appeared in leading journals. His short-story collections include *The Father* (1965) and *A Happy Marriage* (1966). He also published *Writing Fiction* (1963), a manual for authors.

CASSINI, kȧ-sē-nē', an Italian-French family of astronomers, who for four generations dominated the Paris Observatory.

GIOVANNI DOMENICO CASSINI was born in Perinaldo, near Nice, on June 8, 1625. He discovered four of Saturn's satellites, the gap in its ring, and the zodiacal light. While serving as professor of astronomy at the University of Bologna, he proved that Jupiter rotates, observed the shadows cast on that planet by its satellites, and published the first reliable tables of their motions. He was consequently invited to join the Academy of Sciences in France. Calling himself Jean Dominique, Cassini became the dominant personality in the newly established Paris Observatory.

In 1675, Cassini found that Saturn's ring is double; the dark cleavage between the two concentric portions is still known as the "Cassini division." He correctly surmised that the ring is not continuous, but consists of a swarm of tiny satellites, each pursuing its own independent orbit in nearly the same plane.

Cassini obtained a fairly precise measurement of the period in which Mars rotates and compared that planet's white polar caps with the corresponding icy regions on the earth. From observations of Mars made simultaneously on both sides of the Atlantic Ocean, he was able to derive a vastly improved estimate of the distance from the sun to the earth.

Cassini's map of the surface features of the moon remained unsurpassed for more than a century. He was the first to focus attention on the zodiacal light, visible after twilight on a clear moonless evening; it has been explained as a faint beam of sunlight reflected from innumerable tiny particles in the vicinity of the sun. The curve traced by a point moving so that the product of its distances from two fixed points is a constant is called the "Cassinian oval."

He became a French citizen, and thereafter his family were all of that nationality. He died in Paris on Sept. 11, 1712.

Jacques Cassini was born in Paris on Feb. 8, 1677, the son of Jean Dominique. He proved that the so-called fixed stars do not really occupy fixed positions in the heavens. He chose Arcturus, which had been observed from South America more than half a century earlier. Instituting a comparison with similar observations made at Paris in his own time, he showed that Arcturus had shifted southward in the interval. By contrast, another star in the same region of the sky had undergone no such displacement. Therefore, Arcturus has a motion of its own in space, that is, its own proper motion.

He participated in the work of a commission appointed by the Academy of Sciences to measure the speed of sound. The results attained were a marked improvement over previous determinations, particularly in ascertaining the effects of wind velocity as well as atmospheric pressure and temperature.

Jacques Cassini continued the effort of his father, Jean Dominique, to discover the period in which Venus rotates around its axis. Because this planet's surface markings are elusive, he failed to solve this baffling problem. He died in Thury, near Paris, on April 18, 1756.

César François Cassini de Thury was born in Paris on June 17, 1714. He was the first member of the family to receive the official title of director of the Paris Observatory, where his father Jacques and grandfather Jean Dominique had been so prominent. He journeyed to Vienna as a member of the international network of observers cooperatively studying the transit of Venus across the sun's disk in 1761. Such an event, paired with a second transit eight years later, occurs at intervals more than a century apart. Only five transits of Venus have been observed thus far. He died in Paris on Sept. 4, 1784.

Jacques Dominique Cassini was born in Paris on June 30, 1748, the son of Cassini de Thury. He succeeded his father as director and completed the topographical map of France which his father had begun. He published *Voyage to California,* an account of a voyage undertaken to observe the 1769 transit of Venus. He died in Thury on Oct. 18, 1845.

Edward Rosen, *The City College, New York*

CASSINI, kə-sē′nē, **Oleg** (1913–), American fashion designer. He was born in Paris on April 11, 1913, a son of Count Alexander Loiewski-Cassini of Russia. After the Russian Revolution his family eventually settled in Florence, Italy, where his mother opened a couture salon. Cassini attended the Accademia di Belle Arti in Florence, graduating in 1934; the next year he opened his own salon in Rome.

In 1936, Cassini moved to New York City and four years later to Hollywood to design costumes for Paramount Pictures. He interrupted his career in 1942 to volunteer for military service. In 1950 he opened a wholesale dress firm, Oleg Cassini, Inc., in New York City and soon became noted for his elegant designs. In the 1960's he served as couturier for Mrs. John F. Kennedy. He also began designing men's clothes.

CASSINIAN OVAL, kə-sin′ē-ən ō′vəl, the locus of a point the product of whose distances from two fixed points is constant. Also called *Cassian oval* and named for the Italian astronomer Giovanni Cassini, the curve varies in shape as the constant product and the distance between the fixed points are varied, and may break up into two separate but symmetrical parts. Bernoulli's lemniscate is a special case. If the distance between the two fixed points is $2a$ and the constant product is m^2, then the equations of the curve are

$$(x^2 + y^2 + a^2)^2 - 4a^2x^2 = m^4$$

and

$$r^4 - 2a^2r^2 \cos \theta + a^4 = m^4$$

in Cartesian and polar coordinates, respectively.

CASSINO, käs-sē′nō, is a town and commune in the southern part of the Latium region of central Italy, 87 miles (140 km) southeast of Rome. It was an ancient settlement of the Volsci tribe and was known in Latin as Casinum. Because of its location on the inland road from Rome to Naples, Cassino has played an important part in the area throughout its long history.

The pre-Roman and Roman settlement was less than a mile (less than 2 km) southwest of the modern town, on the flanks of Monte Cassino. There, the remains of a Roman amphitheater and of a theater have been excavated, as well as parts of a Roman road and of the town walls. South of the town, the ruins of a bath, built during Roman times, may be seen.

World War II. When, in the fall of 1943, the Allied armies, having taken Naples, began their advance northwest toward Rome, their path was blocked by a series of rivers flowing at right angles to their drive, and by the topography of the region. Much of the land of the area is rugged, and the armies had to follow the main roads. After battles fought on the Volturno River, the way to Rome was open, except for such narrow passages as the one at Cassino. Here, where the Rapido and Liri rivers meet, the Germans made their stand. When the battle was over, in the spring of 1944, both the town of Cassino and the ancient Benedictine monastery that stood on the brow of Monte Cassino, 1500 feet (457 meters) above the town, had been destroyed.

The monastery of Monte Cassino was later completely rebuilt, as was the city of Cassino. The memory of the battle is kept alive by the Polish, British, and American military cemeteries. (See also Monte Cassino.) Population: (1961) of the town, 11,369; (1966 est.) of the commune, 24,332.

George Kish, *University of Michigan*

CASSINO, a card game. See Casino.

CASSIODORUS, kas-ē-ō-dô′rəs (c. 490–c. 580), Roman official under the Ostrogothic kings and important literary figure of the 6th century A. D. Cassiodorus (Flavius Magnus Aurelius Cassiodorus Senator) was born in Scylacium (modern Squillace) in southern Italy no later than 490 A. D. Of noble Roman ancestry, he followed the path of his grandfather and father to high public office. In early youth Cassiodorus was appointed quaestor when his oratorical and literary talents were brought to the attention of the illiterate Ostrogothic emperor, Theodoric. In this office he attended to the diplomatic, legal, and judicial correspondence that went out over the emperor's signature.

Honored with the consulship in 514, Cassiodorus subsequently became Theodoric's master of the offices (chief of the imperial civil service). In 533, after the death of Theodoric, he was elevated to the post of praetorian prefect at the apex of the judiciary. With the decline of the Ostrogoths and the occupation of Italy by the armies of the Byzantine emperor Justinian I, Cassiodorus retired from public life just before 540 in order to found and preside over a new monastery called Vivarium, which was located on his family estate in southern Italy. He lived to be more than 90 years old; 580 A. D. would therefore be the approximate date of his death.

Works. Most of what is known about Cassiodorus is derived from his own voluminous writings. He was a trained rhetorician (not exactly a recommendation in this period), and his style has been condemned as being bad and consisting of "sentence after sentence of verbose and flaccid Latin." Moreover, like many Westerners of this time, his knowledge of Greek was slight and demonstrably inadequate.

As a historian, Cassiodorus composed a *Chronicle* and a *History of the Goths.* The former, which has been preserved, covers the history of mankind from Adam to 519 A. D. in brief annalistic form. Based on the chronicles of the Christian scholars Eusebius and Prosper, it was carelessly done and is completely without merit. The Gothic history in 12 books was a much more pretentious work, but it has not survived. It is known today only in the condensation, presumably inferior to the original, that was made later by Jordanes.

Before retiring to his monastery, Cassiodorus wrote a short philosophic treatise, *On the Soul,* and edited what is probably his most important and certainly his most interesting work, the *Variae.* Again arranged in 12 books, this is a collection of letters written by Cassiodorus himself in the names of Theodoric and other Ostrogothic rulers. It also contains certain form letters of appointment describing the duties of the office to be held.

In the second half of his life Cassiodorus devoted himself to a new kind of literary activity and became the "father of literary monasticism." He and his monks occupied themselves with copying, and thus perpetuating, manuscripts, both Christian and pagan. Cassiodorus also wrote commentaries on the Psalms and on the letters of the apostles as well as a 2-part treatise on the Scriptures and the liberal arts, including grammar, rhetoric, logic, and mathematics. He was past 90 when he put together his last little book, *De orthographia.* This was a treatise on spelling, compiled from the works of 12 earlier grammarians, which Cassiodorus prepared at the request of his monastic scribes.

Tom B. Jones, *University of Minnesota*

CASSIOPEIA, kas-ē-ə-pē′ə, in Greek legend was the wife of Cepheus, king of Ethiopia, and the mother of Andromeda. When Cassiopeia boasted that she was more beautiful than the Nereids (water nymphs), the nymphs became enraged and called for their father, Poseidon (Neptune), to exact vengeance. Poseidon thereupon laid waste the kingdom by a great flood and sent a sea monster to ravage the land. When an oracle declared that the country could be saved only by the sacrifice of Andromeda, her father consented and had her bound to a rock near the sea, where the monster could devour her. Perseus killed the monster and was granted permission from Cepheus to marry Andromeda. Cepheus' brother Phineus, who appeared at the wedding feast, had been betrothed to Andromeda. With several of his followers he would have attacked Perseus, but Perseus put before them the head of the Gorgon Medusa, the sight of which turned them to stone. After Cassiopeia's death she was made a constellation in the Northern Hemisphere.

CASSIOPEIA, kas-ē-ə-pē′ə, in astronomy, is an autumn constellation of the Northern Hemisphere. It is named for the Ethiopian queen in Greek legend who was the wife of Cepheus and mother of Andromeda.

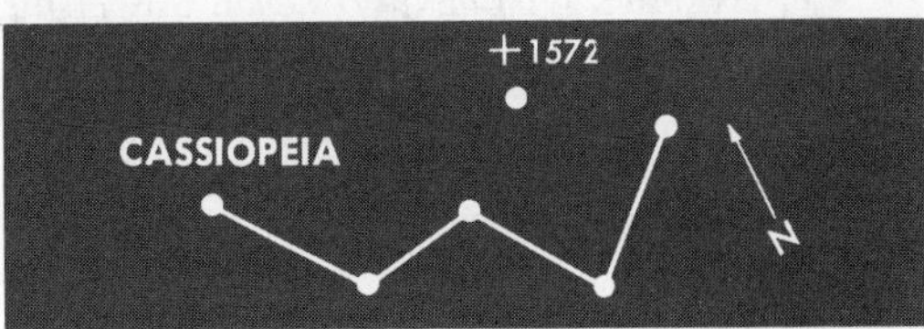

The constellation straddles the Milky Way on the opposite side of the north celestial pole from Ursa Major. Cassiopeia is easily identified by the five 2d- and 3d-magnitude stars it contains, which form a straggling letter W—also known as Cassiopeia's Chair—when the constellation is observed below the pole. In 1572 a famous nova appeared in Cassiopeia and was studied by Tycho Brahe, the Danish astronomer; at its maximum the nova could be seen during the day. See also Constellation.

CASSIRER, kä-sē′rər, **Ernst** (1874–1945), German philosopher, who was an important exponent of neo-Kantian philosophy and was particularly concerned with the function of symbols in human knowledge. He was born at Breslau, Lower Silesia, on July 28, 1874, and studied at the universities of Berlin, Leipzig, and Heidelberg, and at Marburg, where he was a follower of Hermann Cohen's neo-Kantianism. Cassirer became a professor at the University of Hamburg in 1919 and rector in 1930. A Jew, he resigned his post in 1933 and fled Nazi persecution. He taught at Oxford in England, at Göteborg in Sweden, and at Yale and Columbia in the United States. He died in New York City, on April 13, 1945.

Thought and Works. Cassirer accepted Kant's categories of thought as man's way of understanding the universe and also accepted Kant's critical method. He held, however, in *Das Erkenntnisproblem in der Philosophie und Wissenschaft der neueren Zeit* (1906–1920; Eng. tr., *Problem of Knowledge: Philosophy, Science, and History Since Hegel,* 1950) and in *Substanzbegriff und Funktionsbegriff* (1910; Eng. tr., *Substance and Function,* 1923) that Kant's list of categories was incomplete and did not adequately explain the process of perception and that his critical method should be extended to domains of reality not encompassed by Newtonian physics.

Cassirer's major work, *Philosophie der symbolischen Formen* (1923–1927; Eng. tr., *Philosophy of Symbolic Forms,* 1953–1957), and two later works in English, *Essay on Man* (1944) and *Myth of the State* (1946), maintain that man structures his world through the symbolic forms of myth and language. Language especially is the means by which the manifold sense impressions are formed into objects of thought. Therefore, to ask what reality is apart from the forms inherent in language is absurd. Through his use of symbols, Cassirer continued, man is distinguished from animals and creates the peculiarly human phenomenon—culture. Cassirer also explored such aspects of culture as art, science, and historiography in terms of symbolic transformation of experience.

As an intellectual historian, he wrote *Individuum und Kosmos in der Philosophie der Renaissance* (1927; Eng. tr., *Individual and the Cosmos in Renaissance Philosophy*, 1964) and *Philosophie der Aufklärung* (1932; Eng. tr., *Philosophy of the Enlightenment*, 1951).

STEPHEN J. NOREN, *Wesleyan University*

CASSITERITE, kə-sit′ər-īt, a mineral tin dioxide, is the most important ore of tin. It is usually found in massive granular form, but often occurs in the form of crystals as well. Its transparent to translucent crystals are brittle, hard, and have a diamondlike to dull submetallic luster. They are red-brown to black, or rarely, yellowish to white. The mineral usually contains some amount of iron.

Although cassiterite is widespread, there are only a few sites where it is found in sufficient quantities to be mined profitably. The primary sources are in Indonesia, Malaysia, Bolivia, England, Nigeria, and the Congo (Kinshasa).

Composition, SiO_2; hardness, 6–7; specific gravity, 6.8–7.1; crystal system, tetragonal.

CASSIUS LONGINUS, kash′ē-əs lon-jī′nəs, **Gaius** (died 42 B. C.), Roman politician and general, who was the leading assassin of Julius Caesar. Shakespeare's often-quoted description of Cassius as a man with a "lean and hungry look" is based on Plutarch. It seems an apt summation; Cassius was of sour, grim disposition, his words laced with sarcasm and temper. He was frequently impatient with friends and ruthless with enemies. Late in life Cassius became a devotee of Epicurean philosophy, which emphasized simple pleasures and withdrawal from the active life. However, its effect on Cassius was to sharpen his principles and deepen his resolve for tyrannicide.

Military and Political Career. Cassius' first notable appearance in history came in 53 B. C. when he was quaestor, or chief financial assistant, to the commander Marcus Crassus in the ill-fated campaign against Parthia. After the disastrous defeat of the Romans at Carrhae in Mesopotamia, Cassius escaped (or deserted) with the surviving Roman troops and managed to reorganize successful resistance to the Parthians. In 51 he saved the Roman province of Syria from Parthian assault, thereby establishing his military reputation. In 49, Cassius was tribune in Rome when civil war erupted between Caesar and Pompey. The war split many families down the middle. A relative, Quintus Cassius, fled to Caesar and fought under him. But Gaius Cassius joined the forces of Pompey and served as a naval commander. Cassius was among several Pompeian lieutenants who surrendered following Caesar's victory over Pompey at Pharsalus in 48. Caesar could afford to be merciful and generous. Cassius received pardon and then honors befitting his rank. Caesar named him to the praetorship for 44.

But this served only to increase the resentment of the proud and bitter Cassius. He became chief organizer of the plot to assassinate Caesar. The conspiracy included not only ex-Pompeians but even friends of the dictator. Cassius brought unity to this scattered and disparate group by inducing his brother-in-law, the much-admired Marcus Brutus, to join the conspiracy.

Post-Assassination Campaign. Caesar was slain in March 44, but his lieutenant Mark Antony was spared. Brutus had overridden Cassius' insistence than Antony too be killed. This proved to be a fatal mistake. In the succeeding months Antony consolidated his position as the new leader of the Caesarian faction. The conspirators found their support dwindling in Italy and went abroad, Brutus to Macedonia, Cassius to Syria. Cassius still had friends in the East and was able to gather forces and raise money. In 43 he defeated Dolabella, the commander sent to the East by Antony. Cassius expanded his forces with Dolabella's troops. By 42, Cassius had pooled his resources with those of Brutus, who had been equally successful in Macedonia. Together they had at their disposal 19 legions and a multitude of forces from client princes all over the East. The armies of the West, however, had gathered under Antony and Caesar's heir Octavian; 28 legions crossed the Adriatic to face the assassins at Philippi in Thrace in October 42. The battle was inconclusive. Brutus fared better than Cassius, but Cassius despaired. A defect in his eyesight, so it is reported, led him to the mistaken belief that Brutus too had been defeated; as a result Cassius committed suicide. In a subsequent battle, three weeks later, Brutus was indeed beaten and also took his own life. Any hopes of restoring the republic had vanished. But Cassius' memory lived on and his name became synonymous with tyrannicide and republicanism.

The Jurist Cassius. The most famous of Cassius' descendants was also named Gaius Cassius Longinus. A prominent and respected jurist, he reached the consulship in 30 A. D. He inherited his ancestor's severity, rigor, and devotion to Roman traditions. From 45 to 49 he served as governor of Syria.

The emperor Nero, having barely escaped a major attempt on his life in 65, began to crack down on enemies and potential enemies. Cassius' reverence for his ancestor and his general attitude made the emperor suspicious of him, and Nero exiled the legal scholar to Sardinia. But Cassius survived, to be recalled later by the emperor Vespasian, during whose reign (69–79) he died peacefully in Rome. Cassius' writings on Roman law were eventually incorporated into the Justinian code.

ERICH S. GRUEN
University of California at Berkeley

CASSIVELLAUNUS, kas-i-və-lô′nəs, the first British historical personality, led the resistance to Julius Caesar's second invasion of Britain (54 B. C.). He seems to have been king of the Catuvellauni, a Belgic tribe settled a few miles north of London. He had been expanding his power by aggression against surrounding tribes, but the danger of the invasion led to temporary unity against the Romans. Following a defeat in Kent, Cassivellaunus adopted a "scorched earth" policy. The mobility of his 4,000 chariots permitted guerrilla tactics that caused Caesar considerable difficulty. But once across the Thames, Caesar found friends among the Trinovantes of

Essex, who had suffered from Cassivellaunus. The latter's headquarters (perhaps at Wheathampstead) were located and captured, and the king was forced to make peace, pay tribute, and respect the Trinovantes. Though Caesar never completed the subjection of Britain, the episode inaugurated a century of political and commercial contacts with Rome. The dynasty of Cassivellaunus became the chief power in Belgic Britain.

S. S. FRERE, *Oxford University Author of "Britannia"*

CASSOCK, kas'ək, a close-fitting robe with long sleeves, worn by priests, clergy, or laymen when taking part in religious ceremonies. In Latin countries it may also be the ordinary dress of the priest. The color and trim of the cassock vary with ecclesiastical degree. In the Roman Catholic church the pope wears white; cardinals wear scarlet, and archbishops and bishops wear purple cassocks. For everyday use black cassocks trimmed with red or scarlet are worn by the hierarchy, including monsignors, while ordinary clergy wear black untrimmed cassocks. In the Anglican Church black is usually worn by all orders of clergy. See also COSTUME, ECCLESIASTICAL.

CASSOLA, kä-sō'lä, **Carlo** (1917–), Italian author. He was born in Rome on March 17, 1917. He began writing during World War II, and his works reflect his particular interest in the Fascist years in Italy and postwar sociopolitical problems. Cassola's most important nonfictional work, *I minatori della Maremma* (1956), is a study of the conditions of Tuscan miners. His fictional works, realistic and regionalistic, include a collection of short stories, *Il taglio del bosco* (1959), and many novels, among them *Fausto e Anna* (1952) and *Un cuore arido* (1961).

CASSOWARY, kas'ə-wer-ē, any of three species of huge flightless birds that live in the rain forests of New Guinea, its neighboring islands, and northern Australia. They are heavy-bodied birds, from 52 to 65 inches (1.3–1.65 meters) long, and may weigh over 140 pounds (63 kg). Females are larger than males. In adult cassowaries, the coarse, hairlike, long, drooping plumage is black; in the immature birds the plumage is brown.

In all cassowaries the skin of the head and neck is bare and brightly colored in red, blue, purple, and yellow. In two species bright red wattles hang from the foreneck. Cassowaries have characteristic horny casques on their heads and short, narrow, strong bills. The wing feathers are reduced to long, bristlelike spines that curve along the sides. The legs are short, heavy, and well muscled, and the innermost of the three toes has a long sharp claw.

Cassowaries are dangerous and powerful birds that can kill even a full-grown man. They usually leap feet first on their adversary and attack with the sharp claw. Their casques, coarse plumage, and wing quills fend off the undergrowth of the rain forests. Cassowaries are somewhat gregarious outside of the breeding season, but they tend to be pugnacious. In spite of their size, they are hard birds to observe since they are rather shy and are most active at night. They run rapidly, up to 30 miles (48 km) per hour, with the head held forward, and they also swim well. They feed on seeds, berries, and insects.

NEW YORK ZOOLOGICAL SOCIETY

Cassowary

The cassowary's nest is a flat platform of sticks and leaves on the forest floor. The female lays three to eight green eggs. The male incubates the eggs and cares for the striped young.

Cassowaries make up the genus *Casuarius* in the family Casuaridae. With the Australian emus, they comprise the order Casuariiformes.

GEORGE E. WATSON, *Smithsonian Institution*

CAST IRON. See IRON—3. *Cast Iron.*

CASTAGNO, kä-stä'nyō, **Andrea del** (1421?–1457), Florentine painter, a leading master of the early Renaissance. Stylistically, Castagno has more in common with the sculptor Donatello, who greatly influenced his later works, than with other 15th century Florentine painters.

THE YOUTHFUL DAVID (with the slain Goliath), a painting on a leather shield by Andrea del Castagno.

NATIONAL GALLERY OF ART, WASHINGTON, D. C. (WIDENER COLLECTION, 1942)

Life. Castagno was born in the village of Castagno, near Florence. Most of his life was spent in Florence, where the refectory of the Convent of Sant'Apollonia, now a museum, houses many of his major surviving works. In 1440, Castagno painted some figures (now lost) of traitors hanging by their heels on the exterior of the Palazzo del Podestà, Florence, and thereby earned the nickname "Andrew of the Hanged men." A somewhat sinister reputation clung to him for the rest of his life, given support, perhaps, by the brooding intensity of such major works as the *Trinity* fresco (Santissima Annunziata, Florence) and the *Crucifixion*, refectory of Sant'Apollonia). Giorgio Vasari and other 16th century biographers accuse Castagno of murdering his colleague Domenico Veneziano, but research has proved that Domenico outlived Castagno, who died of the plague in Florence, on Aug. 19, 1457.

Work. Castagno's earliest surviving work, painted in 1442, is a fresco of the four Evangelists, with Zachariah and John flanking God the Father (Church of San Zaccaria, Venice). Perhaps his greatest achievement is the cycle of the *Passion of Christ* (1445–1450, refectory of Sant'Apollonia). Castagno's *Last Supper* (refectory of Sant'Apollonia), an immediate forerunner of Leonardo's definitive version of the same subject, is outstanding for its consistent perspective construction, which heightens the dramatic intensity of the painting.

About 1450, Castango executed a series of frescoes (now in the refectory of Sant'Apollonia) of nine exemplary men and women for the Villa Carducci. Another secular work is his equestrian portrait of the military leader Niccola da Tolentino (1456), which stands as a counterpart to Paolo Uccello's portrait of Sir John Hawkwood in the Florence Cathedral.

WAYNE DYNES, *Vassar College*

Further Reading: Richter, George M., *Andrea del Castagno* (Chicago 1943).

CASTALDI, käs-täl'dē, **Pamfilo** (1398–?1490), Italian physician, poet, printer, and humanist. According to the chronicler Bonifacio Pasole, he was born in Feltre on Sept. 22, 1398. He taught literature in Feltre, and it is known that he practiced medicine in Capodistria (now Koper, Yugoslavia).

Documents reveal that he was working in 1472 as a printer in Milan, where one of his pupils was Johann Fust. It has been asserted that Castaldi was the first to print from movable type; that he taught Fust the art; and that the latter imparted Castaldi's secret to Gutenberg. Though nothing is known of Castaldi's life after 1472, it is believed he died in Feltre in 1490.

CASTALIAN SPRING, kas-tā'lē-ən, in Greek mythology, a spring at the foot of Mt. Parnassus sacred to Apollo and the Muses. It is said to be named in honor of the nymph Castalia, daughter of Achelous, who threw herself into the spring and drowned when she was pursued by Apollo. In honor of the spring, the Muses often were known as the Castalides. In Roman times the poets invested the spring with the power to impart poetic inspiration.

CASTANETS, kas-tə-nets', are small, shell-shaped clappers made of hardwood, used for rhythmic accompaniment by Spanish dancers. They are called *castañuelas* in Castilian because of their resemblance to chestnuts (*castañas*). In Andalusia they are known as *palillos*.

The two clappers of castanets are hinged at one end by a string (*pulgarete*, from *pulgar*, "thumb"), which generally is looped around the player's thumb. However, some players, including the Gypsies of Andalusia, prefer to wear the string on the middle finger, which produces a dry "tak" sound that is especially effective in group dances. The dancer holds a pair in each hand, with the lower clapper resting in the palm of the hand. The pair held in the right hand is usually pitched higher (tenor) than that in the left hand (bass). The latter marks the beat, while the former makes trills and counterbeats. A skillful player can make crescendos and diminuendos, besides executing a variety of complex rhythms.

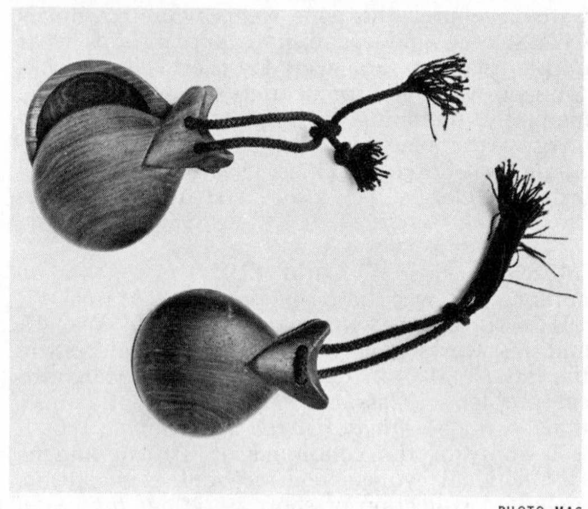

PHOTO MAS

Castanets

Instruments similar to castanets were known in ancient Egypt, Greece, and Rome and in medieval Europe. For the modern orchestra, the castanets have been mechanically adapted to facilitate manipulation by a percussionist.

GILBERT CHASE, *Tulane University*

Further Reading: Chase, Gilbert, *The Music of Spain*, 2d ed. (New York 1962); La Meri, *Spanish Dancing* (New York 1948).

CASTANHEDA, kesh-tə-nyā'thə, **Fernão Lopes de** (c. 1500–1559), Portuguese historian. He was born in Santarém, Portugal, the illegitimate son of Lopo Fernandes de Castanheda. He entered the Dominican order but abandoned the religious life in 1528 to accompany his father to Goa, India, where the elder Castanheda became a magistrate. Ferñao spent about 10 years in India, during which he began writing his monumental 8-volume *História do descobrimento e conquista da Índia pelos Portugueses* (1551–1556). On his return to Portugal he was given a post at the University of Coimbra. He died in Coimbra on March 23, 1559.

Castanheda is noted for his careful scholarship. His history, like those of João de Barros and Diogo do Couto, which it antedates, was useful to Luís Vaz de Camões for background material in writing the epic poem *The Lusiads*. Castenheda's history has been translated into various languages, including English.

GREGORY RABASSA, *Columbia University*

CASTE is a largely static, exclusive social class, membership in which is determined by birth and involves particular customary restrictions and privileges. The word derives from the Portuguese *casta*, meaning "breed," "race," or "kind," and was first used to denote the Hindu social classification on the Indian subcontinent. While this remains the basic connotation, the word "caste" is also used to describe in whole or in part social systems that emerged at various times in other parts of the world.

Generally castes are organized, with a chief and a council acting in concerted authority. Often united in the celebration of certain festivals, the members of a caste are further bound by common occupation and by common customs relating particularly to marriage, food, and questions of pollution by members of lower castes. Thus within a caste, food and drink are restricted, and only members of the same caste may eat together. The caste is, further, a collection of families or groups bearing a common name and quite often claiming common descent from a mythical ancestor, human or divine. Castes are almost invariably endogamous in the sense that a member of the large circle denoted by the common name may not marry outside that circle. Within the circle, however, there are usually a number of smaller circles, each of which is also endogamous.

Castes in India—*Organizational Structure Among the Hindus.* According to some estimates, there are more than 3,000 castes on the Indian subcontinent, greatly varying in size from a few score members to millions. Originally there were only four classifications, which derived from Hindu prescriptions, known as *varnas* (meaning "color" in Sanskrit). The first reference to the varnas is found in the Rig Veda, one of the oldest Indian classics, dating from about 3000 B. C. According to the Rig Veda, society is composed of five hierarchical divisions. The first four, the varnas, are the Brahmans, or priests and scholars; the Kshatriyas, or warriors and rulers; the Vaishyas, or merchants, artisans, and husbandmen; and the Sudras, or servants and slaves. The fifth division is composed of the outvarnas, or untouchables. The members of the first three varnas were said to be twice-born (*dwij*) because they underwent an initiation ceremony after birth. They alone had access to the sacred literature. The Sudras were divided into clean and unclean categories. Food and drink touched by the unclean Sudras were not acceptable to the first three varnas and the clean Sudras.

The varna complex still exists, in more or less modified form, and castes and subcastes still function within the framework of the varna. Each caste operates as a social unit with its own moral and ethical codes. Members may be expelled for violating these codes, and the caste also has the right to readmit expelled members into the fold. The social status of an individual is determined by his caste.

The rights and duties assigned to the different varnas and castes have undergone radical changes. Brahmans as religious authorities and lawgivers have ceased to exist, as have the warrior Kshatriyas. The Vaishyas have evolved a different economic pattern for themselves, and the position of the Sudras has changed considerably, particularly since India gained its independence in 1947. Of course, caste is and always has been subject to change within the system. Occasionally an exogamous group that had grown too large has broken up into smaller groups. Migration to a new settlement generally brings change in caste or subcaste. Change in caste attitudes also occurs as a result of change of occupation or adoption or abandonment of some religious or social customs. Nevertheless, there is no evidence that the caste system as a whole has lost its grip on Indian society. Changes in ritual and ideology, according to which members of a caste or a caste as a whole may gain social prestige, are changes within the system and do not extend beyond the system. The current trend is for each caste to organize itself for social, economic, and political purposes, and parliamentary election contests are being fought on the basis of such caste organizations.

Castes Among Other Groups in India. The caste system in India is not confined only to the Hindus. All important communities, including the Muslims, Christians, and Sikhs, have some sort of caste scheme. These schemes are patterned after the Hindu system, since most of these peoples originally came from Hindu stock. The large-scale conversions that have been going on for centuries have modified Indian caste society. Thus traditional Hindu commensal and connubial rituals and emphasis on inherited social status or rank, though generally rejected in the Islamic or Christian religious ethic, nevertheless operate on a social plane in these societies in India. In India, social rites and customs vary from region to region rather than from religion to religion. Among the Muslims, the Sayid, Sheikh, Pathan, and Momin, among others, function as exclusive, endogamous caste groups. The Christians are divided into a number of groups, including the Chaldean Syrians, Jacobite Syrians, Latin Catholics, Marthomite Syrians, Syrian Catholics, and Protestants. Each of these groups practices endogamy. Among the Catholics, the Syrian Romans and the Latin Romans generally do not intermarry. The Christians have not wholly discarded the idea of food restrictions and pollution by lower caste members. When lower caste Hindus were converted to Christianity a generation or two ago, they were not allowed to sit with high caste Christians in church, and separate churches were erected for them. The Buddhists have their own mutually exclusive sects: three of these sects are the Mahayana, the Hinayana, and the Theravadi.

Origin of the Indian Caste System. There are many theories about the origin of caste in India. The traditional Sanskritic theory ascribes the origin of the four varnas to a mythical deity: the Brahman sprang from his mouth, the Kshatriya from his arms, the Vaishya from his thighs, and the Sudra from his feet. According to the racial approach, caste arose out of race contacts between Aryans and Dravidians. The family and gentile theory states similarities and parallelisms in the ancient Iranian, Roman, and Indian social systems, and the occupational theory describes caste as arising from cultural and occupational differences. Another view attributes the development of the caste system to tribalism and holds that caste is little more than an ordinary class society made rigid. Others base caste on the idea of a morally stratified society, according to which man's caste is his natural and correct place in society. This view holds that caste and class differences in both the East and the West were at first based on merit and only later tended to become hereditary and economic.

Reform Movements. Movements to reform the caste system have been launched from time to time. The impact of Buddhism, Islam, and Christianity on the Hindu social structure encouraged liberalization of the caste system, and on innumerable occasions caste norms have been abandoned to the extent that marriages between Brahmans and untouchables have taken place.

In modern times, a number of reform movements have arisen. Industrialization and technological advances brought to India by Europeans have caused Indian leaders to attempt reform by adapting traditional ideas to the new knowledge. Some founded new sects within which traditional and modern thought might be reconciled. The Brahmo Samaj, a reaction to Christianity, and the Arya Samaj, a reaction to Islam, are among these new sects. The Brahmo Samaj rules out all caste distinctions. But it never spread beyond a limited number of urban educated people. The Arya Samaj, a considerable influence in north India, accepts certain traditional authorities relating to caste but rejects others. It is significant, however, that most of these reform movements sooner or later evolve castes of their own, and despite their initial wish to abolish the system, become, in time, exclusive, endogamous sects. As a result of Mahatma Gandhi's constructive programs, however, which included communal harmony and the removal of caste restrictions, particularly untouchability, caste was at its lowest ebb in India during the struggle for independence, and most of the caste rituals were abolished.

Since independence, increased urbanism and industrialism have accelerated social mobility and have changed the contours of the caste system. New transportation facilities have thrown people of all castes together, eliminating the possibility of maintaining "ceremonial purity." Taboos on food, drink, and personal contacts have been relaxed or in some cases completely eliminated. City factories and slums have forced people of various castes to come into closer contact. In markets, factories, and tea shops, people of all castes work and eat together, defying the ancient restrictions of commensality and exclusive living. Legal equality has already been established for all people of the country, and further changes within the caste system have been reported as a result of government policies and social welfare programs geared toward raising the socioeconomic standards of the backward lower castes. The elimination of occupational specialization among the castes has also affected the caste hierarchy. Some castes have shown a tendency to identify with higher castes, thereby moving up in the social scale. Again, these are changes within the system and are not evidences of a breakdown of the caste system altogether.

In modern India, the forces of Sanskritization and Westernization are working to bring about further changes. Through Sanskritization, by adopting the customs, rites, and beliefs of the Brahmanical scriptures, a low caste can rise to a higher position in the caste hierarchy. Most of the lower castes are vigorously participating in the process of Sanskritization in the effort to obtain upward social mobility. The upper castes are going through a process of Westernization, accepting Western cultural ethos and ideas. When the Sanskritization of a lower caste is complete, it tries to Westernize itself. It may take two generations for a lower caste to Sanskritize, and another two to Westernize. In the course of four to six generations, then, a caste, if fortunate, can move from the bottom to the top in the caste hierarchy.

Westernization and Sanskritization stand for two opposite sets of values; they contradict each other. And yet it appears that for the vast majority of Indians, Westernization is not possible without undergoing Sanskritization.

Caste in Other Areas. Caste is immobile class; class is mobile caste. Every society has this movement from class to caste and vice versa. In ancient Rome patricians and plebeians were almost always engaged in this conflict. Whenever Rome grew economically and militarily, the society permitted free play, and classes could struggle to move up. Whenever this struggle obstructed the maintenance of order in society, and outside pressures grew, the demand for a stable social system was made in the name of justice. Class was often the struggling aspiration of Roman citizens to achieve equality in society. Caste later became an instrument to prevent internal disruption and protect the status quo. This class-caste continuum can be seen in all societies, ancient and modern. When society is dynamic and demands change, the need for expansion gives impetus to the class system. But when society wants to conserve, class may be transformed into caste.

The older social groups of Europe have never been able to lose all elements of their caste system. Even in times of great social mobility, democratic behavior and intermarriage have not been easy or natural. Some social scientists have seen traces of a caste-oriented philosophy in 20th century Europe in both the Bolshevik and Nazi movements, which had as their theoretical aim an egalitarian society. In the United States, on the other hand, while it is difficult to deny the existence of some sort of class system, caste does not exist, aside from such marginal groups as the Boston Brahmins and the sometimes vast distinction between Negro and white.

The Future of the Caste System. Caste springs from two main sources, religious-mythical and economic-political, with much overlapping between the two. Whether myth-oriented or economics-oriented, caste revolves around the concept of the struggle for power. The European caste system was of the economic-political type; the Indian has been of the religious-mythical type, acquiring in recent times some economic-political traits. In Europe there is always the possibility of caste loosening into class and class solidifying into caste. But in India this movement has never completely taken place, since caste in India has always functioned as a powerful myth. Myth is the creation of fact out of a fictitious idea. As a conjectural narrative presented as history, the Hindu basis of the Indian caste system is a perfect example of myth, and is still accepted by a vast majority of Indians, particularly those in rural areas. Nevertheless, caste on the Indian subcontinent is subject to heretofore unfelt pressures from the forces of democracy and modernization, and efforts to break down the success of the mythology of caste are increasing. See also CLASS.

NARMADESHWAR PRASAD
Patna University, India

Further Reading: Ghurye, Govind S., *Caste, Class, and Occupation in India*, 4th rev. ed. (New York 1961); Hutton, John H., *Caste in India: Its Nature, Functions, and Origins* (Cambridge, England, 1952); Prasad, Narmadeshwar, *The Myth of the Caste System* (Patna, India, 1957).

CASTEAU, kas-tō′, is a village in southwestern Belgium, 30 miles (48 km) southwest of Brussels. On March 31, 1967, the Supreme Headquarters of the military arm of the North Atlantic Treaty Organization (NATO), formerly located at Rocquencourt, France, was officially opened there.

The village, with its attractive old farmhouses and the remains of a fortress, is located on the main road between Brussels and Mons. Population: (1961) 1,800.

CASTEL GANDOLFO, käs-tel′ gän-dôl′fō, a town in Italy, in the Alban Hills, 16 miles (25 km) southeast of Rome, has been the summer residence of the popes since the early 17th century. It is situated on a steep spur above the crater Lake of Albano.

The origins of Castel Gandolfo go back before the foundation of Rome. On the site stood the fortress of Alba Longa, built, according to tradition, by Ascanius, the son of Aeneas. In the 1st century A. D., long after the town of Alba Longa had disappeared, the emperor Domitian built a villa here, the ruins of which are still visible. The town's name is attributed to an early feudal owner. Later the Roman family of Savelle ruled it. In the 16th century it became the property of the papacy. See also ALBA LONGA.

The papal residence, or palace, was built between 1624 and 1629 by one of Rome's great architects, Carlo Maderno. Its interior was completely rebuilt after World War II. The main gate is dominated by a balcony, from which the pope gives his blessing to pilgrims and visitors. A large audience hall in the nearby gardens of the Villa Cybo was completed in 1959.

A charming church, designed by Bernini in 1661 and dedicated to St. Thomas of Villanova, and the papal observatory, one of Europe's oldest, are also part of the complex of buildings at Castel Gandolfo. All of the structures are owned by the Holy See. Population: (1961) 2,646.

GEORGE KISH, *University of Michigan*

CASTEL SANT'ANGELO, käs-tel′ sänt-än′jā-lō, is one of the most remarkable and best-preserved monuments of imperial Rome. It was conceived and possibly designed by the emperor Hadrian to be his great tomb and that of his successors.

It was originally built in 135–139 A. D. and called the Moles Hadriani. As Rome declined and became a frequent battleground, Castel Sant'Angelo was turned into a fort. Parts of it became a prison at about the same time and continued to be so used until 1901. Because of its massive fortifications, it was also important as a refuge, and a strong walled passage, some 40 feet (12 meters) above ground level, was built during the Middle Ages to connect it with the Vatican. When the forces of Emperor Charles V sacked Rome in 1527, Pope Clement VII fled to safety in the castle. Because of its function as a prison, Castel Sant'Angelo appears in novels and plays, and its top terrace is the scene of the last act of Puccini's great opera, *Tosca*.

Castel Sant'Angelo rests on Roman foundations, and the visitor can follow a Roman-built inclined circular walk to the funerary chambers of the emperors, in the heart of the edifice. On the four floors above, various popes made many alterations and additions, including the construction of the elegant papal apartments in the 16th century. Some of the rooms are now used as a museum of military history. The top floor of the castle, surmounted by a bronze statue of an angel, provides a magnificent view of Rome.

GEORGE KISH, *University of Michigan*

CASTELAR Y RIPOLL, käs-tā-lär′ ē rē-pôl′yə, **Emilio** (1832–1899), Spanish politician and democratic spokesman, who was premier of Spain in 1873–1874. He was born in Cádiz on Sept. 8, 1832. From 1857 to 1864 he taught history at the Universidad Central in Madrid. In his famous article *El rasgo* (The Deed) he violently attacked the monarchy and he became a leader of the movement to depose Isabella II, which culminated in the revolution of 1868. In the Constituent Assembly of 1869–1870, he made a name for himself as an orator.

In September 1873, Castelar won the premiership. By this time the revolution was verging upon social chaos, and Castelar immediately set the army against the rebellious city cantons. In 1874 he was defeated in his attempt to avert the closing of the Cortes (parliament) by Gen. Manuel Pavia. After the restoration of the monarchy in 1875, Castelar served as a deputy until his death at San Pedro del Pinatar, in Murcia province, on May 25, 1899. It is ironic that his greatest oratorical efforts in behalf of universal suffrage, religious freedom, and democracy took place in the restoration period.

ROBERT W. KERN, *University of Massachusetts*

BERNARD G. SILBERSTEIN, FROM MONKMEYER

CASTEL SANT'ANGELO rises above the Tiber River and Ponte Sant'Angelo (Sant' Angelo Bridge) in Rome. Conceived by the Roman emperor Hadrian as a tomb, the Castel Sant'Angelo has served as a fortress, a refuge, and a prison during its history.

CASTELLAMMARE DI STABIA, käs-tel-läm-mä'rā dē stä'byä, is a city and commune in southern Italy, about 16 miles (26 km) southeast of Naples. It is close to the base of the peninsula of Sorrento. Because of its beautiful location, its excellent beaches, and the variety of its mineral waters (used since Roman times), it is popular with tourists. Macaroni, cement, machinery, soap, textiles, and many other products are manufactured in Castellammare. There are also shipyards in the city.

Of interest among the city's buildings and monuments are the 16th century cathedral, the municipal palace, and a 12th to 13th century castle. Population: (1961) of the city, 49,064; (1966 est.) of the commune, 68,926.

CASTELLANI, käs-tāl-lä'nē, **Aldo** (1878–), Italian physician and microbiologist, best known for his contributions to tropical medicine. In 1903, while in Uganda, Castellani examined the blood and spinal fluid of patients with sleeping sickness and discovered that the parasite *Trypanosoma gambiense* caused the disease. Two years later in Ceylon, he showed that a certain spirochete, or spiral bacteria, *Treponema pertenue,* that is very similar to the organism responsible for syphilis, causes yaws. Later, he also identified *Spirochaeta bronchialis,* which causes hemorrhagic bronchitis. In addition to his work in tropical medicine, Castellani also developed the absorption of agglutinins test, in which antibodies are mixed with unknown bacteria. This test has proved to be an important method for differentiating related strains of bacteria.

Castellani was born in Florence on Sept. 8, 1878. After studying in Florence, Bonn, and London, he did research, studied, and taught in many countries. In 1947 he joined the Institute of Tropical Diseases in Lisbon. Among his writings is *Manual of Tropical Diseases* (1910), a classic text in tropical medicine, coauthored by A. J. Chalmers.

CASTELLIO, kas-tel'ē-ō, **Sebastianus** (1515–1563), French Protestant theologian and humanist. He was born *Sébastien Châtillon* or *Châteillon* in St.-Martin-du-Fresne, Ain, in 1515. He was converted to Protestantism by John Calvin in 1540, and the following year he was made rector of the college in Geneva. Differences regarding questions of religious belief, especially his erotic interpretation of the Song of Solomon, caused him to be denied ordination. In 1545, Castellio was banished to Basel, where he became a professor of Greek at the university in 1552. He died in Basel on Dec. 29, 1563.

In 1554, under the pseudonym of *Martin Bellie,* Castellio published a work in Latin and French (*De Haereticis* and *Traité des hérétiques*). This book made a plea for religious liberty and denounced the execution of Michael Servetus, who was condemned for heresy in Calvinist Geneva. Castellio's most famous work was a translation of the Bible into Latin and French. The Latin version aimed at classical elegance, while the French used the vernacular of the time.

CASTELLÓN DE LA PLANA, käs-tā-lyōn dā lä plä'nä, is the name of a city and province in Spain. The city, which is the capital of the province, is located on a plain (Spanish, *plana*) just in from the Mediterranean coast. The tower of its principal church overlooks the city and its surrounding gardens and cultivated fields. The Reconquest of Spain reached this region in the first half of the 13th century, when the town was established.

Castellón produces a number of manufactured products: *azulejos* (decorative tiles), textiles, cordage, and sandals. There are also sugar refining and olive oil processing plants in the city. Sugar and olive oil, as well as citrus fruits and local wines, are exported from Castellón's adjacent port, El Grao.

The province is in the center of Spain's east coast, on the Mediterranean Sea. It was formerly part of the region of Valencia. It has a fertile coastal plain backed by hills, with mountains in the interior. The light rainfall in Castellón necessitates irrigation systems, such as that of the Mijares River, for carrying out intensive farming, especially of vegetables. Oranges, olives, corn, cotton, grapes, and rice are also grown. Population: (1960) of the province, 339,229; of the city, 62,493.

M. M. Lasley
University of Florida

CASTELNAU, kȧs-tel-nō', **Count de** (1812–1880), French traveler. Francis de La Porte, called the Count de Castelnau, was born in London. Under the sponsorship of the French government he undertook an exploration of equatorial South America in 1843. After returning to France in 1847 he published *Expédition dans les parties centrales de l'Amérique de Sud* (14 vols., 1850–1859). Castelnau later traveled in Arabia and served as consul in several places, including Singapore. At the time of his death—Feb. 4, 1880—he was consul general at Melbourne.

CASTELNAU, kȧs-tel-nō, **Édouard de Curières de** (1851–1944), French general who before World War I assisted the French commander in chief, Gen. Joseph Joffre, in preparing Plan XVII, the design for French operations against Germany. He was born in St.-Affrique, Aveyron, on Dec. 24, 1851. After graduating from St.-Cyr, he saw brief service in the Franco-Prussian War. Radicals hated Castelnau for his noble lineage, suspected royalist leanings, and strong Catholicism. His religious faith, small physique, and dapper appearance prompted Premier Georges Clemenceau to nickname him "Le Capucin Botté" ("Monk in Boots").

As war neared, Joffre named him to command the Second Army, with which Castelnau saved Nancy. Joffre elevated him to command a group of armies and then in 1916 sent him with full powers on a mission to save threatened Verdun. With Joffre's forced retirement late in 1916, Castelnau's active service on the western front ended. After World War I he served in the Chamber of Deputies. He died near Toulouse on March 19, 1944.

Charles B. MacDonald
Deputy Chief Historian, Department of the Army

CASTELNAUDARY, kȧs-tel-nō-dȧ-rē, is a town in France, in the department of Aude, on a height above the Canal du Midi, 22 miles (35 km) west-northwest of Carcassonne. It suffered greatly during the crusade of Simon de Montfort against the Albigenses and was captured in 1212; in 1355 it was almost totally destroyed by Edward the Black Prince. Its Church of St. Michel dates from the 14th century. Population: (1962) 7,944.

CASTELNUOVO-TEDESCO, käs-tāl-nwô′vō tā-dās′kō, **Mario** (1895–1968), Italian composer, was born on April 3, 1895, in Florence, where he studied composition with Ildebrando Pizzetti and piano with Edgardo del Valle de Paz. When only 15, Castelnuovo-Tedesco wrote *Cielo di Settembre* (1910) for piano. During World War I he composed the patriotic song *Fuori i barbari.*

Castelnuovo-Tedesco's compositions are harmonious and noted for fluency of style. Among his works are *Concerto italiano* (1924), *Le danze del re David* (1925), the operas *La Mandragola* (1926) and *Bacco in Toscana* (1931), *Symphonic Variations* (1928), the violin concerto *The Prophets* (1932), the ballet *Birthday of the Infanta* (1942), *Indian Songs and Dances* (1949), and Quintet for Guitar and Orchestra (1950). After moving to the United States in 1939, he wrote sound tracks for films. He died in Los Angeles, Calif., on March 15, 1968.

CASTELO BRANCO, kəsh-te′lo͞o braNNg′ko͞o, **Camilo** (1826–1890), Portuguese writer, who was perhaps Portugal's greatest romantic novelist. A prolific author in many genres, he wrote approximately 80 books. Most of his works are passionate and romantic, but some are realistic, even though he disliked realism and parodied it in his later novels.

An illegitimate child, Castelo Branco was born in Lisbon on March 16, 1826. From the age of 10 he was raised by an aunt in Vila Real, Trás-os-Montes. He married when he was 16 but soon abandoned his wife and daughter. In 1852 he entered a seminary at Oporto but did not take holy orders. Later he was imprisoned for living in adultery with Ana Plácido. During his imprisonment he wrote his best-known work, the novel *Amor de perdição* (1862; *Love of Perdition*), which brought him immediate fame. After his release he continued living with Ana on a farm she had inherited from her husband in 1863. Domestic problems, including an insane child, plus the loss of his sight, drove Castelo Branco to suicide, at São Miguel de Seide, on June 1, 1890.

GREGORY RABASSA, *Columbia University*

CASTELO BRANCO, kəsh-te′lo͞o braNNg′ko͞o, **Humberto de Alencar** (1900–1967), president of Brazil. He was born in Fortaleza, Brazil, on Sept. 20, 1900. He received an army commission in 1921, served in Italy during World War II, and became the Brazilian Army's chief of staff. In 1964, as inflation mounted, military officers combined with local leaders in a military coup that ousted leftist President João Goulart. The civilian Congress chose General Castelo Branco to serve out Goulart's term.

He declared an "institutional act," giving himself power to push laws through Congress. He curtailed political parties and denied the right to hold office to several civilian leaders. His austerity program reduced inflation; his land reform program broke up great estates on the undeveloped frontier. He firmly based the government in the new capital of Brasília. During his three years in power many anticorruption and social reform laws were enacted. In October 1966, Castelo Branco directed Congress to elect a president, and War Minister Artur da Costa e Silva was installed in the office in March 1967. Castelo Branco was killed in an airplane accident near Fortaleza on July 18, 1967.

HELEN M. BAILEY, *East Los Angeles College*

CASTI, käs′tē, **Giovanni Battista** (1724–1803), Italian satirical poet. He was born in Acquapendente on Aug. 29, 1724. After teaching in his youth, he became court poet to Emperor Francis I in Florence in 1764. He was summoned to Vienna in 1769 by Emperor Joseph II, who later exiled him for his *Poema tartaro* (1787), a satirical attack on Catherine II of Russia. In 1798 he settled in Paris, where he died on Feb. 5, 1803. Casti's fame rests chiefly on his *Novelle galanti* (1793), a collection of often licentious verse stories, and *Gli animali parlanti* (1802), an ironic allegory on French social conflicts.

CASTIGLIONE, käs-tē-lyō′nā, **Baldassare** (1478–1529), Italian diplomat and author, who was one of the pivotal figures of the Italian Renaissance. His famous *Libro del cortegiano* (1528; *The Book of the Courtier*), presenting the ideal courtier, helped spread Italian humanism to western Europe and deeply influenced the later concept of what a gentleman must be.

Life. Castiglione was born in Casatico, near Mantua, on Dec. 6, 1478, of an illustrious Lombard family, and lived all his life in princely courts. Schooled in Latin and Greek by humanist professors, he received his knightly training at the court of Ludovico Sforza in Milan and then served Francesco Gonzaga, Marquess of Mantua. In 1504, Castiglione joined the elegant, sophisticated court of Guidobaldo da Montefeltro, Duke of Urbino. After Guidobaldo's death in 1508, Castiglione took part in various Italian wars and was successively an envoy from Urbino and Mantua to the pope. During these years, he wrote *The Courtier*. In 1524, Pope Clement VII sent him to Spain as ambassador to Emperor Charles V. Castiglione died in Toledo, Spain, on Feb. 2, 1529. A portrait by his friend Raphael (in the Louvre, Paris) depicts the tenderness and melancholy that underlay his courtly manner.

The Courtier. The setting of *The Courtier* is

BALDASSARE CASTIGLIONE, in a portrait by Raphael.

GIRAUDON

the court of Urbino, presided over by the duchess, Elisabetta Gonzaga. The work, in four books, is a series of dialogues by her courtiers and her guests, including such prominent nobles and literati as Giuliano de' Medici, Ludovico da Canossa, Pietro Bembo, and Bernardo Bibbiena. In graceful prose touched with humor, the speakers describe the model courtier. He should be nobly born, skilled in military arts, sports, and dancing; well-versed in classical and modern languages, music, and painting; and gracious in conversation. He does everything unaffectedly, with a certain *sprezzatura* (nonchalance), and evinces a decided unwillingness to investigate deep moral issues. His goal is ostensibly to serve his prince, although in many passages it seems to be to acquire the favor of his peers.

The Courtier shows the influence of Cicero's *De oratore*. An immediate success, it was a source of inspiration for Cervantes, Corneille, Edmund Spenser, and Sir Philip Sidney.

JOHN CHARLES NELSON, *Columbia University*

Further Reading: Ady, Julia Cartwright, *Baldassare Castiglione*, 2 vols. (London 1908); Roeder, Ralph, *Man of the Renaissance* (New York 1933).

CASTIGLIONE, käs-tē-lyō'nā, **Giovanni Benedetto** (1605?–?1665), Italian baroque artist, who is noted for his prints and for his religious and genre paintings, in which superbly depicted animals often have a prominent place. He is also credited with the invention of the monotype, a technique by which a single print is taken from a metal plate bearing a design in paint or ink.

Known as Il Grechetto (the Little Greek), Castiglione was born and trained in Genoa. He worked there, in Rome, and in Mantua, where he was court painter from 1648 and where he died.

Castiglione used a variety of media and practiced a style with great variations. He was one of the first Italians to be influenced by the work of Rembrandt, through Rembrandt's etchings, and he was influenced by artists of widely disparate styles, including Van Dyck, Rubens, Poussin, and Bernini. Among his major paintings are those with pastoral or arcadian themes, and large, dramatic religious works, such as *Ancient Sacrifices* (Palazzo Durazzo, Genoa) and *The Immaculate Conception* (Institute of Arts, Minneapolis). He also excelled in sketching in oils thinly brushed on paper. The largest collection of his oil sketches is at Windsor Castle, England.

MILTON LEWINE, *Columbia University*

CASTILE, kas-tēl', is an extensive region of northern and central Spain that is roughly equivalent to the territory of the medieval kingdom of Castile. As a historic region, Castile (Castilla in Spanish) maintains its identity and name, even though it is now divided into 13 provinces.

The Land. Most of Castile consists of an arid, often barren and desolate expanse of tableland averaging more than 2,000 feet (610 meters) in elevation, whose surface is broken by abrupt changes in level and occasionally by mountain ranges. This tableland is known as the meseta, a term that has become synonymous with Castile, where most of Spain's meseta is situated. Rainfall varies, but it is generally insufficient to permit the cultivation of a variety of crops; however, the soil is fertile and produces well under irrigation. The weather is rather severe; temperatures often exceed 100° F (38° C) in summer, and fall below freezing in winter. Castile is essentially an agricultural region, and among the crops that can be grown are wheat and other grains, grapes, and olives. Grass is adequate to support livestock, mostly sheep and goats. The mountain slopes in some areas support cork oak.

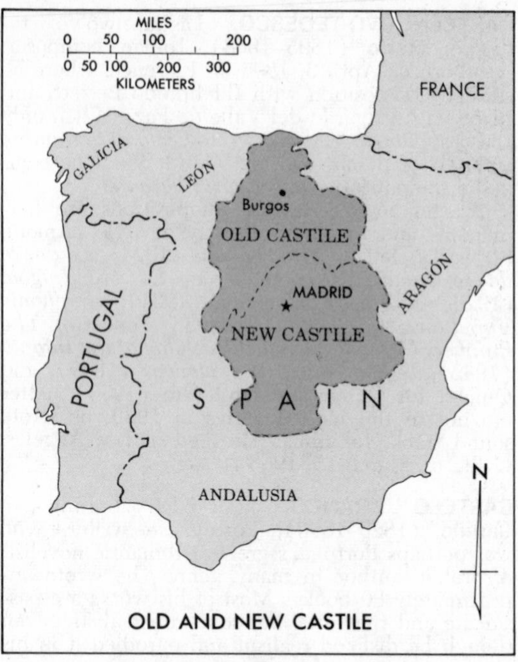

OLD AND NEW CASTILE

The northern edge, which is not typical of Castile, includes the coastline on the Bay of Biscay and is part of the Cantabrian Mountains. Rainfall is high, and corn, potatoes, and beans are grown. This area also has mineral deposits and is part of an industrialized complex.

The northeastern meseta is drained by the Ebro River, which empties into the Mediterranean Sea. The northern portion of the meseta is drained by the Douro (Duero) River, which crosses northern Portugal to enter the Atlantic Ocean. The Guadiana River runs westward through the southern meseta, and in the center is the Tagus River. The last two also empty into the Atlantic Ocean.

The limits of Castile on the east and west are essentially political in origin, there being no natural break in the meseta, which extends into the regions of Aragón in the east and León and Estremadura in the west. The southern limit, however, is the natural barrier of the Sierra Morena mountains, separating Castile from Andalusia. Even though Castile does possess historical and geographical continuity, it is customary to divide the region into Old Castile and New Castile. Chronologically the former precedes the latter in the assumption of the central role in the history of Spain; geographically the meseta is divided into two unequal halves by the central cordillera, formed by the Gredos and Guadarrama ranges.

Old Castile. Northern Castile, called Castilla la Vieja in Spanish, is composed of the present-day provinces of Santander, Burgos, Logroño, Soria, Segovia, Ávila, Palencia, and Valladolid. The last two were part of León in early medieval times but are customarily included in Castile. The name Castile comes from the Latin *castellum*, "fortified camp," or "castle," the type of defended settlement common around Burgos in the early

Middle Ages. With the Battle of Covadonga in 718, the tide of the Muslim invasion was stemmed, and the reconquest of Spain by the Christians began. Along the northern Iberian Peninsula were the centers of resistance and reconquest, kingdoms formed by Romance-speaking Christians. These were, from west to east: Galicia, Asturias, León, Navarre, Aragón, and Catalonia. One of the courtships of León was that of Castile.

Spanish literature begins with epic poems about folk heroes, among whom is Fernán González, the Count of Castile who secured Castile's independence from León in the 10th century. Of even greater stature was the 11th century hero Rodrigo Díaz de Vivar, whose deeds are told in the epic *Poema de Mío Cid*.

The 11th and 12th centuries saw a succession of shifting alliances by marriage and otherwise, among León, Castile, Navarre, and Aragón. In this process Castile steadily acquired prestige and became the leader not only in political matters but also in the nascent Spanish literature.

New Castile. The southern part of Castile, called Castilla la Nueva in Spanish, is made up of the provinces of Toledo, Madrid, Guadalajara, Cuenca, and Ciudad Real. Included in this last province is a large part of La Mancha, a particularly desolate stretch of the meseta made famous by Cervantes in his *Don Quixote*. As was the case with Old Castile, the territory held by the Moors was not densely populated; hence the Christians in the reconquest followed a pattern of capturing the larger towns, encouraging the local inhabitants to continue to live and work in the area, and supplementing the local population with settlers from the north. All of them lived under a set of regional laws, or *fuero*, granted by the king. The slow process of resettlement together with delays caused by political rivalries made the process of reconquest uneven. As early as 1085, Alfonso VI had extended the boundary of Castile and León to Toledo, on the Tagus. But not until 1177 was Cuenca, a city of strategic importance, captured by Alfonso VIII of Castile. This king in 1212 defeated the Moorish Almohads in the decisive battle of Las Navas de Tolosa, in the Sierra Morena. Thus by the early 13th century all of Castile was in effect brought under Christian control, even though the reorganization of the area took several decades.

In 1230, Fernando III finally reunited the kingdoms of Castile and León and pushed the reconquest into Andalusia, reconquering Córdoba (1236), Jaén (1246), and Seville (1248). This advance effectively contained the Moors, although their last stronghold, Granada, did not fall until 1492.

At the end of the 15th century, Spain became a nation; in addition to political and religious unification it had acquired a linguistic unity. As the Castilians had assumed increasing leadership in the reconquest, their dialect had become the language of prestige. Although the other Ibero-Romance dialects have been maintained for local use, Castilian is now the Spanish language.

The medieval kings held court in many towns, but in 1561 Philip II made Madrid, a small town near the center of the country, the permanent capital of Spain. The presence of Madrid, also Spain's largest city, with its converging transportation routes, hydroelectric power, and industry, has been important to the development of the central meseta.

M. M. LASLEY, *University of Florida*

CASTILLA, käs-tē'yä, **Ramón** (1797–1867), Peruvian president and soldier. He was born in Tarapacá, Chile, on Aug. 27, 1797. He fought as an officer in the war for independence (1820–1826) and later in the civil war (1841–1845).

Castilla was president of Peru from 1845 to 1851, and he overthrew José Rufino Echenique in 1855 to become president again until 1862. Castilla's administrations were marked by progress. He developed the country's guano and nitrate resources and used the revenues to reduce the public debt, modernize transportation and communications, foster education, and improve defenses. He abolished Negro slavery and the head tax exacted from the Indians, and promulgated a new constitution in 1860 that remained in force until 1920. Castilla died in Arica (now in Chile) on May 25, 1867.

CASTILLA RUBBER TREE, kas-til'ə, any of 10 species of rubber-bearing trees constituting the genus *Castilla* of the mulberry family (Moraceae). These trees, which attain a height of more than 150 feet (45 meters) and a trunk diameter of 5.5 feet (1.5 meters), possess a system of tubes in the inner bark that carries a milky liquid known as *latex*. After it is drained from the tree, latex can be solidified into crude rubber. *Castilla* trees occur in Mexico, Central America, and southward throughout the Amazon basin.

Tropical American Indians were using primitive rubber products, probably derived from wild *Castilla* trees, long before the arrival of Columbus. The first plantings of rubber trees, carried out in Mexico, also utilized *Castilla*. The invention of vulcanization in 1839 spurred further plantings, both of *Castilla* and the Para rubber tree (*Hevea brasiliensis*). The tropical American plantings of *Castilla*, later abandoned because they could not compete with the Para tree plantings of the Far East, became a significant source of natural rubber during World War II.

The Para rubber tree has almost completely replaced *Castilla* as a plantation tree because it has better latex and greater annual yield; it also yields at a younger age, is cheaper to tap, and requires less space.

LAWRENCE ERBE
University of Southwestern Louisiana

CASTILLEJO, käs-tē-lye'hō, **Cristóbal de** (1490?–1550), Spanish poet, who violently opposed the strong Italian influence in the poetry of his contemporaries Boscán and Garcilaso de la Vega. He expressed his opposition particularly in his *Contra los que dejan los metros castellanos, ...* Castillejo himself retained the traditional, elegant Castilian forms in all his verse, which included songs, ballads, and numerous love poems. He was also noted for his satiric poetry, notably *Diálogo de la vida de corte,* which presented a pointed and witty view of court life.

Castillejo was born in Ciudad Rodrigo, Spain. He was in the service of Archduke Ferdinand (who later became ruler of Austria, Hungary, and Bohemia) throughout most of his life, first as a page and later as a secretary. Castillejo, who had become a Cistercian monk about 1515, lived for many years in Vienna, where he led a rather licentious life. He was constantly plagued by severe financial hardships. He died in Vienna in 1550.

ALVA V. EBERSOLE
Adelphi University

CASTILLEJOS, Marquis de los. See PRIM Y PRATS, JUAN.

CASTILLO, Bernal Díaz del. See DÍAZ DEL CASTILLO, BERNAL.

CASTILLO, käs-tē′yō, **Ramón S.** (1873–1944), president of Argentina. He was born on Nov. 20, 1873, in Catamarca, Argentina, and obtained a law degree at the University of Buenos Aires, where he later was professor of commercial law and dean of the law school (1923–1928). His specialty was bankruptcy law, and he contributed to legal reform in that field.

He served as a senator before he was appointed minister of justice and public instruction in 1936. Elected vice president of Argentina in 1938, Castillo became acting president in July 1940, when the ailing President Roberto Ortiz transferred the functions of the office to him.

Ortiz died in 1942, and Castillo succeeded him. Castillo maintained Argentine neutrality in World War II when other Latin American states broke off relations with or declared war against the Axis powers. In the face of unrest over this neutral policy and over economic dislocations brought on by the war he suspended constitutional guarantees of freedom of speech and assembly, governing by decree. He was overthrown by a military revolt on June 4, 1943. He died in Buenos Aires on Oct. 12, 1944.

JOHN FINAN, *The American University*

CASTILLO ARMAS, käs-tē′yō är′mäs, **Carlos** (1914–1957), Guatemalan soldier and political leader, who overthrew the left-wing constitutional government of President Jacobo Arbenz Guzmán and assumed the presidency in 1954. Born at Santa Lucia Cotzumalguapa, Guatemala, on Nov. 4, 1914, he was a graduate (1936) of the Escuela Politécnica (the nation's military academy). After eight years' service on the academy's faculty, he joined the young officers' revolt against the dictator Gen. Jorge Ubico.

In 1945, after Juan José Arévalo was installed as president, Castillo Armas attended the U. S. Army Command and General Staff School. On his return he was made commandant of the Escuela Politécnica. In 1950, just before Arbenz was elected to succeed Arévalo, Castillo Armas was seriously wounded in a revolt against the government. He spent the next three years in exile in Honduras, gathering men and supplies to overthrow Arbenz' allegedly pro-Communist regime.

Reacting to an intelligence report early in 1954 that a Swedish vessel carrying arms made in Czechoslovakia and shipped from Poland was on its way to Guatemala, the U. S. government sped military equipment to Honduras and Nicaragua. These countries, in turn, released supplies to the CIA-assisted liberation army led by Castillo Armas. On June 17, 1954, his 2,500-man army was launched against the Arbenz regime, and on June 27 the President resigned. After a period of instability and contention among the military officers, Castillo Armas took office as president on Sept. 1, 1954. He quickly reversed the controversial agrarian reform law and encouraged private capital. Elected to a constitutional 5-year term on Oct. 10, 1954, he was assassinated on July 26, 1957 in Guatemala city.

LAURENCE R. BIRNS
The New School for Social Research, New York

CASTILLO NÁJERA, käs-tē′yō nä′hā-rä, **Francisco** (1886–1954), Mexican physician and diplomat. He was born in Durango on Nov. 25, 1886, and received his early education in the *colegio* of that state. Graduated from the medical school of the national university, he pursued further medical study in Paris and Berlin. He served as director of several hospitals, wrote on medicolegal and other topics, and was professor of urology and director of the army medical school before entering on a diplomatic career in 1922.

He was minister to China (1922–1924), Belgium (1927–1930), Holland (1930–1932), and France (1933–1935). From 1935 to 1945 he was both ambassador to the United States and a delegate to the League of Nations and its Council. As ambassador he played a key role in helping Mexico and the United States through the crisis caused by Mexico's expropriation of the foreign-owned petroleum industry, and in maintaining American unity in World War II.

In September 1945 he became foreign secretary of Mexico. He served in that office until he was named ambassador to the United Nations (1946–1950), where he participated in a number of the international conferences that helped shape the international and regional structure of the postwar world. Thereafter he was chairman of Mexico's national insurance commission until his death in Mexico City on Dec. 21, 1954.

HAROLD E. DAVIS, *The American University*

CASTILLON-LA-BATAILLE, kås-tē-yôN′ lä bå-tä′yə, is a town in western France, in the department of Gironde, on the Dordogne River, 26 miles (42 km) east of Bordeaux. It is also known as *Castillon-et-Capitourlain* and *Castillon-sur-Dordogne.* The battle that ended the Hundred Years' War was fought beneath the walls of Castillon on July 17, 1453. The English troops were defeated by the army of Charles VII of France, and the English commander, John Talbot, was killed. This defeat forced the return of Gascony and Guyenne to France, after they had been held by the English for nearly 300 years. Population: (1962) 3,108.

CASTINE, kas-tēn′, is a historic residential town in south central Maine, in Hancock county, about 40 miles (64 km.) south of Bangor. It is situated on the Bagaduce River, which empties into an inlet of Penobscot Bay of the Atlantic Ocean. The Maine Maritime Academy, founded in 1941, is in Castine. Its graduates receive bachelor of science degrees and third officer licenses in the U. S. Merchant Marine; where qualified, they may receive reserve commissions in the U. S. Navy. The training ship *State of Maine* is berthed here. There are many historic sites in the town. Fort George, built by the British in 1770, has been restored.

A trading post was established here in 1626 by the Plymouth Colony of Massachusetts. Later the site was occupied by the French, British, and Dutch. Baron Jean Vincent de St. Castin, for whom the town is named, settled here in 1667. It was settled by the British in 1760. Separated from Penobscot and incorporated in 1796, it became a shire town, but the courts were removed to Ellsworth in 1838. Government is by town meeting. Population: 1,080.

BARBARA M. TROTT
Witherle Memorial Library

CASTING is the process of producing a metal object of a desired shape by pouring molten metal into a mold and allowing the metal to cool and solidify. Man has been making cast metal objects for artistic or practical purposes since very early times, when the first castings probably were made of gold or copper formed in a stone or clay mold. The earliest axes and other useful metal objects were cast in open molds of stone or baked clay. Early art objects were made of cast gold, silver, copper, or bronze; one existing life-sized portrait head in cast bronze from Mesopotamia dates from about 2250 B.C. See also BRONZE AND BRASS IN ART.

The shaping of metals in the liquid state has been in development for centuries. With the growth of industrial societies, the need for metal castings has become very great. In the United States alone the industry produces more than 16 million tons of castings annually, using iron, steel, copper, aluminum, zinc alloys, and magnesium alloys.

Metal castings are vital components of most modern machines and transportation vechicles. Cast metal parts account for more than 50% of the total weight of a tractor and for more than 90% of an automobile engine. High-precision castings are used as turbine vanes and blades in an aircraft jet engine. The reason for the widespread use of castings is that any desired shape or size can be produced economically.

Castings are made by hand-molding operations or by molding machines. Methods for making cast metal parts can be classed in three groups: (1) molding processes that use a permanent pattern of the part and an expendable mold; (2) molding processes that use an expendable pattern and an expendable mold; and (3) molding processes that use a permanent mold. An expendable mold or pattern is one that is used only once.

Permanent Pattern and Expendable Mold. In molding processes that use a permanent pattern and an expendable mold, the mold is made of greensand, dry sand, core sand, plaster of paris, or a resin-sand shell.

Greensand Method. In hand-molding operations, the first step is to make a wood, plastic, or metal pattern that is slightly larger than the final casting to compensate for shrinkage of the hot metal when it cools in the mold. A metal *flask* (molding box) is placed around the pattern, and greensand (93% silica sand, 4% clay, and 3% water) is rammed by hand against the pattern, filling the flask. The flask is then rolled over, and the *parting surface* smoothed with a trowel and cut so that the pattern can later be removed from the mold. Next, another flask is set firmly and precisely in place on top of the first flask. A *sprue pattern* is set in place in this upper flask to provide a passageway (gate) for the metal to enter the mold cavity. After the upper half of the mold is filled with rammed greensand, the sprue pattern is removed, and a *pouring basin* is cut. The top half of the mold (the *cope*) is lifted from the bottom half (the *drag*), and then the pattern is removed from the drag, leaving a shaped space that is the mold cavity. After the cope is replaced over the drag and the halves are clamped together to keep the cope in its proper position, the mold is ready for pouring.

Gray iron, for example, is poured at a temperature of 2500° F (1371° C), which is 300° F (149° C) above the temperature at which the iron starts to solidify. After cooling, the casting is shaken out of the mold and cleaned by sandblast. Metal that solidified in the gate is cut from the casting by using a saw.

ALCOA

Eight-ton aluminum sand castings used as molds for tires for construction and earth-moving equipment.

A hand-molding process is used only when a few castings are needed from a given pattern. For high-volume production, a separate pattern is constructed for each half of the mold, and sand is delivered at high speed and jolted in place by mechanical equipment instead of ramming the sand by hand. Each half of the mold is produced in less than 30 seconds.

Dry-Sand Method. The dry-sand method is similar in all respects to the greensand method except that the mold is baked at about 400° F (204° C) until most of the water is driven off from the sand. This step reduces the reaction of liquid metal with the mold surface and provides a better surface for casting.

Core-Sand Method. In the core-sand method, the sand contains less clay, but oil or resin is added to produce a hard mold after baking at 400° F (204° C). Core sands are also used to produce an internal passage in a casting. To do this, a baked core is inserted and precisely positioned in a greensand mold.

Plaster of Paris Process. In the plaster of paris process, a rubber pattern, which can be very intricate, is surrounded with a plaster of paris slurry. After the slurry sets, the pattern is removed, and the mold is dried. Aluminum, zinc, and other metals that melt below 2400° F (1316° C) can be cast in a plaster mold.

Shell-Molding Method. In shell molding, developed by the Germans during World War II, a metal pattern is heated to 400° F (204° C) and a resin-coated sand is dumped on the pattern. Because the pattern is hot, the layer of sand within 0.25 inch (0.64 cm) of the pattern is bonded by the resin, forming a shell in about 15 seconds. The pattern and the shell are heated for 15 seconds to harden the shell, and then the shell

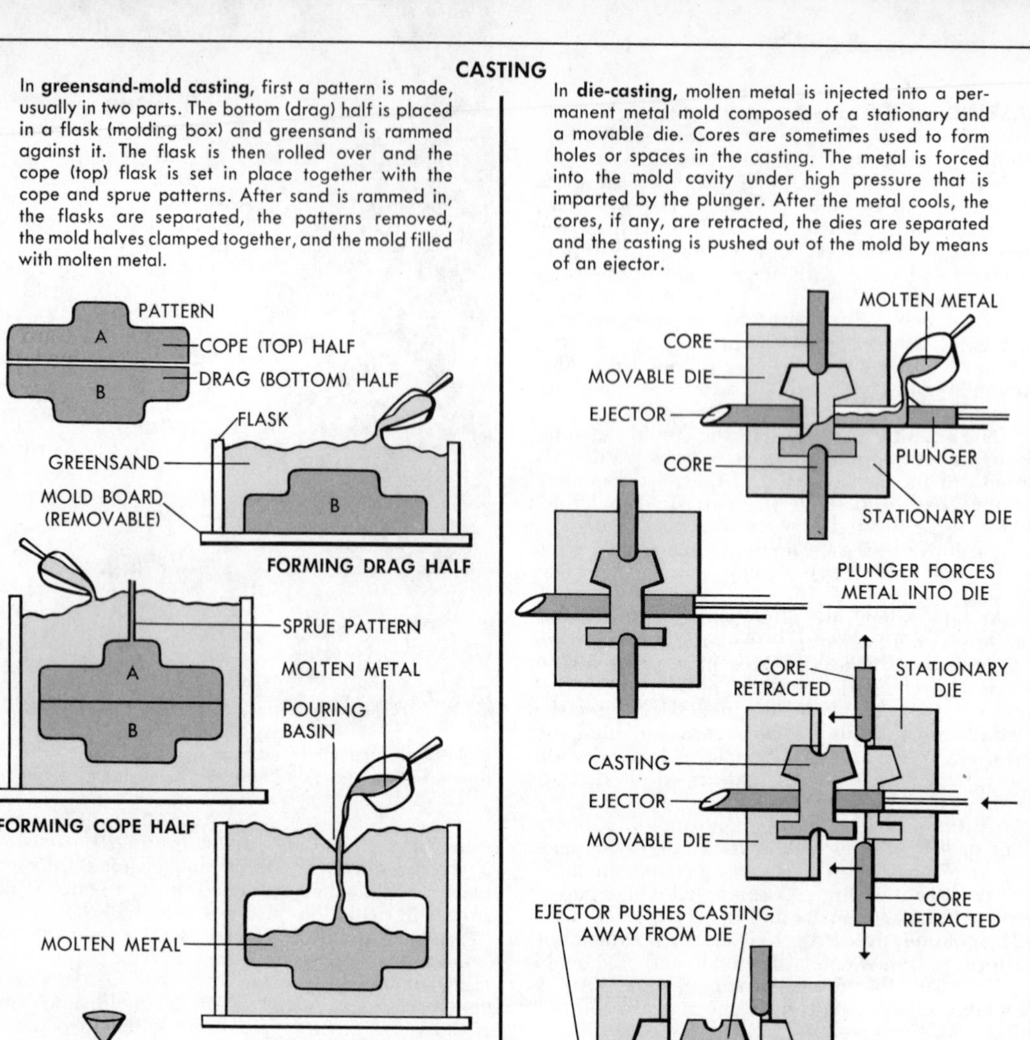

is removed from the pattern by an ejector device. After two shells are made, they are glued together to form a mold cavity for pouring. Shells provide an excellent surface for the making of castings.

Expendable Pattern and Expendable Mold. High precision castings are made by using an expendable pattern and an expendable mold. Patterns are made of such materials as wax, frozen mercury, or polystyrene.

The lost-wax process, used for centuries to produce statuary and jewelry, is now also used for casting dental fillings, gas turbine vanes and blades, and other precision parts. In this process, a wax pattern of the desired part is made, and a wax vertical passageway is attached. The assembly is coated with a ceramic wash, placed in a flask, and surrounded with a slurry containing a heat-resistant material and a binder. After the slurry sets, the wax is burned out at 1800° F (982° C), leaving an accurate, heated cavity into which metal is poured. The dimensions of the final casting can be controlled to 0.003 inch (0.008 cm) per inch (cm), thereby eliminating costly machining. In variations of this process, production-molded polystyrene or frozen mercury patterns are used.

Permanent Mold. In permanent-mold processes, the mold is made of metal or graphite and is reused hundreds of thousands of times, providing high production rates. Methods for making castings by using permanent molds include gravity casting, die casting, and centrifugal casting.

In *gravity casting,* the metal is poured into a vertical passageway leading to the mold cavity. In *die casting,* the liquid metal is injected under pressure into a tightly clamped die. In *centrifugal casting,* the mold is rotated about a horizontal or vertical axis, and the liquid metal is forced against the mold wall by centrifugal force; most cast-iron pipe is made in this way.

RICHARD A. FLINN
University of Michigan

Further Reading: Flinn, Richard A., *Fundamentals of Metal Casting* (Reading, Mass., 1963); Morris, Joe L. *Metal Castings* (Englewood Cliffs, N. J., 1957).

CASTLE, Vernon (1887–1918), British dancer and aviator, who, with his American wife, Irene, formed the most popular dance team of his day. Vernon Castle Blythe was born in Norwich, Norfolk, on May 2, 1887. He was trained in engineering at Birmingham University, but his real interest was the theater. He went to New York City in 1906 and soon became a comic actor. In 1911 he married the dancer Irene Foote (1893?–1969). While they were visiting Paris in 1912 the impoverished newlyweds accepted the invitation of the manager of a nightclub to dance, and soon fame and fortune were theirs. Success followed them to the United States, where they danced in theaters and cabarets and in the film *The Whirl of Life*. By introducing such dances as the Castle walk and the Castle polka, which they originated, and by popularizing other dances, including the maxixe, tango, hesitation waltz, bunny hug, and turkey trot, the Castles set a new style for ballroom dancing. Their book of instruction, *Modern Dancing*, appeared in 1914. Mrs. Castle also popularized bobbed hair.

When World War I broke out, Castle joined a British flying squadron and made many sorties over France. Later he became a flying instructor. He was killed on a training mission on Feb. 15, 1918, in Fort Worth, Texas.

WALTER TERRY, *Author, "The Dance in America"*

CASTLE, William Ernest (1867–1962), American geneticist, who pioneered in the study of mammalian heredity and contributed to the theory of quantitative inheritance. His most famous experiment was on the effects of selective breeding on the amount of black in the black-and-white pattern of hooded rats. From his experiments, he first drew the conclusion that genes might "contaminate" or "modify" each other. Later, he recognized that his experimental results were caused by many genes, each having a very small additive effect. This theory—that some traits are the result of more than one gene—became known as the "multiple factor" or "quantitative inheritance" theory. Castle's last paper, on color in horses, was published in 1960.

Castle was born near Alexandria, Ohio, on October 25, 1867. He studied at Deniston University and at Harvard University, where he received a Ph.D. in zoology in 1895. He spent most of his career at Harvard, rising from an instructor (1897) to professor (1908) and working at the Bussey Institution until his retirement in 1936. After that, he was a research associate at the University of California until his death in Berkeley, Calif., on June 3, 1962.

ALLEN S. FOX, *University of Wisconsin*

Further Reading: Wright, S., "William Ernest Castle," *Genetics*, vol. 48, pp. 1–5 (1963).

CASTLE. See CASTLES AND CHÂTEAUX.

CASTLE, The, an unfinished metaphysical novel by Franz Kafka (q.v.), published posthumously in 1926. Kafka portrays in *The Castle* (German title, *Das Schloss*), as in *The Trial* (1925), the loneliness and isolation of modern man caught up in bureaucracy and unable to find the meaning of life. The helpless hero K. has been sent for by the "divisional chief" of a castle to be a land surveyor. He spends the rest of his life in the nearby village trying to gain access to the castle (representing divine grace) but is always thwarted by officials.

CASTLE CLINTON NATIONAL MONUMENT, in New York City, originally was a fort defending New York Harbor. Circular in shape, it was completed by the federal government in 1811 on a small island off the southwestern tip of Manhattan Island. It was first called West Battery, but was renamed Castle Clinton in 1815 in honor of DeWitt Clinton, mayor of New York. The building was given to the city in 1822, and in 1824 it was remodeled as an entertainment center and its name was changed to Castle Garden. In the 1850's and 1860's, land filling joined the small island to Manhattan. From 1855 until 1890, Castle Garden was a landing depot for immigrants; 7½ million persons entered the United States there. The New York Aquarium occupied the building from 1896 to 1941. The original fort was made a national monument on July 13, 1950.

CASTLE OF OTRANTO, ō-trän'tō, a novel by the English author Horace Walpole, published in 1764. It was the first example of the Gothic novel, characterized by brooding, gloomy settings and supernatural occurrences.

The evil usurper Manfred, prince of Otranto, is determined to retain his power over the realm that he rules illegally. The intricate plot involves his persecuted wife, a handsome young prince in disguise, and two romantic princesses. As Manfred pursues his unsavory course, he is constantly thwarted by weird events, such as a helmet crashing down from heaven into his castle courtyard and an ancestral figure stepping out of a portrait and becoming a ghost. After many difficulties, the forces of good prevail, Manfred is deposed, and the rightful rulers are placed on the throne.

In *Otranto* the "dark" aspects of the imagination found expression. Pale heroines, dark villains, castle prisons, and subterranean escapes create a symbolism of light and shadow, suggesting patterns of psychic conflict that became, in the works of later writers, not traditional antitheses but paradoxical ambiguities. Walpole's immediate successors, the Gothic novelists, notably Ann Radcliffe, exploited only his sensationalism. However, the genre that the book introduced also had an influence on such major authors as the Brontës and Dickens.

JOHN W. LOOFBOUROW, *Boston College*

CASTLE SHANNON, a borough in Pennsylvania, is in Allegheny county, 6 miles (10 km) south of Pittsburgh, of which it is a residential suburb. It was founded in 1782 and was incorporated as a borough in 1918. It is governed by a mayor and council. Population: 11,899.

CASTLEBAR, an urban district in northwestern Ireland, is the county town of Mayo. It is 130 miles (209 km) northwest of Dublin, on the Castlebar River, in a cattle-raising and potato-growing region. In 1641, Parliamentary forces under Sir Henry Bingham surrendered here to Irish Confederates but were later massacred at Shrule, 25 miles (40 km) southeast. Castlebar was the site of the battle known as "Castlebar Races," in which the French general, Jean Humbert, defeated English troops under Gen. Gerald Lake in 1798. Population: (1961) 5,482.

CASTLEMAINE, Countess of. See VILLIERS—*Barbara Villiers*.

CASTLEREAGH, kas′əl-rā, **Viscount** (1769–1822), British statesman. As foreign secretary from 1812 to 1822, Castlereagh managed the Grand Alliance that defeated Napoleon and represented Britain at the Vienna peace conference of 1815.

Castlereagh was born Robert Stewart at Mount Stewart, County Down, Ireland, on June 18, 1769. Descended from Protestant Irish gentry, he derived the titles Viscount Castlereagh and 2d Marquess of Londonderry from his father, who was made a peer in 1789. Castlereagh was educated at Armagh in Ireland and at Cambridge, and entered the Irish House of Commons at 21 and the British Commons at 25. As Irish secretary in 1800 he engineered the Act of Union, which dissolved Ireland's separate Parliament. The "new deal," including Catholic Emancipation, on which he had counted for justification, never materialized, and he was branded a traitor by Irish patriots. He remained outwardly impassive, and the "mask" of Castlereagh was notorious from that time.

Unpopularity in Ireland was no barrier to promotion in England. But Castlereagh's credit as a ruthlessly efficient administrator was wiped out by criticism of his strategy as war minister from 1807 to 1809, and he resigned from office. By challenging his chief critic, Foreign Secretary George Canning, to a duel, in which Canning was wounded, he won some sympathy. But it was the complexity of political bargaining, rather than restored confidence in his capacity, that secured him the foreign secretaryship and the leadership of the House of Commons in 1812.

Damned by the *Times* of London as "the very darling of misfortune," he nevertheless quickly proved an excellent party manager. But his real quality emerged in the diplomacy of war. By winning the confidence and respect of Allied leaders, he created—and by personal contact maintained—the Grand Alliance against Napoleon.

Castlereagh also took the lead in planning for peace. Combining a cool appraisal of national interests with concern for long-term stability in Europe, he moderated his own demands and catered wisely to the susceptibilities of defeated France. Despite its failure to recognize the force of new nationalism, the Vienna peace settlement made useful provision for pacific settlement of international disputes. Ranging far beyond the isolationist views of his government, Castlereagh converted what he called the "sublime mysticism and nonsense" of Czar Alexander of Russia and the dubious pragmatism of Prince Metternich of Austria into a blueprint for diplomacy by summit meetings.

After 1815 he relied on the relations he had established with Metternich and Alexander to preserve Britain's interests without destroying the framework of great power solidarity. But on Aug. 12, 1822, on the eve of a crucial conference, when only his brand of diplomacy could have preserved the Concert of Europe, he committed suicide at his country home, North Cray Place, Kent. The cause of his depression has been ingeniously investigated, but it can be simply explained by the strain of 10 years in office.

Somewhat unjustly labeled a reactionary and long the butt of radical publicists, he was buried amid jeers in Westminster Abbey. Respect for his memory has grown with the development of international organizations; he pioneered the rationalization of consultation procedures.

P. J. V. ROLO, *University of Keele, England*

CASTLES AND CHÂTEAUX, kas′əlz, sha-tōz′, are architectural forms that were originally designed to serve the dual purpose of fortification and habitation. The English word "castle" is derived from the Latin *castellum,* a diminutive of *castrum,* meaning "fort." However, in the Latin of the Vulgate Bible, *castellum* refers to villages whose buildings were fortified. Hence, a castle is essentially a defensible home. The French word *château,* with the same root, has come even more to mean a house, usually a large country house.

The Ancient Castle. Early in the history of Egypt, royal palaces were fortified with towers and parapets, and these structures lingered on in the homes of the ruling class even after their military necessity had disappeared. With the expansion of Egypt up the Nile during the 12th dynasty, there was a need for defense on the southern frontier. There the fort of Semna was built, with heavy brick walls reinforced by bonding members of timber and by massive buttresses.

The ruling caste in Assyria, renowned in literature for its ferocity, was in constant danger from both internal unrest and attack from without. Hence thick walls of mud brick bounded such cities as Khorsabad, with paired towers flanking the city gates and other battlemented towers at intervals along the wall. In case of attack, the Assyrian archers could discharge their arrows from these walls and towers in comparative safety. At one point the city wall was widened into a platform for the palace of Sargon II (reigned late 8th century B.C.), which thus became a bastion to protect Khorsabad. Chariots could drive up ramps to the broad top of the wall and into the courts of the one-story palace. The gates of the palace, its walls, and even its courts were provided at intervals with battlemented towers. The palace was arranged around several courts: the men's or royal court, with its suite of state apartments; a servants' court; a court presumably for women (harem); and finally an area for religious purposes, with its pyramidal tower, or ziggurat, built up in seven stages. Guardian monsters, carved in stone, with the legs and body of a lion or a bull, the wings of an eagle, and the head of a man flanked the main entrance. Friezes sculptured in low relief in the royal apartments commemorated the king's prowess in warfare or in the hunt. Rugs covered the floors, and no doubt textiles were used to help create a sumptuous atmosphere.

The Greek chieftains of the Mycenaean period likewise fortified their palaces. The citadel at Tiryns, built toward the end of the 2d millennium B.C., has walls 26 feet (8 meters) thick, which approximately follow the contours of the hilltop. These walls are built of "Cyclopean" masonry; that is, large blocks of stone of irregular shape fitted together. Narrow passage-like chambers covered by corbel vaults penetrate part of the wall from within and probably served as storage space for provisions and weapons. The chariot entrance led up a ramp so arranged that the fortress wall was on the right of the chariot. Since the Greek warrior carried his shield on his left arm and his spear or sword in his right hand, when he approached the gate his right, or unprotected, side was exposed. If an attacking party succeeded in forcing the first gate, it found itself in a narrow alley flanked on both sides by strong walls with secondary gates at either end—the one on the right leading to the

TOM HOLLYMAN, FROM PHOTO RESEARCHERS

THE ROCK OF CASHEL in Ireland was a fortified stronghold in the Middle Ages. From this height, its defenders dominated the surrounding countryside.

lower ward, or bailey, the other to the palace area. Still another wall divided the palace from the bailey, so that even if the latter were captured the task of the attackers was by no means over. Narrow postern gates, with approaches too steep for chariots, gave secondary access to the lower ward and to the palace proper.

If, however, a peaceful visitor arrived, he might drive his chariot through the gates, through the outer court, and through an entrance pavilion, or propylaea, which separated the outer from the middle court. He could leave his steeds in the middle court and enter through a second propylaea into the inner court in front of the men's suite, or megaron, with its open hearth. The megaron was the center of life in the palace; around it were grouped the quarters for sleeping and other daily activities. Although there was a secondary court and suite of rooms for the women, called the thalamus, which was approached from the megaron by circuitous routes, men and women mingled in the megaron. While waiting for Odysseus' return, Penelope worked at her weaving and entertained her suitors in such a place, but retired at night with her maidens into the thalamus.

Beginning in ancient times, whole cities were fortified. The Acropolis in Athens, a civic and religious center in historic times, offered great natural facilities for defense; its abrupt slopes were further reinforced where necessary by walls. However, as Athens grew, Themistocles walled in the entire city, about 480 B. C.

Rome likewise was defended by walls, parts of which still survive. The city had outgrown the old republican wall before the empire was established, and extensive later walls were added, as for example those built by the Emperor Aurelian, begun in 271 A. D.

In the Roman world, during the centuries of the *Pax Romana* (30 B. C.–235 A. D.), except near the frontiers, no reason existed to mix domestic architecture and provisions for defense. However, although nearly a century was to elapse before the first serious incursion of the barbarians against the Rhenish-Danubian frontier, it is almost symbolic that in the late 3d century Diocletian should have built a defensible palace at Spalato (now Split, Yugoslavia). At least the location brought him closer to the frontier than to Rome.

The plan of Diocletian's palace was influenced by the Roman military camp, which was laid out foursquare, with gates in the center of each side and with straight roads connecting the gates, thus dividing the camp into quarters. Similarly, a square wall enclosed Diocletian's palace, and streets bisected each side of the square. Three of the walls were defended by towers at the corners, in pairs around the gates, and at midpoints between the corners and the gates. The fourth wall, built on the very shore of the Adriatic, needed no defense; it could provide an open gallery along its length as a promenade. This lack of fortification on the sea front suggests that though Diocletian may not have anticipated an actual assault, it was clear that if one should occur, it would come by land, not by sea. The tribes along the Danubian frontier were landsmen.

The Medieval Castle. The heyday of the castle as an architectural form in western Europe was the Middle Ages, from about 1000 to 1500. For this the feudal system was responsible. The weakness of kings and emperors permitted the nobility to become nearly independent in fact if not in theory. The system allowed, if it did not actually encourage, the nobility to plunder their neighbors and the surrounding countryside. Therefore, noble families were compelled to make their homes as nearly impregnable as possible. Because the situation was the same over most of Europe, the basic form of the medieval castle was molded by similar factors in France and Germany, in Spain and England, with the result that the variations in design from country to

PHILIP GENDREAU

DIOCLETIAN'S PALACE in Split, Yugoslavia, was protected against land attack by its strong outer walls.

country are less marked than the similarities.

Although, after the Norman Conquest of 1066, royal power was generally stronger in England than it was on the Continent, the Norman feudal barons required strongholds to control the land and the conquered Saxons. One such stronghold, of great historical interest, is the Tower of London, begun in 1078 by William the Conqueror. Though complicated by extensive later additions, the White Tower, known as the keep because the lord and his garrison lived or "kept" there, was the nucleus of the original structure. Several stories high, with double walls, small windows, and spiral stairs in its corners, the White Tower was quite typical of its day. Perhaps its most interesting feature is the Chapel of St. John, a characteristic small Romanesque church. Such chapels were customary in the larger castles, not only to serve the religious needs of the household, but doubtless also to provide the lord of the castle with space for private conferences, since the hall would rarely be empty of retainers.

Hedingham Castle, Essex, built about 1130 as the home of the de Veres, was one of the most perfect examples of the Norman keeps. (It was gutted by fire during World War I.) Hedingham was solidly built, with double walls of stone 20 feet (6 meters) thick. Its corners were still further reinforced. A flight of steps, arranged like the ramp at Tiryns to expose the unshielded side of an attacker, led up to the door at the level of the second floor. This door entered the great two-storied hall, the center of life for the garrison. Aside from small areas within the thick walls where the meager sanitary facilities of the castle were located, this hall was Hedingham's principal interior. Within it the family and its retainers ate, slept, and lived much of their daily lives. Such light as there was came from a few small windows high up in the wall. These windows, utterly inadequate by modern standards, were necessarily kept to a minimum, not only for defense but for warmth. Since window glass was not available, any warmth in the interior could be preserved only by closing the windows with shutters, thus excluding even the little light these openings might afford. For heating, a fireplace was built in the center of one side of the hall, its chimney rising in one of the middle buttresses of the outer walls. The ceiling was carried on a single great arch that spanned the hall from side to side. The familiar round arch of the Romanesque style, with its characteristic moldings, adorned fireplace, door, windows, and any other feature that required architectural emphasis.

Above the hall was another chamber of the same size, also warmed by a fireplace. Probably the women of the household carried on their activities there, and it may also have served as private quarters for the de Veres. Access to it, as well as to the ground floor, was provided by spiral stairs in one corner of the keep. Since there was no other entrance to the ground floor, this area could have served as a dungeon for prisoners, but it probably was used mostly for storage purposes. If the space provided for the varied purposes of living in Hedingham Castle seems restricted, it was clearly because the necessity for defense superseded comfort. Still, Hedingham was not quite so confined as this description implies; wooden structures that could be destroyed if a siege were imminent once covered the door and the stairway. Traces of the roofs are still visible where they joined the masonry of the keep.

One of the largest of the Norman keeps was Colchester Castle, Essex, of the late 11th century. It measured 152 by 111 feet (46 by 34 meters) exclusive of the towers—so large in fact that walls subdivided the interior. The upper stories at Colchester have been destroyed, but its height can be judged by the keep at Rochester, Kent, begun by Archbishop William of Corbeil (d. 1136), which rises more than 100 feet (30 meters). Built somewhat later, perhaps about 1150, is the small but delightful Castle Rising, Norfolk. In addition to the exceptional richness of its arcades and moldings, Castle Rising affords an example of a fore building designed to enclose the stair. The door at the ground level gave access to the stairs, which led up along the wall of the castle to the main door at the second story.

Perhaps the desire for ampler accommodations contributed to the development of the courtyard castle, whose towered and battlemented walls enclosed a more or less extensive bailey or perhaps more than one. At Pembroke Castle in South Wales, built in the early 13th century, the walls encircling the outer and inner baileys followed the contours of the hilltop, with towers at each change of direction. Within the bailey, whose entrance was guarded by a heavily fortified gatehouse, was ample room both for living quarters and for livestock.

The concept of the keep was not abandoned with the introduction of the courtyard. The keep was simply built either within the bailey, as at Pembroke, or as the strongest point in the castle walls, as at Coucy-le-Château in France. However, the square Norman keep was changed to a circular tower, as were the other towers of the outer walls. This change probably resulted from the Crusades, which brought western Europe into contact with Byzantine architecture and its round towers. These Byzantine forts had already influenced the Saracens in their fortifications of Antioch, Nicaea, and Jerusalem, which offered such formidible resistance to the Crusaders.

Though not large, the early 13th century castle at Coucy-le-Château was an excellent example of the early Gothic castle. Walls, whose angles were reinforced with round towers, surrounded the irregular court and permitted the living quarters of the garrison to be built within and against the walls. Timber galleries might be added atop these walls and projecting from their faces to permit the discharge of missiles on the heads of an attacking party. The keep, or donjon, 210 feet (64 meters) high, was the strongest feature and the point of last resort for the garrison if the bailey should be forced. Actually such castles were rarely taken except by treachery. The one at Coucy never was, and its strength justified the arrogant motto of its lords: "I am not a king, nor a prince, nor a duke, nor even a count; I am the lord of Coucy."

Obviously if the homes of the nobility required such provisions for defense, town dwellers also needed protection. As a result, cities were also walled. If laid out afresh, and if built on level ground, city defenses were as regular as those of a Roman camp. Thus, at Aigues-Mortes in Provence, built in the 13th century, square walls with towers at regular intervals defended the town. The gates, also protected by towers, were in the center of each side. Indeed the only element of asymmetry was the placement of the keep at one corner.

A larger and more famous example of the walled city is Carcassonne. Here the terrain dictated irregularity in the walls, which march up and down the slopes. The builders of the Middle Ages, though not hostile to symmetry, were always willing to abandon it when some requirement, such as the site, suggested a departure. The village of Villeneuve-lès-Avignon, though less well-preserved than Carcassonne, is another example of asymmetrical building. Parts of its old city walls are preserved in many places. Perhaps the best-known English example is Chester, where quite an extensive walk on the walls is still possible.

In the second half of the 13th century, Edward I of England built a series of castles, many of them designed to hold the warlike Welsh in check. Caerphilly Castle (1271) in Glamorganshire, one of the earliest, shows the Edwardian method of designing the castle—with double walls, the inner one enclosing the inner court or bailey, and the second one completely enveloping the first, with space for an outer bailey between them. The presence of more than one gate made the task of blockade by an enemy more difficult, and the presence of additional outworks hindered the attackers still further. Curtain walls punctuated with round towers suggested a derivation from Saracenic fortifications in Palestine. Conway Castle (1285–1287) in North Wales is another excellent example of Edwardian architecture, with its walls following the contours of a high rock on the bank of the Conway River. Still another, Caernarvon Castle (1283–1322), with its hourglass form, is on relatively level ground. Harlech Castle (1285–1290), Merionethshire, had double, or in part even triple, walls that provided for outer, middle, and inner baileys.

GEORGE WHITELEY, FROM PHOTO RESEARCHERS

THE KEEP, which formed the nucleus of the medieval castle, is all that remains of Orford Castle in Suffolk.

Complex as these large royal castles are, they do not provide the clearest illustration of what might normally be required for defense or, more important, of what might be required for the living arrangements of the family and its household. The small but very picturesque Bodiam Castle provides a good example of these requirements.

In 1386 a license was granted to Sir Edward Dalyngrigge "that he may strengthen with a wall of stone and lime and crenellate and may construct and make into a castle his manor house of Bodiam, near the sea, in the county of Sussex, for the defense of the adjacent country and the resistance of our enemies." The rectangular form

WALLED TOWNS, such as Aigues-Mortes in France, adopted the methods of castle fortification for protection.

BERNARD G. SILBERSTEIN, FROM RAPHO GUILLUMETTE

J. ALLAN CASH, FROM RAPHO GUILLUMETTE

WATER-FILLED MOATS, as at Bodiam Castle in Sussex, made it difficult for attackers to reach castle walls.

of Bodiam, with its omission of the concentric walls of Edwardian castles, came into vogue during the Hundred Years' War between France and England.

A moat girdled Bodiam, and the principal approach to the castle was a wooden bridge over the moat to a stone outwork called the barbican. A second bridge led in turn from the barbican to the main gate. In case of attack, these bridges, heavy enough for equestrian traffic, could be destroyed in succession. (The second bridge was demolished only if the barbican was captured or had to be abandoned.) A small bridge, for pedestrian traffic only, crossed the moat to the postern gate at the back of the castle. Round towers defended the corners of Bodiam, and there was a square tower at either side of the main gate and one in the center of each of the remaining sides. Small windows, hardly more than loopholes, were strategically placed in the towers so that fire from them could be brought to bear either on the enemy across the moat or along the walls if the attackers were bold enough to force their way across the water to the base of the wall. In fact, the only window of any considerable size was the chapel window, which was high enough in the wall to be secure. The lower few feet of the walls were battered; that is, sloping outward. The purpose of the batter was less structural than military. If the base of the castle were approached, missiles dropped by the defenders from the top of the wall would be deflected outward by the batter against an attacking party.

Naturally the strongest defenses were reserved for the main gate. Here the towers were not only crenellated (battlemented) but also machicolated. On a machicolated tower the parapet was advanced on brackets beyond the plane of the wall. Between the brackets were openings to permit stones or perhaps boiling water to be dropped on the heads of an assaulting party. (The notion of pouring molten lead on the enemy was more picturesque than practical in view of the value of metal in the Middle Ages.) Loopholes in the parapet wall permitted archers, including crossbowmen, to fire from comparative safety within.

As an added defense for the main gate, the last few feet of the bridge approach formed a drawbridge that could be raised at night or in case of attack. Also, a heavy timber grille, or portcullis, reinforced with iron and held in place by solid masonry on both sides, slid down in front of the door.

Before the days of gunpowder a castle such as Bodiam was practically impregnable if the garrison remained loyal. To besiege such castles required that an army of sufficient strength be kept in the field long enough to starve the defenders into submission. Since these castles were well provisioned and had their own sources of water within the walls—the kitchen tower at Bodiam had an ample well—a siege could be undertaken only at great cost. Although arrows had no effect on the masonry walls, the walls could be undermined. The moat, however, made undermining difficult. It also hindered attackers from bringing up movable towers from whose tops an attacking party might force an entry over the wall. Battering rams and catapults that discharged heavy stones might in time batter down the walls, or incendiary arrows might ignite any inflammable materials within the castle. However, the walls and most of the interior were made of stone, reducing the possibility of capture by forced assault or fire.

A welcome visitor, on the other hand, would ride across the bridges and through the barbican and the main gate. He would then find himself in the court, lined with rooms for the family and

J. ALLEN CASH, FROM RAPHO GUILLUMETTE

EILEAN DONAN CASTLE, in Scotland, was built in the 13th century for protection against the Danes. The original castle was destroyed by naval bombardment in the 18th century, and the present building is a reconstruction made in the 20th century.

GOURSAT, FROM RAPHO GUILLUMETTE

TOWERS AND PARAPETS characterize the 14th-century Château of Pierrefonds, built for the Duke of Valois.

the household. To his left were the family's private chambers, including the castle chapel, which, though small, was adequate for the needs of the establishment. To his right and behind him were retainers' quarters and storage areas. Directly ahead was the door to a passage that led to the postern; to the left was the great hall of the castle, with the solar, or withdrawing room of the lord and the ladies' bower at its further end; to the right was the entrance to the pantry, the buttery, and the kitchen. This arrangement was almost standard in the castles of the later Middle Ages.

Though still the largest single room in the castle, the hall by this time had dwindled in size relative to the space provided for other purposes, when compared, for example, with that at Hedingham Castle. The smaller size reflected the change in living. No longer was it common to sleep in the hall; bedrooms were provided both for the family and for the household. Although the hall was still used for meals, the custom of the family's eating with the retainers was fading. Two quotations indicate the change. In 1235, Robert Grosseteste, bishop of Lincoln, wrote, "As much as ye may, eat ye in the hall afore your many [household] for that shall be to your profit and worship." But by the 1360's, the author of *Piers Plowman* could say, "Dull is the hall each day in the week where neither lord nor lady likes to sit. Now has every kingdom a rule requiring one to eat by himself in a private parlor or in a chamber with a fireplace and to avoid the great hall that was made for men to eat in."

Although the hall usually had its fireplace or a fire kindled in the center of its stone floor, its large size could not but have left it chilly and drafty. Nor could the rough retainers have been suitable companions at all times for the gentler members of the household. On the other hand, the courtyard solved the problem of adequate lighting for the hall and the other rooms of the castle. If for defensive reasons the outer wall of the later castles had only a few small windows like those in Hedingham Castle, large windows could open into the court. Glass, however, remained a luxury until the 15th century and even later, and although oiled paper may have shut out some of the drafts, shutters were still the basic way of closing windows.

The next largest room after the hall was probably the kitchen, which had fireplaces capable of roasting an ox. Space was essential here, in view of the number of mouths to be fed. In addition to the family, the household servants and men-at-arms had to be provided for. Since Bodiam Castle required twenty garderobes (toilets), we may safely assume that a considerable number of persons lived there. The castles also needed extensive storage space for provisions.

Many of the larger and more famous castles resulted from centuries of building and rebuilding. For example, the royal castle at Windsor, begun by Edward III to replace an older castle that in part dated back to the time of William the Conqueror, was much added to later. Another famous English castle is Kenilworth, in Warwickshire, celebrated by Sir Walter Scott. Begun about 1120, it later passed into royal hands, was given by Queen Elizabeth to her favorite, the Earl of Leicester, and was subsequently partly destroyed during the Commonwealth for the sake of its building materials. One of the most imposing of the English castles is Warwick, begun shortly after the Norman Conquest. Probably the most celebrated Irish castle is Blarney, now in ruins but still visited for sentimental reasons. Edinburgh Castle, once a palace for the kings of Scotland, dominates the city.

WILLY PRAGHER, FROM PHOTO RESEARCHERS

CASTLES ON THE RHINE often served their owners in levying tolls on river traffic. Pfalzgrafenstein was built in the 14th century on an island in the river at Kaub.

The elements of military architecture in the Middle Ages and the way of life in the castles were essentially the same on the Continent as in England. The Château de Pierrefonds, for example, (1390–1400) was originally girdled by a moat. Its approximately rectangular curtain wall linked together round towers at the corners and in the middle of each wall; the tower serving as the entrance was larger and stronger than the others. The lower part of the walls was battered, and their tops were provided with machicolated parapets. Quarters for the garrison and retainers lined the courtyard as they had at Bodiam, although the owner, as befitted so high a noble as the duke of Valois, had a nearly independent residence near the gatehouse. Pierrefonds was dismantled in 1617 but restored during the 19th century by Viollet-le-Duc.

Though in ruins, the Château de Gisors, with a circular keep dating from about 1160, is an example of an early type of French castle. The keep was large enough to contain a chapel and was set within a broad bailey defended by a curtain wall with towers at intervals and with its principal gate heavily defended behind a barbican. Also of interest are the ruins of the Château Gaillard, near Les Andelys, built by Richard Coeur de Lion.

Partly because of the weakness of the Holy Roman Empire during the later Middle Ages, the decentralization caused by feudalism was more pronounced in Germany than elsewhere. In consequence, many castles were built by German robber barons to protect their lands or to levy tolls along the waterways and highways. Those along the Rhine from Bingen to Coblenz are especially picturesque because of their sites on hilly ground. Such castles include Drachenfels, near Königswinter, begun by Arnold, archbishop of Cologne, in 1147 and much added to later, and the 12th century castle of Schönburg, near Oberwesel, that is associated with the Lorelei legend.

OUTWARD-SLOPING TURRETS AND WALLS, as at Angers, France, deflected missiles dropped from above.

JEAN ROUBIER, FROM RAPHO GUILLUMETTE

The Moorish conquest of Spain and the centuries-long effort of the Christians to free the country resulted in a wealth of castles in the Iberian Peninsula. The place of religion in that struggle is evident in the 11th century walled city of Ávila, with its 86 towers, where the fortresslike apse of the cathedral, of later date, forms a bastion. The mid-15th century Castillo de Fuensaldaña has a rectangular bailey with a great tower on one side capable of independent defense. The long struggle with the Moors left its mark on the design of many Spanish castles, as, for example, the late 15th century Coca Castle where the Moorish influence is particularly strong. Coca, with the immense batter of its lower walls, its multiple circular and polygonal towers and turrets, and its decorative band of brickwork around the top of its walls, is magnificent architecturally; however, it was constructed so flimsily that it has more the appearance than the reality of military strength. The Alcázar of Segovia, especially the interior, is also Moorish in style. Its tall and slender turrets at the angles, like minarets, make it a picturesque "castle in Spain," though in fact the old fortress was destroyed in the 19th century and the present structure is purely modern.

The Renaissance Châteaux. The medieval castle was almost immune to the weapons and methods of attack of the time. Although gunpowder was known in Europe at least as early as the 14th century, the changes it brought about in fortifications were not felt until the early 16th century, when it became evident that stone walls and towers had lost much of their value. Moreover, with the growth of royal power, the intermittent warfare of feudalism disappeared so that defensibility was no longer essential to houses. Even so, the influence of the medieval castle was destined to linger on for centuries in French building.

The Italian Renaissance involved greater comfort, even luxury, than had existed under the feudal culture of the Middle Ages. Such innovations as upholstered chairs and the use of forks as a normal item of tableware point to the growing sophistication of life in Italy. But up to the end of the 15th century northern Europeans, including the French, remained unaware of these cultural changes. However, in 1494, Charles VIII of France undertook a military expedition into Italy in a futile attempt to establish his claim to the Kingdom of Naples. Though unsuccessful, his venture introduced the culture of Italy to the French aristocracy. Later, with the invasions of Italy by Louis XII and Francis I, French royalty and nobility were stimulated even further to transplant to France the amenities of the Italian Renaissance. For this purpose, they invited Italian artists to Paris and Fontainebleau, and the designs of their châteaux began to show Italianate elements.

The change could not take place overnight. The Louis XII wing (1503) of the Château of Blois, though unfortified, remained predominantly Gothic. Its steep pitched roofs, its window forms, and its traceried parapet at the top of the wall attest to the force of medieval tradition. But around the doorway a few details of carving betray an awareness of Italian forms.

Though built only a few years later, the

GENE HEIL, FROM PHOTO RESEARCHERS

CHENONCEAUX, on the Cher River, France, is characterized by the neo-Gothic detail of its main wing (*at left*) and the classic regularity of the gallery over the river.

Francis I wing (1515–1524) at Blois is even more Italianate. The Italianisms consist essentially of decorative shapes substituted for Gothic details, although there is little change in the larger elements of design. Thus, instead of Gothic pinnacles and a simple gable over the dormer windows, the new designers preferred candelabralike shapes and a tabernacle. In place of Gothic tracery in the parapet, they used heraldic devices and the moldings of a classic cornice. Superposed pilasters created the vertical divisions of the wall. Canopied figures and Italian arabesques adorn the buttresslike supports of the spiral staircase, but the canopies, like the dormers, have been converted to the new forms.

Significantly, these rich Italianisms derive not from the serious examples of Renaissance architecture in Florence but rather from the exuberant detail of such Lombard buildings as the façade of the Certosa at Pavia. Inevitably the French first encountered the north Italian style when they came over the Alps into the plains of Lombardy, and it was the sumptuousness of this style that impressed them. However, aside from these Italian details, the major building forms continued from the French past. The steeply pitched roof, the vertical divisions of the walls, the shape of the windows, and the towerlike projection of the stairway lingered on. The spiral stairs of the medieval castle were placed in turrets that kept the stairs half inside and half outside the building, but the stairs in later structures were larger, and the lack of fortifications permitted them to be open. So, too, the windows in the outer walls are larger. Also, by this time glass for windows had become common so that light could be provided without sacrificing warmth.

The Château of Chambord (1519–1538), having a more unified design, obviously shows the persistence in plan of French tradition even though its architect may have been the Italian Domenico Bernabei of Cortona, nicknamed Il Boccadoro. However, the Italian details were carried out with a certain Rabelaisian exuberance, and the new influence is apparent in the symmetry of the building. The Renaissance laid greater emphasis on symmetry than had the Gothic, even to the extent, at times, of arranging windows and doors to balance regardless of interior requirements.

But if these characteristics pointed to the Renaissance, others perpetuated the traditions of the castle. Chambord's rectangular plan enclosed a court reminiscent of the castle inner baileys. The center of the front of its main unit projects into the court and corresponds to the medieval keep. This part, to be sure, has intersecting axial halls about the great spiral staircase, which is now wholly inside the building, but the long wings that enclose the court are still only one room and a corridor in width, similar to the arrangement within the curtain walls at Bodiam. Towers linked together by other blocks of building compose the façade of Chambord. The derivation from the angle and intermediate towers and curtain walls of the medieval castle is obvious; in design both create an alternation of vertical and horizontal units, of strong accents set off by less emphasized portions. Such accents are almost never found in the Renaissance palaces of Italy. That these towers and links were conceived as semi-independent units is apparent in the arrangement of the visible roofs; conical roofs supporting turrets cover the towers, while each link has its own gable roof hipped at both ends.

Like the exteriors, the interiors of the important rooms in the châteaux of the early 16th century combine medieval forms and Renaissance decoration. Thus the beams and joists that support the floors above were left visible to form the ceiling of the room below, instead of being concealed by plaster or decorative paneling. The large fireplaces were still hooded, but the hood was adorned with Italian arabesques, heraldic emblems, or cartouches.

During the reign of Francis I and his successor, Henry II, many châteaux were built or rebuilt, especially in Touraine and the valley of the Loire. Chenonceaux, begun about 1518, was built on stone piers and arches spanning the river Cher. A smaller example is Azay-le-Rideau (1518–1524), where, despite the symmetry of its façade and the architectural vocabulary of the Renaissance, the visible roofs designed as semi-independent units, the round turrets at each angle, and even the machicolations of medieval military architecture persist. The Château of

LOUIS H. FROHMAN, FROM RAPHO GUILLUMETTE

FRENCH GOVERNMENT TOURIST OFFICE

FRENCH CHÂTEAUX of the 17th century bear little resemblance to the castles of the Middle Ages. Because defense was no longer a consideration, the rooms opened outward through an expanse of glass. The interior of the Château Maisons-Laffitte (*left*), meant for sumptuous living, was given the look of magnificence by its design from classical architectural models. The Château of Vaux-le-Vicomte (*above*) is surrounded by a grand plan of open terraces, steps, and gardens.

Ancy-le-Franc (1538–1546), by the Italian architect Sebastiano Serlio, exhibits a fuller appreciation of the properties of Renaissance architecture. The dormer windows have so dwindled in size as to be unimportant, but the building still encloses a court and retains the towerlike shapes at the corners.

The bitter struggle of the Huguenots and the Catholics during the successive reigns of the three sons of Henry II made the last half of the 16th century architecturally unproductive. Architecture began to revive under Henry IV of Navarre (r. 1589–1610), when the foundations for the later French supremacy in Europe were laid. During the 17th century the last traces of the medieval castle disappeared from the châteaux and palaces, centuries after those forms had lost the military reason for their existence.

The palace of the Luxembourg (1615–1620) in Paris, in the style of Henry IV, was built after his death for his widow, Marie de Médicis. In her childhood she had known the newer parts of the Pitti Palace in Florence, designed by Bartolommeo Ammannati, and to aid her architect, Salomon de Brosse, she had drawings of that edifice sent from Florence. Hence, in the garden front of the Luxembourg there are rusticated orders applied to each of the three floors, with some use of triangular and segmental pediments. On the other hand, pavilions with prominent roofs mark the ends of the façade and create vertical accents to contrast with the adjacent horizontal parts. The central bay of the garden front also projects and has its separate roof, and its verticality is further accented by a special emphasis in its design. Thus the system of towers and curtain walls of the medieval fortress was perpetuated for the rhythm it gave to design. Although most parts of the Luxembourg are still only one room and a corridor in depth, the corner pavilions contain groups of four interconnecting rooms. Like the castle, the Luxembourg encloses a square court, but with a prophetic change. The main part of the palace at the back of the court is three full stories in height, but the wings are only two stories, and the entrance front has been reduced to single story screen with hardly more function than to provide privacy.

The Château of Maisons-Laffitte (1642–1651) near Paris, designed by François Mansart, illustrates the next significant step. Although the plan resembles that of the Luxembourg, the mass of the building is quite different. The court has now vanished as an architectural element, but its location and extent are preserved in landscape design as a terrace with surrounding balustrades. (That age-old feature will henceforth be retained only in the larger *hôtels* within the cities.) The new design eliminated the sense of confinement and gave an opportunity for unhampered circulation of air, perhaps somewhat better lighting, and uninterrupted views of the gardens, bespeaking the changed conditions of life.

But if the enclosed court is gone, the French tradition in other respects is not. The corner rooms of the first and second floors of Maisons-Laffitte project at the ends of the façade and are emphasized in design by pilasters and special treatment of the windows. The central bay also is accented both by its richer architectural treatment and by its three-story height. Separate roofs cover each of these sections. Except for keeping vestiges of the court, Louis Le Vau adopted the scheme of Maisons-Laffitte for the Château of Vaux-le-Vicomte (1657–1660), designed for Nicolas Fouquet, the superintendent of finance during the minority of Louis XIV. Here, however, the plan is two rooms in depth, and the oval salon projects from the façade as the central pavilion.

In the immense palace at Versailles, the last traces of the medieval tradition almost vanish. The palace as a whole, and particularly the suite of state apartments on the garden front, perfectly express the extreme centralization of government and society in the court, with all the formality, pomp, and circumstance characteristic of the age of Louis XIV. The state apartments form a double file, with the Hall of Mirrors occupying most of the main floor. In the center of the garden front, a freestanding colonnade of six shafts at the second floor level rests on an arcaded ground story, while toward, but not at, the ends are similar four-columned pavilions—the last trace of the medieval tower and curtain wall. The pavilions serve no function other than design, and they do not correspond, as did their predecessors at Vaux-le-Vicomte, to separate rooms on the interior. Finally, the pitch of the roof has been so reduced that it is no longer visible from the ground and therefore plays no aesthetic role in the building.

The medieval castle died with the feudal society that brought it into being, but so firmly had it fixed its forms in the minds of the French builders that it took centuries for these forms to disappear. The picturesque appearance of castles and their associations in song and story led to their architectural revival in the late 18th and 19th centuries. An example is Ardoch Castle, Dumbartonshire, with its conscious asymmetry, its towers, and its battlements. However, Ardoch's basic arrangement, like the life it sheltered, was so foreign to the castles of the past that any resemblance to them derives more from sentiment than from architecture.

EVERARD M. UPJOHN
Columbia University

Bibliography

Armitage, Ella S., *The Early Norman Castles of the British Isles* (London 1912).
Braun, Hugh, *The English Castle* (New York 1936).
Cruden, Stewart H., *The Scottish Castle* (Edinburgh 1960).
Debraye, Henry, Touraine and Its Châteaux (London 1926).
Fedden, Henry R., *Crusader Castles* (London 1950).
Fraprie, Frank R., *The Castles and Keeps of Scotland* (Boston 1907).
Gebelin, François, *Les châteaux de France* (Paris 1962).
Holden, Angus H., and Dutton, Ralph, *French Châteaux Open to the Public* (New York 1936).
Hussey, Christopher, *English Country Houses Open to the Public* (London 1953).
Inoue, Munekazu, *Castles of Japan* (Tokyo 1958).
Lawrence, Thomas E., *Crusader Castles* (London 1936).
Leask, Harold G., *Irish Castles and Castellated Houses* (Dundalk, Ireland, 1941).
Mackenzie, William M., *The Mediaeval Castle in Scotland* (London 1927).
Oman, Charles William Chadwick, *Castles* (London 1926).
Rocq, André, *Châteaux de France* (Paris 1963).
Simpson, William D., ed., *Castles from the Air* (London 1949).
Toy, Sidney, *The Castles of Great Britain* (London 1953).
Tuulse, Armin, *Castles of the Western World* (London 1959).
Ward, William H., *French Châteaux and Gardens in the XVIth Century* (London 1909).

For Specialized Study

Bron, Ludovic, *Le lyrisme des pierres: le château* (Paris 1964).
Enaud, François, *Les châteaux forts en France* (Paris 1958).
Gebelin, François, *Les châteaux de la Renaissance* (Paris 1927).
Hotz, Walter, *Kleine Kunstgeschichte der deutschen Burg* (Darmstadt 1965).
Lorck, Carl von, *Burgen, Schlösser, und Gärten in Frankreich* (Frankfurt 1962).
Pillement, Georges, *Palais et châteaux arabes d'Andalousie* (Paris 1951).
Piper, Otto, *Burgenkunde* (Munich 1912).
Ritter, Raymond, *Châteaux, donjons et places fortes* (Paris 1953).
Sarthou Carrerres, Carlos, *Castillos de España* (Madrid 1943).
Schmidt, Richard W., *Burgen des deutschen Mittelalters* (Munich 1959).
Schuchhardt, Karl, *Die Burg im Wandel der Weltgeschichte* (Potsdam 1931).
Terrasse, Charles, *Les châteaux de la Loire* (Paris 1956).
Thompson, Alexander H., *Military Architecture in England During the Middle Ages* (New York 1912).
Tillmann, Curt, *Lexikon der deutschen Burgen und Schlösser*, 4 vols. (Stuttgart 1957–1961).
Toy, Sidney, *A History of Fortification from 3000 B.C. to A.D. 1700* (London 1955).

CASTOR, kas′tər, is a white second-magnitude star in the northern constellation Gemini. It is actually a complex star system. Two components of the system, having magnitudes of 2 and 2.8, complete a revolution around each other in about 340 years. A faint third component, with a magnitude of 10, revolves around the other two once every several thousand years. However, each of these three components is itself a spectroscopic binary, or double star, so that the entire star system called Castor consists of six stars. The system lies at a distance of approximately 47 light years.

See also BINARY STAR; GEMINI.

CASTOR AND POLLUX, kas′tər, pol′əks, in classical mythology, were noted for their brotherly love. They exemplified manly strength, skill, and courage and were inseparable in life and in death. Castor, the mortal, was famed as a horse tamer and charioteer; Pollux, the immortal, was a champion boxer.

Accounts of their origin vary. In one version, Castor was the son of Tyndareus, King of Sparta, and Leda, and the brother of Clytemnestra. Pollux was the son of Zeus (Jupiter) and Leda, and the brother of Helen. In other versions both brothers were the sons of Tyndareus and Leda and were known as *Tyndaridae,* or both were the sons of Zeus and Leda, born with Helen out of an egg, and were known as *Dioscuri.* Because the early Greeks did not understand the phenomenon of twin birth, one son, Pollux (Greek, *Polydeuces,* meaning "very sweet") was regarded as the offspring of a god.

Castor and Pollux took part in a number of heroic exploits. They rescued Helen, who had been abducted by Theseus, and carried off Theseus' mother, Aethra. In the expedition of the Argonauts, Pollux killed Amycus, King of the Bebrycians, in a boxing match. They also figured prominently in the Calydonian Boar Hunt. They had a cult at Sparta, Olympia, and elsewhere, chiefly in Dorian city-states.

At the wedding of their cousins Idas and Lynceus to Phoebe and Hilaira, Castor and Pollux ran off with the girls. In the battle that ensued, all the men were killed except Pollux. In another version, the fight was supposedly over a herd of oxen.

Pollux grieved so for his brother that Zeus allowed him to give up his immortality and rejoin Castor, spending alternate days in the underworld and on Olympus. In another account, the brothers took turns at life and death. In still another, Zeus rewarded their devotion by placing them in the heavens as the constellation Gemini (Twins), the third sign of the zodiac.

Among the Romans, Castor and Pollux were the patrons of the *equites,* a class of warrior knights who were influential in political affairs. In the brothers' temple in the Roman Forum, the Senate convened for many of its meetings. Their prominence in Rome arose partly from the belief that they aided the Romans against the Latins in the Battle of Lake Regillus (449 B.C.). That Castor's prestige was greater can be seen from their occasional name of *Castores.* In another of their attributes, Castor and Pollux were the protectors of sailors, to whom, in legend, they appear in storms as the twin lights of St. Elmo's fire.

URSULA SCHOENHEIM
Queens College, New York

CASTOR AND POLLUX, a tragic opera in five acts by Jean Philippe Rameau (q.v.), first performed at the Paris Opéra on Oct. 24, 1737. Considered to be Rameau's masterpiece, it is part of his revival of French classical opera, which had come under Italian influence after the death of his great predecessor Lully. The libretto, by Pierre Joseph Justin Bernard, is based on the ancient classical myth of Castor and Pollux, twin sons of Zeus and Leda. They are so devoted to each other that Pollux asks Zeus not to let Castor's untimely death in a quarrel separate him from his brother. Except for Télaïre's solemn monologue in Act 1, *Tristes apprêts,* the opera is more important instrumentally than vocally. Rameau used rich harmonies and emphasized orchestral tone color. Particularly noteworthy are the ballet danced by a chorus of demons, the persuasive *Sarabande pour Hébé,* and the funeral music.

CASTOR BEAN, the source of castor oil, is the very poisonous seed of the castor bean plant, *Ricinus communis,* of the spurge family (Euphorbiaceae). The castor bean plant, native to tropical Africa, is a highly variable species. In temperate areas it grows as a coarse annual herb; in the tropics it often becomes a small tree.

Castor oil, a product readily modified by chemical treatment, has a variety of uses. Because of its constant viscosity at high temperatures, it is used as a lubricant for the engines of aircraft and racing cars. Modified castor oil is used in paints and varnishes to increase their quick-drying properties. Castor oil or its derivatives are also used in hydraulic fluids, plastics, fungicides, asphalt tile, explosives, electrical insulation, perfumes, nylon, rayon, biodegradable detergents, urethane foams, and as the well-known purgative.

LAWRENCE ERBE
University of Southwestern Louisiana

A CASTOR BEAN and (*left*) the leaf and flowering seed shoot, with female florets above and male florets below.

(LEFT) THE BAKER CASTOR OIL COMPANY; (RIGHT) USDA

CASTOR OIL is a viscous, pale yellow oil, which is expressed or extracted from the seeds of the castor bean plant, *Ricinus communis.* It has been known since antiquity and was used by the Sumerians to make a crude soap and by the Egyptians in embalming fluid.

Today most castor oil comes from either Brazil or India. The highly refined oil is almost tasteless and odorless, but poorer grades have a very unpleasant taste. Chemically, castor oil is classified as a triglyceride, and it is composed, for the most part, of glycerol and ricinoleic acid. It solidifies at −10°C (14°F) and is soluble in ether, benzene, chloroform, and carbon disulfide.

Castor oil may be taken internally as a cathartic, but if taken too often it may cause severe irritation of the intestine. Castor oil is used industrially in polyurethane foams and plastics. After treatment with sulfuric acid it is used in the dyeing and finishing of textiles. Dehydrated castor oil is used in the varnish and paint industries as a drying oil, and partially dehydrated castor oil is a valuable component in hydraulic fluids and lubricants. Castor oil is a source of sebacic acid, which is used in the production of nylon 610.

ALVIN I. KOSAK, *New York University*

CASTRATION is the removal of the testicles, or sperm-producing organs, from the male. The term "castration" is also used sometimes to denote the removal of the ovaries from the female, but *ovariectomy* and *spaying* are the preferred terms for this procedure. After castration, stallions are known as geldings, bulls as steers, boars as barrows, and rams as wethers.

Reasons for Castration. Many reasons are given for castrating animals: (1) It may be used to sterilize males to prevent propagation of undesirable characteristics and thus facilitate selective breeding. (2) It permits males to be housed together without fighting, and males and females to be housed together without reproducing. (3) It changes the disposition of the male and makes him easier to handle. (4) It enables meat-producing animals to gain more flesh than noncastrated animals. (5) It retards the development of secondary sexual characteristics and causes changes in some internal organs. (6) It permits the normal continuation of life when the testicles are diseased or contain tumors.

Age for Castrating. The age at which animals are castrated varies with the species. Colts are usually castrated at one or two years of age, depending on their intended use and the degree of muscular development or other characteristics desired. Calves are frequently castrated between 6 weeks and 4 months of age, lambs and pigs between 2 and 6 weeks, and dogs and cats between 6 and 12 months.

Methods of Castration. The methods used for castrating animals vary with the species. Surgical removal of the testicles is the method most commonly used in horses. The surgery, under anesthesia, may be performed when the animal is standing or in a recumbent position. Pigs, calves, and lambs are also castrated surgically, but other methods may be employed. In the western United States, range calves and lambs are frequently castrated by the application of rubber bands above the testicles. This causes a cessation of the blood supply to the testicles, and the testicular tissue drops away after a period of time. Occasionally, however, tetanus or lockjaw results from the use of rubber bands. A third method of castration employs the *emasculatome,* an instrument that cuts the spermatic cord leading from the testicles and decreases blood circulation to the testicles. This causes the testicles to shrink and become nonfunctional.

KEITH WAYT, *Colorado State University*

CASTRATO, käs-trä'tō, in music, a male singer who has been emasculated to retain his prepubescent vocal range. Another term is *evirato.* The barbarous practice arose from the Roman Catholic Church's ban on women singing in services. The power and virtuosity of castrato voices created a demand for them for opera as well as for church music. Male sopranos and contraltos flourished in the 17th and 18th centuries, and a castrato sang in the Vatican Choir as late as 1903. The emergence about 1800 of the *musico* (a female contralto singing heroic male roles) indicates that the concept of the castrato persisted after the castrato vogue had waned.

Many castrati won fame and earned huge fees. Farinelli (Carlo Broschi) and Francesco Senesino were idols of Handel's time. Gluck wrote the role of Orfeo for the male contralto Gaetano Guadagni, and Girolamo Crescentini was a favorite singer of Napoleon. The last famous castrato to sing in opera was Giovanni Velluti. His appearance in 1825 in London, where a castrato had not sung for many years, aroused criticism.

The castrato roles pose a major problem for contemporary revivals of operas written for them. They may be given to women, who can sing the music at the original pitch, or to men, for whom the music must be transposed. Neither solution is wholly satisfactory, since the "normal" voice lacks the unique timbre of the castrato.

WILLIAM ASHBROOK, *Author of "Donizetti"*

CASTRES, kȧs'trə, is a city in southern France, in Tarn department, on the Agout River, 45 miles (72 km) east of Toulouse. Castres is a trade center and manufacturing city, specializing in the production of woolen textiles, knitwear and hosiery, machine tools, toys, chemicals, and wood products. It has a small airport and good rail and road facilities.

Castres was the ancient Roman town of Castra Albiensium and was an episcopal see from the early 14th century until the French Revolution. There is a fine 17th century town hall, which houses the city's Goya Museum, devoted primarily to Spanish masters. Behind this building (which once served as the episcopal palace) on the banks of the Agout is a beautiful park and garden in the style of the Tuileries in Paris. There are also many interesting old houses along the river, some of which have authentic medieval features. The churches of St. Benoît and Notre Dame de la Platé and the Hôtel de Nayrac are also of interest. Population: (1962) 32,012.

HOMER PRICE, *Hunter College, New York*

CASTRIES, kȧs-trē', the capital of St. Lucia, in the Caribbean, is situated on the island's northwest coast. The chief port of St. Lucia, it has an excellent landlocked harbor and good docking facilities, handling exports of bananas, sugar and sugar products, and citrus fruits. There is some processing of limes, sugar, rum, and bay oil.

Founded by the French about 1650, Castries became British in 1814. It was largely destroyed by fire in 1948 and subsequently rebuilt. Noteworthy are the square dominated by the Church of the Immaculate Conception, George V Park, and the market. A white, sandy beach stretches to the northwest. Population: (1960) 4,353.

RICHARD E. WEBB
British Information Services, New York

CASTRO, käs'trō, family name of four brothers prominent in Argentine music.

JOSÉ MARÍA CASTRO (1892–1964) was a cellist, conductor, and composer. Born in Buenos Aires on Nov. 17, 1892, he studied music there and began his career as a chamber music performer. From 1933 until shortly before his death he was director of the Municipal Band of Buenos Aires. He composed a concerto grosso (1932); concertos for piano, for cello, and for violin; string quartets; and piano pieces.

JUAN JOSÉ CASTRO (1895–1968), composer and conductor, was the most prominent member of the family. He won the Verdi Prize in 1951 for his opera *Proserpina and the Stranger,* which was produced at La Scala in Milan in 1952.

Juan José Castro was born in Avellaneda, a suburb of Buenos Aires, on March 7, 1895, and studied piano, violin, and theory in Buenos Aires and composition in Paris with Vincent d'Indy. In Buenos Aires he became a conductor at the Teatro Colón (opera) in 1930 and subsequently also of the orchestra of the Asociación Sinfónica. When Juan Perón came to power in 1946, Juan José Castro left Argentina and from 1951 to 1953 was conductor of the Melbourne (Australia) Symphony Orchestra. In 1955 he returned to Buenos Aires as conductor of the National Symphony Orchestra. His compositions include the operas *La zapatera prodigiosa* (1949) and *Bodas de sangre* (1956); *Sinfonía Biblica* (1932), for chorus and orchestra; *Sinfonía Argentina* (1934); concertos for piano and for violin; *Martín Fierro,* a cantata for soli, chorus, and orchestra; and chamber music. He died on Sept. 3, 1968.

LUIS ARNALDO CASTRO (1902–), violinist and musicologist, performed in chamber groups and orchestras in Buenos Aires.

WASHINGTON CASTRO (1909–), cellist, composer, and conductor, directed the Symphony Orchestra of Santa Fe, Argentina, and composed several symphonic and chamber works.

GILBERT CHASE, *Tulane University*

CASTRO, käs'trō, **Cipriano** (1858–1924), Venezuelan dictator. He was the son of an Andean cowboy of Indian blood. As a young cavalryman, Cipriano joined the army of a Venezuelan dictator and became the governor of his native province of Táchira. Following a change in government in Caracas, he was exiled to Colombia. There he amassed a large fortune in illegal cattle trading and hired a personal army of cowboys that enabled him to seize Caracas. On May 23, 1899, he declared himself "supreme military commander of Venezuela," and in February 1902, president. He was finally overthrown by another cowboy general, Juan Vicente Gomez, in 1908.

Castro was constantly involved in uprisings, duels over mistresses, and the imprisonment of political rivals. He leased oil-drilling rights at Maracaibo but made no payments on foreign debts contracted by his predecessors, and in 1902, British, German, and Italian warships set up a blockade to force payment. Theodore Roosevelt intervened diplomatically and implied that the United States was responsible for "policing" the financial arrangements of small Latin American countries with Europe. Ousted from the presidency in 1908, Castro spent his remaining years in exile in Puerto Rico. He died at San Juan on Dec. 4, 1924.

HELEN MILLER BAILEY
East Los Angeles College

CAMERA PRESS—PIX

FIDEL CASTRO, revolutionary premier of Cuba, shown making one of his major political speeches in Havana.

CASTRO, kăsh'trōō, **Eugénio de** (1869–1944), Portuguese poet, who introduced symbolism into Portuguese literature. He was born in Coimbra on March 4, 1869, and was educated in Lisbon. He taught French at the University of Lisbon, and from 1914 to 1939 at the University of Coimbra. Castro's first two volumes of poetry, published in 1884, are traditional in style; but his next two volumes, *Oaristos* (1890) and *Horas* (1891), established him as the first major Portuguese symbolist. In 1895 he helped to found *Arte,* a short-lived symbolist journal. Castro's bleakly impersonal poetry, strict in form, greatly influenced other Portuguese writers. He died in Coimbra on Aug. 17, 1944.

CASTRO, käs'trō, **Fidel** (1926–), Cuban political leader, who transformed his island nation into the first Communist state in the Western hemisphere. His adherents regarded him as the most effective revolutionary leader in Latin America. His enemies charged him with political demagoguery and tyranny. Although unwilling to test his popularity at the polls, Castro reportedly enjoyed considerable support among the Cuban people. Nevertheless, from time to time counterrevolutionary forces became active.

Early Years. Fidel Castro Ruz was born in Birán district, Mayari municipality, Oriente province, Cuba, on Aug. 13, 1926. His father, Ángel Castro, a native of Galicia, Spain, was a moderately wealthy cane planter; his mother, Lina Ruz González, was a native Cuban. After attending a Catholic school in Santiago de Cuba, Fidel graduated from Belén College (a Catholic high school in Havana) and entered the University of Havana as a law student in 1945. More than six feet tall and heavily built, Castro was an outstanding athlete in Belén. Because of his determination to impose his will on his fellow students, however, he was not popular either in Belén or the university. During his university days he joined one of the armed revolutionary groups in the institution, which were warring among themselves.

In 1947, Castro joined the expedition (based on Cayo Confites) prepared by Dominican exiles and Cubans to overthrow Generalissimo Rafael L. Trujillo of the Dominican Republic, but the attempt was broken up by the Cuban government. The following year Castro participated in riots that erupted during the Ninth International Conference of American States in Bogotá.

Road to Power. After graduating from the university with a doctor of law degree in 1950, Castro joined the Ortodoxo party (a reform group) and entered a race for Congress. However, three months before the scheduled elections former president Fulgencio Batista overthrew the government of Carlos Prío Socarrás. On July 26, 1953, Castro led some 160 young revolutionaries in a suicidal attack on the Moncada army post in Santiago de Cuba. Most of them were killed; Castro was sentenced to 15 years' imprisonment, and his younger brother Raúl to 13 years. They were released by the Batista regime in a political amnesty in 1954 and fled to Mexico, where they named their revolutionary movement the "26th of July." About this time Castro's wife, Mirta Díaz Balart, whom he had married in 1948, divorced him; the couple had one son, Fidel.

Castro landed with an armed expedition of 81 men on the southern coast of Oriente province, Cuba, on Dec. 2, 1956. All but 12 of his men were killed or captured by the Batista troops, but he and the other survivors fled into the vastness of the Sierra Maestra. From this headquarters Castro, aided by young revolutionaries throughout the island, waged a propaganda war that, more than his military activities, finally brought him victory.

Batista fled Cuba early on Jan. 1, 1959, and Castro, the undisputed leader of the revolutionary forces, undertook the formation of the new Cuban government. Manuel Urrutia, a former judge, was proclaimed president of the new regime. Castro himself assumed the premiership on February 16; he relinquished that post briefly in July in order to force the ouster of the more moderate Urrutia.

Ruler of Cuba. Promising to establish an honest government, restore the 1940 constitution, guarantee a free press, and respect individual rights and private property, Castro won the support of the majority of the Cuban people. But after he gained power, he boasted to a crowd of peasants that he had deceived his active supporters—who were in the upper and middle property-owning classes—as to his plans for government. (The peasants had remained largely indifferent to Castro until he won.) From the day Castro marched into Havana, he attacked the United States and campaigned against "Yankee imperialism" in an effort to become the leader of the Latin American left. His government confiscated more than $1 billion of American-owned property in Cuba, cut off trade with the United States, imprisoned and executed Americans, and forced most of them to leave the island. The United States broke off diplomatic relations with Cuba on Jan. 3, 1961.

At the same time, the Castro government took over Cuban industry and commerce and allied Cuba with the Communist bloc. It executed more than 1,000 former members of the Batista regime and Castro's own followers who disagreed with his policy of leading the country into the Communist orbit. It deported several hundred Catholic priests, seized all Catholic and other private schools, and began the Communist indoctrination of Cuban youth. In the first nine years of the Castro regime, some 500,000 persons fled Cuba. In 1965, Castro said that anyone who didn't like to live in Cuba could leave. The United States established an airlift, but the number of Cubans seeking to escape the island far exceeded the number that could be accommodated.

Under Castro, Cuba was converted into a fortress, armed with weapons acquired from the Communist countries and administered by a one-party government that exercised dictatorial control over the nation's political and economic life. A vast internal spy network frustrated opponents of the regime. Castro kept up his campaign against the United States and his efforts to encourage Communists throughout Latin America to overthrow their own governments. On Dec. 2, 1961, he threw off his mask of a nationalist and declared to the world: "I am a Marxist-Leninist and will be one until the day I die."

In April 1961, Cuban exiles trained and equipped with U. S. help made an unsuccessful attempt to invade Cuba and overthrow Castro. The exiles expected the U. S. to follow them in with air support but President John F. Kennedy canceled this plan at the last moment. The precipitate failure of the Bay of Pigs landing enhanced Castro's prestige.

In October 1962, U. S. intelligence uncovered the presence of Soviet intermediate-range missiles on Cuban soil. The ensuing showdown between the United States and Russia resulted in the withdrawal of the weapons. In the course of the crisis, Castro's Cuba was exposed as a cold-war pawn, and Castro's prestige was damaged.

The ideological rift between the Soviet Union and Communist China posed a dilemma for Castro. The severity and austerity of his domestic programs and the fervency with which he sought to "export" his revolution to Latin America seemed to place Castro in the Chinese camp. However, the Cuban dictator had to rely heavily on military and economic aid from the Soviet bloc, valued at $1 million a day or more. Castro and the Chinese exchanged sharp words in public in 1966 after the Peking regime allegedly failed to fulfill terms of a trade pact. The Soviet Union regarded Castro as an expensive headache but the best guarantor that communism could maintain a foothold in the Western Hemisphere.

R. HART PHILLIPS
Latin American Correspondent for "Newsday"

Further Reading: Draper, Theodore, *Castroism: Theory and Practice* (New York 1965); Phillips, R. Hart, *The Cuban Dilemma* (New York 1963).

CASTRO, käs'trō, **José María** (1818–1893), Costa Rican president. He was born in San José, Costa Rica, on Sept. 1, 1818. He was elected to a 6-year term as president in 1847. He officially declared his country's independence from the Central American Federation and established the Republic of Costa Rica, earning for himself the title of "Founder of the Republic." After unsuccessful attempts to settle boundary disputes with neighboring Nicaragua and Colombia, he resigned in 1849 and was succeeded by his vice president, Juan Rafael Mora. Returned to the presidency in 1866, Castro served until 1868. He died in San José on April 4, 1893.

CASTRO, käs'trō, **Raúl** (1931–   ), Cuban revolutionary leader, who assisted his older brother Fidel in overthrowing the regime of Fulgencio Batista. He became commander of the Cuban armed forces when Fidel became premier.

Raúl Castro Ruz was born in the Birán district of Oriente province on June 3, 1931. He was educated in Jesuit schools in Santiago de Cuba and attended the University of Havana. On July 26, 1953, Raúl accompanied Fidel in an unsuccessful revolt at Santiago. He and Fidel were imprisoned and then went into exile in Mexico in 1955. After their clandestine landing on the Oriente coast in December 1956, Raúl continued as his brother's loyal subordinate. Because of his reputation for coldness and brutality, he was not as popular as his brother. In 1960, Raúl was made head of the ministry of revolutionary armed forces.

R. HART PHILLIPS, *"Newsday"*

CASTRO, käs'trō, **Rosalía de** (1837–1885), Spanish poet and novelist, who was the greatest modern writer in the Galician dialect. She was born in Santiago on Feb. 21, 1837, and grew up in Padrón, La Coruña province. She began writing verse at the age of 11. In 1856 she went to Madrid, where in 1858 she married the historian Manuel Murguía. Her first book of verse was *La flor* (1857). It was followed by *Cantares gallegos* (1863), which won her fame. She also published four novels. She died in Padrón on July 15, 1885.

Rosalía de Castro's poetry derives from Galician folk poetry but adds formal and metrical innovations. *Cantares gallegos* reflects the spirit of the Galicians; the more personal *Follas novas* (1880) and *En las orillas del Sar* (1884) express a melancholy pessimism. These volumes influenced later Spanish poets, including García Lorca.

CASTRO ALVES, kȧsh'trōō äl'vēs, **Antônio de** (1847–1871), Brazilian poet, whose writings were influential in the abolition of slavery in Brazil. He was born in Curralinho (now Castro Alves) on March 14, 1847. He studied law in Recife and São Paulo, but his studies were cut short by tuberculosis, of which he died in Salvador on July 6, 1871.

Castro Alves published only one book, the verse collection *Espumas flutuantes* (1870; *Floating Foam*). He is better known, however, for the posthumously published volumes *Gonzaga, ou a Revolução de Minas* (1875; *Gonzaga, or the Revolution at Minas*), *Vozes d'Africa* (1880; *Voices of Africa*), and *Os escravos* (1883; *The Slaves*). His poetry, influenced by Victor Hugo, combines strong emotion with verbal opulence. His fiery social conscience led Brazilians to name him "the poet of the slaves."

CASTRO DEL RÍO, käs'trō thel rē'ō, is a town in Spain, in Córdoba province. It is located 22 miles (35 km) southeast of the city of Córdoba, on the Guadajoz River. The town is a market center for agricultural produce, and a number of items are manufactured there, including woolen cloth, soap, and chocolate. The oldest part of the town is surrounded by ruined Moorish fortifications; the modern town lies outside the walls. Old buildings of interest include a 15th century church and a Moorish castle, rebuilt in the late 15th century. Population: (1960) 11,842.

CASTRO VALLEY, kas′trō, is an unincorporated suburban area in western California, in Alameda county, 19 miles (30 km) southeast of San Francisco. It is primarily a residential district. The site was originally part of a Mexican grant made in 1841 to Don Guillermo Castro. Castro dissipated his lands to pay off gambling debts and sold the last of his extensive cattle ranges in 1864. Castro Valley is governed by the Alameda county board of supervisors. Population: 44,760.

PHYLLIS A. PEPPERELL
Castro Valley Branch Library

CASTRO Y BELLVÍS, käs′trō ē bel-yə-vēs′, **Guillén de** (1569–1631), Spanish dramatist, who wrote the plays *Las mocedades del Cid* and *Las hazañas del Cid;* the former served as the model for the tragedy *Le Cid* by the 17th century French playwright Corneille. Castro influenced his contemporary, the great dramatist Lope de Vega, and in turn was influenced by Cervantes, on whose novels he based three of his plays. He was also influenced by the traditional folk ballads of Castile, some of which he incorporated into his historical plays. Among his other major dramas are *La fuerza de la sangre* and *El conde de Alarcos*.

Castro was born in Valencia, Spain, in 1569. After serving as a cavalry captain in the army of Valencia and as a Spanish administrator in the Kingdom of Naples, Italy, he went to Madrid about 1620. There he gained the protection and financial support of the Duke de Osuna and of the Count Duke de Olivares, who was influential in having Castro created a knight of the Order of Santiago. Castro, however, alienated his friends and eventually lost his privileges. He died, a charity case, in a Madrid hospital in 1631.

ALVA V. EBERSOLE, *Adelphi University*

CASUISTRY, kazh′wə-strē, is the reasoned interpretation of the general moral law in terms of a particular instance, or case. The word is derived from the Latin *casus,* meaning "case," and is applied, generally, to theology, although it is pertinent also to jurisprudence and psychology, among other fields. In theology, casuistry pertains to the application of moral principles to singular cases of conscience. It attempts to give the individual some direction in solving his questions of conscience by reducing broad general moral principles to the level of the problems faced in everyday life.

The moral law is essentially abstract. When it must be brought to bear on the specific act, which is unique and singular, moral principles must be defined so that the individual action can be interpreted in terms of its context within the moral law. The particular act, precisely because it can be so complex in its motives, remains difficult to analyze. This analysis is the function of casuistry. It allows the theologian to bridge the gap between the general moral principle and the specific situation. Such situations can then be used as types, or norms, to which the conscience can apply in judging the moral significance of a singular, concrete action.

There is, however, a grave danger that, since casuistry is generally of value for every person in the very same circumstances, it cannot take into account the strictly personal factors present in a particular situation. The danger here is evident. Loosely constructed, casuistry can be made to serve as a substitute for personal responsibility and decision, since only the individual can know all of the factors surrounding a particular case of conscience. It is in this type of application that casuistry has come into disrepute.

Taken, however, in terms of general examples illustrating moral application, the results of casuistry can be of value, even indispensable, for the individual conscience in making specific decisions. In the words of St. Thomas Aquinas' *Summa theologica:* "Anyone who perfectly knew the principles according to all their virtualities (possibilities) would not need any conclusions proposed to him separately. But, because those who know principles do not know them so as to consider everything that is found contained in them, it is necessary that, in the sciences, the conclusions be deduced from principles."

The science of casuistry is not new. It goes back to the origins of Christianity, when Christ sought to solve particular problems of the community (see Luke 20:20–26; Mark 2:23–28). St. Paul used casuistry at great length in his first epistle to the Corinthians to define the moral law on the eating of sacrifical meat, on work, on virginity, and on other practices. The church in both its Catholic and Protestant branches has continued this tradition. Casuistry has often been abused throughout the course of history. However, when casuistry is used well, it remains indispensable in achieving flexibility and awareness in the application of moral principles to the concrete situations of life.

PETER J. RIGA
St. Mary's College, Moraga, Calif.

CASWELL, kaz′wel, **Hollis Leland** (1901–), American educator. Caswell was born in Woodruff, Kans., on Oct. 22, 1901. He was educated at the University of Nebraska and at Columbia University, where he received his Ph. D. in 1929. He served as curriculum consultant to state departments of education and city school systems from 1929 until 1937, when he was appointed professor and head of the department of curriculum and teaching at Columbia's Teachers College. From 1943 to 1948 he was director of demonstration schools and school experimentation. From 1954 to 1962, Caswell was president of Teachers College.

Caswell was an important figure in the reappraisal of public education that took place in the 1950's. He challenged educators to seek new knowledge and more effective means of making education a vital force in the lives of students. He wrote several books, including *Education in the Elementary School,* with A. W. Foshay (rev. ed. 1950), and, with associates, *Curriculum Development in Public School Systems* (1950).

CASWELL, kaz′wel, **Richard** (1729–1789), American politician, who was North Carolina's first governor after independence. He was born in Cecil county, Md., on Aug. 3, 1729. From 1754 to 1771 he was a member of the North Carolina assembly, and during the Revolutionary period he served in the Continental Congress. An officer in the North Carolina militia, he won a decisive victory at Moore's Creek on Feb. 22, 1776. He subsequently held numerous state offices, including the governorship (1776–1780; 1785–1787). He died in Fayetteville, N. C., in November 1789.

CAT

THE ABYSSINIAN, probably the closest living link to the first domesticated cat, is native to the upper Nile Valley.

CAT, Domestic. The domestic cat (*Felis catus*) is a small member of the cat family (Felidae), which also includes lions, tigers, cheetahs, lynxes, and many others (see CAT FAMILY). It has lived in association with man since ancient times and has been widely kept both as a pet and as a mouser.

Modern Popularity. Today the cat enjoys a popularity greater than even many cat admirers realize. Despite the far greater number of dog shows, cats are believed to outnumber dogs by several millions; estimates of the cat population of the United States range as high as 30 million, although a conservative figure of about 25 million seems more valid. In part, the increased popularity of the cat has been brought about by the urbanization of the country, for many people have found cats more convenient apartment pets than dogs. However, even some families that have dogs as pets also keep cats. Indeed, a national survey conducted for the pet food industry found that one-third of the families that owned dogs also had cats, and there was a dog in fully half of all the cat-owning households. Obviously most people have come to realize how little truth there is to the legendary hostility between cat and dog. A few rare souls have even managed to keep uncaged birds and cats together without misfortune befalling the feathered pets—but this is not recommended for most people.

CHARACTERISTICS OF CATS

Anatomy. The zoological order Carnivora, to which cats belong, includes animals whose brains are well developed, whose teeth are generally adapted to shearing meat, whose toes are furnished with claws, and whose clavicles (collarbones) are lacking or incomplete. The sense of smell is the predominant one.

The domestic cat, in general, is not very large, averaging 5 to 6 pounds (about 2.5 kg) in weight. It is, however, muscular and strong for its size. A cat is very well coordinated and supple. With the tail assisting in balance, it usually but not always lands on its feet when falling or being dropped.

The most specialized features of the cat are the teeth and claws. The large canine teeth are used for stabbing and holding the prey; the cutting of the food is done by sharp ridges on the shearing, or carnassial, teeth in the back of the mouth. On each side the upper shearing tooth is the last premolar; in the lower jaw it is the first molar tooth. The lower jaw is attached to the skull in such a way as to permit only up-and-down movement; side-to-side grinding is impossible.

The cat's long, sharp claws are used for catching, holding, and subduing prey. The claws can be retracted into sheaths, and this keeps them from being damaged or dulled by walking. Extension or retraction of the claws is accomplished by tendons attached to the end of the bones of the toes. The front claws are kept sharp by pulling them through tough material like tree bark or cloth. The rear claws are kept sharp by biting and normal wear. The forefeet, unlike the hind feet, possess a fifth claw.

The tabby, or striped, marking is an extremely common one. It is believed to be a direct and persistent throwback to the domestic cat's wild ancestors. Tabby is such a classic marking that it is virtually synonymous with the word "cat." There are two distinct tabby designs: the torquata pattern and the catus, or blotched, pattern. The torquata tabby has narrow stripes transversely, or vertically, arranged on the sides of the body behind the shoulders. Toward the posterior these markings have a tendency to break into shorter stripes or spots. The blotched tabby has broad stripes that usually are looped or spiraled behind the shoulders. There are generally three stripes on the back, running to the root of the tail. These two tabby patterns underlie most of the solid-colored coats in cats, and from time to time a cat will be born on whom the stripes can be seen under the solid color.

Domestic cats display a wide variety of eye colors, including blue, green, yellow, and copper. "Odd-eyed" cats, those having each eye a different color, are not uncommon.

Hunting. The domestic cat is a predator by nature. Like nearly all other members of the cat family, it hunts by stealth and catches its prey with sudden short bursts of speed. The chase response is present even in those cats that live in city apartments and never have the opportunity to get outside. Catching mice and other small animals is part of the outdoor cat's life.

Cats and Birds. There is no question that cats do stalk and kill birds, but cats are an insignificant factor in overall bird mortality. To cite two of a number of biological studies of the stomach contents of cats, only 6 of 50 cats in Wisconsin had eaten birds as their last meal, and birds provided a final repast for only 4% of a group of cats in Oklahoma. Wildlife authorities insist that other birds—jays, for example—kill more birds than do cats. Moreover, cats are themselves the prey of some birds, like the great horned owl.

Nevertheless, it is still popularly believed that cats generally cause serious reductions in the number of birds. One of the usual measures taken to regulate the size and activities of cat population is municipal licenses, as is done with dogs. In vetoing such a bill after it had passed the Illinois state legislature, Gov. Adlai E. Stevenson wrote, "It is the nature of cats to do a certain amount of unescorted roaming. . . . I am afraid this bill could only create discord, recrimination, and enmity. . . . Consider the owner's dilemma: To escort a cat abroad on a leash is against the nature of a cat, and to permit it to venture forth for exercise unattended into a night of new dangers [because of anti-cat laws] is against the nature of the owner. Moreover, cats perform useful service, particularly in rural areas, in combating rodents—work they necessarily perform alone and without regard for property lines. The problem of cat versus bird is as old as time. If we attempt to resolve it by legislation, who knows but what we may be called upon to take sides as well in the age-old problems of dog versus cat, bird versus bird, or even bird versus worm."

Play. Cats are intelligent and freedom-loving creatures. This spirit of independence, attributable to the solitary nature of the cat's wild ancestors, has remained with the cat through several thousand years of domestication. But this independence has in no way diminished the playful nature of the cat. Toys, therefore, should be provided whenever possible. Lightweight balls, wadded paper tied to the end of a string, and items that make some noise create interest in both young and old. Catnip is a stimulant to most cats and should not be used continuously. Boxes, paper bags, and doll houses to crawl into are greatly enjoyed.

Purring. When contented and occasionally when hungry or angry, a cat may make a purring sound. There is some uncertainty as to how this sound is made. One opinion is that it is produced by vibrations of the false vocal cords (membranes lying above the true vocal cords); another is that the hyoid apparatus, a series of small bones between the skull and larynx (voice box), which serves as a support for the tongue, is the source of the purring sound.

Life Cycle. Sexual maturity refers to an animal's ability to reproduce. Male cats (tomcats) mature sexually at about 10 months of age; in the female cat, sexual maturity generally occurs between 7 and 12 months of age. Some female kittens will come into season as early as 4 or 5 months old and are capable of becoming pregnant then. However, the general rule is to breed a female cat only when she has reached physical maturity, at about one year of age. The interval between "seasons," or "heat," varies greatly in individuals. Some cats follow a predictable pattern; others do not.

A female cat in season may alarm her owners by displaying odd behavior. She may roll over, call and moan continually, bend down and tread her hind feet, and appear very loving in every demonstrable way. Cats ordinarily breed two or three times a year with no set breeding season, but breeding usually reaches a peak in late winter and late spring.

Ovulation, the release of the eggs from the ovary, is induced in the female by the sexual act itself. The size of the litter depends on the number of ova that are produced to be fertilized at that time.

Superfetation (the presence of two or more fetuses of different ages in the uterus) has been reported. The occurrence of superfecundity is more common. In this instance, two or more ova liberated at the same ovulation are impregnated during successive acts of mating. Such a litter may have two or more sires; each kitten, of course, will have only one sire.

The gestation period, the time from conception to birth, averages 63 days. This commonly will vary 2 to 3 days either way for a total of 60 to 65 days.

Kittens are born blind, and their eyes open at 7 to 10 days. Weaning occurs between the 4th and 6th week of age. At birth, kittens weigh about 3½ ounces (100 grams), and most will double their birth weight at one week of age. Kittens doing well will gain about 6 to 7 ounces (180 grams) a week.

Kittens learn many things from the mother by her example. They become very adventurous near weaning time, and the mother cat will scold and chirp to keep them in line. At about 8 weeks of age they can be on their own without her supervision.

At 6 months of age, growing cats weigh more than 4 pounds (2 kg). Average maximum growth at 9 to 10 months for the male results in 7 to 11 pounds (3 to 5 kg) of weight. The female weight gain falls off after 6 months, and by 9 months most females will weigh 5 to 6 pounds (about 2.5 kg).

LESTER E. FISHER
Lincoln Park Zoological Gardens

BREEDS

In its travels to every part of the world inhabited by man, the domestic cat has been transformed into a species of almost unbelievable variety in color, size, and structure. Several factors have contributed to these differences. Environmental conditions, especially extremes of heat and cold, played their part; so did the interbreeding of domestic cats with wild felines. Many zoologists theorize that today's longhairs may be traceable to the union of domestic cats with the manul, or Pallas's cat, found in central Asia. But the most significant elements in the development of such diverse breeds have been genetic mutations and their perpetuation by selective breeding. The Manx, Siamese, Himalayan, and Rex breeds originated in this manner.

The principal breeds recognized by most cat fanciers' organizations can be divided into three groups: longhairs, shorthairs, and Rex.

Longhair—*Persian*. These basically solid-color cats have been known in Europe for centuries, but they probably originated in the Middle East. Rather large, short-bodied cats, they have round, massive heads, broad, snub noses, and long, fine, glossy coats. Breeders have developed a remarkable range of colors, including white, black, blue, red, cream, chinchilla (sometimes referred to as silver), shaded silver, smoke, tabby (in silver, brown, blue, or red), cameo (cream background color with shadings, in varieties called shell, shaded, smoke, or tabby), tortoiseshell (a black, orange, and cream combination), tortoiseshell-and-white (also called calico), and blue-cream. Tortoiseshell, tortoiseshell-and-white, and blue-cream males are scarcely ever found, for these are sex-linked colors, carried from generation to generation in the sex-determining chromosome that produces female kittens. The rare males with these colors are usually sterile.

***Peke-Faced*.** Conforming in color, markings, and general type to the red and red-tabby Persians, this cat has a head that closely resembles that of a Pekingese dog, with a very short nose, a depression between the eyes, a wrinkled muzzle, and very round, large, wide-set eyes.

***Himalayan*.** Named not for the Asian mountain range but for the similarly marked Himalayan rabbit, this cat resembles the Persian in body structure and head, but its coloring and markings (points) are like those of the Siamese. The points are the areas of darker color on the mask, ears, paws, and tail. The eyes of the Himalayan are blue. Genetically, the Himalayan demonstrates a partial albinism, as do the Siamese and Burmese breeds. Himalayan cats have the gentle voice of the Persian.

***Balinese*.** This is essentially a Siamese with long hair, just as the Himalayan is a Persian that happens to have Siamese coloring. Produced by inbreeding from Siamese long-coated mutants, the Balinese has a body type that reflects its Siamese ancestry, as do its voice and temperament. Only the fur looks Persian.

Shorthairs—*Domestic Shorthair*. Sometimes labeled "American Shorthair" by cat fanciers but regarded as an "alley cat" by the uninformed, this breed can be found in all the Persian colors. Show cats of this breed have been carefully developed for generations, and they yield place to no other breed in excellence.

***Siamese*.** One of the most popular breeds today, the Siamese probably originated in China but first came to the attention of Europeans in Thailand in the latter half of the 19th century. Playful and "talkative," the Siamese is long, slim, and lithe, with a long, wedge-shaped head. It is not uncommon to see a Siamese with a kinky tail or crossed eyes; although these features often endear the cat to its owner, they are considered serious faults in breeding. Siamese are bred in several colors, including seal point, blue point, chocolate point, lilac point, and albino. The Red Color-point Shorthair, although technically classed as a separate breed, is really a Siamese with a clear white body color and points of dense, deep red.

WALTER CHANDOHA

A MANX CAT bearing the torquata tabby markings. The Manx has no tail, and, with its forelegs shorter than its hind legs, looks rather like a rabbit in motion.

***Burmese*.** The rich, warm, sable brown of this cat, set off by brilliant golden eyes, makes the Burmese one of the most striking of breeds, which probably explains its rapid increase in popularity. It is closely related to the Siamese; the mating of two cats, each carrying genes for both Burmese and Siamese, will produce three Burmese kittens and one Siamese. (Siamese-Burmese hybrids are known as Tonkinese or Honey Siamese.) Very affectionate, the Burmese is also noted for its playfulness.

***Abyssinian*.** This breed, from the upper Nile Valley, is probably the closest living link to the first domesticated cat. Its coat has the protective coloration needed for a desert environment: ruddy brown ticked with various shades of darker brown or black. Exotically handsome, the Abyssinian has never achieved the popularity one might expect it to enjoy.

***Russian Blue*.** In the past sometimes called "Maltese," the Russian Blue is a graceful, noble animal that is too seldom seen. It is gray-blue or slate blue; but the notable feature of its coat is not its beautiful color but its texture, for the Russian Blue's fur is double-coated, somewhat like a seal's, and it is short, thick, and very fine.

***British Blue*.** Almost never seen in the United States, the sturdy British Blue has a coat similar to that of its Russian cousin in color and texture (although it is not as cottony), but its overall appearance is quite different. Whereas the Russian Blue is long and fine-boned, the British Blue is a more compact animal, with shorter legs and a fuller face.

***Manx*.** In some respects this is the most unusual of all the breeds commonly seen: it has a thick double coat, its hind legs are longer than its forelegs, and it has no tail. Believed to have originated in the Far East, the breed has been cultivated for many centuries on the Isle of Man. A Manx in motion looks rather like a rabbit because of the length of its hind legs. For this reason, legend insists—quite erroneously—that the Manx is the result of a cross between a cat and a rabbit. The lack of tail is a gentic mutation, and it is so pronounced that there is actually a depression or hollow where the tail normally would begin. Occasionally a Manx will be born with a very short tail; these cats, ineligible for cat shows, are called "stumpies" to distinguish them from the truly tailless "rumpies." There is a lethal factor accompanying the taillessness: when tailless Manx is bred to tailless, the third generation will be feeble and the fourth generation will be born dead. For that reason, rumpies are often mated with stumpies. All colors can be found in the Manx.

Havana Brown. A relatively new breed developed in Great Britain, the Havana Brown is a sleek, hard, muscular animal of a rich, warm mahogany brown. It is an elegant creature with a somewhat pixieish expression.

Rex. The Rex is a new breed that is regarded as neither longhair nor shorthair. Although its hair is short, it is also wavy, unlike any other cat's. The development of the "rex" coat in cats was not reported until 1953, when it was given the name previously applied to wavy coats in rodents. A mild, gentle cat of almost any color, the Rex has a coat the texture of velvet pile, wavy on the sides and curly like Persian lamb on the abdomen.

Other Breeds. There are many breeds that are unrecognized by official groups and rarely if ever seen in America. Among them are the Korat, an all-gray cat with amber eyes from Thailand; the Burman, a longhair cat with dark mask and rump area, dark legs, white paws, and blue eyes; the curlytailed cats of China; the Mombas cat, an African feline with very short, stiff hair; and the Mexican hairless cat. The Angoras, which derive their name from Ankara, the capital of Turkey, were often seen in America at the turn of the century, but they were soon almost completely supplanted by a somewhat similar longhair type, called Persian. The Maine Coon Cat, a large longhair breed, is considered by some authorities to be of Angora descent and type.

THE CAT FANCY

Cat fanciers, people devoted to the breeding and advancement of cats, make up a group collectively referred to as the "cat fancy." Various organizations within the cat fancy determine and maintain the distinctive qualities of the various cat breeds.

Breed distinctions could not be maintained if there were no organized system for judging specimens to determine how closely they adhered to the ideal (or standard) for the breed. In the American dog fancy one organization governs virtually all breeders and clubs, and in Britain one group, the Governing Council of the Cat Fancy, fills the same role for cats. In Canada the Canadian Cat Association is the governing body. In the United States, however, the cat fancy is splintered. There are seven primary associations: the American Cat Fanciers Association, the American Cat Association, the Cat Fanciers Association, the Crown Cat Fanciers Federation, the Cat Fanciers Federation, the National Cat Fanciers Association, and the United Cat Federation.

Cat Clubs. Every cat club in the United States belongs to one of these seven organizations, which, in addition to maintaining stud (registration) books, also sanction and regulate shows and determine the qualifications of show judges. About 120 cat shows are held annually in the United States. The dates and places of shows and information about the local cat clubs can be obtained from local newspapers, from local cat breeders, from veterinarians, or from the national feline periodicals.

No discussion of the cat fancy would be complete without some reference to the exotic cats —pumas (mountain lions), bobcats, cheetahs, jaguarundis, and, most often, ocelots and margays—that are kept as house pets by a surprising number of people in the United States. Although these cats cannot compete in cat shows, it is not uncommon to see them on display there. The Long Island Ocelot Club represents the owners of these varied exotic cats. It is not limited to ocelot owners, and its membership, despite the name, is national. Most owners of exotic cats are also fanciers of domestic felines.

Cat Shows. What appears to be one cat show may be several shows from an official point of view. One major East Coast show incorporated nine different shows: two all-breed shows and seven specialty shows (shows limited to a specific breed). At most shows there are generally four major categories: kittens (unaltered cats from four to eight months old); championship classes (unaltered animals eight months and older); premiership or peerless classes (altered, or neutered, animals eight months and older); and household pets (cats that do not conform to the standard classifications). It should be noted that unlike most livestock competitions, including dog shows, the cat fancy permits neutered animals to be entered for judging.

The important categories, of course, are the championship classes and, to a lesser extent, the neutered classes. In these two categories, cats, entered within their individual breed-color-sex class, begin as "novices" in their first adult show and advance to "open" after they have received a ribbon indicating best of the class for their breed, color, and sex. A champion (or premier) is a cat that has earned four winner's ribbons under three different judges. The title "Grand Champion" (or "Grand Premier") is bestowed on a cat that has been selected best champion or best-of-opposite-sex champion (or best premier) in enough shows to accumulate a specified number of points.

A cat achieving a championship rating in two cat associations is called a double champion, in three associations, a triple champion, and so on. The American Cat Fanciers Association also awards multiple championships on its own.

Before a cat can be admitted to a show, its owner must produce a veterinary certificate showing that it has been inoculated for enteritis. The cat is then placed in its own cage, where it remains on exhibition when it is not being judged. When its class is about to be judged, a steward removes the cat to one of the cages behind the judging table. The judge examines each cat individually, picking it up and examining it closely. The cat must be examined for type (that is, shape, size, bone, and tail), condition, color, coat, eyes, head, and ears. The household pet class is judged only on beauty and condition. In judging the championship and neuter classes, the judge is guided by a point system and by the standard for the breed.

WILLIAM H. A. CARR
Author of "The Basic Book of the Cat"

YLLA, FROM RAPHO GUILLUMETTE

WALTER CHANDOHA

CATS belonging to recognized breeds include (*clockwise from upper left*) Abyssinian, blue Persian, Himalayan, chinchilla Persian, and Siamese. The Himalayan resembles the Persian in body structure and head, but its markings are like those of the Siamese. The Persian is the most popular longhair breed, and the Siamese is the most popular shorthair breed, with cat fanciers.

WALTER CHANDOHA

YLLA, FROM RAPHO GUILLUMETTE

YLLA, FROM RAPHO GUILLUMETTE

CARE OF CATS

Much research has been directed toward cat diseases. Diagnostic and surgical procedures are continually being refined. The longevity of the cat has steadily increased; the average old age is now 12 to 14 years. Prevention is always better than treatment, so that optimum nutrition, routine immunizations, and prompt medication are recommended.

General Hygiene. The habit of daily grooming is a good one. Healthy cats usually keep themselves clean by constant cleaning or washing with their tongues. Daily use of a comb and brush will help this process, especially in the longhair breeds. Powders like talcum, corn starch, or French chalk can be shaken into the coat before brushing. These powders combine with the natural oil in the hair and act as a good dry cleaner. Regular grooming will minimize the problems of loose hair in the house and the formation of hair balls, which are masses of matted hair that accumulate in the cat's digestive tract as a result of the animal's licking of its fur.

Housecats can have their claws clipped short to minimize scratching damage to household furniture. When clipping the claws, the dewclaw, or thumb, on the inner surface of the front feet should not be forgotten.

Most cats resent regular bathing, and it may take two people to accomplish this safely. A drop of mineral oil or eye ointment placed in the eyes will lessen irritation from soap splashed in the eyes. Drying is especially important because chilling after the bath is a threat to the cat's health. The cat should be wrapped in a towel after the bath; indoors, a blower may be used, if the cat will tolerate it, to help this drying process.

Housebreaking comes easily to most cats. The mother cat takes care of the toilet needs of the newborn; if kittens are orphaned, their bodily functions must be stimulated by gently stroking the belly and anal area, preferably with a ball of absorbent cotton or a piece of soft cloth dampened with warm water.

If kittens have been raised with a mother cat who uses a litter box, they will learn by her example and use the box themselves. Such kittens require no further housebreaking. If a kitten has not used a litter box previously, it can be taught to do so by placing it in the box after each meal and after long naps. Once the kitten begins to use the litter box and recognize its odor, it will use it regularly.

Kittens newly brought into the house should be placed in the litter box first and then allowed to explore their new home from this base. A deep pan or box filled with sand, shredded paper, or a commercial litter makes up the litter box. The litter box should be cleaned at regular, frequent intervals.

The cat's ears should be checked often and cleaned whenever needed. Cotton swabs can be used dry or dipped in oil or alcohol for the purpose.

A special bed is not necessary for the pet cat; a cat will find a place suitable to its needs if given a choice. Most cats, however, do appreciate a soft box or bed to lie in. Areas such as a bed, a living room soft, or a sun parlor window ledge are favorites. Often a dark, quiet corner of a closet or basement will suit the cat best.

Some pet cats will follow their owner about like a puppy and hop on his lap whenever he is seated for a period of time. Other cats may not be seen during the entire daytime period.

Feeding. Until they are 4 weeks old, kittens usually receive all the food they need from their mothers. After that time, however, it is important to begin supplementing the maternal milk with solid food, both to provide sufficient calories and to increase the protein content of the diet. Newly acquired kittens should be fed a diet similar to the one they have been receiving. Gradual changing of the food will minimize digestive upsets. Young kittens should be fed three to four times a day; at 4 months of age, two to three times a day is adequate. Adult cats may be fed once or twice a day. Some authorities recommend free choice, with food available at all times. The feeding habits should be varied with the individual cat's desires as well as those of the owner. Most cats will not overeat with regular feedings.

Kittens will eat about two or three tablespoons of food a day; adult cats will eat 8 to 10 ounces (about 250 grams). Males will eat a little more than females.

Cats that are house pets may be fussy eaters. Milk is not necessary but is a balanced and nutritious food that can be added to the diet. In some individuals the butterfat content of milk may cause loose bowels. Cottage cheese can be an excellent substitute for milk when indicated. In order to maintain health, a varied and balanced diet is important.

In the wild state cats eat small animals in their entirety. This provides the high protein and high caloric diet needed by the cat. Adult cats require over 20% protein in their diet; kittens need more than 30%. Cats also have a great need for the vitamin B complex. Vitamin B is directly related to appetite function and should be supplemented during illness. Fresh water should be available to the cat at all times.

Food can be served in shallow or flat dishes and should be of bite size if possible. Cats do not like to get their noses and muzzles into the food and do not relish food material that sticks to the roof of the mouth. Dried kibble is the product preferred for continual free-choice feeding.

A varied diet is recommended; it prevents the cat from getting used to only one food item, and it makes balancing the diet easier. Food items that most cats like include fish, chicken, liver, kidney, heart, and muscle meats. There are many fine brands of commercial cat food available on the market today.

Vitamin supplements are of value in balancing the diet, and they help with growth in young kittens. Daily use of a multivitamin supplement will do no harm and may minimize danger of dietary deficiencies. Mineral supplements, especially calcium and phosphorus, are important to pregnant cats and growing kittens.

Mineral oil is commonly added to food material once every several weeks to assist with elimination or to prevent hair-ball formation in the intestinal tract.

Older cats may have a diminished sense of taste and smell. Many older cats can be helped by improving the diets and by stimulating the appetite with vitamin B supplements. The injection of hormones by a veterinarian may help the very old cat. If new foods must be used in the

WILLIAM SHAPIRO

Shorthair tabby

CATS

Domestic cats have lived together with man since antiquity, but they carry the sign of their wild ancestry in the tabby—or striped—marking prominent on many cats and microscopically visible even on solid-color cats. The Abyssinian shorthair is an old breed, related to the cats of ancient Egypt. The curly-haired Rex is a new breed, recognized in 1953.

Rex

WALTER CHANDOHA

Abyssinian

MARY ELEANOR BROWNING

Burmese WALTER CHANDOHA

Russian Blue WALTER CHANDOHA

Blue-eyed white Persian WALTER CHANDOHA

PLATE 2

The variety of cat breeds is very large, but there is a basic grouping into longhairs and shorthairs, and, recently, the curly-haired Rex. Both longhairs, such as the Persian, and shorthairs, such as the Burmese, are popular with cat fanciers. The Russian Blue, although not as well known in the Western Hemisphere, is notable both for its thick, double-coated fur and for its graceful bearing.

Silver Persian WALTER CHANDOHA

BROWNING, FROM DE WYS

Seal point Himalayan

PLATE 3

The points referred to in describing a cat's markings are areas of darker coloration on the face, ears, paws, and tail. Similar point markings appear on both longhairs and shorthairs, but there is probably no cat with point markings so well known as those of the shorthaired Siamese.

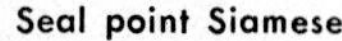

Seal point Siamese

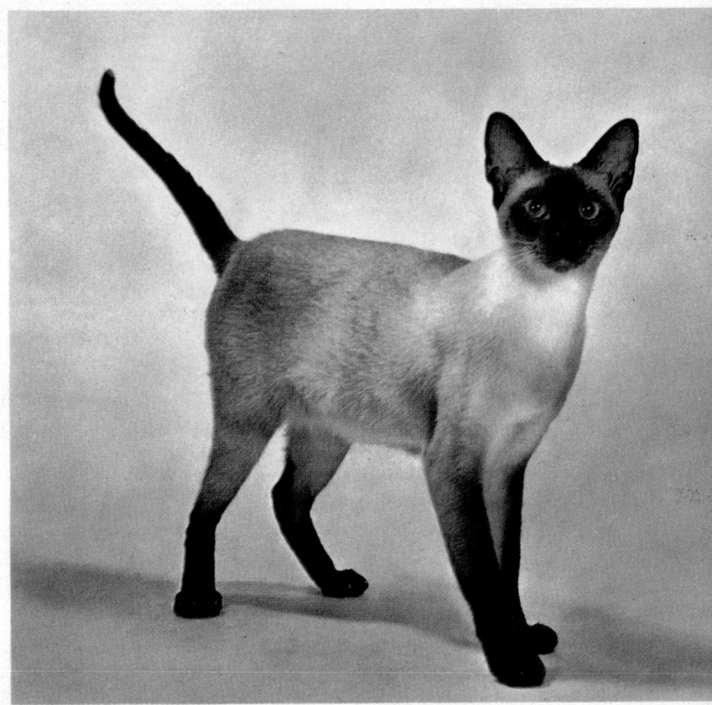

WALTER CHANDOHA

Seal point Himalayan *(left)* with a blue point Siamese.

WALTER CHANDOHA

WALTER CHANDOHA

The calico cat, or tortoiseshell-and-white *(above)*, bears a sex-linked coloration that is usually to be found only in females. Odd-eyed cats *(below)* are not uncommon.

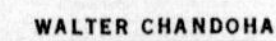

WALTER CHANDOHA

FPG

Careful breeding has perpetuated the tailless Manx *(above)* and the tortoiseshell *(below)*. The Manx, perhaps the most unusual breed, has been cultivated on the Isle of Man.

WALTER CHANDOHA

diet, they can be topped with items that are familiar and have a pleasant taste and flavor. Meat extracts like beef bouillon are good for this purpose.

Ailments. House temperatures are not critical to the cat, since it is a highly adaptable animal. Care should be used, however, to avoid continuous sharp changes in temperature. An adult cat's normal body temperature is 101.5° F (38.5° C), though this may vary either way by 1° F (0.5° C).

Cats are rather hardy animals, but they do have disease problems. A new young kitten should be brought to a veterinarian for a general health checkup. He will determine when to start vaccinations and if there are any other health needs.

Panleukopenia. All serious cat diseases were formerly called "distemper," regardless of symptoms. The first virus isolation was from cats sick with infectious enteritis (inflammation of the intestines). Later the characteristic extensive destruction of the white blood cells was recognized, and the name "panleukopenia" was given to the disease. Panleukopenia is characterized by its sudden and short course, with a very high mortality.

The time it takes for the disease entity to develop following exposure is usually 5 to 6 days. A high fever occurs initially—104° to 105° F (40° to 40.5° C), followed by a drop to normal for 24 hours, then another rise. The cat is very lethargic, and vomiting frequently sets in. Diarrhea occurs several days following onset—if the cat is still alive. Weight loss and dehydration are evident from the onset, and the white blood cell count drops rapidly.

Treatment is aimed at combating the dehydration, preventing secondary infection, and furnishing nourishment. Vaccination against panleukopenia is recommended shortly after weaning (at 7 to 8 weeks of age). Several types of vaccines in single or multiple doses are available commercially and are quite effective.

Pneumonitis. The first sign of pneumonitis is high and usually short-lived fever, accompanied by increased tearing of the eyes; this is followed by a heavy discharge of pus from the eyes and nostrils. Some sneezing and coughing develop. Loss of appetite may develop. Treatment is aimed against secondary bacterial complications, and broad-spectrum antibiotics are used for this. Vaccination is recommended, although it is not specific for all strains of the virus.

Rhinotracheitis. Feline rhinotracheitis has a short incubation time, 2 to 5 days, and the severity of the disease is extremely variable. Fever and sneezing are noted first, followed by salivation (drooling) and sluggishness. The eyes, tongue, and nostrils are involved, and a sinus infection may follow. Treatment is similar to that for pneumonitis. Vaccination is not very effective.

Rabies. Rabies is a contagious disease usually characterized by signs of mental disturbance. It is transmitted by the bite of an infected animal; recent research, however, indicates there may be other means of transmission. Cats are apparently more resistant to the rabies virus than dogs, and the disease is not seen often in pet cats. No treatment is of any value after clinical signs are seen, and once the symptoms appear, death always follows. Vaccination for rabies is recommended for the free-roaming pet cat.

Anemia. The most common anemia in cats is infectious anemia; it is caused by a parasite of the red blood cells. Known as *Hemobartonella felis,* the parasite is a viruslike organism whose classification is still uncertain. Diagnosis is done by microscopic examination of a blood smear, and treatment combines antibiotic therapy along with body-strengthening measures that include whole blood transfusion.

Tumors. Tumors of many different types occur in cats. The tumors are both benign and malignant, with adenocarcinoma (cancer) of the breast quite prevalent. Surgical removal of most tumors is possible, and indications for surgery should be evaluated by the veterinarian.

Abscesses. Primary bacterial infections in cats are not common in the United States. Abscesses, however, may develop in untreated wounds following a fight. The opponent's sharp claws will penetrate the cat's skin and deposit bacteria in the wound. Infection may be evident 3 to 5 days later. Treatment consists of cleansing the wound and applying antibiotics.

Ringworm. Skin diseases are often encountered and range from simple allergies to chronic eczemas. Ringworm, actually a fungus, not only is a stubborn condition but also can be highly contagious to the people in the household. The cat complicates the treating of skin problems because it is continually grooming its skin. Griseofulvin, an antibiotic, has been used successfully in the treatment of ringworm.

Fleas. Parasitic problems, both internal and external, are fairly prevalent. Of the external parasites, fleas and mites are the most commonly encountered. The most difficult problem in ridding the cat of fleas is that the fleas are not all on the host cat at one time. Young (larval) fleas, which may be developing in crevices or corners, represent a continual source of reinfestation. There are many commercial products available that will easily kill the fleas, but only those that are nontoxic for cats can be used, since the cat grooms itself by licking its coat. DDT is essentially harmful to cats.

Worms. There are many internal parasites, but the roundworm and tapeworm are the main medical threats. The new vermifuges (worm killers) available to the veterinarian are efficient and are relatively nontoxic. Microscopic examination will best determine what parasites are present, and both the laboratory examination and prescribed treatment are best done by the veterinarian.

Urinary Stones. The specific cause of frequent stone formation in the urethra of the male cat is not known. The mechanical stoppage constitutes an emergency for the cat and requires immediate treatment by a veterinarian. Otherwise uremic poisoning sets in and causes death. Both drug therapy and surgery are employed in treatment of the condition.

Fractures. Cats living in urban areas are frequently hit by cars and suffer fractures of the skeletal system. In treatment of fractures, splints and other materials are used, and most methods of treatment permit the cat to walk about while wearing a cast. Cats usually have short convalescences after surgical procedures and soon begin walking on their own.

First-aid. Items to keep in the house for first-air treatment of the cat should include a rectal thermometer, bandage material of various widths, adhesive tape, claw clippers, and a mild antiseptic solution. Medication of a sick cat at home may be either easy or difficult, depending on the temperament of the cat and the dexterity of the owner. Cat owners should ask their veterinarians for guidance in home treatment of sick cats and for instruction in techniques to be used in administering the medicine properly and safely.

Neutering. Male cats are usually castrated at less than one year of age. This surgery usually is performed to reduce the male cat's tendency to roam and to minimize odors in the house. A mature, normal tomcat has a very strong urinary odor that can permeate the house even though the best possible absorbent material is used in the litter box. Although a surgical risk is always present, neutering is recommended for most pet cats.

If no kittens are desired, the ovaries and uterus of the female cat are removed by surgery. This procedure is known as "spaying," and it can be done anytime after maturity is reached.

LESTER E. FISHER
Lincoln Park Zoological Gardens

CATS AND MAN

When and where the cat was first domesticated is unknown; the probability is that various small wild felines were tamed in different parts of the world about 5,000 years ago. (For comparison, it might be noted that the dog was domesticated about 50,000 years ago.) There is some statuary evidence that small cats were domesticated in pre-Columbian Florida. There is also reason to believe that the Lake Dwellers of Switzerland kept housecats about 2000 B.C. Sanskrit writings 3,000 years old speak of the cat as a pet in India. Nevertheless, it was in Egypt that the cat first came to the attention of what was then the civilized world.

The household cat of the Egyptians appears to have been closely related to two African wild cats, *Felis ocreata* and *Felis lybica*. The Egyptian cat, looking much like today's Abyssinian but larger, guarded the granaries and homes against rodents. The Egyptians deified the cat as Bast (sometimes given as Pasht, Ubastet, or Bubastis), the goddess of moonlight, fertility, wisdom, and hunting. One of the six major cities of Lower Egypt, Bubastis, was dedicated to the cat goddess. The city appears in the Bible (Ezekiel 30:13,17) under the name Pibeseth. The killing of a cat could be punished by death in Egypt, according to Herodotus. When a cat died, the household went into mourning, and the cat's body was mummified; large numbers of these mummified cats have been unearthed at Tel Basta, and a few of them can be seen today in some American and Egyptian museums.

For many years the Egyptians prohibited the export of cats, but an animal so valuable to man could not be kept under wraps indefinitely. In time the cat appeared in Phoenician cities, whence it ventured with the restless traders to every part of the known world. The Romans adopted the cat wholeheartedly, as any people would who loved cleanliness and order and hated vermin. The only animal admitted to Roman temples was the cat, and the excavations at Pompeii uncovered a woman who had fallen under the volcanic ash while trying to flee with her pet. Eventually the Romans carried their cats with them to Britain, although the British may have tamed some wild cats earlier. The paw prints of cats have been found on tiles from the Roman towns of Silchester and Uriconium, and the skeleton of a cat has been found in the ruins of a Roman villa that burned down at Lullingstone in approximately the year 200.

During the Dark Ages—and, indeed, until the past two centuries—the period of respect for the cat gave way to widespread hatred and persecution, possibly because the cat was associated with the "old religion" (pre-Christian polytheism and animism) and therefore with witchcraft. Demonologists regarded the cat as the favorite witch's "familiar" (supernatural spirit in animal form), and cats often were solemnly put on trial beside their masters or mistresses; they were tortured to make them "confess" and were then burned alive. Even when it was not associated with witchcraft, the cat was treated with incredible cruelty: a condemned man might be drowned in a sack full of cats, which would claw him in their own terror, and public celebrations were often climaxed by the public burning of closed baskets full of cats. Cat burning was particularly popular on religious feast days. To ensure good luck, it was sometimes the custom to seal cats alive in the foundations of buildings. The supposed evil associated with the cat did not prevent Europeans from using its fur to trim coats, nor from eating the flesh of the cat in stews, a taste that is still to be found in some rural areas of Europe.

This detestation of the cat is a Christian phenomenon. In the non-Christian world the cat has never been persecuted on a wide scale. Islamic tradition says that when Mohammed was called away while a beloved cat was sleeping against his arm, he cut off his sleeve to avoid disturbing the pet. Cats have often been treasured in Asia and Africa.

Even in the Western world, moreover, there have always been those who recognized the values of cats and urged that the animals be well treated. The legal code of the Welsh prince Howel the Good, promulgated in 936 A.D., established a high value for a household cat and laid down penalties for its theft or murder. During the Renaissance the cat began to appear incidentally in paintings.

Few people are neutral on the subject of cats; most either hate cats or love them. Goldsmith hated them; so did Boswell, King Henry III of France, Meyerbeer, Ronsard, and Napoleon, among many others. On the other hand, the list of cat lovers is endless, and includes such names as Heine, Samuel Johnson, Samuel Butler, Montaigne, Thoreau, Matthew Arnold, St. Ives, Petrarch, Borodin, Richelieu, St. Gertrude, Hugo, Balzac, Verlaine, Jeremy Bentham, the Brontë sisters, Capek, Gladstone, Darwin, Theodore Roosevelt, Lincoln, and Mark Twain. The attraction of the cat was best expressed, perhaps, by the French satirist Joseph Méry: "God made the cat to give man the pleasure caressing the tiger."

WILLIAM H. A. CARR
Author of "The Basic Book of the Cat"

Further Reading: Carr, William H. A., *The Basic Book of the Cat* (New York 1963); Howey, M. Oldfield, *The Cat in the Mysteries of Religion and Magic* (New York 1956); Mellen, Ida M., *The Science and the Mystery of the Cat* (New York 1949); Van Vechten, Carl, *The Tiger in the House* (New York 1960).

IAN CLEGHORN, FROM PHOTO RESEARCHERS

TWO LIONS rise on their hind legs during a fight in Nairobi National Park, in Kenya. Only male lions have the luxuriant mane on the head and neck. The lion at the right has lost part of his mane in previous fights.

CAT FAMILY, a group of mammals of the order Carnivora, highly adapted for killing and eating warm-blooded animals. The cat family (Felidae) rates among the highest forms of life; the general abilities and intelligence of cats are surpassed only by those of the big bears, elephants, the Old World monkeys, apes, and man. Dogs are generally regarded as more intelligent than cats, but this is because dogs, like men, are organized in social groups, which results in some similarity in communication patterns: man finds it easier to make dogs do what he wants. When trying to teach cats, most people inadvertently treat them "dogwise"—and fail. They conclude that an animal failing to grasp man's meaning must be stupid! However, it is impossible to justly compare the intelligent behavior of widely different species without considering their respective evolutionary histories and ecological adaptations.

Despite the great variation in size, shape, and coloration of cats, they are readily distinguished from other carnivore families, such as the civets, weasels, hyenas, dogs, and bears.

GENERAL CHARACTERISTICS

Size and Shape. The body size of cats varies from that of the 3½-pound (1.5 kg) blackfooted cat to the more than 600-pound (270-kg) tiger.

Cats have five toes on each forefoot and four on each hindfoot, and because of the relatively short jaws, the head is more or less rounded in shape. Fur structure and thickness vary considerably according to the climate.

Coloration. The ground color, or overall color, of cats varies from whitish gray through all shades of buff and yellowish brown to deep orange-brown. Some members of the family have practically no markings except when young; others are vividly marked with stripes, spots, and rosettes. This diversity, however, has been shown to have arisen from one basic pattern.

Unfortunately for a number of cats, man considers their fur durable and very beautiful. This has led to extensive hunting and reduction of several species.

Teeth and Claws. Of all the carnivores, cats have the most specialized teeth for killing other animals quickly and eating them easily. The canine teeth are better developed than in any other carnivore; in the upper jaw they are long and almost straight, like stilettos; in the lower jaw they are hooked to ensure a firm hold on the prey animal's neck.

The last joint of each toe, which carries a sharp, curved claw, is normally bent upwards and backwards, thus keeping the claws well off the ground. In most species the claws are additionally protected by skin sheaths when retracted. The cat can stretch the joint at will and use the claws for climbing, for catching and holding prey, and in fighting. The fifth toe ("thumb") of the forefoot is high up near the wrist and does not touch the ground when the animal is walking. It and its claw, however, play a prominent role in pinning down a small prey animal and in grooming.

Senses. The sense of hearing in cats is very keen, and at least in the smaller species it extends to very high frequencies (40,000 to 50,000 hertz), enabling the animals to hear and locate the ultrasonic utterances of small rodents. Thus a cat knows when a mouse is about to leave the hole, and a cat can catch a mouse covered by litter without seeing it.

The cat's eyes are set in the front of its head, giving the cat a visual field with almost as much overlap, or horopter (seeing the object with the same part of the retina of each eye), as in man and a perfect perception of depth. In most species the curve of the skull profile allows the animal to raise its eyes above cover without showing anything of its body.

Visual acuity is as good or better than that of man. Cats are not completely color blind, but color vision is weak. A layer of reflecting tissue (the tapetum) behind the light-sensitive cells of the retina sends all incoming light back so that it passes through the retina twice. This helps the cat see in very dim light.

In bright daylight the pupils of the eyes contract to mere slits or round pinpoint apertures. Whether the contracted pupil stays round or becomes a slit seems to be correlated with body size. Larger species tend to have round pupils. But there are exceptions: tigers have slits, and the small jaguarundi and Pallas's cat have round pupils.

It is usually assumed that the cat's sense of smell is poorly developed, but few facts are known, and species may differ widely in this respect. Cats are certainly no match for dogs but probably do much better than man.

There has been much speculation about the cat's sense of touch, mainly as operating through its whiskers (vibrissae), but very little research has been done. It seems that cutting off the vibrissae does not make much difference to an otherwise intact cat, but blind animals are much worse off without them.

Distribution. Wild cats are native to all continents except Australia (the so-called native cat is a marsupial) and Antarctica. They range from desert to rain forest and from seacoast to altitudes of 13,000 feet (4,000 meters). Most like warm climates, but some live in very cold habitats (Pallas's cat, snow leopard, Siberian tiger). Most cats are predominantly ground dwellers, but some are especially well adapted to life in trees (margay, marbled cat, and clouded leopard, whose Nepalese name means "tree tiger").

BEHAVIOR

Running and Swimming. Cats are extremely agile animals. They can walk long distances and run faster than any other mammal over short distances. The cheetah attains speeds up to 70 mph (110 kph), but even the lion is able on occasion to reach 60 mph (95 kph). Most also can jump very high and far. Martin Johnson, pioneer American wildlife photographer, quoted reliable reports of lions jumping distances of well over 33 feet (10 meters). But nobody need fear that the average zoo lion would ever exert itself to jump its protecting ditch to feast on the human visitor. It is out of training and condition and would just as certainly fail as would the average bank clerk trying to jump the world record. Besides, contrary to the general opinion, all cats are extremely timid and cautious creatures, and the zoo lion is normally far more afraid of the visitors than they are of it.

The familiar domestic cat, which evolved from the African wild cat and thus is originally adapted to living in rather dry steppe country, has won the whole family an erroneous reputation for being shy of water. Most cats take readily to water, some love it, and all can swim very well. Tigers have been known to cross sea channels 2 or more miles (3 km) wide between islands of the Indonesian archipelago.

Sociality. Cats have a reputation for being solitary animals that live by themselves and are averse to any company of their own kind except when very young or during the mating season. Notable exceptions are the lions, which live in groups—called prides—of up to 30 members, and the cheetahs, which normally live in family groups. However, field studies in the 1960's by George Schaller, American zoologist and author of *The Deer and the Tiger*, produced surprising evidence that the tiger, formerly regarded as the prototype of a solitary animal, is by no means as unsociable as opinion would have it. Schaller even claims that a tiger that has slain prey too big to eat by itself calls its neighbors to share the meal. Further fieldwork may bring many similar surprises, since most of what we read in books about the habits of the smaller cat species in the wild is folklore rather than scientific knowledge. Cats seem to have evolved very elaborate systems of territorial ownership, time schedules, and right-of-way rules in order to avoid unwanted encounters and uncomfortable population densities.

Breeding. Very little is known of the family life of most cat species. Domestic cats are usually thought of as being fairly promiscuous, but this certainly does not mean that they are indiscriminate, and it still remains to be seen how far this is an outcome of domestication. Although in most species of the cat family the partners seem to meet only for brief periods of mating, there is some indication that the same pair may often team up each mating season over many years. Ocelots are said to live in pairs permanently. In captivity the males of the European wild cat and the fishing cat have been observed to carry meat to the den of the nursing female and deposit it there. It is hard to imagine that this should merely have been brought about by conditions of captivity.

The gestation period (pregnancy) varies from 60 to 115 days and is roughly correlated with the size of the species; the larger the species, the longer the gestation period. Litter size varies from one to six, two to three being the average for most species. The young of small species usually open their eyes 9 to 12 days after birth; those of larger species, a few days earlier.

Parental Care. Female cats are famous as good mothers. They usually deliver their litters in some dry and protected spot: a hollow tree, under overhanging rock, or simply under the low branches of dense trees and shrubs. The mother does not leave this simple nest during the first few days after delivery, and after that only for gradually lengthening excursions to feed and drink.

The cleanliness and protectiveness of cat mothers is well known. They defend their litters against even far superior enemies. When the nest is fouled or disturbed, they carry the cubs to another site by the familiar neck grip.

Maturation and Learning. Domestic kittens show a tendency to make brief excursions from the nest at about 3 weeks of age. Their mother encourages them by calling from nearby and sometimes even by pulling them out of the nest if they are too reluctant. However, she makes sure that they do not become too daring too soon and carries them back to the nest if they stray too far.

At about this time the mother starts to carry the remains of partly torn prey animals to the nest, calling the kittens to look and to bite. The kittens are not yet capable of actually biting something off, but they keep chewing and gnawing, and this provides stimuli necessary for the growth and development of the teeth, jaw bones, masticatory muscles, and the skull bones to which the latter are attached. For this reason, when artificially rearing kittens of any kind it is quite wrong to start them exclusively on a diet of minced meat for their first solid food.

It is not until a week later that the first pieces, usually lung, liver, and other soft parts, are actually torn loose and swallowed. In this way the kitten learns that dead animals are something to eat before it starts to kill them itself. If it does not learn this at this precise stage of its development, it usually fails to do so later; it may kill mice and rats but will not eat them.

Hunting behavior (stalking, catching, and killing) in the domestic kitten develops in two well-marked stages. The first stage, beginning during the 5th week of life, when the mother first carries live prey to the nest, is characterized by the maturation of purely innate techniques. If practice is postponed experimentally, maturation reaches its peak toward the end of the 9th week; however, under normal conditions, competition and practice speed up the process, and a healthy kitten should be a perfect killer by the 7th week if not sooner.

During the ensuing second stage the kittens start experimenting with the prey animal and learn a great deal about how to handle it more efficiently and how to cope with situations for which the innate techniques do not allow. There is no sharp termination of this second stage, and there are great individual differences in what a cat will learn and up to what age it will be able to learn new tricks.

Careful analysis, however, has shown one commonly held notion to be entirely wrong: experience and learning do not alter the innate patterns but only add new ones. The cat ends up with two separate repertoires—one innate and never changing, one learned and never quite ceasing to be adaptable—and it can make use of both as the situation requires.

The above timetable for the initiation of domestic kittens into adult cat life cannot be taken as representative for wild cats of similar size, as domestication seems to have made domestic cats early developers. In the big cats the process seems to be slightly different because the mothers usually cannot carry live prey to their young. These therefore start to follow their mother around on hunting trips at a comparatively early age, and the mother assists them in their first attempts to cope with large animals by holding or otherwise hampering or immobilizing them.

Classifications of the Cat Family (Felidae)

	POCOCK SYSTEM (3 subfamilies; 16 genera)	SIMPSON SYSTEM (no subfamilies; 3 genera)
Acinonychinae subfamily		
Cheetah	*Acinonyx*	*Acinonyx*
Pantherinae subfamily		
Lion, tiger, leopard	*Panthera*	*Panthera*
Felinae subfamily		
Wild cats, house cat	*Felis*	*Felis*
Fishing cat, leopard cat	*Prionailurus*	
Golden cats	*Profelis*	
Ocelot, margay	*Leopardus*	
Lynx, bobcat	*Lynx*	
Caracal	*Caracal*	
Mountain lion	*Puma*	
Jaguarundi	*Herpailurus*	
Pampas cat	*Lynchailurus*	
Andean cat	*Oreailurus*	
Pallas's cat	*Otocolobus*	
Clouded leopard	*Neofelis*	
Marbled cat	*Pardofelis*	
Serval	*Leptailurus*	

C. A. W. GUGGISBERG, FROM PHOTO RESEARCHERS

THE LEOPARD, like all cats, is superbly adapted to stalking, killing, and even transporting its prey.

Killing. All cats kill by biting the neck of their victims. Because they innately prefer to approach their prey from behind and above, the first attempts of the uninitiated usually hit the nape of the victim's neck. The cats are then quick to learn that this is also the most efficient way of grasping and killing and to aim for the nape when it is not directly offered. Dissection of prey animals killed by a well-aimed nape bite reveals that, with few exceptions, one of the cat's canine teeth has penetrated the gap between two neck vertebrae—usually the first and second—and severed the spinal cord. In these cases death is practically instantaneous, although nerve reaction within the spinal cord may cause prolonged, spasmodic wriggling of the victim's body. The victim, however, may die in a variety of ways: a mouse may die from sheer exhaustion after a cat has played with it for a long time; many cats throw around small prey of which they are suspicious, often with sufficient force to kill when it is flung against something hard; many of the big cats learn to bring down large, especially horned, prey by the throat and kill by strangulation; cheetahs and servals may kill by beating very hard with their forepaws. In most of these cases, however, it can be observed that the cats do not seem satisfied that they have killed, but apply a formal "killing bite" to the nape of the neck of the already dead animal.

CLASSIFICATION

The classification of mammals is based largely on the characteristics of the skull and teeth of the animals. The members of the cat family, though quite diverse in size, color, overall body structure, and behavior, have rather similar skulls and teeth. This situation has led to uncertainty in classifying the cats. Consequently, various classifications have been proposed, but none has been universally accepted. One of the most compact classifications—that of the American paleontologist George G. Simpson—contains no subfamilies and only three genera; others commonly add one to three genera more. The British zoologist R. I. Pocock has a more expansive classification system: he recognizes 16 genera grouped into three subfamilies.

The author of this article agrees with Simpson in the abolition of subfamilies, but he feels that a thorough revision of the classification of the cats lumped together by Simpson in the genus *Felis* is long overdue. For the time being, Pocock's classification seems more practical, as it does not obscure existing differences and problems. The Pocock and Simpson classifications are summarized on the preceding page.

PAUL LEYHAUSEN
Max Planck Institute for Behavioral Physiology
Wuppertal, Germany

Further Reading: Adamson, Joy, *Born Free* (London 1960); Denis, Armand, *Cats of the World* (London 1964); Schaller, George, *The Deer and the Tiger* (Chicago 1967); Young, Stanley P., and Goldman, Edward A., *The Puma: Mysterious American Cat* (Washington 1946).

CAT ISLAND is in the Bahamas, southeast of Nassau, from which it can be reached by air in less than an hour. It is 45 miles (70 km) long, averages 4 miles (6 km) in width, and has an area of 150 square miles (389 sq km). The island is one of the hilliest and most fertile of the Bahamas. Fruit and vegetables are grown; tomatoes are exported.

Cat Island was settled by Loyalists from the United States in 1783. Pineapple and banana plantations flourished in the 19th century, but they declined after 1900. Extensive real estate development began in the 1960's. Population: (1963) 3,131.

CAT SCRATCH DISEASE is a disorder that is probably caused by a virus and is often contracted through the scratch or bite of a cat. The cat itself is not ill but merely transmits the disease.

A few days after the skin injury a reddish swelling appears. It usually fills with pus and ulcerates. From one to three weeks later, lymph nodes draining the area become greatly enlarged, and the patient becomes feverish. Although the nodes are not tender they may break down and ooze pus. Eventually the nodes recede and the ulcer heals, although it may take weeks or even months. Antibiotics may possibly shorten the course of the disease and prevent the nodes from draining.

LOUIS J. VORHAUS, M. D.
Cornell University Medical College

CATABOLISM. See METABOLISM.

CATACOMBS, kat′ə-kōmz, are subterranean burial places found throughout the Mediterranean world, but chiefly at Rome. Although catacombs are generally thought of as Christian burial places, they were used for burials before the Christian era and were never restricted only to members of the Christian faith. In Italy, the Etruscans buried their dead in underground chambers that were frequently in the shape of houses and often decorated. Hundreds of them have survived and have been explored by archaeologists. Among the Romans, burial was the usual mode of disposing of corpses until cremation replaced it at the beginning of the imperial period. Roman law required that the dead be buried outside the *pomerium,* the vacant strip of land maintained on both sides of the city wall for defense purposes, and graves were protected by law from violation. The graves of some of the great Roman families, for example, the graves of the Scipios, can still be seen today.

The word catacombs is of Greek origin (*kata kymbas*) and first appeared as a designation for the Roman catacombs in the 9th century A. D. The exact meaning of the term is not certain. Greek names were familiar to the Romans, and most scholars accept the view that the term originally referred to a hollow along the Via Appia, one of the main roads connecting Rome with southern Italy, where several underground burial chambers had been constructed. The Latin phrase denoting this place, *ad catacumbas* (at the hollows), came to denote the chambers themselves. It was then transferred from these to other, similar places and became generic.

Christian Catacombs. The first Christians in Rome were buried, like everybody else, in pagan burial places known as *hypogaea.* Christians called these places *koimeteria,* or "sleeping places" (from the Greek *koimeterion,* "bedchamber"), to indicate their conception of death as a transient state before the Resurrection to eternal life. The first apparent reference to the Christian use of *coemeterium* as a burial place is found in the *De anima* by Tertullian (q.v.), an ecclesiastical writer who lived between about 160 and 230 A. D.; the first clearly Christian underground burial chambers date from the middle of the 2d century, when some wealthy converts seem to have opened their family catacombs to fellow believers. During the 3d century, however, the church accepted responsibility for Christian cemeteries; the catacomb of Callistus was named after a deacon (later pope), whom Pope Zephyrinus had appointed their superintendent. Later, the church acquired more areas for the burial of its dead; these catacombs were frequently named after their location (*ad catacumbas*), after a nearby landmark (*ad duas lauros,* "by the two laurels"), for a famous martyr buried there (St. Felicitas), or for a church official (Callistus). Pope Damasus, who began his reign in 366, took the catacombs under his special protection; he repaired damaged sections and had numerous inscriptions placed on the walls.

From about the year 400, but especially after the sack of Rome by the barbarians in 410, the Christians of Rome ceased to bury their dead in the catacombs. These came to assume more and more the character of places for the veneration of martyrs. In the 6th century the catacombs were sacked by the invading Goths, and the lack of security outside the walls of the city in the following centuries made it necessary to transfer the remains of many martyrs from the catacombs outside the city walls to churches and chapels within the city itself. In 817, Pope Paschal I ordered the transfer of 2,300 bodies. With this removal of the remains of most martyrs, the last reason for the continued existence of the catacombs had disappeared, and from the late 9th century only the original underground burial place at the hollow on the Via Appia, now the site of the Church of San Sebastiano, was still visited by the faithful.

Excavation of the Catacombs. Occasionally, people happened on the remains of the ancient catacombs, but the first systematic excavator was Antonio Bosio. His many discoveries, made between 1593 and 1629, are described in a volume published in 1634 (not 1632 as stated on the title), five years after his death. Interest in catacombs was revived, but a lack of understanding of their original purposes led to a number of incorrect inferences (for example, that the catacombs were primarily places of refuge for persecuted Christians, a view that seems to survive all proofs to the contrary) and to the hunt for treasures and (usually fake) relics of martyrs. The first scientific study of the catacombs was started by another great Italian archaeologist, Giovanni Battista de Rossi, who published his *Roma sotterranea cristiana* between 1863 and 1877. Other discoveries were made up through the 1950's, and it is not impossible, though increasingly less likely, that further excavations in the suburban area of Rome or in other places around the Mediterranean may unearth other catacombs. The total length of the galleries of all the catacombs around Rome has been estimated at between 60 and 90 miles (96–144 km), and the number of tombs has been estimated at between 500,000 and 750,000.

Not every type of soil was suitable for the excavation of the sometimes very extensive galleries and chambers that make up the catacombs. There are basically three types of rock to be found in the neighborhood of Rome: (1) *tufa litoide,* a solid stone, too hard for the excavation of extensive catacombs and only rarely used for that purpose, but an excellent construction material for buildings; (2) *tufa granolare,* a granular type of stone soft enough to be worked, yet sufficiently strong to support excavated caves (practically all the catacombs discovered near Rome had been hewn out of this material); and (3) *pozzolana,* a soft material used for the mixing of mortar.

Construction of the Catacombs. Since Roman law required the disposal of dead bodies outside the city limits and protected all burial grounds against violation, there was no need for Christians or other groups to be secretive in the construction of catacombs, even when these groups were considered illegal by the state. Christians and Jews preferred the old custom of burial to the new practice of cremation, believing that burial was more in keeping with the expected resurrection of the dead. The construction of the catacombs had the further advantage that the surface soil could be used for other purposes, either as vineyards or for the construction of churches and other buildings.

A catacomb was started either at the side of a hill, where construction was relatively easy, or on level ground, where the gravediggers (*fossores*) had to build a stairway to a point about 25 feet (7.5 meters) below the surface. From this point on, a main gallery stretched out, frequently with others running parallel to it, interconnected by smaller galleries running at right angles. These galleries are the main characteristic of most catacombs. Originally called *cryptae,* they are now known as *ambulacra.* Most of the *ambulacra* are about 8 feet (2.5 meters) high and usually somewhat less than 3 feet (0.9 meter) wide; the largest ones reach a length of over 600 feet (180 meters).

The walls of the galleries were the most common places for the graves (*loculi*). An area large enough for one, two, three, or more corpses was hewn out of the rock. The bodies were deposited during a short ceremony (*depositio*), and the front of the tomb was closed with bricks or a marble slab. According to the number of corpses

LEONARD VON MATT, FROM RAPHO GUILLUMETTE

BIBLICAL SCENES decorate the arched niche over a tomb in a corridor of the Catacomb of the Jordani, Rome.

deposited in a *loculus,* the graves were called *monosomi, bisomi, trisomi, quadrisomi,* or *polyandria.* The tomb of a martyr was called a *martyrium,* or, in its Latin translation, a *confessio.* To save space, the graves often were arranged around chambers (*cubicula*) of rectangular, hexagonal, or (more rarely) round construction. At a later time, when memorial services for martyrs were held in chambers near their graves and attracted large congregations, it became necessary to provide light and ventilation through a direct connection with the surface (*luminare*). The graves of important persons received a more elaborate treatment than most others. A coffinlike structure was cut out of the rock or built of stone and then closed with a strong marble slab (*tabula, mensa*). These special graves were enclosed by a semicircular niche called an *arcosolium.* In rare cases these niches were rectangular in shape. A grave was also occasionally cut into the floor of a gallery and closed with a horizontal slab called a *forma;* this probably was done only when a corpse was to be buried at a particular spot—for example, near the grave of a martyr—after all the regular *loculi* had been filled.

Catacomb Art and Calligraphy. Since the catacombs contained the graves of many important people, including martyrs and popes, and of rich men, they were frequently decorated. The catacombs are thus another argument against the er-

LEONARD VON MATT, FROM RAPHO GUILLUMETTE

THE DOMITILLA CATACOMB, in Rome, is entered by means of a stairway descending to the burial chambers.

roneous view that the Christian church of Rome during the first three centuries consisted almost exclusively of poor people and slaves. The decorations of the catacombs are important not only as examples of early Christian art, but also because they testify to the beliefs and customs of the Roman Christians.

The exact dating of the catacomb paintings remains unsettled for it depends on an exact date for each catacomb itself. The very earliest paintings, as in the Cubiculum of Amphiatus in the Catacomb of Domitilla, which originated probably in the second half of the 2d century, do not display any particularly Christian characteristics. In later pictures, however, the symbolic representations of the Christian faith are stressed and the Christian character is usually clear, even when the motif had been taken over from pagan tradition. Among the themes most frequently found are the fish (*ichthys*, an anagram of the Greek words *Iēsous Christos Theou yios sōtēr*, "Jesus Christ, Son of God, Saviour"); the *Alpha* and *Omega* ("the beginning and the end," Revelation 1:8; 21:6; 22:13); the good shepherd (John 10:11); the lamb (*Agnus Dei*, John 1:29); the phoenix (ancient symbol of immortality); and the anchor (symbol of hope). Other paintings depict such scenes from the Bible as the raising of Lazarus (John II); Jonah and the great fish (understood by Christians as a symbol of the Resurrection); and Noah in the ark.

The artistic style of these paintings ranges from naturalistic to expressionistic, according to the times in which they were executed. One of the most interesting catacomb paintings (early 3d century) is the earliest known depiction of the Virgin with the Child in the Catacomb of Priscilla. It was natural that a number of catacomb paintings portrayed the person buried there.

Although the dead were usually buried without coffins in the catacombs, sculptured sarcophagi from the 3d and 4th centuries have been found at various places. The oldest sculptures on the sarcophagi depict the deceased in paradise, in the presence of the good shepherd, or in similar religious scenes. The frequently found columnar sarcophagus had been taken over from the pagans. Here, the front is divided into several fields by columns. Each of the fields shows reliefs of scenes, and sometimes includes a portrait, perhaps of a noted Christian.

The catacombs have also yielded a very large number of small art objects. Terra cotta lamps were used to illuminate the galleries underground, and they may also have served a symbolic purpose. These lamps are frequently decorated, usually with the same symbols found in the wall paintings. Among the most interesting objects found are glass disks (sometimes the bottoms of glass containers) overlaid with gold, into which decorations were incised. Since each of the larger catacombs contained a great number of graves, some means of identification for the individual *loculi* became necessary. This seems to have been accomplished by small disks, coins, or medals that were attached to the grave. A number of small glass flasks have been found which sometimes contained traces of red color. This has led to the erroneous view that these flasks had contained the blood of martyrs and that any tomb where such a flask had been discovered was a *martyrium*. Because of this false view many catacomb graves were robbed during the 17th and 18th centuries by people eager to supply the market with relics of martyrs.

The various inscriptions, which range from carefully carved texts over painted words to carelessly produced graffiti, are of great importance to the study of catacombs. Many of the earliest texts are in Greek, a reminder that this was the language of the earliest Christians in Rome. These are usually simple and brief, as, for example, *Dionysias in pace* ("Dionysias rest in peace"). The texts produced by order of Pope Damasus in the second half of the 4th century are easily recognized by their greater length and artful calligraphy.

Jewish and Other Catacombs. Most of the catacombs in Rome were owned by the church, but others were constructed by different religious groups, as is attested by their paintings and inscriptions. Antonio Bosio discovered the first Jewish catacomb in Rome in 1602, and several others were discovered since, both in Rome and elsewhere. As is to be expected, the most frequently found symbols in the Jewish catacombs are those of the *menorah* (7-branched candelabrum) and of the *aron* (ark), containing the tablets of the Jewish Law.

The so-called catacombs of cities like Paris have nothing in common with those discussed in this article. The ones in Paris are former stone quarries which are now used as depositories for the bones from cemeteries no longer in use.

HORST MOEHRING, *Brown University*

Bibliography

Lowrie, Walter, *Art in the Early Church*, 2d rev. ed. (New York 1965).

Marchi, G., *Monumenti delle arti cristiane primitive nella metropoli del Cristianesimo: I—Archittetura della Roma sotterranea* (Rome 1884).

Marucchi, O., *Le catacombe romane* (Rome 1933).

Matt, Leonard von, and Josi, Enrico, *Early Christian Art in Rome* (New York 1961).

Northcote, J. S., and Brownlow, W. F., *Roma sotterranea*, or *An Account of the Roman Catacombs* (London 1879).

Testini, P., *Archeologia cristiana* (Rome 1958).

Volbach, Wolfgang F., *Early Christian Art* (New York 1962).

CATALAN LANGUAGE, kat′ə-lən, one of the nine Romance languages (those derived from Latin). It is used chiefly in the northeast corner of Spain.

General Characteristics and History. The geographic location of Catalan has made it a language bridge between the Gallo-Romance and the Ibero-Romance dialects. Catalan was for many years considered a dialect variant of Provençal, and only around 1925 was there unanimity in placing Catalan in the category of an independent neo-Latin language. It should not be imagined that Catalan is a dialect of Castilian (Spanish) merely because the latter is the official language of all Spain.

There are two opinions as to which of its Romance neighbors Catalan resembles more: one holds that Catalan should be classed with the Gallo-Romances (W. Meyer-Lübke, *Das Katalanische*, 1925); the other, that it be classed with the Ibero-Romances (R. Menéndez Pidal, *Orígenes del español*, 1926). Catalan is fundamentally Hispanic in origin, but because of close political and cultural ties between Catalonia and southern France, it developed many linguistic traits similar to those of Provençal.

Catalan, like all other Romance languages, is based on the Latin spoken by the masses and the Roman middle class. It is sometimes cognate with other Romance languages (Cat. *cova* "cave," Sp. *cueva*, Fr. *caverne*, Lat. *cova*); at other times it has forms cognate with Latin that are not found in other Romance languages (Cat. *desar* "to keep," Sp. *guardar*, Fr. *garder*, Lat. *densare*). The Catalan lexicon was enriched by many contributors besides Vulgar Latin: classical Latin (learned words), Greek (ancient and medieval words, modern technical terms), pre-Romance languages (words from Iberian, Celtic, Ligurian, Phoenician), Germanic (Latinized Germanic words, proper names), and Arabic (many terms and a great number of toponyms). Since its constitution as a language, Catalan has received elements from Provençal, Spanish (and through it, from the American Indian languages), French, Italian, and to a lesser degree English and German.

Catalan is spoken in an area comprising Catalonia, except the Valley of Arán (where Gascon is spoken); Valencia, excepting some regions in the west; the Balearic Islands; almost all the French department of Pyrénées Orientales (formerly Roussillon); Andorra; the city of Alghero (Sardinia); and an eastern strip of the provinces of Huesca, Zaragoza, and Teruel. To the north Catalan is bounded by Provençal and Gascon dialects, and to the west by the surviving forms of Old Aragonese and by Castilian. The total number of Catalan speakers exceeds 6,000,000, including about 5,800,000 in Spain and 260,000 outside Spain.

Catalan is divided into two groups of dialects. The eastern dialects are central (Barcelona, Gerona, Tarragona), Balearic (in the Balearic Islands), Roussillon (in Roussillon, France), and Algherian (Sardinia). The western dialects are Leridan (Lérida) and Valencian (Valencia).

Catalan developed after the decline of the Roman Empire and was the official language of Catalonia until the 18th century. The medieval Catalan of the courts of Barcelona and Valencia was used in literature until the 16th century, when latent dialects began to manifest themselves. By that time the unification of the Spanish provinces gave Spanish a new importance and caused the use of Catalan to decline. A Catalan linguistic and literary revival, accompanying a nationalist movement, took place in the 19th and 20th centuries. Its efforts to purify and fix the literary language have been aided by the holding of language congresses and the publication of Catalan dictionaries, grammars, and texts. Such efforts would serve nothing, however, if the individual speakers of the language felt it to be foreign to them. The success of the revival owes much to the fact that Catalan, despite centuries of decadence and the loss of its position as the official language, has maintained its popular vitality.

Linguistic Features—*Pronunciation*. Catalan distinguishes open *e* from closed *e* and open *o* from closed *o* as separate phonemes. (Castilian has only open and closed variants of the single phonemes *e* and *o*.) In the speech of Barcelona unaccented *a* and *e* are pronounced as an indistinct neutral vowel, and unaccented *o* and *u* are pronounced as *u;* but the western dialects distinguish clearly between *a* and *e* and between *o* and *u*. Catalan has the apico-alveolar articulation of the *s*, as in Castilian (and as opposed to the predorsal *s* in other European languages). It has a series of palatals based on *x* and *j;* an articulation of *l* with strong velar resonance; and the Old Romance affricates *ts, dz, tx, tj*. In syntactic phonetics, voiceless consonants (except occlusives and liquids) become voiced in the final position of a word if the next word begins with a vowel (*els astres* "the stars" is pronounced *elzastres*).

***Phonetics*.** Catalan is distinguished by the absence of spontaneous diphthongization of short Latin vowels: where Castilian has *bien, bueno*, Catalan has *bé, bo* (Lat. *bĕne, bŏnu*). In principle it preserves the original vowels *a, i, o, u;* Vulgar Latin *e*'s produce mixed results, differing according to dialects; the vowels tend to combine with a palatal (the yod) or a velar (the wau) with which they are in contact and close their articulation, thereby reducing the diphthong: Lat. *laicu* gives Cat. *llec* "lay," Lat. *auru* gives Cat. *or* "gold," so that it may be said that there is a vocalic closing due to the effect of the yod or wau. The Catalan consonant system is characterized by the palatalization and assibilation of consonants in contact with the vowels *e* and *i* (Cat. *ciutat* "city," Lat. *civitate*), or in contact with a yod (Cat. *acer* "steel," Lat. *aciariu*); and by the relaxation of consonants whereby the voiceless become voiced (Cat. *nebot* "nephew," Lat. *nepote*), and the voiced consonants at times disappear (Cat. *suor* "sweat," Lat. *sudore*). This relaxation explains the vocalization of the final (or equivalent to final) consonant into *-u* (Cat. *hereu* "heir," Lat. *herede*). In groups of two consonants the first is weakened and at times tends to be assimilated by the second (Cat. *néta* "granddaughter," Lat. *nepta*) and at times tends to be converted to a semivowel *u* or *i;* the semivowel thus formed then either combines with the preceding vowel or is absorbed by it (Cat. *om* "elm," Lat. *ulmu*, which presupposes an intermediate form **oum;* Cat. *fet* "deed," Lat. *factu*, which presupposes **fait*), or it may palatalize the second consonant of the group (Cat. *cunyat* "brother-in-law," Lat. *cognatu*, which presupposes **coinat*). (The asterisk indicates a hypothetical intermediate form.)

***Morphology*.** The derivation of the words from Latin is based on the Latin accusative forms, although there are unquestionably some words derived from other Latin cases, especially from the nominative (*res* "thing"). Latin adjectives with only one form tend to take on a specific ending for the feminine, generalized in a few instances (Cat. *fort, forta* "strong," Lat *forte*), but with greater extension in the popular speech (*fàcil* "easy" has the popular feminine form *fàcila*, not recognized as correct). The article normally comes from Lat. *ille* (*el, la*), but in preliterary Catalan there existed, with wide usage, the article derived from Lat. *ipse* (*es, sa*), still used in the Balearic Islands and on the Costa Brava in Catalonia, and can also be found fossilized in toponyms in much of Catalonia (Collsacabra, St. John Despí). The four Latin conjugations have been preserved in Catalan, although in different proportions: Lat. *cantare* > Cat. *cantar, habēre* > *haver, perdĕre* > *perdre, venire* > *venir.* Characteristic of the Catalan perfect tense is its almost universal replacement by a periphrasis with the present of the verb *anar* "to go" (*vaig* "I go," *vas* "you go"): *vaig cantar* means "I sang" (the same as *cantí*), *vas cantar* "you sang" (as *cantares*).

Syntax. Catalan constructs the determinatives of quantity with a partative: *molt de temps* "much time" (compared to Sp. *mucho tiempo*). Catalan admits some adverbs for the expression of pronominal relations, such as *hi* "in it" (Lat. *ibi*) and *en* "of it" (Lat. *inde*). It distinguishes, as does Spanish, between the two intransitive copulative verbs *ser* and *estar*, but the languages do not coincide in the distinction; for example, temporary state is expressed in Catalan with *ser* and in Spanish with *estar*. In opposition to the use, waxing since the Middle Ages, of the subjunctive mood in Spanish, Catalan prefers other expressions, such as the future (*quan tornaràs* "when you return," Sp. *cuando vuelvas*), the imperfect (*si tu volies* "if you wanted," Sp. *si tu quisieras*), the conditional (*no t'ho hauria dit* "I should not have told you," Sp. *no te lo hubiera dicho*). The past participle in compound tenses, invariable in Spanish, agrees in Catalan with a third-person direct object pronoun: *l'ha conegut* "he has known him," *l'ha coneguda* "he has known her," compared to Spanish *lo* or *lo ha conocido*. See also CATALAN LITERATURE.

A. BADIA MARGARIT
Author of "Gramática catalana"

Further Reading: Badia Margarit, Antonio, *Gramática catalana* (Madrid 1953); Fabra, Pompeu, *Diccionari general de la llengua catalana* (Barcelona 1932); id., *Gramática catalana* (Barcelona 1918); Gili, J. L., *Introductory Catalan Grammar* (London 1943); Moll y Casasnovas, Francisco de Borja, *Gramática histórica catalana* (Madrid 1952).

CATALAN LITERATURE

CATALAN LITERATURE, kat'əl-ən, is a Romance literature produced by writers born in Catalonia, in northeastern Spain, and also from adjacent areas where Catalan is the vernacular, including what were the kingdoms of Majorca and Valencia and the province of Roussillon (now part of France). Catalan literature has two periods of development—the first extending from the beginning of the 13th century to the end of the 15th, before the unification of Spain had been completed; the second beginning about 1830 as part of a Catalonian cultural and political revival.

Background. A collection of sermons, *Homilies d'Organyà*, of the late 12th or early 13th century, is considered the oldest text in Catalan, although its principal value is linguistic rather than literary. In that period, Provençal, a neighboring Romance language, was studiously cultivated in Catalonia by learned or aristocratic Catalan poets, owing to the close political relations between the kings of Aragon (who were also the counts of Barcelona, chief city of Catalonia) and the rulers of southern France. The court of Barcelona received many Provençal troubadours, and as a consequence Catalan courtiers, such as King Alfonso II of Aragon, wrote their verses in Provençal. Among the troubadours born in Catalonia should be mentioned the cynical and brutal Guilhem de Berguedan, the refined and delicate Pons de la Guardia, and Guilhem de Cabestanh, in the 12th century, and the prolific and varied Guilhem de Cervera, called in troubadour fashion Cerverí, in the 13th century. This poetry exercised a strong influence on the learned Catalan poets of the 14th century, who followed faithfully the themes, the style, and in part the language of the classic Provençal troubadours.

Middle Ages and Renaissance. Genuinely Catalan prose reached its greatest perfection in the extensive work of that important figure of the late 13th and early 14th century, the Majorcan Raymond Lully (Cat. Ramón Llull, Lat. Raimundus Lullus). Some 250 authentic works of Lully expound his ideas of philosophy and his missionary zeal. From an exclusively literary point of view he is a true artist of Catalan prose, in which he wrote books on science and philosophy at a time when these subjects were normally treated in Latin. His principal works are his lengthy *Libre de contemplació . . .* (*Book of Contemplation . . .*), an impressive climax to his mystic experiences; his Utopian novels *Libre de meravelles* (*Book of Marvels*) and *Blanquerna;* and his collection of short prayers called *Libre d'Amich e d'Amat* (*Book of the Lover and the Beloved*), an ejaculatory work of Christian lyricism. In his verse Lully used a language closer to Provençal than to Catalan, as can be seen in *Lo Desconhort* (*Despair*), a poem written in a moment of acute pessimism, and in the *Plant de Nostra Dona . . .* (*Lament of Our Lady . . .*), a sort of *Stabat Mater.* A contemporary of Raymond Lully was the famous doctor and visionary from Valencia, Arnáu de Vilanova (Arnaud de Villeneuve), who, although generally using Latin, wrote brief treatises in Catalan in the form of disputes or debates.

Historiography constitutes the most important element of Catalan prose of the 14th century. Four great chronicles stand out: the oldest is the *Libre dels feyts* (*Book of Deeds*), in the redaction of which King James I of Aragon took a leading role (the extant text is a later revision dated between 1313 and 1327). This chronicle narrates principally the Catalan conquests of Majorca and Valencia and is a prose version of epic poems now lost. Bernat Desclot wrote between 1285 and 1295 a *Crònica* devoted for the most part of the deeds of King Pedro III the Great; it is strongly dramatic in the description of early events in the expansion of Aragon through the south of Italy, and especially in describing the war of Catalonia against the invading French. The *Crònica* of Ramón Muntaner, written in 1325, is unforgettable for its familiar and colorful style, as it narrates with detail and emotion the Catalan expedition to Greece and Asia Minor, the chronicler having been one of the leaders of the expedition. The last of the four chief chronicles, finished in 1388, is the work of King Pedro IV the Ceremonious and his collaborators; it has a more political character than the others.

An excellent narrator and writer of pleasant and attractive prose is the 14th century Franciscan friar Francesch Eiximenis, author of *Lo Chrestià*, a monumental encyclopedia similar to the medieval *Summae*. He also wrote the *Libre de les dones* (*Book of Women*), a didactic, colorful work abounding in odd bits of information. The chanceries of the kings of Aragon, thoroughly organized by Pedro IV, formed a sound intellectual center in which the royal secretaries of the end of the 14th century occupied themselves with the editing of Latin manuscripts according to the humanistic principle of returning to a Ciceronian style. This style was immediately adapted to Catalan documents, such chronicles, thereby, giving to the prose an elegant Renaissance form. One notable royal secretary was Bernat Metge of Barcelona, who was much influenced by the Latin works of Petrarch and Boccaccio. In *Lo somni* (*The Dream*), a treatise written in 1398, Metge incorporated the new ideas of the Italian Renaissance and at the same time gave a cultured, measured, humanist elegance to Catalan prose. His many humanist followers, strongly influenced by Italy, were chiefly translators of the Latin classics. Worthy of note towards the end of the 15th century is the Valencian Joan Rois de Corella, an elegant adapter of Ovidian fables in an excessively rhetorical prose style.

Among the prominent lyric poets of the late 14th century were Andreu Febrer and Gilabert de Próxita, who were still influenced by Provençal tastes.

At the beginning of the 15th century the courtly poet Jordi de Sant Jordi united in his work the preciosity of Arnaut Daniel and the tenderness of Petrarch, imitating each at times. The best of the 15th century Catalan lyric poets was the Valencian Auziàs March, falconer to King Alfonso V. March, writing in a Catalan free from Provençalisms, analyzed his fancies and passions according to medieval Scholastic theory in a personal and vigorous style. He put poetry at the service of profoundly tortured and obsessive introspection, which secures for him a position of singular importance in the Romance lyric of the Renaissance. The principal qualities of his style are his many comparisons (frequently referring to the sea) and the proud exalted tone that he acquires on occasion. The 15th century is brightened by a multitude of Catalan poets at times influenced by the Italian or the courtly French lyric; among these are Pere Torroella (who wrote Castilian poetry under the name Pedro Torrellas) and the refined Rois de Corella, already mentioned as a prose writer.

The Catalan novel began with novels of chivalry, versions of French prose texts concerning the Holy Grail and Tristan. In the mid-15th century two important novels of chivalry of Catalan origin appeared: the anonymous *Curial e Güelfa*, revealing French and Italian influences, and *Tirant lo Blanch*. The latter, written by the Valencian knight Johanot Martorell, is one of the most interesting of medieval novels for its realism, its naturalness, and its exactitude in the creation of atmosphere, types, and situations. This novel was known and even imitated to a degree by Ariosto and Cervantes. Within the classification of the novel falls the satiric treatise by the renegade Majorcan Anselm Turmeda entitled *Disputa de l'Ase* (*Dispute of the Ass*), whose original text, written in 1417, has been lost, but which has been preserved through a French version printed in 1544. Although written in narrative verse, *Spill* (1460, *Mirror*), the work of the Valencian Jaume Roig, is really a novel in content: the protagonist, a hapless young man, relates his adventures with bandits and his marital misfortunes; in certain respects *Spill* is a forerunner of the Castilian picaresque novel.

Catalan oratory had many cultivators among the parliamentarians, and outstanding in this field were the discourses delivered by King Martín I. San Vicente Ferrer was an impassioned and popular orator, making frequent references to daily life and customs and not disdaining to use the language of the people. (The Italian orator Bernardino of Siena openly imitated him.) A solemn and learned orator was Felip de Malla, whose extant works include some speeches and a rhetorical, allegorical treatise entitled, *Memorial del pecador remut* (*Memorial of the Redeemed Sinner*).

Decadence and Revival. From the beginning of the 16th century until the middle of the 19th, Catalan letters languished, due chiefly to the disappearance of the court, the real nucleus of medieval Catalan literature. Catalonian and Valencian authors increasingly wrote in Castilian, attracted by the splendor of Golden Age Spanish. However, Catalan continued as the official language in Catalonia with no governmental interference until 1714, when Philip V of Spain, grandson of Louis XIV, imposed complete central authority on Catalonia.

In the following century, romanticism produced a revival of Catalan literature. This revival, called the *Renaixença*, began with the *Oda a la Pàtria* (1833), a perfect ode composed in Madrid by Buenaventura Carlos Aribau. There immediately followed a series of attempts directed toward reviving the ancient Catalan literature and restoring a literary dignity to the language. In this effort Catalonian writers received the collaboration of Majorcans, to a lesser degree of Valencians, and sporadically of writers from Roussillon. Poetry contests, called *Jochs Florals*, were initiated in 1859 and are still held throughout Catalonia. They gave great popularity to the *Renaixença*.

The most important figure of later 19th century Catalan literature was the poet Jacint Verdaguer. His overflowing imagination is evident as much in his epic, exemplified by his poems *L'Atlàntida* (1877, in which he joined classic mythology to the discovery of America) and the *Canigó* (1885, a medieval legend of the Pyrenees), as in his mystic lyrical poems in the Franciscan spirit. The poet Joan Maragall displayed a sincere accent of intimacy in committing his delights, his sorrow, and his impressions to a suitable elevated lyric. The Majorcan poets, especially Joan Alcover and Miquel Costa y Llobera, gave to Catalan poetry of the beginning of the 20th century an exquisite elegance.

The Catalan novel of the end of the 19th and early 20th century is represented by the works of Narcís Oller, Joaquím Ruyra, Víctor Català (pseudonym of the authoress Catalina Albert I Paradís), and especially Eugenio d'Ors. A younger generation includes the novelists Miquel Llor, Sebastià Juan Arbó, and the short-story writers J. E. Martínez Ferrando and Salvador Espriu. The theater suffered from overuse of the popular tone and from routine ruralism. Nevertheless, worthy of note are Angel Guimerà, whose drama *Terra baixa* (1896, *Lowlands*) was an international success and Josep Maria de Sagarra, important also as a lyric and epic poet and author of an excellent translation in verse of the *Divine Comedy*.

Perhaps one of the most significant events in the Catalan literature of the third decade of the 20th century was the surrealist manifesto called the *Full groc* (1928, *Yellow Leaf*), one of whose signers was the painter Salvador Dali. It introduced the ideas of André Breton and was directed against the reactionary popularism of some Catalan authors of that period.

A rich personality characterizes Carles Riba Bracons, who as a poet, beginning with his *Estances*, renewed themes and images and carried the language to a lofty and serene dignity. He maintained these values in his later books, among them *Salvatge cor* (1952, *Savage Heart*). Riba Bracons has exercised a decisive influence over younger generations of poets. A professor of Greek, he has made fine translations of the *Odyssey* (in long verse imitating the Homeric hexameter) as well as the work of Aeschylus, Sophocles, Plutarch, and others. It should be realized that the most cultivated expression of modern Catalan prose is to be found in the translations and adaptations, nearly all of them excellent, of Greek and Latin authors that are published by the Fundació Bernat Metge.

The originality of the poetry of Josep V. Foix is extraordinary. He has managed to join the more positive results of surrealism with a traditional Catalan inspiration (an echo of Raymond Lully and Auzià̀s March) in a full form that is virile and bold as well as disturbingly metaphoric or consciously automatic in expression. His book *Les irreales omegues* (1949, *The Unreal Omegas*) is one of the most important in Catalan lyric poetry of the 20th century. Other outstanding poets of this half century are Josep Carner, "Guerau de Liost" (pseudonym of Jaume Bofill i Mates), Joan Salvat Papasseit, Josep Maria López-Picó, Marià Manent, Tomàs Garcés, Sebastià Sánchez Juan, and the Majorcans Maria Antonia Salvà and Llorenç Riber (also an excellent writer of prose and fine translator of Latin authors).

The creation of many literary awards for the production of books in Catalan (City of Barcelona Prize for Catalan Poetry, established in 1951; Johanot Martorell Prize for the novel, in 1949), the legally sanctioned teaching of Catalan philology and literature in Spanish universities (laws of 1944 and 1952), and the great increase in the editorial output in Catalan since 1947 (part of which is dedicated to the publication of medieval Catalan authors), indicate that in the mid-20th century there has been a new resurgence of this literature in Catalonia proper and in Majorca, and, to a lesser degree, in Valencia. In Roussillon, however, literary production in Catalan is scant, and practically nothing is being published.

See also CATALAN LANGUAGE.

MARTÍN DE RIQUER
Author of "Resumen de literatura catalana"

Further Reading: García Silvestre, Manuel, *Història sumària de la literatura catalana* (Barcelona 1932); Nicolau d' Olwer, Luis, *Resum de literatura catalana* (Barcelona 1927); Riquer, Martín de, *Resumen de literatura catalana* (Barcelona 1947); *Rubió, Jordi, Història general de las literaturas hispánicas,* vol. I (Barcelona 1949).

CATALANI, kä-tä-lä'nē, **Alfredo** (1854–1893), Italian composer of operas in the romantic style. He was born in Lucca on July 19, 1854. After graduating from the Paris Conservatory, he settled in Milan. His operas, including *Elda* (1880), *Dejanire* (1883), and *Edmea* (1886), gained considerable popularity. His most successful opera, *La Wally* (1892), the tragic love story of a peasant girl and a hunter, was performed by the Metropolitan Opera in New York in 1908–1909. Catalani's other works include the Oriental eclogue *La Falce* (1876) and the symphonic poem *Ero e Leandro* (1885). He died in Milan on Aug. 7, 1893.

CATALEPSY, kat'ə-lep-sē. The typical clinical picture of catalepsy is a slight, easily surmountable tension in a patient. The limbs may be put in various postures, and they will remain in the poses in which they have been placed. There is a trancelike state of consciousness as well as the pathological retention of physical attitudes or postures. The condition is seen most often in catatonic schizophrenia and also in certain diseases of the central nervous system in which the pathways between the cerebellum and frontal lobes are impaired (see CATATONIA). The symptoms occur in some cases of hysteria. Investigators have reported that catalepsy may be produced under hypnosis.

The term catalepsy is employed more frequently in traditional, classical neurology and psychiatry than in recent texts. There is a general belief that catalepsy is related to pathology of the central nervous system. There are several neurological conditions in which abnormalities of movement are linked with lack of initiative, usually in diseases that involve the corpus striatum, a part of the upper brainstem. Cataleptic reactions have been reported in postencephalitic patients. Because catalepsy may be shown by some neurotics and may be simulated by normals when under hypnosis, some believe the dynamics of the condition to be psychological rather than neurological.

AUSTIN E. GRIGG, *University of Richmond*

CATALONIA, kat-ə-lō'nyə, is a region in northeast Spain consisting of the interior province of Lérida and the coastal provinces of Gerona, Barcelona, and Tarragona. Catalonia (Spanish, *Cataluña;* also Catalan, *Catalunya*) is bordered on the north by France and Andorra, on the east by the Mediterranean, on the south by the province of Castellón de la Plana, and on the west by the province comprising the historic region of Aragón. A very important if not typical part of Spain, Catalonia has good and varied agricultural production, adequate rainfall, much industry, and a substantial middle class. Catalonia's 4 million inhabitants constitute nearly 13% of Spain's population while occupying only a little over 6% of the country's total area. The only major city in Catalonia is Barcelona, the commercial capital of Spain.

Land and Economy. Rivers play an important role in Catalonia's economy. The Noguera Pallaresa and the Segre unite to supply the extensive irrigation network around Lérida and then join the Ebro, which flows eastward across Tarragona to the Mediterranean. Other rivers, important for irrigation and hydroelectric power, are the Tech, the Fluvia, and the Ter in Gerona, and the Besós and the Llobregat in Barcelona.

CATALONIA contains the rugged coastline called the Costa Brava, where resorts and ports such as Tossa de Mar (*right*) are located.

SPANISH GOVERNMENT TOURIST OFFICE

Catalonia has three natural geographic areas: the Pyrenees, the high central tableland or meseta of the interior, and the coastal plain, backed by hills. With peaks over 10,000 feet (3,000 meters), the Pyrenees are a scenic but formidable natural boundary. They generally mark Spain's border with France. One of the few passes is at Puigcerdá, near Andorra. In the main it is a region of subsistence agriculture, although cereals, vegetables, and even olives are grown on the lower slopes. Streams flow down from the Pyrenees that are vital to Catalonian agriculture and industry.

Lérida province, predominantly high central tableland, has an extensive system of irrigation, including a 90-mile (145-km) long canal, in the area of the city of Lérida, which makes possible good production of cereals, vegetables, fruit, grapes, and olives. There is also extensive grazing of livestock, especially sheep. Mineral wealth in Catalonia is not great and most of it comes from the mountains of the interior. There is lignite, some coal, potassium salts, zinc, a little bauxite, chrome, and manganese.

The most important and productive part of Catalonia is the coastal strip, which includes the low-lying plain and its extension up the river valleys, and the hills near the coast. Here grapes are grown and many good wines are made; olives flourish and the quality of the oil is high; almonds and hazelnuts are grown commercially and flower growing is a minor industry. The *huertas* (intensively cultivated land) and the irrigated valleys provide an abundance of fruits and vegetables; rice is also grown along the coast. Fishing is an important coastal activity.

Although Catalonia is well endowed agriculturally, its industry is more important. While some factories use lignite or coal for power, most use hydroelectricity; consequently, industry is concentrated along river valleys. Textile manufacture, in the many stages from fiber to cloth, is the most important industry; similar diversification of production is found in the paper, iron, and steel industries.

Barcelona is the capital of Catalonia not only historically but also in all aspects of marketing, trade, and industry. Transportation lines converge on the city, which has a good harbor with modern port facilities. Its factories produce textiles, light and heavy machinery, cement, paper, porcelain, pens, typewriters, explosives, salts, soap, paint, glue, dyes, and medicines.

Catalonia's role as an area for tourists is becoming increasingly important. The Pyrenees, called the Spanish Alps, attract visitors and skiers, but the majority of tourists come to Catalonia to go to the beaches. The Costa Brava, the rugged coast of the province of Gerona, has many beaches between rocky headlands that extend to the sea. The coast of the provinces of Barcelona and Tarragona, now called the Costa Dorada (Golden Coast), consists of long wide stretches of sand broken by the deltas of the Llobregat and the Ebro rivers and an occasional rocky cape.

History. In pre-Roman times northeast Spain was inhabited by the Iberians, with coastal colonies held by Phoenicians, Greeks, and Carthaginians. The Romans made Greek Tarragona their provincial capital; Barcelona, named for the Barca family of Carthage, was the capital for the Visigoths. In the 8th century A. D. the Moorish invasion swept over Catalonia.

As a result of the conquest of Catalonia by Charlemagne (785–811), the Spanish March (or Mark), which included the countship of Barcelona, was set up to protect France from invasion. This Christian principality slowly extended its limits to the south, just as the reconquest of Spain was being pushed by León, Castile, and Aragón. Aragón, Catalonia's neighbor to the west, had reached beyond Saragossa by 1137, when Aragón and Catalonia were united through the marriage of the Aragonese Princess Petronilla to Ramón Berenguer IV, count of Barcelona.

In the 13th century James I of Aragón made major reconquests, taking Mallorca (1229), Minorca (1233), Valencia (1238), and Murcia (1266) from the Moors. Aragón ultimately included Sardinia, Sicily, and part of southern Italy. The marriage of Isabel of Castile and León to Ferdinand of Aragón and Catalonia in 1469 was one of the final steps in the formation of Spain as a modern nation.

A separatist movement has on occasion attempted to secure Catalonian independence from Spain, but despite its regional character and the Catalan language (used as well as Spanish), Catalonia continues to be an integral part of Spain. See also CATALAN LANGUAGE; CATALAN LITERATURE.

M. M. LASLEY, *University of Florida*

CATALPA, kə-tal′pə, is a genus of flowering trees of the bignonia family (Bignoniaceae), native to North America and Asia, frequently planted as ornamentals. The catalpas, also known as *cigar trees, toby trees,* and *catawbas,* have large ovate or heart-shaped leaves, which in some species give off a disagreeable odor when crushed. The flowers are white, pinkish, or yellowish in color and are borne on showy, erect clusters (panicles). Catalpa fruits are long, narrow, rather cylindrical pods that look like spikes hanging from the tree. The pods remain on the tree through the winter and open in early spring to expose flat, oblong seeds with a tuft (coma) of hair at each end.

Three of the ten species of *Catalpa* are cultivated as shade and lawn trees and for timber. The common catalpa (*C. bignonioides*), or Indian bean, native to the southeastern United States, grows to 60 feet (18 meters) high and bears handsome white flowers, striped and spotted with yellow and brown. The flowers, each about 2 inches (5 cm) long, are crowded into broad clusters, 6 to 10 inches (15–25 cm) in height. The cylindrical pods are 6 to 15 inches (15–40 cm) long and green in color, ripening into brown. The western catalpa (*C. speciosa*), native to the central United States, grows to 100 feet (30 meters) high and bears white flowers, lightly spotted with yellow, in rather loose, open clusters. Its fruits are 8 to 18 inches (20–45 cm) long and ½ to ¾ inches (13–18 mm) in diameter. *C. ovata,* native to China and widely planted in Japan, grows to 30 feet (9 meters) or more in height and bears large clusters of relatively small, fragrant, yellow flowers.

Catalpa wood is one of the most resistant to decay in contact with the soil, many instances being reported where it has remained free from decay even after 35 to 50 years. The wood thus lends itself to use as poles and posts. Catalpa grown as lumber is set out in rich loam with rather close planting to foster self-pruning.

S. C. Bausor, *California State College, Pa.*

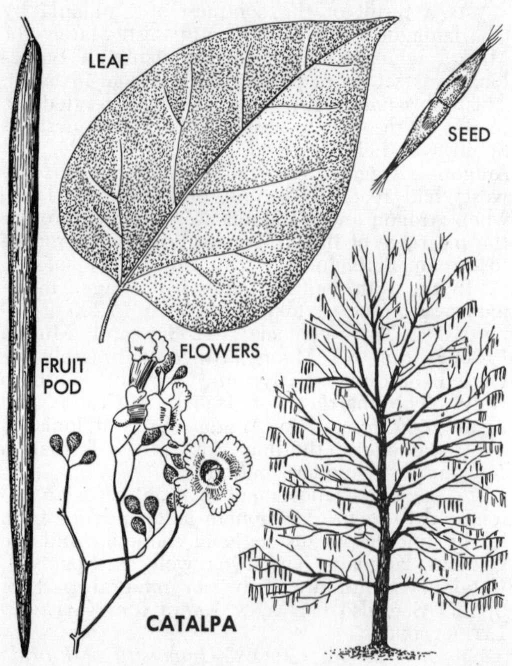

CATALYST, kat′ə-list, a substance that increases the rate of a chemical reaction. The term catalyst was derived in 1835 by the Swedish chemist Jöns Jakob Berzelius from the Greek word *katalysis,* meaning "to loosen or break up." Berzelius assumed that the catalyst acted in some way to loosen the bonds of the reacting substances, thus allowing the reaction to proceed more rapidly. Some catalysts decrease the rate of a reaction; these are referred to as *negative catalysts.* Most catalysts, however, increase reaction rates; unless otherwise specified, the remainder of the article refers to these (*positive*) catalysts.

Characteristics of Catalysts. Any type of substance—solid, liquid, or gas—may act as a catalyst. However, catalytic reactions are very specific, and only certain substances will catalyze certain reactions.

It was first thought that catalysts remained unchanged throughout the reactions in which they participated. It was then realized that some catalysts underwent real changes during the reactions, but that they were then regenerated in their original form and quantity at the end of the reaction. It is now known that some catalysts are permanently altered, at least in form, during the course of a reaction.

Catalysts are generally effective in small quantities. A catalyst may catalyze the reaction of several thousand to a million times it weight in reactants. While catalysts increase the rate of a reaction, they do not affect the equilibrium point of a reversible reaction. The catalyst increases the rate of reaction so that the equilibrium is reached more rapidly, but the relative concentrations of the reactants at the equilibrium point is not changed.

Mechanisms of Catalytic Action. Although the exact mechanism of catalytic action is not known, it is thought in at least some cases to be a surface phenomenon in which reactants are adsorbed onto a small portion of the surface of the catalyst. The formation of such a complex may in some way lessen the amount of energy actually needed for the reaction to begin (activation energy), thereby allowing it to proceed more rapidly. Negative catalysts may act by interfering with a step in a chain reaction, thereby blocking the subsequent steps. For example, the catalyst could combine with one of the intermediates of the reaction, making it impossible for the reaction to continue. Negative catalysts could also function by combining with the positive catalyst, thus stopping its action. Both positive and negative catalysts are subject to the action of various impurities that act as "poisons" and block their action. Such poisons may act by inactivating the active site on the catalyst surface.

Types of Catalysts. Many common catalysts are powders of metals or of metallic compounds, and they may be classified according to the type of compound they are, such as acid, or the type of reaction they catalyze, such as hydrogenation. For example, sulfuric acid catalyzes the isomerization of hydrocarbons, and platinum catalyzes the hydrogenation of double bonds. Enzymes, which are proteins found in plant and animal cells, catalyze the biochemical reactions necessary for life.

CATALYTIC CRACKING. See Petroleum—6. *Petroleum Refining* (Conversion).

CATAMARAN, katʹə-mə-ran, a boat with two hulls connected by crosspieces, driven by sail or engine. The name derives from the word in the Tamil language of India that means tying trees together. Modern catamarans are descended from ancient Polynesian types such as praus. They can be of asymmetrical design, with the outside and inside curves of each hull of differing shapes, or the two hulls can be identical. Powered catamarans are rather rare, but they are useful for operations requiring a stable platform in shallow waters, such as survey work. The most popular application is for racing sailboats, which are very fast. Triple-hulled boats, called *trimarans,* are gaining popularity.

BILL ROBINSON
Editor of "Yachting"

CATAMARCA, kä-tä-märʹkä, is the capital of Catamarca province in northwestern Argentina. It is situated in the foothills of the Andes, about 150 miles (240 km) by road south of Tucumán. Cattle, alfalfa, cotton, and grapes are raised on irrigated farmlands around the city, and Catamarca is an important marketing and processing center. Frozen meat, leather, and textiles are its main industrial products; handwoven ponchos are a specialty of the region. Many pilgrims visit Catamarca's Church of the Virgin of the Valley. The city, founded in 1683, has a cultural institute with a museum. Population: (1960) 49,291.

CATANDUANES, kä-tän-dwäʹnās, the 12th-largest of the Philippine Islands, lies north of Luzon's southeastern extremity, from which it is separated by Lagonoy Gulf and Maqueda Channel. The island is 44 miles (70 km) long on its north-south axis and 22 miles (35 km) wide. Its area is 552 square miles (1,430 sq km). Rolling coastal hills rise toward mountain ridges which reach a maximum elevation of 2,506 feet (764 meters).

Catanduanes is a significant source of abaca (Manila hemp), rice, and coconuts. Other products include cotton, corn, and coal. There is a modern hydroelectric power plant on Balongbong Creek and an airfield located at Virac (1960 population, 34,417), which is the capital of the province of Catanduanes and the chief port for interisland vessels.

From 1901 to 1946, Catanduanes and its surrounding islets were administered as a subprovince of Albay on Luzon. In 1947 Catanduanes became the 50th province of the Philippines. Population: (1965) of the province, 187,000.

LEONARD CASPER
Boston College

CATANIA, kä-täʹnyä, is a commune and the second-largest city on the Italian island of Sicily. The capital of Catania province, it is situated on the east coast of the island, on the southernmost slope of the great volcano, Mt. Etna.

Catania became a Greek city in the 7th century B.C., and came into the possession of Rome some four centuries later. Throughout medieval and early modern times it remained the principal urban center of eastern Sicily, and the marketplace for the produce of the prosperous orchards, vineyards, and farms that line the slopes between Mt. Etna and the sea north of Catania. Retail and wholesale commerce, the business of the port, and a number of small plants engaged in light industry support the economy of the city.

Catania is unique among the larger cities of Italy in the homogeneous character of its baroque architecture. The city was rebuilt after it had been severely damaged by an eruption of Mt. Etna in 1669 and almost completely destroyed by an earthquake in 1693. The Duke of Camastra, viceroy of Sicily, supervised the plan for the new city, which was carried out by the architect Giovanni Battista Vaccarini.

BETHLEHEM STEEL CORPORATION
A catamaran built for oceanographic research.

The principal north-south thoroughfare that provides entrance from the port into the city is called Via Etnea. The great volcanic cone of Etna stands, as it were, at the end of the street, only about 20 miles (32 km) distant. The cathedral square, one of the numerous carefully designed focal points of the city, is dominated by the great church, dedicated to St. Agatha, patron saint of Catania, and by the elegant city hall. Inside the cathedral the tombs of St. Agatha and the composer Vincenzo Bellini, the city's best-known son, provide the highlights.

University square, only two blocks away, provides another fine example of the careful town planning: the main building of the university, San Giuliano Palace, and a church are in perfect balance on the two sides of the square. The street of the crossbearers, Via dei Crociferi, displays a group of lovely baroque churches, all erected during the first half of the 18th century.

At little distance from the center of the city there is the vast Church of St. Nicholas, the largest church in Sicily. Nearby is the former Benedictine monastery, noted for its fine architectural detail; at present it houses an important astrophysical observatory.

Southwest of the center of the city is Ursino Castle, one of the few monuments to survive the earthquake. It was built by Emperor Frederick II in the 13th century and is surrounded by a moat, with imposing medieval towers; it is now the municipal museum. The museum's collections are particularly well known for their ancient Greek and Roman works of art. Population: of the city (1961), 358,700; of the commune (1966 estimate), 401,489.

GEORGE KISH
University of Michigan

CATANZARO, kä-tän-dzä'rō, in southern Italy, is a commune and one of the three principal cities of the region of Calabria. It is the capital of Catanzaro province. It occupies a picturesque site on a mountain spur, overlooking the Ionian Sea. Catanzaro is reached by winding mountain roads.

Catanzaro was one of the early centers of the Italian silk industry, which attracted both Christian and Jewish artisans to the city as early as the 11th century. Only the tradition of fine weaving and embroidering remains, together with some small textile mills. The city is also a center of wholesale and retail trade.

The Corso Mazzini, the principal street of Catanzaro, traverses the greater part of the city and connects the main public buildings. The local museum of archaeology is noted for its collection of prehistoric and Roman antiquities.

Byzantine, Norman, Angevin, and Aragonese overlords at various times ruled the city. In the early 16th century it became part of the domain of the kings of Naples. Population: city (1961), 44,198; commune (1966 estimate), 79,706.

GEORGE KISH, *University of Michigan*

CATAPULT, kat'ə-pult. Although loosely applied to all ancient and medieval projectile-hurling devices, the word "catapult" specifically means the lightest and most flexible Roman siege engine, used from about 200 B.C. to 400 A.D. It threw 6-pound (2.7-kg) javelins. Its power came from energy built up by twisting heavy skeins of fibers of an unknown material. The shooting of a catapult was the same as the shooting of a crossbow, using two horizontal arms, each with its own skein, instead of the bent bow. A rope on a windlass at the rear of the stock drew back the bowstring, 1 inch (2.5 cm) thick, by means of a triggered hook, adding torsion to the skeins. Pulling a lanyard released the stored force against the butt of the javelin, throwing it about 500 yards (460 meters). The javelins often carried flaming tow. Siege engines confused with the catapult are the *ballista,* which was 10 times larger and threw 60-pound (27-kg) stones, and the *onager,* whose single spar moved in a vertical arc to hurl head-size stones. See also ARTILLERY.

EDWIN TUNIS, *Author of "Weapons"*

CATAPULT of a type called the onager hurled a heavy stone in a high trajectory, impelled by twisted cords.

ALINARI—ART REFERENCE BUREAU

CATARACT, kat'ə-rakt, any clouding, or opacity, of the crystalline lens of the eye. The crystalline lens is a small, normally transparent body that lies directly behind the pupil and the iris, the colored portion of the eye.

Cataracts vary greatly in size. Some affect only a small portion of the lens while others involve the entire lens. Some, called punctate cataracts, are collections of many tiny dotlike opacities. Although some cataracts, called stationary cataracts, always remain the same size, many are progressive, becoming larger and larger. The rate of progression, however, is usually not rapid, and it may be many years before treatment becomes necessary.

Causes. Cataracts occur most frequently in older people and are thought to be part of the normal aging process. Almost every person over 60 has some lens opacities. Cataracts that occur earlier in life may be due to many different causes. They are sometimes due to certain diseases, such as diabetes or cholera. They may also result from eye injuries, especially if the fluid-filled chamber in front of the pupil and iris is ruptured and the escaping fluid is absorbed by the lens. A cataract may also be due to an inflammation inside the eye, a dislocation of the lens, or a retinal detachment. Congenital cataracts, those present at birth, may occur if the mother contracted measles or German measles during pregnancy.

The underlying pathological process that produces a cataract is not fully understood, but it is believed to involve a chemical change in the protein of the lens. This chemical change may be caused by several factors, including heat, toxic substances, a degeneration of the lens fibers, and a change in the water content of the lens.

Symptoms and Diagnosis. Because the clouding of the lens usually interferes with the passage of light rays into the eye, the person's vision is often affected. The degree of sight loss, however, is determined by the extent and location of the opacity. A small opacity located in the edge of the lens may not affect vision at all, but the same size opacity in the center of the lens reduces vision considerably, especially in bright light, when the pupil opening is small. In dim light, when the pupil is larger, the person's vision is less affected. Although some patients with cataracts occasionally complain of seeing spots, changes in color may occur only if the lens itself changes color. In some cases it has been known to become amber or brownish.

The diagnosis of a cataract is made by observing the passage of light rays through the lens to determine if the rays are being obstructed. The examination is made with an opthalmoscope or a special microscope called a slit lamp. By examining each layer of the lens, the doctor is able to determine the appearance, extent, and location of the opacity.

Treatment. There are no known treatments, drugs, or manipulations that can cure or arrest the progress of a cataract. The only definitive treatment is the surgical removal of the lens. After the operation, when the patient has fully recovered, his vision may be restored by wearing glasses that perform much of the same functions of the lens.

BERNARD KRONENBERG, M. D.
New York Medical College

CATARACT. See WATERFALL.

CATASAUQUA, kat-ə-sô'kwə, is a borough in eastern Pennsylvania, in Lehigh county, 50 miles (80 km) north of Philadelphia, on the Lehigh River. The borough produces iron and steel products, textiles, household articles, and flour. There are cement works in the vicinity. Catasauqua was the home of George Taylor, signer of the Declaration of Independence. Incorporated in 1853, it is governed by a burgess and council. Population: 5,062.

CATASTROPHISM, kə-tas'trə-fiz-əm, was an anti-evolutionary theory that tried to account for the earth's fossil record by assuming a series of catastrophic geological events, with the creation of new life forms after each event. See GEOLOGY—*Historical Development of Geology*.

CATATONIA, kat-ə-tō'nē-ə, is a psychosis regarded as one of the forms of schizophrenia. The catatonic condition has two major phases: a stuporous phase and an agitated phase. When in a stupor, the patient holds postures for extremely prolonged periods of time, is uncommunicative, and appears to be unresponsive to all outside stimuli. In the other phase the patient is agitated and overly active. The catatonic display contrasting symptoms, stupor and excitement, extreme negativism and extreme compliance.

The stuporous state is regarded as the most characteristic symptom of the illness. The patient sees, hears, records, and retains, but does not act and seems unable to react to external stimulation. Reports from patients indicate that the catatonic stuporous phase is less passive than would appear from a superficial consideration of the condition. The patient refuses to react, but he is aware of what is going on around him. There is vigilance but a lack of movement. Patients report delusions that rationalize their refusal to move. One patient, for example, reported that she believed that if she did not resist all efforts to make her react, her mother would be destroyed. When the patient abandons the uncommunicative stage, his conversation is often difficult to understand because he will break off thoughts in the middle of sentences and will sometimes repeat isolated words.

In the 19th century authorities on mental illness grouped catatonia with several other conditions and placed them under one major class, dementia praecox. More recent writers consider catatonia to be one of the forms of schizophrenia. Harry Stack Sullivan, prominent American authority on schizophrenia, regarded the symptoms of catatonia as part of the acute onset of schizophrenia rather than a stable and permanent subtype of schizophrenia. Medical authorities of the late 19th and early 20th centuries believed that catatonia was most likely related to some disease of the central nervous system. Post-Freudian views hold that catatonia is related to early childhood anxiety, an outgrowth of a psychological disturbance from childhood experiences. Cold and over-demanding parents impose their will on reluctant and pseudocompliant children, who fail to develop the capacity to wish and to act according to their own desires. It is still unknown why some patients who become schizophrenic develop catatnic symptoms while others show symptoms of some other form of schizophrenia.

AUSTIN E. GRIGG
University of Richmond

CATAWBA INDIANS, kə-tô'bə, a tribe of American Indians of the Siouan linguistic stock, formerly living in the area around the Catawba River in what is now North and South Carolina. In the Colonial period, the Catawba were noted for their courage in fighting the Cherokee, the Iroquois, and the "French Indians" from north of the Ohio. They were faithful allies of the English and later of the Americans.

In 1600 the tribe numbered perhaps 5,000 and was the most important of the eastern Siouan groups. Wars and epidemics of smallpox, however, killed so many that the tribe dwindled to about 400 in 1775 and about 100 in the 19th century. A few Catawba joined the North Carolina Cherokee, and others moved to Oklahoma. A remnant stayed on a small reservation in South Carolina until federal trusteeship was terminated in 1962.

CATAWBA RIVER. See WATEREE RIVER.

CATBIRD, kat'bûrd, a common songbird found in the eastern two thirds of North America and in Bermuda. It receives its name from its mewing, catlike alarm note.

About 10 inches (25 cm) long, the catbird is a trim, slender slate-gray bird with a blackish crown and a touch of chestnut beneath its tail. Related to the mockingbird and brown thrasher, it is an accomplished singer as well as a mimic. Its song is bright and varied but somewhat disjointed, with melodious notes intermixed with harsh, squeaky ones.

The catbird lives in bushes or hedges, sometimes close to houses. It feeds on land and water insects in the spring and on small fruits in the summer and winter. Its nest is built of stems and rootlets and is concealed in a bush or dense hedge, usually only a few feet above the ground. Four or five dark grayish or greenish blue eggs are laid. The catbird is migratory in the northern parts of its range.

The catbird belongs to the order of perching birds (Passeriformes) and is in the family Mimidae, which includes the mockingbirds and thrashers. Its species is *Dumetella carolinensis*.

DEAN AMADON
American Museum of Natural History

North American catbird

KARL H. MASLOWSKI, FROM PHOTO RESEARCHERS

CATCH, a kind of round, in which three or more unaccompanied voices, entering successively, sing the same melody. The written music of a catch does not indicate where each new voice starts but leaves it to the singer's skill to take up, or "catch," his part after the agreed upon interval. Originally, in Elizabethan England, "catch" was synonymous with "round," and simple words were used. Later "catch" came to mean only rounds whose words could be mispronounced or interwoven to give a ludicrous effect. During the Restoration, catches were notoriously licentious.

The first published collection of catches was *Pammelia* (1609); the most famous was John Hilton's *Catch That Catch Can* (1652). The Noblemen and Gentlemen's Catch Club, founded in London in 1761, still exists and holds regular competitions for the writing of new catches and other songs.

CATCHER IN THE RYE, a novel by the American writer J. D. Salinger, published in 1951. The book, Salinger's first novel, was an immediate success; it went into 14 printings within a year of publication and continued to have a large sale thereafter. *The Catcher in the Rye* has been compared to *The Adventures of Huckleberry Finn* for its remarkable use of colloquial language, its picaresque form, its implied criticism of American life, and its mixture of comedy and pathos.

Narrated in the first person by Holden Caulfield, a 16-year-old boy who is being dismissed from his prep school for academic failure, the novel relates the boy's adventures during three days alone in New York City. Holden attempts to make contact with a number of people, but is disillusioned when he finds them flawed by hypocrisy, cruelty, or ugliness. The only person in whom he can believe is his younger sister Phoebe, who ultimately persuades him not to run away from home. In the last chapter there is a suggestion that Holden is in a sanatorium and will reenter school in the autumn.

Holden is the "catcher in the rye." He imagines a field of rye atop a cliff, in which children are playing, with Holden standing at the edge of the cliff to catch the children and keep them from falling off. Thus, through this symbolism, Holden's dream of protecting the innocence and integrity of the world of childhood is posed against his inevitable fall into an adult world of self-consciousness and compromise.

JEROME STERN, *Florida State University*

Further Reading: Belcher, William F., and Lee, James W., eds., *J. D. Salinger and the Critics* (Belmont, Calif., 1962); Laser, Marvin, and Fruman, Norman, eds., *Studies in J. D. Salinger* (New York 1963).

CATCHFLY, any of a number of wild flowers with stems that are covered with sticky hairs. The hairs are presumed to trap flies and other small insects that would otherwise take nectar from the flowers. Catchflies, which are frequently cultivated for their attractive red, pink, and white flowers, grow 1 to 3 feet (⅓ to 1 meter) tall and bear alternate leaves. Catchflies are widely distributed throughout the north temperate zone. Because of the ease with which they become established along roadsides and in waste places, many are considered weeds.

Catchflies belong to the genus *Silene* of the family Carophyllaceae.

JOAN E. RAHN, *Lake Forest College, Ill.*

CATEAU-CAMBRÉSIS, Treaty of, kȧ-tō′ kän-brā-zē′, the treaty that ended a long and mutually costly war between France and Spain, concluded on April 3, 1559. England, which had fought briefly on the Spanish side, was also a signatory. By this treaty, France was forced to give up its Italian conquests of Savoy and Piedmont, and with them its claims on Italy, although it retrained the port of Calais against English claims. See also LE CATEAU.

CATECHETICAL SCHOOLS, kat-ə-ket′i-kəl, were centers for preparing adults for baptism in the early Christian church. The term is frequently but incorrectly applied to other institutions, such as the celebrated theological centers that flourished in Alexandria, Antioch, Caesarea, and Edessa in the 2d and 3d centuries, and the schools conducted in Rome by St. Justin Martyr and Tatian. These were private schools, not schools of the Christian community. There is, in fact, no evidence that the early church maintained a school devoted to giving religious or cathechetical instruction.

Alexandria, the closest approximation of a catechetical school, was a Christian academy, a public Hellenistic-Christian university. An official catechetical feature was given the school when Bishop Demetrius (around 202) entrusted Origen, director of the school at the time, with the task of instructing converts. Origen made Heraclas his assistant for instruction of the less educated.

Centers for catechesis, or oral instruction in the faith, were common in the early church. Such instruction is mentioned throughout the New Testament (Luke 1:4; Acts 18:25; Romans 2:18; I Corinthians 14:14); and a baptismal catechesis was the basis for I Peter. At the catechetical centers the pupils were catechumens, and the setting was not a classroom, but rather a liturgical gathering. Catecheses were divided into two classes: prebaptismal and postbaptismal. Outstanding catechetical instructions were written by Cyril of Jerusalem, John Chrysostom, Theodore of Mopsuestia, Nicetas of Remisiana, Hilary of Poitiers, Ambrose, and Augustine. The *Didache*, the oldest church ordo, furnishes directions for instructing catechumens.

ALFRED C. RUSH, C. SS. R.
Catholic University of America

Further Reading: Murphy, Francis X., "Catechetical Schools," *New Catholic Encyclopedia*, vol. 3, p. 219 (Washington 1967); Quasten, Johannes, *Patrology*, vol. 1 (Westminster, Md., 1950).

CATECHISM, kat′ə-kiz-əm, a book that contains a summary of religious teachings. Originally derived from the Greek term *katēchein*, meaning "to resound" or "to proclaim," the term eventually evolved into various technical words designating the teaching process of the Christian church: *catechesis* is the act of teaching religion; *catechist* is the person who teaches; *catechumen* is the recipient of the instruction.

Early Development of Catechesis. The earliest teachings of Christianity were oral catecheses. The word *evangelium* means "good news" and refers to the spoken message proclaimed by Christ to men. The apostles spread this good news by word of mouth. Later, in response to the need for an accurate summation of the words and actions of Christ, the message of the apostles was recorded in the text known as the New Testament or Gospels.

The Gospels are distinguished by their narrative form, exemplifying the teaching methods of Christ. Christ used parables or stories to reveal spiritual mysteries through parallel human experiences. The evangelists, particularly St. Peter and St. Paul, followed Christ's teaching methods by using a Biblical-historical approach and a narrative style in their writing.

In the 1st and 2d centuries, Christian teaching took place mainly at communal worship, where the bishop provided most of the instruction through his homilies. But, the *Didache*, or *Teaching of the Twelve Apostles*, the first handbook of instruction for the catechist, appeared as early as 60–90 A. D. It outlines liturgical practices and presents the Ten Commandments, integrated with the Sermon on the Mount, as the fundamental law of Christian life.

In the 3d century the *catechumenate*—a large community of those desiring baptism—developed. The preparation and instruction of the catechumens lasted for a period of three years, during which they were taught the principles of liturgical worship and the truths of the Christian faith as they were presented in the various creeds. It was for the instruction of the catechumens that St. Augustine wrote *Catechising of the Uninstructed*, one of the most influential of all catechetical works. Augustine outlines the methodology of teaching catechetics as well as a three-point curriculum structure: Biblical narrative, exposition or instruction, and practical application. His work also contains a survey of the Christian message from Genesis to the Last Judgment.

Medieval Catechism. After the conversion of barbarian hordes in the 6th century, infant baptism became the norm, and the catechumenate declined. Consequently, catecheses began to be directed toward the young, and the church placed new emphasis on parental responsibility for the religious education of children. Later in the Middle Ages bishops composed handbooks that local priests used as a basis for pulpit or oral catechesis. This kind of handbook, known as a *catechismus*, helped regulate the doctrinal instruction transmitted verbally to the largely illiterate population of the Middle Ages. At this time also the missionary approach to catechetics ended; Christian environment became viewed as the chief agent of catechetics.

Reformation Period. The Reformation was a fertile period of catechetical endeavor. In 1529, Martin Luther published the *Little Catechism*. Perhaps the most influential book produced by any reformer, it is still the basic text of Lutheranism.

John Calvin's *Instruction and Confession of Faith for the Use of the Church of Geneva* followed in 1541, but it was generally replaced in the Reformed churches by the 1563 edition of the Heidelberg Catechism, which the Synod of Dort revised in 1619. The catechism included in the Book of Common Prayer has been universally used by the Anglican Communion since its ratification in 1549. It was written in the time of King Edward VI of England, probably by Thomas Cranmer.

The Roman Catholic Church issued the Roman Catechism in 1556 at the request of the Council of Trent. It unified and ordered Catholic doctrine, especially emphasized Christian practice, and carefully explained the Lord's Prayer. Intended for adults, especially for pastors, it was primarily apologetic in tone, and the formulas it contained were often lengthy, technical, and involved.

The chief catechism of the Eastern Orthodox Church was compiled by Peter Moghlia, the metropolitan of Kiev, in 1640. Determined to give Orthodoxy definitions as precise as those of Latin Catholicism and Protestantism, Moghlia's *Orthodox Confessions* parallels closely the famous catechism of St. Peter Canisius (*Capita doctrinae Christianae compendio tradita*, 1555). The *Confessions* was later modified and approved by the Council of Constantinople in 1643.

Modern Catechetics. The field of catechetics has undergone vast renewal in modern times. No longer plagued by the fears of the post-Reformation era, Christianity is seeking unity through cooperation. The age of ecumenism stresses what is common among varying faiths; the age of apologetics had stressed the differences between the Christian churches.

The renewal of catechetics began after World War I, when religious education underwent serious reappraisal and was found wanting. It became evident that the traditional approach was too deductive and abstract and lacked imaginative presentation. Thus the formularized question-and-answer doctrinal apologetic that characterized the older catechisms (such as the Roman Catholic Baltimore Catechism of 1884) gradually gave way to a more positive Biblical and liturgical orientation.

This new Christ-centered approach was given great impetus in the Roman Catholic Church by the Second Vatican Council (1962–1965). In its Decree on the Bishops' Pastoral Office, the council stated: "Catechetical training is intended to make men's faith become living, conscious, and active, through the light of instruction. Bishops should see to it that such training be painstakingly given to children, adolescents, young adults, and even grownups. In this instruction a proper sequence should be observed as well as a method appropriate to the matter that is being treated and to the natural disposition, ability, age, and circumstance of life of the listener."

This concern for the psychological, sociological, and educational development of those being taught catechetics has led to various individual and interfaith experimental catechetical projects. New catechetical programs for children include the use of visual aids and music, which special teams of experts have carefully created and evaluated. Adult catechisms are being designed to stimulate thought rather than to transmit knowledge by question and answer.

ALVIN J. ILLEG
C. S. P., Paulist Press

CATECHUMEN, kat-ə-kū′mən, is an adult who, although unbaptized, believes in the doctrines of the Roman Catholic Church and, therefore, is preparing to receive baptism. In the Apostolic Church catechetical instruction frequently followed baptism. By the 3d century, however, the catechumenate, or institution in which catechumens were prepared for baptism, was flourishing. During this training period, which Hippolytus (died about 235) indicates lasted three years, the catechumen was instructed in Sacred Scripture and the writings of Church Fathers. Before being baptized, he was required to undergo an examination, not of his knowledge, but of his everyday practice of Christian virtues. The catechumens were not permitted to participate in the celebration of the Eucharist and were required to leave Mass after the Gospel reading. Consequently the first part of the Mass is sometimes called the Mass of the Catechumens.

After infant baptism became the normal practice in the 6th century, the catechumenate, and the liturgical rites connected with it, disappeared. In its Constitution on the Liturgy, the Second Vatican Council (1962–1965) took steps to renew the catechumenate, which it suggests "is intended as a time of suitable instruction, and may be sanctified by sacred rites to be celebrated at successive intervals."

C. J. McNaspy, S. J.
"America" Magazine

CATEGORICAL, kat-ə-gôr′i-kəl. In traditional logic, a statement is called categorical if it makes a single assertion, unconditionally and without alternatives. Thus, "Columbus discovered America" is a categorical statement, as distinguished from such hypothetical statements as "If the Norse did not arrive first, Columbus discovered America" and the disjunctive statement "Either the Norse discovered America or Columbus did." As may be seen from these illustrations, hypothetical and disjunctive statements contain components which are categorical. In this sense, also, a syllogism is called categorical if its premises and conclusion are categorical statements.

Kant made use of this notion in ethics by dividing injunctions to act, or *imperatives* as he called them, into hypothetical and categorical. A hypothetical imperative gives a command conditionally, on the assumption of a certain aim or purpose. Thus, "If you wish to arrive on time, hurry!" is a hypothetical imperative and has no force for one who does not wish to be on time. Such imperatives can never form the basis of a universal ethics since the injunction can be escaped by denying the aim stated in the condition. If there is to be any ethic binding on all rational beings it must, Kant argues, be based on a categorical imperative, that is, one without conditions. Kant in his *Metaphysic of Ethics* (1785) claims there is such an imperative. It is most frequently stated as follows: 'So act that you could will the maxim of your action to be a universal law." The maxim here is simply the principle on which a person acts and the force of the injunction is to claim that one should act when and only when he could wish that the principle of his action be adopted universally. This command is unconditionally binding and so is categorical.

Paul Henle, *University of Michigan*

CATEGORY, kat′ə-gôr-rē. In the philosophy of Aristotle, categories represent the ultimate types of being. Thus one may say of something that it is a chair, of a chair that it is a piece of furniture, of a piece of furniture that it is an artifact, and so on, going to ever-broader characterizations until one comes to substance. Here one can give no broader description; hence substance is a category. Similarly, one may say of red that it is a color, of color that it is a quality, and here one stops; hence quality is a category. Aristotle gives varying lists of categories; the most complete list in the *Categories* includes: substance, quantity, quality, relation, space, time, situation, state, action, and passion (being acted on). Situation is differentiated from place in that it refers to such characteristics as being right side up or upside down rather than to mere location. Similarly, state (for example, shod) differs from quality (for example, red) in applying most specifically to one part of a whole.

Aristotle's treatment of the categories strikingly differentiates substance from the other categories. It is distinguished from them principally by not being in anything else (that is, by not being a characteristic of anything else) and by its ability to take on contrary characteristics. Thus a chair may have its color changed without ceasing to be the substance chair. Substance, moreover, is divided into two sorts: *primary substance*, or individual things (for example, individual men or chairs), and *secondary substances* (for example, the species, man, or the type, chair). Primary substances may only be subjects of discourse and may never be predicated of anything. Secondary substances may be predicated of primary (for example, one may predicate "man" of Socrates, but one cannot predicate Socrates of anything).

Kantian Categories. Immanuel Kant also made use of the term "category" in reference to a different problem. The British philosophers of the Enlightenment, from Francis Bacon through David Hume, had tried to show that knowledge derives entirely from experience. The attempt was a failure, and in Hume's development, the result was skepticism. Kant accepted Hume's reasoning, and agreed that if experience were the only source of knowledge, the result would be skeptical, but argued that since there is knowledge, it must have some source in addition to experience. This source he found in certain forms of perception and in certain concepts by means of which we organize our experience. These concepts he called categories.

A parallel to Kant's general view of the categories is given by some contemporary accounts of the influence of needs and mental sets upon perception. It is generally admitted that perception is not a simple recording of effects upon the sense organs but rather is influenced by the state of the individual as well. Thus a hungry person is more likely to notice food than a well-fed one, and a coin looks larger to a poor child than to a richer one. In somewhat the same way, Kant claims that our experience of the world is not simply given from without but is the result of a process of organizing our sensations by means of certain concepts. Thus, we think of the world in terms of cause and effect, not because there is any direct sensation of causes in the way that there is of colors and shapes but because causation is one of the ideas which the human mind inevitably uses in the interpretation of experience. Kant holds that causation and the other categories are the same for all people and that the objectivity in our judgments depends upon their use.

In the *Critique of Pure Reason*, Kant sets himself the task of discovering a complete list of categories and of showing that they must apply to all experience. In the former inquiry he discovers 12 categories in all, arranged in four groups of three—the categories of quality, quantity, relation, and modality. Of these, the individual categories of cause and substance are most important. Kant's attempted proof in the "transcendental deduction of the categories," that the categories apply to all experience, is one of the most difficult arguments to be found in any philosophy.

As a result of this doctrine, Kant distinguishes between things as they are in themselves and things as they appear when organized by the categories. The latter he calls *phenomena,* and he argues that scientific knowledge is confined to phenomena.

These two conceptions of category, Aristotle's as the basic types of being and Kant's as basic forms of thought, have been most influential in the history of philosophy. Other views have been intermediate between these. In contemporary philosophy, however, the term is used loosely to refer to any generic concept.

PAUL HENLE, *University of Michigan*

CATENA, kä-tä'nä, **Vincenzo di Biagio** (1470?–1531), Italian painter of the High Renaissance, who was a wealthy Venetian active in humanist circles. Although he was not a major innovator, Catena was able to perpetuate the clarity and order of 15th century painting and at the same time to master the coloristic approach and atmospheric effects of the 16th century Venetians.

Catena's youthful work indicates that he studied with Giovanni Bellini, whose compositions he frequently borrowed, as in the *Madonna and Child with Saints and a Donor* (Walker Gallery, Liverpool). He may have worked in the studio of Giorgione, who refers to Catena as "colleague" in an inscription on the back of a painting of 1505 or 1506. The influence of Giorgione, Titian, Raphael, and Palma Vecchio is also apparent in Catena's mature works. These include the *St. Francis Altarpiece* (Accademia, Venice), *Christ Giving the Keys to St. Peter* (Prado, Madrid), and *Holy Family with St. Anne* (Staatliche Kunstsammlungen, Dresden). Late in his career Catena successfully fused the old and new elements of Venetian Renaissance style, as in his *Warrior Adoring the Infant Christ* (National Gallery, London).

MARTICA SAWIN
Parsons School of Design, New York City

Further Reading: Robertson, Giles, *Vincenzo Catena* (Edinburgh 1954).

CATENARY, kat'ə-ner-ē, the plane curve in which a perfectly flexible cable of uniform thickness and density hangs when suspended from two points. A cable hanging in a catenary curve has the lowest possible center of gravity and therefore the least possible potential energy. The catenary was discovered by the Swiss brothers Jacques and Jean Bernoulli.

The equation of the catenary in rectangular coordinates is

$$y = \left(\frac{a}{2}\right)\left(e^{\frac{x}{a}} + e^{\frac{-x}{a}}\right)$$

where a is the y-intercept of the curve, that is, the point where the curve crosses the y-axis. Since $\frac{1}{2}\left(e^{\frac{x}{a}} + e^{\frac{-x}{a}}\right)$ is equal to $\cosh \frac{x}{a}$, the hyperbolic cosine of $\frac{x}{a}$, the equation may be written $y = a \cosh \frac{x}{a}$.

CATERPILLAR, kat'ə-pil-ər, the young, or larva, of a moth or butterfly. It hatches from the egg and, when fully grown, develops into the pupa or chrysalis, which in turn metamorphoses into an adult moth or butterfly. Caterpillars vary in length from 0.1 to 6 inches (0.25 to 15 cm). Their colors usually are cryptic—that is, they match their environment. See also BUTTERFLIES AND MOTHS.

CATFISH, a large and diversified group of fishes that are widely distributed throughout the world. They vary greatly in size: the largest catfish are over 10 feet (3.3 meters) in length, while others are only a few inches (5 to 10 cm) long. Most catfish are freshwater fishes, but a few species inhabit salt waters.

In North America, catfish extend from the rivers of the Arctic drainage southward through Canada and the United States, especially in the Great Lakes and the Mississippi River. They did not occur naturally in the Pacific drainage of the United States but were introduced successfully into Washington and Oregon during the 1880's. The better-known North American catfish are bullheads, blue cats, yellow cats, mudcats, channel or spotted cats, flatheads, and madtoms.

Description. Catfish have long, whiskerlike barbels, which are sometimes longer than the fish itself; broad mouths; and strong spines on the dorsal and pectoral fins. Some small species, especially the madtom, have single spines, which are often serrated and which contain a poison gland, preceding the dorsal and pectoral fins. The spines, which serve as an effective defense, probably account for the small number of catfish that are eaten by other fishes. Most species have thick, leathery, scaleless skin, but some have a bony, platelike armor over their bodies.

Catfish are most active at night and during cloudy days. One species commonly swims upside down, while another discharges electricity.

JEANNE WHITE, FROM NATIONAL AUDUBON SOCIETY

CATFISH include a freshwater species that is called bullhead

JIM SHERMAN, IOWA STATE CONSERVATION COMMISSION

CHANNEL CATFISH are large catfish found in the deep freshwaters of interior parts of North America.

Some catfish make sounds by vibrating their swim bladders or moving their fins.

Habitat. In general the larger species of catfish inhabit large, rapid rivers, while the smaller species prefer rocky riffles in streams where they can seek protection under rocks when frightened. Many catfish live near the bottom in muddy waters and use their movable barbels to maintain their position in relation to the bottom. The fact that catfish have a tolerance for mud, silt, and pollution, and thus inhabit areas that other fishes shun, protects them from many predator fish.

Some species are gregarious, and most move only short distances in the rivers or lakes that they inhabit. A few species that have accessory breathing apparatus on their gills are able to survive in freshwater ponds that dry up during droughts. Some small species do well in home aquariums.

Feeding Habits. Catfish eat insect larvae, small crustaceans, mollusks, and a variety of other things. One large species in Thailand, over 6 feet (2 meters) long, is a strict vegetarian; it clips algae from rocks and occasionally swallows baseball-size rocks. Still other species are carnivorous and are thought to eat small animals. In South America catfish eat mosquito larvae in freshwater ponds, thus serving to control the number of mosquitoes. Some small marine species of catfish live in the mouths of other catfish, where they irritate the gills, causing bleeding; they then consume the blood.

Catfish rely on their sense of touch and on the taste buds on their barbels to locate food. In one species the entire body, including the tail, is covered with taste buds. In the southern United States catfish feed most heavily when the temperature is about 75° F (24° C); they stop feeding if the temperature is either too hot or too cold.

Care of the Young. Some catfish tend their young very carefully. In some species the male incubates the eggs in his mouth and later protects the young fry in the same way; in some other species the female cares for the young similarly. In one species of bullhead, after the female has prepared the nest and laid the eggs, both parents intermittently take the eggs into their mouths and forcibly blow them out; they continue this process even after the eggs hatch, until the fry can swim freely.

The female of one species develops a spongy skin before she lays her eggs on the river bottom; after laying the eggs, she presses her body against them, and they attach to her spongy skin by means of stalked cups that develop on the abdomen of the female during the breeding season. The eggs remain in the cups, attached to the mother's skin, until they hatch.

Many American catfish build nests for their young in river bottoms or banks and sometimes in empty containers or under logs. Some Australian catfish, after digging nests for their fertilized eggs, cover the nests with stones and abandon them.

Economic Importance. Most of the larger species of freshwater catfish are used for human food. In fact, along the Mississippi River drainage, catfish are among the most important food fishes. The flavor of the blue catfish is delicate, and the meat is firm and flaky. Catfish are caught by traps, nets, and hooks and lines. Although they can be transported safely, most catfish are eaten in the region where they are caught. The two families of catfish that live in marine or brackish waters (Ariidae and Plotosidae) are undesirable as food, and they are occasionally a nuisance to fishermen because their sturdy, serrated spines can easily become entangled in fishing nets.

Classification. As with any large group of fishes, authorities disagree on the classification of catfish. There are about 30 families of catfish in the superorder Ostariophysi. The principal families are Doradidae (dorados), Callichthyidae, and Loricariidae (sucker catfish), all of which are armored; Aspredinidae, banjo catfish; Ariidae and Plotosidae, both marine families; Claridae; Siluridae; Pimelodidae; Bagridae; Trichomycteridae, a parasitic family; Ictaluridae, North American catfish; Schilbeidae; Mochocidae, upside-down catfish; and Malapteruridae, electric catfish.

EDWIN S. IVERSEN, *University of Miami*

CATGUT, or gut, is a tough cord, usually made from the intestines of sheep, used for stringing musical instruments and for making sutures in surgery. Gut was formerly used for stringing tennis, badminton, and other rackets, but it has been replaced for this purpose by synthetic materials such as nylon and by steel wire. The term "catgut" is misleading, because it is doubtful that the intestines of cats were ever used for such cords.

Most gut is manufactured in France and Italy. The number of thicknesses of gut used in the production of the strings for musical instruments varies from three for the smallest violin strings to more than one hundred for a heavy bass viol string.

About 50% of all suturing materials used is gut. Its principal advantage is that it is slowly absorbed by the body after the sutured tissues have healed.

CATHARI, kath′ə-rī, members of a dualistic heretical sect in Europe in the 11th to 13th century. The sect cannot be traced to a particular founder.

The Cathari philosophy originated in dualism, a pre-Christian philosophy that was concerned with the problem of the origins of evil and of the nature of man. Postulating two eternal principles, Good (spirit) and Evil (matter), it demanded an asceticism aimed at liberating the "good" spirit from the "evil" prison of the body. Manichaeanism was one of the earliest examples of dualism. Similar beliefs were held by the 7th century Paulicians of Armenia and the 10th century Bogomils of Bulgaria. Dualism was introduced into the West about 1150 and formed the substratum for Catharism. The sect became particularly strong in northern Italy and in southern France, where the Cathari were called Albigenses. See also ALBIGENSES; MANICHAEANS; PAULICIANS.

The sweeping church reform of Pope Gregory VII (reigned 1073–1085) had spawned sporadic sects demanding clerical reform and apostolic poverty. Impatient of complete success, some, like the Cathari, became anarchistic and repudiated externals: images, property, sacraments, and hierarchy. The Cathari rejected the doctrines of the Incarnation and Resurrection. Their attitude that sex and procreation were evil, their repudiation of authority, and their approval of suicide and usury made them a danger to the social order.

The real Cathari were the so-called "Perfect," who, after a long trial, had received the "Consolamentum"—an imposition of hands that imparted the Spirit. This obliged them to perpetual poverty, continence, and community life, and to extreme asceticism. The Perfect conducted services, preached, dispensed alms, and conducted schools. Those Perfect who failed to live up to the Consolamentum were subjected to a "reconsolation of the soul," or the "endura," a forced death by starvation or asphyxiation. The ordinary believers merely promised to receive the Consolamentum; they lived ordinary lives and were not bound to the severity of the Perfect.

Instruction, correction, threats, a crusade (1209–1229) with brutal cruelties on both sides, and finally the Inquisition were used (1229) as methods of halting the heresy. Ultimately, the Cathari became fragmented and by the end of the 13th century were extinct.

ALFRED C. RUSH, C. S. S. R.
Catholic University of America

Further Reading: Dossat, Y., "Cathari," *New Catholic Encyclopedia*, vol. 3 (New York 1967); Runciman, Steven, *The Medieval Manichee* (Cambridge, England, 1947).

CATHARSIS, kə-thär′sis, in psychology, means a release of emotions. During the early development of psychoanalysis, Sigmund Freud and Josef Breuer employed hypnosis as a means of treating neurotics. Under hypnosis many patients talked freely of their conflicts, and often when they did this, they experienced emotions appropriate to the anecdotes they were relating. On awakening, the patients felt much better and were relieved of their symptoms. This discharge of emotions was called *catharsis*.

Freud and Breuer wrote that the goal of therapy with neurotic patients was to effect a catharsis, or *abreaction*, of repressed feelings. Repressed feelings were viewed as the source of the symptoms. Later they found that catharsis could be achieved without hypnosis. In the permissive setting of the therapeutic interview, the patient tended to bring up anxieties, hostilities, guilts, and other feelings, and often exhibited a reduction of his symptoms as a consequence.

In psychiatry and psychology, catharsis continues to be synonymous with emotional release. The release is a discharge of emotional material associated with repressed events that is achieved by talking about one's experiences and feelings. It is important to differentiate between experiencing emotions during therapy (catharsis) and talking about emotions. Catharsis does not occur when the patient calmly states that he felt a certain way when he had a certain experience. When catharsis occurs, the patient relates some anecdote, and while doing this he actually experiences emotions as events are recalled.

AUSTIN E. GRIGG, *University of Richmond*

CATHARTIC, kə-thär′tik, a drug that promotes the elimination of feces from the intestines. In order of increasing potency, cathartics are known as aperients, laxatives, purgatives, hydragogues, and drastics. Although the term "cathartic" implies a purging action, it is now often used synonymously with the term "laxative."

Types of Modern Cathartics—*Stimulant Cathartics*. Stimulant cathartics increase the peristaltic activity of the intestinal tract by irritating the intestinal mucosa or by acting on the nerves that activate peristalsis. Most usually act only on the large intestine, but some may also act on the small intestine and on the entire digestive tract. All stimulant cathartics cause some intestinal cramps and an increased secretion of mucus from the intestinal tract. The intensity of the effects produced by stimulant cathartics varies with the particular drug, the dosage, and the individual.

Senna and cascara sagrada (containing anthraquinone derivatives) and phenolphthalein, a relatively nontoxic stimulant cathartic widely used in home remedies, act mainly on the large intestine, producing their effects after a time lapse of at least six hours. Castor oil, unlike many other stimulant cathartics, acts mainly on the small intestine and produces thorough evacuation within two to six hours. Other stimulant cathartics include bisacodyl, a relatively new drug administered orally or rectally, and danthron, often combined with a fecal softener.

***Saline Cathartics*.** Saline cathartics are salts that increase the volume of water in the intestine. The resulting increased bulk of the intestinal contents exerts a mechanical stimulus that increases intestinal motility. A semifluid evacuation usually occurs within three to six hours. The common saline cathartics are magnesium sulfate (Epsom salt), milk of magnesia, magnesium citrate, sodium sulfate (Glauber's salt), sodium phosphate, and sodium potassium tartrate (Rochelle salt).

***Bulk-Forming Cathartics*.** Bulk-forming cathartics are natural and semisynthetic polysaccharides and cellulose derivatives that swell in the intestinal fluid to form emollient gels. These gels facilitate the passage of intestinal contents and stimulate peristalsis. The bulk-forming cathartics are derived from agar, plantago seeds (psyllium seeds), kelp (alginates), and plant gums (tragacanth, chondrus, sterculia, and karaya). Synthetic cellulose derivatives are marketed under a variety of trade names, mainly as granules and tablets.

Lubricant Cathartics. Mineral oil and certain digestible plant oils, such as olive oil, lubricate and soften fecal matter by preventing its dehydration and thereby facilitate evacuation.

Other Cathartics. The use of enemas for evacuating the lower bowel dates from antiquity. Tap water, soap suds in water, or solutions of sodium phosphate or sodium citrate injected through the anus add bulk to the intestinal contents and stimulate evacuation. Glycerin suppositories are also effective as a mild cathartic.

Use of Cathartics. Cathartics are used to treat functional constipation which may occur because of faulty personal hygiene, the neglect of response to the bodily urge, faulty eating habits, excessive ingestion of foods (such as processed cheese) that harden the stool, prolonged use of certain drugs (such as aluminum hydroxide, calcium carbonate, and the opiates), and nervous and mental stress. However, cathartics should not be used when an abnormal condition of the intestinal tract causes the constipation. See also CONSTIPATION.

There are few indications for drastic purging today. An exception is the elimination of drug or food poisons from the intestinal tract by the use of saline cathartics. Cathartics may also be used in conjunction with antihelminthics to expel worms from the intestine, and they may be used to create watery stools for microscopic examination. Cathartics should never be used when there is abdominal pain, nausea, vomiting, or other symptoms suggestive of appendicitis.

Cathartic Habit. Prolonged use of cathartics leads to habituation and chronic constipation. Since a cathartic evacuates the bowel completely (while the average bowel movement empties only a portion of the bowel), several days may elapse before a normal bowel movement can occur. The patient, however, often thinks that he is again constipated and takes another dose of a cathartic. His use of increasingly potent cathartics in an attempt to restore regularity leads to persistent overstimulation and irritability of the intestines. To avoid this, cathartics should not be frequently self-administered without the supervision of a physician who will also educate the patient on the importance of adequate diet, correct personal hygiene, and the restoration of normal bowl function.

Harmful Effects of Cathartics. In addition to the harmful effects produced by the cathartic habit, excessive use of cathartics can also cause gastrointestinal disturbances, an excessive loss of fluid, and an imbalance of necessary ions, such as potassium, sodium, and chloride ions, in the body. However, the most serious danger associated with cathartics is their incorrect use when the symptoms of appendicitis are present since cathartic-induced motor activity of the intestinal tract can rupture an inflamed appendix and greatly increase the mortality rate of appendicitis.

Obsolete Cathartics. Cathartics are among the oldest known medicines. For centuries, they have been widely self-administered since almost every culture associated excrement with evil and believed that purging cleansed the body.

Although the use of some of the naturally irritating cathartics, such as croton oil, colocynth, and podophyllum, is practically obsolete, some home remedies still include cathartics that are medically undesirable and should be classified as obsolete. Jalpa, ipomea, gamboge, and elaterin are extremely irritating and acidic. They act on the small intestine and produce extremely watery stools and considerable colic. Their use may lead to nutritional deficiencies, sodium depletion, and dehydration. Another cathartic that was once very popular is calomel (mercurous chloride), a stimulant cathartic that can produce mercury poisoning if it is not quickly eliminated from the body.

GEORGE B. GRIFFENHAGEN
American Pharmaceutical Association

CATHAY, ka-thā′, was the name medieval Europeans used for North China. It derived from the name of a Mongolian people, the Khitan or Ch′i-tan, who overran parts of Mongolia, Manchuria, and North China.

Although the Khitan founded the Liao dynasty (907–1124), their kingdom was often called by their ethnic name. People farther west and the Mongols referred to North China as *Kitai* and to South China as *Mangi*, the "land of the Man." Even after the downfall of the Liao, Kitai continued to be used and is still in use by the Russians and some central Asian peoples.

Franciscan missionaries and Marco Polo visited Karakorum, capital of the Mongol Empire, in the 13th and 14th centuries and transmitted these appellations to Europe. Having only scant knowledge of Asia, Europeans until the turn of the 17th century assumed that Cathay and China were different realms.

HYMAN KUBLIN
The City University of New York